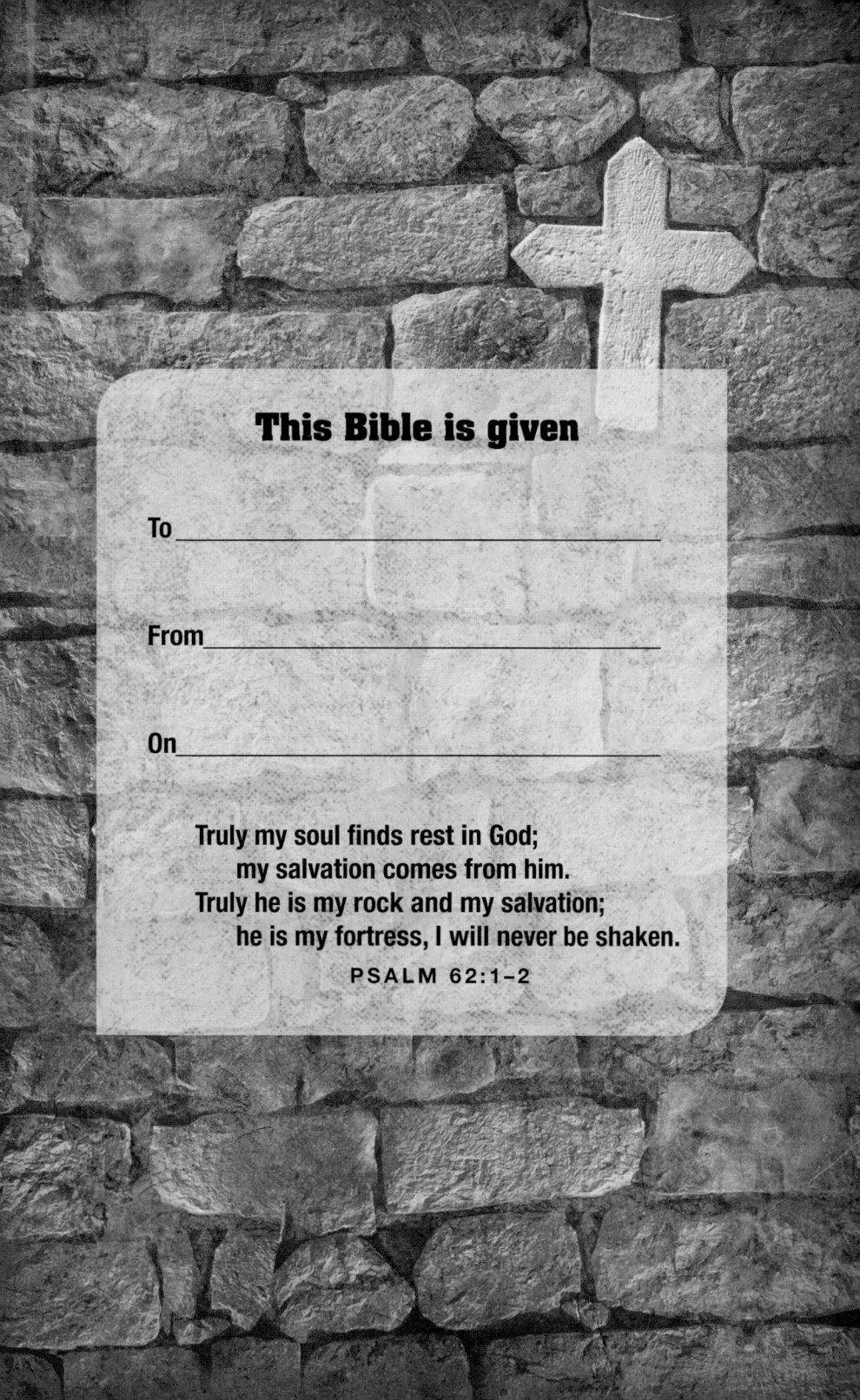

This Bible is given

To _____

From _____

On _____

Truly my soul finds rest in God;
    my salvation comes from him.
Truly he is my rock and my salvation;
    he is my fortress, I will never be shaken.

PSALM 62:1–2

ROCK SOLID FAITH STUDY BIBLE

for teens

NEW INTERNATIONAL VERSION

ROCK SOLID FAITH STUDY BIBLE
for teens

BUILD AND DEFEND YOUR FAITH
BASED ON GOD'S PROMISES

ZONDERVAN®

Table of
Contents

Welcome to the
Rock Solid Faith Study Bible

This Bible was created especially for you to help you grow your faith and find hope for your future. Featuring the complete New International Version text of the Bible and lots of study helps along the way, this Bible will help you to get rooted in the unchanging love, guidance, and promises of God.

Features include:

Book introductions

Rock Solid TRUTHS:
Examines Christian
beliefs and explorations
of other religions

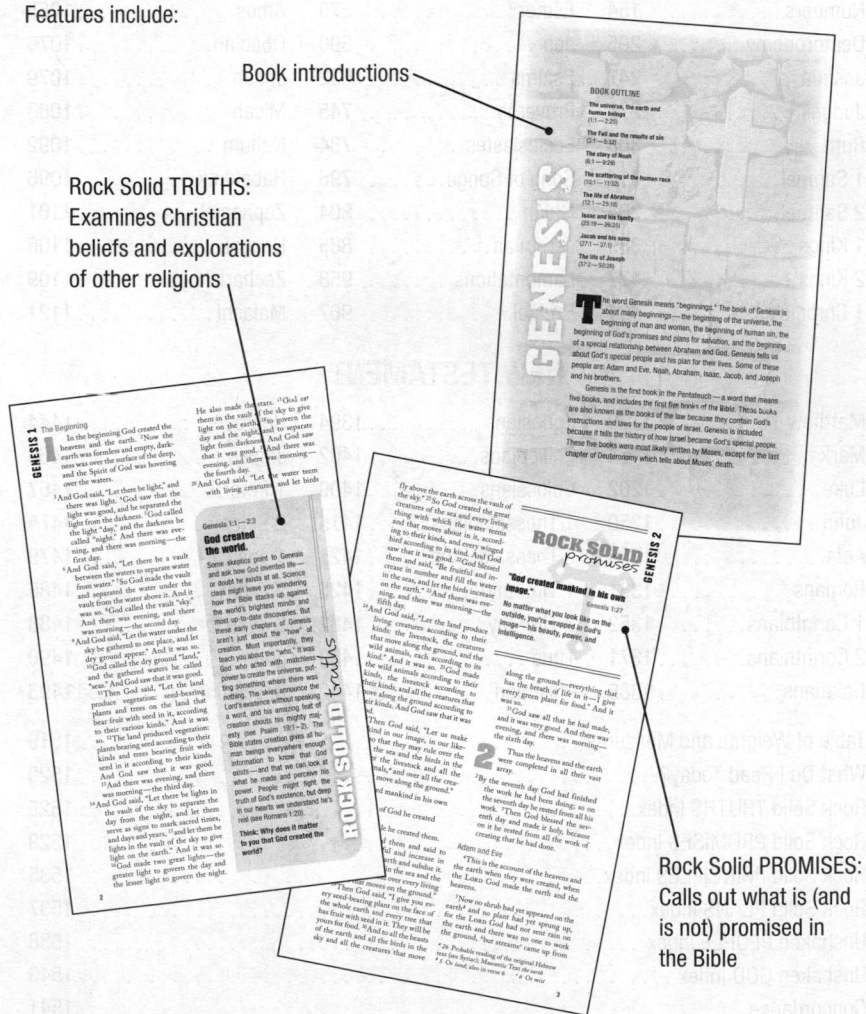

Rock Solid PROMISES:
Calls out what is (and
is not) promised in
the Bible

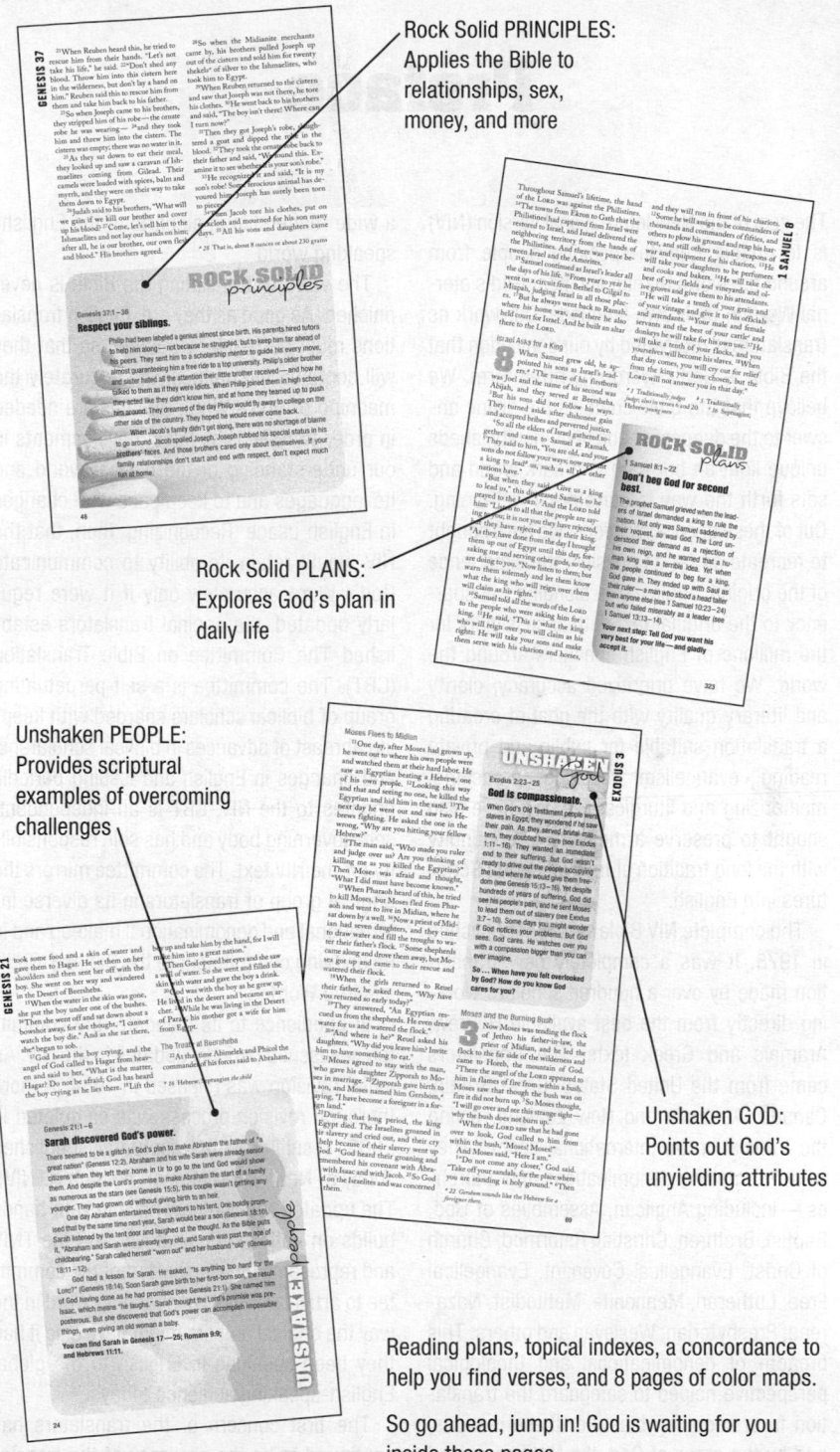

Rock Solid PRINCIPLES: Applies the Bible to relationships, sex, money, and more

Rock Solid PLANS: Explores God's plan in daily life

Unshaken PEOPLE: Provides scriptural examples of overcoming challenges

Unshaken GOD: Points out God's unyielding attributes

Reading plans, topical indexes, a concordance to help you find verses, and 8 pages of color maps.

So go ahead, jump in! God is waiting for you inside these pages.

Preface

The goal of the New International Version (NIV) is to enable English-speaking people from around the world to read and hear God's eternal Word in their own language. Our work as translators is motivated by our conviction that the Bible is God's Word in written form. We believe that the Bible contains the divine answer to the deepest needs of humanity, sheds unique light on our path in a dark world and sets forth the way to our eternal well-being. Out of these deep convictions, we have sought to recreate as far as possible the experience of the original audience — blending transparency to the original text with accessibility for the millions of English speakers around the world. We have prioritized accuracy, clarity and literary quality with the goal of creating a translation suitable for public and private reading, evangelism, teaching, preaching, memorizing and liturgical use. We have also sought to preserve a measure of continuity with the long tradition of translating the Scriptures into English.

The complete NIV Bible was first published in 1978. It was a completely new translation made by over a hundred scholars working directly from the best available Hebrew, Aramaic and Greek texts. The translators came from the United States, Great Britain, Canada, Australia and New Zealand, giving the translation an international scope. They were from many denominations and churches — including Anglican, Assemblies of God, Baptist, Brethren, Christian Reformed, Church of Christ, Evangelical Covenant, Evangelical Free, Lutheran, Mennonite, Methodist, Nazarene, Presbyterian, Wesleyan and others. This breadth of denominational and theological perspective helped to safeguard the translation from sectarian bias. For these reasons, and by the grace of God, the NIV has gained a wide readership in all parts of the English-speaking world.

The work of translating the Bible is never finished. As good as they are, English translations must be regularly updated so that they will continue to communicate accurately the meaning of God's Word. Updates are needed in order to reflect the latest developments in our understanding of the biblical world and its languages and to keep pace with changes in English usage. Recognizing, then, that the NIV would retain its ability to communicate God's Word accurately only if it were regularly updated, the original translators established The Committee on Bible Translation (CBT). The committee is a self-perpetuating group of biblical scholars charged with keeping abreast of advances in biblical scholarship and changes in English and issuing periodic updates to the NIV. CBT is an independent, self-governing body and has sole responsibility for the NIV text. The committee mirrors the original group of translators in its diverse international and denominational makeup and in its unifying commitment to the Bible as God's inspired Word.

In obedience to its mandate, the committee has issued periodic updates to the NIV. An initial revision was released in 1984. A more thorough revision process was completed in 2005, resulting in the separately published Today's New International Version (TNIV). The updated NIV you now have in your hands builds on both the original NIV and the TNIV and represents the latest effort of the committee to articulate God's unchanging Word in the way the original authors might have said it had they been speaking in English to the global English-speaking audience today.

The first concern of the translators has continued to be the accuracy of the translation and its faithfulness to the intended meaning of the biblical writers. This has moved the translators to go beyond a formal word-for-word rendering of the original texts. Because thought patterns and syntax differ from language to language, accurate communication of the meaning of the biblical authors demands constant regard for varied contextual uses of words and idioms and for frequent modifications in sentence structures.

As an aid to the reader, sectional headings have been inserted. They are not to be regarded as part of the biblical text and are not intended for oral reading. It is the committee's hope that these headings may prove more helpful to the reader than the traditional chapter divisions, which were introduced long after the Bible was written.

For the Old Testament the standard Hebrew text, the Masoretic Text as published in the latest edition of *Biblia Hebraica,* has been used throughout. The Masoretic Text tradition contains marginal notations that offer variant readings. These have sometimes been followed instead of the text itself. Because such instances involve variants within the Masoretic tradition, they have not been indicated in the textual notes. In a few cases, words in the basic consonantal text have been divided differently than in the Masoretic Text. Such cases are usually indicated in the textual footnotes. The Dead Sea Scrolls contain biblical texts that represent an earlier stage of the transmission of the Hebrew text. They have been consulted, as have been the Samaritan Pentateuch and the ancient scribal traditions concerning deliberate textual changes. The translators also consulted the more important early versions—the Greek Septuagint, Aquila, Symmachus and Theodotion, the Latin Vulgate, the Syriac Peshitta, the Aramaic Targums and, for the Psalms, the *Juxta Hebraica* of Jerome. Readings from these versions, the Dead Sea Scrolls and the scribal traditions were occasionally followed where the Masoretic Text seemed doubtful and where accepted principles of textual

criticism showed that one or more of these textual witnesses appeared to provide the correct reading. In rare cases, the committee has emended the Hebrew text where it appears to have become corrupted at an even earlier stage of its transmission. These departures from the Masoretic Text are also indicated in the textual footnotes. Sometimes the vowel indicators (which are later additions to the basic consonantal text) found in the Masoretic Text did not, in the judgment of the committee, represent the correct vowels for the original text. Accordingly, some words have been read with a different set of vowels. These instances are usually not indicated in the footnotes.

The Greek text used in translating the New Testament is an eclectic one, based on the latest editions of the Nestle-Aland/United Bible Societies' Greek New Testament. The committee has made its choices among the variant readings in accordance with widely accepted principles of New Testament textual criticism. Footnotes call attention to places where uncertainty remains.

The New Testament authors, writing in Greek, often quote the Old Testament from its ancient Greek version, the Septuagint. This is one reason why some of the Old Testament quotations in the NIV New Testament are not identical to the corresponding passages in the NIV Old Testament. Such quotations in the New Testament are indicated with the footnote "(see Septuagint)."

Other footnotes in this version are of several kinds, most of which need no explanation. Those giving alternative translations begin with "Or" and generally introduce the alternative with the last word preceding it in the text, except when it is a single-word alternative. When poetry is quoted in a footnote, a slash mark indicates a line division.

It should be noted that references to diseases, minerals, flora and fauna, architectural details, clothing, jewelry, musical instruments and other articles cannot always be identified with precision. Also, linear measurements and measures of capacity can only be approximated (see the Table of Weights and Measures). Although *Selah,* used mainly in the Psalms, is probably a musical term, its meaning is uncertain. Since it may interrupt reading and distract the reader, this word has not been kept in the English text, but every occurrence has been signaled by a footnote.

One of the main reasons the task of Bible translation is never finished is the change in our own language, English. Although a basic core of the language remains relatively stable, many diverse and complex linguistic factors continue to bring about subtle shifts in the meanings and/or connotations of even old, well-established words and phrases. One of the shifts that creates particular challenges to writers and translators alike is the manner in which gender is presented. The original NIV (1978) was published in a time when "a man" would naturally be understood, in many contexts, to be referring to a person, whether male or female. But most English speakers today tend to hear a distinctly male connotation in this word. In recognition of this change in English, this edition of the NIV, along with almost all other recent English translations, substitutes other expressions when the original text intends to refer generically to men and women equally. Thus, for instance, the NIV (1984) rendering of 1 Corinthians 8:3, "But the man who loves God is known by God" becomes in this edition "But whoever loves God is known by God." On the other hand, "man" and "mankind," as ways of denoting the human race, are still widely used. This edition of the NIV therefore continues to use these words, along with other expressions, in this way.

A related shift in English creates a greater challenge for modern translations: the move away from using the third-person masculine singular pronouns — "he/him/his" — to refer to men and women equally. This usage does persist at a low level in some forms of English, and this revision therefore occasionally uses these pronouns in a generic sense. But the tendency, recognized in day-to-day usage and

confirmed by extensive research, is away from the generic use of "he," "him" and "his." In recognition of this shift in language and in an effort to translate into the "common" English that people are actually using, this revision of the NIV generally uses other constructions when the biblical text is plainly addressed to men and women equally. The reader will frequently encounter a "they," "them" or "their" to express a generic singular idea. Thus, for instance, Mark 8:36 reads: "What good is it for someone to gain the whole world, yet forfeit their soul?" This generic use of the "indefinite" or "singular" "they/them/their" has a venerable place in English idiom and has quickly become established as standard English, spoken and written, all over the world. Where an individual emphasis is deemed to be present, "anyone" or "everyone" or some other equivalent is generally used as the antecedent of such pronouns.

Sometimes the chapter and/or verse numbering in English translations of the Old Testament differs from that found in published Hebrew texts. This is particularly the case in the Psalms, where the traditional titles are often included in the Hebrew verse numbering. Such differences are indicated in the footnotes at the bottom of the page. In the New Testament, verse numbers that marked off portions of the traditional English text not supported by the best Greek manuscripts now appear in brackets, with a footnote indicating the text that has been omitted (see, for example, Matthew 17:[21]).

Mark 16:9 – 20 and John 7:53 – 8:11, although long accorded virtually equal status with the rest of the Gospels in which they stand, have a very questionable — and confused — standing in the textual history of the New Testament, as noted in the bracketed annotations with which they are set off. A different typeface has been chosen for these passages to indicate even more clearly their uncertain status.

Basic formatting of the text, such as lining the poetry, paragraphing (both prose and poetry), setting up of (administrative-like) lists, indenting letters and lengthy prayers within narratives and the insertion of sectional headings, has been the work of the committee. However, the choice between single-column and double-column formats has been left to the publishers. Also the issuing of "red-letter" editions is a publisher's choice — one the committee does not endorse.

The committee has again been reminded that every human effort is flawed — including this revision of the NIV. We trust, however, that many will find in it an improved representation of the Word of God, through which they hear his call to faith in our Lord Jesus Christ and to service in his kingdom. We offer this version of the Bible to him in whose name and for whose glory it has been made.

The Committee on Bible Translation
September 2010

OLD
TESTAMENT

GENESIS

BOOK OUTLINE

The word Genesis means "beginnings." The book of Genesis is about many beginnings — the beginning of the universe, the beginning of man and woman, the beginning of human sin, the beginning of God's promises and plans for salvation, and the beginning of a special relationship between Abraham and God. Genesis tells us about God's special people and his plan for their lives. Some of these people are: Adam and Eve, Noah, Abraham, Isaac, Jacob, and Joseph and his brothers.

Genesis is the first book in the Pentateuch — a word that means five books, and includes the first five books of the Bible. These books are also known as the books of the law because they contain God's instructions and laws for the people of Israel. Genesis is included because it tells the history of how Israel became God's special people. These five books were most likely written by Moses, except for the last chapter of Deuteronomy which tells about Moses' death.

The Beginning

In the beginning God created the heavens and the earth. ²Now the earth was formless and empty, darkness was over the surface of the deep, and the Spirit of God was hovering over the waters.

³And God said, "Let there be light," and there was light. ⁴God saw that the light was good, and he separated the light from the darkness. ⁵God called the light "day," and the darkness he called "night." And there was evening, and there was morning—the first day.

⁶And God said, "Let there be a vault between the waters to separate water from water." ⁷So God made the vault and separated the water under the vault from the water above it. And it was so. ⁸God called the vault "sky." And there was evening, and there was morning—the second day.

⁹And God said, "Let the water under the sky be gathered to one place, and let dry ground appear." And it was so. ¹⁰God called the dry ground "land," and the gathered waters he called "seas." And God saw that it was good.

¹¹Then God said, "Let the land produce vegetation: seed-bearing plants and trees on the land that bear fruit with seed in it, according to their various kinds." And it was so. ¹²The land produced vegetation: plants bearing seed according to their kinds and trees bearing fruit with seed in it according to their kinds. And God saw that it was good. ¹³And there was evening, and there was morning—the third day.

¹⁴And God said, "Let there be lights in the vault of the sky to separate the day from the night, and let them serve as signs to mark sacred times, and days and years, ¹⁵and let them be lights in the vault of the sky to give light on the earth." And it was so. ¹⁶God made two great lights—the greater light to govern the day and the lesser light to govern the night.

He also made the stars. ¹⁷God set them in the vault of the sky to give light on the earth, ¹⁸to govern the day and the night, and to separate light from darkness. And God saw that it was good. ¹⁹And there was evening, and there was morning—the fourth day.

²⁰And God said, "Let the water teem with living creatures, and let birds

---

Genesis 1:1—2:3

God created the world.

Some skeptics point to Genesis and ask how God invented life—or doubt he exists at all. Science class might leave you wondering how the Bible stacks up against the world's brightest minds and most up-to-date discoveries. But these early chapters of Genesis aren't just about the "how" of creation. Most importantly, they teach you about the "who." It was God who acted with matchless power to create the universe, putting something where there was nothing. The skies announce the Lord's existence without speaking a word, and his amazing feat of creation shouts his mighty majesty (see Psalm 19:1–2). The Bible states creation gives all human beings everywhere enough information to know that God exists—and that we can look at what he made and perceive his power. People might fight the truth of God's existence, but deep in our hearts we understand he's real (see Romans 1:20).

Think: Why does it matter to you that God created the world?

ROCK SOLID truths

fly above the earth across the vault of the sky." ²¹So God created the great creatures of the sea and every living thing with which the water teems and that moves about in it, according to their kinds, and every winged bird according to its kind. And God saw that it was good. ²²God blessed them and said, "Be fruitful and increase in number and fill the water in the seas, and let the birds increase on the earth." ²³And there was evening, and there was morning—the fifth day.

²⁴And God said, "Let the land produce living creatures according to their kinds: the livestock, the creatures that move along the ground, and the wild animals, each according to its kind." And it was so. ²⁵God made the wild animals according to their kinds, the livestock according to their kinds, and all the creatures that move along the ground according to their kinds. And God saw that it was good.

²⁶Then God said, "Let us make mankind in our image, in our likeness, so that they may rule over the fish in the sea and the birds in the sky, over the livestock and all the wild animals,ᵃ and over all the creatures that move along the ground."

²⁷So God created mankind in his own image,
in the image of God he created them;
male and female he created them.

²⁸God blessed them and said to them, "Be fruitful and increase in number; fill the earth and subdue it. Rule over the fish in the sea and the birds in the sky and over every living creature that moves on the ground."

²⁹Then God said, "I give you every seed-bearing plant on the face of the whole earth and every tree that has fruit with seed in it. They will be yours for food. ³⁰And to all the beasts of the earth and all the birds in the sky and all the creatures that move

ROCK SOLID *promises*

"God created mankind in his own image."
Genesis 1:27

No matter what you look like on the outside, you're wrapped in God's image—his beauty, power, and intelligence.

along the ground—everything that has the breath of life in it—I give every green plant for food." And it was so.

³¹God saw all that he had made, and it was very good. And there was evening, and there was morning—the sixth day.

2 Thus the heavens and the earth were completed in all their vast array.

²By the seventh day God had finished the work he had been doing; so on the seventh day he rested from all his work. ³Then God blessed the seventh day and made it holy, because on it he rested from all the work of creating that he had done.

Adam and Eve

⁴This is the account of the heavens and the earth when they were created, when the LORD God made the earth and the heavens.

⁵Now no shrub had yet appeared on the earthᵇ and no plant had yet sprung up, for the LORD God had not sent rain on the earth and there was no one to work the ground, ⁶but streamsᶜ came up from

---

ᵃ *26* Probable reading of the original Hebrew text (see Syriac); Masoretic Text *the earth*
ᵇ *5* Or *land*; also in verse 6   ᶜ *6* Or *mist*

the earth and watered the whole surface of the ground. [7]Then the LORD God formed a man[a] from the dust of the ground and breathed into his nostrils the breath of life, and the man became a living being.

[8]Now the LORD God had planted a garden in the east, in Eden; and there he put the man he had formed. [9]The LORD God made all kinds of trees grow out of the ground—trees that were pleasing to the eye and good for food. In the middle of the garden were the tree of life and the tree of the knowledge of good and evil.

[10]A river watering the garden flowed from Eden; from there it was separated into four headwaters. [11]The name of the first is the Pishon; it winds through the entire land of Havilah, where there is gold. [12](The gold of that land is good; aromatic resin[b] and onyx are also there.) [13]The name of the second river is the Gihon; it winds through the entire land of Cush.[c] [14]The name of the third river is the Tigris; it runs along the east side of Ashur. And the fourth river is the Euphrates.

[15]The LORD God took the man and put him in the Garden of Eden to work it and take care of it. [16]And the LORD God commanded the man, "You are free to eat from any tree in the garden; [17]but you must not eat from the tree of the knowledge of good and evil, for when you eat from it you will certainly die."

[18]The LORD God said, "It is not good for the man to be alone. I will make a helper suitable for him."

[19]Now the LORD God had formed out of the ground all the wild animals and all the birds in the sky. He brought them to the man to see what he would name them; and whatever the man called each living creature, that was its name. [20]So the man gave names to all the livestock, the birds in the sky and all the wild animals.

But for Adam[d] no suitable helper was found. [21]So the LORD God caused the man to fall into a deep sleep; and while he was sleeping, he took one of the man's ribs[e] and then closed up the place with flesh. [22]Then the LORD God made a woman from the rib[f] he had taken out of the man, and he brought her to the man.

[23]The man said,

"This is now bone of my bones
    and flesh of my flesh;
she shall be called 'woman,'
    for she was taken out of man."

[24]That is why a man leaves his father and mother and is united to his wife, and they become one flesh.

[25]Adam and his wife were both naked, and they felt no shame.

The Fall

3 Now the serpent was more crafty than any of the wild animals the LORD God had made. He said to the woman, "Did God really say, 'You must not eat from any tree in the garden'?"

[2]The woman said to the serpent, "We may eat fruit from the trees in the garden, [3]but God did say, 'You must not eat fruit from the tree that is in the middle of the garden, and you must not touch it, or you will die.'"

[4]"You will not certainly die," the serpent said to the woman. [5]"For God knows that when you eat from it your eyes will be opened, and you will be like God, knowing good and evil."

[6]When the woman saw that the fruit of the tree was good for food and pleasing to the eye, and also desirable for gaining wisdom, she took some and ate it. She also gave some to her husband, who was with her, and he ate it. [7]Then the eyes of both of them were opened, and they realized they were naked; so they sewed fig leaves together and made coverings for themselves.

[8]Then the man and his wife heard the sound of the LORD God as he was walking in the garden in the cool of the day, and they hid from the LORD God among the trees of the garden. [9]But the LORD God called to the man, "Where are you?"

---

[a] 7 The Hebrew for *man (adam)* sounds like and may be related to the Hebrew for *ground (adamah)*; it is also the name *Adam* (see verse 20).   [b] 12 Or *good; pearls*
[c] 13 Possibly southeast Mesopotamia
[d] 20 Or *the man*   [e] 21 Or *took part of the man's side*   [f] 22 Or *part*

¹⁰He answered, "I heard you in the garden, and I was afraid because I was naked; so I hid."

¹¹And he said, "Who told you that you were naked? Have you eaten from the tree that I commanded you not to eat from?"

¹²The man said, "The woman you put here with me—she gave me some fruit from the tree, and I ate it."

¹³Then the LORD God said to the woman, "What is this you have done?"

The woman said, "The serpent deceived me, and I ate."

¹⁴So the LORD God said to the serpent, "Because you have done this,

"Cursed are you above all livestock
   and all wild animals!
You will crawl on your belly
   and you will eat dust
   all the days of your life.
¹⁵And I will put enmity
   between you and the woman,
   and between your offspring[a] and
      hers;

he will crush[b] your head,
   and you will strike his heel."

¹⁶To the woman he said,

"I will make your pains in
      childbearing very severe;
   with painful labor you will give
      birth to children.
Your desire will be for your husband,
   and he will rule over you."

¹⁷To Adam he said, "Because you listened to your wife and ate fruit from the tree about which I commanded you, 'You must not eat from it,'

"Cursed is the ground because of you;
   through painful toil you will eat
      food from it
   all the days of your life.
¹⁸It will produce thorns and thistles for
      you,
   and you will eat the plants of the
      field.

a 15 Or *seed*   *b 15* Or *strike*

ROCK SOLID *principles*

Genesis 3:11–14

Don't shift the blame.

"Everyone procrastinates," Matti told herself. "There's no reason to get started when no one else will." But the classmates assigned to work with Matti on a group project had no idea of her plans—or lack of them. While Matti wasted several days streaming videos and polishing her online profile, the other group members couldn't move ahead with their work. Before they could do their parts, Matti had to complete her part. When Matti finally wrapped up the day before the assignment was due, no one else had time to finish. The group failed. And when Matti's partners confronted her, she actually spun the situation around and blamed *them*. "I knew you wouldn't do your parts," she scoffed. "This is all your fault."

Adam and Eve blamed everyone but themselves for breaking God's command not to eat the fruit they saw dangling from "the tree of the knowledge of good and evil" (Genesis 2:17). When a situation goes bad, you don't have to take all the blame. But you need to own up to whatever you did wrong.

¹⁹By the sweat of your brow
    you will eat your food
until you return to the ground,
    since from it you were taken;
for dust you are
    and to dust you will return."

²⁰Adam*ᵃ* named his wife Eve,*ᵇ* because she would become the mother of all the living.

²¹The Lord God made garments of skin for Adam and his wife and clothed them. ²²And the Lord God said, "The man has now become like one of us, knowing good and evil. He must not be allowed to reach out his hand and take also from the tree of life and eat, and live forever." ²³So the Lord God banished him from the Garden of Eden to work the ground from which he had been taken. ²⁴After he drove the man out, he placed on the east side*ᶜ* of the Garden of Eden cherubim and a flaming sword flashing back and forth to guard the way to the tree of life.

Cain and Abel

4 Adam*ᵃ* made love to his wife Eve, and she became pregnant and gave birth to Cain.*ᵈ* She said, "With the help of the Lord I have brought forth*ᵉ* a man." ²Later she gave birth to his brother Abel.

Now Abel kept flocks, and Cain worked the soil. ³In the course of time Cain brought some of the fruits of the soil as an offering to the Lord. ⁴And Abel also brought an offering—fat portions from some of the firstborn of his flock. The Lord looked with favor on Abel and his offering, ⁵but on Cain and his offering he did not look with favor. So Cain was very angry, and his face was downcast.

⁶Then the Lord said to Cain, "Why are you angry? Why is your face downcast? ⁷If you do what is right, will you not be accepted? But if you do not do what is right, sin is crouching at your door; it desires to have you, but you must rule over it."

⁸Now Cain said to his brother Abel, "Let's go out to the field."*ᶠ* While they were in the field, Cain attacked his brother Abel and killed him.

⁹Then the Lord said to Cain, "Where is your brother Abel?"

"I don't know," he replied. "Am I my brother's keeper?"

¹⁰The Lord said, "What have you done? Listen! Your brother's blood cries out to me from the ground. ¹¹Now you are under a curse and driven from the ground, which opened its mouth to receive your brother's blood from your hand. ¹²When you work the ground, it will no longer yield its crops for you. You will be a restless wanderer on the earth."

¹³Cain said to the Lord, "My punishment is more than I can bear. ¹⁴Today you are driving me from the land, and I will be hidden from your presence; I will be a restless wanderer on the earth, and whoever finds me will kill me."

¹⁵But the Lord said to him, "Not so*ᵍ*; anyone who kills Cain will suffer vengeance seven times over." Then the Lord put a mark on Cain so that no one who found him would kill him. ¹⁶So Cain went out from the Lord's presence and lived in the land of Nod,*ᵇ* east of Eden.

¹⁷Cain made love to his wife, and she became pregnant and gave birth to Enoch. Cain was then building a city, and he named it after his son Enoch. ¹⁸To Enoch was born Irad, and Irad was the father of Mehujael, and Mehujael was the father of Methushael, and Methushael was the father of Lamech.

¹⁹Lamech married two women, one named Adah and the other Zillah. ²⁰Adah gave birth to Jabal; he was the father of those who live in tents and raise livestock. ²¹His brother's name was Jubal; he was the father of all who play stringed instruments and pipes. ²²Zillah also had a son, Tubal-Cain, who forged all kinds of tools out of*ⁱ*

ᵃ 20,1 Or *The man*   *ᵇ 20 Eve* probably means *living.*   *ᶜ 24* Or *placed in front*   *ᵈ 1 Cain* sounds like the Hebrew for *brought forth* or *acquired.*   *ᵉ 1* Or *have acquired*
ᶠ 8 Samaritan Pentateuch, Septuagint, Vulgate and Syriac; Masoretic Text does not have *"Let's go out to the field."*   *ᵍ 15* Septuagint, Vulgate and Syriac; Hebrew *Very well*   *ᵇ 16 Nod* means *wandering* (see verses 12 and 14).
ⁱ 22 Or *who instructed all who work in*

bronze and iron. Tubal-Cain's sister was Naamah.

²³Lamech said to his wives,

"Adah and Zillah, listen to me;
　wives of Lamech, hear my words.
I have killed a man for wounding me,
　a young man for injuring me.
²⁴If Cain is avenged seven times,
　then Lamech seventy-seven times."

²⁵Adam made love to his wife again, and she gave birth to a son and named him Seth,ᵃ saying, "God has granted me another child in place of Abel, since Cain killed him." ²⁶Seth also had a son, and he named him Enosh.

At that time people began to call onᵇ the name of the Lᴏʀᴅ.

From Adam to Noah

5 This is the written account of Adam's family line.

When God created mankind, he made them in the likeness of God. ²He created them male and female and blessed them. And he named them "Mankind"ᶜ when they were created.

³When Adam had lived 130 years, he had a son in his own likeness, in his own image; and he named him Seth. ⁴After Seth was born, Adam lived 800 years and had other sons and daughters. ⁵Altogether, Adam lived a total of 930 years, and then he died.

⁶When Seth had lived 105 years, he became the fatherᵈ of Enosh. ⁷After he became the father of Enosh, Seth lived 807 years and had other sons and daughters. ⁸Altogether, Seth lived a total of 912 years, and then he died.

⁹When Enosh had lived 90 years, he became the father of Kenan. ¹⁰After he became the father of Kenan, Enosh lived 815 years and had other sons and daughters. ¹¹Altogether, Enosh lived a total of 905 years, and then he died.

¹²When Kenan had lived 70 years, he became the father of Mahalalel. ¹³After he became the father of Mahalalel, Kenan lived 840 years and had other sons

and daughters. ¹⁴Altogether, Kenan lived a total of 910 years, and then he died.

¹⁵When Mahalalel had lived 65 years, he became the father of Jared. ¹⁶After he became the father of Jared, Mahalalel lived 830 years and had other sons and daughters. ¹⁷Altogether, Mahalalel lived a total of 895 years, and then he died.

¹⁸When Jared had lived 162 years, he became the father of Enoch. ¹⁹After he became the father of Enoch, Jared lived 800 years and had other sons and daughters. ²⁰Altogether, Jared lived a total of 962 years, and then he died.

²¹When Enoch had lived 65 years, he became the father of Methuselah. ²²After he became the father of Methuselah, Enoch walked faithfully with God 300 years and had other sons and daughters. ²³Altogether, Enoch lived a total of 365 years. ²⁴Enoch walked faithfully with God; then he was no more, because God took him away.

²⁵When Methuselah had lived 187 years, he became the father of Lamech. ²⁶After he became the father of Lamech, Methuselah lived 782 years and had other sons and daughters. ²⁷Altogether, Methuselah lived a total of 969 years, and then he died.

²⁸When Lamech had lived 182 years, he had a son. ²⁹He named him Noahᵉ and said, "He will comfort us in the labor and painful toil of our hands caused by the ground the Lᴏʀᴅ has cursed." ³⁰After Noah was born, Lamech lived 595 years and had other sons and daughters. ³¹Altogether, Lamech lived a total of 777 years, and then he died.

³²After Noah was 500 years old, he became the father of Shem, Ham and Japheth.

Wickedness in the World

6 When human beings began to increase in number on the earth and daughters were born to them, ²the

---

ᵃ 25 Seth probably means granted.　ᵇ 26 Or to proclaim　ᶜ 2 Hebrew adam　ᵈ 6 Father may mean ancestor; also in verses 7-26.
ᵉ 29 Noah sounds like the Hebrew for comfort.

sons of God saw that the daughters of humans were beautiful, and they married any of them they chose. ³Then the LORD said, "My Spirit will not contend with*ᵃ* humans forever, for they are mortal*ᵇ*; their days will be a hundred and twenty years."

⁴The Nephilim were on the earth in those days—and also afterward—when the sons of God went to the daughters of humans and had children by them. They were the heroes of old, men of renown.

⁵The LORD saw how great the wickedness of the human race had become on the earth, and that every inclination of the thoughts of the human heart was only evil all the time. ⁶The LORD regretted that he had made human beings on the earth, and his heart was deeply troubled. ⁷So the LORD said, "I will wipe from the face of the earth the human race I have created—and with them the animals, the birds and the creatures that move along the ground—for I regret that I have made them." ⁸But Noah found favor in the eyes of the LORD.

Noah and the Flood

⁹This is the account of Noah and his family.

Noah was a righteous man, blameless among the people of his time, and he walked faithfully with God. ¹⁰Noah had three sons: Shem, Ham and Japheth.

¹¹Now the earth was corrupt in God's sight and was full of violence. ¹²God saw how corrupt the earth had become, for all the people on earth had corrupted their ways. ¹³So God said to Noah, "I am going to put an end to all people, for the earth is filled with violence because of them. I am surely going to destroy both them and the earth. ¹⁴So make yourself an ark of cypress*ᶜ* wood; make rooms in it and coat it with pitch inside and out. ¹⁵This is how you are to build it: The ark is to be three hundred cubits long, fifty cubits wide and thirty cubits high.*ᵈ* ¹⁶Make a roof for it, leaving below the roof an opening one cubit*ᵉ* high all around.*ᶠ* Put a door in the side of the ark and make lower, middle and upper decks. ¹⁷I am going to bring

floodwaters on the earth to destroy all life under the heavens, every creature that has the breath of life in it. Everything on earth will perish. ¹⁸But I will establish my covenant with you, and you will enter the ark—you and your sons and your wife and your sons' wives with you. ¹⁹You are to bring into the ark two of all living creatures, male and female, to keep them alive with you. ²⁰Two of every kind of bird, of every kind of animal and of every kind of creature that moves along the ground will come to you to be kept alive. ²¹You are to take every kind of food that is to be eaten and store it away as food for you and for them."

²²Noah did everything just as God commanded him.

7 The LORD then said to Noah, "Go into the ark, you and your whole family, because I have found you righteous in this generation. ²Take with you seven pairs of every kind of clean animal, a male and its mate, and one pair of every kind of unclean animal, a male and its mate, ³and also seven pairs of every kind of bird, male and female, to keep their various kinds alive throughout the earth. ⁴Seven days from now I will send rain on the earth for forty days and forty nights, and I will wipe from the face of the earth every living creature I have made."

⁵And Noah did all that the LORD commanded him.

⁶Noah was six hundred years old when the floodwaters came on the earth. ⁷And Noah and his sons and his wife and his sons' wives entered the ark to escape the waters of the flood. ⁸Pairs of clean and unclean animals, of birds and of all creatures that move along the ground, ⁹male and female, came to Noah and entered the ark, as God had commanded Noah. ¹⁰And

---

ᵃ 3 Or *My spirit will not remain in*
ᵇ 3 Or *corrupt*   *ᶜ 14* The meaning of the Hebrew for this word is uncertain.   *ᵈ 15* That is, about 450 feet long, 75 feet wide and 45 feet high or about 135 meters long, 23 meters wide and 14 meters high   *ᵉ 16* That is, about 18 inches or about 45 centimeters   *ᶠ 16* The meaning of the Hebrew for this clause is uncertain.

after the seven days the floodwaters came on the earth.

[11] In the six hundredth year of Noah's life, on the seventeenth day of the second month—on that day all the springs of the great deep burst forth, and the floodgates of the heavens were opened. [12] And rain fell on the earth forty days and forty nights.

[13] On that very day Noah and his sons, Shem, Ham and Japheth, together with his wife and the wives of his three sons, entered the ark. [14] They had with them every wild animal according to its kind, all livestock according to their kinds, every creature that moves along the ground according to its kind and every bird according to its kind,

everything with wings. [15] Pairs of all creatures that have the breath of life in them came to Noah and entered the ark. [16] The animals going in were male and female of every living thing, as God had commanded Noah. Then the LORD shut him in.

[17] For forty days the flood kept coming on the earth, and as the waters increased they lifted the ark high above the earth. [18] The waters rose and increased greatly on the earth, and the ark floated on the surface of the water. [19] They rose greatly on the earth, and all the high mountains under the entire heavens were covered. [20] The waters rose and covered the mountains to a depth of more than fifteen

---

Genesis 6:1–22

Noah obeyed God when no one else did.

God looked at Noah's neighbors and noticed they were more than a little bad. He was horrified to look at man and see that "every inclination of the thoughts of the human heart was only evil all the time" (Genesis 6:5). The human race had become so corrupt and violent that the Lord ached that he had ever created people. Everyone was so evil he determined to wipe out humankind with a flood.

Amid all of this badness, Noah stood out as the one good guy. He was "blameless among the people of his time, and he walked faithfully with God" (Genesis 6:9). God warned Noah he was going to flood the earth, instructing him to build an enormous boat and pack it with animals. Noah couldn't just sit still and wait for the Lord to rescue him. He had to choose to obey God even as his neighbors laughed and mocked the guy building a ship far from any sea. Long before a single raindrop fell, Noah trusted God and stayed on task. Scripture says he and his family survived 150 days on the ark and emerged to restart the human race.

The New Testament highlights Noah's faithfulness in the days of great evil, listing him in the great "Hall of Faith" in Hebrews 11. It says, "By faith Noah, when warned about things not yet seen, in holy fear built an ark to save his family" (Hebrews 11:7). When the crowds rebelled, Noah chose to do right.

You can find Noah in Genesis 5—9; Matthew 24:27–28; 1 Peter 3:4; and 2 Peter 2:5.

UNSHAKEN *people*

cubits.[a],[b] [21]Every living thing that moved on land perished—birds, livestock, wild animals, all the creatures that swarm over the earth, and all mankind. [22]Everything on dry land that had the breath of life in its nostrils died. [23]Every living thing on the face of the earth was wiped out; people and animals and the creatures that move along the ground and the birds were wiped from the earth. Only Noah was left, and those with him in the ark.

[24]The waters flooded the earth for a hundred and fifty days.

Genesis 7:1–24

If you do the crime, you'll do the time.

When Adam and Eve ate the forbidden fruit in the Garden of Eden, there was a sudden and serious consequence. The Lord kicked them out of paradise forever (see Genesis 3:23–24). When Cain murdered his brother Abel, he was sentenced to wander the earth until the day he died (see Genesis 4:10–14). As time went on, the sinfulness of humanity reached the point that God looked at man and saw that "every inclination of the thoughts of the human heart was only evil all the time" (Genesis 6:5). The Lord was so pained by the sins of humankind that he decided to wipe out the whole race with a flood. Of all the human beings on earth, only Noah and his family were spared as they took refuge in the ark, an oversized boat. These consequences all demonstrate the New Testament truth that "the wages of sin is death" (Romans 6:23).

Think: Do you believe that God punishes sin? When and how?

ROCK SOLID truths

8 But God remembered Noah and all the wild animals and the livestock that were with him in the ark, and he sent a wind over the earth, and the waters receded. [2]Now the springs of the deep and the floodgates of the heavens had been closed, and the rain had stopped falling from the sky. [3]The water receded steadily from the earth. At the end of the hundred and fifty days the water had gone down, [4]and on the seventeenth day of the seventh month the ark came to rest on the mountains of Ararat. [5]The waters continued to recede until the tenth month, and on the first day of the tenth month the tops of the mountains became visible.

[6]After forty days Noah opened a window he had made in the ark [7]and sent out a raven, and it kept flying back and forth until the water had dried up from the earth. [8]Then he sent out a dove to see if the water had receded from the surface of the ground. [9]But the dove could find nowhere to perch because there was water over all the surface of the earth; so it returned to Noah in the ark. He reached out his hand and took the dove and brought it back to himself in the ark. [10]He waited seven more days and again sent out the dove from the ark. [11]When the dove returned to him in the evening, there in its beak was a freshly plucked olive leaf! Then Noah knew that the water had receded from the earth. [12]He waited seven more days and sent the dove out again, but this time it did not return to him.

[13]By the first day of the first month of Noah's six hundred and first year, the water had dried up from the earth. Noah then removed the covering from the ark and saw that the surface of the ground was dry. [14]By the twenty-seventh day of the second month the earth was completely dry.

[15]Then God said to Noah, [16]"Come out of the ark, you and your wife and your sons and their wives. [17]Bring out every kind of living creature that is with you—the birds, the animals, and all the creatures

---

[a] 20 That is, about 23 feet or about 6.8 meters
[b] 20 Or *rose more than fifteen cubits, and the mountains were covered*

that move along the ground—so they can multiply on the earth and be fruitful and increase in number on it."

¹⁸ So Noah came out, together with his sons and his wife and his sons' wives. ¹⁹ All the animals and all the creatures that move along the ground and all the birds—everything that moves on land—came out of the ark, one kind after another.

²⁰ Then Noah built an altar to the Lord and, taking some of all the clean animals and clean birds, he sacrificed burnt offerings on it. ²¹ The Lord smelled the pleasing aroma and said in his heart: "Never again will I curse the ground because of humans, even though*a* every inclination of the human heart is evil from childhood. And never again will I destroy all living creatures, as I have done.

²² "As long as the earth endures,
seedtime and harvest,
cold and heat,
summer and winter,
day and night
will never cease."

God's Covenant With Noah

9 Then God blessed Noah and his sons, saying to them, "Be fruitful and increase in number and fill the earth. ² The fear and dread of you will fall on all the beasts of the earth, and on all the birds in the sky, on every creature that moves along the ground, and on all the fish in the sea; they are given into your hands. ³ Everything that lives and moves about will be food for you. Just as I gave you the green plants, I now give you everything.

⁴ "But you must not eat meat that has its lifeblood still in it. ⁵ And for your lifeblood I will surely demand an accounting. I will demand an accounting from every animal. And from each human being, too, I will demand an accounting for the life of another human being.

⁶ "Whoever sheds human blood,
by humans shall their blood be
shed;
for in the image of God
has God made mankind.

⁷ As for you, be fruitful and increase in number; multiply on the earth and increase upon it."

⁸ Then God said to Noah and to his sons with him: ⁹ "I now establish my covenant with you and with your descendants after you ¹⁰ and with every living creature that was with you—the birds, the livestock and all the wild animals, all those that came out of the ark with you—every living creature on earth. ¹¹ I establish my covenant with you: Never again will all life be destroyed by the waters of a flood; never again will there be a flood to destroy the earth."

¹² And God said, "This is the sign of the covenant I am making between me and you and every living creature with you, a covenant for all generations to come: ¹³ I have set my rainbow in the clouds, and it will be the sign of the covenant between me and the earth. ¹⁴ Whenever I bring clouds over the earth and the rainbow appears in the clouds, ¹⁵ I will remember my covenant between me and you and all living creatures of every kind. Never again will the waters become a flood to destroy all life. ¹⁶ Whenever the rainbow appears in the clouds, I will see it and remember the everlasting covenant between God and all living creatures of every kind on the earth."

¹⁷ So God said to Noah, "This is the sign of the covenant I have established between me and all life on the earth."

The Sons of Noah

¹⁸ The sons of Noah who came out of the ark were Shem, Ham and Japheth. (Ham was the father of Canaan.) ¹⁹ These were the three sons of Noah, and from them came the people who were scattered over the whole earth.

²⁰ Noah, a man of the soil, proceeded*b* to plant a vineyard. ²¹ When he drank some of its wine, he became drunk and lay uncovered inside his tent. ²² Ham, the father of Canaan, saw his father naked and told his two brothers outside. ²³ But Shem and Japheth took a garment and laid it across their shoulders; then they walked

a 21 Or *humans, for*   *b 20* Or *soil, was the first*

11

in backward and covered their father's naked body. Their faces were turned the other way so that they would not see their father naked.

²⁴When Noah awoke from his wine and found out what his youngest son had done to him, ²⁵he said,

"Cursed be Canaan!
    The lowest of slaves
    will he be to his brothers."

²⁶He also said,

"Praise be to the Lord, the God of
        Shem!
    May Canaan be the slave of Shem.
²⁷May God extend Japheth's*ᵃ territory;
    may Japheth live in the tents of
        Shem,
    and may Canaan be the slave of
        Japheth."

²⁸After the flood Noah lived 350 years. ²⁹Noah lived a total of 950 years, and then he died.

The Table of Nations

10 This is the account of Shem, Ham and Japheth, Noah's sons, who themselves had sons after the flood.

The Japhethites

²The sonsᵇ of Japheth:
    Gomer, Magog, Madai, Javan, Tubal, Meshek and Tiras.
³The sons of Gomer:
    Ashkenaz, Riphath and Togarmah.
⁴The sons of Javan:
    Elishah, Tarshish, the Kittites and the Rodanites.ᶜ ⁵(From these the maritime peoples spread out into their territories by their clans within their nations, each with its own language.)

The Hamites

⁶The sons of Ham:
    Cush, Egypt, Put and Canaan.
⁷The sons of Cush:
    Seba, Havilah, Sabtah, Raamah and Sabteka.

The sons of Raamah:
    Sheba and Dedan.

⁸Cush was the fatherᵈ of Nimrod, who became a mighty warrior on the earth. ⁹He was a mighty hunter before the Lord; that is why it is said, "Like Nimrod, a mighty hunter before the Lord." ¹⁰The first centers of his kingdom were Babylon, Uruk, Akkad and Kalneh, inᵉ Shinar.ᶠ ¹¹From that land he went to Assyria, where he built Nineveh, Rehoboth Ir,ᵍ Calah ¹²and Resen, which is between Nineveh and Calah—which is the great city.

¹³Egypt was the father of
    the Ludites, Anamites, Lehabites, Naphtuhites, ¹⁴Pathrusites, Kasluhites (from whom the Philistines came) and Caphtorites.
¹⁵Canaan was the father of
    Sidon his firstborn,ᵇ and of the Hittites, ¹⁶Jebusites, Amorites, Girgashites, ¹⁷Hivites, Arkites, Sinites, ¹⁸Arvadites, Zemarites and Hamathites.

Later the Canaanite clans scattered ¹⁹and the borders of Canaan reached from Sidon toward Gerar as far as Gaza, and then toward Sodom, Gomorrah, Admah and Zeboyim, as far as Lasha.

²⁰These are the sons of Ham by their clans and languages, in their territories and nations.

The Semites

²¹Sons were also born to Shem, whose older brother wasⁱ Japheth; Shem was the ancestor of all the sons of Eber.

ᵃ 27 *Japheth* sounds like the Hebrew for *extend*.
ᵇ 2 *Sons* may mean *descendants* or *successors* or *nations*; also in verses 3, 4, 6, 7, 20-23, 29 and 31.   ᶜ 4 Some manuscripts of the Masoretic Text and Samaritan Pentateuch (see also Septuagint and 1 Chron. 1:7); most manuscripts of the Masoretic Text *Dodanites*   ᵈ 8 *Father* may mean *ancestor* or *predecessor* or *founder*; also in verses 13, 15, 24 and 26.   ᵉ 10 Or *Uruk and Akkad—all of them in*   ᶠ 10 That is, Babylonia   ᵍ 11 Or *Nineveh with its city squares*   ᵇ 15 Or *of the Sidonians, the foremost*   ⁱ 21 Or *Shem, the older brother of*

²²The sons of Shem:
   Elam, Ashur, Arphaxad, Lud and
   Aram.
²³The sons of Aram:
   Uz, Hul, Gether and Meshek.*
²⁴Arphaxad was the father of* Shelah,
   and Shelah the father of Eber.
²⁵Two sons were born to Eber:
   One was named Peleg,* because in
   his time the earth was divided; his
   brother was named Joktan.
²⁶Joktan was the father of
   Almodad, Sheleph, Hazarmaveth,
   Jerah, ²⁷Hadoram, Uzal, Diklah,
   ²⁸Obal, Abimael, Sheba, ²⁹Ophir,
   Havilah and Jobab. All these were
   sons of Joktan.

³⁰The region where they lived stretched
from Mesha toward Sephar, in the eastern
hill country.
   ³¹These are the sons of Shem by their
clans and languages, in their territories
and nations.

³²These are the clans of Noah's sons,
according to their lines of descent, within their nations. From these the nations
spread out over the earth after the flood.

The Tower of Babel

11 Now the whole world had one
language and a common speech.
²As people moved eastward,*
they found a plain in Shinar* and settled
there.
   ³They said to each other, "Come, let's
make bricks and bake them thoroughly."
They used brick instead of stone, and tar
for mortar. ⁴Then they said, "Come, let
us build ourselves a city, with a tower that
reaches to the heavens, so that we may
make a name for ourselves; otherwise we
will be scattered over the face of the whole
earth."
   ⁵But the LORD came down to see the
city and the tower the people were building. ⁶The LORD said, "If as one people
speaking the same language they have
begun to do this, then nothing they plan
to do will be impossible for them. ⁷Come,
let us go down and confuse their language
so they will not understand each other."

⁸So the LORD scattered them from
there over all the earth, and they stopped
building the city. ⁹That is why it was
called Babel*—because there the LORD
confused the language of the whole world.
From there the LORD scattered them over
the face of the whole earth.

* 23 See Septuagint and 1 Chron. 1:17; Hebrew
Mash.   * 24 Hebrew; Septuagint *father of
Cainan, and Cainan was the father of*
* 25 *Peleg* means *division.*   * 2 Or *from the
east*; or *in the east*   * 2 That is, Babylonia
* 9 That is, Babylon; *Babel* sounds like the
Hebrew for *confused.*

Genesis 11:1–9

Pride triggers pain.

The people at Babel had a plan.
Using baked brick instead of stone
and tar in place of the usual mortar, they would build a tower that
stretched "to the heavens" (Genesis 11:4). But the people of Babel
were undertaking more than a
technologically innovative building project. They plotted to make
a name for themselves, looking
for a way to firmly establish their
prominence and power. God noticed their scheme and saw it for
what it was—an uprising against
him. So he made it more difficult
for the human race to band together. He scrambled human language,
then scattered people across the
face of the earth, breaking up this
proud revolt. Later in time, a new
city grew on the site of Babel. That
city, Babylon, became a symbol
throughout the Bible of rebellion
against God (see Revelation 18:2).

**Think: When have you
experienced pain as a result of
pride—either your own or the
arrogance of another person?**

ROCK SOLID truths

From Shem to Abram

[10]This is the account of Shem's family line.

Two years after the flood, when Shem was 100 years old, he became the father[a] of Arphaxad. [11]And after he became the father of Arphaxad, Shem lived 500 years and had other sons and daughters.

[12]When Arphaxad had lived 35 years, he became the father of Shelah. [13]And after he became the father of Shelah, Arphaxad lived 403 years and had other sons and daughters.[b]

[14]When Shelah had lived 30 years, he became the father of Eber. [15]And after he became the father of Eber, Shelah lived 403 years and had other sons and daughters.

[16]When Eber had lived 34 years, he became the father of Peleg. [17]And after he became the father of Peleg, Eber lived 430 years and had other sons and daughters.

[18]When Peleg had lived 30 years, he became the father of Reu. [19]And after he became the father of Reu, Peleg lived 209 years and had other sons and daughters.

[20]When Reu had lived 32 years, he became the father of Serug. [21]And after he became the father of Serug, Reu lived 207 years and had other sons and daughters.

[22]When Serug had lived 30 years, he became the father of Nahor. [23]And after he became the father of Nahor, Serug lived 200 years and had other sons and daughters.

[24]When Nahor had lived 29 years, he became the father of Terah. [25]And after he became the father of Terah, Nahor lived 119 years and had other sons and daughters.

[26]After Terah had lived 70 years, he became the father of Abram, Nahor and Haran.

Abram's Family

[27]This is the account of Terah's family line.

Terah became the father of Abram, Nahor and Haran. And Haran became the father of Lot. [28]While his father Terah was still alive, Haran died in Ur of the Chaldeans, in the land of his birth. [29]Abram and Nahor both married. The name of Abram's wife was Sarai, and the name of Nahor's wife was Milkah; she was the daughter of Haran, the father of both Milkah and Iskah. [30]Now Sarai was childless because she was not able to conceive.

[31]Terah took his son Abram, his grandson Lot son of Haran, and his daughter-in-law Sarai, the wife of his son Abram, and together they set out from Ur of the Chaldeans to go to Canaan. But when they came to Harran, they settled there.

[32]Terah lived 205 years, and he died in Harran.

The Call of Abram

12 The Lord had said to Abram, "Go from your country, your people and your father's household to the land I will show you.

[2]"I will make you into a great nation,
  and I will bless you;
I will make your name great,
  and you will be a blessing.[c]
[3]I will bless those who bless you,
  and whoever curses you I will curse;
and all peoples on earth
  will be blessed through you."[d]

[4]So Abram went, as the Lord had told him; and Lot went with him. Abram was seventy-five years old when he set out from Harran. [5]He took his wife Sarai, his nephew Lot, all the possessions they had accumulated and the people they had acquired in Harran, and they set out for the land of Canaan, and they arrived there.

---

[a] 10 Father may mean ancestor; also in verses 11-25.   [b] 12,13 Hebrew; Septuagint (see also Luke 3:35, 36 and note at Gen. 10:24) 35 years, he became the father of Cainan. [13]And after he became the father of Cainan, Arphaxad lived 430 years and had other sons and daughters, and then he died. When Cainan had lived 130 years, he became the father of Shelah. And after he became the father of Shelah, Cainan lived 330 years and had other sons and daughters   [c] 2 Or be seen as blessed   [d] 3 Or earth / will use your name in blessings (see 48:20)

ROCK SOLID *promises*

"I will bless you ... and you will be a blessing." Genesis 12:2

God doesn't drop blessings on you just for your benefit. Every gift he gives you creates an opportunity to share and do good to others.

⁶Abram traveled through the land as far as the site of the great tree of Moreh at Shechem. At that time the Canaanites were in the land. ⁷The LORD appeared to Abram and said, "To your offspring*ᵃ* I will give this land." So he built an altar there to the LORD, who had appeared to him.

⁸From there he went on toward the hills east of Bethel and pitched his tent, with Bethel on the west and Ai on the east. There he built an altar to the LORD and called on the name of the LORD.

⁹Then Abram set out and continued toward the Negev.

Abram in Egypt

¹⁰Now there was a famine in the land, and Abram went down to Egypt to live there for a while because the famine was severe. ¹¹As he was about to enter Egypt, he said to his wife Sarai, "I know what a beautiful woman you are. ¹²When the Egyptians see you, they will say, 'This is his wife.' Then they will kill me but will let you live. ¹³Say you are my sister, so that I will be treated well for your sake and my life will be spared because of you."

¹⁴When Abram came to Egypt, the Egyptians saw that Sarai was a very beautiful woman. ¹⁵And when Pharaoh's officials saw her, they praised her to Pharaoh, and she was taken into his palace. ¹⁶He treated Abram well for her sake, and Abram acquired sheep and cattle, male

and female donkeys, male and female servants, and camels.

¹⁷But the LORD inflicted serious diseases on Pharaoh and his household because of Abram's wife Sarai. ¹⁸So Pharaoh summoned Abram. "What have you done to me?" he said. "Why didn't you tell me she was your wife? ¹⁹Why did you say, 'She is my sister,' so that I took her to be my wife? Now then, here is your wife. Take her and go!" ²⁰Then Pharaoh gave orders about Abram to his men, and they sent him on his way, with his wife and everything he had.

Abram and Lot Separate

13 So Abram went up from Egypt to the Negev, with his wife and everything he had, and Lot went with him. ²Abram had become very wealthy in livestock and in silver and gold.

³From the Negev he went from place to place until he came to Bethel, to the place between Bethel and Ai where his tent had been earlier ⁴and where he had first built an altar. There Abram called on the name of the LORD.

⁵Now Lot, who was moving about with Abram, also had flocks and herds and tents. ⁶But the land could not support them while they stayed together, for their possessions were so great that they were not able to stay together. ⁷And quarreling arose between Abram's herders and Lot's. The Canaanites and Perizzites were also living in the land at that time.

⁸So Abram said to Lot, "Let's not have any quarreling between you and me, or between your herders and mine, for we are close relatives. ⁹Is not the whole land before you? Let's part company. If you go to the left, I'll go to the right; if you go to the right, I'll go to the left."

¹⁰Lot looked around and saw that the whole plain of the Jordan toward Zoar was well watered, like the garden of the LORD, like the land of Egypt. (This was before the LORD destroyed Sodom and Gomorrah.) ¹¹So Lot chose for himself the whole plain of the Jordan and set

ᵃ 7 Or *seed*

out toward the east. The two men parted company: ¹²Abram lived in the land of Canaan, while Lot lived among the cities of the plain and pitched his tents near Sodom. ¹³Now the people of Sodom were wicked and were sinning greatly against the Lord.

¹⁴The Lord said to Abram after Lot had parted from him, "Look around from where you are, to the north and south, to the east and west. ¹⁵All the land that you see I will give to you and your offspring*a* forever. ¹⁶I will make your offspring like the dust of the earth, so that if anyone could count the dust, then your offspring could be counted. ¹⁷Go, walk through the length and breadth of the land, for I am giving it to you."

¹⁸So Abram went to live near the great trees of Mamre at Hebron, where he pitched his tents. There he built an altar to the Lord.

Abram Rescues Lot

14 At the time when Amraphel was king of Shinar,*b* Arioch king of Ellasar, Kedorlaomer king of Elam and Tidal king of Goyim, ²these kings went to war against Bera king of Sodom, Birsha king of Gomorrah, Shinab king of Admah, Shemeber king of Zeboyim, and the king of Bela (that is, Zoar). ³All these latter kings joined forces in the Valley of Siddim (that is, the Dead Sea Valley). ⁴For twelve years they had been subject to Kedorlaomer, but in the thirteenth year they rebelled.

⁵In the fourteenth year, Kedorlaomer and the kings allied with him went out and defeated the Rephaites in Ashteroth Karnaim, the Zuzites in Ham, the Emites in Shaveh Kiriathaim ⁶and the Horites in the hill country of Seir, as far as El Paran near the desert. ⁷Then they turned back and went to En Mishpat (that is, Kadesh), and they conquered the whole territory of the Amalekites, as well as the Amorites who were living in Hazezon Tamar.

⁸Then the king of Sodom, the king of Gomorrah, the king of Admah, the king of Zeboyim and the king of Bela (that is,

Zoar) marched out and drew up their battle lines in the Valley of Siddim ⁹against Kedorlaomer king of Elam, Tidal king of Goyim, Amraphel king of Shinar and Arioch king of Ellasar—four kings against five. ¹⁰Now the Valley of Siddim was full of tar pits, and when the kings of Sodom and Gomorrah fled, some of the men fell into them and the rest fled to the hills. ¹¹The four kings seized all the goods of Sodom and Gomorrah and all their food; then they went away. ¹²They also carried off Abram's nephew Lot and his possessions, since he was living in Sodom.

¹³A man who had escaped came and reported this to Abram the Hebrew. Now Abram was living near the great trees of Mamre the Amorite, a brother*c* of Eshkol and Aner, all of whom were allied with Abram. ¹⁴When Abram heard that his relative had been taken captive, he called out the 318 trained men born in his household and went in pursuit as far as Dan. ¹⁵During the night Abram divided his men to attack them and he routed them, pursuing them as far as Hobah, north of Damascus. ¹⁶He recovered all the goods and brought back his relative Lot and his possessions, together with the women and the other people.

¹⁷After Abram returned from defeating Kedorlaomer and the kings allied with him, the king of Sodom came out to meet him in the Valley of Shaveh (that is, the King's Valley).

¹⁸Then Melchizedek king of Salem brought out bread and wine. He was priest of God Most High, ¹⁹and he blessed Abram, saying,

"Blessed be Abram by God Most
    High,
  Creator of heaven and earth.
²⁰And praise be to God Most High,
  who delivered your enemies into
    your hand."

Then Abram gave him a tenth of everything.

---

a 15 Or *seed*; also in verse 16   *b 1* That is, Babylonia; also in verse 9   *c 13* Or *a relative*; or *an ally*

²¹The king of Sodom said to Abram, "Give me the people and keep the goods for yourself."

²²But Abram said to the king of Sodom, "With raised hand I have sworn an oath to the Lord, God Most High, Creator of heaven and earth, ²³that I will accept nothing belonging to you, not even a thread or the strap of a sandal, so that you will never be able to say, 'I made Abram rich.' ²⁴I will accept nothing but what my men have eaten and the share that belongs to the men who went with me—to Aner, Eshkol and Mamre. Let them have their share."

The Lord's Covenant With Abram

15 After this, the word of the Lord came to Abram in a vision:

"Do not be afraid, Abram.
    I am your shield,[a]
    your very great reward.[b]"

²But Abram said, "Sovereign Lord, what can you give me since I remain childless and the one who will inherit[c] my estate is Eliezer of Damascus?" ³And

[a] 1 Or sovereign will be very great   [b] 1 Or shield; / your reward   [c] 2 The meaning of the Hebrew for this phrase is uncertain.

Genesis 15:1–21

Abraham believed God.

If you're looking for the lead character in the plot of the Old Testament, Abraham is the man to watch. He appears early in the book of Genesis, immediately after the Bible's descriptions of creation, the flood, and the tower of Babel in Genesis 1—11. The Lord spoke to Abraham and told him to leave his home and people in the land of Ur and "go ... to the land I will show you" (Genesis 12:1). God not only promised to give him a mysterious new place to live but to make his offspring "a great nation" (Genesis 12:2).

Abraham had to leave behind everything safe and familiar. He was challenged to believe he would father a mighty nation even though he and his wife were childless. Yet Abraham obeyed the Lord without hesitation. When he packed up and embarked on what turned into a thousand-mile walk to Israel, he became a model of how to trust God. The Lord noted Abraham's faith and "credited it to him as righteousness" (Genesis 15:6). His faith made him right with God.

Faith is the most significant thing you can ever learn from Abraham; the entire Bible says faith is how you too can get right with God. When you trust that Jesus died on the cross and rose from the dead for you, the Lord makes you friends with him. The Bible says, "For it is by grace you have been saved, through faith" (Ephesians 2:8). When you believe, it's like Abraham becomes your father in the faith (Galatians 3:6–9).

You can find Abraham in Genesis 11:26—25:11; Romans 4:1–25; and Hebrews 11:8–19.

UNSHAKEN *people*

Abram said, "You have given me no children; so a servant in my household will be my heir."

⁴Then the word of the LORD came to him: "This man will not be your heir, but a son who is your own flesh and blood will be your heir." ⁵He took him outside and said, "Look up at the sky and count the stars—if indeed you can count them." Then he said to him, "So shall your offspring*ᵃ* be."

⁶Abram believed the LORD, and he credited it to him as righteousness.

⁷He also said to him, "I am the LORD, who brought you out of Ur of the Chaldeans to give you this land to take possession of it."

⁸But Abram said, "Sovereign LORD, how can I know that I will gain possession of it?"

⁹So the LORD said to him, "Bring me a heifer, a goat and a ram, each three years old, along with a dove and a young pigeon."

¹⁰Abram brought all these to him, cut them in two and arranged the halves opposite each other; the birds, however, he did not cut in half. ¹¹Then birds of prey came down on the carcasses, but Abram drove them away.

¹²As the sun was setting, Abram fell into a deep sleep, and a thick and dreadful darkness came over him. ¹³Then the LORD said to him, "Know for certain that for four hundred years your descendants will be strangers in a country not their own and that they will be enslaved and mistreated there. ¹⁴But I will punish the nation they serve as slaves, and afterward they will come out with great possessions. ¹⁵You, however, will go to your ancestors in peace and be buried at a good old age. ¹⁶In the fourth generation your descendants will come back here, for the sin of the Amorites has not yet reached its full measure."

¹⁷When the sun had set and darkness had fallen, a smoking firepot with a blazing torch appeared and passed between the pieces. ¹⁸On that day the LORD made a covenant with Abram and said, "To your descendants I give this land, from the Wadi*ᵇ* of Egypt to the great river, the Euphrates— ¹⁹the land of the Kenites,

Kenizzites, Kadmonites, ²⁰Hittites, Perizzites, Rephaites, ²¹Amorites, Canaanites, Girgashites and Jebusites."

Hagar and Ishmael

16 Now Sarai, Abram's wife, had borne him no children. But she had an Egyptian slave named Hagar; ²so she said to Abram, "The LORD has kept me from having children. Go, sleep with my slave; perhaps I can build a family through her."

Abram agreed to what Sarai said. ³So after Abram had been living in Canaan ten years, Sarai his wife took her Egyptian slave Hagar and gave her to her husband to be his wife. ⁴He slept with Hagar, and she conceived.

When she knew she was pregnant, she began to despise her mistress. ⁵Then Sarai said to Abram, "You are responsible for the wrong I am suffering. I put my slave in your arms, and now that she knows she is pregnant, she despises me. May the LORD judge between you and me."

⁶"Your slave is in your hands," Abram said. "Do with her whatever you think best." Then Sarai mistreated Hagar; so she fled from her.

⁷The angel of the LORD found Hagar near a spring in the desert; it was the spring that is beside the road to Shur. ⁸And he said, "Hagar, slave of Sarai, where have you come from, and where are you going?"

"I'm running away from my mistress Sarai," she answered.

⁹Then the angel of the LORD told her, "Go back to your mistress and submit to her." ¹⁰The angel added, "I will increase your descendants so much that they will be too numerous to count."

¹¹The angel of the LORD also said to her:

"You are now pregnant
 and you will give birth to a son.
You shall name him Ishmael,*ᶜ*
 for the LORD has heard of your
  misery.

ᵃ 5 Or *seed*   *ᵇ 18* Or *river*   *ᶜ 11 Ishmael* means *God hears.*

^{12}He will be a wild donkey of a man;
   his hand will be against everyone
   and everyone's hand against him,
  and he will live in hostility
   toward^a all his brothers."

^{13}She gave this name to the LORD who spoke to her: "You are the God who sees me," for she said, "I have now seen^b the One who sees me." ^{14}That is why the well was called Beer Lahai Roi^c; it is still there, between Kadesh and Bered.

^{15}So Hagar bore Abram a son, and Abram gave the name Ishmael to the son she had borne. ^{16}Abram was eighty-six years old when Hagar bore him Ishmael.

The Covenant of Circumcision

17 When Abram was ninety-nine years old, the LORD appeared to him and said, "I am God Almighty^d; walk before me faithfully and be blameless. ^{2}Then I will make my covenant between me and you and will greatly increase your numbers."

^{3}Abram fell facedown, and God said to him, ^{4}"As for me, this is my covenant with you: You will be the father of many nations. ^{5}No longer will you be called Abram^e; your name will be Abraham,^{f} for I have made you a father of many nations. ^{6}I will make you very fruitful; I will make nations of you, and kings will come from you. ^{7}I will establish my covenant as an everlasting covenant between me and you and your descendants after you for the generations to come, to be your God and the God of your descendants after you. ^{8}The whole land of Canaan, where you now reside as a foreigner, I will give as an everlasting possession to you and your descendants after you; and I will be their God."

^{9}Then God said to Abraham, "As for you, you must keep my covenant, you and your descendants after you for the generations to come. ^{10}This is my covenant with you and your descendants after you, the covenant you are to keep: Every male among you shall be circumcised. ^{11}You are to undergo circumcision, and it will be the sign of the covenant between me and you. ^{12}For the generations to come every male among you who is eight days old must be circumcised, including those born in your household or bought with money from a foreigner—those who are not your offspring. ^{13}Whether born in your household or bought with your money, they must be circumcised. My covenant in your flesh is to be an everlasting covenant. ^{14}Any uncircumcised male, who has not been circumcised in the flesh, will be cut off from his people; he has broken my covenant."

^{15}God also said to Abraham, "As for Sarai your wife, you are no longer to call her Sarai; her name will be Sarah. ^{16}I will bless her and will surely give you a son by her. I will bless her so that she will be the mother of nations; kings of peoples will come from her."

^{17}Abraham fell facedown; he laughed and said to himself, "Will a son be born to a man a hundred years old? Will Sarah bear a child at the age of ninety?" ^{18}And Abraham said to God, "If only Ishmael might live under your blessing!"

^{19}Then God said, "Yes, but your wife Sarah will bear you a son, and you will call him Isaac.^{g} I will establish my covenant with him as an everlasting covenant for his descendants after him. ^{20}And as for Ishmael, I have heard you: I will surely bless him; I will make him fruitful and will greatly increase his numbers. He will be the father of twelve rulers, and I will make him into a great nation. ^{21}But my covenant I will establish with Isaac, whom Sarah will bear to you by this time next year." ^{22}When he had finished speaking with Abraham, God went up from him.

^{23}On that very day Abraham took his son Ishmael and all those born in his household or bought with his money, every male in his household, and circumcised them, as God told him. ^{24}Abraham was ninety-nine years old when he was circumcised, ^{25}and his son Ishmael was thirteen; ^{26}Abraham and his son Ishmael

---

^{a} 12 Or *live to the east / of* ^{b} 13 Or *seen the back of* ^{c} 14 *Beer Lahai Roi* means *well of the Living One who sees me.* ^{d} 1 Hebrew *El-Shaddai* ^{e} 5 *Abram* means *exalted father.* ^{f} 5 *Abraham* probably means *father of many.* ^{g} 19 *Isaac* means *he laughs.*

were both circumcised on that very day. ²⁷And every male in Abraham's household, including those born in his household or bought from a foreigner, was circumcised with him.

The Three Visitors

18 The LORD appeared to Abraham near the great trees of Mamre while he was sitting at the entrance to his tent in the heat of the day. ²Abraham looked up and saw three men standing nearby. When he saw them, he hurried from the entrance of his tent to meet them and bowed low to the ground.

³He said, "If I have found favor in your eyes, my lord,ᵃ do not pass your servant by. ⁴Let a little water be brought, and then you may all wash your feet and rest under this tree. ⁵Let me get you something to eat, so you can be refreshed and then go on your way—now that you have come to your servant."

"Very well," they answered, "do as you say."

⁶So Abraham hurried into the tent to Sarah. "Quick," he said, "get three seahsᵇ of the finest flour and knead it and bake some bread."

⁷Then he ran to the herd and selected a choice, tender calf and gave it to a servant, who hurried to prepare it. ⁸He then brought some curds and milk and the calf that had been prepared, and set these before them. While they ate, he stood near them under a tree.

⁹"Where is your wife Sarah?" they asked him.

"There, in the tent," he said.

¹⁰Then one of them said, "I will surely return to you about this time next year, and Sarah your wife will have a son."

Now Sarah was listening at the entrance to the tent, which was behind him. ¹¹Abraham and Sarah were already very old, and Sarah was past the age of childbearing. ¹²So Sarah laughed to herself as she thought, "After I am worn out and my lord is old, will I now have this pleasure?"

¹³Then the LORD said to Abraham, "Why did Sarah laugh and say, 'Will I

really have a child, now that I am old?' ¹⁴Is anything too hard for the LORD? I will return to you at the appointed time next year, and Sarah will have a son."

¹⁵Sarah was afraid, so she lied and said, "I did not laugh."

But he said, "Yes, you did laugh."

Abraham Pleads for Sodom

¹⁶When the men got up to leave, they looked down toward Sodom, and Abraham walked along with them to see them on their way. ¹⁷Then the LORD said, "Shall I hide from Abraham what I am about to do? ¹⁸Abraham will surely become a great and powerful nation, and all nations on earth will be blessed through him.ᶜ ¹⁹For I have chosen him, so that he will direct his children and his household after him to keep the way of the LORD by doing what is right and just, so that the LORD will bring about for Abraham what he has promised him."

ROCK SOLID promises

"The LORD will bring about for Abraham what he has promised him."
Genesis 18:19

God always keeps his promises—even promises that seem too enormous or too difficult to be true.

---

²⁰Then the LORD said, "The outcry against Sodom and Gomorrah is so great and their sin so grievous ²¹that I will go down and see if what they have done is as bad as the outcry that has reached me. If not, I will know."

²²The men turned away and went to-

ᵃ 3 Or *eyes, Lord* ᵇ 6 That is, probably about 36 pounds or about 16 kilograms ᶜ 18 Or *will use his name in blessings* (see 48:20) ward Sodom, but Abraham remained standing before the LORD.ᵃ ²³Then Abraham approached him and said: "Will you sweep away the righteous with the wicked? ²⁴What if there are fifty righteous people in the city? Will you really sweep it away and not spareᵇ the place for the sake of the fifty righteous people in it? ²⁵Far be it from you to do such a thing—to kill the righteous with the wicked, treating the righteous and the wicked alike. Far be it from you! Will not the Judge of all the earth do right?"

²⁶The LORD said, "If I find fifty righteous people in the city of Sodom, I will spare the whole place for their sake."

²⁷Then Abraham spoke up again: "Now that I have been so bold as to speak to the Lord, though I am nothing but dust and ashes, ²⁸what if the number of the righteous is five less than fifty? Will you destroy the whole city for lack of five people?"

"If I find forty-five there," he said, "I will not destroy it."

²⁹Once again he spoke to him, "What if only forty are found there?"

He said, "For the sake of forty, I will not do it."

³⁰Then he said, "May the Lord not be angry, but let me speak. What if only thirty can be found there?"

He answered, "I will not do it if I find thirty there."

³¹Abraham said, "Now that I have been so bold as to speak to the Lord, what if only twenty can be found there?"

He said, "For the sake of twenty, I will not destroy it."

³²Then he said, "May the Lord not be angry, but let me speak just once more. What if only ten can be found there?"

He answered, "For the sake of ten, I will not destroy it."

³³When the LORD had finished speaking with Abraham, he left, and Abraham returned home.

Sodom and Gomorrah Destroyed

19 The two angels arrived at Sodom in the evening, and Lot was sitting in the gateway of the city. When he saw them, he got up to meet them and bowed down with his face to the ground. ²"My lords," he said, "please turn aside to your servant's house. You can wash your feet and spend the night and then go on your way early in the morning."

"No," they answered, "we will spend the night in the square."

³But he insisted so strongly that they did go with him and entered his house. He prepared a meal for them, baking bread without yeast, and they ate. ⁴Before they had gone to bed, all the men from every part of the city of Sodom—both young and old—surrounded the house. ⁵They called to Lot, "Where are the men who came to you tonight? Bring them out to us so that we can have sex with them."

⁶Lot went outside to meet them and shut the door behind him ⁷and said, "No, my friends. Don't do this wicked thing. ⁸Look, I have two daughters who have never slept with a man. Let me bring them out to you, and you can do what you like with them. But don't do anything to these men, for they have come under the protection of my roof."

⁹"Get out of our way," they replied. "This fellow came here as a foreigner, and now he wants to play the judge! We'll treat you worse than them." They kept bringing pressure on Lot and moved forward to break down the door.

¹⁰But the men inside reached out and pulled Lot back into the house and shut the door. ¹¹Then they struck the men who were at the door of the house, young and old, with blindness so that they could not find the door.

¹²The two men said to Lot, "Do you have anyone else here—sons-in-law, sons or daughters, or anyone else in the city who belongs to you? Get them out of here, ¹³because we are going to destroy this place. The outcry to the LORD against its people is so great that he has sent us to destroy it."

ᵃ 22 Masoretic Text; an ancient Hebrew scribal tradition *but the LORD remained standing before Abraham*   ᵇ 24 Or *forgive*; also in verse 26

¹⁴So Lot went out and spoke to his sons-in-law, who were pledged to marry*ᵃ* his daughters. He said, "Hurry and get out of this place, because the LORD is about to destroy the city!" But his sons-in-law thought he was joking.

¹⁵With the coming of dawn, the angels urged Lot, saying, "Hurry! Take your wife and your two daughters who are here, or you will be swept away when the city is punished."

¹⁶When he hesitated, the men grasped his hand and the hands of his wife and of his two daughters and led them safely out of the city, for the LORD was merciful to them. ¹⁷As soon as they had brought them out, one of them said, "Flee for your lives! Don't look back, and don't stop anywhere in the plain! Flee to the mountains or you will be swept away!"

¹⁸But Lot said to them, "No, my lords,*ᵇ* please! ¹⁹Your*ᶜ* servant has found favor in your*ᶜ* eyes, and you*ᶜ* have shown great kindness to me in sparing my life. But I can't flee to the mountains; this disaster will overtake me, and I'll die. ²⁰Look, here is a town near enough to run to, and it is small. Let me flee to it—it is very small, isn't it? Then my life will be spared."

²¹He said to him, "Very well, I will grant this request too; I will not overthrow the town you speak of. ²²But flee there quickly, because I cannot do anything until you reach it." (That is why the town was called Zoar.*ᵈ*)

²³By the time Lot reached Zoar, the sun had risen over the land. ²⁴Then the LORD rained down burning sulfur on Sodom and Gomorrah—from the LORD out of the heavens. ²⁵Thus he overthrew those cities and the entire plain, destroying all those living in the cities—and also the vegetation in the land. ²⁶But Lot's wife looked back, and she became a pillar of salt.

²⁷Early the next morning Abraham got up and returned to the place where he had stood before the LORD. ²⁸He looked down toward Sodom and Gomorrah, toward all the land of the plain, and he saw dense smoke rising from the land, like smoke from a furnace.

²⁹So when God destroyed the cities of the plain, he remembered Abraham, and he brought Lot out of the catastrophe that overthrew the cities where Lot had lived.

Lot and His Daughters

³⁰Lot and his two daughters left Zoar and settled in the mountains, for he was afraid to stay in Zoar. He and his two daughters lived in a cave. ³¹One day the older daughter said to the younger, "Our father is old, and there is no man around here to give us children—as is the custom all over the earth. ³²Let's get our father to drink wine and then sleep with him and preserve our family line through our father."

³³That night they got their father to drink wine, and the older daughter went in and slept with him. He was not aware of it when she lay down or when she got up.

³⁴The next day the older daughter said to the younger, "Last night I slept with my father. Let's get him to drink wine again tonight, and you go in and sleep with him so we can preserve our family line through our father." ³⁵So they got their father to drink wine that night also, and the younger daughter went in and slept with him. Again he was not aware of it when she lay down or when she got up.

³⁶So both of Lot's daughters became pregnant by their father. ³⁷The older daughter had a son, and she named him Moab*ᵉ*; he is the father of the Moabites of today. ³⁸The younger daughter also had a son, and she named him Ben-Ammi*ᶠ*; he is the father of the Ammonites*ᵍ* of today.

Abraham and Abimelek

20 Now Abraham moved on from there into the region of the Negev and lived between Kadesh and Shur. For a while he stayed in Gerar, ²and there Abraham said of his wife Sarah, "She is my sister." Then

---

ᵃ 14 Or *were married to*   *ᵇ 18* Or *No, Lord*; or *No, my lord*   *ᶜ 19* The Hebrew is singular.   *ᵈ 22 Zoar* means *small.*   *ᵉ 37 Moab* sounds like the Hebrew for *from father.*   *ᶠ 38 Ben-Ammi* means *son of my father's people.*   *ᵍ 38* Hebrew *Bene-Ammon*

Abimelek king of Gerar sent for Sarah and took her.

³But God came to Abimelek in a dream one night and said to him, "You are as good as dead because of the woman you have taken; she is a married woman."

⁴Now Abimelek had not gone near her, so he said, "Lord, will you destroy an innocent nation? ⁵Did he not say to me, 'She is my sister,' and didn't she also say, 'He is my brother'? I have done this with a clear conscience and clean hands."

⁶Then God said to him in the dream, "Yes, I know you did this with a clear conscience, and so I have kept you from sinning against me. That is why I did not let you touch her. ⁷Now return the man's wife, for he is a prophet, and he will pray for you and you will live. But if you do not return her, you may be sure that you and all who belong to you will die."

⁸Early the next morning Abimelek summoned all his officials, and when he told them all that had happened, they were very much afraid. ⁹Then Abimelek called Abraham in and said, "What have you done to us? How have I wronged you that you have brought such great guilt upon me and my kingdom? You have done things to me that should never be done." ¹⁰And Abimelek asked Abraham, "What was your reason for doing this?"

¹¹Abraham replied, "I said to myself, 'There is surely no fear of God in this place, and they will kill me because of my wife.' ¹²Besides, she really is my sister, the daughter of my father though not of my mother; and she became my wife. ¹³And when God had me wander from my father's household, I said to her, 'This is how you can show your love to me: Everywhere we go, say of me, "He is my brother."'"

¹⁴Then Abimelek brought sheep and cattle and male and female slaves and gave them to Abraham, and he returned Sarah his wife to him. ¹⁵And Abimelek said, "My land is before you; live wherever you like."

¹⁶To Sarah he said, "I am giving your brother a thousand shekels*a* of silver. This is to cover the offense against you before all who are with you; you are completely vindicated."

¹⁷Then Abraham prayed to God, and God healed Abimelek, his wife and his female slaves so they could have children again, ¹⁸for the LORD had kept all the women in Abimelek's household from conceiving because of Abraham's wife Sarah.

The Birth of Isaac

21 Now the LORD was gracious to Sarah as he had said, and the LORD did for Sarah what he had promised. ²Sarah became pregnant and bore a son to Abraham in his old age, at the very time God had promised him. ³Abraham gave the name Isaac*b* to the son Sarah bore him. ⁴When his son Isaac was eight days old, Abraham circumcised him, as God commanded him. ⁵Abraham was a hundred years old when his son Isaac was born to him.

⁶Sarah said, "God has brought me laughter, and everyone who hears about this will laugh with me." ⁷And she added, "Who would have said to Abraham that Sarah would nurse children? Yet I have borne him a son in his old age."

Hagar and Ishmael Sent Away

⁸The child grew and was weaned, and on the day Isaac was weaned Abraham held a great feast. ⁹But Sarah saw that the son whom Hagar the Egyptian had borne to Abraham was mocking, ¹⁰and she said to Abraham, "Get rid of that slave woman and her son, for that woman's son will never share in the inheritance with my son Isaac."

¹¹The matter distressed Abraham greatly because it concerned his son. ¹²But God said to him, "Do not be so distressed about the boy and your slave woman. Listen to whatever Sarah tells you, because it is through Isaac that your offspring*c* will be reckoned. ¹³I will make the son of the slave into a nation also, because he is your offspring."

¹⁴Early the next morning Abraham

---

a 16 That is, about 25 pounds or about 12 kilograms   *b 3 Isaac* means *he laughs.*
c 12 Or *seed*

took some food and a skin of water and gave them to Hagar. He set them on her shoulders and then sent her off with the boy. She went on her way and wandered in the Desert of Beersheba.

¹⁵When the water in the skin was gone, she put the boy under one of the bushes. ¹⁶Then she went off and sat down about a bowshot away, for she thought, "I cannot watch the boy die." And as she sat there, she*ᵃ* began to sob.

¹⁷God heard the boy crying, and the angel of God called to Hagar from heaven and said to her, "What is the matter, Hagar? Do not be afraid; God has heard the boy crying as he lies there. ¹⁸Lift the boy up and take him by the hand, for I will make him into a great nation."

¹⁹Then God opened her eyes and she saw a well of water. So she went and filled the skin with water and gave the boy a drink. ²⁰God was with the boy as he grew up. He lived in the desert and became an archer. ²¹While he was living in the Desert of Paran, his mother got a wife for him from Egypt.

The Treaty at Beersheba

²²At that time Abimelek and Phicol the commander of his forces said to Abraham,

ᵃ 16 Hebrew; Septuagint the child

Genesis 21:1 – 6

Sarah discovered God's power.

There seemed to be a glitch in God's plan to make Abraham the father of "a great nation" (Genesis 12:2). Abraham and his wife Sarah were already senior citizens when they left their home in Ur to go to the land God would show them. And despite the Lord's promise to make Abraham the start of a family as numerous as the stars (see Genesis 15:5), this couple wasn't getting any younger. They had grown old without giving birth to an heir.

One day Abraham entertained three visitors to his tent. One boldly promised that by the same time next year, Sarah would bear a son (Genesis 18:10). Sarah listened by the tent door and laughed at the thought. As the Bible puts it, "Abraham and Sarah were already very old, and Sarah was past the age of childbearing." Sarah called herself "worn out" and her husband "old" (Genesis 18:11 – 12).

God had a lesson for Sarah. He asked, "Is anything too hard for the LORD?" (Genesis 18:14). Soon Sarah gave birth to her first-born son, the result of God having done as he had promised (see Genesis 21:1). She named him Isaac, which means "he laughs." Sarah thought the Lord's promise was preposterous. But she discovered that God's power can accomplish impossible things, even giving an old woman a baby.

You can find Sarah in Genesis 17 — 25; Romans 9:9; and Hebrews 11:11.

UNSHAKEN people

"God is with you in everything you do. ²³Now swear to me here before God that you will not deal falsely with me or my children or my descendants. Show to me and the country where you now reside as a foreigner the same kindness I have shown to you."

²⁴Abraham said, "I swear it."

²⁵Then Abraham complained to Abimelek about a well of water that Abimelek's servants had seized. ²⁶But Abimelek said, "I don't know who has done this. You did not tell me, and I heard about it only today."

²⁷So Abraham brought sheep and cattle and gave them to Abimelek, and the two men made a treaty. ²⁸Abraham set apart seven ewe lambs from the flock, ²⁹and Abimelek asked Abraham, "What is the meaning of these seven ewe lambs you have set apart by themselves?"

³⁰He replied, "Accept these seven lambs from my hand as a witness that I dug this well."

³¹So that place was called Beersheba,ᵃ because the two men swore an oath there.

³²After the treaty had been made at Beersheba, Abimelek and Phicol the commander of his forces returned to the land of the Philistines. ³³Abraham planted a tamarisk tree in Beersheba, and there he called on the name of the LORD, the Eternal God. ³⁴And Abraham stayed in the land of the Philistines for a long time.

Abraham Tested

22 Some time later God tested Abraham. He said to him, "Abraham!"

"Here I am," he replied.

²Then God said, "Take your son, your only son, whom you love—Isaac—and go to the region of Moriah. Sacrifice him there as a burnt offering on a mountain I will show you."

³Early the next morning Abraham got up and loaded his donkey. He took with him two of his servants and his son Isaac. When he had cut enough wood for the burnt offering, he set out for the place God had told him about. ⁴On the third day Abraham looked up and saw the place in the distance. ⁵He said to his servants, "Stay here with the donkey while I and the boy go over there. We will worship and then we will come back to you."

⁶Abraham took the wood for the burnt offering and placed it on his son Isaac, and he himself carried the fire and the knife. As the two of them went on together, ⁷Isaac spoke up and said to his father Abraham, "Father?"

"Yes, my son?" Abraham replied.

"The fire and wood are here," Isaac said, "but where is the lamb for the burnt offering?"

⁸Abraham answered, "God himself will provide the lamb for the burnt offering, my son." And the two of them went on together.

⁹When they reached the place God had told him about, Abraham built an altar there and arranged the wood on it. He bound his son Isaac and laid him on the altar, on top of the wood. ¹⁰Then he reached out his hand and took the knife to slay his son. ¹¹But the angel of the LORD called out to him from heaven, "Abraham! Abraham!"

"Here I am," he replied.

¹²"Do not lay a hand on the boy," he said. "Do not do anything to him. Now I know that you fear God, because you have not withheld from me your son, your only son."

¹³Abraham looked up and there in a thicket he saw a ramᵇ caught by its horns. He went over and took the ram and sacrificed it as a burnt offering instead of his son. ¹⁴So Abraham called that place The LORD Will Provide. And to this day it is said, "On the mountain of the LORD it will be provided."

¹⁵The angel of the LORD called to Abraham from heaven a second time ¹⁶and said, "I swear by myself, declares the LORD, that because you have done this and have not withheld your son,

---

ᵃ 31 *Beersheba* can mean *well of seven* and *well of the oath.*   ᵇ 13 Many manuscripts of the Masoretic Text, Samaritan Pentateuch, Septuagint and Syriac; most manuscripts of the Masoretic Text *a ram behind him* your only son, [17] I will surely bless you and make your descendants as numerous as the stars in the sky and as the sand on the seashore. Your descendants will take possession of the cities of their enemies, [18] and through your offspring[a] all nations on earth will be blessed,[b] because you have obeyed me."

Genesis 22:1–18

God had a plan to sacrifice his Son.

God gave Abraham strange instructions when he told that Old Testament hero to take his son into the mountains and sacrifice him as a burnt offering. Bible critics point to this scene where Isaac nearly dies as proof that God is hideously evil, calling God's command an example of divine child abuse. But the end of the story shows that God had a plan all along. He was testing Abraham's obedience and faith. The Lord had promised to make Abraham the father of a great nation, and his only son Isaac was how that family was to begin. As Abraham tied Isaac on the altar, Abraham trusted that God knew what he was doing— and that he could fulfill his promise in another way (see Genesis 17:15–22). This scene also points ahead to something far bigger— that one day your heavenly Father would watch his only Son die. He loved the world so much that he would send Jesus as a sacrifice for the sins of all humankind (see John 3:16).

Think: Is this scene an example of child abuse—or a sign of God's amazing plan? Can you explain it?

ROCK SOLID truths

---

[19] Then Abraham returned to his servants, and they set off together for Beersheba. And Abraham stayed in Beersheba.

Nahor's Sons

[20] Some time later Abraham was told, "Milkah is also a mother; she has borne sons to your brother Nahor: [21] Uz the firstborn, Buz his brother, Kemuel (the father of Aram), [22] Kesed, Hazo, Pildash, Jidlaph and Bethuel." [23] Bethuel became the father of Rebekah. Milkah bore these eight sons to Abraham's brother Nahor. [24] His concubine, whose name was Reumah, also had sons: Tebah, Gaham, Tahash and Maakah.

The Death of Sarah

23 Sarah lived to be a hundred and twenty-seven years old. [2] She died at Kiriath Arba (that is, Hebron) in the land of Canaan, and Abraham went to mourn for Sarah and to weep over her.

[3] Then Abraham rose from beside his dead wife and spoke to the Hittites.[c] He said, [4] "I am a foreigner and stranger among you. Sell me some property for a burial site here so I can bury my dead."

[5] The Hittites replied to Abraham, [6] "Sir, listen to us. You are a mighty prince among us. Bury your dead in the choicest of our tombs. None of us will refuse you his tomb for burying your dead."

[7] Then Abraham rose and bowed down before the people of the land, the Hittites. [8] He said to them, "If you are willing to let me bury my dead, then listen to me and intercede with Ephron son of Zohar on my behalf [9] so he will sell me the cave of Machpelah, which belongs to him and is at the end of his field. Ask him to sell it to me for the full price as a burial site among you."

[10] Ephron the Hittite was sitting among his people and he replied to Abraham in the hearing of all the Hittites who had

---

[a] 18 Or seed   [b] 18 Or and all nations on earth will use the name of your offspring in blessings (see 48:20)   [c] 3 Or the descendants of Heth; also in verses 5, 7, 10, 16, 18 and 20

come to the gate of his city. [11]"No, my lord," he said. "Listen to me; I give[a] you the field, and I give[a] you the cave that is in it. I give[a] it to you in the presence of my people. Bury your dead."

[12]Again Abraham bowed down before the people of the land [13]and he said to Ephron in their hearing, "Listen to me, if you will. I will pay the price of the field. Accept it from me so I can bury my dead there."

[14]Ephron answered Abraham, [15]"Listen to me, my lord; the land is worth four hundred shekels[b] of silver, but what is that between you and me? Bury your dead."

[16]Abraham agreed to Ephron's terms and weighed out for him the price he had named in the hearing of the Hittites: four hundred shekels of silver, according to the weight current among the merchants.

[17]So Ephron's field in Machpelah near Mamre—both the field and the cave in it, and all the trees within the borders of the field—was deeded [18]to Abraham as his property in the presence of all the Hittites who had come to the gate of the city. [19]Afterward Abraham buried his wife Sarah in the cave in the field of Machpelah near Mamre (which is at Hebron) in the land of Canaan. [20]So the field and the cave in it were deeded to Abraham by the Hittites as a burial site.

Isaac and Rebekah

24 Abraham was now very old, and the LORD had blessed him in every way. [2]He said to the senior servant in his household, the one in charge of all that he had, "Put your hand under my thigh. [3]I want you to swear by the LORD, the God of heaven and the God of earth, that you will not get a wife for my son from the daughters of the Canaanites, among whom I am living, [4]but will go to my country and my own relatives and get a wife for my son Isaac."

[5]The servant asked him, "What if the woman is unwilling to come back with me to this land? Shall I then take your son back to the country you came from?"

[6]"Make sure that you do not take my son back there," Abraham said. [7]"The LORD, the God of heaven, who brought me out of my father's household and my native land and who spoke to me and promised me on oath, saying, 'To your offspring[c] I will give this land'—he will send his angel before you so that you can get a wife for my son from there. [8]If the woman is unwilling to come back with you, then you will be released from this oath of mine. Only do not take my son back there." [9]So the servant put his hand under the thigh of his master Abraham and swore an oath to him concerning this matter.

[10]Then the servant left, taking with him ten of his master's camels loaded with all kinds of good things from his master. He set out for Aram Naharaim[d] and made his way to the town of Nahor. [11]He had the camels kneel down near the well outside the town; it was toward evening, the time the women go out to draw water.

[12]Then he prayed, "LORD, God of my master Abraham, make me successful today, and show kindness to my master Abraham. [13]See, I am standing beside this spring, and the daughters of the townspeople are coming out to draw water. [14]May it be that when I say to a young woman, 'Please let down your jar that I may have a drink,' and she says, 'Drink, and I'll water your camels too'—let her be the one you have chosen for your servant Isaac. By this I will know that you have shown kindness to my master."

[15]Before he had finished praying, Rebekah came out with her jar on her shoulder. She was the daughter of Bethuel son of Milkah, who was the wife of Abraham's brother Nahor. [16]The woman was very beautiful, a virgin; no man had ever slept with her. She went down to the spring, filled her jar and came up again.

[17]The servant hurried to meet her and said, "Please give me a little water from your jar."

[18]"Drink, my lord," she said, and quickly

---

[a] 11 Or sell   [b] 15 That is, about 10 pounds or about 4.6 kilograms   [c] 7 Or seed
[d] 10 That is, Northwest Mesopotamia

lowered the jar to her hands and gave him a drink.

¹⁹After she had given him a drink, she said, "I'll draw water for your camels too, until they have had enough to drink." ²⁰So she quickly emptied her jar into the trough, ran back to the well to draw more water, and drew enough for all his camels. ²¹Without saying a word, the man watched her closely to learn whether or not the LORD had made his journey successful.

²²When the camels had finished drinking, the man took out a gold nose ring weighing a beka*ᵃ* and two gold bracelets weighing ten shekels.*ᵇ* ²³Then he asked, "Whose daughter are you? Please tell me, is there room in your father's house for us to spend the night?"

²⁴She answered him, "I am the daughter of Bethuel, the son that Milkah bore to Nahor." ²⁵And she added, "We have plenty of straw and fodder, as well as room for you to spend the night."

²⁶Then the man bowed down and worshiped the LORD, ²⁷saying, "Praise be to the LORD, the God of my master Abraham, who has not abandoned his kindness and faithfulness to my master. As for me, the LORD has led me on the journey to the house of my master's relatives."

²⁸The young woman ran and told her mother's household about these things. ²⁹Now Rebekah had a brother named Laban, and he hurried out to the man at the spring. ³⁰As soon as he had seen the nose ring, and the bracelets on his sister's arms, and had heard Rebekah tell what the man said to her, he went out to the man and found him standing by the camels near the spring. ³¹"Come, you who are blessed by the LORD," he said. "Why are you standing out here? I have prepared the house and a place for the camels."

³²So the man went to the house, and the camels were unloaded. Straw and fodder were brought for the camels, and water for him and his men to wash their feet. ³³Then food was set before him, but he said, "I will not eat until I have told you what I have to say."

"Then tell us," Laban said.

³⁴So he said, "I am Abraham's servant. ³⁵The LORD has blessed my master abundantly, and he has become wealthy. He has given him sheep and cattle, silver and gold, male and female servants, and camels and donkeys. ³⁶My master's wife Sarah has borne him a son in her old age, and he has given him everything he owns. ³⁷And my master made me swear an oath, and said, 'You must not get a wife for my son from the daughters of the Canaanites, in whose land I live, ³⁸but go to my father's family and to my own clan, and get a wife for my son.'

³⁹"Then I asked my master, 'What if the woman will not come back with me?'

⁴⁰"He replied, 'The LORD, before whom I have walked faithfully, will send his angel with you and make your journey a success, so that you can get a wife for my son from my own clan and from my father's family. ⁴¹You will be released from my oath if, when you go to my clan, they refuse to give her to you—then you will be released from my oath.'

⁴²"When I came to the spring today, I said, 'LORD, God of my master Abraham, if you will, please grant success to the journey on which I have come. ⁴³See, I am standing beside this spring. If a young woman comes out to draw water and I say to her, "Please let me drink a little water from your jar," ⁴⁴and if she says to me, "Drink, and I'll draw water for your camels too," let her be the one the LORD has chosen for my master's son.'

⁴⁵"Before I finished praying in my heart, Rebekah came out, with her jar on her shoulder. She went down to the spring and drew water, and I said to her, 'Please give me a drink.'

⁴⁶"She quickly lowered her jar from her shoulder and said, 'Drink, and I'll water your camels too.' So I drank, and she watered the camels also.

⁴⁷"I asked her, 'Whose daughter are you?'

"She said, 'The daughter of Bethuel son of Nahor, whom Milkah bore to him.'

ᵃ 22 That is, about 1/5 ounce or about 5.7 grams
ᵇ 22 That is, about 4 ounces or about 115 grams

"Then I put the ring in her nose and the bracelets on her arms, ⁴⁸and I bowed down and worshiped the Lᴏʀᴅ. I praised the Lᴏʀᴅ, the God of my master Abraham, who had led me on the right road to get the granddaughter of my master's brother for his son. ⁴⁹Now if you will show kindness and faithfulness to my master, tell me; and if not, tell me, so I may know which way to turn."

⁵⁰Laban and Bethuel answered, "This is from the Lᴏʀᴅ; we can say nothing to you one way or the other. ⁵¹Here is Rebekah; take her and go, and let her become the wife of your master's son, as the Lᴏʀᴅ has directed."

⁵²When Abraham's servant heard what they said, he bowed down to the ground before the Lᴏʀᴅ. ⁵³Then the servant brought out gold and silver jewelry and articles of clothing and gave them to Rebekah; he also gave costly gifts to her brother and to her mother. ⁵⁴Then he and the men who were with him ate and drank and spent the night there.

When they got up the next morning, he said, "Send me on my way to my master."

⁵⁵But her brother and her mother replied, "Let the young woman remain with us ten days or so; then you^a may go."

^{a} 55 Or she

Genesis 24:1–67

Rebekah made up her own mind.

When Abraham went looking for a wife for his son, he was doing what any ancient dad would do. Actually, this wealthy Old Testament patriarch sent his head servant, Eliezer, searching for a bride for Isaac. Abraham made Eliezer swear he wouldn't consider any of the women near the new family home in Canaan, pointing him instead to his own people and relatives back in Mesopotamia.

Back in that land Eliezer paused with his caravan and prayed for a sign he would discover the right woman. When Rebekah came along and drew water not only for him but also for his long line of camels, he realized God had given him a sign.

Eliezer knew it would be tough to find a wife willing to leave her homeland and marry an unknown man a thousand miles away. But he made the case to Rebekah's father, Laban, explaining how God had answered his prayer for a sign. In an age where fathers exercised complete control over their children, Rebekah's dad quickly agreed to give his daughter in marriage. Eliezer just as quickly unwrapped costly gifts for Rebekah and her family.

But the next morning Laban gave his daughter an unusual choice. He asked if she truly wanted to go. "I will go," Rebekah replied (Genesis 24:58). This ancient woman made up her own mind, daring not only to leave home but also to become part of a family God would use to change the world.

You can find Rebekah in Genesis 24—27.

UNSHAKEN people

⁵⁶But he said to them, "Do not detain me, now that the LORD has granted success to my journey. Send me on my way so I may go to my master."

⁵⁷Then they said, "Let's call the young woman and ask her about it." ⁵⁸So they called Rebekah and asked her, "Will you go with this man?"

"I will go," she said.

⁵⁹So they sent their sister Rebekah on her way, along with her nurse and Abraham's servant and his men. ⁶⁰And they blessed Rebekah and said to her,

> "Our sister, may you increase
>   to thousands upon thousands;
> may your offspring possess
>   the cities of their enemies."

⁶¹Then Rebekah and her attendants got ready and mounted the camels and went back with the man. So the servant took Rebekah and left.

⁶²Now Isaac had come from Beer Lahai Roi, for he was living in the Negev. ⁶³He went out to the field one evening to meditate,ᵃ and as he looked up, he saw camels approaching. ⁶⁴Rebekah also looked up and saw Isaac. She got down from her camel ⁶⁵and asked the servant, "Who is that man in the field coming to meet us?"

"He is my master," the servant answered. So she took her veil and covered herself.

⁶⁶Then the servant told Isaac all he had done. ⁶⁷Isaac brought her into the tent of his mother Sarah, and he married Rebekah. So she became his wife, and he loved her; and Isaac was comforted after his mother's death.

The Death of Abraham

25 Abraham had taken another wife, whose name was Keturah. ²She bore him Zimran, Jokshan, Medan, Midian, Ishbak and Shuah. ³Jokshan was the father of Sheba and Dedan; the descendants of Dedan were the Ashurites, the Letushites and the Leummites. ⁴The sons of Midian were Ephah, Epher, Hanok, Abida and Eldaah. All these were descendants of Keturah.

⁵Abraham left everything he owned to Isaac. ⁶But while he was still living, he gave gifts to the sons of his concubines and sent them away from his son Isaac to the land of the east.

⁷Abraham lived a hundred and seventy-five years. ⁸Then Abraham breathed his last and died at a good old age, an old man and full of years; and he was gathered to his people. ⁹His sons Isaac and Ishmael buried him in the cave of Machpelah near Mamre, in the field of Ephron son of Zohar the Hittite, ¹⁰the field Abraham had bought from the Hittites.ᵇ There Abraham was buried with his wife Sarah. ¹¹After Abraham's death, God blessed his son Isaac, who then lived near Beer Lahai Roi.

Ishmael's Sons

¹²This is the account of the family line of Abraham's son Ishmael, whom Sarah's slave, Hagar the Egyptian, bore to Abraham.

¹³These are the names of the sons of Ishmael, listed in the order of their birth: Nebaioth the firstborn of Ishmael, Kedar, Adbeel, Mibsam, ¹⁴Mishma, Dumah, Massa, ¹⁵Hadad, Tema, Jetur, Naphish and Kedemah. ¹⁶These were the sons of Ishmael, and these are the names of the twelve tribal rulers according to their settlements and camps. ¹⁷Ishmael lived a hundred and thirty-seven years. He breathed his last and died, and he was gathered to his people. ¹⁸His descendants settled in the area from Havilah to Shur, near the eastern border of Egypt, as you go toward Ashur. And they lived in hostility towardᶜ all the tribes related to them.

Jacob and Esau

¹⁹This is the account of the family line of Abraham's son Isaac.

Abraham became the father of Isaac, ²⁰and Isaac was forty years old when he

---

ᵃ 63 The meaning of the Hebrew for this word is uncertain.   ᵇ 10 Or *the descendants of Heth*
ᶜ 18 Or *lived to the east of*

married Rebekah daughter of Bethuel the Aramean from Paddan Aram[a] and sister of Laban the Aramean.

[21] Isaac prayed to the LORD on behalf of his wife, because she was childless. The LORD answered his prayer, and his wife Rebekah became pregnant. [22] The babies jostled each other within her, and she said, "Why is this happening to me?" So she went to inquire of the LORD.

[23] The LORD said to her,

"Two nations are in your womb,
    and two peoples from within you
        will be separated;
one people will be stronger than the
        other,
    and the older will serve the
        younger."

[24] When the time came for her to give birth, there were twin boys in her womb. [25] The first to come out was red, and his whole body was like a hairy garment; so they named him Esau.[b] [26] After this, his brother came out, with his hand grasping Esau's heel; so he was named Jacob.[c] Isaac was sixty years old when Rebekah gave birth to them.

[27] The boys grew up, and Esau became a skillful hunter, a man of the open country, while Jacob was content to stay at home among the tents. [28] Isaac, who had a taste for wild game, loved Esau, but Rebekah loved Jacob.

[29] Once when Jacob was cooking some stew, Esau came in from the open country, famished. [30] He said to Jacob, "Quick, let me have some of that red stew! I'm famished!" (That is why he was also called Edom.[d])

[31] Jacob replied, "First sell me your birthright."

[32] "Look, I am about to die," Esau said. "What good is the birthright to me?"

[33] But Jacob said, "Swear to me first." So he swore an oath to him, selling his birthright to Jacob.

[34] Then Jacob gave Esau some bread and some lentil stew. He ate and drank, and then got up and left.

So Esau despised his birthright.

Isaac and Abimelek

26 Now there was a famine in the land—besides the previous famine in Abraham's time—and Isaac went to Abimelek king of the Philistines in Gerar. [2] The LORD appeared to Isaac and said, "Do not go down to Egypt; live in the land where I tell you to live. [3] Stay in this land for a while, and I will be with you and will bless you. For to you and your descendants I will give all these lands and will confirm the oath I swore to your father Abraham. [4] I will make your descendants as numerous as the stars in the sky and will give them all these lands, and through your offspring[e] all nations on earth will be blessed,[f] [5] because Abraham obeyed me and did everything I required of him, keeping my commands, my decrees and my instructions." [6] So Isaac stayed in Gerar.

[7] When the men of that place asked him about his wife, he said, "She is my sister," because he was afraid to say, "She is my wife." He thought, "The men of this place might kill me on account of Rebekah, because she is beautiful."

[8] When Isaac had been there a long time, Abimelek king of the Philistines looked down from a window and saw Isaac caressing his wife Rebekah. [9] So Abimelek summoned Isaac and said, "She is really your wife! Why did you say, 'She is my sister'?"

Isaac answered him, "Because I thought I might lose my life on account of her."

[10] Then Abimelek said, "What is this you have done to us? One of the men might well have slept with your wife, and you would have brought guilt upon us."

[11] So Abimelek gave orders to all the people: "Anyone who harms this man or his wife shall surely be put to death."

[12] Isaac planted crops in that land and the same year reaped a hundredfold,

---

[a] 20 That is, Northwest Mesopotamia
[b] 25 Esau may mean hairy.   [c] 26 Jacob means he grasps the heel, a Hebrew idiom for he deceives.
[d] 30 Edom means red.   [e] 4 Or seed   [f] 4 Or and all nations on earth will use the name of your offspring in blessings (see 48:20)

because the LORD blessed him. [13]The man became rich, and his wealth continued to grow until he became very wealthy. [14]He had so many flocks and herds and servants that the Philistines envied him. [15]So all the wells that his father's servants had dug in the time of his father Abraham, the Philistines stopped up, filling them with earth.

[16]Then Abimelek said to Isaac, "Move away from us; you have become too powerful for us."

[17]So Isaac moved away from there and encamped in the Valley of Gerar, where he settled. [18]Isaac reopened the wells that had been dug in the time of his father Abraham, which the Philistines had stopped up after Abraham died, and he gave them the same names his father had given them.

[19]Isaac's servants dug in the valley and discovered a well of fresh water there. [20]But the herders of Gerar quarreled with those of Isaac and said, "The water is ours!" So he named the well Esek,[a] because they disputed with him. [21]Then they dug another well, but they quarreled over that one also; so he named it Sitnah.[b] [22]He moved on from there and dug another well, and no one quarreled over it. He named it Rehoboth,[c] saying, "Now the LORD has given us room and we will flourish in the land."

[23]From there he went up to Beersheba. [24]That night the LORD appeared to him and said, "I am the God of your father Abraham. Do not be afraid, for I am with you; I will bless you and will increase the number of your descendants for the sake of my servant Abraham."

[25]Isaac built an altar there and called on the name of the LORD. There he pitched his tent, and there his servants dug a well.

[26]Meanwhile, Abimelek had come to him from Gerar, with Ahuzzath his personal adviser and Phicol the commander of his forces. [27]Isaac asked them, "Why have you come to me, since you were hostile to me and sent me away?"

[28]They answered, "We saw clearly that the LORD was with you; so we said, 'There ought to be a sworn agreement between us'—between us and you. Let us make a treaty with you [29]that you will do us no harm, just as we did not harm you but always treated you well and sent you away peacefully. And now you are blessed by the LORD."

[30]Isaac then made a feast for them, and they ate and drank. [31]Early the next morning the men swore an oath to each other. Then Isaac sent them on their way, and they went away peacefully.

[32]That day Isaac's servants came and told him about the well they had dug. They said, "We've found water!" [33]He called it Shibah,[d] and to this day the name of the town has been Beersheba.[e]

Jacob Takes Esau's Blessing

[34]When Esau was forty years old, he married Judith daughter of Beeri the Hittite, and also Basemath daughter of Elon the Hittite. [35]They were a source of grief to Isaac and Rebekah.

27 When Isaac was old and his eyes were so weak that he could no longer see, he called for Esau his older son and said to him, "My son."

"Here I am," he answered.

---

[a] 20 Esek means dispute.   [b] 21 Sitnah means opposition.   [c] 22 Rehoboth means room.   [d] 33 Shibah can mean oath or seven.   [e] 33 Beersheba can mean well of the oath and well of seven.

ROCK SOLID promises

"Do not be afraid, for I am with you."   Genesis 26:24

Because God is with you, there's nothing to fear. Really. Nothing.

²Isaac said, "I am now an old man and don't know the day of my death. ³Now then, get your equipment—your quiver and bow—and go out to the open country to hunt some wild game for me. ⁴Prepare me the kind of tasty food I like and bring it to me to eat, so that I may give you my blessing before I die."

⁵Now Rebekah was listening as Isaac spoke to his son Esau. When Esau left for the open country to hunt game and bring it back, ⁶Rebekah said to her son Jacob, "Look, I overheard your father say to your brother Esau, ⁷'Bring me some game and prepare me some tasty food to eat, so that I may give you my blessing in the presence of the LORD before I die.' ⁸Now, my son, listen carefully and do what I tell you: ⁹Go out to the flock and bring me two choice young goats, so I can prepare some tasty food for your father, just the way he likes it. ¹⁰Then take it to your father to eat, so that he may give you his blessing before he dies."

¹¹Jacob said to Rebekah his mother, "But my brother Esau is a hairy man while I have smooth skin. ¹²What if my father touches me? I would appear to be tricking him and would bring down a curse on myself rather than a blessing."

¹³His mother said to him, "My son, let the curse fall on me. Just do what I say; go and get them for me."

¹⁴So he went and got them and brought them to his mother, and she prepared some tasty food, just the way his father liked it. ¹⁵Then Rebekah took the best clothes of Esau her older son, which she had in the house, and put them on her younger son Jacob. ¹⁶She also covered his hands and the smooth part of his neck with the goatskins. ¹⁷Then she handed to her son Jacob the tasty food and the bread she had made.

¹⁸He went to his father and said, "My father."

"Yes, my son," he answered. "Who is it?"

¹⁹Jacob said to his father, "I am Esau your firstborn. I have done as you told me. Please sit up and eat some of my game, so that you may give me your blessing."

²⁰Isaac asked his son, "How did you find it so quickly, my son?"

"The LORD your God gave me success," he replied.

²¹Then Isaac said to Jacob, "Come near so I can touch you, my son, to know whether you really are my son Esau or not."

²²Jacob went close to his father Isaac, who touched him and said, "The voice is the voice of Jacob, but the hands are the hands of Esau." ²³He did not recognize him, for his hands were hairy like those of his brother Esau; so he proceeded to bless him. ²⁴"Are you really my son Esau?" he asked.

"I am," he replied.

²⁵Then he said, "My son, bring me some of your game to eat, so that I may give you my blessing."

Jacob brought it to him and he ate; and he brought some wine and he drank. ²⁶Then his father Isaac said to him, "Come here, my son, and kiss me."

²⁷So he went to him and kissed him. When Isaac caught the smell of his clothes, he blessed him and said,

"Ah, the smell of my son
    is like the smell of a field
    that the LORD has blessed.
²⁸May God give you heaven's dew
    and earth's richness—
    an abundance of grain and new
        wine.
²⁹May nations serve you
    and peoples bow down to you.
Be lord over your brothers,
    and may the sons of your mother
        bow down to you.
May those who curse you be cursed
    and those who bless you be blessed."

³⁰After Isaac finished blessing him, and Jacob had scarcely left his father's presence, his brother Esau came in from hunting. ³¹He too prepared some tasty food and brought it to his father. Then he said to him, "My father, please sit up and eat some of my game, so that you may give me your blessing."

³²His father Isaac asked him, "Who are you?"

"I am your son," he answered, "your firstborn, Esau."

³³ Isaac trembled violently and said, "Who was it, then, that hunted game and brought it to me? I ate it just before you came and I blessed him—and indeed he will be blessed!"

³⁴ When Esau heard his father's words, he burst out with a loud and bitter cry and said to his father, "Bless me—me too, my father!"

³⁵ But he said, "Your brother came deceitfully and took your blessing."

³⁶ Esau said, "Isn't he rightly named Jacob*? This is the second time he has taken advantage of me: He took my birthright, and now he's taken my blessing!" Then he asked, "Haven't you reserved any blessing for me?"

³⁷ Isaac answered Esau, "I have made him lord over you and have made all his relatives his servants, and I have sustained him with grain and new wine. So what can I possibly do for you, my son?"

³⁸ Esau said to his father, "Do you have only one blessing, my father? Bless me too, my father!" Then Esau wept aloud.

³⁹ His father Isaac answered him,

"Your dwelling will be
    away from the earth's richness,
    away from the dew of heaven above.
⁴⁰ You will live by the sword
    and you will serve your brother.
But when you grow restless,
    you will throw his yoke
    from off your neck."

⁴¹ Esau held a grudge against Jacob because of the blessing his father had given him. He said to himself, "The days of mourning for my father are near; then I will kill my brother Jacob."

⁴² When Rebekah was told what her older son Esau had said, she sent for her younger son Jacob and said to him, "Your brother Esau is planning to avenge himself by killing you. ⁴³ Now then, my son, do what I say: Flee at once to my brother Laban in Harran. ⁴⁴ Stay with him for a while until your brother's fury subsides. ⁴⁵ When your brother is no longer angry with you

and forgets what you did to him, I'll send word for you to come back from there. Why should I lose both of you in one day?"

⁴⁶ Then Rebekah said to Isaac, "I'm disgusted with living because of these Hittite women. If Jacob takes a wife from among the women of this land, from Hit-

a 36 Jacob means *he grasps the heel*, a Hebrew idiom for *he takes advantage of* or *he deceives*.

Genesis 27:1–46

The Bible describes things you shouldn't do.

King Solomon had several hundred wives, but that doesn't make polygamy right—in fact, those wives led him to worship false gods (see 1 Kings 11:1–15). Gideon was a leader of Israel who tested God's guidance using a dew-soaked piece of cloth, but that doesn't mean putting a fleece blanket on the lawn is the right way to discover the Lord's will (see Judges 6:36–40). And Jacob used treachery and deceit to grab the major portion of the family inheritance. First he convinced his hungry older brother, Esau, to trade his birthright for a bowl of stew (see Genesis 25:27–34). Later he wrapped animal skins on his arms to trick his blind elderly father into thinking he was blessing hairy Esau (see Genesis 27:1–46). Got the point? Just because you read something in the Bible doesn't mean it's okay to do it. God's straightforward commands always tell you the right way to live.

Think: Why did God let the stories of misguided people be told in the Bible?

ROCK SOLID truths

tite women like these, my life will not be worth living."

28

So Isaac called for Jacob and blessed him. Then he commanded him: "Do not marry a Canaanite woman. ²Go at once to Paddan Aram,ᵃ to the house of your mother's father Bethuel. Take a wife for yourself there, from among the daughters of Laban, your mother's brother. ³May God Almightyᵇ bless you and make you fruitful and increase your numbers until you become a community of peoples. ⁴May he give you and your descendants the blessing given to Abraham, so that you may take possession of the land where you now reside as a foreigner, the land God gave to Abraham." ⁵Then Isaac sent Jacob on his way, and he went to Paddan Aram, to Laban son of Bethuel the Aramean, the brother of Rebekah, who was the mother of Jacob and Esau.

⁶Now Esau learned that Isaac had blessed Jacob and had sent him to Paddan Aram to take a wife from there, and that when he blessed him he commanded him, "Do not marry a Canaanite woman," ⁷and that Jacob had obeyed his father and mother and had gone to Paddan Aram. ⁸Esau then realized how displeasing the Canaanite women were to his father Isaac; ⁹so he went to Ishmael and married Mahalath, the sister of Nebaioth and daughter of Ishmael son of Abraham, in addition to the wives he already had.

Jacob's Dream at Bethel

¹⁰Jacob left Beersheba and set out for Harran. ¹¹When he reached a certain place, he stopped for the night because the sun had set. Taking one of the stones there, he put it under his head and lay down to sleep. ¹²He had a dream in which he saw a stairway resting on the earth, with its top reaching to heaven, and the angels of God were ascending and descending on it. ¹³There above itᶜ stood the LORD, and he said: "I am the LORD, the God of your father Abraham and the God of Isaac. I will give you and your descendants the land on which you are lying.

¹⁴Your descendants will be like the dust of the earth, and you will spread out to the west and to the east, to the north and to the south. All peoples on earth will be blessed through you and your offspring.ᵈ ¹⁵I am with you and will watch over you wherever you go, and I will bring you back to this land. I will not leave you until I have done what I have promised you."

¹⁶When Jacob awoke from his sleep, he thought, "Surely the LORD is in this place, and I was not aware of it." ¹⁷He was afraid and said, "How awesome is this place! This is none other than the house of God; this is the gate of heaven."

¹⁸Early the next morning Jacob took the stone he had placed under his head and set it up as a pillar and poured oil on top of it. ¹⁹He called that place Bethel,ᵉ though the city used to be called Luz.

²⁰Then Jacob made a vow, saying, "If God will be with me and will watch over me on this journey I am taking and will give me food to eat and clothes to wear ²¹so that I return safely to my father's household, then the LORDᶠ will be my God ²²andᵍ this stone that I have set up as a pillar will be God's house, and of all that you give me I will give you a tenth."

Jacob Arrives in Paddan Aram

29

Then Jacob continued on his journey and came to the land of the eastern peoples. ²There he saw a well in the open country, with three flocks of sheep lying near it because the flocks were watered from that well. The stone over the mouth of the well was large. ³When all the flocks were gathered there, the shepherds would roll the stone away from the well's mouth and water the sheep. Then they would return the stone to its place over the mouth of the well.

ᵃ 2 That is, Northwest Mesopotamia; also in verses 5, 6 and 7   ᵇ 3 Hebrew *El-Shaddai*
ᶜ 13 Or *There beside him*   ᵈ 14 Or *will use your name and the name of your offspring in blessings* (see 48:20)   ᵉ 19 *Bethel* means *house of God*.
ᶠ 20,21 Or *Since God . . . father's household, the LORD*   ᵍ 21,22 Or *household, and the LORD will be my God,* ²²*then*

⁴Jacob asked the shepherds, "My brothers, where are you from?"

"We're from Harran," they replied.

⁵He said to them, "Do you know Laban, Nahor's grandson?"

"Yes, we know him," they answered.

⁶Then Jacob asked them, "Is he well?"

"Yes, he is," they said, "and here comes his daughter Rachel with the sheep."

⁷"Look," he said, "the sun is still high; it is not time for the flocks to be gathered. Water the sheep and take them back to pasture."

⁸"We can't," they replied, "until all the flocks are gathered and the stone has been rolled away from the mouth of the well. Then we will water the sheep."

⁹While he was still talking with them, Rachel came with her father's sheep, for she was a shepherd. ¹⁰When Jacob saw Rachel daughter of his uncle Laban, and Laban's sheep, he went over and rolled the stone away from the mouth of the well and watered his uncle's sheep. ¹¹Then Jacob kissed Rachel and began to weep aloud. ¹²He had told Rachel that he was a relative of her father and a son of Rebekah. So she ran and told her father.

¹³As soon as Laban heard the news about Jacob, his sister's son, he hurried to

---

Genesis 29:1 – 14

Jacob got in line with God's plan.

Jacob didn't look like good material for a starring role in God's plan to build a nation. First he fooled his brother, Esau, into swapping his honored birthright for a bowl of stew (see Genesis 25:27 – 34). Then he tricked his elderly father into giving him the blessing that belonged to Esau (see Genesis 27:1 – 40). When Esau realized the evil Jacob had done to him, he swore he would kill his brother, and Jacob had to flee to his uncle Laban to avoid his brother's murderous wrath. There Jacob the deceiver finally tasted his own deceit when Laban conned him into working seven years for a wife he didn't want (see Genesis 29:15 – 30).

Despite those years of deceiving and being deceived, Jacob got on track with God. Although Jacob had feared Esau would kill him and his family, the brothers became friends again when Jacob returned and shared his wealth with Esau (see Genesis 32:1 – 21; 33:1 – 20). Along the way the Lord reminded Jacob in a dream that he was indeed part of a great plan to build a nation (see Genesis 28:10 – 22). And in another dream the Lord himself wrestled with this stubborn man, humbling and permanently wounding him (see Genesis 32:22 – 32).

In the end, Jacob watched his own dozen sons battle for supremacy (see Genesis 37; 39 — 50). These sons became the next step in the Lord's plan, founding the 12 tribes that would shape Israel's history for the rest of the Old Testament.

You can find Jacob in Genesis 25 — 37; Acts 7:32; and Hebrews 11:8 – 15.

UNSHAKEN people

meet him. He embraced him and kissed him and brought him to his home, and there Jacob told him all these things. ¹⁴Then Laban said to him, "You are my own flesh and blood."

Jacob Marries Leah and Rachel

After Jacob had stayed with him for a whole month, ¹⁵Laban said to him, "Just because you are a relative of mine, should you work for me for nothing? Tell me what your wages should be."

¹⁶Now Laban had two daughters; the name of the older was Leah, and the name of the younger was Rachel. ¹⁷Leah had weak*ᵃ* eyes, but Rachel had a lovely figure and was beautiful. ¹⁸Jacob was in love with Rachel and said, "I'll work for you seven years in return for your younger daughter Rachel."

¹⁹Laban said, "It's better that I give her to you than to some other man. Stay here with me." ²⁰So Jacob served seven years to get Rachel, but they seemed like only a few days to him because of his love for her.

²¹Then Jacob said to Laban, "Give me my wife. My time is completed, and I want to make love to her."

²²So Laban brought together all the people of the place and gave a feast. ²³But when evening came, he took his daughter Leah and brought her to Jacob, and Jacob made love to her. ²⁴And Laban gave his servant Zilpah to his daughter as her attendant.

²⁵When morning came, there was Leah! So Jacob said to Laban, "What is this you have done to me? I served you for Rachel, didn't I? Why have you deceived me?"

²⁶Laban replied, "It is not our custom here to give the younger daughter in marriage before the older one. ²⁷Finish this daughter's bridal week; then we will give you the younger one also, in return for another seven years of work."

²⁸And Jacob did so. He finished the week with Leah, and then Laban gave him his daughter Rachel to be his wife. ²⁹Laban gave his servant Bilhah to his daughter Rachel as her attendant. ³⁰Jacob made love to Rachel also, and his love for Rachel

was greater than his love for Leah. And he worked for Laban another seven years.

Jacob's Children

³¹When the LORD saw that Leah was not loved, he enabled her to conceive, but Rachel remained childless. ³²Leah became pregnant and gave birth to a son. She named him Reuben,*ᵇ* for she said, "It is because the LORD has seen my misery. Surely my husband will love me now."

³³She conceived again, and when she gave birth to a son she said, "Because the LORD heard that I am not loved, he gave me this one too." So she named him Simeon.*ᶜ*

³⁴Again she conceived, and when she gave birth to a son she said, "Now at last my husband will become attached to me, because I have borne him three sons." So he was named Levi.*ᵈ*

³⁵She conceived again, and when she gave birth to a son she said, "This time I will praise the LORD." So she named him Judah.*ᵉ* Then she stopped having children.

30

When Rachel saw that she was not bearing Jacob any children, she became jealous of her sister. So she said to Jacob, "Give me children, or I'll die!"

²Jacob became angry with her and said, "Am I in the place of God, who has kept you from having children?"

³Then she said, "Here is Bilhah, my servant. Sleep with her so that she can bear children for me and I too can build a family through her."

⁴So she gave him her servant Bilhah as a wife. Jacob slept with her, ⁵and she became pregnant and bore him a son. ⁶Then Rachel said, "God has vindicated me; he has listened to my plea and given me a son." Because of this she named him Dan.*ᶠ*

ᵃ 17 Or *delicate*   *ᵇ 32 Reuben* sounds like the Hebrew for *he has seen my misery*; the name means *see, a son.*   *ᶜ 33 Simeon* probably means *one who hears.*   *ᵈ 34 Levi* sounds like and may be derived from the Hebrew for *attached.*   *ᵉ 35 Judah* sounds like and may be derived from the Hebrew for *praise.*   *ᶠ 6 Dan* here means *he has vindicated.*

⁷Rachel's servant Bilhah conceived again and bore Jacob a second son. ⁸Then Rachel said, "I have had a great struggle with my sister, and I have won." So she named him Naphtali.*

⁹When Leah saw that she had stopped having children, she took her servant Zilpah and gave her to Jacob as a wife. ¹⁰Leah's servant Zilpah bore Jacob a son. ¹¹Then Leah said, "What good fortune!"* So she named him Gad.*

¹²Leah's servant Zilpah bore Jacob a second son. ¹³Then Leah said, "How happy I am! The women will call me happy." So she named him Asher.*

¹⁴During wheat harvest, Reuben went out into the fields and found some mandrake plants, which he brought to his mother Leah. Rachel said to Leah, "Please give me some of your son's mandrakes."

¹⁵But she said to her, "Wasn't it enough that you took away my husband? Will you take my son's mandrakes too?"

"Very well," Rachel said, "he can sleep with you tonight in return for your son's mandrakes."

¹⁶So when Jacob came in from the fields that evening, Leah went out to meet him. "You must sleep with me," she said. "I have hired you with my son's mandrakes." So he slept with her that night.

¹⁷God listened to Leah, and she became pregnant and bore Jacob a fifth son. ¹⁸Then Leah said, "God has rewarded me for giving my servant to my husband." So she named him Issachar.*

¹⁹Leah conceived again and bore Jacob a sixth son. ²⁰Then Leah said, "God has presented me with a precious gift. This time my husband will treat me with honor, because I have borne him six sons." So she named him Zebulun.*

²¹Some time later she gave birth to a daughter and named her Dinah.

²²Then God remembered Rachel; he listened to her and enabled her to conceive. ²³She became pregnant and gave birth to a son and said, "God has taken away my disgrace." ²⁴She named him Joseph,* and said, "May the LORD add to me another son."

Jacob's Flocks Increase

²⁵After Rachel gave birth to Joseph, Jacob said to Laban, "Send me on my way so I can go back to my own homeland. ²⁶Give me my wives and children, for whom I have served you, and I will be on my way. You know how much work I've done for you."

²⁷But Laban said to him, "If I have found favor in your eyes, please stay. I have learned by divination that the LORD has blessed me because of you." ²⁸He added, "Name your wages, and I will pay them."

²⁹Jacob said to him, "You know how I have worked for you and how your livestock has fared under my care. ³⁰The little you had before I came has increased greatly, and the LORD has blessed you wherever I have been. But now, when may I do something for my own household?"

³¹"What shall I give you?" he asked.

"Don't give me anything," Jacob replied. "But if you will do this one thing for me, I will go on tending your flocks and watching over them: ³²Let me go through all your flocks today and remove from them every speckled or spotted sheep, every dark-colored lamb and every spotted or speckled goat. They will be my wages. ³³And my honesty will testify for me in the future, whenever you check on the wages you have paid me. Any goat in my possession that is not speckled or spotted, or any lamb that is not dark-colored, will be considered stolen."

³⁴"Agreed," said Laban. "Let it be as you have said." ³⁵That same day he removed all the male goats that were streaked or spotted, and all the speckled or spotted female goats (all that had white on them) and all the dark-colored lambs, and he placed them in the care of his sons. ³⁶Then he put a three-day journey between himself and Jacob, while Jacob continued to tend the rest of Laban's flocks.

---

a 8 Naphtali means *my struggle.* *b 11 Or "A troop is coming!"* *c 11 Gad* can mean *good fortune* or *a troop.* *d 13 Asher* means *happy.*
e 18 Issachar sounds like the Hebrew for *reward.*
f 20 Zebulun probably means *honor.*
g 24 Joseph means *may he add.*

[37] Jacob, however, took fresh-cut branches from poplar, almond and plane trees and made white stripes on them by peeling the bark and exposing the white inner wood of the branches. [38] Then he placed the peeled branches in all the watering troughs, so that they would be directly in front of the flocks when they came to drink. When the flocks were in heat and came to drink, [39] they mated in front of the branches. And they bore young that were streaked or speckled or spotted. [40] Jacob set apart the young of the flock by themselves, but made the rest face the streaked and dark-colored animals that belonged to Laban. Thus he made separate flocks for himself and did not put them with Laban's animals. [41] Whenever the stronger females were in heat, Jacob would place the branches in the troughs in front of the animals so they would mate near the branches, [42] but if the animals were weak, he would not place them there. So the weak animals went to Laban and the strong ones to Jacob. [43] In this way the man grew exceedingly prosperous and came to own large flocks, and female and male servants, and camels and donkeys.

Jacob Flees From Laban

31 Jacob heard that Laban's sons were saying, "Jacob has taken everything our father owned and has gained all this wealth from what belonged to our father." [2] And Jacob noticed that Laban's attitude toward him was not what it had been.

[3] Then the LORD said to Jacob, "Go back to the land of your fathers and to your relatives, and I will be with you."

[4] So Jacob sent word to Rachel and Leah to come out to the fields where his flocks were. [5] He said to them, "I see that your father's attitude toward me is not what it was before, but the God of my father has been with me. [6] You know that I've worked for your father with all my strength, [7] yet your father has cheated me by changing my wages ten times. However, God has not allowed him to harm me. [8] If he said, 'The speckled ones will be your wages,' then all the flocks gave birth to speckled young; and if he said, 'The streaked ones will be your wages,' then all the flocks bore streaked young. [9] So God has taken away your father's livestock and has given them to me.

[10] "In breeding season I once had a dream in which I looked up and saw that the male goats mating with the flock were streaked, speckled or spotted. [11] The angel of God said to me in the dream, 'Jacob.' I answered, 'Here I am.' [12] And he said, 'Look up and see that all the male goats mating with the flock are streaked, speckled or spotted, for I have seen all that Laban has been doing to you. [13] I am the God of Bethel, where you anointed a pillar and where you made a vow to me. Now leave this land at once and go back to your native land.'"

[14] Then Rachel and Leah replied, "Do we still have any share in the inheritance of our father's estate? [15] Does he not regard us as foreigners? Not only has he sold us, but he has used up what was paid for us. [16] Surely all the wealth that God took away from our father belongs to us and our children. So do whatever God has told you."

[17] Then Jacob put his children and his wives on camels, [18] and he drove all his livestock ahead of him, along with all the goods he had accumulated in Paddan Aram,[a] to go to his father Isaac in the land of Canaan.

[19] When Laban had gone to shear his sheep, Rachel stole her father's household gods. [20] Moreover, Jacob deceived Laban the Aramean by not telling him he was running away. [21] So he fled with all he had, crossed the Euphrates River, and headed for the hill country of Gilead.

Laban Pursues Jacob

[22] On the third day Laban was told that Jacob had fled. [23] Taking his relatives with him, he pursued Jacob for seven days and caught up with him in the hill country of Gilead. [24] Then God came to Laban the Aramean in a dream at night and said to him, "Be careful not to say anything to Jacob, either good or bad."

---

[a] 18 That is, Northwest Mesopotamia

²⁵Jacob had pitched his tent in the hill country of Gilead when Laban overtook him, and Laban and his relatives camped there too. ²⁶Then Laban said to Jacob, "What have you done? You've deceived me, and you've carried off my daughters like captives in war. ²⁷Why did you run off secretly and deceive me? Why didn't you tell me, so I could send you away with joy and singing to the music of timbrels and harps? ²⁸You didn't even let me kiss my grandchildren and my daughters goodbye. You have done a foolish thing. ²⁹I have the power to harm you; but last night the God of your father said to me, 'Be careful not to say anything to Jacob, either good or bad.' ³⁰Now you have gone off because you longed to return to your father's household. But why did you steal my gods?"

³¹Jacob answered Laban, "I was afraid, because I thought you would take your daughters away from me by force. ³²But if you find anyone who has your gods, that person shall not live. In the presence of our relatives, see for yourself whether there is anything of yours here with me; and if so, take it." Now Jacob did not know that Rachel had stolen the gods.

³³So Laban went into Jacob's tent and into Leah's tent and into the tent of the two female servants, but he found nothing. After he came out of Leah's tent, he entered Rachel's tent. ³⁴Now Rachel had taken the household gods and put them inside her camel's saddle and was sitting on them. Laban searched through everything in the tent but found nothing.

³⁵Rachel said to her father, "Don't be angry, my lord, that I cannot stand up in your presence; I'm having my period." So he searched but could not find the household gods.

³⁶Jacob was angry and took Laban to task. "What is my crime?" he asked Laban. "How have I wronged you that you hunt me down? ³⁷Now that you have searched through all my goods, what have you found that belongs to your household? Put it here in front of your relatives and mine, and let them judge between the two of us.

³⁸"I have been with you for twenty years now. Your sheep and goats have not miscarried, nor have I eaten rams from your flocks. ³⁹I did not bring you animals torn by wild beasts; I bore the loss myself. And you demanded payment from me for whatever was stolen by day or night. ⁴⁰This was my situation: The heat consumed me in the daytime and the cold at night, and sleep fled from my eyes. ⁴¹It was like this for the twenty years I was in your household. I worked for you fourteen years for your two daughters and six years for your flocks, and you changed my wages ten times. ⁴²If the God of my father, the God of Abraham and the Fear of Isaac, had not been with me, you would surely have sent me away empty-handed. But God has seen my hardship and the toil of my hands, and last night he rebuked you."

⁴³Laban answered Jacob, "The women are my daughters, the children are my children, and the flocks are my flocks. All you see is mine. Yet what can I do today about these daughters of mine, or about the children they have borne? ⁴⁴Come now, let's make a covenant, you and I, and let it serve as a witness between us."

⁴⁵So Jacob took a stone and set it up as a pillar. ⁴⁶He said to his relatives, "Gather some stones." So they took stones and piled them in a heap, and they ate there by the heap. ⁴⁷Laban called it Jegar Sahadutha, and Jacob called it Galeed.ᵃ

⁴⁸Laban said, "This heap is a witness between you and me today." That is why it was called Galeed. ⁴⁹It was also called Mizpah,ᵇ because he said, "May the LORD keep watch between you and me when we are away from each other. ⁵⁰If you mistreat my daughters or if you take any wives besides my daughters, even though no one is with us, remember that God is a witness between you and me."

⁵¹Laban also said to Jacob, "Here is this heap, and here is this pillar I have set up between you and me. ⁵²This heap is a witness, and this pillar is a witness, that I

ᵃ 47 The Aramaic *Jegar Sahadutha* and the Hebrew *Galeed* both mean *witness heap*.
ᵇ 49 *Mizpah* means *watchtower*.

will not go past this heap to your side to harm you and that you will not go past this heap and pillar to my side to harm me. ⁵³May the God of Abraham and the God of Nahor, the God of their father, judge between us."

So Jacob took an oath in the name of the Fear of his father Isaac. ⁵⁴He offered a sacrifice there in the hill country and invited his relatives to a meal. After they had eaten, they spent the night there.

⁵⁵Early the next morning Laban kissed his grandchildren and his daughters and blessed them. Then he left and returned home.ᵃ

Jacob Prepares to Meet Esau

32ᵇ Jacob also went on his way, and the angels of God met him. ²When Jacob saw them, he said, "This is the camp of God!" So he named that place Mahanaim.ᶜ

³Jacob sent messengers ahead of him to his brother Esau in the land of Seir, the country of Edom. ⁴He instructed them: "This is what you are to say to my lord Esau: 'Your servant Jacob says, I have been staying with Laban and have remained there till now. ⁵I have cattle and donkeys, sheep and goats, male and female servants. Now I am sending this message to my lord, that I may find favor in your eyes.'"

⁶When the messengers returned to Jacob, they said, "We went to your brother Esau, and now he is coming to meet you, and four hundred men are with him."

⁷In great fear and distress Jacob divided the people who were with him into two groups,ᵈ and the flocks and herds and camels as well. ⁸He thought, "If Esau comes and attacks one group,ᵉ the groupᵉ that is left may escape."

⁹Then Jacob prayed, "O God of my father Abraham, God of my father Isaac, Lord, you who said to me, 'Go back to your country and your relatives, and I will make you prosper,' ¹⁰I am unworthy of all the kindness and faithfulness you have shown your servant. I had only my staff when I crossed this Jordan, but now I have become two camps. ¹¹Save me, I

pray, from the hand of my brother Esau, for I am afraid he will come and attack me, and also the mothers with their children. ¹²But you have said, 'I will surely make you prosper and will make your descendants like the sand of the sea, which cannot be counted.'"

¹³He spent the night there, and from what he had with him he selected a gift for his brother Esau: ¹⁴two hundred female goats and twenty male goats, two hundred ewes and twenty rams, ¹⁵thirty female camels with their young, forty cows and ten bulls, and twenty female donkeys and ten male donkeys. ¹⁶He put them in the care of his servants, each herd by itself, and said to his servants, "Go ahead of me, and keep some space between the herds."

¹⁷He instructed the one in the lead: "When my brother Esau meets you and asks, 'Who do you belong to, and where are you going, and who owns all these animals in front of you?' ¹⁸then you are to say, 'They belong to your servant Jacob. They are a gift sent to my lord Esau, and he is coming behind us.'"

¹⁹He also instructed the second, the third and all the others who followed the herds: "You are to say the same thing to Esau when you meet him. ²⁰And be sure to say, 'Your servant Jacob is coming behind us.'" For he thought, "I will pacify him with these gifts I am sending on ahead; later, when I see him, perhaps he will receive me." ²¹So Jacob's gifts went on ahead of him, but he himself spent the night in the camp.

Jacob Wrestles With God

²²That night Jacob got up and took his two wives, his two female servants and his eleven sons and crossed the ford of the Jabbok. ²³After he had sent them across the stream, he sent over all his possessions. ²⁴So Jacob was left alone, and a man wrestled with him till daybreak. ²⁵When the man saw that he could not overpower

---

ᵃ 55 In Hebrew texts this verse (31:55) is numbered 32:1.   ᵇ In Hebrew texts 32:1-32 is numbered 32:2-33.   ᶜ 2 *Mahanaim* means *two camps*.   ᵈ 7 Or *camps*   ᵉ 8 Or *camp* him, he touched the socket of Jacob's hip so that his hip was wrenched as he wrestled with the man. ²⁶Then the man said, "Let me go, for it is daybreak."

But Jacob replied, "I will not let you go unless you bless me."

²⁷The man asked him, "What is your name?"

"Jacob," he answered.

²⁸Then the man said, "Your name will no longer be Jacob, but Israel,ᵃ because you have struggled with God and with humans and have overcome."

²⁹Jacob said, "Please tell me your name."

But he replied, "Why do you ask my name?" Then he blessed him there.

³⁰So Jacob called the place Peniel,ᵇ saying, "It is because I saw God face to face, and yet my life was spared."

³¹The sun rose above him as he passed Peniel,ᶜ and he was limping because of his hip. ³²Therefore to this day the Israelites do not eat the tendon attached to the socket of the hip, because the socket of Jacob's hip was touched near the tendon.

Jacob Meets Esau

33 Jacob looked up and there was Esau, coming with his four hundred men; so he divided the children among Leah, Rachel and the two female servants. ²He put the female servants and their children in front, Leah and her children next, and Rachel and Joseph in the rear. ³He himself went on ahead and bowed down to the ground seven times as he approached his brother.

⁴But Esau ran to meet Jacob and embraced him; he threw his arms around his neck and kissed him. And they wept. ⁵Then Esau looked up and saw the women and children. "Who are these with you?" he asked.

Jacob answered, "They are the children God has graciously given your servant."

⁶Then the female servants and their children approached and bowed down. ⁷Next, Leah and her children came and bowed down. Last of all came Joseph and Rachel, and they too bowed down.

⁸Esau asked, "What's the meaning of all these flocks and herds I met?"

"To find favor in your eyes, my lord," he said.

⁹But Esau said, "I already have plenty, my brother. Keep what you have for yourself."

¹⁰"No, please!" said Jacob. "If I have found favor in your eyes, accept this gift from me. For to see your face is like seeing the face of God, now that you have received me favorably. ¹¹Please accept the present that was brought to you, for God has been gracious to me and I have all I need." And because Jacob insisted, Esau accepted it.

¹²Then Esau said, "Let us be on our way; I'll accompany you."

¹³But Jacob said to him, "My lord knows that the children are tender and

---

UNSHAKEN *God*

Genesis 32:22–32

God is tough.

God must have had enough of Jacob's lifelong scheming and aggression because one day the Lord showed up for a man-on-man wrestling match. Bible experts debate exactly how God appeared in a physical body in this scene, but clearly it was God himself who fought Jacob (see Genesis 32:30). After a long night of wrestling, Jacob refused to surrender. So God reached out and injured Jacob's hip. He used pain to humble Jacob, but he didn't depart without giving Jacob a blessing—a new name probably meaning "he struggles with God." God sometimes uses tough love to teach lessons we won't learn any other way.

So ... When have you shut out something God wanted to say to you?

ᵃ 28 *Israel* probably means *he struggles with God.*
ᵇ 30 *Peniel* means *face of God.*   ᶜ 31 Hebrew *Penuel*, a variant of *Peniel*

that I must care for the ewes and cows that are nursing their young. If they are driven hard just one day, all the animals will die. ¹⁴So let my lord go on ahead of his servant, while I move along slowly at the pace of the flocks and herds before me and the pace of the children, until I come to my lord in Seir."

¹⁵Esau said, "Then let me leave some of my men with you."

"But why do that?" Jacob asked. "Just let me find favor in the eyes of my lord."

¹⁶So that day Esau started on his way back to Seir. ¹⁷Jacob, however, went to Sukkoth, where he built a place for himself and made shelters for his livestock. That is why the place is called Sukkoth.^a

¹⁸After Jacob came from Paddan Aram,^b he arrived safely at the city of Shechem in Canaan and camped within sight of the city. ¹⁹For a hundred pieces of silver,^c he bought from the sons of Hamor, the father of Shechem, the plot of ground where he pitched his tent. ²⁰There he set up an altar and called it El Elohe Israel.^d

Dinah and the Shechemites

34 Now Dinah, the daughter Leah had borne to Jacob, went out to visit the women of the land. ²When Shechem son of Hamor the Hivite, the ruler of that area, saw her, he took her and raped her. ³His heart was drawn to Dinah daughter of Jacob; he loved the young woman and spoke tenderly to her. ⁴And Shechem said to his father Hamor, "Get me this girl as my wife."

⁵When Jacob heard that his daughter Dinah had been defiled, his sons were in the fields with his livestock; so he did nothing about it until they came home.

⁶Then Shechem's father Hamor went out to talk with Jacob. ⁷Meanwhile, Jacob's sons had come in from the fields as soon as they heard what had happened. They were shocked and furious, because Shechem had done an outrageous thing in^e Israel by sleeping with Jacob's daughter—a thing that should not be done.

⁸But Hamor said to them, "My son Shechem has his heart set on your daughter.

Please give her to him as his wife. ⁹Intermarry with us; give us your daughters and take our daughters for yourselves. ¹⁰You can settle among us; the land is open to you. Live in it, trade^f in it, and acquire property in it."

¹¹Then Shechem said to Dinah's father and brothers, "Let me find favor in your eyes, and I will give you whatever you ask. ¹²Make the price for the bride and the gift I am to bring as great as you like, and I'll pay whatever you ask me. Only give me the young woman as my wife."

¹³Because their sister Dinah had been defiled, Jacob's sons replied deceitfully as they spoke to Shechem and his father Hamor. ¹⁴They said to them, "We can't do such a thing; we can't give our sister to a man who is not circumcised. That would be a disgrace to us. ¹⁵We will enter into an agreement with you on one condition only: that you become like us by circumcising all your males. ¹⁶Then we will give you our daughters and take your daughters for ourselves. We'll settle among you and become one people with you. ¹⁷But if you will not agree to be circumcised, we'll take our sister and go."

¹⁸Their proposal seemed good to Hamor and his son Shechem. ¹⁹The young man, who was the most honored of all his father's family, lost no time in doing what they said, because he was delighted with Jacob's daughter. ²⁰So Hamor and his son Shechem went to the gate of their city to speak to the men of their city. ²¹"These men are friendly toward us," they said. "Let them live in our land and trade in it; the land has plenty of room for them. We can marry their daughters and they can marry ours. ²²But the men will agree to live with us as one people only on the condition that our males be circumcised, as they themselves are. ²³Won't their livestock, their property and all their other

---

^a 17 *Sukkoth* means *shelters.*   ^b 18 That is, Northwest Mesopotamia   ^c 19 Hebrew *hundred kesitahs*; a kesitah was a unit of money of unknown weight and value.   ^d 20 *El Elohe Israel* can mean *El is the God of Israel* or *mighty is the God of Israel.*   ^e 7 Or *against* ^f 10 Or *move about freely*; also in verse 21

animals become ours? So let us agree to their terms, and they will settle among us."

²⁴All the men who went out of the city gate agreed with Hamor and his son Shechem, and every male in the city was circumcised.

²⁵Three days later, while all of them were still in pain, two of Jacob's sons, Simeon and Levi, Dinah's brothers, took their swords and attacked the unsuspecting city, killing every male. ²⁶They put Hamor and his son Shechem to the sword and took Dinah from Shechem's house and left. ²⁷The sons of Jacob came upon the dead bodies and looted the city where[a] their sister had been defiled. ²⁸They seized their flocks and herds and donkeys and everything else of theirs in the city and out in the fields. ²⁹They carried off all their wealth and all their women and children, taking as plunder everything in the houses.

³⁰Then Jacob said to Simeon and Levi, "You have brought trouble on me by making me obnoxious to the Canaanites and Perizzites, the people living in this land. We are few in number, and if they join forces against me and attack me, I and my household will be destroyed."

³¹But they replied, "Should he have treated our sister like a prostitute?"

Jacob Returns to Bethel

35 Then God said to Jacob, "Go up to Bethel and settle there, and build an altar there to God, who appeared to you when you were fleeing from your brother Esau."

²So Jacob said to his household and to all who were with him, "Get rid of the foreign gods you have with you, and purify yourselves and change your clothes. ³Then come, let us go up to Bethel, where I will build an altar to God, who answered me in the day of my distress and who has been with me wherever I have gone." ⁴So they gave Jacob all the foreign gods they had and the rings in their ears, and Jacob buried them under the oak at Shechem. ⁵Then they set out, and the terror of God fell on the towns all around them so that no one pursued them.

⁶Jacob and all the people with him came to Luz (that is, Bethel) in the land of Canaan. ⁷There he built an altar, and he called the place El Bethel,[b] because it was there that God revealed himself to him when he was fleeing from his brother.

⁸Now Deborah, Rebekah's nurse, died and was buried under the oak outside Bethel. So it was named Allon Bakuth.[c]

⁹After Jacob returned from Paddan Aram,[d] God appeared to him again and blessed him. ¹⁰God said to him, "Your name is Jacob,[e] but you will no longer be called Jacob; your name will be Israel.[f]" So he named him Israel.

¹¹And God said to him, "I am God Almighty[g]; be fruitful and increase in number. A nation and a community of nations will come from you, and kings will be among your descendants. ¹²The land I gave to Abraham and Isaac I also give to you, and I will give this land to your descendants after you." ¹³Then God went up from him at the place where he had talked with him.

¹⁴Jacob set up a stone pillar at the place where God had talked with him, and he poured out a drink offering on it; he also poured oil on it. ¹⁵Jacob called the place where God had talked with him Bethel.[b]

The Deaths of Rachel and Isaac

¹⁶Then they moved on from Bethel. While they were still some distance from Ephrath, Rachel began to give birth and had great difficulty. ¹⁷And as she was having great difficulty in childbirth, the midwife said to her, "Don't despair, for you have another son." ¹⁸As she breathed her last—for she was dying—she named her son Ben-Oni.[i] But his father named him Benjamin.[j]

¹⁹So Rachel died and was buried on

---

a 27 Or *because*   *b 7 El Bethel* means *God of Bethel.*   *c 8 Allon Bakuth* means *oak of weeping.*
d 9 That is, Northwest Mesopotamia; also in verse 26   *e 10 Jacob* means *he grasps the heel*, a Hebrew idiom for *he deceives.*   *f 10 Israel* probably means *he struggles with God.*
g 11 Hebrew *El-Shaddai*   *b 15 Bethel* means *house of God.*   *i 18 Ben-Oni* means *son of my trouble.*   *j 18 Benjamin* means *son of my right hand.*

Genesis 35:9–15

God never breaks a promise.

Lies. Fibs. Stretching the truth. You can't go a day without hearing people utter dozens of half-truths and outright lies. God, however, is nothing like human beings. He never goes back on his word, a fact you can easily see in how he keeps his "covenants," or "solemn agreements." The Lord swore that he would make Abraham the start of a great nation (see Genesis 12:2). Two generations later (Abraham fathered Isaac, who fathered Jacob), the Lord was still keeping his promise (see Genesis 35:11). God ultimately fulfilled his pledge when Jesus was born to the line of Abraham, making Abraham the spiritual father of everyone who accepts Jesus by faith (see Matthew 1:1; Galatians 4:6–7). All of this adds up to an obvious point: Your God will never lie to you.

Think: Why does it matter to you today that God never breaks a promise?

ROCK SOLID truths

the way to Ephrath (that is, Bethlehem). ²⁰Over her tomb Jacob set up a pillar, and to this day that pillar marks Rachel's tomb.

²¹Israel moved on again and pitched his tent beyond Migdal Eder. ²²While Israel was living in that region, Reuben went in and slept with his father's concubine Bilhah, and Israel heard of it.

Jacob had twelve sons:

²³The sons of Leah:
Reuben the firstborn of Jacob, Simeon, Levi, Judah, Issachar and Zebulun.

²⁴The sons of Rachel:
Joseph and Benjamin.

²⁵The sons of Rachel's servant Bilhah:
Dan and Naphtali.

²⁶The sons of Leah's servant Zilpah:
Gad and Asher.

These were the sons of Jacob, who were born to him in Paddan Aram.

²⁷Jacob came home to his father Isaac in Mamre, near Kiriath Arba (that is, Hebron), where Abraham and Isaac had stayed. ²⁸Isaac lived a hundred and eighty years. ²⁹Then he breathed his last and died and was gathered to his people, old and full of years. And his sons Esau and Jacob buried him.

Esau's Descendants

36 This is the account of the family line of Esau (that is, Edom).

²Esau took his wives from the women of Canaan: Adah daughter of Elon the Hittite, and Oholibamah daughter of Anah and granddaughter of Zibeon the Hivite— ³also Basemath daughter of Ishmael and sister of Nebaioth.

⁴Adah bore Eliphaz to Esau, Basemath bore Reuel, ⁵and Oholibamah bore Jeush, Jalam and Korah. These were the sons of Esau, who were born to him in Canaan.

⁶Esau took his wives and sons and daughters and all the members of his household, as well as his livestock and all his other animals and all the goods he had acquired in Canaan, and moved to a land some distance from his brother Jacob. ⁷Their possessions were too great for them to remain together; the land where they were staying could not support them both because of their livestock. ⁸So Esau (that is, Edom) settled in the hill country of Seir.

⁹This is the account of the family line of Esau the father of the Edomites in the hill country of Seir.

¹⁰These are the names of Esau's sons:
Eliphaz, the son of Esau's wife

Adah, and Reuel, the son of Esau's wife Basemath.
¹¹ The sons of Eliphaz:
Teman, Omar, Zepho, Gatam and Kenaz.
¹² Esau's son Eliphaz also had a concubine named Timna, who bore him Amalek. These were grandsons of Esau's wife Adah.
¹³ The sons of Reuel:
Nahath, Zerah, Shammah and Mizzah. These were grandsons of Esau's wife Basemath.
¹⁴ The sons of Esau's wife Oholibamah daughter of Anah and granddaughter of Zibeon, whom she bore to Esau:
Jeush, Jalam and Korah.

¹⁵ These were the chiefs among Esau's descendants:
The sons of Eliphaz the firstborn of Esau:
Chiefs Teman, Omar, Zepho, Kenaz, ¹⁶ Korah,ᵃ Gatam and Amalek. These were the chiefs descended from Eliphaz in Edom; they were grandsons of Adah.
¹⁷ The sons of Esau's son Reuel:
Chiefs Nahath, Zerah, Shammah and Mizzah. These were the chiefs descended from Reuel in Edom; they were grandsons of Esau's wife Basemath.
¹⁸ The sons of Esau's wife Oholibamah:
Chiefs Jeush, Jalam and Korah. These were the chiefs descended from Esau's wife Oholibamah daughter of Anah.
¹⁹ These were the sons of Esau (that is, Edom), and these were their chiefs.

²⁰ These were the sons of Seir the Horite, who were living in the region:
Lotan, Shobal, Zibeon, Anah, ²¹ Dishon, Ezer and Dishan. These sons of Seir in Edom were Horite chiefs.
²² The sons of Lotan:
Hori and Homam.ᵇ Timna was Lotan's sister.
²³ The sons of Shobal:
Alvan, Manahath, Ebal, Shepho and Onam.

²⁴ The sons of Zibeon:
Aiah and Anah. This is the Anah who discovered the hot springsᶜ in the desert while he was grazing the donkeys of his father Zibeon.
²⁵ The children of Anah:
Dishon and Oholibamah daughter of Anah.
²⁶ The sons of Dishonᵈ:
Hemdan, Eshban, Ithran and Keran.
²⁷ The sons of Ezer:
Bilhan, Zaavan and Akan.
²⁸ The sons of Dishan:
Uz and Aran.
²⁹ These were the Horite chiefs:
Lotan, Shobal, Zibeon, Anah, ³⁰ Dishon, Ezer and Dishan. These were the Horite chiefs, according to their divisions, in the land of Seir.

The Rulers of Edom

³¹ These were the kings who reigned in Edom before any Israelite king reigned:
³² Bela son of Beor became king of Edom. His city was named Dinhabah.
³³ When Bela died, Jobab son of Zerah from Bozrah succeeded him as king.
³⁴ When Jobab died, Husham from the land of the Temanites succeeded him as king.
³⁵ When Husham died, Hadad son of Bedad, who defeated Midian in the country of Moab, succeeded him as king. His city was named Avith.
³⁶ When Hadad died, Samlah from Masrekah succeeded him as king.
³⁷ When Samlah died, Shaul from Rehoboth on the river succeeded him as king.
³⁸ When Shaul died, Baal-Hanan son of Akbor succeeded him as king.

ᵃ 16 Masoretic Text; Samaritan Pentateuch (also verse 11 and 1 Chron. 1:36) does not have *Korah*.
ᵇ 22 Hebrew *Hemam*, a variant of *Homam* (see 1 Chron. 1:39)   ᶜ 24 Vulgate; Syriac *discovered water*; the meaning of the Hebrew for this word is uncertain.   ᵈ 26 Hebrew *Dishan*, a variant of *Dishon*

[39] When Baal-Hanan son of Akbor died, Hadad[a] succeeded him as king. His city was named Pau, and his wife's name was Mehetabel daughter of Matred, the daughter of Me-Zahab.

[40] These were the chiefs descended from Esau, by name, according to their clans and regions:

Timna, Alvah, Jetheth, [41] Oholibamah, Elah, Pinon, [42] Kenaz, Teman, Mibzar, [43] Magdiel and Iram. These were the chiefs of Edom, according to their settlements in the land they occupied.

This is the family line of Esau, the father of the Edomites.

Joseph's Dreams

37 Jacob lived in the land where his father had stayed, the land of Canaan.

[2] This is the account of Jacob's family line.

Joseph, a young man of seventeen, was tending the flocks with his brothers, the sons of Bilhah and the sons of Zilpah, his father's wives, and he brought their father a bad report about them. [3] Now Israel loved Joseph more than any of his other sons, because he had been born to him in his old age; and he made an ornate[b] robe for him. [4] When his brothers saw that their father loved him more than any of them, they hated him and could not speak a kind word to him.

[5] Joseph had a dream, and when he told it to his brothers, they hated him all the more. [6] He said to them, "Listen to this dream I had: [7] We were binding sheaves of grain out in the field when suddenly my sheaf rose and stood upright, while your sheaves gathered around mine and bowed down to it."

[8] His brothers said to him, "Do you intend to reign over us? Will you actually rule us?" And they hated him all the more because of his dream and what he had said.

[9] Then he had another dream, and he told it to his brothers. "Listen," he said, "I had another dream, and this time the sun and moon and eleven stars were bowing down to me."

[10] When he told his father as well as his brothers, his father rebuked him and said, "What is this dream you had? Will your mother and I and your brothers actually come and bow down to the ground before you?" [11] His brothers were jealous of him, but his father kept the matter in mind.

Joseph Sold by His Brothers

[12] Now his brothers had gone to graze their father's flocks near Shechem, [13] and Israel said to Joseph, "As you know, your brothers are grazing the flocks near Shechem. Come, I am going to send you to them."

"Very well," he replied.

[14] So he said to him, "Go and see if all is well with your brothers and with the flocks, and bring word back to me." Then he sent him off from the Valley of Hebron.

When Joseph arrived at Shechem, [15] a man found him wandering around in the fields and asked him, "What are you looking for?"

[16] He replied, "I'm looking for my brothers. Can you tell me where they are grazing their flocks?"

[17] "They have moved on from here," the man answered. "I heard them say, 'Let's go to Dothan.'"

So Joseph went after his brothers and found them near Dothan. [18] But they saw him in the distance, and before he reached them, they plotted to kill him.

[19] "Here comes that dreamer!" they said to each other. [20] "Come now, let's kill him and throw him into one of these cisterns and say that a ferocious animal devoured him. Then we'll see what comes of his dreams."

a 39 Many manuscripts of the Masoretic Text, Samaritan Pentateuch and Syriac (see also 1 Chron. 1:50); most manuscripts of the Masoretic Text *Hadar*   *b 3* The meaning of the Hebrew for this word is uncertain; also in verses 23 and 32.

²¹When Reuben heard this, he tried to rescue him from their hands. "Let's not take his life," he said. ²²"Don't shed any blood. Throw him into this cistern here in the wilderness, but don't lay a hand on him." Reuben said this to rescue him from them and take him back to his father.

²³So when Joseph came to his brothers, they stripped him of his robe—the ornate robe he was wearing— ²⁴and they took him and threw him into the cistern. The cistern was empty; there was no water in it.

²⁵As they sat down to eat their meal, they looked up and saw a caravan of Ishmaelites coming from Gilead. Their camels were loaded with spices, balm and myrrh, and they were on their way to take them down to Egypt.

²⁶Judah said to his brothers, "What will we gain if we kill our brother and cover up his blood? ²⁷Come, let's sell him to the Ishmaelites and not lay our hands on him; after all, he is our brother, our own flesh and blood." His brothers agreed.

²⁸So when the Midianite merchants came by, his brothers pulled Joseph up out of the cistern and sold him for twenty shekels*a* of silver to the Ishmaelites, who took him to Egypt.

²⁹When Reuben returned to the cistern and saw that Joseph was not there, he tore his clothes. ³⁰He went back to his brothers and said, "The boy isn't there! Where can I turn now?"

³¹Then they got Joseph's robe, slaughtered a goat and dipped the robe in the blood. ³²They took the ornate robe back to their father and said, "We found this. Examine it to see whether it is your son's robe."

³³He recognized it and said, "It is my son's robe! Some ferocious animal has devoured him. Joseph has surely been torn to pieces."

³⁴Then Jacob tore his clothes, put on sackcloth and mourned for his son many days. ³⁵All his sons and daughters came

a 28 That is, about 8 ounces or about 230 grams

ROCK SOLID principles

Genesis 37:1 – 36

Respect your siblings.

Philip had been labeled a genius almost since birth. His parents hired tutors to help him along—not because he struggled, but to keep him far ahead of his peers. They sent him to a scholarship mentor to guide his every move, almost guaranteeing him a free ride to a top university. Philip's older brother and sister hated all the attention their little brother received—and how he talked to them as if they were idiots. When Philip joined them in high school, they acted like they didn't know him, and at home they teamed up to push him around. They dreamed of the day Philip would fly away to college on the other side of the country. They hoped he would never come back.

When Jacob's family didn't get along, there was no shortage of blame to go around. Jacob spoiled Joseph. Joseph rubbed his special status in his brothers' faces. And those brothers cared only about themselves. If your family relationships don't start and end with respect, don't expect much fun at home.

to comfort him, but he refused to be comforted. "No," he said, "I will continue to mourn until I join my son in the grave." So his father wept for him.

[36] Meanwhile, the Midianites[a] sold Joseph in Egypt to Potiphar, one of Pharaoh's officials, the captain of the guard.

Judah and Tamar

38 At that time, Judah left his brothers and went down to stay with a man of Adullam named Hirah. [2] There Judah met the daughter of a Canaanite man named Shua. He married her and made love to her; [3] she became pregnant and gave birth to a son, who was named Er. [4] She conceived again and gave birth to a son and named him Onan. [5] She gave birth to still another son and named him Shelah. It was at Kezib that she gave birth to him.

[6] Judah got a wife for Er, his firstborn, and her name was Tamar. [7] But Er, Judah's firstborn, was wicked in the LORD's sight; so the LORD put him to death.

[8] Then Judah said to Onan, "Sleep with your brother's wife and fulfill your duty to her as a brother-in-law to raise up offspring for your brother." [9] But Onan knew that the child would not be his; so whenever he slept with his brother's wife, he spilled his semen on the ground to keep from providing offspring for his brother. [10] What he did was wicked in the LORD's sight; so the LORD put him to death also.

[11] Judah then said to his daughter-in-law Tamar, "Live as a widow in your father's household until my son Shelah grows up." For he thought, "He may die too, just like his brothers." So Tamar went to live in her father's household.

[12] After a long time Judah's wife, the daughter of Shua, died. When Judah had recovered from his grief, he went up to Timnah, to the men who were shearing his sheep, and his friend Hirah the Adullamite went with him.

[13] When Tamar was told, "Your father-in-law is on his way to Timnah to shear his sheep," [14] she took off her widow's clothes, covered herself with a veil to disguise herself, and then sat down at the entrance to Enaim, which is on the road to Timnah. For she saw that, though Shelah had now grown up, she had not been given to him as his wife.

[15] When Judah saw her, he thought she was a prostitute, for she had covered her face. [16] Not realizing that she was his daughter-in-law, he went over to her by the roadside and said, "Come now, let me sleep with you."

"And what will you give me to sleep with you?" she asked.

[17] "I'll send you a young goat from my flock," he said.

"Will you give me something as a pledge until you send it?" she asked.

[18] He said, "What pledge should I give you?"

"Your seal and its cord, and the staff in your hand," she answered. So he gave them to her and slept with her, and she became pregnant by him. [19] After she left, she took off her veil and put on her widow's clothes again.

[20] Meanwhile Judah sent the young goat by his friend the Adullamite in order to get his pledge back from the woman, but he did not find her. [21] He asked the men who lived there, "Where is the shrine prostitute who was beside the road at Enaim?"

"There hasn't been any shrine prostitute here," they said.

[22] So he went back to Judah and said, "I didn't find her. Besides, the men who lived there said, 'There hasn't been any shrine prostitute here.'"

[23] Then Judah said, "Let her keep what she has, or we will become a laughingstock. After all, I did send her this young goat, but you didn't find her."

[24] About three months later Judah was told, "Your daughter-in-law Tamar is guilty of prostitution, and as a result she is now pregnant."

Judah said, "Bring her out and have her burned to death!"

[a] 36 Samaritan Pentateuch, Septuagint, Vulgate and Syriac (see also verse 28); Masoretic Text *Medanites*

²⁵As she was being brought out, she sent a message to her father-in-law. "I am pregnant by the man who owns these," she said. And she added, "See if you recognize whose seal and cord and staff these are." ²⁶Judah recognized them and said, "She is more righteous than I, since I wouldn't give her to my son Shelah." And he did not sleep with her again.

²⁷When the time came for her to give birth, there were twin boys in her womb. ²⁸As she was giving birth, one of them put out his hand; so the midwife took a scarlet thread and tied it on his wrist and said, "This one came out first." ²⁹But when he drew back his hand, his brother came out, and she said, "So this is how you have broken out!" And he was named Perez.ᵃ ³⁰Then his brother, who had the scarlet thread on his wrist, came out. And he was named Zerah.ᵇ

Joseph and Potiphar's Wife

39 Now Joseph had been taken down to Egypt. Potiphar, an Egyptian who was one of Pharaoh's officials, the captain of the guard, bought him from the Ishmaelites who had taken him there.

²The LORD was with Joseph so that he prospered, and he lived in the house of his Egyptian master. ³When his master saw that the LORD was with him and that the LORD gave him success in everything he did, ⁴Joseph found favor in his eyes and became his attendant. Potiphar put him in charge of his household, and he entrusted to his care everything he owned. ⁵From the time he put him in charge of his household and of all that he owned, the LORD blessed the household of the Egyptian because of Joseph. The blessing of the LORD was on everything Potiphar had, both in the house and in the field. ⁶So Potiphar left everything he had in Joseph's care; with Joseph in charge, he did not concern himself with anything except the food he ate.

Now Joseph was well-built and handsome, ⁷and after a while his master's wife took notice of Joseph and said, "Come to bed with me!"

⁸But he refused. "With me in charge," he told her, "my master does not concern himself with anything in the house; everything he owns he has entrusted to my care. ⁹No one is greater in this house than I am. My master has withheld nothing from me except you, because you are his wife. How then could I do such a wicked thing and sin against God?" ¹⁰And though she spoke to Joseph day after day, he refused to go to bed with her or even be with her.

¹¹One day he went into the house to attend to his duties, and none of the household servants was inside. ¹²She caught him by his cloak and said, "Come to bed with me!" But he left his cloak in her hand and ran out of the house.

¹³When she saw that he had left his cloak in her hand and had run out of the house, ¹⁴she called her household servants. "Look," she said to them, "this Hebrew has been brought to us to make sport of us! He came in here to sleep with me, but I screamed. ¹⁵When he heard me scream for help, he left his cloak beside me and ran out of the house."

¹⁶She kept his cloak beside her until his master came home. ¹⁷Then she told him this story: "That Hebrew slave you brought us came to me to make sport of me. ¹⁸But as soon as I screamed for help, he left his cloak beside me and ran out of the house."

¹⁹When his master heard the story his wife told him, saying, "This is how your slave treated me," he burned with anger. ²⁰Joseph's master took him and put him in prison, the place where the king's prisoners were confined.

But while Joseph was there in the prison, ²¹the LORD was with him; he showed him kindness and granted him favor in the eyes of the prison warden. ²²So the warden put Joseph in charge of all those held in the prison, and he was made responsible for all that was done there. ²³The warden paid no attention to anything under Joseph's care, because the LORD was with Joseph and gave him success in whatever he did.

ᵃ 29 *Perez* means *breaking out.* ᵇ 30 *Zerah* can mean *scarlet* or *brightness.*

ROCK SOLID *principles*

Genesis 39:1–15

Flee temptation.

Keenan thought his social life was set forever when he was invited to sit at the popular table at lunch. He ignored his new friends' obnoxiousness when they mocked other students and complained about their parents' unbearable strictness. But he felt uneasy when he met up with the group after school and it was all about lying, swearing, and inventing fresh ways to be cruel. At his first party with his new group, Keenan's eyes gave away his shock when he saw bottles of beer. People told him to get over it and grow up, but Keenan wanted to get out. He ducked into a bathroom and quietly called his parents to come pick him up.

Like Joseph discovered, there's only one way to escape temptation—run away! God always gives you a way out of situations where you feel pulled to sin. The Bible promises, "When you are tempted, he will also provide a way out so that you can endure it" (1 Corinthians 10:13). Your job is to look for the exit. And leave.

The Cupbearer and the Baker

40 Some time later, the cupbearer and the baker of the king of Egypt offended their master, the king of Egypt. ²Pharaoh was angry with his two officials, the chief cupbearer and the chief baker, ³and put them in custody in the house of the captain of the guard, in the same prison where Joseph was confined. ⁴The captain of the guard assigned them to Joseph, and he attended them.

After they had been in custody for some time, ⁵each of the two men—the cupbearer and the baker of the king of Egypt, who were being held in prison—had a dream the same night, and each dream had a meaning of its own.

⁶When Joseph came to them the next morning, he saw that they were dejected. ⁷So he asked Pharaoh's officials who were in custody with him in his master's house, "Why do you look so sad today?"

⁸"We both had dreams," they answered, "but there is no one to interpret them."

Then Joseph said to them, "Do not interpretations belong to God? Tell me your dreams."

⁹So the chief cupbearer told Joseph his dream. He said to him, "In my dream I saw a vine in front of me, ¹⁰and on the vine were three branches. As soon as it budded, it blossomed, and its clusters ripened into grapes. ¹¹Pharaoh's cup was in my hand, and I took the grapes, squeezed them into Pharaoh's cup and put the cup in his hand."

¹²"This is what it means," Joseph said to him. "The three branches are three days. ¹³Within three days Pharaoh will lift up your head and restore you to your position, and you will put Pharaoh's cup in his hand, just as you used to do when you were his cupbearer. ¹⁴But when all goes well with you, remember me and show me kindness; mention me to Pharaoh and get

me out of this prison. ¹⁵I was forcibly carried off from the land of the Hebrews, and even here I have done nothing to deserve being put in a dungeon."

¹⁶When the chief baker saw that Joseph had given a favorable interpretation, he said to Joseph, "I too had a dream: On my head were three baskets of bread.*ᵃ ¹⁷In the top basket were all kinds of baked goods for Pharaoh, but the birds were eating them out of the basket on my head."

¹⁸"This is what it means," Joseph said. "The three baskets are three days. ¹⁹Within three days Pharaoh will lift off your head and impale your body on a pole. And the birds will eat away your flesh."

²⁰Now the third day was Pharaoh's birthday, and he gave a feast for all his officials. He lifted up the heads of the chief cupbearer and the chief baker in the presence of his officials: ²¹He restored the chief cupbearer to his position, so that he once again put the cup into Pharaoh's hand— ²²but he impaled the chief baker, just as Joseph had said to them in his interpretation.

²³The chief cupbearer, however, did not remember Joseph; he forgot him.

Pharaoh's Dreams

41 When two full years had passed, Pharaoh had a dream: He was standing by the Nile, ²when out of the river there came up seven cows, sleek and fat, and they grazed among the reeds. ³After them, seven other cows, ugly and gaunt, came up out of the Nile and stood beside those on the riverbank. ⁴And the cows that were ugly and gaunt ate up the seven sleek, fat cows. Then Pharaoh woke up.

⁵He fell asleep again and had a second dream: Seven heads of grain, healthy and good, were growing on a single stalk. ⁶After them, seven other heads of grain sprouted—thin and scorched by the east wind. ⁷The thin heads of grain swallowed up the seven healthy, full heads. Then Pharaoh woke up; it had been a dream.

⁸In the morning his mind was troubled, so he sent for all the magicians and wise men of Egypt. Pharaoh told them his dreams, but no one could interpret them for him.

⁹Then the chief cupbearer said to Pharaoh, "Today I am reminded of my shortcomings. ¹⁰Pharaoh was once angry with his servants, and he imprisoned me and the chief baker in the house of the captain of the guard. ¹¹Each of us had a dream the same night, and each dream had a meaning of its own. ¹²Now a young Hebrew was there with us, a servant of the captain of the guard. We told him our dreams, and he interpreted them for us, giving each man the interpretation of his dream. ¹³And things turned out exactly as he interpreted them to us: I was restored to my position, and the other man was impaled."

¹⁴So Pharaoh sent for Joseph, and he was quickly brought from the dungeon. When he had shaved and changed his clothes, he came before Pharaoh.

¹⁵Pharaoh said to Joseph, "I had a dream, and no one can interpret it. But I have heard it said of you that when you hear a dream you can interpret it."

¹⁶"I cannot do it," Joseph replied to Pharaoh, "but God will give Pharaoh the answer he desires."

¹⁷Then Pharaoh said to Joseph, "In my dream I was standing on the bank of the Nile, ¹⁸when out of the river there came up seven cows, fat and sleek, and they grazed among the reeds. ¹⁹After them, seven other cows came up—scrawny and very ugly and lean. I had never seen such ugly cows in all the land of Egypt. ²⁰The lean, ugly cows ate up the seven fat cows that came up first. ²¹But even after they ate them, no one could tell that they had done so; they looked just as ugly as before. Then I woke up.

²²"In my dream I saw seven heads of grain, full and good, growing on a single stalk. ²³After them, seven other heads sprouted—withered and thin and scorched by the east wind. ²⁴The thin heads of grain swallowed up the seven good heads. I told this to the magicians, but none of them could explain it to me."

²⁵Then Joseph said to Pharaoh, "The dreams of Pharaoh are one and the same.

ᵃ 16 Or *three wicker baskets*

God has revealed to Pharaoh what he is about to do. [26] The seven good cows are seven years, and the seven good heads of grain are seven years; it is one and the same dream. [27] The seven lean, ugly cows that came up afterward are seven years, and so are the seven worthless heads of grain scorched by the east wind: They are seven years of famine.

[28] "It is just as I said to Pharaoh: God has shown Pharaoh what he is about to do. [29] Seven years of great abundance are coming throughout the land of Egypt, [30] but seven years of famine will follow them. Then all the abundance in Egypt will be forgotten, and the famine will ravage the land. [31] The abundance in the land will not be remembered, because the famine that follows it will be so severe. [32] The reason the dream was given to Pharaoh in two forms is that the matter has been firmly decided by God, and God will do it soon.

[33] "And now let Pharaoh look for a discerning and wise man and put him in charge of the land of Egypt. [34] Let Pharaoh appoint commissioners over the land to take a fifth of the harvest of Egypt during the seven years of abundance. [35] They should collect all the food of these good years that are coming and store up the grain under the authority of Pharaoh, to be kept in the cities for food. [36] This food should be held in reserve for the country, to be used during the seven years of famine that will come upon Egypt, so that the country may not be ruined by the famine."

[37] The plan seemed good to Pharaoh and to all his officials. [38] So Pharaoh asked them, "Can we find anyone like this man, one in whom is the spirit of God[a]?"

[39] Then Pharaoh said to Joseph, "Since God has made all this known to you, there is no one so discerning and wise as you. [40] You shall be in charge of my palace, and all my people are to submit to your orders. Only with respect to the throne will I be greater than you."

Joseph in Charge of Egypt

[41] So Pharaoh said to Joseph, "I hereby put you in charge of the whole land of Egypt." [42] Then Pharaoh took his signet ring from his finger and put it on Joseph's finger. He dressed him in robes of fine linen and put a gold chain around his neck. [43] He had him ride in a chariot as his second-in-command,[b] and people shouted before him, "Make way[c]!" Thus he put him in charge of the whole land of Egypt.

[44] Then Pharaoh said to Joseph, "I am Pharaoh, but without your word no one will lift hand or foot in all Egypt." [45] Pharaoh gave Joseph the name Zaphenath-Paneah and gave him Asenath daughter of Potiphera, priest of On,[d] to be his wife. And Joseph went throughout the land of Egypt.

[46] Joseph was thirty years old when he entered the service of Pharaoh king of Egypt. And Joseph went out from Pharaoh's presence and traveled throughout Egypt. [47] During the seven years of abundance the land produced plentifully. [48] Joseph collected all the food produced in those seven years of abundance in Egypt and stored it in the cities. In each city he put the food grown in the fields surrounding it. [49] Joseph stored up huge quantities of grain, like the sand of the sea; it was so much that he stopped keeping records because it was beyond measure.

[50] Before the years of famine came, two sons were born to Joseph by Asenath daughter of Potiphera, priest of On. [51] Joseph named his firstborn Manasseh[e] and said, "It is because God has made me forget all my trouble and all my father's household." [52] The second son he named Ephraim[f] and said, "It is because God has made me fruitful in the land of my suffering."

[53] The seven years of abundance in Egypt came to an end, [54] and the seven years of famine began, just as Joseph had said. There was famine in all the other lands, but in the whole land of Egypt there

---

[a] 38 Or of the gods   [b] 43 Or in the chariot of his second-in-command; or in his second chariot
[c] 43 Or Bow down   [d] 45 That is, Heliopolis; also in verse 50   [e] 51 Manasseh sounds like and may be derived from the Hebrew for forget.
[f] 52 Ephraim sounds like the Hebrew for twice fruitful.

was food. [55] When all Egypt began to feel the famine, the people cried to Pharaoh for food. Then Pharaoh told all the Egyptians, "Go to Joseph and do what he tells you."

[56] When the famine had spread over the whole country, Joseph opened all the storehouses and sold grain to the Egyptians, for the famine was severe throughout Egypt. [57] And all the world came to Egypt to buy grain from Joseph, because the famine was severe everywhere.

Joseph's Brothers Go to Egypt

42 When Jacob learned that there was grain in Egypt, he said to his sons, "Why do you just keep looking at each other?" [2] He continued, "I have heard that there is grain in Egypt. Go down there and buy some for us, so that we may live and not die."

[3] Then ten of Joseph's brothers went down to buy grain from Egypt. [4] But Jacob did not send Benjamin, Joseph's brother, with the others, because he was afraid that harm might come to him. [5] So Israel's sons were among those who went to buy grain, for there was famine in the land of Canaan also.

[6] Now Joseph was the governor of the land, the person who sold grain to all its people. So when Joseph's brothers arrived, they bowed down to him with their faces to the ground. [7] As soon as Joseph saw his brothers, he recognized them, but he pretended to be a stranger and spoke harshly to them. "Where do you come from?" he asked.

"From the land of Canaan," they replied, "to buy food."

[8] Although Joseph recognized his brothers, they did not recognize him. [9] Then he remembered his dreams about them and said to them, "You are spies! You have come to see where our land is unprotected."

[10] "No, my lord," they answered. "Your servants have come to buy food. [11] We are all the sons of one man. Your servants are honest men, not spies."

[12] "No!" he said to them. "You have come to see where our land is unprotected."

[13] But they replied, "Your servants were twelve brothers, the sons of one man, who lives in the land of Canaan. The youngest is now with our father, and one is no more."

[14] Joseph said to them, "It is just as I told you: You are spies! [15] And this is how you will be tested: As surely as Pharaoh lives, you will not leave this place unless your youngest brother comes here. [16] Send one of your number to get your brother; the rest of you will be kept in prison, so that your words may be tested to see if you are telling the truth. If you are not, then as surely as Pharaoh lives, you are spies!" [17] And he put them all in custody for three days.

[18] On the third day, Joseph said to them, "Do this and you will live, for I fear God: [19] If you are honest men, let one of your brothers stay here in prison, while the rest of you go and take grain back for your starving households. [20] But you must bring your youngest brother to me, so that your words may be verified and that you may not die." This they proceeded to do.

[21] They said to one another, "Surely we are being punished because of our brother. We saw how distressed he was when he pleaded with us for his life, but we would not listen; that's why this distress has come on us."

[22] Reuben replied, "Didn't I tell you not to sin against the boy? But you wouldn't listen! Now we must give an accounting for his blood." [23] They did not realize that Joseph could understand them, since he was using an interpreter.

[24] He turned away from them and began to weep, but then came back and spoke to them again. He had Simeon taken from them and bound before their eyes.

[25] Joseph gave orders to fill their bags with grain, to put each man's silver back in his sack, and to give them provisions for their journey. After this was done for them, [26] they loaded their grain on their donkeys and left.

^{27}At the place where they stopped for the night one of them opened his sack to get feed for his donkey, and he saw his silver in the mouth of his sack. ^{28}"My silver has been returned," he said to his brothers. "Here it is in my sack."

Their hearts sank and they turned to each other trembling and said, "What is this that God has done to us?"

^{29}When they came to their father Jacob in the land of Canaan, they told him all that had happened to them. They said, ^{30}"The man who is lord over the land spoke harshly to us and treated us as though we were spying on the land. ^{31}But we said to him, 'We are honest men; we are not spies. ^{32}We were twelve brothers, sons of one father. One is no more, and the youngest is now with our father in Canaan.'

^{33}"Then the man who is lord over the land said to us, 'This is how I will know whether you are honest men: Leave one of your brothers here with me, and take food for your starving households and go. ^{34}But bring your youngest brother to me so I will know that you are not spies but honest men. Then I will give your brother back to you, and you can trade^a in the land.'"

^{a} 34 Or *move about freely*

Genesis 42:1–38

Joseph put his gifts to good use.

Joseph was the firstborn son of his father's favorite wife. He was gifted. He knew it. And he let everyone else know it. His dad didn't do Joseph any favors by showering him with extra love and an extravagant coat. Joseph's 11 brothers hated him intensely, and Joseph fueled their rage when he told them his dreams that they would all one day bow to him (see Genesis 37:1–36).

At first those jealous brothers plotted to kill Joseph, but they ended up selling him into slavery. In Egypt the captain of the king's guard noticed Joseph's talents and gave him control of his entire household (see Genesis 39:4). After a sad detour in jail for a crime he didn't commit (see Genesis 39:7—40:23), Joseph was summoned by Pharaoh to interpret a baffling dream.

When Joseph said the dream meant Egypt would enjoy seven years of plenty followed by seven years of hunger, Pharaoh dressed him in fine clothes, hung a gold chain around his neck, and promoted him to second-in-command over all of Egypt. The bright 30-year-old ordered the citizens of Egypt to grow and store grain, saving the nation and its neighbors from starvation during a lengthy famine (see Genesis 41:41–57). Even Joseph's jealous brothers came to buy grain from him, although at first they didn't recognize their long-lost brother (see Genesis 42—47).

Joseph was spectacularly gifted, but he could only put his talents to good use when he stopped thinking about himself and employed his gifts for God's purposes.

You can find Joseph in Genesis 37—50; Zechariah 10:6; and Acts 7:9–19.

UNSHAKEN *people*

³⁵As they were emptying their sacks, there in each man's sack was his pouch of silver! When they and their father saw the money pouches, they were frightened. ³⁶Their father Jacob said to them, "You have deprived me of my children. Joseph is no more and Simeon is no more, and now you want to take Benjamin. Everything is against me!"

³⁷Then Reuben said to his father, "You may put both of my sons to death if I do not bring him back to you. Entrust him to my care, and I will bring him back."

³⁸But Jacob said, "My son will not go down there with you; his brother is dead and he is the only one left. If harm comes to him on the journey you are taking, you will bring my gray head down to the grave in sorrow."

The Second Journey to Egypt

43 Now the famine was still severe in the land. ²So when they had eaten all the grain they had brought from Egypt, their father said to them, "Go back and buy us a little more food."

³But Judah said to him, "The man warned us solemnly, 'You will not see my face again unless your brother is with you.' ⁴If you will send our brother along with us, we will go down and buy food for you. ⁵But if you will not send him, we will not go down, because the man said to us, 'You will not see my face again unless your brother is with you.'"

⁶Israel asked, "Why did you bring this trouble on me by telling the man you had another brother?"

⁷They replied, "The man questioned us closely about ourselves and our family. 'Is your father still living?' he asked us. 'Do you have another brother?' We simply answered his questions. How were we to know he would say, 'Bring your brother down here'?"

⁸Then Judah said to Israel his father, "Send the boy along with me and we will go at once, so that we and you and our children may live and not die. ⁹I myself will guarantee his safety; you can hold me personally responsible for him. If I do not bring him back to you and set him here before you, I will bear the blame before you all my life. ¹⁰As it is, if we had not delayed, we could have gone and returned twice."

¹¹Then their father Israel said to them, "If it must be, then do this: Put some of the best products of the land in your bags and take them down to the man as a gift—a little balm and a little honey, some spices and myrrh, some pistachio nuts and almonds. ¹²Take double the amount of silver with you, for you must return the silver that was put back into the mouths of your sacks. Perhaps it was a mistake. ¹³Take your brother also and go back to the man at once. ¹⁴And may God Almighty^a grant you mercy before the man so that he will let your other brother and Benjamin come back with you. As for me, if I am bereaved, I am bereaved."

¹⁵So the men took the gifts and double the amount of silver, and Benjamin also. They hurried down to Egypt and presented themselves to Joseph. ¹⁶When Joseph saw Benjamin with them, he said to the steward of his house, "Take these men to my house, slaughter an animal and prepare a meal; they are to eat with me at noon."

¹⁷The man did as Joseph told him and took the men to Joseph's house. ¹⁸Now the men were frightened when they were taken to his house. They thought, "We were brought here because of the silver that was put back into our sacks the first time. He wants to attack us and overpower us and seize us as slaves and take our donkeys."

¹⁹So they went up to Joseph's steward and spoke to him at the entrance to the house. ²⁰"We beg your pardon, our lord," they said, "we came down here the first time to buy food. ²¹But at the place where we stopped for the night we opened our sacks and each of us found his silver—the exact weight—in the mouth of his sack. So we have brought it back with us. ²²We have also brought additional silver with us to buy food. We don't know who put our silver in our sacks."

^a *14* Hebrew *El-Shaddai*

²³"It's all right," he said. "Don't be afraid. Your God, the God of your father, has given you treasure in your sacks; I received your silver." Then he brought Simeon out to them.

²⁴The steward took the men into Joseph's house, gave them water to wash their feet and provided fodder for their donkeys. ²⁵They prepared their gifts for Joseph's arrival at noon, because they had heard that they were to eat there.

²⁶When Joseph came home, they presented to him the gifts they had brought into the house, and they bowed down before him to the ground. ²⁷He asked them how they were, and then he said, "How is your aged father you told me about? Is he still living?"

²⁸They replied, "Your servant our father is still alive and well." And they bowed down, prostrating themselves before him.

²⁹As he looked about and saw his brother Benjamin, his own mother's son, he asked, "Is this your youngest brother, the one you told me about?" And he said, "God be gracious to you, my son." ³⁰Deeply moved at the sight of his brother, Joseph hurried out and looked for a place to weep. He went into his private room and wept there.

³¹After he had washed his face, he came out and, controlling himself, said, "Serve the food."

³²They served him by himself, the brothers by themselves, and the Egyptians who ate with him by themselves, because Egyptians could not eat with Hebrews, for that is detestable to Egyptians. ³³The men had been seated before him in the order of their ages, from the firstborn to the youngest; and they looked at each other in astonishment. ³⁴When portions were served to them from Joseph's table, Benjamin's portion was five times as much as anyone else's. So they feasted and drank freely with him.

A Silver Cup in a Sack

44 Now Joseph gave these instructions to the steward of his house: "Fill the men's sacks with as much food as they can car-

ry, and put each man's silver in the mouth of his sack. ²Then put my cup, the silver one, in the mouth of the youngest one's sack, along with the silver for his grain." And he did as Joseph said.

³As morning dawned, the men were sent on their way with their donkeys. ⁴They had not gone far from the city when Joseph said to his steward, "Go after those men at once, and when you catch up with them, say to them, 'Why have you repaid good with evil? ⁵Isn't this the cup my master drinks from and also uses for divination? This is a wicked thing you have done.'"

⁶When he caught up with them, he repeated these words to them. ⁷But they said to him, "Why does my lord say such things? Far be it from your servants to do anything like that! ⁸We even brought back to you from the land of Canaan the silver we found inside the mouths of our sacks. So why would we steal silver or gold from your master's house? ⁹If any of your servants is found to have it, he will die; and the rest of us will become my lord's slaves."

¹⁰"Very well, then," he said, "let it be as you say. Whoever is found to have it will become my slave; the rest of you will be free from blame."

¹¹Each of them quickly lowered his sack to the ground and opened it. ¹²Then the steward proceeded to search, beginning with the oldest and ending with the youngest. And the cup was found in Benjamin's sack. ¹³At this, they tore their clothes. Then they all loaded their donkeys and returned to the city.

¹⁴Joseph was still in the house when Judah and his brothers came in, and they threw themselves to the ground before him. ¹⁵Joseph said to them, "What is this you have done? Don't you know that a man like me can find things out by divination?"

¹⁶"What can we say to my lord?" Judah replied. "What can we say? How can we prove our innocence? God has uncovered your servants' guilt. We are now my lord's slaves—we ourselves and the one who was found to have the cup."

¹⁷But Joseph said, "Far be it from me to do such a thing! Only the man who was found to have the cup will become my slave. The rest of you, go back to your father in peace."

¹⁸Then Judah went up to him and said: "Pardon your servant, my lord, let me speak a word to my lord. Do not be angry with your servant, though you are equal to Pharaoh himself. ¹⁹My lord asked his servants, 'Do you have a father or a brother?' ²⁰And we answered, 'We have an aged father, and there is a young son born to him in his old age. His brother is dead, and he is the only one of his mother's sons left, and his father loves him.'

²¹"Then you said to your servants, 'Bring him down to me so I can see him for myself.' ²²And we said to my lord, 'The boy cannot leave his father; if he leaves him, his father will die.' ²³But you told your servants, 'Unless your youngest brother comes down with you, you will not see my face again.' ²⁴When we went back to your servant my father, we told him what my lord had said.

²⁵"Then our father said, 'Go back and buy a little more food.' ²⁶But we said, 'We cannot go down. Only if our youngest brother is with us will we go. We cannot see the man's face unless our youngest brother is with us.'

²⁷"Your servant my father said to us, 'You know that my wife bore me two sons. ²⁸One of them went away from me, and I said, "He has surely been torn to pieces." And I have not seen him since. ²⁹If you take this one from me too and harm comes to him, you will bring my gray head down to the grave in misery.'

³⁰"So now, if the boy is not with us when I go back to your servant my father, and if my father, whose life is closely bound up with the boy's life, ³¹sees that the boy isn't there, he will die. Your servants will bring the gray head of our father down to the grave in sorrow. ³²Your servant guaranteed the boy's safety to my father. I said, 'If I do not bring him back to you, I will bear the blame before you, my father, all my life!'

³³"Now then, please let your servant remain here as my lord's slave in place of the boy, and let the boy return with his brothers. ³⁴How can I go back to my father if the boy is not with me? No! Do not let me see the misery that would come on my father."

Joseph Makes Himself Known

45 Then Joseph could no longer control himself before all his attendants, and he cried out, "Have everyone leave my presence!" So there was no one with Joseph when he made himself known to his brothers. ²And he wept so loudly that the Egyptians heard him, and Pharaoh's household heard about it.

³Joseph said to his brothers, "I am Joseph! Is my father still living?" But his brothers were not able to answer him, because they were terrified at his presence.

⁴Then Joseph said to his brothers, "Come close to me." When they had done so, he said, "I am your brother Joseph, the one you sold into Egypt! ⁵And now, do not be distressed and do not be angry with yourselves for selling me here, because it was to save lives that God sent me ahead of you. ⁶For two years now there has been famine in the land, and for the next five years there will be no plowing and reaping. ⁷But God sent me ahead of you to preserve for you a remnant on earth and to save your lives by a great deliverance.ᵃ

⁸"So then, it was not you who sent me here, but God. He made me father to Pharaoh, lord of his entire household and ruler of all Egypt. ⁹Now hurry back to my father and say to him, 'This is what your son Joseph says: God has made me lord of all Egypt. Come down to me; don't delay. ¹⁰You shall live in the region of Goshen and be near me—you, your children and grandchildren, your flocks and herds, and all you have. ¹¹I will provide for you there, because five years of famine are still to come. Otherwise you and your household and all who belong to you will become destitute.'

ᵃ 7 Or *save you as a great band of survivors*

¹²"You can see for yourselves, and so can my brother Benjamin, that it is really I who am speaking to you. ¹³Tell my father about all the honor accorded me in Egypt and about everything you have seen. And bring my father down here quickly."

¹⁴Then he threw his arms around his brother Benjamin and wept, and Benjamin embraced him, weeping. ¹⁵And he kissed all his brothers and wept over them. Afterward his brothers talked with him.

¹⁶When the news reached Pharaoh's palace that Joseph's brothers had come, Pharaoh and all his officials were pleased. ¹⁷Pharaoh said to Joseph, "Tell your brothers, 'Do this: Load your animals and return to the land of Canaan, ¹⁸and bring your father and your families back to me. I will give you the best of the land of Egypt and you can enjoy the fat of the land.'

¹⁹"You are also directed to tell them, 'Do this: Take some carts from Egypt for your children and your wives, and get your father and come. ²⁰Never mind about your belongings, because the best of all Egypt will be yours.'"

²¹So the sons of Israel did this. Joseph gave them carts, as Pharaoh had commanded, and he also gave them provisions for their journey. ²²To each of them he gave new clothing, but to Benjamin he gave three hundred shekels[a] of silver and five sets of clothes. ²³And this is what he sent to his father: ten donkeys loaded with the best things of Egypt, and ten female donkeys loaded with grain and bread and other provisions for his journey. ²⁴Then he sent his brothers away, and as they were leaving he said to them, "Don't quarrel on the way!"

²⁵So they went up out of Egypt and came to their father Jacob in the land of Canaan. ²⁶They told him, "Joseph is still alive! In fact, he is ruler of all Egypt." Jacob was stunned; he did not believe them.

---

[a] 22 That is, about 7 1/2 pounds or about 3.5 kilograms

ROCK SOLID *principles*

Genesis 44:1 — 45:18

Let people change.

Sophie couldn't hide her glee when the family next door was transferred a thousand miles away because of the dad's job. Sophie and her neighbor Ava had been the closest of friends as preschoolers, but the older they got, the more they grew apart. The day Ava decided to turn the neighborhood girls against Sophie—who knows why—they stopped talking altogether. But two years after Ava moved away, she was suddenly back. Rumors flew that she had returned with her mom because her parents had split. Within a few days Ava was knocking at Sophie's door, saying she wanted the friendship they once had. She was sorry. Sophie wasn't sure what to say.

Joseph's fed-up brothers sold their younger sibling into slavery (see Genesis 37:28). Yet after years of suffering, Joseph attained almost limitless power in Egypt. Then his starving brothers needed his help (see Genesis 42:1 – 7). Joseph had an opportunity to forgive his brothers. His brothers had to realize Joseph had grown into a better man. They could either stay stuck—or give each other a fresh start.

27 But when they told him everything Joseph had said to them, and when he saw the carts Joseph had sent to carry him back, the spirit of their father Jacob revived. 28 And Israel said, "I'm convinced! My son Joseph is still alive. I will go and see him before I die."

Jacob Goes to Egypt

46 So Israel set out with all that was his, and when he reached Beersheba, he offered sacrifices to the God of his father Isaac.

2 And God spoke to Israel in a vision at night and said, "Jacob! Jacob!"

"Here I am," he replied.

3 "I am God, the God of your father," he said. "Do not be afraid to go down to Egypt, for I will make you into a great nation there. 4 I will go down to Egypt with you, and I will surely bring you back again. And Joseph's own hand will close your eyes."

5 Then Jacob left Beersheba, and Israel's sons took their father Jacob and their children and their wives in the carts that Pharaoh had sent to transport him. 6 So Jacob and all his offspring went to Egypt, taking with them their livestock and the possessions they had acquired in Canaan. 7 Jacob brought with him to Egypt his sons and grandsons and his daughters and granddaughters—all his offspring.

8 These are the names of the sons of Israel (Jacob and his descendants) who went to Egypt:

Reuben the firstborn of Jacob.
9 The sons of Reuben:
Hanok, Pallu, Hezron and Karmi.
10 The sons of Simeon:
Jemuel, Jamin, Ohad, Jakin, Zohar and Shaul the son of a Canaanite woman.
11 The sons of Levi:
Gershon, Kohath and Merari.
12 The sons of Judah:
Er, Onan, Shelah, Perez and Zerah (but Er and Onan had died in the land of Canaan).

The sons of Perez:
Hezron and Hamul.
13 The sons of Issachar:
Tola, Puah,[a] Jashub[b] and Shimron.
14 The sons of Zebulun:
Sered, Elon and Jahleel.
15 These were the sons Leah bore to Jacob in Paddan Aram,[c] besides his daughter Dinah. These sons and daughters of his were thirty-three in all.

16 The sons of Gad:
Zephon,[d] Haggi, Shuni, Ezbon, Eri, Arodi and Areli.
17 The sons of Asher:
Imnah, Ishvah, Ishvi and Beriah.
Their sister was Serah.
The sons of Beriah:
Heber and Malkiel.
18 These were the children born to Jacob by Zilpah, whom Laban had given to his daughter Leah—sixteen in all.

19 The sons of Jacob's wife Rachel:
Joseph and Benjamin. 20 In Egypt, Manasseh and Ephraim were born to Joseph by Asenath daughter of Potiphera, priest of On.[e]
21 The sons of Benjamin:
Bela, Beker, Ashbel, Gera, Naaman, Ehi, Rosh, Muppim, Huppim and Ard.
22 These were the sons of Rachel who were born to Jacob—fourteen in all.

23 The son of Dan:
Hushim.
24 The sons of Naphtali:
Jahziel, Guni, Jezer and Shillem.
25 These were the sons born to Jacob by Bilhah, whom Laban had given to his daughter Rachel—seven in all.

26 All those who went to Egypt with Jacob—those who were his direct de-

---

a 13 Samaritan Pentateuch and Syriac (see also 1 Chron. 7:1); Masoretic Text *Puvah*   *b 13* Samaritan Pentateuch and some Septuagint manuscripts (see also Num. 26:24 and 1 Chron. 7:1); Masoretic Text *Iob*   *c 15* That is, Northwest Mesopotamia   *d 16* Samaritan Pentateuch and Septuagint (see also Num. 26:15); Masoretic Text *Ziphion*   *e 20* That is, Heliopolis scendants, not counting his sons' wives—numbered sixty-six persons. [27] With the two sons[a] who had been born to Joseph in Egypt, the members of Jacob's family, which went to Egypt, were seventy[b] in all.

[28] Now Jacob sent Judah ahead of him to Joseph to get directions to Goshen. When they arrived in the region of Goshen, [29] Joseph had his chariot made ready and went to Goshen to meet his father Israel. As soon as Joseph appeared before him, he threw his arms around his father[c] and wept for a long time.

[30] Israel said to Joseph, "Now I am ready to die, since I have seen for myself that you are still alive."

[31] Then Joseph said to his brothers and to his father's household, "I will go up and speak to Pharaoh and will say to him, 'My brothers and my father's household, who were living in the land of Canaan, have come to me. [32] The men are shepherds; they tend livestock, and they have brought along their flocks and herds and everything they own.' [33] When Pharaoh calls you in and asks, 'What is your occupation?' [34] you should answer, 'Your servants have tended livestock from our boyhood on, just as our fathers did.' Then you will be allowed to settle in the region of Goshen, for all shepherds are detestable to the Egyptians."

47 Joseph went and told Pharaoh, "My father and brothers, with their flocks and herds and everything they own, have come from the land of Canaan and are now in Goshen." [2] He chose five of his brothers and presented them before Pharaoh.

[3] Pharaoh asked the brothers, "What is your occupation?"

"Your servants are shepherds," they replied to Pharaoh, "just as our fathers were." [4] They also said to him, "We have come to live here for a while, because the famine is severe in Canaan and your servants' flocks have no pasture. So now, please let your servants settle in Goshen."

[5] Pharaoh said to Joseph, "Your father and your brothers have come to you, [6] and the land of Egypt is before you; settle your

father and your brothers in the best part of the land. Let them live in Goshen. And if you know of any among them with special ability, put them in charge of my own livestock."

[7] Then Joseph brought his father Jacob in and presented him before Pharaoh. After Jacob blessed[d] Pharaoh, [8] Pharaoh asked him, "How old are you?"

[9] And Jacob said to Pharaoh, "The years of my pilgrimage are a hundred and thirty. My years have been few and difficult, and they do not equal the years of the pilgrimage of my fathers." [10] Then Jacob blessed[e] Pharaoh and went out from his presence.

[11] So Joseph settled his father and his brothers in Egypt and gave them property in the best part of the land, the district of Rameses, as Pharaoh directed. [12] Joseph also provided his father and his brothers and all his father's household with food, according to the number of their children.

Joseph and the Famine

[13] There was no food, however, in the whole region because the famine was severe; both Egypt and Canaan wasted away because of the famine. [14] Joseph collected all the money that was to be found in Egypt and Canaan in payment for the grain they were buying, and he brought it to Pharaoh's palace. [15] When the money of the people of Egypt and Canaan was gone, all Egypt came to Joseph and said, "Give us food. Why should we die before your eyes? Our money is all gone."

[16] "Then bring your livestock," said Joseph. "I will sell you food in exchange for your livestock, since your money is gone." [17] So they brought their livestock to Joseph, and he gave them food in exchange for their horses, their sheep and goats, their cattle and donkeys. And he brought them through that year with food in exchange for all their livestock.

[18] When that year was over, they came to

[a] 27 Hebrew; Septuagint *the nine children*
[b] 27 Hebrew (see also Exodus 1:5 and note); Septuagint (see also Acts 7:14) *seventy-five*
[c] 29 Hebrew *around him*   [d] 7 Or *greeted*
[e] 10 Or *said farewell to*

him the following year and said, "We cannot hide from our lord the fact that since our money is gone and our livestock belongs to you, there is nothing left for our lord except our bodies and our land. [19]Why should we perish before your eyes—we and our land as well? Buy us and our land in exchange for food, and we with our land will be in bondage to Pharaoh. Give us seed so that we may live and not die, and that the land may not become desolate."

[20]So Joseph bought all the land in Egypt for Pharaoh. The Egyptians, one and all, sold their fields, because the famine was too severe for them. The land became Pharaoh's, [21]and Joseph reduced the people to servitude,[a] from one end of Egypt to the other. [22]However, he did not buy the land of the priests, because they received a regular allotment from Pharaoh and had food enough from the allotment Pharaoh gave them. That is why they did not sell their land.

[23]Joseph said to the people, "Now that I have bought you and your land today for Pharaoh, here is seed for you so you can plant the ground. [24]But when the crop comes in, give a fifth of it to Pharaoh. The other four-fifths you may keep as seed for the fields and as food for yourselves and your households and your children."

[25]"You have saved our lives," they said. "May we find favor in the eyes of our lord; we will be in bondage to Pharaoh."

[26]So Joseph established it as a law concerning land in Egypt—still in force today—that a fifth of the produce belongs to Pharaoh. It was only the land of the priests that did not become Pharaoh's.

[27]Now the Israelites settled in Egypt in the region of Goshen. They acquired property there and were fruitful and increased greatly in number.

[28]Jacob lived in Egypt seventeen years, and the years of his life were a hundred and forty-seven. [29]When the time drew near for Israel to die, he called for his son Joseph and said to him, "If I have found favor in your eyes, put your hand under my thigh and promise that you will show me kindness and faithfulness. Do not bury

me in Egypt, [30]but when I rest with my fathers, carry me out of Egypt and bury me where they are buried."

"I will do as you say," he said.

[31]"Swear to me," he said. Then Joseph swore to him, and Israel worshiped as he leaned on the top of his staff.[b]

---

[a] 21 Samaritan Pentateuch and Septuagint (see also Vulgate); Masoretic Text *and he moved the people into the cities*   [b] 31 Or *Israel bowed down at the head of his bed*

Genesis 47
The Bible is God's Book.

Many people see the Bible simply as one thick book—and in one way it is. It communicates a unified message from front to back, making us "wise for salvation through faith in Christ Jesus" (2 Timothy 3:15). It informs us that people are sinful and separated from God, but by trusting in the death and resurrection of Jesus we can be friends with God and live forever with him in heaven. Amazingly, the Bible's tight message comes to us through 66 shorter books. These writings came from the pens of at least 36 authors of diverse backgrounds who wrote over an immense span of 1500 years. This unity with diversity signals that the Bible is far more than a human book. The Bible itself claims to be "God-breathed" (2 Timothy 3:16). It records the Lord's own words, the result of authors who "spoke from God as they were carried along by the Holy Spirit" (2 Peter 1:21).

Think: What makes the Bible unique from all other books? Why does that matter?

ROCK SOLID truths

Manasseh and Ephraim

48 Some time later Joseph was told, "Your father is ill." So he took his two sons Manasseh and Ephraim along with him. [2]When Jacob was told, "Your son Joseph has come to you," Israel rallied his strength and sat up on the bed.

[3]Jacob said to Joseph, "God Almighty[a] appeared to me at Luz in the land of Canaan, and there he blessed me [4]and said to me, 'I am going to make you fruitful and increase your numbers. I will make you a community of peoples, and I will give this land as an everlasting possession to your descendants after you.'

[5]"Now then, your two sons born to you in Egypt before I came to you here will be reckoned as mine; Ephraim and Manasseh will be mine, just as Reuben and Simeon are mine. [6]Any children born to you after them will be yours; in the territory they inherit they will be reckoned under the names of their brothers. [7]As I was returning from Paddan,[b] to my sorrow Rachel died in the land of Canaan while we were still on the way, a little distance from Ephrath. So I buried her there beside the road to Ephrath" (that is, Bethlehem).

[8]When Israel saw the sons of Joseph, he asked, "Who are these?"

[9]"They are the sons God has given me here," Joseph said to his father.

Then Israel said, "Bring them to me so I may bless them."

[10]Now Israel's eyes were failing because of old age, and he could hardly see. So Joseph brought his sons close to him, and his father kissed them and embraced them.

[11]Israel said to Joseph, "I never expected to see your face again, and now God has allowed me to see your children too."

[12]Then Joseph removed them from Israel's knees and bowed down with his face to the ground. [13]And Joseph took both of them, Ephraim on his right toward Israel's left hand and Manasseh on his left toward Israel's right hand, and brought them close to him. [14]But Israel reached out his right hand and put it on Ephraim's head, though he was the younger, and crossing his arms, he put his left hand on Manasseh's head, even though Manasseh was the firstborn.

[15]Then he blessed Joseph and said,

"May the God before whom my fathers
    Abraham and Isaac walked faithfully,
the God who has been my shepherd
    all my life to this day,
[16]the Angel who has delivered me from all harm
    —may he bless these boys.
May they be called by my name
    and the names of my fathers
        Abraham and Isaac,
and may they increase greatly
    on the earth."

[17]When Joseph saw his father placing his right hand on Ephraim's head he was displeased; so he took hold of his father's hand to move it from Ephraim's head to Manasseh's head. [18]Joseph said to him, "No, my father, this one is the firstborn; put your right hand on his head."

[19]But his father refused and said, "I know, my son, I know. He too will become a people, and he too will become great. Nevertheless, his younger brother will be greater than he, and his descendants will become a group of nations." [20]He blessed them that day and said,

"In your[c] name will Israel pronounce this blessing:
    'May God make you like Ephraim and Manasseh.'"

So he put Ephraim ahead of Manasseh.

[21]Then Israel said to Joseph, "I am about to die, but God will be with you[d] and take you[d] back to the land of your[d] fathers. [22]And to you I give one more ridge of land[e] than to your brothers, the ridge I took from the Amorites with my sword and my bow."

---

[a] 3 Hebrew *El-Shaddai*   [b] 7 That is, Northwest Mesopotamia   [c] 20 The Hebrew is singular.   [d] 21 The Hebrew is plural.   [e] 22 The Hebrew for *ridge of land* is identical with the place name Shechem.

Jacob Blesses His Sons

49 Then Jacob called for his sons and said: "Gather around so I can tell you what will happen to you in days to come.

² "Assemble and listen, sons of Jacob;
  listen to your father Israel.

³ "Reuben, you are my firstborn,
  my might, the first sign of my
    strength,
  excelling in honor, excelling in
    power.
⁴ Turbulent as the waters, you will no
    longer excel,
  for you went up onto your father's
    bed,
  onto my couch and defiled it.

⁵ "Simeon and Levi are brothers—
  their swords*a* are weapons of
    violence.
⁶ Let me not enter their council,
  let me not join their assembly,
  for they have killed men in their anger
  and hamstrung oxen as they
    pleased.
⁷ Cursed be their anger, so fierce,
  and their fury, so cruel!
  I will scatter them in Jacob
  and disperse them in Israel.

⁸ "Judah,*b* your brothers will praise you;
  your hand will be on the neck of
    your enemies;
  your father's sons will bow down to
    you.
⁹ You are a lion's cub, Judah;
  you return from the prey, my son.
  Like a lion he crouches and lies down,
  like a lioness—who dares to rouse
    him?
¹⁰ The scepter will not depart from
    Judah,
  nor the ruler's staff from between
    his feet,*c*
  until he to whom it belongs*d* shall
    come
  and the obedience of the nations
    shall be his.
¹¹ He will tether his donkey to a vine,
  his colt to the choicest branch;

he will wash his garments in wine,
  his robes in the blood of grapes.
¹² His eyes will be darker than wine,
  his teeth whiter than milk.*e*

¹³ "Zebulun will live by the seashore
  and become a haven for ships;
  his border will extend toward
    Sidon.

¹⁴ "Issachar is a rawboned*f* donkey
  lying down among the sheep pens.*g*
¹⁵ When he sees how good is his resting
    place
  and how pleasant is his land,
  he will bend his shoulder to the burden
  and submit to forced labor.

¹⁶ "Dan*b* will provide justice for his
    people
  as one of the tribes of Israel.
¹⁷ Dan will be a snake by the roadside,
  a viper along the path,
  that bites the horse's heels
  so that its rider tumbles backward.

¹⁸ "I look for your deliverance, LORD.

¹⁹ "Gad*i* will be attacked by a band of
    raiders,
  but he will attack them at their
    heels.

²⁰ "Asher's food will be rich;
  he will provide delicacies fit for a
    king.

²¹ "Naphtali is a doe set free
  that bears beautiful fawns.*j*

²² "Joseph is a fruitful vine,
  a fruitful vine near a spring,
  whose branches climb over a wall.*k*

---

a 5 The meaning of the Hebrew for this word is
uncertain.   *b 8 Judah* sounds like and may be
derived from the Hebrew for *praise.*
c 10 Or *from his descendants*   *d 10* Or *to whom
tribute belongs*; the meaning of the Hebrew for
this phrase is uncertain.   *e 12* Or *will be dull
from wine, / his teeth white from milk*
f 14 Or *strong*   *g 14* Or *the campfires*; or *the
saddlebags*   *b 16 Dan* here means *he provides
justice.*   *i 19 Gad* sounds like the Hebrew for
attack and also for *band of raiders.*
j 21 Or *free; / he utters beautiful words*
k 22 Or *Joseph is a wild colt, / a wild colt near a
spring, / a wild donkey on a terraced hill*

²³With bitterness archers attacked him;
they shot at him with hostility.
²⁴But his bow remained steady,
his strong arms stayed*ᵃ* limber,
because of the hand of the Mighty
One of Jacob,
because of the Shepherd, the Rock
of Israel,

ROCK SOLID
promises

"His bow remained steady . . . because of the hand of the Mighty One."
Genesis 49:24

By yourself you don't have the power to do tough things. God himself makes you strong and steady.

²⁵because of your father's God, who
helps you,
because of the Almighty,*ᵇ* who
blesses you
with blessings of the skies above,
blessings of the deep springs below,
blessings of the breast and womb.
²⁶Your father's blessings are greater
than the blessings of the ancient
mountains,
than*ᶜ* the bounty of the age-old hills.
Let all these rest on the head of
Joseph,
on the brow of the prince among*ᵈ*
his brothers.
²⁷"Benjamin is a ravenous wolf;
in the morning he devours the
prey,
in the evening he divides the
plunder."

²⁸All these are the twelve tribes of Israel, and this is what their father said to
them when he blessed them, giving each
the blessing appropriate to him.

The Death of Jacob

²⁹Then he gave them these instructions: "I am about to be gathered to my people. Bury me with my fathers in the cave in the field of Ephron the Hittite, ³⁰the cave in the field of Machpelah, near Mam-re in Canaan, which Abraham bought along with the field as a burial place from Ephron the Hittite. ³¹There Abraham and his wife Sarah were buried, there Isaac and his wife Rebekah were buried, and there I buried Leah. ³²The field and the cave in it were bought from the Hittites.*ᵉ*"

³³When Jacob had finished giving in-structions to his sons, he drew his feet up into the bed, breathed his last and was gathered to his people.

50 Joseph threw himself on his father and wept over him and kissed him. ²Then Jo-seph directed the physicians in his service to embalm his father Israel. So the physi-cians embalmed him, ³taking a full forty days, for that was the time required for embalming. And the Egyptians mourned for him seventy days.

⁴When the days of mourning had passed, Joseph said to Pharaoh's court, "If I have found favor in your eyes, speak to Phar-aoh for me. Tell him, ⁵'My father made me swear an oath and said, "I am about to die; bury me in the tomb I dug for myself in the land of Canaan." Now let me go up and bury my father; then I will return.'"

⁶Pharaoh said, "Go up and bury your father, as he made you swear to do."

⁷So Joseph went up to bury his fa-ther. All Pharaoh's officials accompanied him—the dignitaries of his court and all the dignitaries of Egypt— ⁸besides all the members of Joseph's household and his brothers and those belonging to his father's household. Only their children and their flocks and herds were left in Go-shen. ⁹Chariots and horsemen*ᶠ* also went up with him. It was a very large company.

*ᵃ 23,24 Or archers will attack . . . will shoot . . .
will remain . . . will stay   ᵇ 25 Hebrew Shaddai
ᶜ 26 Or of my progenitors, / as great as
ᵈ 26 Or of the one separated from   ᵉ 32 Or the
descendants of Heth   ᶠ 9 Or charioteers*

¹⁰When they reached the threshing floor of Atad, near the Jordan, they lamented loudly and bitterly; and there Joseph observed a seven-day period of mourning for his father. ¹¹When the Canaanites who lived there saw the mourning at the threshing floor of Atad, they said, "The Egyptians are holding a solemn ceremony of mourning." That is why that place near the Jordan is called Abel Mizraim.ᵃ

¹²So Jacob's sons did as he had commanded them: ¹³They carried him to the land of Canaan and buried him in the cave in the field of Machpelah, near Mamre, which Abraham had bought along with the field as a burial place from Ephron the Hittite. ¹⁴After burying his father, Joseph returned to Egypt, together with his brothers and all the others who had gone with him to bury his father.

Joseph Reassures His Brothers

¹⁵When Joseph's brothers saw that their father was dead, they said, "What if Joseph holds a grudge against us and pays us back for all the wrongs we did to him?" ¹⁶So they sent word to Joseph, saying, "Your father left these instructions before he died: ¹⁷'This is what you are to say to Joseph: I ask you to forgive your brothers the sins and the wrongs they committed in treating you so badly.' Now please forgive the sins of the servants of the God of your father." When their message came to him, Joseph wept.

¹⁸His brothers then came and threw themselves down before him. "We are your slaves," they said.

¹⁹But Joseph said to them, "Don't be afraid. Am I in the place of God? ²⁰You intended to harm me, but God intended it for good to accomplish what is now being done, the saving of many lives. ²¹So then, don't be afraid. I will provide for you and your children." And he reassured them and spoke kindly to them.

ROCK SOLID *plans*

Genesis 50:20

Count on God to work out his plan for you.

Joseph's brothers hated him so much they plotted to kill him, but they decided instead to sell the teen into slavery (see Genesis 37). Joseph was taken captive to Egypt, and as a slave he was falsely accused of trying to seduce his master's wife and was tossed in prison. But in time he rose to immense power. In the end he saved all of Egypt—and his father and brothers—from starvation. People had evil plans for Joseph, but through it all God was working for Joseph's good.

Your next step: Look for ways that God uses hard times in your life to benefit you or others.

The Death of Joseph

²²Joseph stayed in Egypt, along with all his father's family. He lived a hundred and ten years ²³and saw the third generation of Ephraim's children. Also the children of Makir son of Manasseh were placed at birth on Joseph's knees.ᵇ

²⁴Then Joseph said to his brothers, "I am about to die. But God will surely come to your aid and take you up out of this land to the land he promised on oath to Abraham, Isaac and Jacob." ²⁵And Joseph made the Israelites swear an oath and said, "God will surely come to your aid, and then you must carry my bones up from this place."

²⁶So Joseph died at the age of a hundred and ten. And after they embalmed him, he was placed in a coffin in Egypt.

ᵃ *11 Abel Mizraim* means *mourning of the Egyptians.*   ᵇ *23* That is, were counted as his

BOOK OUTLINE

Moses, God's leader
(1:1 — 4:31)

The contest with Pharaoh
(5:1 — 13:19)

From Egypt to Mount Sinai
(13:20 — 19:2)

God's covenant and laws
(19:3 — 24:8)

The tabernacle for worship
(24:9 — 40:38)

The book of Exodus continues the story of God's people that began with Abraham in the book of Genesis. Exodus means "exit" or "departure." The title of this book comes from the story that demonstrates God's care for his chosen people in the Old Testament—the Israelites as they are freed from slavery and exit Egypt.

From Moses' birth, God chose him for a special task—to lead the Israelites out of Egypt and to the land God had promised them, Canaan. Moses is the main character and author of this book. Although he didn't think he was strong, God made him strong with his power and encouragement (7:6–11). God showed his power to the Israelites and the Egyptians in the ten plagues (7:14–11:10); the last plague made it possible for the Israelites to leave Egypt. Before leaving Egypt they celebrated the Passover (12:1–51).

The Israelites began their journey protected and guided by God in a pillar of cloud during the day and a pillar of fire at night. With Moses leading them they crossed the Red Sea (Sea of Reeds) and settled in the desert at the foot of Mount Sinai for about one year. In the desert of Sinai God set up his covenant with the Israelites by giving them laws to help them live and worship as his holy people.

The covenant between God and Israel began a relationship in which Israel was identified as God's holy nation. God gave his people the Ten Commandments, priests, and the tabernacle to help them live lives that showed they were truly God's people.

The Israelites Oppressed

1 These are the names of the sons of Israel who went to Egypt with Jacob, each with his family: ²Reuben, Simeon, Levi and Judah; ³Issachar, Zebulun and Benjamin; ⁴Dan and Naphtali; Gad and Asher. ⁵The descendants of Jacob numbered seventy*a* in all; Joseph was already in Egypt.

⁶Now Joseph and all his brothers and all that generation died, ⁷but the Israelites were exceedingly fruitful; they multiplied greatly, increased in numbers and became so numerous that the land was filled with them.

⁸Then a new king, to whom Joseph meant nothing, came to power in Egypt. ⁹"Look," he said to his people, "the Israelites have become far too numerous for us. ¹⁰Come, we must deal shrewdly with them or they will become even more numerous and, if war breaks out, will join our enemies, fight against us and leave the country."

¹¹So they put slave masters over them to oppress them with forced labor, and they built Pithom and Rameses as store cities for Pharaoh. ¹²But the more they were oppressed, the more they multiplied and spread; so the Egyptians came to dread the Israelites ¹³and worked them ruthlessly. ¹⁴They made their lives bitter with harsh labor in brick and mortar and with all kinds of work in the fields; in all their harsh labor the Egyptians worked them ruthlessly.

¹⁵The king of Egypt said to the Hebrew midwives, whose names were Shiphrah and Puah, ¹⁶"When you are helping the Hebrew women during childbirth on the delivery stool, if you see that the baby is a boy, kill him; but if it is a girl, let her live." ¹⁷The midwives, however, feared God and did not do what the king of Egypt had told them to do; they let the boys live. ¹⁸Then the king of Egypt summoned the midwives and asked them, "Why have you done this? Why have you let the boys live?"

¹⁹The midwives answered Pharaoh, "Hebrew women are not like Egyptian women; they are vigorous and give birth before the midwives arrive."

²⁰So God was kind to the midwives and the people increased and became even more numerous. ²¹And because the midwives feared God, he gave them families of their own.

²²Then Pharaoh gave this order to all his people: "Every Hebrew boy that is born you must throw into the Nile, but let every girl live."

The Birth of Moses

2 Now a man of the tribe of Levi married a Levite woman, ²and she became pregnant and gave birth to a son. When she saw that he was a fine child, she hid him for three months. ³But when she could hide him no longer, she got a papyrus basket*b* for him and coated it with tar and pitch. Then she placed the child in it and put it among the reeds along the bank of the Nile. ⁴His sister stood at a distance to see what would happen to him.

⁵Then Pharaoh's daughter went down to the Nile to bathe, and her attendants were walking along the riverbank. She saw the basket among the reeds and sent her female slave to get it. ⁶She opened it and saw the baby. He was crying, and she felt sorry for him. "This is one of the Hebrew babies," she said.

⁷Then his sister asked Pharaoh's daughter, "Shall I go and get one of the Hebrew women to nurse the baby for you?"

⁸"Yes, go," she answered. So the girl went and got the baby's mother. ⁹Pharaoh's daughter said to her, "Take this baby and nurse him for me, and I will pay you." So the woman took the baby and nursed him. ¹⁰When the child grew older, she took him to Pharaoh's daughter and he became her son. She named him Moses,*c* saying, "I drew him out of the water."

---

a 5 Masoretic Text (see also Gen. 46:27); Dead Sea Scrolls and Septuagint (see also Acts 7:14 and note at Gen. 46:27) *seventy-five*
b 3 The Hebrew can also mean *ark*, as in Gen. 6:14.   *c 10 Moses* sounds like the Hebrew for *draw out.*

Moses Flees to Midian

[11] One day, after Moses had grown up, he went out to where his own people were and watched them at their hard labor. He saw an Egyptian beating a Hebrew, one of his own people. [12] Looking this way and that and seeing no one, he killed the Egyptian and hid him in the sand. [13] The next day he went out and saw two Hebrews fighting. He asked the one in the wrong, "Why are you hitting your fellow Hebrew?"

[14] The man said, "Who made you ruler and judge over us? Are you thinking of killing me as you killed the Egyptian?" Then Moses was afraid and thought, "What I did must have become known."

[15] When Pharaoh heard of this, he tried to kill Moses, but Moses fled from Pharaoh and went to live in Midian, where he sat down by a well. [16] Now a priest of Midian had seven daughters, and they came to draw water and fill the troughs to water their father's flock. [17] Some shepherds came along and drove them away, but Moses got up and came to their rescue and watered their flock.

[18] When the girls returned to Reuel their father, he asked them, "Why have you returned so early today?"

[19] They answered, "An Egyptian rescued us from the shepherds. He even drew water for us and watered the flock."

[20] "And where is he?" Reuel asked his daughters. "Why did you leave him? Invite him to have something to eat."

[21] Moses agreed to stay with the man, who gave his daughter Zipporah to Moses in marriage. [22] Zipporah gave birth to a son, and Moses named him Gershom,[a] saying, "I have become a foreigner in a foreign land."

[23] During that long period, the king of Egypt died. The Israelites groaned in their slavery and cried out, and their cry for help because of their slavery went up to God. [24] God heard their groaning and he remembered his covenant with Abraham, with Isaac and with Jacob. [25] So God looked on the Israelites and was concerned about them.

UNSHAKEN God

Exodus 2:23–25

God is compassionate.

When God's Old Testament people were slaves in Egypt, they wondered if he saw their pain. As they served brutal masters, they doubted his care (see Exodus 1:11–16). They wanted an immediate end to their suffering, but God wasn't ready to drive out the people occupying the land where he would give them freedom (see Genesis 15:13–16). Yet despite hundreds of years of suffering, God did see his people's pain, and he sent Moses to lead them out of slavery (see Exodus 3:7–10). Some days you might wonder if God notices your problems. But God sees. God cares. He watches over you with a compassion bigger than you can ever imagine.

So ... When have you felt overlooked by God? How do you know God cares for you?

Moses and the Burning Bush

3 Now Moses was tending the flock of Jethro his father-in-law, the priest of Midian, and he led the flock to the far side of the wilderness and came to Horeb, the mountain of God. [2] There the angel of the LORD appeared to him in flames of fire from within a bush. Moses saw that though the bush was on fire it did not burn up. [3] So Moses thought, "I will go over and see this strange sight — why the bush does not burn up."

[4] When the LORD saw that he had gone over to look, God called to him from within the bush, "Moses! Moses!"

And Moses said, "Here I am."

[5] "Do not come any closer," God said. "Take off your sandals, for the place where you are standing is holy ground." [6] Then

---

[a] 22 *Gershom* sounds like the Hebrew for *a foreigner there*.

69

he said, "I am the God of your father,[a] the God of Abraham, the God of Isaac and the God of Jacob." At this, Moses hid his face, because he was afraid to look at God.

[7] The LORD said, "I have indeed seen the misery of my people in Egypt. I have heard them crying out because of their slave drivers, and I am concerned about their suffering. [8] So I have come down to rescue them from the hand of the Egyptians and to bring them up out of that land into a good and spacious land, a land flowing with milk and honey—the home of the Canaanites, Hittites, Amorites, Perizzites, Hivites and Jebusites. [9] And now the cry of the Israelites has reached me, and I have seen the way the Egyptians are oppressing them. [10] So now, go. I am sending you to Pharaoh to bring my people the Israelites out of Egypt."

[11] But Moses said to God, "Who am I that I should go to Pharaoh and bring the Israelites out of Egypt?"

[12] And God said, "I will be with you. And this will be the sign to you that it is I who have sent you: When you have brought the people out of Egypt, you[b] will worship God on this mountain."

[13] Moses said to God, "Suppose I go to the Israelites and say to them, 'The God of your fathers has sent me to you,' and they ask me, 'What is his name?' Then what shall I tell them?"

[14] God said to Moses, "I AM WHO I AM.[c] This is what you are to say to the Israelites: 'I AM has sent me to you.'"

[15] God also said to Moses, "Say to the Israelites, 'The LORD,[d] the God of your fathers—the God of Abraham, the God of Isaac and the God of Jacob—has sent me to you.'

"This is my name forever,
    the name you shall call me
    from generation to generation.

[16] "Go, assemble the elders of Israel and say to them, 'The LORD, the God of your fathers—the God of Abraham, Isaac and Jacob—appeared to me and said: I have watched over you and have seen what has been done to you in Egypt. [17] And I have promised to bring you up out of your mis-

ery in Egypt into the land of the Canaanites, Hittites, Amorites, Perizzites, Hivites and Jebusites—a land flowing with milk and honey.'

[18] "The elders of Israel will listen to you. Then you and the elders are to go to the king of Egypt and say to him, 'The LORD, the God of the Hebrews, has met with us. Let us take a three-day journey into the wilderness to offer sacrifices to the LORD our God.' [19] But I know that the king of Egypt will not let you go unless a mighty hand compels him. [20] So I will stretch out my hand and strike the Egyptians with all the wonders that I will perform among them. After that, he will let you go.

[21] "And I will make the Egyptians fa-

---

[a] 6 Masoretic Text; Samaritan Pentateuch (see Acts 7:32) *fathers*   [b] 12 The Hebrew is plural.
[c] 14 Or *I WILL BE WHAT I WILL BE*
[d] 15 The Hebrew for LORD sounds like and may be related to the Hebrew for *I AM* in verse 14.

UNSHAKEN God

Exodus 3:1–21

God is friendly.

Moses didn't expect to meet God in the desert. After being raised as a prince in the household of Pharaoh, ruler of Egypt, Moses had fled to the wastelands when his true identity as a Hebrew and a murderer was discovered (see Exodus 2:11–15). Yet one day God called to Moses from a flaming bush. Moses was pondering how a shrub could burn yet not be consumed when God revealed his name: "I AM WHO I AM" (Exodus 3:14). With that name the Lord introduced himself as the God who exists from all eternity and who pledges to always be with us. Moses didn't go looking for God. The Lord came looking for Moses—and all of us.

So ... Why does it matter to you that God made a point to introduce himself to Moses?

vorably disposed toward this people, so that when you leave you will not go empty-handed. ²²Every woman is to ask her neighbor and any woman living in her house for articles of silver and gold and for clothing, which you will put on your sons and daughters. And so you will plunder the Egyptians."

Signs for Moses

4 Moses answered, "What if they do not believe me or listen to me and say, 'The LORD did not appear to you'?"

²Then the LORD said to him, "What is that in your hand?"

"A staff," he replied.

³The LORD said, "Throw it on the ground."

Moses threw it on the ground and it became a snake, and he ran from it. ⁴Then the LORD said to him, "Reach out your hand and take it by the tail." So Moses reached out and took hold of the snake and it turned back into a staff in his hand. ⁵"This," said the LORD, "is so that they may believe that the LORD, the God of their fathers—the God of Abraham, the God of Isaac and the God of Jacob—has appeared to you."

⁶Then the LORD said, "Put your hand inside your cloak." So Moses put his hand into his cloak, and when he took it out, the skin was leprous*—it had become as white as snow.

⁷"Now put it back into your cloak," he said. So Moses put his hand back into his cloak, and when he took it out, it was restored, like the rest of his flesh.

⁸Then the LORD said, "If they do not believe you or pay attention to the first sign, they may believe the second. ⁹But if they do not believe these two signs or listen to you, take some water from the Nile and pour it on the dry ground. The water you take from the river will become blood on the ground."

¹⁰Moses said to the LORD, "Pardon your servant, Lord. I have never been eloquent, neither in the past nor since you have spoken to your servant. I am slow of speech and tongue."

¹¹The LORD said to him, "Who gave human beings their mouths? Who makes them deaf or mute? Who gives them sight or makes them blind? Is it not I, the LORD? ¹²Now go; I will help you speak and will teach you what to say."

¹³But Moses said, "Pardon your servant, Lord. Please send someone else."

¹⁴Then the LORD's anger burned against Moses and he said, "What about your brother, Aaron the Levite? I know he can speak well. He is already on his way to meet you, and he will be glad to see you. ¹⁵You shall speak to him and put words in his mouth; I will help both of you speak and will teach you what to do. ¹⁶He will speak to the people for you, and it will be as if he were your mouth and as if you were God to him. ¹⁷But take this staff in your hand so you can perform the signs with it."

Moses Returns to Egypt

¹⁸Then Moses went back to Jethro his father-in-law and said to him, "Let me return to my own people in Egypt to see if any of them are still alive."

Jethro said, "Go, and I wish you well."

¹⁹Now the LORD had said to Moses in Midian, "Go back to Egypt, for all those who wanted to kill you are dead." ²⁰So Moses took his wife and sons, put them on a donkey and started back to Egypt. And he took the staff of God in his hand.

²¹The LORD said to Moses, "When you return to Egypt, see that you perform before Pharaoh all the wonders I have given you the power to do. But I will harden his heart so that he will not let the people go. ²²Then say to Pharaoh, 'This is what the LORD says: Israel is my firstborn son, ²³and I told you, "Let my son go, so he may worship me." But you refused to let him go; so I will kill your firstborn son.'"

²⁴At a lodging place on the way, the LORD met Moses^b and was about to kill him. ²⁵But Zipporah took a flint knife, cut off her son's foreskin and touched Moses'

a 6 The Hebrew word for *leprous* was used for various diseases affecting the skin.
b 24 Hebrew *him*

feet with it.[a] "Surely you are a bridegroom of blood to me," she said. [26]So the LORD let him alone. (At that time she said "bridegroom of blood," referring to circumcision.)

[27]The LORD said to Aaron, "Go into the wilderness to meet Moses." So he met Moses at the mountain of God and kissed him. [28]Then Moses told Aaron everything the LORD had sent him to say, and also about all the signs he had commanded him to perform.

[29]Moses and Aaron brought together all the elders of the Israelites, [30]and Aaron told them everything the LORD had said to Moses. He also performed the signs before the people, [31]and they believed. And when they heard that the LORD was concerned about them and had seen their misery, they bowed down and worshiped.

Bricks Without Straw

5 Afterward Moses and Aaron went to Pharaoh and said, "This is what the LORD, the God of Israel, says: 'Let my people go, so that they may hold a festival to me in the wilderness.'"

[2]Pharaoh said, "Who is the LORD, that I should obey him and let Israel go? I do not know the LORD and I will not let Israel go."

[3]Then they said, "The God of the Hebrews has met with us. Now let us take a three-day journey into the wilderness to offer sacrifices to the LORD our God, or he may strike us with plagues or with the sword."

[4]But the king of Egypt said, "Moses and Aaron, why are you taking the people away from their labor? Get back to your work!" [5]Then Pharaoh said, "Look, the people of the land are now numerous, and you are stopping them from working."

[6]That same day Pharaoh gave this order to the slave drivers and overseers in charge of the people: [7]"You are no longer to supply the people with straw for making bricks; let them go and gather their own straw. [8]But require them to make the same number of bricks as before; don't reduce the quota. They are lazy; that is why they

are crying out, 'Let us go and sacrifice to our God.' [9]Make the work harder for the people so that they keep working and pay no attention to lies."

[10]Then the slave drivers and the overseers went out and said to the people, "This is what Pharaoh says: 'I will not give you any more straw. [11]Go and get your own straw wherever you can find it, but your work will not be reduced at all.'" [12]So the people scattered all over Egypt to gather stubble to use for straw. [13]The slave drivers kept pressing them, saying, "Complete the work required of you for each day, just as when you had straw." [14]And Pharaoh's slave drivers beat the Israelite overseers they had appointed, demanding, "Why haven't you met your quota of bricks yesterday or today, as before?"

[15]Then the Israelite overseers went and appealed to Pharaoh: "Why have you treated your servants this way? [16]Your servants are given no straw, yet we are told, 'Make bricks!' Your servants are being beaten, but the fault is with your own people."

[17]Pharaoh said, "Lazy, that's what you are—lazy! That is why you keep saying, 'Let us go and sacrifice to the LORD.' [18]Now get to work. You will not be given any straw, yet you must produce your full quota of bricks."

[19]The Israelite overseers realized they were in trouble when they were told, "You are not to reduce the number of bricks required of you for each day." [20]When they left Pharaoh, they found Moses and Aaron waiting to meet them, [21]and they said, "May the LORD look on you and judge you! You have made us obnoxious to Pharaoh and his officials and have put a sword in their hand to kill us."

God Promises Deliverance

[22]Moses returned to the LORD and said, "Why, Lord, why have you brought trouble on this people? Is this why you sent me? [23]Ever since I went to Pharaoh to speak in your name, he has brought trou-

[a] 25 The meaning of the Hebrew for this clause is uncertain.

ble on this people, and you have not rescued your people at all."

6 Then the LORD said to Moses, "Now you will see what I will do to Pharaoh: Because of my mighty hand he will let them go; because of my mighty hand he will drive them out of his country."

²God also said to Moses, "I am the LORD. ³I appeared to Abraham, to Isaac and to Jacob as God Almighty,ᵃ but by my name the LORDᵇ I did not make myself fully known to them. ⁴I also established my covenant with them to give them the land of Canaan, where they resided as foreigners. ⁵Moreover, I have heard the groaning of the Israelites, whom the Egyptians are enslaving, and I have remembered my covenant.

⁶"Therefore, say to the Israelites: 'I am the LORD, and I will bring you out from under the yoke of the Egyptians. I will free you from being slaves to them, and I will redeem you with an outstretched arm and with mighty acts of judgment. ⁷I will take you as my own people, and I will be your God. Then you will know that I am the LORD your God, who brought you out from under the yoke of the Egyptians. ⁸And I will bring you to the land I swore

ᵃ 3 Hebrew *El-Shaddai*   ᵇ 3 See note at 3:15.

Exodus 5:1 – 23

Moses led God's people to freedom.

As an infant Moses was nearly murdered when Pharaoh ordered the death of every Hebrew baby boy. But his mother tucked him in a basket and set him afloat on the Nile River where he was found by the Pharaoh's daughter and raised in the king's house (see Exodus 2:5 – 10).

Moses fled to the desert after killing an Egyptian he saw beating a Hebrew slave (see Exodus 2:12). Out in the desert the Lord introduced himself to Moses in a burning bush and told him to return to the palace and demand Pharaoh free the Hebrews (see Exodus 3:1 – 22). Moses did return and announced a series of terrible plagues that finally led to a miraculous escape across the Red Sea. But the people soon proved themselves to be a mass of ungrateful complainers.

The Lord gave Moses the Ten Commandments and told his people how to live for him (see Exodus 20:1 – 17), but their rebellion against God's plans kept almost all of them from entering the land the Lord had given them. For the next 40 years Moses led the people as they wandered the desert.

The Lord had an epic purpose for Moses. He could have lived as a prince of Egypt in the comforts of Pharaoh's palace. Yet Hebrews 11:25 says he "chose to be mistreated along with the people of God rather than to enjoy the fleeting pleasures of sin." Moses stayed true to the Lord and his purposes and led his people to freedom.

You can find Moses from Exodus 1 to his death in Deuteronomy 34:1 – 12, plus Acts 7:17 – 50 and Hebrews 11:23 – 28.

UNSHAKEN people

ROCK SOLID
promises

"I will take you as my own people, and I will be your God." Exodus 6:7

God will never leave you lonely. He makes you his child and promises to be your Lord forever.

with uplifted hand to give to Abraham, to Isaac and to Jacob. I will give it to you as a possession. I am the LORD.'"

⁹Moses reported this to the Israelites, but they did not listen to him because of their discouragement and harsh labor.

¹⁰Then the LORD said to Moses, ¹¹"Go, tell Pharaoh king of Egypt to let the Israelites go out of his country."

¹²But Moses said to the LORD, "If the Israelites will not listen to me, why would Pharaoh listen to me, since I speak with faltering lips*ᵃ*?"

Family Record of Moses and Aaron

¹³Now the LORD spoke to Moses and Aaron about the Israelites and Pharaoh king of Egypt, and he commanded them to bring the Israelites out of Egypt.

¹⁴These were the heads of their families*ᵇ*:

The sons of Reuben the firstborn son of Israel were Hanok and Pallu, Hezron and Karmi. These were the clans of Reuben.

¹⁵The sons of Simeon were Jemuel, Jamin, Ohad, Jakin, Zohar and Shaul the son of a Canaanite woman. These were the clans of Simeon.

¹⁶These were the names of the sons of Levi according to their records: Gershon, Kohath and Merari. Levi lived 137 years.

¹⁷The sons of Gershon, by clans, were Libni and Shimei.

¹⁸The sons of Kohath were Amram, Izhar, Hebron and Uzziel. Kohath lived 133 years.

¹⁹The sons of Merari were Mahli and Mushi.

These were the clans of Levi according to their records.

²⁰Amram married his father's sister Jochebed, who bore him Aaron and Moses. Amram lived 137 years.

²¹The sons of Izhar were Korah, Nepheg and Zikri.

²²The sons of Uzziel were Mishael, Elzaphan and Sithri.

²³Aaron married Elisheba, daughter of Amminadab and sister of Nahshon, and she bore him Nadab and Abihu, Eleazar and Ithamar.

²⁴The sons of Korah were Assir, Elkanah and Abiasaph. These were the Korahite clans.

²⁵Eleazar son of Aaron married one of the daughters of Putiel, and she bore him Phinehas.

These were the heads of the Levite families, clan by clan.

²⁶It was this Aaron and Moses to whom the LORD said, "Bring the Israelites out of Egypt by their divisions." ²⁷They were the ones who spoke to Pharaoh king of Egypt about bringing the Israelites out of Egypt—this same Moses and Aaron.

Aaron to Speak for Moses

²⁸Now when the LORD spoke to Moses in Egypt, ²⁹he said to him, "I am the LORD. Tell Pharaoh king of Egypt everything I tell you."

³⁰But Moses said to the LORD, "Since I speak with faltering lips, why would Pharaoh listen to me?"

7 Then the LORD said to Moses, "See, I have made you like God to Pharaoh, and your brother Aaron will be your prophet. ²You are to say

---

ᵃ 12 Hebrew *I am uncircumcised of lips*; also in verse 30   *ᵇ 14* The Hebrew for *families* here and in verse 25 refers to units larger than clans everything I command you, and your brother Aaron is to tell Pharaoh to let the Israelites go out of his country. [3]But I will harden Pharaoh's heart, and though I multiply my signs and wonders in Egypt, [4]he will not listen to you. Then I will lay my hand on Egypt and with mighty acts of judgment I will bring out my divisions, my people the Israelites. [5]And the Egyptians will know that I am the LORD when I stretch out my hand against Egypt and bring the Israelites out of it."

[6]Moses and Aaron did just as the LORD commanded them. [7]Moses was eighty years old and Aaron eighty-three when they spoke to Pharaoh.

Aaron's Staff Becomes a Snake

[8]The LORD said to Moses and Aaron, [9]"When Pharaoh says to you, 'Perform a miracle,' then say to Aaron, 'Take your staff and throw it down before Pharaoh,' and it will become a snake."

[10]So Moses and Aaron went to Pharaoh and did just as the LORD commanded. Aaron threw his staff down in front of Pharaoh and his officials, and it became a snake. [11]Pharaoh then summoned wise men and sorcerers, and the Egyptian magicians also did the same things by their secret arts: [12]Each one threw down his staff and it became a snake. But Aaron's staff swallowed up their staffs. [13]Yet Pharaoh's heart became hard and he would not listen to them, just as the LORD had said.

The Plague of Blood

[14]Then the LORD said to Moses, "Pharaoh's heart is unyielding; he refuses to let the people go. [15]Go to Pharaoh in the morning as he goes out to the river. Confront him on the bank of the Nile, and take in your hand the staff that was changed into a snake. [16]Then say to him, 'The LORD, the God of the Hebrews, has sent me to say to you: Let my people go, so that they may worship me in the wilderness. But until now you have not listened. [17]This is what the LORD says: By this you will know that I am the LORD: With the staff that is in my hand I will strike the water of the Nile, and it will be changed into blood. [18]The fish in the Nile will die, and the river will stink; the Egyptians will not be able to drink its water.'"

[19]The LORD said to Moses, "Tell Aaron, 'Take your staff and stretch out your hand over the waters of Egypt—over the streams and canals, over the ponds and all the reservoirs—and they will turn to

---

Exodus 7:1–25

Evil sometimes tries to fake God's power.

When Moses and Aaron walked into Pharaoh's court and demanded the Egyptian king free a million Hebrew slaves, onlookers saw some amazing miracles. When Aaron threw his staff to the ground, it changed into a snake and slithered away (see Exodus 7:10). When Aaron stretched out his hand, all the waters of Egypt turned into blood—so that fish died, the river stank, and the Egyptians had nothing to drink (see Exodus 7:20–21). Aaron did these feats through the Lord's miraculous powers, but then a strange thing happened. The magicians in Pharaoh's court duplicated these miracles (see Exodus 7:11 and 22). Pharaoh's "heart became hard" (Exodus 7:22) and he concluded that the God of the Israelites was no one to fear. Satan can give his followers supernatural abilities that can mimic God's own power, but the Lord is infinitely more powerful (see 1 John 4:4). And true miracles are always done for God's glory (see John 11:40).

Think: How can you tell the difference between God's power and supernatural fakes?

ROCK SOLID truths

75

ood.' Blood will be everywhere in Egypt, even in vessels[a] of wood and stone.'"

[20] Moses and Aaron did just as the Lord had commanded. He raised his staff in the presence of Pharaoh and his officials and struck the water of the Nile, and all the water was changed into blood. [21] The fish in the Nile died, and the river smelled so bad that the Egyptians could not drink its water. Blood was everywhere in Egypt.

[22] But the Egyptian magicians did the same things by their secret arts, and Pharaoh's heart became hard; he would not listen to Moses and Aaron, just as the Lord had said. [23] Instead, he turned and went into his palace, and did not take even this to heart. [24] And all the Egyptians dug along the Nile to get drinking water, because they could not drink the water of the river.

The Plague of Frogs

[25] Seven days passed after the Lord struck the Nile. **8**[b] [1] Then the Lord said to Moses, "Go to Pharaoh and say to him, 'This is what the Lord says: Let my people go, so that they may worship me. [2] If you refuse to let them go, I will send a plague of frogs on your whole country. [3] The Nile will teem with frogs. They will come up into your palace and your bedroom and onto your bed, into the houses of your officials and on your people, and into your ovens and kneading troughs. [4] The frogs will come up on you and your people and all your officials.'"

[5] Then the Lord said to Moses, "Tell Aaron, 'Stretch out your hand with your staff over the streams and canals and ponds, and make frogs come up on the land of Egypt.'"

[6] So Aaron stretched out his hand over the waters of Egypt, and the frogs came up and covered the land. [7] But the magicians did the same things by their secret arts; they also made frogs come up on the land of Egypt.

[8] Pharaoh summoned Moses and Aaron and said, "Pray to the Lord to take the frogs away from me and my people, and I will let your people go to offer sacrifices to the Lord."

[9] Moses said to Pharaoh, "I leave to you the honor of setting the time for me to pray for you and your officials and your people that you and your houses may be rid of the frogs, except for those that remain in the Nile."

[10] "Tomorrow," Pharaoh said.

Moses replied, "It will be as you say, so that you may know there is no one like the Lord our God. [11] The frogs will leave you and your houses, your officials and your people; they will remain only in the Nile."

[12] After Moses and Aaron left Pharaoh, Moses cried out to the Lord about the frogs he had brought on Pharaoh. [13] And the Lord did what Moses asked. The frogs died in the houses, in the courtyards and in the fields. [14] They were piled into heaps, and the land reeked of them. [15] But when Pharaoh saw that there was relief, he hardened his heart and would not listen to Moses and Aaron, just as the Lord had said.

The Plague of Gnats

[16] Then the Lord said to Moses, "Tell Aaron, 'Stretch out your staff and strike the dust of the ground,' and throughout the land of Egypt the dust will become gnats." [17] They did this, and when Aaron stretched out his hand with the staff and struck the dust of the ground, gnats came on people and animals. All the dust throughout the land of Egypt became gnats. [18] But when the magicians tried to produce gnats by their secret arts, they could not.

Since the gnats were on people and animals everywhere, [19] the magicians said to Pharaoh, "This is the finger of God." But Pharaoh's heart was hard and he would not listen, just as the Lord had said.

The Plague of Flies

[20] Then the Lord said to Moses, "Get up early in the morning and confront Pharaoh as he goes to the river and say to him, 'This is what the Lord says: Let my people go, so that they may worship me. [21] If you do not let my people go, I will send swarms

---

[a] 19 Or *even on their idols*   [b] In Hebrew texts 8:1-4 is numbered 7:26-29, and 8:5-32 is numbered 8:1-28.

of flies on you and your officials, on your people and into your houses. The houses of the Egyptians will be full of flies; even the ground will be covered with them.

²² "'But on that day I will deal differently with the land of Goshen, where my people live; no swarms of flies will be there, so that you will know that I, the LORD, am in this land. ²³ I will make a distinction^a between my people and your people. This sign will occur tomorrow.'"

²⁴ And the LORD did this. Dense swarms of flies poured into Pharaoh's palace and into the houses of his officials; throughout Egypt the land was ruined by the flies.

²⁵ Then Pharaoh summoned Moses and Aaron and said, "Go, sacrifice to your God here in the land."

²⁶ But Moses said, "That would not be right. The sacrifices we offer the LORD our God would be detestable to the Egyptians. And if we offer sacrifices that are detestable in their eyes, will they not stone us? ²⁷ We must take a three-day journey into the wilderness to offer sacrifices to the LORD our God, as he commands us."

²⁸ Pharaoh said, "I will let you go to offer sacrifices to the LORD your God in the wilderness, but you must not go very far. Now pray for me."

²⁹ Moses answered, "As soon as I leave you, I will pray to the LORD, and tomorrow the flies will leave Pharaoh and his officials and his people. Only let Pharaoh be sure that he does not act deceitfully again by not letting the people go to offer sacrifices to the LORD."

³⁰ Then Moses left Pharaoh and prayed to the LORD, ³¹ and the LORD did what Moses asked. The flies left Pharaoh and his officials and his people; not a fly remained. ³² But this time also Pharaoh hardened his heart and would not let the people go.

The Plague on Livestock

9 Then the LORD said to Moses, "Go to Pharaoh and say to him, 'This is what the LORD, the God of the Hebrews, says: "Let my people go, so that they may worship me." ² If you refuse to let them go and continue to hold them back, ³ the hand of the LORD will bring a terrible plague on your livestock in the field—on your horses, donkeys and camels and on your cattle, sheep and goats. ⁴ But the LORD will make a distinction between the livestock of Israel and that of Egypt, so that no animal belonging to the Israelites will die.'"

⁵ The LORD set a time and said, "Tomorrow the LORD will do this in the land." ⁶ And the next day the LORD did it: All the livestock of the Egyptians died, but not one animal belonging to the Israelites died. ⁷ Pharaoh investigated and found that not even one of the animals of the Israelites had died. Yet his heart was unyielding and he would not let the people go.

The Plague of Boils

⁸ Then the LORD said to Moses and Aaron, "Take handfuls of soot from a furnace and have Moses toss it into the air in the presence of Pharaoh. ⁹ It will become fine dust over the whole land of Egypt, and festering boils will break out on people and animals throughout the land."

¹⁰ So they took soot from a furnace and stood before Pharaoh. Moses tossed it into the air, and festering boils broke out on people and animals. ¹¹ The magicians could not stand before Moses because of the boils that were on them and on all the Egyptians. ¹² But the LORD hardened Pharaoh's heart and he would not listen to Moses and Aaron, just as the LORD had said to Moses.

The Plague of Hail

¹³ Then the LORD said to Moses, "Get up early in the morning, confront Pharaoh and say to him, 'This is what the LORD, the God of the Hebrews, says: Let my people go, so that they may worship me, ¹⁴ or this time I will send the full force of my plagues against you and against your officials and your people, so

^a 23 Septuagint and Vulgate; Hebrew will put a deliverance

you may know that there is no one like me in all the earth. ¹⁵For by now I could have stretched out my hand and struck you and your people with a plague that would have wiped you off the earth. ¹⁶But I have raised you up*a* for this very purpose, that I might show you my power and that my name might be proclaimed in all the earth. ¹⁷You still set yourself against my people and will not let them go. ¹⁸Therefore, at this time tomorrow I will send the worst hailstorm that has ever fallen on Egypt, from the day it was founded till now. ¹⁹Give an order now to bring your livestock and everything you have in the field to a place of shelter, because the hail will fall on every person and animal that has not been brought in and is still out in the field, and they will die.' "

²⁰Those officials of Pharaoh who feared the word of the LORD hurried to bring their slaves and their livestock inside. ²¹But those who ignored the word of the LORD left their slaves and livestock in the field.

²²Then the LORD said to Moses, "Stretch out your hand toward the sky so that hail will fall all over Egypt—on people and animals and on everything growing in the fields of Egypt." ²³When Moses stretched out his staff toward the sky, the LORD sent thunder and hail, and lightning flashed down to the ground. So the LORD rained hail on the land of Egypt; ²⁴hail fell and lightning flashed back and forth. It was the worst storm in all the land of Egypt since it had become a nation. ²⁵Throughout Egypt hail struck everything in the fields—both people and animals; it beat down everything growing in the fields and stripped every tree. ²⁶The only place it did not hail was the land of Goshen, where the Israelites were.

²⁷Then Pharaoh summoned Moses and Aaron. "This time I have sinned," he said to them. "The LORD is in the right, and I and my people are in the wrong. ²⁸Pray to the LORD, for we have had enough thunder and hail. I will let you go; you don't have to stay any longer."

²⁹Moses replied, "When I have gone out of the city, I will spread out my hands in prayer to the LORD. The thunder will stop and there will be no more hail, so you may know that the earth is the LORD's. ³⁰But I know that you and your officials still do not fear the LORD God."

³¹(The flax and barley were destroyed, since the barley had headed and the flax was in bloom. ³²The wheat and spelt, however, were not destroyed, because they ripen later.)

³³Then Moses left Pharaoh and went out of the city. He spread out his hands toward the LORD; the thunder and hail stopped, and the rain no longer poured down on the land. ³⁴When Pharaoh saw that the rain and hail and thunder had stopped, he sinned again: He and his officials hardened their hearts. ³⁵So Pharaoh's heart was hard and he would not let the Israelites go, just as the LORD had said through Moses.

The Plague of Locusts

10 Then the LORD said to Moses, "Go to Pharaoh, for I have hardened his heart and the hearts of his officials so that I may perform these signs of mine among them ²that you may tell your children and grandchildren how I dealt harshly with the Egyptians and how I performed my signs among them, and that you may know that I am the LORD."

³So Moses and Aaron went to Pharaoh and said to him, "This is what the LORD, the God of the Hebrews, says: 'How long will you refuse to humble yourself before me? Let my people go, so that they may worship me. ⁴If you refuse to let them go, I will bring locusts into your country tomorrow. ⁵They will cover the face of the ground so that it cannot be seen. They will devour what little you have left after the hail, including every tree that is growing in your fields. ⁶They will fill your houses and those of all your officials and all the Egyptians—something neither your parents nor your ancestors have ever seen from the day they settled in this land till

a 16 Or *have spared you*

now.'" Then Moses turned and left Pharaoh.

[7] Pharaoh's officials said to him, "How long will this man be a snare to us? Let the people go, so that they may worship the LORD their God. Do you not yet realize that Egypt is ruined?"

[8] Then Moses and Aaron were brought back to Pharaoh. "Go, worship the LORD your God," he said. "But tell me who will be going."

[9] Moses answered, "We will go with our young and our old, with our sons and our daughters, and with our flocks and herds, because we are to celebrate a festival to the LORD."

[10] Pharaoh said, "The LORD be with you—if I let you go, along with your women and children! Clearly you are bent on evil.[a] [11] No! Have only the men go and worship the LORD, since that's what you have been asking for." Then Moses and Aaron were driven out of Pharaoh's presence.

[12] And the LORD said to Moses, "Stretch out your hand over Egypt so that locusts swarm over the land and devour everything growing in the fields, everything left by the hail."

[13] So Moses stretched out his staff over Egypt, and the LORD made an east wind blow across the land all that day and all that night. By morning the wind had brought the locusts; [14] they invaded all Egypt and settled down in every area of the country in great numbers. Never before had there been such a plague of locusts, nor will there ever be again. [15] They covered all the ground until it was black. They devoured all that was left after the hail—everything growing in the fields and the fruit on the trees. Nothing green remained on tree or plant in all the land of Egypt.

[16] Pharaoh quickly summoned Moses and Aaron and said, "I have sinned against the LORD your God and against you. [17] Now forgive my sin once more and pray to the LORD your God to take this deadly plague away from me."

[18] Moses then left Pharaoh and prayed to the LORD. [19] And the LORD changed the wind to a very strong west wind, which caught up the locusts and carried them into the Red Sea.[b] Not a locust was left anywhere in Egypt. [20] But the LORD hardened Pharaoh's heart, and he would not let the Israelites go.

The Plague of Darkness

[21] Then the LORD said to Moses, "Stretch out your hand toward the sky so that darkness spreads over Egypt—darkness that can be felt." [22] So Moses stretched out his hand toward the sky, and total darkness covered all Egypt for three days. [23] No one could see anyone else or move about for three days. Yet all the Israelites had light in the places where they lived.

[24] Then Pharaoh summoned Moses and said, "Go, worship the LORD. Even your women and children may go with you; only leave your flocks and herds behind."

[25] But Moses said, "You must allow us to have sacrifices and burnt offerings to present to the LORD our God. [26] Our livestock too must go with us; not a hoof is to be left behind. We have to use some of them in worshiping the LORD our God, and until we get there we will not know what we are to use to worship the LORD."

[27] But the LORD hardened Pharaoh's heart, and he was not willing to let them go. [28] Pharaoh said to Moses, "Get out of my sight! Make sure you do not appear before me again! The day you see my face you will die."

[29] "Just as you say," Moses replied. "I will never appear before you again."

The Plague on the Firstborn

11 Now the LORD had said to Moses, "I will bring one more plague on Pharaoh and on Egypt. After that, he will let you go from here, and when he does, he will drive you out completely. [2] Tell the people that men and women alike are to ask their neighbors for articles of silver and gold." [3] (The LORD

---

[a] 10 Or *Be careful, trouble is in store for you!*
[b] 19 Or *the Sea of Reeds*

made the Egyptians favorably disposed toward the people, and Moses himself was highly regarded in Egypt by Pharaoh's officials and by the people.)

⁴So Moses said, "This is what the LORD says: 'About midnight I will go throughout Egypt. ⁵Every firstborn son in Egypt will die, from the firstborn son of Pharaoh, who sits on the throne, to the firstborn son of the female slave, who is at her hand mill, and all the firstborn of the cattle as well. ⁶There will be loud wailing throughout Egypt—worse than there has ever been or ever will be again. ⁷But among the Israelites not a dog will bark at any person or animal.' Then you will know that the LORD makes a distinction between Egypt and Israel. ⁸All these officials of yours will come to me, bowing down before me and saying, 'Go, you and all the people who follow you!' After that I will leave." Then Moses, hot with anger, left Pharaoh.

⁹The LORD had said to Moses, "Pharaoh will refuse to listen to you—so that my wonders may be multiplied in Egypt." ¹⁰Moses and Aaron performed all these wonders before Pharaoh, but the LORD hardened Pharaoh's heart, and he would not let the Israelites go out of his country.

The Passover and the Festival of Unleavened Bread

12 The LORD said to Moses and Aaron in Egypt, ²"This month is to be for you the first month, the first month of your year. ³Tell the whole community of Israel that on the tenth day of this month each man is to take a lamb*ᵃ* for his family, one for each household. ⁴If any household is too small for a whole lamb, they must share one with their nearest neighbor, having taken into account the number of people there are. You are to determine the amount of lamb needed in accordance with what each person will eat. ⁵The animals you choose must be year-old males without defect, and you may take them from the sheep or the goats. ⁶Take care of them until the fourteenth day of the month, when all the members

of the community of Israel must slaughter them at twilight. ⁷Then they are to take some of the blood and put it on the sides and tops of the doorframes of the houses where they eat the lambs. ⁸That same night they are to eat the meat roasted over the fire, along with bitter herbs, and bread made without yeast. ⁹Do not eat the meat raw or boiled in water, but roast it over a fire—with the head, legs and internal organs. ¹⁰Do not leave any of it till morning; if some is left till morning, you must burn it. ¹¹This is how you are to eat it: with your cloak tucked into your belt, your sandals on your feet and your staff in your hand. Eat it in haste; it is the LORD's Passover.

¹²"On that same night I will pass through Egypt and strike down every firstborn of both people and animals, and I will bring judgment on all the gods of Egypt. I am the LORD. ¹³The blood will be a sign for you on the houses where you are, and when I see the blood, I will pass over you. No destructive plague will touch you when I strike Egypt.

¹⁴"This is a day you are to commemorate; for the generations to come you shall celebrate it as a festival to the LORD—a lasting ordinance. ¹⁵For seven days you are to eat bread made without yeast. On the first day remove the yeast from your houses, for whoever eats anything with yeast in it from the first day through the seventh must be cut off from Israel. ¹⁶On the first day hold a sacred assembly, and another one on the seventh day. Do no work at all on these days, except to prepare food for everyone to eat; that is all you may do.

¹⁷"Celebrate the Festival of Unleavened Bread, because it was on this very day that I brought your divisions out of Egypt. Celebrate this day as a lasting ordinance for the generations to come. ¹⁸In the first month you are to eat bread made without yeast, from the evening of the fourteenth day until the evening of the twenty-first day. ¹⁹For seven days no yeast is to be found in your houses. And anyone, whether foreigner or native-born,

---

ᵃ 3 The Hebrew word can mean *lamb* or *kid*; also in verse 4.

who eats anything with yeast in it must be cut off from the community of Israel. [20] Eat nothing made with yeast. Wherever you live, you must eat unleavened bread."

[21] Then Moses summoned all the elders of Israel and said to them, "Go at once and select the animals for your families and slaughter the Passover lamb. [22] Take a bunch of hyssop, dip it into the blood in the basin and put some of the blood on the top and on both sides of the doorframe. None of you shall go out of the door of your house until morning. [23] When the LORD goes through the land to strike down the Egyptians, he will see the blood on the top and sides of the doorframe and will pass over that doorway, and he will not permit the destroyer to enter your houses and strike you down.

[24] "Obey these instructions as a lasting ordinance for you and your descendants. [25] When you enter the land that the LORD will give you as he promised, observe this ceremony. [26] And when your children ask you, 'What does this ceremony mean to you?' [27] then tell them, 'It is the Passover sacrifice to the LORD, who passed over the houses of the Israelites in Egypt and spared our homes when he struck down the Egyptians.'" Then the people bowed down and worshiped. [28] The Israelites did just what the LORD commanded Moses and Aaron.

[29] At midnight the LORD struck down all the firstborn in Egypt, from the firstborn of Pharaoh, who sat on the throne, to the firstborn of the prisoner, who was in the dungeon, and the firstborn of all the livestock as well. [30] Pharaoh and all his officials and all the Egyptians got up during the night, and there was loud wailing in Egypt, for there was not a house without someone dead.

The Exodus

[31] During the night Pharaoh summoned Moses and Aaron and said, "Up! Leave my people, you and the Israelites! Go, worship the LORD as you have requested. [32] Take your flocks and herds, as you have said, and go. And also bless me."

[33] The Egyptians urged the people to

ROCK SOLID truths

Exodus 12:1–30

God foreshadowed a Savior.

When Pharaoh stubbornly resisted God's command to free the Hebrew slaves, the Lord declared that an angel of death would kill every firstborn male in Egypt. God also showed his people a path to safety. He instructed each family to slaughter a lamb and use its blood to paint the doorframe of their house. The Lord would see the blood, pass over the house, and spare the people inside. That Passover lamb killed on behalf of the Old Testament Hebrews is a picture of how Jesus would one day free New Testament believers through his death on the cross. When you trust that Jesus died on the cross for your sins, you find safety "under the blood" of the lamb. The apostle Paul says Jesus is the "Passover lamb" sacrificed for us (1 Corinthians 5:7), and because of him, the Lord's judgment passes over you.

Think: Why would God put this clear picture of Jesus in the Old Testament?

hurry and leave the country. "For otherwise," they said, "we will all die!" [34] So the people took their dough before the yeast was added, and carried it on their shoulders in kneading troughs wrapped in clothing. [35] The Israelites did as Moses instructed and asked the Egyptians for articles of silver and gold and for clothing. [36] The LORD had made the Egyptians favorably disposed toward the people, and they gave them what they asked for; so they plundered the Egyptians.

[37] The Israelites journeyed from Rameses

to Sukkoth. There were about six hundred thousand men on foot, besides women and children. [38]Many other people went up with them, and also large droves of livestock, both flocks and herds. [39]With the dough the Israelites had brought from Egypt, they baked loaves of unleavened bread. The dough was without yeast because they had been driven out of Egypt and did not have time to prepare food for themselves.

[40]Now the length of time the Israelite people lived in Egypt[a] was 430 years. [41]At the end of the 430 years, to the very day, all the LORD's divisions left Egypt. [42]Because the LORD kept vigil that night to bring them out of Egypt, on this night all the Israelites are to keep vigil to honor the LORD for the generations to come.

Passover Restrictions

[43]The LORD said to Moses and Aaron, "These are the regulations for the Passover meal:

"No foreigner may eat it. [44]Any slave you have bought may eat it after you have circumcised him, [45]but a temporary resident or a hired worker may not eat it.

[46]"It must be eaten inside the house; take none of the meat outside the house. Do not break any of the bones. [47]The whole community of Israel must celebrate it.

[48]"A foreigner residing among you who wants to celebrate the LORD's Passover must have all the males in his household circumcised; then he may take part like one born in the land. No uncircumcised male may eat it. [49]The same law applies both to the native-born and to the foreigner residing among you."

[50]All the Israelites did just what the LORD had commanded Moses and Aaron. [51]And on that very day the LORD brought the Israelites out of Egypt by their divisions.

Consecration of the Firstborn

13 The LORD said to Moses, [2]"Consecrate to me every firstborn male. The first offspring of every womb among the Israelites belongs to me, whether human or animal."

[3]Then Moses said to the people, "Commemorate this day, the day you came out of Egypt, out of the land of slavery, because the LORD brought you out of it with a mighty hand. Eat nothing containing yeast. [4]Today, in the month of Aviv, you are leaving. [5]When the LORD brings you into the land of the Canaanites, Hittites, Amorites, Hivites and Jebusites—the land he swore to your ancestors to give you, a land flowing with milk and honey—you are to observe this ceremony in this month: [6]For seven days eat bread made without yeast and on the seventh day hold a festival to the LORD. [7]Eat unleavened bread during those seven days; nothing with yeast in it is to be seen among you, nor shall any yeast be seen anywhere within your borders. [8]On that day tell your son, 'I do this because of what the LORD did for me when I came out of Egypt.' [9]This observance will be for you like a sign on your hand and a reminder on your forehead that this law of the LORD is to be on your lips. For the LORD brought you out of Egypt with his mighty hand. [10]You must keep this ordinance at the appointed time year after year.

[11]"After the LORD brings you into the land of the Canaanites and gives it to you, as he promised on oath to you and your ancestors, [12]you are to give over to the LORD the first offspring of every womb. All the firstborn males of your livestock belong to the LORD. [13]Redeem with a lamb every firstborn donkey, but if you do not redeem it, break its neck. Redeem every firstborn among your sons.

[14]"In days to come, when your son asks you, 'What does this mean?' say to him, 'With a mighty hand the LORD brought us out of Egypt, out of the land of slavery. [15]When Pharaoh stubbornly refused to let us go, the LORD killed the firstborn of both people and animals in Egypt. This is why I sacrifice to the LORD the first male offspring of every womb and redeem each of my firstborn sons.' [16]And it will be like a sign on your hand and a symbol on your

<hr>

[a] 40 Masoretic Text; Samaritan Pentateuch and Septuagint *Egypt and Canaan*

forehead that the LORD brought us out of Egypt with his mighty hand."

Crossing the Sea

[17] When Pharaoh let the people go, God did not lead them on the road through the Philistine country, though that was shorter. For God said, "If they face war, they might change their minds and return to Egypt." [18] So God led the people around by the desert road toward the Red Sea.[a] The Israelites went up out of Egypt ready for battle.

[19] Moses took the bones of Joseph with him because Joseph had made the Israelites swear an oath. He had said, "God will surely come to your aid, and then you must carry my bones up with you from this place."[b]

[20] After leaving Sukkoth they camped at Etham on the edge of the desert. [21] By day the LORD went ahead of them in a pillar of cloud to guide them on their way and by night in a pillar of fire to give them light, so that they could travel by day or night. [22] Neither the pillar of cloud by day nor the pillar of fire by night left its place in front of the people.

ROCK SOLID
promises

"The LORD went ahead of them in a pillar of cloud to guide them on their way." Exodus 13:21

When God tells you to do something — to go, to act, to obey — he always goes ahead of you, leading you every step of the way.

14 Then the LORD said to Moses, [2] "Tell the Israelites to turn back and encamp near Pi Hahiroth, between Migdol and the sea. They are to encamp by the sea, directly opposite Baal Zephon. [3] Pharaoh will think, 'The Israelites are wandering around the land

in confusion, hemmed in by the desert.' [4] And I will harden Pharaoh's heart, and he will pursue them. But I will gain glory for myself through Pharaoh and all his army, and the Egyptians will know that I am the LORD." So the Israelites did this.

[5] When the king of Egypt was told that the people had fled, Pharaoh and his officials changed their minds about them and said, "What have we done? We have let the Israelites go and have lost their services!" [6] So he had his chariot made ready and took his army with him. [7] He took six hundred of the best chariots, along with all the other chariots of Egypt, with officers over all of them. [8] The LORD hardened the heart of Pharaoh king of Egypt, so that he pursued the Israelites, who were marching out boldly. [9] The Egyptians — all Pharaoh's horses and chariots, horsemen[c] and troops — pursued the Israelites and overtook them as they camped by the sea near Pi Hahiroth, opposite Baal Zephon.

[10] As Pharaoh approached, the Israelites looked up, and there were the Egyptians, marching after them. They were terrified and cried out to the LORD. [11] They said to Moses, "Was it because there were no graves in Egypt that you brought us to the desert to die? What have you done to us by bringing us out of Egypt? [12] Didn't we say to you in Egypt, 'Leave us alone; let us serve the Egyptians'? It would have been better for us to serve the Egyptians than to die in the desert!"

[13] Moses answered the people, "Do not be afraid. Stand firm and you will see the deliverance the LORD will bring you today. The Egyptians you see today you will never see again. [14] The LORD will fight for you; you need only to be still."

[15] Then the LORD said to Moses, "Why are you crying out to me? Tell the Israelites to move on. [16] Raise your staff and stretch out your hand over the sea to divide the water so that the Israelites can go through the sea on dry ground. [17] I will harden the hearts of the Egyptians so that

[a] 18 Or *the Sea of Reeds* [b] 19 See Gen. 50:25.
[c] 9 Or *charioteers*; also in verses 17, 18, 23, 26 and 28

they will go in after them. And I will gain glory through Pharaoh and all his army, through his chariots and his horsemen. ¹⁸The Egyptians will know that I am the Lord when I gain glory through Pharaoh, his chariots and his horsemen."

¹⁹Then the angel of God, who had been traveling in front of Israel's army, withdrew and went behind them. The pillar of cloud also moved from in front and stood behind them, ²⁰coming between the armies of Egypt and Israel. Throughout the night the cloud brought darkness to the one side and light to the other side; so neither went near the other all night long.

²¹Then Moses stretched out his hand over the sea, and all that night the Lord drove the sea back with a strong east wind and turned it into dry land. The waters were divided, ²²and the Israelites went through the sea on dry ground, with a wall of water on their right and on their left.

²³The Egyptians pursued them, and all Pharaoh's horses and chariots and horsemen followed them into the sea. ²⁴During the last watch of the night the Lord looked down from the pillar of fire and cloud at the Egyptian army and threw it into confusion. ²⁵He jammed[a] the wheels of their chariots so that they had difficulty driving. And the Egyptians said, "Let's get away from the Israelites! The Lord is fighting for them against Egypt."

²⁶Then the Lord said to Moses, "Stretch out your hand over the sea so that the waters may flow back over the Egyptians and their chariots and horsemen." ²⁷Moses stretched out his hand over the sea, and at daybreak the sea went back to its place. The Egyptians were fleeing toward[b] it, and the Lord swept them into the sea. ²⁸The water flowed back and covered the chariots and horsemen—the entire army of Pharaoh that had followed the Israelites into the sea. Not one of them survived.

²⁹But the Israelites went through the sea on dry ground, with a wall of water on their right and on their left. ³⁰That day the Lord saved Israel from the hands of the Egyptians, and Israel saw the Egyptians lying dead on the shore. ³¹And when

ROCK SOLID truths

Exodus 14:1–31

God has real power.

God made an unbreakable pledge to his people. "I am the Lord," he said. "I will bring you out from under the yoke of the Egyptians. I will free you from being slaves to them, and I will redeem you with an outstretched arm and with mighty acts of judgment" (Exodus 6:6). The "exodus" is the event where God kept that strong promise. He struck down the firstborn sons of Egypt, forcing Pharaoh to free the Hebrew slaves. When the slaves escaped into the desert, Pharaoh gave chase to recapture his fleeing slaves. At that moment God showed his enormous might. First he blew a path through the Red Sea to let his people pass safely; then he sent the waters crashing down to destroy Pharaoh and his army. That same power raised Jesus from the dead (see Ephesians 1:19–20) and it also energizes your whole life (see Romans 8:11).

Think: Why does God sometimes visibly show his power—and sometimes not?

the Israelites saw the mighty hand of the Lord displayed against the Egyptians, the people feared the Lord and put their trust in him and in Moses his servant.

The Song of Moses and Miriam

15 Then Moses and the Israelites sang this song to the Lord:

"I will sing to the Lord,
for he is highly exalted.

---

[a] 25 See Samaritan Pentateuch, Septuagint and Syriac; Masoretic Text removed   [b] 27 Or from

Both horse and driver
 he has hurled into the sea.
2 "The Lord is my strength and my
  defense[a];
 he has become my salvation.
He is my God, and I will praise him,
 my father's God, and I will exalt
  him.
3 The Lord is a warrior;
 the Lord is his name.
4 Pharaoh's chariots and his army
 he has hurled into the sea.
The best of Pharaoh's officers
 are drowned in the Red Sea.[b]
5 The deep waters have covered them;
 they sank to the depths like a stone.
6 Your right hand, Lord,
 was majestic in power.
Your right hand, Lord,
 shattered the enemy.

7 "In the greatness of your majesty
 you threw down those who opposed
  you.
You unleashed your burning anger;
 it consumed them like stubble.
8 By the blast of your nostrils
 the waters piled up.
The surging waters stood up like a
  wall;
 the deep waters congealed in the
  heart of the sea.
9 The enemy boasted,
 'I will pursue, I will overtake them.
I will divide the spoils;
 I will gorge myself on them.
I will draw my sword
 and my hand will destroy them.'
10 But you blew with your breath,
 and the sea covered them.
They sank like lead
 in the mighty waters.
11 Who among the gods
 is like you, Lord?
Who is like you—
 majestic in holiness,
awesome in glory,
 working wonders?

12 "You stretch out your right hand,
 and the earth swallows your
  enemies.

13 In your unfailing love you will lead
 the people you have redeemed.
In your strength you will guide them
 to your holy dwelling.
14 The nations will hear and tremble;
 anguish will grip the people of
  Philistia.
15 The chiefs of Edom will be terrified,
 the leaders of Moab will be seized
  with trembling,
the people[c] of Canaan will melt away;
16 terror and dread will fall on them.
By the power of your arm
 they will be as still as a stone—
until your people pass by, Lord,
 until the people you bought[d]
  pass by.
17 You will bring them in and plant them
 on the mountain of your
  inheritance—
the place, Lord, you made for your
  dwelling,
 the sanctuary, Lord, your hands
  established.

18 "The Lord reigns
 for ever and ever."

19 When Pharaoh's horses, chariots and horsemen[e] went into the sea, the Lord brought the waters of the sea back over them, but the Israelites walked through the sea on dry ground. 20 Then Miriam the prophet, Aaron's sister, took a timbrel in her hand, and all the women followed her, with timbrels and dancing. 21 Miriam sang to them:

 "Sing to the Lord,
  for he is highly exalted.
 Both horse and driver
  he has hurled into the sea."

The Waters of Marah and Elim

22 Then Moses led Israel from the Red Sea and they went into the Desert of Shur. For three days they traveled in the desert without finding water. 23 When they came to Marah, they could not drink its water because it was bitter. (That is why the

---

[a] 2 Or *song*   [b] 4 Or *the Sea of Reeds*; also in verse 22   [c] 15 Or *rulers*   [d] 16 Or *created*   [e] 19 Or *charioteers*

place is called Marah.*) ²⁴So the people grumbled against Moses, saying, "What are we to drink?"

²⁵Then Moses cried out to the LORD, and the LORD showed him a piece of wood. He threw it into the water, and the water became fit to drink.

There the LORD issued a ruling and instruction for them and put them to the test. ²⁶He said, "If you listen carefully to the LORD your God and do what is right in his eyes, if you pay attention to his commands and keep all his decrees, I will not bring on you any of the diseases I brought on the Egyptians, for I am the LORD, who heals you."

²⁷Then they came to Elim, where there were twelve springs and seventy palm trees, and they camped there near the water.

Manna and Quail

16 The whole Israelite community set out from Elim and came to the Desert of Sin, which is between Elim and Sinai, on the fifteenth day of the second month after they had come out of Egypt. ²In the desert the whole community grumbled against Moses and Aaron. ³The Israelites said to them, "If only we had died by the LORD's

---

a 23 Marah means *bitter.*

Exodus 15:1–21

Miriam sang to God.

The king of Egypt had grown so fearful of the strong Hebrew slaves multiplying within his kingdom that he ordered the murder of every Hebrew baby boy. But Moses' mother set her little boy afloat in a basket on the Nile River, hoping to save his life. The boy's sister watched Pharaoh's daughter pull Moses from the water, then offered to help the princess find a Hebrew woman to nurse the baby (see Exodus 2:1–10). That protective older sister was Miriam.

Miriam isn't mentioned again until Exodus 15. But without a doubt she was a close observer of the events that set God's people free from hundreds of years of slavery. She knew when her brothers Moses and Aaron went to speak God's command to Pharaoh, "Let my people go!" (see Exodus 5:1). She witnessed the plagues God sent against the Egyptians and the mercy he showed his people through the slaughter of the Passover lamb (see Exodus 7:14—12:30).

This strong sister must have walked with Moses and Aaron at the head of the throng of fleeing slaves as they escaped Egypt and crossed the Red Sea because here in Exodus 15 she led God's people in celebration of their own freedom and the destruction of Pharaoh's army. The Israelite women followed this prophetess as she grabbed a tambourine and sang, "Sing to the LORD, for he is highly exalted" (Exodus 15:21). As the people sang thanks to God for hurling Pharaoh's forces into the sea, Miriam was in the lead.

You can find Miriam in Exodus 2:1–20; Exodus 15:1–21; Numbers 12:1–15; and Numbers 20:1.

UNSHAKEN people

hand in Egypt! There we sat around pots of meat and ate all the food we wanted, but you have brought us out into this desert to starve this entire assembly to death."

⁴Then the LORD said to Moses, "I will rain down bread from heaven for you. The people are to go out each day and gather enough for that day. In this way I will test them and see whether they will follow my instructions. ⁵On the sixth day they are to prepare what they bring in, and that is to be twice as much as they gather on the other days."

⁶So Moses and Aaron said to all the Israelites, "In the evening you will know that it was the LORD who brought you out of Egypt, ⁷and in the morning you will see the glory of the LORD, because he has heard your grumbling against him. Who are we, that you should grumble against us?" ⁸Moses also said, "You will know that it was the LORD when he gives you meat to eat in the evening and all the bread you want in the morning, because he has heard your grumbling against him. Who are we? You are not grumbling against us, but against the LORD."

⁹Then Moses told Aaron, "Say to the entire Israelite community, 'Come before the LORD, for he has heard your grumbling.'"

¹⁰While Aaron was speaking to the whole Israelite community, they looked toward the desert, and there was the glory of the LORD appearing in the cloud.

¹¹The LORD said to Moses, ¹²"I have heard the grumbling of the Israelites. Tell them, 'At twilight you will eat meat, and in the morning you will be filled with bread. Then you will know that I am the LORD your God.'"

¹³That evening quail came and covered the camp, and in the morning there was a layer of dew around the camp. ¹⁴When the dew was gone, thin flakes like frost on the ground appeared on the desert floor. ¹⁵When the Israelites saw it, they said to each other, "What is it?" For they did not know what it was.

Moses said to them, "It is the bread the LORD has given you to eat. ¹⁶This is what the LORD has commanded: 'Everyone is to gather as much as they need. Take an omerᵃ for each person you have in your tent.'"

¹⁷The Israelites did as they were told; some gathered much, some little. ¹⁸And when they measured it by the omer, the one who gathered much did not have too much, and the one who gathered little did not have too little. Everyone had gathered just as much as they needed.

¹⁹Then Moses said to them, "No one is to keep any of it until morning."

²⁰However, some of them paid no attention to Moses; they kept part of it until morning, but it was full of maggots and began to smell. So Moses was angry with them.

²¹Each morning everyone gathered as much as they needed, and when the sun grew hot, it melted away. ²²On the sixth day, they gathered twice as much—two omersᵇ for each person—and the leaders of the community came and reported this to Moses. ²³He said to them, "This is what the LORD commanded: 'Tomorrow is to be a day of sabbath rest, a holy sabbath to the LORD. So bake what you want to bake and boil what you want to boil. Save whatever is left and keep it until morning.'"

²⁴So they saved it until morning, as Moses commanded, and it did not stink or get maggots in it. ²⁵"Eat it today," Moses said, "because today is a sabbath to the LORD. You will not find any of it on the ground today. ²⁶Six days you are to gather it, but on the seventh day, the Sabbath, there will not be any."

²⁷Nevertheless, some of the people went out on the seventh day to gather it, but they found none. ²⁸Then the LORD said to Moses, "How long willyouᶜ refuse to keep my commands and my instructions? ²⁹Bear in mind that the LORD has given you the Sabbath; that is why on the sixth day he gives you bread for two days. Everyone is to stay where they are on the

---

ᵃ *16* That is, possibly about 3 pounds or about 1.4 kilograms; also in verses 18, 32, 33 and 36
ᵇ *22* That is, possibly about 6 pounds or about 2.8 kilograms   ᶜ *28* The Hebrew is plural.

seventh day; no one is to go out." [30] So the people rested on the seventh day.

[31] The people of Israel called the bread manna.[a] It was white like coriander seed and tasted like wafers made with honey. [32] Moses said, "This is what the LORD has commanded: 'Take an omer of manna and keep it for the generations to come, so they can see the bread I gave you to eat in the wilderness when I brought you out of Egypt.'"

[33] So Moses said to Aaron, "Take a jar and put an omer of manna in it. Then place it before the LORD to be kept for the generations to come."

[34] As the LORD commanded Moses, Aaron put the manna with the tablets of the covenant law, so that it might be preserved. [35] The Israelites ate manna forty years, until they came to a land that was settled; they ate manna until they reached the border of Canaan.

[36] (An omer is one-tenth of an ephah.)

UNSHAKEN God

Exodus 16:1–36

God is benevolent.

The Israelites had barely escaped Egypt when they began to grumble against God. It was as if they had forgotten their vicious masters and backbreaking labor, because all they remembered of slavery was sitting around eating all they wanted. A few weeks into a trek toward the promised land, they were sure God had led them into the desert to starve. But the Lord heard their complaints. He had an immediate and miraculous solution, day by day raining down nourishment (manna) that settled like dew on the ground, more than enough for everyone to eat their fill. The people discovered God is thoroughly kind.

So ... When have you worried God was out to get you — but then watched him meet your needs?

Water From the Rock

17 The whole Israelite community set out from the Desert of Sin, traveling from place to place as the LORD commanded. They camped at Rephidim, but there was no water for the people to drink. [2] So they quarreled with Moses and said, "Give us water to drink."

Moses replied, "Why do you quarrel with me? Why do you put the LORD to the test?"

[3] But the people were thirsty for water there, and they grumbled against Moses. They said, "Why did you bring us up out of Egypt to make us and our children and livestock die of thirst?"

[4] Then Moses cried out to the LORD, "What am I to do with these people? They are almost ready to stone me."

[5] The LORD answered Moses, "Go out in front of the people. Take with you some of the elders of Israel and take in your hand the staff with which you struck the Nile, and go. [6] I will stand there before you by the rock at Horeb. Strike the rock, and water will come out of it for the people to drink." So Moses did this in the sight of the elders of Israel. [7] And he called the place Massah[b] and Meribah[c] because the Israelites quarreled and because they tested the LORD saying, "Is the LORD among us or not?"

The Amalekites Defeated

[8] The Amalekites came and attacked the Israelites at Rephidim. [9] Moses said to Joshua, "Choose some of our men and go out to fight the Amalekites. Tomorrow I will stand on top of the hill with the staff of God in my hands."

[10] So Joshua fought the Amalekites as Moses had ordered, and Moses, Aaron and Hur went to the top of the hill. [11] As long as Moses held up his hands, the Israelites were winning, but whenever he lowered his hands, the Amalekites were winning. [12] When Moses' hands grew tired, they took a stone and put it under

---

[a] 31 Manna sounds like the Hebrew for What is it? (see verse 15).   [b] 7 Massah means testing.
[c] 7 Meribah means quarreling.

him and he sat on it. Aaron and Hur held his hands up—one on one side, one on the other—so that his hands remained steady till sunset. ¹³So Joshua overcame the Amalekite army with the sword.

¹⁴Then the LORD said to Moses, "Write this on a scroll as something to be remembered and make sure that Joshua hears it, because I will completely blot out the name of Amalek from under heaven."

¹⁵Moses built an altar and called it The LORD is my Banner. ¹⁶He said, "Because hands were lifted up against^a the throne of the LORD,^b the LORD will be at war against the Amalekites from generation to generation."

Jethro Visits Moses

18 Now Jethro, the priest of Midian and father-in-law of Moses, heard of everything God had done for Moses and for his people Israel, and how the LORD had brought Israel out of Egypt.

²After Moses had sent away his wife Zipporah, his father-in-law Jethro received her ³and her two sons. One son was named Gershom,^c for Moses said, "I have become a foreigner in a foreign land"; ⁴and the other was named Eliezer,^d for he said, "My father's God was my helper; he saved me from the sword of Pharaoh."

⁵Jethro, Moses' father-in-law, together with Moses' sons and wife, came to him in the wilderness, where he was camped near the mountain of God. ⁶Jethro had sent word to him, "I, your father-in-law Jethro, am coming to you with your wife and her two sons."

⁷So Moses went out to meet his father-in-law and bowed down and kissed him. They greeted each other and then went into the tent. ⁸Moses told his father-in-law about everything the LORD had done to Pharaoh and the Egyptians for Israel's sake and about all the hardships they had met along the way and how the LORD had saved them.

⁹Jethro was delighted to hear about all the good things the LORD had done for Israel in rescuing them from the hand of the Egyptians. ¹⁰He said, "Praise be to the LORD, who rescued you from the hand of the Egyptians and of Pharaoh, and who rescued the people from the hand of the Egyptians. ¹¹Now I know that the LORD is greater than all other gods, for he did this to those who had treated Israel arrogantly." ¹²Then Jethro, Moses' father-in-law, brought a burnt offering and other sacrifices to God, and Aaron came with all the elders of Israel to eat a meal with Moses' father-in-law in the presence of God.

¹³The next day Moses took his seat to serve as judge for the people, and they stood around him from morning till evening. ¹⁴When his father-in-law saw all that Moses was doing for the people, he said, "What is this you are doing for the people? Why do you alone sit as judge, while all these people stand around you from morning till evening?"

¹⁵Moses answered him, "Because the people come to me to seek God's will. ¹⁶Whenever they have a dispute, it is brought to me, and I decide between the parties and inform them of God's decrees and instructions."

¹⁷Moses' father-in-law replied, "What you are doing is not good. ¹⁸You and these people who come to you will only wear yourselves out. The work is too heavy for you; you cannot handle it alone. ¹⁹Listen now to me and I will give you some advice, and may God be with you. You must be the people's representative before God and bring their disputes to him. ²⁰Teach them his decrees and instructions, and show them the way they are to live and how they are to behave. ²¹But select capable men from all the people—men who fear God, trustworthy men who hate dishonest gain—and appoint them as officials over thousands, hundreds, fifties and tens. ²²Have them serve as judges for the people at all times, but have them bring every difficult case to you; the simple cases they

---

^a 16 Or to   ^b 16 The meaning of the Hebrew for this clause is uncertain.   ^c 3 Gershom sounds like the Hebrew for a foreigner there.
^d 4 Eliezer means my God is helper.

can decide themselves. That will make your load lighter, because they will share it with you. ²³If you do this and God so commands, you will be able to stand the strain, and all these people will go home satisfied."

²⁴Moses listened to his father-in-law and did everything he said. ²⁵He chose capable men from all Israel and made them leaders of the people, officials over thousands, hundreds, fifties and tens. ²⁶They served as judges for the people at all times. The difficult cases they brought to Moses, but the simple ones they decided themselves.

²⁷Then Moses sent his father-in-law on his way, and Jethro returned to his own country.

At Mount Sinai

19 On the first day of the third month after the Israelites left Egypt—on that very day—they came to the Desert of Sinai. ²After they set out from Rephidim, they entered the Desert of Sinai, and Israel camped there in the desert in front of the mountain.

³Then Moses went up to God, and the LORD called to him from the mountain and said, "This is what you are to say to the descendants of Jacob and what you are to tell the people of Israel: ⁴'You yourselves have seen what I did to Egypt, and how I carried you on eagles' wings and brought you to myself. ⁵Now if you obey me fully and keep my covenant, then out of all nations you will be my treasured possession. Although the whole earth is mine, ⁶you*ᵃ* will be for me a kingdom of priests and a holy nation.' These are the words you are to speak to the Israelites."

⁷So Moses went back and summoned the elders of the people and set before them all the words the LORD had commanded him to speak. ⁸The people all responded together, "We will do everything the LORD has said." So Moses brought their answer back to the LORD.

⁹The LORD said to Moses, "I am going to come to you in a dense cloud, so that the people will hear me speaking with you and will always put their trust in you." Then Moses told the LORD what the people had said.

¹⁰And the LORD said to Moses, "Go to the people and consecrate them today and tomorrow. Have them wash their clothes ¹¹and be ready by the third day, because on that day the LORD will come down on Mount Sinai in the sight of all the people. ¹²Put limits for the people around the mountain and tell them, 'Be careful that you do not approach the mountain or touch the foot of it. Whoever touches the mountain is to be put to death. ¹³They are to be stoned or shot with arrows; not a hand is to be laid on them. No person or animal shall be permitted to live.' Only when the ram's horn sounds a long blast may they approach the mountain."

¹⁴After Moses had gone down the mountain to the people, he consecrated them, and they washed their clothes. ¹⁵Then he said to the people, "Prepare yourselves for the third day. Abstain from sexual relations."

¹⁶On the morning of the third day there was thunder and lightning, with a thick cloud over the mountain, and a very loud trumpet blast. Everyone in the camp trembled. ¹⁷Then Moses led the people out of the camp to meet with God, and they stood at the foot of the mountain. ¹⁸Mount Sinai was covered with smoke, because the LORD descended on it in fire. The smoke billowed up from it like smoke from a furnace, and the whole mountain*ᵇ* trembled violently. ¹⁹As the sound of the trumpet grew louder and louder, Moses spoke and the voice of God answered him.*ᶜ*

²⁰The LORD descended to the top of Mount Sinai and called Moses to the top of the mountain. So Moses went up ²¹and the LORD said to him, "Go down and warn the people so they do not force

---

ᵃ 5,6 Or *possession, for the whole earth is mine.*
⁶You *ᵇ 18* Most Hebrew manuscripts; a few Hebrew manuscripts and Septuagint *and all the people* *ᶜ 19* Or *and God answered him with thunder*

ROCK SOLID *principles*

Exodus 19:16–25

Respect God.

Emilia didn't try to hide the fact that she didn't think much of God. Ever since she was little, an elderly aunt had dragged her to a musty stone church full of silver hair. Not that Emilia didn't love her aunt or other old people, but with no one at church anywhere close to her age, Emilia couldn't relate. She mumbled her way through the words and songs, but once she was back with her friends she couldn't stop ranting about the stupidity of the whole thing. She assumed that God was just an old guy with wispy hair and a frail physique—and that his home must be dark and cold. Emilia saw no reason to respect God or anything about church or faith.

As God prepared to reveal his "Top Ten" Commandments to his people (see Exodus 20:1–21), he once again made his awesomeness clear. Only Moses could come close, while everyone else waited at a safe distance. Respect is the first step to meeting God as he truly is.

their way through to see the Lord and many of them perish. ²²Even the priests, who approach the Lord, must consecrate themselves, or the Lord will break out against them."

²³Moses said to the Lord, "The people cannot come up Mount Sinai, because you yourself warned us, 'Put limits around the mountain and set it apart as holy.'"

²⁴The Lord replied, "Go down and bring Aaron up with you. But the priests and the people must not force their way through to come up to the Lord, or he will break out against them."

²⁵So Moses went down to the people and told them.

The Ten Commandments

20 And God spoke all these words:

²"I am the Lord your God, who brought you out of Egypt, out of the land of slavery.

³"You shall have no other gods before*a* me.

⁴"You shall not make for yourself an image in the form of anything in heaven above or on the earth beneath or in the waters below. ⁵You shall not bow down to them or worship them; for I, the Lord your God, am a jealous God, punishing the children for the sin of the parents to the third and fourth generation of those who hate me, ⁶but showing love to a thousand generations of those who love me and keep my commandments.

⁷"You shall not misuse the name of the Lord your God, for the Lord will not hold anyone guiltless who misuses his name.

⁸"Remember the Sabbath day by keeping it holy. ⁹Six days you shall

a 3 Or besides

labor and do all your work, [10]but the seventh day is a sabbath to the LORD your God. On it you shall not do any work, neither you, nor your son or daughter, nor your male or female servant, nor your animals, nor any foreigner residing in your towns. [11]For in six days the LORD made the heavens and the earth, the sea, and all that is in them, but he rested on the seventh day. Therefore the LORD blessed the Sabbath day and made it holy.

[12]"Honor your father and your mother, so that you may live long in the land the LORD your God is giving you.

[13]"You shall not murder.

[14]"You shall not commit adultery.

[15]"You shall not steal.

[16]"You shall not give false testimony against your neighbor.

[17]"You shall not covet your neighbor's house. You shall not covet your neighbor's wife, or his male or female servant, his ox or donkey, or anything that belongs to your neighbor."

[18]When the people saw the thunder and lightning and heard the trumpet and saw the mountain in smoke, they trembled with fear. They stayed at a distance [19]and said to Moses, "Speak to us yourself and we will listen. But do not have God speak to us or we will die."

[20]Moses said to the people, "Do not be afraid. God has come to test you, so that the fear of God will be with you to keep you from sinning."

[21]The people remained at a distance, while Moses approached the thick darkness where God was.

Idols and Altars

[22]Then the LORD said to Moses, "Tell the Israelites this: 'You have seen for yourselves that I have spoken to you from heaven: [23]Do not make any gods to be alongside me; do not make for yourselves gods of silver or gods of gold.

Exodus 20:1–21

God makes his rules clear.

Like an ancient king telling his subjects the right way to live, God made his top commandments perfectly clear to his people. The Hebrews had barely escaped from slavery in Egypt when God told Moses to climb Mount Sinai. The Lord told the people to stay a safe distance away and promised to reveal his most important rules for their lives (see Exodus 19:1–25). At the top of the Lord's list were the Ten Commandments, instructions on living in a right relationship with God and with others—explaining everything from worshiping the Lord to obeying parents to refusing to crave what other people owned. From the front of the Bible to the back, God always makes his commands known. He never leaves you wondering what he expects. If an issue matters to God, you can be sure he has given a clear command in his Word.

Think: In what area of your life do you need to know God's commands right now? How will you locate his answers in the Bible?

ROCK SOLID truths

---

[24]"'Make an altar of earth for me and sacrifice on it your burnt offerings and fellowship offerings, your sheep and goats and your cattle. Wherever I cause my name to be honored, I will come to you and bless you. [25]If you make an altar of stones for me, do not build it with dressed stones, for you will defile it if you use a tool on it. [26]And do not go up to my altar on steps, or your private parts may be exposed.'

21

"These are the laws you are to set before them:

Hebrew Servants

2 "If you buy a Hebrew servant, he is to serve you for six years. But in the seventh year, he shall go free, without paying anything. 3 If he comes alone, he is to go free alone; but if he has a wife when he comes, she is to go with him. 4 If his master gives him a wife and she bears him sons or daughters, the woman and her children shall belong to her master, and only the man shall go free.

5 "But if the servant declares, 'I love my master and my wife and children and do not want to go free,' 6 then his master must take him before the judges.*a* He shall take him to the door or the doorpost and pierce his ear with an awl. Then he will be his servant for life.

7 "If a man sells his daughter as a servant, she is not to go free as male servants do. 8 If she does not please the master who has selected her for himself,*b* he must let her be redeemed. He has no right to sell her to foreigners, because he has broken faith with her. 9 If he selects her for his son, he must grant her the rights of a daughter. 10 If he marries another woman, he must not deprive the first one of her food, clothing and marital rights. 11 If he does not provide her with these three things, she is to go free, without any payment of money.

Personal Injuries

12 "Anyone who strikes a person with a fatal blow is to be put to death. 13 However, if it is not done intentionally, but God lets it happen, they are to flee to a place I will designate. 14 But if anyone schemes and kills someone deliberately, that person is to be taken from my altar and put to death.

15 "Anyone who attacks*c* their father or mother is to be put to death.

16 "Anyone who kidnaps someone is to be put to death, whether the victim has been sold or is still in the kidnapper's possession.

17 "Anyone who curses their father or mother is to be put to death.

18 "If people quarrel and one person hits another with a stone or with their fist*d* and the victim does not die but is confined to bed, 19 the one who struck the blow will not be held liable if the other can get up and walk around outside with a staff; however, the guilty party must pay the injured person for any loss of time and see that the victim is completely healed.

20 "Anyone who beats their male or female slave with a rod must be punished if the slave dies as a direct result, 21 but they are not to be punished if the slave recovers after a day or two, since the slave is their property.

22 "If people are fighting and hit a pregnant woman and she gives birth prematurely*e* but there is no serious injury, the offender must be fined whatever the woman's husband demands and the court allows. 23 But if there is serious injury, you are to take life for life, 24 eye for eye, tooth for tooth, hand for hand, foot for foot, 25 burn for burn, wound for wound, bruise for bruise.

26 "An owner who hits a male or female slave in the eye and destroys it must let the slave go free to compensate for the eye. 27 And an owner who knocks out the tooth of a male or female slave must let the slave go free to compensate for the tooth.

28 "If a bull gores a man or woman to death, the bull is to be stoned to death, and its meat must not be eaten. But the owner of the bull will not be held responsible. 29 If, however, the bull has had the habit of goring and the owner has been warned but has not kept it penned up and it kills a man or woman, the bull is to be stoned and its owner also is to be put to death. 30 However, if payment is demanded, the owner may redeem his life by the payment of whatever is demanded. 31 This law also applies if the bull gores a son or daughter. 32 If the bull gores a male or female slave, the owner must pay thirty shekels*f* of silver to the master of the slave, and the bull is to be stoned to death.

---

a 6 Or *before God*   *b 8* Or *master so that he does not choose her*   *c 15* Or *kills*   *d 18* Or *with a tool*   *e 22* Or *she has a miscarriage*   *f 32* That is, about 12 ounces or about 345 grams

[33] "If anyone uncovers a pit or digs one and fails to cover it and an ox or a donkey falls into it, [34] the one who opened the pit must pay the owner for the loss and take the dead animal in exchange.

[35] "If anyone's bull injures someone else's bull and it dies, the two parties are to sell the live one and divide both the money and the dead animal equally. [36] However, if it was known that the bull had the habit of goring, yet the owner did not keep it penned up, the owner must pay, animal for animal, and take the dead animal in exchange.

Protection of Property

22 [a] "Whoever steals an ox or a sheep and slaughters it or sells it must pay back five head of cattle for the ox and four sheep for the sheep.

[2] "If a thief is caught breaking in at night and is struck a fatal blow, the defender is not guilty of bloodshed; [3] but if it happens after sunrise, the defender is guilty of bloodshed.

"Anyone who steals must certainly make restitution, but if they have nothing, they must be sold to pay for their theft. [4] If the stolen animal is found alive in their possession—whether ox or donkey or sheep—they must pay back double.

[5] "If anyone grazes their livestock in a field or vineyard and lets them stray and they graze in someone else's field, the offender must make restitution from the best of their own field or vineyard.

[6] "If a fire breaks out and spreads into thornbushes so that it burns shocks of grain or standing grain or the whole field, the one who started the fire must make restitution.

[7] "If anyone gives a neighbor silver or goods for safekeeping and they are stolen from the neighbor's house, the thief, if caught, must pay back double. [8] But if the thief is not found, the owner of the house must appear before the judges, and they must[b] determine whether the owner of the house has laid hands on the other person's property. [9] In all cases of illegal possession of an ox, a donkey, a sheep, a garment, or any other lost property about which somebody says, 'This is mine,' both parties are to bring their cases before the judges.[c] The one whom the judges declare[d] guilty must pay back double to the other.

[10] "If anyone gives a donkey, an ox, a sheep or any other animal to their neighbor for safekeeping and it dies or is injured or is taken away while no one is looking, [11] the issue between them will be settled by the taking of an oath before the LORD that the neighbor did not lay hands on the other person's property. The owner is to accept this, and no restitution is required. [12] But if the animal was stolen from the neighbor, restitution must be made to the owner. [13] If it was torn to pieces by a wild animal, the neighbor shall bring in the remains as evidence and shall not be required to pay for the torn animal.

[14] "If anyone borrows an animal from their neighbor and it is injured or dies while the owner is not present, they must make restitution. [15] But if the owner is with the animal, the borrower will not have to pay. If the animal was hired, the money paid for the hire covers the loss.

Social Responsibility

[16] "If a man seduces a virgin who is not pledged to be married and sleeps with her, he must pay the bride-price, and she shall be his wife. [17] If her father absolutely refuses to give her to him, he must still pay the bride-price for virgins.

[18] "Do not allow a sorceress to live.

[19] "Anyone who has sexual relations with an animal is to be put to death.

[20] "Whoever sacrifices to any god other than the LORD must be destroyed.[e]

[21] "Do not mistreat or oppress a foreigner, for you were foreigners in Egypt.

[22] "Do not take advantage of the widow or the fatherless. [23] If you do and they cry

---

[a] In Hebrew texts 22:1 is numbered 21:37, and 22:2-31 is numbered 22:1-30.   [b] 8 Or before God, and he will   [c] 9 Or before God   [d] 9 Or whom God declares   [e] 20 The Hebrew term refers to the irrevocable giving over of things or persons to the LORD, often by totally destroying them.

out to me, I will certainly hear their cry. ²⁴My anger will be aroused, and I will kill you with the sword; your wives will become widows and your children fatherless.

²⁵"If you lend money to one of my people among you who is needy, do not treat it like a business deal; charge no interest. ²⁶If you take your neighbor's cloak as a pledge, return it by sunset, ²⁷because that cloak is the only covering your neighbor has. What else can they sleep in? When they cry out to me, I will hear, for I am compassionate.

²⁸"Do not blaspheme God*ᵃ* or curse the ruler of your people.

²⁹"Do not hold back offerings from your granaries or your vats.*ᵇ*

"You must give me the firstborn of your sons. ³⁰Do the same with your cattle and your sheep. Let them stay with their mothers for seven days, but give them to me on the eighth day.

³¹"You are to be my holy people. So do not eat the meat of an animal torn by wild beasts; throw it to the dogs.

Laws of Justice and Mercy

23 "Do not spread false reports. Do not help a guilty person by being a malicious witness.

²"Do not follow the crowd in doing wrong. When you give testimony in a lawsuit, do not pervert justice by siding with the crowd, ³and do not show favoritism to a poor person in a lawsuit.

⁴"If you come across your enemy's ox or donkey wandering off, be sure to return it. ⁵If you see the donkey of someone who hates you fallen down under its load, do not leave it there; be sure you help them with it.

⁶"Do not deny justice to your poor people in their lawsuits. ⁷Have nothing to do with a false charge and do not put an innocent or honest person to death, for I will not acquit the guilty.

⁸"Do not accept a bribe, for a bribe blinds those who see and twists the words of the innocent.

⁹"Do not oppress a foreigner; you your-

selves know how it feels to be foreigners, because you were foreigners in Egypt.

Sabbath Laws

¹⁰"For six years you are to sow your fields and harvest the crops, ¹¹but during the seventh year let the land lie unplowed and unused. Then the poor among your people may get food from it, and the wild animals may eat what is left. Do the same with your vineyard and your olive grove.

¹²"Six days do your work, but on the seventh day do not work, so that your ox and your donkey may rest, and so that the slave born in your household and the foreigner living among you may be refreshed.

¹³"Be careful to do everything I have said to you. Do not invoke the names of other gods; do not let them be heard on your lips.

The Three Annual Festivals

¹⁴"Three times a year you are to celebrate a festival to me.

¹⁵"Celebrate the Festival of Unleavened Bread; for seven days eat bread made without yeast, as I commanded you. Do this at the appointed time in the month of Aviv, for in that month you came out of Egypt.

"No one is to appear before me empty-handed.

¹⁶"Celebrate the Festival of Harvest with the firstfruits of the crops you sow in your field.

"Celebrate the Festival of Ingathering at the end of the year, when you gather in your crops from the field.

¹⁷"Three times a year all the men are to appear before the Sovereign LORD.

¹⁸"Do not offer the blood of a sacrifice to me along with anything containing yeast.

"The fat of my festival offerings must not be kept until morning.

¹⁹"Bring the best of the firstfruits of your soil to the house of the LORD your God.

"Do not cook a young goat in its mother's milk.

ᵃ 28 Or *Do not revile the judges*
ᵇ 29 The meaning of the Hebrew for this phrase is uncertain.

God's Angel to Prepare the Way

²⁰"See, I am sending an angel ahead of you to guard you along the way and to bring you to the place I have prepared. ²¹Pay attention to him and listen to what he says. Do not rebel against him; he will not forgive your rebellion, since my Name is in him. ²²If you listen carefully to what he says and do all that I say, I will be an enemy to your enemies and will oppose those who oppose you. ²³My angel will go ahead of you and bring you into the land of the Amorites, Hittites, Perizzites, Canaanites, Hivites and Jebusites, and I will wipe them out. ²⁴Do not bow down before their gods or worship them or follow their practices. You must demolish them and break their sacred stones to pieces. ²⁵Worship the LORD your God, and his blessing will be on your food and water. I will take away sickness from among you, ²⁶and none will miscarry or be barren in your land. I will give you a full life span.

²⁷"I will send my terror ahead of you and throw into confusion every nation you encounter. I will make all your enemies turn their backs and run. ²⁸I will send the hornet ahead of you to drive the Hivites, Canaanites and Hittites out of your way. ²⁹But I will not drive them out in a single year, because the land would become desolate and the wild animals too numerous for you. ³⁰Little by little I will drive them out before you, until you have increased enough to take possession of the land.

³¹"I will establish your borders from the Red Sea*ᵃ* to the Mediterranean Sea,*ᵇ* and from the desert to the Euphrates River. I will give into your hands the people who live in the land, and you will drive them out before you. ³²Do not make a covenant with them or with their gods. ³³Do not let them live in your land or they will cause you to sin against me, because the worship of their gods will certainly be a snare to you."

The Covenant Confirmed

24 Then the LORD said to Moses, "Come up to the LORD, you and Aaron, Nadab and Abihu, and seventy of the elders of Israel. You are to worship at a distance, ²but Moses alone is to approach the LORD; the others must not come near. And the people may not come up with him."

³When Moses went and told the people all the LORD's words and laws, they responded with one voice, "Everything the LORD has said we will do." ⁴Moses then wrote down everything the LORD had said.

He got up early the next morning and built an altar at the foot of the mountain and set up twelve stone pillars representing the twelve tribes of Israel. ⁵Then he sent young Israelite men, and they offered burnt offerings and sacrificed young bulls as fellowship offerings to the LORD. ⁶Moses took half of the blood and put it in bowls, and the other half he splashed against the altar. ⁷Then he took the Book of the Covenant and read it to the people. They responded, "We will do everything the LORD has said; we will obey."

⁸Moses then took the blood, sprinkled it on the people and said, "This is the blood of the covenant that the LORD has made with you in accordance with all these words."

⁹Moses and Aaron, Nadab and Abihu, and the seventy elders of Israel went up ¹⁰and saw the God of Israel. Under his feet was something like a pavement made of lapis lazuli, as bright blue as the sky. ¹¹But God did not raise his hand against these leaders of the Israelites; they saw God, and they ate and drank.

¹²The LORD said to Moses, "Come up to me on the mountain and stay here, and I will give you the tablets of stone with the law and commandments I have written for their instruction."

¹³Then Moses set out with Joshua his aide, and Moses went up on the mountain of God. ¹⁴He said to the elders, "Wait here for us until we come back to you. Aaron and Hur are with you, and anyone involved in a dispute can go to them."

¹⁵When Moses went up on the mountain, the cloud covered it, ¹⁶and the glory

---

ᵃ 31 Or *the Sea of Reeds*   *ᵇ 31* Hebrew *to the Sea of the Philistines* of the Lord settled on Mount Sinai. For six days the cloud covered the mountain, and on the seventh day the Lord called to Moses from within the cloud. [17] To the Israelites the glory of the Lord looked like a consuming fire on top of the mountain. [18] Then Moses entered the cloud as he went on up the mountain. And he stayed on the mountain forty days and forty nights.

Offerings for the Tabernacle

25 The Lord said to Moses, [2] "Tell the Israelites to bring me an offering. You are to receive the offering for me from everyone whose heart prompts them to give. [3] These are the offerings you are to receive from them: gold, silver and bronze; [4] blue, purple and scarlet yarn and fine linen; goat hair; [5] ram skins dyed red and another type of durable leather[a]; acacia wood; [6] olive oil for the light; spices for the anointing oil and for the fragrant incense; [7] and onyx stones and other gems to be mounted on the ephod and breastpiece.

[8] "Then have them make a sanctuary for me, and I will dwell among them. [9] Make this tabernacle and all its furnishings exactly like the pattern I will show you.

The Ark

[10] "Have them make an ark[b] of acacia wood—two and a half cubits long, a cubit and a half wide, and a cubit and a half high.[c] [11] Overlay it with pure gold, both inside and out, and make a gold molding around it. [12] Cast four gold rings for it and fasten them to its four feet, with two rings on one side and two rings on the other. [13] Then make poles of acacia wood and overlay them with gold. [14] Insert the poles into the rings on the sides of the ark to carry it. [15] The poles are to remain in the rings of this ark; they are not to be removed. [16] Then put in the ark the tablets of the covenant law, which I will give you.

[17] "Make an atonement cover of pure gold—two and a half cubits long and a cubit and a half wide. [18] And make two cherubim out of hammered gold at the ends of the cover. [19] Make one cherub on one end and the second cherub on the other; make the cherubim of one piece with the cover, at the two ends. [20] The cherubim are to have their wings spread upward, overshadowing the cover with them. The cherubim are to face each other, looking toward the cover. [21] Place the cover on top of the ark and put in the ark the tablets of the covenant law that I will give you. [22] There, above the cover between the two cherubim that are over the ark of the covenant law, I will meet with you and give you all my commands for the Israelites.

The Table

[23] "Make a table of acacia wood—two cubits long, a cubit wide and a cubit and a half high.[d] [24] Overlay it with pure gold and make a gold molding around it. [25] Also make around it a rim a handbreadth[e] wide and put a gold molding on the rim. [26] Make four gold rings for the table and fasten them to the four corners, where the four legs are. [27] The rings are to be close to the rim to hold the poles used in carrying the table. [28] Make the poles of acacia wood, overlay them with gold and carry the table with them. [29] And make its plates and dishes of pure gold, as well as its pitchers and bowls for the pouring out of offerings. [30] Put the bread of the Presence on this table to be before me at all times.

The Lampstand

[31] "Make a lampstand of pure gold. Hammer out its base and shaft, and make its flowerlike cups, buds and blossoms of one piece with them. [32] Six branches are to extend from the sides of the lampstand—three on one side and three on the other. [33] Three cups shaped like almond flowers with buds and blossoms are to be on one

---

[a] 5 Possibly the hides of large aquatic mammals   [b] 10 That is, a chest   [c] 10 That is, about 3 3/4 feet long and 2 1/4 feet wide and high or about 1.1 meters long and 68 centimeters wide and high; similarly in verse 17   [d] 23 That is, about 3 feet long, 1 1/2 feet wide and 2 1/4 feet high or about 90 centimeters long, 45 centimeters wide and 68 centimeters high   [e] 25 That is, about 3 inches or about 7.5 centimeters

branch, three on the next branch, and the same for all six branches extending from the lampstand. ³⁴And on the lampstand there are to be four cups shaped like almond flowers with buds and blossoms. ³⁵One bud shall be under the first pair of branches extending from the lampstand, a second bud under the second pair, and a third bud under the third pair—six branches in all. ³⁶The buds and branches shall all be of one piece with the lampstand, hammered out of pure gold.

³⁷"Then make its seven lamps and set them up on it so that they light the space in front of it. ³⁸Its wick trimmers and trays are to be of pure gold. ³⁹A talent*a* of pure gold is to be used for the lampstand and all these accessories. ⁴⁰See that you make them according to the pattern shown you on the mountain.

The Tabernacle

26 "Make the tabernacle with ten curtains of finely twisted linen and blue, purple and scarlet yarn, with cherubim woven into them by a skilled worker. ²All the curtains are to be the same size—twenty-eight cubits long and four cubits wide.*b* ³Join five of the curtains together, and do the same with the other five. ⁴Make loops of blue material along the edge of the end curtain in one set, and do the same with the end curtain in the other set. ⁵Make fifty loops on one curtain and fifty loops on the end curtain of the other set, with the loops opposite each other. ⁶Then make fifty gold clasps and use them to fasten the curtains together so that the tabernacle is a unit.

⁷"Make curtains of goat hair for the tent over the tabernacle—eleven altogether. ⁸All eleven curtains are to be the same size—thirty cubits long and four cubits wide.*c* ⁹Join five of the curtains together into one set and the other six into another set. Fold the sixth curtain double at the front of the tent. ¹⁰Make fifty loops along the edge of the end curtain in one set and also along the edge of the end curtain in the other set. ¹¹Then make fifty

bronze clasps and put them in the loops to fasten the tent together as a unit. ¹²As for the additional length of the tent curtains, the half curtain that is left over is to hang down at the rear of the tabernacle. ¹³The tent curtains will be a cubit*d* longer on both sides; what is left will hang over the sides of the tabernacle so as to cover it. ¹⁴Make for the tent a covering of ram skins dyed red, and over that a covering of the other durable leather.*e*

¹⁵"Make upright frames of acacia wood for the tabernacle. ¹⁶Each frame is to be ten cubits long and a cubit and a half wide,*f* ¹⁷with two projections set parallel to each other. Make all the frames of the tabernacle in this way. ¹⁸Make twenty frames for the south side of the tabernacle ¹⁹and make forty silver bases to go under them—two bases for each frame, one under each projection. ²⁰For the other side, the north side of the tabernacle, make twenty frames ²¹and forty silver bases—two under each frame. ²²Make six frames for the far end, that is, the west end of the tabernacle, ²³and make two frames for the corners at the far end. ²⁴At these two corners they must be double from the bottom all the way to the top and fitted into a single ring; both shall be like that. ²⁵So there will be eight frames and sixteen silver bases—two under each frame.

²⁶"Also make crossbars of acacia wood: five for the frames on one side of the tabernacle, ²⁷five for those on the other side, and five for the frames on the west, at the far end of the tabernacle. ²⁸The center crossbar is to extend from end to end at the middle of the frames. ²⁹Overlay the frames with gold and make gold rings to

a 39 That is, about 75 pounds or about 34 kilograms   *b 2* That is, about 42 feet long and 6 feet wide or about 13 meters long and 1.8 meters wide   *c 8* That is, about 45 feet long and 6 feet wide or about 13.5 meters long and 1.8 meters wide   *d 13* That is, about 18 inches or about 45 centimeters   *e 14* Possibly the hides of large aquatic mammals (see 25:5)   *f 16* That is, about 15 feet long and 2 1/4 feet wide or about 4.5 meters long and 68 centimeters wide hold the crossbars. Also overlay the cross-bars with gold.

³⁰"Set up the tabernacle according to the plan shown you on the mountain.

³¹"Make a curtain of blue, purple and scarlet yarn and finely twisted linen, with cherubim woven into it by a skilled worker. ³²Hang it with gold hooks on four posts of acacia wood overlaid with gold and standing on four silver bases. ³³Hang the curtain from the clasps and place the ark of the covenant law behind the curtain. The curtain will separate the Holy Place from the Most Holy Place. ³⁴Put the atonement cover on the ark of the covenant law in the Most Holy Place. ³⁵Place the table outside the curtain on the north side of the tabernacle and put the lampstand opposite it on the south side.

³⁶"For the entrance to the tent make a curtain of blue, purple and scarlet yarn and finely twisted linen—the work of an embroiderer. ³⁷Make gold hooks for this curtain and five posts of acacia wood overlaid with gold. And cast five bronze bases for them.

Exodus 26:1–37

God commands worship.

The Bible says that "Great is the LORD and most worthy of praise" (1 Chronicles 16:25). The Lord not only expects people to perceive his greatness and bow to him, but he actually commands us to worship and to be devoted to no person or thing more than him (see Exodus 20:3–6). In the Old Testament God declared that worship should take place at the tabernacle, and later, in the temple. As you read the elaborate instructions the Lord gave for the design of these structures and their contents, it's obvious that he cares intensely that people worship him well. In the New Testament, Jesus said that worship would no longer be centered on the temple in Jerusalem, but that the Lord looks for people who "worship in the Spirit and in truth," knowing him well and worshiping him fully (John 4:21–24).

Think: Is worship as important to you as it is to God? Why—or why not?

ROCK SOLID truths

The Altar of Burnt Offering

27 "Build an altar of acacia wood, three cubits^a high; it is to be square, five cubits long and five cubits wide.^b ²Make a horn at each of the four corners, so that the horns and the altar are of one piece, and overlay the altar with bronze. ³Make all its utensils of bronze—its pots to remove the ashes, and its shovels, sprinkling bowls, meat forks and firepans. ⁴Make a grating for it, a bronze network, and make a bronze ring at each of the four corners of the network. ⁵Put it under the ledge of the altar so that it is halfway up the altar. ⁶Make poles of acacia wood for the altar and overlay them with bronze. ⁷The poles are to be inserted into the rings so they will be on two sides of the altar when it is carried. ⁸Make the altar hollow, out of boards. It is to be made just as you were shown on the mountain.

The Courtyard

⁹"Make a courtyard for the tabernacle. The south side shall be a hundred cubits^c long and is to have curtains of finely twisted linen, ¹⁰with twenty posts and twenty bronze bases and with silver hooks and bands on the posts. ¹¹The north side shall also be a hundred cubits long and is to have curtains, with twenty posts and twenty bronze bases and with silver hooks and bands on the posts.

^a 1 That is, about 4 1/2 feet or about 1.4 meters
^b 1 That is, about 7 1/2 feet or about 2.3 meters long and wide   ^c 9 That is, about 150 feet or about 45 meters; also in verse 11

¹²"The west end of the courtyard shall be fifty cubits*a* wide and have curtains, with ten posts and ten bases. ¹³On the east end, toward the sunrise, the courtyard shall also be fifty cubits wide. ¹⁴Curtains fifteen cubits*b* long are to be on one side of the entrance, with three posts and three bases, ¹⁵and curtains fifteen cubits long are to be on the other side, with three posts and three bases.

¹⁶"For the entrance to the courtyard, provide a curtain twenty cubits*c* long, of blue, purple and scarlet yarn and finely twisted linen—the work of an embroiderer—with four posts and four bases. ¹⁷All the posts around the courtyard are to have silver bands and hooks, and bronze bases. ¹⁸The courtyard shall be a hundred cubits long and fifty cubits wide,*d* with curtains of finely twisted linen five cubits*e* high, and with bronze bases. ¹⁹All the other articles used in the service of the tabernacle, whatever their function, including all the tent pegs for it and those for the courtyard, are to be of bronze.

Oil for the Lampstand

²⁰"Command the Israelites to bring you clear oil of pressed olives for the light so that the lamps may be kept burning. ²¹In the tent of meeting, outside the curtain that shields the ark of the covenant law, Aaron and his sons are to keep the lamps burning before the LORD from evening till morning. This is to be a lasting ordinance among the Israelites for the generations to come.

The Priestly Garments

28 "Have Aaron your brother brought to you from among the Israelites, along with his sons Nadab and Abihu, Eleazar and Ithamar, so they may serve me as priests. ²Make sacred garments for your brother Aaron to give him dignity and honor. ³Tell all the skilled workers to whom I have given wisdom in such matters that they are to make garments for Aaron, for his consecration, so he may serve me as priest. ⁴These are the garments they are to make:

a breastpiece, an ephod, a robe, a woven tunic, a turban and a sash. They are to make these sacred garments for your brother Aaron and his sons, so they may serve me as priests. ⁵Have them use gold, and blue, purple and scarlet yarn, and fine linen.

The Ephod

⁶"Make the ephod of gold, and of blue, purple and scarlet yarn, and of finely twisted linen—the work of skilled hands. ⁷It is to have two shoulder pieces attached to two of its corners, so it can be fastened. ⁸Its skillfully woven waistband is to be like it—of one piece with the ephod and made with gold, and with blue, purple and scarlet yarn, and with finely twisted linen.

⁹"Take two onyx stones and engrave on them the names of the sons of Israel ¹⁰in the order of their birth—six names on one stone and the remaining six on the other. ¹¹Engrave the names of the sons of Israel on the two stones the way a gem cutter engraves a seal. Then mount the stones in gold filigree settings ¹²and fasten them on the shoulder pieces of the ephod as memorial stones for the sons of Israel. Aaron is to bear the names on his shoulders as a memorial before the LORD. ¹³Make gold filigree settings ¹⁴and two braided chains of pure gold, like a rope, and attach the chains to the settings.

The Breastpiece

¹⁵"Fashion a breastpiece for making decisions—the work of skilled hands. Make it like the ephod: of gold, and of blue, purple and scarlet yarn, and of finely twisted linen. ¹⁶It is to be square—a span*f* long and a span wide—and folded double. ¹⁷Then mount four rows of precious stones on it. The first row shall be carnelian, chrysolite and beryl; ¹⁸the second row shall be turquoise, lapis lazuli and

a 12 That is, about 75 feet or about 23 meters; also in verse 13   *b 14* That is, about 23 feet or about 6.8 meters; also in verse 15   *c 16* That is, about 30 feet or about 9 meters   *d 18* That is, about 150 feet long and 75 feet wide or about 45 meters long and 23 meters wide   *e 18* That is, about 7 1/2 feet or about 2.3 meters   *f 16* That is, about 9 inches or about 23 centimeters emerald; [19] the third row shall be jacinth, agate and amethyst; [20] the fourth row shall be topaz, onyx and jasper.[a] Mount them in gold filigree settings. [21] There are to be twelve stones, one for each of the names of the sons of Israel, each engraved like a seal with the name of one of the twelve tribes.

[22] "For the breastpiece make braided chains of pure gold, like a rope. [23] Make two gold rings for it and fasten them to two corners of the breastpiece. [24] Fasten the two gold chains to the rings at the corners of the breastpiece, [25] and the other ends of the chains to the two settings, attaching them to the shoulder pieces of the ephod at the front. [26] Make two gold rings and attach them to the other two corners of the breastpiece on the inside edge next to the ephod. [27] Make two more gold rings and attach them to the bottom of the shoulder pieces on the front of the ephod, close to the seam just above the waistband of the ephod. [28] The rings of the breastpiece are to be tied to the rings of the ephod with blue cord, connecting it to the waistband, so that the breastpiece will not swing out from the ephod.

[29] "Whenever Aaron enters the Holy Place, he will bear the names of the sons of Israel over his heart on the breastpiece of decision as a continuing memorial before the LORD. [30] Also put the Urim and the Thummim in the breastpiece, so they may be over Aaron's heart whenever he enters the presence of the LORD. Thus Aaron will always bear the means of making decisions for the Israelites over his heart before the LORD.

Other Priestly Garments

[31] "Make the robe of the ephod entirely of blue cloth, [32] with an opening for the head in its center. There shall be a woven edge like a collar[b] around this opening, so that it will not tear. [33] Make pomegranates of blue, purple and scarlet yarn around the hem of the robe, with gold bells between them. [34] The gold bells and the pomegranates are to alternate around the hem of the robe. [35] Aaron must wear it when he ministers. The sound of the bells will be heard when he enters the Holy Place before the LORD and when he comes out, so that he will not die.

[36] "Make a plate of pure gold and engrave on it as on a seal: HOLY TO THE LORD. [37] Fasten a blue cord to it to attach it to the turban; it is to be on the front of the turban. [38] It will be on Aaron's forehead, and he will bear the guilt involved in the sacred gifts the Israelites consecrate, whatever their gifts may be. It will be on Aaron's forehead continually so that they will be acceptable to the LORD.

[39] "Weave the tunic of fine linen and make the turban of fine linen. The sash is to be the work of an embroiderer. [40] Make tunics, sashes and caps for Aaron's sons to give them dignity and honor. [41] After you put these clothes on your brother Aaron and his sons, anoint and ordain them. Consecrate them so they may serve me as priests.

[42] "Make linen undergarments as a covering for the body, reaching from the waist to the thigh. [43] Aaron and his sons must wear them whenever they enter the tent of meeting or approach the altar to minister in the Holy Place, so that they will not incur guilt and die.

"This is to be a lasting ordinance for Aaron and his descendants.

Consecration of the Priests

29 "This is what you are to do to consecrate them, so they may serve me as priests: Take a young bull and two rams without defect. [2] And from the finest wheat flour make round loaves without yeast, thick loaves without yeast and with olive oil mixed in, and thin loaves without yeast and brushed with olive oil. [3] Put them in a basket and present them along with the bull and the two rams. [4] Then bring Aaron and his sons to the entrance to the tent of meeting and wash them with water. [5] Take the garments and dress Aaron with the tunic,

---

[a] 20 The precise identification of some of these precious stones is uncertain.   [b] 32 The meaning of the Hebrew for this word is uncertain.

the robe of the ephod, the ephod itself and the breastpiece. Fasten the ephod on him by its skillfully woven waistband. ⁶Put the turban on his head and attach the sacred emblem to the turban. ⁷Take the anointing oil and anoint him by pouring it on his head. ⁸Bring his sons and dress them in tunics ⁹and fasten caps on them. Then tie sashes on Aaron and his sons.ᵃ The priesthood is theirs by a lasting ordinance.

"Then you shall ordain Aaron and his sons.

¹⁰"Bring the bull to the front of the tent of meeting, and Aaron and his sons shall lay their hands on its head. ¹¹Slaughter it in the Lord's presence at the entrance to the tent of meeting. ¹²Take some of the bull's blood and put it on the horns of the altar with your finger, and pour out the rest of it at the base of the altar. ¹³Then take all the fat on the internal organs, the long lobe of the liver, and both kidneys with the fat on them, and burn them on the altar. ¹⁴But burn the bull's flesh and its hide and its intestines outside the camp. It is a sin offering.ᵇ

¹⁵"Take one of the rams, and Aaron and his sons shall lay their hands on its head. ¹⁶Slaughter it and take the blood and splash it against the sides of the altar. ¹⁷Cut the ram into pieces and wash the internal organs and the legs, putting them with the head and the other pieces. ¹⁸Then burn the entire ram on the altar. It is a burnt offering to the Lord, a pleasing aroma, a food offering presented to the Lord.

¹⁹"Take the other ram, and Aaron and his sons shall lay their hands on its head. ²⁰Slaughter it, take some of its blood and put it on the lobes of the right ears of Aaron and his sons, on the thumbs of their right hands, and on the big toes of their right feet. Then splash blood against the sides of the altar. ²¹And take some blood from the altar and some of the anointing oil and sprinkle it on Aaron and his garments and on his sons and their garments. Then he and his sons and their garments will be consecrated.

²²"Take from this ram the fat, the fat tail, the fat on the internal organs, the long lobe of the liver, both kidneys with the fat on them, and the right thigh. (This is the ram for the ordination.) ²³From the basket of bread made without yeast, which is before the Lord, take one round loaf, one thick loaf with olive oil mixed in, and one thin loaf. ²⁴Put all these in the hands of Aaron and his sons and have them wave them before the Lord as a wave offering. ²⁵Then take them from their hands and burn them on the altar along with the burnt offering for a pleasing aroma to the Lord, a food offering presented to the Lord. ²⁶After you take the breast of the ram for Aaron's ordination, wave it before the Lord as a wave offering, and it will be your share.

²⁷"Consecrate those parts of the ordination ram that belong to Aaron and his sons: the breast that was waved and the thigh that was presented. ²⁸This is always to be the perpetual share from the Israelites for Aaron and his sons. It is the contribution the Israelites are to make to the Lord from their fellowship offerings.

²⁹"Aaron's sacred garments will belong to his descendants so that they can be anointed and ordained in them. ³⁰The son who succeeds him as priest and comes to the tent of meeting to minister in the Holy Place is to wear them seven days.

³¹"Take the ram for the ordination and cook the meat in a sacred place. ³²At the entrance to the tent of meeting, Aaron and his sons are to eat the meat of the ram and the bread that is in the basket. ³³They are to eat these offerings by which atonement was made for their ordination and consecration. But no one else may eat them, because they are sacred. ³⁴And if any of the meat of the ordination ram or any bread is left over till morning, burn it up. It must not be eaten, because it is sacred.

³⁵"Do for Aaron and his sons everything I have commanded you, taking seven days to ordain them. ³⁶Sacrifice a bull each day as a sin offering to make atonement. Purify the altar by making atonement for it, and anoint it to consecrate it. ³⁷For seven days make atonement for the

ᵃ 9 Hebrew; Septuagint *on them*
ᵇ 14 Or *purification offering*; also in verse 36

altar and consecrate it. Then the altar will be most holy, and whatever touches it will be holy.

38 "This is what you are to offer on the altar regularly each day: two lambs a year old. 39 Offer one in the morning and the other at twilight. 40 With the first lamb offer a tenth of an ephah[a] of the finest flour mixed with a quarter of a hin[b] of oil from pressed olives, and a quarter of a hin of wine as a drink offering. 41 Sacrifice the other lamb at twilight with the same grain offering and its drink offering as in the morning—a pleasing aroma, a food offering presented to the LORD.

42 "For the generations to come this burnt offering is to be made regularly at the entrance to the tent of meeting, before the LORD. There I will meet you and speak to you; 43 there also I will meet with the Israelites, and the place will be consecrated by my glory.

44 "So I will consecrate the tent of meeting and the altar and will consecrate Aaron and his sons to serve me as priests. 45 Then I will dwell among the Israelites and be their God. 46 They will know that I am the LORD their God, who brought them out of Egypt so that I might dwell among them. I am the LORD their God.

The Altar of Incense

30 "Make an altar of acacia wood for burning incense. 2 It is to be square, a cubit long and a cubit wide, and two cubits high[c]—its horns of one piece with it. 3 Overlay the top and all the sides and the horns with pure gold, and make a gold molding around it. 4 Make two gold rings for the altar below the molding—two on each of the opposite sides—to hold the poles used to carry it. 5 Make the poles of acacia wood and overlay them with gold. 6 Put the altar in front of the curtain that shields the ark of the covenant law—before the atonement cover that is over the tablets of the covenant law—where I will meet with you.

7 "Aaron must burn fragrant incense on the altar every morning when he tends the

lamps. 8 He must burn incense again when he lights the lamps at twilight so incense will burn regularly before the LORD for the generations to come. 9 Do not offer on this altar any other incense or any burnt offering or grain offering, and do not pour a drink offering on it. 10 Once a year Aaron shall make atonement on its horns. This annual atonement must be made with the blood of the atoning sin offering[d] for the generations to come. It is most holy to the LORD."

Atonement Money

11 Then the LORD said to Moses, 12 "When you take a census of the Israelites

---

UNSHAKEN God

Exodus 29:44–46

God is present.

Even though Old Testament rituals might seem strange or irrelevant to us, God continually used them as amazing revelations of himself. In Exodus 29, God details several of the offerings his people were to bring to him—rams and bulls, plus bread, wine, and oil. As priests burned up these offerings, the people saw a sign that their sins had gone up in smoke. And as the people worshiped the one true God, the Lord fulfilled his promise to "dwell among the Israelites and be their God" (Exodus 29:45). The people saw that God had saved them from slavery and now lived in their midst. Actually, the Lord is never distant. He's always present with his people.

So ... How do you know God is present with you now?

---

a 40 That is, probably about 3 1/2 pounds or about 1.6 kilograms   b 40 That is, probably about 1 quart or about 1 liter   c 2 That is, about 1 1/2 feet long and wide and 3 feet high or about 45 centimeters long and wide and 90 centimeters high   d 10 Or purification offering to count them, each one must pay the LORD a ransom for his life at the time he is counted. Then no plague will come on them when you number them. ¹³Each one who crosses over to those already counted is to give a half shekel,ᵃ according to the sanctuary shekel, which weighs twenty gerahs. This half shekel is an offering to the LORD. ¹⁴All who cross over, those twenty years old or more, are to give an offering to the LORD. ¹⁵The rich are not to give more than a half shekel and the poor are not to give less when you make the offering to the LORD to atone for your lives. ¹⁶Receive the atonement money from the Israelites and use it for the service of the tent of meeting. It will be a memorial for the Israelites before the LORD, making atonement for your lives."

Basin for Washing

¹⁷Then the LORD said to Moses, ¹⁸"Make a bronze basin, with its bronze stand, for washing. Place it between the tent of meeting and the altar, and put water in it. ¹⁹Aaron and his sons are to wash their hands and feet with water from it. ²⁰Whenever they enter the tent of meeting, they shall wash with water so that they will not die. Also, when they approach the altar to minister by presenting a food offering to the LORD, ²¹they shall wash their hands and feet so that they will not die. This is to be a lasting ordinance for Aaron and his descendants for the generations to come."

Anointing Oil

²²Then the LORD said to Moses, ²³"Take the following fine spices: 500 shekelsᵇ of liquid myrrh, half as much (that is, 250 shekels) of fragrant cinnamon, 250 shekelsᶜ of fragrant calamus, ²⁴500 shekels of cassia—all according to the sanctuary shekel—and a hinᵈ of olive oil. ²⁵Make these into a sacred anointing oil, a fragrant blend, the work of a perfumer. It will be the sacred anointing oil. ²⁶Then use it to anoint the tent of meeting, the ark of the covenant law, ²⁷the table and all its articles, the lampstand and its accessories, the altar of incense, ²⁸the altar of burnt offering and all its utensils,

and the basin with its stand. ²⁹You shall consecrate them so they will be most holy, and whatever touches them will be holy.

³⁰"Anoint Aaron and his sons and consecrate them so they may serve me as priests. ³¹Say to the Israelites, 'This is to be my sacred anointing oil for the generations to come. ³²Do not pour it on anyone else's body and do not make any other oil using the same formula. It is sacred, and you are to consider it sacred. ³³Whoever makes perfume like it and puts it on anyone other than a priest must be cut off from their people.'"

Incense

³⁴Then the LORD said to Moses, "Take fragrant spices—gum resin, onycha and galbanum—and pure frankincense, all in equal amounts, ³⁵and make a fragrant blend of incense, the work of a perfumer. It is to be salted and pure and sacred. ³⁶Grind some of it to powder and place it in front of the ark of the covenant law in the tent of meeting, where I will meet with you. It shall be most holy to you. ³⁷Do not make any incense with this formula for yourselves; consider it holy to the LORD. ³⁸Whoever makes incense like it to enjoy its fragrance must be cut off from their people."

Bezalel and Oholiab

31 Then the LORD said to Moses, ²"See, I have chosen Bezalel son of Uri, the son of Hur, of the tribe of Judah, ³and I have filled him with the Spirit of God, with wisdom, with understanding, with knowledge and with all kinds of skills— ⁴to make artistic designs for work in gold, silver and bronze, ⁵to cut and set stones, to work in wood, and to engage in all kinds of crafts. ⁶Moreover, I have appointed Oholiab son of Ahisamak, of the tribe of Dan, to help

---

ᵃ 13 That is, about 1/5 ounce or about 5.8 grams; also in verse 15   ᵇ 23 That is, about 12 1/2 pounds or about 5.8 kilograms; also in verse 24   ᶜ 23 That is, about 6 1/4 pounds or about 2.9 kilograms   ᵈ 24 That is, probably about 1 gallon or about 3.8 liters him. Also I have given ability to all the skilled workers to make everything I have commanded you: [7] the tent of meeting, the ark of the covenant law with the atonement cover on it, and all the other furnishings of the tent— [8] the table and its articles, the pure gold lampstand and all its accessories, the altar of incense, [9] the altar of burnt offering and all its utensils, the basin with its stand— [10] and also the woven garments, both the sacred garments for Aaron the priest and the garments for his sons when they serve as priests, [11] and the anointing oil and fragrant incense for the Holy Place. They are to make them just as I commanded you."

The Sabbath

[12] Then the LORD said to Moses, [13] "Say to the Israelites, 'You must observe my Sabbaths. This will be a sign between me and you for the generations to come, so you may know that I am the LORD, who makes you holy.

[14] "'Observe the Sabbath, because it is holy to you. Anyone who desecrates it is to be put to death; those who do any work on that day must be cut off from their people. [15] For six days work is to be done, but the seventh day is a day of sabbath rest, holy to the LORD. Whoever does any work on the Sabbath day is to be put to death. [16] The Israelites are to observe the Sabbath, celebrating it for the generations to come as a lasting covenant. [17] It will be a sign between me and the Israelites forever, for in six days the LORD made the heavens and the earth, and on the seventh day he rested and was refreshed.'"

[18] When the LORD finished speaking to Moses on Mount Sinai, he gave him the two tablets of the covenant law, the tablets of stone inscribed by the finger of God.

The Golden Calf

32 When the people saw that Moses was so long in coming down from the mountain, they gathered around Aaron and said, "Come, make us gods[a] who will go before us. As for this fellow Moses who

brought us up out of Egypt, we don't know what has happened to him."

[2] Aaron answered them, "Take off the gold earrings that your wives, your sons and your daughters are wearing, and bring them to me." [3] So all the people took off their earrings and brought them to Aaron. [4] He took what they handed him and made it into an idol cast in the shape of a calf, fashioning it with a tool. Then they said, "These are your gods,[b] Israel, who brought you up out of Egypt."

[5] When Aaron saw this, he built an altar in front of the calf and announced, "Tomorrow there will be a festival to the LORD." [6] So the next day the people rose early and sacrificed burnt offerings and presented fellowship offerings. Afterward they sat down to eat and drink and got up to indulge in revelry.

[7] Then the LORD said to Moses, "Go down, because your people, whom you brought up out of Egypt, have become corrupt. [8] They have been quick to turn away from what I commanded them and have made themselves an idol cast in the shape of a calf. They have bowed down to it and sacrificed to it and have said, 'These are your gods, Israel, who brought you up out of Egypt.'

[9] "I have seen these people," the LORD said to Moses, "and they are a stiff-necked people. [10] Now leave me alone so that my anger may burn against them and that I may destroy them. Then I will make you into a great nation."

[11] But Moses sought the favor of the LORD his God. "LORD," he said, "why should your anger burn against your people, whom you brought out of Egypt with great power and a mighty hand? [12] Why should the Egyptians say, 'It was with evil intent that he brought them out, to kill them in the mountains and to wipe them off the face of the earth'? Turn from your fierce anger; relent and do not bring disaster on your people. [13] Remember your servants Abraham, Isaac and Israel, to whom you swore by your own self: 'I will make

---

[a] 1 Or *a god*; also in verses 23 and 31
[b] 4 Or *This is your god*; also in verse 8

your descendants as numerous as the stars in the sky and I will give your descendants all this land I promised them, and it will be their inheritance forever.'" ¹⁴Then the LORD relented and did not bring on his people the disaster he had threatened.

¹⁵Moses turned and went down the mountain with the two tablets of the covenant law in his hands. They were inscribed on both sides, front and back. ¹⁶The tablets were the work of God; the writing was the writing of God, engraved on the tablets.

¹⁷When Joshua heard the noise of the people shouting, he said to Moses, "There is the sound of war in the camp."

¹⁸Moses replied:

"It is not the sound of victory,
    it is not the sound of defeat;
    it is the sound of singing that I hear."

¹⁹When Moses approached the camp and saw the calf and the dancing, his anger burned and he threw the tablets out of his hands, breaking them to pieces at the foot of the mountain. ²⁰And he took the calf the people had made and burned it in the fire; then he ground it to powder, scattered it on the water and made the Israelites drink it.

²¹He said to Aaron, "What did these people do to you, that you led them into such great sin?"

²²"Do not be angry, my lord," Aaron answered. "You know how prone these people are to evil. ²³They said to me, 'Make us gods who will go before us. As for this fellow Moses who brought us up out of Egypt, we don't know what has happened to him.' ²⁴So I told them, 'Whoever has any gold jewelry, take it off.' Then they gave me the gold, and I threw it into the fire, and out came this calf!"

²⁵Moses saw that the people were running wild and that Aaron had let them get out of control and so become a laughingstock to their enemies. ²⁶So he stood at the entrance to the camp and said, "Whoever is for the LORD, come to me." And all the Levites rallied to him.

²⁷Then he said to them, "This is what the LORD, the God of Israel, says: 'Each man strap a sword to his side. Go back and forth through the camp from one end to the other, each killing his brother and friend and neighbor.'" ²⁸The Levites did as Moses commanded, and that day about three thousand of the people died. ²⁹Then Moses said, "You have been set apart to the LORD today, for you were against your own sons and brothers, and he has blessed you this day."

³⁰The next day Moses said to the people, "You have committed a great sin. But

Exodus 32:1 – 35

People mess up at the worst moments.

Moses had met with God atop Mount Sinai and was descending from the mountain when he heard noisy singing in the camp below. In his arms he carried two stone tablets God himself had inscribed with the Ten Commandments (see Exodus 31:18). But Moses was about to discover God's people breaking the law in a big way. Everyone thought Moses was taking too long to come down from the mountain, so they pooled their gold and melted it into two calves, idols similar to the cow and bull worshiped by their neighbors. As God watched people bowing to these false gods, he wanted to destroy them for their stubborn disobedience, and thousands died that day (see Exodus 32:9 – 28). What should have been a peak moment of devotion to the Lord became a catastrophe.

Think: When have you rebelled against God's rules even though you knew the right thing to do?

ROCK SOLID truths

now I will go up to the LORD; perhaps I can make atonement for your sin."

[31] So Moses went back to the LORD and said, "Oh, what a great sin these people have committed! They have made themselves gods of gold. [32] But now, please forgive their sin—but if not, then blot me out of the book you have written."

[33] The LORD replied to Moses, "Whoever has sinned against me I will blot out of my book. [34] Now go, lead the people to the place I spoke of, and my angel will go before you. However, when the time comes for me to punish, I will punish them for their sin."

[35] And the LORD struck the people with a plague because of what they did with the calf Aaron had made.

33

Then the LORD said to Moses, "Leave this place, you and the people you brought up out of Egypt, and go up to the land I promised on oath to Abraham, Isaac and Jacob, saying, 'I will give it to your descendants.' [2] I will send an angel before you and drive out the Canaanites, Amorites, Hittites, Perizzites, Hivites and Jebusites. [3] Go up to the land flowing with milk and honey. But I will not go with you, because you are a stiff-necked people and I might destroy you on the way."

[4] When the people heard these distressing words, they began to mourn and no one put on any ornaments. [5] For the LORD had said to Moses, "Tell the Israelites, 'You are a stiff-necked people. If I were to go with you even for a moment, I might destroy you. Now take off your ornaments and I will decide what to do with you.'" [6] So the Israelites stripped off their ornaments at Mount Horeb.

The Tent of Meeting

[7] Now Moses used to take a tent and pitch it outside the camp some distance away, calling it the "tent of meeting." Anyone inquiring of the LORD would go to the tent of meeting outside the camp. [8] And whenever Moses went out to the tent, all the people rose and stood at the entrances to their tents, watching Moses until he entered the tent. [9] As Moses went into the tent, the pillar of cloud would come down and stay at the entrance, while the LORD spoke with Moses. [10] Whenever the people saw the pillar of cloud standing at the entrance to the tent, they all stood and worshiped, each at the entrance to their tent. [11] The LORD would speak to Moses face to face, as one speaks to a friend. Then Moses would return to the camp, but his young aide Joshua son of Nun did not leave the tent.

Moses and the Glory of the LORD

[12] Moses said to the LORD, "You have been telling me, 'Lead these people,' but you have not let me know whom you will send with me. You have said, 'I know you by name and you have found favor with me.' [13] If you are pleased with me, teach me your ways so I may know you and continue to find favor with you. Remember that this nation is your people."

[14] The LORD replied, "My Presence will go with you, and I will give you rest."

[15] Then Moses said to him, "If your Presence does not go with us, do not send us up from here. [16] How will anyone know that you are pleased with me and with your people unless you go with us? What else will distinguish me and your people from all the other people on the face of the earth?"

[17] And the LORD said to Moses, "I will do the very thing you have asked, because I am pleased with you and I know you by name."

[18] Then Moses said, "Now show me your glory."

[19] And the LORD said, "I will cause all my goodness to pass in front of you, and I will proclaim my name, the LORD, in your presence. I will have mercy on whom I will have mercy, and I will have compassion on whom I will have compassion. [20] But," he said, "you cannot see my face, for no one may see me and live."

[21] Then the LORD said, "There is a place near me where you may stand on a rock. [22] When my glory passes by, I will put you in a cleft in the rock and cover you with

my hand until I have passed by. ²³Then I will remove my hand and you will see my back; but my face must not be seen."

The New Stone Tablets

34 The LORD said to Moses, "Chisel out two stone tablets like the first ones, and I will write on them the words that were on the first tablets, which you broke. ²Be ready in the morning, and then come up on Mount Sinai. Present yourself to me there on top of the mountain. ³No one is to come with you or be seen anywhere on the mountain; not even the flocks and herds may graze in front of the mountain."

⁴So Moses chiseled out two stone tablets like the first ones and went up Mount Sinai early in the morning, as the LORD had commanded him; and he carried the two stone tablets in his hands. ⁵Then the LORD came down in the cloud and stood there with him and proclaimed his name, the LORD. ⁶And he passed in front of Moses, proclaiming, "The LORD, the LORD, the compassionate and gracious God, slow to anger, abounding in love and faithfulness, ⁷maintaining love to thousands, and forgiving wickedness, rebellion and sin. Yet he does not leave the guilty unpunished; he punishes the children and their children for the sin of the parents to the third and fourth generation."

⁸Moses bowed to the ground at once and worshiped. ⁹"Lord," he said, "if I have found favor in your eyes, then let the Lord go with us. Although this is a stiff-necked people, forgive our wickedness and our sin, and take us as your inheritance."

¹⁰Then the LORD said: "I am making a covenant with you. Before all your people I will do wonders never before done in any nation in all the world. The people you live among will see how awesome is the work that I, the LORD, will do for you. ¹¹Obey what I command you today. I will drive out before you the Amorites, Canaanites, Hittites, Perizzites, Hivites and Jebusites. ¹²Be careful not to make a treaty with those who live in the land where you are going, or they will be a snare among

UNSHAKEN God

Exodus 34:4–7

God is angry.

As much as we might want to picture God as a guy who never loses his cool over human sin, that isn't the God of the Bible. The Lord wasn't kidding when he gave Moses the Ten Commandments, his top do's and don'ts of Old Testament faith (see Exodus 20:1–21). He expects his people to keep his rules without exception, and he hates sin. Yet God is slow to anger and overflowing with love. His fury only comes when we continually reject his love, faithfulness, and forgiveness. Even his anger is powered by his loving concern that we honor him and experience his best plans.

So ... How do you explain a God who can be both angry and loving?

you. ¹³Break down their altars, smash their sacred stones and cut down their Asherah poles.ᵃ ¹⁴Do not worship any other god, for the LORD, whose name is Jealous, is a jealous God.

¹⁵"Be careful not to make a treaty with those who live in the land; for when they prostitute themselves to their gods and sacrifice to them, they will invite you and you will eat their sacrifices. ¹⁶And when you choose some of their daughters as wives for your sons and those daughters prostitute themselves to their gods, they will lead your sons to do the same.

¹⁷"Do not make any idols.

¹⁸"Celebrate the Festival of Unleavened Bread. For seven days eat bread made without yeast, as I commanded you. Do this at the appointed time in the month of Aviv, for in that month you came out of Egypt.

¹⁹"The first offspring of every womb

ᵃ 13 That is, wooden symbols of the goddess Asherah

belongs to me, including all the firstborn males of your livestock, whether from herd or flock. ²⁰Redeem the firstborn donkey with a lamb, but if you do not redeem it, break its neck. Redeem all your firstborn sons.

"No one is to appear before me empty-handed.

²¹"Six days you shall labor, but on the seventh day you shall rest; even during the plowing season and harvest you must rest.

²²"Celebrate the Festival of Weeks with the firstfruits of the wheat harvest, and the Festival of Ingathering at the turn of the year.ᵃ ²³Three times a year all your men are to appear before the Sovereign LORD, the God of Israel. ²⁴I will drive out nations before you and enlarge your territory, and no one will covet your land when you go up three times each year to appear before the LORD your God.

²⁵"Do not offer the blood of a sacrifice to me along with anything containing yeast, and do not let any of the sacrifice from the Passover Festival remain until morning.

²⁶"Bring the best of the firstfruits of your soil to the house of the LORD your God.

"Do not cook a young goat in its mother's milk."

²⁷Then the LORD said to Moses, "Write down these words, for in accordance with these words I have made a covenant with you and with Israel." ²⁸Moses was there with the LORD forty days and forty nights without eating bread or drinking water. And he wrote on the tablets the words of the covenant—the Ten Commandments.

The Radiant Face of Moses

²⁹When Moses came down from Mount Sinai with the two tablets of the covenant law in his hands, he was not aware that his face was radiant because he had spoken with the LORD. ³⁰When Aaron and all the Israelites saw Moses, his face was radiant, and they were afraid to come near him. ³¹But Moses called to them; so Aaron and all the leaders of the community came back to him, and he spoke to them. ³²Afterward all the Israelites came near

him, and he gave them all the commands the LORD had given him on Mount Sinai.

³³When Moses finished speaking to them, he put a veil over his face. ³⁴But whenever he entered the LORD's presence to speak with him, he removed the veil until he came out. And when he came out and told the Israelites what he had been commanded, ³⁵they saw that his face was radiant. Then Moses would put the veil back over his face until he went in to speak with the LORD.

Sabbath Regulations

35 Moses assembled the whole Israelite community and said to them, "These are the things the LORD has commanded you to do: ²For six days, work is to be done, but the seventh day shall be your holy day, a day of sabbath rest to the LORD. Whoever does any work on it is to be put to death. ³Do not light a fire in any of your dwellings on the Sabbath day."

Materials for the Tabernacle

⁴Moses said to the whole Israelite community, "This is what the LORD has commanded: ⁵From what you have, take an offering for the LORD. Everyone who is willing is to bring to the LORD an offering of gold, silver and bronze; ⁶blue, purple and scarlet yarn and fine linen; goat hair; ⁷ram skins dyed red and another type of durable leatherᵇ; acacia wood; ⁸olive oil for the light; spices for the anointing oil and for the fragrant incense; ⁹and onyx stones and other gems to be mounted on the ephod and breastpiece.

¹⁰"All who are skilled among you are to come and make everything the LORD has commanded: ¹¹the tabernacle with its tent and its covering, clasps, frames, crossbars, posts and bases; ¹²the ark with its poles and the atonement cover and the curtain that shields it; ¹³the table with its poles and all its articles and the bread of the Presence; ¹⁴the lampstand that is for light with its accessories, lamps and oil for

ᵃ 22 That is, in the autumn   ᵇ 7 Possibly the hides of large aquatic mammals; also in verse 23 the light; [15] the altar of incense with its poles, the anointing oil and the fragrant incense; the curtain for the doorway at the entrance to the tabernacle; [16] the altar of burnt offering with its bronze grating, its poles and all its utensils; the bronze basin with its stand; [17] the curtains of the courtyard with its posts and bases, and the curtain for the entrance to the courtyard; [18] the tent pegs for the tabernacle and for the courtyard, and their ropes; [19] the woven garments worn for ministering in the sanctuary—both the sacred garments for Aaron the priest and the garments for his sons when they serve as priests."

[20] Then the whole Israelite community withdrew from Moses' presence, [21] and everyone who was willing and whose heart moved them came and brought an offering to the LORD for the work on the tent of meeting, for all its service, and for the sacred garments. [22] All who were willing, men and women alike, came and brought gold jewelry of all kinds: brooches, earrings, rings and ornaments. They all presented their gold as a wave offering to the LORD. [23] Everyone who had blue, purple or scarlet yarn or fine linen, or goat hair, ram skins dyed red or the other durable leather brought them. [24] Those presenting an offering of silver or bronze brought it as an offering to the LORD, and everyone who had acacia wood for any part of the work brought it. [25] Every skilled woman spun with her hands and brought what she had spun—blue, purple or scarlet yarn or fine linen. [26] And all the women who were willing and had the skill spun the goat hair. [27] The leaders brought onyx stones and other gems to be mounted on the ephod and breastpiece. [28] They also brought spices and olive oil for the light and for the anointing oil and for the fragrant incense. [29] All the Israelite men and women who were willing brought to the LORD freewill offerings for all the work the LORD through Moses had commanded them to do.

Bezalel and Oholiab

[30] Then Moses said to the Israelites, "See, the LORD has chosen Bezalel son of Uri, the son of Hur, of the tribe of Judah, [31] and he has filled him with the Spirit of God, with wisdom, with understanding, with knowledge and with all kinds of skills— [32] to make artistic designs for work in gold, silver and bronze, [33] to cut and set stones, to work in wood and to engage in all kinds of artistic crafts. [34] And he has given both him and Oholiab son of Ahisamak, of the tribe of Dan, the ability to teach others. [35] He has filled them with skill to do all kinds of work as engravers, designers, embroiderers in blue, purple and scarlet yarn and fine linen, and weavers— all of them skilled workers and designers.

36 [1] So Bezalel, Oholiab and every skilled person to whom the LORD has given skill and ability to know how to carry out all the work of constructing the sanctuary are to do the work just as the LORD has commanded."

[2] Then Moses summoned Bezalel and Oholiab and every skilled person to whom the LORD had given ability and who was willing to come and do the work. [3] They received from Moses all the offerings the Israelites had brought to carry out the work of constructing the sanctuary. And the people continued to bring freewill offerings morning after morning. [4] So all the skilled workers who were doing all the work on the sanctuary left what they were doing [5] and said to Moses, "The people are bringing more than enough for doing the work the LORD commanded to be done."

[6] Then Moses gave an order and they sent this word throughout the camp: "No man or woman is to make anything else as an offering for the sanctuary." And so the people were restrained from bringing more, [7] because what they already had was more than enough to do all the work.

The Tabernacle

[8] All those who were skilled among the workers made the tabernacle with ten curtains of finely twisted linen and blue, purple and scarlet yarn, with cherubim woven into them by expert hands. [9] All the curtains were the same size—twenty-eight

cubits long and four cubits wide.[a] [10]They joined five of the curtains together and did the same with the other five. [11]Then they made loops of blue material along the edge of the end curtain in one set, and the same was done with the end curtain in the other set. [12]They also made fifty loops on one curtain and fifty loops on the end curtain of the other set, with the loops opposite each other. [13]Then they made fifty gold clasps and used them to fasten the two sets of curtains together so that the tabernacle was a unit.

[14]They made curtains of goat hair for the tent over the tabernacle—eleven altogether. [15]All eleven curtains were the same size—thirty cubits long and four cubits wide.[b] [16]They joined five of the curtains into one set and the other six into another set. [17]Then they made fifty loops along the edge of the end curtain in one set and also along the edge of the end curtain in the other set. [18]They made fifty bronze clasps to fasten the tent together as a unit. [19]Then they made for the tent a covering of ram skins dyed red, and over that a covering of the other durable leather.[c]

[20]They made upright frames of acacia wood for the tabernacle. [21]Each frame was ten cubits long and a cubit and a half wide,[d] [22]with two projections set parallel to each other. They made all the frames of the tabernacle in this way. [23]They made twenty frames for the south side of the tabernacle [24]and made forty silver bases to go under them—two bases for each frame, one under each projection. [25]For the other side, the north side of the tabernacle, they made twenty frames [26]and forty silver bases—two under each frame. [27]They made six frames for the far end, that is, the west end of the tabernacle, [28]and two frames were made for the corners of the tabernacle at the far end. [29]At these two corners the frames were double from the bottom all the way to the top and fitted into a single ring; both were made alike. [30]So there were eight frames and sixteen silver bases—two under each frame.

[31]They also made crossbars of acacia wood: five for the frames on one side of the tabernacle, [32]five for those on the other side, and five for the frames on the west, at the far end of the tabernacle. [33]They made the center crossbar so that it extended from end to end at the middle of the frames. [34]They overlaid the frames with gold and made gold rings to hold the crossbars. They also overlaid the crossbars with gold.

[35]They made the curtain of blue, purple and scarlet yarn and finely twisted linen, with cherubim woven into it by a skilled worker. [36]They made four posts of acacia wood for it and overlaid them with gold. They made gold hooks for them and cast their four silver bases. [37]For the entrance to the tent they made a curtain of blue, purple and scarlet yarn and finely twisted linen—the work of an embroiderer; [38]and they made five posts with hooks for them. They overlaid the tops of the posts and their bands with gold and made their five bases of bronze.

The Ark

37 Bezalel made the ark of acacia wood—two and a half cubits long, a cubit and a half wide, and a cubit and a half high.[e] [2]He overlaid it with pure gold, both inside and out, and made a gold molding around it. [3]He cast four gold rings for it and fastened them to its four feet, with two rings on one side and two rings on the other. [4]Then he made poles of acacia wood and overlaid them with gold. [5]And he inserted the poles into the rings on the sides of the ark to carry it.

[6]He made the atonement cover of pure gold—two and a half cubits long and a cubit and a half wide. [7]Then he made two

[a] 9 That is, about 42 feet long and 6 feet wide or about 13 meters long and 1.8 meters wide
[b] 15 That is, about 45 feet long and 6 feet wide or about 14 meters long and 1.8 meters wide
[c] 19 Possibly the hides of large aquatic mammals (see 35:7)   [d] 21 That is, about 15 feet long and 2 1/4 feet wide or about 4.5 meters long and 68 centimeters wide   [e] 1 That is, about 3 3/4 feet long and 2 1/4 feet wide and high or about 1.1 meters long and 68 centimeters wide and high; similarly in verse 6

cherubim out of hammered gold at the ends of the cover. ⁸He made one cherub on one end and the second cherub on the other; at the two ends he made them of one piece with the cover. ⁹The cherubim had their wings spread upward, overshadowing the cover with them. The cherubim faced each other, looking toward the cover.

The Table

¹⁰They*a* made the table of acacia wood—two cubits long, a cubit wide and a cubit and a half high.*b* ¹¹Then they overlaid it with pure gold and made a gold molding around it. ¹²They also made around it a rim a handbreadth*c* wide and put a gold molding on the rim. ¹³They cast four gold rings for the table and fastened them to the four corners, where the four legs were. ¹⁴The rings were put close to the rim to hold the poles used in carrying the table. ¹⁵The poles for carrying the table were made of acacia wood and were overlaid with gold. ¹⁶And they made from pure gold the articles for the table—its plates and dishes and bowls and its pitchers for the pouring out of drink offerings.

The Lampstand

¹⁷They made the lampstand of pure gold. They hammered out its base and shaft, and made its flowerlike cups, buds and blossoms of one piece with them. ¹⁸Six branches extended from the sides of the lampstand—three on one side and three on the other. ¹⁹Three cups shaped like almond flowers with buds and blossoms were on one branch, three on the next branch and the same for all six branches extending from the lampstand. ²⁰And on the lampstand were four cups shaped like almond flowers with buds and blossoms. ²¹One bud was under the first pair of branches extending from the lampstand, a second bud under the second pair, and a third bud under the third pair—six branches in all. ²²The buds and the branches were all of one piece with the lampstand, hammered out of pure gold. ²³They made its seven lamps, as well as its wick trimmers and trays, of pure gold.

²⁴They made the lampstand and all its accessories from one talent*d* of pure gold.

The Altar of Incense

²⁵They made the altar of incense out of acacia wood. It was square, a cubit long and a cubit wide and two cubits high*e*—its horns of one piece with it. ²⁶They overlaid the top and all the sides and the horns with pure gold, and made a gold molding around it. ²⁷They made two gold rings below the molding—two on each of the opposite sides—to hold the poles used to carry it. ²⁸They made the poles of acacia wood and overlaid them with gold.

²⁹They also made the sacred anointing oil and the pure, fragrant incense—the work of a perfumer.

The Altar of Burnt Offering

38 They*f* built the altar of burnt offering of acacia wood, three cubits*g* high; it was square, five cubits long and five cubits wide.*b* ²They made a horn at each of the four corners, so that the horns and the altar were of one piece, and they overlaid the altar with bronze. ³They made all its utensils of bronze—its pots, shovels, sprinkling bowls, meat forks and firepans. ⁴They made a grating for the altar, a bronze network, to be under its ledge, halfway up the altar. ⁵They cast bronze rings to hold the poles for the four corners of the bronze grating. ⁶They made the poles of acacia wood and overlaid them with bronze. ⁷They inserted the poles into the rings so they would be on the sides of the altar for carrying it. They made it hollow, out of boards.

a 10 Or *He*; also in verses 11-29   *b 10* That is, about 3 feet long, 1 1/2 feet wide and 2 1/4 feet high or about 90 centimeters long, 45 centimeters wide and 68 centimeters high   *c 12* That is, about 3 inches or about 7.5 centimeters   *d 24* That is, about 75 pounds or about 34 kilograms   *e 25* That is, about 1 1/2 feet long and wide and 3 feet high or about 45 centimeters long and wide and 90 centimeters high   *f 1* Or *He*; also in verses 2-9   *g 1* That is, about 4 1/2 feet or about 1.4 meters   *b 1* That is, about 7 1/2 feet or about 2.3 meters long and wide

The Basin for Washing

⁸They made the bronze basin and its bronze stand from the mirrors of the women who served at the entrance to the tent of meeting.

The Courtyard

⁹Next they made the courtyard. The south side was a hundred cubits*a* long and had curtains of finely twisted linen, ¹⁰with twenty posts and twenty bronze bases, and with silver hooks and bands on the posts. ¹¹The north side was also a hundred cubits long and had twenty posts and twenty bronze bases, with silver hooks and bands on the posts.

¹²The west end was fifty cubits*b* wide and had curtains, with ten posts and ten bases, with silver hooks and bands on the posts. ¹³The east end, toward the sunrise, was also fifty cubits wide. ¹⁴Curtains fifteen cubits*c* long were on one side of the entrance, with three posts and three bases, ¹⁵and curtains fifteen cubits long were on the other side of the entrance to the courtyard, with three posts and three bases. ¹⁶All the curtains around the courtyard were of finely twisted linen. ¹⁷The bases for the posts were bronze. The hooks and bands on the posts were silver, and their tops were overlaid with silver; so all the posts of the courtyard had silver bands.

¹⁸The curtain for the entrance to the courtyard was made of blue, purple and scarlet yarn and finely twisted linen— the work of an embroiderer. It was twenty cubits*d* long and, like the curtains of the courtyard, five cubits*e* high, ¹⁹with four posts and four bronze bases. Their hooks and bands were silver, and their tops were overlaid with silver. ²⁰All the tent pegs of the tabernacle and of the surrounding courtyard were bronze.

The Materials Used

²¹These are the amounts of the materials used for the tabernacle, the tabernacle of the covenant law, which were recorded at Moses' command by the Levites under the direction of Ithamar son of Aaron, the priest. ²²(Bezalel son of Uri, the son

of Hur, of the tribe of Judah, made everything the Lord commanded Moses; ²³with him was Oholiab son of Ahisamak, of the tribe of Dan—an engraver and designer, and an embroiderer in blue, purple and scarlet yarn and fine linen.) ²⁴The total amount of the gold from the wave offering used for all the work on the sanctuary was 29 talents and 730 shekels,*f* according to the sanctuary shekel.

²⁵The silver obtained from those of the community who were counted in the census was 100 talents*g* and 1,775 shekels,*h* according to the sanctuary shekel— ²⁶one beka per person, that is, half a shekel,*i* according to the sanctuary shekel, from everyone who had crossed over to those counted, twenty years old or more, a total of 603,550 men. ²⁷The 100 talents of silver were used to cast the bases for the sanctuary and for the curtain—100 bases from the 100 talents, one talent for each base. ²⁸They used the 1,775 shekels to make the hooks for the posts, to overlay the tops of the posts, and to make their bands.

²⁹The bronze from the wave offering was 70 talents and 2,400 shekels.*j* ³⁰They used it to make the bases for the entrance to the tent of meeting, the bronze altar with its bronze grating and all its utensils, ³¹the bases for the surrounding courtyard and those for its entrance and all the tent pegs for the tabernacle and those for the surrounding courtyard.

The Priestly Garments

39 From the blue, purple and scarlet yarn they made woven garments for ministering in the sanctuary. They also made

---

a 9 That is, about 150 feet or about 45 meters
b 12 That is, about 75 feet or about 23 meters
c 14 That is, about 22 feet or about 6.8 meters
d 18 That is, about 30 feet or about 9 meters
e 18 That is, about 7 1/2 feet or about 2.3 meters
f 24 The weight of the gold was a little over a ton or about 1 metric ton.   *g 25* That is, about 3 3/4 tons or about 3.4 metric tons; also in verse 27   *h 25* That is, about 44 pounds or about 20 kilograms; also in verse 28   *i 26* That is, about 1/5 ounce or about 5.7 grams
j 29 The weight of the bronze was about 2 1/2 tons or about 2.4 metric tons.

sacred garments for Aaron, as the LORD commanded Moses.

The Ephod

[2] They[a] made the ephod of gold, and of blue, purple and scarlet yarn, and of finely twisted linen. [3] They hammered out thin sheets of gold and cut strands to be worked into the blue, purple and scarlet yarn and fine linen—the work of skilled hands. [4] They made shoulder pieces for the ephod, which were attached to two of its corners, so it could be fastened. [5] Its skillfully woven waistband was like it—of one piece with the ephod and made with gold, and with blue, purple and scarlet yarn, and with finely twisted linen, as the LORD commanded Moses.

[6] They mounted the onyx stones in gold filigree settings and engraved them like a seal with the names of the sons of Israel. [7] Then they fastened them on the shoulder pieces of the ephod as memorial stones for the sons of Israel, as the LORD commanded Moses.

The Breastpiece

[8] They fashioned the breastpiece—the work of a skilled craftsman. They made it like the ephod: of gold, and of blue, purple and scarlet yarn, and of finely twisted linen. [9] It was square—a span[b] long and a span wide—and folded double. [10] Then they mounted four rows of precious stones on it. The first row was carnelian, chrysolite and beryl; [11] the second row was turquoise, lapis lazuli and emerald; [12] the third row was jacinth, agate and amethyst; [13] the fourth row was topaz, onyx and jasper.[c] They were mounted in gold filigree settings. [14] There were twelve stones, one for each of the names of the sons of Israel, each engraved like a seal with the name of one of the twelve tribes.

[15] For the breastpiece they made braided chains of pure gold, like a rope. [16] They made two gold filigree settings and two gold rings, and fastened the rings to two of the corners of the breastpiece. [17] They fastened the two gold chains to the rings at the corners of the breastpiece, [18] and the other ends of the chains to the two settings, attaching them to the shoulder pieces of the ephod at the front. [19] They made two gold rings and attached them to the other two corners of the breastpiece on the inside edge next to the ephod. [20] Then they made two more gold rings and attached them to the bottom of the shoulder pieces on the front of the ephod, close to the seam just above the waistband of the ephod. [21] They tied the rings of the breastpiece to the rings of the ephod with blue cord, connecting it to the waistband so that the breastpiece would not swing out from the ephod—as the LORD commanded Moses.

Other Priestly Garments

[22] They made the robe of the ephod entirely of blue cloth—the work of a weaver— [23] with an opening in the center of the robe like the opening of a collar,[d] and a band around this opening, so that it would not tear. [24] They made pomegranates of blue, purple and scarlet yarn and finely twisted linen around the hem of the robe. [25] And they made bells of pure gold and attached them around the hem between the pomegranates. [26] The bells and pomegranates alternated around the hem of the robe to be worn for ministering, as the LORD commanded Moses.

[27] For Aaron and his sons, they made tunics of fine linen—the work of a weaver— [28] and the turban of fine linen, the linen caps and the undergarments of finely twisted linen. [29] The sash was made of finely twisted linen and blue, purple and scarlet yarn—the work of an embroiderer—as the LORD commanded Moses.

[30] They made the plate, the sacred emblem, out of pure gold and engraved on it, like an inscription on a seal: HOLY TO THE LORD. [31] Then they fastened a blue cord to it to attach it to the turban, as the LORD commanded Moses.

[a] 2 Or He; also in verses 7, 8 and 22   [b] 9 That is, about 9 inches or about 23 centimeters
[c] 13 The precise identification of some of these precious stones is uncertain.
[d] 23 The meaning of the Hebrew for this word is uncertain.

Moses Inspects the Tabernacle

³²So all the work on the tabernacle, the tent of meeting, was completed. The Israelites did everything just as the LORD commanded Moses. ³³Then they brought the tabernacle to Moses: the tent and all its furnishings, its clasps, frames, crossbars, posts and bases; ³⁴the covering of ram skins dyed red and the covering of another durable leather*ᵃ* and the shielding curtain; ³⁵the ark of the covenant law with its poles and the atonement cover; ³⁶the table with all its articles and the bread of the Presence; ³⁷the pure gold lampstand with its row of lamps and all its accessories, and the olive oil for the light; ³⁸the gold altar, the anointing oil, the fragrant incense, and the curtain for the entrance to the tent; ³⁹the bronze altar with its bronze grating, its poles and all its utensils; the basin with its stand; ⁴⁰the curtains of the courtyard with its posts and bases, and the curtain for the entrance to the courtyard; the ropes and tent pegs for the courtyard; all the furnishings for the tabernacle, the tent of meeting; ⁴¹and the woven garments worn for ministering in the sanctuary, both the sacred garments for Aaron the priest and the garments for his sons when serving as priests.

⁴²The Israelites had done all the work just as the LORD had commanded Moses. ⁴³Moses inspected the work and saw that they had done it just as the LORD had commanded. So Moses blessed them.

Setting Up the Tabernacle

40 Then the LORD said to Moses: ²"Set up the tabernacle, the tent of meeting, on the first day of the first month. ³Place the ark of the covenant law in it and shield the ark

ᵃ 34 Possibly the hides of large aquatic mammals

Exodus 39:32

Finish what you start.

Michael was sitting at the kitchen table downing a snack when his dad glanced out the back window. Mr. Garvey was pleased with the look of the lawn—until he spotted the mower sitting in the middle of the yard. And a closer inspection informed him the edges of the lawn hadn't been trimmed. Mr. Garvey didn't get heated, but he pointed to the yard and told Michael to head back outside and finish. "You did 90% of the work, and I appreciate that," he said. "But you didn't finish. That last 10% is the difference between an okay job and a great job. Get out there—and don't come back inside until you're completely done."

God gave the Israelites exceptionally detailed instructions for constructing the tabernacle, or "tent of meeting" (see Exodus 25:1—31:11). It would have been easy to cut corners or leave little things undone. But when Moses inspected their work, he found "the Israelites did everything just as the LORD commanded" (Exodus 39:32). God's people did amazing work. They finished the job they started.

with the curtain. ⁴Bring in the table and set out what belongs on it. Then bring in the lampstand and set up its lamps. ⁵Place the gold altar of incense in front of the ark of the covenant law and put the curtain at the entrance to the tabernacle.

⁶"Place the altar of burnt offering in front of the entrance to the tabernacle, the tent of meeting; ⁷place the basin between the tent of meeting and the altar and put water in it. ⁸Set up the courtyard around it and put the curtain at the entrance to the courtyard.

⁹"Take the anointing oil and anoint the tabernacle and everything in it; consecrate it and all its furnishings, and it will be holy. ¹⁰Then anoint the altar of burnt offering and all its utensils; consecrate the altar, and it will be most holy. ¹¹Anoint the basin and its stand and consecrate them.

¹²"Bring Aaron and his sons to the entrance to the tent of meeting and wash them with water. ¹³Then dress Aaron in the sacred garments, anoint him and consecrate him so he may serve me as priest. ¹⁴Bring his sons and dress them in tunics. ¹⁵Anoint them just as you anointed their father, so they may serve me as priests. Their anointing will be to a priesthood that will continue throughout their generations." ¹⁶Moses did everything just as the Lord commanded him.

¹⁷So the tabernacle was set up on the first day of the first month in the second year. ¹⁸When Moses set up the tabernacle, he put the bases in place, erected the frames, inserted the crossbars and set up the posts. ¹⁹Then he spread the tent over the tabernacle and put the covering over the tent, as the Lord commanded him.

²⁰He took the tablets of the covenant law and placed them in the ark, attached the poles to the ark and put the atonement cover over it. ²¹Then he brought the ark into the tabernacle and hung the shielding curtain and shielded the ark of the covenant law, as the Lord commanded him.

²²Moses placed the table in the tent of meeting on the north side of the tabernacle outside the curtain ²³and set out the bread on it before the Lord, as the Lord commanded him.

²⁴He placed the lampstand in the tent of meeting opposite the table on the south side of the tabernacle ²⁵and set up the lamps before the Lord, as the Lord commanded him.

²⁶Moses placed the gold altar in the tent of meeting in front of the curtain ²⁷and burned fragrant incense on it, as the Lord commanded him.

²⁸Then he put up the curtain at the entrance to the tabernacle. ²⁹He set the altar of burnt offering near the entrance to the tabernacle, the tent of meeting, and offered on it burnt offerings and grain offerings, as the Lord commanded him.

³⁰He placed the basin between the tent of meeting and the altar and put water in it for washing, ³¹and Moses and Aaron and his sons used it to wash their hands and feet. ³²They washed whenever they entered the tent of meeting or approached the altar, as the Lord commanded Moses.

³³Then Moses set up the courtyard around the tabernacle and altar and put up the curtain at the entrance to the courtyard. And so Moses finished the work.

The Glory of the Lord

³⁴Then the cloud covered the tent of meeting, and the glory of the Lord filled the tabernacle. ³⁵Moses could not enter the tent of meeting because the cloud had

ROCK SOLID *promises*

"The glory of the Lord filled the tabernacle."　　　Exodus 40:34

Whenever you worship, God shows up. Watch for his awesome presence.

settled on it, and the glory of the Lord filled the tabernacle.

³⁶ In all the travels of the Israelites, whenever the cloud lifted from above the tabernacle, they would set out; ³⁷ but if the cloud did not lift, they did not set out—until the day it lifted. ³⁸ So the cloud of the Lord was over the tabernacle by day, and fire was in the cloud by night, in the sight of all the Israelites during all their travels.

LEVITICUS

BOOK OUTLINE

Leviticus means "about the Levites." The Levites were God's priests, and the book of Leviticus contains many of the rules they needed to do their work—rules for worshiping God, making sacrifices, and handling everyday problems concerning cleanliness. Although God gave many of the rules only to the Levites, his purpose for giving all the laws was to help the Israelites worship and live as his holy people. A key statement for the entire book is "Be holy, because I am holy" (11:44,45).

The Burnt Offering

1 The Lord called to Moses and spoke to him from the tent of meeting. He said, ²"Speak to the Israelites and say to them: 'When anyone among you brings an offering to the Lord, bring as your offering an animal from either the herd or the flock.

³"'If the offering is a burnt offering from the herd, you are to offer a male without defect. You must present it at the entrance to the tent of meeting so that it will be acceptable to the Lord. ⁴You are to lay your hand on the head of the burnt offering, and it will be accepted on your behalf to make atonement for you. ⁵You are to slaughter the young bull before the Lord, and then Aaron's sons the priests shall bring the blood and splash it against the sides of the altar at the entrance to the tent of meeting. ⁶You are to skin the burnt offering and cut it into pieces. ⁷The sons of Aaron the priest are to put fire on the altar and arrange wood on the fire. ⁸Then Aaron's sons the priests shall arrange the pieces, including the head and the fat, on the wood that is burning on the altar. ⁹You are to wash the internal organs and the legs with water, and the priest is to burn all of it on the altar. It is a burnt offering, a food offering, an aroma pleasing to the Lord.

¹⁰"'If the offering is a burnt offering from the flock, from either the sheep or the goats, you are to offer a male without defect. ¹¹You are to slaughter it at the north side of the altar before the Lord, and Aaron's sons the priests shall splash its blood against the sides of the altar. ¹²You are to cut it into pieces, and the priest shall arrange them, including the head and the fat, on the wood that is burning on the altar. ¹³You are to wash the internal organs and the legs with water, and the priest is to bring all of them and burn them on the altar. It is a burnt offering, a food offering, an aroma pleasing to the Lord.

¹⁴"'If the offering to the Lord is a burnt offering of birds, you are to offer a dove or a young pigeon. ¹⁵The priest shall bring it to the altar, wring off the head and burn it on the altar; its blood shall be drained out on the side of the altar. ¹⁶He is to remove the crop and the feathers[a] and throw them down east of the altar where the ashes are. ¹⁷He shall tear it open by the wings, not dividing it completely, and then the priest shall burn it on the wood that is burning on the altar. It is a burnt offering, a food offering, an aroma pleasing to the Lord.

The Grain Offering

2 "'When anyone brings a grain offering to the Lord, their offering is to be of the finest flour. They are to pour olive oil on it, put incense on it ²and take it to Aaron's sons the priests. The priest shall take a handful of the flour and oil, together with all the incense, and burn this as a memorial[b] portion on the altar, a food offering, an aroma pleasing to the Lord. ³The rest of the grain offering belongs to Aaron and his sons; it is a most holy part of the food offerings presented to the Lord.

⁴"'If you bring a grain offering baked in an oven, it is to consist of the finest flour: either thick loaves made without yeast and with olive oil mixed in or thin loaves made without yeast and brushed with olive oil. ⁵If your grain offering is prepared on a griddle, it is to be made of the finest flour mixed with oil, and without yeast. ⁶Crumble it and pour oil on it; it is a grain offering. ⁷If your grain offering is cooked in a pan, it is to be made of the finest flour and some olive oil. ⁸Bring the grain offering made of these things to the Lord; present it to the priest, who shall take it to the altar. ⁹He shall take out the memorial portion from the grain offering and burn it on the altar as a food offering, an aroma pleasing to the Lord. ¹⁰The rest of the grain offering belongs to Aaron and his sons; it is a most holy part of the food offerings presented to the Lord.

¹¹"'Every grain offering you bring to the Lord must be made without yeast, for you are not to burn any yeast or honey

---

[a] 16 Or *crop with its contents*; the meaning of the Hebrew for this word is uncertain.
[b] 2 Or *representative*; also in verses 9 and 16

in a food offering presented to the Lord. ¹²You may bring them to the Lord as an offering of the firstfruits, but they are not to be offered on the altar as a pleasing aroma. ¹³Season all your grain offerings with salt. Do not leave the salt of the covenant of your God out of your grain offerings; add salt to all your offerings.

¹⁴"If you bring a grain offering of firstfruits to the Lord, offer crushed heads of new grain roasted in the fire. ¹⁵Put oil and incense on it; it is a grain offering. ¹⁶The priest shall burn the memorial portion of the crushed grain and the oil, together with all the incense, as a food offering presented to the Lord.

The Fellowship Offering

3 "If your offering is a fellowship offering, and you offer an animal from the herd, whether male or female, you are to present before the Lord an animal without defect. ²You are to lay your hand on the head of your offering and slaughter it at the entrance to the tent of meeting. Then Aaron's sons the priests shall splash the blood against the sides of the altar. ³From the fellowship offering you are to bring a food offering to the Lord: the internal organs and all the fat that is connected to them, ⁴both kidneys with the fat on them near the loins, and the long lobe of the liver, which you will remove with the kidneys. ⁵Then Aaron's sons are to burn it on the altar on top of the burnt offering that is lying on the burning wood; it is a food offering, an aroma pleasing to the Lord.

⁶"If you offer an animal from the flock as a fellowship offering to the Lord, you are to offer a male or female without defect. ⁷If you offer a lamb, you are to present it before the Lord, ⁸lay your hand on its head and slaughter it in front of the tent of meeting. Then Aaron's sons shall splash its blood against the sides of the altar. ⁹From the fellowship offering you are to bring a food offering to the Lord: its fat, the entire fat tail cut off close to the backbone, the internal organs and all the fat that is connected to them, ¹⁰both kidneys with the fat on them near the loins, and the long lobe of the liver, which you will remove with the kidneys. ¹¹The priest shall burn them on the altar as a food offering presented to the Lord.

¹²"If your offering is a goat, you are to present it before the Lord, ¹³lay your hand on its head and slaughter it in front of the tent of meeting. Then Aaron's sons shall splash its blood against the sides of the altar. ¹⁴From what you offer you are to present this food offering to the Lord: the internal organs and all the fat that is connected to them, ¹⁵both kidneys with the fat on them near the loins, and the long lobe of the liver, which you will remove with the kidneys. ¹⁶The priest shall burn them on the altar as a food offering, a pleasing aroma. All the fat is the Lord's.

¹⁷"This is a lasting ordinance for the generations to come, wherever you live: You must not eat any fat or any blood.'"

The Sin Offering

4 The Lord said to Moses, ²"Say to the Israelites: 'When anyone sins unintentionally and does what is forbidden in any of the Lord's commands—

³"If the anointed priest sins, bringing guilt on the people, he must bring to the Lord a young bull without defect as a sin offering*a* for the sin he has committed. ⁴He is to present the bull at the entrance to the tent of meeting before the Lord. He is to lay his hand on its head and slaughter it there before the Lord. ⁵Then the anointed priest shall take some of the bull's blood and carry it into the tent of meeting. ⁶He is to dip his finger into the blood and sprinkle some of it seven times before the Lord, in front of the curtain of the sanctuary. ⁷The priest shall then put some of the blood on the horns of the altar of fragrant incense that is before the Lord in the tent of meeting. The rest of the bull's blood he shall pour out at the base of the altar of burnt offering at the

---

a 3 Or *purification offering*; here and throughout this chapter

ROCK SOLID *principles*

Leviticus 3:1–17

Bring God the right offering.

Natalie couldn't shake something her youth pastor had said. She sometimes thought Matt was ridiculous, but this time she had to wonder why his words kept popping into her head again and again. "If getting together with other Christians to study the Bible isn't high on your to-do list," he said, "then you're just giving God your rotten leftovers." Natalie felt certain God wanted her to keep up with school, sports, work, and everything else in her schedule. But she also knew that the activities that could help her grow spiritually were the first things she cut when life spun out of control. Maybe Matt was right. Natalie only made time to focus on God when it seemed convenient for her.

Old Testament sacrifices had to be offered correctly down to the last detail for the Lord to accept them. While Christ's death on the cross did away with our need to bring Old Testament sacrifices to make us right with God (see Hebrews 10:12), what you offer him still matters. He wants your best.

entrance to the tent of meeting. [8] He shall remove all the fat from the bull of the sin offering—all the fat that is connected to the internal organs, [9] both kidneys with the fat on them near the loins, and the long lobe of the liver, which he will remove with the kidneys— [10] just as the fat is removed from the ox[a] sacrificed as a fellowship offering. Then the priest shall burn them on the altar of burnt offering. [11] But the hide of the bull and all its flesh, as well as the head and legs, the internal organs and the intestines— [12] that is, all the rest of the bull—he must take outside the camp to a place ceremonially clean, where the ashes are thrown, and burn it there in a wood fire on the ash heap.

[13] "If the whole Israelite community sins unintentionally and does what is forbidden in any of the LORD's commands, even though the community is unaware of the matter, when they realize their guilt [14] and the sin they committed be-

comes known, the assembly must bring a young bull as a sin offering and present it before the tent of meeting. [15] The elders of the community are to lay their hands on the bull's head before the LORD, and the bull shall be slaughtered before the LORD. [16] Then the anointed priest is to take some of the bull's blood into the tent of meeting. [17] He shall dip his finger into the blood and sprinkle it before the LORD seven times in front of the curtain. [18] He is to put some of the blood on the horns of the altar that is before the LORD in the tent of meeting. The rest of the blood he shall pour out at the base of the altar of burnt offering at the entrance to the tent of meeting. [19] He shall remove all the fat from it and burn it on the altar, [20] and do with this bull just as he did with the bull for the sin offering. In this way the priest will make atonement for the community,

[a] *10* The Hebrew word can refer to either male or female.

and they will be forgiven. ²¹Then he shall take the bull outside the camp and burn it as he burned the first bull. This is the sin offering for the community.

²²"'When a leader sins unintentionally and does what is forbidden in any of the commands of the LORD his God, when he realizes his guilt ²³and the sin he has committed becomes known, he must bring as his offering a male goat without defect. ²⁴He is to lay his hand on the goat's head and slaughter it at the place where the burnt offering is slaughtered before the LORD. It is a sin offering. ²⁵Then the priest shall take some of the blood of the sin offering with his finger and put it on the horns of the altar of burnt offering and pour out the rest of the blood at the base of the altar. ²⁶He shall burn all the fat on the altar as he burned the fat of the fellowship offering. In this way the priest will make atonement for the leader's sin, and he will be forgiven.

²⁷"'If any member of the community sins unintentionally and does what is forbidden in any of the LORD's commands, when they realize their guilt ²⁸and the sin they have committed becomes known, they must bring as their offering for the sin they committed a female goat without defect. ²⁹They are to lay their hand on the head of the sin offering and slaughter it at the place of the burnt offering. ³⁰Then the priest is to take some of the blood with his finger and put it on the horns of the altar of burnt offering and pour out the rest of the blood at the base of the altar. ³¹They shall remove all the fat, just as the fat is removed from the fellowship offering, and the priest shall burn it on the altar as an aroma pleasing to the LORD. In this way the priest will make atonement for them, and they will be forgiven.

³²"'If someone brings a lamb as their sin offering, they are to bring a female without defect. ³³They are to lay their hand on its head and slaughter it for a sin offering at the place where the burnt offering is slaughtered. ³⁴Then the priest shall take some of the blood of the sin offering with

his finger and put it on the horns of the altar of burnt offering and pour out the rest of the blood at the base of the altar. ³⁵They shall remove all the fat, just as the fat is removed from the lamb of the fellowship offering, and the priest shall burn it on the altar on top of the food offerings presented to the LORD. In this way the priest will make atonement for them for the sin they have committed, and they will be forgiven.

5 "'If anyone sins because they do not speak up when they hear a public charge to testify regarding something they have seen or learned about, they will be held responsible.

²"'If anyone becomes aware that they are guilty—if they unwittingly touch anything ceremonially unclean (whether the carcass of an unclean animal, wild or domestic, or of any unclean creature that moves along the ground) and they are unaware that they have become unclean, but then they come to realize their guilt; ³or if they touch human uncleanness (anything that would make them unclean) even though they are unaware of it, but then they learn of it and realize their guilt; ⁴or if anyone thoughtlessly takes an oath to do anything, whether good or evil (in any matter one might carelessly swear about) even though they are unaware of it, but then they learn of it and realize their guilt— ⁵when anyone becomes aware that they are guilty in any of these matters, they must confess in what way they have sinned. ⁶As a penalty for the sin they have committed, they must bring to the LORD a female lamb or goat from the flock as a sin offering*ᵃ*; and the priest shall make atonement for them for their sin.

⁷"'Anyone who cannot afford a lamb is to bring two doves or two young pigeons to the LORD as a penalty for their sin—one for a sin offering and the other for a burnt offering. ⁸They are to bring them to the priest, who shall first offer the one for the sin offering. He is to wring its head from

---

ᵃ 6 Or *purification offering*; here and throughout this chapter its neck, not dividing it completely, [9]and is to splash some of the blood of the sin offering against the side of the altar; the rest of the blood must be drained out at the base of the altar. It is a sin offering. [10]The priest shall then offer the other as a burnt offering in the prescribed way and make atonement for them for the sin they have committed, and they will be forgiven.

[11]"'If, however, they cannot afford two doves or two young pigeons, they are to bring as an offering for their sin a tenth of an ephah[a] of the finest flour for a sin offering. They must not put olive oil or incense on it, because it is a sin offering. [12]They are to bring it to the priest, who shall take a handful of it as a memorial[b] portion and burn it on the altar on top of the food offerings presented to the Lord. It is a sin offering. [13]In this way the priest will make atonement for them for any of these sins they have committed, and they will be forgiven. The rest of the offering will belong to the priest, as in the case of the grain offering.'"

The Guilt Offering

[14]The Lord said to Moses: [15]"When anyone is unfaithful to the Lord by sinning unintentionally in regard to any of the Lord's holy things, they are to bring to the Lord as a penalty a ram from the flock, one without defect and of the proper value in silver, according to the sanctuary shekel.[c] It is a guilt offering. [16]They must make restitution for what they have failed to do in regard to the holy things, pay an additional penalty of a fifth of its value and give it all to the priest. The priest will make atonement for them with the ram as a guilt offering, and they will be forgiven.

[17]"If anyone sins and does what is forbidden in any of the Lord's commands, even though they do not know it, they are guilty and will be held responsible. [18]They are to bring to the priest as a guilt offering a ram from the flock, one without defect and of the proper value. In this way the priest will make atonement for them for the wrong they have committed uninten-

tionally, and they will be forgiven. [19]It is a guilt offering; they have been guilty of[d] wrongdoing against the Lord.'"

6 [e] The Lord said to Moses: [2]"If anyone sins and is unfaithful to the Lord by deceiving a neighbor about something entrusted to them or left in their care or about something stolen, or if they cheat their neighbor, [3]or if they find lost property and lie about it, or if they swear falsely about any such sin that people may commit— [4]when they sin in any of these ways and realize their guilt, they must return what they have stolen or taken by extortion, or what was entrusted to them, or the lost property they found, [5]or whatever it was they swore falsely about. They must make restitution in full, add a fifth of the value to it and give it all to the owner on the day they present their guilt offering. [6]And as a penalty they must bring to the priest, that is, to the Lord, their guilt offering, a ram from the flock, one without defect and of the proper value. [7]In this way the priest will make atonement for them before the Lord, and they will be forgiven for any of the things they did that made them guilty."

The Burnt Offering

[8]The Lord said to Moses: [9]"Give Aaron and his sons this command: 'These are the regulations for the burnt offering: The burnt offering is to remain on the altar hearth throughout the night, till morning, and the fire must be kept burning on the altar. [10]The priest shall then put on his linen clothes, with linen undergarments next to his body, and shall remove the ashes of the burnt offering that the fire has consumed on the altar and place them beside the altar. [11]Then he is to take off these clothes and put on others, and carry the ashes outside the camp to a place that is ceremonially clean. [12]The fire on the

---

[a] 11 That is, probably about 3 1/2 pounds or about 1.6 kilograms   [b] 12 Or representative
[c] 15 That is, about 2/5 ounce or about 12 grams
[d] 19 Or offering; atonement has been made for their
[e] In Hebrew texts 6:1-7 is numbered 5:20-26, and 6:8-30 is numbered 6:1-23.

altar must be kept burning; it must not go out. Every morning the priest is to add firewood and arrange the burnt offering on the fire and burn the fat of the fellowship offerings on it. ¹³The fire must be kept burning on the altar continuously; it must not go out.

The Grain Offering

¹⁴"'These are the regulations for the grain offering: Aaron's sons are to bring it before the Lord, in front of the altar. ¹⁵The priest is to take a handful of the finest flour and some olive oil, together with all the incense on the grain offering, and burn the memorial[a] portion on the altar as an aroma pleasing to the Lord. ¹⁶Aaron and his sons shall eat the rest of it, but it is to be eaten without yeast in the sanctuary area; they are to eat it in the courtyard of the tent of meeting. ¹⁷It must not be baked with yeast; I have given it as their share of the food offerings presented to me. Like the sin offering[b] and the guilt offering, it is most holy. ¹⁸Any male descendant of Aaron may eat it. For all generations to come it is his perpetual share of the food offerings presented to the Lord. Whatever touches them will become holy.[c]'"

¹⁹The Lord also said to Moses, ²⁰"This is the offering Aaron and his sons are to bring to the Lord on the day he[d] is anointed: a tenth of an ephah[e] of the finest flour as a regular grain offering, half of it in the morning and half in the evening. ²¹It must be prepared with oil on a griddle; bring it well-mixed and present the grain offering broken[f] in pieces as an aroma pleasing to the Lord. ²²The son who is to succeed him as anointed priest shall prepare it. It is the Lord's perpetual share and is to be burned completely. ²³Every grain offering of a priest shall be burned completely; it must not be eaten."

The Sin Offering

²⁴The Lord said to Moses, ²⁵"Say to Aaron and his sons: 'These are the regulations for the sin offering: The sin offering is to be slaughtered before the Lord in the place the burnt offering is slaughtered; it is

most holy. ²⁶The priest who offers it shall eat it; it is to be eaten in the sanctuary area, in the courtyard of the tent of meeting. ²⁷Whatever touches any of the flesh will become holy, and if any of the blood is spattered on a garment, you must wash it in the sanctuary area. ²⁸The clay pot the meat is cooked in must be broken; but if it is cooked in a bronze pot, the pot is to be scoured and rinsed with water. ²⁹Any male in a priest's family may eat it; it is most holy. ³⁰But any sin offering whose blood is brought into the tent of meeting to make atonement in the Holy Place must not be eaten; it must be burned up.

The Guilt Offering

7 "'These are the regulations for the guilt offering, which is most holy: ²The guilt offering is to be slaughtered in the place where the burnt offering is slaughtered, and its blood is to be splashed against the sides of the altar. ³All its fat shall be offered: the fat tail and the fat that covers the internal organs, ⁴both kidneys with the fat on them near the loins, and the long lobe of the liver, which is to be removed with the kidneys. ⁵The priest shall burn them on the altar as a food offering presented to the Lord. It is a guilt offering. ⁶Any male in a priest's family may eat it, but it must be eaten in the sanctuary area; it is most holy.

⁷"'The same law applies to both the sin offering[g] and the guilt offering: They belong to the priest who makes atonement with them. ⁸The priest who offers a burnt offering for anyone may keep its hide for himself. ⁹Every grain offering baked in an oven or cooked in a pan or on a griddle belongs to the priest who offers it, ¹⁰and every grain offering, whether mixed with olive oil or dry, belongs equally to all the sons of Aaron.

[a] 15 Or representative   [b] 17 Or purification offering; also in verses 25 and 30
[c] 18 Or Whoever touches them must be holy; similarly in verse 27   [d] 20 Or each
[e] 20 That is, probably about 3 1/2 pounds or about 1.6 kilograms   [f] 21 The meaning of the Hebrew for this word is uncertain.
[g] 7 Or purification offering; also in verse 37

The Fellowship Offering

11 "'These are the regulations for the fellowship offering anyone may present to the LORD:

12 "'If they offer it as an expression of thankfulness, then along with this thank offering they are to offer thick loaves made without yeast and with olive oil mixed in, thin loaves made without yeast and brushed with oil, and thick loaves of the finest flour well-kneaded and with oil mixed in. 13 Along with their fellowship offering of thanksgiving they are to present an offering with thick loaves of bread made with yeast. 14 They are to bring one of each kind as an offering, a contribution to the LORD; it belongs to the priest who splashes the blood of the fellowship offering against the altar. 15 The meat of their fellowship offering of thanksgiving must be eaten on the day it is offered; they must leave none of it till morning.

16 "'If, however, their offering is the result of a vow or is a freewill offering, the sacrifice shall be eaten on the day they offer it, but anything left over may be eaten on the next day. 17 Any meat of the sacrifice left over till the third day must be burned up. 18 If any meat of the fellowship offering is eaten on the third day, the one who offered it will not be accepted. It will not be reckoned to their credit, for it has become impure; the person who eats any of it will be held responsible.

19 "'Meat that touches anything ceremonially unclean must not be eaten; it must be burned up. As for other meat, anyone ceremonially clean may eat it. 20 But if anyone who is unclean eats any meat of the fellowship offering belonging to the LORD, they must be cut off from their people. 21 Anyone who touches something unclean—whether human uncleanness or an unclean animal or any unclean creature that moves along the ground[a]—and then eats any of the meat of the fellowship offering belonging to the LORD must be cut off from their people.'"

Eating Fat and Blood Forbidden

22 The LORD said to Moses, 23 "Say to the Israelites: 'Do not eat any of the fat of cattle, sheep or goats. 24 The fat of an animal found dead or torn by wild animals may be used for any other purpose, but you must not eat it. 25 Anyone who eats the fat of an animal from which a food offering may be[b] presented to the LORD must be cut off from their people. 26 And wherever

---

[a] 21 A few Hebrew manuscripts, Samaritan Pentateuch, Syriac and Targum (see 5:2); most Hebrew manuscripts *any unclean, detestable thing*
[b] 25 Or *offering is*

Leviticus 7:1–38

God's rules don't change—usually.

Flipping through the Old Testament might land you in long lists of strange-sounding rules. But God made those rules with a purpose—to teach sinful human beings to serve and obey him. Some rules concern ceremonial parts of religion. Strict regulations about eating and sacrifices, for example, taught the Israelites that the Lord was holy and deserved awe-filled obedience (see Leviticus 10:10). Other rules detailed the moral parts of faith, the rights and wrongs of living. When Jesus came and died on the cross for sin, he did away with the need for old ceremonies of sacrifices and offerings. Because he was the ultimate sacrifice that did away with the old system, those rules don't apply to Christians today (see Hebrews 10:1–25). But we still follow commands that tell us how to fully love God and people. Those really important rules never change.

Think: Why do Christians not follow some Old Testament commands? Which ones?

ROCK SOLID truths

you live, you must not eat the blood of any bird or animal. 27 Anyone who eats blood must be cut off from their people.'"

The Priests' Share

28 The Lord said to Moses, 29 "Say to the Israelites: 'Anyone who brings a fellowship offering to the Lord is to bring part of it as their sacrifice to the Lord. 30 With their own hands they are to present the food offering to the Lord; they are to bring the fat, together with the breast, and wave the breast before the Lord as a wave offering. 31 The priest shall burn the fat on the altar, but the breast belongs to Aaron and his sons. 32 You are to give the right thigh of your fellowship offerings to the priest as a contribution. 33 The son of Aaron who offers the blood and the fat of the fellowship offering shall have the right thigh as his share. 34 From the fellowship offerings of the Israelites, I have taken the breast that is waved and the thigh that is presented and have given them to Aaron the priest and his sons as their perpetual share from the Israelites.'"

35 This is the portion of the food offerings presented to the Lord that were allotted to Aaron and his sons on the day they were presented to serve the Lord as priests. 36 On the day they were anointed, the Lord commanded that the Israelites give this to them as their perpetual share for the generations to come.

37 These, then, are the regulations for the burnt offering, the grain offering, the sin offering, the guilt offering, the ordination offering and the fellowship offering, 38 which the Lord gave Moses at Mount Sinai in the Desert of Sinai on the day he commanded the Israelites to bring their offerings to the Lord.

The Ordination of Aaron and His Sons

8 The Lord said to Moses, 2 "Bring Aaron and his sons, their garments, the anointing oil, the bull for the sin offering,*a* the two rams and the basket containing bread made without yeast, 3 and gather the entire assembly at the entrance to the tent of meeting." 4 Moses did as the Lord commanded him, and the assembly gathered at the entrance to the tent of meeting.

5 Moses said to the assembly, "This is what the Lord has commanded to be done." 6 Then Moses brought Aaron and his sons forward and washed them with water. 7 He put the tunic on Aaron, tied the sash around him, clothed him with the robe and put the ephod on him. He also fastened the ephod with a decorative waistband, which he tied around him. 8 He placed the breastpiece on him and put the Urim and Thummim in the breastpiece. 9 Then he placed the turban on Aaron's head and set the gold plate, the sacred emblem, on the front of it, as the Lord commanded Moses.

10 Then Moses took the anointing oil and anointed the tabernacle and everything in it, and so consecrated them. 11 He sprinkled some of the oil on the altar seven times, anointing the altar and all its utensils and the basin with its stand, to consecrate them. 12 He poured some of the anointing oil on Aaron's head and anointed him to consecrate him. 13 Then he brought Aaron's sons forward, put tunics on them, tied sashes around them and fastened caps on them, as the Lord commanded Moses.

14 He then presented the bull for the sin offering, and Aaron and his sons laid their hands on its head. 15 Moses slaughtered the bull and took some of the blood, and with his finger he put it on all the horns of the altar to purify the altar. He poured out the rest of the blood at the base of the altar. So he consecrated it to make atonement for it. 16 Moses also took all the fat around the internal organs, the long lobe of the liver, and both kidneys and their fat, and burned it on the altar. 17 But the bull with its hide and its flesh and its intestines he burned up outside the camp, as the Lord commanded Moses.

18 He then presented the ram for the burnt offering, and Aaron and his sons laid their hands on its head. 19 Then Moses slaughtered the ram and splashed the

---

a 2 Or *purification offering*; also in verse 14

blood against the sides of the altar. ²⁰He cut the ram into pieces and burned the head, the pieces and the fat. ²¹He washed the internal organs and the legs with water and burned the whole ram on the altar. It was a burnt offering, a pleasing aroma, a food offering presented to the Lord, as the Lord commanded Moses.

²²He then presented the other ram, the ram for the ordination, and Aaron and his sons laid their hands on its head. ²³Moses slaughtered the ram and took some of its blood and put it on the lobe of Aaron's right ear, on the thumb of his right hand and on the big toe of his right foot. ²⁴Moses also brought Aaron's sons forward and put some of the blood on the lobes of their right ears, on the thumbs of their right hands and on the big toes of their right feet. Then he splashed blood against the sides of the altar. ²⁵After that, he took the fat, the fat tail, all the fat around the internal organs, the long lobe of the liver, both kidneys and their fat and the right thigh. ²⁶And from the basket of bread made without yeast, which was before the Lord, he took one thick loaf, one thick loaf with olive oil mixed in, and one thin loaf, and he put these on the fat portions and on the right thigh. ²⁷He put all these in the hands of Aaron and his sons, and they waved them before the Lord as a wave offering. ²⁸Then Moses took them from their hands and burned them on the altar on top of the burnt offering as an ordination offering, a pleasing aroma, a food offering presented to the Lord. ²⁹Moses also took the breast, which was his share of the ordination ram, and waved it before the Lord as a wave offering, as the Lord commanded Moses.

³⁰Then Moses took some of the anointing oil and some of the blood from the altar and sprinkled them on Aaron and his garments and on his sons and their garments. So he consecrated Aaron and his garments and his sons and their garments.

³¹Moses then said to Aaron and his sons, "Cook the meat at the entrance to the tent of meeting and eat it there with the bread from the basket of ordination

offerings, as I was commanded: 'Aaron and his sons are to eat it.' ³²Then burn up the rest of the meat and the bread. ³³Do not leave the entrance to the tent of meeting for seven days, until the days of your ordination are completed, for your ordination will last seven days. ³⁴What has been done today was commanded by the Lord to make atonement for you. ³⁵You must stay at the entrance to the tent of meeting day and night for seven days and do what the Lord requires, so you will not die; for that is what I have been commanded."

³⁶So Aaron and his sons did everything the Lord commanded through Moses.

The Priests Begin Their Ministry

9 On the eighth day Moses summoned Aaron and his sons and the elders of Israel. ²He said to Aaron, "Take a bull calf for your sin offering[a] and a ram for your burnt offering, both without defect, and present them before the Lord. ³Then say to the Israelites: 'Take a male goat for a sin offering, a calf and a lamb—both a year old and without defect—for a burnt offering, ⁴and an ox[b] and a ram for a fellowship offering to sacrifice before the Lord, together with a grain offering mixed with olive oil. For today the Lord will appear to you.'"

⁵They took the things Moses commanded to the front of the tent of meeting, and the entire assembly came near and stood before the Lord. ⁶Then Moses said, "This is what the Lord has commanded you to do, so that the glory of the Lord may appear to you."

⁷Moses said to Aaron, "Come to the altar and sacrifice your sin offering and your burnt offering and make atonement for yourself and the people; sacrifice the offering that is for the people and make atonement for them, as the Lord has commanded."

⁸So Aaron came to the altar and slaughtered the calf as a sin offering for himself. ⁹His sons brought the blood to him, and

---

[a] 2 Or *purification offering*; here and throughout this chapter   [b] 4 The Hebrew word can refer to either male or female; also in verses 18 and 19.

he dipped his finger into the blood and put it on the horns of the altar; the rest of the blood he poured out at the base of the altar. ¹⁰On the altar he burned the fat, the kidneys and the long lobe of the liver from the sin offering, as the LORD commanded Moses; ¹¹the flesh and the hide he burned up outside the camp.

¹²Then he slaughtered the burnt offering. His sons handed him the blood, and he splashed it against the sides of the altar. ¹³They handed him the burnt offering piece by piece, including the head, and he burned them on the altar. ¹⁴He washed the internal organs and the legs and burned them on top of the burnt offering on the altar.

¹⁵Aaron then brought the offering that was for the people. He took the goat for the people's sin offering and slaughtered it and offered it for a sin offering as he did with the first one.

¹⁶He brought the burnt offering and offered it in the prescribed way. ¹⁷He also brought the grain offering, took a handful of it and burned it on the altar in addition to the morning's burnt offering.

¹⁸He slaughtered the ox and the ram as the fellowship offering for the people. His sons handed him the blood, and he splashed it against the sides of the altar. ¹⁹But the fat portions of the ox and the ram—the fat tail, the layer of fat, the kidneys and the long lobe of the liver—²⁰these they laid on the breasts, and then Aaron burned the fat on the altar. ²¹Aaron waved the breasts and the right thigh before the LORD as a wave offering, as Moses commanded.

²²Then Aaron lifted his hands toward the people and blessed them. And having sacrificed the sin offering, the burnt offering and the fellowship offering, he stepped down.

²³Moses and Aaron then went into the tent of meeting. When they came out, they blessed the people; and the glory of the LORD appeared to all the people. ²⁴Fire came out from the presence of the LORD and consumed the burnt offering and the fat portions on the altar. And

when all the people saw it, they shouted for joy and fell facedown.

The Death of Nadab and Abihu

10 Aaron's sons Nadab and Abihu took their censers, put fire in them and added incense; and they offered unauthorized fire before the LORD, contrary to his command. ²So fire came out from the presence of the LORD and consumed them, and they died before the LORD. ³Moses then said to Aaron, "This is what the LORD spoke of when he said:

"'Among those who approach me
    I will be proved holy;
in the sight of all the people
    I will be honored.'"

Aaron remained silent.

ROCK SOLID
promises

"In the sight of all the people I will be honored." Leviticus 10:3

God doesn't tolerate open disrespect forever. When he shows his power in plain sight, he fills people with awe.

---

⁴Moses summoned Mishael and Elzaphan, sons of Aaron's uncle Uzziel, and said to them, "Come here; carry your cousins outside the camp, away from the front of the sanctuary." ⁵So they came and carried them, still in their tunics, outside the camp, as Moses ordered.

⁶Then Moses said to Aaron and his sons Eleazar and Ithamar, "Do not let your hair become unkempt^a and do not tear your clothes, or you will die and the

---

^a 6 Or *Do not uncover your heads*

128

LORD will be angry with the whole community. But your relatives, all the Israelites, may mourn for those the LORD has destroyed by fire. ⁷Do not leave the entrance to the tent of meeting or you will die, because the LORD's anointing oil is on you." So they did as Moses said.

⁸Then the LORD said to Aaron, ⁹"You and your sons are not to drink wine or other fermented drink whenever you go into the tent of meeting, or you will die. This is a lasting ordinance for the generations to come, ¹⁰so that you can distinguish between the holy and the common, between the unclean and the clean, ¹¹and so you can teach the Israelites all the decrees the LORD has given them through Moses."

¹²Moses said to Aaron and his remaining sons, Eleazar and Ithamar, "Take the grain offering left over from the food offerings prepared without yeast and presented to the LORD and eat it beside the altar, for it is most holy. ¹³Eat it in the sanctuary area, because it is your share and your sons' share of the food offerings presented to the LORD; for so I have been commanded. ¹⁴But you and your sons and your daughters may eat the breast that was waved and the thigh that was presented. Eat them in a ceremonially clean place; they have been given to you and your children as your share of the Israelites' fellowship offerings. ¹⁵The thigh that was presented and the breast that was waved must be brought with the fat portions of the food offerings, to be waved before the LORD as a wave offering. This will be the perpetual share for you and your children, as the LORD has commanded."

¹⁶When Moses inquired about the goat of the sin offering[a] and found that it had been burned up, he was angry with Eleazar and Ithamar, Aaron's remaining sons, and asked, ¹⁷"Why didn't you eat the sin offering in the sanctuary area? It is most holy; it was given to you to take away the guilt of the community by making atonement for them before the LORD. ¹⁸Since its blood was not taken into the Holy Place, you should have eaten the goat in the sanctuary area, as I commanded."

¹⁹Aaron replied to Moses, "Today they sacrificed their sin offering and their burnt offering before the LORD, but such things as this have happened to me. Would the LORD have been pleased if I had eaten the sin offering today?" ²⁰When Moses heard this, he was satisfied.

Clean and Unclean Food

11 The LORD said to Moses and Aaron, ²"Say to the Israelites: 'Of all the animals that live on land, these are the ones you may eat: ³You may eat any animal that has a divided hoof and that chews the cud.

⁴"There are some that only chew the cud or only have a divided hoof, but you must not eat them. The camel, though it chews the cud, does not have a divided hoof; it is ceremonially unclean for you. ⁵The hyrax, though it chews the cud, does not have a divided hoof; it is unclean for you. ⁶The rabbit, though it chews the cud, does not have a divided hoof; it is unclean for you. ⁷And the pig, though it has a divided hoof, does not chew the cud; it is unclean for you. ⁸You must not eat their meat or touch their carcasses; they are unclean for you.

⁹"Of all the creatures living in the water of the seas and the streams you may eat any that have fins and scales. ¹⁰But all creatures in the seas or streams that do not have fins and scales—whether among all the swarming things or among all the other living creatures in the water—you are to regard as unclean. ¹¹And since you are to regard them as unclean, you must not eat their meat; you must regard their carcasses as unclean. ¹²Anything living in the water that does not have fins and scales is to be regarded as unclean by you.

¹³"These are the birds you are to regard as unclean and not eat because they are unclean: the eagle,[b] the vulture, the black vulture, ¹⁴the red kite, any kind of black kite, ¹⁵any kind of raven, ¹⁶the horned

---

[a] 16 Or purification offering; also in verses 17 and 19   [b] 13 The precise identification of some of the birds, insects and animals in this chapter is uncertain.

owl, the screech owl, the gull, any kind of hawk, ¹⁷the little owl, the cormorant, the great owl, ¹⁸the white owl, the desert owl, the osprey, ¹⁹the stork, any kind of heron, the hoopoe and the bat.

²⁰"'All flying insects that walk on all fours are to be regarded as unclean by you. ²¹There are, however, some flying insects that walk on all fours that you may eat: those that have jointed legs for hopping on the ground. ²²Of these you may eat any kind of locust, katydid, cricket or grasshopper. ²³But all other flying insects that have four legs you are to regard as unclean.

²⁴"'You will make yourselves unclean by these; whoever touches their carcasses will be unclean till evening. ²⁵Whoever picks up one of their carcasses must wash their clothes, and they will be unclean till evening.

²⁶"'Every animal that does not have a divided hoof or that does not chew the cud is unclean for you; whoever touches the carcass of any of them will be unclean. ²⁷Of all the animals that walk on all fours, those that walk on their paws are unclean for you; whoever touches their carcasses will be unclean till evening. ²⁸Anyone who picks up their carcasses must wash their clothes, and they will be unclean till evening. These animals are unclean for you.

²⁹"'Of the animals that move along the ground, these are unclean for you: the weasel, the rat, any kind of great lizard, ³⁰the gecko, the monitor lizard, the wall lizard, the skink and the chameleon. ³¹Of all those that move along the ground, these are unclean for you. Whoever touches them when they are dead will be unclean till evening. ³²When one of them dies and falls on something, that article, whatever its use, will be unclean, whether it is made of wood, cloth, hide or sackcloth. Put it in water; it will be unclean till evening, and then it will be clean. ³³If one of them falls into a clay pot, everything in it will be unclean, and you must break the pot. ³⁴Any food you are allowed to eat that has come into contact with water from any such pot is unclean, and any liquid that is drunk from such a pot is unclean. ³⁵Any-

thing that one of their carcasses falls on becomes unclean; an oven or cooking pot must be broken up. They are unclean, and you are to regard them as unclean. ³⁶A spring, however, or a cistern for collecting water remains clean, but anyone who touches one of these carcasses is unclean. ³⁷If a carcass falls on any seeds that are to be planted, they remain clean. ³⁸But if water has been put on the seed and a carcass falls on it, it is unclean for you.

³⁹"'If an animal that you are allowed to eat dies, anyone who touches its carcass will be unclean till evening. ⁴⁰Anyone who eats some of its carcass must wash their clothes, and they will be unclean till evening. Anyone who picks up the carcass must wash their clothes, and they will be unclean till evening.

⁴¹"'Every creature that moves along the ground is to be regarded as unclean; it is not to be eaten. ⁴²You are not to eat any creature that moves along the ground, whether it moves on its belly or walks on all fours or on many feet; it is unclean. ⁴³Do not defile yourselves by any of these creatures. Do not make yourselves unclean by means of them or be made unclean by them. ⁴⁴I am the LORD your God; consecrate yourselves and be holy, because I am holy. Do not make yourselves unclean by any creature that moves along the ground. ⁴⁵I am the LORD, who brought you up out of Egypt to be your God; therefore be holy, because I am holy.

⁴⁶"'These are the regulations concerning animals, birds, every living thing that moves about in the water and every creature that moves along the ground. ⁴⁷You must distinguish between the unclean and the clean, between living creatures that may be eaten and those that may not be eaten.'"

Purification After Childbirth

12 The LORD said to Moses, ²"Say to the Israelites: 'A woman who becomes pregnant and gives birth to a son will be ceremonially unclean for seven days, just as she is unclean during her monthly period.

UNSHAKEN God

Leviticus 11:45

God is holy.

You have never faced a challenge like this one: "Be holy," God says, "because I am holy" (Leviticus 11:45). God's holiness means that he is utterly perfect and whole, completely pure and free from evil. Our holiness means we are completely dedicated to him, sharing more and more in his character. So how are you supposed to do that? The New Testament fills out how you begin to reflect God's holiness. Through the death of Jesus, the Lord forgives you and wipes you clean from sin. And he starts a process of changing you so you can think and act like him. You can't ever be holy on your own, but God constantly makes you more and more like him.

So ... Where do you see God's holiness happening in your life?

³On the eighth day the boy is to be circumcised. ⁴Then the woman must wait thirty-three days to be purified from her bleeding. She must not touch anything sacred or go to the sanctuary until the days of her purification are over. ⁵If she gives birth to a daughter, for two weeks the woman will be unclean, as during her period. Then she must wait sixty-six days to be purified from her bleeding.

⁶"When the days of her purification for a son or daughter are over, she is to bring to the priest at the entrance to the tent of meeting a year-old lamb for a burnt offering and a young pigeon or a dove for a sin offering.ᵃ ⁷He shall offer them before the Lord to make atonement for her, and then she will be ceremonially clean from her flow of blood.

"'These are the regulations for the woman who gives birth to a boy or a girl. ⁸But if she cannot afford a lamb, she is to bring two doves or two young pigeons, one for a burnt offering and the other for a sin offering. In this way the priest will make atonement for her, and she will be clean.'"

Regulations About Defiling Skin Diseases

13 The Lord said to Moses and Aaron, ²"When anyone has a swelling or a rash or a shiny spot on their skin that may be a defiling skin disease,ᵇ they must be brought to Aaron the priest or to one of his sonsᶜ who is a priest. ³The priest is to examine the sore on the skin, and if the hair in the sore has turned white and the sore appears to be more than skin deep, it is a defiling skin disease. When the priest examines that person, he shall pronounce them ceremonially unclean. ⁴If the shiny spot on the skin is white but does not appear to be more than skin deep and the hair in it has not turned white, the priest is to isolate the affected person for seven days. ⁵On the seventh day the priest is to examine them, and if he sees that the sore is unchanged and has not spread in the skin, he is to isolate them for another seven days. ⁶On the seventh day the priest is to examine them again, and if the sore has faded and has not spread in the skin, the priest shall pronounce them clean; it is only a rash. They must wash their clothes, and they will be clean. ⁷But if the rash does spread in their skin after they have shown themselves to the priest to be pronounced clean, they must appear before the priest again. ⁸The priest is to examine that person, and if the rash has spread in the skin, he shall pronounce them unclean; it is a defiling skin disease.

⁹"When anyone has a defiling skin disease, they must be brought to the priest. ¹⁰The priest is to examine them, and if there is a white swelling in the skin that has turned the hair white and if there is raw flesh in the swelling, ¹¹it is a chronic

---

ᵃ 6 Or *purification offering*; also in verse 8
ᵇ 2 The Hebrew word for *defiling skin disease*, traditionally translated "leprosy," was used for various diseases affecting the skin; here and throughout verses 3-46.   ᶜ 2 Or *descendants*

skin disease and the priest shall pronounce them unclean. He is not to isolate them, because they are already unclean.

¹²"If the disease breaks out all over their skin and, so far as the priest can see, it covers all the skin of the affected person from head to foot, ¹³the priest is to examine them, and if the disease has covered their whole body, he shall pronounce them clean. Since it has all turned white, they are clean. ¹⁴But whenever raw flesh appears on them, they will be unclean. ¹⁵When the priest sees the raw flesh, he shall pronounce them unclean. The raw flesh is unclean; they have a defiling disease. ¹⁶If the raw flesh changes and turns white, they must go to the priest. ¹⁷The priest is to examine them, and if the sores have turned white, the priest shall pronounce the affected person clean; then they will be clean.

¹⁸"When someone has a boil on their skin and it heals, ¹⁹and in the place where the boil was, a white swelling or reddish-white spot appears, they must present themselves to the priest. ²⁰The priest is to examine it, and if it appears to be more than skin deep and the hair in it has turned white, the priest shall pronounce that person unclean. It is a defiling skin disease that has broken out where the boil was. ²¹But if, when the priest examines it, there is no white hair in it and it is not more than skin deep and has faded, then the priest is to isolate them for seven days. ²²If it is spreading in the skin, the priest shall pronounce them unclean; it is a defiling disease. ²³But if the spot is unchanged and has not spread, it is only a scar from the boil, and the priest shall pronounce them clean.

²⁴"When someone has a burn on their skin and a reddish-white or white spot appears in the raw flesh of the burn, ²⁵the priest is to examine the spot, and if the hair in it has turned white, and it appears to be more than skin deep, it is a defiling disease that has broken out in the burn. The priest shall pronounce them unclean; it is a defiling skin disease. ²⁶But if the priest examines it and there is no white hair in the spot and if it is not more than skin deep and has faded, then the priest is to isolate

them for seven days. ²⁷On the seventh day the priest is to examine that person, and if it is spreading in the skin, the priest shall pronounce them unclean; it is a defiling skin disease. ²⁸If, however, the spot is unchanged and has not spread in the skin but has faded, it is a swelling from the burn, and the priest shall pronounce them clean; it is only a scar from the burn.

²⁹"If a man or woman has a sore on their head or chin, ³⁰the priest is to examine the sore, and if it appears to be more than skin deep and the hair in it is yellow and thin, the priest shall pronounce them unclean; it is a defiling skin disease on the head or chin. ³¹But if, when the priest examines the sore, it does not seem to be more than skin deep and there is no black hair in it, then the priest is to isolate the affected person for seven days. ³²On the seventh day the priest is to examine the sore, and if it has not spread and there is no yellow hair in it and it does not appear to be more than skin deep, ³³then the man or woman must shave themselves, except for the affected area, and the priest is to keep them isolated another seven days. ³⁴On the seventh day the priest is to examine the sore, and if it has not spread in the skin and appears to be no more than skin deep, the priest shall pronounce them clean. They must wash their clothes, and they will be clean. ³⁵But if the sore does spread in the skin after they are pronounced clean, ³⁶the priest is to examine them, and if he finds that the sore has spread in the skin, he does not need to look for yellow hair; they are unclean. ³⁷If, however, the sore is unchanged so far as the priest can see, and if black hair has grown in it, the affected person is healed. They are clean, and the priest shall pronounce them clean.

³⁸"When a man or woman has white spots on the skin, ³⁹the priest is to examine them, and if the spots are dull white, it is a harmless rash that has broken out on the skin; they are clean.

⁴⁰"A man who has lost his hair and is bald is clean. ⁴¹If he has lost his hair from the front of his scalp and has a bald forehead, he is clean. ⁴²But if he has a reddish-

white sore on his bald head or forehead, it is a defiling disease breaking out on his head or forehead. ⁴³The priest is to examine him, and if the swollen sore on his head or forehead is reddish-white like a defiling skin disease, ⁴⁴the man is diseased and is unclean. The priest shall pronounce him unclean because of the sore on his head.

⁴⁵"Anyone with such a defiling disease must wear torn clothes, let their hair be unkempt,ᵃ cover the lower part of their face and cry out, 'Unclean! Unclean!' ⁴⁶As long as they have the disease they remain unclean. They must live alone; they must live outside the camp.

Regulations About Defiling Molds

⁴⁷"As for any fabric that is spoiled with a defiling mold—any woolen or linen clothing, ⁴⁸any woven or knitted material of linen or wool, any leather or anything made of leather— ⁴⁹if the affected area in the fabric, the leather, the woven or knitted material, or any leather article, is greenish or reddish, it is a defiling mold and must be shown to the priest. ⁵⁰The priest is to examine the affected area and isolate the article for seven days. ⁵¹On the seventh day he is to examine it, and if the mold has spread in the fabric, the woven or knitted material, or the leather, whatever its use, it is a persistent defiling mold, the article is unclean. ⁵²He must burn the fabric, the woven or knitted material of wool or linen, or any leather article that has been spoiled; because the defiling mold is persistent, the article must be burned.

⁵³"But if, when the priest examines it, the mold has not spread in the fabric, the woven or knitted material, or the leather article, ⁵⁴he shall order that the spoiled article be washed. Then he is to isolate it for another seven days. ⁵⁵After the article has been washed, the priest is to examine it again, and if the mold has not changed its appearance, even though it has not spread, it is unclean. Burn it, no matter which side of the fabric has been spoiled. ⁵⁶If, when the priest examines it, the mold has faded after the article has been washed, he is to tear the spoiled part out of the fabric, the leather, or the woven or knitted material. ⁵⁷But if it reappears in the fabric, in the woven or knitted material, or in the leather article, it is a spreading mold; whatever has the mold must be burned. ⁵⁸Any fabric, woven or knitted material, or any leather article that has been washed and is rid of the mold, must be washed again. Then it will be clean."

⁵⁹These are the regulations concerning defiling molds in woolen or linen clothing,

---

ᵃ 45 Or *clothes, uncover their head*

Leviticus 13:1–59

The Pentateuch lays down the law.

A glance at the table of contents of your Bible shows an obvious division into two parts, the Old and New Testaments. Yet there are other divisions in the Bible you might spot if you read the Bible from front to back. The first five books of the Old Testament are called the "Pentateuch," from two Greek words meaning "five" and "scroll case." These books outline early human history and the progress of the Israelites toward the promised land. Yet the books of the Pentateuch are best known as "books of the law," because this is where God lays out his rules for right living. He utters commands concerning everything from worship to moral behavior to ceremonial regulations. The law is best summed up in a command found in Deuteronomy 6:5: "Love the LORD your God with all your heart and with all your soul and with all your strength."

Think: What good does the Pentateuch do you today?

ROCK SOLID *truths*

133

woven or knitted material, or any leather article, for pronouncing them clean or unclean.

Cleansing From Defiling Skin Diseases

14 The LORD said to Moses, [2]"These are the regulations for any diseased person at the time of their ceremonial cleansing, when they are brought to the priest: [3]The priest is to go outside the camp and examine them. If they have been healed of their defiling skin disease,[a] [4]the priest shall order that two live clean birds and some cedar wood, scarlet yarn and hyssop be brought for the person to be cleansed. [5]Then the priest shall order that one of the birds be killed over fresh water in a clay pot. [6]He is then to take the live bird and dip it, together with the cedar wood, the scarlet yarn and the hyssop, into the blood of the bird that was killed over the fresh water. [7]Seven times he shall sprinkle the one to be cleansed of the defiling disease, and then pronounce them clean. After that, he is to release the live bird in the open fields.

[8]"The person to be cleansed must wash their clothes, shave off all their hair and bathe with water; then they will be ceremonially clean. After this they may come into the camp, but they must stay outside their tent for seven days. [9]On the seventh day they must shave off all their hair; they must shave their head, their beard, their eyebrows and the rest of their hair. They must wash their clothes and bathe themselves with water, and they will be clean.

[10]"On the eighth day they must bring two male lambs and one ewe lamb a year old, each without defect, along with three-tenths of an ephah[b] of the finest flour mixed with olive oil for a grain offering, and one log[c] of oil. [11]The priest who pronounces them clean shall present both the one to be cleansed and their offerings before the LORD at the entrance to the tent of meeting.

[12]"Then the priest is to take one of the male lambs and offer it as a guilt offering, along with the log of oil; he shall wave them before the LORD as a wave offering. [13]He is to slaughter the lamb in the sanctuary area where the sin offering[d] and the burnt offering are slaughtered. Like the sin offering, the guilt offering belongs to the priest; it is most holy. [14]The priest is to take some of the blood of the guilt offering and put it on the lobe of the right ear of the one to be cleansed, on the thumb of their right hand and on the big toe of their right foot. [15]The priest shall then take some of the log of oil, pour it in the palm of his own left hand, [16]dip his right forefinger into the oil in his palm, and with his finger sprinkle some of it before the LORD seven times. [17]The priest is to put some of the oil remaining in his palm on the lobe of the right ear of the one to be cleansed, on the thumb of their right hand and on the big toe of their right foot, on top of the blood of the guilt offering. [18]The rest of the oil in his palm the priest shall put on the head of the one to be cleansed and make atonement for them before the LORD.

[19]"Then the priest is to sacrifice the sin offering and make atonement for the one to be cleansed from their uncleanness. After that, the priest shall slaughter the burnt offering [20]and offer it on the altar, together with the grain offering, and make atonement for them, and they will be clean.

[21]"If, however, they are poor and cannot afford these, they must take one male lamb as a guilt offering to be waved to make atonement for them, together with a tenth of an ephah[e] of the finest flour mixed with olive oil for a grain offering, a log of oil, [22]and two doves or two young pigeons, such as they can afford, one for a sin offering and the other for a burnt offering.

[a] 3 The Hebrew word for *defiling skin disease*, traditionally translated "leprosy," was used for various diseases affecting the skin; also in verses 7, 32, 54 and 57.   [b] 10 That is, probably about 11 pounds or about 5 kilograms   [c] 10 That is, about 1/3 quart or about 0.3 liter; also in verses 12, 15, 21 and 24   [d] 13 Or *purification offering*; also in verses 19, 22 and 31   [e] 21 That is, probably about 3 1/2 pounds or about 1.6 kilograms

²³"On the eighth day they must bring them for their cleansing to the priest at the entrance to the tent of meeting, before the LORD. ²⁴The priest is to take the lamb for the guilt offering, together with the log of oil, and wave them before the LORD as a wave offering. ²⁵He shall slaughter the lamb for the guilt offering and take some of its blood and put it on the lobe of the right ear of the one to be cleansed, on the thumb of their right hand and on the big toe of their right foot. ²⁶The priest is to pour some of the oil into the palm of his own left hand, ²⁷and with his right forefinger sprinkle some of the oil from his palm seven times before the LORD. ²⁸Some of the oil in his palm he is to put on the same places he put the blood of the guilt offering—on the lobe of the right ear of the one to be cleansed, on the thumb of their right hand and on the big toe of their right foot. ²⁹The rest of the oil in his palm the priest shall put on the head of the one to be cleansed, to make atonement for them before the LORD. ³⁰Then he shall sacrifice the doves or the young pigeons, such as the person can afford, ³¹one as a sin offering and the other as a burnt offering, together with the grain offering. In this way the priest will make atonement before the LORD on behalf of the one to be cleansed."

³²These are the regulations for anyone who has a defiling skin disease and who cannot afford the regular offerings for their cleansing.

Cleansing From Defiling Molds

³³The LORD said to Moses and Aaron, ³⁴"When you enter the land of Canaan, which I am giving you as your possession, and I put a spreading mold in a house in that land, ³⁵the owner of the house must go and tell the priest, 'I have seen something that looks like a defiling mold in my house.' ³⁶The priest is to order the house to be emptied before he goes in to examine the mold, so that nothing in the house will be pronounced unclean. After this the priest is to go in and inspect the house. ³⁷He is to examine the mold on the walls, and if it has greenish or reddish depressions that appear to be deeper than the surface of the wall, ³⁸the priest shall go out the doorway of the house and close it up for seven days. ³⁹On the seventh day the priest shall return to inspect the house. If the mold has spread on the walls, ⁴⁰he is to order that the contaminated stones be torn out and thrown into an unclean place outside the town. ⁴¹He must have all the inside walls of the house scraped and the material that is scraped off dumped into an unclean place outside the town. ⁴²Then they are to take other stones to replace these and take new clay and plaster the house.

⁴³"If the defiling mold reappears in the house after the stones have been torn out and the house scraped and plastered, ⁴⁴the priest is to go and examine it and, if the mold has spread in the house, it is a persistent defiling mold; the house is unclean. ⁴⁵It must be torn down—its stones, timbers and all the plaster—and taken out of the town to an unclean place.

⁴⁶"Anyone who goes into the house while it is closed up will be unclean till evening. ⁴⁷Anyone who sleeps or eats in the house must wash their clothes.

⁴⁸"But if the priest comes to examine it and the mold has not spread after the house has been plastered, he shall pronounce the house clean, because the defiling mold is gone. ⁴⁹To purify the house he is to take two birds and some cedar wood, scarlet yarn and hyssop. ⁵⁰He shall kill one of the birds over fresh water in a clay pot. ⁵¹Then he is to take the cedar wood, the hyssop, the scarlet yarn and the live bird, dip them into the blood of the dead bird and the fresh water, and sprinkle the house seven times. ⁵²He shall purify the house with the bird's blood, the fresh water, the live bird, the cedar wood, the hyssop and the scarlet yarn. ⁵³Then he is to release the live bird in the open fields outside the town. In this way he will make atonement for the house, and it will be clean."

⁵⁴These are the regulations for any defiling skin disease, for a sore, ⁵⁵for defiling

molds in fabric or in a house, ⁵⁶and for a swelling, a rash or a shiny spot, ⁵⁷to determine when something is clean or unclean.

These are the regulations for defiling skin diseases and defiling molds.

Discharges Causing Uncleanness

15 The Lord said to Moses and Aaron, ²"Speak to the Israelites and say to them: 'When any man has an unusual bodily discharge, such a discharge is unclean. ³Whether it continues flowing from his body or is blocked, it will make him unclean. This is how his discharge will bring about uncleanness:

⁴"'Any bed the man with a discharge lies on will be unclean, and anything he sits on will be unclean. ⁵Anyone who touches his bed must wash their clothes and bathe with water, and they will be unclean till evening. ⁶Whoever sits on anything that the man with a discharge sat on must wash their clothes and bathe with water, and they will be unclean till evening.

⁷"'Whoever touches the man who has a discharge must wash their clothes and bathe with water, and they will be unclean till evening.

⁸"'If the man with the discharge spits on anyone who is clean, they must wash their clothes and bathe with water, and they will be unclean till evening.

⁹"'Everything the man sits on when riding will be unclean, ¹⁰and whoever touches any of the things that were under him will be unclean till evening; whoever picks up those things must wash their clothes and bathe with water, and they will be unclean till evening.

¹¹"'Anyone the man with a discharge touches without rinsing his hands with water must wash their clothes and bathe with water, and they will be unclean till evening.

¹²"'A clay pot that the man touches must be broken, and any wooden article is to be rinsed with water.

¹³"'When a man is cleansed from his discharge, he is to count off seven days for his ceremonial cleansing; he must wash his clothes and bathe himself with fresh water, and he will be clean. ¹⁴On the eighth day he must take two doves or two young pigeons and come before the Lord to the entrance to the tent of meeting and give them to the priest. ¹⁵The priest is to sacrifice them, the one for a sin offering*a* and the other for a burnt offering. In this way he will make atonement before the Lord for the man because of his discharge.

¹⁶"'When a man has an emission of semen, he must bathe his whole body with water, and he will be unclean till evening. ¹⁷Any clothing or leather that has semen on it must be washed with water, and it will be unclean till evening. ¹⁸When a man has sexual relations with a woman and there is an emission of semen, both of them must bathe with water, and they will be unclean till evening.

¹⁹"'When a woman has her regular flow of blood, the impurity of her monthly period will last seven days, and anyone who touches her will be unclean till evening.

²⁰"'Anything she lies on during her period will be unclean, and anything she sits on will be unclean. ²¹Anyone who touches her bed will be unclean; they must wash their clothes and bathe with water, and they will be unclean till evening. ²²Anyone who touches anything she sits on will be unclean; they must wash their clothes and bathe with water, and they will be unclean till evening. ²³Whether it is the bed or anything she was sitting on, when anyone touches it, they will be unclean till evening.

²⁴"'If a man has sexual relations with her and her monthly flow touches him, he will be unclean for seven days; any bed he lies on will be unclean.

²⁵"'When a woman has a discharge of blood for many days at a time other than her monthly period or has a discharge that continues beyond her period, she will be unclean as long as she has the discharge, just as in the days of her period. ²⁶Any bed she lies on while her discharge continues will be unclean, as is her bed during

a 15 Or *purification offering; also in verse 30*

her monthly period, and anything she sits on will be unclean, as during her period. ²⁷Anyone who touches them will be unclean; they must wash their clothes and bathe with water, and they will be unclean till evening.

²⁸ "When she is cleansed from her discharge, she must count off seven days, and after that she will be ceremonially clean. ²⁹On the eighth day she must take two doves or two young pigeons and bring them to the priest at the entrance to the tent of meeting. ³⁰The priest is to sacrifice one for a sin offering and the other for a burnt offering. In this way he will make atonement for her before the LORD for the uncleanness of her discharge.

³¹ "'You must keep the Israelites separate from things that make them unclean, so they will not die in their uncleanness for defiling my dwelling place,ᵃ which is among them.'"

³²These are the regulations for a man with a discharge, for anyone made unclean by an emission of semen, ³³for a woman in her monthly period, for a man or a woman with a discharge, and for a man who has sexual relations with a woman who is ceremonially unclean.

The Day of Atonement

16 The LORD spoke to Moses after the death of the two sons of Aaron who died when they approached the LORD. ²The LORD said to Moses: "Tell your brother Aaron that he is not to come whenever he chooses into the Most Holy Place behind the curtain in front of the atonement cover on the ark, or else he will die. For I will appear in the cloud over the atonement cover.

³ "This is how Aaron is to enter the Most Holy Place: He must first bring a young bull for a sin offeringᵇ and a ram for a burnt offering. ⁴He is to put on the sacred linen tunic, with linen undergarments next to his body; he is to tie the linen sash around him and put on the linen turban. These are sacred garments; so he must bathe himself with water before he puts them on. ⁵From the Israelite com-

munity he is to take two male goats for a sin offering and a ram for a burnt offering.

⁶ "Aaron is to offer the bull for his own sin offering to make atonement for himself and his household. ⁷Then he is to take the two goats and present them before the LORD at the entrance to the tent of meeting. ⁸He is to cast lots for the two goats—one lot for the LORD and the other for the scapegoat.ᶜ ⁹Aaron shall bring the goat whose lot falls to the LORD and sacrifice it for a sin offering. ¹⁰But the goat chosen by lot as the scapegoat shall be presented alive before the LORD to be used for making atonement by sending it into the wilderness as a scapegoat.

¹¹ "Aaron shall bring the bull for his own sin offering to make atonement for himself and his household, and he is to slaughter the bull for his own sin offering. ¹²He is to take a censer full of burning coals from the altar before the LORD and two handfuls of finely ground fragrant incense and take them behind the curtain. ¹³He is to put the incense on the fire before the LORD, and the smoke of the incense will conceal the atonement cover above the tablets of the covenant law, so that he will not die. ¹⁴He is to take some of the bull's blood and with his finger sprinkle it on the front of the atonement cover; then he shall sprinkle some of it with his finger seven times before the atonement cover.

¹⁵ "He shall then slaughter the goat for the sin offering for the people and take its blood behind the curtain and do with it as he did with the bull's blood: He shall sprinkle it on the atonement cover and in front of it. ¹⁶In this way he will make atonement for the Most Holy Place because of the uncleanness and rebellion of the Israelites, whatever their sins have been. He is to do the same for the tent of meeting, which is among them in the midst of their uncleanness. ¹⁷No one is to be in the tent of meeting from the time Aaron goes in to make atonement in

---

ᵃ 31 Or *my tabernacle*   ᵇ 3 Or *purification offering*; here and throughout this chapter
ᶜ 8 The meaning of the Hebrew for this word is uncertain; also in verses 10 and 26.

the Most Holy Place until he comes out, having made atonement for himself, his household and the whole community of Israel.

¹⁸ "Then he shall come out to the altar that is before the LORD and make atonement for it. He shall take some of the bull's blood and some of the goat's blood and put it on all the horns of the altar. ¹⁹ He shall sprinkle some of the blood on it with his finger seven times to cleanse it and to consecrate it from the uncleanness of the Israelites.

²⁰ "When Aaron has finished making atonement for the Most Holy Place, the tent of meeting and the altar, he shall bring forward the live goat. ²¹ He is to lay both hands on the head of the live goat and confess over it all the wickedness and rebellion of the Israelites—all their sins—and put them on the goat's head. He shall send the goat away into the wilderness in the care of someone appointed for the task. ²² The goat will carry on itself all their sins to a remote place; and the man shall release it in the wilderness.

²³ "Then Aaron is to go into the tent of meeting and take off the linen garments he put on before he entered the Most Holy Place, and he is to leave them there. ²⁴ He shall bathe himself with water in the sanctuary area and put on his regular garments. Then he shall come out and sacrifice the burnt offering for himself and the burnt offering for the people, to make atonement for himself and for the people. ²⁵ He shall also burn the fat of the sin offering on the altar.

²⁶ "The man who releases the goat as a scapegoat must wash his clothes and bathe himself with water; afterward he may come into the camp. ²⁷ The bull and the goat for the sin offerings, whose blood was brought into the Most Holy Place to make atonement, must be taken outside the camp; their hides, flesh and intestines are to be burned up. ²⁸ The man who burns them must wash his clothes and bathe himself with water; afterward he may come into the camp.

²⁹ "This is to be a lasting ordinance for you: On the tenth day of the seventh month you must deny yourselves*a* and not do any work—whether native-born or a foreigner residing among you— ³⁰ because on this day atonement will be made for you, to cleanse you. Then, before the LORD, you will be clean from all your sins. ³¹ It is a day of sabbath rest, and you must deny yourselves; it is a lasting ordinance. ³² The priest who is anointed and ordained

a 29 Or *must fast*; also in verse 31

Leviticus 16:1–34

Old Testament sacrifices paint a picture.

You're already familiar with sacrifices, even if the only Bible fact you know is that Jesus died on the cross for your sins. His death was the ultimate sacrifice that opened the way for you to know God and have a forever home in heaven (see Hebrews 10:19–22). Yet long before that final New Testament sacrifice, God commanded his people to offer all kinds of sacrifices, details you can read in places like Leviticus 1—7. Each sacrifice had a specific, significant meaning, and the bloodiness or cost of each pointed to the high price of sin. Of all the Old Testament sacrifices, the deadly drama of the Day of Atonement paints the closest picture of the terrible payment Jesus would one day make for our sins. This once-a-year sacrifice displays in living color the awfulness of sin.

Think: What lessons do you take away from the sacrifices described in the Old Testament?

ROCK SOLID truths

to succeed his father as high priest is to make atonement. He is to put on the sacred linen garments [33] and make atonement for the Most Holy Place, for the tent of meeting and the altar, and for the priests and all the members of the community.

[34]"This is to be a lasting ordinance for you: Atonement is to be made once a year for all the sins of the Israelites."

And it was done, as the LORD commanded Moses.

Eating Blood Forbidden

17 The LORD said to Moses, [2]"Speak to Aaron and his sons and to all the Israelites and say to them: 'This is what the LORD has commanded: [3]Any Israelite who sacrifices an ox,[a] a lamb or a goat in the camp or outside of it [4]instead of bringing it to the entrance to the tent of meeting to present it as an offering to the LORD in front of the tabernacle of the LORD—that person shall be considered guilty of bloodshed; they have shed blood and must be cut off from their people. [5]This is so the Israelites will bring to the LORD the sacrifices they are now making in the open fields. They must bring them to the priest, that is, to the LORD, at the entrance to the tent of meeting and sacrifice them as fellowship offerings. [6]The priest is to splash the blood against the altar of the LORD at the entrance to the tent of meeting and burn the fat as an aroma pleasing to the LORD. [7]They must no longer offer any of their sacrifices to the goat idols[b] to whom they prostitute themselves. This is to be a lasting ordinance for them and for the generations to come.'

[8]"Say to them: 'Any Israelite or any foreigner residing among them who offers a burnt offering or sacrifice [9]and does not bring it to the entrance to the tent of meeting to sacrifice it to the LORD must be cut off from the people of Israel.

[10]"'I will set my face against any Israelite or any foreigner residing among them who eats blood, and I will cut them off from the people. [11]For the life of a crea-

ture is in the blood, and I have given it to you to make atonement for yourselves on the altar; it is the blood that makes atonement for one's life.[c] [12]Therefore I say to the Israelites, "None of you may eat blood, nor may any foreigner residing among you eat blood."

[13]"'Any Israelite or any foreigner residing among you who hunts any animal or bird that may be eaten must drain out the blood and cover it with earth, [14]because the life of every creature is its blood. That is why I have said to the Israelites, "You must not eat the blood of any creature, because the life of every creature is its blood; anyone who eats it must be cut off."

[15]"'Anyone, whether native-born or foreigner, who eats anything found dead or torn by wild animals must wash their clothes and bathe with water, and they will be ceremonially unclean till evening; then they will be clean. [16]But if they do not wash their clothes and bathe themselves, they will be held responsible.'"

Unlawful Sexual Relations

18 The LORD said to Moses, [2]"Speak to the Israelites and say to them: 'I am the LORD your God. [3]You must not do as they do in Egypt, where you used to live, and you must not do as they do in the land of Canaan, where I am bringing you. Do not follow their practices. [4]You must obey my laws and be careful to follow my decrees. I am the LORD your God. [5]Keep my decrees and laws, for the person who obeys them will live by them. I am the LORD.

[6]"'No one is to approach any close relative to have sexual relations. I am the LORD.

[7]"'Do not dishonor your father by having sexual relations with your mother. She is your mother; do not have relations with her.

[8]"'Do not have sexual relations with your father's wife; that would dishonor your father.

---

a 3 The Hebrew word can refer to either male or female.   *b 7* Or *the demons*   *c 11* Or *atonement by the life in the blood*

9 " 'Do not have sexual relations with your sister, either your father's daughter or your mother's daughter, whether she was born in the same home or elsewhere.

10 " 'Do not have sexual relations with your son's daughter or your daughter's daughter; that would dishonor you.

11 " 'Do not have sexual relations with the daughter of your father's wife, born to your father; she is your sister.

12 " 'Do not have sexual relations with your father's sister; she is your father's close relative.

13 " 'Do not have sexual relations with your mother's sister, because she is your mother's close relative.

14 " 'Do not dishonor your father's brother by approaching his wife to have sexual relations; she is your aunt.

15 " 'Do not have sexual relations with your daughter-in-law. She is your son's wife; do not have relations with her.

16 " 'Do not have sexual relations with your brother's wife; that would dishonor your brother.

17 " 'Do not have sexual relations with both a woman and her daughter. Do not have sexual relations with either her son's daughter or her daughter's daughter; they are her close relatives. That is wickedness.

18 " 'Do not take your wife's sister as a rival wife and have sexual relations with her while your wife is living.

19 " 'Do not approach a woman to have sexual relations during the uncleanness of her monthly period.

20 " 'Do not have sexual relations with your neighbor's wife and defile yourself with her.

21 " 'Do not give any of your children to be sacrificed to Molek, for you must not profane the name of your God. I am the LORD.

22 " 'Do not have sexual relations with a man as one does with a woman; that is detestable.

23 " 'Do not have sexual relations with an animal and defile yourself with it. A woman must not present herself to an animal to have sexual relations with it; that is a perversion.

24 " 'Do not defile yourselves in any of these ways, because this is how the nations that I am going to drive out before you became defiled. 25 Even the land was defiled; so I punished it for its sin, and the land vomited out its inhabitants. 26 But you must keep my decrees and my laws. The native-born and the foreigners residing among you must not do any of these de-

Leviticus 18:1 – 30

Homosexuality is a sin — and so are lots of other things.

Critics often protest that Christians hate gays, lesbians, transgendered individuals or anyone who doesn't fit the mold of "traditional moral values." But believing a person's behavior is wrong isn't the same thing as hating that person. And despite what some say, the conviction that homosexuality is wrong isn't just based on Old Testament passages — like Leviticus 18:22. The Bible consistently speaks against homosexual behavior, including in New Testament passages like Romans 1:26 – 32 and 1 Corinthians 6:9 – 11. The Bible never paints homosexuality as the worst possible sin, but as one of many things people do wrong. It appears right alongside sins like envy, gossip, lying and disobeying parents (see Romans 1:29 – 30). The belief that homosexuality steps outside God's plans comes from the clear Biblical message that sex is to be enjoyed within the bounds of marriage (see Hebrews 13:4).

Think: Why do you think homosexuality is a sin — or not?

ROCK SOLID truths

testable things, [27] for all these things were done by the people who lived in the land before you, and the land became defiled. [28] And if you defile the land, it will vomit you out as it vomited out the nations that were before you.

[29] "Everyone who does any of these detestable things—such persons must be cut off from their people. [30] Keep my requirements and do not follow any of the detestable customs that were practiced before you came and do not defile yourselves with them. I am the LORD your God.'"

Various Laws

19 The LORD said to Moses, [2] "Speak to the entire assembly of Israel and say to them: 'Be holy because I, the LORD your God, am holy.

[3] "Each of you must respect your mother and father, and you must observe my Sabbaths. I am the LORD your God.

[4] "Do not turn to idols or make metal gods for yourselves. I am the LORD your God.

[5] "When you sacrifice a fellowship offering to the LORD, sacrifice it in such a way that it will be accepted on your behalf. [6] It shall be eaten on the day you sacrifice it or on the next day; anything left over until the third day must be burned up. [7] If any of it is eaten on the third day, it is impure and will not be accepted. [8] Whoever eats it will be held responsible because they have desecrated what is holy to the LORD; they must be cut off from their people.

[9] "When you reap the harvest of your land, do not reap to the very edges of your field or gather the gleanings of your harvest. [10] Do not go over your vineyard a second time or pick up the grapes that have fallen. Leave them for the poor and the foreigner. I am the LORD your God.

[11] "Do not steal.

"Do not lie.

"Do not deceive one another.

[12] "Do not swear falsely by my name

ROCK SOLID principles

Leviticus 19:1–2

Live holy.

Jesus died for my sins, so I can always ask God to forgive me when I do something wrong. Micah used that reasoning to excuse all kinds of behavior. He would only look at one more pornographic video, for example, or copy a friend's homework this time and stop, or wait until tomorrow to quit being so sarcastic. Deep down Micah knew his thinking was messed up, but it took the older guys at church to talk sense into him. Even though Jesus died for all of our sins, they pointed out, doing wrong still hurts his relationship with others, God, and even himself. And if sin is so bad that Jesus had to die for it, that's reason enough to live holy.

God doesn't want you stuck in sinful habits. He commands you to be holy, then does whatever it takes to move you toward that goal. He promises to cut out your stone heart and put a living heart in its place (see Ezekiel 36:26). And that's a heart that wants to be holy like him.

and so profane the name of your God. I am the Lord.

¹³"Do not defraud or rob your neighbor.

"Do not hold back the wages of a hired worker overnight.

¹⁴"Do not curse the deaf or put a stumbling block in front of the blind, but fear your God. I am the Lord.

¹⁵"Do not pervert justice; do not show partiality to the poor or favoritism to the great, but judge your neighbor fairly.

¹⁶"Do not go about spreading slander among your people.

"Do not do anything that endangers your neighbor's life. I am the Lord.

¹⁷"Do not hate a fellow Israelite in your heart. Rebuke your neighbor frankly so you will not share in their guilt.

¹⁸"Do not seek revenge or bear a grudge against anyone among your people, but love your neighbor as yourself. I am the Lord.

¹⁹"Keep my decrees.

"Do not mate different kinds of animals.

"Do not plant your field with two kinds of seed.

"Do not wear clothing woven of two kinds of material.

²⁰"If a man sleeps with a female slave who is promised to another man but who has not been ransomed or given her freedom, there must be due punishment.ᵃ Yet they are not to be put to death, because she had not been freed. ²¹The man, however, must bring a ram to the entrance to the tent of meeting for a guilt offering to the Lord. ²²With the ram of the guilt offering the priest is to make atonement for him before the Lord for the sin he has committed, and his sin will be forgiven.

²³"When you enter the land and plant any kind of fruit tree, regard its fruit as forbidden.ᵇ For three years you are to consider it forbiddenᵇ; it must not be eaten. ²⁴In the fourth year all its fruit will be holy, an offering of praise to the Lord. ²⁵But in the fifth year you may eat its fruit. In this way your harvest will be increased. I am the Lord your God.

²⁶"Do not eat any meat with the blood still in it.

"Do not practice divination or seek omens.

²⁷"Do not cut the hair at the sides of your head or clip off the edges of your beard.

²⁸"Do not cut your bodies for the dead or put tattoo marks on yourselves. I am the Lord.

²⁹"Do not degrade your daughter by making her a prostitute, or the land will turn to prostitution and be filled with wickedness.

³⁰"Observe my Sabbaths and have reverence for my sanctuary. I am the Lord.

³¹"Do not turn to mediums or seek out spiritists, for you will be defiled by them. I am the Lord your God.

³²"Stand up in the presence of the aged, show respect for the elderly and revere your God. I am the Lord.

³³"When a foreigner resides among you in your land, do not mistreat them. ³⁴The foreigner residing among you must be treated as your native-born. Love them as yourself, for you were foreigners in Egypt. I am the Lord your God.

³⁵"Do not use dishonest standards when measuring length, weight or quantity. ³⁶Use honest scales and honest weights, an honest ephahᶜ and an honest hin.ᵈ I am the Lord your God, who brought you out of Egypt.

³⁷"Keep all my decrees and all my laws and follow them. I am the Lord.'"

Punishments for Sin

20 The Lord said to Moses, ²"Say to the Israelites: 'Any Israelite or any foreigner residing in Israel who sacrifices any of his children to Molek is to be put to death. The members of the community are to stone him. ³I myself will set my face against him and will cut him off from his people; for by sacrificing his children to Molek, he has defiled my sanctuary and profaned my holy name. ⁴If the members

ᵃ 20 Or be an inquiry   ᵇ 23 Hebrew uncircumcised   ᶜ 36 An ephah was a dry measure having the capacity of about 3/5 of a bushel or about 22 liters.   ᵈ 36 A hin was a liquid measure having the capacity of about 1 gallon or about 3.8 liters.

of the community close their eyes when that man sacrifices one of his children to Molek and if they fail to put him to death, ⁵ I myself will set my face against him and his family and will cut them off from their people together with all who follow him in prostituting themselves to Molek.

⁶ "'I will set my face against anyone who turns to mediums and spiritists to prostitute themselves by following them, and I will cut them off from their people.

⁷ "'Consecrate yourselves and be holy, because I am the LORD your God. ⁸ Keep my decrees and follow them. I am the LORD, who makes you holy.

⁹ "'Anyone who curses their father or mother is to be put to death. Because they have cursed their father or mother, their blood will be on their own head.

¹⁰ "'If a man commits adultery with another man's wife—with the wife of his neighbor—both the adulterer and the adulteress are to be put to death.

¹¹ "'If a man has sexual relations with his father's wife, he has dishonored his father. Both the man and the woman are to be put to death; their blood will be on their own heads.

¹² "'If a man has sexual relations with his daughter-in-law, both of them are to be put to death. What they have done is a perversion; their blood will be on their own heads.

¹³ "'If a man has sexual relations with a man as one does with a woman, both of them have done what is detestable. They are to be put to death; their blood will be on their own heads.

¹⁴ "'If a man marries both a woman and her mother, it is wicked. Both he and they must be burned in the fire, so that no wickedness will be among you.

¹⁵ "'If a man has sexual relations with an animal, he is to be put to death, and you must kill the animal.

¹⁶ "'If a woman approaches an animal to have sexual relations with it, kill both the woman and the animal. They are to be put to death; their blood will be on their own heads.

¹⁷ "'If a man marries his sister, the daughter of either his father or his mother, and they have sexual relations, it is a disgrace. They are to be publicly removed from their people. He has dishonored his sister and will be held responsible.

¹⁸ "'If a man has sexual relations with a woman during her monthly period, he has exposed the source of her flow, and she has also uncovered it. Both of them are to be cut off from their people.

¹⁹ "'Do not have sexual relations with the sister of either your mother or your father, for that would dishonor a close relative; both of you would be held responsible.

²⁰ "'If a man has sexual relations with his aunt, he has dishonored his uncle. They will be held responsible; they will die childless.

²¹ "'If a man marries his brother's wife, it is an act of impurity; he has dishonored his brother. They will be childless.

²² "'Keep all my decrees and laws and follow them, so that the land where I am bringing you to live may not vomit you out. ²³ You must not live according to the customs of the nations I am going to drive out before you. Because they did all these things, I abhorred them. ²⁴ But I said to you, "You will possess their land; I will give it to you as an inheritance, a land flowing with milk and honey." I am the LORD your God, who has set you apart from the nations.

²⁵ "'You must therefore make a distinction between clean and unclean animals and between unclean and clean birds. Do not defile yourselves by any animal or bird or anything that moves along the ground—those that I have set apart as unclean for you. ²⁶ You are to be holy to me because I, the LORD, am holy, and I have set you apart from the nations to be my own.

²⁷ "'A man or woman who is a medium or spiritist among you must be put to death. You are to stone them; their blood will be on their own heads.'"

Rules for Priests

21 The LORD said to Moses, "Speak to the priests, the sons of Aaron, and say to them: 'A priest must not make himself ceremonially unclean for any of his people who die, ²except for a close relative, such as his mother or father, his son or daughter, his brother, ³or an unmarried sister who is dependent on him since she has no husband—for her he may make himself unclean. ⁴He must not make himself unclean for people related to him by marriage,ᵃ and so defile himself.

⁵"'Priests must not shave their heads or shave off the edges of their beards or cut their bodies. ⁶They must be holy to their God and must not profane the name of their God. Because they present the food offerings to the LORD, the food of their God, they are to be holy.

⁷"'They must not marry women defiled by prostitution or divorced from their husbands, because priests are holy to their God. ⁸Regard them as holy, because they offer up the food of your God. Consider them holy, because I the LORD am holy—I who make you holy.

⁹"'If a priest's daughter defiles herself by becoming a prostitute, she disgraces her father; she must be burned in the fire.

¹⁰"'The high priest, the one among his brothers who has had the anointing oil poured on his head and who has been ordained to wear the priestly garments, must not let his hair become unkemptᵇ or tear his clothes. ¹¹He must not enter a place where there is a dead body. He must not make himself unclean, even for his father or mother, ¹²nor leave the sanctuary of his God or desecrate it, because he has been dedicated by the anointing oil of his God. I am the LORD.

¹³"'The woman he marries must be a virgin. ¹⁴He must not marry a widow, a divorced woman, or a woman defiled by prostitution, but only a virgin from his own people, ¹⁵so that he will not defile his offspring among his people. I am the LORD, who makes him holy.'"

¹⁶The LORD said to Moses, ¹⁷"Say to Aaron: 'For the generations to come none of your descendants who has a defect may come near to offer the food of his God. ¹⁸No man who has any defect may come near: no man who is blind or lame, disfig-ured or deformed; ¹⁹no man with a crippled foot or hand, ²⁰or who is a hunchback or a dwarf, or who has any eye defect, or who has festering or running sores or damaged testicles. ²¹No descendant of Aaron the priest who has any defect is to come near to present the food offerings to the LORD. He has a defect; he must not come near to offer the food of his God. ²²He may eat the most holy food of his God, as well as the holy food; ²³yet because of his defect, he must not go near the curtain or approach the altar, and so desecrate my sanctuary. I am the LORD, who makes them holy.'"

²⁴So Moses told this to Aaron and his sons and to all the Israelites.

22

The LORD said to Moses, ²"Tell Aaron and his sons to treat with respect the sacred offerings the Israelites consecrate to me, so they will not profane my holy name. I am the LORD.

³"Say to them: 'For the generations to come, if any of your descendants is ceremonially unclean and yet comes near the sacred offerings that the Israelites consecrate to the LORD, that person must be cut off from my presence. I am the LORD.

⁴"'If a descendant of Aaron has a defiling skin diseaseᶜ or a bodily discharge, he may not eat the sacred offerings until he is cleansed. He will also be unclean if he touches something defiled by a corpse or by anyone who has an emission of semen, ⁵or if he touches any crawling thing that makes him unclean, or any person who makes him unclean, whatever the uncleanness may be. ⁶The one who touches any such thing will be unclean till evening. He must not eat any of the sacred offerings unless he has bathed himself with water. ⁷When the sun goes down, he will be clean, and after that he may eat the sacred offerings, for they are his food. ⁸He must not eat anything found dead or torn by wild animals, and so become unclean through it. I am the LORD.

ᵃ 4 Or unclean as a leader among his people
ᵇ 10 Or not uncover his head   ᶜ 4 The Hebrew word for defiling skin disease, traditionally translated "leprosy," was used for various diseases affecting the skin.

⁹"'The priests are to perform my service in such a way that they do not become guilty and die for treating it with contempt. I am the LORD, who makes them holy.

¹⁰"'No one outside a priest's family may eat the sacred offering, nor may the guest of a priest or his hired worker eat it. ¹¹But if a priest buys a slave with money, or if slaves are born in his household, they may eat his food. ¹²If a priest's daughter marries anyone other than a priest, she may not eat any of the sacred contributions. ¹³But if a priest's daughter becomes a widow or is divorced, yet has no children, and she returns to live in her father's household as in her youth, she may eat her father's food. No unauthorized person, however, may eat it.

¹⁴"'Anyone who eats a sacred offering by mistake must make restitution to the priest for the offering and add a fifth of the value to it. ¹⁵The priests must not desecrate the sacred offerings the Israelites present to the LORD ¹⁶by allowing them to eat the sacred offerings and so bring upon them guilt requiring payment. I am the LORD, who makes them holy.'"

Unacceptable Sacrifices

¹⁷The LORD said to Moses, ¹⁸"Speak to Aaron and his sons and to all the Israelites and say to them: 'If any of you—whether an Israelite or a foreigner residing in Israel—presents a gift for a burnt offering to the LORD, either to fulfill a vow or as a freewill offering, ¹⁹you must present a male without defect from the cattle, sheep or goats in order that it may be accepted on your behalf. ²⁰Do not bring anything with a defect, because it will not be accepted on your behalf. ²¹When anyone brings from the herd or flock a fellowship offering to the LORD to fulfill a special vow or as a freewill offering, it must be without defect or blemish to be acceptable. ²²Do not offer to the LORD the blind, the injured or the maimed, or anything with warts or festering or running sores. Do not place any of these on the altar as a food offering presented to the LORD. ²³You may, however, present as a freewill offering an ox*a* or a sheep that is deformed or stunted, but it will not be accepted in fulfillment of a vow. ²⁴You must not offer to the LORD an animal whose testicles are bruised, crushed, torn or cut. You must not do this in your own land, ²⁵and you must not accept such animals from the hand of a foreigner and offer them as the food of your God. They will not be accepted on your behalf, because they are deformed and have defects.'"

²⁶The LORD said to Moses, ²⁷"When a calf, a lamb or a goat is born, it is to remain with its mother for seven days. From the eighth day on, it will be acceptable as a food offering presented to the LORD. ²⁸Do not slaughter a cow or a sheep and its young on the same day.

²⁹"When you sacrifice a thank offering to the LORD, sacrifice it in such a way that it will be accepted on your behalf. ³⁰It must be eaten that same day; leave none of it till morning. I am the LORD.

³¹"Keep my commands and follow them. I am the LORD. ³²Do not profane my holy name, for I must be acknowledged as holy by the Israelites. I am the LORD, who made you holy ³³and who brought you out of Egypt to be your God. I am the LORD."

The Appointed Festivals

23 The LORD said to Moses, ²"Speak to the Israelites and say to them: 'These are my appointed festivals, the appointed festivals of the LORD, which you are to proclaim as sacred assemblies.

The Sabbath

³"'There are six days when you may work, but the seventh day is a day of sabbath rest, a day of sacred assembly. You are not to do any work; wherever you live, it is a sabbath to the LORD.

The Passover and the Festival of Unleavened Bread

⁴"'These are the LORD's appointed festivals, the sacred assemblies you are to

---

a 23 The Hebrew word can refer to either male or female.

proclaim at their appointed times: [5]The LORD's Passover begins at twilight on the fourteenth day of the first month. [6]On the fifteenth day of that month the LORD's Festival of Unleavened Bread begins; for seven days you must eat bread made without yeast. [7]On the first day hold a sacred assembly and do no regular work. [8]For seven days present a food offering to the LORD. And on the seventh day hold a sacred assembly and do no regular work.'"

Offering the Firstfruits

[9]The LORD said to Moses, [10]"Speak to the Israelites and say to them: 'When you enter the land I am going to give you and you reap its harvest, bring to the priest a sheaf of the first grain you harvest. [11]He is to wave the sheaf before the LORD so it will be accepted on your behalf; the priest is to wave it on the day after the Sabbath. [12]On the day you wave the sheaf, you must sacrifice as a burnt offering to the LORD a lamb a year old without defect, [13]together with its grain offering of two-tenths of an ephah[a] of the finest flour mixed with olive oil—a food offering presented to the LORD, a pleasing aroma—and its drink offering of a quarter of a hin[b] of wine. [14]You must not eat any bread, or roasted or new grain, until the very day you bring this offering to your God. This is to be a lasting ordinance for the generations to come, wherever you live.

The Festival of Weeks

[15]"'From the day after the Sabbath, the day you brought the sheaf of the wave offering, count off seven full weeks. [16]Count off fifty days up to the day after the seventh Sabbath, and then present an offering of new grain to the LORD. [17]From wherever you live, bring two loaves made of two-tenths of an ephah of the finest flour, baked with yeast, as a wave offering of firstfruits to the LORD. [18]Present with this bread seven male lambs, each a year old and without defect, one young bull and two rams. They will be a burnt offering to the LORD, together with their grain offerings and drink offerings—a food offering, an aroma pleasing to the

LORD. [19]Then sacrifice one male goat for a sin offering[c] and two lambs, each a year old, for a fellowship offering. [20]The priest is to wave the two lambs before the LORD as a wave offering, together with the bread of the firstfruits. They are a sacred offering to the LORD for the priest. [21]On that same day you are to proclaim a sacred assembly and do no regular work. This is to be a lasting ordinance for the generations to come, wherever you live.

[22]"'When you reap the harvest of your land, do not reap to the very edges of your field or gather the gleanings of your harvest. Leave them for the poor and for the foreigner residing among you. I am the LORD your God.'"

The Festival of Trumpets

[23]The LORD said to Moses, [24]"Say to the Israelites: 'On the first day of the seventh month you are to have a day of sabbath rest, a sacred assembly commemorated with trumpet blasts. [25]Do no regular work, but present a food offering to the LORD.'"

The Day of Atonement

[26]The LORD said to Moses, [27]"The tenth day of this seventh month is the Day of Atonement. Hold a sacred assembly and deny yourselves,[d] and present a food offering to the LORD. [28]Do not do any work on that day, because it is the Day of Atonement, when atonement is made for you before the LORD your God. [29]Those who do not deny themselves on that day must be cut off from their people. [30]I will destroy from among their people anyone who does any work on that day. [31]You shall do no work at all. This is to be a lasting ordinance for the generations to come, wherever you live. [32]It is a day of sabbath rest for you, and you must deny yourselves. From the evening of the ninth day of the month until the following evening you are to observe your sabbath."

[a] 13 That is, probably about 7 pounds or about 3.2 kilograms; also in verse 17   [b] 13 That is, about 1 quart or about 1 liter   [c] 19 Or purification offering   [d] 27 Or and fast; similarly in verses 29 and 32

The Festival of Tabernacles

[33] The Lord said to Moses, [34] "Say to the Israelites: 'On the fifteenth day of the seventh month the Lord's Festival of Tabernacles begins, and it lasts for seven days. [35] The first day is a sacred assembly; do no regular work. [36] For seven days present food offerings to the Lord, and on the eighth day hold a sacred assembly and present a food offering to the Lord. It is the closing special assembly; do no regular work.

[37] ("'These are the Lord's appointed festivals, which you are to proclaim as sacred assemblies for bringing food offerings to the Lord—the burnt offerings and grain offerings, sacrifices and drink offerings required for each day. [38] These offerings are in addition to those for the Lord's Sabbaths and[a] in addition to your gifts and whatever you have vowed and all the freewill offerings you give to the Lord.)

[39] "'So beginning with the fifteenth day of the seventh month, after you have gathered the crops of the land, celebrate the festival to the Lord for seven days; the first day is a day of sabbath rest, and the eighth day also is a day of sabbath rest. [40] On the first day you are to take branches from luxuriant trees—from palms, willows and other leafy trees—and rejoice before the Lord your God for seven days. [41] Celebrate this as a festival to the Lord for seven days each year. This is to be a lasting ordinance for the generations to come; celebrate it in the seventh month. [42] Live in temporary shelters for seven days: All native-born Israelites are to live in such shelters [43] so your descendants will know that I had the Israelites live in temporary shelters when I brought them out of Egypt. I am the Lord your God.'"

[44] So Moses announced to the Israelites the appointed festivals of the Lord.

Olive Oil and Bread Set Before the Lord

24 The Lord said to Moses, [2] "Command the Israelites to bring you clear oil of pressed olives for the light so that the lamps may be kept burning continually. [3] Outside the curtain that shields the ark of the covenant law in the tent of meeting, Aaron is to tend the lamps before the Lord from evening till morning, continually. This is to be a lasting ordinance for the generations to come. [4] The lamps on the pure gold lampstand before the Lord must be tended continually.

[5] "Take the finest flour and bake twelve loaves of bread, using two-tenths of an ephah[b] for each loaf. [6] Arrange them in two stacks, six in each stack, on the table of pure gold before the Lord. [7] By each stack put some pure incense as a memorial[c] portion to represent the bread and to be a food offering presented to the Lord. [8] This bread is to be set out before the Lord regularly, Sabbath after Sabbath, on behalf of the Israelites, as a lasting covenant. [9] It belongs to Aaron and his sons, who are to eat it in the sanctuary area, because it is a most holy part of their perpetual share of the food offerings presented to the Lord."

A Blasphemer Put to Death

[10] Now the son of an Israelite mother and an Egyptian father went out among the Israelites, and a fight broke out in the camp between him and an Israelite. [11] The son of the Israelite woman blasphemed the Name with a curse; so they brought him to Moses. (His mother's name was Shelomith, the daughter of Dibri the Danite.) [12] They put him in custody until the will of the Lord should be made clear to them.

[13] Then the Lord said to Moses: [14] "Take the blasphemer outside the camp. All those who heard him are to lay their hands on his head, and the entire assembly is to stone him. [15] Say to the Israelites: 'Anyone who curses their God will be held responsible; [16] anyone who blasphemes the name of the Lord is to be put to death. The entire assembly must stone them. Whether foreigner or native-born, when they blaspheme the Name they are to be put to death.

---

[a] 38 Or These festivals are in addition to the Lord's Sabbaths, and these offerings are
[b] 5 That is, probably about 7 pounds or about 3.2 kilograms   [c] 7 Or representative

17 "'Anyone who takes the life of a human being is to be put to death. 18 Anyone who takes the life of someone's animal must make restitution—life for life. 19 Anyone who injures their neighbor is to be injured in the same manner: 20 fracture for fracture, eye for eye, tooth for tooth. The one who has inflicted the injury must suffer the same injury. 21 Whoever kills an animal must make restitution, but whoever kills a human being is to be put to death. 22 You are to have the same law for the foreigner and the native-born. I am the Lord your God.'"

23 Then Moses spoke to the Israelites, and they took the blasphemer outside the camp and stoned him. The Israelites did as the Lord commanded Moses.

The Sabbath Year

25 The Lord said to Moses at Mount Sinai, 2 "Speak to the Israelites and say to them: 'When you enter the land I am going to give you, the land itself must observe a sabbath to the Lord. 3 For six years sow your fields, and for six years prune your vineyards and gather their crops. 4 But in the seventh year the land is to have a year of sabbath rest, a sabbath to the Lord. Do not sow your fields or prune your vineyards. 5 Do not reap what grows of itself or harvest the grapes of your untended vines. The land is to have a year of rest. 6 Whatever the land yields during the sabbath year will be food for you—for yourself, your male and female servants, and the hired worker and temporary resident who live among you, 7 as well as for your livestock and the wild animals in your land. Whatever the land produces may be eaten.

The Year of Jubilee

8 "'Count off seven sabbath years—seven times seven years—so that the seven sabbath years amount to a period of forty-nine years. 9 Then have the trumpet sounded everywhere on the tenth day of

ROCK SOLID principles

Leviticus 24:17–23

Let God get even.

Angie was screaming inside. She wanted a way to hurt the driver who hurt her mom. Mrs. Perez was minding her own business, driving home late from work, when a big SUV ran a red light and smashed into the driver's side of her shiny little compact. It took an hour for emergency crews just to cut Mrs. Perez free from her car, and now doctors couldn't say if she would ever regain consciousness—or if she did, what brain injuries she might have suffered. As Angie and her family waited for the smallest bit of good news, the drunk who hit her mom was alive, well, and walking free.

The Old Testament gave harsh rules for revenge, like "fracture for fracture" (Leviticus 24:20). But those rules laid down legal codes for a religious society, just like courts now set punishments and penalties. For us as individuals, the New Testament shows the bigger picture when it says to leave revenge to God (see Romans 12:19). Only the perfect God knows the appropriate payback.

the seventh month; on the Day of Atonement sound the trumpet throughout your land. ¹⁰Consecrate the fiftieth year and proclaim liberty throughout the land to all its inhabitants. It shall be a jubilee for you; each of you is to return to your family property and to your own clan. ¹¹The fiftieth year shall be a jubilee for you; do not sow and do not reap what grows of itself or harvest the untended vines. ¹²For it is a jubilee and is to be holy for you; eat only what is taken directly from the fields.

¹³"In this Year of Jubilee everyone is to return to their own property.

¹⁴"If you sell land to any of your own people or buy land from them, do not take advantage of each other. ¹⁵You are to buy from your own people on the basis of the number of years since the Jubilee. And they are to sell to you on the basis of the number of years left for harvesting crops. ¹⁶When the years are many, you are to increase the price, and when the years are few, you are to decrease the price, because what is really being sold to you is the number of crops. ¹⁷Do not take advantage of each other, but fear your God. I am the Lord your God.

¹⁸"Follow my decrees and be careful to obey my laws, and you will live safely in the land. ¹⁹Then the land will yield its fruit, and you will eat your fill and live there in safety. ²⁰You may ask, "What will we eat in the seventh year if we do not plant or harvest our crops?" ²¹I will send you such a blessing in the sixth year that the land will yield enough for three years. ²²While you plant during the eighth year, you will eat from the old crop and will continue to eat from it until the harvest of the ninth year comes in.

²³"The land must not be sold permanently, because the land is mine and you reside in my land as foreigners and strangers. ²⁴Throughout the land that you hold as a possession, you must provide for the redemption of the land.

²⁵"If one of your fellow Israelites becomes poor and sells some of their property, their nearest relative is to come and redeem what they have sold. ²⁶If, however, there is no one to redeem it for them but later on they prosper and acquire sufficient means to redeem it themselves, ²⁷they are to determine the value for the years since they sold it and refund the balance to the one to whom they sold it; they can then go back to their own property. ²⁸But if they do not acquire the means to repay, what was sold will remain in the possession of the buyer until the Year of Jubilee. It will be returned in the Jubilee, and they can then go back to their property.

²⁹"Anyone who sells a house in a walled city retains the right of redemption a full year after its sale. During that time the seller may redeem it. ³⁰If it is not redeemed before a full year has passed, the house in the walled city shall belong permanently to the buyer and the buyer's descendants. It is not to be returned in the Jubilee. ³¹But houses in villages without walls around them are to be considered as belonging to the open country. They can be redeemed, and they are to be returned in the Jubilee.

³²"The Levites always have the right to redeem their houses in the Levitical towns, which they possess. ³³So the property of the Levites is redeemable—that is, a house sold in any town they hold—and is to be returned in the Jubilee, because the houses in the towns of the Levites are their property among the Israelites. ³⁴But the pastureland belonging to their towns must not be sold; it is their permanent possession.

³⁵"If any of your fellow Israelites become poor and are unable to support themselves among you, help them as you would a foreigner and stranger, so they can continue to live among you. ³⁶Do not take interest or any profit from them, but fear your God, so that they may continue to live among you. ³⁷You must not lend them money at interest or sell them food at a profit. ³⁸I am the Lord your God, who brought you out of Egypt to give you the land of Canaan and to be your God.

³⁹"If any of your fellow Israelites become poor and sell themselves to you, do not make them work as slaves. ⁴⁰They are

to be treated as hired workers or temporary residents among you; they are to work for you until the Year of Jubilee. ⁴¹Then they and their children are to be released, and they will go back to their own clans and to the property of their ancestors. ⁴²Because the Israelites are my servants, whom I brought out of Egypt, they must not be sold as slaves. ⁴³Do not rule over them ruthlessly, but fear your God.

⁴⁴"Your male and female slaves are to come from the nations around you; from them you may buy slaves. ⁴⁵You may also buy some of the temporary residents living among you and members of their clans born in your country, and they will become your property. ⁴⁶You can bequeath them to your children as inherited property and can make them slaves for life, but you must not rule over your fellow Israelites ruthlessly.

⁴⁷"If a foreigner residing among you becomes rich and any of your fellow Israelites become poor and sell themselves to the foreigner or to a member of the foreigner's clan, ⁴⁸they retain the right of redemption after they have sold themselves. One of their relatives may redeem them: ⁴⁹An uncle or a cousin or any blood relative in their clan may redeem them. Or if they prosper, they may redeem themselves. ⁵⁰They and their buyer are to count the time from the year they sold themselves up to the Year of Jubilee. The price for their release is to be based on the rate paid to a hired worker for that number of years. ⁵¹If many years remain, they must pay for their redemption a larger share of the price paid for them. ⁵²If only a few years remain until the Year of Jubilee, they are to compute that and pay for their redemption accordingly. ⁵³They are to be treated as workers hired from year to year; you must see to it that those to whom they owe service do not rule over them ruthlessly.

⁵⁴"Even if someone is not redeemed in any of these ways, they and their children are to be released in the Year of Jubilee, ⁵⁵for the Israelites belong to me as servants. They are my servants, whom I brought out of Egypt. I am the LORD your God.

150

Reward for Obedience

26 "'Do not make idols or set up an image or a sacred stone for yourselves, and do not place a carved stone in your land to bow down before it. I am the LORD your God.

²"'Observe my Sabbaths and have reverence for my sanctuary. I am the LORD.

³"'If you follow my decrees and are careful to obey my commands, ⁴I will send you rain in its season, and the ground will yield its crops and the trees their fruit. ⁵Your threshing will continue until grape harvest and the grape harvest will continue until planting, and you will eat all the food you want and live in safety in your land.

⁶"'I will grant peace in the land, and you will lie down and no one will make you afraid. I will remove wild beasts from the land, and the sword will not pass through your country. ⁷You will pursue your enemies, and they will fall by the sword before you. ⁸Five of you will chase a hundred, and a hundred of you will chase ten thousand, and your enemies will fall by the sword before you.

⁹"'I will look on you with favor and make you fruitful and increase your numbers, and I will keep my covenant with you. ¹⁰You will still be eating last year's harvest when you will have to move it out

ROCK SOLID promises

"I will look on you with favor and make you fruitful."

Leviticus 26:9

God's gifts aren't just spiritual or invisible. He meets your every need and multiplies your efforts.

to make room for the new. ¹¹I will put my dwelling place*a* among you, and I will not abhor you. ¹²I will walk among you and be your God, and you will be my people. ¹³I am the LORD your God, who brought you out of Egypt so that you would no longer be slaves to the Egyptians; I broke the bars of your yoke and enabled you to walk with heads held high.

Punishment for Disobedience

¹⁴"'But if you will not listen to me and carry out all these commands, ¹⁵and if you reject my decrees and abhor my laws and fail to carry out all my commands and so violate my covenant, ¹⁶then I will do this to you: I will bring on you sudden terror, wasting diseases and fever that will destroy your sight and sap your strength. You will plant seed in vain, because your enemies will eat it. ¹⁷I will set my face against you so that you will be defeated by your enemies; those who hate you will rule over you, and you will flee even when no one is pursuing you.

¹⁸"'If after all this you will not listen to me, I will punish you for your sins seven times over. ¹⁹I will break down your stubborn pride and make the sky above you like iron and the ground beneath you like bronze. ²⁰Your strength will be spent in vain, because your soil will not yield its crops, nor will the trees of your land yield their fruit.

²¹"'If you remain hostile toward me and refuse to listen to me, I will multiply your afflictions seven times over, as your sins deserve. ²²I will send wild animals against you, and they will rob you of your children, destroy your cattle and make you so few in number that your roads will be deserted.

²³"'If in spite of these things you do not accept my correction but continue to be hostile toward me, ²⁴I myself will be hostile toward you and will afflict you for your sins seven times over. ²⁵And I will bring the sword on you to avenge the breaking of the covenant. When you withdraw into your cities, I will send a plague among you, and you will be given into en-

emy hands. ²⁶When I cut off your supply of bread, ten women will be able to bake your bread in one oven, and they will dole out the bread by weight. You will eat, but you will not be satisfied.

²⁷"'If in spite of this you still do not listen to me but continue to be hostile toward me, ²⁸then in my anger I will be hostile toward you, and I myself will punish you for your sins seven times over. ²⁹You will eat the flesh of your sons and the flesh of your daughters. ³⁰I will destroy your high places, cut down your incense altars and pile your dead bodies*b* on the lifeless forms of your idols, and I will abhor you. ³¹I will turn your cities into ruins and lay waste your sanctuaries, and I will take no delight in the pleasing aroma of your offerings. ³²I myself will lay waste the land, so that your enemies who live there will be appalled. ³³I will scatter you among the nations and will draw out my sword and pursue you. Your land will be laid waste, and your cities will lie in ruins. ³⁴Then the land will enjoy its sabbath years all the time that it lies desolate and you are in the country of your enemies; then the land will rest and enjoy its sabbaths. ³⁵All the time that it lies desolate, the land will have the rest it did not have during the sabbaths you lived in it.

³⁶"'As for those of you who are left, I will make their hearts so fearful in the lands of their enemies that the sound of a windblown leaf will put them to flight. They will run as though fleeing from the sword, and they will fall, even though no one is pursuing them. ³⁷They will stumble over one another as though fleeing from the sword, even though no one is pursuing them. So you will not be able to stand before your enemies. ³⁸You will perish among the nations; the land of your enemies will devour you. ³⁹Those of you who are left will waste away in the lands of their enemies because of their sins; also because of their ancestors' sins they will waste away.

⁴⁰"'But if they will confess their sins

a 11 Or *my tabernacle*   *b 30* Or *your funeral offerings* and the sins of their ancestors—their unfaithfulness and their hostility toward me, ⁴¹which made me hostile toward them so that I sent them into the land of their enemies—then when their uncircumcised hearts are humbled and they pay for their sin, ⁴²I will remember my covenant with Jacob and my covenant with Isaac and my covenant with Abraham, and I will remember the land. ⁴³For the land will be deserted by them and will enjoy its sabbaths while it lies desolate without them. They will pay for their sins because they rejected my laws and abhorred my decrees. ⁴⁴Yet in spite of this, when they are in the land of their enemies, I will not reject them or abhor them so as to destroy them completely, breaking my covenant with them. I am the LORD their God. ⁴⁵But for their sake I will remember the covenant with their ancestors whom I brought out of Egypt in the sight of the nations to be their God. I am the LORD.'"

⁴⁶These are the decrees, the laws and the regulations that the LORD established at Mount Sinai between himself and the Israelites through Moses.

Redeeming What Is the LORD's

27 The LORD said to Moses, ²"Speak to the Israelites and say to them: 'If anyone makes a special vow to dedicate a person to the LORD by giving the equivalent value, ³set the value of a male between the ages of twenty and sixty at fifty shekels*ᵃ* of silver, according to the sanctuary shekel*ᵇ*; ⁴for a female, set her value at thirty shekels*ᶜ*; ⁵for a person between the ages of five and twenty, set the value of a male at twenty shekels*ᵈ* and of a female at ten shekels*ᵉ*; ⁶for a person between one month and five years, set the value of a male at five shekels*ᶠ* of silver and that of a female at three shekels*ᵍ* of silver; ⁷for a person sixty years old or more, set the value of a male at fifteen shekels*ᵇ* and of a female at ten shekels. ⁸If anyone making the vow is too poor to pay the specified amount, the person being dedicated is to be presented to the priest, who will set the value according to what the one making the vow can afford.

⁹"'If what they vowed is an animal that is acceptable as an offering to the LORD, such an animal given to the LORD becomes holy. ¹⁰They must not exchange it or substitute a good one for a bad one, or a bad one for a good one; if they should substitute one animal for another, both it and the substitute become holy. ¹¹If what they vowed is a ceremonially unclean animal—one that is not acceptable as an offering to the LORD—the animal must be presented to the priest, ¹²who will judge its quality as good or bad. Whatever value the priest then sets, that is what it will be. ¹³If the owner wishes to redeem the animal, a fifth must be added to its value.

¹⁴"'If anyone dedicates their house as something holy to the LORD, the priest will judge its quality as good or bad. Whatever value the priest then sets, so it will remain. ¹⁵If the one who dedicates their house wishes to redeem it, they must add a fifth to its value, and the house will again become theirs.

¹⁶"'If anyone dedicates to the LORD part of their family land, its value is to be set according to the amount of seed required for it—fifty shekels of silver to a homer*ⁱ* of barley seed. ¹⁷If they dedicate a field during the Year of Jubilee, the value that has been set remains. ¹⁸But if they dedicate a field after the Jubilee, the priest will determine the value according to the number of years that remain until the next Year of Jubilee, and its set value will be reduced. ¹⁹If the one who dedicates the field wishes to redeem it, they must add a fifth to its value, and the field will again

---

ᵃ 3 That is, about 1 1/4 pounds or about 575 grams; also in verse 16   *ᵇ 3* That is, about 2/5 ounce or about 12 grams; also in verse 25
ᶜ 4 That is, about 12 ounces or about 345 grams
ᵈ 5 That is, about 8 ounces or about 230 grams
ᵉ 5 That is, about 4 ounces or about 115 grams; also in verse 7   *ᶠ 6* That is, about 2 ounces or about 58 grams   *ᵍ 6* That is, about 1 1/4 ounces or about 35 grams   *ᵇ 7* That is, about 6 ounces or about 175 grams   *ⁱ 16* That is, probably about 300 pounds or about 135 kilograms

become theirs. ²⁰If, however, they do not redeem the field, or if they have sold it to someone else, it can never be redeemed. ²¹When the field is released in the Jubilee, it will become holy, like a field devoted to the Lord; it will become priestly property.

²²"If anyone dedicates to the Lord a field they have bought, which is not part of their family land, ²³the priest will determine its value up to the Year of Jubilee, and the owner must pay its value on that day as something holy to the Lord. ²⁴In the Year of Jubilee the field will revert to the person from whom it was bought, the one whose land it was. ²⁵Every value is to be set according to the sanctuary shekel, twenty gerahs to the shekel.

²⁶"No one, however, may dedicate the firstborn of an animal, since the firstborn already belongs to the Lord; whether an ox*a* or a sheep, it is the Lord's. ²⁷If it is one of the unclean animals, it may be bought back at its set value, adding a fifth of the value to it. If it is not redeemed, it is to be sold at its set value.

²⁸"But nothing that a person owns and devotes*b* to the Lord—whether a human being or an animal or family land—may be sold or redeemed; everything so devoted is most holy to the Lord.

²⁹"No person devoted to destruction*c* may be ransomed; they are to be put to death.

³⁰"A tithe of everything from the land, whether grain from the soil or fruit from the trees, belongs to the Lord; it is holy to the Lord. ³¹Whoever would redeem any of their tithe must add a fifth of the value to it. ³²Every tithe of the herd and flock— every tenth animal that passes under the shepherd's rod—will be holy to the Lord. ³³No one may pick out the good from the bad or make any substitution. If anyone does make a substitution, both the animal and its substitute become holy and cannot be redeemed.'"

³⁴These are the commands the Lord gave Moses at Mount Sinai for the Israelites.

---

a 26 The Hebrew word can refer to either male or female.   *b 28* The Hebrew term refers to the irrevocable giving over of things or persons to the Lord.   *c 29* The Hebrew term refers to the irrevocable giving over of things or persons to the Lord, often by totally destroying them.

NUMBERS

Numbers gets its name from the two accounts in chapters 1 and 26 of the numberings or countings of the people of Israel. Moses is the author of this book as well as the leader of the Israelites.

The first part of the book tells about Israel's year while camped at the foot of Mount Sinai. The second part of the book tells of Israel's journey from Mount Sinai to the east side of the Dead Sea. The third part of the book tells of the preparations for entering and conquering the land of Canaan.

Throughout the years of wandering in the desert, the Israelites were constantly reminded of one thing — God's care for them. He miraculously supplied the Israelites with manna, water and quail for their forty years in the desert. God loved and forgave his people continually even though they rebelled against him and their leaders.

The Census

I The LORD spoke to Moses in the tent of meeting in the Desert of Sinai on the first day of the second month of the second year after the Israelites came out of Egypt. He said: ²"Take a census of the whole Israelite community by their clans and families, listing every man by name, one by one. ³You and Aaron are to count according to their divisions all the men in Israel who are twenty years old or more and able to serve in the army. ⁴One man from each tribe, each of them the head of his family, is to help you. ⁵These are the names of the men who are to assist you:

from Reuben, Elizur son of Shedeur;
⁶from Simeon, Shelumiel son of Zurishaddai;
⁷from Judah, Nahshon son of Amminadab;
⁸from Issachar, Nethanel son of Zuar;
⁹from Zebulun, Eliab son of Helon;
¹⁰from the sons of Joseph:
from Ephraim, Elishama son of Ammihud;
from Manasseh, Gamaliel son of Pedahzur;
¹¹from Benjamin, Abidan son of Gideoni;
¹²from Dan, Ahiezer son of Ammishaddai;
¹³from Asher, Pagiel son of Okran;
¹⁴from Gad, Eliasaph son of Deuel;
¹⁵from Naphtali, Ahira son of Enan."

¹⁶These were the men appointed from the community, the leaders of their ancestral tribes. They were the heads of the clans of Israel.

¹⁷Moses and Aaron took these men whose names had been specified, ¹⁸and they called the whole community together on the first day of the second month. The people registered their ancestry by their clans and families, and the men twenty years old or more were listed by name, one by one, ¹⁹as the LORD commanded Moses. And so he counted them in the Desert of Sinai:

²⁰From the descendants of Reuben the firstborn son of Israel:

All the men twenty years old or more who were able to serve in the army were listed by name, one by one, according to the records of their clans and families. ²¹The number from the tribe of Reuben was 46,500.

²²From the descendants of Simeon:

All the men twenty years old or more who were able to serve in the army were counted and listed by name, one by one, according to the records of their clans and families. ²³The number from the tribe of Simeon was 59,300.

²⁴From the descendants of Gad:

All the men twenty years old or more who were able to serve in the army were listed by name, according to the records of their clans and families. ²⁵The number from the tribe of Gad was 45,650.

²⁶From the descendants of Judah:

All the men twenty years old or more who were able to serve in the army were listed by name, according to the records of their clans and families. ²⁷The number from the tribe of Judah was 74,600.

²⁸From the descendants of Issachar:

All the men twenty years old or more who were able to serve in the army were listed by name, according to the records of their clans and families. ²⁹The number from the tribe of Issachar was 54,400.

³⁰From the descendants of Zebulun:

All the men twenty years old or more who were able to serve in the army were listed by name, according to the records of their clans and families. ³¹The number from the tribe of Zebulun was 57,400.

³²From the sons of Joseph:

From the descendants of Ephraim:

All the men twenty years old or more who were able to serve in the army were listed by name, according to the records of their clans and families. ³³The number from the tribe of Ephraim was 40,500.

³⁴From the descendants of Manasseh: All the men twenty years old or more who were able to serve in the army were listed by name, according to the records of their clans and families. ³⁵The number from the tribe of Manasseh was 32,200.

³⁶From the descendants of Benjamin: All the men twenty years old or more who were able to serve in the army were listed by name, according to the records of their clans and families. ³⁷The number from the tribe of Benjamin was 35,400.

³⁸From the descendants of Dan: All the men twenty years old or more who were able to serve in the army were listed by name, according to the records of their clans and families. ³⁹The number from the tribe of Dan was 62,700.

⁴⁰From the descendants of Asher: All the men twenty years old or more who were able to serve in the army were listed by name, according to the records of their clans and families. ⁴¹The number from the tribe of Asher was 41,500.

⁴²From the descendants of Naphtali: All the men twenty years old or more who were able to serve in the army were listed by name, according to the records of their clans and families. ⁴³The number from the tribe of Naphtali was 53,400.

⁴⁴These were the men counted by Moses and Aaron and the twelve leaders of Israel, each one representing his family. ⁴⁵All the Israelites twenty years old or more who were able to serve in Israel's army were counted according to their families. ⁴⁶The total number was 603,550.

⁴⁷The ancestral tribe of the Levites, however, was not counted along with the others. ⁴⁸The LORD had said to Moses: ⁴⁹"You must not count the tribe of Levi or include them in the census of the other

---

Numbers 1:1–46

You can count on the Bible's numbers.

Do the math in the first chapter of Numbers and you discover there were 603,500 men in Israel over the age of 20 who were able to fight in the army (see Numbers 1:45 and 46). But that tally presents a puzzle. That many fighting men means a total population of two or three million, significantly more than the million people archaeologists believe lived in Israel at its peak five hundred years later. Some Christians see this puzzle and accept the numbers in Numbers just as they are stated. Others suggest ancient writers didn't use numbers as we do. They might have rounded the count, or enlarged the numbers to speak of God's mighty power. Whatever we conclude about the data, the Lord's aim of founding a great nation was coming true. He was turning the small family of Abraham into a mighty nation.

Think: Do you think the ancient authors of the Bible used numbers like we do? Why—or why not?

ROCK SOLID truths

Israelites. ⁵⁰Instead, appoint the Levites to be in charge of the tabernacle of the covenant law—over all its furnishings and everything belonging to it. They are to carry the tabernacle and all its furnishings; they are to take care of it and encamp around it. ⁵¹Whenever the tabernacle is to move, the Levites are to take it down, and whenever the tabernacle is to be set up, the Levites shall do it. Anyone else who approaches it is to be put to death. ⁵²The Israelites are to set up their tents by divisions, each of them in their own camp under their standard. ⁵³The Levites, however, are to set up their tents around the tabernacle of the covenant law so that my wrath will not fall on the Israelite community. The Levites are to be responsible for the care of the tabernacle of the covenant law."

⁵⁴The Israelites did all this just as the LORD commanded Moses.

The Arrangement of the Tribal Camps

2 The LORD said to Moses and Aaron: ²"The Israelites are to camp around the tent of meeting some distance from it, each of them under their standard and holding the banners of their family."

³On the east, toward the sunrise, the divisions of the camp of Judah are to encamp under their standard. The leader of the people of Judah is Nahshon son of Amminadab. ⁴His division numbers 74,600.

⁵The tribe of Issachar will camp next to them. The leader of the people of Issachar is Nethanel son of Zuar. ⁶His division numbers 54,400.

⁷The tribe of Zebulun will be next. The leader of the people of Zebulun is Eliab son of Helon. ⁸His division numbers 57,400.

⁹All the men assigned to the camp of Judah, according to their divisions, number 186,400. They will set out first.

¹⁰On the south will be the divisions of the camp of Reuben under their standard. The leader of the people of Reuben is Elizur son of Shedeur. ¹¹His division numbers 46,500.

¹²The tribe of Simeon will camp next to them. The leader of the people of Simeon is Shelumiel son of Zurishaddai. ¹³His division numbers 59,300.

¹⁴The tribe of Gad will be next. The leader of the people of Gad is Eliasaph son of Deuel.^{*a*} ¹⁵His division numbers 45,650.

¹⁶All the men assigned to the camp of Reuben, according to their divisions, number 151,450. They will set out second.

¹⁷Then the tent of meeting and the camp of the Levites will set out in the middle of the camps. They will set out in the same order as they encamp, each in their own place under their standard.

¹⁸On the west will be the divisions of the camp of Ephraim under their standard. The leader of the people of Ephraim is Elishama son of Ammihud. ¹⁹His division numbers 40,500.

²⁰The tribe of Manasseh will be next to them. The leader of the people of Manasseh is Gamaliel son of Pedahzur. ²¹His division numbers 32,200.

²²The tribe of Benjamin will be next. The leader of the people of Benjamin is Abidan son of Gideoni. ²³His division numbers 35,400.

²⁴All the men assigned to the camp of Ephraim, according to their divisions, number 108,100. They will set out third.

²⁵On the north will be the divisions of the camp of Dan under their standard. The leader of the people of Dan is Ahiezer son of Ammishaddai. ²⁶His division numbers 62,700.

²⁷The tribe of Asher will camp next to them. The leader of the people of Asher is Pagiel son of Okran. ²⁸His division numbers 41,500.

²⁹The tribe of Naphtali will be next. The leader of the people of Naphtali is Ahira son of Enan. ³⁰His division numbers 53,400.

³¹All the men assigned to the camp of Dan number 157,600. They will set out last, under their standards.

---

^{*a*} *14* Many manuscripts of the Masoretic Text, Samaritan Pentateuch and Vulgate (see also 1:14); most manuscripts of the Masoretic Text *Reuel*

³²These are the Israelites, counted according to their families. All the men in the camps, by their divisions, number 603,550. ³³The Levites, however, were not counted along with the other Israelites, as the Lord commanded Moses.

³⁴So the Israelites did everything the Lord commanded Moses; that is the way they encamped under their standards, and that is the way they set out, each of them with their clan and family.

The Levites

3 This is the account of the family of Aaron and Moses at the time the Lord spoke to Moses at Mount Sinai.

²The names of the sons of Aaron were Nadab the firstborn and Abihu, Eleazar and Ithamar. ³Those were the names of Aaron's sons, the anointed priests, who were ordained to serve as priests. ⁴Nadab and Abihu, however, died before the Lord when they made an offering with unauthorized fire before him in the Desert of Sinai. They had no sons, so Eleazar and Ithamar served as priests during the lifetime of their father Aaron.

⁵The Lord said to Moses, ⁶"Bring the tribe of Levi and present them to Aaron the priest to assist him. ⁷They are to perform duties for him and for the whole community at the tent of meeting by doing the work of the tabernacle. ⁸They are to take care of all the furnishings of the tent of meeting, fulfilling the obligations of the Israelites by doing the work of the tabernacle. ⁹Give the Levites to Aaron and his sons; they are the Israelites who are to be given wholly to him.[a] ¹⁰Appoint Aaron and his sons to serve as priests; anyone else who approaches the sanctuary is to be put to death."

¹¹The Lord also said to Moses, ¹²"I have taken the Levites from among the Israelites in place of the first male offspring of every Israelite woman. The Levites are mine, ¹³for all the firstborn are mine. When I struck down all the firstborn in Egypt, I set apart for myself every first-born in Israel, whether human or animal. They are to be mine. I am the Lord."

¹⁴The Lord said to Moses in the Desert of Sinai, ¹⁵"Count the Levites by their families and clans. Count every male a month old or more." ¹⁶So Moses counted them, as he was commanded by the word of the Lord.

¹⁷These were the names of the sons of Levi:

Gershon, Kohath and Merari.

¹⁸These were the names of the Gershonite clans:

Libni and Shimei.

¹⁹The Kohathite clans:

Amram, Izhar, Hebron and Uzziel.

²⁰The Merarite clans:

Mahli and Mushi.

These were the Levite clans, according to their families.

²¹To Gershon belonged the clans of the Libnites and Shimeites; these were the Gershonite clans. ²²The number of all the males a month old or more who were counted was 7,500. ²³The Gershonite clans were to camp on the west, behind the tabernacle. ²⁴The leader of the families of the Gershonites was Eliasaph son of Lael. ²⁵At the tent of meeting the Gershonites were responsible for the care of the tabernacle and tent, its coverings, the curtain at the entrance to the tent of meeting, ²⁶the curtains of the courtyard, the curtain at the entrance to the courtyard surrounding the tabernacle and altar, and the ropes—and everything related to their use.

²⁷To Kohath belonged the clans of the Amramites, Izharites, Hebronites and Uzzielites; these were the Kohathite clans. ²⁸The number of all the males a month old or more was 8,600.[b] The Kohathites were responsible for the care of the sanctuary. ²⁹The Kohathite clans were to camp

---

a 9 Most manuscripts of the Masoretic Text; some manuscripts of the Masoretic Text, Samaritan Pentateuch and Septuagint (see also 8:16) *to me*   *b* 28 Hebrew; some Septuagint manuscripts *8,300* on the south side of the tabernacle. ³⁰The leader of the families of the Kohathite clans was Elizaphan son of Uzziel. ³¹They were responsible for the care of the ark, the table, the lampstand, the altars, the articles of the sanctuary used in ministering, the curtain, and everything related to their use. ³²The chief leader of the Levites was Eleazar son of Aaron, the priest. He was appointed over those who were responsible for the care of the sanctuary.

³³To Merari belonged the clans of the Mahlites and the Mushites; these were the Merarite clans. ³⁴The number of all the males a month old or more who were counted was 6,200. ³⁵The leader of the families of the Merarite clans was Zuriel son of Abihail; they were to camp on the north side of the tabernacle. ³⁶The Merarites were appointed to take care of the frames of the tabernacle, its crossbars, posts, bases, all its equipment, and everything related to their use, ³⁷as well as the posts of the surrounding courtyard with their bases, tent pegs and ropes.

³⁸Moses and Aaron and his sons were to camp to the east of the tabernacle, toward the sunrise, in front of the tent of meeting. They were responsible for the care of the sanctuary on behalf of the Israelites. Anyone else who approached the sanctuary was to be put to death.

³⁹The total number of Levites counted at the LORD's command by Moses and Aaron according to their clans, including every male a month old or more, was 22,000.

⁴⁰The LORD said to Moses, "Count all the firstborn Israelite males who are a month old or more and make a list of their names. ⁴¹Take the Levites for me in place of all the firstborn of the Israelites, and the livestock of the Levites in place of all the firstborn of the livestock of the Israelites. I am the LORD."

⁴²So Moses counted all the firstborn of the Israelites, as the LORD command-

ed him. ⁴³The total number of firstborn males a month old or more, listed by name, was 22,273.

⁴⁴The LORD also said to Moses, ⁴⁵"Take the Levites in place of all the firstborn of Israel, and the livestock of the Levites in place of their livestock. The Levites are to be mine. I am the LORD. ⁴⁶To redeem the 273 firstborn Israelites who exceed the number of the Levites, ⁴⁷collect five shekels^a for each one, according to the sanctuary shekel, which weighs twenty gerahs. ⁴⁸Give the money for the redemption of the additional Israelites to Aaron and his sons."

⁴⁹So Moses collected the redemption money from those who exceeded the number redeemed by the Levites. ⁵⁰From the firstborn of the Israelites he collected silver weighing 1,365 shekels,^b according to the sanctuary shekel. ⁵¹Moses gave the redemption money to Aaron and his sons, as he was commanded by the word of the LORD.

The Kohathites

4 The LORD said to Moses and Aaron: ²"Take a census of the Kohathite branch of the Levites by their clans and families. ³Count all the men from thirty to fifty years of age who come to serve in the work at the tent of meeting.

⁴"This is the work of the Kohathites at the tent of meeting: the care of the most holy things. ⁵When the camp is to move, Aaron and his sons are to go in and take down the shielding curtain and put it over the ark of the covenant law. ⁶Then they are to cover the curtain with a durable leather,^c spread a cloth of solid blue over that and put the poles in place.

⁷"Over the table of the Presence they are to spread a blue cloth and put on it the plates, dishes and bowls, and the jars for drink offerings; the bread that is continually there is to remain on it. ⁸They are

^a 47 That is, about 2 ounces or about 58 grams
^b 50 That is, about 35 pounds or about 16 kilograms   ^c 6 Possibly the hides of large aquatic mammals; also in verses 8, 10, 11, 12, 14 and 25

to spread a scarlet cloth over them, cover that with the durable leather and put the poles in place.

⁹"They are to take a blue cloth and cover the lampstand that is for light, together with its lamps, its wick trimmers and trays, and all its jars for the olive oil used to supply it. ¹⁰Then they are to wrap it and all its accessories in a covering of the durable leather and put it on a carrying frame.

¹¹"Over the gold altar they are to spread a blue cloth and cover that with the durable leather and put the poles in place.

¹²"They are to take all the articles used for ministering in the sanctuary, wrap them in a blue cloth, cover that with the durable leather and put them on a carrying frame.

¹³"They are to remove the ashes from the bronze altar and spread a purple cloth over it. ¹⁴Then they are to place on it all the utensils used for ministering at the altar, including the firepans, meat forks, shovels and sprinkling bowls. Over it they are to spread a covering of the durable leather and put the poles in place.

¹⁵"After Aaron and his sons have finished covering the holy furnishings and all the holy articles, and when the camp is ready to move, only then are the Kohathites to come and do the carrying. But they must not touch the holy things or they will die. The Kohathites are to carry those things that are in the tent of meeting.

¹⁶"Eleazar son of Aaron, the priest, is to have charge of the oil for the light, the fragrant incense, the regular grain offering and the anointing oil. He is to be in charge of the entire tabernacle and everything in it, including its holy furnishings and articles."

¹⁷The LORD said to Moses and Aaron, ¹⁸"See that the Kohathite tribal clans are not destroyed from among the Levites. ¹⁹So that they may live and not die when they come near the most holy things, do this for them: Aaron and his sons are to go into the sanctuary and assign to each man his work and what he is to carry. ²⁰But the Kohathites must not go in to look at the holy things, even for a moment, or they will die."

The Gershonites

²¹The LORD said to Moses, ²²"Take a census also of the Gershonites by their families and clans. ²³Count all the men from thirty to fifty years of age who come to serve in the work at the tent of meeting. ²⁴"This is the service of the Gershonite clans in their carrying and their other work: ²⁵They are to carry the curtains of the tabernacle, that is, the tent of meeting, its covering and its outer covering of durable leather, the curtains for the entrance to the tent of meeting, ²⁶the curtains of the courtyard surrounding the tabernacle and altar, the curtain for the entrance to the courtyard, the ropes and all the equipment used in the service of the tent. The Gershonites are to do all that needs to be done with these things. ²⁷All their service, whether carrying or doing other work, is to be done under the direction of Aaron and his sons. You shall assign to them as their responsibility all they are to carry. ²⁸This is the service of the Gershonite clans at the tent of meeting. Their duties are to be under the direction of Ithamar son of Aaron, the priest.

The Merarites

²⁹"Count the Merarites by their clans and families. ³⁰Count all the men from thirty to fifty years of age who come to serve in the work at the tent of meeting. ³¹As part of all their service at the tent, they are to carry the frames of the tabernacle, its crossbars, posts and bases, ³²as well as the posts of the surrounding courtyard with their bases, tent pegs, ropes, all their equipment and everything related to their use. Assign to each man the specific things he is to carry. ³³This is the service of the Merarite clans as they work at the tent of meeting under the direction of Ithamar son of Aaron, the priest."

The Numbering of the Levite Clans

³⁴Moses, Aaron and the leaders of the community counted the Kohathites by their clans and families. ³⁵All the men from thirty to fifty years of age who came to serve in the work at the tent of meeting,

³⁶counted by clans, were 2,750. ³⁷This was the total of all those in the Kohathite clans who served at the tent of meeting. Moses and Aaron counted them according to the LORD's command through Moses.

³⁸The Gershonites were counted by their clans and families. ³⁹All the men from thirty to fifty years of age who came to serve in the work at the tent of meeting, ⁴⁰counted by their clans and families, were 2,630. ⁴¹This was the total of those in the Gershonite clans who served at the tent of meeting. Moses and Aaron counted them according to the LORD's command.

⁴²The Merarites were counted by their clans and families. ⁴³All the men from thirty to fifty years of age who came to serve in the work at the tent of meeting, ⁴⁴counted by their clans, were 3,200. ⁴⁵This was the total of those in the Merarite clans. Moses and Aaron counted them according to the LORD's command through Moses.

⁴⁶So Moses, Aaron and the leaders of Israel counted all the Levites by their clans and families. ⁴⁷All the men from thirty to fifty years of age who came to do the work of serving and carrying the tent of meeting ⁴⁸numbered 8,580. ⁴⁹At the LORD's command through Moses, each was assigned his work and told what to carry.

Thus they were counted, as the LORD commanded Moses.

The Purity of the Camp

5 The LORD said to Moses, ²"Command the Israelites to send away from the camp anyone who has a defiling skin disease^a or a discharge of any kind, or who is ceremonially unclean because of a dead body. ³Send away male and female alike; send them outside the camp so they will not defile their camp, where I dwell among them." ⁴The Israelites did so; they sent them outside the camp. They did just as the LORD had instructed Moses.

Restitution for Wrongs

⁵The LORD said to Moses, ⁶"Say to the Israelites: 'Any man or woman who wrongs another in any way^b and so is unfaithful to the LORD is guilty ⁷and must confess the sin they have committed. They must make full restitution for the wrong they have done, add a fifth of the value to it and give it all to the person they have wronged. ⁸But if that person has no close relative to whom restitution can be made for the wrong, the restitution belongs to the LORD and must be given to the priest, along with the ram with which atonement is made for the wrongdoer. ⁹All the sacred contributions the Israelites bring to a priest will belong to him. ¹⁰Sacred things belong to their owners, but what they give to the priest will belong to the priest.'"

The Test for an Unfaithful Wife

¹¹Then the LORD said to Moses, ¹²"Speak to the Israelites and say to them: 'If a man's wife goes astray and is unfaithful to him ¹³so that another man has sexual relations with her, and this is hidden from her husband and her impurity is undetected (since there is no witness against her and she has not been caught in the act), ¹⁴and if feelings of jealousy come over her husband and he suspects his wife and she is impure—or if he is jealous and suspects her even though she is not impure— ¹⁵then he is to take his wife to the priest. He must also take an offering of a tenth of an ephah^c of barley flour on her behalf. He must not pour olive oil on it or put incense on it, because it is a grain offering for jealousy, a reminder-offering to draw attention to wrongdoing.

¹⁶"'The priest shall bring her and have her stand before the LORD. ¹⁷Then he shall take some holy water in a clay jar and put some dust from the tabernacle floor into the water. ¹⁸After the priest has had the woman stand before the LORD, he shall loosen her hair and place in her hands the reminder-offering, the grain offering for

---

^a 2 The Hebrew word for *defiling skin disease*, traditionally translated "leprosy," was used for various diseases affecting the skin.
^b 6 Or *woman who commits any wrong common to mankind*   ^c 15 That is, probably about 3 1/2 pounds or about 1.6 kilograms

ROCK SOLID
principles

Numbers 5:5–7

Make wrongs right.

Alex bit his lip and tried not to cry. He and his hockey buddies were practicing plays on a community rink when a little girl wandered into his path. Alex knocked her flat on her face, and her lips and chin spilled enough blood to make even a hockey player shiver. Alex said he was sorry, but he wasn't sure what else to do. As he wiped his face, he knew he couldn't undo the accident. But he wanted to fix whatever he could. Before the girl and her parents rushed away for stitches, he got their names and the dad's phone number. Alex decided he had to figure out a way to put a smile back on her face.

You can't undo every bad action—whether it's an accident, mistake, or sin. "Restitution" is acting to make wrongs right to the best of your ability. When you do wrong, start by confessing your fault. Then demonstrate real sorrow by paying back the damages you did—plus more (see Numbers 5:7).

jealousy, while he himself holds the bitter water that brings a curse. ¹⁹Then the priest shall put the woman under oath and say to her, "If no other man has had sexual relations with you and you have not gone astray and become impure while married to your husband, may this bitter water that brings a curse not harm you. ²⁰But if you have gone astray while married to your husband and you have made yourself impure by having sexual relations with a man other than your husband"— ²¹here the priest is to put the woman under this curse—"may the Lord cause you to become a curse*ᵃ* among your people when he makes your womb miscarry and your abdomen swell. ²²May this water that brings a curse enter your body so that your abdomen swells or your womb miscarries."

"'Then the woman is to say, "Amen. So be it."

²³"'The priest is to write these curses on a scroll and then wash them off into the bitter water. ²⁴He shall make the wom-

an drink the bitter water that brings a curse, and this water that brings a curse and causes bitter suffering will enter her. ²⁵The priest is to take from her hands the grain offering for jealousy, wave it before the Lord and bring it to the altar. ²⁶The priest is then to take a handful of the grain offering as a memorial*ᵇ* offering and burn it on the altar; after that, he is to have the woman drink the water. ²⁷If she has made herself impure and been unfaithful to her husband, this will be the result: When she is made to drink the water that brings a curse and causes bitter suffering, it will enter her, her abdomen will swell and her womb will miscarry, and she will become a curse. ²⁸If, however, the woman has not made herself impure, but is clean, she will be cleared of guilt and will be able to have children.

ᵃ 21 That is, may he cause your name to be used in cursing (see Jer. 29:22); or, may others see that you are cursed; similarly in verse 27.
ᵇ 26 Or *representative*

29 "'This, then, is the law of jealousy when a woman goes astray and makes herself impure while married to her husband, 30 or when feelings of jealousy come over a man because he suspects his wife. The priest is to have her stand before the LORD and is to apply this entire law to her. 31 The husband will be innocent of any wrongdoing, but the woman will bear the consequences of her sin.'"

The Nazirite

6 The LORD said to Moses, 2 "Speak to the Israelites and say to them: 'If a man or woman wants to make a special vow, a vow of dedication to the LORD as a Nazirite, 3 they must abstain from wine and other fermented drink and must not drink vinegar made from wine or other fermented drink. They must not drink grape juice or eat grapes or raisins. 4 As long as they remain under their Nazirite vow, they must not eat anything that comes from the grapevine, not even the seeds or skins.

5 "'During the entire period of their Nazirite vow, no razor may be used on their head. They must be holy until the period of their dedication to the LORD is over; they must let their hair grow long.

6 "'Throughout the period of their dedication to the LORD, the Nazirite must not go near a dead body. 7 Even if their own father or mother or brother or sister dies, they must not make themselves ceremonially unclean on account of them, because the symbol of their dedication to God is on their head. 8 Throughout the period of their dedication, they are consecrated to the LORD.

9 "'If someone dies suddenly in the Nazirite's presence, thus defiling the hair that symbolizes their dedication, they must shave their head on the seventh day—the day of their cleansing. 10 Then on the eighth day they must bring two doves or two young pigeons to the priest at the entrance to the tent of meeting. 11 The priest is to offer one as a sin offering[a] and the other as a burnt offering to make atonement for the Nazirite because they sinned by being in the presence of the dead body. That same day they are to consecrate their head again. 12 They must rededicate themselves to the LORD for the same period of dedication and must bring a year-old male lamb as a guilt offering. The previous days do not count, because they became defiled during their period of dedication.

13 "'Now this is the law of the Nazirite when the period of their dedication is over. They are to be brought to the entrance to the tent of meeting. 14 There they are to present their offerings to the LORD: a year-old male lamb without defect for a burnt offering, a year-old ewe lamb without defect for a sin offering, a ram without defect for a fellowship offering, 15 together with their grain offerings and drink offerings, and a basket of bread made with the finest flour and without yeast—thick loaves with olive oil mixed in, and thin loaves brushed with olive oil.

16 "'The priest is to present all these before the LORD and make the sin offering and the burnt offering. 17 He is to present the basket of unleavened bread and is to sacrifice the ram as a fellowship offering to the LORD, together with its grain offering and drink offering.

18 "'Then at the entrance to the tent of meeting, the Nazirite must shave off the hair that symbolizes their dedication. They are to take the hair and put it in the fire that is under the sacrifice of the fellowship offering.

19 "'After the Nazirite has shaved off the hair that symbolizes their dedication, the priest is to place in their hands a boiled shoulder of the ram, and one thick loaf and one thin loaf from the basket, both made without yeast. 20 The priest shall then wave these before the LORD as a wave offering; they are holy and belong to the priest, together with the breast that was waved and the thigh that was presented. After that, the Nazirite may drink wine.

21 "'This is the law of the Nazirite who vows offerings to the LORD in accordance with their dedication, in addition to

^a 11 Or *purification offering*; also in verses 14 and 16

whatever else they can afford. They must fulfill the vows they have made, according to the law of the Nazirite.'"

The Priestly Blessing

²²The Lᴏʀᴅ said to Moses, ²³"Tell Aaron and his sons, 'This is how you are to bless the Israelites. Say to them:

²⁴"'"The Lᴏʀᴅ bless you
and keep you;
²⁵ the Lᴏʀᴅ make his face shine on you
and be gracious to you;
²⁶ the Lᴏʀᴅ turn his face toward you
and give you peace."'

²⁷"So they will put my name on the Israelites, and I will bless them."

ROCK SOLID
promises

"The Lᴏʀᴅ make his face shine on you and be gracious to you."

Numbers 6:25

God isn't the angry guy some people think he is. He reveals himself to you and treats you with kindness you don't deserve.

Offerings at the Dedication of the Tabernacle

7 When Moses finished setting up the tabernacle, he anointed and consecrated it and all its furnishings. He also anointed and consecrated the altar and all its utensils. ²Then the leaders of Israel, the heads of families who were the tribal leaders in charge of those who were counted, made offerings. ³They brought as their gifts before the Lᴏʀᴅ six covered carts and twelve oxen—an ox from each leader and a cart from every two. These they presented before the tabernacle.

⁴The Lᴏʀᴅ said to Moses, ⁵"Accept these from them, that they may be used in the work at the tent of meeting. Give them to the Levites as each man's work requires."

⁶So Moses took the carts and oxen and gave them to the Levites. ⁷He gave two carts and four oxen to the Gershonites, as their work required, ⁸and he gave four carts and eight oxen to the Merarites, as their work required. They were all under the direction of Ithamar son of Aaron, the priest. ⁹But Moses did not give any to the Kohathites, because they were to carry on their shoulders the holy things, for which they were responsible.

¹⁰When the altar was anointed, the leaders brought their offerings for its dedication and presented them before the altar. ¹¹For the Lᴏʀᴅ had said to Moses, "Each day one leader is to bring his offering for the dedication of the altar."

¹²The one who brought his offering on the first day was Nahshon son of Amminadab of the tribe of Judah.

¹³His offering was one silver plate weighing a hundred and thirty shekels[a] and one silver sprinkling bowl weighing seventy shekels,[b] both according to the sanctuary shekel, each filled with the finest flour mixed with olive oil as a grain offering; ¹⁴one gold dish weighing ten shekels,[c] filled with incense; ¹⁵one young bull, one ram and one male lamb a year old for a burnt offering; ¹⁶one male goat for a sin offering[d]; ¹⁷and two oxen, five rams, five male goats and five male lambs a year old to be sacrificed as a fellowship offering. This was the offering of Nahshon son of Amminadab.

¹⁸On the second day Nethanel son of Zuar, the leader of Issachar, brought his offering.

---

[a] *13* That is, about 3 1/4 pounds or about 1.5 kilograms; also elsewhere in this chapter
[b] *13* That is, about 1 3/4 pounds or about 800 grams; also elsewhere in this chapter
[c] *14* That is, about 4 ounces or about 115 grams; also elsewhere in this chapter
[d] *16* Or *purification offering*; also elsewhere in this chapter

[19]The offering he brought was one silver plate weighing a hundred and thirty shekels and one silver sprinkling bowl weighing seventy shekels, both according to the sanctuary shekel, each filled with the finest flour mixed with olive oil as a grain offering; [20]one gold dish weighing ten shekels, filled with incense; [21]one young bull, one ram and one male lamb a year old for a burnt offering; [22]one male goat for a sin offering; [23]and two oxen, five rams, five male goats and five male lambs a year old to be sacrificed as a fellowship offering. This was the offering of Nethanel son of Zuar.

[24]On the third day, Eliab son of Helon, the leader of the people of Zebulun, brought his offering.

[25]His offering was one silver plate weighing a hundred and thirty shekels and one silver sprinkling bowl weighing seventy shekels, both according to the sanctuary shekel, each filled with the finest flour mixed with olive oil as a grain offering; [26]one gold dish weighing ten shekels, filled with incense; [27]one young bull, one ram and one male lamb a year old for a burnt offering; [28]one male goat for a sin offering; [29]and two oxen, five rams, five male goats and five male lambs a year old to be sacrificed as a fellowship offering. This was the offering of Eliab son of Helon.

[30]On the fourth day Elizur son of Shedeur, the leader of the people of Reuben, brought his offering.

[31]His offering was one silver plate weighing a hundred and thirty shekels and one silver sprinkling bowl weighing seventy shekels, both according to the sanctuary shekel, each filled with the finest flour mixed with olive oil as a grain offering; [32]one gold dish weighing ten shekels, filled with incense; [33]one young bull, one ram and one male lamb a year old for a burnt offering; [34]one male goat for a sin offering; [35]and two oxen, five rams, five male goats and five male lambs a year old to be sacrificed as a fellowship offering. This was the offering of Elizur son of Shedeur.

[36]On the fifth day Shelumiel son of Zurishaddai, the leader of the people of Simeon, brought his offering.

[37]His offering was one silver plate weighing a hundred and thirty shekels and one silver sprinkling bowl weighing seventy shekels, both according to the sanctuary shekel, each filled with the finest flour mixed with olive oil as a grain offering; [38]one gold dish weighing ten shekels, filled with incense; [39]one young bull, one ram and one male lamb a year old for a burnt offering; [40]one male goat for a sin offering; [41]and two oxen, five rams, five male goats and five male lambs a year old to be sacrificed as a fellowship offering. This was the offering of Shelumiel son of Zurishaddai.

[42]On the sixth day Eliasaph son of Deuel, the leader of the people of Gad, brought his offering.

[43]His offering was one silver plate weighing a hundred and thirty shekels and one silver sprinkling bowl weighing seventy shekels, both according to the sanctuary shekel, each filled with the finest flour mixed with olive oil as a grain offering; [44]one gold dish weighing ten shekels, filled with incense; [45]one young bull, one ram and one male lamb a year old for a burnt offering; [46]one male goat for a sin offering; [47]and two oxen, five rams, five male goats and five male lambs a year old to be sacrificed as a fellowship offering. This was the offering of Eliasaph son of Deuel.

[48]On the seventh day Elishama son of Ammihud, the leader of the people of Ephraim, brought his offering.

[49]His offering was one silver plate weighing a hundred and thirty shekels and one silver sprinkling bowl

weighing seventy shekels, both according to the sanctuary shekel, each filled with the finest flour mixed with olive oil as a grain offering; ⁵⁰one gold dish weighing ten shekels, filled with incense; ⁵¹one young bull, one ram and one male lamb a year old for a burnt offering; ⁵²one male goat for a sin offering; ⁵³and two oxen, five rams, five male goats and five male lambs a year old to be sacrificed as a fellowship offering. This was the offering of Elishama son of Ammihud.

⁵⁴On the eighth day Gamaliel son of Pedahzur, the leader of the people of Manasseh, brought his offering.

⁵⁵His offering was one silver plate weighing a hundred and thirty shekels and one silver sprinkling bowl weighing seventy shekels, both according to the sanctuary shekel, each filled with the finest flour mixed with olive oil as a grain offering; ⁵⁶one gold dish weighing ten shekels, filled with incense; ⁵⁷one young bull, one ram and one male lamb a year old for a burnt offering; ⁵⁸one male goat for a sin offering; ⁵⁹and two oxen, five rams, five male goats and five male lambs a year old to be sacrificed as a fellowship offering. This was the offering of Gamaliel son of Pedahzur.

⁶⁰On the ninth day Abidan son of Gideoni, the leader of the people of Benjamin, brought his offering.

⁶¹His offering was one silver plate weighing a hundred and thirty shekels and one silver sprinkling bowl weighing seventy shekels, both according to the sanctuary shekel, each filled with the finest flour mixed with olive oil as a grain offering; ⁶²one gold dish weighing ten shekels, filled with incense; ⁶³one young bull, one ram and one male lamb a year old for a burnt offering; ⁶⁴one male goat for a sin offering; ⁶⁵and two oxen, five rams, five male goats

and five male lambs a year old to be sacrificed as a fellowship offering. This was the offering of Abidan son of Gideoni.

⁶⁶On the tenth day Ahiezer son of Ammishaddai, the leader of the people of Dan, brought his offering.

⁶⁷His offering was one silver plate weighing a hundred and thirty shekels and one silver sprinkling bowl weighing seventy shekels, both according to the sanctuary shekel, each filled with the finest flour mixed with olive oil as a grain offering; ⁶⁸one gold dish weighing ten shekels, filled with incense; ⁶⁹one young bull, one ram and one male lamb a year old for a burnt offering; ⁷⁰one male goat for a sin offering; ⁷¹and two oxen, five rams, five male goats and five male lambs a year old to be sacrificed as a fellowship offering. This was the offering of Ahiezer son of Ammishaddai.

⁷²On the eleventh day Pagiel son of Okran, the leader of the people of Asher, brought his offering.

⁷³His offering was one silver plate weighing a hundred and thirty shekels and one silver sprinkling bowl weighing seventy shekels, both according to the sanctuary shekel, each filled with the finest flour mixed with olive oil as a grain offering; ⁷⁴one gold dish weighing ten shekels, filled with incense; ⁷⁵one young bull, one ram and one male lamb a year old for a burnt offering; ⁷⁶one male goat for a sin offering; ⁷⁷and two oxen, five rams, five male goats and five male lambs a year old to be sacrificed as a fellowship offering. This was the offering of Pagiel son of Okran.

⁷⁸On the twelfth day Ahira son of Enan, the leader of the people of Naphtali, brought his offering.

⁷⁹His offering was one silver plate weighing a hundred and thirty shekels and one silver sprinkling bowl weighing seventy shekels, both ac-

cording to the sanctuary shekel, each filled with the finest flour mixed with olive oil as a grain offering; [80]one gold dish weighing ten shekels, filled with incense; [81]one young bull, one ram and one male lamb a year old for a burnt offering; [82]one male goat for a sin offering; [83]and two oxen, five rams, five male goats and five male lambs a year old to be sacrificed as a fellowship offering. This was the offering of Ahira son of Enan.

[84]These were the offerings of the Israelite leaders for the dedication of the altar when it was anointed: twelve silver plates, twelve silver sprinkling bowls and twelve gold dishes. [85]Each silver plate weighed a hundred and thirty shekels, and each sprinkling bowl seventy shekels. Altogether, the silver dishes weighed two thousand four hundred shekels,[a] according to the sanctuary shekel. [86]The twelve gold dishes filled with incense weighed ten shekels each, according to the sanctuary shekel. Altogether, the gold dishes weighed a hundred and twenty shekels.[b] [87]The total number of animals for the burnt offering came to twelve young bulls, twelve rams and twelve male lambs a year old, together with their grain offering. Twelve male goats were used for the sin offering. [88]The total number of animals for the sacrifice of the fellowship offering came to twenty-four oxen, sixty rams, sixty male goats and sixty male lambs a year old. These were the offerings for the dedication of the altar after it was anointed.

[89]When Moses entered the tent of meeting to speak with the LORD, he heard the voice speaking to him from between the two cherubim above the atonement cover on the ark of the covenant law. In this way the LORD spoke to him.

Setting Up the Lamps

8 The LORD said to Moses, [2]"Speak to Aaron and say to him, 'When you set up the lamps, see that all seven light up the area in front of the lampstand.'"

[3]Aaron did so; he set up the lamps so that they faced forward on the lampstand, just as the LORD commanded Moses. [4]This is how the lampstand was made: It was made of hammered gold—from its base to its blossoms. The lampstand was made exactly like the pattern the LORD had shown Moses.

The Setting Apart of the Levites

[5]The LORD said to Moses: [6]"Take the Levites from among all the Israelites and make them ceremonially clean. [7]To purify them, do this: Sprinkle the water of cleansing on them; then have them shave their whole bodies and wash their clothes. And so they will purify themselves. [8]Have them take a young bull with its grain offering of the finest flour mixed with olive oil; then you are to take a second young bull for a sin offering.[c] [9]Bring the Levites to the front of the tent of meeting and assemble the whole Israelite community. [10]You are to bring the Levites before the LORD, and the Israelites are to lay their hands on them. [11]Aaron is to present the Levites before the LORD as a wave offering from the Israelites, so that they may be ready to do the work of the LORD.

[12]"Then the Levites are to lay their hands on the heads of the bulls, using one for a sin offering to the LORD and the other for a burnt offering, to make atonement for the Levites. [13]Have the Levites stand in front of Aaron and his sons and then present them as a wave offering to the LORD. [14]In this way you are to set the Levites apart from the other Israelites, and the Levites will be mine.

[15]"After you have purified the Levites and presented them as a wave offering, they are to come to do their work at the tent of meeting. [16]They are the Israelites who are to be given wholly to me. I have taken them as my own in place of the firstborn, the first male offspring from every Israelite woman. [17]Every firstborn male in

[a] 85 That is, about 60 pounds or about 28 kilograms   [b] 86 That is, about 3 pounds or about 1.4 kilograms   [c] 8 Or purification offering; also in verse 12

Israel, whether human or animal, is mine. When I struck down all the firstborn in Egypt, I set them apart for myself. [18] And I have taken the Levites in place of all the firstborn sons in Israel. [19] From among all the Israelites, I have given the Levites as gifts to Aaron and his sons to do the work at the tent of meeting on behalf of the Israelites and to make atonement for them so that no plague will strike the Israelites when they go near the sanctuary."

[20] Moses, Aaron and the whole Israelite community did with the Levites just as the Lord commanded Moses. [21] The Levites purified themselves and washed their clothes. Then Aaron presented them as a wave offering before the Lord and made atonement for them to purify them. [22] After that, the Levites came to do their work at the tent of meeting under the supervision of Aaron and his sons. They did with the Levites just as the Lord commanded Moses.

[23] The Lord said to Moses, [24] "This applies to the Levites: Men twenty-five years old or more shall come to take part in the work at the tent of meeting, [25] but at the age of fifty, they must retire from their regular service and work no longer. [26] They may assist their brothers in performing their duties at the tent of meeting, but they themselves must not do the work. This, then, is how you are to assign the responsibilities of the Levites."

The Passover

9 The Lord spoke to Moses in the Desert of Sinai in the first month of the second year after they came out of Egypt. He said, [2] "Have the Israelites celebrate the Passover at the appointed time. [3] Celebrate it at the appointed time, at twilight on the fourteenth day of this month, in accordance with all its rules and regulations."

[4] So Moses told the Israelites to celebrate the Passover, [5] and they did so in the Desert of Sinai at twilight on the fourteenth day of the first month. The Israelites did everything just as the Lord commanded Moses.

[6] But some of them could not celebrate the Passover on that day because they were ceremonially unclean on account of a dead body. So they came to Moses and Aaron that same day [7] and said to Moses, "We have become unclean because of a dead body, but why should we be kept from presenting the Lord's offering with the other Israelites at the appointed time?"

[8] Moses answered them, "Wait until I find out what the Lord commands concerning you."

ROCK SOLID promises

"Wait until I find out what the Lord commands concerning you."

Numbers 9:8

God has specific plans for you, and he wants to show them to you.

[9] Then the Lord said to Moses, [10] "Tell the Israelites: 'When any of you or your descendants are unclean because of a dead body or are away on a journey, they are still to celebrate the Lord's Passover, [11] but they are to do it on the fourteenth day of the second month at twilight. They are to eat the lamb, together with unleavened bread and bitter herbs. [12] They must not leave any of it till morning or break any of its bones. When they celebrate the Passover, they must follow all the regulations. [13] But if anyone who is ceremonially clean and not on a journey fails to celebrate the Passover, they must be cut off from their people for not presenting the Lord's offering at the appointed time. They will bear the consequences of their sin.

[14] "'A foreigner residing among you is also to celebrate the Lord's Passover in accordance with its rules and regulations.

You must have the same regulations for both the foreigner and the native-born.'"

The Cloud Above the Tabernacle

¹⁵On the day the tabernacle, the tent of the covenant law, was set up, the cloud covered it. From evening till morning the cloud above the tabernacle looked like fire. ¹⁶That is how it continued to be; the cloud covered it, and at night it looked like fire. ¹⁷Whenever the cloud lifted from above the tent, the Israelites set out; wherever the cloud settled, the Israelites encamped. ¹⁸At the LORD's command the Israelites set out, and at his command they encamped. As long as the cloud stayed over the tabernacle, they remained in camp. ¹⁹When the cloud remained over the tabernacle a long time, the Israelites obeyed the LORD's order and did not set out. ²⁰Sometimes the cloud was over the tabernacle only a few days; at the LORD's command they would encamp, and then at his command they would set out. ²¹Sometimes the cloud stayed only from evening till morning, and when it lifted in the morning, they set out. Whether by day or by night, whenever the cloud lifted, they set out. ²²Whether the cloud stayed over the tabernacle for two days or a month or a year, the Israelites would remain in camp and not set out; but when it lifted, they would set out. ²³At the LORD's command they encamped, and at the LORD's command they set out. They obeyed the LORD's order, in accordance with his command through Moses.

The Silver Trumpets

10 The LORD said to Moses: ²"Make two trumpets of hammered silver, and use them for calling the community together and for having the camps set out. ³When both are sounded, the whole community is to assemble before you at the entrance to the tent of meeting. ⁴If only one is sounded, the leaders—the heads of the clans of Israel—are to assemble before you. ⁵When a trumpet blast is sounded, the tribes camping on the east are to set out. ⁶At

the sounding of a second blast, the camps on the south are to set out. The blast will be the signal for setting out. ⁷To gather the assembly, blow the trumpets, but not with the signal for setting out.

⁸"The sons of Aaron, the priests, are to blow the trumpets. This is to be a lasting ordinance for you and the generations to come. ⁹When you go into battle in your own land against an enemy who is oppressing you, sound a blast on the trumpets. Then you will be remembered by the LORD your God and rescued from your enemies. ¹⁰Also at your times of rejoicing—your appointed festivals and New Moon feasts—you are to sound the trumpets over your burnt offerings and fellowship offerings, and they will be a memorial for you before your God. I am the LORD your God."

The Israelites Leave Sinai

¹¹On the twentieth day of the second month of the second year, the cloud lifted from above the tabernacle of the covenant law. ¹²Then the Israelites set out from the Desert of Sinai and traveled from place to place until the cloud came to rest in the Desert of Paran. ¹³They set out, this first time, at the LORD's command through Moses.

¹⁴The divisions of the camp of Judah went first, under their standard. Nahshon son of Amminadab was in command. ¹⁵Nethanel son of Zuar was over the division of the tribe of Issachar, ¹⁶and Eliab son of Helon was over the division of the tribe of Zebulun. ¹⁷Then the tabernacle was taken down, and the Gershonites and Merarites, who carried it, set out.

¹⁸The divisions of the camp of Reuben went next, under their standard. Elizur son of Shedeur was in command. ¹⁹Shelumiel son of Zurishaddai was over the division of the tribe of Simeon, ²⁰and Eliasaph son of Deuel was over the division of the tribe of Gad. ²¹Then the Kohathites set out, carrying the holy things. The tabernacle was to be set up before they arrived.

²²The divisions of the camp of Ephraim went next, under their standard. Elishama

son of Ammihud was in command. ²³Gamaliel son of Pedahzur was over the division of the tribe of Manasseh, ²⁴and Abidan son of Gideoni was over the division of the tribe of Benjamin.

²⁵Finally, as the rear guard for all the units, the divisions of the camp of Dan set out under their standard. Ahiezer son of Ammishaddai was in command. ²⁶Pagiel son of Okran was over the division of the tribe of Asher, ²⁷and Ahira son of Enan was over the division of the tribe of Naphtali. ²⁸This was the order of march for the Israelite divisions as they set out.

²⁹Now Moses said to Hobab son of Reuel the Midianite, Moses' father-in-law, "We are setting out for the place about which the LORD said, 'I will give it to you.' Come with us and we will treat you well, for the LORD has promised good things to Israel."

³⁰He answered, "No, I will not go; I am going back to my own land and my own people."

³¹But Moses said, "Please do not leave us. You know where we should camp in the wilderness, and you can be our eyes. ³²If you come with us, we will share with you whatever good things the LORD gives us."

³³So they set out from the mountain of the LORD and traveled for three days. The ark of the covenant of the LORD went before them during those three days to find them a place to rest. ³⁴The cloud of the LORD was over them by day when they set out from the camp.

³⁵Whenever the ark set out, Moses said,

"Rise up, LORD!
May your enemies be scattered;
may your foes flee before you."

³⁶Whenever it came to rest, he said,

"Return, LORD,
to the countless thousands of
Israel."

Fire From the LORD

11 Now the people complained about their hardships in the hearing of the LORD, and when he heard them his anger was aroused.

Then fire from the LORD burned among them and consumed some of the outskirts of the camp. ²When the people cried out to Moses, he prayed to the LORD and the fire died down. ³So that place was called Taberah,ᵃ because fire from the LORD had burned among them.

Quail From the LORD

⁴The rabble with them began to crave other food, and again the Israelites started wailing and said, "If only we had meat to eat! ⁵We remember the fish we ate in Egypt at no cost—also the cucumbers, melons, leeks, onions and garlic. ⁶But now we have lost our appetite; we never see anything but this manna!"

⁷The manna was like coriander seed and looked like resin. ⁸The people went around gathering it, and then ground it in a hand mill or crushed it in a mortar. They cooked it in a pot or made it into loaves. And it tasted like something made with olive oil. ⁹When the dew settled on the camp at night, the manna also came down.

¹⁰Moses heard the people of every family wailing at the entrance to their tents. The LORD became exceedingly angry, and Moses was troubled. ¹¹He asked the LORD, "Why have you brought this trouble on your servant? What have I done to displease you that you put the burden of all these people on me? ¹²Did I conceive all these people? Did I give them birth? Why do you tell me to carry them in my arms, as a nurse carries an infant, to the land you promised on oath to their ancestors? ¹³Where can I get meat for all these people? They keep wailing to me, 'Give us meat to eat!' ¹⁴I cannot carry all these people by myself; the burden is too heavy for me. ¹⁵If this is how you are going to treat me, please go ahead and kill me—if I have found favor in your eyes—and do not let me face my own ruin."

¹⁶The LORD said to Moses: "Bring me seventy of Israel's elders who are known to you as leaders and officials among the people. Have them come to the tent of meeting, that they may stand there with

---

ᵃ 3 *Taberah* means *burning*.

you. ¹⁷I will come down and speak with you there, and I will take some of the power of the Spirit that is on you and put it on them. They will share the burden of the people with you so that you will not have to carry it alone.

¹⁸"Tell the people: 'Consecrate yourselves in preparation for tomorrow, when you will eat meat. The LORD heard you when you wailed, "If only we had meat to eat! We were better off in Egypt!" Now the LORD will give you meat, and you will eat it. ¹⁹You will not eat it for just one day, or two days, or five, ten or twenty days, ²⁰but for a whole month—until it comes out of your nostrils and you loathe it—because you have rejected the LORD, who is among you, and have wailed before him, saying, "Why did we ever leave Egypt?"'"

²¹But Moses said, "Here I am among six hundred thousand men on foot, and you say, 'I will give them meat to eat for a whole month!' ²²Would they have enough if flocks and herds were slaughtered for them? Would they have enough if all the fish in the sea were caught for them?"

²³The LORD answered Moses, "Is the LORD's arm too short? Now you will see whether or not what I say will come true for you."

²⁴So Moses went out and told the people what the LORD had said. He brought together seventy of their elders and had them stand around the tent. ²⁵Then the LORD came down in the cloud and spoke with him, and he took some of the power of the Spirit that was on him and put it on the seventy elders. When the Spirit rested on them, they prophesied—but did not do so again.

²⁶However, two men, whose names were Eldad and Medad, had remained in the camp. They were listed among the elders, but did not go out to the tent. Yet the Spirit also rested on them, and they prophesied in the camp. ²⁷A young man ran and told Moses, "Eldad and Medad are prophesying in the camp."

ROCK SOLID principles

Numbers 11:1–35

Smile.

"Why should I act like I'm happy when I'm not?" Kayla wailed. She hated the shift from middle school to high school, and each day seemed worse than the last. "I detest that place. I don't ever see anyone I know. And there's nothing I can do to fix it!" The advice Kayla got wasn't helping—everything from "I'm sure it will get better" to "Toughen up!" Kayla decided that coping was the best she could do—surviving moment by moment, class by class. After a while she had enough tolerable days that she started noticing a few positives about her new school. By the end of the quarter the situation wasn't really any easier. But it was better.

God never said the Israelites couldn't talk about their hardships. But when he grew tired of them attacking his character, he gave them more than they bargained for (see Numbers 11:19–20). Philippians 2:14 says to "Do everything without grumbling or arguing." God never tells you to put on a fake smile. But he expects you to trust his care for you.

²⁸Joshua son of Nun, who had been Moses' aide since youth, spoke up and said, "Moses, my lord, stop them!"

²⁹But Moses replied, "Are you jealous for my sake? I wish that all the LORD's people were prophets and that the LORD would put his Spirit on them!" ³⁰Then Moses and the elders of Israel returned to the camp.

³¹Now a wind went out from the LORD and drove quail in from the sea. It scattered them up to two cubits*a* deep all around the camp, as far as a day's walk in any direction. ³²All that day and night and all the next day the people went out and gathered quail. No one gathered less than ten homers.*b* Then they spread them out all around the camp. ³³But while the meat was still between their teeth and before it could be consumed, the anger of the LORD burned against the people, and he struck them with a severe plague. ³⁴Therefore the place was named Kibroth Hattaavah,*c* because there they buried the people who had craved other food.

³⁵From Kibroth Hattaavah the people traveled to Hazeroth and stayed there.

Miriam and Aaron Oppose Moses

12 Miriam and Aaron began to talk against Moses because of his Cushite wife, for he had married a Cushite. ²"Has the LORD spoken only through Moses?" they asked. "Hasn't he also spoken through us?" And the LORD heard this.

³(Now Moses was a very humble man, more humble than anyone else on the face of the earth.)

⁴At once the LORD said to Moses, Aaron and Miriam, "Come out to the tent of meeting, all three of you." So the three of them went out. ⁵Then the LORD came down in a pillar of cloud; he stood at the entrance to the tent and summoned Aaron and Miriam. When the two of them stepped forward, ⁶he said, "Listen to my words:

"When there is a prophet among you,
    I, the LORD, reveal myself to them
        in visions,
    I speak to them in dreams.

⁷But this is not true of my servant
        Moses;
    he is faithful in all my house.
⁸With him I speak face to face,
    clearly and not in riddles;
    he sees the form of the LORD.
Why then were you not afraid
    to speak against my servant Moses?"

⁹The anger of the LORD burned against them, and he left them.

¹⁰When the cloud lifted from above the tent, Miriam's skin was leprous*d*—it became as white as snow. Aaron turned toward her and saw that she had a defiling skin disease, ¹¹and he said to Moses, "Please, my lord, I ask you not to hold against us the sin we have so foolishly committed. ¹²Do not let her be like a stillborn infant coming from its mother's womb with its flesh half eaten away."

¹³So Moses cried out to the LORD, "Please, God, heal her!"

¹⁴The LORD replied to Moses, "If her father had spit in her face, would she not have been in disgrace for seven days? Confine her outside the camp for seven days; after that she can be brought back." ¹⁵So Miriam was confined outside the camp for seven days, and the people did not move on till she was brought back.

¹⁶After that, the people left Hazeroth and encamped in the Desert of Paran.

Exploring Canaan

13 The LORD said to Moses, ²"Send some men to explore the land of Canaan, which I am giving to the Israelites. From each ancestral tribe send one of its leaders."

³So at the LORD's command Moses sent them out from the Desert of Paran. All of them were leaders of the Israelites. ⁴These are their names:

from the tribe of Reuben, Shammua
    son of Zakkur;

---

a 31 That is, about 3 feet or about 90 centimeters   *b 32* That is, possibly about 1 3/4 tons or about 1.6 metric tons
c 34 *Kibroth Hattaavah* means *graves of craving.*
d 10 The Hebrew for *leprous* was used for various diseases affecting the skin.

⁵from the tribe of Simeon, Shaphat son of Hori;

⁶from the tribe of Judah, Caleb son of Jephunneh;

⁷from the tribe of Issachar, Igal son of Joseph;

⁸from the tribe of Ephraim, Hoshea son of Nun;

⁹from the tribe of Benjamin, Palti son of Raphu;

¹⁰from the tribe of Zebulun, Gaddiel son of Sodi;

¹¹from the tribe of Manasseh (a tribe of Joseph), Gaddi son of Susi;

¹²from the tribe of Dan, Ammiel son of Gemalli;

¹³from the tribe of Asher, Sethur son of Michael;

¹⁴from the tribe of Naphtali, Nahbi son of Vophsi;

¹⁵from the tribe of Gad, Geuel son of Maki.

¹⁶These are the names of the men Moses sent to explore the land. (Moses gave Hoshea son of Nun the name Joshua.)

¹⁷When Moses sent them to explore Canaan, he said, "Go up through the Negev and on into the hill country. ¹⁸See what the land is like and whether the people who live there are strong or weak, few or many. ¹⁹What kind of land do they live in? Is it good or bad? What kind of towns do they live in? Are they unwalled or fortified? ²⁰How is the soil? Is it fertile or poor? Are there trees in it or not? Do your best to bring back some of the fruit of the land." (It was the season for the first ripe grapes.)

²¹So they went up and explored the land from the Desert of Zin as far as Rehob, toward Lebo Hamath. ²²They went up through the Negev and came to Hebron, where Ahiman, Sheshai and Talmai, the descendants of Anak, lived. (Hebron had been built seven years before Zoan in Egypt.) ²³When they reached the Valley of Eshkol,ᵃ they cut off a branch bearing a single cluster of grapes. Two of them carried it on a pole between them, along with some pomegranates and figs. ²⁴That place was called the Valley of Eshkol because of the cluster of grapes the Israelites cut off there. ²⁵At the end of forty days they returned from exploring the land.

Report on the Exploration

²⁶They came back to Moses and Aaron and the whole Israelite community at Kadesh in the Desert of Paran. There they reported to them and to the whole assembly and showed them the fruit of the land. ²⁷They gave Moses this account: "We went into the land to which you sent us, and it does flow with milk and honey! Here is its fruit. ²⁸But the people who live there are powerful, and the cities are fortified and very large. We even saw descendants of Anak there. ²⁹The Amalekites live in the Negev; the Hittites, Jebusites and Amorites live in the hill country; and the Canaanites live near the sea and along the Jordan."

³⁰Then Caleb silenced the people before Moses and said, "We should go up and take possession of the land, for we can certainly do it."

³¹But the men who had gone up with him said, "We can't attack those people; they are stronger than we are." ³²And they spread among the Israelites a bad report about the land they had explored. They said, "The land we explored devours those living in it. All the people we saw there are of great size. ³³We saw the Nephilim there (the descendants of Anak come from the Nephilim). We seemed like grasshoppers in our own eyes, and we looked the same to them."

The People Rebel

14 That night all the members of the community raised their voices and wept aloud. ²All the Israelites grumbled against Moses and Aaron, and the whole assembly said to them, "If only we had died in Egypt! Or in this wilderness! ³Why is the LORD bringing us to this land only to let us fall by the sword? Our wives and children will be taken as plunder. Wouldn't it be better for us to go back to Egypt?" ⁴And they

ᵃ 23 Eshkol means cluster; also in verse 24.

ROCK SOLID *principles*

Numbers 13:26–33

Stand up to the crowd.

At first Brandon could hardly believe someone would pay him just to scoop ice cream, and nothing beat seeing a paycheck from his first job. But then he realized why he landed the job so quickly. No one else wanted it. The hours were long and late. Customers were impatient and rude. And the money didn't add up all that fast. But Brandon refused to roll over like his coworkers. He studied their lazy habits and did the opposite. When customers were scarce, he cleaned up his work space and thumbed through job manuals. And when Brandon felt like he had his job figured out, he started calling out his coworkers' bad attitudes. Their bad habits, he said, were only making the job worse.

Standing up to the crowd doesn't just mean staying drug free or admitting you know Jesus when someone threatens you for your faith. It means doing right wherever God puts you. Joshua and Caleb stood up for God's plan when no one else would (see Numbers 14:30). They weren't trying to make everyone else look bad. They were just being faithful followers.

said to each other, "We should choose a leader and go back to Egypt."

⁵Then Moses and Aaron fell facedown in front of the whole Israelite assembly gathered there. ⁶Joshua son of Nun and Caleb son of Jephunneh, who were among those who had explored the land, tore their clothes ⁷and said to the entire Israelite assembly, "The land we passed through and explored is exceedingly good. ⁸If the LORD is pleased with us, he will lead us into that land, a land flowing with milk and honey, and will give it to us. ⁹Only do not rebel against the LORD. And do not be afraid of the people of the land, because we will devour them. Their protection is gone, but the LORD is with us. Do not be afraid of them."

¹⁰But the whole assembly talked about stoning them. Then the glory of the LORD appeared at the tent of meeting to all the Israelites. ¹¹The LORD said to Moses, "How long will these people treat me with contempt? How long will they re-

fuse to believe in me, in spite of all the signs I have performed among them? ¹²I will strike them down with a plague and destroy them, but I will make you into a nation greater and stronger than they."

¹³Moses said to the LORD, "Then the Egyptians will hear about it! By your power you brought these people up from among them. ¹⁴And they will tell the inhabitants of this land about it. They have already heard that you, LORD, are with these people and that you, LORD, have been seen face to face, that your cloud stays over them, and that you go before them in a pillar of cloud by day and a pillar of fire by night. ¹⁵If you put all these people to death, leaving none alive, the nations who have heard this report about you will say, ¹⁶'The LORD was not able to bring these people into the land he promised them on oath, so he slaughtered them in the wilderness.'

¹⁷"Now may the Lord's strength be displayed, just as you have declared: ¹⁸'The

LORD is slow to anger, abounding in love and forgiving sin and rebellion. Yet he does not leave the guilty unpunished; he punishes the children for the sin of the parents to the third and fourth generation.' ¹⁹In accordance with your great love, forgive the sin of these people, just as you have pardoned them from the time they left Egypt until now."

²⁰The LORD replied, "I have forgiven them, as you asked. ²¹Nevertheless, as surely as I live and as surely as the glory of the LORD fills the whole earth, ²²not one of those who saw my glory and the signs I performed in Egypt and in the wilderness but who disobeyed me and tested me ten times— ²³not one of them will ever see the land I promised on oath to their ancestors. No one who has treated me with contempt will ever see it. ²⁴But because my servant Caleb has a different spirit and follows me wholeheartedly, I will bring him into the land he went to, and his descendants will inherit it. ²⁵Since the Amalekites and the Canaanites are living in the valleys, turn back tomorrow and set out toward the desert along the route to the Red Sea.ᵃ"

²⁶The LORD said to Moses and Aaron: ²⁷"How long will this wicked community grumble against me? I have heard the complaints of these grumbling Israelites. ²⁸So tell them, 'As surely as I live, declares the LORD, I will do to you the very thing I heard you say: ²⁹In this wilderness your bodies will fall—every one of you twenty years old or more who was counted in the census and who has grumbled against me. ³⁰Not one of you will enter the land I swore with uplifted hand to make your home, except Caleb son of Jephunneh and Joshua son of Nun. ³¹As for your children that you said would be taken as plunder, I will bring them in to enjoy the land you have rejected. ³²But as for you, your bodies will fall in this wilderness. ³³Your children will be shepherds here for forty years, suffering for your unfaithfulness, until the last of your bodies lies in the wilderness. ³⁴For forty years—one year for each of the forty days you explored the land—you will suffer for your sins and know what

it is like to have me against you.' ³⁵I, the LORD, have spoken, and I will surely do these things to this whole wicked community, which has banded together against me. They will meet their end in this wilderness; here they will die."

³⁶So the men Moses had sent to explore the land, who returned and made the

ᵃ 25 Or *the Sea of Reeds*

Numbers 14:1 – 45

Sin keeps you from enjoying God's best.

Long before God rescued his people from slavery, he promised Abraham and his descendants a fantastic place to live (see Genesis 12:7). With the freshly escaped slaves poised to conquer their new homeland, a dozen spies scouted the land and saw it was bountiful indeed. But the men also spotted large, heavily fortified cities. Only two of the twelve spies, Joshua and Caleb, trusted the Lord would help the Israelites conquer the land. The rest said the Israelites would be devoured (see Numbers 13:26 – 33). When the Israelites heard this bad news, they wailed and wondered why God led them into the desert to die. Then the crowds got a tough lesson. The Lord is "slow to anger, abounding in love and forgiving sin and rebellion" (Numbers 14:18), yet the consequence for their lack of trust in God was severe. Except for Joshua and Caleb, they would all die before they could enter the promised land.

Think: When has sin caused you to miss out on God's blessing?

ROCK SOLID truths

whole community grumble against him by spreading a bad report about it— ³⁷these men who were responsible for spreading the bad report about the land were struck down and died of a plague before the LORD. ³⁸Of the men who went to explore the land, only Joshua son of Nun and Caleb son of Jephunneh survived.

³⁹When Moses reported this to all the Israelites, they mourned bitterly. ⁴⁰Early the next morning they set out for the highest point in the hill country, saying, "Now we are ready to go up to the land the LORD promised. Surely we have sinned!"

⁴¹But Moses said, "Why are you disobeying the LORD's command? This will not succeed! ⁴²Do not go up, because the LORD is not with you. You will be defeated by your enemies, ⁴³for the Amalekites and the Canaanites will face you there. Because you have turned away from the LORD, he will not be with you and you will fall by the sword."

⁴⁴Nevertheless, in their presumption they went up toward the highest point in the hill country, though neither Moses nor the ark of the LORD's covenant moved from the camp. ⁴⁵Then the Amalekites and the Canaanites who lived in that hill country came down and attacked them and beat them down all the way to Hormah.

Supplementary Offerings

15 The LORD said to Moses, ²"Speak to the Israelites and say to them: 'After you enter the land I am giving you as a home ³and you present to the LORD food offerings from the herd or the flock, as an aroma pleasing to the LORD—whether burnt offerings or sacrifices, for special vows or freewill offerings or festival offerings— ⁴then the person who brings an offering shall present to the LORD a grain offering of a tenth of an ephah*ᵃ* of the finest flour mixed with a quarter of a hin*ᵇ* of olive oil. ⁵With each lamb for the burnt offering or the sacrifice, prepare a quarter of a hin of wine as a drink offering.

⁶"'With a ram prepare a grain offering of two-tenths of an ephah*ᶜ* of the finest flour mixed with a third of a hin*ᵈ* of olive oil, ⁷and a third of a hin of wine as a drink offering. Offer it as an aroma pleasing to the LORD.

⁸"'When you prepare a young bull as a burnt offering or sacrifice, for a special vow or a fellowship offering to the LORD, ⁹bring with the bull a grain offering of three-tenths of an ephah*ᵉ* of the finest flour mixed with half a hin*ᶠ* of olive oil, ¹⁰and also bring half a hin of wine as a drink offering. This will be a food offering, an aroma pleasing to the LORD. ¹¹Each bull or ram, each lamb or young goat, is to be prepared in this manner. ¹²Do this for each one, for as many as you prepare.

¹³"'Everyone who is native-born must do these things in this way when they present a food offering as an aroma pleasing to the LORD. ¹⁴For the generations to come, whenever a foreigner or anyone else living among you presents a food offering as an aroma pleasing to the LORD, they must do exactly as you do. ¹⁵The community is to have the same rules for you and for the foreigner residing among you; this is a lasting ordinance for the generations to come. You and the foreigner shall be the same before the LORD: ¹⁶The same laws and regulations will apply both to you and to the foreigner residing among you.'"

¹⁷The LORD said to Moses, ¹⁸"Speak to the Israelites and say to them: 'When you enter the land to which I am taking you ¹⁹and you eat the food of the land, present a portion as an offering to the LORD. ²⁰Present a loaf from the first of your ground meal and present it as an offering from the threshing floor. ²¹Throughout the generations to come you are to give

ᵃ 4 That is, probably about 3 1/2 pounds or about 1.6 kilograms   *ᵇ 4* That is, about 1 quart or about 1 liter; also in verse 5   *ᶜ 6* That is, probably about 7 pounds or about 3.2 kilograms   *ᵈ 6* That is, about 1 1/3 quarts or about 1.3 liters; also in verse 7   *ᵉ 9* That is, probably about 11 pounds or about 5 kilograms   *ᶠ 9* That is, about 2 quarts or about 1.9 liters; also in verse 10 this offering to the LORD from the first of your ground meal.

Offerings for Unintentional Sins

22 "'Now if you as a community unintentionally fail to keep any of these commands the LORD gave Moses— 23 any of the LORD's commands to you through him, from the day the LORD gave them and continuing through the generations to come— 24 and if this is done unintentionally without the community being aware of it, then the whole community is to offer a young bull for a burnt offering as an aroma pleasing to the LORD, along with its prescribed grain offering and drink offering, and a male goat for a sin offering.*a* 25 The priest is to make atonement for the whole Israelite community, and they will be forgiven, for it was not intentional and they have presented to the LORD for their wrong a food offering and a sin offering. 26 The whole Israelite community and the foreigners residing among them will be forgiven, because all the people were involved in the unintentional wrong.

27 "'But if just one person sins unintentionally, that person must bring a year-old female goat for a sin offering. 28 The priest is to make atonement before the LORD for the one who erred by sinning unintentionally, and when atonement has been made, that person will be forgiven. 29 One and the same law applies to everyone who sins unintentionally, whether a native-born Israelite or a foreigner residing among you.

30 "'But anyone who sins defiantly, whether native-born or foreigner, blasphemes the LORD and must be cut off from the people of Israel. 31 Because they have despised the LORD's word and broken his commands, they must surely be cut off; their guilt remains on them.'"

The Sabbath-Breaker Put to Death

32 While the Israelites were in the wilderness, a man was found gathering wood on the Sabbath day. 33 Those who found him gathering wood brought him to Moses and Aaron and the whole assembly, 34 and they kept him in custody, because it was not clear what should be done to him. 35 Then the LORD said to Moses, "The man must die. The whole assembly must stone him outside the camp." 36 So the assembly took him outside the camp and stoned him to death, as the LORD commanded Moses.

Tassels on Garments

37 The LORD said to Moses, 38 "Speak to the Israelites and say to them: 'Throughout the generations to come you are to make tassels on the corners of your garments, with a blue cord on each tassel. 39 You will have these tassels to look at and so you will remember all the commands of the LORD, that you may obey them and not prostitute yourselves by chasing after the lusts of your own hearts and eyes. 40 Then you will remember to obey all my commands and will be consecrated to your God. 41 I am the LORD your God, who brought you out of Egypt to be your God. I am the LORD your God.'"

Korah, Dathan and Abiram

16 Korah son of Izhar, the son of Kohath, the son of Levi, and certain Reubenites—Dathan and Abiram, sons of Eliab, and On son of Peleth—became insolent*b* 2 and rose up against Moses. With them were 250 Israelite men, well-known community leaders who had been appointed members of the council. 3 They came as a group to oppose Moses and Aaron and said to them, "You have gone too far! The whole community is holy, every one of them, and the LORD is with them. Why then do you set yourselves above the LORD's assembly?"

4 When Moses heard this, he fell facedown. 5 Then he said to Korah and all his followers: "In the morning the LORD will show who belongs to him and who is holy, and he will have that person come near him. The man he chooses he will cause to come near him. 6 You, Korah, and all your followers are to do this: Take censers 7 and tomorrow put burning coals and incense in them before the LORD. The man the

---

a 24 Or *purification offering*; also in verses 25 and 27   *b 1* Or *Peleth—took men*

LORD chooses will be the one who is holy. You Levites have gone too far!"

⁸Moses also said to Korah, "Now listen, you Levites! ⁹Isn't it enough for you that the God of Israel has separated you from the rest of the Israelite community and brought you near himself to do the work at the LORD's tabernacle and to stand before the community and minister to them? ¹⁰He has brought you and all your fellow Levites near himself, but now you are trying to get the priesthood too. ¹¹It is against the LORD that you and all your followers have banded together. Who is Aaron that you should grumble against him?"

¹²Then Moses summoned Dathan and Abiram, the sons of Eliab. But they said, "We will not come! ¹³Isn't it enough that you have brought us up out of a land flowing with milk and honey to kill us in the wilderness? And now you also want to lord it over us! ¹⁴Moreover, you haven't brought us into a land flowing with milk and honey or given us an inheritance of fields and vineyards. Do you want to treat these men like slaves*? No, we will not come!"

¹⁵Then Moses became very angry and said to the LORD, "Do not accept their offering. I have not taken so much as a donkey from them, nor have I wronged any of them."

¹⁶Moses said to Korah, "You and all your followers are to appear before the LORD tomorrow—you and they and Aaron. ¹⁷Each man is to take his censer and put incense in it—250 censers in all—and present it before the LORD. You and Aaron are to present your censers also." ¹⁸So each of them took his censer, put burning coals and incense in it, and stood with Moses and Aaron at the entrance to the tent of meeting. ¹⁹When Korah had gathered all his followers in opposition to them at the entrance to the tent of meeting, the glory of the LORD appeared to the entire assembly. ²⁰The LORD said to Moses and Aaron, ²¹"Separate yourselves from this assembly so I can put an end to them at once."

²²But Moses and Aaron fell facedown and cried out, "O God, the God who gives breath to all living things, will you be angry with the entire assembly when only one man sins?"

²³Then the LORD said to Moses, ²⁴"Say to the assembly, 'Move away from the tents of Korah, Dathan and Abiram.'"

²⁵Moses got up and went to Dathan and Abiram, and the elders of Israel followed him. ²⁶He warned the assembly, "Move back from the tents of these wicked men! Do not touch anything belonging to them, or you will be swept away because of all their sins." ²⁷So they moved away from the tents of Korah, Dathan and Abiram. Dathan and Abiram had come out and were standing with their wives, children and little ones at the entrances to their tents.

²⁸Then Moses said, "This is how you will know that the LORD has sent me to do all these things and that it was not my idea: ²⁹If these men die a natural death and suffer the fate of all mankind, then the LORD has not sent me. ³⁰But if the LORD brings about something totally new, and the earth opens its mouth and swallows them, with everything that belongs to them, and they go down alive into the realm of the dead, then you will know that these men have treated the LORD with contempt."

³¹As soon as he finished saying all this, the ground under them split apart ³²and the earth opened its mouth and swallowed them and their households, and all those associated with Korah, together with their possessions. ³³They went down alive into the realm of the dead, with everything they owned; the earth closed over them, and they perished and were gone from the community. ³⁴At their cries, all the Israelites around them fled, shouting, "The earth is going to swallow us too!"

³⁵And fire came out from the LORD and consumed the 250 men who were offering the incense.

³⁶The LORD said to Moses, ³⁷"Tell Eleazar son of Aaron, the priest, to remove the censers from the charred remains and scatter the coals some distance away, for the censers are holy— ³⁸the censers of the

---

a 14 Or *to deceive these men*; Hebrew *Will you gouge out the eyes of these men*

men who sinned at the cost of their lives. Hammer the censers into sheets to overlay the altar, for they were presented before the LORD and have become holy. Let them be a sign to the Israelites."

³⁹ So Eleazar the priest collected the bronze censers brought by those who had been burned to death, and he had them hammered out to overlay the altar, ⁴⁰ as the LORD directed him through Moses. This was to remind the Israelites that no one except a descendant of Aaron should come to burn incense before the LORD, or he would become like Korah and his followers.

⁴¹ The next day the whole Israelite community grumbled against Moses and Aaron. "You have killed the LORD's people," they said.

⁴² But when the assembly gathered in opposition to Moses and Aaron and turned toward the tent of meeting, suddenly the cloud covered it and the glory of the LORD appeared. ⁴³ Then Moses and Aaron went to the front of the tent of meeting, ⁴⁴ and the LORD said to Moses, ⁴⁵ "Get away from this assembly so I can put an end to them at once." And they fell facedown.

⁴⁶ Then Moses said to Aaron, "Take your censer and put incense in it, along with burning coals from the altar, and hurry to the assembly to make atonement for them. Wrath has come out from the LORD; the plague has started." ⁴⁷ So Aaron did as Moses said, and ran into the midst of the assembly. The plague had already started among the people, but Aaron offered the incense and made atonement for them. ⁴⁸ He stood between the living and the dead, and the plague stopped. ⁴⁹ But 14,700 people died from the plague, in addition to those who had died because of Korah. ⁵⁰ Then Aaron returned to Moses at the entrance to the tent of meeting, for the plague had stopped.ᵃ

ᵃ 50 In Hebrew texts 16:36-50 is numbered 17:1-15.

ROCK SOLID principles

Numbers 16:1–50

Don't be in the wrong place at the wrong time.

There was no escape—and running would have been a bad idea anyway. Kelli was hanging at a park with a random group from school when a couple squad cars rolled up. As the police officers came at Kelli and her classmates, it was clear the officers weren't playing around. A neighbor had complained about teens making noise at the park after hours, and most nights the youth would have been warned and sent home. But when a police dog sniffed marijuana on a guy Kelli barely knew, the whole group got ticketed for disorderly conduct. It didn't matter how much anyone protested. One person's crime upped the consequences for everyone else.

When Korah and his followers lit incense as an offering to God, they stole a holy job belonged to Aaron and his descendants alone (see Numbers 16:40). Not only did Korah and his band of rebels die, but so did their families. Then when grumbling and rebellion spread to the Israelite camp, more died. Sin is contagious, and sometimes consequences are contagious too.

The Budding of Aaron's Staff

17 [a] The LORD said to Moses, [2]"Speak to the Israelites and get twelve staffs from them, one from the leader of each of their ancestral tribes. Write the name of each man on his staff. [3]On the staff of Levi write Aaron's name, for there must be one staff for the head of each ancestral tribe. [4]Place them in the tent of meeting in front of the ark of the covenant law, where I meet with you. [5]The staff belonging to the man I choose will sprout, and I will rid myself of this constant grumbling against you by the Israelites."

[6]So Moses spoke to the Israelites, and their leaders gave him twelve staffs, one for the leader of each of their ancestral tribes, and Aaron's staff was among them. [7]Moses placed the staffs before the LORD in the tent of the covenant law.

[8]The next day Moses entered the tent and saw that Aaron's staff, which represented the tribe of Levi, had not only sprouted but had budded, blossomed and produced almonds. [9]Then Moses brought out all the staffs from the LORD's presence to all the Israelites. They looked at them, and each of the leaders took his own staff. [10]The LORD said to Moses, "Put back Aaron's staff in front of the ark of the covenant law, to be kept as a sign to the rebellious. This will put an end to their grumbling against me, so that they will not die." [11]Moses did just as the LORD commanded him.

[12]The Israelites said to Moses, "We will die! We are lost, we are all lost! [13]Anyone who even comes near the tabernacle of the LORD will die. Are we all going to die?"

Duties of Priests and Levites

18 The LORD said to Aaron, "You, your sons and your family are to bear the responsibility for offenses connected with the sanctuary, and you and your sons alone are to bear the responsibility for offenses connected with the priesthood. [2]Bring your fellow Levites from your ancestral tribe to join you and assist you when you and your sons minister before the tent of the covenant law. [3]They are to be responsible to you and are to perform all the duties of the tent, but they must not go near the furnishings of the sanctuary or the altar. Otherwise both they and you will die. [4]They are to join you and be responsible for the care of the tent of meeting—all the work at the tent—and no one else may come near where you are.

[5]"You are to be responsible for the care of the sanctuary and the altar, so that my wrath will not fall on the Israelites again. [6]I myself have selected your fellow Levites from among the Israelites as a gift to you, dedicated to the LORD to do the work at the tent of meeting. [7]But only you and your sons may serve as priests in connection with everything at the altar and inside the curtain. I am giving you the service of the priesthood as a gift. Anyone else who comes near the sanctuary is to be put to death."

Offerings for Priests and Levites

[8]Then the LORD said to Aaron, "I myself have put you in charge of the offerings presented to me; all the holy offerings the Israelites give me I give to you and your sons as your portion, your perpetual share. [9]You are to have the part of the most holy offerings that is kept from the fire. From all the gifts they bring me as most holy offerings, whether grain or sin[b] or guilt offerings, that part belongs to you and your sons. [10]Eat it as something most holy; every male shall eat it. You must regard it as holy.

[11]"This also is yours: whatever is set aside from the gifts of all the wave offerings of the Israelites. I give this to you and your sons and daughters as your perpetual share. Everyone in your household who is ceremonially clean may eat it.

[12]"I give you all the finest olive oil and all the finest new wine and grain they give the LORD as the firstfruits of their harvest. [13]All the land's firstfruits that they bring to the LORD will be yours. Everyone in

[a] In Hebrew texts 17:1-13 is numbered 17:16-28.
[b] 9 Or *purification*

your household who is ceremonially clean may eat it.

¹⁴"Everything in Israel that is devoted[a] to the LORD is yours. ¹⁵The first offspring of every womb, both human and animal, that is offered to the LORD is yours. But you must redeem every firstborn son and every firstborn male of unclean animals. ¹⁶When they are a month old, you must redeem them at the redemption price set at five shekels[b] of silver, according to the sanctuary shekel, which weighs twenty gerahs.

¹⁷"But you must not redeem the firstborn of a cow, a sheep or a goat; they are holy. Splash their blood against the altar and burn their fat as a food offering, an aroma pleasing to the LORD. ¹⁸Their meat is to be yours, just as the breast of the wave offering and the right thigh are yours. ¹⁹Whatever is set aside from the holy offerings the Israelites present to the LORD I give to you and your sons and daughters as your perpetual share. It is an everlasting covenant of salt before the LORD for both you and your offspring."

²⁰The LORD said to Aaron, "You will have no inheritance in their land, nor will you have any share among them; I am your share and your inheritance among the Israelites.

²¹"I give to the Levites all the tithes in Israel as their inheritance in return for the work they do while serving at the tent of meeting. ²²From now on the Israelites must not go near the tent of meeting, or they will bear the consequences of their sin and will die. ²³It is the Levites who are to do the work at the tent of meeting and bear the responsibility for any offenses they commit against it. This is a lasting ordinance for the generations to come. They will receive no inheritance among the Israelites. ²⁴Instead, I give to the Levites as their inheritance the tithes that the Israelites present as an offering to the LORD. That is why I said concerning them: 'They will have no inheritance among the Israelites.'"

²⁵The LORD said to Moses, ²⁶"Speak to the Levites and say to them: 'When you receive from the Israelites the tithe I give you as your inheritance, you must present a tenth of that tithe as the LORD's offering. ²⁷Your offering will be reckoned to you as grain from the threshing floor or juice from the winepress. ²⁸In this way you also will present an offering to the LORD from all the tithes you receive from the Israelites. From these tithes you must give the LORD's portion to Aaron the priest. ²⁹You must present as the LORD's portion the best and holiest part of everything given to you.'

³⁰"Say to the Levites: 'When you present the best part, it will be reckoned to you as the product of the threshing floor or the winepress. ³¹You and your households may eat the rest of it anywhere, for it is your wages for your work at the tent of meeting. ³²By presenting the best part of it you will not be guilty in this matter; then you will not defile the holy offerings of the Israelites, and you will not die.'"

The Water of Cleansing

19 The LORD said to Moses and Aaron: ²"This is a requirement of the law that the LORD has commanded: Tell the Israelites to bring you a red heifer without defect or blemish and that has never been under a yoke. ³Give it to Eleazar the priest; it is to be taken outside the camp and slaughtered in his presence. ⁴Then Eleazar the priest is to take some of its blood on his finger and sprinkle it seven times toward the front of the tent of meeting. ⁵While he watches, the heifer is to be burned—its hide, flesh, blood and intestines. ⁶The priest is to take some cedar wood, hyssop and scarlet wool and throw them onto the burning heifer. ⁷After that, the priest must wash his clothes and bathe himself with water. He may then come into the camp, but he will be ceremonially unclean till evening. ⁸The man who burns it must also wash his clothes and bathe with water, and he too will be unclean till evening.

---

[a] 14 The Hebrew term refers to the irrevocable giving over of things or persons to the LORD.
[b] 16 That is, about 2 ounces or about 58 grams

⁹"A man who is clean shall gather up the ashes of the heifer and put them in a ceremonially clean place outside the camp. They are to be kept by the Israelite community for use in the water of cleansing; it is for purification from sin. ¹⁰The man who gathers up the ashes of the heifer must also wash his clothes, and he too will be unclean till evening. This will be a lasting ordinance both for the Israelites and for the foreigners residing among them.

¹¹"Whoever touches a human corpse will be unclean for seven days. ¹²They must purify themselves with the water on the third day and on the seventh day; then they will be clean. But if they do not purify themselves on the third and seventh days, they will not be clean. ¹³If they fail to purify themselves after touching a human corpse, they defile the LORD's tabernacle. They must be cut off from Israel. Because the water of cleansing has not been sprinkled on them, they are unclean; their uncleanness remains on them.

¹⁴"This is the law that applies when a person dies in a tent: Anyone who enters the tent and anyone who is in it will be unclean for seven days, ¹⁵and every open container without a lid fastened on it will be unclean.

¹⁶"Anyone out in the open who touches someone who has been killed with a sword or someone who has died a natural death, or anyone who touches a human bone or a grave, will be unclean for seven days.

¹⁷"For the unclean person, put some ashes from the burned purification offering into a jar and pour fresh water over them. ¹⁸Then a man who is ceremonially clean is to take some hyssop, dip it in the water and sprinkle the tent and all the furnishings and the people who were there. He must also sprinkle anyone who has touched a human bone or a grave or anyone who has been killed or anyone who has died a natural death. ¹⁹The man who is clean is to sprinkle those who are unclean on the third and seventh days, and on the seventh day he is to purify them. Those who are being cleansed must wash their clothes and bathe with water, and

that evening they will be clean. ²⁰But if those who are unclean do not purify themselves, they must be cut off from the community, because they have defiled the sanctuary of the LORD. The water of cleansing has not been sprinkled on them, and they are unclean. ²¹This is a lasting ordinance for them.

"The man who sprinkles the water of cleansing must also wash his clothes, and anyone who touches the water of cleansing will be unclean till evening. ²²Anything that an unclean person touches becomes unclean, and anyone who touches it becomes unclean till evening."

Water From the Rock

20 In the first month the whole Israelite community arrived at the Desert of Zin, and they stayed at Kadesh. There Miriam died and was buried.

²Now there was no water for the community, and the people gathered in opposition to Moses and Aaron. ³They quarreled with Moses and said, "If only we had died when our brothers fell dead before the LORD! ⁴Why did you bring the LORD's community into this wilderness, that we and our livestock should die here? ⁵Why did you bring us up out of Egypt to this terrible place? It has no grain or figs, grapevines or pomegranates. And there is no water to drink!"

⁶Moses and Aaron went from the assembly to the entrance to the tent of meeting and fell facedown, and the glory of the LORD appeared to them. ⁷The LORD said to Moses, ⁸"Take the staff, and you and your brother Aaron gather the assembly together. Speak to that rock before their eyes and it will pour out its water. You will bring water out of the rock for the community so they and their livestock can drink."

⁹So Moses took the staff from the LORD's presence, just as he commanded him. ¹⁰He and Aaron gathered the assembly together in front of the rock and Moses said to them, "Listen, you rebels, must we bring you water out of this rock?" ¹¹Then Moses raised his arm and struck the rock

twice with his staff. Water gushed out, and the community and their livestock drank.

¹²But the LORD said to Moses and Aaron, "Because you did not trust in me enough to honor me as holy in the sight of the Israelites, you will not bring this community into the land I give them."

¹³These were the waters of Meribah,ᵃ where the Israelites quarreled with the LORD and where he was proved holy among them.

Edom Denies Israel Passage

¹⁴Moses sent messengers from Kadesh to the king of Edom, saying:

"This is what your brother Israel says: You know about all the hardships that have come on us. ¹⁵Our ancestors went down into Egypt, and we lived there many years. The Egyptians mistreated us and our ancestors, ¹⁶but when we cried out to the LORD, he heard our cry and sent an angel and brought us out of Egypt.

"Now we are here at Kadesh, a town on the edge of your territory. ¹⁷Please let us pass through your country. We will not go through any field or vineyard, or drink water from any well. We will travel along the King's Highway and not turn to the right or to the left until we have passed through your territory."

¹⁸But Edom answered:

"You may not pass through here; if you try, we will march out and attack you with the sword."

¹⁹The Israelites replied:

"We will go along the main road, and if we or our livestock drink any of your water, we will pay for it. We only want to pass through on foot—nothing else."

ᵃ *13 Meribah* means *quarreling.*

ROCK SOLID
principles

Numbers 20:1–13

Keep your cool.

Ben's dad gave him a tough stare. "You can't keep talking to your mom like this," he said. "Having a bad day isn't an excuse for you to take it out on us. You need to find a way to talk things out." Ben knew he had a problem with anger, but he wasn't ready for what his dad said next. "We've talked about this too many times, and I'm done just trying to persuade you. The next time you raise your voice with either one of us, you'll be grounded for the weekend. If you can't be more considerate of us, you need to take some time out and think up a plan to do things differently."

The Lord had told Moses to speak to the rock to make water gush out, but instead Moses hit the rock, acting out of frustration with the people instead of calmly trusting God. That flash of anger brought swift punishment. Because Moses didn't rely on God, the Lord wouldn't let him lead the Israelites into the promised land (see Numbers 20:12). Losing his cool meant Moses lost out on an incredible privilege.

²⁰Again they answered:

"You may not pass through."

Then Edom came out against them with a large and powerful army. ²¹Since Edom refused to let them go through their territory, Israel turned away from them.

The Death of Aaron

²²The whole Israelite community set out from Kadesh and came to Mount Hor. ²³At Mount Hor, near the border of Edom, the Lord said to Moses and Aaron, ²⁴"Aaron will be gathered to his people. He will not enter the land I give the Israelites, because both of you rebelled against my command at the waters of Meribah. ²⁵Get Aaron and his son Eleazar and take them up Mount Hor. ²⁶Remove Aaron's garments and put them on his son Eleazar, for Aaron will be gathered to his people; he will die there."

²⁷Moses did as the Lord commanded: They went up Mount Hor in the sight of the whole community. ²⁸Moses removed Aaron's garments and put them on his son Eleazar. And Aaron died there on top of the mountain. Then Moses and Eleazar came down from the mountain, ²⁹and when the whole community learned that Aaron had died, all the Israelites mourned for him thirty days.

Arad Destroyed

21 When the Canaanite king of Arad, who lived in the Negev, heard that Israel was coming along the road to Atharim, he attacked the Israelites and captured some of them. ²Then Israel made this vow to the Lord: "If you will deliver these people into our hands, we will totally destroy*ᵃ* their cities." ³The Lord listened to Israel's plea and gave the Canaanites over to them. They completely destroyed them and their towns; so the place was named Hormah.*ᵇ*

The Bronze Snake

⁴They traveled from Mount Hor along the route to the Red Sea,*ᶜ* to go around Edom. But the people grew impatient on the way; ⁵they spoke against God and against Moses, and said, "Why have you brought us up out of Egypt to die in the wilderness? There is no bread! There is no water! And we detest this miserable food!"

⁶Then the Lord sent venomous snakes among them; they bit the people and many Israelites died. ⁷The people came to Moses and said, "We sinned when we spoke against the Lord and against you. Pray that the Lord will take the snakes away from us." So Moses prayed for the people.

⁸The Lord said to Moses, "Make a snake and put it up on a pole; anyone who is bitten can look at it and live." ⁹So Moses made a bronze snake and put it up on a pole. Then when anyone was bitten by a snake and looked at the bronze snake, they lived.

The Journey to Moab

¹⁰The Israelites moved on and camped at Oboth. ¹¹Then they set out from Oboth and camped in Iye Abarim, in the wilderness that faces Moab toward the sunrise. ¹²From there they moved on and camped in the Zered Valley. ¹³They set out from there and camped alongside the Arnon, which is in the wilderness extending into Amorite territory. The Arnon is the border of Moab, between Moab and the Amorites. ¹⁴That is why the Book of the Wars of the Lord says:

". . . Zahab*ᵈ* in Suphah and the
    ravines,
  the Arnon ¹⁵and*ᵉ* the slopes of the
    ravines
that lead to the settlement of Ar
  and lie along the border of Moab."

¹⁶From there they continued on to Beer, the well where the Lord said to Moses, "Gather the people together and I will give them water."

¹⁷Then Israel sang this song:

ᵃ 2 The Hebrew term refers to the irrevocable giving over of things or persons to the Lord, often by totally destroying them; also in verse 3.
ᵇ 3 Hormah means *destruction.*   *ᶜ 4* Or *the Sea of Reeds*   *ᵈ 14* Septuagint; Hebrew *Waheb*
ᵉ 14,15 Or *"I have been given from Suphah and the ravines / of the Arnon ¹⁵to*

"Spring up, O well!
  Sing about it,
[18] about the well that the princes dug,
  that the nobles of the people sank—
  the nobles with scepters and staffs."

Then they went from the wilderness to Mattanah, [19] from Mattanah to Nahaliel, from Nahaliel to Bamoth, [20] and from Bamoth to the valley in Moab where the top of Pisgah overlooks the wasteland.

Defeat of Sihon and Og

[21] Israel sent messengers to say to Sihon king of the Amorites:

[22] "Let us pass through your country. We will not turn aside into any field or vineyard, or drink water from any well. We will travel along the King's Highway until we have passed through your territory."

[23] But Sihon would not let Israel pass through his territory. He mustered his entire army and marched out into the wilderness against Israel. When he reached Jahaz, he fought with Israel. [24] Israel, however, put him to the sword and took over his land from the Arnon to the Jabbok, but only as far as the Ammonites, because their border was fortified. [25] Israel captured all the cities of the Amorites and occupied them, including Heshbon and all its surrounding settlements. [26] Heshbon was the city of Sihon king of the Amorites, who had fought against the former king of Moab and had taken from him all his land as far as the Arnon.

[27] That is why the poets say:

"Come to Heshbon and let it be rebuilt;
  let Sihon's city be restored.

[28] "Fire went out from Heshbon,
  a blaze from the city of Sihon.
It consumed Ar of Moab,
  the citizens of Arnon's heights.
[29] Woe to you, Moab!
  You are destroyed, people of
    Chemosh!
He has given up his sons as fugitives
  and his daughters as captives
to Sihon king of the Amorites.

[30] "But we have overthrown them;
  Heshbon's dominion has been
    destroyed all the way to Dibon.
We have demolished them as far as
    Nophah,
  which extends to Medeba."

[31] So Israel settled in the land of the Amorites.

[32] After Moses had sent spies to Jazer, the Israelites captured its surrounding settlements and drove out the Amorites who were there. [33] Then they turned and went up along the road toward Bashan, and Og king of Bashan and his whole army marched out to meet them in battle at Edrei.

[34] The LORD said to Moses, "Do not be afraid of him, for I have delivered him into your hands, along with his whole army and his land. Do to him what you did to Sihon king of the Amorites, who reigned in Heshbon."

[35] So they struck him down, together with his sons and his whole army, leaving them no survivors. And they took possession of his land.

Balak Summons Balaam

22 Then the Israelites traveled to the plains of Moab and camped along the Jordan across from Jericho.

[2] Now Balak son of Zippor saw all that Israel had done to the Amorites, [3] and Moab was terrified because there were so many people. Indeed, Moab was filled with dread because of the Israelites.

[4] The Moabites said to the elders of Midian, "This horde is going to lick up everything around us, as an ox licks up the grass of the field."

So Balak son of Zippor, who was king of Moab at that time, [5] sent messengers to summon Balaam son of Beor, who was at Pethor, near the Euphrates River, in his native land. Balak said:

"A people has come out of Egypt; they cover the face of the land and have settled next to me. [6] Now come and put a curse on these people, because they are too powerful for me.

Perhaps then I will be able to defeat them and drive them out of the land. For I know that whoever you bless is blessed, and whoever you curse is cursed."

⁷The elders of Moab and Midian left, taking with them the fee for divination. When they came to Balaam, they told him what Balak had said.

⁸"Spend the night here," Balaam said to them, "and I will report back to you with the answer the LORD gives me." So the Moabite officials stayed with him.

⁹God came to Balaam and asked, "Who are these men with you?"

¹⁰Balaam said to God, "Balak son of Zippor, king of Moab, sent me this message: ¹¹'A people that has come out of Egypt covers the face of the land. Now come and put a curse on them for me. Perhaps then I will be able to fight them and drive them away.'"

¹²But God said to Balaam, "Do not go with them. You must not put a curse on those people, because they are blessed."

¹³The next morning Balaam got up and said to Balak's officials, "Go back to your own country, for the LORD has refused to let me go with you."

¹⁴So the Moabite officials returned to Balak and said, "Balaam refused to come with us."

¹⁵Then Balak sent other officials, more numerous and more distinguished than the first. ¹⁶They came to Balaam and said:

"This is what Balak son of Zippor says: Do not let anything keep you from coming to me, ¹⁷because I will reward you handsomely and do whatever you say. Come and put a curse on these people for me."

¹⁸But Balaam answered them, "Even if Balak gave me all the silver and gold in his palace, I could not do anything great or small to go beyond the command of the LORD my God. ¹⁹Now spend the night here so that I can find out what else the LORD will tell me."

²⁰That night God came to Balaam and said, "Since these men have come to summon you, go with them, but do only what I tell you."

Balaam's Donkey

²¹Balaam got up in the morning, saddled his donkey and went with the Moabite officials. ²²But God was very angry when he went, and the angel of the LORD stood in the road to oppose him. Balaam was riding on his donkey, and his two servants were with him. ²³When the donkey saw the angel of the LORD standing in the road with a drawn sword in his hand, it turned off the road into a field. Balaam beat it to get it back on the road.

²⁴Then the angel of the LORD stood in a narrow path through the vineyards, with walls on both sides. ²⁵When the donkey saw the angel of the LORD, it pressed close to the wall, crushing Balaam's foot against it. So he beat the donkey again.

²⁶Then the angel of the LORD moved on ahead and stood in a narrow place where there was no room to turn, either to the right or to the left. ²⁷When the donkey saw the angel of the LORD, it lay down under Balaam, and he was angry and beat it with his staff. ²⁸Then the LORD opened the donkey's mouth, and it said to Balaam, "What have I done to you to make you beat me these three times?"

²⁹Balaam answered the donkey, "You have made a fool of me! If only I had a sword in my hand, I would kill you right now."

³⁰The donkey said to Balaam, "Am I not your own donkey, which you have always ridden, to this day? Have I been in the habit of doing this to you?"

"No," he said.

³¹Then the LORD opened Balaam's eyes, and he saw the angel of the LORD standing in the road with his sword drawn. So he bowed low and fell facedown.

³²The angel of the LORD asked him, "Why have you beaten your donkey these three times? I have come here to oppose you because your path is a reckless one before me.ᵃ ³³The donkey saw me and

ᵃ 32 The meaning of the Hebrew for this clause is uncertain.

turned away from me these three times. If it had not turned away, I would certainly have killed you by now, but I would have spared it."

³⁴Balaam said to the angel of the Lord, "I have sinned. I did not realize you were standing in the road to oppose me. Now if you are displeased, I will go back."

³⁵The angel of the Lord said to Balaam, "Go with the men, but speak only what I tell you." So Balaam went with Balak's officials.

³⁶When Balak heard that Balaam was coming, he went out to meet him at the Moabite town on the Arnon border, at the edge of his territory. ³⁷Balak said to Balaam, "Did I not send you an urgent summons? Why didn't you come to me? Am I really not able to reward you?"

³⁸"Well, I have come to you now," Balaam replied. "But I can't say whatever I please. I must speak only what God puts in my mouth."

³⁹Then Balaam went with Balak to Kiriath Huzoth. ⁴⁰Balak sacrificed cattle and sheep, and gave some to Balaam and the officials who were with him. ⁴¹The next morning Balak took Balaam up to Bamoth Baal, and from there he could see the outskirts of the Israelite camp.

Balaam's First Message

23 Balaam said, "Build me seven altars here, and prepare seven bulls and seven rams for me." ²Balak did as Balaam said, and the two of them offered a bull and a ram on each altar.

³Then Balaam said to Balak, "Stay here beside your offering while I go aside. Perhaps the Lord will come to meet with me. Whatever he reveals to me I will tell you." Then he went off to a barren height.

⁴God met with him, and Balaam said, "I have prepared seven altars, and on each altar I have offered a bull and a ram."

⁵The Lord put a word in Balaam's mouth and said, "Go back to Balak and give him this word."

⁶So he went back to him and found him standing beside his offering, with all the Moabite officials. ⁷Then Balaam spoke his message:

> "Balak brought me from Aram,
>   the king of Moab from the eastern
>   mountains.
> 'Come,' he said, 'curse Jacob for me;
>   come, denounce Israel.'
> ⁸How can I curse
>   those whom God has not cursed?
> How can I denounce
>   those whom the Lord has not
>   denounced?
> ⁹From the rocky peaks I see them,
>   from the heights I view them.
> I see a people who live apart
>   and do not consider themselves one
>   of the nations.
> ¹⁰Who can count the dust of Jacob
>   or number even a fourth of Israel?
> Let me die the death of the righteous,
>   and may my final end be like theirs!"

¹¹Balak said to Balaam, "What have you done to me? I brought you to curse my enemies, but you have done nothing but bless them!"

¹²He answered, "Must I not speak what the Lord puts in my mouth?"

Balaam's Second Message

¹³Then Balak said to him, "Come with me to another place where you can see them; you will not see them all but only the outskirts of their camp. And from there, curse them for me." ¹⁴So he took him to the field of Zophim on the top of Pisgah, and there he built seven altars and offered a bull and a ram on each altar.

¹⁵Balaam said to Balak, "Stay here beside your offering while I meet with him over there."

¹⁶The Lord met with Balaam and put a word in his mouth and said, "Go back to Balak and give him this word."

¹⁷So he went to him and found him standing beside his offering, with the Moabite officials. Balak asked him, "What did the Lord say?"

¹⁸Then he spoke his message:

> "Arise, Balak, and listen;
>   hear me, son of Zippor.

¹⁹God is not human, that he should lie,
    not a human being, that he should
        change his mind.
Does he speak and then not act?
    Does he promise and not fulfill?
²⁰I have received a command to bless;
    he has blessed, and I cannot
        change it.

²¹"No misfortune is seen in Jacob,
    no misery observed*ᵃ* in Israel.
The LORD their God is with them;
    the shout of the King is among
        them.
²²God brought them out of Egypt;
    they have the strength of a wild ox.
²³There is no divination against*ᵇ* Jacob,
    no evil omens against*ᵇ* Israel.
It will now be said of Jacob
    and of Israel, 'See what God has
        done!'
²⁴The people rise like a lioness;
    they rouse themselves like a lion
that does not rest till it devours its
        prey
    and drinks the blood of its victims."

²⁵Then Balak said to Balaam, "Neither curse them at all nor bless them at all!"
²⁶Balaam answered, "Did I not tell you I must do whatever the LORD says?"

Balaam's Third Message

²⁷Then Balak said to Balaam, "Come, let me take you to another place. Perhaps it will please God to let you curse them for me from there." ²⁸And Balak took Balaam to the top of Peor, overlooking the wasteland.
²⁹Balaam said, "Build me seven altars here, and prepare seven bulls and seven rams for me." ³⁰Balak did as Balaam had said, and offered a bull and a ram on each altar.

24 Now when Balaam saw that it pleased the LORD to bless Israel, he did not resort to divination as at other times, but turned his face toward the wilderness. ²When Balaam looked out and saw Israel encamped tribe by tribe, the Spirit of God came on him ³and he spoke his message:

UNSHAKEN *God*

Numbers 23:1–30

God is unchanging.

Balak — the king of Moab — wanted the prophet Balaam to curse the Israelites so they couldn't overrun his country. Even though Balaam was a false prophet who once needed a donkey to tell him the right thing to do (Numbers 22:21–30), he occasionally spoke the truth. In this scene Balaam told Balak that God had decided to bless the Israelites, and nothing he could do would change God's mind (see Numbers 23:19). The fact that God is unchanging is one of his most awesome qualities. When God says he loves you, he means it. When he offers forgiveness, he won't back out. Your God is the same "yesterday and today and forever" (Hebrews 13:8).

So ... How is your unchanging God like or unlike people?

"The prophecy of Balaam son of Beor,
    the prophecy of one whose eye sees
        clearly,
⁴the prophecy of one who hears the
        words of God,
who sees a vision from the
        Almighty,*ᶜ*
who falls prostrate, and whose eyes
        are opened:

⁵"How beautiful are your tents, Jacob,
    your dwelling places, Israel!

⁶"Like valleys they spread out,
    like gardens beside a river,
like aloes planted by the LORD,
    like cedars beside the waters.
⁷Water will flow from their buckets;
    their seed will have abundant
        water.

ᵃ 21 Or *He has not looked on Jacob's offenses / or on the wrongs found*   *ᵇ 23* Or *in*   *ᶜ 4* Hebrew *Shaddai; also in verse 16*

"Their king will be greater than
    Agag;
  their kingdom will be exalted.

[8] "God brought them out of Egypt;
  they have the strength of a wild ox.
They devour hostile nations
  and break their bones in pieces;
  with their arrows they pierce them.
[9] Like a lion they crouch and lie down,
  like a lioness—who dares to rouse
    them?

"May those who bless you be blessed
  and those who curse you be cursed!"

[10] Then Balak's anger burned against Balaam. He struck his hands together and said to him, "I summoned you to curse my enemies, but you have blessed them these three times. [11] Now leave at once and go home! I said I would reward you handsomely, but the Lord has kept you from being rewarded."

[12] Balaam answered Balak, "Did I not tell the messengers you sent me, [13] 'Even if Balak gave me all the silver and gold in his palace, I could not do anything of my own accord, good or bad, to go beyond the command of the Lord—and I must say only what the Lord says'? [14] Now I am going back to my people, but come, let me warn you of what this people will do to your people in days to come."

Balaam's Fourth Message

[15] Then he spoke his message:

"The prophecy of Balaam son of
    Beor,
  the prophecy of one whose eye sees
    clearly,
[16] the prophecy of one who hears the
    words of God,
  who has knowledge from the Most
    High,
  who sees a vision from the Almighty,
  who falls prostrate, and whose eyes
    are opened:

[17] "I see him, but not now;
  I behold him, but not near.
A star will come out of Jacob;
  a scepter will rise out of Israel.

He will crush the foreheads of Moab,
  the skulls[a] of[b] all the people of
    Sheth.[c]
[18] Edom will be conquered;
  Seir, his enemy, will be conquered,
  but Israel will grow strong.
[19] A ruler will come out of Jacob
  and destroy the survivors of the city."

Balaam's Fifth Message

[20] Then Balaam saw Amalek and spoke his message:

"Amalek was first among the nations,
  but their end will be utter
    destruction."

Balaam's Sixth Message

[21] Then he saw the Kenites and spoke his message:

"Your dwelling place is secure,
  your nest is set in a rock;
[22] yet you Kenites will be destroyed
  when Ashur takes you captive."

Balaam's Seventh Message

[23] Then he spoke his message:

"Alas! Who can live when God does
    this?[d]
[24] Ships will come from the shores of
    Cyprus;
  they will subdue Ashur and Eber,
  but they too will come to ruin."

[25] Then Balaam got up and returned home, and Balak went his own way.

Moab Seduces Israel

25 While Israel was staying in Shittim, the men began to indulge in sexual immorality with Moabite women, [2] who invited them to the sacrifices to their gods. The people ate the sacrificial meal and bowed

---

[a] 17 Samaritan Pentateuch (see also Jer. 48:45); the meaning of the word in the Masoretic Text is uncertain.   [b] 17 Or possibly *Moab, / batter*   [c] 17 Or *all the noisy boasters*
[d] 23 Masoretic Text; with a different word division of the Hebrew *The people from the islands will gather from the north.*

down before these gods. ³So Israel yoked themselves to the Baal of Peor. And the LORD's anger burned against them.

⁴The LORD said to Moses, "Take all the leaders of these people, kill them and expose them in broad daylight before the LORD, so that the LORD's fierce anger may turn away from Israel."

⁵So Moses said to Israel's judges, "Each of you must put to death those of your people who have yoked themselves to the Baal of Peor."

⁶Then an Israelite man brought into the camp a Midianite woman right before the eyes of Moses and the whole assembly of Israel while they were weeping at the entrance to the tent of meeting. ⁷When Phinehas son of Eleazar, the son of Aaron, the priest, saw this, he left the assembly, took a spear in his hand ⁸and followed the Israelite into the tent. He drove the spear into both of them, right through the Israelite man and into the woman's stomach. Then the plague against the Israelites was stopped; ⁹but those who died in the plague numbered 24,000.

¹⁰The LORD said to Moses, ¹¹"Phinehas son of Eleazar, the son of Aaron, the priest, has turned my anger away from the Israelites. Since he was as zealous for my honor among them as I am, I did not put an end to them in my zeal. ¹²Therefore tell him I am making my covenant of peace with him. ¹³He and his descendants will have a covenant of a lasting priesthood, because he was zealous for the honor of his God and made atonement for the Israelites."

¹⁴The name of the Israelite who was killed with the Midianite woman was Zimri son of Salu, the leader of a Simeonite family. ¹⁵And the name of the Midianite woman who was put to death was Kozbi daughter of Zur, a tribal chief of a Midianite family.

¹⁶The LORD said to Moses, ¹⁷"Treat the Midianites as enemies and kill them. ¹⁸They treated you as enemies when they deceived you in the Peor incident involving their sister Kozbi, the daughter of a Midianite leader, the woman who was

killed when the plague came as a result of that incident."

The Second Census

26 After the plague the LORD said to Moses and Eleazar son of Aaron, the priest, ²"Take a census of the whole Israelite community by families—all those twenty years old or more who are able to serve in the army of Israel." ³So on the plains of Moab by the Jordan across from Jericho, Moses and Eleazar the priest spoke with them and said, ⁴"Take a census of the men twenty years old or more, as the LORD commanded Moses."

These were the Israelites who came out of Egypt:

⁵The descendants of Reuben, the firstborn son of Israel, were:

through Hanok, the Hanokite clan;
through Pallu, the Palluite clan;
⁶through Hezron, the Hezronite clan;
through Karmi, the Karmite clan.

⁷These were the clans of Reuben; those numbered were 43,730.

⁸The son of Pallu was Eliab, ⁹and the sons of Eliab were Nemuel, Dathan and Abiram. The same Dathan and Abiram were the community officials who rebelled against Moses and Aaron and were among Korah's followers when they rebelled against the LORD. ¹⁰The earth opened its mouth and swallowed them along with Korah, whose followers died when the fire devoured the 250 men. And they served as a warning sign. ¹¹The line of Korah, however, did not die out.

¹²The descendants of Simeon by their clans were:

through Nemuel, the Nemuelite clan;
through Jamin, the Jaminite clan;
through Jakin, the Jakinite clan;
¹³through Zerah, the Zerahite clan;
through Shaul, the Shaulite clan.

¹⁴These were the clans of Simeon; those numbered were 22,200.

¹⁵The descendants of Gad by their clans were:

through Zephon, the Zephonite clan;

through Haggi, the Haggite clan;

through Shuni, the Shunite clan;

¹⁶ through Ozni, the Oznite clan;

through Eri, the Erite clan;

¹⁷ through Arodi,ᵃ the Arodite clan;

through Areli, the Arelite clan.

¹⁸ These were the clans of Gad; those numbered were 40,500.

¹⁹ Er and Onan were sons of Judah, but they died in Canaan.

²⁰ The descendants of Judah by their clans were:

through Shelah, the Shelanite clan;

through Perez, the Perezite clan;

through Zerah, the Zerahite clan.

²¹ The descendants of Perez were:

through Hezron, the Hezronite clan;

through Hamul, the Hamulite clan.

²² These were the clans of Judah; those numbered were 76,500.

²³ The descendants of Issachar by their clans were:

through Tola, the Tolaite clan;

through Puah, the Puiteᵇ clan;

²⁴ through Jashub, the Jashubite clan;

through Shimron, the Shimronite clan.

²⁵ These were the clans of Issachar; those numbered were 64,300.

²⁶ The descendants of Zebulun by their clans were:

through Sered, the Seredite clan;

through Elon, the Elonite clan;

through Jahleel, the Jahleelite clan.

²⁷ These were the clans of Zebulun; those numbered were 60,500.

²⁸ The descendants of Joseph by their clans through Manasseh and Ephraim were:

²⁹ The descendants of Manasseh:

through Makir, the Makirite clan (Makir was the father of Gilead);

through Gilead, the Gileadite clan.

³⁰ These were the descendants of Gilead:

through Iezer, the Iezerite clan;

through Helek, the Helekite clan;

³¹ through Asriel, the Asrielite clan;

through Shechem, the Shechemite clan;

³² through Shemida, the Shemidaite clan;

through Hepher, the Hepherite clan.

³³ (Zelophehad son of Hepher had no sons; he had only daughters, whose names were Mahlah, Noah, Hoglah, Milkah and Tirzah.)

³⁴ These were the clans of Manasseh; those numbered were 52,700.

³⁵ These were the descendants of Ephraim by their clans:

through Shuthelah, the Shuthelahite clan;

through Beker, the Bekerite clan;

through Tahan, the Tahanite clan.

³⁶ These were the descendants of Shuthelah:

through Eran, the Eranite clan.

³⁷ These were the clans of Ephraim; those numbered were 32,500.

These were the descendants of Joseph by their clans.

³⁸ The descendants of Benjamin by their clans were:

through Bela, the Belaite clan;

through Ashbel, the Ashbelite clan;

through Ahiram, the Ahiramite clan;

³⁹ through Shupham,ᶜ the Shuphamite clan;

through Hupham, the Huphamite clan.

⁴⁰ The descendants of Bela through Ard and Naaman were:

through Ard,ᵈ the Ardite clan;

ᵃ 17 Samaritan Pentateuch and Syriac (see also Gen. 46:16); Masoretic Text *Arod*

ᵇ 23 Samaritan Pentateuch, Septuagint, Vulgate and Syriac (see also 1 Chron. 7:1); Masoretic Text *through Puvah, the Punite* ᶜ 39 A few manuscripts of the Masoretic Text, Samaritan Pentateuch, Vulgate and Syriac (see also Septuagint); most manuscripts of the Masoretic Text *Shephupham* ᵈ 40 Samaritan Pentateuch and Vulgate (see also Septuagint); Masoretic Text does not have *through Ard*.

191

through Naaman, the Naamite clan.

⁴¹These were the clans of Benjamin; those numbered were 45,600.

⁴²These were the descendants of Dan by their clans:

through Shuham, the Shuhamite clan.

These were the clans of Dan: ⁴³All of them were Shuhamite clans; and those numbered were 64,400.

⁴⁴The descendants of Asher by their clans were:

through Imnah, the Imnite clan;
through Ishvi, the Ishvite clan;
through Beriah, the Beriite clan;
⁴⁵and through the descendants of Beriah:

through Heber, the Heberite clan;
through Malkiel, the Malkielite clan.

⁴⁶(Asher had a daughter named Serah.)
⁴⁷These were the clans of Asher; those numbered were 53,400.

⁴⁸The descendants of Naphtali by their clans were:

through Jahzeel, the Jahzeelite clan;
through Guni, the Gunite clan;
⁴⁹through Jezer, the Jezerite clan;
through Shillem, the Shillemite clan.

⁵⁰These were the clans of Naphtali; those numbered were 45,400.

⁵¹The total number of the men of Israel was 601,730.

⁵²The Lord said to Moses, ⁵³"The land is to be allotted to them as an inheritance based on the number of names. ⁵⁴To a larger group give a larger inheritance, and to a smaller group a smaller one; each is to receive its inheritance according to the number of those listed. ⁵⁵Be sure that the land is distributed by lot. What each group inherits will be according to the names for its ancestral tribe. ⁵⁶Each inheritance is to be distributed by lot among the larger and smaller groups."

⁵⁷These were the Levites who were counted by their clans:

through Gershon, the Gershonite clan;
through Kohath, the Kohathite clan;
through Merari, the Merarite clan.

⁵⁸These also were Levite clans:
the Libnite clan,
the Hebronite clan,
the Mahlite clan,
the Mushite clan,
the Korahite clan.

(Kohath was the forefather of Amram; ⁵⁹the name of Amram's wife was Jochebed, a descendant of Levi, who was born to the Levites*a* in Egypt. To Amram she bore Aaron, Moses and their sister Miriam. ⁶⁰Aaron was the father of Nadab and Abihu, Eleazar and Ithamar. ⁶¹But Nadab and Abihu died when they made an offering before the Lord with unauthorized fire.)

⁶²All the male Levites a month old or more numbered 23,000. They were not counted along with the other Israelites because they received no inheritance among them.

⁶³These are the ones counted by Moses and Eleazar the priest when they counted the Israelites on the plains of Moab by the Jordan across from Jericho. ⁶⁴Not one of them was among those counted by Moses and Aaron the priest when they counted the Israelites in the Desert of Sinai. ⁶⁵For the Lord had told those Israelites they would surely die in the wilderness, and not one of them was left except Caleb son of Jephunneh and Joshua son of Nun.

Zelophehad's Daughters

27 The daughters of Zelophehad son of Hepher, the son of Gilead, the son of Makir, the son of Manasseh, belonged to the clans of Manasseh son of Joseph. The names of the daughters were Mahlah, Noah, Hoglah, Milkah and Tirzah. They came forward ²and stood before Moses, Eleazar the priest, the leaders and the

---

a 59 Or *Jochebed, a daughter of Levi, who was born to Levi* whole assembly at the entrance to the tent of meeting and said, ³"Our father died in the wilderness. He was not among Korah's followers, who banded together against the Lord, but he died for his own sin and left no sons. ⁴Why should our father's name disappear from his clan because he had no son? Give us property among our father's relatives."

⁵So Moses brought their case before the Lord, ⁶and the Lord said to him, ⁷"What Zelophehad's daughters are saying is right. You must certainly give them property as an inheritance among their father's relatives and give their father's inheritance to them.

⁸"Say to the Israelites, 'If a man dies and leaves no son, give his inheritance to his daughter. ⁹If he has no daughter, give his inheritance to his brothers. ¹⁰If he has no brothers, give his inheritance to his father's brothers. ¹¹If his father had no brothers, give his inheritance to the nearest relative in his clan, that he may possess it. This is to have the force of law for the Israelites, as the Lord commanded Moses.'"

Joshua to Succeed Moses

¹²Then the Lord said to Moses, "Go up this mountain in the Abarim Range and see the land I have given the Israelites. ¹³After you have seen it, you too will be gathered to your people, as your brother Aaron was, ¹⁴for when the community rebelled at the waters in the Desert of Zin, both of you disobeyed my command to honor me as holy before their eyes." (These were the waters of Meribah Kadesh, in the Desert of Zin.)

¹⁵Moses said to the Lord, ¹⁶"May the Lord, the God who gives breath to all living things, appoint someone over this community ¹⁷to go out and come in before them, one who will lead them out and bring them in, so the Lord's people will not be like sheep without a shepherd."

¹⁸So the Lord said to Moses, "Take Joshua son of Nun, a man in whom is the spirit of leadership,ᵃ and lay your hand on him. ¹⁹Have him stand before Elea-zar the priest and the entire assembly and commission him in their presence. ²⁰Give him some of your authority so the whole Israelite community will obey him. ²¹He is to stand before Eleazar the priest, who will obtain decisions for him by inquiring of the Urim before the Lord. At his command he and the entire community of the Israelites will go out, and at his command they will come in."

²²Moses did as the Lord commanded him. He took Joshua and had him stand before Eleazar the priest and the whole assembly. ²³Then he laid his hands on him and commissioned him, as the Lord instructed through Moses.

Daily Offerings

28 The Lord said to Moses, ²"Give this command to the Israelites and say to them: 'Make sure that you present to me at the appointed time my food offerings, as an aroma pleasing to me.' ³Say to them: 'This is the food offering you are to present to the Lord: two lambs a year old without defect, as a regular burnt offering each day. ⁴Offer one lamb in the morning and the other at twilight, ⁵together with a grain offering of a tenth of an ephahᵇ of the finest flour mixed with a quarter of a hinᶜ of oil from pressed olives. ⁶This is the regular burnt offering instituted at Mount Sinai as a pleasing aroma, a food offering presented to the Lord. ⁷The accompanying drink offering is to be a quarter of a hin of fermented drink with each lamb. Pour out the drink offering to the Lord at the sanctuary. ⁸Offer the second lamb at twilight, along with the same kind of grain offering and drink offering that you offer in the morning. This is a food offering, an aroma pleasing to the Lord.

Sabbath Offerings

⁹"'On the Sabbath day, make an offering of two lambs a year old without defect,

---

ᵃ 18 Or *the Spirit*   ᵇ 5 That is, probably about 3 1/2 pounds or about 1.6 kilograms; also in verses 13, 21 and 29   ᶜ 5 That is, about 1 quart or about 1 liter; also in verses 7 and 14 together with its drink offering and a grain offering of two-tenths of an ephah*ª* of the finest flour mixed with olive oil. ¹⁰This is the burnt offering for every Sabbath, in addition to the regular burnt offering and its drink offering.

Monthly Offerings

¹¹"'On the first of every month, present to the LORD a burnt offering of two young bulls, one ram and seven male lambs a year old, all without defect. ¹²With each bull there is to be a grain offering of three-tenths of an ephah*ᵇ* of the finest flour mixed with oil; with the ram, a

grain offering of two-tenths of an ephah of the finest flour mixed with oil; ¹³and with each lamb, a grain offering of a tenth of an ephah of the finest flour mixed with oil. This is for a burnt offering, a pleasing aroma, a food offering presented to the LORD. ¹⁴With each bull there is to be a drink offering of half a hin*ᶜ* of wine; with the ram, a third of a hin*ᵈ*; and with

---

ª 9 That is, probably about 7 pounds or about 3.2 kilograms; also in verses 12, 20 and 28

ᵇ 12 That is, probably about 11 pounds or about 5 kilograms; also in verses 20 and 28

ᶜ 14 That is, about 2 quarts or about 1.9 liters

ᵈ 14 That is, about 1 1/3 quarts or about 1.3 liters

Numbers 27:12–23

Joshua lived courageously.

Of a dozen men who scouted the promised land prior to an all-important invasion, only Joshua and Caleb brought back a positive report. The other ten spies saw the bountiful land God had given them, but they claimed God's people were too weak to conquer the giants who lived there (see Numbers 13:26–33).

Joshua was already well known as Moses' chief aide "since youth" (Numbers 11:28). He led a famous battle where God's people gained victory over the Amalekites only as long as Moses kept his hands lifted in prayer (see Exodus 17:8–15). When Moses ascended Mount Sinai to receive the Ten Commandments, Joshua walked part of the distance with Moses (see Exodus 24:13). And whenever the Lord paused to speak with Moses, Joshua worshiped nearby (see Exodus 33:11).

Because Joshua had seen God's power firsthand, he refused to tremble like the spies afraid to take the land. When the Lord said all the people would die without entering the land because of their lack of trust in him, he made an exception for Joshua and Caleb. Of that entire generation, these two men were the only ones who would enter the land (see Numbers 14:30).

Many years later, Joshua assumed leadership of the Israelites when Moses died. He took the lead when it was time for a new generation to storm the promised land. Joshua moved ahead with the Lord's bold promise: "Be strong and courageous. Do not be afraid; do not be discouraged, for the LORD your God will be with you wherever you go" (Joshua 1:9).

You can find Joshua in Numbers 13—14 and 27, throughout the book of Joshua, and Hebrews 4:8.

UNSHAKEN *people*

each lamb, a quarter of a hin. This is the monthly burnt offering to be made at each new moon during the year. ¹⁵Besides the regular burnt offering with its drink offering, one male goat is to be presented to the LORD as a sin offering.^a

The Passover

¹⁶"'On the fourteenth day of the first month the LORD's Passover is to be held. ¹⁷On the fifteenth day of this month there is to be a festival; for seven days eat bread made without yeast. ¹⁸On the first day hold a sacred assembly and do no regular work. ¹⁹Present to the LORD a food offering consisting of a burnt offering of two young bulls, one ram and seven male lambs a year old, all without defect. ²⁰With each bull offer a grain offering of three-tenths of an ephah of the finest flour mixed with oil; with the ram, two-tenths; ²¹and with each of the seven lambs, one-tenth. ²²Include one male goat as a sin offering to make atonement for you. ²³Offer these in addition to the regular morning burnt offering. ²⁴In this way present the food offering every day for seven days as an aroma pleasing to the LORD; it is to be offered in addition to the regular burnt offering and its drink offering. ²⁵On the seventh day hold a sacred assembly and do no regular work.

The Festival of Weeks

²⁶"'On the day of firstfruits, when you present to the LORD an offering of new grain during the Festival of Weeks, hold a sacred assembly and do no regular work. ²⁷Present a burnt offering of two young bulls, one ram and seven male lambs a year old as an aroma pleasing to the LORD. ²⁸With each bull there is to be a grain offering of three-tenths of an ephah of the finest flour mixed with oil; with the ram, two-tenths; ²⁹and with each of the seven lambs, one-tenth. ³⁰Include one male goat to make atonement for you. ³¹Offer these together with their drink offerings, in addition to the regular burnt offering and its grain offering. Be sure the animals are without defect.

The Festival of Trumpets

29 "'On the first day of the seventh month hold a sacred assembly and do no regular work. It is a day for you to sound the trumpets. ²As an aroma pleasing to the LORD, offer a burnt offering of one young bull, one ram and seven male lambs a year old, all without defect. ³With the bull offer a grain offering of three-tenths of an ephah^b of the finest flour mixed with olive oil; with the ram, two-tenths^c; ⁴and with each of the seven lambs, one-tenth.^d ⁵Include one male goat as a sin offering^e to make atonement for you. ⁶These are in addition to the monthly and daily burnt offerings with their grain offerings and drink offerings as specified. They are food offerings presented to the LORD, a pleasing aroma.

The Day of Atonement

⁷"'On the tenth day of this seventh month hold a sacred assembly. You must deny yourselves^f and do no work. ⁸Present as an aroma pleasing to the LORD a burnt offering of one young bull, one ram and seven male lambs a year old, all without defect. ⁹With the bull offer a grain offering of three-tenths of an ephah of the finest flour mixed with oil; with the ram, two-tenths; ¹⁰and with each of the seven lambs, one-tenth. ¹¹Include one male goat as a sin offering, in addition to the sin offering for atonement and the regular burnt offering with its grain offering, and their drink offerings.

The Festival of Tabernacles

¹²"'On the fifteenth day of the seventh month, hold a sacred assembly and do no regular work. Celebrate a festival to the LORD for seven days. ¹³Present as an aroma pleasing to the LORD a food offering

---

^a 15 Or *purification offering*; also in verse 22   ^b 3 That is, probably about 11 pounds or about 5 kilograms; also in verses 9 and 14   ^c 3 That is, probably about 7 pounds or about 3.2 kilograms; also in verses 9 and 14   ^d 4 That is, probably about 3 1/2 pounds or about 1.6 kilograms; also in verses 10 and 15   ^e 5 Or *purification offering*; also elsewhere in this chapter   ^f 7 Or *must fast*

consisting of a burnt offering of thirteen young bulls, two rams and fourteen male lambs a year old, all without defect. [14]With each of the thirteen bulls offer a grain offering of three-tenths of an ephah of the finest flour mixed with oil; with each of the two rams, two-tenths; [15]and with each of the fourteen lambs, one-tenth. [16]Include one male goat as a sin offering, in addition to the regular burnt offering with its grain offering and drink offering.

[17]"'On the second day offer twelve young bulls, two rams and fourteen male lambs a year old, all without defect. [18]With the bulls, rams and lambs, offer their grain offerings and drink offerings according to the number specified. [19]Include one male goat as a sin offering, in addition to the regular burnt offering with its grain offering, and their drink offerings.

[20]"'On the third day offer eleven bulls, two rams and fourteen male lambs a year old, all without defect. [21]With the bulls, rams and lambs, offer their grain offerings and drink offerings according to the number specified. [22]Include one male goat as a sin offering, in addition to the regular burnt offering with its grain offering and drink offering.

[23]"'On the fourth day offer ten bulls, two rams and fourteen male lambs a year old, all without defect. [24]With the bulls, rams and lambs, offer their grain offerings and drink offerings according to the number specified. [25]Include one male goat as a sin offering, in addition to the regular burnt offering with its grain offering and drink offering.

[26]"'On the fifth day offer nine bulls, two rams and fourteen male lambs a year old, all without defect. [27]With the bulls, rams and lambs, offer their grain offerings and drink offerings according to the number specified. [28]Include one male goat as a sin offering, in addition to the regular burnt offering with its grain offering and drink offering.

[29]"'On the sixth day offer eight bulls, two rams and fourteen male lambs a year old, all without defect. [30]With the bulls, rams and lambs, offer their grain offerings

and drink offerings according to the number specified. [31]Include one male goat as a sin offering, in addition to the regular burnt offering with its grain offering and drink offering.

[32]"'On the seventh day offer seven bulls, two rams and fourteen male lambs a year old, all without defect. [33]With the bulls, rams and lambs, offer their grain offerings and drink offerings according to the number specified. [34]Include one male goat as a sin offering, in addition to the regular burnt offering with its grain offering and drink offering.

[35]"'On the eighth day hold a closing special assembly and do no regular work. [36]Present as an aroma pleasing to the Lord a food offering consisting of a burnt offering of one bull, one ram and seven male lambs a year old, all without defect. [37]With the bull, the ram and the lambs, offer their grain offerings and drink offerings according to the number specified. [38]Include one male goat as a sin offering, in addition to the regular burnt offering with its grain offering and drink offering.

[39]"'In addition to what you vow and your freewill offerings, offer these to the Lord at your appointed festivals: your burnt offerings, grain offerings, drink offerings and fellowship offerings.'"

[40]Moses told the Israelites all that the Lord commanded him.[a]

Vows

30 [b] Moses said to the heads of the tribes of Israel: "This is what the Lord commands: [2]When a man makes a vow to the Lord or takes an oath to obligate himself by a pledge, he must not break his word but must do everything he said.

[3]"When a young woman still living in her father's household makes a vow to the Lord or obligates herself by a pledge [4]and her father hears about her vow or pledge but says nothing to her, then all her vows and every pledge by which she obligated

<hr>

[a] 40 In Hebrew texts this verse (29:40) is numbered 30:1.   [b] In Hebrew texts 30:1-16 is numbered 30:2-17.

herself will stand. ⁵But if her father forbids her when he hears about it, none of her vows or the pledges by which she obligated herself will stand; the LORD will release her because her father has forbidden her.

⁶"If she marries after she makes a vow or after her lips utter a rash promise by which she obligates herself ⁷and her husband hears about it but says nothing to her, then her vows or the pledges by which she obligated herself will stand. ⁸But if her husband forbids her when he hears about it, he nullifies the vow that obligates her or the rash promise by which she obligates herself, and the LORD will release her.

⁹"Any vow or obligation taken by a widow or divorced woman will be binding on her.

¹⁰"If a woman living with her husband makes a vow or obligates herself by a pledge under oath ¹¹and her husband hears about it but says nothing to her and does not forbid her, then all her vows or the pledges by which she obligated herself will stand. ¹²But if her husband nullifies them when he hears about them, then none of the vows or pledges that came from her lips will stand. Her husband has nullified them, and the LORD will release her. ¹³Her husband may confirm or nullify any vow she makes or any sworn pledge to deny herself.^a ¹⁴But if her husband says nothing to her about it from day to day, then he confirms all her vows or the pledges binding on her. He confirms them by saying nothing to her when he hears about them. ¹⁵If, however, he nullifies them some time after he hears about them, then he must bear the consequences of her wrongdoing."

¹⁶These are the regulations the LORD gave Moses concerning relationships between a man and his wife, and between a father and his young daughter still living at home.

Vengeance on the Midianites

31 The LORD said to Moses, ²"Take vengeance on the Midianites for the Israelites. After that, you will be gathered to your people."

³So Moses said to the people, "Arm some of your men to go to war against the Midianites so that they may carry out the LORD's vengeance on them. ⁴Send into battle a thousand men from each of the tribes of Israel." ⁵So twelve thousand men armed for battle, a thousand from each tribe, were supplied from the clans of Israel. ⁶Moses sent them into battle, a thousand from each tribe, along with Phinehas son of Eleazar, the priest, who took with him articles from the sanctuary and the trumpets for signaling.

⁷They fought against Midian, as the LORD commanded Moses, and killed every man. ⁸Among their victims were Evi, Rekem, Zur, Hur and Reba—the five kings of Midian. They also killed Balaam son of Beor with the sword. ⁹The Israelites captured the Midianite women and children and took all the Midianite herds, flocks and goods as plunder. ¹⁰They burned all the towns where the Midianites had settled, as well as all their camps. ¹¹They took all the plunder and spoils, including the people and animals, ¹²and brought the captives, spoils and plunder to Moses and Eleazar the priest and the Israelite assembly at their camp on the plains of Moab, by the Jordan across from Jericho.

¹³Moses, Eleazar the priest and all the leaders of the community went to meet them outside the camp. ¹⁴Moses was angry with the officers of the army—the commanders of thousands and commanders of hundreds—who returned from the battle.

¹⁵"Have you allowed all the women to live?" he asked them. ¹⁶"They were the ones who followed Balaam's advice and enticed the Israelites to be unfaithful to the LORD in the Peor incident, so that a plague struck the LORD's people. ¹⁷Now kill all the boys. And kill every woman who has slept with a man, ¹⁸but save for yourselves every girl who has never slept with a man.

¹⁹"Anyone who has killed someone or touched someone who was killed must stay outside the camp seven days. On the third and seventh days you must purify

^a 13 Or to fast

yourselves and your captives. ²⁰Purify every garment as well as everything made of leather, goat hair or wood."

²¹Then Eleazar the priest said to the soldiers who had gone into battle, "This is what is required by the law that the Lord gave Moses: ²²Gold, silver, bronze, iron, tin, lead ²³and anything else that can withstand fire must be put through the fire, and then it will be clean. But it must also be purified with the water of cleansing. And whatever cannot withstand fire must be put through that water. ²⁴On the seventh day wash your clothes and you will be clean. Then you may come into the camp."

Dividing the Spoils

²⁵The Lord said to Moses, ²⁶"You and Eleazar the priest and the family heads of the community are to count all the people and animals that were captured. ²⁷Divide the spoils equally between the soldiers who took part in the battle and the rest of the community. ²⁸From the soldiers who fought in the battle, set apart as tribute for the Lord one out of every five hundred, whether people, cattle, donkeys or sheep. ²⁹Take this tribute from their half share and give it to Eleazar the priest as the Lord's part. ³⁰From the Israelites' half, select one out of every fifty, whether people, cattle, donkeys, sheep or other animals. Give them to the Levites, who are responsible for the care of the Lord's tabernacle."
³¹So Moses and Eleazar the priest did as the Lord commanded Moses.

³²The plunder remaining from the spoils that the soldiers took was 675,000 sheep, ³³72,000 cattle, ³⁴61,000 donkeys ³⁵and 32,000 women who had never slept with a man.

³⁶The half share of those who fought in the battle was:

337,500 sheep, ³⁷of which the tribute for the Lord was 675;
³⁸36,000 cattle, of which the tribute for the Lord was 72;
³⁹30,500 donkeys, of which the tribute for the Lord was 61;
⁴⁰16,000 people, of whom the tribute for the Lord was 32.

⁴¹Moses gave the tribute to Eleazar the priest as the Lord's part, as the Lord commanded Moses.

⁴²The half belonging to the Israelites, which Moses set apart from that of the fighting men— ⁴³the community's half—was 337,500 sheep, ⁴⁴36,000 cattle, ⁴⁵30,500 donkeys ⁴⁶and 16,000 people. ⁴⁷From the Israelites' half, Moses selected one out of every fifty people and animals, as the Lord commanded him, and gave them to the Levites, who were responsible for the care of the Lord's tabernacle.

⁴⁸Then the officers who were over the units of the army—the commanders of thousands and commanders of hundreds—went to Moses ⁴⁹and said to him, "Your servants have counted the soldiers under our command, and not one is missing. ⁵⁰So we have brought as an offering to the Lord the gold articles each of us acquired—armlets, bracelets, signet rings, earrings and necklaces—to make atonement for ourselves before the Lord."

⁵¹Moses and Eleazar the priest accepted from them the gold—all the crafted articles. ⁵²All the gold from the commanders of thousands and commanders of hundreds that Moses and Eleazar presented as a gift to the Lord weighed 16,750 shekels.ᵃ ⁵³Each soldier had taken plunder for himself. ⁵⁴Moses and Eleazar the priest accepted the gold from the commanders of thousands and commanders of hundreds and brought it into the tent of meeting as a memorial for the Israelites before the Lord.

The Transjordan Tribes

32 The Reubenites and Gadites, who had very large herds and flocks, saw that the lands of Jazer and Gilead were suitable for livestock. ²So they came to Moses and Eleazar the priest and to the leaders of the community, and said, ³"Ataroth, Dibon, Jazer, Nimrah, Heshbon, Elealeh, Sebam, Nebo and Beon— ⁴the land the Lord subdued before the people of Israel—are

ᵃ 52 That is, about 420 pounds or about 190 kilograms

suitable for livestock, and your servants have livestock. ⁵If we have found favor in your eyes," they said, "let this land be given to your servants as our possession. Do not make us cross the Jordan."

⁶Moses said to the Gadites and Reubenites, "Should your fellow Israelites go to war while you sit here? ⁷Why do you discourage the Israelites from crossing over into the land the LORD has given them? ⁸This is what your fathers did when I sent them from Kadesh Barnea to look over the land. ⁹After they went up to the Valley of Eshkol and viewed the land, they discouraged the Israelites from entering the land the LORD had given them. ¹⁰The

LORD's anger was aroused that day and he swore this oath: ¹¹'Because they have not followed me wholeheartedly, not one of those who were twenty years old or more when they came up out of Egypt will see the land I promised on oath to Abraham, Isaac and Jacob— ¹²not one except Caleb son of Jephunneh the Kenizzite and Joshua son of Nun, for they followed the LORD wholeheartedly.' ¹³The LORD's anger burned against Israel and he made them wander in the wilderness forty years, until the whole generation of those who had done evil in his sight was gone.

¹⁴"And here you are, a brood of sinners, standing in the place of your fathers and

---

Numbers 32:10–13

Caleb followed God wholeheartedly.

God had freed the slaves from Egypt, bringing them to the brink of entering the promised land. A dozen men stole into the land to scout this miraculous prize. Of the 12 spies, however, only Caleb and Joshua believed God would give his people the might they needed to conquer the land.

Because Joshua was a key aide to Moses—and a Bible book bears his name—you might assume Joshua always took the lead of this dynamic duo. But it was Caleb who first spoke up about the people's dismal disbelief. Numbers 13:30 says, "Then Caleb silenced the people before Moses and said, 'We should go up and take possession of the land, for we can certainly do it.'" Then Caleb and Joshua both argued, "If the LORD is pleased with us, he will lead us into that land, a land flowing with milk and honey, and will give it to us" (Numbers 14:8).

The crowd wanted to exterminate Caleb and Joshua for their bold stand. As Numbers 14:10 reports, "The whole assembly talked about stoning them."

Despite the crowd's violent threats, Caleb never doubted God. He clung to the Lord's promises, believing God's power was stronger than any human force. And God was exceedingly pleased with Caleb and Joshua, because "they followed the LORD wholeheartedly" (Numbers 32:12). Because of their faithfulness, they alone would enter the promised land. God condemned all of the doubters to wander the desert until they died.

You can find Caleb in Numbers 13 and 14; Numbers 32; Deuteronomy 1:36; and Joshua 14:6–14.

UNSHAKEN people

making the Lord even more angry with Israel. [15] If you turn away from following him, he will again leave all this people in the wilderness, and you will be the cause of their destruction."

[16] Then they came up to him and said, "We would like to build pens here for our livestock and cities for our women and children. [17] But we will arm ourselves for battle[a] and go ahead of the Israelites until we have brought them to their place. Meanwhile our women and children will live in fortified cities, for protection from the inhabitants of the land. [18] We will not return to our homes until each of the Israelites has received their inheritance. [19] We will not receive any inheritance with them on the other side of the Jordan, because our inheritance has come to us on the east side of the Jordan."

[20] Then Moses said to them, "If you will do this—if you will arm yourselves before the Lord for battle [21] and if all of you who are armed cross over the Jordan before the Lord until he has driven his enemies out before him— [22] then when the land is subdued before the Lord, you may return and be free from your obligation to the Lord and to Israel. And this land will be your possession before the Lord.

[23] "But if you fail to do this, you will be sinning against the Lord; and you may be sure that your sin will find you out. [24] Build cities for your women and children, and pens for your flocks, but do what you have promised."

[25] The Gadites and Reubenites said to Moses, "We your servants will do as our lord commands. [26] Our children and wives, our flocks and herds will remain here in the cities of Gilead. [27] But your servants, every man who is armed for battle, will cross over to fight before the Lord, just as our lord says."

[28] Then Moses gave orders about them to Eleazar the priest and Joshua son of Nun and to the family heads of the Israelite tribes. [29] He said to them, "If the Gadites and Reubenites, every man armed for battle, cross over the Jordan with you before the Lord, then when the land is subdued before you, you must give them the land of Gilead as their possession. [30] But if they do not cross over with you armed, they must accept their possession with you in Canaan."

[31] The Gadites and Reubenites answered, "Your servants will do what the Lord has said. [32] We will cross over before the Lord into Canaan armed, but the property we inherit will be on this side of the Jordan."

[33] Then Moses gave to the Gadites, the Reubenites and the half-tribe of Manasseh son of Joseph the kingdom of Sihon king of the Amorites and the kingdom of Og king of Bashan—the whole land with its cities and the territory around them.

[34] The Gadites built up Dibon, Ataroth, Aroer, [35] Atroth Shophan, Jazer, Jogbehah, [36] Beth Nimrah and Beth Haran as fortified cities, and built pens for their flocks. [37] And the Reubenites rebuilt Heshbon, Elealeh and Kiriathaim, [38] as well as Nebo and Baal Meon (these names were changed) and Sibmah. They gave names to the cities they rebuilt.

[39] The descendants of Makir son of Manasseh went to Gilead, captured it and drove out the Amorites who were there. [40] So Moses gave Gilead to the Makirites, the descendants of Manasseh, and they settled there. [41] Jair, a descendant of Manasseh, captured their settlements and called them Havvoth Jair.[b] [42] And Nobah captured Kenath and its surrounding settlements and called it Nobah after himself.

Stages in Israel's Journey

33 Here are the stages in the journey of the Israelites when they came out of Egypt by divisions under the leadership of Moses and Aaron. [2] At the Lord's command Moses recorded the stages in their journey. This is their journey by stages:

[3] The Israelites set out from Rameses on the fifteenth day of the first month, the day after the Passover.

---

[a] 17 Septuagint; Hebrew *will be quick to arm ourselves*   [b] 41 Or *them the settlements of Jair*

They marched out defiantly in full view of all the Egyptians, ⁴who were burying all their firstborn, whom the Lord had struck down among them; for the Lord had brought judgment on their gods.

⁵The Israelites left Rameses and camped at Sukkoth.

⁶They left Sukkoth and camped at Etham, on the edge of the desert.

⁷They left Etham, turned back to Pi Hahiroth, to the east of Baal Zephon, and camped near Migdol.

⁸They left Pi Hahiroth*a* and passed through the sea into the desert, and when they had traveled for three days in the Desert of Etham, they camped at Marah.

⁹They left Marah and went to Elim, where there were twelve springs and seventy palm trees, and they camped there.

¹⁰They left Elim and camped by the Red Sea.*b*

¹¹They left the Red Sea and camped in the Desert of Sin.

¹²They left the Desert of Sin and camped at Dophkah.

¹³They left Dophkah and camped at Alush.

¹⁴They left Alush and camped at Rephidim, where there was no water for the people to drink.

¹⁵They left Rephidim and camped in the Desert of Sinai.

¹⁶They left the Desert of Sinai and camped at Kibroth Hattaavah.

¹⁷They left Kibroth Hattaavah and camped at Hazeroth.

¹⁸They left Hazeroth and camped at Rithmah.

¹⁹They left Rithmah and camped at Rimmon Perez.

²⁰They left Rimmon Perez and camped at Libnah.

²¹They left Libnah and camped at Rissah.

²²They left Rissah and camped at Kehelathah.

²³They left Kehelathah and camped at Mount Shepher.

²⁴They left Mount Shepher and camped at Haradah.

²⁵They left Haradah and camped at Makheloth.

²⁶They left Makheloth and camped at Tahath.

²⁷They left Tahath and camped at Terah.

²⁸They left Terah and camped at Mithkah.

²⁹They left Mithkah and camped at Hashmonah.

³⁰They left Hashmonah and camped at Moseroth.

³¹They left Moseroth and camped at Bene Jaakan.

³²They left Bene Jaakan and camped at Hor Haggidgad.

³³They left Hor Haggidgad and camped at Jotbathah.

³⁴They left Jotbathah and camped at Abronah.

³⁵They left Abronah and camped at Ezion Geber.

³⁶They left Ezion Geber and camped at Kadesh, in the Desert of Zin.

³⁷They left Kadesh and camped at Mount Hor, on the border of Edom. ³⁸At the Lord's command Aaron the priest went up Mount Hor, where he died on the first day of the fifth month of the fortieth year after the Israelites came out of Egypt. ³⁹Aaron was a hundred and twenty-three years old when he died on Mount Hor.

⁴⁰The Canaanite king of Arad, who lived in the Negev of Canaan, heard that the Israelites were coming.

⁴¹They left Mount Hor and camped at Zalmonah.

⁴²They left Zalmonah and camped at Punon.

⁴³They left Punon and camped at Oboth.

⁴⁴They left Oboth and camped at Iye Abarim, on the border of Moab.

a 8 Many manuscripts of the Masoretic Text, Samaritan Pentateuch and Vulgate; most manuscripts of the Masoretic Text *left from before Hahiroth*   *b 10* Or *the Sea of Reeds*; also in verse 11

⁴⁵They left Iye Abarim and camped at Dibon Gad.

⁴⁶They left Dibon Gad and camped at Almon Diblathaim.

⁴⁷They left Almon Diblathaim and camped in the mountains of Abarim, near Nebo.

⁴⁸They left the mountains of Abarim and camped on the plains of Moab by the Jordan across from Jericho. ⁴⁹There on the plains of Moab they camped along the Jordan from Beth Jeshimoth to Abel Shittim.

⁵⁰On the plains of Moab by the Jordan across from Jericho the LORD said to Moses, ⁵¹"Speak to the Israelites and say to them: 'When you cross the Jordan into Canaan, ⁵²drive out all the inhabitants of the land before you. Destroy all their carved images and their cast idols, and demolish all their high places. ⁵³Take possession of the land and settle in it, for I have given you the land to possess. ⁵⁴Distribute the land by lot, according to your clans. To a larger group give a larger inheritance, and to a smaller group a smaller one. Whatever falls to them by lot will be theirs. Distribute it according to your ancestral tribes.

⁵⁵"'But if you do not drive out the inhabitants of the land, those you allow to remain will become barbs in your eyes and thorns in your sides. They will give you trouble in the land where you will live. ⁵⁶And then I will do to you what I plan to do to them.'"

Boundaries of Canaan

34 The LORD said to Moses, ²"Command the Israelites and say to them: 'When you enter Canaan, the land that will be allotted to you as an inheritance is to have these boundaries:

³"'Your southern side will include some of the Desert of Zin along the border of Edom. Your southern boundary will start in the east from the southern end of the Dead Sea, ⁴cross south of Scorpion Pass, continue on to Zin and go south of Kadesh Barnea. Then it will go to Hazar Addar and over to Azmon, ⁵where it will turn, join the Wadi of Egypt and end at the Mediterranean Sea.

⁶"'Your western boundary will be the coast of the Mediterranean Sea. This will be your boundary on the west.

⁷"'For your northern boundary, run a line from the Mediterranean Sea to Mount Hor ⁸and from Mount Hor to Lebo Hamath. Then the boundary will go to Zedad, ⁹continue to Ziphron and end at Hazar Enan. This will be your boundary on the north.

¹⁰"'For your eastern boundary, run a line from Hazar Enan to Shepham. ¹¹The boundary will go down from Shepham to Riblah on the east side of Ain and continue along the slopes east of the Sea of Galilee.ᵃ ¹²Then the boundary will go down along the Jordan and end at the Dead Sea.

"'This will be your land, with its boundaries on every side.'"

¹³Moses commanded the Israelites: "Assign this land by lot as an inheritance. The LORD has ordered that it be given to the nine and a half tribes, ¹⁴because the families of the tribe of Reuben, the tribe of Gad and the half-tribe of Manasseh have received their inheritance. ¹⁵These two and a half tribes have received their inheritance east of the Jordan across from Jericho, toward the sunrise."

¹⁶The LORD said to Moses, ¹⁷"These are the names of the men who are to assign the land for you as an inheritance: Eleazar the priest and Joshua son of Nun. ¹⁸And appoint one leader from each tribe to help assign the land. ¹⁹These are their names:

Caleb son of Jephunneh,
    from the tribe of Judah;
²⁰Shemuel son of Ammihud,
    from the tribe of Simeon;
²¹Elidad son of Kislon,
    from the tribe of Benjamin;
²²Bukki son of Jogli,
    the leader from the tribe of Dan;
²³Hanniel son of Ephod,
    the leader from the tribe of Manasseh son of Joseph;

ᵃ 11 Hebrew *Kinnereth*

24 Kemuel son of Shiphtan,
the leader from the tribe of Ephraim son of Joseph;
25 Elizaphan son of Parnak,
the leader from the tribe of Zebulun;
26 Paltiel son of Azzan,
the leader from the tribe of Issachar;
27 Ahihud son of Shelomi,
the leader from the tribe of Asher;
28 Pedahel son of Ammihud,
the leader from the tribe of Naphtali."

29 These are the men the LORD commanded to assign the inheritance to the Israelites in the land of Canaan.

Towns for the Levites

35 On the plains of Moab by the Jordan across from Jericho, the LORD said to Moses, 2 "Command the Israelites to give the Levites towns to live in from the inheritance the Israelites will possess. And give them pasturelands around the towns. 3 Then they will have towns to live in and pasturelands for the cattle they own and all their other animals.

4 "The pasturelands around the towns that you give the Levites will extend a thousand cubits*a* from the town wall. 5 Outside the town, measure two thousand cubits*b* on the east side, two thousand on the south side, two thousand on the west and two thousand on the north, with the town in the center. They will have this area as pastureland for the towns.

Cities of Refuge

6 "Six of the towns you give the Levites will be cities of refuge, to which a person who has killed someone may flee. In addition, give them forty-two other towns. 7 In all you must give the Levites forty-eight towns, together with their pasturelands. 8 The towns you give the Levites from the land the Israelites possess are to be given in proportion to the inheritance of each tribe: Take many towns from a tribe that has many, but few from one that has few."

9 Then the LORD said to Moses: 10 "Speak to the Israelites and say to them: 'When you cross the Jordan into Canaan, 11 select some towns to be your cities of refuge, to which a person who has killed someone accidentally may flee. 12 They will be places of refuge from the avenger, so that anyone accused of murder may not die before they stand trial before the assembly. 13 These six towns you give will be your cities of refuge. 14 Give three on this side of the Jordan and three in Canaan as cities of refuge. 15 These six towns will be a place of refuge for Israelites and for foreigners residing among them, so that anyone who has killed another accidentally can flee there.

16 "'If anyone strikes someone a fatal blow with an iron object, that person is a murderer; the murderer is to be put to death. 17 Or if anyone is holding a stone and strikes someone a fatal blow with it, that person is a murderer; the murderer is to be put to death. 18 Or if anyone is holding a wooden object and strikes someone a fatal blow with it, that person is a murderer; the murderer is to be put to death. 19 The avenger of blood shall put the murderer to death; when the avenger comes upon the murderer, the avenger shall put the murderer to death. 20 If anyone with malice aforethought shoves another or throws something at them intentionally so that they die 21 or if out of enmity one person hits another with their fist so that the other dies, that person is to be put to death; that person is a murderer. The avenger of blood shall put the murderer to death when they meet.

22 "'But if without enmity someone suddenly pushes another or throws something at them unintentionally 23 or, without seeing them, drops on them a stone heavy enough to kill them, and they die, then since that other person was not an enemy and no harm was intended, 24 the assembly must judge between the accused and the avenger of blood according to these

a 4 That is, about 1,500 feet or about 450 meters
b 5 That is, about 3,000 feet or about 900 meters

regulations. ²⁵The assembly must protect the one accused of murder from the avenger of blood and send the accused back to the city of refuge to which they fled. The accused must stay there until the death of the high priest, who was anointed with the holy oil.

²⁶"But if the accused ever goes outside the limits of the city of refuge to which they fled ²⁷and the avenger of blood finds them outside the city, the avenger of blood may kill the accused without being guilty of murder. ²⁸The accused must stay in the city of refuge until the death of the high priest; only after the death of the high priest may they return to their own property.

²⁹"This is to have the force of law for you throughout the generations to come, wherever you live.

³⁰"Anyone who kills a person is to be put to death as a murderer only on the testimony of witnesses. But no one is to be put to death on the testimony of only one witness.

³¹"Do not accept a ransom for the life of a murderer, who deserves to die. They are to be put to death.

³²"Do not accept a ransom for anyone who has fled to a city of refuge and so allow them to go back and live on their own land before the death of the high priest.

³³"Do not pollute the land where you are. Bloodshed pollutes the land, and atonement cannot be made for the land on which blood has been shed, except by the blood of the one who shed it. ³⁴Do not defile the land where you live and where I dwell, for I, the LORD, dwell among the Israelites.'"

Inheritance of Zelophehad's Daughters

36 The family heads of the clan of Gilead son of Makir, the son of Manasseh, who were from the clans of the descendants of Joseph, came and spoke before Moses and the leaders, the heads of the Israelite families. ²They said, "When the LORD commanded my lord to give the land as an inheritance to the Israelites by lot, he ordered you to give the inheritance of our brother Zelophehad to his daughters. ³Now suppose they marry men from other Israelite tribes; then their inheritance will be taken from our ancestral inheritance and added to that of the tribe they marry into. And so part of the inheritance allotted to us will be taken away. ⁴When the Year of Jubilee for the Israelites comes, their inheritance will be added to that of the tribe into which they marry, and their property will be taken from the tribal inheritance of our ancestors."

⁵Then at the LORD's command Moses gave this order to the Israelites: "What the tribe of the descendants of Joseph is saying is right. ⁶This is what the LORD commands for Zelophehad's daughters: They may marry anyone they please as long as they marry within their father's tribal clan. ⁷No inheritance in Israel is to pass from one tribe to another, for every Israelite shall keep the tribal inheritance of their ancestors. ⁸Every daughter who inherits land in any Israelite tribe must marry someone in her father's tribal clan, so that every Israelite will possess the inheritance of their ancestors. ⁹No inheritance may pass from one tribe to another, for each Israelite tribe is to keep the land it inherits."

¹⁰So Zelophehad's daughters did as the LORD commanded Moses. ¹¹Zelophehad's daughters—Mahlah, Tirzah, Hoglah, Milkah and Noah—married their cousins on their father's side. ¹²They married within the clans of the descendants of Manasseh son of Joseph, and their inheritance remained in their father's tribe and clan.

¹³These are the commands and regulations the LORD gave through Moses to the Israelites on the plains of Moab by the Jordan across from Jericho.

DEUTERONOMY

BOOK OUTLINE

Deuteronomy means "second law." After forty years the Israelites were about to enter the promised land of Canaan. But before they did, Moses wanted to remind them of their history, all that God had done for them, and the laws they had to continue to obey as God's chosen people.

His first speech reminded the people of God's goodness to them through their journey and God's gift of the land of Canaan. Moses' second speech was a summary of God's laws including the Ten Commandments. Moses told the people to "love the LORD your God with all your heart and with all your soul and with all your strength" in order to continue to enjoy God's blessing. Moses also emphasized the fact that to keep their relationship right with God, the people had to teach their children to love the Lord and obey his commandments.

Deuteronomy ends with Moses' reminding the people of the covenant God had made with them (29:1 – 29), Joshua's appointment to be the new leader (31:1 – 8), and Moses' death (34:1 – 8). It is generally accepted that Moses wrote Deuteronomy except for the chapter about his death.

The Command to Leave Horeb

1 These are the words Moses spoke to all Israel in the wilderness east of the Jordan—that is, in the Arabah—opposite Suph, between Paran and Tophel, Laban, Hazeroth and Dizahab. ²(It takes eleven days to go from Horeb to Kadesh Barnea by the Mount Seir road.)

³In the fortieth year, on the first day of the eleventh month, Moses proclaimed to the Israelites all that the LORD had commanded him concerning them. ⁴This was after he had defeated Sihon king of the Amorites, who reigned in Heshbon, and at Edrei had defeated Og king of Bashan, who reigned in Ashtaroth.

⁵East of the Jordan in the territory of Moab, Moses began to expound this law, saying:

⁶The LORD our God said to us at Horeb, "You have stayed long enough at this mountain. ⁷Break camp and advance into the hill country of the Amorites; go to all the neighboring peoples in the Arabah, in the mountains, in the western foothills, in the Negev and along the coast, to the land of the Canaanites and to Lebanon, as far as the great river, the Euphrates. ⁸See, I have given you this land. Go in and take possession of the land the LORD swore he would give to your fathers—to Abraham, Isaac and Jacob—and to their descendants after them."

The Appointment of Leaders

⁹At that time I said to you, "You are too heavy a burden for me to carry alone. ¹⁰The LORD your God has increased your numbers so that today you are as numerous as the stars in the sky. ¹¹May the LORD, the God of your ancestors, increase you a thousand times and bless you as he has promised! ¹²But how can I bear your problems and your burdens and your disputes all by myself? ¹³Choose some wise, understanding and respected men from each of your tribes, and I will set them over you."

¹⁴You answered me, "What you propose to do is good."

¹⁵So I took the leading men of your tribes, wise and respected men, and appointed them to have authority over you—as commanders of thousands, of hundreds, of fifties and of tens and as tribal officials. ¹⁶And I charged your judges at that time, "Hear the disputes between your people and judge fairly, whether the case is between two Israelites or between an Israelite and a foreigner residing among you. ¹⁷Do not show partiality in judging; hear both small and great alike. Do not be afraid of anyone, for judgment belongs to God. Bring me any case too hard for you, and I will hear it." ¹⁸And at that time I told you everything you were to do.

Spies Sent Out

¹⁹Then, as the LORD our God commanded us, we set out from Horeb and went toward the hill country of the Amorites through all that vast and dreadful wilderness that you have seen, and so we reached Kadesh Barnea. ²⁰Then I said to you, "You have reached the hill country of the Amorites, which the LORD our God is giving us. ²¹See, the LORD your God has given you the land. Go up and take possession of it as the LORD, the God of your ancestors, told you. Do not be afraid; do not be discouraged."

²²Then all of you came to me and said, "Let us send men ahead to spy out the land for us and bring back a report about the route we are to take and the towns we will come to."

²³The idea seemed good to me; so I selected twelve of you, one man from each tribe. ²⁴They left and went up into the hill country, and came to the Valley of Eshkol and explored it. ²⁵Taking with them some of the fruit of the land, they brought it down to us and reported, "It is a good land that the LORD our God is giving us."

Rebellion Against the LORD

²⁶But you were unwilling to go up; you rebelled against the command of the LORD your God. ²⁷You grumbled in your tents and said, "The LORD hates us; so he brought us out of Egypt to deliver us into the hands of the Amorites to destroy us. ²⁸Where can we go? Our brothers have made our hearts melt in fear. They say,

'The people are stronger and taller than we are; the cities are large, with walls up to the sky. We even saw the Anakites there.'"

²⁹Then I said to you, "Do not be terrified; do not be afraid of them. ³⁰The Lord your God, who is going before you, will fight for you, as he did for you in Egypt, before your very eyes, ³¹and in the wilderness. There you saw how the Lord your God carried you, as a father carries his son, all the way you went until you reached this place."

³²In spite of this, you did not trust in the Lord your God, ³³who went ahead of you on your journey, in fire by night and in a cloud by day, to search out places for you to camp and to show you the way you should go.

³⁴When the Lord heard what you said, he was angry and solemnly swore: ³⁵"No one from this evil generation shall see the good land I swore to give your ancestors, ³⁶except Caleb son of Jephunneh. He will see it, and I will give him and his descendants the land he set his feet on, because he followed the Lord wholeheartedly."

³⁷Because of you the Lord became angry with me also and said, "You shall not enter it, either. ³⁸But your assistant, Joshua son of Nun, will enter it. Encourage him, because he will lead Israel to inherit it. ³⁹And the little ones that you said would be taken captive, your children who do not yet know good from bad—they will enter the land. I will give it to them and they will take possession of it. ⁴⁰But as for you, turn around and set out toward the desert along the route to the Red Sea.ᵃ"

⁴¹Then you replied, "We have sinned against the Lord. We will go up and fight, as the Lord our God commanded us." So every one of you put on his weapons, thinking it easy to go up into the hill country.

⁴²But the Lord said to me, "Tell them, 'Do not go up and fight, because I will not be with you. You will be defeated by your enemies.'"

⁴³So I told you, but you would not listen. You rebelled against the Lord's command and in your arrogance you marched up into the hill country. ⁴⁴The Amorites who lived in those hills came out against you; they chased you like a swarm of bees

and beat you down from Seir all the way to Hormah. ⁴⁵You came back and wept before the Lord, but he paid no attention to your weeping and turned a deaf ear to you. ⁴⁶And so you stayed in Kadesh many days—all the time you spent there.

Wanderings in the Wilderness

2 Then we turned back and set out toward the wilderness along the route to the Red Sea,ᵃ as the Lord had directed me. For a long time we made our way around the hill country of Seir.

²Then the Lord said to me, ³"You have made your way around this hill country long enough; now turn north. ⁴Give the people these orders: 'You are about to pass through the territory of your relatives the descendants of Esau, who live in Seir. They will be afraid of you, but be very careful. ⁵Do not provoke them to war, for I will not give you any of their land, not even enough to put your foot on. I have given Esau the hill country of Seir as his own. ⁶You are to pay them in silver for the food you eat and the water you drink.'"

⁷The Lord your God has blessed you in all the work of your hands. He has watched over your journey through this vast wilderness. These forty years the Lord your God has been with you, and you have not lacked anything.

ᵃ 40,1 Or *the Sea of Reeds*

ROCK SOLID promises

"The Lord your God has been with you, and you have not lacked anything." Deuteronomy 2:7

When you belong to God and lean on him, you will never run short of what you truly need.

⁸So we went on past our relatives the descendants of Esau, who live in Seir. We turned from the Arabah road, which comes up from Elath and Ezion Geber, and traveled along the desert road of Moab.

⁹Then the LORD said to me, "Do not harass the Moabites or provoke them to war, for I will not give you any part of their land. I have given Ar to the descendants of Lot as a possession."

¹⁰(The Emites used to live there—a people strong and numerous, and as tall as the Anakites. ¹¹Like the Anakites, they too were considered Rephaites, but the Moabites called them Emites. ¹²Horites used to live in Seir, but the descendants of Esau drove them out. They destroyed the Horites from before them and settled in their place, just as Israel did in the land the LORD gave them as their possession.)

¹³And the LORD said, "Now get up and cross the Zered Valley." So we crossed the valley.

¹⁴Thirty-eight years passed from the time we left Kadesh Barnea until we crossed the Zered Valley. By then, that entire generation of fighting men had perished from the camp, as the LORD had sworn to them. ¹⁵The LORD's hand was against them until he had completely eliminated them from the camp.

¹⁶Now when the last of these fighting men among the people had died, ¹⁷the LORD said to me, ¹⁸"Today you are to pass by the region of Moab at Ar. ¹⁹When you come to the Ammonites, do not harass them or provoke them to war, for I will not give you possession of any land belonging to the Ammonites. I have given it as a possession to the descendants of Lot."

²⁰(That too was considered a land of the Rephaites, who used to live there; but the Ammonites called them Zamzummites. ²¹They were a people strong and numerous, and as tall as the Anakites. The LORD destroyed them from before the Ammonites, who drove them out and settled in their place. ²²The LORD had done the same for the descendants of Esau, who lived in Seir, when he destroyed the Ho-

rites from before them. They drove them out and have lived in their place to this day. ²³And as for the Avvites who lived in villages as far as Gaza, the Caphtorites coming out from Caphtor*a* destroyed them and settled in their place.)

Defeat of Sihon King of Heshbon

²⁴"Set out now and cross the Arnon Gorge. See, I have given into your hand Sihon the Amorite, king of Heshbon, and his country. Begin to take possession of it and engage him in battle. ²⁵This very day I will begin to put the terror and fear of you on all the nations under heaven. They will hear reports of you and will tremble and be in anguish because of you."

²⁶From the Desert of Kedemoth I sent messengers to Sihon king of Heshbon offering peace and saying, ²⁷"Let us pass through your country. We will stay on the main road; we will not turn aside to the right or to the left. ²⁸Sell us food to eat and water to drink for their price in silver. Only let us pass through on foot— ²⁹as the descendants of Esau, who live in Seir, and the Moabites, who live in Ar, did for us—until we cross the Jordan into the land the LORD our God is giving us." ³⁰But Sihon king of Heshbon refused to let us pass through. For the LORD your God had made his spirit stubborn and his heart obstinate in order to give him into your hands, as he has now done.

³¹The LORD said to me, "See, I have begun to deliver Sihon and his country over to you. Now begin to conquer and possess his land."

³²When Sihon and all his army came out to meet us in battle at Jahaz, ³³the LORD our God delivered him over to us and we struck him down, together with his sons and his whole army. ³⁴At that time we took all his towns and completely destroyed*b* them—men, women and children. We left no survivors. ³⁵But the livestock and the plunder from the towns

---

a 23 That is, Crete   *b 34* The Hebrew term refers to the irrevocable giving over of things or persons to the LORD, often by totally destroying them.

we had captured we carried off for ourselves. [36]From Aroer on the rim of the Arnon Gorge, and from the town in the gorge, even as far as Gilead, not one town was too strong for us. The LORD our God gave us all of them. [37]But in accordance with the command of the LORD our God, you did not encroach on any of the land of the Ammonites, neither the land along the course of the Jabbok nor that around the towns in the hills.

Defeat of Og King of Bashan

3 Next we turned and went up along the road toward Bashan, and Og king of Bashan with his whole army marched out to meet us in battle at Edrei. [2]The LORD said to me, "Do not be afraid of him, for I have delivered him into your hands, along with his whole army and his land. Do to him what you did to Sihon king of the Amorites, who reigned in Heshbon."

[3]So the LORD our God also gave into our hands Og king of Bashan and all his army. We struck them down, leaving no survivors. [4]At that time we took all his cities. There was not one of the sixty cities that we did not take from them—the whole region of Argob, Og's kingdom in Bashan. [5]All these cities were fortified with high walls and with gates and bars, and there were also a great many unwalled villages. [6]We completely destroyed[a] them, as we had done with Sihon king of Heshbon, destroying[a] every city—men, women and children. [7]But all the livestock and the plunder from their cities we carried off for ourselves.

[8]So at that time we took from these two kings of the Amorites the territory east of the Jordan, from the Arnon Gorge as far as Mount Hermon. [9](Hermon is called Sirion by the Sidonians; the Amorites call it Senir.) [10]We took all the towns on the plateau, and all Gilead, and all Bashan as far as Salekah and Edrei, towns of Og's kingdom in Bashan. [11](Og king of Bashan was the last of the Rephaites. His bed was decorated with iron and was more than nine cubits long and four cubits wide.[b] It is still in Rabbah of the Ammonites.)

Division of the Land

[12]Of the land that we took over at that time, I gave the Reubenites and the Gadites the territory north of Aroer by the Arnon Gorge, including half the hill country of Gilead, together with its towns. [13]The rest of Gilead and also all of Bashan, the kingdom of Og, I gave to the half-tribe of Manasseh. (The whole region of Argob in Bashan used to be known as a land of the Rephaites. [14]Jair, a descendant of Manasseh, took the whole region of Argob as far as the border of the Geshurites and the Maakathites; it was named after him, so that to this day Bashan is called Havvoth Jair.[c]) [15]And I gave Gilead to Makir. [16]But to the Reubenites and the Gadites I gave the territory extending from Gilead down to the Arnon Gorge (the middle of the gorge being the border) and out to the Jabbok River, which is the border of the Ammonites. [17]Its western border was the Jordan in the Arabah, from Kinnereth to the Sea of the Arabah (that is, the Dead Sea), below the slopes of Pisgah.

[18]I commanded you at that time: "The LORD your God has given you this land to take possession of it. But all your able-bodied men, armed for battle, must cross over ahead of the other Israelites. [19]However, your wives, your children and your livestock (I know you have much livestock) may stay in the towns I have given you, [20]until the LORD gives rest to your fellow Israelites as he has to you, and they too have taken over the land that the LORD your God is giving them across the Jordan. After that, each of you may go back to the possession I have given you."

Moses Forbidden to Cross the Jordan

[21]At that time I commanded Joshua: "You have seen with your own eyes all that

---

[a] 6 The Hebrew term refers to the irrevocable giving over of things or persons to the LORD, often by totally destroying them.   [b] 11 That is, about 14 feet long and 6 feet wide or about 4 meters long and 1.8 meters wide
[c] 14 Or called the settlements of Jair

the Lord your God has done to these two kings. The Lord will do the same to all the kingdoms over there where you are going. ²²Do not be afraid of them; the Lord your God himself will fight for you."

²³At that time I pleaded with the Lord: ²⁴"Sovereign Lord, you have begun to show to your servant your greatness and your strong hand. For what god is there in heaven or on earth who can do the deeds and mighty works you do? ²⁵Let me go over and see the good land beyond the Jordan—that fine hill country and Lebanon."

²⁶But because of you the Lord was angry with me and would not listen to me. "That is enough," the Lord said. "Do not speak to me anymore about this matter. ²⁷Go up to the top of Pisgah and look west and north and south and east. Look at the land with your own eyes, since you are not going to cross this Jordan. ²⁸But commission Joshua, and encourage and strengthen him, for he will lead this people across and will cause them to inherit the land that you will see." ²⁹So we stayed in the valley near Beth Peor.

Obedience Commanded

4 Now, Israel, hear the decrees and laws I am about to teach you. Follow them so that you may live and may go in and take possession of the land the Lord, the God of your ancestors, is giving you. ²Do not add to what I command you and do not subtract from it, but keep the commands of the Lord your God that I give you.

³You saw with your own eyes what the Lord did at Baal Peor. The Lord your God destroyed from among you everyone who followed the Baal of Peor, ⁴but all of you who held fast to the Lord your God are still alive today.

⁵See, I have taught you decrees and laws as the Lord my God commanded me, so that you may follow them in the land you are entering to take possession of it. ⁶Observe them carefully, for this will show your wisdom and understanding to the nations, who will hear about all these decrees and say, "Surely this great nation is a wise and understanding people." ⁷What other nation is so great as to have their gods near them the way the Lord our God is near us whenever we pray to him? ⁸And what other nation is so great as to have such righteous decrees and laws as this body of laws I am setting before you today?

⁹Only be careful, and watch yourselves closely so that you do not forget the things your eyes have seen or let them fade from your heart as long as you live. Teach them to your children and to their children after them. ¹⁰Remember the day you stood before the Lord your God at Horeb, when he said to me, "Assemble the people before me to hear my words so that they may learn to revere me as long as they live in the land and may teach them to their children." ¹¹You came near and stood at the foot of the mountain while it blazed with fire to the very heavens, with black clouds and deep darkness. ¹²Then the Lord spoke to you out of the fire. You heard the sound of words but saw no form; there was only a voice. ¹³He declared to you his covenant, the Ten Commandments, which he commanded you to follow and then wrote them on two stone tablets. ¹⁴And the Lord directed me at that time to teach you the decrees and laws you are to follow in the land that you are crossing the Jordan to possess.

Idolatry Forbidden

¹⁵You saw no form of any kind the day the Lord spoke to you at Horeb out of the fire. Therefore watch yourselves very carefully, ¹⁶so that you do not become corrupt and make for yourselves an idol, an image of any shape, whether formed like a man or a woman, ¹⁷or like any animal on earth or any bird that flies in the air, ¹⁸or like any creature that moves along the ground or any fish in the waters below. ¹⁹And when you look up to the sky and see the sun, the moon and the stars—all the heavenly array—do not be enticed into bowing down to them and worshiping things the Lord your God has ap-

portioned to all the nations under heaven. [20] But as for you, the LORD took you and brought you out of the iron-smelting furnace, out of Egypt, to be the people of his inheritance, as you now are.

[21] The LORD was angry with me because of you, and he solemnly swore that I would not cross the Jordan and enter the good land the LORD your God is giving you as your inheritance. [22] I will die in this land; I will not cross the Jordan; but you are about to cross over and take possession of that good land. [23] Be careful not to forget the covenant of the LORD your God that he made with you; do not make for yourselves an idol in the form of anything the LORD your God has forbidden. [24] For the LORD your God is a consuming fire, a jealous God.

[25] After you have had children and grandchildren and have lived in the land a long time—if you then become corrupt and make any kind of idol, doing evil in the eyes of the LORD your God and arousing his anger, [26] I call the heavens and the earth as witnesses against you this day that you will quickly perish from the land that you are crossing the Jordan to possess. You will not live there long but will certainly be destroyed. [27] The LORD will scatter you among the peoples, and only a few of you will survive among the nations to which the LORD will drive you. [28] There you will worship man-made gods of wood and stone, which cannot see or hear or eat or smell. [29] But if from there you seek the LORD your God, you will find him if you seek him with all your heart and with all your soul. [30] When you are in distress and all these things have happened to you, then in later days you will return to the LORD your God and obey him. [31] For the LORD your God is a merciful God; he will not abandon or destroy you or forget the covenant with your ancestors, which he confirmed to them by oath.

The LORD Is God

[32] Ask now about the former days, long before your time, from the day God created human beings on the earth; ask from one end of the heavens to the other. Has anything so great as this ever happened, or has anything like it ever been heard of? [33] Has any other people heard the voice of God[a] speaking out of fire, as you have, and lived? [34] Has any god ever tried to take for himself one nation out of another nation, by testings, by signs and wonders, by war, by a mighty hand and an outstretched arm, or by great and awesome deeds, like all the things the LORD your God did for you in Egypt before your very eyes?

[35] You were shown these things so that you might know that the LORD is God; besides him there is no other. [36] From heaven he made you hear his voice to discipline you. On earth he showed you his great fire, and you heard his words from out of the fire. [37] Because he loved your ancestors and chose their descendants after them, he brought you out of Egypt by his

UNSHAKEN *God*

Deuteronomy 4:15–24

God is jealous.

Jealousy doesn't top the list of qualities you want in a friend. But when it comes to God, his jealousy means he's madly in love with you—and he wants you to return that wholehearted affection (see Deuteronomy 4:24). Old Testament nations bowed to the sun, moon, and stars. They worshiped a crazy variety of idols—wood and stone gods shaped to look like earthly creatures. God demands that his people not worship those idols or any other fake god. "The LORD is God," he says, "besides him there is no other" (Deuteronomy 4:35). Take the hint: God alone deserves your total devotion.

So ... Have you ever made God jealous by loving anything more than him? What was it, and what did you do about it?

---

[a] 33 Or *of a god*

Presence and his great strength, [38] to drive out before you nations greater and stronger than you and to bring you into their land to give it to you for your inheritance, as it is today.

[39] Acknowledge and take to heart this day that the LORD is God in heaven above and on the earth below. There is no other. [40] Keep his decrees and commands, which I am giving you today, so that it may go well with you and your children after you and that you may live long in the land the LORD your God gives you for all time.

Cities of Refuge

[41] Then Moses set aside three cities east of the Jordan, [42] to which anyone who had killed a person could flee if they had unintentionally killed a neighbor without malice aforethought. They could flee into one of these cities and save their life. [43] The cities were these: Bezer in the wilderness plateau, for the Reubenites; Ramoth in Gilead, for the Gadites; and Golan in Bashan, for the Manassites.

Introduction to the Law

[44] This is the law Moses set before the Israelites. [45] These are the stipulations, decrees and laws Moses gave them when they came out of Egypt [46] and were in the valley near Beth Peor east of the Jordan, in the land of Sihon king of the Amorites, who reigned in Heshbon and was defeated by Moses and the Israelites as they came out of Egypt. [47] They took possession of his land and the land of Og king of Bashan, the two Amorite kings east of the Jordan. [48] This land extended from Aroer on the rim of the Arnon Gorge to Mount Sirion[a] (that is, Hermon), [49] and included all the Arabah east of the Jordan, as far as the Dead Sea,[b] below the slopes of Pisgah.

The Ten Commandments

5 Moses summoned all Israel and said:

Hear, Israel, the decrees and laws I declare in your hearing today. Learn them and be sure to follow them. [2] The LORD our God made a covenant with us at Horeb. [3] It was not with our ancestors[c] that the LORD made this covenant, but with us, with all of us who are alive here today. [4] The LORD spoke to you face to face out of the fire on the mountain. [5] (At that time I stood between the LORD and you to declare to you the word of the LORD, because you were afraid of the fire and did not go up the mountain.) And he said:

[6] "I am the LORD your God, who brought you out of Egypt, out of the land of slavery.

[7] "You shall have no other gods before[d] me.

[8] "You shall not make for yourself an image in the form of anything in heaven above or on the earth beneath or in the waters below. [9] You shall not bow down to them or worship them; for I, the LORD your God, am a jealous God, punishing the children for the sin of the parents to the third and fourth generation of those who hate me, [10] but showing love to a thousand generations of those who love me and keep my commandments.

[11] "You shall not misuse the name of the LORD your God, for the LORD will not hold anyone guiltless who misuses his name.

[12] "Observe the Sabbath day by keeping it holy, as the LORD your God has commanded you. [13] Six days you shall labor and do all your work, [14] but the seventh day is a sabbath to the LORD your God. On it you shall not do any work, neither you, nor your son or daughter, nor your male or female servant, nor your ox, your donkey or any of your animals, nor any foreigner residing in your towns, so that your male and female servants may rest, as you do. [15] Remember that you

[a] 48 Syriac (see also 3:9); Hebrew *Siyon*
[b] 49 Hebrew *the Sea of the Arabah*   [c] 3 Or *not only with our parents*   [d] 7 Or *besides*

were slaves in Egypt and that the LORD your God brought you out of there with a mighty hand and an outstretched arm. Therefore the LORD your God has commanded you to observe the Sabbath day.

16 "Honor your father and your mother, as the LORD your God has commanded you, so that you may live long and that it may go well with you in the land the LORD your God is giving you.

17 "You shall not murder.

18 "You shall not commit adultery.

19 "You shall not steal.

20 "You shall not give false testimony against your neighbor.

21 "You shall not covet your neighbor's wife. You shall not set your desire on your neighbor's house or land, his male or female servant, his ox or donkey, or anything that belongs to your neighbor."

22 These are the commandments the LORD proclaimed in a loud voice to your whole assembly there on the mountain from out of the fire, the cloud and the deep darkness; and he added nothing more. Then he wrote them on two stone tablets and gave them to me.

23 When you heard the voice out of the darkness, while the mountain was ablaze with fire, all the leaders of your tribes and your elders came to me. 24 And you said, "The LORD our God has shown us his glory and his majesty, and we have heard his voice from the fire. Today we have seen that a person can live even if God speaks with them. 25 But now, why should we die? This great fire will consume us, and we will die if we hear the voice of the LORD our God any longer. 26 For what mortal has ever heard the voice of the living God speaking out of fire, as we have, and survived? 27 Go near and listen to all that the LORD our God says. Then tell us whatever the LORD our God tells you. We will listen and obey."

28 The LORD heard you when you spoke to me, and the LORD said to me, "I have heard what this people said to you. Everything they said was good. 29 Oh, that their hearts would be inclined to fear me and keep all my commands always, so that it might go well with them and their children forever!

30 "Go, tell them to return to their tents. 31 But you stay here with me so that I may give you all the commands, decrees and laws you are to teach them to follow in the land I am giving them to possess."

32 So be careful to do what the LORD your God has commanded you; do not turn aside to the right or to the left. 33 Walk in obedience to all that the LORD your God has commanded you, so that you may live and prosper and prolong your days in the land that you will possess.

Love the LORD Your God

6 These are the commands, decrees and laws the LORD your God directed me to teach you to observe in the land that you are crossing the Jordan to possess, 2 so that you, your children and their children after them may fear the LORD your God as long as you live by keeping all his decrees and commands that I give you, and so that you may enjoy long life. 3 Hear, Israel, and be careful to obey so that it may go well with you and that you may increase greatly in a land flowing with milk and honey, just as the LORD, the God of your ancestors, promised you.

4 Hear, O Israel: The LORD our God, the LORD is one.*a* 5 Love the LORD your God with all your heart and with all your soul and with all your strength. 6 These commandments that I give you today are to be on your hearts. 7 Impress them on your children. Talk about them when you sit at home and when you walk along the road, when you lie down and when you get up. 8 Tie them as symbols on your hands and bind them on your foreheads. 9 Write them on the doorframes of your houses and on your gates.

a 4 Or *The LORD our God is one LORD*; or *The LORD is our God, the LORD is one*; or *The LORD is our God, the LORD alone*

Deuteronomy 6:1–9

Love God totally.

Chloe often laughed inside as she watched her peers at church. Everyone just seemed too into their faith—eager to worship, enthusiastic about serving, happy to study the Bible and just be together. Chloe felt mystified by all of it until a bad situation at home forced her to rely on God like never before. Instead of seeing God as little more than a gatekeeper to heaven and hell, she understood that he constantly watches over the most painful details of life. As Chloe got a larger view of God, her love for the Lord seemed to explode all on its own. She wanted her whole heart to belong to him.

The command to "Love the LORD your God with all your heart and with all your soul and with all your strength" (Deuteronomy 6:5) didn't come out of the blue. God uttered that decree after the people had witnessed his miraculous power and limitless love. You don't have to force yourself to love God. It's a natural response when you notice who he really is.

¹⁰When the LORD your God brings you into the land he swore to your fathers, to Abraham, Isaac and Jacob, to give you—a land with large, flourishing cities you did not build, ¹¹houses filled with all kinds of good things you did not provide, wells you did not dig, and vineyards and olive groves you did not plant—then when you eat and are satisfied, ¹²be careful that you do not forget the LORD, who brought you out of Egypt, out of the land of slavery.

¹³Fear the LORD your God, serve him only and take your oaths in his name. ¹⁴Do not follow other gods, the gods of the peoples around you; ¹⁵for the LORD your God, who is among you, is a jealous God and his anger will burn against you, and he will destroy you from the face of the land. ¹⁶Do not put the LORD your God to the test as you did at Massah. ¹⁷Be sure to keep the commands of the LORD your God and the stipulations and decrees he has given you. ¹⁸Do what is right and good in the LORD's sight, so that it may

go well with you and you may go in and take over the good land the LORD promised on oath to your ancestors, ¹⁹thrusting out all your enemies before you, as the LORD said.

²⁰In the future, when your son asks you, "What is the meaning of the stipulations, decrees and laws the LORD our God has commanded you?" ²¹tell him: "We were slaves of Pharaoh in Egypt, but the LORD brought us out of Egypt with a mighty hand. ²²Before our eyes the LORD sent signs and wonders—great and terrible—on Egypt and Pharaoh and his whole household. ²³But he brought us out from there to bring us in and give us the land he promised on oath to our ancestors. ²⁴The LORD commanded us to obey all these decrees and to fear the LORD our God, so that we might always prosper and be kept alive, as is the case today. ²⁵And if we are careful to obey all this law before the LORD our God, as he has commanded us, that will be our righteousness."

Driving Out the Nations

7 When the Lord your God brings you into the land you are entering to possess and drives out before you many nations—the Hittites, Girgashites, Amorites, Canaanites, Perizzites, Hivites and Jebusites, seven nations larger and stronger than you— ² and when the Lord your God has delivered them over to you and you have defeated them, then you must destroy them totally.ᵃ Make no treaty with them, and show them no mercy. ³ Do not intermarry with them. Do not give your daughters to their sons or take their daughters for your sons, ⁴ for they will turn your children away from following me to serve other gods, and the Lord's anger will burn against you and will quickly destroy you. ⁵ This is what you are to do to them: Break down their altars, smash their sacred stones, cut down their Asherah polesᵇ and burn their idols in the fire. ⁶ For you are a people holy to the Lord your God. The Lord your God has chosen you out of all the peoples on the face of the earth to be his people, his treasured possession.

⁷ The Lord did not set his affection on you and choose you because you were more numerous than other peoples, for you were the fewest of all peoples. ⁸ But it was because the Lord loved you and kept the oath he swore to your ancestors that he brought you out with a mighty hand and redeemed you from the land of slavery, from the power of Pharaoh king of Egypt. ⁹ Know therefore that the Lord your God is God; he is the faithful God, keeping his covenant of love to a thousand generations of those who love him and keep his commandments. ¹⁰ But

those who hate him he will repay to
     their face by destruction;
he will not be slow to repay to their
     face those who hate him.

¹¹ Therefore, take care to follow the commands, decrees and laws I give you today. ¹² If you pay attention to these laws and are careful to follow them, then the Lord your God will keep his covenant of love with you, as he swore to your ancestors. ¹³ He will love you and bless you and increase your numbers. He will bless the fruit of your womb, the crops of your land—your grain, new wine and olive oil—the calves of your herds and the lambs of your flocks in the land he swore to your ancestors to give you. ¹⁴ You will be blessed more than any other people; none of your men or women will be childless, nor will any of your livestock be without young. ¹⁵ The Lord will keep you free from every disease. He will not inflict on you the horrible diseases you knew in Egypt, but he will inflict them on all who hate you. ¹⁶ You must destroy all the peoples the Lord your God gives over to you. Do not look on them with pity and do not serve their gods, for that will be a snare to you.

¹⁷ You may say to yourselves, "These nations are stronger than we are. How can we drive them out?" ¹⁸ But do not be afraid of them; remember well what the Lord your God did to Pharaoh and to all Egypt. ¹⁹ You saw with your own eyes the great trials, the signs and wonders, the mighty hand and outstretched arm, with which the Lord your God brought you out. The Lord your God will do the same to all the peoples you now fear. ²⁰ Moreover, the Lord your God will send the hornet among them until even the survivors who hide from you have perished. ²¹ Do not be terrified by them, for the Lord your God, who is among you, is a great and awesome God. ²² The Lord your God will drive out those nations before you, little by little. You will not be allowed to eliminate them all at once, or the wild animals will multiply around you. ²³ But the Lord your God will deliver them over to you, throwing them into great confusion until they are destroyed. ²⁴ He will give their kings into your hand, and you will wipe out their names from under heaven. No

ᵃ 2 The Hebrew term refers to the irrevocable giving over of things or persons to the Lord, often by totally destroying them; also in verse 26.   ᵇ 5 That is, wooden symbols of the goddess Asherah; here and elsewhere in Deuteronomy one will be able to stand up against you; you will destroy them. ²⁵The images of their gods you are to burn in the fire. Do not covet the silver and gold on them, and do not take it for yourselves, or you will be ensnared by it, for it is detestable to the LORD your God. ²⁶Do not bring a detestable thing into your house or you, like it, will be set apart for destruction. Regard it as vile and utterly detest it, for it is set apart for destruction.

Do Not Forget the LORD

8 Be careful to follow every command I am giving you today, so that you may live and increase and may enter and possess the land the LORD promised on oath to your ancestors. ²Remember how the LORD your God led you all the way in the wilderness these forty years, to humble and test you in order to know what was in your heart, whether or not you would keep his commands. ³He humbled you, causing you to hunger and then feeding you with manna, which neither you nor your ancestors had known, to teach you that man does not live on bread alone but on every word that comes from the mouth of the LORD. ⁴Your clothes did not wear out and your feet did not swell during these forty years. ⁵Know then in your heart that as a man disciplines his son, so the LORD your God disciplines you.

⁶Observe the commands of the LORD your God, walking in obedience to him and revering him. ⁷For the LORD your God is bringing you into a good land— a land with brooks, streams, and deep springs gushing out into the valleys and hills; ⁸a land with wheat and barley, vines and fig trees, pomegranates, olive oil and honey; ⁹a land where bread will not be scarce and you will lack nothing; a land where the rocks are iron and you can dig copper out of the hills.

¹⁰When you have eaten and are satisfied, praise the LORD your God for the good land he has given you. ¹¹Be careful that you do not forget the LORD your God, failing to observe his commands, his laws and his decrees that I am giving you this day. ¹²Otherwise, when you eat and are satisfied, when you build fine houses and settle down, ¹³and when your herds and flocks grow large and your silver and gold increase and all you have is multiplied, ¹⁴then your heart will become proud and you will forget the LORD your God, who brought you out of Egypt, out of the land of slavery. ¹⁵He led you through the vast and dreadful wilderness, that thirsty and waterless land, with its venomous snakes and scorpions. He brought you water out of hard rock. ¹⁶He gave you manna to eat in the wilderness, something your ancestors had never known, to humble and test you so that in the end it might go well with you. ¹⁷You may say to yourself, "My power and the strength of my hands have produced this wealth for me." ¹⁸But remember the LORD your God, for it is he who gives you the ability to produce wealth, and so confirms his covenant, which he swore to your ancestors, as it is today.

¹⁹If you ever forget the LORD your God

ROCK SOLID *plans*

Deuteronomy 8:10–20

Don't forget God when life goes well.

Camped at the edge of the promised land, the Israelites were on the brink of entering a lavish "land flowing with milk and honey" (Exodus 3:8). With a long series of battles ahead of them, they would only succeed with God's help. Yet Moses worried aloud that God's people would sweep the countryside, settle down, then quickly forget the Lord's commands and take credit for their success. As God brought them into a great place, they needed to make a fresh decision to obey him completely (see Deuteronomy 8:10).

Your next step: Thank God for getting you where you are—and tell him you want to follow him more than ever.

and follow other gods and worship and bow down to them, I testify against you today that you will surely be destroyed. [20]Like the nations the Lord destroyed before you, so you will be destroyed for not obeying the Lord your God.

Not Because of Israel's Righteousness

9 Hear, Israel: You are now about to cross the Jordan to go in and dispossess nations greater and stronger than you, with large cities that have walls up to the sky. [2]The people are strong and tall—Anakites! You know about them and have heard it said: "Who can stand up against the Anakites?" [3]But be assured today that the Lord your God is the one who goes across ahead of you like a devouring fire. He will destroy them; he will subdue them before you. And you will drive them out and annihilate them quickly, as the Lord has promised you.

[4]After the Lord your God has driven them out before you, do not say to yourself, "The Lord has brought me here to take possession of this land because of my righteousness." No, it is on account of the wickedness of these nations that the Lord is going to drive them out before you. [5]It is not because of your righteousness or your integrity that you are going in to take possession of their land; but on account of the wickedness of these nations, the Lord your God will drive them out before you, to accomplish what he swore to your fathers, to Abraham, Isaac and Jacob. [6]Understand, then, that it is not because of your righteousness that the Lord your God is giving you this good land to possess, for you are a stiff-necked people.

The Golden Calf

[7]Remember this and never forget how you aroused the anger of the Lord your God in the wilderness. From the day you left Egypt until you arrived here, you have been rebellious against the Lord. [8]At Horeb you aroused the Lord's wrath so that he was angry enough to destroy you. [9]When I went up on the mountain to receive the tablets of stone, the tablets of the covenant that the Lord had made with you, I stayed on the mountain forty days and forty nights; I ate no bread and drank no water. [10]The Lord gave me two stone tablets inscribed by the finger of God. On them were all the commandments the Lord proclaimed to you on the mountain out of the fire, on the day of the assembly.

[11]At the end of the forty days and forty nights, the Lord gave me the two stone tablets, the tablets of the covenant. [12]Then the Lord told me, "Go down from here at once, because your people whom you brought out of Egypt have become corrupt. They have turned away quickly from what I commanded them and have made an idol for themselves."

[13]And the Lord said to me, "I have seen this people, and they are a stiff-necked people indeed! [14]Let me alone, so that I may destroy them and blot out their name from under heaven. And I will make you into a nation stronger and more numerous than they."

[15]So I turned and went down from the mountain while it was ablaze with fire. And the two tablets of the covenant were in my hands. [16]When I looked, I saw that you had sinned against the Lord your God; you had made for yourselves an idol cast in the shape of a calf. You had turned aside quickly from the way that the Lord had commanded you. [17]So I took the two tablets and threw them out of my hands, breaking them to pieces before your eyes.

[18]Then once again I fell prostrate before the Lord for forty days and forty nights; I ate no bread and drank no water, because of all the sin you had committed, doing what was evil in the Lord's sight and so arousing his anger. [19]I feared the anger and wrath of the Lord, for he was angry enough with you to destroy you. But again the Lord listened to me. [20]And the Lord was angry enough with Aaron to destroy him, but at that time I prayed for Aaron too. [21]Also I took that sinful thing of yours, the calf you had made, and burned it in the fire. Then I crushed it and ground it to powder as fine as dust and threw the

dust into a stream that flowed down the mountain.

²²You also made the Lord angry at Taberah, at Massah and at Kibroth Hattaavah.

²³And when the Lord sent you out from Kadesh Barnea, he said, "Go up and take possession of the land I have given you." But you rebelled against the command of the Lord your God. You did not trust him or obey him. ²⁴You have been rebellious against the Lord ever since I have known you.

²⁵I lay prostrate before the Lord those forty days and forty nights because the Lord had said he would destroy you. ²⁶I prayed to the Lord and said, "Sovereign Lord, do not destroy your people, your own inheritance that you redeemed by your great power and brought out of Egypt with a mighty hand. ²⁷Remember your servants Abraham, Isaac and Jacob. Overlook the stubbornness of this people, their wickedness and their sin. ²⁸Otherwise, the country from which you brought us will say, 'Because the Lord was not able to take them into the land he had promised them, and because he hated them, he brought them out to put them to death in the wilderness.' ²⁹But they are your people, your inheritance that you brought out by your great power and your outstretched arm."

Tablets Like the First Ones

10 At that time the Lord said to me, "Chisel out two stone tablets like the first ones and come up to me on the mountain. Also make a wooden ark.ᵃ ²I will write on the tablets the words that were on the first tablets, which you broke. Then you are to put them in the ark."

³So I made the ark out of acacia wood and chiseled out two stone tablets like the first ones, and I went up on the mountain with the two tablets in my hands. ⁴The Lord wrote on these tablets what he had written before, the Ten Commandments he had proclaimed to you on the mountain, out of the fire, on the day of the assembly. And the Lord gave them to me.

⁵Then I came back down the mountain and put the tablets in the ark I had made, as the Lord commanded me, and they are there now.

⁶(The Israelites traveled from the wells of Bene Jaakan to Moserah. There Aaron died and was buried, and Eleazar his son succeeded him as priest. ⁷From there they traveled to Gudgodah and on to Jotbathah, a land with streams of water. ⁸At that time the Lord set apart the tribe of Levi to carry the ark of the covenant of the Lord, to stand before the Lord to minister and to pronounce blessings in his name, as they still do today. ⁹That is why the Levites have no share or inheritance among their fellow Israelites; the Lord is their inheritance, as the Lord your God told them.)

ᵃ 1 That is, a chest

UNSHAKEN God

Deuteronomy 10:17–20

God is impartial.

Consider this fact: God is "God of gods and Lord of lords, the great God, mighty and awesome" (Deuteronomy 10:17). Then ponder this reality: If God were anything like people, he would only mingle with the powerful, rich, and famous. He would offer them attention and favors and expect the same in return. But the Lord is nothing like us. He doesn't play favorites. He won't accept bribes. And he sides with orphans, widows, and foreigners. How does that impact you? God wants you to serve him and show him awe-filled respect. He loves everyone equally and measures everyone by the same high standards (see 1 Peter 1:17–21).

So ... Do you expect God to do you favors because you belong to him? Why—or why not?

¹⁰Now I had stayed on the mountain forty days and forty nights, as I did the first time, and the LORD listened to me at this time also. It was not his will to destroy you. ¹¹"Go," the LORD said to me, "and lead the people on their way, so that they may enter and possess the land I swore to their ancestors to give them."

Fear the LORD

¹²And now, Israel, what does the LORD your God ask of you but to fear the LORD your God, to walk in obedience to him, to love him, to serve the LORD your God with all your heart and with all your soul, ¹³and to observe the LORD's commands and decrees that I am giving you today for your own good?

¹⁴To the LORD your God belong the heavens, even the highest heavens, the earth and everything in it. ¹⁵Yet the LORD set his affection on your ancestors and loved them, and he chose you, their descendants, above all the nations — as it is today. ¹⁶Circumcise your hearts, therefore, and do not be stiff-necked any longer. ¹⁷For the LORD your God is God of gods and Lord of lords, the great God, mighty and awesome, who shows no partiality and accepts no bribes. ¹⁸He defends the cause of the fatherless and the widow, and loves the foreigner residing among you, giving them food and clothing. ¹⁹And you are to love those who are foreigners, for you yourselves were foreigners in Egypt. ²⁰Fear the LORD your God and serve him. Hold fast to him and take your oaths in his name. ²¹He is the one you praise; he is your God, who performed for you those great and awesome wonders you saw with your own eyes. ²²Your ancestors who went down into Egypt were seventy in all, and now the LORD your God has made you as numerous as the stars in the sky.

Love and Obey the LORD

11 Love the LORD your God and keep his requirements, his decrees, his laws and his commands always. ²Remember today that your children were not the ones who saw and ex-

---

ROCK SOLID *promises*

"He is the one you praise; he is your God, who performed for you those great and awesome wonders." Deuteronomy 10:21

God's amazing deeds give you reason to praise him. They prove that your God really cares.

---

perienced the discipline of the LORD your God: his majesty, his mighty hand, his outstretched arm; ³the signs he performed and the things he did in the heart of Egypt, both to Pharaoh king of Egypt and to his whole country; ⁴what he did to the Egyptian army, to its horses and chariots, how he overwhelmed them with the waters of the Red Sea[a] as they were pursuing you, and how the LORD brought lasting ruin on them. ⁵It was not your children who saw what he did for you in the wilderness until you arrived at this place, ⁶and what he did to Dathan and Abiram, sons of Eliab the Reubenite, when the earth opened its mouth right in the middle of all Israel and swallowed them up with their households, their tents and every living thing that belonged to them. ⁷But it was your own eyes that saw all these great things the LORD has done.

⁸Observe therefore all the commands I am giving you today, so that you may have the strength to go in and take over the land that you are crossing the Jordan to possess, ⁹and so that you may live long in the land the LORD swore to your ancestors to give to them and their descendants, a land flowing with milk and honey. ¹⁰The land you are entering to take over is not like the land of Egypt, from which you have come, where you planted your seed

---

a 4 Or *the Sea of Reeds*

and irrigated it by foot as in a vegetable garden. [11]But the land you are crossing the Jordan to take possession of is a land of mountains and valleys that drinks rain from heaven. [12]It is a land the LORD your God cares for; the eyes of the LORD your God are continually on it from the beginning of the year to its end.

[13]So if you faithfully obey the commands I am giving you today—to love the LORD your God and to serve him with all your heart and with all your soul— [14]then I will send rain on your land in its season, both autumn and spring rains, so that you may gather in your grain, new wine and olive oil. [15]I will provide grass in the fields for your cattle, and you will eat and be satisfied.

[16]Be careful, or you will be enticed to turn away and worship other gods and bow down to them. [17]Then the LORD's anger will burn against you, and he will shut up the heavens so that it will not rain and the ground will yield no produce, and you will soon perish from the good land the LORD is giving you. [18]Fix these words of mine in your hearts and minds; tie them as symbols on your hands and bind them on your foreheads. [19]Teach them to your children, talking about them when you sit at home and when you walk along the road, when you lie down and when you get up. [20]Write them on the doorframes of your houses and on your gates, [21]so that your days and the days of your children may be many in the land the LORD swore to give your ancestors, as many as the days that the heavens are above the earth.

[22]If you carefully observe all these commands I am giving you to follow—to love the LORD your God, to walk in obedience to him and to hold fast to him— [23]then the LORD will drive out all these nations before you, and you will dispossess nations larger and stronger than you. [24]Every place where you set your foot will be yours: Your territory will extend from the desert to Lebanon, and from the Euphrates River to the Mediterranean Sea. [25]No one will be able to stand against you. The LORD your God, as he promised you, will put the terror and fear of you on the whole land, wherever you go.

[26]See, I am setting before you today a blessing and a curse— [27]the blessing if you obey the commands of the LORD your God that I am giving you today; [28]the curse if you disobey the commands of the LORD your God and turn from the way that I command you today by following other gods, which you have not known. [29]When the LORD your God has brought you into the land you are entering to possess, you are to proclaim on Mount Gerizim the blessings, and on Mount Ebal the curses. [30]As you know, these mountains are across the Jordan, westward, toward the setting sun, near the great trees of Moreh, in the territory of those Canaanites living in the Arabah in the vicinity of Gilgal. [31]You are about to cross the Jordan to enter and take possession of the land the LORD your God is giving you. When you have taken it over and are living there, [32]be sure that you obey all the decrees and laws I am setting before you today.

The One Place of Worship

12 These are the decrees and laws you must be careful to follow in the land that the LORD, the God of your ancestors, has given you to possess—as long as you live in the land. [2]Destroy completely all the places on the high mountains, on the hills and under every spreading tree, where the nations you are dispossessing worship their gods. [3]Break down their altars, smash their sacred stones and burn their Asherah poles in the fire; cut down the idols of their gods and wipe out their names from those places.

[4]You must not worship the LORD your God in their way. [5]But you are to seek the place the LORD your God will choose from among all your tribes to put his Name there for his dwelling. To that place you must go; [6]there bring your burnt offerings and sacrifices, your tithes and special gifts, what you have vowed to give and your freewill offerings, and the firstborn of your herds and flocks. [7]There, in the presence of the LORD your God, you and

your families shall eat and shall rejoice in everything you have put your hand to, because the Lord your God has blessed you.

[8] You are not to do as we do here today, everyone doing as they see fit, [9] since you have not yet reached the resting place and the inheritance the Lord your God is giving you. [10] But you will cross the Jordan and settle in the land the Lord your God is giving you as an inheritance, and he will give you rest from all your enemies around you so that you will live in safety. [11] Then to the place the Lord your God will choose as a dwelling for his Name— there you are to bring everything I command you: your burnt offerings and sacrifices, your tithes and special gifts, and all the choice possessions you have vowed to the Lord. [12] And there rejoice before the Lord your God—you, your sons and daughters, your male and female servants, and the Levites from your towns who have no allotment or inheritance of their own. [13] Be careful not to sacrifice your burnt offerings anywhere you please. [14] Offer them only at the place the Lord will choose in one of your tribes, and there observe everything I command you.

[15] Nevertheless, you may slaughter your animals in any of your towns and eat as much of the meat as you want, as if it were gazelle or deer, according to the blessing the Lord your God gives you. Both the ceremonially unclean and the clean may eat it. [16] But you must not eat the blood; pour it out on the ground like water. [17] You must not eat in your own towns the tithe of your grain and new wine and olive oil, or the firstborn of your herds and flocks, or whatever you have vowed to give, or your freewill offerings or special gifts. [18] Instead, you are to eat them in the presence of the Lord your God at the place the Lord your God will choose—you, your sons and daughters, your male and female servants, and the Levites from your towns—and you are to rejoice before the Lord your God in everything you put your hand to. [19] Be careful not to neglect the Levites as long as you live in your land.

[20] When the Lord your God has en- larged your territory as he promised you, and you crave meat and say, "I would like some meat," then you may eat as much of it as you want. [21] If the place where the Lord your God chooses to put his Name is too far away from you, you may slaughter animals from the herds and flocks the Lord has given you, as I have commanded you, and in your own towns you may eat as much of them as you want. [22] Eat them as you would gazelle or deer. Both the ceremonially unclean and the clean may eat. [23] But be sure you do not eat the blood, because the blood is the life, and you must not eat the life with the meat. [24] You must not eat the blood; pour it out on the ground like water. [25] Do not eat it, so that it may go well with you and your children after you, because you will be doing what is right in the eyes of the Lord.

[26] But take your consecrated things and whatever you have vowed to give, and go to the place the Lord will choose. [27] Present your burnt offerings on the altar of the Lord your God, both the meat and the blood. The blood of your sacrifices must be poured beside the altar of the Lord your God, but you may eat the meat. [28] Be careful to obey all these regulations I am giving you, so that it may always go well with you and your children after you, because you will be doing what is good and right in the eyes of the Lord your God.

[29] The Lord your God will cut off before you the nations you are about to invade and dispossess. But when you have driven them out and settled in their land, [30] and after they have been destroyed before you, be careful not to be ensnared by inquiring about their gods, saying, "How do these nations serve their gods? We will do the same." [31] You must not worship the Lord your God in their way, because in worshiping their gods, they do all kinds of detestable things the Lord hates. They even burn their sons and daughters in the fire as sacrifices to their gods.

[32] See that you do all I command you; do not add to it or take away from it.[a]

a 32 In Hebrew texts this verse (12:32) is numbered 13:1.

Worshiping Other Gods

13 *a* If a prophet, or one who foretells by dreams, appears among you and announces to you a sign or wonder, ²and if the sign or wonder spoken of takes place, and the prophet says, "Let us follow other gods" (gods you have not known) "and let us worship them," ³you must not listen to the words of that prophet or dreamer. The LORD your God is testing you to find out whether you love him with all your heart and with all your soul. ⁴It is the LORD your God you must follow, and him you must revere. Keep his commands and obey him; serve him and hold fast to him. ⁵That prophet or dreamer must be put to death for inciting rebellion against the LORD your God, who brought you out of Egypt and redeemed you from the land of slavery. That prophet or dreamer tried to turn you from the way the LORD your God commanded you to follow. You must purge the evil from among you.

⁶If your very own brother, or your son or daughter, or the wife you love, or your closest friend secretly entices you, saying, "Let us go and worship other gods" (gods that neither you nor your ancestors have known, ⁷gods of the peoples around you, whether near or far, from one end of the land to the other), ⁸do not yield to them or listen to them. Show them no pity. Do not spare them or shield them. ⁹You must certainly put them to death. Your hand must be the first in putting them to death, and then the hands of all the people. ¹⁰Stone them to death, because they tried to turn you away from the LORD your God, who brought you out of Egypt, out of the land of slavery. ¹¹Then all Israel will hear and be afraid, and no one among you will do such an evil thing again.

¹²If you hear it said about one of the towns the LORD your God is giving you to live in ¹³that troublemakers have arisen among you and have led the people of their town astray, saying, "Let us go and worship other gods" (gods you have not known), ¹⁴then you must inquire, probe and investigate it thoroughly. And if it is true and it has been proved that this detestable thing has been done among you, ¹⁵you must certainly put to the sword all who live in that town. You must destroy it completely,*b* both its people and its livestock. ¹⁶You are to gather all the plunder

a In Hebrew texts 13:1-18 is numbered 13:2-19.
b 15 The Hebrew term refers to the irrevocable giving over of things or persons to the LORD, often by totally destroying them.

Deuteronomy 13:1–18

Liars lead you to death.

When the Israelites escaped from slavery in Egypt, the Lord laid down highly specific laws about how he was to be worshiped. But he knew that deceptive people would come along who would attempt to lead the gullible into worshiping other gods. The person telling spiritual lies could be a false prophet, a family member, or a group of neighbors. God viewed spiritual deception as such a hazard to his people that he prescribed death for anyone who said, "Let us follow other gods ... and let us worship them" (Deuteronomy 13:2). God absolutely doesn't intend for Christians to physically attack people who teach spiritual lies today, because our job is to present our faith with facts and persuasive truths (see 2 Corinthians 10:4). But beware. Following other gods still causes spiritual death.

Think: When have people tried to convince you to follow false gods—to adopt ideas from other religions or to make anything more important than the Lord? What did you do?

ROCK SOLID truths

of the town into the middle of the public square and completely burn the town and all its plunder as a whole burnt offering to the Lord your God. That town is to remain a ruin forever, never to be rebuilt, ¹⁷and none of the condemned things*a* are to be found in your hands. Then the Lord will turn from his fierce anger, will show you mercy, and will have compassion on you. He will increase your numbers, as he promised on oath to your ancestors — ¹⁸because you obey the Lord your God by keeping all his commands that I am giving you today and doing what is right in his eyes.

Clean and Unclean Food

14 You are the children of the Lord your God. Do not cut yourselves or shave the front of your heads for the dead, ²for you are a people holy to the Lord your God. Out of all the peoples on the face of the earth, the Lord has chosen you to be his treasured possession.

³Do not eat any detestable thing. ⁴These are the animals you may eat: the ox, the sheep, the goat, ⁵the deer, the gazelle, the roe deer, the wild goat, the ibex, the antelope and the mountain sheep.*b* ⁶You may eat any animal that has a divided hoof and that chews the cud. ⁷However, of those that chew the cud or that have a divided hoof you may not eat the camel, the rabbit or the hyrax. Although they chew the cud, they do not have a divided hoof; they are ceremonially unclean for you. ⁸The pig is also unclean; although it has a divided hoof, it does not chew the cud. You are not to eat their meat or touch their carcasses.

⁹Of all the creatures living in the water, you may eat any that has fins and scales. ¹⁰But anything that does not have fins and scales you may not eat; for you it is unclean.

¹¹You may eat any clean bird. ¹²But these you may not eat: the eagle, the vulture, the black vulture, ¹³the red kite, the black kite, any kind of falcon, ¹⁴any kind of raven, ¹⁵the horned owl, the screech owl, the gull, any kind of hawk, ¹⁶the little owl, the great owl, the white owl, ¹⁷the desert owl, the osprey, the cormorant, ¹⁸the stork, any kind of heron, the hoopoe and the bat.

¹⁹All flying insects are unclean to you; do not eat them. ²⁰But any winged creature that is clean you may eat.

²¹Do not eat anything you find already dead. You may give it to the foreigner residing in any of your towns, and they may eat it, or you may sell it to any other foreigner. But you are a people holy to the Lord your God.

Do not cook a young goat in its mother's milk.

Tithes

²²Be sure to set aside a tenth of all that your fields produce each year. ²³Eat the tithe of your grain, new wine and olive oil, and the firstborn of your herds and flocks in the presence of the Lord your God at the place he will choose as a dwelling for his Name, so that you may learn to revere the Lord your God always. ²⁴But if that place is too distant and you have been blessed by the Lord your God and cannot carry your tithe (because the place where the Lord will choose to put his Name is so far away), ²⁵then exchange your tithe for silver, and take the silver with you and go to the place the Lord your God will choose. ²⁶Use the silver to buy whatever you like: cattle, sheep, wine or other fermented drink, or anything you wish. Then you and your household shall eat there in the presence of the Lord your God and rejoice. ²⁷And do not neglect the Levites living in your towns, for they have no allotment or inheritance of their own.

²⁸At the end of every three years, bring all the tithes of that year's produce and store it in your towns, ²⁹so that the Levites (who have no allotment or inheritance of their own) and the foreigners, the fatherless and the widows who live in your towns may come and eat and be satisfied, and so that

a 17 The Hebrew term refers to the irrevocable giving over of things or persons to the Lord, often by totally destroying them.   *b 5* The precise identification of some of the birds and animals in this chapter is uncertain.

the Lord your God may bless you in all the work of your hands.

The Year for Canceling Debts

15 At the end of every seven years you must cancel debts. [2]This is how it is to be done: Every creditor shall cancel any loan they have made to a fellow Israelite. They shall not require payment from anyone among their own people, because the Lord's time for canceling debts has been proclaimed. [3]You may require payment from a foreigner, but you must cancel any debt your fellow Israelite owes you. [4]However, there need be no poor people among you, for in the land the Lord your God is giving you to possess as your inheritance, he will richly bless you, [5]if only you fully obey the Lord your God and are careful to follow all these commands I am giving you today. [6]For the Lord your God will bless you as he has promised, and you will lend to many nations but will borrow from none. You will rule over many nations but none will rule over you.

[7]If anyone is poor among your fellow Israelites in any of the towns of the land the Lord your God is giving you, do not be hardhearted or tightfisted toward them. [8]Rather, be openhanded and freely lend them whatever they need. [9]Be careful not to harbor this wicked thought: "The seventh year, the year for canceling debts, is near," so that you do not show ill will toward the needy among your fellow Israelites and give them nothing. They may then appeal to the Lord against you, and you will be found guilty of sin. [10]Give generously to them and do so without a grudging heart; then because of this the Lord your God will bless you in all your work and in everything you put your hand to. [11]There will always be poor people in the land. Therefore I command you to be openhanded toward your fellow Israelites who are poor and needy in your land.

Freeing Servants

[12]If any of your people—Hebrew men or women—sell themselves to you and serve you six years, in the seventh year you must let them go free. [13]And when you release them, do not send them away empty-handed. [14]Supply them liberally from your flock, your threshing floor and your winepress. Give to them as the Lord your God has blessed you. [15]Remember that you were slaves in Egypt and the Lord your God redeemed you. That is why I give you this command today.

[16]But if your servant says to you, "I do not want to leave you," because he loves you and your family and is well off with you, [17]then take an awl and push it through his earlobe into the door, and he will become your servant for life. Do the same for your female servant.

[18]Do not consider it a hardship to set your servant free, because their service to you these six years has been worth twice as much as that of a hired hand. And the Lord your God will bless you in everything you do.

The Firstborn Animals

[19]Set apart for the Lord your God every firstborn male of your herds and flocks. Do not put the firstborn of your cows to work, and do not shear the firstborn of your sheep. [20]Each year you and your family are to eat them in the presence of the Lord your God at the place he will choose. [21]If an animal has a defect, is lame or blind, or has any serious flaw, you must not sacrifice it to the Lord your God. [22]You are to eat it in your own towns. Both the ceremonially unclean and the clean may eat it, as if it were gazelle or deer. [23]But you must not eat the blood; pour it out on the ground like water.

The Passover

16 Observe the month of Aviv and celebrate the Passover of the Lord your God, because in the month of Aviv he brought you out of Egypt by night. [2]Sacrifice as the Passover to the Lord your God an animal from your flock or herd at the place the Lord will choose as a dwelling for his Name. [3]Do not eat it with bread made with yeast, but for seven days eat unleavened bread, the bread of affliction, because you left Egypt in haste—so that all the days of your life you may remember the time of your departure from Egypt. [4]Let no yeast be found in your possession in all your land for seven days. Do not let any of the meat you sacrifice on the evening of the first day remain until morning.

[5]You must not sacrifice the Passover in any town the Lord your God gives you [6]except in the place he will choose as a dwelling for his Name. There you must sacrifice the Passover in the evening, when the sun goes down, on the anniversary[a] of your departure from Egypt. [7]Roast it and eat it at the place the Lord your God will choose. Then in the morning return to your tents. [8]For six days eat unleavened bread and on the seventh day hold an assembly to the Lord your God and do no work.

The Festival of Weeks

[9]Count off seven weeks from the time you begin to put the sickle to the standing grain. [10]Then celebrate the Festival of Weeks to the Lord your God by giving a freewill offering in proportion to the blessings the Lord your God has given you. [11]And rejoice before the Lord your God at the place he will choose as a dwelling for his Name—you, your sons and daughters, your male and female servants, the Levites in your towns, the foreigners, the fatherless and the widows living among you. [12]Remember that you were slaves in Egypt, and follow carefully these decrees.

The Festival of Tabernacles

[13]Celebrate the Festival of Tabernacles for seven days after you have gathered the produce of your threshing floor and your winepress. [14]Be joyful at your festival— you, your sons and daughters, your male and female servants, and the Levites, the foreigners, the fatherless and the widows who live in your towns. [15]For seven days celebrate the festival to the Lord your God at the place the Lord will choose.

For the Lord your God will bless you in all your harvest and in all the work of your hands, and your joy will be complete.

[16]Three times a year all your men must appear before the Lord your God at the place he will choose: at the Festival of Unleavened Bread, the Festival of Weeks and the Festival of Tabernacles. No one should appear before the Lord empty-handed: [17]Each of you must bring a gift in proportion to the way the Lord your God has blessed you.

Judges

[18]Appoint judges and officials for each of your tribes in every town the Lord your God is giving you, and they shall judge the people fairly. [19]Do not pervert justice or show partiality. Do not accept a bribe, for a bribe blinds the eyes of the wise and twists the words of the innocent. [20]Follow justice and justice alone, so that you may live and possess the land the Lord your God is giving you.

Worshiping Other Gods

[21]Do not set up any wooden Asherah pole beside the altar you build to the Lord your God, [22]and do not erect a sacred stone, for these the Lord your God hates.

17

Do not sacrifice to the Lord your God an ox or a sheep that has any defect or flaw in it, for that would be detestable to him.

[2]If a man or woman living among you in one of the towns the Lord gives you is found doing evil in the eyes of the Lord your God in violation of his covenant, [3]and contrary to my command has worshiped other gods, bowing down to them or to the sun or the moon or the stars in the sky, [4]and this has been brought to your attention, then you must investigate it thoroughly. If it is true and it has been proved that this detestable thing has been done in Israel, [5]take the man or woman who has done this evil deed to your city gate and stone that person to death. [6]On the testimony of two or three witnesses a person is to be put to death, but no one is

[a] 6 Or *down, at the time of day*

to be put to death on the testimony of only one witness. [7]The hands of the witnesses must be the first in putting that person to death, and then the hands of all the people. You must purge the evil from among you.

Law Courts

[8]If cases come before your courts that are too difficult for you to judge—whether bloodshed, lawsuits or assaults—take them to the place the LORD your God will choose. [9]Go to the Levitical priests and to the judge who is in office at that time. Inquire of them and they will give you the verdict. [10]You must act according to the decisions they give you at the place the LORD will choose. Be careful to do everything they instruct you to do. [11]Act according to whatever they teach you and the decisions they give you. Do not turn aside from what they tell you, to the right or to the left. [12]Anyone who shows contempt for the judge or for the priest who stands ministering there to the LORD your God is to be put to death. You must purge the evil from Israel. [13]All the people will hear and be afraid, and will not be contemptuous again.

The King

[14]When you enter the land the LORD your God is giving you and have taken possession of it and settled in it, and you say, "Let us set a king over us like all the nations around us," [15]be sure to appoint over you a king the LORD your God chooses. He must be from among your fellow Israelites. Do not place a foreigner over you, one who is not an Israelite. [16]The king, moreover, must not acquire great numbers of horses for himself or make the people return to Egypt to get more of them, for the LORD has told you, "You are not to go back that way again." [17]He must not take many wives, or his heart will be led astray. He must not accumulate large amounts of silver and gold.

[18]When he takes the throne of his kingdom, he is to write for himself on a scroll a copy of this law, taken from that of the Levitical priests. [19]It is to be with him, and he is to read it all the days of his life so that he may learn to revere the LORD his God and follow carefully all the words of this law and these decrees [20]and not consider himself better than his fellow Israelites and turn from the law to the right or to the left. Then he and his descendants will reign a long time over his kingdom in Israel.

Offerings for Priests and Levites

18 The Levitical priests—indeed, the whole tribe of Levi—are to have no allotment or inheritance with Israel. They shall live on the food offerings presented to the LORD, for that is their inheritance. [2]They shall have no inheritance among their fellow Israelites; the LORD is their inheritance, as he promised them.

[3]This is the share due the priests from the people who sacrifice a bull or a sheep: the shoulder, the internal organs and the meat from the head. [4]You are to give them the firstfruits of your grain, new wine and olive oil, and the first wool from the shearing of your sheep, [5]for the LORD your God has chosen them and their descendants out of all your tribes to stand and minister in the LORD's name always.

[6]If a Levite moves from one of your towns anywhere in Israel where he is living, and comes in all earnestness to the place the LORD will choose, [7]he may minister in the name of the LORD his God like all his fellow Levites who serve there in the presence of the LORD. [8]He is to share equally in their benefits, even though he has received money from the sale of family possessions.

Occult Practices

[9]When you enter the land the LORD your God is giving you, do not learn to imitate the detestable ways of the nations there. [10]Let no one be found among you who sacrifices their son or daughter in the fire, who practices divination or sorcery, interprets omens, engages in witchcraft, [11]or casts spells, or who is a medium or

spiritist or who consults the dead. ¹²Anyone who does these things is detestable to the LORD; because of these same detestable practices the LORD your God will drive out those nations before you. ¹³You must be blameless before the LORD your God.

The Prophet

¹⁴The nations you will dispossess listen to those who practice sorcery or divination. But as for you, the LORD your God has not permitted you to do so. ¹⁵The LORD your God will raise up for you a prophet like me from among you, from your fellow Israelites. You must listen to him. ¹⁶For this is what you asked of the LORD your God at Horeb on the day of the assembly when you said, "Let us not hear the voice of the LORD our God nor see this great fire anymore, or we will die."

¹⁷The LORD said to me: "What they say is good. ¹⁸I will raise up for them a prophet like you from among their fellow Israelites, and I will put my words in his mouth. He will tell them everything I command him. ¹⁹I myself will call to account anyone who does not listen to my words that the prophet speaks in my name. ²⁰But a prophet who presumes to speak in my name anything I have not commanded, or a prophet who speaks in the name of other gods, is to be put to death."

²¹You may say to yourselves, "How can we know when a message has not been spoken by the LORD?" ²²If what a prophet proclaims in the name of the LORD does not take place or come true, that is a message the LORD has not spoken. That prophet has spoken presumptuously, so do not be alarmed.

Cities of Refuge

19 When the LORD your God has destroyed the nations whose land he is giving you, and when you have driven them out and settled in their towns and houses, ²then set aside for yourselves three cities in the land the LORD your God is giving you to possess. ³Determine the distances involved and divide into three parts the land the LORD your God is giving you as an inheritance, so that a person who kills someone may flee for refuge to one of these cities.

⁴This is the rule concerning anyone who kills a person and flees there for safety—anyone who kills a neighbor unintentionally, without malice aforethought. ⁵For instance, a man may go into the forest with his neighbor to cut wood, and as he swings his ax to fell a tree, the head

---

Deuteronomy 18:9–13

Magic is out of bounds.

Israel was surrounded by nations that were into "the occult," all kinds of dark spiritual sins. They practiced sorcery and witchcraft, cast spells, looked for omens and attempted to communicate with dead people. God called all of these things "detestable practices" (Deuteronomy 18:12) because they led people away from knowing, trusting and obeying God alone. And the Lord promised to judge Israel's neighbors for these sins. In the New Testament, Acts 19:18–20 shows that magic and other dark arts still go against God's commands. When the people who heard about Jesus understood that evil spirits were behind their occult practices and that only Jesus deserved their loyalty, they gathered their magic books and burned them. People into the dark arts voluntarily took that obvious step when they realized they needed to stop sinning and obey God.

Think: Where do you see people into magic or other spiritual darkness today? How do you respond?

ROCK SOLID truths

may fly off and hit his neighbor and kill him. That man may flee to one of these cities and save his life. ⁶Otherwise, the avenger of blood might pursue him in a rage, overtake him if the distance is too great, and kill him even though he is not deserving of death, since he did it to his neighbor without malice aforethought. ⁷This is why I command you to set aside for yourselves three cities.

⁸If the Lord your God enlarges your territory, as he promised on oath to your ancestors, and gives you the whole land he promised them, ⁹because you carefully follow all these laws I command you to-day—to love the Lord your God and to walk always in obedience to him—then you are to set aside three more cities. ¹⁰Do this so that innocent blood will not be shed in your land, which the Lord your God is giving you as your inheritance, and so that you will not be guilty of bloodshed.

¹¹But if out of hate someone lies in wait, assaults and kills a neighbor, and then flees to one of these cities, ¹²the kill-er shall be sent for by the town elders, be brought back from the city, and be handed over to the avenger of blood to die. ¹³Show no pity. You must purge from Israel the guilt of shedding innocent blood, so that it may go well with you.

¹⁴Do not move your neighbor's bound-ary stone set up by your predecessors in the inheritance you receive in the land the Lord your God is giving you to possess.

Witnesses

¹⁵One witness is not enough to convict anyone accused of any crime or offense they may have committed. A matter must be established by the testimony of two or three witnesses.

¹⁶If a malicious witness takes the stand to accuse someone of a crime, ¹⁷the two people involved in the dispute must stand in the presence of the Lord before the priests and the judges who are in office at the time. ¹⁸The judges must make a thorough investigation, and if the witness proves to be a liar, giving false testimo-ny against a fellow Israelite, ¹⁹then do to the false witness as that witness intended to do to the other party. You must purge the evil from among you. ²⁰The rest of the people will hear of this and be afraid, and never again will such an evil thing be done among you. ²¹Show no pity: life for life, eye for eye, tooth for tooth, hand for hand, foot for foot.

Going to War

20 When you go to war against your enemies and see hors-es and chariots and an army greater than yours, do not be afraid of them, because the Lord your God, who brought you up out of Egypt, will be with you. ²When you are about to go into bat-tle, the priest shall come forward and ad-dress the army. ³He shall say: "Hear, Isra-el: Today you are going into battle against your enemies. Do not be fainthearted or afraid; do not panic or be terrified by them. ⁴For the Lord your God is the one who goes with you to fight for you against your enemies to give you victory."

⁵The officers shall say to the army: "Has anyone built a new house and not yet begun to live in it? Let him go home, or he may die in battle and someone else may begin to live in it. ⁶Has anyone plant-ed a vineyard and not begun to enjoy it? Let him go home, or he may die in bat-tle and someone else enjoy it. ⁷Has any-one become pledged to a woman and not married her? Let him go home, or he may die in battle and someone else marry her." ⁸Then the officers shall add, "Is anyone afraid or fainthearted? Let him go home so that his fellow soldiers will not become dishcartcncd too." ⁹When the officers have finished speaking to the army, they shall appoint commanders over it.

¹⁰When you march up to attack a city, make its people an offer of peace. ¹¹If they accept and open their gates, all the peo-ple in it shall be subject to forced labor and shall work for you. ¹²If they refuse to make peace and they engage you in battle, lay siege to that city. ¹³When the Lord your God delivers it into your hand, put to the sword all the men in it. ¹⁴As for the

women, the children, the livestock and everything else in the city, you may take these as plunder for yourselves. And you may use the plunder the LORD your God gives you from your enemies. [15] This is how you are to treat all the cities that are at a distance from you and do not belong to the nations nearby.

[16] However, in the cities of the nations the LORD your God is giving you as an inheritance, do not leave alive anything that breathes. [17] Completely destroy[a] them — the Hittites, Amorites, Canaanites, Perizzites, Hivites and Jebusites — as the LORD your God has commanded you. [18] Otherwise, they will teach you to follow all the detestable things they do in worshiping their gods, and you will sin against the LORD your God.

[19] When you lay siege to a city for a long time, fighting against it to capture it, do not destroy its trees by putting an ax to them, because you can eat their fruit. Do not cut them down. Are the trees people, that you should besiege them?[b] [20] However, you may cut down trees that you know are not fruit trees and use them to build siege works until the city at war with you falls.

Atonement for an Unsolved Murder

21 If someone is found slain, lying in a field in the land the LORD your God is giving you to possess, and it is not known who the killer was, [2] your elders and judges shall go out and measure the distance from the body to the neighboring towns. [3] Then the elders of the town nearest the body shall take a heifer that has never been worked and has never worn a yoke [4] and lead it down to a valley that has not been plowed or planted and where there is a flowing stream. There in the valley they are to break the heifer's neck. [5] The Levitical priests shall step forward, for the LORD your God has chosen them to minister and to pronounce blessings in the name of the LORD and to decide all cases of dispute and assault. [6] Then all the elders of the town nearest the body shall wash their hands over the heifer whose neck was broken in the valley, [7] and they shall declare: "Our hands did not shed this blood, nor did our eyes see it done. [8] Accept this atonement for your people Israel, whom you have redeemed, LORD, and do not hold your people guilty of the blood of an innocent person." Then the bloodshed will be atoned for, [9] and you will have purged from yourselves the guilt of shedding innocent blood, since you have done what is right in the eyes of the LORD.

Marrying a Captive Woman

[10] When you go to war against your enemies and the LORD your God delivers them into your hands and you take captives, [11] if you notice among the captives a beautiful woman and are attracted to her, you may take her as your wife. [12] Bring her into your home and have her shave her head, trim her nails [13] and put aside the clothes she was wearing when captured. After she has lived in your house and mourned her father and mother for a full month, then you may go to her and be her husband and she shall be your wife. [14] If you are not pleased with her, let her go wherever she wishes. You must not sell her or treat her as a slave, since you have dishonored her.

The Right of the Firstborn

[15] If a man has two wives, and he loves one but not the other, and both bear him sons but the firstborn is the son of the wife he does not love, [16] when he wills his property to his sons, he must not give the rights of the firstborn to the son of the wife he loves in preference to his actual firstborn, the son of the wife he does not love. [17] He must acknowledge the son of his unloved wife as the firstborn by giving him a double share of all he has. That son is the first sign of his father's strength. The right of the firstborn belongs to him.

[a] 17 The Hebrew term refers to the irrevocable giving over of things or persons to the LORD, often by totally destroying them.
[b] 19 Or down to use in the siege, for the fruit trees are for the benefit of people.

A Rebellious Son

[18]If someone has a stubborn and rebellious son who does not obey his father and mother and will not listen to them when they discipline him, [19]his father and mother shall take hold of him and bring him to the elders at the gate of his town. [20]They shall say to the elders, "This son of ours is stubborn and rebellious. He will not obey us. He is a glutton and a drunkard." [21]Then all the men of his town are to stone him to death. You must purge the evil from among you. All Israel will hear of it and be afraid.

Various Laws

[22]If someone guilty of a capital offense is put to death and their body is exposed on a pole, [23]you must not leave the body hanging on the pole overnight. Be sure to bury it that same day, because anyone who is hung on a pole is under God's curse. You must not desecrate the land the LORD your God is giving you as an inheritance.

22 If you see your fellow Israelite's ox or sheep straying, do not ignore it but be sure to take it back to its owner. [2]If they do not live near you or if you do not know who owns it, take it home with you and keep it until they come looking for it. Then give it back. [3]Do the same if you find their donkey or cloak or anything else they have lost. Do not ignore it.

[4]If you see your fellow Israelite's donkey or ox fallen on the road, do not ignore it. Help the owner get it to its feet.

[5]A woman must not wear men's clothing, nor a man wear women's clothing, for the LORD your God detests anyone who does this.

[6]If you come across a bird's nest beside the road, either in a tree or on the ground, and the mother is sitting on the young or on the eggs, do not take the mother with the young. [7]You may take the young, but be sure to let the mother go, so that it may go well with you and you may have a long life.

[8]When you build a new house, make a parapet around your roof so that you may not bring the guilt of bloodshed on your house if someone falls from the roof.

[9]Do not plant two kinds of seed in your vineyard; if you do, not only the crops you plant but also the fruit of the vineyard will be defiled.*a*

[10]Do not plow with an ox and a donkey yoked together.

[11]Do not wear clothes of wool and linen woven together.

[12]Make tassels on the four corners of the cloak you wear.

Marriage Violations

[13]If a man takes a wife and, after sleeping with her, dislikes her [14]and slanders her and gives her a bad name, saying, "I married this woman, but when I approached her, I did not find proof of her virginity," [15]then the young woman's father and mother shall bring to the town elders at the gate proof that she was a virgin. [16]Her father will say to the elders, "I gave my daughter in marriage to this man, but he dislikes her. [17]Now he has slandered her and said, 'I did not find your daughter to be a virgin.' But here is the proof of my daughter's virginity." Then her parents shall display the cloth before the elders of the town, [18]and the elders shall take the man and punish him. [19]They shall fine him a hundred shekels*b* of silver and give them to the young woman's father, because this man has given an Israelite virgin a bad name. She shall continue to be his wife; he must not divorce her as long as he lives.

[20]If, however, the charge is true and no proof of the young woman's virginity can be found, [21]she shall be brought to the door of her father's house and there the men of her town shall stone her to death. She has done an outrageous thing in Israel by being promiscuous while still in her father's house. You must purge the evil from among you.

[22]If a man is found sleeping with another man's wife, both the man who slept with her and the woman must die. You must purge the evil from Israel.

a 9 Or *be forfeited to the sanctuary*   *b 19* That is, about 2 1/2 pounds or about 1.2 kilograms

²³If a man happens to meet in a town a virgin pledged to be married and he sleeps with her, ²⁴you shall take both of them to the gate of that town and stone them to death—the young woman because she was in a town and did not scream for help, and the man because he violated another man's wife. You must purge the evil from among you.

²⁵But if out in the country a man happens to meet a young woman pledged to be married and rapes her, only the man who has done this shall die. ²⁶Do nothing to the woman; she has committed no sin deserving death. This case is like that of someone who attacks and murders a neighbor, ²⁷for the man found the young woman out in the country, and though the betrothed woman screamed, there was no one to rescue her.

²⁸If a man happens to meet a virgin who is not pledged to be married and rapes her and they are discovered, ²⁹he shall pay her father fifty shekels*a* of silver. He must marry the young woman, for he has violated her. He can never divorce her as long as he lives.

³⁰A man is not to marry his father's wife; he must not dishonor his father's bed.*b*

Exclusion From the Assembly

23 *c* No one who has been emasculated by crushing or cutting may enter the assembly of the Lord.

²No one born of a forbidden marriage*d* nor any of their descendants may enter the assembly of the Lord, not even in the tenth generation.

³No Ammonite or Moabite or any of their descendants may enter the assembly of the Lord, not even in the tenth generation. ⁴For they did not come to meet you with bread and water on your way when you came out of Egypt, and they hired Balaam son of Beor from Pethor in Aram Naharaim*e* to pronounce a curse on you. ⁵However, the Lord your God would not listen to Balaam but turned the curse into a blessing for you, because the Lord your

God loves you. ⁶Do not seek a treaty of friendship with them as long as you live.

⁷Do not despise an Edomite, for the Edomites are related to you. Do not despise an Egyptian, because you resided as foreigners in their country. ⁸The third generation of children born to them may enter the assembly of the Lord.

Uncleanness in the Camp

⁹When you are encamped against your enemies, keep away from everything impure. ¹⁰If one of your men is unclean because of a nocturnal emission, he is to go outside the camp and stay there. ¹¹But as evening approaches he is to wash himself, and at sunset he may return to the camp.

¹²Designate a place outside the camp where you can go to relieve yourself. ¹³As part of your equipment have something to dig with, and when you relieve yourself, dig a hole and cover up your excrement. ¹⁴For the Lord your God moves about in your camp to protect you and to deliver your enemies to you. Your camp must be holy, so that he will not see among you anything indecent and turn away from you.

Miscellaneous Laws

¹⁵If a slave has taken refuge with you, do not hand them over to their master. ¹⁶Let them live among you wherever they like and in whatever town they choose. Do not oppress them.

¹⁷No Israelite man or woman is to become a shrine prostitute. ¹⁸You must not bring the earnings of a female prostitute or of a male prostitute*f* into the house of the Lord your God to pay any vow, because the Lord your God detests them both.

¹⁹Do not charge a fellow Israelite interest, whether on money or food or anything else that may earn interest. ²⁰You may charge a foreigner interest, but not a fellow Israelite, so that the Lord your God may bless you in everything you put

a 29 That is, about 1 1/4 pounds or about 575 grams   b 30 In Hebrew texts this verse (22:30) is numbered 23:1.   c In Hebrew texts 23:1-25 is numbered 23:2-26.   d 2 Or one of illegitimate birth   e 4 That is, Northwest Mesopotamia   f 18 Hebrew of a dog your hand to in the land you are entering to possess.

²¹ If you make a vow to the LORD your God, do not be slow to pay it, for the LORD your God will certainly demand it of you and you will be guilty of sin. ²² But if you refrain from making a vow, you will not be guilty. ²³ Whatever your lips utter you must be sure to do, because you made your vow freely to the LORD your God with your own mouth.

²⁴ If you enter your neighbor's vineyard, you may eat all the grapes you want, but do not put any in your basket. ²⁵ If you enter your neighbor's grainfield, you may pick kernels with your hands, but you must not put a sickle to their standing grain.

24

If a man marries a woman who becomes displeasing to him because he finds something indecent about her, and he writes her a certificate of divorce, gives it to her and sends her from his house, ² and if after she leaves his house she becomes the wife of another man, ³ and her second husband dislikes her and writes her a certificate of divorce, gives it to her and sends her from his house, or if he dies, ⁴ then her first husband, who divorced her, is not allowed to marry her again after she has been defiled. That would be detestable in the eyes of the LORD. Do not bring sin upon the land the LORD your God is giving you as an inheritance.

⁵ If a man has recently married, he must not be sent to war or have any other duty laid on him. For one year he is to be free to stay at home and bring happiness to the wife he has married.

⁶ Do not take a pair of millstones—not even the upper one—as security for a debt, because that would be taking a person's livelihood as security.

⁷ If someone is caught kidnapping a fellow Israelite and treating or selling them as a slave, the kidnapper must die. You must purge the evil from among you.

⁸ In cases of defiling skin diseases,ᵃ be very careful to do exactly as the Levitical priests instruct you. You must follow carefully what I have commanded them.

⁹ Remember what the LORD your God did to Miriam along the way after you came out of Egypt.

¹⁰ When you make a loan of any kind to your neighbor, do not go into their house to get what is offered to you as a pledge. ¹¹ Stay outside and let the neighbor to whom you are making the loan bring the pledge out to you. ¹² If the neighbor is poor, do not go to sleep with their pledge in your possession. ¹³ Return their cloak by sunset so that your neighbor may sleep in it. Then they will thank you, and it will be regarded as a righteous act in the sight of the LORD your God.

¹⁴ Do not take advantage of a hired worker who is poor and needy, whether that worker is a fellow Israelite or a foreigner residing in one of your towns. ¹⁵ Pay them their wages each day before sunset, because they are poor and are counting on it. Otherwise they may cry to the LORD against you, and you will be guilty of sin.

¹⁶ Parents are not to be put to death for their children, nor children put to death for their parents; each will die for their own sin.

¹⁷ Do not deprive the foreigner or the fatherless of justice, or take the cloak of the widow as a pledge. ¹⁸ Remember that you were slaves in Egypt and the LORD your God redeemed you from there. That is why I command you to do this.

¹⁹ When you are harvesting in your field and you overlook a sheaf, do not go back to get it. Leave it for the foreigner, the fatherless and the widow, so that the LORD your God may bless you in all the work of your hands. ²⁰ When you beat the olives from your trees, do not go over the branches a second time. Leave what remains for the foreigner, the fatherless and the widow. ²¹ When you harvest the grapes in your vineyard, do not go over the vines again. Leave what remains for the foreigner, the fatherless and the widow. ²² Remember that you were slaves in Egypt. That is why I command you to do this.

ᵃ 8 The Hebrew word for *defiling skin diseases*, traditionally translated "leprosy," was used for various diseases affecting the skin.

ROCK·SOLID *principles*

Deuteronomy 24:1–22

Care about the details.

Ethan felt like he had being a Christian down cold. After all, he went to church every Sunday, youth group most Wednesdays, and signed up for a mission trip every summer. But one day his best friend rattled off a list of points that shouted how much growing Ethan had to do—from filtering his mouth to telling the truth to stepping up his treatment of girls. Mark didn't want to make Ethan feel bad, but he wanted his buddy to see there was more to following Jesus than showing up at church. Every command of God matters—no matter whether his instructions seem big or small.

Page after page of the Old Testament contains rules handed down by God explaining how his people should live. Some people think that makes God picky. Actually, it shows he oversees every major and minor detail of your life. Even though some Old Testament rules don't apply to New Testament believers, the principle behind them still matters: God wants you to pay attention to every detail.

25 When people have a dispute, they are to take it to court and the judges will decide the case, acquitting the innocent and condemning the guilty. ²If the guilty person deserves to be beaten, the judge shall make them lie down and have them flogged in his presence with the number of lashes the crime deserves, ³but the judge must not impose more than forty lashes. If the guilty party is flogged more than that, your fellow Israelite will be degraded in your eyes.

⁴Do not muzzle an ox while it is treading out the grain.

⁵If brothers are living together and one of them dies without a son, his widow must not marry outside the family. Her husband's brother shall take her and marry her and fulfill the duty of a brother-in-law to her. ⁶The first son she bears shall carry on the name of the dead brother so that his name will not be blotted out from Israel.

⁷However, if a man does not want to marry his brother's wife, she shall go to the elders at the town gate and say, "My husband's brother refuses to carry on his brother's name in Israel. He will not fulfill the duty of a brother-in-law to me." ⁸Then the elders of his town shall summon him and talk to him. If he persists in saying, "I do not want to marry her," ⁹his brother's widow shall go up to him in the presence of the elders, take off one of his sandals, spit in his face and say, "This is what is done to the man who will not build up his brother's family line." ¹⁰That man's line shall be known in Israel as The Family of the Unsandaled.

¹¹If two men are fighting and the wife of one of them comes to rescue her husband from his assailant, and she reaches out and seizes him by his private parts, ¹²you shall cut off her hand. Show her no pity.

¹³Do not have two differing weights in your bag—one heavy, one light. ¹⁴Do

not have two differing measures in your house—one large, one small. ¹⁵You must have accurate and honest weights and measures, so that you may live long in the land the Lord your God is giving you. ¹⁶For the Lord your God detests anyone who does these things, anyone who deals dishonestly.

¹⁷Remember what the Amalekites did to you along the way when you came out of Egypt. ¹⁸When you were weary and worn out, they met you on your journey and attacked all who were lagging behind; they had no fear of God. ¹⁹When the Lord your God gives you rest from all the enemies around you in the land he is giving you to possess as an inheritance, you shall blot out the name of Amalek from under heaven. Do not forget!

Firstfruits and Tithes

26 When you have entered the land the Lord your God is giving you as an inheritance and have taken possession of it and settled in it, ²take some of the firstfruits of all that you produce from the soil of the land the Lord your God is giving you and put them in a basket. Then go to the place the Lord your God will choose as a dwelling for his Name ³and say to the priest in office at the time, "I declare today to the Lord your God that I have come to the land the Lord swore to our ancestors to give us." ⁴The priest shall take the basket from your hands and set it down in front of the altar of the Lord your God. ⁵Then you shall declare before the Lord your God: "My father was a wandering Aramean, and he went down into Egypt with a few people and lived there and became a great nation, powerful and numerous. ⁶But the Egyptians mistreated us and made us suffer, subjecting us to harsh labor. ⁷Then we cried out to the Lord, the God of our ancestors, and the Lord heard our voice and saw our misery, toil and oppression. ⁸So the Lord brought us out of Egypt with a mighty hand and an outstretched arm, with great terror and with signs and wonders. ⁹He brought us to this place and gave us this land, a land flowing with milk and honey; ¹⁰and now I bring the firstfruits of the soil that you, Lord, have given me." Place the basket before the Lord your God and bow down before him. ¹¹Then you and the Levites and the foreigners residing among you shall rejoice in all the good things the Lord your God has given to you and your household.

¹²When you have finished setting aside a tenth of all your produce in the third year, the year of the tithe, you shall give it to the Levite, the foreigner, the fatherless and the widow, so that they may eat in your towns and be satisfied. ¹³Then say to the Lord your God: "I have removed from my house the sacred portion and have given it to the Levite, the foreigner, the fatherless and the widow, according to all you commanded. I have not turned aside from your commands nor have I forgotten any of them. ¹⁴I have not eaten any of the sacred portion while I was in mourning, nor have I removed any of it while I was unclean, nor have I offered any of it to the dead. I have obeyed the Lord my God; I have done everything you commanded me. ¹⁵Look down from heaven, your holy dwelling place, and bless your people Israel and the land you have given us as you promised on oath to our ancestors, a land flowing with milk and honey."

Follow the Lord's Commands

¹⁶The Lord your God commands you this day to follow these decrees and laws; carefully observe them with all your heart and with all your soul. ¹⁷You have declared this day that the Lord is your God and that you will walk in obedience to him, that you will keep his decrees, commands and laws—that you will listen to him. ¹⁸And the Lord has declared this day that you are his people, his treasured possession as he promised, and that you are to keep all his commands. ¹⁹He has declared that he will set you in praise, fame and honor high above all the nations he has made and that you will be a people holy to the Lord your God, as he promised.

ROCK SOLID
promises

"You are his people, his treasured possession." Deuteronomy 26:18

God's words are absolute truth, his sworn vow to you. And he declares that he cherishes you.

The Altar on Mount Ebal

27 Moses and the elders of Israel commanded the people: "Keep all these commands that I give you today. ²When you have crossed the Jordan into the land the LORD your God is giving you, set up some large stones and coat them with plaster. ³Write on them all the words of this law when you have crossed over to enter the land the LORD your God is giving you, a land flowing with milk and honey, just as the LORD, the God of your ancestors, promised you. ⁴And when you have crossed the Jordan, set up these stones on Mount Ebal, as I command you today, and coat them with plaster. ⁵Build there an altar to the LORD your God, an altar of stones. Do not use any iron tool on them. ⁶Build the altar of the LORD your God with fieldstones and offer burnt offerings on it to the LORD your God. ⁷Sacrifice fellowship offerings there, eating them and rejoicing in the presence of the LORD your God. ⁸And you shall write very clearly all the words of this law on these stones you have set up."

Curses From Mount Ebal

⁹Then Moses and the Levitical priests said to all Israel, "Be silent, Israel, and listen! You have now become the people of the LORD your God. ¹⁰Obey the LORD your God and follow his commands and decrees that I give you today."

¹¹On the same day Moses commanded the people:

¹²When you have crossed the Jordan, these tribes shall stand on Mount Gerizim to bless the people: Simeon, Levi, Judah, Issachar, Joseph and Benjamin. ¹³And these tribes shall stand on Mount Ebal to pronounce curses: Reuben, Gad, Asher, Zebulun, Dan and Naphtali.

¹⁴The Levites shall recite to all the people of Israel in a loud voice:

¹⁵"Cursed is anyone who makes an idol—a thing detestable to the LORD, the work of skilled hands—and sets it up in secret."

Then all the people shall say, "Amen!"

¹⁶"Cursed is anyone who dishonors their father or mother."

Then all the people shall say, "Amen!"

¹⁷"Cursed is anyone who moves their neighbor's boundary stone."

Then all the people shall say, "Amen!"

¹⁸"Cursed is anyone who leads the blind astray on the road."

Then all the people shall say, "Amen!"

¹⁹"Cursed is anyone who withholds justice from the foreigner, the fatherless or the widow."

Then all the people shall say, "Amen!"

²⁰"Cursed is anyone who sleeps with his father's wife, for he dishonors his father's bed."

Then all the people shall say, "Amen!"

²¹"Cursed is anyone who has sexual relations with any animal."

Then all the people shall say, "Amen!"

²²"Cursed is anyone who sleeps with his sister, the daughter of his father or the daughter of his mother."

Then all the people shall say, "Amen!"

²³"Cursed is anyone who sleeps with his mother-in-law."

Then all the people shall say, "Amen!"

²⁴"Cursed is anyone who kills their neighbor secretly."

Then all the people shall say, "Amen!"

²⁵"Cursed is anyone who accepts a bribe to kill an innocent person."

Then all the people shall say, "Amen!"

²⁶"Cursed is anyone who does not uphold the words of this law by carrying them out."

Then all the people shall say, "Amen!"

Blessings for Obedience

28 If you fully obey the LORD your God and carefully follow all his commands I give you today, the LORD your God will set you high above all the nations on earth. ²All these blessings will come on you and accompany you if you obey the LORD your God:

³You will be blessed in the city and blessed in the country.

⁴The fruit of your womb will be blessed, and the crops of your land and the young of your livestock—the calves of your herds and the lambs of your flocks.

ROCK SOLID promises

"All these blessings will come on you and accompany you if you obey the LORD your God."

Deuteronomy 28:2

You can't earn God's blessings, but you will experience them best when you obey his commands.

⁵Your basket and your kneading trough will be blessed.

⁶You will be blessed when you come in and blessed when you go out.

⁷The LORD will grant that the enemies who rise up against you will be defeated before you. They will come at you from one direction but flee from you in seven.

⁸The LORD will send a blessing on your barns and on everything you put your hand to. The LORD your God will bless you in the land he is giving you.

⁹The LORD will establish you as his holy people, as he promised you on oath, if you keep the commands of the LORD your God and walk in obedience to him. ¹⁰Then all the peoples on earth will see that you are called by the name of the LORD, and they will fear you. ¹¹The LORD will grant you abundant prosperity—in the fruit of your womb, the young of your livestock and the crops of your ground—in the land he swore to your ancestors to give you.

¹²The LORD will open the heavens, the storehouse of his bounty, to send rain on your land in season and to bless all the work of your hands. You will lend to many nations but will borrow from none. ¹³The LORD will make you the head, not the tail. If you pay attention to the commands of the LORD your God that I give you this day and carefully follow them, you will always be at the top, never at the bottom. ¹⁴Do not turn aside from any of the commands I give you today, to the right or to the left, following other gods and serving them.

Curses for Disobedience

¹⁵However, if you do not obey the LORD your God and do not carefully follow all his commands and decrees I am giving you today, all these curses will come on you and overtake you:

¹⁶You will be cursed in the city and cursed in the country.

¹⁷Your basket and your kneading trough will be cursed.

¹⁸The fruit of your womb will be cursed, and the crops of your land,

and the calves of your herds and the lambs of your flocks.

¹⁹You will be cursed when you come in and cursed when you go out.

²⁰The LORD will send on you curses, confusion and rebuke in everything you put your hand to, until you are destroyed and come to sudden ruin because of the evil you have done in forsaking him.ᵃ ²¹The LORD will plague you with diseases until he has destroyed you from the land you are entering to possess. ²²The LORD will strike you with wasting disease, with fever and inflammation, with scorching heat and drought, with blight and mildew, which will plague you until you perish. ²³The sky over your head will be bronze, the ground beneath you iron. ²⁴The LORD will turn the rain of your country into dust and powder; it will come down from the skies until you are destroyed.

²⁵The LORD will cause you to be defeated before your enemies. You will come at them from one direction but flee from them in seven, and you will become a thing of horror to all the kingdoms on earth. ²⁶Your carcasses will be food for all the birds and the wild animals, and there will be no one to frighten them away. ²⁷The LORD will afflict you with the boils of Egypt and with tumors, festering sores and the itch, from which you cannot be cured. ²⁸The LORD will afflict you with madness, blindness and confusion of mind. ²⁹At midday you will grope about like a blind person in the dark. You will be unsuccessful in everything you do; day after day you will be oppressed and robbed, with no one to rescue you.

³⁰You will be pledged to be married to a woman, but another will take her and rape her. You will build a house, but you will not live in it. You will plant a vineyard, but you will not even begin to enjoy its fruit. ³¹Your ox will be slaughtered before your eyes, but you will eat none of it. Your donkey will be forcibly taken from you and will not be returned. Your sheep will be given to your enemies, and no one will rescue them. ³²Your sons and daughters will be given to another nation, and you

will wear out your eyes watching for them day after day, powerless to lift a hand. ³³A people that you do not know will eat what your land and labor produce, and you will have nothing but cruel oppression all your days. ³⁴The sights you see will drive you mad. ³⁵The LORD will afflict your knees and legs with painful boils that cannot be cured, spreading from the soles of your feet to the top of your head.

³⁶The LORD will drive you and the king you set over you to a nation unknown to you or your ancestors. There you will worship other gods, gods of wood and stone. ³⁷You will become a thing of horror, a byword and an object of ridicule among all the peoples where the LORD will drive you.

³⁸You will sow much seed in the field but you will harvest little, because locusts will devour it. ³⁹You will plant vineyards and cultivate them but you will not drink the wine or gather the grapes, because worms will eat them. ⁴⁰You will have olive trees throughout your country but you will not use the oil, because the olives will drop off. ⁴¹You will have sons and daughters but you will not keep them, because they will go into captivity. ⁴²Swarms of locusts will take over all your trees and the crops of your land.

⁴³The foreigners who reside among you will rise above you higher and higher, but you will sink lower and lower. ⁴⁴They will lend to you, but you will not lend to them. They will be the head, but you will be the tail.

⁴⁵All these curses will come on you. They will pursue you and overtake you until you are destroyed, because you did not obey the LORD your God and observe the commands and decrees he gave you. ⁴⁶They will be a sign and a wonder to you and your descendants forever. ⁴⁷Because you did not serve the LORD your God joyfully and gladly in the time of prosperity, ⁴⁸therefore in hunger and thirst, in nakedness and dire poverty, you will serve the enemies the LORD sends against you. He will put an iron yoke on your neck until he has destroyed you.

ᵃ 20 Hebrew me

⁴⁹The LORD will bring a nation against you from far away, from the ends of the earth, like an eagle swooping down, a nation whose language you will not understand, ⁵⁰a fierce-looking nation without respect for the old or pity for the young. ⁵¹They will devour the young of your livestock and the crops of your land until you are destroyed. They will leave you no grain, new wine or olive oil, nor any calves of your herds or lambs of your flocks until you are ruined. ⁵²They will lay siege to all the cities throughout your land until the high fortified walls in which you trust fall down. They will besiege all the cities throughout the land the LORD your God is giving you.

⁵³Because of the suffering your enemy will inflict on you during the siege, you will eat the fruit of the womb, the flesh of the sons and daughters the LORD your God has given you. ⁵⁴Even the most gentle and sensitive man among you will have no compassion on his own brother or the wife he loves or his surviving children, ⁵⁵and he will not give to one of them any of the flesh of his children that he is eating. It will be all he has left because of the suffering your enemy will inflict on you during the siege of all your cities. ⁵⁶The most gentle and sensitive woman among you—so sensitive and gentle that she would not venture to touch the ground with the sole of her foot—will begrudge the husband she loves and her own son or daughter ⁵⁷the afterbirth from her womb and the children she bears. For in her dire need she intends to eat them secretly because of the suffering your enemy will inflict on you during the siege of your cities.

⁵⁸If you do not carefully follow all the words of this law, which are written in this book, and do not revere this glorious and awesome name—the LORD your God— ⁵⁹the LORD will send fearful plagues on you and your descendants, harsh and prolonged disasters, and severe and lingering illnesses. ⁶⁰He will bring on you all the diseases of Egypt that you dreaded, and they will cling to you. ⁶¹The LORD will also bring on you every kind of sickness and disaster not recorded in this Book of the Law, until you are destroyed. ⁶²You who were as numerous as the stars in the sky will be left but few in number, because you did not obey the LORD your God. ⁶³Just as it pleased the LORD to make you prosper and increase in number, so it will please him to ruin and destroy you. You will be uprooted from the land you are entering to possess.

⁶⁴Then the LORD will scatter you among all nations, from one end of the earth to the other. There you will worship other gods—gods of wood and stone, which neither you nor your ancestors have known. ⁶⁵Among those nations you will find no repose, no resting place for the sole of your foot. There the LORD will give you an anxious mind, eyes weary with longing, and a despairing heart. ⁶⁶You will live in constant suspense, filled with dread both night and day, never sure of your life. ⁶⁷In the morning you will say, "If only it were evening!" and in the evening, "If only it were morning!"—because of the terror that will fill your hearts and the sights that your eyes will see. ⁶⁸The LORD will send you back in ships to Egypt on a journey I said you should never make again. There you will offer yourselves for sale to your enemies as male and female slaves, but no one will buy you.

Renewal of the Covenant

29 ᵃ These are the terms of the covenant the LORD commanded Moses to make with the Israelites in Moab, in addition to the covenant he had made with them at Horeb.

²Moses summoned all the Israelites and said to them:

Your eyes have seen all that the LORD did in Egypt to Pharaoh, to all his officials and to all his land. ³With your own eyes you saw those great trials, those signs and great wonders. ⁴But to this day the LORD has not given you a mind that understands

ᵃ In Hebrew texts 29:1 is numbered 28:69, and 29:2-29 is numbered 29:1-28.

or eyes that see or ears that hear. [5] Yet the LORD says, "During the forty years that I led you through the wilderness, your clothes did not wear out, nor did the sandals on your feet. [6] You ate no bread and drank no wine or other fermented drink. I did this so that you might know that I am the LORD your God."

[7] When you reached this place, Sihon king of Heshbon and Og king of Bashan came out to fight against us, but we defeated them. [8] We took their land and gave it as an inheritance to the Reubenites, the Gadites and the half-tribe of Manasseh.

[9] Carefully follow the terms of this covenant, so that you may prosper in everything you do. [10] All of you are standing today in the presence of the LORD your God—your leaders and chief men, your elders and officials, and all the other men of Israel, [11] together with your children and your wives, and the foreigners living in your camps who chop your wood and carry your water. [12] You are standing here in order to enter into a covenant with the LORD your God, a covenant the LORD is making with you this day and sealing with an oath, [13] to confirm you this day as his people, that he may be your God as he promised you and as he swore to your fathers, Abraham, Isaac and Jacob. [14] I am making this covenant, with its oath, not only with you [15] who are standing here with us today in the presence of the LORD our God but also with those who are not here today.

[16] You yourselves know how we lived in Egypt and how we passed through the countries on the way here. [17] You saw among them their detestable images and idols of wood and stone, of silver and gold. [18] Make sure there is no man or woman, clan or tribe among you today whose heart turns away from the LORD our God to go and worship the gods of those nations; make sure there is no root among you that produces such bitter poison.

[19] When such a person hears the words of this oath and they invoke a blessing on themselves, thinking, "I will be safe, even though I persist in going my own way," they will bring disaster on the watered land as well as the dry. [20] The LORD will never be willing to forgive them; his wrath and zeal will burn against them. All the curses written in this book will fall on them, and the LORD will blot out their names from under heaven. [21] The LORD will single them out from all the tribes of Israel for disaster, according to all the curses of the covenant written in this Book of the Law.

[22] Your children who follow you in later generations and foreigners who come from distant lands will see the calamities that have fallen on the land and the diseases with which the LORD has afflicted it. [23] The whole land will be a burning waste of salt and sulfur—nothing planted, nothing sprouting, no vegetation growing on it. It will be like the destruction of Sodom and Gomorrah, Admah and Zeboyim, which the LORD overthrew in fierce anger. [24] All the nations will ask: "Why has the LORD done this to this land? Why this fierce, burning anger?"

[25] And the answer will be: "It is because this people abandoned the covenant of the LORD, the God of their ancestors, the covenant he made with them when he brought them out of Egypt. [26] They went off and worshiped other gods and bowed down to them, gods they did not know, gods he had not given them. [27] Therefore the LORD's anger burned against this land, so that he brought on it all the curses written in this book. [28] In furious anger and in great wrath the LORD uprooted them from their land and thrust them into another land, as it is now."

[29] The secret things belong to the LORD our God, but the things revealed belong to us and to our children forever, that we may follow all the words of this law.

Prosperity After Turning to the LORD

30 When all these blessings and curses I have set before you come on you and you take them to heart wherever the LORD your God disperses you among the nations, [2] and when you and your children return to the LORD your God and obey him with all your heart and with all your soul according to everything I command you today, ³then the LORD your God will restore your fortunes*ᵃ* and have compassion on you and gather you again from all the nations where he scattered you. ⁴Even if you have been banished to the most distant land under the heavens, from there the LORD your God will gather you and bring you back. ⁵He will bring you to the land that belonged to your ancestors, and you will take possession of it. He will make you more prosperous and numerous than your ancestors. ⁶The LORD your God will circumcise your hearts and the hearts of your descendants, so that you may love him with all your heart and with all your soul, and live. ⁷The LORD your God will put all these curses on your enemies who hate and persecute you. ⁸You will again obey the LORD and follow all his commands I am giving you today. ⁹Then the LORD your God will make you most prosperous in all the work of your hands and in the fruit of your womb, the young of your livestock and the crops of your land. The LORD will again delight in you and make you prosperous, just as he delighted in your ancestors, ¹⁰if you obey the LORD your God and keep his commands and decrees that are written in this Book of the Law and turn to the LORD your God with all your heart and with all your soul.

The Offer of Life or Death

¹¹Now what I am commanding you today is not too difficult for you or beyond your reach. ¹²It is not up in heaven, so that you have to ask, "Who will ascend into heaven to get it and proclaim it to us so we may obey it?" ¹³Nor is it beyond the sea, so that you have to ask, "Who will cross the sea to get it and proclaim it to us so we may obey it?" ¹⁴No, the word is very near you; it is in your mouth and in your heart so you may obey it.

¹⁵See, I set before you today life and prosperity, death and destruction. ¹⁶For I command you today to love the LORD your God, to walk in obedience to him,

and to keep his commands, decrees and laws; then you will live and increase, and the LORD your God will bless you in the land you are entering to possess.

¹⁷But if your heart turns away and you are not obedient, and if you are drawn away to bow down to other gods and worship them, ¹⁸I declare to you this day that you will certainly be destroyed. You will not live long in the land you are crossing the Jordan to enter and possess.

¹⁹This day I call the heavens and the earth as witnesses against you that I have set before you life and death, blessings and curses. Now choose life, so that you and your children may live ²⁰and that you may love the LORD your God, listen to his voice, and hold fast to him. For the LORD is your life, and he will give you many years in the land he swore to give to your fathers, Abraham, Isaac and Jacob.

Joshua to Succeed Moses

31 Then Moses went out and spoke these words to all Israel: ²"I am now a hundred and twenty years old and I am no longer able to lead you. The LORD has said to me, 'You shall not cross the Jordan.' ³The LORD your God himself will cross over ahead of you. He will destroy these nations before you, and you will take possession of their land. Joshua also will cross over ahead of you, as the LORD said. ⁴And the LORD will do to them what he did to Sihon and Og, the kings of the Amorites, whom he destroyed along with their land. ⁵The LORD will deliver them to you, and you must do to them all that I have commanded you. ⁶Be strong and courageous. Do not be afraid or terrified because of them, for the LORD your God goes with you; he will never leave you nor forsake you."

⁷Then Moses summoned Joshua and said to him in the presence of all Israel, "Be strong and courageous, for you must go with this people into the land that the LORD swore to their ancestors to give them, and you must divide it among them as their inheritance. ⁸The LORD himself

ᵃ 3 Or will bring you back from captivity

goes before you and will be with you; he will never leave you nor forsake you. Do not be afraid; do not be discouraged."

Public Reading of the Law

⁹So Moses wrote down this law and gave it to the Levitical priests, who carried the ark of the covenant of the Lord, and to all the elders of Israel. ¹⁰Then Moses commanded them: "At the end of every seven years, in the year for canceling debts, during the Festival of Tabernacles, ¹¹when all Israel comes to appear before the Lord your God at the place he will choose, you shall read this law before them in their hearing. ¹²Assemble the people—men, women and children, and the foreigners residing in your towns—so they can listen and learn to fear the Lord your God and follow carefully all the words of this law. ¹³Their children, who do not know this law, must hear it and learn to fear the Lord your God as long as you live in the land you are crossing the Jordan to possess."

Israel's Rebellion Predicted

¹⁴The Lord said to Moses, "Now the day of your death is near. Call Joshua and present yourselves at the tent of meeting, where I will commission him." So Moses and Joshua came and presented themselves at the tent of meeting.

¹⁵Then the Lord appeared at the tent in a pillar of cloud, and the cloud stood over the entrance to the tent. ¹⁶And the Lord said to Moses: "You are going to rest with your ancestors, and these people will soon prostitute themselves to the foreign gods of the land they are entering. They will forsake me and break the covenant I made with them. ¹⁷And in that day I will become angry with them and forsake them; I will hide my face from them, and they will be destroyed. Many disasters and calamities will come on them, and in that day they will ask, 'Have not these disasters come on us because our God is not with us?' ¹⁸And I will certainly hide my face in that day because of all their wickedness in turning to other gods.

¹⁹"Now write down this song and teach it to the Israelites and have them sing it, so that it may be a witness for me against them. ²⁰When I have brought them into the land flowing with milk and honey, the land I promised on oath to their ancestors, and when they eat their fill and thrive, they will turn to other gods and worship them, rejecting me and breaking my covenant. ²¹And when many disasters and calamities come on them, this song will testify against them, because it will not be forgotten by their descendants. I know what they are disposed to do, even before I bring them into the land I promised them on oath." ²²So Moses wrote down this song that day and taught it to the Israelites.

²³The Lord gave this command to Joshua son of Nun: "Be strong and courageous, for you will bring the Israelites into the land I promised them on oath, and I myself will be with you."

²⁴After Moses finished writing in a book the words of this law from beginning to end, ²⁵he gave this command to the Levites who carried the ark of the covenant of the Lord: ²⁶"Take this Book of the Law and place it beside the ark of the covenant of the Lord your God. There it will remain as a witness against you. ²⁷For I know how rebellious and stiff-necked you are. If you have been rebellious against the Lord while I am still alive and with you, how much more will you rebel after I die! ²⁸Assemble before me all the elders of your tribes and all your officials, so that I can speak these words in their hearing and call the heavens and the earth to testify against them. ²⁹For I know that after my death you are sure to become utterly corrupt and to turn from the way I have commanded you. In days to come, disaster will fall on you because you will do evil in the sight of the Lord and arouse his anger by what your hands have made."

The Song of Moses

³⁰And Moses recited the words of this song from beginning to end in the hearing of the whole assembly of Israel:

32

¹ Listen, you heavens, and I will speak;
  hear, you earth, the words of my mouth.
² Let my teaching fall like rain
    and my words descend like dew,
  like showers on new grass,
    like abundant rain on tender plants.

³ I will proclaim the name of the LORD.
    Oh, praise the greatness of our God!
⁴ He is the Rock, his works are perfect,
    and all his ways are just.
  A faithful God who does no wrong,
    upright and just is he.

⁵ They are corrupt and not his children;
    to their shame they are a warped
      and crooked generation.
⁶ Is this the way you repay the LORD,
    you foolish and unwise people?

Is he not your Father, your Creator,ᵃ
    who made you and formed you?
⁷ Remember the days of old;
    consider the generations long past.
  Ask your father and he will tell you,
    your elders, and they will explain to you.
⁸ When the Most High gave the nations their inheritance,
    when he divided all mankind,
  he set up boundaries for the peoples
    according to the number of the sons of Israel.ᵇ
⁹ For the LORD's portion is his people,
    Jacob his allotted inheritance.

¹⁰ In a desert land he found him,
    in a barren and howling waste.
  He shielded him and cared for him;
    he guarded him as the apple of his eye,
¹¹ like an eagle that stirs up its nest
    and hovers over its young,
  that spreads its wings to catch them
    and carries them aloft.
¹² The LORD alone led him;
    no foreign god was with him.

¹³ He made him ride on the heights of the land
    and fed him with the fruit of the fields.
  He nourished him with honey from the rock,
    and with oil from the flinty crag,
¹⁴ with curds and milk from herd and flock
    and with fattened lambs and goats,
  with choice rams of Bashan
    and the finest kernels of wheat.
  You drank the foaming blood of the grape.

¹⁵ Jeshurunᶜ grew fat and kicked;
    filled with food, they became heavy and sleek.
  They abandoned the God who made them
    and rejected the Rock their Savior.

UNSHAKEN God

Deuteronomy 32:4–6

God is just.

As Moses prepared to speak some of his last words before his death, the whole nation of Israel paused to listen. Moses burst out in song, with lyrics that start with the greatness of God. The Lord is the unshakable Rock, the one worth counting on. God astonishes us with his excellence and faithfulness and morality. And more than once Moses calls God "just" (Deuteronomy 32:4–6). It's the Lord's habit of doing what's right, especially his fair treatment of people. People are warped and crooked, but God's actions and decisions and commands are all correct and impartial. People aren't fair, but God is. When your world is unjust, God is constantly fair.

So … How does God's fairness impact how you see the unfairness of life?

ᵃ 6 Or *Father, who bought you*   ᵇ 8 Masoretic Text; Dead Sea Scrolls (see also Septuagint) *sons of God*   ᶜ 15 *Jeshurun* means *the upright one*, that is, Israel.

16 They made him jealous with their
foreign gods
and angered him with their
detestable idols.
17 They sacrificed to false gods, which
are not God—
gods they had not known,
gods that recently appeared,
gods your ancestors did not fear.
18 You deserted the Rock, who fathered
you;
you forgot the God who gave you
birth.

19 The Lord saw this and rejected them
because he was angered by his sons
and daughters.
20 "I will hide my face from them," he
said,
"and see what their end will be;
for they are a perverse generation,
children who are unfaithful.
21 They made me jealous by what is no
god
and angered me with their
worthless idols.
I will make them envious by those
who are not a people;
I will make them angry by a nation
that has no understanding.
22 For a fire will be kindled by my wrath,
one that burns down to the realm of
the dead below.
It will devour the earth and its harvests
and set afire the foundations of the
mountains.

23 "I will heap calamities on them
and spend my arrows against them.
24 I will send wasting famine against them,
consuming pestilence and deadly
plague;
I will send against them the fangs of
wild beasts,
the venom of vipers that glide in the
dust.
25 In the street the sword will make
them childless;
in their homes terror will reign.
The young men and young women
will perish,
the infants and those with gray hair.

26 I said I would scatter them
and erase their name from human
memory,
27 but I dreaded the taunt of the enemy,
lest the adversary misunderstand
and say, 'Our hand has triumphed;
the Lord has not done all this.'"

28 They are a nation without sense,
there is no discernment in them.
29 If only they were wise and would
understand this
and discern what their end will be!
30 How could one man chase a
thousand,
or two put ten thousand to flight,
unless their Rock had sold them,
unless the Lord had given them
up?
31 For their rock is not like our Rock,
as even our enemies concede.
32 Their vine comes from the vine of
Sodom
and from the fields of Gomorrah.
Their grapes are filled with poison,
and their clusters with bitterness.
33 Their wine is the venom of serpents,
the deadly poison of cobras.

34 "Have I not kept this in reserve
and sealed it in my vaults?
35 It is mine to avenge; I will repay.
In due time their foot will slip;
their day of disaster is near
and their doom rushes upon them."

36 The Lord will vindicate his people
and relent concerning his servants
when he sees their strength is gone
and no one is left, slave or free.[a]
37 He will say: "Now where are their
gods,
the rock they took refuge in,
38 the gods who ate the fat of their
sacrifices
and drank the wine of their drink
offerings?
Let them rise up to help you!
Let them give you shelter!

39 "See now that I myself am he!
There is no god besides me.

a 36 Or *and they are without a ruler or leader*

I put to death and I bring to life,
 I have wounded and I will heal,
 and no one can deliver out of my
  hand.
⁴⁰ I lift my hand to heaven and solemnly
  swear:
 As surely as I live forever,
⁴¹ when I sharpen my flashing sword
 and my hand grasps it in judgment,
I will take vengeance on my
  adversaries
 and repay those who hate me.
⁴² I will make my arrows drunk with
  blood,
 while my sword devours flesh:
the blood of the slain and the captives,
 the heads of the enemy leaders.”

⁴³ Rejoice, you nations, with his people,ᵃ,ᵇ
 for he will avenge the blood of his
  servants;
he will take vengeance on his enemies
 and make atonement for his land
  and people.

⁴⁴ Moses came with Joshuaᶜ son of Nun and spoke all the words of this song in the hearing of the people. ⁴⁵ When Moses finished reciting all these words to all Israel, ⁴⁶ he said to them, “Take to heart all the words I have solemnly declared to you this day, so that you may command your children to obey carefully all the words of this law. ⁴⁷ They are not just idle words for you — they are your life. By them you will live long in the land you are crossing the Jordan to possess.”

Moses to Die on Mount Nebo

⁴⁸ On that same day the Lᴏʀᴅ told Moses, ⁴⁹ “Go up into the Abarim Range to Mount Nebo in Moab, across from Jericho, and view Canaan, the land I am giving the Israelites as their own possession. ⁵⁰ There on the mountain that you have climbed you will die and be gathered to your people, just as your brother Aaron died on Mount Hor and was gathered to his people. ⁵¹ This is because both of you broke faith with me in the presence of the Israelites at the waters of Meribah Kadesh in the Desert of Zin and because you did

not uphold my holiness among the Israelites. ⁵² Therefore, you will see the land only from a distance; you will not enter the land I am giving to the people of Israel.”

Moses Blesses the Tribes

33 This is the blessing that Moses the man of God pronounced on the Israelites before his death. ² He said:

“The Lᴏʀᴅ came from Sinai
 and dawned over them from Seir;
 he shone forth from Mount Paran.
He came withᵈ myriads of holy ones
 from the south, from his mountain
  slopes.ᵉ
³ Surely it is you who love the people;
 all the holy ones are in your hand.
At your feet they all bow down,
 and from you receive instruction,
⁴ the law that Moses gave us,
 the possession of the assembly of
  Jacob.
⁵ He was king over Jeshurunᶠ
 when the leaders of the people
  assembled,
 along with the tribes of Israel.

⁶ “Let Reuben live and not die,
 norᵍ his people be few.”

⁷ And this he said about Judah:

“Hear, Lᴏʀᴅ, the cry of Judah;
 bring him to his people.
With his own hands he defends his
  cause.
 Oh, be his help against his foes!”

⁸ About Levi he said:

“Your Thummim and Urim belong
 to your faithful servant.
You tested him at Massah;
 you contended with him at the
  waters of Meribah.

ᵃ 43 Or *Make his people rejoice, you nations*
ᵇ 43 Masoretic Text; Dead Sea Scrolls (see also Septuagint) *people, / and let all the angels worship him, /*   ᶜ 44 Hebrew *Hoshea*, a variant of *Joshua*   ᵈ 2 Or *from*   ᵉ 2 The meaning of the Hebrew for this phrase is uncertain.
ᶠ 5 *Jeshurun* means *the upright one*, that is, Israel; also in verse 26.   ᵍ 6 Or *but let*

⁹He said of his father and mother,
  'I have no regard for them.'
He did not recognize his brothers
  or acknowledge his own children,
but he watched over your word
  and guarded your covenant.
¹⁰He teaches your precepts to Jacob
  and your law to Israel.
He offers incense before you
  and whole burnt offerings on your
    altar.
¹¹Bless all his skills, LORD,
  and be pleased with the work of his
    hands.
Strike down those who rise against
    him,
  his foes till they rise no more."

¹²About Benjamin he said:

"Let the beloved of the LORD rest
    secure in him,
  for he shields him all day long,
  and the one the LORD loves rests
    between his shoulders."

ROCK SOLID *promises*

"Let the beloved of the LORD rest secure in him, for he shields him all day long." Deuteronomy 33:12

If you want to experience God's amazing calm, then trust in his constant love and protection.

¹³About Joseph he said:

"May the LORD bless his land
  with the precious dew from heaven
    above
  and with the deep waters that lie
    below;
¹⁴with the best the sun brings forth
  and the finest the moon can yield;

¹⁵with the choicest gifts of the ancient
    mountains
  and the fruitfulness of the
    everlasting hills;
¹⁶with the best gifts of the earth and its
    fullness
  and the favor of him who dwelt in
    the burning bush.
Let all these rest on the head of Joseph,
  on the brow of the prince among[a]
    his brothers.
¹⁷In majesty he is like a firstborn bull;
  his horns are the horns of a wild ox.
With them he will gore the nations,
  even those at the ends of the earth.
Such are the ten thousands of
    Ephraim;
  such are the thousands of Manasseh."

¹⁸About Zebulun he said:

"Rejoice, Zebulun, in your going out,
  and you, Issachar, in your tents.
¹⁹They will summon peoples to the
    mountain
  and there offer the sacrifices of the
    righteous;
they will feast on the abundance of the
    seas,
  on the treasures hidden in the sand."

²⁰About Gad he said:

"Blessed is he who enlarges Gad's
    domain!
  Gad lives there like a lion,
  tearing at arm or head.
²¹He chose the best land for himself;
  the leader's portion was kept for him.
When the heads of the people
    assembled,
  he carried out the LORD's righteous
    will,
  and his judgments concerning Israel."

²²About Dan he said:

"Dan is a lion's cub,
  springing out of Bashan."

²³About Naphtali he said:

"Naphtali is abounding with the favor
    of the LORD

---

[a] 16 Or *of the one separated from*

and is full of his blessing;
he will inherit southward to the lake."

[24] About Asher he said:

"Most blessed of sons is Asher;
let him be favored by his brothers,
and let him bathe his feet in oil.
[25] The bolts of your gates will be iron
and bronze,
and your strength will equal your
days.

[26] "There is no one like the God of
Jeshurun,
who rides across the heavens to help
you
and on the clouds in his majesty.
[27] The eternal God is your refuge,
and underneath are the everlasting
arms.
He will drive out your enemies before
you,
saying, 'Destroy them!'
[28] So Israel will live in safety;
Jacob will dwell[a] secure
in a land of grain and new wine,
where the heavens drop dew.
[29] Blessed are you, Israel!
Who is like you,
a people saved by the LORD?
He is your shield and helper
and your glorious sword.
Your enemies will cower before you,
and you will tread on their heights."

The Death of Moses

34 Then Moses climbed Mount
Nebo from the plains of
Moab to the top of Pisgah, across from Jericho. There the LORD showed him the whole land—from Gilead to Dan, [2] all of Naphtali, the territory of Ephraim and Manasseh, all the land of Judah as far as the Mediterranean Sea, [3] the Negev and the whole region from the Valley of Jericho, the City of Palms, as far as Zoar. [4] Then the LORD said to him, "This is the land I promised on oath to Abraham, Isaac and Jacob when I said, 'I will give it to your descendants.' I have let you see it with your eyes, but you will not cross over into it."

[5] And Moses the servant of the LORD died there in Moab, as the LORD had said. [6] He buried him[b] in Moab, in the valley opposite Beth Peor, but to this day no one knows where his grave is. [7] Moses was a hundred and twenty years old when he died, yet his eyes were not weak nor his strength gone. [8] The Israelites grieved for Moses in the plains of Moab thirty days, until the time of weeping and mourning was over.

[9] Now Joshua son of Nun was filled with the spirit[c] of wisdom because Moses had laid his hands on him. So the Israelites listened to him and did what the LORD had commanded Moses.

[10] Since then, no prophet has risen in Israel like Moses, whom the LORD knew face to face, [11] who did all those signs and wonders the LORD sent him to do in Egypt—to Pharaoh and to all his officials and to his whole land. [12] For no one has ever shown the mighty power or performed the awesome deeds that Moses did in the sight of all Israel.

---

[a] 28 Septuagint; Hebrew *Jacob's spring is*
[b] 6 Or *He was buried*   [c] 9 Or *Spirit*

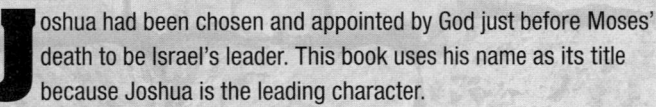

JOSHUA

BOOK OUTLINE

Preparation for possession of Canaan
(1:1 — 5:15)

The conquest of Canaan
(6:1 — 12:24)

The division of land by tribes
(13:1 — 21:45)

Farewell and death of Joshua
(22:1 — 24:33)

Joshua had been chosen and appointed by God just before Moses' death to be Israel's leader. This book uses his name as its title because Joshua is the leading character.

The book of Joshua is the story of both Joshua and Israel as they, with God's help, conquered the promised land—Canaan. The people miraculously crossed the Jordan River and conquered the town of Jericho. Then, with God's help again, they quickly took possession of all the main areas of Canaan.

Before Joshua died, he reminded the people of God's covenant promises to them. He instructed the people to keep on loving and obeying God. Publicly, he spoke of his own willingness to serve God when he said "Choose for yourselves this day whom you will serve ... but as for me and my household, we will serve the LORD" (24:15).

Joshua Installed as Leader

After the death of Moses the servant of the LORD, the LORD said to Joshua son of Nun, Moses' aide: ²"Moses my servant is dead. Now then, you and all these people, get ready to cross the Jordan River into the land I am about to give to them—to the Israelites. ³I will give you every place where you set your foot, as I promised Moses. ⁴Your territory will extend from the desert to Lebanon, and from the great river, the Euphrates—all the Hittite country—to the Mediterranean Sea in the west. ⁵No one will be able to stand against you all the days of your life. As I was with Moses, so I will be with you; I will never leave you nor forsake you. ⁶Be strong and courageous, because you will lead these people to inherit the land I swore to their ancestors to give them.

⁷"Be strong and very courageous. Be careful to obey all the law my servant Moses gave you; do not turn from it to the right or to the left, that you may be successful wherever you go. ⁸Keep this Book of the Law always on your lips; meditate on it day and night, so that you may be careful to do everything written in it. Then you will be prosperous and successful. ⁹Have I not commanded you? Be strong and courageous. Do not be afraid; do not be discouraged, for the LORD your God will be with you wherever you go."

¹⁰So Joshua ordered the officers of the people: ¹¹"Go through the camp and tell the people, 'Get your provisions ready. Three days from now you will cross the Jordan here to go in and take possession of the land the LORD your God is giving you for your own.'"

¹²But to the Reubenites, the Gadites and the half-tribe of Manasseh, Joshua said, ¹³"Remember the command that Moses the servant of the LORD gave you after he said, 'The LORD your God will give you rest by giving you this land.' ¹⁴Your wives, your children and your livestock may stay in the land that Moses

ROCK SOLID
principles

Joshua 1:9

Live boldly.

Samantha wept as she watched her dad's casket being lowered into the ground. Her dad had battled recurring cancer as long as she could remember. She had understood for a long time this day might come, and she had even tried to imagine life without her dad. She and her sister and mom would stay in the same home and school and job. But Samantha already realized it wasn't enough for those outside things to stay the same. She needed fresh strength inside just to do the same old stuff—much less ever do anything new. If Samantha didn't find some courage, her fears would eat at her the same way cancer had consumed her dad. Without courage, she would shrivel up and die.

The Israelites were poised to enter the promised land when God told Joshua to take charge of leading the people forward. A generation before, Joshua had boldly stood and said God would surely give them the land (see Numbers 14:5–11). But Joshua still needed reassurance that God never sends us anywhere without coming along (see Joshua 1:9).

gave you east of the Jordan, but all your fighting men, ready for battle, must cross over ahead of your fellow Israelites. You are to help them ¹⁵until the LORD gives them rest, as he has done for you, and until they too have taken possession of the land the LORD your God is giving them. After that, you may go back and occupy your own land, which Moses the servant of the LORD gave you east of the Jordan toward the sunrise."

¹⁶Then they answered Joshua, "Whatever you have commanded us we will do, and wherever you send us we will go. ¹⁷Just as we fully obeyed Moses, so we will obey you. Only may the LORD your God be with you as he was with Moses. ¹⁸Whoever rebels against your word and does not obey it, whatever you may command them, will be put to death. Only be strong and courageous!"

Rahab and the Spies

2 Then Joshua son of Nun secretly sent two spies from Shittim. "Go, look over the land," he said, "especially Jericho." So they went and entered the house of a prostitute named Rahab and stayed there.

²The king of Jericho was told, "Look, some of the Israelites have come here tonight to spy out the land." ³So the king of Jericho sent this message to Rahab: "Bring out the men who came to you and entered your house, because they have come to spy out the whole land."

⁴But the woman had taken the two men and hidden them. She said, "Yes, the men came to me, but I did not know where they had come from. ⁵At dusk, when it was time to close the city gate, they left. I don't know which way they went. Go after them quickly. You may catch up with them." ⁶(But she had taken them up to the roof and hidden them under the stalks of flax she had laid out on the roof.) ⁷So the men set out in pursuit of the spies on the road that leads to the fords of the Jordan, and as soon as the pursuers had gone out, the gate was shut.

⁸Before the spies lay down for the night, she went up on the roof ⁹and said to them, "I know that the LORD has given you this land and that a great fear of you has fallen on us, so that all who live in this country are melting in fear because of you. ¹⁰We have heard how the LORD dried up the water of the Red Sea[a] for you when you came out of Egypt, and what you did to Sihon and Og, the two kings of the

a 10 Or *the Sea of Reeds*

Joshua 2:1–22

Most moral decisions are easy.

Some people point to the story of Rahab and argue it proves that lying can be a morally good choice. In the Ten Commandments God said, "You shall not give false testimony against your neighbor" (Exodus 20:16), or more simply, "You shall not lie." Yet Rahab lied to protect the lives of two Israelite spies, deceiving their pursuers and saying she didn't know where they were (see Joshua 2:5–6). You might make a case that telling a lie is justified to save a life. You could also argue that Rahab was a prostitute who worshiped false gods and that telling a lie was the least of her problems. But the bigger point is that few decisions about right and wrong are so tough. They aren't up for debate. God's clear commands tell you what to do in most every situation you're likely to face today.

Think: When have you struggled to distinguish right from wrong? Was the debate truly difficult—or were you looking for a way to feel okay about doing something wrong?

ROCK SOLID *truths*

Amorites east of the Jordan, whom you completely destroyed.[a] ¹¹When we heard of it, our hearts melted in fear and everyone's courage failed because of you, for the LORD your God is God in heaven above and on the earth below.

¹²"Now then, please swear to me by the LORD that you will show kindness to my family, because I have shown kindness to you. Give me a sure sign ¹³that you will spare the lives of my father and mother, my brothers and sisters, and all who belong to them—and that you will save us from death."

¹⁴"Our lives for your lives!" the men assured her. "If you don't tell what we are doing, we will treat you kindly and faithfully when the LORD gives us the land."

¹⁵So she let them down by a rope through the window, for the house she lived in was part of the city wall. ¹⁶She said to them, "Go to the hills so the pursuers will not find you. Hide yourselves there three days until they return, and then go on your way."

¹⁷Now the men had said to her, "This oath you made us swear will not be binding on us ¹⁸unless, when we enter the land, you have tied this scarlet cord in the

[a] 10 The Hebrew term refers to the irrevocable giving over of things or persons to the LORD, often by totally destroying them.

Joshua 2:1–24

Rahab met God.

As leader of Israel and a seasoned military commander, Joshua aimed to understand his enemies well. So he sent two spies to scout the strengths and vulnerabilities of a certain walled city, Jericho. The pair found lodging in the home of a prostitute, Rahab.

The king of Jericho soon heard about the spies, and he commanded Rahab to give them up. But this gutsy woman hatched a scheme. She hid the men on her roof, reported they had run off, sent the king's guard on a useless chase, and lowered the spies on a rope hung outside the city wall.

To the king of Jericho, Rahab was a traitor. But this woman was in the process of discovering God. She assisted the spies because she believed God had promised the land to his people. She knew the Lord would enable his people to conquer her city. She even admitted to the Israelite spies that "a great fear of you has fallen on us, so that all who live in this country are melting in fear because of you" (Joshua 2:9). Rahab pleaded with the spies to spare herself and her family when the city came under attack.

Rahab probably wasn't looking for God. But she happened to have more faith than an entire generation that didn't believe the Lord was on their side (see Numbers 14:1–39). She won a spot in the great "Hall of Faith" (see Hebrews 11:31) and many Bible scholars believe this woman is the Rahab who became one of the ancestors of Jesus (see Ruth 4:18–22; Matthew 1:5).

You can find Rahab in Joshua 2; Joshua 6:22–25; and James 2:25.

UNSHAKEN *people*

window through which you let us down, and unless you have brought your father and mother, your brothers and all your family into your house. ¹⁹If any of them go outside your house into the street, their blood will be on their own heads; we will not be responsible. As for those who are in the house with you, their blood will be on our head if a hand is laid on them. ²⁰But if you tell what we are doing, we will be released from the oath you made us swear."

²¹"Agreed," she replied. "Let it be as you say."

So she sent them away, and they departed. And she tied the scarlet cord in the window.

²²When they left, they went into the hills and stayed there three days, until the pursuers had searched all along the road and returned without finding them. ²³Then the two men started back. They went down out of the hills, forded the river and came to Joshua son of Nun and told him everything that had happened to them. ²⁴They said to Joshua, "The Lᴏʀᴅ has surely given the whole land into our hands; all the people are melting in fear because of us."

Crossing the Jordan

3 Early in the morning Joshua and all the Israelites set out from Shittim and went to the Jordan, where they camped before crossing over. ²After three days the officers went throughout the camp, ³giving orders to the people: "When you see the ark of the covenant of the Lᴏʀᴅ your God, and the Levitical priests carrying it, you are to move out from your positions and follow it. ⁴Then you will know which way to go, since you have never been this way before. But keep a distance of about two thousand cubits*ᵃ* between you and the ark; do not go near it."

⁵Joshua told the people, "Consecrate yourselves, for tomorrow the Lᴏʀᴅ will do amazing things among you."

⁶Joshua said to the priests, "Take up the ark of the covenant and pass on ahead of

ROCK SOLID *promises*

"Consecrate yourselves, for tomorrow the Lᴏʀᴅ will do amazing things among you." Joshua 3:5

When you completely commit yourself to God, get set to see his most awe-inspiring acts.

the people." So they took it up and went ahead of them.

⁷And the Lᴏʀᴅ said to Joshua, "Today I will begin to exalt you in the eyes of all Israel, so they may know that I am with you as I was with Moses. ⁸Tell the priests who carry the ark of the covenant: 'When you reach the edge of the Jordan's waters, go and stand in the river.'"

⁹Joshua said to the Israelites, "Come here and listen to the words of the Lᴏʀᴅ your God. ¹⁰This is how you will know that the living God is among you and that he will certainly drive out before you the Canaanites, Hittites, Hivites, Perizzites, Girgashites, Amorites and Jebusites. ¹¹See, the ark of the covenant of the Lord of all the earth will go into the Jordan ahead of you. ¹²Now then, choose twelve men from the tribes of Israel, one from each tribe. ¹³And as soon as the priests who carry the ark of the Lᴏʀᴅ—the Lord of all the earth—set foot in the Jordan, its waters flowing downstream will be cut off and stand up in a heap."

¹⁴So when the people broke camp to cross the Jordan, the priests carrying the ark of the covenant went ahead of them. ¹⁵Now the Jordan is at flood stage all during harvest. Yet as soon as the priests who carried the ark reached the Jordan and

ᵃ 4 That is, about 3,000 feet or about 900 meters

their feet touched the water's edge, ¹⁶the water from upstream stopped flowing. It piled up in a heap a great distance away, at a town called Adam in the vicinity of Zarethan, while the water flowing down to the Sea of the Arabah (that is, the Dead Sea) was completely cut off. So the people crossed over opposite Jericho. ¹⁷The priests who carried the ark of the covenant of the LORD stopped in the middle of the Jordan and stood on dry ground, while all Israel passed by until the whole nation had completed the crossing on dry ground.

4 When the whole nation had finished crossing the Jordan, the LORD said to Joshua, ²"Choose twelve men from among the people, one from each tribe, ³and tell them to take up twelve stones from the middle of the Jordan, from right where the priests are standing, and carry them over with you and put them down at the place where you stay tonight."

⁴So Joshua called together the twelve men he had appointed from the Israelites, one from each tribe, ⁵and said to them, "Go over before the ark of the LORD your God into the middle of the Jordan. Each of you is to take up a stone on his shoulder, according to the number of the tribes of the Israelites, ⁶to serve as a sign among you. In the future, when your children ask you, 'What do these stones mean?' ⁷tell them that the flow of the Jordan was cut off before the ark of the covenant of the LORD. When it crossed the Jordan, the waters of the Jordan were cut off. These stones are to be a memorial to the people of Israel forever."

⁸So the Israelites did as Joshua commanded them. They took twelve stones from the middle of the Jordan, according to the number of the tribes of the Israelites, as the LORD had told Joshua; and they carried them over with them to their camp, where they put them down. ⁹Joshua set up the twelve stones that had been^a in the middle of the Jordan at the spot where the priests who carried the ark of the covenant had stood. And they are there to this day.

¹⁰Now the priests who carried the ark remained standing in the middle of the Jordan until everything the LORD had

ROCK SOLID *plans*

Joshua 4:1–9

Remind yourself of God's amazing acts.

The Israelites were ready to march into the promised land, but the Jordan River blocked their way. So God rolled back the waters and led them across on dry ground. Rather than let that miraculous act fade from memory, the people lifted rocks from the river and piled them up on shore as a permanent reminder of God's power. God had done amazing acts on their behalf, and they didn't want those moments to slip away.

Your next step: Craft a reminder of a time when God helped you — use a picture, sticky note, journal entry, poem, or song. Post it where you will see it regularly.

commanded Joshua was done by the people, just as Moses had directed Joshua. The people hurried over, ¹¹and as soon as all of them had crossed, the ark of the LORD and the priests came to the other side while the people watched. ¹²The men of Reuben, Gad and the half-tribe of Manasseh crossed over, ready for battle, in front of the Israelites, as Moses had directed them. ¹³About forty thousand armed for battle crossed over before the LORD to the plains of Jericho for war.

¹⁴That day the LORD exalted Joshua in the sight of all Israel; and they stood in awe of him all the days of his life, just as they had stood in awe of Moses.

¹⁵Then the LORD said to Joshua, ¹⁶"Command the priests carrying the ark of the covenant law to come up out of the Jordan."

¹⁷So Joshua commanded the priests, "Come up out of the Jordan."

^a 9 Or *Joshua also set up twelve stones*

[18] And the priests came up out of the river carrying the ark of the covenant of the Lord. No sooner had they set their feet on the dry ground than the waters of the Jordan returned to their place and ran at flood stage as before.

[19] On the tenth day of the first month the people went up from the Jordan and camped at Gilgal on the eastern border of Jericho. [20] And Joshua set up at Gilgal the twelve stones they had taken out of the Jordan. [21] He said to the Israelites, "In the future when your descendants ask their parents, 'What do these stones mean?' [22] tell them, 'Israel crossed the Jordan on dry ground.' [23] For the Lord your God dried up the Jordan before you until you had crossed over. The Lord your God did to the Jordan what he had done to the Red Sea[a] when he dried it up before us until we had crossed over. [24] He did this so that all the peoples of the earth might know that the hand of the Lord is powerful and so that you might always fear the Lord your God."

5 Now when all the Amorite kings west of the Jordan and all the Canaanite kings along the coast heard how the Lord had dried up the Jordan before the Israelites until they[b] had crossed over, their hearts melted in fear and they no longer had the courage to face the Israelites.

Circumcision and Passover at Gilgal

[2] At that time the Lord said to Joshua, "Make flint knives and circumcise the Israelites again." [3] So Joshua made flint knives and circumcised the Israelites at Gibeath Haaraloth.[c]

[4] Now this is why he did so: All those who came out of Egypt—all the men of military age—died in the wilderness on the way after leaving Egypt. [5] All the people that came out had been circumcised, but all the people born in the wilderness during the journey from Egypt had not. [6] The Israelites had moved about in the wilderness forty years until all the men who were of military age when they left Egypt had died, since they had not obeyed the Lord. For the Lord had sworn to them that they would not see the land he

had solemnly promised their ancestors to give us, a land flowing with milk and honey. [7] So he raised up their sons in their place, and these were the ones Joshua circumcised. They were still uncircumcised because they had not been circumcised on the way. [8] And after the whole nation had been circumcised, they remained where they were in camp until they were healed.

[9] Then the Lord said to Joshua, "Today I have rolled away the reproach of Egypt from you." So the place has been called Gilgal[d] to this day.

[10] On the evening of the fourteenth day of the month, while camped at Gilgal on the plains of Jericho, the Israelites celebrated the Passover. [11] The day after the Passover, that very day, they ate some of the produce of the land: unleavened bread and roasted grain. [12] The manna stopped the day after[e] they ate this food from the land; there was no longer any manna for the Israelites, but that year they ate the produce of Canaan.

The Fall of Jericho

[13] Now when Joshua was near Jericho, he looked up and saw a man standing in front of him with a drawn sword in his hand. Joshua went up to him and asked, "Are you for us or for our enemies?"

[14] "Neither," he replied, "but as commander of the army of the Lord I have now come." Then Joshua fell facedown to the ground in reverence, and asked him, "What message does my Lord[f] have for his servant?"

[15] The commander of the Lord's army replied, "Take off your sandals, for the place where you are standing is holy." And Joshua did so.

6 Now the gates of Jericho were securely barred because of the Israelites. No one went out and no one came in.

[2] Then the Lord said to Joshua, "See,

---

[a] 23 Or *the Sea of Reeds*   [b] 1 Another textual tradition *we*   [c] 3 *Gibeath Haaraloth* means *the hill of foreskins.*   [d] 9 *Gilgal* sounds like the Hebrew for *roll.*   [e] 12 Or *the day*   [f] 14 Or *lord*

I have delivered Jericho into your hands, along with its king and its fighting men. ³March around the city once with all the armed men. Do this for six days. ⁴Have seven priests carry trumpets of rams' horns in front of the ark. On the seventh day, march around the city seven times, with the priests blowing the trumpets. ⁵When you hear them sound a long blast on the trumpets, have the whole army give a loud shout; then the wall of the city will collapse and the army will go up, everyone straight in."

⁶So Joshua son of Nun called the priests and said to them, "Take up the ark of the covenant of the LORD and have seven priests carry trumpets in front of it." ⁷And he ordered the army, "Advance! March around the city, with an armed guard going ahead of the ark of the LORD."

⁸When Joshua had spoken to the people, the seven priests carrying the seven trumpets before the LORD went forward, blowing their trumpets, and the ark of the LORD's covenant followed them. ⁹The armed guard marched ahead of the priests who blew the trumpets, and the rear guard followed the ark. All this time the trumpets were sounding. ¹⁰But Joshua had commanded the army, "Do not give a war cry, do not raise your voices, do not say a word until the day I tell you to shout. Then shout!" ¹¹So he had the ark of the LORD carried around the city, circling it once. Then the army returned to camp and spent the night there.

¹²Joshua got up early the next morning and the priests took up the ark of the LORD. ¹³The seven priests carrying the seven trumpets went forward, marching before the ark of the LORD and blowing the trumpets. The armed men went ahead of them and the rear guard followed the ark of the LORD, while the trumpets kept sounding. ¹⁴So on the second day they marched around the city once and returned to the camp. They did this for six days.

¹⁵On the seventh day, they got up at daybreak and marched around the city seven times in the same manner, except that on that day they circled the city seven times. ¹⁶The seventh time around, when the priests sounded the trumpet blast, Joshua commanded the army, "Shout! For the LORD has given you the city! ¹⁷The city and all that is in it are to be devoted*ᵃ* to the LORD. Only Rahab the prostitute and all who are with her in her house shall be spared, because she hid the spies we sent. ¹⁸But keep away from the devoted things, so that you will not bring about your own destruction by taking any of them. Otherwise you will make the camp of Israel liable to destruction and bring trouble on it. ¹⁹All the silver and gold and the articles of bronze and iron are sacred to the LORD and must go into his treasury."

²⁰When the trumpets sounded, the army shouted, and at the sound of the trumpet, when the men gave a loud shout, the wall collapsed; so everyone charged straight in, and they took the city. ²¹They devoted the city to the LORD and destroyed with the sword every living thing in it—men and women, young and old, cattle, sheep and donkeys.

²²Joshua said to the two men who had spied out the land, "Go into the prostitute's house and bring her out and all who belong to her, in accordance with your oath to her." ²³So the young men who had done the spying went in and brought out Rahab, her father and mother, her brothers and sisters and all who belonged to her. They brought out her entire family and put them in a place outside the camp of Israel.

²⁴Then they burned the whole city and everything in it, but they put the silver and gold and the articles of bronze and iron into the treasury of the LORD's house. ²⁵But Joshua spared Rahab the prostitute, with her family and all who belonged to her, because she hid the men Joshua had sent as spies to Jericho—and she lives among the Israelites to this day.

ᵃ 17 The Hebrew term refers to the irrevocable giving over of things or persons to the LORD, often by totally destroying them; also in verses 18 and 21.

²⁶At that time Joshua pronounced this solemn oath: "Cursed before the L ORD is the one who undertakes to rebuild this city, Jericho:

"At the cost of his firstborn son
    he will lay its foundations;
at the cost of his youngest
    he will set up its gates."

²⁷So the L ORD was with Joshua, and his fame spread throughout the land.

Achan's Sin

7 But the Israelites were unfaithful in regard to the devoted things*ᵃ*; Achan son of Karmi, the son of Zimri,*ᵇ* the son of Zerah, of the tribe of Judah, took some of them. So the L ORD's anger burned against Israel.

²Now Joshua sent men from Jericho to Ai, which is near Beth Aven to the east of Bethel, and told them, "Go up and spy out the region." So the men went up and spied out Ai.

³When they returned to Joshua, they said, "Not all the army will have to go up against Ai. Send two or three thousand men to take it and do not weary the whole army, for only a few people live there." ⁴So about three thousand went up; but they were routed by the men of Ai, ⁵who killed about thirty six of them. They chased the Israelites from the city gate as far as the stone quarries and struck them down on the slopes. At this the hearts of the people melted in fear and became like water.

⁶Then Joshua tore his clothes and fell facedown to the ground before the ark of the L ORD, remaining there till evening. The elders of Israel did the same, and sprinkled dust on their heads. ⁷And Joshua said, "Alas, Sovereign L ORD, why did you ever bring this people across the Jordan to deliver us into the hands of the Amorites to destroy us? If only we had been content to stay on the other side of the Jordan! ⁸Pardon your servant, Lord. What can I say, now that Israel has been routed by its enemies? ⁹The Canaanites and the other people of the country will hear about this and they will surround us and wipe out our name from the earth. What then will you do for your own great name?"

¹⁰The L ORD said to Joshua, "Stand up! What are you doing down on your face? ¹¹Israel has sinned; they have violated my covenant, which I commanded them to keep. They have taken some of the devoted things; they have stolen, they have lied, they have put them with their own possessions. ¹²That is why the Israelites cannot stand against their enemies; they turn their backs and run because they have been made liable to destruction. I will not be with you anymore unless you destroy whatever among you is devoted to destruction.

¹³"Go, consecrate the people. Tell them, 'Consecrate yourselves in preparation for tomorrow; for this is what the L ORD, the God of Israel, says: There are devoted things among you, Israel. You cannot stand against your enemies until you remove them.

¹⁴"'In the morning, present yourselves tribe by tribe. The tribe the L ORD chooses shall come forward clan by clan; the clan the L ORD chooses shall come forward family by family; and the family the L ORD chooses shall come forward man by man. ¹⁵Whoever is caught with the devoted things shall be destroyed by fire, along with all that belongs to him. He has violated the covenant of the L ORD and has done an outrageous thing in Israel!'"

¹⁶Early the next morning Joshua had Israel come forward by tribes, and Judah was chosen. ¹⁷The clans of Judah came forward, and the Zerahites were chosen. He had the clan of the Zerahites come forward by families, and Zimri was chosen. ¹⁸Joshua had his family come forward man by man, and Achan son of Karmi, the son of Zimri, the son of Zerah, of the tribe of Judah, was chosen. ¹⁹Then Joshua said to Achan, "My son,

---

ᵃ 1 The Hebrew term refers to the irrevocable giving over of things or persons to the L ORD, often by totally destroying them; also in verses 11, 12, 13 and 15.   *ᵇ 1* See Septuagint and 1 Chron. 2:6; Hebrew *Zabdi*; also in verses 17 and 18.

give glory to the LORD, the God of Israel, and honor him. Tell me what you have done; do not hide it from me."

²⁰Achan replied, "It is true! I have sinned against the LORD, the God of Israel. This is what I have done: ²¹When I saw in the plunder a beautiful robe from Babylonia,ᵃ two hundred shekelsᵇ of silver and a bar of gold weighing fifty shekels,ᶜ I coveted them and took them. They are hidden in the ground inside my tent, with the silver underneath."

²²So Joshua sent messengers, and they ran to the tent, and there it was, hidden in his tent, with the silver underneath. ²³They took the things from the tent, brought them to Joshua and all the Israelites and spread them out before the LORD.

²⁴Then Joshua, together with all Israel, took Achan son of Zerah, the silver, the robe, the gold bar, his sons and daughters, his cattle, donkeys and sheep, his tent and all that he had, to the Valley of Achor. ²⁵Joshua said, "Why have you brought this trouble on us? The LORD will bring trouble on you today."

Then all Israel stoned him, and after they had stoned the rest, they burned them. ²⁶Over Achan they heaped up a large pile of rocks, which remains to this day. Then the LORD turned from his fierce anger. Therefore that place has been called the Valley of Achorᵈ ever since.

Ai Destroyed

8 Then the LORD said to Joshua, "Do not be afraid; do not be discouraged. Take the whole army with you, and go up and attack Ai. For I have delivered into your hands the king of Ai, his people, his city and his land. ²You shall do to Ai and its king as you did to Jericho and its king, except that you may carry off their plunder and livestock for yourselves. Set an ambush behind the city."

³So Joshua and the whole army moved out to attack Ai. He chose thirty thousand of his best fighting men and sent them out at night ⁴with these orders: "Listen carefully. You are to set an ambush behind the city. Don't go very far from it. All of you

be on the alert. ⁵I and all those with me will advance on the city, and when the men come out against us, as they did before, we will flee from them. ⁶They will pursue us until we have lured them away from the city, for they will say, 'They are running away from us as they did before.' So when we flee from them, ⁷you are to rise up from ambush and take the city. The LORD your God will give it into your hand. ⁸When you have taken the city, set it on fire. Do what the LORD has commanded. See to it; you have my orders."

⁹Then Joshua sent them off, and they went to the place of ambush and lay in wait between Bethel and Ai, to the west of Ai—but Joshua spent that night with the people.

¹⁰Early the next morning Joshua mustered his army, and he and the leaders of Israel marched before them to Ai. ¹¹The entire force that was with him marched up and approached the city and arrived in front of it. They set up camp north of Ai, with the valley between them and the city. ¹²Joshua had taken about five thousand men and set them in ambush between Bethel and Ai, to the west of the city. ¹³So the soldiers took up their positions—with the main camp to the north of the city and the ambush to the west of it. That night Joshua went into the valley.

¹⁴When the king of Ai saw this, he and all the men of the city hurried out early in the morning to meet Israel in battle at a certain place overlooking the Arabah. But he did not know that an ambush had been set against him behind the city. ¹⁵Joshua and all Israel let themselves be driven back before them, and they fled toward the wilderness. ¹⁶All the men of Ai were called to pursue them, and they pursued Joshua and were lured away from the city. ¹⁷Not a man remained in Ai or Bethel who did not go after Israel. They left the city open and went in pursuit of Israel.

¹⁸Then the LORD said to Joshua, "Hold

ᵃ 21 Hebrew *Shinar*   ᵇ 21 That is, about 5 pounds or about 2.3 kilograms   ᶜ 21 That is, about 1 1/4 pounds or about 575 grams   ᵈ 26 *Achor* means *trouble*.

out toward Ai the javelin that is in your hand, for into your hand I will deliver the city." So Joshua held out toward the city the javelin that was in his hand. ¹⁹As soon as he did this, the men in the ambush rose quickly from their position and rushed forward. They entered the city and captured it and quickly set it on fire.

²⁰The men of Ai looked back and saw the smoke of the city rising up into the sky, but they had no chance to escape in any direction; the Israelites who had been fleeing toward the wilderness had turned back against their pursuers. ²¹For when Joshua and all Israel saw that the ambush had taken the city and that smoke was going up from it, they turned around and attacked the men of Ai. ²²Those in the ambush also came out of the city against them, so that they were caught in the middle, with Israelites on both sides. Israel cut them down, leaving them neither survivors nor fugitives. ²³But they took the king of Ai alive and brought him to Joshua.

²⁴When Israel had finished killing all the men of Ai in the fields and in the wilderness where they had chased them, and when every one of them had been put to the sword, all the Israelites returned to Ai and killed those who were in it. ²⁵Twelve thousand men and women fell that day— all the people of Ai. ²⁶For Joshua did not draw back the hand that held out his javelin until he had destroyed*a* all who lived in Ai. ²⁷But Israel did carry off for themselves the livestock and plunder of this city, as the LORD had instructed Joshua.

²⁸So Joshua burned Ai*b* and made it a permanent heap of ruins, a desolate place to this day. ²⁹He impaled the body of the king of Ai on a pole and left it there until evening. At sunset, Joshua ordered them to take the body from the pole and throw it down at the entrance of the city gate. And they raised a large pile of rocks over it, which remains to this day.

The Covenant Renewed at Mount Ebal

³⁰Then Joshua built on Mount Ebal an altar to the LORD, the God of Israel, ³¹as Moses the servant of the LORD had commanded the Israelites. He built it according to what is written in the Book of the Law of Moses—an altar of uncut stones, on which no iron tool had been used. On it they offered to the LORD burnt offerings and sacrificed fellowship offerings. ³²There, in the presence of the Israelites, Joshua wrote on stones a copy of the law of Moses. ³³All the Israelites, with their elders, officials and judges, were standing on both sides of the ark of the covenant of the LORD, facing the Levitical priests who carried it. Both the foreigners living among them and the native-born were there. Half of the people stood in front of Mount Gerizim and half of them in front of Mount Ebal, as Moses the servant of the LORD had formerly commanded when he gave instructions to bless the people of Israel.

³⁴Afterward, Joshua read all the words of the law—the blessings and the curses—just as it is written in the Book of the Law. ³⁵There was not a word of all that Moses had commanded that Joshua did not read to the whole assembly of Israel, including the women and children, and the foreigners who lived among them.

The Gibeonite Deception

9 Now when all the kings west of the Jordan heard about these things— the kings in the hill country, in the western foothills, and along the entire coast of the Mediterranean Sea as far as Lebanon (the kings of the Hittites, Amorites, Canaanites, Perizzites, Hivites and Jebusites)— ²they came together to wage war against Joshua and Israel.

³However, when the people of Gibeon heard what Joshua had done to Jericho and Ai, ⁴they resorted to a ruse: They went as a delegation whose donkeys were loaded*c* with worn-out sacks and old wineskins, cracked and mended. ⁵They put worn and patched sandals on their feet and wore old

a 26 The Hebrew term refers to the irrevocable giving over of things or persons to the LORD, often by totally destroying them.   *b 28 Ai* means *the ruin.*   *c 4* Most Hebrew manuscripts; some Hebrew manuscripts, Vulgate and Syriac (see also Septuagint) *They prepared provisions and loaded their donkeys* clothes. All the bread of their food supply was dry and moldy. [6]Then they went to Joshua in the camp at Gilgal and said to him and the Israelites, "We have come from a distant country; make a treaty with us."

[7]The Israelites said to the Hivites, "But perhaps you live near us, so how can we make a treaty with you?"

[8]"We are your servants," they said to Joshua.

But Joshua asked, "Who are you and where do you come from?"

[9]They answered: "Your servants have come from a very distant country because of the fame of the LORD your God. For we have heard reports of him: all that he did in Egypt, [10]and all that he did to the two kings of the Amorites east of the Jordan—Sihon king of Heshbon, and Og king of Bashan, who reigned in Ashtaroth. [11]And our elders and all those living in our country said to us, 'Take provisions for your journey; go and meet them and say to them, "We are your servants; make a treaty with us."' [12]This bread of ours was warm when we packed it at home on the day we left to come to you. But now see how dry and moldy it is. [13]And these wineskins that we filled were new, but see how cracked they are. And our clothes and sandals are worn out by the very long journey."

[14]The Israelites sampled their provisions but did not inquire of the LORD. [15]Then Joshua made a treaty of peace with them to let them live, and the leaders of the assembly ratified it by oath.

[16]Three days after they made the treaty with the Gibeonites, the Israelites heard that they were neighbors, living near them. [17]So the Israelites set out and on the third day came to their cities: Gibeon, Kephirah, Beeroth and Kiriath Jearim. [18]But the Israelites did not attack them, because the leaders of the assembly had sworn an oath to them by the LORD, the God of Israel.

The whole assembly grumbled against the leaders, [19]but all the leaders answered, "We have given them our oath by the LORD, the God of Israel, and we cannot touch them now. [20]This is what we will do to them: We will let them live, so that

God's wrath will not fall on us for breaking the oath we swore to them." [21]They continued, "Let them live, but let them be woodcutters and water carriers in the service of the whole assembly." So the leaders' promise to them was kept.

[22]Then Joshua summoned the Gibeonites and said, "Why did you deceive us by saying, 'We live a long way from you,' while actually you live near us? [23]You are now under a curse: You will never be released from service as woodcutters and water carriers for the house of my God."

[24]They answered Joshua, "Your servants were clearly told how the LORD your God had commanded his servant Moses to give you the whole land and to wipe out all its inhabitants from before you. So we feared for our lives because of you, and that is why we did this. [25]We are now in your hands. Do to us whatever seems good and right to you."

[26]So Joshua saved them from the Israelites, and they did not kill them. [27]That day he made the Gibeonites woodcutters and water carriers for the assembly, to provide for the needs of the altar of the LORD at the place the LORD would choose. And that is what they are to this day.

The Sun Stands Still

10 Now Adoni-Zedek king of Jerusalem heard that Joshua had taken Ai and totally destroyed[a] it, doing to Ai and its king as he had done to Jericho and its king, and that the people of Gibeon had made a treaty of peace with Israel and had become their allies. [2]He and his people were very much alarmed at this, because Gibeon was an important city, like one of the royal cities; it was larger than Ai, and all its men were good fighters. [3]So Adoni-Zedek king of Jerusalem appealed to Hoham king of Hebron, Piram king of Jarmuth, Japhia king of Lachish and Debir king of Eglon. [4]"Come up and help me attack Gibeon,"

[a] 1 The Hebrew term refers to the irrevocable giving over of things or persons to the LORD, often by totally destroying them; also in verses 28, 35, 37, 39 and 40.

he said, "because it has made peace with Joshua and the Israelites."

⁵Then the five kings of the Amorites—the kings of Jerusalem, Hebron, Jarmuth, Lachish and Eglon—joined forces. They moved up with all their troops and took up positions against Gibeon and attacked it.

⁶The Gibeonites then sent word to Joshua in the camp at Gilgal: "Do not abandon your servants. Come up to us quickly and save us! Help us, because all the Amorite kings from the hill country have joined forces against us."

⁷So Joshua marched up from Gilgal with his entire army, including all the best fighting men. ⁸The Lord said to Joshua, "Do not be afraid of them; I have given them into your hand. Not one of them will be able to withstand you."

⁹After an all-night march from Gilgal, Joshua took them by surprise. ¹⁰The Lord threw them into confusion before Israel, so Joshua and the Israelites defeated them completely at Gibeon. Israel pursued them along the road going up to Beth Horon and cut them down all the way to Azekah and Makkedah. ¹¹As they fled before Israel on the road down from Beth Horon to Azekah, the Lord hurled large hailstones down on them, and more of them died from the hail than were killed by the swords of the Israelites.

¹²On the day the Lord gave the Amorites over to Israel, Joshua said to the Lord in the presence of Israel:

"Sun, stand still over Gibeon,
  and you, moon, over the Valley of Aijalon."
¹³So the sun stood still,
  and the moon stopped,
  till the nation avenged itself on[a] its enemies,

as it is written in the Book of Jashar.

The sun stopped in the middle of the sky and delayed going down about a full day. ¹⁴There has never been a day like it before or since, a day when the Lord listened to a human being. Surely the Lord was fighting for Israel!

¹⁵Then Joshua returned with all Israel to the camp at Gilgal.

Joshua 10:1–15
You can believe in miracles.

Of all the miracles of the Bible, one of the biggest happens in Joshua 10. As the Israelites waged a fierce battle against the Amorites, they needed more time to completely rout the enemy. So Joshua prayed for God to make the sun stand still. And "the sun stopped in the middle of the sky and delayed going down about a full day" (Joshua 10:13). That miracle requires the earth to stop spinning—or some other major intervention in the natural order. If you're trying to demonstrate the truthfulness of Bible miracles, it's tough to begin an argument using that ancient story. Your best proof for Bible miracles begins with evidence that Jesus really rose from the dead—like the detail that hundreds of people saw him alive (see 1 Corinthians 15:3–8). If the astonishing miracle of the resurrection is true, then we have reason to believe the Bible's other amazing accounts.

Think: Do you believe the Bible's miracles? Why—or why not?

ROCK SOLID *truths*

Five Amorite Kings Killed

¹⁶Now the five kings had fled and hidden in the cave at Makkedah. ¹⁷When Joshua was told that the five kings had been found hiding in the cave at Makkedah, ¹⁸he said, "Roll large rocks up to the mouth of the cave, and post some men there to guard it. ¹⁹But don't stop; pursue your enemies! Attack them from the rear and don't let them reach their cities, for

a 13 Or *nation triumphed over*

the LORD your God has given them into your hand."

²⁰ So Joshua and the Israelites defeated them completely, but a few survivors managed to reach their fortified cities. ²¹ The whole army then returned safely to Joshua in the camp at Makkedah, and no one uttered a word against the Israelites.

²² Joshua said, "Open the mouth of the cave and bring those five kings out to me." ²³ So they brought the five kings out of the cave—the kings of Jerusalem, Hebron, Jarmuth, Lachish and Eglon. ²⁴ When they had brought these kings to Joshua, he summoned all the men of Israel and said to the army commanders who had come with him, "Come here and put your feet on the necks of these kings." So they came forward and placed their feet on their necks.

²⁵ Joshua said to them, "Do not be afraid; do not be discouraged. Be strong and courageous. This is what the LORD will do to all the enemies you are going to fight." ²⁶ Then Joshua put the kings to death and exposed their bodies on five poles, and they were left hanging on the poles until evening.

²⁷ At sunset Joshua gave the order and they took them down from the poles and threw them into the cave where they had been hiding. At the mouth of the cave they placed large rocks, which are there to this day.

Southern Cities Conquered

²⁸ That day Joshua took Makkedah. He put the city and its king to the sword and totally destroyed everyone in it. He left no survivors. And he did to the king of Makkedah as he had done to the king of Jericho.

²⁹ Then Joshua and all Israel with him moved on from Makkedah to Libnah and attacked it. ³⁰ The LORD also gave that city and its king into Israel's hand. The city and everyone in it Joshua put to the sword. He left no survivors there. And he did to its king as he had done to the king of Jericho.

³¹ Then Joshua and all Israel with him

moved on from Libnah to Lachish; he took up positions against it and attacked it. ³² The LORD gave Lachish into Israel's hands, and Joshua took it on the second day. The city and everyone in it he put to the sword, just as he had done to Libnah. ³³ Meanwhile, Horam king of Gezer had come up to help Lachish, but Joshua defeated him and his army—until no survivors were left.

³⁴ Then Joshua and all Israel with him moved on from Lachish to Eglon; they took up positions against it and attacked it. ³⁵ They captured it that same day and put it to the sword and totally destroyed everyone in it, just as they had done to Lachish.

³⁶ Then Joshua and all Israel with him went up from Eglon to Hebron and attacked it. ³⁷ They took the city and put it to the sword, together with its king, its villages and everyone in it. They left no survivors. Just as at Eglon, they totally destroyed it and everyone in it.

³⁸ Then Joshua and all Israel with him turned around and attacked Debir. ³⁹ They took the city, its king and its villages, and put them to the sword. Everyone in it they totally destroyed. They left no survivors. They did to Debir and its king as they had done to Libnah and its king and to Hebron.

⁴⁰ So Joshua subdued the whole region, including the hill country, the Negev, the western foothills and the mountain slopes, together with all their kings. He left no survivors. He totally destroyed all who breathed, just as the LORD, the God of Israel, had commanded. ⁴¹ Joshua subdued them from Kadesh Barnea to Gaza and from the whole region of Goshen to Gibeon. ⁴² All these kings and their lands Joshua conquered in one campaign, because the LORD, the God of Israel, fought for Israel.

⁴³ Then Joshua returned with all Israel to the camp at Gilgal.

Northern Kings Defeated

11 When Jabin king of Hazor heard of this, he sent word to Jobab king of Madon, to the kings of Shimron and Akshaph, ² and to the northern kings who were in the mountains, in the Arabah south of Kinnereth, in the western foothills and in Naphoth Dor on the west; ³to the Canaanites in the east and west; to the Amorites, Hittites, Perizzites and Jebusites in the hill country; and to the Hivites below Hermon in the region of Mizpah. ⁴They came out with all their troops and a large number of horses and chariots—a huge army, as numerous as the sand on the seashore. ⁵All these kings joined forces and made camp together at the Waters of Merom to fight against Israel.

⁶The Lord said to Joshua, "Do not be afraid of them, because by this time tomorrow I will hand all of them, slain, over to Israel. You are to hamstring their horses and burn their chariots."

⁷So Joshua and his whole army came against them suddenly at the Waters of Merom and attacked them, ⁸and the Lord gave them into the hand of Israel. They defeated them and pursued them all the way to Greater Sidon, to Misrephoth Maim, and to the Valley of Mizpah on the east, until no survivors were left. ⁹Joshua did to them as the Lord had directed: He hamstrung their horses and burned their chariots.

¹⁰At that time Joshua turned back and captured Hazor and put its king to the sword. (Hazor had been the head of all these kingdoms.) ¹¹Everyone in it they put to the sword. They totally destroyed*a* them, not sparing anyone that breathed, and he burned Hazor itself.

¹²Joshua took all these royal cities and their kings and put them to the sword. He totally destroyed them, as Moses the servant of the Lord had commanded. ¹³Yet Israel did not burn any of the cities built on their mounds—except Hazor, which Joshua burned. ¹⁴The Israelites carried off for themselves all the plunder and livestock of these cities, but all the people they put to the sword until they completely destroyed them, not sparing anyone that breathed. ¹⁵As the Lord commanded his servant Moses, so Moses commanded Joshua, and Joshua did it; he left nothing undone of all that the Lord commanded Moses.

¹⁶So Joshua took this entire land: the hill country, all the Negev, the whole region of Goshen, the western foothills, the Arabah and the mountains of Israel with their foothills, ¹⁷from Mount Halak, which rises toward Seir, to Baal Gad in the Valley of Lebanon below Mount Hermon. He captured all their kings and put them to death. ¹⁸Joshua waged war against all these kings for a long time. ¹⁹Except for the Hivites living in Gibeon, not one city made a treaty of peace with the Israelites, who took them all in battle. ²⁰For it was the Lord himself who hardened their hearts to wage war against Israel, so that he might destroy them totally, exterminating them without mercy, as the Lord had commanded Moses.

²¹At that time Joshua went and destroyed the Anakites from the hill country: from Hebron, Debir and Anab, from all the hill country of Judah, and from all the hill country of Israel. Joshua totally destroyed them and their towns. ²²No Anakites were left in Israelite territory; only in Gaza, Gath and Ashdod did any survive.

²³So Joshua took the entire land, just as the Lord had directed Moses, and he gave it as an inheritance to Israel according to their tribal divisions. Then the land had rest from war.

List of Defeated Kings

12 These are the kings of the land whom the Israelites had defeated and whose territory they took over east of the Jordan, from the Arnon Gorge to Mount Hermon, including all the eastern side of the Arabah:

²Sihon king of the Amorites, who reigned in Heshbon.

He ruled from Aroer on the rim of the Arnon Gorge—from the middle of the gorge—to the Jabbok

---

a 11 The Hebrew term refers to the irrevocable giving over of things or persons to the Lord, often by totally destroying them; also in verses 12, 20 and 21.

River, which is the border of the Ammonites. This included half of Gilead. ³He also ruled over the eastern Arabah from the Sea of Galilee*a* to the Sea of the Arabah (that is, the Dead Sea), to Beth Jeshimoth, and then southward below the slopes of Pisgah.

⁴And the territory of Og king of Bashan, one of the last of the Rephaites, who reigned in Ashtaroth and Edrei. ⁵He ruled over Mount Hermon, Salekah, all of Bashan to the border of the people of Geshur and Maakah, and half of Gilead to the border of Sihon king of Heshbon.

⁶Moses, the servant of the LORD, and the Israelites conquered them. And Moses the servant of the LORD gave their land to the Reubenites, the Gadites and the half-tribe of Manasseh to be their possession.

⁷Here is a list of the kings of the land that Joshua and the Israelites conquered on the west side of the Jordan, from Baal Gad in the Valley of Lebanon to Mount Halak, which rises toward Seir. Joshua gave their lands as an inheritance to the tribes of Israel according to their tribal divisions. ⁸The lands included the hill country, the western foothills, the Arabah, the mountain slopes, the wilderness and the Negev. These were the lands of the Hittites, Amorites, Canaanites, Perizzites, Hivites and Jebusites. These were the kings:

⁹the king of Jericho	one
the king of Ai (near Bethel)	one
¹⁰the king of Jerusalem	one
the king of Hebron	one
¹¹the king of Jarmuth	one
the king of Lachish	one
¹²the king of Eglon	one
the king of Gezer	one
¹³the king of Debir	one
the king of Geder	one
¹⁴the king of Hormah	one
the king of Arad	one
¹⁵the king of Libnah	one
the king of Adullam	one
¹⁶the king of Makkedah	one
the king of Bethel	one
¹⁷the king of Tappuah	one
the king of Hepher	one
¹⁸the king of Aphek	one
the king of Lasharon	one
¹⁹the king of Madon	one
the king of Hazor	one
²⁰the king of Shimron Meron	one
the king of Akshaph	one
²¹the king of Taanach	one
the king of Megiddo	one
²²the king of Kedesh	one
the king of Jokneam in Carmel	one
²³the king of Dor (in Naphoth Dor)	one
the king of Goyim in Gilgal	one
²⁴the king of Tirzah	one
thirty-one kings in all.	

Land Still to Be Taken

13 When Joshua had grown old, the LORD said to him, "You are now very old, and there are still very large areas of land to be taken over.

²"This is the land that remains: all the regions of the Philistines and Geshurites, ³from the Shihor River on the east of Egypt to the territory of Ekron on the north, all of it counted as Canaanite though held by the five Philistine rulers in Gaza, Ashdod, Ashkelon, Gath and Ekron; the territory of the Avvites ⁴on the south; all the land of the Canaanites, from Arah of the Sidonians as far as Aphek and the border of the Amorites; ⁵the area of Byblos; and all Lebanon to the east, from Baal Gad below Mount Hermon to Lebo Hamath.

⁶"As for all the inhabitants of the mountain regions from Lebanon to Misrephoth Maim, that is, all the Sidonians, I myself will drive them out before the Israelites. Be sure to allocate this land to Israel for an inheritance, as I have instructed you, ⁷and divide it as an inheritance among the nine tribes and half of the tribe of Manasseh."

a 3 Hebrew *Kinnereth*

Division of the Land East of the Jordan

[8] The other half of Manasseh,[a] the Reubenites and the Gadites had received the inheritance that Moses had given them east of the Jordan, as he, the servant of the LORD, had assigned it to them.

[9] It extended from Aroer on the rim of the Arnon Gorge, and from the town in the middle of the gorge, and included the whole plateau of Medeba as far as Dibon, [10] and all the towns of Sihon king of the Amorites, who ruled in Heshbon, out to the border of the Ammonites. [11] It also included Gilead, the territory of the people of Geshur and Maakah, all of Mount Hermon and all Bashan as far as Salekah— [12] that is, the whole kingdom of Og in Bashan, who had reigned in Ashtaroth and Edrei. (He was the last of the Rephaites.) Moses had defeated them and taken over their land. [13] But the Israelites did not drive out the people of Geshur and Maakah, so they continue to live among the Israelites to this day.

[14] But to the tribe of Levi he gave no inheritance, since the food offerings presented to the LORD, the God of Israel, are their inheritance, as he promised them.

[15] This is what Moses had given to the tribe of Reuben, according to its clans:

[16] The territory from Aroer on the rim of the Arnon Gorge, and from the town in the middle of the gorge, and the whole plateau past Medeba [17] to Heshbon and all its towns on the plateau, including Dibon, Bamoth Baal, Beth Baal Meon, [18] Jahaz, Kedemoth, Mephaath, [19] Kiriathaim, Sibmah, Zereth Shahar on the hill in the valley, [20] Beth Peor, the slopes of Pisgah, and Beth Jeshimoth— [21] all the towns on the plateau and the entire realm of Sihon king of the Amorites, who ruled at Heshbon. Moses had defeated him and the Midianite chiefs, Evi, Rekem, Zur, Hur and Reba—princes allied with Sihon—who lived in that country. [22] In addition to those slain in battle, the Israelites had put to the sword Balaam son of Beor, who practiced divination. [23] The boundary of the Reubenites was the bank of the Jordan. These towns and their villages were the inheritance of the Reubenites, according to their clans.

[24] This is what Moses had given to the tribe of Gad, according to its clans:

[25] The territory of Jazer, all the towns of Gilead and half the Ammonite country as far as Aroer, near Rabbah; [26] and from Heshbon to Ramath Mizpah and Betonim, and from Mahanaim to the territory of Debir; [27] and in the valley, Beth Haram, Beth Nimrah, Sukkoth and Zaphon with the rest of the realm of Sihon king of Heshbon (the east side of the Jordan, the territory up to the end of the Sea of Galilee[b]). [28] These towns and their villages were the inheritance of the Gadites, according to their clans.

[29] This is what Moses had given to the half-tribe of Manasseh, that is, to half the family of the descendants of Manasseh, according to its clans:

[30] The territory extending from Mahanaim and including all of Bashan, the entire realm of Og king of Bashan—all the settlements of Jair in Bashan, sixty towns, [31] half of Gilead, and Ashtaroth and Edrei (the royal cities of Og in Bashan). This was for the descendants of Makir son of Manasseh—for half of the sons of Makir, according to their clans.

[32] This is the inheritance Moses had given when he was in the plains of Moab across the Jordan east of Jericho. [33] But to the tribe of Levi, Moses had given no inheritance; the LORD, the God of Israel, is their inheritance, as he promised them.

---

a 8 Hebrew *With it* (that is, with the other half of Manasseh)   *b 27* Hebrew *Kinnereth*

Division of the Land West of the Jordan

14 Now these are the areas the Israelites received as an inheritance in the land of Canaan, which Eleazar the priest, Joshua son of Nun and the heads of the tribal clans of Israel allotted to them. [2] Their inheritances were assigned by lot to the nine and a half tribes, as the Lord had commanded through Moses. [3] Moses had granted the two and a half tribes their inheritance east of the Jordan but had not granted the Levites an inheritance among the rest, [4] for Joseph's descendants had become two tribes—Manasseh and Ephraim. The Levites received no share of the land but only towns to live in, with pasturelands for their flocks and herds. [5] So the Israelites divided the land, just as the Lord had commanded Moses.

Allotment for Caleb

[6] Now the people of Judah approached Joshua at Gilgal, and Caleb son of Jephunneh the Kenizzite said to him, "You know what the Lord said to Moses the man of God at Kadesh Barnea about you and me. [7] I was forty years old when Moses the servant of the Lord sent me from Kadesh Barnea to explore the land. And I brought him back a report according to my convictions, [8] but my fellow Israelites who went up with me made the hearts of the people melt in fear. I, however, followed the Lord my God wholeheartedly. [9] So on that day Moses swore to me, 'The land on which your feet have walked will be your inheritance and that of your children forever, because you have followed the Lord my God wholeheartedly.'[a]

[10] "Now then, just as the Lord promised, he has kept me alive for forty-five years since the time he said this to Moses, while Israel moved about in the wilderness. So here I am today, eighty-five years old! [11] I am still as strong today as the day Moses sent me out; I'm just as vigorous to go out to battle now as I was then. [12] Now give me this hill country that the Lord promised me that day. You yourself heard then that the Anakites were there and their cities were large and fortified, but,

the Lord helping me, I will drive them out just as he said."

[13] Then Joshua blessed Caleb son of Jephunneh and gave him Hebron as his inheritance. [14] So Hebron has belonged to Caleb son of Jephunneh the Kenizzite ever since, because he followed the Lord, the God of Israel, wholeheartedly. [15] (Hebron used to be called Kiriath Arba after Arba, who was the greatest man among the Anakites.)

Then the land had rest from war.

ROCK SOLID *promises*

"Then the land had rest from war."
Joshua 14:15

Life's terrors might seem never-ending, but God will bring you peace.

Allotment for Judah

15 The allotment for the tribe of Judah, according to its clans, extended down to the territory of Edom, to the Desert of Zin in the extreme south.

[2] Their southern boundary started from the bay at the southern end of the Dead Sea, [3] crossed south of Scorpion Pass, continued on to Zin and went over to the south of Kadesh Barnea. Then it ran past Hezron up to Addar and curved around to Karka. [4] It then passed along to Azmon and joined the Wadi of Egypt, ending at the Mediterranean Sea. This is their[b] southern boundary.

[5] The eastern boundary is the Dead Sea as far as the mouth of the Jordan.

[a] 9 Deut. 1:36   [b] 4 Septuagint; Hebrew *your*

The northern boundary started from the bay of the sea at the mouth of the Jordan, ⁶went up to Beth Hoglah and continued north of Beth Arabah to the Stone of Bohan son of Reuben. ⁷The boundary then went up to Debir from the Valley of Achor and turned north to Gilgal, which faces the Pass of Adummim south of the gorge. It continued along to the waters of En Shemesh and came out at En Rogel. ⁸Then it ran up the Valley of Ben Hinnom along the southern slope of the Jebusite city (that is, Jerusalem). From there it climbed to the top of the hill west of the Hinnom Valley at the northern end of the Valley of Rephaim. ⁹From the hilltop the boundary headed toward the spring of the waters of Nephtoah, came out at the towns of Mount Ephron and went down toward Baalah (that is, Kiriath Jearim). ¹⁰Then it curved westward from Baalah to Mount Seir, ran along the northern slope of Mount Jearim (that is, Kesalon), continued down to Beth Shemesh and crossed to Timnah. ¹¹It went to the northern slope of Ekron, turned toward Shikkeron, passed along to Mount Baalah and reached Jabneel. The boundary ended at the sea.

¹²The western boundary is the coastline of the Mediterranean Sea.

These are the boundaries around the people of Judah by their clans.

¹³In accordance with the LORD's command to him, Joshua gave to Caleb son of Jephunneh a portion in Judah — Kiriath Arba, that is, Hebron. (Arba was the forefather of Anak.) ¹⁴From Hebron Caleb drove out the three Anakites — Sheshai, Ahiman and Talmai, the sons of Anak. ¹⁵From there he marched against the people living in Debir (formerly called Kiriath Sepher). ¹⁶And Caleb said, "I will give my daughter Aksah in marriage to the man who attacks and captures Kiriath Sepher." ¹⁷Othniel son of Kenaz, Caleb's brother, took it; so Caleb gave his daughter Aksah to him in marriage.

Joshua 15:1–12

The Bible records Israel's history.

It's not tough to spot the break in the Bible between the Old and New Testaments. But there are other smaller collections within the 66 books in God's Word. The "historical books" is a label given to the books of Joshua, Judges, Ruth, 1 and 2 Samuel, 1 and 2 Kings, 1 and 2 Chronicles, Ezra, Nehemiah, and Esther. These books focus on the story of Israel from conquering the promised land ... to the rise of great kings like David and Solomon ... to the fall of Israel to foreign armies ... to the rebuilding of Jerusalem and its temple. All of these Old Testament books do more than record human history. They show God's program to build a people that belongs to him (see Exodus 6:7). And they don't just relate dusty ancient facts about who lived where. They are "holy history," showing God at work in your world.

Think: What does the history of Israel have to do with your life today?

ROCK SOLID *truths*

¹⁸One day when she came to Othniel, she urged himᵃ to ask her father for a field. When she got off her donkey, Caleb asked her, "What can I do for you?"

¹⁹She replied, "Do me a special favor. Since you have given me land in the Negev, give me also springs of water." So Caleb gave her the upper and lower springs.

²⁰This is the inheritance of the tribe of Judah, according to its clans:

ᵃ 18 Hebrew and some Septuagint manuscripts; other Septuagint manuscripts (see also note at Judges 1:14) *Othniel, he urged her*

²¹The southernmost towns of the tribe of Judah in the Negev toward the boundary of Edom were:

Kabzeel, Eder, Jagur, ²²Kinah, Dimonah, Adadah, ²³Kedesh, Hazor, Ithnan, ²⁴Ziph, Telem, Bealoth, ²⁵Hazor Hadattah, Kerioth Hezron (that is, Hazor), ²⁶Amam, Shema, Moladah, ²⁷Hazar Gaddah, Heshmon, Beth Pelet, ²⁸Hazar Shual, Beersheba, Biziothiah, ²⁹Baalah, Iyim, Ezem, ³⁰Eltolad, Kesil, Hormah, ³¹Ziklag, Madmannah, Sansannah, ³²Lebaoth, Shilhim, Ain and Rimmon—a total of twenty-nine towns and their villages.

³³In the western foothills:

Eshtaol, Zorah, Ashnah, ³⁴Zanoah, En Gannim, Tappuah, Enam, ³⁵Jarmuth, Adullam, Sokoh, Azekah, ³⁶Shaaraim, Adithaim and Gederah (or Gederothaim)ᵃ—fourteen towns and their villages.

³⁷Zenan, Hadashah, Migdal Gad, ³⁸Dilean, Mizpah, Joktheel, ³⁹Lachish, Bozkath, Eglon, ⁴⁰Kabbon, Lahmas, Kitlish, ⁴¹Gederoth, Beth Dagon, Naamah and Makkedah—sixteen towns and their villages.

⁴²Libnah, Ether, Ashan, ⁴³Iphtah, Ashnah, Nezib, ⁴⁴Keilah, Akzib and Mareshah—nine towns and their villages.

⁴⁵Ekron, with its surrounding settlements and villages; ⁴⁶west of Ekron, all that were in the vicinity of Ashdod, together with their villages; ⁴⁷Ashdod, its surrounding settlements and villages; and Gaza, its settlements and villages, as far as the Wadi of Egypt and the coastline of the Mediterranean Sea.

⁴⁸In the hill country:

Shamir, Jattir, Sokoh, ⁴⁹Dannah, Kiriath Sannah (that is, Debir), ⁵⁰Anab, Eshtemoh, Anim, ⁵¹Goshen, Holon and Giloh—eleven towns and their villages.

⁵²Arab, Dumah, Eshan, ⁵³Janim, Beth Tappuah, Aphekah, ⁵⁴Humtah, Kiriath Arba (that is, Hebron) and Zior—nine towns and their villages.

⁵⁵Maon, Carmel, Ziph, Juttah, ⁵⁶Jezreel, Jokdeam, Zanoah, ⁵⁷Kain, Gibeah and Timnah—ten towns and their villages.

⁵⁸Halhul, Beth Zur, Gedor, ⁵⁹Maarath, Beth Anoth and Eltekon—six towns and their villages.ᵇ

⁶⁰Kiriath Baal (that is, Kiriath Jearim) and Rabbah—two towns and their villages.

⁶¹In the wilderness:

Beth Arabah, Middin, Sekakah, ⁶²Nibshan, the City of Salt and En Gedi—six towns and their villages.

⁶³Judah could not dislodge the Jebusites, who were living in Jerusalem; to this day the Jebusites live there with the people of Judah.

Allotment for Ephraim and Manasseh

16 The allotment for Joseph began at the Jordan, east of the springs of Jericho, and went up from there through the desert into the hill country of Bethel. ²It went on from Bethel (that is, Luz),ᶜ crossed over to the territory of the Arkites in Ataroth, ³descended westward to the territory of the Japhletites as far as the region of Lower Beth Horon and on to Gezer, ending at the Mediterranean Sea.

⁴So Manasseh and Ephraim, the descendants of Joseph, received their inheritance.

⁵This was the territory of Ephraim, according to its clans:

The boundary of their inheritance went from Ataroth Addar in the east to Upper Beth Horon ⁶and continued to the Mediterranean Sea. From Mikmethath on the north it curved eastward to Taanath Shiloh, passing by it to Janoah on the east. ⁷Then it went down from Janoah to

---

ᵃ 36 Or *Gederah and Gederothaim*   ᵇ 59 The Septuagint adds another district of eleven towns, including Tekoa and Ephrathah (Bethlehem).
ᶜ 2 Septuagint; Hebrew *Bethel to Luz*

Ataroth and Naarah, touched Jericho and came out at the Jordan. ⁸From Tappuah the border went west to the Kanah Ravine and ended at the Mediterranean Sea. This was the inheritance of the tribe of the Ephraimites, according to its clans. ⁹It also included all the towns and their villages that were set aside for the Ephraimites within the inheritance of the Manassites.

¹⁰They did not dislodge the Canaanites living in Gezer; to this day the Canaanites live among the people of Ephraim but are required to do forced labor.

17 This was the allotment for the tribe of Manasseh as Joseph's firstborn, that is, for Makir, Manasseh's firstborn. Makir was the ancestor of the Gileadites, who had received Gilead and Bashan because the Makirites were great soldiers. ²So this allotment was for the rest of the people of Manasseh—the clans of Abiezer, Helek, Asriel, Shechem, Hepher and Shemida. These are the other male descendants of Manasseh son of Joseph by their clans.

³Now Zelophehad son of Hepher, the son of Gilead, the son of Makir, the son of Manasseh, had no sons but only daughters, whose names were Mahlah, Noah, Hoglah, Milkah and Tirzah. ⁴They went to Eleazar the priest, Joshua son of Nun, and the leaders and said, "The LORD commanded Moses to give us an inheritance among our relatives." So Joshua gave them an inheritance along with the brothers of their father, according to the LORD's command. ⁵Manasseh's share consisted of ten tracts of land besides Gilead and Bashan east of the Jordan, ⁶because the daughters of the tribe of Manasseh received an inheritance among the sons. The land of Gilead belonged to the rest of the descendants of Manasseh.

⁷The territory of Manasseh extended from Asher to Mikmethath east of Shechem. The boundary ran southward from there to include the people living at En Tappuah. ⁸(Manasseh had the land of Tappuah, but Tappuah itself, on the boundary of Manasseh, belonged to the Ephraimites.) ⁹Then the boundary continued south to the Kanah Ravine. There were towns belonging to Ephraim lying among the towns of Manasseh, but the boundary of Manasseh was the northern side of the ravine and ended at the Mediterranean Sea. ¹⁰On the south the land belonged to Ephraim, on the north to Manasseh. The territory of Manasseh reached the Mediterranean Sea and bordered Asher on the north and Issachar on the east.

¹¹Within Issachar and Asher, Manasseh also had Beth Shan, Ibleam and the people of Dor, Endor, Taanach and Megiddo, together with their surrounding settlements (the third in the list is Naphoth[a]).

¹²Yet the Manassites were not able to occupy these towns, for the Canaanites were determined to live in that region. ¹³However, when the Israelites grew stronger, they subjected the Canaanites to forced labor but did not drive them out completely.

¹⁴The people of Joseph said to Joshua, "Why have you given us only one allotment and one portion for an inheritance? We are a numerous people, and the LORD has blessed us abundantly."

¹⁵"If you are so numerous," Joshua answered, "and if the hill country of Ephraim is too small for you, go up into the forest and clear land for yourselves there in the land of the Perizzites and Rephaites."

¹⁶The people of Joseph replied, "The hill country is not enough for us, and all the Canaanites who live in the plain have chariots fitted with iron, both those in Beth Shan and its settlements and those in the Valley of Jezreel."

¹⁷But Joshua said to the tribes of Joseph—to Ephraim and Manasseh—"You are numerous and very powerful. You will have not only one allotment ¹⁸but the forested hill country as well. Clear it, and its farthest limits will be yours; though the Canaanites have chariots fitted with iron

---

a 11 That is, Naphoth Dor

and though they are strong, you can drive them out."

Division of the Rest of the Land

18 The whole assembly of the Israelites gathered at Shiloh and set up the tent of meeting there. The country was brought under their control, ²but there were still seven Israelite tribes who had not yet received their inheritance.

³ So Joshua said to the Israelites: "How long will you wait before you begin to take possession of the land that the LORD, the God of your ancestors, has given you? ⁴Appoint three men from each tribe. I will send them out to make a survey of the land and to write a description of it, according to the inheritance of each. Then they will return to me. ⁵You are to divide the land into seven parts. Judah is to remain in its territory on the south and the tribes of Joseph in their territory on the north. ⁶After you have written descriptions of the seven

parts of the land, bring them here to me and I will cast lots for you in the presence of the LORD our God. ⁷The Levites, however, do not get a portion among you, because the priestly service of the LORD is their inheritance. And Gad, Reuben and the half-tribe of Manasseh have already received their inheritance on the east side of the Jordan. Moses the servant of the LORD gave it to them."

⁸As the men started on their way to map out the land, Joshua instructed them, "Go and make a survey of the land and write a description of it. Then return to me, and I will cast lots for you here at Shiloh in the presence of the LORD." ⁹So the men left and went through the land. They wrote its description on a scroll, town by town, in seven parts, and returned to Joshua in the camp at Shiloh. ¹⁰Joshua then cast lots for them in Shiloh in the presence of the LORD, and there he distributed the land to the Israelites according to their tribal divisions.

ROCK SOLID principles

Joshua 18:1–10

Do what you know.

Every day after school Ryan walked past a community center that served free suppers each evening. For a long time he didn't even know the center was there. Ryan lived in a middle class suburb of a major city, and no one he knew was going hungry. But a speaker at school said there were hundreds of elderly people and other hidden poor nearby without enough to eat. Ryan thought it might be cool to help out—good for the people, and interesting for him. But something always held him back. Tomorrow seemed like a better time. So he just kept walking. A good thing to do was right in front of him, but he didn't choose to do it.

By the time of Joshua 18, the Israelites had conquered much of the land God had promised them. But they had yet to move in and settle down. So Joshua asked them, "How long will you wait?" (Joshua 18:3). When God gives you a command, he doesn't intend for you to lounge around. He expects you to live up to what you know.

Allotment for Benjamin

¹¹The first lot came up for the tribe of Benjamin according to its clans. Their allotted territory lay between the tribes of Judah and Joseph:

¹²On the north side their boundary began at the Jordan, passed the northern slope of Jericho and headed west into the hill country, coming out at the wilderness of Beth Aven. ¹³From there it crossed to the south slope of Luz (that is, Bethel) and went down to Ataroth Addar on the hill south of Lower Beth Horon.

¹⁴From the hill facing Beth Horon on the south the boundary turned south along the western side and came out at Kiriath Baal (that is, Kiriath Jearim), a town of the people of Judah. This was the western side.

¹⁵The southern side began at the outskirts of Kiriath Jearim on the west, and the boundary came out at the spring of the waters of Nephtoah. ¹⁶The boundary went down to the foot of the hill facing the Valley of Ben Hinnom, north of the Valley of Rephaim. It continued down the Hinnom Valley along the southern slope of the Jebusite city and so to En Rogel. ¹⁷It then curved north, went to En Shemesh, continued to Geliloth, which faces the Pass of Adummim, and ran down to the Stone of Bohan son of Reuben. ¹⁸It continued to the northern slope of Beth Arabah[a] and on down into the Arabah. ¹⁹It then went to the northern slope of Beth Hoglah and came out at the northern bay of the Dead Sea, at the mouth of the Jordan in the south. This was the southern boundary. ²⁰The Jordan formed the boundary on the eastern side.

These were the boundaries that marked out the inheritance of the clans of Benjamin on all sides.

²¹The tribe of Benjamin, according to its clans, had the following towns:

Jericho, Beth Hoglah, Emek Keziz, ²²Beth Arabah, Zemaraim, Bethel, ²³Avvim, Parah, Ophrah, ²⁴Kephar Ammoni, Ophni and Geba—twelve towns and their villages.

²⁵Gibeon, Ramah, Beeroth, ²⁶Mizpah, Kephirah, Mozah, ²⁷Rekem, Irpeel, Taralah, ²⁸Zelah, Haeleph, the Jebusite city (that is, Jerusalem), Gibeah and Kiriath—fourteen towns and their villages.

This was the inheritance of Benjamin for its clans.

Allotment for Simeon

19 The second lot came out for the tribe of Simeon according to its clans. Their inheritance lay within the territory of Judah. ²It included:

Beersheba (or Sheba),[b] Moladah, ³Hazar Shual, Balah, Ezem, ⁴Eltolad, Bethul, Hormah, ⁵Ziklag, Beth Markaboth, Hazar Susah, ⁶Beth Lebaoth and Sharuhen—thirteen towns and their villages;

⁷Ain, Rimmon, Ether and Ashan—four towns and their villages— ⁸and all the villages around these towns as far as Baalath Beer (Ramah in the Negev).

This was the inheritance of the tribe of the Simeonites, according to its clans. ⁹The inheritance of the Simeonites was taken from the share of Judah, because Judah's portion was more than they needed. So the Simeonites received their inheritance within the territory of Judah.

Allotment for Zebulun

¹⁰The third lot came up for Zebulun according to its clans:

The boundary of their inheritance went as far as Sarid. ¹¹Going west it ran to Maralah, touched Dabbesheth, and extended to the ravine near Jokneam. ¹²It turned east from Sarid toward the sunrise to the territory of Kisloth Tabor and went on to Daberath and up to Japhia. ¹³Then

---

a 18 Septuagint; Hebrew *slope facing the Arabah*
b 2 Or *Beersheba, Sheba*; 1 Chron. 4:28 does not have *Sheba*.

it continued eastward to Gath Hepher and Eth Kazin; it came out at Rimmon and turned toward Neah. ¹⁴There the boundary went around on the north to Hannathon and ended at the Valley of Iphtah El. ¹⁵Included were Kattath, Nahalal, Shimron, Idalah and Bethlehem. There were twelve towns and their villages. ¹⁶These towns and their villages were the inheritance of Zebulun, according to its clans.

Allotment for Issachar

¹⁷The fourth lot came out for Issachar according to its clans. ¹⁸Their territory included:

Jezreel, Kesulloth, Shunem, ¹⁹Hapharaim, Shion, Anaharath, ²⁰Rabbith, Kishion, Ebez, ²¹Remeth, En Gannim, En Haddah and Beth Pazzez. ²²The boundary touched Tabor, Shahazumah and Beth Shemesh, and ended at the Jordan. There were sixteen towns and their villages. ²³These towns and their villages were the inheritance of the tribe of Issachar, according to its clans.

Allotment for Asher

²⁴The fifth lot came out for the tribe of Asher according to its clans. ²⁵Their territory included:

Helkath, Hali, Beten, Akshaph, ²⁶Allammelek, Amad and Mishal. On the west the boundary touched Carmel and Shihor Libnath. ²⁷It then turned east toward Beth Dagon, touched Zebulun and the Valley of Iphtah El, and went north to Beth Emek and Neiel, passing Kabul on the left. ²⁸It went to Abdon,^a Rehob, Hammon and Kanah, as far as Greater Sidon. ²⁹The boundary then turned back toward Ramah and went to the fortified city of Tyre, turned toward Hosah and came out at the Mediterranean Sea in the region of Akzib, ³⁰Ummah, Aphek and Rehob. There were twenty-two towns and their villages.

³¹These towns and their villages were the inheritance of the tribe of Asher, according to its clans.

Allotment for Naphtali

³²The sixth lot came out for Naphtali according to its clans:

³³Their boundary went from Heleph and the large tree in Zaanannim, passing Adami Nekeb and Jabneel to Lakkum and ending at the Jordan. ³⁴The boundary ran west through Aznoth Tabor and came out at Hukkok. It touched Zebulun on the south, Asher on the west and the Jordan^b on the east. ³⁵The fortified towns were Ziddim, Zer, Hammath, Rakkath, Kinnereth, ³⁶Adamah, Ramah, Hazor, ³⁷Kedesh, Edrei, En Hazor, ³⁸Iron, Migdal El, Horem, Beth Anath and Beth Shemesh. There were nineteen towns and their villages. ³⁹These towns and their villages were the inheritance of the tribe of Naphtali, according to its clans.

Allotment for Dan

⁴⁰The seventh lot came out for the tribe of Dan according to its clans. ⁴¹The territory of their inheritance included:

Zorah, Eshtaol, Ir Shemesh, ⁴²Shaalabbin, Aijalon, Ithlah, ⁴³Elon, Timnah, Ekron, ⁴⁴Eltekeh, Gibbethon, Baalath, ⁴⁵Jehud, Bene Berak, Gath Rimmon, ⁴⁶Me Jarkon and Rakkon, with the area facing Joppa.

⁴⁷(When the territory of the Danites was lost to them, they went up and attacked Leshem, took it, put it to the sword and occupied it. They settled in Leshem and named it Dan after their ancestor.) ⁴⁸These towns and their villages were the inheritance of the tribe of Dan, according to its clans.

Allotment for Joshua

⁴⁹When they had finished dividing the land into its allotted portions, the Isra-

---

^a 28 Some Hebrew manuscripts (see also 21:30); most Hebrew manuscripts *Ebron*
^b 34 Septuagint; Hebrew *west, and Judah, the Jordan,*

elites gave Joshua son of Nun an inheritance among them, ⁵⁰as the LORD had commanded. They gave him the town he asked for—Timnath Serah^a in the hill country of Ephraim. And he built up the town and settled there.

⁵¹These are the territories that Eleazar the priest, Joshua son of Nun and the heads of the tribal clans of Israel assigned by lot at Shiloh in the presence of the LORD at the entrance to the tent of meeting. And so they finished dividing the land.

Cities of Refuge

20 Then the LORD said to Joshua: ²"Tell the Israelites to designate the cities of refuge, as I instructed you through Moses, ³so that anyone who kills a person accidentally and unintentionally may flee there and find protection from the avenger of blood. ⁴When they flee to one of these cities, they are to stand in the entrance of the city gate and state their case before the elders of that city. Then the elders are to admit the fugitive into their city and provide a place to live among them. ⁵If the avenger of blood comes in pursuit, the elders must not surrender the fugitive, because the fugitive killed their neighbor unintentionally and without malice aforethought. ⁶They are to stay in that city until they have stood trial before the assembly and until the death of the high priest who is serving at that time. Then they may go back to their own home in the town from which they fled."

⁷So they set apart Kedesh in Galilee in the hill country of Naphtali, Shechem in the hill country of Ephraim, and Kiriath Arba (that is, Hebron) in the hill country of Judah. ⁸East of the Jordan (on the other side from Jericho) they designated Bezer in the wilderness on the plateau in the tribe of Reuben, Ramoth in Gilead in the tribe of Gad, and Golan in Bashan in the tribe of Manasseh. ⁹Any of the Israelites or any foreigner residing among them who killed someone accidentally could flee to these designated cities and

not be killed by the avenger of blood prior to standing trial before the assembly.

Towns for the Levites

21 Now the family heads of the Levites approached Eleazar the priest, Joshua son of Nun, and the heads of the other tribal families of Israel ²at Shiloh in Canaan and said to them, "The LORD commanded through Moses that you give us towns to live in, with pasturelands for our livestock." ³So, as the LORD had commanded, the Israelites gave the Levites the following towns and pasturelands out of their own inheritance:

⁴The first lot came out for the Kohathites, according to their clans. The Levites who were descendants of Aaron the priest were allotted thirteen towns from the tribes of Judah, Simeon and Benjamin. ⁵The rest of Kohath's descendants were allotted ten towns from the clans of the tribes of Ephraim, Dan and half of Manasseh.

⁶The descendants of Gershon were allotted thirteen towns from the clans of the tribes of Issachar, Asher, Naphtali and the half-tribe of Manasseh in Bashan.

⁷The descendants of Merari, according to their clans, received twelve towns from the tribes of Reuben, Gad and Zebulun.

⁸So the Israelites allotted to the Levites these towns and their pasturelands, as the LORD had commanded through Moses.

⁹From the tribes of Judah and Simeon they allotted the following towns by name ¹⁰(these towns were assigned to the descendants of Aaron who were from the Kohathite clans of the Levites, because the first lot fell to them):

¹¹They gave them Kiriath Arba (that is, Hebron), with its surrounding pastureland, in the hill country of Judah. (Arba was the forefather of Anak.) ¹²But the fields and villages around the city they had given to Caleb son of Jephunneh as his possession.

^a 50 Also known as *Timnath Heres* (see Judges 2:9)

¹³So to the descendants of Aaron the priest they gave Hebron (a city of refuge for one accused of murder), Libnah, ¹⁴Jattir, Eshtemoa, ¹⁵Holon, Debir, ¹⁶Ain, Juttah and Beth Shemesh, together with their pasturelands—nine towns from these two tribes.

¹⁷And from the tribe of Benjamin they gave them Gibeon, Geba, ¹⁸Anathoth and Almon, together with their pasturelands—four towns.

¹⁹The total number of towns for the priests, the descendants of Aaron, came to thirteen, together with their pasturelands.

²⁰The rest of the Kohathite clans of the Levites were allotted towns from the tribe of Ephraim:

²¹In the hill country of Ephraim they were given Shechem (a city of refuge for one accused of murder) and Gezer, ²²Kibzaim and Beth Horon, together with their pasturelands—four towns.

²³Also from the tribe of Dan they received Eltekeh, Gibbethon, ²⁴Aijalon and Gath Rimmon, together with their pasturelands—four towns.

²⁵From half the tribe of Manasseh they received Taanach and Gath Rimmon, together with their pasturelands—two towns.

²⁶All these ten towns and their pasturelands were given to the rest of the Kohathite clans.

²⁷The Levite clans of the Gershonites were given:

from the half-tribe of Manasseh,
Golan in Bashan (a city of refuge for one accused of murder) and Be Eshterah, together with their pasturelands—two towns;
²⁸from the tribe of Issachar,
Kishion, Daberath, ²⁹Jarmuth and En Gannim, together with their pasturelands—four towns;
³⁰from the tribe of Asher,
Mishal, Abdon, ³¹Helkath and Rehob, together with their pasturelands—four towns;

³²from the tribe of Naphtali,
Kedesh in Galilee (a city of refuge for one accused of murder), Hammoth Dor and Kartan, together with their pasturelands—three towns.
³³The total number of towns of the Gershonite clans came to thirteen, together with their pasturelands.

³⁴The Merarite clans (the rest of the Levites) were given:

from the tribe of Zebulun,
Jokneam, Kartah, ³⁵Dimnah and Nahalal, together with their pasturelands—four towns;
³⁶from the tribe of Reuben,
Bezer, Jahaz, ³⁷Kedemoth and Mephaath, together with their pasturelands—four towns;
³⁸from the tribe of Gad,
Ramoth in Gilead (a city of refuge for one accused of murder), Mahanaim, ³⁹Heshbon and Jazer, together with their pasturelands—four towns in all.

⁴⁰The total number of towns allotted to the Merarite clans, who were the rest of the Levites, came to twelve.

⁴¹The towns of the Levites in the territory held by the Israelites were forty-eight in all, together with their pasturelands. ⁴²Each of these towns had pasturelands surrounding it; this was true for all these towns.

⁴³So the LORD gave Israel all the land he had sworn to give their ancestors, and they took possession of it and settled there. ⁴⁴The LORD gave them rest on every side, just as he had sworn to their ancestors. Not one of their enemies withstood them; the LORD gave all their enemies into their hands. ⁴⁵Not one of all the LORD's good promises to Israel failed; every one was fulfilled.

Eastern Tribes Return Home

22 Then Joshua summoned the Reubenites, the Gadites and the half-tribe of Manasseh ²and said to them, "You have done all that Moses the servant of the LORD command-

ROCK SOLID *plans*

Joshua 21:43–45

Get what God has promised you.

God's people were still slaves in Egypt when they first heard the Lord promise to give them a homeland full of everything they needed to prosper (see Exodus 3:8). Yet that promise didn't take away the need for them to do their part. God wasn't simply going to hand them their new property. So the Israelites did everything God commanded. They went to battle, taking possession of the land the Lord had promised them. The people didn't expect *God* to do what he required *them* to do.

Your next step: Write down one of God's goals for your life—and the actions *you* need to take to get there.

with large herds of livestock, with silver, gold, bronze and iron, and a great quantity of clothing—and divide the plunder from your enemies with your fellow Israelites."

⁹So the Reubenites, the Gadites and the half-tribe of Manasseh left the Israelites at Shiloh in Canaan to return to Gilead, their own land, which they had acquired in accordance with the command of the LORD through Moses.

¹⁰When they came to Geliloth near the Jordan in the land of Canaan, the Reubenites, the Gadites and the half-tribe of Manasseh built an imposing altar there by the Jordan. ¹¹And when the Israelites heard that they had built the altar on the border of Canaan at Geliloth near the Jordan on the Israelite side, ¹²the whole assembly of Israel gathered at Shiloh to go to war against them.

¹³So the Israelites sent Phinehas son of Eleazar, the priest, to the land of Gilead—to Reuben, Gad and the half-tribe of Manasseh. ¹⁴With him they sent ten of the chief men, one from each of the tribes of Israel, each the head of a family division among the Israelite clans.

¹⁵When they went to Gilead—to Reuben, Gad and the half-tribe of Manasseh—they said to them: ¹⁶"The whole assembly of the LORD says: 'How could you break faith with the God of Israel like this? How could you turn away from the LORD and build yourselves an altar in rebellion against him now? ¹⁷Was not the sin of Peor enough for us? Up to this very day we have not cleansed ourselves from that sin, even though a plague fell on the community of the LORD! ¹⁸And are you now turning away from the LORD?

"'If you rebel against the LORD today, tomorrow he will be angry with the whole community of Israel. ¹⁹If the land you possess is defiled, come over to the LORD's land, where the LORD's tabernacle stands, and share the land with us. But do not rebel against the LORD or against us by building an altar for yourselves, other than the altar of the LORD our God. ²⁰When Achan son of Zerah was unfaithful in

ed, and you have obeyed me in everything I commanded. ³For a long time now—to this very day—you have not deserted your fellow Israelites but have carried out the mission the LORD your God gave you. ⁴Now that the LORD your God has given them rest as he promised, return to your homes in the land that Moses the servant of the LORD gave you on the other side of the Jordan. ⁵But be very careful to keep the commandment and the law that Moses the servant of the LORD gave you: to love the LORD your God, to walk in obedience to him, to keep his commands, to hold fast to him and to serve him with all your heart and with all your soul."

⁶Then Joshua blessed them and sent them away, and they went to their homes. ⁷(To the half-tribe of Manasseh Moses had given land in Bashan, and to the other half of the tribe Joshua gave land on the west side of the Jordan along with their fellow Israelites.) When Joshua sent them home, he blessed them, ⁸saying, "Return to your homes with your great wealth—

regard to the devoted things,[a] did not wrath come on the whole community of Israel? He was not the only one who died for his sin.'"

²¹Then Reuben, Gad and the half-tribe of Manasseh replied to the heads of the clans of Israel: ²²"The Mighty One, God, the LORD! The Mighty One, God, the LORD! He knows! And let Israel know! If this has been in rebellion or disobedience to the LORD, do not spare us this day. ²³If we have built our own altar to turn away from the LORD and to offer burnt offerings and grain offerings, or to sacrifice fellowship offerings on it, may the LORD himself call us to account.

²⁴"No! We did it for fear that some day your descendants might say to ours, 'What do you have to do with the LORD, the God of Israel? ²⁵The LORD has made the Jordan a boundary between us and you— you Reubenites and Gadites! You have no share in the LORD.' So your descendants might cause ours to stop fearing the LORD.

²⁶"That is why we said, 'Let us get ready and build an altar—but not for burnt offerings or sacrifices.' ²⁷On the contrary, it is to be a witness between us and you and the generations that follow, that we will worship the LORD at his sanctuary with our burnt offerings, sacrifices and fellowship offerings. Then in the future your descendants will not be able to say to ours, 'You have no share in the LORD.'

²⁸"And we said, 'If they ever say this to us, or to our descendants, we will answer: Look at the replica of the LORD's altar, which our ancestors built, not for burnt offerings and sacrifices, but as a witness between us and you.'

²⁹"Far be it from us to rebel against the LORD and turn away from him today by building an altar for burnt offerings, grain offerings and sacrifices, other than the altar of the LORD our God that stands before his tabernacle."

³⁰When Phinehas the priest and the leaders of the community—the heads of the clans of the Israelites—heard what Reuben, Gad and Manasseh had to say, they were pleased. ³¹And Phinehas son of Eleazar, the priest, said to Reuben, Gad and Manasseh, "Today we know that the LORD is with us, because you have not been unfaithful to the LORD in this matter. Now you have rescued the Israelites from the LORD's hand."

³²Then Phinehas son of Eleazar, the priest, and the leaders returned to Canaan from their meeting with the Reubenites and Gadites in Gilead and reported to the Israelites. ³³They were glad to hear the report and praised God. And they talked no more about going to war against them to devastate the country where the Reubenites and the Gadites lived.

³⁴And the Reubenites and the Gadites gave the altar this name: A Witness Between Us—that the LORD is God.

Joshua's Farewell to the Leaders

23 After a long time had passed and the LORD had given Israel rest from all their enemies around them, Joshua, by then a very old man, ²summoned all Israel—their elders, leaders, judges and officials—and said to them: "I am very old. ³You yourselves have seen everything the LORD your God has done to all these nations for your sake; it was the LORD your God who fought for you. ⁴Remember how I have allotted as an inheritance for your tribes all the land of the nations that remain—the nations I conquered—between the Jordan and the Mediterranean Sea in the west. ⁵The LORD your God himself will push them out for your sake. He will drive them out before you, and you will take possession of their land, as the LORD your God promised you.

⁶"Be very strong; be careful to obey all that is written in the Book of the Law of Moses, without turning aside to the right or to the left. ⁷Do not associate with these nations that remain among you; do not invoke the names of their gods or swear by them. You must not serve them or bow down to them. ⁸But you are to hold fast

---

[a] 20 The Hebrew term refers to the irrevocable giving over of things or persons to the LORD, often by totally destroying them.

to the Lord your God, as you have until now.

⁹"The Lord has driven out before you great and powerful nations; to this day no one has been able to withstand you. ¹⁰One of you routs a thousand, because the Lord your God fights for you, just as he promised. ¹¹So be very careful to love the Lord your God.

¹²"But if you turn away and ally yourselves with the survivors of these nations that remain among you and if you intermarry with them and associate with them, ¹³then you may be sure that the Lord your God will no longer drive out these nations before you. Instead, they will become snares and traps for you, whips on your backs and thorns in your eyes, until you perish from this good land, which the Lord your God has given you.

¹⁴"Now I am about to go the way of all the earth. You know with all your heart and soul that not one of all the good promises the Lord your God gave you has failed. Every promise has been fulfilled; not one has failed. ¹⁵But just as

---

ROCK SOLID promises

"Not one of all the good promises the Lord your God gave you has failed."   Joshua 23:14

God proves his care for you by keeping his promises. Every one of them. Always. For the rest of your life.

---

all the good things the Lord your God has promised you have come to you, so he will bring on you all the evil things he has threatened, until the Lord your God has destroyed you from this good land he has given you. ¹⁶If you violate the covenant of the Lord your God, which he

commanded you, and go and serve other gods and bow down to them, the Lord's anger will burn against you, and you will quickly perish from the good land he has given you."

The Covenant Renewed at Shechem

24 Then Joshua assembled all the tribes of Israel at Shechem. He summoned the elders, leaders, judges and officials of Israel, and they presented themselves before God.

²Joshua said to all the people, "This is what the Lord, the God of Israel, says: 'Long ago your ancestors, including Terah the father of Abraham and Nahor, lived beyond the Euphrates River and worshiped other gods. ³But I took your father Abraham from the land beyond the Euphrates and led him throughout Canaan and gave him many descendants. I gave him Isaac, ⁴and to Isaac I gave Jacob and Esau. I assigned the hill country of Seir to Esau, but Jacob and his family went down to Egypt.

⁵"'Then I sent Moses and Aaron, and I afflicted the Egyptians by what I did there, and I brought you out. ⁶When I brought your people out of Egypt, you came to the sea, and the Egyptians pursued them with chariots and horsemen[a] as far as the Red Sea.[b] ⁷But they cried to the Lord for help, and he put darkness between you and the Egyptians; he brought the sea over them and covered them. You saw with your own eyes what I did to the Egyptians. Then you lived in the wilderness for a long time.

⁸"'I brought you to the land of the Amorites who lived east of the Jordan. They fought against you, but I gave them into your hands. I destroyed them from before you, and you took possession of their land. ⁹When Balak son of Zippor, the king of Moab, prepared to fight against Israel, he sent for Balaam son of Beor to put a curse on you. ¹⁰But I would not listen to Balaam, so he blessed you again and again, and I delivered you out of his hand.

---

a 6 Or charioteers   *b 6 Or the Sea of Reeds*

11 "Then you crossed the Jordan and came to Jericho. The citizens of Jericho fought against you, as did also the Amorites, Perizzites, Canaanites, Hittites, Girgashites, Hivites and Jebusites, but I gave them into your hands. 12 I sent the hornet ahead of you, which drove them out before you—also the two Amorite kings. You did not do it with your own sword and bow. 13 So I gave you a land on which you did not toil and cities you did not build; and you live in them and eat from vineyards and olive groves that you did not plant.'

14 "Now fear the LORD and serve him with all faithfulness. Throw away the gods your ancestors worshiped beyond the Euphrates River and in Egypt, and serve the LORD. 15 But if serving the LORD seems undesirable to you, then choose for yourselves this day whom you will serve, whether the gods your ancestors served beyond the Euphrates, or the gods of the Amorites, in whose land you are living. But as for me and my household, we will serve the LORD."

16 Then the people answered, "Far be it from us to forsake the LORD to serve other gods! 17 It was the LORD our God himself who brought us and our parents up out of Egypt, from that land of slavery, and performed those great signs before our eyes. He protected us on our entire journey and among all the nations through which we traveled. 18 And the LORD drove out before us all the nations, including the Amorites, who lived in the land. We too will serve the LORD, because he is our God."

19 Joshua said to the people, "You are not able to serve the LORD. He is a holy God; he is a jealous God. He will not forgive your rebellion and your sins. 20 If you forsake the LORD and serve foreign gods, he will turn and bring disaster on you and make an end of you, after he has been good to you."

ROCK SOLID principles

Joshua 24:14–27

Choose to follow God today.

"The easiest thing in the world is to get pumped up about God when you're on a retreat," Sara's youth pastor explained. "We're away from our normal routine, and we've made time to get to know God and each other. We're away from the temptations we face at home. So here's the big choice. You need to make a decision—a real decision—to keep living for God when you get home. You need to make it today, and keep making it every minute back in your real world. Because if you can't or won't or don't make the choice right now when it's easy, you'll never make it when life gets hard."

Joshua didn't believe the Israelites when they said they would follow God. The Lord had rescued them from slavery in Egypt with his miraculous power. He gave them an amazing land to call home. But Joshua knew people would be tempted to follow false gods. So he challenged them to make a choice to follow God totally ... today ... and to never turn back (see Joshua 24:15).

²¹But the people said to Joshua, "No! We will serve the LORD."

²²Then Joshua said, "You are witnesses against yourselves that you have chosen to serve the LORD."

"Yes, we are witnesses," they replied.

²³"Now then," said Joshua, "throw away the foreign gods that are among you and yield your hearts to the LORD, the God of Israel."

²⁴And the people said to Joshua, "We will serve the LORD our God and obey him."

²⁵On that day Joshua made a covenant for the people, and there at Shechem he reaffirmed for them decrees and laws. ²⁶And Joshua recorded these things in the Book of the Law of God. Then he took a large stone and set it up there under the oak near the holy place of the LORD.

²⁷"See!" he said to all the people. "This stone will be a witness against us. It has heard all the words the LORD has said to us. It will be a witness against you if you are untrue to your God."

²⁸Then Joshua dismissed the people, each to their own inheritance.

Buried in the Promised Land

²⁹After these things, Joshua son of Nun, the servant of the LORD, died at the age of a hundred and ten. ³⁰And they buried him in the land of his inheritance, at Timnath Serah^a in the hill country of Ephraim, north of Mount Gaash.

³¹Israel served the LORD throughout the lifetime of Joshua and of the elders who outlived him and who had experienced everything the LORD had done for Israel.

³²And Joseph's bones, which the Israelites had brought up from Egypt, were buried at Shechem in the tract of land that Jacob bought for a hundred pieces of silver^b from the sons of Hamor, the father of Shechem. This became the inheritance of Joseph's descendants.

³³And Eleazar son of Aaron died and was buried at Gibeah, which had been allotted to his son Phinehas in the hill country of Ephraim.

^a 30 Also known as *Timnath Heres* (see Judges 2:9)   ^b 32 Hebrew *hundred kesitahs*; a kesitah was a unit of money of unknown weight and value.

JUDGES

BOOK OUTLINE

**Conditions during the time
of the judges**
(1:1 — 3:6)

**Conquering nations and
ruling judges**
(3:7 — 16:31)

Idolatry and civil war
(17:1 — 21:35)

The book of Judges tells the stories of Israel's history for the years between the death of Joshua and the ministry of Samuel. This time period was known for its heroes—called judges— who ruled the tribes of Israel. A total of fifteen judges are listed for their leadership. The best-known judges are Deborah, Gideon and Samson.

The events in Judges followed a certain pattern:

1. The Israelites lived in peace while serving and loving God.
2. The Israelites forgot God and worshiped idols.
3. God punished his people by sending a neighboring nation to fight and rule over them.
4. The Israelites turned to God and asked for forgiveness.
5. God forgave his people and saved them by sending a judge to help conquer their enemy.

This pattern of events repeated itself over and over during this time in Israel's history.

Israel Fights the Remaining Canaanites

After the death of Joshua, the Israelites asked the LORD, "Who of us is to go up first to fight against the Canaanites?"

²The LORD answered, "Judah shall go up; I have given the land into their hands."

³The men of Judah then said to the Simeonites their fellow Israelites, "Come up with us into the territory allotted to us, to fight against the Canaanites. We in turn will go with you into yours." So the Simeonites went with them.

⁴When Judah attacked, the LORD gave the Canaanites and Perizzites into their hands, and they struck down ten thousand men at Bezek. ⁵It was there that they found Adoni-Bezek and fought against him, putting to rout the Canaanites and Perizzites. ⁶Adoni-Bezek fled, but they chased him and caught him, and cut off his thumbs and big toes.

⁷Then Adoni-Bezek said, "Seventy kings with their thumbs and big toes cut off have picked up scraps under my table. Now God has paid me back for what I did to them." They brought him to Jerusalem, and he died there.

⁸The men of Judah attacked Jerusalem also and took it. They put the city to the sword and set it on fire.

⁹After that, Judah went down to fight against the Canaanites living in the hill country, the Negev and the western foothills. ¹⁰They advanced against the Canaanites living in Hebron (formerly called Kiriath Arba) and defeated Sheshai, Ahiman and Talmai. ¹¹From there they advanced against the people living in Debir (formerly called Kiriath Sepher).

¹²And Caleb said, "I will give my daughter Aksah in marriage to the man who attacks and captures Kiriath Sepher." ¹³Othniel son of Kenaz, Caleb's younger brother, took it; so Caleb gave his daughter Aksah to him in marriage.

¹⁴One day when she came to Othniel, she urged him[a] to ask her father for a field. When she got off her donkey, Caleb asked her, "What can I do for you?"

¹⁵She replied, "Do me a special favor. Since you have given me land in the Negev, give me also springs of water." So Caleb gave her the upper and lower springs.

¹⁶The descendants of Moses' father-in-law, the Kenite, went up from the City of Palms[b] with the people of Judah to live among the inhabitants of the Desert of Judah in the Negev near Arad.

¹⁷Then the men of Judah went with the Simeonites their fellow Israelites and attacked the Canaanites living in Zephath, and they totally destroyed[c] the city. Therefore it was called Hormah.[d] ¹⁸Judah also took[e] Gaza, Ashkelon and Ekron—each city with its territory.

¹⁹The LORD was with the men of Judah. They took possession of the hill country, but they were unable to drive the people from the plains, because they had chariots fitted with iron. ²⁰As Moses had promised, Hebron was given to Caleb, who drove from it the three sons of Anak. ²¹The Benjamites, however, did not drive out the Jebusites, who were living in Jerusalem; to this day the Jebusites live there with the Benjamites.

²²Now the tribes of Joseph attacked Bethel, and the LORD was with them. ²³When they sent men to spy out Bethel (formerly called Luz), ²⁴the spies saw a man coming out of the city and they said to him, "Show us how to get into the city and we will see that you are treated well." ²⁵So he showed them, and they put the city to the sword but spared the man and his whole family. ²⁶He then went to the land of the Hittites, where he built a city and called it Luz, which is its name to this day.

²⁷But Manasseh did not drive out the people of Beth Shan or Taanach or Dor or Ibleam or Megiddo and their surrounding settlements, for the Canaanites were determined to live in that land. ²⁸When Israel became strong, they pressed the Canaanites into forced labor but never drove them

---

[a] 14 Hebrew; Septuagint and Vulgate *Othniel, he urged her*   [b] 16 That is, Jericho

[c] 17 The Hebrew term refers to the irrevocable giving over of things or persons to the LORD, often by totally destroying them.

[d] 17 *Hormah* means *destruction*.

[e] 18 Hebrew; Septuagint *Judah did not take*

out completely. ²⁹Nor did Ephraim drive out the Canaanites living in Gezer, but the Canaanites continued to live there among them. ³⁰Neither did Zebulun drive out the Canaanites living in Kitron or Nahalol, so these Canaanites lived among them, but Zebulun did subject them to forced labor. ³¹Nor did Asher drive out those living in Akko or Sidon or Ahlab or Akzib or Helbah or Aphek or Rehob. ³²The Asherites lived among the Canaanite inhabitants of the land because they did not drive them out. ³³Neither did Naphtali drive out those living in Beth Shemesh or Beth Anath; but the Naphtalites too lived among the Canaanite inhabitants of the land, and those living in Beth Shemesh and Beth Anath became forced laborers for them. ³⁴The Amorites confined the Danites to the hill country, not allowing them to come down into the plain. ³⁵And the Amorites were determined also to hold out in Mount Heres, Aijalon and Shaalbim, but when the power of the tribes of Joseph increased, they too were pressed into forced labor. ³⁶The boundary of the Amorites was from Scorpion Pass to Sela and beyond.

The Angel of the LORD at Bokim

2 The angel of the LORD went up from Gilgal to Bokim and said, "I brought you up out of Egypt and led you into the land I swore to give to your ancestors. I said, 'I will never break my covenant with you, ²and you shall not make a covenant with the people of this land, but you shall break down their altars.' Yet you have disobeyed me. Why have you done this? ³And I have also said, 'I will not drive them out before you; they will become traps for you, and their gods will become snares to you.'"

⁴When the angel of the LORD had spoken these things to all the Israelites, the people wept aloud, ⁵and they called that place Bokim.ᵃ There they offered sacrifices to the LORD.

Disobedience and Defeat

⁶After Joshua had dismissed the Israelites, they went to take possession of the land, each to their own inheritance. ⁷The people served the LORD throughout the lifetime of Joshua and of the elders who outlived him and who had seen all the great things the LORD had done for Israel.

⁸Joshua son of Nun, the servant of the LORD, died at the age of a hundred and ten. ⁹And they buried him in the land of his inheritance, at Timnath Heresᵇ in the hill country of Ephraim, north of Mount Gaash.

¹⁰After that whole generation had been gathered to their ancestors, another generation grew up who knew neither the LORD nor what he had done for Israel. ¹¹Then the Israelites did evil in the eyes of the LORD and served the Baals. ¹²They forsook the LORD, the God of their ancestors, who had brought them out of Egypt. They followed and worshiped various gods of the peoples around them. They aroused the LORD's anger ¹³because they forsook him and served Baal and the Ashtoreths. ¹⁴In his anger against Israel the LORD gave them into the hands of raiders who plundered them. He sold them into the hands of their enemies all around, whom they were no longer able to resist. ¹⁵Whenever Israel went out to fight, the hand of the LORD was against them to defeat them, just as he had sworn to them. They were in great distress.

¹⁶Then the LORD raised up judges,ᶜ who saved them out of the hands of these raiders. ¹⁷Yet they would not listen to their judges but prostituted themselves to other gods and worshiped them. They quickly turned from the ways of their ancestors, who had been obedient to the LORD's commands. ¹⁸Whenever the LORD raised up a judge for them, he was with the judge and saved them out of the hands of their enemies as long as the judge lived; for the LORD relented because of their groaning under those who oppressed and afflicted them. ¹⁹But when the judge died, the people returned to ways even more corrupt than those of their ancestors, following

---

ᵃ 5 Bokim means weepers.   ᵇ 9 Also known as Timnath Serah (see Joshua 19:50 and 24:30)
ᶜ 16 Or leaders; similarly in verses 17-19

other gods and serving and worshiping them. They refused to give up their evil practices and stubborn ways.

²⁰Therefore the LORD was very angry with Israel and said, "Because this nation has violated the covenant I ordained for their ancestors and has not listened to me, ²¹I will no longer drive out before them any of the nations Joshua left when he died. ²²I will use them to test Israel and see whether they will keep the way of the LORD and walk in it as their ancestors did." ²³The LORD had allowed those nations to remain; he did not drive them out at once by giving them into the hands of Joshua.

3 These are the nations the LORD left to test all those Israelites who had not experienced any of the wars in Canaan ²(he did this only to teach warfare to the descendants of the Israelites who had not had previous battle experience): ³the five rulers of the Philistines, all the Canaanites, the Sidonians, and the Hivites living in the Lebanon mountains from Mount Baal Hermon to Lebo Hamath. ⁴They were left to test the Israelites to see whether they would obey the LORD's commands, which he had given their ancestors through Moses.

⁵The Israelites lived among the Canaanites, Hittites, Amorites, Perizzites, Hivites and Jebusites. ⁶They took their daughters in marriage and gave their own daughters to their sons, and served their gods.

Othniel

⁷The Israelites did evil in the eyes of the LORD; they forgot the LORD their God and served the Baals and the Asherahs. ⁸The anger of the LORD burned against Israel so that he sold them into the hands of Cushan-Rishathaim king of Aram Naharaim,^a to whom the Israelites were subject for eight years. ⁹But when they cried

^a 8 That is, Northwest Mesopotamia

ROCK SOLID principles

Judges 2:6–23

Make faith your own.

Every Sunday morning when Rachel was small her mom pulled her out of bed and nudged her toward the shower. By the time Rachel was dressed, the kitchen table was spread with a breakfast of everything she liked. Mom and Rachel both enjoyed the drive to church—it was their time to talk. And as Rachel grew up, her mom decided to explain why she went to so much work to make Sunday special. "I want you to see that this time is about God," she started. "I want you to know he loves you even more than I do. And I want you to follow Jesus for yourself—because you want to, not because I make you."

Joshua and the Israelites who marched into the promised land had seen God's powerful acts on their behalf. But when that generation died, "another generation grew up who knew neither the LORD nor what he had done for Israel" (Judges 2:10). The next generation did evil because they lived off their parents' religion. They never made that faith their own.

out to the Lord, he raised up for them a deliverer, Othniel son of Kenaz, Caleb's younger brother, who saved them. [10] The Spirit of the Lord came on him, so that he became Israel's judge[a] and went to war. The Lord gave Cushan-Rishathaim king of Aram into the hands of Othniel, who overpowered him. [11] So the land had peace for forty years, until Othniel son of Kenaz died.

Ehud

[12] Again the Israelites did evil in the eyes of the Lord, and because they did this evil the Lord gave Eglon king of Moab power over Israel. [13] Getting the Ammonites and Amalekites to join him, Eglon came and attacked Israel, and they took possession of the City of Palms.[b] [14] The Israelites were subject to Eglon king of Moab for eighteen years.

[15] Again the Israelites cried out to the Lord, and he gave them a deliverer—Ehud, a left-handed man, the son of Gera the Benjamite. The Israelites sent him with tribute to Eglon king of Moab. [16] Now Ehud had made a double-edged sword about a cubit[c] long, which he strapped to his right thigh under his clothing. [17] He presented the tribute to Eglon king of Moab, who was a very fat man. [18] After Ehud had presented the tribute, he sent on their way those who had carried it. [19] But on reaching the stone images near Gilgal he himself went back to Eglon and said, "Your Majesty, I have a secret message for you."

The king said to his attendants, "Leave us!" And they all left.

[20] Ehud then approached him while he was sitting alone in the upper room of his palace[d] and said, "I have a message from God for you." As the king rose from his seat, [21] Ehud reached with his left hand, drew the sword from his right thigh and plunged it into the king's belly. [22] Even the handle sank in after the blade, and his bowels discharged. Ehud did not pull the sword out, and the fat closed in over it. [23] Then Ehud went out to the porch[e]; he shut the doors of the upper room behind him and locked them.

[24] After he had gone, the servants came and found the doors of the upper room locked. They said, "He must be relieving himself in the inner room of the palace." [25] They waited to the point of embarrass-

---

[a] 10 Or *leader*   [b] 13 That is, Jericho
[c] 16 That is, about 18 inches or about 45 centimeters   [d] 20 The meaning of the Hebrew for this word is uncertain; also in verse 24.   [e] 23 The meaning of the Hebrew for this word is uncertain.

Judges 3:1–31

God isn't bloodthirsty.

You might be unfamiliar with the Bible story about the king who died by the sword—a guy so large that his belly fat swallowed the handle of the blade (see Judges 3:21–22). Or the account of an army commander killed by a stake pounded through his head (see Judges 4:21). You might read these scenes and get the impression that God is all about blood and gore. But the violence the Israelites inflicted on others was payback for sin. God had condemned the inhabitants of the promised land more than 400 years before, and when the Israelites conquered the land they executed the Lord's judgment on sinful people (Genesis 14:14–16). The Lord had given the Canaanites centuries to repent, but they ignored his patient mercy and continued their habits of child sacrifice, adultery, incest, homosexuality, and bestiality (see Leviticus 18). God isn't driven by an urge to violence, but he does put a stop to sin.

Think: Is your image of God one that includes anger and violence? Why—or why not?

ROCK SOLID truths

ment, but when he did not open the doors of the room, they took a key and unlocked them. There they saw their lord fallen to the floor, dead.

²⁶While they waited, Ehud got away. He passed by the stone images and escaped to Seirah. ²⁷When he arrived there, he blew a trumpet in the hill country of Ephraim, and the Israelites went down with him from the hills, with him leading them.

²⁸"Follow me," he ordered, "for the LORD has given Moab, your enemy, into your hands." So they followed him down and took possession of the fords of the Jordan that led to Moab; they allowed no one to cross over. ²⁹At that time they struck down about ten thousand Moabites, all vigorous and strong; not one escaped. ³⁰That day Moab was made subject to Israel, and the land had peace for eighty years.

Shamgar

³¹After Ehud came Shamgar son of Anath, who struck down six hundred Philistines with an oxgoad. He too saved Israel.

Deborah

4 Again the Israelites did evil in the eyes of the LORD, now that Ehud was dead. ²So the LORD sold them into the hands of Jabin king of Canaan, who reigned in Hazor. Sisera, the commander of his army, was based in Harosheth Haggoyim. ³Because he had nine hundred chariots fitted with iron and had cruelly oppressed the Israelites for twenty years, they cried to the LORD for help.

⁴Now Deborah, a prophet, the wife of Lappidoth, was leading*a* Israel at that time. ⁵She held court under the Palm of Deborah between Ramah and Bethel in the hill country of Ephraim, and the Israelites went up to her to have their disputes decided. ⁶She sent for Barak son of Abinoam from Kedesh in Naphtali and said to him, "The LORD, the God of Israel, commands you: 'Go, take with you ten thousand men of Naphtali and Zebulun and lead them up to Mount Tabor. ⁷I

will lead Sisera, the commander of Jabin's army, with his chariots and his troops to the Kishon River and give him into your hands.'"

⁸Barak said to her, "If you go with me, I will go; but if you don't go with me, I won't go."

⁹"Certainly I will go with you," said Deborah. "But because of the course you are taking, the honor will not be yours, for the LORD will deliver Sisera into the hands of a woman." So Deborah went with Barak to Kedesh. ¹⁰There Barak summoned Zebulun and Naphtali, and ten thousand men went up under his command. Deborah also went up with him.

¹¹Now Heber the Kenite had left the other Kenites, the descendants of Hobab, Moses' brother-in-law,*b* and pitched his tent by the great tree in Zaanannim near Kedesh.

¹²When they told Sisera that Barak son of Abinoam had gone up to Mount Tabor, ¹³Sisera summoned from Harosheth Haggoyim to the Kishon River all his men and his nine hundred chariots fitted with iron.

¹⁴Then Deborah said to Barak, "Go! This is the day the LORD has given Sisera into your hands. Has not the LORD gone ahead of you?" So Barak went down Mount Tabor, with ten thousand men following him. ¹⁵At Barak's advance, the LORD routed Sisera and all his chariots and army by the sword, and Sisera got down from his chariot and fled on foot.

¹⁶Barak pursued the chariots and army as far as Harosheth Haggoyim, and all Sisera's troops fell by the sword; not a man was left. ¹⁷Sisera, meanwhile, fled on foot to the tent of Jael, the wife of Heber the Kenite, because there was an alliance between Jabin king of Hazor and the family of Heber the Kenite.

¹⁸Jael went out to meet Sisera and said to him, "Come, my lord, come right in. Don't be afraid." So he entered her tent, and she covered him with a blanket.

¹⁹"I'm thirsty," he said. "Please give me some water." She opened a skin of milk, gave him a drink, and covered him up.

a 4 Traditionally judging   *b 11 Or father-in-law*

20"Stand in the doorway of the tent," he told her. "If someone comes by and asks you, 'Is anyone in there?' say 'No.'"

21But Jael, Heber's wife, picked up a tent peg and a hammer and went quietly to him while he lay fast asleep, exhausted. She drove the peg through his temple into the ground, and he died.

22Just then Barak came by in pursuit of Sisera, and Jael went out to meet him. "Come," she said, "I will show you the man you're looking for." So he went in with her, and there lay Sisera with the tent peg through his temple—dead.

23On that day God subdued Jabin king of Canaan before the Israelites. 24And the hand of the Israelites pressed harder and harder against Jabin king of Canaan until they destroyed him.

The Song of Deborah

5 On that day Deborah and Barak son of Abinoam sang this song:

2"When the princes in Israel take the lead,
    when the people willingly offer themselves—
    praise the LORD!

3"Hear this, you kings! Listen, you rulers!

Judges 4:1–23

Deborah exercised leadership.

No one told Deborah she should stay home and keep out of trouble. And that's a good thing.

Deborah was well known for giving wise rulings while sitting under "the Palm of Deborah" (Judges 4:5). One day the Lord spoke to her. He said that Barak, an Israelite man, should call together 10,000 Israelite warriors and head to Mount Tabor. God would lure in the armies of a Canaanite king, Jabin, and hand them over to Israel. Barak refused because he was frightened of the commander of Jabin's army, Sisera, a man who had employed his 900 chariots to torment the Israelites for 20 years. Barak finally agreed to go to war, but only if Deborah went with him. The prophetess said yes, but she noted that credit for the victory would go not to Barak but to herself, a woman.

Deborah and Barak mustered 10,000 fighting men from the tribes of Naphtali and Zebulun and made their way to Mount Tabor. When Barak and the Israelites charged, they destroyed the entire enemy army. Sisera alone lived to flee, but when he stopped to rest, a woman named Jael pounded a tent stake through his head. Credit for this significant military victory went not just to one woman but to two.

Deborah listened to God. She obeyed his word when few people followed the Lord. And of all the judges remembered in the Bible, she gets more praise than any other. This "mother of Israel" celebrated her victory in the "Song of Deborah," an early example of Hebrew poetry (Judges 5:1–31).

You can find Deborah in Judges 4 and 5.

UNSHAKEN people

I, even I, will sing to^a the Lord;
  I will praise the Lord, the God of
    Israel, in song.

⁴"When you, Lord, went out from
    Seir,
  when you marched from the land of
    Edom,
the earth shook, the heavens poured,
  the clouds poured down water.
⁵The mountains quaked before the
    Lord, the One of Sinai,
  before the Lord, the God of Israel.

⁶"In the days of Shamgar son of Anath,
  in the days of Jael, the highways
    were abandoned;
  travelers took to winding paths.
⁷Villagers in Israel would not fight;
  they held back until I, Deborah,
    arose,
  until I arose, a mother in Israel.
⁸God chose new leaders
  when war came to the city gates,
but not a shield or spear was seen
  among forty thousand in Israel.
⁹My heart is with Israel's princes,
  with the willing volunteers among
    the people.
  Praise the Lord!

¹⁰"You who ride on white donkeys,
  sitting on your saddle blankets,
  and you who walk along the road,
consider ¹¹the voice of the singers^b at
  the watering places.
  They recite the victories of the
    Lord,
  the victories of his villagers in Israel.

"Then the people of the Lord
  went down to the city gates.
¹²'Wake up, wake up, Deborah!
  Wake up, wake up, break out in
    song!
  Arise, Barak!
  Take captive your captives, son of
    Abinoam.'
¹³"The remnant of the nobles came
    down;
  the people of the Lord came down
    to me against the mighty.

¹⁴Some came from Ephraim, whose
    roots were in Amalek;
  Benjamin was with the people who
    followed you.
  From Makir captains came down,
  from Zebulun those who bear a
    commander's^b staff.
¹⁵The princes of Issachar were with
    Deborah;
  yes, Issachar was with Barak,
  sent under his command into the
    valley.
In the districts of Reuben
  there was much searching of heart.
¹⁶Why did you stay among the sheep
    pens^c
  to hear the whistling for the flocks?
In the districts of Reuben
  there was much searching of heart.
¹⁷Gilead stayed beyond the Jordan.
  And Dan, why did he linger by the
    ships?
Asher remained on the coast
  and stayed in his coves.
¹⁸The people of Zebulun risked their
    very lives;
  so did Naphtali on the terraced
    fields.

¹⁹"Kings came, they fought,
  the kings of Canaan fought.
At Taanach, by the waters of Megiddo,
  they took no plunder of silver.
²⁰From the heavens the stars fought,
  from their courses they fought
    against Sisera.
²¹The river Kishon swept them away,
  the age-old river, the river Kishon.
  March on, my soul; be strong!
²²Then thundered the horses' hooves —
  galloping, galloping go his mighty
    steeds.
²³'Curse Meroz,' said the angel of the
    Lord.
  'Curse its people bitterly,
  because they did not come to help the
    Lord,
  to help the Lord against the
    mighty.'

---

^a 3 Or of   ^b 11,14 The meaning of the
Hebrew for this word is uncertain.
^c 16 Or the campfires; or the saddlebags

²⁴"Most blessed of women be Jael,
    the wife of Heber the Kenite,
    most blessed of tent-dwelling
    women.
²⁵He asked for water, and she gave him
    milk;
    in a bowl fit for nobles she brought
    him curdled milk.
²⁶Her hand reached for the tent peg,
    her right hand for the workman's
    hammer.
She struck Sisera, she crushed his
    head,
    she shattered and pierced his temple.
²⁷At her feet he sank,
    he fell; there he lay.
At her feet he sank, he fell;
    where he sank, there he fell—dead.

²⁸"Through the window peered Sisera's
    mother;
    behind the lattice she cried out,
'Why is his chariot so long in coming?
    Why is the clatter of his chariots
    delayed?'
²⁹The wisest of her ladies answer her;
    indeed, she keeps saying to herself,
³⁰'Are they not finding and dividing the
    spoils:
    a woman or two for each man,
colorful garments as plunder for
    Sisera,
    colorful garments embroidered,
highly embroidered garments for my
    neck—
    all this as plunder?'

³¹"So may all your enemies perish,
    LORD!
But may all who love you be like the
    sun
    when it rises in its strength."

Then the land had peace forty years.

Gideon

6 The Israelites did evil in the eyes of the LORD, and for seven years he gave them into the hands of the Midianites. ²Because the power of Midian was so oppressive, the Israelites prepared shelters for themselves in mountain clefts, caves and strongholds. ³Whenever the Israelites planted their crops, the Midianites, Amalekites and other eastern peoples invaded the country. ⁴They camped on the land and ruined the crops all the way to Gaza and did not spare a living thing for Israel, neither sheep nor cattle nor donkeys. ⁵They came up with their livestock and their tents like swarms of locusts. It was impossible to count them or their camels; they invaded the land to ravage it. ⁶Midian so impoverished the Israelites that they cried out to the LORD for help.

⁷When the Israelites cried out to the LORD because of Midian, ⁸he sent them a prophet, who said, "This is what the LORD, the God of Israel, says: I brought you up out of Egypt, out of the land of slavery. ⁹I rescued you from the hand of the Egyptians. And I delivered you from the hand of all your oppressors; I drove them out before you and gave you their land. ¹⁰I said to you, 'I am the LORD your God; do not worship the gods of the Amorites, in whose land you live.' But you have not listened to me."

¹¹The angel of the LORD came and sat down under the oak in Ophrah that belonged to Joash the Abiezrite, where his son Gideon was threshing wheat in a winepress to keep it from the Midianites. ¹²When the angel of the LORD appeared to Gideon, he said, "The LORD is with you, mighty warrior."

ROCK SOLID promises

"May all who love you be like the sun when it rises in its strength."
Judges 5:31

If you love God, your life will shine with the scorching heat of a desert sun.

[13]"Pardon me, my lord," Gideon replied, "but if the LORD is with us, why has all this happened to us? Where are all his wonders that our ancestors told us about when they said, 'Did not the LORD bring us up out of Egypt?' But now the LORD has abandoned us and given us into the hand of Midian."

[14]The LORD turned to him and said, "Go in the strength you have and save Israel out of Midian's hand. Am I not sending you?"

[15]"Pardon me, my lord," Gideon replied, "but how can I save Israel? My clan is the weakest in Manasseh, and I am the least in my family."

[16]The LORD answered, "I will be with you, and you will strike down all the Midianites, leaving none alive."

[17]Gideon replied, "If now I have found favor in your eyes, give me a sign that it is really you talking to me. [18]Please do not go away until I come back and bring my offering and set it before you."

And the LORD said, "I will wait until you return."

[19]Gideon went inside, prepared a young goat, and from an ephah[a] of flour he made bread without yeast. Putting the meat in a basket and its broth in a pot, he brought them out and offered them to him under the oak.

[20]The angel of God said to him, "Take the meat and the unleavened bread, place them on this rock, and pour out the broth." And Gideon did so. [21]Then the angel of the LORD touched the meat and the unleavened bread with the tip of the staff that was in his hand. Fire flared from the rock, consuming the meat and the bread. And the angel of the LORD disappeared. [22]When Gideon realized that it was the angel of the LORD, he exclaimed, "Alas, Sovereign LORD! I have seen the angel of the LORD face to face!"

[23]But the LORD said to him, "Peace! Do not be afraid. You are not going to die."

[24]So Gideon built an altar to the LORD there and called it The LORD Is Peace. To this day it stands in Ophrah of the Abiezrites.

[25]That same night the LORD said to him, "Take the second bull from your father's herd, the one seven years old.[b] Tear down your father's altar to Baal and cut down the Asherah pole[c] beside it. [26]Then build a proper kind of[d] altar to the LORD your God on the top of this height. Using the wood of the Asherah pole that you cut down, offer the second[e] bull as a burnt offering."

[27]So Gideon took ten of his servants and did as the LORD told him. But because he was afraid of his family and the townspeople, he did it at night rather than in the daytime.

[28]In the morning when the people of the town got up, there was Baal's altar, demolished, with the Asherah pole beside it cut down and the second bull sacrificed on the newly built altar!

[29]They asked each other, "Who did this?"

When they carefully investigated, they were told, "Gideon son of Joash did it."

[30]The people of the town demanded of Joash, "Bring out your son. He must die, because he has broken down Baal's altar and cut down the Asherah pole beside it."

[31]But Joash replied to the hostile crowd around him, "Are you going to plead Baal's cause? Are you trying to save him? Whoever fights for him shall be put to death by morning! If Baal really is a god, he can defend himself when someone breaks down his altar." [32]So because Gideon broke down Baal's altar, they gave him the name Jerub-Baal[f] that day, saying, "Let Baal contend with him."

[33]Now all the Midianites, Amalekites and other eastern peoples joined forces and crossed over the Jordan and camped in the Valley of Jezreel. [34]Then the Spirit of the LORD came on Gideon, and he blew a trumpet, summoning the Abiezrites to follow him. [35]He sent messengers throughout Manasseh, calling them to arms, and also

[a] 19 That is, probably about 36 pounds or about 16 kilograms   [b] 25 Or Take a full-grown, mature bull from your father's herd   [c] 25 That is, a wooden symbol of the goddess Asherah; also in verses 26, 28 and 30   [d] 26 Or build with layers of stone an   [e] 26 Or full-grown; also in verse 28   [f] 32 Jerub-Baal probably means let Baal contend.

into Asher, Zebulun and Naphtali, so that they too went up to meet them.

³⁶ Gideon said to God, "If you will save Israel by my hand as you have promised— ³⁷ look, I will place a wool fleece on the threshing floor. If there is dew only on the fleece and all the ground is dry, then I will know that you will save Israel by my hand, as you said." ³⁸ And that is what happened. Gideon rose early the next day; he squeezed the fleece and wrung out the dew—a bowlful of water.

³⁹ Then Gideon said to God, "Do not be angry with me. Let me make just one more request. Allow me one more test with the fleece, but this time make the fleece dry and let the ground be covered with dew." ⁴⁰ That night God did so. Only the fleece was dry; all the ground was covered with dew.

Gideon Defeats the Midianites

7 Early in the morning, Jerub-Baal (that is, Gideon) and all his men camped at the spring of Harod. The camp of Midian was north of them in the valley near the hill of Moreh. ² The Lord said to Gideon, "You have too many men. I cannot deliver Midian into their hands, or Israel would boast against me, 'My own strength has saved me.' ³ Now announce to the army, 'Anyone who trembles with fear may turn back and leave Mount Gilead.'" So twenty-two thousand men left, while ten thousand remained.

⁴ But the Lord said to Gideon, "There are still too many men. Take them down to the water, and I will thin them out for you there. If I say, 'This one shall go with you,' he shall go; but if I say, 'This one shall not go with you,' he shall not go."

⁵ So Gideon took the men down to the water. There the Lord told him, "Separate those who lap the water with their tongues as a dog laps from those who kneel down to drink." ⁶ Three hundred of them drank from cupped hands, lapping like dogs. All the rest got down on their knees to drink.

⁷ The Lord said to Gideon, "With the three hundred men that lapped I will save you and give the Midianites into your

hands. Let all the others go home." ⁸ So Gideon sent the rest of the Israelites home but kept the three hundred, who took over the provisions and trumpets of the others.

Now the camp of Midian lay below him in the valley. ⁹ During that night the Lord said to Gideon, "Get up, go down against the camp, because I am going to give it into your hands. ¹⁰ If you are afraid to attack, go down to the camp with your servant Purah ¹¹ and listen to what they are saying. Afterward, you will be encouraged to attack the camp." So he and Purah his servant went down to the outposts of the camp. ¹² The Midianites, the Amalekites and all the other eastern peoples had settled in the valley, thick as locusts. Their camels could no more be counted than the sand on the seashore.

¹³ Gideon arrived just as a man was telling a friend his dream. "I had a dream," he was saying. "A round loaf of barley bread came tumbling into the Midianite camp. It struck the tent with such force that the tent overturned and collapsed."

¹⁴ His friend responded, "This can be nothing other than the sword of Gideon son of Joash, the Israelite. God has given the Midianites and the whole camp into his hands."

¹⁵ When Gideon heard the dream and its interpretation, he bowed down and worshiped. He returned to the camp of Israel and called out, "Get up! The Lord has given the Midianite camp into your hands." ¹⁶ Dividing the three hundred men into three companies, he placed trumpets and empty jars in the hands of all of them, with torches inside.

¹⁷ "Watch me," he told them. "Follow my lead. When I get to the edge of the camp, do exactly as I do. ¹⁸ When I and all who are with me blow our trumpets, then from all around the camp blow yours and shout, 'For the Lord and for Gideon.'"

¹⁹ Gideon and the hundred men with him reached the edge of the camp at the beginning of the middle watch, just after they had changed the guard. They blew their trumpets and broke the jars that were in their hands. ²⁰ The three compa-

nies blew the trumpets and smashed the jars. Grasping the torches in their left hands and holding in their right hands the trumpets they were to blow, they shouted, "A sword for the LORD and for Gideon!" ²¹While each man held his position around the camp, all the Midianites ran, crying out as they fled.

²²When the three hundred trumpets sounded, the LORD caused the men throughout the camp to turn on each other with their swords. The army fled to Beth Shittah toward Zererah as far as the border of Abel Meholah near Tabbath. ²³Israelites from Naphtali, Asher and all Manasseh were called out, and they pursued the Midianites. ²⁴Gideon sent messengers throughout the hill country of Ephraim, saying, "Come down against the Midianites and seize the waters of the Jordan ahead of them as far as Beth Barah."

So all the men of Ephraim were called out and they seized the waters of the Jordan as far as Beth Barah. ²⁵They also captured two of the Midianite leaders, Oreb and Zeeb. They killed Oreb at the rock of Oreb, and Zeeb at the winepress of Zeeb. They pursued the Midianites and brought the heads of Oreb and Zeeb to Gideon, who was by the Jordan.

Judges 7:1–25

Gideon got God's strength.

Gideon was threshing wheat in a winepress, hiding it from his Midianite enemies, a distant clan that descended onto the land on camels to steal from the Israelites. That's when the "angel of the LORD" came and sat under an oak tree and spoke to Gideon. This was God himself, and he greeted Gideon enthusiastically. "The LORD is with you, mighty warrior," he said (Judges 6:12).

Gideon wasn't so thrilled. If God were with him, he wondered, why did he need to hide from his enemies? When the Lord promised to give Gideon strength to fend off the attackers, Gideon protested. "My Lord," he asked, "How can I save Israel? My clan is the weakest in Manasseh, and I am the least in my family" (Judges 6:15). The Lord promised to go with Gideon, empowering him to strike down the Midianites. God even gave Gideon a sign, torching a rock where he had placed meat and bread.

Gideon believed God. After gathering a few servants and tearing down his father's backyard altar to the false god Baal (see Judges 6:25–32), he called for men to fight the Midianites—and 32,000 showed up. God said such a large crowd would take credit for defeating the Midianites. He eventually sent Gideon into battle with only 300 men on his side.

The large Midianite force was defeated so soundly that the nation never again harassed Israel (see Judges 8:28). And Gideon stopped worrying about feeling weak. God himself was all the strength he needed.

You can find Gideon in Judges 6:1—8:32 and Hebrews 11:32.

UNSHAKEN *people*

Zebah and Zalmunna

8 Now the Ephraimites asked Gideon, "Why have you treated us like this? Why didn't you call us when you went to fight Midian?" And they challenged him vigorously.

² But he answered them, "What have I accomplished compared to you? Aren't the gleanings of Ephraim's grapes better than the full grape harvest of Abiezer? ³ God gave Oreb and Zeeb, the Midianite leaders, into your hands. What was I able to do compared to you?" At this, their resentment against him subsided.

⁴ Gideon and his three hundred men, exhausted yet keeping up the pursuit, came to the Jordan and crossed it. ⁵ He said to the men of Sukkoth, "Give my troops some bread; they are worn out, and I am still pursuing Zebah and Zalmunna, the kings of Midian."

⁶ But the officials of Sukkoth said, "Do you already have the hands of Zebah and Zalmunna in your possession? Why should we give bread to your troops?"

⁷ Then Gideon replied, "Just for that, when the LORD has given Zebah and Zalmunna into my hand, I will tear your flesh with desert thorns and briers."

⁸ From there he went up to Peniel*a* and made the same request of them, but they answered as the men of Sukkoth had. ⁹ So he said to the men of Peniel, "When I return in triumph, I will tear down this tower."

¹⁰ Now Zebah and Zalmunna were in Karkor with a force of about fifteen thousand men, all that were left of the armies of the eastern peoples; a hundred and twenty thousand swordsmen had fallen. ¹¹ Gideon went up by the route of the nomads east of Nobah and Jogbehah and attacked the unsuspecting army. ¹² Zebah and Zalmunna, the two kings of Midian, fled, but he pursued them and captured them, routing their entire army.

¹³ Gideon son of Joash then returned from the battle by the Pass of Heres. ¹⁴ He caught a young man of Sukkoth and questioned him, and the young man wrote down for him the names of the seventy-seven officials of Sukkoth, the elders of the town. ¹⁵ Then Gideon came and said to the men of Sukkoth, "Here are Zebah and Zalmunna, about whom you taunted me by saying, 'Do you already have the hands of Zebah and Zalmunna in your possession? Why should we give bread to your exhausted men?'" ¹⁶ He took the elders of the town and taught the men of Sukkoth a lesson by punishing them with desert thorns and briers. ¹⁷ He also pulled down the tower of Peniel and killed the men of the town.

¹⁸ Then he asked Zebah and Zalmunna, "What kind of men did you kill at Tabor?"

"Men like you," they answered, "each one with the bearing of a prince."

¹⁹ Gideon replied, "Those were my brothers, the sons of my own mother. As surely as the LORD lives, if you had spared their lives, I would not kill you." ²⁰ Turning to Jether, his oldest son, he said, "Kill them!" But Jether did not draw his sword, because he was only a boy and was afraid.

²¹ Zebah and Zalmunna said, "Come, do it yourself. 'As is the man, so is his strength.'" So Gideon stepped forward and killed them, and took the ornaments off their camels' necks.

Gideon's Ephod

²² The Israelites said to Gideon, "Rule over us—you, your son and your grandson—because you have saved us from the hand of Midian."

²³ But Gideon told them, "I will not rule over you, nor will my son rule over you. The LORD will rule over you." ²⁴ And he said, "I do have one request, that each of you give me an earring from your share of the plunder." (It was the custom of the Ishmaelites to wear gold earrings.)

²⁵ They answered, "We'll be glad to give them." So they spread out a garment, and each of them threw a ring from his plunder onto it. ²⁶ The weight of the gold rings he asked for came to seventeen hundred shekels,*b* not counting the ornaments, the pendants and the purple garments worn by the kings of Midian or the chains that were

a 8 Hebrew *Penuel*, a variant of *Peniel*; also in verses 9 and 17   *b* 26 That is, about 43 pounds or about 20 kilograms

ROCK SOLID
promises

"The LORD will rule over you."

Judges 8:23

No human being can ever be your ultimate boss. God is your one real master, now and forever.

---

on their camels' necks. ²⁷Gideon made the gold into an ephod, which he placed in Ophrah, his town. All Israel prostituted themselves by worshiping it there, and it became a snare to Gideon and his family.

Gideon's Death

²⁸Thus Midian was subdued before the Israelites and did not raise its head again. During Gideon's lifetime, the land had peace forty years.

²⁹Jerub-Baal son of Joash went back home to live. ³⁰He had seventy sons of his own, for he had many wives. ³¹His concubine, who lived in Shechem, also bore him a son, whom he named Abimelek. ³²Gideon son of Joash died at a good old age and was buried in the tomb of his father Joash in Ophrah of the Abiezrites.

³³No sooner had Gideon died than the Israelites again prostituted themselves to the Baals. They set up Baal-Berith as their god ³⁴and did not remember the LORD their God, who had rescued them from the hands of all their enemies on every side. ³⁵They also failed to show any loyalty to the family of Jerub-Baal (that is, Gideon) in spite of all the good things he had done for them.

Abimelek

9 Abimelek son of Jerub-Baal went to his mother's brothers in Shechem and said to them and to all his mother's clan, ²"Ask all the citizens

of Shechem, 'Which is better for you: to have all seventy of Jerub-Baal's sons rule over you, or just one man?' Remember, I am your flesh and blood."

³When the brothers repeated all this to the citizens of Shechem, they were inclined to follow Abimelek, for they said, "He is related to us." ⁴They gave him seventy shekels*a* of silver from the temple of Baal-Berith, and Abimelek used it to hire reckless scoundrels, who became his followers. ⁵He went to his father's home in Ophrah and on one stone murdered his seventy brothers, the sons of Jerub-Baal. But Jotham, the youngest son of Jerub-Baal, escaped by hiding. ⁶Then all the citizens of Shechem and Beth Millo gathered beside the great tree at the pillar in Shechem to crown Abimelek king.

⁷When Jotham was told about this, he climbed up on the top of Mount Gerizim and shouted to them, "Listen to me, citizens of Shechem, so that God may listen to you. ⁸One day the trees went out to anoint a king for themselves. They said to the olive tree, 'Be our king.'

⁹"But the olive tree answered, 'Should I give up my oil, by which both gods and humans are honored, to hold sway over the trees?'

¹⁰"Next, the trees said to the fig tree, 'Come and be our king.'

¹¹"But the fig tree replied, 'Should I give up my fruit, so good and sweet, to hold sway over the trees?'

¹²"Then the trees said to the vine, 'Come and be our king.'

¹³"But the vine answered, 'Should I give up my wine, which cheers both gods and humans, to hold sway over the trees?'

¹⁴"Finally all the trees said to the thornbush, 'Come and be our king.'

¹⁵"The thornbush said to the trees, 'If you really want to anoint me king over you, come and take refuge in my shade; but if not, then let fire come out of the thornbush and consume the cedars of Lebanon!'

¹⁶"Have you acted honorably and in good faith by making Abimelek king?

a 4 That is, about 1 3/4 pounds or about 800 grams

Have you been fair to Jerub-Baal and his family? Have you treated him as he deserves? [17] Remember that my father fought for you and risked his life to rescue you from the hand of Midian. [18] But today you have revolted against my father's family. You have murdered his seventy sons on a single stone and have made Abimelek, the son of his female slave, king over the citizens of Shechem because he is related to you. [19] So have you acted honorably and in good faith toward Jerub-Baal and his family today? If you have, may Abimelek be your joy, and may you be his, too! [20] But if you have not, let fire come out from Abimelek and consume you, the citizens of Shechem and Beth Millo, and let fire come out from you, the citizens of Shechem and Beth Millo, and consume Abimelek!"

[21] Then Jotham fled, escaping to Beer, and he lived there because he was afraid of his brother Abimelek.

[22] After Abimelek had governed Israel three years, [23] God stirred up animosity between Abimelek and the citizens of Shechem so that they acted treacherously against Abimelek. [24] God did this in order that the crime against Jerub-Baal's seventy sons, the shedding of their blood, might be avenged on their brother Abimelek and on the citizens of Shechem, who had helped him murder his brothers. [25] In opposition to him these citizens of Shechem set men on the hilltops to ambush and rob everyone who passed by, and this was reported to Abimelek.

[26] Now Gaal son of Ebed moved with his clan into Shechem, and its citizens put their confidence in him. [27] After they had gone out into the fields and gathered the grapes and trodden them, they held a festival in the temple of their god. While they were eating and drinking, they cursed Abimelek. [28] Then Gaal son of Ebed said, "Who is Abimelek, and why should we Shechemites be subject to him? Isn't he Jerub-Baal's son, and isn't Zebul his deputy? Serve the family of Hamor, Shechem's father! Why should we serve Abimelek? [29] If only this people were under my command! Then I would get rid of

him. I would say to Abimelek, 'Call out your whole army!'" [a]

[30] When Zebul the governor of the city heard what Gaal son of Ebed said, he was very angry. [31] Under cover he sent messengers to Abimelek, saying, "Gaal son of Ebed and his clan have come to Shechem and are stirring up the city against you. [32] Now then, during the night you and your men should come and lie in wait in the fields. [33] In the morning at sunrise, advance against the city. When Gaal and his men come out against you, seize the opportunity to attack them."

[34] So Abimelek and all his troops set out by night and took up concealed positions near Shechem in four companies. [35] Now Gaal son of Ebed had gone out and was standing at the entrance of the city gate just as Abimelek and his troops came out from their hiding place.

[36] When Gaal saw them, he said to Zebul, "Look, people are coming down from the tops of the mountains!"

Zebul replied, "You mistake the shadows of the mountains for men."

[37] But Gaal spoke up again: "Look, people are coming down from the central hill, [b] and a company is coming from the direction of the diviners' tree."

[38] Then Zebul said to him, "Where is your big talk now, you who said, 'Who is Abimelek that we should be subject to him?' Aren't these the men you ridiculed? Go out and fight them!"

[39] So Gaal led out [c] the citizens of Shechem and fought Abimelek. [40] Abimelek chased him all the way to the entrance of the gate, and many were killed as they fled. [41] Then Abimelek stayed in Arumah, and Zebul drove Gaal and his clan out of Shechem.

[42] The next day the people of Shechem went out to the fields, and this was reported to Abimelek. [43] So he took his men, divided them into three companies and set an ambush in the fields. When he saw the peo-

---

a 29 Septuagint; Hebrew *him." Then he said to Abimelek, "Call out your whole army!"*   *b 37* The Hebrew for this phrase means *the navel of the earth.*   *c 39* Or *Gaal went out in the sight of* ple coming out of the city, he rose to attack them. ⁴⁴Abimelek and the companies with him rushed forward to a position at the entrance of the city gate. Then two companies attacked those in the fields and struck them down. ⁴⁵All that day Abimelek pressed his attack against the city until he had captured it and killed its people. Then he destroyed the city and scattered salt over it.

⁴⁶On hearing this, the citizens in the tower of Shechem went into the stronghold of the temple of El-Berith. ⁴⁷When Abimelek heard that they had assembled there, ⁴⁸he and all his men went up Mount Zalmon. He took an ax and cut off some branches, which he lifted to his shoulders. He ordered the men with him, "Quick! Do what you have seen me do!" ⁴⁹So all the men cut branches and followed Abimelek. They piled them against the stronghold and set it on fire with the people still inside. So all the people in the tower of Shechem, about a thousand men and women, also died.

⁵⁰Next Abimelek went to Thebez and besieged it and captured it. ⁵¹Inside the city, however, was a strong tower, to which all the men and women—all the people of the city—had fled. They had locked themselves in and climbed up on the tower roof. ⁵²Abimelek went to the tower and attacked it. But as he approached the entrance to the tower to set it on fire, ⁵³a woman dropped an upper millstone on his head and cracked his skull.

⁵⁴Hurriedly he called to his armor-bearer, "Draw your sword and kill me, so that they can't say, 'A woman killed him.'" So his servant ran him through, and he died. ⁵⁵When the Israelites saw that Abimelek was dead, they went home.

⁵⁶Thus God repaid the wickedness that Abimelek had done to his father by murdering his seventy brothers. ⁵⁷God also made the people of Shechem pay for all their wickedness. The curse of Jotham son of Jerub-Baal came on them.

Tola

10 After the time of Abimelek, a man of Issachar named Tola son of Puah, the son of Dodo, rose to save Israel. He lived in Shamir, in

the hill country of Ephraim. ²He led[a] Israel twenty-three years; then he died, and was buried in Shamir.

Jair

³He was followed by Jair of Gilead, who led Israel twenty-two years. ⁴He had thirty sons, who rode thirty donkeys. They controlled thirty towns in Gilead, which to this day are called Havvoth Jair.[b] ⁵When Jair died, he was buried in Kamon.

Jephthah

⁶Again the Israelites did evil in the eyes of the LORD. They served the Baals and the Ashtoreths, and the gods of Aram, the gods of Sidon, the gods of Moab, the gods of the Ammonites and the gods of the Philistines. And because the Israelites forsook the LORD and no longer served him, ⁷he became angry with them. He sold them into the hands of the Philistines and the Ammonites, ⁸who that year shattered and crushed them. For eighteen years they oppressed all the Israelites on the east side of the Jordan in Gilead, the land of the Amorites. ⁹The Ammonites also crossed the Jordan to fight against Judah, Benjamin and Ephraim; Israel was in great distress. ¹⁰Then the Israelites cried out to the LORD, "We have sinned against you, forsaking our God and serving the Baals."

¹¹The LORD replied, "When the Egyptians, the Amorites, the Ammonites, the Philistines, ¹²the Sidonians, the Amalekites and the Maonites[c] oppressed you and you cried to me for help, did I not save you from their hands? ¹³But you have forsaken me and served other gods, so I will no longer save you. ¹⁴Go and cry out to the gods you have chosen. Let them save you when you are in trouble!"

¹⁵But the Israelites said to the LORD, "We have sinned. Do with us whatever you think best, but please rescue us now." ¹⁶Then they got rid of the foreign gods

[a] 2 Traditionally *judged*; also in verse 3
[b] 4 Or *called the settlements of Jair*
[c] 12 Hebrew; some Septuagint manuscripts *Midianites*

among them and served the Lord. And he could bear Israel's misery no longer.

¹⁷When the Ammonites were called to arms and camped in Gilead, the Israelites assembled and camped at Mizpah. ¹⁸The leaders of the people of Gilead said to each other, "Whoever will take the lead in attacking the Ammonites will be head over all who live in Gilead."

11 Jephthah the Gileadite was a mighty warrior. His father was Gilead; his mother was a prostitute. ²Gilead's wife also bore him sons, and when they were grown up, they drove Jephthah away. "You are not going to get any inheritance in our family," they said, "because you are the son of another woman." ³So Jephthah fled from his brothers and settled in the land of Tob, where a gang of scoundrels gathered around him and followed him.

⁴Some time later, when the Ammonites were fighting against Israel, ⁵the elders of Gilead went to get Jephthah from the land of Tob. ⁶"Come," they said, "be our commander, so we can fight the Ammonites."

⁷Jephthah said to them, "Didn't you hate me and drive me from my father's house? Why do you come to me now, when you're in trouble?"

⁸The elders of Gilead said to him, "Nevertheless, we are turning to you now; come with us to fight the Ammonites, and you will be head over all of us who live in Gilead."

⁹Jephthah answered, "Suppose you take me back to fight the Ammonites and the Lord gives them to me—will I really be your head?"

¹⁰The elders of Gilead replied, "The Lord is our witness; we will certainly do as you say." ¹¹So Jephthah went with the elders of Gilead, and the people made him head and commander over them. And he repeated all his words before the Lord in Mizpah.

¹²Then Jephthah sent messengers to the Ammonite king with the question: "What do you have against me that you have attacked my country?"

¹³The king of the Ammonites answered Jephthah's messengers, "When Israel came up out of Egypt, they took away my land from the Arnon to the Jabbok, all the way to the Jordan. Now give it back peaceably."

¹⁴Jephthah sent back messengers to the Ammonite king, ¹⁵saying:

"This is what Jephthah says: Israel did not take the land of Moab or the land of the Ammonites. ¹⁶But when they came up out of Egypt, Israel went through the wilderness to the Red Sea[a] and on to Kadesh. ¹⁷Then Israel sent messengers to the king of Edom, saying, 'Give us permission to go through your country,' but the king of Edom would not listen. They sent also to the king of Moab, and he refused. So Israel stayed at Kadesh.

¹⁸"Next they traveled through the wilderness, skirted the lands of Edom and Moab, passed along the eastern side of the country of Moab, and camped on the other side of the Arnon. They did not enter the territory of Moab, for the Arnon was its border.

¹⁹"Then Israel sent messengers to Sihon king of the Amorites, who ruled in Heshbon, and said to him, 'Let us pass through your country to our own place.' ²⁰Sihon, however, did not trust Israel[b] to pass through his territory. He mustered all his troops and encamped at Jahaz and fought with Israel.

²¹"Then the Lord, the God of Israel, gave Sihon and his whole army into Israel's hands, and they defeated them. Israel took over all the land of the Amorites who lived in that country, ²²capturing all of it from the Arnon to the Jabbok and from the desert to the Jordan.

²³"Now since the Lord, the God of Israel, has driven the Amorites out before his people Israel, what right have you to take it over? ²⁴Will you

---

a 16 Or *the Sea of Reeds*   *b 20* Or *however, would not make an agreement for Israel* not take what your god Chemosh gives you? Likewise, whatever the LORD our God has given us, we will possess. ²⁵Are you any better than Balak son of Zippor, king of Moab? Did he ever quarrel with Israel or fight with them? ²⁶For three hundred years Israel occupied Heshbon, Aroer, the surrounding settlements and all the towns along the Arnon. Why didn't you retake them during that time? ²⁷I have not wronged you, but you are doing me wrong by waging war against me. Let the LORD, the Judge, decide the dispute this day between the Israelites and the Ammonites."

²⁸The king of Ammon, however, paid no attention to the message Jephthah sent him.

²⁹Then the Spirit of the LORD came on Jephthah. He crossed Gilead and Manasseh, passed through Mizpah of Gilead, and from there he advanced against the Ammonites. ³⁰And Jephthah made a vow to the LORD: "If you give the Ammonites into my hands, ³¹whatever comes out of the door of my house to meet me when I return in triumph from the Ammonites will be the LORD's, and I will sacrifice it as a burnt offering."

³²Then Jephthah went over to fight the Ammonites, and the LORD gave them into his hands. ³³He devastated twenty towns from Aroer to the vicinity of Minnith, as far as Abel Keramim. Thus Israel subdued Ammon.

³⁴When Jephthah returned to his home in Mizpah, who should come out to meet him but his daughter, dancing to the sound of timbrels! She was an only child. Except for her he had neither son nor daughter. ³⁵When he saw her, he tore his clothes and cried, "Oh no, my daughter! You have brought me down and I am devastated. I have made a vow to the LORD that I cannot break."

³⁶"My father," she replied, "you have given your word to the LORD. Do to me just as you promised, now that the LORD has avenged you of your enemies, the Ammonites. ³⁷But grant me this one request," she said. "Give me two months to roam the hills and weep with my friends, because I will never marry."

³⁸"You may go," he said. And he let her go for two months. She and her friends went into the hills and wept because she would never marry. ³⁹After the two months, she returned to her father, and he did to her as he had vowed. And she was a virgin.

From this comes the Israelite tradition ⁴⁰that each year the young women of Israel go out for four days to commemorate the daughter of Jephthah the Gileadite.

Jephthah and Ephraim

12 The Ephraimite forces were called out, and they crossed over to Zaphon. They said to Jephthah, "Why did you go to fight the Ammonites without calling us to go with you? We're going to burn down your house over your head."

²Jephthah answered, "I and my people were engaged in a great struggle with the Ammonites, and although I called, you didn't save me out of their hands. ³When I saw that you wouldn't help, I took my life in my hands and crossed over to fight the Ammonites, and the LORD gave me the victory over them. Now why have you come up today to fight me?"

⁴Jephthah then called together the men of Gilead and fought against Ephraim. The Gileadites struck them down because the Ephraimites had said, "You Gileadites are renegades from Ephraim and Manasseh." ⁵The Gileadites captured the fords of the Jordan leading to Ephraim, and whenever a survivor of Ephraim said, "Let me cross over," the men of Gilead asked him, "Are you an Ephraimite?" If he replied, "No," ⁶they said, "All right, say 'Shibboleth.'" If he said, "Sibboleth," because he could not pronounce the word correctly, they seized him and killed him at the fords of the Jordan. Forty-two thousand Ephraimites were killed at that time.

⁷Jephthah led^a Israel six years. Then

^a 7 Traditionally *judged*; also in verses 8-14

Jephthah the Gileadite died and was buried in a town in Gilead.

Ibzan, Elon and Abdon

⁸ After him, Ibzan of Bethlehem led Israel. ⁹ He had thirty sons and thirty daughters. He gave his daughters away in marriage to those outside his clan, and for his sons he brought in thirty young women as wives from outside his clan. Ibzan led Israel seven years. ¹⁰ Then Ibzan died and was buried in Bethlehem.

¹¹ After him, Elon the Zebulunite led Israel ten years. ¹² Then Elon died and was buried in Aijalon in the land of Zebulun.

¹³ After him, Abdon son of Hillel, from Pirathon, led Israel. ¹⁴ He had forty sons and thirty grandsons, who rode on seventy donkeys. He led Israel eight years. ¹⁵ Then Abdon son of Hillel died and was buried at Pirathon in Ephraim, in the hill country of the Amalekites.

The Birth of Samson

13 Again the Israelites did evil in the eyes of the LORD, so the LORD delivered them into the hands of the Philistines for forty years.

² A certain man of Zorah, named Manoah, from the clan of the Danites, had a wife who was childless, unable to give birth. ³ The angel of the LORD appeared to her and said, "You are barren and childless, but you are going to become pregnant and give birth to a son. ⁴ Now see to it that you drink no wine or other fermented drink and that you do not eat anything unclean. ⁵ You will become pregnant and have a son whose head is never to be touched by a razor because the boy is to be a Nazirite, dedicated to God from the womb. He will take the lead in delivering Israel from the hands of the Philistines."

⁶ Then the woman went to her husband and told him, "A man of God came to me. He looked like an angel of God, very awesome. I didn't ask him where he came from, and he didn't tell me his name. ⁷ But he said to me, 'You will become pregnant and have a son. Now then, drink no wine or other fermented drink and do not eat anything unclean, because the boy will be a Nazirite of God from the womb until the day of his death.'"

⁸ Then Manoah prayed to the LORD: "Pardon your servant, Lord. I beg you to let the man of God you sent to us come again to teach us how to bring up the boy who is to be born."

⁹ God heard Manoah, and the angel of God came again to the woman while she was out in the field; but her husband Manoah was not with her. ¹⁰ The woman hurried to tell her husband, "He's here! The man who appeared to me the other day!"

¹¹ Manoah got up and followed his wife. When he came to the man, he said, "Are you the man who talked to my wife?"

"I am," he said.

¹² So Manoah asked him, "When your words are fulfilled, what is to be the rule that governs the boy's life and work?"

¹³ The angel of the LORD answered, "Your wife must do all that I have told her. ¹⁴ She must not eat anything that comes from the grapevine, nor drink any wine or other fermented drink nor eat anything unclean. She must do everything I have commanded her."

¹⁵ Manoah said to the angel of the LORD, "We would like you to stay until we prepare a young goat for you."

¹⁶ The angel of the LORD replied, "Even though you detain me, I will not eat any of your food. But if you prepare a burnt offering, offer it to the LORD." (Manoah did not realize that it was the angel of the LORD.)

¹⁷ Then Manoah inquired of the angel of the LORD, "What is your name, so that we may honor you when your word comes true?"

¹⁸ He replied, "Why do you ask my name? It is beyond understanding.*" ¹⁹ Then Manoah took a young goat, together with the grain offering, and sacrificed it on a rock to the LORD. And the LORD did an amazing thing while Manoah and his wife watched: ²⁰ As the flame blazed up from the altar toward heaven, the angel of the LORD ascended in the flame. Seeing this, Manoah and his wife fell with their faces to the

---

a 18 Or is wonderful

ROCK SOLID *plans*

Judges 13:1–24

Live up to your potential.

Even before Samson was born, God chose him to rescue Israel from its brutal enemies, the Philistines. Samson's mother dedicated her boy to God as a Nazirite—a special vow of purity—and she begged the Lord for wisdom to raise him right (see Judges 13:8). God gave Samson superhuman strength, but Samson wasted his energies chasing ungodly women, and he let his enemies overpower him. Although Samson came back to God at the end of his life (see Judges 16:28), he never became the hero God had planned.

Your next step: Think about what you are doing—or not doing—that makes you less than what God has planned for you. How can you change this?

ground. ²¹When the angel of the LORD did not show himself again to Manoah and his wife, Manoah realized that it was the angel of the LORD.

²²"We are doomed to die!" he said to his wife. "We have seen God!"

²³But his wife answered, "If the LORD had meant to kill us, he would not have accepted a burnt offering and grain offering from our hands, nor shown us all these things or now told us this."

²⁴The woman gave birth to a boy and named him Samson. He grew and the LORD blessed him, ²⁵and the Spirit of the LORD began to stir him while he was in Mahaneh Dan, between Zorah and Eshtaol.

Samson's Marriage

14 Samson went down to Timnah and saw there a young Philistine woman. ²When he returned, he said to his father and mother, "I have seen a Philistine woman in Timnah; now get her for me as my wife."

³His father and mother replied, "Isn't there an acceptable woman among your relatives or among all our people? Must you go to the uncircumcised Philistines to get a wife?"

But Samson said to his father, "Get her for me. She's the right one for me." ⁴(His parents did not know that this was from the LORD, who was seeking an occasion to confront the Philistines; for at that time they were ruling over Israel.)

⁵Samson went down to Timnah together with his father and mother. As they approached the vineyards of Timnah, suddenly a young lion came roaring toward him. ⁶The Spirit of the LORD came powerfully upon him so that he tore the lion apart with his bare hands as he might have torn a young goat. But he told neither his father nor his mother what he had done. ⁷Then he went down and talked with the woman, and he liked her.

⁸Some time later, when he went back to marry her, he turned aside to look at the lion's carcass, and in it he saw a swarm of bees and some honey. ⁹He scooped out the honey with his hands and ate as he went along. When he rejoined his parents, he gave them some, and they too ate it. But he did not tell them that he had taken the honey from the lion's carcass.

¹⁰Now his father went down to see the woman. And there Samson held a feast, as was customary for young men. ¹¹When the people saw him, they chose thirty men to be his companions.

¹²"Let me tell you a riddle," Samson said to them. "If you can give me the answer within the seven days of the feast, I will give you thirty linen garments and thirty sets of clothes. ¹³If you can't tell me the answer, you must give me thirty linen garments and thirty sets of clothes."

"Tell us your riddle," they said. "Let's hear it."

¹⁴He replied,

"Out of the eater, something to eat;
out of the strong, something sweet."

For three days they could not give the answer.

¹⁵On the fourth[a] day, they said to Samson's wife, "Coax your husband into explaining the riddle for us, or we will burn you and your father's household to death. Did you invite us here to steal our property?"

¹⁶Then Samson's wife threw herself on him, sobbing, "You hate me! You don't really love me. You've given my people a riddle, but you haven't told me the answer."

"I haven't even explained it to my father or mother," he replied, "so why should I explain it to you?" ¹⁷She cried the whole seven days of the feast. So on the seventh day he finally told her, because she continued to press him. She in turn explained the riddle to her people.

¹⁸Before sunset on the seventh day the men of the town said to him,

"What is sweeter than honey?
What is stronger than a lion?"

Samson said to them,

"If you had not plowed with my heifer,
    you would not have solved my
        riddle."

¹⁹Then the Spirit of the LORD came powerfully upon him. He went down to Ashkelon, struck down thirty of their men, stripped them of everything and gave their clothes to those who had explained the riddle. Burning with anger, he returned to his father's home. ²⁰And Samson's wife was given to one of his companions who had attended him at the feast.

Samson's Vengeance on the Philistines

15 Later on, at the time of wheat harvest, Samson took a young goat and went to visit his wife. He said, "I'm going to my wife's room." But her father would not let him go in.

²"I was so sure you hated her," he said, "that I gave her to your companion. Isn't her younger sister more attractive? Take her instead."

³Samson said to them, "This time I have a right to get even with the Philistines; I will really harm them." ⁴So he went out and caught three hundred foxes and tied them tail to tail in pairs. He then fastened a torch to every pair of tails, ⁵lit the torches and let the foxes loose in the standing grain of the Philistines. He burned up the shocks and standing grain, together with the vineyards and olive groves.

⁶When the Philistines asked, "Who did this?" they were told, "Samson, the Timnite's son-in-law, because his wife was given to his companion."

So the Philistines went up and burned her and her father to death. ⁷Samson said to them, "Since you've acted like this, I swear that I won't stop until I get my revenge on you." ⁸He attacked them viciously and slaughtered many of them. Then he went down and stayed in a cave in the rock of Etam.

⁹The Philistines went up and camped in Judah, spreading out near Lehi. ¹⁰The people of Judah asked, "Why have you come to fight us?"

"We have come to take Samson prisoner," they answered, "to do to him as he did to us."

¹¹Then three thousand men from Judah went down to the cave in the rock of Etam and said to Samson, "Don't you realize that the Philistines are rulers over us? What have you done to us?"

He answered, "I merely did to them what they did to me."

¹²They said to him, "We've come to tie you up and hand you over to the Philistines."

Samson said, "Swear to me that you won't kill me yourselves."

¹³"Agreed," they answered. "We will only tie you up and hand you over to them. We will not kill you." So they bound him with two new ropes and led him up from the rock. ¹⁴As he approached Lehi, the Philistines came toward him shouting. The Spirit of the LORD came powerfully upon him. The ropes on his arms became like charred flax, and the bindings dropped from his hands. ¹⁵Finding a fresh jawbone of a donkey, he grabbed it and struck down a thousand men.

---

[a] 15 Some Septuagint manuscripts and Syriac; Hebrew *seventh*

¹⁶Then Samson said,

"With a donkey's jawbone
I have made donkeys of them.ᵃ
With a donkey's jawbone
I have killed a thousand men."

¹⁷When he finished speaking, he threw away the jawbone; and the place was called Ramath Lehi.ᵇ

¹⁸Because he was very thirsty, he cried out to the LORD, "You have given your servant this great victory. Must I now die of thirst and fall into the hands of the uncircumcised?" ¹⁹Then God opened up the hollow place in Lehi, and water came out of it. When Samson drank, his strength returned and he revived. So the spring was called En Hakkore,ᶜ and it is still there in Lehi.

²⁰Samson ledᵈ Israel for twenty years in the days of the Philistines.

Samson and Delilah

16 One day Samson went to Gaza, where he saw a prostitute. He went in to spend the night with her. ²The people of Gaza were told, "Samson is here!" So they surrounded the place and lay in wait for him all night at the city gate. They made no move during the night, saying, "At dawn we'll kill him."

³But Samson lay there only until the middle of the night. Then he got up and took hold of the doors of the city gate, together with the two posts, and tore them loose, bar and all. He lifted them to his shoulders and carried them to the top of the hill that faces Hebron.

⁴Some time later, he fell in love with a woman in the Valley of Sorek whose name was Delilah. ⁵The rulers of the Philistines went to her and said, "See if you can lure him into showing you the secret of his great strength and how we can overpower him so we may tie him up and subdue him. Each one of us will give you eleven hundred shekelsᵉ of silver."

⁶So Delilah said to Samson, "Tell me the secret of your great strength and how you can be tied up and subdued."

⁷Samson answered her, "If anyone ties me with seven fresh bowstrings that have not been dried, I'll become as weak as any other man."

⁸Then the rulers of the Philistines brought her seven fresh bowstrings that had not been dried, and she tied him with them. ⁹With men hidden in the room, she called to him, "Samson, the Philistines are upon you!" But he snapped the bowstrings as easily as a piece of string snaps when it comes close to a flame. So the secret of his strength was not discovered.

¹⁰Then Delilah said to Samson, "You have made a fool of me; you lied to me. Come now, tell me how you can be tied."

¹¹He said, "If anyone ties me securely with new ropes that have never been used, I'll become as weak as any other man."

¹²So Delilah took new ropes and tied him with them. Then, with men hidden in the room, she called to him, "Samson, the Philistines are upon you!" But he snapped the ropes off his arms as if they were threads.

¹³Delilah then said to Samson, "All this time you have been making a fool of me and lying to me. Tell me how you can be tied."

He replied, "If you weave the seven braids of my head into the fabric on the loom and tighten it with the pin, I'll become as weak as any other man." So while he was sleeping, Delilah took the seven braids of his head, wove them into the fabric ¹⁴andᶠ tightened it with the pin.

Again she called to him, "Samson, the Philistines are upon you!" He awoke from his sleep and pulled up the pin and the loom, with the fabric.

¹⁵Then she said to him, "How can you say, 'I love you,' when you won't confide in me? This is the third time you have made a fool of me and haven't told me the secret

---

ᵃ 16 Or *made a heap or two*; the Hebrew for *donkey* sounds like the Hebrew for *heap*.
ᵇ 17 *Ramath Lehi* means *jawbone hill*.
ᶜ 19 *En Hakkore* means *caller's spring*.
ᵈ 20 Traditionally *judged*   ᵉ 5 That is, about 28 pounds or about 13 kilograms
ᶠ 13,14 Some Septuagint manuscripts; Hebrew replied, "I can if you weave the seven braids of my head into the fabric on the loom." ¹⁴So she

of your great strength." [16]With such nagging she prodded him day after day until he was sick to death of it.

[17]So he told her everything. "No razor has ever been used on my head," he said, "because I have been a Nazirite dedicated to God from my mother's womb. If my head were shaved, my strength would leave me, and I would become as weak as any other man."

[18]When Delilah saw that he had told her everything, she sent word to the rulers of the Philistines, "Come back once more; he has told me everything." So the rulers of the Philistines returned with the silver in their hands. [19]After putting him to sleep on her lap, she called for someone to shave off the seven braids of his hair, and so began to subdue him.[a] And his strength left him.

[20]Then she called, "Samson, the Philistines are upon you!"

He awoke from his sleep and thought, "I'll go out as before and shake myself free." But he did not know that the LORD had left him.

[21]Then the Philistines seized him, gouged out his eyes and took him down to Gaza. Binding him with bronze shackles, they set him to grinding grain in the prison. [22]But the hair on his head began to grow again after it had been shaved.

The Death of Samson

[23]Now the rulers of the Philistines assembled to offer a great sacrifice to Dagon their god and to celebrate, saying, "Our god has delivered Samson, our enemy, into our hands."

[24]When the people saw him, they praised their god, saying,

"Our god has delivered our enemy
    into our hands,
the one who laid waste our land
    and multiplied our slain."

[25]While they were in high spirits, they shouted, "Bring out Samson to entertain us." So they called Samson out of the prison, and he performed for them.

When they stood him among the pillars, [26]Samson said to the servant who held his hand, "Put me where I can feel the pillars that support the temple, so that I may lean against them." [27]Now the temple was crowded with men and women; all the rulers of the Philistines were there, and on the roof were about three thousand men and women watching Samson perform. [28]Then Samson prayed to the LORD, "Sovereign LORD, remember me. Please, God, strengthen me just once more, and let me with one blow get revenge on the Philistines for my two eyes." [29]Then Samson reached toward the two central pillars on which the temple stood. Bracing himself against them, his right hand on the one and his left hand on the other, [30]Samson said, "Let me die with the Philistines!" Then he pushed with all his might, and down came the temple on the rulers and all the people in it. Thus he killed many more when he died than while he lived.

[31]Then his brothers and his father's whole family went down to get him. They brought him back and buried him between Zorah and Eshtaol in the tomb of Manoah his father. He had led[b] Israel twenty years.

Micah's Idols

17 Now a man named Micah from the hill country of Ephraim [2]said to his mother, "The eleven hundred shekels[c] of silver that were taken from you and about which I heard you utter a curse—I have that silver with me; I took it."

Then his mother said, "The LORD bless you, my son!"

[3]When he returned the eleven hundred shekels of silver to his mother, she said, "I solemnly consecrate my silver to the LORD for my son to make an image overlaid with silver. I will give it back to you."

[4]So after he returned the silver to his mother, she took two hundred shekels[d] of silver and gave them to a silversmith, who

[a] 19 Hebrew; some Septuagint manuscripts *and he began to weaken*   [b] 31 Traditionally *judged*   [c] 2 That is, about 28 pounds or about 13 kilograms   [d] 4 That is, about 5 pounds or about 2.3 kilograms

used them to make the idol. And it was put in Micah's house.

⁵Now this man Micah had a shrine, and he made an ephod and some household gods and installed one of his sons as his priest. ⁶In those days Israel had no king; everyone did as they saw fit.

⁷A young Levite from Bethlehem in Judah, who had been living within the clan of Judah, ⁸left that town in search of some other place to stay. On his way*a* he came to Micah's house in the hill country of Ephraim.

⁹Micah asked him, "Where are you from?"

"I'm a Levite from Bethlehem in Ju-dah," he said, "and I'm looking for a place to stay."

¹⁰Then Micah said to him, "Live with me and be my father and priest, and I'll give you ten shekels*b* of silver a year, your clothes and your food." ¹¹So the Levite agreed to live with him, and the young man became like one of his sons to him. ¹²Then Micah installed the Levite, and the young man became his priest and lived in his house. ¹³And Micah said, "Now I know that the LORD will be good to me, since this Levite has become my priest."

a 8 Or *To carry on his profession*   *b 10* That is, about 4 ounces or about 115 grams

---

Judges 16:23–31

Samson learned from his mistakes.

Samson showed huge promise as a future defender of Israel. Right from the start his mom dedicated him to God, and the angel of the Lord appeared to his parents to confirm his choice of Samson. The boy would grow up as a Nazirite, never cutting his hair or drinking wine—and one day he would rescue Israel from its brutal Philistine neighbors. Samson's mother even passionately prayed to know how to raise her boy for God (see Judges 13:1–25).

Samson wasn't wise when he told his parents he wanted to marry a Philistine woman. But the Lord used the situation to provoke a fight that left 30 Philistine men dead and naked (see Judges 14:1–20). Later Samson torched Philistine crops and killed a thousand of his enemies for murdering his wife (see Judges 15:1–20). One day Samson made a truly unwise move, revealing that his long hair was the secret behind his superhuman strength. He had paired up with a Philistine woman, Delilah, and as he slept she cut his hair, making him as weak as a normal man. His enemies led him away, gouged out his eyes, and forced him to grind grain like an animal (see Judges 16:1–22).

But Samson learned from his mistakes. His enemies took him to the temple of their god, Dagon, so crowds could mock him. Samson turned back to God, praying for one last burst of strength. With a mighty push on the supporting pillars of the temple, he brought down the entire structure, crushing thousands of Israel's enemies.

You can find Samson in Judges 13—16 and Hebrews 11:32.

UNSHAKEN *people*

The Danites Settle in Laish

18 In those days Israel had no king. And in those days the tribe of the Danites was seeking a place of their own where they might settle, because they had not yet come into an inheritance among the tribes of Israel. [2] So the Danites sent five of their leading men from Zorah and Eshtaol to spy out the land and explore it. These men represented all the Danites. They told them, "Go, explore the land."

So they entered the hill country of Ephraim and came to the house of Micah, where they spent the night. [3] When they were near Micah's house, they recognized the voice of the young Levite; so they turned in there and asked him, "Who brought you here? What are you doing in this place? Why are you here?"

[4] He told them what Micah had done for him, and said, "He has hired me and I am his priest."

[5] Then they said to him, "Please inquire of God to learn whether our journey will be successful."

[6] The priest answered them, "Go in peace. Your journey has the LORD's approval."

[7] So the five men left and came to Laish, where they saw that the people were living in safety, like the Sidonians, at peace and secure. And since their land lacked nothing, they were prosperous.[a] Also, they lived a long way from the Sidonians and had no relationship with anyone else.[b]

[8] When they returned to Zorah and Eshtaol, their fellow Danites asked them, "How did you find things?"

[9] They answered, "Come on, let's attack them! We have seen the land, and it is very good. Aren't you going to do something? Don't hesitate to go there and take it over. [10] When you get there, you will find an unsuspecting people and a spacious land that God has put into your hands, a land that lacks nothing whatever."

[11] Then six hundred men of the Danites, armed for battle, set out from Zorah and Eshtaol. [12] On their way they set up camp near Kiriath Jearim in Judah. This is why the place west of Kiriath Jearim is called Mahaneh Dan[c] to this day. [13] From there they went on to the hill country of Ephraim and came to Micah's house.

[14] Then the five men who had spied out the land of Laish said to their fellow Danites, "Do you know that one of these houses has an ephod, some household gods and an image overlaid with silver? Now you know what to do." [15] So they turned in there and went to the house of the young Levite at Micah's place and greeted him. [16] The six hundred Danites, armed for battle, stood at the entrance of the gate. [17] The five men who had spied out the land went inside and took the idol, the ephod and the household gods while the priest and the six hundred armed men stood at the entrance of the gate.

[18] When the five men went into Micah's house and took the idol, the ephod and the household gods, the priest said to them, "What are you doing?"

[19] They answered him, "Be quiet! Don't say a word. Come with us, and be our father and priest. Isn't it better that you serve a tribe and clan in Israel as priest rather than just one man's household?" [20] The priest was very pleased. He took the ephod, the household gods and the idol and went along with the people. [21] Putting their little children, their livestock and their possessions in front of them, they turned away and left.

[22] When they had gone some distance from Micah's house, the men who lived near Micah were called together and overtook the Danites. [23] As they shouted after them, the Danites turned and said to Micah, "What's the matter with you that you called out your men to fight?"

[24] He replied, "You took the gods I made, and my priest, and went away. What else do I have? How can you ask, 'What's the matter with you?'"

[25] The Danites answered, "Don't argue with us, or some of the men may get angry

[a] 7 The meaning of the Hebrew for this clause is uncertain.   [b] 7 Hebrew; some Septuagint manuscripts *with the Arameans*   [c] 12 *Mahaneh Dan* means *Dan's camp.*

and attack you, and you and your family will lose your lives." ²⁶So the Danites went their way, and Micah, seeing that they were too strong for him, turned around and went back home.

²⁷Then they took what Micah had made, and his priest, and went on to Laish, against a people at peace and secure. They attacked them with the sword and burned down their city. ²⁸There was no one to rescue them because they lived a long way from Sidon and had no relationship with anyone else. The city was in a valley near Beth Rehob.

The Danites rebuilt the city and settled there. ²⁹They named it Dan after their ancestor Dan, who was born to Israel—though the city used to be called Laish. ³⁰There the Danites set up for themselves the idol, and Jonathan son of Gershom, the son of Moses,^a and his sons were priests for the tribe of Dan until the time of the captivity of the land. ³¹They continued to use the idol Micah had made, all the time the house of God was in Shiloh.

A Levite and His Concubine

19 In those days Israel had no king. Now a Levite who lived in a remote area in the hill country of Ephraim took a concubine from Bethlehem in Judah. ²But she was unfaithful to him. She left him and went back to her parents' home in Bethlehem, Judah. After she had been there four months, ³her husband went to her to persuade her to return. He had with him his servant and two donkeys. She took him into her parents' home, and when her father saw him, he gladly welcomed him. ⁴His father-in-law, the woman's father, prevailed on him to stay; so he remained with him three days, eating and drinking, and sleeping there.

⁵On the fourth day they got up early and he prepared to leave, but the woman's father said to his son-in-law, "Refresh yourself with something to eat; then you can go." ⁶So the two of them sat down to eat and drink together. Afterward the woman's father said, "Please stay tonight and enjoy yourself." ⁷And when the man

got up to go, his father-in-law persuaded him, so he stayed there that night. ⁸On the morning of the fifth day, when he rose to go, the woman's father said, "Refresh yourself. Wait till afternoon!" So the two of them ate together.

⁹Then when the man, with his concubine and his servant, got up to leave, his father-in-law, the woman's father, said, "Now look, it's almost evening. Spend the night here; the day is nearly over. Stay and enjoy yourself. Early tomorrow morning you can get up and be on your way home." ¹⁰But, unwilling to stay another night, the man left and went toward Jebus (that is, Jerusalem), with his two saddled donkeys and his concubine.

¹¹When they were near Jebus and the day was almost gone, the servant said to his master, "Come, let's stop at this city of the Jebusites and spend the night." ¹²His master replied, "No. We won't go into any city whose people are not Israelites. We will go on to Gibeah." ¹³He added, "Come, let's try to reach Gibeah or Ramah and spend the night in one of those places." ¹⁴So they went on, and the sun set as they neared Gibeah in Benjamin. ¹⁵There they stopped to spend the night. They went and sat in the city square, but no one took them in for the night.

¹⁶That evening an old man from the hill country of Ephraim, who was living in Gibeah (the inhabitants of the place were Benjamites), came in from his work in the fields. ¹⁷When he looked and saw the traveler in the city square, the old man asked, "Where are you going? Where did you come from?"

¹⁸He answered, "We are on our way from Bethlehem in Judah to a remote area in the hill country of Ephraim where I live. I have been to Bethlehem in Judah and now I am going to the house of the LORD.^b No one has taken me in for the

---

^a 30 Many Hebrew manuscripts, some Septuagint manuscripts and Vulgate; many other Hebrew manuscripts and some other Septuagint manuscripts *Manasseh*
^b 18 Hebrew, Vulgate, Syriac and Targum; Septuagint *going home*

night. [19]We have both straw and fodder for our donkeys and bread and wine for ourselves your servants—me, the woman and the young man with us. We don't need anything."

[20]"You are welcome at my house," the old man said. "Let me supply whatever you need. Only don't spend the night in the square." [21]So he took him into his house and fed his donkeys. After they had washed their feet, they had something to eat and drink.

[22]While they were enjoying themselves, some of the wicked men of the city surrounded the house. Pounding on the door, they shouted to the old man who owned the house, "Bring out the man who came to your house so we can have sex with him."

[23]The owner of the house went outside and said to them, "No, my friends, don't be so vile. Since this man is my guest, don't do this outrageous thing. [24]Look, here is my virgin daughter, and his concubine. I will bring them out to you now, and you can use them and do to them whatever you wish. But as for this man, don't do such an outrageous thing."

[25]But the men would not listen to him. So the man took his concubine and sent her outside to them, and they raped her and abused her throughout the night, and at dawn they let her go. [26]At daybreak the woman went back to the house where her master was staying, fell down at the door and lay there until daylight.

[27]When her master got up in the morning and opened the door of the house and stepped out to continue on his way, there lay his concubine, fallen in the doorway of the house, with her hands on the threshold. [28]He said to her, "Get up; let's go." But there was no answer. Then the man put her on his donkey and set out for home.

[29]When he reached home, he took a knife and cut up his concubine, limb by limb, into twelve parts and sent them into all the areas of Israel. [30]Everyone who saw it was saying to one another, "Such a thing has never been seen or done, not since the

UNSHAKEN God

Judges 19:1–30

God is street smart.

You might worry that God is like a sheltered kid who doesn't understand your tough world. But God has witnessed more evil than we can imagine, including this sickening story of a temple assistant and his female servant. This account spanning Judges 19 to 21 describes a time when "everyone did as they saw fit" (Judges 21:25). The world of the Bible was likely a place far more hazardous than anyplace you live, home to every kind of sin and violence, including child sacrifice (see Jeremiah 7:31). So God knows and feels whatever goes on in your neighborhood. It's the world Jesus came to die for.

So ... Do you believe that God understands the roughest parts of life? Why does that matter to you—or not?

day the Israelites came up out of Egypt. Just imagine! We must do something! So speak up!"

The Israelites Punish the Benjamites

20 Then all Israel from Dan to Beersheba and from the land of Gilead came together as one and assembled before the LORD in Mizpah. [2]The leaders of all the people of the tribes of Israel took their places in the assembly of God's people, four hundred thousand men armed with swords. [3](The Benjamites heard that the Israelites had gone up to Mizpah.) Then the Israelites said, "Tell us how this awful thing happened."

[4]So the Levite, the husband of the murdered woman, said, "I and my concubine came to Gibeah in Benjamin to spend the night. [5]During the night the men of Gib-

eah came after me and surrounded the house, intending to kill me. They raped my concubine, and she died. [6]I took my concubine, cut her into pieces and sent one piece to each region of Israel's inheritance, because they committed this lewd and outrageous act in Israel. [7]Now, all you Israelites, speak up and tell me what you have decided to do."

[8]All the men rose up together as one, saying, "None of us will go home. No, not one of us will return to his house. [9]But now this is what we'll do to Gibeah: We'll go up against it in the order decided by casting lots. [10]We'll take ten men out of every hundred from all the tribes of Israel, and a hundred from a thousand, and a thousand from ten thousand, to get provisions for the army. Then, when the army arrives at Gibeah[a] in Benjamin, it can give them what they deserve for this outrageous act done in Israel." [11]So all the Israelites got together and united as one against the city.

[12]The tribes of Israel sent messengers throughout the tribe of Benjamin, saying, "What about this awful crime that was committed among you? [13]Now turn those wicked men of Gibeah over to us so that we may put them to death and purge the evil from Israel."

But the Benjamites would not listen to their fellow Israelites. [14]From their towns they came together at Gibeah to fight against the Israelites. [15]At once the Benjamites mobilized twenty-six thousand swordsmen from their towns, in addition to seven hundred able young men from those living in Gibeah. [16]Among all these soldiers there were seven hundred select troops who were left-handed, each of whom could sling a stone at a hair and not miss.

[17]Israel, apart from Benjamin, mustered four hundred thousand swordsmen, all of them fit for battle.

[18]The Israelites went up to Bethel[b] and inquired of God. They said, "Who of us is to go up first to fight against the Benjamites?"

The Lord replied, "Judah shall go first."

[19]The next morning the Israelites got up and pitched camp near Gibeah. [20]The Israelites went out to fight the Benjamites and took up battle positions against them at Gibeah. [21]The Benjamites came out of Gibeah and cut down twenty-two thousand Israelites on the battlefield that day. [22]But the Israelites encouraged one another and again took up their positions where they had stationed themselves the first day. [23]The Israelites went up and wept before the Lord until evening, and they inquired of the Lord. They said, "Shall we go up again to fight against the Benjamites, our fellow Israelites?"

The Lord answered, "Go up against them."

[24]Then the Israelites drew near to Benjamin the second day. [25]This time, when the Benjamites came out from Gibeah to oppose them, they cut down another eighteen thousand Israelites, all of them armed with swords.

[26]Then all the Israelites, the whole army, went up to Bethel, and there they sat weeping before the Lord. They fasted that day until evening and presented burnt offerings and fellowship offerings to the Lord. [27]And the Israelites inquired of the Lord. (In those days the ark of the covenant of God was there, [28]with Phinehas son of Eleazar, the son of Aaron, ministering before it.) They asked, "Shall we go up again to fight against the Benjamites, our fellow Israelites, or not?"

The Lord responded, "Go, for tomorrow I will give them into your hands."

[29]Then Israel set an ambush around Gibeah. [30]They went up against the Benjamites on the third day and took up positions against Gibeah as they had done before. [31]The Benjamites came out to meet them and were drawn away from the city. They began to inflict casualties on the Israelites as before, so that about thirty men fell in the open field and on the roads—the one leading to Bethel and the other to Gibeah. [32]While the Benjamites

[a] 10 One Hebrew manuscript; most Hebrew manuscripts Geba, a variant of Gibeah
[b] 18 Or to the house of God; also in verse 26

were saying, "We are defeating them as before," the Israelites were saying, "Let's retreat and draw them away from the city to the roads."

³³All the men of Israel moved from their places and took up positions at Baal Tamar, and the Israelite ambush charged out of its place on the west*a* of Gibeah.*b* ³⁴Then ten thousand of Israel's able young men made a frontal attack on Gibeah. The fighting was so heavy that the Benjamites did not realize how near disaster was. ³⁵The LORD defeated Benjamin before Israel, and on that day the Israelites struck down 25,100 Benjamites, all armed with swords. ³⁶Then the Benjamites saw that they were beaten.

Now the men of Israel had given way before Benjamin, because they relied on the ambush they had set near Gibeah. ³⁷Those who had been in ambush made a sudden dash into Gibeah, spread out and put the whole city to the sword. ³⁸The Israelites had arranged with the ambush that they should send up a great cloud of smoke from the city, ³⁹and then the Israelites would counterattack.

The Benjamites had begun to inflict casualties on the Israelites (about thirty), and they said, "We are defeating them as in the first battle." ⁴⁰But when the column of smoke began to rise from the city, the Benjamites turned and saw the whole city going up in smoke. ⁴¹Then the Israelites counterattacked, and the Benjamites were terrified, because they realized that disaster had come on them. ⁴²So they fled before the Israelites in the direction of the wilderness, but they could not escape the battle. And the Israelites who came out of the towns cut them down there. ⁴³They surrounded the Benjamites, chased them and easily*c* overran them in the vicinity of Gibeah on the east. ⁴⁴Eighteen thousand Benjamites fell, all of them valiant fighters. ⁴⁵As they turned and fled toward the wilderness to the rock of Rimmon, the Israelites cut down five thousand men along the roads. They kept pressing after the Benjamites as far as Gidom and struck down two thousand more.

⁴⁶On that day twenty-five thousand Benjamite swordsmen fell, all of them valiant fighters. ⁴⁷But six hundred of them turned and fled into the wilderness to the rock of Rimmon, where they stayed four months. ⁴⁸The men of Israel went back to Benjamin and put all the towns to the sword, including the animals and everything else they found. All the towns they came across they set on fire.

Wives for the Benjamites

21 The men of Israel had taken an oath at Mizpah: "Not one of us will give his daughter in marriage to a Benjamite."

²The people went to Bethel,*d* where they sat before God until evening, raising their voices and weeping bitterly. ³"LORD, God of Israel," they cried, "why has this happened to Israel? Why should one tribe be missing from Israel today?"

⁴Early the next day the people built an altar and presented burnt offerings and fellowship offerings.

⁵Then the Israelites asked, "Who from all the tribes of Israel has failed to assemble before the LORD?" For they had taken a solemn oath that anyone who failed to assemble before the LORD at Mizpah was to be put to death.

⁶Now the Israelites grieved for the tribe of Benjamin, their fellow Israelites. "Today one tribe is cut off from Israel," they said. ⁷"How can we provide wives for those who are left, since we have taken an oath by the LORD not to give them any of our daughters in marriage?" ⁸Then they asked, "Which one of the tribes of Israel failed to assemble before the LORD at Mizpah?" They discovered that no one from Jabesh Gilead had come to the camp for the assembly. ⁹For when they counted the people, they found that none of the people of Jabesh Gilead were there.

a 33 Some Septuagint manuscripts and Vulgate; the meaning of the Hebrew for this word is uncertain.   *b 33* Hebrew *Geba*, a variant of *Gibeah*   *c 43* The meaning of the Hebrew for this word is uncertain.   *d 2* Or *to the house of God*

¹⁰So the assembly sent twelve thousand fighting men with instructions to go to Jabesh Gilead and put to the sword those living there, including the women and children. ¹¹"This is what you are to do," they said. "Kill every male and every woman who is not a virgin." ¹²They found among the people living in Jabesh Gilead four hundred young women who had never slept with a man, and they took them to the camp at Shiloh in Canaan.

¹³Then the whole assembly sent an offer of peace to the Benjamites at the rock of Rimmon. ¹⁴So the Benjamites returned at that time and were given the women of Jabesh Gilead who had been spared. But there were not enough for all of them.

¹⁵The people grieved for Benjamin, because the Lord had made a gap in the tribes of Israel. ¹⁶And the elders of the assembly said, "With the women of Benjamin destroyed, how shall we provide wives for the men who are left? ¹⁷The Benjamite survivors must have heirs," they said, "so that a tribe of Israel will not be wiped out. ¹⁸We can't give them our daughters as wives, since we Israelites have taken this oath: 'Cursed be anyone who gives a wife to a Benjamite.' ¹⁹But look, there is the annual festival of the Lord in Shiloh, which lies north of Bethel, east of the road that goes from Bethel to Shechem, and south of Lebonah."

²⁰So they instructed the Benjamites, saying, "Go and hide in the vineyards ²¹and watch. When the young women of Shiloh come out to join in the dancing, rush from the vineyards and each of you seize one of them to be your wife. Then return to the land of Benjamin. ²²When their fathers or brothers complain to us, we will say to them, 'Do us the favor of helping them, because we did not get wives for them during the war. You will not be guilty of breaking your oath because you did not give your daughters to them.'"

²³So that is what the Benjamites did. While the young women were dancing, each man caught one and carried her off to be his wife. Then they returned to their inheritance and rebuilt the towns and settled in them.

²⁴At that time the Israelites left that place and went home to their tribes and clans, each to his own inheritance.

²⁵In those days Israel had no king; everyone did as they saw fit.

Judges 21:25

People aren't qualified to make the rules.

Judges 21 recounts a ghastly story of mass killing and kidnapping, but it's just another chapter in a whole book that describes what happens when people forget about God. Judges begins by noting that after the great leader Joshua died, "another generation grew up who knew neither the Lord nor what he had done for Israel" (Judges 2:10). Israel began to pick up the evil habits of their neighbors, especially their sinful worship of false gods. During this era Israel sometimes obeyed God, but they often rebelled. By the end of Judges, the nation has fallen into chaos for one main reason: "Everyone did as they saw fit" (Judges 21:25). Instead of following God's commands, people made up their own rules of right and wrong. It's an ancient example of "moral relativism," the belief that people ultimately define good and evil. It's a tempting approach to life, but when people make the rules, everything falls apart.

Think: How do you see people trying to make up their own rules of right and wrong? What is the result?

ROCK SOLID truths

307

BOOK OUTLINE

**Naomi's departure from Israel
and her return**
(1:1–22)

Ruth's welcome
(2:1 — 3:18)

Boaz and Ruth
(4:1–22)

RUTH

The book of Ruth is named after the leading character whose story is told here. It may have been written during the reign of David, whose ancestry is traced in the final verses to his great-grandfather Boaz, whose wife was Ruth.

The story begins with an Israelite couple who moved to Moab during a famine in Canaan. The husband and his two sons died, leaving the mother (Naomi) alone with her two daughters-in-law (Orpah and Ruth). Naomi decided to move back to Israel, and Ruth insisted on going back with her. Back in Israel they looked to their relative Boaz for help, and Ruth finally married Boaz. The royal family of King David and the Messiah, Jesus Christ, came from their family.

This book teaches us about love and devotion. It also teaches us of God's concern for our everyday needs and that he is working out his plan for salvation.

Naomi Loses Her Husband and Sons

In the days when the judges ruled,[a] there was a famine in the land. So a man from Bethlehem in Judah, together with his wife and two sons, went to live for a while in the country of Moab. [2]The man's name was Elimelek, his wife's name was Naomi, and the names of his two sons were Mahlon and Kilion. They were Ephrathites from Bethlehem, Judah. And they went to Moab and lived there.

[3]Now Elimelek, Naomi's husband, died, and she was left with her two sons. [4]They married Moabite women, one named Orpah and the other Ruth. After they had lived there about ten years, [5]both Mahlon and Kilion also died, and Naomi was left without her two sons and her husband.

Naomi and Ruth Return to Bethlehem

[6]When Naomi heard in Moab that the LORD had come to the aid of his people by providing food for them, she and her daughters-in-law prepared to return home from there. [7]With her two daughters-in-law she left the place where she had been living and set out on the road that would take them back to the land of Judah.

[8]Then Naomi said to her two daughters-in-law, "Go back, each of you, to your mother's home. May the LORD show you kindness, as you have shown kindness to your dead husbands and to me. [9]May the LORD grant that each of you will find rest in the home of another husband."

Then she kissed them goodbye and they wept aloud [10]and said to her, "We will go back with you to your people."

[11]But Naomi said, "Return home, my daughters. Why would you come with me? Am I going to have any more sons, who could become your husbands? [12]Return home, my daughters; I am too old to have another husband. Even if I thought there was still hope for me — even if I had a husband tonight and then gave birth to sons — [13]would you wait until they grew up? Would you remain unmarried for them? No, my daughters. It is more bitter for me than for you, because the LORD's hand has turned against me!"

[14]At this they wept aloud again. Then Orpah kissed her mother-in-law goodbye, but Ruth clung to her.

[15]"Look," said Naomi, "your sister-in-law is going back to her people and her gods. Go back with her."

[16]But Ruth replied, "Don't urge me to leave you or to turn back from you. Where you go I will go, and where you stay I will stay. Your people will be my people and your God my God. [17]Where you die I will die, and there I will be buried. May the LORD deal with me, be it ever so severely, if even death separates you and me." [18]When Naomi realized that Ruth was determined to go with her, she stopped urging her.

[19]So the two women went on until they came to Bethlehem. When they arrived in Bethlehem, the whole town was stirred because of them, and the women exclaimed, "Can this be Naomi?"

[20]"Don't call me Naomi,[b]" she told them. "Call me Mara,[c] because the Almighty[d] has made my life very bitter. [21]I went away full, but the LORD has brought me back empty. Why call me Naomi? The LORD has afflicted[e] me; the Almighty has brought misfortune upon me."

[22]So Naomi returned from Moab accompanied by Ruth the Moabite, her daughter-in-law, arriving in Bethlehem as the barley harvest was beginning.

Ruth Meets Boaz in the Grain Field

Now Naomi had a relative on her husband's side, a man of standing from the clan of Elimelek, whose name was Boaz.

[2]And Ruth the Moabite said to Naomi, "Let me go to the fields and pick up the leftover grain behind anyone in whose eyes I find favor."

Naomi said to her, "Go ahead, my daughter." [3]So she went out, entered a field and began to glean behind the harvesters. As it turned out, she was working in a field

---

[a] 1 Traditionally *judged*   [b] 20 *Naomi* means *pleasant*.   [c] 20 *Mara* means *bitter*.
[d] 20 Hebrew *Shaddai*; also in verse 21
[e] 21 Or *has testified against*

belonging to Boaz, who was from the clan of Elimelek.

⁴Just then Boaz arrived from Bethlehem and greeted the harvesters, "The LORD be with you!"

"The LORD bless you!" they answered.

⁵Boaz asked the overseer of his harvesters, "Who does that young woman belong to?"

⁶The overseer replied, "She is the Moabite who came back from Moab with Naomi. ⁷She said, 'Please let me glean and gather among the sheaves behind the harvesters.' She came into the field and has remained here from morning till now, except for a short rest in the shelter."

⁸So Boaz said to Ruth, "My daughter, listen to me. Don't go and glean in another field and don't go away from here. Stay here with the women who work for me. ⁹Watch the field where the men are harvesting, and follow along after the women. I have told the men not to lay a hand on you. And whenever you are thirsty, go and get a drink from the water jars the men have filled."

¹⁰At this, she bowed down with her face to the ground. She asked him, "Why have I found such favor in your eyes that you notice me—a foreigner?"

¹¹Boaz replied, "I've been told all about what you have done for your mother-in-law since the death of your husband—how you left your father and mother and your homeland and came to live with a people you did not know before. ¹²May the LORD repay you for what you have done. May you be richly rewarded by the LORD, the God of Israel, under whose wings you have come to take refuge."

¹³"May I continue to find favor in your eyes, my lord," she said. "You have put me at ease by speaking kindly to your servant—though I do not have the standing of one of your servants."

¹⁴At mealtime Boaz said to her, "Come over here. Have some bread and dip it in the wine vinegar."

When she sat down with the harvesters, he offered her some roasted grain. She ate all she wanted and had some left over.

¹⁵As she got up to glean, Boaz gave orders to his men, "Let her gather among the sheaves and don't reprimand her. ¹⁶Even pull out some stalks for her from the bundles and leave them for her to pick up, and don't rebuke her."

¹⁷So Ruth gleaned in the field until evening. Then she threshed the barley she had gathered, and it amounted to about an ephah.ᵃ ¹⁸She carried it back to town, and her mother-in-law saw how much she had gathered. Ruth also brought out and gave her what she had left over after she had eaten enough.

¹⁹Her mother-in-law asked her, "Where did you glean today? Where did you work? Blessed be the man who took notice of you!"

Then Ruth told her mother-in-law about the one at whose place she had been working. "The name of the man I worked with today is Boaz," she said.

²⁰"The LORD bless him!" Naomi said to her daughter-in-law. "He has not stopped showing his kindness to the living and the dead." She added, "That man is our close relative; he is one of our guardian-redeemers.ᵇ"

²¹Then Ruth the Moabite said, "He even said to me, 'Stay with my workers until they finish harvesting all my grain.'"

²²Naomi said to Ruth her daughter-in-law, "It will be good for you, my daughter, to go with the women who work for him, because in someone else's field you might be harmed."

²³So Ruth stayed close to the women of Boaz to glean until the barley and wheat harvests were finished. And she lived with her mother-in-law.

Ruth and Boaz at the Threshing Floor

3 One day Ruth's mother-in-law Naomi said to her, "My daughter, I must find a homeᶜ for you, where you will be well provided for. ²Now Boaz,

---

ᵃ 17 That is, probably about 30 pounds or about 13 kilograms   ᵇ 20 The Hebrew word for *guardian-redeemer* is a legal term for one who has the obligation to redeem a relative in serious difficulty (see Lev. 25:25-55).   ᶜ 1 Hebrew *find rest* (see 1:9) with whose women you have worked, is a relative of ours. Tonight he will be winnowing barley on the threshing floor. ³Wash, put on perfume, and get dressed in your best clothes. Then go down to the threshing floor, but don't let him know you are there until he has finished eating and drinking. ⁴When he lies down, note the place where he is lying. Then go and uncover his feet and lie down. He will tell you what to do."

⁵"I will do whatever you say," Ruth answered. ⁶So she went down to the threshing floor and did everything her mother-in-law told her to do.

⁷When Boaz had finished eating and drinking and was in good spirits, he went over to lie down at the far end of the grain pile. Ruth approached quietly, uncovered his feet and lay down. ⁸In the middle of the night something startled the man; he turned—and there was a woman lying at his feet!

⁹"Who are you?" he asked.

"I am your servant Ruth," she said. "Spread the corner of your garment over me, since you are a guardian-redeemer*ᵃ* of our family."

ᵃ 9 The Hebrew word for *guardian-redeemer* is a legal term for one who has the obligation to redeem a relative in serious difficulty (see Lev. 25:25-55); also in verses 12 and 13.

Ruth 3:1–8

Ruth stayed true to family.

Ruth had every reason to stay in her homeland. Ten years earlier, her husband's family had migrated to her country, Moab, to escape famine in Israel. Now all three men in that family were dead. Suddenly young Ruth was a widow, along with her Moabite sister-in-law, Orpah, and her Israelite mother-in-law, Naomi. Beaten down and bitter, Naomi decided to return home to Israel, instructing Ruth and Orpah to stay behind with their own people.

Orpah made a levelheaded decision to stay home. But at that instant Ruth made a daring choice. She decided to stick with Naomi, making her mother-in-law an amazing promise: "Where you go I will go," she said. "And where you stay I will stay. Your people will be my people and your God my God" (Ruth 1:16).

Widows in ancient times often starved to death or became prostitutes to survive, but Ruth bound herself to care for Naomi until death. And as Ruth chose to show Naomi compassion, both women discovered God's enormous provision. In Israel Ruth fell in love with a wealthy man, Boaz, who kindly cared for both Ruth and her mother-in-law.

Ruth's new family connection ultimately made her grandmother to King David, the greatest-ever king of Israel (see Ruth 4:17). Even more significantly, Ruth became an ancestor to Jesus, who hundreds of years later was born to the line of David (see 2 Samuel 7:16; Matthew 1:5). Through sacrificial faithfulness to her family, Ruth experienced God's blessings beyond her dreams.

You can find Ruth throughout the book of Ruth and in Matthew 1:5.

UNSHAKEN *people*

¹⁰"The LORD bless you, my daughter," he replied. "This kindness is greater than that which you showed earlier: You have not run after the younger men, whether rich or poor. ¹¹And now, my daughter, don't be afraid. I will do for you all you ask. All the people of my town know that you are a woman of noble character. ¹²Although it is true that I am a guardian-redeemer of our family, there is another who is more closely related than I. ¹³Stay here for the night, and in the morning if he wants to do his duty as your guardian-redeemer, good; let him redeem you. But if he is not willing, as surely as the LORD lives I will do it. Lie here until morning."

¹⁴So she lay at his feet until morning, but got up before anyone could be recognized; and he said, "No one must know that a woman came to the threshing floor."

¹⁵He also said, "Bring me the shawl you are wearing and hold it out." When she did so, he poured into it six measures of barley and placed the bundle on her. Then he^a went back to town.

¹⁶When Ruth came to her mother-in-law, Naomi asked, "How did it go, my daughter?"

Then she told her everything Boaz had done for her ¹⁷and added, "He gave me these six measures of barley, saying, 'Don't go back to your mother-in-law empty-handed.'"

¹⁸Then Naomi said, "Wait, my daughter, until you find out what happens. For the man will not rest until the matter is settled today."

Boaz Marries Ruth

4 Meanwhile Boaz went up to the town gate and sat down there just as the guardian-redeemer^b he had mentioned came along. Boaz said, "Come over here, my friend, and sit down." So he went over and sat down.

²Boaz took ten of the elders of the town and said, "Sit here," and they did so. ³Then he said to the guardian-redeemer, "Naomi, who has come back from Moab, is selling the piece of land that belonged to our relative Elimelek. ⁴I thought I should bring the matter to your attention and suggest that you buy it in the presence of these seated here and in the presence of the elders of my people. If you will redeem it, do so. But if you^c will not, tell me, so I will know. For no one has the right to do it except you, and I am next in line."

"I will redeem it," he said.

⁵Then Boaz said, "On the day you buy the land from Naomi, you also acquire Ruth the Moabite, the^d dead man's widow, in order to maintain the name of the dead with his property."

⁶At this, the guardian-redeemer said, "Then I cannot redeem it because I might endanger my own estate. You redeem it yourself. I cannot do it."

⁷(Now in earlier times in Israel, for the redemption and transfer of property to become final, one party took off his sandal and gave it to the other. This was the method of legalizing transactions in Israel.)

⁸So the guardian-redeemer said to Boaz, "Buy it yourself." And he removed his sandal.

⁹Then Boaz announced to the elders and all the people, "Today you are witnesses that I have bought from Naomi all the property of Elimelek, Kilion and Mahlon. ¹⁰I have also acquired Ruth the Moabite, Mahlon's widow, as my wife, in order to maintain the name of the dead with his property, so that his name will not disappear from among his family or from his hometown. Today you are witnesses!"

¹¹Then the elders and all the people at the gate said, "We are witnesses. May the LORD make the woman who is coming

^a 15 Most Hebrew manuscripts; many Hebrew manuscripts, Vulgate and Syriac *she*   ^b 1 The Hebrew word for *guardian-redeemer* is a legal term for one who has the obligation to redeem a relative in serious difficulty (see Lev. 25:25-55); also in verses 3, 6, 8 and 14.   ^c 4 Many Hebrew manuscripts, Septuagint, Vulgate and Syriac; most Hebrew manuscripts *he*
^d 5 Vulgate and Syriac; Hebrew (see also Septuagint) *Naomi and from Ruth the Moabite, you acquire the*

into your home like Rachel and Leah, who together built up the family of Israel. May you have standing in Ephrathah and be famous in Bethlehem. ¹²Through the offspring the Lord gives you by this young woman, may your family be like that of Perez, whom Tamar bore to Judah."

Naomi Gains a Son

¹³So Boaz took Ruth and she became his wife. When he made love to her, the Lord enabled her to conceive, and she gave birth to a son. ¹⁴The women said to Naomi: "Praise be to the Lord, who this day has not left you without a guardian-redeemer. May he become famous throughout Israel! ¹⁵He will renew your life and sustain you in your old age. For your daughter-in-law, who loves you and who is better to you than seven sons, has given him birth."

¹⁶Then Naomi took the child in her arms and cared for him. ¹⁷The women living there said, "Naomi has a son!" And they named him Obed. He was the father of Jesse, the father of David.

The Genealogy of David

¹⁸This, then, is the family line of Perez:

Perez was the father of Hezron,
¹⁹Hezron the father of Ram,
    Ram the father of Amminadab,
²⁰Amminadab the father of Nahshon,
    Nahshon the father of Salmon,[a]

RUTH 4

ROCK SOLID *plans*

Ruth 4:13–22

Trust God — not chance.

As a young wife, Ruth endured her husband's death and left her own country and people to live in the foreign land of Israel. She was awestruck when one of the most caring men she had ever met took her as his wife. But there was more to this ancient love story than good luck. Behind the drama God was working his plan. Ruth ultimately became the great-grandmother of King David and an important member of Jesus' family line. With God in charge, there's no such thing as chance.

Your next step: Tell God you count on him to direct your life even when life feels random.

²¹Salmon the father of Boaz,
    Boaz the father of Obed,
²²Obed the father of Jesse,
    and Jesse the father of David.

a 20 A few Hebrew manuscripts, some Septuagint manuscripts and Vulgate (see also verse 21 and Septuagint of 1 Chron. 2:11); most Hebrew manuscripts *Salma*

BOOK OUTLINE

Eli as priest and judge
(1:1 — 4:22)

Samuel as leader of Israel
(5:1 — 8:22)

Saul as the first king of Israel
(9:1 — 15:35)

David and Saul
(16:1 — 30:31)

Death of Saul
(31:1 – 13)

1 SAMUEL

The book of 1 Samuel records the lives of Samuel and Saul, and much of the life of David. First Samuel begins with the birth of Samuel and his training in the house of the LORD. It describes how he led Israel as prophet, priest and judge.

When the people of Israel demanded a king, Samuel, by God's leading, anointed Saul to be the first king of Israel. But Saul was disobedient to God and God rejected him as king. Then Samuel secretly anointed David to take Saul's place. The struggles between Saul and David make up the rest of this book. Although the stories of these people's disobedience are included, there is a stronger emphasis on their goodness and obedience to God.

Samuel, as prophet, priest and judge, had a great deal of influence throughout this time period. During this part of Israel's history the nation changed from the leadership of judges to the leadership of a king, which is what the people wanted. The Israelites were now ruled like their neighboring nations.

The Birth of Samuel

There was a certain man from Ramathaim, a Zuphite[a] from the hill country of Ephraim, whose name was Elkanah son of Jeroham, the son of Elihu, the son of Tohu, the son of Zuph, an Ephraimite. ²He had two wives; one was called Hannah and the other Peninnah. Peninnah had children, but Hannah had none.

³Year after year this man went up from his town to worship and sacrifice to the Lord Almighty at Shiloh, where Hophni and Phinehas, the two sons of Eli, were priests of the Lord. ⁴Whenever the day came for Elkanah to sacrifice, he would give portions of the meat to his wife Peninnah and to all her sons and daughters. ⁵But to Hannah he gave a double portion because he loved her, and the Lord had closed her womb. ⁶Because the Lord had closed Hannah's womb, her rival kept provoking her in order to irritate her. ⁷This went on year after year. Whenever Hannah went up to the house of the Lord, her rival provoked her till she wept and would not eat. ⁸Her husband Elkanah would say to her, "Hannah, why are you weeping? Why don't you eat? Why are you downhearted? Don't I mean more to you than ten sons?"

⁹Once when they had finished eating and drinking in Shiloh, Hannah stood up. Now Eli the priest was sitting on his chair by the doorpost of the Lord's house. ¹⁰In her deep anguish Hannah prayed to the Lord, weeping bitterly. ¹¹And she made a vow, saying, "Lord Almighty, if you will only look on your servant's misery and remember me, and not forget your servant but give her a son, then I will give him to the Lord for all the days of his life, and no razor will ever be used on his head."

¹²As she kept on praying to the Lord, Eli observed her mouth. ¹³Hannah was praying in her heart, and her lips were moving but her voice was not heard. Eli thought she was drunk ¹⁴and said to her, "How long are you going to stay drunk? Put away your wine."

¹⁵"Not so, my lord," Hannah replied, "I am a woman who is deeply troubled. I have not been drinking wine or beer; I was pouring out my soul to the Lord. ¹⁶Do not take your servant for a wicked woman; I have been praying here out of my great anguish and grief."

¹⁷Eli answered, "Go in peace, and may the God of Israel grant you what you have asked of him."

¹⁸She said, "May your servant find favor in your eyes." Then she went her way and ate something, and her face was no longer downcast.

¹⁹Early the next morning they arose and worshiped before the Lord and then went back to their home at Ramah. Elkanah made love to his wife Hannah, and the Lord remembered her. ²⁰So in the course of time Hannah became pregnant and gave birth to a son. She named him Samuel,[b] saying, "Because I asked the Lord for him."

Hannah Dedicates Samuel

²¹When her husband Elkanah went up with all his family to offer the annual sacrifice to the Lord and to fulfill his vow, ²²Hannah did not go. She said to her husband, "After the boy is weaned, I will take him and present him before the Lord, and he will live there always."[c]

²³"Do what seems best to you," her husband Elkanah told her. "Stay here until you have weaned him; only may the Lord make good his[d] word." So the woman stayed at home and nursed her son until she had weaned him.

²⁴After he was weaned, she took the boy with her, young as he was, along with a three-year-old bull,[e] an ephah[f] of flour and a skin of wine, and brought him to house of the Lord at Shiloh. ²⁵When the bull had been sacrificed, they brought the boy to Eli, ²⁶and she said to him, "Pardon

---

a 1 See Septuagint and 1 Chron. 6:26-27,33-35; or *from Ramathaim Zuphim.* *b 20 Samuel* sounds like the Hebrew for *heard by God.*
c 22 Masoretic Text; Dead Sea Scrolls *always. I have dedicated him as a Nazirite — all the days of his life." d 23* Masoretic Text; Dead Sea Scrolls, Septuagint and Syriac *your*
e 24 Dead Sea Scrolls, Septuagint and Syriac; Masoretic Text *with three bulls f 24* That is, probably about 36 pounds or about 16 kilograms

me, my lord. As surely as you live, I am the woman who stood here beside you praying to the LORD. ²⁷ I prayed for this child, and the LORD has granted me what I asked of him. ²⁸ So now I give him to the LORD. For his whole life he will be given over to the LORD." And he worshiped the LORD there.

Hannah's Prayer

2 Then Hannah prayed and said:

"My heart rejoices in the LORD;
   in the LORD my horn^a is lifted high.
My mouth boasts over my enemies,
   for I delight in your deliverance.

² "There is no one holy like the LORD;
   there is no one besides you;
   there is no Rock like our God.

³ "Do not keep talking so proudly
   or let your mouth speak such arrogance,
for the LORD is a God who knows,
   and by him deeds are weighed.

⁴ "The bows of the warriors are broken,
   but those who stumbled are armed with strength.
⁵ Those who were full hire themselves out for food,

---

^a *1 Horn* here symbolizes strength; also in verse 10.

---

1 Samuel 1:1–28

Hannah prayed her heart out.

When Hannah showed up at the house of the Lord to pray, the head priest thought she was drunk. Hannah ached with grief because she was childless, a condition interpreted in that day as a sign of God's anger. Her husband, Elkanah, loved her deeply, but his other wife, Peninnah, mocked her inability to conceive. Hannah vowed that if God gave her a son, she would dedicate his whole life to God.

The priest Eli saw her weeping and mumbling and told her to get rid of her wine. Hannah protested she was only pouring her heart out to God. Great anguish drove her prayers. Eli must have felt sobered when he answered, "Go in peace, and may the God of Israel grant you what you have asked of him" (1 Samuel 1:17). God indeed gave Hannah what she requested, and she called her son Samuel, a name that sounds like the Hebrew words "heard by God."

Samuel was just a small boy when Hannah presented him at the temple, and this loving mom continued to pray her heart out, speaking thankful words recorded in 1 Samuel 2:1–10. Her boy "continued to grow in stature and in favor with the LORD and with people" (1 Samuel 2:26), and as time passed he grew into a great judge and prophet. Samuel was the last leader of Israel before the Lord appointed Saul as Israel's first king. Samuel was a perfect answer to Hannah's prayers.

You can find Hannah in 1 Samuel 1—2.

UNSHAKEN *people*

ROCK SOLID *principles*

1 Samuel 2:3

Walk the talk.

Madison had the ugliest reputation of any girl in her grade. Not that she had done anything amazingly evil. But she was a phony—a total fake—and everyone knew it. Madison drew fish designs on her book covers and posted Bible verses in her locker and sometimes carried a Bible to class. She made big noises about Jesus on her profile online and posted updates when she was on church outings. But despite the nice show, Madison was the meanest girl anyone had ever met. There wasn't a person in school she hadn't verbally shredded at one time or another. She was a phony—a total fake—and everyone knew it.

Hannah dedicated Samuel to God from his earliest years (see 1 Samuel 1:21–28). More than anything this mom wanted her son to obey God. She knew that the Lord knows everything—and he sees every action (see 1 Samuel 2:3). God can't be fooled by pretty words or good intentions. He wants obedience that shows up in real life.

but those who were hungry are
  hungry no more.
She who was barren has borne seven
  children,
  but she who has had many sons
  pines away.
6 "The Lord brings death and makes
  alive;
  he brings down to the grave and
  raises up.
7 The Lord sends poverty and wealth;
  he humbles and he exalts.
8 He raises the poor from the dust
  and lifts the needy from the ash
  heap;
  he seats them with princes
  and has them inherit a throne of
  honor.
"For the foundations of the earth are
  the Lord's;
  on them he has set the world.
9 He will guard the feet of his faithful
  servants,

but the wicked will be silenced in
  the place of darkness.

"It is not by strength that one
  prevails;
10   those who oppose the Lord will be
  broken.
The Most High will thunder from
  heaven;
  the Lord will judge the ends of the
  earth.

"He will give strength to his king
  and exalt the horn of his anointed."

11 Then Elkanah went home to Ramah,
but the boy ministered before the Lord
under Eli the priest.

Eli's Wicked Sons

12 Eli's sons were scoundrels; they had
no regard for the Lord. 13 Now it was
the practice of the priests that, whenever any of the people offered a sacrifice,
the priest's servant would come with a

three-pronged fork in his hand while the meat was being boiled ^{14}and would plunge the fork into the pan or kettle or caldron or pot. Whatever the fork brought up the priest would take for himself. This is how they treated all the Israelites who came to Shiloh. ^{15}But even before the fat was burned, the priest's servant would come and say to the person who was sacrificing, "Give the priest some meat to roast; he won't accept boiled meat from you, but only raw."

^{16}If the person said to him, "Let the fat be burned first, and then take whatever you want," the servant would answer, "No, hand it over now; if you don't, I'll take it by force."

^{17}This sin of the young men was very great in the Lord's sight, for they^a were treating the Lord's offering with contempt.

^{18}But Samuel was ministering before the Lord—a boy wearing a linen ephod. ^{19}Each year his mother made him a little robe and took it to him when she went up with her husband to offer the annual sacrifice. ^{20}Eli would bless Elkanah and his wife, saying, "May the Lord give you children by this woman to take the place of the one she prayed for and gave to^b the Lord." Then they would go home. ^{21}And the Lord was gracious to Hannah; she gave birth to three sons and two daughters. Meanwhile, the boy Samuel grew up in the presence of the Lord.

^{22}Now Eli, who was very old, heard about everything his sons were doing to all Israel and how they slept with the women who served at the entrance to the tent of meeting. ^{23}So he said to them, "Why do you do such things? I hear from all the people about these wicked deeds of yours. ^{24}No, my sons; the report I hear spreading among the Lord's people is not good. ^{25}If one person sins against another, God^c may mediate for the offender; but if anyone sins against the Lord, who will intercede for them?" His sons, however, did not listen to their father's rebuke, for it was the Lord's will to put them to death.

^{26}And the boy Samuel continued to grow in stature and in favor with the Lord and with people.

Prophecy Against the House of Eli

^{27}Now a man of God came to Eli and said to him, "This is what the Lord says: 'Did I not clearly reveal myself to your ancestor's family when they were in Egypt under Pharaoh? ^{28}I chose your ancestor out of all the tribes of Israel to be my priest, to go up to my altar, to burn incense, and to wear an ephod in my presence. I also gave your ancestor's family all the food offerings presented by the Israelites. ^{29}Why do you^d scorn my sacrifice and offering that I prescribed for my dwelling? Why do you honor your sons more than me by fattening yourselves on the choice parts of every offering made by my people Israel?'

^{30}"Therefore the Lord, the God of Israel, declares: 'I promised that members of your family would minister before me forever.' But now the Lord declares: 'Far be it from me! Those who honor me I will honor, but those who despise me will be disdained. ^{31}The time is coming when I will cut short your strength and the strength of your priestly house, so that no one in it will reach old age, ^{32}and you will see distress in my dwelling. Although good will be done to Israel, no one in your family line will ever reach old age. ^{33}Every one of you that I do not cut off from serving at my altar I will spare only to destroy your sight and sap your strength, and all your descendants will die in the prime of life.

^{34}"'And what happens to your two sons, Hophni and Phinehas, will be a sign to you—they will both die on the same day. ^{35}I will raise up for myself a faithful priest, who will do according to what is in my heart and mind. I will firmly establish his priestly house, and they will minister before my anointed one always. ^{36}Then everyone left in your family line will come and bow down before him for a piece of silver and a loaf of bread and

^{a} 17 Dead Sea Scrolls and Septuagint; Masoretic Text people ^{b} 20 Dead Sea Scrolls; Masoretic Text and asked from ^{c} 25 Or the judges ^{d} 29 The Hebrew is plural.

plead, "Appoint me to some priestly office so I can have food to eat."'"

The LORD Calls Samuel

3 The boy Samuel ministered before the LORD under Eli. In those days the word of the LORD was rare; there were not many visions.

²One night Eli, whose eyes were becoming so weak that he could barely see, was lying down in his usual place. ³The lamp of God had not yet gone out, and Samuel was lying down in the house of the LORD, where the ark of God was. ⁴Then the LORD called Samuel.

Samuel answered, "Here I am." ⁵And he ran to Eli and said, "Here I am; you called me."

But Eli said, "I did not call; go back and lie down." So he went and lay down.

⁶Again the LORD called, "Samuel!" And Samuel got up and went to Eli and said, "Here I am; you called me."

"My son," Eli said, "I did not call; go back and lie down."

⁷Now Samuel did not yet know the LORD: The word of the LORD had not yet been revealed to him.

⁸A third time the LORD called, "Samuel!" And Samuel got up and went to Eli and said, "Here I am; you called me."

Then Eli realized that the LORD was calling the boy. ⁹So Eli told Samuel, "Go and lie down, and if he calls you, say, 'Speak, LORD, for your servant is listening.'" So Samuel went and lay down in his place.

¹⁰The LORD came and stood there, calling as at the other times, "Samuel! Samuel!"

Then Samuel said, "Speak, for your servant is listening."

¹¹And the LORD said to Samuel: "See, I am about to do something in Israel that will make the ears of everyone who hears about it tingle. ¹²At that time I will carry out against Eli everything I spoke against his family—from beginning to end. ¹³For I told him that I would judge his family forever because of the sin he knew about; his sons blasphemed God,ᵃ and he failed to restrain them. ¹⁴Therefore I swore to the house of Eli, 'The guilt of Eli's house will never be atoned for by sacrifice or offering.'"

¹⁵Samuel lay down until morning and then opened the doors of the house of the LORD. He was afraid to tell Eli the vision, ¹⁶but Eli called him and said, "Samuel, my son."

Samuel answered, "Here I am."

¹⁷"What was it he said to you?" Eli asked. "Do not hide it from me. May God deal with you, be it ever so severely, if you hide from me anything he told you." ¹⁸So Samuel told him everything, hiding nothing from him. Then Eli said, "He is the LORD; let him do what is good in his eyes."

¹⁹The LORD was with Samuel as he grew up, and he let none of Samuel's words fall to the ground. ²⁰And all Israel from Dan to Beersheba recognized that Samuel was attested as a prophet of the LORD. ²¹The LORD continued to appear at Shiloh, and there he revealed himself to Samuel through his word.

4 And Samuel's word came to all Israel.

The Philistines Capture the Ark

Now the Israelites went out to fight against the Philistines. The Israelites camped at Ebenezer, and the Philistines at Aphek. ²The Philistines deployed their forces to meet Israel, and as the battle spread, Israel was defeated by the Philistines, who killed about four thousand of them on the battlefield. ³When the soldiers returned to camp, the elders of Israel asked, "Why did the LORD bring defeat on us today before the Philistines? Let us bring the ark of the LORD's covenant from Shiloh, so that he may go with us and save us from the hand of our enemies."

⁴So the people sent men to Shiloh, and they brought back the ark of the covenant of the LORD Almighty, who is enthroned between the cherubim. And Eli's two sons, Hophni and Phinehas, were there with the ark of the covenant of God.

ᵃ *13* An ancient Hebrew scribal tradition (see also Septuagint); Masoretic Text *sons made themselves contemptible*

⁵When the ark of the Lord's covenant came into the camp, all Israel raised such a great shout that the ground shook. ⁶Hearing the uproar, the Philistines asked, "What's all this shouting in the Hebrew camp?"

When they learned that the ark of the Lord had come into the camp, ⁷the Philistines were afraid. "A god has*ᵃ* come into the camp," they said. "Oh no! Nothing like this has happened before. ⁸We're doomed! Who will deliver us from the hand of these mighty gods? They are the gods who struck the Egyptians with all kinds of plagues in the wilderness. ⁹Be strong, Philistines! Be men, or you will be subject to the Hebrews, as they have been to you. Be men, and fight!"

¹⁰So the Philistines fought, and the Israelites were defeated and every man fled to his tent. The slaughter was very great; Israel lost thirty thousand foot soldiers. ¹¹The ark of God was captured, and Eli's two sons, Hophni and Phinehas, died.

Death of Eli

¹²That same day a Benjamite ran from the battle line and went to Shiloh with his clothes torn and dust on his head. ¹³When he arrived, there was Eli sitting on his chair by the side of the road, watching, because his heart feared for the ark of God. When the man entered the town and told what had happened, the whole town sent up a cry.

¹⁴Eli heard the outcry and asked, "What is the meaning of this uproar?"

The man hurried over to Eli, ¹⁵who was ninety-eight years old and whose eyes had failed so that he could not see. ¹⁶He told Eli, "I have just come from the battle line; I fled from it this very day."

Eli asked, "What happened, my son?"

¹⁷The man who brought the news replied, "Israel fled before the Philistines, and the army has suffered heavy losses. Also your two sons, Hophni and Phinehas, are dead, and the ark of God has been captured."

¹⁸When he mentioned the ark of God, Eli fell backward off his chair by the side of the gate. His neck was broken and he died, for he was an old man, and he was heavy. He had led*ᵇ* Israel forty years.

¹⁹His daughter-in-law, the wife of Phinehas, was pregnant and near the time of delivery. When she heard the news that the ark of God had been captured and that her father-in-law and her husband were dead, she went into labor and gave birth, but was overcome by her labor pains. ²⁰As she was dying, the women attending her said, "Don't despair; you have given birth to a son." But she did not respond or pay any attention.

²¹She named the boy Ichabod,*ᶜ* saying, "The Glory has departed from Israel"— because of the capture of the ark of God and the deaths of her father-in-law and her husband. ²²She said, "The Glory has departed from Israel, for the ark of God has been captured."

The Ark in Ashdod and Ekron

5 After the Philistines had captured the ark of God, they took it from Ebenezer to Ashdod. ²Then they carried the ark into Dagon's temple and set it beside Dagon. ³When the people of Ashdod rose early the next day, there was Dagon, fallen on his face on the ground before the ark of the Lord! They took Dagon and put him back in his place. ⁴But the following morning when they rose, there was Dagon, fallen on his face on the ground before the ark of the Lord! His head and hands had been broken off and were lying on the threshold; only his body remained. ⁵That is why to this day neither the priests of Dagon nor any others who enter Dagon's temple at Ashdod step on the threshold.

⁶The Lord's hand was heavy on the people of Ashdod and its vicinity; he brought devastation on them and afflicted them with tumors.*ᵈ* ⁷When the people of Ashdod saw what was happening, they

---

ᵃ 7 Or *"Gods have* (see Septuagint)
ᵇ 18 Traditionally *judged* *ᶜ 21 Ichabod* means *no glory.* *ᵈ 6* Hebrew; Septuagint and Vulgate *tumors. And rats appeared in their land, and there was death and destruction throughout the city*

said, "The ark of the god of Israel must not stay here with us, because his hand is heavy on us and on Dagon our god." ⁸So they called together all the rulers of the Philistines and asked them, "What shall we do with the ark of the god of Israel?"

They answered, "Have the ark of the god of Israel moved to Gath." So they moved the ark of the God of Israel.

⁹But after they had moved it, the LORD's hand was against that city, throwing it into a great panic. He afflicted the people of the city, both young and old, with an outbreak of tumors.ᵃ ¹⁰So they sent the ark of God to Ekron.

As the ark of God was entering Ekron, the people of Ekron cried out, "They have brought the ark of the god of Israel around to us to kill us and our people." ¹¹So they called together all the rulers of the Philistines and said, "Send the ark of the god of Israel away; let it go back to its own place, or itᵇ will kill us and our people." For death had filled the city with panic; God's hand was very heavy on it. ¹²Those who did not die were afflicted with tumors, and the outcry of the city went up to heaven.

The Ark Returned to Israel

6 When the ark of the LORD had been in Philistine territory seven months, ²the Philistines called for the priests and the diviners and said, "What shall we do with the ark of the LORD? Tell us how we should send it back to its place."

³They answered, "If you return the ark of the god of Israel, do not send it back to him without a gift; by all means send a guilt offering to him. Then you will be healed, and you will know why his hand has not been lifted from you."

⁴The Philistines asked, "What guilt offering should we send to him?"

They replied, "Five gold tumors and five gold rats, according to the number of the Philistine rulers, because the same plague has struck both you and your rulers. ⁵Make models of the tumors and of the rats that are destroying the country, and give glory to Israel's god. Perhaps

he will lift his hand from you and your gods and your land. ⁶Why do you harden your hearts as the Egyptians and Pharaoh did? When Israel's god dealt harshly with them, did they not send the Israelites out so they could go on their way?

⁷"Now then, get a new cart ready, with two cows that have calved and have never been yoked. Hitch the cows to the cart, but take their calves away and pen them up. ⁸Take the ark of the LORD and put it on the cart, and in a chest beside it put the gold objects you are sending back to him as a guilt offering. Send it on its way, ⁹but keep watching it. If it goes up to its own territory, toward Beth Shemesh, then the LORD has brought this great disaster on us. But if it does not, then we will know that it was not his hand that struck us but that it happened to us by chance."

¹⁰So they did this. They took two such cows and hitched them to the cart and penned up their calves. ¹¹They placed the ark of the LORD on the cart and along with it the chest containing the gold rats and the models of the tumors. ¹²Then the cows went straight up toward Beth Shemesh, keeping on the road and lowing all the way; they did not turn to the right or to the left. The rulers of the Philistines followed them as far as the border of Beth Shemesh.

¹³Now the people of Beth Shemesh were harvesting their wheat in the valley, and when they looked up and saw the ark, they rejoiced at the sight. ¹⁴The cart came to the field of Joshua of Beth Shemesh, and there it stopped beside a large rock. The people chopped up the wood of the cart and sacrificed the cows as a burnt offering to the LORD. ¹⁵The Levites took down the ark of the LORD, together with the chest containing the gold objects, and placed them on the large rock. On that day the people of Beth Shemesh offered burnt offerings and made sacrifices to the LORD. ¹⁶The five rulers of the Philistines saw all this and then returned that same day to Ekron.

ᵃ 9 Or with tumors in the groin (see Septuagint)
ᵇ 11 Or he

[17]These are the gold tumors the Philistines sent as a guilt offering to the LORD—one each for Ashdod, Gaza, Ashkelon, Gath and Ekron. [18]And the number of the gold rats was according to the number of Philistine towns belonging to the five rulers—the fortified towns with their country villages. The large rock on which the Levites set the ark of the LORD is a witness to this day in the field of Joshua of Beth Shemesh.

[19]But God struck down some of the inhabitants of Beth Shemesh, putting seventy[a] of them to death because they looked into the ark of the LORD. The people mourned because of the heavy blow the LORD had dealt them. [20]And the people of Beth Shemesh asked, "Who can stand in the presence of the LORD, this holy God? To whom will the ark go up from here?"

[21]Then they sent messengers to the people of Kiriath Jearim, saying, "The Philistines have returned the ark of the LORD. Come down and take it up to your town."

7 [1]So the men of Kiriath Jearim came and took up the ark of the LORD. They brought it to Abinadab's house on the hill and consecrated Eleazar his son to guard the ark of the LORD. [2]The ark remained at Kiriath Jearim a long time—twenty years in all.

Samuel Subdues the Philistines at Mizpah

Then all the people of Israel turned back to the LORD. [3]So Samuel said to all the Israelites, "If you are returning to the LORD with all your hearts, then rid yourselves of the foreign gods and the Ashtoreths and commit yourselves to the LORD and serve him only, and he will deliver you out of the hand of the Philistines." [4]So the Israelites put away their Baals and Ashtoreths, and served the LORD only.

[5]Then Samuel said, "Assemble all Israel at Mizpah, and I will intercede with the LORD for you." [6]When they had assembled at Mizpah, they drew water and poured it out before the LORD. On that day they fasted and there they confessed, "We have sinned against the LORD." Now

ROCK SOLID *promises*

"Commit yourselves to the LORD and serve him only, and he will deliver you." 1 Samuel 7:3

Don't expect the Lord to rescue you if you chase other gods—if you let anything become more important than him.

Samuel was serving as leader[b] of Israel at Mizpah.

[7]When the Philistines heard that Israel had assembled at Mizpah, the rulers of the Philistines came up to attack them. When the Israelites heard of it, they were afraid because of the Philistines. [8]They said to Samuel, "Do not stop crying out to the LORD our God for us, that he may rescue us from the hand of the Philistines." [9]Then Samuel took a suckling lamb and sacrificed it as a whole burnt offering to the LORD. He cried out to the LORD on Israel's behalf, and the LORD answered him.

[10]While Samuel was sacrificing the burnt offering, the Philistines drew near to engage Israel in battle. But that day the LORD thundered with loud thunder against the Philistines and threw them into such a panic that they were routed before the Israelites. [11]The men of Israel rushed out of Mizpah and pursued the Philistines, slaughtering them along the way to a point below Beth Kar.

[12]Then Samuel took a stone and set it up between Mizpah and Shen. He named it Ebenezer,[c] saying, "Thus far the LORD has helped us."

[13]So the Philistines were subdued and they stopped invading Israel's territory.

[a] 19 A few Hebrew manuscripts; most Hebrew manuscripts and Septuagint 50,070
[b] 6 Traditionally judge; also in verse 15
[c] 12 Ebenezer means stone of help.

Throughout Samuel's lifetime, the hand of the LORD was against the Philistines. [14]The towns from Ekron to Gath that the Philistines had captured from Israel were restored to Israel, and Israel delivered the neighboring territory from the hands of the Philistines. And there was peace between Israel and the Amorites.

[15]Samuel continued as Israel's leader all the days of his life. [16]From year to year he went on a circuit from Bethel to Gilgal to Mizpah, judging Israel in all those places. [17]But he always went back to Ramah, where his home was, and there he also held court for Israel. And he built an altar there to the LORD.

Israel Asks for a King

8 When Samuel grew old, he appointed his sons as Israel's leaders.[a] [2]The name of his firstborn was Joel and the name of his second was Abijah, and they served at Beersheba. [3]But his sons did not follow his ways. They turned aside after dishonest gain and accepted bribes and perverted justice.

[4]So all the elders of Israel gathered together and came to Samuel at Ramah. [5]They said to him, "You are old, and your sons do not follow your ways; now appoint a king to lead[b] us, such as all the other nations have."

[6]But when they said, "Give us a king to lead us," this displeased Samuel; so he prayed to the LORD. [7]And the LORD told him: "Listen to all that the people are saying to you; it is not you they have rejected, but they have rejected me as their king. [8]As they have done from the day I brought them up out of Egypt until this day, forsaking me and serving other gods, so they are doing to you. [9]Now listen to them; but warn them solemnly and let them know what the king who will reign over them will claim as his rights."

[10]Samuel told all the words of the LORD to the people who were asking him for a king. [11]He said, "This is what the king who will reign over you will claim as his rights: He will take your sons and make them serve with his chariots and horses,

and they will run in front of his chariots. [12]Some he will assign to be commanders of thousands and commanders of fifties, and others to plow his ground and reap his harvest, and still others to make weapons of war and equipment for his chariots. [13]He will take your daughters to be perfumers and cooks and bakers. [14]He will take the best of your fields and vineyards and olive groves and give them to his attendants. [15]He will take a tenth of your grain and of your vintage and give it to his officials and attendants. [16]Your male and female servants and the best of your cattle[c] and donkeys he will take for his own use. [17]He will take a tenth of your flocks, and you yourselves will become his slaves. [18]When that day comes, you will cry out for relief from the king you have chosen, but the LORD will not answer you in that day."

a 1 Traditionally *judges*   *b 5* Traditionally *judge*; also in verses 6 and 20   *c 16* Septuagint; Hebrew *young men*

ROCK SOLID *plans*

1 Samuel 8:1–22

Don't beg God for second best.

The prophet Samuel grieved when the leaders of Israel demanded a king to rule the nation. Not only was Samuel saddened by their request, so was God. The Lord understood their demand as a rejection of his own reign, and he warned that a human king was a terrible idea. Yet when the people continued to beg for a king, God gave in. They ended up with Saul as their ruler—a man who stood a head taller than anyone else (see 1 Samuel 10:23–24) but who failed miserably as a leader (see 1 Samuel 13:13–14).

Your next step: Tell God you want his very best for your life—and gladly accept it.

¹⁹But the people refused to listen to Samuel. "No!" they said. "We want a king over us. ²⁰Then we will be like all the other nations, with a king to lead us and to go out before us and fight our battles."

²¹When Samuel heard all that the people said, he repeated it before the Lord. ²²The Lord answered, "Listen to them and give them a king."

Then Samuel said to the Israelites, "Everyone go back to your own town."

Samuel Anoints Saul

9 There was a Benjamite, a man of standing, whose name was Kish son of Abiel, the son of Zeror, the son of Bekorath, the son of Aphiah of Benjamin. ²Kish had a son named Saul, as handsome a young man as could be found anywhere in Israel, and he was a head taller than anyone else.

³Now the donkeys belonging to Saul's father Kish were lost, and Kish said to his son Saul, "Take one of the servants with you and go and look for the donkeys." ⁴So he passed through the hill country of Ephraim and through the area around Shalisha, but they did not find them. They went on into the district of Shaalim, but the donkeys were not there. Then he passed through the territory of Benjamin, but they did not find them.

⁵When they reached the district of Zuph, Saul said to the servant who was with him, "Come, let's go back, or my father will stop thinking about the donkeys and start worrying about us."

⁶But the servant replied, "Look, in this town there is a man of God; he is highly respected, and everything he says comes true. Let's go there now. Perhaps he will tell us what way to take."

⁷Saul said to his servant, "If we go, what can we give the man? The food in our sacks is gone. We have no gift to take to the man of God. What do we have?"

⁸The servant answered him again. "Look," he said, "I have a quarter of a shekel^a of silver. I will give it to the man of God so that he will tell us what way to take." ⁹(Formerly in Israel, if someone

went to inquire of God, they would say, "Come, let us go to the seer," because the prophet of today used to be called a seer.)

¹⁰"Good," Saul said to his servant. "Come, let's go." So they set out for the town where the man of God was.

¹¹As they were going up the hill to the town, they met some young women coming out to draw water, and they asked them, "Is the seer here?"

¹²"He is," they answered. "He's ahead of you. Hurry now; he has just come to our town today, for the people have a sacrifice at the high place. ¹³As soon as you enter the town, you will find him before he goes up to the high place to eat. The people will not begin eating until he comes, because he must bless the sacrifice; afterward, those who are invited will eat. Go up now; you should find him about this time."

¹⁴They went up to the town, and as they were entering it, there was Samuel, coming toward them on his way up to the high place.

¹⁵Now the day before Saul came, the Lord had revealed this to Samuel: ¹⁶"About this time tomorrow I will send you a man from the land of Benjamin. Anoint him ruler over my people Israel; he will deliver them from the hand of the Philistines. I have looked on my people, for their cry has reached me."

¹⁷When Samuel caught sight of Saul, the Lord said to him, "This is the man I spoke to you about; he will govern my people."

¹⁸Saul approached Samuel in the gateway and asked, "Would you please tell me where the seer's house is?"

¹⁹"I am the seer," Samuel replied. "Go up ahead of me to the high place, for today you are to eat with me, and in the morning I will send you on your way and will tell you all that is in your heart. ²⁰As for the donkeys you lost three days ago, do not worry about them; they have been found. And to whom is all the desire of Israel turned, if not to you and your whole family line?"

²¹Saul answered, "But am I not a Benja-

^a 8 That is, about 1/10 ounce or about 3 grams

mite, from the smallest tribe of Israel, and is not my clan the least of all the clans of the tribe of Benjamin? Why do you say such a thing to me?"

²²Then Samuel brought Saul and his servant into the hall and seated them at the head of those who were invited—about thirty in number. ²³Samuel said to the cook, "Bring the piece of meat I gave you, the one I told you to lay aside."

²⁴So the cook took up the thigh with what was on it and set it in front of Saul. Samuel said, "Here is what has been kept for you. Eat, because it was set aside for you for this occasion from the time I said, 'I have invited guests.'" And Saul dined with Samuel that day.

²⁵After they came down from the high place to the town, Samuel talked with Saul on the roof of his house. ²⁶They rose about daybreak, and Samuel called to Saul on the roof, "Get ready, and I will send you on your way." When Saul got ready, he and Samuel went outside together. ²⁷As they were going down to the edge of the town, Samuel said to Saul, "Tell the servant to go on ahead of us"—and the servant did so—"but you stay here for a while, so that I may give you a message from God."

10 Then Samuel took a flask of olive oil and poured it on Saul's head and kissed him, saying, "Has not the LORD anointed you ruler over his inheritance?*a* ²When you leave me today, you will meet two men near Rachel's tomb, at Zelzah on the border of Benjamin. They will say to you, 'The donkeys you set out to look for have been found. And now your father has stopped thinking about them and is worried about you. He is asking, "What shall I do about my son?"'

³"Then you will go on from there until you reach the great tree of Tabor. Three men going up to worship God at Bethel will meet you there. One will be carrying three young goats, another three loaves of bread, and another a skin of wine. ⁴They will greet you and offer you two loaves of bread, which you will accept from them.

⁵"After that you will go to Gibeah of God, where there is a Philistine outpost. As you approach the town, you will meet a procession of prophets coming down from the high place with lyres, timbrels, pipes and harps being played before them, and they will be prophesying. ⁶The Spirit of the LORD will come powerfully upon you, and you will prophesy with them; and you will be changed into a different person. ⁷Once these signs are fulfilled, do whatever your hand finds to do, for God is with you.

⁸"Go down ahead of me to Gilgal. I will surely come down to you to sacrifice burnt offerings and fellowship offerings, but you must wait seven days until I come to you and tell you what you are to do."

Saul Made King

⁹As Saul turned to leave Samuel, God changed Saul's heart, and all these signs were fulfilled that day. ¹⁰When he and his servant arrived at Gibeah, a procession of prophets met him; the Spirit of God came powerfully upon him, and he joined in their prophesying. ¹¹When all those who had formerly known him saw him prophesying with the prophets, they asked each other, "What is this that has happened to the son of Kish? Is Saul also among the prophets?"

¹²A man who lived there answered, "And who is their father?" So it became a saying: "Is Saul also among the prophets?" ¹³After Saul stopped prophesying, he went to the high place.

¹⁴Now Saul's uncle asked him and his servant, "Where have you been?"

"Looking for the donkeys," he said. "But when we saw they were not to be found, we went to Samuel."

¹⁵Saul's uncle said, "Tell me what Samuel said to you."

¹⁶Saul replied, "He assured us that the donkeys had been found." But he did not

a 1 Hebrew; Septuagint and Vulgate over his people Israel? You will reign over the LORD's people and save them from the power of their enemies round about. And this will be a sign to you that the LORD has anointed you ruler over his inheritance:

tell his uncle what Samuel had said about the kingship.

[17]Samuel summoned the people of Israel to the LORD at Mizpah [18]and said to them, "This is what the LORD, the God of Israel, says: 'I brought Israel up out of Egypt, and I delivered you from the power of Egypt and all the kingdoms that oppressed you.' [19]But you have now rejected your God, who saves you out of all your disasters and calamities. And you have said, 'No, appoint a king over us.' So now present yourselves before the LORD by your tribes and clans."

[20]When Samuel had all Israel come forward by tribes, the tribe of Benjamin was taken by lot. [21]Then he brought forward the tribe of Benjamin, clan by clan, and Matri's clan was taken. Finally Saul son of Kish was taken. But when they looked for him, he was not to be found. [22]So they inquired further of the LORD, "Has the man come here yet?"

And the LORD said, "Yes, he has hidden himself among the supplies."

[23]They ran and brought him out, and as he stood among the people he was a head taller than any of the others. [24]Samuel said to all the people, "Do you see the man the LORD has chosen? There is no one like him among all the people."

Then the people shouted, "Long live the king!"

[25]Samuel explained to the people the rights and duties of kingship. He wrote them down on a scroll and deposited it before the LORD. Then Samuel dismissed the people to go to their own homes.

[26]Saul also went to his home in Gibeah, accompanied by valiant men whose hearts God had touched. [27]But some scoundrels said, "How can this fellow save us?" They despised him and brought him no gifts. But Saul kept silent.

Saul Rescues the City of Jabesh

11 Nahash[a] the Ammonite went up and besieged Jabesh Gilead. And all the men of Jabesh said to him, "Make a treaty with us, and we will be subject to you."

[2]But Nahash the Ammonite replied, "I

ROCK SOLID truths

1 Samuel 10:9–27

Looks aren't everything.

The people of Israel were convinced that having a king to lead them in war would make them as brawny and triumphant as their pagan neighbors (see 1 Samuel 8:1–22). And they liked the guy destined to become their first king. Saul was "as handsome a young man as could be found anywhere in Israel, and he was a head taller than anyone else" (1 Samuel 9:2). But Israel was about to discover that looks aren't everything. In this comic scene, the whole nation waits to meet the new king, only to have the Lord himself have to point out that the giant guy is hiding under a pile of baggage (see 1 Samuel 10:22). Saul repeatedly rejected God's commands, including keeping goods taken in war for himself rather than destroying them as the Lord had instructed (see 1 Samuel 15:14–21). Good looks might have made Saul popular, but they did nothing for his ability to be a smart and committed follower of God.

Think: Where do you see people adored for how they look on the outside? How do you deal with that?

---

[a] *1 Masoretic Text; Dead Sea Scrolls gifts. Now Nahash king of the Ammonites oppressed the Gadites and Reubenites severely. He gouged out all their right eyes and struck terror and dread in Israel. Not a man remained among the Israelites beyond the Jordan whose right eye was not gouged out by Nahash king of the Ammonites, except that seven thousand men fled from the Ammonites and entered Jabesh Gilead. About a month later,* [1]*Nahash*

will make a treaty with you only on the condition that I gouge out the right eye of every one of you and so bring disgrace on all Israel."

³The elders of Jabesh said to him, "Give us seven days so we can send messengers throughout Israel; if no one comes to rescue us, we will surrender to you."

⁴When the messengers came to Gibeah of Saul and reported these terms to the people, they all wept aloud. ⁵Just then Saul was returning from the fields, behind his oxen, and he asked, "What is wrong with everyone? Why are they weeping?" Then they repeated to him what the men of Jabesh had said.

⁶When Saul heard their words, the Spirit of God came powerfully upon him, and he burned with anger. ⁷He took a pair of oxen, cut them into pieces, and sent the pieces by messengers throughout Israel, proclaiming, "This is what will be done to the oxen of anyone who does not follow Saul and Samuel." Then the terror of the LORD fell on the people, and they came out together as one. ⁸When Saul mustered them at Bezek, the men of Israel numbered three hundred thousand and those of Judah thirty thousand.

⁹They told the messengers who had come, "Say to the men of Jabesh Gilead, 'By the time the sun is hot tomorrow, you will be rescued.'" When the messengers went and reported this to the men of Jabesh, they were elated. ¹⁰They said to the Ammonites, "Tomorrow we will surrender to you, and you can do to us whatever you like."

¹¹The next day Saul separated his men into three divisions; during the last watch of the night they broke into the camp of the Ammonites and slaughtered them until the heat of the day. Those who survived were scattered, so that no two of them were left together.

Saul Confirmed as King

¹²The people then said to Samuel, "Who was it that asked, 'Shall Saul reign over us?' Turn these men over to us so that we may put them to death."

¹³But Saul said, "No one will be put to death today, for this day the LORD has rescued Israel."

¹⁴Then Samuel said to the people, "Come, let us go to Gilgal and there renew the kingship." ¹⁵So all the people went to Gilgal and made Saul king in the presence of the LORD. There they sacrificed fellowship offerings before the LORD, and Saul and all the Israelites held a great celebration.

Samuel's Farewell Speech

12 Samuel said to all Israel, "I have listened to everything you said to me and have set a king over you. ²Now you have a king as your leader. As for me, I am old and gray, and my sons are here with you. I have been your leader from my youth until this day. ³Here I stand. Testify against me in the presence of the LORD and his anointed. Whose ox have I taken? Whose donkey have I taken? Whom have I cheated? Whom have I oppressed? From whose hand have I accepted a bribe to make me shut my eyes? If I have done any of these things, I will make it right."

⁴"You have not cheated or oppressed us," they replied. "You have not taken anything from anyone's hand."

⁵Samuel said to them, "The LORD is witness against you, and also his anointed is witness this day, that you have not found anything in my hand."

"He is witness," they said.

⁶Then Samuel said to the people, "It is the LORD who appointed Moses and Aaron and brought your ancestors up out of Egypt. ⁷Now then, stand here, because I am going to confront you with evidence before the LORD as to all the righteous acts performed by the LORD for you and your ancestors.

⁸"After Jacob entered Egypt, they cried to the LORD for help, and the LORD sent Moses and Aaron, who brought your ancestors out of Egypt and settled them in this place.

⁹"But they forgot the LORD their God; so he sold them into the hand of Sisera,

the commander of the army of Hazor, and into the hands of the Philistines and the king of Moab, who fought against them. [10]They cried out to the LORD and said, 'We have sinned; we have forsaken the LORD and served the Baals and the Ashtoreths. But now deliver us from the hands of our enemies, and we will serve you.' [11]Then the LORD sent Jerub-Baal,[a] Barak,[b] Jephthah and Samuel,[c] and he delivered you from the hands of your enemies all around you, so that you lived in safety.

[12]"But when you saw that Nahash king of the Ammonites was moving against you, you said to me, 'No, we want a king to rule over us'—even though the LORD your God was your king. [13]Now here is the king you have chosen, the one you asked for; see, the LORD has set a king over you. [14]If you fear the LORD and serve and obey him and do not rebel against his commands, and if both you and the king who reigns over you follow the LORD your God—good! [15]But if you do not obey the LORD, and if you rebel against his com-

[a] 11 Also called *Gideon*   [b] 11 Some Septuagint manuscripts and Syriac; Hebrew *Bedan*   [c] 11 Hebrew; some Septuagint manuscripts and Syriac *Samson*

---

1 Samuel 12:1–25

Samuel lived his whole life for God.

Samuel was a miracle baby, born to Hannah, a woman long unable to conceive a child. As this godly woman prayed in the house of the Lord year after year, God honored her request. He granted her a son, whom she promised to dedicate absolutely to him. She kept her vow, presenting her little boy to serve in God's house and declaring that "his whole life he will be given over to the LORD" (1 Samuel 1:28).

Samuel lived up to his mother's pledge. From the start he "worshiped the LORD" (1 Samuel 1:28) and "ministered before the LORD" (1 Samuel 3:1). One night young Samuel was lying in the temple near the ark of God, a focused place of the Lord's presence. Samuel heard a voice calling him and assumed it was Eli, the head priest. But it was the Lord himself, warning he was about to carry out judgment against Eli and his evil sons (see 1 Samuel 3:1–18). People soon recognized Samuel was a prophet, because the Lord "let none of Samuel's words fall to the ground" (1 Samuel 3:19).

Samuel anointed Saul as Israel's first king (see 1 Samuel 10:1) and David as his successor (see 1 Samuel 16:1–13), and he spoke a passionate farewell speech that listed his service to God (see 1 Samuel 12). Even long after his death Samuel was esteemed as one of Israel's great leaders (see Jeremiah 15:1). This is a guy famed for giving his whole life to God.

You can find Samuel in 1 Samuel 1—16; 1 Samuel 25:1; 1 Samuel 28:3–16; Acts 13:20; and Hebrews 11:32.

UNSHAKEN people

mands, his hand will be against you, as it was against your ancestors.

¹⁶ "Now then, stand still and see this great thing the LORD is about to do before your eyes! ¹⁷ Is it not wheat harvest now? I will call on the LORD to send thunder and rain. And you will realize what an evil thing you did in the eyes of the LORD when you asked for a king."

¹⁸ Then Samuel called on the LORD, and that same day the LORD sent thunder and rain. So all the people stood in awe of the LORD and of Samuel.

¹⁹ The people all said to Samuel, "Pray to the LORD your God for your servants so that we will not die, for we have added to all our other sins the evil of asking for a king."

²⁰ "Do not be afraid," Samuel replied. "You have done all this evil; yet do not turn away from the LORD, but serve the LORD with all your heart. ²¹ Do not turn away after useless idols. They can do you no good, nor can they rescue you, because they are useless. ²² For the sake of his great name the LORD will not reject his people, because the LORD was pleased to make you his own. ²³ As for me, far be it from me that I should sin against the LORD by failing to pray for you. And I will teach you the way that is good and right. ²⁴ But be sure to fear the LORD and serve him faithfully with all your heart; consider what great things he has done for you. ²⁵ Yet if you persist in doing evil, both you and your king will perish."

Samuel Rebukes Saul

13 Saul was thirty^a years old when he became king, and he reigned over Israel forty-^b two years.

² Saul chose three thousand men from Israel; two thousand were with him at Mikmash and in the hill country of Bethel, and a thousand were with Jonathan at Gibeah in Benjamin. The rest of the men he sent back to their homes.

³ Jonathan attacked the Philistine outpost at Geba, and the Philistines heard about it. Then Saul had the trumpet blown throughout the land and said, "Let the Hebrews hear!" ⁴ So all Israel heard the news: "Saul has attacked the Philistine outpost, and now Israel has become obnoxious to the Philistines." And the people were summoned to join Saul at Gilgal.

⁵ The Philistines assembled to fight Israel, with three thousand^c chariots, six thousand charioteers, and soldiers as numerous as the sand on the seashore. They went up and camped at Mikmash, east of Beth Aven. ⁶ When the Israelites saw that their situation was critical and that their army was hard pressed, they hid in caves and thickets, among the rocks, and in pits and cisterns. ⁷ Some Hebrews even crossed the Jordan to the land of Gad and Gilead.

Saul remained at Gilgal, and all the troops with him were quaking with fear. ⁸ He waited seven days, the time set by Samuel; but Samuel did not come to Gilgal, and Saul's men began to scatter. ⁹ So he said, "Bring me the burnt offering and the fellowship offerings." And Saul offered up the burnt offering. ¹⁰ Just as he finished making the offering, Samuel arrived, and Saul went out to greet him.

¹¹ "What have you done?" asked Samuel.

Saul replied, "When I saw that the men were scattering, and that you did not come at the set time, and that the Philistines were assembling at Mikmash, ¹² I thought, 'Now the Philistines will come down against me at Gilgal, and I have not sought the LORD's favor.' So I felt compelled to offer the burnt offering."

¹³ "You have done a foolish thing," Samuel said. "You have not kept the command the LORD your God gave you; if you had, he would have established your kingdom over Israel for all time. ¹⁴ But now your kingdom will not endure; the LORD has sought out a man after his own heart and appointed him ruler of

---

^a 1 A few late manuscripts of the Septuagint; Hebrew does not have *thirty*.   ^b 1 Probable reading of the original Hebrew text (see Acts 13:21); Masoretic Text does not have *forty-*.
^c 5 Some Septuagint manuscripts and Syriac; Hebrew *thirty thousand*

his people, because you have not kept the Lord's command."

¹⁵Then Samuel left Gilgal*ᵃ* and went up to Gibeah in Benjamin, and Saul counted the men who were with him. They numbered about six hundred.

ROCK SOLID
promises

"The Lord has sought out a man after his own heart." 1 Samuel 13:14

God eagerly puts his real followers to work. He's looking for you to passionately obey his commands.

Israel Without Weapons

¹⁶Saul and his son Jonathan and the men with them were staying in Gibeah*ᵇ* in Benjamin, while the Philistines camped at Mikmash. ¹⁷Raiding parties went out from the Philistine camp in three detachments. One turned toward Ophrah in the vicinity of Shual, ¹⁸another toward Beth Horon, and the third toward the borderland overlooking the Valley of Zeboyim facing the wilderness.

¹⁹Not a blacksmith could be found in the whole land of Israel, because the Philistines had said, "Otherwise the Hebrews will make swords or spears!" ²⁰So all Israel went down to the Philistines to have their plow points, mattocks, axes and sickles*ᶜ* sharpened. ²¹The price was two-thirds of a shekel*ᵈ* for sharpening plow points and mattocks, and a third of a shekel*ᵉ* for sharpening forks and axes and for repointing goads. ²²So on the day of the battle not a soldier with Saul and Jonathan had a sword or spear in his hand; only Saul and his son Jonathan had them.

Jonathan Attacks the Philistines

²³Now a detachment of Philistines had gone out to the pass at Mikmash.

14 ¹One day Jonathan son of Saul said to his young armor-bearer, "Come, let's go over to the Philistine outpost on the other side." But he did not tell his father.

²Saul was staying on the outskirts of Gibeah under a pomegranate tree in Migron. With him were about six hundred men, ³among whom was Ahijah, who was wearing an ephod. He was a son of Ichabod's brother Ahitub son of Phinehas, the son of Eli, the Lord's priest in Shiloh. No one was aware that Jonathan had left.

⁴On each side of the pass that Jonathan intended to cross to reach the Philistine outpost was a cliff; one was called Bozez and the other Seneh. ⁵One cliff stood to the north toward Mikmash, the other to the south toward Geba.

⁶Jonathan said to his young armor-bearer, "Come, let's go over to the outpost of those uncircumcised men. Perhaps the Lord will act in our behalf. Nothing can hinder the Lord from saving, whether by many or by few."

⁷"Do all that you have in mind," his armor-bearer said. "Go ahead; I am with you heart and soul."

⁸Jonathan said, "Come on, then; we will cross over toward them and let them see us. ⁹If they say to us, 'Wait there until we come to you,' we will stay where we are and not go up to them. ¹⁰But if they say, 'Come up to us,' we will climb up, because that will be our sign that the Lord has given them into our hands."

¹¹So both of them showed themselves to the Philistine outpost. "Look!" said the Philistines. "The Hebrews are crawling out of the holes they were hiding in." ¹²The men of the outpost shouted to Jon-

---

ᵃ 15 Hebrew; Septuagint *Gilgal and went his way; the rest of the people went after Saul to meet the army, and they went out of Gilgal*
ᵇ 16 Two Hebrew manuscripts; most Hebrew manuscripts *Geba,* a variant of *Gibeah*
ᶜ 20 Septuagint; Hebrew *plow points*
ᵈ 21 That is, about 1/4 ounce or about 8 grams
ᵉ 21 That is, about 1/8 ounce or about 4 grams

athan and his armor-bearer, "Come up to us and we'll teach you a lesson."

So Jonathan said to his armor-bearer, "Climb up after me; the LORD has given them into the hand of Israel."

[13]Jonathan climbed up, using his hands and feet, with his armor-bearer right behind him. The Philistines fell before Jonathan, and his armor-bearer followed and killed behind him. [14]In that first attack Jonathan and his armor-bearer killed some twenty men in an area of about half an acre.

Israel Routs the Philistines

[15]Then panic struck the whole army—those in the camp and field, and those in the outposts and raiding parties—and the ground shook. It was a panic sent by God.[a]

[16]Saul's lookouts at Gibeah in Benjamin saw the army melting away in all directions. [17]Then Saul said to the men who were with him, "Muster the forces and see who has left us." When they did, it was Jonathan and his armor-bearer who were not there.

[18]Saul said to Ahijah, "Bring the ark of God." (At that time it was with the Israelites.)[b] [19]While Saul was talking to the priest, the tumult in the Philistine camp increased more and more. So Saul said to the priest, "Withdraw your hand."

[20]Then Saul and all his men assembled and went to the battle. They found the Philistines in total confusion, striking each other with their swords. [21]Those Hebrews who had previously been with the Philistines and had gone up with them to their camp went over to the Israelites who were with Saul and Jonathan. [22]When all the Israelites who had hidden in the hill country of Ephraim heard that the Philistines were on the run, they joined the battle in hot pursuit. [23]So on that day the LORD saved Israel, and the battle moved on beyond Beth Aven.

Jonathan Eats Honey

[24]Now the Israelites were in distress that day, because Saul had bound the people under an oath, saying, "Cursed be anyone who eats food before evening comes, before I have avenged myself on my enemies!" So none of the troops tasted food.

[25]The entire army entered the woods, and there was honey on the ground. [26]When they went into the woods, they saw the honey oozing out; yet no one put his hand to his mouth, because they feared the oath. [27]But Jonathan had not heard that his father had bound the people with the oath, so he reached out the end of the staff that was in his hand and dipped it into the honeycomb. He raised his hand to his mouth, and his eyes brightened.[c] [28]Then one of the soldiers told him, "Your father bound the army under a strict oath, saying, 'Cursed be anyone who eats food today!' That is why the men are faint."

[29]Jonathan said, "My father has made trouble for the country. See how my eyes brightened when I tasted a little of this honey. [30]How much better it would have been if the men had eaten today some of the plunder they took from their enemies. Would not the slaughter of the Philistines have been even greater?"

[31]That day, after the Israelites had struck down the Philistines from Mikmash to Aijalon, they were exhausted. [32]They pounced on the plunder and, taking sheep, cattle and calves, they butchered them on the ground and ate them, together with the blood. [33]Then someone said to Saul, "Look, the men are sinning against the LORD by eating meat that has blood in it."

"You have broken faith," he said. "Roll a large stone over here at once." [34]Then he said, "Go out among the men and tell them, 'Each of you bring me your cattle and sheep, and slaughter them here and eat them. Do not sin against the LORD by eating meat with blood still in it.'"

So everyone brought his ox that night and slaughtered it there. [35]Then Saul built an altar to the LORD; it was the first time he had done this.

[36]Saul said, "Let us go down and pursue the Philistines by night and plunder them till dawn, and let us not leave one of them alive."

[a] 15 Or *a terrible panic*   [b] 18 Hebrew; Septuagint *"Bring the ephod." (At that time he wore the ephod before the Israelites.)*   [c] 27 Or *his strength was renewed*; similarly in verse 29

"Do whatever seems best to you," they replied.

But the priest said, "Let us inquire of God here."

37 So Saul asked God, "Shall I go down and pursue the Philistines? Will you give them into Israel's hand?" But God did not answer him that day.

38 Saul therefore said, "Come here, all you who are leaders of the army, and let us find out what sin has been committed today. 39 As surely as the LORD who rescues Israel lives, even if the guilt lies with my son Jonathan, he must die." But not one of them said a word.

40 Saul then said to all the Israelites, "You stand over there; I and Jonathan my son will stand over here."

"Do what seems best to you," they replied.

41 Then Saul prayed to the LORD, the God of Israel, "Why have you not answered your servant today? If the fault is in me or my son Jonathan, respond with Urim, but if the men of Israel are at fault,[a] respond with Thummim." Jonathan and Saul were taken by lot, and the men were cleared. 42 Saul said, "Cast the lot between me and Jonathan my son." And Jonathan was taken.

43 Then Saul said to Jonathan, "Tell me what you have done."

So Jonathan told him, "I tasted a little honey with the end of my staff. And now I must die!"

44 Saul said, "May God deal with me, be it ever so severely, if you do not die, Jonathan."

45 But the men said to Saul, "Should Jonathan die — he who has brought about this great deliverance in Israel? Never! As surely as the LORD lives, not a hair of his head will fall to the ground, for he did this today with God's help." So the men rescued Jonathan, and he was not put to death.

46 Then Saul stopped pursuing the Philistines, and they withdrew to their own land.

47 After Saul had assumed rule over Israel, he fought against their enemies on every side: Moab, the Ammonites, Edom, the kings[b] of Zobah, and the Philistines.

Wherever he turned, he inflicted punishment on them.[c] 48 He fought valiantly and defeated the Amalekites, delivering Israel from the hands of those who had plundered them.

Saul's Family

49 Saul's sons were Jonathan, Ishvi and Malki-Shua. The name of his older daughter was Merab, and that of the younger was Michal. 50 His wife's name was Ahinoam daughter of Ahimaaz. The name of the commander of Saul's army was Abner son of Ner, and Ner was Saul's uncle. 51 Saul's father Kish and Abner's father Ner were sons of Abiel.

52 All the days of Saul there was bitter war with the Philistines, and whenever Saul saw a mighty or brave man, he took him into his service.

The LORD Rejects Saul as King

15 Samuel said to Saul, "I am the one the LORD sent to anoint you king over his people Israel; so listen now to the message from the LORD. 2 This is what the LORD Almighty says: 'I will punish the Amalekites for what they did to Israel when they waylaid them as they came up from Egypt. 3 Now go, attack the Amalekites and totally destroy[d] all that belongs to them. Do not spare them; put to death men and women, children and infants, cattle and sheep, camels and donkeys.'"

4 So Saul summoned the men and mustered them at Telaim — two hundred thousand foot soldiers and ten thousand from Judah. 5 Saul went to the city of Amalek and set an ambush in the ravine. 6 Then he said to the Kenites, "Go away, leave the Amalekites so that I do not destroy you along with them; for you showed kindness to all the Israelites when they

---

a 41 Septuagint; Hebrew does not have *"Why . . . at fault.*   *b 47* Masoretic Text; Dead Sea Scrolls and Septuagint *king*   *c 47* Hebrew; Septuagint *he was victorious*   *d 3* The Hebrew term refers to the irrevocable giving over of things or persons to the LORD, often by totally destroying them; also in verses 8, 9, 15, 18, 20 and 21.

came up out of Egypt." So the Kenites moved away from the Amalekites.

[7] Then Saul attacked the Amalekites all the way from Havilah to Shur, near the eastern border of Egypt. [8] He took Agag king of the Amalekites alive, and all his people he totally destroyed with the sword. [9] But Saul and the army spared Agag and the best of the sheep and cattle, the fat calves[a] and lambs—everything that was good. These they were unwilling to destroy completely, but everything that was despised and weak they totally destroyed.

[10] Then the word of the LORD came to Samuel: [11] "I regret that I have made Saul king, because he has turned away from me and has not carried out my instructions." Samuel was angry, and he cried out to the LORD all that night.

[12] Early in the morning Samuel got up and went to meet Saul, but he was told, "Saul has gone to Carmel. There he has set up a monument in his own honor and has turned and gone on down to Gilgal."

[13] When Samuel reached him, Saul said, "The LORD bless you! I have carried out the LORD's instructions."

[14] But Samuel said, "What then is this bleating of sheep in my ears? What is this lowing of cattle that I hear?"

[15] Saul answered, "The soldiers brought them from the Amalekites; they spared the best of the sheep and cattle to sacrifice to the LORD your God, but we totally destroyed the rest."

[16] "Enough!" Samuel said to Saul. "Let me tell you what the LORD said to me last night."

"Tell me," Saul replied.

[17] Samuel said, "Although you were once small in your own eyes, did you not become the head of the tribes of Israel? The LORD anointed you king over Israel. [18] And he sent you on a mission, saying, 'Go and completely destroy those wicked people, the Amalekites; wage war against them until you have wiped them out.' [19] Why did you not obey the LORD? Why did you pounce on the plunder and do evil in the eyes of the LORD?"

[20] "But I did obey the LORD," Saul said.

"I went on the mission the LORD assigned me. I completely destroyed the Amalekites and brought back Agag their king. [21] The soldiers took sheep and cattle from the plunder, the best of what was devoted to God, in order to sacrifice them to the LORD your God at Gilgal."

[22] But Samuel replied:

"Does the LORD delight in burnt offerings and sacrifices
    as much as in obeying the LORD?
To obey is better than sacrifice,
    and to heed is better than the fat of rams.
[23] For rebellion is like the sin of divination,
    and arrogance like the evil of idolatry.
Because you have rejected the word of the LORD,
    he has rejected you as king."

[24] Then Saul said to Samuel, "I have sinned. I violated the LORD's command and your instructions. I was afraid of the men and so I gave in to them. [25] Now I beg you, forgive my sin and come back with me, so that I may worship the LORD."

[26] But Samuel said to him, "I will not go back with you. You have rejected the word of the LORD, and the LORD has rejected you as king over Israel!"

[27] As Samuel turned to leave, Saul caught hold of the hem of his robe, and it tore. [28] Samuel said to him, "The LORD has torn the kingdom of Israel from you today and has given it to one of your neighbors—to one better than you. [29] He who is the Glory of Israel does not lie or change his mind; for he is not a human being, that he should change his mind."

[30] Saul replied, "I have sinned. But please honor me before the elders of my people and before Israel; come back with me, so that I may worship the LORD your God." [31] So Samuel went back with Saul, and Saul worshiped the LORD.

[32] Then Samuel said, "Bring me Agag king of the Amalekites."

Agag came to him in chains.[b] And he

---

[a] 9 Or *the grown bulls*; the meaning of the Hebrew for this phrase is uncertain.
[b] 32 The meaning of the Hebrew for this phrase is uncertain.

thought, "Surely the bitterness of death is past."

³³But Samuel said,

"As your sword has made women
    childless,
  so will your mother be childless
    among women."

And Samuel put Agag to death before the Lord at Gilgal.

³⁴Then Samuel left for Ramah, but Saul went up to his home in Gibeah of Saul. ³⁵Until the day Samuel died, he did not go to see Saul again, though Samuel mourned for him. And the Lord regretted that he had made Saul king over Israel.

Samuel Anoints David

16 The Lord said to Samuel, "How long will you mourn for Saul, since I have rejected him as king over Israel? Fill your horn with oil and be on your way; I am sending you to Jesse of Bethlehem. I have chosen one of his sons to be king."

²But Samuel said, "How can I go? If Saul hears about it, he will kill me."

The Lord said, "Take a heifer with you and say, 'I have come to sacrifice to the Lord.' ³Invite Jesse to the sacrifice, and I will show you what to do. You are to anoint for me the one I indicate."

⁴Samuel did what the Lord said. When he arrived at Bethlehem, the elders of the town trembled when they met him. They asked, "Do you come in peace?"

⁵Samuel replied, "Yes, in peace; I have come to sacrifice to the Lord. Consecrate yourselves and come to the sacrifice with me." Then he consecrated Jesse and his sons and invited them to the sacrifice.

⁶When they arrived, Samuel saw Eliab and thought, "Surely the Lord's anointed stands here before the Lord."

⁷But the Lord said to Samuel, "Do not consider his appearance or his height, for I have rejected him. The Lord does not look at the things people look at. People look at the outward appearance, but the Lord looks at the heart."

ROCK SOLID *promises*

"People look at the outward appearance, but the Lord looks at the heart." 1 Samuel 16:7

God isn't putting on a beauty pageant or a popularity contest. He sees what matters most.

⁸Then Jesse called Abinadab and had him pass in front of Samuel. But Samuel said, "The Lord has not chosen this one either." ⁹Jesse then had Shammah pass by, but Samuel said, "Nor has the Lord chosen this one." ¹⁰Jesse had seven of his sons pass before Samuel, but Samuel said to him, "The Lord has not chosen these." ¹¹So he asked Jesse, "Are these all the sons you have?"

"There is still the youngest," Jesse answered. "He is tending the sheep."

Samuel said, "Send for him; we will not sit down until he arrives."

¹²So he sent for him and had him brought in. He was glowing with health and had a fine appearance and handsome features.

Then the Lord said, "Rise and anoint him; this is the one."

¹³So Samuel took the horn of oil and anointed him in the presence of his brothers, and from that day on the Spirit of the Lord came powerfully upon David. Samuel then went to Ramah.

David in Saul's Service

¹⁴Now the Spirit of the Lord had departed from Saul, and an evil^a spirit from the Lord tormented him.

¹⁵Saul's attendants said to him, "See,

^a 14 Or *and a harmful*; similarly in verses 15, 16 and 23

an evil spirit from God is tormenting you. [16] Let our lord command his servants here to search for someone who can play the lyre. He will play when the evil spirit from God comes on you, and you will feel better."

[17] So Saul said to his attendants, "Find someone who plays well and bring him to me."

[18] One of the servants answered, "I have seen a son of Jesse of Bethlehem who knows how to play the lyre. He is a brave man and a warrior. He speaks well and is a fine-looking man. And the LORD is with him."

[19] Then Saul sent messengers to Jesse and said, "Send me your son David, who is with the sheep." [20] So Jesse took a donkey loaded with bread, a skin of wine and a young goat and sent them with his son David to Saul.

[21] David came to Saul and entered his service. Saul liked him very much, and David became one of his armor-bearers. [22] Then Saul sent word to Jesse, saying, "Allow David to remain in my service, for I am pleased with him."

[23] Whenever the spirit from God came on Saul, David would take up his lyre and play. Then relief would come to Saul; he would feel better, and the evil spirit would leave him.

David and Goliath

17 Now the Philistines gathered their forces for war and assembled at Sokoh in Judah. They pitched camp at Ephes Dammim, between Sokoh and Azekah. [2] Saul and the Israelites assembled and camped in the Valley of Elah and drew up their battle line to meet the Philistines. [3] The Philistines occupied one hill and the Israelites another, with the valley between them.

[4] A champion named Goliath, who was from Gath, came out of the Philistine camp. His height was six cubits and a span.[a] [5] He had a bronze helmet on his head and wore a coat of scale armor of bronze weighing five thousand shekels[b]; [6] on his legs he wore bronze greaves, and a

bronze javelin was slung on his back. [7] His spear shaft was like a weaver's rod, and its iron point weighed six hundred shekels.[c] His shield bearer went ahead of him.

[8] Goliath stood and shouted to the ranks of Israel, "Why do you come out and line up for battle? Am I not a Philistine, and are you not the servants of Saul? Choose a man and have him come down to me. [9] If he is able to fight and kill me, we will become your subjects; but if I overcome him and kill him, you will become our subjects and serve us." [10] Then the Philistine said, "This day I defy the armies of Israel! Give me a man and let us fight each other." [11] On hearing the Philistine's words, Saul and all the Israelites were dismayed and terrified.

[12] Now David was the son of an Ephrathite named Jesse, who was from Bethlehem in Judah. Jesse had eight sons, and in Saul's time he was very old. [13] Jesse's three oldest sons had followed Saul to the war: The firstborn was Eliab; the second, Abinadab; and the third, Shammah. [14] David was the youngest. The three oldest followed Saul, [15] but David went back and forth from Saul to tend his father's sheep at Bethlehem.

[16] For forty days the Philistine came forward every morning and evening and took his stand.

[17] Now Jesse said to his son David, "Take this ephah[d] of roasted grain and these ten loaves of bread for your brothers and hurry to their camp. [18] Take along these ten cheeses to the commander of their unit. See how your brothers are and bring back some assurance[e] from them. [19] They are with Saul and all the men of Israel in the Valley of Elah, fighting against the Philistines."

[20] Early in the morning David left the flock in the care of a shepherd, loaded up and set out, as Jesse had directed. He reached the camp as the army was going

---

[a] 4 That is, about 9 feet 9 inches or about 3 meters   [b] 5 That is, about 125 pounds or about 58 kilograms   [c] 7 That is, about 15 pounds or about 6.9 kilograms   [d] 17 That is, probably about 36 pounds or about 16 kilograms   [e] 18 Or *some token*; or *some pledge of spoils*

out to its battle positions, shouting the war cry. ²¹Israel and the Philistines were drawing up their lines facing each other. ²²David left his things with the keeper of supplies, ran to the battle lines and asked his brothers how they were. ²³As he was talking with them, Goliath, the Philistine champion from Gath, stepped out from his lines and shouted his usual defiance, and David heard it. ²⁴Whenever the Israelites saw the man, they all fled from him in great fear.

²⁵Now the Israelites had been saying, "Do you see how this man keeps coming out? He comes out to defy Israel. The king will give great wealth to the man who kills him. He will also give him his daughter in marriage and will exempt his family from taxes in Israel."

²⁶David asked the men standing near him, "What will be done for the man who kills this Philistine and removes this disgrace from Israel? Who is this uncircumcised Philistine that he should defy the armies of the living God?"

²⁷They repeated to him what they had been saying and told him, "This is what will be done for the man who kills him."

²⁸When Eliab, David's oldest brother, heard him speaking with the men, he burned with anger at him and asked, "Why have you come down here? And with whom did you leave those few sheep in the wilderness? I know how conceited you are and how wicked your heart is; you came down only to watch the battle."

²⁹"Now what have I done?" said David. "Can't I even speak?" ³⁰He then turned away to someone else and brought up the same matter, and the men answered him as before. ³¹What David said was overheard and reported to Saul, and Saul sent for him.

³²David said to Saul, "Let no one lose heart on account of this Philistine; your servant will go and fight him."

³³Saul replied, "You are not able to go out against this Philistine and fight him; you are only a young man, and he has been a warrior from his youth."

³⁴But David said to Saul, "Your servant has been keeping his father's sheep. When a lion or a bear came and carried off a sheep from the flock, ³⁵I went after it, struck it and rescued the sheep from its mouth. When it turned on me, I seized it by its hair, struck it and killed it. ³⁶Your servant has killed both the lion and the bear; this uncircumcised Philistine will be like one of them, because he has defied the armies of the living God. ³⁷The Lord who rescued me from the paw of the lion and the paw of the bear will rescue me from the hand of this Philistine."

Saul said to David, "Go, and the Lord be with you."

³⁸Then Saul dressed David in his own tunic. He put a coat of armor on him and a bronze helmet on his head. ³⁹David fastened on his sword over the tunic and tried walking around, because he was not used to them.

"I cannot go in these," he said to Saul, "because I am not used to them." So he took them off. ⁴⁰Then he took his staff in his hand, chose five smooth stones from the stream, put them in the pouch of his shepherd's bag and, with his sling in his hand, approached the Philistine.

⁴¹Meanwhile, the Philistine, with his shield bearer in front of him, kept coming closer to David. ⁴²He looked David over and saw that he was little more than a boy, glowing with health and handsome, and he despised him. ⁴³He said to David, "Am I a dog, that you come at me with sticks?" And the Philistine cursed David by his gods. ⁴⁴"Come here," he said, "and I'll give your flesh to the birds and the wild animals!"

⁴⁵David said to the Philistine, "You come against me with sword and spear and javelin, but I come against you in the name of the Lord Almighty, the God of the armies of Israel, whom you have defied. ⁴⁶This day the Lord will deliver you into my hands, and I'll strike you down and cut off your head. This very day I will give the carcasses of the Philistine army to the birds and the wild animals, and the whole world will know that there is a God in Israel. ⁴⁷All those gathered here will know that it is not by sword or spear that the Lord saves; for the battle is the

Lord's, and he will give all of you into our hands."

⁴⁸ As the Philistine moved closer to attack him, David ran quickly toward the battle line to meet him. ⁴⁹ Reaching into his bag and taking out a stone, he slung it and struck the Philistine on the forehead. The stone sank into his forehead, and he fell facedown on the ground.

⁵⁰ So David triumphed over the Philistine with a sling and a stone; without a sword in his hand he struck down the Philistine and killed him.

⁵¹ David ran and stood over him. He took hold of the Philistine's sword and drew it from the sheath. After he killed him, he cut off his head with the sword.

When the Philistines saw that their hero was dead, they turned and ran. ⁵² Then the men of Israel and Judah surged forward with a shout and pursued the Philistines to the entrance of Gath*a* and to the gates of Ekron. Their dead were strewn along the Shaaraim road to Gath and Ekron. ⁵³ When the Israelites returned from chasing the Philistines, they plundered their camp.

⁵⁴ David took the Philistine's head and brought it to Jerusalem; he put the Philistine's weapons in his own tent.

⁵⁵ As Saul watched David going out to meet the Philistine, he said to Abner, commander of the army, "Abner, whose son is that young man?"

Abner replied, "As surely as you live, Your Majesty, I don't know."

⁵⁶ The king said, "Find out whose son this young man is."

⁵⁷ As soon as David returned from killing the Philistine, Abner took him and brought him before Saul, with David still holding the Philistine's head.

⁵⁸ "Whose son are you, young man?" Saul asked him.

David said, "I am the son of your servant Jesse of Bethlehem."

---

a 52 Some Septuagint manuscripts; Hebrew *of a valley*

ROCK SOLID *principles*

1 Samuel 17:1–58

Count on God to be with you.

Anthony had grown up watching his dad drink. His dad would stay sober for a few months, then fall back into a nightmare of alcohol abuse. His dad's off-and-on drinking made it impossible for him to keep a job for long, so Anthony and his dad and little brother had to move to yet another city ... neighborhood ... job ... school. Anthony prided himself on his ability to roll with the punches. But his brother kept reminding him that they couldn't do anything all by themselves. That crazy kid prayed out loud for Anthony and himself and their dad each day before school and every night before bed. They weren't alone, he would say, because God was with them.

David could have claimed credit for his legendary fighting skills, but he knew his ability to defend sheep against wild animals came straight from God. He looked to the Lord for the same large help to deal with Goliath (see 1 Samuel 17:37). When you face giant-sized problems, remember that "the battle is the Lord's" (1 Samuel 17:47).

Saul's Growing Fear of David

18 After David had finished talking with Saul, Jonathan became one in spirit with David, and he loved him as himself. ² From that day Saul kept David with him and did not let him return home to his family. ³ And Jonathan made a covenant with David because he loved him as himself. ⁴ Jonathan took off the robe he was wearing and gave it to David, along with his tunic, and even his sword, his bow and his belt.

⁵ Whatever mission Saul sent him on, David was so successful that Saul gave him a high rank in the army. This pleased all the troops, and Saul's officers as well.

⁶ When the men were returning home after David had killed the Philistine, the women came out from all the towns of Israel to meet King Saul with singing and dancing, with joyful songs and with timbrels and lyres. ⁷ As they danced, they sang:

"Saul has slain his thousands,
and David his tens of thousands."

⁸ Saul was very angry; this refrain displeased him greatly. "They have credited David with tens of thousands," he thought, "but me with only thousands. What more can he get but the kingdom?" ⁹ And from that time on Saul kept a close eye on David.

¹⁰ The next day an evil*ᵃ* spirit from God came forcefully on Saul. He was prophesying in his house, while David was playing the lyre, as he usually did. Saul had a spear in his hand ¹¹ and he hurled it, saying to himself, "I'll pin David to the wall." But David eluded him twice.

¹² Saul was afraid of David, because the LORD was with David but had departed from Saul. ¹³ So he sent David away from him and gave him command over a thousand men, and David led the troops in their campaigns. ¹⁴ In everything he did he had great success, because the LORD was with him. ¹⁵ When Saul saw how successful he was, he was afraid of him. ¹⁶ But all Israel and Judah loved David, because he led them in their campaigns.

¹⁷ Saul said to David, "Here is my older daughter Merab. I will give her to you in marriage; only serve me bravely and fight the battles of the LORD." For Saul said to himself, "I will not raise a hand against him. Let the Philistines do that!"

¹⁸ But David said to Saul, "Who am I, and what is my family or my clan in Israel, that I should become the king's son-in-law?" ¹⁹ So*ᵇ* when the time came for Merab, Saul's daughter, to be given to David, she was given in marriage to Adriel of Meholah.

²⁰ Now Saul's daughter Michal was in love with David, and when they told Saul about it, he was pleased. ²¹ "I will give her to him," he thought, "so that she may be a snare to him and so that the hand of the Philistines may be against him." So Saul said to David, "Now you have a second opportunity to become my son-in-law."

²² Then Saul ordered his attendants: "Speak to David privately and say, 'Look, the king likes you, and his attendants all love you; now become his son-in-law.'"

²³ They repeated these words to David. But David said, "Do you think it is a small matter to become the king's son-in-law? I'm only a poor man and little known."

²⁴ When Saul's servants told him what David had said, ²⁵ Saul replied, "Say to David, 'The king wants no other price for the bride than a hundred Philistine foreskins, to take revenge on his enemies.'" Saul's plan was to have David fall by the hands of the Philistines.

²⁶ When the attendants told David these things, he was pleased to become the king's son-in-law. So before the allotted time elapsed, ²⁷ David took his men with him and went out and killed two hundred Philistines and brought back their foreskins. They counted out the full number to the king so that David might become the king's son-in-law. Then Saul gave him his daughter Michal in marriage.

²⁸ When Saul realized that the LORD was with David and that his daughter Michal loved David, ²⁹ Saul became still more afraid of him, and he remained his enemy the rest of his days.

ᵃ 10 Or *a harmful*   *ᵇ 19* Or *However,*

³⁰The Philistine commanders continued to go out to battle, and as often as they did, David met with more success than the rest of Saul's officers, and his name became well known.

Saul Tries to Kill David

19 Saul told his son Jonathan and all the attendants to kill David. But Jonathan had taken a great liking to David ²and warned him, "My father Saul is looking for a chance to kill you. Be on your guard tomorrow morning; go into hiding and stay there. ³I will go out and stand with my father in the field where you are. I'll speak to him about you and will tell you what I find out."

⁴Jonathan spoke well of David to Saul his father and said to him, "Let not the king do wrong to his servant David; he has not wronged you, and what he has done has benefited you greatly. ⁵He took his life in his hands when he killed the Philistine. The LORD won a great victory for all Israel, and you saw it and were glad. Why then would you do wrong to an innocent man like David by killing him for no reason?"

⁶Saul listened to Jonathan and took this oath: "As surely as the LORD lives, David will not be put to death."

⁷So Jonathan called David and told him the whole conversation. He brought him to Saul, and David was with Saul as before.

⁸Once more war broke out, and David went out and fought the Philistines. He struck them with such force that they fled before him.

⁹But an evil*a* spirit from the LORD came on Saul as he was sitting in his house with his spear in his hand. While David was playing the lyre, ¹⁰Saul tried to pin him to the wall with his spear, but David eluded him as Saul drove the spear into the wall. That night David made good his escape.

¹¹Saul sent men to David's house to watch it and to kill him in the morning. But Michal, David's wife, warned him, "If you don't run for your life tonight, tomorrow you'll be killed." ¹²So Michal let David down through a window, and he fled and escaped. ¹³Then Michal took an idol and laid it on the bed, covering it with a garment and putting some goats' hair at the head.

¹⁴When Saul sent the men to capture David, Michal said, "He is ill."

¹⁵Then Saul sent the men back to see David and told them, "Bring him up to me in his bed so that I may kill him." ¹⁶But when the men entered, there was the idol in the bed, and at the head was some goats' hair.

¹⁷Saul said to Michal, "Why did you deceive me like this and send my enemy away so that he escaped?"

Michal told him, "He said to me, 'Let me get away. Why should I kill you?'"

¹⁸When David had fled and made his escape, he went to Samuel at Ramah and told him all that Saul had done to him. Then he and Samuel went to Naioth and stayed there. ¹⁹Word came to Saul: "David is in Naioth at Ramah"; ²⁰so he sent men to capture him. But when they saw a group of prophets prophesying, with Samuel standing there as their leader, the Spirit of God came on Saul's men, and they also prophesied. ²¹Saul was told about it, and he sent more men, and they prophesied too. Saul sent men a third time, and they also prophesied. ²²Finally, he himself left for Ramah and went to the great cistern at Seku. And he asked, "Where are Samuel and David?"

"Over in Naioth at Ramah," they said.

²³So Saul went to Naioth at Ramah. But the Spirit of God came even on him, and he walked along prophesying until he came to Naioth. ²⁴He stripped off his garments, and he too prophesied in Samuel's presence. He lay naked all that day and all that night. This is why people say, "Is Saul also among the prophets?"

David and Jonathan

20 Then David fled from Naioth at Ramah and went to Jonathan and asked, "What have I done? What is my crime? How have

---

a 9 Or *But a harmful*

I wronged your father, that he is trying to kill me?"

²"Never!" Jonathan replied. "You are not going to die! Look, my father doesn't do anything, great or small, without letting me know. Why would he hide this from me? It isn't so!"

³But David took an oath and said, "Your father knows very well that I have found favor in your eyes, and he has said to himself, 'Jonathan must not know this or he will be grieved.' Yet as surely as the LORD lives and as you live, there is only a step between me and death."

⁴Jonathan said to David, "Whatever you want me to do, I'll do for you."

⁵So David said, "Look, tomorrow is the New Moon feast, and I am supposed to dine with the king; but let me go and hide in the field until the evening of the day after tomorrow. ⁶If your father misses me at all, tell him, 'David earnestly asked my permission to hurry to Bethlehem, his hometown, because an annual sacrifice is being made there for his whole clan.' ⁷If he says, 'Very well,' then your servant is safe. But if he loses his temper, you can be sure that he is determined to harm me. ⁸As for you, show kindness to your servant, for you have brought him into a covenant with you before the LORD. If I am guilty, then kill me yourself! Why hand me over to your father?"

⁹"Never!" Jonathan said. "If I had the least inkling that my father was determined to harm you, wouldn't I tell you?"

¹⁰David asked, "Who will tell me if your father answers you harshly?"

¹¹"Come," Jonathan said, "let's go out into the field." So they went there together.

¹²Then Jonathan said to David, "I swear by the LORD, the God of Israel, that I will surely sound out my father by this time the day after tomorrow! If he is favorably disposed toward you, will I not send you word and let you know? ¹³But if my father intends to harm you, may the LORD deal with Jonathan, be it ever so severely, if I do not let you know and send you away in peace. May the LORD be with you as he has been with my father. ¹⁴But show me unfailing kindness like the LORD's kindness as long as I live, so that I may not be killed, ¹⁵and do not ever cut off your kindness from my family—not even when the LORD has cut off every one of David's enemies from the face of the earth."

¹⁶So Jonathan made a covenant with the house of David, saying, "May the LORD call David's enemies to account." ¹⁷And Jonathan had David reaffirm his oath out of love for him, because he loved him as he loved himself.

¹⁸Then Jonathan said to David, "Tomorrow is the New Moon feast. You will be missed, because your seat will be empty. ¹⁹The day after tomorrow, toward evening, go to the place where you hid when this trouble began, and wait by the stone Ezel. ²⁰I will shoot three arrows to the side of it, as though I were shooting at a target. ²¹Then I will send a boy and say, 'Go, find the arrows.' If I say to him, 'Look, the arrows are on this side of you; bring them here,' then come, because, as surely as the LORD lives, you are safe; there is no danger. ²²But if I say to the boy, 'Look, the arrows are beyond you,' then you must go, because the LORD has sent you away. ²³And about the matter you and I discussed—remember, the LORD is witness between you and me forever."

²⁴So David hid in the field, and when the New Moon feast came, the king sat down to eat. ²⁵He sat in his customary place by the wall, opposite Jonathan,ᵃ and Abner sat next to Saul, but David's place was empty. ²⁶Saul said nothing that day, for he thought, "Something must have happened to David to make him ceremonially unclean—surely he is unclean." ²⁷But the next day, the second day of the month, David's place was empty again. Then Saul said to his son Jonathan, "Why hasn't the son of Jesse come to the meal, either yesterday or today?"

²⁸Jonathan answered, "David earnestly asked me for permission to go to Bethlehem. ²⁹He said, 'Let me go, because our family is observing a sacrifice in the town and my brother has ordered me to be

ᵃ 25 Septuagint; Hebrew wall. Jonathan arose

there. If I have found favor in your eyes, let me get away to see my brothers.' That is why he has not come to the king's table."

³⁰Saul's anger flared up at Jonathan and he said to him, "You son of a perverse and rebellious woman! Don't I know that you have sided with the son of Jesse to your own shame and to the shame of the mother who bore you? ³¹As long as the son of Jesse lives on this earth, neither you nor your kingdom will be established. Now send someone to bring him to me, for he must die!"

³²"Why should he be put to death? What has he done?" Jonathan asked his father. ³³But Saul hurled his spear at him to kill him. Then Jonathan knew that his father intended to kill David.

³⁴Jonathan got up from the table in fierce anger; on that second day of the feast he did not eat, because he was grieved at his father's shameful treatment of David.

³⁵In the morning Jonathan went out to the field for his meeting with David. He had a small boy with him, ³⁶and he said to the boy, "Run and find the arrows I shoot." As the boy ran, he shot an arrow beyond him. ³⁷When the boy came to the place where Jonathan's arrow had fallen, Jonathan called out after him, "Isn't the arrow beyond you?" ³⁸Then he shouted,

1 Samuel 20:1–42

Jonathan stuck with his friend.

When God decided he was fed up with Saul's sins as Israel's first king (see 1 Samuel 15:28), he sent the prophet Samuel to anoint David as the next ruler of Israel (see 1 Samuel 16:1–13). David became Saul's armor bearer, the guy who carried a large shield and other weapons for the king, and he often played his harp to calm the edgy king (see 1 Samuel 16:21–23). Saul knew firsthand of David's bravery in his battle with Goliath (see 1 Samuel 17:57–58).

Saul liked David "very much" (1 Samuel 16:21). But that was all before Saul grew jealous of the praise David began to receive from the crowds. In the meantime David had become close friends with Jonathan, Saul's son, sharing a relationship so tight that "Jonathan became one in spirit with David, and he loved him as himself" (1 Samuel 18:1).

If David was a threat to Saul, then he was also a danger to Jonathan, who would expect to one day inherit his father's throne (see 1 Samuel 20:30–31). These two young men should have been sworn enemies, yet Jonathan decided his friendship with David was more important than the throne. He gave David his robe, sword, bow, and belt—a sign not only of friendship but of a handover of royal power. Saul repeatedly tried to kill David (see 1 Samuel 18:25; 19:2; 20:33) so that David had to flee. But Jonathan continued to side with David over his father. The two friends wept as they parted, promising their descendants would always get along.

You can find Jonathan in 1 Samuel 13—14, 18—20 and 2 Samuel 1.

UNSHAKEN people

"Hurry! Go quickly! Don't stop!" The boy picked up the arrow and returned to his master. ³⁹(The boy knew nothing about all this; only Jonathan and David knew.) ⁴⁰Then Jonathan gave his weapons to the boy and said, "Go, carry them back to town."

⁴¹After the boy had gone, David got up from the south side of the stone and bowed down before Jonathan three times, with his face to the ground. Then they kissed each other and wept together—but David wept the most.

⁴²Jonathan said to David, "Go in peace, for we have sworn friendship with each other in the name of the LORD, saying, 'The LORD is witness between you and me, and between your descendants and my descendants forever.'" Then David left, and Jonathan went back to the town.ᵃ

David at Nob

21 ᵇ David went to Nob, to Ahimelek the priest. Ahimelek trembled when he met him, and asked, "Why are you alone? Why is no one with you?"

²David answered Ahimelek the priest, "The king sent me on a mission and said to me, 'No one is to know anything about the mission I am sending you on.' As for my men, I have told them to meet me at a certain place. ³Now then, what do you have on hand? Give me five loaves of bread, or whatever you can find."

⁴But the priest answered David, "I don't have any ordinary bread on hand; however, there is some consecrated bread here—provided the men have kept themselves from women."

⁵David replied, "Indeed women have been kept from us, as usual wheneverᶜ I set out. The men's bodies are holy even on missions that are not holy. How much more so today!" ⁶So the priest gave him the consecrated bread, since there was no bread there except the bread of the Presence that had been removed from before the LORD and replaced by hot bread on the day it was taken away.

⁷Now one of Saul's servants was there

that day, detained before the LORD; he was Doeg the Edomite, Saul's chief shepherd.

⁸David asked Ahimelek, "Don't you have a spear or a sword here? I haven't brought my sword or any other weapon, because the king's mission was urgent."

⁹The priest replied, "The sword of Goliath the Philistine, whom you killed in the Valley of Elah, is here; it is wrapped in a cloth behind the ephod. If you want it, take it; there is no sword here but that one."

David said, "There is none like it; give it to me."

David at Gath

¹⁰That day David fled from Saul and went to Achish king of Gath. ¹¹But the servants of Achish said to him, "Isn't this David, the king of the land? Isn't he the one they sing about in their dances:

"'Saul has slain his thousands,
    and David his tens of thousands'?"

¹²David took these words to heart and was very much afraid of Achish king of Gath. ¹³So he pretended to be insane in their presence; and while he was in their hands he acted like a madman, making marks on the doors of the gate and letting saliva run down his beard.

¹⁴Achish said to his servants, "Look at the man! He is insane! Why bring him to me? ¹⁵Am I so short of madmen that you have to bring this fellow here to carry on like this in front of me? Must this man come into my house?"

David at Adullam and Mizpah

22 David left Gath and escaped to the cave of Adullam. When his brothers and his father's household heard about it, they went down to him there. ²All those who were in distress or in debt or discontented gathered around him, and he became their commander. About four hundred men were with him.

ᵃ 42 In Hebrew texts this sentence (20:42b) is numbered 21:1.   ᵇ In Hebrew texts 21:1-15 is numbered 21:2-16.   ᶜ 5 Or *from us in the past few days since*

³From there David went to Mizpah in Moab and said to the king of Moab, "Would you let my father and mother come and stay with you until I learn what God will do for me?" ⁴So he left them with the king of Moab, and they stayed with him as long as David was in the stronghold.

⁵But the prophet Gad said to David, "Do not stay in the stronghold. Go into the land of Judah." So David left and went to the forest of Hereth.

Saul Kills the Priests of Nob

⁶Now Saul heard that David and his men had been discovered. And Saul was seated, spear in hand, under the tamarisk tree on the hill at Gibeah, with all his officials standing at his side. ⁷He said to them, "Listen, men of Benjamin! Will the son of Jesse give all of you fields and vineyards? Will he make all of you commanders of thousands and commanders of hundreds? ⁸Is that why you have all conspired against me? No one tells me when my son makes a covenant with the son of Jesse. None of you is concerned about me or tells me that my son has incited my servant to lie in wait for me, as he does today."

⁹But Doeg the Edomite, who was standing with Saul's officials, said, "I saw the son of Jesse come to Ahimelek son of Ahitub at Nob. ¹⁰Ahimelek inquired of the Lord for him; he also gave him provisions and the sword of Goliath the Philistine."

¹¹Then the king sent for the priest Ahimelek son of Ahitub and all the men of his family, who were the priests at Nob, and they all came to the king. ¹²Saul said, "Listen now, son of Ahitub."

"Yes, my lord," he answered.

¹³Saul said to him, "Why have you conspired against me, you and the son of Jesse, giving him bread and a sword and inquiring of God for him, so that he has rebelled against me and lies in wait for me, as he does today?"

¹⁴Ahimelek answered the king, "Who of all your servants is as loyal as David, the king's son-in-law, captain of your bodyguard and highly respected in your household? ¹⁵Was that day the first time I inquired of God for him? Of course not! Let not the king accuse your servant or any of his father's family, for your servant knows nothing at all about this whole affair."

¹⁶But the king said, "You will surely die, Ahimelek, you and your whole family."

¹⁷Then the king ordered the guards at his side: "Turn and kill the priests of the Lord, because they too have sided with David. They knew he was fleeing, yet they did not tell me."

But the king's officials were unwilling to raise a hand to strike the priests of the Lord.

¹⁸The king then ordered Doeg, "You turn and strike down the priests." So Doeg the Edomite turned and struck them down. That day he killed eighty-five men who wore the linen ephod. ¹⁹He also put to the sword Nob, the town of the priests, with its men and women, its children and infants, and its cattle, donkeys and sheep.

²⁰But one son of Ahimelek son of Ahitub, named Abiathar, escaped and fled to join David. ²¹He told David that Saul had killed the priests of the Lord. ²²Then David said to Abiathar, "That day, when Doeg the Edomite was there, I knew he would be sure to tell Saul. I am responsible for the death of your whole family. ²³Stay with me; don't be afraid. The man who wants to kill you is trying to kill me too. You will be safe with me."

David Saves Keilah

23 When David was told, "Look, the Philistines are fighting against Keilah and are looting the threshing floors," ²he inquired of the Lord, saying, "Shall I go and attack these Philistines?"

The Lord answered him, "Go, attack the Philistines and save Keilah."

³But David's men said to him, "Here in Judah we are afraid. How much more, then, if we go to Keilah against the Philistine forces!"

⁴Once again David inquired of the Lord, and the Lord answered him, "Go down to Keilah, for I am going to give

the Philistines into your hand." ⁵So David and his men went to Keilah, fought the Philistines and carried off their livestock. He inflicted heavy losses on the Philistines and saved the people of Keilah. ⁶(Now Abiathar son of Ahimelek had brought the ephod down with him when he fled to David at Keilah.)

Saul Pursues David

⁷Saul was told that David had gone to Keilah, and he said, "God has delivered him into my hands, for David has imprisoned himself by entering a town with gates and bars." ⁸And Saul called up all his forces for battle, to go down to Keilah to besiege David and his men.

⁹When David learned that Saul was plotting against him, he said to Abiathar the priest, "Bring the ephod." ¹⁰David said, "LORD, God of Israel, your servant has heard definitely that Saul plans to come to Keilah and destroy the town on account of me. ¹¹Will the citizens of Keilah surrender me to him? Will Saul come down, as your servant has heard? LORD, God of Israel, tell your servant."

And the LORD said, "He will."

¹²Again David asked, "Will the citizens of Keilah surrender me and my men to Saul?"

And the LORD said, "They will."

¹³So David and his men, about six hundred in number, left Keilah and kept moving from place to place. When Saul was told that David had escaped from Keilah, he did not go there.

¹⁴David stayed in the wilderness strongholds and in the hills of the Desert of Ziph. Day after day Saul searched for him, but God did not give David into his hands.

¹⁵While David was at Horesh in the Desert of Ziph, he learned that*a* Saul had come out to take his life. ¹⁶And Saul's son Jonathan went to David at Horesh and helped him find strength in God. ¹⁷"Don't be afraid," he said. "My father Saul will not lay a hand on you. You will be king over Israel, and I will be second to you. Even my father Saul knows this." ¹⁸The two of them made a covenant before

the LORD. Then Jonathan went home, but David remained at Horesh.

¹⁹The Ziphites went up to Saul at Gibeah and said, "Is not David hiding among us in the strongholds at Horesh, on the hill of Hakilah, south of Jeshimon? ²⁰Now, Your Majesty, come down whenever it pleases you to do so, and we will be responsible for giving him into your hands."

²¹Saul replied, "The LORD bless you for your concern for me. ²²Go and get more information. Find out where David usually goes and who has seen him there. They tell me he is very crafty. ²³Find out about all the hiding places he uses and come back to me with definite information. Then I will go with you; if he is in the area, I will track him down among all the clans of Judah."

²⁴So they set out and went to Ziph ahead of Saul. Now David and his men were in the Desert of Maon, in the Arabah south of Jeshimon. ²⁵Saul and his men began the search, and when David was told about it, he went down to the rock and stayed in the Desert of Maon. When Saul heard this, he went into the Desert of Maon in pursuit of David.

²⁶Saul was going along one side of the mountain, and David and his men were on the other side, hurrying to get away from Saul. As Saul and his forces were closing in on David and his men to capture them, ²⁷a messenger came to Saul, saying, "Come quickly! The Philistines are raiding the land." ²⁸Then Saul broke off his pursuit of David and went to meet the Philistines. That is why they call this place Sela Hammahlekoth.*b* ²⁹And David went up from there and lived in the strongholds of En Gedi.*c*

David Spares Saul's Life

24 *d* After Saul returned from pursuing the Philistines, he was told, "David is in the Desert of En Gedi." ²So Saul took

---

a 15 Or *he was afraid because*   *b 28 Sela Hammahlekoth* means *rock of parting.*   *c 29* In Hebrew texts this verse (23:29) is numbered 24:1.   *d* In Hebrew texts 24:1-22 is numbered 24:2-23.

three thousand able young men from all Israel and set out to look for David and his men near the Crags of the Wild Goats.

³He came to the sheep pens along the way; a cave was there, and Saul went in to relieve himself. David and his men were far back in the cave. ⁴The men said, "This is the day the LORD spoke of when he said[a] to you, 'I will give your enemy into your hands for you to deal with as you wish.'" Then David crept up unnoticed and cut off a corner of Saul's robe.

⁵Afterward, David was conscience-stricken for having cut off a corner of his robe. ⁶He said to his men, "The LORD forbid that I should do such a thing to my master, the LORD's anointed, or lay my hand on him; for he is the anointed of the LORD." ⁷With these words David sharply rebuked his men and did not allow them to attack Saul. And Saul left the cave and went his way.

⁸Then David went out of the cave and called out to Saul, "My lord the king!" When Saul looked behind him, David bowed down and prostrated himself with his face to the ground. ⁹He said to Saul, "Why do you listen when men say, 'David is bent on harming you'? ¹⁰This day you have seen with your own eyes how the LORD delivered you into my hands in the cave. Some urged me to kill you, but I spared you; I said, 'I will not lay my hand on my lord, because he is the LORD's anointed.' ¹¹See, my father, look at this piece of your robe in my hand! I cut off the corner of your robe but did not kill you. See that there is nothing in my hand to indicate that I am guilty of wrongdoing or rebellion. I have not wronged you, but you are hunting me down to take my life. ¹²May the LORD judge between you and me. And may the LORD avenge the wrongs you have done to me, but my hand will not touch you. ¹³As the old saying goes, 'From evildoers come evil deeds,' so my hand will not touch you.

¹⁴"Against whom has the king of Israel come out? Who are you pursuing? A dead dog? A flea? ¹⁵May the LORD be our judge and decide between us. May he consider my cause and uphold it; may he vindicate me by delivering me from your hand."

¹⁶When David finished saying this, Saul asked, "Is that your voice, David my son?" And he wept aloud. ¹⁷"You are more righteous than I," he said. "You have treated me well, but I have treated you badly. ¹⁸You have just now told me about the good you did to me; the LORD delivered me into your hands, but you did not kill me. ¹⁹When a man finds his enemy, does he let him get away unharmed? May the LORD reward you well for the way you treated me today. ²⁰I know that you will surely be king and that the kingdom of Israel will be established in your hands. ²¹Now swear to me by the LORD that you will not kill off my descendants or wipe out my name from my father's family."

²²So David gave his oath to Saul. Then Saul returned home, but David and his men went up to the stronghold.

David, Nabal and Abigail

25 Now Samuel died, and all Israel assembled and mourned for him; and they buried him at his home in Ramah. Then David moved down into the Desert of Paran.[b]

²A certain man in Maon, who had property there at Carmel, was very wealthy. He had a thousand goats and three thousand sheep, which he was shearing in Carmel. ³His name was Nabal and his wife's name was Abigail. She was an intelligent and beautiful woman, but her husband was surly and mean in his dealings—he was a Calebite.

⁴While David was in the wilderness, he heard that Nabal was shearing sheep. ⁵So he sent ten young men and said to them, "Go up to Nabal at Carmel and greet him in my name. ⁶Say to him: 'Long life to you! Good health to you and your household! And good health to all that is yours!

⁷"'Now I hear that it is sheep-shearing time. When your shepherds were with us,

---

a 4 Or *"Today the LORD is saying*   *b 1* Hebrew and some Septuagint manuscripts; other Septuagint manuscripts *Maon* we did not mistreat them, and the whole time they were at Carmel nothing of theirs was missing. [8] Ask your own servants and they will tell you. Therefore be favorable toward my men, since we come at a festive time. Please give your servants and your son David whatever you can find for them.'"

[9] When David's men arrived, they gave Nabal this message in David's name. Then they waited.

[10] Nabal answered David's servants, "Who is this David? Who is this son of Jesse? Many servants are breaking away from their masters these days. [11] Why should I take my bread and water, and the meat I have slaughtered for my shearers, and give it to men coming from who knows where?"

[12] David's men turned around and went back. When they arrived, they reported every word. [13] David said to his men, "Each of you strap on your sword!" So they did, and David strapped his on as well. About four hundred men went up with David, while two hundred stayed with the supplies.

[14] One of the servants told Abigail, Nabal's wife, "David sent messengers from the wilderness to give our master his greetings, but he hurled insults at them. [15] Yet these men were very good to us. They did not mistreat us, and the whole time we were out in the fields near them nothing was missing. [16] Night and day they were a wall around us the whole time we were herding our sheep near them. [17] Now think it over and see what you can do, because disaster is hanging over our master and his whole household. He is such a wicked man that no one can talk to him."

[18] Abigail acted quickly. She took two hundred loaves of bread, two skins of wine, five dressed sheep, five seahs[a] of roasted grain, a hundred cakes of raisins and two hundred cakes of pressed figs, and loaded them on donkeys. [19] Then she told her servants, "Go on ahead; I'll follow you." But she did not tell her husband Nabal.

[20] As she came riding her donkey into a mountain ravine, there were David and his men descending toward her, and she met them. [21] David had just said, "It's been useless—all my watching over this fellow's property in the wilderness so that nothing of his was missing. He has paid me back evil for good. [22] May God deal with David,[b] be it ever so severely, if by morning I leave alive one male of all who belong to him!"

[23] When Abigail saw David, she quickly got off her donkey and bowed down before David with her face to the ground. [24] She fell at his feet and said: "Pardon your servant, my lord, and let me speak to you; hear what your servant has to say. [25] Please pay no attention, my lord, to that wicked man Nabal. He is just like his name—his name means Fool, and folly goes with him. And as for me, your servant, I did not see the men my lord sent. [26] And now, my lord, as surely as the LORD your God lives and as you live, since the LORD has kept you from bloodshed and from avenging yourself with your own hands, may your enemies and all who are intent on harming my lord be like Nabal. [27] And let this gift, which your servant has brought to my lord, be given to the men who follow you.

[28] "Please forgive your servant's presumption. The LORD your God will certainly make a lasting dynasty for my lord, because you fight the LORD's battles, and no wrongdoing will be found in you as long as you live. [29] Even though someone is pursuing you to take your life, the life of my lord will be bound securely in the bundle of the living by the LORD your God, but the lives of your enemies he will hurl away as from the pocket of a sling. [30] When the LORD has fulfilled for my lord every good thing he promised concerning him and has appointed him ruler over Israel, [31] my lord will not have on his conscience the staggering burden of needless bloodshed or of having avenged himself. And when the LORD your God has brought my lord success, remember your servant."

---

[a] 18 That is, probably about 60 pounds or about 27 kilograms   [b] 22 Some Septuagint manuscripts; Hebrew *with David's enemies*

³²David said to Abigail, "Praise be to the LORD, the God of Israel, who has sent you today to meet me. ³³May you be blessed for your good judgment and for keeping me from bloodshed this day and from avenging myself with my own hands. ³⁴Otherwise, as surely as the LORD, the God of Israel, lives, who has kept me from harming you, if you had not come quickly to meet me, not one male belonging to Nabal would have been left alive by daybreak."

³⁵Then David accepted from her hand what she had brought him and said, "Go home in peace. I have heard your words and granted your request."

³⁶When Abigail went to Nabal, he was in the house holding a banquet like that of a king. He was in high spirits and very drunk. So she told him nothing at all until daybreak. ³⁷Then in the morning, when Nabal was sober, his wife told him all these things, and his heart failed him and he became like a stone. ³⁸About ten days later, the LORD struck Nabal and he died.

³⁹When David heard that Nabal was dead, he said, "Praise be to the LORD, who has upheld my cause against Nabal for treating me with contempt. He has kept his servant from doing wrong and has brought Nabal's wrongdoing down on his own head."

---

1 Samuel 25

Abigail acted wisely.

Abigail was married to a truly unwise man, Nabal, a rich, roaring drunk. In those days King Saul had pushed David and his warriors into the wilderness of Judah. Running for their lives, they were low on food and water. So David sent a plea for help from Nabal, who owned thousands of sheep and goats.

David wasn't begging. He was looking for compensation for having protected Nabal's flocks and servants as his men camped nearby. But Nabal rudely rejected the request. So David said to himself, "It's been useless—all my watching over this fellow's property in the wilderness so that nothing of his was missing. He has paid me back evil for good" (1 Samuel 25:21). David swore he would avenge the insult by killing Nabal and every man in his household.

David ordered 400 of his fighting men to strap on their swords. But before they could reach Nabal, Abigail loaded up a train of animals with ample bread and meat for David and his men. She rode out to greet him and fell on her face before him. Abigail's thorough apology and abundant generosity swayed David to relent.

Abigail couldn't fix every problem created by her arrogant husband, but in this instance her wisdom halted what would have been a bloody attack. Days later Nabal died, struck by God, and David took this smart woman as his wife.

You can find Abigail in 1 Samuel 25; 1 Samuel 30:5; and 2 Samuel 2:2.

UNSHAKEN *people*

Then David sent word to Abigail, asking her to become his wife. [40]His servants went to Carmel and said to Abigail, "David has sent us to you to take you to become his wife."

[41]She bowed down with her face to the ground and said, "I am your servant and am ready to serve you and wash the feet of my lord's servants." [42]Abigail quickly got on a donkey and, attended by her five female servants, went with David's messengers and became his wife. [43]David had also married Ahinoam of Jezreel, and they both were his wives. [44]But Saul had given his daughter Michal, David's wife, to Paltiel[a] son of Laish, who was from Gallim.

David Again Spares Saul's Life

26 The Ziphites went to Saul at Gibeah and said, "Is not David hiding on the hill of Hakilah, which faces Jeshimon?"

[2]So Saul went down to the Desert of Ziph, with his three thousand select Israelite troops, to search there for David. [3]Saul made his camp beside the road on the hill of Hakilah facing Jeshimon, but David stayed in the wilderness. When he saw that Saul had followed him there, [4]he sent out scouts and learned that Saul had definitely arrived.

[5]Then David set out and went to the place where Saul had camped. He saw where Saul and Abner son of Ner, the commander of the army, had lain down. Saul was lying inside the camp, with the army encamped around him.

[6]David then asked Ahimelek the Hittite and Abishai son of Zeruiah, Joab's brother, "Who will go down into the camp with me to Saul?"

"I'll go with you," said Abishai.

[7]So David and Abishai went to the army by night, and there was Saul, lying asleep inside the camp with his spear stuck in the ground near his head. Abner and the soldiers were lying around him.

[8]Abishai said to David, "Today God has delivered your enemy into your hands. Now let me pin him to the ground with one thrust of the spear; I won't strike him twice."

[9]But David said to Abishai, "Don't destroy him! Who can lay a hand on the LORD's anointed and be guiltless? [10]As surely as the LORD lives," he said, "the LORD himself will strike him, or his time will come and he will die, or he will go into battle and perish. [11]But the LORD forbid that I should lay a hand on the LORD's anointed. Now get the spear and water jug that are near his head, and let's go."

[12]So David took the spear and water jug near Saul's head, and they left. No one saw or knew about it, nor did anyone wake up. They were all sleeping, because the LORD had put them into a deep sleep.

[13]Then David crossed over to the other side and stood on top of the hill some distance away; there was a wide space between them. [14]He called out to the army and to Abner son of Ner, "Aren't you going to answer me, Abner?"

Abner replied, "Who are you who calls to the king?"

[15]David said, "You're a man, aren't you? And who is like you in Israel? Why didn't you guard your lord the king? Someone came to destroy your lord the king. [16]What you have done is not good. As surely as the LORD lives, you and your men must die, because you did not guard your master, the LORD's anointed. Look around you. Where are the king's spear and water jug that were near his head?"

[17]Saul recognized David's voice and said, "Is that your voice, David my son?"

David replied, "Yes it is, my lord the king." [18]And he added, "Why is my lord pursuing his servant? What have I done, and what wrong am I guilty of? [19]Now let my lord the king listen to his servant's words. If the LORD has incited you against me, then may he accept an offering. If, however, people have done it, may they be cursed before the LORD! They have driven me today from my share in the LORD's inheritance and have said, 'Go, serve other gods.' [20]Now do not let my blood fall to the ground far from the presence of the

---

[a] 44 Hebrew *Palti*, a variant of *Paltiel*

LORD. The king of Israel has come out to look for a flea—as one hunts a partridge in the mountains."

²¹Then Saul said, "I have sinned. Come back, David my son. Because you considered my life precious today, I will not try to harm you again. Surely I have acted like a fool and have been terribly wrong."

²²"Here is the king's spear," David answered. "Let one of your young men come over and get it. ²³The LORD rewards everyone for their righteousness and faithfulness. The LORD delivered you into my hands today, but I would not lay a hand on the LORD's anointed. ²⁴As surely as I valued your life today, so may the LORD value my life and deliver me from all trouble."

²⁵Then Saul said to David, "May you be blessed, David my son; you will do great things and surely triumph."

So David went on his way, and Saul returned home.

David Among the Philistines

27 But David thought to himself, "One of these days I will be destroyed by the hand of Saul. The best thing I can do is to escape to the land of the Philistines. Then Saul will give up searching for me anywhere in Israel, and I will slip out of his hand."

²So David and the six hundred men with him left and went over to Achish son of Maok king of Gath. ³David and his men settled in Gath with Achish. Each man had his family with him, and David had his two wives: Ahinoam of Jezreel and Abigail of Carmel, the widow of Nabal. ⁴When Saul was told that David had fled to Gath, he no longer searched for him.

⁵Then David said to Achish, "If I have found favor in your eyes, let a place be assigned to me in one of the country towns, that I may live there. Why should your servant live in the royal city with you?"

⁶So on that day Achish gave him Ziklag, and it has belonged to the kings of Judah ever since. ⁷David lived in Philistine territory a year and four months.

⁸Now David and his men went up and raided the Geshurites, the Girzites and the Amalekites. (From ancient times these peoples had lived in the land extending to Shur and Egypt.) ⁹Whenever David attacked an area, he did not leave a man or woman alive, but took sheep and cattle, donkeys and camels, and clothes. Then he returned to Achish.

¹⁰When Achish asked, "Where did you go raiding today?" David would say, "Against the Negev of Judah" or "Against the Negev of Jerahmeel" or "Against the Negev of the Kenites." ¹¹He did not leave a man or woman alive to be brought to Gath, for he thought, "They might inform on us and say, 'This is what David did.'" And such was his practice as long as he lived in Philistine territory. ¹²Achish trusted David and said to himself, "He has become so obnoxious to his people, the Israelites, that he will be my servant for life."

28 In those days the Philistines gathered their forces to fight against Israel. Achish said to David, "You must understand that you and your men will accompany me in the army."

²David said, "Then you will see for yourself what your servant can do."

Achish replied, "Very well, I will make you my bodyguard for life."

Saul and the Medium at Endor

³Now Samuel was dead, and all Israel had mourned for him and buried him in his own town of Ramah. Saul had expelled the mediums and spiritists from the land.

⁴The Philistines assembled and came and set up camp at Shunem, while Saul gathered all Israel and set up camp at Gilboa. ⁵When Saul saw the Philistine army, he was afraid; terror filled his heart. ⁶He inquired of the LORD, but the LORD did not answer him by dreams or Urim or prophets. ⁷Saul then said to his attendants, "Find me a woman who is a medium, so I may go and inquire of her."

"There is one in Endor," they said.

⁸So Saul disguised himself, putting on other clothes, and at night he and two

men went to the woman. "Consult a spirit for me," he said, "and bring up for me the one I name."

[9] But the woman said to him, "Surely you know what Saul has done. He has cut off the mediums and spiritists from the land. Why have you set a trap for my life to bring about my death?"

[10] Saul swore to her by the LORD, "As surely as the LORD lives, you will not be punished for this."

[11] Then the woman asked, "Whom shall I bring up for you?"

"Bring up Samuel," he said.

[12] When the woman saw Samuel, she cried out at the top of her voice and said to Saul, "Why have you deceived me? You are Saul!"

[13] The king said to her, "Don't be afraid. What do you see?"

The woman said, "I see a ghostly figure[a] coming up out of the earth."

[14] "What does he look like?" he asked.

"An old man wearing a robe is coming up," she said.

Then Saul knew it was Samuel, and he bowed down and prostrated himself with his face to the ground.

[15] Samuel said to Saul, "Why have you disturbed me by bringing me up?"

"I am in great distress," Saul said. "The Philistines are fighting against me, and God has departed from me. He no longer answers me, either by prophets or by dreams. So I have called on you to tell me what to do."

[16] Samuel said, "Why do you consult me, now that the LORD has departed from you and become your enemy? [17] The LORD has done what he predicted through me. The LORD has torn the kingdom out of your hands and given it to one of your neighbors—to David. [18] Because you did not obey the LORD or carry out his fierce wrath against the Amalekites, the LORD has done this to you today. [19] The LORD will deliver both Israel and you into the hands of the Philistines, and tomorrow you and your sons will be with me. The LORD will also give the army of Israel into the hands of the Philistines."

[20] Immediately Saul fell full length on the ground, filled with fear because of Samuel's words. His strength was gone, for he had eaten nothing all that day and all that night.

[21] When the woman came to Saul and saw that he was greatly shaken, she said, "Look, your servant has obeyed you. I took my life in my hands and did what you told me to do. [22] Now please listen to your servant and let me give you some food so you may eat and have the strength to go on your way."

a 13 Or *see spirits*; or *see gods*

1 Samuel 28:1–25

Truth comes from God.

Saul didn't want the news he was about to hear. When the king saw the Philistine army gathering against him, he was terrified. He asked God for guidance, but the Lord was silent. So he sought out a medium, a woman who claimed to talk to the deceased. When God caused the dead prophet Samuel to appear, the medium jumped. And instead of being assured he would be a success in battle, Saul learned he and his sons would die the next day. Notice that the Lord was silent because he had already decided Saul was no longer fit to be king (see 1 Samuel 15:28). But Saul missed the bigger point that all truth comes from God, and that turning anywhere else would only lead to his undoing. Wherever you find truth, you can be sure God is the ultimate source.

Think: Who or what do you trust to tell you the truth? Why?

ROCK SOLID truths

²³He refused and said, "I will not eat."

But his men joined the woman in urging him, and he listened to them. He got up from the ground and sat on the couch. ²⁴The woman had a fattened calf at the house, which she butchered at once. She took some flour, kneaded it and baked bread without yeast. ²⁵Then she set it before Saul and his men, and they ate. That same night they got up and left.

Achish Sends David Back to Ziklag

29 The Philistines gathered all their forces at Aphek, and Israel camped by the spring in Jezreel. ²As the Philistine rulers marched with their units of hundreds and thousands, David and his men were marching at the rear with Achish. ³The commanders of the Philistines asked, "What about these Hebrews?"

Achish replied, "Is this not David, who was an officer of Saul king of Israel? He has already been with me for over a year, and from the day he left Saul until now, I have found no fault in him."

⁴But the Philistine commanders were angry with Achish and said, "Send the man back, that he may return to the place you assigned him. He must not go with us into battle, or he will turn against us during the fighting. How better could he regain his master's favor than by taking the heads of our own men? ⁵Isn't this the David they sang about in their dances:

" 'Saul has slain his thousands,
  and David his tens of thousands'?"

⁶So Achish called David and said to him, "As surely as the LORD lives, you have been reliable, and I would be pleased to have you serve with me in the army. From the day you came to me until today, I have found no fault in you, but the rulers don't approve of you. ⁷Now turn back and go in peace; do nothing to displease the Philistine rulers."

⁸"But what have I done?" asked David. "What have you found against your servant from the day I came to you until now? Why can't I go and fight against the enemies of my lord the king?"

⁹Achish answered, "I know that you have been as pleasing in my eyes as an angel of God; nevertheless, the Philistine commanders have said, 'He must not go up with us into battle.' ¹⁰Now get up early, along with your master's servants who have come with you, and leave in the morning as soon as it is light."

¹¹So David and his men got up early in the morning to go back to the land of the Philistines, and the Philistines went up to Jezreel.

David Destroys the Amalekites

30 David and his men reached Ziklag on the third day. Now the Amalekites had raided the Negev and Ziklag. They had attacked Ziklag and burned it, ²and had taken captive the women and everyone else in it, both young and old. They killed none of them, but carried them off as they went on their way.

³When David and his men reached Ziklag, they found it destroyed by fire and their wives and sons and daughters taken captive. ⁴So David and his men wept aloud until they had no strength left to weep. ⁵David's two wives had been captured—Ahinoam of Jezreel and Abigail, the widow of Nabal of Carmel. ⁶David was greatly distressed because the men were talking of stoning him; each one was bitter in spirit because of his sons and daughters. But David found strength in the LORD his God.

⁷Then David said to Abiathar the priest, the son of Ahimelek, "Bring me the ephod." Abiathar brought it to him, ⁸and David inquired of the LORD, "Shall I pursue this raiding party? Will I overtake them?"

"Pursue them," he answered. "You will certainly overtake them and succeed in the rescue."

⁹David and the six hundred men with him came to the Besor Valley, where some stayed behind. ¹⁰Two hundred of them were too exhausted to cross the valley, but David and the other four hundred continued the pursuit.

[11] They found an Egyptian in a field and brought him to David. They gave him water to drink and food to eat— [12] part of a cake of pressed figs and two cakes of raisins. He ate and was revived, for he had not eaten any food or drunk any water for three days and three nights.

[13] David asked him, "Who do you belong to? Where do you come from?"

He said, "I am an Egyptian, the slave of an Amalekite. My master abandoned me when I became ill three days ago. [14] We raided the Negev of the Kerethites, some territory belonging to Judah and the Negev of Caleb. And we burned Ziklag."

[15] David asked him, "Can you lead me down to this raiding party?"

He answered, "Swear to me before God that you will not kill me or hand me over to my master, and I will take you down to them."

[16] He led David down, and there they were, scattered over the countryside, eating, drinking and reveling because of the great amount of plunder they had taken from the land of the Philistines and from Judah. [17] David fought them from dusk until the evening of the next day, and none of them got away, except four hundred young men who rode off on camels and fled. [18] David recovered everything the Amalekites had taken, including his two wives. [19] Nothing was missing: young or old, boy or girl, plunder or anything else they had taken. David brought everything back. [20] He took all the flocks and herds, and his men drove them ahead of the other livestock, saying, "This is David's plunder."

[21] Then David came to the two hundred men who had been too exhausted to follow him and who were left behind at the Besor Valley. They came out to meet David and the men with him. As David and his men approached, he asked them how they were. [22] But all the evil men and troublemakers among David's followers said, "Because they did not go out with us, we will not share with them the plunder we recovered. However, each man may take his wife and children and go."

[23] David replied, "No, my brothers, you must not do that with what the LORD has given us. He has protected us and delivered into our hands the raiding party that came against us. [24] Who will listen to what you say? The share of the man who stayed with the supplies is to be the same as that of him who went down to the battle. All will share alike." [25] David made this a statute and ordinance for Israel from that day to this.

[26] When David reached Ziklag, he sent some of the plunder to the elders of Judah, who were his friends, saying, "Here is a gift for you from the plunder of the LORD's enemies."

[27] David sent it to those who were in Bethel, Ramoth Negev and Jattir; [28] to those in Aroer, Siphmoth, Eshtemoa [29] and Rakal; to those in the towns of the Jerahmeelites and the Kenites; [30] to those in Hormah, Bor Ashan, Athak [31] and Hebron; and to those in all the other places where he and his men had roamed.

Saul Takes His Life

31 Now the Philistines fought against Israel; the Israelites fled before them, and many fell dead on Mount Gilboa. [2] The Philistines were in hot pursuit of Saul and his sons, and they killed his sons Jonathan, Abinadab and Malki-Shua. [3] The fighting grew fierce around Saul, and when the archers overtook him, they wounded him critically.

[4] Saul said to his armor-bearer, "Draw your sword and run me through, or these uncircumcised fellows will come and run me through and abuse me."

But his armor-bearer was terrified and would not do it; so Saul took his own sword and fell on it. [5] When the armor-bearer saw that Saul was dead, he too fell on his sword and died with him. [6] So Saul and his three sons and his armor-bearer and all his men died together that same day.

[7] When the Israelites along the valley and those across the Jordan saw that the Israelite army had fled and that Saul and

his sons had died, they abandoned their towns and fled. And the Philistines came and occupied them.

⁸The next day, when the Philistines came to strip the dead, they found Saul and his three sons fallen on Mount Gilboa. ⁹They cut off his head and stripped off his armor, and they sent messengers throughout the land of the Philistines to proclaim the news in the temple of their idols and among their people. ¹⁰They put his armor in the temple of the Ashtoreths and fastened his body to the wall of Beth Shan.

¹¹When the people of Jabesh Gilead heard what the Philistines had done to Saul, ¹²all their valiant men marched through the night to Beth Shan. They took down the bodies of Saul and his sons from the wall of Beth Shan and went to Jabesh, where they burned them. ¹³Then they took their bones and buried them under a tamarisk tree at Jabesh, and they fasted seven days.

2 SAMUEL

BOOK OUTLINE

David as king of Judah
(1:1 — 4:12)

David unites Israel
(5:1 — 24:25)

Second Samuel continues the story of the kingdom of Israel. It begins with the death of the very first king, King Saul. Then it describes David's forty-year reign. Some of the best-known stories are the capture of Jerusalem, David's sin with Bathsheba, and Absalom's rebellion.

David Hears of Saul's Death

After the death of Saul, David returned from striking down the Amalekites and stayed in Ziklag two days. **2** On the third day a man arrived from Saul's camp with his clothes torn and dust on his head. When he came to David, he fell to the ground to pay him honor.

3 "Where have you come from?" David asked him.

He answered, "I have escaped from the Israelite camp."

4 "What happened?" David asked. "Tell me."

"The men fled from the battle," he replied. "Many of them fell and died. And Saul and his son Jonathan are dead."

5 Then David said to the young man who brought him the report, "How do you know that Saul and his son Jonathan are dead?"

6 "I happened to be on Mount Gilboa," the young man said, "and there was Saul, leaning on his spear, with the chariots and their drivers in hot pursuit. **7** When he turned around and saw me, he called out to me, and I said, 'What can I do?'

8 "He asked me, 'Who are you?'

"'An Amalekite,' I answered.

9 "Then he said to me, 'Stand here by me and kill me! I'm in the throes of death, but I'm still alive.'

10 "So I stood beside him and killed him, because I knew that after he had fallen he could not survive. And I took the crown that was on his head and the band on his arm and have brought them here to my lord."

11 Then David and all the men with him took hold of their clothes and tore them. **12** They mourned and wept and fasted till evening for Saul and his son Jonathan, and for the army of the LORD and for the nation of Israel, because they had fallen by the sword.

13 David said to the young man who brought him the report, "Where are you from?"

ROCK SOLID principles

2 Samuel 1:1 – 12

Grieve your losses.

Jason had a hard time thinking about any of it. One night after supper his older sister had gone out with friends, her usual happy self. Just a few hours later, his parents were called to the hospital. By the time they arrived, Nicole was gone — dead from rare bleeding on her brain. Jason watched his parents cry and question and lash out in anger, and he didn't want to add to their pain. So he vowed to keep it together, not even crying at Nicole's funeral. Months later, Jason looked fine on the outside, but inside all he felt was sadness. He was starting to crack.

You would think David would rejoice at the death of his enemy, King Saul. But this tough warrior was able to express true sadness. David not only mourned and wept, but he also followed other customs of his day, tearing his clothes and going without food (see 2 Samuel 1:11 – 12). David even wrote a song to remember the fallen king (see 2 Samuel 1:17 – 27).

"I am the son of a foreigner, an Amalekite," he answered.

¹⁴David asked him, "Why weren't you afraid to lift your hand to destroy the Lord's anointed?"

¹⁵Then David called one of his men and said, "Go, strike him down!" So he struck him down, and he died. ¹⁶For David had said to him, "Your blood be on your own head. Your own mouth testified against you when you said, 'I killed the Lord's anointed.'"

David's Lament for Saul and Jonathan

¹⁷David took up this lament concerning Saul and his son Jonathan, ¹⁸and he ordered that the people of Judah be taught this lament of the bow (it is written in the Book of Jashar):

¹⁹"A gazelle*a* lies slain on your heights,
    Israel.
  How the mighty have fallen!

²⁰"Tell it not in Gath,
    proclaim it not in the streets of
      Ashkelon,
  lest the daughters of the Philistines be
    glad,
  lest the daughters of the
    uncircumcised rejoice.

²¹"Mountains of Gilboa,
    may you have neither dew nor rain,
    may no showers fall on your
      terraced fields.*b*
For there the shield of the mighty was
    despised,
    the shield of Saul—no longer
      rubbed with oil.

²²"From the blood of the slain,
    from the flesh of the mighty,
  the bow of Jonathan did not turn back,
    the sword of Saul did not return
      unsatisfied.

²³Saul and Jonathan—
    in life they were loved and admired,
    and in death they were not parted.
They were swifter than eagles,
    they were stronger than lions.

²⁴"Daughters of Israel,
    weep for Saul,

who clothed you in scarlet and finery,
  who adorned your garments with
    ornaments of gold.

²⁵"How the mighty have fallen in battle!
    Jonathan lies slain on your heights.
²⁶I grieve for you, Jonathan my brother;
    you were very dear to me.
Your love for me was wonderful,
    more wonderful than that of
      women.

²⁷"How the mighty have fallen!
    The weapons of war have perished!"

David Anointed King Over Judah

2 In the course of time, David inquired of the Lord. "Shall I go up to one of the towns of Judah?" he asked.

The Lord said, "Go up."

David asked, "Where shall I go?"

"To Hebron," the Lord answered.

²So David went up there with his two wives, Ahinoam of Jezreel and Abigail, the widow of Nabal of Carmel. ³David also took the men who were with him, each with his family, and they settled in Hebron and its towns. ⁴Then the men of Judah came to Hebron, and there they anointed David king over the tribe of Judah.

When David was told that it was the men from Jabesh Gilead who had buried Saul, ⁵he sent messengers to them to say to them, "The Lord bless you for showing this kindness to Saul your master by burying him. ⁶May the Lord now show you kindness and faithfulness, and I too will show you the same favor because you have done this. ⁷Now then, be strong and brave, for Saul your master is dead, and the people of Judah have anointed me king over them."

War Between the Houses of David and Saul

⁸Meanwhile, Abner son of Ner, the commander of Saul's army, had taken Ish-Bosheth son of Saul and brought him over

---

a 19 *Gazelle* here symbolizes a human dignitary.
b 21 Or / *nor fields that yield grain for offerings*

to Mahanaim. ⁹He made him king over Gilead, Ashuri and Jezreel, and also over Ephraim, Benjamin and all Israel.

¹⁰Ish-Bosheth son of Saul was forty years old when he became king over Israel, and he reigned two years. The tribe of Judah, however, remained loyal to David. ¹¹The length of time David was king in Hebron over Judah was seven years and six months.

¹²Abner son of Ner, together with the men of Ish-Bosheth son of Saul, left Mahanaim and went to Gibeon. ¹³Joab son of Zeruiah and David's men went out and met them at the pool of Gibeon. One group sat down on one side of the pool and one group on the other side.

¹⁴Then Abner said to Joab, "Let's have some of the young men get up and fight hand to hand in front of us."

"All right, let them do it," Joab said.

¹⁵So they stood up and were counted off—twelve men for Benjamin and Ish-Bosheth son of Saul, and twelve for David. ¹⁶Then each man grabbed his opponent by the head and thrust his dagger into his opponent's side, and they fell down together. So that place in Gibeon was called Helkath Hazzurim.[a]

¹⁷The battle that day was very fierce, and Abner and the Israelites were defeated by David's men.

¹⁸The three sons of Zeruiah were there: Joab, Abishai and Asahel. Now Asahel was as fleet-footed as a wild gazelle. ¹⁹He chased Abner, turning neither to the right nor to the left as he pursued him. ²⁰Abner looked behind him and asked, "Is that you, Asahel?"

"It is," he answered.

²¹Then Abner said to him, "Turn aside to the right or to the left; take on one of the young men and strip him of his weapons." But Asahel would not stop chasing him.

²²Again Abner warned Asahel, "Stop chasing me! Why should I strike you down? How could I look your brother Joab in the face?"

²³But Asahel refused to give up the pursuit; so Abner thrust the butt of his spear into Asahel's stomach, and the spear came out through his back. He fell there and died on the spot. And every man stopped when he came to the place where Asahel had fallen and died.

²⁴But Joab and Abishai pursued Abner, and as the sun was setting, they came to the hill of Ammah, near Giah on the way to the wasteland of Gibeon. ²⁵Then the men of Benjamin rallied behind Abner. They formed themselves into a group and took their stand on top of a hill.

²⁶Abner called out to Joab, "Must the sword devour forever? Don't you realize that this will end in bitterness? How long before you order your men to stop pursuing their fellow Israelites?"

²⁷Joab answered, "As surely as God lives, if you had not spoken, the men would have continued pursuing them until morning."

²⁸So Joab blew the trumpet, and all the troops came to a halt; they no longer pursued Israel, nor did they fight anymore.

²⁹All that night Abner and his men marched through the Arabah. They crossed the Jordan, continued through the morning hours[b] and came to Mahanaim.

³⁰Then Joab stopped pursuing Abner and assembled the whole army. Besides Asahel, nineteen of David's men were found missing. ³¹But David's men had killed three hundred and sixty Benjamites who were with Abner. ³²They took Asahel and buried him in his father's tomb at Bethlehem. Then Joab and his men marched all night and arrived at Hebron by daybreak.

3 The war between the house of Saul and the house of David lasted a long time. David grew stronger and stronger, while the house of Saul grew weaker and weaker.

²Sons were born to David in Hebron:

His firstborn was Amnon the son of Ahinoam of Jezreel;

³his second, Kileab the son of Abigail the widow of Nabal of Carmel;

---

[a] 16 *Helkath Hazzurim* means *field of daggers* or *field of hostilities.*   [b] 29 See Septuagint; the meaning of the Hebrew for this phrase is uncertain.

the third, Absalom the son of Maakah daughter of Talmai king of
Geshur;

[4] the fourth, Adonijah the son of
Haggith;
the fifth, Shephatiah the son of
Abital;

[5] and the sixth, Ithream the son of
David's wife Eglah.
These were born to David in He-
bron.

Abner Goes Over to David

[6] During the war between the house of
Saul and the house of David, Abner had
been strengthening his own position in the
house of Saul. [7] Now Saul had had a concubine named Rizpah daughter of Aiah. And
Ish-Bosheth said to Abner, "Why did you
sleep with my father's concubine?"

[8] Abner was very angry because of what
Ish-Bosheth said. So he answered, "Am I
a dog's head—on Judah's side? This very
day I am loyal to the house of your father
Saul and to his family and friends. I haven't
handed you over to David. Yet now you accuse me of an offense involving this woman! [9] May God deal with Abner, be it ever
so severely, if I do not do for David what the
LORD promised him on oath [10] and transfer
the kingdom from the house of Saul and establish David's throne over Israel and Judah
from Dan to Beersheba." [11] Ish-Bosheth did
not dare to say another word to Abner, because he was afraid of him.

[12] Then Abner sent messengers on his
behalf to say to David, "Whose land is it?
Make an agreement with me, and I will
help you bring all Israel over to you."

[13] "Good," said David. "I will make an
agreement with you. But I demand one
thing of you: Do not come into my presence unless you bring Michal daughter of
Saul when you come to see me." [14] Then
David sent messengers to Ish-Bosheth son
of Saul, demanding, "Give me my wife Michal, whom I betrothed to myself for the
price of a hundred Philistine foreskins."

[15] So Ish-Bosheth gave orders and had
her taken away from her husband Paltiel son of Laish. [16] Her husband, however,
went with her, weeping behind her all the
way to Bahurim. Then Abner said to him,
"Go back home!" So he went back.

[17] Abner conferred with the elders of
Israel and said, "For some time you have
wanted to make David your king. [18] Now
do it! For the LORD promised David, 'By
my servant David I will rescue my people
Israel from the hand of the Philistines and
from the hand of all their enemies.'"

[19] Abner also spoke to the Benjamites
in person. Then he went to Hebron to
tell David everything that Israel and the
whole tribe of Benjamin wanted to do.
[20] When Abner, who had twenty men
with him, came to David at Hebron, David prepared a feast for him and his men.
[21] Then Abner said to David, "Let me go
at once and assemble all Israel for my lord
the king, so that they may make a covenant with you, and that you may rule over
all that your heart desires." So David sent
Abner away, and he went in peace.

Joab Murders Abner

[22] Just then David's men and Joab returned from a raid and brought with them
a great deal of plunder. But Abner was no
longer with David in Hebron, because
David had sent him away, and he had gone
in peace. [23] When Joab and all the soldiers
with him arrived, he was told that Abner
son of Ner had come to the king and that
the king had sent him away and that he
had gone in peace.

[24] So Joab went to the king and said,
"What have you done? Look, Abner came
to you. Why did you let him go? Now he
is gone! [25] You know Abner son of Ner;
he came to deceive you and observe your
movements and find out everything you
are doing."

[26] Joab then left David and sent messengers after Abner, and they brought him
back from the cistern at Sirah. But David did not know it. [27] Now when Abner
returned to Hebron, Joab took him aside
into an inner chamber, as if to speak with
him privately. And there, to avenge the
blood of his brother Asahel, Joab stabbed
him in the stomach, and he died.

[28] Later, when David heard about this, he said, "I and my kingdom are forever innocent before the LORD concerning the blood of Abner son of Ner. [29] May his blood fall on the head of Joab and on his whole family! May Joab's family never be without someone who has a running sore or leprosy[a] or who leans on a crutch or who falls by the sword or who lacks food."

[30] (Joab and his brother Abishai murdered Abner because he had killed their brother Asahel in the battle at Gibeon.)

[31] Then David said to Joab and all the people with him, "Tear your clothes and put on sackcloth and walk in mourning in front of Abner." King David himself walked behind the bier. [32] They buried Abner in Hebron, and the king wept aloud at Abner's tomb. All the people wept also.

[33] The king sang this lament for Abner:

"Should Abner have died as the
      lawless die?
[34]   Your hands were not bound,
      your feet were not fettered.
   You fell as one falls before the wicked."

And all the people wept over him again. [35] Then they all came and urged David to eat something while it was still day; but David took an oath, saying, "May God deal with me, be it ever so severely, if I taste bread or anything else before the sun sets!"

[36] All the people took note and were pleased; indeed, everything the king did pleased them. [37] So on that day all the people there and all Israel knew that the king had no part in the murder of Abner son of Ner.

[38] Then the king said to his men, "Do you not realize that a commander and a great man has fallen in Israel this day? [39] And today, though I am the anointed king, I am weak, and these sons of Zeruiah are too strong for me. May the LORD repay the evildoer according to his evil deeds!"

Ish-Bosheth Murdered

4 When Ish-Bosheth son of Saul heard that Abner had died in Hebron, he lost courage, and all Israel became alarmed. [2] Now Saul's son had two men who were leaders of raiding bands. One was named Baanah and the other Rekab; they were sons of Rimmon the Beerothite from the tribe of Benjamin — Beeroth is considered part of Benjamin, [3] because the people of Beeroth fled to Gittaim and have resided there as foreigners to this day.

[4] (Jonathan son of Saul had a son who was lame in both feet. He was five years old when the news about Saul and Jonathan came from Jezreel. His nurse picked him up and fled, but as she hurried to leave, he fell and became disabled. His name was Mephibosheth.)

[5] Now Rekab and Baanah, the sons of Rimmon the Beerothite, set out for the house of Ish-Bosheth, and they arrived there in the heat of the day while he was taking his noonday rest. [6] They went into the inner part of the house as if to get some wheat, and they stabbed him in the stomach. Then Rekab and his brother Baanah slipped away.

[7] They had gone into the house while he was lying on the bed in his bedroom. After they stabbed and killed him, they cut off his head. Taking it with them, they traveled all night by way of the Arabah. [8] They brought the head of Ish-Bosheth to David at Hebron and said to the king, "Here is the head of Ish-Bosheth son of Saul, your enemy, who tried to kill you. This day the LORD has avenged my lord the king against Saul and his offspring."

[9] David answered Rekab and his brother Baanah, the sons of Rimmon the Beerothite, "As surely as the LORD lives, who has delivered me out of every trouble, [10] when someone told me, 'Saul is dead,' and thought he was bringing good news, I seized him and put him to death in Ziklag. That was the reward I gave him for his news! [11] How much more — when wicked men have killed an innocent man in his own house and on his own bed — should I not now demand his blood from your hand and rid the earth of you!"

[12] So David gave an order to his men,

---

[a] 29 The Hebrew for *leprosy* was used for various diseases affecting the skin.

and they killed them. They cut off their hands and feet and hung the bodies by the pool in Hebron. But they took the head of Ish-Bosheth and buried it in Abner's tomb at Hebron.

David Becomes King Over Israel

5 All the tribes of Israel came to David at Hebron and said, "We are your own flesh and blood. ²In the past, while Saul was king over us, you were the one who led Israel on their military campaigns. And the LORD said to you, 'You will shepherd my people Israel, and you will become their ruler.'"

³When all the elders of Israel had come to King David at Hebron, the king made a covenant with them at Hebron before the LORD, and they anointed David king over Israel.

⁴David was thirty years old when he became king, and he reigned forty years. ⁵In Hebron he reigned over Judah seven years and six months, and in Jerusalem he reigned over all Israel and Judah thirty-three years.

David Conquers Jerusalem

⁶The king and his men marched to Jerusalem to attack the Jebusites, who lived there. The Jebusites said to David, "You will not get in here; even the blind and

---

2 Samuel 5

David had God's heart.

David almost got overlooked. When the prophet Samuel went hunting for a replacement for King Saul, he watched the tall and handsome sons of Jesse parade before him, certain that one of them was the next king. But God was looking for something more. As Jesse's oldest son strolled by, the Lord said, "Do not consider his appearance or his height, for I have rejected him. The LORD does not look at the things people look at. People look at the outward appearance, but the LORD looks at the heart" (1 Samuel 16:7).

Then Samuel met David, the youngest son. The Lord picked David as the next king, saying he was "a man after my own heart" who would do "everything I want him to do" (Acts 13:22).

As a young man David skillfully guarded his father's flocks, killing bears and lions to protect the sheep. He rose to serve God in spectacular ways. He defended God's honor by felling Goliath, a Philistine giant who mocked God (see 1 Samuel 17). He built a political kingdom and laid plans to construct a magnificent temple for the Lord (see 1 Chronicles 28:1 – 10). And he led Israel in worship, composing at least half of the songs in the book of Psalms.

David wasn't perfect. He sinned by stealing another man's wife and sending that husband to die in battle. But even then this spiritual giant displayed his heart for God, writing Psalm 51 to ask God to forgive his sin.

You can find David in 1 Samuel 16 to 1 Kings 2; 1 Chronicles 11 — 29; Matthew 1:1; and Luke 2:11.

UNSHAKEN *people*

the lame can ward you off." They thought, "David cannot get in here." [7]Nevertheless, David captured the fortress of Zion—which is the City of David.

[8]On that day David had said, "Anyone who conquers the Jebusites will have to use the water shaft to reach those 'lame and blind' who are David's enemies.[a]" That is why they say, "The 'blind and lame' will not enter the palace."

[9]David then took up residence in the fortress and called it the City of David. He built up the area around it, from the terraces[b] inward. [10]And he became more and more powerful, because the Lord God Almighty was with him.

[11]Now Hiram king of Tyre sent envoys to David, along with cedar logs and carpenters and stonemasons, and they built a palace for David. [12]Then David knew that the Lord had established him as king over Israel and had exalted his kingdom for the sake of his people Israel.

[13]After he left Hebron, David took more concubines and wives in Jerusalem, and more sons and daughters were born to him. [14]These are the names of the children born to him there: Shammua, Shobab, Nathan, Solomon, [15]Ibhar, Elishua, Nepheg, Japhia, [16]Elishama, Eliada and Eliphelet.

David Defeats the Philistines

[17]When the Philistines heard that David had been anointed king over Israel, they went up in full force to search for him, but David heard about it and went down to the stronghold. [18]Now the Philistines had come and spread out in the Valley of Rephaim; [19]so David inquired of the Lord, "Shall I go and attack the Philistines? Will you deliver them into my hands?"

The Lord answered him, "Go, for I will surely deliver the Philistines into your hands."

[20]So David went to Baal Perazim, and there he defeated them. He said, "As waters break out, the Lord has broken out against my enemies before me." So that place was called Baal Perazim.[c] [21]The

Philistines abandoned their idols there, and David and his men carried them off.

[22]Once more the Philistines came up and spread out in the Valley of Rephaim; [23]so David inquired of the Lord, and he answered, "Do not go straight up, but circle around behind them and attack them in front of the poplar trees. [24]As soon as you hear the sound of marching in the tops of the poplar trees, move quickly, because that will mean the Lord has gone out in front of you to strike the Philistine army." [25]So David did as the Lord commanded him, and he struck down the Philistines all the way from Gibeon[d] to Gezer.

The Ark Brought to Jerusalem

6 David again brought together all the able young men of Israel—thirty thousand. [2]He and all his men went to Baalah[e] in Judah to bring up from there the ark of God, which is called by the Name,[f] the name of the Lord Almighty, who is enthroned between the cherubim on the ark. [3]They set the ark of God on a new cart and brought it from the house of Abinadab, which was on the hill. Uzzah and Ahio, sons of Abinadab, were guiding the new cart [4]with the ark of God on it,[g] and Ahio was walking in front of it. [5]David and all Israel were celebrating with all their might before the Lord, with castanets,[h] harps, lyres, timbrels, sistrums and cymbals.

[6]When they came to the threshing floor of Nakon, Uzzah reached out and took hold of the ark of God, because the oxen stumbled. [7]The Lord's anger burned against Uzzah because of his irreverent

---

[a] 8 Or are hated by David   [b] 9 Or the Millo
[c] 20 Baal Perazim means the lord who breaks out.
[d] 25 Septuagint (see also 1 Chron. 14:16); Hebrew Geba   [e] 2 That is, Kiriath Jearim (see 1 Chron. 13:6)   [f] 2 Hebrew; Septuagint and Vulgate do not have the Name.   [g] 3,4 Dead Sea Scrolls and some Septuagint manuscripts; Masoretic Text cart [4]and they brought it with the ark of God from the house of Abinadab, which was on the hill   [h] 5 Masoretic Text; Dead Sea Scrolls and Septuagint (see also 1 Chron. 13:8) songs

act; therefore God struck him down, and he died there beside the ark of God.

⁸Then David was angry because the Lord's wrath had broken out against Uzzah, and to this day that place is called Perez Uzzah.ᵃ

⁹David was afraid of the Lord that day and said, "How can the ark of the Lord ever come to me?" ¹⁰He was not willing to take the ark of the Lord to be with him in the City of David. Instead, he took it to the house of Obed-Edom the Gittite. ¹¹The ark of the Lord remained in the house of Obed-Edom the Gittite for three months, and the Lord blessed him and his entire household.

¹²Now King David was told, "The Lord has blessed the household of Obed-Edom and everything he has, because of the ark of God." So David went to bring up the ark of God from the house of Obed-Edom to the City of David with rejoicing. ¹³When those who were carrying the ark of the Lord had taken six steps, he sacrificed a bull and a fattened calf. ¹⁴Wearing a linen ephod, David was dancing before the Lord with all his might, ¹⁵while he and all Israel were bringing up the ark of the Lord with shouts and the sound of trumpets.

¹⁶As the ark of the Lord was entering the City of David, Michal daughter of Saul watched from a window. And when she saw King David leaping and dancing before the Lord, she despised him in her heart.

¹⁷They brought the ark of the Lord and set it in its place inside the tent that David had pitched for it, and David sacrificed burnt offerings and fellowship offerings before the Lord. ¹⁸After he had finished sacrificing the burnt offerings and fellowship offerings, he blessed the people in the name of the Lord Almighty. ¹⁹Then he gave a loaf of bread, a cake of dates and a cake of raisins to each person in the whole crowd of Israelites, both men and women. And all the people went to their homes.

²⁰When David returned home to bless his household, Michal daughter of Saul came out to meet him and said, "How the king of Israel has distinguished himself today, going around half-naked in full view of the slave girls of his servants as any vulgar fellow would!"

²¹David said to Michal, "It was before the Lord, who chose me rather than your father or anyone from his house when he appointed me ruler over the Lord's people Israel—I will celebrate before the Lord. ²²I will become even more undignified than this, and I will be humiliated in my own eyes. But by these slave girls you spoke of, I will be held in honor."

²³And Michal daughter of Saul had no children to the day of her death.

God's Promise to David

7 After the king was settled in his palace and the Lord had given him rest from all his enemies around him, ²he said to Nathan the prophet, "Here I am, living in a house of cedar, while the ark of God remains in a tent."

³Nathan replied to the king, "Whatever you have in mind, go ahead and do it, for the Lord is with you."

⁴But that night the word of the Lord came to Nathan, saying:

⁵"Go and tell my servant David, 'This is what the Lord says: Are you the one to build me a house to dwell in? ⁶I have not dwelt in a house from the day I brought the Israelites up out of Egypt to this day. I have been moving from place to place with a tent as my dwelling. ⁷Wherever I have moved with all the Israelites, did I ever say to any of their rulers whom I commanded to shepherd my people Israel, "Why have you not built me a house of cedar?"'

⁸"Now then, tell my servant David, 'This is what the Lord Almighty says: I took you from the pasture, from tending the flock, and appointed you ruler over my people Israel. ⁹I have been with you wherever you have gone, and I have cut off all your enemies from before you.

ᵃ 8 *Perez Uzzah* means *outbreak against Uzzah.*

Now I will make your name great, like the names of the greatest men on earth. [10] And I will provide a place for my people Israel and will plant them so that they can have a home of their own and no longer be disturbed. Wicked people will not oppress them anymore, as they did at the beginning [11] and have done ever since the time I appointed leaders[a] over my people Israel. I will also give you rest from all your enemies.

"'The Lord declares to you that the Lord himself will establish a house for you: [12] When your days are over and you rest with your ancestors, I will raise up your offspring to succeed you, your own flesh and blood, and I will establish his kingdom. [13] He is the one who will build a house for my Name, and I will establish the throne of his kingdom forever. [14] I will be his father, and he will be my son. When he does wrong, I will punish him with a rod wielded by men, with floggings inflicted by human hands. [15] But my love will never be taken away from him, as I took it away from Saul, whom I removed from before you. [16] Your house and your kingdom will endure forever before me[b]; your throne will be established forever.'"

[17] Nathan reported to David all the words of this entire revelation.

David's Prayer

[18] Then King David went in and sat before the Lord, and he said:

"Who am I, Sovereign Lord, and what is my family, that you have brought me this far? [19] And as if this were not enough in your sight, Sovereign Lord, you have also spoken about the future of the house of your servant—and this decree, Sovereign Lord, is for a mere human![c]

[20] "What more can David say to you? For you know your servant, Sovereign Lord. [21] For the sake of your word and according to your will, you have done this great thing and made it known to your servant.

[22] "How great you are, Sovereign Lord! There is no one like you, and there is no God but you, as we have heard with our own ears. [23] And who is like your people Israel—the one nation on earth that God went out to redeem as a people for himself, and to make a name for himself, and to perform great and awesome wonders by driving out nations and their gods from before your people, whom you redeemed from Egypt?[d] [24] You have

[a] 11 Traditionally *judges*   [b] 16 Some Hebrew manuscripts and Septuagint; most Hebrew manuscripts *you*   [c] 19 Or *for the human race*   [d] 23 See Septuagint and 1 Chron. 17:21; Hebrew *wonders for your land and before your people, whom you redeemed from Egypt, from the nations and their gods.*

UNSHAKEN God

2 Samuel 7:22

God is unique.

God had just spoken a unique promise to King David, pledging that he would establish a royal house for David, and not just for a little while. God said David's throne "will be established forever," a prophecy that Jesus would one day be born to David's line (2 Samuel 7:16). David responds by noting God's own uniqueness. He calls God great, the "Sovereign Lord," the one who rules with unlimited power. David declares that no one else is like God. No one even comes close. The Lord is one of a kind. Your world is full of imposters competing to prove their importance and win your love. But you serve the only real God.

So ... What makes God different from people who claim to be really important?

established your people Israel as your very own forever, and you, LORD, have become their God.

25 "And now, LORD God, keep forever the promise you have made concerning your servant and his house. Do as you promised, 26 so that your name will be great forever. Then people will say, 'The LORD Almighty is God over Israel!' And the house of your servant David will be established in your sight.

27 "LORD Almighty, God of Israel, you have revealed this to your servant, saying, 'I will build a house for you.' So your servant has found courage to pray this prayer to you. 28 Sovereign LORD, you are God! Your covenant is trustworthy, and you have promised these good things to your servant. 29 Now be pleased to bless the house of your servant, that it may continue forever in your sight; for you, Sovereign LORD, have spoken, and with your blessing the house of your servant will be blessed forever."

David's Victories

8 In the course of time, David defeated the Philistines and subdued them, and he took Metheg Ammah from the control of the Philistines.

2 David also defeated the Moabites. He made them lie down on the ground and measured them off with a length of cord. Every two lengths of them were put to death, and the third length was allowed to live. So the Moabites became subject to David and brought him tribute.

3 Moreover, David defeated Hadadezer son of Rehob, king of Zobah, when he went to restore his monument at[a] the Euphrates River. 4 David captured a thousand of his chariots, seven thousand charioteers[b] and twenty thousand foot soldiers. He hamstrung all but a hundred of the chariot horses.

5 When the Arameans of Damascus came to help Hadadezer king of Zobah, David struck down twenty-two thousand of them. 6 He put garrisons in the Arame-

an kingdom of Damascus, and the Arameans became subject to him and brought tribute. The LORD gave David victory wherever he went.

7 David took the gold shields that belonged to the officers of Hadadezer and brought them to Jerusalem. 8 From Tebah[c] and Berothai, towns that belonged to Hadadezer, King David took a great quantity of bronze.

9 When Tou[d] king of Hamath heard that David had defeated the entire army of Hadadezer, 10 he sent his son Joram[e] to King David to greet him and congratulate him on his victory in battle over Hadadezer, who had been at war with Tou. Joram brought with him articles of silver, of gold and of bronze.

11 King David dedicated these articles to the LORD, as he had done with the silver and gold from all the nations he had subdued: 12 Edom[f] and Moab, the Ammonites and the Philistines, and Amalek. He also dedicated the plunder taken from Hadadezer son of Rehob, king of Zobah.

13 And David became famous after he returned from striking down eighteen thousand Edomites[g] in the Valley of Salt.

14 He put garrisons throughout Edom, and all the Edomites became subject to David. The LORD gave David victory wherever he went.

David's Officials

15 David reigned over all Israel, doing what was just and right for all his people. 16 Joab son of Zeruiah was over the army; Jehoshaphat son of Ahilud was recorder; 17 Zadok son of Ahitub and Ahimelek son

---

a 3 Or *his control along*   *b 4* Septuagint (see also Dead Sea Scrolls and 1 Chron. 18:4); Masoretic Text *captured seventeen hundred of his charioteers*   *c 8* See some Septuagint manuscripts (see also 1 Chron. 18:8); Hebrew *Betah*.   *d 9* Hebrew *Toi*, a variant of *Tou*; also in verse 10   *e 10* A variant of *Hadoram* *f 12* Some Hebrew manuscripts, Septuagint and Syriac (see also 1 Chron. 18:11); most Hebrew manuscripts *Aram*   *g 13* A few Hebrew manuscripts, Septuagint and Syriac (see also 1 Chron. 18:12); most Hebrew manuscripts *Aram* (that is, Arameans) of Abiathar were priests; Seraiah was secretary; [18]Benaiah son of Jehoiada was over the Kerethites and Pelethites; and David's sons were priests.[a]

David and Mephibosheth

9 David asked, "Is there anyone still left of the house of Saul to whom I can show kindness for Jonathan's sake?"

[2]Now there was a servant of Saul's household named Ziba. They summoned him to appear before David, and the king said to him, "Are you Ziba?"

"At your service," he replied.

[3]The king asked, "Is there no one still alive from the house of Saul to whom I can show God's kindness?"

Ziba answered the king, "There is still a son of Jonathan; he is lame in both feet."

[4]"Where is he?" the king asked.

Ziba answered, "He is at the house of Makir son of Ammiel in Lo Debar."

[5]So King David had him brought from Lo Debar, from the house of Makir son of Ammiel.

[6]When Mephibosheth son of Jonathan, the son of Saul, came to David, he bowed down to pay him honor.

David said, "Mephibosheth!"

"At your service," he replied.

[7]"Don't be afraid," David said to him, "for I will surely show you kindness for the sake of your father Jonathan. I will restore to you all the land that belonged to your grandfather Saul, and you will always eat at my table."

[8]Mephibosheth bowed down and said, "What is your servant, that you should notice a dead dog like me?"

[9]Then the king summoned Ziba, Saul's steward, and said to him, "I have given your master's grandson everything that belonged to Saul and his family. [10]You and your sons and your servants are to farm the land for him and bring in the crops, so that your master's grandson may be provided for. And Mephibosheth, grandson of your master, will always eat at my table." (Now Ziba had fifteen sons and twenty servants.)

[11]Then Ziba said to the king, "Your servant will do whatever my lord the king commands his servant to do." So Mephibosheth ate at David's[b] table like one of the king's sons.

[12]Mephibosheth had a young son named Mika, and all the members of Ziba's household were servants of Mephibosheth. [13]And Mephibosheth lived in Jerusalem, because he always ate at the king's table; he was lame in both feet.

David Defeats the Ammonites

10 In the course of time, the king of the Ammonites died, and his son Hanun succeeded him as king. [2]David thought, "I will show kindness to Hanun son of Nahash, just as his father showed kindness to me." So David sent a delegation to express his sympathy to Hanun concerning his father.

When David's men came to the land of the Ammonites, [3]the Ammonite commanders said to Hanun their lord, "Do you think David is honoring your father by sending envoys to you to express sympathy? Hasn't David sent them to you only to explore the city and spy it out and overthrow it?" [4]So Hanun seized David's envoys, shaved off half of each man's beard, cut off their garments at the buttocks, and sent them away.

[5]When David was told about this, he sent messengers to meet the men, for they were greatly humiliated. The king said, "Stay at Jericho till your beards have grown, and then come back."

[6]When the Ammonites realized that they had become obnoxious to David, they hired twenty thousand Aramean foot soldiers from Beth Rehob and Zobah, as well as the king of Maakah with a thousand men, and also twelve thousand men from Tob.

[7]On hearing this, David sent Joab out with the entire army of fighting men. [8]The Ammonites came out and drew up in battle formation at the entrance of their city gate,

---

[a] *18* Or *were chief officials* (see Septuagint and Targum; see also 1 Chron. 18:17)
[b] *11* Septuagint; Hebrew *my*

while the Arameans of Zobah and Rehob and the men of Tob and Maakah were by themselves in the open country.

⁹Joab saw that there were battle lines in front of him and behind him; so he selected some of the best troops in Israel and deployed them against the Arameans. ¹⁰He put the rest of the men under the command of Abishai his brother and deployed them against the Ammonites. ¹¹Joab said, "If the Arameans are too strong for me, then you are to come to my rescue; but if the Ammonites are too strong for you, then I will come to rescue you. ¹²Be strong, and let us fight bravely for our people and the cities of our God. The LORD will do what is good in his sight."

¹³Then Joab and the troops with him advanced to fight the Arameans, and they fled before him. ¹⁴When the Ammonites realized that the Arameans were fleeing, they fled before Abishai and went inside the city. So Joab returned from fighting the Ammonites and came to Jerusalem.

¹⁵After the Arameans saw that they had been routed by Israel, they regrouped. ¹⁶Hadadezer had Arameans brought from beyond the Euphrates River; they went to Helam, with Shobak the commander of Hadadezer's army leading them.

¹⁷When David was told of this, he gathered all Israel, crossed the Jordan and went to Helam. The Arameans formed their battle lines to meet David and fought against him. ¹⁸But they fled before Israel, and David killed seven hundred of their charioteers and forty thousand of their foot soldiers.ᵃ He also struck down Shobak the commander of their army, and he died there. ¹⁹When all the kings who were vassals of Hadadezer saw that they had been routed by Israel, they made peace with the Israelites and became subject to them.

So the Arameans were afraid to help the Ammonites anymore.

David and Bathsheba

11 In the spring, at the time when kings go off to war, David sent Joab out with the king's men and the whole Israelite army. They destroyed the Ammonites and besieged Rabbah. But David remained in Jerusalem.

²One evening David got up from his bed and walked around on the roof of the palace. From the roof he saw a woman bathing. The woman was very beautiful, ³and David sent someone to find out about her. The man said, "She is Bathsheba, the daughter of Eliam and the wife of Uriah the Hittite." ⁴Then David sent messengers to get her. She came to him, and he slept with her. (Now she was purifying herself from her monthly uncleanness.) Then she went back home. ⁵The woman conceived and sent word to David, saying, "I am pregnant."

⁶So David sent this word to Joab: "Send me Uriah the Hittite." And Joab sent him to David. ⁷When Uriah came to him, David asked him how Joab was, how the soldiers were and how the war was going. ⁸Then David said to Uriah, "Go down to your house and wash your feet." So Uriah left the palace, and a gift from the king was sent after him. ⁹But Uriah slept at the entrance to the palace with all his master's servants and did not go down to his house.

¹⁰David was told, "Uriah did not go home." So he asked Uriah, "Haven't you just come from a military campaign? Why didn't you go home?"

¹¹Uriah said to David, "The ark and Israel and Judah are staying in tents,ᵇ and my commander Joab and my lord's men are camped in the open country. How could I go to my house to eat and drink and make love to my wife? As surely as you live, I will not do such a thing!"

¹²Then David said to him, "Stay here one more day, and tomorrow I will send you back." So Uriah remained in Jerusalem that day and the next. ¹³At David's invitation, he ate and drank with him, and David made him drunk. But in the evening Uriah went out to sleep on his mat among his master's servants; he did not go home.

¹⁴In the morning David wrote a letter to Joab and sent it with Uriah. ¹⁵In it he

---

ᵃ 18 Some Septuagint manuscripts (see also 1 Chron. 19:18); Hebrew *horsemen*
ᵇ 11 Or *staying at Sukkoth*

wrote, "Put Uriah out in front where the fighting is fiercest. Then withdraw from him so he will be struck down and die."

¹⁶So while Joab had the city under siege, he put Uriah at a place where he knew the strongest defenders were. ¹⁷When the men of the city came out and fought against Joab, some of the men in David's army fell; moreover, Uriah the Hittite died.

¹⁸Joab sent David a full account of the battle. ¹⁹He instructed the messenger: "When you have finished giving the king this account of the battle, ²⁰the king's anger may flare up, and he may ask you, 'Why did you get so close to the city to fight? Didn't you know they would shoot arrows from the wall? ²¹Who killed Abimelek son of Jerub-Besheth*? Didn't a woman drop an upper millstone on him from the wall, so that he died in Thebez? Why did you get so close to the wall?' If he asks you this, then say to him, 'Moreover, your servant Uriah the Hittite is dead.'"

²²The messenger set out, and when he arrived he told David everything Joab had sent him to say. ²³The messenger said to David, "The men overpowered us and came out against us in the open, but we drove them back to the entrance of the city gate. ²⁴Then the archers shot arrows at your servants from the wall, and some of the king's men died. Moreover, your servant Uriah the Hittite is dead."

²⁵David told the messenger, "Say this to Joab: 'Don't let this upset you; the sword devours one as well as another. Press the attack against the city and destroy it.' Say this to encourage Joab."

²⁶When Uriah's wife heard that her husband was dead, she mourned for him. ²⁷After the time of mourning was over, David had her brought to his house, and she became his wife and bore him a son. But the thing David had done displeased the LORD.

Nathan Rebukes David

12 The LORD sent Nathan to David. When he came to him, he said, "There were two men in a certain town, one rich and the other poor. ²The rich man had a very large number of sheep and cattle, ³but the poor man had nothing except one little ewe lamb he had bought. He raised it, and it grew up with him and his children. It shared his food, drank from his cup and even slept in his arms. It was like a daughter to him.

⁴"Now a traveler came to the rich man, but the rich man refrained from taking one of his own sheep or cattle to prepare a meal for the traveler who had come to him. Instead, he took the ewe lamb that belonged to the poor man and prepared it for the one who had come to him."

⁵David burned with anger against the man and said to Nathan, "As surely as the LORD lives, the man who did this must die! ⁶He must pay for that lamb four times over, because he did such a thing and had no pity."

⁷Then Nathan said to David, "You are the man! This is what the LORD, the God of Israel, says: 'I anointed you king over Israel, and I delivered you from the hand of Saul. ⁸I gave your master's house to you, and your master's wives into your arms. I gave you all Israel and Judah. And if all this had been too little, I would have given you even more. ⁹Why did you despise the word of the LORD by doing what is evil in his eyes? You struck down Uriah the Hittite with the sword and took his wife to be your own. You killed him with the sword of the Ammonites. ¹⁰Now, therefore, the sword will never depart from your house, because you despised me and took the wife of Uriah the Hittite to be your own.'

¹¹"This is what the LORD says: 'Out of your own household I am going to bring calamity on you. Before your very eyes I will take your wives and give them to one who is close to you, and he will sleep with your wives in broad daylight. ¹²You did it in secret, but I will do this thing in broad daylight before all Israel.'"

¹³Then David said to Nathan, "I have sinned against the LORD."

Nathan replied, "The LORD has taken away your sin. You are not going to

---

ᵃ 21 Also known as *Jerub-Baal* (that is, Gideon)

die. [14]But because by doing this you have shown utter contempt for[a] the LORD, the son born to you will die."

[15]After Nathan had gone home, the LORD struck the child that Uriah's wife had borne to David, and he became ill. [16]David pleaded with God for the child. He fasted and spent the nights lying in sackcloth[b] on the ground. [17]The elders of his household stood beside him to get him up from the ground, but he refused, and he would not eat any food with them.

[18]On the seventh day the child died. David's attendants were afraid to tell him that the child was dead, for they thought, "While the child was still living, he wouldn't listen to us when we spoke to him. How can we now tell him the child is dead? He may do something desperate."

[19]David noticed that his attendants were whispering among themselves, and he realized the child was dead. "Is the child dead?" he asked.

"Yes," they replied, "he is dead."

[20]Then David got up from the ground. After he had washed, put on lotions and changed his clothes, he went into the house of the LORD and worshiped. Then

[a] 14 An ancient Hebrew scribal tradition; Masoretic Text *for the enemies of*   [b] 16 Dead Sea Scrolls and Septuagint; Masoretic Text does not have *in sackcloth*.

2 Samuel 12

Nathan stood up to the king.

King David must have been an intimidating man. He started his life as the youngest of eight brothers, a boy given the humble job of watching his father's sheep. But he dropped Goliath the giant with a single rock from his sling. He escaped King Saul's constant plots to murder him. He gathered hundreds of warriors around him and conquered the city of Jerusalem, and his kingdom and power expanded until he was respected by his people and feared by his enemies.

But David wasn't perfect, and the job fell to Nathan the prophet to keep him in check. David had lusted after the beautiful Bathsheba and ordered her to the palace. When she became pregnant, David sent her husband, Uriah, to die in battle.

Nathan slyly told the story of a poor man who had a single small lamb he had raised like his own child, sharing his food and cup and cradling it in his arms. But a man with many sheep came along and stole that lone sheep. David was rightly outraged at the rich man. Then he discovered the point of the story. "You are the man!" Nathan said (2 Samuel 12:7).

The prophet surely didn't enjoy telling David what the consequences of his sin would be—from the death of the child he had conceived with Bathsheba to the violence that would plague his kingdom. But when David most needed correction, Nathan stepped up. He stood up to the king.

You can find Nathan in 2 Samuel 7 and 12; 1 Kings 1; and in the heading of Psalm 51.

UNSHAKEN *people*

he went to his own house, and at his request they served him food, and he ate.

²¹His attendants asked him, "Why are you acting this way? While the child was alive, you fasted and wept, but now that the child is dead, you get up and eat!"

²²He answered, "While the child was still alive, I fasted and wept. I thought, 'Who knows? The LORD may be gracious to me and let the child live.' ²³But now that he is dead, why should I go on fasting? Can I bring him back again? I will go to him, but he will not return to me."

²⁴Then David comforted his wife Bathsheba, and he went to her and made love to her. She gave birth to a son, and they named him Solomon. The LORD loved him; ²⁵and because the LORD loved him, he sent word through Nathan the prophet to name him Jedidiah.ᵃ

²⁶Meanwhile Joab fought against Rabbah of the Ammonites and captured the royal citadel. ²⁷Joab then sent messengers to David, saying, "I have fought against Rabbah and taken its water supply. ²⁸Now muster the rest of the troops and besiege the city and capture it. Otherwise I will take the city, and it will be named after me."

²⁹So David mustered the entire army and went to Rabbah, and attacked and captured it. ³⁰David took the crown from their king'sᵇ head, and it was placed on his own head. It weighed a talentᶜ of gold, and it was set with precious stones. David took a great quantity of plunder from the city ³¹and brought out the people who were there, consigning them to labor with saws and with iron picks and axes, and he made them work at brickmaking.ᵈ David did this to all the Ammonite towns. Then he and his entire army returned to Jerusalem.

Amnon and Tamar

13 In the course of time, Amnon son of David fell in love with Tamar, the beautiful sister of Absalom son of David.

²Amnon became so obsessed with his sister Tamar that he made himself ill. She was a virgin, and it seemed impossible for him to do anything to her.

³Now Amnon had an adviser named Jonadab son of Shimeah, David's brother. Jonadab was a very shrewd man. ⁴He asked Amnon, "Why do you, the king's son, look so haggard morning after morning? Won't you tell me?"

Amnon said to him, "I'm in love with Tamar, my brother Absalom's sister."

---

2 Samuel 12:1–25

Sin will find you out.

God called David "a man after his own heart" (1 Samuel 13:14), but that didn't mean he never messed up. In fact, this man who lived out loud for God blew it in a major way, taking another man's wife as his own and sending her husband to die in battle. David surely thought he got away with his crime, because he was caught by surprise when the prophet Nathan told a pointed story that exposed his sin. We might think we can do wrong without anyone knowing, but God sees everything. And like Moses warned long ago, "You will be sinning against the LORD; and you may be sure that your sin will find you out" (Numbers 32:23). Despite his horrible failure, David modeled exactly what to do next. He admitted to Nathan, "I have sinned against the LORD," and God forgave him (2 Samuel 12:13).

Think: When have you thought you got away with a sin—only to be caught?

ROCK SOLID truths

ᵃ 25 Jedidiah means loved by the LORD.
ᵇ 30 Or from Milkom's (that is, Molek's)
ᶜ 30 That is, about 75 pounds or about 34 kilograms   ᵈ 31 The meaning of the Hebrew for this clause is uncertain.

5 "Go to bed and pretend to be ill," Jonadab said. "When your father comes to see you, say to him, 'I would like my sister Tamar to come and give me something to eat. Let her prepare the food in my sight so I may watch her and then eat it from her hand.'"

6 So Amnon lay down and pretended to be ill. When the king came to see him, Amnon said to him, "I would like my sister Tamar to come and make some special bread in my sight, so I may eat from her hand."

7 David sent word to Tamar at the palace: "Go to the house of your brother Amnon and prepare some food for him." 8 So Tamar went to the house of her brother Amnon, who was lying down. She took some dough, kneaded it, made the bread in his sight and baked it. 9 Then she took the pan and served him the bread, but he refused to eat.

"Send everyone out of here," Amnon said. So everyone left him. 10 Then Amnon said to Tamar, "Bring the food here into my bedroom so I may eat from your hand." And Tamar took the bread she had prepared and brought it to her brother Amnon in his bedroom. 11 But when she took it to him to eat, he grabbed her and said, "Come to bed with me, my sister."

12 "No, my brother!" she said to him. "Don't force me! Such a thing should not be done in Israel! Don't do this wicked thing. 13 What about me? Where could I get rid of my disgrace? And what about you? You would be like one of the wicked fools in Israel. Please speak to the king; he will not keep me from being married to you." 14 But he refused to listen to her, and since he was stronger than she, he raped her.

15 Then Amnon hated her with intense hatred. In fact, he hated her more than he had loved her. Amnon said to her, "Get up and get out!"

16 "No!" she said to him. "Sending me away would be a greater wrong than what you have already done to me."

But he refused to listen to her. 17 He called his personal servant and said, "Get this woman out of my sight and bolt the door after her." 18 So his servant put her out and bolted the door after her. She was wearing an ornate*a* robe, for this was the kind of garment the virgin daughters of the king wore. 19 Tamar put ashes on her head and tore the ornate robe she was wearing. She put her hands on her head and went away, weeping aloud as she went.

20 Her brother Absalom said to her, "Has that Amnon, your brother, been with you? Be quiet for now, my sister; he is your brother. Don't take this thing to heart." And Tamar lived in her brother Absalom's house, a desolate woman.

21 When King David heard all this, he was furious. 22 And Absalom never said a word to Amnon, either good or bad; he hated Amnon because he had disgraced his sister Tamar.

Absalom Kills Amnon

23 Two years later, when Absalom's sheepshearers were at Baal Hazor near the border of Ephraim, he invited all the king's sons to come there. 24 Absalom went to the king and said, "Your servant has had shearers come. Will the king and his attendants please join me?"

25 "No, my son," the king replied. "All of us should not go; we would only be a burden to you." Although Absalom urged him, he still refused to go but gave him his blessing.

26 Then Absalom said, "If not, please let my brother Amnon come with us."

The king asked him, "Why should he go with you?" 27 But Absalom urged him, so he sent with him Amnon and the rest of the king's sons.

28 Absalom ordered his men, "Listen! When Amnon is in high spirits from drinking wine and I say to you, 'Strike Amnon down,' then kill him. Don't be afraid. Haven't I given you this order? Be strong and brave." 29 So Absalom's men did to Amnon what Absalom had ordered. Then all the king's sons got up, mounted their mules and fled.

a 18 The meaning of the Hebrew for this word is uncertain; also in verse 19.

³⁰While they were on their way, the report came to David: "Absalom has struck down all the king's sons; not one of them is left." ³¹The king stood up, tore his clothes and lay down on the ground; and all his attendants stood by with their clothes torn.

³²But Jonadab son of Shimeah, David's brother, said, "My lord should not think that they killed all the princes; only Amnon is dead. This has been Absalom's express intention ever since the day Amnon raped his sister Tamar. ³³My lord the king should not be concerned about the report that all the king's sons are dead. Only Amnon is dead."

³⁴Meanwhile, Absalom had fled.

Now the man standing watch looked up and saw many people on the road west of him, coming down the side of the hill. The watchman went and told the king, "I see men in the direction of Horonaim, on the side of the hill."ᵃ

³⁵Jonadab said to the king, "See, the king's sons have come; it has happened just as your servant said."

³⁶As he finished speaking, the king's sons came in, wailing loudly. The king, too, and all his attendants wept very bitterly.

³⁷Absalom fled and went to Talmai son of Ammihud, the king of Geshur. But King David mourned many days for his son.

³⁸After Absalom fled and went to Geshur, he stayed there three years. ³⁹And King David longed to go to Absalom, for he was consoled concerning Amnon's death.

Absalom Returns to Jerusalem

14 Joab son of Zeruiah knew that the king's heart longed for Absalom. ²So Joab sent someone to Tekoa and had a wise woman brought from there. He said to her, "Pretend you are in mourning. Dress in mourning clothes, and don't use any cosmetic lotions. Act like a woman who has spent many days grieving for the dead. ³Then go to the king and speak these words to him." And Joab put the words in her mouth.

⁴When the woman from Tekoa wentᵇ to the king, she fell with her face to the ground to pay him honor, and she said, "Help me, Your Majesty!"

⁵The king asked her, "What is troubling you?"

She said, "I am a widow; my husband is dead. ⁶I your servant had two sons. They got into a fight with each other in the field, and no one was there to separate them. One struck the other and killed him. ⁷Now the whole clan has risen up against your servant; they say, 'Hand over the one who struck his brother down, so that we may put him to death for the life of his brother whom he killed; then we will get rid of the heir as well.' They would put out the only burning coal I have left, leaving my husband neither name nor descendant on the face of the earth."

⁸The king said to the woman, "Go home, and I will issue an order in your behalf."

⁹But the woman from Tekoa said to him, "Let my lord the king pardon me and my family, and let the king and his throne be without guilt."

¹⁰The king replied, "If anyone says anything to you, bring them to me, and they will not bother you again."

¹¹She said, "Then let the king invoke the Lord his God to prevent the avenger of blood from adding to the destruction, so that my son will not be destroyed."

"As surely as the Lord lives," he said, "not one hair of your son's head will fall to the ground."

¹²Then the woman said, "Let your servant speak a word to my lord the king."

"Speak," he replied.

¹³The woman said, "Why then have you devised a thing like this against the people of God? When the king says this, does he not convict himself, for the king has not brought back his banished son? ¹⁴Like water spilled on the ground, which cannot be recovered, so we must die. But

ᵃ 34 Septuagint; Hebrew does not have this sentence.   ᵇ 4 Many Hebrew manuscripts, Septuagint, Vulgate and Syriac; most Hebrew manuscripts *spoke* that is not what God desires; rather, he devises ways so that a banished person does not remain banished from him.

15 "And now I have come to say this to my lord the king because the people have made me afraid. Your servant thought, 'I will speak to the king; perhaps he will grant his servant's request. 16 Perhaps the king will agree to deliver his servant from the hand of the man who is trying to cut off both me and my son from God's inheritance.'

17 "And now your servant says, 'May the word of my lord the king secure my inheritance, for my lord the king is like an angel of God in discerning good and evil. May the LORD your God be with you.'"

18 Then the king said to the woman, "Don't keep from me the answer to what I am going to ask you."

"Let my lord the king speak," the woman said.

19 The king asked, "Isn't the hand of Joab with you in all this?"

The woman answered, "As surely as you live, my lord the king, no one can turn to the right or to the left from anything my lord the king says. Yes, it was your servant Joab who instructed me to do this and who put all these words into the mouth of your servant. 20 Your servant Joab did this to change the present situation. My lord has wisdom like that of an angel of God—he knows everything that happens in the land."

21 The king said to Joab, "Very well, I will do it. Go, bring back the young man Absalom."

22 Joab fell with his face to the ground to pay him honor, and he blessed the king. Joab said, "Today your servant knows that he has found favor in your eyes, my lord the king, because the king has granted his servant's request."

23 Then Joab went to Geshur and brought Absalom back to Jerusalem. 24 But the king said, "He must go to his own house; he must not see my face." So Absalom went to his own house and did not see the face of the king.

25 In all Israel there was not a man so highly praised for his handsome appearance as Absalom. From the top of his head to the sole of his foot there was no blemish in him. 26 Whenever he cut the hair of his head—he used to cut his hair once a year because it became too heavy for him—he would weigh it, and its weight was two hundred shekels[a] by the royal standard.

27 Three sons and a daughter were born to Absalom. His daughter's name was Tamar, and she became a beautiful woman.

28 Absalom lived two years in Jerusalem without seeing the king's face. 29 Then Absalom sent for Joab in order to send him to the king, but Joab refused to come to him. So he sent a second time, but he refused to come. 30 Then he said to his servants, "Look, Joab's field is next to mine, and he has barley there. Go and set it on fire." So Absalom's servants set the field on fire.

31 Then Joab did go to Absalom's house, and he said to him, "Why have your servants set my field on fire?"

32 Absalom said to Joab, "Look, I sent word to you and said, 'Come here so I can send you to the king to ask, "Why have I come from Geshur? It would be better for me if I were still there!"' Now then, I want to see the king's face, and if I am guilty of anything, let him put me to death."

33 So Joab went to the king and told him this. Then the king summoned Absalom, and he came in and bowed down with his face to the ground before the king. And the king kissed Absalom.

Absalom's Conspiracy

15 In the course of time, Absalom provided himself with a chariot and horses and with fifty men to run ahead of him. 2 He would get up early and stand by the side of the road leading to the city gate. Whenever anyone came with a complaint to be placed before the king for a decision, Absalom would call out to him, "What town are you from?" He would answer, "Your servant is from one of the tribes of Israel." 3 Then Absalom would say to him, "Look, your claims are

---

a 26 That is, about 5 pounds or about 2.3 kilograms

valid and proper, but there is no representative of the king to hear you." [4] And Absalom would add, "If only I were appointed judge in the land! Then everyone who has a complaint or case could come to me and I would see that they receive justice."

[5] Also, whenever anyone approached him to bow down before him, Absalom would reach out his hand, take hold of him and kiss him. [6] Absalom behaved in this way toward all the Israelites who came to the king asking for justice, and so he stole the hearts of the people of Israel.

[7] At the end of four[a] years, Absalom said to the king, "Let me go to Hebron and fulfill a vow I made to the LORD. [8] While your servant was living at Geshur in Aram, I made this vow: 'If the LORD takes me back to Jerusalem, I will worship the LORD in Hebron.[b]'"

[9] The king said to him, "Go in peace." So he went to Hebron.

[10] Then Absalom sent secret messengers throughout the tribes of Israel to say, "As soon as you hear the sound of the trumpets, then say, 'Absalom is king in Hebron.'" [11] Two hundred men from Jerusalem had accompanied Absalom. They had been invited as guests and went quite innocently, knowing nothing about the matter. [12] While Absalom was offering sacrifices, he also sent for Ahithophel the Gilonite, David's counselor, to come from Giloh, his hometown. And so the conspiracy gained strength, and Absalom's following kept on increasing.

David Flees

[13] A messenger came and told David, "The hearts of the people of Israel are with Absalom."

[14] Then David said to all his officials who were with him in Jerusalem, "Come! We must flee, or none of us will escape from Absalom. We must leave immediately, or he will move quickly to overtake us and bring ruin on us and put the city to the sword."

[15] The king's officials answered him, "Your servants are ready to do whatever our lord the king chooses."

[16] The king set out, with his entire household following him; but he left ten concubines to take care of the palace. [17] So the king set out, with all the people following him, and they halted at the edge of the city. [18] All his men marched past him, along with all the Kerethites and Pelethites; and all the six hundred Gittites who had accompanied him from Gath marched before the king.

[19] The king said to Ittai the Gittite, "Why should you come along with us? Go back and stay with King Absalom. You are a foreigner, an exile from your homeland. [20] You came only yesterday. And today shall I make you wander about with us, when I do not know where I am going? Go back, and take your people with you. May the LORD show you kindness and faithfulness."[c]

[21] But Ittai replied to the king, "As surely as the LORD lives, and as my lord the king lives, wherever my lord the king may be, whether it means life or death, there will your servant be."

[22] David said to Ittai, "Go ahead, march on." So Ittai the Gittite marched on with all his men and the families that were with him.

[23] The whole countryside wept aloud as all the people passed by. The king also crossed the Kidron Valley, and all the people moved on toward the wilderness.

[24] Zadok was there, too, and all the Levites who were with him were carrying the ark of the covenant of God. They set down the ark of God, and Abiathar offered sacrifices until all the people had finished leaving the city.

[25] Then the king said to Zadok, "Take the ark of God back into the city. If I find favor in the LORD's eyes, he will bring me back and let me see it and his dwelling place again. [26] But if he says, 'I am not pleased with you,' then I am ready; let him do to me whatever seems good to him."

---

[a] 7 Some Septuagint manuscripts, Syriac and Josephus; Hebrew *forty*   [b] 8 Some Septuagint manuscripts; Hebrew does not have *in Hebron*.   [c] 20 Septuagint; Hebrew *May kindness and faithfulness be with you*

²⁷The king also said to Zadok the priest, "Do you understand? Go back to the city with my blessing. Take your son Ahimaaz with you, and also Abiathar's son Jonathan. You and Abiathar return with your two sons. ²⁸I will wait at the fords in the wilderness until word comes from you to inform me." ²⁹So Zadok and Abiathar took the ark of God back to Jerusalem and stayed there.

³⁰But David continued up the Mount of Olives, weeping as he went; his head was covered and he was barefoot. All the people with him covered their heads too and were weeping as they went up. ³¹Now David had been told, "Ahithophel is among the conspirators with Absalom." So David prayed, "Lᴏʀᴅ, turn Ahithophel's counsel into foolishness."

³²When David arrived at the summit, where people used to worship God, Hushai the Arkite was there to meet him, his robe torn and dust on his head. ³³David said to him, "If you go with me, you will be a burden to me. ³⁴But if you return to the city and say to Absalom, 'Your Majesty, I will be your servant; I was your father's servant in the past, but now I will be your servant,' then you can help me by frustrating Ahithophel's advice. ³⁵Won't the priests Zadok and Abiathar be there with you? Tell them anything you hear in the king's palace. ³⁶Their two sons, Ahimaaz son of Zadok and Jonathan son of Abiathar, are there with them. Send them to me with anything you hear."

³⁷So Hushai, David's confidant, arrived at Jerusalem as Absalom was entering the city.

David and Ziba

16 When David had gone a short distance beyond the summit, there was Ziba, the steward of Mephibosheth, waiting to meet him. He had a string of donkeys saddled and loaded with two hundred loaves of bread, a hundred cakes of raisins, a hundred cakes of figs and a skin of wine.

²The king asked Ziba, "Why have you brought these?"

Ziba answered, "The donkeys are for the king's household to ride on, the bread and fruit are for the men to eat, and the wine is to refresh those who become exhausted in the wilderness."

³The king then asked, "Where is your master's grandson?"

Ziba said to him, "He is staying in Jerusalem, because he thinks, 'Today the Israelites will restore to me my grandfather's kingdom.'"

⁴Then the king said to Ziba, "All that belonged to Mephibosheth is now yours."

"I humbly bow," Ziba said. "May I find favor in your eyes, my lord the king."

Shimei Curses David

⁵As King David approached Bahurim, a man from the same clan as Saul's family came out from there. His name was Shimei son of Gera, and he cursed as he came out. ⁶He pelted David and all the king's officials with stones, though all the troops and the special guard were on David's right and left. ⁷As he cursed, Shimei said, "Get out, get out, you murderer, you scoundrel! ⁸The Lᴏʀᴅ has repaid you for all the blood you shed in the household of Saul, in whose place you have reigned. The Lᴏʀᴅ has given the kingdom into the hands of your son Absalom. You have come to ruin because you are a murderer!"

⁹Then Abishai son of Zeruiah said to the king, "Why should this dead dog curse my lord the king? Let me go over and cut off his head."

¹⁰But the king said, "What does this have to do with you, you sons of Zeruiah? If he is cursing because the Lᴏʀᴅ said to him, 'Curse David,' who can ask, 'Why do you do this?'"

¹¹David then said to Abishai and all his officials, "My son, my own flesh and blood, is trying to kill me. How much more, then, this Benjamite! Leave him alone; let him curse, for the Lᴏʀᴅ has told him to. ¹²It may be that the Lᴏʀᴅ will look upon my misery and restore to me his covenant blessing instead of his curse today."

¹³So David and his men continued

along the road while Shimei was going along the hillside opposite him, cursing as he went and throwing stones at him and showering him with dirt. ¹⁴The king and all the people with him arrived at their destination exhausted. And there he refreshed himself.

The Advice of Ahithophel and Hushai

¹⁵Meanwhile, Absalom and all the men of Israel came to Jerusalem, and Ahithophel was with him. ¹⁶Then Hushai the Arkite, David's confidant, went to Absalom and said to him, "Long live the king! Long live the king!"

¹⁷Absalom said to Hushai, "So this is the love you show your friend? If he's your friend, why didn't you go with him?"

¹⁸Hushai said to Absalom, "No, the one chosen by the LORD, by these people, and by all the men of Israel—his I will be, and I will remain with him. ¹⁹Furthermore, whom should I serve? Should I not serve the son? Just as I served your father, so I will serve you."

²⁰Absalom said to Ahithophel, "Give us your advice. What should we do?"

²¹Ahithophel answered, "Sleep with your father's concubines whom he left to take care of the palace. Then all Israel will hear that you have made yourself obnoxious to your father, and the hands of everyone with you will be more resolute." ²²So they pitched a tent for Absalom on the roof, and he slept with his father's concubines in the sight of all Israel.

²³Now in those days the advice Ahithophel gave was like that of one who inquires of God. That was how both David and Absalom regarded all of Ahithophel's advice.

17 Ahithophel said to Absalom, "I would^a choose twelve thousand men and set out tonight in pursuit of David. ²I would attack him while he is weary and weak. I would strike him with terror, and then all the people with him will flee. I would strike down only the king ³and bring all the people back to you. The death of the man you seek will mean the return of all; all the people will

be unharmed." ⁴This plan seemed good to Absalom and to all the elders of Israel.

⁵But Absalom said, "Summon also Hushai the Arkite, so we can hear what he has to say as well." ⁶When Hushai came to him, Absalom said, "Ahithophel has given this advice. Should we do what he says? If not, give us your opinion."

⁷Hushai replied to Absalom, "The advice Ahithophel has given is not good this time. ⁸You know your father and his men; they are fighters, and as fierce as a wild bear robbed of her cubs. Besides, your father is an experienced fighter; he will not spend the night with the troops. ⁹Even now, he is hidden in a cave or some other place. If he should attack your troops first,^b whoever hears about it will say, 'There has been a slaughter among the troops who follow Absalom.' ¹⁰Then even the bravest soldier, whose heart is like the heart of a lion, will melt with fear, for all Israel knows that your father is a fighter and that those with him are brave.

¹¹"So I advise you: Let all Israel, from Dan to Beersheba—as numerous as the sand on the seashore—be gathered to you, with you yourself leading them into battle. ¹²Then we will attack him wherever he may be found, and we will fall on him as dew settles on the ground. Neither he nor any of his men will be left alive. ¹³If he withdraws into a city, then all Israel will bring ropes to that city, and we will drag it down to the valley until not so much as a pebble is left."

¹⁴Absalom and all the men of Israel said, "The advice of Hushai the Arkite is better than that of Ahithophel." For the LORD had determined to frustrate the good advice of Ahithophel in order to bring disaster on Absalom.

¹⁵Hushai told Zadok and Abiathar, the priests, "Ahithophel has advised Absalom and the elders of Israel to do such and such, but I have advised them to do so and so. ¹⁶Now send a message at once and tell David, 'Do not spend the night at the fords in the wilderness; cross over

---

^a 1 Or Let me   ^b 9 Or When some of the men fall at the first attack

without fail, or the king and all the people with him will be swallowed up.'"

[17] Jonathan and Ahimaaz were staying at En Rogel. A female servant was to go and inform them, and they were to go and tell King David, for they could not risk being seen entering the city. [18] But a young man saw them and told Absalom. So the two of them left at once and went to the house of a man in Bahurim. He had a well in his courtyard, and they climbed down into it. [19] His wife took a covering and spread it out over the opening of the well and scattered grain over it. No one knew anything about it.

[20] When Absalom's men came to the woman at the house, they asked, "Where are Ahimaaz and Jonathan?"

The woman answered them, "They crossed over the brook."[a] The men searched but found no one, so they returned to Jerusalem.

[21] After they had gone, the two climbed out of the well and went to inform King David. They said to him, "Set out and cross the river at once; Ahithophel has advised such and such against you." [22] So David and all the people with him set out and crossed the Jordan. By daybreak, no one was left who had not crossed the Jordan.

[23] When Ahithophel saw that his advice had not been followed, he saddled his donkey and set out for his house in his hometown. He put his house in order and then hanged himself. So he died and was buried in his father's tomb.

Absalom's Death

[24] David went to Mahanaim, and Absalom crossed the Jordan with all the men of Israel. [25] Absalom had appointed Amasa over the army in place of Joab. Amasa was the son of Jether,[b] an Ishmaelite[c] who had married Abigail,[d] the daughter of Nahash and sister of Zeruiah the mother of Joab. [26] The Israelites and Absalom camped in the land of Gilead.

[27] When David came to Mahanaim, Shobi son of Nahash from Rabbah of the Ammonites, and Makir son of Ammiel from Lo Debar, and Barzillai the Gileadite from Rogelim [28] brought bedding and bowls and articles of pottery. They also brought wheat and barley, flour and roasted grain, beans and lentils,[e] [29] honey and curds, sheep, and cheese from cows' milk for David and his people to eat. For they said, "The people have become exhausted and hungry and thirsty in the wilderness."

18 David mustered the men who were with him and appointed over them commanders of thousands and commanders of hundreds. [2] David sent out his troops, a third under the command of Joab, a third under Joab's brother Abishai son of Zeruiah, and a third under Ittai the Gittite. The king told the troops, "I myself will surely march out with you."

[3] But the men said, "You must not go out; if we are forced to flee, they won't care about us. Even if half of us die, they won't care; but you are worth ten thousand of us.[f] It would be better now for you to give us support from the city."

[4] The king answered, "I will do whatever seems best to you."

So the king stood beside the gate while all his men marched out in units of hundreds and of thousands. [5] The king commanded Joab, Abishai and Ittai, "Be gentle with the young man Absalom for my sake." And all the troops heard the king giving orders concerning Absalom to each of the commanders.

[6] David's army marched out of the city to fight Israel, and the battle took place in the forest of Ephraim. [7] There Israel's troops were routed by David's men, and the casualties that day were great—twenty thousand men. [8] The battle spread out over the whole countryside, and the forest

---

[a] 20 Or "They passed by the sheep pen toward the water." [b] 25 Hebrew Ithra, a variant of Jether [c] 25 Some Septuagint manuscripts (see also 1 Chron. 2:17); Hebrew and other Septuagint manuscripts Israelite [d] 25 Hebrew Abigal, a variant of Abigail [e] 28 Most Septuagint manuscripts and Syriac; Hebrew lentils, and roasted grain [f] 3 Two Hebrew manuscripts, some Septuagint manuscripts and Vulgate; most Hebrew manuscripts care; for now there are ten thousand like us

swallowed up more men that day than the sword.

⁹Now Absalom happened to meet David's men. He was riding his mule, and as the mule went under the thick branches of a large oak, Absalom's hair got caught in the tree. He was left hanging in mid-air, while the mule he was riding kept on going.

¹⁰When one of the men saw what had happened, he told Joab, "I just saw Absalom hanging in an oak tree."

¹¹Joab said to the man who had told him this, "What! You saw him? Why didn't you strike him to the ground right there? Then I would have had to give you ten shekels*ᵃ* of silver and a warrior's belt."

¹²But the man replied, "Even if a thousand shekels*ᵇ* were weighed out into my hands, I would not lay a hand on the king's son. In our hearing the king commanded you and Abishai and Ittai, 'Protect the young man Absalom for my sake.'*ᶜ* ¹³And if I had put my life in jeopardy*ᵈ*—and

nothing is hidden from the king—you would have kept your distance from me."

¹⁴Joab said, "I'm not going to wait like this for you." So he took three javelins in his hand and plunged them into Absalom's heart while Absalom was still alive in the oak tree. ¹⁵And ten of Joab's armor-bearers surrounded Absalom, struck him and killed him.

¹⁶Then Joab sounded the trumpet, and the troops stopped pursuing Israel, for Joab halted them. ¹⁷They took Absalom, threw him into a big pit in the forest and piled up a large heap of rocks over him. Meanwhile, all the Israelites fled to their homes.

¹⁸During his lifetime Absalom had taken a pillar and erected it in the King's

---

ᵃ 11 That is, about 4 ounces or about 115 grams   *ᵇ 12* That is, about 25 pounds or about 12 kilograms   *ᶜ 12* A few Hebrew manuscripts, Septuagint, Vulgate and Syriac; most Hebrew manuscripts may be translated *Absalom, whoever you may be.*   *ᵈ 13* Or *Otherwise, if I had acted treacherously toward him*

ROCK SOLID principles

2 Samuel 18:1–18

Work through your family issues.

Amber didn't think the problems at home were any worse than anything she heard about from her friends. Her dad had a temper, her mom was a hovering control freak, her older sister always broke curfew, and Amber just tried to make everyone smile. But apparently their family problems were bad enough to land them all in counseling, because that's where Amber found herself every Thursday night. She thought the therapist was nerdy. He constantly blathered that they needed to pull together or life would pull them apart. But it couldn't hurt the family to sit down each week to talk. And the therapist was a good referee.

David's son Absalom took justice into his own hands when he killed Amnon to avenge the rape of his sister Tamar (see 2 Samuel 13:23–39). For two entire years after that killing, David refused to see his son (see 2 Samuel 14:24). A rift opened between father and son that provoked Absalom to try to seize the throne. David had to flee his palace, and Absalom ended up dead. A little communication could have made a big difference.

Valley as a monument to himself, for he thought, "I have no son to carry on the memory of my name." He named the pillar after himself, and it is called Absalom's Monument to this day.

David Mourns

¹⁹Now Ahimaaz son of Zadok said, "Let me run and take the news to the king that the LORD has vindicated him by delivering him from the hand of his enemies."

²⁰"You are not the one to take the news today," Joab told him. "You may take the news another time, but you must not do so today, because the king's son is dead."

²¹Then Joab said to a Cushite, "Go, tell the king what you have seen." The Cushite bowed down before Joab and ran off.

²²Ahimaaz son of Zadok again said to Joab, "Come what may, please let me run behind the Cushite."

But Joab replied, "My son, why do you want to go? You don't have any news that will bring you a reward."

²³He said, "Come what may, I want to run."

So Joab said, "Run!" Then Ahimaaz ran by way of the plain*a* and outran the Cushite.

²⁴While David was sitting between the inner and outer gates, the watchman went up to the roof of the gateway by the wall. As he looked out, he saw a man running alone. ²⁵The watchman called out to the king and reported it.

The king said, "If he is alone, he must have good news." And the runner came closer and closer.

²⁶Then the watchman saw another runner, and he called down to the gatekeeper, "Look, another man running alone!"

The king said, "He must be bringing good news, too."

²⁷The watchman said, "It seems to me that the first one runs like Ahimaaz son of Zadok."

"He's a good man," the king said. "He comes with good news."

²⁸Then Ahimaaz called out to the king, "All is well!" He bowed down before the king with his face to the ground and said,

"Praise be to the LORD your God! He has delivered up those who lifted their hands against my lord the king."

²⁹The king asked, "Is the young man Absalom safe?"

Ahimaaz answered, "I saw great confusion just as Joab was about to send the king's servant and me, your servant, but I don't know what it was."

³⁰The king said, "Stand aside and wait here." So he stepped aside and stood there.

³¹Then the Cushite arrived and said, "My lord the king, hear the good news! The LORD has vindicated you today by delivering you from the hand of all who rose up against you."

³²The king asked the Cushite, "Is the young man Absalom safe?"

The Cushite replied, "May the enemies of my lord the king and all who rise up to harm you be like that young man."

³³The king was shaken. He went up to the room over the gateway and wept. As he went, he said: "O my son Absalom! My son, my son Absalom! If only I had died instead of you—O Absalom, my son, my son!"*b*

19 *c*Joab was told, "The king is weeping and mourning for Absalom." ²And for the whole army the victory that day was turned into mourning, because on that day the troops heard it said, "The king is grieving for his son." ³The men stole into the city that day as men steal in who are ashamed when they flee from battle. ⁴The king covered his face and cried aloud, "O my son Absalom! O Absalom, my son, my son!"

⁵Then Joab went into the house to the king and said, "Today you have humiliated all your men, who have just saved your life and the lives of your sons and daughters and the lives of your wives and concubines. ⁶You love those who hate you and hate those who love you. You have made it clear today that the commanders and their men mean nothing to you. I see

---

a 23 That is, the plain of the Jordan   *b 33* In Hebrew texts this verse (18:33) is numbered 19:1.   *c* In Hebrew texts 19:1-43 is numbered 19:2-44.

that you would be pleased if Absalom were alive today and all of us were dead. ⁷Now go out and encourage your men. I swear by the Lᴏʀᴅ that if you don't go out, not a man will be left with you by nightfall. This will be worse for you than all the calamities that have come on you from your youth till now."

⁸So the king got up and took his seat in the gateway. When the men were told, "The king is sitting in the gateway," they all came before him.

Meanwhile, the Israelites had fled to their homes.

David Returns to Jerusalem

⁹Throughout the tribes of Israel, all the people were arguing among themselves, saying, "The king delivered us from the hand of our enemies; he is the one who rescued us from the hand of the Philistines. But now he has fled the country to escape from Absalom; ¹⁰and Absalom, whom we anointed to rule over us, has died in battle. So why do you say nothing about bringing the king back?"

¹¹King David sent this message to Zadok and Abiathar, the priests: "Ask the elders of Judah, 'Why should you be the last to bring the king back to his palace, since what is being said throughout Israel has reached the king at his quarters? ¹²You are my relatives, my own flesh and blood. So why should you be the last to bring back the king?' ¹³And say to Amasa, 'Are you not my own flesh and blood? May God deal with me, be it ever so severely, if you are not the commander of my army for life in place of Joab.'"

¹⁴He won over the hearts of the men of Judah so that they were all of one mind. They sent word to the king, "Return, you and all your men." ¹⁵Then the king returned and went as far as the Jordan.

Now the men of Judah had come to Gilgal to go out and meet the king and bring him across the Jordan. ¹⁶Shimei son of Gera, the Benjamite from Bahurim, hurried down with the men of Judah to meet King David. ¹⁷With him were a thousand Benjamites, along with Ziba,

the steward of Saul's household, and his fifteen sons and twenty servants. They rushed to the Jordan, where the king was. ¹⁸They crossed at the ford to take the king's household over and to do whatever he wished.

When Shimei son of Gera crossed the Jordan, he fell prostrate before the king ¹⁹and said to him, "May my lord not hold me guilty. Do not remember how your servant did wrong on the day my lord the king left Jerusalem. May the king put it out of his mind. ²⁰For I your servant know that I have sinned, but today I have come here as the first from the tribes of Joseph to come down and meet my lord the king."

²¹Then Abishai son of Zeruiah said, "Shouldn't Shimei be put to death for this? He cursed the Lᴏʀᴅ's anointed."

²²David replied, "What does this have to do with you, you sons of Zeruiah? What right do you have to interfere? Should anyone be put to death in Israel today? Don't I know that today I am king over Israel?" ²³So the king said to Shimei, "You shall not die." And the king promised him on oath.

²⁴Mephibosheth, Saul's grandson, also went down to meet the king. He had not taken care of his feet or trimmed his mustache or washed his clothes from the day the king left until the day he returned safely. ²⁵When he came from Jerusalem to meet the king, the king asked him, "Why didn't you go with me, Mephibosheth?"

²⁶He said, "My lord the king, since I your servant am lame, I said, 'I will have my donkey saddled and will ride on it, so I can go with the king.' But Ziba my servant betrayed me. ²⁷And he has slandered your servant to my lord the king. My lord the king is like an angel of God; so do whatever you wish. ²⁸All my grandfather's descendants deserved nothing but death from my lord the king, but you gave your servant a place among those who eat at your table. So what right do I have to make any more appeals to the king?"

²⁹The king said to him, "Why say more? I order you and Ziba to divide the land."

³⁰Mephibosheth said to the king, "Let him take everything, now that my lord the king has returned home safely."

³¹Barzillai the Gileadite also came down from Rogelim to cross the Jordan with the king and to send him on his way from there. ³²Now Barzillai was very old, eighty years of age. He had provided for the king during his stay in Mahanaim, for he was a very wealthy man. ³³The king said to Barzillai, "Cross over with me and stay with me in Jerusalem, and I will provide for you."

³⁴But Barzillai answered the king, "How many more years will I live, that I should go up to Jerusalem with the king? ³⁵I am now eighty years old. Can I tell the difference between what is enjoyable and what is not? Can your servant taste what he eats and drinks? Can I still hear the voices of male and female singers? Why should your servant be an added burden to my lord the king? ³⁶Your servant will cross over the Jordan with the king for a short distance, but why should the king reward me in this way? ³⁷Let your servant return, that I may die in my own town near the tomb of my father and mother. But here is your servant Kimham. Let him cross over with my lord the king. Do for him whatever you wish."

³⁸The king said, "Kimham shall cross over with me, and I will do for him whatever you wish. And anything you desire from me I will do for you."

³⁹So all the people crossed the Jordan, and then the king crossed over. The king kissed Barzillai and bid him farewell, and Barzillai returned to his home.

⁴⁰When the king crossed over to Gilgal, Kimham crossed with him. All the troops of Judah and half the troops of Israel had taken the king over.

⁴¹Soon all the men of Israel were coming to the king and saying to him, "Why did our brothers, the men of Judah, steal the king away and bring him and his household across the Jordan, together with all his men?"

ROCK SOLID *principles*

2 Samuel 19:24–30

Let go of bitterness.

"I can't stay stuck in the past," Karissa said. "It honestly doesn't do any good. I hang onto the few nice moments and let go of the rest. My past has been basically awful, so I better focus on my present and my future." Back in elementary school, Karissa watched her parents pitch an epic divorce battle. In middle school most nights she cried herself to sleep. By high school she decided enough was enough. She didn't have to forget the tough lessons she had learned, but staying angry at her parents wasn't doing her any good. In a few months she was moving out and onward.

Getting accidentally dropped as a child left Mephibosheth crippled for life (see 2 Samuel 4:4), making him an easy target for abuse. Mephibosheth even expected to be killed as revenge for his family's past when David became king of Israel. David instead invited him to eat at the royal table. Mephibosheth had many reasons to be bitter, but he let go and lived life.

⁴²All the men of Judah answered the men of Israel, "We did this because the king is closely related to us. Why are you angry about it? Have we eaten any of the king's provisions? Have we taken anything for ourselves?"

⁴³Then the men of Israel answered the men of Judah, "We have ten shares in the king; so we have a greater claim on David than you have. Why then do you treat us with contempt? Weren't we the first to speak of bringing back our king?"

But the men of Judah pressed their claims even more forcefully than the men of Israel.

Sheba Rebels Against David

20 Now a troublemaker named Sheba son of Bikri, a Benjamite, happened to be there. He sounded the trumpet and shouted,

"We have no share in David,
    no part in Jesse's son!
Every man to his tent, Israel!"

²So all the men of Israel deserted David to follow Sheba son of Bikri. But the men of Judah stayed by their king all the way from the Jordan to Jerusalem.

³When David returned to his palace in Jerusalem, he took the ten concubines he had left to take care of the palace and put them in a house under guard. He provided for them but had no sexual relations with them. They were kept in confinement till the day of their death, living as widows.

⁴Then the king said to Amasa, "Summon the men of Judah to come to me within three days, and be here yourself." ⁵But when Amasa went to summon Judah, he took longer than the time the king had set for him.

⁶David said to Abishai, "Now Sheba son of Bikri will do us more harm than Absalom did. Take your master's men and pursue him, or he will find fortified cities and escape from us."ᵃ ⁷So Joab's men and the Kerethites and Pelethites and all the mighty warriors went out under the command of Abishai. They marched out from Jerusalem to pursue Sheba son of Bikri.

⁸While they were at the great rock in Gibeon, Amasa came to meet them. Joab was wearing his military tunic, and strapped over it at his waist was a belt with a dagger in its sheath. As he stepped forward, it dropped out of its sheath.

⁹Joab said to Amasa, "How are you, my brother?" Then Joab took Amasa by the beard with his right hand to kiss him. ¹⁰Amasa was not on his guard against the dagger in Joab's hand, and Joab plunged it into his belly, and his intestines spilled out on the ground. Without being stabbed again, Amasa died. Then Joab and his brother Abishai pursued Sheba son of Bikri.

¹¹One of Joab's men stood beside Amasa and said, "Whoever favors Joab, and whoever is for David, let him follow Joab!" ¹²Amasa lay wallowing in his blood in the middle of the road, and the man saw that all the troops came to a halt there. When he realized that everyone who came up to Amasa stopped, he dragged him from the road into a field and threw a garment over him. ¹³After Amasa had been removed from the road, everyone went on with Joab to pursue Sheba son of Bikri.

¹⁴Sheba passed through all the tribes of Israel to Abel Beth Maakah and through the entire region of the Bikrites,ᵇ who gathered together and followed him. ¹⁵All the troops with Joab came and besieged Sheba in Abel Beth Maakah. They built a siege ramp up to the city, and it stood against the outer fortifications. While they were battering the wall to bring it down, ¹⁶a wise woman called from the city, "Listen! Listen! Tell Joab to come here so I can speak to him." ¹⁷He went toward her, and she asked, "Are you Joab?"

"I am," he answered.

She said, "Listen to what your servant has to say."

"I'm listening," he said.

¹⁸She continued, "Long ago they used to say, 'Get your answer at Abel,' and that settled it. ¹⁹We are the peaceful and faithful in Israel. You are trying to destroy a

ᵃ 6 Or *and do us serious injury*   ᵇ 14 See Septuagint and Vulgate; Hebrew *Berites.*

381

city that is a mother in Israel. Why do you want to swallow up the LORD's inheritance?"

20 "Far be it from me!" Joab replied, "Far be it from me to swallow up or destroy! 21 That is not the case. A man named Sheba son of Bikri, from the hill country of Ephraim, has lifted up his hand against the king, against David. Hand over this one man, and I'll withdraw from the city."

The woman said to Joab, "His head will be thrown to you from the wall."

22 Then the woman went to all the people with her wise advice, and they cut off the head of Sheba son of Bikri and threw it to Joab. So he sounded the trumpet, and his men dispersed from the city, each returning to his home. And Joab went back to the king in Jerusalem.

David's Officials

23 Joab was over Israel's entire army; Benaiah son of Jehoiada was over the Kerethites and Pelethites; 24 Adoniram*a* was in charge of forced labor; Jehoshaphat son of Ahilud was recorder; 25 Sheva was secretary; Zadok and Abiathar were priests; 26 and Ira the Jairite*b* was David's priest.

The Gibeonites Avenged

21 During the reign of David, there was a famine for three successive years; so David sought the face of the LORD. The LORD said, "It is on account of Saul and his blood-stained house; it is because he put the Gibeonites to death."

2 The king summoned the Gibeonites and spoke to them. (Now the Gibeonites were not a part of Israel but were survivors of the Amorites; the Israelites had sworn to spare them, but Saul in his zeal for Israel and Judah had tried to annihilate them.) 3 David asked the Gibeonites, "What shall I do for you? How shall I make atonement so that you will bless the LORD's inheritance?"

4 The Gibeonites answered him, "We have no right to demand silver or gold from Saul or his family, nor do we have the right to put anyone in Israel to death."

"What do you want me to do for you?" David asked.

5 They answered the king, "As for the man who destroyed us and plotted against us so that we have been decimated and have no place anywhere in Israel, 6 let seven of his male descendants be given to us to be killed and their bodies exposed before the LORD at Gibeah of Saul—the LORD's chosen one."

So the king said, "I will give them to you."

7 The king spared Mephibosheth son of Jonathan, the son of Saul, because of the oath before the LORD between David and Jonathan son of Saul. 8 But the king took Armoni and Mephibosheth, the two sons of Aiah's daughter Rizpah, whom she had borne to Saul, together with the five sons of Saul's daughter Merab,*c* whom she had borne to Adriel son of Barzillai the Meholathite. 9 He handed them over to the Gibeonites, who killed them and exposed their bodies on a hill before the LORD. All seven of them fell together; they were put to death during the first days of the harvest, just as the barley harvest was beginning.

10 Rizpah daughter of Aiah took sackcloth and spread it out for herself on a rock. From the beginning of the harvest till the rain poured down from the heavens on the bodies, she did not let the birds touch them by day or the wild animals by night. 11 When David was told what Aiah's daughter Rizpah, Saul's concubine, had done, 12 he went and took the bones of Saul and his son Jonathan from the citizens of Jabesh Gilead. (They had stolen their bodies from the public square at Beth Shan, where the Philistines had hung them after they struck Saul down on Gilboa.) 13 David brought the bones of Saul and his son Jonathan from there, and

a 24 Some Septuagint manuscripts (see also 1 Kings 4:6 and 5:14); Hebrew *Adoram*
b 26 Hebrew; some Septuagint manuscripts and Syriac (see also 23:38) *Ithrite*   *c 8* Two Hebrew manuscripts, some Septuagint manuscripts and Syriac (see also 1 Samuel 18:19); most Hebrew and Septuagint manuscripts *Michal*

the bones of those who had been killed and exposed were gathered up.

[14] They buried the bones of Saul and his son Jonathan in the tomb of Saul's father Kish, at Zela in Benjamin, and did everything the king commanded. After that, God answered prayer in behalf of the land.

Wars Against the Philistines

[15] Once again there was a battle between the Philistines and Israel. David went down with his men to fight against the Philistines, and he became exhausted. [16] And Ishbi-Benob, one of the descendants of Rapha, whose bronze spearhead weighed three hundred shekels[a] and who was armed with a new sword, said he would kill David. [17] But Abishai son of Zeruiah came to David's rescue; he struck the Philistine down and killed him. Then David's men swore to him, saying, "Never again will you go out with us to battle, so that the lamp of Israel will not be extinguished."

[18] In the course of time, there was another battle with the Philistines, at Gob. At that time Sibbekai the Hushathite killed Saph, one of the descendants of Rapha.

[19] In another battle with the Philistines at Gob, Elhanan son of Jair[b] the Bethlehemite killed the brother of[c] Goliath the Gittite, who had a spear with a shaft like a weaver's rod.

[20] In still another battle, which took place at Gath, there was a huge man with six fingers on each hand and six toes on each foot—twenty-four in all. He also was descended from Rapha. [21] When he taunted Israel, Jonathan son of Shimeah, David's brother, killed him.

[22] These four were descendants of Rapha in Gath, and they fell at the hands of David and his men.

David's Song of Praise

22 David sang to the LORD the words of this song when the LORD delivered him from the hand of all his enemies and from the hand of Saul. [2] He said:

"The LORD is my rock, my fortress
    and my deliverer;
[3] my God is my rock, in whom I take
    refuge,
my shield[d] and the horn[e] of my
    salvation.
He is my stronghold, my refuge and
    my savior—
from violent people you save me.

[4] "I called to the LORD, who is worthy
    of praise,
    and have been saved from my
    enemies.
[5] The waves of death swirled about me;
    the torrents of destruction
    overwhelmed me.
[6] The cords of the grave coiled around
    me;
    the snares of death confronted me.

[7] "In my distress I called to the LORD;
    I called out to my God.
From his temple he heard my voice;
    my cry came to his ears.
[8] The earth trembled and quaked,
    the foundations of the heavens[f]
    shook;
    they trembled because he was angry.
[9] Smoke rose from his nostrils;
    consuming fire came from his
    mouth,
    burning coals blazed out of it.
[10] He parted the heavens and came
    down;
    dark clouds were under his feet.
[11] He mounted the cherubim and flew;
    he soared[g] on the wings of the
    wind.
[12] He made darkness his canopy around
    him—
    the dark[h] rain clouds of the sky.

---

[a] 16 That is, about 7 1/2 pounds or about 3.5 kilograms   [b] 19 See 1 Chron. 20:5; Hebrew *Jaare-Oregim.*   [c] 19 See 1 Chron. 20:5; Hebrew does not have *the brother of.*   [d] 3 Or *sovereign*   [e] 3 *Horn* here symbolizes strength.   [f] 8 Hebrew; Vulgate and Syriac (see also Psalm 18:7) *mountains*   [g] 11 Many Hebrew manuscripts (see also Psalm 18:10); most Hebrew manuscripts *appeared*   [h] 12 Septuagint (see also Psalm 18:11); Hebrew *massed*

¹³ Out of the brightness of his presence
  bolts of lightning blazed forth.
¹⁴ The LORD thundered from heaven;
  the voice of the Most High
  resounded.
¹⁵ He shot his arrows and scattered the
  enemy,
  with great bolts of lightning he
  routed them.
¹⁶ The valleys of the sea were exposed
  and the foundations of the earth
  laid bare
  at the rebuke of the LORD,
  at the blast of breath from his
  nostrils.

¹⁷ "He reached down from on high and
  took hold of me;
  he drew me out of deep waters.
¹⁸ He rescued me from my powerful
  enemy,
  from my foes, who were too strong
  for me.
¹⁹ They confronted me in the day of my
  disaster,
  but the LORD was my support.
²⁰ He brought me out into a spacious
  place;
  he rescued me because he delighted
  in me.

²¹ "The LORD has dealt with me
  according to my righteousness;
  according to the cleanness of my
  hands he has rewarded me.
²² For I have kept the ways of the
  LORD;
  I am not guilty of turning from my
  God.
²³ All his laws are before me;
  I have not turned away from his
  decrees.
²⁴ I have been blameless before him
  and have kept myself from sin.
²⁵ The LORD has rewarded me according
  to my righteousness,
  according to my cleanness*ᵃ in his
  sight.

²⁶ "To the faithful you show yourself
  faithful,
  to the blameless you show yourself
  blameless,

²⁷ to the pure you show yourself pure,
  but to the devious you show yourself
  shrewd.
²⁸ You save the humble,
  but your eyes are on the haughty to
  bring them low.
²⁹ You, LORD, are my lamp;
  the LORD turns my darkness into
  light.
³⁰ With your help I can advance against
  a troop*ᵇ;
  with my God I can scale a wall.

³¹ "As for God, his way is perfect:
  The LORD's word is flawless;
  he shields all who take refuge in
  him.

ᵃ 25 Hebrew; Septuagint and Vulgate (see also
Psalm 18:24) *to the cleanness of my hands*
ᵇ 30 Or *can run through a barricade*

UNSHAKEN God

2 Samuel 22:27

God is shrewd.

David had plenty to say to God. This famous king had finally triumphed over his enemies, especially Saul, the previous ruler—a guy who had traveled down a bad road from vast popularity to disastrous spiritual rebellion. In 2 Samuel 22, David burst into song, declaring that God is superior to every evildoer. The Lord can thunder from heaven and shoot bolts of lightning to scatter his enemies (see 2 Samuel 22:14–15). And even though evildoers are crooked or twisted, God is "shrewd" (2 Samuel 22:27), smart enough to make them look like fools. Your God is never surprised by people intent on doing wrong. He outsmarts them every time.

So ... Do you really think God can outwit the evildoers you know? Why—or why not?

ROCK SOLID *promises*

**"As for God, his way is perfect:
the Lord's word is flawless."**

2 Samuel 22:31

**There's nothing defective, evil, or mean
in anything God says or does.**

³² For who is God besides the Lord?
 And who is the Rock except our
 God?
³³ It is God who arms me with strength^a
 and keeps my way secure.
³⁴ He makes my feet like the feet of a
 deer;
 he causes me to stand on the
 heights.
³⁵ He trains my hands for battle;
 my arms can bend a bow of bronze.
³⁶ You make your saving help my shield;
 your help has made^b me great.
³⁷ You provide a broad path for my feet,
 so that my ankles do not give way.

³⁸ "I pursued my enemies and crushed
 them;
 I did not turn back till they were
 destroyed.
³⁹ I crushed them completely, and they
 could not rise;
 they fell beneath my feet.
⁴⁰ You armed me with strength for
 battle;
 you humbled my adversaries before
 me.
⁴¹ You made my enemies turn their backs
 in flight,
 and I destroyed my foes.
⁴² They cried for help, but there was no
 one to save them—
 to the Lord, but he did not answer.

⁴³ I beat them as fine as the dust of the
 earth;
 I pounded and trampled them like
 mud in the streets.
⁴⁴ "You have delivered me from the
 attacks of the peoples;
 you have preserved me as the head
 of nations.
People I did not know now serve me,
⁴⁵ foreigners cower before me;
 as soon as they hear of me, they
 obey me.
⁴⁶ They all lose heart;
 they come trembling^c from their
 strongholds.

⁴⁷ "The Lord lives! Praise be to my
 Rock!
 Exalted be my God, the Rock, my
 Savior!
⁴⁸ He is the God who avenges me,
 who puts the nations under me,
⁴⁹ who sets me free from my enemies.
You exalted me above my foes;
 from a violent man you rescued me.
⁵⁰ Therefore I will praise you, Lord,
 among the nations;
 I will sing the praises of your name.

⁵¹ "He gives his king great victories;
 he shows unfailing kindness to his
 anointed,
 to David and his descendants
 forever."

David's Last Words

23 These are the last words of
 David:

"The inspired utterance of David son
 of Jesse,
 the utterance of the man exalted by
 the Most High,
the man anointed by the God of Jacob,
 the hero of Israel's songs:

^a *33* Dead Sea Scrolls, some Septuagint
manuscripts, Vulgate and Syriac (see also Psalm
18:32); Masoretic Text *who is my strong refuge*
^b *36* Dead Sea Scrolls; Masoretic Text *shield; /
you stoop down to make*   ^c *46* Some Septuagint
manuscripts and Vulgate (see also Psalm 18:45);
Masoretic Text *they arm themselves*

2 "The Spirit of the LORD spoke
　　through me;
　his word was on my tongue.
3 The God of Israel spoke,
　　the Rock of Israel said to me:
'When one rules over people in
　　righteousness,
　when he rules in the fear of God,
4 he is like the light of morning at
　　sunrise
　on a cloudless morning,
　like the brightness after rain
　　that brings grass from the earth.'

5 "If my house were not right with
　　God,
　surely he would not have made with
　　me an everlasting covenant,
　arranged and secured in every
　　part;
　surely he would not bring to fruition
　　my salvation
　and grant me my every desire.
6 But evil men are all to be cast aside
　　like thorns,
　which are not gathered with the
　　hand.
7 Whoever touches thorns
　uses a tool of iron or the shaft of a
　　spear;
　they are burned up where they lie."

David's Mighty Warriors

8 These are the names of David's mighty
warriors:

Josheb-Basshebeth,[a] a Tahkemonite,[b]
was chief of the Three; he raised his
spear against eight hundred men, whom
he killed[c] in one encounter.

9 Next to him was Eleazar son of Dodai
the Ahohite. As one of the three mighty
warriors, he was with David when they
taunted the Philistines gathered at Pas
Dammim[d] for battle. Then the Israelites
retreated, 10 but Eleazar stood his ground
and struck down the Philistines till his
hand grew tired and froze to the sword.
The LORD brought about a great victory
that day. The troops returned to Eleazar,
but only to strip the dead.

11 Next to him was Shammah son of
Agee the Hararite. When the Philistines

banded together at a place where there
was a field full of lentils, Israel's troops
fled from them. 12 But Shammah took his
stand in the middle of the field. He defended it and struck the Philistines down,
and the LORD brought about a great victory.

13 During harvest time, three of the
thirty chief warriors came down to David at the cave of Adullam, while a band
of Philistines was encamped in the Valley
of Rephaim. 14 At that time David was in
the stronghold, and the Philistine garrison was at Bethlehem. 15 David longed
for water and said, "Oh, that someone
would get me a drink of water from the
well near the gate of Bethlehem!" 16 So the
three mighty warriors broke through the
Philistine lines, drew water from the well
near the gate of Bethlehem and carried it
back to David. But he refused to drink it;
instead, he poured it out before the LORD.
17 "Far be it from me, LORD, to do this!"
he said. "Is it not the blood of men who
went at the risk of their lives?" And David
would not drink it.

Such were the exploits of the three
mighty warriors.

18 Abishai the brother of Joab son of
Zeruiah was chief of the Three.[e] He
raised his spear against three hundred
men, whom he killed, and so he became
as famous as the Three. 19 Was he not held
in greater honor than the Three? He became their commander, even though he
was not included among them.

20 Benaiah son of Jehoiada, a valiant
fighter from Kabzeel, performed great
exploits. He struck down Moab's two
mightiest warriors. He also went down
into a pit on a snowy day and killed a

---

[a] 8 Hebrew; some Septuagint manuscripts
suggest Ish-Bosheth, that is, Esh-Baal (see also
1 Chron. 11:11 Jashobeam).　　[b] 8 Probably a
variant of Hakmonite (see 1 Chron. 11:11)
[c] 8 Some Septuagint manuscripts (see also
1 Chron. 11:11); Hebrew and other Septuagint
manuscripts Three; it was Adino the Eznite who
killed eight hundred men　　[d] 9 See 1 Chron.
11:13; Hebrew gathered there.　　[e] 18 Most
Hebrew manuscripts (see also 1 Chron. 11:20);
two Hebrew manuscripts and Syriac Thirty

lion. ²¹And he struck down a huge Egyptian. Although the Egyptian had a spear in his hand, Benaiah went against him with a club. He snatched the spear from the Egyptian's hand and killed him with his own spear. ²²Such were the exploits of Benaiah son of Jehoiada; he too was as famous as the three mighty warriors. ²³He was held in greater honor than any of the Thirty, but he was not included among the Three. And David put him in charge of his bodyguard.

²⁴Among the Thirty were:
Asahel the brother of Joab,
Elhanan son of Dodo from Bethlehem,
²⁵Shammah the Harodite,
Elika the Harodite,
²⁶Helez the Paltite,
Ira son of Ikkesh from Tekoa,
²⁷Abiezer from Anathoth,
Sibbekai^a the Hushathite,
²⁸Zalmon the Ahohite,
Maharai the Netophathite,
²⁹Heled^b son of Baanah the Netophathite,
Ithai son of Ribai from Gibeah in Benjamin,
³⁰Benaiah the Pirathonite,
Hiddai^c from the ravines of Gaash,
³¹Abi-Albon the Arbathite,
Azmaveth the Barhumite,
³²Eliahba the Shaalbonite,
the sons of Jashen,
Jonathan ³³son of^d Shammah the Hararite,
Ahiam son of Sharar^e the Hararite,
³⁴Eliphelet son of Ahasbai the Maakathite,
Eliam son of Ahithophel the Gilonite,
³⁵Hezro the Carmelite,
Paarai the Arbite,
³⁶Igal son of Nathan from Zobah,
the son of Hagri,^f
³⁷Zelek the Ammonite,
Naharai the Beerothite, the armorbearer of Joab son of Zeruiah,
³⁸Ira the Ithrite,
Gareb the Ithrite

³⁹and Uriah the Hittite.
There were thirty-seven in all.

David Enrolls the Fighting Men

24 Again the anger of the LORD burned against Israel, and he incited David against them, saying, "Go and take a census of Israel and Judah."

²So the king said to Joab and the army commanders^g with him, "Go throughout the tribes of Israel from Dan to Beersheba and enroll the fighting men, so that I may know how many there are."

³But Joab replied to the king, "May the LORD your God multiply the troops a hundred times over, and may the eyes of my lord the king see it. But why does my lord the king want to do such a thing?"

⁴The king's word, however, overruled Joab and the army commanders; so they left the presence of the king to enroll the fighting men of Israel.

⁵After crossing the Jordan, they camped near Aroer, south of the town in the gorge, and then went through Gad and on to Jazer. ⁶They went to Gilead and the region of Tahtim Hodshi, and on to Dan Jaan and around toward Sidon. ⁷Then they went toward the fortress of Tyre and all the towns of the Hivites and Canaanites. Finally, they went on to Beersheba in the Negev of Judah.

⁸After they had gone through the entire land, they came back to Jerusalem at the end of nine months and twenty days.

⁹Joab reported the number of the fighting men to the king: In Israel there were eight hundred thousand able-bodied men

^a 27 Some Septuagint manuscripts (see also 21:18; 1 Chron. 11:29); Hebrew *Mebunnai*   ^b 29 Some Hebrew manuscripts and Vulgate (see also 1 Chron. 11:30); most Hebrew manuscripts *Heleb*   ^c 30 Hebrew; some Septuagint manuscripts (see also 1 Chron. 11:32) *Hurai*   ^d 33 Some Septuagint manuscripts (see also 1 Chron. 11:34); Hebrew does not have *son of.*   ^e 33 Hebrew; some Septuagint manuscripts (see also 1 Chron. 11:35) *Sakar*   ^f 36 Some Septuagint manuscripts (see also 1 Chron. 11:38); Hebrew *Haggadi*   ^g 2 Septuagint (see also verse 4 and 1 Chron. 21:2); Hebrew *Joab the army commander*

who could handle a sword, and in Judah five hundred thousand.

[10] David was conscience-stricken after he had counted the fighting men, and he said to the LORD, "I have sinned greatly in what I have done. Now, LORD, I beg you, take away the guilt of your servant. I have done a very foolish thing."

[11] Before David got up the next morning, the word of the LORD had come to Gad the prophet, David's seer: [12] "Go and tell David, 'This is what the LORD says: I am giving you three options. Choose one of them for me to carry out against you.'"

[13] So Gad went to David and said to him, "Shall there come on you three[a] years of famine in your land? Or three months of fleeing from your enemies while they pursue you? Or three days of plague in your land? Now then, think it over and decide how I should answer the one who sent me."

[14] David said to Gad, "I am in deep distress. Let us fall into the hands of the LORD, for his mercy is great; but do not let me fall into human hands."

[15] So the LORD sent a plague on Israel from that morning until the end of the time designated, and seventy thousand of the people from Dan to Beersheba died. [16] When the angel stretched out his hand to destroy Jerusalem, the LORD relented concerning the disaster and said to the angel who was afflicting the people, "Enough! Withdraw your hand." The angel of the LORD was then at the threshing floor of Araunah the Jebusite.

[17] When David saw the angel who was striking down the people, he said to the LORD, "I have sinned; I, the shepherd,[b] have done wrong. These are but sheep. What have they done? Let your hand fall on me and my family."

David Builds an Altar

[18] On that day Gad went to David and said to him, "Go up and build an altar to the LORD on the threshing floor of Araunah the Jebusite." [19] So David went up, as the LORD had commanded through Gad. [20] When Araunah looked and saw the king and his officials coming toward him, he went out and bowed down before the king with his face to the ground.

[21] Araunah said, "Why has my lord the king come to his servant?"

"To buy your threshing floor," David answered, "so I can build an altar to the LORD, that the plague on the people may be stopped."

[22] Araunah said to David, "Let my lord the king take whatever he wishes and offer it up. Here are oxen for the burnt offering, and here are threshing sledges and ox yokes for the wood. [23] Your Majesty, Araunah[c] gives all this to the king." Araunah also said to him, "May the LORD your God accept you."

[24] But the king replied to Araunah, "No, I insist on paying you for it. I will not sacrifice to the LORD my God burnt offerings that cost me nothing."

So David bought the threshing floor and the oxen and paid fifty shekels[d] of silver for them. [25] David built an altar to the LORD there and sacrificed burnt offerings and fellowship offerings. Then the LORD answered his prayer in behalf of the land, and the plague on Israel was stopped.

[a] 13 Septuagint (see also 1 Chron. 21:12); Hebrew *seven*   [b] 17 Dead Sea Scrolls and Septuagint; Masoretic Text does not have *the shepherd*.   [c] 23 Some Hebrew manuscripts and Septuagint; most Hebrew manuscripts *King Araunah*   [d] 24 That is, about 1 1/4 pounds or about 575 grams

1 KINGS

Beginning with Solomon's reign (about 971 BC) 1 Kings records the history of Israel through the divided kingdom to the death of Ahaziah, the son of Ahab. Chapters 3 through 11 describe Solomon's reign, including the building of the temple and the palace in Jerusalem.

Rehoboam, Solomon's son, took the throne after Solomon's death but lost the northern part of the kingdom to Jeroboam. After this the northern kingdom was known as Israel, and the southern kingdom was called Judah. The last chapters of 1 Kings tell about the evil King Ahab and God's prophet Elijah, who condemned Ahab's wickedness and Israel's disobedience.

Because the author of 1 and 2 Kings was interested in Israel's faithfulness to God and his covenant he recorded how each king was faithful or unfaithful to God. The author often used the phrase, "did what was right in the eyes of the LORD," or "did evil in the eyes of the LORD," to describe the goodness or wickedness of the king.

The author observes that the same pattern as in the time of the judges repeats itself during the time of the kings: God brought peace to the land when Israel was obedient, but Israel suffered wars and other disasters when the people were disobedient and worshiped idols.

Adonijah Sets Himself Up as King

When King David was very old, he could not keep warm even when they put covers over him. ²So his attendants said to him, "Let us look for a young virgin to serve the king and take care of him. She can lie beside him so that our lord the king may keep warm."

³Then they searched throughout Israel for a beautiful young woman and found Abishag, a Shunammite, and brought her to the king. ⁴The woman was very beautiful; she took care of the king and waited on him, but the king had no sexual relations with her.

⁵Now Adonijah, whose mother was Haggith, put himself forward and said, "I will be king." So he got chariots and horses[a] ready, with fifty men to run ahead of him. ⁶(His father had never rebuked him by asking, "Why do you behave as you do?" He was also very handsome and was born next after Absalom.)

⁷Adonijah conferred with Joab son of Zeruiah and with Abiathar the priest, and they gave him their support. ⁸But Zadok the priest, Benaiah son of Jehoiada, Nathan the prophet, Shimei and Rei and David's special guard did not join Adonijah.

⁹Adonijah then sacrificed sheep, cattle and fattened calves at the Stone of Zoheleth near En Rogel. He invited all his brothers, the king's sons, and all the royal officials of Judah, ¹⁰but he did not invite Nathan the prophet or Benaiah or the special guard or his brother Solomon.

¹¹Then Nathan asked Bathsheba, Solomon's mother, "Have you not heard that Adonijah, the son of Haggith, has become king, and our lord David knows nothing about it? ¹²Now then, let me advise you how you can save your own life and the life of your son Solomon. ¹³Go in to King David and say to him, 'My lord the king, did you not swear to me your servant: "Surely Solomon your son shall be king after me, and he will sit on my throne"? Why then has Adonijah become king?' ¹⁴While you are still there talking to the king, I will come in and add my word to what you have said."

¹⁵So Bathsheba went to see the aged king in his room, where Abishag the Shunammite was attending him. ¹⁶Bathsheba bowed down, prostrating herself before the king.

"What is it you want?" the king asked.

¹⁷She said to him, "My lord, you yourself swore to me your servant by the Lord your God: 'Solomon your son shall be king after me, and he will sit on my throne.' ¹⁸But now Adonijah has become king, and you, my lord the king, do not know about it. ¹⁹He has sacrificed great numbers of cattle, fattened calves, and sheep, and has invited all the king's sons, Abiathar the priest and Joab the commander of the army, but he has not invited Solomon your servant. ²⁰My lord the king, the eyes of all Israel are on you, to learn from you who will sit on the throne of my lord the king after him. ²¹Otherwise, as soon as my lord the king is laid to rest with his ancestors, I and my son Solomon will be treated as criminals."

²²While she was still speaking with the king, Nathan the prophet arrived. ²³And the king was told, "Nathan the prophet is here." So he went before the king and bowed with his face to the ground.

²⁴Nathan said, "Have you, my lord the king, declared that Adonijah shall be king after you, and that he will sit on your throne? ²⁵Today he has gone down and sacrificed great numbers of cattle, fattened calves, and sheep. He has invited all the king's sons, the commanders of the army and Abiathar the priest. Right now they are eating and drinking with him and saying, 'Long live King Adonijah!' ²⁶But me your servant, and Zadok the priest, and Benaiah son of Jehoiada, and your servant Solomon he did not invite. ²⁷Is this something my lord the king has done without letting his servants know who should sit on the throne of my lord the king after him?"

David Makes Solomon King

²⁸Then King David said, "Call in Bathsheba." So she came into the king's presence and stood before him.

---

[a] 5 Or *charioteers*

²⁹The king then took an oath: "As surely as the Lord lives, who has delivered me out of every trouble, ³⁰I will surely carry out this very day what I swore to you by the Lord, the God of Israel: Solomon your son shall be king after me, and he will sit on my throne in my place."

³¹Then Bathsheba bowed down with her face to the ground, prostrating herself before the king, and said, "May my lord King David live forever!"

³²King David said, "Call in Zadok the priest, Nathan the prophet and Benaiah son of Jehoiada." When they came before the king, ³³he said to them: "Take your lord's servants with you and have Solomon my son mount my own mule and take him down to Gihon. ³⁴There have Zadok the priest and Nathan the prophet anoint him king over Israel. Blow the trumpet and shout, 'Long live King Solomon!' ³⁵Then you are to go up with him, and he is to come and sit on my throne and reign in my place. I have appointed him ruler over Israel and Judah."

³⁶Benaiah son of Jehoiada answered the king, "Amen! May the Lord, the God of my lord the king, so declare it. ³⁷As the Lord was with my lord the king, so may he be with Solomon to make his throne even greater than the throne of my lord King David!"

³⁸So Zadok the priest, Nathan the prophet, Benaiah son of Jehoiada, the Kerethites and the Pelethites went down and had Solomon mount King David's mule, and they escorted him to Gihon. ³⁹Zadok the priest took the horn of oil from the sacred tent and anointed Solomon. Then they sounded the trumpet and all the people shouted, "Long live King Solomon!" ⁴⁰And all the people went up after him, playing pipes and rejoicing greatly, so that the ground shook with the sound.

⁴¹Adonijah and all the guests who were with him heard it as they were finishing their feast. On hearing the sound of the trumpet, Joab asked, "What's the meaning of all the noise in the city?"

⁴²Even as he was speaking, Jonathan son of Abiathar the priest arrived. Ado-nijah said, "Come in. A worthy man like you must be bringing good news."

⁴³"Not at all!" Jonathan answered. "Our lord King David has made Solomon king. ⁴⁴The king has sent with him Zadok the priest, Nathan the prophet, Benaiah son of Jehoiada, the Kerethites and the Pelethites, and they have put him on the king's mule, ⁴⁵and Zadok the priest and Nathan the prophet have anointed him king at Gihon. From there they have gone up cheering, and the city resounds with it. That's the noise you hear. ⁴⁶Moreover, Solomon has taken his seat on the royal throne. ⁴⁷Also, the royal officials have come to congratulate our lord King David, saying, 'May your God make Solomon's name more famous than yours and his throne greater than yours!' And the king bowed in worship on his bed ⁴⁸and said, 'Praise be to the Lord, the God of Israel, who has allowed my eyes to see a successor on my throne today.'"

⁴⁹At this, all Adonijah's guests rose in alarm and dispersed. ⁵⁰But Adonijah, in fear of Solomon, went and took hold of the horns of the altar. ⁵¹Then Solomon was told, "Adonijah is afraid of King Solomon and is clinging to the horns of the altar. He says, 'Let King Solomon swear to me today that he will not put his servant to death with the sword.'"

⁵²Solomon replied, "If he shows himself to be worthy, not a hair of his head will fall to the ground; but if evil is found in him, he will die." ⁵³Then King Solomon sent men, and they brought him down from the altar. And Adonijah came and bowed down to King Solomon, and Solomon said, "Go to your home."

David's Charge to Solomon

2 When the time drew near for David to die, he gave a charge to Solomon his son.

²"I am about to go the way of all the earth," he said. "So be strong, act like a man, ³and observe what the Lord your God requires: Walk in obedience to him, and keep his decrees and commands, his laws and regulations, as written in the

Law of Moses. Do this so that you may prosper in all you do and wherever you go ⁴and that the LORD may keep his promise to me: 'If your descendants watch how they live, and if they walk faithfully before me with all their heart and soul, you will never fail to have a successor on the throne of Israel.'

ROCK SOLID
promises

"Walk in obedience to him ... so that you may prosper in all you do and wherever you go."

1 Kings 2:3

By obeying God you're choosing to live in a zone where he is free to bless you.

---

⁵"Now you yourself know what Joab son of Zeruiah did to me—what he did to the two commanders of Israel's armies, Abner son of Ner and Amasa son of Jether. He killed them, shedding their blood in peacetime as if in battle, and with that blood he stained the belt around his waist and the sandals on his feet. ⁶Deal with him according to your wisdom, but do not let his gray head go down to the grave in peace.

⁷"But show kindness to the sons of Barzillai of Gilead and let them be among those who eat at your table. They stood by me when I fled from your brother Absalom.

⁸"And remember, you have with you Shimei son of Gera, the Benjamite from Bahurim, who called down bitter curses on me the day I went to Mahanaim. When he came down to meet me at the Jordan, I swore to him by the LORD: 'I will not put you to death by the sword.' ⁹But now, do not consider him innocent. You are a man of wisdom; you will know what to do to him. Bring his gray head down to the grave in blood."

¹⁰Then David rested with his ancestors and was buried in the City of David. ¹¹He had reigned forty years over Israel—seven years in Hebron and thirty-three in Jerusalem. ¹²So Solomon sat on the throne of his father David, and his rule was firmly established.

Solomon's Throne Established

¹³Now Adonijah, the son of Haggith, went to Bathsheba, Solomon's mother. Bathsheba asked him, "Do you come peacefully?"

He answered, "Yes, peacefully." ¹⁴Then he added, "I have something to say to you."

"You may say it," she replied.

¹⁵"As you know," he said, "the kingdom was mine. All Israel looked to me as their king. But things changed, and the kingdom has gone to my brother; for it has come to him from the LORD. ¹⁶Now I have one request to make of you. Do not refuse me."

"You may make it," she said.

¹⁷So he continued, "Please ask King Solomon—he will not refuse you—to give me Abishag the Shunammite as my wife."

¹⁸"Very well," Bathsheba replied, "I will speak to the king for you."

¹⁹When Bathsheba went to King Solomon to speak to him for Adonijah, the king stood up to meet her, bowed down to her and sat down on his throne. He had a throne brought for the king's mother, and she sat down at his right hand.

²⁰"I have one small request to make of you," she said. "Do not refuse me."

The king replied, "Make it, my mother; I will not refuse you."

²¹So she said, "Let Abishag the Shunammite be given in marriage to your brother Adonijah."

²²King Solomon answered his mother, "Why do you request Abishag the Shunammite for Adonijah? You might as well request the kingdom for him—after all, he is my older brother—yes, for him and for Abiathar the priest and Joab son of Zeruiah!"

²³Then King Solomon swore by the LORD: "May God deal with me, be it ever

so severely, if Adonijah does not pay with his life for this request! 24 And now, as surely as the LORD lives—he who has established me securely on the throne of my father David and has founded a dynasty for me as he promised—Adonijah shall be put to death today!" 25 So King Solomon gave orders to Benaiah son of Jehoiada, and he struck down Adonijah and he died.

26 To Abiathar the priest the king said, "Go back to your fields in Anathoth. You deserve to die, but I will not put you to death now, because you carried the ark of the Sovereign LORD before my father David and shared all my father's hardships." 27 So Solomon removed Abiathar from the priesthood of the LORD, fulfilling the word the LORD had spoken at Shiloh about the house of Eli.

28 When the news reached Joab, who had conspired with Adonijah though not with Absalom, he fled to the tent of the LORD and took hold of the horns of the altar. 29 King Solomon was told that Joab had fled to the tent of the LORD and was beside the altar. Then Solomon ordered Benaiah son of Jehoiada, "Go, strike him down!"

30 So Benaiah entered the tent of the LORD and said to Joab, "The king says, 'Come out!'"

But he answered, "No, I will die here."

Benaiah reported to the king, "This is how Joab answered me."

31 Then the king commanded Benaiah, "Do as he says. Strike him down and bury him, and so clear me and my whole family of the guilt of the innocent blood that Joab shed. 32 The LORD will repay him for the blood he shed, because without my father David knowing it he attacked two men and killed them with the sword. Both of them—Abner son of Ner, commander of Israel's army, and Amasa son of Jether, commander of Judah's army—were better men and more upright than he. 33 May the guilt of their blood rest on the head of Joab and his descendants forever. But on David and his descendants, his house and his throne, may there be the LORD's peace forever."

34 So Benaiah son of Jehoiada went up and struck down Joab and killed him, and he was buried at his home out in the country. 35 The king put Benaiah son of Jehoiada over the army in Joab's position and replaced Abiathar with Zadok the priest.

36 Then the king sent for Shimei and said to him, "Build yourself a house in Jerusalem and live there, but do not go anywhere else. 37 The day you leave and cross the Kidron Valley, you can be sure you will die; your blood will be on your own head."

38 Shimei answered the king, "What you say is good. Your servant will do as my lord the king has said." And Shimei stayed in Jerusalem for a long time.

39 But three years later, two of Shimei's slaves ran off to Achish son of Maakah, king of Gath, and Shimei was told, "Your slaves are in Gath." 40 At this, he saddled his donkey and went to Achish at Gath in search of his slaves. So Shimei went away and brought the slaves back from Gath.

41 When Solomon was told that Shimei had gone from Jerusalem to Gath and had returned, 42 the king summoned Shimei and said to him, "Did I not make you swear by the LORD and warn you, 'On the day you leave to go anywhere else, you can be sure you will die'? At that time you said to me, 'What you say is good. I will obey.' 43 Why then did you not keep your oath to the LORD and obey the command I gave you?"

44 The king also said to Shimei, "You know in your heart all the wrong you did to my father David. Now the LORD will repay you for your wrongdoing. 45 But King Solomon will be blessed, and David's throne will remain secure before the LORD forever."

46 Then the king gave the order to Benaiah son of Jehoiada, and he went out and struck Shimei down and he died.

The kingdom was now established in Solomon's hands.

Solomon Asks for Wisdom

3 Solomon made an alliance with Pharaoh king of Egypt and married his daughter. He brought her to the City of David until he finished building his palace and the temple of the LORD, and the wall around Jerusalem. ²The people, however, were still sacrificing at the high places, because a temple had not yet been built for the Name of the LORD. ³Solomon showed his love for the LORD by walking according to the instructions given him by his father David, except that he offered sacrifices and burned incense on the high places.

⁴The king went to Gibeon to offer sacrifices, for that was the most important high place, and Solomon offered a thousand burnt offerings on that altar. ⁵At Gibeon the LORD appeared to Solomon during the night in a dream, and God said, "Ask for whatever you want me to give you."

⁶Solomon answered, "You have shown great kindness to your servant, my father David, because he was faithful to you and righteous and upright in heart. You have continued this great kindness to him and have given him a son to sit on his throne this very day.

⁷"Now, LORD my God, you have made your servant king in place of my father David. But I am only a little child and do not know how to carry out my duties. ⁸Your servant is here among the people you have chosen, a great people, too numerous to count or number. ⁹So give your servant a discerning heart to govern your people and to distinguish between right and wrong. For who is able to govern this great people of yours?"

¹⁰The Lord was pleased that Solomon had asked for this. ¹¹So God said to him, "Since you have asked for this and not for long life or wealth for yourself, nor have asked for the death of your enemies but for discernment in administering justice, ¹²I will do what you have asked. I will give you a wise and discerning heart, so that there will never have been anyone like you, nor will there ever be. ¹³Moreover, I will give you what you have not asked for—both wealth and honor—so that in your lifetime you will have no equal among kings. ¹⁴And if you walk in obedience to me and keep my decrees and commands as David

your father did, I will give you a long life." ¹⁵Then Solomon awoke—and he realized it had been a dream.

He returned to Jerusalem, stood before the ark of the Lord's covenant and sacrificed burnt offerings and fellowship offerings. Then he gave a feast for all his court.

A Wise Ruling

¹⁶Now two prostitutes came to the king and stood before him. ¹⁷One of them said, "Pardon me, my lord. This woman and I live in the same house, and I had a baby while she was there with me. ¹⁸The third day after my child was born, this woman also had a baby. We were alone; there was no one in the house but the two of us.

¹⁹"During the night this woman's son died because she lay on him. ²⁰So she got up in the middle of the night and took my son from my side while I your servant was asleep. She put him by her breast and put her dead son by my breast. ²¹The next morning, I got up to nurse my son—and he was dead! But when I looked at him closely in the morning light, I saw that it wasn't the son I had borne."

²²The other woman said, "No! The living one is my son; the dead one is yours."

But the first one insisted, "No! The dead one is yours; the living one is mine." And so they argued before the king.

²³The king said, "This one says, 'My son is alive and your son is dead,' while that one says, 'No! Your son is dead and mine is alive.'"

²⁴Then the king said, "Bring me a sword." So they brought a sword for the king. ²⁵He then gave an order: "Cut the living child in two and give half to one and half to the other."

²⁶The woman whose son was alive was deeply moved out of love for her son and said to the king, "Please, my lord, give her the living baby! Don't kill him!"

But the other said, "Neither I nor you shall have him. Cut him in two!"

²⁷Then the king gave his ruling: "Give the living baby to the first woman. Do not kill him; she is his mother."

²⁸When all Israel heard the verdict the

king had given, they held the king in awe, because they saw that he had wisdom from God to administer justice.

Solomon's Officials and Governors

4 So King Solomon ruled over all Israel. ²And these were his chief officials:

Azariah son of Zadok—the priest;
³Elihoreph and Ahijah, sons of Shisha—secretaries;
Jehoshaphat son of Ahilud—recorder;
⁴Benaiah son of Jehoiada—commander in chief;
Zadok and Abiathar—priests;
⁵Azariah son of Nathan—in charge of the district governors;
Zabud son of Nathan—a priest and adviser to the king;
⁶Ahishar—palace administrator;
Adoniram son of Abda—in charge of forced labor.

⁷Solomon had twelve district governors over all Israel, who supplied provisions for the king and the royal household. Each one had to provide supplies for one month in the year. ⁸These are their names:

Ben-Hur—in the hill country of Ephraim;
⁹Ben-Deker—in Makaz, Shaalbim, Beth Shemesh and Elon Bethhanan;
¹⁰Ben-Hesed—in Arubboth (Sokoh and all the land of Hepher were his);
¹¹Ben-Abinadab—in Naphoth Dor (he was married to Taphath daughter of Solomon);
¹²Baana son of Ahilud—in Taanach and Megiddo, and in all of Beth Shan next to Zarethan below Jezreel, from Beth Shan to Abel Meholah across to Jokmeam;
¹³Ben-Geber—in Ramoth Gilead (the settlements of Jair son of Manasseh in Gilead were his, as well as the region of Argob in Bashan and its sixty large walled cities with bronze gate bars);
¹⁴Ahinadab son of Iddo—in Mahanaim;
¹⁵Ahimaaz—in Naphtali (he had married Basemath daughter of Solomon);
¹⁶Baana son of Hushai—in Asher and in Aloth;
¹⁷Jehoshaphat son of Paruah—in Issachar;
¹⁸Shimei son of Ela—in Benjamin;
¹⁹Geber son of Uri—in Gilead (the country of Sihon king of the Amorites and the country of Og king of Bashan). He was the only governor over the district.

Solomon's Daily Provisions

²⁰The people of Judah and Israel were as numerous as the sand on the seashore; they ate, they drank and they were happy. ²¹And Solomon ruled over all the kingdoms from the Euphrates River to the land of the Philistines, as far as the border of Egypt. These countries brought tribute and were Solomon's subjects all his life.

²²Solomon's daily provisions were thirty cors[a] of the finest flour and sixty cors[b] of meal, ²³ten head of stall-fed cattle, twenty of pasture-fed cattle and a hundred sheep and goats, as well as deer, gazelles, roebucks and choice fowl. ²⁴For he ruled over all the kingdoms west of the Euphrates River, from Tiphsah to Gaza, and had peace on all sides. ²⁵During Solomon's lifetime Judah and Israel, from Dan to Beersheba, lived in safety, everyone under their own vine and under their own fig tree.

²⁶Solomon had four[c] thousand stalls for chariot horses, and twelve thousand horses.[d] ²⁷The district governors, each in his month, supplied provisions for King Solomon and all who came to the king's table. They saw to it that nothing was lacking. ²⁸They also brought to the proper place their quotas of barley and straw for the chariot horses and the other horses.

---

[a] 22 That is, probably about 5 1/2 tons or about 5 metric tons   [b] 22 That is, probably about 11 tons or about 10 metric tons   [c] 26 Some Septuagint manuscripts (see also 2 Chron. 9:25); Hebrew *forty*   [d] 26 Or *charioteers*

Solomon's Wisdom

29 God gave Solomon wisdom and very great insight, and a breadth of understanding as measureless as the sand on the seashore. 30 Solomon's wisdom was greater than the wisdom of all the people of the East, and greater than all the wisdom of Egypt. 31 He was wiser than anyone else, including Ethan the Ezrahite—wiser than Heman, Kalkol and Darda, the sons of Mahol. And his fame spread to all the surrounding nations. 32 He spoke three thousand proverbs and his songs numbered a thousand and five. 33 He spoke about plant life, from the cedar of Lebanon to the hyssop that grows out of walls. He also spoke about animals and birds, reptiles and fish. 34 From all nations people came to listen to Solomon's wisdom, sent by all the kings of the world, who had heard of his wisdom.*a*

1 Kings 4:20–34

Archaeology backs up the Bible.

The book of 1 Kings paints a breathtaking picture of Solomon's kingdom. The people of the southern and northern parts of the kingdom were "as numerous as the sand on the seashore" (1 Kings 4:20). Solomon's kingdom ranged far in every direction, and neighboring peoples were counted among the king's subjects. The king himself was famed for his vast wealth and wisdom. So for years skeptical archaeologists wondered why they hadn't found indisputable evidence of this significant kingdom. Yet in 1994, a carved stone was discovered in the far north of Israel that mentions "the House of David." This "Tel Dan Inscription" dates to approximately 150 years after David's death. It proves that David was a real historical figure ... that he founded a royal dynasty continued by Solomon and his descendants ... and that you can count on the history presented in the Bible.

Think: Why does it matter that researchers can find evidence for the existence of Bible history?

ROCK SOLID *truths*

Preparations for Building the Temple

5 *b* When Hiram king of Tyre heard that Solomon had been anointed king to succeed his father David, he sent his envoys to Solomon, because he had always been on friendly terms with David. 2 Solomon sent back this message to Hiram:

3 "You know that because of the wars waged against my father David from all sides, he could not build a temple for the Name of the LORD his God until the LORD put his enemies under his feet. 4 But now the LORD my God has given me rest on every side, and there is no adversary or disaster. 5 I intend, therefore, to build a temple for the Name of the LORD my God, as the LORD told my father David, when he said, 'Your son whom I will put on the throne in your place will build the temple for my Name.'

6 "So give orders that cedars of Lebanon be cut for me. My men will work with yours, and I will pay you for your men whatever wages you set. You know that we have no one so skilled in felling timber as the Sidonians."

7 When Hiram heard Solomon's message, he was greatly pleased and said, "Praise be to the LORD today, for he has given David a wise son to rule over this great nation."

8 So Hiram sent word to Solomon:

a 34 In Hebrew texts 4:21-34 is numbered 5:1-14.   *b* In Hebrew texts 5:1-18 is numbered 5:15-32.

"I have received the message you sent me and will do all you want in providing the cedar and juniper logs. ⁹My men will haul them down from Lebanon to the Mediterranean Sea, and I will float them as rafts by sea to the place you specify. There I will separate them and you can take them away. And you are to grant my wish by providing food for my royal household."

¹⁰In this way Hiram kept Solomon supplied with all the cedar and juniper logs he wanted, ¹¹and Solomon gave Hiram twenty thousand cors*a* of wheat as food for his household, in addition to twenty thousand baths*b,c* of pressed olive oil. Solomon continued to do this for Hiram year after year. ¹²The LORD gave Solomon wisdom, just as he had promised him. There were peaceful relations between Hiram and Solomon, and the two of them made a treaty.

¹³King Solomon conscripted laborers from all Israel—thirty thousand men. ¹⁴He sent them off to Lebanon in shifts of ten thousand a month, so that they spent one month in Lebanon and two months at home. Adoniram was in charge of the forced labor. ¹⁵Solomon had seventy thousand carriers and eighty thousand stonecutters in the hills, ¹⁶as well as thirty-three hundred*d* foremen who supervised the project and directed the workers. ¹⁷At the king's command they removed from the quarry large blocks of high-grade stone to provide a foundation of dressed stone for the temple. ¹⁸The craftsmen of Solomon and Hiram and workers from Byblos cut and prepared the timber and stone for the building of the temple.

a 11 That is, probably about 3,600 tons or about 3,250 metric tons   *b 11* Septuagint (see also 2 Chron. 2:10); Hebrew *twenty cors*   *c 11* That is, about 120,000 gallons or about 440,000 liters   *d 16* Hebrew; some Septuagint manuscripts (see also 2 Chron. 2:2,18) *thirty-six hundred*

ROCK SOLID principles

1 Kings 5:1–18

Show respect to followers of other faiths.

Bekka couldn't understand her new chemistry lab partner—as in Bekka could barely decipher a word she said. Sufia had arrived from Somalia only months before. It didn't take long to figure out Sufia was smart—she paid better attention in class than Bekka, and sometimes outscored her. Still, Bekka worried how the two would work together, and she wondered about being paired with a Muslim. Sufia's dark skin and long dresses made her different from anyone else at school, and almost everyone ignored her. Bekka decided not to shun Sufia, even outside of lab. Sufia was nice. And if Bekka didn't befriend her, she was sure no one else would.

Solomon and the king of Tyre didn't worship the same God, so you might expect them to be enemies. Yet these two powerful leaders shared a long family friendship. They traded goods and laborers, and the king of Tyre even supported Solomon's drive to build a temple to the God of Israel. Despite their differences, each respected the other. They figured out how to get along.

Solomon Builds the Temple

6 In the four hundred and eightieth[a] year after the Israelites came out of Egypt, in the fourth year of Solomon's reign over Israel, in the month of Ziv, the second month, he began to build the temple of the LORD.

[2] The temple that King Solomon built for the LORD was sixty cubits long, twenty wide and thirty high.[b] [3] The portico at the front of the main hall of the temple extended the width of the temple, that is twenty cubits,[c] and projected ten cubits[d] from the front of the temple. [4] He made narrow windows high up in the temple walls. [5] Against the walls of the main hall and inner sanctuary he built a structure around the building, in which there were side rooms. [6] The lowest floor was five cubits[e] wide, the middle floor six cubits[f] and the third floor seven.[g] He made offset ledges around the outside of the temple so that nothing would be inserted into the temple walls.

[7] In building the temple, only blocks dressed at the quarry were used, and no hammer, chisel or any other iron tool was heard at the temple site while it was being built.

[8] The entrance to the lowest[h] floor was on the south side of the temple; a stairway led up to the middle level and from there to the third. [9] So he built the temple and completed it, roofing it with beams and cedar planks. [10] And he built the side rooms all along the temple. The height of each was five cubits, and they were attached to the temple by beams of cedar.

[11] The word of the LORD came to Solomon: [12] "As for this temple you are building, if you follow my decrees, observe my laws and keep all my commands and obey them, I will fulfill through you the promise I gave to David your father. [13] And I will live among the Israelites and will not abandon my people Israel."

[14] So Solomon built the temple and completed it. [15] He lined its interior walls with cedar boards, paneling them from the floor of the temple to the ceiling, and covered the floor of the temple with planks of juniper. [16] He partitioned off twenty cubits at the rear of the temple with cedar boards from floor to ceiling to form within the temple an inner sanctuary, the Most Holy Place. [17] The main hall in front of this room was forty cubits[i] long. [18] The inside of the temple was cedar, carved with gourds and open flowers. Everything was cedar; no stone was to be seen.

[19] He prepared the inner sanctuary within the temple to set the ark of the covenant of the LORD there. [20] The inner sanctuary was twenty cubits long, twenty wide and twenty high. He overlaid the inside with pure gold, and he also overlaid the altar of cedar. [21] Solomon covered the inside of the temple with pure gold, and he extended gold chains across the front of the inner sanctuary, which was overlaid with gold. [22] So he overlaid the whole interior with gold. He also overlaid with gold the altar that belonged to the inner sanctuary.

[23] For the inner sanctuary he made a pair of cherubim out of olive wood, each ten cubits high. [24] One wing of the first cherub was five cubits long, and the other wing five cubits—ten cubits from wing tip to wing tip. [25] The second cherub also measured ten cubits, for the two cherubim were identical in size and shape. [26] The height of each cherub was ten cubits. [27] He placed the cherubim inside the innermost room of the temple, with their wings spread out. The wing of one cherub touched one wall, while the wing of the other touched the other wall, and their wings touched each other in the middle of the room. [28] He overlaid the cherubim with gold.

[29] On the walls all around the temple, in

---

[a] 1 Hebrew; Septuagint *four hundred and fortieth* [b] 2 That is, about 90 feet long, 30 feet wide and 45 feet high or about 27 meters long, 9 meters wide and 14 meters high [c] 3 That is, about 30 feet or about 9 meters; also in verses 16 and 20 [d] 3 That is, about 15 feet or about 4.5 meters; also in verses 23-26 [e] 6 That is, about 7 1/2 feet or about 2.3 meters; also in verses 10 and 24 [f] 6 That is, about 9 feet or about 2.7 meters [g] 6 That is, about 11 feet or about 3.2 meters [h] 8 Septuagint; Hebrew *middle* [i] 17 That is, about 60 feet or about 18 meters

both the inner and outer rooms, he carved cherubim, palm trees and open flowers. [30] He also covered the floors of both the inner and outer rooms of the temple with gold.

[31] For the entrance to the inner sanctuary he made doors out of olive wood that were one fifth of the width of the sanctuary. [32] And on the two olive-wood doors he carved cherubim, palm trees and open flowers, and overlaid the cherubim and palm trees with hammered gold. [33] In the same way, for the entrance to the main hall he made doorframes out of olive wood that were one fourth of the width of the hall. [34] He also made two doors out of juniper wood, each having two leaves that turned in sockets. [35] He carved cherubim, palm trees and open flowers on them and overlaid them with gold hammered evenly over the carvings.

[36] And he built the inner courtyard of three courses of dressed stone and one course of trimmed cedar beams.

[37] The foundation of the temple of the LORD was laid in the fourth year, in the month of Ziv. [38] In the eleventh year in the month of Bul, the eighth month, the temple was finished in all its details according to its specifications. He had spent seven years building it.

Solomon Builds His Palace

7 It took Solomon thirteen years, however, to complete the construction of his palace. [2] He built the Palace of the Forest of Lebanon a hundred cubits long, fifty wide and thirty high,[a] with four rows of cedar columns supporting trimmed cedar beams. [3] It was roofed with cedar above the beams that rested on the columns—forty-five beams, fifteen to a row. [4] Its windows were placed high in sets of three, facing each other. [5] All the doorways had rectangular frames; they were in the front part in sets of three, facing each other.[b]

[6] He made a colonnade fifty cubits long and thirty wide.[c] In front of it was a portico, and in front of that were pillars and an overhanging roof.

[7] He built the throne hall, the Hall of Justice, where he was to judge, and he covered it with cedar from floor to ceiling.[d] [8] And the palace in which he was to live, set farther back, was similar in design. Solomon also made a palace like this hall for Pharaoh's daughter, whom he had married.

[9] All these structures, from the outside to the great courtyard and from foundation to eaves, were made of blocks of high-grade stone cut to size and smoothed on their inner and outer faces. [10] The foundations were laid with large stones of good quality, some measuring ten cubits[e] and some eight.[f] [11] Above were high-grade stones, cut to size, and cedar beams. [12] The great courtyard was surrounded by a wall of three courses of dressed stone and one course of trimmed cedar beams, as was the inner courtyard of the temple of the LORD with its portico.

The Temple's Furnishings

[13] King Solomon sent to Tyre and brought Huram,[g] [14] whose mother was a widow from the tribe of Naphtali and whose father was from Tyre and a skilled craftsman in bronze. Huram was filled with wisdom, with understanding and with knowledge to do all kinds of bronze work. He came to King Solomon and did all the work assigned to him.

[15] He cast two bronze pillars, each eighteen cubits high and twelve cubits in circumference.[b] [16] He also made two capitals of cast bronze to set on the tops of the pillars; each capital was five cubits[i] high. [17] A

[a] 2 That is, about 150 feet long, 75 feet wide and 45 feet high or about 45 meters long, 23 meters wide and 14 meters high   [b] 5 The meaning of the Hebrew for this verse is uncertain.
[c] 6 That is, about 75 feet long and 45 feet wide or about 23 meters long and 14 meters wide
[d] 7 Vulgate and Syriac; Hebrew *floor*
[e] 10 That is, about 15 feet or about 4.5 meters; also in verse 23   [f] 10 That is, about 12 feet or about 3.6 meters   [g] 13 Hebrew *Hiram*, a variant of *Huram*; also in verses 40 and 45
[b] 15 That is, about 27 feet high and 18 feet in circumference or about 8.1 meters high and 5.4 meters in circumference   [i] 16 That is, about 7 1/2 feet or about 2.3 meters; also in verse 23

network of interwoven chains adorned the capitals on top of the pillars, seven for each capital. [18] He made pomegranates in two rows[a] encircling each network to decorate the capitals on top of the pillars.[b] He did the same for each capital. [19] The capitals on top of the pillars in the portico were in the shape of lilies, four cubits[c] high. [20] On the capitals of both pillars, above the bowl-shaped part next to the network, were the two hundred pomegranates in rows all around. [21] He erected the pillars at the portico of the temple. The pillar to the south he named Jakin[d] and the one to the north Boaz.[e] [22] The capitals on top were in the shape of lilies. And so the work on the pillars was completed.

[23] He made the Sea of cast metal, circular in shape, measuring ten cubits from rim to rim and five cubits high. It took a line of thirty cubits[f] to measure around it. [24] Below the rim, gourds encircled it — ten to a cubit. The gourds were cast in two rows in one piece with the Sea.

[25] The Sea stood on twelve bulls, three facing north, three facing west, three facing south and three facing east. The Sea rested on top of them, and their hindquarters were toward the center. [26] It was a handbreadth[g] in thickness, and its rim was like the rim of a cup, like a lily blossom. It held two thousand baths.[b]

[27] He also made ten movable stands of bronze; each was four cubits long, four wide and three high.[i] [28] This is how the stands were made: They had side panels attached to uprights. [29] On the panels between the uprights were lions, bulls and cherubim — and on the uprights as well. Above and below the lions and bulls were wreaths of hammered work. [30] Each stand had four bronze wheels with bronze axles, and each had a basin resting on four supports, cast with wreaths on each side. [31] On the inside of the stand there was an opening that had a circular frame one cubit[j] deep. This opening was round, and with its basework it measured a cubit and a half.[k] Around its opening there was engraving. The panels of the stands were square, not round. [32] The four wheels were under the panels, and the axles of the wheels were attached to the stand. The diameter of each wheel was a cubit and a half. [33] The wheels were made like chariot wheels; the axles, rims, spokes and hubs were all of cast metal.

[34] Each stand had four handles, one on each corner, projecting from the stand. [35] At the top of the stand there was a circular band half a cubit[l] deep. The supports and panels were attached to the top of the stand. [36] He engraved cherubim, lions and palm trees on the surfaces of the supports and on the panels, in every available space, with wreaths all around. [37] This is the way he made the ten stands. They were all cast in the same molds and were identical in size and shape.

[38] He then made ten bronze basins, each holding forty baths[m] and measuring four cubits across, one basin to go on each of the ten stands. [39] He placed five of the stands on the south side of the temple and five on the north. He placed the Sea on the south side, at the southeast corner of the temple. [40] He also made the pots[n] and shovels and sprinkling bowls.

So Huram finished all the work he had undertaken for King Solomon in the temple of the LORD:

[a] 18 Two Hebrew manuscripts and Septuagint; most Hebrew manuscripts *made the pillars, and there were two rows*   [b] 18 Many Hebrew manuscripts and Syriac; most Hebrew manuscripts *pomegranates*   [c] 19 That is, about 6 feet or about 1.8 meters; also in verse 38   [d] 21 *Jakin* probably means *he establishes.*   [e] 21 *Boaz* probably means *in him is strength.*   [f] 23 That is, about 45 feet or about 14 meters   [g] 26 That is, about 3 inches or about 7.5 centimeters   [b] 26 That is, about 12,000 gallons or about 44,000 liters; the Septuagint does not have this sentence.   [i] 27 That is, about 6 feet long and wide and about 4 1/2 feet high or about 1.8 meters long and wide and 1.4 meters high   [j] 31 That is, about 18 inches or about 45 centimeters   [k] 31 That is, about 2 1/4 feet or about 68 centimeters; also in verse 32   [l] 35 That is, about 9 inches or about 23 centimeters   [m] 38 That is, about 240 gallons or about 880 liters   [n] 40 Many Hebrew manuscripts, Septuagint, Syriac and Vulgate (see also verse 45 and 2 Chron. 4:11); many other Hebrew manuscripts *basins*

41 the two pillars;

the two bowl-shaped capitals on top of the pillars;

the two sets of network decorating the two bowl-shaped capitals on top of the pillars;

42 the four hundred pomegranates for the two sets of network (two rows of pomegranates for each network decorating the bowl-shaped capitals on top of the pillars);

43 the ten stands with their ten basins;

44 the Sea and the twelve bulls under it;

45 the pots, shovels and sprinkling bowls.

All these objects that Huram made for King Solomon for the temple of the LORD were of burnished bronze. 46 The king had them cast in clay molds in the plain of the Jordan between Sukkoth and Zarethan. 47 Solomon left all these things unweighed, because there were so many; the weight of the bronze was not determined.

48 Solomon also made all the furnishings that were in the LORD's temple:

the golden altar;

the golden table on which was the bread of the Presence;

49 the lampstands of pure gold (five on the right and five on the left, in front of the inner sanctuary);

the gold floral work and lamps and tongs;

50 the pure gold basins, wick trimmers, sprinkling bowls, dishes and censers;

and the gold sockets for the doors of the innermost room, the Most Holy Place, and also for the doors of the main hall of the temple.

51 When all the work King Solomon had done for the temple of the LORD was finished, he brought in the things his father David had dedicated—the silver and gold and the furnishings—and he placed them in the treasuries of the LORD's temple.

The Ark Brought to the Temple

8 Then King Solomon summoned into his presence at Jerusalem the elders of Israel, all the heads of the tribes and the chiefs of the Israelite families, to bring up the ark of the LORD's covenant from Zion, the City of David. 2 All the Israelites came together to King Solomon at the time of the festival in the month of Ethanim, the seventh month.

3 When all the elders of Israel had arrived, the priests took up the ark, 4 and they brought up the ark of the LORD and the tent of meeting and all the sacred furnishings in it. The priests and Levites carried them up, 5 and King Solomon and the entire assembly of Israel that had gathered about him were before the ark, sacrificing so many sheep and cattle that they could not be recorded or counted.

6 The priests then brought the ark of the LORD's covenant to its place in the inner sanctuary of the temple, the Most Holy Place, and put it beneath the wings of the cherubim. 7 The cherubim spread their wings over the place of the ark and overshadowed the ark and its carrying poles. 8 These poles were so long that their ends could be seen from the Holy Place in front of the inner sanctuary, but not from outside the Holy Place; and they are still there today. 9 There was nothing in the ark except the two stone tablets that Moses had placed in it at Horeb, where the LORD made a covenant with the Israelites after they came out of Egypt.

10 When the priests withdrew from the Holy Place, the cloud filled the temple of the LORD. 11 And the priests could not perform their service because of the cloud, for the glory of the LORD filled his temple.

12 Then Solomon said, "The LORD has said that he would dwell in a dark cloud; 13 I have indeed built a magnificent temple for you, a place for you to dwell forever."

14 While the whole assembly of Israel was standing there, the king turned around and blessed them. 15 Then he said:

"Praise be to the LORD, the God of Israel, who with his own hand has fulfilled what he promised with his own mouth to my father David. For he said, 16 'Since the day I brought my people Israel out of Egypt, I have not chosen a city in any tribe of Israel to have a temple built so that my Name might be there, but I have chosen David to rule my people Israel.'

¹⁷"My father David had it in his heart to build a temple for the Name of the LORD, the God of Israel. ¹⁸But the LORD said to my father David, 'You did well to have it in your heart to build a temple for my Name. ¹⁹Nevertheless, you are not the one to build the temple, but your son, your own flesh and blood—he is the one who will build the temple for my Name.'

²⁰"The LORD has kept the promise he made: I have succeeded David my father and now I sit on the throne of Israel, just as the LORD promised, and I have built the temple for the Name of the LORD, the God of Israel. ²¹I have provided a place there for the ark, in which is the covenant of the LORD that he made with our ancestors when he brought them out of Egypt."

Solomon's Prayer of Dedication

²²Then Solomon stood before the altar of the LORD in front of the whole assembly of Israel, spread out his hands toward heaven ²³and said:

"LORD, the God of Israel, there is no God like you in heaven above or on earth below—you who keep your covenant of love with your servants who continue wholeheartedly in your way. ²⁴You have kept your promise to your servant David my father; with your mouth you have promised and with your hand you have fulfilled it—as it is today.

²⁵"Now LORD, the God of Israel, keep for your servant David my father the promises you made to him when you said, 'You shall never fail to have a successor to sit before me on the throne of Israel, if only your descendants are careful in all they do to walk before me faithfully as you have done.' ²⁶And now, God of Israel, let your word that you promised your servant David my father come true.

²⁷"But will God really dwell on earth? The heavens, even the highest heaven, cannot contain you. How much less this temple I have built! ²⁸Yet give attention to your servant's prayer and his plea for mercy, LORD my God. Hear the cry and the prayer that your servant is praying in your presence this day. ²⁹May your eyes be open toward this temple night and day, this place of which you said, 'My Name shall be there,' so that you will hear the prayer your servant prays toward this place. ³⁰Hear the supplication of your servant and of your people Israel when they pray toward this place. Hear from heaven, your dwelling place, and when you hear, forgive.

³¹"When anyone wrongs their neighbor and is required to take an

UNSHAKEN God

1 Kings 8:27–30

God is all-present.

God had given Solomon the privilege not only of succeeding his father David as king of Israel but also of building a permanent house of worship, the temple in Jerusalem. Even though the temple was a place of God's intense presence (see 2 Chronicles 5:14), Solomon knew the temple could never contain God. The earth is too small to hold him, and even the highest heavens won't do (see 1 Kings 8:27). Solomon describes a key characteristic of God, that he is "omnipresent" or "all-present," able to be everywhere at once. There isn't a place in the universe where your immense God isn't there. No matter where you go, God is right there with you.

So ... What difference will it make for you today that God is everywhere?

oath and they come and swear the oath before your altar in this temple, ³² then hear from heaven and act. Judge between your servants, condemning the guilty by bringing down on their heads what they have done, and vindicating the innocent by treating them in accordance with their innocence.

³³ "When your people Israel have been defeated by an enemy because they have sinned against you, and when they turn back to you and give praise to your name, praying and making supplication to you in this temple, ³⁴ then hear from heaven and forgive the sin of your people Israel and bring them back to the land you gave to their ancestors.

³⁵ "When the heavens are shut up and there is no rain because your people have sinned against you, and when they pray toward this place and give praise to your name and turn from their sin because you have afflicted them, ³⁶ then hear from heaven and forgive the sin of your servants, your people Israel. Teach them the right way to live, and send rain on the land you gave your people for an inheritance.

³⁷ "When famine or plague comes to the land, or blight or mildew, locusts or grasshoppers, or when an enemy besieges them in any of their cities, whatever disaster or disease may come, ³⁸ and when a prayer or plea is made by anyone among your people Israel—being aware of the afflictions of their own hearts, and spreading out their hands toward this temple— ³⁹ then hear from heaven, your dwelling place. Forgive and act; deal with everyone according to all they do, since you know their hearts (for you alone know every human heart), ⁴⁰ so that they will fear you all the time they live in the land you gave our ancestors.

⁴¹ "As for the foreigner who does not belong to your people Israel but has come from a distant land because of your name— ⁴² for they will hear of your great name and your mighty hand and your outstretched arm— when they come and pray toward this temple, ⁴³ then hear from heaven, your dwelling place. Do whatever the foreigner asks of you, so that all the peoples of the earth may know your name and fear you, as do your own people Israel, and may know that this house I have built bears your Name.

⁴⁴ "When your people go to war against their enemies, wherever you send them, and when they pray to the LORD toward the city you have chosen and the temple I have built for your Name, ⁴⁵ then hear from heaven their prayer and their plea, and uphold their cause.

⁴⁶ "When they sin against you— for there is no one who does not sin—and you become angry with them and give them over to their enemies, who take them captive to their own lands, far away or near; ⁴⁷ and if they have a change of heart in the land where they are held captive, and repent and plead with you in the land of their captors and say, 'We have sinned, we have done wrong, we have acted wickedly'; ⁴⁸ and if they turn back to you with all their heart and soul in the land of their enemies who took them captive, and pray to you toward the land you gave their ancestors, toward the city you have chosen and the temple I have built for your Name; ⁴⁹ then from heaven, your dwelling place, hear their prayer and their plea, and uphold their cause. ⁵⁰ And forgive your people, who have sinned against you; forgive all the offenses they have committed against you, and cause their captors to show them mercy; ⁵¹ for they are your people and your inheritance, whom you brought out of Egypt, out of that iron-smelting furnace.

⁵² "May your eyes be open to your servant's plea and to the plea of your

people Israel, and may you listen to them whenever they cry out to you. ⁵³For you singled them out from all the nations of the world to be your own inheritance, just as you declared through your servant Moses when you, Sovereign LORD, brought our ancestors out of Egypt."

⁵⁴When Solomon had finished all these prayers and supplications to the LORD, he rose from before the altar of the LORD, where he had been kneeling with his hands spread out toward heaven. ⁵⁵He stood and blessed the whole assembly of Israel in a loud voice, saying:

⁵⁶"Praise be to the LORD, who has given rest to his people Israel just as he promised. Not one word has failed of all the good promises he gave through his servant Moses. ⁵⁷May the LORD our God be with us as he was with our ancestors; may he never leave us nor forsake us. ⁵⁸May he turn our hearts to him, to walk in obedience to him and keep the commands, decrees and laws he gave our ancestors. ⁵⁹And may these words of mine, which I have prayed before the LORD, be near to the LORD our God day and night, that he may uphold the cause of his servant and the cause of his people Israel according to each day's need, ⁶⁰so that all the peoples of the earth may know that the LORD is God and that there is no other. ⁶¹And may your hearts be fully committed to the LORD our God, to live by his decrees and obey his commands, as at this time."

The Dedication of the Temple

⁶²Then the king and all Israel with him offered sacrifices before the LORD. ⁶³Solomon offered a sacrifice of fellowship offerings to the LORD: twenty-two thousand cattle and a hundred and twenty thousand sheep and goats. So the king and all the Israelites dedicated the temple of the LORD.

⁶⁴On that same day the king conse-crated the middle part of the courtyard in front of the temple of the LORD, and there he offered burnt offerings, grain offerings and the fat of the fellowship offerings, because the bronze altar that stood before the LORD was too small to hold the burnt offerings, the grain offerings and the fat of the fellowship offerings.

⁶⁵So Solomon observed the festival at that time, and all Israel with him—a vast assembly, people from Lebo Hamath to the Wadi of Egypt. They celebrated it before the LORD our God for seven days and seven days more, fourteen days in all. ⁶⁶On the following day he sent the people away. They blessed the king and then went home, joyful and glad in heart for all the good things the LORD had done for his servant David and his people Israel.

The LORD Appears to Solomon

9 When Solomon had finished building the temple of the LORD and the royal palace, and had achieved all he had desired to do, ²the LORD appeared to him a second time, as he had appeared to him at Gibeon. ³The LORD said to him:

"I have heard the prayer and plea you have made before me; I have consecrated this temple, which you have built, by putting my Name there forever. My eyes and my heart will always be there.

⁴"As for you, if you walk before me faithfully with integrity of heart and uprightness, as David your father did, and do all I command and observe my decrees and laws, ⁵I will establish your royal throne over Israel forever, as I promised David your father when I said, 'You shall never fail to have a successor on the throne of Israel.'

⁶"But if you*ᵃ* or your descendants turn away from me and do not observe the commands and decrees I have given you*ᵃ* and go off to serve other gods and worship them, ⁷then

---

ᵃ 6 The Hebrew is plural.

I will cut off Israel from the land I have given them and will reject this temple I have consecrated for my Name. Israel will then become a byword and an object of ridicule among all peoples. ⁸This temple will become a heap of rubble. All*a* who pass by will be appalled and will scoff and say, 'Why has the LORD done such a thing to this land and to this temple?' ⁹People will answer, 'Because they have forsaken the LORD their God, who brought their ancestors out of Egypt, and have embraced other gods, worshiping and serving them—that is why the LORD brought all this disaster on them.'"

Solomon's Other Activities

¹⁰At the end of twenty years, during which Solomon built these two buildings—the temple of the LORD and the royal palace— ¹¹King Solomon gave twenty towns in Galilee to Hiram king of Tyre, because Hiram had supplied him with all the cedar and juniper and gold he wanted. ¹²But when Hiram went from Tyre to see the towns that Solomon had given him, he was not pleased with them. ¹³"What kind of towns are these you have given me, my brother?" he asked. And he called them the Land of Kabul,*b* a name they have to this day. ¹⁴Now Hiram had sent to the king 120 talents*c* of gold.

¹⁵Here is the account of the forced labor King Solomon conscripted to build the LORD's temple, his own palace, the terraces,*d* the wall of Jerusalem, and Hazor, Megiddo and Gezer. ¹⁶(Pharaoh king of Egypt had attacked and captured Gezer. He had set it on fire. He killed its Canaanite inhabitants and then gave it as a wedding gift to his daughter, Solomon's wife. ¹⁷And Solomon rebuilt Gezer.) He built up Lower Beth Horon, ¹⁸Baalath, and Tadmor*e* in the desert, within his land, ¹⁹as well as all his store cities and the towns for his chariots and for his horses*f*—whatever he desired to build in Jerusalem, in Lebanon and throughout all the territory he ruled.

²⁰There were still people left from the Amorites, Hittites, Perizzites, Hivites and Jebusites (these peoples were not Israelites). ²¹Solomon conscripted the descendants of all these peoples remaining in the land—whom the Israelites could not exterminate*g*—to serve as slave labor, as it is to this day. ²²But Solomon did not make slaves of any of the Israelites; they were his fighting men, his government officials, his officers, his captains, and the commanders of his chariots and charioteers. ²³They were also the chief officials in charge of Solomon's projects—550 officials supervising those who did the work.

²⁴After Pharaoh's daughter had come up from the City of David to the palace Solomon had built for her, he constructed the terraces.

²⁵Three times a year Solomon sacrificed burnt offerings and fellowship offerings on the altar he had built for the LORD, burning incense before the LORD along with them, and so fulfilled the temple obligations.

²⁶King Solomon also built ships at Ezion Geber, which is near Elath in Edom, on the shore of the Red Sea.*b* ²⁷And Hiram sent his men—sailors who knew the sea—to serve in the fleet with Solomon's men. ²⁸They sailed to Ophir and brought back 420 talents*i* of gold, which they delivered to King Solomon.

The Queen of Sheba Visits Solomon

10 When the queen of Sheba heard about the fame of Solomon and his relationship to the LORD, she came to test Solomon with hard questions. ²Arriving at Jerusalem with

---

a 8 See some Septuagint manuscripts, Old Latin, Syriac, Arabic and Targum; Hebrew *And though this temple is now imposing, all*
b 13 *Kabul* sounds like the Hebrew for *good-for-nothing.* *c* 14 That is, about 4 1/2 tons or about 4 metric tons *d* 15 Or *the Millo*; also in verse 24 *e* 18 The Hebrew may also be read *Tamar.* *f* 19 Or *charioteers* *g* 21 The Hebrew term refers to the irrevocable giving over of things or persons to the LORD, often by totally destroying them. *b* 26 Or *the Sea of Reeds* *i* 28 That is, about 16 tons or about 14 metric tons

a very great caravan—with camels carrying spices, large quantities of gold, and precious stones—she came to Solomon and talked with him about all that she had on her mind. ³Solomon answered all her questions; nothing was too hard for the king to explain to her. ⁴When the queen of Sheba saw all the wisdom of Solomon and the palace he had built, ⁵the food on his table, the seating of his officials, the attending servants in their robes, his cupbearers, and the burnt offerings he made at*ᵃ* the temple of the Lord, she was overwhelmed.

⁶She said to the king, "The report I heard in my own country about your achievements and your wisdom is true. ⁷But I did not believe these things until I came and saw with my own eyes. Indeed, not even half was told me; in wisdom and wealth you have far exceeded the report I heard. ⁸How happy your people must be! How happy your officials, who continually stand before you and hear your wisdom! ⁹Praise be to the Lord your God, who has delighted in you and placed you on the throne of Israel. Because of the Lord's eternal love for Israel, he has made you king to maintain justice and righteousness."

¹⁰And she gave the king 120 talents*ᵇ* of gold, large quantities of spices, and precious stones. Never again were so many spices brought in as those the queen of Sheba gave to King Solomon.

¹¹(Hiram's ships brought gold from Ophir; and from there they brought great cargoes of almugwood*ᶜ* and precious stones. ¹²The king used the almugwood to make supports*ᵈ* for the temple of the Lord and for the royal palace, and to make harps and lyres for the musicians. So much almugwood has never been imported or seen since that day.)

¹³King Solomon gave the queen of Sheba all she desired and asked for, besides what he had given her out of his royal bounty. Then she left and returned with her retinue to her own country.

Solomon's Splendor

¹⁴The weight of the gold that Solomon received yearly was 666 talents,*ᵉ* ¹⁵not including the revenues from merchants and traders and from all the Arabian kings and the governors of the territories.

¹⁶King Solomon made two hundred large shields of hammered gold; six hundred shekels*ᶠ* of gold went into each shield. ¹⁷He also made three hundred small shields of hammered gold, with three minas*ᵍ* of gold in each shield. The king put them in the Palace of the Forest of Lebanon.

¹⁸Then the king made a great throne covered with ivory and overlaid with fine gold. ¹⁹The throne had six steps, and its back had a rounded top. On both sides of the seat were armrests, with a lion standing beside each of them. ²⁰Twelve lions stood on the six steps, one at either end of each step. Nothing like it had ever been made for any other kingdom. ²¹All King Solomon's goblets were gold, and all the household articles in the Palace of the Forest of Lebanon were pure gold. Nothing was made of silver, because silver was considered of little value in Solomon's days. ²²The king had a fleet of trading ships*ᵇ* at sea along with the ships of Hiram. Once every three years it returned, carrying gold, silver and ivory, and apes and baboons.

²³King Solomon was greater in riches and wisdom than all the other kings of the earth. ²⁴The whole world sought audience with Solomon to hear the wisdom God had put in his heart. ²⁵Year after year, everyone who came brought a gift—articles of silver and gold, robes, weapons and spices, and horses and mules.

²⁶Solomon accumulated chariots and horses; he had fourteen hundred chariots and twelve thousand horses,*ⁱ* which

---

ᵃ 5 Or *the ascent by which he went up to*
ᵇ 10 That is, about 4 1/2 tons or about 4 metric tons   *ᶜ 11* Probably a variant of *algumwood*; also in verse 12   *ᵈ 12* The meaning of the Hebrew for this word is uncertain.   *ᵉ 14* That is, about 25 tons or about 23 metric tons
ᶠ 16 That is, about 15 pounds or about 6.9 kilograms; also in verse 29   *ᵍ 17* That is, about 3 3/4 pounds or about 1.7 kilograms; or perhaps reference is to double minas, that is, about 7 1/2 pounds or about 3.5 kilograms.   *ᵇ 22* Hebrew *of ships of Tarshish*   *ⁱ 26* Or *charioteers*

he kept in the chariot cities and also with him in Jerusalem. ²⁷The king made silver as common in Jerusalem as stones, and cedar as plentiful as sycamore-fig trees in the foothills. ²⁸Solomon's horses were imported from Egypt and from Kue[a]—the royal merchants purchased them from Kue at the current price. ²⁹They imported a chariot from Egypt for six hundred shekels of silver, and a horse for a hundred and fifty.[b] They also exported them to all the kings of the Hittites and of the Arameans.

Solomon's Wives

11 King Solomon, however, loved many foreign women besides Pharaoh's daughter—Moabites, Ammonites, Edomites, Sidonians and Hittites. ²They were from nations about which the LORD had told the Israelites, "You must not intermarry with them, because they will surely turn your hearts after their gods." Nevertheless, Solomon held fast to them in love. ³He had seven hundred wives of royal birth and three hundred concubines, and his wives led him astray. ⁴As Solomon grew old, his wives turned his heart after other gods, and his heart was not fully devoted to the LORD his God, as the heart of David his father had been. ⁵He followed Ashtoreth the goddess of the Sidonians, and Molek the detestable god of the Ammonites. ⁶So Solomon did evil in the eyes of the LORD; he did not follow the LORD completely, as David his father had done.

⁷On a hill east of Jerusalem, Solomon built a high place for Chemosh the detestable god of Moab, and for Molek the detestable god of the Ammonites. ⁸He did the same for all his foreign wives, who burned incense and offered sacrifices to their gods.

⁹The LORD became angry with Solomon because his heart had turned away from the LORD, the God of Israel, who had appeared to him twice. ¹⁰Although he had forbidden Solomon to follow other gods, Solomon did not keep the LORD's command. ¹¹So the LORD said to Solomon, "Since this is your attitude and you have not kept my covenant and my decrees, which I commanded you, I will most certainly tear the kingdom away from you and give it to one of your subordinates. ¹²Nevertheless, for the sake of David your father, I will not do it during your lifetime. I will tear it out of the hand of your son. ¹³Yet I will not tear the whole kingdom from him, but will give him one tribe for the sake of David my servant and for the sake of Jerusalem, which I have chosen."

Solomon's Adversaries

¹⁴Then the LORD raised up against Solomon an adversary, Hadad the Edomite, from the royal line of Edom. ¹⁵Earlier when David was fighting with Edom, Joab the commander of the army, who had gone up to bury the dead, had struck down all the men in Edom. ¹⁶Joab and all the Israelites stayed there for six months, until they had destroyed all the men in Edom. ¹⁷But Hadad, still only a boy, fled to Egypt with some Edomite officials who had served his father. ¹⁸They set out from Midian and went to Paran. Then taking people from Paran with them, they went to Egypt, to Pharaoh king of Egypt, who gave Hadad a house and land and provided him with food.

¹⁹Pharaoh was so pleased with Hadad that he gave him a sister of his own wife, Queen Tahpenes, in marriage. ²⁰The sister of Tahpenes bore him a son named Genubath, whom Tahpenes brought up in the royal palace. There Genubath lived with Pharaoh's own children.

²¹While he was in Egypt, Hadad heard that David rested with his ancestors and that Joab the commander of the army was also dead. Then Hadad said to Pharaoh, "Let me go, that I may return to my own country."

²²"What have you lacked here that you want to go back to your own country?" Pharaoh asked.

"Nothing," Hadad replied, "but do let me go!"

---

^a 28 Probably *Cilicia*   ^b 29 That is, about 3 3/4 pounds or about 1.7 kilograms

²³And God raised up against Solomon another adversary, Rezon son of Eliada, who had fled from his master, Hadadezer king of Zobah. ²⁴When David destroyed Zobah's army, Rezon gathered a band of men around him and became their leader; they went to Damascus, where they settled and took control. ²⁵Rezon was Israel's adversary as long as Solomon lived, adding to the trouble caused by Hadad. So Rezon ruled in Aram and was hostile toward Israel.

Jeroboam Rebels Against Solomon

²⁶Also, Jeroboam son of Nebat rebelled against the king. He was one of Solomon's officials, an Ephraimite from Zeredah, and his mother was a widow named Zeruah.

²⁷Here is the account of how he rebelled against the king: Solomon had built the terraces*a* and had filled in the gap in the wall of the city of David his father. ²⁸Now Jeroboam was a man of standing, and when Solomon saw how well the young man did his work, he put him in charge of the whole labor force of the tribes of Joseph.

²⁹About that time Jeroboam was going

a 27 Or *the Millo*

1 Kings 11:1–13

Solomon asked for God's best.

Solomon was barely out of his teens when he was crowned king of Israel. Under the remarkable leadership of David, his father, the kingdom had grown wealthy and spiritually strong. Solomon knew he would need extraordinary skill to live up to his father's grand accomplishments. One night the Lord appeared to Solomon in a dream and said, "Ask for whatever you want me to give you." The young king replied, "I am only a little child and do not know how to carry out my duties." Then Solomon asked for "a discerning heart to govern your people and to distinguish between right and wrong" (1 Kings 3:5–9).

Solomon could have asked for wealth or long life or the death of his enemies, but he chose wisdom. God was so pleased with his request that he not only gave Solomon more insight than anyone on earth, but he also showered the king with riches and fame (see 1 Kings 3:10–14). Solomon's reputation for wisdom spread throughout the world, and the book of Proverbs records many of his pithy sayings.

Sadly, this uniquely wise man sometimes acted like a fool. Solomon took hundreds of foreign wives and concubines in clear disobedience to God. Those women enticed him to worship their false gods, and as Solomon strayed from doing good, the Lord declared he would lose most of his kingdom.

You can find Solomon in 1 Kings 1—11 as well as 1 Chronicles 22 to 2 Chronicles 9. His writings are found in Proverbs, Ecclesiastes, and the Song of Songs.

UNSHAKEN *people*

out of Jerusalem, and Ahijah the prophet of Shiloh met him on the way, wearing a new cloak. The two of them were alone out in the country, ³⁰ and Ahijah took hold of the new cloak he was wearing and tore it into twelve pieces. ³¹ Then he said to Jeroboam, "Take ten pieces for yourself, for this is what the LORD, the God of Israel, says: 'See, I am going to tear the kingdom out of Solomon's hand and give you ten tribes. ³² But for the sake of my servant David and the city of Jerusalem, which I have chosen out of all the tribes of Israel, he will have one tribe. ³³ I will do this because they have[a] forsaken me and worshiped Ashtoreth the goddess of the Sidonians, Chemosh the god of the Moabites, and Molek the god of the Ammonites, and have not walked in obedience to me, nor done what is right in my eyes, nor kept my decrees and laws as David, Solomon's father, did.

³⁴ "'But I will not take the whole kingdom out of Solomon's hand; I have made him ruler all the days of his life for the sake of David my servant, whom I chose and who obeyed my commands and decrees. ³⁵ I will take the kingdom from his son's hands and give you ten tribes. ³⁶ I will give one tribe to his son so that David my servant may always have a lamp before me in Jerusalem, the city where I chose to put my Name. ³⁷ However, as for you, I will take you, and you will rule over all that your heart desires; you will be king over Israel. ³⁸ If you do whatever I command you and walk in obedience to me and do what is right in my eyes by obeying my decrees and commands, as David my servant did, I will be with you. I will build you a dynasty as enduring as the one I built for David and will give Israel to you. ³⁹ I will humble David's descendants because of this, but not forever.'"

⁴⁰ Solomon tried to kill Jeroboam, but Jeroboam fled to Egypt, to Shishak the king, and stayed there until Solomon's death.

Solomon's Death

⁴¹ As for the other events of Solomon's reign—all he did and the wisdom he dis-played—are they not written in the book of the annals of Solomon? ⁴² Solomon reigned in Jerusalem over all Israel forty years. ⁴³ Then he rested with his ancestors and was buried in the city of David his father. And Rehoboam his son succeeded him as king.

Israel Rebels Against Rehoboam

12 Rehoboam went to Shechem, for all Israel had gone there to make him king. ² When Jeroboam son of Nebat heard this (he was still in Egypt, where he had fled from King Solomon), he returned from[b] Egypt. ³ So they sent for Jeroboam, and he and the whole assembly of Israel went to Rehoboam and said to him: ⁴ "Your father put a heavy yoke on us, but now lighten the harsh labor and the heavy yoke he put on us, and we will serve you."

⁵ Rehoboam answered, "Go away for three days and then come back to me." So the people went away.

⁶ Then King Rehoboam consulted the elders who had served his father Solomon during his lifetime. "How would you advise me to answer these people?" he asked.

⁷ They replied, "If today you will be a servant to these people and serve them and give them a favorable answer, they will always be your servants."

⁸ But Rehoboam rejected the advice the elders gave him and consulted the young men who had grown up with him and were serving him. ⁹ He asked them, "What is your advice? How should we answer these people who say to me, 'Lighten the yoke your father put on us'?"

¹⁰ The young men who had grown up with him replied, "These people have said to you, 'Your father put a heavy yoke on us, but make our yoke lighter.' Now tell them, 'My little finger is thicker than my father's waist. ¹¹ My father laid on you a heavy yoke; I will make it even heavier. My father scourged you with whips; I will scourge you with scorpions.'"

¹² Three days later Jeroboam and all the

---

a 33 Hebrew; Septuagint, Vulgate and Syriac *because he has*   *b 2* Or *he remained in* people returned to Rehoboam, as the king had said, "Come back to me in three days." [13] The king answered the people harshly. Rejecting the advice given him by the elders, [14] he followed the advice of the young men and said, "My father made your yoke heavy; I will make it even heavier. My father scourged you with whips; I will scourge you with scorpions." [15] So the king did not listen to the people, for this turn of events was from the LORD, to fulfill the word the LORD had spoken to Jeroboam son of Nebat through Ahijah the Shilonite.

[16] When all Israel saw that the king refused to listen to them, they answered the king:

"What share do we have in David,
    what part in Jesse's son?
To your tents, Israel!
    Look after your own house, David!"

So the Israelites went home. [17] But as for the Israelites who were living in the towns of Judah, Rehoboam still ruled over them.

[18] King Rehoboam sent out Adoniram,[a] who was in charge of forced labor, but all Israel stoned him to death. King Rehoboam, however, managed to get into his chariot and escape to Jerusalem. [19] So Israel has been in rebellion against the house of David to this day.

[20] When all the Israelites heard that Jeroboam had returned, they sent and called him to the assembly and made him king over all Israel. Only the tribe of Judah remained loyal to the house of David.

[21] When Rehoboam arrived in Jerusalem, he mustered all Judah and the tribe of Benjamin—a hundred and eighty thousand able young men—to go to war against Israel and to regain the kingdom for Rehoboam son of Solomon.

[22] But this word of God came to Shemaiah the man of God: [23] "Say to Rehoboam son of Solomon king of Judah, to all Judah and Benjamin, and to the rest of the people, [24] 'This is what the LORD says: Do not go up to fight against your brothers, the Israelites. Go home, every one of you, for this is my doing.'" So they obeyed the word of the LORD and went home again, as the LORD had ordered.

Golden Calves at Bethel and Dan

[25] Then Jeroboam fortified Shechem in the hill country of Ephraim and lived there. From there he went out and built up Peniel.[b]

[26] Jeroboam thought to himself, "The kingdom will now likely revert to the house of David. [27] If these people go up to offer sacrifices at the temple of the LORD in Jerusalem, they will again give their allegiance to their lord, Rehoboam king of Judah. They will kill me and return to King Rehoboam."

[28] After seeking advice, the king made two golden calves. He said to the people, "It is too much for you to go up to Jerusalem. Here are your gods, Israel, who brought you up out of Egypt." [29] One he set up in Bethel, and the other in Dan. [30] And this thing became a sin; the people came to worship the one at Bethel and went as far as Dan to worship the other.[c]

[31] Jeroboam built shrines on high places and appointed priests from all sorts of people, even though they were not Levites. [32] He instituted a festival on the fifteenth day of the eighth month, like the festival held in Judah, and offered sacrifices on the altar. This he did in Bethel, sacrificing to the calves he had made. And at Bethel he also installed priests at the high places he had made. [33] On the fifteenth day of the eighth month, a month of his own choosing, he offered sacrifices on the altar he had built at Bethel. So he instituted the festival for the Israelites and went up to the altar to make offerings.

The Man of God From Judah

13 By the word of the LORD a man of God came from Judah to Bethel, as Jeroboam was standing by the altar to make an offering. [2] By the word of the LORD he cried out against the altar: "Altar, altar! This is what the LORD says: 'A son named Josiah will

---

[a] 18 Some Septuagint manuscripts and Syriac (see also 4:6 and 5:14); Hebrew *Adoram*
[b] 25 Hebrew *Penuel*, a variant of *Peniel*
[c] 30 Probable reading of the original Hebrew text; Masoretic Text *people went to the one as far as Dan*

be born to the house of David. On you he will sacrifice the priests of the high places who make offerings here, and human bones will be burned on you.'" ³That same day the man of God gave a sign: "This is the sign the LORD has declared: The altar will be split apart and the ashes on it will be poured out."

⁴When King Jeroboam heard what the man of God cried out against the altar at Bethel, he stretched out his hand from the altar and said, "Seize him!" But the hand he stretched out toward the man shriveled up, so that he could not pull it back. ⁵Also, the altar was split apart and its ashes poured out according to the sign given by the man of God by the word of the LORD.

⁶Then the king said to the man of God, "Intercede with the LORD your God and pray for me that my hand may be restored." So the man of God interceded with the LORD, and the king's hand was restored and became as it was before.

⁷The king said to the man of God, "Come home with me for a meal, and I will give you a gift."

⁸But the man of God answered the king, "Even if you were to give me half your possessions, I would not go with you, nor would I eat bread or drink water here. ⁹For I was commanded by the word of the LORD: 'You must not eat bread or drink water or return by the way you came.'" ¹⁰So he took another road and did not return by the way he had come to Bethel.

¹¹Now there was a certain old prophet living in Bethel, whose sons came and told him all that the man of God had done there that day. They also told their father what he had said to the king. ¹²Their father asked them, "Which way did he go?" And his sons showed him which road the man of God from Judah had taken. ¹³So he said to his sons, "Saddle the donkey for me." And when they had saddled the donkey for him, he mounted it ¹⁴and rode after the man of God. He found him sitting under an oak tree and asked, "Are you the man of God who came from Judah?"

"I am," he replied.

¹⁵So the prophet said to him, "Come home with me and eat."

¹⁶The man of God said, "I cannot turn back and go with you, nor can I eat bread or drink water with you in this place. ¹⁷I have been told by the word of the LORD: 'You must not eat bread or drink water there or return by the way you came.'"

¹⁸The old prophet answered, "I too am a prophet, as you are. And an angel said to me by the word of the LORD: 'Bring him back with you to your house so that he may eat bread and drink water.'" (But he was lying to him.) ¹⁹So the man of God returned with him and ate and drank in his house.

²⁰While they were sitting at the table, the word of the LORD came to the old prophet who had brought him back. ²¹He cried out to the man of God who had come from Judah, "This is what the LORD says: 'You have defied the word of the LORD and have not kept the command the LORD your God gave you. ²²You came back and ate bread and drank water in the place where he told you not to eat or drink. Therefore your body will not be buried in the tomb of your ancestors.'"

²³When the man of God had finished eating and drinking, the prophet who had brought him back saddled his donkey for him. ²⁴As he went on his way, a lion met him on the road and killed him, and his body was left lying on the road, with both the donkey and the lion standing beside it. ²⁵Some people who passed by saw the body lying there, with the lion standing beside the body, and they went and reported it in the city where the old prophet lived.

²⁶When the prophet who had brought him back from his journey heard of it, he said, "It is the man of God who defied the word of the LORD. The LORD has given him over to the lion, which has mauled him and killed him, as the word of the LORD had warned him."

²⁷The prophet said to his sons, "Saddle the donkey for me," and they did so. ²⁸Then he went out and found the body lying on the road, with the donkey and the

lion standing beside it. The lion had neither eaten the body nor mauled the donkey. ²⁹So the prophet picked up the body of the man of God, laid it on the donkey, and brought it back to his own city to mourn for him and bury him. ³⁰Then he laid the body in his own tomb, and they mourned over him and said, "Alas, my brother!"

³¹After burying him, he said to his sons, "When I die, bury me in the grave where the man of God is buried; lay my bones beside his bones. ³²For the message he declared by the word of the LORD against the altar in Bethel and against all the shrines on the high places in the towns of Samaria will certainly come true."

³³Even after this, Jeroboam did not change his evil ways, but once more appointed priests for the high places from all sorts of people. Anyone who wanted to become a priest he consecrated for the high places. ³⁴This was the sin of the house of Jeroboam that led to its downfall and to its destruction from the face of the earth.

Ahijah's Prophecy Against Jeroboam

14 At that time Abijah son of Jeroboam became ill, ²and Jeroboam said to his wife, "Go, disguise yourself, so you won't be recognized as the wife of Jeroboam. Then go to Shiloh. Ahijah the prophet is there—the one who told me I would be king over this people. ³Take ten loaves of bread with you, some cakes and a jar of honey, and go to him. He will tell you what will happen to the boy." ⁴So Jeroboam's wife did what he said and went to Ahijah's house in Shiloh.

Now Ahijah could not see; his sight was gone because of his age. ⁵But the LORD had told Ahijah, "Jeroboam's wife is coming to ask you about her son, for he is ill, and you are to give her such and such an answer. When she arrives, she will pretend to be someone else."

⁶So when Ahijah heard the sound of her footsteps at the door, he said, "Come in, wife of Jeroboam. Why this pretense? I have been sent to you with bad news. ⁷Go, tell Jeroboam that this is what the LORD, the God of Israel, says: 'I raised you up from among the people and appointed you ruler over my people Israel. ⁸I tore the kingdom away from the house of David and gave it to you, but you have not been like my servant David, who kept my commands and followed me with all his heart, doing only what was right in my eyes. ⁹You have done more evil than all who lived before you. You have made for yourself other gods, idols made of metal; you have aroused my anger and turned your back on me.

¹⁰"'Because of this, I am going to bring disaster on the house of Jeroboam. I will cut off from Jeroboam every last male in Israel—slave or free.ᵃ I will burn up the house of Jeroboam as one burns dung, until it is all gone. ¹¹Dogs will eat those belonging to Jeroboam who die in the city, and the birds will feed on those who die in the country. The LORD has spoken!'

¹²"As for you, go back home. When you set foot in your city, the boy will die. ¹³All Israel will mourn for him and bury him. He is the only one belonging to Jeroboam who will be buried, because he is the only one in the house of Jeroboam in whom the LORD, the God of Israel, has found anything good.

¹⁴"The LORD will raise up for himself a king over Israel who will cut off the family of Jeroboam. Even now this is beginning to happen.ᵇ ¹⁵And the LORD will strike Israel, so that it will be like a reed swaying in the water. He will uproot Israel from this good land that he gave to their ancestors and scatter them beyond the Euphrates River, because they aroused the LORD's anger by making Asherah poles.ᶜ ¹⁶And he will give Israel up because of the sins Jeroboam has committed and has caused Israel to commit."

¹⁷Then Jeroboam's wife got up and left and went to Tirzah. As soon as she stepped over the threshold of the house,

ᵃ 10 Or Israel—every ruler or leader
ᵇ 14 The meaning of the Hebrew for this sentence is uncertain.   ᶜ 15 That is, wooden symbols of the goddess Asherah; here and elsewhere in 1 Kings

the boy died. ¹⁸They buried him, and all Israel mourned for him, as the LORD had said through his servant the prophet Ahijah.

¹⁹The other events of Jeroboam's reign, his wars and how he ruled, are written in the book of the annals of the kings of Israel. ²⁰He reigned for twenty-two years and then rested with his ancestors. And Nadab his son succeeded him as king.

Rehoboam King of Judah

²¹Rehoboam son of Solomon was king in Judah. He was forty-one years old when he became king, and he reigned seventeen years in Jerusalem, the city the LORD had chosen out of all the tribes of Israel in which to put his Name. His mother's name was Naamah; she was an Ammonite.

²²Judah did evil in the eyes of the LORD. By the sins they committed they stirred up his jealous anger more than those who were before them had done. ²³They also set up for themselves high places, sacred stones and Asherah poles on every high hill and under every spreading tree. ²⁴There were even male shrine prostitutes in the land; the people engaged in all the detestable practices of the nations the LORD had driven out before the Israelites.

²⁵In the fifth year of King Rehoboam, Shishak king of Egypt attacked Jerusalem. ²⁶He carried off the treasures of the temple of the LORD and the treasures of the royal palace. He took everything, including all the gold shields Solomon had made. ²⁷So King Rehoboam made bronze shields to replace them and assigned these to the commanders of the guard on duty at the entrance to the royal palace. ²⁸Whenever the king went to the LORD's temple, the guards bore the shields, and afterward they returned them to the guardroom.

²⁹As for the other events of Rehoboam's reign, and all he did, are they not written in the book of the annals of the kings of Judah? ³⁰There was continual warfare between Rehoboam and Jeroboam. ³¹And Rehoboam rested with his ancestors and was buried with them in the City of Da-

vid. His mother's name was Naamah; she was an Ammonite. And Abijah*ᵃ* his son succeeded him as king.

Abijah King of Judah

15 In the eighteenth year of the reign of Jeroboam son of Nebat, Abijah*ᵇ* became king of Judah, ²and he reigned in Jerusalem three years. His mother's name was Maakah daughter of Abishalom.*ᶜ*

³He committed all the sins his father had done before him; his heart was not fully devoted to the LORD his God, as the heart of David his forefather had been. ⁴Nevertheless, for David's sake the LORD his God gave him a lamp in Jerusalem by raising up a son to succeed him and by making Jerusalem strong. ⁵For David had done what was right in the eyes of the LORD and had not failed to keep any of the LORD's commands all the days of his life — except in the case of Uriah the Hittite.

⁶There was war between Abijah*ᵈ* and Jeroboam throughout Abijah's lifetime. ⁷As for the other events of Abijah's reign, and all he did, are they not written in the book of the annals of the kings of Judah? There was war between Abijah and Jeroboam. ⁸And Abijah rested with his ancestors and was buried in the City of David. And Asa his son succeeded him as king.

Asa King of Judah

⁹In the twentieth year of Jeroboam king of Israel, Asa became king of Judah, ¹⁰and he reigned in Jerusalem forty-one years. His grandmother's name was Maakah daughter of Abishalom.

¹¹Asa did what was right in the eyes of the LORD, as his father David had done. ¹²He expelled the male shrine prostitutes

ᵃ 31 Some Hebrew manuscripts and Septuagint (see also 2 Chron. 12:16); most Hebrew manuscripts *Abijam*   *ᵇ 1* Some Hebrew manuscripts and Septuagint (see also 2 Chron. 12:16); most Hebrew manuscripts *Abijam*; also in verses 7 and 8   *ᶜ 2* A variant of *Absalom*; also in verse 10   *ᵈ 6* Some Hebrew manuscripts and Syriac *Abijam* (that is, Abijah); most Hebrew manuscripts *Rehoboam*

1 Kings 15:5

No one is above God's rules.

Royal histories don't often record the failures of kings and queens. So a key lesson jumps out of 1 Kings 15:5: "David had done what was right in the eyes of the LORD and had not failed to keep any of the LORD's commands all the days of his life—except in the case of Uriah the Hittite." King David excelled at obeying God in every area of his life—except a major sin that involved sleeping with a man's wife and sending the man to die in battle (see 2 Samuel 11:2—12:25). David was famed for his devotion to God—but that didn't excuse him from needing to follow God's commands. He was the Lord's chosen king—but he still had to obey the law. Powerful people often think they can do what they want and escape unpunished. But God doesn't work that way. He expects everyone to follow the rules—no exceptions.

Think: When have you seen people act like rules don't apply to them? When have you fallen into that trap?

ROCK SOLID *truths*

from the land and got rid of all the idols his ancestors had made. ¹³He even deposed his grandmother Maakah from her position as queen mother, because she had made a repulsive image for the worship of Asherah. Asa cut it down and burned it in the Kidron Valley. ¹⁴Although he did not remove the high places, Asa's heart was fully committed to the LORD all his life. ¹⁵He brought into the temple of the LORD the silver and gold and the articles that he and his father had dedicated.

¹⁶There was war between Asa and Baasha king of Israel throughout their reigns. ¹⁷Baasha king of Israel went up against Judah and fortified Ramah to prevent anyone from leaving or entering the territory of Asa king of Judah.

¹⁸Asa then took all the silver and gold that was left in the treasuries of the LORD's temple and of his own palace. He entrusted it to his officials and sent them to Ben-Hadad son of Tabrimmon, the son of Hezion, the king of Aram, who was ruling in Damascus. ¹⁹"Let there be a treaty between me and you," he said, "as there was between my father and your father. See, I am sending you a gift of silver and gold. Now break your treaty with Baasha king of Israel so he will withdraw from me."

²⁰Ben-Hadad agreed with King Asa and sent the commanders of his forces against the towns of Israel. He conquered Ijon, Dan, Abel Beth Maakah and all Kinnereth in addition to Naphtali. ²¹When Baasha heard this, he stopped building Ramah and withdrew to Tirzah. ²²Then King Asa issued an order to all Judah—no one was exempt—and they carried away from Ramah the stones and timber Baasha had been using there. With them King Asa built up Geba in Benjamin, and also Mizpah.

²³As for all the other events of Asa's reign, all his achievements, all he did and the cities he built, are they not written in the book of the annals of the kings of Judah? In his old age, however, his feet became diseased. ²⁴Then Asa rested with his ancestors and was buried with them in the city of his father David. And Jehoshaphat his son succeeded him as king.

Nadab King of Israel

²⁵Nadab son of Jeroboam became king of Israel in the second year of Asa king of Judah, and he reigned over Israel two years. ²⁶He did evil in the eyes of the LORD, following the ways of his father and committing the same sin his father had caused Israel to commit. ²⁷Baasha son of Ahijah from the tribe

of Issachar plotted against him, and he struck him down at Gibbethon, a Philistine town, while Nadab and all Israel were besieging it. ²⁸Baasha killed Nadab in the third year of Asa king of Judah and succeeded him as king.

²⁹As soon as he began to reign, he killed Jeroboam's whole family. He did not leave Jeroboam anyone that breathed, but destroyed them all, according to the word of the LORD given through his servant Ahijah the Shilonite. ³⁰This happened because of the sins Jeroboam had committed and had caused Israel to commit, and because he aroused the anger of the LORD, the God of Israel.

³¹As for the other events of Nadab's reign, and all he did, are they not written in the book of the annals of the kings of Israel? ³²There was war between Asa and Baasha king of Israel throughout their reigns.

Baasha King of Israel

³³In the third year of Asa king of Judah, Baasha son of Ahijah became king of all Israel in Tirzah, and he reigned twenty-four years. ³⁴He did evil in the eyes of the LORD, following the ways of Jeroboam and committing the same sin Jeroboam had caused Israel to commit.

16 Then the word of the LORD came to Jehu son of Hanani concerning Baasha: ²"I lifted you up from the dust and appointed you ruler over my people Israel, but you followed the ways of Jeroboam and caused my people Israel to sin and to arouse my anger by their sins. ³So I am about to wipe out Baasha and his house, and I will make your house like that of Jeroboam son of Nebat. ⁴Dogs will eat those belonging to Baasha who die in the city, and birds will feed on those who die in the country."

⁵As for the other events of Baasha's reign, what he did and his achievements, are they not written in the book of the annals of the kings of Israel? ⁶Baasha rested with his ancestors and was buried in Tirzah. And Elah his son succeeded him as king.

⁷Moreover, the word of the LORD came through the prophet Jehu son of Hanani to Baasha and his house, because of all the evil he had done in the eyes of the LORD, arousing his anger by the things he did, becoming like the house of Jeroboam—and also because he destroyed it.

Elah King of Israel

⁸In the twenty-sixth year of Asa king of Judah, Elah son of Baasha became king of Israel, and he reigned in Tirzah two years.

⁹Zimri, one of his officials, who had command of half his chariots, plotted against him. Elah was in Tirzah at the time, getting drunk in the home of Arza, the palace administrator at Tirzah. ¹⁰Zimri came in, struck him down and killed him in the twenty-seventh year of Asa king of Judah. Then he succeeded him as king.

¹¹As soon as he began to reign and was seated on the throne, he killed off Baasha's whole family. He did not spare a single male, whether relative or friend. ¹²So Zimri destroyed the whole family of Baasha, in accordance with the word of the LORD spoken against Baasha through the prophet Jehu— ¹³because of all the sins Baasha and his son Elah had committed and had caused Israel to commit, so that they aroused the anger of the LORD, the God of Israel, by their worthless idols.

¹⁴As for the other events of Elah's reign, and all he did, are they not written in the book of the annals of the kings of Israel?

Zimri King of Israel

¹⁵In the twenty-seventh year of Asa king of Judah, Zimri reigned in Tirzah seven days. The army was encamped near Gibbethon, a Philistine town. ¹⁶When the Israelites in the camp heard that Zimri had plotted against the king and murdered him, they proclaimed Omri, the commander of the army, king over Israel that very day there in the camp. ¹⁷Then Omri and all the Israelites with him withdrew from Gibbethon and laid siege to Tirzah. ¹⁸When Zimri saw that the city was taken, he went into the citadel of the royal

palace and set the palace on fire around him. So he died, [19]because of the sins he had committed, doing evil in the eyes of the LORD and following the ways of Jeroboam and committing the same sin Jeroboam had caused Israel to commit.

[20]As for the other events of Zimri's reign, and the rebellion he carried out, are they not written in the book of the annals of the kings of Israel?

Omri King of Israel

[21]Then the people of Israel were split into two factions; half supported Tibni son of Ginath for king, and the other half supported Omri. [22]But Omri's followers proved stronger than those of Tibni son of Ginath. So Tibni died and Omri became king.

[23]In the thirty-first year of Asa king of Judah, Omri became king of Israel, and he reigned twelve years, six of them in Tirzah. [24]He bought the hill of Samaria from Shemer for two talents[a] of silver and built a city on the hill, calling it Samaria, after Shemer, the name of the former owner of the hill.

[25]But Omri did evil in the eyes of the LORD and sinned more than all those before him. [26]He followed completely the ways of Jeroboam son of Nebat, committing the same sin Jeroboam had caused Israel to commit, so that they aroused the anger of the LORD, the God of Israel, by their worthless idols.

[27]As for the other events of Omri's reign, what he did and the things he achieved, are they not written in the book of the annals of the kings of Israel? [28]Omri rested with his ancestors and was buried in Samaria. And Ahab his son succeeded him as king.

Ahab Becomes King of Israel

[29]In the thirty-eighth year of Asa king of Judah, Ahab son of Omri became king of Israel, and he reigned in Samaria over Israel twenty-two years. [30]Ahab son of Omri did more evil in the eyes of the LORD than any of those before him. [31]He not only considered it trivial to commit the sins of Jeroboam son of Nebat, but he also married Jezebel daughter of Ethbaal king of the Sidonians, and began to serve Baal and worship him. [32]He set up an altar for Baal in the temple of Baal that he built in Samaria. [33]Ahab also made an Asherah pole and did more to arouse the anger of the LORD, the God of Israel, than did all the kings of Israel before him.

[34]In Ahab's time, Hiel of Bethel rebuilt Jericho. He laid its foundations at the cost of his firstborn son Abiram, and he set up its gates at the cost of his youngest son Segub, in accordance with the word of the LORD spoken by Joshua son of Nun.

Elijah Announces a Great Drought

17 Now Elijah the Tishbite, from Tishbe[b] in Gilead, said to Ahab, "As the LORD, the God of Israel, lives, whom I serve, there will be neither dew nor rain in the next few years except at my word."

Elijah Fed by Ravens

[2]Then the word of the LORD came to Elijah: [3]"Leave here, turn eastward and hide in the Kerith Ravine, east of the Jordan. [4]You will drink from the brook, and I have directed the ravens to supply you with food there."

[5]So he did what the LORD had told him. He went to the Kerith Ravine, east of the Jordan, and stayed there. [6]The ravens brought him bread and meat in the morning and bread and meat in the evening, and he drank from the brook.

Elijah and the Widow at Zarephath

[7]Some time later the brook dried up because there had been no rain in the land. [8]Then the word of the LORD came to him: [9]"Go at once to Zarephath in the region of Sidon and stay there. I have directed a widow there to supply you with food." [10]So he went to Zarephath. When he came to the town gate, a widow was there gathering sticks. He called to her and asked, "Would you bring me a little

---

[a] 24 That is, about 150 pounds or about 68 kilograms   [b] 1 Or *Tishbite, of the settlers*

water in a jar so I may have a drink?" [11] As she was going to get it, he called, "And bring me, please, a piece of bread."

[12] "As surely as the LORD your God lives," she replied, "I don't have any bread—only a handful of flour in a jar and a little olive oil in a jug. I am gathering a few sticks to take home and make a meal for myself and my son, that we may eat it—and die."

[13] Elijah said to her, "Don't be afraid. Go home and do as you have said. But first make a small loaf of bread for me from what you have and bring it to me, and then make something for yourself and your son. [14] For this is what the LORD, the God of Israel, says: 'The jar of flour will not be used up and the jug of oil will not run dry until the day the LORD sends rain on the land.'"

[15] She went away and did as Elijah had told her. So there was food every day for Elijah and for the woman and her family. [16] For the jar of flour was not used up and the jug of oil did not run dry, in keeping with the word of the LORD spoken by Elijah.

[17] Some time later the son of the woman who owned the house became ill. He grew worse and worse, and finally stopped breathing. [18] She said to Elijah, "What do you have against me, man of God? Did you come to remind me of my sin and kill my son?"

[19] "Give me your son," Elijah replied. He took him from her arms, carried him to the upper room where he was staying, and laid him on his bed. [20] Then he cried out to the LORD, "LORD my God, have you brought tragedy even on this widow I am staying with, by causing her son to die?" [21] Then he stretched himself out on the boy three times and cried out to the LORD, "LORD my God, let this boy's life return to him!"

[22] The LORD heard Elijah's cry, and the boy's life returned to him, and he lived. [23] Elijah picked up the child and carried him down from the room into the house. He gave him to his mother and said, "Look, your son is alive!"

[24] Then the woman said to Elijah, "Now I know that you are a man of God and that the word of the LORD from your mouth is the truth."

Elijah and Obadiah

18 After a long time, in the third year, the word of the LORD came to Elijah: "Go and present yourself to Ahab, and I will send rain on the land." [2] So Elijah went to present himself to Ahab.

Now the famine was severe in Samaria, [3] and Ahab had summoned Obadiah, his palace administrator. (Obadiah was a devout believer in the LORD. [4] While Jezebel was killing off the LORD's prophets, Obadiah had taken a hundred prophets and hidden them in two caves, fifty in each, and had supplied them with food and water.) [5] Ahab had said to Obadiah, "Go through the land to all the springs and valleys. Maybe we can find some grass to keep the horses and mules alive so we will not have to kill any of our animals." [6] So they divided the land they were to cover, Ahab going in one direction and Obadiah in another.

[7] As Obadiah was walking along, Elijah met him. Obadiah recognized him, bowed down to the ground, and said, "Is it really you, my lord Elijah?"

[8] "Yes," he replied. "Go tell your master, 'Elijah is here.'"

[9] "What have I done wrong," asked Obadiah, "that you are handing your servant over to Ahab to be put to death? [10] As surely as the LORD your God lives, there is not a nation or kingdom where my master has not sent someone to look for you. And whenever a nation or kingdom claimed you were not there, he made them swear they could not find you. [11] But now you tell me to go to my master and say, 'Elijah is here.' [12] I don't know where the Spirit of the LORD may carry you when I leave you. If I go and tell Ahab and he doesn't find you, he will kill me. Yet I your servant have worshiped the LORD since my youth. [13] Haven't you heard, my lord, what I did while Jezebel was killing the prophets of

the LORD? I hid a hundred of the LORD's prophets in two caves, fifty in each, and supplied them with food and water. ¹⁴And now you tell me to go to my master and say, 'Elijah is here.' He will kill me!"

¹⁵Elijah said, "As the LORD Almighty lives, whom I serve, I will surely present myself to Ahab today."

Elijah on Mount Carmel

¹⁶So Obadiah went to meet Ahab and told him, and Ahab went to meet Elijah. ¹⁷When he saw Elijah, he said to him, "Is that you, you troubler of Israel?"

¹⁸"I have not made trouble for Israel," Elijah replied. "But you and your father's family have. You have abandoned the LORD's commands and have followed the Baals. ¹⁹Now summon the people from all over Israel to meet me on Mount Carmel. And bring the four hundred and fifty prophets of Baal and the four hundred prophets of Asherah, who eat at Jezebel's table."

²⁰So Ahab sent word throughout all Israel and assembled the prophets on Mount Carmel. ²¹Elijah went before the people and said, "How long will you waver between two opinions? If the LORD is God, follow him; but if Baal is God, follow him."

But the people said nothing.

²²Then Elijah said to them, "I am the only one of the LORD's prophets left, but Baal has four hundred and fifty prophets. ²³Get two bulls for us. Let Baal's prophets choose one for themselves, and let them cut it into pieces and put it on the wood but not set fire to it. I will prepare the other bull and put it on the wood but not set fire to it. ²⁴Then you call on the name of your god, and I will call on the name of the LORD. The god who answers by fire—he is God."

Then all the people said, "What you say is good."

²⁵Elijah said to the prophets of Baal, "Choose one of the bulls and prepare it first, since there are so many of you. Call on the name of your god, but do not light the fire." ²⁶So they took the bull given them and prepared it.

Then they called on the name of Baal from morning till noon. "Baal, answer us!" they shouted. But there was no response; no one answered. And they danced around the altar they had made.

²⁷At noon Elijah began to taunt them. "Shout louder!" he said. "Surely he is a god! Perhaps he is deep in thought, or busy, or traveling. Maybe he is sleeping and must be awakened." ²⁸So they shouted louder and slashed themselves with swords and spears, as was their custom, until their blood flowed. ²⁹Midday passed, and they continued their frantic prophesying until the time for the evening sacrifice. But there was no response, no one answered, no one paid attention.

³⁰Then Elijah said to all the people, "Come here to me." They came to him, and he repaired the altar of the LORD, which had been torn down. ³¹Elijah took twelve stones, one for each of the tribes descended from Jacob, to whom the word of the LORD had come, saying, "Your name shall be Israel." ³²With the stones he built an altar in the name of the LORD, and he dug a trench around it large enough to hold two seahs*ᵃ* of seed. ³³He arranged the wood, cut the bull into pieces and laid it on the wood. Then he said to them, "Fill four large jars with water and pour it on the offering and on the wood."

³⁴"Do it again," he said, and they did it again.

"Do it a third time," he ordered, and they did it the third time. ³⁵The water ran down around the altar and even filled the trench.

³⁶At the time of sacrifice, the prophet Elijah stepped forward and prayed: "LORD, the God of Abraham, Isaac and Israel, let it be known today that you are God in Israel and that I am your servant and have done all these things at your command. ³⁷Answer me, LORD, answer me, so these people will know that you, LORD, are God, and that you are turning their hearts back again."

ᵃ 32 That is, probably about 24 pounds or about 11 kilograms

ROCK SOLID
promises

"Answer me, so these people will know that you, LORD, are God."

1 Kings 18:37

Don't pray for spectacular answers just for your own sake. Invite God to show everyone he is real.

---

38 Then the fire of the LORD fell and burned up the sacrifice, the wood, the stones and the soil, and also licked up the water in the trench.

39 When all the people saw this, they fell prostrate and cried, "The LORD—he is God! The LORD—he is God!"

40 Then Elijah commanded them, "Seize the prophets of Baal. Don't let anyone get away!" They seized them, and Elijah had them brought down to the Kishon Valley and slaughtered there.

41 And Elijah said to Ahab, "Go, eat and drink, for there is the sound of a heavy rain." 42 So Ahab went off to eat and drink, but Elijah climbed to the top of Carmel, bent down to the ground and put his face between his knees.

43 "Go and look toward the sea," he told his servant. And he went up and looked.

"There is nothing there," he said.

Seven times Elijah said, "Go back."

44 The seventh time the servant reported, "A cloud as small as a man's hand is rising from the sea."

So Elijah said, "Go and tell Ahab, 'Hitch up your chariot and go down before the rain stops you.'"

45 Meanwhile, the sky grew black with clouds, the wind rose, a heavy rain started falling and Ahab rode off to Jezreel. 46 The power of the LORD came on Elijah and, tucking his cloak into his belt, he ran ahead of Ahab all the way to Jezreel.

Elijah Flees to Horeb

19 Now Ahab told Jezebel everything Elijah had done and how he had killed all the prophets with the sword. 2 So Jezebel sent a messenger to Elijah to say, "May the gods deal with me, be it ever so severely, if by this time tomorrow I do not make your life like that of one of them."

3 Elijah was afraid[a] and ran for his life. When he came to Beersheba in Judah, he left his servant there, 4 while he himself went a day's journey into the wilderness. He came to a broom bush, sat down under it and prayed that he might die. "I have had enough, LORD," he said. "Take my life; I am no better than my ancestors." 5 Then he lay down under the bush and fell asleep.

All at once an angel touched him and said, "Get up and eat." 6 He looked around, and there by his head was some bread baked over hot coals, and a jar of water. He ate and drank and then lay down again.

7 The angel of the LORD came back a second time and touched him and said, "Get up and eat, for the journey is too much for you." 8 So he got up and ate and drank. Strengthened by that food, he traveled forty days and forty nights until he reached Horeb, the mountain of God. 9 There he went into a cave and spent the night.

The LORD Appears to Elijah

And the word of the LORD came to him: "What are you doing here, Elijah?"

10 He replied, "I have been very zealous for the LORD God Almighty. The Israelites have rejected your covenant, torn down your altars, and put your prophets to death with the sword. I am the only one left, and now they are trying to kill me too."

11 The LORD said, "Go out and stand on the mountain in the presence of the LORD, for the LORD is about to pass by."

Then a great and powerful wind tore the mountains apart and shattered the

---

a 3 Or Elijah saw

rocks before the Lord, but the Lord was not in the wind. After the wind there was an earthquake, but the Lord was not in the earthquake. ¹²After the earthquake came a fire, but the Lord was not in the fire. And after the fire came a gentle whisper. ¹³When Elijah heard it, he pulled his cloak over his face and went out and stood at the mouth of the cave.

Then a voice said to him, "What are you doing here, Elijah?"

¹⁴He replied, "I have been very zealous for the Lord God Almighty. The Israelites have rejected your covenant, torn down your altars, and put your prophets to death with the sword. I am the only one left, and now they are trying to kill me too."

¹⁵The Lord said to him, "Go back the way you came, and go to the Desert of Damascus. When you get there, anoint Hazael king over Aram. ¹⁶Also, anoint Jehu son of Nimshi king over Israel, and anoint Elisha son of Shaphat from Abel Meholah to succeed you as prophet. ¹⁷Jehu will put to death any who escape the sword of Hazael, and Elisha will put to death any who escape the sword of Jehu. ¹⁸Yet I reserve seven thousand in Israel—all whose knees have not bowed down to Baal and whose mouths have not kissed him."

The Call of Elisha

¹⁹So Elijah went from there and found Elisha son of Shaphat. He was plowing with twelve yoke of oxen, and he himself was driving the twelfth pair. Elijah went up to him and threw his cloak around him. ²⁰Elisha then left his oxen and ran after Elijah. "Let me kiss my father and mother goodbye," he said, "and then I will come with you."

"Go back," Elijah replied. "What have I done to you?"

²¹So Elisha left him and went back. He took his yoke of oxen and slaughtered them. He burned the plowing equipment to cook the meat and gave it to the people,

ROCK SOLID principles

1 Kings 19:9–18

Lean on God when you're lonely.

A couple months ago, Lauren thought she had her friends all figured out. She knew her friendships would get weird after middle school—when half of her classmates moved to high school with her, while the other half headed to a rival school miles away. But Lauren still watched, stunned as her friendships disintegrated. Old friends had stopped calling, and Lauren hadn't really made any new friends to take their place. Everyone else seemed to be rapidly adjusting to the change, but Lauren felt stuck in slow motion. Every night and weekend was a struggle to find something to do. And all too often nothing worked out and Lauren just sat home alone.

Elijah prayed down fire from heaven, proving the Lord's ultimate power over the false god Baal. But when the wicked queen Jezebel threatened retaliation, Elijah ran for his life (see 1 Kings 19:3). He felt so battered and isolated that he wanted to die. But God doesn't let us suffer alone. He might not show up and shatter rocks, but he is always with us (see Matthew 28:20).

and they ate. Then he set out to follow Elijah and became his servant.

Ben-Hadad Attacks Samaria

20 Now Ben-Hadad king of Aram mustered his entire army. Accompanied by thirty-two kings with their horses and chariots, he went up and besieged Samaria and attacked it. ²He sent messengers into the city to Ahab king of Israel, saying, "This is what Ben-Hadad says: ³'Your silver and gold are mine, and the best of your wives and children are mine.'"

⁴The king of Israel answered, "Just as you say, my lord the king. I and all I have are yours."

⁵The messengers came again and said, "This is what Ben-Hadad says: 'I sent to demand your silver and gold, your wives and your children. ⁶But about this time tomorrow I am going to send my officials to search your palace and the houses of your officials. They will seize everything you value and carry it away.'"

⁷The king of Israel summoned all the elders of the land and said to them, "See how this man is looking for trouble! When he sent for my wives and my children, my silver and my gold, I did not refuse him."

⁸The elders and the people all answered, "Don't listen to him or agree to his demands."

⁹So he replied to Ben-Hadad's messengers, "Tell my lord the king, 'Your servant will do all you demanded the first time, but this demand I cannot meet.'" They left and took the answer back to Ben-Hadad.

¹⁰Then Ben-Hadad sent another message to Ahab: "May the gods deal with me, be it ever so severely, if enough dust remains in Samaria to give each of my men a handful."

¹¹The king of Israel answered, "Tell him: 'One who puts on his armor should not boast like one who takes it off.'"

¹²Ben-Hadad heard this message while he and the kings were drinking in their tents,ᵃ and he ordered his men: "Prepare to attack." So they prepared to attack the city.

Ahab Defeats Ben-Hadad

¹³Meanwhile a prophet came to Ahab king of Israel and announced, "This is what the LORD says: 'Do you see this vast army? I will give it into your hand today, and then you will know that I am the LORD.'"

¹⁴"But who will do this?" asked Ahab.

The prophet replied, "This is what the LORD says: 'The junior officers under the provincial commanders will do it.'"

"And who will start the battle?" he asked.

The prophet answered, "You will."

¹⁵So Ahab summoned the 232 junior officers under the provincial commanders. Then he assembled the rest of the Israelites, 7,000 in all. ¹⁶They set out at noon while Ben-Hadad and the 32 kings allied with him were in their tents getting drunk. ¹⁷The junior officers under the provincial commanders went out first.

Now Ben-Hadad had dispatched scouts, who reported, "Men are advancing from Samaria."

¹⁸He said, "If they have come out for peace, take them alive; if they have come out for war, take them alive."

¹⁹The junior officers under the provincial commanders marched out of the city with the army behind them ²⁰and each one struck down his opponent. At that, the Arameans fled, with the Israelites in pursuit. But Ben-Hadad king of Aram escaped on horseback with some of his horsemen. ²¹The king of Israel advanced and overpowered the horses and chariots and inflicted heavy losses on the Arameans.

²²Afterward, the prophet came to the king of Israel and said, "Strengthen your position and see what must be done, because next spring the king of Aram will attack you again."

²³Meanwhile, the officials of the king of Aram advised him, "Their gods are gods of the hills. That is why they were too strong for us. But if we fight them on the plains, surely we will be stronger than they. ²⁴Do this: Remove all the kings

ᵃ 12 Or *in Sukkoth*; also in verse 16

from their commands and replace them with other officers. ²⁵You must also raise an army like the one you lost—horse for horse and chariot for chariot—so we can fight Israel on the plains. Then surely we will be stronger than they." He agreed with them and acted accordingly.

²⁶The next spring Ben-Hadad mustered the Arameans and went up to Aphek to fight against Israel. ²⁷When the Israelites were also mustered and given provisions, they marched out to meet them. The Israelites camped opposite them like two small flocks of goats, while the Arameans covered the countryside.

²⁸The man of God came up and told the king of Israel, "This is what the LORD says: 'Because the Arameans think the LORD is a god of the hills and not a god of the valleys, I will deliver this vast army into your hands, and you will know that I am the LORD.'"

²⁹For seven days they camped opposite each other, and on the seventh day the battle was joined. The Israelites inflicted a hundred thousand casualties on the Aramean foot soldiers in one day. ³⁰The rest of them escaped to the city of Aphek, where the wall collapsed on twenty-seven thousand of them. And Ben-Hadad fled to the city and hid in an inner room.

³¹His officials said to him, "Look, we have heard that the kings of Israel are merciful. Let us go to the king of Israel with sackcloth around our waists and ropes around our heads. Perhaps he will spare your life."

³²Wearing sackcloth around their waists and ropes around their heads, they went to the king of Israel and said, "Your servant Ben-Hadad says: 'Please let me live.'"

The king answered, "Is he still alive? He is my brother."

³³The men took this as a good sign and were quick to pick up his word. "Yes, your brother Ben-Hadad!" they said.

"Go and get him," the king said. When Ben-Hadad came out, Ahab had him come up into his chariot.

³⁴"I will return the cities my father took from your father," Ben-Hadad offered.

"You may set up your own market areas in Damascus, as my father did in Samaria."

Ahab said, "On the basis of a treaty I will set you free." So he made a treaty with him, and let him go.

A Prophet Condemns Ahab

³⁵By the word of the LORD one of the company of the prophets said to his companion, "Strike me with your weapon," but he refused.

³⁶So the prophet said, "Because you have not obeyed the LORD, as soon as you leave me a lion will kill you." And after the man went away, a lion found him and killed him.

³⁷The prophet found another man and said, "Strike me, please." So the man struck him and wounded him. ³⁸Then the prophet went and stood by the road waiting for the king. He disguised himself with his headband down over his eyes. ³⁹As the king passed by, the prophet called out to him, "Your servant went into the thick of the battle, and someone came to me with a captive and said, 'Guard this man. If he is missing, it will be your life for his life, or you must pay a talent[a] of silver.' ⁴⁰While your servant was busy here and there, the man disappeared."

"That is your sentence," the king of Israel said. "You have pronounced it yourself."

⁴¹Then the prophet quickly removed the headband from his eyes, and the king of Israel recognized him as one of the prophets. ⁴²He said to the king, "This is what the LORD says: 'You have set free a man I had determined should die.[b] Therefore it is your life for his life, your people for his people.'" ⁴³Sullen and angry, the king of Israel went to his palace in Samaria.

Naboth's Vineyard

21 Some time later there was an incident involving a vineyard belonging to Naboth the Jezreelite. The vineyard was in Jezreel, close

---

^a 39 That is, about 75 pounds or about 34 kilograms   ^b 42 The Hebrew term refers to the irrevocable giving over of things or persons to the LORD, often by totally destroying them.

to the palace of Ahab king of Samaria. ²Ahab said to Naboth, "Let me have your vineyard to use for a vegetable garden, since it is close to my palace. In exchange I will give you a better vineyard or, if you prefer, I will pay you whatever it is worth." ³But Naboth replied, "The LORD forbid that I should give you the inheritance of my ancestors."

⁴So Ahab went home, sullen and angry because Naboth the Jezreelite had said, "I will not give you the inheritance of my ancestors." He lay on his bed sulking and refused to eat.

⁵His wife Jezebel came in and asked him, "Why are you so sullen? Why won't you eat?"

⁶He answered her, "Because I said to Naboth the Jezreelite, 'Sell me your vineyard; or if you prefer, I will give you another vineyard in its place.' But he said, 'I will not give you my vineyard.'"

⁷Jezebel his wife said, "Is this how you act as king over Israel? Get up and eat! Cheer up. I'll get you the vineyard of Naboth the Jezreelite."

⁸So she wrote letters in Ahab's name, placed his seal on them, and sent them to the elders and nobles who lived in Naboth's city with him. ⁹In those letters she wrote:

> "Proclaim a day of fasting and seat Naboth in a prominent place among the people. ¹⁰But seat two scoundrels opposite him and have them bring charges that he has cursed both God and the king. Then take him out and stone him to death."

¹¹So the elders and nobles who lived in Naboth's city did as Jezebel directed in the letters she had written to them. ¹²They proclaimed a fast and seated Naboth in a prominent place among the people. ¹³Then two scoundrels came and sat opposite him and brought charges against Naboth before the people, saying, "Naboth has cursed both God and the king." So they took him outside the city and stoned him to death. ¹⁴Then they sent word to Jezebel: "Naboth has been stoned to death."

¹⁵As soon as Jezebel heard that Naboth had been stoned to death, she said to Ahab, "Get up and take possession of the vineyard of Naboth the Jezreelite that he refused to sell you. He is no longer alive, but dead." ¹⁶When Ahab heard that Naboth was dead, he got up and went down to take possession of Naboth's vineyard.

¹⁷Then the word of the LORD came to Elijah the Tishbite: ¹⁸"Go down to meet Ahab king of Israel, who rules in Samaria. He is now in Naboth's vineyard, where he has gone to take possession of it. ¹⁹Say to him, 'This is what the LORD says: Have you not murdered a man and seized his property?' Then say to him, 'This is what the LORD says: In the place where dogs licked up Naboth's blood, dogs will lick up your blood—yes, yours!'"

²⁰Ahab said to Elijah, "So you have found me, my enemy!"

"I have found you," he answered, "because you have sold yourself to do evil in the eyes of the LORD. ²¹He says, 'I am going to bring disaster on you. I will wipe out your descendants and cut off from Ahab every last male in Israel—slave or free.ᵃ ²²I will make your house like that of Jeroboam son of Nebat and that of Baasha son of Ahijah, because you have aroused my anger and have caused Israel to sin.'

²³"And also concerning Jezebel the LORD says: 'Dogs will devour Jezebel by the wall ofᵇ Jezreel.'

²⁴"Dogs will eat those belonging to Ahab who die in the city, and the birds will feed on those who die in the country."

²⁵(There was never anyone like Ahab, who sold himself to do evil in the eyes of the LORD, urged on by Jezebel his wife. ²⁶He behaved in the vilest manner by going after idols, like the Amorites the LORD drove out before Israel.)

²⁷When Ahab heard these words, he tore his clothes, put on sackcloth and fasted. He lay in sackcloth and went around meekly.

ᵃ 21 Or *Israel—every ruler or leader*
ᵇ 23 Most Hebrew manuscripts; a few Hebrew manuscripts, Vulgate and Syriac (see also 2 Kings 9:26) *the plot of ground at*

²⁸Then the word of the LORD came to Elijah the Tishbite: ²⁹"Have you noticed how Ahab has humbled himself before me? Because he has humbled himself, I will not bring this disaster in his day, but I will bring it on his house in the days of his son."

Micaiah Prophesies Against Ahab

22 For three years there was no war between Aram and Israel. ²But in the third year Jehoshaphat king of Judah went down to see the king of Israel. ³The king of Israel had said to his officials, "Don't you know that Ramoth Gilead belongs to us and yet we are doing nothing to retake it from the king of Aram?"

⁴So he asked Jehoshaphat, "Will you go with me to fight against Ramoth Gilead?"

Jehoshaphat replied to the king of Israel, "I am as you are, my people as your people, my horses as your horses." ⁵But Jehoshaphat also said to the king of Israel, "First seek the counsel of the LORD."

⁶So the king of Israel brought together the prophets—about four hundred men—and asked them, "Shall I go to war against Ramoth Gilead, or shall I refrain?"

"Go," they answered, "for the Lord will give it into the king's hand."

⁷But Jehoshaphat asked, "Is there no longer a prophet of the LORD here whom we can inquire of?"

⁸The king of Israel answered Jehoshaphat, "There is still one prophet through whom we can inquire of the LORD, but I hate him because he never prophesies anything good about me, but always bad. He is Micaiah son of Imlah."

"The king should not say such a thing," Jehoshaphat replied.

⁹So the king of Israel called one of his officials and said, "Bring Micaiah son of Imlah at once."

¹⁰Dressed in their royal robes, the king of Israel and Jehoshaphat king of Judah were sitting on their thrones at the threshing floor by the entrance of the gate of Samaria, with all the prophets prophesying before them. ¹¹Now Zedekiah son of Kenaanah had made iron horns and he declared, "This is what the LORD says: 'With these you will gore the Arameans until they are destroyed.'"

¹²All the other prophets were prophesying the same thing. "Attack Ramoth Gilead and be victorious," they said, "for the LORD will give it into the king's hand."

¹³The messenger who had gone to summon Micaiah said to him, "Look, the other prophets without exception are predicting success for the king. Let your word agree with theirs, and speak favorably."

¹⁴But Micaiah said, "As surely as the LORD lives, I can tell him only what the LORD tells me."

¹⁵When he arrived, the king asked him, "Micaiah, shall we go to war against Ramoth Gilead, or not?"

"Attack and be victorious," he answered, "for the LORD will give it into the king's hand."

¹⁶The king said to him, "How many times must I make you swear to tell me nothing but the truth in the name of the LORD?"

¹⁷Then Micaiah answered, "I saw all Israel scattered on the hills like sheep without a shepherd, and the LORD said, 'These people have no master. Let each one go home in peace.'"

¹⁸The king of Israel said to Jehoshaphat, "Didn't I tell you that he never prophesies anything good about me, but only bad?"

¹⁹Micaiah continued, "Therefore hear the word of the LORD: I saw the LORD sitting on his throne with all the multitudes of heaven standing around him on his right and on his left. ²⁰And the LORD said, 'Who will entice Ahab into attacking Ramoth Gilead and going to his death there?'

"One suggested this, and another that. ²¹Finally, a spirit came forward, stood before the LORD and said, 'I will entice him.'

²²"'By what means?' the LORD asked.

"'I will go out and be a deceiving spirit in the mouths of all his prophets,' he said.

"'You will succeed in enticing him,' said the LORD. 'Go and do it.'

²³"So now the LORD has put a deceiving

spirit in the mouths of all these prophets of yours. The LORD has decreed disaster for you."

24Then Zedekiah son of Kenaanah went up and slapped Micaiah in the face. "Which way did the spirit from*a* the LORD go when he went from me to speak to you?" he asked.

25Micaiah replied, "You will find out on the day you go to hide in an inner room."

26The king of Israel then ordered, "Take Micaiah and send him back to Amon the ruler of the city and to Joash the king's son 27and say, 'This is what the king says: Put this fellow in prison and give him nothing but bread and water until I return safely.'"

28Micaiah declared, "If you ever return safely, the LORD has not spoken through me." Then he added, "Mark my words, all you people!"

Ahab Killed at Ramoth Gilead

29So the king of Israel and Jehoshaphat king of Judah went up to Ramoth Gilead. 30The king of Israel said to Jehoshaphat, "I will enter the battle in disguise, but you wear your royal robes." So the king of Israel disguised himself and went into battle.

31Now the king of Aram had ordered his thirty-two chariot commanders, "Do not fight with anyone, small or great, except the king of Israel." 32When the chariot commanders saw Jehoshaphat, they thought, "Surely this is the king of Israel." So they turned to attack him, but when Jehoshaphat cried out, 33the chariot commanders saw that he was not the king of Israel and stopped pursuing him.

34But someone drew his bow at random and hit the king of Israel between the sections of his armor. The king told his chariot driver, "Wheel around and get me out of the fighting. I've been wounded." 35All day long the battle raged, and the king was propped up in his chariot facing the Arameans. The blood from his wound ran onto the floor of the chariot, and that evening he died. 36As the sun was setting, a cry spread through the army: "Every man to his town. Every man to his land!"

37So the king died and was brought to Samaria, and they buried him there. 38They washed the chariot at a pool in Samaria (where the prostitutes bathed),*b* and the dogs licked up his blood, as the word of the LORD had declared.

39As for the other events of Ahab's reign, including all he did, the palace he built and adorned with ivory, and the cities he fortified, are they not written in the book of the annals of the kings of Israel? 40Ahab rested with his ancestors. And Ahaziah his son succeeded him as king.

Jehoshaphat King of Judah

41Jehoshaphat son of Asa became king of Judah in the fourth year of Ahab king of Israel. 42Jehoshaphat was thirty-five years old when he became king, and he reigned in Jerusalem twenty-five years. His mother's name was Azubah daughter of Shilhi. 43In everything he followed the ways of his father Asa and did not stray from them; he did what was right in the eyes of the LORD. The high places, however, were not removed, and the people continued to offer sacrifices and burn incense there.*c* 44Jehoshaphat was also at peace with the king of Israel.

45As for the other events of Jehoshaphat's reign, the things he achieved and his military exploits, are they not written in the book of the annals of the kings of Judah? 46He rid the land of the rest of the male shrine prostitutes who remained there even after the reign of his father Asa. 47There was then no king in Edom; a provincial governor ruled.

48Now Jehoshaphat built a fleet of trading ships*d* to go to Ophir for gold, but they never set sail—they were wrecked at Ezion Geber. 49At that time Ahaziah son of Ahab said to Jehoshaphat, "Let my men sail with yours," but Jehoshaphat refused.

50Then Jehoshaphat rested with his

---

a 24 Or *Spirit of*   *b 38* Or *Samaria and cleaned the weapons*   *c 43* In Hebrew texts this sentence (22:43b) is numbered 22:44, and 22:44-53 is numbered 22:45-54.   *d 48* Hebrew *of ships of Tarshish* ancestors and was buried with them in the city of David his father. And Jehoram his son succeeded him as king.

Ahaziah King of Israel

51 Ahaziah son of Ahab became king of Israel in Samaria in the seventeenth year of Jehoshaphat king of Judah, and he reigned over Israel two years. 52 He did evil in the eyes of the LORD, because he followed the ways of his father and mother and of Jeroboam son of Nebat, who caused Israel to sin. 53 He served and worshiped Baal and aroused the anger of the LORD, the God of Israel, just as his father had done.

2 KINGS

BOOK OUTLINE

Elijah and Elisha
(1:1 — 8:15)

Kings of Israel and Judah
(8:16 — 17:6)

Israel taken captive to Assyria
(17:7 — 41)

Judah survives Assyrian rule
(18:1 — 23:37)

Judah taken captive to Babylonia
(24:1 — 25:30)

Second Kings continues the stories of the great prophets Elijah and Elisha. It records the history of the northern kingdom of Israel and the southern kingdom of Judah until they were both finally conquered. Israel was conquered by Assyria in 722 BC and Judah was conquered by the Babylonians in 586 BC. In both kingdoms God's prophets continually warned the people that God would punish them if they did not repent from their sins.

The Lord's Judgment on Ahaziah

After Ahab's death, Moab rebelled against Israel. ²Now Ahaziah had fallen through the lattice of his upper room in Samaria and injured himself. So he sent messengers, saying to them, "Go and consult Baal-Zebub, the god of Ekron, to see if I will recover from this injury."

³But the angel of the Lord said to Elijah the Tishbite, "Go up and meet the messengers of the king of Samaria and ask them, 'Is it because there is no God in Israel that you are going off to consult Baal-Zebub, the god of Ekron?' ⁴Therefore this is what the Lord says: 'You will not leave the bed you are lying on. You will certainly die!'" So Elijah went.

⁵When the messengers returned to the king, he asked them, "Why have you come back?"

⁶"A man came to meet us," they replied. "And he said to us, 'Go back to the king who sent you and tell him, "This is what the Lord says: Is it because there is no God in Israel that you are sending messengers to consult Baal-Zebub, the god of Ekron? Therefore you will not leave the bed you are lying on. You will certainly die!"'"

⁷The king asked them, "What kind of man was it who came to meet you and told you this?"

⁸They replied, "He had a garment of hairᵃ and had a leather belt around his waist."

The king said, "That was Elijah the Tishbite."

⁹Then he sent to Elijah a captain with his company of fifty men. The captain went up to Elijah, who was sitting on the top of a hill, and said to him, "Man of God, the king says, 'Come down!'"

¹⁰Elijah answered the captain, "If I am a man of God, may fire come down from heaven and consume you and your fifty men!" Then fire fell from heaven and consumed the captain and his men.

¹¹At this the king sent to Elijah another captain with his fifty men. The captain said to him, "Man of God, this is what the king says, 'Come down at once!'"

¹²"If I am a man of God," Elijah replied, "may fire come down from heaven and consume you and your fifty men!" Then the fire of God fell from heaven and consumed him and his fifty men.

¹³So the king sent a third captain with his fifty men. This third captain went up and fell on his knees before Elijah. "Man of God," he begged, "please have respect for my life and the lives of these fifty men, your servants! ¹⁴See, fire has fallen from heaven and consumed the first two captains and all their men. But now have respect for my life!"

¹⁵The angel of the Lord said to Elijah, "Go down with him; do not be afraid of him." So Elijah got up and went down with him to the king.

¹⁶He told the king, "This is what the Lord says: Is it because there is no God in Israel for you to consult that you have sent messengers to consult Baal-Zebub, the god of Ekron? Because you have done this, you will never leave the bed you are lying on. You will certainly die!" ¹⁷So he died, according to the word of the Lord that Elijah had spoken.

Because Ahaziah had no son, Joramᵇ succeeded him as king in the second year of Jehoram son of Jehoshaphat king of Judah. ¹⁸As for all the other events of Ahaziah's reign, and what he did, are they not written in the book of the annals of the kings of Israel?

Elijah Taken Up to Heaven

When the Lord was about to take Elijah up to heaven in a whirlwind, Elijah and Elisha were on their way from Gilgal. ²Elijah said to Elisha, "Stay here; the Lord has sent me to Bethel."

But Elisha said, "As surely as the Lord lives and as you live, I will not leave you." So they went down to Bethel.

³The company of the prophets at Bethel came out to Elisha and asked, "Do you know that the Lord is going to take your master from you today?"

ᵃ 8 Or *He was a hairy man*   ᵇ 17 Hebrew *Jehoram*, a variant of *Joram*

"Yes, I know," Elisha replied, "so be quiet."

⁴Then Elijah said to him, "Stay here, Elisha; the LORD has sent me to Jericho."

And he replied, "As surely as the LORD lives and as you live, I will not leave you." So they went to Jericho.

⁵The company of the prophets at Jericho went up to Elisha and asked him, "Do you know that the LORD is going to take your master from you today?"

"Yes, I know," he replied, "so be quiet."

⁶Then Elijah said to him, "Stay here; the LORD has sent me to the Jordan."

And he replied, "As surely as the LORD

lives and as you live, I will not leave you." So the two of them walked on.

⁷Fifty men from the company of the prophets went and stood at a distance, facing the place where Elijah and Elisha had stopped at the Jordan. ⁸Elijah took his cloak, rolled it up and struck the water with it. The water divided to the right and to the left, and the two of them crossed over on dry ground.

⁹When they had crossed, Elijah said to Elisha, "Tell me, what can I do for you before I am taken from you?"

"Let me inherit a double portion of your spirit," Elisha replied.

2 Kings 1:1–18
Elijah stood up to a sinful nation.

Elijah began his ministry as a prophet by starting a whopping fight. He walked into the courts of one of Israel's most evil kings and declared no rain would fall until he himself prayed to God to send rain (1 Kings 17:1). His proclamation was all the more daring because Ahab worshiped a false god, Baal, who was believed to control the rain (see 1 Kings 31–32).

Three years later not a drop of rain had fallen, and Elijah challenged hundreds of Baal's prophets to a showdown on top of Mount Carmel. Each side was to pray down fire from heaven to consume a sacrifice, a public test to prove whether God or Baal was more powerful. Baal's prophets danced up a sweat with no success, but a simple prayer from Elijah brought down holy fire that burned up not only the sacrifice but also a rock altar. The people of Israel rose up and slaughtered Baal's priests, and God immediately sent rain (see 1 Kings 18:16–46).

Elijah is remembered as one of Israel's most significant prophets because he boldly stood against some of the nation's worst rulers. Despite his important calling, Elijah sometimes slipped into deep depression, complaining at one point that he was the only Israelite left who followed God (see 1 Kings 19:9–19).

At the end of his life, Elijah was swept up to God in a whirlwind (see 2 Kings 2:1–12). And in the New Testament, Elijah stood alongside Moses as Jesus shone with heavenly brilliance (see Matthew 17:3).

You can find Elijah in 1 Kings 17 to 2 Kings 2; Matthew 16:14; John 1:21; Romans 11:2; and James 5:17.

UNSHAKEN people

¹⁰"You have asked a difficult thing," Elijah said, "yet if you see me when I am taken from you, it will be yours—otherwise, it will not."

¹¹As they were walking along and talking together, suddenly a chariot of fire and horses of fire appeared and separated the two of them, and Elijah went up to heaven in a whirlwind. ¹²Elisha saw this and cried out, "My father! My father! The chariots and horsemen of Israel!" And Elisha saw him no more. Then he took hold of his garment and tore it in two.

¹³Elisha then picked up Elijah's cloak that had fallen from him and went back and stood on the bank of the Jordan. ¹⁴He took the cloak that had fallen from Elijah and struck the water with it. "Where now is the LORD, the God of Elijah?" he asked. When he struck the water, it divided to the right and to the left, and he crossed over.

¹⁵The company of the prophets from Jericho, who were watching, said, "The spirit of Elijah is resting on Elisha." And they went to meet him and bowed to the ground before him. ¹⁶"Look," they said, "we your servants have fifty able men. Let them go and look for your master. Perhaps the Spirit of the LORD has picked him up and set him down on some mountain or in some valley."

"No," Elisha replied, "do not send them."

¹⁷But they persisted until he was too embarrassed to refuse. So he said, "Send them." And they sent fifty men, who searched for three days but did not find him. ¹⁸When they returned to Elisha, who was staying in Jericho, he said to them, "Didn't I tell you not to go?"

Healing of the Water

¹⁹The people of the city said to Elisha, "Look, our lord, this town is well situated, as you can see, but the water is bad and the land is unproductive."

²⁰"Bring me a new bowl," he said, "and put salt in it." So they brought it to him.

ROCK SOLID principles

2 Kings 2:1–17

Find partners in ministry.

Hunter dreamed of doing something about the racial divides he saw in his urban school. His classmates spoke a couple dozen languages—and came from nearly three dozen nations. Yet everyone shuffled through school in their own ethnic groups, never interacting except for accidental bumps and occasional fights. One day Hunter mumbled in social studies how sad it was that the school's groups barely knew each other. He didn't say it, but he also thought that as a Christian he should be reaching out to people different than himself. When Hunter saw nothing but blank faces, he assumed his thoughts had fallen with a thud to the floor. Then Tristan stopped him after class. He wanted to talk.

When Elijah was at his most lost and lonely, God promised him a helper. The Lord sent Elisha to work alongside Elijah and one day take his place (see 1 Kings 19:16). Elijah discovered God doesn't expect us to serve him alone. If it feels like you are the only one serving God, pray for help. Then look around for God's answer.

²¹Then he went out to the spring and threw the salt into it, saying, "This is what the Lord says: 'I have healed this water. Never again will it cause death or make the land unproductive.'" ²²And the water has remained pure to this day, according to the word Elisha had spoken.

Elisha Is Jeered

²³From there Elisha went up to Bethel. As he was walking along the road, some boys came out of the town and jeered at him. "Get out of here, baldy!" they said. "Get out of here, baldy!" ²⁴He turned around, looked at them and called down a curse on them in the name of the Lord. Then two bears came out of the woods and mauled forty-two of the boys. ²⁵And he went on to Mount Carmel and from there returned to Samaria.

Moab Revolts

3 Joram*a* son of Ahab became king of Israel in Samaria in the eighteenth year of Jehoshaphat king of Judah, and he reigned twelve years. ²He did evil in the eyes of the Lord, but not as his father and mother had done. He got rid of the sacred stone of Baal that his father had made. ³Nevertheless he clung to the sins of Jeroboam son of Nebat, which he had caused Israel to commit; he did not turn away from them.

⁴Now Mesha king of Moab raised sheep, and he had to pay the king of Israel a tribute of a hundred thousand lambs and the wool of a hundred thousand rams. ⁵But after Ahab died, the king of Moab rebelled against the king of Israel. ⁶So at that time King Joram set out from Samaria and mobilized all Israel. ⁷He also sent this message to Jehoshaphat king of Judah: "The king of Moab has rebelled against me. Will you go with me to fight against Moab?"

"I will go with you," he replied. "I am as you are, my people as your people, my horses as your horses."

⁸"By what route shall we attack?" he asked.

"Through the Desert of Edom," he answered.

⁹So the king of Israel set out with the king of Judah and the king of Edom. After a roundabout march of seven days, the army had no more water for themselves or for the animals with them.

¹⁰"What!" exclaimed the king of Israel. "Has the Lord called us three kings together only to deliver us into the hands of Moab?"

¹¹But Jehoshaphat asked, "Is there no prophet of the Lord here, through whom we may inquire of the Lord?"

An officer of the king of Israel answered, "Elisha son of Shaphat is here. He used to pour water on the hands of Elijah.*b*"

¹²Jehoshaphat said, "The word of the Lord is with him." So the king of Israel and Jehoshaphat and the king of Edom went down to him.

¹³Elisha said to the king of Israel, "Why do you want to involve me? Go to the prophets of your father and the prophets of your mother."

"No," the king of Israel answered, "because it was the Lord who called us three kings together to deliver us into the hands of Moab."

¹⁴Elisha said, "As surely as the Lord Almighty lives, whom I serve, if I did not have respect for the presence of Jehoshaphat king of Judah, I would not pay any attention to you. ¹⁵But now bring me a harpist."

While the harpist was playing, the hand of the Lord came on Elisha ¹⁶and he said, "This is what the Lord says: I will fill this valley with pools of water. ¹⁷For this is what the Lord says: You will see neither wind nor rain, yet this valley will be filled with water, and you, your cattle and your other animals will drink. ¹⁸This is an easy thing in the eyes of the Lord; he will also deliver Moab into your hands. ¹⁹You will overthrow every fortified city and every major town. You will cut down every good tree, stop up all the springs, and ruin every good field with stones."

---

a 1 Hebrew *Jehoram*, a variant of *Joram*; also in verse 6   *b 11* That is, he was Elijah's personal servant.

²⁰The next morning, about the time for offering the sacrifice, there it was—water flowing from the direction of Edom! And the land was filled with water.

²¹Now all the Moabites had heard that the kings had come to fight against them; so every man, young and old, who could bear arms was called up and stationed on the border. ²²When they got up early in the morning, the sun was shining on the water. To the Moabites across the way, the water looked red—like blood. ²³"That's blood!" they said. "Those kings must have fought and slaughtered each other. Now to the plunder, Moab!"

²⁴But when the Moabites came to the camp of Israel, the Israelites rose up and fought them until they fled. And the Israelites invaded the land and slaughtered the Moabites. ²⁵They destroyed the towns, and each man threw a stone on every good field until it was covered. They stopped up all the springs and cut down every good tree. Only Kir Hareseth was left with its stones in place, but men armed with slings surrounded it and attacked it.

²⁶When the king of Moab saw that the battle had gone against him, he took with him seven hundred swordsmen to break through to the king of Edom, but they failed. ²⁷Then he took his firstborn son, who was to succeed him as king, and offered him as a sacrifice on the city wall. The fury against Israel was great; they withdrew and returned to their own land.

The Widow's Olive Oil

4 The wife of a man from the company of the prophets cried out to Elisha, "Your servant my husband is dead, and you know that he revered the Lord. But now his creditor is coming to take my two boys as his slaves."

²Elisha replied to her, "How can I help you? Tell me, what do you have in your house?"

"Your servant has nothing there at all," she said, "except a small jar of olive oil."

³Elisha said, "Go around and ask all your neighbors for empty jars. Don't ask for just a few. ⁴Then go inside and shut the door behind you and your sons. Pour oil into all the jars, and as each is filled, put it to one side."

⁵She left him and shut the door behind her and her sons. They brought the jars to her and she kept pouring. ⁶When all the jars were full, she said to her son, "Bring me another one."

But he replied, "There is not a jar left." Then the oil stopped flowing.

⁷She went and told the man of God, and he said, "Go, sell the oil and pay your debts. You and your sons can live on what is left."

The Shunammite's Son Restored to Life

⁸One day Elisha went to Shunem. And a well-to-do woman was there, who urged him to stay for a meal. So whenever he came by, he stopped there to eat. ⁹She said to her husband, "I know that this man who often comes our way is a holy man of God. ¹⁰Let's make a small room on the roof and put in it a bed and a table, a chair and a lamp for him. Then he can stay there whenever he comes to us."

¹¹One day when Elisha came, he went up to his room and lay down there. ¹²He said to his servant Gehazi, "Call the Shunammite." So he called her, and she stood before him. ¹³Elisha said to him, "Tell her, 'You have gone to all this trouble for us. Now what can be done for you? Can we speak on your behalf to the king or the commander of the army?'"

She replied, "I have a home among my own people."

¹⁴"What can be done for her?" Elisha asked.

Gehazi said, "She has no son, and her husband is old."

¹⁵Then Elisha said, "Call her." So he called her, and she stood in the doorway. ¹⁶"About this time next year," Elisha said, "you will hold a son in your arms."

"No, my lord!" she objected. "Please, man of God, don't mislead your servant!"

¹⁷But the woman became pregnant, and the next year about that same time she gave birth to a son, just as Elisha had told her.

¹⁸The child grew, and one day he went out to his father, who was with the reapers. ¹⁹He said to his father, "My head! My head!"

His father told a servant, "Carry him to his mother." ²⁰After the servant had lifted him up and carried him to his mother, the boy sat on her lap until noon, and then he died. ²¹She went up and laid him on the bed of the man of God, then shut the door and went out.

²²She called her husband and said, "Please send me one of the servants and a donkey so I can go to the man of God quickly and return."

²³"Why go to him today?" he asked. "It's not the New Moon or the Sabbath."

"That's all right," she said.

²⁴She saddled the donkey and said to her servant, "Lead on; don't slow down for me unless I tell you." ²⁵So she set out and came to the man of God at Mount Carmel.

When he saw her in the distance, the man of God said to his servant Gehazi, "Look! There's the Shunammite! ²⁶Run to meet her and ask her, 'Are you all right? Is your husband all right? Is your child all right?'"

"Everything is all right," she said.

²⁷When she reached the man of God at the mountain, she took hold of his feet. Gehazi came over to push her away, but the man of God said, "Leave her alone! She is in bitter distress, but the LORD has hidden it from me and has not told me why."

²⁸"Did I ask you for a son, my lord?" she said. "Didn't I tell you, 'Don't raise my hopes'?"

²⁹Elisha said to Gehazi, "Tuck your cloak into your belt, take my staff in your hand and run. Don't greet anyone you meet, and if anyone greets you, do not answer. Lay my staff on the boy's face."

³⁰But the child's mother said, "As surely as the LORD lives and as you live, I will not leave you." So he got up and followed her.

³¹Gehazi went on ahead and laid the staff on the boy's face, but there was no sound or response. So Gehazi went back to meet Elisha and told him, "The boy has not awakened."

³²When Elisha reached the house, there was the boy lying dead on his couch. ³³He went in, shut the door on the two of them and prayed to the LORD. ³⁴Then he got on the bed and lay on the boy, mouth to mouth, eyes to eyes, hands to hands. As he stretched himself out on him, the boy's body grew warm. ³⁵Elisha turned away and walked back and forth in the room and then got on the bed and stretched out on him once more. The boy sneezed seven times and opened his eyes.

³⁶Elisha summoned Gehazi and said, "Call the Shunammite." And he did. When she came, he said, "Take your son." ³⁷She came in, fell at his feet and bowed to the ground. Then she took her son and went out.

Death in the Pot

³⁸Elisha returned to Gilgal and there was a famine in that region. While the company of the prophets was meeting with him, he said to his servant, "Put on the large pot and cook some stew for these prophets."

³⁹One of them went out into the fields to gather herbs and found a wild vine and picked as many of its gourds as his garment could hold. When he returned, he cut them up into the pot of stew, though no one knew what they were. ⁴⁰The stew was poured out for the men, but as they began to eat it, they cried out, "Man of God, there is death in the pot!" And they could not eat it.

⁴¹Elisha said, "Get some flour." He put it into the pot and said, "Serve it to the people to eat." And there was nothing harmful in the pot.

Feeding of a Hundred

⁴²A man came from Baal Shalishah, bringing the man of God twenty loaves of barley bread baked from the first ripe grain, along with some heads of new grain. "Give it to the people to eat," Elisha said.

⁴³"How can I set this before a hundred men?" his servant asked.

But Elisha answered, "Give it to the

people to eat. For this is what the LORD says: 'They will eat and have some left over.'" ⁴⁴Then he set it before them, and they ate and had some left over, according to the word of the LORD.

Naaman Healed of Leprosy

5 Now Naaman was commander of the army of the king of Aram. He was a great man in the sight of his master and highly regarded, because through him the LORD had given victory to Aram. He was a valiant soldier, but he had leprosy.ᵃ

²Now bands of raiders from Aram had gone out and had taken captive a young girl from Israel, and she served Naaman's wife. ³She said to her mistress, "If only my master would see the prophet who is in Samaria! He would cure him of his leprosy."

⁴Naaman went to his master and told him what the girl from Israel had said. ⁵"By all means, go," the king of Aram replied. "I will send a letter to the king of Israel." So Naaman left, taking with him ten talentsᵇ of silver, six thousand shekelsᶜ of gold and ten sets of clothing. ⁶The letter that he took to the king of Israel read: "With this letter I am sending my servant Naaman to you so that you may cure him of his leprosy."

⁷As soon as the king of Israel read the letter, he tore his robes and said, "Am I God? Can I kill and bring back to life? Why does this fellow send someone to me to be cured of his leprosy? See how he is trying to pick a quarrel with me!"

⁸When Elisha the man of God heard that the king of Israel had torn his robes, he sent him this message: "Why have you torn your robes? Have the man come to me and he will know that there is a prophet in Israel." ⁹So Naaman went with his horses and chariots and stopped at the door of Elisha's house. ¹⁰Elisha sent a messenger to say to him, "Go, wash yourself seven times in the Jordan, and your flesh will be restored and you will be cleansed."

¹¹But Naaman went away angry and said, "I thought that he would surely come out to me and stand and call on the name of the LORD his God, wave his hand over the spot and cure me of my leprosy. ¹²Are not Abana and Pharpar, the rivers of Damascus, better than all the waters of Israel? Couldn't I wash in them and be cleansed?" So he turned and went off in a rage.

¹³Naaman's servants went to him and said, "My father, if the prophet had told you to do some great thing, would you not have done it? How much more, then, when he tells you, 'Wash and be cleansed'!" ¹⁴So he went down and dipped himself in the Jordan seven times, as the man of God had told him, and his flesh was restored and became clean like that of a young boy.

¹⁵Then Naaman and all his attendants went back to the man of God. He stood before him and said, "Now I know that there is no God in all the world except in Israel. So please accept a gift from your servant."

¹⁶The prophet answered, "As surely as the LORD lives, whom I serve, I will not accept a thing." And even though Naaman urged him, he refused.

¹⁷"If you will not," said Naaman, "please let me, your servant, be given as much earth as a pair of mules can carry, for your servant will never again make burnt offerings and sacrifices to any other god but the LORD. ¹⁸But may the LORD forgive your servant for this one thing: When my master enters the temple of Rimmon to bow down and he is leaning on my arm and I have to bow there also—when I bow down in the temple of Rimmon, may the LORD forgive your servant for this."

¹⁹"Go in peace," Elisha said.

After Naaman had traveled some distance, ²⁰Gehazi, the servant of Elisha the man of God, said to himself, "My master was too easy on Naaman, this Aramean, by not accepting from him what he brought. As surely as the LORD lives, I will run after him and get something from him."

ᵃ *1* The Hebrew for *leprosy* was used for various diseases affecting the skin; also in verses 3, 6, 7, 11 and 27.   ᵇ *5* That is, about 750 pounds or about 340 kilograms   ᶜ *5* That is, about 150 pounds or about 69 kilograms

2 Kings 5:1–19

God's commands aren't as crazy as they sound.

Naaman was furious. He was commander of the entire army of the nation of Aram, and he had traveled to Israel with an enormous fortune intending to buy a cure to his leprosy, a terrible skin condition. He showed up with his chariot and horses at Elisha's door, but the prophet wouldn't even speak to Naaman. Instead of saying a mighty prayer, Elisha sent the general to wash in the murky Jordan River. Naaman wanted nothing to do with what seemed like a ridiculous command—until his servants persuaded him to give the instructions a try. And Naaman was shocked when he was suddenly healed. That's how it often works with God's commands. Obeying the Lord can seem absolutely foolish, until you try to do life God's way—and find out it works.

Think: When has one of God's commands seemed crazy to you—but you obeyed anyway? What happened?

ROCK SOLID *truths*

21 So Gehazi hurried after Naaman. When Naaman saw him running toward him, he got down from the chariot to meet him. "Is everything all right?" he asked.

22 "Everything is all right," Gehazi answered. "My master sent me to say, 'Two young men from the company of the prophets have just come to me from the hill country of Ephraim. Please give them a talent*a* of silver and two sets of clothing.'"

23 "By all means, take two talents," said Naaman. He urged Gehazi to accept them, and then tied up the two talents of silver in two bags, with two sets of clothing. He gave them to two of his servants, and they carried them ahead of Gehazi. 24 When Gehazi came to the hill, he took the things from the servants and put them away in the house. He sent the men away and they left.

25 When he went in and stood before his master, Elisha asked him, "Where have you been, Gehazi?"

"Your servant didn't go anywhere," Gehazi answered.

26 But Elisha said to him, "Was not my spirit with you when the man got down from his chariot to meet you? Is this the time to take money or to accept clothes— or olive groves and vineyards, or flocks and herds, or male and female slaves? 27 Naaman's leprosy will cling to you and to your descendants forever." Then Gehazi went from Elisha's presence and his skin was leprous—it had become as white as snow.

An Axhead Floats

6 The company of the prophets said to Elisha, "Look, the place where we meet with you is too small for us. 2 Let us go to the Jordan, where each of us can get a pole; and let us build a place there for us to meet."

And he said, "Go."

3 Then one of them said, "Won't you please come with your servants?"

"I will," Elisha replied. 4 And he went with them.

They went to the Jordan and began to cut down trees. 5 As one of them was cutting down a tree, the iron axhead fell into the water. "Oh no, my lord!" he cried out. "It was borrowed!"

6 The man of God asked, "Where did it fall?" When he showed him the place, Elisha cut a stick and threw it there, and made the iron float. 7 "Lift it out," he said. Then the man reached out his hand and took it.

Elisha Traps Blinded Arameans

8 Now the king of Aram was at war with Israel. After conferring with his officers,

a 22 That is, about 75 pounds or about 34 kilograms

he said, "I will set up my camp in such and such a place."

⁹The man of God sent word to the king of Israel: "Beware of passing that place, because the Arameans are going down there." ¹⁰So the king of Israel checked on the place indicated by the man of God. Time and again Elisha warned the king, so that he was on his guard in such places.

¹¹This enraged the king of Aram. He summoned his officers and demanded of them, "Tell me! Which of us is on the side of the king of Israel?"

¹²"None of us, my lord the king," said one of his officers, "but Elisha, the prophet who is in Israel, tells the king of Israel the very words you speak in your bedroom."

¹³"Go, find out where he is," the king ordered, "so I can send men and capture him." The report came back: "He is in Dothan." ¹⁴Then he sent horses and chariots and a strong force there. They went by night and surrounded the city.

¹⁵When the servant of the man of God got up and went out early the next morning, an army with horses and chariots had surrounded the city. "Oh no, my lord! What shall we do?" the servant asked.

¹⁶"Don't be afraid," the prophet answered. "Those who are with us are more than those who are with them."

¹⁷And Elisha prayed, "Open his eyes, LORD, so that he may see." Then the LORD opened the servant's eyes, and he looked and saw the hills full of horses and chariots of fire all around Elisha.

¹⁸As the enemy came down toward him, Elisha prayed to the LORD, "Strike this army with blindness." So he struck them with blindness, as Elisha had asked.

¹⁹Elisha told them, "This is not the road and this is not the city. Follow me, and I will lead you to the man you are looking for." And he led them to Samaria.

²⁰After they entered the city, Elisha said, "LORD, open the eyes of these men so they can see." Then the LORD opened their eyes and they looked, and there they were, inside Samaria.

²¹When the king of Israel saw them, he asked Elisha, "Shall I kill them, my father? Shall I kill them?"

²²"Do not kill them," he answered. "Would you kill those you have captured with your own sword or bow? Set food and water before them so that they may eat and drink and then go back to their master." ²³So he prepared a great feast for them, and after they had finished eating and drinking, he sent them away, and they returned to their master. So the bands from Aram stopped raiding Israel's territory.

2 Kings 6:8–22

Angels protect you.

You might picture angels as bright glittery beings floating around making the world a better place. Or maybe as chubby little guys shooting love arrows on Valentine's Day. But the Bible presents angels as real, powerful beings active in your world. When the prophet Elisha and his servant saw they were surrounded by an angry army from Aram, they could have panicked. Yet Elisha spotted an even stronger army on their side, with "the hills full of horses and chariots of fire all around Elisha" (2 Kings 6:17). The Lord sent those angels to guard Elisha, just as he appoints angels to watch over you. Psalm 91:11 promises the Lord "will command his angels concerning you to guard you in all your ways." And Hebrews 1:14 says, "Are not all angels ministering spirits sent to serve those who will inherit salvation?"

Think: Do you believe angels exist as an important part of your world? Why—or why not?

ROCK SOLID truths

Famine in Besieged Samaria

²⁴Some time later, Ben-Hadad king of Aram mobilized his entire army and marched up and laid siege to Samaria. ²⁵There was a great famine in the city; the siege lasted so long that a donkey's head sold for eighty shekels^a of silver, and a quarter of a cab^b of seed pods^c for five shekels.^d

²⁶As the king of Israel was passing by on the wall, a woman cried to him, "Help me, my lord the king!"

²⁷The king replied, "If the LORD does not help you, where can I get help for you? From the threshing floor? From the winepress?" ²⁸Then he asked her, "What's the matter?"

She answered, "This woman said to me, 'Give up your son so we may eat him today, and tomorrow we'll eat my son.' ²⁹So we cooked my son and ate him. The next day I said to her, 'Give up your son so we may eat him,' but she had hidden him."

³⁰When the king heard the woman's words, he tore his robes. As he went along the wall, the people looked, and they saw that, under his robes, he had sackcloth on his body. ³¹He said, "May God deal with me, be it ever so severely, if the head of Elisha son of Shaphat remains on his shoulders today!"

³²Now Elisha was sitting in his house, and the elders were sitting with him. The king sent a messenger ahead, but before he arrived, Elisha said to the elders, "Don't you see how this murderer is sending someone to cut off my head? Look, when the messenger comes, shut the door and hold it shut against him. Is not the sound of his master's footsteps behind him?" ³³While he was still talking to them, the messenger came down to him.

The king said, "This disaster is from the LORD. Why should I wait for the LORD any longer?"

7 Elisha replied, "Hear the word of the LORD. This is what the LORD says: About this time tomorrow, a seah^e of the finest flour will sell for a shekel^f and two seahs^g of barley for a shekel at the gate of Samaria."

²The officer on whose arm the king was leaning said to the man of God, "Look, even if the LORD should open the floodgates of the heavens, could this happen?"

"You will see it with your own eyes," answered Elisha, "but you will not eat any of it!"

The Siege Lifted

³Now there were four men with leprosy^h at the entrance of the city gate. They said to each other, "Why stay here until we die? ⁴If we say, 'We'll go into the city'—the famine is there, and we will die. And if we stay here, we will die. So let's go over to the camp of the Arameans and surrender. If they spare us, we live; if they kill us, then we die."

⁵At dusk they got up and went to the camp of the Arameans. When they reached the edge of the camp, no one was there, ⁶for the Lord had caused the Arameans to hear the sound of chariots and horses and a great army, so that they said to one another, "Look, the king of Israel has hired the Hittite and Egyptian kings to attack us!" ⁷So they got up and fled in the dusk and abandoned their tents and their horses and donkeys. They left the camp as it was and ran for their lives.

⁸The men who had leprosy reached the edge of the camp, entered one of the tents and ate and drank. Then they took silver, gold and clothes, and went off and hid them. They returned and entered another tent and took some things from it and hid them also.

⁹Then they said to each other, "What we're doing is not right. This is a day of good news and we are keeping it to

---

^a 25 That is, about 2 pounds or about 920 grams
^b 25 That is, probably about 1/4 pound or about 100 grams   ^c 25 Or *of doves' dung*
^d 25 That is, about 2 ounces or about 58 grams
^e 1 That is, probably about 12 pounds or about 5.5 kilograms of flour; also in verses 16 and 18
^f 1 That is, about 2/5 ounce or about 12 grams; also in verses 16 and 18   ^g 1 That is, probably about 20 pounds or about 9 kilograms of barley; also in verses 16 and 18   ^h 3 The Hebrew for *leprosy* was used for various diseases affecting the skin; also in verse 8.

ourselves. If we wait until daylight, punishment will overtake us. Let's go at once and report this to the royal palace."

¹⁰So they went and called out to the city gatekeepers and told them, "We went into the Aramean camp and no one was there—not a sound of anyone—only tethered horses and donkeys, and the tents left just as they were." ¹¹The gatekeepers shouted the news, and it was reported within the palace.

¹²The king got up in the night and said to his officers, "I will tell you what the Arameans have done to us. They know we are starving; so they have left the camp to hide in the countryside, thinking, 'They will surely come out, and then we will take them alive and get into the city.'"

¹³One of his officers answered, "Have some men take five of the horses that are left in the city. Their plight will be like that of all the Israelites left here—yes, they will only be like all these Israelites who are doomed. So let us send them to find out what happened."

¹⁴So they selected two chariots with their horses, and the king sent them after the Aramean army. He commanded the drivers, "Go and find out what has happened." ¹⁵They followed them as far as the Jordan, and they found the whole road strewn with the clothing and equipment the Arameans had thrown away in their headlong flight. So the messengers returned and reported to the king. ¹⁶Then the people went out and plundered the camp of the Arameans. So a seah of the finest flour sold for a shekel, and two seahs of barley sold for a shekel, as the Lord had said.

¹⁷Now the king had put the officer on whose arm he leaned in charge of the gate, and the people trampled him in the gateway, and he died, just as the man of God had foretold when the king came down to his house. ¹⁸It happened as the man of God had said to the king: "About this time tomorrow, a seah of the finest flour will sell for a shekel and two seahs of barley for a shekel at the gate of Samaria."

¹⁹The officer had said to the man of God, "Look, even if the Lord should open the floodgates of the heavens, could this happen?" The man of God had replied, "You will see it with your own eyes, but you will not eat any of it!" ²⁰And that is exactly what happened to him, for the people trampled him in the gateway, and he died.

The Shunammite's Land Restored

8 Now Elisha had said to the woman whose son he had restored to life, "Go away with your family and stay for a while wherever you can, because the Lord has decreed a famine in the land that will last seven years." ²The woman proceeded to do as the man of God said. She and her family went away and stayed in the land of the Philistines seven years.

³At the end of the seven years she came back from the land of the Philistines and went to appeal to the king for her house and land. ⁴The king was talking to Gehazi, the servant of the man of God, and had said, "Tell me about all the great things Elisha has done." ⁵Just as Gehazi was telling the king how Elisha had restored the dead to life, the woman whose son Elisha had brought back to life came to appeal to the king for her house and land.

Gehazi said, "This is the woman, my lord the king, and this is her son whom Elisha restored to life." ⁶The king asked the woman about it, and she told him.

Then he assigned an official to her case and said to him, "Give back everything that belonged to her, including all the income from her land from the day she left the country until now."

Hazael Murders Ben-Hadad

⁷Elisha went to Damascus, and Ben-Hadad king of Aram was ill. When the king was told, "The man of God has come all the way up here," ⁸he said to Hazael, "Take a gift with you and go to meet the man of God. Consult the Lord through him; ask him, 'Will I recover from this illness?'"

⁹Hazael went to meet Elisha, taking with him as a gift forty camel-loads of all

the finest wares of Damascus. He went in and stood before him, and said, "Your son Ben-Hadad king of Aram has sent me to ask, 'Will I recover from this illness?'"

¹⁰Elisha answered, "Go and say to him, 'You will certainly recover.' Nevertheless,ᵃ the LORD has revealed to me that he will in fact die." ¹¹He stared at him with a fixed gaze until Hazael was embarrassed. Then the man of God began to weep.

¹²"Why is my lord weeping?" asked Hazael.

"Because I know the harm you will do to the Israelites," he answered. "You will set fire to their fortified places, kill their young men with the sword, dash their little children to the ground, and rip open their pregnant women."

¹³Hazael said, "How could your servant, a mere dog, accomplish such a feat?"

"The LORD has shown me that you will become king of Aram," answered Elisha.

¹⁴Then Hazael left Elisha and returned to his master. When Ben-Hadad asked, "What did Elisha say to you?" Hazael replied, "He told me that you would certainly recover." ¹⁵But the next day he took a thick cloth, soaked it in water and spread it over the king's face, so that he died. Then Hazael succeeded him as king.

Jehoram King of Judah

¹⁶In the fifth year of Joram son of Ahab king of Israel, when Jehoshaphat was king of Judah, Jehoram son of Jehoshaphat began his reign as king of Judah. ¹⁷He was thirty-two years old when he became king, and he reigned in Jerusalem eight years. ¹⁸He followed the ways of the kings of Israel, as the house of Ahab had done, for he married a daughter of Ahab. He did evil in the eyes of the LORD. ¹⁹Nevertheless, for the sake of his servant David, the LORD was not willing to destroy Judah. He had promised to maintain a lamp for David and his descendants forever.

²⁰In the time of Jehoram, Edom rebelled against Judah and set up its own king. ²¹So Jehoramᵇ went to Zair with all his chariots. The Edomites surrounded him and his chariot commanders, but he rose up and broke through by night; his army, however, fled back home. ²²To this day Edom has been in rebellion against Judah. Libnah revolted at the same time.

²³As for the other events of Jehoram's reign, and all he did, are they not written in the book of the annals of the kings of Judah? ²⁴Jehoram rested with his ancestors and was buried with them in the City of David. And Ahaziah his son succeeded him as king.

Ahaziah King of Judah

²⁵In the twelfth year of Joram son of Ahab king of Israel, Ahaziah son of Jehoram king of Judah began to reign. ²⁶Ahaziah was twenty-two years old when he became king, and he reigned in Jerusalem one year. His mother's name was Athaliah, a granddaughter of Omri king of Israel. ²⁷He followed the ways of the house of Ahab and did evil in the eyes of the LORD, as the house of Ahab had done, for he was related by marriage to Ahab's family.

²⁸Ahaziah went with Joram son of Ahab to war against Hazael king of Aram at Ramoth Gilead. The Arameans wounded Joram; ²⁹so King Joram returned to Jezreel to recover from the wounds the Arameans had inflicted on him at Ramothᶜ in his battle with Hazael king of Aram.

Then Ahaziah son of Jehoram king of Judah went down to Jezreel to see Joram son of Ahab, because he had been wounded.

Jehu Anointed King of Israel

9 The prophet Elisha summoned a man from the company of the prophets and said to him, "Tuck your cloak into your belt, take this flask of olive oil with you and go to Ramoth Gilead. ²When you get there, look for Jehu son of Jehoshaphat, the son of Nimshi. Go to him, get him away from his companions and take him into an inner room. ³Then take the flask and pour the oil on his head

---

ᵃ 10 The Hebrew may also be read *Go and say, 'You will certainly not recover,' for.*
ᵇ 21 Hebrew *Joram*, a variant of *Jehoram*; also in verses 23 and 24   ᶜ 29 Hebrew *Ramah*, a variant of *Ramoth*

and declare, 'This is what the LORD says: I anoint you king over Israel.' Then open the door and run; don't delay!"

⁴So the young prophet went to Ramoth Gilead. ⁵When he arrived, he found the army officers sitting together. "I have a message for you, commander," he said.

"For which of us?" asked Jehu.

"For you, commander," he replied.

⁶Jehu got up and went into the house. Then the prophet poured the oil on Jehu's head and declared, "This is what the LORD, the God of Israel, says: 'I anoint you king over the LORD's people Israel. ⁷You are to destroy the house of Ahab your master, and I will avenge the blood of my servants the prophets and the blood of all the LORD's servants shed by Jezebel. ⁸The whole house of Ahab will perish. I will cut off from Ahab every last male in Israel—slave or free.ᵃ ⁹I will make the house of Ahab like the house of Jeroboam son of Nebat and like the house of Baasha son of Ahijah. ¹⁰As for Jezebel, dogs will devour her on the plot of ground at Jezreel, and no one will bury her.'" Then he opened the door and ran.

¹¹When Jehu went out to his fellow officers, one of them asked him, "Is everything all right? Why did this maniac come to you?"

"You know the man and the sort of things he says," Jehu replied.

¹²"That's not true!" they said. "Tell us."

Jehu said, "Here is what he told me: 'This is what the LORD says: I anoint you king over Israel.'"

¹³They quickly took their cloaks and spread them under him on the bare steps. Then they blew the trumpet and shouted, "Jehu is king!"

Jehu Kills Joram and Ahaziah

¹⁴So Jehu son of Jehoshaphat, the son of Nimshi, conspired against Joram. (Now Joram and all Israel had been defending Ramoth Gilead against Hazael king of Aram, ¹⁵but King Joramᵇ had returned to Jezreel to recover from the wounds the Arameans had inflicted on him in the battle with Hazael king of Aram.) Jehu said,

"If you desire to make me king, don't let anyone slip out of the city to go and tell the news in Jezreel." ¹⁶Then he got into his chariot and rode to Jezreel, because Joram was resting there and Ahaziah king of Judah had gone down to see him.

¹⁷When the lookout standing on the tower in Jezreel saw Jehu's troops approaching, he called out, "I see some troops coming."

"Get a horseman," Joram ordered. "Send him to meet them and ask, 'Do you come in peace?'"

¹⁸The horseman rode off to meet Jehu and said, "This is what the king says: 'Do you come in peace?'"

"What do you have to do with peace?" Jehu replied. "Fall in behind me."

The lookout reported, "The messenger has reached them, but he isn't coming back."

¹⁹So the king sent out a second horseman. When he came to them he said, "This is what the king says: 'Do you come in peace?'"

Jehu replied, "What do you have to do with peace? Fall in behind me."

²⁰The lookout reported, "He has reached them, but he isn't coming back either. The driving is like that of Jehu son of Nimshi—he drives like a maniac."

²¹"Hitch up my chariot," Joram ordered. And when it was hitched up, Joram king of Israel and Ahaziah king of Judah rode out, each in his own chariot, to meet Jehu. They met him at the plot of ground that had belonged to Naboth the Jezreelite. ²²When Joram saw Jehu he asked, "Have you come in peace, Jehu?"

"How can there be peace," Jehu replied, "as long as all the idolatry and witchcraft of your mother Jezebel abound?"

²³Joram turned about and fled, calling out to Ahaziah, "Treachery, Ahaziah!"

²⁴Then Jehu drew his bow and shot Joram between the shoulders. The arrow pierced his heart and he slumped down in his chariot. ²⁵Jehu said to Bidkar, his

---

ᵃ 8 Or *Israel—every ruler or leader*
ᵇ 15 Hebrew *Jehoram*, a variant of *Joram*; also in verses 17 and 21-24

chariot officer, "Pick him up and throw him on the field that belonged to Naboth the Jezreelite. Remember how you and I were riding together in chariots behind Ahab his father when the LORD spoke this prophecy against him: ²⁶'Yesterday I saw the blood of Naboth and the blood of his sons, declares the LORD, and I will surely make you pay for it on this plot of ground, declares the LORD.'ᵃ Now then, pick him up and throw him on that plot, in accordance with the word of the LORD."

²⁷When Ahaziah king of Judah saw what had happened, he fled up the road to Beth Haggan.ᵇ Jehu chased him, shouting, "Kill him too!" They wounded him in his chariot on the way up to Gur near Ibleam, but he escaped to Megiddo and died there. ²⁸His servants took him by chariot to Jerusalem and buried him with his ancestors in his tomb in the City of David. ²⁹(In the eleventh year of Joram son of Ahab, Ahaziah had become king of Judah.)

Jezebel Killed

³⁰Then Jehu went to Jezreel. When Jezebel heard about it, she put on eye makeup, arranged her hair and looked out of a window. ³¹As Jehu entered the gate, she asked, "Have you come in peace, you Zimri, you murderer of your master?"ᶜ

³²He looked up at the window and called out, "Who is on my side? Who?" Two or three eunuchs looked down at him. ³³"Throw her down!" Jehu said. So they threw her down, and some of her blood spattered the wall and the horses as they trampled her underfoot.

³⁴Jehu went in and ate and drank. "Take care of that cursed woman," he said, "and bury her, for she was a king's daughter." ³⁵But when they went out to bury her, they found nothing except her skull, her feet and her hands. ³⁶They went back and told Jehu, who said, "This is the word of the LORD that he spoke through his servant Elijah the Tishbite: On the plot of ground at Jezreel dogs will devour Jezebel's flesh.ᵈ ³⁷Jezebel's body will be like dung on the ground in the plot at Jezreel, so that no one will be able to say, 'This is Jezebel.'"

Ahab's Family Killed

10 Now there were in Samaria seventy sons of the house of Ahab. So Jehu wrote letters and sent them to Samaria: to the officials of Jezreel,ᵉ to the elders and to the guardians of Ahab's children. He said, ²"You have your master's sons with you and you have chariots and horses, a fortified city and weapons. Now as soon as this letter reaches you, ³choose the best and most worthy of your master's sons and set him on his father's throne. Then fight for your master's house."

⁴But they were terrified and said, "If two kings could not resist him, how can we?"

⁵So the palace administrator, the city governor, the elders and the guardians sent this message to Jehu: "We are your servants and we will do anything you say. We will not appoint anyone as king; you do whatever you think best."

⁶Then Jehu wrote them a second letter, saying, "If you are on my side and will obey me, take the heads of your master's sons and come to me in Jezreel by this time tomorrow."

Now the royal princes, seventy of them, were with the leading men of the city, who were rearing them. ⁷When the letter arrived, these men took the princes and slaughtered all seventy of them. They put their heads in baskets and sent them to Jehu in Jezreel. ⁸When the messenger arrived, he told Jehu, "They have brought the heads of the princes."

Then Jehu ordered, "Put them in two piles at the entrance of the city gate until morning."

⁹The next morning Jehu went out. He stood before all the people and said, "You are innocent. It was I who conspired against my master and killed him, but who killed all these? ¹⁰Know, then, that not a word the LORD has spoken against

---

ᵃ 26 See 1 Kings 21:19.   ᵇ 27 Or fled by way of the garden house   ᶜ 31 Or "Was there peace for Zimri, who murdered his master?"   ᵈ 36 See 1 Kings 21:23.   ᵉ 1 Hebrew; some Septuagint manuscripts and Vulgate of the city the house of Ahab will fail. The LORD has done what he announced through his servant Elijah." ¹¹So Jehu killed everyone in Jezreel who remained of the house of Ahab, as well as all his chief men, his close friends and his priests, leaving him no survivor.

¹²Jehu then set out and went toward Samaria. At Beth Eked of the Shepherds, ¹³he met some relatives of Ahaziah king of Judah and asked, "Who are you?"

They said, "We are relatives of Ahaziah, and we have come down to greet the families of the king and of the queen mother."

¹⁴"Take them alive!" he ordered. So they took them alive and slaughtered them by the well of Beth Eked—forty-two of them. He left no survivor.

¹⁵After he left there, he came upon Jehonadab son of Rekab, who was on his way to meet him. Jehu greeted him and said, "Are you in accord with me, as I am with you?"

"I am," Jehonadab answered.

"If so," said Jehu, "give me your hand." So he did, and Jehu helped him up into the chariot. ¹⁶Jehu said, "Come with me and see my zeal for the LORD." Then he had him ride along in his chariot.

¹⁷When Jehu came to Samaria, he killed all who were left there of Ahab's family; he destroyed them, according to the word of the LORD spoken to Elijah.

Servants of Baal Killed

¹⁸Then Jehu brought all the people together and said to them, "Ahab served Baal a little; Jehu will serve him much. ¹⁹Now summon all the prophets of Baal, all his servants and all his priests. See that no one is missing, because I am going to hold a great sacrifice for Baal. Anyone who fails to come will no longer live." But Jehu was acting deceptively in order to destroy the servants of Baal.

²⁰Jehu said, "Call an assembly in honor of Baal." So they proclaimed it. ²¹Then he sent word throughout Israel, and all the servants of Baal came; not one stayed away. They crowded into the temple of Baal until it was full from one end to the other. ²²And Jehu said to the keeper of the wardrobe, "Bring robes for all the servants of Baal." So he brought out robes for them.

²³Then Jehu and Jehonadab son of Rekab went into the temple of Baal. Jehu said to the servants of Baal, "Look around and see that no one who serves the LORD is here with you—only servants of Baal." ²⁴So they went in to make sacrifices and burnt offerings. Now Jehu had posted eighty men outside with this warning: "If one of you lets any of the men I am placing in your hands escape, it will be your life for his life."

²⁵As soon as Jehu had finished making the burnt offering, he ordered the guards and officers: "Go in and kill them; let no one escape." So they cut them down with the sword. The guards and officers threw the bodies out and then entered the inner shrine of the temple of Baal. ²⁶They brought the sacred stone out of the temple of Baal and burned it. ²⁷They demolished the sacred stone of Baal and tore down the temple of Baal, and people have used it for a latrine to this day.

²⁸So Jehu destroyed Baal worship in Israel. ²⁹However, he did not turn away from the sins of Jeroboam son of Nebat, which he had caused Israel to commit—the worship of the golden calves at Bethel and Dan.

³⁰The LORD said to Jehu, "Because you have done well in accomplishing what is right in my eyes and have done to the house of Ahab all I had in mind to do, your descendants will sit on the throne of Israel to the fourth generation." ³¹Yet Jehu was not careful to keep the law of the LORD, the God of Israel, with all his heart. He did not turn away from the sins of Jeroboam, which he had caused Israel to commit.

³²In those days the LORD began to reduce the size of Israel. Hazael overpowered the Israelites throughout their territory ³³east of the Jordan in all the land of Gilead (the region of Gad, Reuben and Manasseh), from Aroer by the Arnon Gorge through Gilead to Bashan.

³⁴As for the other events of Jehu's reign, all he did, and all his achievements, are

ROCK SOLID *plans*

2 Kings 10:28–33

Aim to be truly great.

As king of Israel, Jehu cleansed the nation of wicked leaders and crushed priests of the false god Baal. He built a royal dynasty that lasted a century. But for all the good Jehu did, he fell far short of true greatness. Even though Jehu loudly declared his devotion to God (see 2 Kings 10:16), he allowed the nation to continue worshiping idols — two golden calves propped up as gods. In the end, God condemned Jehu for not keeping the law of the Lord with all of his heart.

Your next step: Look at your life for ways you half-heartedly follow God's commands — and then choose to obey God all the way.

they not written in the book of the annals of the kings of Israel?

³⁵Jehu rested with his ancestors and was buried in Samaria. And Jehoahaz his son succeeded him as king. ³⁶The time that Jehu reigned over Israel in Samaria was twenty-eight years.

Athaliah and Joash

11 When Athaliah the mother of Ahaziah saw that her son was dead, she proceeded to destroy the whole royal family. ²But Jehosheba, the daughter of King Jehoram^a and sister of Ahaziah, took Joash son of Ahaziah and stole him away from among the royal princes, who were about to be murdered. She put him and his nurse in a bedroom to hide him from Athaliah; so he was not killed. ³He remained hidden with his nurse at the temple of the Lord for six years while Athaliah ruled the land.

⁴In the seventh year Jehoiada sent for the commanders of units of a hundred, the Carites and the guards and had them brought to him at the temple of the Lord.

He made a covenant with them and put them under oath at the temple of the Lord. Then he showed them the king's son. ⁵He commanded them, saying, "This is what you are to do: You who are in the three companies that are going on duty on the Sabbath — a third of you guarding the royal palace, ⁶a third at the Sur Gate, and a third at the gate behind the guard, who take turns guarding the temple — ⁷and you who are in the other two companies that normally go off Sabbath duty are all to guard the temple for the king. ⁸Station yourselves around the king, each of you with weapon in hand. Anyone who approaches your ranks^b is to be put to death. Stay close to the king wherever he goes."

⁹The commanders of units of a hundred did just as Jehoiada the priest ordered. Each one took his men — those who were going on duty on the Sabbath and those who were going off duty — and came to Jehoiada the priest. ¹⁰Then he gave the commanders the spears and shields that had belonged to King David and that were in the temple of the Lord. ¹¹The guards, each with weapon in hand, stationed themselves around the king — near the altar and the temple, from the south side to the north side of the temple.

¹²Jehoiada brought out the king's son and put the crown on him; he presented him with a copy of the covenant and proclaimed him king. They anointed him, and the people clapped their hands and shouted, "Long live the king!"

¹³When Athaliah heard the noise made by the guards and the people, she went to the people at the temple of the Lord. ¹⁴She looked and there was the king, standing by the pillar, as the custom was. The officers and the trumpeters were beside the king, and all the people of the land were rejoicing and blowing trumpets. Then Athaliah tore her robes and called out, "Treason! Treason!"

¹⁵Jehoiada the priest ordered the commanders of units of a hundred, who were in charge of the troops: "Bring her out

^a 2 Hebrew *Joram*, a variant of *Jehoram*
^b 8 Or *approaches the precincts*

between the ranks[a] and put to the sword anyone who follows her." For the priest had said, "She must not be put to death in the temple of the Lord." [16]So they seized her as she reached the place where the horses enter the palace grounds, and there she was put to death.

[17]Jehoiada then made a covenant between the Lord and the king and people that they would be the Lord's people. He also made a covenant between the king and the people. [18]All the people of the land went to the temple of Baal and tore it down. They smashed the altars and idols to pieces and killed Mattan the priest of Baal in front of the altars.

Then Jehoiada the priest posted guards at the temple of the Lord. [19]He took with him the commanders of hundreds, the Carites, the guards and all the people of the land, and together they brought the king down from the temple of the Lord and went into the palace, entering by way of the gate of the guards. The king then took his place on the royal throne. [20]All the people of the land rejoiced, and the city was calm, because Athaliah had been slain with the sword at the palace.

[21]Joash[b] was seven years old when he began to reign.[c]

Joash Repairs the Temple

12 [d] In the seventh year of Jehu, Joash[e] became king, and he reigned in Jerusalem forty years. His mother's name was Zibiah; she was from Beersheba. [2]Joash did what was right in the eyes of the Lord all the years Jehoiada the priest instructed him. [3]The high places, however, were not removed; the people continued to offer sacrifices and burn incense there.

[4]Joash said to the priests, "Collect all the money that is brought as sacred offerings to the temple of the Lord—the money collected in the census, the money received from personal vows and the money brought voluntarily to the temple. [5]Let every priest receive the money from one of the treasurers, then use it to repair whatever damage is found in the temple."

[6]But by the twenty-third year of King Joash the priests still had not repaired the temple. [7]Therefore King Joash summoned Jehoiada the priest and the other priests and asked them, "Why aren't you repairing the damage done to the temple? Take no more money from your treasurers, but hand it over for repairing the temple." [8]The priests agreed that they would not collect any more money from the people and that they would not repair the temple themselves.

[9]Jehoiada the priest took a chest and bored a hole in its lid. He placed it beside the altar, on the right side as one enters the temple of the Lord. The priests who guarded the entrance put into the chest all the money that was brought to the temple of the Lord. [10]Whenever they saw that there was a large amount of money in the chest, the royal secretary and the high priest came, counted the money that had been brought into the temple of the Lord and put it into bags. [11]When the amount had been determined, they gave the money to the men appointed to supervise the work on the temple. With it they paid those who worked on the temple of the Lord—the carpenters and builders, [12]the masons and stonecutters. They purchased timber and blocks of dressed stone for the repair of the temple of the Lord, and met all the other expenses of restoring the temple.

[13]The money brought into the temple was not spent for making silver basins, wick trimmers, sprinkling bowls, trumpets or any other articles of gold or silver for the temple of the Lord; [14]it was paid to the workers, who used it to repair the temple. [15]They did not require an accounting from those to whom they gave the money to pay the workers, because they acted with complete honesty. [16]The money from the guilt offerings and sin offerings[f] was not brought into the

---

[a] 15 Or *out from the precincts*   [b] 21 Hebrew *Jehoash*, a variant of *Joash*   [c] 21 In Hebrew texts this verse (11:21) is numbered 12:1.   [d] In Hebrew texts 12:1-21 is numbered 12:2-22.   [e] 1 Hebrew *Jehoash*, a variant of *Joash*; also in verses 2, 4, 6, 7 and 18   [f] 16 Or *purification offerings*

temple of the LORD; it belonged to the priests. ¹⁷About this time Hazael king of Aram went up and attacked Gath and captured it. Then he turned to attack Jerusalem. ¹⁸But Joash king of Judah took all the sacred objects dedicated by his predecessors—Jehoshaphat, Jehoram and Ahaziah, the kings of Judah—and the gifts he himself had dedicated and all the gold found in the treasuries of the temple of the LORD and of the royal palace, and he sent them to Hazael king of Aram, who then withdrew from Jerusalem.

¹⁹As for the other events of the reign of Joash, and all he did, are they not written in the book of the annals of the kings of Judah? ²⁰His officials conspired against him and assassinated him at Beth Millo, on the road down to Silla. ²¹The officials who murdered him were Jozabad son of Shimeath and Jehozabad son of Shomer. He died and was buried with his ancestors in the City of David. And Amaziah his son succeeded him as king.

Jehoahaz King of Israel

13 In the twenty-third year of Joash son of Ahaziah king of Judah, Jehoahaz son of Jehu became king of Israel in Samaria, and he reigned seventeen years. ²He did evil in the eyes of the LORD by following the sins of Jeroboam son of Nebat, which he had caused Israel to commit, and he did not turn away from them. ³So the LORD's anger burned against Israel, and for a long time he kept them under the power of Hazael king of Aram and Ben-Hadad his son.

⁴Then Jehoahaz sought the LORD's favor, and the LORD listened to him, for he saw how severely the king of Aram was oppressing Israel. ⁵The LORD provided a deliverer for Israel, and they escaped from the power of Aram. So the Israelites lived in their own homes as they had before. ⁶But they did not turn away from the sins of the house of Jeroboam, which he had caused Israel to commit; they continued in them. Also, the Asherah pole*a* remained standing in Samaria.

⁷Nothing had been left of the army of Jehoahaz except fifty horsemen, ten chariots and ten thousand foot soldiers, for the king of Aram had destroyed the rest and made them like the dust at threshing time.

⁸As for the other events of the reign of Jehoahaz, all he did and his achievements, are they not written in the book of the annals of the kings of Israel? ⁹Jehoahaz rested with his ancestors and was buried in Samaria. And Jehoash*b* his son succeeded him as king.

Jehoash King of Israel

¹⁰In the thirty-seventh year of Joash king of Judah, Jehoash son of Jehoahaz became king of Israel in Samaria, and he reigned sixteen years. ¹¹He did evil in the eyes of the LORD and did not turn away from any of the sins of Jeroboam son of Nebat, which he had caused Israel to commit; he continued in them.

¹²As for the other events of the reign of Jehoash, all he did and his achievements, including his war against Amaziah king of Judah, are they not written in the book of the annals of the kings of Israel? ¹³Jehoash rested with his ancestors, and Jeroboam succeeded him on the throne. Jehoash was buried in Samaria with the kings of Israel.

¹⁴Now Elisha had been suffering from the illness from which he died. Jehoash king of Israel went down to see him and wept over him. "My father! My father!" he cried. "The chariots and horsemen of Israel!"

¹⁵Elisha said, "Get a bow and some arrows," and he did so. ¹⁶"Take the bow in your hands," he said to the king of Israel. When he had taken it, Elisha put his hands on the king's hands.

¹⁷"Open the east window," he said, and he opened it. "Shoot!" Elisha said, and he shot. "The LORD's arrow of victory, the arrow of victory over Aram!" Elisha declared. "You will completely destroy the Arameans at Aphek."

---

a 6 That is, a wooden symbol of the goddess Asherah; here and elsewhere in 2 Kings
b 9 Hebrew *Joash*, a variant of *Jehoash*; also in verses 12-14 and 25

18 Then he said, "Take the arrows," and the king took them. Elisha told him, "Strike the ground." He struck it three times and stopped. 19 The man of God was angry with him and said, "You should have struck the ground five or six times; then you would have defeated Aram and completely destroyed it. But now you will defeat it only three times."

20 Elisha died and was buried.

Now Moabite raiders used to enter the country every spring. 21 Once while some Israelites were burying a man, suddenly they saw a band of raiders; so they threw the man's body into Elisha's tomb. When the body touched Elisha's bones, the man came to life and stood up on his feet.

22 Hazael king of Aram oppressed Israel throughout the reign of Jehoahaz. 23 But the Lord was gracious to them and had compassion and showed concern for them because of his covenant with Abraham, Isaac and Jacob. To this day he has been unwilling to destroy them or banish them from his presence.

24 Hazael king of Aram died, and Ben-Hadad his son succeeded him as king. 25 Then Jehoash son of Jehoahaz recaptured from Ben-Hadad son of Hazael the towns he had taken in battle from his father Jehoahaz. Three times Jehoash defeated him, and so he recovered the Israelite towns.

Amaziah King of Judah

14 In the second year of Jehoash[a] son of Jehoahaz king of Israel, Amaziah son of Joash king of Judah began to reign. 2 He was twenty-five years old when he became king, and he reigned in Jerusalem twenty-nine years. His mother's name was Jehoaddan; she was from Jerusalem. 3 He did what was right in the eyes of the Lord, but not as his father David had done. In everything he followed the example of his father Joash. 4 The high places, however, were not removed; the people continued to offer sacrifices and burn incense there.

5 After the kingdom was firmly in his grasp, he executed the officials who had murdered his father the king. 6 Yet he did not put the children of the assassins to death, in accordance with what is written in the Book of the Law of Moses where the Lord commanded: "Parents are not to be put to death for their children, nor children put to death for their parents; each will die for their own sin."[b]

7 He was the one who defeated ten thousand Edomites in the Valley of Salt and captured Sela in battle, calling it Joktheel, the name it has to this day.

8 Then Amaziah sent messengers to Jehoash son of Jehoahaz, the son of Jehu, king of Israel, with the challenge: "Come, let us face each other in battle."

9 But Jehoash king of Israel replied to Amaziah king of Judah: "A thistle in Lebanon sent a message to a cedar in Lebanon, 'Give your daughter to my son in marriage.' Then a wild beast in Lebanon came along and trampled the thistle underfoot. 10 You have indeed defeated Edom and now you are arrogant. Glory in your victory, but stay at home! Why ask for trouble and cause your own downfall and that of Judah also?"

11 Amaziah, however, would not listen, so Jehoash king of Israel attacked. He and Amaziah king of Judah faced each other at Beth Shemesh in Judah. 12 Judah was routed by Israel, and every man fled to his home. 13 Jehoash king of Israel captured Amaziah king of Judah, the son of Joash, the son of Ahaziah, at Beth Shemesh. Then Jehoash went to Jerusalem and broke down the wall of Jerusalem from the Ephraim Gate to the Corner Gate—a section about four hundred cubits long.[c] 14 He took all the gold and silver and all the articles found in the temple of the Lord and in the treasuries of the royal palace. He also took hostages and returned to Samaria.

15 As for the other events of the reign of Jehoash, what he did and his achievements, including his war against Amaziah king of Judah, are they not written in the

---

[a] 1 Hebrew Joash, a variant of Jehoash; also in verses 13, 23 and 27   [b] 6 Deut. 24:16
[c] 13 That is, about 600 feet or about 180 meters

book of the annals of the kings of Israel? [16]Jehoash rested with his ancestors and was buried in Samaria with the kings of Israel. And Jeroboam his son succeeded him as king.

[17]Amaziah son of Joash king of Judah lived for fifteen years after the death of Jehoash son of Jehoahaz king of Israel. [18]As for the other events of Amaziah's reign, are they not written in the book of the annals of the kings of Judah?

[19]They conspired against him in Jerusalem, and he fled to Lachish, but they sent men after him to Lachish and killed him there. [20]He was brought back by horse and was buried in Jerusalem with his ancestors, in the City of David.

[21]Then all the people of Judah took Azariah,[a] who was sixteen years old, and made him king in place of his father Amaziah. [22]He was the one who rebuilt Elath and restored it to Judah after Amaziah rested with his ancestors.

Jeroboam II King of Israel

[23]In the fifteenth year of Amaziah son of Joash king of Judah, Jeroboam son of Jehoash king of Israel became king in Samaria, and he reigned forty-one years. [24]He did evil in the eyes of the LORD and did not turn away from any of the sins of Jeroboam son of Nebat, which he had caused Israel to commit. [25]He was the one who restored the boundaries of Israel from Lebo Hamath to the Dead Sea,[b] in accordance with the word of the LORD, the God of Israel, spoken through his servant Jonah son of Amittai, the prophet from Gath Hepher.

[26]The LORD had seen how bitterly everyone in Israel, whether slave or free, was suffering;[c] there was no one to help them. [27]And since the LORD had not said he would blot out the name of Israel from under heaven, he saved them by the hand of Jeroboam son of Jehoash.

[28]As for the other events of Jeroboam's reign, all he did, and his military achievements, including how he recovered for Israel both Damascus and Hamath, which had belonged to Judah, are they not writ-

ten in the book of the annals of the kings of Israel? [29]Jeroboam rested with his ancestors, the kings of Israel. And Zechariah his son succeeded him as king.

Azariah King of Judah

15 In the twenty-seventh year of Jeroboam king of Israel, Azariah[d] son of Amaziah king of Judah began to reign. [2]He was sixteen years old when he became king, and he reigned in Jerusalem fifty-two years. His mother's name was Jekoliah; she was from Jerusalem. [3]He did what was right in the eyes of the LORD, just as his father Amaziah had done. [4]The high places, however, were not removed; the people continued to offer sacrifices and burn incense there.

[5]The LORD afflicted the king with leprosy[e] until the day he died, and he lived in a separate house.[f] Jotham the king's son had charge of the palace and governed the people of the land.

[6]As for the other events of Azariah's reign, and all he did, are they not written in the book of the annals of the kings of Judah? [7]Azariah rested with his ancestors and was buried near them in the City of David. And Jotham his son succeeded him as king.

Zechariah King of Israel

[8]In the thirty-eighth year of Azariah king of Judah, Zechariah son of Jeroboam became king of Israel in Samaria, and he reigned six months. [9]He did evil in the eyes of the LORD, as his predecessors had done. He did not turn away from the sins of Jeroboam son of Nebat, which he had caused Israel to commit.

[10]Shallum son of Jabesh conspired against Zechariah. He attacked him in front of the people,[g] assassinated him

---

[a] 21 Also called *Uzziah*   [b] 25 Hebrew *the Sea of the Arabah*   [c] 26 Or *Israel was suffering. They were without a ruler or leader, and*
[d] 1 Also called *Uzziah*; also in verses 6, 7, 8, 17, 23 and 27   [e] 5 The Hebrew for *leprosy* was used for various diseases affecting the skin.
[f] 5 Or *in a house where he was relieved of responsibilities*   [g] 10 Hebrew; some Septuagint manuscripts *in Ibleam*

447

and succeeded him as king. [11] The other events of Zechariah's reign are written in the book of the annals of the kings of Israel. [12] So the word of the LORD spoken to Jehu was fulfilled: "Your descendants will sit on the throne of Israel to the fourth generation."[a]

Shallum King of Israel

[13] Shallum son of Jabesh became king in the thirty-ninth year of Uzziah king of Judah, and he reigned in Samaria one month. [14] Then Menahem son of Gadi went from Tirzah up to Samaria. He attacked Shallum son of Jabesh in Samaria, assassinated him and succeeded him as king.

[15] The other events of Shallum's reign, and the conspiracy he led, are written in the book of the annals of the kings of Israel.

[16] At that time Menahem, starting out from Tirzah, attacked Tiphsah and everyone in the city and its vicinity, because they refused to open their gates. He sacked Tiphsah and ripped open all the pregnant women.

Menahem King of Israel

[17] In the thirty-ninth year of Azariah king of Judah, Menahem son of Gadi became king of Israel, and he reigned in Samaria ten years. [18] He did evil in the eyes of the LORD. During his entire reign he did not turn away from the sins of Jeroboam son of Nebat, which he had caused Israel to commit.

[19] Then Pul[b] king of Assyria invaded the land, and Menahem gave him a thousand talents[c] of silver to gain his support and strengthen his own hold on the kingdom. [20] Menahem exacted this money from Israel. Every wealthy person had to contribute fifty shekels[d] of silver to be given to the king of Assyria. So the king of Assyria withdrew and stayed in the land no longer.

[21] As for the other events of Menahem's reign, and all he did, are they not written in the book of the annals of the kings of Israel? [22] Menahem rested with his ancestors. And Pekahiah his son succeeded him as king.

Pekahiah King of Israel

[23] In the fiftieth year of Azariah king of Judah, Pekahiah son of Menahem became king of Israel in Samaria, and he reigned two years. [24] Pekahiah did evil in the eyes of the LORD. He did not turn away from the sins of Jeroboam son of Nebat, which he had caused Israel to commit. [25] One of his chief officers, Pekah son of Remaliah, conspired against him. Taking fifty men of Gilead with him, he assassinated Pekahiah, along with Argob and Arieh, in the citadel of the royal palace at Samaria. So Pekah killed Pekahiah and succeeded him as king.

[26] The other events of Pekahiah's reign, and all he did, are written in the book of the annals of the kings of Israel.

Pekah King of Israel

[27] In the fifty-second year of Azariah king of Judah, Pekah son of Remaliah became king of Israel in Samaria, and he reigned twenty years. [28] He did evil in the eyes of the LORD. He did not turn away from the sins of Jeroboam son of Nebat, which he had caused Israel to commit.

[29] In the time of Pekah king of Israel, Tiglath-Pileser king of Assyria came and took Ijon, Abel Beth Maakah, Janoah, Kedesh and Hazor. He took Gilead and Galilee, including all the land of Naphtali, and deported the people to Assyria. [30] Then Hoshea son of Elah conspired against Pekah son of Remaliah. He attacked and assassinated him, and then succeeded him as king in the twentieth year of Jotham son of Uzziah.

[31] As for the other events of Pekah's reign, and all he did, are they not written in the book of the annals of the kings of Israel?

Jotham King of Judah

[32] In the second year of Pekah son of Remaliah king of Israel, Jotham son of Uzziah king of Judah began to reign.

---

[a] 12 2 Kings 10:30   [b] 19 Also called Tiglath-Pileser   [c] 19 That is, about 38 tons or about 34 metric tons   [d] 20 That is, about 1 1/4 pounds or about 575 grams

³³He was twenty-five years old when he became king, and he reigned in Jerusalem sixteen years. His mother's name was Jerusha daughter of Zadok. ³⁴He did what was right in the eyes of the LORD, just as his father Uzziah had done. ³⁵The high places, however, were not removed; the people continued to offer sacrifices and burn incense there. Jotham rebuilt the Upper Gate of the temple of the LORD.

³⁶As for the other events of Jotham's reign, and what he did, are they not written in the book of the annals of the kings of Judah? ³⁷(In those days the LORD began to send Rezin king of Aram and Pekah son of Remaliah against Judah.) ³⁸Jotham rested with his ancestors and was buried with them in the City of David, the city of his father. And Ahaz his son succeeded him as king.

Ahaz King of Judah

16 In the seventeenth year of Pekah son of Remaliah, Ahaz son of Jotham king of Judah began to reign. ²Ahaz was twenty years old when he became king, and he reigned in Jerusalem sixteen years. Unlike David his father, he did not do what was right in the eyes of the LORD his God. ³He followed the ways of the kings of Israel and even sacrificed his son in the fire, engaging in the detestable practices of the nations the LORD had driven out before the Israelites. ⁴He offered sacrifices and burned incense at the high places, on the hilltops and under every spreading tree.

⁵Then Rezin king of Aram and Pekah son of Remaliah king of Israel marched up to fight against Jerusalem and besieged Ahaz, but they could not overpower him. ⁶At that time, Rezin king of Aram recovered Elath for Aram by driving out the people of Judah. Edomites then moved into Elath and have lived there to this day. ⁷Ahaz sent messengers to say to Tiglath-Pileser king of Assyria, "I am your servant and vassal. Come up and save me out of the hand of the king of Aram and of the king of Israel, who are attacking me." ⁸And Ahaz took the silver and gold found in the temple of the LORD and in the treasuries of the royal palace and sent it as a gift to the king of Assyria. ⁹The king of Assyria complied by attacking Damascus and capturing it. He deported its inhabitants to Kir and put Rezin to death.

¹⁰Then King Ahaz went to Damascus to meet Tiglath-Pileser king of Assyria. He saw an altar in Damascus and sent to Uriah the priest a sketch of the altar, with detailed plans for its construction. ¹¹So Uriah the priest built an altar in accordance with all the plans that King Ahaz had sent from Damascus and finished it before King Ahaz returned. ¹²When the king came back from Damascus and saw the altar, he approached it and presented offerings[a] on it. ¹³He offered up his burnt offering and grain offering, poured out his drink offering, and splashed the blood of his fellowship offerings against the altar. ¹⁴As for the bronze altar that stood before the LORD, he brought it from the front of the temple—from between the new altar and the temple of the LORD—and put it on the north side of the new altar.

¹⁵King Ahaz then gave these orders to Uriah the priest: "On the large new altar, offer the morning burnt offering and the evening grain offering, the king's burnt offering and his grain offering, and the burnt offering of all the people of the land, and their grain offering and their drink offering. Splash against this altar the blood of all the burnt offerings and sacrifices. But I will use the bronze altar for seeking guidance." ¹⁶And Uriah the priest did just as King Ahaz had ordered.

¹⁷King Ahaz cut off the side panels and removed the basins from the movable stands. He removed the Sea from the bronze bulls that supported it and set it on a stone base. ¹⁸He took away the Sabbath canopy[b] that had been built at the temple and removed the royal entryway outside the temple of the LORD, in deference to the king of Assyria.

¹⁹As for the other events of the reign of Ahaz, and what he did, are they not

---

ᵃ 12 Or *and went up*   ᵇ 18 Or *the dais of his throne* (see Septuagint) written in the book of the annals of the kings of Judah? [20] Ahaz rested with his ancestors and was buried with them in the City of David. And Hezekiah his son succeeded him as king.

Hoshea Last King of Israel

17 In the twelfth year of Ahaz king of Judah, Hoshea son of Elah became king of Israel in Samaria, and he reigned nine years. [2] He did evil in the eyes of the LORD, but not like the kings of Israel who preceded him.

[3] Shalmaneser king of Assyria came up to attack Hoshea, who had been Shalmaneser's vassal and had paid him tribute. [4] But the king of Assyria discovered that Hoshea was a traitor, for he had sent envoys to So[a] king of Egypt, and he no longer paid tribute to the king of Assyria, as he had done year by year. Therefore Shalmaneser seized him and put him in prison. [5] The king of Assyria invaded the entire land, marched against Samaria and laid siege to it for three years. [6] In the ninth year of Hoshea, the king of Assyria captured Samaria and deported the Israelites to Assyria. He settled them in Halah, in Gozan on the Habor River and in the towns of the Medes.

Israel Exiled Because of Sin

[7] All this took place because the Israelites had sinned against the LORD their God, who had brought them up out of Egypt from under the power of Pharaoh king of Egypt. They worshiped other gods [8] and followed the practices of the nations the LORD had driven out before them, as well as the practices that the kings of Israel had introduced. [9] The Israelites secretly did things against the LORD their God that were not right. From watchtower to fortified city they built themselves high places in all their towns. [10] They set up sacred stones and Asherah poles on every high hill and under every spreading tree. [11] At every high place they burned incense, as the nations whom the LORD had driven out before them had done. They did wicked things that aroused the LORD's anger.

[12] They worshiped idols, though the LORD had said, "You shall not do this."[b] [13] The LORD warned Israel and Judah through all his prophets and seers: "Turn from your evil ways. Observe my commands and decrees, in accordance with the entire Law that I commanded your ancestors to obey and that I delivered to you through my servants the prophets."

[14] But they would not listen and were as stiff-necked as their ancestors, who did not trust in the LORD their God. [15] They rejected his decrees and the covenant he had made with their ancestors and the statutes he had warned them to keep. They followed worthless idols and themselves became worthless. They imitated the nations around them although the LORD had ordered them, "Do not do as they do."

[16] They forsook all the commands of the LORD their God and made for themselves two idols cast in the shape of calves, and an Asherah pole. They bowed down to all the starry hosts, and they worshiped Baal. [17] They sacrificed their sons and daughters in the fire. They practiced divination and sought omens and sold themselves to do evil in the eyes of the LORD, arousing his anger.

[18] So the LORD was very angry with Israel and removed them from his presence. Only the tribe of Judah was left, [19] and even Judah did not keep the commands of the LORD their God. They followed the practices Israel had introduced. [20] Therefore the LORD rejected all the people of Israel; he afflicted them and gave them into the hands of plunderers, until he thrust them from his presence.

[21] When he tore Israel away from the house of David, they made Jeroboam son of Nebat their king. Jeroboam enticed Israel away from following the LORD and caused them to commit a great sin. [22] The Israelites persisted in all the sins of Jeroboam and did not turn away from them [23] until the LORD removed them from his presence, as he had warned through all his

---

[a] *4 So* is probably an abbreviation for *Osorkon*.
[b] *12* Exodus 20:4,5

servants the prophets. So the people of Israel were taken from their homeland into exile in Assyria, and they are still there.

Samaria Resettled

²⁴The king of Assyria brought people from Babylon, Kuthah, Avva, Hamath and Sepharvaim and settled them in the towns of Samaria to replace the Israelites. They took over Samaria and lived in its towns. ²⁵When they first lived there, they did not worship the Lord; so he sent lions among them and they killed some of the people. ²⁶It was reported to the king of Assyria: "The people you deported and resettled in the towns of Samaria do not know what the god of that country requires. He has sent lions among them, which are killing them off, because the people do not know what he requires."

²⁷Then the king of Assyria gave this order: "Have one of the priests you took captive from Samaria go back to live there and teach the people what the god of the land requires." ²⁸So one of the priests who had been exiled from Samaria came to live in Bethel and taught them how to worship the Lord.

²⁹Nevertheless, each national group made its own gods in the several towns where they settled, and set them up in the shrines the people of Samaria had made at the high places. ³⁰The people from Babylon made Sukkoth Benoth, those from Kuthah made Nergal, and those from Hamath made Ashima; ³¹the Avvites made Nibhaz and Tartak, and the Sepharvites burned their children in the fire as sacrifices to Adrammelek and Anammelek, the gods of Sepharvaim. ³²They worshiped the Lord, but they also appointed all sorts of their own people to officiate for them as priests in the shrines at the high places. ³³They worshiped the Lord, but they also served their own gods in accordance with the customs of the nations from which they had been brought.

³⁴To this day they persist in their former practices. They neither worship the Lord nor adhere to the decrees and regulations, the laws and commands that the Lord gave the descendants of Jacob, whom he named Israel. ³⁵When the Lord made a covenant with the Israelites, he commanded them: "Do not worship any other gods or bow down to them, serve them or sacrifice to them. ³⁶But the Lord, who brought you up out of Egypt with mighty power and outstretched arm, is the one you must worship. To him you shall bow down and to him offer sacrifices. ³⁷You must always be careful to keep the decrees

---

2 Kings 17:7–40

God's patience doesn't last forever.

The Lord made clear right from the start that he was to be his people's one and only God. "I will take you as my own people," he promised, "and I will be your God" (Exodus 6:7). For centuries God was patient when his people wandered from him. But their sin became constant, including building "high places" and "sacred stones" and "Asherah poles" to worship false gods (2 Kings 17:9–10). So the Lord gave his people a huge dose of discipline. He allowed them to be conquered by foreign armies and carried off to captivity. The northern kingdom of Israel fell first—to the Assyrians in 722 BC. Then the southern kingdom of Judah was conquered—by the Babylonians in 586 BC. "The Lord is slow to anger, abounding in love and forgiving sin and rebellion" (Numbers 14:18), but he won't be patient forever. Sometimes he lets his people hit hard times until they come back to him.

Think: Do you think God gets impatient with us when we continue to sin—or not?

ROCK SOLID truths

and regulations, the laws and commands he wrote for you. Do not worship other gods. [38] Do not forget the covenant I have made with you, and do not worship other gods. [39] Rather, worship the LORD your God; it is he who will deliver you from the hand of all your enemies."

[40] They would not listen, however, but persisted in their former practices. [41] Even while these people were worshiping the LORD, they were serving their idols. To this day their children and grandchildren continue to do as their ancestors did.

Hezekiah King of Judah

18 In the third year of Hoshea son of Elah king of Israel, Hezekiah son of Ahaz king of Judah began to reign. [2] He was twenty-five years old when he became king, and he reigned in Jerusalem twenty-nine years. His mother's name was Abijah[a] daughter of Zechariah. [3] He did what was right in the eyes of the LORD, just as his father David had done. [4] He removed the high places, smashed the sacred stones and cut down the Asherah poles. He broke into pieces the bronze snake Moses had made, for up to that time the Israelites had been burning incense to it. (It was called Nehushtan.[b])

[5] Hezekiah trusted in the LORD, the God of Israel. There was no one like him among all the kings of Judah, either before him or after him. [6] He held fast to the LORD and did not stop following him; he kept the commands the LORD had given Moses. [7] And the LORD was with him; he was successful in whatever he undertook. He rebelled against the king of Assyria and did not serve him. [8] From watchtower to fortified city, he defeated the Philistines, as far as Gaza and its territory.

[9] In King Hezekiah's fourth year, which was the seventh year of Hoshea son of Elah king of Israel, Shalmaneser king of Assyria marched against Samaria and laid siege to it. [10] At the end of three years the Assyrians took it. So Samaria was captured in Hezekiah's sixth year, which was the ninth year of Hoshea king of Israel.

[11] The king of Assyria deported Israel to Assyria and settled them in Halah, in Gozan on the Habor River and in towns of the Medes. [12] This happened because they had not obeyed the LORD their God, but had violated his covenant—all that Moses the servant of the LORD commanded. They neither listened to the commands nor carried them out.

[13] In the fourteenth year of King Hezekiah's reign, Sennacherib king of Assyria attacked all the fortified cities of Judah and captured them. [14] So Hezekiah king of Judah sent this message to the king of Assyria at Lachish: "I have done wrong. Withdraw from me, and I will pay whatever you demand of me." The king of Assyria exacted from Hezekiah king of Judah three hundred talents[c] of silver and thirty talents[d] of gold. [15] So Hezekiah gave him all the silver that was found in the temple of the LORD and in the treasuries of the royal palace.

[16] At this time Hezekiah king of Judah stripped off the gold with which he had covered the doors and doorposts of the temple of the LORD, and gave it to the king of Assyria.

Sennacherib Threatens Jerusalem

[17] The king of Assyria sent his supreme commander, his chief officer and his field commander with a large army, from Lachish to King Hezekiah at Jerusalem. They came up to Jerusalem and stopped at the aqueduct of the Upper Pool, on the road to the Washerman's Field. [18] They called for the king; and Eliakim son of Hilkiah the palace administrator, Shebna the secretary, and Joah son of Asaph the recorder went out to them.

[19] The field commander said to them, "Tell Hezekiah:

"'This is what the great king, the king of Assyria, says: On what are you basing this confidence of

---

[a] 2 Hebrew *Abi*, a variant of *Abijah*
[b] 4 *Nehushtan* sounds like the Hebrew for both *bronze* and *snake*.   [c] 14 That is, about 11 tons or about 10 metric tons   [d] 14 That is, about 1 ton or about 1 metric ton

yours? ²⁰You say you have the counsel and the might for war—but you speak only empty words. On whom are you depending, that you rebel against me? ²¹Look, I know you are depending on Egypt, that splintered reed of a staff, which pierces the hand of anyone who leans on it! Such is Pharaoh king of Egypt to all who depend on him. ²²But if you say to me, "We are depending on the Lord our God"—isn't he the one whose high places and altars Hezekiah removed, saying to Judah and Jerusalem, "You must worship before this altar in Jerusalem"?

²³"Come now, make a bargain with my master, the king of Assyria: I will give you two thousand horses—if you can put riders on them! ²⁴How can you repulse one officer of the least of my master's officials, even though you are depending on Egypt for chariots and horsemen*? ²⁵Furthermore, have I come to attack and destroy this place without word from the Lord? The Lord himself told me to march against this country and destroy it.'"

²⁶Then Eliakim son of Hilkiah, and Shebna and Joah said to the field commander, "Please speak to your servants in Aramaic, since we understand it. Don't speak to us in Hebrew in the hearing of the people on the wall."

²⁷But the commander replied, "Was it only to your master and you that my master sent me to say these things, and not to the people sitting on the wall—who, like you, will have to eat their own excrement and drink their own urine?"

²⁸Then the commander stood and called out in Hebrew, "Hear the word of the great king, the king of Assyria! ²⁹This is what the king says: Do not let Hezekiah deceive you. He cannot deliver you from my hand. ³⁰Do not let Hezekiah persuade you to trust in the Lord when he says, 'The Lord will surely deliver us; this city will not be given into the hand of the king of Assyria.'

³¹"Do not listen to Hezekiah. This is what the king of Assyria says: Make peace with me and come out to me. Then each of you will eat fruit from your own vine and fig tree and drink water from your own cistern, ³²until I come and take you to a land like your own—a land of grain and new wine, a land of bread and vineyards, a land of olive trees and honey. Choose life and not death!

"Do not listen to Hezekiah, for he is misleading you when he says, 'The Lord will deliver us.' ³³Has the god of any nation ever delivered his land from the hand of the king of Assyria? ³⁴Where are the gods of Hamath and Arpad? Where are the gods of Sepharvaim, Hena and Ivvah? Have they rescued Samaria from my hand? ³⁵Who of all the gods of these countries has been able to save his land from me? How then can the Lord deliver Jerusalem from my hand?"

³⁶But the people remained silent and said nothing in reply, because the king had commanded, "Do not answer him."

³⁷Then Eliakim son of Hilkiah the palace administrator, Shebna the secretary, and Joah son of Asaph the recorder went to Hezekiah, with their clothes torn, and told him what the field commander had said.

Jerusalem's Deliverance Foretold

19 When King Hezekiah heard this, he tore his clothes and put on sackcloth and went into the temple of the Lord. ²He sent Eliakim the palace administrator, Shebna the secretary and the leading priests, all wearing sackcloth, to the prophet Isaiah son of Amoz. ³They told him, "This is what Hezekiah says: This day is a day of distress and rebuke and disgrace, as when children come to the moment of birth and there is no strength to deliver them. ⁴It may be that the Lord your God will hear all the words of the field commander, whom his master, the king of Assyria, has sent to ridicule the living God, and that he will rebuke him for the words the Lord your God has

^a 24 Or *charioteers*

heard. Therefore pray for the remnant that still survives.'"

[5] When King Hezekiah's officials came to Isaiah, [6] Isaiah said to them, "Tell your master, 'This is what the LORD says: Do not be afraid of what you have heard— those words with which the underlings of the king of Assyria have blasphemed me. [7] Listen! When he hears a certain report, I will make him want to return to his own country, and there I will have him cut down with the sword.'"

ROCK SOLID promises

"Do not be afraid of what you have heard."
2 Kings 19:6

Don't let human threats scare you. Listen hard to God and trust him.

---

[8] When the field commander heard that the king of Assyria had left Lachish, he withdrew and found the king fighting against Libnah.

[9] Now Sennacherib received a report that Tirhakah, the king of Cush,[a] was marching out to fight against him. So he again sent messengers to Hezekiah with this word: [10] "Say to Hezekiah king of Judah: Do not let the god you depend on deceive you when he says, 'Jerusalem will not be given into the hands of the king of Assyria.' [11] Surely you have heard what the kings of Assyria have done to all the countries, destroying them completely. And will you be delivered? [12] Did the gods of the nations that were destroyed by my predecessors deliver them—the gods of Gozan, Harran, Rezeph and the people of Eden who were in Tel Assar? [13] Where is the king of Hamath or the king of Arpad? Where are the kings of Lair, Sepharvaim, Hena and Ivvah?"

Hezekiah's Prayer

[14] Hezekiah received the letter from the messengers and read it. Then he went up to the temple of the LORD and spread it out before the LORD. [15] And Hezekiah prayed to the LORD: "LORD, the God of Israel, enthroned between the cherubim, you alone are God over all the kingdoms of the earth. You have made heaven and earth. [16] Give ear, LORD, and hear; open your eyes, LORD, and see; listen to the words Sennacherib has sent to ridicule the living God.

[17] "It is true, LORD, that the Assyrian kings have laid waste these nations and their lands. [18] They have thrown their gods into the fire and destroyed them, for they were not gods but only wood and stone, fashioned by human hands. [19] Now, LORD our God, deliver us from his hand, so that all the kingdoms of the earth may know that you alone, LORD, are God."

Isaiah Prophesies Sennacherib's Fall

[20] Then Isaiah son of Amoz sent a message to Hezekiah: "This is what the LORD, the God of Israel, says: I have heard your prayer concerning Sennacherib king of Assyria. [21] This is the word that the LORD has spoken against him:

"'Virgin Daughter Zion
despises you and mocks you.
Daughter Jerusalem
tosses her head as you flee.
[22] Who is it you have ridiculed and
blasphemed?
Against whom have you raised your
voice
and lifted your eyes in pride?
Against the Holy One of Israel!
[23] By your messengers
you have ridiculed the Lord.
And you have said,
"With my many chariots
I have ascended the heights of the
mountains,
the utmost heights of Lebanon.

---

[a] 9 That is, the upper Nile region

I have cut down its tallest cedars,
  the choicest of its junipers.
I have reached its remotest parts,
  the finest of its forests.
²⁴I have dug wells in foreign lands
  and drunk the water there.
With the soles of my feet
  I have dried up all the streams of
    Egypt."

²⁵"'Have you not heard?
  Long ago I ordained it.
In days of old I planned it;
  now I have brought it to pass,
that you have turned fortified cities
  into piles of stone.
²⁶Their people, drained of power,
  are dismayed and put to shame.
They are like plants in the field,
  like tender green shoots,
like grass sprouting on the roof,
  scorched before it grows up.

²⁷"'But I know where you are
  and when you come and go
  and how you rage against me.
²⁸Because you rage against me
  and because your insolence has
    reached my ears,
I will put my hook in your nose
  and my bit in your mouth,
and I will make you return
  by the way you came.'

²⁹"This will be the sign for you, Hezekiah:

"This year you will eat what grows by
    itself,
  and the second year what springs
    from that.
But in the third year sow and reap,
  plant vineyards and eat their fruit.
³⁰Once more a remnant of the kingdom
    of Judah
  will take root below and bear fruit
    above.
³¹For out of Jerusalem will come a
    remnant,
  and out of Mount Zion a band of
    survivors.

"The zeal of the LORD Almighty will accomplish this.

³²"Therefore this is what the LORD says concerning the king of Assyria:

"'He will not enter this city
  or shoot an arrow here.
He will not come before it with shield
  or build a siege ramp against it.
³³By the way that he came he will
    return;
  he will not enter this city,
            declares the LORD.
³⁴I will defend this city and save it,
  for my sake and for the sake of
    David my servant.'"

³⁵That night the angel of the LORD went out and put to death a hundred and eighty-five thousand in the Assyrian camp. When the people got up the next morning—there were all the dead bodies! ³⁶So Sennacherib king of Assyria broke camp and withdrew. He returned to Nineveh and stayed there.

³⁷One day, while he was worshiping in the temple of his god Nisrok, his sons Adrammelek and Sharezer killed him with the sword, and they escaped to the land of Ararat. And Esarhaddon his son succeeded him as king.

Hezekiah's Illness

20 In those days Hezekiah became ill and was at the point of death. The prophet Isaiah son of Amoz went to him and said, "This is what the LORD says: Put your house in order, because you are going to die; you will not recover."

²Hezekiah turned his face to the wall and prayed to the LORD, ³"Remember, LORD, how I have walked before you faithfully and with wholehearted devotion and have done what is good in your eyes." And Hezekiah wept bitterly.

⁴Before Isaiah had left the middle court, the word of the LORD came to him: ⁵"Go back and tell Hezekiah, the ruler of my people, 'This is what the LORD, the God of your father David, says: I have heard your prayer and seen your tears; I will heal you. On the third day from now you will go up to the temple of the LORD.

⁶I will add fifteen years to your life. And I will deliver you and this city from the hand of the king of Assyria. I will defend this city for my sake and for the sake of my servant David.'"

⁷Then Isaiah said, "Prepare a poultice of figs." They did so and applied it to the boil, and he recovered.

⁸Hezekiah had asked Isaiah, "What will be the sign that the LORD will heal me and that I will go up to the temple of the LORD on the third day from now?"

⁹Isaiah answered, "This is the LORD's sign to you that the LORD will do what he has promised: Shall the shadow go forward ten steps, or shall it go back ten steps?"

¹⁰"It is a simple matter for the shadow to go forward ten steps," said Hezekiah. "Rather, have it go back ten steps."

¹¹Then the prophet Isaiah called on the LORD, and the LORD made the shadow go back the ten steps it had gone down on the stairway of Ahaz.

Envoys From Babylon

¹²At that time Marduk-Baladan son of Baladan king of Babylon sent Hezekiah letters and a gift, because he had heard of Hezekiah's illness. ¹³Hezekiah received the envoys and showed them all that was in his storehouses—the silver, the gold, the spices and the fine olive oil—his armory and everything found among his treasures. There was nothing in his palace or in all his kingdom that Hezekiah did not show them.

¹⁴Then Isaiah the prophet went to King Hezekiah and asked, "What did those men say, and where did they come from?"

"From a distant land," Hezekiah replied. "They came from Babylon."

¹⁵The prophet asked, "What did they see in your palace?"

"They saw everything in my palace," Hezekiah said. "There is nothing among my treasures that I did not show them."

¹⁶Then Isaiah said to Hezekiah, "Hear

ROCK SOLID principles

2 Kings 20:1–11

Start with prayer.

Ayla always felt like praying was pointless. She knew the Bible said she should pray. She had read where Jesus taught his disciples to pray simple words telling the Lord their everyday needs (see Matthew 6:9–14). But she felt like the world was full of too many terrible problems for God to bother with her prayers about boys and homework and finding a part-time job. So prayer never made sense to Ayla—until she had a request she thought was big enough to get God's attention. She needed God to protect her brother, who struggled with depression. When Ayla started praying, she felt a huge rush of relief. She got the impression God had been waiting to talk with her for a long time.

Hezekiah was one of Judah's greatest kings, famed for his devotion to God. He fell ill, and even God said he would die. But when Hezekiah sought God in prayer, the Lord granted Hezekiah another 15 years of life. For Hezekiah, prayer wasn't a last resort. Talking to God was the first place he turned.

the word of the LORD: ¹⁷The time will surely come when everything in your palace, and all that your predecessors have stored up until this day, will be carried off to Babylon. Nothing will be left, says the LORD. ¹⁸And some of your descendants, your own flesh and blood who will be born to you, will be taken away, and they will become eunuchs in the palace of the king of Babylon."

¹⁹"The word of the LORD you have spoken is good," Hezekiah replied. For he thought, "Will there not be peace and security in my lifetime?"

²⁰As for the other events of Hezekiah's reign, all his achievements and how he made the pool and the tunnel by which he brought water into the city, are they not written in the book of the annals of the kings of Judah? ²¹Hezekiah rested with his ancestors. And Manasseh his son succeeded him as king.

Manasseh King of Judah

21 Manasseh was twelve years old when he became king, and he reigned in Jerusalem fifty-five years. His mother's name was Hephzibah. ²He did evil in the eyes of the LORD, following the detestable practices of the nations the LORD had driven out before the Israelites. ³He rebuilt the high places his father Hezekiah had destroyed; he also erected altars to Baal and made an Asherah pole, as Ahab king of Israel had done. He bowed down to all the starry hosts and worshiped them. ⁴He built altars in the temple of the LORD, of which the LORD had said, "In Jerusalem I will put my Name." ⁵In the two courts of the temple of the LORD, he built altars to all the starry hosts. ⁶He sacrificed his own son in the fire, practiced divination, sought omens, and consulted mediums and spiritists. He did much evil in the eyes of the LORD, arousing his anger.

⁷He took the carved Asherah pole he had made and put it in the temple, of which the LORD had said to David and to his son Solomon, "In this temple and in Jerusalem, which I have chosen out of all the tribes of Israel, I will put my Name forever. ⁸I will not again make the feet of the Israelites wander from the land I gave their ancestors, if only they will be careful to do everything I commanded them and will keep the whole Law that my servant Moses gave them." ⁹But the people did not listen. Manasseh led them astray, so that they did more evil than the nations the LORD had destroyed before the Israelites.

¹⁰The LORD said through his servants the prophets: ¹¹"Manasseh king of Judah has committed these detestable sins. He has done more evil than the Amorites who preceded him and has led Judah into sin with his idols. ¹²Therefore this is what the LORD, the God of Israel, says: I am going to bring such disaster on Jerusalem and Judah that the ears of everyone who hears of it will tingle. ¹³I will stretch out over Jerusalem the measuring line used against Samaria and the plumb line used against the house of Ahab. I will wipe out Jerusalem as one wipes a dish, wiping it and turning it upside down. ¹⁴I will forsake the remnant of my inheritance and give them into the hands of enemies. They will be looted and plundered by all their enemies; ¹⁵they have done evil in my eyes and have aroused my anger from the day their ancestors came out of Egypt until this day."

¹⁶Moreover, Manasseh also shed so much innocent blood that he filled Jerusalem from end to end—besides the sin that he had caused Judah to commit, so that they did evil in the eyes of the LORD.

¹⁷As for the other events of Manasseh's reign, and all he did, including the sin he committed, are they not written in the book of the annals of the kings of Judah? ¹⁸Manasseh rested with his ancestors and was buried in his palace garden, the garden of Uzza. And Amon his son succeeded him as king.

Amon King of Judah

¹⁹Amon was twenty-two years old when he became king, and he reigned in Jerusalem two years. His mother's name was Meshullemeth daughter of Haruz; she was from Jotbah. ²⁰He did evil in the eyes of the LORD, as his father Manasseh had done. ²¹He followed completely the ways of his father, worshiping the idols his

father had worshiped, and bowing down to them. ²²He forsook the LORD, the God of his ancestors, and did not walk in obedience to him.

²³Amon's officials conspired against him and assassinated the king in his palace. ²⁴Then the people of the land killed all who had plotted against King Amon, and they made Josiah his son king in his place.

²⁵As for the other events of Amon's reign, and what he did, are they not written in the book of the annals of the kings of Judah? ²⁶He was buried in his tomb in the garden of Uzza. And Josiah his son succeeded him as king.

The Book of the Law Found

22 Josiah was eight years old when he became king, and he reigned in Jerusalem thirty-one years. His mother's name was Jedidah daughter of Adaiah; she was from Bozkath. ²He did what was right in the eyes of the LORD and followed completely the ways of his father David, not turning aside to the right or to the left.

³In the eighteenth year of his reign, King Josiah sent the secretary, Shaphan son of Azaliah, the son of Meshullam, to the temple of the LORD. He said: ⁴"Go up to Hilkiah the high priest and have him get ready the money that has been brought into the temple of the LORD, which the doorkeepers have collected from the people. ⁵Have them entrust it to the men appointed to supervise the work on the temple. And have these men pay the workers who repair the temple of the LORD— ⁶the carpenters, the builders and the masons. Also have them purchase timber and dressed stone to repair the temple. ⁷But they need not account for the money entrusted to them, because they are honest in their dealings."

⁸Hilkiah the high priest said to Shaphan the secretary, "I have found the Book of the Law in the temple of the LORD." He gave it to Shaphan, who read it. ⁹Then Shaphan the secretary went to the king and reported to him: "Your officials have paid out the money that was in the temple of the LORD and have entrusted it to the workers and supervisors at the temple."

¹⁰Then Shaphan the secretary informed the king, "Hilkiah the priest has given me a book." And Shaphan read from it in the presence of the king.

¹¹When the king heard the words of the Book of the Law, he tore his robes. ¹²He gave these orders to Hilkiah the priest, Ahikam son of Shaphan, Akbor son of Micaiah, Shaphan the secretary and Asaiah the king's attendant: ¹³"Go and inquire of the LORD for me and for the people and for all Judah about what is written in this book that has been found. Great is the LORD's anger that burns against us because those who have gone before us have not obeyed the words of this book; they have not acted in accordance with all that is written there concerning us."

¹⁴Hilkiah the priest, Ahikam, Akbor, Shaphan and Asaiah went to speak to the prophet Huldah, who was the wife of Shallum son of Tikvah, the son of Harhas, keeper of the wardrobe. She lived in Jerusalem, in the New Quarter.

¹⁵She said to them, "This is what the LORD, the God of Israel, says: Tell the man who sent you to me, ¹⁶'This is what the LORD says: I am going to bring disaster on this place and its people, according to everything written in the book the king of Judah has read. ¹⁷Because they have forsaken me and burned incense to other gods and aroused my anger by all the idols their hands have made,ᵃ my anger will burn against this place and will not be quenched.' ¹⁸Tell the king of Judah, who sent you to inquire of the LORD, 'This is what the LORD, the God of Israel, says concerning the words you heard: ¹⁹Because your heart was responsive and you humbled yourself before the LORD when you heard what I have spoken against this place and its people—that they would become a curseᵇ and be laid waste—and because you tore your robes and wept in my presence, I also have heard you, declares the LORD. ²⁰Therefore I will gather you to your ancestors, and you will be buried

---

ᵃ 17 Or *by everything they have done*
ᵇ 19 That is, their names would be used in cursing (see Jer. 29:22); or, others would see that they are cursed.

in peace. Your eyes will not see all the disaster I am going to bring on this place.'"

So they took her answer back to the king.

Josiah Renews the Covenant

23 Then the king called together all the elders of Judah and Jerusalem. ²He went up to the temple of the Lord with the people of Judah, the inhabitants of Jerusalem, the priests and the prophets—all the people from the least to the greatest. He read in their hearing all the words of the Book of the Covenant, which had been found in the temple of the Lord. ³The king stood by the pillar and renewed the covenant in the presence of the Lord—to follow the Lord and keep his commands, statutes and decrees with all his heart and all his soul, thus confirming the words of the covenant written in this book. Then all the people pledged themselves to the covenant.

⁴The king ordered Hilkiah the high priest, the priests next in rank and the doorkeepers to remove from the temple of the Lord all the articles made for Baal and Asherah and all the starry hosts. He burned them outside Jerusalem in the fields of the Kidron Valley and took the ashes to Bethel. ⁵He did away with the idolatrous priests appointed by the kings of Judah to burn incense on the high places of the towns of Judah and on those around Jerusalem—those who burned incense to Baal, to the sun and moon, to the constellations and to all the starry hosts. ⁶He took the Asherah pole from the temple of the Lord to the Kidron Valley outside Jerusalem and burned it there. He ground it to powder and scattered the dust over the graves of the common people. ⁷He also tore down the quarters of the male shrine prostitutes that were in the temple of the Lord, the quarters where women did weaving for Asherah.

⁸Josiah brought all the priests from the towns of Judah and desecrated the high places, from Geba to Beersheba, where the priests had burned incense. He broke down the gateway at the entrance of the Gate of Joshua, the city governor, which was on the left of the city gate. ⁹Although the priests of the high places did not serve at the altar of the Lord in Jerusalem, they ate unleavened bread with their fellow priests.

¹⁰He desecrated Topheth, which was in the Valley of Ben Hinnom, so no one could use it to sacrifice their son or daughter in the fire to Molek. ¹¹He removed from the entrance to the temple of the Lord the horses that the kings of Judah had dedicated to the sun. They were in the court*a* near the room of an official named Nathan-Melek. Josiah then burned the chariots dedicated to the sun.

¹²He pulled down the altars the kings of Judah had erected on the roof near the upper room of Ahaz, and the altars Manasseh had built in the two courts of the temple of the Lord. He removed them from there, smashed them to pieces and threw the rubble into the Kidron Valley. ¹³The king also desecrated the high places that were east of Jerusalem on the south of the Hill of Corruption—the ones Solomon king of Israel had built for Ashtoreth the vile goddess of the Sidonians, for Chemosh the vile god of Moab, and for Molek the detestable god of the people of Ammon. ¹⁴Josiah smashed the sacred stones and cut down the Asherah poles and covered the sites with human bones.

¹⁵Even the altar at Bethel, the high place made by Jeroboam son of Nebat, who had caused Israel to sin—even that altar and high place he demolished. He burned the high place and ground it to powder, and burned the Asherah pole also. ¹⁶Then Josiah looked around, and when he saw the tombs that were there on the hillside, he had the bones removed from them and burned on the altar to defile it, in accordance with the word of the Lord proclaimed by the man of God who foretold these things.

¹⁷The king asked, "What is that tombstone I see?"

The people of the city said, "It marks the tomb of the man of God who came from Judah and pronounced against the altar of Bethel the very things you have done to it."

¹⁸"Leave it alone," he said. "Don't let

---

a 11 The meaning of the Hebrew for this word is uncertain.

anyone disturb his bones." So they spared his bones and those of the prophet who had come from Samaria.

¹⁹Just as he had done at Bethel, Josiah removed all the shrines at the high places that the kings of Israel had built in the towns of Samaria and that had aroused the LORD's anger. ²⁰Josiah slaughtered all the priests of those high places on the altars and burned human bones on them. Then he went back to Jerusalem.

²¹The king gave this order to all the people: "Celebrate the Passover to the LORD your God, as it is written in this Book of the Covenant." ²²Neither in the days of the judges who led Israel nor in the days of the kings of Israel and the kings of Judah had any such Passover been observed. ²³But in the eighteenth year of King Josiah, this Passover was celebrated to the LORD in Jerusalem.

²⁴Furthermore, Josiah got rid of the mediums and spiritists, the household gods, the idols and all the other detestable things seen in Judah and Jerusalem. This he did to fulfill the requirements of the law written in the book that Hilkiah the priest had discovered in the temple of the LORD. ²⁵Neither before nor after Josiah was there a king like him who turned to the LORD as he did—with all his heart and with all his soul and with

---

2 Kings 23:25

Josiah revived true worship.

Scripture calls Manasseh the country's most evil king ever (see 2 Kings 21:9). He worshiped Baal and Asherah along with the sun, moon, and stars, and he even sacrificed his son to the god Molech (see 2 Kings 21:6). At the end of his life Manasseh repented and tried to abolish idolatry, but his reforms were undone by his evil son Amon, who ruled just two years (see 2 Chronicles 33:11 – 24).

Enter Josiah, crowned king at the age of eight, put on his father's throne when Amon was assassinated. He was sixteen when he "began to seek the God of his father David" (2 Chronicles 34:3) and just twenty when he began to thoroughly destroy any sign of the worship of pagan gods in Jerusalem and throughout Judah. Not only did he do away with false worship, but he encouraged respect for the one true God. He ordered the temple to be restored, and during that process Hilkiah the priest rediscovered the "Book of the Law" that described all the ways the people should obey God.

This young king tore his clothes with grief that the Lord's law had been misplaced for so long. He suddenly understood that spiritual rebellion was the reason so much tragedy had struck the nation. He renewed his commitment to following all of the Lord's commands, and as long as Josiah lived, all the people of Israel "did not fail to follow the LORD" (2 Chronicles 34:33).

You can find Josiah in 2 Kings 21 — 23; 2 Chronicles 33 — 35; Jeremiah 1:1 – 2; Zephaniah 1:1; and Matthew 1:10.

UNSHAKEN people

all his strength, in accordance with all the Law of Moses.

²⁶Nevertheless, the LORD did not turn away from the heat of his fierce anger, which burned against Judah because of all that Manasseh had done to arouse his anger. ²⁷So the LORD said, "I will remove Judah also from my presence as I removed Israel, and I will reject Jerusalem, the city I chose, and this temple, about which I said, 'My Name shall be there.'*"

²⁸As for the other events of Josiah's reign, and all he did, are they not written in the book of the annals of the kings of Judah?

²⁹While Josiah was king, Pharaoh Necho king of Egypt went up to the Euphrates River to help the king of Assyria. King Josiah marched out to meet him in battle, but Necho faced him and killed him at Megiddo. ³⁰Josiah's servants brought his body in a chariot from Megiddo to Jerusalem and buried him in his own tomb. And the people of the land took Jehoahaz son of Josiah and anointed him and made him king in place of his father.

Jehoahaz King of Judah

³¹Jehoahaz was twenty-three years old when he became king, and he reigned in Jerusalem three months. His mother's name was Hamutal daughter of Jeremiah; she was from Libnah. ³²He did evil in the eyes of the LORD, just as his predecessors had done. ³³Pharaoh Necho put him in chains at Riblah in the land of Hamath so that he might not reign in Jerusalem, and he imposed on Judah a levy of a hundred talents*ᵇ* of silver and a talent*ᶜ* of gold. ³⁴Pharaoh Necho made Eliakim son of Josiah king in place of his father Josiah and changed Eliakim's name to Jehoiakim. But he took Jehoahaz and carried him off to Egypt, and there he died. ³⁵Jehoiakim paid Pharaoh Necho the silver and gold he demanded. In order to do so, he taxed the land and exacted the silver and gold from the people of the land according to their assessments.

Jehoiakim King of Judah

³⁶Jehoiakim was twenty-five years old when he became king, and he reigned in

Jerusalem eleven years. His mother's name was Zebidah daughter of Pedaiah; she was from Rumah. ³⁷And he did evil in the eyes of the LORD, just as his predecessors had done.

24 During Jehoiakim's reign, Nebuchadnezzar king of Babylon invaded the land, and Jehoiakim became his vassal for three years. But then he turned against Nebuchadnezzar and rebelled. ²The LORD sent Babylonian,*ᵈ* Aramean, Moabite and Ammonite raiders against him to destroy Judah, in accordance with the word of the LORD proclaimed by his servants the prophets. ³Surely these things happened to Judah according to the LORD's command, in order to remove them from his presence because of the sins of Manasseh and all he had done, ⁴including the shedding of innocent blood. For he had filled Jerusalem with innocent blood, and the LORD was not willing to forgive.

⁵As for the other events of Jehoiakim's reign, and all he did, are they not written in the book of the annals of the kings of Judah? ⁶Jehoiakim rested with his ancestors. And Jehoiachin his son succeeded him as king.

⁷The king of Egypt did not march out from his own country again, because the king of Babylon had taken all his territory, from the Wadi of Egypt to the Euphrates River.

Jehoiachin King of Judah

⁸Jehoiachin was eighteen years old when he became king, and he reigned in Jerusalem three months. His mother's name was Nehushta daughter of Elnathan; she was from Jerusalem. ⁹He did evil in the eyes of the LORD, just as his father had done.

¹⁰At that time the officers of Nebuchadnezzar king of Babylon advanced on Jerusalem and laid siege to it, ¹¹and Nebuchadnezzar himself came up to the city while his officers were besieging it.

ᵃ 27 1 Kings 8:29   *ᵇ 33* That is, about 3 3/4 tons or about 3.4 metric tons   *ᶜ 33* That is, about 75 pounds or about 34 kilograms   *ᵈ 2* Or *Chaldean*

¹²Jehoiachin king of Judah, his mother, his attendants, his nobles and his officials all surrendered to him.

In the eighth year of the reign of the king of Babylon, he took Jehoiachin prisoner. ¹³As the Lord had declared, Nebuchadnezzar removed the treasures from the temple of the Lord and from the royal palace, and cut up the gold articles that Solomon king of Israel had made for the temple of the Lord. ¹⁴He carried all Jerusalem into exile: all the officers and fighting men, and all the skilled workers and artisans—a total of ten thousand. Only the poorest people of the land were left.

¹⁵Nebuchadnezzar took Jehoiachin captive to Babylon. He also took from Jerusalem to Babylon the king's mother, his wives, his officials and the prominent people of the land. ¹⁶The king of Babylon also deported to Babylon the entire force of seven thousand fighting men, strong and fit for war, and a thousand skilled workers and artisans. ¹⁷He made Mattaniah, Jehoiachin's uncle, king in his place and changed his name to Zedekiah.

Zedekiah King of Judah

¹⁸Zedekiah was twenty-one years old when he became king, and he reigned in Jerusalem eleven years. His mother's name was Hamutal daughter of Jeremiah; she was from Libnah. ¹⁹He did evil in the eyes of the Lord, just as Jehoiakim had done. ²⁰It was because of the Lord's anger that all this happened to Jerusalem and Judah, and in the end he thrust them from his presence.

The Fall of Jerusalem

Now Zedekiah rebelled against the king of Babylon.

25 So in the ninth year of Zedekiah's reign, on the tenth day of the tenth month, Nebuchadnezzar king of Babylon marched against Jerusalem with his whole army. He encamped outside the city and built siege works all around it. ²The city was kept under siege until the eleventh year of King Zedekiah.

³By the ninth day of the fourth[a] month the famine in the city had become so severe that there was no food for the people to eat. ⁴Then the city wall was broken through, and the whole army fled at night through the gate between the two walls near the king's garden, though the Babylonians[b] were surrounding the city. They fled toward the Arabah,[c] ⁵but the Babylonian[d] army pursued the king and overtook him in the plains of Jericho. All his soldiers were separated from him and scattered, ⁶and he was captured.

He was taken to the king of Babylon at Riblah, where sentence was pronounced on him. ⁷They killed the sons of Zedekiah before his eyes. Then they put out his eyes, bound him with bronze shackles and took him to Babylon.

⁸On the seventh day of the fifth month, in the nineteenth year of Nebuchadnezzar king of Babylon, Nebuzaradan commander of the imperial guard, an official of the king of Babylon, came to Jerusalem. ⁹He set fire to the temple of the Lord, the royal palace and all the houses of Jerusalem. Every important building he burned down. ¹⁰The whole Babylonian army under the commander of the imperial guard broke down the walls around Jerusalem. ¹¹Nebuzaradan the commander of the guard carried into exile the people who remained in the city, along with the rest of the populace and those who had deserted to the king of Babylon. ¹²But the commander left behind some of the poorest people of the land to work the vineyards and fields.

¹³The Babylonians broke up the bronze pillars, the movable stands and the bronze Sea that were at the temple of the Lord and they carried the bronze to Babylon. ¹⁴They also took away the pots, shovels, wick trimmers, dishes and all the bronze articles used in the temple service. ¹⁵The commander of the imperial guard took

---

a 3 Probable reading of the original Hebrew text (see Jer. 52:6); Masoretic Text does not have *fourth.*   *b 4* Or *Chaldeans*; also in verses 13, 25 and 26   *c 4* Or *the Jordan Valley*   *d 5* Or *Chaldean*; also in verses 10 and 24 away the censers and sprinkling bowls—all that were made of pure gold or silver.

¹⁶The bronze from the two pillars, the Sea and the movable stands, which Solomon had made for the temple of the LORD, was more than could be weighed. ¹⁷Each pillar was eighteen cubits*a* high. The bronze capital on top of one pillar was three cubits*b* high and was decorated with a network and pomegranates of bronze all around. The other pillar, with its network, was similar.

¹⁸The commander of the guard took as prisoners Seraiah the chief priest, Zephaniah the priest next in rank and the three doorkeepers. ¹⁹Of those still in the city, he took the officer in charge of the fighting men, and five royal advisers. He also took the secretary who was chief officer in charge of conscripting the people of the land and sixty of the conscripts who were found in the city. ²⁰Nebuzaradan the commander took them all and brought them to the king of Babylon at Riblah. ²¹There at Riblah, in the land of Hamath, the king had them executed.

So Judah went into captivity, away from her land.

²²Nebuchadnezzar king of Babylon appointed Gedaliah son of Ahikam, the son of Shaphan, to be over the people he had left behind in Judah. ²³When all the army officers and their men heard that the king of Babylon had appointed Gedaliah as governor, they came to Gedaliah at Mizpah—Ishmael son of Nethaniah, Johanan son of Kareah, Seraiah son of Tanhumeth the Netophathite, Jaazaniah the son of the Maakathite, and their men. ²⁴Gedaliah took an oath to reassure them and their men. "Do not be afraid of the Babylonian officials," he said. "Settle down in the land and serve the king of Babylon, and it will go well with you."

²⁵In the seventh month, however, Ishmael son of Nethaniah, the son of Elishama, who was of royal blood, came with ten men and assassinated Gedaliah and also the men of Judah and the Babylonians who were with him at Mizpah. ²⁶At this, all the people from the least to the greatest, together with the army officers, fled to Egypt for fear of the Babylonians.

Jehoiachin Released

²⁷In the thirty-seventh year of the exile of Jehoiachin king of Judah, in the year Awel-Marduk became king of Babylon, he released Jehoiachin king of Judah from prison. He did this on the twenty-seventh day of the twelfth month. ²⁸He spoke kindly to him and gave him a seat of honor higher than those of the other kings who were with him in Babylon. ²⁹So Jehoiachin put aside his prison clothes and for the rest of his life ate regularly at the king's table. ³⁰Day by day the king gave Jehoiachin a regular allowance as long as he lived.

a 17 That is, about 27 feet or about 8.1 meters
b 17 That is, about 4 1/2 feet or about 1.4 meters

1 CHRONICLES

BOOK OUTLINE

List of generations
(1:1 — 9:44)

The reign of David
(10:1 — 29:30)

Although the books of Chronicles seem like a repeat of Samuel and Kings, they aren't. The Chronicles were written for the exiles who had returned to Israel after the Babylonian captivity to remind them they were from the royal line of David and were God's chosen people. The main theme is that God is always faithful to his covenant.

For these reasons 1 Chronicles begins with an outline of history from Adam through the death of King Saul. The rest of the book is about the reign of King David. These books serve as both a warning and encouragement to the Jews to be faithful to the covenant.

Historical Records From Adam to Abraham

To Noah's Sons

Adam, Seth, Enosh, [2]Kenan, Mahalalel, Jared, [3]Enoch, Methuselah, Lamech, Noah.

[4]The sons of Noah:[a]
Shem, Ham and Japheth.

The Japhethites

[5]The sons[b] of Japheth:
Gomer, Magog, Madai, Javan, Tubal, Meshek and Tiras.
[6]The sons of Gomer:
Ashkenaz, Riphath[c] and Togarmah.
[7]The sons of Javan:
Elishah, Tarshish, the Kittites and the Rodanites.

The Hamites

[8]The sons of Ham:
Cush, Egypt, Put and Canaan.
[9]The sons of Cush:
Seba, Havilah, Sabta, Raamah and Sabteka.
The sons of Raamah:
Sheba and Dedan.
[10]Cush was the father[d] of
Nimrod, who became a mighty warrior on earth.
[11]Egypt was the father of
the Ludites, Anamites, Lehabites, Naphtuhites, [12]Pathrusites, Kasluhites (from whom the Philistines came) and Caphtorites.
[13]Canaan was the father of
Sidon his firstborn,[e] and of the Hittites, [14]Jebusites, Amorites, Girgashites, [15]Hivites, Arkites, Sinites, [16]Arvadites, Zemarites and Hamathites.

The Semites

[17]The sons of Shem:
Elam, Ashur, Arphaxad, Lud and Aram.
The sons of Aram:[f]
Uz, Hul, Gether and Meshek.
[18]Arphaxad was the father of Shelah, and Shelah the father of Eber.
[19]Two sons were born to Eber:
One was named Peleg,[g] because in his time the earth was divided; his brother was named Joktan.
[20]Joktan was the father of
Almodad, Sheleph, Hazarmaveth, Jerah, [21]Hadoram, Uzal, Diklah, [22]Obal,[b] Abimael, Sheba, [23]Ophir, Havilah and Jobab. All these were sons of Joktan.

[24]Shem, Arphaxad,[i] Shelah,
[25]Eber, Peleg, Reu,
[26]Serug, Nahor, Terah
[27]and Abram (that is, Abraham).

The Family of Abraham

[28]The sons of Abraham:
Isaac and Ishmael.

Descendants of Hagar

[29]These were their descendants:
Nebaioth the firstborn of Ishmael, Kedar, Adbeel, Mibsam, [30]Mishma, Dumah, Massa, Hadad, Tema, [31]Jetur, Naphish and Kedemah. These were the sons of Ishmael.

Descendants of Keturah

[32]The sons born to Keturah, Abraham's concubine:
Zimran, Jokshan, Medan, Midian, Ishbak and Shuah.
The sons of Jokshan:
Sheba and Dedan.
[33]The sons of Midian:

---

[a] 4 Septuagint; Hebrew does not have this line.
[b] 5 *Sons* may mean *descendants* or *successors* or *nations*; also in verses 6-9, 17 and 23.
[c] 6 Many Hebrew manuscripts and Vulgate (see also Septuagint and Gen. 10:3); most Hebrew manuscripts *Diphath*   [d] 10 *Father* may mean *ancestor* or *predecessor* or *founder*; also in verses 11, 13, 18 and 20.   [e] 13 Or *of the Sidonians, the foremost*   [f] 17 One Hebrew manuscript and some Septuagint manuscripts (see also Gen. 10:23); most Hebrew manuscripts do not have this line.   [g] 19 *Peleg* means *division*.
[h] 22 Some Hebrew manuscripts and Syriac (see also Gen. 10:28); most Hebrew manuscripts *Ebal*   [i] 24 Hebrew; some Septuagint manuscripts *Arphaxad, Cainan* (see also note at Gen. 11:10)

Ephah, Epher, Hanok, Abida and Eldaah.
All these were descendants of Keturah.

Descendants of Sarah

³⁴Abraham was the father of Isaac.
The sons of Isaac:
Esau and Israel.

Esau's Sons

³⁵The sons of Esau:
Eliphaz, Reuel, Jeush, Jalam and Korah.
³⁶The sons of Eliphaz:
Teman, Omar, Zepho,[a] Gatam and Kenaz;
by Timna: Amalek.[b]
³⁷The sons of Reuel:
Nahath, Zerah, Shammah and Mizzah.

The People of Seir in Edom

³⁸The sons of Seir:
Lotan, Shobal, Zibeon, Anah, Dishon, Ezer and Dishan.
³⁹The sons of Lotan:
Hori and Homam. Timna was Lotan's sister.
⁴⁰The sons of Shobal:
Alvan,[c] Manahath, Ebal, Shepho and Onam.
The sons of Zibeon:
Aiah and Anah.
⁴¹The son of Anah:
Dishon.
The sons of Dishon:
Hemdan,[d] Eshban, Ithran and Keran.
⁴²The sons of Ezer:
Bilhan, Zaavan and Akan.[e]
The sons of Dishan[f]:
Uz and Aran.

The Rulers of Edom

⁴³These were the kings who reigned in Edom before any Israelite king reigned:
Bela son of Beor, whose city was named Dinhabah.
⁴⁴When Bela died, Jobab son of Zerah from Bozrah succeeded him as king.
⁴⁵When Jobab died, Husham from the land of the Temanites succeeded him as king.
⁴⁶When Husham died, Hadad son of Bedad, who defeated Midian in the country of Moab, succeeded him as king. His city was named Avith.
⁴⁷When Hadad died, Samlah from Masrekah succeeded him as king.
⁴⁸When Samlah died, Shaul from Rehoboth on the river[g] succeeded him as king.
⁴⁹When Shaul died, Baal-Hanan son of Akbor succeeded him as king.
⁵⁰When Baal-Hanan died, Hadad succeeded him as king. His city was named Pau,[h] and his wife's name was Mehetabel daughter of Matred, the daughter of Me-Zahab.
⁵¹Hadad also died.

The chiefs of Edom were:
Timna, Alvah, Jetheth, ⁵²Oholibamah, Elah, Pinon, ⁵³Kenaz, Teman, Mibzar, ⁵⁴Magdiel and Iram. These were the chiefs of Edom.

Israel's Sons

2 These were the sons of Israel:
Reuben, Simeon, Levi, Judah, Issachar, Zebulun, ²Dan, Joseph, Benjamin, Naphtali, Gad and Asher.

---

[a] 36 Many Hebrew manuscripts, some Septuagint manuscripts and Syriac (see also Gen. 36:11); most Hebrew manuscripts *Zephi*
[b] 36 Some Septuagint manuscripts (see also Gen. 36:12); Hebrew *Gatam, Kenaz, Timna and Amalek*   [c] 40 Many Hebrew manuscripts and some Septuagint manuscripts (see also Gen. 36:23); most Hebrew manuscripts *Alian*
[d] 41 Many Hebrew manuscripts and some Septuagint manuscripts (see also Gen. 36:26); most Hebrew manuscripts *Hamran*
[e] 42 Many Hebrew and Septuagint manuscripts (see also Gen. 36:27); most Hebrew manuscripts *Zaavan, Jaakan*   [f] 42 See Gen. 36:28; Hebrew *Dishon*, a variant of *Dishan*
[g] 48 Possibly the Euphrates   [h] 50 Many Hebrew manuscripts, some Septuagint manuscripts, Vulgate and Syriac (see also Gen. 36:39); most Hebrew manuscripts *Pai*

Judah
To Hezron's Sons

³ The sons of Judah:

Er, Onan and Shelah. These three were born to him by a Canaanite woman, the daughter of Shua. Er, Judah's firstborn, was wicked in the Lord's sight; so the Lord put him to death. ⁴Judah's daughter-in-law Tamar bore Perez and Zerah to Judah. He had five sons in all.

⁵ The sons of Perez:

Hezron and Hamul.

⁶ The sons of Zerah:

Zimri, Ethan, Heman, Kalkol and Darda*ᵃ*—five in all.

⁷ The son of Karmi:

Achar,*ᵇ* who brought trouble on Israel by violating the ban on taking devoted things.*ᶜ*

⁸ The son of Ethan:

Azariah.

⁹ The sons born to Hezron were:

Jerahmeel, Ram and Caleb.*ᵈ*

From Ram Son of Hezron

¹⁰ Ram was the father of

Amminadab, and Amminadab the father of Nahshon, the leader of the people of Judah. ¹¹Nahshon was the father of Salmon,*ᵉ* Salmon the father of Boaz, ¹²Boaz the father of Obed and Obed the father of Jesse.

¹³ Jesse was the father of

Eliab his firstborn; the second son was Abinadab, the third Shimea, ¹⁴the fourth Nethanel, the fifth Raddai, ¹⁵the sixth Ozem and the seventh David. ¹⁶Their sisters were Zeruiah and Abigail. Zeruiah's three sons were Abishai, Joab and Asahel. ¹⁷Abigail was the mother of Amasa, whose father was Jether the Ishmaelite.

Caleb Son of Hezron

¹⁸ Caleb son of Hezron had children by his wife Azubah (and by Jerioth). These were her sons: Jesher, Sho-bab and Ardon. ¹⁹When Azubah died, Caleb married Ephrath, who bore him Hur. ²⁰Hur was the father of Uri, and Uri the father of Bezalel.

²¹ Later, Hezron, when he was sixty years old, married the daughter of Makir the father of Gilead. He made love to her, and she bore him Segub. ²²Segub was the father of Jair, who controlled twenty-three towns in Gilead. ²³(But Geshur and Aram captured Havvoth Jair,*ᶠ* as well as Kenath with its surrounding settlements—sixty towns.) All these were descendants of Makir the father of Gilead.

²⁴ After Hezron died in Caleb Ephrathah, Abijah the wife of Hezron bore him Ashhur the father*ᵍ* of Tekoa.

Jerahmeel Son of Hezron

²⁵ The sons of Jerahmeel the firstborn of Hezron:

Ram his firstborn, Bunah, Oren, Ozem and*ᵇ* Ahijah. ²⁶Jerahmeel had another wife, whose name was Atarah; she was the mother of Onam.

²⁷ The sons of Ram the firstborn of Jerahmeel:

Maaz, Jamin and Eker.

²⁸ The sons of Onam:

Shammai and Jada.

The sons of Shammai:

Nadab and Abishur.

²⁹ Abishur's wife was named Abihail, who bore him Ahban and Molid.

ᵃ 6 Many Hebrew manuscripts, some Septuagint manuscripts and Syriac (see also 1 Kings 4:31); most Hebrew manuscripts *Dara*   *ᵇ 7 Achar* means *trouble*; *Achar* is called *Achan* in Joshua.   *ᶜ 7* The Hebrew term refers to the irrevocable giving over of things or persons to the Lord, often by totally destroying them.   *ᵈ 9* Hebrew *Kelubai,* a variant of *Caleb*   *ᵉ 11* Septuagint (see also Ruth 4:21); Hebrew *Salma*   *ᶠ 23* Or *captured the settlements of Jair*   *ᵍ 24 Father* may mean *civic leader* or *military leader;* also in verses 42, 45, 49-52 and possibly elsewhere.   *ᵇ 25* Or *Oren and Ozem, by*

³⁰The sons of Nadab:
Seled and Appaim. Seled died without children.
³¹The son of Appaim:
Ishi, who was the father of Sheshan.
Sheshan was the father of Ahlai.
³²The sons of Jada, Shammai's brother:
Jether and Jonathan. Jether died without children.
³³The sons of Jonathan:
Peleth and Zaza.
These were the descendants of Jerahmeel.
³⁴Sheshan had no sons—only daughters.
He had an Egyptian servant named Jarha. ³⁵Sheshan gave his daughter in marriage to his servant Jarha, and she bore him Attai.
³⁶Attai was the father of Nathan,
Nathan the father of Zabad,
³⁷Zabad the father of Ephlal,
Ephlal the father of Obed,
³⁸Obed the father of Jehu,
Jehu the father of Azariah,
³⁹Azariah the father of Helez,
Helez the father of Eleasah,
⁴⁰Eleasah the father of Sismai,
Sismai the father of Shallum,
⁴¹Shallum the father of Jekamiah,
and Jekamiah the father of Elishama.

The Clans of Caleb

⁴²The sons of Caleb the brother of Jerahmeel:
Mesha his firstborn, who was the father of Ziph, and his son Mareshah,ᵃ who was the father of Hebron.
⁴³The sons of Hebron:
Korah, Tappuah, Rekem and Shema. ⁴⁴Shema was the father of Raham, and Raham the father of Jorkeam. Rekem was the father of Shammai. ⁴⁵The son of Shammai was Maon, and Maon was the father of Beth Zur.
⁴⁶Caleb's concubine Ephah was the mother of Haran, Moza and Gazez. Haran was the father of Gazez.

⁴⁷The sons of Jahdai:
Regem, Jotham, Geshan, Pelet, Ephah and Shaaph.
⁴⁸Caleb's concubine Maakah was the mother of Sheber and Tirhanah. ⁴⁹She also gave birth to Shaaph the father of Madmannah and to Sheva the father of Makbenah and Gibea. Caleb's daughter was Aksah. ⁵⁰These were the descendants of Caleb.

The sons of Hur the firstborn of Ephrathah:
Shobal the father of Kiriath Jearim, ⁵¹Salma the father of Bethlehem, and Hareph the father of Beth Gader.
⁵²The descendants of Shobal the father of Kiriath Jearim were:
Haroeh, half the Manahathites, ⁵³and the clans of Kiriath Jearim: the Ithrites, Puthites, Shumathites and Mishraites. From these descended the Zorathites and Eshtaolites.
⁵⁴The descendants of Salma:
Bethlehem, the Netophathites, Atroth Beth Joab, half the Manahathites, the Zorites, ⁵⁵and the clans of scribesᵇ who lived at Jabez: the Tirathites, Shimeathites and Sucathites. These are the Kenites who came from Hammath, the father of the Rekabites.ᶜ

The Sons of David

3 These were the sons of David born to him in Hebron:
The firstborn was Amnon the son of Ahinoam of Jezreel;
the second, Daniel the son of Abigail of Carmel;
²the third, Absalom the son of Maakah daughter of Talmai king of Geshur;
the fourth, Adonijah the son of Haggith;

ᵃ 42 The meaning of the Hebrew for this phrase is uncertain.   ᵇ 55 Or of the Sopherites   ᶜ 55 Or father of Beth Rekab

³the fifth, Shephatiah the son of Abital;
and the sixth, Ithream, by his wife Eglah.
⁴These six were born to David in Hebron, where he reigned seven years and six months.

David reigned in Jerusalem thirty-three years, ⁵and these were the children born to him there:

Shammua,ᵃ Shobab, Nathan and Solomon. These four were by Bathshebaᵇ daughter of Ammiel. ⁶There were also Ibhar, Elishua,ᶜ Eliphelet, ⁷Nogah, Nepheg, Japhia, ⁸Elishama, Eliada and Eliphelet—nine in all. ⁹All these were the sons of David, besides his sons by his concubines. And Tamar was their sister.

The Kings of Judah

¹⁰Solomon's son was Rehoboam,
Abijah his son,
Asa his son,

ᵃ 5 Hebrew *Shimea,* a variant of *Shammua*
ᵇ 5 One Hebrew manuscript and Vulgate (see also Septuagint and 2 Samuel 11:3); most Hebrew manuscripts *Bathshua*   ᶜ 6 Two Hebrew manuscripts (see also 2 Samuel 5:15 and 1 Chron. 14:5); most Hebrew manuscripts *Elishama*

1 Chronicles 3:5

Bathsheba put her life back together.

The Bible doesn't say what Bathsheba thought when King David summoned her to his palace. The king had spotted the woman bathing from his rooftop, and the Bible only says she was "very beautiful" (2 Samuel 11:2). David himself was "glowing with health and had a fine appearance and handsome features" (1 Samuel 16:12).

David asked his servants about her identity and availability, then ignored that she was a married woman and beckoned her to his bed. Maybe Bathsheba came eagerly, but she might simply have obeyed the command of a king with nearly unlimited powers.

Whatever the circumstance, Bathsheba already had a husband, a one-of-a-kind man. Uriah was one of David's own mighty men (see 2 Samuel 23:39). When David called Uriah back from the front so he could sleep with his wife—to cover up the fact that David had gotten Bathsheba pregnant—Uriah refused to spend the night with his wife as long as his comrades were at war (see 2 Samuel 11:13).

Bathsheba is forever remembered as the female half of this sexual scandal, but she was more than that. She gave birth to five of David's children, and she ensured their son Solomon became king, as God had chosen (see 1 Kings 1:1 – 53). The New Testament lists her among the ancestors of Jesus (see Matthew 1:6). We would understand Bathsheba better if the Bible told us exactly what she thought and felt. But we do know she overcame a tough situation to live her life for God.

You can find Bathsheba in 2 Samuel 11 — 12; 1 Kings 1 — 2; and the heading of Psalm 51.

UNSHAKEN *people*

Jehoshaphat his son,
11 Jehoram[a] his son,
   Ahaziah his son,
   Joash his son,
12 Amaziah his son,
   Azariah his son,
   Jotham his son,
13 Ahaz his son,
   Hezekiah his son,
   Manasseh his son,
14 Amon his son,
   Josiah his son.
15 The sons of Josiah:
   Johanan the firstborn,
   Jehoiakim the second son,
   Zedekiah the third,
   Shallum the fourth.
16 The successors of Jehoiakim:
   Jehoiachin[b] his son,
   and Zedekiah.

The Royal Line After the Exile

17 The descendants of Jehoiachin the captive:
   Shealtiel his son, 18 Malkiram, Pedaiah, Shenazzar, Jekamiah, Hoshama and Nedabiah.
19 The sons of Pedaiah:
   Zerubbabel and Shimei.
   The sons of Zerubbabel:
   Meshullam and Hananiah.
   Shelomith was their sister.
20 There were also five others:
   Hashubah, Ohel, Berekiah, Hasadiah and Jushab-Hesed.
21 The descendants of Hananiah:
   Pelatiah and Jeshaiah, and the sons of Rephaiah, of Arnan, of Obadiah and of Shekaniah.
22 The descendants of Shekaniah:
   Shemaiah and his sons:
   Hattush, Igal, Bariah, Neariah and Shaphat—six in all.
23 The sons of Neariah:
   Elioenai, Hizkiah and Azrikam—three in all.
24 The sons of Elioenai:
   Hodaviah, Eliashib, Pelaiah, Akkub, Johanan, Delaiah and Anani—seven in all.

Other Clans of Judah

4 The descendants of Judah:
   Perez, Hezron, Karmi, Hur and Shobal.

2 Reaiah son of Shobal was the father of Jahath, and Jahath the father of Ahumai and Lahad. These were the clans of the Zorathites.

3 These were the sons[c] of Etam:
   Jezreel, Ishma and Idbash. Their sister was named Hazzelelponi.
4 Penuel was the father of Gedor, and Ezer the father of Hushah.

These were the descendants of Hur, the firstborn of Ephrathah and father[d] of Bethlehem.

5 Ashhur the father of Tekoa had two wives, Helah and Naarah.

6 Naarah bore him Ahuzzam, Hepher, Temeni and Haahashtari. These were the descendants of Naarah.

7 The sons of Helah:
   Zereth, Zohar, Ethnan, 8 and Koz, who was the father of Anub and Hazzobebah and of the clans of Aharhel son of Harum.

9 Jabez was more honorable than his brothers. His mother had named him Jabez,[e] saying, "I gave birth to him in pain." 10 Jabez cried out to the God of Israel, "Oh, that you would bless me and enlarge my territory! Let your hand be with me, and keep me from harm so that I will be free from pain." And God granted his request.

11 Kelub, Shuhah's brother, was the father of Mehir, who was the father of Eshton. 12 Eshton was the father of Beth Rapha, Paseah and Tehinnah the father of Ir Nahash.[f] These were the men of Rekah.

13 The sons of Kenaz:
   Othniel and Seraiah.

---

a 11 Hebrew Joram, a variant of Jehoram
b 16 Hebrew Jeconiah, a variant of Jehoiachin;
also in verse 17   c 3 Some Septuagint
manuscripts (see also Vulgate); Hebrew father
d 4 Father may mean civic leader or military
leader; also in verses 12, 14, 17, 18 and possibly
elsewhere.   e 9 Jabez sounds like the Hebrew
for pain.   f 12 Or of the city of Nahash

The sons of Othniel:

Hathath and Meonothai.* ¹⁴Meonothai was the father of Ophrah.

Seraiah was the father of Joab,
the father of Ge Harashim.ᵇ It was called this because its people were skilled workers.

¹⁵The sons of Caleb son of Jephunneh:
Iru, Elah and Naam.

The son of Elah:
Kenaz.

¹⁶The sons of Jehallelel:
Ziph, Ziphah, Tiria and Asarel.

¹⁷The sons of Ezrah:
Jether, Mered, Epher and Jalon. One of Mered's wives gave birth to Miriam, Shammai and Ishbah the father of Eshtemoa. ¹⁸(His wife from the tribe of Judah gave birth to Jered the father of Gedor, Heber the father of Soko, and Jekuthiel the father of Zanoah.) These were the children of Pharaoh's daughter Bithiah, whom Mered had married.

¹⁹The sons of Hodiah's wife, the sister of Naham:
the father of Keilah the Garmite, and Eshtemoa the Maakathite.

²⁰The sons of Shimon:
Amnon, Rinnah, Ben-Hanan and Tilon.

The descendants of Ishi:
Zoheth and Ben-Zoheth.

²¹The sons of Shelah son of Judah:
Er the father of Lekah, Laadah the father of Mareshah and the clans of the linen workers at Beth Ashbea, ²²Jokim, the men of Kozeba, and Joash and Saraph, who ruled in Moab and Jashubi Lehem. (These records are from ancient times.) ²³They were the potters who lived at Netaim and Gederah; they stayed there and worked for the king.

Simeon

²⁴The descendants of Simeon:
Nemuel, Jamin, Jarib, Zerah and Shaul;

²⁵Shallum was Shaul's son, Mibsam his son and Mishma his son.
²⁶The descendants of Mishma:
Hammuel his son, Zakkur his son and Shimei his son.
²⁷Shimei had sixteen sons and six daughters, but his brothers did not have many children; so their entire clan did not become as numerous as the people of Judah. ²⁸They lived in Beersheba, Moladah, Hazar Shual, ²⁹Bilhah, Ezem, Tolad, ³⁰Bethuel, Hormah, Ziklag, ³¹Beth Markaboth, Hazar Susim, Beth Biri and Shaaraim. These were their towns until the reign of David. ³²Their surrounding villages were Etam, Ain, Rimmon, Token and Ashan—five towns— ³³and all the villages around these towns as far as Baalath.ᶜ These were their settlements. And they kept a genealogical record.

³⁴Meshobab, Jamlech, Joshah son of Amaziah, ³⁵Joel, Jehu son of Joshibiah, the son of Seraiah, the son of Asiel, ³⁶also Elioenai, Jaakobah, Jeshohaiah, Asaiah, Adiel, Jesimiel, Benaiah, ³⁷and Ziza son of Shiphi, the son of Allon, the son of Jedaiah, the son of Shimri, the son of Shemaiah.

³⁸The men listed above by name were leaders of their clans. Their families increased greatly, ³⁹and they went to the outskirts of Gedor to the east of the valley in search of pasture for their flocks. ⁴⁰They found rich, good pasture, and the land was spacious, peaceful and quiet. Some Hamites had lived there formerly.

⁴¹The men whose names were listed came in the days of Hezekiah king of Judah. They attacked the Hamites in their dwellings and also the Meunites who were there and completely destroyedᵈ them, as is evident to this day. Then they settled in

---

ᵃ 13 Some Septuagint manuscripts and Vulgate; Hebrew does not have *and Meonothai.*
ᵇ 14 Ge Harashim means *valley of skilled workers.*
ᶜ 33 Some Septuagint manuscripts (see also Joshua 19:8); Hebrew *Baal*   ᵈ 41 The Hebrew term refers to the irrevocable giving over of things or persons to the LORD, often by totally destroying them.

their place, because there was pasture for their flocks. ⁴²And five hundred of these Simeonites, led by Pelatiah, Neariah, Rephaiah and Uzziel, the sons of Ishi, invaded the hill country of Seir. ⁴³They killed the remaining Amalekites who had escaped, and they have lived there to this day.

Reuben

5 The sons of Reuben the firstborn of Israel (he was the firstborn, but when he defiled his father's marriage bed, his rights as firstborn were given to the sons of Joseph son of Israel; so he could not be listed in the genealogical record in accordance with his birthright, ²and though Judah was the strongest of his brothers and a ruler came from him, the rights of the firstborn belonged to Joseph)— ³the sons of Reuben the firstborn of Israel:

Hanok, Pallu, Hezron and Karmi.
⁴The descendants of Joel:
Shemaiah his son, Gog his son, Shimei his son, ⁵Micah his son, Reaiah his son, Baal his son, ⁶and Beerah his son, whom Tiglath-Pileser*a* king of Assyria took into exile. Beerah was a leader of the Reubenites.

⁷Their relatives by clans, listed according to their genealogical records:
Jeiel the chief, Zechariah, ⁸and Bela son of Azaz, the son of Shema, the son of Joel. They settled in the area from Aroer to Nebo and Baal Meon. ⁹To the east they occupied the land up to the edge of the desert that extends to the Euphrates River, because their livestock had increased in Gilead.

¹⁰During Saul's reign they waged war against the Hagrites, who were defeated at their hands; they occupied the dwellings of the Hagrites throughout the entire region east of Gilead.

Gad

¹¹The Gadites lived next to them in Bashan, as far as Salekah:

¹²Joel was the chief, Shapham the second, then Janai and Shaphat, in Bashan.

¹³Their relatives, by families, were:
Michael, Meshullam, Sheba, Jorai, Jakan, Zia and Eber—seven in all. ¹⁴These were the sons of Abihail son of Huri, the son of Jaroah, the son of Gilead, the son of Michael, the son of Jeshishai, the son of Jahdo, the son of Buz.

¹⁵Ahi son of Abdiel, the son of Guni, was head of their family.

¹⁶The Gadites lived in Gilead, in Bashan and its outlying villages, and on all the pasturelands of Sharon as far as they extended.

¹⁷All these were entered in the genealogical records during the reigns of Jotham king of Judah and Jeroboam king of Israel.

¹⁸The Reubenites, the Gadites and the half-tribe of Manasseh had 44,760 men ready for military service—able-bodied men who could handle shield and sword, who could use a bow, and who were trained for battle. ¹⁹They waged war against the Hagrites, Jetur, Naphish and Nodab. ²⁰They were helped in fighting them, and God delivered the Hagrites and all their allies into their hands, because they cried out to him during the battle. He answered their prayers, because they trusted in him. ²¹They seized the livestock of the Hagrites—fifty thousand camels, two hundred fifty thousand sheep and two thousand donkeys. They also took one hundred thousand people captive, ²²and many others fell slain, because the battle was God's. And they occupied the land until the exile.

The Half-Tribe of Manasseh

²³The people of the half-tribe of Manasseh were numerous; they settled in the land from Bashan to Baal Hermon, that is, to Senir (Mount Hermon).

²⁴These were the heads of their fami-

a 6 Hebrew *Tilgath-Pilneser*, a variant of *Tiglath-Pileser*; also in verse 26 lies: Epher, Ishi, Eliel, Azriel, Jeremiah, Hodaviah and Jahdiel. They were brave warriors, famous men, and heads of their families. ²⁵ But they were unfaithful to the God of their ancestors and prostituted themselves to the gods of the peoples of the land, whom God had destroyed before them. ²⁶ So the God of Israel stirred up the spirit of Pul king of Assyria (that is, Tiglath-Pileser king of Assyria), who took the Reubenites, the Gadites and the half-tribe of Manasseh into exile. He took them to Halah, Habor, Hara and the river of Gozan, where they are to this day.

Levi

6 ^a The sons of Levi:
Gershon, Kohath and Merari.
² The sons of Kohath:
Amram, Izhar, Hebron and Uzziel.
³ The children of Amram:
Aaron, Moses and Miriam.
The sons of Aaron:
Nadab, Abihu, Eleazar and Ithamar.
⁴ Eleazar was the father of Phinehas,
Phinehas the father of Abishua,
⁵ Abishua the father of Bukki,
Bukki the father of Uzzi,
⁶ Uzzi the father of Zerahiah,
Zerahiah the father of Meraioth,
⁷ Meraioth the father of Amariah,
Amariah the father of Ahitub,
⁸ Ahitub the father of Zadok,
Zadok the father of Ahimaaz,
⁹ Ahimaaz the father of Azariah,
Azariah the father of Johanan,
¹⁰ Johanan the father of Azariah (it was he who served as priest in the temple Solomon built in Jerusalem),
¹¹ Azariah the father of Amariah,
Amariah the father of Ahitub,
¹² Ahitub the father of Zadok,
Zadok the father of Shallum,
¹³ Shallum the father of Hilkiah,
Hilkiah the father of Azariah,
¹⁴ Azariah the father of Seraiah,
and Seraiah the father of Jozadak.^b

¹⁵ Jozadak was deported when the LORD sent Judah and Jerusalem into exile by the hand of Nebuchadnezzar.

¹⁶ The sons of Levi:
Gershon,^c Kohath and Merari.
¹⁷ These are the names of the sons of Gershon:
Libni and Shimei.
¹⁸ The sons of Kohath:
Amram, Izhar, Hebron and Uzziel.
¹⁹ The sons of Merari:
Mahli and Mushi.
These are the clans of the Levites listed according to their fathers:
²⁰ Of Gershon:
Libni his son, Jahath his son,
Zimmah his son, ²¹ Joah his son,
Iddo his son, Zerah his son
and Jeatherai his son.
²² The descendants of Kohath:
Amminadab his son, Korah his son,
Assir his son, ²³ Elkanah his son,
Ebiasaph his son, Assir his son,
²⁴ Tahath his son, Uriel his son,
Uzziah his son and Shaul his son.
²⁵ The descendants of Elkanah:
Amasai, Ahimoth,
²⁶ Elkanah his son,^d Zophai his son,
Nahath his son, ²⁷ Eliab his son,
Jeroham his son, Elkanah his son
and Samuel his son.^e
²⁸ The sons of Samuel:
Joel^f the firstborn
and Abijah the second son.
²⁹ The descendants of Merari:
Mahli, Libni his son,

^a In Hebrew texts 6:1-15 is numbered 5:27-41, and 6:16-81 is numbered 6:1-66.
^b 14 Hebrew *Jehozadak*, a variant of *Jozadak*; also in verse 15   ^c 16 Hebrew *Gershom*, a variant of *Gershon*; also in verses 17, 20, 43, 62 and 71   ^d 26 Some Hebrew manuscripts, Septuagint and Syriac; most Hebrew manuscripts *Ahimoth* ²⁶ *and Elkanah. The sons of Elkanah:*   ^e 27 Some Septuagint manuscripts (see also 1 Samuel 1:19,20 and 1 Chron. 6:33,34); Hebrew does not have *and Samuel his son.*   ^f 28 Some Septuagint manuscripts and Syriac (see also 1 Samuel 8:2 and 1 Chron. 6:33); Hebrew does not have *Joel.*

Shimei his son, Uzzah his son,
³⁰ Shimea his son, Haggiah his son
and Asaiah his son.

The Temple Musicians

³¹ These are the men David put in charge of the music in the house of the LORD after the ark came to rest there. ³² They ministered with music before the tabernacle, the tent of meeting, until Solomon built the temple of the LORD in Jerusalem. They performed their duties according to the regulations laid down for them.

³³ Here are the men who served, together with their sons:

From the Kohathites:
  Heman, the musician,
  the son of Joel, the son of Samuel,
³⁴ the son of Elkanah, the son of Jeroham,
  the son of Eliel, the son of Toah,
³⁵ the son of Zuph, the son of Elkanah,
  the son of Mahath, the son of Amasai,
³⁶ the son of Elkanah, the son of Joel,
  the son of Azariah, the son of Zephaniah,
³⁷ the son of Tahath, the son of Assir,
  the son of Ebiasaph, the son of Korah,
³⁸ the son of Izhar, the son of Kohath,
  the son of Levi, the son of Israel;
³⁹ and Heman's associate Asaph, who served at his right hand:
  Asaph son of Berekiah, the son of Shimea,
⁴⁰ the son of Michael, the son of Baaseiah,ᵃ
  the son of Malkijah, ⁴¹ the son of Ethni,
  the son of Zerah, the son of Adaiah,
⁴² the son of Ethan, the son of Zimmah,
  the son of Shimei, ⁴³ the son of Jahath,
  the son of Gershon, the son of Levi;

⁴⁴ and from their associates, the Merarites, at his left hand:
  Ethan son of Kishi, the son of Abdi,
  the son of Malluk, ⁴⁵ the son of Hashabiah,
  the son of Amaziah, the son of Hilkiah,
⁴⁶ the son of Amzi, the son of Bani,
  the son of Shemer, ⁴⁷ the son of Mahli,
  the son of Mushi, the son of Merari,
  the son of Levi.

⁴⁸ Their fellow Levites were assigned to all the other duties of the tabernacle, the house of God. ⁴⁹ But Aaron and his descendants were the ones who presented offerings on the altar of burnt offering and on the altar of incense in connection with all that was done in the Most Holy Place, making atonement for Israel, in accordance with all that Moses the servant of God had commanded.

⁵⁰ These were the descendants of Aaron:
  Eleazar his son, Phinehas his son,
  Abishua his son, ⁵¹ Bukki his son,
  Uzzi his son, Zerahiah his son,
⁵² Meraioth his son, Amariah his son,
  Ahitub his son, ⁵³ Zadok his son
  and Ahimaaz his son.

⁵⁴ These were the locations of their settlements allotted as their territory (they were assigned to the descendants of Aaron who were from the Kohathite clan, because the first lot was for them):
⁵⁵ They were given Hebron in Judah with its surrounding pasturelands. ⁵⁶ But the fields and villages around the city were given to Caleb son of Jephunneh. ⁵⁷ So the descendants of Aaron were given Hebron (a city of refuge), and Libnah,ᵇ Jattir, Eshtemoa,

---

ᵃ 40 Most Hebrew manuscripts; some Hebrew manuscripts, one Septuagint manuscript and Syriac *Maaseiah*   ᵇ 57 See Joshua 21:13; Hebrew *given the cities of refuge: Hebron, Libnah.*

⁵⁸Hilen, Debir, ⁵⁹Ashan, Juttah*ᵃ* and Beth Shemesh, together with their pasturelands. ⁶⁰And from the tribe of Benjamin they were given Gibeon,*ᵇ* Geba, Alemeth and Anathoth, together with their pasturelands.

The total number of towns distributed among the Kohathite clans came to thirteen.

⁶¹The rest of Kohath's descendants were allotted ten towns from the clans of half the tribe of Manasseh.

⁶²The descendants of Gershon, clan by clan, were allotted thirteen towns from the tribes of Issachar, Asher and Naphtali, and from the part of the tribe of Manasseh that is in Bashan.

⁶³The descendants of Merari, clan by clan, were allotted twelve towns from the tribes of Reuben, Gad and Zebulun.

⁶⁴So the Israelites gave the Levites these towns and their pasturelands. ⁶⁵From the tribes of Judah, Simeon and Benjamin they allotted the previously named towns.

⁶⁶Some of the Kohathite clans were given as their territory towns from the tribe of Ephraim.

⁶⁷In the hill country of Ephraim they were given Shechem (a city of refuge), and Gezer,*ᶜ* ⁶⁸Jokmeam, Beth Horon, ⁶⁹Aijalon and Gath Rimmon, together with their pasturelands.

⁷⁰And from half the tribe of Manasseh the Israelites gave Aner and Bileam, together with their pasturelands, to the rest of the Kohathite clans.

⁷¹The Gershonites received the following:

From the clan of the half-tribe of Manasseh

they received Golan in Bashan and also Ashtaroth, together with their pasturelands;

⁷²from the tribe of Issachar

they received Kedesh, Daberath, ⁷³Ramoth and Anem, together with their pasturelands;

⁷⁴from the tribe of Asher

they received Mashal, Abdon, ⁷⁵Hukok and Rehob, together with their pasturelands;

⁷⁶and from the tribe of Naphtali

they received Kedesh in Galilee, Hammon and Kiriathaim, together with their pasturelands.

⁷⁷The Merarites (the rest of the Levites) received the following:

From the tribe of Zebulun

they received Jokneam, Kartah,*ᵈ* Rimmono and Tabor, together with their pasturelands;

⁷⁸from the tribe of Reuben across the Jordan east of Jericho

they received Bezer in the wilderness, Jahzah, ⁷⁹Kedemoth and Mephaath, together with their pasturelands;

⁸⁰and from the tribe of Gad

they received Ramoth in Gilead, Mahanaim, ⁸¹Heshbon and Jazer, together with their pasturelands.

Issachar

7 The sons of Issachar:

Tola, Puah, Jashub and Shimron—four in all.

²The sons of Tola:

Uzzi, Rephaiah, Jeriel, Jahmai, Ibsam and Samuel—heads of their families. During the reign of David, the descendants of Tola listed as fighting men in their genealogy numbered 22,600.

³The son of Uzzi:

Izrahiah.

The sons of Izrahiah:

Michael, Obadiah, Joel and Ishiah. All five of them were chiefs. ⁴According to their family genealogy, they had 36,000 men ready for battle, for they had many wives and children.

⁵The relatives who were fighting men

ᵃ 59 Syriac (see also Septuagint and Joshua 21:16); Hebrew does not have *Juttah.*
ᵇ 60 See Joshua 21:17; Hebrew does not have *Gibeon.*   *ᶜ 67* See Joshua 21:21; Hebrew *given the cities of refuge: Shechem, Gezer.*   *ᵈ 77* See Septuagint and Joshua 21:34; Hebrew does not have *Jokneam, Kartah.*

belonging to all the clans of Issachar, as listed in their genealogy, were 87,000 in all.

Benjamin

[6] Three sons of Benjamin:
Bela, Beker and Jediael.
[7] The sons of Bela:
Ezbon, Uzzi, Uzziel, Jerimoth and Iri, heads of families—five in all. Their genealogical record listed 22,034 fighting men.
[8] The sons of Beker:
Zemirah, Joash, Eliezer, Elioenai, Omri, Jeremoth, Abijah, Anathoth and Alemeth. All these were the sons of Beker. [9] Their genealogical record listed the heads of families and 20,200 fighting men.
[10] The son of Jediael:
Bilhan.

The sons of Bilhan:
Jeush, Benjamin, Ehud, Kenaanah, Zethan, Tarshish and Ahishahar. [11] All these sons of Jediael were heads of families. There were 17,200 fighting men ready to go out to war. [12] The Shuppites and Huppites were the descendants of Ir, and the Hushites[a] the descendants of Aher.

Naphtali

[13] The sons of Naphtali:
Jahziel, Guni, Jezer and Shillem[b]—the descendants of Bilhah.

Manasseh

[14] The descendants of Manasseh:
Asriel was his descendant through his Aramean concubine. She gave birth to Makir the father of Gilead. [15] Makir took a wife from among the Huppites and Shuppites. His sister's name was Maakah.

Another descendant was named Zelophehad, who had only daughters.

[16] Makir's wife Maakah gave birth to a son and named him Peresh. His brother was named Sheresh, and his sons were Ulam and Rakem.
[17] The son of Ulam:
Bedan.

These were the sons of Gilead son of Makir, the son of Manasseh. [18] His sister Hammoleketh gave birth to Ishhod, Abiezer and Mahlah.
[19] The sons of Shemida were:
Ahian, Shechem, Likhi and Aniam.

Ephraim

[20] The descendants of Ephraim:
Shuthelah, Bered his son,
Tahath his son, Eleadah his son,
Tahath his son, [21] Zabad his son
and Shuthelah his son.

Ezer and Elead were killed by the native-born men of Gath, when they went down to seize their livestock. [22] Their father Ephraim mourned for them many days, and his relatives came to comfort him. [23] Then he made love to his wife again, and she became pregnant and gave birth to a son. He named him Beriah,[c] because there had been misfortune in his family. [24] His daughter was Sheerah, who built Lower and Upper Beth Horon as well as Uzzen Sheerah.
[25] Rephah was his son, Resheph his son,[d]
Telah his son, Tahan his son,
[26] Ladan his son, Ammihud his son,
Elishama his son, [27] Nun his son
and Joshua his son.

[28] Their lands and settlements included Bethel and its surrounding villages, Naaran to the east, Gezer and its villages to the west, and Shechem and its villages all the way to Ayyah and its villages. [29] Along the borders of Manasseh were Beth Shan, Taanach, Megiddo and Dor, together with their villages. The descendants of Joseph son of Israel lived in these towns.

---

[a] 12 Or *Ir. The sons of Dan: Hushim,* (see Gen. 46:23); Hebrew does not have *The sons of Dan.*
[b] 13 Some Hebrew and Septuagint manuscripts (see also Gen. 46:24 and Num. 26:49); most Hebrew manuscripts *Shallum*   [c] 23 *Beriah* sounds like the Hebrew for *misfortune.*
[d] 25 Some Septuagint manuscripts; Hebrew does not have *his son.*

Asher

30 The sons of Asher:

Imnah, Ishvah, Ishvi and Beriah. Their sister was Serah.

31 The sons of Beriah:

Heber and Malkiel, who was the father of Birzaith.

32 Heber was the father of Japhlet, Shomer and Hotham and of their sister Shua.

33 The sons of Japhlet:

Pasak, Bimhal and Ashvath. These were Japhlet's sons.

34 The sons of Shomer:

Ahi, Rohgah,*a* Hubbah and Aram.

35 The sons of his brother Helem:

Zophah, Imna, Shelesh and Amal.

36 The sons of Zophah:

Suah, Harnepher, Shual, Beri, Imrah, 37 Bezer, Hod, Shamma, Shilshah, Ithran*b* and Beera.

38 The sons of Jether:

Jephunneh, Pispah and Ara.

39 The sons of Ulla:

Arah, Hanniel and Rizia.

40 All these were descendants of Asher—heads of families, choice men, brave warriors and outstanding leaders. The number of men ready for battle, as listed in their genealogy, was 26,000.

The Genealogy of Saul the Benjamite

8 Benjamin was the father of Bela his firstborn,

Ashbel the second son, Aharah the third,

2 Nohah the fourth and Rapha the fifth.

3 The sons of Bela were:

Addar, Gera, Abihud,*c* 4 Abishua, Naaman, Ahoah, 5 Gera, Shephuphan and Huram.

6 These were the descendants of Ehud, who were heads of families of those living in Geba and were deported to Manahath:

7 Naaman, Ahijah, and Gera, who deported them and who was the father of Uzza and Ahihud.

8 Sons were born to Shaharaim in Moab after he had divorced his wives Hushim and Baara. 9 By his wife Hodesh he had Jobab, Zibia, Mesha, Malkam, 10 Jeuz, Sakia and Mirmah. These were his sons, heads of families. 11 By Hushim he had Abitub and Elpaal.

12 The sons of Elpaal:

Eber, Misham, Shemed (who

---

a 34 Or *of his brother Shomer: Rohgah*
b 37 Possibly a variant of *Jether*   *c* 3 Or *Gera the father of Ehud*

---

1 Chronicles 7:1–40

Even dry parts of the Bible make a point.

Family trees can tell you a ton, especially if you're part of the family. As a believer you're a member of God's big family. So you should know why the Bible includes several dense sections of your spiritual family history. These genealogies are a quick sketch of your roots, a reminder of deep family connections that extend for generations. But these ancient lists served practical functions too. They organized tribes for military duties (see Numbers 1:2–4) and determined taxes and temple contributions (see Numbers 7:11–89). They detailed the division of the promised land, with each tribe receiving a specific parcel of land (Joshua 16—19). And genealogies have one more essential job. They traced the birth of Jesus to the line of David (see Isaiah 11:1), a sign that Jesus was the genuine Savior sent from God.

Think: What parts of the Bible do you find boring? Why do you think God included those parts in his flawless Word?

ROCK SOLID truths

built Ono and Lod with its surrounding villages), ¹³and Beriah
and Shema, who were heads of
families of those living in Aijalon
and who drove out the inhabitants
of Gath.

¹⁴Ahio, Shashak, Jeremoth, ¹⁵Zebadi-
ah, Arad, Eder, ¹⁶Michael, Ishpah
and Joha were the sons of Beriah.

¹⁷Zebadiah, Meshullam, Hizki, He-
ber, ¹⁸Ishmerai, Izliah and Jobab
were the sons of Elpaal.

¹⁹Jakim, Zikri, Zabdi, ²⁰Elienai, Zille-
thai, Eliel, ²¹Adaiah, Beraiah and
Shimrath were the sons of Shimei.

²²Ishpan, Eber, Eliel, ²³Abdon, Zikri,
Hanan, ²⁴Hananiah, Elam, An-
thothijah, ²⁵Iphdeiah and Penuel
were the sons of Shashak.

²⁶Shamsherai, Shehariah, Athaliah,
²⁷Jaareshiah, Elijah and Zikri were
the sons of Jeroham.

²⁸All these were heads of families,
chiefs as listed in their genealogy, and they
lived in Jerusalem.

²⁹Jeiel[a] the father[b] of Gibeon lived in
Gibeon.
His wife's name was Maakah,
³⁰and his firstborn son was Ab-
don, followed by Zur, Kish, Baal,
Ner,[c] Nadab, ³¹Gedor, Ahio, Ze-
ker ³²and Mikloth, who was the
father of Shimeah. They too lived
near their relatives in Jerusalem.

³³Ner was the father of Kish, Kish the
father of Saul, and Saul the father
of Jonathan, Malki-Shua, Abinadab and Esh-Baal.[d]

³⁴The son of Jonathan:
Merib-Baal,[e] who was the father
of Micah.

³⁵The sons of Micah:
Pithon, Melek, Tarea and Ahaz.

³⁶Ahaz was the father of Jehoaddah,
Jehoaddah was the father of Ale-
meth, Azmaveth and Zimri, and
Zimri was the father of Moza.
³⁷Moza was the father of Binea;
Raphah was his son, Eleasah his
son and Azel his son.

³⁸Azel had six sons, and these were
their names:
Azrikam, Bokeru, Ishmael, Sheariah, Obadiah and Hanan. All
these were the sons of Azel.

³⁹The sons of his brother Eshek:
Ulam his firstborn, Jeush the second son and Eliphelet the third.
⁴⁰The sons of Ulam were brave
warriors who could handle the
bow. They had many sons and
grandsons—150 in all.

All these were the descendants of
Benjamin.

9 All Israel was listed in the genealogies recorded in the book of the
kings of Israel and Judah. They
were taken captive to Babylon because of
their unfaithfulness.

The People in Jerusalem

²Now the first to resettle on their own
property in their own towns were some
Israelites, priests, Levites and temple servants.

³Those from Judah, from Benjamin,
and from Ephraim and Manasseh who
lived in Jerusalem were:

⁴Uthai son of Ammihud, the son of
Omri, the son of Imri, the son of
Bani, a descendant of Perez son of
Judah.

⁵Of the Shelanites[f]:
Asaiah the firstborn and his sons.

⁶Of the Zerahites:
Jeuel.
The people from Judah numbered
690.

⁷Of the Benjamites:
Sallu son of Meshullam, the son of
Hodaviah, the son of Hassenuah;
⁸Ibneiah son of Jeroham; Elah son
of Uzzi, the son of Mikri; and Me-

---

[a] 29 Some Septuagint manuscripts (see also
9:35); Hebrew does not have *Jeiel.*
[b] 29 *Father* may mean *civic leader* or *military
leader.*   [c] 30 Some Septuagint manuscripts
(see also 9:36); Hebrew does not have *Ner.*
[d] 33 Also known as *Ish-Bosheth*   [e] 34 Also
known as *Mephibosheth*   [f] 5 See Num. 26:20;
Hebrew *Shilonites.*

shullam son of Shephatiah, the son of Reuel, the son of Ibnijah.

⁹The people from Benjamin, as listed in their genealogy, numbered 956. All these men were heads of their families.

¹⁰Of the priests:

Jedaiah; Jehoiarib; Jakin;

¹¹Azariah son of Hilkiah, the son of Meshullam, the son of Zadok, the son of Meraioth, the son of Ahitub, the official in charge of the house of God;

¹²Adaiah son of Jeroham, the son of Pashhur, the son of Malkijah; and Maasai son of Adiel, the son of Jahzerah, the son of Meshullam, the son of Meshillemith, the son of Immer.

¹³The priests, who were heads of families, numbered 1,760. They were able men, responsible for ministering in the house of God.

¹⁴Of the Levites:

Shemaiah son of Hasshub, the son of Azrikam, the son of Hashabiah, a Merarite; ¹⁵Bakbakkar, Heresh, Galal and Mattaniah son of Mika, the son of Zikri, the son of Asaph; ¹⁶Obadiah son of Shemaiah, the son of Galal, the son of Jeduthun; and Berekiah son of Asa, the son of Elkanah, who lived in the villages of the Netophathites.

¹⁷The gatekeepers:

Shallum, Akkub, Talmon, Ahiman and their fellow Levites, Shallum their chief ¹⁸being stationed at the King's Gate on the east, up to the present time. These were the gatekeepers belonging to the camp of the Levites. ¹⁹Shallum son of Kore, the son of Ebiasaph, the son of Korah, and his fellow gatekeepers from his family (the Korahites) were responsible for guarding the thresholds of the tent just as their ancestors had been responsible for guarding the entrance to the dwelling of the LORD. ²⁰In earlier times Phinehas

son of Eleazar was the official in charge of the gatekeepers, and the LORD was with him. ²¹Zechariah son of Meshelemiah was the gatekeeper at the entrance to the tent of meeting.

²²Altogether, those chosen to be gatekeepers at the thresholds numbered 212. They were registered by genealogy in their villages. The gatekeepers had been assigned to their positions of trust by David and Samuel the seer. ²³They and their descendants were in charge of guarding the gates of the house of the LORD—the house called the tent of meeting. ²⁴The gatekeepers were on the four sides: east, west, north and south. ²⁵Their fellow Levites in their villages had to come from time to time and share their duties for seven-day periods. ²⁶But the four principal gatekeepers, who were Levites, were entrusted with the responsibility for the rooms and treasuries in the house of God. ²⁷They would spend the night stationed around the house of God, because they had to guard it; and they had charge of the key for opening it each morning.

²⁸Some of them were in charge of the articles used in the temple service; they counted them when they were brought in and when they were taken out. ²⁹Others were assigned to take care of the furnishings and all the other articles of the sanctuary, as well as the special flour and wine, and the olive oil, incense and spices. ³⁰But some of the priests took care of mixing the spices. ³¹A Levite named Mattithiah, the firstborn son of Shallum the Korahite, was entrusted with the responsibility for baking the offering bread. ³²Some of the Kohathites, their fellow Levites, were in charge of preparing for every Sabbath the bread set out on the table.

³³Those who were musicians, heads of Levite families, stayed in the rooms of the temple and were exempt from other duties because they were responsible for the work day and night.

³⁴All these were heads of Levite families, chiefs as listed in their genealogy, and they lived in Jerusalem.

The Genealogy of Saul

35 Jeiel the father[a] of Gibeon lived in Gibeon.

His wife's name was Maakah, 36 and his firstborn son was Abdon, followed by Zur, Kish, Baal, Ner, Nadab, 37 Gedor, Ahio, Zechariah and Mikloth. 38 Mikloth was the father of Shimeam. They too lived near their relatives in Jerusalem.

39 Ner was the father of Kish, Kish the father of Saul, and Saul the father of Jonathan, Malki-Shua, Abinadab and Esh-Baal.[b]

40 The son of Jonathan:
Merib-Baal,[c] who was the father of Micah.

41 The sons of Micah:
Pithon, Melek, Tahrea and Ahaz.[d]

42 Ahaz was the father of Jadah, Jadah[e] was the father of Alemeth, Azmaveth and Zimri, and Zimri was the father of Moza. 43 Moza was the father of Binea; Rephaiah was his son, Eleasah his son and Azel his son.

44 Azel had six sons, and these were their names:
Azrikam, Bokeru, Ishmael, Sheariah, Obadiah and Hanan. These were the sons of Azel.

Saul Takes His Life

10 Now the Philistines fought against Israel; the Israelites fled before them, and many fell dead on Mount Gilboa. 2 The Philistines were in hot pursuit of Saul and his sons, and they killed his sons Jonathan, Abinadab and Malki-Shua. 3 The fighting grew fierce around Saul, and when the archers overtook him, they wounded him.

4 Saul said to his armor-bearer, "Draw your sword and run me through, or these uncircumcised fellows will come and abuse me."

But his armor-bearer was terrified and would not do it; so Saul took his own sword and fell on it. 5 When the armor-bearer saw that Saul was dead, he too fell on his sword and died. 6 So Saul and his three sons died, and all his house died together.

7 When all the Israelites in the valley saw that the army had fled and that Saul and his sons had died, they abandoned their towns and fled. And the Philistines came and occupied them.

8 The next day, when the Philistines came to strip the dead, they found Saul and his sons fallen on Mount Gilboa. 9 They stripped him and took his head and his armor, and sent messengers throughout the land of the Philistines to proclaim the news among their idols and their people. 10 They put his armor in the temple of their gods and hung up his head in the temple of Dagon.

11 When all the inhabitants of Jabesh Gilead heard what the Philistines had done to Saul, 12 all their valiant men went and took the bodies of Saul and his sons and brought them to Jabesh. Then they buried their bones under the great tree in Jabesh, and they fasted seven days.

13 Saul died because he was unfaithful to the LORD; he did not keep the word of the LORD and even consulted a medium for guidance, 14 and did not inquire of the LORD. So the LORD put him to death and turned the kingdom over to David son of Jesse.

David Becomes King Over Israel

11 All Israel came together to David at Hebron and said, "We are your own flesh and blood. 2 In the past, even while Saul was king, you were the one who led Israel on their military campaigns. And the LORD your God said to you, 'You will shepherd my people Israel, and you will become their ruler.'"

3 When all the elders of Israel had come to King David at Hebron, he made a covenant with them at Hebron before the

---

[a] 35 *Father* may mean *civic leader* or *military leader.*   [b] 39 Also known as *Ish-Bosheth*
[c] 40 Also known as *Mephibosheth*
[d] 41 Vulgate and Syriac (see also Septuagint and 8:35); Hebrew does not have *and Ahaz.*
[e] 42 Some Hebrew manuscripts and Septuagint (see also 8:36); most Hebrew manuscripts *Jarah, Jarah*

[7]David then took up residence in the fortress, and so it was called the City of David. [8]He built up the city around it, from the terraces[a] to the surrounding wall, while Joab restored the rest of the city. [9]And David became more and more powerful, because the LORD Almighty was with him.

David's Mighty Warriors

[10]These were the chiefs of David's mighty warriors—they, together with all Israel, gave his kingship strong support to extend it over the whole land, as the LORD had promised— [11]this is the list of David's mighty warriors:

Jashobeam,[b] a Hakmonite, was chief of the officers[c]; he raised his spear against three hundred men, whom he killed in one encounter.

[12]Next to him was Eleazar son of Dodai the Ahohite, one of the three mighty warriors. [13]He was with David at Pas Dammim when the Philistines gathered there for battle. At a place where there was a field full of barley, the troops fled from the Philistines. [14]But they took their stand in the middle of the field. They defended it and struck the Philistines down, and the LORD brought about a great victory.

[15]Three of the thirty chiefs came down to David to the rock at the cave of Adullam, while a band of Philistines was encamped in the Valley of Rephaim. [16]At that time David was in the stronghold, and the Philistine garrison was at Bethlehem. [17]David longed for water and said, "Oh, that someone would get me a drink of water from the well near the gate of Bethlehem!" [18]So the Three broke through the Philistine lines, drew water from the well near the gate of Bethlehem and carried it back to David. But he refused to drink it; instead, he poured it out to the LORD. [19]"God forbid that I should do this!" he said. "Should I drink the blood of these men who went at the risk of their lives?" Because they risked their lives to bring it back, David would not drink it.

[a] 8 Or the Millo   [b] 11 Possibly a variant of Jashob-Baal   [c] 11 Or Thirty; some Septuagint manuscripts Three (see also 2 Samuel 23:8)

ROCK SOLID truths

1 Chronicles 10:1–14

Sin means missing the mark.

Saul was the good-looking guy picked as Israel's first king. But the man who stood a head taller than everyone else in Israel didn't amount to much. God wanted Saul to carefully follow his commands, but he "did not keep the word of the LORD." In the end Saul died "because he was unfaithful to the LORD" (1 Chronicles 10:13). He didn't live up to the standard God set. In fact, his life is a concrete example of sin, a word that in New Testament Greek literally means "missing the mark," like an archer shooting an arrow and failing to hit a target. That image tells us God expects us to aim for his very best. He doesn't want us to settle for barely nicking the target. He wants us to nail the bull's-eye—every time—by obeying him completely.

Think: What makes an attitude or behavior a sin?

LORD, and they anointed David king over Israel, as the LORD had promised through Samuel.

David Conquers Jerusalem

[4]David and all the Israelites marched to Jerusalem (that is, Jebus). The Jebusites who lived there [5]said to David, "You will not get in here." Nevertheless, David captured the fortress of Zion—which is the City of David.

[6]David had said, "Whoever leads the attack on the Jebusites will become commander-in-chief." Joab son of Zeruiah went up first, and so he received the command.

Such were the exploits of the three mighty warriors.

²⁰ Abishai the brother of Joab was chief of the Three. He raised his spear against three hundred men, whom he killed, and so he became as famous as the Three. ²¹ He was doubly honored above the Three and became their commander, even though he was not included among them.

²² Benaiah son of Jehoiada, a valiant fighter from Kabzeel, performed great exploits. He struck down Moab's two mightiest warriors. He also went down into a pit on a snowy day and killed a lion. ²³ And he struck down an Egyptian who was five cubits*a* tall. Although the Egyptian had a spear like a weaver's rod in his hand, Benaiah went against him with a club. He snatched the spear from the Egyptian's hand and killed him with his own spear. ²⁴ Such were the exploits of Benaiah son of Jehoiada; he too was as famous as the three mighty warriors. ²⁵ He was held in greater honor than any of the Thirty, but he was not included among the Three. And David put him in charge of his bodyguard.

²⁶ The mighty warriors were:

Asahel the brother of Joab,
Elhanan son of Dodo from Bethlehem,
²⁷ Shammoth the Harorite,
Helez the Pelonite,
²⁸ Ira son of Ikkesh from Tekoa,
Abiezer from Anathoth,
²⁹ Sibbekai the Hushathite,
Ilai the Ahohite,
³⁰ Maharai the Netophathite,
Heled son of Baanah the Netophathite,
³¹ Ithai son of Ribai from Gibeah in Benjamin,
Benaiah the Pirathonite,
³² Hurai from the ravines of Gaash,
Abiel the Arbathite,
³³ Azmaveth the Baharumite,
Eliahba the Shaalbonite,
³⁴ the sons of Hashem the Gizonite,
Jonathan son of Shagee the Hararite,
³⁵ Ahiam son of Sakar the Hararite,

Eliphal son of Ur,
³⁶ Hepher the Mekerathite,
Ahijah the Pelonite,
³⁷ Hezro the Carmelite,
Naarai son of Ezbai,
³⁸ Joel the brother of Nathan,
Mibhar son of Hagri,
³⁹ Zelek the Ammonite,
Naharai the Berothite, the armor-bearer of Joab son of Zeruiah,
⁴⁰ Ira the Ithrite,
Gareb the Ithrite,
⁴¹ Uriah the Hittite,
Zabad son of Ahlai,
⁴² Adina son of Shiza the Reubenite, who was chief of the Reubenites, and the thirty with him,
⁴³ Hanan son of Maakah,
Joshaphat the Mithnite,
⁴⁴ Uzzia the Ashterathite,
Shama and Jeiel the sons of Hotham the Aroerite,
⁴⁵ Jediael son of Shimri,
his brother Joha the Tizite,
⁴⁶ Eliel the Mahavite,
Jeribai and Joshaviah the sons of Elnaam,
Ithmah the Moabite,
⁴⁷ Eliel, Obed and Jaasiel the Mezobaite.

Warriors Join David

12 These were the men who came to David at Ziklag, while he was banished from the presence of Saul son of Kish (they were among the warriors who helped him in battle; ² they were armed with bows and were able to shoot arrows or to sling stones right-handed or left-handed; they were relatives of Saul from the tribe of Benjamin):

³ Ahiezer their chief and Joash the sons of Shemaah the Gibeathite; Jeziel and Pelet the sons of Azmaveth; Berakah, Jehu the Anathothite, ⁴ and Ishmaiah the Gibeonite, a mighty warrior among the Thirty, who was a leader of the Thirty; Jeremiah, Ja-

---

a 23 That is, about 7 feet 6 inches or about 2.3 meters

haziel, Johanan, Jozabad the Gederathite,[a] [5]Eluzai, Jerimoth, Bealiah, Shemariah and Shephatiah the Haruphite; [6]Elkanah, Ishiah, Azarel, Joezer and Jashobeam the Korahites; [7]and Joelah and Zebadiah the sons of Jeroham from Gedor.

[8]Some Gadites defected to David at his stronghold in the wilderness. They were brave warriors, ready for battle and able to handle the shield and spear. Their faces were the faces of lions, and they were as swift as gazelles in the mountains.

[9]Ezer was the chief,
Obadiah the second in command, Eliab the third,
[10]Mishmannah the fourth, Jeremiah the fifth,
[11]Attai the sixth, Eliel the seventh,
[12]Johanan the eighth, Elzabad the ninth,
[13]Jeremiah the tenth and Makbannai the eleventh.

[14]These Gadites were army commanders; the least was a match for a hundred, and the greatest for a thousand. [15]It was they who crossed the Jordan in the first month when it was overflowing all its banks, and they put to flight everyone living in the valleys, to the east and to the west.

[16]Other Benjamites and some men from Judah also came to David in his stronghold. [17]David went out to meet them and said to them, "If you have come to me in peace to help me, I am ready for you to join me. But if you have come to betray me to my enemies when my hands are free from violence, may the God of our ancestors see it and judge you."

[18]Then the Spirit came on Amasai, chief of the Thirty, and he said:

"We are yours, David!
We are with you, son of Jesse!
Success, success to you,
and success to those who help you,
for your God will help you."

So David received them and made them leaders of his raiding bands.

[19]Some of the tribe of Manasseh defected to David when he went with the Philistines to fight against Saul. (He and his men did not help the Philistines because, after consultation, their rulers sent him away. They said, "It will cost us our heads if he deserts to his master Saul.") [20]When David went to Ziklag, these were the men of Manasseh who defected to him: Adnah, Jozabad, Jediael, Michael, Jozabad, Elihu and Zillethai, leaders of units of a thousand in Manasseh. [21]They helped David against raiding bands, for all of them were brave warriors, and they were commanders in his army. [22]Day after day men came to help David, until he had a great army, like the army of God.[b]

Others Join David at Hebron

[23]These are the numbers of the men armed for battle who came to David at Hebron to turn Saul's kingdom over to him, as the Lord had said:

[24]from Judah, carrying shield and spear—6,800 armed for battle;
[25]from Simeon, warriors ready for battle—7,100;
[26]from Levi—4,600, [27]including Jehoiada, leader of the family of Aaron, with 3,700 men, [28]and Zadok, a brave young warrior, with 22 officers from his family;
[29]from Benjamin, Saul's tribe—3,000, most of whom had remained loyal to Saul's house until then;
[30]from Ephraim, brave warriors, famous in their own clans—20,800;
[31]from half the tribe of Manasseh, designated by name to come and make David king—18,000;
[32]from Issachar, men who understood the times and knew what Israel should do—200 chiefs, with all their relatives under their command;
[33]from Zebulun, experienced soldiers prepared for battle with every type of weapon, to help David with undivided loyalty—50,000;

---

[a] 4 In Hebrew texts the second half of this verse (*Jeremiah . . . Gederathite*) is numbered 12:5, and 12:5-40 is numbered 12:6-41.   [b] 22 Or *a great and mighty army*

[34] from Naphtali—1,000 officers, together with 37,000 men carrying shields and spears;

[35] from Dan, ready for battle—28,600;

[36] from Asher, experienced soldiers prepared for battle—40,000;

[37] and from east of the Jordan, from Reuben, Gad and the half-tribe of Manasseh, armed with every type of weapon—120,000.

[38] All these were fighting men who volunteered to serve in the ranks. They came to Hebron fully determined to make David king over all Israel. All the rest of the Israelites were also of one mind to make David king. [39] The men spent three days there with David, eating and drinking, for their families had supplied provisions for them. [40] Also, their neighbors from as far away as Issachar, Zebulun and Naphtali came bringing food on donkeys, camels, mules and oxen. There were plentiful supplies of flour, fig cakes, raisin cakes, wine, olive oil, cattle and sheep, for there was joy in Israel.

Bringing Back the Ark

13 David conferred with each of his officers, the commanders of thousands and commanders of hundreds. [2] He then said to the whole assembly of Israel, "If it seems good to you and if it is the will of the LORD our God, let us send word far and wide to the rest of our people throughout the territories of Israel, and also to the priests and Levites who are with them in their towns and pasturelands, to come and join us. [3] Let us bring the ark of our God back to us, for we did not inquire of[a] it[b] during the reign of Saul." [4] The whole assembly agreed to do this, because it seemed right to all the people.

[5] So David assembled all Israel, from the Shihor River in Egypt to Lebo Hamath, to bring the ark of God from Kiriath Jearim. [6] David and all Israel went to Baalah of Judah (Kiriath Jearim) to bring up from there the ark of God the LORD, who is enthroned between the cherubim—the ark that is called by the Name.

[7] They moved the ark of God from Abinadab's house on a new cart, with Uzzah and Ahio guiding it. [8] David and all the Israelites were celebrating with all their might before God, with songs and with harps, lyres, timbrels, cymbals and trumpets.

[9] When they came to the threshing floor of Kidon, Uzzah reached out his hand to steady the ark, because the oxen stumbled. [10] The LORD's anger burned against Uzzah, and he struck him down because he had put his hand on the ark. So he died there before God.

[11] Then David was angry because the LORD's wrath had broken out against Uzzah, and to this day that place is called Perez Uzzah.[c]

[12] David was afraid of God that day and asked, "How can I ever bring the ark of God to me?" [13] He did not take the ark to be with him in the City of David. Instead, he took it to the house of Obed-Edom the Gittite. [14] The ark of God remained with the family of Obed-Edom in his house for three months, and the LORD blessed his household and everything he had.

David's House and Family

14 Now Hiram king of Tyre sent messengers to David, along with cedar logs, stonemasons and carpenters to build a palace for him. [2] And David knew that the LORD had established him as king over Israel and that his kingdom had been highly exalted for the sake of his people Israel.

[3] In Jerusalem David took more wives and became the father of more sons and daughters. [4] These are the names of the children born to him there: Shammua, Shobab, Nathan, Solomon, [5] Ibhar, Elishua, Elpelet, [6] Nogah, Nepheg, Japhia, [7] Elishama, Beeliada[d] and Eliphelet.

David Defeats the Philistines

[8] When the Philistines heard that David had been anointed king over all Isra-

---

[a] 3 Or *we neglected*   [b] 3 Or *him*   [c] 11 *Perez Uzzah* means *outbreak against Uzzah*.
[d] 7 A variant of *Eliada*

el, they went up in full force to search for him, but David heard about it and went out to meet them. ⁹Now the Philistines had come and raided the Valley of Rephaim; ¹⁰so David inquired of God: "Shall I go and attack the Philistines? Will you deliver them into my hands?"

The Lord answered him, "Go, I will deliver them into your hands."

¹¹So David and his men went up to Baal Perazim, and there he defeated them. He said, "As waters break out, God has broken out against my enemies by my hand." So that place was called Baal Perazim.ᵃ ¹²The Philistines had abandoned their gods there, and David gave orders to burn them in the fire.

¹³Once more the Philistines raided the valley; ¹⁴so David inquired of God again, and God answered him, "Do not go directly after them, but circle around them and attack them in front of the poplar trees. ¹⁵As soon as you hear the sound of marching in the tops of the poplar trees, move out to battle, because that will mean God has gone out in front of you to strike the Philistine army." ¹⁶So David did as God commanded him, and they struck down the Philistine army, all the way from Gibeon to Gezer.

¹⁷So David's fame spread throughout every land, and the Lord made all the nations fear him.

The Ark Brought to Jerusalem

15 After David had constructed buildings for himself in the City of David, he prepared a place for the ark of God and pitched a tent for it. ²Then David said, "No one but the Levites may carry the ark of God, because the Lord chose them to carry the ark of the Lord and to minister before him forever."

³David assembled all Israel in Jerusalem to bring up the ark of the Lord to the place he had prepared for it. ⁴He called together the descendants of Aaron and the Levites:

⁵From the descendants of Kohath,
Uriel the leader and 120 relatives;

⁶from the descendants of Merari,
Asaiah the leader and 220 relatives;

⁷from the descendants of Gershon,ᵇ
Joel the leader and 130 relatives;

⁸from the descendants of Elizaphan,
Shemaiah the leader and 200 relatives;

⁹from the descendants of Hebron,
Eliel the leader and 80 relatives;

¹⁰from the descendants of Uzziel,
Amminadab the leader and 112 relatives.

¹¹Then David summoned Zadok and Abiathar the priests, and Uriel, Asaiah, Joel, Shemaiah, Eliel and Amminadab the Levites. ¹²He said to them, "You are the heads of the Levitical families; you and your fellow Levites are to consecrate yourselves and bring up the ark of the Lord, the God of Israel, to the place I have prepared for it. ¹³It was because you, the Levites, did not bring it up the first time that the Lord our God broke out in anger against us. We did not inquire of him about how to do it in the prescribed way." ¹⁴So the priests and Levites consecrated themselves in order to bring up the ark of the Lord, the God of Israel. ¹⁵And the Levites carried the ark of God with the poles on their shoulders, as Moses had commanded in accordance with the word of the Lord.

¹⁶David told the leaders of the Levites to appoint their fellow Levites as musicians to make a joyful sound with musical instruments: lyres, harps and cymbals.

¹⁷So the Levites appointed Heman son of Joel; from his relatives, Asaph son of Berekiah; and from their relatives the Merarites, Ethan son of Kushaiah; ¹⁸and with them their relatives next in rank: Zechariah,ᶜ Jaaziel, Shemiramoth, Jehiel, Unni, Eliab, Benaiah, Maaseiah, Mattithiah, Eliphelehu, Mikneiah, Obed-Edom and Jeiel,ᵈ the gatekeepers.

ᵃ 11 Baal Perazim means the lord who breaks out.
ᵇ 7 Hebrew Gershom, a variant of Gershon
ᶜ 18 Three Hebrew manuscripts and most Septuagint manuscripts (see also verse 20 and 16:5); most Hebrew manuscripts Zechariah son and or Zechariah, Ben and   ᵈ 18 Hebrew; Septuagint (see also verse 21) Jeiel and Azaziah

[19]The musicians Heman, Asaph and Ethan were to sound the bronze cymbals; [20]Zechariah, Jaaziel,[a] Shemiramoth, Jehiel, Unni, Eliab, Maaseiah and Benaiah were to play the lyres according to *alamoth,*[b] [21]and Mattithiah, Eliphelehu, Mikneiah, Obed-Edom, Jeiel and Azaziah were to play the harps, directing according to *sheminith.*[b] [22]Kenaniah the head Levite was in charge of the singing; that was his responsibility because he was skillful at it.

[23]Berekiah and Elkanah were to be doorkeepers for the ark. [24]Shebaniah, Joshaphat, Nethanel, Amasai, Zechariah, Benaiah and Eliezer the priests were to blow trumpets before the ark of God. Obed-Edom and Jehiah were also to be doorkeepers for the ark.

[25]So David and the elders of Israel and the commanders of units of a thousand went to bring up the ark of the covenant of the LORD from the house of Obed-Edom, with rejoicing. [26]Because God had helped the Levites who were carrying the ark of the covenant of the LORD, seven bulls and seven rams were sacrificed. [27]Now David was clothed in a robe of fine linen, as were all the Levites who were carrying the ark, and as were the musicians, and Kenaniah, who was in charge of the singing of the choirs. David also wore a linen ephod. [28]So all Israel brought up the ark of the covenant of the LORD with shouts, with the sounding of rams' horns and trumpets, and of cymbals, and the playing of lyres and harps.

[29]As the ark of the covenant of the LORD was entering the City of David, Michal daughter of Saul watched from a window. And when she saw King David dancing and celebrating, she despised him in her heart.

---

[a] *20* See verse 18; Hebrew *Aziel*, a variant of *Jaaziel.*   [b] *20,21* Probably a musical term

ROCK SOLID *principles*

1 Chronicles 15:23–29

Dance for God.

Nora grabbed little Mateo by the hands and spun him around, lifting him into the air in a whirl. *This is fun,* she thought. After spending almost a month far from home caring for children at an orphanage, she couldn't imagine anywhere she would rather be. She had seen God at work in a place so different from home—a place where people were desperately poor yet so trusting in God. What she liked most of all was the chance to attend worship services at a small local church. When the worship band got going, she and her mission trip teammates joined in the singing, shouting, and dancing. They couldn't help but catch the contagious joy.

The "ark of God" (1 Chronicles 15:1) was an ornate box, a focused place of God's presence. Israel's enemies had captured the ark and carried it away (see 1 Samuel 4:1–11). David was so overjoyed that the ark was on its way back to Jerusalem that he called for a parade and danced in celebration. When God makes you happy, don't be afraid to show it.

Ministering Before the Ark

16 They brought the ark of God and set it inside the tent that David had pitched for it, and they presented burnt offerings and fellowship offerings before God. ²After David had finished sacrificing the burnt offerings and fellowship offerings, he blessed the people in the name of the LORD. ³Then he gave a loaf of bread, a cake of dates and a cake of raisins to each Israelite man and woman.

⁴He appointed some of the Levites to minister before the ark of the LORD, to extol,ᵃ thank, and praise the LORD, the God of Israel: ⁵Asaph was the chief, and next to him in rank were Zechariah, then Jaaziel,ᵇ Shemiramoth, Jehiel, Mattithiah, Eliab, Benaiah, Obed-Edom and Jeiel. They were to play the lyres and harps, Asaph was to sound the cymbals, ⁶and Benaiah and Jahaziel the priests were to blow the trumpets regularly before the ark of the covenant of God.

⁷That day David first appointed Asaph and his associates to give praise to the LORD in this manner:

⁸Give praise to the LORD, proclaim his
     name;
  make known among the nations
     what he has done.
⁹Sing to him, sing praise to him;
  tell of all his wonderful acts.
¹⁰Glory in his holy name;
  let the hearts of those who seek the
     LORD rejoice.
¹¹Look to the LORD and his strength;
  seek his face always.

¹²Remember the wonders he has
     done,
  his miracles, and the judgments he
     pronounced,
¹³you his servants, the descendants of
     Israel,
  his chosen ones, the children of
     Jacob.
¹⁴He is the LORD our God;
  his judgments are in all the
     earth.

¹⁵He remembersᶜ his covenant forever,
  the promise he made, for a
     thousand generations,
¹⁶the covenant he made with Abraham,
  the oath he swore to Isaac.
¹⁷He confirmed it to Jacob as a decree,
  to Israel as an everlasting covenant:
¹⁸"To you I will give the land of Canaan
  as the portion you will inherit."

¹⁹When they were but few in number,
  few indeed, and strangers in it,
²⁰theyᵈ wandered from nation to nation,
  from one kingdom to another.
²¹He allowed no one to oppress them;
  for their sake he rebuked kings:
²²"Do not touch my anointed ones;
  do my prophets no harm."

²³Sing to the LORD, all the earth;
  proclaim his salvation day after day.
²⁴Declare his glory among the nations,
  his marvelous deeds among all
     peoples.

²⁵For great is the LORD and most
     worthy of praise;
  he is to be feared above all gods.

ᵃ *4* Or *petition*; or *invoke*   ᵇ *5* See 15:18,20; Hebrew *Jeiel*, possibly another name for *Jaaziel*.   ᶜ *15* Some Septuagint manuscripts (see also Psalm 105:8); Hebrew *Remember*   ᵈ *18-20* One Hebrew manuscript, Septuagint and Vulgate (see also Psalm 105:12); most Hebrew manuscripts *inherit, / ¹⁹though you are but few in number, / few indeed, and strangers in it." / ²⁰They*

ROCK SOLID
promises

"Great is the LORD and most worthy of praise; he is to be feared above all gods."   1 Chronicles 16:25

Fake gods aim to steal your allegiance. The Lord alone deserves your awe-filled respect.

²⁶For all the gods of the nations are
    idols,
  but the Lord made the heavens.
²⁷Splendor and majesty are before him;
  strength and joy are in his dwelling
    place.
²⁸Ascribe to the Lord, all you families
    of nations,
  ascribe to the Lord glory and
    strength.
²⁹Ascribe to the Lord the glory due his
    name;
  bring an offering and come before
    him.
Worship the Lord in the splendor of
    his*a* holiness.
³⁰ Tremble before him, all the earth!
  The world is firmly established; it
    cannot be moved.

³¹Let the heavens rejoice, let the earth
    be glad;
  let them say among the nations,
    "The Lord reigns!"
³²Let the sea resound, and all that is in it;
  let the fields be jubilant, and
    everything in them!
³³Let the trees of the forest sing,
  let them sing for joy before the
    Lord,
  for he comes to judge the earth.
³⁴Give thanks to the Lord, for he is
    good;
  his love endures forever.
³⁵Cry out, "Save us, God our Savior;
  gather us and deliver us from the
    nations,
that we may give thanks to your holy
    name,
  and glory in your praise."
³⁶Praise be to the Lord, the God of
    Israel,
  from everlasting to everlasting.

Then all the people said "Amen" and
"Praise the Lord."

³⁷David left Asaph and his associates
before the ark of the covenant of the Lord
to minister there regularly, according to
each day's requirements. ³⁸He also left
Obed-Edom and his sixty-eight associates
to minister with them. Obed-Edom son
of Jeduthun, and also Hosah, were gatekeepers.

³⁹David left Zadok the priest and his
fellow priests before the tabernacle of the
Lord at the high place in Gibeon ⁴⁰to
present burnt offerings to the Lord on the
altar of burnt offering regularly, morning
and evening, in accordance with everything written in the Law of the Lord,
which he had given Israel. ⁴¹With them
were Heman and Jeduthun and the rest
of those chosen and designated by name
to give thanks to the Lord, "for his love
endures forever." ⁴²Heman and Jeduthun
were responsible for the sounding of the
trumpets and cymbals and for the playing
of the other instruments for sacred song.
The sons of Jeduthun were stationed at
the gate.

⁴³Then all the people left, each for their
own home, and David returned home to
bless his family.

God's Promise to David

17 After David was settled in his
palace, he said to Nathan the
prophet, "Here I am, living in
a house of cedar, while the ark of the covenant of the Lord is under a tent."

²Nathan replied to David, "Whatever
you have in mind, do it, for God is with
you."

³But that night the word of God came
to Nathan, saying:

⁴"Go and tell my servant David,
'This is what the Lord says: You
are not the one to build me a house
to dwell in. ⁵I have not dwelt in a
house from the day I brought Israel
up out of Egypt to this day. I have
moved from one tent site to another,
from one dwelling place to another.
⁶Wherever I have moved with all
the Israelites, did I ever say to any of
their leaders*b* whom I commanded to
shepherd my people, "Why have you
not built me a house of cedar?" '

---

a 29 Or Lord *with the splendor of*
b 6 Traditionally *judges*; also in verse 10

⁷"Now then, tell my servant David, 'This is what the LORD Almighty says: I took you from the pasture, from tending the flock, and appointed you ruler over my people Israel. ⁸I have been with you wherever you have gone, and I have cut off all your enemies from before you. Now I will make your name like the names of the greatest men on earth. ⁹And I will provide a place for my people Israel and will plant them so that they can have a home of their own and no longer be disturbed. Wicked people will not oppress them anymore, as they did at the beginning ¹⁰and have done ever since the time I appointed leaders over my people Israel. I will also subdue all your enemies.

"'I declare to you that the LORD will build a house for you: ¹¹When your days are over and you go to be with your ancestors, I will raise up your offspring to succeed you, one of your own sons, and I will establish his kingdom. ¹²He is the one who will build a house for me, and I will establish his throne forever. ¹³I will be his father, and he will be my son. I will never take my love away from him, as I took it away from your predecessor. ¹⁴I will set him over my house and my kingdom forever; his throne will be established forever.'"

¹⁵Nathan reported to David all the words of this entire revelation.

David's Prayer

¹⁶Then King David went in and sat before the LORD, and he said:

"Who am I, LORD God, and what is my family, that you have brought me this far? ¹⁷And as if this were not enough in your sight, my God, you have spoken about the future of the house of your servant. You, LORD God, have looked on me as though I were the most exalted of men.

¹⁸"What more can David say to you for honoring your servant? For you know your servant, ¹⁹LORD. For the sake of your servant and according to your will, you have done this great thing and made known all these great promises.

²⁰"There is no one like you, LORD, and there is no God but you, as we have heard with our own ears. ²¹And who is like your people Israel—the one nation on earth whose God went out to redeem a people for himself, and to make a name for yourself, and to perform great and awesome wonders by driving out nations from before your people, whom you redeemed from Egypt? ²²You made your people Israel your very own forever, and you, LORD, have become their God.

²³"And now, LORD, let the promise you have made concerning your servant and his house be established forever. Do as you promised, ²⁴so that it will be established and that your name will be great forever. Then people will say, 'The LORD Almighty, the God over Israel, is Israel's God!' And the house of your servant David will be established before you.

²⁵"You, my God, have revealed to your servant that you will build a house for him. So your servant has found courage to pray to you. ²⁶You, LORD, are God! You have promised these good things to your servant. ²⁷Now you have been pleased to bless the house of your servant, that it may continue forever in your sight; for you, LORD, have blessed it, and it will be blessed forever."

David's Victories

18 In the course of time, David defeated the Philistines and subdued them, and he took Gath and its surrounding villages from the control of the Philistines.

²David also defeated the Moabites, and they became subject to him and brought him tribute.

³Moreover, David defeated Hadadezer king of Zobah, in the vicinity of Hamath, when he went to set up his monument at*a* the Euphrates River. ⁴David captured a thousand of his chariots, seven thousand charioteers and twenty thousand foot soldiers. He hamstrung all but a hundred of the chariot horses.

⁵When the Arameans of Damascus came to help Hadadezer king of Zobah, David struck down twenty-two thousand of them. ⁶He put garrisons in the Aramean kingdom of Damascus, and the Arameans became subject to him and brought him tribute. The LORD gave David victory wherever he went.

⁷David took the gold shields carried by the officers of Hadadezer and brought them to Jerusalem. ⁸From Tebah*b* and Kun, towns that belonged to Hadadezer, David took a great quantity of bronze, which Solomon used to make the bronze Sea, the pillars and various bronze articles.

⁹When Tou king of Hamath heard that David had defeated the entire army of Hadadezer king of Zobah, ¹⁰he sent his son Hadoram to King David to greet him and congratulate him on his victory in battle over Hadadezer, who had been at war with Tou. Hadoram brought all kinds of articles of gold, of silver and of bronze.

¹¹King David dedicated these articles to the LORD, as he had done with the silver and gold he had taken from all these nations: Edom and Moab, the Ammonites and the Philistines, and Amalek.

¹²Abishai son of Zeruiah struck down eighteen thousand Edomites in the Valley of Salt. ¹³He put garrisons in Edom, and all the Edomites became subject to David. The LORD gave David victory wherever he went.

David's Officials

¹⁴David reigned over all Israel, doing what was just and right for all his people. ¹⁵Joab son of Zeruiah was over the army; Jehoshaphat son of Ahilud was recorder; ¹⁶Zadok son of Ahitub and Ahimelek*c* son of Abiathar were priests; Shavsha was secretary; ¹⁷Benaiah son of Jehoiada was over the Kerethites and Pelethites; and David's sons were chief officials at the king's side.

David Defeats the Ammonites

19 In the course of time, Nahash king of the Ammonites died, and his son succeeded him as king. ²David thought, "I will show kindness to Hanun son of Nahash, because his father showed kindness to me." So David sent a delegation to express his sympathy to Hanun concerning his father.

When David's envoys came to Hanun in the land of the Ammonites to express sympathy to him, ³the Ammonite commanders said to Hanun, "Do you think David is honoring your father by sending envoys to you to express sympathy? Haven't his envoys come to you only to explore and spy out the country and overthrow it?" ⁴So Hanun seized David's envoys, shaved them, cut off their garments at the buttocks, and sent them away.

⁵When someone came and told David about the men, he sent messengers to meet them, for they were greatly humiliated. The king said, "Stay at Jericho till your beards have grown, and then come back."

⁶When the Ammonites realized that they had become obnoxious to David, Hanun and the Ammonites sent a thousand talents*d* of silver to hire chariots and charioteers from Aram Naharaim,*e* Aram Maakah and Zobah. ⁷They hired thirty-two thousand chariots and charioteers, as well as the king of Maakah with his troops, who came and camped near Medeba, while the Ammonites were mustered from their towns and moved out for battle.

⁸On hearing this, David sent Joab out with the entire army of fighting men. ⁹The Ammonites came out and drew up in battle formation at the entrance to their

---

a 3 Or *to restore his control over*   *b 8* Hebrew *Tibhath,* a variant of *Tebah*   *c 16* Some Hebrew manuscripts, Vulgate and Syriac (see also 2 Samuel 8:17); most Hebrew manuscripts *Abimelek*   *d 6* That is, about 38 tons or about 34 metric tons   *e 6* That is, Northwest Mesopotamia city, while the kings who had come were by themselves in the open country.

[10]Joab saw that there were battle lines in front of him and behind him; so he selected some of the best troops in Israel and deployed them against the Arameans. [11]He put the rest of the men under the command of Abishai his brother, and they were deployed against the Ammonites. [12]Joab said, "If the Arameans are too strong for me, then you are to rescue me; but if the Ammonites are too strong for you, then I will rescue you. [13]Be strong, and let us fight bravely for our people and the cities of our God. The LORD will do what is good in his sight."

[14]Then Joab and the troops with him advanced to fight the Arameans, and they fled before him. [15]When the Ammonites realized that the Arameans were fleeing, they too fled before his brother Abishai and went inside the city. So Joab went back to Jerusalem.

[16]After the Arameans saw that they had been routed by Israel, they sent messengers and had Arameans brought from beyond the Euphrates River, with Shophak the commander of Hadadezer's army leading them.

[17]When David was told of this, he gathered all Israel and crossed the Jordan; he advanced against them and formed his battle lines opposite them. David formed his lines to meet the Arameans in battle, and they fought against him. [18]But they fled before Israel, and David killed seven thousand of their charioteers and forty thousand of their foot soldiers. He also killed Shophak the commander of their army.

[19]When the vassals of Hadadezer saw that they had been routed by Israel, they made peace with David and became subject to him.

So the Arameans were not willing to help the Ammonites anymore.

The Capture of Rabbah

20 In the spring, at the time when kings go off to war, Joab led out the armed forces. He laid waste the land of the Ammon-ites and went to Rabbah and besieged it, but David remained in Jerusalem. Joab attacked Rabbah and left it in ruins. [2]David took the crown from the head of their king[a]—its weight was found to be a talent[b] of gold, and it was set with precious stones—and it was placed on David's head. He took a great quantity of plunder from the city [3]and brought out the people who were there, consigning them to labor with saws and with iron picks and axes. David did this to all the Ammonite towns. Then David and his entire army returned to Jerusalem.

War With the Philistines

[4]In the course of time, war broke out with the Philistines, at Gezer. At that time Sibbekai the Hushathite killed Sippai, one of the descendants of the Rephaites, and the Philistines were subjugated.

[5]In another battle with the Philistines, Elhanan son of Jair killed Lahmi the brother of Goliath the Gittite, who had a spear with a shaft like a weaver's rod.

[6]In still another battle, which took place at Gath, there was a huge man with six fingers on each hand and six toes on each foot—twenty-four in all. He also was descended from Rapha. [7]When he taunted Israel, Jonathan son of Shimea, David's brother, killed him.

[8]These were descendants of Rapha in Gath, and they fell at the hands of David and his men.

David Counts the Fighting Men

21 Satan rose up against Israel and incited David to take a census of Israel. [2]So David said to Joab and the commanders of the troops, "Go and count the Israelites from Beersheba to Dan. Then report back to me so that I may know how many there are."

[3]But Joab replied, "May the LORD multiply his troops a hundred times over. My lord the king, are they not all my lord's subjects? Why does my lord want to do this? Why should he bring guilt on Israel?"

---

[a] 2 Or *of Milkom*, that is, Molek   [b] 2 That is, about 75 pounds or about 34 kilograms

⁴The king's word, however, overruled Joab; so Joab left and went throughout Israel and then came back to Jerusalem. ⁵Joab reported the number of the fighting men to David: In all Israel there were one million one hundred thousand men who could handle a sword, including four hundred and seventy thousand in Judah.

⁶But Joab did not include Levi and Benjamin in the numbering, because the king's command was repulsive to him. ⁷This command was also evil in the sight of God; so he punished Israel.

⁸Then David said to God, "I have sinned greatly by doing this. Now, I beg you, take away the guilt of your servant. I have done a very foolish thing."

⁹The LORD said to Gad, David's seer, ¹⁰"Go and tell David, 'This is what the LORD says: I am giving you three options. Choose one of them for me to carry out against you.'"

¹¹So Gad went to David and said to him, "This is what the LORD says: 'Take your choice: ¹²three years of famine, three months of being swept away*ᵃ* before your enemies, with their swords overtaking you, or three days of the sword of the LORD—days of plague in the land, with the angel of the LORD ravaging every part of Israel.' Now then, decide how I should answer the one who sent me."

¹³David said to Gad, "I am in deep distress. Let me fall into the hands of the LORD, for his mercy is very great; but do not let me fall into human hands."

¹⁴So the LORD sent a plague on Israel, and seventy thousand men of Israel fell dead. ¹⁵And God sent an angel to destroy Jerusalem. But as the angel was doing so, the LORD saw it and relented concerning the disaster and said to the angel who was destroying the people, "Enough! Withdraw your hand." The angel of the LORD was then standing at the threshing floor of Araunah*ᵇ* the Jebusite.

¹⁶David looked up and saw the angel of the LORD standing between heaven and earth, with a drawn sword in his hand extended over Jerusalem. Then David and the elders, clothed in sackcloth, fell facedown.

¹⁷David said to God, "Was it not I who ordered the fighting men to be counted? I, the shepherd,*ᶜ* have sinned and done wrong. These are but sheep. What have they done? LORD my God, let your hand fall on me and my family, but do not let this plague remain on your people."

David Builds an Altar

¹⁸Then the angel of the LORD ordered Gad to tell David to go up and build an altar to the LORD on the threshing floor of Araunah the Jebusite. ¹⁹So David went up in obedience to the word that Gad had spoken in the name of the LORD.

²⁰While Araunah was threshing wheat, he turned and saw the angel; his four sons who were with him hid themselves. ²¹Then David approached, and when Araunah looked and saw him, he left the threshing floor and bowed down before David with his face to the ground.

²²David said to him, "Let me have the site of your threshing floor so I can build an altar to the LORD, that the plague on the people may be stopped. Sell it to me at the full price."

²³Araunah said to David, "Take it! Let my lord the king do whatever pleases him. Look, I will give the oxen for the burnt offerings, the threshing sledges for the wood, and the wheat for the grain offering. I will give all this."

²⁴But King David replied to Araunah, "No, I insist on paying the full price. I will not take for the LORD what is yours, or sacrifice a burnt offering that costs me nothing."

²⁵So David paid Araunah six hundred shekels*ᵈ* of gold for the site. ²⁶David built an altar to the LORD there and sacrificed burnt offerings and fellowship offerings. He called on the LORD, and the LORD answered him with fire from heaven on the altar of burnt offering.

ᵃ 12 Hebrew; Septuagint and Vulgate (see also 2 Samuel 24:13) *of fleeing*   *ᵇ 15* Hebrew *Ornan,* a variant of *Araunah;* also in verses 18-28   *ᶜ 17* Probable reading of the original Hebrew text (see 2 Samuel 24:17 and note); Masoretic Text does not have *the shepherd.*   *ᵈ 25* That is, about 15 pounds or about 6.9 kilograms

²⁷Then the LORD spoke to the angel, and he put his sword back into its sheath. ²⁸At that time, when David saw that the LORD had answered him on the threshing floor of Araunah the Jebusite, he offered sacrifices there. ²⁹The tabernacle of the LORD, which Moses had made in the wilderness, and the altar of burnt offering were at that time on the high place at Gibeon. ³⁰But David could not go before it to inquire of God, because he was afraid of the sword of the angel of the LORD.

1 Chronicles 21:1–30
The devil didn't make you do it.

This scene isn't the first time someone claimed "the devil made me do it." Back in the Garden of Eden, Adam and Eve ate a piece of forbidden fruit. When God confronted the world's first couple, Adam said "the woman you put here" made him sin (Genesis 3:12). Eve said "the serpent deceived me," putting blame on the devil himself (Genesis 3:13). In this 1 Chronicles 21 scene it says "Satan rose up against Israel and incited David to take a census of Israel" (1 Chronicles 21:1). While it might not seem sinful for a king to want to count the people in his kingdom, it meant David was planning to rely on people rather than the Lord to win his battles. God grew hot and struck down 70,000 men. Spot this point: Even though the devil influenced David's decision, David was fully responsible for his sin (see 1 Chronicles 21:17). He didn't use the devil as an excuse.

Think: How do you think the devil influences people to sin?

ROCK SOLID truths

22

Then David said, "The house of the LORD God is to be here, and also the altar of burnt offering for Israel."

Preparations for the Temple

²So David gave orders to assemble the foreigners residing in Israel, and from among them he appointed stonecutters to prepare dressed stone for building the house of God. ³He provided a large amount of iron to make nails for the doors of the gateways and for the fittings, and more bronze than could be weighed. ⁴He also provided more cedar logs than could be counted, for the Sidonians and Tyrians had brought large numbers of them to David.

⁵David said, "My son Solomon is young and inexperienced, and the house to be built for the LORD should be of great magnificence and fame and splendor in the sight of all the nations. Therefore I will make preparations for it." So David made extensive preparations before his death.

⁶Then he called for his son Solomon and charged him to build a house for the LORD, the God of Israel. ⁷David said to Solomon: "My son, I had it in my heart to build a house for the Name of the LORD my God. ⁸But this word of the LORD came to me: 'You have shed much blood and have fought many wars. You are not to build a house for my Name, because you have shed much blood on the earth in my sight. ⁹But you will have a son who will be a man of peace and rest, and I will give him rest from all his enemies on every side. His name will be Solomon,[a] and I will grant Israel peace and quiet during his reign. ¹⁰He is the one who will build a house for my Name. He will be my son, and I will be his father. And I will establish the throne of his kingdom over Israel forever.'

¹¹"Now, my son, the LORD be with you, and may you have success and build the house of the LORD your God, as he said you would. ¹²May the LORD give you

[a] 9 Solomon sounds like and may be derived from the Hebrew for peace.

discretion and understanding when he puts you in command over Israel, so that you may keep the law of the LORD your God. ¹³Then you will have success if you are careful to observe the decrees and laws that the LORD gave Moses for Israel. Be strong and courageous. Do not be afraid or discouraged.

¹⁴"I have taken great pains to provide for the temple of the LORD a hundred thousand talents*a* of gold, a million talents*b* of silver, quantities of bronze and iron too great to be weighed, and wood and stone. And you may add to them. ¹⁵You have many workers: stonecutters, masons and carpenters, as well as those skilled in every kind of work ¹⁶in gold and silver, bronze and iron—craftsmen beyond number. Now begin the work, and the LORD be with you."

¹⁷Then David ordered all the leaders of Israel to help his son Solomon. ¹⁸He said to them, "Is not the LORD your God with you? And has he not granted you rest on every side? For he has given the inhabitants of the land into my hands, and the land is subject to the LORD and to his people. ¹⁹Now devote your heart and soul to seeking the LORD your God. Begin to build the sanctuary of the LORD God, so that you may bring the ark of the covenant of the LORD and the sacred articles belonging to God into the temple that will be built for the Name of the LORD."

The Levites

23 When David was old and full of years, he made his son Solomon king over Israel.

²He also gathered together all the leaders of Israel, as well as the priests and Levites. ³The Levites thirty years old or more were counted, and the total number of men was thirty-eight thousand. ⁴David said, "Of these, twenty-four thousand are to be in charge of the work of the temple of the LORD and six thousand are to be officials and judges. ⁵Four thousand are to be gatekeepers and four thousand are to praise the LORD with the musical instruments I have provided for that purpose."

⁶David separated the Levites into divisions corresponding to the sons of Levi: Gershon, Kohath and Merari.

Gershonites

⁷Belonging to the Gershonites:
Ladan and Shimei.

⁸The sons of Ladan:
Jehiel the first, Zetham and Joel—three in all.

⁹The sons of Shimei:
Shelomoth, Haziel and Haran—three in all.
These were the heads of the families of Ladan.

¹⁰And the sons of Shimei:
Jahath, Ziza,*c* Jeush and Beriah.
These were the sons of Shimei—four in all.

¹¹Jahath was the first and Ziza the second, but Jeush and Beriah did not have many sons; so they were counted as one family with one assignment.

Kohathites

¹²The sons of Kohath:
Amram, Izhar, Hebron and Uzziel—four in all.

¹³The sons of Amram:
Aaron and Moses.
Aaron was set apart, he and his descendants forever, to consecrate the most holy things, to offer sacrifices before the LORD, to minister before him and to pronounce blessings in his name forever. ¹⁴The sons of Moses the man of God were counted as part of the tribe of Levi.

¹⁵The sons of Moses:
Gershom and Eliezer.

¹⁶The descendants of Gershom:
Shubael was the first.

¹⁷The descendants of Eliezer:
Rehabiah was the first.

a 14 That is, about 3,750 tons or about 3,400 metric tons   *b 14* That is, about 37,500 tons or about 34,000 metric tons   *c 10* One Hebrew manuscript, Septuagint and Vulgate (see also verse 11); most Hebrew manuscripts *Zina*

Eliezer had no other sons, but the sons of Rehabiah were very numerous.

¹⁸The sons of Izhar:
Shelomith was the first.

¹⁹The sons of Hebron:
Jeriah the first, Amariah the second, Jahaziel the third and Jekameam the fourth.

²⁰The sons of Uzziel:
Micah the first and Ishiah the second.

Merarites

²¹The sons of Merari:
Mahli and Mushi.
The sons of Mahli:
Eleazar and Kish.

²²Eleazar died without having sons: he had only daughters. Their cousins, the sons of Kish, married them.

²³The sons of Mushi:
Mahli, Eder and Jerimoth—three in all.

²⁴These were the descendants of Levi by their families—the heads of families as they were registered under their names and counted individually, that is, the workers twenty years old or more who served in the temple of the LORD. ²⁵For David had said, "Since the LORD, the God of Israel, has granted rest to his people and has come to dwell in Jerusalem forever, ²⁶the Levites no longer need to carry the tabernacle or any of the articles used in its service." ²⁷According to the last instructions of David, the Levites were counted from those twenty years old or more.

²⁸The duty of the Levites was to help Aaron's descendants in the service of the temple of the LORD: to be in charge of the courtyards, the side rooms, the purification of all sacred things and the performance of other duties at the house of God. ²⁹They were in charge of the bread set out on the table, the special flour for the grain offerings, the thin loaves made without yeast, the baking and the mixing, and all measurements of quantity and size. ³⁰They were also to stand every morning to thank and praise the LORD. They were to do the same in the evening ³¹and whenever burnt offerings were presented to the LORD on the Sabbaths, at the New Moon feasts and at the appointed festivals. They were to serve before the LORD regularly in the proper number and in the way prescribed for them.

³²And so the Levites carried out their responsibilities for the tent of meeting, for the Holy Place and, under their relatives the descendants of Aaron, for the service of the temple of the LORD.

The Divisions of Priests

24 These were the divisions of the descendants of Aaron:

The sons of Aaron were Nadab, Abihu, Eleazar and Ithamar. ²But Nadab and Abihu died before their father did, and they had no sons; so Eleazar and Ithamar served as the priests. ³With the help of Zadok a descendant of Eleazar and Ahimelek a descendant of Ithamar, David separated them into divisions for their appointed order of ministering. ⁴A larger number of leaders were found among Eleazar's descendants than among Ithamar's, and they were divided accordingly: sixteen heads of families from Eleazar's descendants and eight heads of families from Ithamar's descendants. ⁵They divided them impartially by casting lots, for there were officials of the sanctuary and officials of God among the descendants of both Eleazar and Ithamar.

⁶The scribe Shemaiah son of Nethanel, a Levite, recorded their names in the presence of the king and of the officials: Zadok the priest, Ahimelek son of Abiathar and the heads of families of the priests and of the Levites—one family being taken from Eleazar and then one from Ithamar.

⁷The first lot fell to Jehoiarib,
the second to Jedaiah,
⁸the third to Harim,
the fourth to Seorim,
⁹the fifth to Malkijah,
the sixth to Mijamin,
¹⁰the seventh to Hakkoz,
the eighth to Abijah,

¹¹ the ninth to Jeshua,
the tenth to Shekaniah,
¹² the eleventh to Eliashib,
the twelfth to Jakim,
¹³ the thirteenth to Huppah,
the fourteenth to Jeshebeab,
¹⁴ the fifteenth to Bilgah,
the sixteenth to Immer,
¹⁵ the seventeenth to Hezir,
the eighteenth to Happizzez,
¹⁶ the nineteenth to Pethahiah,
the twentieth to Jehezkel,
¹⁷ the twenty-first to Jakin,
the twenty-second to Gamul,
¹⁸ the twenty-third to Delaiah
and the twenty-fourth to Maaziah.

¹⁹ This was their appointed order of ministering when they entered the temple of the Lord, according to the regulations prescribed for them by their ancestor Aaron, as the Lord, the God of Israel, had commanded him.

The Rest of the Levites

²⁰ As for the rest of the descendants of Levi:
from the sons of Amram: Shubael;
from the sons of Shubael: Jehdeiah.
²¹ As for Rehabiah, from his sons:
Ishiah was the first.
²² From the Izharites: Shelomoth;
from the sons of Shelomoth: Jahath.
²³ The sons of Hebron: Jeriah the first,^a Amariah the second, Jahaziel the third and Jekameam the fourth.
²⁴ The son of Uzziel: Micah;
from the sons of Micah: Shamir.
²⁵ The brother of Micah: Ishiah;
from the sons of Ishiah: Zechariah.
²⁶ The sons of Merari: Mahli and Mushi.
The son of Jaaziah: Beno.
²⁷ The sons of Merari:
from Jaaziah: Beno, Shoham, Zakkur and Ibri.
²⁸ From Mahli: Eleazar, who had no sons.
²⁹ From Kish: the son of Kish: Jerahmeel.

³⁰ And the sons of Mushi: Mahli, Eder and Jerimoth.

These were the Levites, according to their families. ³¹ They also cast lots, just as their relatives the descendants of Aaron did, in the presence of King David and of Zadok, Ahimelek, and the heads of families of the priests and of the Levites. The families of the oldest brother were treated the same as those of the youngest.

The Musicians

25 David, together with the commanders of the army, set apart some of the sons of Asaph, Heman and Jeduthun for the ministry of prophesying, accompanied by harps, lyres and cymbals. Here is the list of the men who performed this service:

² From the sons of Asaph:
Zakkur, Joseph, Nethaniah and Asarelah. The sons of Asaph were under the supervision of Asaph, who prophesied under the king's supervision.
³ As for Jeduthun, from his sons:
Gedaliah, Zeri, Jeshaiah, Shimei,^b Hashabiah and Mattithiah, six in all, under the supervision of their father Jeduthun, who prophesied, using the harp in thanking and praising the Lord.
⁴ As for Heman, from his sons:
Bukkiah, Mattaniah, Uzziel, Shubael and Jerimoth; Hananiah, Hanani, Eliathah, Giddalti and Romamti-Ezer; Joshbekashah, Mallothi, Hothir and Mahazioth. ⁵ (All these were sons of Heman the king's seer. They were given him through the promises of God to exalt him. God gave Heman fourteen sons and three daughters.)

⁶ All these men were under the supervision of their father for the music of the

^a 23 Two Hebrew manuscripts and some Septuagint manuscripts (see also 23:19); most Hebrew manuscripts *The sons of Jeriah:*
^b 3 One Hebrew manuscript and some Septuagint manuscripts (see also verse 17); most Hebrew manuscripts do not have *Shimei.*

temple of the LORD, with cymbals, lyres and harps, for the ministry at the house of God.

Asaph, Jeduthun and Heman were under the supervision of the king. ⁷Along with their relatives—all of them trained and skilled in music for the LORD—they numbered 288. ⁸Young and old alike, teacher as well as student, cast lots for their duties.

⁹The first lot, which was for
  Asaph, fell to Joseph,
  his sons and relatives*   12*
the second to Gedaliah,
  him and his relatives
  and sons   12
¹⁰the third to Zakkur,
  his sons and relatives   12
¹¹the fourth to Izri,*
  his sons and relatives   12
¹²the fifth to Nethaniah,
  his sons and relatives   12
¹³the sixth to Bukkiah,
  his sons and relatives   12
¹⁴the seventh to Jesarelah,*
  his sons and relatives   12
¹⁵the eighth to Jeshaiah,
  his sons and relatives   12
¹⁶the ninth to Mattaniah,
  his sons and relatives   12
¹⁷the tenth to Shimei,
  his sons and relatives   12
¹⁸the eleventh to Azarel,*
  his sons and relatives   12
¹⁹the twelfth to Hashabiah,
  his sons and relatives   12
²⁰the thirteenth to Shubael,
  his sons and relatives   12
²¹the fourteenth to Mattithiah,
  his sons and relatives   12
²²the fifteenth to Jerimoth,
  his sons and relatives   12
²³the sixteenth to Hananiah,
  his sons and relatives   12
²⁴the seventeenth to Joshbekashah,
  his sons and relatives   12
²⁵the eighteenth to Hanani,
  his sons and relatives   12
²⁶the nineteenth to Mallothi,
  his sons and relatives   12
²⁷the twentieth to Eliathah,
  his sons and relatives   12
²⁸the twenty-first to Hothir,
  his sons and relatives   12
²⁹the twenty-second to Giddalti,
  his sons and relatives   12
³⁰the twenty-third to Mahazioth,
  his sons and relatives   12
³¹the twenty-fourth to
  Romamti-Ezer,
  his sons and relatives   12.

The Gatekeepers

26 The divisions of the gatekeepers:

From the Korahites: Meshelemiah son of Kore, one of the sons of Asaph.

²Meshelemiah had sons:
  Zechariah the firstborn,
  Jediael the second,
  Zebadiah the third,
  Jathniel the fourth,
  ³Elam the fifth,
  Jehohanan the sixth
  and Eliehoenai the seventh.
⁴Obed-Edom also had sons:
  Shemaiah the firstborn,
  Jehozabad the second,
  Joah the third,
  Sakar the fourth,
  Nethanel the fifth,
  ⁵Ammiel the sixth,
  Issachar the seventh
  and Peullethai the eighth.
  (For God had blessed Obed-Edom.)

⁶Obed-Edom's son Shemaiah also had sons, who were leaders in their father's family because they were very capable men. ⁷The sons of Shemaiah: Othni, Rephael, Obed and Elzabad; his relatives Elihu and Semakiah were also able men. ⁸All these were descendants of Obed-Edom; they and their

---

*a 9 See Septuagint; Hebrew does not have *his sons and relatives*.   b 9 See the total in verse 7; Hebrew does not have *twelve*.   c 11 A variant of *Zeri*   d 14 A variant of *Asarelah*   e 18 A variant of *Uzziel* sons and their relatives were capable men with the strength to do the work—descendants of Obed-Edom, 62 in all. ⁹Meshelemiah had sons and relatives, who were able men—18 in all.

¹⁰Hosah the Merarite had sons: Shimri the first (although he was not the firstborn, his father had appointed him the first), ¹¹Hilkiah the second, Tabaliah the third and Zechariah the fourth. The sons and relatives of Hosah were 13 in all.

¹²These divisions of the gatekeepers, through their leaders, had duties for ministering in the temple of the LORD, just as their relatives had. ¹³Lots were cast for each gate, according to their families, young and old alike.

¹⁴The lot for the East Gate fell to Shelemiah.ᵃ Then lots were cast for his son Zechariah, a wise counselor, and the lot for the North Gate fell to him. ¹⁵The lot for the South Gate fell to Obed-Edom, and the lot for the storehouse fell to his sons. ¹⁶The lots for the West Gate and the Shalleketh Gate on the upper road fell to Shuppim and Hosah.

Guard was alongside of guard: ¹⁷There were six Levites a day on the east, four a day on the north, four a day on the south and two at a time at the storehouse. ¹⁸As for the courtᵇ to the west, there were four at the road and two at the courtᵇ itself.

¹⁹These were the divisions of the gatekeepers who were descendants of Korah and Merari.

The Treasurers and Other Officials

²⁰Their fellow Levites wereᶜ in charge of the treasuries of the house of God and the treasuries for the dedicated things. ²¹The descendants of Ladan, who were Gershonites through Ladan and who were heads of families belonging to Ladan the Gershonite, were Jehieli, ²²the sons of Jehieli, Zetham and his brother Joel. They were in charge of the treasuries of the temple of the LORD.

²³From the Amramites, the Izharites, the Hebronites and the Uzzielites:

²⁴Shubael, a descendant of Gershom son of Moses, was the official in charge of the treasuries. ²⁵His relatives through Eliezer: Rehabiah his son, Jeshaiah his son, Joram his son, Zikri his son and Shelomith his son. ²⁶Shelomith and his relatives were in charge of all the treasuries for the things dedicated by King David, by the heads of families who were the commanders of thousands and commanders of hundreds, and by the other army commanders. ²⁷Some of the plunder taken in battle they dedicated for the repair of the temple of the LORD. ²⁸And everything dedicated by Samuel the seer and by Saul son of Kish, Abner son of Ner and Joab son of Zeruiah, and all the other dedicated things were in the care of Shelomith and his relatives.

²⁹From the Izharites: Kenaniah and his sons were assigned duties away from the temple, as officials and judges over Israel.

³⁰From the Hebronites: Hashabiah and his relatives—seventeen hundred able men—were responsible in Israel west of the Jordan for all the work of the LORD and for the king's service. ³¹As for the Hebronites, Jeriah was their chief according to the genealogical records of their families. In the fortieth year of David's reign a search was made in the records, and capable men among the Hebronites were found at Jazer in Gilead. ³²Jeriah had twenty-seven hundred relatives, who were able men and heads of families, and King David put them in charge of the Reubenites, the Gadites and the half-tribe of Manasseh for every matter pertaining to God and for the affairs of the king.

ᵃ 14 A variant of *Meshelemiah*   ᵇ 18 The meaning of the Hebrew for this word is uncertain.   ᶜ 20 Septuagint; Hebrew *As for the Levites, Ahijah was*

Army Divisions

27 This is the list of the Israelites—heads of families, commanders of thousands and commanders of hundreds, and their officers, who served the king in all that concerned the army divisions that were on duty month by month throughout the year. Each division consisted of 24,000 men.

²In charge of the first division, for the first month, was Jashobeam son of Zabdiel. There were 24,000 men in his division. ³He was a descendant of Perez and chief of all the army officers for the first month.

⁴In charge of the division for the second month was Dodai the Ahohite; Mikloth was the leader of his division. There were 24,000 men in his division.

⁵The third army commander, for the third month, was Benaiah son of Jehoiada the priest. He was chief and there were 24,000 men in his division. ⁶This was the Benaiah who was a mighty warrior among the Thirty and was over the Thirty. His son Ammizabad was in charge of his division.

⁷The fourth, for the fourth month, was Asahel the brother of Joab; his son Zebadiah was his successor. There were 24,000 men in his division.

⁸The fifth, for the fifth month, was the commander Shamhuth the Izrahite. There were 24,000 men in his division.

⁹The sixth, for the sixth month, was Ira the son of Ikkesh the Tekoite. There were 24,000 men in his division.

¹⁰The seventh, for the seventh month, was Helez the Pelonite, an Ephraimite. There were 24,000 men in his division.

¹¹The eighth, for the eighth month, was Sibbekai the Hushathite, a Zerahite. There were 24,000 men in his division.

¹²The ninth, for the ninth month, was Abiezer the Anathothite, a Benjamite. There were 24,000 men in his division.

¹³The tenth, for the tenth month, was Maharai the Netophathite, a Zerahite. There were 24,000 men in his division.

¹⁴The eleventh, for the eleventh month, was Benaiah the Pirathonite, an Ephraimite. There were 24,000 men in his division.

¹⁵The twelfth, for the twelfth month, was Heldai the Netophathite, from the family of Othniel. There were 24,000 men in his division.

Leaders of the Tribes

¹⁶The leaders of the tribes of Israel:

over the Reubenites: Eliezer son of Zikri;

over the Simeonites: Shephatiah son of Maakah;

¹⁷over Levi: Hashabiah son of Kemuel;

over Aaron: Zadok;

¹⁸over Judah: Elihu, a brother of David;

over Issachar: Omri son of Michael;

¹⁹over Zebulun: Ishmaiah son of Obadiah;

over Naphtali: Jerimoth son of Azriel;

²⁰over the Ephraimites: Hoshea son of Azaziah;

over half the tribe of Manasseh: Joel son of Pedaiah;

²¹over the half-tribe of Manasseh in Gilead: Iddo son of Zechariah;

over Benjamin: Jaasiel son of Abner;

²²over Dan: Azarel son of Jeroham.

These were the leaders of the tribes of Israel.

²³David did not take the number of the men twenty years old or less, because the LORD had promised to make Israel as numerous as the stars in the sky. ²⁴Joab son of Zeruiah began to count the men but did not finish. God's wrath came on Israel on account of this numbering, and the number was not entered in the book* of the annals of King David.

*24 Septuagint; Hebrew *number*

The King's Overseers

²⁵Azmaveth son of Adiel was in charge of the royal storehouses.

Jonathan son of Uzziah was in charge of the storehouses in the outlying districts, in the towns, the villages and the watchtowers.

²⁶Ezri son of Kelub was in charge of the workers who farmed the land.

²⁷Shimei the Ramathite was in charge of the vineyards.

Zabdi the Shiphmite was in charge of the produce of the vineyards for the wine vats.

²⁸Baal-Hanan the Gederite was in charge of the olive and sycamore-fig trees in the western foothills.

Joash was in charge of the supplies of olive oil.

²⁹Shitrai the Sharonite was in charge of the herds grazing in Sharon.

Shaphat son of Adlai was in charge of the herds in the valleys.

³⁰Obil the Ishmaelite was in charge of the camels.

Jehdeiah the Meronothite was in charge of the donkeys.

³¹Jaziz the Hagrite was in charge of the flocks.

All these were the officials in charge of King David's property.

³²Jonathan, David's uncle, was a counselor, a man of insight and a scribe. Jehiel son of Hakmoni took care of the king's sons.

³³Ahithophel was the king's counselor.

Hushai the Arkite was the king's confidant. ³⁴Ahithophel was succeeded by Jehoiada son of Benaiah and by Abiathar.

Joab was the commander of the royal army.

David's Plans for the Temple

28 David summoned all the officials of Israel to assemble at Jerusalem: the officers over the tribes, the commanders of the divisions in the service of the king, the commanders of thousands and commanders of hundreds, and the officials in charge of all the property and livestock belonging to the king and his sons, together with the palace officials, the warriors and all the brave fighting men.

²King David rose to his feet and said: "Listen to me, my fellow Israelites, my people. I had it in my heart to build a house as a place of rest for the ark of the covenant of the LORD, for the footstool of our God, and I made plans to build it. ³But God said to me, 'You are not to build a house for my Name, because you are a warrior and have shed blood.'

⁴"Yet the LORD, the God of Israel, chose me from my whole family to be king over Israel forever. He chose Judah as leader, and from the tribe of Judah he chose my family, and from my father's sons he was pleased to make me king over all Israel. ⁵Of all my sons—and the LORD has given me many—he has chosen my son Solomon to sit on the throne of the kingdom of the LORD over Israel. ⁶He said to me: 'Solomon your son is the one who will build my house and my courts, for I have chosen him to be my son, and I will be his father. ⁷I will establish his kingdom forever if he is unswerving in carrying out my commands and laws, as is being done at this time.'

⁸"So now I charge you in the sight of all Israel and of the assembly of the LORD, and in the hearing of our God: Be careful to follow all the commands of the LORD your God, that you may possess this good land and pass it on as an inheritance to your descendants forever.

⁹"And you, my son Solomon, acknowledge the God of your father, and serve him with wholehearted devotion and with a willing mind, for the LORD searches every heart and understands every desire and every thought. If you seek him, he will be found by you; but if you forsake him, he will reject you forever. ¹⁰Consider now, for the LORD has chosen you to build a house as the sanctuary. Be strong and do the work."

¹¹Then David gave his son Solomon the plans for the portico of the temple, its buildings, its storerooms, its upper parts, its inner rooms and the place of atonement. ¹²He gave him the plans of all that the Spirit had put in his mind for the courts of the

temple of the Lord and all the surrounding rooms, for the treasuries of the temple of God and for the treasuries for the dedicated things. ¹³He gave him instructions for the divisions of the priests and Levites, and for all the work of serving in the temple of the Lord, as well as for all the articles to be used in its service. ¹⁴He designated the weight of gold for all the gold articles to be used in various kinds of service, and the weight of silver for all the silver articles to be used in various kinds of service: ¹⁵the weight of gold for the gold lampstands and their lamps, with the weight for each lampstand and its lamps; and the weight of silver for each silver lampstand and its lamps, according to the use of each lampstand; ¹⁶the weight of gold for each table for consecrated bread; the weight of silver for the silver tables; ¹⁷the weight of pure gold for the forks, sprinkling bowls and pitchers; the weight of gold for each gold dish; the weight of silver for each silver dish; ¹⁸and the weight of the refined gold for the altar of incense. He also gave him the plan for the chariot, that is, the cherubim of gold that spread their wings and overshadow the ark of the covenant of the Lord.

¹⁹"All this," David said, "I have in writing as a result of the Lord's hand on me, and he enabled me to understand all the details of the plan."

²⁰David also said to Solomon his son, "Be strong and courageous, and do the work. Do not be afraid or discouraged, for the Lord God, my God, is with you. He will not fail you or forsake you until all the work for the service of the temple of the Lord is finished. ²¹The divisions of the priests and Levites are ready for all the work on the temple of God, and every willing person skilled in any craft will help you in all the work. The officials and all the people will obey your every command."

Gifts for Building the Temple

29 Then King David said to the whole assembly: "My son Solomon, the one whom God has chosen, is young and inexperi-enced. The task is great, because this palatial structure is not for man but for the Lord God. ²With all my resources I have provided for the temple of my God—gold for the gold work, silver for the silver, bronze for the bronze, iron for the iron and wood for the wood, as well as onyx for the settings, turquoise,ᵃ stones of various colors, and all kinds of fine stone and marble—all of these in large quantities. ³Besides, in my devotion to the temple of my God I now give my personal treasures of gold and silver for the temple of my God, over and above everything I have provided for this holy temple: ⁴three thousand talentsᵇ of gold (gold of Ophir) and seven thousand talentsᶜ of refined silver, for the overlaying of the walls of the buildings, ⁵for the gold work and the silver work, and for all the work to be done by the

ᵃ 2 The meaning of the Hebrew for this word is uncertain. ᵇ 4 That is, about 110 tons or about 100 metric tons ᶜ 4 That is, about 260 tons or about 235 metric tons

ROCK SOLID plans

1 Chronicles 29:1–25

Keep your parents close.

God chose Solomon to rule Israel after his father, the famed King David. The Lord even gave Solomon the weighty responsibility of building a permanent house of worship—a magnificent temple. Solomon could have taken the throne and pushed David to the side, but he continued to look to his father as a resource God had put in his life. Because Solomon counted on his father's advice and assistance, the people praised God and supported Solomon—and God gave Solomon more power and splendor than any other king (see 1 Chronicles 29:25).

Your next step: Ask your parents for their help with an important, right-now choice.

craftsmen. Now, who is willing to conse-crate themselves to the LORD today?"

⁶Then the leaders of families, the offi-cers of the tribes of Israel, the command-ers of thousands and commanders of hun-dreds, and the officials in charge of the king's work gave willingly. ⁷They gave to-ward the work on the temple of God five thousand talents*a* and ten thousand dar-ics*b* of gold, ten thousand talents*c* of silver, eighteen thousand talents*d* of bronze and a hundred thousand talents*e* of iron. ⁸Any-one who had precious stones gave them to the treasury of the temple of the LORD in the custody of Jehiel the Gershonite. ⁹The people rejoiced at the willing response of their leaders, for they had given freely and wholeheartedly to the LORD. David the king also rejoiced greatly.

David's Prayer

¹⁰David praised the LORD in the pres-ence of the whole assembly, saying,

"Praise be to you, LORD,
    the God of our father Israel,
    from everlasting to everlasting.
¹¹Yours, LORD, is the greatness and the
        power
    and the glory and the majesty and
        the splendor,
    for everything in heaven and earth
        is yours.
Yours, LORD, is the kingdom;
    you are exalted as head over all.
¹²Wealth and honor come from you;
    you are the ruler of all things.
In your hands are strength and power
    to exalt and give strength to all.
¹³Now, our God, we give you thanks,
    and praise your glorious name.

¹⁴"But who am I, and who are my peo-ple, that we should be able to give as gen-erously as this? Everything comes from you, and we have given you only what comes from your hand. ¹⁵We are foreign-ers and strangers in your sight, as were all our ancestors. Our days on earth are like a shadow, without hope. ¹⁶LORD our God, all this abundance that we have provided for building you a temple for your Holy

---

UNSHAKEN God

1 Chronicles 29:10 – 13

God is majestic.

As Solomon rolled out plans to build the temple in Jerusalem, his goal was to create a temple fit for a king — the King of the Universe, that is. The people of Israel contributed jaw-dropping amounts of gold and silver, exotic woods and pre-cious stones like onyx and turquoise (see 1 Chronicles 29:1 – 9). Seeing this generous outpouring, King David loudly praised the Lord, proclaiming God's "greatness … power … glory … maj-esty … splendor" (1 Chronicles 29:11). God is infinitely more majestic than any earthly ruler. He possesses overwhelm-ing dignity and loftiness and grandeur. He is King of Everything.

So … How will you worship your King today?

Name comes from your hand, and all of it belongs to you. ¹⁷I know, my God, that you test the heart and are pleased with integrity. All these things I have given willingly and with honest intent. And now I have seen with joy how willingly your people who are here have given to you. ¹⁸LORD, the God of our fathers Abra-ham, Isaac and Israel, keep these desires and thoughts in the hearts of your people forever, and keep their hearts loyal to you. ¹⁹And give my son Solomon the whole-hearted devotion to keep your commands, statutes and decrees and to do everything to build the palatial structure for which I have provided."

²⁰Then David said to the whole assem-

---

a 7 That is, about 190 tons or about 170 metric tons
b 7 That is, about 185 pounds or about 84 kilograms   *c* 7 That is, about 380 tons or about 340 metric tons   *d* 7 That is, about 675 tons or about 610 metric tons   *e* 7 That is, about 3,800 tons or about 3,400 metric tons

bly, "Praise the LORD your God." So they all praised the LORD, the God of their fathers; they bowed down, prostrating themselves before the LORD and the king.

Solomon Acknowledged as King

²¹ The next day they made sacrifices to the LORD and presented burnt offerings to him: a thousand bulls, a thousand rams and a thousand male lambs, together with their drink offerings, and other sacrifices in abundance for all Israel. ²² They ate and drank with great joy in the presence of the LORD that day.

Then they acknowledged Solomon son of David as king a second time, anointing him before the LORD to be ruler and Zadok to be priest. ²³ So Solomon sat on the throne of the LORD as king in place of his father David. He prospered and all Israel obeyed him. ²⁴ All the officers and warriors, as well as all of King David's sons, pledged their submission to King Solomon.

²⁵ The LORD highly exalted Solomon in the sight of all Israel and bestowed on him royal splendor such as no king over Israel ever had before.

The Death of David

²⁶ David son of Jesse was king over all Israel. ²⁷ He ruled over Israel forty years — seven in Hebron and thirty-three in Jerusalem. ²⁸ He died at a good old age, having enjoyed long life, wealth and honor. His son Solomon succeeded him as king.

²⁹ As for the events of King David's reign, from beginning to end, they are written in the records of Samuel the seer, the records of Nathan the prophet and the records of Gad the seer, ³⁰ together with the details of his reign and power, and the circumstances that surrounded him and Israel and the kingdoms of all the other lands.

BOOK OUTLINE

The reign of Solomon
(1:1 — 9:31)

The kings of Judah
(10:1 — 36:14)

The destruction of Jerusalem
(36:15 – 23)

2 CHRONICLES

Second Chronicles continues the history of David's royal line. Chapters 1 – 9 describe the building of the temple during Solomon's reign. Chapters 10 – 36 follow the history of the southern kingdom of Judah to the final destruction of Jerusalem and the people being captured and taken to Babylon.

This book, like 1 Chronicles, shows that the people's relationship to God was most important. When the author wrote about the kings, he measured them on the basis of their faithfulness to God. The reigns of evil kings are reported by the author quickly, while the reigns of good kings are described in more detail.

Solomon Asks for Wisdom

1 Solomon son of David established himself firmly over his kingdom, for the LORD his God was with him and made him exceedingly great.

[2] Then Solomon spoke to all Israel—to the commanders of thousands and commanders of hundreds, to the judges and to all the leaders in Israel, the heads of families— [3] and Solomon and the whole assembly went to the high place at Gibeon, for God's tent of meeting was there, which Moses the LORD's servant had made in the wilderness. [4] Now David had brought up the ark of God from Kiriath Jearim to the place he had prepared for it, because he had pitched a tent for it in Jerusalem. [5] But the bronze altar that Bezalel son of Uri, the son of Hur, had made was in Gibeon in front of the tabernacle of the LORD; so Solomon and the assembly inquired of him there. [6] Solomon went up to the bronze altar before the LORD in the tent of meeting and offered a thousand burnt offerings on it.

[7] That night God appeared to Solomon and said to him, "Ask for whatever you want me to give you."

[8] Solomon answered God, "You have shown great kindness to David my father and have made me king in his place. [9] Now, LORD God, let your promise to my father David be confirmed, for you have made me king over a people who are as numerous as the dust of the earth. [10] Give me wisdom and knowledge, that I may lead this people, for who is able to govern this great people of yours?"

[11] God said to Solomon, "Since this is your heart's desire and you have not asked for wealth, possessions or honor, nor for the death of your enemies, and since you have not asked for a long life but for wisdom and knowledge to govern my people over whom I have made you king, [12] therefore wisdom and knowledge will be given you. And I will also give you wealth, possessions and honor, such as no king who was before you ever had and none after you will have."

[13] Then Solomon went to Jerusalem from the high place at Gibeon, from before the tent of meeting. And he reigned over Israel.

[14] Solomon accumulated chariots and horses; he had fourteen hundred chariots and twelve thousand horses,[a] which he kept in the chariot cities and also with him in Jerusalem. [15] The king made silver and gold as common in Jerusalem as stones, and cedar as plentiful as sycamore-fig trees in the foothills. [16] Solomon's horses were imported from Egypt and from Kue[b]—the royal merchants purchased them from Kue at the current price. [17] They imported a chariot from Egypt for six hundred shekels[c] of silver, and a horse for a hundred and fifty.[d] They also exported them to all the kings of the Hittites and of the Arameans.

Preparations for Building the Temple

2[e] Solomon gave orders to build a temple for the Name of the LORD and a royal palace for himself. [2] He conscripted 70,000 men as carriers and 80,000 as stonecutters in the hills and 3,600 as foremen over them.

[3] Solomon sent this message to Hiram[f] king of Tyre:

"Send me cedar logs as you did for my father David when you sent him cedar to build a palace to live in. [4] Now I am about to build a temple for the Name of the LORD my God and to dedicate it to him for burning fragrant incense before him, for setting out the consecrated bread regularly, and for making burnt offerings every morning and evening and on the Sabbaths, at the New Moons and at the appointed festivals of the LORD our God. This is a lasting ordinance for Israel.

[5] "The temple I am going to build

---

[a] 14 Or *charioteers*   [b] 16 Probably Cilicia
[c] 17 That is, about 15 pounds or about 6.9 kilograms   [d] 17 That is, about 3 3/4 pounds or about 1.7 kilograms   [e] In Hebrew texts 2:1 is numbered 1:18, and 2:2-18 is numbered 2:1-17.   [f] 3 Hebrew *Huram,* a variant of *Hiram;* also in verses 11 and 12

will be great, because our God is greater than all other gods. ⁶But who is able to build a temple for him, since the heavens, even the highest heavens, cannot contain him? Who then am I to build a temple for him, except as a place to burn sacrifices before him?

⁷"Send me, therefore, a man skilled to work in gold and silver, bronze and iron, and in purple, crimson and blue yarn, and experienced in the art of engraving, to work in Judah and Jerusalem with my skilled workers, whom my father David provided.

⁸"Send me also cedar, juniper and algum*^a* logs from Lebanon, for I know that your servants are skilled in cutting timber there. My servants will work with yours ⁹to provide me with plenty of lumber, because the temple I build must be large and magnificent. ¹⁰I will give your servants, the woodsmen who cut the timber, twenty thousand cors*^b* of ground wheat, twenty thousand cors*^c* of barley, twenty thousand baths*^d* of wine and twenty thousand baths of olive oil."

¹¹Hiram king of Tyre replied by letter to Solomon:

"Because the LORD loves his people, he has made you their king."

¹²And Hiram added:

"Praise be to the LORD, the God of Israel, who made heaven and earth! He has given King David a wise son, endowed with intelligence and discernment, who will build a temple for the LORD and a palace for himself.

¹³"I am sending you Huram-Abi, a man of great skill, ¹⁴whose mother was from Dan and whose father was from Tyre. He is trained to work in gold and silver, bronze and iron, stone and wood, and with purple and blue and crimson yarn and fine linen. He is experienced in all kinds of engraving and can execute any design

given to him. He will work with your skilled workers and with those of my lord, David your father.

¹⁵"Now let my lord send his servants the wheat and barley and the olive oil and wine he promised, ¹⁶and we will cut all the logs from Lebanon that you need and will float them as rafts by sea down to Joppa. You can then take them up to Jerusalem."

¹⁷Solomon took a census of all the foreigners residing in Israel, after the census his father David had taken; and they were found to be 153,600. ¹⁸He assigned 70,000 of them to be carriers and 80,000 to be stonecutters in the hills, with 3,600 foremen over them to keep the people working.

Solomon Builds the Temple

3 Then Solomon began to build the temple of the LORD in Jerusalem on Mount Moriah, where the LORD had appeared to his father David. It was on the threshing floor of Araunah*^e* the Jebusite, the place provided by David. ²He began building on the second day of the second month in the fourth year of his reign.

³The foundation Solomon laid for building the temple of God was sixty cubits long and twenty cubits wide*^f* (using the cubit of the old standard). ⁴The portico at the front of the temple was twenty cubits*^g* long across the width of the building and twenty*^h* cubits high.

He overlaid the inside with pure gold. ⁵He paneled the main hall with juniper and covered it with fine gold and decorated it with palm tree and chain designs.

---

^a 8 Probably a variant of *almug*   *^b 10* That is, probably about 3,600 tons or about 3,200 metric tons of wheat   *^c 10* That is, probably about 3,000 tons or about 2,700 metric tons of barley   *^d 10* That is, about 120,000 gallons or about 440,000 liters   *^e 1* Hebrew *Ornan*, a variant of *Araunah*   *^f 3* That is, about 90 feet long and 30 feet wide or about 27 meters long and 9 meters wide   *^g 4* That is, about 30 feet or about 9 meters; also in verses 8, 11 and 13   *^h 4* Some Septuagint and Syriac manuscripts; Hebrew *and a hundred and twenty*

[6]He adorned the temple with precious stones. And the gold he used was gold of Parvaim. [7]He overlaid the ceiling beams, doorframes, walls and doors of the temple with gold, and he carved cherubim on the walls.

[8]He built the Most Holy Place, its length corresponding to the width of the temple — twenty cubits long and twenty cubits wide. He overlaid the inside with six hundred talents[a] of fine gold. [9]The gold nails weighed fifty shekels.[b] He also overlaid the upper parts with gold.

[10]For the Most Holy Place he made a pair of sculptured cherubim and overlaid them with gold. [11]The total wingspan of the cherubim was twenty cubits. One wing of the first cherub was five cubits[c] long and touched the temple wall, while its other wing, also five cubits long, touched the wing of the other cherub. [12]Similarly one wing of the second cherub was five cubits long and touched the other temple wall, and its other wing, also five cubits long, touched the wing of the first cherub. [13]The wings of these cherubim extended twenty cubits. They stood on their feet, facing the main hall.[d]

[14]He made the curtain of blue, purple and crimson yarn and fine linen, with cherubim worked into it.

[15]For the front of the temple he made two pillars, which together were thirty-five cubits[e] long, each with a capital five cubits high. [16]He made interwoven chains[f] and put them on top of the pillars. He also made a hundred pomegranates and attached them to the chains. [17]He erected the pillars in the front of the temple, one to the south and one to the north. The one to the south he named Jakin[g] and the one to the north Boaz.[h]

The Temple's Furnishings

4 He made a bronze altar twenty cubits long, twenty cubits wide and ten cubits high.[i] [2]He made the Sea of cast metal, circular in shape, measuring ten cubits from rim to rim and five cubits[j] high. It took a line of thirty cubits[k] to measure around it. [3]Below the rim, figures of bulls encircled it — ten to a cubit.[l] The bulls were cast in two rows in one piece with the Sea.

[4]The Sea stood on twelve bulls, three facing north, three facing west, three facing south and three facing east. The Sea rested on top of them, and their hindquarters were toward the center. [5]It was a handbreadth[m] in thickness, and its rim was like the rim of a cup, like a lily blossom. It held three thousand baths.[n]

[6]He then made ten basins for washing and placed five on the south side and five on the north. In them the things to be used for the burnt offerings were rinsed, but the Sea was to be used by the priests for washing.

[7]He made ten gold lampstands according to the specifications for them and placed them in the temple, five on the south side and five on the north.

[8]He made ten tables and placed them in the temple, five on the south side and five on the north. He also made a hundred gold sprinkling bowls.

[9]He made the courtyard of the priests, and the large court and the doors for the court, and overlaid the doors with bronze. [10]He placed the Sea on the south side, at the southeast corner.

[11]And Huram also made the pots and shovels and sprinkling bowls.

So Huram finished the work he had undertaken for King Solomon in the temple of God:

---

[a] 8 That is, about 23 tons or about 21 metric tons   [b] 9 That is, about 1 1/4 pounds or about 575 grams   [c] 11 That is, about 7 1/2 feet or about 2.3 meters; also in verse 15   [d] 13 Or *facing inward*   [e] 15 That is, about 53 feet or about 16 meters   [f] 16 Or possibly *made chains in the inner sanctuary*; the meaning of the Hebrew for this phrase is uncertain.   [g] 17 *Jakin* probably means *he establishes.*   [h] 17 *Boaz* probably means *in him is strength.*   [i] 1 That is, about 30 feet long and wide and 15 feet high or about 9 meters long and wide and 4.5 meters high   [j] 2 That is, about 7 1/2 feet or about 2.3 meters   [k] 2 That is, about 45 feet or about 14 meters   [l] 3 That is, about 18 inches or about 45 centimeters   [m] 5 That is, about 3 inches or about 7.5 centimeters   [n] 5 That is, about 18,000 gallons or about 66,000 liters

¹²the two pillars;

the two bowl-shaped capitals on top of the pillars;

the two sets of network decorating the two bowl-shaped capitals on top of the pillars;

¹³the four hundred pomegranates for the two sets of network (two rows of pomegranates for each network, decorating the bowl-shaped capitals on top of the pillars);

¹⁴the stands with their basins;

¹⁵the Sea and the twelve bulls under it;

¹⁶the pots, shovels, meat forks and all related articles.

All the objects that Huram-Abi made for King Solomon for the temple of the LORD were of polished bronze. ¹⁷The king had them cast in clay molds in the plain of the Jordan between Sukkoth and Zarethan.ᵃ ¹⁸All these things that Solomon made amounted to so much that the weight of the bronze could not be calculated.

¹⁹Solomon also made all the furnishings that were in God's temple:

the golden altar;

the tables on which was the bread of the Presence;

²⁰the lampstands of pure gold with their lamps, to burn in front of the inner sanctuary as prescribed;

²¹the gold floral work and lamps and tongs (they were solid gold);

²²the pure gold wick trimmers, sprinkling bowls, dishes and censers; and the gold doors of the temple: the inner doors to the Most Holy Place and the doors of the main hall.

5 When all the work Solomon had done for the temple of the LORD was finished, he brought in the things his father David had dedicated—the silver and gold and all the furnishings—and he placed them in the treasuries of God's temple.

The Ark Brought to the Temple

²Then Solomon summoned to Jerusalem the elders of Israel, all the heads of the tribes and the chiefs of the Israelite families, to bring up the ark of the LORD's covenant from Zion, the City of David. ³And all the Israelites came together to the king at the time of the festival in the seventh month.

⁴When all the elders of Israel had arrived, the Levites took up the ark, ⁵and they brought up the ark and the tent of meeting and all the sacred furnishings in it. The Levitical priests carried them up; ⁶and King Solomon and the entire assembly of Israel that had gathered about him were before the ark, sacrificing so many sheep and cattle that they could not be recorded or counted.

⁷The priests then brought the ark of the LORD's covenant to its place in the inner sanctuary of the temple, the Most Holy Place, and put it beneath the wings of the

---

UNSHAKEN God

2 Chronicles 4:1–22

God is artistic.

There was nothing plain about the temple that Solomon built as a house of worship for the one true God. The interior was overlaid with gold and adorned with precious stones. The walls were carved with angels. The most sacred room of the temple was veiled with a curtain of magnificent yarn and fine linen (see 2 Chronicles 3:4–14). And the temple was furnished with every kind of golden decoration. You might have the impression that God is all about brilliant white and nothing more. But you can see his originality in creation, and the temple reflected his beauty. Your God isn't bland. Every bit of him is an artist.

So ... How do you use artistry—beautiful things, words, songs—to worship God?

ᵃ 17 Hebrew *Zeredatha*, a variant of *Zarethan*

cherubim. [8]The cherubim spread their wings over the place of the ark and covered the ark and its carrying poles. [9]These poles were so long that their ends, extending from the ark, could be seen from in front of the inner sanctuary, but not from outside the Holy Place; and they are still there today. [10]There was nothing in the ark except the two tablets that Moses had placed in it at Horeb, where the LORD made a covenant with the Israelites after they came out of Egypt.

[11]The priests then withdrew from the Holy Place. All the priests who were there had consecrated themselves, regardless of their divisions. [12]All the Levites who were musicians—Asaph, Heman, Jeduthun and their sons and relatives—stood on the east side of the altar, dressed in fine linen and playing cymbals, harps and lyres. They were accompanied by 120 priests sounding trumpets. [13]The trumpeters and musicians joined in unison to give praise and thanks to the LORD. Accompanied by trumpets, cymbals and other instruments, the singers raised their voices in praise to the LORD and sang:

"He is good;
    his love endures forever."

Then the temple of the LORD was filled with the cloud, [14]and the priests could not perform their service because of the cloud, for the glory of the LORD filled the temple of God.

6 Then Solomon said, "The LORD has said that he would dwell in a dark cloud; [2]I have built a magnificent temple for you, a place for you to dwell forever."

[3]While the whole assembly of Israel was standing there, the king turned around and blessed them. [4]Then he said:

"Praise be to the LORD, the God of Israel, who with his hands has fulfilled what he promised with his mouth to my father David. For he said, [5]'Since the day I brought my people out of Egypt, I have not chosen a city in any tribe of Israel to have a temple built so that my Name might

be there, nor have I chosen anyone to be ruler over my people Israel. [6]But now I have chosen Jerusalem for my Name to be there, and I have chosen David to rule my people Israel.'

[7]"My father David had it in his heart to build a temple for the Name of the LORD, the God of Israel. [8]But the LORD said to my father David, 'You did well to have it in your heart to build a temple for my Name. [9]Nevertheless, you are not the one to build the temple, but your son, your own flesh and blood—he is the one who will build the temple for my Name.'

[10]"The LORD has kept the promise he made. I have succeeded David my father and now I sit on the throne of Israel, just as the LORD promised, and I have built the temple for the Name of the LORD, the God of Israel. [11]There I have placed the ark, in which is the covenant of the LORD that he made with the people of Israel."

Solomon's Prayer of Dedication

[12]Then Solomon stood before the altar of the LORD in front of the whole assembly of Israel and spread out his hands. [13]Now he had made a bronze platform, five cubits long, five cubits wide and three cubits high,[a] and had placed it in the center of the outer court. He stood on the platform and then knelt down before the whole assembly of Israel and spread out his hands toward heaven. [14]He said:

"LORD, the God of Israel, there is no God like you in heaven or on earth—you who keep your covenant of love with your servants who continue wholeheartedly in your way. [15]You have kept your promise to your servant David my father; with your mouth you have promised and with your hand you have fulfilled it—as it is today.

[16]"Now, LORD, the God of Israel,

---

[a] 13 That is, about 7 1/2 feet long and wide and 4 1/2 feet high or about 2.3 meters long and wide and 1.4 meters high

keep for your servant David my father the promises you made to him when you said, 'You shall never fail to have a successor to sit before me on the throne of Israel, if only your descendants are careful in all they do to walk before me according to my law, as you have done.' [17] And now, Lord, the God of Israel, let your word that you promised your servant David come true.

[18] "But will God really dwell on earth with humans? The heavens, even the highest heavens, cannot contain you. How much less this temple I have built! [19] Yet, Lord my God, give attention to your servant's prayer and his plea for mercy. Hear the cry and the prayer that your servant is praying in your presence. [20] May your eyes be open toward this temple day and night, this place of which you said you would put your Name there. May you hear the prayer your servant prays toward this place. [21] Hear the supplications of your servant and of your people Israel when they pray toward this place. Hear from heaven, your dwelling place; and when you hear, forgive.

[22] "When anyone wrongs their neighbor and is required to take an oath and they come and swear the oath before your altar in this temple, [23] then hear from heaven and act. Judge between your servants, condemning the guilty and bringing down on their heads what they have done, and vindicating the innocent by treating them in accordance with their innocence.

[24] "When your people Israel have been defeated by an enemy because they have sinned against you and when they turn back and give praise to your name, praying and making supplication before you in this temple, [25] then hear from heaven and forgive the sin of your people Israel and bring them back to the land you gave to them and their ancestors.

[26] "When the heavens are shut up and there is no rain because your people have sinned against you, and when they pray toward this place and give praise to your name and turn from their sin because you have afflicted them, [27] then hear from heaven and forgive the sin of your servants, your people Israel. Teach them the right way to live, and send rain on the land you gave your people for an inheritance.

[28] "When famine or plague comes to the land, or blight or mildew, locusts or grasshoppers, or when enemies besiege them in any of their cities, whatever disaster or disease may come, [29] and when a prayer or plea is made by anyone among your people Israel—being aware of their afflictions and pains, and spreading out their hands toward this temple— [30] then hear from heaven, your dwelling place. Forgive, and deal with everyone according to all they do, since you know their hearts (for you alone know the human heart), [31] so that they will fear you and walk in obedience to you all the time they live in the land you gave our ancestors.

[32] "As for the foreigner who does not belong to your people Israel but has come from a distant land because of your great name and your mighty hand and your outstretched arm—when they come and pray toward this temple, [33] then hear from heaven, your dwelling place. Do whatever the foreigner asks of you, so that all the peoples of the earth may know your name and fear you, as do your own people Israel, and may know that this house I have built bears your Name.

[34] "When your people go to war against their enemies, wherever you send them, and when they pray to you toward this city you have chosen and the temple I have built for your Name, [35] then hear from heaven their prayer and their plea, and uphold their cause.

³⁶"When they sin against you— for there is no one who does not sin—and you become angry with them and give them over to the enemy, who takes them captive to a land far away or near; ³⁷ and if they have a change of heart in the land where they are held captive, and repent and plead with you in the land of their captivity and say, 'We have sinned, we have done wrong and acted wickedly'; ³⁸ and if they turn back to you with all their heart and soul in the land of their captivity where they were taken, and pray toward the land you gave their ancestors, toward the city you have chosen and toward the temple I have built for your Name; ³⁹ then from heaven, your dwelling place, hear their prayer and their pleas, and uphold their cause. And forgive your people, who have sinned against you.

⁴⁰"Now, my God, may your eyes be open and your ears attentive to the prayers offered in this place.

⁴¹"Now arise, Lord God, and
    come to your resting
    place,
  you and the ark of your might.
May your priests, Lord God, be
    clothed with salvation,
  may your faithful people
    rejoice in your goodness.
⁴² Lord God, do not reject your
    anointed one.
  Remember the great love
    promised to David your
    servant."

The Dedication of the Temple

7 When Solomon finished praying, fire came down from heaven and consumed the burnt offering and the sacrifices, and the glory of the Lord filled the temple. ² The priests could not enter the temple of the Lord because the glory of the Lord filled it. ³ When all the Israelites saw the fire coming down and the glory of the Lord above the temple, they knelt on the pavement with their fac-

es to the ground, and they worshiped and gave thanks to the Lord, saying,

"He is good;
  his love endures forever."

⁴ Then the king and all the people offered sacrifices before the Lord. ⁵ And King Solomon offered a sacrifice of twenty-two thousand head of cattle and a hundred and twenty thousand sheep and goats. So the king and all the people dedicated the temple of God. ⁶ The priests took their positions, as did the Levites with the Lord's musical instruments, which King David had made for praising the Lord and which were used when he gave thanks, saying, "His love endures forever." Opposite the Levites, the priests blew their trumpets, and all the Israelites were standing.

⁷ Solomon consecrated the middle part of the courtyard in front of the temple of the Lord, and there he offered burnt offerings and the fat of the fellowship offerings, because the bronze altar he had made could not hold the burnt offerings, the grain offerings and the fat portions.

⁸ So Solomon observed the festival at that time for seven days, and all Israel with him—a vast assembly, people from Lebo Hamath to the Wadi of Egypt. ⁹ On the eighth day they held an assembly, for they had celebrated the dedication of the altar for seven days and the festival for seven days more. ¹⁰ On the twenty-third day of the seventh month he sent the people to their homes, joyful and glad in heart for the good things the Lord had done for David and Solomon and for his people Israel.

The Lord Appears to Solomon

¹¹ When Solomon had finished the temple of the Lord and the royal palace, and had succeeded in carrying out all he had in mind to do in the temple of the Lord and in his own palace, ¹² the Lord appeared to him at night and said:

"I have heard your prayer and have chosen this place for myself as a temple for sacrifices.

13 "When I shut up the heavens so that there is no rain, or command locusts to devour the land or send a plague among my people, 14 if my people, who are called by my name, will humble themselves and pray and seek my face and turn from their wicked ways, then I will hear from heaven, and I will forgive their sin and will heal their land. 15 Now my eyes will be open and my ears attentive to the prayers offered in this place. 16 I have chosen and consecrated this temple so that my Name may be there forever. My eyes and my heart will always be there.

17 "As for you, if you walk before me faithfully as David your father did, and do all I command, and observe my decrees and laws, 18 I will establish your royal throne, as I covenanted with David your father when I said, 'You shall never fail to have a successor to rule over Israel.'

19 "But if you*a* turn away and forsake the decrees and commands I have given you*a* and go off to serve other gods and worship them, 20 then I will uproot Israel from my land, which I have given them, and will reject this temple I have consecrated for my Name. I will make it a byword and an object of ridicule among all peoples. 21 This temple will become a heap of rubble. All*b* who pass by will be appalled and say, 'Why has the LORD done such a thing to this land and to this temple?' 22 People will answer, 'Because they have forsaken the LORD, the God of their ancestors, who brought them out of Egypt, and have embraced other gods, worshiping and serving them — that is why he brought all this disaster on them.'"

a 19 The Hebrew is plural.   *b 21* See some Septuagint manuscripts, Old Latin, Syriac, Arabic and Targum; Hebrew *And though this temple is now so imposing, all*

ROCK SOLID *principles*

2 Chronicles 7:14–16

Repent.

Shawna felt sick. At first her online rants made everyone laugh. A few times a week she posted her most sarcastic thoughts on whatever topic popped into her head. But when Shawna ran out of things to write about, she turned her wicked humor on girls at school and church and her neighborhood, tearing into anyone who stood out as different. When Shawna heard that one of her targets had sought help from a counselor because of the vicious attacks, she had to admit what she had become — a cyber bully. Shawna deleted her posts and wrote an online apology. She prayed for forgiveness. But now she had to figure out how to reach out to the girls one-by-one and make things right.

Hundreds of years before Solomon, Joshua had predicted God's people would wander away from the Lord (see Joshua 24:14–27). But God always gives us a way back. He wants us to "repent," or turn away from sin. He promises to hear us ... to forgive us ... and heal us. It's one of the Lord's most amazing promises.

Solomon's Other Activities

8 At the end of twenty years, during which Solomon built the temple of the LORD and his own palace, ²Solomon rebuilt the villages that Hiram*ᵃ* had given him, and settled Israelites in them. ³Solomon then went to Hamath Zobah and captured it. ⁴He also built up Tadmor in the desert and all the store cities he had built in Hamath. ⁵He rebuilt Upper Beth Horon and Lower Beth Horon as fortified cities, with walls and with gates and bars, ⁶as well as Baalath and all his store cities, and all the cities for his chariots and for his horses*ᵇ*—whatever he desired to build in Jerusalem, in Lebanon and throughout all the territory he ruled.

⁷There were still people left from the Hittites, Amorites, Perizzites, Hivites and Jebusites (these people were not Israelites). ⁸Solomon conscripted the descendants of all these people remaining in the land—whom the Israelites had not destroyed—to serve as slave labor, as it is to this day. ⁹But Solomon did not make slaves of the Israelites for his work; they were his fighting men, commanders of his captains, and commanders of his chariots and charioteers. ¹⁰They were also King Solomon's chief officials—two hundred and fifty officials supervising the men.

¹¹Solomon brought Pharaoh's daughter up from the City of David to the palace he had built for her, for he said, "My wife must not live in the palace of David king of Israel, because the places the ark of the LORD has entered are holy."

¹²On the altar of the LORD that he had built in front of the portico, Solomon sacrificed burnt offerings to the LORD, ¹³according to the daily requirement for offerings commanded by Moses for the Sabbaths, the New Moons and the three annual festivals—the Festival of Unleavened Bread, the Festival of Weeks and the Festival of Tabernacles. ¹⁴In keeping with the ordinance of his father David, he appointed the divisions of the priests for their duties, and the Levites to lead the praise and to assist the priests according to each day's requirement. He also appointed the gatekeepers by divisions for the various gates, because this was what David the man of God had ordered. ¹⁵They did not deviate from the king's commands to the priests or to the Levites in any matter, including that of the treasuries.

¹⁶All Solomon's work was carried out, from the day the foundation of the temple of the LORD was laid until its completion. So the temple of the LORD was finished.

¹⁷Then Solomon went to Ezion Geber and Elath on the coast of Edom. ¹⁸And Hiram sent him ships commanded by his own men, sailors who knew the sea. These, with Solomon's men, sailed to Ophir and brought back four hundred and fifty talents*ᶜ* of gold, which they delivered to King Solomon.

The Queen of Sheba Visits Solomon

9 When the queen of Sheba heard of Solomon's fame, she came to Jerusalem to test him with hard questions. Arriving with a very great caravan—with camels carrying spices, large quantities of gold, and precious stones—she came to Solomon and talked with him about all she had on her mind. ²Solomon answered all her questions; nothing was too hard for him to explain to her. ³When the queen of Sheba saw the wisdom of Solomon, as well as the palace he had built, ⁴the food on his table, the seating of his officials, the attending servants in their robes, the cupbearers in their robes and the burnt offerings he made at*ᵈ* the temple of the LORD, she was overwhelmed.

⁵She said to the king, "The report I heard in my own country about your achievements and your wisdom is true. ⁶But I did not believe what they said until I came and saw with my own eyes. Indeed, not even half the greatness of your wisdom was told me; you have far exceeded the report I heard. ⁷How happy your people must be! How happy your officials, who continually stand before you and hear your

---

ᵃ 2 Hebrew *Huram,* a variant of *Hiram*; also in verse 18   *ᵇ 6* Or *charioteers*   *ᶜ 18* That is, about 17 tons or about 15 metric tons
ᵈ 4 Or *and the ascent by which he went up to*

wisdom! [8] Praise be to the LORD your God, who has delighted in you and placed you on his throne as king to rule for the LORD your God. Because of the love of your God for Israel and his desire to uphold them forever, he has made you king over them, to maintain justice and righteousness."

[9] Then she gave the king 120 talents[a] of gold, large quantities of spices, and precious stones. There had never been such spices as those the queen of Sheba gave to King Solomon.

[10] (The servants of Hiram and the servants of Solomon brought gold from Ophir; they also brought algumwood[b] and precious stones. [11] The king used the algumwood to make steps for the temple of the LORD and for the royal palace, and to make harps and lyres for the musicians. Nothing like them had ever been seen in Judah.)

[12] King Solomon gave the queen of Sheba all she desired and asked for; he gave her more than she had brought to him.

Then she left and returned with her retinue to her own country.

Solomon's Splendor

[13] The weight of the gold that Solomon received yearly was 666 talents,[c] [14] not including the revenues brought in by merchants and traders. Also all the kings of Arabia and the governors of the territories brought gold and silver to Solomon.

[15] King Solomon made two hundred large shields of hammered gold; six hundred shekels[d] of hammered gold went into each shield. [16] He also made three hundred small shields of hammered gold, with three hundred shekels[e] of gold in each shield. The king put them in the Palace of the Forest of Lebanon.

[a] 9 That is, about 4 1/2 tons or about 4 metric tons   [b] 10 Probably a variant of almugwood   [c] 13 That is, about 25 tons or about 23 metric tons   [d] 15 That is, about 15 pounds or about 6.9 kilograms   [e] 16 That is, about 7 1/2 pounds or about 3.5 kilograms

ROCK SOLID principles

2 Chronicles 9:1–12

Check the facts for yourself.

Aaron didn't know what to say. His English teacher had raised some tough questions. How could Aaron know that God made the world? Why allow a dusty book like the Bible to dictate his life? And how could anyone believe that Jesus actually rose from the dead? Aaron didn't have answers for Mr. Norton. But the questions drove Aaron to read his Bible more and start asking questions at church. He found books that showed that plenty of smart people had asked and answered the same questions Mr. Norton posed. Aaron wasn't able to persuade his teacher of much, but at least Aaron was learning to think hard about his faith.

The queen of Sheba ruled the land that is now Ethiopia. She had heard of Solomon's fame, and she came bearing gifts appropriate for the richest guy in the world. But the most significant thing she brought was tough questions, asking "all she had on her mind" (2 Chronicles 9:1). The queen dug for real answers and checked the facts for herself.

¹⁷Then the king made a great throne covered with ivory and overlaid with pure gold. ¹⁸The throne had six steps, and a footstool of gold was attached to it. On both sides of the seat were armrests, with a lion standing beside each of them. ¹⁹Twelve lions stood on the six steps, one at either end of each step. Nothing like it had ever been made for any other kingdom. ²⁰All King Solomon's goblets were gold, and all the household articles in the Palace of the Forest of Lebanon were pure gold. Nothing was made of silver, because silver was considered of little value in Solomon's day. ²¹The king had a fleet of trading ships^a manned by Hiram's^b servants. Once every three years it returned, carrying gold, silver and ivory, and apes and baboons.

²²King Solomon was greater in riches and wisdom than all the other kings of the earth. ²³All the kings of the earth sought audience with Solomon to hear the wisdom God had put in his heart. ²⁴Year after year, everyone who came brought a gift—articles of silver and gold, and robes, weapons and spices, and horses and mules.

²⁵Solomon had four thousand stalls for horses and chariots, and twelve thousand horses,^c which he kept in the chariot cities and also with him in Jerusalem. ²⁶He ruled over all the kings from the Euphrates River to the land of the Philistines, as far as the border of Egypt. ²⁷The king made silver as common in Jerusalem as stones, and cedar as plentiful as sycamore-fig trees in the foothills. ²⁸Solomon's horses were imported from Egypt and from all other countries.

Solomon's Death

²⁹As for the other events of Solomon's reign, from beginning to end, are they not written in the records of Nathan the prophet, in the prophecy of Ahijah the Shilonite and in the visions of Iddo the seer concerning Jeroboam son of Nebat? ³⁰Solomon reigned in Jerusalem over all Israel forty years. ³¹Then he rested with his ancestors and was buried in the city of David his father. And Rehoboam his son succeeded him as king.

Israel Rebels Against Rehoboam

10 Rehoboam went to Shechem, for all Israel had gone there to make him king. ²When Jeroboam son of Nebat heard this (he was in Egypt, where he had fled from King Solomon), he returned from Egypt. ³So they sent for Jeroboam, and he and all Israel went to Rehoboam and said to him: ⁴"Your father put a heavy yoke on us, but now lighten the harsh labor and the heavy yoke he put on us, and we will serve you."

⁵Rehoboam answered, "Come back to me in three days." So the people went away.

⁶Then King Rehoboam consulted the elders who had served his father Solomon during his lifetime. "How would you advise me to answer these people?" he asked.

⁷They replied, "If you will be kind to these people and please them and give them a favorable answer, they will always be your servants."

⁸But Rehoboam rejected the advice the elders gave him and consulted the young men who had grown up with him and were serving him. ⁹He asked them, "What is your advice? How should we answer these people who say to me, 'Lighten the yoke your father put on us'?"

¹⁰The young men who had grown up with him replied, "The people have said to you, 'Your father put a heavy yoke on us, but make our yoke lighter.' Now tell them, 'My little finger is thicker than my father's waist. ¹¹My father laid on you a heavy yoke; I will make it even heavier. My father scourged you with whips; I will scourge you with scorpions.'"

¹²Three days later Jeroboam and all the people returned to Rehoboam, as the king had said, "Come back to me in three days." ¹³The king answered them harshly. Rejecting the advice of the elders, ¹⁴he followed the advice of the young men and said, "My father made your yoke heavy; I will make it even heavier. My father scourged you with whips; I will scourge you with scorpions." ¹⁵So the king did

^a 21 Hebrew *of ships that could go to Tarshish*
^b 21 Hebrew *Huram*, a variant of *Hiram*
^c 25 Or *charioteers*

not listen to the people, for this turn of events was from God, to fulfill the word the LORD had spoken to Jeroboam son of Nebat through Ahijah the Shilonite.

¹⁶When all Israel saw that the king refused to listen to them, they answered the king:

"What share do we have in David,
    what part in Jesse's son?
To your tents, Israel!
    Look after your own house, David!"

So all the Israelites went home. ¹⁷But as for the Israelites who were living in the towns of Judah, Rehoboam still ruled over them.

¹⁸King Rehoboam sent out Adoniram,ᵃ who was in charge of forced labor, but the Israelites stoned him to death. King Rehoboam, however, managed to get into his chariot and escape to Jerusalem. ¹⁹So Israel has been in rebellion against the house of David to this day.

11 When Rehoboam arrived in Jerusalem, he mustered Judah and Benjamin—a hundred and eighty thousand able young men—to go to war against Israel and to regain the kingdom for Rehoboam.

²But this word of the LORD came to Shemaiah the man of God: ³"Say to Rehoboam son of Solomon king of Judah and to all Israel in Judah and Benjamin, ⁴'This is what the LORD says: Do not go up to fight against your fellow Israelites. Go home, every one of you, for this is my doing.'" So they obeyed the words of the LORD and turned back from marching against Jeroboam.

Rehoboam Fortifies Judah

⁵Rehoboam lived in Jerusalem and built up towns for defense in Judah: ⁶Bethlehem, Etam, Tekoa, ⁷Beth Zur, Soko, Adullam, ⁸Gath, Mareshah, Ziph, ⁹Adoraim, Lachish, Azekah, ¹⁰Zorah, Aijalon and Hebron. These were fortified cities in Judah and Benjamin. ¹¹He strengthened their defenses and put commanders in them, with supplies of food, olive oil and wine. ¹²He put shields and spears in all the cities, and made them very strong. So Judah and Benjamin were his.

¹³The priests and Levites from all their districts throughout Israel sided with him. ¹⁴The Levites even abandoned their pasturelands and property and came to Judah and Jerusalem, because Jeroboam and his sons had rejected them as priests of the LORD ¹⁵when he appointed his own priests for the high places and for the goat and calf idols he had made. ¹⁶Those from every tribe of Israel who set their hearts on seeking the LORD, the God of Israel, followed the Levites to Jerusalem to offer sacrifices to the LORD, the God of their ancestors. ¹⁷They strengthened the kingdom of Judah and supported Rehoboam son of Solomon three years, following the ways of David and Solomon during this time.

Rehoboam's Family

¹⁸Rehoboam married Mahalath, who was the daughter of David's son Jerimoth and of Abihail, the daughter of Jesse's son Eliab. ¹⁹She bore him sons: Jeush, Shemariah and Zaham. ²⁰Then he married Maakah daughter of Absalom, who bore him Abijah, Attai, Ziza and Shelomith. ²¹Rehoboam loved Maakah daughter of Absalom more than any of his other wives and concubines. In all, he had eighteen wives and sixty concubines, twenty-eight sons and sixty daughters.

²²Rehoboam appointed Abijah son of Maakah as crown prince among his brothers, in order to make him king. ²³He acted wisely, dispersing some of his sons throughout the districts of Judah and Benjamin, and to all the fortified cities. He gave them abundant provisions and took many wives for them.

Shishak Attacks Jerusalem

12 After Rehoboam's position as king was established and he had become strong, he and all Israelᵇ with him abandoned the law of the LORD. ²Because they had been unfaithful to the LORD, Shishak king of Egypt at-

---

ᵃ *18* Hebrew *Hadoram*, a variant of *Adoniram*
ᵇ *1* That is, Judah, as frequently in 2 Chronicles

tacked Jerusalem in the fifth year of King Rehoboam. ³With twelve hundred chariots and sixty thousand horsemen and the innumerable troops of Libyans, Sukkites and Cushites*ᵃ* that came with him from Egypt, ⁴he captured the fortified cities of Judah and came as far as Jerusalem.

⁵Then the prophet Shemaiah came to Rehoboam and to the leaders of Judah who had assembled in Jerusalem for fear of Shishak, and he said to them, "This is what the LORD says, 'You have abandoned me; therefore, I now abandon you to Shishak.'"

⁶The leaders of Israel and the king humbled themselves and said, "The LORD is just."

⁷When the LORD saw that they humbled themselves, this word of the LORD came to Shemaiah: "Since they have humbled themselves, I will not destroy them but will soon give them deliverance. My wrath will not be poured out on Jerusalem through Shishak. ⁸They will, however, become subject to him, so that they may learn the difference between serving me and serving the kings of other lands."

⁹When Shishak king of Egypt attacked Jerusalem, he carried off the treasures of the temple of the LORD and the treasures of the royal palace. He took everything, including the gold shields Solomon had made. ¹⁰So King Rehoboam made bronze shields to replace them and assigned these to the commanders of the guard on duty at the entrance to the royal palace. ¹¹Whenever the king went to the LORD's temple, the guards went with him, bearing the shields, and afterward they returned them to the guardroom.

¹²Because Rehoboam humbled himself, the LORD's anger turned from him, and he was not totally destroyed. Indeed, there was some good in Judah.

¹³King Rehoboam established himself firmly in Jerusalem and continued as king. He was forty-one years old when he became king, and he reigned seventeen years in Jerusalem, the city the LORD had chosen out of all the tribes of Israel in which to put his Name. His mother's name was Naamah; she was an Ammonite. ¹⁴He did evil because he had not set his heart on seeking the LORD.

¹⁵As for the events of Rehoboam's reign, from beginning to end, are they not written in the records of Shemaiah the prophet and of Iddo the seer that deal with genealogies? There was continual warfare between Rehoboam and Jeroboam. ¹⁶Rehoboam rested with his ancestors and was buried in the City of David. And Abijah his son succeeded him as king.

Abijah King of Judah

13 In the eighteenth year of the reign of Jeroboam, Abijah became king of Judah, ²and he reigned in Jerusalem three years. His mother's name was Maakah,*ᵇ* a daughter*ᶜ* of Uriel of Gibeah.

There was war between Abijah and Jeroboam. ³Abijah went into battle with an army of four hundred thousand able fighting men, and Jeroboam drew up a battle line against him with eight hundred thousand able troops.

⁴Abijah stood on Mount Zemaraim, in the hill country of Ephraim, and said, "Jeroboam and all Israel, listen to me! ⁵Don't you know that the LORD, the God of Israel, has given the kingship of Israel to David and his descendants forever by a covenant of salt? ⁶Yet Jeroboam son of Nebat, an official of Solomon son of David, rebelled against his master. ⁷Some worthless scoundrels gathered around him and opposed Rehoboam son of Solomon when he was young and indecisive and not strong enough to resist them.

⁸"And now you plan to resist the kingdom of the LORD, which is in the hands of David's descendants. You are indeed a vast army and have with you the golden calves that Jeroboam made to be your gods. ⁹But didn't you drive out the priests of the LORD, the sons of Aaron, and the Levites, and make priests of your own as

---

ᵃ 3 That is, people from the upper Nile region
ᵇ 2 Most Septuagint manuscripts and Syriac (see also 11:20 and 1 Kings 15:2); Hebrew *Micaiah*   *ᶜ 2* Or *granddaughter*

the peoples of other lands do? Whoever comes to consecrate himself with a young bull and seven rams may become a priest of what are not gods.

¹⁰"As for us, the Lord is our God, and we have not forsaken him. The priests who serve the Lord are sons of Aaron, and the Levites assist them. ¹¹Every morning and evening they present burnt offerings and fragrant incense to the Lord. They set out the bread on the ceremonially clean table and light the lamps on the gold lampstand every evening. We are observing the requirements of the Lord our God. But you have forsaken him. ¹²God is with us; he is our leader. His priests with their trumpets will sound the battle cry against you. People of Israel, do not fight against the Lord, the God of your ancestors, for you will not succeed."

¹³Now Jeroboam had sent troops around to the rear, so that while he was in front of Judah the ambush was behind them. ¹⁴Judah turned and saw that they were being attacked at both front and rear. Then they cried out to the Lord. The priests blew their trumpets ¹⁵and the men of Judah raised the battle cry. At the sound of their battle cry, God routed Jeroboam and all Israel before Abijah and Judah. ¹⁶The Israelites fled before Judah, and God delivered them into their hands. ¹⁷Abijah and his troops inflicted heavy losses on them, so that there were five hundred thousand casualties among Israel's able men. ¹⁸The Israelites were subdued on that occasion, and the people of Judah were victorious because they relied on the Lord, the God of their ancestors.

¹⁹Abijah pursued Jeroboam and took from him the towns of Bethel, Jeshanah and Ephron, with their surrounding villages. ²⁰Jeroboam did not regain power during the time of Abijah. And the Lord struck him down and he died.

²¹But Abijah grew in strength. He married fourteen wives and had twenty-two sons and sixteen daughters.

²²The other events of Abijah's reign, what he did and what he said, are written in the annotations of the prophet Iddo.

14 ᵃ And Abijah rested with his ancestors and was buried in the City of David. Asa his son succeeded him as king, and in his days the country was at peace for ten years.

Asa King of Judah

²Asa did what was good and right in the eyes of the Lord his God. ³He removed the foreign altars and the high places, smashed the sacred stones and cut down the Asherah poles.ᵇ ⁴He commanded Judah to seek the Lord, the God of their ancestors, and to obey his laws and commands. ⁵He removed the high places and incense altars in every town in Judah, and the kingdom was at peace under him. ⁶He built up the fortified cities of Judah, since the land was at peace. No one was at war with him during those years, for the Lord gave him rest.

⁷"Let us build up these towns," he said to Judah, "and put walls around them, with towers, gates and bars. The land is still ours, because we have sought the Lord our God; we sought him and he has given us rest on every side." So they built and prospered.

⁸Asa had an army of three hundred thousand men from Judah, equipped with large shields and with spears, and two hundred and eighty thousand from Benjamin, armed with small shields and with bows. All these were brave fighting men.

⁹Zerah the Cushite marched out against them with an army of thousands upon thousands and three hundred chariots, and came as far as Mareshah. ¹⁰Asa went out to meet him, and they took up battle positions in the Valley of Zephathah near Mareshah.

¹¹Then Asa called to the Lord his God and said, "Lord, there is no one like you to help the powerless against the mighty. Help us, Lord our God, for we rely on you, and in your name we have come against this vast army. Lord, you are

---

ᵃ In Hebrew texts 14:1 is numbered 13:23, and 14:2-15 is numbered 14:1-14.   ᵇ 3 That is, wooden symbols of the goddess Asherah; here and elsewhere in 2 Chronicles our God; do not let mere mortals prevail against you."

[12]The Lord struck down the Cushites before Asa and Judah. The Cushites fled, [13]and Asa and his army pursued them as far as Gerar. Such a great number of Cushites fell that they could not recover; they were crushed before the Lord and his forces. The men of Judah carried off a large amount of plunder. [14]They destroyed all the villages around Gerar, for the terror of the Lord had fallen on them. They looted all these villages, since there was much plunder there. [15]They also attacked the camps of the herders and carried off droves of sheep and goats and camels. Then they returned to Jerusalem.

Asa's Reform

15 The Spirit of God came on Azariah son of Oded. [2]He went out to meet Asa and said to him, "Listen to me, Asa and all Judah and Benjamin. The Lord is with you when you are with him. If you seek him, he will be found by you, but if you forsake him, he will forsake you. [3]For a long time Israel was without the true God, without a priest to teach and without the law. [4]But in their distress they turned to the Lord, the God of Israel, and sought him, and he was found by them. [5]In those days it was not safe to travel about, for all the inhabitants of the lands were in great turmoil. [6]One nation was being crushed by another and one city by another, because God was troubling them with every kind of distress. [7]But as for you, be strong and do not give up, for your work will be rewarded."

[8]When Asa heard these words and the prophecy of Azariah son of[a] Oded the prophet, he took courage. He removed the detestable idols from the whole land of Judah and Benjamin and from the towns he had captured in the hills of Ephraim. He repaired the altar of the Lord that was in front of the portico of the Lord's temple.

[9]Then he assembled all Judah and Benjamin and the people from Ephraim, Manasseh and Simeon who had settled among them, for large numbers had come

ROCK SOLID *promises*

"Be strong and do not give up, for your work will be rewarded."

2 Chronicles 15:7

God notices your love and loyalty. He will make your hard work worthwhile.

over to him from Israel when they saw that the Lord his God was with him.

[10]They assembled at Jerusalem in the third month of the fifteenth year of Asa's reign. [11]At that time they sacrificed to the Lord seven hundred head of cattle and seven thousand sheep and goats from the plunder they had brought back. [12]They entered into a covenant to seek the Lord, the God of their ancestors, with all their heart and soul. [13]All who would not seek the Lord, the God of Israel, were to be put to death, whether small or great, man or woman. [14]They took an oath to the Lord with loud acclamation, with shouting and with trumpets and horns. [15]All Judah rejoiced about the oath because they had sworn it wholeheartedly. They sought God eagerly, and he was found by them. So the Lord gave them rest on every side.

[16]King Asa also deposed his grandmother Maakah from her position as queen mother, because she had made a repulsive image for the worship of Asherah. Asa cut it down, broke it up and burned it in the Kidron Valley. [17]Although he did not remove the high places from Israel, Asa's heart was fully committed to the Lord all his life. [18]He brought into the temple of God the silver and gold and the articles that he and his father had dedicated.

[a] 8 Vulgate and Syriac (see also Septuagint and verse 1); Hebrew does not have *Azariah son of*.

¹⁹There was no more war until the thirty-fifth year of Asa's reign.

Asa's Last Years

16 In the thirty-sixth year of Asa's reign Baasha king of Israel went up against Judah and fortified Ramah to prevent anyone from leaving or entering the territory of Asa king of Judah.

²Asa then took the silver and gold out of the treasuries of the LORD's temple and of his own palace and sent it to Ben-Hadad king of Aram, who was ruling in Damascus. ³"Let there be a treaty between me and you," he said, "as there was between my father and your father. See, I am sending you silver and gold. Now break your treaty with Baasha king of Israel so he will withdraw from me."

⁴Ben-Hadad agreed with King Asa and sent the commanders of his forces against the towns of Israel. They conquered Ijon, Dan, Abel Maim*ᵃ* and all the store cities of Naphtali. ⁵When Baasha heard this, he stopped building Ramah and abandoned his work. ⁶Then King Asa brought all the men of Judah, and they carried away from Ramah the stones and timber Baasha had been using. With them he built up Geba and Mizpah.

⁷At that time Hanani the seer came to Asa king of Judah and said to him: "Because you relied on the king of Aram and not on the LORD your God, the army of the king of Aram has escaped from your hand. ⁸Were not the Cushites*ᵇ* and Libyans a mighty army with great numbers of chariots and horsemen*ᶜ*? Yet when you relied on the LORD, he delivered them into your hand. ⁹For the eyes of the LORD range throughout the earth to strengthen those whose hearts are fully committed to him. You have done a foolish thing, and from now on you will be at war."

¹⁰Asa was angry with the seer because of this; he was so enraged that he put him in prison. At the same time Asa brutally oppressed some of the people.

¹¹The events of Asa's reign, from beginning to end, are written in the book of the kings of Judah and Israel. ¹²In the thirty-ninth year of his reign Asa was afflicted with a disease in his feet. Though his disease was severe, even in his illness he did not seek help from the LORD, but only from the physicians. ¹³Then in the forty-first year of his reign Asa died and rested with his ancestors. ¹⁴They buried him in the tomb that he had cut out for himself in the City of David. They laid him on a bier covered with spices and various blended perfumes, and they made a huge fire in his honor.

Jehoshaphat King of Judah

17 Jehoshaphat his son succeeded him as king and strengthened himself against Israel. ²He stationed troops in all the fortified cities of

ᵃ 4 Also known as *Abel Beth Maakah*
ᵇ 8 That is, people from the upper Nile region
ᶜ 8 Or *charioteers*

UNSHAKEN God

2 Chronicles 16:1–10

God is supportive.

Asa king of Judah learned the hard way that God is always looking for people to help. Asa, instead of relying on God when he came under attack, turned to the pagan king of Aram, emptying gold and silver from the temple and palace as payment for help. The prophet Hanani showed up and reminded Asa that God had been willing to help all along—he was ready to chase off Asa's enemy. Because Asa didn't look to God, he would spend the rest of his life at war. Got it? If your heart is fully committed to God, the Lord is eager to make you strong (see 2 Chronicles 16:9).

So … How are you relying on others in a way that pushes God out of the situation?

520

Judah and put garrisons in Judah and in the towns of Ephraim that his father Asa had captured.

³The LORD was with Jehoshaphat because he followed the ways of his father David before him. He did not consult the Baals ⁴but sought the God of his father and followed his commands rather than the practices of Israel. ⁵The LORD established the kingdom under his control; and all Judah brought gifts to Jehoshaphat, so that he had great wealth and honor. ⁶His heart was devoted to the ways of the LORD; furthermore, he removed the high places and the Asherah poles from Judah.

⁷In the third year of his reign he sent his officials Ben-Hail, Obadiah, Zechariah, Nethanel and Micaiah to teach in the towns of Judah. ⁸With them were certain Levites—Shemaiah, Nethaniah, Zebadiah, Asahel, Shemiramoth, Jehonathan, Adonijah, Tobijah and Tob-Adonijah—and the priests Elishama and Jehoram. ⁹They taught throughout Judah, taking with them the Book of the Law of the LORD; they went around to all the towns of Judah and taught the people.

¹⁰The fear of the LORD fell on all the kingdoms of the lands surrounding Judah, so that they did not go to war against Jehoshaphat. ¹¹Some Philistines brought Jehoshaphat gifts and silver as tribute, and the Arabs brought him flocks: seven thousand seven hundred rams and seven thousand seven hundred goats.

¹²Jehoshaphat became more and more powerful; he built forts and store cities in Judah ¹³and had large supplies in the towns of Judah. He also kept experienced fighting men in Jerusalem. ¹⁴Their enrollment by families was as follows:

From Judah, commanders of units of 1,000:
Adnah the commander, with 300,000 fighting men;
¹⁵next, Jehohanan the commander, with 280,000;
¹⁶next, Amasiah son of Zikri, who volunteered himself for the service of the LORD, with 200,000.

¹⁷From Benjamin:
Eliada, a valiant soldier, with 200,000 men armed with bows and shields;
¹⁸next, Jehozabad, with 180,000 men armed for battle.

¹⁹These were the men who served the king, besides those he stationed in the fortified cities throughout Judah.

Micaiah Prophesies Against Ahab

18 Now Jehoshaphat had great wealth and honor, and he allied himself with Ahab by marriage. ²Some years later he went down to see Ahab in Samaria. Ahab slaughtered many sheep and cattle for him and the people with him and urged him to attack Ramoth Gilead. ³Ahab king of Israel asked Jehoshaphat king of Judah, "Will you go with me against Ramoth Gilead?"

Jehoshaphat replied, "I am as you are, and my people as your people; we will join you in the war." ⁴But Jehoshaphat also said to the king of Israel, "First seek the counsel of the LORD."

⁵So the king of Israel brought together the prophets—four hundred men—and asked them, "Shall we go to war against Ramoth Gilead, or shall I not?"

"Go," they answered, "for God will give it into the king's hand."

⁶But Jehoshaphat asked, "Is there no longer a prophet of the LORD here whom we can inquire of?"

⁷The king of Israel answered Jehoshaphat, "There is still one prophet through whom we can inquire of the LORD, but I hate him because he never prophesies anything good about me, but always bad. He is Micaiah son of Imlah."

"The king should not say such a thing," Jehoshaphat replied.

⁸So the king of Israel called one of his officials and said, "Bring Micaiah son of Imlah at once."

⁹Dressed in their royal robes, the king of Israel and Jehoshaphat king of Judah were sitting on their thrones at the threshing floor by the entrance of the gate of Samaria, with all the prophets prophesying

before them. ¹⁰Now Zedekiah son of Kenaanah had made iron horns, and he declared, "This is what the LORD says: 'With these you will gore the Arameans until they are destroyed.'"

¹¹All the other prophets were prophesying the same thing. "Attack Ramoth Gilead and be victorious," they said, "for the LORD will give it into the king's hand."

¹²The messenger who had gone to summon Micaiah said to him, "Look, the other prophets without exception are predicting success for the king. Let your word agree with theirs, and speak favorably."

¹³But Micaiah said, "As surely as the LORD lives, I can tell him only what my God says."

¹⁴When he arrived, the king asked him, "Micaiah, shall we go to war against Ramoth Gilead, or shall I not?"

"Attack and be victorious," he answered, "for they will be given into your hand."

¹⁵The king said to him, "How many times must I make you swear to tell me nothing but the truth in the name of the LORD?"

¹⁶Then Micaiah answered, "I saw all Israel scattered on the hills like sheep without a shepherd, and the LORD said, 'These people have no master. Let each one go home in peace.'"

¹⁷The king of Israel said to Jehoshaphat, "Didn't I tell you that he never prophesies anything good about me, but only bad?"

¹⁸Micaiah continued, "Therefore hear the word of the LORD: I saw the LORD sitting on his throne with all the multitudes of heaven standing on his right and on his left. ¹⁹And the LORD said, 'Who will entice Ahab king of Israel into attacking Ramoth Gilead and going to his death there?'

"One suggested this, and another that. ²⁰Finally, a spirit came forward, stood before the LORD and said, 'I will entice him.'

"'By what means?' the LORD asked.

²¹"'I will go and be a deceiving spirit in the mouths of all his prophets,' he said.

"'You will succeed in enticing him,' said the LORD. 'Go and do it.'

²²"So now the LORD has put a deceiv-ing spirit in the mouths of these prophets of yours. The LORD has decreed disaster for you."

²³Then Zedekiah son of Kenaanah went up and slapped Micaiah in the face. "Which way did the spirit from*ᵃ* the LORD go when he went from me to speak to you?" he asked.

²⁴Micaiah replied, "You will find out on the day you go to hide in an inner room."

²⁵The king of Israel then ordered, "Take Micaiah and send him back to Amon the ruler of the city and to Joash the king's son, ²⁶and say, 'This is what the king says: Put this fellow in prison and give him nothing but bread and water until I return safely.'"

²⁷Micaiah declared, "If you ever return safely, the LORD has not spoken through me." Then he added, "Mark my words, all you people!"

ᵃ 23 Or Spirit of

ROCK SOLID *plans*

2 Chronicles 18:1–34

Listen to tough advice.

Ahab had a well-earned reputation as Israel's most evil king ever, a man who got his advice from 400 corrupt prophets of the Canaanite goddess Asherah. As Ahab plotted to go to war, he enlisted help from King Jehoshaphat of Judah. When Jehoshaphat called for guidance from an authentic prophet of God, Ahab complained that the prophet never had anything good to say (see 2 Chronicles 18:7). As expected, Micaiah arrived and warned against war. Ahab rejected God's tough word, went to battle anyway and wound up dead (see 2 Chronicles 18:33–34).

Your next step: Choose carefully who you listen to—and make a habit of taking even the toughest (yet wise) advice.

Ahab Killed at Ramoth Gilead

²⁸ So the king of Israel and Jehoshaphat king of Judah went up to Ramoth Gilead. ²⁹ The king of Israel said to Jehoshaphat, "I will enter the battle in disguise, but you wear your royal robes." So the king of Israel disguised himself and went into battle.

³⁰ Now the king of Aram had ordered his chariot commanders, "Do not fight with anyone, small or great, except the king of Israel." ³¹ When the chariot commanders saw Jehoshaphat, they thought, "This is the king of Israel." So they turned to attack him, but Jehoshaphat cried out, and the LORD helped him. God drew them away from him, ³² for when the chariot commanders saw that he was not the king of Israel, they stopped pursuing him.

³³ But someone drew his bow at random and hit the king of Israel between the breastplate and the scale armor. The king told the chariot driver, "Wheel around and get me out of the fighting. I've been wounded." ³⁴ All day long the battle raged, and the king of Israel propped himself up in his chariot facing the Arameans until evening. Then at sunset he died.

19 When Jehoshaphat king of Judah returned safely to his palace in Jerusalem, ²Jehu the seer, the son of Hanani, went out to meet him and said to the king, "Should you help the wicked and love*ᵃ* those who hate the LORD? Because of this, the wrath of the LORD is on you. ³There is, however, some good in you, for you have rid the land of the Asherah poles and have set your heart on seeking God."

Jehoshaphat Appoints Judges

⁴ Jehoshaphat lived in Jerusalem, and he went out again among the people from Beersheba to the hill country of Ephraim and turned them back to the LORD, the God of their ancestors. ⁵ He appointed judges in the land, in each of the fortified cities of Judah. ⁶ He told them, "Consider carefully what you do, because you are not judging for mere mortals but for the LORD, who is with you whenever you give a verdict. ⁷ Now let the fear of the LORD be on you.

Judge carefully, for with the LORD our God there is no injustice or partiality or bribery."

⁸ In Jerusalem also, Jehoshaphat appointed some of the Levites, priests and heads of Israelite families to administer the law of the LORD and to settle disputes. And they lived in Jerusalem. ⁹ He gave them these orders: "You must serve faithfully and wholeheartedly in the fear of the LORD. ¹⁰ In every case that comes before you from your people who live in the cities—whether bloodshed or other concerns of the law, commands, decrees or regulations—you are to warn them not to sin against the LORD; otherwise his wrath will come on you and your people. Do this, and you will not sin.

¹¹ "Amariah the chief priest will be over you in any matter concerning the LORD, and Zebadiah son of Ishmael, the leader of the tribe of Judah, will be over you in any matter concerning the king, and the Levites will serve as officials before you. Act with courage, and may the LORD be with those who do well."

ROCK SOLID
promises

"Act with courage, and may the LORD be with those who do well."

2 Chronicles 19:11

When God commands you to do something, expect his help to do it boldly and do it well.

Jehoshaphat Defeats Moab and Ammon

20 After this, the Moabites and Ammonites with some of the Meunites*ᵇ* came to wage war against Jehoshaphat.

ᵃ 2 Or *and make alliances with*   *ᵇ 1* Some Septuagint manuscripts; Hebrew *Ammonites*

²Some people came and told Jehoshaphat, "A vast army is coming against you from Edom,ᵃ from the other side of the Dead Sea. It is already in Hazezon Tamar" (that is, En Gedi). ³Alarmed, Jehoshaphat resolved to inquire of the Lᴏʀᴅ, and he proclaimed a fast for all Judah. ⁴The people of Judah came together to seek help from the Lᴏʀᴅ; indeed, they came from every town in Judah to seek him.

⁵Then Jehoshaphat stood up in the assembly of Judah and Jerusalem at the temple of the Lᴏʀᴅ in the front of the new courtyard ⁶and said:

"Lᴏʀᴅ, the God of our ancestors, are you not the God who is in heaven? You rule over all the kingdoms of the nations. Power and might are in your hand, and no one can withstand you. ⁷Our God, did you not drive out the inhabitants of this land before your people Israel and give it forever to the descendants of Abraham your friend? ⁸They have lived in it and have built in it a sanctuary for your Name, saying, ⁹'If calamity comes upon us, whether the sword of judgment, or plague or famine, we will stand in your presence before this temple that bears your Name and will cry out to you in our distress, and you will hear us and save us.'

¹⁰"But now here are men from Ammon, Moab and Mount Seir, whose territory you would not allow Israel to invade when they came from Egypt; so they turned away from them and did not destroy them. ¹¹See how they are repaying us by coming to drive us out of the possession you gave us as an inheritance. ¹²Our God, will you not judge them? For we have no power to face this vast army that is attacking us. We do not know what to do, but our eyes are on you."

¹³All the men of Judah, with their wives and children and little ones, stood there before the Lᴏʀᴅ.

¹⁴Then the Spirit of the Lᴏʀᴅ came on Jahaziel son of Zechariah, the son of Benaiah, the son of Jeiel, the son of Mattaniah, a Levite and descendant of Asaph, as he stood in the assembly.

¹⁵He said: "Listen, King Jehoshaphat and all who live in Judah and Jerusalem! This is what the Lᴏʀᴅ says to you: 'Do not be afraid or discouraged because of this vast army. For the battle is not yours, but God's. ¹⁶Tomorrow march down against them. They will be climbing up by the Pass of Ziz, and you will find them at the end of the gorge in the Desert of Jeruel. ¹⁷You will not have to fight this battle. Take up your positions; stand firm and see the deliverance the Lᴏʀᴅ will give you, Judah and Jerusalem. Do not be afraid; do not be discouraged. Go out to face them tomorrow, and the Lᴏʀᴅ will be with you.'"

¹⁸Jehoshaphat bowed down with his face to the ground, and all the people of Judah and Jerusalem fell down in worship before the Lᴏʀᴅ. ¹⁹Then some Levites from the Kohathites and Korahites stood up and praised the Lᴏʀᴅ, the God of Israel, with a very loud voice.

²⁰Early in the morning they left for the Desert of Tekoa. As they set out, Jehoshaphat stood and said, "Listen to me, Judah and people of Jerusalem! Have faith in the Lᴏʀᴅ your God and you will be upheld; have faith in his prophets and you will be successful." ²¹After consulting the people, Jehoshaphat appointed men to sing to the Lᴏʀᴅ and to praise him for the splendor of hisᵇ holiness as they went out at the head of the army, saying:

"Give thanks to the Lᴏʀᴅ,
    for his love endures forever."

²²As they began to sing and praise, the Lᴏʀᴅ set ambushes against the men of Ammon and Moab and Mount Seir who were invading Judah, and they were defeated. ²³The Ammonites and Moabites rose up against the men from Mount Seir to destroy and annihilate them. After they finished slaughtering the men from Seir, they helped to destroy one another.

ᵃ 2 One Hebrew manuscript; most Hebrew manuscripts, Septuagint and Vulgate *Aram*
ᵇ 21 Or *him with the splendor of*

²⁴When the men of Judah came to the place that overlooks the desert and looked toward the vast army, they saw only dead bodies lying on the ground; no one had escaped. ²⁵So Jehoshaphat and his men went to carry off their plunder, and they found among them a great amount of equipment and clothing*a* and also articles of value—more than they could take away. There was so much plunder that it took three days to collect it. ²⁶On the fourth day they assembled in the Valley of Berakah, where they praised the Lord. This is why it is called the Valley of Berakah*b* to this day.

²⁷Then, led by Jehoshaphat, all the men of Judah and Jerusalem returned joyfully to Jerusalem, for the Lord had given them cause to rejoice over their enemies. ²⁸They entered Jerusalem and went to the temple of the Lord with harps and lyres and trumpets.

²⁹The fear of God came on all the surrounding kingdoms when they heard how the Lord had fought against the enemies of Israel. ³⁰And the kingdom of Jehoshaphat was at peace, for his God had given him rest on every side.

The End of Jehoshaphat's Reign

³¹So Jehoshaphat reigned over Judah. He was thirty-five years old when he became king of Judah, and he reigned in Jerusalem twenty-five years. His mother's name was Azubah daughter of Shilhi. ³²He followed the ways of his father Asa and did not stray from them; he did what was right in the eyes of the Lord. ³³The high places, however, were not removed, and the people still had not set their hearts on the God of their ancestors.

³⁴The other events of Jehoshaphat's reign, from beginning to end, are written in the annals of Jehu son of Hanani, which are recorded in the book of the kings of Israel.

³⁵Later, Jehoshaphat king of Judah made an alliance with Ahaziah king of Israel, whose ways were wicked. ³⁶He agreed with him to construct a fleet of trading ships.*c* After these were built at Ezion Geber, ³⁷Eliezer son of Dodavahu of Mareshah prophesied against Jehoshaphat, saying,

"Because you have made an alliance with Ahaziah, the Lord will destroy what you have made." The ships were wrecked and were not able to set sail to trade.*d*

21 Then Jehoshaphat rested with his ancestors and was buried with them in the City of David. And Jehoram his son succeeded him as king. ²Jehoram's brothers, the sons of Jehoshaphat, were Azariah, Jehiel, Zechariah, Azariahu, Michael and Shephatiah. All these were sons of Jehoshaphat king of Israel.*e* ³Their father had given them many gifts of silver and gold and articles of value, as well as fortified cities in Judah, but he had given the kingdom to Jehoram because he was his firstborn son.

Jehoram King of Judah

⁴When Jehoram established himself firmly over his father's kingdom, he put all his brothers to the sword along with some of the officials of Israel. ⁵Jehoram was thirty-two years old when he became king, and he reigned in Jerusalem eight years. ⁶He followed the ways of the kings of Israel, as the house of Ahab had done, for he married a daughter of Ahab. He did evil in the eyes of the Lord. ⁷Nevertheless, because of the covenant the Lord had made with David, the Lord was not willing to destroy the house of David. He had promised to maintain a lamp for him and his descendants forever.

⁸In the time of Jehoram, Edom rebelled against Judah and set up its own king. ⁹So Jehoram went there with his officers and all his chariots. The Edomites surrounded him and his chariot commanders, but he rose up and broke through by night. ¹⁰To this day Edom has been in rebellion against Judah.

Libnah revolted at the same time, because Jehoram had forsaken the Lord, the God of his ancestors. ¹¹He had also built high places on the hills of Judah and had

a 25 Some Hebrew manuscripts and Vulgate; most Hebrew manuscripts *corpses*
b 26 Berakah means *praise.* *c 36* Hebrew *of ships that could go to Tarshish* *d 37* Hebrew *sail for Tarshish* *e 2* That is, Judah, as frequently in 2 Chronicles

caused the people of Jerusalem to prostitute themselves and had led Judah astray.

¹²Jehoram received a letter from Elijah the prophet, which said:

"This is what the LORD, the God of your father David, says: 'You have not followed the ways of your father Jehoshaphat or of Asa king of Judah. ¹³But you have followed the ways of the kings of Israel, and you have led Judah and the people of Jerusalem to prostitute themselves, just as the house of Ahab did. You have also murdered your own brothers, members of your own family, men who were better than you. ¹⁴So now the LORD is about to strike your people, your sons, your wives and everything that is yours, with a heavy blow. ¹⁵You yourself will be very ill with a lingering disease of the bowels, until the disease causes your bowels to come out.'"

¹⁶The LORD aroused against Jehoram the hostility of the Philistines and of the Arabs who lived near the Cushites. ¹⁷They attacked Judah, invaded it and carried off all the goods found in the king's palace, together with his sons and wives. Not a son was left to him except Ahaziah,ᵃ the youngest.

¹⁸After all this, the LORD afflicted Jehoram with an incurable disease of the bowels. ¹⁹In the course of time, at the end of the second year, his bowels came out because of the disease, and he died in great pain. His people made no funeral fire in his honor, as they had for his predecessors.

²⁰Jehoram was thirty-two years old when he became king, and he reigned in Jerusalem eight years. He passed away, to no one's regret, and was buried in the City of David, but not in the tombs of the kings.

Ahaziah King of Judah

22 The people of Jerusalem made Ahaziah, Jehoram's youngest son, king in his place, since the raiders, who came with the Arabs into the camp, had killed all the older sons. So Ahaziah son of Jehoram king of Judah began to reign.

²Ahaziah was twenty-twoᵇ years old when he became king, and he reigned in Jerusalem one year. His mother's name was Athaliah, a granddaughter of Omri.

³He too followed the ways of the house of Ahab, for his mother encouraged him to act wickedly. ⁴He did evil in the eyes of the LORD, as the house of Ahab had done, for after his father's death they became his advisers, to his undoing. ⁵He also followed their counsel when he went with Joramᶜ son of Ahab king of Israel to wage war against Hazael king of Aram at Ramoth Gilead. The Arameans wounded Joram; ⁶so he returned to Jezreel to recover from the wounds they had inflicted on him at Ramothᵈ in his battle with Hazael king of Aram.

Then Ahaziahᵉ son of Jehoram king of Judah went down to Jezreel to see Joram son of Ahab because he had been wounded.

⁷Through Ahaziah's visit to Joram, God brought about Ahaziah's downfall. When Ahaziah arrived, he went out with Joram to meet Jehu son of Nimshi, whom the LORD had anointed to destroy the house of Ahab. ⁸While Jehu was executing judgment on the house of Ahab, he found the officials of Judah and the sons of Ahaziah's relatives, who had been attending Ahaziah, and he killed them. ⁹He then went in search of Ahaziah, and his men captured him while he was hiding in Samaria. He was brought to Jehu and put to death. They buried him, for they said, "He was a son of Jehoshaphat, who sought the LORD with all his heart." So there was no one in the house of Ahaziah powerful enough to retain the kingdom.

ᵃ 17 Hebrew *Jehoahaz*, a variant of *Ahaziah*
ᵇ 2 Some Septuagint manuscripts and Syriac (see also 2 Kings 8:26); Hebrew *forty-two*
ᶜ 5 Hebrew *Jehoram*, a variant of *Joram*; also in verses 6 and 7   ᵈ 6 Hebrew *Ramah*, a variant of *Ramoth*   ᵉ 6 Some Hebrew manuscripts, Septuagint, Vulgate and Syriac (see also 2 Kings 8:29); most Hebrew manuscripts *Azariah*

Athaliah and Joash

¹⁰When Athaliah the mother of Ahaziah saw that her son was dead, she proceeded to destroy the whole royal family of the house of Judah. ¹¹But Jehosheba,ᵃ the daughter of King Jehoram, took Joash son of Ahaziah and stole him away from among the royal princes who were about to be murdered and put him and his nurse in a bedroom. Because Jehosheba,ᵃ the daughter of King Jehoram and wife of the priest Jehoiada, was Ahaziah's sister, she hid the child from Athaliah so she could not kill him. ¹²He remained hidden with them at the temple of God for six years while Athaliah ruled the land.

23 In the seventh year Jehoiada showed his strength. He made a covenant with the commanders of units of a hundred: Azariah son of Jeroham, Ishmael son of Jehohanan, Azariah son of Obed, Maaseiah son of Adaiah, and Elishaphat son of Zikri. ²They went throughout Judah and gathered the Levites and the heads of Israelite families from all the towns. When they came to Jerusalem, ³the whole assembly made a covenant with the king at the temple of God.

Jehoiada said to them, "The king's son shall reign, as the LORD promised concerning the descendants of David. ⁴Now this is what you are to do: A third of you priests and Levites who are going on duty on the Sabbath are to keep watch at the doors, ⁵a third of you at the royal palace and a third at the Foundation Gate, and all the others are to be in the courtyards of the temple of the LORD. ⁶No one is to enter the temple of the LORD except the priests and Levites on duty; they may enter because they are consecrated, but all the others are to observe the LORD's command not to enter.ᵇ ⁷The Levites are to station themselves around the king, each with weapon in hand. Anyone who enters the temple is to be put to death. Stay close to the king wherever he goes."

⁸The Levites and all the men of Judah did just as Jehoiada the priest ordered. Each one took his men—those who were going on duty on the Sabbath and those who were going off duty—for Jehoiada the priest had not released any of the divisions. ⁹Then he gave the commanders of units of a hundred the spears and the large and small shields that had belonged to King David and that were in the temple of God. ¹⁰He stationed all the men, each with his weapon in his hand, around the king—near the altar and the temple, from the south side to the north side of the temple.

¹¹Jehoiada and his sons brought out the king's son and put the crown on him; they presented him with a copy of the covenant and proclaimed him king. They anointed him and shouted, "Long live the king!"

¹²When Athaliah heard the noise of the people running and cheering the king, she went to them at the temple of the LORD. ¹³She looked, and there was the king, standing by his pillar at the entrance. The officers and the trumpeters were beside the king, and all the people of the land were rejoicing and blowing trumpets, and musicians with their instruments were leading the praises. Then Athaliah tore her robes and shouted, "Treason! Treason!"

¹⁴Jehoiada the priest sent out the commanders of units of a hundred, who were in charge of the troops, and said to them: "Bring her out between the ranksᶜ and put to the sword anyone who follows her." For the priest had said, "Do not put her to death at the temple of the LORD." ¹⁵So they seized her as she reached the entrance of the Horse Gate on the palace grounds, and there they put her to death.

¹⁶Jehoiada then made a covenant that he, the people and the kingᵈ would be the LORD's people. ¹⁷All the people went to the temple of Baal and tore it down. They smashed the altars and idols and killed Mattan the priest of Baal in front of the altars.

ᵃ 11 Hebrew *Jehoshabeath*, a variant of *Jehosheba*
ᵇ 6 Or *are to stand guard where the LORD has assigned them*   ᶜ 14 Or *out from the precincts*
ᵈ 16 Or *covenant between the LORD and the people and the king that they* (see 2 Kings 11:17)

¹⁸Then Jehoiada placed the oversight of the temple of the Lord in the hands of the Levitical priests, to whom David had made assignments in the temple, to present the burnt offerings of the Lord as written in the Law of Moses, with rejoicing and singing, as David had ordered. ¹⁹He also stationed gatekeepers at the gates of the Lord's temple so that no one who was in any way unclean might enter.

²⁰He took with him the commanders of hundreds, the nobles, the rulers of the people and all the people of the land and brought the king down from the temple of the Lord. They went into the palace through the Upper Gate and seated the king on the royal throne. ²¹All the people of the land rejoiced, and the city was calm, because Athaliah had been slain with the sword.

Joash Repairs the Temple

24 Joash was seven years old when he became king, and he reigned in Jerusalem forty years. His mother's name was Zibiah; she was from Beersheba. ²Joash did what was right in the eyes of the Lord all the years of Jehoiada the priest. ³Jehoiada chose two wives for him, and he had sons and daughters.

⁴Some time later Joash decided to restore the temple of the Lord. ⁵He called together the priests and Levites and said to them, "Go to the towns of Judah and collect the money due annually from all Israel, to repair the temple of your God. Do it now." But the Levites did not act at once.

⁶Therefore the king summoned Jehoiada the chief priest and said to him, "Why haven't you required the Levites to bring in from Judah and Jerusalem the tax imposed by Moses the servant of the Lord and by the assembly of Israel for the tent of the covenant law?"

⁷Now the sons of that wicked woman Athaliah had broken into the temple of God and had used even its sacred objects for the Baals.

⁸At the king's command, a chest was made and placed outside, at the gate of the temple of the Lord. ⁹A proclamation was then issued in Judah and Jerusalem that they should bring to the Lord the tax that Moses the servant of God had required of Israel in the wilderness. ¹⁰All the officials and all the people brought their contributions gladly, dropping them into the chest until it was full. ¹¹Whenever the chest was brought in by the Levites to the king's officials and they saw that there was a large amount of money, the royal secretary and the officer of the chief priest would come and empty the chest and carry it back to its place. They did this regularly and collected a great amount of money. ¹²The king and Jehoiada gave it to those who carried out the work required for the temple of the Lord. They hired masons and carpenters to restore the Lord's temple, and also workers in iron and bronze to repair the temple.

¹³The men in charge of the work were diligent, and the repairs progressed under them. They rebuilt the temple of God according to its original design and reinforced it. ¹⁴When they had finished, they brought the rest of the money to the king and Jehoiada, and with it were made articles for the Lord's temple: articles for the service and for the burnt offerings, and also dishes and other objects of gold and silver. As long as Jehoiada lived, burnt offerings were presented continually in the temple of the Lord.

¹⁵Now Jehoiada was old and full of years, and he died at the age of a hundred and thirty. ¹⁶He was buried with the kings in the City of David, because of the good he had done in Israel for God and his temple.

The Wickedness of Joash

¹⁷After the death of Jehoiada, the officials of Judah came and paid homage to the king, and he listened to them. ¹⁸They abandoned the temple of the Lord, the God of their ancestors, and worshiped Asherah poles and idols. Because of their guilt, God's anger came on Judah and Jerusalem. ¹⁹Although the Lord sent prophets to the people to bring them back

to him, and though they testified against them, they would not listen.

²⁰Then the Spirit of God came on Zechariah son of Jehoiada the priest. He stood before the people and said, "This is what God says: 'Why do you disobey the LORD's commands? You will not prosper. Because you have forsaken the LORD, he has forsaken you.'"

²¹But they plotted against him, and by order of the king they stoned him to death in the courtyard of the LORD's temple. ²²King Joash did not remember the kindness Zechariah's father Jehoiada had shown him but killed his son, who said as he lay dying, "May the LORD see this and call you to account."

²³At the turn of the year,^a the army of Aram marched against Joash; it invaded Judah and Jerusalem and killed all the leaders of the people. They sent all the plunder to their king in Damascus. ²⁴Although the Aramean army had come with only a few men, the LORD delivered into their hands a much larger army. Because Judah had forsaken the LORD, the God of their ancestors, judgment was executed on Joash. ²⁵When the Arameans withdrew, they left Joash severely wounded. His officials conspired against him for murdering the son of Jehoiada the priest, and they killed him in his bed. So he died and was buried in the City of David, but not in the tombs of the kings.

²⁶Those who conspired against him were Zabad,^b son of Shimeath an Ammonite woman, and Jehozabad, son of Shimrith^c a Moabite woman. ²⁷The account of his sons, the many prophecies about him, and the record of the restoration of the temple of God are written in the annotations on the book of the kings. And Amaziah his son succeeded him as king.

Amaziah King of Judah

25 Amaziah was twenty-five years old when he became king, and he reigned in Jerusalem twenty-nine years. His mother's name was Jehoaddan; she was from Je-

rusalem. ²He did what was right in the eyes of the LORD, but not wholeheartedly. ³After the kingdom was firmly in his control, he executed the officials who had murdered his father the king. ⁴Yet he did not put their children to death, but acted in accordance with what is written in the Law, in the Book of Moses, where the LORD commanded: "Parents shall not be put to death for their children, nor children be put to death for their parents; each will die for their own sin."^d

⁵Amaziah called the people of Judah together and assigned them according to their families to commanders of thousands and commanders of hundreds for all Judah and Benjamin. He then mustered those twenty years old or more and found that there were three hundred thousand men fit for military service, able to handle the spear and shield. ⁶He also hired a hundred thousand fighting men from Israel for a hundred talents^e of silver.

⁷But a man of God came to him and said, "Your Majesty, these troops from Israel must not march with you, for the LORD is not with Israel—not with any of the people of Ephraim. ⁸Even if you go and fight courageously in battle, God will overthrow you before the enemy, for God has the power to help or to overthrow."

⁹Amaziah asked the man of God, "But what about the hundred talents I paid for these Israelite troops?"

The man of God replied, "The LORD can give you much more than that."

¹⁰So Amaziah dismissed the troops who had come to him from Ephraim and sent them home. They were furious with Judah and left for home in a great rage.

¹¹Amaziah then marshaled his strength and led his army to the Valley of Salt, where he killed ten thousand men of Seir. ¹²The army of Judah also captured ten thousand men alive, took them to the top of a cliff and threw them down so that all were dashed to pieces.

^a 23 Probably in the spring   ^b 26 A variant of *Jozabad*   ^c 26 A variant of *Shomer*   ^d 4 Deut. 24:16   ^e 6 That is, about 3 3/4 tons or about 3.4 metric tons; also in verse 9

¹³Meanwhile the troops that Amaziah had sent back and had not allowed to take part in the war raided towns belonging to Judah from Samaria to Beth Horon. They killed three thousand people and carried off great quantities of plunder.

¹⁴When Amaziah returned from slaughtering the Edomites, he brought back the gods of the people of Seir. He set them up as his own gods, bowed down to them and burned sacrifices to them. ¹⁵The anger of the LORD burned against Amaziah, and he sent a prophet to him, who said, "Why do you consult this people's gods, which could not save their own people from your hand?"

¹⁶While he was still speaking, the king said to him, "Have we appointed you an adviser to the king? Stop! Why be struck down?"

So the prophet stopped but said, "I know that God has determined to destroy you, because you have done this and have not listened to my counsel."

¹⁷After Amaziah king of Judah consulted his advisers, he sent this challenge to Jehoash[a] son of Jehoahaz, the son of Jehu, king of Israel: "Come, let us face each other in battle."

¹⁸But Jehoash king of Israel replied to Amaziah king of Judah: "A thistle in Lebanon sent a message to a cedar in Lebanon, 'Give your daughter to my son in marriage.' Then a wild beast in Lebanon came along and trampled the thistle underfoot. ¹⁹You say to yourself that you have defeated Edom, and now you are arrogant and proud. But stay at home! Why ask for trouble and cause your own downfall and that of Judah also?"

²⁰Amaziah, however, would not listen, for God so worked that he might deliver them into the hands of Jehoash, because they sought the gods of Edom. ²¹So Jehoash king of Israel attacked. He and Amaziah king of Judah faced each other at Beth Shemesh in Judah. ²²Judah was routed by Israel, and every man fled to his home. ²³Jehoash king of Israel captured Amaziah king of Judah, the son of Joash, the son of Ahaziah,[b] at Beth

Shemesh. Then Jehoash brought him to Jerusalem and broke down the wall of Jerusalem from the Ephraim Gate to the Corner Gate—a section about four hundred cubits[c] long. ²⁴He took all the gold and silver and all the articles found in the temple of God that had been in the care of Obed-Edom, together with the palace treasures and the hostages, and returned to Samaria.

²⁵Amaziah son of Joash king of Judah lived for fifteen years after the death of Jehoash son of Jehoahaz king of Israel. ²⁶As for the other events of Amaziah's reign, from beginning to end, are they not written in the book of the kings of Judah and Israel? ²⁷From the time that Amaziah turned away from following the LORD, they conspired against him in Jerusalem and he fled to Lachish, but they sent men after him to Lachish and killed him there. ²⁸He was brought back by horse and was buried with his ancestors in the City of Judah.[d]

Uzziah King of Judah

26 Then all the people of Judah took Uzziah,[e] who was sixteen years old, and made him king in place of his father Amaziah. ²He was the one who rebuilt Elath and restored it to Judah after Amaziah rested with his ancestors.

³Uzziah was sixteen years old when he became king, and he reigned in Jerusalem fifty-two years. His mother's name was Jekoliah; she was from Jerusalem. ⁴He did what was right in the eyes of the LORD, just as his father Amaziah had done. ⁵He sought God during the days of Zechariah, who instructed him in the fear[f] of God. As long as he sought the LORD, God gave him success.

a 17 Hebrew *Joash,* a variant of *Jehoash;* also in verses 18, 21, 23 and 25   *b 23* Hebrew *Jehoahaz,* a variant of *Ahaziah*   *c 23* That is, about 600 feet or about 180 meters   *d 28* Most Hebrew manuscripts; some Hebrew manuscripts, Septuagint, Vulgate and Syriac (see also 2 Kings 14:20) *David*   *e 1* Also called *Azariah*   *f 5* Many Hebrew manuscripts, Septuagint and Syriac; other Hebrew manuscripts *vision*

⁶He went to war against the Philistines and broke down the walls of Gath, Jabneh and Ashdod. He then rebuilt towns near Ashdod and elsewhere among the Philistines. ⁷God helped him against the Philistines and against the Arabs who lived in Gur Baal and against the Meunites. ⁸The Ammonites brought tribute to Uzziah, and his fame spread as far as the border of Egypt, because he had become very powerful.

⁹Uzziah built towers in Jerusalem at the Corner Gate, at the Valley Gate and at the angle of the wall, and he fortified them. ¹⁰He also built towers in the wilderness and dug many cisterns, because he had much livestock in the foothills and in the plain. He had people working his fields and vineyards in the hills and in the fertile lands, for he loved the soil.

¹¹Uzziah had a well-trained army, ready to go out by divisions according to their numbers as mustered by Jeiel the secretary and Maaseiah the officer under the direction of Hananiah, one of the royal officials. ¹²The total number of family leaders over the fighting men was 2,600. ¹³Under their command was an army of 307,500 men trained for war, a powerful force to support the king against his enemies. ¹⁴Uzziah provided shields, spears, helmets, coats of armor, bows and slingstones for the entire army. ¹⁵In Jerusalem he made devices invented for use on the towers and on the corner defenses so that soldiers could shoot arrows and hurl large stones from the walls. His fame spread far and wide, for he was greatly helped until he became powerful.

¹⁶But after Uzziah became powerful, his pride led to his downfall. He was unfaithful to the Lord his God, and entered the temple of the Lord to burn incense on the altar of incense. ¹⁷Azariah the priest with eighty other courageous priests of the Lord followed him in. ¹⁸They confronted King Uzziah and said, "It is not right for you, Uzziah, to burn incense to the Lord. That is for the priests, the descendants of Aaron, who have been consecrated to burn incense. Leave the sanctuary, for you have

been unfaithful; and you will not be honored by the Lord God."

¹⁹Uzziah, who had a censer in his hand ready to burn incense, became angry. While he was raging at the priests in their presence before the incense altar in the Lord's temple, leprosy*a* broke out on his forehead. ²⁰When Azariah the chief priest and all the other priests looked at him, they saw that he had leprosy on his forehead, so they hurried him out. Indeed, he himself was eager to leave, because the Lord had afflicted him.

²¹King Uzziah had leprosy until the day he died. He lived in a separate house*b* — leprous, and banned from the temple of the Lord. Jotham his son had charge of the palace and governed the people of the land.

²²The other events of Uzziah's reign,

a 19 The Hebrew for *leprosy* was used for various diseases affecting the skin; also in verses 20, 21 and 23.   *b 21* Or *in a house where he was relieved of responsibilities*

ROCK SOLID *plans*

2 Chronicles 26:1–23

Don't let power go to your head.

Uzziah was just 16 years old when he took the throne of Judah. He "did what was right" and "sought God" and "God gave him success" (2 Chronicles 26:4–5). Yet as Uzziah grew powerful, he became proud and unfaithful to God (see 2 Chronicles 26:16). He stole the job of a temple priest and burned incense on a sacred altar. God struck Uzziah with leprosy, a skin condition that excluded him from both public worship and continuing as king. Because Uzziah let power go to his head, he lost everything.

Your next step: Ask a friend to point out when you let pride or popularity impact your actions.

from beginning to end, are recorded by the prophet Isaiah son of Amoz. ²³Uzziah rested with his ancestors and was buried near them in a cemetery that belonged to the kings, for people said, "He had leprosy." And Jotham his son succeeded him as king.

Jotham King of Judah

27 Jotham was twenty-five years old when he became king, and he reigned in Jerusalem sixteen years. His mother's name was Jerusha daughter of Zadok. ²He did what was right in the eyes of the LORD, just as his father Uzziah had done, but unlike him he did not enter the temple of the LORD. The people, however, continued their corrupt practices. ³Jotham rebuilt the Upper Gate of the temple of the LORD and did extensive work on the wall at the hill of Ophel. ⁴He built towns in the hill country of Judah and forts and towers in the wooded areas.

⁵Jotham waged war against the king of the Ammonites and conquered them. That year the Ammonites paid him a hundred talents*a* of silver, ten thousand cors*b* of wheat and ten thousand cors*c* of barley. The Ammonites brought him the same amount also in the second and third years.

⁶Jotham grew powerful because he walked steadfastly before the LORD his God.

⁷The other events in Jotham's reign, including all his wars and the other things he did, are written in the book of the kings of Israel and Judah. ⁸He was twenty-five years old when he became king, and he reigned in Jerusalem sixteen years. ⁹Jotham rested with his ancestors and was buried in the City of David. And Ahaz his son succeeded him as king.

Ahaz King of Judah

28 Ahaz was twenty years old when he became king, and he reigned in Jerusalem sixteen years. Unlike David his father, he did not do what was right in the eyes of the LORD. ²He followed the ways of the kings of Israel and also made idols for worshiping the Baals. ³He burned sacrifices in the Valley of Ben Hinnom and sacrificed his children in the fire, engaging in the detestable practices of the nations the LORD had driven out before the Israelites. ⁴He offered sacrifices and burned incense at the high places, on the hilltops and under every spreading tree.

⁵Therefore the LORD his God delivered him into the hands of the king of Aram. The Arameans defeated him and took many of his people as prisoners and brought them to Damascus.

He was also given into the hands of the king of Israel, who inflicted heavy casualties on him. ⁶In one day Pekah son of Remaliah killed a hundred and twenty thousand soldiers in Judah—because Judah had forsaken the LORD, the God of their ancestors. ⁷Zikri, an Ephraimite warrior, killed Maaseiah the king's son, Azrikam the officer in charge of the palace, and Elkanah, second to the king. ⁸The men of Israel took captive from their fellow Israelites who were from Judah two hundred thousand wives, sons and daughters. They also took a great deal of plunder, which they carried back to Samaria.

⁹But a prophet of the LORD named Oded was there, and he went out to meet the army when it returned to Samaria. He said to them, "Because the LORD, the God of your ancestors, was angry with Judah, he gave them into your hand. But you have slaughtered them in a rage that reaches to heaven. ¹⁰And now you intend to make the men and women of Judah and Jerusalem your slaves. But aren't you also guilty of sins against the LORD your God? ¹¹Now listen to me! Send back your fellow Israelites you have taken as prisoners, for the LORD's fierce anger rests on you."

¹²Then some of the leaders in Ephraim—Azariah son of Jehohanan, Berekiah son of Meshillemoth, Jehizkiah son

a 5 That is, about 3 3/4 tons or about 3.4 metric tons   *b* 5 That is, probably about 1,800 tons or about 1,600 metric tons of wheat   *c* 5 That is, probably about 1,500 tons or about 1,350 metric tons of barley of Shallum, and Amasa son of Hadlai—confronted those who were arriving from the war. ¹³"You must not bring those prisoners here," they said, "or we will be guilty before the Lord. Do you intend to add to our sin and guilt? For our guilt is already great, and his fierce anger rests on Israel."

¹⁴So the soldiers gave up the prisoners and plunder in the presence of the officials and all the assembly. ¹⁵The men designated by name took the prisoners, and from the plunder they clothed all who were naked. They provided them with clothes and sandals, food and drink, and healing balm. All those who were weak they put on donkeys. So they took them back to their fellow Israelites at Jericho, the City of Palms, and returned to Samaria.

¹⁶At that time King Ahaz sent to the kings[a] of Assyria for help. ¹⁷The Edomites had again come and attacked Judah and carried away prisoners, ¹⁸while the Philistines had raided towns in the foothills and in the Negev of Judah. They captured and occupied Beth Shemesh, Aijalon and Gederoth, as well as Soko, Timnah and Gimzo, with their surrounding villages. ¹⁹The Lord had humbled Judah because of Ahaz king of Israel,[b] for he had promoted wickedness in Judah and had been most unfaithful to the Lord. ²⁰Tiglath-Pileser[c] king of Assyria came to him, but he gave him trouble instead of help. ²¹Ahaz took some of the things from the temple of the Lord and from the royal palace and from the officials and presented them to the king of Assyria, but that did not help him.

²²In his time of trouble King Ahaz became even more unfaithful to the Lord. ²³He offered sacrifices to the gods of Damascus, who had defeated him; for he thought, "Since the gods of the kings of Aram have helped them, I will sacrifice to them so they will help me." But they were his downfall and the downfall of all Israel.

²⁴Ahaz gathered together the furnishings from the temple of God and cut them in pieces. He shut the doors of the Lord's temple and set up altars at every street corner in Jerusalem. ²⁵In every town in Judah

he built high places to burn sacrifices to other gods and aroused the anger of the Lord, the God of his ancestors.

²⁶The other events of his reign and all his ways, from beginning to end, are written in the book of the kings of Judah and Israel. ²⁷Ahaz rested with his ancestors and was buried in the city of Jerusalem, but he was not placed in the tombs of the kings of Israel. And Hezekiah his son succeeded him as king.

Hezekiah Purifies the Temple

29 Hezekiah was twenty-five years old when he became king, and he reigned in Jerusalem twenty-nine years. His mother's name was Abijah daughter of Zechariah. ²He did what was right in the eyes of the Lord, just as his father David had done.

³In the first month of the first year of his reign, he opened the doors of the temple of the Lord and repaired them. ⁴He brought in the priests and the Levites, assembled them in the square on the east side ⁵and said: "Listen to me, Levites! Consecrate yourselves now and consecrate the temple of the Lord, the God of your ancestors. Remove all defilement from the sanctuary. ⁶Our parents were unfaithful; they did evil in the eyes of the Lord our God and forsook him. They turned their faces away from the Lord's dwelling place and turned their backs on him. ⁷They also shut the doors of the portico and put out the lamps. They did not burn incense or present any burnt offerings at the sanctuary to the God of Israel. ⁸Therefore, the anger of the Lord has fallen on Judah and Jerusalem; he has made them an object of dread and horror and scorn, as you can see with your own eyes. ⁹This is why our fathers have fallen by the sword and why our sons and daughters and our wives are in captivity. ¹⁰Now I intend to make a covenant with the Lord, the God of Israel, so

---

[a] 16 Most Hebrew manuscripts; one Hebrew manuscript, Septuagint and Vulgate (see also 2 Kings 16:7) king   [b] 19 That is, Judah, as frequently in 2 Chronicles   [c] 20 Hebrew *Tilgath-Pilneser*, a variant of *Tiglath-Pileser*

that his fierce anger will turn away from us. ¹¹My sons, do not be negligent now, for the LORD has chosen you to stand before him and serve him, to minister before him and to burn incense."

¹²Then these Levites set to work:

from the Kohathites,
Mahath son of Amasai and Joel son of Azariah;
from the Merarites,
Kish son of Abdi and Azariah son of Jehallelel;
from the Gershonites,
Joah son of Zimmah and Eden son of Joah;
¹³from the descendants of Elizaphan,
Shimri and Jeiel;
from the descendants of Asaph,
Zechariah and Mattaniah;
¹⁴from the descendants of Heman,
Jehiel and Shimei;
from the descendants of Jeduthun,
Shemaiah and Uzziel.

¹⁵When they had assembled their fellow Levites and consecrated themselves, they went in to purify the temple of the LORD, as the king had ordered, following the word of the LORD. ¹⁶The priests went into the sanctuary of the LORD to purify it. They brought out to the courtyard of the LORD's temple everything unclean that they found in the temple of the LORD. The Levites took it and carried it out to the Kidron Valley. ¹⁷They began the consecration on the first day of the first month, and by the eighth day of the month they reached the portico of the LORD. For eight more days they consecrated the temple of the LORD itself, finishing on the sixteenth day of the first month.

¹⁸Then they went in to King Hezekiah and reported: "We have purified the entire temple of the LORD, the altar of burnt offering with all its utensils, and the table for setting out the consecrated bread, with all its articles. ¹⁹We have prepared and consecrated all the articles that King Ahaz removed in his unfaithfulness while he was king. They are now in front of the LORD's altar."

²⁰Early the next morning King Hezekiah gathered the city officials together and went up to the temple of the LORD. ²¹They brought seven bulls, seven rams, seven male lambs and seven male goats as a sin offering[a] for the kingdom, for the sanctuary and for Judah. The king commanded the priests, the descendants of Aaron, to offer these on the altar of the LORD. ²²So they slaughtered the bulls, and the priests took the blood and splashed it against the altar; next they slaughtered the rams and splashed their blood against the altar; then they slaughtered the lambs and splashed their blood against the altar. ²³The goats for the sin offering were brought before the king and the assembly, and they laid their hands on them. ²⁴The priests then slaughtered the goats and presented their blood on the altar for a sin offering to atone for all Israel, because the king had ordered the burnt offering and the sin offering for all Israel.

²⁵He stationed the Levites in the temple of the LORD with cymbals, harps and lyres in the way prescribed by David and Gad the king's seer and Nathan the prophet; this was commanded by the LORD through his prophets. ²⁶So the Levites stood ready with David's instruments, and the priests with their trumpets.

²⁷Hezekiah gave the order to sacrifice the burnt offering on the altar. As the offering began, singing to the LORD began also, accompanied by trumpets and the instruments of David king of Israel. ²⁸The whole assembly bowed in worship, while the musicians played and the trumpets sounded. All this continued until the sacrifice of the burnt offering was completed.

²⁹When the offerings were finished, the king and everyone present with him knelt down and worshiped. ³⁰King Hezekiah and his officials ordered the Levites to praise the LORD with the words of David and of Asaph the seer. So they sang praises with gladness and bowed down and worshiped.

³¹Then Hezekiah said, "You have now dedicated yourselves to the LORD. Come

---

a 21 Or *purification offering*; also in verses 23 and 24

and bring sacrifices and thank offerings to the temple of the Lord." So the assembly brought sacrifices and thank offerings, and all whose hearts were willing brought burnt offerings.

³²The number of burnt offerings the assembly brought was seventy bulls, a hundred rams and two hundred male lambs—all of them for burnt offerings to the Lord. ³³The animals consecrated as sacrifices amounted to six hundred bulls and three thousand sheep and goats. ³⁴The priests, however, were too few to skin all the burnt offerings; so their relatives the Levites helped them until the task was finished and until other priests had been consecrated, for the Levites had been more conscientious in consecrating themselves than the priests had been. ³⁵There were burnt offerings in abundance, together with the fat of the fellowship offerings and the drink offerings that accompanied the burnt offerings.

So the service of the temple of the Lord was reestablished. ³⁶Hezekiah and all the people rejoiced at what God had brought about for his people, because it was done so quickly.

Hezekiah Celebrates the Passover

30 Hezekiah sent word to all Israel and Judah and also wrote letters to Ephraim and Manasseh, inviting them to come to the temple of the Lord in Jerusalem and celebrate the Passover to the Lord, the God of Israel. ²The king and his officials and the whole assembly in Jerusalem decided to celebrate the Passover in the second month. ³They had not been able to celebrate it at the regular time because not enough priests had consecrated themselves and the people had not assembled in Jerusalem. ⁴The plan seemed right both to the king and to the whole assembly. ⁵They decided to send a proclamation throughout Israel, from Beersheba to Dan, calling the people to come to Jerusalem and celebrate the Passover to the Lord, the God of Israel. It had not been celebrated in large numbers according to what was written.

⁶At the king's command, couriers went throughout Israel and Judah with letters from the king and from his officials, which read:

"People of Israel, return to the Lord, the God of Abraham, Isaac and Israel, that he may return to you who are left, who have escaped from the hand of the kings of Assyria. ⁷Do not be like your parents and your fellow Israelites, who were unfaithful to the Lord, the God of their ancestors, so that he made them an object of horror, as you see. ⁸Do not be stiff-necked, as your ancestors were; submit to the Lord. Come to his sanctuary, which he has consecrated forever. Serve the Lord your God, so that his fierce anger will turn away from you. ⁹If you return to the Lord, then your fellow Israelites and your children will be shown compassion by their captors and will return to this land, for the Lord your God is gracious and compassionate. He will not turn his face from you if you return to him."

¹⁰The couriers went from town to town in Ephraim and Manasseh, as far as Zebulun, but people scorned and ridiculed them. ¹¹Nevertheless, some from Asher, Manasseh and Zebulun humbled themselves and went to Jerusalem. ¹²Also in Judah the hand of God was on the people to give them unity of mind to carry out what the king and his officials had ordered, following the word of the Lord.

¹³A very large crowd of people assembled in Jerusalem to celebrate the Festival of Unleavened Bread in the second month. ¹⁴They removed the altars in Jerusalem and cleared away the incense altars and threw them into the Kidron Valley.

¹⁵They slaughtered the Passover lamb on the fourteenth day of the second month. The priests and the Levites were ashamed and consecrated themselves and brought burnt offerings to the temple of the Lord. ¹⁶Then they took up their regular positions as prescribed in the Law of Moses

the man of God. The priests splashed against the altar the blood handed to them by the Levites. [17] Since many in the crowd had not consecrated themselves, the Levites had to kill the Passover lambs for all those who were not ceremonially clean and could not consecrate their lambs[a] to the LORD. [18] Although most of the many people who came from Ephraim, Manasseh, Issachar and Zebulun had not purified themselves, yet they ate the Passover, contrary to what was written. But Hezekiah prayed for them, saying, "May the LORD, who is good, pardon everyone [19] who sets their heart on seeking God—the LORD, the God of their ancestors—even if they are not clean according to the rules of the sanctuary." [20] And the LORD heard Hezekiah and healed the people.

[21] The Israelites who were present in Jerusalem celebrated the Festival of Unleavened Bread for seven days with great rejoicing, while the Levites and priests praised the LORD every day with resounding instruments dedicated to the LORD.[b]

[22] Hezekiah spoke encouragingly to all the Levites, who showed good understanding of the service of the LORD. For the seven days they ate their assigned portion and offered fellowship offerings and praised[c] the LORD, the God of their ancestors.

[23] The whole assembly then agreed to celebrate the festival seven more days; so for another seven days they celebrated joyfully. [24] Hezekiah king of Judah provided a thousand bulls and seven thousand sheep and goats for the assembly, and the officials provided them with a thousand bulls and ten thousand sheep and goats. A great number of priests consecrated themselves. [25] The entire assembly of Judah rejoiced, along with the priests and Levites and all who had assembled from Israel, including the foreigners who had come from Israel and also those who resided in Judah. [26] There was great joy in Jerusalem, for since the days of Solomon son of David king of Israel there had been nothing like this in Jerusalem. [27] The priests and the Levites stood to bless the people, and God heard them, for their prayer reached heaven, his holy dwelling place.

31 When all this had ended, the Israelites who were there went out to the towns of Judah, smashed the sacred stones and cut down the Asherah poles. They destroyed the high places and the altars throughout Judah and Benjamin and in Ephraim and Manasseh. After they had destroyed all of them, the Israelites returned to their own towns and to their own property.

Contributions for Worship

[2] Hezekiah assigned the priests and Levites to divisions—each of them according to their duties as priests or Le-

---

UNSHAKEN *God*

2 Chronicles 30:1–20

God is forgiving.

The people of Israel were down and out, distant from God, not worshiping or enjoying the Lord as he commanded. Among other sins, they had failed to keep the Passover, the celebration of their rescue from slavery in Egypt. King Hezekiah invited people back to God. He called their ancestors unfaithful, stubborn and stiff-necked, objects of horror to God. But God is gracious and compassionate. The king promised that if the people returned home to God, the Lord would welcome them (see 2 Chronicles 30:9). That's your God. He's forgiving. If you confess your sins, he forgives you and cleanses the wrongs you have done (see 1 John 1:9).

So ... How have you wandered away from God? Ask his forgiveness. And come home.

---

[a] 17 Or *consecrate themselves*   [b] 21 Or *priests sang to the LORD every day, accompanied by the LORD's instruments of praise*   [c] 22 Or *and confessed their sins to*

vites — to offer burnt offerings and fellowship offerings, to minister, to give thanks and to sing praises at the gates of the Lord's dwelling. ³The king contributed from his own possessions for the morning and evening burnt offerings and for the burnt offerings on the Sabbaths, at the New Moons and at the appointed festivals as written in the Law of the Lord. ⁴He ordered the people living in Jerusalem to give the portion due the priests and Levites so they could devote themselves to the Law of the Lord. ⁵As soon as the order went out, the Israelites generously gave the firstfruits of their grain, new wine, olive oil and honey and all that the fields produced. They brought a great amount, a tithe of everything. ⁶The people of Israel and Judah who lived in the towns of Judah also brought a tithe of their herds and flocks and a tithe of the holy things dedicated to the Lord their God, and they piled them in heaps. ⁷They began doing this in the third month and finished in the seventh month. ⁸When Hezekiah and his officials came and saw the heaps, they praised the Lord and blessed his people Israel.

⁹Hezekiah asked the priests and Levites about the heaps; ¹⁰and Azariah the chief priest, from the family of Zadok, answered, "Since the people began to bring their contributions to the temple of the Lord, we have had enough to eat and plenty to spare, because the Lord has blessed his people, and this great amount is left over."

¹¹Hezekiah gave orders to prepare storerooms in the temple of the Lord, and this was done. ¹²Then they faithfully brought in the contributions, tithes and dedicated gifts. Konaniah, a Levite, was the overseer in charge of these things, and his brother Shimei was next in rank. ¹³Jehiel, Azaziah, Nahath, Asahel, Jerimoth, Jozabad, Eliel, Ismakiah, Mahath and Benaiah were assistants of Konaniah and Shimei his brother. All these served by appointment of King Hezekiah and Azariah the official in charge of the temple of God.

¹⁴Kore son of Imnah the Levite, keeper of the East Gate, was in charge of the freewill offerings given to God, distributing the contributions made to the Lord and also the consecrated gifts. ¹⁵Eden, Miniamin, Jeshua, Shemaiah, Amariah and Shekaniah assisted him faithfully in the towns of the priests, distributing to their fellow priests according to their divisions, old and young alike.

¹⁶In addition, they distributed to the males three years old or more whose names were in the genealogical records — all who would enter the temple of the Lord to perform the daily duties of their various tasks, according to their responsibilities and their divisions. ¹⁷And they distributed to the priests enrolled by their families in the genealogical records and likewise to the Levites twenty years old or more, according to their responsibilities and their divisions. ¹⁸They included all the little ones, the wives, and the sons and daughters of the whole community listed in these genealogical records. For they were faithful in consecrating themselves.

¹⁹As for the priests, the descendants of Aaron, who lived on the farmlands around their towns or in any other towns, men were designated by name to distribute portions to every male among them and to all who were recorded in the genealogies of the Levites.

²⁰This is what Hezekiah did throughout Judah, doing what was good and right and faithful before the Lord his God. ²¹In everything that he undertook in the service of God's temple and in obedience to the law and the commands, he sought his God and worked wholeheartedly. And so he prospered.

Sennacherib Threatens Jerusalem

32 After all that Hezekiah had so faithfully done, Sennacherib king of Assyria came and invaded Judah. He laid siege to the fortified cities, thinking to conquer them for himself. ²When Hezekiah saw that Sennacherib had come and that he intended to wage war against Jerusalem,

³he consulted with his officials and military staff about blocking off the water from the springs outside the city, and they helped him. ⁴They gathered a large group of people who blocked all the springs and the stream that flowed through the land. "Why should the kings^a of Assyria come and find plenty of water?" they said. ⁵Then he worked hard repairing all the broken sections of the wall and building towers on it. He built another wall outside that one and reinforced the terraces^b of the City of David. He also made large numbers of weapons and shields.

⁶He appointed military officers over the people and assembled them before him in the square at the city gate and encouraged them with these words: ⁷"Be strong and courageous. Do not be afraid or discouraged because of the king of Assyria and the vast army with him, for there is a greater power with us than with him. ⁸With him is only the arm of flesh, but with us is the Lord our God to help us and to fight our battles." And the people gained confidence from what Hezekiah the king of Judah said.

ROCK SOLID promises

"There is a greater power with us than with him ... With us is the Lord our God to help us and to fight our battles." 2 Chronicles 32:7-8

No matter how impressive your enemies look, God is more potent than all of them put together.

⁹Later, when Sennacherib king of Assyria and all his forces were laying siege to Lachish, he sent his officers to Jerusalem with this message for Hezekiah king of Judah and for all the people of Judah who were there:

¹⁰"This is what Sennacherib king of Assyria says: On what are you basing your confidence, that you remain in Jerusalem under siege? ¹¹When Hezekiah says, 'The Lord our God will save us from the hand of the king of Assyria,' he is misleading you, to let you die of hunger and thirst. ¹²Did not Hezekiah himself remove this god's high places and altars, saying to Judah and Jerusalem, 'You must worship before one altar and burn sacrifices on it'?

¹³"Do you not know what I and my predecessors have done to all the peoples of the other lands? Were the gods of those nations ever able to deliver their land from my hand? ¹⁴Who of all the gods of these nations that my predecessors destroyed has been able to save his people from me? How then can your god deliver you from my hand? ¹⁵Now do not let Hezekiah deceive you and mislead you like this. Do not believe him, for no god of any nation or kingdom has been able to deliver his people from my hand or the hand of my predecessors. How much less will your god deliver you from my hand!"

¹⁶Sennacherib's officers spoke further against the Lord God and against his servant Hezekiah. ¹⁷The king also wrote letters ridiculing the Lord, the God of Israel, and saying this against him: "Just as the gods of the peoples of the other lands did not rescue their people from my hand, so the god of Hezekiah will not rescue his people from my hand." ¹⁸Then they called out in Hebrew to the people of Jerusalem who were on the wall, to terrify them and make them afraid in order to capture the city. ¹⁹They spoke about the God of Jerusalem as they did about the gods of the other peoples of the world—the work of human hands.

²⁰King Hezekiah and the prophet Isaiah son of Amoz cried out in prayer to

^a 4 Hebrew; Septuagint and Syriac king
^b 5 Or the Millo

heaven about this. ²¹And the LORD sent an angel, who annihilated all the fighting men and the commanders and officers in the camp of the Assyrian king. So he withdrew to his own land in disgrace. And when he went into the temple of his god, some of his sons, his own flesh and blood, cut him down with the sword.

²²So the LORD saved Hezekiah and the people of Jerusalem from the hand of Sennacherib king of Assyria and from the hand of all others. He took care of them*a* on every side. ²³Many brought offerings to Jerusalem for the LORD and valuable gifts for Hezekiah king of Judah. From then on he was highly regarded by all the nations.

Hezekiah's Pride, Success and Death

²⁴In those days Hezekiah became ill and was at the point of death. He prayed to the LORD, who answered him and gave him a miraculous sign. ²⁵But Hezekiah's heart was proud and he did not respond to the kindness shown him; therefore the LORD's wrath was on him and on Judah and Jerusalem. ²⁶Then Hezekiah repented of the pride of his heart, as did the people of Jerusalem; therefore the LORD's wrath did not come on them during the days of Hezekiah.

²⁷Hezekiah had very great wealth and honor, and he made treasuries for his silver and gold and for his precious stones, spices, shields and all kinds of valuables. ²⁸He also made buildings to store the harvest of grain, new wine and olive oil; and he made stalls for various kinds of cattle, and pens for the flocks. ²⁹He built villages and acquired great numbers of flocks and herds, for God had given him very great riches.

³⁰It was Hezekiah who blocked the upper outlet of the Gihon spring and channeled the water down to the west side of the City of David. He succeeded in everything he undertook. ³¹But when envoys were sent by the rulers of Babylon to ask him about the miraculous sign that had occurred in the land, God left him to test him and to know everything that was in his heart.

³²The other events of Hezekiah's reign and his acts of devotion are written in the vision of the prophet Isaiah son of Amoz in the book of the kings of Judah and Israel. ³³Hezekiah rested with his ancestors and was buried on the hill where the tombs of David's descendants are. All Judah and the people of Jerusalem honored him when he died. And Manasseh his son succeeded him as king.

Manasseh King of Judah

33 Manasseh was twelve years old when he became king, and he reigned in Jerusalem fifty-five years. ²He did evil in the eyes of the LORD, following the detestable practices of the nations the LORD had driven out before the Israelites. ³He rebuilt the high places his father Hezekiah had demolished; he also erected altars to the Baals and made Asherah poles. He bowed down to all the starry hosts and worshiped them. ⁴He built altars in the temple of the LORD, of which the LORD had said, "My Name will remain in Jerusalem forever." ⁵In both courts of the temple of the LORD, he built altars to all the starry hosts. ⁶He sacrificed his children in the fire in the Valley of Ben Hinnom, practiced divination and witchcraft, sought omens, and consulted mediums and spiritists. He did much evil in the eyes of the LORD, arousing his anger.

⁷He took the image he had made and put it in God's temple, of which God had said to David and to his son Solomon, "In this temple and in Jerusalem, which I have chosen out of all the tribes of Israel, I will put my Name forever. ⁸I will not again make the feet of the Israelites leave the land I assigned to your ancestors, if only they will be careful to do everything I commanded them concerning all the laws, decrees and regulations given through Moses." ⁹But Manasseh led Judah and the people of Jerusalem astray, so that they did more evil than the nations the LORD had destroyed before the Israelites.

¹⁰The LORD spoke to Manasseh and his

---

a 22 Hebrew; Septuagint and Vulgate *He gave them rest*

people, but they paid no attention. ¹¹So the LORD brought against them the army commanders of the king of Assyria, who took Manasseh prisoner, put a hook in his nose, bound him with bronze shackles and took him to Babylon. ¹²In his distress he sought the favor of the LORD his God and humbled himself greatly before the God of his ancestors. ¹³And when he prayed to him, the LORD was moved by his entreaty and listened to his plea; so he brought him back to Jerusalem and to his kingdom. Then Manasseh knew that the LORD is God.

¹⁴Afterward he rebuilt the outer wall of the City of David, west of the Gihon spring in the valley, as far as the entrance of the Fish Gate and encircling the hill of Ophel; he also made it much higher. He stationed military commanders in all the fortified cities in Judah.

¹⁵He got rid of the foreign gods and removed the image from the temple of the LORD, as well as all the altars he had built on the temple hill and in Jerusalem; and he threw them out of the city. ¹⁶Then he restored the altar of the LORD and sacrificed fellowship offerings and thank offerings on it, and told Judah to serve the LORD, the God of Israel. ¹⁷The people, however, continued to sacrifice at the high places, but only to the LORD their God.

2 Chronicles 33:1–20
Manasseh started over with God.

There can only be one baddest of the bad, and among the evil kings of Judah, the Bible says Manasseh was the worst. He led the people of God so far astray that they acted even more evil than the sinful peoples the Lord had driven out of the promised land (see 2 Kings 21:9).

Manasseh ascended to the throne at age 12 and ruled for 55 years, longer than any other Israelite king. He succeeded his father Hezekiah, who had boldly turned the nation back to God. But Manasseh undid all the good things his godly father accomplished. He rebuilt altars to false gods, worshiped Baal and Asherah, put pagan altars in the temple, practiced sorcery, talked to mediums, and burned his son as a sacrifice (see 2 Kings 21:3–6). He "shed so much innocent blood that he filled Jerusalem from end to end" (2 Kings 21:16). Tradition holds him responsible for having the great prophet Isaiah sawn in two (see Hebrews 11:37).

But Manasseh changed. Toward the end of his life, foreign armies dragged him to captivity in Babylon. After a short period there he repented, and "Manasseh knew that the LORD is God" (2 Chronicles 33:13). He returned to Jerusalem a humbled, changed man. He rid the nation of foreign gods and destroyed their altars. He restored real worship and ordered the people to obey God. After many terrible years of disobeying God, Manasseh got a fresh start.

You can find Manasseh in 2 Kings 20—24; 1 Chronicles 33; Jeremiah 15:4; and Matthew 1:10.

UNSHAKEN people

[18] The other events of Manasseh's reign, including his prayer to his God and the words the seers spoke to him in the name of the LORD, the God of Israel, are written in the annals of the kings of Israel.[a] [19] His prayer and how God was moved by his entreaty, as well as all his sins and unfaithfulness, and the sites where he built high places and set up Asherah poles and idols before he humbled himself—all these are written in the records of the seers.[b] [20] Manasseh rested with his ancestors and was buried in his palace. And Amon his son succeeded him as king.

Amon King of Judah

[21] Amon was twenty-two years old when he became king, and he reigned in Jerusalem two years. [22] He did evil in the eyes of the LORD, as his father Manasseh had done. Amon worshiped and offered sacrifices to all the idols Manasseh had made. [23] But unlike his father Manasseh, he did not humble himself before the LORD; Amon increased his guilt.

[24] Amon's officials conspired against him and assassinated him in his palace. [25] Then the people of the land killed all who had plotted against King Amon, and they made Josiah his son king in his place.

Josiah's Reforms

34 Josiah was eight years old when he became king, and he reigned in Jerusalem thirty-one years. [2] He did what was right in the eyes of the LORD and followed the ways of his father David, not turning aside to the right or to the left.

[3] In the eighth year of his reign, while he was still young, he began to seek the God of his father David. In his twelfth year he began to purge Judah and Jerusalem of high places, Asherah poles and idols. [4] Under his direction the altars of the Baals were torn down; he cut to pieces the incense altars that were above them, and smashed the Asherah poles and the idols. These he broke to pieces and scattered over the graves of those who had sacrificed to them. [5] He burned the bones of the priests on their altars, and so he purged Judah and Jerusalem. [6] In the towns of Manasseh, Ephraim and Simeon, as far as Naphtali, and in the ruins around them, [7] he tore down the altars and the Asherah poles and crushed the idols to powder and cut to pieces all the incense altars throughout Israel. Then he went back to Jerusalem.

[8] In the eighteenth year of Josiah's reign, to purify the land and the temple, he sent Shaphan son of Azaliah and Maaseiah the ruler of the city, with Joah son of Joahaz, the recorder, to repair the temple of the LORD his God.

[9] They went to Hilkiah the high priest and gave him the money that had been brought into the temple of God, which the Levites who were the gatekeepers had collected from the people of Manasseh, Ephraim and the entire remnant of Israel and from all the people of Judah and Benjamin and the inhabitants of Jerusalem. [10] Then they entrusted it to the men appointed to supervise the work on the LORD's temple. These men paid the workers who repaired and restored the temple. [11] They also gave money to the carpenters and builders to purchase dressed stone, and timber for joists and beams for the buildings that the kings of Judah had allowed to fall into ruin.

[12] The workers labored faithfully. Over them to direct them were Jahath and Obadiah, Levites descended from Merari, and Zechariah and Meshullam, descended from Kohath. The Levites—all who were skilled in playing musical instruments— [13] had charge of the laborers and supervised all the workers from job to job. Some of the Levites were secretaries, scribes and gatekeepers.

The Book of the Law Found

[14] While they were bringing out the money that had been taken into the temple of the LORD, Hilkiah the priest found

[a] 18 That is, Judah, as frequently in 2 Chronicles   [b] 19 One Hebrew manuscript and Septuagint; most Hebrew manuscripts of Hozai

the Book of the Law of the Lord that had been given through Moses. ¹⁵Hilkiah said to Shaphan the secretary, "I have found the Book of the Law in the temple of the Lord." He gave it to Shaphan.

¹⁶Then Shaphan took the book to the king and reported to him: "Your officials are doing everything that has been committed to them. ¹⁷They have paid out the money that was in the temple of the Lord and have entrusted it to the supervisors and workers." ¹⁸Then Shaphan the secretary informed the king, "Hilkiah the priest has given me a book." And Shaphan read from it in the presence of the king.

¹⁹When the king heard the words of the Law, he tore his robes. ²⁰He gave these orders to Hilkiah, Ahikam son of Shaphan, Abdon son of Micah,ᵃ Shaphan the secretary and Asaiah the king's attendant: ²¹"Go and inquire of the Lord for me and for the remnant in Israel and Judah about what is written in this book that has been found. Great is the Lord's anger that is poured out on us because those who have gone before us have not kept the word of the Lord; they have not acted in accordance with all that is written in this book."

²²Hilkiah and those the king had sent with himᵇ went to speak to the prophet Huldah, who was the wife of Shallum son of Tokhath,ᶜ the son of Hasrah,ᵈ keeper of the wardrobe. She lived in Jerusalem, in the New Quarter.

²³She said to them, "This is what the Lord, the God of Israel, says: Tell the man who sent you to me, ²⁴'This is what the Lord says: I am going to bring disaster on this place and its people—all the curses written in the book that has been read in the presence of the king of Judah. ²⁵Because they have forsaken me and burned incense to other gods and aroused my anger by all that their hands have made,ᵉ my anger will be poured out on this place and will not be quenched.' ²⁶Tell the king of Judah, who sent you to inquire of the Lord, 'This is what the Lord, the God of Israel, says concerning the words you heard: ²⁷Because your heart was responsive and you humbled yourself

before God when you heard what he spoke against this place and its people, and because you humbled yourself before me and tore your robes and wept in my presence, I have heard you, declares the Lord. ²⁸Now I will gather you to your ancestors, and

ᵃ 20 Also called *Akbor son of Micaiah*
ᵇ 22 One Hebrew manuscript, Vulgate and Syriac; most Hebrew manuscripts do not have *had sent with him.*   ᶜ 22 Also called *Tikvah*
ᵈ 22 Also called *Harhas*   ᵉ 25 Or *by everything they have done*

---

2 Chronicles 34:14–33

God guards the Bible.

Josiah became king of Judah at the wee age of eight, inheriting a kingdom of subjects dedicated to doing wrong, especially worshiping false gods. As a teen, Josiah got serious about following God, and soon the young king tore down pagan altars and restarted true worship at the temple of Jerusalem. During repairs of the temple, the high priest of Israel uncovered a lost "Book of the Law," possibly a portion of the Old Testament book of Deuteronomy. Josiah tore his clothes in grief that God's Word had been neglected, then used what the book taught him to lead his kingdom even closer to the Lord. This scene demonstrates God's amazing care for the Bible throughout history. Even in a period of rampant sin, the Lord didn't let his Word slip away. He had a copy safely stowed, waiting for someone willing to hear and obey his commands.

Think: Have you ever misplaced the Bible from the core of your life? What did you do to make things right?

ROCK SOLID truths

you will be buried in peace. Your eyes will not see all the disaster I am going to bring on this place and on those who live here.'"

So they took her answer back to the king.

²⁹Then the king called together all the elders of Judah and Jerusalem. ³⁰He went up to the temple of the LORD with the people of Judah, the inhabitants of Jerusalem, the priests and the Levites—all the people from the least to the greatest. He read in their hearing all the words of the Book of the Covenant, which had been found in the temple of the LORD. ³¹The king stood by his pillar and renewed the covenant in the presence of the LORD—to follow the LORD and keep his commands, statutes and decrees with all his heart and all his soul, and to obey the words of the covenant written in this book.

³²Then he had everyone in Jerusalem and Benjamin pledge themselves to it; the people of Jerusalem did this in accordance with the covenant of God, the God of their ancestors.

³³Josiah removed all the detestable idols from all the territory belonging to the Israelites, and he had all who were present in Israel serve the LORD their God. As long as he lived, they did not fail to follow the LORD, the God of their ancestors.

Josiah Celebrates the Passover

35 Josiah celebrated the Passover to the LORD in Jerusalem, and the Passover lamb was slaughtered on the fourteenth day of the first month. ²He appointed the priests to their duties and encouraged them in the service of the LORD's temple. ³He said to the Levites, who instructed all Israel and who had been consecrated to the LORD: "Put the sacred ark in the temple that Solomon son of David king of Israel built. It is not to be carried about on your shoulders. Now serve the LORD your God and his people Israel. ⁴Prepare yourselves by families in your divisions, according to the instructions written by David king of Israel and by his son Solomon.

⁵"Stand in the holy place with a group

of Levites for each subdivision of the families of your fellow Israelites, the lay people. ⁶Slaughter the Passover lambs, consecrate yourselves and prepare the lambs for your fellow Israelites, doing what the LORD commanded through Moses."

⁷Josiah provided for all the lay people who were there a total of thirty thousand lambs and goats for the Passover offerings, and also three thousand cattle—all from the king's own possessions.

⁸His officials also contributed voluntarily to the people and the priests and Levites. Hilkiah, Zechariah and Jehiel, the officials in charge of God's temple, gave the priests twenty-six hundred Passover offerings and three hundred cattle. ⁹Also Konaniah along with Shemaiah and Nethanel, his brothers, and Hashabiah, Jeiel and Jozabad, the leaders of the Levites, provided five thousand Passover offerings and five hundred head of cattle for the Levites.

¹⁰The service was arranged and the priests stood in their places with the Levites in their divisions as the king had ordered. ¹¹The Passover lambs were slaughtered, and the priests splashed against the altar the blood handed to them, while the Levites skinned the animals. ¹²They set aside the burnt offerings to give them to the subdivisions of the families of the people to offer to the LORD, as it is written in the Book of Moses. They did the same with the cattle. ¹³They roasted the Passover animals over the fire as prescribed, and boiled the holy offerings in pots, caldrons and pans and served them quickly to all the people. ¹⁴After this, they made preparations for themselves and for the priests, because the priests, the descendants of Aaron, were sacrificing the burnt offerings and the fat portions until nightfall. So the Levites made preparations for themselves and for the Aaronic priests.

¹⁵The musicians, the descendants of Asaph, were in the places prescribed by David, Asaph, Heman and Jeduthun the king's seer. The gatekeepers at each gate did not need to leave their posts, because their fellow Levites made the preparations for them.

¹⁶So at that time the entire service of the Lord was carried out for the celebration of the Passover and the offering of burnt offerings on the altar of the Lord, as King Josiah had ordered. ¹⁷The Israelites who were present celebrated the Passover at that time and observed the Festival of Unleavened Bread for seven days. ¹⁸The Passover had not been observed like this in Israel since the days of the prophet Samuel; and none of the kings of Israel had ever celebrated such a Passover as did Josiah, with the priests, the Levites and all Judah and Israel who were there with the people of Jerusalem. ¹⁹This Passover was celebrated in the eighteenth year of Josiah's reign.

The Death of Josiah

²⁰After all this, when Josiah had set the temple in order, Necho king of Egypt went up to fight at Carchemish on the Euphrates, and Josiah marched out to meet him in battle. ²¹But Necho sent messengers to him, saying, "What quarrel is there, king of Judah, between you and me? It is not you I am attacking at this time, but the house with which I am at war. God has told me to hurry; so stop opposing God, who is with me, or he will destroy you."

²²Josiah, however, would not turn away from him, but disguised himself to engage him in battle. He would not listen to what Necho had said at God's command but went to fight him on the plain of Megiddo.

²³Archers shot King Josiah, and he told his officers, "Take me away; I am badly wounded." ²⁴So they took him out of his chariot, put him in his other chariot and brought him to Jerusalem, where he died. He was buried in the tombs of his ancestors, and all Judah and Jerusalem mourned for him.

²⁵Jeremiah composed laments for Josiah, and to this day all the male and female singers commemorate Josiah in the laments. These became a tradition in Israel and are written in the Laments.

²⁶The other events of Josiah's reign and his acts of devotion in accordance with what is written in the Law of the Lord— ²⁷all the events, from beginning to end, are written in the book of the kings of Israel and Judah.

36

¹And the people of the land took Jehoahaz son of Josiah and made him king in Jerusalem in place of his father.

Jehoahaz King of Judah

²Jehoahaz^a was twenty-three years old when he became king, and he reigned in Jerusalem three months. ³The king of Egypt dethroned him in Jerusalem and imposed on Judah a levy of a hundred talents^b of silver and a talent^c of gold. ⁴The king of Egypt made Eliakim, a brother of Jehoahaz, king over Judah and Jerusalem and changed Eliakim's name to Jehoiakim. But Necho took Eliakim's brother Jehoahaz and carried him off to Egypt.

Jehoiakim King of Judah

⁵Jehoiakim was twenty-five years old when he became king, and he reigned in Jerusalem eleven years. He did evil in the eyes of the Lord his God. ⁶Nebuchadnezzar king of Babylon attacked him and bound him with bronze shackles to take him to Babylon. ⁷Nebuchadnezzar also took to Babylon articles from the temple of the Lord and put them in his temple^d there.

⁸The other events of Jehoiakim's reign, the detestable things he did and all that was found against him, are written in the book of the kings of Israel and Judah. And Jehoiachin his son succeeded him as king.

Jehoiachin King of Judah

⁹Jehoiachin was eighteen^e years old when he became king, and he reigned in Jerusalem three months and ten days. He did evil in the eyes of the Lord. ¹⁰In the

^a 2 Hebrew *Joahaz*, a variant of *Jehoahaz*; also in verse 4   ^b 3 That is, about 3 3/4 tons or about 3.4 metric tons   ^c 3 That is, about 75 pounds or about 34 kilograms   ^d 7 Or *palace*   ^e 9 One Hebrew manuscript, some Septuagint manuscripts and Syriac (see also 2 Kings 24:8); most Hebrew manuscripts *eight*

spring, King Nebuchadnezzar sent for him and brought him to Babylon, together with articles of value from the temple of the LORD, and he made Jehoiachin's uncle,*ᵃ* Zedekiah, king over Judah and Jerusalem.

Zedekiah King of Judah

¹¹Zedekiah was twenty-one years old when he became king, and he reigned in Jerusalem eleven years. ¹²He did evil in the eyes of the LORD his God and did not humble himself before Jeremiah the prophet, who spoke the word of the LORD. ¹³He also rebelled against King Nebuchadnezzar, who had made him take an oath in God's name. He became stiff-necked and hardened his heart and would not turn to the LORD, the God of Israel. ¹⁴Furthermore, all the leaders of the priests and the people became more and more unfaithful, following all the detestable practices of the nations and defiling the temple of the LORD, which he had consecrated in Jerusalem.

The Fall of Jerusalem

¹⁵The LORD, the God of their ancestors, sent word to them through his messengers again and again, because he had pity on his people and on his dwelling place. ¹⁶But they mocked God's messengers, despised his words and scoffed at his prophets until the wrath of the LORD was aroused against his people and there was no remedy. ¹⁷He brought up against them the king of the Babylonians,*ᵇ* who killed their young men with the sword in the

sanctuary, and did not spare young men or young women, the elderly or the infirm. God gave them all into the hands of Nebuchadnezzar. ¹⁸He carried to Babylon all the articles from the temple of God, both large and small, and the treasures of the LORD's temple and the treasures of the king and his officials. ¹⁹They set fire to God's temple and broke down the wall of Jerusalem; they burned all the palaces and destroyed everything of value there.

²⁰He carried into exile to Babylon the remnant, who escaped from the sword, and they became servants to him and his successors until the kingdom of Persia came to power. ²¹The land enjoyed its sabbath rests; all the time of its desolation it rested, until the seventy years were completed in fulfillment of the word of the LORD spoken by Jeremiah.

²²In the first year of Cyrus king of Persia, in order to fulfill the word of the LORD spoken by Jeremiah, the LORD moved the heart of Cyrus king of Persia to make a proclamation throughout his realm and also to put it in writing:

²³"This is what Cyrus king of Persia says:

"'The LORD, the God of heaven, has given me all the kingdoms of the earth and he has appointed me to build a temple for him at Jerusalem in Judah. Any of his people among you may go up, and may the LORD their God be with them.'"

ᵃ 10 Hebrew *brother,* that is, relative (see 2 Kings 24:17)   *ᵇ 17* Or *Chaldeans*

EZRA

The book of Ezra tells about the return of the Jews from exile in Babylon. It begins in 539 BC with the decree of Cyrus, king of Persia, which allowed the people to go back to Jerusalem under the leadership of Zerubbabel. The people enthusiastically began rebuilding the temple and resumed making sacrifices. But for eighteen years they were delayed by their enemies from the north. Finally, in 521 BC a decree from Darius, king of Persia, let them continue the building project. The people completed and dedicated the temple in 515 BC.

In 458 BC, Ezra, the priest, returned to Jerusalem with another group of Babylonian exiles. He taught the people the law and reformed their religious life so the other nations around them could see they were God's chosen nation.

Ezra is the author of the books of Ezra and Nehemiah.

Cyrus Helps the Exiles to Return

1 In the first year of Cyrus king of Persia, in order to fulfill the word of the LORD spoken by Jeremiah, the LORD moved the heart of Cyrus king of Persia to make a proclamation throughout his realm and also to put it in writing:

2 "This is what Cyrus king of Persia says:

"'The LORD, the God of heaven, has given me all the kingdoms of the earth and he has appointed me to build a temple for him at Jerusalem in Judah. 3 Any of his people among you may go up to Jerusalem in Judah and build the temple of the LORD, the God of Israel, the God who is in Jerusalem, and may their God be with them. 4 And in any locality where survivors may now be living, the people are to provide them with silver and gold, with goods and livestock, and with freewill offerings for the temple of God in Jerusalem.'"

5 Then the family heads of Judah and Benjamin, and the priests and Levites — everyone whose heart God had moved — prepared to go up and build the house of the LORD in Jerusalem. 6 All their neighbors assisted them with articles of silver and gold, with goods and livestock, and with valuable gifts, in addition to all the freewill offerings.

7 Moreover, King Cyrus brought out the articles belonging to the temple of the LORD, which Nebuchadnezzar had carried away from Jerusalem and had placed in the temple of his god.ᵃ 8 Cyrus king of Persia had them brought by Mithredath the treasurer, who counted them out to Sheshbazzar the prince of Judah.

9 This was the inventory:

gold dishes	30
silver dishes	1,000
silver pansᵇ	29
10 gold bowls	30
matching silver bowls	410
other articles	1,000

11 In all, there were 5,400 articles of gold and of silver. Sheshbazzar brought all these along with the exiles when they came up from Babylon to Jerusalem.

The List of the Exiles Who Returned

2 Now these are the people of the province who came up from the captivity of the exiles, whom Nebuchadnezzar king of Babylon had taken captive to Babylon (they returned to Jerusalem and Judah, each to their own town, 2 in company with Zerubbabel, Joshua, Nehemiah, Seraiah, Reelaiah, Mordecai, Bilshan, Mispar, Bigvai, Rehum and Baanah):

The list of the men of the people of Israel:

3 the descendants of Parosh	2,172
4 of Shephatiah	372

UNSHAKEN God

Ezra 1:1 – 4

God is all-knowing.

In his first year as king of Persia, Cyrus made a bold announcement. The people of God — who decades before had been dragged away from Judah as captives — could go back to their homeland. Not only could they live in freedom, but they could build a new temple in Jerusalem. That kingly proclamation was even more amazing because God had foretold long ago it would happen. More than a century before, the prophet Isaiah prophesied that a ruler named Cyrus would issue that decree (see Isaiah 44:28; 45:1). It's a small but stunning sign that your God is "omniscient," or "all-knowing." He knows every fact, even before it happens.

So ... God knows everything, everywhere, at every time. Is that good or bad? Why?

ᵃ 7 Or *gods*   ᵇ 9 The meaning of the Hebrew for this word is uncertain.

⁵ of Arah   775
⁶ of Pahath-Moab (through
the line of Jeshua and
Joab)   2,812
⁷ of Elam   1,254
⁸ of Zattu   945
⁹ of Zakkai   760
¹⁰ of Bani   642
¹¹ of Bebai   623
¹² of Azgad   1,222
¹³ of Adonikam   666
¹⁴ of Bigvai   2,056
¹⁵ of Adin   454
¹⁶ of Ater (through
Hezekiah)   98
¹⁷ of Bezai   323
¹⁸ of Jorah   112
¹⁹ of Hashum   223
²⁰ of Gibbar   95

²¹ the men of Bethlehem   123
²² of Netophah   56
²³ of Anathoth   128
²⁴ of Azmaveth   42
²⁵ of Kiriath Jearim,ᵃ
Kephirah and Beeroth   743
²⁶ of Ramah and Geba   621
²⁷ of Mikmash   122
²⁸ of Bethel and Ai   223
²⁹ of Nebo   52
³⁰ of Magbish   156
³¹ of the other Elam   1,254
³² of Harim   320
³³ of Lod, Hadid and Ono   725
³⁴ of Jericho   345
³⁵ of Senaah   3,630

³⁶ The priests:

the descendants of Jedaiah
(through the family
of Jeshua)   973
³⁷ of Immer   1,052
³⁸ of Pashhur   1,247
³⁹ of Harim   1,017

⁴⁰ The Levites:

the descendants of Jeshua
and Kadmiel (of the line
of Hodaviah)   74

⁴¹ The musicians:

the descendants of Asaph   128

⁴² The gatekeepers of the temple:

the descendants of
Shallum, Ater, Talmon,
Akkub, Hatita and
Shobai   139

⁴³ The temple servants:

the descendants of
Ziha, Hasupha, Tabbaoth,
⁴⁴ Keros, Siaha, Padon,
⁴⁵ Lebanah, Hagabah, Akkub,
⁴⁶ Hagab, Shalmai, Hanan,
⁴⁷ Giddel, Gahar, Reaiah,
⁴⁸ Rezin, Nekoda, Gazzam,
⁴⁹ Uzza, Paseah, Besai,
⁵⁰ Asnah, Meunim, Nephusim,
⁵¹ Bakbuk, Hakupha, Harhur,
⁵² Bazluth, Mehida, Harsha,
⁵³ Barkos, Sisera, Temah,
⁵⁴ Neziah and Hatipha

⁵⁵ The descendants of the servants of
Solomon:

the descendants of
Sotai, Hassophereth, Peruda,
⁵⁶ Jaala, Darkon, Giddel,
⁵⁷ Shephatiah, Hattil,
Pokereth-Hazzebaim and Ami

⁵⁸ The temple servants and the
descendants of the servants
of Solomon   392

⁵⁹ The following came up from
the towns of Tel Melah, Tel Harsha,
Kerub, Addon and Immer, but they
could not show that their families
were descended from Israel:

⁶⁰ The descendants of
Delaiah, Tobiah and
Nekoda   652

⁶¹ And from among the priests:

The descendants of
Hobaiah, Hakkoz and
Barzillai (a man who had
married a daughter of Barzillai
the Gileadite and was called by
that name).

ᵃ 25 See Septuagint (see also Neh. 7:29);
Hebrew *Kiriath Arim.*

⁶²These searched for their family records, but they could not find them and so were excluded from the priesthood as unclean. ⁶³The governor ordered them not to eat any of the most sacred food until there was a priest ministering with the Urim and Thummim.

⁶⁴The whole company numbered 42,360, ⁶⁵besides their 7,337 male and female slaves; and they also had 200 male and female singers. ⁶⁶They had 736 horses, 245 mules, ⁶⁷435 camels and 6,720 donkeys.

⁶⁸When they arrived at the house of the LORD in Jerusalem, some of the heads of the families gave freewill offerings toward the rebuilding of the house of God on its site. ⁶⁹According to their ability they gave to the treasury for this work 61,000 darics*a* of gold, 5,000 minas*b* of silver and 100 priestly garments.

⁷⁰The priests, the Levites, the musicians, the gatekeepers and the temple servants settled in their own towns, along with some of the other people, and the rest of the Israelites settled in their towns.

Rebuilding the Altar

3 When the seventh month came and the Israelites had settled in their towns, the people assembled together as one in Jerusalem. ²Then Joshua son of Jozadak and his fellow priests and Zerubbabel son of Shealtiel and his associates began to build the altar of the God of Israel to sacrifice burnt offerings on it, in accordance with what is written in the Law of Moses the man of God. ³Despite their fear of the peoples around them, they built the altar on its foundation and sacrificed burnt offerings on it to the LORD, both the morning and evening sacrifices. ⁴Then in accordance with what is written, they celebrated the Festival of Tabernacles with the required number of burnt offerings prescribed for each day. ⁵After that, they presented the regular burnt offerings, the New Moon sacrifices and the sacrifices for all the appointed sacred festivals of the LORD, as well as those brought as freewill offerings to the LORD. ⁶On the first day of the seventh month they began to offer burnt offerings to the LORD, though the foundation of the LORD's temple had not yet been laid.

Rebuilding the Temple

⁷Then they gave money to the masons and carpenters, and gave food and drink and olive oil to the people of Sidon and Tyre, so that they would bring cedar logs by sea from Lebanon to Joppa, as authorized by Cyrus king of Persia.

⁸In the second month of the second year after their arrival at the house of God in Jerusalem, Zerubbabel son of Shealtiel, Joshua son of Jozadak and the rest of the people (the priests and the Levites and all who had returned from the captivity to Jerusalem) began the work. They appointed Levites twenty years old and older to supervise the building of the house of the LORD. ⁹Joshua and his sons and brothers and Kadmiel and his sons (descendants of Hodaviah*c*) and the sons of Henadad and their sons and brothers—all Levites—joined together in supervising those working on the house of God.

¹⁰When the builders laid the foundation of the temple of the LORD, the priests in their vestments and with trumpets, and the Levites (the sons of Asaph) with cymbals, took their places to praise the LORD, as prescribed by David king of Israel. ¹¹With praise and thanksgiving they sang to the LORD:

"He is good;
    his love toward Israel endures
        forever."

And all the people gave a great shout of praise to the LORD, because the foundation of the house of the LORD was laid. ¹²But many of the older priests and Levites and family heads, who had seen the former temple, wept aloud when they saw the foundation of this temple being laid,

---

a 69 That is, about 1,100 pounds or about 500 kilograms   *b 69* That is, about 3 tons or about 2.8 metric tons   *c 9* Hebrew *Yehudah,* a variant of *Hodaviah* while many others shouted for joy. ¹³No one could distinguish the sound of the shouts of joy from the sound of weeping, because the people made so much noise. And the sound was heard far away.

Opposition to the Rebuilding

4 When the enemies of Judah and Benjamin heard that the exiles were building a temple for the LORD, the God of Israel, ²they came to Zerubbabel and to the heads of the families and said, "Let us help you build because, like you, we seek your God and have been sacrificing to him since the time of Esarhaddon king of Assyria, who brought us here."

³But Zerubbabel, Joshua and the rest of the heads of the families of Israel answered, "You have no part with us in building a temple to our God. We alone will build it for the LORD, the God of Israel, as King Cyrus, the king of Persia, commanded us."

⁴Then the peoples around them set out to discourage the people of Judah and make them afraid to go on building.ᵃ ⁵They bribed officials to work against them and frustrate their plans during the entire reign of Cyrus king of Persia and down to the reign of Darius king of Persia.

Later Opposition Under Xerxes and Artaxerxes

⁶At the beginning of the reign of Xerxes,ᵇ they lodged an accusation against the people of Judah and Jerusalem.

⁷And in the days of Artaxerxes king of Persia, Bishlam, Mithredath, Tabeel and the rest of his associates wrote a letter to Artaxerxes. The letter was written in Aramaic script and in the Aramaic language.ᶜ,ᵈ

⁸Rehum the commanding officer and Shimshai the secretary wrote a letter against Jerusalem to Artaxerxes the king as follows:

⁹Rehum the commanding officer and Shimshai the secretary, together with the rest of their associates—the judges, officials and administrators over the people from Persia, Uruk and

Babylon, the Elamites of Susa, ¹⁰and the other people whom the great and honorable Ashurbanipal deported and settled in the city of Samaria and elsewhere in Trans-Euphrates.

¹¹(This is a copy of the letter they sent him.)

ᵃ 4 Or *and troubled them as they built*
ᵇ 6 Hebrew *Ahasuerus*   ᶜ 7 Or *written in Aramaic and translated*   ᵈ 7 The text of 4:8 – 6:18 is in Aramaic.

Ezra 4:1 – 5

You can expect opposition to God's work.

Zerubbabel's refusal of help to rebuild the temple in Jerusalem sounded harsh. These volunteers, after all, sounded so eager to help. They claimed that they too worshiped the Lord, the God of Israel. But Zerubbabel shut them out completely. Why? Because these potential workers were the offspring of Israelites who had married foreigners. They were guilty of mixing true worship of the one real God with their own false religions, the sin that caused God to send his people into captivity (see 2 Kings 17:9 – 10). So Zerubbabel saw their help as an effort to undo authentic, whole-hearted commitment to God. That's the kind of opposition you can expect when you attempt to accomplish something for God. Some people might outright oppose your efforts. But others just want to sneak in and mess you up.

Think: Why do people trying to do good things to honor God often encounter opposition?

ROCK SOLID truths

To King Artaxerxes,

From your servants in Trans-Euphrates:

¹²The king should know that the people who came up to us from you have gone to Jerusalem and are rebuilding that rebellious and wicked city. They are restoring the walls and repairing the foundations.

¹³Furthermore, the king should know that if this city is built and its walls are restored, no more taxes, tribute or duty will be paid, and eventually the royal revenues will suffer.ᵃ ¹⁴Now since we are under obligation to the palace and it is not proper for us to see the king dishonored, we are sending this message to inform the king, ¹⁵so that a search may be made in the archives of your predecessors. In these records you will find that this city is a rebellious city, troublesome to kings and provinces, a place with a long history of sedition. That is why this city was destroyed. ¹⁶We inform the king that if this city is built and its walls are restored, you will be left with nothing in Trans-Euphrates.

¹⁷The king sent this reply:

To Rehum the commanding officer, Shimshai the secretary and the rest of their associates living in Samaria and elsewhere in Trans-Euphrates:

Greetings.

¹⁸The letter you sent us has been read and translated in my presence. ¹⁹I issued an order and a search was made, and it was found that this city has a long history of revolt against kings and has been a place of rebellion and sedition. ²⁰Jerusalem has had powerful kings ruling over the whole of Trans-Euphrates, and taxes, tribute and duty were paid to them. ²¹Now issue an order to these men to stop work, so that this city will not be rebuilt until I so order. ²²Be careful

not to neglect this matter. Why let this threat grow, to the detriment of the royal interests?

²³As soon as the copy of the letter of King Artaxerxes was read to Rehum and Shimshai the secretary and their associates, they went immediately to the Jews in Jerusalem and compelled them by force to stop.

²⁴Thus the work on the house of God in Jerusalem came to a standstill until the second year of the reign of Darius king of Persia.

Tattenai's Letter to Darius

5 Now Haggai the prophet and Zechariah the prophet, a descendant of Iddo, prophesied to the Jews in Judah and Jerusalem in the name of the God of Israel, who was over them. ²Then Zerubbabel son of Shealtiel and Joshua son of Jozadak set to work to rebuild the house of God in Jerusalem. And the prophets of God were with them, supporting them.

³At that time Tattenai, governor of Trans-Euphrates, and Shethar-Bozenai and their associates went to them and asked, "Who authorized you to rebuild this temple and to finish it?" ⁴Theyᵇ also asked, "What are the names of those who are constructing this building?" ⁵But the eye of their God was watching over the elders of the Jews, and they were not stopped until a report could go to Darius and his written reply be received.

⁶This is a copy of the letter that Tattenai, governor of Trans-Euphrates, and Shethar-Bozenai and their associates, the officials of Trans-Euphrates, sent to King Darius. ⁷The report they sent him read as follows:

To King Darius:

Cordial greetings.

⁸The king should know that we went to the district of Judah, to the

---

ᵃ 13 The meaning of the Aramaic for this clause is uncertain.   ᵇ 4 See Septuagint; Aramaic We.

temple of the great God. The people are building it with large stones and placing the timbers in the walls. The work is being carried on with diligence and is making rapid progress under their direction.

⁹We questioned the elders and asked them, "Who authorized you to rebuild this temple and to finish it?" ¹⁰We also asked them their names, so that we could write down the names of their leaders for your information.

¹¹This is the answer they gave us:

"We are the servants of the God of heaven and earth, and we are rebuilding the temple that was built many years ago, one that a great king of Israel built and finished. ¹²But because our ancestors angered the God of heaven, he gave them into the hands of Nebuchadnezzar the Chaldean, king of Babylon, who destroyed this temple and deported the people to Babylon.

¹³"However, in the first year of Cyrus king of Babylon, King Cyrus issued a decree to rebuild this house of God. ¹⁴He even removed from the temple*ᵃ* of Babylon the gold and silver articles of the house of God, which Nebuchadnezzar had taken from the temple in Jerusalem and brought to the temple*ᵃ* in Babylon. Then King Cyrus gave them to a man named Sheshbazzar, whom he had appointed governor, ¹⁵and he told him, 'Take these articles and go and deposit them in the temple in Jerusalem. And rebuild the house of God on its site.'

¹⁶"So this Sheshbazzar came and laid the foundations of the house of God in Jerusalem. From that day to the present it has been under construction but is not yet finished."

¹⁷Now if it pleases the king, let a search be made in the royal archives of Babylon to see if King Cyrus did in fact issue a decree to rebuild this house of God in Jerusalem. Then let the king send us his decision in this matter.

The Decree of Darius

6 King Darius then issued an order, and they searched in the archives stored in the treasury at Babylon. ²A scroll was found in the citadel of Ecbatana in the province of Media, and this was written on it:

Memorandum:

³In the first year of King Cyrus, the king issued a decree concerning the temple of God in Jerusalem:

Let the temple be rebuilt as a place to present sacrifices, and let its foundations be laid. It is to be sixty cubits*ᵇ* high and sixty cubits wide, ⁴with three courses of large stones and one of timbers. The costs are to be paid by the royal treasury. ⁵Also, the gold and silver articles of the house of God, which Nebuchadnezzar took from the temple in Jerusalem and brought to Babylon, are to be returned to their places in the temple in Jerusalem; they are to be deposited in the house of God.

⁶Now then, Tattenai, governor of Trans-Euphrates, and Shethar-Bozenai and you other officials of that province, stay away from there. ⁷Do not interfere with the work on this temple of God. Let the governor of the Jews and the Jewish elders rebuild this house of God on its site.

⁸Moreover, I hereby decree what you are to do for these elders of the Jews in the construction of this house of God:

Their expenses are to be fully paid out of the royal treasury, from the revenues of Trans-Euphrates, so that the work will not stop. ⁹Whatever is needed—young bulls, rams, male lambs for burnt offerings to the God of heaven, and wheat, salt, wine and

---

ᵃ 14 Or *palace*   *ᵇ 3* That is, about 90 feet or about 27 meters olive oil, as requested by the priests in Jerusalem—must be given them daily without fail, [10] so that they may offer sacrifices pleasing to the God of heaven and pray for the well-being of the king and his sons.

[11] Furthermore, I decree that if anyone defies this edict, a beam is to be pulled from their house and they are to be impaled on it. And for this crime their house is to be made a pile of rubble. [12] May God, who has caused his Name to dwell there, overthrow any king or people who lifts a hand to change this decree or to destroy this temple in Jerusalem.

I Darius have decreed it. Let it be carried out with diligence.

Completion and Dedication of the Temple

[13] Then, because of the decree King Darius had sent, Tattenai, governor of Trans-Euphrates, and Shethar-Bozenai and their associates carried it out with diligence. [14] So the elders of the Jews continued to build and prosper under the preaching of Haggai the prophet and Zechariah, a descendant of Iddo. They finished building the temple according to the command of the God of Israel and the decrees of Cyrus, Darius and Artaxerxes, kings of Persia. [15] The temple was completed on the third day of the month Adar, in the sixth year of the reign of King Darius.

[16] Then the people of Israel—the priests, the Levites and the rest of the exiles—celebrated the dedication of the house of God with joy. [17] For the dedication of this house of God they offered a hundred bulls, two hundred rams, four hundred male lambs and, as a sin offering[a] for all Israel, twelve male goats, one for each of the tribes of Israel. [18] And they installed the priests in their divisions and the Levites in their groups for the service of God at Jerusalem, according to what is written in the Book of Moses.

The Passover

[19] On the fourteenth day of the first month, the exiles celebrated the Pass-

over. [20] The priests and Levites had purified themselves and were all ceremonially clean. The Levites slaughtered the Passover lamb for all the exiles, for their relatives the priests and for themselves. [21] So the Israelites who had returned from the exile ate it, together with all who had separated themselves from the unclean practices of their Gentile neighbors in order to seek the LORD, the God of Israel. [22] For seven days they celebrated with joy the Festival of Unleavened Bread, because the LORD had filled them with joy by changing the attitude of the king of Assyria so that he assisted them in the work on the house of God, the God of Israel.

Ezra Comes to Jerusalem

7 After these things, during the reign of Artaxerxes king of Persia, Ezra son of Seraiah, the son of Azariah, the son of Hilkiah, [2] the son of Shallum, the son of Zadok, the son of Ahitub, [3] the son of Amariah, the son of Azariah, the son of Meraioth, [4] the son of Zerahiah, the son of Uzzi, the son of Bukki, [5] the son of Abishua, the son of Phinehas, the son of Eleazar, the son of Aaron the chief priest— [6] this Ezra came up from Babylon. He was a teacher well versed in the Law of Moses, which the LORD, the God of Israel, had given. The king had granted him everything he asked, for the hand of the LORD his God was on him. [7] Some of the Israelites, including priests, Levites, musicians, gatekeepers and temple servants, also came up to Jerusalem in the seventh year of King Artaxerxes.

[8] Ezra arrived in Jerusalem in the fifth month of the seventh year of the king. [9] He had begun his journey from Babylon on the first day of the first month, and he arrived in Jerusalem on the first day of the fifth month, for the gracious hand of his God was on him. [10] For Ezra had devoted himself to the study and observance of the Law of the LORD, and to teaching its decrees and laws in Israel.

---

[a] 17 Or *purification offering*

King Artaxerxes' Letter to Ezra

[11] This is a copy of the letter King Artaxerxes had given to Ezra the priest, a teacher of the Law, a man learned in matters concerning the commands and decrees of the LORD for Israel:

[12] Artaxerxes, king of kings,

To Ezra the priest, teacher of the Law of the God of heaven:

Greetings.

[13] Now I decree that any of the Israelites in my kingdom, including priests and Levites, who volunteer to go to Jerusalem with you, may go. [14] You are sent by the king and his seven advisers to inquire about Judah and Jerusalem with regard to the Law of your God, which is in your hand. [15] Moreover, you are to take with you the silver and gold that the king and his advisers have freely given to the God of Israel, whose dwelling is in Jerusalem, [16] together with all the silver and gold you may obtain from the province of Babylon, as well as the freewill offerings of the people and priests for the temple of their God in Jerusalem. [17] With this money be sure to buy bulls, rams and male lambs, together with their grain offerings and drink offerings, and sacrifice them on the altar of the temple of your God in Jerusalem.

[18] You and your fellow Israelites may then do whatever seems best with the rest of the silver and gold, in accordance with the will of your God. [19] Deliver to the God of Jerusalem all the articles entrusted to you for worship in the temple of your God. [20] And anything else needed for the temple of your God that you are responsible to supply, you may provide from the royal treasury.

[21] Now I, King Artaxerxes, decree that all the treasurers of Trans-Euphrates are to provide with diligence whatever Ezra the priest, the teacher of the Law of the God of heaven,

may ask of you— [22] up to a hundred talents[a] of silver, a hundred cors[b] of wheat, a hundred baths[c] of wine, a hundred baths[c] of olive oil, and salt without limit. [23] Whatever the God of heaven has prescribed, let it be done with diligence for the temple of the God of heaven. Why should his wrath fall on the realm of the king and of his sons? [24] You are also to know that you have no authority to impose taxes, tribute or duty on any of the priests, Levites, musicians, gatekeepers, temple servants or other workers at this house of God.

[25] And you, Ezra, in accordance with the wisdom of your God, which you possess, appoint magistrates and judges to administer justice to all the people of Trans-Euphrates—all who know the laws of your God. And you are to teach any who do not know them. [26] Whoever does not obey the law of your God and the law of the king must surely be punished by death, banishment, confiscation of property, or imprisonment.[d]

[27] Praise be to the LORD, the God of our ancestors, who has put it into the king's heart to bring honor to the house of the LORD in Jerusalem in this way [28] and who has extended his good favor to me before the king and his advisers and all the king's powerful officials. Because the hand of the LORD my God was on me, I took courage and gathered leaders from Israel to go up with me.

List of the Family Heads Returning With Ezra

8 These are the family heads and those registered with them who came up with me from Babylon during the reign of King Artaxerxes:

[2] of the descendants of Phinehas, Gershom;

---

[a] 22 That is, about 3 3/4 tons or about 3.4 metric tons   [b] 22 That is, probably about 18 tons or about 16 metric tons   [c] 22 That is, about 600 gallons or about 2,200 liters
[d] 26 The text of 7:12-26 is in Aramaic.

of the descendants of Ithamar, Daniel;

of the descendants of David, Hattush ³of the descendants of Shekaniah;

of the descendants of Parosh, Zechariah, and with him were registered 150 men;

⁴of the descendants of Pahath-Moab, Eliehoenai son of Zerahiah, and with him 200 men;

⁵of the descendants of Zattu,ª Shekaniah son of Jahaziel, and with him 300 men;

⁶of the descendants of Adin, Ebed son of Jonathan, and with him 50 men;

⁷of the descendants of Elam, Jeshaiah son of Athaliah, and with him 70 men;

⁸of the descendants of Shephatiah, Zebadiah son of Michael, and with him 80 men;

⁹of the descendants of Joab, Obadiah son of Jehiel, and with him 218 men;

¹⁰of the descendants of Bani,ᵇ Shelomith son of Josiphiah, and with him 160 men;

¹¹of the descendants of Bebai, Zechariah son of Bebai, and with him 28 men;

¹²of the descendants of Azgad, Johanan son of Hakkatan, and with him 110 men;

¹³of the descendants of Adonikam, the last ones, whose names were Eliphelet, Jeuel and Shemaiah, and with them 60 men;

¹⁴of the descendants of Bigvai, Uthai and Zakkur, and with them 70 men.

The Return to Jerusalem

¹⁵I assembled them at the canal that flows toward Ahava, and we camped there three days. When I checked among the people and the priests, I found no Levites there. ¹⁶So I summoned Eliezer, Ariel, Shemaiah, Elnathan, Jarib, Elnathan, Nathan, Zechariah and Meshullam, who were leaders, and Joiarib and Elnathan, who were men of learning, ¹⁷and I ordered them to go to Iddo, the leader in

Kasiphia. I told them what to say to Iddo and his fellow Levites, the temple servants in Kasiphia, so that they might bring attendants to us for the house of our God. ¹⁸Because the gracious hand of our God was on us, they brought us Sherebiah, a capable man, from the descendants of Mahli son of Levi, the son of Israel, and Sherebiah's sons and brothers, 18 in all; ¹⁹and Hashabiah, together with Jeshaiah from the descendants of Merari, and his brothers and nephews, 20 in all. ²⁰They also brought 220 of the temple servants—a body that David and the officials had established to assist the Levites. All were registered by name.

²¹There, by the Ahava Canal, I proclaimed a fast, so that we might humble ourselves before our God and ask him for a safe journey for us and our children, with all our possessions. ²²I was ashamed to ask the king for soldiers and horsemen to protect us from enemies on the road, because we had told the king, "The gracious hand of our God is on everyone who looks to him, but his great anger is against all who forsake him." ²³So we fasted and petitioned our God about this, and he answered our prayer.

ª 5 Some Septuagint manuscripts (also 1 Esdras 8:32); Hebrew does not have *Zattu.*
ᵇ 10 Some Septuagint manuscripts (also 1 Esdras 8:36); Hebrew does not have *Bani.*

ROCK SOLID
promises

"The gracious hand of our God is on everyone who looks to him."

Ezra 8:22

When you depend on God alone, he will give you more than you can ever deserve or imagine.

²⁴Then I set apart twelve of the leading priests, namely, Sherebiah, Hashabiah and ten of their brothers, ²⁵and I weighed out to them the offering of silver and gold and the articles that the king, his advisers, his officials and all Israel present there had donated for the house of our God. ²⁶I weighed out to them 650 talents*ᵃ* of silver, silver articles weighing 100 talents,*ᵇ* 100 talents*ᵇ* of gold, ²⁷20 bowls of gold valued at 1,000 darics,*ᶜ* and two fine articles of polished bronze, as precious as gold.

²⁸I said to them, "You as well as these articles are consecrated to the LORD. The silver and gold are a freewill offering to the LORD, the God of your ancestors. ²⁹Guard them carefully until you weigh them out in the chambers of the house of the LORD in Jerusalem before the leading priests and the Levites and the family heads of Israel." ³⁰Then the priests and Levites received the silver and gold and sacred articles that had been weighed out to be taken to the house of our God in Jerusalem.

³¹On the twelfth day of the first month we set out from the Ahava Canal to go to Jerusalem. The hand of our God was on us, and he protected us from enemies and bandits along the way. ³²So we arrived in Jerusalem, where we rested three days.

³³On the fourth day, in the house of our God, we weighed out the silver and gold and the sacred articles into the hands of Meremoth son of Uriah, the priest. Eleazar son of Phinehas was with him, and so were the Levites Jozabad son of Jeshua and Noadiah son of Binnui. ³⁴Everything was accounted for by number and weight, and the entire weight was recorded at that time.

³⁵Then the exiles who had returned from captivity sacrificed burnt offerings to the God of Israel: twelve bulls for all Israel, ninety-six rams, seventy-seven male lambs and, as a sin offering,*ᵈ* twelve male goats. All this was a burnt offering to the LORD. ³⁶They also delivered the king's orders to the royal satraps and to the governors of Trans-Euphrates, who then gave assistance to the people and to the house of God.

Ezra's Prayer About Intermarriage

9 After these things had been done, the leaders came to me and said, "The people of Israel, including the priests and the Levites, have not kept themselves separate from the neighboring peoples with their detestable practices, like those of the Canaanites, Hittites, Perizzites, Jebusites, Ammonites, Moabites, Egyptians and Amorites. ²They have taken some of their daughters as wives for themselves and their sons, and have mingled the holy race with the peoples around them. And the leaders and officials have led the way in this unfaithfulness."

³When I heard this, I tore my tunic and cloak, pulled hair from my head and beard and sat down appalled. ⁴Then everyone who trembled at the words of the God of Israel gathered around me because of this unfaithfulness of the exiles. And I sat there appalled until the evening sacrifice.

⁵Then, at the evening sacrifice, I rose from my self-abasement, with my tunic and cloak torn, and fell on my knees with my hands spread out to the LORD my God ⁶and prayed:

"I am too ashamed and disgraced, my God, to lift up my face to you, because our sins are higher than our heads and our guilt has reached to the heavens. ⁷From the days of our ancestors until now, our guilt has been great. Because of our sins, we and our kings and our priests have been subjected to the sword and captivity, to pillage and humiliation at the hand of foreign kings, as it is today.

⁸"But now, for a brief moment, the LORD our God has been gracious in leaving us a remnant and giving us a firm place*ᵉ* in his sanctuary, and so our God gives light to our eyes and a little relief in our bondage. ⁹Though we are slaves, our God has not forsaken us in our bondage. He

---

ᵃ 26 That is, about 24 tons or about 22 metric tons   *ᵇ 26* That is, about 3 3/4 tons or about 3.4 metric tons   *ᶜ 27* That is, about 19 pounds or about 8.4 kilograms   *ᵈ 35* Or *purification offering*   *ᵉ 8* Or *a foothold* has shown us kindness in the sight of the kings of Persia: He has granted us new life to rebuild the house of our God and repair its ruins, and he has given us a wall of protection in Judah and Jerusalem.

¹⁰"But now, our God, what can we say after this? For we have forsaken the commands ¹¹you gave through your servants the prophets when you said: 'The land you are entering to possess is a land polluted by the corruption of its peoples. By their detestable practices they have filled it with their impurity from one end to the other. ¹²Therefore, do not give your daughters in marriage to their sons or take their daughters for your sons. Do not seek a treaty of friendship with them at any time, that you may be strong and eat the good things of the land and leave it to your children as an everlasting inheritance.'

¹³"What has happened to us is a result of our evil deeds and our great guilt, and yet, our God, you have punished us less than our sins deserved and have given us a remnant like this. ¹⁴Shall we then break your commands again and intermarry with the peoples who commit such detestable practices? Would you not be angry enough with us to destroy us, leaving us no remnant or survivor? ¹⁵LORD, the God of Israel, you are righteous! We are left this day as a remnant. Here we are before you in our guilt, though because of it not one of us can stand in your presence."

The People's Confession of Sin

10 While Ezra was praying and confessing, weeping and throwing himself down before the house of God, a large crowd of Israelites—men, women and children— gathered around him. They too wept bitterly. ²Then Shekaniah son of Jehiel, one

ROCK SOLID principles

Ezra 9:1–15

Pick a Christian spouse.

Grant never went to church until his best soccer friend invited him. When Grant started getting interested in girls, his parents said he could date anyone he wanted and they weren't going to lay down any rules. But Grant had heard at church that he should only go out with girls who were authentic followers of Christ. So now Grant faced a choice. He could chase whatever girl he wanted and do whatever he thought was fun, or he could deliberately limit his options to girls who also wanted to trust in God and stay pure. No one was going to make up his mind for him. Grant had to choose.

God gave strict instructions to his people when they entered the promised land: Don't marry the people living in the land, because pagan spouses would lead people away from the one true God (see Judges 3:1–6). By the time of Ezra, an enormous sin had to be undone. The Lord has the same expectation today—that you pick a spouse devoted to him (see 1 Corinthians 6:14–17).

of the descendants of Elam, said to Ezra, "We have been unfaithful to our God by marrying foreign women from the peoples around us. But in spite of this, there is still hope for Israel. ³Now let us make a covenant before our God to send away all these women and their children, in accordance with the counsel of my lord and of those who fear the commands of our God. Let it be done according to the Law. ⁴Rise up; this matter is in your hands. We will support you, so take courage and do it."

⁵So Ezra rose up and put the leading priests and Levites and all Israel under oath to do what had been suggested. And they took the oath. ⁶Then Ezra withdrew from before the house of God and went to the room of Jehohanan son of Eliashib. While he was there, he ate no food and drank no water, because he continued to mourn over the unfaithfulness of the exiles.

⁷A proclamation was then issued throughout Judah and Jerusalem for all the exiles to assemble in Jerusalem. ⁸Anyone who failed to appear within three days would forfeit all his property, in accordance with the decision of the officials and elders, and would himself be expelled from the assembly of the exiles.

⁹Within the three days, all the men of Judah and Benjamin had gathered in Jerusalem. And on the twentieth day of the ninth month, all the people were sitting in the square before the house of God, greatly distressed by the occasion and because of the rain. ¹⁰Then Ezra the priest stood up and said to them, "You have been unfaithful; you have married foreign women, adding to Israel's guilt. ¹¹Now honor*a* the Lord, the God of your ancestors, and do his will. Separate yourselves from the peoples around you and from your foreign wives."

¹²The whole assembly responded with a loud voice: "You are right! We must do as you say. ¹³But there are many people here and it is the rainy season; so we cannot stand outside. Besides, this matter cannot be taken care of in a day or two, because we have sinned greatly in this thing. ¹⁴Let our officials act for the whole assembly. Then let everyone in our towns who has married a foreign woman come at a set time, along with the elders and judges of each town, until the fierce anger of our God in this matter is turned away from us." ¹⁵Only Jonathan son of Asahel and Jahzeiah son of Tikvah, supported by Meshullam and Shabbethai the Levite, opposed this.

¹⁶So the exiles did as was proposed. Ezra the priest selected men who were family heads, one from each family division, and all of them designated by name. On the first day of the tenth month they sat down to investigate the cases, ¹⁷and by the first day of the first month they finished dealing with all the men who had married foreign women.

Those Guilty of Intermarriage

¹⁸Among the descendants of the priests, the following had married foreign women:

From the descendants of Joshua son of Jozadak, and his brothers: Maaseiah, Eliezer, Jarib and Gedaliah. ¹⁹(They all gave their hands in pledge to put away their wives, and for their guilt they each presented a ram from the flock as a guilt offering.)

²⁰From the descendants of Immer: Hanani and Zebadiah.

²¹From the descendants of Harim: Maaseiah, Elijah, Shemaiah, Jehiel and Uzziah.

²²From the descendants of Pashhur: Elioenai, Maaseiah, Ishmael, Nethanel, Jozabad and Elasah.

²³Among the Levites:

Jozabad, Shimei, Kelaiah (that is, Kelita), Pethahiah, Judah and Eliezer.

²⁴From the musicians: Eliashib.

From the gatekeepers: Shallum, Telem and Uri.

a 11 Or *Now make confession to*

25 And among the other Israelites:

From the descendants of Parosh:
Ramiah, Izziah, Malkijah, Mijamin,
Eleazar, Malkijah and Benaiah.

26 From the descendants of Elam:
Mattaniah, Zechariah, Jehiel,
Abdi, Jeremoth and Elijah.

27 From the descendants of Zattu:
Elioenai, Eliashib, Mattaniah, Jeremoth, Zabad and Aziza.

28 From the descendants of Bebai:
Jehohanan, Hananiah, Zabbai and
Athlai.

29 From the descendants of Bani:
Meshullam, Malluk, Adaiah, Jashub, Sheal and Jeremoth.

30 From the descendants of Pahath-Moab:
Adna, Kelal, Benaiah, Maaseiah,
Mattaniah, Bezalel, Binnui and
Manasseh.

31 From the descendants of Harim:
Eliezer, Ishijah, Malkijah, Shemaiah, Shimeon, 32 Benjamin, Malluk
and Shemariah.

33 From the descendants of Hashum:
Mattenai, Mattattah, Zabad,
Eliphelet, Jeremai, Manasseh and
Shimei.

34 From the descendants of Bani:
Maadai, Amram, Uel, 35 Benaiah,
Bedeiah, Keluhi, 36 Vaniah, Meremoth, Eliashib, 37 Mattaniah,
Mattenai and Jaasu.

38 From the descendants of Binnui:*a*
Shimei, 39 Shelemiah, Nathan,
Adaiah, 40 Maknadebai, Shashai,
Sharai, 41 Azarel, Shelemiah,
Shemariah, 42 Shallum, Amariah
and Joseph.

43 From the descendants of Nebo:
Jeiel, Mattithiah, Zabad, Zebina,
Jaddai, Joel and Benaiah.

44 All these had married foreign women,
and some of them had children by these
wives.*b*

a 37,38 See Septuagint (also 1 Esdras 9:34);
Hebrew *Jaasu 38 and Bani and Binnui,*
b 44 Or *and they sent them away with their
children*

BOOK OUTLINE

Nehemiah rebuilds the walls
(1:1 — 7:3)

Change under Ezra
(7:4 — 10:39)

Nehemiah's plans
(11:1 — 13:31)

NEHEMIAH

The book of Nehemiah continues the history of the Jews who returned from exile in Babylon. Nehemiah gave up his job as cupbearer to Artaxerxes, the Persian king, to become governor of Jerusalem. Nehemiah went to Jerusalem in 444 BC, almost 100 years after the return of the first exiles. Nehemiah led the people in repairing the walls of Jerusalem and with Ezra provided leadership for the people. An important part of this book is the description of the importance of prayer to Nehemiah.

Nehemiah's Prayer

1 The words of Nehemiah son of Hakaliah:

In the month of Kislev in the twentieth year, while I was in the citadel of Susa, ²Hanani, one of my brothers, came from Judah with some other men, and I questioned them about the Jewish remnant that had survived the exile, and also about Jerusalem.

³They said to me, "Those who survived the exile and are back in the province are in great trouble and disgrace. The wall of Jerusalem is broken down, and its gates have been burned with fire."

⁴When I heard these things, I sat down and wept. For some days I mourned and fasted and prayed before the God of heaven. ⁵Then I said:

"LORD, the God of heaven, the great and awesome God, who keeps his covenant of love with those who love him and keep his commandments, ⁶let your ear be attentive and your eyes open to hear the prayer your servant is praying before you day and night for your servants, the people of Israel. I confess the sins we Israelites, including myself and my father's family, have committed against you. ⁷We have acted very wickedly toward you. We have not obeyed the commands, decrees and laws you gave your servant Moses.

⁸"Remember the instruction you gave your servant Moses, saying, 'If you are unfaithful, I will scatter you among the nations, ⁹but if you return to me and obey my commands, then even if your exiled people are at the farthest horizon, I will gather them from there and bring them to the place I have chosen as a dwelling for my Name.'

¹⁰"They are your servants and your people, whom you redeemed by your great strength and your mighty hand. ¹¹Lord, let your ear be attentive to the prayer of this your servant and the prayer of your servants who delight in revering your name. Give your servant success today by granting him favor in the presence of this man."

I was cupbearer to the king.

Artaxerxes Sends Nehemiah to Jerusalem

2 In the month of Nisan in the twentieth year of King Artaxerxes, when wine was brought for him, I took the wine and gave it to the king. I had not been sad in his presence before, ²so the king asked me, "Why does your face look so sad when you are not ill? This can be nothing but sadness of heart."

I was very much afraid, ³but I said to the king, "May the king live forever! Why should my face not look sad when the city where my ancestors are buried lies in ruins, and its gates have been destroyed by fire?"

⁴The king said to me, "What is it you want?"

Then I prayed to the God of heaven, ⁵and I answered the king, "If it pleases the king and if your servant has found favor in his sight, let him send me to the city in Judah where my ancestors are buried so that I can rebuild it."

⁶Then the king, with the queen sitting beside him, asked me, "How long will your journey take, and when will you get back?" It pleased the king to send me; so I set a time.

⁷I also said to him, "If it pleases the king, may I have letters to the governors of Trans-Euphrates, so that they will provide me safe-conduct until I arrive in Judah? ⁸And may I have a letter to Asaph, keeper of the royal park, so he will give me timber to make beams for the gates of the citadel by the temple and for the city wall and for the residence I will occupy?" And because the gracious hand of my God was on me, the king granted my requests. ⁹So I went to the governors of Trans-Euphrates and gave them the king's letters. The king had also sent army officers and cavalry with me.

¹⁰When Sanballat the Horonite and Tobiah the Ammonite official heard about this, they were very much disturbed that someone had come to promote the welfare of the Israelites.

Nehemiah Inspects Jerusalem's Walls

¹¹I went to Jerusalem, and after staying there three days ¹²I set out during the night with a few others. I had not told anyone what my God had put in my heart to do for Jerusalem. There were no mounts with me except the one I was riding on.

¹³By night I went out through the Valley Gate toward the Jackal* Well and the Dung Gate, examining the walls of Jerusalem, which had been broken down, and its gates, which had been destroyed by fire. ¹⁴Then I moved on toward the Fountain Gate and the King's Pool, but there was not enough room for my mount to get through; ¹⁵so I went up the valley by night, examining the wall. Finally, I turned back and reentered through the Valley Gate. ¹⁶The officials did not know where I had gone or what I was doing, because as yet I had said nothing to the Jews or the priests or nobles or officials or any others who would be doing the work.

¹⁷Then I said to them, "You see the trouble we are in: Jerusalem lies in ruins, and its gates have been burned with fire. Come, let us rebuild the wall of Jerusalem, and we will no longer be in disgrace." ¹⁸I also told them about the gracious hand of my God on me and what the king had said to me.

They replied, "Let us start rebuilding." So they began this good work.

¹⁹But when Sanballat the Horonite, Tobiah the Ammonite official and Geshem the Arab heard about it, they mocked and ridiculed us. "What is this you are doing?" they asked. "Are you rebelling against the king?"

²⁰I answered them by saying, "The God of heaven will give us success. We his servants will start rebuilding, but as for you, you have no share in Jerusalem or any claim or historic right to it."

ROCK SOLID
promises

"The God of heaven will give us success." Nehemiah 2:20

When God gives you a task to do, he also gives you everything you need to get it done.

Builders of the Wall

3 Eliashib the high priest and his fellow priests went to work and rebuilt the Sheep Gate. They dedicated it and set its doors in place, building as far as the Tower of the Hundred, which they dedicated, and as far as the Tower of Hananel. ²The men of Jericho built the adjoining section, and Zakkur son of Imri built next to them.

³The Fish Gate was rebuilt by the sons of Hassenaah. They laid its beams and put its doors and bolts and bars in place. ⁴Meremoth son of Uriah, the son of Hakkoz, repaired the next section. Next to him Meshullam son of Berekiah, the son of Meshezabel, made repairs, and next to him Zadok son of Baana also made repairs. ⁵The next section was repaired by the men of Tekoa, but their nobles would not put their shoulders to the work under their supervisors.*

⁶The Jeshanah* Gate was repaired by Joiada son of Paseah and Meshullam son of Besodeiah. They laid its beams and put its doors with their bolts and bars in place. ⁷Next to them, repairs were made by men from Gibeon and Mizpah—Melatiah of Gibeon and Jadon of Meronoth—places under the authority of the governor of

---

ᵃ 13 Or Serpent or Fig   ᵇ 5 Or their Lord or the governor   ᶜ 6 Or Old

Trans-Euphrates. [8]Uzziel son of Harhaiah, one of the goldsmiths, repaired the next section; and Hananiah, one of the perfume-makers, made repairs next to that. They restored Jerusalem as far as the Broad Wall. [9]Rephaiah son of Hur, ruler of a half-district of Jerusalem, repaired the next section. [10]Adjoining this, Jedaiah son of Harumaph made repairs opposite his house, and Hattush son of Hashabneiah made repairs next to him. [11]Malkijah son of Harim and Hasshub son of Pahath-Moab repaired another section and the Tower of the Ovens. [12]Shallum son of Hallohesh, ruler of a half-district of Jerusalem, repaired the next section with the help of his daughters.

[13]The Valley Gate was repaired by Hanun and the residents of Zanoah. They rebuilt it and put its doors with their bolts and bars in place. They also repaired a thousand cubits[a] of the wall as far as the Dung Gate.

[14]The Dung Gate was repaired by Malkijah son of Rekab, ruler of the district of Beth Hakkerem. He rebuilt it and put its doors with their bolts and bars in place.

[15]The Fountain Gate was repaired by Shallun son of Kol-Hozeh, ruler of the district of Mizpah. He rebuilt it, roofing it over and putting its doors and bolts and bars in place. He also repaired the wall of the Pool of Siloam,[b] by the King's Garden, as far as the steps going down from the City of David. [16]Beyond him, Nehemiah son of Azbuk, ruler of a half-district of Beth Zur, made repairs up to a point opposite the tombs[c] of David, as far as the artificial pool and the House of the Heroes.

[17]Next to him, the repairs were made by the Levites under Rehum son of Bani. Beside him, Hashabiah, ruler of half the district of Keilah, carried out repairs for his district. [18]Next to him, the repairs were made by their fellow Levites under Binnui[d] son of Henadad, ruler of the other half-district of Keilah. [19]Next to him, Ezer son of Jeshua, ruler of Mizpah, repaired another section, from a point facing the ascent to the armory as far as the angle of the wall. [20]Next to him, Baruch son of Zabbai zealously repaired another section, from the angle to the entrance of the house of Eliashib the high priest. [21]Next to him, Meremoth son of Uriah, the son of Hakkoz, repaired another section, from the entrance of Eliashib's house to the end of it.

[22]The repairs next to him were made by the priests from the surrounding region. [23]Beyond them, Benjamin and Hasshub made repairs in front of their house; and next to them, Azariah son of Maaseiah, the son of Ananiah, made repairs beside his house. [24]Next to him, Binnui son of Henadad repaired another section, from Azariah's house to the angle and the corner, [25]and Palal son of Uzai worked opposite the angle and the tower projecting from the upper palace near the court of the guard. Next to him, Pedaiah son of Parosh [26]and the temple servants living on the hill of Ophel made repairs up to a point opposite the Water Gate toward the east and the projecting tower. [27]Next to them, the men of Tekoa repaired another section, from the great projecting tower to the wall of Ophel.

[28]Above the Horse Gate, the priests made repairs, each in front of his own house. [29]Next to them, Zadok son of Immer made repairs opposite his house. Next to him, Shemaiah son of Shekaniah, the guard at the East Gate, made repairs. [30]Next to him, Hananiah son of Shelemiah, and Hanun, the sixth son of Zalaph, repaired another section. Next to them, Meshullam son of Berekiah made repairs opposite his living quarters. [31]Next to him, Malkijah, one of the goldsmiths, made repairs as far as the house of the temple servants and the merchants, opposite the Inspection Gate, and as far as

---

[a] 13 That is, about 1,500 feet or about 450 meters   [b] 15 Hebrew Shelah, a variant of Shiloah, that is, Siloam   [c] 16 Hebrew; Septuagint, some Vulgate manuscripts and Syriac tomb   [d] 18 Two Hebrew manuscripts and Syriac (see also Septuagint and verse 24); most Hebrew manuscripts Bavvai

the room above the corner; [32]and between the room above the corner and the Sheep Gate the goldsmiths and merchants made repairs.

Opposition to the Rebuilding

4 [a] When Sanballat heard that we were rebuilding the wall, he became angry and was greatly incensed. He ridiculed the Jews, [2]and in the presence of his associates and the army of Samaria, he said, "What are those feeble Jews doing? Will they restore their wall? Will they offer sacrifices? Will they finish in a day? Can they bring the stones back to life from those heaps of rubble—burned as they are?"

[3]Tobiah the Ammonite, who was at his side, said, "What they are building—even a fox climbing up on it would break down their wall of stones!"

[4]Hear us, our God, for we are despised. Turn their insults back on their own heads. Give them over as plunder in a land of captivity. [5]Do not cover up their guilt or blot out their sins from your sight, for they have thrown insults in the face of[b] the builders.

[6]So we rebuilt the wall till all of it reached half its height, for the people worked with all their heart.

[7]But when Sanballat, Tobiah, the Arabs, the Ammonites and the people of Ashdod heard that the repairs to Jerusalem's walls had gone ahead and that the gaps were being closed, they were very angry. [8]They all plotted together to come and fight against Jerusalem and stir up trouble against it. [9]But we prayed to our God and posted a guard day and night to meet this threat.

[10]Meanwhile, the people in Judah said, "The strength of the laborers is giving out,

[a] In Hebrew texts 4:1-6 is numbered 3:33-38, and 4:7-23 is numbered 4:1-17.   [b] 5 Or *have aroused your anger before*

ROCK SOLID principles

Nehemiah 4:6

Work hard.

"Breeann is in bed," Jen told Mrs. Taylor when she called to check in. "She went to sleep a couple hours ago." Jen loved her job as a babysitter. Wherever she went she had a standard routine. She played one board game, sat the kids in front of a stack of movies while she went online or chatted with friends, then put the children to bed as early as possible. Tonight when the Taylors returned home and checked on Breeann, her mom came back in a huff. "Jen, Breeann had a nosebleed. Her pillow is covered with blood," Mrs. Taylor said. "She always wakes up when that happens. She must have cried herself back to sleep. Why didn't you hear her? What were you doing?"

Nehemiah was brokenhearted at the thought of the crumbled wall around Jerusalem, a city unprotected from its enemies (see Nehemiah 1:3—4). But the wall was rebuilt as the people "worked with all their heart" (Nehemiah 4:6). They accomplished the task "with the help of our God" (Nehemiah 6:16). Hard work done in God's power is always a plan for success.

and there is so much rubble that we cannot rebuild the wall.”

¹¹Also our enemies said, “Before they know it or see us, we will be right there among them and will kill them and put an end to the work.”

¹²Then the Jews who lived near them came and told us ten times over, “Wherever you turn, they will attack us.”

¹³Therefore I stationed some of the people behind the lowest points of the wall at the exposed places, posting them by families, with their swords, spears and bows. ¹⁴After I looked things over, I stood up and said to the nobles, the officials and the rest of the people, “Don’t be afraid of them. Remember the Lord, who is great and awesome, and fight for your families, your sons and your daughters, your wives and your homes.”

¹⁵When our enemies heard that we were aware of their plot and that God had frustrated it, we all returned to the wall, each to our own work.

¹⁶From that day on, half of my men did the work, while the other half were equipped with spears, shields, bows and armor. The officers posted themselves behind all the people of Judah ¹⁷who were building the wall. Those who carried materials did their work with one hand and held a weapon in the other, ¹⁸and each of the builders wore his sword at his side as he worked. But the man who sounded the trumpet stayed with me.

¹⁹Then I said to the nobles, the officials and the rest of the people, “The work is extensive and spread out, and we are widely separated from each other along the wall. ²⁰Wherever you hear the sound of the trumpet, join us there. Our God will fight for us!”

²¹So we continued the work with half the men holding spears, from the first light of dawn till the stars came out. ²²At that time I also said to the people, “Have every man and his helper stay inside Jerusalem at night, so they can serve us as guards by night and as workers by day.” ²³Neither I nor my brothers nor my men nor the guards with me took off our clothes; each had his weapon, even when he went for water.*

Nehemiah Helps the Poor

5 Now the men and their wives raised a great outcry against their fellow Jews. ²Some were saying, “We and our sons and daughters are numerous; in order for us to eat and stay alive, we must get grain.”

³Others were saying, “We are mortgaging our fields, our vineyards and our homes to get grain during the famine.”

⁴Still others were saying, “We have had to borrow money to pay the king’s tax on our fields and vineyards. ⁵Although we are of the same flesh and blood as our fellow Jews and though our children are as good as theirs, yet we have to subject our sons and daughters to slavery. Some of our daughters have already been enslaved, but we are powerless, because our fields and our vineyards belong to others.”

⁶When I heard their outcry and these charges, I was very angry. ⁷I pondered them in my mind and then accused the nobles and officials. I told them, “You are charging your own people interest!” So I called together a large meeting to deal with them ⁸and said: “As far as possible, we have bought back our fellow Jews who were sold to the Gentiles. Now you are selling your own people, only for them to be sold back to us!” They kept quiet, because they could find nothing to say.

⁹So I continued, “What you are doing is not right. Shouldn’t you walk in the fear of our God to avoid the reproach of our Gentile enemies? ¹⁰I and my brothers and my men are also lending the people money and grain. But let us stop charging interest! ¹¹Give back to them immediately their fields, vineyards, olive groves and houses, and also the interest you are charging them—one percent of the money, grain, new wine and olive oil.”

¹²“We will give it back,” they said. “And we will not demand anything more from them. We will do as you say.”

---

a 23 The meaning of the Hebrew for this clause is uncertain.

Then I summoned the priests and made the nobles and officials take an oath to do what they had promised. ¹³I also shook out the folds of my robe and said, "In this way may God shake out of their house and possessions anyone who does not keep this promise. So may such a person be shaken out and emptied!"

At this the whole assembly said, "Amen," and praised the LORD. And the people did as they had promised.

¹⁴Moreover, from the twentieth year of King Artaxerxes, when I was appointed to be their governor in the land of Judah, until his thirty-second year—twelve years—neither I nor my brothers ate the food allotted to the governor. ¹⁵But the earlier governors—those preceding me—placed a heavy burden on the people and took forty shekels*a* of silver from them in addition to food and wine. Their assistants also lorded it over the people. But out of reverence for God I did not act like that. ¹⁶Instead, I devoted myself to the work on this wall. All my men were assembled there for the work; we*b* did not acquire any land.

¹⁷Furthermore, a hundred and fifty Jews and officials ate at my table, as well as those who came to us from the surrounding nations. ¹⁸Each day one ox, six choice sheep and some poultry were prepared for me, and every ten days an abundant supply of wine of all kinds. In spite of all this, I never demanded the food allotted to the governor, because the demands were heavy on these people.

¹⁹Remember me with favor, my God, for all I have done for these people.

Further Opposition to the Rebuilding

6 When word came to Sanballat, Tobiah, Geshem the Arab and the rest of our enemies that I had rebuilt the wall and not a gap was left in it—though up to that time I had not set the doors in the gates— ²Sanballat and Geshem sent me this message: "Come, let us meet together in one of the villages*c* on the plain of Ono."

But they were scheming to harm me; ³so I sent messengers to them with this reply: "I am carrying on a great project and cannot go down. Why should the work stop while I leave it and go down to you?" ⁴Four times they sent me the same message, and each time I gave them the same answer.

⁵Then, the fifth time, Sanballat sent his aide to me with the same message, and in his hand was an unsealed letter ⁶in which was written:

"It is reported among the nations—and Geshem*d* says it is true—that you and the Jews are plotting to revolt, and therefore you are building the wall. Moreover, according to these reports you are about to become their king ⁷and have even appointed prophets to make this proclamation about you in Jerusalem: 'There is a king in Judah!' Now this report will get back to the king; so come, let us meet together."

⁸I sent him this reply: "Nothing like what you are saying is happening; you are just making it up out of your head."

⁹They were all trying to frighten us, thinking, "Their hands will get too weak for the work, and it will not be completed."

But I prayed, "Now strengthen my hands."

¹⁰One day I went to the house of Shemaiah son of Delaiah, the son of Mehetabel, who was shut in at his home. He said, "Let us meet in the house of God, inside the temple, and let us close the temple doors, because men are coming to kill you—by night they are coming to kill you."

¹¹But I said, "Should a man like me run away? Or should someone like me go into the temple to save his life? I will not go!" ¹²I realized that God had not sent him, but that he had prophesied against me because Tobiah and Sanballat had hired

---

a 15 That is, about 1 pound or about 460 grams
b 16 Most Hebrew manuscripts; some Hebrew manuscripts, Septuagint, Vulgate and Syriac *I*
c 2 Or *in Kephirim*   *d 6* Hebrew *Gashmu*, a variant of *Geshem*

him. ¹³He had been hired to intimidate me so that I would commit a sin by doing this, and then they would give me a bad name to discredit me.

¹⁴Remember Tobiah and Sanballat, my God, because of what they have done; remember also the prophet Noadiah and how she and the rest of the prophets have been trying to intimidate me. ¹⁵So the wall was completed on the twenty-fifth of Elul, in fifty-two days.

Opposition to the Completed Wall

¹⁶When all our enemies heard about this, all the surrounding nations were afraid and lost their self-confidence, because they realized that this work had been done with the help of our God.

ROCK SOLID *promises*

"This work had been done with the help of our God." Nehemiah 6:16

God gets the credit for everything you accomplish, no matter whether the job felt easy or hard.

¹⁷Also, in those days the nobles of Judah were sending many letters to Tobiah, and replies from Tobiah kept coming to them. ¹⁸For many in Judah were under oath to him, since he was son-in-law to Shekaniah son of Arah, and his son Jehohanan had married the daughter of Meshullam son of Berekiah. ¹⁹Moreover, they kept reporting to me his good deeds and then telling him what I said. And Tobiah sent letters to intimidate me.

7 After the wall had been rebuilt and I had set the doors in place, the gatekeepers, the musicians and the Levites were appointed. ²I put in

charge of Jerusalem my brother Hanani, along with Hananiah the commander of the citadel, because he was a man of integrity and feared God more than most people do. ³I said to them, "The gates of Jerusalem are not to be opened until the sun is hot. While the gatekeepers are still on duty, have them shut the doors and bar them. Also appoint residents of Jerusalem as guards, some at their posts and some near their own houses."

The List of the Exiles Who Returned

⁴Now the city was large and spacious, but there were few people in it, and the houses had not yet been rebuilt. ⁵So my God put it into my heart to assemble the nobles, the officials and the common people for registration by families. I found the genealogical record of those who had been the first to return. This is what I found written there:

⁶These are the people of the province who came up from the captivity of the exiles whom Nebuchadnezzar king of Babylon had taken captive (they returned to Jerusalem and Judah, each to his own town, ⁷in company with Zerubbabel, Joshua, Nehemiah, Azariah, Raamiah, Nahamani, Mordecai, Bilshan, Mispereth, Bigvai, Nehum and Baanah):

The list of the men of Israel:

⁸the descendants of Parosh	2,172
⁹of Shephatiah	372
¹⁰of Arah	652
¹¹of Pahath-Moab (through the line of Jeshua and Joab)	2,818
¹²of Elam	1,254
¹³of Zattu	845
¹⁴of Zakkai	760
¹⁵of Binnui	648
¹⁶of Bebai	628
¹⁷of Azgad	2,322
¹⁸of Adonikam	667
¹⁹of Bigvai	2,067
²⁰of Adin	655
²¹of Ater (through Hezekiah)	98

22 of Hashum   328
23 of Bezai   324
24 of Hariph   112
25 of Gibeon   95

26 the men of Bethlehem and
     Netophah   188
27 of Anathoth   128
28 of Beth Azmaveth   42
29 of Kiriath Jearim,
     Kephirah and Beeroth   743
30 of Ramah and Geba   621
31 of Mikmash   122
32 of Bethel and Ai   123
33 of the other Nebo   52
34 of the other Elam   1,254
35 of Harim   320
36 of Jericho   345
37 of Lod, Hadid and Ono   721
38 of Senaah   3,930

39 The priests:

the descendants of Jedaiah
     (through the family of
     Jeshua)   973
40 of Immer   1,052
41 of Pashhur   1,247
42 of Harim   1,017

43 The Levites:

the descendants of Jeshua
     (through Kadmiel through
     the line of Hodaviah)   74

44 The musicians:

the descendants of Asaph   148

45 The gatekeepers:

the descendants of
     Shallum, Ater, Talmon,
     Akkub, Hatita and Shobai   138

46 The temple servants:

the descendants of
     Ziha, Hasupha, Tabbaoth,
47 Keros, Sia, Padon,
48 Lebana, Hagaba, Shalmai,
49 Hanan, Giddel, Gahar,
50 Reaiah, Rezin, Nekoda,
51 Gazzam, Uzza, Paseah,
52 Besai, Meunim, Nephusim,
53 Bakbuk, Hakupha, Harhur,
54 Bazluth, Mehida, Harsha,
55 Barkos, Sisera, Temah,
56 Neziah and Hatipha

57 The descendants of the servants of
Solomon:

the descendants of
     Sotai, Sophereth, Perida,
58 Jaala, Darkon, Giddel,
59 Shephatiah, Hattil,
     Pokereth-Hazzebaim and
     Amon

60 The temple servants and the
     descendants of the servants
     of Solomon   392

61 The following came up from
the towns of Tel Melah, Tel Harsha,
Kerub, Addon and Immer, but they
could not show that their families
were descended from Israel:

62 the descendants of
     Delaiah, Tobiah and
     Nekoda   642

63 And from among the priests:

the descendants of
     Hobaiah, Hakkoz and
     Barzillai (a man who had
     married a daughter of Barzillai
     the Gileadite and was called by
     that name).

64 These searched for their family records, but they could not find them and so were excluded from the priesthood as unclean. 65 The governor, therefore, ordered them not to eat any of the most sacred food until there should be a priest ministering with the Urim and Thummim.

66 The whole company numbered 42,360, 67 besides their 7,337 male and female slaves; and they also had 245 male and female singers. 68 There were 736 horses, 245 mules,[a] 69 435 camels and 6,720 donkeys.

70 Some of the heads of the families contributed to the work. The gover-

---

[a] 68 Some Hebrew manuscripts (see also Ezra 2:66); most Hebrew manuscripts do not have this verse.

nor gave to the treasury 1,000 darics[a] of gold, 50 bowls and 530 garments for priests. [71]Some of the heads of the families gave to the treasury for the work 20,000 darics[b] of gold and 2,200 minas[c] of silver. [72]The total given by the rest of the people was 20,000 darics of gold, 2,000 minas[d] of silver and 67 garments for priests.

[73]The priests, the Levites, the gatekeepers, the musicians and the temple servants, along with certain of the people and the rest of the Israelites, settled in their own towns.

Ezra Reads the Law

When the seventh month came and the Israelites had settled in their towns, [1]all the people came together as one in the square before the Water Gate. They told Ezra the teacher of the Law to bring out the Book of the Law of Moses, which the LORD had commanded for Israel.

[2]So on the first day of the seventh month Ezra the priest brought the Law before the assembly, which was made up of men and women and all who were able to understand. [3]He read it aloud from daybreak till noon as he faced the square before the Water Gate in the presence of the men, women and others who could understand. And all the people listened attentively to the Book of the Law.

[4]Ezra the teacher of the Law stood on a high wooden platform built for the occasion. Beside him on his right stood Mattithiah, Shema, Anaiah, Uriah, Hilkiah and Maaseiah; and on his left were Pedaiah, Mishael, Malkijah, Hashum, Hashbaddanah, Zechariah and Meshullam.

[5]Ezra opened the book. All the people could see him because he was standing above them; and as he opened it, the people all stood up. [6]Ezra praised the LORD, the great God; and all the people lifted their hands and responded, "Amen! Amen!" Then they bowed down and worshiped the LORD with their faces to the ground.

[7]The Levites—Jeshua, Bani, Sherebiah, Jamin, Akkub, Shabbethai, Hodiah, Maaseiah, Kelita, Azariah, Jozabad, Hanan and Pelaiah—instructed the people in the Law while the people were standing there. [8]They read from the Book of the Law of God, making it clear[e] and giving

[a] 70 That is, about 19 pounds or about 8.4 kilograms   [b] 71 That is, about 375 pounds or about 170 kilograms; also in verse 72   [c] 71 That is, about 1 1/3 tons or about 1.2 metric tons   [d] 72 That is, about 1 1/4 tons or about 1.1 metric tons   [e] 8 Or God, translating it

Nehemiah 8:1–12

God's Word is worth celebrating.

You likely haven't been in a church service like this. Nehemiah and his fellow citizens had finished rebuilding the protective wall around Jerusalem. Some had settled back in their hometowns. But now everyone gathered to hear Ezra the priest read the Law. He read aloud "from daybreak till noon" (Nehemiah 8:3). Everyone lifted their hands and shouted "Amen!" They bowed face down in worship. Others also read from the Law, explaining its meaning so everyone could understand. As the crowds listened to God's Word, they wept. They had fallen so short of God's standards they couldn't help being pierced to the heart. But the leaders told the people not to weep. They even told the crowds to go and celebrate with feasting, because they finally had a grasp of God's Word. And "the joy of the LORD" would be their strength (Nehemiah 8:10).

Think: When does reading the Bible make you sad? When does it make you happy?

ROCK SOLID truths

the meaning so that the people understood what was being read.

⁹Then Nehemiah the governor, Ezra the priest and teacher of the Law, and the Levites who were instructing the people said to them all, "This day is holy to the LORD your God. Do not mourn or weep." For all the people had been weeping as they listened to the words of the Law.

¹⁰Nehemiah said, "Go and enjoy choice food and sweet drinks, and send some to those who have nothing prepared. This day is holy to our Lord. Do not grieve, for the joy of the LORD is your strength."

¹¹The Levites calmed all the people, saying, "Be still, for this is a holy day. Do not grieve."

¹²Then all the people went away to eat and drink, to send portions of food and to celebrate with great joy, because they now understood the words that had been made known to them.

¹³On the second day of the month, the heads of all the families, along with the priests and the Levites, gathered around Ezra the teacher to give attention to the words of the Law. ¹⁴They found written in the Law, which the LORD had commanded through Moses, that the Israelites were to live in temporary shelters during the festival of the seventh month ¹⁵and that they should proclaim this word and spread it throughout their towns and in Jerusalem: "Go out into the hill country and bring back branches from olive and wild olive trees, and from myrtles, palms and shade trees, to make temporary shelters"—as it is written.ᵃ

¹⁶So the people went out and brought back branches and built themselves temporary shelters on their own roofs, in their courtyards, in the courts of the house of God and in the square by the Water Gate and the one by the Gate of Ephraim. ¹⁷The whole company that had returned from exile built temporary shelters and lived in them. From the days of Joshua son of Nun until that day, the Israelites had not celebrated it like this. And their joy was very great.

¹⁸Day after day, from the first day to the last, Ezra read from the Book of the Law of God. They celebrated the festival for seven days, and on the eighth day, in accordance with the regulation, there was an assembly.

The Israelites Confess Their Sins

9 On the twenty-fourth day of the same month, the Israelites gathered together, fasting and wearing sackcloth and putting dust on their heads. ²Those of Israelite descent had separated themselves from all foreigners. They stood in their places and confessed their sins and the sins of their ancestors. ³They stood where they were and read from the Book of the Law of the LORD their God for a quarter of the day, and spent another quarter in confession and in worshiping the LORD their God. ⁴Standing on the stairs of the Levites were Jeshua, Bani, Kadmiel, Shebaniah, Bunni, Sherebiah, Bani and Kenani. They cried out with loud voices to the LORD their God. ⁵And the Levites—Jeshua, Kadmiel, Bani, Hashabneiah, Sherebiah, Hodiah, Shebaniah and Pethahiah—said: "Stand up and praise the LORD your God, who is from everlasting to everlasting.ᵇ"

"Blessed be your glorious name, and may it be exalted above all blessing and praise. ⁶You alone are the LORD. You made the heavens, even the highest heavens, and all their starry host, the earth and all that is on it, the seas and all that is in them. You give life to everything, and the multitudes of heaven worship you.

⁷"You are the LORD God, who chose Abram and brought him out of Ur of the Chaldeans and named him Abraham. ⁸You found his heart faithful to you, and you made a covenant with him to give to his descendants the land of the Canaanites, Hittites, Amorites, Perizzites, Jebusites and Girgashites. You have kept your promise because you are righteous.

ᵃ 15 See Lev. 23:37-40.   ᵇ 5 Or *God for ever and ever*

⁹"You saw the suffering of our ancestors in Egypt; you heard their cry at the Red Sea.ᵃ ¹⁰You sent signs and wonders against Pharaoh, against all his officials and all the people of his land, for you knew how arrogantly the Egyptians treated them. You made a name for yourself, which remains to this day. ¹¹You divided the sea before them, so that they passed through it on dry ground, but you hurled their pursuers into the depths, like a stone into mighty waters. ¹²By day you led them with a pillar of cloud, and by night with a pillar of fire to give them light on the way they were to take.

¹³"You came down on Mount Sinai; you spoke to them from heaven. You gave them regulations and laws that are just and right, and decrees and commands that are good. ¹⁴You made known to them your holy Sabbath and gave them commands, decrees and laws through your servant Moses. ¹⁵In their hunger you gave them bread from heaven and in their thirst you brought them water from the rock; you told them to go in and take possession of the land you had sworn with uplifted hand to give them.

¹⁶"But they, our ancestors, became arrogant and stiff-necked, and they did not obey your commands. ¹⁷They refused to listen and failed to remember the miracles you performed among them. They became stiff-necked and in their rebellion appointed a leader in order to return to their slavery. But you are a forgiving God, gracious and compassionate, slow to anger and abounding in love. Therefore you did not desert them, ¹⁸even when they cast for themselves an image of a calf and said, 'This is your god, who brought you up out of Egypt,' or when they committed awful blasphemies.

¹⁹"Because of your great compassion you did not abandon them in the wilderness. By day the pillar of cloud did not fail to guide them on their path, nor the pillar of fire by night to shine on the way they were to take. ²⁰You gave your good Spirit to instruct them. You did not withhold your manna from their mouths, and you gave them water for their thirst. ²¹For forty years you sustained them in the wilderness; they lacked nothing, their clothes did not wear out nor did their feet become swollen.

²²"You gave them kingdoms and nations, allotting to them even the remotest frontiers. They took over the country of Sihonᵇ king of Heshbon and the country of Og king of Bashan. ²³You made their children as numerous as the stars in the sky, and you brought them into the land that you told their parents to enter and possess. ²⁴Their children went in and took possession of the land. You subdued before them the Canaanites, who lived in the land; you gave the Canaanites into their hands, along with their kings and the peoples of the land, to deal with them as they pleased. ²⁵They captured fortified cities and fertile land; they took possession of houses filled with all kinds of good things, wells already dug, vineyards, olive groves and fruit trees in abundance. They ate to the full and were well-nourished; they reveled in your great goodness.

²⁶"But they were disobedient and rebelled against you; they turned their backs on your law. They killed your prophets, who had warned them in order to turn them back to you; they committed awful blasphemies. ²⁷So you delivered them into the hands of their enemies, who oppressed them. But when they were oppressed they cried out to you. From heaven you heard them, and in your great compassion you gave

---

ᵃ 9 Or *the Sea of Reeds*   ᵇ 22 One Hebrew manuscript and Septuagint; most Hebrew manuscripts *Sihon, that is, the country of the* them deliverers, who rescued them from the hand of their enemies.

28 "But as soon as they were at rest, they again did what was evil in your sight. Then you abandoned them to the hand of their enemies so that they ruled over them. And when they cried out to you again, you heard from heaven, and in your compassion you delivered them time after time.

29 "You warned them in order to turn them back to your law, but they became arrogant and disobeyed your commands. They sinned against your ordinances, of which you said, 'The person who obeys them will live by them.' Stubbornly they turned their backs on you, became stiff-necked and refused to listen. 30 For many years you were patient with them. By your Spirit you warned them through your prophets. Yet they paid no attention, so you gave them into the hands of the neighboring peoples. 31 But in your great mercy you did not put an end to them or abandon them, for you are a gracious and merciful God.

32 "Now therefore, our God, the great God, mighty and awesome, who keeps his covenant of love, do not let all this hardship seem trifling in your eyes—the hardship that has come on us, on our kings and leaders, on our priests and prophets, on our ancestors and all your people, from the days of the kings of Assyria until today. 33 In all that has happened to us, you have remained righteous; you have acted faithfully, while we acted wickedly. 34 Our kings, our leaders, our priests and our ancestors did not follow your law; they did not pay attention to your commands or the statutes you warned them to keep. 35 Even while they were in their kingdom, enjoying your great goodness to them in the spacious and fertile land you gave them, they did not serve you or turn from their evil ways.

36 "But see, we are slaves today, slaves in the land you gave our ancestors so they could eat its fruit and the other good things it produces. 37 Because of our sins, its abundant harvest goes to the kings you have placed over us. They rule over our bodies and our cattle as they please. We are in great distress.

The Agreement of the People

38 "In view of all this, we are making a binding agreement, putting it in writing, and our leaders, our Levites and our priests are affixing their seals to it."[a]

10 [b] Those who sealed it were:

Nehemiah the governor, the son of Hakaliah.

Zedekiah, 2 Seraiah, Azariah, Jeremiah,
3 Pashhur, Amariah, Malkijah,
4 Hattush, Shebaniah, Malluk,
5 Harim, Meremoth, Obadiah,
6 Daniel, Ginnethon, Baruch,
7 Meshullam, Abijah, Mijamin,
8 Maaziah, Bilgai and Shemaiah.
These were the priests.

9 The Levites:

Jeshua son of Azaniah, Binnui of the sons of Henadad, Kadmiel,
10 and their associates: Shebaniah, Hodiah, Kelita, Pelaiah, Hanan,
11 Mika, Rehob, Hashabiah,
12 Zakkur, Sherebiah, Shebaniah,
13 Hodiah, Bani and Beninu.

14 The leaders of the people:

Parosh, Pahath Moab, Elam, Zattu, Bani,
15 Bunni, Azgad, Bebai,
16 Adonijah, Bigvai, Adin,
17 Ater, Hezekiah, Azzur,
18 Hodiah, Hashum, Bezai,
19 Hariph, Anathoth, Nebai,
20 Magpiash, Meshullam, Hezir,
21 Meshezabel, Zadok, Jaddua,

---

a 38 In Hebrew texts this verse (9:38) is numbered 10:1.   b In Hebrew texts 10:1-39 is numbered 10:2-40.

²²Pelatiah, Hanan, Anaiah,
²³Hoshea, Hananiah, Hasshub,
²⁴Hallohesh, Pilha, Shobek,
²⁵Rehum, Hashabnah, Maaseiah,
²⁶Ahiah, Hanan, Anan,
²⁷Malluk, Harim and Baanah.

²⁸"The rest of the people—priests, Levites, gatekeepers, musicians, temple servants and all who separated themselves from the neighboring peoples for the sake of the Law of God, together with their wives and all their sons and daughters who are able to understand— ²⁹all these now join their fellow Israelites the nobles, and bind themselves with a curse and an oath to follow the Law of God given through Moses the servant of God and to obey carefully all the commands, regulations and decrees of the LORD our Lord.

³⁰"We promise not to give our daughters in marriage to the peoples around us or take their daughters for our sons.

³¹"When the neighboring peoples bring merchandise or grain to sell on the Sabbath, we will not buy from them on the Sabbath or on any holy day. Every seventh year we will forgo working the land and will cancel all debts.

³²"We assume the responsibility for carrying out the commands to give a third of a shekel*ᵃ* each year for the service of the house of our God: ³³for the bread set out on the table; for the regular grain offerings and burnt offerings; for the offerings on the Sabbaths, at the New Moon feasts and at the appointed festivals; for the holy offerings; for sin offerings*ᵇ* to make atonement for Israel; and for all the duties of the house of our God.

³⁴"We—the priests, the Levites and the people—have cast lots to determine when each of our families is to bring to the house of our God at set times each year a contribution of wood to burn on the altar of the LORD our God, as it is written in the Law.

³⁵"We also assume responsibility for bringing to the house of the LORD each year the firstfruits of our crops and of every fruit tree.

³⁶"As it is also written in the Law, we will bring the firstborn of our sons and of our cattle, of our herds and of our flocks to the house of our God, to the priests ministering there.

³⁷"Moreover, we will bring to the storerooms of the house of our God, to the priests, the first of our ground meal, of our grain offerings, of the fruit of all our trees and of our new wine and olive oil. And we will bring a tithe of our crops to the Levites, for it is the Levites who collect the tithes in all the towns where we work. ³⁸A priest descended from Aaron is to accompany the Levites when they receive the tithes, and the Levites are to bring a tenth of the tithes up to the house of our God, to the storerooms of the treasury. ³⁹The people of Israel, including the Levites, are to bring their contributions of grain, new wine and olive oil to the storerooms, where the articles for the sanctuary and for the ministering priests, the gatekeepers and the musicians are also kept.

"We will not neglect the house of our God."

The New Residents of Jerusalem

11 Now the leaders of the people settled in Jerusalem. The rest of the people cast lots to bring one out of every ten of them to live in Jerusalem, the holy city, while the remaining nine were to stay in their own towns. ²The people commended all who volunteered to live in Jerusalem.

³These are the provincial leaders who settled in Jerusalem (now some Israelites, priests, Levites, temple servants and

---

ᵃ 32 That is, about 1/8 ounce or about 4 grams
ᵇ 33 Or *purification offerings*

descendants of Solomon's servants lived in the towns of Judah, each on their own property in the various towns, ⁴while other people from both Judah and Benjamin lived in Jerusalem):

From the descendants of Judah:

Athaiah son of Uzziah, the son of Zechariah, the son of Amariah, the son of Shephatiah, the son of Mahalalel, a descendant of Perez; ⁵and Maaseiah son of Baruch, the son of Kol-Hozeh, the son of Hazaiah, the son of Adaiah, the son of Joiarib, the son of Zechariah, a descendant of Shelah. ⁶The descendants of Perez

who lived in Jerusalem totaled 468 men of standing.

⁷From the descendants of Benjamin:

Sallu son of Meshullam, the son of Joed, the son of Pedaiah, the son of Kolaiah, the son of Maaseiah, the son of Ithiel, the son of Jeshaiah, ⁸and his followers, Gabbai and Sallai—928 men. ⁹Joel son of Zikri was their chief officer, and Judah son of Hassenuah was over the New Quarter of the city.

¹⁰From the priests:

Jedaiah; the son of Joiarib; Jakin; ¹¹Seraiah son of Hilkiah, the son of

Nehemiah 11
Nehemiah got the job done.

Nehemiah had a comfortable job as the trusted wine taster in the court of Artaxerxes, emperor of Persia. He lived far from his homeland in Jerusalem, but he wept when he heard a report of the destruction of that holy city, with its broken down walls and burned out gates. He fasted and prayed, admitting not only his own sins but the evil deeds of the entire nation. And then he pleaded with God to lead him back to his homeland (see Nehemiah 1:1–11).

The fact that Jerusalem stood defenseless consumed Nehemiah, and his boss the king read the concern on his face. When Nehemiah asked the king for permission to return to Jerusalem, the king not only let him go but sent him on his way with letters ensuring safe passage and supplies for rebuilding (see Nehemiah 2:1–10).

Nehemiah arrived in the city and secretly surveyed the problem. He gathered helpers and told them his plan. He stationed them around the wall, putting some to work on repairs and ordering others to stand guard. He fended off opponents who tried to distract them and spread rumors that Nehemiah was plotting a rebellion. When the wall was completed, everyone could see "this work had been done with the help of our God" (Nehemiah 6:16).

Nehemiah didn't just start a job. He got it done. And this daring leader didn't just rebuild the wall. He forced nobles to give away land and stop impoverishing their fellow Israelites (see Nehemiah 5:1–13). He also called the nation back to spiritual reforms and godly marriages (see Nehemiah 13:4–31).

You can find Nehemiah in Ezra 2:2 and throughout the book of Nehemiah.

UNSHAKEN people

Meshullam, the son of Zadok, the son of Meraioth, the son of Ahitub, the official in charge of the house of God, ¹²and their associates, who carried on work for the temple—822 men; Adaiah son of Jeroham, the son of Pelaliah, the son of Amzi, the son of Zechariah, the son of Pashhur, the son of Malkijah, ¹³and his associates, who were heads of families—242 men; Amashsai son of Azarel, the son of Ahzai, the son of Meshillemoth, the son of Immer, ¹⁴and his^a associates, who were men of standing—128. Their chief officer was Zabdiel son of Haggedolim.

¹⁵From the Levites:

Shemaiah son of Hasshub, the son of Azrikam, the son of Hashabiah, the son of Bunni; ¹⁶Shabbethai and Jozabad, two of the heads of the Levites, who had charge of the outside work of the house of God; ¹⁷Mattaniah son of Mika, the son of Zabdi, the son of Asaph, the director who led in thanksgiving and prayer; Bakbukiah, second among his associates; and Abda son of Shammua, the son of Galal, the son of Jeduthun. ¹⁸The Levites in the holy city totaled 284.

¹⁹The gatekeepers:

Akkub, Talmon and their associates, who kept watch at the gates—172 men.

²⁰The rest of the Israelites, with the priests and Levites, were in all the towns of Judah, each on their ancestral property.
²¹The temple servants lived on the hill of Ophel, and Ziha and Gishpa were in charge of them.
²²The chief officer of the Levites in Jerusalem was Uzzi son of Bani, the son of Hashabiah, the son of Mattaniah, the son of Mika. Uzzi was one of Asaph's descendants, who were the musicians responsible for the service of the house of God. ²³The musicians were under the king's orders, which regulated their daily activity.
²⁴Pethahiah son of Meshezabel, one of the descendants of Zerah son of Judah, was the king's agent in all affairs relating to the people.

²⁵As for the villages with their fields, some of the people of Judah lived in Kiriath Arba and its surrounding settlements, in Dibon and its settlements, in Jekabzeel and its villages, ²⁶in Jeshua, in Moladah, in Beth Pelet, ²⁷in Hazar Shual, in Beersheba and its settlements, ²⁸in Ziklag, in Mekonah and its settlements, ²⁹in En Rimmon, in Zorah, in Jarmuth, ³⁰Zanoah, Adullam and their villages, in Lachish and its fields, and in Azekah and its settlements. So they were living all the way from Beersheba to the Valley of Hinnom.

³¹The descendants of the Benjamites from Geba lived in Mikmash, Aija, Bethel and its settlements, ³²in Anathoth, Nob and Ananiah, ³³in Hazor, Ramah and Gittaim, ³⁴in Hadid, Zeboim and Neballat, ³⁵in Lod and Ono, and in Ge Harashim.

³⁶Some of the divisions of the Levites of Judah settled in Benjamin.

Priests and Levites

12 These were the priests and Levites who returned with Zerubbabel son of Shealtiel and with Joshua:

Seraiah, Jeremiah, Ezra,
²Amariah, Malluk, Hattush,
³Shekaniah, Rehum, Meremoth,
⁴Iddo, Ginnethon,^b Abijah,
⁵Mijamin,^c Moadiah, Bilgah,
⁶Shemaiah, Joiarib, Jedaiah,
⁷Sallu, Amok, Hilkiah and Jedaiah.
These were the leaders of the priests and their associates in the days of Joshua.

⁸The Levites were Jeshua, Binnui, Kadmiel, Sherebiah, Judah, and also Mattaniah, who, together with his associates, was in charge of the songs of thanksgiving. ⁹Bakbukiah and Unni, their associates, stood opposite them in the services.
¹⁰Joshua was the father of Joiakim,

---

^a 14 Most Septuagint manuscripts; Hebrew *their*   ^b 4 Many Hebrew manuscripts and Vulgate (see also verse 16); most Hebrew manuscripts *Ginnethoi*   ^c 5 A variant of *Miniamin*

Joiakim the father of Eliashib, Eliashib the father of Joiada, ¹¹Joiada the father of Jonathan, and Jonathan the father of Jaddua.

¹²In the days of Joiakim, these were the heads of the priestly families:

of Seraiah's family, Meraiah;

of Jeremiah's, Hananiah;

¹³of Ezra's, Meshullam;

of Amariah's, Jehohanan;

¹⁴of Malluk's, Jonathan;

of Shekaniah's,ᵃ Joseph;

¹⁵of Harim's, Adna;

of Meremoth's,ᵇ Helkai;

¹⁶of Iddo's, Zechariah;

of Ginnethon's, Meshullam;

¹⁷of Abijah's, Zikri;

of Miniamin's and of Moadiah's, Piltai;

¹⁸of Bilgah's, Shammua;

of Shemaiah's, Jehonathan;

¹⁹of Joiarib's, Mattenai;

of Jedaiah's, Uzzi;

²⁰of Sallu's, Kallai;

of Amok's, Eber;

²¹of Hilkiah's, Hashabiah;

of Jedaiah's, Nethanel.

²²The family heads of the Levites in the days of Eliashib, Joiada, Johanan and Jaddua, as well as those of the priests, were recorded in the reign of Darius the Persian. ²³The family heads among the descendants of Levi up to the time of Johanan son of Eliashib were recorded in the book of the annals. ²⁴And the leaders of the Levites were Hashabiah, Sherebiah, Jeshua son of Kadmiel, and their associates, who stood opposite them to give praise and thanksgiving, one section responding to the other, as prescribed by David the man of God.

²⁵Mattaniah, Bakbukiah, Obadiah, Meshullam, Talmon and Akkub were gatekeepers who guarded the storerooms at the gates. ²⁶They served in the days of Joiakim son of Joshua, the son of Jozadak, and in the days of Nehemiah the governor and of Ezra the priest, the teacher of the Law.

Dedication of the Wall of Jerusalem

²⁷At the dedication of the wall of Jerusalem, the Levites were sought out from where they lived and were brought to Jerusalem to celebrate joyfully the dedication with songs of thanksgiving and with the music of cymbals, harps and lyres. ²⁸The musicians also were brought together from the region around Jerusalem—from the villages of the Netophathites, ²⁹from Beth Gilgal, and from the area of Geba and Azmaveth, for the musicians had built villages for themselves around Jerusalem. ³⁰When the priests and Levites had purified themselves ceremonially, they purified the people, the gates and the wall.

³¹I had the leaders of Judah go up on top ofᶜ the wall. I also assigned two large choirs to give thanks. One was to proceed on top ofᵈ the wall to the right, toward the Dung Gate. ³²Hoshaiah and half the leaders of Judah followed them, ³³along with Azariah, Ezra, Meshullam, ³⁴Judah, Benjamin, Shemaiah, Jeremiah, ³⁵as well as some priests with trumpets, and also Zechariah son of Jonathan, the son of Shemaiah, the son of Mattaniah, the son of Micaiah, the son of Zakkur, the son of Asaph, ³⁶and his associates—Shemaiah, Azarel, Milalai, Gilalai, Maai, Nethanel, Judah and Hanani—with musical instruments prescribed by David the man of God. Ezra the teacher of the Law led the procession. ³⁷At the Fountain Gate they continued directly up the steps of the City of David on the ascent to the wall and passed above the site of David's palace to the Water Gate on the east.

³⁸The second choir proceeded in the opposite direction. I followed them on top ofᵉ the wall, together with half the people—past the Tower of the Ovens to the Broad Wall, ³⁹over the Gate of Ephraim, the Jeshanahᶠ Gate, the Fish Gate, the Tower of Hananel and the Tower of the Hundred, as far as the Sheep Gate. At the Gate of the Guard they stopped.

⁴⁰The two choirs that gave thanks then

ᵃ 14 Very many Hebrew manuscripts, some Septuagint manuscripts and Syriac (see also verse 3); most Hebrew manuscripts *Shebaniah's*
ᵇ 15 Some Septuagint manuscripts (see also verse 3); Hebrew *Meraioth's*   ᶜ 31 Or *go alongside*   ᵈ 31 Or *proceed alongside*
ᵉ 38 Or *them alongside*   ᶠ 39 Or *Old*

took their places in the house of God; so did I, together with half the officials, [41] as well as the priests—Eliakim, Maaseiah, Miniamin, Micaiah, Elioenai, Zechariah and Hananiah with their trumpets— [42] and also Maaseiah, Shemaiah, Eleazar, Uzzi, Jehohanan, Malkijah, Elam and Ezer. The choirs sang under the direction of Jezrahiah. [43] And on that day they offered great sacrifices, rejoicing because God had given them great joy. The women and children also rejoiced. The sound of rejoicing in Jerusalem could be heard far away.

[44] At that time men were appointed to be in charge of the storerooms for the contributions, firstfruits and tithes. From the fields around the towns they were to bring into the storerooms the portions required by the Law for the priests and the Levites, for Judah was pleased with the ministering priests and Levites. [45] They performed the service of their God and the service of purification, as did also the musicians and gatekeepers, according to the commands of David and his son Solomon. [46] For long ago, in the days of David and Asaph, there had been directors for the musicians and for the songs of praise and thanksgiving to God. [47] So in the days of Zerubbabel and of Nehemiah, all Israel contributed the daily portions for the musicians and the gatekeepers. They also set aside the portion for the other Levites, and the Levites set aside the portion for the descendants of Aaron.

Nehemiah's Final Reforms

13 On that day the Book of Moses was read aloud in the hearing of the people and there it was found written that no Ammonite or Moabite should ever be admitted into the assembly of God, [2] because they had not met the Israelites with food and water but had hired Balaam to call a curse down on them. (Our God, however, turned the curse into a blessing.) [3] When the people heard this law, they excluded from Israel all who were of foreign descent.

[4] Before this, Eliashib the priest had

been put in charge of the storerooms of the house of our God. He was closely associated with Tobiah, [5] and he had provided him with a large room formerly used to store the grain offerings and incense and temple articles, and also the tithes of grain, new wine and olive oil prescribed for the Levites, musicians and gatekeepers, as well as the contributions for the priests.

[6] But while all this was going on, I was not in Jerusalem, for in the thirty-second year of Artaxerxes king of Babylon I had returned to the king. Some time later I asked his permission [7] and came back to Jerusalem. Here I learned about the evil thing Eliashib had done in providing Tobiah a room in the courts of the house of God. [8] I was greatly displeased and threw all Tobiah's household goods out of the room. [9] I gave orders to purify the rooms, and then I put back into them the equipment of the house of God, with the grain offerings and the incense.

[10] I also learned that the portions assigned to the Levites had not been given to them, and that all the Levites and musicians responsible for the service had gone back to their own fields. [11] So I rebuked the officials and asked them, "Why is the house of God neglected?" Then I called them together and stationed them at their posts.

[12] All Judah brought the tithes of grain, new wine and olive oil into the storerooms. [13] I put Shelemiah the priest, Zadok the scribe, and a Levite named Pedaiah in charge of the storerooms and made Hanan son of Zakkur, the son of Mattaniah, their assistant, because they were considered trustworthy. They were made responsible for distributing the supplies to their fellow Levites.

[14] Remember me for this, my God, and do not blot out what I have so faithfully done for the house of my God and its services.

[15] In those days I saw people in Judah treading winepresses on the Sabbath and bringing in grain and loading it on donkeys, together with wine, grapes, figs and

all other kinds of loads. And they were bringing all this into Jerusalem on the Sabbath. Therefore I warned them against selling food on that day. [16]People from Tyre who lived in Jerusalem were bringing in fish and all kinds of merchandise and selling them in Jerusalem on the Sabbath to the people of Judah. [17]I rebuked the nobles of Judah and said to them, "What is this wicked thing you are doing—desecrating the Sabbath day? [18]Didn't your ancestors do the same things, so that our God brought all this calamity on us and on this city? Now you are stirring up more wrath against Israel by desecrating the Sabbath."

[19]When evening shadows fell on the gates of Jerusalem before the Sabbath, I ordered the doors to be shut and not opened until the Sabbath was over. I stationed some of my own men at the gates so that no load could be brought in on the Sabbath day. [20]Once or twice the merchants and sellers of all kinds of goods spent the night outside Jerusalem. [21]But I warned them and said, "Why do you spend the night by the wall? If you do this again, I will arrest you." From that time on they no longer came on the Sabbath. [22]Then I commanded the Levites to purify themselves and go and guard the gates in order to keep the Sabbath day holy.

Remember me for this also, my God, and show mercy to me according to your great love.

[23]Moreover, in those days I saw men of Judah who had married women from Ashdod, Ammon and Moab. [24]Half of their children spoke the language of Ashdod or the language of one of the other peoples, and did not know how to speak the language of Judah. [25]I rebuked them and called curses down on them. I beat some of the men and pulled out their hair. I made them take an oath in God's name and said: "You are not to give your daughters in marriage to their sons, nor are you to take their daughters in marriage for your sons or for yourselves. [26]Was it not because of marriages like these that Solomon king of Israel sinned? Among the many nations there was no king like him. He was loved by his God, and God made him king over all Israel, but even he was led into sin by foreign women. [27]Must we hear now that you too are doing all this terrible wickedness and are being unfaithful to our God by marrying foreign women?"

[28]One of the sons of Joiada son of Eliashib the high priest was son-in-law to Sanballat the Horonite. And I drove him away from me.

[29]Remember them, my God, because they defiled the priestly office and the covenant of the priesthood and of the Levites.

[30]So I purified the priests and the Levites of everything foreign, and assigned them duties, each to his own task. [31]I also made provision for contributions of wood at designated times, and for the firstfruits.

Remember me with favor, my God.

BOOK OUTLINE

Esther made queen
(1:1 — 2:23)

Haman's plot to destroy the Jews
(3:1 — 5:14)

The Jews win
(6:1 — 10:3)

ESTHER

The setting for the book of Esther is Susa, the capital city of Persia. It takes place during the time of King Xerxes, who ruled Persia from 486 to 465 BC. The book tells the story of a beautiful Jewish girl whom King Xerxes chose to be his queen. When Haman plotted to murder all the Jews, Queen Esther's cousin Mordecai persuaded Esther to try to save her people. Risking her own life, she appealed to the king and rescued the Jews.

Although the name of God does not appear in this book, his care for his chosen people is clearly shown. The annual days of Purim celebrate this exciting story of the rescue of the Jews. During the days of celebration the Jews read the book of Esther out loud.

Queen Vashti Deposed

1 This is what happened during the time of Xerxes,[a] the Xerxes who ruled over 127 provinces stretching from India to Cush[b]: [2]At that time King Xerxes reigned from his royal throne in the citadel of Susa, [3]and in the third year of his reign he gave a banquet for all his nobles and officials. The military leaders of Persia and Media, the princes, and the nobles of the provinces were present.

[4]For a full 180 days he displayed the vast wealth of his kingdom and the splendor and glory of his majesty. [5]When these days were over, the king gave a banquet, lasting seven days, in the enclosed garden of the king's palace, for all the people from the least to the greatest who were in the citadel of Susa. [6]The garden had hangings of white and blue linen, fastened with cords of white linen and purple material to silver rings on marble pillars. There were couches of gold and silver on a mosaic pavement of porphyry, marble, mother-of-pearl and other costly stones. [7]Wine was served in goblets of gold, each one different from the other, and the royal wine was abundant, in keeping with the king's liberality. [8]By the king's command each guest was allowed to drink with no restrictions, for the king instructed all the wine stewards to serve each man what he wished.

[9]Queen Vashti also gave a banquet for the women in the royal palace of King Xerxes.

[10]On the seventh day, when King Xerxes was in high spirits from wine, he commanded the seven eunuchs who served him—Mehuman, Biztha, Harbona, Bigtha, Abagtha, Zethar and Karkas— [11]to bring before him Queen Vashti, wearing her royal crown, in order to display her beauty to the people and nobles, for she was lovely to look at. [12]But when the attendants delivered the king's command, Queen Vashti refused to come. Then the king became furious and burned with anger.

[13]Since it was customary for the king to consult experts in matters of law and justice, he spoke with the wise men who understood the times [14]and were closest to the king—Karshena, Shethar, Admatha, Tarshish, Meres, Marsena and Memukan, the seven nobles of Persia and Media who had special access to the king and were highest in the kingdom.

[15]"According to law, what must be done to Queen Vashti?" he asked. "She has not obeyed the command of King Xerxes that the eunuchs have taken to her."

[16]Then Memukan replied in the presence of the king and the nobles, "Queen Vashti has done wrong, not only against the king but also against all the nobles and the peoples of all the provinces of King Xerxes. [17]For the queen's conduct will become known to all the women, and so they will despise their husbands and say, 'King Xerxes commanded Queen Vashti to be brought before him, but she would not come.' [18]This very day the Persian and Median women of the nobility who have heard about the queen's conduct will respond to all the king's nobles in the same way. There will be no end of disrespect and discord.

[19]"Therefore, if it pleases the king, let him issue a royal decree and let it be written in the laws of Persia and Media, which cannot be repealed, that Vashti is never again to enter the presence of King Xerxes. Also let the king give her royal position to someone else who is better than she. [20]Then when the king's edict is proclaimed throughout all his vast realm, all the women will respect their husbands, from the least to the greatest."

[21]The king and his nobles were pleased with this advice, so the king did as Memukan proposed. [22]He sent dispatches to all parts of the kingdom, to each province in its own script and to each people in their own language, proclaiming that every man should be ruler over his own household, using his native tongue.

Esther Made Queen

2 Later when King Xerxes' fury had subsided, he remembered Vashti and what she had done and what he had decreed about her. [2]Then the

---

[a] *1* Hebrew *Ahasuerus*; here and throughout Esther   [b] *1* That is, the upper Nile region

king's personal attendants proposed, "Let a search be made for beautiful young virgins for the king. ³Let the king appoint commissioners in every province of his realm to bring all these beautiful young women into the harem at the citadel of Susa. Let them be placed under the care of Hegai, the king's eunuch, who is in charge of the women; and let beauty treatments be given to them. ⁴Then let the young woman who pleases the king be queen instead of Vashti." This advice appealed to the king, and he followed it.

⁵Now there was in the citadel of Susa a Jew of the tribe of Benjamin, named Mordecai son of Jair, the son of Shimei, the son of Kish, ⁶who had been carried into exile from Jerusalem by Nebuchadnezzar king of Babylon, among those taken captive with Jehoiachin*ᵃ* king of Judah. ⁷Mordecai had a cousin named Hadassah, whom he had brought up because she had neither father nor mother. This young woman, who was also known as Esther, had a lovely figure and was beautiful. Mordecai had taken her as his own daughter when her father and mother died.

⁸When the king's order and edict had been proclaimed, many young women were brought to the citadel of Susa and put under the care of Hegai. Esther also was taken to the king's palace and entrusted to Hegai, who had charge of the harem. ⁹She pleased him and won his favor. Immediately he provided her with her beauty treatments and special food. He assigned to her seven female attendants selected from the king's palace and moved her and her attendants into the best place in the harem.

¹⁰Esther had not revealed her nationality and family background, because Mordecai had forbidden her to do so. ¹¹Every day he walked back and forth near the courtyard of the harem to find out how Esther was and what was happening to her.

¹²Before a young woman's turn came to go in to King Xerxes, she had to complete twelve months of beauty treatments prescribed for the women, six months with oil of myrrh and six with perfumes and cosmetics. ¹³And this is how she would go to the king: Anything she wanted was given her to take with her from the harem to the king's palace. ¹⁴In the evening she would go there and in the morning return to another part of the harem to the care of Shaashgaz, the king's eunuch who was in charge of the concubines. She would not return to the king unless he was pleased with her and summoned her by name.

¹⁵When the turn came for Esther (the young woman Mordecai had adopted, the daughter of his uncle Abihail) to go to the king, she asked for nothing other than what Hegai, the king's eunuch who was in charge of the harem, suggested. And Esther won the favor of everyone who saw her. ¹⁶She was taken to King Xerxes in the royal residence in the tenth month, the month of Tebeth, in the seventh year of his reign.

¹⁷Now the king was attracted to Esther more than to any of the other women, and she won his favor and approval more than any of the other virgins. So he set a royal crown on her head and made her queen instead of Vashti. ¹⁸And the king gave a great banquet, Esther's banquet, for all his nobles and officials. He proclaimed a holiday throughout the provinces and distributed gifts with royal liberality.

Mordecai Uncovers a Conspiracy

¹⁹When the virgins were assembled a second time, Mordecai was sitting at the king's gate. ²⁰But Esther had kept secret her family background and nationality just as Mordecai had told her to do, for she continued to follow Mordecai's instructions as she had done when he was bringing her up.

²¹During the time Mordecai was sitting at the king's gate, Bigthana*ᵇ* and Teresh, two of the king's officers who guarded the doorway, became angry and conspired to assassinate King Xerxes. ²²But Mordecai found out about the plot and told Queen Esther, who in turn reported it to the

---

ᵃ 6 Hebrew *Jeconiah*, a variant of *Jehoiachin*
ᵇ 21 Hebrew *Bigthan*, a variant of *Bigthana*

king, giving credit to Mordecai. ²³And when the report was investigated and found to be true, the two officials were impaled on poles. All this was recorded in the book of the annals in the presence of the king.

Haman's Plot to Destroy the Jews

3 After these events, King Xerxes honored Haman son of Hammedatha, the Agagite, elevating him and giving him a seat of honor higher than that of all the other nobles. ²All the royal officials at the king's gate knelt down and paid honor to Haman, for the king had commanded this concerning him. But Mordecai would not kneel down or pay him honor.

³Then the royal officials at the king's gate asked Mordecai, "Why do you disobey the king's command?" ⁴Day after day they spoke to him but he refused to comply. Therefore they told Haman about it

to see whether Mordecai's behavior would be tolerated, for he had told them he was a Jew.

⁵When Haman saw that Mordecai would not kneel down or pay him honor, he was enraged. ⁶Yet having learned who Mordecai's people were, he scorned the idea of killing only Mordecai. Instead Haman looked for a way to destroy all Mordecai's people, the Jews, throughout the whole kingdom of Xerxes.

⁷In the twelfth year of King Xerxes, in the first month, the month of Nisan, the *pur* (that is, the lot) was cast in the presence of Haman to select a day and month. And the lot fell on^a the twelfth month, the month of Adar.

⁸Then Haman said to King Xerxes, "There is a certain people dispersed among the peoples in all the provinces of your kingdom who keep themselves sep-

---

^a 7 Septuagint; Hebrew does not have *And the lot fell on.*

ROCK SOLID *principles*

Esther 3:1–15

Don't tolerate racism.

"Don't tell me where I can or can't sit!" Stephanie fumed. "I'm done with you!" Since middle school Stephanie had been part of a tight group that frowned on its members spending time with people outside the clique — especially if that outsider looked different from them. When Stephanie started hanging out with Danielle, she found out her group was not only insecure and clingy but prejudiced as well. Stephanie didn't advertise her study sessions with Danielle. But she didn't hide an invitation to their lunch table. Stephanie saw no reason she shouldn't eat with her new friend. In fact, she suddenly saw plenty of reasons she wanted a new place to sit.

Haman the noble was so enraged when Esther's older cousin Mordecai refused to bow to him that he looked for a way to destroy every Jew in the kingdom (Esther 3:6). He said the Jews were different ... intolerable ... deserving destruction (see Esther 3:8). If you don't deal with your fear of people different from you, racism can be the result.

arate. Their customs are different from those of all other people, and they do not obey the king's laws; it is not in the king's best interest to tolerate them. ⁹If it pleases the king, let a decree be issued to destroy them, and I will give ten thousand talents*ᵃ* of silver to the king's administrators for the royal treasury."

¹⁰So the king took his signet ring from his finger and gave it to Haman son of Hammedatha, the Agagite, the enemy of the Jews. ¹¹"Keep the money," the king said to Haman, "and do with the people as you please."

¹²Then on the thirteenth day of the first month the royal secretaries were summoned. They wrote out in the script of each province and in the language of each people all Haman's orders to the king's satraps, the governors of the various provinces and the nobles of the various peoples. These were written in the name of King Xerxes himself and sealed with his own ring. ¹³Dispatches were sent by couriers to all the king's provinces with the order to destroy, kill and annihilate all the Jews—young and old, women and children—on a single day, the thirteenth day of the twelfth month, the month of Adar, and to plunder their goods. ¹⁴A copy of the text of the edict was to be issued as law in every province and made known to the people of every nationality so they would be ready for that day.

¹⁵The couriers went out, spurred on by the king's command, and the edict was issued in the citadel of Susa. The king and Haman sat down to drink, but the city of Susa was bewildered.

Mordecai Persuades Esther to Help

4 When Mordecai learned of all that had been done, he tore his clothes, put on sackcloth and ashes, and went out into the city, wailing loudly and bitterly. ²But he went only as far as the king's gate, because no one clothed in sackcloth was allowed to enter it. ³In every province to which the edict and order of the king came, there was great mourning among the Jews, with fasting, weeping

and wailing. Many lay in sackcloth and ashes.

⁴When Esther's eunuchs and female attendants came and told her about Mordecai, she was in great distress. She sent clothes for him to put on instead of his sackcloth, but he would not accept them. ⁵Then Esther summoned Hathak, one of the king's eunuchs assigned to attend her, and ordered him to find out what was troubling Mordecai and why.

⁶So Hathak went out to Mordecai in the open square of the city in front of the king's gate. ⁷Mordecai told him everything that had happened to him, including the exact amount of money Haman had promised to pay into the royal treasury for the destruction of the Jews. ⁸He also gave him a copy of the text of the edict for their annihilation, which had been published in Susa, to show to Esther and explain it to her, and he told him to instruct her to go into the king's presence to beg for mercy and plead with him for her people.

⁹Hathak went back and reported to Esther what Mordecai had said. ¹⁰Then she instructed him to say to Mordecai, ¹¹"All the king's officials and the people of the royal provinces know that for any man or woman who approaches the king in the inner court without being summoned the king has but one law: that they be put to death unless the king extends the gold scepter to them and spares their lives. But thirty days have passed since I was called to go to the king."

¹²When Esther's words were reported to Mordecai, ¹³he sent back this answer: "Do not think that because you are in the king's house you alone of all the Jews will escape. ¹⁴For if you remain silent at this time, relief and deliverance for the Jews will arise from another place, but you and your father's family will perish. And who knows but that you have come to your royal position for such a time as this?"

¹⁵Then Esther sent this reply to Mordecai: ¹⁶"Go, gather together all the Jews

ᵃ 9 That is, about 375 tons or about 340 metric tons

ROCK SOLID *plans*

Esther 4:13

Step up at the right time.

Esther hid her faith in the God of Israel even as she was swept into the palace of one of the most powerful rulers on earth, Xerxes of Persia, and was chosen to be queen. Yet when a royal decree threatened all of the Jews in the kingdom with slaughter, she risked her life to speak up. Esther revealed her identity and pleaded for her people's safety. She stood against evil when no one else could. Esther was God's right person in God's right place — and she stepped up at God's right time.

Your next step: Look for opportunities to boldly stand for God — with others or on your own.

who are in Susa, and fast for me. Do not eat or drink for three days, night or day. I and my attendants will fast as you do. When this is done, I will go to the king, even though it is against the law. And if I perish, I perish."

¹⁷So Mordecai went away and carried out all of Esther's instructions.

Esther's Request to the King

5 On the third day Esther put on her royal robes and stood in the inner court of the palace, in front of the king's hall. The king was sitting on his royal throne in the hall, facing the entrance. ²When he saw Queen Esther standing in the court, he was pleased with her and held out to her the gold scepter that was in his hand. So Esther approached and touched the tip of the scepter.

³Then the king asked, "What is it, Queen Esther? What is your request? Even up to half the kingdom, it will be given you."

⁴"If it pleases the king," replied Esther, "let the king, together with Haman, come today to a banquet I have prepared for him."

⁵"Bring Haman at once," the king said, "so that we may do what Esther asks."

So the king and Haman went to the banquet Esther had prepared. ⁶As they were drinking wine, the king again asked Esther, "Now what is your petition? It will be given you. And what is your request? Even up to half the kingdom, it will be granted."

⁷Esther replied, "My petition and my request is this: ⁸If the king regards me with favor and if it pleases the king to grant my petition and fulfill my request, let the king and Haman come tomorrow to the banquet I will prepare for them. Then I will answer the king's question."

Haman's Rage Against Mordecai

⁹Haman went out that day happy and in high spirits. But when he saw Mordecai at the king's gate and observed that he neither rose nor showed fear in his presence, he was filled with rage against Mordecai. ¹⁰Nevertheless, Haman restrained himself and went home.

Calling together his friends and Zeresh, his wife, ¹¹Haman boasted to them about his vast wealth, his many sons, and all the ways the king had honored him and how he had elevated him above the other nobles and officials. ¹²"And that's not all," Haman added. "I'm the only person Queen Esther invited to accompany the king to the banquet she gave. And she has invited me along with the king tomorrow. ¹³But all this gives me no satisfaction as long as I see that Jew Mordecai sitting at the king's gate."

¹⁴His wife Zeresh and all his friends said to him, "Have a pole set up, reaching to a height of fifty cubits,^a and ask the king in the morning to have Mordecai impaled on it. Then go with the king to the banquet and enjoy yourself." This suggestion delighted Haman, and he had the pole set up.

^a *14* That is, about 75 feet or about 23 meters

Mordecai Honored

6 That night the king could not sleep; so he ordered the book of the chronicles, the record of his reign, to be brought in and read to him. ²It was found recorded there that Mordecai had exposed Bigthana and Teresh, two of the king's officers who guarded the doorway, who had conspired to assassinate King Xerxes.

³"What honor and recognition has Mordecai received for this?" the king asked.

"Nothing has been done for him," his attendants answered.

⁴The king said, "Who is in the court?" Now Haman had just entered the outer court of the palace to speak to the king about impaling Mordecai on the pole he had set up for him.

⁵His attendants answered, "Haman is standing in the court."

"Bring him in," the king ordered.

⁶When Haman entered, the king asked him, "What should be done for the man the king delights to honor?"

Now Haman thought to himself, "Who is there that the king would rather honor than me?" ⁷So he answered the king, "For the man the king delights to honor, ⁸have them bring a royal robe the king has worn and a horse the king has ridden, one with a royal crest placed on its head. ⁹Then let the robe and horse be entrusted to one of the king's most noble princes. Let them robe the man the king delights to honor, and lead him on the horse through the city streets, proclaiming before him, 'This is what is done for the man the king delights to honor!'"

¹⁰"Go at once," the king commanded Haman. "Get the robe and the horse and do just as you have suggested for Mordecai the Jew, who sits at the king's gate. Do not neglect anything you have recommended."

¹¹So Haman got the robe and the horse. He robed Mordecai, and led him on horseback through the city streets, proclaiming before him, "This is what is done for the man the king delights to honor!"

¹²Afterward Mordecai returned to the king's gate. But Haman rushed home, with his head covered in grief, ¹³and told Zeresh his wife and all his friends everything that had happened to him.

His advisers and his wife Zeresh said to him, "Since Mordecai, before whom your downfall has started, is of Jewish origin, you cannot stand against him—you will surely come to ruin!" ¹⁴While they were still talking with him, the king's eunuchs arrived and hurried Haman away to the banquet Esther had prepared.

Haman Impaled

7 So the king and Haman went to Queen Esther's banquet, ²and as they were drinking wine on the second day, the king again asked, "Queen Esther, what is your petition? It will be given you. What is your request? Even up to half the kingdom, it will be granted."

³Then Queen Esther answered, "If I have found favor with you, Your Majesty, and if it pleases you, grant me my life—this is my petition. And spare my people—this is my request. ⁴For I and my people have been sold to be destroyed, killed and annihilated. If we had merely been sold as male and female slaves, I would have kept quiet, because no such distress would justify disturbing the king.*"

⁵King Xerxes asked Queen Esther, "Who is he? Where is he—the man who has dared to do such a thing?"

⁶Esther said, "An adversary and enemy! This vile Haman!"

Then Haman was terrified before the king and queen. ⁷The king got up in a rage, left his wine and went out into the palace garden. But Haman, realizing that the king had already decided his fate, stayed behind to beg Queen Esther for his life.

⁸Just as the king returned from the palace garden to the banquet hall, Haman was falling on the couch where Esther was reclining.

The king exclaimed, "Will he even molest the queen while she is with me in the house?"

As soon as the word left the king's

ᵃ 4 Or quiet, but the compensation our adversary offers cannot be compared with the loss the king would suffer mouth, they covered Haman's face. ⁹Then Harbona, one of the eunuchs attending the king, said, "A pole reaching to a height of fifty cubits*ᵃ* stands by Haman's house. He had it set up for Mordecai, who spoke up to help the king."

The king said, "Impale him on it!" ¹⁰So they impaled Haman on the pole he had set up for Mordecai. Then the king's fury subsided.

The King's Edict in Behalf of the Jews

8 That same day King Xerxes gave Queen Esther the estate of Haman, the enemy of the Jews. And Mordecai came into the presence of the king, for Esther had told how he was related to her. ²The king took off his signet ring, which he had reclaimed from Haman, and presented it to Mordecai. And Esther appointed him over Haman's estate.

³Esther again pleaded with the king, falling at his feet and weeping. She begged him to put an end to the evil plan of Haman the Agagite, which he had devised against the Jews. ⁴Then the king extended the gold scepter to Esther and she arose and stood before him.

⁵"If it pleases the king," she said, "and

ᵃ 9 That is, about 75 feet or about 23 meters

Esther 8

Esther fulfilled God's purpose.

Esther started life in the king's palace as a beauty queen, but she ended up saving her people. Her family came from Judah, part of the large population dragged to captivity in Babylon by King Nebuchadnezzar. She was somehow orphaned—the Bible doesn't give any details—and raised by her older cousin Mordecai.

At that time King Xerxes of Persia was searching for a new wife after Queen Vashti refused his command to parade before some drunken guests. Because Esther "had a lovely figure and was beautiful" (Esther 2:7), she was gathered with crowds of other girls and taken to the royal city of Susa. After 12 months of oils, perfumes and cosmetics, she went to the king, where "she won his favor and approval more than any of the other virgins" (Esther 2:17).

Xerxes immediately crowned her queen, but all the while she kept her nationality a secret. Outside the palace, however, her people (the Jews) were being threatened with execution. When Mordecai told her to speak up, she protested that she could be killed for entering the king's presence uninvited. Her older cousin replied that if she remained silent she would die—and that perhaps God had brought her to the throne for "such a time as this" (Esther 4:14).

Esther took a strange path to power. But this beautiful woman proved she had courage and brains. Her bold plan prevented the slaughter of the Jews, fulfilling the Lord's purpose not just for her own life but for her entire people.

You can find Esther throughout the book named for her.

UNSHAKEN people

if he regards me with favor and thinks it the right thing to do, and if he is pleased with me, let an order be written overruling the dispatches that Haman son of Hammedatha, the Agagite, devised and wrote to destroy the Jews in all the king's provinces. [6] For how can I bear to see disaster fall on my people? How can I bear to see the destruction of my family?"

[7] King Xerxes replied to Queen Esther and to Mordecai the Jew, "Because Haman attacked the Jews, I have given his estate to Esther, and they have impaled him on the pole he set up. [8] Now write another decree in the king's name in behalf of the Jews as seems best to you, and seal it with the king's signet ring—for no document written in the king's name and sealed with his ring can be revoked."

[9] At once the royal secretaries were summoned—on the twenty-third day of the third month, the month of Sivan. They wrote out all Mordecai's orders to the Jews, and to the satraps, governors and nobles of the 127 provinces stretching from India to Cush.[a] These orders were written in the script of each province and the language of each people and also to the Jews in their own script and language. [10] Mordecai wrote in the name of King Xerxes, sealed the dispatches with the king's signet ring, and sent them by mounted couriers, who rode fast horses especially bred for the king.

[11] The king's edict granted the Jews in every city the right to assemble and protect themselves; to destroy, kill and annihilate the armed men of any nationality or province who might attack them and their women and children,[b] and to plunder the property of their enemies. [12] The day appointed for the Jews to do this in all the provinces of King Xerxes was the thirteenth day of the twelfth month, the month of Adar. [13] A copy of the text of the edict was to be issued as law in every province and made known to the people of every nationality so that the Jews would be ready on that day to avenge themselves on their enemies.

[14] The couriers, riding the royal horses, went out, spurred on by the king's command, and the edict was issued in the citadel of Susa.

The Triumph of the Jews

[15] When Mordecai left the king's presence, he was wearing royal garments of blue and white, a large crown of gold and a purple robe of fine linen. And the city of Susa held a joyous celebration. [16] For the Jews it was a time of happiness and joy, gladness and honor. [17] In every province and in every city to which the edict of the king came, there was joy and gladness among the Jews, with feasting and celebrating. And many people of other nationalities became Jews because fear of the Jews had seized them.

9 On the thirteenth day of the twelfth month, the month of Adar, the edict commanded by the king was to be carried out. On this day the enemies of the Jews had hoped to overpower them, but now the tables were turned and the Jews got the upper hand over those who hated them. [2] The Jews assembled in their cities in all the provinces of King Xerxes to attack those determined to destroy them. No one could stand against them, because the people of all the other nationalities were afraid of them. [3] And all the nobles of the provinces, the satraps, the governors and the king's administrators helped the Jews, because fear of Mordecai had seized them. [4] Mordecai was prominent in the palace; his reputation spread throughout the provinces, and he became more and more powerful.

[5] The Jews struck down all their enemies with the sword, killing and destroying them, and they did what they pleased to those who hated them. [6] In the citadel of Susa, the Jews killed and destroyed five hundred men. [7] They also killed Parshandatha, Dalphon, Aspatha, [8] Poratha, Adalia, Aridatha, [9] Parmashta, Arisai, Aridai and Vaizatha, [10] the ten sons of Haman son of Hammedatha, the enemy of the

Jews. But they did not lay their hands on the plunder.

¹¹The number of those killed in the citadel of Susa was reported to the king that same day. ¹²The king said to Queen Esther, "The Jews have killed and destroyed five hundred men and the ten sons of Haman in the citadel of Susa. What have they done in the rest of the king's provinces? Now what is your petition? It will be given you. What is your request? It will also be granted."

¹³"If it pleases the king," Esther answered, "give the Jews in Susa permission to carry out this day's edict tomorrow also, and let Haman's ten sons be impaled on poles."

¹⁴So the king commanded that this be done. An edict was issued in Susa, and they impaled the ten sons of Haman. ¹⁵The Jews in Susa came together on the fourteenth day of the month of Adar, and they put to death in Susa three hundred men, but they did not lay their hands on the plunder.

¹⁶Meanwhile, the remainder of the Jews who were in the king's provinces also assembled to protect themselves and get relief from their enemies. They killed seventy-five thousand of them but did not lay their hands on the plunder. ¹⁷This happened on the thirteenth day of the month of Adar, and on the fourteenth they rested and made it a day of feasting and joy.

¹⁸The Jews in Susa, however, had assembled on the thirteenth and fourteenth, and then on the fifteenth they rested and made it a day of feasting and joy.

¹⁹That is why rural Jews—those living in villages—observe the fourteenth of the month of Adar as a day of joy and feasting, a day for giving presents to each other.

Purim Established

²⁰Mordecai recorded these events, and he sent letters to all the Jews throughout the provinces of King Xerxes, near and far, ²¹to have them celebrate annually the fourteenth and fifteenth days of the month of Adar ²²as the time when the Jews got relief from their enemies, and as

Esther 9:1–17

God is heroic.

The people of God looked doomed. Even though Queen Esther had risked her life to speak up for her people, the Jews were still in danger. King Xerxes had been duped into signing a law that all Jews could be killed and their property seized, and that law couldn't be undone (see Esther 3:1–15). But God is a rescuer … a protector … a hero. A new royal decree was issued that the Jews could assemble together and fight back against their attackers (see Esther 8:11). Instead of being annihilated, the Jews destroyed their enemies. God's people weren't spared because of their own ingenuity or power, but because the Lord came to their side and saved them from their enemies.

So … When has God rescued you when you felt doomed?

the month when their sorrow was turned into joy and their mourning into a day of celebration. He wrote them to observe the days as days of feasting and joy and giving presents of food to one another and gifts to the poor.

²³So the Jews agreed to continue the celebration they had begun, doing what Mordecai had written to them. ²⁴For Haman son of Hammedatha, the Agagite, the enemy of all the Jews, had plotted against the Jews to destroy them and had cast the *pur* (that is, the lot) for their ruin and destruction. ²⁵But when the plot came to the king's attention,ᵃ he issued written orders that the evil scheme Haman had devised against the Jews should come back onto his own head, and that he and his sons should be impaled on

---

ᵃ 25 Or *when Esther came before the king*

poles. ²⁶(Therefore these days were called Purim, from the word *pur*.) Because of everything written in this letter and because of what they had seen and what had happened to them, ²⁷the Jews took it on themselves to establish the custom that they and their descendants and all who join them should without fail observe these two days every year, in the way prescribed and at the time appointed. ²⁸These days should be remembered and observed in every generation by every family, and in every province and in every city. And these days of Purim should never fail to be celebrated by the Jews—nor should the memory of these days die out among their descendants.

²⁹So Queen Esther, daughter of Abihail, along with Mordecai the Jew, wrote with full authority to confirm this second letter concerning Purim. ³⁰And Mordecai sent letters to all the Jews in the 127 provinces of Xerxes' kingdom—words of goodwill and assurance— ³¹to establish these days of Purim at their designated times, as Mordecai the Jew and Queen Esther had decreed for them, and as they had established for themselves and their descendants in regard to their times of fasting and lamentation. ³²Esther's decree confirmed these regulations about Purim, and it was written down in the records.

The Greatness of Mordecai

10 King Xerxes imposed tribute throughout the empire, to its distant shores. ²And all his acts of power and might, together with a full account of the greatness of Mordecai, whom the king had promoted, are they not written in the book of the annals of the kings of Media and Persia? ³Mordecai the Jew was second in rank to King Xerxes, preeminent among the Jews, and held in high esteem by his many fellow Jews, because he worked for the good of his people and spoke up for the welfare of all the Jews.

JOB

BOOK OUTLINE

The book of Job is named for its main character, a righteous man who was very rich. Even after losing everything he owned and suffering from a terrible sickness, Job still confessed his love for God.

The book questions the reasons for suffering, especially why good people or those who love God suffer. Job's friends insist he was suffering as punishment for his sin. Job defends himself by insisting that he has done nothing seriously wrong and then expresses his trust in God.

Finally God speaks and shows his mighty power. Job then admits that God is too great and wonderful for us to understand. Because Job remains faithful to God through his ordeal, God blesses him and rebuilds his family and restores his wealth.

Prologue

In the land of Uz there lived a man whose name was Job. This man was blameless and upright; he feared God and shunned evil. ²He had seven sons and three daughters, ³and he owned seven thousand sheep, three thousand camels, five hundred yoke of oxen and five hundred donkeys, and had a large number of servants. He was the greatest man among all the people of the East.

⁴His sons used to hold feasts in their homes on their birthdays, and they would invite their three sisters to eat and drink with them. ⁵When a period of feasting had run its course, Job would make arrangements for them to be purified. Early in the morning he would sacrifice a burnt offering for each of them, thinking, "Perhaps my children have sinned and cursed God in their hearts." This was Job's regular custom.

⁶One day the angels*a* came to present themselves before the Lord, and Satan*b* also came with them. ⁷The Lord said to Satan, "Where have you come from?"

Satan answered the Lord, "From roaming throughout the earth, going back and forth on it."

⁸Then the Lord said to Satan, "Have you considered my servant Job? There is no one on earth like him; he is blameless and upright, a man who fears God and shuns evil."

⁹"Does Job fear God for nothing?" Satan replied. ¹⁰"Have you not put a hedge around him and his household and everything he has? You have blessed the work of his hands, so that his flocks and herds are spread throughout the land. ¹¹But now stretch out your hand and strike everything he has, and he will surely curse you to your face."

¹²The Lord said to Satan, "Very well, then, everything he has is in your power, but on the man himself do not lay a finger." Then Satan went out from the presence of the Lord.

¹³One day when Job's sons and daughters were feasting and drinking wine at the oldest brother's house, ¹⁴a messenger came to Job and said, "The oxen were plowing and the donkeys were grazing nearby, ¹⁵and the Sabeans attacked and made off with them. They put the servants to the sword, and I am the only one who has escaped to tell you!"

¹⁶While he was still speaking, another messenger came and said, "The fire of God fell from the heavens and burned up the sheep and the servants, and I am the only one who has escaped to tell you!"

¹⁷While he was still speaking, another messenger came and said, "The Chaldeans

---

a 6 Hebrew *the sons of God*   *b* 6 Hebrew *satan* means *adversary*.

Job 1:6–22

Satan lives.

The Bible never portrays Satan as a cartoon figure wearing red tights and wielding a pitchfork. At the start of the Bible he appears as the snake in the Garden of Eden, luring humankind into rebellion against God (see Genesis 3:1–7). In the back of the Bible he's the leader of worldwide evil, a being who gets tossed in the lake of fire (see Revelation 20:10). And in the middle he "prowls around like a roaring lion looking for someone to devour" (1 Peter 5:8). Here in Job Satan talks with God in heaven, complaining that he can't shake Job's faith because the Lord protects the devout man too well. Catch these facts about Satan: He's real. He wants to pull you into whatever sin he can. And he's an enemy to resist, but we know that other believers all around the world have to face the same kind of testing (see 1 Peter 5:9).

Think: How do you see Satan active in your world?

ROCK SOLID *truths*

formed three raiding parties and swept down on your camels and made off with them. They put the servants to the sword, and I am the only one who has escaped to tell you!"

¹⁸While he was still speaking, yet another messenger came and said, "Your sons and daughters were feasting and drinking wine at the oldest brother's house, ¹⁹when suddenly a mighty wind swept in from the desert and struck the four corners of the house. It collapsed on them and they are dead, and I am the only one who has escaped to tell you!"

²⁰At this, Job got up and tore his robe and shaved his head. Then he fell to the ground in worship ²¹and said:

> "Naked I came from my mother's
>   womb,
>   and naked I will depart.ᵃ
> The Lord gave and the Lord has
>   taken away;
>   may the name of the Lord be
>   praised."

²²In all this, Job did not sin by charging God with wrongdoing.

2 On another day the angelsᵇ came to present themselves before the Lord, and Satan also came with them to present himself before him. ²And the Lord said to Satan, "Where have you come from?"

Satan answered the Lord, "From roaming throughout the earth, going back and forth on it."

³Then the Lord said to Satan, "Have you considered my servant Job? There is no one on earth like him; he is blameless and upright, a man who fears God and shuns evil. And he still maintains his integrity, though you incited me against him to ruin him without any reason."

⁴"Skin for skin!" Satan replied. "A man will give all he has for his own life. ⁵But now stretch out your hand and strike his flesh and bones, and he will surely curse you to your face."

⁶The Lord said to Satan, "Very well, then, he is in your hands; but you must spare his life."

⁷So Satan went out from the presence of the Lord and afflicted Job with painful sores from the soles of his feet to the crown of his head. ⁸Then Job took a piece of broken pottery and scraped himself with it as he sat among the ashes.

⁹His wife said to him, "Are you still maintaining your integrity? Curse God and die!"

¹⁰He replied, "You are talking like a foolishᶜ woman. Shall we accept good from God, and not trouble?"

In all this, Job did not sin in what he said.

¹¹When Job's three friends, Eliphaz the Temanite, Bildad the Shuhite and Zophar the Naamathite, heard about all the troubles that had come upon him, they set out from their homes and met together by agreement to go and sympathize with him and comfort him. ¹²When they saw him from a distance, they could hardly recognize him; they began to weep aloud, and they tore their robes and sprinkled dust on their heads. ¹³Then they sat on the ground with him for seven days and seven nights. No one said a word to him, because they saw how great his suffering was.

Job Speaks

3 After this, Job opened his mouth and cursed the day of his birth. ²He said:

> ³"May the day of my birth perish,
>   and the night that said, 'A boy is
>   conceived!'
> ⁴That day—may it turn to darkness;
>   may God above not care about it;
>   may no light shine on it.
> ⁵May gloom and utter darkness claim it
>   once more;
>   may a cloud settle over it;
>   may blackness overwhelm it.
> ⁶That night—may thick darkness
>   seize it;
>   may it not be included among the
>   days of the year
>   nor be entered in any of the months.

ᵃ 21 Or *will return there*   ᵇ 1 Hebrew *the sons of God*   ᶜ 10 The Hebrew word rendered *foolish* denotes moral deficiency.

ROCK SOLID
principles

Job 2:11–13

Sometimes it's best to shut up.

Adam had a place near his house where he hid when life got difficult. Nothing he faced was out-and-out terrible, but almost everything was more than a little bad. It all pushed him into a funk he had to work hard to shake. But he always liked the spot where a small creek dumped into a wide marsh. No matter the season, there was scenery to soak in and wildlife to spot. Sometimes his buddies joined him. They tried to talk about Adam's problems, but he told them to be quiet. There were times he wanted to talk. But not here. Not now. When Adam was down by the marsh, he just wanted the world to stop for a while.

Much of the book of Job records the words of Job's friends Eliphaz, Bildad, and Zophar. Their long speeches end up doing Job more harm than good. They should have kept their mouths shut—like they did when they first saw his pain (see Job 2:13). Sometimes sitting in silence with a suffering friend is the kindest thing you can do.

^{7}May that night be barren;
  may no shout of joy be heard in it.
^{8}May those who curse days^a curse that day,
  those who are ready to rouse Leviathan.
^{9}May its morning stars become dark;
  may it wait for daylight in vain
  and not see the first rays of dawn,
^{10}for it did not shut the doors of the womb on me
  to hide trouble from my eyes.

^{11}"Why did I not perish at birth,
  and die as I came from the womb?
^{12}Why were there knees to receive me
  and breasts that I might be nursed?
^{13}For now I would be lying down in peace;
  I would be asleep and at rest
^{14}with kings and rulers of the earth,
  who built for themselves places now lying in ruins,
^{15}with princes who had gold,
  who filled their houses with silver.

^{16}Or why was I not hidden away in the ground like a stillborn child,
  like an infant who never saw the light of day?
^{17}There the wicked cease from turmoil,
  and there the weary are at rest.
^{18}Captives also enjoy their ease;
  they no longer hear the slave driver's shout.
^{19}The small and the great are there,
  and the slaves are freed from their owners.

^{20}"Why is light given to those in misery,
  and life to the bitter of soul,
^{21}to those who long for death that does not come,
  who search for it more than for hidden treasure,
^{22}who are filled with gladness
  and rejoice when they reach the grave?

^{a} 8 Or *curse the sea*

²³ Why is life given to a man
  whose way is hidden,
  whom God has hedged in?
²⁴ For sighing has become my daily food;
  my groans pour out like water.
²⁵ What I feared has come upon me;
  what I dreaded has happened to me.
²⁶ I have no peace, no quietness;
  I have no rest, but only turmoil."

Eliphaz

4 Then Eliphaz the Temanite replied:

² "If someone ventures a word with you,
  will you be impatient?
  But who can keep from speaking?
³ Think how you have instructed many,
  how you have strengthened feeble
  hands.
⁴ Your words have supported those who
  stumbled;
  you have strengthened faltering
  knees.
⁵ But now trouble comes to you, and
  you are discouraged;
  it strikes you, and you are dismayed.
⁶ Should not your piety be your
  confidence
  and your blameless ways your hope?

⁷ "Consider now: Who, being innocent,
  has ever perished?
  Where were the upright ever
  destroyed?
⁸ As I have observed, those who plow
  evil
  and those who sow trouble reap it.
⁹ At the breath of God they perish;
  at the blast of his anger they are no
  more.
¹⁰ The lions may roar and growl,
  yet the teeth of the great lions are
  broken.
¹¹ The lion perishes for lack of prey,
  and the cubs of the lioness are
  scattered.

¹² "A word was secretly brought to me,
  my ears caught a whisper of it.
¹³ Amid disquieting dreams in the night,
  when deep sleep falls on people,

¹⁴ fear and trembling seized me
  and made all my bones shake.
¹⁵ A spirit glided past my face,
  and the hair on my body stood on end.
¹⁶ It stopped,
  but I could not tell what it was.
  A form stood before my eyes,
  and I heard a hushed voice:
¹⁷ 'Can a mortal be more righteous than
  God?
  Can even a strong man be more
  pure than his Maker?
¹⁸ If God places no trust in his servants,
  if he charges his angels with error,
¹⁹ how much more those who live in
  houses of clay,
  whose foundations are in the dust,
  who are crushed more readily than a
  moth!
²⁰ Between dawn and dusk they are
  broken to pieces;
  unnoticed, they perish forever.
²¹ Are not the cords of their tent pulled
  up,
  so that they die without wisdom?'

5 "Call if you will, but who will
  answer you?
  To which of the holy ones will
  you turn?
² Resentment kills a fool,
  and envy slays the simple.
³ I myself have seen a fool taking root,
  but suddenly his house was cursed.
⁴ His children are far from safety,
  crushed in court without a defender.
⁵ The hungry consume his harvest,
  taking it even from among thorns,
  and the thirsty pant after his
  wealth.
⁶ For hardship does not spring from the
  soil,
  nor does trouble sprout from the
  ground.
⁷ Yet man is born to trouble
  as surely as sparks fly upward.

⁸ "But if I were you, I would appeal to
  God;
  I would lay my cause before him.
⁹ He performs wonders that cannot be
  fathomed,

miracles that cannot be counted.
¹⁰ He provides rain for the earth;
 he sends water on the countryside.
¹¹ The lowly he sets on high,
 and those who mourn are lifted to
 safety.
¹² He thwarts the plans of the crafty,
 so that their hands achieve no
 success.
¹³ He catches the wise in their craftiness,
 and the schemes of the wily are
 swept away.
¹⁴ Darkness comes upon them in the
 daytime;
 at noon they grope as in the night.
¹⁵ He saves the needy from the sword in
 their mouth;
 he saves them from the clutches of
 the powerful.
¹⁶ So the poor have hope,
 and injustice shuts its mouth.

¹⁷ "Blessed is the one whom God
 corrects;
 so do not despise the discipline of
 the Almighty.ᵃ

ROCK SOLID promises

"Blessed is the one whom God corrects." Job 5:17

Correction often feels like a curse, but God's discipline proves his astonishing love for you.

¹⁸ For he wounds, but he also binds up;
 he injures, but his hands also heal.
¹⁹ From six calamities he will rescue you;
 in seven no harm will touch you.
²⁰ In famine he will deliver you from
 death,
 and in battle from the stroke of the
 sword.

²¹ You will be protected from the lash of
 the tongue,
 and need not fear when destruction
 comes.
²² You will laugh at destruction and
 famine,
 and need not fear the wild animals.
²³ For you will have a covenant with the
 stones of the field,
 and the wild animals will be at
 peace with you.
²⁴ You will know that your tent is secure;
 you will take stock of your property
 and find nothing missing.
²⁵ You will know that your children will
 be many,
 and your descendants like the grass
 of the earth.
²⁶ You will come to the grave in full
 vigor,
 like sheaves gathered in season.

²⁷ "We have examined this, and it is true.
 So hear it and apply it to yourself."

Job

6 Then Job replied:

² "If only my anguish could be
 weighed
 and all my misery be placed on the
 scales!
³ It would surely outweigh the sand of
 the seas—
 no wonder my words have been
 impetuous.
⁴ The arrows of the Almighty are in
 me,
 my spirit drinks in their poison;
 God's terrors are marshaled against
 me.
⁵ Does a wild donkey bray when it has
 grass,
 or an ox bellow when it has fodder?
⁶ Is tasteless food eaten without salt,
 or is there flavor in the sap of the
 mallowᵇ?
⁷ I refuse to touch it;
 such food makes me ill.

ᵃ 17 Hebrew Shaddai; here and throughout Job
ᵇ 6 The meaning of the Hebrew for this phrase
is uncertain.

8 "Oh, that I might have my request,
　　that God would grant what I hope
　　for,
9 that God would be willing to crush me,
　　to let loose his hand and cut off my
　　life!
10 Then I would still have this
　　consolation—
　　my joy in unrelenting pain—
　　that I had not denied the words of
　　the Holy One.

11 "What strength do I have, that I
　　should still hope?
　　What prospects, that I should be
　　patient?
12 Do I have the strength of stone?
　　Is my flesh bronze?
13 Do I have any power to help myself,
　　now that success has been driven
　　from me?

14 "Anyone who withholds kindness
　　from a friend
　　forsakes the fear of the Almighty.
15 But my brothers are as undependable
　　as intermittent streams,
　　as the streams that overflow
16 when darkened by thawing ice
　　and swollen with melting snow,
17 but that stop flowing in the dry
　　season,
　　and in the heat vanish from their
　　channels.
18 Caravans turn aside from their routes;
　　they go off into the wasteland and
　　perish.
19 The caravans of Tema look for water,
　　the traveling merchants of Sheba
　　look in hope.
20 They are distressed, because they had
　　been confident;
　　they arrive there, only to be
　　disappointed.
21 Now you too have proved to be of no
　　help;
　　you see something dreadful and are
　　afraid.
22 Have I ever said, 'Give something on
　　my behalf,
　　pay a ransom for me from your
　　wealth,
23 deliver me from the hand of the enemy,
　　rescue me from the clutches of the
　　ruthless'?

24 "Teach me, and I will be quiet;
　　show me where I have been wrong.
25 How painful are honest words!
　　But what do your arguments prove?
26 Do you mean to correct what I say,
　　and treat my desperate words as wind?
27 You would even cast lots for the
　　fatherless
　　and barter away your friend.

28 "But now be so kind as to look at me.
　　Would I lie to your face?
29 Relent, do not be unjust;
　　reconsider, for my integrity is at
　　stake.ᵃ
30 Is there any wickedness on my lips?
　　Can my mouth not discern malice?

7 "Do not mortals have hard service
　　on earth?
　　Are not their days like those of
　　hired laborers?
2 Like a slave longing for the evening
　　shadows,
　　or a hired laborer waiting to be paid,
3 so I have been allotted months of
　　futility,
　　and nights of misery have been
　　assigned to me.
4 When I lie down I think, 'How long
　　before I get up?'
　　The night drags on, and I toss and
　　turn until dawn.
5 My body is clothed with worms and
　　scabs,
　　my skin is broken and festering.

6 "My days are swifter than a weaver's
　　shuttle,
　　and they come to an end without
　　hope.
7 Remember, O God, that my life is but
　　a breath;
　　my eyes will never see happiness again.
8 The eye that now sees me will see me
　　no longer;
　　you will look for me, but I will be
　　no more.

ᵃ 29 Or *my righteousness still stands*

⁹As a cloud vanishes and is gone,
  so one who goes down to the grave
    does not return.
¹⁰He will never come to his house again;
  his place will know him no more.

¹¹"Therefore I will not keep silent;
  I will speak out in the anguish of
    my spirit,
  I will complain in the bitterness of
    my soul.
¹²Am I the sea, or the monster of the
    deep,
  that you put me under guard?
¹³When I think my bed will comfort me
  and my couch will ease my
    complaint,
¹⁴even then you frighten me with
    dreams
  and terrify me with visions,
¹⁵so that I prefer strangling and death,
  rather than this body of mine.
¹⁶I despise my life; I would not live
    forever.
  Let me alone; my days have no
    meaning.

¹⁷"What is mankind that you make so
    much of them,
  that you give them so much
    attention,
¹⁸that you examine them every morning
  and test them every moment?
¹⁹Will you never look away from me,
  or let me alone even for an instant?
²⁰If I have sinned, what have I done to
    you,
  you who see everything we do?
  Why have you made me your target?
  Have I become a burden to you?ᵃ
²¹Why do you not pardon my offenses
  and forgive my sins?
  For I will soon lie down in the dust;
  you will search for me, but I will be
    no more."

Bildad

8 Then Bildad the Shuhite replied:

²"How long will you say such
    things?
  Your words are a blustering wind.

³Does God pervert justice?
  Does the Almighty pervert what is
    right?
⁴When your children sinned against him,
  he gave them over to the penalty of
    their sin.
⁵But if you will seek God earnestly
  and plead with the Almighty,
⁶if you are pure and upright,
  even now he will rouse himself on
    your behalf
  and restore you to your prosperous
    state.
⁷Your beginnings will seem humble,
  so prosperous will your future be.

⁸"Ask the former generation
  and find out what their ancestors
    learned,
⁹for we were born only yesterday and
    know nothing,
  and our days on earth are but a
    shadow.
¹⁰Will they not instruct you and tell you?
  Will they not bring forth words
    from their understanding?
¹¹Can papyrus grow tall where there is
    no marsh?
  Can reeds thrive without water?
¹²While still growing and uncut,
  they wither more quickly than
    grass.
¹³Such is the destiny of all who forget
    God;
  so perishes the hope of the godless.
¹⁴What they trust in is fragileᵇ;
  what they rely on is a spider's web.
¹⁵They lean on the web, but it gives way;
  they cling to it, but it does not hold.
¹⁶They are like a well-watered plant in
    the sunshine,
  spreading its shoots over the garden;
¹⁷it entwines its roots around a pile of
    rocks
  and looks for a place among the
    stones.

ᵃ 20 A few manuscripts of the Masoretic Text,
an ancient Hebrew scribal tradition and
Septuagint; most manuscripts of the Masoretic
Text *I have become a burden to myself.*   ᵇ 14 The
meaning of the Hebrew for this word is
uncertain.

¹⁸ But when it is torn from its spot,
   that place disowns it and says, 'I
      never saw you.'
¹⁹ Surely its life withers away,
   and*ᵃ* from the soil other plants
      grow.

²⁰ "Surely God does not reject one who is
      blameless
   or strengthen the hands of
      evildoers.
²¹ He will yet fill your mouth with
      laughter
   and your lips with shouts of joy.
²² Your enemies will be clothed in shame,
   and the tents of the wicked will be
      no more."

ROCK SOLID
promises

"He will yet fill your mouth with laughter and your lips with shouts of joy."   **Job 8:21**

Don't stop hoping when you feel less than happy, because God will bring back your smile.

Job

9

Then Job replied:

² "Indeed, I know that this is
      true.
   But how can mere mortals prove
      their innocence before God?
³ Though they wished to dispute with
      him,
   they could not answer him one time
      out of a thousand.
⁴ His wisdom is profound, his power is
      vast.
   Who has resisted him and come out
      unscathed?

⁵ He moves mountains without their
      knowing it
   and overturns them in his anger.
⁶ He shakes the earth from its place
   and makes its pillars tremble.
⁷ He speaks to the sun and it does not
      shine;
   he seals off the light of the stars.
⁸ He alone stretches out the heavens
   and treads on the waves of the sea.
⁹ He is the Maker of the Bear*ᵇ* and
      Orion,
   the Pleiades and the constellations
      of the south.
¹⁰ He performs wonders that cannot be
      fathomed,
   miracles that cannot be counted.
¹¹ When he passes me, I cannot see him;
   when he goes by, I cannot perceive
      him.
¹² If he snatches away, who can stop
      him?
   Who can say to him, 'What are you
      doing?'
¹³ God does not restrain his anger;
   even the cohorts of Rahab cowered
      at his feet.

¹⁴ "How then can I dispute with him?
   How can I find words to argue with
      him?
¹⁵ Though I were innocent, I could not
      answer him;
   I could only plead with my Judge
      for mercy.
¹⁶ Even if I summoned him and he
      responded,
   I do not believe he would give me a
      hearing.
¹⁷ He would crush me with a storm
   and multiply my wounds for no
      reason.
¹⁸ He would not let me catch my breath
   but would overwhelm me with
      misery.
¹⁹ If it is a matter of strength, he is
      mighty!
   And if it is a matter of justice, who
      can challenge him*ᶜ*?

ᵃ 19 Or *Surely all the joy it has / is that*   *ᵇ 9* Or *of Leo*   *ᶜ 19* See Septuagint; Hebrew *me.*

²⁰Even if I were innocent, my mouth
would condemn me;
if I were blameless, it would
pronounce me guilty.

²¹"Although I am blameless,
I have no concern for myself;
I despise my own life.
²²It is all the same; that is why I say,
'He destroys both the blameless and
the wicked.'
²³When a scourge brings sudden death,
he mocks the despair of the
innocent.
²⁴When a land falls into the hands of
the wicked,
he blindfolds its judges.
If it is not he, then who is it?

²⁵"My days are swifter than a runner;
they fly away without a glimpse of
joy.
²⁶They skim past like boats of papyrus,
like eagles swooping down on their
prey.
²⁷If I say, 'I will forget my complaint,
I will change my expression, and
smile,'
²⁸I still dread all my sufferings,
for I know you will not hold me
innocent.
²⁹Since I am already found guilty,
why should I struggle in vain?
³⁰Even if I washed myself with soap
and my hands with cleansing powder,
³¹you would plunge me into a slime pit
so that even my clothes would
detest me.

³²"He is not a mere mortal like me that
I might answer him,
that we might confront each other
in court.
³³If only there were someone to mediate
between us,
someone to bring us together,
³⁴someone to remove God's rod from me,
so that his terror would frighten me
no more.
³⁵Then I would speak up without fear of
him,
but as it now stands with me, I
cannot.

10

"I loathe my very life;
therefore I will give free rein
to my complaint
and speak out in the bitterness of
my soul.
²I say to God: Do not declare me
guilty,
but tell me what charges you have
against me.
³Does it please you to oppress me,
to spurn the work of your hands,
while you smile on the plans of the
wicked?
⁴Do you have eyes of flesh?
Do you see as a mortal sees?
⁵Are your days like those of a mortal
or your years like those of a strong
man,
⁶that you must search out my faults
and probe after my sin—
⁷though you know that I am not guilty
and that no one can rescue me from
your hand?

⁸"Your hands shaped me and made me.
Will you now turn and destroy me?
⁹Remember that you molded me like
clay.
Will you now turn me to dust again?
¹⁰Did you not pour me out like milk
and curdle me like cheese,
¹¹clothe me with skin and flesh
and knit me together with bones
and sinews?
¹²You gave me life and showed me
kindness,
and in your providence watched
over my spirit.

¹³"But this is what you concealed in
your heart,
and I know that this was in your
mind:
¹⁴If I sinned, you would be watching me
and would not let my offense go
unpunished.
¹⁵If I am guilty—woe to me!
Even if I am innocent, I cannot lift
my head,
for I am full of shame
and drowned in^a my affliction.

^a 15 Or *and aware of*

16 If I hold my head high, you stalk me
      like a lion
   and again display your awesome
      power against me.
17 You bring new witnesses against me
      and increase your anger toward me;
   your forces come against me wave
      upon wave.

18 "Why then did you bring me out of
      the womb?
   I wish I had died before any eye saw
      me.
19 If only I had never come into being,
      or had been carried straight from
      the womb to the grave!
20 Are not my few days almost over?
   Turn away from me so I can have a
      moment's joy
21 before I go to the place of no return,
      to the land of gloom and utter
      darkness,
22 to the land of deepest night,
      of utter darkness and disorder,
   where even the light is like
      darkness."

Zophar

11 Then Zophar the Naamathite
      replied:

2 "Are all these words to go
      unanswered?
   Is this talker to be vindicated?
3 Will your idle talk reduce others to
      silence?
   Will no one rebuke you when you
      mock?
4 You say to God, 'My beliefs are
      flawless
   and I am pure in your sight.'
5 Oh, how I wish that God would
      speak,
   that he would open his lips against
      you
6 and disclose to you the secrets of
      wisdom,
   for true wisdom has two sides.
   Know this: God has even forgotten
      some of your sin.

7 "Can you fathom the mysteries of
      God?
   Can you probe the limits of the
      Almighty?
8 They are higher than the heavens
      above — what can you do?
   They are deeper than the depths
      below — what can you know?
9 Their measure is longer than the earth
      and wider than the sea.

10 "If he comes along and confines you in
      prison
   and convenes a court, who can
      oppose him?
11 Surely he recognizes deceivers;
   and when he sees evil, does he not
      take note?
12 But the witless can no more become
      wise
   than a wild donkey's colt can be
      born human.*a*

UNSHAKEN *God*

Job 10:1 – 22
God is thick skinned.

Job's life had been ripped from him —
his wealth destroyed, his family killed
and his health ruined (see Job 1:6 – 22).
Even the friends who came to support him turned out to be tormenters.
Throughout his shocking troubles, however, Job found one comfort. Although
he had come to hate his life, Job could
speak freely to God (see Job 10:1 – 2).
Job discovered that God is thick-skinned,
able to handle our darkest words and
deepest complaints. Job talked about his
hurt, his loss of hope and his confusion
about God's seeming lack of care. One
day Job would learn that he didn't have
all the answers (see Job 38:1 – 3). But for
now, God didn't shut him up.

**So ... What hurts do you have that
no one else knows about? What do
you want to tell God about them?**

---

a 12 Or *wild donkey can be born tame*

¹³ "Yet if you devote your heart to him
　　and stretch out your hands to him,
¹⁴ if you put away the sin that is in your
　　hand
　　and allow no evil to dwell in your
　　tent,
¹⁵ then, free of fault, you will lift up your
　　face;
　　you will stand firm and without
　　fear.
¹⁶ You will surely forget your trouble,
　　recalling it only as waters gone by.
¹⁷ Life will be brighter than noonday,
　　and darkness will become like
　　morning.
¹⁸ You will be secure, because there is
　　hope;
　　you will look about you and take
　　your rest in safety.
¹⁹ You will lie down, with no one to
　　make you afraid,
　　and many will court your favor.
²⁰ But the eyes of the wicked will fail,
　　and escape will elude them;
　　their hope will become a dying
　　gasp."

Job

12

Then Job replied:

² "Doubtless you are the only
　　people who matter,
　　and wisdom will die with you!
³ But I have a mind as well as you;
　　I am not inferior to you.
　　Who does not know all these things?

⁴ "I have become a laughingstock to my
　　friends,
　　though I called on God and he
　　answered—
　　a mere laughingstock, though
　　righteous and blameless!
⁵ Those who are at ease have contempt
　　for misfortune
　　as the fate of those whose feet are
　　slipping.
⁶ The tents of marauders are
　　undisturbed,
　　and those who provoke God are
　　secure—
　　those God has in his hand.^a

⁷ "But ask the animals, and they will
　　teach you,
　　or the birds in the sky, and they will
　　tell you;
⁸ or speak to the earth, and it will teach
　　you,
　　or let the fish in the sea inform you.
⁹ Which of all these does not know
　　that the hand of the LORD has done
　　this?
¹⁰ In his hand is the life of every
　　creature
　　and the breath of all mankind.
¹¹ Does not the ear test words
　　as the tongue tastes food?
¹² Is not wisdom found among the aged?
　　Does not long life bring
　　understanding?

¹³ "To God belong wisdom and power;
　　counsel and understanding are his.

ROCK SOLID
promises

"To God belong wisdom and power; counsel and understanding are his." Job 12:13

There's no bigger or better wisdom in the universe than what you can get from God.

¹⁴ What he tears down cannot be rebuilt;
　　those he imprisons cannot be
　　released.
¹⁵ If he holds back the waters, there is
　　drought;
　　if he lets them loose, they devastate
　　the land.
¹⁶ To him belong strength and insight;
　　both deceived and deceiver are his.
¹⁷ He leads rulers away stripped
　　and makes fools of judges.

^a 6 Or *those whose god is in their own hand*

¹⁸ He takes off the shackles put on by
    kings
        and ties a loincloth*a* around their
        waist.
¹⁹ He leads priests away stripped
        and overthrows officials long
        established.
²⁰ He silences the lips of trusted advisers
        and takes away the discernment of
        elders.
²¹ He pours contempt on nobles
        and disarms the mighty.
²² He reveals the deep things of darkness
        and brings utter darkness into the
        light.
²³ He makes nations great, and destroys
        them;
        he enlarges nations, and disperses
        them.
²⁴ He deprives the leaders of the earth of
        their reason;
        he makes them wander in a
        trackless waste.
²⁵ They grope in darkness with no light;
        he makes them stagger like
        drunkards.

13

"My eyes have seen all this,
        my ears have heard and
        understood it.
² What you know, I also know;
        I am not inferior to you.
³ But I desire to speak to the Almighty
        and to argue my case with God.
⁴ You, however, smear me with lies;
        you are worthless physicians, all of
        you!
⁵ If only you would be altogether silent!
        For you, that would be wisdom.
⁶ Hear now my argument;
        listen to the pleas of my lips.
⁷ Will you speak wickedly on God's
        behalf?
        Will you speak deceitfully for him?
⁸ Will you show him partiality?
        Will you argue the case for God?
⁹ Would it turn out well if he examined
        you?
        Could you deceive him as you
        might deceive a mortal?
¹⁰ He would surely call you to account
        if you secretly showed partiality.

¹¹ Would not his splendor terrify you?
        Would not the dread of him fall on
        you?
¹² Your maxims are proverbs of ashes;
        your defenses are defenses of clay.

¹³ "Keep silent and let me speak;
        then let come to me what may.
¹⁴ Why do I put myself in jeopardy
        and take my life in my hands?
¹⁵ Though he slay me, yet will I hope in
        him;
        I will surely*b* defend my ways to his
        face.
¹⁶ Indeed, this will turn out for my
        deliverance,
        for no godless person would dare
        come before him!
¹⁷ Listen carefully to what I say;
        let my words ring in your ears.
¹⁸ Now that I have prepared my case,
        I know I will be vindicated.
¹⁹ Can anyone bring charges against me?
        If so, I will be silent and die.

²⁰ "Only grant me these two things,
        God,
        and then I will not hide from you:
²¹ Withdraw your hand far from me,
        and stop frightening me with your
        terrors.
²² Then summon me and I will answer,
        or let me speak, and you reply
        to me.
²³ How many wrongs and sins have I
        committed?
        Show me my offense and my sin.
²⁴ Why do you hide your face
        and consider me your enemy?
²⁵ Will you torment a windblown leaf?
        Will you chase after dry chaff?
²⁶ For you write down bitter things
        against me
        and make me reap the sins of my
        youth.
²⁷ You fasten my feet in shackles;
        you keep close watch on all my
        paths
        by putting marks on the soles of my
        feet.

---

a 18 Or *shackles of kings / and ties a belt*   *b* 15 Or
He will surely slay me; I have no hope — / yet I will

UNSHAKEN God

Job 13:1–28

God is trustworthy.

Job couldn't understand how such bad things could happen to such a good guy. After the loss of his wealth, his family, and his health, Job breathed countless words of protest to God and defended himself against the mean comments of his so-called friends. Yet through all of his trials, Job never forgot that God was just. Even though Job couldn't understand God's ways, he didn't question the Lord's character. He would keep trusting even to the point of death at God's hands: "Though he slay me," Job sighed, "yet will I hope in him" (Job 13:15). Whatever happens to you today, God deserves your trust.

So ... When have you had a hard time trusting God? How did you get through it?

28 "So man wastes away like something
rotten,
like a garment eaten by moths.

14 "Mortals, born of woman,
are of few days and full of
trouble.
2 They spring up like flowers and
wither away;
like fleeting shadows, they do not
endure.
3 Do you fix your eye on them?
Will you bring them[a] before you for
judgment?
4 Who can bring what is pure from the
impure?
No one!
5 A person's days are determined;
you have decreed the number of his
months
and have set limits he cannot
exceed.

6 So look away from him and let him
alone,
till he has put in his time like a
hired laborer.
7 "At least there is hope for a tree:
If it is cut down, it will sprout
again,
and its new shoots will not fail.
8 Its roots may grow old in the
ground
and its stump die in the soil,
9 yet at the scent of water it will bud
and put forth shoots like a plant.
10 But a man dies and is laid low;
he breathes his last and is no more.
11 As the water of a lake dries up
or a riverbed becomes parched and
dry,
12 so he lies down and does not rise;
till the heavens are no more, people
will not awake
or be roused from their sleep.

13 "If only you would hide me in the
grave
and conceal me till your anger has
passed!
If only you would set me a time
and then remember me!
14 If someone dies, will they live again?
All the days of my hard service
I will wait for my renewal[b] to
come.
15 You will call and I will answer you;
you will long for the creature your
hands have made.
16 Surely then you will count my steps
but not keep track of my sin.
17 My offenses will be sealed up in
a bag;
you will cover over my sin.

18 "But as a mountain erodes and
crumbles
and as a rock is moved from its
place,
19 as water wears away stones
and torrents wash away the soil,
so you destroy a person's hope.

a 3 Septuagint, Vulgate and Syriac; Hebrew me
b 14 Or release

²⁰You overpower them once for all, and they are gone;
　　you change their countenance and send them away.
²¹If their children are honored, they do not know it;
　　if their offspring are brought low, they do not see it.
²²They feel but the pain of their own bodies
　　and mourn only for themselves."

Job 14:1–22

Life here doesn't last forever.

Job's cry sounds like a colossal downer. He says the few days people live are packed with trouble (see Job 14:1). People are like withering flowers and fleeting shadows (see Job 14:2). God has determined how long each person will live, and we mark our time like a worker watching the clock (see Job 14:5–6). While those laments are tough to hear, Job is right that life doesn't last forever, and you don't have to have a terrible illness to get smart to that truth. Plus there is an upside to that realization. Knowing your life (on earth) won't last forever can push you to search for better ways to spend your days, and you can learn to hope in God like Job did: "You will call and I will answer you; you will long for the creature your hands have made" (Job 14:15). Your life on earth might be long or short, but it isn't the end.

Think: How does it change the way you live when you realize your life on earth won't last forever?

ROCK SOLID truths

Eliphaz

15 Then Eliphaz the Temanite replied:

²"Would a wise person answer with empty notions
　　or fill their belly with the hot east wind?
³Would they argue with useless words,
　　with speeches that have no value?
⁴But you even undermine piety
　　and hinder devotion to God.
⁵Your sin prompts your mouth;
　　you adopt the tongue of the crafty.
⁶Your own mouth condemns you, not mine;
　　your own lips testify against you.

⁷"Are you the first man ever born?
　　Were you brought forth before the hills?
⁸Do you listen in on God's council?
　　Do you have a monopoly on wisdom?
⁹What do you know that we do not know?
　　What insights do you have that we do not have?
¹⁰The gray-haired and the aged are on our side,
　　men even older than your father.
¹¹Are God's consolations not enough for you,
　　words spoken gently to you?
¹²Why has your heart carried you away,
　　and why do your eyes flash,
¹³so that you vent your rage against God
　　and pour out such words from your mouth?

¹⁴"What are mortals, that they could be pure,
　　or those born of woman, that they could be righteous?
¹⁵If God places no trust in his holy ones,
　　if even the heavens are not pure in his eyes,
¹⁶how much less mortals, who are vile and corrupt,
　　who drink up evil like water!

¹⁷"Listen to me and I will explain to you;
　　let me tell you what I have seen,

¹⁸ what the wise have declared,
hiding nothing received from their
ancestors
¹⁹ (to whom alone the land was given
when no foreigners moved among
them):
²⁰ All his days the wicked man suffers
torment,
the ruthless man through all the
years stored up for him.
²¹ Terrifying sounds fill his ears;
when all seems well, marauders
attack him.
²² He despairs of escaping the realm of
darkness;
he is marked for the sword.
²³ He wanders about for food like a
vulture;
he knows the day of darkness is at
hand.
²⁴ Distress and anguish fill him with
terror;
troubles overwhelm him, like a king
poised to attack,
²⁵ because he shakes his fist at God
and vaunts himself against the
Almighty,
²⁶ defiantly charging against him
with a thick, strong shield.

²⁷ "Though his face is covered with fat
and his waist bulges with flesh,
²⁸ he will inhabit ruined towns
and houses where no one lives,
houses crumbling to rubble.
²⁹ He will no longer be rich and his
wealth will not endure,
nor will his possessions spread over
the land.
³⁰ He will not escape the darkness;
a flame will wither his shoots,
and the breath of God's mouth will
carry him away.
³¹ Let him not deceive himself by
trusting what is worthless,
for he will get nothing in return.
³² Before his time he will wither,
and his branches will not flourish.
³³ He will be like a vine stripped of its
unripe grapes,
like an olive tree shedding its
blossoms.

³⁴ For the company of the godless will be
barren,
and fire will consume the tents of
those who love bribes.
³⁵ They conceive trouble and give birth
to evil;
their womb fashions deceit."

Job

16

Then Job replied:

² "I have heard many things
like these;
you are miserable comforters, all of
you!
³ Will your long-winded speeches never
end?
What ails you that you keep on
arguing?
⁴ I also could speak like you,
if you were in my place;
I could make fine speeches against
you
and shake my head at you.
⁵ But my mouth would encourage you;
comfort from my lips would bring
you relief.

⁶ "Yet if I speak, my pain is not relieved;
and if I refrain, it does not go away.
⁷ Surely, God, you have worn me out;
you have devastated my entire
household.
⁸ You have shriveled me up — and it has
become a witness;
my gauntness rises up and testifies
against me.
⁹ God assails me and tears me in his
anger
and gnashes his teeth at me;
my opponent fastens on me his
piercing eyes.
¹⁰ People open their mouths to jeer at me;
they strike my cheek in scorn
and unite together against me.
¹¹ God has turned me over to the ungodly
and thrown me into the clutches of
the wicked.
¹² All was well with me, but he shattered
me;
he seized me by the neck and
crushed me.

He has made me his target;
¹³ his archers surround me.
Without pity, he pierces my kidneys
and spills my gall on the ground.
¹⁴ Again and again he bursts upon me;
he rushes at me like a warrior.

¹⁵ "I have sewed sackcloth over my skin
and buried my brow in the dust.
¹⁶ My face is red with weeping,
dark shadows ring my eyes;
¹⁷ yet my hands have been free of
violence
and my prayer is pure.

¹⁸ "Earth, do not cover my blood;
may my cry never be laid to rest!
¹⁹ Even now my witness is in heaven;
my advocate is on high.
²⁰ My intercessor is my friend[a]
as my eyes pour out tears to God;
²¹ on behalf of a man he pleads with
God
as one pleads for a friend.

²² "Only a few years will pass
before I take the path of no return.

17

¹ My spirit is broken,
my days are cut short,
the grave awaits me.
² Surely mockers surround me;
my eyes must dwell on their
hostility.

³ "Give me, O God, the pledge you
demand.
Who else will put up security for
me?
⁴ You have closed their minds to
understanding;
therefore you will not let them
triumph.
⁵ If anyone denounces their friends for
reward,
the eyes of their children will fail.

⁶ "God has made me a byword to
everyone,
a man in whose face people spit.
⁷ My eyes have grown dim with grief;
my whole frame is but a shadow.
⁸ The upright are appalled at this;
the innocent are aroused against the
ungodly.

⁹ Nevertheless, the righteous will hold
to their ways,
and those with clean hands will
grow stronger.

¹⁰ "But come on, all of you, try again!
I will not find a wise man among
you.
¹¹ My days have passed, my plans are
shattered.
Yet the desires of my heart
¹² turn night into day;
in the face of the darkness light is
near.
¹³ If the only home I hope for is the
grave,
if I spread out my bed in the realm
of darkness,
¹⁴ if I say to corruption, 'You are my
father,'
and to the worm, 'My mother' or
'My sister,'
¹⁵ where then is my hope—
who can see any hope for me?
¹⁶ Will it go down to the gates of death?
Will we descend together into the
dust?"

Bildad

18

Then Bildad the Shuhite replied:

² "When will you end these speeches?
Be sensible, and then we can talk.
³ Why are we regarded as cattle
and considered stupid in your sight?
⁴ You who tear yourself to pieces in your
anger,
is the earth to be abandoned for
your sake?
Or must the rocks be moved from
their place?

⁵ "The lamp of a wicked man is snuffed
out;
the flame of his fire stops burning.
⁶ The light in his tent becomes dark;
the lamp beside him goes out.
⁷ The vigor of his step is weakened;
his own schemes throw him down.
⁸ His feet thrust him into a net;

---

[a] 20 Or *My friends treat me with scorn*

he wanders into its mesh.
⁹ A trap seizes him by the heel;
a snare holds him fast.
¹⁰ A noose is hidden for him on the
ground;
a trap lies in his path.
¹¹ Terrors startle him on every side
and dog his every step.
¹² Calamity is hungry for him;
disaster is ready for him when he
falls.
¹³ It eats away parts of his skin;
death's firstborn devours his limbs.
¹⁴ He is torn from the security of his
tent
and marched off to the king of
terrors.
¹⁵ Fire resides*a* in his tent;
burning sulfur is scattered over his
dwelling.
¹⁶ His roots dry up below
and his branches wither above.
¹⁷ The memory of him perishes from the
earth;
he has no name in the land.
¹⁸ He is driven from light into the realm
of darkness
and is banished from the world.
¹⁹ He has no offspring or descendants
among his people,
no survivor where once he lived.
²⁰ People of the west are appalled at his
fate;
those of the east are seized with
horror.
²¹ Surely such is the dwelling of an evil
man;
such is the place of one who does
not know God."

Job

19

Then Job replied:

² "How long will you torment
me
and crush me with words?
³ Ten times now you have reproached
me;
shamelessly you attack me.
⁴ If it is true that I have gone astray,
my error remains my concern alone.

⁵ If indeed you would exalt yourselves
above me
and use my humiliation against me,
⁶ then know that God has wronged me
and drawn his net around me.

⁷ "Though I cry, 'Violence!' I get no
response;
though I call for help, there is no
justice.
⁸ He has blocked my way so I cannot
pass;
he has shrouded my paths in darkness.
⁹ He has stripped me of my honor
and removed the crown from my
head.
¹⁰ He tears me down on every side till I
am gone;
he uproots my hope like a tree.
¹¹ His anger burns against me;
he counts me among his enemies.
¹² His troops advance in force;
they build a siege ramp against me
and encamp around my tent.

¹³ "He has alienated my family from me;
my acquaintances are completely
estranged from me.
¹⁴ My relatives have gone away;
my closest friends have forgotten me.
¹⁵ My guests and my female servants
count me a foreigner;
they look on me as on a stranger.
¹⁶ I summon my servant, but he does not
answer,
though I beg him with my own
mouth.
¹⁷ My breath is offensive to my wife;
I am loathsome to my own family.
¹⁸ Even the little boys scorn me;
when I appear, they ridicule me.
¹⁹ All my intimate friends detest me;
those I love have turned against me.
²⁰ I am nothing but skin and bones;
I have escaped only by the skin of
my teeth.*b*

²¹ "Have pity on me, my friends, have
pity,
for the hand of God has struck me.

a 15 Or *Nothing he had remains*   *b 20* Or *only
by my gums*

²²Why do you pursue me as God does?
  Will you never get enough of my flesh?

²³"Oh, that my words were recorded,
  that they were written on a scroll,
²⁴that they were inscribed with an iron
    tool on[a] lead,
  or engraved in rock forever!
²⁵I know that my redeemer[b] lives,
  and that in the end he will stand on
    the earth.[c]

ROCK SOLID promises

"I know that my redeemer lives."

Job 19:25

**The God who rescues you truly exists.
When troubles overwhelm you, he's real
and ready to help.**

---

²⁶And after my skin has been destroyed,
    yet[d] in[e] my flesh I will see God;
²⁷I myself will see him
  with my own eyes—I, and not
    another.
  How my heart yearns within me!

²⁸"If you say, 'How we will hound him,
  since the root of the trouble lies in
    him,'[f]
²⁹you should fear the sword yourselves;
  for wrath will bring punishment by
    the sword,
  and then you will know that there is
    judgment.[g]

Zophar

20 Then Zophar the Naamathite replied:

²"My troubled thoughts prompt me to
    answer
  because I am greatly disturbed.

³I hear a rebuke that dishonors me,
  and my understanding inspires me
    to reply.

⁴"Surely you know how it has been
    from of old,
  ever since mankind[b] was placed on
    the earth,
⁵that the mirth of the wicked is brief,
  the joy of the godless lasts but a
    moment.
⁶Though the pride of the godless
    person reaches to the heavens
  and his head touches the clouds,
⁷he will perish forever, like his own
    dung;
  those who have seen him will say,
    'Where is he?'
⁸Like a dream he flies away, no more to
    be found,
  banished like a vision of the night.
⁹The eye that saw him will not see him
    again;
  his place will look on him no more.
¹⁰His children must make amends to
    the poor;
  his own hands must give back his
    wealth.
¹¹The youthful vigor that fills his bones
  will lie with him in the dust.

¹²"Though evil is sweet in his mouth
  and he hides it under his tongue,
¹³though he cannot bear to let it go
  and lets it linger in his mouth,
¹⁴yet his food will turn sour in his
    stomach;
  it will become the venom of
    serpents within him.
¹⁵He will spit out the riches he
    swallowed;
  God will make his stomach vomit
    them up.
¹⁶He will suck the poison of serpents;
  the fangs of an adder will kill him.

---

a 24 Or *and*   *b 25* Or *vindicator*   *c 25* Or
on my grave   *d 26* Or *And after I awake, /
though this body has been destroyed, / then*
e 26 Or *destroyed, / apart from*   *f 28* Many
Hebrew manuscripts, Septuagint and Vulgate;
most Hebrew manuscripts *me*   *g 29* Or *sword,
/ that you may come to know the Almighty*   *b 4* Or
Adam

¹⁷He will not enjoy the streams,
  the rivers flowing with honey and
    cream.
¹⁸What he toiled for he must give back
    uneaten;
  he will not enjoy the profit from his
    trading.
¹⁹For he has oppressed the poor and left
    them destitute;
  he has seized houses he did not
    build.

²⁰"Surely he will have no respite from
    his craving;
  he cannot save himself by his treasure.
²¹Nothing is left for him to devour;
  his prosperity will not endure.
²²In the midst of his plenty, distress will
    overtake him;
  the full force of misery will come
    upon him.
²³When he has filled his belly,
  God will vent his burning anger
    against him
  and rain down his blows on him.
²⁴Though he flees from an iron weapon,
  a bronze-tipped arrow pierces him.
²⁵He pulls it out of his back,
  the gleaming point out of his liver.
  Terrors will come over him;
²⁶ total darkness lies in wait for his
    treasures.
  A fire unfanned will consume him
  and devour what is left in his tent.
²⁷The heavens will expose his guilt;
  the earth will rise up against him.
²⁸A flood will carry off his house,
  rushing waters^a on the day of God's
    wrath.
²⁹Such is the fate God allots the wicked,
  the heritage appointed for them by
    God."

Job

21 Then Job replied:

²"Listen carefully to my
    words;
  let this be the consolation you
    give me.
³Bear with me while I speak,
  and after I have spoken, mock on.

⁴"Is my complaint directed to a human
    being?
  Why should I not be impatient?
⁵Look at me and be appalled;
  clap your hand over your mouth.
⁶When I think about this, I am
    terrified;
  trembling seizes my body.
⁷Why do the wicked live on,
  growing old and increasing in
    power?
⁸They see their children established
    around them,
  their offspring before their eyes.
⁹Their homes are safe and free from
    fear;
  the rod of God is not on them.
¹⁰Their bulls never fail to breed;
  their cows calve and do not
    miscarry.
¹¹They send forth their children as a
    flock;
  their little ones dance about.
¹²They sing to the music of timbrel and
    lyre;
  they make merry to the sound of
    the pipe.
¹³They spend their years in prosperity
  and go down to the grave in peace.^b
¹⁴Yet they say to God, 'Leave us alone!
  We have no desire to know your
    ways.
¹⁵Who is the Almighty, that we should
    serve him?
  What would we gain by praying to
    him?'
¹⁶But their prosperity is not in their own
    hands,
  so I stand aloof from the plans of
    the wicked.

¹⁷"Yet how often is the lamp of the
    wicked snuffed out?
  How often does calamity come
    upon them,
  the fate God allots in his anger?
¹⁸How often are they like straw before
    the wind,
  like chaff swept away by a gale?

---

^a 28 Or *The possessions in his house will be carried
off, / washed away*   ^b 13 Or *in an instant*

¹⁹ It is said, 'God stores up the punishment of the wicked for their children.'
Let him repay the wicked, so that they themselves will experience it!

²⁰ Let their own eyes see their destruction;
let them drink the cup of the wrath of the Almighty.

²¹ For what do they care about the families they leave behind
when their allotted months come to an end?

²² "Can anyone teach knowledge to God, since he judges even the highest?

²³ One person dies in full vigor, completely secure and at ease,

²⁴ well nourished in body,ᵃ bones rich with marrow.

²⁵ Another dies in bitterness of soul, never having enjoyed anything good.

²⁶ Side by side they lie in the dust, and worms cover them both.

²⁷ "I know full well what you are thinking,
the schemes by which you would wrong me.

²⁸ You say, 'Where now is the house of the great,
the tents where the wicked lived?'

²⁹ Have you never questioned those who travel?
Have you paid no regard to their accounts—

³⁰ that the wicked are spared from the day of calamity,
that they are delivered fromᵇ the day of wrath?

³¹ Who denounces their conduct to their face?
Who repays them for what they have done?

³² They are carried to the grave, and watch is kept over their tombs.

³³ The soil in the valley is sweet to them; everyone follows after them,
and a countless throng goesᶜ before them.

³⁴ "So how can you console me with your nonsense?
Nothing is left of your answers but falsehood!"

Eliphaz

22 Then Eliphaz the Temanite replied:

² "Can a man be of benefit to God?
Can even a wise person benefit him?

³ What pleasure would it give the Almighty if you were righteous?
What would he gain if your ways were blameless?

⁴ "Is it for your piety that he rebukes you
and brings charges against you?

⁵ Is not your wickedness great?
Are not your sins endless?

⁶ You demanded security from your relatives for no reason;
you stripped people of their clothing, leaving them naked.

⁷ You gave no water to the weary
and you withheld food from the hungry,

⁸ though you were a powerful man, owning land—
an honored man, living on it.

⁹ And you sent widows away empty-handed
and broke the strength of the fatherless.

¹⁰ That is why snares are all around you, why sudden peril terrifies you,

¹¹ why it is so dark you cannot see, and why a flood of water covers you.

¹² "Is not God in the heights of heaven?
And see how lofty are the highest stars!

¹³ Yet you say, 'What does God know?
Does he judge through such darkness?

ᵃ *24* The meaning of the Hebrew for this word is uncertain.   ᵇ *30* Or *wicked are reserved for the day of calamity, / that they are brought forth to*   ᶜ *33* Or *them, / as a countless throng went*

¹⁴Thick clouds veil him, so he does not see us
   as he goes about in the vaulted heavens.'
¹⁵Will you keep to the old path
   that the wicked have trod?
¹⁶They were carried off before their time,
   their foundations washed away by a flood.
¹⁷They said to God, 'Leave us alone!
   What can the Almighty do to us?'
¹⁸Yet it was he who filled their houses with good things,
   so I stand aloof from the plans of the wicked.
¹⁹The righteous see their ruin and rejoice;
   the innocent mock them, saying,
²⁰'Surely our foes are destroyed,
   and fire devours their wealth.'

²¹"Submit to God and be at peace with him;
   in this way prosperity will come to you.
²²Accept instruction from his mouth
   and lay up his words in your heart.
²³If you return to the Almighty, you will be restored:
   If you remove wickedness far from your tent
²⁴and assign your nuggets to the dust,
   your gold of Ophir to the rocks in the ravines,
²⁵then the Almighty will be your gold,
   the choicest silver for you.
²⁶Surely then you will find delight in the Almighty
   and will lift up your face to God.
²⁷You will pray to him, and he will hear you,
   and you will fulfill your vows.
²⁸What you decide on will be done,
   and light will shine on your ways.
²⁹When people are brought low and you say, 'Lift them up!'
   then he will save the downcast.
³⁰He will deliver even one who is not innocent,
   who will be delivered through the cleanness of your hands."

ROCK SOLID truths

Job 22:1–30

Bad things happen to good people.

At first Eliphaz seems to make sense. This friend says poor Job suffers because of hidden sins. How could God let harm come to someone who really lives for him? As Eliphaz points out, "Is it for your piety that he rebukes you and brings charges against you? Is not your wickedness great? Are not your sins endless?" (Job 22:4–5). While Eliphaz is correct that every person on earth has sins they need to admit and quit, in the end the Lord says that Eliphaz doesn't really understand much (see Job 42:7). Suffering is more complicated than the philosophy that bad things happen as payback for being bad. In fact, there is plenty of evidence that really nasty things happen to really good people. But when you experience suffering, take the time to ask God if he is trying to point out something you're doing wrong—yet know that sometimes bad things just happen, even to good people.

Think: Why do you think good people suffer?

Job

23

Then Job replied:

² "Even today my complaint is bitter;
   his hand*a* is heavy in spite of*b* my groaning.
³If only I knew where to find him;
   if only I could go to his dwelling!

a 2 Septuagint and Syriac; Hebrew / *the hand on me*   *b 2* Or *heavy on me in*

⁴I would state my case before him
and fill my mouth with arguments.
⁵I would find out what he would
answer me,
and consider what he would say to
me.
⁶Would he vigorously oppose me?
No, he would not press charges
against me.
⁷There the upright can establish their
innocence before him,
and there I would be delivered
forever from my judge.

⁸"But if I go to the east, he is not there;
if I go to the west, I do not find
him.
⁹When he is at work in the north, I do
not see him;
when he turns to the south, I catch
no glimpse of him.
¹⁰But he knows the way that I take;
when he has tested me, I will come
forth as gold.

ROCK SOLID *promises*

**"When he has tested me, I will
come forth as gold."** Job 23:10

You can't escape rough situations, but
every trial is a chance to prove you are
faithful to God.

---

¹¹My feet have closely followed his
steps;
I have kept to his way without
turning aside.
¹²I have not departed from the
commands of his lips;
I have treasured the words of his
mouth more than my daily
bread.

¹³"But he stands alone, and who can
oppose him?
He does whatever he pleases.
¹⁴He carries out his decree against me,
and many such plans he still has in
store.
¹⁵That is why I am terrified before
him;
when I think of all this, I fear him.
¹⁶God has made my heart faint;
the Almighty has terrified me.
¹⁷Yet I am not silenced by the darkness,
by the thick darkness that covers
my face.

24 "Why does the Almighty
not set times for judgment?
Why must those who
know him look in vain for such
days?
²There are those who move boundary
stones;
they pasture flocks they have
stolen.
³They drive away the orphan's donkey
and take the widow's ox in pledge.
⁴They thrust the needy from the path
and force all the poor of the land
into hiding.
⁵Like wild donkeys in the desert,
the poor go about their labor of
foraging food;
the wasteland provides food for
their children.
⁶They gather fodder in the fields
and glean in the vineyards of the
wicked.
⁷Lacking clothes, they spend the night
naked;
they have nothing to cover
themselves in the cold.
⁸They are drenched by mountain rains
and hug the rocks for lack of
shelter.
⁹The fatherless child is snatched from
the breast;
the infant of the poor is seized for a
debt.
¹⁰Lacking clothes, they go about
naked;
they carry the sheaves, but still go
hungry.

¹¹They crush olives among the terraces*;
 they tread the winepresses, yet
   suffer thirst.
¹²The groans of the dying rise from the
   city,
 and the souls of the wounded cry
   out for help.
 But God charges no one with
   wrongdoing.

¹³"There are those who rebel against the
   light,
 who do not know its ways
 or stay in its paths.
¹⁴When daylight is gone, the murderer
   rises up,
 kills the poor and needy,
 and in the night steals forth like a
   thief.
¹⁵The eye of the adulterer watches for
   dusk;
 he thinks, 'No eye will see me,'
 and he keeps his face concealed.
¹⁶In the dark, thieves break into houses,
 but by day they shut themselves in;
 they want nothing to do with the
   light.
¹⁷For all of them, midnight is their
   morning;
 they make friends with the terrors
   of darkness.

¹⁸"Yet they are foam on the surface of
   the water;
 their portion of the land is cursed,
 so that no one goes to the vineyards.
¹⁹As heat and drought snatch away the
   melted snow,
 so the grave snatches away those
   who have sinned.
²⁰The womb forgets them,
 the worm feasts on them;
 the wicked are no longer remembered
 but are broken like a tree.
²¹They prey on the barren and childless
   woman,
 and to the widow they show no
   kindness.
²²But God drags away the mighty by his
   power;
 though they become established,
 they have no assurance of life.

²³He may let them rest in a feeling of
   security,
 but his eyes are on their ways.
²⁴For a little while they are exalted, and
   then they are gone;
 they are brought low and gathered
   up like all others;
 they are cut off like heads of grain.

²⁵"If this is not so, who can prove me
   false
 and reduce my words to nothing?"

Bildad

25 Then Bildad the Shuhite
replied:

²"Dominion and awe belong to God;
 he establishes order in the heights
   of heaven.
³Can his forces be numbered?
 On whom does his light not rise?
⁴How then can a mortal be righteous
   before God?
 How can one born of woman be
   pure?
⁵If even the moon is not bright
 and the stars are not pure in his
   eyes,
⁶how much less a mortal, who is but a
   maggot—
 a human being, who is only a
   worm!"

Job

26 Then Job replied:

²"How you have helped the
powerless!
 How you have saved the arm that is
   feeble!
³What advice you have offered to one
   without wisdom!
 And what great insight you have
   displayed!
⁴Who has helped you utter these
   words?
 And whose spirit spoke from your
   mouth?

a 11 The meaning of the Hebrew for this word
is uncertain.

⁵ "The dead are in deep anguish,
  those beneath the waters and all
    that live in them.
⁶ The realm of the dead is naked before
    God;
  Destruction^a lies uncovered.
⁷ He spreads out the northern skies over
    empty space;
  he suspends the earth over nothing.
⁸ He wraps up the waters in his clouds,
  yet the clouds do not burst under
    their weight.
⁹ He covers the face of the full moon,
  spreading his clouds over it.
¹⁰ He marks out the horizon on the face
    of the waters
  for a boundary between light and
    darkness.
¹¹ The pillars of the heavens quake,
  aghast at his rebuke.
¹² By his power he churned up the sea;
  by his wisdom he cut Rahab to
    pieces.
¹³ By his breath the skies became fair;
  his hand pierced the gliding
    serpent.
¹⁴ And these are but the outer fringe of
    his works;
  how faint the whisper we hear of him!
  Who then can understand the
    thunder of his power?"

Job's Final Word to His Friends

27 And Job continued his discourse:

² "As surely as God lives, who has
    denied me justice,
  the Almighty, who has made my
    life bitter,
³ as long as I have life within me,
  the breath of God in my nostrils,
⁴ my lips will not say anything wicked,
  and my tongue will not utter lies.
⁵ I will never admit you are in the right;
  till I die, I will not deny my
    integrity.
⁶ I will maintain my innocence and
    never let go of it;
  my conscience will not reproach me
    as long as I live.

⁷ "May my enemy be like the wicked,
  my adversary like the unjust!
⁸ For what hope have the godless when
    they are cut off,
  when God takes away their life?
⁹ Does God listen to their cry
  when distress comes upon them?
¹⁰ Will they find delight in the
    Almighty?
  Will they call on God at all times?

¹¹ "I will teach you about the power of
    God;
  the ways of the Almighty I will not
    conceal.
¹² You have all seen this yourselves.
  Why then this meaningless talk?

¹³ "Here is the fate God allots to the
    wicked,
  the heritage a ruthless man receives
    from the Almighty:
¹⁴ However many his children, their fate
    is the sword;
  his offspring will never have enough
    to eat.
¹⁵ The plague will bury those who
    survive him,
  and their widows will not weep for
    them.
¹⁶ Though he heaps up silver like dust
  and clothes like piles of clay,
¹⁷ what he lays up the righteous will
    wear,
  and the innocent will divide his
    silver.
¹⁸ The house he builds is like a moth's
    cocoon,
  like a hut made by a watchman.
¹⁹ He lies down wealthy, but will do so
    no more;
  when he opens his eyes, all is gone.
²⁰ Terrors overtake him like a flood;
  a tempest snatches him away in the
    night.
²¹ The east wind carries him off, and he
    is gone;
  it sweeps him out of his place.
²² It hurls itself against him without
    mercy
  as he flees headlong from its power.

---

^a 6 Hebrew *Abaddon*

23 It claps its hands in derision
　　and hisses him out of his place."

Interlude: Where Wisdom Is Found

28
There is a mine for silver
and a place where gold is
refined.
2 Iron is taken from the earth,
　　and copper is smelted from ore.
3 Mortals put an end to the darkness;
　　they search out the farthest recesses
　　for ore in the blackest darkness.
4 Far from human dwellings they cut a
　　　shaft,
　　in places untouched by human feet;
　　far from other people they dangle
　　　and sway.
5 The earth, from which food comes,
　　is transformed below as by fire;
6 lapis lazuli comes from its rocks,
　　and its dust contains nuggets of
　　　gold.
7 No bird of prey knows that hidden path,
　　no falcon's eye has seen it.
8 Proud beasts do not set foot on it,
　　and no lion prowls there.
9 People assault the flinty rock with
　　　their hands
　　and lay bare the roots of the
　　　mountains.
10 They tunnel through the rock;
　　their eyes see all its treasures.
11 They search*a* the sources of the rivers
　　and bring hidden things to light.

12 But where can wisdom be found?
　　Where does understanding dwell?
13 No mortal comprehends its worth;
　　it cannot be found in the land of the
　　　living.
14 The deep says, "It is not in me";
　　the sea says, "It is not with me."
15 It cannot be bought with the finest
　　　gold,
　　nor can its price be weighed out in
　　　silver.
16 It cannot be bought with the gold of
　　　Ophir,
　　with precious onyx or lapis lazuli.
17 Neither gold nor crystal can compare
　　　with it,
　　nor can it be had for jewels of gold.

18 Coral and jasper are not worthy of
　　　mention;
　　the price of wisdom is beyond rubies.
19 The topaz of Cush cannot compare
　　　with it;
　　it cannot be bought with pure gold.

20 Where then does wisdom come from?
　　Where does understanding dwell?
21 It is hidden from the eyes of every
　　　living thing,
　　concealed even from the birds in the
　　　sky.

a 11 Septuagint, Aquila and Vulgate; Hebrew
They dam up

Job 28:1–28

You don't have to have all the answers.

This is deep stuff. Job says that no matter how deep human beings dig, they never discover wisdom. People know how to hunt for silver and gold. They can cut a shaft into the earth—all the way to the place where heat creates brilliant sapphires and gold. Humans manage to unearth all kinds of treasures. But when it comes to wisdom, they can't locate it on their own. Actually, people don't even understand why it's worth searching for. But listen to this good news. You don't have to find the answers on your own. Job says, "God understands the way to it and he alone knows where it dwells" (Job 28:23). God has all the wisdom in the world, and he's more than willing to share. Wisdom starts with living with an awe-filled respect for God (see Job 28:28).

Think: Do you honestly believe God is smarter than you? Why—or why not?

ROCK SOLID truths

²²Destruction*a* and Death say,
  "Only a rumor of it has reached our
    ears."
²³God understands the way to it
  and he alone knows where it
    dwells,
²⁴for he views the ends of the earth
  and sees everything under the
    heavens.
²⁵When he established the force of the
    wind
  and measured out the waters,
²⁶when he made a decree for the rain
  and a path for the thunderstorm,
²⁷then he looked at wisdom and
    appraised it;
  he confirmed it and tested it.
²⁸And he said to the human race,
  "The fear of the Lord—that is
    wisdom,
  and to shun evil is understanding."

Job's Final Defense

29 Job continued his discourse:

²"How I long for the
    months gone by,
  for the days when God watched
    over me,
³when his lamp shone on my head
  and by his light I walked through
    darkness!
⁴Oh, for the days when I was in my
    prime,
  when God's intimate friendship
    blessed my house,
⁵when the Almighty was still with me
  and my children were around me,
⁶when my path was drenched with
    cream
  and the rock poured out for me
    streams of olive oil.

⁷"When I went to the gate of the city
  and took my seat in the public
    square,
⁸the young men saw me and stepped
    aside
  and the old men rose to their feet;
⁹the chief men refrained from speaking
  and covered their mouths with their
    hands;

¹⁰the voices of the nobles were hushed,
  and their tongues stuck to the roof
    of their mouths.
¹¹Whoever heard me spoke well of me,
  and those who saw me commended
    me,
¹²because I rescued the poor who cried
    for help,
  and the fatherless who had none to
    assist them.
¹³The one who was dying blessed me;
  I made the widow's heart sing.
¹⁴I put on righteousness as my
    clothing;
  justice was my robe and my turban.
¹⁵I was eyes to the blind
  and feet to the lame.
¹⁶I was a father to the needy;
  I took up the case of the stranger.
¹⁷I broke the fangs of the wicked
  and snatched the victims from their
    teeth.

¹⁸"I thought, 'I will die in my own
    house,
  my days as numerous as the grains
    of sand.
¹⁹My roots will reach to the water,
  and the dew will lie all night on my
    branches.
²⁰My glory will not fade;
  the bow will be ever new in my hand.'

²¹"People listened to me expectantly,
  waiting in silence for my counsel.
²²After I had spoken, they spoke no
    more;
  my words fell gently on their ears.
²³They waited for me as for showers
  and drank in my words as the spring
    rain.
²⁴When I smiled at them, they scarcely
    believed it;
  the light of my face was precious to
    them.*b*
²⁵I chose the way for them and sat as
    their chief;
  I dwelt as a king among his troops;
  I was like one who comforts
    mourners.

---

a 22 Hebrew *Abaddon*   *b* 24 The meaning of
the Hebrew for this clause is uncertain.

30

"But now they mock me,
  men younger than I,
  whose fathers I would have
    disdained
  to put with my sheep dogs.
2 Of what use was the strength of their
    hands to me,
  since their vigor had gone from
    them?
3 Haggard from want and hunger,
  they roamed^a the parched land
  in desolate wastelands at night.
4 In the brush they gathered salt herbs,
  and their food^b was the root of the
    broom bush.
5 They were banished from human
    society,
  shouted at as if they were thieves.
6 They were forced to live in the dry
    stream beds,
  among the rocks and in holes in the
    ground.
7 They brayed among the bushes
  and huddled in the undergrowth.
8 A base and nameless brood,
  they were driven out of the land.

9 "And now those young men mock me
    in song;
  I have become a byword among them.
10 They detest me and keep their
    distance;
  they do not hesitate to spit in my
    face.
11 Now that God has unstrung my bow
    and afflicted me,
  they throw off restraint in my
    presence.
12 On my right the tribe^c attacks;
  they lay snares for my feet,
  they build their siege ramps against
    me.
13 They break up my road;
  they succeed in destroying me.
  'No one can help him,' they say.
14 They advance as through a gaping
    breach;
  amid the ruins they come rolling in.
15 Terrors overwhelm me;
  my dignity is driven away as by the
    wind,
  my safety vanishes like a cloud.

16 "And now my life ebbs away;
  days of suffering grip me.
17 Night pierces my bones;
  my gnawing pains never rest.
18 In his great power God becomes like
    clothing to me^d;
  he binds me like the neck of my
    garment.
19 He throws me into the mud,
  and I am reduced to dust and ashes.

20 "I cry out to you, God, but you do not
    answer;
  I stand up, but you merely look at me.
21 You turn on me ruthlessly;
  with the might of your hand you
    attack me.
22 You snatch me up and drive me before
    the wind;
  you toss me about in the storm.
23 I know you will bring me down to
    death,
  to the place appointed for all the
    living.

24 "Surely no one lays a hand on a broken
    man
  when he cries for help in his
    distress.
25 Have I not wept for those in trouble?
  Has not my soul grieved for the
    poor?
26 Yet when I hoped for good, evil came;
  when I looked for light, then came
    darkness.
27 The churning inside me never stops;
  days of suffering confront me.
28 I go about blackened, but not by the
    sun;
  I stand up in the assembly and cry
    for help.
29 I have become a brother of jackals,
  a companion of owls.
30 My skin grows black and peels;
  my body burns with fever.
31 My lyre is tuned to mourning,
  and my pipe to the sound of
    wailing.

^{a} 3 Or gnawed ^{b} 4 Or fuel ^{c} 12 The
meaning of the Hebrew for this word is
uncertain. ^{d} 18 Hebrew; Septuagint power
he grasps my clothing

31

"I made a covenant with my eyes
    not to look lustfully at a
    young woman.
²For what is our lot from God above,
    our heritage from the Almighty on
    high?
³Is it not ruin for the wicked,
    disaster for those who do wrong?
⁴Does he not see my ways
    and count my every step?

⁵"If I have walked with falsehood
    or my foot has hurried after
    deceit—
⁶let God weigh me in honest scales
    and he will know that I am
    blameless—
⁷if my steps have turned from the
    path,
    if my heart has been led by my eyes,
    or if my hands have been defiled,
⁸then may others eat what I have
    sown,
    and may my crops be uprooted.

⁹"If my heart has been enticed by a
    woman,
    or if I have lurked at my neighbor's
    door,
¹⁰then may my wife grind another man's
    grain,
    and may other men sleep with her.
¹¹For that would have been wicked,
    a sin to be judged.
¹²It is a fire that burns to Destruction[a];
    it would have uprooted my harvest.

¹³"If I have denied justice to any of my
    servants,
    whether male or female,
    when they had a grievance against me,
¹⁴what will I do when God confronts me?
    What will I answer when called to
    account?
¹⁵Did not he who made me in the womb
    make them?
    Did not the same one form us both
    within our mothers?

---

[a] 12 Hebrew *Abaddon*

ROCK SOLID *principles*

Job 31:1–12

Purify your mind.

What started as giggling with the guys at photos they saw online had become a sexual obsession that ran Colton's life. His parents thought they had his computer locked down tight, but he still found ways to spend hours surfing pornographic websites. The images and videos Colton saw warped how he saw real-world girls. He ranked them by their physical features and whether he caught a sexual tease in how they carried themselves. Colton knew he was in a bad spot, but he wasn't sure he wanted to do anything to fix it.

When Job blurts out his promise "not to look lustfully at a young woman" (Job 31:1), it shows he understands the serious sin of wanting a woman who isn't his wife. After all, he didn't want other men lusting for Mrs. Job (see Job 31:9–11). Lust might seem like it doesn't hurt anyone. But whether it goes on in the mind of a guy or a girl, it's "a fire that burns to Destruction" (Job 31:12), causing unplanned and uncontrolled damage.

16 "If I have denied the desires of the poor
    or let the eyes of the widow grow
      weary,
17 if I have kept my bread to myself,
    not sharing it with the fatherless—
18 but from my youth I reared them as a
      father would,
    and from my birth I guided the
      widow—
19 if I have seen anyone perishing for
      lack of clothing,
    or the needy without garments,
20 and their hearts did not bless me
    for warming them with the fleece
      from my sheep,
21 if I have raised my hand against the
      fatherless,
    knowing that I had influence in
      court,
22 then let my arm fall from the shoulder,
    let it be broken off at the joint.
23 For I dreaded destruction from God,
    and for fear of his splendor I could
      not do such things.

24 "If I have put my trust in gold
    or said to pure gold, 'You are my
      security,'
25 if I have rejoiced over my great wealth,
    the fortune my hands had gained,
26 if I have regarded the sun in its
      radiance
    or the moon moving in splendor,
27 so that my heart was secretly enticed
    and my hand offered them a kiss of
      homage,
28 then these also would be sins to be
      judged,
    for I would have been unfaithful to
      God on high.

29 "If I have rejoiced at my enemy's
      misfortune
    or gloated over the trouble that
      came to him—
30 I have not allowed my mouth to sin
    by invoking a curse against their
      life—
31 if those of my household have never
      said,
    'Who has not been filled with Job's
      meat?'—

32 but no stranger had to spend the night
      in the street,
    for my door was always open to the
      traveler—
33 if I have concealed my sin as people
      do,*a*
    by hiding my guilt in my heart
34 because I so feared the crowd
    and so dreaded the contempt of the
      clans
    that I kept silent and would not go
      outside—

35 ("Oh, that I had someone to hear me!
    I sign now my defense—let the
      Almighty answer me;
    let my accuser put his indictment in
      writing.
36 Surely I would wear it on my
      shoulder,
    I would put it on like a crown.
37 I would give him an account of my
      every step;
    I would present it to him as to a
      ruler.)—

38 "if my land cries out against me
    and all its furrows are wet with
      tears,
39 if I have devoured its yield without
      payment
    or broken the spirit of its tenants,
40 then let briers come up instead of
      wheat
    and stinkweed instead of barley."

The words of Job are ended.

Elihu

32 So these three men stopped answering Job, because he was righteous in his own eyes. 2 But Elihu son of Barakel the Buzite, of the family of Ram, became very angry with Job for justifying himself rather than God. 3 He was also angry with the three friends, because they had found no way to refute Job, and yet had condemned him.*b* 4 Now Elihu had waited before speaking to Job because they were older than he. 5 But

a 33 Or *as Adam did*   *b 3* Masoretic Text; an ancient Hebrew scribal tradition *Job, and so had condemned God* when he saw that the three men had nothing more to say, his anger was aroused.

⁶So Elihu son of Barakel the Buzite said:

"I am young in years,
    and you are old;
that is why I was fearful,
    not daring to tell you what I know.
⁷I thought, 'Age should speak;
    advanced years should teach
        wisdom.'
⁸But it is the spirit*ᵃ* in a person,
    the breath of the Almighty, that
        gives them understanding.
⁹It is not only the old*ᵇ* who are wise,
    not only the aged who understand
        what is right.

¹⁰"Therefore I say: Listen to me;
    I too will tell you what I know.
¹¹I waited while you spoke,
    I listened to your reasoning;
while you were searching for words,
¹²   I gave you my full attention.
But not one of you has proved Job
        wrong;
    none of you has answered his
        arguments.
¹³Do not say, 'We have found wisdom;
    let God, not a man, refute him.'
¹⁴But Job has not marshaled his words
        against me,
    and I will not answer him with your
        arguments.

¹⁵"They are dismayed and have no more
        to say;
    words have failed them.
¹⁶Must I wait, now that they are silent,
    now that they stand there with no
        reply?
¹⁷I too will have my say;
    I too will tell what I know.
¹⁸For I am full of words,
    and the spirit within me compels
        me;
¹⁹inside I am like bottled-up wine,
    like new wineskins ready to burst.
²⁰I must speak and find relief;
    I must open my lips and reply.
²¹I will show no partiality,
    nor will I flatter anyone;

²²for if I were skilled in flattery,
    my Maker would soon take me away.

33 "But now, Job, listen to my
        words;
    pay attention to everything
        I say.
²I am about to open my mouth;
    my words are on the tip of my
        tongue.
³My words come from an upright
        heart;
    my lips sincerely speak what I know.
⁴The Spirit of God has made me;
    the breath of the Almighty gives me
        life.
⁵Answer me then, if you can;
    stand up and argue your case before
        me.
⁶I am the same as you in God's sight;
    I too am a piece of clay.
⁷No fear of me should alarm you,
    nor should my hand be heavy on
        you.

⁸"But you have said in my hearing—
    I heard the very words—
⁹'I am pure, I have done no wrong;
    I am clean and free from sin.
¹⁰Yet God has found fault with me;
    he considers me his enemy.
¹¹He fastens my feet in shackles;
    he keeps close watch on all my
        paths.'

¹²"But I tell you, in this you are not
        right,
    for God is greater than any mortal.
¹³Why do you complain to him
    that he responds to no one's words*ᶜ*?
¹⁴For God does speak—now one way,
        now another—
    though no one perceives it.
¹⁵In a dream, in a vision of the night,
    when deep sleep falls on people
        as they slumber in their beds,
¹⁶he may speak in their ears
    and terrify them with warnings,
¹⁷to turn them from wrongdoing
    and keep them from pride,

ᵃ 8 Or *Spirit*; also in verse 18   *ᵇ 9* Or *many*;
or *great*   *ᶜ 13* Or *that he does not answer for any
of his actions*

¹⁸ to preserve them from the pit,
  their lives from perishing by the
    sword.*

¹⁹ "Or someone may be chastened on a
    bed of pain
  with constant distress in their bones,
²⁰ so that their body finds food repulsive
  and their soul loathes the choicest
    meal.
²¹ Their flesh wastes away to nothing,
  and their bones, once hidden, now
    stick out.
²² They draw near to the pit,
  and their life to the messengers of
    death.*

²³ Yet if there is an angel at their side,
  a messenger, one out of a thousand,
    sent to tell them how to be upright,
²⁴ and he is gracious to that person and
    says to God,
  'Spare them from going down to
    the pit;
  I have found a ransom for them—
²⁵ let their flesh be renewed like a child's;
  let them be restored as in the days
    of their youth'—
²⁶ then that person can pray to God and
    find favor with him,
  they will see God's face and shout
    for joy;
  he will restore them to full well-
    being.
²⁷ And they will go to others and say,
  'I have sinned, I have perverted
    what is right,
  but I did not get what I deserved.
²⁸ God has delivered me from going
    down to the pit,
  and I shall live to enjoy the light of
    life.'

²⁹ "God does all these things to a
    person—
  twice, even three times—
³⁰ to turn them back from the pit,
  that the light of life may shine on
    them.

³¹ "Pay attention, Job, and listen to me;
  be silent, and I will speak.
³² If you have anything to say, answer me;
  speak up, for I want to vindicate you.

³³ But if not, then listen to me;
  be silent, and I will teach you
    wisdom."

34

Then Elihu said:

² "Hear my words, you wise
    men;
  listen to me, you men of learning.
³ For the ear tests words
  as the tongue tastes food.
⁴ Let us discern for ourselves what is
    right;
  let us learn together what is good.

⁵ "Job says, 'I am innocent,
  but God denies me justice.
⁶ Although I am right,
  I am considered a liar;
  although I am guiltless,
  his arrow inflicts an incurable
    wound.'
⁷ Is there anyone like Job,
  who drinks scorn like water?
⁸ He keeps company with evildoers;
  he associates with the wicked.
⁹ For he says, 'There is no profit
  in trying to please God.'

¹⁰ "So listen to me, you men of
    understanding.
  Far be it from God to do evil,
  from the Almighty to do wrong.
¹¹ He repays everyone for what they
    have done;
  he brings on them what their
    conduct deserves.
¹² It is unthinkable that God would do
    wrong,
  that the Almighty would pervert
    justice.
¹³ Who appointed him over the earth?
  Who put him in charge of the
    whole world?
¹⁴ If it were his intention
  and he withdrew his spirit^c and
    breath,
¹⁵ all humanity would perish together
  and mankind would return to the
    dust.

---

a 18 Or *from crossing the river*   *b 22* Or *to the place of the dead*   *c 14* Or *Spirit*

16 "If you have understanding, hear this;
  listen to what I say.
17 Can someone who hates justice
    govern?
  Will you condemn the just and
    mighty One?
18 Is he not the One who says to kings,
    'You are worthless,'
  and to nobles, 'You are wicked,'
19 who shows no partiality to princes
  and does not favor the rich over the
    poor,
  for they are all the work of his hands?
20 They die in an instant, in the middle
    of the night;

the people are shaken and they pass
    away;
  the mighty are removed without
    human hand.

21 "His eyes are on the ways of
    mortals;
  he sees their every step.
22 There is no deep shadow, no utter
    darkness,
  where evildoers can hide.
23 God has no need to examine people
    further,
  that they should come before him
    for judgment.

Job 34

Job struggled to understand.

Fire fell from the sky and torched 7,000 of Job's sheep. A house collapsed and killed all of his sons and daughters. His body broke out in ugly wounds "from the soles of his feet to the crown of his head" (Job 2:7). All Job could do was sit and scrape his painful sores with a piece of broken pottery.

Hurting. Puzzled. Dazed. Confused. Job suffered the loss of most everything that meant anything to him — his wealth, his children, and his own health. Of all the problems Job faced, however, the toughest was something happening inside himself. He struggled to understand the reason for his suffering.

Job's friends tried to explain his plight, but their answers didn't help. His wife told him he should curse God and die. Job loudly told the Lord he didn't deserve such a brutal life. But this tormented man couldn't see events going on behind the scenes. He didn't know he was undergoing a cosmic test, that Satan was trying to cause him so much pain he would give up on God. Lacking that crucial bit of information, Job would never understand.

Job had to admit he couldn't make sense of anything. He told the Lord, "I spoke of things I did not understand, things too wonderful for me to know" (Job 42:3). God didn't expect Job to figure things out. He just wanted this good man to trust him.

You can find Job in the book named for him as well as in Ezekiel 14:14.

UNSHAKEN people

²⁴Without inquiry he shatters the
mighty
and sets up others in their place.
²⁵Because he takes note of their deeds,
he overthrows them in the night
and they are crushed.
²⁶He punishes them for their wickedness
where everyone can see them,
²⁷because they turned from following
him
and had no regard for any of his ways.
²⁸They caused the cry of the poor to
come before him,
so that he heard the cry of the
needy.
²⁹But if he remains silent, who can
condemn him?
If he hides his face, who can see
him?
Yet he is over individual and nation
alike,
³⁰   to keep the godless from ruling,
from laying snares for the people.

³¹"Suppose someone says to God,
'I am guilty but will offend no more.
³²Teach me what I cannot see;
if I have done wrong, I will not do
so again.'
³³Should God then reward you on your
terms,
when you refuse to repent?
You must decide, not I;
so tell me what you know.

³⁴"Men of understanding declare,
wise men who hear me say to me,
³⁵'Job speaks without knowledge;
his words lack insight.'
³⁶Oh, that Job might be tested to the
utmost
for answering like a wicked man!
³⁷To his sin he adds rebellion;
scornfully he claps his hands
among us
and multiplies his words against
God."

35

Then Elihu said:

²"Do you think this is just?
You say, 'I am in the right, not God.'
³Yet you ask him, 'What profit is it to
me,^a
and what do I gain by not sinning?'

⁴"I would like to reply to you
and to your friends with you.
⁵Look up at the heavens and see;
gaze at the clouds so high above
you.
⁶If you sin, how does that affect him?
If your sins are many, what does
that do to him?
⁷If you are righteous, what do you give
to him,
or what does he receive from your
hand?
⁸Your wickedness only affects humans
like yourself,
and your righteousness only other
people.

⁹"People cry out under a load of
oppression;
they plead for relief from the arm of
the powerful.
¹⁰But no one says, 'Where is God my
Maker,
who gives songs in the night,
¹¹who teaches us more than he teaches^b
the beasts of the earth
and makes us wiser than^c the birds
in the sky?'
¹²He does not answer when people cry
out
because of the arrogance of the
wicked.
¹³Indeed, God does not listen to their
empty plea;
the Almighty pays no attention to it.
¹⁴How much less, then, will he listen
when you say that you do not see
him,
that your case is before him
and you must wait for him,
¹⁵and further, that his anger never
punishes
and he does not take the least notice
of wickedness.^d

^a 3 Or you   ^b 10,11 Or night, / ¹¹who teaches
us by   ^c 11 Or us wise by   ^d 15 Symmachus,
Theodotion and Vulgate; the meaning of the
Hebrew for this word is uncertain.

16 So Job opens his mouth with empty
talk;
without knowledge he multiplies
words."

36

Elihu continued:

2 "Bear with me a little
longer and I will show you
that there is more to be said in
God's behalf.
3 I get my knowledge from afar;
I will ascribe justice to my Maker.
4 Be assured that my words are not false;
one who has perfect knowledge is
with you.

5 "God is mighty, but despises no one;
he is mighty, and firm in his
purpose.

ROCK SOLID promises

"God is mighty, but despises no one."
Job 36:5

God could crush humankind with a whisper, but he instead sees each of us as his uniquely valuable creation.

---

6 He does not keep the wicked alive
but gives the afflicted their rights.
7 He does not take his eyes off the
righteous;
he enthrones them with kings
and exalts them forever.
8 But if people are bound in chains,
held fast by cords of affliction,
9 he tells them what they have done—
that they have sinned arrogantly.
10 He makes them listen to correction
and commands them to repent of
their evil.

11 If they obey and serve him,
they will spend the rest of their days
in prosperity
and their years in contentment.
12 But if they do not listen,
they will perish by the sword[a]
and die without knowledge.

13 "The godless in heart harbor
resentment;
even when he fetters them, they do
not cry for help.
14 They die in their youth,
among male prostitutes of the
shrines.
15 But those who suffer he delivers in
their suffering;
he speaks to them in their
affliction.

16 "He is wooing you from the jaws of
distress
to a spacious place free from
restriction,
to the comfort of your table laden
with choice food.
17 But now you are laden with the
judgment due the wicked;
judgment and justice have taken
hold of you.
18 Be careful that no one entices you by
riches;
do not let a large bribe turn you
aside.
19 Would your wealth or even all your
mighty efforts
sustain you so you would not be in
distress?
20 Do not long for the night,
to drag people away from their
homes.[b]
21 Beware of turning to evil,
which you seem to prefer to
affliction.

22 "God is exalted in his power.
Who is a teacher like him?
23 Who has prescribed his ways for him,
or said to him, 'You have done
wrong'?

---

[a] 12 Or *will cross the river*   [b] 20 The meaning
of the Hebrew for verses 18-20 is uncertain.

²⁴ Remember to extol his work,
    which people have praised in song.
²⁵ All humanity has seen it;
    mortals gaze on it from afar.
²⁶ How great is God—beyond our
        understanding!
    The number of his years is past
        finding out.

²⁷ "He draws up the drops of water,
    which distill as rain to the streams*ᵃ*;
²⁸ the clouds pour down their moisture
    and abundant showers fall on
        mankind.
²⁹ Who can understand how he spreads
        out the clouds,
    how he thunders from his pavilion?
³⁰ See how he scatters his lightning
        about him,
    bathing the depths of the sea.
³¹ This is the way he governs*ᵇ* the
        nations
    and provides food in abundance.
³² He fills his hands with lightning
    and commands it to strike its mark.
³³ His thunder announces the coming
        storm;
    even the cattle make known its
        approach.*ᶜ*

37

"At this my heart pounds
    and leaps from its place.
² Listen! Listen to the roar
    of his voice,
to the rumbling that comes from his
        mouth.
³ He unleashes his lightning beneath
        the whole heaven
    and sends it to the ends of the earth.
⁴ After that comes the sound of his roar;
    he thunders with his majestic voice.
When his voice resounds,
    he holds nothing back.
⁵ God's voice thunders in marvelous ways;
    he does great things beyond our
        understanding.
⁶ He says to the snow, 'Fall on the earth,'
    and to the rain shower, 'Be a mighty
        downpour.'
⁷ So that everyone he has made may
        know his work,
    he stops all people from their labor.*ᵈ*

⁸ The animals take cover;
    they remain in their dens.
⁹ The tempest comes out from its
        chamber,
    the cold from the driving winds.
¹⁰ The breath of God produces ice,
    and the broad waters become
        frozen.
¹¹ He loads the clouds with moisture;
    he scatters his lightning through
        them.
¹² At his direction they swirl around
    over the face of the whole earth
    to do whatever he commands them.
¹³ He brings the clouds to punish
        people,
    or to water his earth and show his
        love.

¹⁴ "Listen to this, Job;
    stop and consider God's wonders.
¹⁵ Do you know how God controls the
        clouds
    and makes his lightning flash?
¹⁶ Do you know how the clouds hang
        poised,
    those wonders of him who has
        perfect knowledge?
¹⁷ You who swelter in your clothes
    when the land lies hushed under the
        south wind,
¹⁸ can you join him in spreading out the
        skies,
    hard as a mirror of cast bronze?

¹⁹ "Tell us what we should say to him;
    we cannot draw up our case because
        of our darkness.
²⁰ Should he be told that I want to
        speak?
    Would anyone ask to be swallowed
        up?
²¹ Now no one can look at the sun,
    bright as it is in the skies
    after the wind has swept them clean.
²² Out of the north he comes in golden
        splendor;
    God comes in awesome majesty.

ᵃ 27 Or *distill from the mist as rain*   *ᵇ 31* Or
nourishes   *ᶜ 33* Or *announces his coming—* / *the
One zealous against evil*   *ᵈ 7* Or *work,* / *he fills
all people with fear by his power*

²³ The Almighty is beyond our reach
and exalted in power;
in his justice and great
righteousness, he does not
oppress.
²⁴ Therefore, people revere him,
for does he not have regard for all
the wise in heart?ᵃ"

The Lord Speaks

38 Then the Lord spoke to Job
out of the storm. He said:

² "Who is this that obscures my plans
with words without knowledge?
³ Brace yourself like a man;
I will question you,
and you shall answer me.

⁴ "Where were you when I laid the
earth's foundation?
Tell me, if you understand.

⁵ Who marked off its dimensions?
Surely you know!
Who stretched a measuring line
across it?
⁶ On what were its footings set,
or who laid its cornerstone—
⁷ while the morning stars sang together
and all the angelsᵇ shouted for joy?

⁸ "Who shut up the sea behind doors
when it burst forth from the womb,
⁹ when I made the clouds its garment
and wrapped it in thick darkness,
¹⁰ when I fixed limits for it
and set its doors and bars in place,
¹¹ when I said, 'This far you may come
and no farther;
here is where your proud waves
halt'?

¹² "Have you ever given orders to the
morning,
or shown the dawn its place,
¹³ that it might take the earth by the
edges
and shake the wicked out of it?
¹⁴ The earth takes shape like clay under
a seal;
its features stand out like those of a
garment.
¹⁵ The wicked are denied their light,
and their upraised arm is broken.

¹⁶ "Have you journeyed to the springs of
the sea
or walked in the recesses of the
deep?
¹⁷ Have the gates of death been shown to
you?
Have you seen the gates of the
deepest darkness?
¹⁸ Have you comprehended the vast
expanses of the earth?
Tell me, if you know all this.

¹⁹ "What is the way to the abode of
light?
And where does darkness reside?
²⁰ Can you take them to their places?
Do you know the paths to their
dwellings?

UNSHAKEN God

Job 38:1–4

God is mysterious.

Job wasn't trying to pick a fight with God. He understood that no mortal could claim to be righteous before God, and no mere human mind could answer God "one time out of a thousand" (Job 9:3). God never stopped Job when he mourned his painful losses. But in the end Job needed a reminder that we can never fully understand God's thoughts and actions. The Lord told Job to brace himself like a man, then blasted Job with fact after fact that Job couldn't comprehend (see Job 38–41). Because God is greater than we can ever fully know, there's no end to what we can learn about him. The Lord will always be part mystery.

So ... How do you plan to go deeper in your understanding of God?

ᵃ 24 Or *for he does not have regard for any who think they are wise.*   ᵇ 7 Hebrew *the sons of God*

²¹ Surely you know, for you were already
　　born!
　　You have lived so many years!

²² "Have you entered the storehouses of
　　the snow
　　or seen the storehouses of the hail,
²³ which I reserve for times of trouble,
　　for days of war and battle?
²⁴ What is the way to the place where
　　the lightning is dispersed,
　　or the place where the east winds
　　are scattered over the earth?
²⁵ Who cuts a channel for the torrents of
　　rain,
　　and a path for the thunderstorm,
²⁶ to water a land where no one lives,
　　an uninhabited desert,
²⁷ to satisfy a desolate wasteland
　　and make it sprout with grass?
²⁸ Does the rain have a father?
　　Who fathers the drops of dew?
²⁹ From whose womb comes the ice?
　　Who gives birth to the frost from
　　the heavens
³⁰ when the waters become hard as stone,
　　when the surface of the deep is
　　frozen?

³¹ "Can you bind the chains*ᵃ* of the
　　Pleiades?
　　Can you loosen Orion's belt?
³² Can you bring forth the constellations
　　in their seasons*ᵇ*
　　or lead out the Bear*ᶜ* with its cubs?
³³ Do you know the laws of the heavens?
　　Can you set up God's*ᵈ* dominion
　　over the earth?

³⁴ "Can you raise your voice to the clouds
　　and cover yourself with a flood of
　　water?
³⁵ Do you send the lightning bolts on
　　their way?
　　Do they report to you, 'Here we are'?
³⁶ Who gives the ibis wisdom*ᵉ*
　　or gives the rooster understanding?*ᶠ*
³⁷ Who has the wisdom to count the
　　clouds?
　　Who can tip over the water jars of
　　the heavens
³⁸ when the dust becomes hard
　　and the clods of earth stick together?

³⁹ "Do you hunt the prey for the lioness
　　and satisfy the hunger of the lions
⁴⁰ when they crouch in their dens
　　or lie in wait in a thicket?
⁴¹ Who provides food for the raven
　　when its young cry out to God
　　and wander about for lack of food?

39 "Do you know when the
　　mountain goats give birth?
　　Do you watch when the
　　doe bears her fawn?
² Do you count the months till they
　　bear?
　　Do you know the time they give
　　birth?
³ They crouch down and bring forth
　　their young;
　　their labor pains are ended.
⁴ Their young thrive and grow strong in
　　the wilds;
　　they leave and do not return.

⁵ "Who let the wild donkey go free?
　　Who untied its ropes?
⁶ I gave it the wasteland as its home,
　　the salt flats as its habitat.
⁷ It laughs at the commotion in the
　　town;
　　it does not hear a driver's shout.
⁸ It ranges the hills for its pasture
　　and searches for any green thing.

⁹ "Will the wild ox consent to serve
　　you?
　　Will it stay by your manger at
　　night?
¹⁰ Can you hold it to the furrow with a
　　harness?
　　Will it till the valleys behind you?
¹¹ Will you rely on it for its great
　　strength?
　　Will you leave your heavy work to
　　it?
¹² Can you trust it to haul in your grain
　　and bring it to your threshing
　　floor?

ᵃ 31 Septuagint; Hebrew *beauty*　　*ᵇ 32* Or
the morning star in its season　　*ᶜ 32* Or *out Leo*
ᵈ 33 Or *their*　　*ᵉ 36* That is, wisdom about
the flooding of the Nile　　*ᶠ 36* That is,
understanding of when to crow; the meaning
of the Hebrew for this verse is uncertain.

¹³ "The wings of the ostrich flap
  joyfully,
  though they cannot compare
  with the wings and feathers of the
    stork.
¹⁴ She lays her eggs on the ground
  and lets them warm in the sand,
¹⁵ unmindful that a foot may crush
    them,
  that some wild animal may trample
    them.
¹⁶ She treats her young harshly, as if they
    were not hers;
  she cares not that her labor was in
    vain,
¹⁷ for God did not endow her with
    wisdom
  or give her a share of good sense.
¹⁸ Yet when she spreads her feathers to
    run,
  she laughs at horse and rider.

¹⁹ "Do you give the horse its strength
  or clothe its neck with a flowing
    mane?
²⁰ Do you make it leap like a locust,
  striking terror with its proud
    snorting?
²¹ It paws fiercely, rejoicing in its
    strength,
  and charges into the fray.
²² It laughs at fear, afraid of nothing;
  it does not shy away from the
    sword.
²³ The quiver rattles against its side,
  along with the flashing spear and
    lance.
²⁴ In frenzied excitement it eats up the
    ground;
  it cannot stand still when the
    trumpet sounds.
²⁵ At the blast of the trumpet it snorts,
    'Aha!'
  It catches the scent of battle from
    afar,
  the shout of commanders and the
    battle cry.

²⁶ "Does the hawk take flight by your
    wisdom
  and spread its wings toward the
    south?

²⁷ Does the eagle soar at your
    command
  and build its nest on high?
²⁸ It dwells on a cliff and stays there at
    night;
  a rocky crag is its stronghold.
²⁹ From there it looks for food;
  its eyes detect it from afar.
³⁰ Its young ones feast on blood,
  and where the slain are, there it is."

40

The LORD said to Job:

² "Will the one who
  contends with the Almighty
  correct him?
  Let him who accuses God answer
    him!"

³ Then Job answered the LORD:

⁴ "I am unworthy—how can I reply to
    you?
  I put my hand over my mouth.
⁵ I spoke once, but I have no answer—
  twice, but I will say no more."

⁶ Then the LORD spoke to Job out of the
storm:

⁷ "Brace yourself like a man;
  I will question you,
  and you shall answer me.

⁸ "Would you discredit my justice?
  Would you condemn me to justify
    yourself?
⁹ Do you have an arm like God's,
  and can your voice thunder like his?
¹⁰ Then adorn yourself with glory and
    splendor,
  and clothe yourself in honor and
    majesty.
¹¹ Unleash the fury of your wrath,
  look at all who are proud and bring
    them low,
¹² look at all who are proud and humble
    them,
  crush the wicked where they stand.
¹³ Bury them all in the dust together;
  shroud their faces in the grave.
¹⁴ Then I myself will admit to you
  that your own right hand can save
    you.

15 "Look at Behemoth,
   which I made along with you
   and which feeds on grass like an ox.
16 What strength it has in its loins,
   what power in the muscles of its
      belly!
17 Its tail sways like a cedar;
   the sinews of its thighs are close-
      knit.
18 Its bones are tubes of bronze,
   its limbs like rods of iron.
19 It ranks first among the works of
      God,
   yet its Maker can approach it with
      his sword.
20 The hills bring it their produce,
   and all the wild animals play
      nearby.
21 Under the lotus plants it lies,
   hidden among the reeds in the
      marsh.
22 The lotuses conceal it in their
      shadow;
   the poplars by the stream
      surround it.
23 A raging river does not alarm it;
   it is secure, though the Jordan
      should surge against its
      mouth.
24 Can anyone capture it by the eyes,
   or trap it and pierce its nose?

41 *a* "Can you pull in Leviathan
   with a fishhook
   or tie down its tongue with
   a rope?
2 Can you put a cord through its nose
   or pierce its jaw with a hook?
3 Will it keep begging you for mercy?
   Will it speak to you with gentle
      words?
4 Will it make an agreement with you
   for you to take it as your slave for
      life?
5 Can you make a pet of it like a bird
   or put it on a leash for the young
      women in your house?
6 Will traders barter for it?
   Will they divide it up among the
      merchants?
7 Can you fill its hide with harpoons
   or its head with fishing spears?

8 If you lay a hand on it,
   you will remember the struggle and
      never do it again!
9 Any hope of subduing it is false;
   the mere sight of it is overpowering.
10 No one is fierce enough to rouse it.
   Who then is able to stand
      against me?
11 Who has a claim against me that I
      must pay?
   Everything under heaven belongs
      to me.

12 "I will not fail to speak of Leviathan's
      limbs,
   its strength and its graceful form.
13 Who can strip off its outer coat?
   Who can penetrate its double coat
      of armor*b*?
14 Who dares open the doors of its
      mouth,
   ringed about with fearsome teeth?
15 Its back has*c* rows of shields
   tightly sealed together;
16 each is so close to the next
   that no air can pass between.
17 They are joined fast to one another;
   they cling together and cannot be
      parted.
18 Its snorting throws out flashes of
      light;
   its eyes are like the rays of dawn.
19 Flames stream from its mouth;
   sparks of fire shoot out.
20 Smoke pours from its nostrils
   as from a boiling pot over burning
      reeds.
21 Its breath sets coals ablaze,
   and flames dart from its mouth.
22 Strength resides in its neck;
   dismay goes before it.
23 The folds of its flesh are tightly joined;
   they are firm and immovable.
24 Its chest is hard as rock,
   hard as a lower millstone.
25 When it rises up, the mighty are
      terrified;
   they retreat before its thrashing.

a In Hebrew texts 41:1-8 is numbered 40:25-32,
and 41:9-34 is numbered 41:1-26.
b 13 Septuagint; Hebrew *double bridle*
c 15 Or *Its pride is its*

26 The sword that reaches it has no
effect,
nor does the spear or the dart or the
javelin.
27 Iron it treats like straw
and bronze like rotten wood.
28 Arrows do not make it flee;
slingstones are like chaff to it.
29 A club seems to it a piece of straw;
it laughs at the rattling of the lance.
30 Its undersides are jagged potsherds,
leaving a trail in the mud like a
threshing sledge.
31 It makes the depths churn like a
boiling caldron
and stirs up the sea like a pot of
ointment.
32 It leaves a glistening wake behind it;
one would think the deep had white
hair.
33 Nothing on earth is its equal—
a creature without fear.
34 It looks down on all that are haughty;
it is king over all that are proud.”

Job

42

Then Job replied to the
Lord:

2 “I know that you can do all things;
no purpose of yours can be thwarted.
3 You asked, ‘Who is this that obscures
my plans without knowledge?’
Surely I spoke of things I did not
understand,
things too wonderful for me to know.
4 “You said, ‘Listen now, and I will
speak;
I will question you,
and you shall answer me.’
5 My ears had heard of you
but now my eyes have seen you.
6 Therefore I despise myself
and repent in dust and ashes.”

Epilogue

7 After the Lord had said these things
to Job, he said to Eliphaz the Teman-

ROCK SOLID principles

Job 42:1 – 17

Humble yourself.

Mom stars in a symphony orchestra. Dad directs college choirs. And Mariah began playing violin before she started kindergarten. On top of all of her natural talent, Mariah has heaped years of rigorous lessons and hours of daily practice that come before anything else. She has every reason to be proud of her stand-out accomplishments. Mariah likes to bow her head and pray before she plays, but others just see it as another part of the show. Her attitude suggests that she somehow overlooks the fact that God gave her both talent and the perseverance to succeed. Mariah is great and will only get better. But the Lord will forever be the best.

Job couldn't stop talking about his own goodness—until the Lord spoke up and stumped him with an encyclopedia of his infinite power and knowledge. Job covered himself in ashes to demonstrate remorse, but the Lord didn't leave him in the dirt. The end of Job's story sounds like the promise in James 4:10: “Humble yourselves before the Lord, and he will lift you up.”

ite, "I am angry with you and your two friends, because you have not spoken the truth about me, as my servant Job has. ⁸ So now take seven bulls and seven rams and go to my servant Job and sacrifice a burnt offering for yourselves. My servant Job will pray for you, and I will accept his prayer and not deal with you according to your folly. You have not spoken the truth about me, as my servant Job has." ⁹ So Eliphaz the Temanite, Bildad the Shuhite and Zophar the Naamathite did what the LORD told them; and the LORD accepted Job's prayer.

¹⁰ After Job had prayed for his friends, the LORD restored his fortunes and gave him twice as much as he had before. ¹¹ All his brothers and sisters and everyone who had known him before came and ate with him in his house. They comforted and consoled him over all the trouble the LORD had brought on him, and each one gave him a piece of silver*a* and a gold ring. ¹² The LORD blessed the latter part of Job's life more than the former part. He had fourteen thousand sheep, six thousand camels, a thousand yoke of oxen and a thousand donkeys. ¹³ And he also had seven sons and three daughters. ¹⁴ The first daughter he named Jemimah, the second Keziah and the third Keren-Happuch. ¹⁵ Nowhere in all the land were there found women as beautiful as Job's daughters, and their father granted them an inheritance along with their brothers.

¹⁶ After this, Job lived a hundred and forty years; he saw his children and their children to the fourth generation. ¹⁷ And so Job died, an old man and full of years.

a 11 Hebrew *him a kesitah*; a kesitah was a unit of money of unknown weight and value.

BOOK OUTLINE

PSALMS

The Psalms are poems or songs of praise, worship, thankfulness and repentance. They show a variety of emotions, attitudes and interests, and vary in length from a few verses (Psalm 117) to many parts with 176 verses (Psalm 119). Hebrew poetry often uses pairs of lines. The second line either repeats the thought of the first or gives an opposite. Look for these pairs of lines as you read the Psalms.

Of the 150 Psalms, one hundred of them are thought to be written by the following authors: David—73; Asaph—12; Sons of Korah—10; Moses—1; Heman the Ezrahite—1; Ethan the Ezrahite—1; and one or two by Solomon. The rest of the Psalms have no recorded author.

These poems have a world-wide appeal and are familiar and loved by many people because they were written by many authors, from different time periods, and show a variety of emotions.

BOOK I

Psalms 1–41

Psalm 1

¹ Blessed is the one
who does not walk in step with the
wicked
or stand in the way that sinners take
or sit in the company of mockers,
² but whose delight is in the law of the
LORD,
and who meditates on his law day
and night.
³ That person is like a tree planted by
streams of water,
which yields its fruit in season
and whose leaf does not wither—
whatever they do prospers.

⁴ Not so the wicked!
They are like chaff
that the wind blows away.

⁵ Therefore the wicked will not stand in
the judgment,
nor sinners in the assembly of the
righteous.

⁶ For the LORD watches over the way of
the righteous,
but the way of the wicked leads to
destruction.

Psalm 2

¹ Why do the nations conspire[a]
and the peoples plot in vain?
² The kings of the earth rise up
and the rulers band together
against the LORD and against his
anointed, saying,
³ "Let us break their chains
and throw off their shackles."

⁴ The One enthroned in heaven laughs;
the Lord scoffs at them.

[a] 1 Hebrew; Septuagint rage

PSALM 2

ROCK SOLID principles

Psalm 1:1–6

Get blessed.

Wyatt enjoyed his status as the popular starting quarterback of his high school football team. He gave credit to God for his abilities, seeing them as a gift straight from above. But he couldn't figure out why God didn't come to his side when he broke curfew and got benched for a game. Or when he partied with friends and got booted from the squad for failing a breathalyzer test. Wyatt thought God would always keep blessing him. He assumed the Lord's plan to save his high school was doomed without a Christian at the head of the football team. But Wyatt's choices had clearly taken him out of bounds.

God doesn't bless you as payback for your good behavior. He gives you good gifts because of his grace—favor you can't earn. But running down sinful paths often takes you out of his blessings. You head to rough and rocky places where you're bound to get hurt. If you want to experience the best life possible, stay close to God.

633

⁵He rebukes them in his anger
   and terrifies them in his wrath,
     saying,
⁶"I have installed my king
   on Zion, my holy mountain."

⁷I will proclaim the LORD's decree:

He said to me, "You are my son;
   today I have become your father.
⁸Ask me,
   and I will make the nations your
     inheritance,
   the ends of the earth your
     possession.
⁹You will break them with a rod of
     iron*ᵃ*;
   you will dash them to pieces like
     pottery."

¹⁰Therefore, you kings, be wise;
   be warned, you rulers of the earth.
¹¹Serve the LORD with fear
   and celebrate his rule with
     trembling.
¹²Kiss his son, or he will be angry
   and your way will lead to your
     destruction,
for his wrath can flare up in a
     moment.
   Blessed are all who take refuge in
     him.

Psalm 3 *ᵇ*

A psalm of David. When he fled
from his son Absalom.

¹LORD, how many are my foes!
   How many rise up against me!
²Many are saying of me,
   "God will not deliver him."*ᶜ*

³But you, LORD, are a shield around
     me,
   my glory, the One who lifts my
     head high.
⁴I call out to the LORD,
   and he answers me from his holy
     mountain.
⁵I lie down and sleep;
   I wake again, because the LORD
     sustains me.

⁶I will not fear though tens of
     thousands
   assail me on every side.

⁷Arise, LORD!
   Deliver me, my God!
Strike all my enemies on the jaw;
   break the teeth of the wicked.

⁸From the LORD comes deliverance.
   May your blessing be on your
     people.

Psalm 4 *ᵈ*

For the director of music. With stringed
instruments. A psalm of David.

¹Answer me when I call to you,
   my righteous God.
Give me relief from my distress;
   have mercy on me and hear my
     prayer.

²How long will you people turn my
     glory into shame?
How long will you love delusions
   and seek false gods*ᵉ*?*ᶠ*
³Know that the LORD has set apart his
     faithful servant for himself;
   the LORD hears when I call to
     him.

⁴Tremble and*ᵍ* do not sin;
   when you are on your beds,
   search your hearts and be silent.
⁵Offer the sacrifices of the righteous
   and trust in the LORD.

⁶Many, LORD, are asking, "Who will
     bring us prosperity?"
   Let the light of your face shine
     on us.
⁷Fill my heart with joy
   when their grain and new wine
     abound.

ᵃ 9 Or *will rule them with an iron scepter* (see
Septuagint and Syriac)   *ᵇ* In Hebrew texts
3:1-8 is numbered 3:2-9.   *ᶜ 2* The Hebrew has
Selah (a word of uncertain meaning) here and at
the end of verses 4 and 8.   *ᵈ* In Hebrew texts
4:1-8 is numbered 4:2-9.   *ᵉ 2* Or *seek lies*
ᶠ 2 The Hebrew has *Selah* (a word of uncertain
meaning) here and at the end of verse 4.
ᵍ 4 Or *In your anger* (see Septuagint)

8 In peace I will lie down and sleep,
  for you alone, LORD,
  make me dwell in safety.

ROCK SOLID
promises

"In peace I will lie down and sleep, for you alone, LORD, make me dwell in safety." Psalm 4:8

When you recall that God protects you, you don't have to go to bed uptight.

Psalm 5 [a]

For the director of music. For pipes.
A psalm of David.

1 Listen to my words, LORD,
  consider my lament.
2 Hear my cry for help,
  my King and my God,
  for to you I pray.

3 In the morning, LORD, you hear my
    voice;
  in the morning I lay my requests
    before you
  and wait expectantly.
4 For you are not a God who is pleased
    with wickedness;
  with you, evil people are not
    welcome.
5 The arrogant cannot stand
  in your presence.
  You hate all who do wrong;
6   you destroy those who tell lies.
  The bloodthirsty and deceitful
  you, LORD, detest.
7 But I, by your great love,
  can come into your house;
  in reverence I bow down
  toward your holy temple.

PSALM 5

8 Lead me, LORD, in your righteousness
    because of my enemies—
  make your way straight before me.
9 Not a word from their mouth can be
    trusted;
  their heart is filled with malice.
  Their throat is an open grave;
  with their tongues they tell lies.
10 Declare them guilty, O God!
  Let their intrigues be their
    downfall.
  Banish them for their many sins,
  for they have rebelled against you.
11 But let all who take refuge in you be
    glad;
  let them ever sing for joy.
  Spread your protection over them,
  that those who love your name may
    rejoice in you.

12 Surely, LORD, you bless the righteous;
  you surround them with your favor
  as with a shield.

[a] In Hebrew texts 5:1-12 is numbered 5:2-13.

ROCK SOLID
plans

Psalm 5:3

Start every day with God.

No one knows whether David had been crowned king of Israel when he wrote this psalm. But whatever was going on in David's life at the time, he wasn't rolling over in the morning and lazily drifting back to sleep. His enemies and difficulties felt so heavy that he immediately went to prayer—listing his needs, worshiping God's holiness, and pleading for mercy, blessing, and protection. David could have jumped into his day and tried to handle his problems by himself. Instead he started by talking with God.

Your next step: Build a habit of talking with God at the beginning of each day.

Psalm 6[a]

For the director of music. With stringed
instruments. According to *sheminith.*[b]
A psalm of David.

[1] Lord, do not rebuke me in your anger
or discipline me in your wrath.
[2] Have mercy on me, Lord, for I am
faint;
heal me, Lord, for my bones are in
agony.
[3] My soul is in deep anguish.
How long, Lord, how long?

[4] Turn, Lord, and deliver me;
save me because of your unfailing
love.
[5] Among the dead no one proclaims
your name.
Who praises you from the grave?

[6] I am worn out from my groaning.

All night long I flood my bed with
weeping
and drench my couch with tears.
[7] My eyes grow weak with sorrow;
they fail because of all my foes.

[8] Away from me, all you who do evil,
for the Lord has heard my weeping.
[9] The Lord has heard my cry for mercy;
the Lord accepts my prayer.
[10] All my enemies will be overwhelmed
with shame and anguish;
they will turn back and suddenly be
put to shame.

Psalm 7[c]

A *shiggaion*[d] of David, which he sang to the
Lord concerning Cush, a Benjamite.

[1] Lord my God, I take refuge in you;
save and deliver me from all who
pursue me,
[2] or they will tear me apart like a lion
and rip me to pieces with no one to
rescue me.

[3] Lord my God, if I have done this
and there is guilt on my hands—
[4] if I have repaid my ally with evil
or without cause have robbed my
foe—

[5] then let my enemy pursue and
overtake me;
let him trample my life to the
ground
and make me sleep in the dust.[e]

[6] Arise, Lord, in your anger;
rise up against the rage of my
enemies.
Awake, my God; decree justice.
[7] Let the assembled peoples gather
around you,
while you sit enthroned over them
on high.
[8]   Let the Lord judge the peoples.
Vindicate me, Lord, according to my
righteousness,
according to my integrity, O Most
High.
[9] Bring to an end the violence of the
wicked
and make the righteous secure—
you, the righteous God
who probes minds and hearts.

[10] My shield[f] is God Most High,
who saves the upright in heart.
[11] God is a righteous judge,
a God who displays his wrath every
day.
[12] If he does not relent,
he[g] will sharpen his sword;
he will bend and string his bow.
[13] He has prepared his deadly weapons;
he makes ready his flaming
arrows.

[14] Whoever is pregnant with evil
conceives trouble and gives birth to
disillusionment.
[15] Whoever digs a hole and scoops it out
falls into the pit they have made.
[16] The trouble they cause recoils on
them;
their violence comes down on their
own heads.

---

[a] In Hebrew texts 6:1-10 is numbered 6:2-11.
[b] Title: Probably a musical term   [c] In Hebrew
texts 7:1-17 is numbered 7:2-18.   [d] Title:
Probably a literary or musical term   [e] 5 The
Hebrew has *Selah* (a word of uncertain meaning)
here.   [f] 10 Or *sovereign*   [g] 12 Or *If anyone
does not repent, / God*

[17] I will give thanks to the LORD because
of his righteousness;
I will sing the praises of the name
of the LORD Most High.

Psalm 8[a]

For the director of music. According to
gittith.[b] A psalm of David.

[1] LORD, our Lord,
how majestic is your name in all the
earth!

You have set your glory
in the heavens.
[2] Through the praise of children and
infants

you have established a stronghold
against your enemies,
to silence the foe and the avenger.
[3] When I consider your heavens,
the work of your fingers,
the moon and the stars,
which you have set in place,
[4] what is mankind that you are mindful
of them,
human beings that you care for them?[c]

[5] You have made them[d] a little lower
than the angels[e]
and crowned them[d] with glory and
honor.
[6] You made them rulers over the works
of your hands;
you put everything under their[f] feet:
[7] all flocks and herds,
and the animals of the wild,
[8] the birds in the sky,
and the fish in the sea,
all that swim the paths of the seas.

[9] LORD, our Lord,
how majestic is your name in all the
earth!

Psalm 9[g,h]

For the director of music. To the tune
of "The Death of the Son."
A psalm of David.

[1] I will give thanks to you, LORD, with
all my heart;
I will tell of all your wonderful
deeds.
[2] I will be glad and rejoice in you;
I will sing the praises of your name,
O Most High.

[3] My enemies turn back;
they stumble and perish before you.

Psalm 8:1–9

God made people spectacular.

God's majesty spreads over the earth like a royal robe. His bright glory reaches higher than the skies. Even the lips of kids and babies sing his praise. Compared to God, you can't help but conclude human beings don't matter much. But that's not the end of the story. You might feel small when you stand under the moon and stars the Lord hung in the sky, but God infused you with some of his own glory and honor. In the social pecking order of the universe, the Lord ranked you just a little below angels (see Psalm 8:5), and he put you on earth to rule over creation. When the Bible says God's name is majestic "in all the earth" (Psalm 8:1 and 9), you are part of that impressive display.

Think: Do you feel like you are part of God's majestic creation? How can you remind yourself of that fact today?

ROCK SOLID *truths*

---

[a] In Hebrew texts 8:1-9 is numbered 8:2-10.
[b] Title: Probably a musical term   [c] 4 Or *what is a human being that you are mindful of him, / a son of man that you care for him?*   [d] 5 Or *him*   [e] 5 Or *than God*   [f] 6 Or *made him ruler . . . ; / . . . his*   [g] Psalms 9 and 10 may originally have been a single acrostic poem in which alternating lines began with the successive letters of the Hebrew alphabet. In the Septuagint they constitute one psalm.   [h] In Hebrew texts 9:1-20 is numbered 9:2-21.

⁴For you have upheld my right and my
cause,
sitting enthroned as the righteous
judge.
⁵You have rebuked the nations and
destroyed the wicked;
you have blotted out their name for
ever and ever.
⁶Endless ruin has overtaken my enemies,
you have uprooted their cities;
even the memory of them has
perished.

⁷The Lord reigns forever;
he has established his throne for
judgment.
⁸He rules the world in righteousness
and judges the peoples with equity.
⁹The Lord is a refuge for the
oppressed,
a stronghold in times of trouble.
¹⁰Those who know your name trust in
you,
for you, Lord, have never forsaken
those who seek you.

¹¹Sing the praises of the Lord,
enthroned in Zion;
proclaim among the nations what
he has done.
¹²For he who avenges blood remembers;
he does not ignore the cries of the
afflicted.

¹³Lord, see how my enemies persecute
me!
Have mercy and lift me up from the
gates of death,
¹⁴that I may declare your praises
in the gates of Daughter Zion,
and there rejoice in your salvation.

¹⁵The nations have fallen into the pit
they have dug;
their feet are caught in the net they
have hidden.
¹⁶The Lord is known by his acts of
justice;
the wicked are ensnared by the
work of their hands.ᵃ
¹⁷The wicked go down to the realm of
the dead,
all the nations that forget God.

¹⁸But God will never forget the needy;
the hope of the afflicted will never
perish.

¹⁹Arise, Lord, do not let mortals
triumph;
let the nations be judged in your
presence.
²⁰Strike them with terror, Lord;
let the nations know they are only
mortal.

Psalm 10ᵇ

¹Why, Lord, do you stand far off?
Why do you hide yourself in times
of trouble?

²In his arrogance the wicked man
hunts down the weak,
who are caught in the schemes he
devises.
³He boasts about the cravings of his
heart;
he blesses the greedy and reviles the
Lord.
⁴In his pride the wicked man does not
seek him;
in all his thoughts there is no room
for God.
⁵His ways are always prosperous;
your laws are rejected byᶜ him;
he sneers at all his enemies.
⁶He says to himself, "Nothing will ever
shake me."
He swears, "No one will ever do me
harm."

⁷His mouth is full of lies and threats;
trouble and evil are under his tongue.
⁸He lies in wait near the villages;
from ambush he murders the
innocent.
His eyes watch in secret for his victims;
⁹   like a lion in cover he lies in wait.

ᵃ 16 The Hebrew has *Higgaion* and *Selah* (words
of uncertain meaning) here; *Selah* occurs also
at the end of verse 20.   ᵇ Psalms 9 and 10
may originally have been a single acrostic poem
in which alternating lines began with the
successive letters of the Hebrew alphabet. In
the Septuagint they constitute one psalm.
ᶜ 5 See Septuagint; Hebrew / *they are haughty,
and your laws are far from*

He lies in wait to catch the helpless;
  he catches the helpless and drags
    them off in his net.
¹⁰His victims are crushed, they collapse;
  they fall under his strength.
¹¹He says to himself, "God will never
    notice;
  he covers his face and never sees."

¹²Arise, Lᴏʀᴅ! Lift up your hand,
  O God.
  Do not forget the helpless.
¹³Why does the wicked man revile
    God?
  Why does he say to himself,
  "He won't call me to account"?
¹⁴But you, God, see the trouble of the
    afflicted;
  you consider their grief and take it
    in hand.
  The victims commit themselves to you;
  you are the helper of the fatherless.
¹⁵Break the arm of the wicked man;
  call the evildoer to account for his
    wickedness
  that would not otherwise be found
    out.

¹⁶The Lᴏʀᴅ is King for ever and ever;
  the nations will perish from his
    land.
¹⁷You, Lᴏʀᴅ, hear the desire of the
    afflicted;
  you encourage them, and you listen
    to their cry,

ROCK SOLID promises

"You, Lᴏʀᴅ, hear the desire of the afflicted; you encourage them, and you listen to their cry."

Psalm 10:17

It might feel like God ignores your requests, but you can be sure he hears your every cry.

¹⁸defending the fatherless and the
    oppressed,
  so that mere earthly mortals
  will never again strike terror.

Psalm 11

For the director of music. Of David.

¹In the Lᴏʀᴅ I take refuge.
  How then can you say to me:
  "Flee like a bird to your mountain.
²For look, the wicked bend their
    bows;
  they set their arrows against the
    strings
to shoot from the shadows
  at the upright in heart.
³When the foundations are being
    destroyed,
  what can the righteous do?"

⁴The Lᴏʀᴅ is in his holy temple;
  the Lᴏʀᴅ is on his heavenly
    throne.
He observes everyone on earth;
  his eyes examine them.
⁵The Lᴏʀᴅ examines the righteous,
  but the wicked, those who love
    violence,
  he hates with a passion.
⁶On the wicked he will rain
  fiery coals and burning sulfur;
  a scorching wind will be their lot.

⁷For the Lᴏʀᴅ is righteous,
  he loves justice;
  the upright will see his face.

Psalm 12ᵃ

For the director of music. According
to *sheminith.*ᵇ A psalm of David.

¹Help, Lᴏʀᴅ, for no one is faithful
    anymore;
  those who are loyal have vanished
    from the human race.
²Everyone lies to their neighbor;
  they flatter with their lips
  but harbor deception in their
    hearts.

ᵃ In Hebrew texts 12:1-8 is numbered 12:2-9.
ᵇ Title: Probably a musical term

³May the LORD silence all flattering
    lips
  and every boastful tongue—
⁴those who say,
  "By our tongues we will prevail;
  our own lips will defend us—who
    is lord over us?"

⁵"Because the poor are plundered and
    the needy groan,
  I will now arise," says the LORD.
  "I will protect them from those who
    malign them."
⁶And the words of the LORD are
    flawless,
  like silver purified in a crucible,
  like gold*a* refined seven times.

⁷You, LORD, will keep the needy safe
  and will protect us forever from the
    wicked,
⁸who freely strut about
  when what is vile is honored by the
    human race.

Psalm 13*b*

For the director of music. A psalm of David.

¹How long, LORD? Will you forget me
    forever?
  How long will you hide your face
    from me?
²How long must I wrestle with my
    thoughts
  and day after day have sorrow in my
    heart?
  How long will my enemy triumph
    over me?

³Look on me and answer, LORD my God.
  Give light to my eyes, or I will sleep
    in death,
⁴and my enemy will say, "I have
    overcome him,"
  and my foes will rejoice when I fall.

a 6 Probable reading of the original Hebrew
text; Masoretic Text *earth*   *b* In Hebrew texts
13:1-6 is numbered 13:2-6.

ROCK SOLID
principles

Psalm 12:1–8

Choose your words carefully.

It was already suppertime one Friday evening, and Kaitlin still didn't know what she was doing that night. As friends hit her with calls and texts, she was trying to put together a complicated social schedule where she needed her parents to give her several rides throughout the evening. When her parents nudged her to lock down her plans, she blew. "Well, fine!" she said. "I'll stay home by myself tonight!" They asked if Kaitlin was sure that's what she wanted. It was. By the time she cooled down, it was too late to take back her words. Her parents told her not to act so surprised. "You know the rule," they said. "Say what you mean, and mean what you say."

The people around David had a habit of speaking freely, saying whatever they wanted. They owned their lips, after all, and no one could master them. But when those folks aimed their evil words at the weak and poor, God decided to rise up and help. Sooner or later God always shuts down bad words.

⁵ But I trust in your unfailing love;
  my heart rejoices in your salvation.
⁶ I will sing the LORD's praise,
  for he has been good to me.

Psalm 14

For the director of music. Of David.

¹ The fool*a* says in his heart,
  "There is no God."
They are corrupt, their deeds are vile;
  there is no one who does good.

² The LORD looks down from heaven
  on all mankind
to see if there are any who understand,
  any who seek God.
³ All have turned away, all have become
    corrupt;
  there is no one who does good,
    not even one.

⁴ Do all these evildoers know nothing?

They devour my people as though
    eating bread;
  they never call on the LORD.
⁵ But there they are, overwhelmed with
    dread,
  for God is present in the company
    of the righteous.
⁶ You evildoers frustrate the plans of the
    poor,
  but the LORD is their refuge.

⁷ Oh, that salvation for Israel would
    come out of Zion!
  When the LORD restores his people,
  let Jacob rejoice and Israel be glad!

Psalm 15

A psalm of David.

¹ LORD, who may dwell in your sacred
    tent?
  Who may live on your holy mountain?

² The one whose walk is blameless,
  who does what is righteous,
  who speaks the truth from their
    heart;
³ whose tongue utters no slander,
  who does no wrong to a neighbor,
  and casts no slur on others;

Psalm 14:1–7

Atheists don't know the truth about God.

Christians often quote Psalm 14 to thump people who say "there is no God" (Psalm 14:1). It's true that atheists don't realize the truth about God. Neither do "practical atheists," people who claim to believe in God but act like he doesn't exist. Both are fools (see Psalm 14:1), not short on intellectual capacity but in spiritual sensitivity. But Psalm 14 makes a point for all of us. Each of us is part fool. When God studies humankind, he sees that "all have turned away." Every one of us is "corrupt," a Hebrew word that means "soured," like bad milk. Not one of us does good, "not even one" (Psalm 14:3). The solution to our problem comes in verse 4, which hints that we all need to pray to God. As we count on God as our shelter, we figure out who he really is and that he really exists.

Think: Do you ever doubt God's existence? How can you find the answers you need?

ROCK SOLID *truths*

---

⁴ who despises a vile person
  but honors those who fear the
    LORD;
who keeps an oath even when it hurts,
  and does not change their mind;
⁵ who lends money to the poor without
    interest;
  who does not accept a bribe against
    the innocent.

Whoever does these things
  will never be shaken.

---

a 1 The Hebrew words rendered *fool* in Psalms denote one who is morally deficient.

Psalm 16

A *miktam*[a] of David.

[1] Keep me safe, my God,
   for in you I take refuge.

[2] I say to the LORD, "You are my Lord;
   apart from you I have no good thing."
[3] I say of the holy people who are in the
      land,
   "They are the noble ones in whom
      is all my delight."
[4] Those who run after other gods will
      suffer more and more.
   I will not pour out libations of
      blood to such gods
   or take up their names on my lips.

[5] LORD, you alone are my portion and
      my cup;
   you make my lot secure.
[6] The boundary lines have fallen for me
      in pleasant places;
   surely I have a delightful
      inheritance.
[7] I will praise the LORD, who counsels
      me;
   even at night my heart instructs me.
[8] I keep my eyes always on the LORD.
   With him at my right hand, I will
      not be shaken.

[9] Therefore my heart is glad and my
      tongue rejoices;
   my body also will rest secure,
[10] because you will not abandon me to
      the realm of the dead,
   nor will you let your faithful[b] one
      see decay.
[11] You make known to me the path of
      life;
   you will fill me with joy in your
      presence,
   with eternal pleasures at your right
      hand.

Psalm 17

A prayer of David.

[1] Hear me, LORD, my plea is just;
   listen to my cry.
   Hear my prayer—
   it does not rise from deceitful lips.

ROCK SOLID *promises*

"You make known to me the path of life; you will fill me with joy in your presence." Psalm 16:11

The path to real life leads straight to God, and in his presence is the happiest place you can ever be.

[2] Let my vindication come from you;
   may your eyes see what is right.

[3] Though you probe my heart,
   though you examine me at night
      and test me,
   you will find that I have planned no
      evil;
   my mouth has not transgressed.
[4] Though people tried to bribe me,
   I have kept myself from the ways of
      the violent
   through what your lips have
      commanded.
[5] My steps have held to your paths;
   my feet have not stumbled.

[6] I call on you, my God, for you will
      answer me;
   turn your ear to me and hear my
      prayer.
[7] Show me the wonders of your great
      love,
   you who save by your right hand
   those who take refuge in you from
      their foes.
[8] Keep me as the apple of your eye;
   hide me in the shadow of your wings
[9] from the wicked who are out to
      destroy me,
   from my mortal enemies who
      surround me.

[a] Title: Probably a literary or musical term
[b] 10 Or *holy*

10 They close up their callous hearts,
and their mouths speak with
arrogance.
11 They have tracked me down, they now
surround me,
with eyes alert, to throw me to the
ground.
12 They are like a lion hungry for prey,
like a fierce lion crouching in
cover.

13 Rise up, Lord, confront them, bring
them down;
with your sword rescue me from the
wicked.
14 By your hand save me from such
people, Lord,
from those of this world whose
reward is in this life.
May what you have stored up for the
wicked fill their bellies;
may their children gorge themselves
on it,
and may there be leftovers for their
little ones.

15 As for me, I will be vindicated and
will see your face;
when I awake, I will be satisfied
with seeing your likeness.

Psalm 18[a]

For the director of music. Of David the
servant of the Lord. He sang to the Lord
the words of this song when the Lord
delivered him from the hand of all his
enemies and from the hand of Saul. He said:

1 I love you, Lord, my strength.

2 The Lord is my rock, my fortress and
my deliverer;
my God is my rock, in whom I take
refuge,
my shield[b] and the horn[c] of my
salvation, my stronghold.
3 I called to the Lord, who is worthy of
praise,
and I have been saved from my
enemies.
4 The cords of death entangled me;
the torrents of destruction
overwhelmed me.

5 The cords of the grave coiled around
me;
the snares of death confronted me.

6 In my distress I called to the Lord;
I cried to my God for help.
From his temple he heard my voice;
my cry came before him, into his
ears.
7 The earth trembled and quaked,
and the foundations of the
mountains shook;
they trembled because he was
angry.
8 Smoke rose from his nostrils;
consuming fire came from his
mouth,
burning coals blazed out of it.
9 He parted the heavens and came
down;
dark clouds were under his feet.
10 He mounted the cherubim and flew;
he soared on the wings of the wind.
11 He made darkness his covering, his
canopy around him—
the dark rain clouds of the sky.
12 Out of the brightness of his presence
clouds advanced,
with hailstones and bolts of
lightning.
13 The Lord thundered from heaven;
the voice of the Most High
resounded.[d]
14 He shot his arrows and scattered the
enemy,
with great bolts of lightning he
routed them.
15 The valleys of the sea were exposed
and the foundations of the earth
laid bare
at your rebuke, Lord,
at the blast of breath from your
nostrils.

16 He reached down from on high and
took hold of me;
he drew me out of deep waters.

a In Hebrew texts 18:1-50 is numbered 18:2-51.
b 2 Or sovereign   c 2 Horn here symbolizes
strength.   d 13 Some Hebrew manuscripts
and Septuagint (see also 2 Samuel 22:14); most
Hebrew manuscripts resounded, / amid hailstones
and bolts of lightning

17 He rescued me from my powerful
        enemy,
    from my foes, who were too strong
        for me.
18 They confronted me in the day of my
        disaster,
    but the LORD was my support.
19 He brought me out into a spacious
        place;
    he rescued me because he delighted
        in me.

20 The LORD has dealt with me
        according to my righteousness;
    according to the cleanness of my
        hands he has rewarded me.
21 For I have kept the ways of the LORD;
    I am not guilty of turning from my
        God.
22 All his laws are before me;
    I have not turned away from his
        decrees.
23 I have been blameless before him
    and have kept myself from sin.
24 The LORD has rewarded me according
        to my righteousness,
    according to the cleanness of my
        hands in his sight.

25 To the faithful you show yourself
        faithful,
    to the blameless you show yourself
        blameless,
26 to the pure you show yourself pure,
    but to the devious you show yourself
        shrewd.
27 You save the humble
    but bring low those whose eyes are
        haughty.
28 You, LORD, keep my lamp burning;
    my God turns my darkness into
        light.
29 With your help I can advance against
        a troop[a];
    with my God I can scale a wall.

30 As for God, his way is perfect:
    The LORD's word is flawless;
    he shields all who take refuge in
        him.
31 For who is God besides the LORD?
    And who is the Rock except our
        God?

UNSHAKEN God

Psalm 18:1–50

God is perfect.

David sang to God when the Lord saved him from his adversary, King Saul of Israel. All of Psalm 18 captures God's best points, especially his power over deadly enemies. But David sums up God with this sweet description: "As for God, his way is perfect; the LORD's word is flawless" (Psalm 18:30). God is more than we can hope for, better than any other being in the universe. His actions are perfect. His words are perfect. The Lord is perfect in every way we could ever think of. When people disappoint you … when your favorite possessions break … when experiences don't live up to the hype … God is perfect.

So … What about God's perfection is worth singing about?

32 It is God who arms me with strength
    and keeps my way secure.
33 He makes my feet like the feet of a
        deer;
    he causes me to stand on the
        heights.
34 He trains my hands for battle;
    my arms can bend a bow of bronze.
35 You make your saving help my shield,
    and your right hand sustains me;
    your help has made me great.
36 You provide a broad path for my feet,
    so that my ankles do not give way.
37 I pursued my enemies and overtook
        them;
    I did not turn back till they were
        destroyed.
38 I crushed them so that they could not
        rise;
    they fell beneath my feet.

a 29 Or *can run through a barricade*

³⁹ You armed me with strength for
battle;
you humbled my adversaries before
me.
⁴⁰ You made my enemies turn their backs
in flight,
and I destroyed my foes.
⁴¹ They cried for help, but there was no
one to save them—
to the LORD, but he did not answer.
⁴² I beat them as fine as windblown
dust;
I trampled them*ᵃ* like mud in the
streets.
⁴³ You have delivered me from the
attacks of the people;
you have made me the head of
nations.
People I did not know now serve me,
⁴⁴ foreigners cower before me;
as soon as they hear of me, they
obey me.
⁴⁵ They all lose heart;
they come trembling from their
strongholds.
⁴⁶ The LORD lives! Praise be to my
Rock!
Exalted be God my Savior!
⁴⁷ He is the God who avenges me,
who subdues nations under me,
⁴⁸ who saves me from my enemies.
You exalted me above my foes;
from a violent man you rescued me.
⁴⁹ Therefore I will praise you, LORD,
among the nations;
I will sing the praises of your
name.
⁵⁰ He gives his king great victories;
he shows unfailing love to his
anointed,
to David and to his descendants
forever.

Psalm 19*ᵇ*

For the director of music.
A psalm of David.

¹ The heavens declare the glory of God;
the skies proclaim the work of his
hands.

² Day after day they pour forth speech;
night after night they reveal
knowledge.
³ They have no speech, they use no words;
no sound is heard from them.
⁴ Yet their voice*ᶜ* goes out into all the
earth,
their words to the ends of the world.

ᵃ 42 Many Hebrew manuscripts, Septuagint,
Syriac and Targum (see also 2 Samuel 22:43);
Masoretic Text *I poured them out*   *ᵇ* In
Hebrew texts 19:1-14 is numbered 19:2-15.
ᶜ 4 Septuagint, Jerome and Syriac; Hebrew
measuring line

Psalm 19:1–11

The world is evidence of God's existence.

You probably rely on the Bible to give all the information you need to conclude that God is real—and that Jesus is the Son of God and Savior of the world. But the Bible itself says there is another crucial source of knowledge about God. If you have ever tried to out-argue someone who says "I see God in nature," Psalm 19 might make you squirm. Because those folks are partly right. People get a good glimpse of God in the world he made. We can look up and observe his glory stretched across the heavens. We can hear the skies declare his artistry and power. The facts about God beat down on earth like hot rays from the sun. While the created universe doesn't give the total picture of God like we get from the Bible, it's a starting point for everyone who wonders if God is real.

Think: What does the physical universe teach us about God? What can't it tell us?

ROCK SOLID truths

In the heavens God has pitched a tent
    for the sun.
5   It is like a bridegroom coming out
        of his chamber,
    like a champion rejoicing to run his
        course.
⁶ It rises at one end of the heavens
    and makes its circuit to the other;
    nothing is deprived of its warmth.

⁷ The law of the LORD is perfect,
    refreshing the soul.
The statutes of the LORD are
        trustworthy,
    making wise the simple.
⁸ The precepts of the LORD are right,
    giving joy to the heart.
The commands of the LORD are
        radiant,
    giving light to the eyes.
⁹ The fear of the LORD is pure,
    enduring forever.
The decrees of the LORD are firm,
    and all of them are righteous.

¹⁰ They are more precious than gold,
    than much pure gold;
they are sweeter than honey,
    than honey from the honeycomb.
¹¹ By them your servant is warned;
    in keeping them there is great
        reward.
¹² But who can discern their own
        errors?
    Forgive my hidden faults.
¹³ Keep your servant also from willful
        sins;
    may they not rule over me.
Then I will be blameless,
    innocent of great transgression.

¹⁴ May these words of my mouth and
        this meditation of my heart
    be pleasing in your sight,
    LORD, my Rock and my Redeemer.

Psalm 20 *a*

For the director of music. A psalm of David.

¹ May the LORD answer you when you
        are in distress;
    may the name of the God of Jacob
        protect you.

² May he send you help from the
        sanctuary
    and grant you support from Zion.
³ May he remember all your sacrifices
    and accept your burnt offerings. *b*
⁴ May he give you the desire of your
        heart
    and make all your plans succeed.
⁵ May we shout for joy over your victory
    and lift up our banners in the name
        of our God.

May the LORD grant all your requests.

⁶ Now this I know:
    The LORD gives victory to his
        anointed.
He answers him from his heavenly
        sanctuary
    with the victorious power of his
        right hand.
⁷ Some trust in chariots and some in
        horses,
    but we trust in the name of the
        LORD our God.
⁸ They are brought to their knees and
        fall,
    but we rise up and stand firm.
⁹ LORD, give victory to the king!
    Answer us when we call!

Psalm 21 *c*

For the director of music. A psalm of David.

¹ The king rejoices in your strength,
        LORD.
    How great is his joy in the victories
        you give!

² You have granted him his heart's desire
    and have not withheld the request
        of his lips. *b*
³ You came to greet him with rich
        blessings
    and placed a crown of pure gold on
        his head.
⁴ He asked you for life, and you gave it
        to him—
    length of days, for ever and ever.

---

a In Hebrew texts 20:1-9 is numbered 20:2-10.
b 3,2 The Hebrew has *Selah* (a word of uncertain
meaning) here.   *c* In Hebrew texts 21:1-13 is
numbered 21:2-14.

⁵Through the victories you gave, his
glory is great;
you have bestowed on him splendor
and majesty.
⁶Surely you have granted him unending
blessings
and made him glad with the joy of
your presence.
⁷For the king trusts in the Lord;
through the unfailing love of the
Most High
he will not be shaken.

⁸Your hand will lay hold on all your
enemies;
your right hand will seize your foes.
⁹When you appear for battle,
you will burn them up as in a
blazing furnace.
The Lord will swallow them up in
his wrath,
and his fire will consume them.
¹⁰You will destroy their descendants
from the earth,
their posterity from mankind.
¹¹Though they plot evil against you
and devise wicked schemes, they
cannot succeed.
¹²You will make them turn their backs
when you aim at them with drawn
bow.

¹³Be exalted in your strength, Lord;
we will sing and praise your might.

Psalm 22 *a*

For the director of music. To the tune of "The
Doe of the Morning." A psalm of David.

¹My God, my God, why have you
forsaken me?
Why are you so far from saving me,
so far from my cries of anguish?
²My God, I cry out by day, but you do
not answer,
by night, but I find no rest.*b*

³Yet you are enthroned as the Holy
One;
you are the one Israel praises.*c*
⁴In you our ancestors put their trust;
they trusted and you delivered
them.

⁵To you they cried out and were saved;
in you they trusted and were not put
to shame.
⁶But I am a worm and not a man,
scorned by everyone, despised by
the people.
⁷All who see me mock me;
they hurl insults, shaking their
heads.
⁸"He trusts in the Lord," they say,
"let the Lord rescue him.
Let him deliver him,
since he delights in him."

⁹Yet you brought me out of the womb;
you made me trust in you, even at
my mother's breast.
¹⁰From birth I was cast on you;
from my mother's womb you have
been my God.

¹¹Do not be far from me,
for trouble is near
and there is no one to help.

¹²Many bulls surround me;
strong bulls of Bashan encircle me.
¹³Roaring lions that tear their prey
open their mouths wide against me.
¹⁴I am poured out like water,
and all my bones are out of joint.
My heart has turned to wax;
it has melted within me.
¹⁵My mouth*d* is dried up like a potsherd,
and my tongue sticks to the roof of
my mouth;
you lay me in the dust of death.

¹⁶Dogs surround me,
a pack of villains encircles me;
they pierce*e* my hands and my feet.
¹⁷All my bones are on display;
people stare and gloat over me.
¹⁸They divide my clothes among them
and cast lots for my garment.

---

a In Hebrew texts 22:1-31 is numbered 22:2-32.
b 2 Or *night, and am not silent*   *c* 3 Or *Yet you
are holy, / enthroned on the praises of Israel*
d 15 Probable reading of the original Hebrew
text; Masoretic Text *strength*   *e* 16 Dead Sea
Scrolls and some manuscripts of the Masoretic
Text, Septuagint and Syriac; most manuscripts
of the Masoretic Text *me, / like a lion*

¹⁹ But you, LORD, do not be far from me.
  You are my strength; come quickly
    to help me.
²⁰ Deliver me from the sword,
  my precious life from the power of
    the dogs.
²¹ Rescue me from the mouth of the
    lions;
  save me from the horns of the wild
    oxen.

²² I will declare your name to my
    people;
  in the assembly I will praise you.
²³ You who fear the LORD, praise him!
  All you descendants of Jacob, honor
    him!
  Revere him, all you descendants of
    Israel!
²⁴ For he has not despised or scorned
    the suffering of the afflicted one;
  he has not hidden his face from him
    but has listened to his cry for help.

²⁵ From you comes the theme of my
    praise in the great assembly;
  before those who fear you[a] I will
    fulfill my vows.
²⁶ The poor will eat and be satisfied;
  those who seek the LORD will
    praise him—
  may your hearts live forever!

²⁷ All the ends of the earth
  will remember and turn to the
    LORD,
  and all the families of the nations
  will bow down before him,
²⁸ for dominion belongs to the LORD
  and he rules over the nations.

²⁹ All the rich of the earth will feast and
    worship;
  all who go down to the dust will
    kneel before him—
  those who cannot keep themselves
    alive.
³⁰ Posterity will serve him;
  future generations will be told about
    the Lord.
³¹ They will proclaim his righteousness,
  declaring to a people yet unborn:
  He has done it!

Psalm 23

A psalm of David.

¹ The LORD is my shepherd, I lack
    nothing.
² He makes me lie down in green
    pastures,
  he leads me beside quiet waters,
³ he refreshes my soul.
  He guides me along the right paths
    for his name's sake.
⁴ Even though I walk
    through the darkest valley,[b]
  I will fear no evil,
    for you are with me;
  your rod and your staff,
    they comfort me.

⁵ You prepare a table before me
  in the presence of my enemies.

---

[a] 25 Hebrew *him*   [b] 4 Or *the valley of the shadow of death*

UNSHAKEN *god*

Psalm 23:1–6

God is caring.

Consider this creepy possibility: There is a significant chance that someday a loved one will read Psalm 23 at your memorial service—hopefully a some-day eight or nine decades from now. Yet these words couldn't be any more essential to you right now. After all, this song of David contains some of the most comforting thoughts in the Bible. You might know nothing about sheep, but you can still understand the picture of a shepherd who cares so completely for his flock that he would do anything to protect and provide for it. Jesus made this image his own when he called himself "the good shepherd" who "lays down his life for the sheep" (John 10:11).

So … How can you get comfort from Psalm 23 today?

You anoint my head with oil;
my cup overflows.
6 Surely your goodness and love will
follow me
all the days of my life,
and I will dwell in the house of the LORD
forever.

Psalm 24

Of David. A psalm.

1 The earth is the LORD's, and
everything in it,
the world, and all who live in it;
2 for he founded it on the seas
and established it on the waters.

3 Who may ascend the mountain of the
LORD?
Who may stand in his holy place?
4 The one who has clean hands and a
pure heart,
who does not trust in an idol
or swear by a false god.*a*

5 They will receive blessing from the LORD
and vindication from God their
Savior.
6 Such is the generation of those who
seek him,
who seek your face, God of Jacob.*b,c*

7 Lift up your heads, you gates;
be lifted up, you ancient doors,
that the King of glory may come in.
8 Who is this King of glory?
The LORD strong and mighty,
the LORD mighty in battle.
9 Lift up your heads, you gates;
lift them up, you ancient doors,
that the King of glory may come in.
10 Who is he, this King of glory?
The LORD Almighty—
he is the King of glory.

Psalm 25*d*

Of David.

1 In you, LORD my God,
I put my trust.

2 I trust in you;
do not let me be put to shame,
nor let my enemies triumph over me.

Psalm 24:1–10

God doesn't tolerate evil.

God doesn't let unholy people into his presence. Psalm 24:3–6 says he requires perfect purity—spotless actions, an uncontaminated heart, a soul that doesn't make anything more important than him, a tongue that never lies, and a life focused on chasing after God. We could thumb through the Bible and add even more ways we have to be perfect to get near God. If that were the whole story, we could all crawl under a giant rock and never again try to get near God—because we all do have a problem. Each of us sins (see Romans 3:23), and "without holiness no one will see the Lord" (Hebrews 12:14). But the Bible gives us a solution. Because of the death of Jesus we can "draw near to God" (Hebrews 10:22). God doesn't tolerate evil, but Jesus opens the door and lets us in.

Think: Why does God seem so uptight about evil?

ROCK SOLID *truths*

3 No one who hopes in you
will ever be put to shame,
but shame will come on those
who are treacherous without cause.

4 Show me your ways, LORD,
teach me your paths.

a 4 Or *swear falsely*   *b* 6 Two Hebrew manuscripts and Syriac (see also Septuagint); most Hebrew manuscripts *face, Jacob*   *c* 6 The Hebrew has *Selah* (a word of uncertain meaning) here and at the end of verse 10.   *d* This psalm is an acrostic poem, the verses of which begin with the successive letters of the Hebrew alphabet.

5 Guide me in your truth and teach me,
    for you are God my Savior,
    and my hope is in you all day long.
6 Remember, Lord, your great mercy
        and love,
    for they are from of old.
7 Do not remember the sins of my youth
    and my rebellious ways;
    according to your love remember me,
    for you, Lord, are good.

ROCK SOLID *promises*

"Do not remember the sins of my youth and my rebellious ways."

Psalm 25:7

God's love for you is infinitely bigger than your failures. If you admit your sins to him, you get a fresh start.

8 Good and upright is the Lord;
    therefore he instructs sinners in his
        ways.
9 He guides the humble in what is right
    and teaches them his way.
10 All the ways of the Lord are loving
        and faithful
    toward those who keep the
        demands of his covenant.
11 For the sake of your name, Lord,
    forgive my iniquity, though it is great.

12 Who, then, are those who fear the
        Lord?
    He will instruct them in the ways
        they should choose.[a]
13 They will spend their days in prosperity,
    and their descendants will inherit
        the land.
14 The Lord confides in those who fear
        him;
    he makes his covenant known to
        them.

15 My eyes are ever on the Lord,
    for only he will release my feet from
        the snare.

16 Turn to me and be gracious to me,
    for I am lonely and afflicted.
17 Relieve the troubles of my heart
    and free me from my anguish.
18 Look on my affliction and my
        distress
    and take away all my sins.
19 See how numerous are my enemies
    and how fiercely they hate me!

20 Guard my life and rescue me;
    do not let me be put to shame,
    for I take refuge in you.
21 May integrity and uprightness protect
        me,
    because my hope, Lord,[b] is in you.

22 Deliver Israel, O God,
    from all their troubles!

Psalm 26

Of David.

1 Vindicate me, Lord,
    for I have led a blameless life;
I have trusted in the Lord
    and have not faltered.
2 Test me, Lord, and try me,
    examine my heart and my mind;
3 for I have always been mindful of
        your unfailing love
    and have lived in reliance on your
        faithfulness.

4 I do not sit with the deceitful,
    nor do I associate with hypocrites.
5 I abhor the assembly of evildoers
    and refuse to sit with the wicked.
6 I wash my hands in innocence,
    and go about your altar, Lord,
7 proclaiming aloud your praise
    and telling of all your wonderful
        deeds.

8 Lord, I love the house where you
        live,
    the place where your glory dwells.

a 12 Or *ways he chooses*   b 21 Septuagint;
Hebrew does not have Lord.

⁹Do not take away my soul along with
  sinners,
  my life with those who are
  bloodthirsty,
¹⁰in whose hands are wicked schemes,
  whose right hands are full of bribes.
¹¹I lead a blameless life;
  deliver me and be merciful to me.

¹²My feet stand on level ground;
  in the great congregation I will
  praise the LORD.

Psalm 27

Of David.

¹The LORD is my light and my
  salvation—
  whom shall I fear?
The LORD is the stronghold of my
  life—
  of whom shall I be afraid?

ROCK SOLID *promises*

**"The LORD is my light and my
salvation—whom shall I fear?"**

Psalm 27:1

**God rescues you from darkness, and he
scares away your enemies.**

---

²When the wicked advance against me
  to devour*ᵃ* me,
  it is my enemies and my foes
  who will stumble and fall.
³Though an army besiege me,
  my heart will not fear;
  though war break out against me,
  even then I will be confident.

⁴One thing I ask from the LORD,
  this only do I seek:

that I may dwell in the house of the
  LORD
  all the days of my life,
to gaze on the beauty of the LORD
  and to seek him in his temple.
⁵For in the day of trouble
  he will keep me safe in his dwelling;
he will hide me in the shelter of his
  sacred tent
  and set me high upon a rock.

⁶Then my head will be exalted
  above the enemies who surround me;
at his sacred tent I will sacrifice with
  shouts of joy;
  I will sing and make music to the
  LORD.

⁷Hear my voice when I call, LORD;
  be merciful to me and answer me.
⁸My heart says of you, "Seek his face!"
  Your face, LORD, I will seek.
⁹Do not hide your face from me,
  do not turn your servant away in
  anger;
  you have been my helper.
Do not reject me or forsake me,
  God my Savior.
¹⁰Though my father and mother forsake
  me,
  the LORD will receive me.
¹¹Teach me your way, LORD;
  lead me in a straight path
  because of my oppressors.
¹²Do not turn me over to the desire of
  my foes,
  for false witnesses rise up against me,
  spouting malicious accusations.

¹³I remain confident of this:
  I will see the goodness of the LORD
  in the land of the living.
¹⁴Wait for the LORD;
  be strong and take heart
  and wait for the LORD.

Psalm 28

Of David.

¹To you, LORD, I call;
  you are my Rock,
  do not turn a deaf ear to me.

ᵃ 2 Or *slander*

For if you remain silent,
    I will be like those who go down to
        the pit.
2 Hear my cry for mercy
    as I call to you for help,
as I lift up my hands
    toward your Most Holy Place.

3 Do not drag me away with the
      wicked,
    with those who do evil,
who speak cordially with their
      neighbors
    but harbor malice in their hearts.
4 Repay them for their deeds
    and for their evil work;
repay them for what their hands have
      done
    and bring back on them what they
      deserve.

5 Because they have no regard for the
      deeds of the LORD
    and what his hands have done,
he will tear them down
    and never build them up again.

6 Praise be to the LORD,
    for he has heard my cry for
      mercy.
7 The LORD is my strength and my
      shield;
    my heart trusts in him, and he
      helps me.
My heart leaps for joy,
    and with my song I praise him.

8 The LORD is the strength of his
      people,
    a fortress of salvation for his
      anointed one.
9 Save your people and bless your
      inheritance;
    be their shepherd and carry them
      forever.

Psalm 29

A psalm of David.

1 Ascribe to the LORD, you heavenly
      beings,
    ascribe to the LORD glory and
      strength.

2 Ascribe to the LORD the glory due his
      name;
    worship the LORD in the splendor
      of his*a* holiness.

3 The voice of the LORD is over the
      waters;
    the God of glory thunders,
    the LORD thunders over the mighty
      waters.
4 The voice of the LORD is powerful;
    the voice of the LORD is majestic.
5 The voice of the LORD breaks the
      cedars;
    the LORD breaks in pieces the
      cedars of Lebanon.
6 He makes Lebanon leap like a calf,
    Sirion*b* like a young wild ox.
7 The voice of the LORD strikes
    with flashes of lightning.
8 The voice of the LORD shakes the
      desert;
    the LORD shakes the Desert of
      Kadesh.
9 The voice of the LORD twists the oaks*c*
    and strips the forests bare.
And in his temple all cry, "Glory!"

10 The LORD sits enthroned over the
      flood;
    the LORD is enthroned as King
      forever.
11 The LORD gives strength to his
      people;
    the LORD blesses his people with
      peace.

Psalm 30*d*

A psalm. A song. For the dedication
    of the temple.*e* Of David.

1 I will exalt you, LORD,
    for you lifted me out of the depths
    and did not let my enemies gloat
      over me.
2 LORD my God, I called to you for
      help,
    and you healed me.

a 2 Or *LORD with the splendor of*   *b* 6 That is,
Mount Hermon   *c* 9 Or *LORD makes the deer
give birth*   *d* In Hebrew texts 30:1-12 is
numbered 30:2-13.   *e* Title: Or *palace*

³You, Lord, brought me up from the
  realm of the dead;
  you spared me from going down to
  the pit.

⁴Sing the praises of the Lord, you his
  faithful people;
  praise his holy name.
⁵For his anger lasts only a moment,
  but his favor lasts a lifetime;
  weeping may stay for the night,
  but rejoicing comes in the
  morning.

⁶When I felt secure, I said,
  "I will never be shaken."
⁷Lord, when you favored me,
  you made my royal mountain*ᵃ*
  stand firm;
  but when you hid your face,
  I was dismayed.

⁸To you, Lord, I called;
  to the Lord I cried for mercy:
⁹"What is gained if I am silenced,
  if I go down to the pit?
  Will the dust praise you?
  Will it proclaim your faithfulness?
¹⁰Hear, Lord, and be merciful to me;
  Lord, be my help."

¹¹You turned my wailing into
  dancing;
  you removed my sackcloth and
  clothed me with joy,

ROCK SOLID
promises

**"You turned my wailing into
dancing ... that my heart may sing
your praises and not be silent."**

Psalm 30:11 – 12

**Even in your most dire moments, God
gives you reason to worship him.**

---

¹²that my heart may sing your praises
  and not be silent.
  Lord my God, I will praise you
  forever.

Psalm 31*ᵇ*

For the director of music.
A psalm of David.

¹In you, Lord, I have taken refuge;
  let me never be put to shame;
  deliver me in your righteousness.
²Turn your ear to me,
  come quickly to my rescue;
  be my rock of refuge,
  a strong fortress to save me.
³Since you are my rock and my fortress,
  for the sake of your name lead and
  guide me.
⁴Keep me free from the trap that is set
  for me,
  for you are my refuge.
⁵Into your hands I commit my spirit;
  deliver me, Lord, my faithful God.

⁶I hate those who cling to worthless idols;
  as for me, I trust in the Lord.
⁷I will be glad and rejoice in your love,
  for you saw my affliction
  and knew the anguish of my soul.
⁸You have not given me into the hands
  of the enemy
  but have set my feet in a spacious
  place.

⁹Be merciful to me, Lord, for I am in
  distress;
  my eyes grow weak with sorrow,
  my soul and body with grief.
¹⁰My life is consumed by anguish
  and my years by groaning;
  my strength fails because of my
  affliction,*ᶜ*
  and my bones grow weak.
¹¹Because of all my enemies,
  I am the utter contempt of my
  neighbors
  and an object of dread to my closest
  friends—
  those who see me on the street flee
  from me.

ᵃ 7 That is, Mount Zion   *ᵇ* In Hebrew texts
31:1-24 is numbered 31:2-25.   *ᶜ 10* Or *guilt*

¹²I am forgotten as though I were
    dead;
  I have become like broken pottery.
¹³For I hear many whispering,
    "Terror on every side!"
  They conspire against me
    and plot to take my life.

¹⁴But I trust in you, Lord;
    I say, "You are my God."
¹⁵My times are in your hands;
    deliver me from the hands of my
      enemies,
  from those who pursue me.
¹⁶Let your face shine on your servant;
  save me in your unfailing love.
¹⁷Let me not be put to shame, Lord,
    for I have cried out to you;
  but let the wicked be put to shame
    and be silent in the realm of the
      dead.
¹⁸Let their lying lips be silenced,
    for with pride and contempt
    they speak arrogantly against the
      righteous.

¹⁹How abundant are the good things
    that you have stored up for those
      who fear you,
  that you bestow in the sight of all,
    on those who take refuge in you.
²⁰In the shelter of your presence you
    hide them
    from all human intrigues;
  you keep them safe in your dwelling
    from accusing tongues.

²¹Praise be to the Lord,
    for he showed me the wonders of
      his love
  when I was in a city under siege.
²²In my alarm I said,
    "I am cut off from your sight!"
  Yet you heard my cry for mercy
    when I called to you for help.

²³Love the Lord, all his faithful
    people!
  The Lord preserves those who are
    true to him,
  but the proud he pays back in full.
²⁴Be strong and take heart,
    all you who hope in the Lord.

Psalm 32

Of David. A *maskil.*[a]

¹Blessed is the one
  whose transgressions are forgiven,
  whose sins are covered.
²Blessed is the one
  whose sin the Lord does not count
    against them
  and in whose spirit is no deceit.

³When I kept silent,
  my bones wasted away
  through my groaning all day long.
⁴For day and night
  your hand was heavy on me;
  my strength was sapped
  as in the heat of summer.[b]

⁵Then I acknowledged my sin to you
  and did not cover up my iniquity.
  I said, "I will confess
    my transgressions to the Lord."
  And you forgave
    the guilt of my sin.

⁶Therefore let all the faithful pray to you
  while you may be found;
  surely the rising of the mighty waters
  will not reach them.
⁷You are my hiding place;
  you will protect me from trouble
  and surround me with songs of
    deliverance.

⁸I will instruct you and teach you in
    the way you should go;
  I will counsel you with my loving
    eye on you.
⁹Do not be like the horse or the mule,
  which have no understanding
  but must be controlled by bit and
    bridle
  or they will not come to you.
¹⁰Many are the woes of the wicked,
  but the Lord's unfailing love
  surrounds the one who trusts in him.

¹¹Rejoice in the Lord and be glad, you
    righteous;
  sing, all you who are upright in heart!

---

[a] Title: Probably a literary or musical term
[b] 4 The Hebrew has *Selah* (a word of uncertain meaning) here and at the end of verses 5 and 7.

ROCK SOLID *principles*

Psalm 32:8–11

Quit being so stubborn.

Jackie had done everything she knew to discover whether God wanted her to go out with a guy at church three grades older than her. She prayed and asked God to show her the right thing to do. She scanned her Bible and studied anything it said about guy-girl relationships. And she asked her parents and Bible study leader at church for input. Jackie didn't like what she heard. Everything said that—for now—having more than a friendship with Mark wasn't a good idea. Jackie decided she didn't want to fight what God was saying loud and clear. She knew it wasn't smart to be stubborn.

You probably don't like being compared to a mule so stubborn and stupid that it needs a bit in its mouth to tell it where to go. But that's how dense we are whenever we choose to do our own thing. We can go through life having to learn things the hard way. Or we can get smart and obey willingly.

Psalm 33

1 Sing joyfully to the LORD, you righteous;
it is fitting for the upright to praise him.
2 Praise the LORD with the harp;
make music to him on the ten-stringed lyre.
3 Sing to him a new song;
play skillfully, and shout for joy.

4 For the word of the LORD is right and true;
he is faithful in all he does.
5 The LORD loves righteousness and justice;
the earth is full of his unfailing love.

6 By the word of the LORD the heavens were made,
their starry host by the breath of his mouth.

7 He gathers the waters of the sea into jars[a];
he puts the deep into storehouses.
8 Let all the earth fear the LORD;
let all the people of the world revere him.
9 For he spoke, and it came to be;
he commanded, and it stood firm.

10 The LORD foils the plans of the nations;
he thwarts the purposes of the peoples.
11 But the plans of the LORD stand firm forever,
the purposes of his heart through all generations.

12 Blessed is the nation whose God is the LORD,
the people he chose for his inheritance.

[a] 7 Or *sea as into a heap*

¹³ From heaven the LORD looks down
and sees all mankind;
¹⁴ from his dwelling place he watches
all who live on earth—
¹⁵ he who forms the hearts of all,
who considers everything they do.

¹⁶ No king is saved by the size of his
army;
no warrior escapes by his great
strength.
¹⁷ A horse is a vain hope for deliverance;
despite all its great strength it
cannot save.
¹⁸ But the eyes of the LORD are on those
who fear him,
on those whose hope is in his
unfailing love,
¹⁹ to deliver them from death
and keep them alive in famine.

²⁰ We wait in hope for the LORD;
he is our help and our shield.
²¹ In him our hearts rejoice,
for we trust in his holy name.
²² May your unfailing love be with us,
LORD,
even as we put our hope in you.

Psalm 34 *a,b*

Of David. When he pretended to be
insane before Abimelek, who drove
him away, and he left.

¹ I will extol the LORD at all times;
his praise will always be on my lips.
² I will glory in the LORD;
let the afflicted hear and rejoice.
³ Glorify the LORD with me;
let us exalt his name together.

⁴ I sought the LORD, and he answered
me;
he delivered me from all my fears.
⁵ Those who look to him are radiant;
their faces are never covered with
shame.
⁶ This poor man called, and the LORD
heard him;
he saved him out of all his troubles.
⁷ The angel of the LORD encamps
around those who fear him,
and he delivers them.

⁸ Taste and see that the LORD is good;
blessed is the one who takes refuge
in him.
⁹ Fear the LORD, you his holy people,
for those who fear him lack
nothing.
¹⁰ The lions may grow weak and hungry,
but those who seek the LORD lack
no good thing.
¹¹ Come, my children, listen to me;
I will teach you the fear of the
LORD.
¹² Whoever of you loves life
and desires to see many good days,
¹³ keep your tongue from evil
and your lips from telling lies.
¹⁴ Turn from evil and do good;
seek peace and pursue it.

¹⁵ The eyes of the LORD are on the
righteous,
and his ears are attentive to their
cry;
¹⁶ but the face of the LORD is against
those who do evil,
to blot out their name from the
earth.

¹⁷ The righteous cry out, and the LORD
hears them;
he delivers them from all their
troubles.
¹⁸ The LORD is close to the brokenhearted
and saves those who are crushed in
spirit.

¹⁹ The righteous person may have many
troubles,
but the LORD delivers him from
them all;
²⁰ he protects all his bones,
not one of them will be broken.

²¹ Evil will slay the wicked;
the foes of the righteous will be
condemned.
²² The LORD will rescue his servants;
no one who takes refuge in him will
be condemned.

a This psalm is an acrostic poem, the verses of
which begin with the successive letters of the
Hebrew alphabet.   *b* In Hebrew texts 34:1-22
is numbered 34:2-23.

God invites people to try him out.

It might sound strange to "Taste and see that the LORD is good" (Psalm 34:8), like you're taking a car for a spin before you buy. Or trying on clothes before handing over your money. Or sampling a spoonful before you commit to a whole bowl of ice cream. It's true that God isn't looking for on-again-off-again followers. Jesus tells us that to be his disciples we need to count the cost of following him (see Luke 14:28), give up our selfish selves and take up our cross (Mark 8:34), and obey him without looking back (see Luke 9:62). Even Jesus' first followers had to get to know him and learn about his purpose on earth. God is not offended by your questions. So don't be afraid to try God out. Let him demonstrate to you today that he is good.

Think: What does it mean to "taste God"? Who do you know who needs to try God?

ROCK SOLID truths

Psalm 35

Of David.

¹ Contend, LORD, with those who
contend with me;
fight against those who fight
against me.
² Take up shield and armor;
arise and come to my aid.
³ Brandish spear and javelin*ᵃ*
against those who pursue me.
Say to me,
"I am your salvation."

⁴ May those who seek my life
be disgraced and put to shame;

may those who plot my ruin
be turned back in dismay.
⁵ May they be like chaff before the
wind,
with the angel of the LORD driving
them away;
⁶ may their path be dark and slippery,
with the angel of the LORD
pursuing them.

⁷ Since they hid their net for me
without cause
and without cause dug a pit for me,
⁸ may ruin overtake them by surprise—
may the net they hid entangle
them,
may they fall into the pit, to their
ruin.
⁹ Then my soul will rejoice in the LORD
and delight in his salvation.
¹⁰ My whole being will exclaim,
"Who is like you, LORD?
You rescue the poor from those too
strong for them,
the poor and needy from those who
rob them."

¹¹ Ruthless witnesses come forward;
they question me on things I know
nothing about.
¹² They repay me evil for good
and leave me like one bereaved.
¹³ Yet when they were ill, I put on
sackcloth
and humbled myself with fasting.
When my prayers returned to me
unanswered,
¹⁴ I went about mourning
as though for my friend or brother.
I bowed my head in grief
as though weeping for my mother.
¹⁵ But when I stumbled, they gathered in
glee;
assailants gathered against me
without my knowledge.
They slandered me without ceasing.
¹⁶ Like the ungodly they maliciously
mocked;*ᵇ*
they gnashed their teeth at me.

ᵃ 3 Or *and block the way*   *ᵇ 16* Septuagint;
Hebrew may mean *Like an ungodly circle of
mockers,*

17 How long, Lord, will you look on?
   Rescue me from their ravages,
   my precious life from these
      lions.
18 I will give you thanks in the great
      assembly;
   among the throngs I will praise
      you.
19 Do not let those gloat over me
   who are my enemies without
      cause;
   do not let those who hate me without
      reason
   maliciously wink the eye.
20 They do not speak peaceably,
   but devise false accusations
   against those who live quietly in
      the land.
21 They sneer at me and say, "Aha! Aha!
   With our own eyes we have
      seen it."

22 Lord, you have seen this; do not be
      silent.
   Do not be far from me, Lord.
23 Awake, and rise to my defense!
   Contend for me, my God and
      Lord.
24 Vindicate me in your righteousness,
   Lord my God;
   do not let them gloat over me.
25 Do not let them think, "Aha, just
      what we wanted!"
   or say, "We have swallowed
      him up."

26 May all who gloat over my distress
   be put to shame and confusion;
   may all who exalt themselves over me
   be clothed with shame and
      disgrace.
27 May those who delight in my
      vindication
   shout for joy and gladness;
   may they always say, "The Lord be
      exalted,
   who delights in the well-being of
      his servant."

28 My tongue will proclaim your
      righteousness,
   your praises all day long.

Psalm 36[a]

For the director of music. Of David
the servant of the Lord.

1 I have a message from God in my
      heart
   concerning the sinfulness of the
      wicked:[b]
   There is no fear of God
      before their eyes.

2 In their own eyes they flatter themselves
   too much to detect or hate their sin.
3 The words of their mouths are wicked
      and deceitful;
   they fail to act wisely or do good.
4 Even on their beds they plot evil;
   they commit themselves to a sinful
      course
   and do not reject what is wrong.

5 Your love, Lord, reaches to the
      heavens,
   your faithfulness to the skies.
6 Your righteousness is like the highest
      mountains,
   your justice like the great deep.
   You, Lord, preserve both people
      and animals.
7 How priceless is your unfailing love,
      O God!
   People take refuge in the shadow of
      your wings.
8 They feast on the abundance of your
      house;
   you give them drink from your river
      of delights.
9 For with you is the fountain of life;
   in your light we see light.

10 Continue your love to those who know
      you,
   your righteousness to the upright in
      heart.
11 May the foot of the proud not come
      against me,
   nor the hand of the wicked drive me
      away.
12 See how the evildoers lie fallen—
   thrown down, not able to rise!

a In Hebrew texts 36:1-12 is numbered 36:2-13.
b 1 Or A message from God: The transgression of
the wicked / resides in their hearts.

Psalm 37[a]

Of David.

1 Do not fret because of those who are
evil
  or be envious of those who do
  wrong;
2 for like the grass they will soon wither,
  like green plants they will soon die
  away.

3 Trust in the Lord and do good;
  dwell in the land and enjoy safe
  pasture.
4 Take delight in the Lord,
  and he will give you the desires of
  your heart.

5 Commit your way to the Lord;
  trust in him and he will do this:
6 He will make your righteous reward
  shine like the dawn,
  your vindication like the noonday
  sun.

7 Be still before the Lord
  and wait patiently for him;

do not fret when people succeed in
their ways,
  when they carry out their wicked
  schemes.

8 Refrain from anger and turn from
wrath;
  do not fret—it leads only to evil.
9 For those who are evil will be
destroyed,
  but those who hope in the Lord
  will inherit the land.

10 A little while, and the wicked will be
no more;
  though you look for them, they will
  not be found.
11 But the meek will inherit the land
  and enjoy peace and prosperity.

12 The wicked plot against the
righteous
  and gnash their teeth at them;
13 but the Lord laughs at the wicked,
  for he knows their day is coming.

14 The wicked draw the sword
  and bend the bow
to bring down the poor and needy,
  to slay those whose ways are
  upright.
15 But their swords will pierce their own
hearts,
  and their bows will be broken.

16 Better the little that the righteous
have
  than the wealth of many wicked;
17 for the power of the wicked will be
broken,
  but the Lord upholds the
  righteous.

18 The blameless spend their days under
the Lord's care,
  and their inheritance will endure
  forever.
19 In times of disaster they will not
wither;
  in days of famine they will enjoy
  plenty.

ROCK SOLID *plans*

Psalm 37:1–7

Commit your path to God.

People deep into evil can push you to do things you shouldn't—or they can pull you in by selling you on the advantages of sin. Yet one day those people will dry up and die like grass. God invites you to trust him, do good, and make him your biggest desire. When you do, he promises to satisfy your heart and make your rightness shine as bright as the sun. "Observe the upright," David says. "A future awaits those who seek peace" (Psalm 37:37).

Your next step: Make up your mind right now to follow God's path—while you're not feeling the push and pull of sin.

[a] This psalm is an acrostic poem, the stanzas of which begin with the successive letters of the Hebrew alphabet.

²⁰ But the wicked will perish:
Though the LORD's enemies are like
the flowers of the field,
they will be consumed, they will go
up in smoke.
²¹ The wicked borrow and do not repay,
but the righteous give generously;
²² those the LORD blesses will inherit the
land,
but those he curses will be
destroyed.

²³ The LORD makes firm the steps
of the one who delights in him;
²⁴ though he may stumble, he will not
fall,
for the LORD upholds him with his
hand.

²⁵ I was young and now I am old,
yet I have never seen the righteous
forsaken
or their children begging bread.
²⁶ They are always generous and lend
freely;
their children will be a blessing.^a

²⁷ Turn from evil and do good;
then you will dwell in the land
forever.
²⁸ For the LORD loves the just
and will not forsake his faithful
ones.

Wrongdoers will be completely
destroyed^b;
the offspring of the wicked will
perish.
²⁹ The righteous will inherit the land
and dwell in it forever.

³⁰ The mouths of the righteous utter
wisdom,
and their tongues speak what is just.
³¹ The law of their God is in their
hearts;
their feet do not slip.

³² The wicked lie in wait for the
righteous,
intent on putting them to death;
³³ but the LORD will not leave them in
the power of the wicked

or let them be condemned when
brought to trial.
³⁴ Hope in the LORD
and keep his way.
He will exalt you to inherit the land;
when the wicked are destroyed, you
will see it.

³⁵ I have seen a wicked and ruthless man
flourishing like a luxuriant native
tree,
³⁶ but he soon passed away and was no
more;
though I looked for him, he could
not be found.

³⁷ Consider the blameless, observe the
upright;
a future awaits those who seek
peace.^c
³⁸ But all sinners will be destroyed;
there will be no future^d for the
wicked.

³⁹ The salvation of the righteous comes
from the LORD;
he is their stronghold in time of
trouble.
⁴⁰ The LORD helps them and delivers
them;
he delivers them from the wicked
and saves them,
because they take refuge in him.

Psalm 38^e

A psalm of David. A petition.

¹ LORD, do not rebuke me in your anger
or discipline me in your wrath.
² Your arrows have pierced me,
and your hand has come down on
me.
³ Because of your wrath there is no
health in my body;
there is no soundness in my bones
because of my sin.

---

^a 26 Or freely; / the names of their children will be
used in blessings (see Gen. 48:20); or freely; / others
will see that their children are blessed   ^b 28 See
Septuagint; Hebrew They will be protected forever
^c 37 Or upright; / those who seek peace will have
posterity   ^d 38 Or posterity   ^e In Hebrew
texts 38:1-22 is numbered 38:2-23.

⁴My guilt has overwhelmed me
  like a burden too heavy to bear.

⁵My wounds fester and are loathsome
  because of my sinful folly.
⁶I am bowed down and brought very low;
  all day long I go about mourning.
⁷My back is filled with searing pain;
  there is no health in my body.
⁸I am feeble and utterly crushed;
  I groan in anguish of heart.

⁹All my longings lie open before you,
    Lord;
  my sighing is not hidden from you.
¹⁰My heart pounds, my strength fails me;
  even the light has gone from my
    eyes.
¹¹My friends and companions avoid me
  because of my wounds;
  my neighbors stay far away.
¹²Those who want to kill me set their
    traps,
  those who would harm me talk of
    my ruin;
  all day long they scheme and lie.

¹³I am like the deaf, who cannot hear,
  like the mute, who cannot speak;
¹⁴I have become like one who does not
    hear,
  whose mouth can offer no reply.
¹⁵Lord, I wait for you;
  you will answer, Lord my God.
¹⁶For I said, "Do not let them gloat
  or exalt themselves over me when
    my feet slip."

¹⁷For I am about to fall,
  and my pain is ever with me.
¹⁸I confess my iniquity;
  I am troubled by my sin.
¹⁹Many have become my enemies
    without cause*;
  those who hate me without reason
    are numerous.
²⁰Those who repay my good with evil
  lodge accusations against me,
  though I seek only to do what is good.

²¹Lord, do not forsake me;
  do not be far from me, my God.
²²Come quickly to help me,
  my Lord and my Savior.

Psalm 39ᵇ

For the director of music.
For Jeduthun. A psalm of David.

¹I said, "I will watch my ways
  and keep my tongue from sin;
  I will put a muzzle on my mouth
  while in the presence of the wicked."
²So I remained utterly silent,
  not even saying anything good.
  But my anguish increased;
³ my heart grew hot within me.
  While I meditated, the fire burned;
  then I spoke with my tongue:

⁴"Show me, Lord, my life's end
  and the number of my days;
  let me know how fleeting my life is.
⁵You have made my days a mere
    handbreadth;
  the span of my years is as nothing
    before you.
  Everyone is but a breath,
  even those who seem secure.ᶜ

⁶"Surely everyone goes around like a
    mere phantom;
  in vain they rush about, heaping up
    wealth
  without knowing whose it will
    finally be.

⁷"But now, Lord, what do I look for?
  My hope is in you.
⁸Save me from all my transgressions;
  do not make me the scorn of fools.
⁹I was silent; I would not open my
    mouth,
  for you are the one who has done
    this.
¹⁰Remove your scourge from me;
  I am overcome by the blow of your
    hand.
¹¹When you rebuke and discipline
    anyone for their sin,
  you consume their wealth like a
    moth—
  surely everyone is but a breath.

ᵃ 19 One Dead Sea Scrolls manuscript;
Masoretic Text *my vigorous enemies*   ᵇ In
Hebrew texts 39:1-13 is numbered 39:2-14.
ᶜ 5 The Hebrew has *Selah* (a word of uncertain
meaning) here and at the end of verse 11.

12 "Hear my prayer, LORD,
   listen to my cry for help;
   do not be deaf to my weeping.
I dwell with you as a foreigner,
   a stranger, as all my ancestors were.
13 Look away from me, that I may enjoy
      life again
   before I depart and am no more."

Psalm 40 [a]

For the director of music. Of David. A psalm.

1 I waited patiently for the LORD;
   he turned to me and heard my cry.
2 He lifted me out of the slimy pit,
   out of the mud and mire;
he set my feet on a rock
   and gave me a firm place to stand.
3 He put a new song in my mouth,
   a hymn of praise to our God.
Many will see and fear the LORD
   and put their trust in him.

4 Blessed is the one
   who trusts in the LORD,

who does not look to the proud,
   to those who turn aside to false
      gods. [b]
5 Many, LORD my God,
   are the wonders you have done,
   the things you planned for us.
None can compare with you;
   were I to speak and tell of your deeds,
   they would be too many to declare.

6 Sacrifice and offering you did not
      desire—
   but my ears you have opened [c]—
   burnt offerings and sin offerings [d]
      you did not require.
7 Then I said, "Here I am, I have
      come—
   it is written about me in the scroll. [e]
8 I desire to do your will, my God;
   your law is within my heart."

---

[a] In Hebrew texts 40:1-17 is numbered 40:2-18.
[b] 4 Or to lies   [c] 6 Hebrew; some Septuagint
manuscripts *but a body you have prepared for me*
[d] 6 Or *purification offerings*   [e] 7 Or *come /
with the scroll written for me*

ROCK SOLID principles

Psalm 40:1–6

Wait for God.

Almost everyone craves summer vacation, but Josiah was taking crave to another level. He felt trapped and alone, like his world would never get better. His friends had moved on to new people, all but abandoning him. School was simultaneously hard and boring, and youth group was small and struggling. His boss was a jerk. And when Josiah tried out for his favorite sport, B squad was the best he could do. Hardest of all was the fact that God seemed to have exited his life. No matter how hard Josiah looked and prayed and tried to trust, it seemed like God was nowhere to be found.

When you cry out to God and he seems slow to reply, don't give up. God rescues in his time and his way, putting you on solid ground and striking awe in everyone who sees him act. And he's worth waiting for. Turning to "false gods" (Psalm 40:4) means counting on someone or something else to do what only God can do. But ultimate help comes from your potent and loving God.

⁹ I proclaim your saving acts in the
   great assembly;
   I do not seal my lips, Lord,
   as you know.
¹⁰ I do not hide your righteousness in
   my heart;
   I speak of your faithfulness and
   your saving help.
   I do not conceal your love and your
   faithfulness
   from the great assembly.

¹¹ Do not withhold your mercy from
   me, Lord;
   may your love and faithfulness
   always protect me.
¹² For troubles without number
   surround me;
   my sins have overtaken me, and I
   cannot see.
   They are more than the hairs of my
   head,
   and my heart fails within me.
¹³ Be pleased to save me, Lord;
   come quickly, Lord, to help me.

¹⁴ May all who want to take my life
   be put to shame and confusion;
   may all who desire my ruin
   be turned back in disgrace.
¹⁵ May those who say to me,
   "Aha! Aha!"
   be appalled at their own shame.
¹⁶ But may all who seek you
   rejoice and be glad in you;
   may those who long for your saving
   help always say,
   "The Lord is great!"

¹⁷ But as for me, I am poor and needy;
   may the Lord think of me.
   You are my help and my deliverer;
   you are my God, do not delay.

Psalm 41 ᵃ

For the director of music.
A psalm of David.

¹ Blessed are those who have regard for
   the weak;
   the Lord delivers them in times of
   trouble.

² The Lord protects and preserves
   them —
   they are counted among the blessed
   in the land —
   he does not give them over to the
   desire of their foes.
³ The Lord sustains them on their
   sickbed
   and restores them from their bed of
   illness.

⁴ I said, "Have mercy on me, Lord;
   heal me, for I have sinned against
   you."
⁵ My enemies say of me in malice,
   "When will he die and his name
   perish?"
⁶ When one of them comes to see me,
   he speaks falsely, while his heart
   gathers slander;
   then he goes out and spreads it
   around.

⁷ All my enemies whisper together
   against me;
   they imagine the worst for me,
   saying,
⁸ "A vile disease has afflicted him;
   he will never get up from the place
   where he lies."
⁹ Even my close friend,
   someone I trusted,
   one who shared my bread,
   has turned ᵇ against me.

¹⁰ But may you have mercy on me,
   Lord;
   raise me up, that I may repay them.
¹¹ I know that you are pleased with me,
   for my enemy does not triumph
   over me.
¹² Because of my integrity you
   uphold me
   and set me in your presence
   forever.

¹³ Praise be to the Lord, the God of
   Israel,
   from everlasting to everlasting.
   Amen and Amen.

ᵃ In Hebrew texts 41:1-13 is numbered 41:2-14.
ᵇ 9 Hebrew *has lifted up his heel*

BOOK II

Psalms 42–72

Psalm 42[a,b]

For the director of music. A *maskil*[c]
of the Sons of Korah.

[1] As the deer pants for streams of water,
   so my soul pants for you, my God.
[2] My soul thirsts for God, for the living
      God.
   When can I go and meet with God?
[3] My tears have been my food
      day and night,
   while people say to me all day long,
      "Where is your God?"
[4] These things I remember
      as I pour out my soul:
   how I used to go to the house of God
      under the protection of the Mighty
         One[d]
   with shouts of joy and praise
      among the festive throng.

[5] Why, my soul, are you downcast?
      Why so disturbed within me?
   Put your hope in God,
      for I will yet praise him,
      my Savior and my God.

[6] My soul is downcast within me;
      therefore I will remember you
   from the land of the Jordan,
      the heights of Hermon—from
         Mount Mizar.
[7] Deep calls to deep
      in the roar of your waterfalls;
   all your waves and breakers
      have swept over me.

[8] By day the LORD directs his love,
      at night his song is with me—
   a prayer to the God of my life.

[9] I say to God my Rock,
      "Why have you forgotten me?
   Why must I go about mourning,
      oppressed by the enemy?"
[10] My bones suffer mortal agony
      as my foes taunt me,
   saying to me all day long,
      "Where is your God?"

UNSHAKEN God

Psalm 42:1–9

God is desirable.

The ancient Israelites knew the feeling of real thirst. Those desert-dwellers understood that drinkable water was desperately valuable—and an entire city could live or die by its water supply (see 2 Kings 2:20–22). This song by the Sons of Korah describes a deer on the hunt for a life-giving stream, searching instinctively for a clean flowing brook to quench its thirst. That's the same panting desire you can have for God. It's not a desire you have to force yourself to feel but a natural response that comes when you appreciate God's true worth. Once you have had a deep drink of God, you won't stop wanting more.

So ... How much do you thirst for God? How can you increase your thirst?

[11] Why, my soul, are you downcast?
      Why so disturbed within me?
   Put your hope in God,
      for I will yet praise him,
      my Savior and my God.

Psalm 43[a]

[1] Vindicate me, my God,
      and plead my cause
      against an unfaithful nation.
   Rescue me from those who are
      deceitful and wicked.
[2] You are God my stronghold.
      Why have you rejected me?
   Why must I go about mourning,
      oppressed by the enemy?

---

[a] In many Hebrew manuscripts Psalms 42 and 43 constitute one psalm.   [b] In Hebrew texts 42:1-11 is numbered 42:2-12.   [c] Title: Probably a literary or musical term   [d] 4 See Septuagint and Syriac; the meaning of the Hebrew for this line is uncertain.

³ Send me your light and your faithful
    care,
  let them lead me;
  let them bring me to your holy
    mountain,
    to the place where you dwell.

ROCK SOLID
promises

**"Send me your light and your
faithful care, let them lead me."**

Psalm 43:3

**God will light up dark situations and
clear up your confusion. Then you will
know what to do.**

⁴ Then I will go to the altar of God,
  to God, my joy and my delight.
  I will praise you with the lyre,
  O God, my God.
⁵ Why, my soul, are you downcast?
  Why so disturbed within me?
  Put your hope in God,
  for I will yet praise him,
  my Savior and my God.

Psalm 44ᵃ

For the director of music. Of the
Sons of Korah. A *maskil.ᵇ*

¹ We have heard it with our ears, O God;
  our ancestors have told us
what you did in their days,
  in days long ago.
² With your hand you drove out the
    nations
  and planted our ancestors;
you crushed the peoples
  and made our ancestors flourish.
³ It was not by their sword that they
    won the land,
  nor did their arm bring them
    victory;

it was your right hand, your arm,
  and the light of your face, for you
    loved them.
⁴ You are my King and my God,
  who decreesᶜ victories for Jacob.
⁵ Through you we push back our
    enemies;
  through your name we trample our
    foes.
⁶ I put no trust in my bow,
  my sword does not bring me
    victory;
⁷ but you give us victory over our
    enemies,
  you put our adversaries to shame.
⁸ In God we make our boast all day
    long,
  and we will praise your name
    forever.ᵈ

⁹ But now you have rejected and
    humbled us;
  you no longer go out with our
    armies.
¹⁰ You made us retreat before the enemy,
  and our adversaries have plundered
    us.
¹¹ You gave us up to be devoured like
    sheep
  and have scattered us among the
    nations.
¹² You sold your people for a pittance,
  gaining nothing from their sale.

¹³ You have made us a reproach to our
    neighbors,
  the scorn and derision of those
    around us.
¹⁴ You have made us a byword among
    the nations;
  the peoples shake their heads at us.
¹⁵ I live in disgrace all day long,
  and my face is covered with shame
¹⁶ at the taunts of those who reproach
    and revile me,
  because of the enemy, who is bent
    on revenge.

ᵃ In Hebrew texts 44:1-26 is numbered 44:2-27.
ᵇ Title: Probably a literary or musical term
ᶜ 4 Septuagint, Aquila and Syriac; Hebrew
King, O God; / command   ᵈ 8 The Hebrew has
Selah (a word of uncertain meaning) here.

17 All this came upon us,
    though we had not forgotten
        you;
    we had not been false to your
        covenant.
18 Our hearts had not turned back;
    our feet had not strayed from your
        path.
19 But you crushed us and made us a
        haunt for jackals;
    you covered us over with deep
        darkness.

20 If we had forgotten the name of our
        God
    or spread out our hands to a
        foreign god,
21 would not God have discovered it,
    since he knows the secrets of the
        heart?
22 Yet for your sake we face death all
        day long;
    we are considered as sheep to be
        slaughtered.

23 Awake, Lord! Why do you sleep?
    Rouse yourself! Do not reject us
        forever.
24 Why do you hide your face
    and forget our misery and
        oppression?

25 We are brought down to the dust;
    our bodies cling to the ground.
26 Rise up and help us;
    rescue us because of your unfailing
        love.

Psalm 45[a]

For the director of music. To the
tune of "Lilies." Of the Sons of Korah.
A *maskil*.[b] A wedding song.

1 My heart is stirred by a noble theme
    as I recite my verses for the king;
    my tongue is the pen of a skillful
        writer.

2 You are the most excellent of men
    and your lips have been anointed
        with grace,
    since God has blessed you
        forever.

3 Gird your sword on your side, you
        mighty one;
    clothe yourself with splendor and
        majesty.
4 In your majesty ride forth victoriously
    in the cause of truth, humility and
        justice;
    let your right hand achieve awesome
        deeds.
5 Let your sharp arrows pierce the
        hearts of the king's enemies;
    let the nations fall beneath your
        feet.
6 Your throne, O God,[c] will last for ever
        and ever;
    a scepter of justice will be the
        scepter of your kingdom.
7 You love righteousness and hate
        wickedness;
    therefore God, your God, has set
        you above your companions
    by anointing you with the oil of
        joy.
8 All your robes are fragrant with myrrh
        and aloes and cassia;
    from palaces adorned with ivory
    the music of the strings makes you
        glad.
9 Daughters of kings are among your
        honored women;
    at your right hand is the royal bride
        in gold of Ophir.

10 Listen, daughter, and pay careful
        attention:
    Forget your people and your father's
        house.
11 Let the king be enthralled by your
        beauty;
    honor him, for he is your lord.
12 The city of Tyre will come with a
        gift,[d]
    people of wealth will seek your
        favor.
13 All glorious is the princess within her
        chamber;
    her gown is interwoven with gold.

[a] In Hebrew texts 45:1-17 is numbered 45:2-18.
[b] Title: Probably a literary or musical term
[c] 6 Here the king is addressed as God's
representative.   [d] 12 Or *A Tyrian robe is
among the gifts*

14 In embroidered garments she is led to
the king;
her virgin companions follow her—
those brought to be with her.
15 Led in with joy and gladness,
they enter the palace of the king.

16 Your sons will take the place of your
fathers;
you will make them princes
throughout the land.

17 I will perpetuate your memory
through all generations;
therefore the nations will praise you
for ever and ever.

Psalm 46[a]

For the director of music. Of the Sons
of Korah. According to *alamoth*.[b] A song.

1 God is our refuge and strength,
an ever-present help in trouble.
2 Therefore we will not fear, though the
earth give way
and the mountains fall into the
heart of the sea,

ROCK SOLID
promises

**"God is our refuge and strength,
an ever-present help in trouble.
Therefore we will not fear."**

Psalm 46:1–2

**Be still. Calm down. God will protect and
help you, whatever you face.**

3 though its waters roar and foam
and the mountains quake with their
surging.[c]

4 There is a river whose streams make
glad the city of God,
the holy place where the Most High
dwells.

5 God is within her, she will not fall;
God will help her at break of day.
6 Nations are in uproar, kingdoms fall;
he lifts his voice, the earth melts.

7 The LORD Almighty is with us;
the God of Jacob is our fortress.

8 Come and see what the LORD has
done,
the desolations he has brought on
the earth.
9 He makes wars cease
to the ends of the earth.
He breaks the bow and shatters the
spear;
he burns the shields[d] with fire.
10 He says, "Be still, and know that I am
God;
I will be exalted among the nations,
I will be exalted in the earth."

11 The LORD Almighty is with us;
the God of Jacob is our fortress.

Psalm 47[e]

For the director of music. Of the Sons
of Korah. A psalm.

1 Clap your hands, all you nations;
shout to God with cries of joy.

2 For the LORD Most High is awesome,
the great King over all the earth.
3 He subdued nations under us,
peoples under our feet.
4 He chose our inheritance for us,
the pride of Jacob, whom he loved.[f]

5 God has ascended amid shouts of joy,
the LORD amid the sounding of
trumpets.
6 Sing praises to God, sing praises;
sing praises to our King, sing
praises.
7 For God is the King of all the earth;
sing to him a psalm of praise.

[a] In Hebrew texts 46:1-11 is numbered 46:2-12.
[b] Title: Probably a musical term   [c] 3 The
Hebrew has Selah (a word of uncertain meaning)
here and at the end of verses 7 and 11.
[d] 9 Or chariots   [e] In Hebrew texts 47:1-9 is
numbered 47:2-10.   [f] 4 The Hebrew has
Selah (a word of uncertain meaning) here.

Psalm 47:1-9

God rules the whole world.

Israel's Old Testament neighbors believed their gods were local deities whose power was limited to a small place and select group of people, like Baal was lord over the land of Canaan, or Molech was god of the Phoenicians. Then God came along and revealed himself to Abraham and promised "all peoples on earth will be blessed through you" (Genesis 12:3). That was just the start of God revealing to everyone that he rules not just a clan in ancient Israel but the whole world. He is "LORD Most High ... the great King over all the earth" (Psalm 47:2). He "reigns over the nations" (Psalm 47:8). So "all you nations" can clap and shout to God with joy (Psalm 47:1). Everyone and everything in the world belongs to him.

Think: Suppose it's true that God rules the whole world. How does that change how you will live today?

ROCK SOLID truths

⁸God reigns over the nations;
   God is seated on his holy throne.
⁹The nobles of the nations assemble
   as the people of the God of Abraham,
for the kings*a* of the earth belong to God;
   he is greatly exalted.

Psalm 48*b*

A song. A psalm of the Sons of Korah.

¹Great is the LORD, and most worthy of praise,
   in the city of our God, his holy mountain.

²Beautiful in its loftiness,
   the joy of the whole earth,
like the heights of Zaphon*c* is Mount Zion,
   the city of the Great King.
³God is in her citadels;
   he has shown himself to be her fortress.

⁴When the kings joined forces,
   when they advanced together,
⁵they saw her and were astounded;
   they fled in terror.
⁶Trembling seized them there,
   pain like that of a woman in labor.
⁷You destroyed them like ships of Tarshish
   shattered by an east wind.

⁸As we have heard,
   so we have seen
in the city of the LORD Almighty,
   in the city of our God:
God makes her secure forever.*d*

⁹Within your temple, O God,
   we meditate on your unfailing love.
¹⁰Like your name, O God,
   your praise reaches to the ends of the earth;
   your right hand is filled with righteousness.
¹¹Mount Zion rejoices,
   the villages of Judah are glad
   because of your judgments.

¹²Walk about Zion, go around her,
   count her towers,
¹³consider well her ramparts,
   view her citadels,
that you may tell of them
   to the next generation.

¹⁴For this God is our God for ever and ever;
   he will be our guide even to the end.

a 9 Or *shields*   *b* In Hebrew texts 48:1-14 is numbered 48:2-15.   *c 2 Zaphon* was the most sacred mountain of the Canaanites.   *d 8* The Hebrew has *Selah* (a word of uncertain meaning) here.

For the director of music. Of the
Sons of Korah. A psalm.

¹ Hear this, all you peoples;
    listen, all who live in this world,
² both low and high,
    rich and poor alike:
³ My mouth will speak words of
    wisdom;
    the meditation of my heart will give
    you understanding.
⁴ I will turn my ear to a proverb;
    with the harp I will expound my
    riddle:

⁵ Why should I fear when evil days
    come,
    when wicked deceivers surround
    me —
⁶ those who trust in their wealth
    and boast of their great riches?
⁷ No one can redeem the life of another
    or give to God a ransom for
    them —
⁸ the ransom for a life is costly,
    no payment is ever enough —
⁹ so that they should live on forever
    and not see decay.
¹⁰ For all can see that the wise die,
    that the foolish and the senseless
    also perish,
    leaving their wealth to others.
¹¹ Their tombs will remain their houses^b
    forever,
    their dwellings for endless
    generations,
    though they had^c named lands after
    themselves.

¹² People, despite their wealth, do not
    endure;
    they are like the beasts that perish.

¹³ This is the fate of those who trust in
    themselves,
    and of their followers, who approve
    their sayings.^d
¹⁴ They are like sheep and are destined
    to die;
    death will be their shepherd
    (but the upright will prevail over
    them in the morning).

Their forms will decay in the grave,
    far from their princely mansions.
¹⁵ But God will redeem me from the
    realm of the dead;
    he will surely take me to himself.
¹⁶ Do not be overawed when others grow
    rich,
    when the splendor of their houses
    increases;
¹⁷ for they will take nothing with them
    when they die,
    their splendor will not descend with
    them.
¹⁸ Though while they live they count
    themselves blessed —
    and people praise you when you
    prosper —
¹⁹ they will join those who have gone
    before them,
    who will never again see the light of
    life.

²⁰ People who have wealth but lack
    understanding
    are like the beasts that perish.

Psalm 50

A psalm of Asaph.

¹ The Mighty One, God, the LORD,
    speaks and summons the earth
    from the rising of the sun to where
    it sets.
² From Zion, perfect in beauty,
    God shines forth.
³ Our God comes
    and will not be silent;
    a fire devours before him,
    and around him a tempest rages.
⁴ He summons the heavens above,
    and the earth, that he may judge his
    people:
⁵ "Gather to me this consecrated
    people,
    who made a covenant with me by
    sacrifice."

^a In Hebrew texts 49:1-20 is numbered 49:2-21.
^b 11 Septuagint and Syriac; Hebrew *In their
thoughts their houses will remain*   ^c 11 Or
generations, / for they have   ^d 13 The Hebrew
has *Selah* (a word of uncertain meaning) here
and at the end of verse 15.

[6] And the heavens proclaim his
   righteousness,
      for he is a God of justice.[a,b]

[7] "Listen, my people, and I will speak;
   I will testify against you, Israel:
      I am God, your God.
[8] I bring no charges against you
      concerning your sacrifices
   or concerning your burnt offerings,
      which are ever before me.
[9] I have no need of a bull from your stall
   or of goats from your pens,
[10] for every animal of the forest is mine,
   and the cattle on a thousand hills.
[11] I know every bird in the mountains,
   and the insects in the fields are
      mine.
[12] If I were hungry I would not tell you,
   for the world is mine, and all that is
      in it.
[13] Do I eat the flesh of bulls
   or drink the blood of goats?

UNSHAKEN God

Psalm 50:12

God is independent.

God has a flawless grasp of the inner workings of your heart and mind. He wants to be closer than close with you. But don't miss the fact that as God, he is the one "independent" or "self-sufficient" being in the universe, having everything he needs in himself. Put simply, God doesn't need us at all. And that's a good thing. When God created human beings, he wasn't designing a collection of action figures to entertain himself. He didn't make us because he was lonely. He gave us life because he wanted to show us his love and share his goodness and glory.

So ... Explain it in your own words—what's the connection between God's independence and his love for you?

[14] "Sacrifice thank offerings to God,
   fulfill your vows to the Most High,
[15] and call on me in the day of trouble;
   I will deliver you, and you will
      honor me."

[16] But to the wicked person, God says:

"What right have you to recite my
      laws
   or take my covenant on your lips?
[17] You hate my instruction
   and cast my words behind you.
[18] When you see a thief, you join with
      him;
   you throw in your lot with
      adulterers.
[19] You use your mouth for evil
   and harness your tongue to deceit.
[20] You sit and testify against your
      brother
   and slander your own mother's son.
[21] When you did these things and I kept
      silent,
   you thought I was exactly[c] like you.
But I now arraign you
   and set my accusations before you.

[22] "Consider this, you who forget God,
   or I will tear you to pieces, with no
      one to rescue you:
[23] Those who sacrifice thank offerings
      honor me,
   and to the blameless[d] I will show
      my salvation."

Psalm 51[e]

For the director of music. A psalm of David. When the prophet Nathan came to him after David had committed adultery with Bathsheba.

[1] Have mercy on me, O God,
   according to your unfailing love;
according to your great compassion
   blot out my transgressions.

[a] 6 With a different word division of the Hebrew; Masoretic Text *for God himself is judge*   [b] 6 The Hebrew has *Selah* (a word of uncertain meaning) here.   [c] 21 Or *thought the 'I AM' was*   [d] 23 Probable reading of the original Hebrew text; the meaning of the Masoretic Text for this phrase is uncertain.   [e] In Hebrew texts 51:1-19 is numbered 51:3-21.

²Wash away all my iniquity
 and cleanse me from my sin.

³For I know my transgressions,
 and my sin is always before me.
⁴Against you, you only, have I sinned
 and done what is evil in your
 sight;
 so you are right in your verdict
 and justified when you judge.
⁵Surely I was sinful at birth,
 sinful from the time my mother
 conceived me.
⁶Yet you desired faithfulness even in
 the womb;
 you taught me wisdom in that secret
 place.

⁷Cleanse me with hyssop, and I will be
 clean;
 wash me, and I will be whiter than
 snow.
⁸Let me hear joy and gladness;
 let the bones you have crushed
 rejoice.

⁹Hide your face from my sins
 and blot out all my iniquity.
¹⁰Create in me a pure heart, O God,
 and renew a steadfast spirit within
 me.
¹¹Do not cast me from your presence
 or take your Holy Spirit from me.
¹²Restore to me the joy of your
 salvation
 and grant me a willing spirit, to
 sustain me.

¹³Then I will teach transgressors your
 ways,
 so that sinners will turn back to
 you.
¹⁴Deliver me from the guilt of
 bloodshed, O God,
 you who are God my Savior,
 and my tongue will sing of your
 righteousness.
¹⁵Open my lips, Lord,
 and my mouth will declare your
 praise.

ROCK SOLID principles

Psalm 51:1–19

Confess your sins.

Ella wasn't so dumb that she stole from the cash registers—that would be too easily detected. She didn't rip off customer credit card numbers—that was too high risk. But she did take advantage of her job at a huge discount chain to pocket whatever cosmetics she needed. Lipstick, eye liner, mascara—they all slipped easily into her pocket and then into her purse. Ella knew she was done for, however, when the store's loss prevention officer called her over to watch a few clips of surveillance video. While the store didn't press charges, Ella was instantly out of a job. She knew her manager wasn't happy with her behavior, and she was sure God wasn't either.

The prophet Nathan didn't let David get away with stealing another man's wife and getting the man killed in battle (see 2 Samuel 12:1–14). Psalm 51 captures David's words coming clean about this awful sin. Borrow these words when you need to admit your sins to God. You can be confident that when you confess, God forgives (see 1 John 1:9).

16 You do not delight in sacrifice, or I
would bring it;
  you do not take pleasure in burnt
  offerings.
17 My sacrifice, O God, is[a] a broken
spirit;
  a broken and contrite heart
  you, God, will not despise.

18 May it please you to prosper Zion,
  to build up the walls of
  Jerusalem.
19 Then you will delight in the sacrifices
of the righteous,
  in burnt offerings offered whole;
  then bulls will be offered on your
  altar.

Psalm 52[b]

For the director of music. A *maskil*[c]
of David. When Doeg the Edomite
had gone to Saul and told him: "David
has gone to the house of Ahimelek."

1 Why do you boast of evil, you mighty
hero?
  Why do you boast all day long,
  you who are a disgrace in the eyes of
  God?
2 You who practice deceit,
  your tongue plots destruction;
  it is like a sharpened razor.
3 You love evil rather than good,
  falsehood rather than speaking the
  truth.[d]
4 You love every harmful word,
  you deceitful tongue!

5 Surely God will bring you down to
everlasting ruin:
  He will snatch you up and pluck
  you from your tent;
  he will uproot you from the land of
  the living.
6 The righteous will see and fear;
  they will laugh at you, saying,
7 "Here now is the man
  who did not make God his
  stronghold
  but trusted in his great wealth
  and grew strong by destroying
  others!"

8 But I am like an olive tree
flourishing in the house of God;
  I trust in God's unfailing love
  for ever and ever.
9 For what you have done I will always
praise you
  in the presence of your faithful
  people.
  And I will hope in your name,
  for your name is good.

Psalm 53[e]

For the director of music. According
to *mahalath*.[f] A *maskil*[c] of David.

1 The fool says in his heart,
  "There is no God."
They are corrupt, and their ways are
vile;
  there is no one who does good.

2 God looks down from heaven
  on all mankind
to see if there are any who understand,
  any who seek God.
3 Everyone has turned away, all have
become corrupt;
  there is no one who does good,
  not even one.

4 Do all these evildoers know nothing?

They devour my people as though
eating bread;
  they never call on God.
5 But there they are, overwhelmed with
dread,
  where there was nothing to dread.
God scattered the bones of those who
attacked you;
  you put them to shame, for God
  despised them.

6 Oh, that salvation for Israel would
come out of Zion!
  When God restores his people,
  let Jacob rejoice and Israel be glad!

[a] 17 Or *The sacrifices of God are*   [b] In Hebrew
texts 52:1-9 is numbered 52:3-11.   [c] Title:
Probably a literary or musical term   [d] 3 The
Hebrew has *Selah* (a word of uncertain meaning)
here and at the end of verse 5.   [e] In Hebrew
texts 53:1-6 is numbered 53:2-7.   [f] Title:
Probably a musical term

Psalm 54[a]

For the director of music. With stringed instruments. A *maskil*[b] of David. When the Ziphites had gone to Saul and said, "Is not David hiding among us?"

¹ Save me, O God, by your name;
    vindicate me by your might.
² Hear my prayer, O God;
    listen to the words of my mouth.

³ Arrogant foes are attacking me;
    ruthless people are trying to kill me—
    people without regard for God.[c]

⁴ Surely God is my help;
    the Lord is the one who sustains me.

⁵ Let evil recoil on those who slander me;
    in your faithfulness destroy them.

⁶ I will sacrifice a freewill offering to you;
    I will praise your name, Lord, for it is good.
⁷ You have delivered me from all my troubles,
    and my eyes have looked in triumph on my foes.

Psalm 55[d]

For the director of music. With stringed instruments. A *maskil*[b] of David.

¹ Listen to my prayer, O God,
    do not ignore my plea;
²   hear me and answer me.
My thoughts trouble me and I am distraught
³   because of what my enemy is saying,
    because of the threats of the wicked;
for they bring down suffering on me
    and assail me in their anger.

⁴ My heart is in anguish within me;
    the terrors of death have fallen on me.
⁵ Fear and trembling have beset me;
    horror has overwhelmed me.
⁶ I said, "Oh, that I had the wings of a dove!
    I would fly away and be at rest.
⁷ I would flee far away
    and stay in the desert;[e]

⁸ I would hurry to my place of shelter,
    far from the tempest and storm."

⁹ Lord, confuse the wicked, confound their words,
    for I see violence and strife in the city.
¹⁰ Day and night they prowl about on its walls;
    malice and abuse are within it.
¹¹ Destructive forces are at work in the city;
    threats and lies never leave its streets.

¹² If an enemy were insulting me,
    I could endure it;
if a foe were rising against me,
    I could hide.
¹³ But it is you, a man like myself,
    my companion, my close friend,
¹⁴ with whom I once enjoyed sweet fellowship
    at the house of God,
as we walked about
    among the worshipers.

¹⁵ Let death take my enemies by surprise;
    let them go down alive to the realm of the dead,
    for evil finds lodging among them.

¹⁶ As for me, I call to God,
    and the Lord saves me.
¹⁷ Evening, morning and noon
    I cry out in distress,
    and he hears my voice.
¹⁸ He rescues me unharmed
    from the battle waged against me,
    even though many oppose me.
¹⁹ God, who is enthroned from of old,
    who does not change—
he will hear them and humble them,
    because they have no fear of God.

²⁰ My companion attacks his friends;
    he violates his covenant.

[a] In Hebrew texts 54:1-7 is numbered 54:3-9.
[b] Title: Probably a literary or musical term
[c] 3 The Hebrew has *Selah* (a word of uncertain meaning) here.   [d] In Hebrew texts 55:1-23 is numbered 55:2-24.   [e] 7 The Hebrew has *Selah* (a word of uncertain meaning) here and in the middle of verse 19.

Psalm 55:12–14

Friends can turn on you.

You can't help but feel for David as he lists all of his heartaches at the start of Psalm 55. He has enemies outside. Anguish inside. And he has to plead with God not to ignore his prayer. But the real stab comes when you read a bit further. It's not just any old foe opposing David. It's his "companion" and "close friend" (Psalm 55:13). Many believers see a picture here of the betrayal Jesus felt when his disciple Judas turned on him and handed him over to the Romans (see Luke 22:47–48). Judas, after all, started out as one of the Lord's handpicked friends and followers. If people like David and Jesus were sold out by close friends, it shouldn't surprise you when acquaintances ... and classmates ... and significant others ... and even close friends or family members ... turn and bite you.

Think: How does it help you to know that David and Jesus felt betrayed by their closest friends?

ROCK SOLID truths

²¹ His talk is smooth as butter,
    yet war is in his heart;
his words are more soothing than
        oil,
    yet they are drawn swords.

²² Cast your cares on the LORD
    and he will sustain you;
he will never let
    the righteous be shaken.

²³ But you, God, will bring down the
        wicked
    into the pit of decay;

the bloodthirsty and deceitful
    will not live out half their days.

But as for me, I trust in you.

Psalm 56ᵃ

For the director of music. To the tune of "A Dove on Distant Oaks." Of David. A *miktam*.ᵇ When the Philistines had seized him in Gath.

¹ Be merciful to me, my God,
    for my enemies are in hot pursuit;
    all day long they press their attack.
² My adversaries pursue me all day
        long;
    in their pride many are attacking me.

³ When I am afraid, I put my trust in
        you.
⁴   In God, whose word I praise—
    in God I trust and am not afraid.
    What can mere mortals do to me?

⁵ All day long they twist my words;
    all their schemes are for my ruin.
⁶ They conspire, they lurk,
    they watch my steps,
    hoping to take my life.
⁷ Because of their wickedness do notᶜ let
        them escape;
    in your anger, God, bring the
        nations down.

⁸ Record my misery;
    list my tears on your scrollᵈ—
    are they not in your record?
⁹ Then my enemies will turn back
    when I call for help.
    By this I will know that God is
        for me.

¹⁰ In God, whose word I praise,
    in the LORD, whose word I praise—
¹¹ in God I trust and am not afraid.
    What can man do to me?

¹² I am under vows to you, my God;
    I will present my thank offerings to
        you.

ᵃ In Hebrew texts 56:1-13 is numbered 56:2-14.
ᵇ Title: Probably a literary or musical term
ᶜ 7 Probable reading of the original Hebrew text; Masoretic Text does not have *do not*.
ᵈ 8 Or *misery; / put my tears in your wineskin*

¹³ For you have delivered me from death
and my feet from stumbling,
that I may walk before God
in the light of life.

Psalm 57 [a]

For the director of music. To the tune of "Do
Not Destroy." Of David. A *miktam.* [b] When
he had fled from Saul into the cave.

¹ Have mercy on me, my God, have
mercy on me,
for in you I take refuge.
I will take refuge in the shadow of
your wings
until the disaster has passed.

² I cry out to God Most High,
to God, who vindicates me.
³ He sends from heaven and saves me,
rebuking those who hotly pursue
me— [c]
God sends forth his love and his
faithfulness.

⁴ I am in the midst of lions;
I am forced to dwell among
ravenous beasts—
men whose teeth are spears and arrows,
whose tongues are sharp swords.

⁵ Be exalted, O God, above the heavens;
let your glory be over all the earth.

⁶ They spread a net for my feet—
I was bowed down in distress.
They dug a pit in my path—
but they have fallen into it
themselves.

⁷ My heart, O God, is steadfast,
my heart is steadfast;
I will sing and make music.
⁸ Awake, my soul!
Awake, harp and lyre!
I will awaken the dawn.

⁹ I will praise you, Lord, among the
nations;
I will sing of you among the
peoples.
¹⁰ For great is your love, reaching to the
heavens;
your faithfulness reaches to the
skies.

ROCK SOLID *promises*

**"For great is your love, reaching
to the heavens; your faithfulness
reaches to the skies."** Psalm 57:10

**There are no limits to God's love. There's
no end to his commitment to you. His
care stretches to the sky.**

¹¹ Be exalted, O God, above the heavens;
let your glory be over all the earth.

Psalm 58 [d]

For the director of music. To
the tune of "Do Not Destroy."
Of David. A *miktam.* [b]

¹ Do you rulers indeed speak justly?
Do you judge people with equity?
² No, in your heart you devise injustice,
and your hands mete out violence
on the earth.

³ Even from birth the wicked go astray;
from the womb they are wayward,
spreading lies.
⁴ Their venom is like the venom of a
snake,
like that of a cobra that has stopped
its ears,
⁵ that will not heed the tune of the
charmer,
however skillful the enchanter
may be.

⁶ Break the teeth in their mouths,
O God;
LORD, tear out the fangs of those
lions!

[a] In Hebrew texts 57:1-11 is numbered 57:2-12.
[b] Title: Probably a literary or musical term
[c] 3 The Hebrew has *Selah* (a word of uncertain
meaning) here and at the end of verse 6.   [d] In
Hebrew texts 58:1-11 is numbered 58:2-12.

⁷Let them vanish like water that flows
away;
when they draw the bow, let their
arrows fall short.
⁸May they be like a slug that melts
away as it moves along,
like a stillborn child that never sees
the sun.

⁹Before your pots can feel the heat of
the thorns—
whether they be green or dry—the
wicked will be swept away.ᵃ
¹⁰The righteous will be glad when they
are avenged,
when they dip their feet in the
blood of the wicked.
¹¹Then people will say,
"Surely the righteous still are
rewarded;
surely there is a God who judges
the earth."

Psalm 59ᵇ

For the director of music. To the tune
of "Do Not Destroy." Of David. A *miktam*.ᶜ
When Saul had sent men to watch
David's house in order to kill him.

¹Deliver me from my enemies,
O God;
be my fortress against those who are
attacking me.
²Deliver me from evildoers
and save me from those who are
after my blood.

³See how they lie in wait for me!
Fierce men conspire against me
for no offense or sin of mine,
LORD.
⁴I have done no wrong, yet they are
ready to attack me.
Arise to help me; look on my plight!
⁵You, LORD God Almighty,
you who are the God of Israel,
rouse yourself to punish all the
nations;
show no mercy to wicked traitors.ᵈ

⁶They return at evening,
snarling like dogs,
and prowl about the city.

⁷See what they spew from their
mouths—
the words from their lips are sharp
as swords,
and they think, "Who can
hear us?"
⁸But you laugh at them, LORD;
you scoff at all those nations.

⁹You are my strength, I watch for you;
you, God, are my fortress,
¹⁰   my God on whom I can rely.

God will go before me
and will let me gloat over those
who slander me.
¹¹But do not kill them, Lord our
shield,ᵉ
or my people will forget.
In your might uproot them
and bring them down.
¹²For the sins of their mouths,
for the words of their lips,
let them be caught in their pride.
For the curses and lies they utter,
¹³   consume them in your wrath,
consume them till they are no
more.
Then it will be known to the ends of
the earth
that God rules over Jacob.

¹⁴They return at evening,
snarling like dogs,
and prowl about the city.
¹⁵They wander about for food
and howl if not satisfied.
¹⁶But I will sing of your strength,
in the morning I will sing of your
love;
for you are my fortress,
my refuge in times of trouble.

¹⁷You are my strength, I sing praise to
you;
you, God, are my fortress,
my God on whom I can rely.

ᵃ 9 The meaning of the Hebrew for this verse is
uncertain.   ᵇ In Hebrew texts 59:1-17 is
numbered 59:2-18.   ᶜ Title: Probably a literary
or musical term   ᵈ 5 The Hebrew has *Selah* (a
word of uncertain meaning) here and at the end
of verse 13.   ᵉ 11 Or *sovereign*

Psalm 60[a]

For the director of music. To the tune of "The Lily of the Covenant." A *miktam*[b] of David. For teaching. When he fought Aram Naharaim[c] and Aram Zobah,[d] and when Joab returned and struck down twelve thousand Edomites in the Valley of Salt.

[1] You have rejected us, God, and burst upon us;
    you have been angry—now restore us!
[2] You have shaken the land and torn it open;
    mend its fractures, for it is quaking.
[3] You have shown your people desperate times;
    you have given us wine that makes us stagger.
[4] But for those who fear you, you have raised a banner
    to be unfurled against the bow.[e]

[5] Save us and help us with your right hand,
    that those you love may be delivered.
[6] God has spoken from his sanctuary:
    "In triumph I will parcel out Shechem
    and measure off the Valley of Sukkoth.
[7] Gilead is mine, and Manasseh is mine;
    Ephraim is my helmet,
    Judah is my scepter.
[8] Moab is my washbasin,
    on Edom I toss my sandal;
    over Philistia I shout in triumph."

[9] Who will bring me to the fortified city?
    Who will lead me to Edom?
[10] Is it not you, God, you who have now rejected us
    and no longer go out with our armies?
[11] Give us aid against the enemy,
    for human help is worthless.
[12] With God we will gain the victory,
    and he will trample down our enemies.

Psalm 61[f]

For the director of music. With stringed instruments. Of David.

[1] Hear my cry, O God;
    listen to my prayer.

[2] From the ends of the earth I call to you,
    I call as my heart grows faint;
    lead me to the rock that is higher than I.
[3] For you have been my refuge,
    a strong tower against the foe.

ROCK SOLID *promises*

"You have been my refuge, a strong tower against the foe." Psalm 61:3

When enemies rage against you, God gives you shelter. You can run to him and hide in his constant care.

[4] I long to dwell in your tent forever
    and take refuge in the shelter of your wings.[e]

[5] For you, God, have heard my vows;
    you have given me the heritage of those who fear your name.

[6] Increase the days of the king's life,
    his years for many generations.
[7] May he be enthroned in God's presence forever;
    appoint your love and faithfulness to protect him.

[a] In Hebrew texts 60:1-12 is numbered 60:3-14.   [b] Title: Probably a literary or musical term   [c] Title: That is, Arameans of Northwest Mesopotamia   [d] Title: That is, Arameans of central Syria   [e] 4 The Hebrew has *Selah* (a word of uncertain meaning) here.   [f] In Hebrew texts 61:1-8 is numbered 61:2-9.

8 Then I will ever sing in praise of your
name
and fulfill my vows day after day.

Psalm 62 [a]

For the director of music. For Jeduthun.
A psalm of David.

1 Truly my soul finds rest in God;
my salvation comes from him.
2 Truly he is my rock and my salvation;
he is my fortress, I will never be
shaken.

3 How long will you assault me?
Would all of you throw me down—
this leaning wall, this tottering
fence?
4 Surely they intend to topple me
from my lofty place;
they take delight in lies.
With their mouths they bless,
but in their hearts they curse. [b]

5 Yes, my soul, find rest in God;
my hope comes from him.
6 Truly he is my rock and my salvation;
he is my fortress, I will not be
shaken.
7 My salvation and my honor depend on
God [c];
he is my mighty rock, my refuge.
8 Trust in him at all times, you people;
pour out your hearts to him,
for God is our refuge.

9 Surely the lowborn are but a breath,
the highborn are but a lie.
If weighed on a balance, they are
nothing;
together they are only a breath.
10 Do not trust in extortion
or put vain hope in stolen goods;
though your riches increase,
do not set your heart on them.

11 One thing God has spoken,
two things I have heard:
"Power belongs to you, God,
12 and with you, Lord, is unfailing
love";
and, "You reward everyone
according to what they have done."

Psalm 62:1–12

Salvation only comes from God.

King David expects to get salvation only from God. Period. Nowhere else. As he writes this song the kind of salvation he needs is a rescue from enemies. They push on him like a tipping fence, using lies and curses to topple him. But David has a reason to trust God. He has hung out with the Lord enough to say, "Power belongs to you, God, and with you, Lord, is unfailing love" (Psalm 62:11–12). If David had confidence God would save him from earthly enemies, we can be even surer that God will give us an even bigger salvation—rescue from sin and a forever home in heaven. The apostle Peter was talking about Jesus when he said, "Salvation is found in no one else, for there is no other name under heaven given to mankind by which we must be saved" (Acts 4:12). We get eternal salvation only from Jesus. Period. Nowhere else.

Think: Do you think your God is the only way to real happiness and a home in heaven? Why—or why not?

ROCK SOLID truths

Psalm 63 [d]

A psalm of David. When he was
in the Desert of Judah.

1 You, God, are my God,
earnestly I seek you;

[a] In Hebrew texts 62:1-12 is numbered 62:2-13.
[b] 4 The Hebrew has *Selah* (a word of uncertain meaning) here and at the end of verse 8.   [c] 7 Or
/ *God Most High is my salvation and my honor*
[d] In Hebrew texts 63:1-11 is numbered 63:2-12.

I thirst for you,
my whole being longs for you,
in a dry and parched land
where there is no water.

2 I have seen you in the sanctuary
and beheld your power and your
glory.
3 Because your love is better than life,
my lips will glorify you.
4 I will praise you as long as I live,
and in your name I will lift up my
hands.
5 I will be fully satisfied as with the
richest of foods;
with singing lips my mouth will
praise you.

6 On my bed I remember you;
I think of you through the watches
of the night.
7 Because you are my help,
I sing in the shadow of your
wings.

8 I cling to you;
your right hand upholds me.

9 Those who want to kill me will be
destroyed;
they will go down to the depths of
the earth.
10 They will be given over to the sword
and become food for jackals.

11 But the king will rejoice in God;
all who swear by God will glory in
him,
while the mouths of liars will be
silenced.

Psalm 64[a]

For the director of music. A psalm of David.

1 Hear me, my God, as I voice my
complaint;
protect my life from the threat of
the enemy.

2 Hide me from the conspiracy of the
wicked,
from the plots of evildoers.
3 They sharpen their tongues like
swords
and aim cruel words like deadly
arrows.
4 They shoot from ambush at the
innocent;
they shoot suddenly, without fear.

5 They encourage each other in evil
plans,
they talk about hiding their snares;
they say, "Who will see it[b]?"
6 They plot injustice and say,
"We have devised a perfect plan!"
Surely the human mind and heart
are cunning.

7 But God will shoot them with his
arrows;
they will suddenly be struck down.
8 He will turn their own tongues
against them
and bring them to ruin;
all who see them will shake their
heads in scorn.

UNSHAKEN God

Psalm 63:2

God is glorious.

God surely wants to be your best friend in all the world—forever. But that doesn't make him your pal, buddy, or peer. In Psalm 63, David glimpses God "in the sanctuary," the Old Testament tabernacle where God promised to be intensely present with his people (see Exodus 29:45). What David spots is God's glory, his bright shining majesty, the weightiness that makes him God. It's tempting to turn the Lord into a mini-god you tuck in your pocket and ignore until you need him. But God wants you to see him glowing in all of his heavenly glory—and be filled with awe.

So … When have you treated God like a peer? How can you give him the awe-filled respect he deserves?

a In Hebrew texts 64:1-10 is numbered 64:2-11.
b 5 Or us

⁹All people will fear;
   they will proclaim the works of God
   and ponder what he has done.

¹⁰The righteous will rejoice in the Lord
   and take refuge in him;
   all the upright in heart will glory in
      him!

Psalm 65ᵃ

For the director of music.
A psalm of David. A song.

¹Praise awaitsᵇ you, our God, in Zion;
   to you our vows will be fulfilled.
²You who answer prayer,
   to you all people will come.
³When we were overwhelmed by sins,
   you forgaveᶜ our transgressions.
⁴Blessed are those you choose
   and bring near to live in your courts!
We are filled with the good things of
      your house,
   of your holy temple.

⁵You answer us with awesome and
      righteous deeds,
   God our Savior,
the hope of all the ends of the earth
   and of the farthest seas,
⁶who formed the mountains by your
      power,
   having armed yourself with
      strength,
⁷who stilled the roaring of the seas,
   the roaring of their waves,
   and the turmoil of the nations.
⁸The whole earth is filled with awe at
      your wonders;
   where morning dawns, where
      evening fades,
   you call forth songs of joy.

⁹You care for the land and water it;
   you enrich it abundantly.
The streams of God are filled with
      water
   to provide the people with grain,
   for so you have ordained it.ᵈ
¹⁰You drench its furrows and level its
      ridges;
   you soften it with showers and bless
      its crops.

¹¹You crown the year with your bounty,
   and your carts overflow with
      abundance.
¹²The grasslands of the wilderness
      overflow;
   the hills are clothed with
      gladness.
¹³The meadows are covered with flocks
   and the valleys are mantled with
      grain;
   they shout for joy and sing.

Psalm 66

For the director of music.
A song. A psalm.

¹Shout for joy to God, all the earth!
²   Sing the glory of his name;
   make his praise glorious.
³Say to God, "How awesome are your
      deeds!
So great is your power
   that your enemies cringe before you.
⁴All the earth bows down to you;
   they sing praise to you,
   they sing the praises of your
      name."ᵉ

⁵Come and see what God has done,
   his awesome deeds for mankind!
⁶He turned the sea into dry land,
   they passed through the waters on
      foot—
   come, let us rejoice in him.
⁷He rules forever by his power,
   his eyes watch the nations—
   let not the rebellious rise up against
      him.

⁸Praise our God, all peoples,
   let the sound of his praise be
      heard;
⁹he has preserved our lives
   and kept our feet from slipping.
¹⁰For you, God, tested us;
   you refined us like silver.

ᵃ In Hebrew texts 65:1-13 is numbered 65:2-14.
ᵇ 1 Or *befits*; the meaning of the Hebrew for
this word is uncertain.   ᶜ 3 Or *made*
atonement for   ᵈ 9 Or *for that is how you*
prepare the land   ᵉ 4 The Hebrew has *Selah* (a
word of uncertain meaning) here and at the end
of verses 7 and 15.

¹¹You brought us into prison
    and laid burdens on our backs.
¹²You let people ride over our heads;
    we went through fire and water,
    but you brought us to a place of
        abundance.

¹³I will come to your temple with burnt
        offerings
    and fulfill my vows to you—
¹⁴vows my lips promised and my mouth
        spoke
    when I was in trouble.

¹⁵I will sacrifice fat animals to you
    and an offering of rams;
    I will offer bulls and goats.

¹⁶Come and hear, all you who fear
        God;
    let me tell you what he has done
        for me.
¹⁷I cried out to him with my mouth;
    his praise was on my tongue.
¹⁸If I had cherished sin in my heart,
    the Lord would not have listened;
¹⁹but God has surely listened
    and has heard my prayer.
²⁰Praise be to God,
    who has not rejected my prayer
    or withheld his love from me!

Psalm 67ᵃ

For the director of music. With stringed
    instruments. A psalm. A song.

¹May God be gracious to us and
        bless us
    and make his face shine on us—ᵇ
²so that your ways may be known on
        earth,
    your salvation among all nations.

³May the peoples praise you, God;
    may all the peoples praise you.
⁴May the nations be glad and sing for
        joy,
    for you rule the peoples with
        equity
    and guide the nations of the earth.
⁵May the peoples praise you, God;
    may all the peoples praise you.

⁶The land yields its harvest;
    God, our God, blesses us.

UNSHAKEN God

Psalm 67:1–7

God is absolute.

Plenty of people picture God as a harsh judge waiting to send people to hell. That caricature misses the Lord's love and compassion, but God truly is the ultimate and absolute judge, the final moral authority. Psalm 9:7–8 says "The LORD reigns forever; he has established his throne for judgment. He rules the world in righteousness and judges the peoples with equity." And Psalm 67 fills out that picture of God as total ruler of the universe. He blesses … shows us the right way to live … sends salvation … makes the world glad … rules justly … and guides every nation on earth. Because God reigns as judge he will one day put an end to every kind of evil. That's a very good thing.

So … God rules as judge of the world. Is that good or bad? Why?

⁷May God bless us still,
    so that all the ends of the earth will
        fear him.

Psalm 68ᶜ

For the director of music.
    Of David. A psalm. A song.

¹May God arise, may his enemies be
        scattered;
    may his foes flee before him.
²May you blow them away like smoke—
    as wax melts before the fire,
    may the wicked perish before God.
³But may the righteous be glad
    and rejoice before God;
    may they be happy and joyful.

ᵃ In Hebrew texts 67:1-7 is numbered 67:2-8.
ᵇ 1 The Hebrew has *Selah* (a word of uncertain meaning) here and at the end of verse 4.   ᶜ In Hebrew texts 68:1-35 is numbered 68:2-36.

⁴Sing to God, sing in praise of his
name,
extol him who rides on the clouds^a;
rejoice before him—his name is the
Lord.
⁵A father to the fatherless, a defender
of widows,
is God in his holy dwelling.
⁶God sets the lonely in families,^b
he leads out the prisoners with
singing;
but the rebellious live in a sun-
scorched land.

⁷When you, God, went out before your
people,
when you marched through the
wilderness,^c
⁸the earth shook, the heavens poured
down rain,
before God, the One of Sinai,
before God, the God of Israel.
⁹You gave abundant showers, O God;
you refreshed your weary
inheritance.
¹⁰Your people settled in it,
and from your bounty, God, you
provided for the poor.

¹¹The Lord announces the word,
and the women who proclaim it are
a mighty throng:
¹²"Kings and armies flee in haste;
the women at home divide the
plunder.
¹³Even while you sleep among the sheep
pens,^d
the wings of my dove are sheathed
with silver,
its feathers with shining gold."
¹⁴When the Almighty^e scattered the
kings in the land,
it was like snow fallen on Mount
Zalmon.

¹⁵Mount Bashan, majestic mountain,
Mount Bashan, rugged mountain,
¹⁶why gaze in envy, you rugged
mountain,
at the mountain where God chooses
to reign,
where the Lord himself will dwell
forever?

¹⁷The chariots of God are tens of
thousands
and thousands of thousands;
the Lord has come from Sinai into
his sanctuary.^f
¹⁸When you ascended on high,
you took many captives;
you received gifts from people,
even from^g the rebellious—
that you,^h Lord God, might dwell
there.

¹⁹Praise be to the Lord, to God our
Savior,
who daily bears our burdens.
²⁰Our God is a God who saves;
from the Sovereign Lord comes
escape from death.
²¹Surely God will crush the heads of his
enemies,
the hairy crowns of those who go
on in their sins.
²²The Lord says, "I will bring them
from Bashan;
I will bring them from the depths
of the sea,
²³that your feet may wade in the blood
of your foes,
while the tongues of your dogs have
their share."

²⁴Your procession, God, has come into
view,
the procession of my God and King
into the sanctuary.
²⁵In front are the singers, after them the
musicians;
with them are the young women
playing the timbrels.
²⁶Praise God in the great
congregation;
praise the Lord in the assembly of
Israel.

^a 4 Or name, / prepare the way for him who rides
through the deserts   ^b 6 Or the desolate in a
homeland   ^c 7 The Hebrew has Selah (a word
of uncertain meaning) here and at the end of
verses 19 and 32.   ^d 13 Or the campfires;
or the saddlebags   ^e 14 Hebrew Shaddai
^f 17 Probable reading of the original Hebrew
text; Masoretic Text Lord is among them at Sinai
in holiness   ^g 18 Or gifts for people, / even
^h 18 Or they

27 There is the little tribe of Benjamin,
leading them,
there the great throng of Judah's
princes,
and there the princes of Zebulun
and of Naphtali.

28 Summon your power, God*a*;
show us your strength, our God, as
you have done before.
29 Because of your temple at
Jerusalem
kings will bring you gifts.
30 Rebuke the beast among the reeds,
the herd of bulls among the calves
of the nations.
Humbled, may the beast bring bars
of silver.
Scatter the nations who delight in
war.
31 Envoys will come from Egypt;
Cush*b* will submit herself to God.

32 Sing to God, you kingdoms of the
earth,
sing praise to the Lord,
33 to him who rides across the highest
heavens, the ancient
heavens,
who thunders with mighty voice.
34 Proclaim the power of God,
whose majesty is over Israel,
whose power is in the heavens.
35 You, God, are awesome in your
sanctuary;
the God of Israel gives power and
strength to his people.

Praise be to God!

Psalm 69*c*

For the director of music. To the
tune of "Lilies." Of David.

1 Save me, O God,
for the waters have come up to
my neck.
2 I sink in the miry depths,
where there is no foothold.
I have come into the deep waters;
the floods engulf me.
3 I am worn out calling for help;
my throat is parched.

My eyes fail,
looking for my God.
4 Those who hate me without reason
outnumber the hairs of my head;
many are my enemies without cause,
those who seek to destroy me.
I am forced to restore
what I did not steal.

5 You, God, know my folly;
my guilt is not hidden from you.

6 Lord, the LORD Almighty,
may those who hope in you
not be disgraced because of me;
God of Israel,
may those who seek you
not be put to shame because of me.
7 For I endure scorn for your sake,
and shame covers my face.
8 I am a foreigner to my own family,
a stranger to my own mother's
children;
9 for zeal for your house consumes me,
and the insults of those who insult
you fall on me.
10 When I weep and fast,
I must endure scorn;
11 when I put on sackcloth,
people make sport of me.
12 Those who sit at the gate mock me,
and I am the song of the
drunkards.

13 But I pray to you, LORD,
in the time of your favor;
in your great love, O God,
answer me with your sure salvation.
14 Rescue me from the mire,
do not let me sink;
deliver me from those who hate me,
from the deep waters.
15 Do not let the floodwaters engulf me
or the depths swallow me up
or the pit close its mouth over me.

16 Answer me, LORD, out of the
goodness of your love;
in your great mercy turn to me.

a 28 Many Hebrew manuscripts, Septuagint and
Syriac; most Hebrew manuscripts *Your God has
summoned power for you* *b 31* That is, the
upper Nile region *c* In Hebrew texts 69:1-36
is numbered 69:2-37.

¹⁷ Do not hide your face from your
    servant;
  answer me quickly, for I am in
    trouble.
¹⁸ Come near and rescue me;
  deliver me because of my foes.

¹⁹ You know how I am scorned,
    disgraced and shamed;
  all my enemies are before you.
²⁰ Scorn has broken my heart
    and has left me helpless;
  I looked for sympathy, but there was
    none,
  for comforters, but I found none.
²¹ They put gall in my food
  and gave me vinegar for my thirst.

²² May the table set before them become
    a snare;
  may it become retribution andᵃ a
    trap.
²³ May their eyes be darkened so they
    cannot see,
  and their backs be bent forever.
²⁴ Pour out your wrath on them;
  let your fierce anger overtake them.
²⁵ May their place be deserted;
  let there be no one to dwell in their
    tents.
²⁶ For they persecute those you wound
  and talk about the pain of those you
    hurt.
²⁷ Charge them with crime upon crime;
  do not let them share in your
    salvation.
²⁸ May they be blotted out of the book of
    life
  and not be listed with the righteous.

²⁹ But as for me, afflicted and in pain—
  may your salvation, God, protect
    me.

³⁰ I will praise God's name in song
  and glorify him with thanksgiving.
³¹ This will please the LORD more than
    an ox,
  more than a bull with its horns and
    hooves.
³² The poor will see and be glad—
  you who seek God, may your hearts
    live!

³³ The LORD hears the needy
  and does not despise his captive
    people.
³⁴ Let heaven and earth praise him,
  the seas and all that move in them,
³⁵ for God will save Zion
  and rebuild the cities of Judah.
Then people will settle there and
    possess it;
³⁶ the children of his servants will
    inherit it,
  and those who love his name will
    dwell there.

Psalm 70ᵇ

For the director of music. Of David.
A petition.

¹ Hasten, O God, to save me;
  come quickly, LORD, to help me.

² May those who want to take my life
  be put to shame and confusion;
may all who desire my ruin
  be turned back in disgrace.
³ May those who say to me, "Aha! Aha!"
  turn back because of their shame.
⁴ But may all who seek you
  rejoice and be glad in you;
may those who long for your saving
    help always say,
  "The LORD is great!"

⁵ But as for me, I am poor and needy;
  come quickly to me, O God.
You are my help and my deliverer;
  LORD, do not delay.

Psalm 71

¹ In you, LORD, I have taken refuge;
  let me never be put to shame.
² In your righteousness, rescue me and
    deliver me;
  turn your ear to me and save me.
³ Be my rock of refuge,
  to which I can always go;
give the command to save me,
  for you are my rock and my
    fortress.

ᵃ 22 Or snare / and their fellowship become   ᵇ In
Hebrew texts 70:1-5 is numbered 70:2-6.

⁴Deliver me, my God, from the hand
    of the wicked,
    from the grasp of those who are evil
    and cruel.
⁵For you have been my hope, Sovereign
    Lord,
    my confidence since my youth.

ROCK SOLID
promises

**"You have been my hope, Sovereign
Lord, my confidence since my
youth."**   Psalm 71:5

**God deserves your entire life, starting
now and reaching to the day he takes you
home to heaven.**

⁶From birth I have relied on you;
    you brought me forth from my
    mother's womb.
    I will ever praise you.
⁷I have become a sign to many;
    you are my strong refuge.
⁸My mouth is filled with your praise,
    declaring your splendor all day
    long.

⁹Do not cast me away when I am old;
    do not forsake me when my
    strength is gone.
¹⁰For my enemies speak against me;
    those who wait to kill me conspire
    together.
¹¹They say, "God has forsaken him;
    pursue him and seize him,
    for no one will rescue him."
¹²Do not be far from me, my God;
    come quickly, God, to help me.
¹³May my accusers perish in shame;
    may those who want to harm me
    be covered with scorn and disgrace.

¹⁴As for me, I will always have hope;
    I will praise you more and more.

¹⁵My mouth will tell of your righteous
    deeds,
    of your saving acts all day long—
    though I know not how to relate
    them all.
¹⁶I will come and proclaim your mighty
    acts, Sovereign Lord;
    I will proclaim your righteous
    deeds, yours alone.
¹⁷Since my youth, God, you have taught
    me,
    and to this day I declare your
    marvelous deeds.
¹⁸Even when I am old and gray,
    do not forsake me, my God,
    till I declare your power to the next
    generation,
    your mighty acts to all who are to
    come.

¹⁹Your righteousness, God, reaches to
    the heavens,
    you who have done great things.
    Who is like you, God?
²⁰Though you have made me see
    troubles,
    many and bitter,
    you will restore my life again;
    from the depths of the earth
    you will again bring me up.
²¹You will increase my honor
    and comfort me once more.

²²I will praise you with the harp
    for your faithfulness, my God;
    I will sing praise to you with the lyre,
    Holy One of Israel.
²³My lips will shout for joy
    when I sing praise to you—
    I whom you have delivered.
²⁴My tongue will tell of your righteous
    acts
    all day long,
    for those who wanted to harm me
    have been put to shame and confusion.

Psalm 72

Of Solomon.

¹Endow the king with your justice,
    O God,
    the royal son with your righteousness.

²May he judge your people in
  righteousness,
    your afflicted ones with justice.

³May the mountains bring prosperity
  to the people,
    the hills the fruit of righteousness.
⁴May he defend the afflicted among
  the people
    and save the children of the needy;
    may he crush the oppressor.
⁵May he endure*a* as long as the sun,
  as long as the moon, through all
  generations.
⁶May he be like rain falling on a mown
  field,
    like showers watering the earth.
⁷In his days may the righteous flourish
  and prosperity abound till the moon
  is no more.

⁸May he rule from sea to sea
  and from the River*b* to the ends of
  the earth.
⁹May the desert tribes bow before him
  and his enemies lick the dust.
¹⁰May the kings of Tarshish and of
  distant shores
    bring tribute to him.
  May the kings of Sheba and Seba
    present him gifts.
¹¹May all kings bow down to him
  and all nations serve him.

¹²For he will deliver the needy who cry
  out,
    the afflicted who have no one to
    help.
¹³He will take pity on the weak and the
  needy
    and save the needy from death.
¹⁴He will rescue them from oppression
  and violence,
    for precious is their blood in his
    sight.

¹⁵Long may he live!
  May gold from Sheba be given him.
  May people ever pray for him
  and bless him all day long.
¹⁶May grain abound throughout the
  land;
    on the tops of the hills may it sway.

May the crops flourish like Lebanon
  and thrive*c* like the grass of the
  field.
¹⁷May his name endure forever;
  may it continue as long as the sun.

Then all nations will be blessed
  through him,*d*
    and they will call him blessed.

¹⁸Praise be to the Lᴏʀᴅ God, the God
  of Israel,
    who alone does marvelous deeds.
¹⁹Praise be to his glorious name
  forever;
    may the whole earth be filled with
    his glory.
      Amen and Amen.

²⁰This concludes the prayers of David
  son of Jesse.

BOOK III

Psalms 73–89

Psalm 73

A psalm of Asaph.

¹Surely God is good to Israel,
  to those who are pure in heart.

²But as for me, my feet had almost
  slipped;
    I had nearly lost my foothold.
³For I envied the arrogant
  when I saw the prosperity of the
  wicked.

⁴They have no struggles;
  their bodies are healthy and
  strong.*e*
⁵They are free from common human
  burdens;
    they are not plagued by human ills.

---

a 5 Septuagint; Hebrew *You will be feared*
b 8 That is, the Euphrates   *c 16* Probable
reading of the original Hebrew text; Masoretic
Text *Lebanon, / from the city*   *d 17* Or *will use
his name in blessings* (see Gen. 48:20)
e 4 With a different word division of the
Hebrew; Masoretic Text *struggles at their death; /
their bodies are healthy*

⁶Therefore pride is their necklace;
  they clothe themselves with
    violence.
⁷From their callous hearts comes
    iniquity*ᵃ*;
  their evil imaginations have no
    limits.
⁸They scoff, and speak with malice;
  with arrogance they threaten
    oppression.
⁹Their mouths lay claim to heaven,
  and their tongues take possession of
    the earth.
¹⁰Therefore their people turn to them
  and drink up waters in abundance.*ᵇ*
¹¹They say, "How would God know?
  Does the Most High know
    anything?"

¹²This is what the wicked are like—
  always free of care, they go on
    amassing wealth.

¹³Surely in vain I have kept my heart
    pure
  and have washed my hands in
    innocence.
¹⁴All day long I have been afflicted,
  and every morning brings new
    punishments.

¹⁵If I had spoken out like that,
  I would have betrayed your
    children.
¹⁶When I tried to understand all this,
  it troubled me deeply
¹⁷till I entered the sanctuary of God;
  then I understood their final
    destiny.

¹⁸Surely you place them on slippery
    ground;
  you cast them down to ruin.
¹⁹How suddenly are they destroyed,
  completely swept away by terrors!
²⁰They are like a dream when one
    awakes;
  when you arise, Lord,
  you will despise them as fantasies.

²¹When my heart was grieved
  and my spirit embittered,
²²I was senseless and ignorant;
  I was a brute beast before you.

²³Yet I am always with you;
  you hold me by my right hand.
²⁴You guide me with your counsel,
  and afterward you will take me into
    glory.
²⁵Whom have I in heaven but you?
  And earth has nothing I desire
    besides you.
²⁶My flesh and my heart may fail,
  but God is the strength of my heart
  and my portion forever.

ᵃ 7 Syriac (see also Septuagint); Hebrew *Their eyes bulge with fat*   *ᵇ 10* The meaning of the Hebrew for this verse is uncertain.

Psalm 73:1–28

Those who do evil ultimately lose.

The author of this song admits that his faith in God nearly crashed and burned. Asaph was just minding his own business when he noticed that wicked people prosper. They never struggle. They enjoy an easy life. And their endless stream of successes means they sport pride as a necklace and wear violence like comfy old jeans. Asaph wondered if he should turn against God and do evil, especially when God seemed to be doing nothing to halt sin. But then this good man begins to understand what God has in store for evildoers. He sets them on slippery spots, so sooner or later the wicked slide to ruin. In the end Asaph concludes he doesn't have to get upset about evil people. God has a firm grip with his hand. And the Lord is all Asaph needs.

Think: How do you feel when you see bad people succeed? What do you do about it?

ROCK SOLID truths

²⁷ Those who are far from you will
   perish;
   you destroy all who are unfaithful
   to you.
²⁸ But as for me, it is good to be near
   God.
   I have made the Sovereign LORD
   my refuge;
   I will tell of all your deeds.

Psalm 74

A *maskil*^a of Asaph.

¹ O God, why have you rejected us
   forever?
   Why does your anger smolder
   against the sheep of your
   pasture?
² Remember the nation you purchased
   long ago,
   the people of your inheritance,
   whom you redeemed—
   Mount Zion, where you dwelt.
³ Turn your steps toward these
   everlasting ruins,
   all this destruction the enemy has
   brought on the sanctuary.
⁴ Your foes roared in the place where
   you met with us;
   they set up their standards as signs.
⁵ They behaved like men wielding axes
   to cut through a thicket of trees.
⁶ They smashed all the carved paneling
   with their axes and hatchets.
⁷ They burned your sanctuary to the
   ground;
   they defiled the dwelling place of
   your Name.
⁸ They said in their hearts, "We will
   crush them completely!"
   They burned every place where God
   was worshiped in the land.

⁹ We are given no signs from God;
   no prophets are left,
   and none of us knows how long this
   will be.
¹⁰ How long will the enemy mock you,
   God?
   Will the foe revile your name
   forever?

¹¹ Why do you hold back your hand,
   your right hand?
   Take it from the folds of your
   garment and destroy them!

¹² But God is my King from long ago;
   he brings salvation on the earth.

¹³ It was you who split open the sea by
   your power;
   you broke the heads of the monster
   in the waters.
¹⁴ It was you who crushed the heads of
   Leviathan
   and gave it as food to the creatures
   of the desert.
¹⁵ It was you who opened up springs and
   streams;
   you dried up the ever-flowing
   rivers.
¹⁶ The day is yours, and yours also the
   night;
   you established the sun and moon.
¹⁷ It was you who set all the boundaries
   of the earth;
   you made both summer and
   winter.

¹⁸ Remember how the enemy has
   mocked you, LORD,
   how foolish people have reviled
   your name.
¹⁹ Do not hand over the life of your dove
   to wild beasts;
   do not forget the lives of your
   afflicted people forever.
²⁰ Have regard for your covenant,
   because haunts of violence fill the
   dark places of the land.
²¹ Do not let the oppressed retreat in
   disgrace;
   may the poor and needy praise your
   name.
²² Rise up, O God, and defend your
   cause;
   remember how fools mock you all
   day long.
²³ Do not ignore the clamor of your
   adversaries,
   the uproar of your enemies, which
   rises continually.

^a Title: Probably a literary or musical term

Psalm 75[a]

For the director of music. To the tune of "Do Not Destroy." A psalm of Asaph. A song.

[1] We praise you, God,
    we praise you, for your Name is
       near;
    people tell of your wonderful deeds.

[2] You say, "I choose the appointed time;
    it is I who judge with equity.
[3] When the earth and all its people
       quake,
    it is I who hold its pillars firm.[b]
[4] To the arrogant I say, 'Boast no more,'
    and to the wicked, 'Do not lift up
       your horns.[c]
[5] Do not lift your horns against
       heaven;
    do not speak so defiantly.'"

[6] No one from the east or the west
    or from the desert can exalt
       themselves.
[7] It is God who judges:
    He brings one down, he exalts
       another.
[8] In the hand of the LORD is a cup
    full of foaming wine mixed with
       spices;
    he pours it out, and all the wicked of
       the earth
    drink it down to its very dregs.

[9] As for me, I will declare this forever;
    I will sing praise to the God of
       Jacob,
[10] who says, "I will cut off the horns of
       all the wicked,
    but the horns of the righteous will
       be lifted up."

Psalm 76[d]

For the director of music. With stringed instruments. A psalm of Asaph. A song.

[1] God is renowned in Judah;
    in Israel his name is great.
[2] His tent is in Salem,
    his dwelling place in Zion.
[3] There he broke the flashing arrows,
    the shields and the swords, the
       weapons of war.[e]

[4] You are radiant with light,
    more majestic than mountains rich
       with game.
[5] The valiant lie plundered,
    they sleep their last sleep;
    not one of the warriors
    can lift his hands.
[6] At your rebuke, God of Jacob,
    both horse and chariot lie still.

[7] It is you alone who are to be feared.
    Who can stand before you when
       you are angry?
[8] From heaven you pronounced
       judgment,
    and the land feared and was quiet—
[9] when you, God, rose up to judge,
    to save all the afflicted of the land.
[10] Surely your wrath against mankind
       brings you praise,
    and the survivors of your wrath are
       restrained.[f]

[11] Make vows to the LORD your God
    and fulfill them;
    let all the neighboring lands
    bring gifts to the One to be feared.
[12] He breaks the spirit of rulers;
    he is feared by the kings of the
       earth.

Psalm 77[g]

For the director of music. For Jeduthun. Of Asaph. A psalm.

[1] I cried out to God for help;
    I cried out to God to hear me.
[2] When I was in distress, I sought the
       Lord;
    at night I stretched out untiring
       hands,
    and I would not be comforted.

[a] In Hebrew texts 75:1-10 is numbered 75:2-11.
[b] 3 The Hebrew has *Selah* (a word of uncertain meaning) here.   [c] 4 *Horns* here symbolize strength; also in verses 5 and 10.   [d] In Hebrew texts 76:1-12 is numbered 76:2-13.
[e] 3 The Hebrew has *Selah* (a word of uncertain meaning) here and at the end of verse 9.
[f] 10 Or *Surely the wrath of mankind brings you praise, / and with the remainder of wrath you arm yourself*   [g] In Hebrew texts 77:1-20 is numbered 77:2-21.

³I remembered you, God, and I
  groaned;
  I meditated, and my spirit grew faint.ᵃ
⁴You kept my eyes from closing;
  I was too troubled to speak.
⁵I thought about the former days,
  the years of long ago;
⁶I remembered my songs in the night.
  My heart meditated and my spirit
    asked:

⁷"Will the Lord reject forever?
  Will he never show his favor again?
⁸Has his unfailing love vanished
    forever?
  Has his promise failed for all time?
⁹Has God forgotten to be merciful?
  Has he in anger withheld his
    compassion?"

¹⁰Then I thought, "To this I will appeal:
  the years when the Most High
    stretched out his right hand.
¹¹I will remember the deeds of the Lᴏʀᴅ;
  yes, I will remember your miracles
    of long ago.
¹²I will consider all your works
  and meditate on all your mighty
    deeds."

¹³Your ways, God, are holy.
  What god is as great as our God?
¹⁴You are the God who performs miracles;
  you display your power among the
    peoples.

ROCK SOLID
promises

**"You are the God who performs
miracles; you display your power
among the peoples."** Psalm 77:14

**God does astonishing acts beyond human
understanding. He does extraordinary
deeds so everyone can see he is God.**

¹⁵With your mighty arm you redeemed
    your people,
  the descendants of Jacob and Joseph.

¹⁶The waters saw you, God,
  the waters saw you and writhed;
  the very depths were convulsed.
¹⁷The clouds poured down water,
  the heavens resounded with
    thunder;
  your arrows flashed back and forth.
¹⁸Your thunder was heard in the
    whirlwind,
  your lightning lit up the world;
  the earth trembled and quaked.
¹⁹Your path led through the sea,
  your way through the mighty
    waters,
  though your footprints were not
    seen.

²⁰You led your people like a flock
  by the hand of Moses and Aaron.

Psalm 78

A *maskil*ᵇ of Asaph.

¹My people, hear my teaching;
  listen to the words of my mouth.
²I will open my mouth with a parable;
  I will utter hidden things, things
    from of old—
³things we have heard and known,
  things our ancestors have told us.
⁴We will not hide them from their
    descendants;
  we will tell the next generation
  the praiseworthy deeds of the Lᴏʀᴅ,
    his power, and the wonders he has
      done.
⁵He decreed statutes for Jacob
  and established the law in Israel,
  which he commanded our ancestors
    to teach their children,
⁶so the next generation would know
    them,
  even the children yet to be born,
  and they in turn would tell their
    children.

ᵃ 3 The Hebrew has *Selah* (a word of uncertain
meaning) here and at the end of verses 9 and 15.
ᵇ Title: Probably a literary or musical term

⁷Then they would put their trust in God
and would not forget his deeds
but would keep his commands.
⁸They would not be like their
ancestors—
a stubborn and rebellious
generation,
whose hearts were not loyal to God,
whose spirits were not faithful to him.

⁹The men of Ephraim, though armed
with bows,
turned back on the day of battle;
¹⁰they did not keep God's covenant
and refused to live by his law.
¹¹They forgot what he had done,
the wonders he had shown them.
¹²He did miracles in the sight of their
ancestors
in the land of Egypt, in the region
of Zoan.
¹³He divided the sea and led them
through;
he made the water stand up like a
wall.
¹⁴He guided them with the cloud by day
and with light from the fire all
night.
¹⁵He split the rocks in the wilderness
and gave them water as abundant as
the seas;
¹⁶he brought streams out of a rocky crag
and made water flow down like
rivers.

¹⁷But they continued to sin against him,
rebelling in the wilderness against
the Most High.
¹⁸They willfully put God to the test
by demanding the food they craved.
¹⁹They spoke against God;
they said, "Can God really
spread a table in the wilderness?
²⁰True, he struck the rock,
and water gushed out,
streams flowed abundantly,
but can he also give us bread?
Can he supply meat for his people?"
²¹When the LORD heard them, he was
furious;
his fire broke out against Jacob,
and his wrath rose against Israel,

²²for they did not believe in God
or trust in his deliverance.
²³Yet he gave a command to the skies
above
and opened the doors of the
heavens;
²⁴he rained down manna for the people
to eat,
he gave them the grain of heaven.
²⁵Human beings ate the bread of
angels;
he sent them all the food they could
eat.
²⁶He let loose the east wind from the
heavens
and by his power made the south
wind blow.
²⁷He rained meat down on them like
dust,
birds like sand on the seashore.
²⁸He made them come down inside
their camp,
all around their tents.
²⁹They ate till they were gorged—
he had given them what they
craved.
³⁰But before they turned from what they
craved,
even while the food was still in
their mouths,
³¹God's anger rose against them;
he put to death the sturdiest among
them,
cutting down the young men of
Israel.

³²In spite of all this, they kept on
sinning;
in spite of his wonders, they did not
believe.
³³So he ended their days in futility
and their years in terror.
³⁴Whenever God slew them, they would
seek him;
they eagerly turned to him again.
³⁵They remembered that God was their
Rock,
that God Most High was their
Redeemer.
³⁶But then they would flatter him with
their mouths,
lying to him with their tongues;

³⁷ their hearts were not loyal to him,
    they were not faithful to his covenant.
³⁸ Yet he was merciful;
    he forgave their iniquities
    and did not destroy them.
  Time after time he restrained his anger
    and did not stir up his full wrath.
³⁹ He remembered that they were but
    flesh,
    a passing breeze that does not return.

⁴⁰ How often they rebelled against him
    in the wilderness
    and grieved him in the wasteland!
⁴¹ Again and again they put God to the
    test;
    they vexed the Holy One of Israel.
⁴² They did not remember his power—
    the day he redeemed them from the
    oppressor,
⁴³ the day he displayed his signs in
    Egypt,
    his wonders in the region of Zoan.
⁴⁴ He turned their river into blood;
    they could not drink from their
    streams.
⁴⁵ He sent swarms of flies that devoured
    them,
    and frogs that devastated them.
⁴⁶ He gave their crops to the
    grasshopper,
    their produce to the locust.
⁴⁷ He destroyed their vines with hail
    and their sycamore-figs with sleet.
⁴⁸ He gave over their cattle to the hail,
    their livestock to bolts of lightning.
⁴⁹ He unleashed against them his hot
    anger,
    his wrath, indignation and
    hostility—
    a band of destroying angels.
⁵⁰ He prepared a path for his anger;
    he did not spare them from death
    but gave them over to the plague.
⁵¹ He struck down all the firstborn of
    Egypt,
    the firstfruits of manhood in the
    tents of Ham.
⁵² But he brought his people out like a
    flock;
    he led them like sheep through the
    wilderness.

⁵³ He guided them safely, so they were
    unafraid;
    but the sea engulfed their enemies.
⁵⁴ And so he brought them to the border
    of his holy land,
    to the hill country his right hand
    had taken.
⁵⁵ He drove out nations before them
    and allotted their lands to them as
    an inheritance;
    he settled the tribes of Israel in
    their homes.

⁵⁶ But they put God to the test
    and rebelled against the Most
    High;
    they did not keep his statutes.
⁵⁷ Like their ancestors they were disloyal
    and faithless,
    as unreliable as a faulty bow.
⁵⁸ They angered him with their high
    places;
    they aroused his jealousy with their
    idols.
⁵⁹ When God heard them, he was
    furious;
    he rejected Israel completely.
⁶⁰ He abandoned the tabernacle of
    Shiloh,
    the tent he had set up among
    humans.
⁶¹ He sent the ark of his might into
    captivity,
    his splendor into the hands of the
    enemy.
⁶² He gave his people over to the
    sword;
    he was furious with his inheritance.
⁶³ Fire consumed their young men,
    and their young women had no
    wedding songs;
⁶⁴ their priests were put to the sword,
    and their widows could not weep.

⁶⁵ Then the Lord awoke as from sleep,
    as a warrior wakes from the stupor
    of wine.
⁶⁶ He beat back his enemies;
    he put them to everlasting shame.
⁶⁷ Then he rejected the tents of Joseph,
    he did not choose the tribe of
    Ephraim;

ROCK SOLID *principles*

Psalm 78:1–72

Remember God's acts.

It felt like a birthday, and Gabriel wasn't sure why. His mom made him save the night for a family supper, his sister cooked his favorite foods, and his dad had a stack of family videos piled next to his spot at the dinner table. "I'm sure you don't remember why this date is important, Gabe," his dad started. "But ten years ago today you had your last heart surgery. For the first five years of your life, we weren't sure if you were going to live or die. But we know God finally healed you through the doctors that day. Tonight we want to celebrate you and remember God's faithfulness."

Psalm 78 is like a family video so old you remember the video more than the actual moment. You might not track with all the details in this psalm, but that's the whole point. This song and all the Bible's historical accounts are reminders of God's mighty acts. Read them again and again to help you remember his deeds and keep his commands (see Psalm 78:7).

⁶⁸but he chose the tribe of Judah,
    Mount Zion, which he loved.
⁶⁹He built his sanctuary like the heights,
    like the earth that he established
        forever.
⁷⁰He chose David his servant
    and took him from the sheep pens;
⁷¹from tending the sheep he brought
        him
    to be the shepherd of his people
        Jacob,
    of Israel his inheritance.
⁷²And David shepherded them with
        integrity of heart;
    with skillful hands he led them.

Psalm 79

A psalm of Asaph.

¹O God, the nations have invaded your
        inheritance;
    they have defiled your holy temple,
    they have reduced Jerusalem to
        rubble.
²They have left the dead bodies of your
        servants
    as food for the birds of the sky,
    the flesh of your own people for the
        animals of the wild.
³They have poured out blood like water
    all around Jerusalem,
    and there is no one to bury the
        dead.
⁴We are objects of contempt to our
        neighbors,
    of scorn and derision to those
        around us.

⁵How long, Lord? Will you be angry
        forever?
    How long will your jealousy burn
        like fire?
⁶Pour out your wrath on the nations
    that do not acknowledge you,
    on the kingdoms
    that do not call on your name;
⁷for they have devoured Jacob
    and devastated his homeland.

693

⁸Do not hold against us the sins of past
generations;
    may your mercy come quickly to
meet us,
    for we are in desperate need.
⁹Help us, God our Savior,
    for the glory of your name;
deliver us and forgive our sins
    for your name's sake.
¹⁰Why should the nations say,
    "Where is their God?"

Before our eyes, make known among
the nations
    that you avenge the outpoured
blood of your servants.
¹¹May the groans of the prisoners come
before you;
    with your strong arm preserve those
condemned to die.
¹²Pay back into the laps of our neighbors
seven times
    the contempt they have hurled at
you, Lord.
¹³Then we your people, the sheep of
your pasture,
    will praise you forever;
from generation to generation
    we will proclaim your praise.

Psalm 80[a]

For the director of music. To the
tune of "The Lilies of the Covenant."
Of Asaph. A psalm.

¹Hear us, Shepherd of Israel,
    you who lead Joseph like a flock.
You who sit enthroned between the
cherubim,
    shine forth ²before Ephraim,
Benjamin and Manasseh.
Awaken your might;
    come and save us.

³Restore us, O God;
    make your face shine on us,
    that we may be saved.

⁴How long, Lord God Almighty,
    will your anger smolder
    against the prayers of your people?
⁵You have fed them with the bread of
tears;

you have made them drink tears by
the bowlful.
⁶You have made us an object of
derision[b] to our neighbors,
    and our enemies mock us.

⁷Restore us, God Almighty;
    make your face shine on us,
    that we may be saved.

⁸You transplanted a vine from Egypt;
    you drove out the nations and
planted it.
⁹You cleared the ground for it,
    and it took root and filled the land.
¹⁰The mountains were covered with its
shade,
    the mighty cedars with its branches.
¹¹Its branches reached as far as the Sea,[c]
    its shoots as far as the River.[d]

¹²Why have you broken down its walls
    so that all who pass by pick its
grapes?
¹³Boars from the forest ravage it,
    and insects from the fields feed
on it.
¹⁴Return to us, God Almighty!
    Look down from heaven and see!
Watch over this vine,
¹⁵   the root your right hand has
planted,
    the son[e] you have raised up for
yourself.

¹⁶Your vine is cut down, it is burned
with fire;
    at your rebuke your people perish.
¹⁷Let your hand rest on the man at your
right hand,
    the son of man you have raised up
for yourself.
¹⁸Then we will not turn away from you;
    revive us, and we will call on your
name.

¹⁹Restore us, Lord God Almighty;
    make your face shine on us,
    that we may be saved.

a In Hebrew texts 80:1-19 is numbered 80:2-20.
b 6 Probable reading of the original Hebrew
text; Masoretic Text *contention*   *c* 11 Probably
the Mediterranean   *d* 11 That is, the
Euphrates   *e* 15 Or *branch*

Psalm 81[a]

For the director of music. According to *gittith*.[b] Of Asaph.

1 Sing for joy to God our strength;
   shout aloud to the God of Jacob!
2 Begin the music, strike the timbrel,
   play the melodious harp and lyre.

3 Sound the ram's horn at the New Moon,
   and when the moon is full, on the
      day of our festival;
4 this is a decree for Israel,
   an ordinance of the God of Jacob.
5 When God went out against Egypt,
   he established it as a statute for
      Joseph.

I heard an unknown voice say:

6 "I removed the burden from their
      shoulders;
   their hands were set free from the
      basket.
7 In your distress you called and I
      rescued you,
   I answered you out of a
      thundercloud;
   I tested you at the waters of
      Meribah.[c]
8 Hear me, my people, and I will warn
      you—
   if you would only listen to me,
      Israel!
9 You shall have no foreign god among
      you;
   you shall not worship any god other
      than me.
10 I am the LORD your God,
   who brought you up out of Egypt.
   Open wide your mouth and I will fill it.

11 "But my people would not listen to me;
   Israel would not submit to me.
12 So I gave them over to their stubborn
      hearts
   to follow their own devices.

13 "If my people would only listen to me,
   if Israel would only follow my ways,
14 how quickly I would subdue their
      enemies
   and turn my hand against their
      foes!

ROCK SOLID *promises*

"I am the LORD your God, who brought you up out of Egypt. Open wide your mouth and I will fill it."

Psalm 81:10

God didn't rescue his people from slavery in Egypt to make them miserable. And God saves you to lead you to his good life.

---

15 Those who hate the LORD would
      cringe before him,
   and their punishment would last
      forever.
16 But you would be fed with the finest
      of wheat;
   with honey from the rock I would
      satisfy you."

Psalm 82

A psalm of Asaph.

1 God presides in the great assembly;
   he renders judgment among the
      "gods":

2 "How long will you[d] defend the unjust
   and show partiality to the wicked?[c]
3 Defend the weak and the fatherless;
   uphold the cause of the poor and
      the oppressed.
4 Rescue the weak and the needy;
   deliver them from the hand of the
      wicked.

5 "The 'gods' know nothing, they
      understand nothing.
   They walk about in darkness;
   all the foundations of the earth are
      shaken.

[a] In Hebrew texts 81:1-16 is numbered 81:2-17.
[b] Title: Probably a musical term   [c] 7,2 The
Hebrew has *Selah* (a word of uncertain meaning)
here.   [d] 2 The Hebrew is plural.

⁶"I said, 'You are "gods";
  you are all sons of the Most High.'
⁷But you will die like mere mortals;
  you will fall like every other ruler."

⁸Rise up, O God, judge the earth,
  for all the nations are your
    inheritance.

Psalm 83^a

A song. A psalm of Asaph.

¹O God, do not remain silent;
  do not turn a deaf ear,
  do not stand aloof, O God.
²See how your enemies growl,
  how your foes rear their heads.
³With cunning they conspire against
    your people;
  they plot against those you cherish.
⁴"Come," they say, "let us destroy them
    as a nation,
  so that Israel's name is remembered
    no more."

⁵With one mind they plot together;
  they form an alliance against you—
⁶the tents of Edom and the Ishmaelites,
  of Moab and the Hagrites,
⁷Byblos, Ammon and Amalek,
  Philistia, with the people of Tyre.
⁸Even Assyria has joined them
  to reinforce Lot's descendants.^b

⁹Do to them as you did to Midian,
  as you did to Sisera and Jabin at the
    river Kishon,
¹⁰who perished at Endor
  and became like dung on the
    ground.
¹¹Make their nobles like Oreb and Zeeb,
  all their princes like Zebah and
    Zalmunna,
¹²who said, "Let us take possession
  of the pasturelands of God."

¹³Make them like tumbleweed, my God,
  like chaff before the wind.
¹⁴As fire consumes the forest
  or a flame sets the mountains
    ablaze,
¹⁵so pursue them with your tempest
  and terrify them with your storm.

¹⁶Cover their faces with shame, Lord,
  so that they will seek your name.

¹⁷May they ever be ashamed and
    dismayed;
  may they perish in disgrace.
¹⁸Let them know that you, whose name
    is the Lord—
  that you alone are the Most High
    over all the earth.

Psalm 84^c

For the director of music.
According to *gittith*.^d Of the Sons
of Korah. A psalm.

¹How lovely is your dwelling place,
  Lord Almighty!
²My soul yearns, even faints,
  for the courts of the Lord;
my heart and my flesh cry out
  for the living God.
³Even the sparrow has found a home,
  and the swallow a nest for herself,
  where she may have her young—
a place near your altar,
  Lord Almighty, my King and my
    God.
⁴Blessed are those who dwell in your
    house;
  they are ever praising you.^e

⁵Blessed are those whose strength is in
    you,
  whose hearts are set on pilgrimage.
⁶As they pass through the Valley of
    Baka,
  they make it a place of springs;
  the autumn rains also cover it with
    pools.^f
⁷They go from strength to strength,
  till each appears before God in Zion.

⁸Hear my prayer, Lord God
    Almighty;
  listen to me, God of Jacob.

---

^a In Hebrew texts 83:1-18 is numbered 83:2-19.
^b 8 The Hebrew has *Selah* (a word of uncertain
meaning) here.   ^c In Hebrew texts 84:1-12 is
numbered 84:2-13.   ^d Title: Probably a
musical term   ^e 4 The Hebrew has *Selah* (a
word of uncertain meaning) here and at the end
of verse 8.   ^f 6 Or *blessings*

⁹Look on our shield,ᵃ O God;
　look with favor on your anointed one.

¹⁰Better is one day in your courts
　than a thousand elsewhere;
I would rather be a doorkeeper in the
　house of my God
　than dwell in the tents of the
　wicked.
¹¹For the Lᴏʀᴅ God is a sun and shield;
　the Lᴏʀᴅ bestows favor and honor;
no good thing does he withhold
　from those whose walk is blameless.
¹²Lᴏʀᴅ Almighty,
　blessed is the one who trusts in you.

Psalm 84:1 – 12

Living for God is always better than sinning.

The top of Psalm 84 credits the song to the sons of Korah, a group of men in the family occupation of guarding the gates of the temple (see 1 Chronicles 26:1) and leading "the music in the house of the Lᴏʀᴅ" (1 Chronicles 6:31 and 37). These guys knew the temple. They understood worship. And they decided that being close to God was the best place they could ever be. Check out their reasoning: The temple courts are beautiful … God's altar is a safe shelter … even the desert trek to worship in Jerusalem gushes with refreshing springs … and life with God is so good that they would rather stand at the temple door than live close to evildoers. That's an astonishing image. Being near to the Lord is always better than sin.

Think: Be honest. Is living for God better than doing wrong? Why — or why not?

ROCK SOLID truths

Psalm 85ᵇ

For the director of music. Of the Sons
　of Korah. A psalm.

¹You, Lᴏʀᴅ, showed favor to your land;
　you restored the fortunes of Jacob.
²You forgave the iniquity of your
　people
　and covered all their sins.ᶜ
³You set aside all your wrath
　and turned from your fierce anger.

⁴Restore us again, God our Savior,
　and put away your displeasure
　　toward us.
⁵Will you be angry with us forever?
　Will you prolong your anger
　　through all generations?
⁶Will you not revive us again,
　that your people may rejoice in you?
⁷Show us your unfailing love, Lᴏʀᴅ,
　and grant us your salvation.

⁸I will listen to what God the Lᴏʀᴅ
　says;
　he promises peace to his people, his
　　faithful servants —
　but let them not turn to folly.
⁹Surely his salvation is near those who
　fear him,
　that his glory may dwell in our land.

¹⁰Love and faithfulness meet together;
　righteousness and peace kiss each
　　other.
¹¹Faithfulness springs forth from the
　earth,
　and righteousness looks down from
　　heaven.
¹²The Lᴏʀᴅ will indeed give what is
　good,
　and our land will yield its harvest.
¹³Righteousness goes before him
　and prepares the way for his steps.

Psalm 86

A prayer of David.

¹Hear me, Lᴏʀᴅ, and answer me,
　for I am poor and needy.

ᵃ 9 Or *sovereign*　ᵇ In Hebrew texts 85:1-13
is numbered 85:2-14.　ᶜ 2 The Hebrew has
Selah (a word of uncertain meaning) here.

²Guard my life, for I am faithful to
  you;
    save your servant who trusts in you.
  You are my God; ³have mercy on me,
    Lord,
      for I call to you all day long.
⁴Bring joy to your servant, Lord,
  for I put my trust in you.

⁵You, Lord, are forgiving and good,
  abounding in love to all who call to
    you.
⁶Hear my prayer, Lord;
  listen to my cry for mercy.
⁷When I am in distress, I call to you,
  because you answer me.

⁸Among the gods there is none like
  you, Lord;
    no deeds can compare with yours.
⁹All the nations you have made
  will come and worship before you,
    Lord;
      they will bring glory to your name.
¹⁰For you are great and do marvelous
  deeds;
    you alone are God.

¹¹Teach me your way, Lord,
  that I may rely on your faithfulness;
    give me an undivided heart,
      that I may fear your name.
¹²I will praise you, Lord my God, with
  all my heart;
    I will glorify your name forever.
¹³For great is your love toward me;
  you have delivered me from the
    depths,
      from the realm of the dead.

¹⁴Arrogant foes are attacking me, O God;
  ruthless people are trying to kill
    me—
      they have no regard for you.
¹⁵But you, Lord, are a compassionate
  and gracious God,
    slow to anger, abounding in love
      and faithfulness.
¹⁶Turn to me and have mercy on me;
  show your strength in behalf of
    your servant;
      save me, because I serve you
        just as my mother did.

UNSHAKEN God

Psalm 86:1 – 17

God is gracious.

David ruled as Israel's greatest king ever, yet he called himself "poor and needy" and prayed for God's help (Psalm 86:1). He longed for protection from his enemies, guidance for life, and forgiveness of his sins. David counted on God to give him all those good things and more because the Lord is "a compassionate and gracious God, slow to anger, abounding in love and faithfulness" (Psalm 86:15). To be gracious means that God freely gives us grace, favor we don't deserve. He gives us every kind of help, meeting our practical needs and heaping forgiveness on us. God's graciousness isn't a one-time offer. It's the pattern of how he relates to each of us.

So ... How has God been gracious toward you?

¹⁷Give me a sign of your goodness,
  that my enemies may see it and be
    put to shame,
      for you, Lord, have helped me and
        comforted me.

Psalm 87

Of the Sons of Korah. A psalm. A song.

¹He has founded his city on the holy
  mountain.
²The Lord loves the gates of Zion
  more than all the other dwellings of
    Jacob.

³Glorious things are said of you,
  city of God:^a
⁴"I will record Rahab^b and Babylon
  among those who acknowledge me—

^a 3 The Hebrew has *Selah* (a word of uncertain
meaning) here and at the end of verse 6.
^b 4 A poetic name for Egypt

Philistia too, and Tyre, along with
  Cush[a]—
  and will say, 'This one was born in
  Zion.'"[b]
[5] Indeed, of Zion it will be said,
  "This one and that one were born in
  her,
  and the Most High himself will
  establish her."
[6] The LORD will write in the register of
  the peoples:
  "This one was born in Zion."

[7] As they make music they will sing,
  "All my fountains are in you."

Psalm 88[c]

A song. A psalm of the Sons of Korah.
For the director of music. According
to *mahalath leannoth*.[d] A *maskil*[e]
of Heman the Ezrahite.

[1] LORD, you are the God who saves me;
  day and night I cry out to you.
[2] May my prayer come before you;
  turn your ear to my cry.

[3] I am overwhelmed with troubles
  and my life draws near to death.
[4] I am counted among those who go
  down to the pit;
  I am like one without strength.
[5] I am set apart with the dead,
  like the slain who lie in the grave,
  whom you remember no more,
  who are cut off from your care.

[6] You have put me in the lowest pit,
  in the darkest depths.
[7] Your wrath lies heavily on me;
  you have overwhelmed me with all
  your waves.[f]
[8] You have taken from me my closest
  friends
  and have made me repulsive to
  them.
  I am confined and cannot escape;
[9]   my eyes are dim with grief.

  I call to you, LORD, every day;
  I spread out my hands to you.
[10] Do you show your wonders to the dead?
  Do their spirits rise up and praise
  you?

[11] Is your love declared in the grave,
  your faithfulness in Destruction[g]?
[12] Are your wonders known in the place
  of darkness,
  or your righteous deeds in the land
  of oblivion?

[13] But I cry to you for help, LORD;
  in the morning my prayer comes
  before you.
[14] Why, LORD, do you reject me
  and hide your face from me?

[15] From my youth I have suffered and
  been close to death;
  I have borne your terrors and am in
  despair.
[16] Your wrath has swept over me;
  your terrors have destroyed me.
[17] All day long they surround me like a
  flood;
  they have completely engulfed me.
[18] You have taken from me friend and
  neighbor—
  darkness is my closest friend.

Psalm 89[b]

A *maskil*[e] of Ethan the Ezrahite.

[1] I will sing of the LORD's great love
  forever;
  with my mouth I will make your
  faithfulness known
  through all generations.
[2] I will declare that your love stands
  firm forever,
  that you have established your
  faithfulness in heaven itself.
[3] You said, "I have made a covenant
  with my chosen one,
  I have sworn to David my
  servant,

[a] 4 That is, the upper Nile region   [b] 4 Or "I
will record concerning those who acknowledge me: /
'This one was born in Zion.' / Hear this, Rahab and
Babylon, / and you too, Philistia, Tyre and Cush."
[c] In Hebrew texts 88:1-18 is numbered 88:2-19.
[d] Title: Possibly a tune, "The Suffering of
Affliction"   [e] Title: Probably a literary or
musical term   [f] 7 The Hebrew has *Selah* (a
word of uncertain meaning) here and at the end
of verse 10.   [g] 11 Hebrew *Abaddon*   [b] In
Hebrew texts 89:1-52 is numbered 89:2-53.

⁴'I will establish your line forever
  and make your throne firm through
    all generations.'" *a*

⁵The heavens praise your wonders,
    Lord,
  your faithfulness too, in the
    assembly of the holy ones.
⁶For who in the skies above can
    compare with the Lord?
  Who is like the Lord among the
    heavenly beings?
⁷In the council of the holy ones God is
    greatly feared;
  he is more awesome than all who
    surround him.
⁸Who is like you, Lord God
    Almighty?
  You, Lord, are mighty, and your
    faithfulness surrounds you.

⁹You rule over the surging sea;
  when its waves mount up, you still
    them.
¹⁰You crushed Rahab like one of the
    slain;
  with your strong arm you scattered
    your enemies.
¹¹The heavens are yours, and yours also
    the earth;
  you founded the world and all that
    is in it.
¹²You created the north and the south;
  Tabor and Hermon sing for joy at
    your name.
¹³Your arm is endowed with power;
  your hand is strong, your right hand
    exalted.

¹⁴Righteousness and justice are the
    foundation of your throne;
  love and faithfulness go before
    you.
¹⁵Blessed are those who have learned to
    acclaim you,
  who walk in the light of your
    presence, Lord.
¹⁶They rejoice in your name all day
    long;
  they celebrate your righteousness.
¹⁷For you are their glory and strength,
  and by your favor you exalt our
    horn. *b*

ROCK SOLID *promises*

"Blessed are those who have learned to acclaim you, who walk in the light of your presence, Lord."

Psalm 89:15

You experience God's best when you dedicate your words and your life to him.

¹⁸Indeed, our shield *c* belongs to the Lord,
  our king to the Holy One of Israel.

¹⁹Once you spoke in a vision,
  to your faithful people you said:
  "I have bestowed strength on a warrior;
    I have raised up a young man from
      among the people.
²⁰I have found David my servant;
  with my sacred oil I have anointed
    him.
²¹My hand will sustain him;
  surely my arm will strengthen him.
²²The enemy will not get the better of
    him;
  the wicked will not oppress him.
²³I will crush his foes before him
  and strike down his adversaries.
²⁴My faithful love will be with him,
  and through my name his horn *d*
    will be exalted.
²⁵I will set his hand over the sea,
  his right hand over the rivers.
²⁶He will call out to me, 'You are my
    Father,
  my God, the Rock my Savior.'
²⁷And I will appoint him to be my
    firstborn,
  the most exalted of the kings of the
    earth.

a 4 The Hebrew has *Selah* (a word of uncertain meaning) here and at the end of verses 37, 45 and 48.   *b 17 Horn* here symbolizes strong one.   *c 18* Or *sovereign*   *d 24 Horn* here symbolizes strength.

28 I will maintain my love to him forever,
    and my covenant with him will
      never fail.
29 I will establish his line forever,
    his throne as long as the heavens
      endure.

30 "If his sons forsake my law
    and do not follow my statutes,
31 if they violate my decrees
    and fail to keep my commands,
32 I will punish their sin with the rod,
    their iniquity with flogging;
33 but I will not take my love from him,
    nor will I ever betray my
      faithfulness.
34 I will not violate my covenant
    or alter what my lips have uttered.
35 Once for all, I have sworn by my
      holiness—
    and I will not lie to David—
36 that his line will continue forever
    and his throne endure before me
      like the sun;
37 it will be established forever like the
      moon,
    the faithful witness in the sky."

38 But you have rejected, you have
      spurned,
    you have been very angry with your
      anointed one.
39 You have renounced the covenant with
      your servant
    and have defiled his crown in the
      dust.
40 You have broken through all his walls
    and reduced his strongholds to
      ruins.
41 All who pass by have plundered him;
    he has become the scorn of his
      neighbors.
42 You have exalted the right hand of his
      foes;
    you have made all his enemies
      rejoice.
43 Indeed, you have turned back the edge
      of his sword
    and have not supported him in
      battle.
44 You have put an end to his splendor
    and cast his throne to the ground.

45 You have cut short the days of his
      youth;
    you have covered him with a mantle
      of shame.
46 How long, Lord? Will you hide
      yourself forever?
    How long will your wrath burn like
      fire?
47 Remember how fleeting is my life.
    For what futility you have created
      all humanity!
48 Who can live and not see death,
    or who can escape the power of the
      grave?
49 Lord, where is your former great love,
    which in your faithfulness you
      swore to David?
50 Remember, Lord, how your servant
      hasª been mocked,
    how I bear in my heart the taunts of
      all the nations,
51 the taunts with which your enemies,
      Lord, have mocked,
    with which they have mocked every
      step of your anointed one.

52 Praise be to the Lord forever!
    Amen and Amen.

BOOK IV

Psalms 90–106

Psalm 90

A prayer of Moses the man of God.

1 Lord, you have been our dwelling
      place
    throughout all generations.
2 Before the mountains were born
    or you brought forth the whole world,
    from everlasting to everlasting you
      are God.

3 You turn people back to dust,
    saying, "Return to dust, you mortals."
4 A thousand years in your sight
    are like a day that has just gone by,
    or like a watch in the night.

ª 50 Or *your servants have*

UNSHAKEN *God*

Psalm 90:1–2

God is eternal.

Moses wasn't overflowing with happy thoughts when he wrote Psalm 90. He notes that God turns people back to dust. Humans live 70 years—sometimes 80. In the end we wither like grass. Yet there is a truth about God that gives us hope. The Lord has reigned "from everlasting to everlasting." He existed before he "brought forth the whole world." And he has been our shelter "throughout all generations" (Psalm 90:1–2). Even though our lives last only a blink, God is eternal. He's beyond time. Outside of time. Always existing. And because God is eternal, he's there for us whenever we need him. Now and forever, he's our Lord and Savior.

So ... What good does it do you that God is eternal?

5 Yet you sweep people away in the sleep of death—
  they are like the new grass of the morning:
6 In the morning it springs up new,
  but by evening it is dry and withered.

7 We are consumed by your anger
  and terrified by your indignation.
8 You have set our iniquities before you,
  our secret sins in the light of your presence.
9 All our days pass away under your wrath;
  we finish our years with a moan.
10 Our days may come to seventy years,
  or eighty, if our strength endures;
yet the best of them are but trouble and sorrow,
  for they quickly pass, and we fly away.

11 If only we knew the power of your anger!
  Your wrath is as great as the fear that is your due.
12 Teach us to number our days,
  that we may gain a heart of wisdom.
13 Relent, LORD! How long will it be?
  Have compassion on your servants.
14 Satisfy us in the morning with your unfailing love,
  that we may sing for joy and be glad all our days.
15 Make us glad for as many days as you have afflicted us,
  for as many years as we have seen trouble.
16 May your deeds be shown to your servants,
  your splendor to their children.

17 May the favor[a] of the Lord our God rest on us;
  establish the work of our hands for us—
  yes, establish the work of our hands.

Psalm 91

1 Whoever dwells in the shelter of the Most High
  will rest in the shadow of the Almighty.[b]
2 I will say of the LORD, "He is my refuge and my fortress,
  my God, in whom I trust."

3 Surely he will save you
  from the fowler's snare
  and from the deadly pestilence.
4 He will cover you with his feathers,
  and under his wings you will find refuge;
  his faithfulness will be your shield and rampart.
5 You will not fear the terror of night,
  nor the arrow that flies by day,
6 nor the pestilence that stalks in the darkness,
  nor the plague that destroys at midday.

a 17 Or *beauty* *b* 1 Hebrew *Shaddai*

⁷A thousand may fall at your side,
  ten thousand at your right hand,
  but it will not come near you.
⁸You will only observe with your eyes
  and see the punishment of the
    wicked.

⁹If you say, "The Lord is my refuge,"
  and you make the Most High your
    dwelling,
¹⁰no harm will overtake you,
  no disaster will come near your tent.
¹¹For he will command his angels
    concerning you
  to guard you in all your ways;

¹²they will lift you up in their hands,
  so that you will not strike your foot
    against a stone.
¹³You will tread on the lion and the cobra;
  you will trample the great lion and
    the serpent.

¹⁴"Because heᵃ loves me," says the
    Lord, "I will rescue him;
  I will protect him, for he
    acknowledges my name.
¹⁵He will call on me, and I will answer
    him;
  I will be with him in trouble,
  I will deliver him and honor him.
¹⁶With long life I will satisfy him
  and show him my salvation."

Psalm 92ᵇ

A psalm. A song. For the Sabbath day.

¹It is good to praise the Lord
  and make music to your name,
    O Most High,
²proclaiming your love in the morning
  and your faithfulness at night,
³to the music of the ten-stringed lyre
  and the melody of the harp.

⁴For you make me glad by your deeds,
    Lord;
  I sing for joy at what your hands
    have done.
⁵How great are your works, Lord,
  how profound your thoughts!
⁶Senseless people do not know,
  fools do not understand,
⁷that though the wicked spring up like
    grass
  and all evildoers flourish,
  they will be destroyed forever.

⁸But you, Lord, are forever exalted.

⁹For surely your enemies, Lord,
  surely your enemies will perish;
  all evildoers will be scattered.
¹⁰You have exalted my hornᶜ like that of
    a wild ox;
  fine oils have been poured on me.

Psalm 91:1–16

God watches over you.

Psalm 91 reads like the script of an action movie where the hero meets nonstop explosive dangers but in the end emerges unharmed. The songwriter tells about deadly diseases, night terrors, whizzing arrows, and more death and disease—topped off by 10,000 people dropping dead. Yet he claims that "If you say 'The Lord is my refuge,' and you make the Most High your dwelling, no harm will overtake you" (Psalm 91:9–10). That promise might sound too good to be true. But consider what it actually says. The Lord doesn't say your life will be free of chaos and danger, or even disease and death. But he does pledge to watch over you as you dart through an obstacle course full of every kind of hazard. If you love him and acknowledge him as God, he promises to protect you.

Think: What does it mean that God will rescue and protect you?

ROCK SOLID truths

ᵃ 14 That is, probably the king   ᵇ In Hebrew texts 92:1-15 is numbered 92:2-16.   ᶜ 10 Horn here symbolizes strength.

11 My eyes have seen the defeat of my
  adversaries;
 my ears have heard the rout of my
  wicked foes.

12 The righteous will flourish like a palm
  tree,
 they will grow like a cedar of
  Lebanon;
13 planted in the house of the Lord,
 they will flourish in the courts of
  our God.
14 They will still bear fruit in old age,
 they will stay fresh and green,
15 proclaiming, "The Lord is upright;
 he is my Rock, and there is no
  wickedness in him."

Psalm 93

1 The Lord reigns, he is robed in majesty;
 the Lord is robed in majesty and
  armed with strength;
 indeed, the world is established,
  firm and secure.
2 Your throne was established long ago;
 you are from all eternity.

3 The seas have lifted up, Lord,
 the seas have lifted up their voice;
 the seas have lifted up their
  pounding waves.
4 Mightier than the thunder of the great
  waters,
 mightier than the breakers of the
  sea—
 the Lord on high is mighty.

5 Your statutes, Lord, stand firm;
 holiness adorns your house
 for endless days.

Psalm 94

1 The Lord is a God who avenges.
 O God who avenges, shine forth.
2 Rise up, Judge of the earth;
 pay back to the proud what they
  deserve.
3 How long, Lord, will the wicked,
 how long will the wicked be jubilant?

4 They pour out arrogant words;
 all the evildoers are full of boasting.

5 They crush your people, Lord;
 they oppress your inheritance.
6 They slay the widow and the foreigner;
 they murder the fatherless.
7 They say, "The Lord does not see;
 the God of Jacob takes no notice."

8 Take notice, you senseless ones among
  the people;
 you fools, when will you become
  wise?
9 Does he who fashioned the ear not hear?
 Does he who formed the eye not see?
10 Does he who disciplines nations not
  punish?
 Does he who teaches mankind lack
  knowledge?
11 The Lord knows all human plans;
 he knows that they are futile.

12 Blessed is the one you discipline, Lord,
 the one you teach from your law;
13 you grant them relief from days of
  trouble,
 till a pit is dug for the wicked.
14 For the Lord will not reject his people;
 he will never forsake his
  inheritance.
15 Judgment will again be founded on
  righteousness,
 and all the upright in heart will
  follow it.

16 Who will rise up for me against the
  wicked?
 Who will take a stand for me
  against evildoers?
17 Unless the Lord had given me help,
 I would soon have dwelt in the
  silence of death.
18 When I said, "My foot is slipping,"
 your unfailing love, Lord,
  supported me.
19 When anxiety was great within me,
 your consolation brought me joy.

20 Can a corrupt throne be allied with
  you—
 a throne that brings on misery by its
  decrees?
21 The wicked band together against the
  righteous
 and condemn the innocent to death.

²²But the LORD has become my fortress,
  and my God the rock in whom I
    take refuge.
²³He will repay them for their sins
  and destroy them for their
    wickedness;
  the LORD our God will destroy
    them.

Psalm 95

¹Come, let us sing for joy to the LORD;
  let us shout aloud to the Rock of
    our salvation.
²Let us come before him with
    thanksgiving
  and extol him with music and song.

³For the LORD is the great God,
  the great King above all gods.
⁴In his hand are the depths of the earth,
  and the mountain peaks belong to
    him.
⁵The sea is his, for he made it,
  and his hands formed the dry land.

⁶Come, let us bow down in worship,
  let us kneel before the LORD our
    Maker;
⁷for he is our God
  and we are the people of his pasture,
    the flock under his care.

Today, if only you would hear his voice,
⁸"Do not harden your hearts as you did
    at Meribah,ᵃ
  as you did that day at Massahᵇ in
    the wilderness,
⁹where your ancestors tested me;
  they tried me, though they had seen
    what I did.
¹⁰For forty years I was angry with that
    generation;
  I said, 'They are a people whose
    hearts go astray,
  and they have not known my ways.'
¹¹So I declared on oath in my anger,
  'They shall never enter my rest.'"

ᵃ 8 *Meribah* means *quarreling.*   ᵇ 8 *Massah* means *testing.*

ROCK SOLID
principles

Psalm 95:1–11

Praise God.

Hailey knew what her old pastor meant when he talked about having "a hard heart." It's when you stop trusting and loving God, and your spiritual passion gets replaced with rock-hard disinterest. That's how Hailey had been feeling for the past year. She had always been so enthusiastic about God, like her heart was soft thumping flesh. She hadn't faced anything traumatic, but she found herself wondering if God really cared about her life. But maybe her heart wasn't completely cold and dead, because as her pastor preached she remembered how she used to feel about God. Maybe it was just a flash of emotion, but she started to tell God how much she missed him. And loved him. And how great he is.

"Meribah" and "Massah" (Psalm 95:8) are names that mean "quarreling" and "testing." It's two descriptions of a single place where the Israelites questioned if God really cared for them (see Exodus 17:7). Praise is the opposite of that kind of doubt. Praise is remembering and saying out loud all the reasons God deserves your worship.

¹ Sing to the LORD a new song;
  sing to the LORD, all the earth.
² Sing to the LORD, praise his name;
  proclaim his salvation day after
    day.
³ Declare his glory among the nations,
  his marvelous deeds among all
    peoples.

⁴ For great is the LORD and most
    worthy of praise;
  he is to be feared above all gods.
⁵ For all the gods of the nations are
    idols,
  but the LORD made the heavens.
⁶ Splendor and majesty are before him;
  strength and glory are in his
    sanctuary.

⁷ Ascribe to the LORD, all you families
    of nations,
  ascribe to the LORD glory and
    strength.
⁸ Ascribe to the LORD the glory due his
    name;
  bring an offering and come into his
    courts.
⁹ Worship the LORD in the splendor of
    his*ᵃ holiness;
  tremble before him, all the earth.
¹⁰ Say among the nations, "The LORD
    reigns."
  The world is firmly established, it
    cannot be moved;
  he will judge the peoples with
    equity.

¹¹ Let the heavens rejoice, let the earth
    be glad;
  let the sea resound, and all that is
    in it.
¹² Let the fields be jubilant, and
    everything in them;
  let all the trees of the forest sing for
    joy.
¹³ Let all creation rejoice before the
    LORD, for he comes,
  he comes to judge the earth.
  He will judge the world in
    righteousness
  and the peoples in his faithfulness.

¹ The LORD reigns, let the earth be glad;
  let the distant shores rejoice.
² Clouds and thick darkness surround
    him;
  righteousness and justice are the
    foundation of his throne.
³ Fire goes before him
  and consumes his foes on every side.
⁴ His lightning lights up the world;
  the earth sees and trembles.
⁵ The mountains melt like wax before
    the LORD,
  before the Lord of all the earth.
⁶ The heavens proclaim his
    righteousness,
  and all peoples see his glory.

⁷ All who worship images are put to shame,
  those who boast in idols—
  worship him, all you gods!

⁸ Zion hears and rejoices
  and the villages of Judah are glad
  because of your judgments, LORD.
⁹ For you, LORD, are the Most High
    over all the earth;
  you are exalted far above all gods.
¹⁰ Let those who love the LORD hate evil,
  for he guards the lives of his faithful
    ones
  and delivers them from the hand of
    the wicked.

ᵃ 9 Or LORD with the splendor of

ROCK SOLID promises

"Let those who love the LORD hate evil, for he guards the lives of his faithful ones." Psalm 97:10

The more you understand God's care, the more reasons you have to love him. And the more you love him, the less you will crave evil.

¹¹ Light shines*ᵃ* on the righteous
  and joy on the upright in heart.
¹² Rejoice in the Lᴏʀᴅ, you who are
    righteous,
  and praise his holy name.

Psalm 98

A psalm.

¹ Sing to the Lᴏʀᴅ a new song,
  for he has done marvelous things;
his right hand and his holy arm
  have worked salvation for him.
² The Lᴏʀᴅ has made his salvation
    known
  and revealed his righteousness to
    the nations.
³ He has remembered his love
  and his faithfulness to Israel;
all the ends of the earth have seen
  the salvation of our God.

⁴ Shout for joy to the Lᴏʀᴅ, all the
    earth,
  burst into jubilant song with music;
⁵ make music to the Lᴏʀᴅ with the
    harp,
  with the harp and the sound of
    singing,
⁶ with trumpets and the blast of the
    ram's horn—
  shout for joy before the Lᴏʀᴅ, the
    King.

⁷ Let the sea resound, and everything
    in it,
  the world, and all who live in it.
⁸ Let the rivers clap their hands,
  let the mountains sing together for
    joy;
⁹ let them sing before the Lᴏʀᴅ,
  for he comes to judge the earth.
He will judge the world in
    righteousness
  and the peoples with equity.

Psalm 99

¹ The Lᴏʀᴅ reigns,
  let the nations tremble;
he sits enthroned between the
    cherubim,
  let the earth shake.

² Great is the Lᴏʀᴅ in Zion;
  he is exalted over all the nations.
³ Let them praise your great and
    awesome name—
  he is holy.

⁴ The King is mighty, he loves
    justice—
  you have established equity;
in Jacob you have done
  what is just and right.
⁵ Exalt the Lᴏʀᴅ our God
  and worship at his footstool;
  he is holy.

⁶ Moses and Aaron were among his
    priests,
  Samuel was among those who
    called on his name;
they called on the Lᴏʀᴅ
  and he answered them.
⁷ He spoke to them from the pillar of
    cloud;
  they kept his statutes and the
    decrees he gave them.

⁸ Lᴏʀᴅ our God,
  you answered them;
you were to Israel a forgiving God,
  though you punished their
    misdeeds.ᵇ
⁹ Exalt the Lᴏʀᴅ our God
  and worship at his holy mountain,
  for the Lᴏʀᴅ our God is holy.

Psalm 100

A psalm. For giving grateful praise.

¹ Shout for joy to the Lᴏʀᴅ, all the
    earth.
² Worship the Lᴏʀᴅ with gladness;
  come before him with joyful
    songs.
³ Know that the Lᴏʀᴅ is God.
  It is he who made us, and we are
    hisᶜ;
  we are his people, the sheep of his
    pasture.

ᵃ 11 One Hebrew manuscript and ancient
versions (see also 112:4); most Hebrew
manuscripts *Light is sown*   ᵇ 8 Or *God, / an
avenger of the wrongs done to them*   ᶜ 3 Or *and
not we ourselves*

⁴Enter his gates with thanksgiving
and his courts with praise;
give thanks to him and praise his
name.
⁵For the LORD is good and his love
endures forever;
his faithfulness continues through
all generations.

ROCK SOLID *promises*

"The LORD is good and his love endures forever." Psalm 100:5

God's kindness and love for you will never wear out, run out, or die out.

Psalm 101

Of David. A psalm.

¹I will sing of your love and justice;
to you, LORD, I will sing praise.
²I will be careful to lead a blameless
life—
when will you come to me?

I will conduct the affairs of my house
with a blameless heart.
³I will not look with approval
on anything that is vile.

I hate what faithless people do;
I will have no part in it.
⁴The perverse of heart shall be far from
me;
I will have nothing to do with what
is evil.

⁵Whoever slanders their neighbor in
secret,
I will put to silence;
whoever has haughty eyes and a proud
heart,
I will not tolerate.

⁶My eyes will be on the faithful in the
land,
that they may dwell with me;
the one whose walk is blameless
will minister to me.

⁷No one who practices deceit
will dwell in my house;
no one who speaks falsely
will stand in my presence.

⁸Every morning I will put to silence
all the wicked in the land;
I will cut off every evildoer
from the city of the LORD.

Psalm 102^a

A prayer of an afflicted person who has
grown weak and pours out a lament
before the LORD.

¹Hear my prayer, LORD;
let my cry for help come to you.
²Do not hide your face from me
when I am in distress.
Turn your ear to me;
when I call, answer me quickly.

³For my days vanish like smoke;
my bones burn like glowing
embers.
⁴My heart is blighted and withered like
grass;
I forget to eat my food.
⁵In my distress I groan aloud
and am reduced to skin and bones.
⁶I am like a desert owl,
like an owl among the ruins.
⁷I lie awake; I have become
like a bird alone on a roof.
⁸All day long my enemies taunt me;
those who rail against me use my
name as a curse.
⁹For I eat ashes as my food
and mingle my drink with tears
¹⁰because of your great wrath,
for you have taken me up and
thrown me aside.
¹¹My days are like the evening
shadow;
I wither away like grass.

^a In Hebrew texts 102:1-28 is numbered
102:2-29.

¹²But you, LORD, sit enthroned forever;
  your renown endures through all
    generations.
¹³You will arise and have compassion on
    Zion,
  for it is time to show favor to her;
  the appointed time has come.
¹⁴For her stones are dear to your
    servants;
  her very dust moves them to pity.
¹⁵The nations will fear the name of the
    LORD,
  all the kings of the earth will revere
    your glory.
¹⁶For the LORD will rebuild Zion
  and appear in his glory.
¹⁷He will respond to the prayer of the
    destitute;
  he will not despise their plea.

¹⁸Let this be written for a future
    generation,
  that a people not yet created may
    praise the LORD:
¹⁹"The LORD looked down from his
    sanctuary on high,
  from heaven he viewed the earth,
²⁰to hear the groans of the prisoners
  and release those condemned to
    death."
²¹So the name of the LORD will be
    declared in Zion
  and his praise in Jerusalem
²²when the peoples and the kingdoms
  assemble to worship the LORD.

²³In the course of my life*a* he broke my
    strength;
  he cut short my days.
²⁴So I said:
  "Do not take me away, my God, in the
    midst of my days;
  your years go on through all
    generations.
²⁵In the beginning you laid the
    foundations of the earth,
  and the heavens are the work of
    your hands.
²⁶They will perish, but you remain;
  they will all wear out like a garment.
  Like clothing you will change them
  and they will be discarded.

UNSHAKEN *God*

Psalm 102:25–28

God is infinite.

You can't count to infinity. You can't wrap your mind around the concept. But you can nevertheless relate to the infinite God. To be "infinite" means that God is outside the world we know—a realm of time and space. The Lord exists outside of what we can see, having "laid the foundations of the earth" (Psalm 102:25). He is so far beyond us that we couldn't perceive or understand him if we hadn't chosen to reveal himself to us. But God shows us his power in the world he made (Romans 1:20). And in Jesus he shows us the depths of who is (John 1:14). God lives beyond our human limits, but he reveals himself so we can understand him.

So ... How impressed are you that God is infinite? Why—or why not?

²⁷But you remain the same,
  and your years will never end.
²⁸The children of your servants will live
    in your presence;
  their descendants will be
    established before you."

Psalm 103

Of David.

¹Praise the LORD, my soul;
  all my inmost being, praise his holy
    name.
²Praise the LORD, my soul,
  and forget not all his benefits—
³who forgives all your sins
  and heals all your diseases,
⁴who redeems your life from the pit
  and crowns you with love and
    compassion,

---

a 23 Or *By his power*

⁵who satisfies your desires with good
things
so that your youth is renewed like
the eagle's.

⁶The Lord works righteousness
and justice for all the oppressed.

⁷He made known his ways to Moses,
his deeds to the people of Israel:
⁸The Lord is compassionate and
gracious,
slow to anger, abounding in love.
⁹He will not always accuse,
nor will he harbor his anger
forever;
¹⁰he does not treat us as our sins deserve
or repay us according to our
iniquities.
¹¹For as high as the heavens are above
the earth,
so great is his love for those who
fear him;
¹²as far as the east is from the west,
so far has he removed our
transgressions from us.

¹³As a father has compassion on his
children,
so the Lord has compassion on
those who fear him;
¹⁴for he knows how we are formed,
he remembers that we are dust.
¹⁵The life of mortals is like grass,
they flourish like a flower of the
field;
¹⁶the wind blows over it and it is gone,
and its place remembers it no more.
¹⁷But from everlasting to everlasting
the Lord's love is with those who
fear him,
and his righteousness with their
children's children—
¹⁸with those who keep his covenant
and remember to obey his precepts.

¹⁹The Lord has established his throne
in heaven,
and his kingdom rules over all.

²⁰Praise the Lord, you his angels,
you mighty ones who do his
bidding,
who obey his word.

Psalm 103:1–22

You can't thrive without God.

God has a grip on the best and worst parts of your days. Whether you soar high or sink low, God gives you the support you need to get through life. In this song David details all the ways God is good to human beings. He forgives sin … heals diseases … lifts you from the pit … fills you up with love … satisfies your desires. Since before the days of Moses, the Lord has demonstrated he is compassionate … gracious … slow to anger … loving … merciful … forgiving. And why? Because God is like a kind dad. He "knows how we are formed, he remembers that we are dust" (Psalm 103:14). People are like grass. They tumble away in the wind, and no one recalls they were ever there. But God shows his everlasting love to everyone who respects him. Without him, you can't exist at all.

Think: What all does God do for you to allow you to survive— and thrive?

ROCK SOLID *truths*

²¹Praise the Lord, all his heavenly
hosts,
you his servants who do his will.
²²Praise the Lord, all his works
everywhere in his dominion.

Praise the Lord, my soul.

Psalm 104

¹Praise the Lord, my soul.

Lord my God, you are very great;
you are clothed with splendor and
majesty.

² The Lord wraps himself in light as
    with a garment;
  he stretches out the heavens like a
    tent
³ and lays the beams of his upper
    chambers on their waters.
He makes the clouds his chariot
  and rides on the wings of the wind.
⁴ He makes winds his messengers,ᵃ
  flames of fire his servants.

⁵ He set the earth on its foundations;
  it can never be moved.
⁶ You covered it with the watery depths
    as with a garment;
  the waters stood above the
    mountains.
⁷ But at your rebuke the waters fled,
  at the sound of your thunder they
    took to flight;
⁸ they flowed over the mountains,
  they went down into the valleys,
  to the place you assigned for them.
⁹ You set a boundary they cannot cross;
  never again will they cover the
    earth.

¹⁰ He makes springs pour water into the
    ravines;
  it flows between the mountains.
¹¹ They give water to all the beasts of the
    field;
  the wild donkeys quench their
    thirst.
¹² The birds of the sky nest by the
    waters;
  they sing among the branches.
¹³ He waters the mountains from his
    upper chambers;
  the land is satisfied by the fruit of
    his work.
¹⁴ He makes grass grow for the cattle,
  and plants for people to cultivate—
  bringing forth food from the earth:
¹⁵ wine that gladdens human hearts,
  oil to make their faces shine,
  and bread that sustains their hearts.
¹⁶ The trees of the Lord are well
    watered,
  the cedars of Lebanon that he
    planted.
¹⁷ There the birds make their nests;

  the stork has its home in the
    junipers.
¹⁸ The high mountains belong to the
    wild goats;
  the crags are a refuge for the hyrax.

¹⁹ He made the moon to mark the
    seasons,
  and the sun knows when to go
    down.
²⁰ You bring darkness, it becomes night,
  and all the beasts of the forest
    prowl.
²¹ The lions roar for their prey
  and seek their food from God.
²² The sun rises, and they steal away;
  they return and lie down in their
    dens.
²³ Then people go out to their work,
  to their labor until evening.

²⁴ How many are your works, Lord!
  In wisdom you made them all;
  the earth is full of your creatures.
²⁵ There is the sea, vast and spacious,
  teeming with creatures beyond
    number—
  living things both large and small.
²⁶ There the ships go to and fro,
  and Leviathan, which you formed
    to frolic there.

²⁷ All creatures look to you
  to give them their food at the
    proper time.
²⁸ When you give it to them,
  they gather it up;
  when you open your hand,
  they are satisfied with good things.
²⁹ When you hide your face,
  they are terrified;
  when you take away their breath,
  they die and return to the dust.
³⁰ When you send your Spirit,
  they are created,
  and you renew the face of the
    ground.
³¹ May the glory of the Lord endure
    forever;
  may the Lord rejoice in his
    works—

ᵃ 4 Or *angels*

³²he who looks at the earth, and it
  trembles,
  who touches the mountains, and
  they smoke.
³³I will sing to the LORD all my life;
  I will sing praise to my God as long
  as I live.
³⁴May my meditation be pleasing to him,
  as I rejoice in the LORD.
³⁵But may sinners vanish from the earth
  and the wicked be no more.

Praise the LORD, my soul.

Praise the LORD.ᵃ

Psalm 105

¹Give praise to the LORD, proclaim his
  name;
  make known among the nations
  what he has done.
²Sing to him, sing praise to him;
  tell of all his wonderful acts.
³Glory in his holy name;
  let the hearts of those who seek the
  LORD rejoice.
⁴Look to the LORD and his strength;
  seek his face always.

⁵Remember the wonders he has done,
  his miracles, and the judgments he
  pronounced,
⁶you his servants, the descendants of
  Abraham,
  his chosen ones, the children of
  Jacob.
⁷He is the LORD our God;
  his judgments are in all the earth.

⁸He remembers his covenant forever,
  the promise he made, for a
  thousand generations,
⁹the covenant he made with Abraham,
  the oath he swore to Isaac.
¹⁰He confirmed it to Jacob as a decree,
  to Israel as an everlasting covenant:
¹¹"To you I will give the land of Canaan
  as the portion you will inherit."

¹²When they were but few in number,
  few indeed, and strangers in it,
¹³they wandered from nation to nation,
  from one kingdom to another.

UNSHAKEN *God*

Psalm 105:8–11

God is faithful.

It's probably no shock that the all-knowing God can remember something "for a thousand generations" (Psalm 105:8). What the Lord recalls in Psalm 105 is a "promise he made." He recalls his "covenant," his pledge to give the Israelite slaves the promised land (see Psalm 105:11). That's more than an amazing feat of memory. It demonstrates God's faithfulness—his flawless dependability. Faithfulness means the Lord never lets you down, no matter how long it takes for his promises to be fulfilled. Sometimes it can feel like God has forgotten you. But he never fails to keep his word. Like Lamentations 3:23 says, "Great is [his] faithfulness."

So ... When have you doubted God's faithfulness? What do you think now?

¹⁴He allowed no one to oppress them;
  for their sake he rebuked kings:
¹⁵"Do not touch my anointed ones;
  do my prophets no harm."

¹⁶He called down famine on the land
  and destroyed all their supplies of
  food;
¹⁷and he sent a man before them—
  Joseph, sold as a slave.
¹⁸They bruised his feet with shackles,
  his neck was put in irons,
¹⁹till what he foretold came to pass,
  till the word of the LORD proved
  him true.
²⁰The king sent and released him,
  the ruler of peoples set him free.
²¹He made him master of his household,
  ruler over all he possessed,

ᵃ 35 Hebrew *Hallelu Yah*; in the Septuagint this
line stands at the beginning of Psalm 105.

PSALM 106

22 to instruct his princes as he pleased
and teach his elders wisdom.

23 Then Israel entered Egypt;
Jacob resided as a foreigner in the
land of Ham.
24 The LORD made his people very
fruitful;
he made them too numerous for
their foes,
25 whose hearts he turned to hate his
people,
to conspire against his servants.
26 He sent Moses his servant,
and Aaron, whom he had chosen.
27 They performed his signs among
them,
his wonders in the land of Ham.
28 He sent darkness and made the land
dark—
for had they not rebelled against his
words?
29 He turned their waters into blood,
causing their fish to die.
30 Their land teemed with frogs,
which went up into the bedrooms of
their rulers.
31 He spoke, and there came swarms of
flies,
and gnats throughout their country.
32 He turned their rain into hail,
with lightning throughout their
land;
33 he struck down their vines and fig
trees
and shattered the trees of their
country.
34 He spoke, and the locusts came,
grasshoppers without number;
35 they ate up every green thing in their
land,
ate up the produce of their soil.
36 Then he struck down all the firstborn
in their land,
the firstfruits of all their manhood.
37 He brought out Israel, laden with
silver and gold,
and from among their tribes no one
faltered.
38 Egypt was glad when they left,
because dread of Israel had fallen on
them.

39 He spread out a cloud as a covering,
and a fire to give light at night.
40 They asked, and he brought them
quail;
he fed them well with the bread of
heaven.
41 He opened the rock, and water gushed
out;
it flowed like a river in the desert.

42 For he remembered his holy promise
given to his servant Abraham.
43 He brought out his people with
rejoicing,
his chosen ones with shouts of joy;
44 he gave them the lands of the nations,
and they fell heir to what others had
toiled for—
45 that they might keep his precepts
and observe his laws.

Praise the LORD.ᵃ

Psalm 106

1 Praise the LORD.ᵇ

Give thanks to the LORD, for he is
good;
his love endures forever.

2 Who can proclaim the mighty acts of
the LORD
or fully declare his praise?
3 Blessed are those who act justly,
who always do what is right.

4 Remember me, LORD, when you show
favor to your people,
come to my aid when you save
them,
5 that I may enjoy the prosperity of your
chosen ones,
that I may share in the joy of your
nation
and join your inheritance in giving
praise.

6 We have sinned, even as our ancestors
did;
we have done wrong and acted
wickedly.

ᵃ 45 Hebrew *Hallelu Yah*   ᵇ 1 Hebrew *Hallelu Yah*; also in verse 48

5713

⁷When our ancestors were in Egypt,
  they gave no thought to your
    miracles;
  they did not remember your many
    kindnesses,
  and they rebelled by the sea, the
    Red Sea.ᵃ
⁸Yet he saved them for his name's sake,
  to make his mighty power known.
⁹He rebuked the Red Sea, and it dried
    up;
  he led them through the depths as
    through a desert.
¹⁰He saved them from the hand of the foe;
  from the hand of the enemy he
    redeemed them.
¹¹The waters covered their adversaries;
  not one of them survived.
¹²Then they believed his promises
  and sang his praise.

¹³But they soon forgot what he had done
  and did not wait for his plan to
    unfold.
¹⁴In the desert they gave in to their
    craving;
  in the wilderness they put God to
    the test.
¹⁵So he gave them what they asked for,
  but sent a wasting disease among
    them.

¹⁶In the camp they grew envious of Moses
  and of Aaron, who was consecrated
    to the LORD.
¹⁷The earth opened up and swallowed
    Dathan;
  it buried the company of Abiram.
¹⁸Fire blazed among their followers;
  a flame consumed the wicked.
¹⁹At Horeb they made a calf
  and worshiped an idol cast from
    metal.
²⁰They exchanged their glorious God
  for an image of a bull, which eats
    grass.
²¹They forgot the God who saved them,
  who had done great things in Egypt,
²²miracles in the land of Ham
  and awesome deeds by the Red Sea.
²³So he said he would destroy them—
  had not Moses, his chosen one,

stood in the breach before him
  to keep his wrath from destroying
    them.

²⁴Then they despised the pleasant land;
  they did not believe his promise.
²⁵They grumbled in their tents
  and did not obey the LORD.
²⁶So he swore to them with uplifted
    hand
  that he would make them fall in the
    wilderness,
²⁷make their descendants fall among the
    nations
  and scatter them throughout the
    lands.

²⁸They yoked themselves to the Baal of
    Peor
  and ate sacrifices offered to lifeless
    gods;
²⁹they aroused the LORD's anger by their
    wicked deeds,
  and a plague broke out among
    them.
³⁰But Phinehas stood up and
    intervened,
  and the plague was checked.
³¹This was credited to him as
    righteousness
  for endless generations to come.
³²By the waters of Meribah they
    angered the LORD,
  and trouble came to Moses because
    of them;
³³for they rebelled against the Spirit of
    God,
  and rash words came from Moses'
    lips.ᵇ

³⁴They did not destroy the peoples
  as the LORD had commanded them,
³⁵but they mingled with the nations
  and adopted their customs.
³⁶They worshiped their idols,
  which became a snare to them.
³⁷They sacrificed their sons
  and their daughters to false gods.
³⁸They shed innocent blood,
  the blood of their sons and daughters,

ᵃ 7 Or *the Sea of Reeds*; also in verses 9 and 22
ᵇ 33 Or *against his spirit, / and rash words came
from his lips*

whom they sacrificed to the idols of
Canaan,
and the land was desecrated by their
blood.
³⁹ They defiled themselves by what they
did;
by their deeds they prostituted
themselves.

⁴⁰ Therefore the LORD was angry with
his people
and abhorred his inheritance.
⁴¹ He gave them into the hands of the
nations,
and their foes ruled over them.
⁴² Their enemies oppressed them
and subjected them to their power.
⁴³ Many times he delivered them,
but they were bent on rebellion
and they wasted away in their sin.
⁴⁴ Yet he took note of their distress
when he heard their cry;
⁴⁵ for their sake he remembered his
covenant
and out of his great love he relented.
⁴⁶ He caused all who held them captive
to show them mercy.

⁴⁷ Save us, LORD our God,
and gather us from the nations,
that we may give thanks to your holy
name
and glory in your praise.

⁴⁸ Praise be to the LORD, the God of
Israel,
from everlasting to everlasting.

Let all the people say, "Amen!"

Praise the LORD.

BOOK V

Psalms 107–150

Psalm 107

¹ Give thanks to the LORD, for he is good;
his love endures forever.

² Let the redeemed of the LORD tell
their story—
those he redeemed from the hand of
the foe,

³ those he gathered from the lands,
from east and west, from north and
south.ᵃ

⁴ Some wandered in desert wastelands,
finding no way to a city where they
could settle.
⁵ They were hungry and thirsty,
and their lives ebbed away.
⁶ Then they cried out to the LORD in
their trouble,
and he delivered them from their
distress.
⁷ He led them by a straight way
to a city where they could settle.
⁸ Let them give thanks to the LORD for
his unfailing love
and his wonderful deeds for
mankind,
⁹ for he satisfies the thirsty
and fills the hungry with good things.

¹⁰ Some sat in darkness, in utter
darkness,
prisoners suffering in iron chains,
¹¹ because they rebelled against God's
commands
and despised the plans of the Most
High.
¹² So he subjected them to bitter labor;
they stumbled, and there was no
one to help.
¹³ Then they cried to the LORD in their
trouble,
and he saved them from their
distress.
¹⁴ He brought them out of darkness, the
utter darkness,
and broke away their chains.
¹⁵ Let them give thanks to the LORD for
his unfailing love
and his wonderful deeds for mankind,
¹⁶ for he breaks down gates of bronze
and cuts through bars of iron.

¹⁷ Some became fools through their
rebellious ways
and suffered affliction because of
their iniquities.
¹⁸ They loathed all food
and drew near the gates of death.

ᵃ 3 Hebrew *north and the sea*

19 Then they cried to the LORD in their
     trouble,
   and he saved them from their
     distress.
20 He sent out his word and healed them;
   he rescued them from the grave.
21 Let them give thanks to the LORD for
     his unfailing love
   and his wonderful deeds for
     mankind.
22 Let them sacrifice thank offerings
   and tell of his works with songs of
     joy.

23 Some went out on the sea in ships;
   they were merchants on the mighty
     waters.
24 They saw the works of the LORD,
   his wonderful deeds in the deep.
25 For he spoke and stirred up a tempest
   that lifted high the waves.
26 They mounted up to the heavens and
     went down to the depths;
   in their peril their courage melted
     away.
27 They reeled and staggered like
     drunkards;
   they were at their wits' end.
28 Then they cried out to the LORD in
     their trouble,
   and he brought them out of their
     distress.
29 He stilled the storm to a whisper;
   the waves of the sea*a* were hushed.

30 They were glad when it grew calm,
   and he guided them to their desired
     haven.
31 Let them give thanks to the LORD for
     his unfailing love
   and his wonderful deeds for
     mankind.
32 Let them exalt him in the assembly of
     the people
   and praise him in the council of the
     elders.

33 He turned rivers into a desert,
   flowing springs into thirsty ground,
34 and fruitful land into a salt waste,
   because of the wickedness of those
     who lived there.
35 He turned the desert into pools of
     water
   and the parched ground into
     flowing springs;
36 there he brought the hungry to live,
   and they founded a city where they
     could settle.
37 They sowed fields and planted
     vineyards
   that yielded a fruitful harvest;
38 he blessed them, and their numbers
     greatly increased,
   and he did not let their herds
     diminish.

39 Then their numbers decreased, and
     they were humbled
   by oppression, calamity and sorrow;
40 he who pours contempt on nobles
   made them wander in a trackless
     waste.
41 But he lifted the needy out of their
     affliction
   and increased their families like
     flocks.
42 The upright see and rejoice,
   but all the wicked shut their
     mouths.

43 Let the one who is wise heed these
     things
   and ponder the loving deeds of the
     LORD.

a 29 Dead Sea Scrolls; Masoretic Text / *their
waves*

ROCK SOLID *promises*

**"He stilled the storm to a whisper;
the waves of the sea were hushed."**

Psalm 107:29

**God controls every force on earth. He
does seemingly impossible things.**

Psalm 108[a]

A song. A psalm of David.

[1] My heart, O God, is steadfast;
   I will sing and make music with all
      my soul.
[2] Awake, harp and lyre!
   I will awaken the dawn.
[3] I will praise you, Lord, among the
      nations;
   I will sing of you among the peoples.
[4] For great is your love, higher than the
      heavens;
   your faithfulness reaches to the skies.
[5] Be exalted, O God, above the heavens;
   let your glory be over all the earth.

[6] Save us and help us with your right
      hand,
   that those you love may be delivered.
[7] God has spoken from his sanctuary:
   "In triumph I will parcel out
      Shechem
   and measure off the Valley of
      Sukkoth.
[8] Gilead is mine, Manasseh is mine;
   Ephraim is my helmet,
   Judah is my scepter.
[9] Moab is my washbasin,
   on Edom I toss my sandal;
   over Philistia I shout in triumph."

[10] Who will bring me to the fortified city?
   Who will lead me to Edom?
[11] Is it not you, God, you who have
      rejected us
   and no longer go out with our armies?
[12] Give us aid against the enemy,
   for human help is worthless.
[13] With God we will gain the victory,
   and he will trample down our
      enemies.

Psalm 109

For the director of music. Of David. A psalm.

[1] My God, whom I praise,
   do not remain silent,
[2] for people who are wicked and deceitful
   have opened their mouths against me;
   they have spoken against me with
      lying tongues.
[3] With words of hatred they surround me;
   they attack me without cause.
[4] In return for my friendship they
      accuse me,
   but I am a man of prayer.
[5] They repay me evil for good,
   and hatred for my friendship.

[6] Appoint someone evil to oppose my
      enemy;
   let an accuser stand at his right hand.
[7] When he is tried, let him be found
      guilty,
   and may his prayers condemn him.
[8] May his days be few;
   may another take his place of
      leadership.
[9] May his children be fatherless
   and his wife a widow.
[10] May his children be wandering
      beggars;
   may they be driven[b] from their
      ruined homes.
[11] May a creditor seize all he has;
   may strangers plunder the fruits of
      his labor.
[12] May no one extend kindness to him
   or take pity on his fatherless
      children.
[13] May his descendants be cut off,
   their names blotted out from the
      next generation.
[14] May the iniquity of his fathers be
      remembered before the Lord;
   may the sin of his mother never be
      blotted out.
[15] May their sins always remain before
      the Lord,
   that he may blot out their name
      from the earth.

[16] For he never thought of doing a
      kindness,
   but hounded to death the poor
   and the needy and the
      brokenhearted.
[17] He loved to pronounce a curse—
   may it come back on him.
   He found no pleasure in blessing—
   may it be far from him.

[a] In Hebrew texts 108:1-13 is numbered 108:2-
14.   [b] 10 Septuagint; Hebrew sought

¹⁸ He wore cursing as his garment;
   it entered into his body like water,
   into his bones like oil.
¹⁹ May it be like a cloak wrapped about
      him,
   like a belt tied forever around him.
²⁰ May this be the LORD's payment to
      my accusers,
   to those who speak evil of me.

²¹ But you, Sovereign LORD,
   help me for your name's sake;
   out of the goodness of your love,
      deliver me.
²² For I am poor and needy,
   and my heart is wounded within me.
²³ I fade away like an evening shadow;
   I am shaken off like a locust.
²⁴ My knees give way from fasting;
   my body is thin and gaunt.
²⁵ I am an object of scorn to my accusers;
   when they see me, they shake their
      heads.

²⁶ Help me, LORD my God;
   save me according to your unfailing
      love.
²⁷ Let them know that it is your hand,
   that you, LORD, have done it.
²⁸ While they curse, may you bless;
   may those who attack me be put to
      shame,
   but may your servant rejoice.
²⁹ May my accusers be clothed with
      disgrace
   and wrapped in shame as in a cloak.

³⁰ With my mouth I will greatly extol
      the LORD;
   in the great throng of worshipers I
      will praise him.
³¹ For he stands at the right hand of the
      needy,
   to save their lives from those who
      would condemn them.

Psalm 110

Of David. A psalm.

¹ The LORD says to my lord:ᵃ

"Sit at my right hand
   until I make your enemies
   a footstool for your feet."

² The LORD will extend your mighty
      scepter from Zion, saying,
   "Rule in the midst of your enemies!"
³ Your troops will be willing
   on your day of battle.
Arrayed in holy splendor,
   your young men will come to you
   like dew from the morning's womb.ᵇ

⁴ The LORD has sworn
   and will not change his mind:
"You are a priest forever,
   in the order of Melchizedek."

⁵ The Lord is at your right handᶜ;
   he will crush kings on the day of his
      wrath.
⁶ He will judge the nations, heaping up
      the dead
   and crushing the rulers of the whole
      earth.
⁷ He will drink from a brook along the
      way,ᵈ
   and so he will lift his head high.

Psalm 111ᵉ

¹ Praise the LORD.ᶠ

I will extol the LORD with all my
      heart
   in the council of the upright and in
      the assembly.

² Great are the works of the LORD;
   they are pondered by all who
      delight in them.
³ Glorious and majestic are his deeds,
   and his righteousness endures
      forever.
⁴ He has caused his wonders to be
      remembered;
   the LORD is gracious and
      compassionate.
⁵ He provides food for those who fear
      him;
   he remembers his covenant forever.

ᵃ 1 Or *Lord*   ᵇ 3 The meaning of the Hebrew
for this sentence is uncertain.   ᶜ 5 Or *My lord
is at your right hand, LORD*   ᵈ 7 The meaning
of the Hebrew for this clause is uncertain.
ᵉ This psalm is an acrostic poem, the lines of
which begin with the successive letters of the
Hebrew alphabet.   ᶠ 1 Hebrew *Hallelu Yah*

⁶He has shown his people the power of
his works,
giving them the lands of other
nations.
⁷The works of his hands are faithful
and just;
all his precepts are trustworthy.
⁸They are established for ever and ever,
enacted in faithfulness and
uprightness.
⁹He provided redemption for his people;
he ordained his covenant forever—
holy and awesome is his name.

¹⁰The fear of the LORD is the beginning
of wisdom;
all who follow his precepts have
good understanding.
To him belongs eternal praise.

Psalm 112ᵃ

¹Praise the LORD.ᵇ

Blessed are those who fear the LORD,
who find great delight in his
commands.

²Their children will be mighty in the
land;
the generation of the upright will be
blessed.
³Wealth and riches are in their houses,
and their righteousness endures
forever.
⁴Even in darkness light dawns for the
upright,
for those who are gracious and
compassionate and righteous.
⁵Good will come to those who are
generous and lend freely,
who conduct their affairs with
justice.

⁶Surely the righteous will never be
shaken;
they will be remembered forever.
⁷They will have no fear of bad news;
their hearts are steadfast, trusting
in the LORD.
⁸Their hearts are secure, they will have
no fear;
in the end they will look in triumph
on their foes.

⁹They have freely scattered their gifts
to the poor,
their righteousness endures forever;
their hornᶜ will be lifted high in
honor.
¹⁰The wicked will see and be vexed,
they will gnash their teeth and
waste away;
the longings of the wicked will
come to nothing.

ROCK SOLID promises

"The longings of the wicked will come to nothing." Psalm 112:10

If you set your heart on doing evil, God
will dash your hopes.

Psalm 113

¹Praise the LORD.ᵈ

Praise the LORD, you his servants;
praise the name of the LORD.
²Let the name of the LORD be praised,
both now and forevermore.
³From the rising of the sun to the place
where it sets,
the name of the LORD is to be
praised.

⁴The LORD is exalted over all the
nations,
his glory above the heavens.
⁵Who is like the LORD our God,
the One who sits enthroned on
high,

ᵃ This psalm is an acrostic poem, the lines of
which begin with the successive letters of the
Hebrew alphabet.   ᵇ 1 Hebrew Hallelu Yah
ᶜ 9 Horn here symbolizes dignity.
ᵈ 1 Hebrew Hallelu Yah; also in verse 9

⁶who stoops down to look
on the heavens and the earth?

⁷He raises the poor from the dust
and lifts the needy from the ash
heap;
⁸he seats them with princes,
with the princes of his people.
⁹He settles the childless woman in her
home
as a happy mother of children.

Praise the LORD.

Psalm 114

¹When Israel came out of Egypt,
Jacob from a people of foreign
tongue,
²Judah became God's sanctuary,
Israel his dominion.

³The sea looked and fled,
the Jordan turned back;
⁴the mountains leaped like rams,
the hills like lambs.

⁵Why was it, sea, that you fled?
Why, Jordan, did you turn back?
⁶Why, mountains, did you leap like rams,
you hills, like lambs?

⁷Tremble, earth, at the presence of the
Lord,
at the presence of the God of
Jacob,
⁸who turned the rock into a pool,
the hard rock into springs of
water.

Psalm 115

¹Not to us, LORD, not to us
but to your name be the glory,
because of your love and
faithfulness.

²Why do the nations say,
"Where is their God?"
³Our God is in heaven;
he does whatever pleases him.
⁴But their idols are silver and gold,
made by human hands.
⁵They have mouths, but cannot speak,
eyes, but cannot see.

⁶They have ears, but cannot hear,
noses, but cannot smell.
⁷They have hands, but cannot feel,
feet, but cannot walk,
nor can they utter a sound with their
throats.
⁸Those who make them will be like
them,
and so will all who trust in them.

⁹All you Israelites, trust in the
LORD—
he is their help and shield.
¹⁰House of Aaron, trust in the LORD—
he is their help and shield.
¹¹You who fear him, trust in the
LORD—
he is their help and shield.

¹²The LORD remembers us and will
bless us:
He will bless his people Israel,
he will bless the house of Aaron,
¹³he will bless those who fear the
LORD—
small and great alike.

¹⁴May the LORD cause you to
flourish,
both you and your children.
¹⁵May you be blessed by the LORD,
the Maker of heaven and earth.

¹⁶The highest heavens belong to the
LORD,
but the earth he has given to
mankind.
¹⁷It is not the dead who praise the
LORD,
those who go down to the place of
silence;
¹⁸it is we who extol the LORD,
both now and forevermore.

Praise the LORD.ᵃ

Psalm 116

¹I love the LORD, for he heard my
voice;
he heard my cry for mercy.
²Because he turned his ear to me,
I will call on him as long as I live.

ᵃ 18 Hebrew *Hallelu Yah*

ROCK SOLID principles

Psalm 115:1–11

Give God the credit.

Always the biggest kid anywhere in his grade, Gavin looked destined to be a state champion wrestler by the time he hit high school. In the meantime, however, he was working hard at being the most annoying guy in the universe. With the ego of a professional wrestler who isn't happy unless he is shouting into a microphone to an arena full of fans, Gavin strolled through school and expected crowds to part and make way. He made a hobby out of intimidating smaller kids—which was everyone. And he possessed the kind of ferocious temper that made his classmates wonder if someday he would snap an opponent in two. Gavin was big. Enormously big. And he knew it.

Old Testament idols were hunks of metal or wood carved into made-up gods. The world is still jam-packed with idols, because we create a false god whenever we make something more important than the Lord. Sometimes we even idolize ourselves, congratulating ourselves for anything good we do. But God is the one who really deserves the credit.

3 The cords of death entangled me,
  the anguish of the grave came over me;
  I was overcome by distress and
    sorrow.
4 Then I called on the name of the Lord:
  "Lord, save me!"

5 The Lord is gracious and righteous;
  our God is full of compassion.
6 The Lord protects the unwary;
  when I was brought low, he saved me.

7 Return to your rest, my soul,
  for the Lord has been good to you.

8 For you, Lord, have delivered me
    from death,
  my eyes from tears,
  my feet from stumbling,
9 that I may walk before the Lord
  in the land of the living.

10 I trusted in the Lord when I said,
  "I am greatly afflicted";
11 in my alarm I said,
  "Everyone is a liar."

12 What shall I return to the Lord
  for all his goodness to me?
13 I will lift up the cup of salvation
  and call on the name of the Lord.
14 I will fulfill my vows to the Lord
  in the presence of all his people.

15 Precious in the sight of the Lord
  is the death of his faithful
    servants.
16 Truly I am your servant, Lord;
  I serve you just as my mother did;
  you have freed me from my chains.

17 I will sacrifice a thank offering to you
  and call on the name of the Lord.
18 I will fulfill my vows to the Lord
  in the presence of all his people,
19 in the courts of the house of the
    Lord—
  in your midst, Jerusalem.

Praise the Lord.[a]

[a] 19 Hebrew Hallelu Yah

Psalm 117

¹ Praise the LORD, all you nations;
    extol him, all you peoples.
² For great is his love toward us,
    and the faithfulness of the LORD
        endures forever.

Praise the LORD.ᵃ

Psalm 118

¹ Give thanks to the LORD, for he is
        good;
    his love endures forever.

² Let Israel say:
    "His love endures forever."
³ Let the house of Aaron say:
    "His love endures forever."
⁴ Let those who fear the LORD say:
    "His love endures forever."

⁵ When hard pressed, I cried to the
        LORD;
    he brought me into a spacious place.
⁶ The LORD is with me; I will not be
        afraid.
    What can mere mortals do to me?
⁷ The LORD is with me; he is my helper.
    I look in triumph on my enemies.

⁸ It is better to take refuge in the LORD
    than to trust in humans.
⁹ It is better to take refuge in the LORD
    than to trust in princes.
¹⁰ All the nations surrounded me,
    but in the name of the LORD I cut
        them down.
¹¹ They surrounded me on every side,
    but in the name of the LORD I cut
        them down.
¹² They swarmed around me like bees,
    but they were consumed as quickly
        as burning thorns;
    in the name of the LORD I cut them
        down.
¹³ I was pushed back and about to fall,
    but the LORD helped me.
¹⁴ The LORD is my strength and my
        defenseᵇ;
    he has become my salvation.

¹⁵ Shouts of joy and victory
    resound in the tents of the righteous:

"The LORD's right hand has done
        mighty things!
¹⁶   The LORD's right hand is lifted
        high;
    the LORD's right hand has done
        mighty things!"
¹⁷ I will not die but live,
    and will proclaim what the LORD
        has done.
¹⁸ The LORD has chastened me severely,
    but he has not given me over to
        death.
¹⁹ Open for me the gates of the
        righteous;
    I will enter and give thanks to the
        LORD.
²⁰ This is the gate of the LORD
    through which the righteous may
        enter.
²¹ I will give you thanks, for you
        answered me;
    you have become my salvation.

²² The stone the builders rejected
    has become the cornerstone;
²³ the LORD has done this,
    and it is marvelous in our eyes.
²⁴ The LORD has done it this very day;
    let us rejoice today and be glad.

²⁵ LORD, save us!
    LORD, grant us success!

²⁶ Blessed is he who comes in the name
        of the LORD.
    From the house of the LORD we
        bless you.ᶜ
²⁷ The LORD is God,
    and he has made his light shine on
        us.
With boughs in hand, join in the
        festal procession
    upᵈ to the horns of the altar.

²⁸ You are my God, and I will praise you;
    you are my God, and I will exalt
        you.

²⁹ Give thanks to the LORD, for he is
        good;
    his love endures forever.

ᵃ 2 Hebrew *Hallelu Yah*   ᵇ 14 Or *song*
ᶜ 26 The Hebrew is plural.   ᵈ 27 Or *Bind the
festal sacrifice with ropes / and take it*

Psalm 119[a]

א Aleph

1 Blessed are those whose ways are
blameless,
who walk according to the law of
the Lord.
2 Blessed are those who keep his statutes
and seek him with all their heart—
3 they do no wrong
but follow his ways.
4 You have laid down precepts
that are to be fully obeyed.
5 Oh, that my ways were steadfast
in obeying your decrees!
6 Then I would not be put to shame
when I consider all your commands.
7 I will praise you with an upright heart
as I learn your righteous laws.
8 I will obey your decrees;
do not utterly forsake me.

ב Beth

9 How can a young person stay on the
path of purity?
By living according to your word.
10 I seek you with all my heart;
do not let me stray from your
commands.
11 I have hidden your word in my heart
that I might not sin against you.
12 Praise be to you, Lord;
teach me your decrees.

ROCK SOLID
promises

**"I have hidden your word in my
heart that I might not sin against
you."** Psalm 119:11

**God's truth has the power to teach and
encourage you to choose to stay true to
him.**

---

13 With my lips I recount
all the laws that come from your
mouth.
14 I rejoice in following your statutes
as one rejoices in great riches.
15 I meditate on your precepts
and consider your ways.
16 I delight in your decrees;
I will not neglect your word.

ג Gimel

17 Be good to your servant while I live,
that I may obey your word.
18 Open my eyes that I may see
wonderful things in your law.
19 I am a stranger on earth;
do not hide your commands from me.
20 My soul is consumed with longing
for your laws at all times.
21 You rebuke the arrogant, who are
accursed,
those who stray from your
commands.
22 Remove from me their scorn and
contempt,
for I keep your statutes.
23 Though rulers sit together and
slander me,
your servant will meditate on your
decrees.
24 Your statutes are my delight;
they are my counselors.

ד Daleth

25 I am laid low in the dust;
preserve my life according to your
word.
26 I gave an account of my ways and you
answered me;
teach me your decrees.
27 Cause me to understand the way of
your precepts,
that I may meditate on your
wonderful deeds.
28 My soul is weary with sorrow;
strengthen me according to your
word.

[a] This psalm is an acrostic poem, the stanzas of
which begin with successive letters of the Hebrew
alphabet; moreover, the verses of each stanza begin
with the same letter of the Hebrew alphabet.

²⁹Keep me from deceitful ways;
 be gracious to me and teach me
 your law.
³⁰I have chosen the way of faithfulness;
 I have set my heart on your laws.
³¹I hold fast to your statutes, Lord;
 do not let me be put to shame.
³²I run in the path of your commands,
 for you have broadened my
 understanding.

ה He

³³Teach me, Lord, the way of your
 decrees,
 that I may follow it to the end.^a
³⁴Give me understanding, so that I may
 keep your law
 and obey it with all my heart.
³⁵Direct me in the path of your
 commands,
 for there I find delight.
³⁶Turn my heart toward your statutes
 and not toward selfish gain.
³⁷Turn my eyes away from worthless
 things;
 preserve my life according to your
 word.^b
³⁸Fulfill your promise to your servant,
 so that you may be feared.
³⁹Take away the disgrace I dread,
 for your laws are good.
⁴⁰How I long for your precepts!
 In your righteousness preserve my
 life.

ו Waw

⁴¹May your unfailing love come to me,
 Lord,
 your salvation, according to your
 promise;
⁴²then I can answer anyone who taunts
 me,
 for I trust in your word.
⁴³Never take your word of truth from
 my mouth,
 for I have put my hope in your
 laws.
⁴⁴I will always obey your law,
 for ever and ever.
⁴⁵I will walk about in freedom,
 for I have sought out your precepts.

⁴⁶I will speak of your statutes before
 kings
 and will not be put to shame,
⁴⁷for I delight in your commands
 because I love them.
⁴⁸I reach out for your commands, which
 I love,
 that I may meditate on your
 decrees.

ז Zayin

⁴⁹Remember your word to your servant,
 for you have given me hope.
⁵⁰My comfort in my suffering is this:
 Your promise preserves my life.
⁵¹The arrogant mock me unmercifully,
 but I do not turn from your law.
⁵²I remember, Lord, your ancient laws,
 and I find comfort in them.
⁵³Indignation grips me because of the
 wicked,
 who have forsaken your law.
⁵⁴Your decrees are the theme of my song
 wherever I lodge.
⁵⁵In the night, Lord, I remember your
 name,
 that I may keep your law.
⁵⁶This has been my practice:
 I obey your precepts.

ח Heth

⁵⁷You are my portion, Lord;
 I have promised to obey your words.
⁵⁸I have sought your face with all my
 heart;
 be gracious to me according to your
 promise.
⁵⁹I have considered my ways
 and have turned my steps to your
 statutes.
⁶⁰I will hasten and not delay
 to obey your commands.
⁶¹Though the wicked bind me with
 ropes,
 I will not forget your law.
⁶²At midnight I rise to give you thanks
 for your righteous laws.

^a 33 Or *follow it for its reward*   ^b 37 Two
manuscripts of the Masoretic Text and Dead Sea
Scrolls; most manuscripts of the Masoretic Text
life in your way

⁶³ I am a friend to all who fear you,
  to all who follow your precepts.
⁶⁴ The earth is filled with your love,
  LORD;
  teach me your decrees.

ט Teth

⁶⁵ Do good to your servant
  according to your word, LORD.
⁶⁶ Teach me knowledge and good
  judgment,
  for I trust your commands.
⁶⁷ Before I was afflicted I went astray,
  but now I obey your word.
⁶⁸ You are good, and what you do is
  good;
  teach me your decrees.
⁶⁹ Though the arrogant have smeared me
  with lies,
  I keep your precepts with all my
  heart.
⁷⁰ Their hearts are callous and unfeeling,
  but I delight in your law.
⁷¹ It was good for me to be afflicted
  so that I might learn your decrees.
⁷² The law from your mouth is more
  precious to me
  than thousands of pieces of silver
  and gold.

י Yodh

⁷³ Your hands made me and formed me;
  give me understanding to learn your
  commands.
⁷⁴ May those who fear you rejoice when
  they see me,
  for I have put my hope in your word.
⁷⁵ I know, LORD, that your laws are
  righteous,
  and that in faithfulness you have
  afflicted me.
⁷⁶ May your unfailing love be my
  comfort,
  according to your promise to your
  servant.
⁷⁷ Let your compassion come to me that
  I may live,
  for your law is my delight.
⁷⁸ May the arrogant be put to shame for
  wronging me without cause;
  but I will meditate on your precepts.

⁷⁹ May those who fear you turn to me,
  those who understand your statutes.
⁸⁰ May I wholeheartedly follow your
  decrees,
  that I may not be put to shame.

כ Kaph

⁸¹ My soul faints with longing for your
  salvation,
  but I have put my hope in your word.
⁸² My eyes fail, looking for your promise;
  I say, "When will you comfort me?"
⁸³ Though I am like a wineskin in the
  smoke,
  I do not forget your decrees.
⁸⁴ How long must your servant wait?
  When will you punish my
  persecutors?
⁸⁵ The arrogant dig pits to trap me,
  contrary to your law.
⁸⁶ All your commands are trustworthy;
  help me, for I am being persecuted
  without cause.
⁸⁷ They almost wiped me from the earth,
  but I have not forsaken your
  precepts.
⁸⁸ In your unfailing love preserve my life,
  that I may obey the statutes of your
  mouth.

ל Lamedh

⁸⁹ Your word, LORD, is eternal;
  it stands firm in the heavens.
⁹⁰ Your faithfulness continues through
  all generations;
  you established the earth, and it
  endures.
⁹¹ Your laws endure to this day,
  for all things serve you.
⁹² If your law had not been my delight,
  I would have perished in my
  affliction.
⁹³ I will never forget your precepts,
  for by them you have preserved my
  life.
⁹⁴ Save me, for I am yours;
  I have sought out your precepts.
⁹⁵ The wicked are waiting to destroy me,
  but I will ponder your statutes.
⁹⁶ To all perfection I see a limit,
  but your commands are boundless.

מ Mem

⁹⁷Oh, how I love your law!
  I meditate on it all day long.
⁹⁸Your commands are always with me
  and make me wiser than my
    enemies.
⁹⁹I have more insight than all my teachers,
  for I meditate on your statutes.
¹⁰⁰I have more understanding than the
    elders,
  for I obey your precepts.
¹⁰¹I have kept my feet from every evil
    path
  so that I might obey your word.
¹⁰²I have not departed from your laws,
  for you yourself have taught me.
¹⁰³How sweet are your words to my taste,
  sweeter than honey to my mouth!
¹⁰⁴I gain understanding from your
    precepts;
  therefore I hate every wrong path.

נ Nun

¹⁰⁵Your word is a lamp for my feet,
  a light on my path.

ROCK SOLID plans

Psalm 119:105

Read the manual.

Not only does Psalm 119 form a highly structured poem where each line in a section starts with the same letter of the Hebrew alphabet, but this longest chapter in the Bible spans 176 verses detailing the greatness of God's Word. Read the entire psalm and you will discover that every statement recaps a simple fact: God's Word teaches you how to stay tightly connected to him. God didn't give you the Bible to sit on your shelf. He designed it to be your complete and reliable handbook for life.

Your next step: Plan how you can use the Bible each day to keep you from stumbling through life.

¹⁰⁶I have taken an oath and confirmed it,
  that I will follow your righteous
    laws.
¹⁰⁷I have suffered much;
  preserve my life, LORD, according
    to your word.
¹⁰⁸Accept, LORD, the willing praise of
    my mouth,
  and teach me your laws.
¹⁰⁹Though I constantly take my life in
    my hands,
  I will not forget your law.
¹¹⁰The wicked have set a snare for me,
  but I have not strayed from your
    precepts.
¹¹¹Your statutes are my heritage forever;
  they are the joy of my heart.
¹¹²My heart is set on keeping your
    decrees
  to the very end.ᵃ

ס Samekh

¹¹³I hate double-minded people,
  but I love your law.
¹¹⁴You are my refuge and my shield;
  I have put my hope in your word.
¹¹⁵Away from me, you evildoers,
  that I may keep the commands of
    my God!
¹¹⁶Sustain me, my God, according to
    your promise, and I will live;
  do not let my hopes be dashed.
¹¹⁷Uphold me, and I will be delivered;
  I will always have regard for your
    decrees.
¹¹⁸You reject all who stray from your
    decrees,
  for their delusions come to nothing.
¹¹⁹All the wicked of the earth you
    discard like dross;
  therefore I love your statutes.
¹²⁰My flesh trembles in fear of you;
  I stand in awe of your laws.

ע Ayin

¹²¹I have done what is righteous and just;
  do not leave me to my oppressors.
¹²²Ensure your servant's well-being;
  do not let the arrogant oppress me.

ᵃ 112 Or *decrees / for their enduring reward*

¹²³My eyes fail, looking for your
salvation,
looking for your righteous promise.
¹²⁴Deal with your servant according to
your love
and teach me your decrees.
¹²⁵I am your servant; give me discernment
that I may understand your statutes.
¹²⁶It is time for you to act, Lord;
your law is being broken.
¹²⁷Because I love your commands
more than gold, more than pure
gold,
¹²⁸and because I consider all your
precepts right,
I hate every wrong path.

פ Pe

¹²⁹Your statutes are wonderful;
therefore I obey them.
¹³⁰The unfolding of your words gives
light;
it gives understanding to the simple.
¹³¹I open my mouth and pant,
longing for your commands.
¹³²Turn to me and have mercy on me,
as you always do to those who love
your name.
¹³³Direct my footsteps according to your
word;
let no sin rule over me.
¹³⁴Redeem me from human oppression,
that I may obey your precepts.
¹³⁵Make your face shine on your servant
and teach me your decrees.
¹³⁶Streams of tears flow from my eyes,
for your law is not obeyed.

צ Tsadhe

¹³⁷You are righteous, Lord,
and your laws are right.
¹³⁸The statutes you have laid down are
righteous;
they are fully trustworthy.
¹³⁹My zeal wears me out,
for my enemies ignore your words.
¹⁴⁰Your promises have been thoroughly
tested,
and your servant loves them.
¹⁴¹Though I am lowly and despised,
I do not forget your precepts.

¹⁴²Your righteousness is everlasting
and your law is true.
¹⁴³Trouble and distress have come
upon me,
but your commands give me delight.
¹⁴⁴Your statutes are always righteous;
give me understanding that I may
live.

ק Qoph

¹⁴⁵I call with all my heart; answer me,
Lord,
and I will obey your decrees.
¹⁴⁶I call out to you; save me
and I will keep your statutes.
¹⁴⁷I rise before dawn and cry for help;
I have put my hope in your word.
¹⁴⁸My eyes stay open through the
watches of the night,
that I may meditate on your
promises.
¹⁴⁹Hear my voice in accordance with
your love;
preserve my life, Lord, according
to your laws.
¹⁵⁰Those who devise wicked schemes are
near,
but they are far from your law.
¹⁵¹Yet you are near, Lord,
and all your commands are true.
¹⁵²Long ago I learned from your statutes
that you established them to last
forever.

ר Resh

¹⁵³Look on my suffering and deliver me,
for I have not forgotten your law.
¹⁵⁴Defend my cause and redeem me;
preserve my life according to your
promise.
¹⁵⁵Salvation is far from the wicked,
for they do not seek out your
decrees.
¹⁵⁶Your compassion, Lord, is great;
preserve my life according to your
laws.
¹⁵⁷Many are the foes who persecute me,
but I have not turned from your
statutes.
¹⁵⁸I look on the faithless with loathing,
for they do not obey your word.

¹⁵⁹See how I love your precepts;
    preserve my life, Lord, in
        accordance with your love.
¹⁶⁰All your words are true;
    all your righteous laws are
        eternal.

ש Sin and Shin

¹⁶¹Rulers persecute me without cause,
    but my heart trembles at your
        word.
¹⁶²I rejoice in your promise
    like one who finds great spoil.
¹⁶³I hate and detest falsehood
    but I love your law.
¹⁶⁴Seven times a day I praise you
    for your righteous laws.

Psalm 119:160

The Bible is true.

Many people want a solid reason to pick up the Bible. It takes an even bigger motivation to make a habit of reading it. And if you're ever going to put the Bible into action, you need to be fairly well convinced you will reap real benefits. Psalm 119 lays out nearly a couple hundred reasons you can commit your life to the teachings of the Bible, and Psalm 119:160 offers you one of the best: "All your words are true." God's Word is the only book you will ever read that doesn't contain mistakes or inaccuracies or half-truths. It tells you everything you need to navigate your world, especially how to enjoy God, live smart, and spend forever in heaven (see 2 Timothy 3:16–17). You can count on the Bible because it's true.

Think: How does the total truth of the Bible motivate you to read and live out its words?

ROCK SOLID truths

---

¹⁶⁵Great peace have those who love your
    law,
    and nothing can make them
        stumble.
¹⁶⁶I wait for your salvation, Lord,
    and I follow your commands.
¹⁶⁷I obey your statutes,
    for I love them greatly.
¹⁶⁸I obey your precepts and your
        statutes,
    for all my ways are known to you.

ת Taw

¹⁶⁹May my cry come before you, Lord;
    give me understanding according to
        your word.
¹⁷⁰May my supplication come before
        you;
    deliver me according to your
        promise.
¹⁷¹May my lips overflow with praise,
    for you teach me your decrees.
¹⁷²May my tongue sing of your word,
    for all your commands are
        righteous.
¹⁷³May your hand be ready to help me,
    for I have chosen your precepts.
¹⁷⁴I long for your salvation, Lord,
    and your law gives me delight.
¹⁷⁵Let me live that I may praise you,
    and may your laws sustain me.
¹⁷⁶I have strayed like a lost sheep.
    Seek your servant,
    for I have not forgotten your
        commands.

Psalm 120

A song of ascents.

¹I call on the Lord in my distress,
    and he answers me.
²Save me, Lord,
    from lying lips
    and from deceitful tongues.

³What will he do to you,
    and what more besides,
    you deceitful tongue?
⁴He will punish you with a warrior's
        sharp arrows,
    with burning coals of the broom
        bush.

⁵Woe to me that I dwell in Meshek,
  that I live among the tents of
    Kedar!
⁶Too long have I lived
  among those who hate peace.
⁷I am for peace;
  but when I speak, they are for war.

Psalm 121

A song of ascents.

¹I lift up my eyes to the
    mountains—
  where does my help come from?
²My help comes from the Lord,
  the Maker of heaven and earth.

³He will not let your foot slip—
  he who watches over you will not
    slumber;
⁴indeed, he who watches over Israel
  will neither slumber nor sleep.

⁵The Lord watches over you—
  the Lord is your shade at your
    right hand;
⁶the sun will not harm you by day,
  nor the moon by night.

⁷The Lord will keep you from all
    harm—
  he will watch over your life;
⁸the Lord will watch over your
    coming and going
  both now and forevermore.

ROCK SOLID
promises

"The Lord will watch over your coming and going both now and forevermore." Psalm 121:8

Wherever you go and whatever you do, God looks out for you. He never lets you wander out of his sight.

Psalm 122

A song of ascents. Of David.

¹I rejoiced with those who said to me,
  "Let us go to the house of the
    Lord."
²Our feet are standing
  in your gates, Jerusalem.

³Jerusalem is built like a city
  that is closely compacted together.
⁴That is where the tribes go up—
  the tribes of the Lord—
to praise the name of the Lord
  according to the statute given to
    Israel.
⁵There stand the thrones for
    judgment,
  the thrones of the house of David.

⁶Pray for the peace of Jerusalem:
  "May those who love you be secure.
⁷May there be peace within your
    walls
  and security within your citadels."
⁸For the sake of my family and
    friends,
  I will say, "Peace be within you."
⁹For the sake of the house of the Lord
    our God,
  I will seek your prosperity.

Psalm 123

A song of ascents.

¹I lift up my eyes to you,
  to you who sit enthroned in
    heaven.
²As the eyes of slaves look to the hand
    of their master,
  as the eyes of a female slave look to
    the hand of her mistress,
so our eyes look to the Lord our
    God,
  till he shows us his mercy.

³Have mercy on us, Lord, have mercy
    on us,
  for we have endured no end of
    contempt.
⁴We have endured no end
  of ridicule from the arrogant,
  of contempt from the proud.

ROCK·SOLID principles

Psalm 122:1–9

Go to church with your friends.

Shanise felt a little embarrassed riding shotgun with her mom in the family minivan every Wednesday evening. But she was glad her mom was willing to tool around the neighborhood picking up friends for church. Some of Shanise's friends were deep into trouble most evenings of the week, but she was glad to have her mid-week youth group to introduce them to God and show them a better way to live. The pick-up rounds were just the start of the fun because every week Shanise's youth pastor managed to plan an evening of worship, study, and activities that pumped everyone up for another week. For Shanise, church was never a nuisance. It was as good as good gets.

Psalm 122 is a "psalm of ascent," a song sung as people trekked to worship God in Jerusalem. While a trip to church might not seem like much of a reason to sing, getting together to worship with other believers should be a party. There's nothing better than being near God and hanging with all your "family and friends" (Psalm 122:8).

Psalm 124

A song of ascents. Of David.

1 If the Lord had not been on our
side—
let Israel say—
2 if the Lord had not been on our side
when people attacked us,
3 they would have swallowed us alive
when their anger flared against us;
4 the flood would have engulfed us,
the torrent would have swept over
us,
5 the raging waters
would have swept us away.

6 Praise be to the Lord,
who has not let us be torn by their
teeth.
7 We have escaped like a bird
from the fowler's snare;
the snare has been broken,
and we have escaped.
8 Our help is in the name of the Lord,
the Maker of heaven and earth.

Psalm 125

A song of ascents.

1 Those who trust in the Lord are like
Mount Zion,
which cannot be shaken but endures
forever.
2 As the mountains surround Jerusalem,
so the Lord surrounds his people
both now and forevermore.

3 The scepter of the wicked will not
remain
over the land allotted to the
righteous,
for then the righteous might use
their hands to do evil.

4 Lord, do good to those who are
good,
to those who are upright in heart.
5 But those who turn to crooked ways
the Lord will banish with the
evildoers.

Peace be on Israel.

Psalm 126

A song of ascents.

¹ When the Lord restored the fortunes
of ᵃ Zion,
we were like those who dreamed.ᵇ
² Our mouths were filled with laughter,
our tongues with songs of joy.
Then it was said among the nations,
"The Lord has done great things
for them."
³ The Lord has done great things for us,
and we are filled with joy.

⁴ Restore our fortunes,ᶜ Lord,
like streams in the Negev.
⁵ Those who sow with tears
will reap with songs of joy.
⁶ Those who go out weeping,
carrying seed to sow,
will return with songs of joy,
carrying sheaves with them.

Psalm 127

A song of ascents. Of Solomon.

¹ Unless the Lord builds the house,
the builders labor in vain.
Unless the Lord watches over the city,
the guards stand watch in vain.
² In vain you rise early
and stay up late,
toiling for food to eat —
for he grants sleep toᵈ those he
loves.

³ Children are a heritage from the
Lord,
offspring a reward from him.
⁴ Like arrows in the hands of a warrior
are children born in one's youth.
⁵ Blessed is the man
whose quiver is full of them.
They will not be put to shame
when they contend with their
opponents in court.

Psalm 128

A song of ascents.

¹ Blessed are all who fear the Lord,
who walk in obedience to him.

UNSHAKEN God

Psalm 127:1 – 2

God is practical.

Critics say religion fills people's heads with heavenly thoughts that do no good on earth. But your God is highly practical. He notices your everyday needs and fills them. The Lord knows you require basics like food and clothing (see Matthew 6:31 – 32), and he promises to meet "all your needs according to the riches of his glory in Christ Jesus" (Philippians 4:19). God cares so much about strong homes that he works alongside builders. He considers neighborhood safety so essential that he stands watch with human guards (see Psalm 127:1). God even warns you against overworking and commands you to get enough sleep at night (see Psalm 127:2). You serve a get-it-done kind of God.

So ... Why does God care about your practical needs?

² You will eat the fruit of your labor;
blessings and prosperity will be
yours.
³ Your wife will be like a fruitful vine
within your house;
your children will be like olive shoots
around your table.
⁴ Yes, this will be the blessing
for the man who fears the Lord.

⁵ May the Lord bless you from Zion;
may you see the prosperity of
Jerusalem
all the days of your life.
⁶ May you live to see your children's
children —
peace be on Israel.

ᵃ 1 Or Lord brought back the captives to
ᵇ 1 Or those restored to health   ᶜ 4 Or Bring
back our captives   ᵈ 2 Or eat — / for while they
sleep he provides for

Psalm 129

A song of ascents.

1 "They have greatly oppressed me from
my youth,"
let Israel say;
2 "they have greatly oppressed me from
my youth,
but they have not gained the victory
over me.
3 Plowmen have plowed my back
and made their furrows long.
4 But the Lord is righteous;
he has cut me free from the cords of
the wicked."

5 May all who hate Zion
be turned back in shame.
6 May they be like grass on the roof,
which withers before it can grow;
7 a reaper cannot fill his hands with it,
nor one who gathers fill his arms.
8 May those who pass by not say to them,
"The blessing of the Lord be on you;
we bless you in the name of the
Lord."

Psalm 130

A song of ascents.

1 Out of the depths I cry to you, Lord;
2   Lord, hear my voice.
Let your ears be attentive
to my cry for mercy.

3 If you, Lord, kept a record of sins,
Lord, who could stand?
4 But with you there is forgiveness,
so that we can, with reverence,
serve you.

5 I wait for the Lord, my whole being
waits,
and in his word I put my hope.
6 I wait for the Lord
more than watchmen wait for the
morning,
more than watchmen wait for the
morning.

7 Israel, put your hope in the Lord,
for with the Lord is unfailing love
and with him is full redemption.

8 He himself will redeem Israel
from all their sins.

Psalm 131

A song of ascents. Of David.

1 My heart is not proud, Lord,
my eyes are not haughty;
I do not concern myself with great
matters
or things too wonderful for me.
2 But I have calmed and quieted myself,
I am like a weaned child with its
mother;
like a weaned child I am content.

3 Israel, put your hope in the Lord
both now and forevermore.

Psalm 132

A song of ascents.

1 Lord, remember David
and all his self-denial.

2 He swore an oath to the Lord,
he made a vow to the Mighty One
of Jacob:
3 "I will not enter my house
or go to my bed,
4 I will allow no sleep to my eyes
or slumber to my eyelids,
5 till I find a place for the Lord,
a dwelling for the Mighty One of
Jacob."

6 We heard it in Ephrathah,
we came upon it in the fields of Jaar:*a*
7 "Let us go to his dwelling place,
let us worship at his footstool,
saying,
8 'Arise, Lord, and come to your
resting place,
you and the ark of your might.
9 May your priests be clothed with your
righteousness;
may your faithful people sing for joy.' "

10 For the sake of your servant David,
do not reject your anointed one.

*a 6 Or heard of it in Ephrathah, / we found it in
the fields of Jearim. (See 1 Chron. 13:5,6) (And
no quotation marks around verses 7-9)*

¹¹ The Lᴏʀᴅ swore an oath to David,
  a sure oath he will not revoke:
  "One of your own descendants
  I will place on your throne.
¹² If your sons keep my covenant
  and the statutes I teach them,
  then their sons will sit
  on your throne for ever and ever."

¹³ For the Lᴏʀᴅ has chosen Zion,
  he has desired it for his dwelling,
  saying,
¹⁴ "This is my resting place for ever and
  ever;
  here I will sit enthroned, for I have
  desired it.
¹⁵ I will bless her with abundant provisions;
  her poor I will satisfy with food.
¹⁶ I will clothe her priests with salvation,
  and her faithful people will ever
  sing for joy.

¹⁷ "Here I will make a horn^a grow for
  David
  and set up a lamp for my anointed one.
¹⁸ I will clothe his enemies with shame,
  but his head will be adorned with a
  radiant crown."

Psalm 133

A song of ascents. Of David.

¹ How good and pleasant it is
  when God's people live together in
  unity!

ROCK SOLID promises

"How good and pleasant it is when God's people live together in unity!" Psalm 133:1

You won't find a sweeter spot than living at peace with your spiritual brothers and sisters.

---

² It is like precious oil poured on the
  head,
  running down on the beard,
  running down on Aaron's beard,
  down on the collar of his robe.
³ It is as if the dew of Hermon
  were falling on Mount Zion.
  For there the Lᴏʀᴅ bestows his
  blessing,
  even life forevermore.

Psalm 134

A song of ascents.

¹ Praise the Lᴏʀᴅ, all you servants of
  the Lᴏʀᴅ
  who minister by night in the house
  of the Lᴏʀᴅ.
² Lift up your hands in the sanctuary
  and praise the Lᴏʀᴅ.

³ May the Lᴏʀᴅ bless you from Zion,
  he who is the Maker of heaven and
  earth.

Psalm 135

¹ Praise the Lᴏʀᴅ.^b

Praise the name of the Lᴏʀᴅ;
  praise him, you servants of the
  Lᴏʀᴅ,
² you who minister in the house of the
  Lᴏʀᴅ,
  in the courts of the house of our
  God.

³ Praise the Lᴏʀᴅ, for the Lᴏʀᴅ is
  good;
  sing praise to his name, for that is
  pleasant.
⁴ For the Lᴏʀᴅ has chosen Jacob to be
  his own,
  Israel to be his treasured possession.

⁵ I know that the Lᴏʀᴅ is great,
  that our Lord is greater than all
  gods.
⁶ The Lᴏʀᴅ does whatever pleases him,
  in the heavens and on the earth,
  in the seas and all their depths.

---

^a 17 Horn here symbolizes strong one, that is,
king. ^b 1 Hebrew Hallelu Yah; also in verses
3 and 21

⁷He makes clouds rise from the ends of
the earth;
he sends lightning with the rain
and brings out the wind from his
storehouses.

⁸He struck down the firstborn of Egypt,
the firstborn of people and animals.
⁹He sent his signs and wonders into
your midst, Egypt,
against Pharaoh and all his servants.
¹⁰He struck down many nations
and killed mighty kings—
¹¹Sihon king of the Amorites,
Og king of Bashan,
and all the kings of Canaan—
¹²and he gave their land as an inheritance,
an inheritance to his people Israel.

¹³Your name, LORD, endures forever,
your renown, LORD, through all
generations.
¹⁴For the LORD will vindicate his people
and have compassion on his servants.

¹⁵The idols of the nations are silver and
gold,
made by human hands.
¹⁶They have mouths, but cannot speak,
eyes, but cannot see.
¹⁷They have ears, but cannot hear,
nor is there breath in their mouths.
¹⁸Those who make them will be like
them,
and so will all who trust in them.

¹⁹All you Israelites, praise the LORD;
house of Aaron, praise the LORD;
²⁰house of Levi, praise the LORD;
you who fear him, praise the LORD.
²¹Praise be to the LORD from Zion,
to him who dwells in Jerusalem.

Praise the LORD.

Psalm 136

¹Give thanks to the LORD, for he is
good.
His love endures forever.
²Give thanks to the God of gods.
His love endures forever.
³Give thanks to the Lord of lords:
His love endures forever.

⁴to him who alone does great wonders,
His love endures forever.
⁵who by his understanding made the
heavens,
His love endures forever.
⁶who spread out the earth upon the
waters,
His love endures forever.
⁷who made the great lights—
His love endures forever.
⁸the sun to govern the day,
His love endures forever.
⁹the moon and stars to govern the
night;
His love endures forever.

¹⁰to him who struck down the firstborn
of Egypt
His love endures forever.
¹¹and brought Israel out from among
them
His love endures forever.
¹²with a mighty hand and outstretched
arm;
His love endures forever.

¹³to him who divided the Red Sea*ᵃ*
asunder
His love endures forever.
¹⁴and brought Israel through the midst
of it,
His love endures forever.
¹⁵but swept Pharaoh and his army into
the Red Sea;
His love endures forever.

¹⁶to him who led his people through the
wilderness;
His love endures forever.

¹⁷to him who struck down great kings,
His love endures forever.
¹⁸and killed mighty kings—
His love endures forever.
¹⁹Sihon king of the Amorites
His love endures forever.
²⁰and Og king of Bashan—
His love endures forever.
²¹and gave their land as an inheritance,
His love endures forever.
²²an inheritance to his servant Israel.
His love endures forever.

ᵃ 13 Or *the Sea of Reeds*; also in verse 15

23 He remembered us in our low estate
His love endures forever.
24 and freed us from our enemies.
His love endures forever.
25 He gives food to every creature.
His love endures forever.

26 Give thanks to the God of heaven.
His love endures forever.

Psalm 137

1 By the rivers of Babylon we sat and
wept
when we remembered Zion.
2 There on the poplars
we hung our harps,
3 for there our captors asked us for songs,
our tormentors demanded songs of
joy;
they said, "Sing us one of the songs
of Zion!"

UNSHAKEN *God*

Psalm 136:1 – 26

God is merciful.

You aren't paying attention if you miss
the main point of Psalm 136: "*His love
endures forever . . .* " That word "love"
is a particular brand of caring. It's the
compassion God shows to people stuck
in a miserable situation — his "mercy."
The Lord shows mercy when people get
hurt because of their own actions, like
when we mess up our lives through sin.
He shows mercy to people who suffer
as a result of things they didn't cause,
like accidents or illness. This ancient
song lists examples of God's blessings
and his mighty acts of creation. It highlights episodes where God rescued his
people from dire circumstances. There's
a power behind the Lord's every kind act.
It's his huge merciful heart.

**So . . . When do you need mercy from
God?**

4 How can we sing the songs of the
Lord
while in a foreign land?
5 If I forget you, Jerusalem,
may my right hand forget its
skill.
6 May my tongue cling to the roof of
my mouth
if I do not remember you,
if I do not consider Jerusalem
my highest joy.

7 Remember, Lord, what the
Edomites did
on the day Jerusalem fell.
"Tear it down," they cried,
"tear it down to its foundations!"
8 Daughter Babylon, doomed to
destruction,
happy is the one who repays you
according to what you have done
to us.
9 Happy is the one who seizes your
infants
and dashes them against the
rocks.

Psalm 138

Of David.

1 I will praise you, Lord, with all my
heart;
before the "gods" I will sing your
praise.
2 I will bow down toward your holy
temple
and will praise your name
for your unfailing love and your
faithfulness,
for you have so exalted your solemn
decree
that it surpasses your fame.
3 When I called, you answered me;
you greatly emboldened me.

4 May all the kings of the earth praise
you, Lord,
when they hear what you have
decreed.
5 May they sing of the ways of the
Lord,
for the glory of the Lord is great.

6Though the LORD is exalted, he looks
    kindly on the lowly;
  though lofty, he sees them from
    afar.
7Though I walk in the midst of
    trouble,
  you preserve my life.
You stretch out your hand against the
    anger of my foes;
  with your right hand you save me.
8The LORD will vindicate me;
  your love, LORD, endures
    forever—
  do not abandon the works of your
    hands.

Psalm 138:6–8

God won't stop working until he's done with you.

You might not like the feeling of anyone running your life. But you really need your parents to launch you to adulthood. And you truly need your wise and loving God as he works out his plan for your life. The Lord passionately cares about everything he wants to do in and through you. "The LORD will vindicate me," this song promises (Psalm 138:8). The New Testament says the same thing, that "He who began a good work in you will carry it on to completion until the day of Christ Jesus" (Philippians 1:6). God sees all the moves he has mapped out for you (see Psalm 139:16). He pays attention to the smallest details of your life (see Luke 12:7). The Lord won't ever give up on you. Your job is to never give up on him.

Think: What do you think God wants to do in your life today?

ROCK SOLID *truths*

Psalm 139

For the director of music.
Of David. A psalm.

1You have searched me, LORD,
  and you know me.
2You know when I sit and when I rise;
  you perceive my thoughts from afar.
3You discern my going out and my
    lying down;
  you are familiar with all my ways.
4Before a word is on my tongue
  you, LORD, know it completely.
5You hem me in behind and before,
  and you lay your hand upon me.
6Such knowledge is too wonderful for me,
  too lofty for me to attain.

7Where can I go from your Spirit?
  Where can I flee from your
    presence?
8If I go up to the heavens, you are there;
  if I make my bed in the depths, you
    are there.
9If I rise on the wings of the dawn,
  if I settle on the far side of the sea,
10even there your hand will guide me,
  your right hand will hold me fast.
11If I say, "Surely the darkness will
    hide me
  and the light become night around
    me,"
12even the darkness will not be dark to
    you;
  the night will shine like the day,
  for darkness is as light to you.

13For you created my inmost being;
  you knit me together in my mother's
    womb.
14I praise you because I am fearfully and
    wonderfully made;
  your works are wonderful,
  I know that full well.
15My frame was not hidden from you
  when I was made in the secret place,
  when I was woven together in the
    depths of the earth.
16Your eyes saw my unformed body;
  all the days ordained for me were
    written in your book
  before one of them came to be.

ROCK SOLID
promises

"All the days ordained for me were written in your book before one of them came to be." **Psalm 139:16**

God has a plan for you. Keep the major commands you already know, and he will fill you in on the minor details.

---

17 How precious to me are your
    thoughts,*a* God!
    How vast is the sum of them!
18 Were I to count them,
    they would outnumber the grains of
        sand—
    when I awake, I am still with you.

19 If only you, God, would slay the
        wicked!
    Away from me, you who are
        bloodthirsty!
20 They speak of you with evil intent;
    your adversaries misuse your name.
21 Do I not hate those who hate you,
    LORD,
    and abhor those who are in
        rebellion against you?
22 I have nothing but hatred for them;
    I count them my enemies.
23 Search me, God, and know my heart;
    test me and know my anxious
        thoughts.
24 See if there is any offensive way in me,
    and lead me in the way everlasting.

Psalm 140*b*

For the director of music.
A psalm of David.

1 Rescue me, LORD, from evildoers;
    protect me from the violent,
2 who devise evil plans in their hearts
    and stir up war every day.

3 They make their tongues as sharp as a
        serpent's;
    the poison of vipers is on their lips.*c*

4 Keep me safe, LORD, from the hands
        of the wicked;
    protect me from the violent,
    who devise ways to trip my feet.
5 The arrogant have hidden a snare for
        me;
    they have spread out the cords of
        their net
    and have set traps for me along my
        path.

6 I say to the LORD, "You are my God."
    Hear, LORD, my cry for mercy.
7 Sovereign LORD, my strong deliverer,
    you shield my head in the day of
        battle.

a 17 Or *How amazing are your thoughts concerning me*   *b* In Hebrew texts 140:1-13 is numbered 140:2-14.   *c 3* The Hebrew has *Selah* (a word of uncertain meaning) here and at the end of verses 5 and 8.

ROCK SOLID
plans

Psalm 139:1 – 24

Count on God's one-of-a-kind love.

No human will ever know you like God does. He shaped you in your mother's womb and scripted your life before you were born. He sees your steps, reads your thoughts, and hears your words. His ability to track your every move means you can never escape his love. So you can be bold and can bare every part of your soul to him because he already knows you inside and out. He's the one who knows you the best and loves you the most.

Your next step: Sum up in your own words the most encouraging statements in Psalm 139. Post them where you will see them often.

⁸ Do not grant the wicked their desires,
    Lord;
    do not let their plans succeed.

⁹ Those who surround me proudly rear
    their heads;
    may the mischief of their lips engulf
    them.

¹⁰ May burning coals fall on them;
    may they be thrown into the fire,
    into miry pits, never to rise.

¹¹ May slanderers not be established in
    the land;
    may disaster hunt down the violent.

¹² I know that the Lord secures justice
    for the poor
    and upholds the cause of the needy.

¹³ Surely the righteous will praise your
    name,
    and the upright will live in your
    presence.

Psalm 141

A psalm of David.

¹ I call to you, Lord, come quickly to
    me;
    hear me when I call to you.

² May my prayer be set before you like
    incense;
    may the lifting up of my hands be
    like the evening sacrifice.

³ Set a guard over my mouth, Lord;
    keep watch over the door of my lips.

⁴ Do not let my heart be drawn to what
    is evil
    so that I take part in wicked deeds
    along with those who are evildoers;
    do not let me eat their delicacies.

⁵ Let a righteous man strike me—that
    is a kindness;
    let him rebuke me—that is oil on
    my head.
    My head will not refuse it,
    for my prayer will still be against
    the deeds of evildoers.

⁶ Their rulers will be thrown down
    from the cliffs,
    and the wicked will learn that my
    words were well spoken.

⁷ They will say, "As one plows and
    breaks up the earth,
    so our bones have been scattered at
    the mouth of the grave."

⁸ But my eyes are fixed on you,
    Sovereign Lord;
    in you I take refuge—do not give
    me over to death.

⁹ Keep me safe from the traps set by
    evildoers,
    from the snares they have laid for
    me.

¹⁰ Let the wicked fall into their own
    nets,
    while I pass by in safety.

Psalm 142ᵃ

A maskilᵇ of David. When he was
    in the cave. A prayer.

¹ I cry aloud to the Lord;
    I lift up my voice to the Lord for
    mercy.

² I pour out before him my complaint;
    before him I tell my trouble.

³ When my spirit grows faint within
    me,
    it is you who watch over my way.
    In the path where I walk
    people have hidden a snare for me.

⁴ Look and see, there is no one at my
    right hand;
    no one is concerned for me.
    I have no refuge;
    no one cares for my life.

⁵ I cry to you, Lord;
    I say, "You are my refuge,
    my portion in the land of the living."

⁶ Listen to my cry,
    for I am in desperate need;
    rescue me from those who pursue me,
    for they are too strong for me.

⁷ Set me free from my prison,
    that I may praise your name.
    Then the righteous will gather
    about me
    because of your goodness to me.

ᵃ In Hebrew texts 142:1-7 is numbered 142:2-8.
ᵇ Title: Probably a literary or musical term

Psalm 143

A psalm of David.

[1] Lord, hear my prayer,
   listen to my cry for mercy;
 in your faithfulness and righteousness
   come to my relief.
[2] Do not bring your servant into
     judgment,
   for no one living is righteous before
     you.
[3] The enemy pursues me,
   he crushes me to the ground;
 he makes me dwell in the darkness
   like those long dead.
[4] So my spirit grows faint within me;
   my heart within me is dismayed.
[5] I remember the days of long ago;
   I meditate on all your works
   and consider what your hands have
     done.
[6] I spread out my hands to you;
   I thirst for you like a parched land.[a]

[7] Answer me quickly, Lord;
   my spirit fails.
 Do not hide your face from me
   or I will be like those who go down
     to the pit.
[8] Let the morning bring me word of
     your unfailing love,
   for I have put my trust in you.
 Show me the way I should go,
   for to you I entrust my life.

ROCK SOLID promises

**"Show me the way I should go, for
to you I entrust my life."**

Psalm 143:8

**God will never say "no" when you
commit every part of you to him — and
ask him to show you how to do life.**

---

[9] Rescue me from my enemies, Lord,
   for I hide myself in you.
[10] Teach me to do your will,
   for you are my God;
 may your good Spirit
   lead me on level ground.

[11] For your name's sake, Lord, preserve
     my life;
   in your righteousness, bring me out
     of trouble.
[12] In your unfailing love, silence my
     enemies;
   destroy all my foes,
   for I am your servant.

Psalm 144

Of David.

[1] Praise be to the Lord my Rock,
   who trains my hands for war,
   my fingers for battle.
[2] He is my loving God and my fortress,
   my stronghold and my deliverer,
 my shield, in whom I take refuge,
   who subdues peoples[b] under me.

[3] Lord, what are human beings that
     you care for them,
   mere mortals that you think of
     them?
[4] They are like a breath;
   their days are like a fleeting
     shadow.

[5] Part your heavens, Lord, and come
     down;
   touch the mountains, so that they
     smoke.
[6] Send forth lightning and scatter the
     enemy;
   shoot your arrows and rout them.
[7] Reach down your hand from on high;
   deliver me and rescue me
 from the mighty waters,
   from the hands of foreigners
[8] whose mouths are full of lies,
   whose right hands are deceitful.

---

[a] 6 The Hebrew has *Selah* (a word of uncertain
meaning) here.   [b] 2 Many manuscripts of the
Masoretic Text, Dead Sea Scrolls, Aquila,
Jerome and Syriac; most manuscripts of the
Masoretic Text *subdues my people*

⁹I will sing a new song to you, my God;
  on the ten-stringed lyre I will make
    music to you,
¹⁰to the One who gives victory to kings,
  who delivers his servant David.

From the deadly sword ¹¹deliver me;
  rescue me from the hands of
    foreigners
whose mouths are full of lies,
  whose right hands are deceitful.

¹²Then our sons in their youth
  will be like well-nurtured plants,
and our daughters will be like pillars
  carved to adorn a palace.
¹³Our barns will be filled
  with every kind of provision.
Our sheep will increase by thousands,
  by tens of thousands in our fields;
¹⁴ our oxen will draw heavy loads.ᵃ
There will be no breaching of walls,
  no going into captivity,
  no cry of distress in our streets.
¹⁵Blessed is the people of whom this is
    true;
  blessed is the people whose God is
    the Lord.

Psalm 145ᵇ

A psalm of praise. Of David.

¹I will exalt you, my God the King;
  I will praise your name for ever and
    ever.
²Every day I will praise you
  and extol your name for ever and
    ever.
³Great is the Lord and most worthy of
    praise;
  his greatness no one can fathom.
⁴One generation commends your works
    to another;
  they tell of your mighty acts.
⁵They speak of the glorious splendor of
    your majesty—
  and I will meditate on your
    wonderful works.ᶜ
⁶They tell of the power of your
    awesome works—
  and I will proclaim your great
    deeds.

⁷They celebrate your abundant
    goodness
  and joyfully sing of your
    righteousness.

⁸The Lord is gracious and
    compassionate,
  slow to anger and rich in love.

⁹The Lord is good to all;
  he has compassion on all he has
    made.
¹⁰All your works praise you, Lord;
  your faithful people extol you.
¹¹They tell of the glory of your kingdom
  and speak of your might,
¹²so that all people may know of your
    mighty acts
  and the glorious splendor of your
    kingdom.
¹³Your kingdom is an everlasting
    kingdom,
  and your dominion endures through
    all generations.

The Lord is trustworthy in all he
    promises
  and faithful in all he does.ᵈ
¹⁴The Lord upholds all who fall
  and lifts up all who are bowed down.
¹⁵The eyes of all look to you,
  and you give them their food at the
    proper time.
¹⁶You open your hand
  and satisfy the desires of every
    living thing.

¹⁷The Lord is righteous in all his ways
  and faithful in all he does.
¹⁸The Lord is near to all who call on
    him,
  to all who call on him in truth.

ᵃ 14 Or *our chieftains will be firmly established*
ᵇ This psalm is an acrostic poem, the verses of
which (including verse 13b) begin with the
successive letters of the Hebrew alphabet.
ᶜ 5 Dead Sea Scrolls and Syriac (see also
Septuagint); Masoretic Text *On the glorious
splendor of your majesty / and on your wonderful
works I will meditate*   ᵈ 13 One manuscript of
the Masoretic Text, Dead Sea Scrolls and Syriac
(see also Septuagint); most manuscripts of the
Masoretic Text do not have the last two lines of
verse 13.

⁴ When their spirit departs, they return
to the ground;
on that very day their plans come to
nothing.
⁵ Blessed are those whose help is the
God of Jacob,
whose hope is in the LORD their
God.

⁶ He is the Maker of heaven and earth,
the sea, and everything in them—
he remains faithful forever.
⁷ He upholds the cause of the
oppressed
and gives food to the hungry.
The LORD sets prisoners free,
⁸ the LORD gives sight to the blind,
the LORD lifts up those who are
bowed down,
the LORD loves the righteous.
⁹ The LORD watches over the foreigner
and sustains the fatherless and the
widow,
but he frustrates the ways of the
wicked.

¹⁰ The LORD reigns forever,
your God, O Zion, for all
generations.

Praise the LORD.

UNSHAKEN *God*

Psalm 145:1–21

God is good.

God sometimes puts conditions on experiencing his blessings—like if you want to enjoy the best possible guy-girl relationships, you don't want to ignore his commands about sexual purity. But God isn't just kind to his followers. He's unconditionally good "to all" (Psalm 145:9). God goes out of his way to do good to his entire creation. According to this song, he shares his compassion, glory, and might with everyone. He's loving toward "all he has made" and satisfies "every living thing" (Psalm 145:9 and 16). So never let anyone fool you into thinking God has an evil attitude toward this planet. God is totally good.

So ... In what ways do you see God being good to everyone on earth?

¹⁹ He fulfills the desires of those who
fear him;
he hears their cry and saves them.
²⁰ The LORD watches over all who love
him,
but all the wicked he will destroy.
²¹ My mouth will speak in praise of the
LORD.
Let every creature praise his holy
name
for ever and ever.

Psalm 146

¹ Praise the LORD.^{*a*}

Praise the LORD, my soul.

² I will praise the LORD all my life;
I will sing praise to my God as long
as I live.
³ Do not put your trust in princes,
in human beings, who cannot save.

Psalm 147

¹ Praise the LORD.^{*b*}

How good it is to sing praises to our
God,
how pleasant and fitting to praise
him!

² The LORD builds up Jerusalem;
he gathers the exiles of Israel.
³ He heals the brokenhearted
and binds up their wounds.
⁴ He determines the number of the stars
and calls them each by name.
⁵ Great is our Lord and mighty in
power;
his understanding has no limit.
⁶ The LORD sustains the humble
but casts the wicked to the ground.

^{*a*} *1* Hebrew *Hallelu Yah*; also in verse 10
^{*b*} *1* Hebrew *Hallelu Yah*; also in verse 20

ROCK SOLID *promises*

"He heals the brokenhearted and binds up their wounds."

Psalm 147:3

God wants to heal your pains inside and out. Tell him where it hurts.

---

⁷ Sing to the LORD with grateful praise;
    make music to our God on the harp.

⁸ He covers the sky with clouds;
    he supplies the earth with rain
    and makes grass grow on the hills.
⁹ He provides food for the cattle
    and for the young ravens when they
        call.

¹⁰ His pleasure is not in the strength of
        the horse,
    nor his delight in the legs of the
        warrior;
¹¹ the LORD delights in those who fear him,
    who put their hope in his unfailing
        love.

¹² Extol the LORD, Jerusalem;
    praise your God, Zion.
¹³ He strengthens the bars of your gates
    and blesses your people within you.
¹⁴ He grants peace to your borders
    and satisfies you with the finest of
        wheat.

¹⁵ He sends his command to the earth;
    his word runs swiftly.
¹⁶ He spreads the snow like wool
    and scatters the frost like ashes.
¹⁷ He hurls down his hail like pebbles.
    Who can withstand his icy blast?
¹⁸ He sends his word and melts them;
    he stirs up his breezes, and the
        waters flow.

¹⁹ He has revealed his word to Jacob,
    his laws and decrees to Israel.
²⁰ He has done this for no other nation;
    they do not know his laws.ᵃ

Praise the LORD.

Psalm 148

¹ Praise the LORD.ᵇ

Praise the LORD from the heavens;
    praise him in the heights above.
² Praise him, all his angels;
    praise him, all his heavenly hosts.
³ Praise him, sun and moon;
    praise him, all you shining stars.
⁴ Praise him, you highest heavens
    and you waters above the skies.

⁵ Let them praise the name of the
        LORD,
    for at his command they were
        created,
⁶ and he established them for ever and
        ever—
    he issued a decree that will never
        pass away.

⁷ Praise the LORD from the earth,
    you great sea creatures and all ocean
        depths,
⁸ lightning and hail, snow and clouds,
    stormy winds that do his bidding,
⁹ you mountains and all hills,
    fruit trees and all cedars,
¹⁰ wild animals and all cattle,
    small creatures and flying birds,
¹¹ kings of the earth and all nations,
    you princes and all rulers on earth,
¹² young men and women,
    old men and children.

¹³ Let them praise the name of the
        LORD,
    for his name alone is exalted;
    his splendor is above the earth and
        the heavens.
¹⁴ And he has raised up for his people a
        horn,ᶜ

ᵃ *20* Masoretic Text; Dead Sea Scrolls and
Septuagint *nation; / he has not made his laws
known to them*   ᵇ *1* Hebrew *Hallelu Yah*; also in
verse 14   ᶜ *14 Horn* here symbolizes strength.

the praise of all his faithful servants,
of Israel, the people close to his
heart.

Praise the LORD.

Psalm 149

¹ Praise the LORD.ᵃ

Sing to the LORD a new song,
his praise in the assembly of his
faithful people.

² Let Israel rejoice in their Maker;
let the people of Zion be glad in
their King.
³ Let them praise his name with dancing
and make music to him with
timbrel and harp.
⁴ For the LORD takes delight in his
people;
he crowns the humble with victory.
⁵ Let his faithful people rejoice in this
honor
and sing for joy on their beds.

⁶ May the praise of God be in their
mouths
and a double-edged sword in their
hands,
⁷ to inflict vengeance on the nations
and punishment on the peoples,
⁸ to bind their kings with fetters,
their nobles with shackles of
iron,
⁹ to carry out the sentence written
against them—
this is the glory of all his faithful
people.

Praise the LORD.

Psalm 150

¹ Praise the LORD.ᵇ

Praise God in his sanctuary;
praise him in his mighty
heavens.

ᵃ 1 Hebrew *Hallelu Yah*; also in verse 9
ᵇ 1 Hebrew *Hallelu Yah*; also in verse 6

ROCK SOLID principles

Psalm 150:1–6

Rock for God.

Lindsay adored her older brother. When he offered to loan her one of his electric guitars and teach her to play, she was completely hooked. Lindsay studied chord charts and tabs and scales, and whenever she had a free moment she was hammering out a new guitar part. In a few months her brother called her abilities "respectable," about as large a compliment as his coolness would allow him to give. Even though Lindsay had some classmates looking to put together a band, she wanted a different place to use her new skills. After trying out and failing a couple times, she was invited to join a worship band at her church. Lindsay didn't just want to rock. She wanted to rock for God.

Don't believe people who think worship is an hour of sour-faced silence. Real worship reaches all the way from the "sanctuary" to the Lord's "mighty heavens" to everywhere between (Psalm 150:1). And real worship isn't tame. It can rock every kind of noisy instrument to praise God's unbeatable clout. If you can breath, praise the Lord.

² Praise him for his acts of power;
  praise him for his surpassing greatness.
³ Praise him with the sounding of the
    trumpet,
  praise him with the harp and lyre,
⁴ praise him with timbrel and dancing,
  praise him with the strings and pipe,

⁵ praise him with the clash of cymbals,
  praise him with resounding
    cymbals.

⁶ Let everything that has breath praise
    the LORD.

Praise the LORD.

PROVERBS

BOOK OUTLINE

Proverbs is a collection of wise sayings and good advice for daily living. The author begins by reminding us that "The fear of the LORD is the beginning of knowledge" (1:7). The first four chapters discuss the importance of wisdom.

The author also includes a collection of short and powerful two-line sayings that cover many different subjects including marriage, social behavior, friendship, justice, folly, poverty, wealth, family, love, laziness, and warnings against drinking and adultery.

Many of these proverbs were written by King Solomon. Others were copied by the men of Hezekiah. Agur and Lemuel wrote the last two chapters.

Purpose and Theme

The proverbs of Solomon son of David, king of Israel:

² for gaining wisdom and instruction;
for understanding words of insight;
³ for receiving instruction in prudent behavior,
doing what is right and just and fair;
⁴ for giving prudence to those who are simple,*ᵃ*
knowledge and discretion to the young—
⁵ let the wise listen and add to their learning,
and let the discerning get guidance—
⁶ for understanding proverbs and parables,
the sayings and riddles of the wise.*ᵇ*

⁷ The fear of the LORD is the beginning of knowledge,
but fools*ᶜ* despise wisdom and instruction.

Prologue: Exhortations to Embrace Wisdom

Warning Against the Invitation of Sinful Men

⁸ Listen, my son, to your father's instruction
and do not forsake your mother's teaching.
⁹ They are a garland to grace your head
and a chain to adorn your neck.

¹⁰ My son, if sinful men entice you,
do not give in to them.
¹¹ If they say, "Come along with us;
let's lie in wait for innocent blood,
let's ambush some harmless soul;
¹² let's swallow them alive, like the grave,
and whole, like those who go down to the pit;
¹³ we will get all sorts of valuable things
and fill our houses with plunder;
¹⁴ cast lots with us;
we will all share the loot"—

¹⁵ my son, do not go along with them,
do not set foot on their paths;
¹⁶ for their feet rush into evil,
they are swift to shed blood.
¹⁷ How useless to spread a net
where every bird can see it!
¹⁸ These men lie in wait for their own blood;
they ambush only themselves!
¹⁹ Such are the paths of all who go after ill-gotten gain;
it takes away the life of those who get it.

Wisdom's Rebuke

²⁰ Out in the open wisdom calls aloud,
she raises her voice in the public square;
²¹ on top of the wall*ᵈ* she cries out,
at the city gate she makes her speech:

²² "How long will you who are simple
love your simple ways?
How long will mockers delight in mockery
and fools hate knowledge?
²³ Repent at my rebuke!
Then I will pour out my thoughts to you,
I will make known to you my teachings.
²⁴ But since you refuse to listen when I call
and no one pays attention when I stretch out my hand,
²⁵ since you disregard all my advice
and do not accept my rebuke,
²⁶ I in turn will laugh when disaster strikes you;
I will mock when calamity overtakes you—

ᵃ 4 The Hebrew word rendered *simple* in Proverbs denotes a person who is gullible, without moral direction and inclined to evil.
ᵇ 6 Or *understanding a proverb, namely, a parable, / and the sayings of the wise, their riddles*
ᶜ 7 The Hebrew words rendered *fool* in Proverbs, and often elsewhere in the Old Testament, denote a person who is morally deficient.
ᵈ 21 Septuagint; Hebrew / *at noisy street corners*

²⁷when calamity overtakes you like a
    storm,
  when disaster sweeps over you like a
    whirlwind,
  when distress and trouble
    overwhelm you.

²⁸"Then they will call to me but I will
    not answer;
  they will look for me but will not
    find me,
²⁹since they hated knowledge
  and did not choose to fear the Lord.
³⁰Since they would not accept my advice
  and spurned my rebuke,
³¹they will eat the fruit of their ways
  and be filled with the fruit of their
    schemes.
³²For the waywardness of the simple
    will kill them,
  and the complacency of fools will
    destroy them;
³³but whoever listens to me will live in
    safety
  and be at ease, without fear of harm."

Moral Benefits of Wisdom

2 My son, if you accept my words
  and store up my commands
    within you,
²turning your ear to wisdom
  and applying your heart to
    understanding—
³indeed, if you call out for insight
  and cry aloud for understanding,
⁴and if you look for it as for silver
  and search for it as for hidden
    treasure,
⁵then you will understand the fear of
    the Lord
  and find the knowledge of God.
⁶For the Lord gives wisdom;
  from his mouth come knowledge
    and understanding.
⁷He holds success in store for the upright,
  he is a shield to those whose walk is
    blameless,
⁸for he guards the course of the just
  and protects the way of his faithful
    ones.

ROCK SOLID *principles*

Proverbs 2:1–11

Get smart.

Maybe it was because Dylan was the oldest child in his family, but he always charged into life headfirst, insisting on learning everything the hard way. When his parents told him to clean up his room, he made a bigger mess. When a teacher said an assignment was due on Friday, he never turned it in until the following Wednesday. And when the whole world tried to convince him that drugs were a dumb idea, Dylan had to check it out for himself. His younger brother Logan watched all this and lived the motto, "Dylan's pain, my gain." Dylan gave Logan a steady stream of lessons in how to steer clear of stupidity.

The hard knocks of life give you a schooling when you least expect it. But it's far better to go hunting for wisdom, actively asking God to teach you his instructions for the best life possible. The Lord himself is the source of all insights, and if you search for his wisdom with the passion you devote to hunting for treasure, he guarantees you will find it.

⁹Then you will understand what is
    right and just
    and fair—every good path.
¹⁰For wisdom will enter your heart,
    and knowledge will be pleasant to
    your soul.
¹¹Discretion will protect you,
    and understanding will guard you.

¹²Wisdom will save you from the ways
    of wicked men,
    from men whose words are
    perverse,
¹³who have left the straight paths
    to walk in dark ways,
¹⁴who delight in doing wrong
    and rejoice in the perverseness of
    evil,
¹⁵whose paths are crooked
    and who are devious in their ways.

¹⁶Wisdom will save you also from the
    adulterous woman,
    from the wayward woman with her
    seductive words,
¹⁷who has left the partner of her youth
    and ignored the covenant she made
    before God.ᵃ
¹⁸Surely her house leads down to death
    and her paths to the spirits of the
    dead.
¹⁹None who go to her return
    or attain the paths of life.

²⁰Thus you will walk in the ways of the
    good
    and keep to the paths of the
    righteous.
²¹For the upright will live in the land,
    and the blameless will remain in it;
²²but the wicked will be cut off from the
    land,
    and the unfaithful will be torn
    from it.

Wisdom Bestows Well-Being

3 My son, do not forget my
    teaching,
    but keep my commands in your
    heart,
²for they will prolong your life many
    years
    and bring you peace and prosperity.

³Let love and faithfulness never leave
    you;
    bind them around your neck,
    write them on the tablet of your
    heart.
⁴Then you will win favor and a good
    name
    in the sight of God and man.

⁵Trust in the LORD with all your heart
    and lean not on your own
    understanding;
⁶in all your ways submit to him,
    and he will make your paths
    straight.ᵇ

⁷Do not be wise in your own eyes;
    fear the LORD and shun evil.
⁸This will bring health to your body
    and nourishment to your bones.

⁹Honor the LORD with your wealth,
    with the firstfruits of all your
    crops;

ᵃ 17 Or covenant of her God   ᵇ 6 Or will direct
your paths

ROCK SOLID plans

Proverbs 3:1–8

Let God steer your life.

Every voice in your world might shout
that you should go your own way and do
your own thing, but God's plan in Proverbs
3:1–8 is better: Remember his teaching.
Keep his commands. And trust the facts
of his love and faithfulness. God's instruction is wise: Lean on him wholeheartedly.
Don't think you're smarter than him. Admit
you need him. And invite him to direct you.
God's promise is sure: Respect him always.
Run from evil. And expect him to make every part of you stronger than strong.

**Your next step: In what specific areas
of life are you going your own way—
rather than going through life God's
way? Get help to change.**

¹⁰ then your barns will be filled to
overflowing,
and your vats will brim over with
new wine.

¹¹ My son, do not despise the LORD's
discipline,
and do not resent his rebuke,
¹² because the LORD disciplines those he
loves,
as a father the son he delights in.*ᵃ*

¹³ Blessed are those who find wisdom,
those who gain understanding,
¹⁴ for she is more profitable than silver
and yields better returns than gold.
¹⁵ She is more precious than rubies;
nothing you desire can compare
with her.
¹⁶ Long life is in her right hand;
in her left hand are riches and honor.
¹⁷ Her ways are pleasant ways,
and all her paths are peace.
¹⁸ She is a tree of life to those who take
hold of her;
those who hold her fast will be
blessed.

¹⁹ By wisdom the LORD laid the earth's
foundations,
by understanding he set the heavens
in place;
²⁰ by his knowledge the watery depths
were divided,
and the clouds let drop the dew.

²¹ My son, do not let wisdom and
understanding out of your
sight,
preserve sound judgment and
discretion;
²² they will be life for you,
an ornament to grace your neck.
²³ Then you will go on your way in
safety,
and your foot will not stumble.
²⁴ When you lie down, you will not be
afraid;
when you lie down, your sleep will
be sweet.
²⁵ Have no fear of sudden disaster
or of the ruin that overtakes the
wicked,

²⁶ for the LORD will be at your side
and will keep your foot from being
snared.

²⁷ Do not withhold good from those to
whom it is due,
when it is in your power to act.
²⁸ Do not say to your neighbor,
"Come back tomorrow and I'll give
it to you"—
when you already have it with you.
²⁹ Do not plot harm against your
neighbor,
who lives trustfully near you.
³⁰ Do not accuse anyone for no reason—
when they have done you no harm.

³¹ Do not envy the violent
or choose any of their ways.
³² For the LORD detests the perverse
but takes the upright into his
confidence.
³³ The LORD's curse is on the house of
the wicked,
but he blesses the home of the
righteous.
³⁴ He mocks proud mockers
but shows favor to the humble and
oppressed.
³⁵ The wise inherit honor,
but fools get only shame.

Get Wisdom at Any Cost

4 Listen, my sons, to a father's
instruction;
pay attention and gain
understanding.
² I give you sound learning,
so do not forsake my teaching.
³ For I too was a son to my father,
still tender, and cherished by my
mother.
⁴ Then he taught me, and he said to me,
"Take hold of my words with all
your heart;
keep my commands, and you will live.
⁵ Get wisdom, get understanding;
do not forget my words or turn away
from them.

ᵃ 12 Hebrew; Septuagint *loves, / and he chastens
everyone he accepts as his child*

⁶Do not forsake wisdom, and she will
    protect you;
  love her, and she will watch over
    you.
⁷The beginning of wisdom is this: Get*a*
    wisdom.
  Though it cost all you have,*b* get
    understanding.
⁸Cherish her, and she will exalt you;
  embrace her, and she will honor
    you.
⁹She will give you a garland to grace
    your head
  and present you with a glorious
    crown."

¹⁰Listen, my son, accept what I say,
  and the years of your life will be
    many.
¹¹I instruct you in the way of wisdom
  and lead you along straight paths.
¹²When you walk, your steps will not be
    hampered;
  when you run, you will not stumble.
¹³Hold on to instruction, do not let it go;
  guard it well, for it is your life.
¹⁴Do not set foot on the path of the
    wicked
  or walk in the way of evildoers.
¹⁵Avoid it, do not travel on it;
  turn from it and go on your way.
¹⁶For they cannot rest until they do evil;
  they are robbed of sleep till they
    make someone stumble.
¹⁷They eat the bread of wickedness
  and drink the wine of violence.

¹⁸The path of the righteous is like the
    morning sun,
  shining ever brighter till the full
    light of day.
¹⁹But the way of the wicked is like deep
    darkness;
  they do not know what makes them
    stumble.

²⁰My son, pay attention to what I say;
  turn your ear to my words.
²¹Do not let them out of your sight,
  keep them within your heart;
²²for they are life to those who find
    them
  and health to one's whole body.

²³Above all else, guard your heart,
  for everything you do flows from it.
²⁴Keep your mouth free of perversity;
  keep corrupt talk far from your lips.
²⁵Let your eyes look straight ahead;
  fix your gaze directly before you.
²⁶Give careful thought to the*c* paths for
    your feet
  and be steadfast in all your ways.
²⁷Do not turn to the right or the left;
  keep your foot from evil.

Warning Against Adultery

5 My son, pay attention to my
    wisdom,
  turn your ear to my words of
    insight,
²that you may maintain discretion
  and your lips may preserve
    knowledge.
³For the lips of the adulterous woman
    drip honey,
  and her speech is smoother than
    oil;
⁴but in the end she is bitter as gall,
  sharp as a double-edged sword.
⁵Her feet go down to death;
  her steps lead straight to the grave.
⁶She gives no thought to the way of
    life;
  her paths wander aimlessly, but she
    does not know it.

⁷Now then, my sons, listen to me;
  do not turn aside from what I say.
⁸Keep to a path far from her,
  do not go near the door of her
    house,
⁹lest you lose your honor to others
  and your dignity*d* to one who is
    cruel,
¹⁰lest strangers feast on your wealth
  and your toil enrich the house of
    another.
¹¹At the end of your life you will groan,
  when your flesh and body are
    spent.
¹²You will say, "How I hated discipline!
  How my heart spurned correction!

a 7 Or *Wisdom is supreme; therefore get*
b 7 Or *wisdom. / Whatever else you get*
c 26 Or *Make level*   *d* 9 Or *years*

¹³ I would not obey my teachers
  or turn my ear to my instructors.
¹⁴ And I was soon in serious trouble
  in the assembly of God's people."

¹⁵ Drink water from your own cistern,
  running water from your own well.
¹⁶ Should your springs overflow in the
    streets,
  your streams of water in the public
    squares?
¹⁷ Let them be yours alone,
  never to be shared with strangers.
¹⁸ May your fountain be blessed,
  and may you rejoice in the wife of
    your youth.
¹⁹ A loving doe, a graceful deer—
  may her breasts satisfy you always,
  may you ever be intoxicated with
    her love.
²⁰ Why, my son, be intoxicated with
    another man's wife?
  Why embrace the bosom of a
    wayward woman?

²¹ For your ways are in full view of the
    LORD,
  and he examines all your paths.
²² The evil deeds of the wicked ensnare
    them;
  the cords of their sins hold them
    fast.
²³ For lack of discipline they will die,
  led astray by their own great
    folly.

Warnings Against Folly

6 My son, if you have put up
    security for your neighbor,
  if you have shaken hands in
    pledge for a stranger,
² you have been trapped by what you
    said,
  ensnared by the words of your
    mouth.
³ So do this, my son, to free yourself,
  since you have fallen into your
    neighbor's hands:

ROCK SOLID *principles*

Proverbs 5:1–23

Save yourself for the best.

Nikki stood across the street, half hidden by a massive oak tree. She stared at the front door of her boyfriend's house, debating with herself whether to walk over and go inside. Nikki and Zach had been going out for months, and they had even used the L-word to say how they felt about each other. Zach told Nikki to come over at 9:00 one Friday night, because his parents would be out for a late dinner and movie with friends. They wouldn't be home for hours, so the pair would have the house to themselves. Nikki didn't have to guess what Zach wanted because he had told her. But at 8:55 she was still making up her mind whether she wanted that too.

God's blunt insights about sex shock anyone who thinks the Lord is down on sex. You get the real picture in Proverbs 5. The Lord invented sex for more than breeding the human species, and physical love is at its happiest within the boundaries he designed. Sex outside marriage leads "straight to the grave" (Proverbs 5:5).

Go—to the point of exhaustion—[a]
and give your neighbor no rest!
⁴ Allow no sleep to your eyes,
no slumber to your eyelids.
⁵ Free yourself, like a gazelle from the
hand of the hunter,
like a bird from the snare of the
fowler.

⁶ Go to the ant, you sluggard;
consider its ways and be wise!
⁷ It has no commander,
no overseer or ruler,
⁸ yet it stores its provisions in summer
and gathers its food at harvest.

⁹ How long will you lie there, you
sluggard?
When will you get up from your
sleep?
¹⁰ A little sleep, a little slumber,
a little folding of the hands to
rest—
¹¹ and poverty will come on you like a
thief
and scarcity like an armed man.

¹² A troublemaker and a villain,
who goes about with a corrupt
mouth,
¹³ who winks maliciously with his eye,
signals with his feet
and motions with his fingers,
¹⁴ who plots evil with deceit in his
heart—
he always stirs up conflict.
¹⁵ Therefore disaster will overtake him
in an instant;
he will suddenly be destroyed—
without remedy.

¹⁶ There are six things the Lord hates,
seven that are detestable to him:
¹⁷ haughty eyes,
a lying tongue,
hands that shed innocent blood,
¹⁸ a heart that devises wicked
schemes,
feet that are quick to rush into
evil,
¹⁹ a false witness who pours out lies
and a person who stirs up conflict
in the community.

Warning Against Adultery

²⁰ My son, keep your father's command
and do not forsake your mother's
teaching.
²¹ Bind them always on your heart;
fasten them around your neck.
²² When you walk, they will guide you;
when you sleep, they will watch
over you;
when you awake, they will speak to
you.
²³ For this command is a lamp,
this teaching is a light,
and correction and instruction
are the way to life,
²⁴ keeping you from your neighbor's
wife,
from the smooth talk of a wayward
woman.

²⁵ Do not lust in your heart after her
beauty
or let her captivate you with her eyes.

²⁶ For a prostitute can be had for a loaf of
bread,
but another man's wife preys on
your very life.
²⁷ Can a man scoop fire into his lap
without his clothes being burned?
²⁸ Can a man walk on hot coals
without his feet being scorched?
²⁹ So is he who sleeps with another
man's wife;
no one who touches her will go
unpunished.

³⁰ People do not despise a thief if he
steals
to satisfy his hunger when he is
starving.
³¹ Yet if he is caught, he must pay
sevenfold,
though it costs him all the wealth of
his house.
³² But a man who commits adultery has
no sense;
whoever does so destroys himself.
³³ Blows and disgrace are his lot,
and his shame will never be wiped
away.

[a] 3 Or *Go and humble yourself,*

34 For jealousy arouses a husband's fury,
  and he will show no mercy when he
    takes revenge.
35 He will not accept any compensation;
  he will refuse a bribe, however great
    it is.

Warning Against the Adulterous Woman

7 My son, keep my words
  and store up my commands
    within you.
2 Keep my commands and you will live;
  guard my teachings as the apple of
    your eye.
3 Bind them on your fingers;
  write them on the tablet of your
    heart.
4 Say to wisdom, "You are my sister,"
  and to insight, "You are my
    relative."
5 They will keep you from the
    adulterous woman,
  from the wayward woman with her
    seductive words.

6 At the window of my house
  I looked down through the lattice.
7 I saw among the simple,
  I noticed among the young men,
  a youth who had no sense.
8 He was going down the street near her
    corner,
  walking along in the direction of
    her house
9 at twilight, as the day was fading,
  as the dark of night set in.

10 Then out came a woman to meet him,
  dressed like a prostitute and with
    crafty intent.
11 (She is unruly and defiant,
  her feet never stay at home;
12 now in the street, now in the squares,
  at every corner she lurks.)
13 She took hold of him and kissed him
  and with a brazen face she said:

14 "Today I fulfilled my vows,
  and I have food from my fellowship
    offering at home.
15 So I came out to meet you;
  I looked for you and have found
    you!

16 I have covered my bed
  with colored linens from Egypt.
17 I have perfumed my bed
  with myrrh, aloes and cinnamon.
18 Come, let's drink deeply of love till
    morning;
  let's enjoy ourselves with love!
19 My husband is not at home;
  he has gone on a long journey.
20 He took his purse filled with money
  and will not be home till full moon."

21 With persuasive words she led him
    astray;
  she seduced him with her smooth
    talk.
22 All at once he followed her
  like an ox going to the slaughter,
  like a deer*a* stepping into a noose*b*
23   till an arrow pierces his liver,
  like a bird darting into a snare,
  little knowing it will cost him his life.

24 Now then, my sons, listen to me;
  pay attention to what I say.
25 Do not let your heart turn to her ways
  or stray into her paths.
26 Many are the victims she has brought
    down;
  her slain are a mighty throng.
27 Her house is a highway to the grave,
  leading down to the chambers of
    death.

Wisdom's Call

8 Does not wisdom call out?
  Does not understanding raise her
    voice?
2 At the highest point along the way,
  where the paths meet, she takes her
    stand;
3 beside the gate leading into the city,
  at the entrance, she cries aloud:
4 "To you, O people, I call out;
  I raise my voice to all mankind.
5 You who are simple, gain prudence;
  you who are foolish, set your hearts
    on it.*c*

a 22 Syriac (see also Septuagint); Hebrew *fool*
b 22 The meaning of the Hebrew for this line is
uncertain.   *c* 5 Septuagint; Hebrew *foolish,
instruct your minds*

753

⁶Listen, for I have trustworthy things
   to say;
   I open my lips to speak what is right.
⁷My mouth speaks what is true,
   for my lips detest wickedness.
⁸All the words of my mouth are just;
   none of them is crooked or perverse.
⁹To the discerning all of them are right;
   they are upright to those who have
   found knowledge.
¹⁰Choose my instruction instead of silver,
   knowledge rather than choice gold,
¹¹for wisdom is more precious than
   rubies,
   and nothing you desire can compare
   with her.

¹²"I, wisdom, dwell together with
   prudence;
   I possess knowledge and discretion.
¹³To fear the Lord is to hate evil;
   I hate pride and arrogance,
   evil behavior and perverse speech.
¹⁴Counsel and sound judgment are mine;
   I have insight, I have power.
¹⁵By me kings reign
   and rulers issue decrees that are
   just;
¹⁶by me princes govern,
   and nobles—all who rule on earth.ᵃ
¹⁷I love those who love me,
   and those who seek me find me.
¹⁸With me are riches and honor,
   enduring wealth and prosperity.
¹⁹My fruit is better than fine gold;
   what I yield surpasses choice silver.
²⁰I walk in the way of righteousness,
   along the paths of justice,
²¹bestowing a rich inheritance on those
   who love me
   and making their treasuries full.

²²"The Lord brought me forth as the
   first of his works,ᵇ,ᶜ
   before his deeds of old;
²³I was formed long ages ago,
   at the very beginning, when the
   world came to be.
²⁴When there were no watery depths, I
   was given birth,
   when there were no springs
   overflowing with water;

²⁵before the mountains were settled in
   place,
   before the hills, I was given birth,
²⁶before he made the world or its
   fields
   or any of the dust of the earth.
²⁷I was there when he set the heavens in
   place,
   when he marked out the horizon on
   the face of the deep,
²⁸when he established the clouds above
   and fixed securely the fountains of
   the deep,
²⁹when he gave the sea its boundary
   so the waters would not overstep his
   command,
   and when he marked out the
   foundations of the earth.
³⁰   Then I was constantlyᵈ at his side.
   I was filled with delight day after day,
   rejoicing always in his presence,
³¹rejoicing in his whole world
   and delighting in mankind.

³²"Now then, my children, listen to me;
   blessed are those who keep my
   ways.
³³Listen to my instruction and be wise;
   do not disregard it.
³⁴Blessed are those who listen to me,
   watching daily at my doors,
   waiting at my doorway.
³⁵For those who find me find life
   and receive favor from the Lord.
³⁶But those who fail to find me harm
   themselves;
   all who hate me love death."

Invitations of Wisdom and Folly

9 Wisdom has built her house;
   she has set upᵉ its seven pillars.
²She has prepared her meat and
   mixed her wine;
   she has also set her table.

ᵃ *16* Some Hebrew manuscripts and Septuagint;
other Hebrew manuscripts *all righteous rulers*
ᵇ *22* Or *way*; or *dominion*   ᶜ *22* Or *The Lord
possessed me at the beginning of his work*; or *The
Lord brought me forth at the beginning of his work*
ᵈ *30* Or *was the artisan*; or *was a little child*
ᵉ *1* Septuagint, Syriac and Targum; Hebrew *has
hewn out*

³She has sent out her servants, and she
calls
from the highest point of the city,
⁴ "Let all who are simple come to my
house!"
To those who have no sense she says,
⁵ "Come, eat my food
and drink the wine I have mixed.
⁶Leave your simple ways and you will
live;
walk in the way of insight."

⁷Whoever corrects a mocker invites
insults;
whoever rebukes the wicked incurs
abuse.
⁸Do not rebuke mockers or they will
hate you;
rebuke the wise and they will love
you.
⁹Instruct the wise and they will be
wiser still;
teach the righteous and they will
add to their learning.

¹⁰The fear of the LORD is the beginning
of wisdom,
and knowledge of the Holy One is
understanding.
¹¹For through wisdom*a* your days will
be many,
and years will be added to your life.
¹²If you are wise, your wisdom will
reward you;
if you are a mocker, you alone will
suffer.

¹³Folly is an unruly woman;
she is simple and knows nothing.
¹⁴She sits at the door of her house,
on a seat at the highest point of the
city,
¹⁵calling out to those who pass by,
who go straight on their way,
¹⁶ "Let all who are simple come to my
house!"
To those who have no sense she says,
¹⁷ "Stolen water is sweet;
food eaten in secret is delicious!"
¹⁸But little do they know that the dead
are there,
that her guests are deep in the
realm of the dead.

Proverbs 9:1–10

Fearing God is the start of wisdom.

Teachers and parents and peers try to size up your intelligence in all kinds of ways. But the Bible provides just one way to score your true smarts. Proverbs 9:10 says, "The fear of the LORD is the beginning of wisdom, and knowledge of the Holy One is understanding." That word "fear" doesn't mean "fright" or "terror" but an awe-filled respect for the Lord. This kind of fear is how you get wise. And throughout the Bible the "fear of the Lord" is a healthy understanding of God that leads to happy obedience (see Proverbs 14:27; Isaiah 11:3; Acts 9:31). Here in Proverbs 9, wisdom is pictured as a woman who has built a strong house and set a fine spread of food. She's shouting, "Come and get it!" She dares you to come inside and eat—or stand outside and look stupid.

Think: How will your life be better today if you live in "the fear of the Lord"?

ROCK SOLID truths

Proverbs of Solomon

10 The proverbs of Solomon:

A wise son brings joy to his
father,
but a foolish son brings grief to his
mother.

²Ill-gotten treasures have no lasting
value,
but righteousness delivers from
death.

a 11 Septuagint, Syriac and Targum;
Hebrew *me*

755

³ The LORD does not let the righteous
  go hungry,
  but he thwarts the craving of the
  wicked.

⁴ Lazy hands make for poverty,
  but diligent hands bring wealth.

⁵ He who gathers crops in summer is a
  prudent son,
  but he who sleeps during harvest is
  a disgraceful son.

⁶ Blessings crown the head of the
  righteous,
  but violence overwhelms the mouth
  of the wicked.ᵃ

⁷ The name of the righteous is used in
  blessings,ᵇ
  but the name of the wicked will rot.

⁸ The wise in heart accept commands,
  but a chattering fool comes to ruin.

⁹ Whoever walks in integrity walks
  securely,
  but whoever takes crooked paths
  will be found out.

¹⁰ Whoever winks maliciously causes
  grief,
  and a chattering fool comes to
  ruin.

¹¹ The mouth of the righteous is a
  fountain of life,
  but the mouth of the wicked
  conceals violence.

¹² Hatred stirs up conflict,
  but love covers over all wrongs.

¹³ Wisdom is found on the lips of the
  discerning,
  but a rod is for the back of one who
  has no sense.

¹⁴ The wise store up knowledge,
  but the mouth of a fool invites ruin.

¹⁵ The wealth of the rich is their
  fortified city,
  but poverty is the ruin of the poor.

¹⁶ The wages of the righteous is life,
  but the earnings of the wicked are
  sin and death.

¹⁷ Whoever heeds discipline shows the
  way to life,
  but whoever ignores correction
  leads others astray.

¹⁸ Whoever conceals hatred with lying
  lips
  and spreads slander is a fool.

¹⁹ Sin is not ended by multiplying words,
  but the prudent hold their tongues.

²⁰ The tongue of the righteous is choice
  silver,
  but the heart of the wicked is of
  little value.

²¹ The lips of the righteous nourish many,
  but fools die for lack of sense.

²² The blessing of the LORD brings wealth,
  without painful toil for it.

²³ A fool finds pleasure in wicked
  schemes,
  but a person of understanding
  delights in wisdom.

²⁴ What the wicked dread will overtake
  them;
  what the righteous desire will be
  granted.

²⁵ When the storm has swept by, the
  wicked are gone,
  but the righteous stand firm forever.

²⁶ As vinegar to the teeth and smoke to
  the eyes,
  so are sluggards to those who send
  them.

²⁷ The fear of the LORD adds length to
  life,
  but the years of the wicked are cut
  short.

²⁸ The prospect of the righteous is joy,
  but the hopes of the wicked come to
  nothing.

²⁹ The way of the LORD is a refuge for
  the blameless,
  but it is the ruin of those who do
  evil.

ᵃ 6 Or *righteous, / but the mouth of the wicked
conceals violence*   ᵇ 7 See Gen. 48:20.

³⁰ The righteous will never be uprooted,
but the wicked will not remain in
the land.

³¹ From the mouth of the righteous
comes the fruit of wisdom,
but a perverse tongue will be
silenced.

³² The lips of the righteous know what
finds favor,
but the mouth of the wicked only
what is perverse.

11 The Lᴏʀᴅ detests dishonest
scales,
but accurate weights find favor
with him.

² When pride comes, then comes
disgrace,
but with humility comes wisdom.

³ The integrity of the upright guides
them,
but the unfaithful are destroyed by
their duplicity.

⁴ Wealth is worthless in the day of wrath,
but righteousness delivers from death.

⁵ The righteousness of the blameless
makes their paths straight,
but the wicked are brought down by
their own wickedness.

⁶ The righteousness of the upright
delivers them,
but the unfaithful are trapped by
evil desires.

⁷ Hopes placed in mortals die with them;
all the promise ofᵃ their power
comes to nothing.

⁸ The righteous person is rescued from
trouble,
and it falls on the wicked instead.

⁹ With their mouths the godless destroy
their neighbors,
but through knowledge the
righteous escape.

¹⁰ When the righteous prosper, the city
rejoices;
when the wicked perish, there are
shouts of joy.

¹¹ Through the blessing of the upright a
city is exalted,
but by the mouth of the wicked it is
destroyed.

¹² Whoever derides their neighbor has
no sense,
but the one who has understanding
holds their tongue.

¹³ A gossip betrays a confidence,
but a trustworthy person keeps a
secret.

¹⁴ For lack of guidance a nation falls,
but victory is won through many
advisers.

¹⁵ Whoever puts up security for a
stranger will surely suffer,
but whoever refuses to shake hands
in pledge is safe.

¹⁶ A kindhearted woman gains honor,
but ruthless men gain only wealth.

¹⁷ Those who are kind benefit
themselves,
but the cruel bring ruin on
themselves.

¹⁸ A wicked person earns deceptive
wages,
but the one who sows righteousness
reaps a sure reward.

¹⁹ Truly the righteous attain life,
but whoever pursues evil finds
death.

²⁰ The Lᴏʀᴅ detests those whose hearts
are perverse,
but he delights in those whose ways
are blameless.

²¹ Be sure of this: The wicked will not
go unpunished,
but those who are righteous will go
free.

²² Like a gold ring in a pig's snout
is a beautiful woman who shows no
discretion.

ᵃ 7 Two Hebrew manuscripts; most Hebrew
manuscripts, Vulgate, Syriac and Targum *When
the wicked die, their hope perishes; / all they expected
from*

23 The desire of the righteous ends only
    in good,
  but the hope of the wicked only in
    wrath.

24 One person gives freely, yet gains even
    more;
  another withholds unduly, but
    comes to poverty.

25 A generous person will prosper;
  whoever refreshes others will be
    refreshed.

26 People curse the one who hoards
    grain,
  but they pray God's blessing on the
    one who is willing to sell.

27 Whoever seeks good finds favor,
  but evil comes to one who searches
    for it.

28 Those who trust in their riches will
    fall,
  but the righteous will thrive like a
    green leaf.

29 Whoever brings ruin on their family
    will inherit only wind,
  and the fool will be servant to the
    wise.

30 The fruit of the righteous is a tree of
    life,
  and the one who is wise saves lives.

31 If the righteous receive their due on
    earth,
  how much more the ungodly and
    the sinner!

12 Whoever loves discipline
    loves knowledge,
  but whoever hates correction
    is stupid.

2 Good people obtain favor from the
    LORD,
  but he condemns those who devise
    wicked schemes.

3 No one can be established through
    wickedness,
  but the righteous cannot be uprooted.

ROCK SOLID principles

Proverbs 12:1

Love correction.

Owen constantly struggled with his dad. He couldn't get through a chore without his dad pointing out a superior method for the task. Owen didn't care if the lawn would grow better if he avoided mowing in the same pattern week after week. He didn't like scraping and spackling and sanding and priming to get the house painted to his dad's tough standards. Mr. Brooks could be gruff, but that didn't mean he wasn't a sensitive guy. He just looked for opportunities to teach Owen and get him ready for life. And Mr. Brooks actually enjoyed seeing Owen spin a situation around and teach him a thing or two, because anyone smart learns to love correction.

You get graded at school so you get smarter. You endure reviews at work so you do a better job. You get judged in sports and music and art so you perfect your skills. God wants to give you that same beneficial feedback on how you do life, using both people and his Word to make you wise. Hating his correction turns you stupid.

⁴A wife of noble character is her
    husband's crown,
  but a disgraceful wife is like decay
    in his bones.

⁵The plans of the righteous are just,
  but the advice of the wicked is
    deceitful.

⁶The words of the wicked lie in wait for
    blood,
  but the speech of the upright
    rescues them.

⁷The wicked are overthrown and are
    no more,
  but the house of the righteous
    stands firm.

⁸A person is praised according to their
    prudence,
  and one with a warped mind is
    despised.

⁹Better to be a nobody and yet have a
    servant
  than pretend to be somebody and
    have no food.

¹⁰The righteous care for the needs of
    their animals,
  but the kindest acts of the wicked
    are cruel.

¹¹Those who work their land will have
    abundant food,
  but those who chase fantasies have
    no sense.

¹²The wicked desire the stronghold of
    evildoers,
  but the root of the righteous
    endures.

¹³Evildoers are trapped by their sinful
    talk,
  and so the innocent escape trouble.

¹⁴From the fruit of their lips people are
    filled with good things,
  and the work of their hands brings
    them reward.

¹⁵The way of fools seems right to them,
  but the wise listen to advice.

¹⁶Fools show their annoyance at once,
  but the prudent overlook an insult.

¹⁷An honest witness tells the truth,
  but a false witness tells lies.

¹⁸The words of the reckless pierce like
    swords,
  but the tongue of the wise brings
    healing.

¹⁹Truthful lips endure forever,
  but a lying tongue lasts only a
    moment.

²⁰Deceit is in the hearts of those who
    plot evil,
  but those who promote peace have
    joy.

²¹No harm overtakes the righteous,
  but the wicked have their fill of
    trouble.

²²The LORD detests lying lips,
  but he delights in people who are
    trustworthy.

²³The prudent keep their knowledge to
    themselves,
  but a fool's heart blurts out folly.

²⁴Diligent hands will rule,
  but laziness ends in forced labor.

²⁵Anxiety weighs down the heart,
  but a kind word cheers it up.

²⁶The righteous choose their friends
    carefully,
  but the way of the wicked leads
    them astray.

²⁷The lazy do not roast*a* any game,
  but the diligent feed on the riches
    of the hunt.

²⁸In the way of righteousness there is life;
  along that path is immortality.

13 A wise son heeds his father's
    instruction,
  but a mocker does not
    respond to rebukes.

²From the fruit of their lips people
    enjoy good things,
  but the unfaithful have an appetite
    for violence.

a 27 The meaning of the Hebrew for this word
is uncertain.

³Those who guard their lips preserve
    their lives,
  but those who speak rashly will
    come to ruin.

⁴A sluggard's appetite is never filled,
  but the desires of the diligent are
    fully satisfied.

⁵The righteous hate what is false,
  but the wicked make themselves a
    stench
  and bring shame on themselves.

⁶Righteousness guards the person of
    integrity,
  but wickedness overthrows the
    sinner.

⁷One person pretends to be rich, yet
    has nothing;
  another pretends to be poor, yet has
    great wealth.

⁸A person's riches may ransom their life,
  but the poor cannot respond to
    threatening rebukes.

⁹The light of the righteous shines
    brightly,
  but the lamp of the wicked is
    snuffed out.

¹⁰Where there is strife, there is pride,
  but wisdom is found in those who
    take advice.

¹¹Dishonest money dwindles away,
  but whoever gathers money little by
    little makes it grow.

¹²Hope deferred makes the heart sick,
  but a longing fulfilled is a tree of
    life.

¹³Whoever scorns instruction will pay
    for it,
  but whoever respects a command is
    rewarded.

¹⁴The teaching of the wise is a fountain
    of life,
  turning a person from the snares of
    death.

¹⁵Good judgment wins favor,
  but the way of the unfaithful leads
    to their destruction.ᵃ

¹⁶All who are prudent act withᵇ
    knowledge,
  but fools expose their folly.

¹⁷A wicked messenger falls into
    trouble,
  but a trustworthy envoy brings
    healing.

¹⁸Whoever disregards discipline comes
    to poverty and shame,
  but whoever heeds correction is
    honored.

¹⁹A longing fulfilled is sweet to the
    soul,
  but fools detest turning from evil.

²⁰Walk with the wise and become wise,
  for a companion of fools suffers
    harm.

²¹Trouble pursues the sinner,
  but the righteous are rewarded with
    good things.

ᵃ 15 Septuagint and Syriac; the meaning of the
Hebrew for this phrase is uncertain.
ᵇ 16 Or *prudent protect themselves through*

ROCK SOLID *plans*

Proverbs 13:20

Get solid advice.

No one makes it in life by going it alone.
And no one gets anywhere good by asking directions from people who are lost and
wandering. The Bible points out that there's
only one smart path — walking alongside
people unmistakably wiser than you. Wisdom in the Bible doesn't mean you have the
brightest mind in the room. Wisdom starts
with showing God the awe-filled respect he
deserves (see Proverbs 9:10). And wisdom
grows when you do life with as many wise
people as you can find (see Proverbs 24:6).

**Your next step: Find a mature Christian
willing to help you follow God wisely
wherever you go.**

²²A good person leaves an inheritance
　　for their children's children,
　　but a sinner's wealth is stored up for
　　the righteous.

²³An unplowed field produces food for
　　the poor,
　　but injustice sweeps it away.

²⁴Whoever spares the rod hates their
　　children,
　　but the one who loves their children
　　is careful to discipline them.

²⁵The righteous eat to their hearts'
　　content,
　　but the stomach of the wicked goes
　　hungry.

14 The wise woman builds her
　　house,
　　but with her own hands the
　　foolish one tears hers down.

²Whoever fears the LORD walks
　　uprightly,
　　but those who despise him are
　　devious in their ways.

³A fool's mouth lashes out with pride,
　　but the lips of the wise protect
　　them.

⁴Where there are no oxen, the manger
　　is empty,
　　but from the strength of an ox come
　　abundant harvests.

⁵An honest witness does not deceive,
　　but a false witness pours out lies.

⁶The mocker seeks wisdom and finds
　　none,
　　but knowledge comes easily to the
　　discerning.

⁷Stay away from a fool,
　　for you will not find knowledge on
　　their lips.

⁸The wisdom of the prudent is to give
　　thought to their ways,
　　but the folly of fools is deception.

⁹Fools mock at making amends for sin,
　　but goodwill is found among the
　　upright.

¹⁰Each heart knows its own bitterness,
　　and no one else can share its joy.

¹¹The house of the wicked will be
　　destroyed,
　　but the tent of the upright will
　　flourish.

¹²There is a way that appears to be
　　right,
　　but in the end it leads to death.

¹³Even in laughter the heart may ache,
　　and rejoicing may end in grief.

¹⁴The faithless will be fully repaid for
　　their ways,
　　and the good rewarded for theirs.

¹⁵The simple believe anything,
　　but the prudent give thought to
　　their steps.

¹⁶The wise fear the LORD and shun
　　evil,
　　but a fool is hotheaded and yet feels
　　secure.

¹⁷A quick-tempered person does foolish
　　things,
　　and the one who devises evil
　　schemes is hated.

¹⁸The simple inherit folly,
　　but the prudent are crowned with
　　knowledge.

¹⁹Evildoers will bow down in the
　　presence of the good,
　　and the wicked at the gates of the
　　righteous.

²⁰The poor are shunned even by their
　　neighbors,
　　but the rich have many friends.

²¹It is a sin to despise one's neighbor,
　　but blessed is the one who is kind to
　　the needy.

²²Do not those who plot evil go astray?
　　But those who plan what is good
　　find*ᵃ* love and faithfulness.

²³All hard work brings a profit,
　　but mere talk leads only to poverty.

ᵃ 22 Or *show*

²⁴ The wealth of the wise is their crown,
    but the folly of fools yields folly.

²⁵ A truthful witness saves lives,
    but a false witness is deceitful.

²⁶ Whoever fears the Lord has a secure
    fortress,
    and for their children it will be a
    refuge.

²⁷ The fear of the Lord is a fountain of
    life,
    turning a person from the snares of
    death.

²⁸ A large population is a king's glory,
    but without subjects a prince is
    ruined.

²⁹ Whoever is patient has great
    understanding,
    but one who is quick-tempered
    displays folly.

³⁰ A heart at peace gives life to the body,
    but envy rots the bones.

³¹ Whoever oppresses the poor shows
    contempt for their Maker,
    but whoever is kind to the needy
    honors God.

³² When calamity comes, the wicked are
    brought down,
    but even in death the righteous seek
    refuge in God.

³³ Wisdom reposes in the heart of the
    discerning
    and even among fools she lets
    herself be known.ᵃ

³⁴ Righteousness exalts a nation,
    but sin condemns any people.

³⁵ A king delights in a wise servant,
    but a shameful servant arouses his
    fury.

15 A gentle answer turns away
    wrath,
    but a harsh word stirs up anger.

² The tongue of the wise adorns
    knowledge,
    but the mouth of the fool gushes
    folly.

³ The eyes of the Lord are
    everywhere,
    keeping watch on the wicked and
    the good.

⁴ The soothing tongue is a tree of life,
    but a perverse tongue crushes the
    spirit.

⁵ A fool spurns a parent's discipline,
    but whoever heeds correction shows
    prudence.

⁶ The house of the righteous contains
    great treasure,
    but the income of the wicked brings
    ruin.

⁷ The lips of the wise spread
    knowledge,
    but the hearts of fools are not
    upright.

⁸ The Lord detests the sacrifice of the
    wicked,
    but the prayer of the upright pleases
    him.

⁹ The Lord detests the way of the
    wicked,
    but he loves those who pursue
    righteousness.

¹⁰ Stern discipline awaits anyone who
    leaves the path;
    the one who hates correction will
    die.

¹¹ Death and Destructionᵇ lie open
    before the Lord—
    how much more do human
    hearts!

¹² Mockers resent correction,
    so they avoid the wise.

¹³ A happy heart makes the face
    cheerful,
    but heartache crushes the spirit.

¹⁴ The discerning heart seeks
    knowledge,
    but the mouth of a fool feeds on
    folly.

ᵃ *33* Hebrew; Septuagint and Syriac *discerning /
but in the heart of fools she is not known*
ᵇ *11* Hebrew *Abaddon*

15 All the days of the oppressed are
 wretched,
  but the cheerful heart has a
  continual feast.

16 Better a little with the fear of the Lord
 than great wealth with turmoil.

17 Better a small serving of vegetables
 with love
  than a fattened calf with hatred.

18 A hot-tempered person stirs up
 conflict,
  but the one who is patient calms a
  quarrel.

19 The way of the sluggard is blocked
 with thorns,
  but the path of the upright is a
  highway.

20 A wise son brings joy to his father,
  but a foolish man despises his
  mother.

21 Folly brings joy to one who has no
 sense,
  but whoever has understanding
  keeps a straight course.

22 Plans fail for lack of counsel,
  but with many advisers they
  succeed.

23 A person finds joy in giving an apt
 reply—
  and how good is a timely word!

24 The path of life leads upward for the
 prudent
  to keep them from going down to
  the realm of the dead.

25 The Lord tears down the house of
 the proud,
  but he sets the widow's boundary
  stones in place.

26 The Lord detests the thoughts of the
 wicked,
  but gracious words are pure in his
  sight.

27 The greedy bring ruin to their
 households,
  but the one who hates bribes will
  live.

28 The heart of the righteous weighs its
 answers,
  but the mouth of the wicked gushes
  evil.

29 The Lord is far from the wicked,
  but he hears the prayer of the
  righteous.

30 Light in a messenger's eyes brings joy
 to the heart,
  and good news gives health to the
  bones.

31 Whoever heeds life-giving correction
 will be at home among the wise.

32 Those who disregard discipline
 despise themselves,
  but the one who heeds correction
  gains understanding.

33 Wisdom's instruction is to fear the
 Lord,
  and humility comes before honor.

16 To humans belong the plans
 of the heart,
  but from the Lord comes the
  proper answer of the tongue.

2 All a person's ways seem pure to
 them,
  but motives are weighed by the
  Lord.

3 Commit to the Lord whatever you do,
  and he will establish your plans.

4 The Lord works out everything to its
 proper end—
  even the wicked for a day of
  disaster.

5 The Lord detests all the proud of
 heart.
  Be sure of this: They will not go
  unpunished.

6 Through love and faithfulness sin is
 atoned for;
  through the fear of the Lord evil is
  avoided.

7 When the Lord takes pleasure in
 anyone's way,
  he causes their enemies to make
  peace with them.

⁸ Better a little with righteousness
than much gain with injustice.

⁹ In their hearts humans plan their course,
but the LORD establishes their steps.

ROCK SOLID *promises*

"In their hearts humans plan their course, but the LORD establishes their steps." **Proverbs 16:9**

You can draw a map of the place you think you're headed, but God ultimately takes you where he wants you to go.

¹⁰ The lips of a king speak as an oracle,
and his mouth does not betray justice.

¹¹ Honest scales and balances belong to
the LORD;
all the weights in the bag are of his
making.

¹² Kings detest wrongdoing,
for a throne is established through
righteousness.

¹³ Kings take pleasure in honest lips;
they value the one who speaks what
is right.

¹⁴ A king's wrath is a messenger of death,
but the wise will appease it.

¹⁵ When a king's face brightens, it means
life;
his favor is like a rain cloud in spring.

¹⁶ How much better to get wisdom than
gold,
to get insight rather than silver!

¹⁷ The highway of the upright avoids evil;
those who guard their ways preserve
their lives.

¹⁸ Pride goes before destruction,
a haughty spirit before a fall.

¹⁹ Better to be lowly in spirit along with
the oppressed
than to share plunder with the
proud.

²⁰ Whoever gives heed to instruction
prospers,[a]
and blessed is the one who trusts in
the LORD.

²¹ The wise in heart are called discerning,
and gracious words promote
instruction.[b]

²² Prudence is a fountain of life to the
prudent,
but folly brings punishment to fools.

²³ The hearts of the wise make their
mouths prudent,
and their lips promote instruction.[c]

²⁴ Gracious words are a honeycomb,
sweet to the soul and healing to the
bones.

²⁵ There is a way that appears to be right,
but in the end it leads to death.

²⁶ The appetite of laborers works for them;
their hunger drives them on.

²⁷ A scoundrel plots evil,
and on their lips it is like a
scorching fire.

²⁸ A perverse person stirs up conflict,
and a gossip separates close friends.

²⁹ A violent person entices their neighbor
and leads them down a path that is
not good.

³⁰ Whoever winks with their eye is
plotting perversity;
whoever purses their lips is bent on
evil.

³¹ Gray hair is a crown of splendor;
it is attained in the way of
righteousness.

³² Better a patient person than a warrior,
one with self-control than one who
takes a city.

[a] 20 Or *whoever speaks prudently finds what is good*   [b] 21 Or *words make a person persuasive*
[c] 23 Or *prudent / and make their lips persuasive*

³³The lot is cast into the lap,
  but its every decision is from the
    LORD.

17 Better a dry crust with peace
and quiet
  than a house full of feasting,
    with strife.

²A prudent servant will rule over a
    disgraceful son
  and will share the inheritance as
    one of the family.

³The crucible for silver and the furnace
    for gold,
  but the LORD tests the heart.

⁴A wicked person listens to deceitful
    lips;
  a liar pays attention to a destructive
    tongue.

⁵Whoever mocks the poor shows
    contempt for their Maker;
  whoever gloats over disaster will not
    go unpunished.

⁶Children's children are a crown to the
    aged,
  and parents are the pride of their
    children.

⁷Eloquent lips are unsuited to a godless
    fool—
  how much worse lying lips to a ruler!

⁸A bribe is seen as a charm by the one
    who gives it;
  they think success will come at
    every turn.

⁹Whoever would foster love covers over
    an offense,
  but whoever repeats the matter
    separates close friends.

¹⁰A rebuke impresses a discerning person
  more than a hundred lashes a fool.

¹¹Evildoers foster rebellion against God;
  the messenger of death will be sent
    against them.

¹²Better to meet a bear robbed of her cubs
  than a fool bent on folly.

¹³Evil will never leave the house
  of one who pays back evil for good.

¹⁴Starting a quarrel is like breaching a
    dam;
  so drop the matter before a dispute
    breaks out.

¹⁵Acquitting the guilty and condemning
    the innocent—
  the LORD detests them both.

¹⁶Why should fools have money in hand
    to buy wisdom,
  when they are not able to
    understand it?

¹⁷A friend loves at all times,
  and a brother is born for a time of
    adversity.

¹⁸One who has no sense shakes hands in
    pledge
  and puts up security for a neighbor.

¹⁹Whoever loves a quarrel loves sin;
  whoever builds a high gate invites
    destruction.

²⁰One whose heart is corrupt does not
    prosper;
  one whose tongue is perverse falls
    into trouble.

²¹To have a fool for a child brings grief;
  there is no joy for the parent of a
    godless fool.

²²A cheerful heart is good medicine,
  but a crushed spirit dries up the
    bones.

ROCK SOLID
promises

"A cheerful heart is good medicine." Proverbs 17:22

Thinking about God and all of his kind gifts doesn't just make you happy. It heals your whole body.

²³ The wicked accept bribes in secret
  to pervert the course of justice.

²⁴ A discerning person keeps wisdom in
    view,
  but a fool's eyes wander to the ends
    of the earth.

²⁵ A foolish son brings grief to his
    father
  and bitterness to the mother who
    bore him.

²⁶ If imposing a fine on the innocent is
    not good,
  surely to flog honest officials is not
    right.

²⁷ The one who has knowledge uses
    words with restraint,
  and whoever has understanding is
    even-tempered.

²⁸ Even fools are thought wise if they
    keep silent,
  and discerning if they hold their
    tongues.

18 An unfriendly person pursues
    selfish ends
  and against all sound
    judgment starts quarrels.

² Fools find no pleasure in
    understanding
  but delight in airing their own
    opinions.

³ When wickedness comes, so does
    contempt,
  and with shame comes reproach.

⁴ The words of the mouth are deep
    waters,
  but the fountain of wisdom is a
    rushing stream.

⁵ It is not good to be partial to the
    wicked
  and so deprive the innocent of
    justice.

⁶ The lips of fools bring them strife,
  and their mouths invite a beating.

⁷ The mouths of fools are their undoing,
  and their lips are a snare to their
    very lives.

Proverbs 18:1-2
No one can do life solo.

You might sit by yourself in the library because you need space to think—that's great. Or you might retreat to your room when you feel beat up and need time to heal—nothing wrong with that. But the Bible warns against a pattern of cutting ourselves off from others. Being unfriendly can be a sign of selfishness, and listening only to your own voice will make you crazy. The Bible constantly points out that we can't get through life without each other. Ecclesiastes 4:10 says, "Pity anyone who falls and has no one to help them up." And in the New Testament the apostle Paul compares Christians to a living body. The body can't function if a single part stops working, and no body part can decide to go it alone (1 Corinthians 12:15-22). Watch out when you only want to hang out with yourself, because you need people. And people need you.

Think: Why is it dangerous to cut yourself off from people?

ROCK SOLID truths

⁸ The words of a gossip are like choice
    morsels;
  they go down to the inmost parts.

⁹ One who is slack in his work
  is brother to one who destroys.

¹⁰ The name of the LORD is a fortified
    tower;
  the righteous run to it and are safe.

¹¹ The wealth of the rich is their
    fortified city;
  they imagine it a wall too high to
    scale.

¹²Before a downfall the heart is
    haughty,
  but humility comes before honor.

¹³To answer before listening—
  that is folly and shame.

¹⁴The human spirit can endure in
    sickness,
  but a crushed spirit who can bear?

¹⁵The heart of the discerning acquires
    knowledge,
  for the ears of the wise seek it out.

¹⁶A gift opens the way
  and ushers the giver into the
    presence of the great.

¹⁷In a lawsuit the first to speak seems
    right,
  until someone comes forward and
    cross-examines.

¹⁸Casting the lot settles disputes
  and keeps strong opponents apart.

¹⁹A brother wronged is more unyielding
    than a fortified city;
  disputes are like the barred gates of
    a citadel.

²⁰From the fruit of their mouth a
    person's stomach is filled;
  with the harvest of their lips they
    are satisfied.

²¹The tongue has the power of life and
    death,
  and those who love it will eat its
    fruit.

²²He who finds a wife finds what is
    good
  and receives favor from the Lord.

²³The poor plead for mercy,
  but the rich answer harshly.

²⁴One who has unreliable friends soon
    comes to ruin,
  but there is a friend who sticks
    closer than a brother.

19 Better the poor whose walk is
    blameless
  than a fool whose lips are
    perverse.

²Desire without knowledge is not
    good—
  how much more will hasty feet miss
    the way!

³A person's own folly leads to their
    ruin,
  yet their heart rages against the
    Lord.

⁴Wealth attracts many friends,
  but even the closest friend of the
    poor person deserts them.

⁵A false witness will not go
    unpunished,
  and whoever pours out lies will not
    go free.

⁶Many curry favor with a ruler,
  and everyone is the friend of one
    who gives gifts.

⁷The poor are shunned by all their
    relatives—
  how much more do their friends
    avoid them!
Though the poor pursue them with
    pleading,
  they are nowhere to be found.ᵃ

⁸The one who gets wisdom loves life;
  the one who cherishes understanding
    will soon prosper.

⁹A false witness will not go
    unpunished,
  and whoever pours out lies will
    perish.

¹⁰It is not fitting for a fool to live in
    luxury—
  how much worse for a slave to rule
    over princes!

¹¹A person's wisdom yields patience;
  it is to one's glory to overlook an
    offense.

¹²A king's rage is like the roar of a lion,
  but his favor is like dew on the grass.

¹³A foolish child is a father's ruin,
  and a quarrelsome wife is like
    the constant dripping of a leaky roof.

ᵃ 7 The meaning of the Hebrew for this
sentence is uncertain.

¹⁴Houses and wealth are inherited from
parents,
but a prudent wife is from the
LORD.

¹⁵Laziness brings on deep sleep,
and the shiftless go hungry.

¹⁶Whoever keeps commandments keeps
their life,
but whoever shows contempt for
their ways will die.

¹⁷Whoever is kind to the poor lends to
the LORD,
and he will reward them for what
they have done.

¹⁸Discipline your children, for in that
there is hope;
do not be a willing party to their
death.

¹⁹A hot-tempered person must pay the
penalty;
rescue them, and you will have to
do it again.

²⁰Listen to advice and accept discipline,
and at the end you will be counted
among the wise.

²¹Many are the plans in a person's heart,
but it is the LORD's purpose that
prevails.

²²What a person desires is unfailing
love^a;
better to be poor than a liar.

²³The fear of the LORD leads to life;
then one rests content, untouched
by trouble.

²⁴A sluggard buries his hand in the dish;
he will not even bring it back to his
mouth!

²⁵Flog a mocker, and the simple will
learn prudence;
rebuke the discerning, and they will
gain knowledge.

²⁶Whoever robs their father and drives
out their mother
is a child who brings shame and
disgrace.

²⁷Stop listening to instruction, my son,
and you will stray from the words of
knowledge.

²⁸A corrupt witness mocks at justice,
and the mouth of the wicked gulps
down evil.

²⁹Penalties are prepared for mockers,
and beatings for the backs of fools.

20 Wine is a mocker and beer
a brawler;
whoever is led astray by
them is not wise.

²A king's wrath strikes terror like the
roar of a lion;
those who anger him forfeit their
lives.

³It is to one's honor to avoid strife,
but every fool is quick to quarrel.

⁴Sluggards do not plow in season;
so at harvest time they look but find
nothing.

⁵The purposes of a person's heart are
deep waters,
but one who has insight draws them
out.

⁶Many claim to have unfailing love,
but a faithful person who can find?

⁷The righteous lead blameless lives;
blessed are their children after
them.

⁸When a king sits on his throne to
judge,
he winnows out all evil with his
eyes.

⁹Who can say, "I have kept my heart
pure;
I am clean and without sin"?

¹⁰Differing weights and differing
measures—
the LORD detests them both.

¹¹Even small children are known by
their actions,
so is their conduct really pure and
upright?

^a 22 Or *Greed is a person's shame*

¹²Ears that hear and eyes that see—
the LORD has made them both.

¹³Do not love sleep or you will grow
poor;
stay awake and you will have food
to spare.

¹⁴"It's no good, it's no good!" says the
buyer—
then goes off and boasts about the
purchase.

¹⁵Gold there is, and rubies in abundance,
but lips that speak knowledge are a
rare jewel.

¹⁶Take the garment of one who puts up
security for a stranger;
hold it in pledge if it is done for an
outsider.

¹⁷Food gained by fraud tastes sweet,
but one ends up with a mouth full
of gravel.

¹⁸Plans are established by seeking advice;
so if you wage war, obtain guidance.

¹⁹A gossip betrays a confidence;
so avoid anyone who talks too much.

²⁰If someone curses their father or
mother,
their lamp will be snuffed out in
pitch darkness.

²¹An inheritance claimed too soon
will not be blessed at the end.

²²Do not say, "I'll pay you back for this
wrong!"
Wait for the LORD, and he will
avenge you.

²³The LORD detests differing weights,
and dishonest scales do not please
him.

²⁴A person's steps are directed by the
LORD.
How then can anyone understand
their own way?

²⁵It is a trap to dedicate something
rashly
and only later to consider one's
vows.

²⁶A wise king winnows out the wicked;
he drives the threshing wheel over
them.

²⁷The human spirit is*a* the lamp of the
LORD
that sheds light on one's inmost
being.

²⁸Love and faithfulness keep a king
safe;
through love his throne is made
secure.

²⁹The glory of young men is their
strength,
gray hair the splendor of the old.

³⁰Blows and wounds scrub away evil,
and beatings purge the inmost
being.

21 In the LORD's hand the king's
heart is a stream of water
that he channels toward all
who please him.

²A person may think their own ways
are right,
but the LORD weighs the heart.

³To do what is right and just
is more acceptable to the LORD than
sacrifice.

⁴Haughty eyes and a proud heart—
the unplowed field of the wicked—
produce sin.

⁵The plans of the diligent lead to profit
as surely as haste leads to poverty.

⁶A fortune made by a lying tongue
is a fleeting vapor and a deadly
snare.*b*

⁷The violence of the wicked will drag
them away,
for they refuse to do what is right.

⁸The way of the guilty is devious,
but the conduct of the innocent is
upright.

a 27 Or *A person's words are*   *b 6* Some
Hebrew manuscripts, Septuagint and Vulgate;
most Hebrew manuscripts *vapor for those who
seek death*

⁹Better to live on a corner of the roof
than share a house with a
quarrelsome wife.

¹⁰The wicked crave evil;
their neighbors get no mercy from
them.

¹¹When a mocker is punished, the
simple gain wisdom;
by paying attention to the wise they
get knowledge.

¹²The Righteous One*a* takes note of the
house of the wicked
and brings the wicked to ruin.

¹³Whoever shuts their ears to the cry of
the poor
will also cry out and not be
answered.

¹⁴A gift given in secret soothes anger,
and a bribe concealed in the cloak
pacifies great wrath.

¹⁵When justice is done, it brings joy to
the righteous
but terror to evildoers.

¹⁶Whoever strays from the path of
prudence
comes to rest in the company of the
dead.

¹⁷Whoever loves pleasure will become
poor;
whoever loves wine and olive oil
will never be rich.

¹⁸The wicked become a ransom for the
righteous,
and the unfaithful for the upright.

¹⁹Better to live in a desert
than with a quarrelsome and
nagging wife.

²⁰The wise store up choice food and
olive oil,
but fools gulp theirs down.

²¹Whoever pursues righteousness and
love
finds life, prosperity*b* and honor.

²²One who is wise can go up against the
city of the mighty

and pull down the stronghold in
which they trust.

²³Those who guard their mouths and
their tongues
keep themselves from calamity.

²⁴The proud and arrogant person—
"Mocker" is his name—
behaves with insolent fury.

²⁵The craving of a sluggard will be the
death of him,
because his hands refuse to work.

²⁶All day long he craves for more,
but the righteous give without
sparing.

²⁷The sacrifice of the wicked is
detestable—
how much more so when brought
with evil intent!

²⁸A false witness will perish,
but a careful listener will testify
successfully.

²⁹The wicked put up a bold front,
but the upright give thought to their
ways.

³⁰There is no wisdom, no insight, no
plan
that can succeed against the Lord.

³¹The horse is made ready for the day of
battle,
but victory rests with the Lord.

22 A good name is more
desirable than great riches;
to be esteemed is better
than silver or gold.

²Rich and poor have this in common:
The Lord is the Maker of them all.

³The prudent see danger and take
refuge,
but the simple keep going and pay
the penalty.

⁴Humility is the fear of the Lord;
its wages are riches and honor and
life.

a 12 Or *The righteous person*
b 21 Or *righteousness*

ROCK SOLID *principles*

Protect your reputation.

Mia and her family were best friends with another family who had a boy her age, Noah. The two had been like brother and sister since way back in the day. But after the families returned from a spring break together at the beach, rumors flew at school that Mia and Noah were in a relationship. To Mia that was just plain weird. But the story also said that Mia had gotten drunk with Noah—and who knows what else happened. The only reason the talk faded quickly was everyone was clear on the fact that Mia didn't drink—or mess around with guys. She had a solid reputation that could stand up to attacks.

You would put up a fight if someone tried to beat you bloody. Or you would yell for help before you let someone steal your most treasured possessions. Your reputation deserves that same do-or-die kind of protection. You can build a reputation that can stand up to scrutiny. Or you can hand people reasons to talk about you like trash.

⁵ In the paths of the wicked are snares
  and pitfalls,
  but those who would preserve their
    life stay far from them.

⁶ Start children off on the way they
    should go,
  and even when they are old they
    will not turn from it.

⁷ The rich rule over the poor,
  and the borrower is slave to the
    lender.

⁸ Whoever sows injustice reaps
    calamity,
  and the rod they wield in fury will
    be broken.

⁹ The generous will themselves be
    blessed,
  for they share their food with the
    poor.

¹⁰ Drive out the mocker, and out goes
    strife;
  quarrels and insults are ended.

¹¹ One who loves a pure heart and who
    speaks with grace
  will have the king for a friend.

¹² The eyes of the LORD keep watch over
    knowledge,
  but he frustrates the words of the
    unfaithful.

¹³ The sluggard says, "There's a lion
    outside!
  I'll be killed in the public square!"

¹⁴ The mouth of an adulterous woman is
    a deep pit;
  a man who is under the LORD's
    wrath falls into it.

¹⁵ Folly is bound up in the heart of a
    child,
  but the rod of discipline will drive it
    far away.

¹⁶ One who oppresses the poor to
    increase his wealth
  and one who gives gifts to the
    rich—both come to poverty.

Thirty Sayings of the Wise

Saying 1

¹⁷ Pay attention and turn your ear to the
    sayings of the wise;
    apply your heart to what I teach,
¹⁸ for it is pleasing when you keep them
    in your heart
    and have all of them ready on your
      lips.
¹⁹ So that your trust may be in the
    LORD,
    I teach you today, even you.
²⁰ Have I not written thirty sayings for
    you,
    sayings of counsel and knowledge,
²¹ teaching you to be honest and to speak
    the truth,
    so that you bring back truthful
      reports
    to those you serve?

Saying 2

²² Do not exploit the poor because they
    are poor
    and do not crush the needy in court,
²³ for the LORD will take up their case
    and will exact life for life.

Saying 3

²⁴ Do not make friends with a hot-
    tempered person,
    do not associate with one easily
      angered,
²⁵ or you may learn their ways
    and get yourself ensnared.

Saying 4

²⁶ Do not be one who shakes hands in
    pledge
    or puts up security for debts;
²⁷ if you lack the means to pay,
    your very bed will be snatched from
      under you.

Saying 5

²⁸ Do not move an ancient boundary stone
    set up by your ancestors.

Saying 6

²⁹ Do you see someone skilled in their
    work?

They will serve before kings;
    they will not serve before officials
      of low rank.

Saying 7

23 When you sit to dine with
    a ruler,
    note well what*ᵃ* is before you,
² and put a knife to your throat
    if you are given to gluttony.
³ Do not crave his delicacies,
    for that food is deceptive.

Saying 8

⁴ Do not wear yourself out to get rich;
    do not trust your own cleverness.
⁵ Cast but a glance at riches, and they
    are gone,
    for they will surely sprout wings
    and fly off to the sky like an
      eagle.

Saying 9

⁶ Do not eat the food of a begrudging
    host,
    do not crave his delicacies;
⁷ for he is the kind of person
    who is always thinking about the
      cost.*ᵇ*
    "Eat and drink," he says to you,
    but his heart is not with you.
⁸ You will vomit up the little you have
    eaten
    and will have wasted your
      compliments.

Saying 10

⁹ Do not speak to fools,
    for they will scorn your prudent
      words.

Saying 11

¹⁰ Do not move an ancient boundary
    stone
    or encroach on the fields of the
      fatherless,
¹¹ for their Defender is strong;
    he will take up their case against
      you.

ᵃ 1 Or *who*   *ᵇ 7* Or *for as he thinks within
himself, / so he is*; or *for as he puts on a feast, / so he is*

Saying 12

12 Apply your heart to instruction
and your ears to words of
knowledge.

Saying 13

13 Do not withhold discipline from a
child;
if you punish them with the rod,
they will not die.
14 Punish them with the rod
and save them from death.

Saying 14

15 My son, if your heart is wise,
then my heart will be glad indeed;
16 my inmost being will rejoice
when your lips speak what is right.

Saying 15

17 Do not let your heart envy sinners,
but always be zealous for the fear of
the Lord.
18 There is surely a future hope for you,
and your hope will not be cut off.

Saying 16

19 Listen, my son, and be wise,
and set your heart on the right path:
20 Do not join those who drink too much
wine
or gorge themselves on meat,
21 for drunkards and gluttons become
poor,
and drowsiness clothes them in rags.

Saying 17

22 Listen to your father, who gave you
life,
and do not despise your mother
when she is old.
23 Buy the truth and do not sell it —
wisdom, instruction and insight as
well.
24 The father of a righteous child has
great joy;
a man who fathers a wise son
rejoices in him.
25 May your father and mother rejoice;
may she who gave you birth be
joyful!

Saying 18

26 My son, give me your heart
and let your eyes delight in my ways,
27 for an adulterous woman is a deep pit,
and a wayward wife is a narrow
well.
28 Like a bandit she lies in wait
and multiplies the unfaithful among
men.

Saying 19

29 Who has woe? Who has sorrow?
Who has strife? Who has
complaints?
Who has needless bruises? Who
has bloodshot eyes?
30 Those who linger over wine,
who go to sample bowls of mixed
wine.
31 Do not gaze at wine when it is red,
when it sparkles in the cup,
when it goes down smoothly!
32 In the end it bites like a snake
and poisons like a viper.
33 Your eyes will see strange sights,
and your mind will imagine
confusing things.
34 You will be like one sleeping on the
high seas,
lying on top of the rigging.
35 "They hit me," you will say, "but I'm
not hurt!
They beat me, but I don't feel it!
When will I wake up
so I can find another drink?"

Saying 20

24 Do not envy the wicked,
do not desire their
company;
2 for their hearts plot violence,
and their lips talk about making
trouble.

Saying 21

3 By wisdom a house is built,
and through understanding it is
established;
4 through knowledge its rooms are
filled
with rare and beautiful treasures.

ROCK SOLID *principles*

Proverbs 23:29–35

Don't get drunk.

For Conner the last few months felt like a scene from a health class video about the dangers of drinking. Like every elementary school kid he ever knew, Conner had once sworn he would never abuse alcohol—and he got a t-shirt to prove it. But nothing was that easy when he showed up at a party and saw all of his best friends with beer in hand. Conner grabbed a bottle—just to fit in—but he soon decided he was both cooler and more comical if he actually drank. Alcohol became a habit. One weekend Conner found out there was nothing fresh or funny about getting a citation for underage consumption. He was so busted—in so many ways.

Don't let anyone tell you that abusing alcohol is no big deal. Drinking has been around as long as people have been alive, and God long ago explained its impact. Alcohol might go down smooth, but it bites with fangs full of deadly venom. See substance abuse for what it is—a quick way to get "needless bruises" (Proverbs 23:29).

Saying 22

⁵The wise prevail through great
power,
and those who have knowledge
muster their strength.
⁶Surely you need guidance to wage war,
and victory is won through many
advisers.

Saying 23

⁷Wisdom is too high for fools;
in the assembly at the gate they
must not open their mouths.

Saying 24

⁸Whoever plots evil
will be known as a schemer.
⁹The schemes of folly are sin,
and people detest a mocker.

Saying 25

¹⁰If you falter in a time of trouble,
how small is your strength!

¹¹Rescue those being led away to
death;
hold back those staggering toward
slaughter.
¹²If you say, "But we knew nothing
about this,"
does not he who weighs the heart
perceive it?
Does not he who guards your life
know it?
Will he not repay everyone
according to what they have
done?

Saying 26

¹³Eat honey, my son, for it is good;
honey from the comb is sweet to
your taste.
¹⁴Know also that wisdom is like honey
for you:
If you find it, there is a future hope
for you,
and your hope will not be cut off.

Saying 27

¹⁵ Do not lurk like a thief near the house
of the righteous,
do not plunder their dwelling place;
¹⁶ for though the righteous fall seven
times, they rise again,
but the wicked stumble when
calamity strikes.

Saying 28

¹⁷ Do not gloat when your enemy falls;
when they stumble, do not let your
heart rejoice,
¹⁸ or the LORD will see and disapprove
and turn his wrath away from them.

Saying 29

¹⁹ Do not fret because of evildoers
or be envious of the wicked,
²⁰ for the evildoer has no future hope,
and the lamp of the wicked will be
snuffed out.

Saying 30

²¹ Fear the LORD and the king, my son,
and do not join with rebellious
officials,
²² for those two will send sudden
destruction on them,
and who knows what calamities
they can bring?

Further Sayings of the Wise

²³ These also are sayings of the wise:

To show partiality in judging is not
good:
²⁴ Whoever says to the guilty, "You are
innocent,"
will be cursed by peoples and
denounced by nations.
²⁵ But it will go well with those who
convict the guilty,
and rich blessing will come on
them.

²⁶ An honest answer
is like a kiss on the lips.

²⁷ Put your outdoor work in order
and get your fields ready;
after that, build your house.

²⁸ Do not testify against your neighbor
without cause—
would you use your lips to mislead?
²⁹ Do not say, "I'll do to them as they
have done to me;
I'll pay them back for what they did."

³⁰ I went past the field of a sluggard,
past the vineyard of someone who
has no sense;
³¹ thorns had come up everywhere,
the ground was covered with weeds,
and the stone wall was in ruins.
³² I applied my heart to what I observed
and learned a lesson from what I
saw:
³³ A little sleep, a little slumber,
a little folding of the hands to rest—
³⁴ and poverty will come on you like a
thief
and scarcity like an armed man.

More Proverbs of Solomon

25 These are more proverbs of
Solomon, compiled by the
men of Hezekiah king of
Judah:

² It is the glory of God to conceal a
matter;
to search out a matter is the glory of
kings.
³ As the heavens are high and the earth
is deep,
so the hearts of kings are
unsearchable.

⁴ Remove the dross from the silver,
and a silversmith can produce a
vessel;
⁵ remove wicked officials from the
king's presence,
and his throne will be established
through righteousness.

⁶ Do not exalt yourself in the king's
presence,
and do not claim a place among his
great men;
⁷ it is better for him to say to you,
"Come up here,"
than for him to humiliate you
before his nobles.

What you have seen with your eyes
  8   do not bring*a* hastily to court,
for what will you do in the end
  if your neighbor puts you to shame?

⁹ If you take your neighbor to court,
  do not betray another's confidence,
¹⁰ or the one who hears it may shame you
  and the charge against you will
    stand.

¹¹ Like apples*b* of gold in settings of silver
  is a ruling rightly given.
¹² Like an earring of gold or an
    ornament of fine gold
  is the rebuke of a wise judge to a
    listening ear.

¹³ Like a snow-cooled drink at harvest
    time
  is a trustworthy messenger to the
    one who sends him;
  he refreshes the spirit of his master.
¹⁴ Like clouds and wind without rain
  is one who boasts of gifts never
    given.

¹⁵ Through patience a ruler can be
    persuaded,
  and a gentle tongue can break a
    bone.

¹⁶ If you find honey, eat just enough—
  too much of it, and you will vomit.
¹⁷ Seldom set foot in your neighbor's
    house—
  too much of you, and they will hate
    you.

¹⁸ Like a club or a sword or a sharp arrow
  is one who gives false testimony
    against a neighbor.
¹⁹ Like a broken tooth or a lame foot
  is reliance on the unfaithful in a
    time of trouble.
²⁰ Like one who takes away a garment on
    a cold day,
  or like vinegar poured on a wound,
  is one who sings songs to a heavy
    heart.

²¹ If your enemy is hungry, give him
    food to eat;
  if he is thirsty, give him water to
    drink.

²² In doing this, you will heap burning
    coals on his head,
  and the LORD will reward you.

²³ Like a north wind that brings
    unexpected rain
  is a sly tongue—which provokes a
    horrified look.

²⁴ Better to live on a corner of the roof
  than share a house with a
    quarrelsome wife.

²⁵ Like cold water to a weary soul
  is good news from a distant land.
²⁶ Like a muddied spring or a polluted
    well
  are the righteous who give way to
    the wicked.

²⁷ It is not good to eat too much honey,
  nor is it honorable to search out
    matters that are too deep.

²⁸ Like a city whose walls are broken
    through
  is a person who lacks self-control.

26 Like snow in summer or
    rain in harvest,
    honor is not fitting for
    a fool.
² Like a fluttering sparrow or a darting
    swallow,
  an undeserved curse does not come
    to rest.
³ A whip for the horse, a bridle for the
    donkey,
  and a rod for the backs of fools!
⁴ Do not answer a fool according to his
    folly,
  or you yourself will be just like him.
⁵ Answer a fool according to his folly,
  or he will be wise in his own eyes.
⁶ Sending a message by the hands of a
    fool
  is like cutting off one's feet or
    drinking poison.
⁷ Like the useless legs of one who is lame
  is a proverb in the mouth of a fool.
⁸ Like tying a stone in a sling
  is the giving of honor to a fool.

a 7,8 Or *nobles / on whom you had set your eyes. /
⁸Do not go*   *b 11* Or possibly *apricots*

⁹ Like a thornbush in a drunkard's
    hand
    is a proverb in the mouth of a fool.
¹⁰ Like an archer who wounds at random
    is one who hires a fool or any
    passer-by.
¹¹ As a dog returns to its vomit,
    so fools repeat their folly.
¹² Do you see a person wise in their own
    eyes?
    There is more hope for a fool than
    for them.

¹³ A sluggard says, "There's a lion in the
    road,
    a fierce lion roaming the streets!"
¹⁴ As a door turns on its hinges,
    so a sluggard turns on his bed.
¹⁵ A sluggard buries his hand in the
    dish;
    he is too lazy to bring it back to his
    mouth.
¹⁶ A sluggard is wiser in his own eyes
    than seven people who answer
    discreetly.

¹⁷ Like one who grabs a stray dog by the
    ears
    is someone who rushes into a
    quarrel not their own.

¹⁸ Like a maniac shooting
    flaming arrows of death
¹⁹ is one who deceives their neighbor
    and says, "I was only joking!"

²⁰ Without wood a fire goes out;
    without a gossip a quarrel dies
    down.
²¹ As charcoal to embers and as wood to
    fire,
    so is a quarrelsome person for
    kindling strife.
²² The words of a gossip are like choice
    morsels;
    they go down to the inmost parts.

²³ Like a coating of silver dross on
    earthenware
    are fervent*ᵃ* lips with an evil heart.
²⁴ Enemies disguise themselves with
    their lips,
    but in their hearts they harbor
    deceit.

²⁵ Though their speech is charming, do
    not believe them,
    for seven abominations fill their
    hearts.
²⁶ Their malice may be concealed by
    deception,
    but their wickedness will be
    exposed in the assembly.
²⁷ Whoever digs a pit will fall into it;
    if someone rolls a stone, it will roll
    back on them.
²⁸ A lying tongue hates those it hurts,
    and a flattering mouth works ruin.

27 Do not boast about
    tomorrow,
    for you do not know what a
    day may bring.

² Let someone else praise you, and not
    your own mouth;
    an outsider, and not your own lips.

³ Stone is heavy and sand a burden,
    but a fool's provocation is heavier
    than both.

⁴ Anger is cruel and fury overwhelming,
    but who can stand before jealousy?

⁵ Better is open rebuke
    than hidden love.

⁶ Wounds from a friend can be trusted,
    but an enemy multiplies kisses.

ᵃ 23 Hebrew; Septuagint *smooth*

ROCK SOLID
promises

"Wounds from a friend can be trusted."   **Proverbs 27:6**

Hard words from a friend's mouth can help you grow.

⁷One who is full loathes honey from
the comb,
but to the hungry even what is
bitter tastes sweet.

⁸Like a bird that flees its nest
is anyone who flees from home.

⁹Perfume and incense bring joy to the
heart,
and the pleasantness of a friend
springs from their heartfelt advice.

¹⁰Do not forsake your friend or a friend
of your family,
and do not go to your relative's
house when disaster strikes
you—
better a neighbor nearby than a
relative far away.

¹¹Be wise, my son, and bring joy to my
heart;
then I can answer anyone who
treats me with contempt.

¹²The prudent see danger and take
refuge,
but the simple keep going and pay
the penalty.

¹³Take the garment of one who puts up
security for a stranger;
hold it in pledge if it is done for an
outsider.

¹⁴If anyone loudly blesses their neighbor
early in the morning,
it will be taken as a curse.

¹⁵A quarrelsome wife is like the
dripping
of a leaky roof in a rainstorm;
¹⁶restraining her is like restraining the
wind
or grasping oil with the hand.

¹⁷As iron sharpens iron,
so one person sharpens another.

¹⁸The one who guards a fig tree will eat
its fruit,
and whoever protects their master
will be honored.

¹⁹As water reflects the face,
so one's life reflects the heart.ᵃ

²⁰Death and Destructionᵇ are never
satisfied,
and neither are human eyes.

²¹The crucible for silver and the furnace
for gold,
but people are tested by their praise.

²²Though you grind a fool in a mortar,
grinding them like grain with a
pestle,
you will not remove their folly from
them.

²³Be sure you know the condition of
your flocks,
give careful attention to your herds;
²⁴for riches do not endure forever,
and a crown is not secure for all
generations.
²⁵When the hay is removed and new
growth appears
and the grass from the hills is
gathered in,
²⁶the lambs will provide you with
clothing,
and the goats with the price of a field.
²⁷You will have plenty of goats' milk to
feed your family
and to nourish your female servants.

28 The wicked flee though no
one pursues,
but the righteous are as
bold as a lion.

²When a country is rebellious, it has
many rulers,
but a ruler with discernment and
knowledge maintains order.

³A rulerᶜ who oppresses the poor
is like a driving rain that leaves no
crops.

⁴Those who forsake instruction praise
the wicked,
but those who heed it resist them.

⁵Evildoers do not understand what is
right,
but those who seek the LORD
understand it fully.

ᵃ 19 Or *so others reflect your heart back to you*
ᵇ 20 Hebrew *Abaddon*   ᶜ 3 Or *A poor person*

⁶Better the poor whose walk is blameless
 than the rich whose ways are perverse.

⁷A discerning son heeds instruction,
 but a companion of gluttons
  disgraces his father.

⁸Whoever increases wealth by taking
  interest or profit from the
  poor
 amasses it for another, who will be
  kind to the poor.

⁹If anyone turns a deaf ear to my
  instruction,
 even their prayers are detestable.

¹⁰Whoever leads the upright along an
  evil path
 will fall into their own trap,
 but the blameless will receive a
  good inheritance.

¹¹The rich are wise in their own eyes;
 one who is poor and discerning sees
  how deluded they are.

¹²When the righteous triumph, there is
  great elation;
 but when the wicked rise to power,
  people go into hiding.

¹³Whoever conceals their sins does not
  prosper,
 but the one who confesses and
  renounces them finds mercy.

¹⁴Blessed is the one who always
  trembles before God,
 but whoever hardens their heart
  falls into trouble.

¹⁵Like a roaring lion or a charging
  bear
 is a wicked ruler over a helpless
  people.

¹⁶A tyrannical ruler practices extortion,
 but one who hates ill-gotten gain
  will enjoy a long reign.

¹⁷Anyone tormented by the guilt of
  murder
 will seek refuge in the grave;
 let no one hold them back.

¹⁸The one whose walk is blameless is
  kept safe,

but the one whose ways are perverse
 will fall into the pit.ᵃ

¹⁹Those who work their land will have
  abundant food,
 but those who chase fantasies will
  have their fill of poverty.

²⁰A faithful person will be richly blessed,
 but one eager to get rich will not go
  unpunished.

²¹To show partiality is not good—
 yet a person will do wrong for a
  piece of bread.

²²The stingy are eager to get rich
 and are unaware that poverty awaits
  them.

²³Whoever rebukes a person will in the
  end gain favor
 rather than one who has a flattering
  tongue.

²⁴Whoever robs their father or mother
 and says, "It's not wrong,"
 is partner to one who destroys.

²⁵The greedy stir up conflict,
 but those who trust in the LORD
  will prosper.

²⁶Those who trust in themselves are fools,
 but those who walk in wisdom are
  kept safe.

²⁷Those who give to the poor will lack
  nothing,
 but those who close their eyes to
  them receive many curses.

²⁸When the wicked rise to power,
  people go into hiding;
 but when the wicked perish, the
  righteous thrive.

29 Whoever remains stiff-
  necked after many rebukes
  will suddenly be
  destroyed—without remedy.

²When the righteous thrive, the people
  rejoice;
 when the wicked rule, the people
  groan.

ᵃ 18 Syriac (see Septuagint); Hebrew *into one*

³A man who loves wisdom brings joy to
  his father,
  but a companion of prostitutes
    squanders his wealth.

⁴By justice a king gives a country
    stability,
  but those who are greedy for*ᵃ bribes
    tear it down.

⁵Those who flatter their neighbors
  are spreading nets for their feet.

⁶Evildoers are snared by their own sin,
  but the righteous shout for joy and
    are glad.

⁷The righteous care about justice for
    the poor,
  but the wicked have no such
    concern.

⁸Mockers stir up a city,
  but the wise turn away anger.

⁹If a wise person goes to court with a
    fool,
  the fool rages and scoffs, and there
    is no peace.

¹⁰The bloodthirsty hate a person of
    integrity
  and seek to kill the upright.

¹¹Fools give full vent to their rage,
  but the wise bring calm in the end.

¹²If a ruler listens to lies,
  all his officials become wicked.

¹³The poor and the oppressor have this
    in common:
  The Lord gives sight to the eyes of
    both.

¹⁴If a king judges the poor with
    fairness,
  his throne will be established
    forever.

¹⁵A rod and a reprimand impart
    wisdom,
  but a child left undisciplined
    disgraces its mother.

¹⁶When the wicked thrive, so does sin,
  but the righteous will see their
    downfall.

¹⁷Discipline your children, and they will
    give you peace;
  they will bring you the delights you
    desire.

¹⁸Where there is no revelation, people
    cast off restraint;
  but blessed is the one who heeds
    wisdom's instruction.

¹⁹Servants cannot be corrected by mere
    words;
  though they understand, they will
    not respond.

²⁰Do you see someone who speaks in
    haste?
  There is more hope for a fool than
    for them.

²¹A servant pampered from youth
  will turn out to be insolent.

²²An angry person stirs up conflict,
  and a hot-tempered person commits
    many sins.

²³Pride brings a person low,
  but the lowly in spirit gain honor.

²⁴The accomplices of thieves are their
    own enemies;
  they are put under oath and dare
    not testify.

²⁵Fear of man will prove to be a snare,
  but whoever trusts in the Lord is
    kept safe.

²⁶Many seek an audience with a ruler,
  but it is from the Lord that one
    gets justice.

²⁷The righteous detest the dishonest;
  the wicked detest the upright.

Sayings of Agur

30 The sayings of Agur son of
    Jakeh—an inspired utterance.

This man's utterance to Ithiel:

"I am weary, God,
  but I can prevail.*ᵇ

ᵃ 4 Or *who give*   *ᵇ 1* With a different word
division of the Hebrew; Masoretic Text *utterance
to Ithiel, / to Ithiel and Ukal:*

² Surely I am only a brute, not a man;
    I do not have human understanding.
³ I have not learned wisdom,
    nor have I attained to the
        knowledge of the Holy One.
⁴ Who has gone up to heaven and come
        down?
    Whose hands have gathered up the
        wind?
    Who has wrapped up the waters in a
        cloak?
    Who has established all the ends of
        the earth?
    What is his name, and what is the
        name of his son?
    Surely you know!

⁵ "Every word of God is flawless;
    he is a shield to those who take
        refuge in him.

ROCK SOLID promises

"Every word of God is flawless."

Proverbs 30:5

Don't expect perfection from human words. Only the God-inspired words of the Bible are totally correct.

---

⁶ Do not add to his words,
    or he will rebuke you and prove you
        a liar.

⁷ "Two things I ask of you, LORD;
    do not refuse me before I die:
⁸ Keep falsehood and lies far from me;
    give me neither poverty nor riches,
    but give me only my daily bread.
⁹ Otherwise, I may have too much and
        disown you
    and say, 'Who is the LORD?'
    Or I may become poor and steal,
        and so dishonor the name of my God.

¹⁰ "Do not slander a servant to their
        master,
    or they will curse you, and you will
        pay for it.

¹¹ "There are those who curse their
        fathers
    and do not bless their mothers;
¹² those who are pure in their own eyes
    and yet are not cleansed of their
        filth;
¹³ those whose eyes are ever so haughty,
    whose glances are so disdainful;
¹⁴ those whose teeth are swords
    and whose jaws are set with knives
    to devour the poor from the earth
    and the needy from among
        mankind.

¹⁵ "The leech has two daughters.
    'Give! Give!' they cry.

"There are three things that are never
        satisfied,
    four that never say, 'Enough!':
¹⁶ the grave, the barren womb,
    land, which is never satisfied with
        water,
    and fire, which never says,
        'Enough!'

¹⁷ "The eye that mocks a father,
    that scorns an aged mother,
    will be pecked out by the ravens of the
        valley,
    will be eaten by the vultures.

¹⁸ "There are three things that are too
        amazing for me,
    four that I do not understand:
¹⁹ the way of an eagle in the sky,
    the way of a snake on a rock,
    the way of a ship on the high seas,
    and the way of a man with a young
        woman.

²⁰ "This is the way of an adulterous
        woman:
    She eats and wipes her mouth
    and says, 'I've done nothing
        wrong.'

²¹ "Under three things the earth
        trembles,
    under four it cannot bear up:

²² a servant who becomes king,
　a godless fool who gets plenty to
　　eat,
²³ a contemptible woman who gets
　　married,
　and a servant who displaces her
　　mistress.

²⁴ "Four things on earth are small,
　yet they are extremely wise:
²⁵ Ants are creatures of little strength,
　yet they store up their food in the
　　summer;
²⁶ hyraxes are creatures of little power,
　yet they make their home in the
　　crags;
²⁷ locusts have no king,
　yet they advance together in
　　ranks;
²⁸ a lizard can be caught with the hand,
　yet it is found in kings' palaces.

²⁹ "There are three things that are stately
　　in their stride,
　four that move with stately
　　bearing:
³⁰ a lion, mighty among beasts,
　who retreats before nothing;
³¹ a strutting rooster, a he-goat,
　and a king secure against revolt.ᵃ

³² "If you play the fool and exalt yourself,
　or if you plan evil,
　clap your hand over your mouth!
³³ For as churning cream produces
　　butter,
　and as twisting the nose produces
　　blood,
　so stirring up anger produces
　　strife."

Sayings of King Lemuel

31 The sayings of King Lemuel—an inspired utterance his
mother taught him.

² Listen, my son! Listen, son of my
　womb!
　Listen, my son, the answer to my
　　prayers!
³ Do not spend your strengthᵇ on
　　women,
　your vigor on those who ruin kings.

⁴ It is not for kings, Lemuel—
　it is not for kings to drink wine,
　not for rulers to crave beer,
⁵ lest they drink and forget what has
　　been decreed,
　and deprive all the oppressed of
　　their rights.
⁶ Let beer be for those who are
　　perishing,
　wine for those who are in anguish!
⁷ Let them drink and forget their
　　poverty
　and remember their misery no
　　more.

⁸ Speak up for those who cannot speak
　　for themselves,
　for the rights of all who are
　　destitute.
⁹ Speak up and judge fairly;
　defend the rights of the poor and
　　needy.

Epilogue: The Wife of Noble Character

¹⁰ ᶜ A wife of noble character who can
　　find?
　She is worth far more than rubies.
¹¹ Her husband has full confidence in
　　her
　and lacks nothing of value.
¹² She brings him good, not harm,
　all the days of her life.
¹³ She selects wool and flax
　and works with eager hands.
¹⁴ She is like the merchant ships,
　bringing her food from afar.
¹⁵ She gets up while it is still night;
　she provides food for her family
　and portions for her female
　　servants.
¹⁶ She considers a field and buys it;
　out of her earnings she plants a
　　vineyard.
¹⁷ She sets about her work vigorously;
　her arms are strong for her tasks.

ᵃ 31 The meaning of the Hebrew for this phrase
is uncertain.　ᵇ 3 Or *wealth*　ᶜ 10 Verses
10-31 are an acrostic poem, the verses of which
begin with the successive letters of the Hebrew
alphabet.

18 She sees that her trading is profitable,
   and her lamp does not go out at
   night.
19 In her hand she holds the distaff
   and grasps the spindle with her
   fingers.
20 She opens her arms to the poor
   and extends her hands to the needy.
21 When it snows, she has no fear for her
   household;
   for all of them are clothed in
   scarlet.
22 She makes coverings for her bed;
   she is clothed in fine linen and
   purple.
23 Her husband is respected at the city
   gate,
   where he takes his seat among the
   elders of the land.
24 She makes linen garments and sells
   them,
   and supplies the merchants with
   sashes.

25 She is clothed with strength and
   dignity;
   she can laugh at the days to come.
26 She speaks with wisdom,
   and faithful instruction is on her
   tongue.
27 She watches over the affairs of her
   household
   and does not eat the bread of
   idleness.
28 Her children arise and call her
   blessed;
   her husband also, and he praises her:
29 "Many women do noble things,
   but you surpass them all."
30 Charm is deceptive, and beauty is
   fleeting;
   but a woman who fears the LORD is
   to be praised.
31 Honor her for all that her hands have
   done,
   and let her works bring her praise at
   the city gate.

ROCK SOLID principles

Proverbs 31:10–31

Look inside.

Eric and Mackenzie were perfectly paired—like the Ken and Barbie of their rural town. Eric could bench press his weight, and Mackenzie was an obvious pick for captain of the cheerleading squad. But for all the pair had going for them on the outside, there was nothing but air on the inside. When their classmates got to vote for homecoming court, they chose the couple everyone actually liked—a couple everyone would describe with words like "smart" and "nice." Eric and Mackenzie thought they would be taking their place as prince and princess at the 50 yard line. But for once they were left standing on the sidelines.

The "wife of noble character" (Proverbs 31:10) isn't an empty-headed shell. She not only oversees her family but also excels in business. She not only works hard with her hands but also easily dispenses wisdom. Her greatest attribute is her respect for God (see Proverbs 31:30). When you set your sights on a significant other, make sure you look deeper than skin.

ECCLESIASTES

BOOK OUTLINE

Ecclesiastes studies the meaning of life. The Teacher looks at wisdom, pleasure, work, power, riches, religion and other things. All of these have some value and are useful in the proper time and place, but they have lasting value only if God is at the center of a person's life. Reverence and respect for God and a real devotion in serving God are the most important to make life meaningful. Without God, the Teacher says, "Everything is meaningless" (1:2).

Everything Is Meaningless

1 The words of the Teacher,[a] son of David, king in Jerusalem:

² "Meaningless! Meaningless!"
  says the Teacher.
"Utterly meaningless!
  Everything is meaningless."

³ What do people gain from all their labors
  at which they toil under the sun?
⁴ Generations come and generations go,
  but the earth remains forever.
⁵ The sun rises and the sun sets,
  and hurries back to where it rises.
⁶ The wind blows to the south
  and turns to the north;
round and round it goes,
  ever returning on its course.
⁷ All streams flow into the sea,
  yet the sea is never full.
To the place the streams come from,
  there they return again.
⁸ All things are wearisome,
  more than one can say.
The eye never has enough of seeing,
  nor the ear its fill of hearing.
⁹ What has been will be again,
  what has been done will be done again;
  there is nothing new under the sun.
¹⁰ Is there anything of which one can say,
  "Look! This is something new"?
It was here already, long ago;
  it was here before our time.
¹¹ No one remembers the former generations,
  and even those yet to come
will not be remembered
  by those who follow them.

Wisdom Is Meaningless

¹² I, the Teacher, was king over Israel in Jerusalem. ¹³ I applied my mind to study and to explore by wisdom all that is done under the heavens. What a heavy burden God has laid on mankind! ¹⁴ I have seen all the things that are done under the sun; all of them are meaningless, a chasing after the wind.

¹⁵ What is crooked cannot be straightened;
  what is lacking cannot be counted.

¹⁶ I said to myself, "Look, I have increased in wisdom more than anyone who has ruled over Jerusalem before me; I have experienced much of wisdom and knowledge." ¹⁷ Then I applied myself to the understanding of wisdom, and also of madness and folly, but I learned that this, too, is a chasing after the wind.

¹⁸ For with much wisdom comes much sorrow;
  the more knowledge, the more grief.

Pleasures Are Meaningless

2 I said to myself, "Come now, I will test you with pleasure to find out what is good." But that also proved to be meaningless. ² "Laughter," I said, "is madness. And what does pleasure accomplish?" ³ I tried cheering myself with wine, and embracing folly—my mind still guiding me with wisdom. I wanted to see what was good for people to do under the heavens during the few days of their lives.

⁴ I undertook great projects: I built houses for myself and planted vineyards. ⁵ I made gardens and parks and planted all kinds of fruit trees in them. ⁶ I made reservoirs to water groves of flourishing trees. ⁷ I bought male and female slaves and had other slaves who were born in my house. I also owned more herds and flocks than anyone in Jerusalem before me. ⁸ I amassed silver and gold for myself, and the treasure of kings and provinces. I acquired male and female singers, and a harem[b] as well—the delights of a man's heart. ⁹ I became greater by far than anyone in Jerusalem before me. In all this my wisdom stayed with me.

¹⁰ I denied myself nothing my eyes desired;
  I refused my heart no pleasure.
My heart took delight in all my labor,
  and this was the reward for all my toil.

---

a 1 Or *the leader of the assembly*; also in verses 2 and 12   *b 8* The meaning of the Hebrew for this phrase is uncertain.

¹¹Yet when I surveyed all that my hands
had done
and what I had toiled to achieve,
everything was meaningless, a chasing
after the wind;
nothing was gained under the sun.

Wisdom and Folly Are Meaningless

¹²Then I turned my thoughts to
consider wisdom,
and also madness and folly.
What more can the king's successor do
than what has already been done?
¹³I saw that wisdom is better than folly,
just as light is better than darkness.
¹⁴The wise have eyes in their heads,
while the fool walks in the darkness;
but I came to realize
that the same fate overtakes them
both.

¹⁵Then I said to myself,

"The fate of the fool will overtake me
also.
What then do I gain by being wise?"
I said to myself,
"This too is meaningless."
¹⁶For the wise, like the fool, will not be
long remembered;
the days have already come when
both have been forgotten.
Like the fool, the wise too must die!

Toil Is Meaningless

¹⁷So I hated life, because the work that
is done under the sun was grievous to me.
All of it is meaningless, a chasing after
the wind. ¹⁸I hated all the things I had
toiled for under the sun, because I must
leave them to the one who comes after
me. ¹⁹And who knows whether that person will be wise or foolish? Yet they will
have control over all the fruit of my toil
into which I have poured my effort and
skill under the sun. This too is meaningless. ²⁰So my heart began to despair over
all my toilsome labor under the sun. ²¹For a
person may labor with wisdom, knowledge
and skill, and then they must leave all they
own to another who has not toiled for it.
This too is meaningless and a great misfortune. ²²What do people get for all the
toil and anxious striving with which they
labor under the sun? ²³All their days their
work is grief and pain; even at night their
minds do not rest. This too is meaningless.

²⁴A person can do nothing better than
to eat and drink and find satisfaction in
their own toil. This too, I see, is from
the hand of God, ²⁵for without him, who
can eat or find enjoyment? ²⁶To the person who pleases him, God gives wisdom,
knowledge and happiness, but to the sinner he gives the task of gathering and stor-

---

Ecclesiastes 2:24–26

Life without God is empty.

The pages of Ecclesiastes read like the journal of a desperate man. Solomon dove headfirst into a search for the meaning of life. He studied so hard he accumulated more wisdom than anyone ever had, but he discovered that knowledge only gave him grief (see Ecclesiastes 1:18). He grew rich and indulged in every kind of pleasure, but no matter how much wealth his hard work gained for him, he would leave everything behind when he died (see Ecclesiastes 2:10–11). You can sense Solomon's sweet relief when he decides there is nothing better in life than enjoying what the Lord gives him—things like food, drink and satisfying work. Plus wisdom, knowledge and happiness. And a life centered on pleasing God. Without those gifts from the Lord, life is "meaningless, a chasing after the wind" (Ecclesiastes 2:26).

Think: How do people try to make their lives meaningful apart from God? How well does it work?

ROCK SOLID truths

ing up wealth to hand it over to the one who pleases God. This too is meaningless, a chasing after the wind.

A Time for Everything

3 There is a time for everything, and a season for every activity under the heavens:

2 a time to be born and a time to die,
a time to plant and a time to uproot,
3 a time to kill and a time to heal,
a time to tear down and a time to build,
4 a time to weep and a time to laugh,
a time to mourn and a time to dance,
5 a time to scatter stones and a time to gather them,
a time to embrace and a time to refrain from embracing,
6 a time to search and a time to give up,
a time to keep and a time to throw away,
7 a time to tear and a time to mend,
a time to be silent and a time to speak,
8 a time to love and a time to hate,
a time for war and a time for peace.

9 What do workers gain from their toil? 10 I have seen the burden God has laid on the human race. 11 He has made everything beautiful in its time. He has also set eternity in the human heart; yet[a] no one can fathom what God has done from beginning to end. 12 I know that there is nothing better for people than to be happy and to do good while they live. 13 That each of them may eat and drink, and find satisfaction in all their toil—this is the gift of God. 14 I know that everything God does will endure forever; nothing can be added to it and nothing taken from it. God does it so that people will fear him.

15 Whatever is has already been,
and what will be has been before;
and God will call the past to account.[b]

16 And I saw something else under the sun:

In the place of judgment—wickedness was there,
in the place of justice—wickedness was there.

17 I said to myself,

"God will bring into judgment
both the righteous and the wicked,
for there will be a time for every activity,
a time to judge every deed."

18 I also said to myself, "As for humans, God tests them so that they may see that they are like the animals. 19 Surely the fate of human beings is like that of the animals; the same fate awaits them both: As one dies, so dies the other. All have the same breath[c]; humans have no advantage over animals. Everything is meaningless. 20 All go to the same place; all come from dust, and to dust all return. 21 Who knows if the human spirit rises upward and if the spirit of the animal goes down into the earth?"

22 So I saw that there is nothing better for a person than to enjoy their work, because that is their lot. For who can bring them to see what will happen after them?

Oppression, Toil, Friendlessness

4 Again I looked and saw all the oppression that was taking place under the sun:

I saw the tears of the oppressed—
and they have no comforter;
power was on the side of their oppressors—
and they have no comforter.
2 And I declared that the dead,
who had already died,
are happier than the living,
who are still alive.
3 But better than both
is the one who has never been born,
who has not seen the evil
that is done under the sun.

---

[a] 11 Or *also placed ignorance in the human heart, so that* [b] 15 Or *God calls back the past*
[c] 19 Or *spirit*

⁴And I saw that all toil and all achievement spring from one person's envy of another. This too is meaningless, a chasing after the wind.

⁵Fools fold their hands
    and ruin themselves.
⁶Better one handful with tranquillity
    than two handfuls with toil
    and chasing after the wind.

⁷Again I saw something meaningless under the sun:

⁸There was a man all alone;
    he had neither son nor brother.
There was no end to his toil,
    yet his eyes were not content with
        his wealth.
"For whom am I toiling," he asked,
    "and why am I depriving myself of
        enjoyment?"
This too is meaningless—
    a miserable business!

⁹Two are better than one,
    because they have a good return for
        their labor:
¹⁰If either of them falls down,
    one can help the other up.
But pity anyone who falls
    and has no one to help them up.
¹¹Also, if two lie down together, they
        will keep warm.
    But how can one keep warm alone?
¹²Though one may be overpowered,
    two can defend themselves.
A cord of three strands is not quickly
        broken.

Advancement Is Meaningless

¹³Better a poor but wise youth than an old but foolish king who no longer knows how to heed a warning. ¹⁴The youth may have come from prison to the kingship, or he may have been born in poverty within his kingdom. ¹⁵I saw that all who lived and walked under the sun followed the youth, the king's successor. ¹⁶There was no end to all the people who were before them. But those who came later were not pleased with the successor. This too is meaningless, a chasing after the wind.

788

ROCK SOLID *promises*

"A cord of three strands is not quickly broken." Ecclesiastes 4:12

Two are better than one. Three are even better. Two people plus God is almost indestructible.

Fulfill Your Vow to God

5 ᵃ Guard your steps when you go to the house of God. Go near to listen rather than to offer the sacrifice of fools, who do not know that they do wrong.

²Do not be quick with your mouth,
    do not be hasty in your heart
    to utter anything before God.
God is in heaven
    and you are on earth,
    so let your words be few.
³A dream comes when there are many
        cares,
    and many words mark the speech of
        a fool.

⁴When you make a vow to God, do not delay to fulfill it. He has no pleasure in fools; fulfill your vow. ⁵It is better not to make a vow than to make one and not fulfill it. ⁶Do not let your mouth lead you into sin. And do not protest to the temple messenger, "My vow was a mistake." Why should God be angry at what you say and destroy the work of your hands? ⁷Much dreaming and many words are meaningless. Therefore fear God.

Riches Are Meaningless

⁸If you see the poor oppressed in a district, and justice and rights denied, do not

ᵃ In Hebrew texts 5:1 is numbered 4:17, and 5:2-20 is numbered 5:1-19.

be surprised at such things; for one official is eyed by a higher one, and over them both are others higher still. ⁹The increase from the land is taken by all; the king himself profits from the fields.

¹⁰Whoever loves money never has
enough;
whoever loves wealth is never
satisfied with their income.
This too is meaningless.

¹¹As goods increase,
so do those who consume them.
And what benefit are they to the owners
except to feast their eyes on them?

¹²The sleep of a laborer is sweet,
whether they eat little or much,
but as for the rich, their abundance
permits them no sleep.

¹³I have seen a grievous evil under the sun:

wealth hoarded to the harm of its
owners,
¹⁴ or wealth lost through some
misfortune,
so that when they have children
there is nothing left for them to
inherit.
¹⁵Everyone comes naked from their
mother's womb,
and as everyone comes, so they
depart.
They take nothing from their toil
that they can carry in their hands.

¹⁶This too is a grievous evil:

As everyone comes, so they depart,
and what do they gain,
since they toil for the wind?
¹⁷All their days they eat in darkness,
with great frustration, affliction
and anger.

¹⁸This is what I have observed to be good: that it is appropriate for a person to eat, to drink and to find satisfaction in their toilsome labor under the sun during the few days of life God has given them— for this is their lot. ¹⁹Moreover, when God gives someone wealth and possessions, and the ability to enjoy them, to accept their lot and be happy in their toil—this is a gift of God. ²⁰They seldom reflect on the days of their life, because God keeps them occupied with gladness of heart.

6 I have seen another evil under the sun, and it weighs heavily on mankind: ²God gives some people wealth, possessions and honor, so that they lack nothing their hearts desire, but God does not grant them the ability to enjoy them, and strangers enjoy them instead. This is meaningless, a grievous evil.

³A man may have a hundred children and live many years; yet no matter how long he lives, if he cannot enjoy his prosperity and does not receive proper burial, I say that a stillborn child is better off than he. ⁴It comes without meaning, it departs in darkness, and in darkness its name is shrouded. ⁵Though it never saw the sun or knew anything, it has more rest than does that man— ⁶even if he lives a thousand

---

UNSHAKEN *God*

Ecclesiastes 5:10–12

God is satisfying.

Solomon would have fit well in our world. The richest guy of his day (1 Kings 3:13), this king of Israel wrote about nonstop pressure to get more. And you know how it goes. You buy something ... anything ... and before long you realize there is a must-have list of accessories, add-ons, and upgrades. That pressure to get more often comes from your surroundings, but much of it starts inside of you. Once you fall in love with money and material stuff, you won't ever be satisfied with what you have. The problem isn't owning or enjoying things, but is instead loving them more than people and God, the most important things ever.

So ... How can you tell the difference between enjoying things ... and loving them too much?

years twice over but fails to enjoy his prosperity. Do not all go to the same place?

⁷Everyone's toil is for their mouth,
  yet their appetite is never
    satisfied.
⁸What advantage have the wise over
    fools?
  What do the poor gain
    by knowing how to conduct
      themselves before others?
⁹Better what the eye sees
    than the roving of the appetite.
  This too is meaningless,
    a chasing after the wind.

¹⁰Whatever exists has already been
    named,
  and what humanity is has been
    known;
  no one can contend
    with someone who is stronger.
¹¹The more the words,
    the less the meaning,
  and how does that profit anyone?

¹²For who knows what is good for a person in life, during the few and meaningless days they pass through like a shadow?
Who can tell them what will happen under the sun after they are gone?

Wisdom

7 A good name is better than fine
    perfume,
  and the day of death better than
    the day of birth.
²It is better to go to a house of
    mourning
  than to go to a house of feasting,
  for death is the destiny of everyone;
    the living should take this to
      heart.
³Frustration is better than laughter,
    because a sad face is good for the
      heart.
⁴The heart of the wise is in the house
    of mourning,
  but the heart of fools is in the house
    of pleasure.
⁵It is better to heed the rebuke of a wise
    person
  than to listen to the song of fools.

⁶Like the crackling of thorns under the
    pot,
  so is the laughter of fools.
  This too is meaningless.

⁷Extortion turns a wise person into a
    fool,
  and a bribe corrupts the heart.

⁸The end of a matter is better than its
    beginning,
  and patience is better than pride.
⁹Do not be quickly provoked in your
    spirit,
  for anger resides in the lap of fools.

¹⁰Do not say, "Why were the old days
    better than these?"
  For it is not wise to ask such
    questions.

¹¹Wisdom, like an inheritance, is a good
    thing
  and benefits those who see the sun.
¹²Wisdom is a shelter
  as money is a shelter,
  but the advantage of knowledge is
    this:
  Wisdom preserves those who have it.

¹³Consider what God has done:

  Who can straighten
    what he has made crooked?
¹⁴When times are good, be happy;
  but when times are bad, consider
    this:
  God has made the one
    as well as the other.
  Therefore, no one can discover
    anything about their future.

¹⁵In this meaningless life of mine I have
seen both of these:

  the righteous perishing in their
    righteousness,
  and the wicked living long in their
    wickedness.
¹⁶Do not be overrighteous,
  neither be overwise—
  why destroy yourself?
¹⁷Do not be overwicked,
  and do not be a fool—
  why die before your time?

¹⁸It is good to grasp the one
and not let go of the other.
Whoever fears God will avoid all
extremes.^a

¹⁹Wisdom makes one wise person more
powerful
than ten rulers in a city.

²⁰Indeed, there is no one on earth who
is righteous,
no one who does what is right and
never sins.

²¹Do not pay attention to every word
people say,
or you may hear your servant
cursing you—
²²for you know in your heart
that many times you yourself have
cursed others.

²³All this I tested by wisdom and I said,

"I am determined to be wise"—
but this was beyond me.
²⁴Whatever exists is far off and most
profound—
who can discover it?
²⁵So I turned my mind to understand,
to investigate and to search out
wisdom and the scheme of
things
and to understand the stupidity of
wickedness
and the madness of folly.

²⁶I find more bitter than death
the woman who is a snare,
whose heart is a trap
and whose hands are chains.
The man who pleases God will escape
her,
but the sinner she will ensnare.

²⁷"Look," says the Teacher,^b "this is
what I have discovered:

"Adding one thing to another to
discover the scheme of
things—
²⁸ while I was still searching
but not finding—
I found one upright man among a
thousand,

but not one upright woman among
them all.
²⁹This only have I found:
God created mankind upright,
but they have gone in search of
many schemes."

8 Who is like the wise?
Who knows the explanation of
things?
A person's wisdom brightens their face
and changes its hard appearance.

Obey the King

²Obey the king's command, I say, be-
cause you took an oath before God. ³Do
not be in a hurry to leave the king's presence. Do not stand up for a bad cause, for
he will do whatever he pleases. ⁴Since a
king's word is supreme, who can say to
him, "What are you doing?"

⁵Whoever obeys his command will
come to no harm,
and the wise heart will know the
proper time and procedure.
⁶For there is a proper time and
procedure for every matter,
though a person may be weighed
down by misery.

⁷Since no one knows the future,
who can tell someone else what is to
come?
⁸As no one has power over the wind to
contain it,
so^c no one has power over the time
of their death.
As no one is discharged in time of war,
so wickedness will not release those
who practice it.

⁹All this I saw, as I applied my mind to
everything done under the sun. There is a
time when a man lords it over others to his
own^d hurt. ¹⁰Then too, I saw the wicked
buried—those who used to come and go
from the holy place and receive praise^e in

---

^a 18 Or *will follow them both*   ^b 27 Or *the leader
of the assembly*   ^c 8 Or *over the human spirit to
retain it, / and so*   ^d 9 Or *to their*   ^e 10 Some
Hebrew manuscripts and Septuagint (Aquila);
most Hebrew manuscripts *and are forgotten*

the city where they did this. This too is meaningless.

[11] When the sentence for a crime is not quickly carried out, people's hearts are filled with schemes to do wrong. [12] Although a wicked person who commits a hundred crimes may live a long time, I know that it will go better with those who fear God, who are reverent before him. [13] Yet because the wicked do not fear God, it will not go well with them, and their days will not lengthen like a shadow.

[14] There is something else meaningless that occurs on earth: the righteous who get what the wicked deserve, and the wicked who get what the righteous deserve. This too, I say, is meaningless. [15] So I commend the enjoyment of life, because there is nothing better for a person under the sun than to eat and drink and be glad. Then joy will accompany them in their toil all the days of the life God has given them under the sun.

[16] When I applied my mind to know wisdom and to observe the labor that is done on earth—people getting no sleep day or night— [17] then I saw all that God has done. No one can comprehend what goes on under the sun. Despite all their efforts to search it out, no one can discover its meaning. Even if the wise claim they know, they cannot really comprehend it.

A Common Destiny for All

9 So I reflected on all this and concluded that the righteous and the wise and what they do are in God's hands, but no one knows whether love or hate awaits them. [2] All share a common destiny—the righteous and the wicked, the good and the bad,[a] the clean and the unclean, those who offer sacrifices and those who do not.

As it is with the good,
    so with the sinful;
as it is with those who take oaths,
    so with those who are afraid to take
        them.

[3] This is the evil in everything that happens under the sun: The same destiny overtakes all. The hearts of people, moreover, are full of evil and there is madness in their hearts while they live, and afterward they join the dead. [4] Anyone who is among the living has hope[b]—even a live dog is better off than a dead lion!

[5] For the living know that they will die,
    but the dead know nothing;
they have no further reward,
    and even their name is forgotten.
[6] Their love, their hate
    and their jealousy have long since
        vanished;
never again will they have a part
    in anything that happens under the
        sun.

[7] Go, eat your food with gladness, and drink your wine with a joyful heart, for God has already approved what you do. [8] Always be clothed in white, and always anoint your head with oil. [9] Enjoy life with your wife, whom you love, all the days of this meaningless life that God has given you under the sun—all your meaningless days. For this is your lot in life and in your toilsome labor under the sun. [10] Whatever your hand finds to do, do it with all your might, for in the realm of the dead, where you are going, there is neither working nor planning nor knowledge nor wisdom.

[11] I have seen something else under the sun:

The race is not to the swift
    or the battle to the strong,
nor does food come to the wise
    or wealth to the brilliant
    or favor to the learned;
but time and chance happen to them
    all.

[12] Moreover, no one knows when their hour will come:

As fish are caught in a cruel net,
    or birds are taken in a snare,
so people are trapped by evil times
    that fall unexpectedly upon them.

a 2 Septuagint (Aquila), Vulgate and Syriac; Hebrew does not have *and the bad.*   *b* 4 Or *What then is to be chosen? With all who live, there is hope*

ROCK SOLID *principles*

Ecclesiastes 9:7–12

Enjoy the simple things of life.

Bryan sometimes wanted to have all the things his friends had. He didn't have to pull out a measuring tape to know his house was smaller. The entertainment system downstairs didn't gather a crowd. His parents drove cars that sported some rust and sometimes made odd and unexpected noises in public. But Bryan could count on plenty of good food on the table when he invited friends to stay for supper. He had no doubt his parents would always be in love. And in his house both parents and kids knew how to work for the few extras they enjoyed. Bryan could have wished for more. But not really.

King Solomon had limitless riches, unmatched wisdom, and countless servants. But he discovered that real happiness comes from simple things like good food, true love, and hard work. Don't miss his point: You don't have to kill yourself to get the best of everything. Be happy with the best things of life.

Wisdom Better Than Folly

¹³ I also saw under the sun this example of wisdom that greatly impressed me: ¹⁴ There was once a small city with only a few people in it. And a powerful king came against it, surrounded it and built huge siege works against it. ¹⁵ Now there lived in that city a man poor but wise, and he saved the city by his wisdom. But nobody remembered that poor man. ¹⁶ So I said, "Wisdom is better than strength." But the poor man's wisdom is despised, and his words are no longer heeded.

¹⁷ The quiet words of the wise are more
to be heeded
than the shouts of a ruler of fools.
¹⁸ Wisdom is better than weapons of war,
but one sinner destroys much good.

10

As dead flies give perfume a
bad smell,
so a little folly outweighs
wisdom and honor.

² The heart of the wise inclines to the
right,
but the heart of the fool to the left.
³ Even as fools walk along the road,
they lack sense
and show everyone how stupid they
are.
⁴ If a ruler's anger rises against you,
do not leave your post;
calmness can lay great offenses to
rest.

⁵ There is an evil I have seen under the
sun,
the sort of error that arises from a
ruler:
⁶ Fools are put in many high positions,
while the rich occupy the low ones.
⁷ I have seen slaves on horseback,
while princes go on foot like slaves.

⁸ Whoever digs a pit may fall into it;
whoever breaks through a wall may
be bitten by a snake.

⁹Whoever quarries stones may be
   injured by them;
 whoever splits logs may be
   endangered by them.

¹⁰If the ax is dull
   and its edge unsharpened,
 more strength is needed,
   but skill will bring success.

¹¹If a snake bites before it is charmed,
   the charmer receives no fee.

¹²Words from the mouth of the wise are
   gracious,
 but fools are consumed by their own
   lips.

¹³At the beginning their words are folly;
   at the end they are wicked
   madness—

¹⁴   and fools multiply words.

 No one knows what is coming—
   who can tell someone else what will
   happen after them?

¹⁵The toil of fools wearies them;
   they do not know the way to town.

¹⁶Woe to the land whose king was a
   servant*a*
 and whose princes feast in the
   morning.

¹⁷Blessed is the land whose king is of
   noble birth
 and whose princes eat at a proper
   time—
 for strength and not for
   drunkenness.

¹⁸Through laziness, the rafters sag;
   because of idle hands, the house
   leaks.

¹⁹A feast is made for laughter,
   wine makes life merry,
 and money is the answer for
   everything.

²⁰Do not revile the king even in your
   thoughts,
 or curse the rich in your bedroom,
 because a bird in the sky may carry
   your words,
 and a bird on the wing may report
   what you say.

Invest in Many Ventures

11 Ship your grain across the sea;
   after many days you may receive
   a return.

²Invest in seven ventures, yes, in eight;
   you do not know what disaster may
   come upon the land.

³If clouds are full of water,
   they pour rain on the earth.
 Whether a tree falls to the south or to
   the north,
 in the place where it falls, there it
   will lie.

⁴Whoever watches the wind will not
   plant;
 whoever looks at the clouds will not
   reap.

⁵As you do not know the path of the
   wind,
 or how the body is formed*b* in a
   mother's womb,
 so you cannot understand the work of
   God,
 the Maker of all things.

⁶Sow your seed in the morning,
   and at evening let your hands not be
   idle,
 for you do not know which will
   succeed,
 whether this or that,
 or whether both will do equally
   well.

Remember Your Creator While Young

⁷Light is sweet,
   and it pleases the eyes to see the
   sun.
⁸However many years anyone may live,
   let them enjoy them all.
 But let them remember the days of
   darkness,
 for there will be many.
 Everything to come is meaningless.

⁹You who are young, be happy while
   you are young,
 and let your heart give you joy in
   the days of your youth.

---

a 16 Or *king is a child*   *b* 5 Or *know how life*
(or *the spirit*) / *enters the body being formed*

Follow the ways of your heart
   and whatever your eyes see,
but know that for all these things
   God will bring you into judgment.
¹⁰ So then, banish anxiety from your
      heart
   and cast off the troubles of your
      body,
   for youth and vigor are meaningless.

12 Remember your Creator
   in the days of your youth,
   before the days of trouble
   come
and the years approach when you
   will say,
   "I find no pleasure in them"—
² before the sun and the light
   and the moon and the stars grow
      dark,
   and the clouds return after the rain;
³ when the keepers of the house
      tremble,
   and the strong men stoop,
when the grinders cease because they
   are few,
   and those looking through the
      windows grow dim;
⁴ when the doors to the street are closed
   and the sound of grinding fades;
when people rise up at the sound of
   birds,
   but all their songs grow faint;
⁵ when people are afraid of heights
   and of dangers in the streets;
when the almond tree blossoms
   and the grasshopper drags itself
      along
   and desire no longer is stirred.
Then people go to their eternal home
   and mourners go about the streets.

⁶ Remember him—before the silver
      cord is severed,
   and the golden bowl is broken;
   before the pitcher is shattered at the
      spring,
   and the wheel broken at the well,
⁷ and the dust returns to the ground it
      came from,
   and the spirit returns to God who
      gave it.

⁸ "Meaningless! Meaningless!" says the
      Teacher.^a
   "Everything is meaningless!"

The Conclusion of the Matter

⁹ Not only was the Teacher wise, but he
also imparted knowledge to the people.
He pondered and searched out and set
in order many proverbs. ¹⁰ The Teacher
searched to find just the right words, and
what he wrote was upright and true.

¹¹ The words of the wise are like goads,
their collected sayings like firmly embed-
ded nails—given by one shepherd.^b ¹² Be
warned, my son, of anything in addition
to them.

Of making many books there is no end,
and much study wearies the body.

¹³ Now all has been heard;
   here is the conclusion of the matter:
Fear God and keep his
      commandments,
   for this is the duty of all mankind.
¹⁴ For God will bring every deed into
      judgment,
   including every hidden thing,
   whether it is good or evil.

---

^a 8 Or *the leader of the assembly*; also in verses 9
and 10   ^b 11 Or *Shepherd*

SONG OF SONGS

BOOK OUTLINE

The bride and the bridegroom
(1:1—2:7)

The praise of her beloved
(2:8—3:5)

In praise of the bride
(3:6—5:1)

A troubled love
(5:2—7:9)

The unbroken communion
(7:10—8:14)

Although some scholars view Song of Songs as being a picture of Christ's love for his people, the more accepted view of Song of Songs is that it is a collection of love poems between a man and a woman. It is a beautiful picture of ideal human love and marriage.

1

Solomon's Song of Songs.

She[a]

2 Let him kiss me with the kisses of his
mouth—
for your love is more delightful than
wine.
3 Pleasing is the fragrance of your
perfumes;
your name is like perfume poured
out.
No wonder the young women love
you!
4 Take me away with you—let us hurry!
Let the king bring me into his
chambers.

Friends

We rejoice and delight in you[b];
we will praise your love more than
wine.

She

How right they are to adore you!

5 Dark am I, yet lovely,
daughters of Jerusalem,
dark like the tents of Kedar,
like the tent curtains of Solomon.[c]
6 Do not stare at me because I am dark,
because I am darkened by the sun.
My mother's sons were angry with me
and made me take care of the
vineyards;
my own vineyard I had to neglect.
7 Tell me, you whom I love,
where you graze your flock
and where you rest your sheep at
midday.
Why should I be like a veiled woman
beside the flocks of your friends?

Friends

8 If you do not know, most beautiful of
women,
follow the tracks of the sheep
and graze your young goats
by the tents of the shepherds.

He

9 I liken you, my darling, to a mare
among Pharaoh's chariot horses.

10 Your cheeks are beautiful with
earrings,
your neck with strings of jewels.
11 We will make you earrings of gold,
studded with silver.

She

12 While the king was at his table,
my perfume spread its fragrance.
13 My beloved is to me a sachet of myrrh
resting between my breasts.
14 My beloved is to me a cluster of henna
blossoms
from the vineyards of En Gedi.

He

15 How beautiful you are, my darling!
Oh, how beautiful!
Your eyes are doves.

She

16 How handsome you are, my beloved!
Oh, how charming!
And our bed is verdant.

He

17 The beams of our house are cedars;
our rafters are firs.

She[d]

2

I am a rose[e] of Sharon,
a lily of the valleys.

He

2 Like a lily among thorns
is my darling among the young
women.

She

3 Like an apple[f] tree among the trees of
the forest
is my beloved among the young men.

---

[a] The main male and female speakers (identified
primarily on the basis of the gender of the
relevant Hebrew forms) are indicated by the
captions *He* and *She* respectively. The words of
others are marked *Friends*. In some instances the
divisions and their captions are debatable.
[b] 4 The Hebrew is masculine singular.
[c] 5 Or *Salma*   [d] Or *He*   [e] 1 Probably a
member of the crocus family   [f] 3 Or possibly
apricot; here and elsewhere in Song of Songs

I delight to sit in his shade,
  and his fruit is sweet to my taste.
⁴Let him lead me to the banquet hall,
  and let his banner over me be love.
⁵Strengthen me with raisins,
  refresh me with apples,
  for I am faint with love.
⁶His left arm is under my head,
  and his right arm embraces me.
⁷Daughters of Jerusalem, I charge you
  by the gazelles and by the does of
    the field:
Do not arouse or awaken love
  until it so desires.

⁸Listen! My beloved!
  Look! Here he comes,
leaping across the mountains,
  bounding over the hills.
⁹My beloved is like a gazelle or a young
    stag.
  Look! There he stands behind our
    wall,
gazing through the windows,
  peering through the lattice.
¹⁰My beloved spoke and said to me,
  "Arise, my darling,
  my beautiful one, come with me.
¹¹See! The winter is past;
  the rains are over and gone.
¹²Flowers appear on the earth;
  the season of singing has come,
  the cooing of doves
  is heard in our land.
¹³The fig tree forms its early fruit;
  the blossoming vines spread their
    fragrance.
  Arise, come, my darling;
  my beautiful one, come with me."

He

¹⁴My dove in the clefts of the rock,
  in the hiding places on the
    mountainside,
show me your face,
  let me hear your voice;
for your voice is sweet,
  and your face is lovely.
¹⁵Catch for us the foxes,
  the little foxes
that ruin the vineyards,
  our vineyards that are in bloom.

She

¹⁶My beloved is mine and I am his;
  he browses among the lilies.
¹⁷Until the day breaks
  and the shadows flee,
turn, my beloved,
  and be like a gazelle
or like a young stag
  on the rugged hills.ᵃ

3 All night long on my bed
  I looked for the one my heart
    loves;
  I looked for him but did not find
    him.
²I will get up now and go about the city,
  through its streets and squares;
  I will search for the one my heart
    loves.
  So I looked for him but did not find
    him.
³The watchmen found me
  as they made their rounds in the
    city.
  "Have you seen the one my heart
    loves?"
⁴Scarcely had I passed them
  when I found the one my heart
    loves.
  I held him and would not let him go
    till I had brought him to my
      mother's house,
  to the room of the one who
    conceived me.
⁵Daughters of Jerusalem, I charge you
  by the gazelles and by the does of
    the field:
Do not arouse or awaken love
  until it so desires.

⁶Who is this coming up from the
    wilderness
  like a column of smoke,
perfumed with myrrh and incense
  made from all the spices of the
    merchant?
⁷Look! It is Solomon's carriage,
  escorted by sixty warriors,
  the noblest of Israel,
⁸all of them wearing the sword,
  all experienced in battle,

ᵃ 17 Or *the hills of Bether*

ROCK·SOLID *principles*

Wait.

Savannah rolled her eyes and shot a look that said, "Mom, I don't want to talk about it." Yet Mrs. Harris wasn't about to shut up. That day at work a close friend had shared that her 14-year-old daughter had a sexually transmitted disease that might mean she would never have children. "It's not just about having or not having kids, Savannah," her mom said. "Waiting for sex until marriage isn't a rule meant to ruin your life. It's a plan you choose to help you enjoy true love at the right time. When couples go too far, girls always blame guys, and guys always blame girls. We each need to take responsibility for our own actions."

Solomon's wife-to-be was "a lily among thorns" (Song of Songs 2:2). Her man was "an apple tree among the trees of the forest" (Song of Songs 2:3). But this pair waits to "arouse or awaken love" until the proper time (Song of Songs 2:7). The woman's friends even promise to guard her purity until "the day she is spoken for" (Song of Songs 8:8 – 9). This couple is wild with love, yet they choose to wait.

---

each with his sword at his side,
    prepared for the terrors of the night.
[9] King Solomon made for himself the
      carriage;
    he made it of wood from Lebanon.
[10] Its posts he made of silver,
    its base of gold.
Its seat was upholstered with purple,
    its interior inlaid with love.
Daughters of Jerusalem, [11] come out,
    and look, you daughters of Zion.
Look[a] on King Solomon wearing a
      crown,
    the crown with which his mother
      crowned him
on the day of his wedding,
    the day his heart rejoiced.

He

4

How beautiful you are, my
    darling!
    Oh, how beautiful!
Your eyes behind your veil are
    doves.

Your hair is like a flock of goats
    descending from the hills of
      Gilead.
[2] Your teeth are like a flock of sheep
      just shorn,
    coming up from the washing.
Each has its twin;
    not one of them is alone.
[3] Your lips are like a scarlet ribbon;
    your mouth is lovely.
Your temples behind your veil
    are like the halves of a
      pomegranate.
[4] Your neck is like the tower of David,
    built with courses of stone[b];
on it hang a thousand shields,
    all of them shields of warriors.
[5] Your breasts are like two fawns,
    like twin fawns of a gazelle
    that browse among the lilies.

---

[a] 10,11 Or *interior lovingly inlaid / by the daughters of Jerusalem. / [11]Come out, you daughters of Zion, / and look*   [b] 4 The meaning of the Hebrew for this phrase is uncertain.

⁶Until the day breaks
  and the shadows flee,
I will go to the mountain of myrrh
  and to the hill of incense.
⁷You are altogether beautiful, my darling;
  there is no flaw in you.

⁸Come with me from Lebanon, my
    bride,
  come with me from Lebanon.
Descend from the crest of Amana,
  from the top of Senir, the summit
    of Hermon,
from the lions' dens
  and the mountain haunts of leopards.
⁹You have stolen my heart, my sister,
    my bride;
  you have stolen my heart
with one glance of your eyes,
  with one jewel of your necklace.
¹⁰How delightful is your love, my sister,
    my bride!
  How much more pleasing is your
    love than wine,
and the fragrance of your perfume
  more than any spice!
¹¹Your lips drop sweetness as the
    honeycomb, my bride;
  milk and honey are under your
    tongue.
The fragrance of your garments
  is like the fragrance of Lebanon.
¹²You are a garden locked up, my sister,
    my bride;
  you are a spring enclosed, a sealed
    fountain.
¹³Your plants are an orchard of
    pomegranates
  with choice fruits,
  with henna and nard,
¹⁴ nard and saffron,
  calamus and cinnamon,
  with every kind of incense tree,
  with myrrh and aloes
  and all the finest spices.
¹⁵You are*ᵃ* a garden fountain,
  a well of flowing water
  streaming down from Lebanon.

She

¹⁶Awake, north wind,
  and come, south wind!

Blow on my garden,
  that its fragrance may spread
    everywhere.
Let my beloved come into his garden
  and taste its choice fruits.

He

5 I have come into my garden, my
  sister, my bride;
  I have gathered my myrrh with
  my spice.
I have eaten my honeycomb and my
  honey;
  I have drunk my wine and my milk.

Friends

Eat, friends, and drink;
  drink your fill of love.

She

²I slept but my heart was awake.
  Listen! My beloved is knocking:
"Open to me, my sister, my darling,
  my dove, my flawless one.
My head is drenched with dew,
  my hair with the dampness of the
    night."
³I have taken off my robe—
  must I put it on again?
I have washed my feet—
  must I soil them again?
⁴My beloved thrust his hand through
    the latch-opening;
  my heart began to pound for him.
⁵I arose to open for my beloved,
  and my hands dripped with myrrh,
my fingers with flowing myrrh,
  on the handles of the bolt.
⁶I opened for my beloved,
  but my beloved had left; he was
    gone.
  My heart sank at his departure.*ᵇ*
I looked for him but did not find him.
  I called him but he did not answer.
⁷The watchmen found me
  as they made their rounds in the city.
They beat me, they bruised me;
  they took away my cloak,
  those watchmen of the walls!

ᵃ 15 Or *I am* (spoken by *She*)   *ᵇ 6* Or *heart
had gone out to him when he spoke*

⁸Daughters of Jerusalem, I charge
you—
if you find my beloved,
what will you tell him?
Tell him I am faint with love.

Friends

⁹How is your beloved better than
others,
most beautiful of women?
How is your beloved better than
others,
that you so charge us?

She

¹⁰My beloved is radiant and ruddy,
outstanding among ten thousand.
¹¹His head is purest gold;
his hair is wavy
and black as a raven.
¹²His eyes are like doves
by the water streams,
washed in milk,
mounted like jewels.
¹³His cheeks are like beds of spice
yielding perfume.
His lips are like lilies
dripping with myrrh.
¹⁴His arms are rods of gold
set with topaz.
His body is like polished ivory
decorated with lapis lazuli.
¹⁵His legs are pillars of marble
set on bases of pure gold.
His appearance is like Lebanon,
choice as its cedars.
¹⁶His mouth is sweetness itself;
he is altogether lovely.
This is my beloved, this is my friend,
daughters of Jerusalem.

Friends

6 Where has your beloved gone,
most beautiful of women?
Which way did your beloved
turn,
that we may look for him with you?

She

²My beloved has gone down to his
garden,
to the beds of spices,

Song of Songs 5

Wisdom books do more than make you wise.

There are other divisions in the Bible besides the Old and New Testament. The Old Testament's first five books, the Pentateuch, spell out the laws God gave to Israel. The books of "History" record Israel's story, and the "Prophets" relate the words God uttered through his spokespeople. That leaves five books in the middle of the Bible—Job, Psalms, Proverbs, Ecclesiastes, and the Song of Songs. While it's tough to find a label that fits all five writings, scholars have settled on calling them "Wisdom" books. These books can contain lengthy teachings or short wise sayings (like Proverbs and Ecclesiastes), songs and prayers (like the Psalms) or narratives to make you think (like Job and Song of Songs). Wherever you turn in the Wisdom books, you will find clear, understandable language. So dive in.

Think: How often do you read the Wisdom books of the Bible? What do they teach you?

ROCK SOLID truths

to browse in the gardens
and to gather lilies.
³I am my beloved's and my beloved is
mine;
he browses among the lilies.

He

⁴You are as beautiful as Tirzah, my
darling,
as lovely as Jerusalem,
as majestic as troops with banners.

⁵Turn your eyes from me;
    they overwhelm me.
Your hair is like a flock of goats
    descending from Gilead.
⁶Your teeth are like a flock of sheep
    coming up from the washing.
Each has its twin,
    not one of them is missing.
⁷Your temples behind your veil
    are like the halves of a pomegranate.
⁸Sixty queens there may be,
    and eighty concubines,
    and virgins beyond number;
⁹but my dove, my perfect one, is unique,
    the only daughter of her mother,
    the favorite of the one who bore her.
The young women saw her and called
        her blessed;
    the queens and concubines praised
        her.

Friends

¹⁰Who is this that appears like the dawn,
    fair as the moon, bright as the sun,
    majestic as the stars in procession?

He

¹¹I went down to the grove of nut trees
    to look at the new growth in the
        valley,
to see if the vines had budded
    or the pomegranates were in bloom.
¹²Before I realized it,
    my desire set me among the royal
        chariots of my people.*a*

Friends

¹³Come back, come back,
        O Shulammite;
    come back, come back, that we may
        gaze on you!

He

Why would you gaze on the
        Shulammite
    as on the dance of Mahanaim?*b*

7 *c* How beautiful your sandaled
        feet,
        O prince's daughter!
Your graceful legs are like jewels,
    the work of an artist's hands.

²Your navel is a rounded goblet
    that never lacks blended wine.
Your waist is a mound of wheat
    encircled by lilies.
³Your breasts are like two fawns,
    like twin fawns of a gazelle.
⁴Your neck is like an ivory tower.
Your eyes are the pools of Heshbon
    by the gate of Bath Rabbim.
Your nose is like the tower of Lebanon
    looking toward Damascus.
⁵Your head crowns you like Mount
        Carmel.
Your hair is like royal tapestry;
    the king is held captive by its tresses.
⁶How beautiful you are and how
        pleasing,
    my love, with your delights!
⁷Your stature is like that of the palm,
    and your breasts like clusters of
        fruit.
⁸I said, "I will climb the palm tree;
    I will take hold of its fruit."
May your breasts be like clusters of
        grapes on the vine,
    the fragrance of your breath like
        apples,
⁹   and your mouth like the best wine.

She

May the wine go straight to my
        beloved,
    flowing gently over lips and teeth.*d*
¹⁰I belong to my beloved,
    and his desire is for me.
¹¹Come, my beloved, let us go to the
        countryside,
    let us spend the night in the
        villages.*e*
¹²Let us go early to the vineyards
    to see if the vines have budded,
if their blossoms have opened,
    and if the pomegranates are in
        bloom—
    there I will give you my love.

a 12 Or *among the chariots of Amminadab*; or
among the chariots of the people of the prince
b 13 In Hebrew texts this verse (6:13) is
numbered 7:1.   *c* In Hebrew texts 7:1-13 is
numbered 7:2-14.   *d 9* Septuagint, Aquila,
Vulgate and Syriac; Hebrew *lips of sleepers*
e 11 Or *the henna bushes*

13 The mandrakes send out their
      fragrance,
   and at our door is every delicacy,
both new and old,
   that I have stored up for you, my
      beloved.

8 If only you were to me like a
      brother,
   who was nursed at my mother's
      breasts!
Then, if I found you outside,
   I would kiss you,
   and no one would despise me.
2 I would lead you
   and bring you to my mother's
      house—
   she who has taught me.
I would give you spiced wine to
      drink,
   the nectar of my pomegranates.
3 His left arm is under my head
   and his right arm embraces me.
4 Daughters of Jerusalem, I charge you:
   Do not arouse or awaken love
   until it so desires.

Friends

5 Who is this coming up from the
      wilderness
   leaning on her beloved?

She

   Under the apple tree I roused you;
      there your mother conceived you,
      there she who was in labor gave you
         birth.
6 Place me like a seal over your heart,
   like a seal on your arm;
for love is as strong as death,
   its jealousy*a* unyielding as the
      grave.
It burns like blazing fire,
   like a mighty flame.*b*
7 Many waters cannot quench love;
   rivers cannot sweep it away.

If one were to give
   all the wealth of one's house for love,
   it*c* would be utterly scorned.

Friends

8 We have a little sister,
   and her breasts are not yet grown.
What shall we do for our sister
   on the day she is spoken for?
9 If she is a wall,
   we will build towers of silver on her.
If she is a door,
   we will enclose her with panels of
      cedar.

She

10 I am a wall,
   and my breasts are like towers.
Thus I have become in his eyes
   like one bringing contentment.
11 Solomon had a vineyard in Baal
      Hamon;
   he let out his vineyard to tenants.
Each was to bring for its fruit
   a thousand shekels*d* of silver.
12 But my own vineyard is mine to give;
   the thousand shekels are for you,
      Solomon,
   and two hundred*e* are for those who
      tend its fruit.

He

13 You who dwell in the gardens
   with friends in attendance,
   let me hear your voice!

She

14 Come away, my beloved,
   and be like a gazelle
   or like a young stag
   on the spice-laden mountains.

a 6 Or *ardor*   *b* 6 Or *fire, / like the very flame
of the* LORD   *c* 7 Or *he*   *d* 11 That is, about
25 pounds or about 12 kilograms; also in
verse 12   *e* 12 That is, about 5 pounds or
about 2.3 kilograms

ISAIAH

BOOK OUTLINE

Isaiah prophesied in Judah during the reigns of Kings Uzziah, Jotham, Ahaz and Hezekiah. According to tradition Isaiah was martyred under Manasseh, the wicked son of Hezekiah, about 680 BC.

Isaiah repeatedly warned the people that Jerusalem and Judah would be judged because of their wickedness. In chapter 39 he predicted the Babylonian exile. But he also held to the hope that the kingdom would be restored again.

Beginning in chapter 40 Isaiah offered comfort with these promises from God: (1) Babylonian exiles would be allowed to return to Jerusalem; (2) a righteous, suffering servant would bring salvation; (3) God would set up a new, righteous kingdom.

The vision concerning Judah and Jerusalem that Isaiah son of Amoz saw during the reigns of Uzziah, Jotham, Ahaz and Hezekiah, kings of Judah.

A Rebellious Nation

2 Hear me, you heavens! Listen, earth!
   For the Lord has spoken:
"I reared children and brought them
       up,
   but they have rebelled against me.
3 The ox knows its master,
       the donkey its owner's manger,
   but Israel does not know,
       my people do not understand."

4 Woe to the sinful nation,
       a people whose guilt is great,
   a brood of evildoers,
       children given to corruption!
   They have forsaken the Lord;
       they have spurned the Holy One of
           Israel
       and turned their backs on him.

5 Why should you be beaten anymore?
       Why do you persist in rebellion?
   Your whole head is injured,
       your whole heart afflicted.
6 From the sole of your foot to the top
       of your head
   there is no soundness—
       only wounds and welts
       and open sores,
   not cleansed or bandaged
       or soothed with olive oil.

7 Your country is desolate,
       your cities burned with fire;
   your fields are being stripped by
           foreigners
       right before you,
   laid waste as when overthrown by
           strangers.
8 Daughter Zion is left
       like a shelter in a vineyard,
   like a hut in a cucumber field,
       like a city under siege.
9 Unless the Lord Almighty
       had left us some survivors,
   we would have become like Sodom,
       we would have been like Gomorrah.

10 Hear the word of the Lord,
       you rulers of Sodom;
   listen to the instruction of our God,
       you people of Gomorrah!
11 "The multitude of your sacrifices—
       what are they to me?" says the
           Lord.
   "I have more than enough of burnt
           offerings,
       of rams and the fat of fattened
           animals;
   I have no pleasure
       in the blood of bulls and lambs and
           goats.
12 When you come to appear before me,
       who has asked this of you,
       this trampling of my courts?
13 Stop bringing meaningless offerings!
       Your incense is detestable to me.
   New Moons, Sabbaths and
           convocations—
       I cannot bear your worthless
           assemblies.
14 Your New Moon feasts and your
           appointed festivals
       I hate with all my being.
   They have become a burden to me;
       I am weary of bearing them.
15 When you spread out your hands in
           prayer,
       I hide my eyes from you;
   even when you offer many prayers,
       I am not listening.

   Your hands are full of blood!

16 Wash and make yourselves clean.
       Take your evil deeds out of my
           sight;
       stop doing wrong.
17 Learn to do right; seek justice.
       Defend the oppressed.*a*
   Take up the cause of the fatherless;
       plead the case of the widow.

18 "Come now, let us settle the matter,"
       says the Lord.
   "Though your sins are like scarlet,
       they shall be as white as snow;
   though they are red as crimson,
       they shall be like wool.

a 17 Or justice. / Correct the oppressor

ROCK SOLID
promises

"Though your sins are like scarlet, they shall be as white as snow."

Isaiah 1:18

Sin colors your heart like a deep stain, but God will scrub you clean.

---

¹⁹ If you are willing and obedient,
  you will eat the good things of the land;
²⁰ but if you resist and rebel,
  you will be devoured by the sword."
    For the mouth of the LORD
      has spoken.

²¹ See how the faithful city
  has become a prostitute!
She once was full of justice;
  righteousness used to dwell in her—
  but now murderers!
²² Your silver has become dross,
  your choice wine is diluted with water.
²³ Your rulers are rebels,
  partners with thieves;
they all love bribes
  and chase after gifts.
They do not defend the cause of the fatherless;
  the widow's case does not come before them.

²⁴ Therefore the Lord, the LORD Almighty,
  the Mighty One of Israel, declares:
"Ah! I will vent my wrath on my foes
  and avenge myself on my enemies.
²⁵ I will turn my hand against you;ᵃ
  I will thoroughly purge away your dross
  and remove all your impurities.

²⁶ I will restore your leaders as in days of old,
  your rulers as at the beginning.
Afterward you will be called
  the City of Righteousness,
  the Faithful City."

²⁷ Zion will be delivered with justice,
  her penitent ones with righteousness.
²⁸ But rebels and sinners will both be broken,
  and those who forsake the LORD
  will perish.

²⁹ "You will be ashamed because of the sacred oaks
  in which you have delighted;
you will be disgraced because of the gardens
  that you have chosen.
³⁰ You will be like an oak with fading leaves,
  like a garden without water.
³¹ The mighty man will become tinder
  and his work a spark;
both will burn together,
  with no one to quench the fire."

The Mountain of the LORD

2 This is what Isaiah son of Amoz saw concerning Judah and Jerusalem:

² In the last days

the mountain of the LORD's temple
  will be established
  as the highest of the mountains;
it will be exalted above the hills,
  and all nations will stream to it.

³ Many peoples will come and say,

"Come, let us go up to the mountain of the LORD,
  to the temple of the God of Jacob.
He will teach us his ways,
  so that we may walk in his paths."
The law will go out from Zion,
  the word of the LORD from Jerusalem.
⁴ He will judge between the nations
  and will settle disputes for many peoples.

ᵃ 25 That is, against Jerusalem

They will beat their swords into
plowshares
and their spears into pruning hooks.
Nation will not take up sword against
nation,
nor will they train for war anymore.

⁵Come, descendants of Jacob,
let us walk in the light of the LORD.

The Day of the LORD

⁶You, LORD, have abandoned your
people,
the descendants of Jacob.
They are full of superstitions from the
East;
they practice divination like the
Philistines
and embrace pagan customs.
⁷Their land is full of silver and gold;
there is no end to their treasures.
Their land is full of horses;
there is no end to their chariots.
⁸Their land is full of idols;
they bow down to the work of their
hands,
to what their fingers have made.
⁹So people will be brought low
and everyone humbled—
do not forgive them.ᵃ

¹⁰Go into the rocks, hide in the ground
from the fearful presence of the
LORD
and the splendor of his majesty!
¹¹The eyes of the arrogant will be
humbled
and human pride brought low;
the LORD alone will be exalted in that
day.

¹²The LORD Almighty has a day in
store
for all the proud and lofty,
for all that is exalted
(and they will be humbled),
¹³for all the cedars of Lebanon, tall and
lofty,
and all the oaks of Bashan,
¹⁴for all the towering mountains
and all the high hills,
¹⁵for every lofty tower
and every fortified wall,

¹⁶for every trading shipᵇ
and every stately vessel.
¹⁷The arrogance of man will be brought
low
and human pride humbled;
the LORD alone will be exalted in that
day,
¹⁸   and the idols will totally disappear.

¹⁹People will flee to caves in the rocks
and to holes in the ground
from the fearful presence of the LORD
and the splendor of his majesty,
when he rises to shake the earth.
²⁰In that day people will throw away
to the moles and bats
their idols of silver and idols of gold,
which they made to worship.
²¹They will flee to caverns in the rocks
and to the overhanging crags
from the fearful presence of the LORD
and the splendor of his majesty,
when he rises to shake the earth.

²²Stop trusting in mere humans,
who have but a breath in their
nostrils.
Why hold them in esteem?

Judgment on Jerusalem and Judah

3 See now, the Lord,
the LORD Almighty,
is about to take from Jerusalem
and Judah
both supply and support:
all supplies of food and all supplies of
water,
²   the hero and the warrior,
the judge and the prophet,
the diviner and the elder,
³the captain of fifty and the man of
rank,
the counselor, skilled craftsman and
clever enchanter.

⁴"I will make mere youths their officials;
children will rule over them."

⁵People will oppress each other—
man against man, neighbor against
neighbor.

ᵃ 9 Or *not raise them up*   ᵇ 16 Hebrew *every
ship of Tarshish*

The young will rise up against the old,
the nobody against the honored.

⁶A man will seize one of his brothers
in his father's house, and say,
"You have a cloak, you be our leader;
take charge of this heap of ruins!"
⁷But in that day he will cry out,
"I have no remedy.
I have no food or clothing in my
house;
do not make me the leader of the
people."

⁸Jerusalem staggers,
Judah is falling;
their words and deeds are against the
Lord,
defying his glorious presence.
⁹The look on their faces testifies
against them;
they parade their sin like Sodom;
they do not hide it.
Woe to them!
They have brought disaster upon
themselves.

¹⁰Tell the righteous it will be well with
them,
for they will enjoy the fruit of their
deeds.
¹¹Woe to the wicked!
Disaster is upon them!
They will be paid back
for what their hands have done.

ROCK SOLID promises

"Tell the righteous it will be well with them, for they will enjoy the fruit of their deeds."

Isaiah 3:10

Doing good can feel worthless, but God will make sure you see good results.

¹²Youths oppress my people,
women rule over them.
My people, your guides lead you astray;
they turn you from the path.

¹³The Lord takes his place in court;
he rises to judge the people.
¹⁴The Lord enters into judgment
against the elders and leaders of his
people:
"It is you who have ruined my vineyard;
the plunder from the poor is in your
houses.
¹⁵What do you mean by crushing my
people
and grinding the faces of the poor?"
declares the Lord,
the Lord Almighty.

¹⁶The Lord says,
"The women of Zion are haughty,
walking along with outstretched necks,
flirting with their eyes,
strutting along with swaying hips,
with ornaments jingling on their
ankles.
¹⁷Therefore the Lord will bring sores
on the heads of the women of
Zion;
the Lord will make their scalps
bald."

¹⁸In that day the Lord will snatch away
their finery: the bangles and headbands
and crescent necklaces, ¹⁹the earrings and
bracelets and veils, ²⁰the headdresses and
anklets and sashes, the perfume bottles
and charms, ²¹the signet rings and nose
rings, ²²the fine robes and the capes and
cloaks, the purses ²³and mirrors, and the
linen garments and tiaras and shawls.

²⁴Instead of fragrance there will be a
stench;
instead of a sash, a rope;
instead of well-dressed hair, baldness;
instead of fine clothing, sackcloth;
instead of beauty, branding.
²⁵Your men will fall by the sword,
your warriors in battle.
²⁶The gates of Zion will lament and
mourn;
destitute, she will sit on the ground.

4

¹In that day seven women
will take hold of one man
and say, "We will eat our own food
and provide our own clothes;
only let us be called by your name.
Take away our disgrace!"

The Branch of the LORD

²In that day the Branch of the LORD
will be beautiful and glorious, and the
fruit of the land will be the pride and glory of the survivors in Israel. ³Those who
are left in Zion, who remain in Jerusalem,
will be called holy, all who are recorded
among the living in Jerusalem. ⁴The Lord
will wash away the filth of the women of
Zion; he will cleanse the bloodstains from
Jerusalem by a spirit*ᵃ* of judgment and a
spirit*ᵃ* of fire. ⁵Then the LORD will create over all of Mount Zion and over those
who assemble there a cloud of smoke by
day and a glow of flaming fire by night;
over everything the glory*ᵇ* will be a canopy. ⁶It will be a shelter and shade from the
heat of the day, and a refuge and hiding
place from the storm and rain.

The Song of the Vineyard

5

I will sing for the one I love
a song about his vineyard:
My loved one had a vineyard
on a fertile hillside.
²He dug it up and cleared it of stones
and planted it with the choicest
vines.
He built a watchtower in it
and cut out a winepress as well.
Then he looked for a crop of good
grapes,
but it yielded only bad fruit.

³"Now you dwellers in Jerusalem and
people of Judah,
judge between me and my vineyard.
⁴What more could have been done for
my vineyard
than I have done for it?
When I looked for good grapes,
why did it yield only bad?
⁵Now I will tell you
what I am going to do to my
vineyard:

I will take away its hedge,
and it will be destroyed;
I will break down its wall,
and it will be trampled.
⁶I will make it a wasteland,
neither pruned nor cultivated,
and briers and thorns will grow there.
I will command the clouds
not to rain on it."

⁷The vineyard of the LORD Almighty
is the nation of Israel,
and the people of Judah
are the vines he delighted in.
And he looked for justice, but saw
bloodshed;
for righteousness, but heard cries of
distress.

Woes and Judgments

⁸Woe to you who add house to house
and join field to field
till no space is left
and you live alone in the land.

⁹The LORD Almighty has declared in
my hearing:

"Surely the great houses will become
desolate,
the fine mansions left without
occupants.
¹⁰A ten-acre vineyard will produce only
a bath*ᶜ* of wine;
a homer*ᵈ* of seed will yield only an
ephah*ᵉ* of grain."

¹¹Woe to those who rise early in the
morning
to run after their drinks,
who stay up late at night
till they are inflamed with wine.
¹²They have harps and lyres at their
banquets,
pipes and timbrels and wine,
but they have no regard for the deeds
of the LORD,
no respect for the work of his hands.

ᵃ 4 Or *the Spirit*   *ᵇ 5* Or *over all the glory there*
ᶜ 10 That is, about 6 gallons or about 22 liters
ᵈ 10 That is, probably about 360 pounds or
about 160 kilograms   *ᵉ 10* That is, probably
about 36 pounds or about 16 kilograms

¹³Therefore my people will go into exile
for lack of understanding;
those of high rank will die of hunger
and the common people will be
parched with thirst.
¹⁴Therefore Death expands its jaws,
opening wide its mouth;
into it will descend their nobles and
masses
with all their brawlers and revelers.
¹⁵So people will be brought low
and everyone humbled,
the eyes of the arrogant humbled.
¹⁶But the Lord Almighty will be
exalted by his justice,
and the holy God will be proved
holy by his righteous acts.
¹⁷Then sheep will graze as in their own
pasture;
lambs will feed*a* among the ruins of
the rich.

¹⁸Woe to those who draw sin along with
cords of deceit,
and wickedness as with cart ropes,
¹⁹to those who say, "Let God hurry;
let him hasten his work
so we may see it.
The plan of the Holy One of Israel—
let it approach, let it come into
view,
so we may know it."

²⁰Woe to those who call evil good
and good evil,
who put darkness for light
and light for darkness,
who put bitter for sweet
and sweet for bitter.

²¹Woe to those who are wise in their
own eyes
and clever in their own sight.

²²Woe to those who are heroes at
drinking wine
and champions at mixing drinks,
²³who acquit the guilty for a bribe,
but deny justice to the innocent.
²⁴Therefore, as tongues of fire lick up
straw
and as dry grass sinks down in the
flames,
so their roots will decay
and their flowers blow away like dust;
for they have rejected the law of the
Lord Almighty
and spurned the word of the Holy
One of Israel.
²⁵Therefore the Lord's anger burns
against his people;
his hand is raised and he strikes
them down.
The mountains shake,
and the dead bodies are like refuse
in the streets.

Yet for all this, his anger is not turned
away,
his hand is still upraised.

²⁶He lifts up a banner for the distant
nations,
he whistles for those at the ends of
the earth.
Here they come,
swiftly and speedily!
²⁷Not one of them grows tired or
stumbles,
not one slumbers or sleeps;
not a belt is loosened at the waist,
not a sandal strap is broken.
²⁸Their arrows are sharp,
all their bows are strung;
their horses' hooves seem like flint,
their chariot wheels like a
whirlwind.
²⁹Their roar is like that of the lion,
they roar like young lions;
they growl as they seize their prey
and carry it off with no one to
rescue.
³⁰In that day they will roar over it
like the roaring of the sea.
And if one looks at the land,
there is only darkness and distress;
even the sun will be darkened by
clouds.

Isaiah's Commission

6 In the year that King Uzziah died,
I saw the Lord, high and exalted,
seated on a throne; and the train
of his robe filled the temple. ²Above him

---

a 17 Septuagint; Hebrew / *strangers will eat*

were seraphim, each with six wings: With two wings they covered their faces, with two they covered their feet, and with two they were flying. ³And they were calling to one another:

"Holy, holy, holy is the LORD
  Almighty;
  the whole earth is full of his glory."

⁴At the sound of their voices the doorposts and thresholds shook and the temple was filled with smoke.

⁵"Woe to me!" I cried. "I am ruined! For I am a man of unclean lips, and I live among a people of unclean lips, and my eyes have seen the King, the LORD Almighty."

⁶Then one of the seraphim flew to me with a live coal in his hand, which he had taken with tongs from the altar. ⁷With it he touched my mouth and said, "See, this has touched your lips; your guilt is taken away and your sin atoned for."

⁸Then I heard the voice of the Lord saying, "Whom shall I send? And who will go for us?"

And I said, "Here am I. Send me!"

⁹He said, "Go and tell this people:

"'Be ever hearing, but never
    understanding;
  be ever seeing, but never
    perceiving.'
¹⁰Make the heart of this people
    calloused;
  make their ears dull
    and close their eyes.^a
Otherwise they might see with their
    eyes,
  hear with their ears,
  understand with their hearts,
and turn and be healed."

¹¹Then I said, "For how long, Lord?"

And he answered:

"Until the cities lie ruined
    and without inhabitant,
until the houses are left deserted
    and the fields ruined and ravaged,
¹²until the LORD has sent everyone far
    away
    and the land is utterly forsaken.

UNSHAKEN *God*

Isaiah 6:1–10

God is exalted.

To be "exalted" means to be "elevated" or "raised," in status or character. So when the prophet Isaiah saw "the Lord, high and exalted, seated on a throne" (Isaiah 6:1), he had spotted God's absolute superiority over anything and everything else. Isaiah had a vision of the Lord seated on his heavenly throne enjoying the worship of angels, and the prophet's human reaction was a crushing sense of his own lowliness and sinfulness. God not only reached out and forgave Isaiah's sin, but he also appointed Isaiah as his spokesperson. While nothing we can do will ever make the Lord any greater, we "exalt God" when we recognize his greatness and give him the worship he deserves.

So … When and how do you exalt God?

¹³And though a tenth remains in the
    land,
  it will again be laid waste.
But as the terebinth and oak
  leave stumps when they are cut
    down,
  so the holy seed will be the stump
    in the land."

The Sign of Immanuel

7 When Ahaz son of Jotham, the son of Uzziah, was king of Judah, King Rezin of Aram and Pekah son of Remaliah king of Israel marched up to fight against Jerusalem, but they could not overpower it.

^a *9,10 Hebrew; Septuagint 'You will be ever hearing, but never understanding; / you will be ever seeing, but never perceiving.' / ¹⁰This people's heart has become calloused; / they hardly hear with their ears, / and they have closed their eyes*

[2]Now the house of David was told, "Aram has allied itself with[a] Ephraim"; so the hearts of Ahaz and his people were shaken, as the trees of the forest are shaken by the wind.

[3]Then the LORD said to Isaiah, "Go out, you and your son Shear-Jashub,[b] to meet Ahaz at the end of the aqueduct of the Upper Pool, on the road to the Launderer's Field. [4]Say to him, 'Be careful, keep calm and don't be afraid. Do not lose heart because of these two smoldering stubs of firewood—because of the fierce anger of Rezin and Aram and of the son of Remaliah. [5]Aram, Ephraim and Remaliah's son have plotted your ruin, saying, [6]"Let us invade Judah; let us tear it apart and divide it among ourselves, and make the son of Tabeel king over it." [7]Yet this is what the Sovereign LORD says:

"'It will not take place,
    it will not happen,
[8]for the head of Aram is Damascus,
    and the head of Damascus is only
      Rezin.
Within sixty-five years
    Ephraim will be too shattered to be
      a people.
[9]The head of Ephraim is Samaria,
    and the head of Samaria is only
      Remaliah's son.
If you do not stand firm in your faith,
    you will not stand at all.'"

[10]Again the LORD spoke to Ahaz, [11]"Ask the LORD your God for a sign, whether in the deepest depths or in the highest heights."

[12]But Ahaz said, "I will not ask; I will not put the LORD to the test."

[13]Then Isaiah said, "Hear now, you house of David! Is it not enough to try the patience of humans? Will you try the patience of my God also? [14]Therefore the Lord himself will give you[c] a sign: The virgin[d] will conceive and give birth to a son, and[e] will call him Immanuel.[f] [15]He will be eating curds and honey when he knows enough to reject the wrong and choose the right, [16]for before the boy knows enough to reject the wrong and

choose the right, the land of the two kings you dread will be laid waste. [17]The LORD will bring on you and on your people and on the house of your father a time unlike any since Ephraim broke away from Judah—he will bring the king of Assyria."

Assyria, the LORD's Instrument

[18]In that day the LORD will whistle for flies from the Nile delta in Egypt and for bees from the land of Assyria. [19]They will all come and settle in the steep ravines and in the crevices in the rocks, on all the thornbushes and at all the water holes. [20]In that day the Lord will use a razor hired from beyond the Euphrates River—the king of Assyria—to shave your head and private parts, and to cut off your beard also. [21]In that day, a person will keep alive a young cow and two goats. [22]And because of the abundance of the milk they give, there will be curds to eat. All who remain in the land will eat curds and honey. [23]In that day, in every place where there were a thousand vines worth a thousand silver shekels,[g] there will be only briers and thorns. [24]Hunters will go there with bow and arrow, for the land will be covered with briers and thorns. [25]As for all the hills once cultivated by the hoe, you will no longer go there for fear of the briers and thorns; they will become places where cattle are turned loose and where sheep run.

Isaiah and His Children as Signs

8 The LORD said to me, "Take a large scroll and write on it with an ordinary pen: Maher-Shal-al-Hash-Baz.[b] [2]So I called in Uriah the priest and Zechariah son of Jeberekiah as reliable witnesses for me. [3]Then I made love to the prophetess, and she conceived

---

[a] *2* Or *has set up camp in*   [b] *3* Shear-Jashub means *a remnant will return.*   [c] *14* The Hebrew is plural.   [d] *14* Or *young woman*   [e] *14* Masoretic Text; Dead Sea Scrolls *son, and he* or *son, and they*   [f] *14* Immanuel means *God with us.*   [g] *23* That is, about 25 pounds or about 12 kilograms   [b] *1* Maher-Shalal-Hash-Baz means *quick to the plunder, swift to the spoil*; also in verse 3.

and gave birth to a son. And the Lord said to me, "Name him Maher-Shalal-Hash-Baz. ⁴For before the boy knows how to say 'My father' or 'My mother,' the wealth of Damascus and the plunder of Samaria will be carried off by the king of Assyria."

⁵The Lord spoke to me again:

⁶"Because this people has rejected
    the gently flowing waters of Shiloah
and rejoices over Rezin
    and the son of Remaliah,
⁷therefore the Lord is about to bring
    against them
    the mighty floodwaters of the
      Euphrates—
    the king of Assyria with all his
      pomp.
It will overflow all its channels,
    run over all its banks
⁸and sweep on into Judah, swirling
    over it,
    passing through it and reaching up
      to the neck.
Its outspread wings will cover the
    breadth of your land,
    Immanuel*ᵃ!"

⁹Raise the war cry,ᵇ you nations, and be
    shattered!
Listen, all you distant lands.
Prepare for battle, and be shattered!
Prepare for battle, and be shattered!
¹⁰Devise your strategy, but it will be
    thwarted;
    propose your plan, but it will not
      stand,
    for God is with us.ᶜ

¹¹This is what the Lord says to me with his strong hand upon me, warning me not to follow the way of this people:

¹²"Do not call conspiracy
    everything this people calls a
      conspiracy;
    do not fear what they fear,
    and do not dread it.
¹³The Lord Almighty is the one you
    are to regard as holy,
    he is the one you are to fear,
    he is the one you are to dread.

¹⁴He will be a holy place;
    for both Israel and Judah he will be
a stone that causes people to stumble
    and a rock that makes them fall.
And for the people of Jerusalem he
    will be
    a trap and a snare.
¹⁵Many of them will stumble;
    they will fall and be broken,
    they will be snared and captured."

¹⁶Bind up this testimony of warning
    and seal up God's instruction
      among my disciples.
¹⁷I will wait for the Lord,
    who is hiding his face from the
      descendants of Jacob.
I will put my trust in him.

¹⁸Here am I, and the children the Lord has given me. We are signs and symbols in Israel from the Lord Almighty, who dwells on Mount Zion.

The Darkness Turns to Light

¹⁹When someone tells you to consult mediums and spiritists, who whisper and mutter, should not a people inquire of their God? Why consult the dead on behalf of the living? ²⁰Consult God's instruction and the testimony of warning. If anyone does not speak according to this word, they have no light of dawn. ²¹Distressed and hungry, they will roam through the land; when they are famished, they will become enraged and, looking upward, will curse their king and their God. ²²Then they will look toward the earth and see only distress and darkness and fearful gloom, and they will be thrust into utter darkness.

9 ᵈ Nevertheless, there will be no more gloom for those who were in distress. In the past he humbled the land of Zebulun and the land of Naphtali, but in the future he will honor Galilee of the nations, by the Way of the Sea, beyond the Jordan—

ᵃ 8 *Immanuel* means *God with us.*   ᵇ 9 Or *Do your worst*   ᶜ 10 Hebrew *Immanuel*   ᵈ In Hebrew texts 9:1 is numbered 8:23, and 9:2-21 is numbered 9:1-20.

²The people walking in darkness
   have seen a great light;
on those living in the land of deep
   darkness
   a light has dawned.
³You have enlarged the nation
   and increased their joy;
they rejoice before you
   as people rejoice at the harvest,
as warriors rejoice
   when dividing the plunder.
⁴For as in the day of Midian's defeat,
   you have shattered
the yoke that burdens them,
   the bar across their shoulders,
   the rod of their oppressor.
⁵Every warrior's boot used in battle
   and every garment rolled in blood
will be destined for burning,
   will be fuel for the fire.
⁶For to us a child is born,
   to us a son is given,
   and the government will be on his
     shoulders.
And he will be called
   Wonderful Counselor, Mighty
     God,
   Everlasting Father, Prince of Peace.
⁷Of the greatness of his government
     and peace
   there will be no end.
He will reign on David's throne
   and over his kingdom,
establishing and upholding it
   with justice and righteousness
   from that time on and forever.
The zeal of the Lord Almighty
   will accomplish this.

The Lord's Anger Against Israel

⁸The Lord has sent a message against
     Jacob;
   it will fall on Israel.
⁹All the people will know it—
   Ephraim and the inhabitants of
     Samaria—
who say with pride
   and arrogance of heart,
¹⁰"The bricks have fallen down,
   but we will rebuild with dressed
     stone;

Isaiah 9:6–7

God promised a Savior.

If Jesus had shown up on earth unannounced, people might have mistaken him for any other baby. But God sent angels to announce his birth to shepherds (see Luke 2:8–20). He brought curious wise men from faraway lands to investigate the newborn king (see Matthew 2:1–2). And for hundreds of years before Jesus was born in Bethlehem, the Lord detailed how we could recognize Jesus and exactly what he would accomplish. This rescuer would come as a child and reign over the world. And his names would capture his extraordinary character. He would be called "Wonderful Counselor, Mighty God, Everlasting Father, Prince of Peace" (Isaiah 9:6). Of all the prophets in the Bible, Isaiah brought the most stunning news of the coming Savior. Look for Jesus in Isaiah 7:14; 11:2; 53:2–5; and 61:1–2.

Think: How do these prophecies about Jesus spoken hundreds of years before his birth help show you he is the Savior sent from God?

ROCK SOLID truths

---

the fig trees have been felled,
   but we will replace them with
     cedars."
¹¹But the Lord has strengthened
     Rezin's foes against them
   and has spurred their enemies on.
¹²Arameans from the east and
     Philistines from the west
have devoured Israel with open
     mouth.

Yet for all this, his anger is not turned
away,
his hand is still upraised.

¹³ But the people have not returned to
him who struck them,
nor have they sought the Lord
Almighty.
¹⁴ So the Lord will cut off from Israel
both head and tail,
both palm branch and reed in a
single day;
¹⁵ the elders and dignitaries are the head,
the prophets who teach lies are the
tail.
¹⁶ Those who guide this people mislead
them,
and those who are guided are led
astray.
¹⁷ Therefore the Lord will take no
pleasure in the young men,
nor will he pity the fatherless and
widows,
for everyone is ungodly and wicked,
every mouth speaks folly.

Yet for all this, his anger is not turned
away,
his hand is still upraised.

¹⁸ Surely wickedness burns like a fire;
it consumes briers and thorns,
it sets the forest thickets ablaze,
so that it rolls upward in a column
of smoke.
¹⁹ By the wrath of the Lord Almighty
the land will be scorched
and the people will be fuel for the fire;
they will not spare one another.
²⁰ On the right they will devour,
but still be hungry;
on the left they will eat,
but not be satisfied.
Each will feed on the flesh of their
own offspring^a:
²¹   Manasseh will feed on Ephraim,
and Ephraim on Manasseh;
together they will turn against
Judah.

Yet for all this, his anger is not turned
away,
his hand is still upraised.

10 Woe to those who make
unjust laws,
to those who issue oppressive
decrees,
² to deprive the poor of their rights
and withhold justice from the
oppressed of my people,
making widows their prey
and robbing the fatherless.
³ What will you do on the day of
reckoning,
when disaster comes from afar?
To whom will you run for help?
Where will you leave your riches?
⁴ Nothing will remain but to cringe
among the captives
or fall among the slain.

Yet for all this, his anger is not turned
away,
his hand is still upraised.

God's Judgment on Assyria

⁵ "Woe to the Assyrian, the rod of my
anger,
in whose hand is the club of my
wrath!
⁶ I send him against a godless nation,
I dispatch him against a people who
anger me,
to seize loot and snatch plunder,
and to trample them down like mud
in the streets.
⁷ But this is not what he intends,
this is not what he has in mind;
his purpose is to destroy,
to put an end to many nations.
⁸ 'Are not my commanders all kings?' he
says.
⁹   'Has not Kalno fared like
Carchemish?
Is not Hamath like Arpad,
and Samaria like Damascus?
¹⁰ As my hand seized the kingdoms of
the idols,
kingdoms whose images excelled those
of Jerusalem and Samaria—
¹¹ shall I not deal with Jerusalem and her
images
as I dealt with Samaria and her idols?'"

^a 20 Or arm

¹²When the Lord has finished all his work against Mount Zion and Jerusalem, he will say, "I will punish the king of Assyria for the willful pride of his heart and the haughty look in his eyes. ¹³For he says:

"'By the strength of my hand I have
      done this,
   and by my wisdom, because I have
      understanding.
I removed the boundaries of nations,
   I plundered their treasures;
   like a mighty one I subdued*a* their
      kings.
¹⁴As one reaches into a nest,
   so my hand reached for the wealth
      of the nations;
as people gather abandoned eggs,
   so I gathered all the countries;
not one flapped a wing,
   or opened its mouth to chirp.'"

¹⁵Does the ax raise itself above the
      person who swings it,
   or the saw boast against the one
      who uses it?
As if a rod were to wield the person
      who lifts it up,
   or a club brandish the one who is
      not wood!
¹⁶Therefore, the Lord, the LORD
      Almighty,
   will send a wasting disease upon his
      sturdy warriors;
under his pomp a fire will be kindled
   like a blazing flame.
¹⁷The Light of Israel will become a fire,
   their Holy One a flame;
in a single day it will burn and
      consume
   his thorns and his briers.
¹⁸The splendor of his forests and fertile
      fields
   it will completely destroy,
   as when a sick person wastes away.
¹⁹And the remaining trees of his forests
      will be so few
   that a child could write them down.

The Remnant of Israel

²⁰In that day the remnant of Israel,
   the survivors of Jacob,
will no longer rely on him
   who struck them down
but will truly rely on the LORD,
   the Holy One of Israel.
²¹A remnant will return,*b* a remnant of
      Jacob
   will return to the Mighty God.
²²Though your people be like the sand
      by the sea, Israel,
   only a remnant will return.
Destruction has been decreed,
   overwhelming and righteous.
²³The Lord, the LORD Almighty, will
      carry out
   the destruction decreed upon the
      whole land.

²⁴Therefore this is what the Lord, the
LORD Almighty, says:

"My people who live in Zion,
   do not be afraid of the Assyrians,
who beat you with a rod
   and lift up a club against you, as
      Egypt did.
²⁵Very soon my anger against you will
      end
   and my wrath will be directed to
      their destruction."
²⁶The LORD Almighty will lash them
      with a whip,
   as when he struck down Midian at
      the rock of Oreb;
and he will raise his staff over the waters,
   as he did in Egypt.
²⁷In that day their burden will be lifted
      from your shoulders,
   their yoke from your neck;
the yoke will be broken
   because you have grown so fat.*c*

²⁸They enter Aiath;
   they pass through Migron;
   they store supplies at Mikmash.
²⁹They go over the pass, and say,
   "We will camp overnight at Geba."
Ramah trembles;
   Gibeah of Saul flees.

---

a 13 Or *treasures; / I subdued the mighty,*
b 21 Hebrew *shear-jashub* (see 7:3 and note); also
in verse 22   *c* 27 Hebrew; Septuagint *broken /
from your shoulders*

³⁰ Cry out, Daughter Gallim!
    Listen, Laishah!
    Poor Anathoth!
³¹ Madmenah is in flight;
    the people of Gebim take cover.
³² This day they will halt at Nob;
    they will shake their fist
at the mount of Daughter Zion,
    at the hill of Jerusalem.

³³ See, the Lord, the LORD Almighty,
    will lop off the boughs with great
        power.
The lofty trees will be felled,
    the tall ones will be brought low.
³⁴ He will cut down the forest thickets
    with an ax;
    Lebanon will fall before the Mighty
        One.

The Branch From Jesse

11 A shoot will come up from the
    stump of Jesse;
    from his roots a Branch will
        bear fruit.
² The Spirit of the LORD will rest on
    him—
    the Spirit of wisdom and of
        understanding,
    the Spirit of counsel and of
        might,
    the Spirit of the knowledge and
        fear of the LORD—
³ and he will delight in the fear of the
    LORD.

He will not judge by what he sees with
    his eyes,
    or decide by what he hears with his
        ears;
⁴ but with righteousness he will judge
    the needy,
    with justice he will give decisions
        for the poor of the earth.
He will strike the earth with the rod
    of his mouth;
    with the breath of his lips he will
        slay the wicked.
⁵ Righteousness will be his belt
    and faithfulness the sash around his
        waist.

⁶ The wolf will live with the lamb,
    the leopard will lie down with the
        goat,
    the calf and the lion and the yearling*ᵃ*
        together;
    and a little child will lead them.
⁷ The cow will feed with the bear,
    their young will lie down together,
    and the lion will eat straw like the ox.
⁸ The infant will play near the cobra's
    den,
    and the young child will put its
        hand into the viper's nest.
⁹ They will neither harm nor destroy
    on all my holy mountain,
for the earth will be filled with the
    knowledge of the LORD
    as the waters cover the sea.

¹⁰ In that day the Root of Jesse will stand
as a banner for the peoples; the nations
will rally to him, and his resting place will
be glorious. ¹¹ In that day the Lord will
reach out his hand a second time to re-
claim the surviving remnant of his people
from Assyria, from Lower Egypt, from
Upper Egypt, from Cush,*ᵇ* from Elam,
from Babylonia,*ᶜ* from Hamath and from
the islands of the Mediterranean.

¹² He will raise a banner for the nations
    and gather the exiles of Israel;
he will assemble the scattered people
    of Judah
from the four quarters of the earth.
¹³ Ephraim's jealousy will vanish,
    and Judah's enemies*ᵈ* will be
        destroyed;
Ephraim will not be jealous of Judah,
    nor Judah hostile toward Ephraim.
¹⁴ They will swoop down on the slopes
    of Philistia to the west;
    together they will plunder the
        people to the east.
They will subdue Edom and Moab,
    and the Ammonites will be subject
        to them.
¹⁵ The LORD will dry up
    the gulf of the Egyptian sea;

ᵃ 6 Hebrew; Septuagint *lion will feed*
ᵇ 11 That is, the upper Nile region
ᶜ 11 Hebrew *Shinar*   *ᵈ 13* Or *hostility*

with a scorching wind he will sweep
his hand
over the Euphrates River.
He will break it up into seven streams
so that anyone can cross over in
sandals.
16 There will be a highway for the
remnant of his people
that is left from Assyria,
as there was for Israel
when they came up from Egypt.

Songs of Praise

12 In that day you will say:

"I will praise you, LORD.
Although you were angry with me,
your anger has turned away
and you have comforted me.
2 Surely God is my salvation;
I will trust and not be afraid.
The LORD, the LORD himself, is my
strength and my defense*a*;
he has become my salvation."

ROCK SOLID promises

**"The LORD ... is my strength and
my defense; he has become my
salvation."** **Isaiah 12:2**

**Make God the theme song of your life. He
will save you and make you unshakable.**

3 With joy you will draw water
from the wells of salvation.

4 In that day you will say:

"Give praise to the LORD, proclaim
his name;
make known among the nations
what he has done,
and proclaim that his name is exalted.

5 Sing to the LORD, for he has done
glorious things;
let this be known to all the world.
6 Shout aloud and sing for joy, people of
Zion,
for great is the Holy One of Israel
among you."

A Prophecy Against Babylon

13 A prophecy against Babylon
that Isaiah son of Amoz saw:

2 Raise a banner on a bare hilltop,
shout to them;
beckon to them
to enter the gates of the nobles.
3 I have commanded those I prepared
for battle;
I have summoned my warriors to
carry out my wrath—
those who rejoice in my triumph.

4 Listen, a noise on the mountains,
like that of a great multitude!
Listen, an uproar among the
kingdoms,
like nations massing together!
The LORD Almighty is mustering
an army for war.
5 They come from faraway lands,
from the ends of the heavens—
the LORD and the weapons of his
wrath—
to destroy the whole country.

6 Wail, for the day of the LORD is near;
it will come like destruction from
the Almighty.*b*
7 Because of this, all hands will go
limp,
every heart will melt with fear.
8 Terror will seize them,
pain and anguish will grip them;
they will writhe like a woman in
labor.
They will look aghast at each other,
their faces aflame.
9 See, the day of the LORD is coming
—a cruel day, with wrath and
fierce anger—

a 2 Or *song*   *b 6* Hebrew *Shaddai*

to make the land desolate
and destroy the sinners within it.
¹⁰ The stars of heaven and their
constellations
will not show their light.
The rising sun will be darkened
and the moon will not give its
light.
¹¹ I will punish the world for its evil,
the wicked for their sins.
I will put an end to the arrogance of
the haughty
and will humble the pride of the
ruthless.
¹² I will make people scarcer than pure
gold,
more rare than the gold of Ophir.
¹³ Therefore I will make the heavens
tremble;
and the earth will shake from its
place
at the wrath of the LORD Almighty,
in the day of his burning anger.

¹⁴ Like a hunted gazelle,
like sheep without a shepherd,
they will all return to their own
people,
they will flee to their native land.
¹⁵ Whoever is captured will be thrust
through;
all who are caught will fall by the
sword.
¹⁶ Their infants will be dashed to pieces
before their eyes;
their houses will be looted and their
wives violated.

¹⁷ See, I will stir up against them the
Medes,
who do not care for silver
and have no delight in gold.
¹⁸ Their bows will strike down the
young men;
they will have no mercy on infants,
nor will they look with compassion
on children.
¹⁹ Babylon, the jewel of kingdoms,
the pride and glory of the
Babylonians,[a]
will be overthrown by God
like Sodom and Gomorrah.

²⁰ She will never be inhabited
or lived in through all generations;
there no nomads will pitch their tents,
there no shepherds will rest their
flocks.
²¹ But desert creatures will lie there,
jackals will fill her houses;
there the owls will dwell,
and there the wild goats will leap
about.
²² Hyenas will inhabit her strongholds,
jackals her luxurious palaces.
Her time is at hand,
and her days will not be prolonged.

14 The LORD will have
compassion on Jacob;
once again he will choose
Israel
and will settle them in their own
land.
Foreigners will join them
and unite with the descendants of
Jacob.
² Nations will take them
and bring them to their own place.
And Israel will take possession of the
nations
and make them male and female
servants in the LORD's land.
They will make captives of their
captors
and rule over their oppressors.

³ On the day the LORD gives you relief from your suffering and turmoil and from the harsh labor forced on you, ⁴ you will take up this taunt against the king of Babylon:

How the oppressor has come to an end!
How his fury[b] has ended!
⁵ The LORD has broken the rod of the
wicked,
the scepter of the rulers,
⁶ which in anger struck down peoples
with unceasing blows,
and in fury subdued nations
with relentless aggression.

^a 19 Or *Chaldeans*   ^b 4 Dead Sea Scrolls,
Septuagint and Syriac; the meaning of the word
in the Masoretic Text is uncertain.

⁷All the lands are at rest and at peace;
  they break into singing.
⁸Even the junipers and the cedars of
    Lebanon
  gloat over you and say,
"Now that you have been laid low,
  no one comes to cut us down."

⁹The realm of the dead below is all
    astir
  to meet you at your coming;
it rouses the spirits of the departed to
    greet you—
  all those who were leaders in the
    world;
it makes them rise from their
    thrones—
  all those who were kings over the
    nations.
¹⁰They will all respond,
  they will say to you,
"You also have become weak, as we
    are;
  you have become like us."
¹¹All your pomp has been brought down
    to the grave,
  along with the noise of your harps;
maggots are spread out beneath you
  and worms cover you.

¹²How you have fallen from heaven,
  morning star, son of the dawn!
You have been cast down to the
    earth,
  you who once laid low the nations!
¹³You said in your heart,
  "I will ascend to the heavens;
I will raise my throne
  above the stars of God;
I will sit enthroned on the mount of
    assembly,
  on the utmost heights of Mount
    Zaphon.ᵃ
¹⁴I will ascend above the tops of the
    clouds;
  I will make myself like the Most
    High."
¹⁵But you are brought down to the
    realm of the dead,
  to the depths of the pit.

¹⁶Those who see you stare at you,
  they ponder your fate:

"Is this the man who shook the earth
  and made kingdoms tremble,
¹⁷the man who made the world a
    wilderness,
  who overthrew its cities
  and would not let his captives go
    home?"

¹⁸All the kings of the nations lie in state,
  each in his own tomb.

ᵃ 13 Or *of the north*; Zaphon was the most sacred
mountain of the Canaanites.

Isaiah 14:12–21

Satan wants to take God's place.

While this scene continues a description of the arrogant king of Babylon (Isaiah 14:4), believers since the early church have also seen in this passage a description of Satan, a supernatural being who has attempted to outshine God since before the world began. The name "morning star" in Isaiah 14:12 means "day star." This poetic verse says that this "star" wanted to climb to the peak of the heavens, even higher than God's throne. Satan taunts God when he says, "I will ascend above the tops of the clouds; I will make myself like the Most High" (Isaiah 14:14). One thing is certain: Satan is doomed not to succeed. Jesus said he saw Satan "fall like lightning from heaven" (Luke 10:18), and this passage promises Lucifer will go "down to the realm of the dead, to the depths of the pit" (Isaiah 14:15). Hell is where Satan winds up at the end of time (Revelation 20:7–10).

Think: How do people try to be more important than God?

ROCK SOLID truths

¹⁹ But you are cast out of your tomb
   like a rejected branch;
you are covered with the slain,
   with those pierced by the sword,
   those who descend to the stones of
      the pit.
Like a corpse trampled underfoot,
²⁰   you will not join them in burial,
   for you have destroyed your land
      and killed your people.

Let the offspring of the wicked
   never be mentioned again.
²¹ Prepare a place to slaughter his
      children
   for the sins of their ancestors;
they are not to rise to inherit the land
   and cover the earth with their cities.

²² "I will rise up against them,"
   declares the LORD Almighty.
"I will wipe out Babylon's name and
      survivors,
   her offspring and descendants,"
                  declares the LORD.
²³ "I will turn her into a place for owls
   and into swampland;
I will sweep her with the broom of
      destruction,"
   declares the LORD Almighty.

²⁴ The LORD Almighty has sworn,

"Surely, as I have planned, so it will
      be,
   and as I have purposed, so it will
      happen.
²⁵ I will crush the Assyrian in my land;
   on my mountains I will trample
      him down.
His yoke will be taken from my
      people,
   and his burden removed from their
      shoulders."

²⁶ This is the plan determined for the
      whole world;
   this is the hand stretched out over
      all nations.
²⁷ For the LORD Almighty has purposed,
      and who can thwart him?
   His hand is stretched out, and who
      can turn it back?

UNSHAKEN *God*

Isaiah 14:24–27

God is sovereign.

To be "sovereign" means to have supreme rank or power. A human king or queen is "sovereign" over a nation, and saying that God is sovereign means he rules the universe. God ultimately controls everything. In Isaiah 24 God displays that clout when he predicts the mercy he will show Israel and the judgments he will pour out on its neighbors. Because God is sovereign, nothing can halt the Lord's plans. He says, "Surely, as I have planned, so it will be, and as I have purposed, so it will happen" (Isaiah 14:24). As ruler of all, God oversees not only the rise and fall of nations but the smallest details of our lives.

So ... How does it feel that God ultimately controls the world?

A Prophecy Against the Philistines

²⁸ This prophecy came in the year King Ahaz died:

²⁹ Do not rejoice, all you Philistines,
   that the rod that struck you is
      broken;
from the root of that snake will spring
      up a viper,
   its fruit will be a darting, venomous
      serpent.
³⁰ The poorest of the poor will find
      pasture,
   and the needy will lie down in
      safety.
But your root I will destroy by famine;
   it will slay your survivors.

³¹ Wail, you gate! Howl, you city!
   Melt away, all you Philistines!
A cloud of smoke comes from the
      north,
   and there is not a straggler in its
      ranks.

³²What answer shall be given
to the envoys of that nation?
"The LORD has established Zion,
and in her his afflicted people will
find refuge."

A Prophecy Against Moab

15 A prophecy against Moab:

Ar in Moab is ruined,
destroyed in a night!
Kir in Moab is ruined,
destroyed in a night!
²Dibon goes up to its temple,
to its high places to weep;
Moab wails over Nebo and
Medeba.
Every head is shaved
and every beard cut off.
³In the streets they wear sackcloth;
on the roofs and in the public
squares
they all wail,
prostrate with weeping.
⁴Heshbon and Elealeh cry out,
their voices are heard all the way to
Jahaz.
Therefore the armed men of Moab cry
out,
and their hearts are faint.

⁵My heart cries out over Moab;
her fugitives flee as far as Zoar,
as far as Eglath Shelishiyah.
They go up the hill to Luhith,
weeping as they go;
on the road to Horonaim
they lament their destruction.
⁶The waters of Nimrim are dried up
and the grass is withered;
the vegetation is gone
and nothing green is left.
⁷So the wealth they have acquired and
stored up
they carry away over the Ravine of
the Poplars.
⁸Their outcry echoes along the border
of Moab;
their wailing reaches as far as
Eglaim,
their lamentation as far as Beer
Elim.

⁹The waters of Dimon^a are full of
blood,
but I will bring still more upon
Dimon^a—
a lion upon the fugitives of Moab
and upon those who remain in the
land.

16 Send lambs as tribute
to the ruler of the land,
from Sela, across the desert,
to the mount of Daughter Zion.
²Like fluttering birds
pushed from the nest,
so are the women of Moab
at the fords of the Arnon.

³"Make up your mind," Moab says.
"Render a decision.
Make your shadow like night—
at high noon.
Hide the fugitives,
do not betray the refugees.
⁴Let the Moabite fugitives stay with
you;
be their shelter from the destroyer."

The oppressor will come to an end,
and destruction will cease;
the aggressor will vanish from the
land.
⁵In love a throne will be established;
in faithfulness a man will sit
on it—
one from the house^b of David—
one who in judging seeks justice
and speeds the cause of
righteousness.

⁶We have heard of Moab's pride—
how great is her arrogance!—
of her conceit, her pride and her
insolence;
but her boasts are empty.
⁷Therefore the Moabites wail,
they wail together for Moab.
Lament and grieve
for the raisin cakes of Kir Hareseth.
⁸The fields of Heshbon wither,
the vines of Sibmah also.

^a 9 *Dimon*, a wordplay on *Dibon* (see verse 2),
sounds like the Hebrew for *blood*.
^b 5 Hebrew *tent*

The rulers of the nations
  have trampled down the choicest
    vines,
which once reached Jazer
  and spread toward the desert.
Their shoots spread out
  and went as far as the sea.*

⁹ So I weep, as Jazer weeps,
  for the vines of Sibmah.
Heshbon and Elealeh,
  I drench you with tears!
The shouts of joy over your ripened
    fruit
  and over your harvests have been
    stilled.
¹⁰ Joy and gladness are taken away from
    the orchards;
  no one sings or shouts in the
    vineyards;
  no one treads out wine at the presses,
    for I have put an end to the
    shouting.
¹¹ My heart laments for Moab like a
    harp,
  my inmost being for Kir Hareseth.
¹² When Moab appears at her high
    place,
  she only wears herself out;
when she goes to her shrine to pray,
  it is to no avail.

¹³ This is the word the LORD has already spoken concerning Moab. ¹⁴ But now the LORD says: "Within three years, as a servant bound by contract would count them, Moab's splendor and all her many people will be despised, and her survivors will be very few and feeble."

A Prophecy Against Damascus

17 A prophecy against Damascus:

"See, Damascus will no
    longer be a city
  but will become a heap of ruins.
² The cities of Aroer will be deserted
  and left to flocks, which will lie
    down,
  with no one to make them afraid.
³ The fortified city will disappear from
    Ephraim,
  and royal power from Damascus;

the remnant of Aram will be
  like the glory of the Israelites,"
    declares the LORD Almighty.

⁴ "In that day the glory of Jacob will
    fade;
  the fat of his body will waste away.
⁵ It will be as when reapers harvest the
    standing grain,
  gathering the grain in their
    arms—
as when someone gleans heads of
    grain
  in the Valley of Rephaim.
⁶ Yet some gleanings will remain,
  as when an olive tree is beaten,
leaving two or three olives on the
    topmost branches,
  four or five on the fruitful boughs,"
    declares the LORD,
      the God of Israel.

⁷ In that day people will look to their
    Maker
  and turn their eyes to the Holy One
    of Israel.
⁸ They will not look to the altars,
  the work of their hands,
and they will have no regard for the
    Asherah poles*
  and the incense altars their fingers
    have made.

⁹ In that day their strong cities, which they left because of the Israelites, will be like places abandoned to thickets and undergrowth. And all will be desolation.

¹⁰ You have forgotten God your Savior;
  you have not remembered the Rock,
    your fortress.
Therefore, though you set out the
    finest plants
  and plant imported vines,
¹¹ though on the day you set them out,
  you make them grow,
  and on the morning when you plant
    them, you bring them to bud,
yet the harvest will be as nothing
  in the day of disease and incurable
    pain.

---

a 8 Probably the Dead Sea   *b 8* That is, wooden symbols of the goddess Asherah

¹²Woe to the many nations that rage—
    they rage like the raging sea!
Woe to the peoples who roar—
    they roar like the roaring of great
        waters!
¹³Although the peoples roar like the
        roar of surging waters,
    when he rebukes them they flee far
        away,
    driven before the wind like chaff on
        the hills,
    like tumbleweed before a gale.
¹⁴In the evening, sudden terror!
    Before the morning, they are gone!
This is the portion of those who loot
        us,
    the lot of those who plunder us.

A Prophecy Against Cush

18 Woe to the land of whirring
    wings[a]
    along the rivers of Cush,[b]
²which sends envoys by sea
    in papyrus boats over the water.

Go, swift messengers,
to a people tall and smooth-skinned,
    to a people feared far and wide,
an aggressive nation of strange speech,
    whose land is divided by rivers.

³All you people of the world,
    you who live on the earth,
when a banner is raised on the
        mountains,
    you will see it,
and when a trumpet sounds,
    you will hear it.
⁴This is what the LORD says to me:
    "I will remain quiet and will look
        on from my dwelling place,
like shimmering heat in the sunshine,
    like a cloud of dew in the heat of
        harvest."
⁵For, before the harvest, when the
        blossom is gone
    and the flower becomes a ripening
        grape,
he will cut off the shoots with pruning
        knives,
    and cut down and take away the
        spreading branches.

⁶They will all be left to the mountain
        birds of prey
    and to the wild animals;
the birds will feed on them all summer,
    the wild animals all winter.

⁷At that time gifts will be brought to
the LORD Almighty

from a people tall and smooth-skinned,
    from a people feared far and wide,

---

a 1 Or *of locusts*   *b 1* That is, the upper Nile
region

Isaiah 18

The prophets spoke for God.

Along with the Pentateuch (or "Law"), History books and Wisdom books, "the Prophets" make up one of the four main groups of Old Testament books. The prophetic books split into the "Major Prophets" (Isaiah, Jeremiah, Lamentations, Ezekiel, and Daniel) and the "Minor Prophets" (Hosea through Malachi). Prophets were God's spokespeople, bringing the Lord's messages to his own people. They didn't hesitate to preach against evils going on in the nations around them, as Isaiah did when he prophesied against Cush, the land south of Egypt. While some of the prophets' words ("prophecies") describe the future, most address issues of good and evil happening at that moment. And even though these messages were pointed at people long ago, they still teach us today. They tell us how to live wholeheartedly for God.

Think: How can you use the Bible's prophetic books to grow today?

ROCK SOLID truths

an aggressive nation of strange speech,
whose land is divided by rivers—

the gifts will be brought to Mount Zion,
the place of the Name of the LORD Almighty.

A Prophecy Against Egypt

19 A prophecy against Egypt:

See, the LORD rides on a
swift cloud
and is coming to Egypt.
The idols of Egypt tremble before
him,
and the hearts of the Egyptians
melt with fear.

2 "I will stir up Egyptian against
Egyptian—
brother will fight against brother,
neighbor against neighbor,
city against city,
kingdom against kingdom.
3 The Egyptians will lose heart,
and I will bring their plans to
nothing;
they will consult the idols and the
spirits of the dead,
the mediums and the spiritists.
4 I will hand the Egyptians over
to the power of a cruel master,
and a fierce king will rule over them,"
declares the Lord, the LORD
Almighty.

5 The waters of the river will dry up,
and the riverbed will be parched
and dry.
6 The canals will stink;
the streams of Egypt will dwindle
and dry up.
The reeds and rushes will wither,
7   also the plants along the Nile,
at the mouth of the river.
Every sown field along the Nile
will become parched, will blow
away and be no more.
8 The fishermen will groan and lament,
all who cast hooks into the Nile;
those who throw nets on the water
will pine away.

9 Those who work with combed flax
will despair,
the weavers of fine linen will lose
hope.
10 The workers in cloth will be dejected,
and all the wage earners will be sick
at heart.

11 The officials of Zoan are nothing but
fools;
the wise counselors of Pharaoh give
senseless advice.
How can you say to Pharaoh,
"I am one of the wise men,
a disciple of the ancient kings"?

12 Where are your wise men now?
Let them show you and make known
what the LORD Almighty
has planned against Egypt.
13 The officials of Zoan have become
fools,
the leaders of Memphis are
deceived;
the cornerstones of her peoples
have led Egypt astray.
14 The LORD has poured into them
a spirit of dizziness;
they make Egypt stagger in all that
she does,
as a drunkard staggers around in his
vomit.
15 There is nothing Egypt can do—
head or tail, palm branch or reed.

16 In that day the Egyptians will become
weaklings. They will shudder with fear at
the uplifted hand that the LORD Almighty
raises against them. 17 And the land of Judah will bring terror to the Egyptians; everyone to whom Judah is mentioned will
be terrified, because of what the LORD
Almighty is planning against them.

18 In that day five cities in Egypt will
speak the language of Canaan and swear
allegiance to the LORD Almighty. One of
them will be called the City of the Sun.ᵃ

19 In that day there will be an altar to
the LORD in the heart of Egypt, and a

ᵃ 18 Some manuscripts of the Masoretic Text,
Dead Sea Scrolls, Symmachus and Vulgate;
most manuscripts of the Masoretic Text *City of
Destruction*

monument to the Lord at its border. ²⁰It will be a sign and witness to the Lord Almighty in the land of Egypt. When they cry out to the Lord because of their oppressors, he will send them a savior and defender, and he will rescue them. ²¹So the Lord will make himself known to the Egyptians, and in that day they will acknowledge the Lord. They will worship with sacrifices and grain offerings; they will make vows to the Lord and keep them. ²²The Lord will strike Egypt with a plague; he will strike them and heal them. They will turn to the Lord, and he will respond to their pleas and heal them.

²³In that day there will be a highway from Egypt to Assyria. The Assyrians will go to Egypt and the Egyptians to Assyria. The Egyptians and Assyrians will worship together. ²⁴In that day Israel will be the third, along with Egypt and Assyria, a blessing*a* on the earth. ²⁵The Lord Almighty will bless them, saying, "Blessed be Egypt my people, Assyria my handiwork, and Israel my inheritance."

A Prophecy Against Egypt and Cush

20 In the year that the supreme commander, sent by Sargon king of Assyria, came to Ashdod and attacked and captured it— ²at that time the Lord spoke through Isaiah son of Amoz. He said to him, "Take off the sackcloth from your body and the sandals from your feet." And he did so, going around stripped and barefoot.

³Then the Lord said, "Just as my servant Isaiah has gone stripped and barefoot for three years, as a sign and portent against Egypt and Cush,*b* ⁴so the king of Assyria will lead away stripped and barefoot the Egyptian captives and Cushite exiles, young and old, with buttocks bared—to Egypt's shame. ⁵Those who trusted in Cush and boasted in Egypt will be dismayed and put to shame. ⁶In that day the people who live on this coast will say, 'See what has happened to those we relied on, those we fled to for help and deliverance from the king of Assyria! How then can we escape?'"

A Prophecy Against Babylon

21 A prophecy against the Desert by the Sea:

Like whirlwinds sweeping through
    the southland,
an invader comes from the desert,
    from a land of terror.

²A dire vision has been shown to me:
    The traitor betrays, the looter takes
      loot.
Elam, attack! Media, lay siege!
    I will bring to an end all the
      groaning she caused.

³At this my body is racked with pain,
    pangs seize me, like those of a
      woman in labor;
I am staggered by what I hear,
    I am bewildered by what I see.
⁴My heart falters,
    fear makes me tremble;
the twilight I longed for
    has become a horror to me.

⁵They set the tables,
    they spread the rugs,
    they eat, they drink!
Get up, you officers,
    oil the shields!

⁶This is what the Lord says to me:

"Go, post a lookout
    and have him report what he sees.
⁷When he sees chariots
    with teams of horses,
riders on donkeys
    or riders on camels,
let him be alert,
    fully alert."

⁸And the lookout*c* shouted,

"Day after day, my lord, I stand on the
    watchtower;
every night I stay at my post.
⁹Look, here comes a man in a chariot
    with a team of horses.

---

a 24 Or *Assyria, whose names will be used in blessings* (see Gen. 48:20); or *Assyria, who will be seen by others as blessed*   *b 3* That is, the upper Nile region; also in verse 5   *c 8* Dead Sea Scrolls and Syriac; Masoretic Text *A lion*

And he gives back the answer:
'Babylon has fallen, has fallen!
All the images of its gods
lie shattered on the ground!'"

¹⁰My people who are crushed on the
threshing floor,
I tell you what I have heard
from the LORD Almighty,
from the God of Israel.

A Prophecy Against Edom

¹¹A prophecy against Dumah*ᵃ:

Someone calls to me from Seir,
"Watchman, what is left of the night?
Watchman, what is left of the night?"
¹²The watchman replies,
"Morning is coming, but also the
night.
If you would ask, then ask;
and come back yet again."

A Prophecy Against Arabia

¹³A prophecy against Arabia:

You caravans of Dedanites,
who camp in the thickets of Arabia,
¹⁴   bring water for the thirsty;
you who live in Tema,
bring food for the fugitives.
¹⁵They flee from the sword,
from the drawn sword,
from the bent bow
and from the heat of battle.

¹⁶This is what the Lord says to me:
"Within one year, as a servant bound by
contract would count it, all the splendor of
Kedar will come to an end. ¹⁷The survivors of the archers, the warriors of Kedar,
will be few." The LORD, the God of Israel,
has spoken.

A Prophecy About Jerusalem

22 A prophecy against the Valley of Vision:

What troubles you now,
that you have all gone up on the
roofs,
²you town so full of commotion,
you city of tumult and revelry?

Your slain were not killed by the
sword,
nor did they die in battle.
³All your leaders have fled together;
they have been captured without
using the bow.
All you who were caught were taken
prisoner together,
having fled while the enemy was
still far away.
⁴Therefore I said, "Turn away from me;
let me weep bitterly.
Do not try to console me
over the destruction of my people."

⁵The Lord, the LORD Almighty, has a
day
of tumult and trampling and terror
in the Valley of Vision,
a day of battering down walls
and of crying out to the mountains.
⁶Elam takes up the quiver,
with her charioteers and horses;
Kir uncovers the shield.
⁷Your choicest valleys are full of
chariots,
and horsemen are posted at the city
gates.

⁸The Lord stripped away the defenses
of Judah,
and you looked in that day
to the weapons in the Palace of the
Forest.
⁹You saw that the walls of the City of
David
were broken through in many
places;
you stored up water
in the Lower Pool.
¹⁰You counted the buildings in Jerusalem
and tore down houses to strengthen
the wall.
¹¹You built a reservoir between the two
walls
for the water of the Old Pool,
but you did not look to the One who
made it,
or have regard for the One who
planned it long ago.

ᵃ 11 Dumah, a wordplay on Edom, means silence
or stillness.

¹²The Lord, the LORD Almighty,
  called you on that day
to weep and to wail,
  to tear out your hair and put on
    sackcloth.
¹³But see, there is joy and revelry,
  slaughtering of cattle and killing of
    sheep,
  eating of meat and drinking of wine!
"Let us eat and drink," you say,
  "for tomorrow we die!"

¹⁴The LORD Almighty has revealed this
in my hearing: "Till your dying day this
sin will not be atoned for," says the Lord,
the LORD Almighty.

¹⁵This is what the Lord, the LORD Almighty, says:

"Go, say to this steward,
  to Shebna the palace administrator:
¹⁶What are you doing here and who
    gave you permission
  to cut out a grave for yourself here,
hewing your grave on the height
  and chiseling your resting place in
    the rock?

¹⁷"Beware, the LORD is about to take
    firm hold of you
  and hurl you away, you mighty man.
¹⁸He will roll you up tightly like a ball
  and throw you into a large country.
There you will die
  and there the chariots you were so
    proud of
  will become a disgrace to your
    master's house.
¹⁹I will depose you from your office,
  and you will be ousted from your
    position.

²⁰"In that day I will summon my servant, Eliakim son of Hilkiah. ²¹I will
clothe him with your robe and fasten your
sash around him and hand your authority
over to him. He will be a father to those
who live in Jerusalem and to the people of
Judah. ²²I will place on his shoulder the
key to the house of David; what he opens
no one can shut, and what he shuts no one
can open. ²³I will drive him like a peg
into a firm place; he will become a seat*ᵃ*

of honor for the house of his father. ²⁴All
the glory of his family will hang on him:
its offspring and offshoots—all its lesser
vessels, from the bowls to all the jars.

²⁵"In that day," declares the LORD Almighty, "the peg driven into the firm place
will give way; it will be sheared off and
will fall, and the load hanging on it will be
cut down." The LORD has spoken.

A Prophecy Against Tyre

23 A prophecy against Tyre:

Wail, you ships of Tarshish!
For Tyre is destroyed
  and left without house or harbor.
From the land of Cyprus
  word has come to them.

²Be silent, you people of the island
  and you merchants of Sidon,
  whom the seafarers have enriched.
³On the great waters
  came the grain of the Shihor;
the harvest of the Nile*ᵇ* was the
    revenue of Tyre,
  and she became the marketplace of
    the nations.

⁴Be ashamed, Sidon, and you fortress
    of the sea,
  for the sea has spoken:
"I have neither been in labor nor given
    birth;
  I have neither reared sons nor
    brought up daughters."
⁵When word comes to Egypt,
  they will be in anguish at the report
    from Tyre.

⁶Cross over to Tarshish;
  wail, you people of the island.
⁷Is this your city of revelry,
  the old, old city,
whose feet have taken her
  to settle in far-off lands?
⁸Who planned this against Tyre,
  the bestower of crowns,

ᵃ 23 Or *throne*   *ᵇ 2,3* Masoretic Text; Dead
Sea Scrolls *Sidon, / who cross over the sea; / your
envoys* ³*are on the great waters. / The grain of the
Shihor, / the harvest of the Nile,*

whose merchants are princes,
whose traders are renowned in the
earth?
⁹ The LORD Almighty planned it,
to bring down her pride in all her
splendor
and to humble all who are
renowned on the earth.

¹⁰ Till*a* your land as they do along the Nile,
Daughter Tarshish,
for you no longer have a harbor.
¹¹ The LORD has stretched out his hand
over the sea
and made its kingdoms tremble.

He has given an order concerning
Phoenicia
that her fortresses be destroyed.
¹² He said, "No more of your reveling,
Virgin Daughter Sidon, now
crushed!

"Up, cross over to Cyprus;
even there you will find no rest."
¹³ Look at the land of the Babylonians,*b*
this people that is now of no
account!

a 10 Dead Sea Scrolls and some Septuagint
manuscripts; Masoretic Text *Go through*
b 13 Or *Chaldeans*

Isaiah 22
Isaiah called out God's people.

Details about Old Testament prophets are sometimes fuzzy. But in the case of Isaiah, we know his ministry dates to the year King Uzziah died (see Isaiah 6:1). He began preaching in the year 740 BC.

The story behind Isaiah's ministry is just as clear. Isaiah had a stunning vision of God sitting high upon his heavenly throne, surrounded by hovering angels calling out in worship, "Holy, holy, holy is the LORD Almighty; the whole earth is full of his glory" (Isaiah 6:3). Isaiah cried out that he was too sinful to stand before God. But the Lord forgave his sins and offered him a job. Isaiah was supposed to "Go and tell this people …" (Isaiah 6:9).

Isaiah spent almost the next 60 years going and telling people what God told him to say. Much of the time this powerful preacher delivered a message of judgment, hammering on details of how the people fell short of God's expectations. But he also said a Messiah would be born to the line of David. This Savior would reign forever (see Isaiah 9:6–7) and suffer for the sins of the world, a clear prediction of Jesus' death on the cross (see Isaiah 53:1–12).

The people of Israel must have grown fed up with Isaiah's correction. Tradition says he was sawn in half by Manasseh, the most evil king to ever rule Judah.

You can find Isaiah in 2 Kings 19–20; 2 Chronicles 26:22 and 32:32; and the book that bears his name, as well as many quotations in the New Testament, such as Matthew 3:3.

UNSHAKEN people

The Assyrians have made it
a place for desert creatures;
they raised up their siege towers,
they stripped its fortresses bare
and turned it into a ruin.
¹⁴Wail, you ships of Tarshish;
your fortress is destroyed!

¹⁵At that time Tyre will be forgotten
for seventy years, the span of a king's life.
But at the end of these seventy years, it
will happen to Tyre as in the song of the
prostitute:

¹⁶"Take up a harp, walk through the
city,
you forgotten prostitute;
play the harp well, sing many a song,
so that you will be remembered."

¹⁷At the end of seventy years, the Lord
will deal with Tyre. She will return to her
lucrative prostitution and will ply her trade
with all the kingdoms on the face of the
earth. ¹⁸Yet her profit and her earnings
will be set apart for the Lord; they will
not be stored up or hoarded. Her profits
will go to those who live before the Lord,
for abundant food and fine clothes.

The Lord's Devastation of the Earth

24 See, the Lord is going to
lay waste the earth
and devastate it;
he will ruin its face
and scatter its inhabitants—
²it will be the same
for priest as for people,
for the master as for his servant,
for the mistress as for her servant,
for seller as for buyer,
for borrower as for lender,
for debtor as for creditor.
³The earth will be completely laid
waste
and totally plundered.

The Lord has spoken
this word.

⁴The earth dries up and withers,
the world languishes and withers,
the heavens languish with the
earth.

⁵The earth is defiled by its people;
they have disobeyed the laws,
violated the statutes
and broken the everlasting
covenant.
⁶Therefore a curse consumes the earth;
its people must bear their guilt.
Therefore earth's inhabitants are
burned up,
and very few are left.
⁷The new wine dries up and the vine
withers;
all the merrymakers groan.
⁸The joyful timbrels are stilled,
the noise of the revelers has stopped,
the joyful harp is silent.
⁹No longer do they drink wine with a
song;
the beer is bitter to its drinkers.
¹⁰The ruined city lies desolate;
the entrance to every house is
barred.
¹¹In the streets they cry out for wine;
all joy turns to gloom,
all joyful sounds are banished from
the earth.
¹²The city is left in ruins,
its gate is battered to pieces.
¹³So will it be on the earth
and among the nations,
as when an olive tree is beaten,
or as when gleanings are left after
the grape harvest.

¹⁴They raise their voices, they shout for
joy;
from the west they acclaim the
Lord's majesty.
¹⁵Therefore in the east give glory to the
Lord;
exalt the name of the Lord, the
God of Israel,
in the islands of the sea.
¹⁶From the ends of the earth we hear
singing:
"Glory to the Righteous One."

But I said, "I waste away, I waste away!
Woe to me!
The treacherous betray!
With treachery the treacherous
betray!"

17 Terror and pit and snare await you,
   people of the earth.
18 Whoever flees at the sound of terror
   will fall into a pit;
whoever climbs out of the pit
   will be caught in a snare.

The floodgates of the heavens are
   opened,
   the foundations of the earth shake.
19 The earth is broken up,
   the earth is split asunder,
   the earth is violently shaken.
20 The earth reels like a drunkard,
   it sways like a hut in the wind;
so heavy upon it is the guilt of its
   rebellion
   that it falls—never to rise again.

21 In that day the LORD will punish
   the powers in the heavens above
   and the kings on the earth below.
22 They will be herded together
   like prisoners bound in a dungeon;
they will be shut up in prison
   and be punished[a] after many days.
23 The moon will be dismayed,
   the sun ashamed;
for the LORD Almighty will reign
   on Mount Zion and in Jerusalem,
   and before its elders—with great
   glory.

Praise to the LORD

25 LORD, you are my God;
   I will exalt you and praise
   your name,
for in perfect faithfulness
   you have done wonderful things,
   things planned long ago.
2 You have made the city a heap of rubble,
   the fortified town a ruin,
the foreigners' stronghold a city no
   more;
   it will never be rebuilt.
3 Therefore strong peoples will honor
   you;
   cities of ruthless nations will revere
   you.
4 You have been a refuge for the poor,
   a refuge for the needy in their
   distress,

a shelter from the storm
   and a shade from the heat.
For the breath of the ruthless
   is like a storm driving against a
   wall
5   and like the heat of the desert.
You silence the uproar of foreigners;
   as heat is reduced by the shadow of
   a cloud,
   so the song of the ruthless is stilled.

6 On this mountain the LORD Almighty
   will prepare
   a feast of rich food for all peoples,
a banquet of aged wine—
   the best of meats and the finest of
   wines.
7 On this mountain he will destroy
   the shroud that enfolds all peoples,
the sheet that covers all nations;
8   he will swallow up death forever.
The Sovereign LORD will wipe away
   the tears
   from all faces;
he will remove his people's disgrace
   from all the earth.
                  The LORD has spoken.

9 In that day they will say,

"Surely this is our God;
   we trusted in him, and he saved us.
This is the LORD, we trusted in him;
   let us rejoice and be glad in his
   salvation."

10 The hand of the LORD will rest on
   this mountain;
   but Moab will be trampled in their
   land
   as straw is trampled down in the
   manure.
11 They will stretch out their hands in it,
   as swimmers stretch out their hands
   to swim.
God will bring down their pride
   despite the cleverness[b] of their
   hands.
12 He will bring down your high
   fortified walls
   and lay them low;

[a] 22 Or released   [b] 11 The meaning of the
Hebrew for this word is uncertain.

he will bring them down to the ground,
to the very dust.

A Song of Praise

26 In that day this song will be
sung in the land of Judah:

We have a strong city;
God makes salvation
its walls and ramparts.
² Open the gates
that the righteous nation may enter,
the nation that keeps faith.
³ You will keep in perfect peace
those whose minds are steadfast,
because they trust in you.

ROCK SOLID
promises

"You will keep in perfect peace those whose minds are steadfast, because they trust in you."

Isaiah 26:3

If you want to experience peace that calms you to the core, listen to God's promises until you're convinced he cares.

---

⁴ Trust in the LORD forever,
for the LORD, the LORD himself, is
the Rock eternal.
⁵ He humbles those who dwell on high,
he lays the lofty city low;
he levels it to the ground
and casts it down to the dust.
⁶ Feet trample it down —
the feet of the oppressed,
the footsteps of the poor.

⁷ The path of the righteous is level;
you, the Upright One, make the
way of the righteous smooth.
⁸ Yes, LORD, walking in the way of your
laws,ᵃ
we wait for you;

your name and renown
are the desire of our hearts.
⁹ My soul yearns for you in the night;
in the morning my spirit longs for
you.
When your judgments come upon the
earth,
the people of the world learn
righteousness.
¹⁰ But when grace is shown to the wicked,
they do not learn righteousness;
even in a land of uprightness they go
on doing evil
and do not regard the majesty of the
LORD.
¹¹ LORD, your hand is lifted high,
but they do not see it.
Let them see your zeal for your people
and be put to shame;
let the fire reserved for your
enemies consume them.

¹² LORD, you establish peace for us;
all that we have accomplished you
have done for us.
¹³ LORD our God, other lords besides
you have ruled over us,
but your name alone do we honor.
¹⁴ They are now dead, they live no more;
their spirits do not rise.
You punished them and brought them
to ruin;
you wiped out all memory of them.
¹⁵ You have enlarged the nation, LORD;
you have enlarged the nation.
You have gained glory for yourself;
you have extended all the borders of
the land.

¹⁶ LORD, they came to you in their
distress;
when you disciplined them,
they could barely whisper a prayer.ᵇ
¹⁷ As a pregnant woman about to give
birth
writhes and cries out in her pain,
so were we in your presence, LORD.
¹⁸ We were with child, we writhed in
labor,
but we gave birth to wind.

ᵃ 8 Or *judgments*   ᵇ 16 The meaning of the
Hebrew for this clause is uncertain.

We have not brought salvation to the
earth,
and the people of the world have
not come to life.

19 But your dead will live, Lord;
their bodies will rise —
let those who dwell in the dust
wake up and shout for joy —
your dew is like the dew of the morning;
the earth will give birth to her dead.

20 Go, my people, enter your rooms
and shut the doors behind you;
hide yourselves for a little while
until his wrath has passed by.
21 See, the Lord is coming out of his
dwelling
to punish the people of the earth for
their sins.
The earth will disclose the blood shed
on it;
the earth will conceal its slain no
longer.

Deliverance of Israel

27 In that day,

the Lord will punish with
his sword —
his fierce, great and powerful
sword —
Leviathan the gliding serpent,
Leviathan the coiling serpent;
he will slay the monster of the sea.

2 In that day —

"Sing about a fruitful vineyard:
3   I, the Lord, watch over it;
I water it continually.
I guard it day and night
so that no one may harm it.
4   I am not angry.
If only there were briers and thorns
confronting me!
I would march against them in
battle;
I would set them all on fire.
5 Or else let them come to me for
refuge;
let them make peace with me,
yes, let them make peace with me."

6 In days to come Jacob will take root,
Israel will bud and blossom
and fill all the world with fruit.

7 Has the Lord struck her
as he struck down those who struck
her?
Has she been killed
as those were killed who killed
her?
8 By warfare*a* and exile you contend
with her —
with his fierce blast he drives her
out,
as on a day the east wind blows.
9 By this, then, will Jacob's guilt be
atoned for,
and this will be the full fruit of the
removal of his sin:
When he makes all the altar stones
to be like limestone crushed to
pieces,
no Asherah poles*b* or incense altars
will be left standing.
10 The fortified city stands desolate,
an abandoned settlement, forsaken
like the wilderness;
there the calves graze,
there they lie down;
they strip its branches bare.
11 When its twigs are dry, they are
broken off
and women come and make fires
with them.
For this is a people without
understanding;
so their Maker has no compassion
on them,
and their Creator shows them no
favor.

12 In that day the Lord will thresh
from the flowing Euphrates to the Wadi
of Egypt, and you, Israel, will be gathered up one by one. 13 And in that day a
great trumpet will sound. Those who were
perishing in Assyria and those who were
exiled in Egypt will come and worship the
Lord on the holy mountain in Jerusalem.

a 8 See Septuagint; the meaning of the Hebrew
for this word is uncertain.   *b 9* That is,
wooden symbols of the goddess Asherah

Woe to the Leaders of Ephraim and Judah

28

Woe to that wreath,
the pride of Ephraim's
drunkards,
to the fading flower, his glorious
beauty,
set on the head of a fertile valley—
to that city, the pride of those laid
low by wine!
² See, the Lord has one who is powerful
and strong.
Like a hailstorm and a destructive
wind,
like a driving rain and a flooding
downpour,
he will throw it forcefully to the
ground.
³ That wreath, the pride of Ephraim's
drunkards,
will be trampled underfoot.
⁴ That fading flower, his glorious
beauty,
set on the head of a fertile valley,
will be like figs ripe before harvest—
as soon as people see them and take
them in hand,
they swallow them.

⁵ In that day the Lord Almighty
will be a glorious crown,
a beautiful wreath
for the remnant of his people.
⁶ He will be a spirit of justice
to the one who sits in judgment,
a source of strength
to those who turn back the battle at
the gate.

⁷ And these also stagger from wine
and reel from beer:
Priests and prophets stagger from beer
and are befuddled with wine;
they reel from beer,
they stagger when seeing visions,
they stumble when rendering
decisions.
⁸ All the tables are covered with vomit
and there is not a spot without filth.

⁹ "Who is it he is trying to teach?
To whom is he explaining his
message?
To children weaned from their
milk,
to those just taken from the
breast?
¹⁰ For it is:
Do this, do that,
a rule for this, a rule for that*ᵃ*;
a little here, a little there."

¹¹ Very well then, with foreign lips and
strange tongues
God will speak to this people,
¹² to whom he said,
"This is the resting place, let the
weary rest";
and, "This is the place of repose"—
but they would not listen.
¹³ So then, the word of the Lord to
them will become:
Do this, do that,
a rule for this, a rule for that;
a little here, a little there—
so that as they go they will fall
backward;
they will be injured and snared and
captured.

¹⁴ Therefore hear the word of the Lord,
you scoffers
who rule this people in Jerusalem.
¹⁵ You boast, "We have entered into a
covenant with death,
with the realm of the dead we have
made an agreement.
When an overwhelming scourge
sweeps by,
it cannot touch us,
for we have made a lie our refuge
and falsehoodᵇ our hiding place."

¹⁶ So this is what the Sovereign Lord
says:

"See, I lay a stone in Zion, a tested
stone,
a precious cornerstone for a sure
foundation;
the one who relies on it
will never be stricken with panic.

ᵃ 10 Hebrew / *sav lasav sav lasav / kav lakav kav
lakav* (probably meaningless sounds mimicking
the prophet's words); also in verse 13
ᵇ 15 Or *false gods*

¹⁷I will make justice the measuring line
  and righteousness the plumb line;
hail will sweep away your refuge, the
    lie,
  and water will overflow your hiding
    place.
¹⁸Your covenant with death will be
    annulled;
  your agreement with the realm of
    the dead will not stand.
When the overwhelming scourge
    sweeps by,
  you will be beaten down by it.
¹⁹As often as it comes it will carry you
    away;
  morning after morning, by day and
    by night,
  it will sweep through."

The understanding of this message
  will bring sheer terror.
²⁰The bed is too short to stretch out on,
  the blanket too narrow to wrap
    around you.
²¹The LORD will rise up as he did at
    Mount Perazim,
  he will rouse himself as in the
    Valley of Gibeon—
to do his work, his strange work,
  and perform his task, his alien
    task.
²²Now stop your mocking,
  or your chains will become
    heavier;
the Lord, the LORD Almighty, has
    told me
  of the destruction decreed against
    the whole land.

²³Listen and hear my voice;
  pay attention and hear what I say.
²⁴When a farmer plows for planting,
  does he plow continually?
Does he keep on breaking up and
    working the soil?
²⁵When he has leveled the surface,
  does he not sow caraway and
    scatter cumin?
Does he not plant wheat in its
    place,^a
  barley in its plot,^a
  and spelt in its field?

²⁶His God instructs him
  and teaches him the right way.

²⁷Caraway is not threshed with a sledge,
  nor is the wheel of a cart rolled over
    cumin;
caraway is beaten out with a rod,
  and cumin with a stick.
²⁸Grain must be ground to make
    bread;
  so one does not go on threshing it
    forever.
The wheels of a threshing cart may be
    rolled over it,
  but one does not use horses to grind
    grain.
²⁹All this also comes from the LORD
    Almighty,
  whose plan is wonderful,
  whose wisdom is magnificent.

Woe to David's City

29 Woe to you, Ariel, Ariel,
  the city where David
    settled!
Add year to year
  and let your cycle of festivals go on.
²Yet I will besiege Ariel;
  she will mourn and lament,
  she will be to me like an altar
    hearth.^b
³I will encamp against you on all
    sides;
  I will encircle you with towers
  and set up my siege works against
    you.
⁴Brought low, you will speak from the
    ground;
  your speech will mumble out of the
    dust.
Your voice will come ghostlike from
    the earth;
  out of the dust your speech will
    whisper.

⁵But your many enemies will become
    like fine dust,
  the ruthless hordes like blown
    chaff.

^a 25 The meaning of the Hebrew for this word
is uncertain.   ^b 2 The Hebrew for *altar hearth*
sounds like the Hebrew for *Ariel*.

Suddenly, in an instant,
6   the LORD Almighty will come
with thunder and earthquake and
        great noise,
    with windstorm and tempest and
        flames of a devouring fire.
7 Then the hordes of all the nations that
        fight against Ariel,
    that attack her and her fortress and
        besiege her,
will be as it is with a dream,
    with a vision in the night—
8 as when a hungry person dreams of
        eating,
    but awakens hungry still;
as when a thirsty person dreams of
        drinking,
    but awakens faint and thirsty still.
So will it be with the hordes of all the
        nations
    that fight against Mount Zion.

9 Be stunned and amazed,
    blind yourselves and be sightless;
be drunk, but not from wine,
    stagger, but not from beer.
10 The LORD has brought over you a
        deep sleep:
    He has sealed your eyes (the
        prophets);
    he has covered your heads (the seers).

11 For you this whole vision is nothing
but words sealed in a scroll. And if you
give the scroll to someone who can read,
and say, "Read this, please," they will answer, "I can't; it is sealed." 12 Or if you give
the scroll to someone who cannot read,
and say, "Read this, please," they will answer, "I don't know how to read."

13 The Lord says:

"These people come near to me with
        their mouth
    and honor me with their lips,
    but their hearts are far from me.
Their worship of me
    is based on merely human rules they
        have been taught.*
14 Therefore once more I will astound
        these people
    with wonder upon wonder;

the wisdom of the wise will perish,
    the intelligence of the intelligent
        will vanish."
15 Woe to those who go to great depths
        to hide their plans from the LORD,
    who do their work in darkness and
        think,
    "Who sees us? Who will know?"
16 You turn things upside down,
    as if the potter were thought to be
        like the clay!
Shall what is formed say to the one
        who formed it,
    "You did not make me"?
Can the pot say to the potter,
    "You know nothing"?

17 In a very short time, will not
        Lebanon be turned into a
        fertile field
    and the fertile field seem like a
        forest?
18 In that day the deaf will hear the
        words of the scroll,
    and out of gloom and darkness
        the eyes of the blind will see.
19 Once more the humble will rejoice in
        the LORD;
    the needy will rejoice in the Holy
        One of Israel.
20 The ruthless will vanish,
    the mockers will disappear,
    and all who have an eye for evil will
        be cut down—
21 those who with a word make someone
        out to be guilty,
    who ensnare the defender in court
    and with false testimony deprive the
        innocent of justice.

22 Therefore this is what the LORD, who
redeemed Abraham, says to the descendants of Jacob:

"No longer will Jacob be ashamed;
    no longer will their faces grow
        pale.
23 When they see among them their
        children,
    the work of my hands,

_____
*a 13 Hebrew; Septuagint They worship me in
vain; / their teachings are merely human rules_

they will keep my name holy;
they will acknowledge the holiness
of the Holy One of Jacob,
and will stand in awe of the God of
Israel.
²⁴Those who are wayward in spirit will
gain understanding;
those who complain will accept
instruction."

Woe to the Obstinate Nation

30 "Woe to the obstinate
children,"
declares the Lord,
"to those who carry out plans that are
not mine,
forming an alliance, but not by my
Spirit,
heaping sin upon sin;
²who go down to Egypt
without consulting me;
who look for help to Pharaoh's
protection,
to Egypt's shade for refuge.
³But Pharaoh's protection will be to
your shame,
Egypt's shade will bring you
disgrace.
⁴Though they have officials in Zoan
and their envoys have arrived in
Hanes,
⁵everyone will be put to shame
because of a people useless to them,
who bring neither help nor advantage,
but only shame and disgrace."

⁶A prophecy concerning the animals of
the Negev:

Through a land of hardship and
distress,
of lions and lionesses,
of adders and darting snakes,
the envoys carry their riches on
donkeys' backs,
their treasures on the humps of
camels,
to that unprofitable nation,
⁷ to Egypt, whose help is utterly
useless.
Therefore I call her
Rahab the Do-Nothing.

⁸Go now, write it on a tablet for them,
inscribe it on a scroll,
that for the days to come
it may be an everlasting witness.
⁹For these are rebellious people,
deceitful children,
children unwilling to listen to the
Lord's instruction.
¹⁰They say to the seers,
"See no more visions!"
and to the prophets,
"Give us no more visions of what is
right!
Tell us pleasant things,
prophesy illusions.
¹¹Leave this way,
get off this path,
and stop confronting us
with the Holy One of Israel!"

¹²Therefore this is what the Holy One
of Israel says:

"Because you have rejected this
message,
relied on oppression
and depended on deceit,
¹³this sin will become for you
like a high wall, cracked and
bulging,
that collapses suddenly, in an
instant.
¹⁴It will break in pieces like pottery,
shattered so mercilessly
that among its pieces not a fragment
will be found
for taking coals from a hearth
or scooping water out of a cistern."

¹⁵This is what the Sovereign Lord, the
Holy One of Israel, says:

"In repentance and rest is your
salvation,
in quietness and trust is your
strength,
but you would have none of it.
¹⁶You said, 'No, we will flee on horses.'
Therefore you will flee!
You said, 'We will ride off on swift
horses.'
Therefore your pursuers will be
swift!

¹⁷ A thousand will flee
at the threat of one;
at the threat of five
you will all flee away,
till you are left
like a flagstaff on a mountaintop,
like a banner on a hill."

¹⁸ Yet the LORD longs to be gracious to
you;
therefore he will rise up to show you
compassion.
For the LORD is a God of justice.
Blessed are all who wait for him!

¹⁹ People of Zion, who live in Jerusalem,
you will weep no more. How gracious he
will be when you cry for help! As soon as
he hears, he will answer you. ²⁰ Although
the Lord gives you the bread of adversity
and the water of affliction, your teachers
will be hidden no more; with your own
eyes you will see them. ²¹ Whether you
turn to the right or to the left, your ears
will hear a voice behind you, saying, "This
is the way; walk in it." ²² Then you will

ROCK SOLID *plans*

Isaiah 30:21

Listen for God to speak.

Moses heard God speak from a burning
bush (see Exodus 3:4). The little boy Samuel listened to God calling in the night (see
1 Samuel 3:10). And prophets throughout
the Bible relayed God's words in speeches,
songs, and letters. Christians today debate
whether God still speaks out loud, but the
Lord nevertheless promises you will hear
him. Listen for him whenever you open the
Bible, or hear a sermon at church, or chat
with Christian friends—wherever you hear
his truth. When you wonder where to go,
God will make sure you hear him say, "This
is the way; walk in it."

**Your next step: Ask God to help you
hear him leading you.**

desecrate your idols overlaid with silver
and your images covered with gold; you
will throw them away like a menstrual
cloth and say to them, "Away with you!"

²³ He will also send you rain for the
seed you sow in the ground, and the food
that comes from the land will be rich and
plentiful. In that day your cattle will graze
in broad meadows. ²⁴ The oxen and donkeys that work the soil will eat fodder and
mash, spread out with fork and shovel.
²⁵ In the day of great slaughter, when the
towers fall, streams of water will flow on
every high mountain and every lofty hill.
²⁶ The moon will shine like the sun, and
the sunlight will be seven times brighter,
like the light of seven full days, when the
LORD binds up the bruises of his people
and heals the wounds he inflicted.

²⁷ See, the Name of the LORD comes
from afar,
with burning anger and dense
clouds of smoke;
his lips are full of wrath,
and his tongue is a consuming fire.
²⁸ His breath is like a rushing torrent,
rising up to the neck.
He shakes the nations in the sieve of
destruction;
he places in the jaws of the peoples
a bit that leads them astray.
²⁹ And you will sing
as on the night you celebrate a holy
festival;
your hearts will rejoice
as when people playing pipes go up
to the mountain of the LORD,
to the Rock of Israel.
³⁰ The LORD will cause people to hear
his majestic voice
and will make them see his arm
coming down
with raging anger and consuming
fire,
with cloudburst, thunderstorm and
hail.
³¹ The voice of the LORD will shatter
Assyria;
with his rod he will strike them
down.

³²Every stroke the Lord lays on them
  with his punishing club
will be to the music of timbrels and
  harps,
    as he fights them in battle with the
      blows of his arm.
³³Topheth has long been prepared;
  it has been made ready for the
    king.
Its fire pit has been made deep and
  wide,
    with an abundance of fire and
      wood;
the breath of the Lord,
  like a stream of burning sulfur,
  sets it ablaze.

Woe to Those Who Rely on Egypt

31 Woe to those who go down
    to Egypt for help,
    who rely on horses,
who trust in the multitude of their
  chariots
and in the great strength of their
  horsemen,
but do not look to the Holy One of
  Israel,
  or seek help from the Lord.
²Yet he too is wise and can bring
  disaster;
  he does not take back his words.
He will rise up against that wicked
  nation,
  against those who help evildoers.
³But the Egyptians are mere mortals
  and not God;
  their horses are flesh and not
    spirit.
When the Lord stretches out his
  hand,
  those who help will stumble,
  those who are helped will fall;
  all will perish together.

⁴This is what the Lord says to me:

"As a lion growls,
  a great lion over its prey—
and though a whole band of shepherds
  is called together against it,
it is not frightened by their shouts
  or disturbed by their clamor—

so the Lord Almighty will come
  down
    to do battle on Mount Zion and on
      its heights.
⁵Like birds hovering overhead,
  the Lord Almighty will shield
    Jerusalem;
he will shield it and deliver it,
  he will 'pass over' it and will rescue
    it."

⁶Return, you Israelites, to the One you
have so greatly revolted against. ⁷For in
that day every one of you will reject the
idols of silver and gold your sinful hands
have made.

⁸"Assyria will fall by no human sword;
  a sword, not of mortals, will devour
    them.
They will flee before the sword
  and their young men will be put to
    forced labor.
⁹Their stronghold will fall because of
    terror;
  at the sight of the battle standard
    their commanders will panic,"
declares the Lord,
  whose fire is in Zion,
  whose furnace is in Jerusalem.

The Kingdom of Righteousness

32 See, a king will reign in
    righteousness
    and rulers will rule with
      justice.
²Each one will be like a shelter from
    the wind
  and a refuge from the storm,
like streams of water in the desert
  and the shadow of a great rock in a
    thirsty land.

³Then the eyes of those who see will no
    longer be closed,
  and the ears of those who hear will
    listen.
⁴The fearful heart will know and
    understand,
  and the stammering tongue will be
    fluent and clear.
⁵No longer will the fool be called noble
  nor the scoundrel be highly respected.

⁶For fools speak folly,
  their hearts are bent on evil:
They practice ungodliness
  and spread error concerning the Lord;
the hungry they leave empty
  and from the thirsty they withhold
    water.
⁷Scoundrels use wicked methods,
  they make up evil schemes
to destroy the poor with lies,
  even when the plea of the needy is
    just.
⁸But the noble make noble plans,
  and by noble deeds they stand.

The Women of Jerusalem

⁹You women who are so complacent,
  rise up and listen to me;
you daughters who feel secure,
  hear what I have to say!
¹⁰In little more than a year
  you who feel secure will tremble;
the grape harvest will fail,
  and the harvest of fruit will not come.
¹¹Tremble, you complacent women;
  shudder, you daughters who feel
    secure!
Strip off your fine clothes
  and wrap yourselves in rags.
¹²Beat your breasts for the pleasant fields,
  for the fruitful vines
¹³and for the land of my people,
  a land overgrown with thorns and
    briers—
yes, mourn for all houses of merriment
  and for this city of revelry.
¹⁴The fortress will be abandoned,
  the noisy city deserted;
citadel and watchtower will become a
    wasteland forever,
  the delight of donkeys, a pasture for
    flocks,
¹⁵till the Spirit is poured on us from on
    high,
  and the desert becomes a fertile field,
  and the fertile field seems like a
    forest.
¹⁶The Lord's justice will dwell in the
    desert,
  his righteousness live in the fertile
    field.

¹⁷The fruit of that righteousness will be
    peace;
  its effect will be quietness and
    confidence forever.
¹⁸My people will live in peaceful
    dwelling places,
  in secure homes,
  in undisturbed places of rest.
¹⁹Though hail flattens the forest
  and the city is leveled completely,
²⁰how blessed you will be,
  sowing your seed by every stream,
  and letting your cattle and donkeys
    range free.

Isaiah 32:15–20

Doing right brings good results.

Isaiah doesn't hold back the harsh words God told him to speak. He calls the women of Jerusalem "complacent" and "secure" but says they should "shudder" and put on ugly "rags" (Isaiah 32:9–11). These women were content with their cozy lives, but their happy world was about to be shattered. Their lives won't be right again until God shows up and pours out his Spirit. When the Lord comes, evil will no longer rule the land. His justice will reach even the desert. And get this: The effect of righteousness "will be quietness and confidence forever" (Isaiah 32:17). Those ancient women loved their lives of comfort, but true life only comes when we obey God's commands. The Lord is the real source of everything we really want—peace, security and blessing.

Think: How does obeying God bring you good results?

ROCK SOLID truths

Distress and Help

33 Woe to you, destroyer,
you who have not been
destroyed!
Woe to you, betrayer,
   you who have not been betrayed!
When you stop destroying,
   you will be destroyed;
when you stop betraying,
   you will be betrayed.

2 Lord, be gracious to us;
   we long for you.
Be our strength every morning,
   our salvation in time of distress.
3 At the uproar of your army, the
      peoples flee;
   when you rise up, the nations scatter.
4 Your plunder, O nations, is harvested
      as by young locusts;
   like a swarm of locusts people
      pounce on it.

5 The Lord is exalted, for he dwells on
      high;
   he will fill Zion with his justice and
      righteousness.
6 He will be the sure foundation for
      your times,
   a rich store of salvation and wisdom
      and knowledge;
   the fear of the Lord is the key to
      this treasure.ᵃ

7 Look, their brave men cry aloud in the
      streets;
   the envoys of peace weep bitterly.
8 The highways are deserted,
   no travelers are on the roads.
The treaty is broken,
   its witnessesᵇ are despised,
   no one is respected.
9 The land dries up and wastes away,
   Lebanon is ashamed and withers;
Sharon is like the Arabah,
   and Bashan and Carmel drop their
      leaves.

10 "Now will I arise," says the Lord.
   "Now will I be exalted;
   now will I be lifted up.
11 You conceive chaff,
   you give birth to straw;

your breath is a fire that consumes
   you.
12 The peoples will be burned to ashes;
   like cut thornbushes they will be set
      ablaze."

13 You who are far away, hear what I
      have done;
   you who are near, acknowledge my
      power!
14 The sinners in Zion are terrified;
   trembling grips the godless:
"Who of us can dwell with the
      consuming fire?
   Who of us can dwell with
      everlasting burning?"
15 Those who walk righteously
   and speak what is right,
who reject gain from extortion
   and keep their hands from
      accepting bribes,
who stop their ears against plots of
      murder
   and shut their eyes against
      contemplating evil—
16 they are the ones who will dwell on
      the heights,
   whose refuge will be the mountain
      fortress.
Their bread will be supplied,
   and water will not fail them.

17 Your eyes will see the king in his beauty
   and view a land that stretches afar.
18 In your thoughts you will ponder the
      former terror:
   "Where is that chief officer?
Where is the one who took the revenue?
   Where is the officer in charge of
      the towers?"
19 You will see those arrogant people no
      more,
   people whose speech is obscure,
   whose language is strange and
      incomprehensible.

20 Look on Zion, the city of our festivals;
   your eyes will see Jerusalem,
   a peaceful abode, a tent that will
      not be moved;

ᵃ 6 Or *is a treasure from him*   ᵇ 8 Dead Sea
Scrolls; Masoretic Text / *the cities*

its stakes will never be pulled up,
nor any of its ropes broken.
²¹ There the Lord will be our Mighty
One.
It will be like a place of broad rivers
and streams.
No galley with oars will ride them,
no mighty ship will sail them.
²² For the Lord is our judge,
the Lord is our lawgiver,
the Lord is our king;
it is he who will save us.

²³ Your rigging hangs loose:
The mast is not held secure,
the sail is not spread.
Then an abundance of spoils will be
divided
and even the lame will carry off
plunder.
²⁴ No one living in Zion will say, "I am
ill";
and the sins of those who dwell
there will be forgiven.

Judgment Against the Nations

34 Come near, you nations,
and listen;
pay attention, you peoples!
Let the earth hear, and all that is in it,
the world, and all that comes out of
it!
² The Lord is angry with all nations;
his wrath is on all their armies.
He will totally destroy*a* them,
he will give them over to slaughter.
³ Their slain will be thrown out,
their dead bodies will stink;
the mountains will be soaked with
their blood.
⁴ All the stars in the sky will be
dissolved
and the heavens rolled up like a
scroll;
all the starry host will fall
like withered leaves from the vine,
like shriveled figs from the fig tree.

⁵ My sword has drunk its fill in the
heavens;
see, it descends in judgment on
Edom,
the people I have totally destroyed.

⁶ The sword of the Lord is bathed in
blood,
it is covered with fat—
the blood of lambs and goats,
fat from the kidneys of rams.
For the Lord has a sacrifice in
Bozrah
and a great slaughter in the land of
Edom.
⁷ And the wild oxen will fall with them,
the bull calves and the great bulls.
Their land will be drenched with
blood,
and the dust will be soaked with fat.

⁸ For the Lord has a day of vengeance,
a year of retribution, to uphold
Zion's cause.
⁹ Edom's streams will be turned into
pitch,
her dust into burning sulfur;
her land will become blazing pitch!
¹⁰ It will not be quenched night or day;
its smoke will rise forever.
From generation to generation it will
lie desolate;
no one will ever pass through it
again.
¹¹ The desert owl*b* and screech owl*b* will
possess it;
the great owl*b* and the raven will
nest there.
God will stretch out over Edom
the measuring line of chaos
and the plumb line of desolation.
¹² Her nobles will have nothing there to
be called a kingdom,
all her princes will vanish away.
¹³ Thorns will overrun her citadels,
nettles and brambles her
strongholds.
She will become a haunt for jackals,
a home for owls.
¹⁴ Desert creatures will meet with
hyenas,
and wild goats will bleat to each
other;

---

a 2 The Hebrew term refers to the irrevocable
giving over of things or persons to the Lord,
often by totally destroying them; also in verse 5.
b 11 The precise identification of these birds is
uncertain.

there the night creatures will also lie
  down
  and find for themselves places of rest.
[15] The owl will nest there and lay eggs,
  she will hatch them, and care for
    her young
  under the shadow of her wings;
  there also the falcons will gather,
    each with its mate.

[16] Look in the scroll of the LORD and read:

None of these will be missing,
  not one will lack her mate.
For it is his mouth that has given the
    order,
  and his Spirit will gather them
    together.
[17] He allots their portions;
  his hand distributes them by measure.
They will possess it forever
  and dwell there from generation to
    generation.

Joy of the Redeemed

35 The desert and the parched
land will be glad;
  the wilderness will rejoice
and blossom.
Like the crocus, [2] it will burst into
    bloom;
  it will rejoice greatly and shout for
    joy.
The glory of Lebanon will be given
    to it,
  the splendor of Carmel and Sharon;
they will see the glory of the LORD,
  the splendor of our God.

[3] Strengthen the feeble hands,
  steady the knees that give way;
[4] say to those with fearful hearts,
  "Be strong, do not fear;
your God will come,
  he will come with vengeance;
with divine retribution
  he will come to save you."

[5] Then will the eyes of the blind be
    opened
  and the ears of the deaf unstopped.
[6] Then will the lame leap like a deer,
  and the mute tongue shout for joy.

Water will gush forth in the
    wilderness
  and streams in the desert.
[7] The burning sand will become a pool,
  the thirsty ground bubbling springs.
In the haunts where jackals once lay,
  grass and reeds and papyrus will
    grow.

[8] And a highway will be there;
  it will be called the Way of Holiness;
  it will be for those who walk on that
    Way.
The unclean will not journey on it;
  wicked fools will not go about on it.
[9] No lion will be there,
  nor any ravenous beast;
  they will not be found there.
But only the redeemed will walk there,
[10]   and those the LORD has rescued
    will return.
They will enter Zion with singing;
  everlasting joy will crown their
    heads.
Gladness and joy will overtake them,
  and sorrow and sighing will flee
    away.

Sennacherib Threatens Jerusalem

36 In the fourteenth year of
King Hezekiah's reign, Sennacherib king of Assyria at-
tacked all the fortified cities of Judah and
captured them. [2] Then the king of Assyria sent his field commander with a large
army from Lachish to King Hezekiah at
Jerusalem. When the commander stopped
at the aqueduct of the Upper Pool, on the
road to the Launderer's Field, [3] Eliakim
son of Hilkiah the palace administrator,
Shebna the secretary, and Joah son of
Asaph the recorder went out to him.
[4] The field commander said to them,
"Tell Hezekiah:

"'This is what the great king, the
king of Assyria, says: On what are
you basing this confidence of yours?
[5] You say you have counsel and might
for war—but you speak only empty
words. On whom are you depending,
that you rebel against me? [6] Look, I

know you are depending on Egypt, that splintered reed of a staff, which pierces the hand of anyone who leans on it! Such is Pharaoh king of Egypt to all who depend on him. [7]But if you say to me, "We are depending on the LORD our God"—isn't he the one whose high places and altars Hezekiah removed, saying to Judah and Jerusalem, "You must worship before this altar"?

[8]"'Come now, make a bargain with my master, the king of Assyria: I will give you two thousand horses—if you can put riders on them! [9]How then can you repulse one officer of the least of my master's officials, even though you are depending on Egypt for chariots and horsemen[a]? [10]Furthermore, have I come to attack and destroy this land without the LORD? The LORD himself told me to march against this country and destroy it.'"

[11]Then Eliakim, Shebna and Joah said to the field commander, "Please speak to your servants in Aramaic, since we understand it. Don't speak to us in Hebrew in the hearing of the people on the wall."

[12]But the commander replied, "Was it only to your master and you that my master sent me to say these things, and not to the people sitting on the wall—who, like you, will have to eat their own excrement and drink their own urine?"

[13]Then the commander stood and called out in Hebrew, "Hear the words of the great king, the king of Assyria! [14]This is what the king says: Do not let Hezekiah deceive you. He cannot deliver you! [15]Do not let Hezekiah persuade you to trust in the LORD when he says, 'The LORD will surely deliver us; this city will not be given into the hand of the king of Assyria.'

[16]"Do not listen to Hezekiah. This is what the king of Assyria says: Make peace with me and come out to me. Then each of you will eat fruit from your own vine and fig tree and drink water from your own cistern, [17]until I come and take you to a land like your own—a land of grain and new wine, a land of bread and vineyards.

[18]"Do not let Hezekiah mislead you when he says, 'The LORD will deliver us.' Have the gods of any nations ever delivered their lands from the hand of the king of Assyria? [19]Where are the gods of Hamath and Arpad? Where are the gods of Sepharvaim? Have they rescued Samaria from my hand? [20]Who of all the gods of these countries have been able to save their lands from me? How then can the LORD deliver Jerusalem from my hand?"

[21]But the people remained silent and said nothing in reply, because the king had commanded, "Do not answer him."

[22]Then Eliakim son of Hilkiah the palace administrator, Shebna the secretary and Joah son of Asaph the recorder went to Hezekiah, with their clothes torn, and told him what the field commander had said.

Jerusalem's Deliverance Foretold

37 When King Hezekiah heard this, he tore his clothes and put on sackcloth and went into the temple of the LORD. [2]He sent Eliakim the palace administrator, Shebna the secretary, and the leading priests, all wearing sackcloth, to the prophet Isaiah son of Amoz. [3]They told him, "This is what Hezekiah says: This day is a day of distress and rebuke and disgrace, as when children come to the moment of birth and there is no strength to deliver them. [4]It may be that the LORD your God will hear the words of the field commander, whom his master, the king of Assyria, has sent to ridicule the living God, and that he will rebuke him for the words the LORD your God has heard. Therefore pray for the remnant that still survives."

[5]When King Hezekiah's officials came to Isaiah, [6]Isaiah said to them, "Tell your master, 'This is what the LORD says: Do not be afraid of what you have heard—those words with which the underlings of the king of Assyria have blasphemed me. [7]Listen! When he hears a certain report, I will make him want to return to his own country, and there I will have him cut down with the sword.'"

[a] 9 Or *charioteers*

[8]When the field commander heard that the king of Assyria had left Lachish, he withdrew and found the king fighting against Libnah.

[9]Now Sennacherib received a report that Tirhakah, the king of Cush,[a] was marching out to fight against him. When he heard it, he sent messengers to Hezekiah with this word: [10]"Say to Hezekiah king of Judah: Do not let the god you depend on deceive you when he says, 'Jerusalem will not be given into the hands of the king of Assyria.' [11]Surely you have heard what the kings of Assyria have done to all the countries, destroying them completely. And will you be delivered? [12]Did the gods of the nations that were destroyed by my predecessors deliver them—the gods of Gozan, Harran, Rezeph and the people of Eden who were in Tel Assar? [13]Where is the king of Hamath or the king of Arpad? Where are the kings of Lair, Sepharvaim, Hena and Ivvah?"

Hezekiah's Prayer

[14]Hezekiah received the letter from the messengers and read it. Then he went up to the temple of the LORD and spread it out before the LORD. [15]And Hezekiah prayed to the LORD: [16]"LORD Almighty, the God of Israel, enthroned between the cherubim, you alone are God over all the kingdoms of the earth. You have made heaven and earth. [17]Give ear, LORD, and hear; open your eyes, LORD, and see; listen to all the words Sennacherib has sent to ridicule the living God.

[18]"It is true, LORD, that the Assyrian kings have laid waste all these peoples and their lands. [19]They have thrown their gods into the fire and destroyed them, for they were not gods but only wood and stone, fashioned by human hands. [20]Now, LORD our God, deliver us from his hand, so that all the kingdoms of the earth may know that you, LORD, are the only God.[b]"

Sennacherib's Fall

[21]Then Isaiah son of Amoz sent a message to Hezekiah: "This is what the LORD, the God of Israel, says: Because you have prayed to me concerning Sennacherib king of Assyria, [22]this is the word the LORD has spoken against him:

"Virgin Daughter Zion
    despises and mocks you.
Daughter Jerusalem
    tosses her head as you flee.
[23]Who is it you have ridiculed and
        blasphemed?
    Against whom have you raised your
        voice
and lifted your eyes in pride?
    Against the Holy One of Israel!
[24]By your messengers
    you have ridiculed the Lord.
And you have said,
    'With my many chariots
I have ascended the heights of the
        mountains,
    the utmost heights of Lebanon.
I have cut down its tallest cedars,
    the choicest of its junipers.
I have reached its remotest
        heights,
    the finest of its forests.
[25]I have dug wells in foreign lands[c]
    and drunk the water there.
With the soles of my feet
    I have dried up all the streams of
        Egypt.'

[26]"Have you not heard?
    Long ago I ordained it.
In days of old I planned it;
    now I have brought it to pass,
that you have turned fortified cities
    into piles of stone.
[27]Their people, drained of power,
    are dismayed and put to shame.
They are like plants in the field,
    like tender green shoots,
like grass sprouting on the roof,
    scorched[d] before it grows up.

---

[a] 9 That is, the upper Nile region   [b] 20 Dead Sea Scrolls (see also 2 Kings 19:19); Masoretic Text *you alone are the* LORD   [c] 25 Dead Sea Scrolls (see also 2 Kings 19:24); Masoretic Text does not have *in foreign lands.*   [d] 27 Some manuscripts of the Masoretic Text, Dead Sea Scrolls and some Septuagint manuscripts (see also 2 Kings 19:26); most manuscripts of the Masoretic Text *roof / and terraced fields*

28 "But I know where you are
   and when you come and go
   and how you rage against me.
29 Because you rage against me
   and because your insolence has
      reached my ears,
I will put my hook in your nose
   and my bit in your mouth,
and I will make you return
   by the way you came.

30 "This will be the sign for you, Hezekiah:

"This year you will eat what grows by
   itself,
   and the second year what springs
      from that.

But in the third year sow and reap,
   plant vineyards and eat their
      fruit.
31 Once more a remnant of the kingdom
      of Judah
   will take root below and bear fruit
      above.
32 For out of Jerusalem will come a
      remnant,
   and out of Mount Zion a band of
      survivors.

The zeal of the LORD Almighty
   will accomplish this.

33 "Therefore this is what the LORD says
concerning the king of Assyria:

Isaiah 36:1 — 37:20

Hezekiah prayed to God.

Hezekiah was six years into his reign over the southern kingdom of Judah when the northern kingdom of Israel was defeated by the Assyrians and its people dragged into captivity. God had predicted long before that he would judge his people if they didn't abandon their sins, threatening to send them into captivity as punishment for their worship of false gods (see 2 Kings 17:5 – 23). When judgment came, the people of Israel were taken to Assyria and conquered peoples from other nations settled on their land.

Hezekiah saw what happened to the north, and he feared his kingdom could face the same swift judgment. Only a few years later, in fact, Sennacherib king of Assyria conquered all the walled cities of Judah — all except for Jerusalem. From outside the wall he taunted that he would soon destroy the holy city.

Rather than give up, Hezekiah prayed. He worshiped God as king of the entire earth. He told the Lord not to ignore all the insults Sennacherib was spewing at heaven. He reminded the Lord that the Assyrians had conquered the peoples around them and dethroned their idols. And then Hezekiah asked that God would save them, "so that all the kingdoms of the earth may know that you, LORD, are the only God" (Isaiah 37:20).

When Hezekiah prayed, the Lord answered. He put to death 185,000 foreign soldiers, forcing Sennacherib to withdraw. And while the Assyrian king was back home worshiping his god Nisroch, his sons caught and murdered him (see Isaiah 37:36 – 38).

You can find Hezekiah in 2 Kings 18 – 20; 2 Chronicles 29 – 33; Isaiah 36 – 39; and Matthew 1:9.

UNSHAKEN people

"He will not enter this city
    or shoot an arrow here.
He will not come before it with shield
    or build a siege ramp against it.
³⁴By the way that he came he will
      return;
    he will not enter this city,"
                declares the LORD.
³⁵"I will defend this city and save it,
    for my sake and for the sake of
      David my servant!"

³⁶Then the angel of the LORD went out and put to death a hundred and eighty-five thousand in the Assyrian camp. When the people got up the next morning—there were all the dead bodies! ³⁷So Sennacherib king of Assyria broke camp and withdrew. He returned to Nineveh and stayed there.

³⁸One day, while he was worshiping in the temple of his god Nisrok, his sons Adrammelek and Sharezer killed him with the sword, and they escaped to the land of Ararat. And Esarhaddon his son succeeded him as king.

Hezekiah's Illness

38 In those days Hezekiah became ill and was at the point of death. The prophet Isaiah son of Amoz went to him and said, "This is what the LORD says: Put your house in order, because you are going to die; you will not recover."

²Hezekiah turned his face to the wall and prayed to the LORD, ³"Remember, LORD, how I have walked before you faithfully and with wholehearted devotion and have done what is good in your eyes." And Hezekiah wept bitterly.

⁴Then the word of the LORD came to Isaiah: ⁵"Go and tell Hezekiah, 'This is what the LORD, the God of your father David, says: I have heard your prayer and seen your tears; I will add fifteen years to your life. ⁶And I will deliver you and this city from the hand of the king of Assyria. I will defend this city.

⁷"'This is the LORD's sign to you that the LORD will do what he has promised: ⁸I will make the shadow cast by the sun go back the ten steps it has gone down on the stairway of Ahaz.'" So the sunlight went back the ten steps it had gone down.

⁹A writing of Hezekiah king of Judah after his illness and recovery:

¹⁰I said, "In the prime of my life
    must I go through the gates of
      death
    and be robbed of the rest of my
      years?"
¹¹I said, "I will not again see the LORD
      himself
    in the land of the living;
no longer will I look on my fellow
      man,
    or be with those who now dwell in
      this world.
¹²Like a shepherd's tent my house
    has been pulled down and taken
      from me.
Like a weaver I have rolled up my life,
    and he has cut me off from the
      loom;
    day and night you made an end of
      me.
¹³I waited patiently till dawn,
    but like a lion he broke all my
      bones;
    day and night you made an end of
      me.
¹⁴I cried like a swift or thrush,
    I moaned like a mourning dove.
My eyes grew weak as I looked to the
      heavens.
    I am being threatened; Lord, come
      to my aid!"

¹⁵But what can I say?
    He has spoken to me, and he
      himself has done this.
I will walk humbly all my years
    because of this anguish of my soul.
¹⁶Lord, by such things people live;
    and my spirit finds life in them too.
You restored me to health
    and let me live.
¹⁷Surely it was for my benefit
    that I suffered such anguish.
In your love you kept me
    from the pit of destruction;
you have put all my sins
    behind your back.

ROCK SOLID
promises

"You have put all my sins behind your back." Isaiah 38:17

When you confess your sins, God disposes of them and won't dig them up.

---

[18] For the grave cannot praise you,
    death cannot sing your praise;
those who go down to the pit
    cannot hope for your faithfulness.
[19] The living, the living—they praise you,
    as I am doing today;
parents tell their children
    about your faithfulness.

[20] The LORD will save me,
    and we will sing with stringed
        instruments
all the days of our lives
    in the temple of the LORD.

[21] Isaiah had said, "Prepare a poultice of figs and apply it to the boil, and he will recover." [22] Hezekiah had asked, "What will be the sign that I will go up to the temple of the LORD?"

Envoys From Babylon

39 At that time Marduk-Baladan son of Baladan king of Babylon sent Hezekiah letters and a gift, because he had heard of his illness and recovery. [2] Hezekiah received the envoys gladly and showed them what was in his storehouses—the silver, the gold, the spices, the fine olive oil— his entire armory and everything found among his treasures. There was nothing in his palace or in all his kingdom that Hezekiah did not show them.

848

[3] Then Isaiah the prophet went to King Hezekiah and asked, "What did those men say, and where did they come from?"

"From a distant land," Hezekiah replied. "They came to me from Babylon."

[4] The prophet asked, "What did they see in your palace?"

"They saw everything in my palace," Hezekiah said. "There is nothing among my treasures that I did not show them."

[5] Then Isaiah said to Hezekiah, "Hear the word of the LORD Almighty: [6] The time will surely come when everything in your palace, and all that your predecessors have stored up until this day, will be carried off to Babylon. Nothing will be left, says the LORD. [7] And some of your descendants, your own flesh and blood who will be born to you, will be taken away, and they will become eunuchs in the palace of the king of Babylon."

[8] "The word of the LORD you have spoken is good," Hezekiah replied. For he thought, "There will be peace and security in my lifetime."

Comfort for God's People

40 Comfort, comfort my people,
        says your God.
[2] Speak tenderly to Jerusalem,
    and proclaim to her
that her hard service has been
        completed,
    that her sin has been paid for,
    that she has received from the LORD's
        hand
    double for all her sins.

[3] A voice of one calling:
"In the wilderness prepare
    the way for the LORD[a];
make straight in the desert
    a highway for our God.[b]
[4] Every valley shall be raised up,
    every mountain and hill made low;
the rough ground shall become level,
    the rugged places a plain.

---

[a] 3 Or *A voice of one calling in the wilderness: / "Prepare the way for the LORD*   [b] 3 Hebrew; Septuagint *make straight the paths of our God*

⁵And the glory of the Lord will be
    revealed,
    and all people will see it together.
                For the mouth of the
                Lord has spoken."

⁶A voice says, "Cry out."
    And I said, "What shall I cry?"

"All people are like grass,
    and all their faithfulness is like the
    flowers of the field.
⁷The grass withers and the flowers
    fall,
    because the breath of the Lord
    blows on them.
    Surely the people are grass.
⁸The grass withers and the flowers
    fall,
    but the word of our God endures
    forever."

⁹You who bring good news to Zion,
    go up on a high mountain.
You who bring good news to
    Jerusalem,ᵃ
    lift up your voice with a shout,
lift it up, do not be afraid;
    say to the towns of Judah,
    "Here is your God!"
¹⁰See, the Sovereign Lord comes with
    power,
    and he rules with a mighty arm.
See, his reward is with him,
    and his recompense accompanies
    him.
¹¹He tends his flock like a shepherd:
    He gathers the lambs in his arms
and carries them close to his heart;
    he gently leads those that have
    young.

¹²Who has measured the waters in the
    hollow of his hand,
    or with the breadth of his hand
    marked off the heavens?
Who has held the dust of the earth in
    a basket,
    or weighed the mountains on the
    scales
    and the hills in a balance?
¹³Who can fathom the Spiritᵇ of the
    Lord,

or instruct the Lord as his
    counselor?
¹⁴Whom did the Lord consult to
    enlighten him,
    and who taught him the right way?
Who was it that taught him
    knowledge,
    or showed him the path of
    understanding?

¹⁵Surely the nations are like a drop in a
    bucket;
    they are regarded as dust on the
    scales;
    he weighs the islands as though
    they were fine dust.
¹⁶Lebanon is not sufficient for altar
    fires,
    nor its animals enough for burnt
    offerings.
¹⁷Before him all the nations are as
    nothing;
    they are regarded by him as
    worthless
    and less than nothing.

¹⁸With whom, then, will you compare
    God?
    To what image will you liken him?
¹⁹As for an idol, a metalworker casts it,
    and a goldsmith overlays it with
    gold
    and fashions silver chains for it.
²⁰A person too poor to present such an
    offering
    selects wood that will not rot;
    they look for a skilled worker
    to set up an idol that will not
    topple.

²¹Do you not know?
    Have you not heard?
Has it not been told you from the
    beginning?
    Have you not understood since the
    earth was founded?
²²He sits enthroned above the circle of
    the earth,
    and its people are like grasshoppers.

ᵃ 9 Or Zion, bringer of good news, / go up on a high
mountain. / Jerusalem, bringer of good news
ᵇ 13 Or mind

He stretches out the heavens like a
canopy,
and spreads them out like a tent to
live in.
²³ He brings princes to naught
and reduces the rulers of this world
to nothing.
²⁴ No sooner are they planted,
no sooner are they sown,
no sooner do they take root in the
ground,
than he blows on them and they
wither,
and a whirlwind sweeps them away
like chaff.

²⁵ "To whom will you compare me?
Or who is my equal?" says the Holy
One.
²⁶ Lift up your eyes and look to the
heavens:
Who created all these?
He who brings out the starry host one
by one
and calls forth each of them by
name.
Because of his great power and mighty
strength,
not one of them is missing.

²⁷ Why do you complain, Jacob?
Why do you say, Israel,
"My way is hidden from the LORD;
my cause is disregarded by my
God"?
²⁸ Do you not know?
Have you not heard?
The LORD is the everlasting God,
the Creator of the ends of the earth.
He will not grow tired or weary,
and his understanding no one can
fathom.
²⁹ He gives strength to the weary
and increases the power of the
weak.
³⁰ Even youths grow tired and weary,
and young men stumble and fall;
³¹ but those who hope in the LORD
will renew their strength.
They will soar on wings like eagles;
they will run and not grow weary,
they will walk and not be faint.

850

ROCK SOLID *promises*

"Those who hope in the LORD will renew their strength. They will soar on wings like eagles."

Isaiah 40:31

Trusting God puts wind beneath your wings.

The Helper of Israel

41 "Be silent before me, you
islands!
Let the nations renew their
strength!
Let them come forward and speak;
let us meet together at the place of
judgment.

² "Who has stirred up one from the east,
calling him in righteousness to his
service[a]?
He hands nations over to him
and subdues kings before him.
He turns them to dust with his sword,
to windblown chaff with his bow.
³ He pursues them and moves on
unscathed,
by a path his feet have not traveled
before.
⁴ Who has done this and carried it
through,
calling forth the generations from
the beginning?
I, the LORD—with the first of them
and with the last—I am he."

⁵ The islands have seen it and fear;
the ends of the earth tremble.
They approach and come forward;
⁶ they help each other
and say to their companions, "Be
strong!"

[a] 2 Or *east, / whom victory meets at every step*

⁷The metalworker encourages the
    goldsmith,
and the one who smooths with the
    hammer
spurs on the one who strikes the
    anvil.
One says of the welding, "It is good."
    The other nails down the idol so it
    will not topple.

⁸"But you, Israel, my servant,
    Jacob, whom I have chosen,
    you descendants of Abraham my
    friend,
⁹I took you from the ends of the earth,
    from its farthest corners I called you.
I said, 'You are my servant';
    I have chosen you and have not
    rejected you.
¹⁰So do not fear, for I am with you;
    do not be dismayed, for I am your
    God.
I will strengthen you and help you;
    I will uphold you with my righteous
    right hand.

¹¹"All who rage against you
    will surely be ashamed and disgraced;
those who oppose you
    will be as nothing and perish.
¹²Though you search for your enemies,
    you will not find them.
Those who wage war against you
    will be as nothing at all.
¹³For I am the LORD your God
    who takes hold of your right hand
and says to you, Do not fear;
    I will help you.
¹⁴Do not be afraid, you worm Jacob,
    little Israel, do not fear,
for I myself will help you," declares
    the LORD,
    your Redeemer, the Holy One of
    Israel.
¹⁵"See, I will make you into a threshing
    sledge,
    new and sharp, with many teeth.
You will thresh the mountains and
    crush them,
    and reduce the hills to chaff.

ROCK SOLID principles

Isaiah 41:8–14

Fear no one.

Emily shook at the thought of auditioning for the spring play, but she still wanted to try. She didn't want any kind of a big part—just a chance to meet people, find out if she liked drama, and overcome her dread of being up in front of a crowd. Emily's fears weren't exactly soothed when a couple of theatre regulars told her she didn't have a chance of making the cast. When it came time for auditions, all of Emily's breathing exercises just weren't enough. She didn't calm down until she realized God was with her on stage ... and in the auditorium seats ... and sitting right next to the director. Just like he promised, God was there.

The kingdom of Israel felt small and vulnerable amid dominant neighboring nations who threatened death and disgrace. But God reminded Israel that he chose them. He promised to grab them by the hand and protect them. His promise isn't just nice words. Whether or not you feel God nearby, he really is there to help. So let go of your fear.

¹⁶ You will winnow them, the wind will
pick them up,
and a gale will blow them away.
But you will rejoice in the LORD
and glory in the Holy One of Israel.

¹⁷ "The poor and needy search for water,
but there is none;
their tongues are parched with
thirst.
But I the LORD will answer them;
I, the God of Israel, will not forsake
them.
¹⁸ I will make rivers flow on barren
heights,
and springs within the valleys.
I will turn the desert into pools of
water,
and the parched ground into springs.
¹⁹ I will put in the desert
the cedar and the acacia, the myrtle
and the olive.
I will set junipers in the wasteland,
the fir and the cypress together,
²⁰ so that people may see and know,
may consider and understand,
that the hand of the LORD has done
this,
that the Holy One of Israel has
created it.

²¹ "Present your case," says the LORD.
"Set forth your arguments," says
Jacob's King.
²² "Tell us, you idols,
what is going to happen.
Tell us what the former things were,
so that we may consider them
and know their final outcome.
Or declare to us the things to come,
²³ tell us what the future holds,
so we may know that you are gods.
Do something, whether good or bad,
so that we will be dismayed and
filled with fear.
²⁴ But you are less than nothing
and your works are utterly worthless;
whoever chooses you is detestable.

²⁵ "I have stirred up one from the north,
and he comes—
one from the rising sun who calls on
my name.

He treads on rulers as if they were
mortar,
as if he were a potter treading the
clay.
²⁶ Who told of this from the beginning,
so we could know,
or beforehand, so we could say, 'He
was right'?
No one told of this,
no one foretold it,
no one heard any words from you.
²⁷ I was the first to tell Zion, 'Look, here
they are!'
I gave to Jerusalem a messenger of
good news.
²⁸ I look but there is no one—
no one among the gods to give
counsel,
no one to give answer when I ask
them.
²⁹ See, they are all false!
Their deeds amount to nothing;
their images are but wind and
confusion.

The Servant of the LORD

42 "Here is my servant, whom
I uphold,
my chosen one in whom I
delight;
I will put my Spirit on him,
and he will bring justice to the
nations.
² He will not shout or cry out,
or raise his voice in the streets.
³ A bruised reed he will not break,
and a smoldering wick he will not
snuff out.
In faithfulness he will bring forth
justice;
⁴ he will not falter or be discouraged
till he establishes justice on earth.
In his teaching the islands will put
their hope."

⁵ This is what God the LORD says—
the Creator of the heavens, who
stretches them out,
who spreads out the earth with all
that springs from it,
who gives breath to its people,
and life to those who walk on it:

⁶ "I, the LORD, have called you in
    righteousness;
  I will take hold of your hand.
I will keep you and will make you
    to be a covenant for the people
    and a light for the Gentiles,
⁷ to open eyes that are blind,
    to free captives from prison
    and to release from the dungeon
      those who sit in darkness.

⁸ "I am the LORD; that is my name!
  I will not yield my glory to
      another
    or my praise to idols.
⁹ See, the former things have taken
      place,
    and new things I declare;
  before they spring into being
    I announce them to you."

Song of Praise to the LORD

¹⁰ Sing to the LORD a new song,
    his praise from the ends of the
      earth,
  you who go down to the sea, and all
      that is in it,
    you islands, and all who live in
      them.
¹¹ Let the wilderness and its towns raise
      their voices;
    let the settlements where Kedar
      lives rejoice.
  Let the people of Sela sing for joy;
    let them shout from the
      mountaintops.
¹² Let them give glory to the LORD
    and proclaim his praise in the
      islands.
¹³ The LORD will march out like a
      champion,
    like a warrior he will stir up his
      zeal;
  with a shout he will raise the battle
      cry
    and will triumph over his enemies.

¹⁴ "For a long time I have kept silent,
    I have been quiet and held myself
      back.
  But now, like a woman in childbirth,
    I cry out, I gasp and pant.

¹⁵ I will lay waste the mountains and
      hills
    and dry up all their vegetation;
  I will turn rivers into islands
    and dry up the pools.
¹⁶ I will lead the blind by ways they have
      not known,
    along unfamiliar paths I will guide
      them;
  I will turn the darkness into light
      before them
    and make the rough places smooth.
  These are the things I will do;
    I will not forsake them.
¹⁷ But those who trust in idols,
    who say to images, 'You are our
      gods,'
    will be turned back in utter shame.

Israel Blind and Deaf

¹⁸ "Hear, you deaf;
    look, you blind, and see!
¹⁹ Who is blind but my servant,
    and deaf like the messenger I send?
  Who is blind like the one in covenant
      with me,
    blind like the servant of the LORD?
²⁰ You have seen many things, but you
      pay no attention;
    your ears are open, but you do not
      listen."

²¹ It pleased the LORD
    for the sake of his righteousness
    to make his law great and glorious.
²² But this is a people plundered and
      looted,
    all of them trapped in pits
    or hidden away in prisons.
  They have become plunder,
    with no one to rescue them;
  they have been made loot,
    with no one to say, "Send them
      back."

²³ Which of you will listen to this
    or pay close attention in time to
      come?
²⁴ Who handed Jacob over to become
      loot,
    and Israel to the plunderers?
  Was it not the LORD,
    against whom we have sinned?

For they would not follow his ways;
    they did not obey his law.
²⁵ So he poured out on them his burning
        anger,
    the violence of war.
It enveloped them in flames, yet they
        did not understand;
    it consumed them, but they did not
        take it to heart.

Israel's Only Savior

43 But now, this is what the
    LORD says—
he who created you, Jacob,
he who formed you, Israel:
"Do not fear, for I have redeemed you;
    I have summoned you by name; you
        are mine.

ROCK SOLID *promises*

**"I have summoned you by name;
you are mine."** Isaiah 43:1

God not only knows who you are but he
calls you by name. He aches to remind
you that you belong to him.

² When you pass through the waters,
    I will be with you;
and when you pass through the rivers,
    they will not sweep over you.
When you walk through the fire,
    you will not be burned;
    the flames will not set you ablaze.
³ For I am the LORD your God,
    the Holy One of Israel, your
        Savior;
I give Egypt for your ransom,
    Cush*ᵃ* and Seba in your stead.
⁴ Since you are precious and honored in
        my sight,
    and because I love you,

I will give people in exchange for
        you,
    nations in exchange for your life.
⁵ Do not be afraid, for I am with you;
    I will bring your children from the
        east
    and gather you from the west.
⁶ I will say to the north, 'Give them
        up!'
    and to the south, 'Do not hold them
        back.'
Bring my sons from afar
    and my daughters from the ends of
        the earth—
⁷ everyone who is called by my name,
    whom I created for my glory,
    whom I formed and made."

⁸ Lead out those who have eyes but are
        blind,
    who have ears but are deaf.
⁹ All the nations gather together
    and the peoples assemble.
Which of their gods foretold this
    and proclaimed to us the former
        things?
Let them bring in their witnesses to
        prove they were right,
    so that others may hear and say, "It
        is true."
¹⁰ "You are my witnesses," declares the
        LORD,
    "and my servant whom I have
        chosen,
so that you may know and believe me
    and understand that I am he.
Before me no god was formed,
    nor will there be one after me.
¹¹ I, even I, am the LORD,
    and apart from me there is no
        savior.
¹² I have revealed and saved and
        proclaimed—
    I, and not some foreign god among
        you.
You are my witnesses," declares the
    LORD, "that I am God.
¹³   Yes, and from ancient days I am he.
No one can deliver out of my hand.
    When I act, who can reverse it?"

ᵃ 3 That is, the upper Nile region

God's Mercy and Israel's Unfaithfulness

¹⁴This is what the LORD says—
  your Redeemer, the Holy One of
    Israel:
"For your sake I will send to Babylon
  and bring down as fugitives all the
    Babylonians,ª
  in the ships in which they took
    pride.
¹⁵I am the LORD, your Holy One,
  Israel's Creator, your King."

¹⁶This is what the LORD says—
  he who made a way through the sea,
  a path through the mighty waters,
¹⁷who drew out the chariots and horses,
  the army and reinforcements
    together,
  and they lay there, never to rise again,
  extinguished, snuffed out like a
    wick:
¹⁸"Forget the former things;
  do not dwell on the past.
¹⁹See, I am doing a new thing!
  Now it springs up; do you not
    perceive it?
I am making a way in the wilderness
  and streams in the wasteland.
²⁰The wild animals honor me,
  the jackals and the owls,
because I provide water in the
    wilderness
  and streams in the wasteland,
to give drink to my people, my chosen,
²¹ the people I formed for myself
  that they may proclaim my praise.

²²"Yet you have not called on me, Jacob,
  you have not wearied yourselves forᵇ
    me, Israel.
²³You have not brought me sheep for
    burnt offerings,
  nor honored me with your
    sacrifices.
I have not burdened you with grain
    offerings
  nor wearied you with demands for
    incense.
²⁴You have not bought any fragrant
    calamus for me,
  or lavished on me the fat of your
    sacrifices.

But you have burdened me with your
    sins
  and wearied me with your offenses.

²⁵"I, even I, am he who blots out
  your transgressions, for my own
    sake,
  and remembers your sins no more.
²⁶Review the past for me,
  let us argue the matter together;
  state the case for your innocence.
²⁷Your first father sinned;
  those I sent to teach you rebelled
    against me.
²⁸So I disgraced the dignitaries of your
    temple;
  I consigned Jacob to destructionᶜ
  and Israel to scorn.

ª 14 Or *Chaldeans*   ᵇ 22 Or *Jacob; / surely you
have grown weary of*   ᶜ 28 The Hebrew term
refers to the irrevocable giving over of things or
persons to the LORD, often by totally destroying
them.

UNSHAKEN God

Isaiah 43:25

God is forgetful.

God is all-knowing or "omniscient,"
knowing every possible detail of who you
are and what you think, say, and do (see
Psalm 139:2). So he can't literally forget
something you do wrong. But the Lord
explains what he does with your sins—
his attitude toward them. He "blots out
your transgressions," that is, he covers
them up—but only after you uncover
and confess them. He "remembers your
sins no more"—but only after you recall
and admit what you did wrong (Isaiah
43:25). Amazingly, the Lord forgives and
forgets your sins. He won't bring them up
again. Every time you admit your sins to
God, he forgives you (see 1 John 1:8–9).

**So ... Why remember and learn from
your sins? When and why should
you forget them?**

Israel the Chosen

44 "But now listen, Jacob, my servant,
Israel, whom I have chosen.
² This is what the LORD says—
he who made you, who formed you
in the womb,
and who will help you:
Do not be afraid, Jacob, my servant,
Jeshurun,^a whom I have chosen.
³ For I will pour water on the thirsty
land,
and streams on the dry ground;
I will pour out my Spirit on your
offspring,
and my blessing on your
descendants.
⁴ They will spring up like grass in a
meadow,
like poplar trees by flowing streams.
⁵ Some will say, 'I belong to the LORD';
others will call themselves by the
name of Jacob;
still others will write on their hand,
'The LORD's,'
and will take the name Israel.

The LORD, Not Idols

⁶ "This is what the LORD says—
Israel's King and Redeemer, the
LORD Almighty:
I am the first and I am the last;
apart from me there is no God.
⁷ Who then is like me? Let him
proclaim it.
Let him declare and lay out before me
what has happened since I established
my ancient people,
and what is yet to come—
yes, let them foretell what will come.
⁸ Do not tremble, do not be afraid.
Did I not proclaim this and foretell
it long ago?
You are my witnesses. Is there any
God besides me?
No, there is no other Rock; I know
not one."

⁹ All who make idols are nothing,
and the things they treasure are
worthless.

Those who would speak up for them
are blind;
they are ignorant, to their own
shame.
¹⁰ Who shapes a god and casts an idol,
which can profit nothing?
¹¹ People who do that will be put to
shame;
such craftsmen are only human
beings.
Let them all come together and take
their stand;
they will be brought down to terror
and shame.

¹² The blacksmith takes a tool
and works with it in the coals;
he shapes an idol with hammers,
he forges it with the might of his arm.
He gets hungry and loses his strength;
he drinks no water and grows faint.
¹³ The carpenter measures with a line
and makes an outline with a
marker;
he roughs it out with chisels
and marks it with compasses.
He shapes it in human form,
human form in all its glory,
that it may dwell in a shrine.
¹⁴ He cut down cedars,
or perhaps took a cypress or oak.
He let it grow among the trees of the
forest,
or planted a pine, and the rain made
it grow.
¹⁵ It is used as fuel for burning;
some of it he takes and warms
himself,
he kindles a fire and bakes bread.
But he also fashions a god and
worships it;
he makes an idol and bows down
to it.
¹⁶ Half of the wood he burns in the fire;
over it he prepares his meal,
he roasts his meat and eats his fill.
He also warms himself and says,
"Ah! I am warm; I see the fire."
¹⁷ From the rest he makes a god, his idol;
he bows down to it and worships.

^a 2 *Jeshurun* means *the upright one,* that is, Israel.

He prays to it and says,
"Save me! You are my god!"
18 They know nothing, they understand
nothing;
their eyes are plastered over so they
cannot see,
and their minds closed so they
cannot understand.
19 No one stops to think,
no one has the knowledge or
understanding to say,
"Half of it I used for fuel;
I even baked bread over its coals,
I roasted meat and I ate.
Shall I make a detestable thing from
what is left?
Shall I bow down to a block of wood?"
20 Such a person feeds on ashes; a
deluded heart misleads him;
he cannot save himself, or say,
"Is not this thing in my right hand a
lie?"

21 "Remember these things, Jacob,
for you, Israel, are my servant.
I have made you, you are my servant;
Israel, I will not forget you.
22 I have swept away your offenses like a
cloud,
your sins like the morning mist.
Return to me,
for I have redeemed you."

23 Sing for joy, you heavens, for the
LORD has done this;
shout aloud, you earth beneath.
Burst into song, you mountains,
you forests and all your trees,
for the LORD has redeemed Jacob,
he displays his glory in Israel.

Jerusalem to Be Inhabited

24 "This is what the LORD says—
your Redeemer, who formed you in
the womb:

I am the LORD,
the Maker of all things,
who stretches out the heavens,
who spreads out the earth by
myself,
25 who foils the signs of false prophets
and makes fools of diviners,

Isaiah 44:10–23
No one made God.

You can almost see God smile like a stand-up comic as he mocks the foolishness of idols and people who worship them. He describes how a blacksmith bangs out an idol with a hammer. He details how a carpenter carves a god out of a log and uses the leftover wood to build a fire. The man bows to half of a hunk of wood, and he bakes bread with the other half. And no one pauses to realize how stupid this is. The Lord says, "Remember these things . . . I have made you" (Isaiah 44:21). People think they can make a god. But God made people. And no one made God. The Lord drove home this point from the first moment he told humankind his name. He called himself "I AM WHO I AM," or "Yahweh," the one who has always existed (Exodus 3:14).

Think: How would you answer someone who asked you, "Who made God?"

ROCK SOLID truths

who overthrows the learning of the
wise
and turns it into nonsense,
26 who carries out the words of his
servants
and fulfills the predictions of his
messengers,

who says of Jerusalem, 'It shall be
inhabited,'
of the towns of Judah, 'They shall
be rebuilt,'
and of their ruins, 'I will restore
them,'
27 who says to the watery deep, 'Be dry,
and I will dry up your streams,'

²⁸who says of Cyrus, 'He is my shepherd
and will accomplish all that I
please;
he will say of Jerusalem, "Let it be
rebuilt,"
and of the temple, "Let its
foundations be laid."'

45

"This is what the LORD
says to his anointed,
to Cyrus, whose right hand
I take hold of
to subdue nations before him
and to strip kings of their armor,
to open doors before him
so that gates will not be shut:
²I will go before you
and will level the mountains*;
I will break down gates of bronze
and cut through bars of iron.
³I will give you hidden treasures,
riches stored in secret places,
so that you may know that I am the
LORD,
the God of Israel, who summons
you by name.
⁴For the sake of Jacob my servant,
of Israel my chosen,
I summon you by name
and bestow on you a title of honor,
though you do not acknowledge me.
⁵I am the LORD, and there is no other;
apart from me there is no God.
I will strengthen you,
though you have not acknowledged
me,
⁶so that from the rising of the sun
to the place of its setting
people may know there is none besides
me.
I am the LORD, and there is no
other.
⁷I form the light and create darkness,
I bring prosperity and create
disaster;
I, the LORD, do all these things.

⁸"You heavens above, rain down my
righteousness;
let the clouds shower it down.
Let the earth open wide,
let salvation spring up,

let righteousness flourish with it;
I, the LORD, have created it.

⁹"Woe to those who quarrel with their
Maker,
those who are nothing but
potsherds
among the potsherds on the ground.
Does the clay say to the potter,
'What are you making?'
Does your work say,
'The potter has no hands'?
¹⁰Woe to the one who says to a father,
'What have you begotten?'
or to a mother,
'What have you brought to birth?'

¹¹"This is what the LORD says—
the Holy One of Israel, and its
Maker:
Concerning things to come,
do you question me about my
children,
or give me orders about the work of
my hands?
¹²It is I who made the earth
and created mankind on it.
My own hands stretched out the
heavens;
I marshaled their starry hosts.
¹³I will raise up Cyrusᵇ in my
righteousness:
I will make all his ways straight.
He will rebuild my city
and set my exiles free,
but not for a price or reward,
says the LORD Almighty."

¹⁴This is what the LORD says:

"The products of Egypt and the
merchandise of Cush,ᶜ
and those tall Sabeans—
they will come over to you
and will be yours;
they will trudge behind you,
coming over to you in chains.
They will bow down before you
and plead with you, saying,

―――――――――

ᵃ 2 Dead Sea Scrolls and Septuagint; the
meaning of the word in the Masoretic Text is
uncertain.   *ᵇ 13* Hebrew *him*   *ᶜ 14* That is,
the upper Nile region

'Surely God is with you, and there is
no other;
there is no other god.'"

¹⁵Truly you are a God who has been
hiding himself,
the God and Savior of Israel.
¹⁶All the makers of idols will be put to
shame and disgraced;
they will go off into disgrace
together.
¹⁷But Israel will be saved by the Lord
with an everlasting salvation;
you will never be put to shame or
disgraced,
to ages everlasting.

¹⁸For this is what the Lord says—
he who created the heavens,
he is God;
he who fashioned and made the earth,
he founded it;
he did not create it to be empty,
but formed it to be inhabited—
he says:
"I am the Lord,
and there is no other.
¹⁹I have not spoken in secret,
from somewhere in a land of
darkness;
I have not said to Jacob's descendants,
'Seek me in vain.'
I, the Lord, speak the truth;
I declare what is right.

²⁰"Gather together and come;
assemble, you fugitives from the
nations.
Ignorant are those who carry about
idols of wood,
who pray to gods that cannot save.
²¹Declare what is to be, present it—
let them take counsel together.
Who foretold this long ago,
who declared it from the distant
past?
Was it not I, the Lord?
And there is no God apart from me,
a righteous God and a Savior;
there is none but me.

²²"Turn to me and be saved,
all you ends of the earth;
for I am God, and there is no other.
²³By myself I have sworn,
my mouth has uttered in all
integrity
a word that will not be revoked:
Before me every knee will bow;
by me every tongue will swear.
²⁴They will say of me, 'In the Lord
alone
are deliverance and strength.'"
All who have raged against him
will come to him and be put to
shame.
²⁵But all the descendants of Israel
will find deliverance in the Lord
and will make their boast in him.

Gods of Babylon

46 Bel bows down, Nebo
stoops low;
their idols are borne by
beasts of burden.^a
The images that are carried about are
burdensome,
a burden for the weary.
²They stoop and bow down together;
unable to rescue the burden,
they themselves go off into captivity.

³"Listen to me, you descendants of
Jacob,
all the remnant of the people of
Israel,

ROCK SOLID promises

**"I have not spoken in secret, from
somewhere in a land of darkness."**

Isaiah 45:19

**God doesn't whisper his point. He speaks
loud and clear so you can hear.**

^a 1 Or *are but beasts and cattle*

you whom I have upheld since your
birth,
and have carried since you were
born.
⁴ Even to your old age and gray hairs
I am he, I am he who will sustain
you.
I have made you and I will carry you;
I will sustain you and I will rescue
you.

⁵ "With whom will you compare me or
count me equal?
To whom will you liken me that we
may be compared?
⁶ Some pour out gold from their bags
and weigh out silver on the scales;
they hire a goldsmith to make it into a
god,
and they bow down and worship it.
⁷ They lift it to their shoulders and
carry it;
they set it up in its place, and there
it stands.
From that spot it cannot move.
Even though someone cries out to it, it
cannot answer;
it cannot save them from their
troubles.

⁸ "Remember this, keep it in mind,
take it to heart, you rebels.
⁹ Remember the former things, those of
long ago;
I am God, and there is no other;
I am God, and there is none like me.
¹⁰ I make known the end from the
beginning,
from ancient times, what is still to
come.
I say, 'My purpose will stand,
and I will do all that I please.'
¹¹ From the east I summon a bird of
prey;
from a far-off land, a man to fulfill
my purpose.
What I have said, that I will bring
about;
what I have planned, that I will do.
¹² Listen to me, you stubborn-hearted,
you who are now far from my
righteousness.

¹³ I am bringing my righteousness near,
it is not far away;
and my salvation will not be
delayed.
I will grant salvation to Zion,
my splendor to Israel.

The Fall of Babylon

47 "Go down, sit in the dust,
Virgin Daughter Babylon;
sit on the ground without a
throne,
queen city of the Babylonians.ᵃ
No more will you be called
tender or delicate.
² Take millstones and grind flour;
take off your veil.
Lift up your skirts, bare your legs,
and wade through the streams.
³ Your nakedness will be exposed
and your shame uncovered.
I will take vengeance;
I will spare no one."

⁴ Our Redeemer—the LORD Almighty
is his name—
is the Holy One of Israel.

⁵ "Sit in silence, go into darkness,
queen city of the Babylonians;
no more will you be called
queen of kingdoms.
⁶ I was angry with my people
and desecrated my inheritance;
I gave them into your hand,
and you showed them no mercy.
Even on the aged
you laid a very heavy yoke.
⁷ You said, 'I am forever—
the eternal queen!'
But you did not consider these
things
or reflect on what might happen.

⁸ "Now then, listen, you lover of
pleasure,
lounging in your security
and saying to yourself,
'I am, and there is none besides me.
I will never be a widow
or suffer the loss of children.'

ᵃ 1 Or *Chaldeans*; also in verse 5

860

⁹Both of these will overtake you
  in a moment, on a single day:
  loss of children and widowhood.
They will come upon you in full
    measure,
  in spite of your many sorceries
  and all your potent spells.
¹⁰You have trusted in your wickedness
  and have said, 'No one sees me.'
Your wisdom and knowledge mislead you
  when you say to yourself,
  'I am, and there is none besides me.'
¹¹Disaster will come upon you,
  and you will not know how to
    conjure it away.
A calamity will fall upon you
  that you cannot ward off with a
    ransom;
a catastrophe you cannot foresee
  will suddenly come upon you.

¹²"Keep on, then, with your magic spells
  and with your many sorceries,
  which you have labored at since
    childhood.
Perhaps you will succeed,
  perhaps you will cause terror.
¹³All the counsel you have received has
    only worn you out!
Let your astrologers come forward,
  those stargazers who make predictions
    month by month,
  let them save you from what is
    coming upon you.
¹⁴Surely they are like stubble;
  the fire will burn them up.
They cannot even save themselves
  from the power of the flame.
These are not coals for warmth;
  this is not a fire to sit by.
¹⁵That is all they are to you—
  these you have dealt with
  and labored with since childhood.
All of them go on in their error;
  there is not one that can save you.

Stubborn Israel

48 "Listen to this, you
    descendants of Jacob,
  you who are called by the
    name of Israel
and come from the line of Judah,
you who take oaths in the name of the
    LORD
  and invoke the God of Israel—
  but not in truth or righteousness—
²you who call yourselves citizens of the
    holy city
  and claim to rely on the God of
    Israel—
  the LORD Almighty is his name:
³I foretold the former things long
    ago,
  my mouth announced them and I
    made them known;
  then suddenly I acted, and they
    came to pass.
⁴For I knew how stubborn you were;
  your neck muscles were iron,
  your forehead was bronze.
⁵Therefore I told you these things long
    ago;
  before they happened I announced
    them to you
so that you could not say,
  'My images brought them about;
  my wooden image and metal god
    ordained them.'
⁶You have heard these things; look at
    them all.
  Will you not admit them?

"From now on I will tell you of new
    things,
  of hidden things unknown to you.
⁷They are created now, and not long
    ago;
  you have not heard of them before
    today.
So you cannot say,
  'Yes, I knew of them.'
⁸You have neither heard nor
    understood;
  from of old your ears have not been
    open.
Well do I know how treacherous you
    are;
  you were called a rebel from
    birth.
⁹For my own name's sake I delay my
    wrath;
  for the sake of my praise I hold it
    back from you,
  so as not to destroy you completely.

¹⁰ See, I have refined you, though not as
    silver;
  I have tested you in the furnace of
    affliction.
¹¹ For my own sake, for my own sake, I
    do this.
  How can I let myself be defamed?
  I will not yield my glory to
    another.

Israel Freed

¹² "Listen to me, Jacob,
  Israel, whom I have called:
I am he;
  I am the first and I am the last.
¹³ My own hand laid the foundations of
    the earth,
  and my right hand spread out the
    heavens;
when I summon them,
  they all stand up together.

¹⁴ "Come together, all of you, and
    listen:
  Which of the idols has foretold
    these things?
The LORD's chosen ally
  will carry out his purpose against
    Babylon;
  his arm will be against the
    Babylonians.*^a
¹⁵ I, even I, have spoken;
  yes, I have called him.
I will bring him,
  and he will succeed in his mission.

¹⁶ "Come near me and listen to this:

"From the first announcement I have
    not spoken in secret;
  at the time it happens, I am there."

And now the Sovereign LORD has sent
    me,
  endowed with his Spirit.

¹⁷ This is what the LORD says —
  your Redeemer, the Holy One of
    Israel:
"I am the LORD your God,
  who teaches you what is best for
    you,
  who directs you in the way you
    should go.

Isaiah 48:17

God knows best.

The Lord knows all. Really. Unlike "know-it-alls" who act smart and make sure everyone knows it, God literally knows everything. And instead of rubbing our faces in his infinite wisdom, he aims to share it with us and make our lives better. God listed for Israel the good results that come from following his commands. The people could enjoy peace like a flowing river, goodness as forceful as ocean waves, and families that live long and prosper. But Israel missed out on those blessings because of their sin. God cries, "If only you had listened to me!" When you're tempted to think you know better than God, remind yourself of the Lord's awesomeness. He says, "I am the LORD your God, who teaches you what is best for you, who directs you in the way you should go" (Isaiah 48:17). Your Heavenly Father really does know best.

Think: When have you worried God isn't smart — or doesn't have your best interests in mind?

ROCK SOLID truths

---

¹⁸ If only you had paid attention to my
    commands,
  your peace would have been like a
    river,
  your well-being like the waves of
    the sea.
¹⁹ Your descendants would have been
    like the sand,
  your children like its numberless
    grains;
  their name would never be blotted out
    nor destroyed from before me."

---

^a *14* Or *Chaldeans*; also in verse 20

²⁰Leave Babylon,
 flee from the Babylonians!
Announce this with shouts of joy
 and proclaim it.
Send it out to the ends of the earth;
 say, "The LORD has redeemed his
 servant Jacob."
²¹They did not thirst when he led them
 through the deserts;
 he made water flow for them from
 the rock;
he split the rock
 and water gushed out.

²²"There is no peace," says the LORD,
 "for the wicked."

The Servant of the LORD

49

Listen to me, you islands;
 hear this, you distant
 nations:
Before I was born the LORD called me;
 from my mother's womb he has
 spoken my name.
²He made my mouth like a sharpened
 sword,
 in the shadow of his hand he hid
 me;
he made me into a polished arrow
 and concealed me in his quiver.
³He said to me, "You are my servant,
 Israel, in whom I will display my
 splendor."
⁴But I said, "I have labored in vain;
 I have spent my strength for
 nothing at all.
Yet what is due me is in the LORD's
 hand,
 and my reward is with my God."

⁵And now the LORD says—
 he who formed me in the womb to
 be his servant
to bring Jacob back to him
 and gather Israel to himself,
for I am^a honored in the eyes of the
 LORD
 and my God has been my
 strength—
⁶he says:
"It is too small a thing for you to be
 my servant

to restore the tribes of Jacob
 and bring back those of Israel I have
 kept.
I will also make you a light for the
 Gentiles,
 that my salvation may reach to the
 ends of the earth."

⁷This is what the LORD says—
 the Redeemer and Holy One of
 Israel—
to him who was despised and abhorred
 by the nation,
 to the servant of rulers:
"Kings will see you and stand up,
 princes will see and bow down,
because of the LORD, who is
 faithful,
 the Holy One of Israel, who has
 chosen you."

^a 5 Or *him, / but Israel would not be gathered; / yet
I will he*

UNSHAKEN God

Isaiah 49:6–7

God is sacrificial.

Running through the book of Isaiah is a stream of what Bible scholars call "servant songs," passages describing a Savior to come. Here in Isaiah 49:6–7, you discover it would be "too small a thing" if this Savior only rescued Israel. Isaiah prophesied that the Savior will also come for the sake of "the Gentiles," all non-Jews. The rest of the Bible unfolds the story of how the Savior will light the darkness and save the world. God himself will come in the flesh, born as Jesus at Bethlehem. Jesus will die and rise. God is willing to take our punishment and get hurt to the point of death in order to help us. He volunteers to make the ultimate sacrifice.

So … How does God's sacrificial love make you feel?

Restoration of Israel

⁸This is what the LORD says:

"In the time of my favor I will answer
you,
and in the day of salvation I will
help you;
I will keep you and will make you
to be a covenant for the people,
to restore the land
and to reassign its desolate
inheritances,
⁹to say to the captives, 'Come out,'
and to those in darkness, 'Be free!'

"They will feed beside the roads
and find pasture on every barren
hill.
¹⁰They will neither hunger nor
thirst,
nor will the desert heat or the sun
beat down on them.
He who has compassion on them will
guide them
and lead them beside springs of
water.
¹¹I will turn all my mountains into
roads,
and my highways will be raised up.
¹²See, they will come from afar—
some from the north, some from
the west,
some from the region of Aswan.ᵃ"

¹³Shout for joy, you heavens;
rejoice, you earth;
burst into song, you mountains!
For the LORD comforts his people
and will have compassion on his
afflicted ones.

¹⁴But Zion said, "The LORD has
forsaken me,
the Lord has forgotten me."

¹⁵"Can a mother forget the baby at her
breast
and have no compassion on the
child she has borne?
Though she may forget,
I will not forget you!
¹⁶See, I have engraved you on the palms
of my hands;
your walls are ever before me.

¹⁷Your children hasten back,
and those who laid you waste depart
from you.
¹⁸Lift up your eyes and look around;
all your children gather and come to
you.
As surely as I live," declares the LORD,
"you will wear them all as
ornaments;
you will put them on, like a bride.

¹⁹"Though you were ruined and made
desolate
and your land laid waste,
now you will be too small for your
people,
and those who devoured you will be
far away.
²⁰The children born during your
bereavement
will yet say in your hearing,
'This place is too small for us;
give us more space to live in.'
²¹Then you will say in your heart,
'Who bore me these?
I was bereaved and barren;
I was exiled and rejected.
Who brought these up?
I was left all alone,
but these—where have they come
from?'"

²²This is what the Sovereign LORD says:

"See, I will beckon to the nations,
I will lift up my banner to the
peoples;
they will bring your sons in their
arms
and carry your daughters on their
hips.
²³Kings will be your foster fathers,
and their queens your nursing
mothers.
They will bow down before you with
their faces to the ground;
they will lick the dust at your feet.
Then you will know that I am the
LORD;
those who hope in me will not be
disappointed."

ᵃ 12 Dead Sea Scrolls; Masoretic Text *Sinim*

²⁴Can plunder be taken from warriors,
  or captives be rescued from the
    fierce*?

²⁵But this is what the Lord says:

"Yes, captives will be taken from
    warriors,
  and plunder retrieved from the
    fierce;
I will contend with those who contend
    with you,
  and your children I will save.
²⁶I will make your oppressors eat their
    own flesh;
  they will be drunk on their own
    blood, as with wine.
Then all mankind will know
  that I, the Lord, am your Savior,
  your Redeemer, the Mighty One of
    Jacob."

Israel's Sin and the Servant's Obedience

50 This is what the Lord says:

"Where is your mother's
    certificate of divorce
  with which I sent her away?
Or to which of my creditors
  did I sell you?
Because of your sins you were sold;
  because of your transgressions your
    mother was sent away.
²When I came, why was there no one?
  When I called, why was there no
    one to answer?
Was my arm too short to deliver you?
  Do I lack the strength to rescue
    you?
By a mere rebuke I dry up the sea,
  I turn rivers into a desert;
their fish rot for lack of water
  and die of thirst.
³I clothe the heavens with darkness
  and make sackcloth its
    covering."

⁴The Sovereign Lord has given me a
    well-instructed tongue,
  to know the word that sustains the
    weary.

He wakens me morning by morning,
  wakens my ear to listen like one
    being instructed.
⁵The Sovereign Lord has opened my
    ears;
  I have not been rebellious,
  I have not turned away.
⁶I offered my back to those who beat
    me,
  my cheeks to those who pulled out
    my beard;
I did not hide my face
  from mocking and spitting.
⁷Because the Sovereign Lord helps
    me,
  I will not be disgraced.
Therefore have I set my face like
    flint,
  and I know I will not be put to
    shame.
⁸He who vindicates me is near.
  Who then will bring charges
    against me?
  Let us face each other!
Who is my accuser?
  Let him confront me!
⁹It is the Sovereign Lord who helps
    me.
  Who will condemn me?
They will all wear out like a
    garment;
  the moths will eat them up.

¹⁰Who among you fears the Lord
  and obeys the word of his
    servant?
Let the one who walks in the dark,
  who has no light,
trust in the name of the Lord
  and rely on their God.
¹¹But now, all you who light fires
  and provide yourselves with flaming
    torches,
go, walk in the light of your fires
  and of the torches you have set
    ablaze.
This is what you shall receive from my
    hand:
  You will lie down in torment.

ᵃ 24 Dead Sea Scrolls, Vulgate and Syriac (see also Septuagint and verse 25); Masoretic Text *righteous*

Everlasting Salvation for Zion

51 "Listen to me, you who
pursue righteousness
and who seek the LORD:
Look to the rock from which you were
cut
and to the quarry from which you
were hewn;
2 look to Abraham, your father,
and to Sarah, who gave you birth.
When I called him he was only one
man,
and I blessed him and made him
many.
3 The LORD will surely comfort Zion
and will look with compassion on
all her ruins;
he will make her deserts like Eden,
her wastelands like the garden of
the LORD.
Joy and gladness will be found in her,
thanksgiving and the sound of
singing.

4 "Listen to me, my people;
hear me, my nation:
Instruction will go out from me;
my justice will become a light to the
nations.
5 My righteousness draws near
speedily,
my salvation is on the way,
and my arm will bring justice to the
nations.
The islands will look to me
and wait in hope for my arm.
6 Lift up your eyes to the heavens,
look at the earth beneath;
the heavens will vanish like smoke,
the earth will wear out like a
garment
and its inhabitants die like flies.
But my salvation will last forever,
my righteousness will never fail.

7 "Hear me, you who know what is
right,
you people who have taken my
instruction to heart:
Do not fear the reproach of mere
mortals
or be terrified by their insults.

8 For the moth will eat them up like a
garment;
the worm will devour them like
wool.
But my righteousness will last forever,
my salvation through all
generations."

9 Awake, awake, arm of the LORD,
clothe yourself with strength!
Awake, as in days gone by,
as in generations of old.
Was it not you who cut Rahab to
pieces,
who pierced that monster through?
10 Was it not you who dried up the sea,
the waters of the great deep,
who made a road in the depths of the
sea
so that the redeemed might cross
over?
11 Those the LORD has rescued will
return.
They will enter Zion with singing;
everlasting joy will crown their
heads.
Gladness and joy will overtake them,
and sorrow and sighing will flee
away.

12 "I, even I, am he who comforts you.
Who are you that you fear mere
mortals,
human beings who are but grass,
13 that you forget the LORD your Maker,
who stretches out the heavens
and who lays the foundations of the
earth,
that you live in constant terror every
day
because of the wrath of the oppressor,
who is bent on destruction?
For where is the wrath of the
oppressor?
14 The cowering prisoners will soon be
set free;
they will not die in their dungeon,
nor will they lack bread.
15 For I am the LORD your God,
who stirs up the sea so that its
waves roar —
the LORD Almighty is his name.

¹⁶ I have put my words in your mouth
and covered you with the shadow of
my hand—
I who set the heavens in place,
who laid the foundations of the
earth,
and who say to Zion, 'You are my
people.'"

The Cup of the LORD's Wrath

¹⁷ Awake, awake!
Rise up, Jerusalem,
you who have drunk from the hand of
the LORD
the cup of his wrath,
you who have drained to its dregs
the goblet that makes people
stagger.
¹⁸ Among all the children she bore
there was none to guide her;
among all the children she reared
there was none to take her by the
hand.
¹⁹ These double calamities have come
upon you—
who can comfort you?—
ruin and destruction, famine and
sword—
who can^a console you?
²⁰ Your children have fainted;
they lie at every street corner,
like antelope caught in a net.
They are filled with the wrath of the
LORD,
with the rebuke of your God.

²¹ Therefore hear this, you afflicted one,
made drunk, but not with wine.
²² This is what your Sovereign LORD says,
your God, who defends his people:
"See, I have taken out of your hand
the cup that made you stagger;
from that cup, the goblet of my wrath,
you will never drink again.
²³ I will put it into the hands of your
tormentors,
who said to you,
'Fall prostrate that we may walk on
you.'
And you made your back like the
ground,
like a street to be walked on."

52 Awake, awake, Zion,
clothe yourself with
strength!
Put on your garments of splendor,
Jerusalem, the holy city.
The uncircumcised and defiled
will not enter you again.
² Shake off your dust;
rise up, sit enthroned, Jerusalem.
Free yourself from the chains on your
neck,
Daughter Zion, now a captive.

³ For this is what the LORD says:

"You were sold for nothing,
and without money you will be
redeemed."

⁴ For this is what the Sovereign LORD
says:

"At first my people went down to
Egypt to live;
lately, Assyria has oppressed them.

⁵ "And now what do I have here?" declares the LORD.

"For my people have been taken away
for nothing,
and those who rule them mock,^b"
declares the LORD.
"And all day long
my name is constantly blasphemed.
⁶ Therefore my people will know my
name;
therefore in that day they will know
that it is I who foretold it.
Yes, it is I."

⁷ How beautiful on the mountains
are the feet of those who bring good
news,
who proclaim peace,
who bring good tidings,
who proclaim salvation,
who say to Zion,
"Your God reigns!"
⁸ Listen! Your watchmen lift up their
voices;
together they shout for joy.

---

^a *19* Dead Sea Scrolls, Septuagint, Vulgate and
Syriac; Masoretic Text / *how can I*   ^b *5* Dead
Sea Scrolls and Vulgate; Masoretic Text *wail*

When the Lord returns to Zion,
  they will see it with their own eyes.
⁹Burst into songs of joy together,
  you ruins of Jerusalem,
for the Lord has comforted his people,
  he has redeemed Jerusalem.
¹⁰The Lord will lay bare his holy arm
  in the sight of all the nations,
and all the ends of the earth will see
  the salvation of our God.

¹¹Depart, depart, go out from there!
  Touch no unclean thing!
Come out from it and be pure,
  you who carry the articles of the
    Lord's house.
¹²But you will not leave in haste
  or go in flight;
for the Lord will go before you,
  the God of Israel will be your rear
    guard.

The Suffering and Glory of the Servant

¹³See, my servant will act wisely[a];
  he will be raised and lifted up and
    highly exalted.
¹⁴Just as there were many who were
    appalled at him[b]—
  his appearance was so disfigured
    beyond that of any human
    being
  and his form marred beyond human
    likeness—
¹⁵so he will sprinkle many nations,[c]
  and kings will shut their mouths
    because of him.
For what they were not told, they will
    see,
  and what they have not heard, they
    will understand.

53 Who has believed our
  message
  and to whom has the arm
  of the Lord been revealed?
²He grew up before him like a tender
    shoot,
  and like a root out of dry ground.
He had no beauty or majesty to attract
    us to him,
  nothing in his appearance that we
    should desire him.

³He was despised and rejected by
    mankind,
  a man of suffering, and familiar
    with pain.
Like one from whom people hide their
    faces
  he was despised, and we held him in
    low esteem.

⁴Surely he took up our pain
  and bore our suffering,
yet we considered him punished by
    God,
  stricken by him, and afflicted.
⁵But he was pierced for our
    transgressions,
  he was crushed for our iniquities;
the punishment that brought us peace
    was on him,
  and by his wounds we are healed.
⁶We all, like sheep, have gone astray,
  each of us has turned to our own
    way;
and the Lord has laid on him
  the iniquity of us all.

⁷He was oppressed and afflicted,
  yet he did not open his mouth;
he was led like a lamb to the slaughter,
  and as a sheep before its shearers is
    silent,
  so he did not open his mouth.
⁸By oppression[d] and judgment he was
    taken away.
  Yet who of his generation protested?
For he was cut off from the land of the
    living;
  for the transgression of my people
    he was punished.[e]
⁹He was assigned a grave with the
    wicked,
  and with the rich in his death,
though he had done no violence,
  nor was any deceit in his mouth.

¹⁰Yet it was the Lord's will to crush
    him and cause him to suffer,

---

^a 13 Or *will prosper*   ^b 14 Hebrew *you*
^c 15 Or *so will many nations be amazed at him*
(see also Septuagint)   ^d 8 Or *From arrest*
^e 8 Or *generation considered / that he was cut off
from the land of the living, / that he was punished
for the transgression of my people?*

and though the LORD makes[a] his
life an offering for sin,
he will see his offspring and prolong
his days,
and the will of the LORD will
prosper in his hand.
¹¹ After he has suffered,
he will see the light of life[b] and be
satisfied[c];
by his knowledge[d] my righteous
servant will justify many,
and he will bear their iniquities.

¹² Therefore I will give him a portion
among the great,[e]
and he will divide the spoils with
the strong,[f]
because he poured out his life unto
death,
and was numbered with the
transgressors.
For he bore the sin of many,
and made intercession for the
transgressors.

The Future Glory of Zion

54 "Sing, barren woman,
you who never bore a child;
burst into song, shout for joy,
you who were never in labor;
because more are the children of the
desolate woman
than of her who has a husband,"
says the LORD.
² "Enlarge the place of your tent,
stretch your tent curtains wide,
do not hold back;
lengthen your cords,
strengthen your stakes.
³ For you will spread out to the right
and to the left;
your descendants will dispossess
nations
and settle in their desolate cities.

⁴ "Do not be afraid; you will not be put
to shame.
Do not fear disgrace; you will not
be humiliated.
You will forget the shame of your
youth
and remember no more the reproach
of your widowhood.
⁵ For your Maker is your husband —
the LORD Almighty is his name —
the Holy One of Israel is your
Redeemer;
he is called the God of all the earth.

Isaiah 53:4–12

The Bible foreshadowed the cross.

If you printed out this passage and asked people who it talks about, lots of people would say, "Jesus." But most would be surprised that this description of a suffering Savior comes from the book of Isaiah — and that these words were spoken many hundreds of years before Jesus arrived on earth. Isaiah prophesied in detail what Jesus would experience on the cross. He would be "pierced for our transgressions" and "crushed for our iniquities." His punishment would bring us peace, and "by his wounds we are healed." And Jesus bore "the iniquity of us all" (Isaiah 53:5–6). If you want to understand what Jesus did for you, study this passage line by line. If you want to be amazed at the Lord's love for you, don't forget that long ago God had a plan to rescue you from sin.

Think: How does it make you feel that God told about the cross long before it happened?

ROCK SOLID truths

---

^a 10 Hebrew *though you make*   ^b 11 Dead Sea
Scrolls (see also Septuagint); Masoretic Text
does not have *the light of life.*   ^c 11 Or (with
Masoretic Text) ¹¹*He will see the fruit of his
suffering / and will be satisfied*   ^d 11 Or *by
knowledge of him*   ^e 12 Or *many*
^f 12 Or *numerous*

⁶"The Lord will call you back
as if you were a wife deserted and
distressed in spirit—
a wife who married young,
only to be rejected," says your God.
⁷"For a brief moment I abandoned you,
but with deep compassion I will
bring you back.
⁸In a surge of anger
I hid my face from you for a moment,
but with everlasting kindness
I will have compassion on you,"
says the Lord your Redeemer.

⁹"To me this is like the days of Noah,
when I swore that the waters of
Noah would never again cover
the earth.
So now I have sworn not to be angry
with you,
never to rebuke you again.
¹⁰Though the mountains be shaken
and the hills be removed,
yet my unfailing love for you will not
be shaken
nor my covenant of peace be
removed,"
says the Lord, who has compassion
on you.

ROCK SOLID *promises*

"Though the mountains be shaken and the hills be removed, yet my unfailing love for you will not be shaken." Isaiah 54:10

Your whole world might be tossed, rocked, and broken, but God's love for you can't be shaken.

¹¹"Afflicted city, lashed by storms and
not comforted,
I will rebuild you with stones of
turquoise,ᵃ
your foundations with lapis lazuli.

¹²I will make your battlements of rubies,
your gates of sparkling jewels,
and all your walls of precious
stones.
¹³All your children will be taught by the
Lord,
and great will be their peace.
¹⁴In righteousness you will be
established:
Tyranny will be far from you;
you will have nothing to fear.
Terror will be far removed;
it will not come near you.
¹⁵If anyone does attack you, it will not
be my doing;
whoever attacks you will surrender
to you.

¹⁶"See, it is I who created the
blacksmith
who fans the coals into flame
and forges a weapon fit for its work.
And it is I who have created the
destroyer to wreak havoc;
¹⁷ no weapon forged against you will
prevail,
and you will refute every tongue
that accuses you.
This is the heritage of the servants of
the Lord,
and this is their vindication from me,"
declares the Lord.

Invitation to the Thirsty

55 "Come, all you who are
thirsty,
come to the waters;
and you who have no money,
come, buy and eat!
Come, buy wine and milk
without money and without cost.
²Why spend money on what is not
bread,
and your labor on what does not
satisfy?
Listen, listen to me, and eat what is
good,
and you will delight in the richest of
fare.

ᵃ *11* The meaning of the Hebrew for this word
is uncertain.

³Give ear and come to me;
  listen, that you may live.
I will make an everlasting covenant
    with you,
  my faithful love promised to David.
⁴See, I have made him a witness to the
    peoples,
  a ruler and commander of the
    peoples.
⁵Surely you will summon nations you
    know not,
  and nations you do not know will
    come running to you,
because of the Lord your God,
  the Holy One of Israel,
  for he has endowed you with
    splendor."

⁶Seek the Lord while he may be found;
  call on him while he is near.
⁷Let the wicked forsake their ways
  and the unrighteous their thoughts.
Let them turn to the Lord, and he
    will have mercy on them,
  and to our God, for he will freely
    pardon.

⁸"For my thoughts are not your
    thoughts,
  neither are your ways my ways,"
            declares the Lord.
⁹"As the heavens are higher than the
    earth,
  so are my ways higher than your ways
  and my thoughts than your thoughts.
¹⁰As the rain and the snow
  come down from heaven,
and do not return to it
  without watering the earth
and making it bud and flourish,
  so that it yields seed for the sower
    and bread for the eater,
¹¹so is my word that goes out from my
    mouth:
  It will not return to me empty,
but will accomplish what I desire
  and achieve the purpose for which I
    sent it.
¹²You will go out in joy
  and be led forth in peace;
the mountains and hills
  will burst into song before you,

and all the trees of the field
  will clap their hands.
¹³Instead of the thornbush will grow the
    juniper,
  and instead of briers the myrtle will
    grow.
This will be for the Lord's renown,
  for an everlasting sign,
  that will endure forever."

Salvation for Others

56 This is what the Lord says:

  "Maintain justice
and do what is right,
for my salvation is close at hand
  and my righteousness will soon be
    revealed.
²Blessed is the one who does this—
  the person who holds it fast,
who keeps the Sabbath without
    desecrating it,
  and keeps their hands from doing
    any evil."

³Let no foreigner who is bound to the
    Lord say,
  "The Lord will surely exclude me
    from his people."
And let no eunuch complain,
  "I am only a dry tree."

⁴For this is what the Lord says:

"To the eunuchs who keep my
    Sabbaths,
  who choose what pleases me
  and hold fast to my covenant—
⁵to them I will give within my temple
    and its walls
  a memorial and a name
  better than sons and daughters;
I will give them an everlasting
    name
  that will endure forever.
⁶And foreigners who bind themselves
    to the Lord
  to minister to him,
to love the name of the Lord,
  and to be his servants,
all who keep the Sabbath without
    desecrating it
  and who hold fast to my covenant—

⁷these I will bring to my holy mountain
    and give them joy in my house of
        prayer.
Their burnt offerings and sacrifices
    will be accepted on my altar;
for my house will be called
    a house of prayer for all nations."
⁸The Sovereign LORD declares—
    he who gathers the exiles of
        Israel:
"I will gather still others to them
    besides those already gathered."

God's Accusation Against the Wicked

⁹Come, all you beasts of the field,
    come and devour, all you beasts of
        the forest!
¹⁰Israel's watchmen are blind,
    they all lack knowledge;
they are all mute dogs,
    they cannot bark;
they lie around and dream,
    they love to sleep.
¹¹They are dogs with mighty appetites;
    they never have enough.
They are shepherds who lack
        understanding;
    they all turn to their own way,
        they seek their own gain.
¹²"Come," each one cries, "let me get
        wine!
Let us drink our fill of beer!
And tomorrow will be like today,
    or even far better."

57 The righteous perish,
    and no one takes it to heart;
    the devout are taken away,
and no one understands
that the righteous are taken away
    to be spared from evil.
²Those who walk uprightly
    enter into peace;
    they find rest as they lie in death.

³"But you—come here, you children of
        a sorceress,
    you offspring of adulterers and
        prostitutes!
⁴Who are you mocking?
    At whom do you sneer
    and stick out your tongue?

Are you not a brood of rebels,
    the offspring of liars?
⁵You burn with lust among the oaks
    and under every spreading tree;
you sacrifice your children in the
        ravines
    and under the overhanging crags.
⁶The idols among the smooth stones of
        the ravines are your portion;
    indeed, they are your lot.
Yes, to them you have poured out
        drink offerings
    and offered grain offerings.
    In view of all this, should I relent?
⁷You have made your bed on a high and
        lofty hill;
    there you went up to offer your
        sacrifices.
⁸Behind your doors and your doorposts
    you have put your pagan symbols.
Forsaking me, you uncovered your bed,
    you climbed into it and opened it
        wide;
you made a pact with those whose
        beds you love,
    and you looked with lust on their
        naked bodies.
⁹You went to Molek*ᵃ* with olive oil
    and increased your perfumes.
You sent your ambassadors*ᵇ* far away;
    you descended to the very realm of
        the dead!
¹⁰You wearied yourself by such going
        about,
    but you would not say, 'It is hopeless.'
You found renewal of your strength,
    and so you did not faint.

¹¹"Whom have you so dreaded and
        feared
    that you have not been true to me,
    and have neither remembered me
        nor taken this to heart?
Is it not because I have long been silent
    that you do not fear me?
¹²I will expose your righteousness and
        your works,
    and they will not benefit you.
¹³When you cry out for help,
    let your collection of idols save you!

ᵃ 9 Or *to the king*   *ᵇ* 9 Or *idols*

The wind will carry all of them off,
  a mere breath will blow them away.
But whoever takes refuge in me
  will inherit the land
  and possess my holy mountain."

Comfort for the Contrite

¹⁴ And it will be said:

"Build up, build up, prepare the road!
  Remove the obstacles out of the way
    of my people."

¹⁵ For this is what the high and exalted
    One says—
  he who lives forever, whose name is
    holy:
"I live in a high and holy place,
  but also with the one who is contrite
    and lowly in spirit,
to revive the spirit of the lowly
  and to revive the heart of the contrite.
¹⁶ I will not accuse them forever,
  nor will I always be angry,
for then they would faint away because
    of me—
  the very people I have created.
¹⁷ I was enraged by their sinful greed;
  I punished them, and hid my face in
    anger,
  yet they kept on in their willful ways.
¹⁸ I have seen their ways, but I will heal
    them;
  I will guide them and restore
    comfort to Israel's mourners,
¹⁹   creating praise on their lips.
Peace, peace, to those far and near,"
  says the LORD. "And I will heal
    them."
²⁰ But the wicked are like the tossing sea,
  which cannot rest,
  whose waves cast up mire and mud.
²¹ "There is no peace," says my God, "for
    the wicked."

True Fasting

58

"Shout it aloud, do not
  hold back.
Raise your voice like a
  trumpet.
Declare to my people their rebellion
  and to the descendants of Jacob
    their sins.

² For day after day they seek me out;
  they seem eager to know my ways,
as if they were a nation that does what
    is right
  and has not forsaken the commands
    of its God.
They ask me for just decisions
  and seem eager for God to come
    near them.
³ 'Why have we fasted,' they say,
  'and you have not seen it?
Why have we humbled ourselves,
  and you have not noticed?'

"Yet on the day of your fasting, you do
    as you please
  and exploit all your workers.
⁴ Your fasting ends in quarreling and
    strife,
  and in striking each other with
    wicked fists.
You cannot fast as you do today
  and expect your voice to be heard
    on high.
⁵ Is this the kind of fast I have chosen,
  only a day for people to humble
    themselves?
Is it only for bowing one's head like a
    reed
  and for lying in sackcloth and
    ashes?
Is that what you call a fast,
  a day acceptable to the LORD?

⁶ "Is not this the kind of fasting I have
    chosen:
to loose the chains of injustice
  and untie the cords of the yoke,
to set the oppressed free
  and break every yoke?
⁷ Is it not to share your food with the
    hungry
  and to provide the poor wanderer
    with shelter—
when you see the naked, to clothe
    them,
  and not to turn away from your own
    flesh and blood?
⁸ Then your light will break forth like
    the dawn,
  and your healing will quickly
    appear;

then your righteousness*a* will go
before you,
and the glory of the LORD will be
your rear guard.
⁹Then you will call, and the LORD will
answer;
you will cry for help, and he will
say: Here am I.

"If you do away with the yoke of
oppression,
with the pointing finger and
malicious talk,
¹⁰and if you spend yourselves in behalf
of the hungry
and satisfy the needs of the
oppressed,
then your light will rise in the darkness,
and your night will become like the
noonday.
¹¹The LORD will guide you always;
he will satisfy your needs in a sun-
scorched land
and will strengthen your frame.
You will be like a well-watered garden,
like a spring whose waters never fail.
¹²Your people will rebuild the ancient
ruins
and will raise up the age-old
foundations;
you will be called Repairer of Broken
Walls,
Restorer of Streets with Dwellings.

¹³"If you keep your feet from breaking
the Sabbath
and from doing as you please on my
holy day,
if you call the Sabbath a delight
and the LORD's holy day honorable,
and if you honor it by not going your
own way
and not doing as you please or
speaking idle words,
¹⁴then you will find your joy in the LORD,
and I will cause you to ride in
triumph on the heights of the
land
and to feast on the inheritance of
your father Jacob."
For the mouth of the
LORD has spoken.

Sin, Confession and Redemption

59 Surely the arm of the LORD
is not too short to save,
nor his ear too dull to hear.
²But your iniquities have separated
you from your God;
your sins have hidden his face from you,
so that he will not hear.
³For your hands are stained with blood,
your fingers with guilt.
Your lips have spoken falsely,
and your tongue mutters wicked
things.
⁴No one calls for justice;
no one pleads a case with integrity.
They rely on empty arguments, they
utter lies;
they conceive trouble and give birth
to evil.
⁵They hatch the eggs of vipers
and spin a spider's web.
Whoever eats their eggs will die,
and when one is broken, an adder is
hatched.
⁶Their cobwebs are useless for clothing;
they cannot cover themselves with
what they make.
Their deeds are evil deeds,
and acts of violence are in their
hands.
⁷Their feet rush into sin;
they are swift to shed innocent
blood.
They pursue evil schemes;
acts of violence mark their ways.
⁸The way of peace they do not know;
there is no justice in their paths.
They have turned them into crooked
roads;
no one who walks along them will
know peace.

⁹So justice is far from us,
and righteousness does not reach us.
We look for light, but all is darkness;
for brightness, but we walk in deep
shadows.
¹⁰Like the blind we grope along the wall,
feeling our way like people without
eyes.

---

a 8 Or *your righteous One*

874

At midday we stumble as if it were
twilight;
among the strong, we are like the
dead.
[11] We all growl like bears;
we moan mournfully like doves.
We look for justice, but find none;
for deliverance, but it is far away.

[12] For our offenses are many in your
sight,
and our sins testify against us.
Our offenses are ever with us,
and we acknowledge our iniquities:

[13] rebellion and treachery against the
LORD,
turning our backs on our God,
inciting revolt and oppression,
uttering lies our hearts have
conceived.
[14] So justice is driven back,
and righteousness stands at a
distance;
truth has stumbled in the streets,
honesty cannot enter.
[15] Truth is nowhere to be found,
and whoever shuns evil becomes a
prey.

The LORD looked and was displeased
that there was no justice.
[16] He saw that there was no one,
he was appalled that there was no
one to intervene;
so his own arm achieved salvation for
him,
and his own righteousness sustained
him.
[17] He put on righteousness as his
breastplate,
and the helmet of salvation on his
head;
he put on the garments of vengeance
and wrapped himself in zeal as in a
cloak.
[18] According to what they have done,
so will he repay
wrath to his enemies
and retribution to his foes;
he will repay the islands their due.
[19] From the west, people will fear the
name of the LORD,
and from the rising of the sun, they
will revere his glory.
For he will come like a pent-up flood
that the breath of the LORD drives
along.[a]

[20] "The Redeemer will come to Zion,
to those in Jacob who repent of
their sins,"
declares the LORD.

[21] "As for me, this is my covenant with
them," says the LORD. "My Spirit, who is

Isaiah 59:1–13

Sin makes God feel far away.

The slogans slapped on Christian bumper stickers can make your faith sound cheesy. But here's one that speaks truth: "If God seems far away, who moved?" That sums up what Isaiah meant when he said, "Your iniquities have separated you from your God" (Isaiah 59:2). Sin makes the Lord seem far away. In fact, separation from God is the biggest consequence of doing wrong. Every time you sin—whether by doing wrong or failing to do right—it's like you put another brick on a wall between you and God. Jesus came and knocked down that wall so you can live close to God now and forever (see Hebrews 10:19–22). But people who keep piling up those bricks will one day find themselves walled up in a cell, cut off from God. That separation from God is what hell is all about.

Think: Do you feel far from God when you sin? What are you going to do about that?

ROCK SOLID truths

---

[a] 19 Or *When enemies come in like a flood, / the Spirit of the LORD will put them to flight*

on you, will not depart from you, and my words that I have put in your mouth will always be on your lips, on the lips of your children and on the lips of their descendants—from this time on and forever," says the LORD.

The Glory of Zion

60

"Arise, shine, for your light has come,
and the glory of the LORD rises upon you.
² See, darkness covers the earth
and thick darkness is over the peoples,
but the LORD rises upon you
and his glory appears over you.

ROCK SOLID
promises

"Arise, shine, for your light has come, and the glory of the LORD rises upon you." Isaiah 60:1

Darkness envelops the earth, but God will light up your world and shine through you.

---

³ Nations will come to your light,
and kings to the brightness of your dawn.

⁴ "Lift up your eyes and look about you:
All assemble and come to you;
your sons come from afar,
and your daughters are carried on the hip.
⁵ Then you will look and be radiant,
your heart will throb and swell with joy;
the wealth on the seas will be brought to you,
to you the riches of the nations will come.

⁶ Herds of camels will cover your land,
young camels of Midian and Ephah.
And all from Sheba will come,
bearing gold and incense
and proclaiming the praise of the LORD.
⁷ All Kedar's flocks will be gathered to you,
the rams of Nebaioth will serve you;
they will be accepted as offerings on my altar,
and I will adorn my glorious temple.

⁸ "Who are these that fly along like clouds,
like doves to their nests?
⁹ Surely the islands look to me;
in the lead are the ships of Tarshish,ᵃ
bringing your children from afar,
with their silver and gold,
to the honor of the LORD your God,
the Holy One of Israel,
for he has endowed you with splendor.

¹⁰ "Foreigners will rebuild your walls,
and their kings will serve you.
Though in anger I struck you,
in favor I will show you compassion.
¹¹ Your gates will always stand open,
they will never be shut, day or night,
so that people may bring you the wealth of the nations—
their kings led in triumphal procession.
¹² For the nation or kingdom that will not serve you will perish;
it will be utterly ruined.

¹³ "The glory of Lebanon will come to you,
the juniper, the fir and the cypress together,
to adorn my sanctuary;
and I will glorify the place for my feet.
¹⁴ The children of your oppressors will come bowing before you;

ᵃ 9 Or *the trading ships*

all who despise you will bow down
at your feet
and will call you the City of the LORD,
Zion of the Holy One of Israel.

15 "Although you have been forsaken and
hated,
with no one traveling through,
I will make you the everlasting pride
and the joy of all generations.
16 You will drink the milk of nations
and be nursed at royal breasts.
Then you will know that I, the LORD,
am your Savior,
your Redeemer, the Mighty One of
Jacob.
17 Instead of bronze I will bring you
gold,
and silver in place of iron.
Instead of wood I will bring you
bronze,
and iron in place of stones.
I will make peace your governor
and well-being your ruler.
18 No longer will violence be heard in
your land,
nor ruin or destruction within your
borders,
but you will call your walls Salvation
and your gates Praise.
19 The sun will no more be your light by
day,
nor will the brightness of the moon
shine on you,
for the LORD will be your everlasting
light,
and your God will be your glory.
20 Your sun will never set again,
and your moon will wane no more;
the LORD will be your everlasting light,
and your days of sorrow will end.
21 Then all your people will be righteous
and they will possess the land
forever.
They are the shoot I have planted,
the work of my hands,
for the display of my splendor.
22 The least of you will become a
thousand,
the smallest a mighty nation.
I am the LORD;
in its time I will do this swiftly."

The Year of the LORD's Favor

61 The Spirit of the Sovereign
LORD is on me,
because the LORD has
anointed me
to proclaim good news to the poor.
He has sent me to bind up the
brokenhearted,
to proclaim freedom for the captives
and release from darkness for the
prisoners,[a]
2 to proclaim the year of the LORD's
favor
and the day of vengeance of our God,
to comfort all who mourn,
3   and provide for those who grieve in
Zion —
to bestow on them a crown of beauty
instead of ashes,

a 1 Hebrew; Septuagint *the blind*

UNSHAKEN *God*

Isaiah 61:1 – 3

God is healing.

When Adam and Eve sinned, they kicked off what became a bad human habit. Our sinfulness has shattered the good world God created. But the Lord has a plan to put everything back together again. The prophet Isaiah sums up how God aims to heal us — by serving the poor, the brokenhearted, and the captive ... by comforting mourners ... by lifting people from despair (see Isaiah 61:1 – 3). Jesus stood up in his hometown house of worship, read this passage aloud and declared it was talking about him. His neighbors were so upset they chased him out of town to toss him from a cliff (see Luke 4:14 – 30). They didn't grasp that Jesus is at the heart of God's plan to heal us.

So ... What kind of healing do you need from God?

the oil of joy
    instead of mourning,
and a garment of praise
    instead of a spirit of despair.
They will be called oaks of
    righteousness,
    a planting of the Lord
for the display of his splendor.

⁴ They will rebuild the ancient ruins
    and restore the places long
      devastated;
they will renew the ruined cities
    that have been devastated for
      generations.
⁵ Strangers will shepherd your flocks;
    foreigners will work your fields and
      vineyards.
⁶ And you will be called priests of the
    Lord,
    you will be named ministers of our
      God.
You will feed on the wealth of nations,
    and in their riches you will boast.

⁷ Instead of your shame
    you will receive a double portion,
and instead of disgrace
    you will rejoice in your inheritance.
And so you will inherit a double
    portion in your land,
    and everlasting joy will be yours.

⁸ "For I, the Lord, love justice;
    I hate robbery and wrongdoing.
In my faithfulness I will reward my
    people
    and make an everlasting covenant
      with them.
⁹ Their descendants will be known
    among the nations
    and their offspring among the
      peoples.
All who see them will acknowledge
    that they are a people the Lord has
      blessed."

¹⁰ I delight greatly in the Lord;
    my soul rejoices in my God.
For he has clothed me with garments
    of salvation
and arrayed me in a robe of his
    righteousness,
as a bridegroom adorns his head like a
    priest,
    and as a bride adorns herself with
      her jewels.
¹¹ For as the soil makes the sprout
    come up
    and a garden causes seeds to grow,
so the Sovereign Lord will make
    righteousness
    and praise spring up before all
      nations.

Zion's New Name

62 For Zion's sake I will not
    keep silent,
    for Jerusalem's sake I will
    not remain quiet,
till her vindication shines out like the
    dawn,
    her salvation like a blazing torch.
² The nations will see your vindication,
    and all kings your glory;
you will be called by a new name
    that the mouth of the Lord will
      bestow.
³ You will be a crown of splendor in the
    Lord's hand,
    a royal diadem in the hand of your
      God.
⁴ No longer will they call you Deserted,
    or name your land Desolate.
But you will be called Hephzibah,ᵃ
    and your land Beulahᵇ;
for the Lord will take delight in you,
    and your land will be married.
⁵ As a young man marries a young
    woman,
    so will your Builder marry you;
as a bridegroom rejoices over his bride,
    so will your God rejoice over you.

⁶ I have posted watchmen on your walls,
    Jerusalem;
    they will never be silent day or night.
You who call on the Lord,
    give yourselves no rest,
⁷ and give him no rest till he establishes
    Jerusalem
    and makes her the praise of the
      earth.

ᵃ 4 *Hephzibah* means *my delight is in her.*
ᵇ 4 *Beulah* means *married.*

8 The LORD has sworn by his right
hand
and by his mighty arm:
"Never again will I give your grain
as food for your enemies,
and never again will foreigners drink
the new wine
for which you have toiled;
9 but those who harvest it will eat it
and praise the LORD,
and those who gather the grapes will
drink it
in the courts of my sanctuary."

10 Pass through, pass through the gates!
Prepare the way for the people.
Build up, build up the highway!
Remove the stones.
Raise a banner for the nations.

11 The LORD has made proclamation
to the ends of the earth:
"Say to Daughter Zion,
'See, your Savior comes!
See, his reward is with him,
and his recompense accompanies
him.'"
12 They will be called the Holy People,
the Redeemed of the LORD;
and you will be called Sought After,
the City No Longer Deserted.

God's Day of Vengeance and Redemption

63 Who is this coming from
Edom,
from Bozrah, with his
garments stained crimson?
Who is this, robed in splendor,
striding forward in the greatness of
his strength?

"It is I, proclaiming victory,
mighty to save."

2 Why are your garments red,
like those of one treading the
winepress?

3 "I have trodden the winepress alone;
from the nations no one was with
me.
I trampled them in my anger
and trod them down in my wrath;

their blood spattered my garments,
and I stained all my clothing.
4 It was for me the day of vengeance;
the year for me to redeem had come.
5 I looked, but there was no one to help,
I was appalled that no one gave
support;
so my own arm achieved salvation
for me,
and my own wrath sustained me.
6 I trampled the nations in my anger;
in my wrath I made them drunk
and poured their blood on the
ground."

Praise and Prayer

7 I will tell of the kindnesses of the
LORD,
the deeds for which he is to be
praised,
according to all the LORD has done
for us—
yes, the many good things
he has done for Israel,
according to his compassion and
many kindnesses.
8 He said, "Surely they are my people,
children who will be true to me";
and so he became their Savior.
9 In all their distress he too was
distressed,
and the angel of his presence saved
them.*a*
In his love and mercy he redeemed
them;
he lifted them up and carried them
all the days of old.
10 Yet they rebelled
and grieved his Holy Spirit.
So he turned and became their enemy
and he himself fought against them.

11 Then his people recalled*b* the days of
old,
the days of Moses and his people—
where is he who brought them
through the sea,
with the shepherd of his flock?

*a 9 Or Savior 9in their distress. / It was no envoy
or angel / but his own presence that saved them
b 11 Or But may he recall*

Where is he who set
 his Holy Spirit among them,
[12] who sent his glorious arm of power
 to be at Moses' right hand,
who divided the waters before them,
 to gain for himself everlasting
  renown,
[13] who led them through the depths?
Like a horse in open country,
 they did not stumble;
[14] like cattle that go down to the plain,
 they were given rest by the Spirit of
  the Lord.
This is how you guided your people
 to make for yourself a glorious name.

[15] Look down from heaven and see,
 from your lofty throne, holy and
  glorious.
Where are your zeal and your might?
 Your tenderness and compassion are
  withheld from us.
[16] But you are our Father,
 though Abraham does not know us
 or Israel acknowledge us;
you, Lord, are our Father,
 our Redeemer from of old is your
  name.
[17] Why, Lord, do you make us wander
 from your ways
 and harden our hearts so we do not
  revere you?
Return for the sake of your servants,
 the tribes that are your inheritance.
[18] For a little while your people
 possessed your holy place,
but now our enemies have trampled
 down your sanctuary.
[19] We are yours from of old;
 but you have not ruled over them,
 they have not been called[a] by your
  name.

64

[b] Oh, that you would rend
the heavens and come
down,
 that the mountains would tremble
  before you!
[2] As when fire sets twigs ablaze
 and causes water to boil,
come down to make your name known
 to your enemies

and cause the nations to quake
 before you!
[3] For when you did awesome things that
 we did not expect,
 you came down, and the mountains
  trembled before you.
[4] Since ancient times no one has heard,
 no ear has perceived,
no eye has seen any God besides you,
 who acts on behalf of those who
  wait for him.
[5] You come to the help of those who
 gladly do right,
 who remember your ways.
But when we continued to sin against
 them,
 you were angry.
How then can we be saved?
[6] All of us have become like one who is
 unclean,
 and all our righteous acts are like
  filthy rags;
we all shrivel up like a leaf,
 and like the wind our sins sweep us
  away.
[7] No one calls on your name
 or strives to lay hold of you;
for you have hidden your face from us
 and have given us over to[c] our sins.

[8] Yet you, Lord, are our Father.
 We are the clay, you are the potter;
 we are all the work of your hand.
[9] Do not be angry beyond measure,
 Lord;
 do not remember our sins forever.
Oh, look on us, we pray,
 for we are all your people.
[10] Your sacred cities have become a
 wasteland;
 even Zion is a wasteland, Jerusalem
  a desolation.
[11] Our holy and glorious temple, where
 our ancestors praised you,
has been burned with fire,
 and all that we treasured lies in
  ruins.

a 19 Or *We are like those you have never ruled, /
like those never called*   *b* In Hebrew texts 64:1 is
numbered 63:19b, and 64:2-12 is numbered
64:1-11.   *c 7* Septuagint, Syriac and Targum;
Hebrew *have made us melt because of*

¹²After all this, Lord, will you hold
   yourself back?
 Will you keep silent and punish us
   beyond measure?

Judgment and Salvation

65 "I revealed myself to those
   who did not ask for me;
   I was found by those who
   did not seek me.
 To a nation that did not call on my
   name,
   I said, 'Here am I, here am I.'
²All day long I have held out my hands
   to an obstinate people,
 who walk in ways not good,
   pursuing their own imaginations—
³a people who continually provoke me
   to my very face,
 offering sacrifices in gardens

and burning incense on altars of
   brick;
⁴who sit among the graves
   and spend their nights keeping
   secret vigil;
 who eat the flesh of pigs,
   and whose pots hold broth of
   impure meat;
⁵who say, 'Keep away; don't come near
   me,
   for I am too sacred for you!'
 Such people are smoke in my nostrils,
   a fire that keeps burning all day.

⁶"See, it stands written before me:
   I will not keep silent but will pay
   back in full;
   I will pay it back into their laps—
⁷both your sins and the sins of your
   ancestors,"
 says the Lord.
"Because they burned sacrifices on the
   mountains
   and defied me on the hills,
 I will measure into their laps
   the full payment for their former
   deeds."

⁸This is what the Lord says:

"As when juice is still found in a
   cluster of grapes
   and people say, 'Don't destroy it,
   there is still a blessing in it,'
 so will I do in behalf of my servants;
   I will not destroy them all.
⁹I will bring forth descendants from
   Jacob,
   and from Judah those who will
   possess my mountains;
 my chosen people will inherit them,
   and there will my servants live.
¹⁰Sharon will become a pasture for
   flocks,
   and the Valley of Achor a resting
   place for herds,
 for my people who seek me.

¹¹"But as for you who forsake the Lord
   and forget my holy mountain,
 who spread a table for Fortune
   and fill bowls of mixed wine for
   Destiny,

UNSHAKEN God

Isaiah 64:1–12

God is awesome.

The prophet Isaiah was so upset by the sins of Israel's enemies that he begged for God to "rend the heavens and come down" (Isaiah 64:1). Inviting the Lord to come and judge the world might sound like asking to get grounded—or worse—but only if you have done something wrong. Isaiah admits that God's people have sinned. They have endured his punishment. But now he asks the Lord to halt his anger and forgive them (see Isaiah 64:8–9,12). And he begs for God to unleash ferocious power against his enemies (see Isaiah 64:2). Isaiah understood the awesomeness of God. God is awesome in both forgiveness and fury.

So ... Suppose your awesome God came down into your world right now. What would he do?

¹²I will destine you for the sword,
 and all of you will fall in the
  slaughter;
for I called but you did not answer,
 I spoke but you did not listen.
You did evil in my sight
 and chose what displeases me."

¹³Therefore this is what the Sovereign
Lord says:

"My servants will eat,
 but you will go hungry;
my servants will drink,
 but you will go thirsty;
my servants will rejoice,
 but you will be put to shame.
¹⁴My servants will sing
 out of the joy of their hearts,
but you will cry out
 from anguish of heart
 and wail in brokenness of spirit.
¹⁵You will leave your name
 for my chosen ones to use in their
  curses;
the Sovereign Lord will put you to
  death,
 but to his servants he will give
  another name.
¹⁶Whoever invokes a blessing in the
  land
 will do so by the one true God;
whoever takes an oath in the land
 will swear by the one true God.
For the past troubles will be forgotten
 and hidden from my eyes.

New Heavens and a New Earth

¹⁷"See, I will create
 new heavens and a new earth.
The former things will not be
  remembered,
 nor will they come to mind.
¹⁸But be glad and rejoice forever
 in what I will create,
for I will create Jerusalem to be a
  delight
 and its people a joy.
¹⁹I will rejoice over Jerusalem
 and take delight in my people;
the sound of weeping and of crying
 will be heard in it no more.

²⁰"Never again will there be in it
 an infant who lives but a few days,
 or an old man who does not live out
  his years;
the one who dies at a hundred
 will be thought a mere child;
the one who fails to reach^a a hundred
 will be considered accursed.
²¹They will build houses and dwell in
  them;
 they will plant vineyards and eat
  their fruit.
²²No longer will they build houses and
  others live in them,
 or plant and others eat.
For as the days of a tree,
 so will be the days of my people;
my chosen ones will long enjoy
 the work of their hands.
²³They will not labor in vain,
 nor will they bear children doomed
  to misfortune;
for they will be a people blessed by the
  Lord,
 they and their descendants with
  them.
²⁴Before they call I will answer;
 while they are still speaking I will
  hear.
²⁵The wolf and the lamb will feed
  together,
 and the lion will eat straw like the
  ox,
 and dust will be the serpent's food.
They will neither harm nor destroy
 on all my holy mountain,"
                    says the Lord.

Judgment and Hope

66 This is what the Lord says:

"Heaven is my throne,
 and the earth is my footstool.
Where is the house you will build for
  me?
 Where will my resting place be?
²Has not my hand made all these
  things,
 and so they came into being?"
                    declares the Lord.

^a 20 Or *the sinner who reaches*

"These are the ones I look on with
favor:
those who are humble and contrite
in spirit,
and who tremble at my word.
³ But whoever sacrifices a bull
is like one who kills a person,
and whoever offers a lamb
is like one who breaks a dog's neck;
whoever makes a grain offering
is like one who presents pig's blood,
and whoever burns memorial incense
is like one who worships an idol.
They have chosen their own ways,
and they delight in their
abominations;
⁴ so I also will choose harsh treatment
for them
and will bring on them what they
dread.
For when I called, no one answered,
when I spoke, no one listened.
They did evil in my sight
and chose what displeases me."

⁵ Hear the word of the LORD,
you who tremble at his word:
"Your own people who hate you,
and exclude you because of my
name, have said,
'Let the LORD be glorified,
that we may see your joy!'
Yet they will be put to shame.
⁶ Hear that uproar from the city,
hear that noise from the temple!
It is the sound of the LORD
repaying his enemies all they
deserve.

⁷ "Before she goes into labor,
she gives birth;
before the pains come upon her,
she delivers a son.
⁸ Who has ever heard of such things?
Who has ever seen things like this?
Can a country be born in a day
or a nation be brought forth in a
moment?
Yet no sooner is Zion in labor
than she gives birth to her children.
⁹ Do I bring to the moment of birth
and not give delivery?" says the LORD.

"Do I close up the womb
when I bring to delivery?" says your
God.
¹⁰ "Rejoice with Jerusalem and be glad
for her,
all you who love her;
rejoice greatly with her,
all you who mourn over her.
¹¹ For you will nurse and be satisfied
at her comforting breasts;
you will drink deeply
and delight in her overflowing
abundance."

¹² For this is what the LORD says:

"I will extend peace to her like a river,
and the wealth of nations like a
flooding stream;
you will nurse and be carried on her
arm
and dandled on her knees.
¹³ As a mother comforts her child,
so will I comfort you;
and you will be comforted over
Jerusalem."

¹⁴ When you see this, your heart will
rejoice
and you will flourish like grass;
the hand of the LORD will be made
known to his servants,
but his fury will be shown to his
foes.
¹⁵ See, the LORD is coming with fire,
and his chariots are like a
whirlwind;
he will bring down his anger with
fury,
and his rebuke with flames of fire.
¹⁶ For with fire and with his sword
the LORD will execute judgment on
all people,
and many will be those slain by the
LORD.

¹⁷ "Those who consecrate and purify
themselves to go into the gardens, following one who is among those who eat
the flesh of pigs, rats and other unclean
things—they will meet their end together with the one they follow," declares the
LORD.

¹⁸"And I, because of what they have planned and done, am about to come^a and gather the people of all nations and languages, and they will come and see my glory.

¹⁹"I will set a sign among them, and I will send some of those who survive to the nations—to Tarshish, to the Libyans^b and Lydians (famous as archers), to Tubal and Greece, and to the distant islands that have not heard of my fame or seen my glory. They will proclaim my glory among the nations. ²⁰And they will bring all your people, from all the nations, to my holy mountain in Jerusalem as an offering to the LORD—on horses, in chariots and wagons, and on mules and camels," says the LORD. "They will bring them, as the Israelites bring their grain offerings, to the temple of the LORD in ceremonially clean vessels. ²¹And I will select some of them also to be priests and Levites," says the LORD.

²²"As the new heavens and the new earth that I make will endure before me," declares the LORD, "so will your name and descendants endure. ²³From one New Moon to another and from one Sabbath to another, all mankind will come and bow down before me," says the LORD. ²⁴"And they will go out and look on the dead bodies of those who rebelled against me; the worms that eat them will not die, the fire that burns them will not be quenched, and they will be loathsome to all mankind."

^a 18 The meaning of the Hebrew for this clause is uncertain.   ^b 19 Some Septuagint manuscripts Put (Libyans); Hebrew Pul

JEREMIAH

BOOK OUTLINE

Jeremiah, like Isaiah, was a young man called by God to warn Judah about its wickedness. He spent the first twenty years of his ministry under Josiah, a good king who tried to bring the people of Judah back to God. Jeremiah was often in danger from political and religious leaders who were angry because of his messages. Through this entire ordeal God protected Jeremiah so he could continue to warn the wicked and comfort those who trusted in God.

After Jerusalem was destroyed in 586 BC, Jeremiah chose to remain with the people, and eventually went with them to Egypt.

Since the messages of Jeremiah are not arranged in chronological order, it is helpful to read the history of Judah as found in Kings and Chronicles to better understand Jeremiah's messages.

1

The words of Jeremiah son of Hilkiah, one of the priests at Anathoth in the territory of Benjamin. ²The word of the LORD came to him in the thirteenth year of the reign of Josiah son of Amon king of Judah, ³and through the reign of Jehoiakim son of Josiah king of Judah, down to the fifth month of the eleventh year of Zedekiah son of Josiah king of Judah, when the people of Jerusalem went into exile.

The Call of Jeremiah

⁴The word of the LORD came to me, saying,

⁵"Before I formed you in the womb I
    knew*ᵃ* you,
    before you were born I set you
        apart;
    I appointed you as a prophet to the
        nations."

⁶"Alas, Sovereign LORD," I said, "I do not know how to speak; I am too young."

⁷But the LORD said to me, "Do not say, 'I am too young.' You must go to everyone I send you to and say whatever I command you. ⁸Do not be afraid of them, for I am with you and will rescue you," declares the LORD.

⁹Then the LORD reached out his hand and touched my mouth and said to me, "I have put my words in your mouth. ¹⁰See, today I appoint you over nations and kingdoms to uproot and tear down, to destroy and overthrow, to build and to plant."

¹¹The word of the LORD came to me: "What do you see, Jeremiah?"

"I see the branch of an almond tree," I replied.

¹²The LORD said to me, "You have seen correctly, for I am watching*ᵇ* to see that my word is fulfilled."

¹³The word of the LORD came to me again: "What do you see?"

"I see a pot that is boiling," I answered. "It is tilting toward us from the north."

¹⁴The LORD said to me, "From the north disaster will be poured out on all who live in the land. ¹⁵I am about to summon all the peoples of the northern kingdoms," declares the LORD.

"Their kings will come and set up
    their thrones
    in the entrance of the gates of
        Jerusalem;
they will come against all her
    surrounding walls
and against all the towns of
    Judah.
¹⁶I will pronounce my judgments on
    my people
    because of their wickedness in
        forsaking me,
in burning incense to other gods
    and in worshiping what their hands
        have made.

¹⁷"Get yourself ready! Stand up and say to them whatever I command you. Do not be terrified by them, or I will terrify you before them. ¹⁸Today I have made you a fortified city, an iron pillar and a bronze wall to stand against the whole land— against the kings of Judah, its officials, its priests and the people of the land. ¹⁹They will fight against you but will not overcome you, for I am with you and will rescue you," declares the LORD.

Israel Forsakes God

2

The word of the LORD came to me: ²"Go and proclaim in the hearing of Jerusalem:

"This is what the LORD says:

"'I remember the devotion of your
    youth,
    how as a bride you loved me
and followed me through the
    wilderness,
    through a land not sown.
³Israel was holy to the LORD,
    the firstfruits of his harvest;
all who devoured her were held
    guilty,
    and disaster overtook them,'"
                        declares the LORD.

⁴Hear the word of the LORD, you
    descendants of Jacob,
    all you clans of Israel.

ᵃ 5 Or *chose*   *ᵇ 12* The Hebrew for *watching* sounds like the Hebrew for *almond tree.*

⁵This is what the LORD says:

"What fault did your ancestors find in
    me,
    that they strayed so far from me?
They followed worthless idols
    and became worthless themselves.
⁶They did not ask, 'Where is the LORD,
    who brought us up out of Egypt
and led us through the barren
    wilderness,
    through a land of deserts and ravines,
a land of drought and utter darkness,
    a land where no one travels and no
        one lives?'
⁷I brought you into a fertile land
    to eat its fruit and rich produce.
But you came and defiled my land
    and made my inheritance
        detestable.
⁸The priests did not ask,
    'Where is the LORD?'
Those who deal with the law did not
        know me;
    the leaders rebelled against me.
The prophets prophesied by Baal,
    following worthless idols.

⁹"Therefore I bring charges against you
        again,"
                        declares the LORD.
    "And I will bring charges against
        your children's children.
¹⁰Cross over to the coasts of Cyprus and
        look,
    send to Kedar*ᵃ* and observe closely;
    see if there has ever been anything
        like this:
¹¹Has a nation ever changed its gods?
    (Yet they are not gods at all.)
But my people have exchanged their
        glorious God
    for worthless idols.
¹²Be appalled at this, you heavens,
    and shudder with great horror,"
                        declares the LORD.
¹³"My people have committed two sins:
They have forsaken me,
    the spring of living water,
and have dug their own cisterns,
    broken cisterns that cannot hold
        water.

ROCK SOLID truths

Jeremiah 2:1–11

The whole human race is guilty.

God's words hit hard. Israel was "holy to the LORD," chosen and dedicated to him (Jeremiah 2:3). When God's people first broke free from slavery they followed God in the desert like a young bride chases after a groom. But soon Israel ran fast and far in the opposite direction. They worshiped other gods and became worthless. God asks, "What fault did your ancestors find in me, that they strayed so far from me?" (Jeremiah 2:5). That's the same pointed truth God has to bring up with humankind again and again. Isaiah declared, "We all, like sheep, have gone astray, each of us has turned to our own way" (Isaiah 53:6). The apostle Paul wrote, "All have sinned and fall short of the glory of God" (Romans 3:23). God leaves no doubt. Human beings are sinful. We all need a Savior.

Think: Do you agree that all people are sinful — and need God's forgiveness and help to change? Why or why not?

---

¹⁴Is Israel a servant, a slave by birth?
    Why then has he become
        plunder?
¹⁵Lions have roared;
    they have growled at him.
They have laid waste his land;
    his towns are burned and
        deserted.
¹⁶Also, the men of Memphis and
        Tahpanhes
    have cracked your skull.

ᵃ 10 In the Syro-Arabian desert

¹⁷ Have you not brought this on
    yourselves
    by forsaking the Lord your God
    when he led you in the way?
¹⁸ Now why go to Egypt
    to drink water from the Nile*ᵃ*?
    And why go to Assyria
    to drink water from the Euphrates?
¹⁹ Your wickedness will punish you;
    your backsliding will rebuke you.
    Consider then and realize
    how evil and bitter it is for you
when you forsake the Lord your God
    and have no awe of me,"
               declares the Lord,
           the Lord Almighty.

²⁰ "Long ago you broke off your yoke
    and tore off your bonds;
    you said, 'I will not serve you!'
Indeed, on every high hill
    and under every spreading tree
    you lay down as a prostitute.
²¹ I had planted you like a choice vine
    of sound and reliable stock.
How then did you turn against me
    into a corrupt, wild vine?
²² Although you wash yourself with
    soap
    and use an abundance of cleansing
    powder,
    the stain of your guilt is still before
    me,"
          declares the Sovereign Lord.
²³ "How can you say, 'I am not defiled;
    I have not run after the Baals'?
See how you behaved in the valley;
    consider what you have done.
You are a swift she-camel
    running here and there,
²⁴ a wild donkey accustomed to the
    desert,
    sniffing the wind in her craving—
    in her heat who can restrain her?
Any males that pursue her need not
    tire themselves;
    at mating time they will find her.
²⁵ Do not run until your feet are bare
    and your throat is dry.
But you said, 'It's no use!
    I love foreign gods,
    and I must go after them.'

²⁶ "As a thief is disgraced when he is
    caught,
    so the people of Israel are
    disgraced—
they, their kings and their officials,
    their priests and their prophets.
²⁷ They say to wood, 'You are my father,'
    and to stone, 'You gave me birth.'
They have turned their backs to me
    and not their faces;
    yet when they are in trouble, they say,
    'Come and save us!'
²⁸ Where then are the gods you made for
    yourselves?
    Let them come if they can save you
    when you are in trouble!
For you, Judah, have as many gods
    as you have towns.

²⁹ "Why do you bring charges against me?
    You have all rebelled against me,"
              declares the Lord.
³⁰ "In vain I punished your people;
    they did not respond to correction.
Your sword has devoured your
    prophets
    like a ravenous lion.

³¹ "You of this generation, consider the
word of the Lord:

"Have I been a desert to Israel
    or a land of great darkness?
Why do my people say, 'We are free to
    roam;
    we will come to you no more'?
³² Does a young woman forget her
    jewelry,
    a bride her wedding ornaments?
Yet my people have forgotten me,
    days without number.
³³ How skilled you are at pursuing love!
    Even the worst of women can learn
    from your ways.
³⁴ On your clothes is found
    the lifeblood of the innocent poor,
    though you did not catch them
    breaking in.
Yet in spite of all this
³⁵   you say, 'I am innocent;
    he is not angry with me.'

ᵃ 18 Hebrew *Shihor*; that is, a branch of the Nile

But I will pass judgment on you
  because you say, 'I have not sinned.'
³⁶ Why do you go about so much,
  changing your ways?
You will be disappointed by Egypt
  as you were by Assyria.
³⁷ You will also leave that place
  with your hands on your head,
for the Lord has rejected those you
    trust;
  you will not be helped by them.

3 "If a man divorces his wife
  and she leaves him and marries
    another man,
should he return to her again?
  Would not the land be completely
    defiled?
But you have lived as a prostitute with
    many lovers—
  would you now return to me?"
                    declares the Lord.
² "Look up to the barren heights and see.
  Is there any place where you have
    not been ravished?
By the roadside you sat waiting for
    lovers,
  sat like a nomad in the desert.
You have defiled the land
  with your prostitution and
    wickedness.
³ Therefore the showers have been
    withheld,
  and no spring rains have fallen.
Yet you have the brazen look of a
    prostitute;
  you refuse to blush with shame.
⁴ Have you not just called to me:
  'My Father, my friend from my
    youth,
⁵ will you always be angry?
  Will your wrath continue forever?'
This is how you talk,
  but you do all the evil you can."

Unfaithful Israel

⁶ During the reign of King Josiah, the Lord said to me, "Have you seen what faithless Israel has done? She has gone up on every high hill and under every spreading tree and has committed adultery there.

⁷ I thought that after she had done all this she would return to me but she did not, and her unfaithful sister Judah saw it. ⁸ I gave faithless Israel her certificate of divorce and sent her away because of all her adulteries. Yet I saw that her unfaithful sister Judah had no fear; she also went out and committed adultery. ⁹ Because Israel's immorality mattered so little to her, she defiled the land and committed adultery with stone and wood. ¹⁰ In spite of all this, her unfaithful sister Judah did not return to me with all her heart, but only in pretense," declares the Lord.

¹¹ The Lord said to me, "Faithless Israel is more righteous than unfaithful Judah. ¹² Go, proclaim this message toward the north:

"'Return, faithless Israel,' declares the
    Lord,
  'I will frown on you no longer,
for I am faithful,' declares the Lord,
  'I will not be angry forever.
¹³ Only acknowledge your guilt—
  you have rebelled against the Lord
    your God,
you have scattered your favors to
    foreign gods
  under every spreading tree,
  and have not obeyed me,'"
                    declares the Lord.

¹⁴ "Return, faithless people," declares the Lord, "for I am your husband. I will choose you—one from a town and two from a clan—and bring you to Zion. ¹⁵ Then I will give you shepherds after my own heart, who will lead you with knowledge and understanding. ¹⁶ In those days, when your numbers have increased greatly in the land," declares the Lord, "people will no longer say, 'The ark of the covenant of the Lord.' It will never enter their minds or be remembered; it will not be missed, nor will another one be made. ¹⁷ At that time they will call Jerusalem The Throne of the Lord, and all nations will gather in Jerusalem to honor the name of the Lord. No longer will they follow the stubbornness of their evil hearts. ¹⁸ In those days the people of Judah will join

the people of Israel, and together they will come from a northern land to the land I gave your ancestors as an inheritance.

¹⁹ "I myself said,

"'How gladly would I treat you like
my children
and give you a pleasant land,
the most beautiful inheritance of
any nation.'
I thought you would call me 'Father'
and not turn away from following me.
²⁰ But like a woman unfaithful to her
husband,
so you, Israel, have been unfaithful
to me,"
declares the LORD.

²¹ A cry is heard on the barren heights,
the weeping and pleading of the
people of Israel,
because they have perverted their ways
and have forgotten the LORD their
God.

²² "Return, faithless people;
I will cure you of backsliding."

"Yes, we will come to you,
for you are the LORD our God.

ROCK SOLID
promises

"Return, faithless people; I will cure you of backsliding."

Jeremiah 3:22

God will not only forgive you and give you a do-over when you fail, but he will give you power to live his way.

---

²³ Surely the idolatrous commotion on
the hills
and mountains is a deception;
surely in the LORD our God
is the salvation of Israel.

²⁴ From our youth shameful gods have
consumed
the fruits of our ancestors' labor—
their flocks and herds,
their sons and daughters.
²⁵ Let us lie down in our shame,
and let our disgrace cover us.
We have sinned against the LORD our
God,
both we and our ancestors;
from our youth till this day
we have not obeyed the LORD our
God."

4 "If you, Israel, will return,
then return to me,"
declares the LORD.
"If you put your detestable idols out of
my sight
and no longer go astray,
² and if in a truthful, just and righteous
way
you swear, 'As surely as the LORD
lives,'
then the nations will invoke blessings
by him
and in him they will boast."

³ This is what the LORD says to the people of Judah and to Jerusalem:

"Break up your unplowed ground
and do not sow among thorns.
⁴ Circumcise yourselves to the LORD,
circumcise your hearts,
you people of Judah and inhabitants
of Jerusalem,
or my wrath will flare up and burn
like fire
because of the evil you have
done—
burn with no one to quench it.

Disaster From the North

⁵ "Announce in Judah and proclaim in
Jerusalem and say:
'Sound the trumpet throughout the
land!'
Cry aloud and say:
'Gather together!
Let us flee to the fortified cities!'
⁶ Raise the signal to go to Zion!
Flee for safety without delay!

For I am bringing disaster from the
north,
even terrible destruction."

7 A lion has come out of his lair;
a destroyer of nations has set out.
He has left his place
to lay waste your land.
Your towns will lie in ruins
without inhabitant.
8 So put on sackcloth,
lament and wail,
for the fierce anger of the LORD
has not turned away from us.

9 "In that day," declares the LORD,
"the king and the officials will lose
heart,
the priests will be horrified,
and the prophets will be appalled."

10 Then I said, "Alas, Sovereign LORD!
How completely you have deceived this people and Jerusalem by saying, 'You will have
peace,' when the sword is at our throats!"

11 At that time this people and Jerusalem will be told, "A scorching wind from
the barren heights in the desert blows
toward my people, but not to winnow or
cleanse; 12 a wind too strong for that comes
from me. Now I pronounce my judgments
against them."

13 Look! He advances like the clouds,
his chariots come like a whirlwind,
his horses are swifter than eagles.
Woe to us! We are ruined!
14 Jerusalem, wash the evil from your
heart and be saved.
How long will you harbor wicked
thoughts?
15 A voice is announcing from Dan,
proclaiming disaster from the hills
of Ephraim.
16 "Tell this to the nations,
proclaim concerning Jerusalem:
'A besieging army is coming from a
distant land,
raising a war cry against the cities
of Judah.
17 They surround her like men guarding
a field,
because she has rebelled against me,'"
declares the LORD.

18 "Your own conduct and actions
have brought this on you.
This is your punishment.
How bitter it is!
How it pierces to the heart!"

19 Oh, my anguish, my anguish!
I writhe in pain.
Oh, the agony of my heart!
My heart pounds within me,
I cannot keep silent.
For I have heard the sound of the
trumpet;
I have heard the battle cry.
20 Disaster follows disaster;
the whole land lies in ruins.
In an instant my tents are destroyed,
my shelter in a moment.
21 How long must I see the battle
standard
and hear the sound of the trumpet?

22 "My people are fools;
they do not know me.
They are senseless children;
they have no understanding.
They are skilled in doing evil;
they know not how to do good."

23 I looked at the earth,
and it was formless and empty;
and at the heavens,
and their light was gone.
24 I looked at the mountains,
and they were quaking;
all the hills were swaying.
25 I looked, and there were no people;
every bird in the sky had flown away.
26 I looked, and the fruitful land was a
desert;
all its towns lay in ruins
before the LORD, before his fierce
anger.

27 This is what the LORD says:

"The whole land will be ruined,
though I will not destroy it
completely.
28 Therefore the earth will mourn
and the heavens above grow dark,
because I have spoken and will not
relent,
I have decided and will not turn back."

²⁹ At the sound of horsemen and archers
    every town takes to flight.
Some go into the thickets;
    some climb up among the rocks.
All the towns are deserted;
    no one lives in them.

³⁰ What are you doing, you devastated
    one?
Why dress yourself in scarlet
    and put on jewels of gold?
Why highlight your eyes with
    makeup?
You adorn yourself in vain.
Your lovers despise you;
    they want to kill you.

³¹ I hear a cry as of a woman in labor,
    a groan as of one bearing her first
      child—
the cry of Daughter Zion gasping for
    breath,
    stretching out her hands and
      saying,
"Alas! I am fainting;
    my life is given over to murderers."

Not One Is Upright

5 "Go up and down the streets of
    Jerusalem,
    look around and consider,
    search through her squares.
If you can find but one person
    who deals honestly and seeks the
      truth,
    I will forgive this city.
² Although they say, 'As surely as the
    Lord lives,'
    still they are swearing falsely."

³ Lord, do not your eyes look for truth?
    You struck them, but they felt no
      pain;
    you crushed them, but they refused
      correction.
They made their faces harder than
    stone
    and refused to repent.
⁴ I thought, "These are only the poor;
    they are foolish,
for they do not know the way of the
    Lord,
    the requirements of their God.

⁵ So I will go to the leaders
    and speak to them;
surely they know the way of the Lord,
    the requirements of their God."
But with one accord they too had
    broken off the yoke
    and torn off the bonds.
⁶ Therefore a lion from the forest will
    attack them,
    a wolf from the desert will ravage
      them,
    a leopard will lie in wait near their
      towns
    to tear to pieces any who venture
      out,
for their rebellion is great
    and their backslidings many.

⁷ "Why should I forgive you?
    Your children have forsaken me
    and sworn by gods that are not
      gods.
I supplied all their needs,
    yet they committed adultery
    and thronged to the houses of
      prostitutes.
⁸ They are well-fed, lusty stallions,
    each neighing for another man's
      wife.
⁹ Should I not punish them for this?"
    declares the Lord.
"Should I not avenge myself
    on such a nation as this?

¹⁰ "Go through her vineyards and ravage
    them,
    but do not destroy them completely.
Strip off her branches,
    for these people do not belong to
      the Lord.
¹¹ The people of Israel and the people of
    Judah
    have been utterly unfaithful to me,"
          declares the Lord.

¹² They have lied about the Lord;
    they said, "He will do nothing!
No harm will come to us;
    we will never see sword or famine.
¹³ The prophets are but wind
    and the word is not in them;
    so let what they say be done to
      them."

¹⁴Therefore this is what the Lord God Almighty says:

"Because the people have spoken these
    words,
  I will make my words in your
      mouth a fire
  and these people the wood it
      consumes.
¹⁵People of Israel," declares the Lord,
  "I am bringing a distant nation
      against you—
  an ancient and enduring nation,
    a people whose language you do not
        know,
    whose speech you do not
        understand.
¹⁶Their quivers are like an open grave;
    all of them are mighty warriors.
¹⁷They will devour your harvests and
        food,
    devour your sons and daughters;
  they will devour your flocks and
        herds,
    devour your vines and fig trees.
  With the sword they will destroy
    the fortified cities in which you
        trust.

¹⁸"Yet even in those days," declares the Lord, "I will not destroy you completely. ¹⁹And when the people ask, 'Why has the Lord our God done all this to us?' you will tell them, 'As you have forsaken me and served foreign gods in your own land, so now you will serve foreigners in a land not your own.'

²⁰"Announce this to the descendants of
        Jacob
    and proclaim it in Judah:
²¹Hear this, you foolish and senseless
        people,
    who have eyes but do not see,
    who have ears but do not hear:
²²Should you not fear me?" declares the
        Lord.
    "Should you not tremble in my
        presence?
  I made the sand a boundary for the
        sea,
    an everlasting barrier it cannot
        cross.

  The waves may roll, but they cannot
        prevail;
    they may roar, but they cannot
        cross it.
²³But these people have stubborn and
        rebellious hearts;
    they have turned aside and gone
        away.
²⁴They do not say to themselves,
    'Let us fear the Lord our God,
  who gives autumn and spring rains in
        season,
    who assures us of the regular weeks
        of harvest.'
²⁵Your wrongdoings have kept these
        away;
    your sins have deprived you of good.

²⁶"Among my people are the wicked
    who lie in wait like men who snare
        birds
    and like those who set traps to catch
        people.
²⁷Like cages full of birds,
    their houses are full of deceit;
  they have become rich and powerful
²⁸   and have grown fat and sleek.
  Their evil deeds have no limit;
    they do not seek justice.
  They do not promote the case of the
        fatherless;
    they do not defend the just cause of
        the poor.
²⁹Should I not punish them for this?"
        declares the Lord.
    "Should I not avenge myself
    on such a nation as this?

³⁰"A horrible and shocking thing
    has happened in the land:
³¹The prophets prophesy lies,
    the priests rule by their own authority,
  and my people love it this way.
    But what will you do in the end?

Jerusalem Under Siege

6 "Flee for safety, people of
        Benjamin!
    Flee from Jerusalem!
  Sound the trumpet in Tekoa!
    Raise the signal over Beth
        Hakkerem!

For disaster looms out of the north,
 even terrible destruction.
² I will destroy Daughter Zion,
 so beautiful and delicate.
³ Shepherds with their flocks will come
  against her;
 they will pitch their tents around
  her,
 each tending his own portion."

⁴ "Prepare for battle against her!
 Arise, let us attack at noon!
But, alas, the daylight is fading,
 and the shadows of evening grow
  long.
⁵ So arise, let us attack at night
 and destroy her fortresses!"

⁶ This is what the LORD Almighty says:

"Cut down the trees
 and build siege ramps against
  Jerusalem.
This city must be punished;
 it is filled with oppression.
⁷ As a well pours out its water,
 so she pours out her wickedness.
Violence and destruction resound in
  her;
 her sickness and wounds are ever
  before me.
⁸ Take warning, Jerusalem,
 or I will turn away from you
and make your land desolate
 so no one can live in it."

⁹ This is what the LORD Almighty says:

"Let them glean the remnant of Israel
 as thoroughly as a vine;
pass your hand over the branches
  again,
 like one gathering grapes."

¹⁰ To whom can I speak and give
  warning?
 Who will listen to me?
Their ears are closed^a
 so they cannot hear.
The word of the LORD is offensive to
  them;
 they find no pleasure in it.
¹¹ But I am full of the wrath of the LORD,
 and I cannot hold it in.

"Pour it out on the children in the
  street
 and on the young men gathered
  together;
both husband and wife will be caught
  in it,
 and the old, those weighed down
  with years.
¹² Their houses will be turned over to
  others,
 together with their fields and their
  wives,
when I stretch out my hand
 against those who live in the land,"
       declares the LORD.
¹³ "From the least to the greatest,
 all are greedy for gain;
prophets and priests alike,
 all practice deceit.
¹⁴ They dress the wound of my people
 as though it were not serious.
'Peace, peace,' they say,
 when there is no peace.
¹⁵ Are they ashamed of their detestable
  conduct?
 No, they have no shame at all;
 they do not even know how to
  blush.
So they will fall among the fallen;
 they will be brought down when I
  punish them,"
       says the LORD.

¹⁶ This is what the LORD says:

"Stand at the crossroads and look;
 ask for the ancient paths,
ask where the good way is, and walk
  in it,
 and you will find rest for your
  souls.
But you said, 'We will not walk
  in it.'
¹⁷ I appointed watchmen over you and
  said,
 'Listen to the sound of the
  trumpet!'
But you said, 'We will not listen.'
¹⁸ Therefore hear, you nations;
 you who are witnesses,
 observe what will happen to them.

---

^a 10 Hebrew *uncircumcised*

ROCK SOLID
promises

"Ask where the good way is, and walk in it, and you will find rest for your souls." Jeremiah 6:16

Peace comes from walking in God's commands, not from running fast to escape them.

¹⁹Hear, you earth:
    I am bringing disaster on this
        people,
    the fruit of their schemes,
because they have not listened to my
        words
    and have rejected my law.
²⁰What do I care about incense from
        Sheba
    or sweet calamus from a distant
        land?
Your burnt offerings are not
        acceptable;
    your sacrifices do not please me."

²¹Therefore this is what the Lord says:

"I will put obstacles before this people.
    Parents and children alike will
        stumble over them;
    neighbors and friends will perish."

²²This is what the Lord says:

"Look, an army is coming
    from the land of the north;
a great nation is being stirred up
    from the ends of the earth.
²³They are armed with bow and spear;
    they are cruel and show no mercy.
They sound like the roaring sea
    as they ride on their horses;
they come like men in battle
        formation
    to attack you, Daughter Zion."

²⁴We have heard reports about them,
    and our hands hang limp.
Anguish has gripped us,
    pain like that of a woman in labor.
²⁵Do not go out to the fields
    or walk on the roads,
for the enemy has a sword,
    and there is terror on every side.
²⁶Put on sackcloth, my people,
    and roll in ashes;
mourn with bitter wailing
    as for an only son,
for suddenly the destroyer
    will come upon us.

²⁷"I have made you a tester of metals
    and my people the ore,
that you may observe
    and test their ways.
²⁸They are all hardened rebels,
    going about to slander.
They are bronze and iron;
    they all act corruptly.
²⁹The bellows blow fiercely
    to burn away the lead with fire,
but the refining goes on in vain;
    the wicked are not purged out.
³⁰They are called rejected silver,
    because the Lord has rejected
        them."

False Religion Worthless

7 This is the word that came to Jeremiah from the Lord: ²"Stand at the gate of the Lord's house and there proclaim this message:

"'Hear the word of the Lord, all you people of Judah who come through these gates to worship the Lord. ³This is what the Lord Almighty, the God of Israel, says: Reform your ways and your actions, and I will let you live in this place. ⁴Do not trust in deceptive words and say, "This is the temple of the Lord, the temple of the Lord, the temple of the Lord!" ⁵If you really change your ways and your actions and deal with each other justly, ⁶if you do not oppress the foreigner, the fatherless or the widow and do not shed innocent blood in this place, and if you do not follow other gods to your own harm, ⁷then I will let you live in this place, in the land I gave your ancestors for ever and ever. ⁸But look, you are trusting in deceptive words that are worthless.

⁹"'Will you steal and murder, commit adultery and perjury,ᵃ burn incense to Baal and follow other gods you have not known, ¹⁰and then come and stand before me in this house, which bears my Name, and say, "We are safe"—safe to do all these detestable things? ¹¹Has this house, which bears my Name, become a den of robbers to you? But I have been watching! declares the LORD.

¹²"'Go now to the place in Shiloh where I first made a dwelling for my Name, and see what I did to it because of the wickedness of my people Israel. ¹³While you were doing all these things, declares the LORD, I spoke to you again and again, but you did not listen; I called you, but you did not answer. ¹⁴Therefore, what I did to Shiloh I will now do to the house that bears my Name, the temple you trust in, the place I gave to you and your ancestors. ¹⁵I will thrust you from my presence, just as I did all your fellow Israelites, the people of Ephraim.'

¹⁶"So do not pray for this people nor offer any plea or petition for them; do not plead with me, for I will not listen to you. ¹⁷Do you not see what they are doing in the towns of Judah and in the streets of Jerusalem? ¹⁸The children gather wood, the fathers light the fire, and the women knead the dough and make cakes to offer to the Queen of Heaven. They pour out drink offerings to other gods to arouse my anger. ¹⁹But am I the one they are provoking? declares the LORD. Are they not rather harming themselves, to their own shame?

²⁰"'Therefore this is what the Sovereign LORD says: My anger and my wrath will be poured out on this place—on man and beast, on the trees of the field and on the crops of your land—and it will burn and not be quenched.

²¹"This is what the LORD Almighty, the God of Israel, says: Go ahead, add your burnt offerings to your other sacrifices and eat the meat yourselves! ²²For when I brought your ancestors out of Egypt and spoke to them, I did not just give them commands about burnt offerings and sacrifices, ²³but I gave them this command: Obey me, and I will be your God and you will be my people. Walk in obedience to all I command you, that it may go well with you. ²⁴But they did not listen or pay attention; instead, they followed the stubborn inclinations of their evil hearts. They went backward and not forward. ²⁵From the time your ancestors left Egypt until now, day after day, again and again I sent you my servants the prophets. ²⁶But they did not listen to me or pay attention. They were stiff-necked and did more evil than their ancestors.'

²⁷"When you tell them all this, they will not listen to you; when you call to them, they will not answer. ²⁸Therefore say to them, 'This is the nation that has not obeyed the LORD its God or responded to correction. Truth has perished; it has vanished from their lips.

²⁹"'Cut off your hair and throw it away; take up a lament on the barren heights, for the LORD has rejected and abandoned this generation that is under his wrath.

The Valley of Slaughter

³⁰"'The people of Judah have done evil in my eyes, declares the LORD. They have set up their detestable idols in the house that bears my Name and have defiled it. ³¹They have built the high places of Topheth in the Valley of Ben Hinnom to burn their sons and daughters in the fire—something I did not command, nor did it enter my mind. ³²So beware, the days are coming, declares the LORD, when people will no longer call it Topheth or the Valley of Ben Hinnom, but the Valley of Slaughter, for they will bury the dead in Topheth until there is no more room. ³³Then the carcasses of this people will become food for the birds and the wild animals, and there will be no one to frighten them away. ³⁴I will bring an end to the sounds of joy and gladness and to the voices of bride and bridegroom in the towns

ᵃ 9 Or *and swear by false gods*

of Judah and the streets of Jerusalem, for the land will become desolate.

8

"'At that time, declares the LORD, the bones of the kings and officials of Judah, the bones of the priests and prophets, and the bones of the people of Jerusalem will be removed from their graves. ²They will be exposed to the sun and the moon and all the stars of the heavens, which they have loved and served and which they have followed and consulted and worshiped. They will not be gathered up or buried, but will be like dung lying on the ground. ³Wherever I banish them, all the survivors of this evil nation will prefer death to life, declares the LORD Almighty.'

Sin and Punishment

⁴"Say to them, 'This is what the LORD says:

"'When people fall down, do they not get up?
    When someone turns away, do they not return?
⁵Why then have these people turned away?
    Why does Jerusalem always turn away?
They cling to deceit;
    they refuse to return.
⁶I have listened attentively,
    but they do not say what is right.
None of them repent of their wickedness,
    saying, "What have I done?"
Each pursues their own course
    like a horse charging into battle.
⁷Even the stork in the sky
    knows her appointed seasons,
and the dove, the swift and the thrush
    observe the time of their migration.
But my people do not know
    the requirements of the LORD.

⁸"'How can you say, "We are wise,
    for we have the law of the LORD,"
when actually the lying pen of the scribes
    has handled it falsely?

⁹The wise will be put to shame;
    they will be dismayed and trapped.
Since they have rejected the word of the LORD,
    what kind of wisdom do they have?
¹⁰Therefore I will give their wives to other men
    and their fields to new owners.
From the least to the greatest,
    all are greedy for gain;
prophets and priests alike,
    all practice deceit.
¹¹They dress the wound of my people
    as though it were not serious.
"Peace, peace," they say,
    when there is no peace.
¹²Are they ashamed of their detestable conduct?
    No, they have no shame at all;
    they do not even know how to blush.
So they will fall among the fallen;
    they will be brought down when they are punished,
        says the LORD.

¹³"'I will take away their harvest,
        declares the LORD.
    There will be no grapes on the vine.
There will be no figs on the tree,
    and their leaves will wither.
What I have given them
    will be taken from them.ᵃ'"

¹⁴Why are we sitting here?
    Gather together!
Let us flee to the fortified cities
    and perish there!
For the LORD our God has doomed us to perish
    and given us poisoned water to drink,
    because we have sinned against him.
¹⁵We hoped for peace
    but no good has come,
for a time of healing
    but there is only terror.
¹⁶The snorting of the enemy's horses
    is heard from Dan;

ᵃ 13 The meaning of the Hebrew for this sentence is uncertain.

897

at the neighing of their stallions
 the whole land trembles.
They have come to devour
 the land and everything in it,
 the city and all who live there.

¹⁷ "See, I will send venomous snakes
  among you,
 vipers that cannot be charmed,
 and they will bite you,"
  declares the Lord.

¹⁸ You who are my Comforter^a in sorrow,
 my heart is faint within me.
¹⁹ Listen to the cry of my people
 from a land far away:
 "Is the Lord not in Zion?
 Is her King no longer there?"

"Why have they aroused my anger
 with their images,
 with their worthless foreign idols?"

²⁰ "The harvest is past,
 the summer has ended,
 and we are not saved."

²¹ Since my people are crushed, I am
  crushed;
 I mourn, and horror grips me.
²² Is there no balm in Gilead?
 Is there no physician there?
 Why then is there no healing
 for the wound of my people?

9 ^b ¹ Oh, that my head were a spring
  of water
 and my eyes a fountain of tears!
I would weep day and night
 for the slain of my people.
² Oh, that I had in the desert
 a lodging place for travelers,
so that I might leave my people
 and go away from them;
for they are all adulterers,
 a crowd of unfaithful people.

³ "They make ready their tongue
 like a bow, to shoot lies;
it is not by truth
 that they triumph^c in the land.
They go from one sin to another;
 they do not acknowledge me,"
  declares the Lord.
⁴ "Beware of your friends;
 do not trust anyone in your clan.

For every one of them is a deceiver,^d
 and every friend a slanderer.
⁵ Friend deceives friend,
 and no one speaks the truth.
They have taught their tongues to lie;
 they weary themselves with
  sinning.
⁶ You^e live in the midst of deception;
 in their deceit they refuse to
  acknowledge me,"
  declares the Lord.

⁷ Therefore this is what the Lord Almighty says:

"See, I will refine and test them,
 for what else can I do
 because of the sin of my people?
⁸ Their tongue is a deadly arrow;
 it speaks deceitfully.
With their mouths they all speak
  cordially to their neighbors,
 but in their hearts they set traps for
  them.
⁹ Should I not punish them for this?"
 declares the Lord.
"Should I not avenge myself
 on such a nation as this?"

¹⁰ I will weep and wail for the mountains
 and take up a lament concerning
  the wilderness grasslands.
They are desolate and untraveled,
 and the lowing of cattle is not
  heard.
The birds have all fled
 and the animals are gone.

¹¹ "I will make Jerusalem a heap of ruins,
 a haunt of jackals;
 and I will lay waste the towns of Judah
 so no one can live there."

¹² Who is wise enough to understand this? Who has been instructed by the Lord and can explain it? Why has the land been ruined and laid waste like a desert that no one can cross?

---

^a *18* The meaning of the Hebrew for this word is uncertain. ^b In Hebrew texts 9:1 is numbered 8:23, and 9:2-26 is numbered 9:1-25. ^c *3* Or *lies; / they are not valiant for truth* ^d *4* Or *a deceiving Jacob* ^e *6* That is, Jeremiah (the Hebrew is singular)

¹³The Lord said, "It is because they have forsaken my law, which I set before them; they have not obeyed me or followed my law. ¹⁴Instead, they have followed the stubbornness of their hearts; they have followed the Baals, as their ancestors taught them." ¹⁵Therefore this is what the Lord Almighty, the God of Israel, says: "See, I will make this people eat bitter food and drink poisoned water. ¹⁶I will scatter them among nations that neither they nor their ancestors have known, and I will pursue them with the sword until I have made an end of them."

¹⁷This is what the Lord Almighty says:

"Consider now! Call for the wailing
        women to come;
    send for the most skillful of them.
¹⁸Let them come quickly
        and wail over us
    till our eyes overflow with tears
        and water streams from our
            eyelids.
¹⁹The sound of wailing is heard from
            Zion,
    'How ruined we are!
    How great is our shame!
    We must leave our land
        because our houses are in ruins.'"

²⁰Now, you women, hear the word of
            the Lord;
    open your ears to the words of his
        mouth.
Teach your daughters how to wail;
    teach one another a lament.
²¹Death has climbed in through our
        windows
    and has entered our fortresses;
it has removed the children from the
        streets
    and the young men from the public
        squares.

²²Say, "This is what the Lord declares:

"'Dead bodies will lie
    like dung on the open field,
like cut grain behind the reaper,
    with no one to gather them.'"

²³This is what the Lord says:

"Let not the wise boast of their wisdom
    or the strong boast of their strength
    or the rich boast of their riches,
²⁴but let the one who boasts boast about
        this:
    that they have the understanding to
        know me,
    that I am the Lord, who exercises
        kindness,
    justice and righteousness on earth,
    for in these I delight,"
                declares the Lord.

²⁵"The days are coming," declares the Lord, "when I will punish all who are circumcised only in the flesh — ²⁶Egypt, Judah, Edom, Ammon, Moab and all who live in the wilderness in distant places.*a* For all these nations are really uncircumcised, and even the whole house of Israel is uncircumcised in heart."

God and Idols

10 Hear what the Lord says to you, people of Israel. ²This is what the Lord says:

"Do not learn the ways of the nations
    or be terrified by signs in the
        heavens,
    though the nations are terrified by
        them.
³For the practices of the peoples are
        worthless;
    they cut a tree out of the forest,
    and a craftsman shapes it with his
        chisel.
⁴They adorn it with silver and gold;
    they fasten it with hammer and nails
    so it will not totter.
⁵Like a scarecrow in a cucumber field,
    their idols cannot speak;
they must be carried
    because they cannot walk.
Do not fear them;
    they can do no harm
    nor can they do any good."

⁶No one is like you, Lord;
    you are great,
    and your name is mighty in power.

---

a 26 Or *wilderness and who clip the hair by their foreheads*

ROCK SOLID *principles*

Jeremiah 9:23–24

Brag about God.

Carlos easily qualified for placement in his school's gifted program, but something about special classes for smart kids made him and his parents uneasy. Carlos outscored almost all of his peers in the gifted program, so he had nothing to prove to anyone. He liked his regular teachers, who gave him challenging assignments that fit his interests. But the biggest reason Carlos decided to stay in his regular classes was he didn't want to be locked up with classmates who acted like they were the most incredibly special people in the world. Carlos didn't think his brainpower made him better than his classmates. His intelligence was just a gift from God that he wanted to use to help others.

You have to be blindfolded not to spot these people as they roam your world—the guys or girls who show off their brains, flex their muscles for all to see, or flash their wealth in ways no one can miss. But you have something even better to be proud of. You know God. And he's smartest . . . and strongest . . . and richest.

⁷Who should not fear you,
 King of the nations?
 This is your due.
Among all the wise leaders of the
  nations
 and in all their kingdoms,
 there is no one like you.

⁸They are all senseless and foolish;
 they are taught by worthless
  wooden idols.
⁹Hammered silver is brought from
  Tarshish
 and gold from Uphaz.
What the craftsman and goldsmith
  have made
 is then dressed in blue and purple—
 all made by skilled workers.
¹⁰But the LORD is the true God;
 he is the living God, the eternal
  King.
When he is angry, the earth trembles;
 the nations cannot endure his
  wrath.

¹¹"Tell them this: 'These gods, who did not make the heavens and the earth, will perish from the earth and from under the heavens.'"ᵃ

¹²But God made the earth by his power;
 he founded the world by his wisdom
 and stretched out the heavens by his
  understanding.
¹³When he thunders, the waters in the
  heavens roar;
 he makes clouds rise from the ends
  of the earth.
He sends lightning with the rain
 and brings out the wind from his
  storehouses.

¹⁴Everyone is senseless and without
  knowledge;
 every goldsmith is shamed by his
  idols.
The images he makes are a fraud;
 they have no breath in them.

ᵃ 11 The text of this verse is in Aramaic.

¹⁵ They are worthless, the objects of
   mockery;
   when their judgment comes, they
      will perish.
¹⁶ He who is the Portion of Jacob is not
   like these,
   for he is the Maker of all things,
      including Israel, the people of his
         inheritance—
      the LORD Almighty is his name.

God is smarter than people.

Fake gods are as good as "a scarecrow in a cucumber field" (Jeremiah 10:5). They can't speak. They can't walk. There is no reason to fear them. And they don't do anyone any good. Time after time God had told the Israelites never to worship other gods. It was the very first of his Ten Commandments (see Exodus 20:3). And now the prophet Jeremiah offers good reasons the Lord expects to be worshiped. "No one is like you, LORD; you are great" (Jeremiah 10:6). "Among all the wise leaders of the nations … there is no one like you" (Jeremiah 10:7). "God made the earth by his power" (Jeremiah 10:12). In spite of the Lord's obvious amazingness, people continue to bow before idols. And so God reaches a logical conclusion. "Everyone is senseless and without knowledge" (Jeremiah 10:14). That's another way of saying that sometimes human beings aren't very bright.

Think: If God is so smart and good, why are we so slow to live for him?

ROCK SOLID truths

Coming Destruction

¹⁷ Gather up your belongings to leave
   the land,
   you who live under siege.
¹⁸ For this is what the LORD says:
   "At this time I will hurl out
      those who live in this land;
   I will bring distress on them
      so that they may be captured."

¹⁹ Woe to me because of my injury!
   My wound is incurable!
   Yet I said to myself,
   "This is my sickness, and I must
      endure it."
²⁰ My tent is destroyed;
   all its ropes are snapped.
   My children are gone from me and are
      no more;
   no one is left now to pitch my tent
      or to set up my shelter.
²¹ The shepherds are senseless
      and do not inquire of the LORD;
   so they do not prosper
      and all their flock is scattered.
²² Listen! The report is coming—
      a great commotion from the land of
         the north!
   It will make the towns of Judah desolate,
      a haunt of jackals.

Jeremiah's Prayer

²³ LORD, I know that people's lives are
      not their own;
   it is not for them to direct their steps.
²⁴ Discipline me, LORD, but only in due
         measure—
   not in your anger,
      or you will reduce me to nothing.
²⁵ Pour out your wrath on the nations
      that do not acknowledge you,
   on the peoples who do not call on
      your name.
   For they have devoured Jacob;
      they have devoured him completely
         and destroyed his homeland.

The Covenant Is Broken

11 This is the word that came to Jeremiah from the LORD: ²"Listen to the terms of this covenant and tell them to the people of Judah and to those who live in Jerusalem. ³Tell them that this is what the LORD, the God of Israel, says: 'Cursed is the one who does not obey the terms of this covenant— ⁴the terms I commanded your ancestors when I brought them out of Egypt, out of the iron-smelting furnace.' I said, 'Obey me and do everything I command you, and you will be my people, and I will be your God. ⁵Then I will fulfill the oath I swore to your ancestors, to give them a land flowing with milk and honey'—the land you possess today."

I answered, "Amen, LORD."

⁶The LORD said to me, "Proclaim all these words in the towns of Judah and in the streets of Jerusalem: 'Listen to the terms of this covenant and follow them. ⁷From the time I brought your ancestors up from Egypt until today, I warned them again and again, saying, "Obey me." ⁸But they did not listen or pay attention; instead, they followed the stubbornness of their evil hearts. So I brought on them all the curses of the covenant I had commanded them to follow but that they did not keep.'"

⁹Then the LORD said to me, "There is a conspiracy among the people of Judah and those who live in Jerusalem. ¹⁰They have returned to the sins of their ancestors, who refused to listen to my words. They have followed other gods to serve them. Both Israel and Judah have broken the covenant I made with their ancestors. ¹¹Therefore this is what the LORD says: 'I will bring on them a disaster they cannot escape. Although they cry out to me, I will not listen to them. ¹²The towns of Judah and the people of Jerusalem will go and cry out to the gods to whom they burn incense, but they will not help them at all when disaster strikes. ¹³You, Judah, have as many gods as you have towns; and the altars you have set up to burn incense to that shameful god Baal are as many as the streets of Jerusalem.'

¹⁴"Do not pray for this people or offer any plea or petition for them, because I will not listen when they call to me in the time of their distress.

¹⁵"What is my beloved doing in my temple
  as she, with many others, works out her evil schemes?
Can consecrated meat avert your punishment?
When you engage in your wickedness,
  then you rejoice.ᵃ"

¹⁶The LORD called you a thriving olive tree
  with fruit beautiful in form.
But with the roar of a mighty storm he will set it on fire,
  and its branches will be broken.

¹⁷The LORD Almighty, who planted you, has decreed disaster for you, because the people of both Israel and Judah have done evil and aroused my anger by burning incense to Baal.

Plot Against Jeremiah

¹⁸Because the LORD revealed their plot to me, I knew it, for at that time he showed me what they were doing. ¹⁹I had been like a gentle lamb led to the slaughter; I did not realize that they had plotted against me, saying,

"Let us destroy the tree and its fruit;
  let us cut him off from the land of the living,
  that his name be remembered no more."
²⁰But you, LORD Almighty, who judge righteously
  and test the heart and mind,
let me see your vengeance on them,
  for to you I have committed my cause.

²¹Therefore this is what the LORD says about the people of Anathoth who are threatening to kill you, saying, "Do not prophesy in the name of the LORD or you will die by our hands"— ²²therefore this is what the LORD Almighty says: "I will punish them. Their young men will die by the sword, their sons and daughters by

---

ᵃ 15 Or *Could consecrated meat avert your punishment? / Then you would rejoice* famine. ²³Not even a remnant will be left to them, because I will bring disaster on the people of Anathoth in the year of their punishment."

Jeremiah's Complaint

12 You are always righteous,
Lord,
 when I bring a case before
  you.
Yet I would speak with you about your
  justice:
Why does the way of the wicked
  prosper?
Why do all the faithless live at ease?
²You have planted them, and they have
  taken root;
 they grow and bear fruit.
You are always on their lips
 but far from their hearts.
³Yet you know me, Lord;
 you see me and test my thoughts
  about you.
Drag them off like sheep to be
  butchered!
 Set them apart for the day of
  slaughter!
⁴How long will the land lie parched
 and the grass in every field be
  withered?
Because those who live in it are
  wicked,
 the animals and birds have
  perished.
Moreover, the people are saying,
 "He will not see what happens to us."

God's Answer

⁵"If you have raced with men on foot
 and they have worn you out,
  how can you compete with horses?
If you stumble^a in safe country,
 how will you manage in the thickets
  by^b the Jordan?
⁶Your relatives, members of your own
  family—
 even they have betrayed you;
 they have raised a loud cry against
  you.
Do not trust them,
 though they speak well of you.

⁷"I will forsake my house,
 abandon my inheritance;
I will give the one I love
 into the hands of her enemies.
⁸My inheritance has become to me
 like a lion in the forest.
She roars at me;
 therefore I hate her.
⁹Has not my inheritance become to me
 like a speckled bird of prey
 that other birds of prey surround
  and attack?
Go and gather all the wild beasts;
 bring them to devour.
¹⁰Many shepherds will ruin my vineyard
 and trample down my field;
they will turn my pleasant field
 into a desolate wasteland.
¹¹It will be made a wasteland,
 parched and desolate before me;
the whole land will be laid waste
 because there is no one who cares.
¹²Over all the barren heights in the
  desert
 destroyers will swarm,
for the sword of the Lord will devour
 from one end of the land to the
  other;
 no one will be safe.
¹³They will sow wheat but reap thorns;
 they will wear themselves out but
  gain nothing.
They will bear the shame of their
  harvest
 because of the Lord's fierce anger."

¹⁴This is what the Lord says: "As for all my wicked neighbors who seize the inheritance I gave my people Israel, I will uproot them from their lands and I will uproot the people of Judah from among them. ¹⁵But after I uproot them, I will again have compassion and will bring each of them back to their own inheritance and their own country. ¹⁶And if they learn well the ways of my people and swear by my name, saying, 'As surely as the Lord lives'—even as they once taught my people to swear by Baal—then they will be established among my people. ¹⁷But if any

---

^a 5 Or *you feel secure only*   ^b 5 Or *the flooding of*

nation does not listen, I will completely uproot and destroy it," declares the LORD.

A Linen Belt

13 This is what the LORD said to me: "Go and buy a linen belt and put it around your waist, but do not let it touch water." ²So I bought a belt, as the LORD directed, and put it around my waist.

³Then the word of the LORD came to me a second time: ⁴"Take the belt you bought and are wearing around your waist, and go now to Perath*ᵃ* and hide it there in a crevice in the rocks." ⁵So I went and hid it at Perath, as the LORD told me.

⁶Many days later the LORD said to me, "Go now to Perath and get the belt I told you to hide there." ⁷So I went to Perath and dug up the belt and took it from the place where I had hidden it, but now it was ruined and completely useless.

⁸Then the word of the LORD came to me: ⁹"This is what the LORD says: 'In the same way I will ruin the pride of Judah and the great pride of Jerusalem. ¹⁰These wicked people, who refuse to listen to my words, who follow the stubbornness of their hearts and go after other gods to serve and worship them, will be like this belt—completely useless! ¹¹For as a belt is bound around the waist, so I bound all the people of Israel and all the people of Judah to me,' declares the LORD, 'to be my people for my renown and praise and honor. But they have not listened.'

Wineskins

¹²"Say to them: 'This is what the LORD, the God of Israel, says: Every wineskin should be filled with wine.' And if they say to you, 'Don't we know that every wineskin should be filled with wine?' ¹³then tell them, 'This is what the LORD says: I am going to fill with drunkenness all who live in this land, including the kings who sit on David's throne, the priests, the prophets and all those living in Jerusalem. ¹⁴I will smash them one against the other, parents and children alike, declares the LORD. I will allow no pity or mercy or compassion to keep me from destroying them.'"

Threat of Captivity

¹⁵Hear and pay attention,
    do not be arrogant,
    for the LORD has spoken.
¹⁶Give glory to the LORD your God
    before he brings the darkness,
before your feet stumble
    on the darkening hills.
You hope for light,
    but he will turn it to utter darkness
    and change it to deep gloom.
¹⁷If you do not listen,
    I will weep in secret
    because of your pride;
my eyes will weep bitterly,
    overflowing with tears,
because the LORD's flock will be
    taken captive.

¹⁸Say to the king and to the queen
        mother,
    "Come down from your thrones,
for your glorious crowns
    will fall from your heads."
¹⁹The cities in the Negev will be shut up,
    and there will be no one to open
        them.
All Judah will be carried into exile,
    carried completely away.

²⁰Look up and see
    those who are coming from the
        north.
Where is the flock that was entrusted
        to you,
    the sheep of which you boasted?
²¹What will you say when the LORD sets
        over you
    those you cultivated as your special
        allies?
Will not pain grip you
    like that of a woman in labor?
²²And if you ask yourself,
    "Why has this happened to me?"—
it is because of your many sins
    that your skirts have been torn off
    and your body mistreated.

ᵃ 4 Or possibly *to the Euphrates*; similarly in verses 5-7

²³Can an Ethiopian*^a change his skin
⁣ or a leopard its spots?
Neither can you do good
⁣ who are accustomed to doing evil.

²⁴"I will scatter you like chaff
⁣ driven by the desert wind.
²⁵This is your lot,
⁣ the portion I have decreed for you,"
⁣⁣⁣⁣ declares the LORD,
"because you have forgotten me
⁣ and trusted in false gods.
²⁶I will pull up your skirts over your face
⁣ that your shame may be seen—
²⁷your adulteries and lustful neighings,
⁣ your shameless prostitution!
I have seen your detestable acts
⁣ on the hills and in the fields.
Woe to you, Jerusalem!
⁣ How long will you be unclean?"

Drought, Famine, Sword

14 This is the word of the LORD that came to Jeremiah concerning the drought:

²"Judah mourns,
⁣ her cities languish;
they wail for the land,
⁣ and a cry goes up from Jerusalem.
³The nobles send their servants for
⁣⁣⁣⁣ water;
⁣ they go to the cisterns
⁣ but find no water.
They return with their jars unfilled;
⁣ dismayed and despairing,
⁣ they cover their heads.
⁴The ground is cracked
⁣ because there is no rain in the land;
the farmers are dismayed
⁣ and cover their heads.
⁵Even the doe in the field
⁣ deserts her newborn fawn
because there is no grass.
⁶Wild donkeys stand on the barren
⁣⁣⁣⁣ heights
⁣ and pant like jackals;
their eyes fail
⁣ for lack of food."

⁷Although our sins testify against us,
⁣ do something, LORD, for the sake of
⁣⁣⁣⁣ your name.

For we have often rebelled;
⁣ we have sinned against you.
⁸You who are the hope of Israel,
⁣ its Savior in times of distress,
why are you like a stranger in the land,
⁣ like a traveler who stays only a
⁣⁣⁣⁣ night?
⁹Why are you like a man taken by
⁣⁣⁣⁣ surprise,
⁣ like a warrior powerless to save?
You are among us, LORD,
⁣ and we bear your name;
⁣ do not forsake us!

¹⁰This is what the LORD says about this people:

"They greatly love to wander;
⁣ they do not restrain their feet.
So the LORD does not accept them;
⁣ he will now remember their
⁣⁣⁣⁣ wickedness
⁣ and punish them for their sins."

¹¹Then the LORD said to me, "Do not pray for the well-being of this people. ¹²Although they fast, I will not listen to their cry; though they offer burnt offerings and grain offerings, I will not accept them. Instead, I will destroy them with the sword, famine and plague."

¹³But I said, "Alas, Sovereign LORD! The prophets keep telling them, 'You will not see the sword or suffer famine. Indeed, I will give you lasting peace in this place.'"

¹⁴Then the LORD said to me, "The prophets are prophesying lies in my name. I have not sent them or appointed them or spoken to them. They are prophesying to you false visions, divinations, idolatries*^b and the delusions of their own minds. ¹⁵Therefore this is what the LORD says about the prophets who are prophesying in my name: I did not send them, yet they are saying, 'No sword or famine will touch this land.' Those same prophets will perish by sword and famine. ¹⁶And the people they are prophesying to will be thrown out into the streets of Jerusalem because of the famine and sword. There will be no one

---

^a 23 Hebrew *Cushite* (probably a person from the upper Nile region) *^b 14* Or *visions, worthless divinations*

to bury them, their wives, their sons and their daughters. I will pour out on them the calamity they deserve.

17 "Speak this word to them:

"'Let my eyes overflow with tears
    night and day without ceasing;
for the Virgin Daughter, my people,
    has suffered a grievous wound,
    a crushing blow.
18 If I go into the country,
    I see those slain by the sword;
if I go into the city,
    I see the ravages of famine.
Both prophet and priest
    have gone to a land they know not.'"

19 Have you rejected Judah completely?
    Do you despise Zion?
Why have you afflicted us
    so that we cannot be healed?
We hoped for peace
    but no good has come,
for a time of healing
    but there is only terror.

20 We acknowledge our wickedness,
    LORD,
    and the guilt of our ancestors;
    we have indeed sinned against you.
21 For the sake of your name do not
    despise us;
    do not dishonor your glorious
    throne.
Remember your covenant with us
    and do not break it.
22 Do any of the worthless idols of the
    nations bring rain?
    Do the skies themselves send down
    showers?
No, it is you, LORD our God.
    Therefore our hope is in you,
    for you are the one who does all
    this.

15 Then the LORD said to me: "Even if Moses and Samuel were to stand before me, my heart would not go out to this people. Send them away from my presence! Let them go! 2 And if they ask you, 'Where

---

ROCK SOLID
principles

Jeremiah 14:14–16

Beware of people who twist God's words.

Sierra was wowed the moment she walked into her friend's church. The worship band was as tight as any group she had ever seen in person, and the talks made her feel like God was involved in every bit of her life. The pastor was so sure of what he said. He did spout a lot of negative comments about other churches—not just a few churches he thought were mixed up in what they taught, but all churches everywhere, except his. And it seemed like the pastor talked far more about his thoughts and his plans for the church than he did about the Bible or about Jesus. It took a while for Sierra to see through his words, but he sure wasn't speaking for God.

Some people claim to speak for God, but they lie. They say they have visions, but they really hallucinate. Wise up to this reality: Some people who say they have a message from God are more messed up than you can imagine. So don't swallow human words whole. Test them against the Bible, the one message that comes straight from God.

shall we go?' tell them, 'This is what the LORD says:

> "'Those destined for death, to death;
> those for the sword, to the sword;
> those for starvation, to starvation;
> those for captivity, to captivity.'

³"I will send four kinds of destroyers against them," declares the LORD, "the sword to kill and the dogs to drag away and the birds and the wild animals to devour and destroy. ⁴I will make them abhorrent to all the kingdoms of the earth because of what Manasseh son of Hezekiah king of Judah did in Jerusalem.

> ⁵"Who will have pity on you,
> Jerusalem?
> Who will mourn for you?
> Who will stop to ask how you are?
> ⁶You have rejected me," declares the
> LORD.
> "You keep on backsliding.
> So I will reach out and destroy you;
> I am tired of holding back.
> ⁷I will winnow them with a winnowing
> fork
> at the city gates of the land.
> I will bring bereavement and
> destruction on my people,
> for they have not changed their ways.
> ⁸I will make their widows more
> numerous
> than the sand of the sea.
> At midday I will bring a destroyer
> against the mothers of their young
> men;
> suddenly I will bring down on them
> anguish and terror.
> ⁹The mother of seven will grow faint
> and breathe her last.
> Her sun will set while it is still day;
> she will be disgraced and
> humiliated.
> I will put the survivors to the sword
> before their enemies,"
>   declares the LORD.

> ¹⁰Alas, my mother, that you gave me
> birth,
> a man with whom the whole land
> strives and contends!

> I have neither lent nor borrowed,
> yet everyone curses me.

¹¹The LORD said,

> "Surely I will deliver you for a good
> purpose;
> surely I will make your enemies
> plead with you
> in times of disaster and times of
> distress.

> ¹²"Can a man break iron—
> iron from the north—or bronze?

> ¹³"Your wealth and your treasures
> I will give as plunder, without
> charge,
> because of all your sins
> throughout your country.
> ¹⁴I will enslave you to your enemies
> in*ᵃ* a land you do not know,
> for my anger will kindle a fire
> that will burn against you."

> ¹⁵LORD, you understand;
> remember me and care for me.
> Avenge me on my persecutors.
> You are long-suffering—do not take
> me away;
> think of how I suffer reproach for
> your sake.
> ¹⁶When your words came, I ate them;
> they were my joy and my heart's
> delight,
> for I bear your name,
> LORD God Almighty.
> ¹⁷I never sat in the company of revelers,
> never made merry with them;
> I sat alone because your hand was on me
> and you had filled me with
> indignation.
> ¹⁸Why is my pain unending
> and my wound grievous and
> incurable?
> You are to me like a deceptive brook,
> like a spring that fails.

¹⁹Therefore this is what the LORD says:

> "If you repent, I will restore you
> that you may serve me;

ᵃ 14 Some Hebrew manuscripts, Septuagint and Syriac (see also 17:4); most Hebrew manuscripts I will cause your enemies to bring you / into

if you utter worthy, not worthless,
> words,
you will be my spokesman.
Let this people turn to you,
> but you must not turn to them.
20 I will make you a wall to this people,
> a fortified wall of bronze;
they will fight against you
> but will not overcome you,
for I am with you
> to rescue and save you,"
>> declares the LORD.
21 "I will save you from the hands of the
> wicked
and deliver you from the grasp of
> the cruel."

Day of Disaster

16 Then the word of the LORD came to me: 2 "You must not marry and have sons or daughters in this place." 3 For this is what the LORD says about the sons and daughters born in this land and about the women who are their mothers and the men who are their fathers: 4 "They will die of deadly diseases. They will not be mourned or buried but will be like dung lying on the ground. They will perish by sword and famine, and their dead bodies will become food for the birds and the wild animals."

5 For this is what the LORD says: "Do not enter a house where there is a funeral meal; do not go to mourn or show sympathy, because I have withdrawn my blessing, my love and my pity from this people," declares the LORD. 6 "Both high and low will die in this land. They will not be buried or mourned, and no one will cut themselves or shave their head for the dead. 7 No one will offer food to comfort those who mourn for the dead—not even for a father or a mother—nor will anyone give them a drink to console them.

8 "And do not enter a house where there is feasting and sit down to eat and drink. 9 For this is what the LORD Almighty, the God of Israel, says: Before your eyes and in your days I will bring an end to the sounds of joy and gladness and to the voices of bride and bridegroom in this place.

10 "When you tell these people all this and they ask you, 'Why has the LORD decreed such a great disaster against us? What wrong have we done? What sin have we committed against the LORD our God?' 11 then say to them, 'It is because your ancestors forsook me,' declares the LORD, 'and followed other gods and served and worshiped them. They forsook me and did not keep my law. 12 But you have behaved more wickedly than your ancestors. See how all of you are following the stubbornness of your evil hearts instead of obeying me. 13 So I will throw you out of this land into a land neither you nor your ancestors have known, and there you will serve other gods day and night, for I will show you no favor.'

14 "However, the days are coming," declares the LORD, "when it will no longer be said, 'As surely as the LORD lives, who brought the Israelites up out of Egypt,' 15 but it will be said, 'As surely as the LORD lives, who brought the Israelites up out of the land of the north and out of all the countries where he had banished them.' For I will restore them to the land I gave their ancestors.

16 "But now I will send for many fishermen," declares the LORD, "and they will catch them. After that I will send for many hunters, and they will hunt them down on every mountain and hill and from the crevices of the rocks. 17 My eyes are on all their ways; they are not hidden from me, nor is their sin concealed from my eyes. 18 I will repay them double for their wickedness and their sin, because they have defiled my land with the lifeless forms of their vile images and have filled my inheritance with their detestable idols."

19 LORD, my strength and my fortress,
> my refuge in time of distress,
to you the nations will come
> from the ends of the earth and say,
"Our ancestors possessed nothing but
> false gods,
worthless idols that did them no
> good.
20 Do people make their own gods?
> Yes, but they are not gods!"

21 "Therefore I will teach them—
this time I will teach them
my power and might.
Then they will know
that my name is the LORD.

17 "Judah's sin is engraved with
an iron tool,
inscribed with a flint point,
on the tablets of their hearts
and on the horns of their altars.
2 Even their children remember
their altars and Asherah poles[a]
beside the spreading trees
and on the high hills.
3 My mountain in the land
and your[b] wealth and all your
treasures
I will give away as plunder,
together with your high places,
because of sin throughout your
country.
4 Through your own fault you will lose
the inheritance I gave you.
I will enslave you to your enemies
in a land you do not know,
for you have kindled my anger,
and it will burn forever."

5 This is what the LORD says:

"Cursed is the one who trusts in man,
who draws strength from mere flesh
and whose heart turns away from
the LORD.
6 That person will be like a bush in the
wastelands;
they will not see prosperity when it
comes.
They will dwell in the parched places
of the desert,
in a salt land where no one lives.

7 "But blessed is the one who trusts in
the LORD,
whose confidence is in him.
8 They will be like a tree planted by the
water
that sends out its roots by the stream.
It does not fear when heat comes;
its leaves are always green.
It has no worries in a year of drought
and never fails to bear fruit."

9 The heart is deceitful above all things
and beyond cure.
Who can understand it?

10 "I the LORD search the heart
and examine the mind,
to reward each person according to
their conduct,
according to what their deeds deserve."

11 Like a partridge that hatches eggs it
did not lay
are those who gain riches by unjust
means.
When their lives are half gone, their
riches will desert them,
and in the end they will prove to be
fools.

12 A glorious throne, exalted from the
beginning,
is the place of our sanctuary.
13 LORD, you are the hope of Israel;
all who forsake you will be put to
shame.
Those who turn away from you will be
written in the dust
because they have forsaken the LORD,
the spring of living water.

14 Heal me, LORD, and I will be healed;
save me and I will be saved,
for you are the one I praise.

[a] 2 That is, wooden symbols of the goddess
Asherah   [b] 2,3 Or hills / 3 and the mountains
of the land. / Your

ROCK SOLID *promises*

"Heal me, LORD, and I will be healed." Jeremiah 17:14

People who turn away from God will turn to dust. But God will put your body, heart, and mind back together.

15 They keep saying to me,
"Where is the word of the LORD?
Let it now be fulfilled!"
16 I have not run away from being your
shepherd;
you know I have not desired the day
of despair.
What passes my lips is open before
you.
17 Do not be a terror to me;
you are my refuge in the day of
disaster.
18 Let my persecutors be put to
shame,
but keep me from shame;
let them be terrified,
but keep me from terror.
Bring on them the day of disaster;
destroy them with double
destruction.

Keeping the Sabbath Day Holy

19 This is what the LORD said to me:
"Go and stand at the Gate of the People,*a* through which the kings of Judah
go in and out; stand also at all the other
gates of Jerusalem. 20 Say to them, 'Hear
the word of the LORD, you kings of Judah
and all people of Judah and everyone living in Jerusalem who come through these
gates. 21 This is what the LORD says: Be
careful not to carry a load on the Sabbath day or bring it through the gates of
Jerusalem. 22 Do not bring a load out of
your houses or do any work on the Sabbath, but keep the Sabbath day holy, as
I commanded your ancestors. 23 Yet they
did not listen or pay attention; they were
stiff-necked and would not listen or respond to discipline. 24 But if you are careful to obey me, declares the LORD, and
bring no load through the gates of this
city on the Sabbath, but keep the Sabbath day holy by not doing any work on
it, 25 then kings who sit on David's throne
will come through the gates of this city
with their officials. They and their officials will come riding in chariots and on
horses, accompanied by the men of Judah
and those living in Jerusalem, and this
city will be inhabited forever. 26 People

will come from the towns of Judah and
the villages around Jerusalem, from the
territory of Benjamin and the western
foothills, from the hill country and the
Negev, bringing burnt offerings and sacrifices, grain offerings and incense, and
bringing thank offerings to the house of
the LORD. 27 But if you do not obey me to
keep the Sabbath day holy by not carrying
any load as you come through the gates
of Jerusalem on the Sabbath day, then I
will kindle an unquenchable fire in the
gates of Jerusalem that will consume her
fortresses.'"

At the Potter's House

18 This is the word that came
to Jeremiah from the LORD:
2 "Go down to the potter's
house, and there I will give you my message." 3 So I went down to the potter's
house, and I saw him working at the
wheel. 4 But the pot he was shaping from
the clay was marred in his hands; so the
potter formed it into another pot, shaping
it as seemed best to him.

5 Then the word of the LORD came to
me. 6 He said, "Can I not do with you,
Israel, as this potter does?" declares the
LORD. "Like clay in the hand of the
potter, so are you in my hand, Israel.
7 If at any time I announce that a nation or kingdom is to be uprooted, torn
down and destroyed, 8 and if that nation
I warned repents of its evil, then I will
relent and not inflict on it the disaster I
had planned. 9 And if at another time I
announce that a nation or kingdom is to
be built up and planted, 10 and if it does
evil in my sight and does not obey me,
then I will reconsider the good I had intended to do for it.

11 "Now therefore say to the people of
Judah and those living in Jerusalem, 'This
is what the LORD says: Look! I am preparing a disaster for you and devising a plan
against you. So turn from your evil ways,
each one of you, and reform your ways and
your actions.' 12 But they will reply, 'It's no
use. We will continue with our own plans;

a 19 Or *Army*

we will all follow the stubbornness of our evil hearts.'"

13 Therefore this is what the Lord says:

"Inquire among the nations:
Who has ever heard anything like
  this?
A most horrible thing has been done
  by Virgin Israel.
14 Does the snow of Lebanon
  ever vanish from its rocky slopes?
Do its cool waters from distant
  sources
  ever stop flowing?[a]
15 Yet my people have forgotten me;
  they burn incense to worthless
  idols,
which made them stumble in their
  ways,
  in the ancient paths.
They made them walk in byways,
  on roads not built up.
16 Their land will be an object of horror
  and of lasting scorn;
all who pass by will be appalled
  and will shake their heads.
17 Like a wind from the east,
  I will scatter them before their
  enemies;
I will show them my back and not my
  face
  in the day of their disaster."

18 They said, "Come, let's make plans against Jeremiah; for the teaching of the law by the priest will not cease, nor will counsel from the wise, nor the word from the prophets. So come, let's attack him with our tongues and pay no attention to anything he says."

19 Listen to me, Lord;
  hear what my accusers are saying!
20 Should good be repaid with evil?
  Yet they have dug a pit for me.
Remember that I stood before you
  and spoke in their behalf
  to turn your wrath away from
  them.
21 So give their children over to famine;
  hand them over to the power of the
  sword.

Let their wives be made childless and
  widows;
  let their men be put to death,
  their young men slain by the sword
  in battle.
22 Let a cry be heard from their houses
  when you suddenly bring invaders
  against them,
for they have dug a pit to capture me
  and have hidden snares for my feet.
23 But you, Lord, know
  all their plots to kill me.
Do not forgive their crimes
  or blot out their sins from your
  sight.
Let them be overthrown before you;
  deal with them in the time of your
  anger.

19 This is what the Lord says: "Go and buy a clay jar from a potter. Take along some of the elders of the people and of the priests 2 and go out to the Valley of Ben Hinnom, near the entrance of the Potsherd Gate. There proclaim the words I tell you, 3 and say, 'Hear the word of the Lord, you kings of Judah and people of Jerusalem. This is what the Lord Almighty, the God of Israel, says: Listen! I am going to bring a disaster on this place that will make the ears of everyone who hears of it tingle. 4 For they have forsaken me and made this a place of foreign gods; they have burned incense in it to gods that neither they nor their ancestors nor the kings of Judah ever knew, and they have filled this place with the blood of the innocent. 5 They have built the high places of Baal to burn their children in the fire as offerings to Baal— something I did not command or mention, nor did it enter my mind. 6 So beware, the days are coming, declares the Lord, when people will no longer call this place Topheth or the Valley of Ben Hinnom, but the Valley of Slaughter.

7 "'In this place I will ruin[b] the plans of

[a] 14 The meaning of the Hebrew for this sentence is uncertain.   [b] 7 The Hebrew for ruin sounds like the Hebrew for jar (see verses 1 and 10).

Judah and Jerusalem. I will make them fall by the sword before their enemies, at the hands of those who want to kill them, and I will give their carcasses as food to the birds and the wild animals. ⁸I will devastate this city and make it an object of horror and scorn; all who pass by will be appalled and will scoff because of all its wounds. ⁹I will make them eat the flesh of their sons and daughters, and they will eat one another's flesh because their enemies will press the siege so hard against them to destroy them.'

¹⁰"Then break the jar while those who go with you are watching, ¹¹and say to them, 'This is what the Lord Almighty says: I will smash this nation and this city just as this potter's jar is smashed and cannot be repaired. They will bury the dead in Topheth until there is no more room. ¹²This is what I will do to this place and to those who live here, declares the Lord. I will make this city like Topheth. ¹³The houses in Jerusalem and those of the kings of Judah will be defiled like this place, Topheth—all the houses where they burned incense on the roofs to all the starry hosts and poured out drink offerings to other gods.'"

¹⁴Jeremiah then returned from Topheth, where the Lord had sent him to prophesy, and stood in the court of the Lord's temple and said to all the people, ¹⁵"This is what the Lord Almighty, the God of Israel, says: 'Listen! I am going to bring on this city and all the villages around it every disaster I pronounced against them, because they were stiff-necked and would not listen to my words.'"

Jeremiah and Pashhur

20 When the priest Pashhur son of Immer, the official in charge of the temple of the Lord, heard Jeremiah prophesying these things, ²he had Jeremiah the prophet beaten and put in the stocks at the Upper Gate of Benjamin at the Lord's temple. ³The next day, when Pashhur released him from the stocks, Jeremiah said to him, "The Lord's name for you is not Pashhur, but

Terror on Every Side. ⁴For this is what the Lord says: 'I will make you a terror to yourself and to all your friends; with your own eyes you will see them fall by the sword of their enemies. I will give all Judah into the hands of the king of Babylon, who will carry them away to Babylon or put them to the sword. ⁵I will deliver all the wealth of this city into the hands of their enemies—all its products, all its valuables and all the treasures of the kings of Judah. They will take it away as plunder and carry it off to Babylon. ⁶And you, Pashhur, and all who live in your house will go into exile to Babylon. There you will die and be buried, you and all your friends to whom you have prophesied lies.'"

Jeremiah's Complaint

⁷You deceived*ᵃ* me, Lord, and I was
      deceived*ᵃ*;
   you overpowered me and prevailed.
I am ridiculed all day long;
   everyone mocks me.
⁸Whenever I speak, I cry out
   proclaiming violence and
      destruction.
So the word of the Lord has brought
      me
   insult and reproach all day long.
⁹But if I say, "I will not mention his
      word
   or speak anymore in his name,"
his word is in my heart like a fire,
   a fire shut up in my bones.
I am weary of holding it in;
   indeed, I cannot.
¹⁰I hear many whispering,
   "Terror on every side!
   Denounce him! Let's denounce him!"
All my friends
   are waiting for me to slip, saying,
"Perhaps he will be deceived;
   then we will prevail over him
   and take our revenge on him."

¹¹But the Lord is with me like a mighty
      warrior;
   so my persecutors will stumble and
      not prevail.

ᵃ 7 Or persuaded

They will fail and be thoroughly
disgraced;
their dishonor will never be forgotten.

They will fail and be thoroughly
disgraced;
their dishonor will never be forgotten.
¹²Lord Almighty, you who examine the
righteous
and probe the heart and mind,
let me see your vengeance on them,
for to you I have committed my
cause.

¹³Sing to the Lord!
Give praise to the Lord!
He rescues the life of the needy
from the hands of the wicked.

¹⁴Cursed be the day I was born!
May the day my mother bore me
not be blessed!
¹⁵Cursed be the man who brought my
father the news,
who made him very glad, saying,
"A child is born to you—a son!"
¹⁶May that man be like the towns
the Lord overthrew without pity.
May he hear wailing in the morning,
a battle cry at noon.
¹⁷For he did not kill me in the womb,
with my mother as my grave,
her womb enlarged forever.
¹⁸Why did I ever come out of the womb
to see trouble and sorrow
and to end my days in shame?

God Rejects Zedekiah's Request

21 The word came to Jeremiah
from the Lord when King
Zedekiah sent to him Pashhur
son of Malkijah and the priest Zephani-
ah son of Maaseiah. They said: ²"Inquire
now of the Lord for us because Nebuchadnezzar*a* king of Babylon is attacking
us. Perhaps the Lord will perform wonders for us as in times past so that he will
withdraw from us."

³But Jeremiah answered them, "Tell
Zedekiah, ⁴'This is what the Lord, the
God of Israel, says: I am about to turn
against you the weapons of war that are
in your hands, which you are using to fight
the king of Babylon and the Babylonians*b*
who are outside the wall besieging you.
And I will gather them inside this city.

⁵I myself will fight against you with an
outstretched hand and a mighty arm in
furious anger and in great wrath. ⁶I will
strike down those who live in this city—
both man and beast—and they will die
of a terrible plague. ⁷After that, declares
the Lord, I will give Zedekiah king of
Judah, his officials and the people in this
city who survive the plague, sword and
famine, into the hands of Nebuchadnezzar king of Babylon and to their enemies
who want to kill them. He will put them
to the sword; he will show them no mercy
or pity or compassion.'

⁸"Furthermore, tell the people, 'This
is what the Lord says: See, I am setting
before you the way of life and the way of
death. ⁹Whoever stays in this city will die
by the sword, famine or plague. But who-
ever goes out and surrenders to the Babylonians who are besieging you will live;
they will escape with their lives. ¹⁰I have
determined to do this city harm and not
good, declares the Lord. It will be given
into the hands of the king of Babylon, and
he will destroy it with fire.'

¹¹"Moreover, say to the royal house of
Judah, 'Hear the word of the Lord. ¹²This
is what the Lord says to you, house of
David:

"'Administer justice every morning;
rescue from the hand of the
oppressor
the one who has been robbed,
or my wrath will break out and burn
like fire
because of the evil you have done—
burn with no one to quench it.
¹³I am against you, Jerusalem,
you who live above this valley
on the rocky plateau, declares the
Lord—
you who say, "Who can come against us?
Who can enter our refuge?"
¹⁴I will punish you as your deeds
deserve,
declares the Lord.

I will kindle a fire in your forests
    that will consume everything
    around you.'"

Judgment Against Wicked Kings

22 This is what the LORD says:
"Go down to the palace of
the king of Judah and pro-
claim this message there: ²'Hear the word
of the LORD to you, king of Judah, you
who sit on David's throne—you, your officials and your people who come through
these gates. ³This is what the LORD says:
Do what is just and right. Rescue from
the hand of the oppressor the one who has
been robbed. Do no wrong or violence to
the foreigner, the fatherless or the widow, and do not shed innocent blood in
this place. ⁴For if you are careful to carry
out these commands, then kings who sit
on David's throne will come through the
gates of this palace, riding in chariots and
on horses, accompanied by their officials
and their people. ⁵But if you do not obey
these commands, declares the LORD, I
swear by myself that this palace will become a ruin.'"

⁶For this is what the LORD says about
the palace of the king of Judah:

"Though you are like Gilead to me,
    like the summit of Lebanon,
I will surely make you like a
    wasteland,
    like towns not inhabited.
⁷I will send destroyers against you,
    each man with his weapons,
and they will cut up your fine cedar
    beams
    and throw them into the fire.

⁸"People from many nations will pass by
this city and will ask one another, 'Why
has the LORD done such a thing to this
great city?' ⁹And the answer will be: 'Because they have forsaken the covenant of
the LORD their God and have worshiped
and served other gods.'"

¹⁰Do not weep for the dead king or
    mourn his loss;
    rather, weep bitterly for him who is
    exiled,

because he will never return
    nor see his native land again.

¹¹For this is what the LORD says about
Shallum[a] son of Josiah, who succeeded his
father as king of Judah but has gone from
this place: "He will never return. ¹²He will
die in the place where they have led him
captive; he will not see this land again."

¹³"Woe to him who builds his palace by
    unrighteousness,
    his upper rooms by injustice,
making his own people work for
    nothing,
    not paying them for their labor.
¹⁴He says, 'I will build myself a great
    palace
    with spacious upper rooms.'
So he makes large windows in it,
    panels it with cedar
    and decorates it in red.

¹⁵"Does it make you a king
    to have more and more cedar?
Did not your father have food and
    drink?
    He did what was right and just,
    so all went well with him.
¹⁶He defended the cause of the poor and
    needy,
    and so all went well.
Is that not what it means to know me?"
    declares the LORD.
¹⁷"But your eyes and your heart
    are set only on dishonest gain,
on shedding innocent blood
    and on oppression and extortion."

¹⁸Therefore this is what the LORD says about
Jehoiakim son of Josiah king of Judah:

"They will not mourn for him:
    'Alas, my brother! Alas, my sister!'
They will not mourn for him:
    'Alas, my master! Alas, his
    splendor!'
¹⁹He will have the burial of a donkey—
    dragged away and thrown
    outside the gates of Jerusalem."

²⁰"Go up to Lebanon and cry out,
    let your voice be heard in Bashan,

---

a 11 Also called *Jehoahaz*

cry out from Abarim,
for all your allies are crushed.
²¹ I warned you when you felt secure,
but you said, 'I will not listen!'
This has been your way from your youth;
you have not obeyed me.
²² The wind will drive all your shepherds
away,
and your allies will go into exile.
Then you will be ashamed and
disgraced
because of all your wickedness.
²³ You who live in 'Lebanon,'*ᵃ*
who are nestled in cedar buildings,
how you will groan when pangs come
upon you,
pain like that of a woman in labor!

²⁴ "As surely as I live," declares the LORD,
"even if you, Jehoiachin*ᵇ* son of Jehoiakim
king of Judah, were a signet ring on my
right hand, I would still pull you off. ²⁵ I
will deliver you into the hands of those who
want to kill you, those you fear—Nebuchadnezzar
king of Babylon and the Babylonians.*ᶜ* ²⁶ I will hurl you and the mother
who gave you birth into another country,
where neither of you was born, and there
you both will die. ²⁷ You will never come
back to the land you long to return to."

²⁸ Is this man Jehoiachin a despised,
broken pot,
an object no one wants?
Why will he and his children be
hurled out,
cast into a land they do not know?
²⁹ O land, land, land,
hear the word of the LORD!
³⁰ This is what the LORD says:
"Record this man as if childless,
a man who will not prosper in his
lifetime,
for none of his offspring will prosper,
none will sit on the throne of David
or rule anymore in Judah."

The Righteous Branch

23 "Woe to the shepherds who
are destroying and scattering
the sheep of my pasture!" declares the LORD. ² Therefore this
is what the LORD, the God of Israel, says
to the shepherds who tend my people:
"Because you have scattered my flock and
driven them away and have not bestowed
care on them, I will bestow punishment
on you for the evil you have done," declares
the LORD. ³ "I myself will gather the
remnant of my flock out of all the countries
where I have driven them and will
bring them back to their pasture, where
they will be fruitful and increase in number. ⁴ I will place shepherds over them who
will tend them, and they will no longer be
afraid or terrified, nor will any be missing,"
declares the LORD.

⁵ "The days are coming," declares the
LORD,
"when I will raise up for David*ᵈ* a
righteous Branch,
a King who will reign wisely
and do what is just and right in the
land.
⁶ In his days Judah will be saved
and Israel will live in safety.
This is the name by which he will be
called:
The LORD Our Righteous Savior.

⁷ "So then, the days are coming," declares
the LORD, "when people will no longer say,
'As surely as the LORD lives, who brought
the Israelites up out of Egypt,' ⁸ but they
will say, 'As surely as the LORD lives, who
brought the descendants of Israel up out
of the land of the north and out of all the
countries where he had banished them.'
Then they will live in their own land."

Lying Prophets

⁹ Concerning the prophets:

My heart is broken within me;
all my bones tremble.
I am like a drunken man,
like a strong man overcome by
wine,
because of the LORD
and his holy words.

ᵃ 23 That is, the palace in Jerusalem (see 1 Kings
7:2)   *ᵇ 24* Hebrew *Koniah,* a variant of
Jehoiachin; also in verse 28   *ᶜ 25* Or *Chaldeans*
ᵈ 5 Or *up from David's line*

¹⁰The land is full of adulterers;
  because of the curse*ᵃ* the land lies
    parched
  and the pastures in the wilderness
    are withered.
The prophets follow an evil course
  and use their power unjustly.

¹¹"Both prophet and priest are godless;
  even in my temple I find their
    wickedness,"
          declares the LORD.
¹²"Therefore their path will become
    slippery;
  they will be banished to darkness
  and there they will fall.
I will bring disaster on them
  in the year they are punished,"
          declares the LORD.

¹³"Among the prophets of Samaria
  I saw this repulsive thing:
They prophesied by Baal
  and led my people Israel astray.
¹⁴And among the prophets of Jerusalem
  I have seen something horrible:
They commit adultery and live
    a lie.
They strengthen the hands of
    evildoers,
  so that not one of them turns from
    their wickedness.
They are all like Sodom to me;
  the people of Jerusalem are like
    Gomorrah."

¹⁵Therefore this is what the LORD Almighty says concerning the prophets:

"I will make them eat bitter food
  and drink poisoned water,
because from the prophets of
    Jerusalem
  ungodliness has spread throughout
    the land."

¹⁶This is what the LORD Almighty says:

"Do not listen to what the prophets
  are prophesying to you;
  they fill you with false hopes.
They speak visions from their own
    minds,
  not from the mouth of the LORD.

¹⁷They keep saying to those who despise
    me,
  'The LORD says: You will have
    peace.'
And to all who follow the
    stubbornness of their hearts
  they say, 'No harm will come to
    you.'
¹⁸But which of them has stood in the
    council of the LORD
  to see or to hear his word?
Who has listened and heard his
    word?
¹⁹See, the storm of the LORD
  will burst out in wrath,
a whirlwind swirling down
  on the heads of the wicked.
²⁰The anger of the LORD will not turn
    back
  until he fully accomplishes
    the purposes of his heart.
In days to come
  you will understand it clearly.
²¹I did not send these prophets,
  yet they have run with their message;
I did not speak to them,
  yet they have prophesied.
²²But if they had stood in my council,
  they would have proclaimed my
    words to my people
and would have turned them from
    their evil ways
  and from their evil deeds.

²³"Am I only a God nearby,"
          declares the LORD,
  "and not a God far away?
²⁴Who can hide in secret places
  so that I cannot see them?"
          declares the LORD.
"Do not I fill heaven and earth?"
          declares the LORD.

²⁵"I have heard what the prophets say
who prophesy lies in my name. They say, 'I
had a dream! I had a dream!' ²⁶How long
will this continue in the hearts of these
lying prophets, who prophesy the delusions of their own minds? ²⁷They think
the dreams they tell one another will
make my people forget my name, just as

ᵃ 10 Or because of these things

916

their ancestors forgot my name through Baal worship. ²⁸ Let the prophet who has a dream recount the dream, but let the one who has my word speak it faithfully. For what has straw to do with grain?" declares the LORD. ²⁹ "Is not my word like fire," declares the LORD, "and like a hammer that breaks a rock in pieces?

³⁰ "Therefore," declares the LORD, "I am against the prophets who steal from one another words supposedly from me. ³¹ Yes," declares the LORD, "I am against the prophets who wag their own tongues and yet declare, 'The LORD declares.' ³² Indeed, I am against those who prophesy false dreams," declares the LORD. "They

tell them and lead my people astray with their reckless lies, yet I did not send or appoint them. They do not benefit these people in the least," declares the LORD.

False Prophecy

³³ "When these people, or a prophet or a priest, ask you, 'What is the message from the LORD?' say to them, 'What message? I will forsake you, declares the LORD.' ³⁴ If a prophet or a priest or anyone else claims, 'This is a message from the LORD,' I will punish them and their household. ³⁵ This is what each of you keeps saying to your friends and other Israelites: 'What is the LORD's answer?' or 'What has the LORD

Jeremiah 23

Jeremiah cried for his peers.

Jeremiah is well known as "the weeping prophet" because of the constant pain he felt for his peers. You can feel this guy's grief as he prayed, "Oh, that my head were a spring of water and my eyes a fountain of tears! I would weep day and night for the slain of my people" (Jeremiah 9:1).

When the Lord called him to preach, Jeremiah protested he was too young to speak for God. His words, "Alas, Sovereign LORD" actually mean, "No, Lord God!" (Jeremiah 1:6). But the Lord wouldn't let Jeremiah wiggle free. He had plans for Jeremiah that stretched back to his days in his mother's womb. That's when the Lord appointed him a prophet to the nations, and now the Lord promised to give him all the words he needed to speak, giving him the task of both uprooting and planting nations (see Jeremiah 1:4 – 10).

Jeremiah preached to the last five kings of Judah, often slamming them with harsh words. He prophesied even after the southern kingdom was conquered by the Babylonians. Here in Jeremiah 23, he hits the leaders and false prophets who led the people away from God.

The prophet's words flowed from persistent concern for his people, a depth of distress that would make a grown man cry. He called his pain "unending" and his wound "grievous and incurable" (Jeremiah 15:18). But he continued to point out sin and call the nation to repent.

You can find Jeremiah throughout the book named for him, as well as in 2 Chronicles 35 – 36; Matthew 2:18; and Matthew 27:9.

UNSHAKEN *people*

spoken?' ³⁶But you must not mention 'a message from the LORD' again, because each one's word becomes their own message. So you distort the words of the living God, the LORD Almighty, our God. ³⁷This is what you keep saying to a prophet: 'What is the LORD's answer to you?' or 'What has the LORD spoken?' ³⁸Although you claim, 'This is a message from the LORD,' this is what the LORD says: You used the words, 'This is a message from the LORD,' even though I told you that you must not claim, 'This is a message from the LORD.' ³⁹Therefore, I will surely forget you and cast you out of my presence along with the city I gave to you and your ancestors. ⁴⁰I will bring on you everlasting disgrace—everlasting shame that will not be forgotten."

Two Baskets of Figs

24 After Jehoiachin*ᵃ* son of Jehoiakim king of Judah and the officials, the skilled workers and the artisans of Judah were carried into exile from Jerusalem to Babylon by Nebuchadnezzar king of Babylon, the LORD showed me two baskets of figs placed in front of the temple of the LORD. ²One basket had very good figs, like those that ripen early; the other basket had very bad figs, so bad they could not be eaten.

³Then the LORD asked me, "What do you see, Jeremiah?"

"Figs," I answered. "The good ones are very good, but the bad ones are so bad they cannot be eaten."

⁴Then the word of the LORD came to me: ⁵"This is what the LORD, the God of Israel, says: 'Like these good figs, I regard as good the exiles from Judah, whom I sent away from this place to the land of the Babylonians.*ᵇ* ⁶My eyes will watch over them for their good, and I will bring them back to this land. I will build them up and not tear them down; I will plant them and not uproot them. ⁷I will give them a heart to know me, that I am the LORD. They will be my people, and I will be their God, for they will return to me with all their heart.

⁸"'But like the bad figs, which are so bad they cannot be eaten,' says the LORD, 'so will I deal with Zedekiah king of Judah, his officials and the survivors from Jerusalem, whether they remain in this land or live in Egypt. ⁹I will make them abhorrent and an offense to all the kingdoms of the earth, a reproach and a byword, a curse*ᶜ* and an object of ridicule, wherever I banish them. ¹⁰I will send the sword, famine and plague against them until they are destroyed from the land I gave to them and their ancestors.'"

Seventy Years of Captivity

25 The word came to Jeremiah concerning all the people of Judah in the fourth year of Jehoiakim son of Josiah king of Judah, which was the first year of Nebuchadnezzar king of Babylon. ²So Jeremiah the prophet said to all the people of Judah and to all those living in Jerusalem: ³For twenty-three years—from the thirteenth year of Josiah son of Amon king of Judah until this very day—the word of the LORD has come to me and I have spoken to you again and again, but you have not listened.

⁴And though the LORD has sent all his servants the prophets to you again and again, you have not listened or paid any attention. ⁵They said, "Turn now, each of you, from your evil ways and your evil practices, and you can stay in the land the LORD gave to you and your ancestors for ever and ever. ⁶Do not follow other gods to serve and worship them; do not arouse my anger with what your hands have made. Then I will not harm you."

⁷"But you did not listen to me," declares the LORD, "and you have aroused my anger with what your hands have made, and you have brought harm to yourselves."

⁸Therefore the LORD Almighty says this: "Because you have not listened to my words, ⁹I will summon all the peoples of the north and my servant Nebu-

---

ᵃ 1 Hebrew *Jeconiah,* a variant of *Jehoiachin*
ᵇ 5 Or *Chaldeans*   *ᶜ 9* That is, their names will be used in cursing (see 29:22); or, others will see that they are cursed.

chadnezzar king of Babylon," declares the LORD, "and I will bring them against this land and its inhabitants and against all the surrounding nations. I will completely destroy*a* them and make them an object of horror and scorn, and an everlasting ruin. [10]I will banish from them the sounds of joy and gladness, the voices of bride and bridegroom, the sound of millstones and the light of the lamp. [11]This whole country will become a desolate wasteland, and these nations will serve the king of Babylon seventy years.

[12]"But when the seventy years are fulfilled, I will punish the king of Babylon and his nation, the land of the Babylonians,*b* for their guilt," declares the LORD, "and will make it desolate forever. [13]I will bring on that land all the things I have spoken against it, all that are written in this book and prophesied by Jeremiah against all the nations. [14]They themselves will be enslaved by many nations and great kings; I will repay them according to their deeds and the work of their hands."

The Cup of God's Wrath

[15]This is what the LORD, the God of Israel, said to me: "Take from my hand this cup filled with the wine of my wrath and make all the nations to whom I send you drink it. [16]When they drink it, they will stagger and go mad because of the sword I will send among them."

[17]So I took the cup from the LORD's hand and made all the nations to whom he sent me drink it: [18]Jerusalem and the towns of Judah, its kings and officials, to make them a ruin and an object of horror and scorn, a curse*c*—as they are today; [19]Pharaoh king of Egypt, his attendants, his officials and all his people, [20]and all the foreign people there; all the kings of Uz; all the kings of the Philistines (those of Ashkelon, Gaza, Ekron, and the people left at Ashdod); [21]Edom, Moab and Ammon; [22]all the kings of Tyre and Sidon; the kings of the coastlands across the sea; [23]Dedan, Tema, Buz and all who are in distant places*d*; [24]all the kings of Arabia and all the kings of the foreign people

who live in the wilderness; [25]all the kings of Zimri, Elam and Media; [26]and all the kings of the north, near and far, one after the other—all the kingdoms on the face of the earth. And after all of them, the king of Sheshak*e* will drink it too.

[27]"Then tell them, 'This is what the LORD Almighty, the God of Israel, says: Drink, get drunk and vomit, and fall to rise no more because of the sword I will send among you.' [28]But if they refuse to take the cup from your hand and drink, tell them, 'This is what the LORD Almighty says: You must drink it! [29]See, I am beginning to bring disaster on the city that bears my Name, and will you indeed go unpunished? You will not go unpunished, for I am calling down a sword on all who live on the earth, declares the LORD Almighty.'

[30]"Now prophesy all these words against them and say to them:

"'The LORD will roar from on high;
　he will thunder from his holy
　　dwelling
　and roar mightily against his land.
He will shout like those who tread the
　　grapes,
　shout against all who live on the
　　earth.
[31]The tumult will resound to the ends
　　of the earth,
　for the LORD will bring charges
　　against the nations;
he will bring judgment on all
　　mankind
　and put the wicked to the sword,'"
　　　　　　　declares the LORD.

[32]This is what the LORD Almighty says:

"Look! Disaster is spreading
　from nation to nation;
a mighty storm is rising
　from the ends of the earth."

---

a 9 The Hebrew term refers to the irrevocable giving over of things or persons to the LORD, often by totally destroying them.
b 12 Or *Chaldeans*　　*c 18* That is, their names to be used in cursing (see 29:22); or, to be seen by others as cursed　　*d 23* Or *who clip the hair by their foreheads*　　*e 26* Sheshak is a cryptogram for Babylon.

33 At that time those slain by the Lord will be everywhere—from one end of the earth to the other. They will not be mourned or gathered up or buried, but will be like dung lying on the ground.

34 Weep and wail, you shepherds;
    roll in the dust, you leaders of the
      flock.
For your time to be slaughtered has
    come;
    you will fall like the best of the
      rams.*a*
35 The shepherds will have nowhere to
    flee,
    the leaders of the flock no place to
      escape.
36 Hear the cry of the shepherds,
    the wailing of the leaders of the
      flock,
for the Lord is destroying their
    pasture.
37 The peaceful meadows will be laid
    waste
    because of the fierce anger of the
      Lord.
38 Like a lion he will leave his lair,
    and their land will become desolate
because of the sword*b* of the oppressor
    and because of the Lord's fierce
      anger.

Jeremiah Threatened With Death

26 Early in the reign of Jehoiakim son of Josiah king of Judah, this word came from the Lord: 2 "This is what the Lord says: Stand in the courtyard of the Lord's house and speak to all the people of the towns of Judah who come to worship in the house of the Lord. Tell them everything I command you; do not omit a word. 3 Perhaps they will listen and each will turn from their evil ways. Then I will relent and not inflict on them the disaster I was planning because of the evil they have done. 4 Say to them, 'This is what the Lord says: If you do not listen to me and follow my law, which I have set before you, 5 and if you do not listen to the words of my servants the prophets, whom I have sent to you again and again (though you have not listened),

6 then I will make this house like Shiloh and this city a curse*c* among all the nations of the earth.'"

7 The priests, the prophets and all the people heard Jeremiah speak these words in the house of the Lord. 8 But as soon as Jeremiah finished telling all the people everything the Lord had commanded him to say, the priests, the prophets and all the people seized him and said, "You must die! 9 Why do you prophesy in the Lord's name that this house will be like Shiloh and this city will be desolate and deserted?" And all the people crowded around Jeremiah in the house of the Lord.

10 When the officials of Judah heard about these things, they went up from the royal palace to the house of the Lord and took their places at the entrance of the New Gate of the Lord's house. 11 Then the priests and the prophets said to the officials and all the people, "This man should be sentenced to death because he has prophesied against this city. You have heard it with your own ears!"

12 Then Jeremiah said to all the officials and all the people: "The Lord sent me to prophesy against this house and this city all the things you have heard. 13 Now reform your ways and your actions and obey the Lord your God. Then the Lord will relent and not bring the disaster he has pronounced against you. 14 As for me, I am in your hands; do with me whatever you think is good and right. 15 Be assured, however, that if you put me to death, you will bring the guilt of innocent blood on yourselves and on this city and on those who live in it, for in truth the Lord has sent me to you to speak all these words in your hearing."

16 Then the officials and all the people said to the priests and the prophets, "This man should not be sentenced to death! He has spoken to us in the name of the Lord our God."

a 34 Septuagint; Hebrew *fall and be shattered like fine pottery*   *b 38* Some Hebrew manuscripts and Septuagint (see also 46:16 and 50:16); most Hebrew manuscripts *anger*   *c 6* That is, its name will be used in cursing (see 29:22); or, others will see that it is cursed.

¹⁷Some of the elders of the land stepped forward and said to the entire assembly of people, ¹⁸"Micah of Moresheth prophesied in the days of Hezekiah king of Judah. He told all the people of Judah, 'This is what the LORD Almighty says:

"'Zion will be plowed like a field,
Jerusalem will become a heap of
rubble,
the temple hill a mound overgrown
with thickets.'ᵃ

¹⁹"Did Hezekiah king of Judah or anyone else in Judah put him to death? Did not Hezekiah fear the LORD and seek his favor? And did not the LORD relent, so that he did not bring the disaster he pronounced against them? We are about to bring a terrible disaster on ourselves!"

²⁰(Now Uriah son of Shemaiah from Kiriath Jearim was another man who prophesied in the name of the LORD; he prophesied the same things against this city and this land as Jeremiah did. ²¹When King Jehoiakim and all his officers and officials heard his words, the king was determined to put him to death. But Uriah heard of it and fled in fear to Egypt. ²²King Jehoiakim, however, sent Elnathan son of Akbor to Egypt, along with some other men. ²³They brought Uriah out of Egypt and took him to King Jehoiakim, who had him struck down with a sword and his body thrown into the burial place of the common people.)

²⁴Furthermore, Ahikam son of Shaphan supported Jeremiah, and so he was not handed over to the people to be put to death.

Judah to Serve Nebuchadnezzar

27 Early in the reign of Zedekiahᵇ son of Josiah king of Judah, this word came to Jeremiah from the LORD: ²This is what the LORD said to me: "Make a yoke out of straps and crossbars and put it on your neck. ³Then send word to the kings of Edom, Moab, Ammon, Tyre and Sidon through the envoys who have come to Jerusalem to Zedekiah king of Judah. ⁴Give them a message for their masters and say, 'This is what the LORD Almighty, the God of Israel, says: "Tell this to your masters: ⁵With my great power and outstretched arm I made the earth and its people and the animals that are on it, and I give it to anyone I please. ⁶Now I will give all your countries into the hands of my servant Nebuchadnezzar king of Babylon; I will make even the wild animals subject to him. ⁷All nations will serve him and his son and his grandson until the time for his land comes; then many nations and great kings will subjugate him.

⁸"'"If, however, any nation or kingdom will not serve Nebuchadnezzar king of Babylon or bow its neck under his yoke, I will punish that nation with the sword, famine and plague, declares the LORD, until I destroy it by his hand. ⁹So do not listen to your prophets, your diviners, your interpreters of dreams, your mediums or your sorcerers who tell you, 'You will not serve the king of Babylon.' ¹⁰They prophesy lies to you that will only serve to remove you far from your lands; I will banish you and you will perish. ¹¹But if any nation will bow its neck under the yoke of the king of Babylon and serve him, I will let that nation remain in its own land to till it and to live there, declares the LORD."'"

¹²I gave the same message to Zedekiah king of Judah. I said, "Bow your neck under the yoke of the king of Babylon; serve him and his people, and you will live. ¹³Why will you and your people die by the sword, famine and plague with which the LORD has threatened any nation that will not serve the king of Babylon? ¹⁴Do not listen to the words of the prophets who say to you, 'You will not serve the king of Babylon,' for they are prophesying lies to you. ¹⁵'I have not sent them,' declares the LORD. 'They are prophesying lies in my name. Therefore, I will banish you and

---

ᵃ 18 Micah 3:12   ᵇ 1 A few Hebrew manuscripts and Syriac (see also 27:3,12 and 28:1); most Hebrew manuscripts *Jehoiakim* (Most Septuagint manuscripts do not have this verse.)

you will perish, both you and the prophets who prophesy to you.'"

¹⁶Then I said to the priests and all these people, "This is what the LORD says: Do not listen to the prophets who say, 'Very soon now the articles from the LORD's house will be brought back from Babylon.' They are prophesying lies to you. ¹⁷Do not listen to them. Serve the king of Babylon, and you will live. Why should this city become a ruin? ¹⁸If they are prophets and have the word of the LORD, let them plead with the LORD Almighty that the articles remaining in the house of the LORD and in the palace of the king of Judah and in Jerusalem not be taken to Babylon. ¹⁹For this is what the LORD Almighty says about the pillars, the bronze Sea, the movable stands and the other articles that are left in this city, ²⁰which Nebuchadnezzar king of Babylon did not take away when he carried Jehoiachin*a* son of Jehoiakim king of Judah into exile from Jerusalem to Babylon, along with all the nobles of Judah and Jerusalem— ²¹yes, this is what the LORD Almighty, the God of Israel, says about the things that are left in the house of the LORD and in the palace of the king of Judah and in Jerusalem: ²²'They will be taken to Babylon and there they will remain until the day I come for them,' declares the LORD. 'Then I will bring them back and restore them to this place.'"

The False Prophet Hananiah

28 In the fifth month of that same year, the fourth year, early in the reign of Zedekiah king of Judah, the prophet Hananiah son of Azzur, who was from Gibeon, said to me in the house of the LORD in the presence of the priests and all the people: ²"This is what the LORD Almighty, the God of Israel, says: 'I will break the yoke of the king of Babylon. ³Within two years I will bring back to this place all the articles of the LORD's house that Nebuchadnezzar king of Babylon removed from here and took to Babylon. ⁴I will also bring back to this place Jehoiachin*a* son of Jehoiakim king of Judah and all the other

exiles from Judah who went to Babylon,' declares the LORD, 'for I will break the yoke of the king of Babylon.'"

⁵Then the prophet Jeremiah replied to the prophet Hananiah before the priests and all the people who were standing in the house of the LORD. ⁶He said, "Amen! May the LORD do so! May the LORD fulfill the words you have prophesied by bringing the articles of the LORD's house and all the exiles back to this place from Babylon. ⁷Nevertheless, listen to what I have to say in your hearing and in the hearing of all the people: ⁸From early times the prophets who preceded you and me have prophesied war, disaster and plague against many countries and great kingdoms. ⁹But the prophet who prophesies peace will be recognized as one truly sent by the LORD only if his prediction comes true."

¹⁰Then the prophet Hananiah took the yoke off the neck of the prophet Jeremiah and broke it, ¹¹and he said before all the people, "This is what the LORD says: 'In the same way I will break the yoke of Nebuchadnezzar king of Babylon off the neck of all the nations within two years.'" At this, the prophet Jeremiah went on his way.

¹²After the prophet Hananiah had broken the yoke off the neck of the prophet Jeremiah, the word of the LORD came to Jeremiah: ¹³"Go and tell Hananiah, 'This is what the LORD says: You have broken a wooden yoke, but in its place you will get a yoke of iron. ¹⁴This is what the LORD Almighty, the God of Israel, says: I will put an iron yoke on the necks of all these nations to make them serve Nebuchadnezzar king of Babylon, and they will serve him. I will even give him control over the wild animals.'"

¹⁵Then the prophet Jeremiah said to Hananiah the prophet, "Listen, Hananiah! The LORD has not sent you, yet you have persuaded this nation to trust in lies. ¹⁶Therefore this is what the LORD says: 'I am about to remove you from the face of the earth. This very year you are going to

a 20,4 Hebrew *Jeconiah,* a variant of *Jehoiachin*

die, because you have preached rebellion against the LORD.'"

[17] In the seventh month of that same year, Hananiah the prophet died.

A Letter to the Exiles

29 This is the text of the letter that the prophet Jeremiah sent from Jerusalem to the surviving elders among the exiles and to the priests, the prophets and all the other people Nebuchadnezzar had carried into exile from Jerusalem to Babylon. [2] (This was after King Jehoiachin[a] and the queen mother, the court officials and the leaders of Judah and Jerusalem, the skilled workers and the artisans had gone into exile from Jerusalem.) [3] He entrusted the letter to Elasah son of Shaphan and to Gemariah son of Hilkiah, whom Zedekiah king of Judah sent to King Nebuchadnezzar in Babylon. It said:

[4] This is what the LORD Almighty, the God of Israel, says to all those I carried into exile from Jerusalem to Babylon: [5] "Build houses and settle down; plant gardens and eat what they produce. [6] Marry and have sons and daughters; find wives for your sons and give your daughters in marriage, so that they too may have sons and daughters. Increase in number there; do not decrease. [7] Also, seek the peace and prosperity of the city to which I have carried you into exile. Pray to the LORD for it, because if it prospers, you too will prosper." [8] Yes, this is what the LORD Almighty, the God of Israel, says: "Do not let the prophets and diviners among you deceive you. Do not listen to the dreams you encourage them to have. [9] They are prophesying lies to you in my name. I have not sent them," declares the LORD.

[10] This is what the LORD says: "When seventy years are completed for Babylon, I will come to you and fulfill my good promise to bring you back to this place. [11] For I know the plans I have for you," declares the

LORD, "plans to prosper you and not to harm you, plans to give you hope and a future. [12] Then you will call on me and come and pray to me, and I will listen to you. [13] You will seek me and find me when you seek me with all your heart. [14] I will be found by you," declares the LORD, "and will bring you back from captivity.[b] I will gather you from all the nations and places where I have banished you," declares the LORD, "and will bring you back to the place from which I carried you into exile."

ROCK SOLID promises

"'I know the plans I have for you,' declares the LORD, 'plans to prosper you and not to harm you, plans to give you hope and a future.'"
Jeremiah 29:11

The Lord's plans for you surpass anything you can dream up. He doesn't plan to wreck your life but to lead you to good places.

[15] You may say, "The LORD has raised up prophets for us in Babylon," [16] but this is what the LORD says about the king who sits on David's throne and all the people who remain in this city, your fellow citizens who did not go with you into exile— [17] yes, this is what the LORD Almighty says: "I will send the sword, famine and plague against them and I will make them like figs that are so bad they cannot be eaten. [18] I will pursue them with the sword, famine and plague and will make them abhorrent to all the

---

[a] 2 Hebrew *Jeconiah*, a variant of *Jehoiachin*
[b] 14 Or *will restore your fortunes*

kingdoms of the earth, a curse[a] and an object of horror, of scorn and reproach, among all the nations where I drive them. [19]For they have not listened to my words," declares the LORD, "words that I sent to them again and again by my servants the prophets. And you exiles have not listened either," declares the LORD.

[20]Therefore, hear the word of the LORD, all you exiles whom I have sent away from Jerusalem to Babylon. [21]This is what the LORD Almighty, the God of Israel, says about Ahab son of Kolaiah and Zedekiah son of Maaseiah, who are prophesying lies to you in my name: "I will deliver them into the hands of Nebuchadnezzar king of Babylon, and he will put them to death before your very eyes. [22]Because of them, all the exiles from Judah who are in Babylon will use this curse: 'May the LORD treat you like Zedekiah and Ahab, whom the king of Babylon burned in the fire.' [23]For they have done outrageous things in Israel; they have committed adultery with their neighbors' wives, and in my name they have uttered lies—which I did not authorize. I know it and am a witness to it," declares the LORD.

Message to Shemaiah

[24]Tell Shemaiah the Nehelamite, [25]"This is what the LORD Almighty, the God of Israel, says: You sent letters in your own name to all the people in Jerusalem, to the priest Zephaniah son of Maaseiah, and to all the other priests. You said to Zephaniah, [26]'The LORD has appointed you priest in place of Jehoiada to be in charge of the house of the LORD; you should put any maniac who acts like a prophet into the stocks and neck-irons. [27]So why have you not reprimanded Jeremiah from Anathoth, who poses as a prophet among you? [28]He has sent this message to us in Babylon: It will be a long time. Therefore build houses and settle down; plant gardens and eat what they produce.'"

[29]Zephaniah the priest, however, read the letter to Jeremiah the prophet. [30]Then the word of the LORD came to Jeremiah: [31]"Send this message to all the exiles: 'This is what the LORD says about Shemaiah the Nehelamite: Because Shemaiah has prophesied to you, even though I did not send him, and has persuaded you to trust in lies, [32]this is what the LORD says: I will surely punish Shemaiah the Nehelamite and his descendants. He will have no one left among this people, nor will he see the good things I will do for my people, declares the LORD, because he has preached rebellion against me.'"

Restoration of Israel

30 This is the word that came to Jeremiah from the LORD: [2]"This is what the LORD, the God of Israel, says: 'Write in a book all the words I have spoken to you. [3]The days are coming,' declares the LORD, 'when I will bring my people Israel and Judah back from captivity[b] and restore them to the land I gave their ancestors to possess,' says the LORD."

[4]These are the words the LORD spoke concerning Israel and Judah: [5]"This is what the LORD says:

"'Cries of fear are heard—
    terror, not peace.
[6]Ask and see:
    Can a man bear children?
Then why do I see every strong man
    with his hands on his stomach like a
        woman in labor,
    every face turned deathly pale?
[7]How awful that day will be!
    No other will be like it.
It will be a time of trouble for Jacob,
    but he will be saved out of it.

[8]"'In that day,' declares the LORD
        Almighty,
    'I will break the yoke off their
        necks

---

[a] 18 That is, their names will be used in cursing (see verse 22); or, others will see that they are cursed.   [b] 3 Or *will restore the fortunes of my people Israel and Judah*

and will tear off their bonds;
no longer will foreigners enslave
them.
⁹ Instead, they will serve the LORD their
God
and David their king,
whom I will raise up for them.

¹⁰ "'So do not be afraid, Jacob my
servant;
do not be dismayed, Israel,'
declares the LORD.
'I will surely save you out of a distant
place,
your descendants from the land of
their exile.
Jacob will again have peace and
security,
and no one will make him afraid.
¹¹ I am with you and will save you,'
declares the LORD.
'Though I completely destroy all the
nations
among which I scatter you,
I will not completely destroy you.
I will discipline you but only in due
measure;
I will not let you go entirely
unpunished.'

¹² "This is what the LORD says:

"'Your wound is incurable,
your injury beyond healing.
¹³ There is no one to plead your cause,
no remedy for your sore,
no healing for you.
¹⁴ All your allies have forgotten you;
they care nothing for you.
I have struck you as an enemy would
and punished you as would the
cruel,
because your guilt is so great
and your sins so many.
¹⁵ Why do you cry out over your wound,
your pain that has no cure?
Because of your great guilt and many
sins
I have done these things to you.

¹⁶ "'But all who devour you will be
devoured;
all your enemies will go into exile.

Those who plunder you will be
plundered;
all who make spoil of you I will
despoil.
¹⁷ But I will restore you to health
and heal your wounds,'
declares the LORD,
'because you are called an outcast,
Zion for whom no one cares.'

¹⁸ "This is what the LORD says:

"'I will restore the fortunes of Jacob's
tents
and have compassion on his
dwellings;
the city will be rebuilt on her ruins,
and the palace will stand in its
proper place.
¹⁹ From them will come songs of
thanksgiving
and the sound of rejoicing.
I will add to their numbers,
and they will not be decreased;
I will bring them honor,
and they will not be disdained.
²⁰ Their children will be as in days of
old,
and their community will be
established before me;
I will punish all who oppress them.
²¹ Their leader will be one of their own;
their ruler will arise from among
them.
I will bring him near and he will come
close to me—
for who is he who will devote
himself
to be close to me?'
declares the LORD.
²² "'So you will be my people,
and I will be your God.'"

²³ See, the storm of the LORD
will burst out in wrath,
a driving wind swirling down
on the heads of the wicked.
²⁴ The fierce anger of the LORD will not
turn back
until he fully accomplishes
the purposes of his heart.
In days to come
you will understand this.

31

"At that time," declares the LORD, "I will be the God of all the families of Israel, and they will be my people."

[2] This is what the LORD says:

"The people who survive the sword
    will find favor in the wilderness;
    I will come to give rest to Israel."

[3] The LORD appeared to us in the past,[a] saying:

"I have loved you with an everlasting love;
    I have drawn you with unfailing kindness.
[4] I will build you up again,
    and you, Virgin Israel, will be rebuilt.
Again you will take up your timbrels
    and go out to dance with the joyful.
[5] Again you will plant vineyards
    on the hills of Samaria;
the farmers will plant them
    and enjoy their fruit.
[6] There will be a day when watchmen cry out
    on the hills of Ephraim,
'Come, let us go up to Zion,
    to the LORD our God.'"

[7] This is what the LORD says:

"Sing with joy for Jacob;
    shout for the foremost of the nations.
Make your praises heard, and say,
    'LORD, save your people,
    the remnant of Israel.'
[8] See, I will bring them from the land of the north
    and gather them from the ends of the earth.
Among them will be the blind and the lame,
    expectant mothers and women in labor;
    a great throng will return.
[9] They will come with weeping;
    they will pray as I bring them back.
I will lead them beside streams of water
    on a level path where they will not stumble,
because I am Israel's father,
    and Ephraim is my firstborn son.

[10] "Hear the word of the LORD, you nations;
    proclaim it in distant coastlands:
'He who scattered Israel will gather them
    and will watch over his flock like a shepherd.'
[11] For the LORD will deliver Jacob
    and redeem them from the hand of those stronger than they.
[12] They will come and shout for joy on the heights of Zion;
    they will rejoice in the bounty of the LORD—
the grain, the new wine and the olive oil,
    the young of the flocks and herds.
They will be like a well-watered garden,
    and they will sorrow no more.
[13] Then young women will dance and be glad,
    young men and old as well.
I will turn their mourning into gladness;
    I will give them comfort and joy instead of sorrow.
[14] I will satisfy the priests with abundance,
    and my people will be filled with my bounty,"
            declares the LORD.

[15] This is what the LORD says:

"A voice is heard in Ramah,
    mourning and great weeping,
Rachel weeping for her children
    and refusing to be comforted,
    because they are no more."

[16] This is what the LORD says:

"Restrain your voice from weeping
    and your eyes from tears,
for your work will be rewarded,"
            declares the LORD.
    "They will return from the land of the enemy.

---

[a] 3 Or LORD has appeared to us from afar

17 So there is hope for your descendants,"
    declares the Lord.
"Your children will return to their
    own land.

18 "I have surely heard Ephraim's moaning:
    'You disciplined me like an unruly
        calf,
    and I have been disciplined.
Restore me, and I will return,
    because you are the Lord my God.
19 After I strayed,
    I repented;
after I came to understand,
    I beat my breast.
I was ashamed and humiliated
    because I bore the disgrace of my
        youth.'
20 Is not Ephraim my dear son,
    the child in whom I delight?
Though I often speak against him,
    I still remember him.
Therefore my heart yearns for him;
    I have great compassion for him,"
        declares the Lord.

21 "Set up road signs;
    put up guideposts.
Take note of the highway,
    the road that you take.
Return, Virgin Israel,
    return to your towns.
22 How long will you wander,
    unfaithful Daughter Israel?
The Lord will create a new thing on
        earth—
    the woman will return to*a* the man."

23 This is what the Lord Almighty, the
God of Israel, says: "When I bring them
back from captivity,*b* the people in the land
of Judah and in its towns will once again
use these words: 'The Lord bless you,
you prosperous city, you sacred mountain.'
24 People will live together in Judah and all
its towns—farmers and those who move
about with their flocks. 25 I will refresh the
weary and satisfy the faint."

26 At this I awoke and looked around.
My sleep had been pleasant to me.
27 "The days are coming," declares the
Lord, "when I will plant the kingdoms
of Israel and Judah with the offspring of

people and of animals. 28 Just as I watched
over them to uproot and tear down, and
to overthrow, destroy and bring disaster,
so I will watch over them to build and to
plant," declares the Lord. 29 "In those days
people will no longer say,

'The parents have eaten sour grapes,
    and the children's teeth are set on
        edge.'

30 Instead, everyone will die for their own
sin; whoever eats sour grapes—their own
teeth will be set on edge.

31 "The days are coming," declares the
        Lord,
    "when I will make a new covenant
with the people of Israel
    and with the people of Judah.
32 It will not be like the covenant
    I made with their ancestors
when I took them by the hand
    to lead them out of Egypt,
because they broke my covenant,
    though I was a husband to*c* them,*d*"
        declares the Lord.
33 "This is the covenant I will make with
        the people of Israel
    after that time," declares the Lord.
"I will put my law in their minds
    and write it on their hearts.
I will be their God,
    and they will be my people.
34 No longer will they teach their
        neighbor,
    or say to one another, 'Know the
        Lord,'
because they will all know me,
    from the least of them to the greatest,"
        declares the Lord.
"For I will forgive their wickedness
    and will remember their sins no more."

35 This is what the Lord says,

he who appoints the sun
    to shine by day,
who decrees the moon and stars
    to shine by night,

---

a 22 Or *will protect*   *b 23* Or *I restore their
fortunes*   *c 32* Hebrew; Septuagint and Syriac
/ *and I turned away from*   *d 32* Or *was their
master*

God changes people from the inside out.

God commands you to obey him. You might wish you could. But you can't. Not on your own anyway. That's the first point God makes in this passage. When the Lord rescued his people from slavery in Egypt, he made a "covenant" or "solemn agreement" with them where he loved them like crazy, gave them the Ten Commandments and the rest of the law, and required them to obey. But God has a second point. He's making a new agreement. This time he won't write his rules on stone. He plans to etch his laws on our hearts and minds. And that will make all the difference. Instead of rules coming at us from the outside, the Lord himself will change us from the inside. He promises to transform us by putting his Spirit inside us (see Ezekiel 36:26–27). Get it? Now you can obey God. Just don't try to do it on your own.

Think: How do you suppose God writes his law on your heart?

ROCK SOLID *truths*

who stirs up the sea
   so that its waves roar—
   the LORD Almighty is his name:
36 "Only if these decrees vanish from my
      sight,"
   declares the LORD,
"will Israel ever cease
   being a nation before me."

37 This is what the LORD says:

"Only if the heavens above can be
      measured

and the foundations of the earth
      below be searched out
will I reject all the descendants of
      Israel
   because of all they have done,"
         declares the LORD.

38 "The days are coming," declares the LORD, "when this city will be rebuilt for me from the Tower of Hananel to the Corner Gate. 39 The measuring line will stretch from there straight to the hill of Gareb and then turn to Goah. 40 The whole valley where dead bodies and ashes are thrown, and all the terraces out to the Kidron Valley on the east as far as the corner of the Horse Gate, will be holy to the LORD. The city will never again be uprooted or demolished."

Jeremiah Buys a Field

32 This is the word that came to Jeremiah from the LORD in the tenth year of Zedekiah king of Judah, which was the eighteenth year of Nebuchadnezzar. 2 The army of the king of Babylon was then besieging Jerusalem, and Jeremiah the prophet was confined in the courtyard of the guard in the royal palace of Judah.

3 Now Zedekiah king of Judah had imprisoned him there, saying, "Why do you prophesy as you do? You say, 'This is what the LORD says: I am about to give this city into the hands of the king of Babylon, and he will capture it. 4 Zedekiah king of Judah will not escape the Babylonians*a* but will certainly be given into the hands of the king of Babylon, and will speak with him face to face and see him with his own eyes. 5 He will take Zedekiah to Babylon, where he will remain until I deal with him, declares the LORD. If you fight against the Babylonians, you will not succeed.'"

6 Jeremiah said, "The word of the LORD came to me: 7 Hanamel son of Shallum your uncle is going to come to you and say, 'Buy my field at Anathoth, because as nearest relative it is your right and duty to buy it.'

a 4 Or *Chaldeans*; also in verses 5, 24, 25, 28, 29 and 43

[8]"Then, just as the LORD had said, my cousin Hanamel came to me in the courtyard of the guard and said, 'Buy my field at Anathoth in the territory of Benjamin. Since it is your right to redeem it and possess it, buy it for yourself.'

"I knew that this was the word of the LORD; [9]so I bought the field at Anathoth from my cousin Hanamel and weighed out for him seventeen shekels[a] of silver. [10]I signed and sealed the deed, had it witnessed, and weighed out the silver on the scales. [11]I took the deed of purchase — the sealed copy containing the terms and conditions, as well as the unsealed copy — [12]and I gave this deed to Baruch son of Neriah, the son of Mahseiah, in the presence of my cousin Hanamel and of the witnesses who had signed the deed and of all the Jews sitting in the courtyard of the guard.

[13]"In their presence I gave Baruch these instructions: [14]'This is what the LORD Almighty, the God of Israel, says: Take these documents, both the sealed and unsealed copies of the deed of purchase, and put them in a clay jar so they will last a long time. [15]For this is what the LORD Almighty, the God of Israel, says: Houses, fields and vineyards will again be bought in this land.'

[16]"After I had given the deed of purchase to Baruch son of Neriah, I prayed to the LORD:

[17]"Ah, Sovereign LORD, you have made the heavens and the earth by your great power and outstretched arm. Nothing is too hard for you. [18]You show love to thousands but bring the punishment for the parents' sins into the laps of their children after them. Great and mighty God, whose name is the LORD Almighty, [19]great are your purposes and mighty are your deeds. Your eyes are open to the ways of all mankind; you reward each person according to their conduct and as their deeds deserve. [20]You performed signs and wonders in Egypt and have continued them to this day, in Israel and among all mankind, and have gained the renown that is still yours. [21]You brought your people Israel out of Egypt with signs and wonders, by a mighty hand and an outstretched arm and with great terror. [22]You gave them this land you had sworn to give their ancestors, a land flowing with milk and honey. [23]They came in and took possession of it, but they did not obey you or follow your law; they did not do what you commanded them to do. So you brought all this disaster on them.

[24]"See how the siege ramps are built up to take the city. Because of the sword, famine and plague, the city will be given into the hands of the Babylonians who are attacking

---

[a] 9 That is, about 7 ounces or about 200 grams

UNSHAKEN God

Jeremiah 32:17

God is all-powerful.

The prophet Jeremiah had warned again and again that the king of Babylon — Nebuchadnezzar — would ravage the city of Jerusalem and carry its people away as slaves. And yet the Lord made an astounding promise. After a period of slavery, the captives would come back to the land (see Jeremiah 32:15). Everyone called Jeremiah the weeping prophet (see Jeremiah 9:1), but suddenly he had reason to cheer. "Ah, Sovereign LORD," he prayed, "Nothing is too hard for you" (Jeremiah 32:17). What an opening line. Despite all the problems God's people faced, the Lord is still "omnipotent," or "all powerful." Nothing — not a thing — is too difficult for him.

So ... When have you seen God do powerful things no one else could do?

it. What you said has happened, as you now see. ²⁵And though the city will be given into the hands of the Babylonians, you, Sovereign LORD, say to me, 'Buy the field with silver and have the transaction witnessed.'"

²⁶Then the word of the LORD came to Jeremiah: ²⁷"I am the LORD, the God of all mankind. Is anything too hard for me? ²⁸Therefore this is what the LORD says: I am about to give this city into the hands of the Babylonians and to Nebuchadnezzar king of Babylon, who will capture it. ²⁹The Babylonians who are attacking this city will come in and set it on fire; they will burn it down, along with the houses where the people aroused my anger by burning incense on the roofs to Baal and by pouring out drink offerings to other gods.

³⁰"The people of Israel and Judah have done nothing but evil in my sight from their youth; indeed, the people of Israel have done nothing but arouse my anger with what their hands have made, declares the LORD. ³¹From the day it was built until now, this city has so aroused my anger and wrath that I must remove it from my sight. ³²The people of Israel and Judah have provoked me by all the evil they have done—they, their kings and officials, their priests and prophets, the people of Judah and those living in Jerusalem. ³³They turned their backs to me and not their faces; though I taught them again and again, they would not listen or respond to discipline. ³⁴They set up their vile images in the house that bears my Name and defiled it. ³⁵They built high places for Baal in the Valley of Ben Hinnom to sacrifice their sons and daughters to Molek, though I never commanded—nor did it enter my mind—that they should do such a detestable thing and so make Judah sin.

³⁶"You are saying about this city, 'By the sword, famine and plague it will be given into the hands of the king of Babylon'; but this is what the LORD, the God of Israel, says: ³⁷I will surely gather them from all the lands where I banish them in my fu-rious anger and great wrath; I will bring them back to this place and let them live in safety. ³⁸They will be my people, and I will be their God. ³⁹I will give them singleness of heart and action, so that they will always fear me and that all will then go well for them and for their children after them. ⁴⁰I will make an everlasting covenant with them: I will never stop doing good to them, and I will inspire them to fear me, so that they will never turn away from me. ⁴¹I will rejoice in doing them good and will assuredly plant them in this land with all my heart and soul.

⁴²"This is what the LORD says: As I have brought all this great calamity on this people, so I will give them all the prosperity I have promised them. ⁴³Once more fields will be bought in this land of which you say, 'It is a desolate waste, without people or animals, for it has been given into the hands of the Babylonians.' ⁴⁴Fields will be bought for silver, and deeds will be signed, sealed and witnessed in the territory of Benjamin, in the villages around Jerusalem, in the towns of Judah and in the towns of the hill country, of the western foothills and of the Negev, because I will restore their fortunes,[a] declares the LORD."

Promise of Restoration

33 While Jeremiah was still confined in the courtyard of the guard, the word of the LORD came to him a second time: ²"This is what the LORD says, he who made the earth, the LORD who formed it and established it—the LORD is his name: ³'Call to me and I will answer you and tell you great and unsearchable things you do not know.' ⁴For this is what the LORD, the God of Israel, says about the houses in this city and the royal palaces of Judah that have been torn down to be used against the siege ramps and the sword ⁵in the fight with the Babylonians[b]: 'They will be filled with the dead bodies of the people I will slay in my anger and wrath. I will hide

---

[a] 44 Or *will bring them back from captivity*
[b] 5 Or *Chaldeans*

my face from this city because of all its wickedness.

⁶"Nevertheless, I will bring health and healing to it; I will heal my people and will let them enjoy abundant peace and security. ⁷I will bring Judah and Israel back from captivity[a] and will rebuild them as they were before. ⁸I will cleanse them from all the sin they have committed against me and will forgive all their sins of rebellion against me. ⁹Then this city will bring me renown, joy, praise and honor before all nations on earth that hear of all the good things I do for it; and they will be in awe and will tremble at the abundant prosperity and peace I provide for it.'

¹⁰"This is what the LORD says: 'You say about this place, "It is a desolate waste, without people or animals." Yet in the towns of Judah and the streets of Jerusalem that are deserted, inhabited by neither people nor animals, there will be heard once more ¹¹the sounds of joy and gladness, the voices of bride and bridegroom, and the voices of those who bring thank offerings to the house of the LORD, saying,

"Give thanks to the LORD Almighty,
    for the LORD is good;
    his love endures forever."

For I will restore the fortunes of the land as they were before,' says the LORD.

¹²"This is what the LORD Almighty says: 'In this place, desolate and without people or animals—in all its towns there will again be pastures for shepherds to rest their flocks. ¹³In the towns of the hill country, of the western foothills and of the Negev, in the territory of Benjamin, in the villages around Jerusalem and in the towns of Judah, flocks will again pass under the hand of the one who counts them,' says the LORD.

¹⁴"'The days are coming,' declares the LORD, 'when I will fulfill the good promise I made to the people of Israel and Judah.

¹⁵"'In those days and at that time
    I will make a righteous Branch
        sprout from David's line;
    he will do what is just and right in
        the land.

¹⁶In those days Judah will be saved
    and Jerusalem will live in safety.
This is the name by which it[b] will be
        called:
    The LORD Our Righteous Savior.'

¹⁷For this is what the LORD says: 'David will never fail to have a man to sit on the throne of Israel, ¹⁸nor will the Levitical priests ever fail to have a man to stand before me continually to offer burnt offerings, to burn grain offerings and to present sacrifices.'"

¹⁹The word of the LORD came to Jeremiah: ²⁰"This is what the LORD says: 'If you can break my covenant with the day and my covenant with the night, so that day and night no longer come at their appointed time, ²¹then my covenant with David my servant—and my covenant with the Levites who are priests ministering before me—can be broken and David will no longer have a descendant to reign on his throne. ²²I will make the descendants of David my servant and the Levites who minister before me as countless as the stars in the sky and as measureless as the sand on the seashore.'"

²³The word of the LORD came to Jeremiah: ²⁴"Have you not noticed that these people are saying, 'The LORD has rejected the two kingdoms[c] he chose'? So they despise my people and no longer regard them as a nation. ²⁵This is what the LORD says: 'If I have not made my covenant with day and night and established the laws of heaven and earth, ²⁶then I will reject the descendants of Jacob and David my servant and will not choose one of his sons to rule over the descendants of Abraham, Isaac and Jacob. For I will restore their fortunes[d] and have compassion on them.'"

Warning to Zedekiah

34 While Nebuchadnezzar king of Babylon and all his army and all the kingdoms and peoples in the empire he ruled were fighting

---

[a] 7 Or *will restore the fortunes of Judah and Israel*   [b] 16 Or *he*   [c] 24 Or *families*   [d] 26 Or *will bring them back from captivity*

against Jerusalem and all its surrounding towns, this word came to Jeremiah from the LORD: [2]"This is what the LORD, the God of Israel, says: Go to Zedekiah king of Judah and tell him, 'This is what the LORD says: I am about to give this city into the hands of the king of Babylon, and he will burn it down. [3]You will not escape from his grasp but will surely be captured and given into his hands. You will see the king of Babylon with your own eyes, and he will speak with you face to face. And you will go to Babylon.

[4]"'Yet hear the LORD's promise to you, Zedekiah king of Judah. This is what the LORD says concerning you: You will not die by the sword; [5]you will die peacefully. As people made a funeral fire in honor of your predecessors, the kings who ruled before you, so they will make a fire in your honor and lament, "Alas, master!" I myself make this promise, declares the LORD.'"

[6]Then Jeremiah the prophet told all this to Zedekiah king of Judah, in Jerusalem, [7]while the army of the king of Babylon was fighting against Jerusalem and the other cities of Judah that were still holding out—Lachish and Azekah. These were the only fortified cities left in Judah.

Freedom for Slaves

[8]The word came to Jeremiah from the LORD after King Zedekiah had made a covenant with all the people in Jerusalem to proclaim freedom for the slaves. [9]Everyone was to free their Hebrew slaves, both male and female; no one was to hold a fellow Hebrew in bondage. [10]So all the officials and people who entered into this covenant agreed that they would free their male and female slaves and no longer hold them in bondage. They agreed, and set them free. [11]But afterward they changed their minds and took back the slaves they had freed and enslaved them again.

[12]Then the word of the LORD came to Jeremiah: [13]"This is what the LORD, the God of Israel, says: I made a covenant with your ancestors when I brought them out of Egypt, out of the land of slavery. I said, [14]'Every seventh year each of you

must free any fellow Hebrews who have sold themselves to you. After they have served you six years, you must let them go free.'[a] Your ancestors, however, did not listen to me or pay attention to me. [15]Recently you repented and did what is right in my sight: Each of you proclaimed freedom to your own people. You even made a covenant before me in the house that bears my Name. [16]But now you have turned around and profaned my name; each of you has taken back the male and female slaves you had set free to go where they wished. You have forced them to become your slaves again.

[17]"Therefore this is what the LORD says: You have not obeyed me; you have not proclaimed freedom to your own people. So I now proclaim 'freedom' for you, declares the LORD—'freedom' to fall by the sword, plague and famine. I will make you abhorrent to all the kingdoms of the earth. [18]Those who have violated my covenant and have not fulfilled the terms of the covenant they made before me, I will treat like the calf they cut in two and then walked between its pieces. [19]The leaders of Judah and Jerusalem, the court officials, the priests and all the people of the land who walked between the pieces of the calf, [20]I will deliver into the hands of their enemies who want to kill them. Their dead bodies will become food for the birds and the wild animals.

[21]"I will deliver Zedekiah king of Judah and his officials into the hands of their enemies who want to kill them, to the army of the king of Babylon, which has withdrawn from you. [22]I am going to give the order, declares the LORD, and I will bring them back to this city. They will fight against it, take it and burn it down. And I will lay waste the towns of Judah so no one can live there."

The Rekabites

35 This is the word that came to Jeremiah from the LORD during the reign of Jehoiakim son of Josiah king of Judah: [2]"Go to

[a] 14 Deut. 15:12

the Rekabite family and invite them to come to one of the side rooms of the house of the LORD and give them wine to drink."

³So I went to get Jaazaniah son of Jeremiah, the son of Habazziniah, and his brothers and all his sons—the whole family of the Rekabites. ⁴I brought them into the house of the LORD, into the room of the sons of Hanan son of Igdaliah the man of God. It was next to the room of the officials, which was over that of Maaseiah son of Shallum the doorkeeper. ⁵Then I set bowls full of wine and some cups before the Rekabites and said to them, "Drink some wine."

⁶But they replied, "We do not drink wine, because our forefather Jehonadab*ᵃ* son of Rekab gave us this command: 'Neither you nor your descendants must ever drink wine. ⁷Also you must never build houses, sow seed or plant vineyards; you must never have any of these things, but must always live in tents. Then you will live a long time in the land where you are nomads.' ⁸We have obeyed everything our forefather Jehonadab son of Rekab commanded us. Neither we nor our wives nor our sons and daughters have ever drunk wine ⁹or built houses to live in or had vineyards, fields or crops. ¹⁰We have lived in tents and have fully obeyed everything our forefather Jehonadab commanded us. ¹¹But when Nebuchadnezzar king of Babylon invaded this land, we said, 'Come, we must go to Jerusalem to escape the Babylonian*ᵇ* and Aramean armies.' So we have remained in Jerusalem."

¹²Then the word of the LORD came to Jeremiah, saying: ¹³"This is what the LORD Almighty, the God of Israel, says: Go and tell the people of Judah and those living in Jerusalem, 'Will you not learn a lesson and obey my words?' declares the LORD. ¹⁴'Jehonadab son of Rekab ordered his descendants not to drink wine and this command has been kept. To this day they do not drink wine, because they obey their forefather's command. But I have spoken to you again and again, yet you have not obeyed me. ¹⁵Again and again I sent all my servants the prophets to you. They said,

"Each of you must turn from your wicked ways and reform your actions; do not follow other gods to serve them. Then you will live in the land I have given to you and your ancestors." But you have not paid attention or listened to me. ¹⁶The descendants of Jehonadab son of Rekab have carried out the command their forefather gave them, but these people have not obeyed me.'

¹⁷"Therefore this is what the LORD God Almighty, the God of Israel, says: 'Listen! I am going to bring on Judah and on everyone living in Jerusalem every disaster I pronounced against them. I spoke to them, but they did not listen; I called to them, but they did not answer.'"

¹⁸Then Jeremiah said to the family of the Rekabites, "This is what the LORD Almighty, the God of Israel, says: 'You have obeyed the command of your forefather Jehonadab and have followed all his instructions and have done everything he ordered.' ¹⁹Therefore this is what the LORD Almighty, the God of Israel, says: 'Jehonadab son of Rekab will never fail to have a descendant to serve me.'"

Jehoiakim Burns Jeremiah's Scroll

36 In the fourth year of Jehoiakim son of Josiah king of Judah, this word came to Jeremiah from the LORD: ²"Take a scroll and write on it all the words I have spoken to you concerning Israel, Judah and all the other nations from the time I began speaking to you in the reign of Josiah till now. ³Perhaps when the people of Judah hear about every disaster I plan to inflict on them, they will each turn from their wicked ways; then I will forgive their wickedness and their sin."

⁴So Jeremiah called Baruch son of Neriah, and while Jeremiah dictated all the words the LORD had spoken to him, Baruch wrote them on the scroll. ⁵Then Jeremiah told Baruch, "I am restricted; I am not allowed to go to the LORD's temple. ⁶So you go to the house of the LORD on a day of fasting and read to the people from

---

ᵃ 6 Hebrew Jonadab, a variant of Jehonadab; here and often in this chapter   ᵇ 11 Or Chaldean the scroll the words of the LORD that you wrote as I dictated. Read them to all the people of Judah who come in from their towns. ⁷Perhaps they will bring their petition before the LORD and will each turn from their wicked ways, for the anger and wrath pronounced against this people by the LORD are great."

⁸Baruch son of Neriah did everything Jeremiah the prophet told him to do; at the LORD's temple he read the words of the LORD from the scroll. ⁹In the ninth month of the fifth year of Jehoiakim son of Josiah king of Judah, a time of fasting before the LORD was proclaimed for all the people in Jerusalem and those who had come from the towns of Judah. ¹⁰From the room of Gemariah son of Shaphan the secretary, which was in the upper courtyard at the entrance of the New Gate of the temple, Baruch read to all the people at the LORD's temple the words of Jeremiah from the scroll.

¹¹When Micaiah son of Gemariah, the son of Shaphan, heard all the words of the LORD from the scroll, ¹²he went down to the secretary's room in the royal palace, where all the officials were sitting: Elishama the secretary, Delaiah son of Shemaiah, Elnathan son of Akbor, Gemariah son of Shaphan, Zedekiah son of Hananiah, and all the other officials. ¹³After Micaiah told them everything he had heard Baruch read to the people from the scroll, ¹⁴all the officials sent Jehudi son of Nethaniah, the son of Shelemiah, the son of Cushi, to say to Baruch, "Bring the scroll from which you have read to the people and come." So Baruch son of Neriah went to them with the scroll in his hand. ¹⁵They said to him, "Sit down, please, and read it to us."

So Baruch read it to them. ¹⁶When they heard all these words, they looked at each other in fear and said to Baruch, "We must report all these words to the king." ¹⁷Then they asked Baruch, "Tell us, how did you come to write all this? Did Jeremiah dictate it?"

¹⁸"Yes," Baruch replied, "he dictated all these words to me, and I wrote them in ink on the scroll."

¹⁹Then the officials said to Baruch, "You and Jeremiah, go and hide. Don't let anyone know where you are."

²⁰After they put the scroll in the room of Elishama the secretary, they went to the king in the courtyard and reported everything to him. ²¹The king sent Jehudi to get the scroll, and Jehudi brought it from the room of Elishama the secretary and read it to the king and all the officials standing beside him. ²²It was the ninth month and the king was sitting in the winter apartment, with a fire burning in the firepot in front of him. ²³Whenever Jehudi had read three or four columns of the scroll, the king cut them off with a scribe's knife and threw them into the firepot, until the entire scroll was burned in the fire. ²⁴The king and all his attendants who heard all these words showed no fear, nor did they tear their clothes. ²⁵Even though Elnathan, Delaiah and Gemariah urged the king not to burn the scroll, he would not listen to them. ²⁶Instead, the king commanded Jerahmeel, a son of the king, Seraiah son of Azriel and Shelemiah son of Abdeel to arrest Baruch the scribe and Jeremiah the prophet. But the LORD had hidden them.

²⁷After the king burned the scroll containing the words that Baruch had written at Jeremiah's dictation, the word of the LORD came to Jeremiah: ²⁸"Take another scroll and write on it all the words that were on the first scroll, which Jehoiakim king of Judah burned up. ²⁹Also tell Jehoiakim king of Judah, 'This is what the LORD says: You burned that scroll and said, "Why did you write on it that the king of Babylon would certainly come and destroy this land and wipe from it both man and beast?" ³⁰Therefore this is what the LORD says about Jehoiakim king of Judah: He will have no one to sit on the throne of David; his body will be thrown out and exposed to the heat by day and the frost by night. ³¹I will punish him and his children and his attendants for their wickedness; I will bring on them and those living in Jerusalem and the people of Judah every disaster I pro-

nounced against them, because they have not listened.'"

[32] So Jeremiah took another scroll and gave it to the scribe Baruch son of Neriah, and as Jeremiah dictated, Baruch wrote on it all the words of the scroll that Jehoiakim king of Judah had burned in the fire. And many similar words were added to them.

Jeremiah in Prison

37 Zedekiah son of Josiah was made king of Judah by Nebuchadnezzar king of Babylon; he reigned in place of Jehoiachin[a] son of Jehoiakim. [2] Neither he nor his attendants nor the people of the land paid any attention to the words the LORD had spoken through Jeremiah the prophet.

[3] King Zedekiah, however, sent Jehukal son of Shelemiah with the priest Zephaniah son of Maaseiah to Jeremiah the prophet with this message: "Please pray to the LORD our God for us."

[4] Now Jeremiah was free to come and go among the people, for he had not yet been put in prison. [5] Pharaoh's army had marched out of Egypt, and when the Babylonians[b] who were besieging Jerusalem heard the report about them, they withdrew from Jerusalem.

[6] Then the word of the LORD came to Jeremiah the prophet: [7] "This is what the LORD, the God of Israel, says: Tell the king of Judah, who sent you to inquire of me, 'Pharaoh's army, which has marched out to support you, will go back to its own land, to Egypt. [8] Then the Babylonians will return and attack this city; they will capture it and burn it down.'

[9] "This is what the LORD says: Do not deceive yourselves, thinking, 'The Babylonians will surely leave us.' They will not! [10] Even if you were to defeat the entire Babylonian[c] army that is attacking you and only wounded men were left in their tents, they would come out and burn this city down."

[11] After the Babylonian army had withdrawn from Jerusalem because of Pharaoh's army, [12] Jeremiah started to leave the city to go to the territory of Benjamin to get his share of the property among the people there. [13] But when he reached the Benjamin Gate, the captain of the guard, whose name was Irijah son of Shelemiah, the son of Hananiah, arrested him and said, "You are deserting to the Babylonians!"

[14] "That's not true!" Jeremiah said. "I am not deserting to the Babylonians." But Irijah would not listen to him; instead, he arrested Jeremiah and brought him to the officials. [15] They were angry with Jeremiah and had him beaten and imprisoned in the house of Jonathan the secretary, which they had made into a prison.

[16] Jeremiah was put into a vaulted cell in a dungeon, where he remained a long time. [17] Then King Zedekiah sent for him and had him brought to the palace, where he asked him privately, "Is there any word from the LORD?"

"Yes," Jeremiah replied, "you will be delivered into the hands of the king of Babylon."

[18] Then Jeremiah said to King Zedekiah, "What crime have I committed against you or your attendants or this people, that you have put me in prison? [19] Where are your prophets who prophesied to you, 'The king of Babylon will not attack you or this land'? [20] But now, my lord the king, please listen. Let me bring my petition before you: Do not send me back to the house of Jonathan the secretary, or I will die there."

[21] King Zedekiah then gave orders for Jeremiah to be placed in the courtyard of the guard and given a loaf of bread from the street of the bakers each day until all the bread in the city was gone. So Jeremiah remained in the courtyard of the guard.

Jeremiah Thrown Into a Cistern

38 Shephatiah son of Mattan, Gedaliah son of Pashhur, Jehukal[d] son of Shelemiah, and Pashhur son of Malkijah heard what

---

[a] 1 Hebrew *Koniah*, a variant of *Jehoiachin*
[b] 5 Or *Chaldeans*; also in verses 8, 9, 13 and 14
[c] 10 Or *Chaldean*; also in verse 11
[d] 1 Hebrew *Jukal*, a variant of *Jehukal*

Jeremiah was telling all the people when he said, ²"This is what the LORD says: 'Whoever stays in this city will die by the sword, famine or plague, but whoever goes over to the Babylonians*a* will live. They will escape with their lives; they will live.' ³And this is what the LORD says: 'This city will certainly be given into the hands of the army of the king of Babylon, who will capture it.'"

⁴Then the officials said to the king, "This man should be put to death. He is discouraging the soldiers who are left in this city, as well as all the people, by the things he is saying to them. This man is not seeking the good of these people but their ruin."

⁵"He is in your hands," King Zedekiah answered. "The king can do nothing to oppose you."

⁶So they took Jeremiah and put him into the cistern of Malkijah, the king's son, which was in the courtyard of the guard. They lowered Jeremiah by ropes into the cistern; it had no water in it, only mud, and Jeremiah sank down into the mud.

⁷But Ebed-Melek, a Cushite,*b* an official*c* in the royal palace, heard that they had put Jeremiah into the cistern. While the king was sitting in the Benjamin Gate, ⁸Ebed-Melek went out of the palace and said to him, ⁹"My lord the king, these men have acted wickedly in all they have done to Jeremiah the prophet. They have thrown him into a cistern, where he will starve to death when there is no longer any bread in the city."

¹⁰Then the king commanded Ebed-Melek the Cushite, "Take thirty men from here with you and lift Jeremiah the prophet out of the cistern before he dies."

¹¹So Ebed-Melek took the men with him and went to a room under the treasury in the palace. He took some old rags and worn-out clothes from there and let them down with ropes to Jeremiah in the cistern. ¹²Ebed-Melek the Cushite said to Jeremiah, "Put these old rags and worn-out clothes under your arms to pad the ropes." Jeremiah did so, ¹³and they pulled him up with the ropes and lifted him out of the cistern. And Jeremiah remained in the courtyard of the guard.

Zedekiah Questions Jeremiah Again

¹⁴Then King Zedekiah sent for Jeremiah the prophet and had him brought to the third entrance to the temple of the LORD. "I am going to ask you something," the king said to Jeremiah. "Do not hide anything from me."

¹⁵Jeremiah said to Zedekiah, "If I give you an answer, will you not kill me? Even if I did give you counsel, you would not listen to me."

¹⁶But King Zedekiah swore this oath secretly to Jeremiah: "As surely as the LORD lives, who has given us breath, I will neither kill you nor hand you over to those who want to kill you."

¹⁷Then Jeremiah said to Zedekiah, "This is what the LORD God Almighty, the God of Israel, says: 'If you surrender to the officers of the king of Babylon, your life will be spared and this city will not be burned down; you and your family will live. ¹⁸But if you will not surrender to the officers of the king of Babylon, this city will be given into the hands of the Babylonians and they will burn it down; you yourself will not escape from them.'"

¹⁹King Zedekiah said to Jeremiah, "I am afraid of the Jews who have gone over to the Babylonians, for the Babylonians may hand me over to them and they will mistreat me."

²⁰"They will not hand you over," Jeremiah replied. "Obey the LORD by doing what I tell you. Then it will go well with you, and your life will be spared. ²¹But if you refuse to surrender, this is what the LORD has revealed to me: ²²All the women left in the palace of the king of Judah will be brought out to the officials of the king of Babylon. Those women will say to you:

"'They misled you and overcame
    you—
  those trusted friends of yours.

---

a 2 Or *Chaldeans*; also in verses 18, 19 and 23
b 7 Probably from the upper Nile region
c 7 Or *a eunuch*

Your feet are sunk in the mud;
your friends have deserted you.'

²³"All your wives and children will be brought out to the Babylonians. You yourself will not escape from their hands but will be captured by the king of Babylon; and this city will*a* be burned down."

²⁴Then Zedekiah said to Jeremiah, "Do not let anyone know about this conversation, or you may die. ²⁵If the officials hear that I talked with you, and they come to you and say, 'Tell us what you said to the king and what the king said to you; do not hide it from us or we will kill you,' ²⁶then tell them, 'I was pleading with the king not to send me back to Jonathan's house to die there.'"

²⁷All the officials did come to Jeremiah and question him, and he told them everything the king had ordered him to say. So they said no more to him, for no one had heard his conversation with the king.

²⁸And Jeremiah remained in the courtyard of the guard until the day Jerusalem was captured.

The Fall of Jerusalem

39 This is how Jerusalem was taken: ¹In the ninth year of Zedekiah king of Judah, in the tenth month, Nebuchadnezzar king of Babylon marched against Jerusalem with his whole army and laid siege to it. ²And on the ninth day of the fourth month of Zedekiah's eleventh year, the city wall was broken through. ³Then all the officials of the king of Babylon came and took seats in the Middle Gate: Nergal-Sharezer of Samgar, Nebo-Sarsekim a chief officer, Nergal-Sharezer a high official and all the other officials of the king of Babylon. ⁴When Zedekiah king of Judah and all the soldiers saw them, they fled; they left the city at night by way of the king's garden, through the gate between the two walls, and headed toward the Arabah.*b*

⁵But the Babylonian*c* army pursued them and overtook Zedekiah in the plains of Jericho. They captured him and took him to Nebuchadnezzar king of Babylon

at Riblah in the land of Hamath, where he pronounced sentence on him. ⁶There at Riblah the king of Babylon slaughtered the sons of Zedekiah before his eyes and also killed all the nobles of Judah. ⁷Then he put out Zedekiah's eyes and bound him with bronze shackles to take him to Babylon.

⁸The Babylonians*d* set fire to the royal palace and the houses of the people and broke down the walls of Jerusalem. ⁹Nebuzaradan commander of the imperial guard carried into exile to Babylon the

a 23 Or *and you will cause this city to*   *b 4* Or *the Jordan Valley*   *c 5* Or *Chaldean*   *d 8* Or *Chaldeans*

Jeremiah 39:1–8

Sin makes you weak.

If you want a visual reminder of the badness of disobeying God, picture the conquered city of Jerusalem. It was God's sacred city, capital of the southern kingdom and site of the holy temple. It was the place of worship for every Old Testament saint. But in 586 BC the city was attacked and destroyed. An army led by King Nebuchadnezzar of Babylon hunted down King Zedekiah of Judah and put his eyes out, then burned the palace, temple and city walls. The people of Jerusalem were led as prisoners to Babylon, a thousand-mile walk. The book of Lamentations describes the destruction of the city, bluntly explaining why the city fell. Jerusalem had invited God's anger by sinning greatly (see Lamentations 1:8). Obeying God made Jerusalem powerful. Disobeying the Lord made the city blow apart.

Think: How does sin make you feeble?

ROCK SOLID truths

people who remained in the city, along with those who had gone over to him, and the rest of the people. [10]But Nebuzaradan the commander of the guard left behind in the land of Judah some of the poor people, who owned nothing; and at that time he gave them vineyards and fields.

[11]Now Nebuchadnezzar king of Babylon had given these orders about Jeremiah through Nebuzaradan commander of the imperial guard: [12]"Take him and look after him; don't harm him but do for him whatever he asks." [13]So Nebuzaradan the commander of the guard, Nebushazban a chief officer, Nergal-Sharezer a high official and all the other officers of the king of Babylon [14]sent and had Jeremiah taken out of the courtyard of the guard. They turned him over to Gedaliah son of Ahikam, the son of Shaphan, to take him back to his home. So he remained among his own people.

[15]While Jeremiah had been confined in the courtyard of the guard, the word of the Lord came to him: [16]"Go and tell Ebed-Melek the Cushite, 'This is what the Lord Almighty, the God of Israel, says: I am about to fulfill my words against this city—words concerning disaster, not prosperity. At that time they will be fulfilled before your eyes. [17]But I will rescue you on that day, declares the Lord; you will not be given into the hands of those you fear. [18]I will save you; you will not fall by the sword but will escape with your life, because you trust in me, declares the Lord.'"

Jeremiah Freed

40 The word came to Jeremiah from the Lord after Nebuzaradan commander of the imperial guard had released him at Ramah. He had found Jeremiah bound in chains among all the captives from Jerusalem and Judah who were being carried into exile to Babylon. [2]When the commander of the guard found Jeremiah, he said to him, "The Lord your God decreed this disaster for this place. [3]And now the Lord has brought it about; he has done

just as he said he would. All this happened because you people sinned against the Lord and did not obey him. [4]But today I am freeing you from the chains on your wrists. Come with me to Babylon, if you like, and I will look after you; but if you do not want to, then don't come. Look, the whole country lies before you; go wherever you please." [5]However, before Jeremiah turned to go,[a] Nebuzaradan added, "Go back to Gedaliah son of Ahikam, the son of Shaphan, whom the king of Babylon has appointed over the towns of Judah, and live with him among the people, or go anywhere else you please."

Then the commander gave him provisions and a present and let him go. [6]So Jeremiah went to Gedaliah son of Ahikam at Mizpah and stayed with him among the people who were left behind in the land.

Gedaliah Assassinated

[7]When all the army officers and their men who were still in the open country heard that the king of Babylon had appointed Gedaliah son of Ahikam as governor over the land and had put him in charge of the men, women and children who were the poorest in the land and who had not been carried into exile to Babylon, [8]they came to Gedaliah at Mizpah—Ishmael son of Nethaniah, Johanan and Jonathan the sons of Kareah, Seraiah son of Tanhumeth, the sons of Ephai the Netophathite, and Jaazaniah[b] the son of the Maakathite, and their men. [9]Gedaliah son of Ahikam, the son of Shaphan, took an oath to reassure them and their men. "Do not be afraid to serve the Babylonians,[c]" he said. "Settle down in the land and serve the king of Babylon, and it will go well with you. [10]I myself will stay at Mizpah to represent you before the Babylonians who come to us, but you are to harvest the wine, summer fruit and olive oil, and put them in your storage jars, and live in the towns you have taken over."

[11]When all the Jews in Moab, Ammon,

---

[a] 5 Or *Jeremiah answered*   [b] 8 Hebrew *Jezaniah*, a variant of *Jaazaniah*
[c] 9 Or *Chaldeans*; also in verse 10

Edom and all the other countries heard that the king of Babylon had left a remnant in Judah and had appointed Gedaliah son of Ahikam, the son of Shaphan, as governor over them, ¹²they all came back to the land of Judah, to Gedaliah at Mizpah, from all the countries where they had been scattered. And they harvested an abundance of wine and summer fruit.

¹³Johanan son of Kareah and all the army officers still in the open country came to Gedaliah at Mizpah ¹⁴and said to him, "Don't you know that Baalis king of the Ammonites has sent Ishmael son of Nethaniah to take your life?" But Gedaliah son of Ahikam did not believe them.

¹⁵Then Johanan son of Kareah said privately to Gedaliah in Mizpah, "Let me go and kill Ishmael son of Nethaniah, and no one will know it. Why should he take your life and cause all the Jews who are gathered around you to be scattered and the remnant of Judah to perish?"

¹⁶But Gedaliah son of Ahikam said to Johanan son of Kareah, "Don't do such a thing! What you are saying about Ishmael is not true."

41 In the seventh month Ishmael son of Nethaniah, the son of Elishama, who was of royal blood and had been one of the king's officers, came with ten men to Gedaliah son of Ahikam at Mizpah. While they were eating together there, ²Ishmael son of Nethaniah and the ten men who were with him got up and struck down Gedaliah son of Ahikam, the son of Shaphan, with the sword, killing the one whom the king of Babylon had appointed as governor over the land. ³Ishmael also killed all the men of Judah who were with Gedaliah at Mizpah, as well as the Babylonian*ᵃ* soldiers who were there.

⁴The day after Gedaliah's assassination, before anyone knew about it, ⁵eighty men who had shaved off their beards, torn their clothes and cut themselves came from Shechem, Shiloh and Samaria, bringing grain offerings and incense with them to the house of the LORD. ⁶Ishmael son of Nethaniah went out from Mizpah to meet them, weeping as he went. When he met them, he said, "Come to Gedaliah son of Ahikam." ⁷When they went into the city, Ishmael son of Nethaniah and the men who were with him slaughtered them and threw them into a cistern. ⁸But ten of them said to Ishmael, "Don't kill us! We have wheat and barley, olive oil and honey, hidden in a field." So he let them alone and did not kill them with the others. ⁹Now the cistern where he threw all the bodies of the men he had killed along with Gedaliah was the one King Asa had made as part of his defense against Baasha king of Israel. Ishmael son of Nethaniah filled it with the dead.

¹⁰Ishmael made captives of all the rest of the people who were in Mizpah—the king's daughters along with all the others who were left there, over whom Nebuzaradan commander of the imperial guard had appointed Gedaliah son of Ahikam. Ishmael son of Nethaniah took them captive and set out to cross over to the Ammonites.

¹¹When Johanan son of Kareah and all the army officers who were with him heard about all the crimes Ishmael son of Nethaniah had committed, ¹²they took all their men and went to fight Ishmael son of Nethaniah. They caught up with him near the great pool in Gibeon. ¹³When all the people Ishmael had with him saw Johanan son of Kareah and the army officers who were with him, they were glad. ¹⁴All the people Ishmael had taken captive at Mizpah turned and went over to Johanan son of Kareah. ¹⁵But Ishmael son of Nethaniah and eight of his men escaped from Johanan and fled to the Ammonites.

Flight to Egypt

¹⁶Then Johanan son of Kareah and all the army officers who were with him led away all the people of Mizpah who had survived, whom Johanan had recovered from Ishmael son of Nethaniah after Ishmael had assassinated Gedaliah son of Ahikam—the soldiers, women, children and court officials he had recovered from

ᵃ 3 Or Chaldean

Gibeon. ¹⁷And they went on, stopping at Geruth Kimham near Bethlehem on their way to Egypt ¹⁸to escape the Babylonians.ᵃ They were afraid of them because Ishmael son of Nethaniah had killed Gedaliah son of Ahikam, whom the king of Babylon had appointed as governor over the land.

42 Then all the army officers, including Johanan son of Kareah and Jezaniahᵇ son of Hoshaiah, and all the people from the least to the greatest approached ²Jeremiah the prophet and said to him, "Please hear our petition and pray to the LORD your God for this entire remnant. For as you now see, though we were once many, now only a few are left. ³Pray that the LORD your God will tell us where we should go and what we should do."

⁴"I have heard you," replied Jeremiah the prophet. "I will certainly pray to the LORD your God as you have requested; I will tell you everything the LORD says and will keep nothing back from you."

⁵Then they said to Jeremiah, "May the LORD be a true and faithful witness against us if we do not act in accordance with everything the LORD your God sends you to tell us. ⁶Whether it is favorable or unfavorable, we will obey the LORD our God, to whom we are sending you, so that it will go well with us, for we will obey the LORD our God."

⁷Ten days later the word of the LORD came to Jeremiah. ⁸So he called together Johanan son of Kareah and all the army officers who were with him and all the people from the least to the greatest. ⁹He said to them, "This is what the LORD, the God of Israel, to whom you sent me to present your petition, says: ¹⁰'If you stay in this land, I will build you up and not tear you down; I will plant you and not uproot you, for I have relented concerning the disaster I have inflicted on you. ¹¹Do not be afraid of the king of Babylon, whom you now fear. Do not be afraid of him, declares the LORD, for I am with you and will save you and deliver you from his hands. ¹²I will show you compassion so that he will

have compassion on you and restore you to your land.'

¹³"However, if you say, 'We will not stay in this land,' and so disobey the LORD your God, ¹⁴and if you say, 'No, we will go and live in Egypt, where we will not see war or hear the trumpet or be hungry for bread,' ¹⁵then hear the word of the LORD, you remnant of Judah. This is what the LORD Almighty, the God of Israel, says: 'If you are determined to go to Egypt and you do go to settle there, ¹⁶then the sword you fear will overtake you there, and the famine you dread will follow you into Egypt, and there you will die. ¹⁷Indeed, all who are determined to go to Egypt to settle there will die by the sword, famine and plague; not one of them will survive or escape the disaster I will bring on them.' ¹⁸This is what the LORD Almighty, the God of Israel, says: 'As my anger and wrath have been poured out on those who lived in Jerusalem, so will my wrath be poured out on you when you go to Egypt. You will be a curseᶜ and an object of horror, a curseᶜ and an object of reproach; you will never see this place again.'

¹⁹"Remnant of Judah, the LORD has told you, 'Do not go to Egypt.' Be sure of this: I warn you today ²⁰that you made a fatal mistake when you sent me to the LORD your God and said, 'Pray to the LORD our God for us; tell us everything he says and we will do it.' ²¹I have told you today, but you still have not obeyed the LORD your God in all he sent me to tell you. ²²So now, be sure of this: You will die by the sword, famine and plague in the place where you want to go to settle."

43 When Jeremiah had finished telling the people all the words of the LORD their God—everything the LORD had sent him to tell them— ²Azariah son of Hoshaiah and Johanan son of Kareah and all the arrogant men said to Jeremiah, "You are lying! The LORD our God has not sent you

---

ᵃ *18* Or *Chaldeans*   ᵇ *1* Hebrew; Septuagint (see also 43:2) *Azariah*   ᶜ *18* That is, your name will be used in cursing (see 29:22); or, others will see that you are cursed.

to say, 'You must not go to Egypt to settle there.' ³But Baruch son of Neriah is inciting you against us to hand us over to the Babylonians,ᵃ so they may kill us or carry us into exile to Babylon."

⁴So Johanan son of Kareah and all the army officers and all the people disobeyed the LORD's command to stay in the land of Judah. ⁵Instead, Johanan son of Kareah and all the army officers led away all the remnant of Judah who had come back to live in the land of Judah from all the nations where they had been scattered. ⁶They also led away all those whom Nebuzaradan commander of the imperial guard had left with Gedaliah son of Ahikam, the son of Shaphan—the men, the women, the children and the king's daughters. And they took Jeremiah the prophet and Baruch son of Neriah along with them. ⁷So they entered Egypt in disobedience to the LORD and went as far as Tahpanhes.

⁸In Tahpanhes the word of the LORD came to Jeremiah: ⁹"While the Jews are watching, take some large stones with you and bury them in clay in the brick pavement at the entrance to Pharaoh's palace in Tahpanhes. ¹⁰Then say to them, 'This is what the LORD Almighty, the God of Israel, says: I will send for my servant Nebuchadnezzar king of Babylon, and I will set his throne over these stones I have buried here; he will spread his royal canopy above them. ¹¹He will come and attack Egypt, bringing death to those destined for death, captivity to those destined for captivity, and the sword to those destined for the sword. ¹²He will set fire to the temples of the gods of Egypt; he will burn their temples and take their gods captive. As a shepherd picks his garment clean of lice, so he will pick Egypt clean and depart. ¹³There in the temple of the sunᵇ in Egypt he will demolish the sacred pillars and will burn down the temples of the gods of Egypt.'"

Disaster Because of Idolatry

44 This word came to Jeremiah concerning all the Jews living in Lower Egypt—in Migdol, Tahpanhes and Memphis—and

in Upper Egypt: ²"This is what the LORD Almighty, the God of Israel, says: You saw the great disaster I brought on Jerusalem and on all the towns of Judah. Today they lie deserted and in ruins ³because of the evil they have done. They aroused my anger by burning incense to and worshiping other gods that neither they nor you nor your ancestors ever knew. ⁴Again and again I sent my servants the prophets, who said, 'Do not do this detestable thing that I hate!' ⁵But they did not listen or pay attention; they did not turn from their wickedness or stop burning incense to other gods. ⁶Therefore, my fierce anger was poured out; it raged against the towns of Judah and the streets of Jerusalem and made them the desolate ruins they are today.

⁷"Now this is what the LORD God Almighty, the God of Israel, says: Why bring such great disaster on yourselves by cutting off from Judah the men and women, the children and infants, and so leave yourselves without a remnant? ⁸Why arouse my anger with what your hands have made, burning incense to other gods in Egypt, where you have come to live? You will destroy yourselves and make yourselves a curseᶜ and an object of reproach among all the nations on earth. ⁹Have you forgotten the wickedness committed by your ancestors and by the kings and queens of Judah and the wickedness committed by you and your wives in the land of Judah and the streets of Jerusalem? ¹⁰To this day they have not humbled themselves or shown reverence, nor have they followed my law and the decrees I set before you and your ancestors.

¹¹"Therefore this is what the LORD Almighty, the God of Israel, says: I am determined to bring disaster on you and to destroy all Judah. ¹²I will take away the remnant of Judah who were determined to go to Egypt to settle there. They will all perish in Egypt; they will fall by the sword or die from famine. From the least to the greatest, they will die by sword or

---

ᵃ *3* Or *Chaldeans*   ᵇ *13* Or *in Heliopolis*
ᶜ *8* That is, your name will be used in cursing (see 29:22); or, others will see that you are cursed; also in verse 12; similarly in verse 22.

famine. They will become a curse and an object of horror, a curse and an object of reproach. [13]I will punish those who live in Egypt with the sword, famine and plague, as I punished Jerusalem. [14]None of the remnant of Judah who have gone to live in Egypt will escape or survive to return to the land of Judah, to which they long to return and live; none will return except a few fugitives."

[15]Then all the men who knew that their wives were burning incense to other gods, along with all the women who were present—a large assembly—and all the people living in Lower and Upper Egypt, said to Jeremiah, [16]"We will not listen to the message you have spoken to us in the name of the LORD! [17]We will certainly do everything we said we would: We will burn incense to the Queen of Heaven and will pour out drink offerings to her just as we and our ancestors, our kings and our officials did in the towns of Judah and in the streets of Jerusalem. At that time we had plenty of food and were well off and suffered no harm. [18]But ever since we stopped burning incense to the Queen of Heaven and pouring out drink offerings to her, we have had nothing and have been perishing by sword and famine."

[19]The women added, "When we burned incense to the Queen of Heaven and poured out drink offerings to her, did not our husbands know that we were making cakes impressed with her image and pouring out drink offerings to her?"

[20]Then Jeremiah said to all the people, both men and women, who were answering him, [21]"Did not the LORD remember and call to mind the incense burned in the towns of Judah and the streets of Jerusalem by you and your ancestors, your kings and your officials and the people of the land? [22]When the LORD could no longer endure your wicked actions and the detestable things you did, your land became a curse and a desolate waste without inhabitants, as it is today. [23]Because you have burned incense and have sinned against the LORD and have not obeyed him or followed his law or his decrees or his stipulations, this disaster has come upon you, as you now see."

[24]Then Jeremiah said to all the people, including the women, "Hear the word of the LORD, all you people of Judah in Egypt. [25]This is what the LORD Almighty, the God of Israel, says: You and your wives have done what you said you would do when you promised, 'We will certainly carry out the vows we made to burn incense and pour out drink offerings to the Queen of Heaven.'

"Go ahead then, do what you promised!

Jeremiah 44:1–30

Sin doesn't get you what you want.

God and his people had a disagreement that was no little thing. After the Babylonians conquered the holy city of Jerusalem, many Jews fled to Egypt to avoid being taken captive to Babylon. Now the prophet Jeremiah was in a fight with that group. The people thought they had experienced good times because they had burned incense to "the Queen of Heaven," an Egyptian goddess, and they assumed they were now suffering because they had stopped honoring the goddess. Jeremiah argued that the opposite was true. The people were stricken and starving because of the years they had worshiped idols. So when the people told Jeremiah they were once again going to worship the Queen of Heaven, the prophet threatened God would destroy them for their sin. It's not a happy story. But sooner or later sin brings disaster.

Think: When have you thought sinning would get you what you wanted? What happened?

ROCK SOLID truths

Keep your vows! ²⁶But hear the word of the LORD, all you Jews living in Egypt: 'I swear by my great name,' says the LORD, 'that no one from Judah living anywhere in Egypt will ever again invoke my name or swear, "As surely as the Sovereign LORD lives." ²⁷For I am watching over them for harm, not for good; the Jews in Egypt will perish by sword and famine until they are all destroyed. ²⁸Those who escape the sword and return to the land of Judah from Egypt will be very few. Then the whole remnant of Judah who came to live in Egypt will know whose word will stand—mine or theirs.

²⁹"'This will be the sign to you that I will punish you in this place,' declares the LORD, 'so that you will know that my threats of harm against you will surely stand.' ³⁰This is what the LORD says: 'I am going to deliver Pharaoh Hophra king of Egypt into the hands of his enemies who want to kill him, just as I gave Zedekiah king of Judah into the hands of Nebuchadnezzar king of Babylon, the enemy who wanted to kill him.'"

A Message to Baruch

45 When Baruch son of Neriah wrote on a scroll the words Jeremiah the prophet dictated in the fourth year of Jehoiakim son of Josiah king of Judah, Jeremiah said this to Baruch: ²"This is what the LORD, the God of Israel, says to you, Baruch: ³You said, 'Woe to me! The LORD has added sorrow to my pain; I am worn out with groaning and find no rest.' ⁴But the LORD has told me to say to you, 'This is what the LORD says: I will overthrow what I have built and uproot what I have planted, throughout the earth. ⁵Should you then seek great things for yourself? Do not seek them. For I will bring disaster on all people, declares the LORD, but wherever you go I will let you escape with your life.'"

A Message About Egypt

46 This is the word of the LORD that came to Jeremiah the prophet concerning the nations:

²Concerning Egypt:

This is the message against the army of Pharaoh Necho king of Egypt, which was defeated at Carchemish on the Euphrates River by Nebuchadnezzar king of Babylon in the fourth year of Jehoiakim son of Josiah king of Judah:

³"Prepare your shields, both large and small,
and march out for battle!
⁴Harness the horses,
mount the steeds!
Take your positions
with helmets on!
Polish your spears,
put on your armor!
⁵What do I see?
They are terrified,
they are retreating,
their warriors are defeated.
They flee in haste
without looking back,
and there is terror on every side,"
declares the LORD.
⁶"The swift cannot flee
nor the strong escape.
In the north by the River Euphrates
they stumble and fall.

⁷"Who is this that rises like the Nile,
like rivers of surging waters?
⁸Egypt rises like the Nile,
like rivers of surging waters.
She says, 'I will rise and cover the earth;
I will destroy cities and their people.'
⁹Charge, you horses!
Drive furiously, you charioteers!
March on, you warriors—men of Cush^a and Put who carry shields,
men of Lydia who draw the bow.
¹⁰But that day belongs to the Lord, the LORD Almighty—
a day of vengeance, for vengeance on his foes.
The sword will devour till it is satisfied,
till it has quenched its thirst with blood.

^a 9 That is, the upper Nile region

For the Lord, the LORD Almighty,
  will offer sacrifice
in the land of the north by the River
  Euphrates.
11 "Go up to Gilead and get balm,
  Virgin Daughter Egypt.
But you try many medicines in vain;
  there is no healing for you.
12 The nations will hear of your shame;
  your cries will fill the earth.
One warrior will stumble over
    another;
  both will fall down together."

13 This is the message the LORD spoke to Jeremiah the prophet about the coming of Nebuchadnezzar king of Babylon to attack Egypt:

14 "Announce this in Egypt, and
    proclaim it in Migdol;
  proclaim it also in Memphis and
    Tahpanhes:
  'Take your positions and get ready,
    for the sword devours those around
      you.'
15 Why will your warriors be laid low?
  They cannot stand, for the LORD
    will push them down.
16 They will stumble repeatedly;
  they will fall over each other.
They will say, 'Get up, let us go back
  to our own people and our native
    lands,
  away from the sword of the oppressor.'
17 There they will exclaim,
  'Pharaoh king of Egypt is only a
    loud noise;
  he has missed his opportunity.'

18 "As surely as I live," declares the King,
  whose name is the LORD Almighty,
  "one will come who is like Tabor
    among the mountains,
  like Carmel by the sea.
19 Pack your belongings for exile,
  you who live in Egypt,
for Memphis will be laid waste
  and lie in ruins without inhabitant.

20 "Egypt is a beautiful heifer,
  but a gadfly is coming
  against her from the north.
21 The mercenaries in her ranks
  are like fattened calves.
They too will turn and flee together,
  they will not stand their ground,
for the day of disaster is coming upon
    them,
  the time for them to be punished.
22 Egypt will hiss like a fleeing serpent
  as the enemy advances in force;
they will come against her with axes,
  like men who cut down trees.
23 They will chop down her forest,"
                    declares the LORD,
  "dense though it be.
They are more numerous than
    locusts,
  they cannot be counted.
24 Daughter Egypt will be put to shame,
  given into the hands of the people
    of the north."

25 The LORD Almighty, the God of Israel, says: "I am about to bring punishment on Amon god of Thebes, on Pharaoh, on Egypt and her gods and her kings, and on those who rely on Pharaoh. 26 I will give them into the hands of those who want to kill them—Nebuchadnezzar king of Babylon and his officers. Later, however, Egypt will be inhabited as in times past," declares the LORD.

27 "Do not be afraid, Jacob my servant;
  do not be dismayed, Israel.
I will surely save you out of a distant
    place,
  your descendants from the land of
    their exile.
Jacob will again have peace and
    security,
  and no one will make him afraid.
28 Do not be afraid, Jacob my servant,
  for I am with you," declares the
    LORD.
"Though I completely destroy all the
    nations
  among which I scatter you,
  I will not completely destroy you.
I will discipline you but only in due
    measure;
  I will not let you go entirely
    unpunished."

A Message About the Philistines

47 This is the word of the LORD that came to Jeremiah the prophet concerning the Philistines before Pharaoh attacked Gaza:

²This is what the LORD says:

"See how the waters are rising in the
  north;
  they will become an overflowing
    torrent.
They will overflow the land and
  everything in it,
  the towns and those who live in
    them.
The people will cry out;
  all who dwell in the land will wail
³at the sound of the hooves of galloping
  steeds,
  at the noise of enemy chariots
  and the rumble of their wheels.
Parents will not turn to help their
  children;
  their hands will hang limp.
⁴For the day has come
  to destroy all the Philistines
and to remove all survivors
  who could help Tyre and Sidon.
The LORD is about to destroy the
  Philistines,
  the remnant from the coasts of
    Caphtor.ᵃ
⁵Gaza will shave her head in
  mourning;
  Ashkelon will be silenced.
You remnant on the plain,
  how long will you cut yourselves?

⁶"'Alas, sword of the LORD,
  how long till you rest?
Return to your sheath;
  cease and be still.'
⁷But how can it rest
  when the LORD has commanded it,
when he has ordered it
  to attack Ashkelon and the coast?"

A Message About Moab

48 Concerning Moab:

This is what the LORD Almighty, the God of Israel, says:

"Woe to Nebo, for it will be ruined.
  Kiriathaim will be disgraced and
    captured;
  the strongholdᵇ will be disgraced
    and shattered.
²Moab will be praised no more;
  in Heshbonᶜ people will plot her
    downfall:
  'Come, let us put an end to that
    nation.'
You, the people of Madmen,ᵈ will also
  be silenced;
  the sword will pursue you.
³Cries of anguish arise from Horonaim,
  cries of great havoc and destruction.
⁴Moab will be broken;
  her little ones will cry out.ᵉ
⁵They go up the hill to Luhith,
  weeping bitterly as they go;
on the road down to Horonaim
  anguished cries over the destruction
    are heard.
⁶Flee! Run for your lives;
  become like a bushᶠ in the desert.
⁷Since you trust in your deeds and
  riches,
  you too will be taken captive,
and Chemosh will go into exile,
  together with his priests and
    officials.
⁸The destroyer will come against every
  town,
  and not a town will escape.
The valley will be ruined
  and the plateau destroyed,
  because the LORD has spoken.
⁹Put salt on Moab,
  for she will be laid wasteᵍ;
her towns will become desolate,
  with no one to live in them.

¹⁰"A curse on anyone who is lax in doing
  the LORD's work!
A curse on anyone who keeps their
  sword from bloodshed!

ᵃ 4 That is, Crete   ᵇ 1 Or captured; / Misgab
ᶜ 2 The Hebrew for Heshbon sounds like the
Hebrew for plot.   ᵈ 2 The name of the
Moabite town Madmen sounds like the Hebrew
for be silenced.   ᵉ 4 Hebrew; Septuagint
/ proclaim it to Zoar   ᶠ 6 Or like Aroer
ᵍ 9 Or Give wings to Moab, / for she will fly away

¹¹ "Moab has been at rest from youth,
  like wine left on its dregs,
not poured from one jar to another —
  she has not gone into exile.
So she tastes as she did,
  and her aroma is unchanged.
¹² But days are coming,"
  declares the LORD,
"when I will send men who pour from
    pitchers,
  and they will pour her out;
they will empty her pitchers
  and smash her jars.
¹³ Then Moab will be ashamed of
    Chemosh,
  as Israel was ashamed
  when they trusted in Bethel.

¹⁴ "How can you say, 'We are warriors,
  men valiant in battle'?
¹⁵ Moab will be destroyed and her towns
    invaded;
  her finest young men will go down
    in the slaughter,"
  declares the King, whose name is
    the LORD Almighty.
¹⁶ "The fall of Moab is at hand;
  her calamity will come quickly.
¹⁷ Mourn for her, all who live around
    her,
  all who know her fame;
say, 'How broken is the mighty
    scepter,
  how broken the glorious staff!'

¹⁸ "Come down from your glory
  and sit on the parched ground,
  you inhabitants of Daughter
    Dibon,
for the one who destroys Moab
  will come up against you
  and ruin your fortified cities.
¹⁹ Stand by the road and watch,
  you who live in Aroer.
Ask the man fleeing and the woman
    escaping,
  ask them, 'What has happened?'
²⁰ Moab is disgraced, for she is
    shattered.
  Wail and cry out!
Announce by the Arnon
  that Moab is destroyed.

²¹ Judgment has come to the plateau —
  to Holon, Jahzah and Mephaath,
²² to Dibon, Nebo and Beth
    Diblathaim,
²³ to Kiriathaim, Beth Gamul and
    Beth Meon,
²⁴ to Kerioth and Bozrah —
  to all the towns of Moab, far and
    near.
²⁵ Moab's horn*ᵃ* is cut off;
  her arm is broken,"
            declares the LORD.

²⁶ "Make her drunk,
  for she has defied the LORD.
Let Moab wallow in her vomit;
  let her be an object of ridicule.
²⁷ Was not Israel the object of your
    ridicule?
  Was she caught among thieves,
that you shake your head in scorn
  whenever you speak of her?
²⁸ Abandon your towns and dwell among
    the rocks,
  you who live in Moab.
Be like a dove that makes its nest
  at the mouth of a cave.

²⁹ "We have heard of Moab's pride —
  how great is her arrogance! —
of her insolence, her pride, her conceit
  and the haughtiness of her heart.
³⁰ I know her insolence but it is futile,"
            declares the LORD,
  "and her boasts accomplish nothing.
³¹ Therefore I wail over Moab,
  for all Moab I cry out,
  I moan for the people of Kir
    Hareseth.
³² I weep for you, as Jazer weeps,
  you vines of Sibmah.
Your branches spread as far as the sea*ᵇ*;
  they reached as far as*ᶜ* Jazer.
The destroyer has fallen
  on your ripened fruit and grapes.
³³ Joy and gladness are gone
  from the orchards and fields of
    Moab.

ᵃ 25 Horn here symbolizes strength.
ᵇ 32 Probably the Dead Sea   *ᶜ 32* Two
Hebrew manuscripts and Septuagint; most
Hebrew manuscripts *as far as the Sea of*

I have stopped the flow of wine from
the presses;
no one treads them with shouts of
joy.
Although there are shouts,
they are not shouts of joy.

34 "The sound of their cry rises
from Heshbon to Elealeh and
Jahaz,
from Zoar as far as Horonaim and
Eglath Shelishiyah,
for even the waters of Nimrim are
dried up.
35 In Moab I will put an end
to those who make offerings on the
high places
and burn incense to their gods,"
declares the LORD.
36 "So my heart laments for Moab like
the music of a pipe;
it laments like a pipe for the people
of Kir Hareseth.
The wealth they acquired is gone.
37 Every head is shaved
and every beard cut off;
every hand is slashed
and every waist is covered with
sackcloth.
38 On all the roofs in Moab
and in the public squares
there is nothing but mourning,
for I have broken Moab
like a jar that no one wants,"
declares the LORD.
39 "How shattered she is! How they wail!
How Moab turns her back in
shame!
Moab has become an object of
ridicule,
an object of horror to all those
around her."

40 This is what the LORD says:

"Look! An eagle is swooping down,
spreading its wings over Moab.
41 Kerioth*a* will be captured
and the strongholds taken.
In that day the hearts of Moab's
warriors
will be like the heart of a woman in
labor.

42 Moab will be destroyed as a nation
because she defied the LORD.
43 Terror and pit and snare await you,
you people of Moab,"
declares the LORD.
44 "Whoever flees from the terror
will fall into a pit,
whoever climbs out of the pit
will be caught in a snare;
for I will bring on Moab
the year of her punishment,"
declares the LORD.

45 "In the shadow of Heshbon
the fugitives stand helpless,
for a fire has gone out from Heshbon,
a blaze from the midst of Sihon;
it burns the foreheads of Moab,
the skulls of the noisy boasters.
46 Woe to you, Moab!
The people of Chemosh are
destroyed;
your sons are taken into exile
and your daughters into captivity.

47 "Yet I will restore the fortunes of Moab
in days to come,"
declares the LORD.

Here ends the judgment on Moab.

A Message About Ammon

49

Concerning the Ammonites:

This is what the LORD says:

"Has Israel no sons?
Has Israel no heir?
Why then has Molek*b* taken
possession of Gad?
Why do his people live in its towns?
2 But the days are coming,"
declares the LORD,
"when I will sound the battle cry
against Rabbah of the Ammonites;
it will become a mound of ruins,
and its surrounding villages will be
set on fire.
Then Israel will drive out
those who drove her out,"
says the LORD.

a 41 Or *The cities*   *b 1* Or *their king*; also in
verse 3

³"Wail, Heshbon, for Ai is destroyed!
　Cry out, you inhabitants of Rabbah!
Put on sackcloth and mourn;
　rush here and there inside the walls,
for Molek will go into exile,
　together with his priests and
　　officials.
⁴Why do you boast of your valleys,
　boast of your valleys so fruitful?
Unfaithful Daughter Ammon,
　you trust in your riches and say,
'Who will attack me?'
⁵I will bring terror on you
　from all those around you,"
　　　　　declares the Lord,
　　　　　the Lord Almighty.
"Every one of you will be driven away,
　and no one will gather the fugitives.

⁶"Yet afterward, I will restore the
　fortunes of the Ammonites,"
　　　　　declares the Lord.

A Message About Edom

⁷Concerning Edom:

This is what the Lord Almighty says:

"Is there no longer wisdom in Teman?
　Has counsel perished from the
　　prudent?
　Has their wisdom decayed?
⁸Turn and flee, hide in deep caves,
　you who live in Dedan,
for I will bring disaster on Esau
　at the time when I punish him.
⁹If grape pickers came to you,
　would they not leave a few grapes?
If thieves came during the night,
　would they not steal only as much
　　as they wanted?
¹⁰But I will strip Esau bare;
　I will uncover his hiding places,
　so that he cannot conceal himself.
His armed men are destroyed,
　also his allies and neighbors,
　so there is no one to say,
¹¹'Leave your fatherless children; I will
　　keep them alive.
　Your widows too can depend on me.'"

¹²This is what the Lord says: "If those
who do not deserve to drink the cup must
drink it, why should you go unpunished?
You will not go unpunished, but must
drink it. ¹³I swear by myself," declares the
Lord, "that Bozrah will become a ruin
and a curse,ᵃ an object of horror and reproach; and all its towns will be in ruins
forever."

¹⁴I have heard a message from the
　　Lord;
　an envoy was sent to the nations to
　　say,
"Assemble yourselves to attack it!
　Rise up for battle!"

¹⁵"Now I will make you small among
　　the nations,
　despised by mankind.
¹⁶The terror you inspire
　and the pride of your heart have
　　deceived you,
you who live in the clefts of the rocks,
　who occupy the heights of the hill.
Though you build your nest as high as
　　the eagle's,
　from there I will bring you down,"
　　　　　declares the Lord.
¹⁷"Edom will become an object of
　　horror;
　all who pass by will be appalled and
　　will scoff
because of all its wounds.
¹⁸As Sodom and Gomorrah were
　　overthrown,
　along with their neighboring towns,"
　　　　　says the Lord,
"so no one will live there;
　no people will dwell in it.

¹⁹"Like a lion coming up from Jordan's
　　thickets
　to a rich pastureland,
I will chase Edom from its land in an
　　instant.
　Who is the chosen one I will
　　appoint for this?
Who is like me and who can challenge
　　me?
　And what shepherd can stand
　　against me?"

ᵃ 13 That is, its name will be used in cursing
(see 29:22); or, others will see that it is cursed.

²⁰ Therefore, hear what the LORD has
    planned against Edom,
what he has purposed against those
    who live in Teman:
The young of the flock will be
    dragged away;
    their pasture will be appalled at
        their fate.
²¹ At the sound of their fall the earth
    will tremble;
    their cry will resound to the Red Sea.*a*
²² Look! An eagle will soar and swoop
    down,
    spreading its wings over Bozrah.
In that day the hearts of Edom's
    warriors
    will be like the heart of a woman in
        labor.

A Message About Damascus

²³ Concerning Damascus:

"Hamath and Arpad are dismayed,
    for they have heard bad news.
They are disheartened,
    troubled like*b* the restless sea.
²⁴ Damascus has become feeble,
    she has turned to flee
    and panic has gripped her;
anguish and pain have seized her,
    pain like that of a woman in labor.
²⁵ Why has the city of renown not been
    abandoned,
    the town in which I delight?
²⁶ Surely, her young men will fall in the
    streets;
    all her soldiers will be silenced in
        that day,"
            declares the LORD Almighty.
²⁷ "I will set fire to the walls of
    Damascus;
    it will consume the fortresses of
        Ben-Hadad."

A Message About Kedar and Hazor

²⁸ Concerning Kedar and the kingdoms
of Hazor, which Nebuchadnezzar king of
Babylon attacked:

This is what the LORD says:

"Arise, and attack Kedar
    and destroy the people of the East.

²⁹ Their tents and their flocks will be
    taken;
    their shelters will be carried off
    with all their goods and camels.
People will shout to them,
    'Terror on every side!'
³⁰ "Flee quickly away!
    Stay in deep caves, you who live in
        Hazor,"
            declares the LORD.
"Nebuchadnezzar king of Babylon has
    plotted against you;
    he has devised a plan against you.

³¹ "Arise and attack a nation at ease,
    which lives in confidence,"
            declares the LORD,
"a nation that has neither gates nor
    bars;
    its people live far from danger.
³² Their camels will become plunder,
    and their large herds will be spoils
        of war.
I will scatter to the winds those who
    are in distant places*c*
    and will bring disaster on them
        from every side,"
            declares the LORD.
³³ "Hazor will become a haunt of
    jackals,
    a desolate place forever.
No one will live there;
    no people will dwell in it."

A Message About Elam

³⁴ This is the word of the LORD that
came to Jeremiah the prophet concerning
Elam, early in the reign of Zedekiah king
of Judah:

³⁵ This is what the LORD Almighty says:

"See, I will break the bow of Elam,
    the mainstay of their might.
³⁶ I will bring against Elam the four
    winds
    from the four quarters of heaven;
I will scatter them to the four winds,
    and there will not be a nation
    where Elam's exiles do not go.

a 21 Or *the Sea of Reeds*   *b* 23 Hebrew *on* or
by   *c* 32 Or *who clip the hair by their foreheads*

³⁷ I will shatter Elam before their foes,
    before those who want to kill them;
I will bring disaster on them,
    even my fierce anger,"
                declares the Lord.
"I will pursue them with the sword
    until I have made an end of them.
³⁸ I will set my throne in Elam
    and destroy her king and officials,"
                declares the Lord.

³⁹ "Yet I will restore the fortunes of Elam
    in days to come,"
                declares the Lord.

A Message About Babylon

50 This is the word the Lord spoke through Jeremiah the prophet concerning Babylon and the land of the Babylonians*ᵃ*:

² "Announce and proclaim among the
    nations,
lift up a banner and proclaim it;
    keep nothing back, but say,
'Babylon will be captured;
    Bel will be put to shame,
    Marduk filled with terror.
Her images will be put to shame
    and her idols filled with terror.'
³ A nation from the north will attack her
    and lay waste her land.
No one will live in it;
    both people and animals will flee
        away.

⁴ "In those days, at that time,"
    declares the Lord,
"the people of Israel and the people of
    Judah together
will go in tears to seek the Lord
    their God.
⁵ They will ask the way to Zion
    and turn their faces toward it.
They will come and bind themselves
    to the Lord
in an everlasting covenant
    that will not be forgotten.

⁶ "My people have been lost sheep;
    their shepherds have led them astray
and caused them to roam on the
    mountains.

They wandered over mountain and
    hill
    and forgot their own resting place.
⁷ Whoever found them devoured them;
    their enemies said, 'We are not guilty,
for they sinned against the Lord,
    their verdant pasture,
the Lord, the hope of their
    ancestors.'

⁸ "Flee out of Babylon;
    leave the land of the Babylonians,
and be like the goats that lead the
    flock.
⁹ For I will stir up and bring against
    Babylon
an alliance of great nations from the
    land of the north.
They will take up their positions
    against her,
and from the north she will be
    captured.
Their arrows will be like skilled
    warriors
who do not return empty-handed.
¹⁰ So Babyloniaᵇ will be plundered;
    all who plunder her will have their
        fill,"
                declares the Lord.

¹¹ "Because you rejoice and are glad,
    you who pillage my inheritance,
because you frolic like a heifer
    threshing grain
and neigh like stallions,
¹² your mother will be greatly ashamed;
    she who gave you birth will be
        disgraced.
She will be the least of the nations—
    a wilderness, a dry land, a desert.
¹³ Because of the Lord's anger she will
    not be inhabited
but will be completely desolate.
All who pass Babylon will be appalled;
    they will scoff because of all her
        wounds.
¹⁴ "Take up your positions around
    Babylon,
all you who draw the bow.

ᵃ *1* Or *Chaldeans*; also in verses 8, 25, 35 and 45
ᵇ *10* Or *Chaldea*

Shoot at her! Spare no arrows,
    for she has sinned against the
      Lord.
¹⁵ Shout against her on every side!
    She surrenders, her towers fall,
      her walls are torn down.
Since this is the vengeance of the
      Lord,
    take vengeance on her;
    do to her as she has done to others.
¹⁶ Cut off from Babylon the sower,
    and the reaper with his sickle at
      harvest.
Because of the sword of the oppressor
    let everyone return to their own
      people,
    let everyone flee to their own land.

¹⁷ "Israel is a scattered flock
    that lions have chased away.
The first to devour them
    was the king of Assyria;
the last to crush their bones
    was Nebuchadnezzar king of
      Babylon."

¹⁸ Therefore this is what the Lord Almighty, the God of Israel, says:

"I will punish the king of Babylon and
    his land
    as I punished the king of Assyria.
¹⁹ But I will bring Israel back to their
    own pasture,
    and they will graze on Carmel and
      Bashan;
their appetite will be satisfied
    on the hills of Ephraim and
      Gilead.
²⁰ In those days, at that time,"
    declares the Lord,
"search will be made for Israel's guilt,
    but there will be none,
and for the sins of Judah,
    but none will be found,
for I will forgive the remnant I
    spare.

²¹ "Attack the land of Merathaim
    and those who live in Pekod.
Pursue, kill and completely destroy^a
    them,"
              declares the Lord.

"Do everything I have commanded
    you.
²² The noise of battle is in the land,
    the noise of great destruction!
²³ How broken and shattered
    is the hammer of the whole earth!
How desolate is Babylon
    among the nations!
²⁴ I set a trap for you, Babylon,
    and you were caught before you
      knew it;
you were found and captured
    because you opposed the Lord.
²⁵ The Lord has opened his arsenal
    and brought out the weapons of his
      wrath,
for the Sovereign Lord Almighty has
    work to do
    in the land of the Babylonians.
²⁶ Come against her from afar.
    Break open her granaries;
    pile her up like heaps of grain.
Completely destroy her
    and leave her no remnant.
²⁷ Kill all her young bulls;
    let them go down to the slaughter!
Woe to them! For their day has come,
    the time for them to be punished.
²⁸ Listen to the fugitives and refugees
      from Babylon
    declaring in Zion
how the Lord our God has taken
    vengeance,
    vengeance for his temple.

²⁹ "Summon archers against Babylon,
    all those who draw the bow.
Encamp all around her;
    let no one escape.
Repay her for her deeds;
    do to her as she has done.
For she has defied the Lord,
    the Holy One of Israel.
³⁰ Therefore, her young men will fall in
    the streets;
    all her soldiers will be silenced in
      that day,"
              declares the Lord.

^a 21 The Hebrew term refers to the irrevocable
giving over of things or persons to the Lord,
often by totally destroying them; also in
verse 26.

31 "See, I am against you, you arrogant
        one,"
    declares the Lord, the LORD
        Almighty,
    "for your day has come,
        the time for you to be punished.
32 The arrogant one will stumble and fall
        and no one will help her up;
    I will kindle a fire in her towns
        that will consume all who are
        around her."

33 This is what the LORD Almighty says:

    "The people of Israel are oppressed,
        and the people of Judah as well.
    All their captors hold them fast,
        refusing to let them go.
34 Yet their Redeemer is strong;
        the LORD Almighty is his name.
    He will vigorously defend their cause
        so that he may bring rest to their
        land,
    but unrest to those who live in
        Babylon.

ROCK SOLID
promises

"Their Redeemer is strong; the LORD Almighty is his name."

Jeremiah 50:34

People can tie you up tight, but the one who will rescue you from bondage is all-powerful.

35 "A sword against the Babylonians!"
        declares the LORD—
    "against those who live in Babylon
        and against her officials and wise
        men!
36 A sword against her false prophets!
        They will become fools.
    A sword against her warriors!
        They will be filled with terror.

37 A sword against her horses and
        chariots
    and all the foreigners in her ranks!
        They will become weaklings.
    A sword against her treasures!
        They will be plundered.
38 A drought on[a] her waters!
        They will dry up.
    For it is a land of idols,
        idols that will go mad with terror.

39 "So desert creatures and hyenas will
        live there,
    and there the owl will dwell.
    It will never again be inhabited
        or lived in from generation to
        generation.
40 As I overthrew Sodom and Gomorrah
        along with their neighboring towns,"
            declares the LORD,
    "so no one will live there;
        no people will dwell in it.

41 "Look! An army is coming from the
        north;
    a great nation and many kings
        are being stirred up from the ends
        of the earth.
42 They are armed with bows and spears;
        they are cruel and without mercy.
    They sound like the roaring sea
        as they ride on their horses;
    they come like men in battle
        formation
        to attack you, Daughter Babylon.
43 The king of Babylon has heard reports
        about them,
    and his hands hang limp.
    Anguish has gripped him,
        pain like that of a woman in labor.
44 Like a lion coming up from Jordan's
        thickets
    to a rich pastureland,
    I will chase Babylon from its land in
        an instant.
    Who is the chosen one I will
        appoint for this?
    Who is like me and who can challenge
        me?
    And what shepherd can stand
        against me?"

a 38 Or A sword against

45 Therefore, hear what the Lord has
    planned against Babylon,
  what he has purposed against the
    land of the Babylonians:
The young of the flock will be
    dragged away;
  their pasture will be appalled at
    their fate.
46 At the sound of Babylon's capture the
    earth will tremble;
  its cry will resound among the
    nations.

51 This is what the Lord says:

  "See, I will stir up the spirit
    of a destroyer
  against Babylon and the people of
    Leb Kamai.ᵃ
2 I will send foreigners to Babylon
    to winnow her and to devastate her
    land;
  they will oppose her on every side
    in the day of her disaster.
3 Let not the archer string his bow,
    nor let him put on his armor.
  Do not spare her young men;
    completely destroyᵇ her army.
4 They will fall down slain in Babylon,ᶜ
    fatally wounded in her streets.
5 For Israel and Judah have not been
    forsaken
  by their God, the Lord Almighty,
  though their landᵈ is full of guilt
    before the Holy One of Israel.

6 "Flee from Babylon!
    Run for your lives!
  Do not be destroyed because of her
    sins.
  It is time for the Lord's vengeance;
    he will repay her what she deserves.
7 Babylon was a gold cup in the Lord's
    hand;
  she made the whole earth drunk.
  The nations drank her wine;
    therefore they have now gone mad.
8 Babylon will suddenly fall and be
    broken.
  Wail over her!
  Get balm for her pain;
    perhaps she can be healed.

9 "'We would have healed Babylon,
    but she cannot be healed;
  let us leave her and each go to our own
    land,
  for her judgment reaches to the
    skies,
    it rises as high as the heavens.'

10 "'The Lord has vindicated us;
    come, let us tell in Zion
  what the Lord our God has done.'

11 "Sharpen the arrows,
    take up the shields!
  The Lord has stirred up the kings of
    the Medes,
  because his purpose is to destroy
    Babylon.
  The Lord will take vengeance,
    vengeance for his temple.
12 Lift up a banner against the walls of
    Babylon!
  Reinforce the guard,
  station the watchmen,
    prepare an ambush!
  The Lord will carry out his purpose,
    his decree against the people of
    Babylon.
13 You who live by many waters
    and are rich in treasures,
  your end has come,
    the time for you to be destroyed.
14 The Lord Almighty has sworn by
    himself:
  I will surely fill you with troops, as
    with a swarm of locusts,
  and they will shout in triumph over
    you.

15 "He made the earth by his power;
    he founded the world by his wisdom
  and stretched out the heavens by his
    understanding.
16 When he thunders, the waters in the
    heavens roar;
  he makes clouds rise from the ends
    of the earth.

ᵃ 1 *Leb Kamai* is a cryptogram for Chaldea, that
is, Babylonia.   ᵇ 3 The Hebrew term refers to
the irrevocable giving over of things or persons
to the Lord, often by totally destroying them.
ᶜ 4 Or *Chaldea*   ᵈ 5 Or *Almighty, / and the
land of the Babylonians*

He sends lightning with the rain
  and brings out the wind from his
    storehouses.

17 "Everyone is senseless and without
    knowledge;
  every goldsmith is shamed by his
    idols.
The images he makes are a fraud;
  they have no breath in them.
18 They are worthless, the objects of
    mockery;
  when their judgment comes, they
    will perish.
19 He who is the Portion of Jacob is not
    like these,
  for he is the Maker of all things,
including the people of his
    inheritance—
  the Lord Almighty is his name.

20 "You are my war club,
  my weapon for battle—
with you I shatter nations,
  with you I destroy kingdoms,
21 with you I shatter horse and rider,
  with you I shatter chariot and
    driver,
22 with you I shatter man and woman,
  with you I shatter old man and
    youth,
  with you I shatter young man and
    young woman,
23 with you I shatter shepherd and flock,
  with you I shatter farmer and oxen,
  with you I shatter governors and
    officials.

24 "Before your eyes I will repay Babylon
and all who live in Babylonia*a* for all the
wrong they have done in Zion," declares
the Lord.

25 "I am against you, you destroying
    mountain,
  you who destroy the whole earth,"
    declares the Lord.
"I will stretch out my hand against you,
  roll you off the cliffs,
  and make you a burned-out
    mountain.
26 No rock will be taken from you for a
    cornerstone,

nor any stone for a foundation,
  for you will be desolate forever,"
    declares the Lord.

27 "Lift up a banner in the land!
  Blow the trumpet among the nations!
Prepare the nations for battle against
    her;
  summon against her these
    kingdoms:
  Ararat, Minni and Ashkenaz.
Appoint a commander against her;
  send up horses like a swarm of
    locusts.
28 Prepare the nations for battle against
    her—
  the kings of the Medes,
their governors and all their officials,
  and all the countries they rule.
29 The land trembles and writhes,
  for the Lord's purposes against
    Babylon stand—
to lay waste the land of Babylon
  so that no one will live there.
30 Babylon's warriors have stopped
    fighting;
  they remain in their strongholds.
Their strength is exhausted;
  they have become weaklings.
Her dwellings are set on fire;
  the bars of her gates are broken.
31 One courier follows another
  and messenger follows messenger
to announce to the king of Babylon
  that his entire city is captured,
32 the river crossings seized,
  the marshes set on fire,
  and the soldiers terrified."

33 This is what the Lord Almighty, the
God of Israel, says:

"Daughter Babylon is like a threshing
    floor
  at the time it is trampled;
  the time to harvest her will soon
    come."

34 "Nebuchadnezzar king of Babylon has
    devoured us,
  he has thrown us into confusion,
  he has made us an empty jar.

a 24 Or *Chaldea*; also in verse 35

Like a serpent he has swallowed us
and filled his stomach with our
delicacies,
and then has spewed us out.
³⁵ May the violence done to our flesh*ᵃ* be
on Babylon,"
say the inhabitants of Zion.
"May our blood be on those who live
in Babylonia,"
says Jerusalem.

³⁶ Therefore this is what the LORD says:

"See, I will defend your cause
and avenge you;
I will dry up her sea
and make her springs dry.
³⁷ Babylon will be a heap of ruins,
a haunt of jackals,
an object of horror and scorn,
a place where no one lives.
³⁸ Her people all roar like young
lions,
they growl like lion cubs.
³⁹ But while they are aroused,
I will set out a feast for them
and make them drunk,
so that they shout with laughter—
then sleep forever and not
awake,"
declares the LORD.
⁴⁰ "I will bring them down
like lambs to the slaughter,
like rams and goats.

⁴¹ "How Sheshak*ᵇ* will be captured,
the boast of the whole earth
seized!
How desolate Babylon will be
among the nations!
⁴² The sea will rise over Babylon;
its roaring waves will cover her.
⁴³ Her towns will be desolate,
a dry and desert land,
a land where no one lives,
through which no one travels.
⁴⁴ I will punish Bel in Babylon
and make him spew out what he has
swallowed.
The nations will no longer stream to
him.
And the wall of Babylon will fall.

⁴⁵ "Come out of her, my people!
Run for your lives!
Run from the fierce anger of the
LORD.
⁴⁶ Do not lose heart or be afraid
when rumors are heard in the land;
one rumor comes this year, another
the next,
rumors of violence in the land
and of ruler against ruler.
⁴⁷ For the time will surely come
when I will punish the idols of
Babylon;
her whole land will be disgraced
and her slain will all lie fallen
within her.
⁴⁸ Then heaven and earth and all that is
in them
will shout for joy over Babylon,
for out of the north
destroyers will attack her,"
declares the LORD.

⁴⁹ "Babylon must fall because of Israel's
slain,
just as the slain in all the earth
have fallen because of Babylon.
⁵⁰ You who have escaped the sword,
leave and do not linger!
Remember the LORD in a distant
land,
and call to mind Jerusalem."

⁵¹ "We are disgraced,
for we have been insulted
and shame covers our faces,
because foreigners have entered
the holy places of the LORD's
house."

⁵² "But days are coming," declares the
LORD,
"when I will punish her idols,
and throughout her land
the wounded will groan.
⁵³ Even if Babylon ascends to the
heavens
and fortifies her lofty stronghold,
I will send destroyers against her,"
declares the LORD.

ᵃ *35* Or *done to us and to our children*
ᵇ *41* *Sheshak* is a cryptogram for Babylon.

⁵⁴"The sound of a cry comes from
Babylon,
the sound of great destruction
from the land of the Babylonians.^a
⁵⁵The LORD will destroy Babylon;
he will silence her noisy din.
Waves of enemies will rage like great
waters;
the roar of their voices will resound.
⁵⁶A destroyer will come against
Babylon;
her warriors will be captured,
and their bows will be broken.
For the LORD is a God of retribution;
he will repay in full.
⁵⁷I will make her officials and wise men
drunk,
her governors, officers and warriors
as well;
they will sleep forever and not awake,"
declares the King, whose name is
the LORD Almighty.

⁵⁸This is what the LORD Almighty says:

"Babylon's thick wall will be leveled
and her high gates set on fire;
the peoples exhaust themselves for
nothing,
the nations' labor is only fuel for the
flames."

⁵⁹This is the message Jeremiah the
prophet gave to the staff officer Seraiah
son of Neriah, the son of Mahseiah, when
he went to Babylon with Zedekiah king
of Judah in the fourth year of his reign.
⁶⁰Jeremiah had written on a scroll about
all the disasters that would come upon
Babylon—all that had been recorded
concerning Babylon. ⁶¹He said to Seraiah, "When you get to Babylon, see that
you read all these words aloud. ⁶²Then say,
'LORD, you have said you will destroy this
place, so that neither people nor animals
will live in it; it will be desolate forever.'
⁶³When you finish reading this scroll, tie
a stone to it and throw it into the Euphrates. ⁶⁴Then say, 'So will Babylon sink to
rise no more because of the disaster I will
bring on her. And her people will fall.'"

The words of Jeremiah end here.

The Fall of Jerusalem

52 Zedekiah was twenty-one
years old when he became
king, and he reigned in Jerusalem eleven years. His mother's name
was Hamutal daughter of Jeremiah; she
was from Libnah. ²He did evil in the eyes
of the LORD, just as Jehoiakim had done.
³It was because of the LORD's anger that
all this happened to Jerusalem and Judah,
and in the end he thrust them from his
presence.

Now Zedekiah rebelled against the
king of Babylon.

⁴So in the ninth year of Zedekiah's
reign, on the tenth day of the tenth month,
Nebuchadnezzar king of Babylon marched
against Jerusalem with his whole army.
They encamped outside the city and built
siege works all around it. ⁵The city was
kept under siege until the eleventh year of
King Zedekiah.

⁶By the ninth day of the fourth month
the famine in the city had become so severe
that there was no food for the people to eat.
⁷Then the city wall was broken through,
and the whole army fled. They left the city
at night through the gate between the two
walls near the king's garden, though the
Babylonians^b were surrounding the city.
They fled toward the Arabah,^c ⁸but the
Babylonian^d army pursued King Zedekiah
and overtook him in the plains of Jericho.
All his soldiers were separated from him
and scattered, ⁹and he was captured.

He was taken to the king of Babylon
at Riblah in the land of Hamath, where
he pronounced sentence on him. ¹⁰There
at Riblah the king of Babylon killed the
sons of Zedekiah before his eyes; he also
killed all the officials of Judah. ¹¹Then he
put out Zedekiah's eyes, bound him with
bronze shackles and took him to Babylon,
where he put him in prison till the day of
his death.

¹²On the tenth day of the fifth month,
in the nineteenth year of Nebuchadnezzar
king of Babylon, Nebuzaradan command-

---

^a 54 Or *Chaldeans*   ^b 7 Or *Chaldeans*; also in
verse 17   ^c 7 Or *the Jordan Valley*   ^d 8 Or
Chaldean; also in verse 14

er of the imperial guard, who served the king of Babylon, came to Jerusalem. ¹³He set fire to the temple of the Lord, the royal palace and all the houses of Jerusalem. Every important building he burned down. ¹⁴The whole Babylonian army, under the commander of the imperial guard, broke down all the walls around Jerusalem. ¹⁵Nebuzaradan the commander of the guard carried into exile some of the poorest people and those who remained in the city, along with the rest of the craftsmen*a* and those who had deserted to the king of Babylon. ¹⁶But Nebuzaradan left behind the rest of the poorest people of the land to work the vineyards and fields.

¹⁷The Babylonians broke up the bronze pillars, the movable stands and the bronze Sea that were at the temple of the Lord and they carried all the bronze to Babylon. ¹⁸They also took away the pots, shovels, wick trimmers, sprinkling bowls, dishes and all the bronze articles used in the temple service. ¹⁹The commander of the imperial guard took away the basins, censers, sprinkling bowls, pots, lampstands, dishes and bowls used for drink offerings—all that were made of pure gold or silver.

²⁰The bronze from the two pillars, the Sea and the twelve bronze bulls under it, and the movable stands, which King Solomon had made for the temple of the Lord, was more than could be weighed. ²¹Each pillar was eighteen cubits high and twelve cubits in circumference*b*; each was four fingers thick, and hollow. ²²The bronze capital on top of one pillar was five cubits*c* high and was decorated with a network and pomegranates of bronze all around. The other pillar, with its pomegranates, was similar. ²³There were ninety-six pomegranates on the sides; the total number of pomegranates above the surrounding network was a hundred.

²⁴The commander of the guard took as prisoners Seraiah the chief priest, Zephaniah the priest next in rank and the three doorkeepers. ²⁵Of those still in the city, he took the officer in charge of the fighting men, and seven royal advisers. He also took the secretary who was chief officer in charge of conscripting the people of the land, sixty of whom were found in the city. ²⁶Nebuzaradan the commander took them all and brought them to the king of Babylon at Riblah. ²⁷There at Riblah, in the land of Hamath, the king had them executed.

So Judah went into captivity, away from her land. ²⁸This is the number of the people Nebuchadnezzar carried into exile:

in the seventh year, 3,023 Jews;
²⁹in Nebuchadnezzar's eighteenth year,
    832 people from Jerusalem;
³⁰in his twenty-third year,
    745 Jews taken into exile by Nebuzaradan the commander of the imperial guard.
There were 4,600 people in all.

Jehoiachin Released

³¹In the thirty-seventh year of the exile of Jehoiachin king of Judah, in the year Awel-Marduk became king of Babylon, on the twenty-fifth day of the twelfth month, he released Jehoiachin king of Judah and freed him from prison. ³²He spoke kindly to him and gave him a seat of honor higher than those of the other kings who were with him in Babylon. ³³So Jehoiachin put aside his prison clothes and for the rest of his life ate regularly at the king's table. ³⁴Day by day the king of Babylon gave Jehoiachin a regular allowance as long as he lived, till the day of his death.

a 15 Or *the populace*   *b* 21 That is, about 27 feet high and 18 feet in circumference or about 8.1 meters high and 5.4 meters in circumference
c 22 That is, about 7 1/2 feet or about 2.3 meters

LAMENTATIONS

BOOK OUTLINE

Jerusalem's total destruction
(1:1–22)

God's anger—search for comfort
(2:1–22)

Thoughts on suffering—hope in God
(3:1–66)

The old glory of Jerusalem—present misery
(4:1–22)

A prayer for God's mercy
(5:1–22)

The title of this book means "funeral songs." The author was probably Jeremiah, who was grieving about the destruction of Jerusalem.

In the original language, Hebrew, the twenty-two verses in each of chapters 1, 2, and 4 use the twenty-two letters of the Hebrew alphabet to start the verse. The third chapter has sixty-six verses and every third verse starts a new letter of the Hebrew alphabet. This is called an acrostic.

In this book Jeremiah reflects on the destruction of Jerusalem and the temple. But he recognizes that this disaster is the judgment of a righteous God. Knowing that God is merciful he appeals for mercy in prayer to God.

^a How deserted lies the city,
once so full of people!
How like a widow is she,
who once was great among the
nations!
She who was queen among the
provinces
has now become a slave.

² Bitterly she weeps at night,
tears are on her cheeks.
Among all her lovers
there is no one to comfort her.
All her friends have betrayed her;
they have become her enemies.

³ After affliction and harsh labor,
Judah has gone into exile.
She dwells among the nations;
she finds no resting place.
All who pursue her have overtaken her
in the midst of her distress.

⁴ The roads to Zion mourn,
for no one comes to her appointed
festivals.
All her gateways are desolate,
her priests groan,
her young women grieve,
and she is in bitter anguish.

⁵ Her foes have become her masters;
her enemies are at ease.
The LORD has brought her grief
because of her many sins.
Her children have gone into exile,
captive before the foe.

⁶ All the splendor has departed
from Daughter Zion.
Her princes are like deer
that find no pasture;
in weakness they have fled
before the pursuer.

⁷ In the days of her affliction and
wandering
Jerusalem remembers all the
treasures
that were hers in days of old.
When her people fell into enemy hands,
there was no one to help her.
Her enemies looked at her
and laughed at her destruction.

⁸ Jerusalem has sinned greatly
and so has become unclean.
All who honored her despise her,
for they have all seen her naked;
she herself groans
and turns away.

⁹ Her filthiness clung to her skirts;
she did not consider her future.
Her fall was astounding;
there was none to comfort her.
"Look, LORD, on my affliction,
for the enemy has triumphed."

¹⁰ The enemy laid hands
on all her treasures;
she saw pagan nations
enter her sanctuary—
those you had forbidden
to enter your assembly.

¹¹ All her people groan
as they search for bread;
they barter their treasures for food
to keep themselves alive.
"Look, LORD, and consider,
for I am despised."

¹² "Is it nothing to you, all you who pass
by?
Look around and see.
Is any suffering like my suffering
that was inflicted on me,
that the LORD brought on me
in the day of his fierce anger?

¹³ "From on high he sent fire,
sent it down into my bones.
He spread a net for my feet
and turned me back.
He made me desolate,
faint all the day long.

¹⁴ "My sins have been bound into a yoke^b;
by his hands they were woven
together.
They have been hung on my neck,
and the Lord has sapped my
strength.

^a This chapter is an acrostic poem, the verses of
which begin with the successive letters of the
Hebrew alphabet.   ^b 14 Most Hebrew
manuscripts; many Hebrew manuscripts and
Septuagint *He kept watch over my sins*

He has given me into the hands
of those I cannot withstand.

¹⁵"The Lord has rejected
all the warriors in my midst;
he has summoned an army against me
to*ᵃ* crush my young men.
In his winepress the Lord has
trampled
Virgin Daughter Judah.

¹⁶"This is why I weep
and my eyes overflow with tears.
No one is near to comfort me,
no one to restore my spirit.
My children are destitute
because the enemy has prevailed."

¹⁷Zion stretches out her hands,
but there is no one to comfort her.
The Lord has decreed for Jacob
that his neighbors become his foes;
Jerusalem has become
an unclean thing among them.

¹⁸"The Lord is righteous,
yet I rebelled against his
command.
Listen, all you peoples;
look on my suffering.
My young men and young women
have gone into exile.

¹⁹"I called to my allies
but they betrayed me.
My priests and my elders
perished in the city
while they searched for food
to keep themselves alive.

²⁰"See, Lord, how distressed I am!
I am in torment within,
and in my heart I am disturbed,
for I have been most rebellious.
Outside, the sword bereaves;
inside, there is only death.

²¹"People have heard my groaning,
but there is no one to comfort me.
All my enemies have heard of my
distress;
they rejoice at what you have done.
May you bring the day you have
announced
so they may become like me.

²²"Let all their wickedness come before
you;
deal with them
as you have dealt with me
because of all my sins.
My groans are many
and my heart is faint."

2 *ᵇ* How the Lord has covered
Daughter Zion
with the cloud of his anger*ᶜ*!
He has hurled down the splendor of
Israel
from heaven to earth;
he has not remembered his footstool
in the day of his anger.

²Without pity the Lord has swallowed up
all the dwellings of Jacob;
in his wrath he has torn down
the strongholds of Daughter Judah.
He has brought her kingdom and its
princes
down to the ground in dishonor.

³In fierce anger he has cut off
every horn*ᵈ,ᵉ* of Israel.
He has withdrawn his right hand
at the approach of the enemy.
He has burned in Jacob like a flaming
fire
that consumes everything around it.

⁴Like an enemy he has strung his bow;
his right hand is ready.
Like a foe he has slain
all who were pleasing to the eye;
he has poured out his wrath like fire
on the tent of Daughter Zion.

⁵The Lord is like an enemy;
he has swallowed up Israel.
He has swallowed up all her palaces
and destroyed her strongholds.
He has multiplied mourning and
lamentation
for Daughter Judah.

ᵃ 15 Or *has set a time for me / when he will*
ᵇ This chapter is an acrostic poem, the verses of
which begin with the successive letters of the
Hebrew alphabet.   *ᶜ 1* Or *How the Lord in his
anger / has treated Daughter Zion with contempt*
ᵈ 3 Or *off / all the strength*; or *every king*
ᵉ 3 Horn here symbolizes strength.

⁶He has laid waste his dwelling like a
    garden;
  he has destroyed his place of
    meeting.
The Lord has made Zion forget
  her appointed festivals and her
    Sabbaths;
in his fierce anger he has spurned
  both king and priest.

⁷The Lord has rejected his altar
  and abandoned his sanctuary.
He has given the walls of her palaces
  into the hands of the enemy;
they have raised a shout in the house
    of the Lord
  as on the day of an appointed
    festival.

⁸The Lord determined to tear down
  the wall around Daughter Zion.
He stretched out a measuring line
  and did not withhold his hand from
    destroying.
He made ramparts and walls lament;
  together they wasted away.

⁹Her gates have sunk into the ground;
  their bars he has broken and
    destroyed.
Her king and her princes are exiled
    among the nations,
  the law is no more,
and her prophets no longer find
  visions from the Lord.

¹⁰The elders of Daughter Zion
  sit on the ground in silence;
they have sprinkled dust on their
    heads
  and put on sackcloth.
The young women of Jerusalem
  have bowed their heads to the
    ground.

¹¹My eyes fail from weeping,
  I am in torment within;
my heart is poured out on the ground
  because my people are destroyed,
because children and infants faint
  in the streets of the city.

¹²They say to their mothers,
  "Where is bread and wine?"

as they faint like the wounded
  in the streets of the city,
as their lives ebb away
  in their mothers' arms.

¹³What can I say for you?
  With what can I compare you,
    Daughter Jerusalem?
To what can I liken you,
  that I may comfort you,
    Virgin Daughter Zion?
Your wound is as deep as the sea.
  Who can heal you?

¹⁴The visions of your prophets
  were false and worthless;
they did not expose your sin
  to ward off your captivity.
The prophecies they gave you
  were false and misleading.

¹⁵All who pass your way
  clap their hands at you;
they scoff and shake their heads
  at Daughter Jerusalem:
"Is this the city that was called
  the perfection of beauty,
  the joy of the whole earth?"

¹⁶All your enemies open their mouths
  wide against you;
they scoff and gnash their teeth
  and say, "We have swallowed her
    up.
This is the day we have waited for;
  we have lived to see it."

¹⁷The Lord has done what he
    planned;
  he has fulfilled his word,
  which he decreed long ago.
He has overthrown you without pity,
  he has let the enemy gloat over you,
  he has exalted the horn^a of your
    foes.

¹⁸The hearts of the people
  cry out to the Lord.
You walls of Daughter Zion,
  let your tears flow like a river
  day and night;
give yourself no relief,
  your eyes no rest.

^a 17 Horn here symbolizes strength.

¹⁹ Arise, cry out in the night,
    as the watches of the night begin;
pour out your heart like water
    in the presence of the Lord.
Lift up your hands to him
    for the lives of your children,
who faint from hunger
    at every street corner.

²⁰ "Look, Lord, and consider:
    Whom have you ever treated like
        this?
Should women eat their offspring,
    the children they have cared for?
Should priest and prophet be
        killed
    in the sanctuary of the Lord?

²¹ "Young and old lie together
    in the dust of the streets;
my young men and young women
    have fallen by the sword.
You have slain them in the day of your
        anger;
    you have slaughtered them without
        pity.

²² "As you summon to a feast day,
    so you summoned against me
        terrors on every side.
In the day of the Lord's anger
    no one escaped or survived;
those I cared for and reared
    my enemy has destroyed."

3 ᵃ I am the man who has seen
        affliction
    by the rod of the Lord's wrath.
² He has driven me away and made me
        walk
    in darkness rather than light;
³ indeed, he has turned his hand against
        me
    again and again, all day long.

⁴ He has made my skin and my flesh
        grow old
    and has broken my bones.
⁵ He has besieged me and surrounded
        me
    with bitterness and hardship.
⁶ He has made me dwell in darkness
    like those long dead.

⁷ He has walled me in so I cannot
        escape;
    he has weighed me down with chains.
⁸ Even when I call out or cry for help,
    he shuts out my prayer.
⁹ He has barred my way with blocks of
        stone;
    he has made my paths crooked.

¹⁰ Like a bear lying in wait,
    like a lion in hiding,
¹¹ he dragged me from the path and
        mangled me
    and left me without help.
¹² He drew his bow
    and made me the target for his
        arrows.

¹³ He pierced my heart
    with arrows from his quiver.
¹⁴ I became the laughingstock of all my
        people;
    they mock me in song all day long.
¹⁵ He has filled me with bitter herbs
    and given me gall to drink.

¹⁶ He has broken my teeth with gravel;
    he has trampled me in the dust.
¹⁷ I have been deprived of peace;
    I have forgotten what prosperity is.
¹⁸ So I say, "My splendor is gone
    and all that I had hoped from the
        Lord."

¹⁹ I remember my affliction and my
        wandering,
    the bitterness and the gall.
²⁰ I well remember them,
    and my soul is downcast within me.
²¹ Yet this I call to mind
    and therefore I have hope:

²² Because of the Lord's great love we
        are not consumed,
    for his compassions never fail.
²³ They are new every morning;
    great is your faithfulness.
²⁴ I say to myself, "The Lord is my
        portion;
    therefore I will wait for him."

ᵃ This chapter is an acrostic poem; the verses of
each stanza begin with the successive letters of
the Hebrew alphabet, and the verses within each
stanza begin with the same letter.

²⁵The Lord is good to those whose
hope is in him,
to the one who seeks him;
²⁶it is good to wait quietly
for the salvation of the Lord.
²⁷It is good for a man to bear the yoke
while he is young.

²⁸Let him sit alone in silence,
for the Lord has laid it on him.
²⁹Let him bury his face in the dust—
there may yet be hope.
³⁰Let him offer his cheek to one who
would strike him,
and let him be filled with disgrace.

³¹For no one is cast off
by the Lord forever.
³²Though he brings grief, he will show
compassion,
so great is his unfailing love.
³³For he does not willingly bring
affliction
or grief to anyone.

³⁴To crush underfoot
all prisoners in the land,
³⁵to deny people their rights
before the Most High,
³⁶to deprive them of justice—
would not the Lord see such
things?

³⁷Who can speak and have it happen
if the Lord has not decreed it?
³⁸Is it not from the mouth of the Most
High
that both calamities and good
things come?
³⁹Why should the living complain
when punished for their sins?

⁴⁰Let us examine our ways and test
them,
and let us return to the Lord.
⁴¹Let us lift up our hearts and our hands
to God in heaven, and say:
⁴²"We have sinned and rebelled
and you have not forgiven.

ROCK SOLID *principles*

Lamentations 3:19–26

Look up when you're down.

It was 3 a.m. when a nurse made her rounds and woke Steven to check his temperature and blood pressure. Steven wrestled away, tired and dopey from medication. After a week in the hospital, he felt trapped by day and lonely at night. His doctors said he was getting better and predicted he might go home in a few days. By the time the nurse was done, Steven was wide awake. He stared at the ceiling, exhausted and alone, thinking about flipping on the TV to watch infomercials. Instead he shut his eyes and prayed. Steven never prayed much before he got sick. Now it was the one thing that kept him going.

The people of Israel couldn't have felt more distant from God. Held captive in a foreign country, they were so sad they hung up their harps and cried (see Psalm 137:1–9). But God spared them from total destruction. His compassion was fresh every morning. When you feel like everything good has been ripped from you, know that you still have the Lord.

ROCK SOLID
promises

"Because of the LORD's great love we are not consumed, for his compassions never fail."

Lamentations 3:22

God's love sees you when you're getting eaten alive. He will wrap you in his merciful care.

43 "You have covered yourself with anger
and pursued us;
you have slain without pity.
44 You have covered yourself with a cloud
so that no prayer can get through.
45 You have made us scum and refuse
among the nations.

46 "All our enemies have opened their
mouths
wide against us.
47 We have suffered terror and pitfalls,
ruin and destruction."
48 Streams of tears flow from my eyes
because my people are destroyed.

49 My eyes will flow unceasingly,
without relief,
50 until the LORD looks down
from heaven and sees.
51 What I see brings grief to my soul
because of all the women of my city.

52 Those who were my enemies without
cause
hunted me like a bird.
53 They tried to end my life in a pit
and threw stones at me;
54 the waters closed over my head,
and I thought I was about to perish.

55 I called on your name, LORD,
from the depths of the pit.
56 You heard my plea: "Do not close your
ears
to my cry for relief."

57 You came near when I called you,
and you said, "Do not fear."
58 You, Lord, took up my case;
you redeemed my life.
59 LORD, you have seen the wrong done
to me.
Uphold my cause!
60 You have seen the depth of their
vengeance,
all their plots against me.

61 LORD, you have heard their insults,
all their plots against me—
62 what my enemies whisper and mutter
against me all day long.
63 Look at them! Sitting or standing,
they mock me in their songs.

64 Pay them back what they deserve,
LORD,
for what their hands have done.
65 Put a veil over their hearts,
and may your curse be on them!
66 Pursue them in anger and destroy
them
from under the heavens of the
LORD.

4 *a* How the gold has lost its luster,
the fine gold become dull!
The sacred gems are scattered
at every street corner.

2 How the precious children of Zion,
once worth their weight in gold,
are now considered as pots of clay,
the work of a potter's hands!

3 Even jackals offer their breasts
to nurse their young,
but my people have become
heartless
like ostriches in the desert.

4 Because of thirst the infant's tongue
sticks to the roof of its mouth;
the children beg for bread,
but no one gives it to them.

5 Those who once ate delicacies
are destitute in the streets.

a This chapter is an acrostic poem, the verses of
which begin with the successive letters of the
Hebrew alphabet.

Those brought up in royal purple
    now lie on ash heaps.

⁶The punishment of my people
    is greater than that of Sodom,
which was overthrown in a moment
    without a hand turned to help her.

⁷Their princes were brighter than snow
    and whiter than milk,
their bodies more ruddy than rubies,
    their appearance like lapis lazuli.

⁸But now they are blacker than soot;
    they are not recognized in the
        streets.
Their skin has shriveled on their
        bones;
    it has become as dry as a stick.

⁹Those killed by the sword are better
        off
    than those who die of famine;
racked with hunger, they waste away
    for lack of food from the field.

¹⁰With their own hands compassionate
        women
    have cooked their own children,
who became their food
    when my people were destroyed.

¹¹The LORD has given full vent to his
        wrath;
    he has poured out his fierce anger.
He kindled a fire in Zion
    that consumed her foundations.

¹²The kings of the earth did not
        believe,
    nor did any of the peoples of the
        world,
that enemies and foes could enter
    the gates of Jerusalem.

¹³But it happened because of the sins of
        her prophets
    and the iniquities of her priests,
who shed within her
    the blood of the righteous.

¹⁴Now they grope through the streets
    as if they were blind.
They are so defiled with blood
    that no one dares to touch their
        garments.

¹⁵"Go away! You are unclean!" people
    cry to them.
"Away! Away! Don't touch us!"
When they flee and wander about,
    people among the nations say,
"They can stay here no longer."

¹⁶The LORD himself has scattered them;
    he no longer watches over them.
The priests are shown no honor,
    the elders no favor.

¹⁷Moreover, our eyes failed,
    looking in vain for help;
from our towers we watched
    for a nation that could not save us.

¹⁸People stalked us at every step,
    so we could not walk in our streets.
Our end was near, our days were
        numbered,
    for our end had come.

¹⁹Our pursuers were swifter
    than eagles in the sky;
they chased us over the mountains
    and lay in wait for us in the desert.

²⁰The LORD's anointed, our very life
        breath,
    was caught in their traps.
We thought that under his shadow
    we would live among the nations.

²¹Rejoice and be glad, Daughter Edom,
    you who live in the land of Uz.
But to you also the cup will be passed;
    you will be drunk and stripped
        naked.

²²Your punishment will end, Daughter
        Zion;
    he will not prolong your exile.
But he will punish your sin, Daughter
        Edom,
    and expose your wickedness.

5 Remember, LORD, what has
        happened to us;
    look, and see our disgrace.
²Our inheritance has been turned over
        to strangers,
    our homes to foreigners.
³We have become fatherless,
    our mothers are widows.

⁴We must buy the water we drink;
  our wood can be had only at a
    price.
⁵Those who pursue us are at our heels;
  we are weary and find no rest.
⁶We submitted to Egypt and Assyria
  to get enough bread.
⁷Our ancestors sinned and are no more,
  and we bear their punishment.
⁸Slaves rule over us,
  and there is no one to free us from
    their hands.
⁹We get our bread at the risk of our
    lives
  because of the sword in the desert.
¹⁰Our skin is hot as an oven,
  feverish from hunger.
¹¹Women have been violated in Zion,
  and virgins in the towns of Judah.
¹²Princes have been hung up by their
    hands;
  elders are shown no respect.
¹³Young men toil at the millstones;
  boys stagger under loads of wood.

¹⁴The elders are gone from the city gate;
  the young men have stopped their
    music.
¹⁵Joy is gone from our hearts;
  our dancing has turned to
    mourning.
¹⁶The crown has fallen from our head.
  Woe to us, for we have sinned!
¹⁷Because of this our hearts are faint,
  because of these things our eyes
    grow dim
¹⁸for Mount Zion, which lies desolate,
  with jackals prowling over it.

¹⁹You, LORD, reign forever;
  your throne endures from
    generation to generation.
²⁰Why do you always forget us?
  Why do you forsake us so long?
²¹Restore us to yourself, LORD, that we
    may return;
  renew our days as of old
²²unless you have utterly rejected us
  and are angry with us beyond
    measure.

EZEKIEL

This book is named after the prophet Ezekiel, whose name means "God is strong." He wrote this message between the years 593 and 571 BC for his fellow exiles in Babylonian captivity.

Born in 623 BC to a priestly family, Ezekiel grew up in the surroundings of the temple in Jerusalem. In 597 BC he was included in a group of people taken as captives to Babylon. In 593 BC God called him in a divine revelation to be a prophet.

During the first part of his ministry, Ezekiel proclaimed a similar message to Jeremiah's—Jerusalem and the temple were doomed to destruction because of the sinfulness and idolatry of the people.

After the news reached Babylon that Jerusalem actually had been destroyed in 586 BC, Ezekiel proclaimed a new message of hope and restoration—God would re-gather the Israelites from the ends of the earth and re-establish them in their own land. The nations who challenged Israel's return would be defeated and judged.

In my thirtieth year, in the fourth month on the fifth day, while I was among the exiles by the Kebar River, the heavens were opened and I saw visions of God.

² On the fifth of the month — it was the fifth year of the exile of King Jehoiachin — ³ the word of the LORD came to Ezekiel the priest, the son of Buzi, by the Kebar River in the land of the Babylonians.*ᵃ* There the hand of the LORD was on him.

⁴ I looked, and I saw a windstorm coming out of the north — an immense cloud with flashing lightning and surrounded by brilliant light. The center of the fire looked like glowing metal, ⁵ and in the fire was what looked like four living creatures. In appearance their form was human, ⁶ but each of them had four faces and four wings. ⁷ Their legs were straight; their feet were like those of a calf and gleamed like burnished bronze. ⁸ Under their wings on their four sides they had human hands. All four of them had faces and wings, ⁹ and the wings of one touched the wings of another. Each one went straight ahead; they did not turn as they moved.

¹⁰ Their faces looked like this: Each of the four had the face of a human being, and on the right side each had the face of a lion, and on the left the face of an ox; each also had the face of an eagle. ¹¹ Such were their faces. They each had two wings spreading out upward, each wing touching that of the creature on either side; and each had two other wings covering its body. ¹² Each one went straight ahead. Wherever the spirit would go, they would go, without turning as they went. ¹³ The appearance of the living creatures was like burning coals of fire or like torches. Fire moved back and forth among the creatures; it was bright, and lightning flashed out of it. ¹⁴ The creatures sped back and forth like flashes of lightning.

¹⁵ As I looked at the living creatures, I saw a wheel on the ground beside each creature with its four faces. ¹⁶ This was the appearance and structure of the wheels: They sparkled like topaz, and all four looked alike. Each appeared to be made like a wheel intersecting a wheel. ¹⁷ As they moved, they would go in any one of the four directions the creatures faced; the wheels did not change direction as the creatures went. ¹⁸ Their rims were high and awesome, and all four rims were full of eyes all around.

¹⁹ When the living creatures moved, the wheels beside them moved; and when the living creatures rose from the ground, the wheels also rose. ²⁰ Wherever the spirit would go, they would go, and the wheels would rise along with them, because the spirit of the living creatures was in the wheels. ²¹ When the creatures moved, they also moved; when the creatures stood still, they also stood still; and when the creatures rose from the ground, the wheels rose along with them, because the spirit of the living creatures was in the wheels.

²² Spread out above the heads of the living creatures was what looked something like a vault, sparkling like crystal, and awesome. ²³ Under the vault their wings were stretched out one toward the other, and each had two wings covering its body. ²⁴ When the creatures moved, I heard the sound of their wings, like the roar of rushing waters, like the voice of the Almighty,*ᵇ* like the tumult of an army. When they stood still, they lowered their wings.

²⁵ Then there came a voice from above the vault over their heads as they stood with lowered wings. ²⁶ Above the vault over their heads was what looked like a throne of lapis lazuli, and high above on the throne was a figure like that of a man. ²⁷ I saw that from what appeared to be his waist up he looked like glowing metal, as if full of fire, and that from there down he looked like fire; and brilliant light surrounded him. ²⁸ Like the appearance of a rainbow in the clouds on a rainy day, so was the radiance around him.

This was the appearance of the likeness of the glory of the LORD. When I saw it, I fell facedown, and I heard the voice of one speaking.

ᵃ 3 Or *Chaldeans*   *ᵇ 24* Hebrew *Shaddai*

Ezekiel's Call to Be a Prophet

2 He said to me, "Son of man,*a* stand up on your feet and I will speak to you." ²As he spoke, the Spirit came into me and raised me to my feet, and I heard him speaking to me.

³He said: "Son of man, I am sending you to the Israelites, to a rebellious nation that has rebelled against me; they and their ancestors have been in revolt against me to this very day. ⁴The people to whom I am sending you are obstinate and stubborn. Say to them, 'This is what the Sovereign LORD says.' ⁵And whether they listen or fail to listen—for they are a rebellious people—they will know that a prophet has been among them. ⁶And you, son of man, do not be afraid of them or their words. Do not be afraid, though briers and thorns are all around you and you live among scorpions. Do not be afraid of what they say or be terrified by them, though they are a rebellious people. ⁷You must speak my words to them, whether they listen or fail to listen, for they are rebellious. ⁸But you, son of man, listen to what I say to you. Do not rebel like that rebellious people; open your mouth and eat what I give you."

⁹Then I looked, and I saw a hand stretched out to me. In it was a scroll, ¹⁰which he unrolled before me. On both sides of it were written words of lament and mourning and woe.

3 And he said to me, "Son of man, eat what is before you, eat this scroll; then go and speak to the people of Israel." ²So I opened my mouth, and he gave me the scroll to eat.

³Then he said to me, "Son of man, eat this scroll I am giving you and fill your stomach with it." So I ate it, and it tasted as sweet as honey in my mouth.

a 1 The Hebrew phrase *ben adam* means *human being*. The phrase *son of man* is retained as a form of address here and throughout Ezekiel because of its possible association with "Son of Man" in the New Testament.

ROCK SOLID *principles*

Ezekiel 2:1–9

Speak up.

"Jeremy, your partying is hurting yourself—and it's hurting other people too," Megan said quietly. "I know life hasn't been easy. I know people think you should figure out your issues yourself. But I need to tell you about the damage you're causing." Jeremy had always been an example to everyone at church. After his parents split he gradually stopped coming to youth group. Then he started drinking. A couple guys who had been on the fence about following Jesus decided to follow his lead and dive into partying. "Jeremy," Megan continued, "I'm going to remind you of what you know is right—even if you hate me for it."

People won't listen for long if you offer an opinion on everything. But when you pay attention to God, he will give you the right words at the right time for the right situation. You don't have to be an Old Testament prophet to speak the truth in love (see Ephesians 4:15). You know words come from God when they build up people who hear them (see Ephesians 4:29).

[4]He then said to me: "Son of man, go now to the people of Israel and speak my words to them. [5]You are not being sent to a people of obscure speech and strange language, but to the people of Israel— [6]not to many peoples of obscure speech and strange language, whose words you cannot understand. Surely if I had sent you to them, they would have listened to you. [7]But the people of Israel are not willing to listen to you because they are not willing to listen to me, for all the Israelites are hardened and obstinate. [8]But I will make you as unyielding and hardened as they are. [9]I will make your forehead like the hardest stone, harder than flint. Do not be afraid of them or terrified by them, though they are a rebellious people."

[10]And he said to me, "Son of man, listen carefully and take to heart all the words I speak to you. [11]Go now to your people in exile and speak to them. Say to them, 'This is what the Sovereign Lord says,' whether they listen or fail to listen."

[12]Then the Spirit lifted me up, and I heard behind me a loud rumbling sound as the glory of the Lord rose from the place where it was standing.[a] [13]It was the sound of the wings of the living creatures brushing against each other and the sound of the wheels beside them, a loud rumbling sound. [14]The Spirit then lifted me up and took me away, and I went in bitterness and in the anger of my spirit, with the strong hand of the Lord on me. [15]I came to the exiles who lived at Tel Aviv near the Kebar River. And there, where they were living, I sat among them for seven days—deeply distressed.

Ezekiel's Task as Watchman

[16]At the end of seven days the word of the Lord came to me: [17]"Son of man, I have made you a watchman for the people of Israel; so hear the word I speak and give them warning from me. [18]When I say to a wicked person, 'You will surely die,' and you do not warn them or speak out to dissuade them from their evil ways in order to save their life, that wicked person will die for[b] their sin, and I will hold you ac-

countable for their blood. [19]But if you do warn the wicked person and they do not turn from their wickedness or from their evil ways, they will die for their sin; but you will have saved yourself.

[20]"Again, when a righteous person turns from their righteousness and does evil, and I put a stumbling block before them, they will die. Since you did not warn them, they will die for their sin. The righteous things that person did will not be remembered, and I will hold you accountable for their blood. [21]But if you do warn the righteous person not to sin and they do not sin, they will surely live because they took warning, and you will have saved yourself."

[22]The hand of the Lord was on me there, and he said to me, "Get up and go out to the plain, and there I will speak to you." [23]So I got up and went out to the plain. And the glory of the Lord was standing there, like the glory I had seen by the Kebar River, and I fell facedown. [24]Then the Spirit came into me and raised me to my feet. He spoke to me and said: "Go, shut yourself inside your house. [25]And you, son of man, they will tie with ropes; you will be bound so that you cannot go out among the people. [26]I will make your tongue stick to the roof of your mouth so that you will be silent and unable to rebuke them, for they are a rebellious people. [27]But when I speak to you, I will open your mouth and you shall say to them, 'This is what the Sovereign Lord says.' Whoever will listen let them listen, and whoever will refuse let them refuse; for they are a rebellious people.

Siege of Jerusalem Symbolized

4 "Now, son of man, take a block of clay, put it in front of you and draw the city of Jerusalem on it. [2]Then lay siege to it: Erect siege works against it, build a ramp up to it, set up camps against it and put battering rams around it. [3]Then

---

[a] 12 Probable reading of the original Hebrew text; Masoretic Text *sound—may the glory of the Lord be praised from his place* [b] 18 Or *in*; also in verses 19 and 20

take an iron pan, place it as an iron wall between you and the city and turn your face toward it. It will be under siege, and you shall besiege it. This will be a sign to the people of Israel.

⁴"Then lie on your left side and put the sin of the people of Israel upon yourself.ᵃ You are to bear their sin for the number of days you lie on your side. ⁵I have assigned you the same number of days as the years of their sin. So for 390 days you will bear the sin of the people of Israel.

⁶"After you have finished this, lie down again, this time on your right side, and bear the sin of the people of Judah. I have assigned you 40 days, a day for each year. ⁷Turn your face toward the siege of Jerusalem and with bared arm prophesy against her. ⁸I will tie you up with ropes so that you cannot turn from one side to the other until you have finished the days of your siege.

⁹"Take wheat and barley, beans and lentils, millet and spelt; put them in a storage jar and use them to make bread for yourself. You are to eat it during the 390 days you lie on your side. ¹⁰Weigh out twenty shekelsᵇ of food to eat each day and eat it at set times. ¹¹Also measure out a sixth of a hinᶜ of water and drink it at set times. ¹²Eat the food as you would a loaf of barley bread; bake it in the sight of the people, using human excrement for fuel." ¹³The LORD said, "In this way the people of Israel will eat defiled food among the nations where I will drive them."

¹⁴Then I said, "Not so, Sovereign LORD! I have never defiled myself. From my youth until now I have never eaten anything found dead or torn by wild animals. No impure meat has ever entered my mouth."

¹⁵"Very well," he said, "I will let you bake your bread over cow dung instead of human excrement."

¹⁶He then said to me: "Son of man, I am about to cut off the food supply in Jerusalem. The people will eat rationed food in anxiety and drink rationed water in despair, ¹⁷for food and water will be scarce. They will be appalled at the sight of each other and will waste away because ofᵈ their sin.

God's Razor of Judgment

5 "Now, son of man, take a sharp sword and use it as a barber's razor to shave your head and your beard. Then take a set of scales and divide up the hair. ²When the days of your siege come to an end, burn a third of the hair inside the city. Take a third and strike it with the sword all around the city. And scatter a third to the wind. For I will pursue them with drawn sword. ³But take a few hairs and tuck them away in the folds of your garment. ⁴Again, take a few of these and throw them into the fire and burn them up. A fire will spread from there to all Israel.

⁵"This is what the Sovereign LORD says: This is Jerusalem, which I have set in the center of the nations, with countries all around her. ⁶Yet in her wickedness she has rebelled against my laws and decrees more than the nations and countries around her. She has rejected my laws and has not followed my decrees.

⁷"Therefore this is what the Sovereign LORD says: You have been more unruly than the nations around you and have not followed my decrees or kept my laws. You have not evenᵉ conformed to the standards of the nations around you.

⁸"Therefore this is what the Sovereign LORD says: I myself am against you, Jerusalem, and I will inflict punishment on you in the sight of the nations. ⁹Because of all your detestable idols, I will do to you what I have never done before and will never do again. ¹⁰Therefore in your midst parents will eat their children, and children will eat their parents. I will inflict punishment on you and will scatter all your survivors to the winds. ¹¹Therefore as surely as I live, declares the Sovereign LORD, because you have defiled my

---

ᵃ 4 Or *upon your side*   ᵇ 10 That is, about 8 ounces or about 230 grams   ᶜ 11 That is, about 2/3 quart or about 0.6 liter   ᵈ 17 Or *away in*   ᵉ 7 Most Hebrew manuscripts; some Hebrew manuscripts and Syriac *You have* sanctuary with all your vile images and detestable practices, I myself will shave you; I will not look on you with pity or spare you. ¹²A third of your people will die of the plague or perish by famine inside you; a third will fall by the sword outside your walls; and a third I will scatter to the winds and pursue with drawn sword.

¹³"Then my anger will cease and my wrath against them will subside, and I will be avenged. And when I have spent my wrath on them, they will know that I the LORD have spoken in my zeal.

¹⁴"I will make you a ruin and a reproach among the nations around you, in the sight of all who pass by. ¹⁵You will be a reproach and a taunt, a warning and an object of horror to the nations around you when I inflict punishment on you in anger and in wrath and with stinging rebuke. I the LORD have spoken. ¹⁶When I shoot at you with my deadly and destructive arrows of famine, I will shoot to destroy you. I will bring more and more famine upon you and cut off your supply of food. ¹⁷I will send famine and wild beasts against you, and they will leave you childless. Plague and bloodshed will sweep through you, and I will bring the sword against you. I the LORD have spoken."

Doom for the Mountains of Israel

6 The word of the LORD came to me: ²"Son of man, set your face against the mountains of Israel; prophesy against them ³and say: 'You mountains of Israel, hear the word of the Sovereign LORD. This is what the Sovereign LORD says to the mountains and hills, to the ravines and valleys: I am about to bring a sword against you, and I will destroy your high places. ⁴Your altars will be demolished and your incense altars will be smashed; and I will slay your people in front of your idols. ⁵I will lay the dead bodies of the Israelites in front of their idols, and I will scatter your bones around your altars. ⁶Wherever you live, the towns will be laid waste and the high places demolished, so that your altars will be laid waste and devastated, your idols

smashed and ruined, your incense altars broken down, and what you have made wiped out. ⁷Your people will fall slain among you, and you will know that I am the LORD.

⁸"'But I will spare some, for some of you will escape the sword when you are scattered among the lands and nations. ⁹Then in the nations where they have been carried captive, those who escape will remember me—how I have been grieved by their adulterous hearts, which have turned away from me, and by their eyes, which have lusted after their idols. They will loathe themselves for the evil they have done and for all their detestable practices. ¹⁰And they will know that I am the LORD; I did not threaten in vain to bring this calamity on them.

¹¹"'This is what the Sovereign LORD says: Strike your hands together and stamp your feet and cry out "Alas!" because of all the wicked and detestable practices of the people of Israel, for they will fall by the sword, famine and plague. ¹²One who is far away will die of the plague, and one who is near will fall by the sword, and anyone who survives and is spared will die of famine. So will I pour out my wrath on them. ¹³And they will know that I am the LORD, when their people lie slain among their idols around their altars, on every high hill and on all the mountaintops, under every spreading tree and every leafy oak—places where they offered fragrant incense to all their idols. ¹⁴And I will stretch out my hand against them and make the land a desolate waste from the desert to Diblah*—wherever they live. Then they will know that I am the LORD.'"

The End Has Come

7 The word of the LORD came to me: ²"Son of man, this is what the Sovereign LORD says to the land of Israel:

"'The end! The end has come
    upon the four corners of the land!

ᵃ 14 Most Hebrew manuscripts; a few Hebrew manuscripts *Riblah*

God doesn't make idle threats.

It sounds odd to hear God threaten doom and destruction against the mountains of Israel—until you realize what was going on up top. The "high places" (Ezekiel 6:3) were hilltop sites of worship to fake deities like the goddess Asherah. Idol worship sometimes was mixed in the high places with worship of the one true God, but that didn't excuse the rampant practice of idolatry. These evil sites had plagued Israel even after King Josiah had wiped them from the land (see 2 Chronicles 34:1–7). So now the Lord threatened to destroy these high places, slay sinful people, and drop their dead bodies in front of their idols. And he wants everyone to be sure he isn't blowing smoke: "They will know that I am the Lord," he says. "I did not threaten in vain to bring this calamity on them" (Ezekiel 6:10).

Think: Why does a good God threaten and punish bad people?

ROCK SOLID *truths*

³The end is now upon you,
    and I will unleash my anger against
        you.
I will judge you according to your
        conduct
    and repay you for all your detestable
        practices.
⁴I will not look on you with pity;
    I will not spare you.
I will surely repay you for your
        conduct
    and for the detestable practices
        among you.

"'Then you will know that I am the Lord.'

⁵"This is what the Sovereign Lord says:

"'Disaster! Unheard-of[a] disaster!
    See, it comes!
⁶The end has come!
    The end has come!
It has roused itself against you.
    See, it comes!
⁷Doom has come upon you,
    upon you who dwell in the land.
The time has come! The day is near!
    There is panic, not joy, on the
        mountains.
⁸I am about to pour out my wrath on
        you
    and spend my anger against you.
I will judge you according to your
        conduct
    and repay you for all your detestable
        practices.
⁹I will not look on you with pity;
    I will not spare you.
I will repay you for your conduct
    and for the detestable practices
        among you.

"'Then you will know that it is I the Lord
who strikes you.

¹⁰"'See, the day!
    See, it comes!
Doom has burst forth,
    the rod has budded,
    arrogance has blossomed!
¹¹Violence has arisen,[b]
    a rod to punish the wicked.
None of the people will be left,
    none of that crowd—
none of their wealth,
    nothing of value.
¹²The time has come!
    The day has arrived!
Let not the buyer rejoice
    nor the seller grieve,
    for my wrath is on the whole crowd.
¹³The seller will not recover
    the property that was sold—
    as long as both buyer and seller live.

---

[a] 5 Most Hebrew manuscripts; some Hebrew
manuscripts and Syriac *Disaster after*
[b] 11 Or *The violent one has become*

For the vision concerning the whole
  crowd
    will not be reversed.
Because of their sins, not one of them
    will preserve their life.

[14] "They have blown the trumpet,
    they have made all things ready,
but no one will go into battle,
    for my wrath is on the whole crowd.
[15] Outside is the sword;
    inside are plague and famine.
Those in the country
    will die by the sword;
those in the city
    will be devoured by famine and
      plague.
[16] The fugitives who escape
    will flee to the mountains.
Like doves of the valleys,
    they will all moan,
    each for their own sins.
[17] Every hand will go limp;
    every leg will be wet with urine.
[18] They will put on sackcloth
    and be clothed with terror.
Every face will be covered with shame,
    and every head will be shaved.

[19] "They will throw their silver into the
    streets,
    and their gold will be treated as a
      thing unclean.
Their silver and gold
    will not be able to deliver them
    in the day of the Lord's wrath.
It will not satisfy their hunger
    or fill their stomachs,
    for it has caused them to stumble
      into sin.
[20] They took pride in their beautiful
    jewelry
    and used it to make their detestable
      idols.
They made it into vile images;
    therefore I will make it a thing
      unclean for them.
[21] I will give their wealth as plunder to
    foreigners
    and as loot to the wicked of the
      earth,
    who will defile it.

[22] I will turn my face away from the
    people,
    and robbers will desecrate the place
      I treasure.
They will enter it
    and will defile it.

[23] "Prepare chains!
For the land is full of bloodshed,
    and the city is full of violence.
[24] I will bring the most wicked of nations
    to take possession of their houses.
I will put an end to the pride of the
    mighty,
    and their sanctuaries will be
      desecrated.
[25] When terror comes,
    they will seek peace in vain.
[26] Calamity upon calamity will come,
    and rumor upon rumor.
They will go searching for a vision
    from the prophet,
    priestly instruction in the law will
      cease,
    the counsel of the elders will come
      to an end.
[27] The king will mourn,
    the prince will be clothed with
      despair,
    and the hands of the people of the
      land will tremble.
I will deal with them according to
    their conduct,
    and by their own standards I will
      judge them.

" 'Then they will know that I am the
Lord.' "

Idolatry in the Temple

8 In the sixth year, in the sixth
month on the fifth day, while I
was sitting in my house and the
elders of Judah were sitting before me, the
hand of the Sovereign Lord came on me
there. [2] I looked, and I saw a figure like
that of a man.[a] From what appeared to be
his waist down he was like fire, and from
there up his appearance was as bright as
glowing metal. [3] He stretched out what
looked like a hand and took me by the

---

[a] 2 Or *saw a fiery figure*

hair of my head. The Spirit lifted me up between earth and heaven and in visions of God he took me to Jerusalem, to the entrance of the north gate of the inner court, where the idol that provokes to jealousy stood. ⁴And there before me was the glory of the God of Israel, as in the vision I had seen in the plain.

⁵Then he said to me, "Son of man, look toward the north." So I looked, and in the entrance north of the gate of the altar I saw this idol of jealousy.

⁶And he said to me, "Son of man, do you see what they are doing—the utterly detestable things the Israelites are doing here, things that will drive me far from my sanctuary? But you will see things that are even more detestable."

⁷Then he brought me to the entrance to the court. I looked, and I saw a hole in the wall. ⁸He said to me, "Son of man, now dig into the wall." So I dug into the wall and saw a doorway there.

⁹And he said to me, "Go in and see the wicked and detestable things they are doing here." ¹⁰So I went in and looked, and I saw portrayed all over the walls all kinds of crawling things and unclean animals and all the idols of Israel. ¹¹In front of them stood seventy elders of Israel, and Jaazaniah son of Shaphan was standing among them. Each had a censer in his hand, and a fragrant cloud of incense was rising.

¹²He said to me, "Son of man, have you seen what the elders of Israel are doing in the darkness, each at the shrine of his own idol? They say, 'The Lord does not see us; the Lord has forsaken the land.'"

¹³Again, he said, "You will see them doing things that are even more detestable."

¹⁴Then he brought me to the entrance of the north gate of the house of the Lord, and I saw women sitting there, mourning the god Tammuz. ¹⁵He said to me, "Do you see this, son of man? You will see things that are even more detestable than this."

¹⁶He then brought me into the inner court of the house of the Lord, and there at the entrance to the temple, between the portico and the altar, were about twenty-five men. With their backs toward the temple of the Lord and their faces toward the east, they were bowing down to the sun in the east.

¹⁷He said to me, "Have you seen this, son of man? Is it a trivial matter for the people of Judah to do the detestable things they are doing here? Must they also fill the land with violence and continually arouse my anger? Look at them putting the branch to their nose! ¹⁸Therefore I will deal with them in anger; I will not look on them with pity or spare them. Although they shout in my ears, I will not listen to them."

Judgment on the Idolaters

9 Then I heard him call out in a loud voice, "Bring near those who are appointed to execute judgment on the city, each with a weapon in his hand." ²And I saw six men coming from the direction of the upper gate, which faces north, each with a deadly weapon in his hand. With them was a man clothed in linen who had a writing kit at his side. They came in and stood beside the bronze altar.

³Now the glory of the God of Israel went up from above the cherubim, where it had been, and moved to the threshold of the temple. Then the Lord called to the man clothed in linen who had the writing kit at his side ⁴and said to him, "Go throughout the city of Jerusalem and put a mark on the foreheads of those who grieve and lament over all the detestable things that are done in it."

⁵As I listened, he said to the others, "Follow him through the city and kill, without showing pity or compassion. ⁶Slaughter the old men, the young men and women, the mothers and children, but do not touch anyone who has the mark. Begin at my sanctuary." So they began with the old men who were in front of the temple.

⁷Then he said to them, "Defile the temple and fill the courts with the slain. Go!" So they went out and began killing throughout the city. ⁸While they were killing and I was left alone, I fell facedown, crying out, "Alas, Sovereign Lord! Are you going to destroy the entire

remnant of Israel in this outpouring of your wrath on Jerusalem?"

⁹He answered me, "The sin of the people of Israel and Judah is exceedingly great; the land is full of bloodshed and the city is full of injustice. They say, 'The LORD has forsaken the land; the LORD does not see.' ¹⁰So I will not look on them with pity or spare them, but I will bring down on their own heads what they have done."

¹¹Then the man in linen with the writing kit at his side brought back word, saying, "I have done as you commanded."

God's Glory Departs From the Temple

10 I looked, and I saw the likeness of a throne of lapis lazuli above the vault that was over the heads of the cherubim. ²The LORD said to the man clothed in linen, "Go in among the wheels beneath the cherubim. Fill your hands with burning coals from among the cherubim and scatter them over the city." And as I watched, he went in.

³Now the cherubim were standing on the south side of the temple when the man went in, and a cloud filled the inner court. ⁴Then the glory of the LORD rose from above the cherubim and moved to the threshold of the temple. The cloud filled the temple, and the court was full of the radiance of the glory of the LORD. ⁵The sound of the wings of the cherubim could be heard as far away as the outer court, like the voice of God Almighty*ᵃ* when he speaks.

⁶When the LORD commanded the man in linen, "Take fire from among the wheels, from among the cherubim," the man went in and stood beside a wheel. ⁷Then one of the cherubim reached out his hand to the fire that was among them. He took up some of it and put it into the hands of the man in linen, who took it and went out. ⁸(Under the wings of the cherubim could be seen what looked like human hands.)

⁹I looked, and I saw beside the cherubim four wheels, one beside each of the cherubim; the wheels sparkled like topaz. ¹⁰As for their appearance, the four of them looked alike; each was like a wheel inter-secting a wheel. ¹¹As they moved, they would go in any one of the four directions the cherubim faced; the wheels did not turn about*ᵇ* as the cherubim went. The cherubim went in whatever direction the head faced, without turning as they went. ¹²Their entire bodies, including their backs, their hands and their wings, were completely full of eyes, as were their four wheels. ¹³I heard the wheels being called "the whirling wheels." ¹⁴Each of the cherubim had four faces: One face was that of a cherub, the second the face of a human being, the third the face of a lion, and the fourth the face of an eagle.

¹⁵Then the cherubim rose upward. These were the living creatures I had seen by the Kebar River. ¹⁶When the cherubim moved, the wheels beside them moved; and when the cherubim spread their wings to rise from the ground, the wheels did not leave their side. ¹⁷When the cherubim stood still, they also stood still; and when the cherubim rose, they rose with them, because the spirit of the living creatures was in them.

¹⁸Then the glory of the LORD departed from over the threshold of the temple and stopped above the cherubim. ¹⁹While I watched, the cherubim spread their wings and rose from the ground, and as they went, the wheels went with them. They stopped at the entrance of the east gate of the LORD's house, and the glory of the God of Israel was above them.

²⁰These were the living creatures I had seen beneath the God of Israel by the Kebar River, and I realized that they were cherubim. ²¹Each had four faces and four wings, and under their wings was what looked like human hands. ²²Their faces had the same appearance as those I had seen by the Kebar River. Each one went straight ahead.

God's Sure Judgment on Jerusalem

11 Then the Spirit lifted me up and brought me to the gate of the house of the LORD that faces east. There at the entrance of the gate

---

ᵃ 5 Hebrew *El-Shaddai*   *ᵇ 11* Or *aside*

were twenty-five men, and I saw among them Jaazaniah son of Azzur and Pelatiah son of Benaiah, leaders of the people. ²The Lord said to me, "Son of man, these are the men who are plotting evil and giving wicked advice in this city. ³They say, 'Haven't our houses been recently rebuilt? This city is a pot, and we are the meat in it.' ⁴Therefore prophesy against them; prophesy, son of man."

⁵Then the Spirit of the Lord came on me, and he told me to say: "This is what the Lord says: That is what you are saying, you leaders in Israel, but I know what is going through your mind. ⁶You have killed many people in this city and filled its streets with the dead.

⁷"Therefore this is what the Sovereign Lord says: The bodies you have thrown there are the meat and this city is the pot, but I will drive you out of it. ⁸You fear the sword, and the sword is what I will bring against you, declares the Sovereign Lord. ⁹I will drive you out of the city and deliver you into the hands of foreigners and inflict punishment on you. ¹⁰You will fall by the sword, and I will execute judgment on you at the borders of Israel. Then you will know that I am the Lord. ¹¹This city will not be a pot for you, nor will you be the meat in it; I will execute judgment on you at the borders of Israel. ¹²And you will know that I am the Lord, for you have not followed my decrees or kept my laws but have conformed to the standards of the nations around you."

¹³Now as I was prophesying, Pelatiah son of Benaiah died. Then I fell facedown and cried out in a loud voice, "Alas, Sovereign Lord! Will you completely destroy the remnant of Israel?"

The Promise of Israel's Return

¹⁴The word of the Lord came to me: ¹⁵"Son of man, the people of Jerusalem have said of your fellow exiles and all the other Israelites, 'They are far away from the Lord; this land was given to us as our possession.'

¹⁶"Therefore say: 'This is what the Sovereign Lord says: Although I sent them far away among the nations and scattered them among the countries, yet for a little while I have been a sanctuary for them in the countries where they have gone.'

¹⁷"Therefore say: 'This is what the Sovereign Lord says: I will gather you from the nations and bring you back from the countries where you have been scattered, and I will give you back the land of Israel again.'

¹⁸"They will return to it and remove all its vile images and detestable idols. ¹⁹I will give them an undivided heart and put a new spirit in them; I will remove from them their heart of stone and give them a heart of flesh. ²⁰Then they will follow my decrees and be careful to keep my laws. They will be my people, and I will be their God. ²¹But as for those whose hearts are devoted to their vile images and detestable idols, I will bring down on their own heads what they have done, declares the Sovereign Lord."

ROCK SOLID *promises*

"I will remove from them their heart of stone and give them a heart of flesh." **Ezekiel 11:19**

God promises to change you from the inside out. He will help you obey him because you want to, not because you have to.

²²Then the cherubim, with the wheels beside them, spread their wings, and the glory of the God of Israel was above them. ²³The glory of the Lord went up from within the city and stopped above the mountain east of it. ²⁴The Spirit lifted me up and brought me to the exiles in Babylonia*ᵃ* in the vision given by the Spirit of God.

ᵃ 24 Or *Chaldea*

Then the vision I had seen went up from me, [25] and I told the exiles everything the Lord had shown me.

The Exile Symbolized

12 The word of the Lord came to me: [2] "Son of man, you are living among a rebellious people. They have eyes to see but do not see and ears to hear but do not hear, for they are a rebellious people.

[3] "Therefore, son of man, pack your belongings for exile and in the daytime, as they watch, set out and go from where you are to another place. Perhaps they will understand, though they are a rebellious people. [4] During the daytime, while they watch, bring out your belongings packed for exile. Then in the evening, while they are watching, go out like those who go into exile. [5] While they watch, dig through the wall and take your belongings out through it. [6] Put them on your shoulder as they are watching and carry them out at dusk. Cover your face so that you cannot see the land, for I have made you a sign to the Israelites."

[7] So I did as I was commanded. During the day I brought out my things packed for exile. Then in the evening I dug through the wall with my hands. I took my belongings out at dusk, carrying them on my shoulders while they watched.

[8] In the morning the word of the Lord came to me: [9] "Son of man, did not the Israelites, that rebellious people, ask you, 'What are you doing?'

[10] "Say to them, 'This is what the Sovereign Lord says: This prophecy concerns the prince in Jerusalem and all the Israelites who are there.' [11] Say to them, 'I am a sign to you.'

"As I have done, so it will be done to them. They will go into exile as captives.

[12] "The prince among them will put his things on his shoulder at dusk and leave, and a hole will be dug in the wall for him to go through. He will cover his face so that he cannot see the land. [13] I will spread my net for him, and he will be caught in my snare; I will bring him to Babylonia, the land of the Chaldeans, but he will not

see it, and there he will die. [14] I will scatter to the winds all those around him—his staff and all his troops—and I will pursue them with drawn sword.

[15] "They will know that I am the Lord, when I disperse them among the nations and scatter them through the countries. [16] But I will spare a few of them from the sword, famine and plague, so that in the nations where they go they may acknowledge all their detestable practices. Then they will know that I am the Lord."

[17] The word of the Lord came to me: [18] "Son of man, tremble as you eat your food, and shudder in fear as you drink your water. [19] Say to the people of the land: 'This is what the Sovereign Lord says about those living in Jerusalem and in the land of Israel: They will eat their food in anxiety and drink their water in despair, for their land will be stripped of everything in it because of the violence of all who live there. [20] The inhabited towns will be laid waste and the land will be desolate. Then you will know that I am the Lord.'"

There Will Be No Delay

[21] The word of the Lord came to me: [22] "Son of man, what is this proverb you have in the land of Israel: 'The days go by and every vision comes to nothing'? [23] Say to them, 'This is what the Sovereign Lord says: I am going to put an end to this proverb, and they will no longer quote it in Israel.' Say to them, 'The days are near when every vision will be fulfilled. [24] For there will be no more false visions or flattering divinations among the people of Israel. [25] But I the Lord will speak what I will, and it shall be fulfilled without delay. For in your days, you rebellious people, I will fulfill whatever I say, declares the Sovereign Lord.'"

[26] The word of the Lord came to me: [27] "Son of man, the Israelites are saying, 'The vision he sees is for many years from now, and he prophesies about the distant future.'

[28] "Therefore say to them, 'This is what the Sovereign Lord says: None of my words will be delayed any longer; what-

ever I say will be fulfilled, declares the Sovereign LORD.'"

False Prophets Condemned

13 The word of the LORD came to me: ²"Son of man, prophesy against the prophets of Israel who are now prophesying. Say to those who prophesy out of their own imagination: 'Hear the word of the LORD! ³This is what the Sovereign LORD says: Woe to the foolish^a prophets who follow their own spirit and have seen nothing! ⁴Your prophets, Israel, are like jackals among ruins. ⁵You have not gone up to the breaches in the wall to repair it for the people of Israel so that it will stand firm in the battle on the day of the LORD. ⁶Their visions are false and their divinations a lie. Even though the LORD has not sent them, they say, "The LORD declares," and expect him to fulfill their words. ⁷Have you not seen false visions and uttered lying divinations when you say, "The LORD declares," though I have not spoken?

⁸"'Therefore this is what the Sovereign LORD says: Because of your false words and lying visions, I am against you, declares the Sovereign LORD. ⁹My hand will be against the prophets who see false visions and utter lying divinations. They will not belong to the council of my people or be listed in the records of Israel, nor will they enter the land of Israel. Then you will know that I am the Sovereign LORD.

¹⁰"'Because they lead my people astray, saying, "Peace," when there is no peace, and because, when a flimsy wall is built, they cover it with whitewash, ¹¹therefore tell those who cover it with whitewash that it is going to fall. Rain will come in torrents, and I will send hailstones hurtling down, and violent winds will burst forth. ¹²When the wall collapses, will people not ask you, "Where is the whitewash you covered it with?"

¹³"'Therefore this is what the Sovereign LORD says: In my wrath I will unleash a violent wind, and in my anger hailstones and torrents of rain will fall with destructive fury. ¹⁴I will tear down the wall you

have covered with whitewash and will level it to the ground so that its foundation will be laid bare. When it^b falls, you will be destroyed in it; and you will know that I am the LORD. ¹⁵So I will pour out my wrath against the wall and against those who covered it with whitewash. I will say to you, "The wall is gone and so are those who whitewashed it, ¹⁶those prophets of Israel who prophesied to Jerusalem and saw visions of peace for her when there was no peace, declares the Sovereign LORD."'

¹⁷"Now, son of man, set your face against the daughters of your people who prophesy out of their own imagination. Prophesy against them ¹⁸and say, 'This is what the Sovereign LORD says: Woe to the women who sew magic charms on all their wrists and make veils of various lengths for their heads in order to ensnare people. Will you ensnare the lives of my people but preserve your own? ¹⁹You have profaned me among my people for a few handfuls of barley and scraps of bread. By lying to my people, who listen to lies, you have killed those who should not have died and have spared those who should not live.

²⁰"'Therefore this is what the Sovereign LORD says: I am against your magic charms with which you ensnare people like birds and I will tear them from your arms; I will set free the people that you ensnare like birds. ²¹I will tear off your veils and save my people from your hands, and they will no longer fall prey to your power. Then you will know that I am the LORD. ²²Because you disheartened the righteous with your lies, when I had brought them no grief, and because you encouraged the wicked not to turn from their evil ways and so save their lives, ²³therefore you will no longer see false visions or practice divination. I will save my people from your hands. And then you will know that I am the LORD.'"

Idolaters Condemned

14 Some of the elders of Israel came to me and sat down in front of me. ²Then the word of the LORD came to me: ³"Son of man,

^a 3 Or *wicked*   ^b 14 Or *the city*

these men have set up idols in their hearts and put wicked stumbling blocks before their faces. Should I let them inquire of me at all? ⁴Therefore speak to them and tell them, 'This is what the Sovereign Lord says: When any of the Israelites set up idols in their hearts and put a wicked stumbling block before their faces and then go to a prophet, I the Lord will answer them myself in keeping with their great idolatry. ⁵I will do this to recapture the hearts of the people of Israel, who have all deserted me for their idols.'

⁶"Therefore say to the people of Israel, 'This is what the Sovereign Lord says: Repent! Turn from your idols and renounce all your detestable practices!

⁷"When any of the Israelites or any foreigner residing in Israel separate themselves from me and set up idols in their hearts and put a wicked stumbling block before their faces and then go to a prophet to inquire of me, I the Lord will answer them myself. ⁸I will set my face against them and make them an example and a byword. I will remove them from my people. Then you will know that I am the Lord.

⁹"And if the prophet is enticed to utter a prophecy, I the Lord have enticed that prophet, and I will stretch out my hand against him and destroy him from among my people Israel. ¹⁰They will bear their guilt—the prophet will be as guilty as the one who consults him. ¹¹Then the people of Israel will no longer stray from me, nor will they defile themselves anymore with all their sins. They will be my people, and I will be their God, declares the Sovereign Lord.'"

Jerusalem's Judgment Inescapable

¹²The word of the Lord came to me: ¹³"Son of man, if a country sins against me by being unfaithful and I stretch out my hand against it to cut off its food supply and send famine upon it and kill its people and their animals, ¹⁴even if these three men—Noah, Daniel*a* and Job—were in it, they could save only themselves by their righteousness, declares the Sovereign Lord.

¹⁵"Or if I send wild beasts through that country and they leave it childless and it becomes desolate so that no one can pass through it because of the beasts, ¹⁶as surely as I live, declares the Sovereign Lord, even if these three men were in it, they could not save their own sons or daughters. They alone would be saved, but the land would be desolate.

¹⁷"Or if I bring a sword against that country and say, 'Let the sword pass throughout the land,' and I kill its people and their animals, ¹⁸as surely as I live, declares the Sovereign Lord, even if these three men were in it, they could not save their own sons or daughters. They alone would be saved.

¹⁹"Or if I send a plague into that land and pour out my wrath on it through bloodshed, killing its people and their animals, ²⁰as surely as I live, declares the Sovereign Lord, even if Noah, Daniel and Job were in it, they could save neither son nor daughter. They would save only themselves by their righteousness.

²¹"For this is what the Sovereign Lord says: How much worse will it be when I send against Jerusalem my four dreadful judgments—sword and famine and wild beasts and plague—to kill its men and their animals! ²²Yet there will be some survivors—sons and daughters who will be brought out of it. They will come to you, and when you see their conduct and their actions, you will be consoled regarding the disaster I have brought on Jerusalem—every disaster I have brought on it. ²³You will be consoled when you see their conduct and their actions, for you will know that I have done nothing in it without cause, declares the Sovereign Lord."

Jerusalem as a Useless Vine

15 The word of the Lord came to me: ²"Son of man, how is the wood of a vine different from that of a branch from any of the trees in the forest? ³Is wood ever taken from it to

---

a 14 Or *Danel*, a man of renown in ancient literature; also in verse 20 make anything useful? Do they make pegs from it to hang things on? [4]And after it is thrown on the fire as fuel and the fire burns both ends and chars the middle, is it then useful for anything? [5]If it was not useful for anything when it was whole, how much less can it be made into something useful when the fire has burned it and it is charred?

[6]"Therefore this is what the Sovereign LORD says: As I have given the wood of the vine among the trees of the forest as fuel for the fire, so will I treat the people living in Jerusalem. [7]I will set my face against them. Although they have come out of the fire, the fire will yet consume them. And when I set my face against them, you will know that I am the LORD. [8]I will make the land desolate because they have been unfaithful, declares the Sovereign LORD."

Jerusalem as an Adulterous Wife

16 The word of the LORD came to me: [2]"Son of man, confront Jerusalem with her detestable practices [3]and say, 'This is what the Sovereign LORD says to Jerusalem: Your ancestry and birth were in the land of the Canaanites; your father was an Amorite and your mother a Hittite. [4]On the day you were born your cord was not cut, nor were you washed with water to make you clean, nor were you rubbed with salt or wrapped in cloths. [5]No one looked on you with pity or had compassion enough to do any of these things for you. Rather, you were thrown out into the open field, for on the day you were born you were despised.

[6]"Then I passed by and saw you kicking about in your blood, and as you lay there in your blood I said to you, "Live!"[a] [7]I made you grow like a plant of the field. You grew and developed and entered puberty. Your breasts had formed and your hair had grown, yet you were stark naked.

[8]"Later I passed by, and when I looked at you and saw that you were old enough for love, I spread the corner of my garment over you and covered your naked body. I gave you my solemn oath and entered into a covenant with you, declares the Sovereign LORD, and you became mine.

[9]"'I bathed you with water and washed the blood from you and put ointments on you. [10]I clothed you with an embroidered dress and put sandals of fine leather on you. I dressed you in fine linen and covered you with costly garments. [11]I adorned you with jewelry: I put bracelets on your arms and a necklace around your neck, [12]and I put a ring on your nose, earrings on your ears and a beautiful crown on your head. [13]So you were adorned with gold and silver; your clothes were of fine linen and costly fabric and embroidered cloth. Your food was honey, olive oil and the finest flour. You became very beautiful and rose to be a queen. [14]And your fame spread among the nations on account of your beauty, because the splendor I had given you made your beauty perfect, declares the Sovereign LORD.

[15]"'But you trusted in your beauty and used your fame to become a prostitute. You lavished your favors on anyone who passed by and your beauty became his. [16]You took some of your garments to make gaudy high places, where you carried on your prostitution. You went to him, and he possessed your beauty.[b] [17]You also took the fine jewelry I gave you, the jewelry made of my gold and silver, and you made for yourself male idols and engaged in prostitution with them. [18]And you took your embroidered clothes to put on them, and you offered my oil and incense before them. [19]Also the food I provided for you—the flour, olive oil and honey I gave you to eat—you offered as fragrant incense before them. That is what happened, declares the Sovereign LORD.

[20]"'And you took your sons and daughters whom you bore to me and sacrificed them as food to the idols. Was your prostitution not enough? [21]You slaughtered my children and sacrificed them to the idols.

---

[a] 6 A few Hebrew manuscripts, Septuagint and Syriac; most Hebrew manuscripts repeat *and as you lay there in your blood I said to you, "Live!"*
[b] 16 The meaning of the Hebrew for this sentence is uncertain.

²²In all your detestable practices and your prostitution you did not remember the days of your youth, when you were naked and bare, kicking about in your blood.

²³"'Woe! Woe to you, declares the Sovereign Lord. In addition to all your other wickedness, ²⁴you built a mound for yourself and made a lofty shrine in every public square. ²⁵At every street corner you built your lofty shrines and degraded your beauty, spreading your legs with increasing promiscuity to anyone who passed by. ²⁶You engaged in prostitution with the Egyptians, your neighbors with large genitals, and aroused my anger with your increasing promiscuity. ²⁷So I stretched out my hand against you and reduced your territory; I gave you over to the greed of your enemies, the daughters of the Philistines, who were shocked by your lewd conduct. ²⁸You engaged in prostitution with the Assyrians too, because you were insatiable; and even after that, you still were not satisfied. ²⁹Then you increased your promiscuity to include Babylonia,ᵃ a land of merchants, but even with this you were not satisfied.

³⁰"'I am filled with fury against you,ᵇ declares the Sovereign Lord, when you do all these things, acting like a brazen prostitute! ³¹When you built your mounds at every street corner and made your lofty shrines in every public square, you were unlike a prostitute, because you scorned payment.

³²"'You adulterous wife! You prefer strangers to your own husband! ³³All prostitutes receive gifts, but you give gifts to all your lovers, bribing them to come to you from everywhere for your illicit favors. ³⁴So in your prostitution you are the opposite of others; no one runs after you for your favors. You are the very opposite, for you give payment and none is given to you.

³⁵"'Therefore, you prostitute, hear the word of the Lord! ³⁶This is what the Sovereign Lord says: Because you poured out your lust and exposed your naked body in your promiscuity with your lovers, and because of all your detestable idols, and because you gave them your children's blood, ³⁷therefore I am going to gather all your lovers, with whom you found pleasure, those you loved as well as those you hated. I will gather them against you from all around and will strip you in front of them, and they will see you stark naked. ³⁸I will sentence you to the punishment of women who commit adultery and who shed blood; I will bring on you the blood vengeance of my wrath and jealous anger. ³⁹Then I will deliver you into the hands of your lovers, and they will tear down your mounds and destroy your lofty shrines. They will strip you of your clothes and take your fine jewelry and leave you stark naked. ⁴⁰They will bring a mob against you, who will stone you and hack you to pieces with their swords. ⁴¹They will burn down your houses and inflict punishment on you in the sight of many women. I will put a stop to your prostitution, and you will no longer pay your lovers. ⁴²Then my wrath against you will subside and my jealous anger will turn away from you; I will be calm and no longer angry.

⁴³"'Because you did not remember the days of your youth but enraged me with all these things, I will surely bring down on your head what you have done, declares the Sovereign Lord. Did you not add lewdness to all your other detestable practices?

⁴⁴"'Everyone who quotes proverbs will quote this proverb about you: "Like mother, like daughter." ⁴⁵You are a true daughter of your mother, who despised her husband and her children; and you are a true sister of your sisters, who despised their husbands and their children. Your mother was a Hittite and your father an Amorite. ⁴⁶Your older sister was Samaria, who lived to the north of you with her daughters; and your younger sister, who lived to the south of you with her daughters, was Sodom. ⁴⁷You not only followed their ways and copied their detestable practices, but in all your ways you soon became more depraved than they. ⁴⁸As surely as I live, declares the Sovereign Lord, your sister

---

ᵃ 29 Or *Chaldea*   ᵇ 30 Or *How feverish is your heart,*

Sodom and her daughters never did what you and your daughters have done.

⁴⁹ "'Now this was the sin of your sister Sodom: She and her daughters were arrogant, overfed and unconcerned; they did not help the poor and needy. ⁵⁰ They were haughty and did detestable things before me. Therefore I did away with them as you have seen. ⁵¹ Samaria did not commit half the sins you did. You have done more detestable things than they, and have made your sisters seem righteous by all these things you have done. ⁵² Bear your disgrace, for you have furnished some justification for your sisters. Because your sins were more vile than theirs, they appear more righteous than you. So then, be ashamed and bear your disgrace, for you have made your sisters appear righteous.

⁵³ "'However, I will restore the fortunes of Sodom and her daughters and of Samaria and her daughters, and your fortunes along with them, ⁵⁴ so that you may bear your disgrace and be ashamed of all you have done in giving them comfort. ⁵⁵ And your sisters, Sodom with her daughters and Samaria with her daughters, will return to what they were before; and you and your daughters will return to what you were before. ⁵⁶ You would not even mention your sister Sodom in the day of your pride, ⁵⁷ before your wickedness was uncovered. Even so, you are now scorned by the daughters of Edom*ᵃ* and all her neighbors and the daughters of the Philistines—all those around you who despise you. ⁵⁸ You will bear the consequences of your lewdness and your detestable practices, declares the LORD.

⁵⁹ "'This is what the Sovereign LORD says: I will deal with you as you deserve, because you have despised my oath by breaking the covenant. ⁶⁰ Yet I will remember the covenant I made with you in the days of your youth, and I will establish an everlasting covenant with you. ⁶¹ Then you will remember your ways and be ashamed when you receive your sisters, both those who are older than you and those who are younger. I will give them to you as daughters, but not on the basis

of my covenant with you. ⁶² So I will establish my covenant with you, and you will know that I am the LORD. ⁶³ Then, when I make atonement for you for all you have done, you will remember and be ashamed and never again open your mouth because of your humiliation, declares the Sovereign LORD.'"

Two Eagles and a Vine

17 The word of the LORD came to me: ² "Son of man, set forth an allegory and tell it to the Israelites as a parable. ³ Say to them, 'This is what the Sovereign LORD says: A great eagle with powerful wings, long feathers and full plumage of varied colors came to Lebanon. Taking hold of the top of a cedar, ⁴ he broke off its topmost shoot and carried it away to a land of merchants, where he planted it in a city of traders.

⁵ "'He took one of the seedlings of the land and put it in fertile soil. He planted it like a willow by abundant water, ⁶ and it sprouted and became a low, spreading vine. Its branches turned toward him, but its roots remained under it. So it became a vine and produced branches and put out leafy boughs.

⁷ "'But there was another great eagle with powerful wings and full plumage. The vine now sent out its roots toward him from the plot where it was planted and stretched out its branches to him for water. ⁸ It had been planted in good soil by abundant water so that it would produce branches, bear fruit and become a splendid vine.'

⁹ "Say to them, 'This is what the Sovereign LORD says: Will it thrive? Will it not be uprooted and stripped of its fruit so that it withers? All its new growth will wither. It will not take a strong arm or many people to pull it up by the roots. ¹⁰ It has been planted, but will it thrive? Will it not wither completely when the east wind strikes it—wither away in the plot where it grew?'"

ᵃ 57 Many Hebrew manuscripts and Syriac; most Hebrew manuscripts, Septuagint and Vulgate *Aram*

¹¹Then the word of the LORD came to me: ¹²"Say to this rebellious people, 'Do you not know what these things mean?' Say to them: 'The king of Babylon went to Jerusalem and carried off her king and her nobles, bringing them back with him to Babylon. ¹³Then he took a member of the royal family and made a treaty with him, putting him under oath. He also carried away the leading men of the land, ¹⁴so that the kingdom would be brought low, unable to rise again, surviving only by keeping his treaty. ¹⁵But the king rebelled against him by sending his envoys to Egypt to get horses and a large army. Will he succeed? Will he who does such things escape? Will he break the treaty and yet escape?

¹⁶"'As surely as I live, declares the Sovereign LORD, he shall die in Babylon, in the land of the king who put him on the throne, whose oath he despised and whose treaty he broke. ¹⁷Pharaoh with his mighty army and great horde will be of no help to him in war, when ramps are built and siege works erected to destroy many lives. ¹⁸He despised the oath by breaking the covenant. Because he had given his hand in pledge and yet did all these things, he shall not escape.

¹⁹"'Therefore this is what the Sovereign LORD says: As surely as I live, I will repay him for despising my oath and breaking my covenant. ²⁰I will spread my net for him, and he will be caught in my snare. I will bring him to Babylon and execute judgment on him there because he was unfaithful to me. ²¹All his choice troops will fall by the sword, and the survivors will be scattered to the winds. Then you will know that I the LORD have spoken.

²²"'This is what the Sovereign LORD says: I myself will take a shoot from the very top of a cedar and plant it; I will break off a tender sprig from its topmost shoots and plant it on a high and lofty mountain. ²³On the mountain heights of Israel I will plant it; it will produce branches and bear fruit and become a splendid cedar. Birds of every kind will nest in it; they will find shelter in the shade of its branches. ²⁴All

the trees of the forest will know that I the LORD bring down the tall tree and make the low tree grow tall. I dry up the green tree and make the dry tree flourish.

"'I the LORD have spoken, and I will do it.'"

The One Who Sins Will Die

18 The word of the LORD came to me: ²"What do you people mean by quoting this proverb about the land of Israel:

"'The parents eat sour grapes,
   and the children's teeth are set on
   edge'?

³"As surely as I live, declares the Sovereign LORD, you will no longer quote this proverb in Israel. ⁴For everyone belongs to me, the parent as well as the child—both alike belong to me. The one who sins is the one who will die.

UNSHAKEN *God*

Ezekiel 18:1–4

God is fair.

The crowds raged at God. They kept quoting an old saying that means "the fathers sin ... and the children pay for it" (see Ezekiel 18:2). When the Lord overheard their grumbling, he exploded. He swore people would no longer quote that saying. He said people die for their own sins, not the sins of others. God then goes on to explain what good living looks like. He declares that he gets no pleasure from watching wicked people die. And this sharp exchange proves that God treats people with extraordinary fairness. Ironically, God would one day come in the person of Jesus to suffer and die for sins he didn't commit—all the sins of humankind. Talk about unfair.

So ... Does God seem fair—or more than fair?

⁵"Suppose there is a righteous man
  who does what is just and right.
⁶He does not eat at the mountain
    shrines
  or look to the idols of Israel.
He does not defile his neighbor's wife
  or have sexual relations with a
    woman during her period.
⁷He does not oppress anyone,
  but returns what he took in pledge
    for a loan.
He does not commit robbery
  but gives his food to the hungry
  and provides clothing for the naked.
⁸He does not lend to them at interest
  or take a profit from them.
He withholds his hand from doing
    wrong
  and judges fairly between two
    parties.
⁹He follows my decrees
  and faithfully keeps my laws.
That man is righteous;
  he will surely live,
      declares the Sovereign LORD.

¹⁰"Suppose he has a violent son, who
sheds blood or does any of these other things* ¹¹(though the father has done
none of them):

"He eats at the mountain shrines.
He defiles his neighbor's wife.
¹²He oppresses the poor and needy.
He commits robbery.
He does not return what he took in
    pledge.
He looks to the idols.
He does detestable things.
¹³He lends at interest and takes a profit.

Will such a man live? He will not! Because
he has done all these detestable things, he
is to be put to death; his blood will be on
his own head.

¹⁴"But suppose this son has a son who
sees all the sins his father commits, and
though he sees them, he does not do such
things:

¹⁵"He does not eat at the mountain
    shrines
  or look to the idols of Israel.

He does not defile his neighbor's wife.
¹⁶He does not oppress anyone
  or require a pledge for a loan.
He does not commit robbery
  but gives his food to the hungry
  and provides clothing for the naked.
¹⁷He withholds his hand from
    mistreating the poor
  and takes no interest or profit from
    them.
He keeps my laws and follows my
    decrees.

He will not die for his father's sin; he will
surely live.. ¹⁸But his father will die for
his own sin, because he practiced extortion, robbed his brother and did what was
wrong among his people.

¹⁹"Yet you ask, 'Why does the son not
share the guilt of his father?' Since the son
has done what is just and right and has
been careful to keep all my decrees, he
will surely live. ²⁰The one who sins is the
one who will die. The child will not share
the guilt of the parent, nor will the parent share the guilt of the child. The righteousness of the righteous will be credited
to them, and the wickedness of the wicked
will be charged against them.

²¹"But if a wicked person turns away
from all the sins they have committed
and keeps all my decrees and does what is
just and right, that person will surely live;
they will not die. ²²None of the offenses
they have committed will be remembered
against them. Because of the righteous
things they have done, they will live.
²³Do I take any pleasure in the death of
the wicked? declares the Sovereign LORD.
Rather, am I not pleased when they turn
from their ways and live?

²⁴"But if a righteous person turns from
their righteousness and commits sin and
does the same detestable things the wicked person does, will they live? None of the
righteous things that person has done will
be remembered. Because of the unfaithfulness they are guilty of and because of the
sins they have committed, they will die.

²⁵"Yet you say, 'The way of the Lord is

a 10 Or things to a brother

985

not just.' Hear, you Israelites: Is my way unjust? Is it not your ways that are unjust? 26 If a righteous person turns from their righteousness and commits sin, they will die for it; because of the sin they have committed they will die. 27 But if a wicked person turns away from the wickedness they have committed and does what is just and right, they will save their life. 28 Because they consider all the offenses they have committed and turn away from them, that person will surely live; they will not die. 29 Yet the Israelites say, 'The way of the Lord is not just.' Are my ways unjust, people of Israel? Is it not your ways that are unjust?

30 "Therefore, you Israelites, I will judge each of you according to your own ways, declares the Sovereign Lord. Repent! Turn away from all your offenses; then sin will not be your downfall. 31 Rid yourselves of all the offenses you have committed, and get a new heart and a new spirit. Why will you die, people of Israel? 32 For I take no pleasure in the death of anyone, declares the Sovereign Lord. Repent and live!

A Lament Over Israel's Princes

19 "Take up a lament concerning the princes of Israel 2 and say:

" 'What a lioness was your mother
    among the lions!
She lay down among them
    and reared her cubs.
3 She brought up one of her cubs,
    and he became a strong lion.
He learned to tear the prey
    and he became a man-eater.
4 The nations heard about him,
    and he was trapped in their pit.
They led him with hooks
    to the land of Egypt.

5 " 'When she saw her hope unfulfilled,
    her expectation gone,
she took another of her cubs
    and made him a strong lion.
6 He prowled among the lions,
    for he was now a strong lion.
He learned to tear the prey
    and he became a man-eater.

7 He broke down[a] their strongholds
    and devastated their towns.
The land and all who were in it
    were terrified by his roaring.
8 Then the nations came against him,
    those from regions round about.
They spread their net for him,
    and he was trapped in their pit.
9 With hooks they pulled him into a cage
    and brought him to the king of
        Babylon.
They put him in prison,
    so his roar was heard no longer
        on the mountains of Israel.

10 " 'Your mother was like a vine in your
        vineyard[b]
    planted by the water;
it was fruitful and full of branches
    because of abundant water.
11 Its branches were strong,
    fit for a ruler's scepter.
It towered high
    above the thick foliage,
conspicuous for its height
    and for its many branches.
12 But it was uprooted in fury
    and thrown to the ground.
The east wind made it shrivel,
    it was stripped of its fruit;
its strong branches withered
    and fire consumed them.
13 Now it is planted in the desert,
    in a dry and thirsty land.
14 Fire spread from one of its main[c]
        branches
    and consumed its fruit.
No strong branch is left on it
    fit for a ruler's scepter.'

"This is a lament and is to be used as a lament."

Rebellious Israel Purged

20 In the seventh year, in the fifth month on the tenth day, some of the elders of Israel came to inquire of the Lord, and they sat down in front of me.

---

a 7 Targum (see Septuagint); Hebrew *He knew*
b 10 Two Hebrew manuscripts; most Hebrew manuscripts *your blood*   c 14 Or *from under its*

²Then the word of the LORD came to me: ³"Son of man, speak to the elders of Israel and say to them, 'This is what the Sovereign LORD says: Have you come to inquire of me? As surely as I live, I will not let you inquire of me, declares the Sovereign LORD.'

⁴"Will you judge them? Will you judge them, son of man? Then confront them with the detestable practices of their ancestors ⁵and say to them: 'This is what the Sovereign LORD says: On the day I chose Israel, I swore with uplifted hand to the descendants of Jacob and revealed myself to them in Egypt. With uplifted hand I said to them, "I am the LORD your God." ⁶On that day I swore to them that I would bring them out of Egypt into a land I had searched out for them, a land flowing with milk and honey, the most beautiful of all lands. ⁷And I said to them, "Each of you, get rid of the vile images you have set your eyes on, and do not defile yourselves with the idols of Egypt. I am the LORD your God."

⁸"'But they rebelled against me and would not listen to me; they did not get rid of the vile images they had set their eyes on, nor did they forsake the idols of Egypt. So I said I would pour out my wrath on them and spend my anger against them in Egypt. ⁹But for the sake of my name, I brought them out of Egypt. I did it to keep my name from being profaned in the eyes of the nations among whom they lived and in whose sight I had revealed myself to the Israelites. ¹⁰Therefore I led them out of Egypt and brought them into the wilderness. ¹¹I gave them my decrees and made known to them my laws, by which the person who obeys them will live. ¹²Also I gave them my Sabbaths as a sign between us, so they would know that I the LORD made them holy.

¹³"'Yet the people of Israel rebelled against me in the wilderness. They did not follow my decrees but rejected my laws—by which the person who obeys them will live—and they utterly desecrated my Sabbaths. So I said I would pour out my wrath on them and destroy them in the wilderness. ¹⁴But for the sake of my name I did what would keep it from being profaned in the eyes of the nations in whose sight I had brought them out. ¹⁵Also with uplifted hand I swore to them in the wilderness that I would not bring them into the land I had given them—a land flowing with milk and honey, the most beautiful of all lands— ¹⁶because they rejected my laws and did not follow my decrees and desecrated my Sabbaths. For their hearts were devoted to their idols. ¹⁷Yet I looked on them with pity and did not destroy them or put an end to them in the wilderness. ¹⁸I said to their children in the wilderness, "Do not follow the statutes of your parents or keep their laws or defile yourselves with their idols. ¹⁹I am the LORD your God; follow my decrees and be careful to keep my laws. ²⁰Keep my Sabbaths holy, that they may be a sign between us. Then you will know that I am the LORD your God."

²¹"'But the children rebelled against me: They did not follow my decrees, they were not careful to keep my laws, of which I said, "The person who obeys them will live by them," and they desecrated my Sabbaths. So I said I would pour out my wrath on them and spend my anger against them in the wilderness. ²²But I withheld my hand, and for the sake of my name I did what would keep it from being profaned in the eyes of the nations in whose sight I had brought them out. ²³Also with uplifted hand I swore to them in the wilderness that I would disperse them among the nations and scatter them through the countries, ²⁴because they had not obeyed my laws but had rejected my decrees and desecrated my Sabbaths, and their eyes lusted after their parents' idols. ²⁵So I gave them other statutes that were not good and laws through which they could not live; ²⁶I defiled them through their gifts—the sacrifice of every firstborn—that I might fill them with horror so they would know that I am the LORD.'

²⁷"Therefore, son of man, speak to the people of Israel and say to them, 'This is what the Sovereign LORD says: In this also your ancestors blasphemed me by being unfaithful to me: ²⁸When I brought them

into the land I had sworn to give them and they saw any high hill or any leafy tree, there they offered their sacrifices, made offerings that aroused my anger, presented their fragrant incense and poured out their drink offerings. ²⁹Then I said to them: What is this high place you go to?'" (It is called Bamah*ᵃ* to this day.)

Rebellious Israel Renewed

³⁰"Therefore say to the Israelites: 'This is what the Sovereign LORD says: Will you defile yourselves the way your ancestors did and lust after their vile images? ³¹When you offer your gifts—the sacrifice of your children in the fire—you continue to defile yourselves with all your idols to this day. Am I to let you inquire of me, you Israelites? As surely as I live, declares the Sovereign LORD, I will not let you inquire of me.

³²"'You say, "We want to be like the nations, like the peoples of the world, who serve wood and stone." But what you have in mind will never happen. ³³As surely as I live, declares the Sovereign LORD, I will reign over you with a mighty hand and an outstretched arm and with outpoured wrath. ³⁴I will bring you from the nations and gather you from the countries where you have been scattered—with a mighty hand and an outstretched arm and with outpoured wrath. ³⁵I will bring you into the wilderness of the nations and there, face to face, I will execute judgment upon you. ³⁶As I judged your ancestors in the wilderness of the land of Egypt, so I will judge you, declares the Sovereign LORD. ³⁷I will take note of you as you pass under my rod, and I will bring you into the bond of the covenant. ³⁸I will purge you of those who revolt and rebel against me. Although I will bring them out of the land where they are living, yet they will not enter the land of Israel. Then you will know that I am the LORD.

³⁹"'As for you, people of Israel, this is what the Sovereign LORD says: Go and serve your idols, every one of you! But afterward you will surely listen to me and no longer profane my holy name with your gifts and idols. ⁴⁰For on my holy mountain,

the high mountain of Israel, declares the Sovereign LORD, there in the land all the people of Israel will serve me, and there I will accept them. There I will require your offerings and your choice gifts,*ᵇ* along with all your holy sacrifices. ⁴¹I will accept you as fragrant incense when I bring you out from the nations and gather you from the countries where you have been scattered, and I will be proved holy through you in the sight of the nations. ⁴²Then you will know that I am the LORD, when I bring you into the land of Israel, the land I had sworn with uplifted hand to give to your ancestors. ⁴³There you will remember your conduct and all the actions by which you have defiled yourselves, and you will loathe yourselves for all the evil you have done. ⁴⁴You will know that I am the LORD, when I deal with you for my name's sake and not according to your evil ways and your corrupt practices, you people of Israel, declares the Sovereign LORD.'"

Prophecy Against the South

⁴⁵The word of the LORD came to me: ⁴⁶"Son of man, set your face toward the south; preach against the south and prophesy against the forest of the southland. ⁴⁷Say to the southern forest: 'Hear the word of the LORD. This is what the Sovereign LORD says: I am about to set fire to you, and it will consume all your trees, both green and dry. The blazing flame will not be quenched, and every face from south to north will be scorched by it. ⁴⁸Everyone will see that I the LORD have kindled it; it will not be quenched.'"

⁴⁹Then I said, "Sovereign LORD, they are saying of me, 'Isn't he just telling parables?'"*ᶜ*

Babylon as God's Sword of Judgment

21ᵈ The word of the LORD came to me: ²"Son of man, set your face against Jerusalem and preach against the sanctuary. Prophesy

---

ᵃ 29 Bamah means *high place.* *ᵇ 40* Or *and the gifts of your firstfruits* *ᶜ 49* In Hebrew texts 20:45-49 is numbered 21:1-5. *ᵈ* In Hebrew texts 21:1-32 is numbered 21:6-37.

against the land of Israel ³and say to her: 'This is what the LORD says: I am against you. I will draw my sword from its sheath and cut off from you both the righteous and the wicked. ⁴Because I am going to cut off the righteous and the wicked, my sword will be unsheathed against everyone from south to north. ⁵Then all people will know that I the LORD have drawn my sword from its sheath; it will not return again.'

⁶"Therefore groan, son of man! Groan before them with broken heart and bitter grief. ⁷And when they ask you, 'Why are you groaning?' you shall say, 'Because of the news that is coming. Every heart will melt with fear and every hand go limp; every spirit will become faint and every leg will be wet with urine.' It is coming! It will surely take place, declares the Sovereign LORD."

⁸The word of the LORD came to me: ⁹"Son of man, prophesy and say, 'This is what the Lord says:

" 'A sword, a sword,
    sharpened and polished—
¹⁰sharpened for the slaughter,
    polished to flash like lightning!

" 'Shall we rejoice in the scepter of my royal son? The sword despises every such stick.

¹¹" 'The sword is appointed to be
        polished,
    to be grasped with the hand;
it is sharpened and polished,
    made ready for the hand of the slayer.
¹²Cry out and wail, son of man,
    for it is against my people;
    it is against all the princes of Israel.
They are thrown to the sword
    along with my people.
Therefore beat your breast.

¹³" 'Testing will surely come. And what if even the scepter, which the sword despises, does not continue? declares the Sovereign LORD.'

¹⁴"So then, son of man, prophesy
    and strike your hands together.
Let the sword strike twice,
    even three times.

It is a sword for slaughter—
    a sword for great slaughter,
    closing in on them from every side.
¹⁵So that hearts may melt with fear
    and the fallen be many,
I have stationed the sword for
        slaughterᵃ
    at all their gates.
Look! It is forged to strike like
        lightning,
    it is grasped for slaughter.
¹⁶Slash to the right, you sword,
    then to the left,
    wherever your blade is turned.
¹⁷I too will strike my hands together,
    and my wrath will subside.
I the LORD have spoken."

¹⁸The word of the LORD came to me: ¹⁹"Son of man, mark out two roads for the sword of the king of Babylon to take, both starting from the same country. Make a signpost where the road branches off to the city. ²⁰Mark out one road for the sword to come against Rabbah of the Ammonites and another against Judah and fortified Jerusalem. ²¹For the king of Babylon will stop at the fork in the road, at the junction of the two roads, to seek an omen: He will cast lots with arrows, he will consult his idols, he will examine the liver. ²²Into his right hand will come the lot for Jerusalem, where he is to set up battering rams, to give the command to slaughter, to sound the battle cry, to set battering rams against the gates, to build a ramp and to erect siege works. ²³It will seem like a false omen to those who have sworn allegiance to him, but he will remind them of their guilt and take them captive.

²⁴"Therefore this is what the Sovereign LORD says: 'Because you people have brought to mind your guilt by your open rebellion, revealing your sins in all that you do—because you have done this, you will be taken captive.

²⁵" 'You profane and wicked prince of Israel, whose day has come, whose time of punishment has reached its climax, ²⁶this

---

ᵃ 15 Septuagint; the meaning of the Hebrew for this word is uncertain.

is what the Sovereign LORD says: Take off the turban, remove the crown. It will not be as it was: The lowly will be exalted and the exalted will be brought low. ²⁷A ruin! A ruin! I will make it a ruin! The crown will not be restored until he to whom it rightfully belongs shall come; to him I will give it.'

²⁸"And you, son of man, prophesy and say, 'This is what the Sovereign LORD says about the Ammonites and their insults:

"'A sword, a sword,
    drawn for the slaughter,
polished to consume
    and to flash like lightning!
²⁹Despite false visions concerning you
    and lying divinations about you,
it will be laid on the necks
    of the wicked who are to be slain,
whose day has come,
    whose time of punishment has
        reached its climax.

³⁰"'Let the sword return to its sheath.
    In the place where you were created,
in the land of your ancestry,
    I will judge you.
³¹I will pour out my wrath on you
    and breathe out my fiery anger
        against you;
I will deliver you into the hands of
        brutal men,
    men skilled in destruction.
³²You will be fuel for the fire,
    your blood will be shed in your
        land,
you will be remembered no more;
    for I the LORD have spoken.'"

Judgment on Jerusalem's Sins

22 The word of the LORD came to me:

²"Son of man, will you judge her? Will you judge this city of bloodshed? Then confront her with all her detestable practices ³and say: 'This is what the Sovereign LORD says: You city that brings on herself doom by shedding blood in her midst and defiles herself by making idols, ⁴you have become guilty because of the blood you have shed and have become defiled by the idols you have made. You have brought your days to a close, and the end of your years has come. Therefore I will make you an object of scorn to the nations and a laughingstock to all the countries. ⁵Those who are near and those who are far away will mock you, you infamous city, full of turmoil.

⁶"'See how each of the princes of Israel who are in you uses his power to shed blood. ⁷In you they have treated father and mother with contempt; in you they have oppressed the foreigner and mistreated the fatherless and the widow. ⁸You have despised my holy things and desecrated my Sabbaths. ⁹In you are slanderers who are bent on shedding blood; in you are those who eat at the mountain shrines and commit lewd acts. ¹⁰In you are those who dishonor their father's bed; in you are those who violate women during their period, when they are ceremonially unclean. ¹¹In you one man commits a detestable offense with his neighbor's wife, another shamefully defiles his daughter-in-law, and another violates his sister, his own father's daughter. ¹²In you are people who accept bribes to shed blood; you take interest and make a profit from the poor. You extort unjust gain from your neighbors. And you have forgotten me, declares the Sovereign LORD.

¹³"'I will surely strike my hands together at the unjust gain you have made and at the blood you have shed in your midst. ¹⁴Will your courage endure or your hands be strong in the day I deal with you? I the LORD have spoken, and I will do it. ¹⁵I will disperse you among the nations and scatter you through the countries; and I will put an end to your uncleanness. ¹⁶When you have been defiled*a* in the eyes of the nations, you will know that I am the LORD.'"

¹⁷Then the word of the LORD came to me: ¹⁸"Son of man, the people of Israel have become dross to me; all of them are the copper, tin, iron and lead left inside a furnace. They are but the dross of silver. ¹⁹Therefore this is what the Sovereign LORD says: 'Because you have all become

---

a 16 Or When I have allotted you your inheritance

dross, I will gather you into Jerusalem. [20] As silver, copper, iron, lead and tin are gathered into a furnace to be melted with a fiery blast, so will I gather you in my anger and my wrath and put you inside the city and melt you. [21] I will gather you and I will blow on you with my fiery wrath, and you will be melted inside her. [22] As silver is melted in a furnace, so you will be melted inside her, and you will know that I the LORD have poured out my wrath on you.'"

[23] Again the word of the LORD came to me: [24] "Son of man, say to the land, 'You are a land that has not been cleansed or rained on in the day of wrath.' [25] There is a conspiracy of her princes[a] within her like a roaring lion tearing its prey; they devour people, take treasures and precious things and make many widows within her. [26] Her priests do violence to my law and profane my holy things; they do not distinguish between the holy and the common; they teach that there is no difference between the unclean and the clean; and they shut their eyes to the keeping of my Sabbaths, so that I am profaned among them. [27] Her officials within her are like wolves tearing their prey; they shed blood and kill people to make unjust gain. [28] Her prophets whitewash these deeds for them by false visions and lying divinations. They say, 'This is what the Sovereign LORD says'— when the LORD has not spoken. [29] The people of the land practice extortion and commit robbery; they oppress the poor and needy and mistreat the foreigner, denying them justice.

[30] "I looked for someone among them who would build up the wall and stand before me in the gap on behalf of the land so I would not have to destroy it, but I found no one. [31] So I will pour out my wrath on them and consume them with my fiery anger, bringing down on their own heads all they have done, declares the Sovereign LORD."

[a] 25 Septuagint; Hebrew *prophets*

ROCK SOLID *principles*

Ezekiel 22:1–31

Stand in the gap.

Cody knew that most people pray—but they don't really pray. Their prayers are like tossing a wish into the air, hoping God will hear their requests and maybe help out. "Real prayer," he told his Bible study group, "expects God to keep his promises—like Acts 1:8, which says the Holy Spirit will give us power to tell people about Jesus." Cody saw astonishing pain among his non-Christian friends, but he and his Christian friends were doing nothing about that hurt. "I think we need to start praying for our friends," he added. "We can pray that they would want to know God. And we can pray to know how to explain Christ to them."

The prophet Ezekiel saw rampant and violent sin all around him. Worse yet, false prophets said those behaviors were okay. God was searching for someone to stand up for right among his people, like a soldier guarding a gap in a broken city wall (see Ezekiel 22:30). You stand in the gap when you act and talk right—and when you pray for mercy for the people around you.

Two Adulterous Sisters

23 The word of the LORD came to me: [2]"Son of man, there were two women, daughters of the same mother. [3]They became prostitutes in Egypt, engaging in prostitution from their youth. In that land their breasts were fondled and their virgin bosoms caressed. [4]The older was named Oholah, and her sister was Oholibah. They were mine and gave birth to sons and daughters. Oholah is Samaria, and Oholibah is Jerusalem.

[5]"Oholah engaged in prostitution while she was still mine; and she lusted after her lovers, the Assyrians—warriors [6]clothed in blue, governors and commanders, all of them handsome young men, and mounted horsemen. [7]She gave herself as a prostitute to all the elite of the Assyrians and defiled herself with all the idols of everyone she lusted after. [8]She did not give up the prostitution she began in Egypt, when during her youth men slept with her, caressed her virgin bosom and poured out their lust on her.

[9]"Therefore I delivered her into the hands of her lovers, the Assyrians, for whom she lusted. [10]They stripped her naked, took away her sons and daughters and killed her with the sword. She became a byword among women, and punishment was inflicted on her.

[11]"Her sister Oholibah saw this, yet in her lust and prostitution she was more depraved than her sister. [12]She too lusted after the Assyrians—governors and commanders, warriors in full dress, mounted horsemen, all handsome young men. [13]I saw that she too defiled herself; both of them went the same way.

[14]"But she carried her prostitution still further. She saw men portrayed on a wall, figures of Chaldeans[a] portrayed in red, [15]with belts around their waists and flowing turbans on their heads; all of them looked like Babylonian chariot officers, natives of Chaldea.[b] [16]As soon as she saw them, she lusted after them and sent messengers to them in Chaldea. [17]Then the Babylonians came to her, to the bed of love, and in their lust they defiled her. After she had been defiled by them, she turned away from them in disgust. [18]When she carried on her prostitution openly and exposed her naked body, I turned away from her in disgust, just as I had turned away from her sister. [19]Yet she became more and more promiscuous as she recalled the days of her youth, when she was a prostitute in Egypt. [20]There she lusted after her lovers, whose genitals were like those of donkeys and whose emission was like that of horses. [21]So you longed for the lewdness of your youth, when in Egypt your bosom was caressed and your young breasts fondled.[c]

[22]"Therefore, Oholibah, this is what the Sovereign LORD says: I will stir up your lovers against you, those you turned away from in disgust, and I will bring them against you from every side— [23]the Babylonians and all the Chaldeans, the men of Pekod and Shoa and Koa, and all the Assyrians with them, handsome young men, all of them governors and commanders, chariot officers and men of high rank, all mounted on horses. [24]They will come against you with weapons,[d] chariots and wagons and with a throng of people; they will take up positions against you on every side with large and small shields and with helmets. I will turn you over to them for punishment, and they will punish you according to their standards. [25]I will direct my jealous anger against you, and they will deal with you in fury. They will cut off your noses and your ears, and those of you who are left will fall by the sword. They will take away your sons and daughters, and those of you who are left will be consumed by fire. [26]They will also strip you of your clothes and take your fine jewelry. [27]So I will put a stop to the lewdness and prostitution you began in Egypt. You will not look on these things with longing or remember Egypt anymore.

[28]"For this is what the Sovereign LORD says: I am about to deliver you into the

---

[a] 14 Or *Babylonians*   [b] 15 Or *Babylonia*; also in verse 16   [c] 21 Syriac (see also verse 3); Hebrew *caressed because of your young breasts*
[d] 24 The meaning of the Hebrew for this word is uncertain.

hands of those you hate, to those you turned away from in disgust. ²⁹They will deal with you in hatred and take away everything you have worked for. They will leave you stark naked, and the shame of your prostitution will be exposed. Your lewdness and promiscuity ³⁰have brought this on you, because you lusted after the nations and defiled yourself with their idols. ³¹You have gone the way of your sister; so I will put her cup into your hand.

³²"This is what the Sovereign LORD says:

"You will drink your sister's cup,
    a cup large and deep;
it will bring scorn and derision,
    for it holds so much.
³³You will be filled with drunkenness
        and sorrow,
    the cup of ruin and desolation,
    the cup of your sister Samaria.
³⁴You will drink it and drain it dry
    and chew on its pieces—
    and you will tear your breasts.

I have spoken, declares the Sovereign LORD.

³⁵"Therefore this is what the Sovereign LORD says: Since you have forgotten me and turned your back on me, you must bear the consequences of your lewdness and prostitution."

³⁶The LORD said to me: "Son of man, will you judge Oholah and Oholibah? Then confront them with their detestable practices, ³⁷for they have committed adultery and blood is on their hands. They committed adultery with their idols; they even sacrificed their children, whom they bore to me, as food for them. ³⁸They have also done this to me: At that same time they defiled my sanctuary and desecrated my Sabbaths. ³⁹On the very day they sacrificed their children to their idols, they entered my sanctuary and desecrated it. That is what they did in my house.

⁴⁰"They even sent messengers for men who came from far away, and when they arrived you bathed yourself for them, applied eye makeup and put on your jewelry. ⁴¹You sat on an elegant couch, with a table spread before it on which you had placed the incense and olive oil that belonged to me.

⁴²"The noise of a carefree crowd was around her; drunkards were brought from the desert along with men from the rabble, and they put bracelets on the wrists of the woman and her sister and beautiful crowns on their heads. ⁴³Then I said about the one worn out by adultery, 'Now let them use her as a prostitute, for that is all she is.' ⁴⁴And they slept with her. As men sleep with a prostitute, so they slept with those lewd women, Oholah and Oholibah. ⁴⁵But righteous judges will sentence them to the punishment of women who commit adultery and shed blood, because they are adulterous and blood is on their hands.

⁴⁶"This is what the Sovereign LORD says: Bring a mob against them and give them over to terror and plunder. ⁴⁷The mob will stone them and cut them down with their swords; they will kill their sons and daughters and burn down their houses.

⁴⁸"So I will put an end to lewdness in the land, that all women may take warning and not imitate you. ⁴⁹You will suffer the penalty for your lewdness and bear the consequences of your sins of idolatry. Then you will know that I am the Sovereign LORD."

Jerusalem as a Cooking Pot

24 In the ninth year, in the tenth month on the tenth day, the word of the LORD came to me: ²"Son of man, record this date, this very date, because the king of Babylon has laid siege to Jerusalem this very day. ³Tell this rebellious people a parable and say to them: 'This is what the Sovereign LORD says:

"'Put on the cooking pot; put it on
    and pour water into it.
⁴Put into it the pieces of meat,
    all the choice pieces—the leg and
        the shoulder.
Fill it with the best of these bones;
⁵   take the pick of the flock.
Pile wood beneath it for the bones;
    bring it to a boil
    and cook the bones in it.

⁶"'For this is what the Sovereign Lᴏʀᴅ says:

"'Woe to the city of bloodshed,
to the pot now encrusted,
whose deposit will not go away!
Take the meat out piece by piece
in whatever order it comes.

⁷"'For the blood she shed is in her
midst:
She poured it on the bare rock;
she did not pour it on the ground,
where the dust would cover it.
⁸To stir up wrath and take revenge
I put her blood on the bare rock,
so that it would not be covered.

⁹"'Therefore this is what the Sovereign Lᴏʀᴅ says:

"'Woe to the city of bloodshed!
I, too, will pile the wood high.
¹⁰So heap on the wood
and kindle the fire.
Cook the meat well,
mixing in the spices;
and let the bones be charred.
¹¹Then set the empty pot on the coals
till it becomes hot and its copper
glows,
so that its impurities may be melted
and its deposit burned away.
¹²It has frustrated all efforts;
its heavy deposit has not been
removed,
not even by fire.

¹³"'Now your impurity is lewdness. Because I tried to cleanse you but you would not be cleansed from your impurity, you will not be clean again until my wrath against you has subsided.

¹⁴"'I the Lᴏʀᴅ have spoken. The time has come for me to act. I will not hold back; I will not have pity, nor will I relent. You will be judged according to your conduct and your actions, declares the Sovereign Lᴏʀᴅ.'"

Ezekiel's Wife Dies

¹⁵The word of the Lᴏʀᴅ came to me: ¹⁶"Son of man, with one blow I am about to take away from you the delight of your eyes. Yet do not lament or weep or shed any tears. ¹⁷Groan quietly; do not mourn for the dead. Keep your turban fastened and your sandals on your feet; do not cover your mustache and beard or eat the customary food of mourners."

¹⁸So I spoke to the people in the morning, and in the evening my wife died. The next morning I did as I had been commanded.

¹⁹Then the people asked me, "Won't you tell us what these things have to do with us? Why are you acting like this?"

²⁰So I said to them, "The word of the Lᴏʀᴅ came to me: ²¹Say to the people of Israel, 'This is what the Sovereign Lᴏʀᴅ says: I am about to desecrate my sanctuary—the stronghold in which you take pride, the delight of your eyes, the object of your affection. The sons and daughters you left behind will fall by the sword. ²²And you will do as I have done. You will not cover your mustache and beard or eat the customary food of mourners. ²³You will keep your turbans on your heads and your sandals on your feet. You will not mourn or weep but will waste away because of*ᵃ* your sins and groan among yourselves. ²⁴Ezekiel will be a sign to you; you will do just as he has done. When this happens, you will know that I am the Sovereign Lᴏʀᴅ.'

²⁵"And you, son of man, on the day I take away their stronghold, their joy and glory, the delight of their eyes, their heart's desire, and their sons and daughters as well— ²⁶on that day a fugitive will come to tell you the news. ²⁷At that time your mouth will be opened; you will speak with him and will no longer be silent. So you will be a sign to them, and they will know that I am the Lᴏʀᴅ."

A Prophecy Against Ammon

25 The word of the Lᴏʀᴅ came to me: ²"Son of man, set your face against the Ammonites and prophesy against them. ³Say to them, 'Hear the word of the Sov-

---

ᵃ 23 Or away in

reign LORD. This is what the Sovereign LORD says: Because you said "Aha!" over my sanctuary when it was desecrated and over the land of Israel when it was laid waste and over the people of Judah when they went into exile, [4]therefore I am going to give you to the people of the East as a possession. They will set up their camps and pitch their tents among you; they will eat your fruit and drink your milk. [5]I will turn Rabbah into a pasture for camels and Ammon into a resting place for sheep. Then you will know that I am the LORD. [6]For this is what the Sovereign LORD says: Because you have clapped your hands and stamped your feet, rejoicing with all the malice of your heart against the land of Israel, [7]therefore I will stretch out my hand against you and give you as plunder to the nations. I will wipe you out from among the nations and exterminate you from the countries. I will destroy you, and you will know that I am the LORD.'"

A Prophecy Against Moab

[8]"This is what the Sovereign LORD says: 'Because Moab and Seir said, "Look, Judah has become like all the other nations," [9]therefore I will expose the flank of Moab, beginning at its frontier towns— Beth Jeshimoth, Baal Meon and Kiriathaim—the glory of that land. [10]I will give Moab along with the Ammonites to the people of the East as a possession, so that the Ammonites will not be remembered among the nations; [11]and I will inflict punishment on Moab. Then they will know that I am the LORD.'"

A Prophecy Against Edom

[12]"This is what the Sovereign LORD says: 'Because Edom took revenge on Judah and became very guilty by doing so, [13]therefore this is what the Sovereign LORD says: I will stretch out my hand against Edom and kill both man and beast. I will lay it waste, and from Teman to Dedan they will fall by the sword. [14]I will take vengeance on Edom by the hand of my people Israel, and they will deal with Edom in accordance with my

anger and my wrath; they will know my vengeance, declares the Sovereign LORD.'"

A Prophecy Against Philistia

[15]"This is what the Sovereign LORD says: 'Because the Philistines acted in vengeance and took revenge with malice in their hearts, and with ancient hostility sought to destroy Judah, [16]therefore this is what the Sovereign LORD says: I am about to stretch out my hand against the Philistines, and I will wipe out the Kerethites and destroy those remaining along the coast. [17]I will carry out great vengeance on them and punish them in my wrath. Then they will know that I am the LORD, when I take vengeance on them.'"

A Prophecy Against Tyre

26 In the eleventh month of the twelfth[a] year, on the first day of the month, the word of the LORD came to me: [2]"Son of man, because Tyre has said of Jerusalem, 'Aha! The gate to the nations is broken, and its doors have swung open to me; now that she lies in ruins I will prosper,' [3]therefore this is what the Sovereign LORD says: I am against you, Tyre, and I will bring many nations against you, like the sea casting up its waves. [4]They will destroy the walls of Tyre and pull down her towers; I will scrape away her rubble and make her a bare rock. [5]Out in the sea she will become a place to spread fishnets, for I have spoken, declares the Sovereign LORD. She will become plunder for the nations, [6]and her settlements on the mainland will be ravaged by the sword. Then they will know that I am the LORD.

[7]"For this is what the Sovereign LORD says: From the north I am going to bring against Tyre Nebuchadnezzar[b] king of Babylon, king of kings, with horses and chariots, with horsemen and a great army. [8]He will ravage your settlements on the

---

[a] 1 Probable reading of the original Hebrew text; Masoretic Text does not have *month of the twelfth*.   [b] 7 Hebrew *Nebuchadrezzar*, of which *Nebuchadnezzar* is a variant; here and often in Ezekiel and Jeremiah

mainland with the sword; he will set up siege works against you, build a ramp up to your walls and raise his shields against you. ⁹He will direct the blows of his battering rams against your walls and demolish your towers with his weapons. ¹⁰His horses will be so many that they will cover you with dust. Your walls will tremble at the noise of the warhorses, wagons and chariots when he enters your gates as men enter a city whose walls have been broken through. ¹¹The hooves of his horses will trample all your streets; he will kill your people with the sword, and your strong pillars will fall to the ground. ¹²They will plunder your wealth and loot your merchandise; they will break down your walls and demolish your fine houses and throw your stones, timber and rubble into the sea. ¹³I will put an end to your noisy songs, and the music of your harps will be heard no more. ¹⁴I will make you a bare rock, and you will become a place to spread fishnets. You will never be rebuilt, for I the LORD have spoken, declares the Sovereign LORD.

¹⁵"This is what the Sovereign LORD says to Tyre: Will not the coastlands tremble at the sound of your fall, when the wounded groan and the slaughter takes place in you? ¹⁶Then all the princes of the coast will step down from their thrones and lay aside their robes and take off their embroidered garments. Clothed with terror, they will sit on the ground, trembling every moment, appalled at you. ¹⁷Then they will take up a lament concerning you and say to you:

"'How you are destroyed, city of renown,
      peopled by men of the sea!
You were a power on the seas,
      you and your citizens;
you put your terror
      on all who lived there.
¹⁸Now the coastlands tremble
      on the day of your fall;
the islands in the sea
      are terrified at your collapse.'

¹⁹"This is what the Sovereign LORD says: When I make you a desolate city, like cities no longer inhabited, and when I bring the ocean depths over you and its vast waters cover you, ²⁰then I will bring you down with those who go down to the pit, to the people of long ago. I will make you dwell in the earth below, as in ancient ruins, with those who go down to the pit, and you will not return or take your place*a* in the land of the living. ²¹I will bring you to a horrible end and you will be no more. You will be sought, but you will never again be found, declares the Sovereign LORD."

A Lament Over Tyre

27 The word of the LORD came to me: ²"Son of man, take up a lament concerning Tyre. ³Say to Tyre, situated at the gateway to the sea, merchant of peoples on many coasts, 'This is what the Sovereign LORD says:

"'You say, Tyre,
      "I am perfect in beauty."
⁴Your domain was on the high seas;
      your builders brought your beauty
            to perfection.
⁵They made all your timbers
      of juniper from Senir*b*;
they took a cedar from Lebanon
      to make a mast for you.
⁶Of oaks from Bashan
      they made your oars;
of cypress wood*c* from the coasts of
            Cyprus
they made your deck, adorned with
            ivory.
⁷Fine embroidered linen from Egypt
            was your sail
      and served as your banner;
your awnings were of blue and
            purple
      from the coasts of Elishah.
⁸Men of Sidon and Arvad were your
            oarsmen;
      your skilled men, Tyre, were aboard
            as your sailors.

a 20 Septuagint; Hebrew *return, and I will give glory*   *b 5* That is, Mount Hermon
c 6 Targum; the Masoretic Text has a different division of the consonants.

⁹Veteran craftsmen of Byblos were on board
  as shipwrights to caulk your seams.
All the ships of the sea and their sailors
  came alongside to trade for your wares.

¹⁰"Men of Persia, Lydia and Put
  served as soldiers in your army.
They hung their shields and helmets
  on your walls,
  bringing you splendor.
¹¹Men of Arvad and Helek
  guarded your walls on every side;
men of Gammad
  were in your towers.
They hung their shields around your
  walls;
  they brought your beauty to
    perfection.

¹²"Tarshish did business with you because of your great wealth of goods; they exchanged silver, iron, tin and lead for your merchandise.

¹³"Greece, Tubal and Meshek did business with you; they traded human beings and articles of bronze for your wares.

¹⁴"Men of Beth Togarmah exchanged chariot horses, cavalry horses and mules for your merchandise.

¹⁵"The men of Rhodes*ᵃ* traded with you, and many coastlands were your customers; they paid you with ivory tusks and ebony.

¹⁶"Aram*ᵇ* did business with you because of your many products; they exchanged turquoise, purple fabric, embroidered work, fine linen, coral and rubies for your merchandise.

¹⁷"Judah and Israel traded with you; they exchanged wheat from Minnith and confections,*ᶜ* honey, olive oil and balm for your wares.

¹⁸"Damascus did business with you because of your many products and great wealth of goods. They offered wine from Helbon, wool from Zahar ¹⁹and casks of wine from Izal in exchange for your wares: wrought iron, cassia and calamus.

²⁰"Dedan traded in saddle blankets with you.

²¹"'Arabia and all the princes of Kedar were your customers; they did business with you in lambs, rams and goats.

²²"'The merchants of Sheba and Raamah traded with you; for your merchandise they exchanged the finest of all kinds of spices and precious stones, and gold.

²³"'Harran, Kanneh and Eden and merchants of Sheba, Ashur and Kilmad traded with you. ²⁴In your marketplace they traded with you beautiful garments, blue fabric, embroidered work and multicolored rugs with cords twisted and tightly knotted.

²⁵"'The ships of Tarshish serve
  as carriers for your wares.
You are filled with heavy cargo
  as you sail the sea.
²⁶Your oarsmen take you
  out to the high seas.
But the east wind will break you to
    pieces
  far out at sea.
²⁷Your wealth, merchandise and wares,
  your mariners, sailors and
    shipwrights,
your merchants and all your
    soldiers,
  and everyone else on board
will sink into the heart of the sea
  on the day of your shipwreck.
²⁸The shorelands will quake
  when your sailors cry out.
²⁹All who handle the oars
  will abandon their ships;
the mariners and all the sailors
  will stand on the shore.
³⁰They will raise their voice
  and cry bitterly over you;
they will sprinkle dust on their heads
  and roll in ashes.
³¹They will shave their heads because of
    you
  and will put on sackcloth.
They will weep over you with anguish
    of soul
  and with bitter mourning.

ᵃ 15 Septuagint; Hebrew *Dedan*   *ᵇ 16* Most Hebrew manuscripts; some Hebrew manuscripts and Syriac *Edom*   *ᶜ 17* The meaning of the Hebrew for this word is uncertain.

³² As they wail and mourn over you,
  they will take up a lament
    concerning you:
"Who was ever silenced like Tyre,
  surrounded by the sea?"
³³ When your merchandise went out on
    the seas,
  you satisfied many nations;
with your great wealth and your wares
  you enriched the kings of the earth.
³⁴ Now you are shattered by the sea
  in the depths of the waters;
your wares and all your company
  have gone down with you.
³⁵ All who live in the coastlands
  are appalled at you;
their kings shudder with horror
  and their faces are distorted with fear.
³⁶ The merchants among the nations
    scoff at you;
  you have come to a horrible end
  and will be no more.'"

A Prophecy Against the King of Tyre

28 The word of the Lord came
to me: ²"Son of man, say to
the ruler of Tyre, 'This is
what the Sovereign Lord says:

"'In the pride of your heart
  you say, "I am a god;
I sit on the throne of a god
  in the heart of the seas."
But you are a mere mortal and not a
    god,
  though you think you are as wise as
    a god.
³ Are you wiser than Daniel*ᵃ*?
  Is no secret hidden from you?
⁴ By your wisdom and understanding
  you have gained wealth for yourself
and amassed gold and silver
  in your treasuries.
⁵ By your great skill in trading
  you have increased your wealth,
and because of your wealth
  your heart has grown proud.

⁶ "'Therefore this is what the Sovereign
Lord says:

"'Because you think you are wise,
  as wise as a god,

⁷ I am going to bring foreigners against
    you,
  the most ruthless of nations;
they will draw their swords against
    your beauty and wisdom
  and pierce your shining splendor.
⁸ They will bring you down to the pit,
  and you will die a violent death
  in the heart of the seas.
⁹ Will you then say, "I am a god,"
  in the presence of those who kill you?
You will be but a mortal, not a god,
  in the hands of those who slay you.
¹⁰ You will die the death of the
    uncircumcised
  at the hands of foreigners.

I have spoken, declares the Sovereign
Lord.'"

¹¹ The word of the Lord came to me:
¹² "Son of man, take up a lament concerning the king of Tyre and say to him: 'This is what the Sovereign Lord says:

"'You were the seal of perfection,
  full of wisdom and perfect in beauty.
¹³ You were in Eden,
  the garden of God;
every precious stone adorned you:
  carnelian, chrysolite and emerald,
  topaz, onyx and jasper,
  lapis lazuli, turquoise and beryl.*ᵇ*
Your settings and mountings*ᶜ* were
    made of gold;
  on the day you were created they
    were prepared.
¹⁴ You were anointed as a guardian
    cherub,
  for so I ordained you.
You were on the holy mount of God;
  you walked among the fiery stones.
¹⁵ You were blameless in your ways
  from the day you were created
  till wickedness was found in you.
¹⁶ Through your widespread trade
  you were filled with violence,
  and you sinned.

ᵃ 3 Or *Danel,* a man of renown in ancient
literature   *ᵇ 13* The precise identification of
some of these precious stones is uncertain.
ᶜ 13 The meaning of the Hebrew for this phrase
is uncertain.

So I drove you in disgrace from the
mount of God,
and I expelled you, guardian cherub,
from among the fiery stones.
¹⁷ Your heart became proud
on account of your beauty,
and you corrupted your wisdom
because of your splendor.
So I threw you to the earth;
I made a spectacle of you before
kings.
¹⁸ By your many sins and dishonest trade
you have desecrated your
sanctuaries.

So I made a fire come out from you,
and it consumed you,
and I reduced you to ashes on the
ground
in the sight of all who were
watching.
¹⁹ All the nations who knew you
are appalled at you;
you have come to a horrible end
and will be no more.'"

A Prophecy Against Sidon

²⁰ The word of the LORD came to me:
²¹ "Son of man, set your face against Sidon;

Ezekiel 28

Ezekiel was odd for God.

Ezekiel wasn't content just to speak the Lord's messages. He had to act them out. In the process of following the Lord's dramatic directions, he sometimes looked incredibly odd for God.

Look back to Ezekiel 4, for example. The prophet took a clay tablet and sketched a picture of Jerusalem under attack, including details like battering rams, siege ramps and camped-out soldiers. He added an iron pan and acted out the story. Next he laid on his left side for 390 days, a day for each year of sins committed by Israel. Then he flipped to his right side for 40 days, a day for each year of Judah's sins. The Lord even gave Ezekiel precise directions for grains he should eat, including instructions about cooking his food over human excrement, a sign of the defiled food God's people would be forced to eat in captivity.

The prophet followed other strange instructions from God. He shaved his head bald (see Ezekiel 5:1 – 4). He locked himself in his house (see Ezekiel 3:24). And he didn't grieve when his wife died (see Ezekiel 24:15 – 19).

If God weren't the inspiration for these strange dramas, we might see Ezekiel as a very strange street preacher. But at the start of his ministry Ezekiel said, "The heavens were opened and I saw visions of God" (Ezekiel 1:1). This prophet's world was full of colorful visions of God and divine plans to rebuild Israel. This man was willing to do whatever it took to make sure everyone got his point.

You can find Ezekiel in the book named after him.

UNSHAKEN *people*

prophesy against her ²²and say: 'This is what the Sovereign LORD says:

> "'I am against you, Sidon,
>> and among you I will display my
>>> glory.
> You will know that I am the LORD,
>> when I inflict punishment on you
>> and within you am proved to be
>>> holy.
> ²³I will send a plague upon you
>> and make blood flow in your
>>> streets.
> The slain will fall within you,
>> with the sword against you on every
>>> side.
> Then you will know that I am the
>> LORD.

²⁴"'No longer will the people of Israel have malicious neighbors who are painful briers and sharp thorns. Then they will know that I am the Sovereign LORD.

²⁵"'This is what the Sovereign LORD says: When I gather the people of Israel from the nations where they have been scattered, I will be proved holy through them in the sight of the nations. Then they will live in their own land, which I gave to my servant Jacob. ²⁶They will live there in safety and will build houses and plant vineyards; they will live in safety when I inflict punishment on all their neighbors who maligned them. Then they will know that I am the LORD their God.'"

A Prophecy Against Egypt
Judgment on Pharaoh

29 In the tenth year, in the tenth month on the twelfth day, the word of the LORD came to me: ²"Son of man, set your face against Pharaoh king of Egypt and prophesy against him and against all Egypt. ³Speak to him and say: 'This is what the Sovereign LORD says:

> "'I am against you, Pharaoh king of
>> Egypt,
>> you great monster lying among your
>>> streams.
> You say, "The Nile belongs to me;
>> I made it for myself."

> ⁴But I will put hooks in your jaws
>> and make the fish of your streams
>>> stick to your scales.
> I will pull you out from among your
>>> streams,
>> with all the fish sticking to your
>>> scales.
> ⁵I will leave you in the desert,
>> you and all the fish of your streams.
> You will fall on the open field
>> and not be gathered or picked up.
> I will give you as food
>> to the beasts of the earth and the
>>> birds of the sky.

⁶Then all who live in Egypt will know that I am the LORD.

> "'You have been a staff of reed for the people of Israel. ⁷When they grasped you with their hands, you splintered and you tore open their shoulders; when they leaned on you, you broke and their backs were wrenched.^a

⁸"'Therefore this is what the Sovereign LORD says: I will bring a sword against you and kill both man and beast. ⁹Egypt will become a desolate wasteland. Then they will know that I am the LORD.

> "'Because you said, "The Nile is mine; I made it," ¹⁰therefore I am against you and against your streams, and I will make the land of Egypt a ruin and a desolate waste from Migdol to Aswan, as far as the border of Cush.^b ¹¹The foot of neither man nor beast will pass through it; no one will live there for forty years. ¹²I will make the land of Egypt desolate among devastated lands, and her cities will lie desolate forty years among ruined cities. And I will disperse the Egyptians among the nations and scatter them through the countries.

¹³"'Yet this is what the Sovereign LORD says: At the end of forty years I will gather the Egyptians from the nations where they were scattered. ¹⁴I will bring them back from captivity and return them to Upper Egypt, the land of their ancestry. There they will be a lowly kingdom. ¹⁵It

---

^a 7 Syriac (see also Septuagint and Vulgate);
Hebrew *and you caused their backs to stand*
^b 10 That is, the upper Nile region

will be the lowliest of kingdoms and will never again exalt itself above the other nations. I will make it so weak that it will never again rule over the nations. ¹⁶ Egypt will no longer be a source of confidence for the people of Israel but will be a reminder of their sin in turning to her for help. Then they will know that I am the Sovereign Lord.'"

Nebuchadnezzar's Reward

¹⁷ In the twenty-seventh year, in the first month on the first day, the word of the Lord came to me: ¹⁸ "Son of man, Nebuchadnezzar king of Babylon drove his army in a hard campaign against Tyre; every head was rubbed bare and every shoulder made raw. Yet he and his army got no reward from the campaign he led against Tyre. ¹⁹ Therefore this is what the Sovereign Lord says: I am going to give Egypt to Nebuchadnezzar king of Babylon, and he will carry off its wealth. He will loot and plunder the land as pay for his army. ²⁰ I have given him Egypt as a reward for his efforts because he and his army did it for me, declares the Sovereign Lord. ²¹ "On that day I will make a horn^a grow for the Israelites, and I will open your mouth among them. Then they will know that I am the Lord."

A Lament Over Egypt

30 The word of the Lord came to me: ² "Son of man, prophesy and say: 'This is what the Sovereign Lord says:

"'Wail and say,
  "Alas for that day!"
³ For the day is near,
  the day of the Lord is near—
a day of clouds,
  a time of doom for the nations.
⁴ A sword will come against Egypt,
  and anguish will come upon Cush.^b
When the slain fall in Egypt,
  her wealth will be carried away
  and her foundations torn down.

⁵ Cush and Libya, Lydia and all Arabia, Kub and the people of the covenant land will fall by the sword along with Egypt.

⁶ "'This is what the Lord says:

"'The allies of Egypt will fall
  and her proud strength will fail.
From Migdol to Aswan
  they will fall by the sword within her,
    declares the Sovereign Lord.
⁷ "'They will be desolate
  among desolate lands,
and their cities will lie
  among ruined cities.
⁸ Then they will know that I am the
  Lord,
when I set fire to Egypt
  and all her helpers are crushed.

⁹ "'On that day messengers will go out from me in ships to frighten Cush out of her complacency. Anguish will take hold of them on the day of Egypt's doom, for it is sure to come.

¹⁰ "'This is what the Sovereign Lord says:

"'I will put an end to the hordes of
  Egypt
  by the hand of Nebuchadnezzar
    king of Babylon.
¹¹ He and his army—the most ruthless
  of nations—
  will be brought in to destroy the
    land.
They will draw their swords against
  Egypt
  and fill the land with the slain.
¹² I will dry up the waters of the Nile
  and sell the land to an evil nation;
by the hand of foreigners
  I will lay waste the land and
    everything in it.

I the Lord have spoken.

¹³ "'This is what the Sovereign Lord says:

"'I will destroy the idols
  and put an end to the images in
    Memphis.
No longer will there be a prince in
  Egypt,
  and I will spread fear throughout
    the land.

^a 21 Horn here symbolizes strength.
^b 4 That is, the upper Nile region; also in verses 5 and 9

1001

¹⁴I will lay waste Upper Egypt,
　　set fire to Zoan
　　and inflict punishment on Thebes.
¹⁵I will pour out my wrath on Pelusium,
　　the stronghold of Egypt,
　　and wipe out the hordes of Thebes.
¹⁶I will set fire to Egypt;
　　Pelusium will writhe in agony.
Thebes will be taken by storm;
　　Memphis will be in constant
　　　distress.
¹⁷The young men of Heliopolis and
　　　Bubastis
　　will fall by the sword,
　　and the cities themselves will go
　　　into captivity.
¹⁸Dark will be the day at Tahpanhes
　　when I break the yoke of Egypt;
　　there her proud strength will come
　　　to an end.
She will be covered with clouds,
　　and her villages will go into
　　　captivity.
¹⁹So I will inflict punishment on Egypt,
　　and they will know that I am the
　　　LORD.'"

Pharaoh's Arms Are Broken

²⁰In the eleventh year, in the first month on the seventh day, the word of the LORD came to me: ²¹"Son of man, I have broken the arm of Pharaoh king of Egypt. It has not been bound up to be healed or put in a splint so that it may become strong enough to hold a sword. ²²Therefore this is what the Sovereign LORD says: I am against Pharaoh king of Egypt. I will break both his arms, the good arm as well as the broken one, and make the sword fall from his hand. ²³I will disperse the Egyptians among the nations and scatter them through the countries. ²⁴I will strengthen the arms of the king of Babylon and put my sword in his hand, but I will break the arms of Pharaoh, and he will groan before him like a mortally wounded man. ²⁵I will strengthen the arms of the king of Babylon, but the arms of Pharaoh will fall limp. Then they will know that I am the LORD, when I put my sword into the hand of the king of Babylon and he brandish-

es it against Egypt. ²⁶I will disperse the Egyptians among the nations and scatter them through the countries. Then they will know that I am the LORD."

Pharaoh as a Felled Cedar of Lebanon

31 In the eleventh year, in the third month on the first day, the word of the LORD came to me: ²"Son of man, say to Pharaoh king of Egypt and to his hordes:

"'Who can be compared with you in
　　majesty?
³Consider Assyria, once a cedar in
　　Lebanon,
　　with beautiful branches
　　　overshadowing the forest;
it towered on high,
　　its top above the thick foliage.
⁴The waters nourished it,
　　deep springs made it grow tall;
their streams flowed
　　all around its base
and sent their channels
　　to all the trees of the field.
⁵So it towered higher
　　than all the trees of the field;
its boughs increased
　　and its branches grew long,
　　spreading because of abundant
　　　waters.
⁶All the birds of the sky
　　nested in its boughs,
all the animals of the wild
　　gave birth under its branches;
all the great nations
　　lived in its shade.
⁷It was majestic in beauty,
　　with its spreading boughs,
for its roots went down
　　to abundant waters.
⁸The cedars in the garden of God
　　could not rival it,
nor could the junipers
　　equal its boughs,
nor could the plane trees
　　compare with its branches—
no tree in the garden of God
　　could match its beauty.
⁹I made it beautiful
　　with abundant branches,

the envy of all the trees of Eden
  in the garden of God.

10 "'Therefore this is what the Sovereign Lord says: Because the great cedar towered over the thick foliage, and because it was proud of its height, 11 I gave it into the hands of the ruler of the nations, for him to deal with according to its wickedness. I cast it aside, 12 and the most ruthless of foreign nations cut it down and left it. Its boughs fell on the mountains and in all the valleys; its branches lay broken in all the ravines of the land. All the nations of the earth came out from under its shade and left it. 13 All the birds settled on the fallen tree, and all the wild animals lived among its branches. 14 Therefore no other trees by the waters are ever to tower proudly on high, lifting their tops above the thick foliage. No other trees so well-watered are ever to reach such a height; they are all destined for death, for the earth below, among mortals who go down to the realm of the dead.

15 "'This is what the Sovereign Lord says: On the day it was brought down to the realm of the dead I covered the deep springs with mourning for it; I held back its streams, and its abundant waters were restrained. Because of it I clothed Lebanon with gloom, and all the trees of the field withered away. 16 I made the nations tremble at the sound of its fall when I brought it down to the realm of the dead to be with those who go down to the pit. Then all the trees of Eden, the choicest and best of Lebanon, the well-watered trees, were consoled in the earth below. 17 They too, like the great cedar, had gone down to the realm of the dead, to those killed by the sword, along with the armed men who lived in its shade among the nations.

18 "'Which of the trees of Eden can be compared with you in splendor and majesty? Yet you, too, will be brought down with the trees of Eden to the earth below; you will lie among the uncircumcised, with those killed by the sword.

"'This is Pharaoh and all his hordes, declares the Sovereign Lord.'"

A Lament Over Pharaoh

32 In the twelfth year, in the twelfth month on the first day, the word of the Lord came to me: 2 "Son of man, take up a lament concerning Pharaoh king of Egypt and say to him:

"'You are like a lion among the
    nations;
  you are like a monster in the seas
thrashing about in your streams,
  churning the water with your feet
  and muddying the streams.

3 "'This is what the Sovereign Lord says:

"'With a great throng of people
  I will cast my net over you,
  and they will haul you up in my net.
4 I will throw you on the land
  and hurl you on the open field.
I will let all the birds of the sky settle
    on you
  and all the animals of the wild
    gorge themselves on you.
5 I will spread your flesh on the
    mountains
  and fill the valleys with your
    remains.
6 I will drench the land with your
    flowing blood
  all the way to the mountains,
  and the ravines will be filled with
    your flesh.
7 When I snuff you out, I will cover the
    heavens
  and darken their stars;
I will cover the sun with a cloud,
  and the moon will not give its
    light.
8 All the shining lights in the heavens
  I will darken over you;
  I will bring darkness over your land,
    declares the Sovereign Lord.
9 I will trouble the hearts of many
    peoples
  when I bring about your destruction
    among the nations,
  among[a] lands you have not known.

a 9 Hebrew; Septuagint *bring you into captivity among the nations, / to*

¹⁰ I will cause many peoples to be
appalled at you,
and their kings will shudder with
horror because of you
when I brandish my sword before
them.
On the day of your downfall
each of them will tremble
every moment for his life.

¹¹ "'For this is what the Sovereign Lord
says:

"'The sword of the king of Babylon
will come against you.
¹² I will cause your hordes to fall
by the swords of mighty men—
the most ruthless of all nations.
They will shatter the pride of Egypt,
and all her hordes will be
overthrown.
¹³ I will destroy all her cattle
from beside abundant waters
no longer to be stirred by the foot of
man
or muddied by the hooves of cattle.
¹⁴ Then I will let her waters settle
and make her streams flow like oil,
declares the Sovereign Lord.
¹⁵ When I make Egypt desolate
and strip the land of everything
in it,
when I strike down all who live there,
then they will know that I am the
Lord.'

¹⁶ "This is the lament they will chant
for her. The daughters of the nations will
chant it; for Egypt and all her hordes
they will chant it, declares the Sovereign
Lord."

Egypt's Descent Into the Realm of the Dead

¹⁷ In the twelfth year, on the fifteenth
day of the month, the word of the Lord
came to me: ¹⁸ "Son of man, wail for the
hordes of Egypt and consign to the earth
below both her and the daughters of
mighty nations, along with those who go
down to the pit. ¹⁹ Say to them, 'Are you
more favored than others? Go down and
be laid among the uncircumcised.' ²⁰ They
will fall among those killed by the sword.

The sword is drawn; let her be dragged
off with all her hordes. ²¹ From within the
realm of the dead the mighty leaders will
say of Egypt and her allies, 'They have
come down and they lie with the uncircumcised, with those killed by the sword.'

²² "Assyria is there with her whole army;
she is surrounded by the graves of all her
slain, all who have fallen by the sword.
²³ Their graves are in the depths of the pit
and her army lies around her grave. All
who had spread terror in the land of the
living are slain, fallen by the sword.

²⁴ "Elam is there, with all her hordes
around her grave. All of them are slain,
fallen by the sword. All who had spread
terror in the land of the living went down
uncircumcised to the earth below. They
bear their shame with those who go down
to the pit. ²⁵ A bed is made for her among
the slain, with all her hordes around her
grave. All of them are uncircumcised,
killed by the sword. Because their terror
had spread in the land of the living, they
bear their shame with those who go down
to the pit; they are laid among the slain.

²⁶ "Meshek and Tubal are there, with
all their hordes around their graves. All
of them are uncircumcised, killed by the
sword because they spread their terror in
the land of the living. ²⁷ But they do not lie
with the fallen warriors of old,^a who went
down to the realm of the dead with their
weapons of war—their swords placed un-
der their heads and their shields^b resting
on their bones—though these warriors
also had terrorized the land of the living.

²⁸ "You too, Pharaoh, will be broken and
will lie among the uncircumcised, with
those killed by the sword.

²⁹ "Edom is there, her kings and all her
princes; despite their power, they are laid
with those killed by the sword. They lie
with the uncircumcised, with those who
go down to the pit.

³⁰ "All the princes of the north and all
the Sidonians are there; they went down

^a 27 Septuagint; Hebrew *warriors who were
uncircumcised*   ^b 27 Probable reading of the
original Hebrew text; Masoretic Text
punishment

with the slain in disgrace despite the terror caused by their power. They lie uncircumcised with those killed by the sword and bear their shame with those who go down to the pit.

³¹"Pharaoh—he and all his army—will see them and he will be consoled for all his hordes that were killed by the sword, declares the Sovereign LORD. ³²Although I had him spread terror in the land of the living, Pharaoh and all his hordes will be laid among the uncircumcised, with those killed by the sword, declares the Sovereign LORD."

Renewal of Ezekiel's Call as Watchman

33 The word of the LORD came to me: ²"Son of man, speak to your people and say to them: 'When I bring the sword against a land, and the people of the land choose one of their men and make him their watchman, ³and he sees the sword coming against the land and blows the trumpet to warn the people, ⁴then if anyone hears the trumpet but does not heed the warning and the sword comes and takes their life, their blood will be on their own head. ⁵Since they heard the sound of the trumpet but did not heed the warning, their blood will be on their own head. If they had heeded the warning, they would have saved themselves. ⁶But if the watchman sees the sword coming and does not blow the trumpet to warn the people and the sword comes and takes someone's life, that person's life will be taken because of their sin, but I will hold the watchman accountable for their blood.'

⁷"Son of man, I have made you a watchman for the people of Israel; so hear the word I speak and give them warning from me. ⁸When I say to the wicked, 'You wicked person, you will surely die,' and you do not speak out to dissuade them from their ways, that wicked person will die forᵃ their sin, and I will hold you accountable for their blood. ⁹But if you do warn the wicked person to turn from their ways and they do not do so, they will die for their sin, though you yourself will be saved.

¹⁰"Son of man, say to the Israelites, 'This is what you are saying: "Our offenses and sins weigh us down, and we are wasting away because ofᵇ them. How then can we live?"' ¹¹Say to them, 'As surely as I live, declares the Sovereign LORD, I take no pleasure in the death of the wicked, but rather that they turn from their ways and live. Turn! Turn from your evil ways! Why will you die, people of Israel?'

¹²"Therefore, son of man, say to your people, 'If someone who is righteous disobeys, that person's former righteousness will count for nothing. And if someone who is wicked repents, that person's former wickedness will not bring condemnation. The righteous person who sins will not be allowed to live even though they were formerly righteous.' ¹³If I tell a righteous person that they will surely live, but then they trust in their righteousness and do evil, none of the righteous things that person has done will be remembered; they will die for the evil they have done. ¹⁴And if I say to a wicked person, 'You will surely die,' but they then turn away from their sin and do what is just and right— ¹⁵if they give back what they took in pledge for a loan, return what they have stolen, follow the decrees that give life, and do no evil—that person will surely live; they will not die. ¹⁶None of the sins that person has committed will be remembered against them. They have done what is just and right; they will surely live.

¹⁷"Yet your people say, 'The way of the Lord is not just.' But it is their way that is not just. ¹⁸If a righteous person turns from their righteousness and does evil, they will die for it. ¹⁹And if a wicked person turns away from their wickedness and does what is just and right, they will live by doing so. ²⁰Yet you Israelites say, 'The way of the Lord is not just.' But I will judge each of you according to your own ways."

Jerusalem's Fall Explained

²¹In the twelfth year of our exile, in the tenth month on the fifth day, a man who had escaped from Jerusalem came to me

ᵃ 8 Or *in*; also in verse 9   ᵇ 10 Or *away in*

and said, "The city has fallen!" ²²Now the evening before the man arrived, the hand of the Lord was on me, and he opened my mouth before the man came to me in the morning. So my mouth was opened and I was no longer silent.

²³Then the word of the Lord came to me: ²⁴"Son of man, the people living in those ruins in the land of Israel are saying, 'Abraham was only one man, yet he possessed the land. But we are many; surely the land has been given to us as our possession.' ²⁵Therefore say to them, 'This is what the Sovereign Lord says: Since you eat meat with the blood still in it and look to your idols and shed blood, should you then possess the land? ²⁶You rely on your sword, you do detestable things, and each of you defiles his neighbor's wife. Should you then possess the land?'

²⁷"Say this to them: 'This is what the Sovereign Lord says: As surely as I live, those who are left in the ruins will fall by the sword, those out in the country I will give to the wild animals to be devoured, and those in strongholds and caves will die of a plague. ²⁸I will make the land a desolate waste, and her proud strength will come to an end, and the mountains of Israel will become desolate so that no one will cross them. ²⁹Then they will know that I am the Lord, when I have made the land a desolate waste because of all the detestable things they have done.'

³⁰"As for you, son of man, your people are talking together about you by the walls and at the doors of the houses, saying to each other, 'Come and hear the message that has come from the Lord.' ³¹My people come to you, as they usually do, and sit before you to hear your words, but they do not put them into practice. Their mouths speak of love, but their hearts are greedy for unjust gain. ³²Indeed, to them you are nothing more than one who sings love songs with a beautiful voice and plays an instrument well, for they hear your words but do not put them into practice.

³³"When all this comes true—and it surely will—then they will know that a prophet has been among them."

The Lord Will Be Israel's Shepherd

34 The word of the Lord came to me: ²"Son of man, prophesy against the shepherds of Israel; prophesy and say to them: 'This is what the Sovereign Lord says: Woe to you shepherds of Israel who only take care of yourselves! Should not shepherds take care of the flock? ³You eat the curds, clothe yourselves with the wool and slaughter the choice animals, but you do not take care of the flock. ⁴You have not strengthened the weak or healed the sick or bound up the injured. You have not brought back the strays or searched for the lost. You have ruled them harshly and brutally. ⁵So they were scattered because there was no shepherd, and when they were scattered they became food for all the wild animals. ⁶My sheep wandered over all the mountains and on every high hill. They were scattered over the whole earth, and no one searched or looked for them.

⁷"'Therefore, you shepherds, hear the word of the Lord: ⁸As surely as I live, declares the Sovereign Lord, because my flock lacks a shepherd and so has been plundered and has become food for all the wild animals, and because my shepherds did not search for my flock but cared for themselves rather than for my flock, ⁹therefore, you shepherds, hear the word of the Lord: ¹⁰This is what the Sovereign Lord says: I am against the shepherds and will hold them accountable for my flock. I will remove them from tending the flock so that the shepherds can no longer feed themselves. I will rescue my flock from their mouths, and it will no longer be food for them.

¹¹"'For this is what the Sovereign Lord says: I myself will search for my sheep and look after them. ¹²As a shepherd looks after his scattered flock when he is with them, so will I look after my sheep. I will rescue them from all the places where they were scattered on a day of clouds and darkness. ¹³I will bring them out from the nations and gather them from the countries, and I will bring them into their own land. I will pasture them on the moun-

tains of Israel, in the ravines and in all the settlements in the land. ¹⁴I will tend them in a good pasture, and the mountain heights of Israel will be their grazing land. There they will lie down in good grazing land, and there they will feed in a rich pasture on the mountains of Israel. ¹⁵I myself will tend my sheep and have them lie down, declares the Sovereign LORD. ¹⁶I will search for the lost and bring back the strays. I will bind up the injured and strengthen the weak, but the sleek and the strong I will destroy. I will shepherd the flock with justice.

¹⁷"'As for you, my flock, this is what the Sovereign LORD says: I will judge between one sheep and another, and between rams and goats. ¹⁸Is it not enough for you to feed on the good pasture? Must you also trample the rest of your pasture with your feet? Is it not enough for you to drink clear water? Must you also muddy the rest with your feet? ¹⁹Must my flock feed on what you have trampled and drink what you have muddied with your feet?

²⁰"'Therefore this is what the Sovereign LORD says to them: See, I myself will judge between the fat sheep and the lean sheep. ²¹Because you shove with flank and shoulder, butting all the weak sheep with your horns until you have driven them away, ²²I will save my flock, and they will no longer be plundered. I will judge between one sheep and another. ²³I will place over them one shepherd, my servant David, and he will tend them; he will tend them and be their shepherd. ²⁴I the LORD will be their God, and my servant David will be prince among them. I the LORD have spoken.

²⁵"'I will make a covenant of peace with them and rid the land of savage beasts so that they may live in the wilderness and sleep in the forests in safety. ²⁶I will make them and the places surrounding my hill a blessing.ᵃ I will send down showers in season; there will be showers of blessing. ²⁷The trees will yield their fruit and the ground will yield its crops; the people will be secure in their land. They will know that I am the LORD, when I break the

ROCK SOLID promises

"I will send down showers in season; there will be showers of blessing." Ezekiel 34:26

God knows exactly what kind of refreshment you need and when you need it. Expect his blessings.

bars of their yoke and rescue them from the hands of those who enslaved them. ²⁸They will no longer be plundered by the nations, nor will wild animals devour them. They will live in safety, and no one will make them afraid. ²⁹I will provide for them a land renowned for its crops, and they will no longer be victims of famine in the land or bear the scorn of the nations. ³⁰Then they will know that I, the LORD their God, am with them and that they, the Israelites, are my people, declares the Sovereign LORD. ³¹You are my sheep, the sheep of my pasture, and I am your God, declares the Sovereign LORD.'"

A Prophecy Against Edom

35 The word of the LORD came to me: ²"Son of man, set your face against Mount Seir; prophesy against it ³and say: 'This is what the Sovereign LORD says: I am against you, Mount Seir, and I will stretch out my hand against you and make you a desolate waste. ⁴I will turn your towns into ruins and you will be desolate. Then you will know that I am the LORD.

⁵"'Because you harbored an ancient hostility and delivered the Israelites over to the sword at the time of their calamity,

ᵃ 26 Or I will cause them and the places surrounding my hill to be named in blessings (see Gen. 48:20); or I will cause them and the places surrounding my hill to be seen as blessed the time their punishment reached its climax, [6]therefore as surely as I live, declares the Sovereign Lord, I will give you over to bloodshed and it will pursue you. Since you did not hate bloodshed, bloodshed will pursue you. [7]I will make Mount Seir a desolate waste and cut off from it all who come and go. [8]I will fill your mountains with the slain; those killed by the sword will fall on your hills and in your valleys and in all your ravines. [9]I will make you desolate forever; your towns will not be inhabited. Then you will know that I am the Lord.

[10]"'Because you have said, "These two nations and countries will be ours and we will take possession of them," even though I the Lord was there, [11]therefore as surely as I live, declares the Sovereign Lord, I will treat you in accordance with the anger and jealousy you showed in your hatred of them and I will make myself known among them when I judge you. [12]Then you will know that I the Lord have heard all the contemptible things you have said against the mountains of Israel. You said, "They have been laid waste and have been given over to us to devour." [13]You boasted against me and spoke against me without restraint, and I heard it. [14]This is what the Sovereign Lord says: While the whole earth rejoices, I will make you desolate. [15]Because you rejoiced when the inheritance of Israel became desolate, that is how I will treat you. You will be desolate, Mount Seir, you and all of Edom. Then they will know that I am the Lord.'"

Hope for the Mountains of Israel

36 "Son of man, prophesy to the mountains of Israel and say, 'Mountains of Israel, hear the word of the Lord. [2]This is what the Sovereign Lord says: The enemy said of you, "Aha! The ancient heights have become our possession."' [3]Therefore prophesy and say, 'This is what the Sovereign Lord says: Because they ravaged and crushed you from every side so that you became the possession of the rest of the nations and the object of people's mali-

cious talk and slander, [4]therefore, mountains of Israel, hear the word of the Sovereign Lord: This is what the Sovereign Lord says to the mountains and hills, to the ravines and valleys, to the desolate ruins and the deserted towns that have been plundered and ridiculed by the rest of the nations around you— [5]this is what the Sovereign Lord says: In my burning zeal I have spoken against the rest of the nations, and against all Edom, for with glee and with malice in their hearts they made my land their own possession so that they might plunder its pastureland.' [6]Therefore prophesy concerning the land of Israel and say to the mountains and hills, to the ravines and valleys: 'This is what the Sovereign Lord says: I speak in my jealous wrath because you have suffered the scorn of the nations. [7]Therefore this is what the Sovereign Lord says: I swear with uplifted hand that the nations around you will also suffer scorn.

[8]"'But you, mountains of Israel, will produce branches and fruit for my people Israel, for they will soon come home. [9]I am concerned for you and will look on you with favor; you will be plowed and sown, [10]and I will cause many people to live on you—yes, all of Israel. The towns will be inhabited and the ruins rebuilt. [11]I will increase the number of people and animals living on you, and they will be fruitful and become numerous. I will settle people on you as in the past and will make you prosper more than before. Then you will know that I am the Lord. [12]I will cause people, my people Israel, to live on you. They will possess you, and you will be their inheritance; you will never again deprive them of their children.

[13]"'This is what the Sovereign Lord says: Because some say to you, "You devour people and deprive your nation of its children," [14]therefore you will no longer devour people or make your nation childless, declares the Sovereign Lord. [15]No longer will I make you hear the taunts of the nations, and no longer will you suffer the scorn of the peoples or cause your nation to fall, declares the Sovereign Lord.'"

Israel's Restoration Assured

¹⁶Again the word of the Lord came to me: ¹⁷"Son of man, when the people of Israel were living in their own land, they defiled it by their conduct and their actions. Their conduct was like a woman's monthly uncleanness in my sight. ¹⁸So I poured out my wrath on them because they had shed blood in the land and because they had defiled it with their idols. ¹⁹I dispersed them among the nations, and they were scattered through the countries; I judged them according to their conduct and their actions. ²⁰And wherever they went among the nations they profaned my holy name, for it was said of them, 'These are the Lord's people, and yet they had to leave his land.' ²¹I had concern for my holy name, which the people of Israel profaned among the nations where they had gone.

²²"Therefore say to the Israelites, 'This is what the Sovereign Lord says: It is not for your sake, people of Israel, that I am going to do these things, but for the sake of my holy name, which you have profaned among the nations where you have gone. ²³I will show the holiness of my great name, which has been profaned among the nations, the name you have profaned among them. Then the nations will know that I am the Lord, declares the Sovereign Lord, when I am proved holy through you before their eyes.

²⁴"'For I will take you out of the nations; I will gather you from all the countries and bring you back into your own land. ²⁵I will sprinkle clean water on you, and you will be clean; I will cleanse you from all your impurities and from all your idols. ²⁶I will give you a new heart and put a new spirit in you; I will remove from you your heart of stone and give you a heart of flesh. ²⁷And I will put my Spirit in you and move you to follow my decrees and be careful to keep my laws. ²⁸Then you will live in the land I gave your ancestors; you will be my people, and I will be your God. ²⁹I will save you from all your uncleanness. I will call for the grain and make it plentiful and will not bring famine upon you. ³⁰I will increase the fruit of the trees and the crops of the field, so that you will no longer suffer disgrace among the nations because of famine. ³¹Then you will remember your evil ways and wicked deeds, and you will loathe yourselves for your sins and detestable practices. ³²I want you to know that I am not doing this for your sake, declares the Sovereign Lord. Be ashamed and disgraced for your conduct, people of Israel!

³³"'This is what the Sovereign Lord says: On the day I cleanse you from all your sins, I will resettle your towns, and the ruins will be rebuilt. ³⁴The desolate land will be cultivated instead of lying desolate in the sight of all who pass through it. ³⁵They will say, "This land that was laid waste has become like the garden of Eden; the cities that were lying in ruins, desolate and destroyed, are now fortified and inhabited." ³⁶Then the nations around you that remain will know that I the Lord have rebuilt what was destroyed and have replanted what was desolate. I the Lord have spoken, and I will do it.'

³⁷"This is what the Sovereign Lord says: Once again I will yield to Israel's plea and do this for them: I will make their people as numerous as sheep, ³⁸as numerous as the flocks for offerings at Jerusalem during her appointed festivals. So will the ruined cities be filled with flocks of people. Then they will know that I am the Lord."

The Valley of Dry Bones

37 The hand of the Lord was on me, and he brought me out by the Spirit of the Lord and set me in the middle of a valley; it was full of bones. ²He led me back and forth among them, and I saw a great many bones on the floor of the valley, bones that were very dry. ³He asked me, "Son of man, can these bones live?"

I said, "Sovereign Lord, you alone know."

⁴Then he said to me, "Prophesy to these bones and say to them, 'Dry bones, hear the word of the Lord! ⁵This is what the Sovereign Lord says to these bones: I will

make breath[a] enter you, and you will come to life. [6]I will attach tendons to you and make flesh come upon you and cover you with skin; I will put breath in you, and you will come to life. Then you will know that I am the LORD.'"

[7]So I prophesied as I was commanded. And as I was prophesying, there was a noise, a rattling sound, and the bones came together, bone to bone. [8]I looked, and tendons and flesh appeared on them and skin covered them, but there was no breath in them.

[9]Then he said to me, "Prophesy to the breath; prophesy, son of man, and say to it, 'This is what the Sovereign LORD says: Come, breath, from the four winds and breathe into these slain, that they may live.'" [10]So I prophesied as he commanded me, and breath entered them; they came to life and stood up on their feet—a vast army.

[11]Then he said to me: "Son of man, these bones are the people of Israel. They say, 'Our bones are dried up and our hope is gone; we are cut off.' [12]Therefore prophesy and say to them: 'This is what the Sovereign LORD says: My people, I am going to open your graves and bring you up from them; I will bring you back to the land of Israel. [13]Then you, my people, will know that I am the LORD, when I open your graves and bring you up from them. [14]I will put my Spirit in you and you will live, and I will settle you in your own land. Then you will know that I the LORD have spoken, and I have done it, declares the LORD.'"

One Nation Under One King

[15]The word of the LORD came to me: [16]"Son of man, take a stick of wood and write on it, 'Belonging to Judah and the Israelites associated with him.' Then take another stick of wood, and write on it, 'Belonging to Joseph (that is, to Ephraim) and all the Israelites associated with him.' [17]Join them together into one stick so that they will become one in your hand.

[18]"When your people ask you, 'Won't you tell us what you mean by this?' [19]say

ROCK SOLID *promises*

"I will put my Spirit in you and you will live."
Ezekiel 37:14

You can't create spiritual life in yourself any more than you could decide to be born. God's Spirit gives you power.

to them, 'This is what the Sovereign LORD says: I am going to take the stick of Joseph—which is in Ephraim's hand—and of the Israelite tribes associated with him, and join it to Judah's stick. I will make them into a single stick of wood, and they will become one in my hand.' [20]Hold before their eyes the sticks you have written on [21]and say to them, 'This is what the Sovereign LORD says: I will take the Israelites out of the nations where they have gone. I will gather them from all around and bring them back into their own land. [22]I will make them one nation in the land, on the mountains of Israel. There will be one king over all of them and they will never again be two nations or be divided into two kingdoms. [23]They will no longer defile themselves with their idols and vile images or with any of their offenses, for I will save them from all their sinful backsliding,[b] and I will cleanse them. They will be my people, and I will be their God.

[24]"'My servant David will be king over them, and they will all have one shepherd. They will follow my laws and be careful to keep my decrees. [25]They will live in the land I gave to my servant Jacob, the land where your ancestors lived. They and their

---

[a] 5 The Hebrew for this word can also mean *wind* or *spirit* (see verses 6-14).   [b] 23 Many Hebrew manuscripts (see also Septuagint); most Hebrew manuscripts *all their dwelling places where they sinned*

children and their children's children will live there forever, and David my servant will be their prince forever. ²⁶I will make a covenant of peace with them; it will be an everlasting covenant. I will establish them and increase their numbers, and I will put my sanctuary among them forever. ²⁷My dwelling place will be with them; I will be their God, and they will be my people. ²⁸Then the nations will know that I the LORD make Israel holy, when my sanctuary is among them forever.'"

The LORD's Great Victory Over the Nations

38 The word of the LORD came to me: ²"Son of man, set your face against Gog, of the land of Magog, the chief prince of*ᵃ* Meshek and Tubal; prophesy against him ³and say: 'This is what the Sovereign LORD says: I am against you, Gog, chief prince of*ᵇ* Meshek and Tubal. ⁴I will turn you around, put hooks in your jaws and bring you out with your whole army—your horses, your horsemen fully armed, and a great horde with large and small shields, all of them brandishing their swords. ⁵Persia, Cush*ᶜ* and Put will be with them, all with shields and helmets, ⁶also Gomer with all its troops, and Beth Togarmah from the far north with all its troops—the many nations with you.

⁷"'Get ready; be prepared, you and all the hordes gathered about you, and take command of them. ⁸After many days you will be called to arms. In future years you will invade a land that has recovered from war, whose people were gathered from many nations to the mountains of Israel, which had long been desolate. They had been brought out from the nations, and now all of them live in safety. ⁹You and all your troops and the many nations with you will go up, advancing like a storm; you will be like a cloud covering the land.

¹⁰"'This is what the Sovereign LORD says: On that day thoughts will come into your mind and you will devise an evil scheme. ¹¹You will say, "I will invade a land of unwalled villages; I will attack a peaceful and unsuspecting people—all of them living without walls and without gates and bars. ¹²I will plunder and loot and turn my hand against the resettled ruins and the people gathered from the nations, rich in livestock and goods, living at the center of the land.*ᵈ*" ¹³Sheba and Dedan and the merchants of Tarshish and all her villages*ᵉ* will say to you, "Have you come to plunder? Have you gathered your hordes to loot, to carry off silver and gold, to take away livestock and goods and to seize much plunder?"'

¹⁴"Therefore, son of man, prophesy and say to Gog: 'This is what the Sovereign LORD says: In that day, when my people Israel are living in safety, will you not take notice of it? ¹⁵You will come from your place in the far north, you and many nations with you, all of them riding on horses, a great horde, a mighty army. ¹⁶You will advance against my people Israel like a cloud that covers the land. In days to come, Gog, I will bring you against my land, so that the nations may know me when I am proved holy through you before their eyes.

¹⁷"'This is what the Sovereign LORD says: You are the one I spoke of in former days by my servants the prophets of Israel. At that time they prophesied for years that I would bring you against them. ¹⁸This is what will happen in that day: When Gog attacks the land of Israel, my hot anger will be aroused, declares the Sovereign LORD. ¹⁹In my zeal and fiery wrath I declare that at that time there shall be a great earthquake in the land of Israel. ²⁰The fish in the sea, the birds in the sky, the beasts of the field, every creature that moves along the ground, and all the people on the face of the earth will tremble at my presence. The mountains will be overturned, the cliffs will crumble and every wall will fall to the ground. ²¹I will summon a sword against Gog on all my mountains, declares the Sovereign LORD. Every

---

ᵃ 2 Or *the prince of Rosh,*   *ᵇ 3* Or *Gog, prince of Rosh,*   *ᶜ 5* That is, the upper Nile region   *ᵈ 12* The Hebrew for this phrase means *the navel of the earth.*   *ᵉ 13* Or *her strong lions* man's sword will be against his brother. ²²I will execute judgment on him with plague and bloodshed; I will pour down torrents of rain, hailstones and burning sulfur on him and on his troops and on the many nations with him. ²³And so I will show my greatness and my holiness, and I will make myself known in the sight of many nations. Then they will know that I am the LORD.'

39 "Son of man, prophesy against Gog and say: 'This is what the Sovereign LORD says: I am against you, Gog, chief prince of*ᵃ* Meshek and Tubal. ²I will turn you around and drag you along. I will bring you from the far north and send you against the mountains of Israel. ³Then I will strike your bow from your left hand and make your arrows drop from your right hand. ⁴On the mountains of Israel you will fall, you and all your troops and the nations with you. I will give you as food to all kinds of carrion birds and to the wild animals. ⁵You will fall in the open field, for I have spoken, declares the Sovereign LORD. ⁶I will send fire on Magog and on those who live in safety in the coastlands, and they will know that I am the LORD.

⁷"'I will make known my holy name among my people Israel. I will no longer let my holy name be profaned, and the nations will know that I the LORD am the Holy One in Israel. ⁸It is coming! It will surely take place, declares the Sovereign LORD. This is the day I have spoken of.

⁹"'Then those who live in the towns of Israel will go out and use the weapons for fuel and burn them up — the small and large shields, the bows and arrows, the war clubs and spears. For seven years they will use them for fuel. ¹⁰They will not need to gather wood from the fields or cut it from the forests, because they will use the weapons for fuel. And they will plunder those who plundered them and loot those who looted them, declares the Sovereign LORD.

¹¹"'On that day I will give Gog a burial place in Israel, in the valley of those who travel east of the Sea. It will block the way of travelers, because Gog and all his hordes will be buried there. So it will be called the Valley of Hamon Gog.*ᵇ*

¹²"'For seven months the Israelites will be burying them in order to cleanse the land. ¹³All the people of the land will bury them, and the day I display my glory will be a memorable day for them, declares the Sovereign LORD. ¹⁴People will be continually employed in cleansing the land. They will spread out across the land and, along with others, they will bury any bodies that are lying on the ground.

"'After the seven months they will carry out a more detailed search. ¹⁵As they go through the land, anyone who sees a human bone will leave a marker beside it until the gravediggers bury it in the Valley of Hamon Gog, ¹⁶near a town called Hamonah.*ᶜ* And so they will cleanse the land.'

¹⁷"Son of man, this is what the Sovereign LORD says: Call out to every kind of bird and all the wild animals: 'Assemble and come together from all around to the sacrifice I am preparing for you, the great sacrifice on the mountains of Israel. There you will eat flesh and drink blood. ¹⁸You will eat the flesh of mighty men and drink the blood of the princes of the earth as if they were rams and lambs, goats and bulls — all of them fattened animals from Bashan. ¹⁹At the sacrifice I am preparing for you, you will eat fat till you are glutted and drink blood till you are drunk. ²⁰At my table you will eat your fill of horses and riders, mighty men and soldiers of every kind,' declares the Sovereign LORD.

²¹"I will display my glory among the nations, and all the nations will see the punishment I inflict and the hand I lay on them. ²²From that day forward the people of Israel will know that I am the LORD their God. ²³And the nations will know that the people of Israel went into exile for their sin, because they were unfaithful to me. So I hid my face from them and handed them over to their enemies, and they all fell by

---

ᵃ 1 Or *Gog, prince of Rosh,*   *ᵇ 11 Hamon Gog* means *hordes of Gog.*   *ᶜ 16 Hamonah* means *horde.*

the sword. ²⁴I dealt with them according to their uncleanness and their offenses, and I hid my face from them.

²⁵"Therefore this is what the Sovereign Lord says: I will now restore the fortunes of Jacob[a] and will have compassion on all the people of Israel, and I will be zealous for my holy name. ²⁶They will forget their shame and all the unfaithfulness they showed toward me when they lived in safety in their land with no one to make them afraid. ²⁷When I have brought them back from the nations and have gathered them from the countries of their enemies, I will be proved holy through them in the sight of many nations. ²⁸Then they will know that I am the Lord their God, for though I sent them into exile among the nations, I will gather them to their own land, not leaving any behind. ²⁹I will no longer hide my face from them, for I will pour out my Spirit on the people of Israel, declares the Sovereign Lord."

The Temple Area Restored

40 In the twenty-fifth year of our exile, at the beginning of the year, on the tenth of the month, in the fourteenth year after the fall of the city—on that very day the hand of the Lord was on me and he took me there. ²In visions of God he took me to the land of Israel and set me on a very high mountain, on whose south side were some buildings that looked like a city. ³He took me there, and I saw a man whose appearance was like bronze; he was standing in the gateway with a linen cord and a measuring rod in his hand. ⁴The man said to me, "Son of man, look carefully and listen closely and pay attention to everything I am going to show you, for that is why you have been brought here. Tell the people of Israel everything you see."

The East Gate to the Outer Court

⁵I saw a wall completely surrounding the temple area. The length of the measuring rod in the man's hand was six long cubits,[b] each of which was a cubit and a handbreadth. He measured the wall; it was one measuring rod thick and one rod high.

⁶Then he went to the east gate. He climbed its steps and measured the threshold of the gate; it was one rod deep.

[a] 25 Or *now bring Jacob back from captivity*
[b] 5 That is, about 11 feet or about 3.2 meters; also in verse 12. The long cubit of about 21 inches or about 53 centimeters is the basic unit of measurement of length throughout chapters 40–48.

Ezekiel 40:1–4

The temple shows true worship.

King Solomon built the first temple in Jerusalem. Famed for its intricate detail and careful craftsmanship, it showed off not only God's glory but also the material wealth of the nation. Yet the temple was more than just a building. While no structure on earth could ever contain the Lord, the temple was the place where God was especially present on earth, the site where people worshiped him and brought the sacrifices he commanded (see 1 Kings 8:22–25). So it's no surprise Ezekiel felt horror when he had a vision of the Lord's presence leaving the temple, as if God had totally abandoned his people (see Ezekiel 10:19). But now in Ezekiel 40:1—43:12, Ezekiel envisions a stunning new temple and God's brilliant arrival. Christians see this scene as a picture of how God fills our lives when he comes to live in us through his Holy Spirit (see Romans 8:11).

Think: Why was the temple so crucial for Old Testament faith? Why is it not important now?

ROCK SOLID truths

[7] The alcoves for the guards were one rod long and one rod wide, and the projecting walls between the alcoves were five cubits[a] thick. And the threshold of the gate next to the portico facing the temple was one rod deep.

[8] Then he measured the portico of the gateway; [9] it[b] was eight cubits[c] deep and its jambs were two cubits[d] thick. The portico of the gateway faced the temple.

[10] Inside the east gate were three alcoves on each side; the three had the same measurements, and the faces of the projecting walls on each side had the same measurements. [11] Then he measured the width of the entrance of the gateway; it was ten cubits and its length was thirteen cubits.[e] [12] In front of each alcove was a wall one cubit high, and the alcoves were six cubits square. [13] Then he measured the gateway from the top of the rear wall of one alcove to the top of the opposite one; the distance was twenty-five cubits[f] from one parapet opening to the opposite one. [14] He measured along the faces of the projecting walls all around the inside of the gateway—sixty cubits.[g] The measurement was up to the portico[h] facing the courtyard.[i] [15] The distance from the entrance of the gateway to the far end of its portico was fifty cubits.[j] [16] The alcoves and the projecting walls inside the gateway were surmounted by narrow parapet openings all around, as was the portico; the openings all around faced inward. The faces of the projecting walls were decorated with palm trees.

The Outer Court

[17] Then he brought me into the outer court. There I saw some rooms and a pavement that had been constructed all around the court; there were thirty rooms along the pavement. [18] It abutted the sides of the gateways and was as wide as they were long; this was the lower pavement. [19] Then he measured the distance from the inside of the lower gateway to the outside of the inner court; it was a hundred cubits[k] on the east side as well as on the north.

The North Gate

[20] Then he measured the length and width of the north gate, leading into the outer court. [21] Its alcoves—three on each side—its projecting walls and its portico had the same measurements as those of the first gateway. It was fifty cubits long and twenty-five cubits wide. [22] Its openings, its portico and its palm tree decorations had the same measurements as those of the gate facing east. Seven steps led up to it, with its portico opposite them. [23] There was a gate to the inner court facing the north gate, just as there was on the east. He measured from one gate to the opposite one; it was a hundred cubits.

The South Gate

[24] Then he led me to the south side and I saw the south gate. He measured its jambs and its portico, and they had the same measurements as the others. [25] The gateway and its portico had narrow openings all around, like the openings of the others. It was fifty cubits long and twenty-five cubits wide. [26] Seven steps led up to it, with its portico opposite them; it had palm tree decorations on the faces of the projecting walls on each side. [27] The inner court also had a gate facing south, and he measured from this gate to the outer gate on the south side; it was a hundred cubits.

---

[a] 7 That is, about 8 3/4 feet or about 2.7 meters; also in verse 48   [b] 8,9 Many Hebrew manuscripts, Septuagint, Vulgate and Syriac; most Hebrew manuscripts *gateway facing the temple; it was one rod deep.* [9] *Then he measured the portico of the gateway; it*   [c] 9 That is, about 14 feet or about 4.2 meters   [d] 9 That is, about 3 1/2 feet or about 1 meter   [e] 11 That is, about 18 feet wide and 23 feet long or about 5.3 meters wide and 6.9 meters long   [f] 13 That is, about 44 feet or about 13 meters; also in verses 21, 25, 29, 30, 33 and 36   [g] 14 That is, about 105 feet or about 32 meters   [h] 14 Septuagint; Hebrew *projecting wall*   [i] 14 The meaning of the Hebrew for this verse is uncertain.   [j] 15 That is, about 88 feet or about 27 meters; also in verses 21, 25, 29, 33 and 36   [k] 19 That is, about 175 feet or about 53 meters; also in verses 23, 27 and 47

The Gates to the Inner Court

[28] Then he brought me into the inner court through the south gate, and he measured the south gate; it had the same measurements as the others. [29] Its alcoves, its projecting walls and its portico had the same measurements as the others. The gateway and its portico had openings all around. It was fifty cubits long and twenty-five cubits wide. [30] (The porticoes of the gateways around the inner court were twenty-five cubits wide and five cubits deep.) [31] Its portico faced the outer court; palm trees decorated its jambs, and eight steps led up to it.

[32] Then he brought me to the inner court on the east side, and he measured the gateway; it had the same measurements as the others. [33] Its alcoves, its projecting walls and its portico had the same measurements as the others. The gateway and its portico had openings all around. It was fifty cubits long and twenty-five cubits wide. [34] Its portico faced the outer court; palm trees decorated the jambs on either side, and eight steps led up to it.

[35] Then he brought me to the north gate and measured it. It had the same measurements as the others, [36] as did its alcoves, its projecting walls and its portico, and it had openings all around. It was fifty cubits long and twenty-five cubits wide. [37] Its portico[a] faced the outer court; palm trees decorated the jambs on either side, and eight steps led up to it.

The Rooms for Preparing Sacrifices

[38] A room with a doorway was by the portico in each of the inner gateways, where the burnt offerings were washed. [39] In the portico of the gateway were two tables on each side, on which the burnt offerings, sin offerings[b] and guilt offerings were slaughtered. [40] By the outside wall of the portico of the gateway, near the steps at the entrance of the north gateway were two tables, and on the other side of the steps were two tables. [41] So there were four tables on one side of the gateway and four on the other—eight tables in all—on which the sacrifices were slaughtered. [42] There were also four tables of dressed stone for the burnt offerings, each a cubit and a half long, a cubit and a half wide and a cubit high.[c] On them were placed the utensils for slaughtering the burnt offerings and the other sacrifices. [43] And double-pronged hooks, each a handbreadth[d] long, were attached to the wall all around. The tables were for the flesh of the offerings.

The Rooms for the Priests

[44] Outside the inner gate, within the inner court, were two rooms, one[e] at the side of the north gate and facing south, and another at the side of the south[f] gate and facing north. [45] He said to me, "The room facing south is for the priests who guard the temple, [46] and the room facing north is for the priests who guard the altar. These are the sons of Zadok, who are the only Levites who may draw near to the LORD to minister before him."

[47] Then he measured the court: It was square—a hundred cubits long and a hundred cubits wide. And the altar was in front of the temple.

The New Temple

[48] He brought me to the portico of the temple and measured the jambs of the portico; they were five cubits wide on either side. The width of the entrance was fourteen cubits[g] and its projecting walls were[h] three cubits[i] wide on either side. [49] The portico was twenty cubits[j] wide, and twelve[k] cubits[l] from front to back. It was reached by a flight of stairs,[m] and there were pillars on each side of the jambs.

[a] 37 Septuagint (see also verses 31 and 34); Hebrew *jambs*   [b] 39 Or *purification offerings*   [c] 42 That is, about 2 2/3 feet long and wide and 21 inches high or about 80 centimeters long and wide and 53 centimeters high   [d] 43 That is, about 3 1/2 inches or about 9 centimeters   [e] 44 Septuagint; Hebrew *were rooms for singers, which were*   [f] 44 Septuagint; Hebrew *east*   [g] 48 That is, about 25 feet or about 7.4 meters   [h] 48 Septuagint; Hebrew *entrance was*   [i] 48 That is, about 5 1/4 feet or about 1.6 meters   [j] 49 That is, about 35 feet or about 11 meters   [k] 49 Septuagint; Hebrew *eleven*   [l] 49 That is, about 21 feet or about 6.4 meters   [m] 49 Hebrew; Septuagint *Ten steps led up to it*

41

Then the man brought me to the main hall and measured the jambs; the width of the jambs was six cubits*a* on each side.*b* 2The entrance was ten cubits*c* wide, and the projecting walls on each side of it were five cubits*d* wide. He also measured the main hall; it was forty cubits long and twenty cubits wide.*e*

3Then he went into the inner sanctuary and measured the jambs of the entrance; each was two cubits*f* wide. The entrance was six cubits wide, and the projecting walls on each side of it were seven cubits*g* wide. 4And he measured the length of the inner sanctuary; it was twenty cubits, and its width was twenty cubits across the end of the main hall. He said to me, "This is the Most Holy Place."

5Then he measured the wall of the temple; it was six cubits thick, and each side room around the temple was four cubits*b* wide. 6The side rooms were on three levels, one above another, thirty on each level. There were ledges all around the wall of the temple to serve as supports for the side rooms, so that the supports were not inserted into the wall of the temple. 7The side rooms all around the temple were wider at each successive level. The structure surrounding the temple was built in ascending stages, so that the rooms widened as one went upward. A stairway went up from the lowest floor to the top floor through the middle floor.

8I saw that the temple had a raised base all around it, forming the foundation of the side rooms. It was the length of the rod, six long cubits. 9The outer wall of the side rooms was five cubits thick. The open area between the side rooms of the temple 10and the priests' rooms was twenty cubits wide all around the temple. 11There were entrances to the side rooms from the open area, one on the north and another on the south; and the base adjoining the open area was five cubits wide all around.

12The building facing the temple courtyard on the west side was seventy cubits*i* wide. The wall of the building was five cubits thick all around, and its length was ninety cubits.*j*

13Then he measured the temple; it was a hundred cubits*k* long, and the temple courtyard and the building with its walls were also a hundred cubits long. 14The width of the temple courtyard on the east, including the front of the temple, was a hundred cubits.

15Then he measured the length of the building facing the courtyard at the rear of the temple, including its galleries on each side; it was a hundred cubits.

The main hall, the inner sanctuary and the portico facing the court, 16as well as the thresholds and the narrow windows and galleries around the three of them—everything beyond and including the threshold was covered with wood. The floor, the wall up to the windows, and the windows were covered. 17In the space above the outside of the entrance to the inner sanctuary and on the walls at regular intervals all around the inner and outer sanctuary 18were carved cherubim and palm trees. Palm trees alternated with cherubim. Each cherub had two faces: 19the face of a human being toward the palm tree on one side and the face of a lion toward the palm tree on the other. They were carved all around the whole temple. 20From the floor to the area above the entrance, cherubim and palm trees were carved on the wall of the main hall.

21The main hall had a rectangular doorframe, and the one at the front of the Most Holy Place was similar. 22There was

---

a 1 That is, about 11 feet or about 3.2 meters; also in verses 3, 5 and 8   *b 1* One Hebrew manuscript and Septuagint; most Hebrew manuscripts *side, the width of the tent*
c 2 That is, about 18 feet or about 5.3 meters
d 2 That is, about 8 3/4 feet or about 2.7 meters; also in verses 9, 11 and 12   *e 2* That is, about 70 feet long and 35 feet wide or about 21 meters long and 11 meters wide   *f 3* That is, about 3 1/2 feet or about 1.1 meters; also in verse 22
g 3 That is, about 12 feet or about 3.7 meters
b 5 That is, about 7 feet or about 2.1 meters
i 12 That is, about 123 feet or about 37 meters
j 12 That is, about 158 feet or about 48 meters
k 13 That is, about 175 feet or about 53 meters; also in verses 14 and 15

a wooden altar three cubits*a* high and two cubits square*b*; its corners, its base*c* and its sides were of wood. The man said to me, "This is the table that is before the LORD." ²³Both the main hall and the Most Holy Place had double doors. ²⁴Each door had two leaves—two hinged leaves for each door. ²⁵And on the doors of the main hall were carved cherubim and palm trees like those carved on the walls, and there was a wooden overhang on the front of the portico. ²⁶On the sidewalls of the portico were narrow windows with palm trees carved on each side. The side rooms of the temple also had overhangs.

The Rooms for the Priests

42 Then the man led me northward into the outer court and brought me to the rooms opposite the temple courtyard and opposite the outer wall on the north side. ²The building whose door faced north was a hundred cubits long and fifty cubits wide.*d* ³Both in the section twenty cubits*e* from the inner court and in the section opposite the pavement of the outer court, gallery faced gallery at the three levels. ⁴In front of the rooms was an inner passageway ten cubits wide and a hundred cubits*f* long.*g* Their doors were on the north. ⁵Now the upper rooms were narrower, for the galleries took more space from them than from the rooms on the lower and middle floors of the building. ⁶The rooms on the top floor had no pillars, as the courts had; so they were smaller in floor space than those on the lower and middle floors. ⁷There was an outer wall parallel to the rooms and the outer court; it extended in front of the rooms for fifty cubits. ⁸While the row of rooms on the side next to the outer court was fifty cubits long, the row on the side nearest the sanctuary was a hundred cubits long. ⁹The lower rooms had an entrance on the east side as one enters them from the outer court.

¹⁰On the south side*h* along the length of the wall of the outer court, adjoining temple courtyard and opposite the outer wall, were rooms ¹¹with a passageway in front of them. These were like the rooms on the north; they had the same length and width, with similar exits and dimensions. Similar to the doorways on the north ¹²were the doorways of the rooms on the south. There was a doorway at the beginning of the passageway that was parallel to the corresponding wall extending eastward, by which one enters the rooms.

¹³Then he said to me, "The north and south rooms facing the temple courtyard are the priests' rooms, where the priests who approach the LORD will eat the most holy offerings. There they will put the most holy offerings—the grain offerings, the sin offerings*i* and the guilt offerings— for the place is holy. ¹⁴Once the priests enter the holy precincts, they are not to go into the outer court until they leave behind the garments in which they minister, for these are holy. They are to put on other clothes before they go near the places that are for the people."

¹⁵When he had finished measuring what was inside the temple area, he led me out by the east gate and measured the area all around: ¹⁶He measured the east side with the measuring rod; it was five hundred cubits.*j,k* ¹⁷He measured the north side; it was five hundred cubits*l* by the measuring rod. ¹⁸He measured the south side; it was five hundred cubits by the measuring rod. ¹⁹Then he turned to the west side and measured; it was five hundred cubits by the measuring rod. ²⁰So he measured the area on all four sides. It

a 22 That is, about 5 1/4 feet or about 1.5 meters   *b 22* Septuagint; Hebrew *long*
c 22 Septuagint; Hebrew *length*   *d 2* That is, about 175 feet long and 88 feet wide or about 53 meters long and 27 meters wide   *e 3* That is, about 35 feet or about 11 meters
f 4 Septuagint and Syriac; Hebrew *and one cubit*   *g 4* That is, about 18 feet wide and 175 feet long or about 5.3 meters wide and 53 meters long   *h 10* Septuagint; Hebrew *Eastward*   *i 13* Or *purification offerings*
j 16 See Septuagint of verse 17; Hebrew *rods*; also in verses 18 and 19.   *k 16* Five hundred cubits equal about 875 feet or about 265 meters; also in verses 17, 18 and 19.   *l 17* Septuagint; Hebrew *rods*

had a wall around it, five hundred cubits long and five hundred cubits wide, to separate the holy from the common.

God's Glory Returns to the Temple

43 Then the man brought me to the gate facing east, [2] and I saw the glory of the God of Israel coming from the east. His voice was like the roar of rushing waters, and the land was radiant with his glory. [3] The vision I saw was like the vision I had seen when he[a] came to destroy the city and like the visions I had seen by the Kebar River, and I fell facedown. [4] The glory of the LORD entered the temple through the gate facing east. [5] Then the Spirit lifted me up and brought me into the inner court, and the glory of the LORD filled the temple.

[6] While the man was standing beside me, I heard someone speaking to me from inside the temple. [7] He said: "Son of man, this is the place of my throne and the place for the soles of my feet. This is where I will live among the Israelites forever. The people of Israel will never again defile my holy name—neither they nor their kings—by their prostitution and the funeral offerings[b] for their kings at their death.[c] [8] When they placed their threshold next to my threshold and their doorposts beside my doorposts, with only a wall between me and them, they defiled my holy name by their detestable practices. So I destroyed them in my anger. [9] Now let them put away from me their prostitution and the funeral offerings for their kings, and I will live among them forever.

[10] "Son of man, describe the temple to the people of Israel, that they may be ashamed of their sins. Let them consider its perfection, [11] and if they are ashamed of all they have done, make known to them the design of the temple—its arrangement, its exits and entrances—its whole design and all its regulations[d] and laws. Write these down before them so that they may be faithful to its design and follow all its regulations.

[12] "This is the law of the temple: All the surrounding area on top of the mountain will be most holy. Such is the law of the temple.

The Great Altar Restored

[13] "These are the measurements of the altar in long cubits,[e] that cubit being a cubit and a handbreadth: Its gutter is a cubit deep and a cubit wide, with a rim of one span[f] around the edge. And this is the height of the altar: [14] From the gutter on the ground up to the lower ledge that goes around the altar it is two cubits high, and the ledge is a cubit wide.[g] From this lower ledge to the upper ledge that goes around the altar it is four cubits high, and that ledge is also a cubit wide.[b] [15] Above that, the altar hearth is four cubits high, and four horns project upward from the hearth. [16] The altar hearth is square, twelve cubits[i] long and twelve cubits wide. [17] The upper ledge also is square, fourteen cubits[j] long and fourteen cubits wide. All around the altar is a gutter of one cubit with a rim of half a cubit.[f] The steps of the altar face east."

[18] Then he said to me, "Son of man, this is what the Sovereign LORD says: These will be the regulations for sacrificing burnt offerings and splashing blood against the altar when it is built: [19] You are to give a young bull as a sin offering[k] to the Levitical priests of the family of Zadok, who come near to minister before me, declares the Sovereign LORD. [20] You

---

[a] 3 Some Hebrew manuscripts and Vulgate; most Hebrew manuscripts *I*   [b] 7 Or *the memorial monuments*; also in verse 9
[c] 7 Or *their high places*   [d] 11 Some Hebrew manuscripts and Septuagint; most Hebrew manuscripts *regulations and its whole design*
[e] 13 That is, about 21 inches or about 53 centimeters; also in verses 14 and 17. The long cubit is the basic unit for linear measurement throughout Ezekiel 40–48.   [f] 13,17 That is, about 11 inches or about 27 centimeters
[g] 14 That is, about 3 1/2 feet high and 1 3/4 feet wide or about 105 centimeters high and 53 centimeters wide   [b] 14 That is, about 7 feet high and 1 3/4 feet wide or about 2.1 meters high and 53 centimeters wide   [i] 16 That is, about 21 feet or about 6.4 meters   [j] 17 That is, about 25 feet or about 7.4 meters   [k] 19 Or *purification offering*; also in verses 21, 22 and 25

are to take some of its blood and put it on the four horns of the altar and on the four corners of the upper ledge and all around the rim, and so purify the altar and make atonement for it. ²¹You are to take the bull for the sin offering and burn it in the designated part of the temple area outside the sanctuary.

²²"On the second day you are to offer a male goat without defect for a sin offering, and the altar is to be purified as it was purified with the bull. ²³When you have finished purifying it, you are to offer a young bull and a ram from the flock, both without defect. ²⁴You are to offer them before the Lord, and the priests are to sprinkle salt on them and sacrifice them as a burnt offering to the Lord.

²⁵"For seven days you are to provide a male goat daily for a sin offering; you are also to provide a young bull and a ram from the flock, both without defect. ²⁶For seven days they are to make atonement for the altar and cleanse it; thus they will dedicate it. ²⁷At the end of these days, from the eighth day on, the priests are to present your burnt offerings and fellowship offerings on the altar. Then I will accept you, declares the Sovereign Lord."

The Priesthood Restored

44 Then the man brought me back to the outer gate of the sanctuary, the one facing east, and it was shut. ²The Lord said to me, "This gate is to remain shut. It must not be opened; no one may enter through it. It is to remain shut because the Lord, the God of Israel, has entered through it. ³The prince himself is the only one who may sit inside the gateway to eat in the presence of the Lord. He is to enter by way of the portico of the gateway and go out the same way."

⁴Then the man brought me by way of the north gate to the front of the temple. I looked and saw the glory of the Lord filling the temple of the Lord, and I fell facedown.

⁵The Lord said to me, "Son of man, look carefully, listen closely and give at-

tention to everything I tell you concerning all the regulations and instructions regarding the temple of the Lord. Give attention to the entrance to the temple and all the exits of the sanctuary. ⁶Say to rebellious Israel, 'This is what the Sovereign Lord says: Enough of your detestable practices, people of Israel! ⁷In addition to all your other detestable practices, you brought foreigners uncircumcised in heart and flesh into my sanctuary, desecrating my temple while you offered me food, fat and blood, and you broke my covenant. ⁸Instead of carrying out your duty in regard to my holy things, you put others in charge of my sanctuary. ⁹This is what the Sovereign Lord says: No foreigner uncircumcised in heart and flesh is to enter my sanctuary, not even the foreigners who live among the Israelites.

¹⁰"'The Levites who went far from me when Israel went astray and who wandered from me after their idols must bear the consequences of their sin. ¹¹They may serve in my sanctuary, having charge of the gates of the temple and serving in it; they may slaughter the burnt offerings and sacrifices for the people and stand before the people and serve them. ¹²But because they served them in the presence of their idols and made the people of Israel fall into sin, therefore I have sworn with uplifted hand that they must bear the consequences of their sin, declares the Sovereign Lord. ¹³They are not to come near to serve me as priests or come near any of my holy things or my most holy offerings; they must bear the shame of their detestable practices. ¹⁴And I will appoint them to guard the temple for all the work that is to be done in it.

¹⁵"'But the Levitical priests, who are descendants of Zadok and who guarded my sanctuary when the Israelites went astray from me, are to come near to minister before me; they are to stand before me to offer sacrifices of fat and blood, declares the Sovereign Lord. ¹⁶They alone are to enter my sanctuary; they alone are to come near to my table to minister before me and serve me as guards.

¹⁷"'When they enter the gates of the inner court, they are to wear linen clothes; they must not wear any woolen garment while ministering at the gates of the inner court or inside the temple. ¹⁸They are to wear linen turbans on their heads and linen undergarments around their waists. They must not wear anything that makes them perspire. ¹⁹When they go out into the outer court where the people are, they are to take off the clothes they have been ministering in and are to leave them in the sacred rooms, and put on other clothes, so that the people are not consecrated through contact with their garments.

²⁰"'They must not shave their heads or let their hair grow long, but they are to keep the hair of their heads trimmed. ²¹No priest is to drink wine when he enters the inner court. ²²They must not marry widows or divorced women; they may marry only virgins of Israelite descent or widows of priests. ²³They are to teach my people the difference between the holy and the common and show them how to distinguish between the unclean and the clean.

²⁴"'In any dispute, the priests are to serve as judges and decide it according to my ordinances. They are to keep my laws and my decrees for all my appointed festivals, and they are to keep my Sabbaths holy.

²⁵"'A priest must not defile himself by going near a dead person; however, if the dead person was his father or mother, son or daughter, brother or unmarried sister, then he may defile himself. ²⁶After he is cleansed, he must wait seven days. ²⁷On the day he goes into the inner court of the sanctuary to minister in the sanctuary, he is to offer a sin offering[a] for himself, declares the Sovereign LORD.

²⁸"'I am to be the only inheritance the priests have. You are to give them no possession in Israel; I will be their possession. ²⁹They will eat the grain offerings, the sin offerings and the guilt offerings; and everything in Israel devoted[b] to the LORD will belong to them. ³⁰The best of all the firstfruits and of all your special gifts will belong to the priests. You are to give them the first portion of your ground meal so that a blessing may rest on your household. ³¹The priests must not eat anything, whether bird or animal, found dead or torn by wild animals.

Israel Fully Restored

45 "'When you allot the land as an inheritance, you are to present to the LORD a portion of the land as a sacred district, 25,000 cubits[c] long and 20,000[d] cubits[e] wide; the entire area will be holy. ²Of this, a section 500 cubits[f] square is to be for the sanctuary, with 50 cubits[g] around it for open land. ³In the sacred district, measure off a section 25,000 cubits long and 10,000 cubits[b] wide. In it will be the sanctuary, the Most Holy Place. ⁴It will be the sacred portion of the land for the priests, who minister in the sanctuary and who draw near to minister before the LORD. It will be a place for their houses as well as a holy place for the sanctuary. ⁵An area 25,000 cubits long and 10,000 cubits wide will belong to the Levites, who serve in the temple, as their possession for towns to live in.[i]

⁶"'You are to give the city as its property an area 5,000 cubits[j] wide and 25,000 cubits long, adjoining the sacred portion; it will belong to all Israel.

⁷"'The prince will have the land bordering each side of the area formed by the sacred district and the property of the city. It will extend westward from the west side and eastward from the east side, running lengthwise from the western to the eastern

---

a 27 Or *purification offering*; also in verse 29
b 29 The Hebrew term refers to the irrevocable giving over of things or persons to the LORD.
c 1 That is, about 8 miles or about 13 kilometers; also in verses 3, 5 and 6
d 1 Septuagint (see also verses 3 and 5 and 48:9); Hebrew *10,000*   *e 1* That is, about 6 1/2 miles or about 11 kilometers   *f 2* That is, about 875 feet or about 265 meters   *g 2* That is, about 88 feet or about 27 meters   *b 3* That is, about 3 1/3 miles or about 5.3 kilometers; also in verse 5   *i 5* Septuagint; Hebrew *temple; they will have as their possession 20 rooms*
j 6 That is, about 1 2/3 miles or about 2.7 kilometers

border parallel to one of the tribal portions. [8]This land will be his possession in Israel. And my princes will no longer oppress my people but will allow the people of Israel to possess the land according to their tribes.

[9]"'This is what the Sovereign LORD says: You have gone far enough, princes of Israel! Give up your violence and oppression and do what is just and right. Stop dispossessing my people, declares the Sovereign LORD. [10]You are to use accurate scales, an accurate ephah[a] and an accurate bath.[b] [11]The ephah and the bath are to be the same size, the bath containing a tenth of a homer and the ephah a tenth of a homer; the homer is to be the standard measure for both. [12]The shekel[c] is to consist of twenty gerahs. Twenty shekels plus twenty-five shekels plus fifteen shekels equal one mina.[d]

[13]"'This is the special gift you are to offer: a sixth of an ephah[e] from each homer of wheat and a sixth of an ephah[f] from each homer of barley. [14]The prescribed portion of olive oil, measured by the bath, is a tenth of a bath[g] from each cor (which consists of ten baths or one homer, for ten baths are equivalent to a homer). [15]Also one sheep is to be taken from every flock of two hundred from the well-watered pastures of Israel. These will be used for the grain offerings, burnt offerings and fellowship offerings to make atonement for the people, declares the Sovereign LORD. [16]All the people of the land will be required to give this special offering to the prince in Israel. [17]It will be the duty of the prince to provide the burnt offerings, grain offerings and drink offerings at the festivals, the New Moons and the Sabbaths—at all the appointed festivals of Israel. He will provide the sin offerings,[b] grain offerings, burnt offerings and fellowship offerings to make atonement for the Israelites.

[18]"'This is what the Sovereign LORD says: In the first month on the first day you are to take a young bull without defect and purify the sanctuary. [19]The priest is to take some of the blood of the sin offering and put it on the doorposts of the temple,

on the four corners of the upper ledge of the altar and on the gateposts of the inner court. [20]You are to do the same on the seventh day of the month for anyone who sins unintentionally or through ignorance; so you are to make atonement for the temple.

[21]"'In the first month on the fourteenth day you are to observe the Passover, a festival lasting seven days, during which you shall eat bread made without yeast. [22]On that day the prince is to provide a bull as a sin offering for himself and for all the people of the land. [23]Every day during the seven days of the festival he is to provide seven bulls and seven rams without defect as a burnt offering to the LORD, and a male goat for a sin offering. [24]He is to provide as a grain offering an ephah for each bull and an ephah for each ram, along with a hin[i] of olive oil for each ephah.

[25]"'During the seven days of the festival, which begins in the seventh month on the fifteenth day, he is to make the same provision for sin offerings, burnt offerings, grain offerings and oil.

46

"'This is what the Sovereign LORD says: The gate of the inner court facing east is to be shut on the six working days, but on the Sabbath day and on the day of the New Moon it is to be opened. [2]The prince is to enter from the outside through the portico of the gateway and stand by the gatepost. The priests are to sacrifice his burnt offering and his fellowship offerings. He is to bow down in worship at the threshold of the gateway and then go out, but the gate will not be shut until evening. [3]On the Sabbaths and New Moons

---

[a] 10 An ephah was a dry measure having the capacity of about 3/5 bushel or about 22 liters.
[b] 10 A bath was a liquid measure equaling about 6 gallons or about 22 liters.   [c] 12 A shekel weighed about 2/5 ounce or about 12 grams.
[d] 12 That is, 60 shekels; the common mina was 50 shekels. Sixty shekels were about 1 1/2 pounds or about 690 grams.   [e] 13 That is, probably about 6 pounds or about 2.7 kilograms
[f] 13 That is, probably about 5 pounds or about 2.3 kilograms   [g] 14 That is, about 2 1/2 quarts or about 2.2 liters   [b] 17 Or *purification offerings*; also in verses 19, 22, 23 and 25
[i] 24 That is, about 1 gallon or about 3.8 liters

the people of the land are to worship in the presence of the LORD at the entrance of that gateway. ⁴The burnt offering the prince brings to the LORD on the Sabbath day is to be six male lambs and a ram, all without defect. ⁵The grain offering given with the ram is to be an ephah,ᵃ and the grain offering with the lambs is to be as much as he pleases, along with a hinᵇ of olive oil for each ephah. ⁶On the day of the New Moon he is to offer a young bull, six lambs and a ram, all without defect. ⁷He is to provide as a grain offering one ephah with the bull, one ephah with the ram, and with the lambs as much as he wants to give, along with a hin of oil for each ephah. ⁸When the prince enters, he is to go in through the portico of the gateway, and he is to come out the same way.

⁹"'When the people of the land come before the LORD at the appointed festivals, whoever enters by the north gate to worship is to go out the south gate; and whoever enters by the south gate is to go out the north gate. No one is to return through the gate by which they entered, but each is to go out the opposite gate. ¹⁰The prince is to be among them, going in when they go in and going out when they go out. ¹¹At the feasts and the appointed festivals, the grain offering is to be an ephah with a bull, an ephah with a ram, and with the lambs as much as he pleases, along with a hin of oil for each ephah.

¹²"'When the prince provides a freewill offering to the LORD—whether a burnt offering or fellowship offerings—the gate facing east is to be opened for him. He shall offer his burnt offering or his fellowship offerings as he does on the Sabbath day. Then he shall go out, and after he has gone out, the gate will be shut.

¹³"'Every day you are to provide a year-old lamb without defect for a burnt offering to the LORD; morning by morning you shall provide it. ¹⁴You are also to provide with it morning by morning a grain offering, consisting of a sixth of an ephahᶜ with a third of a hinᵈ of oil to moisten the flour. The presenting of this grain offering to the LORD is a lasting ordinance. ¹⁵So the

lamb and the grain offering and the oil shall be provided morning by morning for a regular burnt offering.

¹⁶"'This is what the Sovereign LORD says: If the prince makes a gift from his inheritance to one of his sons, it will also belong to his descendants; it is to be their property by inheritance. ¹⁷If, however, he makes a gift from his inheritance to one of his servants, the servant may keep it until the year of freedom; then it will revert to the prince. His inheritance belongs to his sons only; it is theirs. ¹⁸The prince must not take any of the inheritance of the people, driving them off their property. He is to give his sons their inheritance out of his own property, so that not one of my people will be separated from their property.'"

¹⁹Then the man brought me through the entrance at the side of the gate to the sacred rooms facing north, which belonged to the priests, and showed me a place at the western end. ²⁰He said to me, "This is the place where the priests are to cook the guilt offering and the sin offeringᵉ and bake the grain offering, to avoid bringing them into the outer court and consecrating the people."

²¹He then brought me to the outer court and led me around to its four corners, and I saw in each corner another court. ²²In the four corners of the outer court were enclosedᶠ courts, forty cubits long and thirty cubits wide;ᵍ each of the courts in the four corners was the same size. ²³Around the inside of each of the four courts was a ledge of stone, with places for fire built all around under the ledge. ²⁴He said to me, "These are the kitchens where those who minister at the temple are to cook the sacrifices of the people."

ᵃ 5 That is, probably about 35 pounds or about 16 kilograms; also in verses 7 and 11
ᵇ 5 That is, about 1 gallon or about 3.8 liters; also in verses 7 and 11   ᶜ 14 That is, probably about 6 pounds or about 2.7 kilograms
ᵈ 14 That is, about 1 1/2 quarts or about 1.3 liters   ᵉ 20 Or purification offering
ᶠ 22 The meaning of the Hebrew for this word is uncertain.   ᵍ 22 That is, about 70 feet long and 53 feet wide or about 21 meters long and 16 meters wide

The River From the Temple

47 The man brought me back to the entrance to the temple, and I saw water coming out from under the threshold of the temple toward the east (for the temple faced east). The water was coming down from under the south side of the temple, south of the altar. ²He then brought me out through the north gate and led me around the outside to the outer gate facing east, and the water was trickling from the south side.

³As the man went eastward with a measuring line in his hand, he measured off a thousand cubits*a* and then led me through water that was ankle-deep. ⁴He measured off another thousand cubits and led me through water that was knee-deep. He measured off another thousand and led me through water that was up to the waist. ⁵He measured off another thousand, but now it was a river that I could not cross, because the water had risen and was deep enough to swim in—a river that no one could cross. ⁶He asked me, "Son of man, do you see this?"

Then he led me back to the bank of the river. ⁷When I arrived there, I saw a great number of trees on each side of the river. ⁸He said to me, "This water flows toward the eastern region and goes down into the Arabah,*b* where it enters the Dead Sea. When it empties into the sea, the salty water there becomes fresh. ⁹Swarms of living creatures will live wherever the river flows. There will be large numbers of fish, because this water flows there and makes the salt water fresh; so where the river flows everything will live. ¹⁰Fishermen will stand along the shore; from En Gedi to En Eglaim there will be places for spreading nets. The fish will be of many kinds—like the fish of the Mediterranean Sea. ¹¹But the swamps and marshes will not become fresh; they will be left for salt. ¹²Fruit trees of all kinds will grow on both banks of the river. Their leaves will not wither, nor will their fruit fail. Every month they will bear fruit, because the water from the sanctuary flows to them. Their fruit will serve for food and their leaves for healing."

The Boundaries of the Land

¹³This is what the Sovereign LORD says: "These are the boundaries of the land that you will divide among the twelve tribes of Israel as their inheritance, with two portions for Joseph. ¹⁴You are to divide it equally among them. Because I swore with uplifted hand to give it to your ancestors, this land will become your inheritance.

¹⁵"This is to be the boundary of the land:

"On the north side it will run from the Mediterranean Sea by the Hethlon road past Lebo Hamath to Zedad, ¹⁶Berothah*c* and Sibraim (which lies on the border between Damascus and Hamath), as far as Hazer Hattikon, which is on the border of Hauran. ¹⁷The boundary will extend from the sea to Hazar Enan,*d* along the northern border of Damascus, with the border of Hamath to the north. This will be the northern boundary. ¹⁸"On the east side the boundary will run between Hauran and Damascus, along the Jordan between Gilead and the land of Israel, to the Dead Sea and as far as Tamar.*e* This will be the eastern boundary. ¹⁹"On the south side it will run from Tamar as far as the waters of Meribah Kadesh, then along the Wadi of Egypt to the Mediterranean Sea. This will be the southern boundary. ²⁰"On the west side, the Mediterranean Sea will be the boundary to a point opposite Lebo Hamath. This will be the western boundary.

²¹"You are to distribute this land among yourselves according to the tribes of Israel. ²²You are to allot it as an inheritance for yourselves and for the foreigners residing among you and who have children. You

---

a 3 That is, about 1,700 feet or about 530 meters   *b 8* Or *the Jordan Valley*   *c 15,16* See Septuagint and 48:1; Hebrew *road to go into Zedad,* ¹⁶*Hamath, Berothah.*   *d 17* Hebrew *Enon,* a variant of *Enan*   *e 18* See Syriac; Hebrew *Israel. You will measure to the Dead Sea.*

are to consider them as native-born Israelites; along with you they are to be allotted an inheritance among the tribes of Israel. ²³ In whatever tribe a foreigner resides, there you are to give them their inheritance," declares the Sovereign LORD.

The Division of the Land

48 "These are the tribes, listed by name: At the northern frontier, Dan will have one portion; it will follow the Hethlon road to Lebo Hamath; Hazar Enan and the northern border of Damascus next to Hamath will be part of its border from the east side to the west side.

² "Asher will have one portion; it will border the territory of Dan from east to west.

³ "Naphtali will have one portion; it will border the territory of Asher from east to west.

⁴ "Manasseh will have one portion; it will border the territory of Naphtali from east to west.

⁵ "Ephraim will have one portion; it will border the territory of Manasseh from east to west.

⁶ "Reuben will have one portion; it will border the territory of Ephraim from east to west.

⁷ "Judah will have one portion; it will border the territory of Reuben from east to west.

⁸ "Bordering the territory of Judah from east to west will be the portion you are to present as a special gift. It will be 25,000 cubits*ᵃ* wide, and its length from east to west will equal one of the tribal portions; the sanctuary will be in the center of it.

⁹ "The special portion you are to offer to the LORD will be 25,000 cubits long and 10,000 cubits*ᵇ* wide. ¹⁰ This will be the sacred portion for the priests. It will be 25,000 cubits long on the north side, 10,000 cubits wide on the west side, 10,000 cubits wide on the east side and 25,000 cubits long on the south side. In the center of it will be the sanctuary of the LORD. ¹¹ This will be for the consecrated

priests, the Zadokites, who were faithful in serving me and did not go astray as the Levites did when the Israelites went astray. ¹² It will be a special gift to them from the sacred portion of the land, a most holy portion, bordering the territory of the Levites.

¹³ "Alongside the territory of the priests, the Levites will have an allotment 25,000 cubits long and 10,000 cubits wide. Its total length will be 25,000 cubits and its width 10,000 cubits. ¹⁴ They must not sell or exchange any of it. This is the best of the land and must not pass into other hands, because it is holy to the LORD.

¹⁵ "The remaining area, 5,000 cubits*ᶜ* wide and 25,000 cubits long, will be for the common use of the city, for houses and for pastureland. The city will be in the center of it ¹⁶ and will have these measurements: the north side 4,500 cubits,*ᵈ* the south side 4,500 cubits, the east side 4,500 cubits, and the west side 4,500 cubits. ¹⁷ The pastureland for the city will be 250 cubits*ᵉ* on the north, 250 cubits on the south, 250 cubits on the east, and 250 cubits on the west. ¹⁸ What remains of the area, bordering on the sacred portion and running the length of it, will be 10,000 cubits on the east side and 10,000 cubits on the west side. Its produce will supply food for the workers of the city. ¹⁹ The workers from the city who farm it will come from all the tribes of Israel. ²⁰ The entire portion will be a square, 25,000 cubits on each side. As a special gift you will set aside the sacred portion, along with the property of the city.

²¹ "What remains on both sides of the area formed by the sacred portion and the property of the city will belong to the prince. It will extend eastward from the 25,000 cubits of the sacred portion

---

ᵃ 8 That is, about 8 miles or about 13 kilometers; also in verses 9, 10, 13, 15, 20 and 21   *ᵇ 9* That is, about 3 1/3 miles or about 5.3 kilometers; also in verses 10, 13 and 18   *ᶜ 15* That is, about 1 2/3 miles or about 2.7 kilometers   *ᵈ 16* That is, about 1 1/2 miles or about 2.4 kilometers; also in verses 30, 32, 33 and 34   *ᵉ 17* That is, about 440 feet or about 135 meters to the eastern border, and westward from the 25,000 cubits to the western border. Both these areas running the length of the tribal portions will belong to the prince, and the sacred portion with the temple sanctuary will be in the center of them. [22] So the property of the Levites and the property of the city will lie in the center of the area that belongs to the prince. The area belonging to the prince will lie between the border of Judah and the border of Benjamin.

[23] "As for the rest of the tribes: Benjamin will have one portion; it will extend from the east side to the west side.

[24] "Simeon will have one portion; it will border the territory of Benjamin from east to west.

[25] "Issachar will have one portion; it will border the territory of Simeon from east to west.

[26] "Zebulun will have one portion; it will border the territory of Issachar from east to west.

[27] "Gad will have one portion; it will border the territory of Zebulun from east to west.

[28] "The southern boundary of Gad will run south from Tamar to the waters of Meribah Kadesh, then along the Wadi of Egypt to the Mediterranean Sea.

[29] "This is the land you are to allot as an inheritance to the tribes of Israel, and these will be their portions," declares the Sovereign Lord.

The Gates of the New City

[30] "These will be the exits of the city: Beginning on the north side, which is 4,500 cubits long, [31] the gates of the city will be named after the tribes of Israel. The three gates on the north side will be the gate of Reuben, the gate of Judah and the gate of Levi.

[32] "On the east side, which is 4,500 cubits long, will be three gates: the gate of Joseph, the gate of Benjamin and the gate of Dan.

[33] "On the south side, which measures 4,500 cubits, will be three gates: the gate of Simeon, the gate of Issachar and the gate of Zebulun.

[34] "On the west side, which is 4,500 cubits long, will be three gates: the gate of Gad, the gate of Asher and the gate of Naphtali.

[35] "The distance all around will be 18,000 cubits.[a]

"And the name of the city from that time on will be:

THE LORD IS THERE."

[a] 35 That is, about 6 miles or about 9.5 kilometers

BOOK OUTLINE

Daniel has traditionally been named the author of this book. The entire book tells of the experiences of Daniel and his friends as captives in Babylon and the divine revelation that came to Daniel in dreams and visions during his lifetime (about 605 – 530 BC).

Daniel was taken hostage from Jerusalem in 605 BC to the Babylonian court. After retelling and interpreting Nebuchadnezzar's dream Daniel was given a position of power. He wrote this book during Israel's captivity to encourage the people to trust in God who controls all of history.

In the last six chapters of this book, Daniel describes his visions of the rise and fall of earthly kingdoms and finally the rise of an everlasting kingdom.

Daniel's Training in Babylon

In the third year of the reign of Jehoiakim king of Judah, Nebuchadnezzar king of Babylon came to Jerusalem and besieged it. ²And the Lord delivered Jehoiakim king of Judah into his hand, along with some of the articles from the temple of God. These he carried off to the temple of his god in Babylonia[a] and put in the treasure house of his god.

³Then the king ordered Ashpenaz, chief of his court officials, to bring into the king's service some of the Israelites from the royal family and the nobility— ⁴young men without any physical defect, handsome, showing aptitude for every kind of learning, well informed, quick to understand, and qualified to serve in the king's palace. He was to teach them the language and literature of the Babylonians.[b] ⁵The king assigned them a daily amount of food and wine from the king's table. They were to be trained for three years, and after that they were to enter the king's service.

⁶Among those who were chosen were some from Judah: Daniel, Hananiah, Mishael and Azariah. ⁷The chief official gave them new names: to Daniel, the name Belteshazzar; to Hananiah, Shadrach; to Mishael, Meshach; and to Azariah, Abednego.

⁸But Daniel resolved not to defile himself with the royal food and wine, and he asked the chief official for permission not to defile himself this way. ⁹Now God had caused the official to show favor and compassion to Daniel, ¹⁰but the official told Daniel, "I am afraid of my lord the king, who has assigned your[c] food and drink. Why should he see you looking worse than the other young men your age? The king would then have my head because of you."

¹¹Daniel then said to the guard whom the chief official had appointed over Daniel, Hananiah, Mishael and Azariah, ¹²"Please test your servants for ten days: Give us nothing but vegetables to eat and water to drink. ¹³Then compare our appearance with that of the young men who eat the royal food, and treat your servants in accordance with what you see." ¹⁴So he agreed to this and tested them for ten days.

¹⁵At the end of the ten days they looked healthier and better nourished than any of the young men who ate the royal food. ¹⁶So the guard took away their choice food and the wine they were to drink and gave them vegetables instead.

¹⁷To these four young men God gave knowledge and understanding of all kinds of literature and learning. And Daniel could understand visions and dreams of all kinds.

¹⁸At the end of the time set by the king to bring them into his service, the chief official presented them to Nebuchadnezzar. ¹⁹The king talked with them, and he found none equal to Daniel, Hananiah, Mishael and Azariah; so they entered the king's service. ²⁰In every matter of wisdom and understanding about which the king questioned them, he found them ten times better than all the magicians and enchanters in his whole kingdom.

²¹And Daniel remained there until the first year of King Cyrus.

Nebuchadnezzar's Dream

In the second year of his reign, Nebuchadnezzar had dreams; his mind was troubled and he could not sleep. ²So the king summoned the magicians, enchanters, sorcerers and astrologers[d] to tell him what he had dreamed. When they came in and stood before the king, ³he said to them, "I have had a dream that troubles me and I want to know what it means.[e]"

⁴Then the astrologers answered the king,[f] "May the king live forever! Tell your servants the dream, and we will interpret it."

⁵The king replied to the astrologers,

---

[a] 2 Hebrew *Shinar*   [b] 4 Or *Chaldeans*
[c] 10 The Hebrew for *your* and *you* in this verse is plural.   [d] 2 Or *Chaldeans*; also in verses 4, 5 and 10   [e] 3 Or *was*   [f] 4 At this point the Hebrew text has *in Aramaic*, indicating that the text from here through the end of chapter 7 is in Aramaic.

"This is what I have firmly decided: If you do not tell me what my dream was and interpret it, I will have you cut into pieces and your houses turned into piles of rubble. ⁶But if you tell me the dream and explain it, you will receive from me gifts and rewards and great honor. So tell me the dream and interpret it for me."

⁷Once more they replied, "Let the king tell his servants the dream, and we will interpret it."

⁸Then the king answered, "I am certain that you are trying to gain time, because you realize that this is what I have firmly decided: ⁹If you do not tell me the dream, there is only one penalty for you. You have conspired to tell me misleading and wicked things, hoping the situation will change. So then, tell me the dream, and I will know that you can interpret it for me."

¹⁰The astrologers answered the king, "There is no one on earth who can do what the king asks! No king, however great and mighty, has ever asked such a thing of any magician or enchanter or astrologer. ¹¹What the king asks is too difficult. No one can reveal it to the king except the gods, and they do not live among humans."

¹²This made the king so angry and furious that he ordered the execution of all the wise men of Babylon. ¹³So the decree was issued to put the wise men to death, and men were sent to look for Daniel and his friends to put them to death.

¹⁴When Arioch, the commander of the king's guard, had gone out to put to death the wise men of Babylon, Daniel spoke to him with wisdom and tact. ¹⁵He asked the king's officer, "Why did the king issue such a harsh decree?" Arioch then explained the matter to Daniel. ¹⁶At this, Daniel went in to the king and asked for time, so that he might interpret the dream for him.

¹⁷Then Daniel returned to his house and explained the matter to his friends Hananiah, Mishael and Azariah. ¹⁸He urged them to plead for mercy from the God of heaven concerning this mystery, so that he and his friends might not be executed with the rest of the wise men of Babylon. ¹⁹During the night the mystery was revealed to Daniel in a vision. Then Daniel praised the God of heaven ²⁰and said:

"Praise be to the name of God for ever and ever;
    wisdom and power are his.
²¹He changes times and seasons;
    he deposes kings and raises up others.
He gives wisdom to the wise
    and knowledge to the discerning.
²²He reveals deep and hidden things;
    he knows what lies in darkness,
    and light dwells with him.
²³I thank and praise you, God of my ancestors:
    You have given me wisdom and power,
you have made known to me what we asked of you,
    you have made known to us the dream of the king."

Daniel Interprets the Dream

²⁴Then Daniel went to Arioch, whom the king had appointed to execute the wise men of Babylon, and said to him, "Do not execute the wise men of Babylon. Take me to the king, and I will interpret his dream for him."

²⁵Arioch took Daniel to the king at once and said, "I have found a man among the exiles from Judah who can tell the king what his dream means."

²⁶The king asked Daniel (also called Belteshazzar), "Are you able to tell me what I saw in my dream and interpret it?"

²⁷Daniel replied, "No wise man, enchanter, magician or diviner can explain to the king the mystery he has asked about, ²⁸but there is a God in heaven who reveals mysteries. He has shown King Nebuchadnezzar what will happen in days to come. Your dream and the visions that passed through your mind as you were lying in bed are these:

²⁹"As Your Majesty was lying there, your mind turned to things to come, and the revealer of mysteries showed you what

is going to happen. ³⁰As for me, this mystery has been revealed to me, not because I have greater wisdom than anyone else alive, but so that Your Majesty may know the interpretation and that you may understand what went through your mind.

³¹"Your Majesty looked, and there before you stood a large statue—an enormous, dazzling statue, awesome in appearance. ³²The head of the statue was made of pure gold, its chest and arms of silver, its belly and thighs of bronze, ³³its legs of iron, its feet partly of iron and partly of baked clay. ³⁴While you were watching, a rock was cut out, but not by human hands. It struck the statue on its feet of iron and clay and smashed them. ³⁵Then the iron, the clay, the bronze, the silver and the gold were all broken to pieces and became like chaff on a threshing floor in the summer. The wind swept them away without leaving a trace. But the rock that struck the statue became a huge mountain and filled the whole earth.

³⁶"This was the dream, and now we will interpret it to the king. ³⁷Your Majesty, you are the king of kings. The God of heaven has given you dominion and power and might and glory; ³⁸in your hands he has placed all mankind and the beasts of the field and the birds in the sky. Wherever they live, he has made you ruler over them all. You are that head of gold.

³⁹"After you, another kingdom will arise, inferior to yours. Next, a third kingdom, one of bronze, will rule over the whole earth. ⁴⁰Finally, there will be a fourth kingdom, strong as iron—for iron breaks and smashes everything—and as iron breaks things to pieces, so it will crush and break all the others. ⁴¹Just as you saw that the feet and toes were partly of baked clay and partly of iron, so this will be a divided kingdom; yet it will have some of the strength of iron in it, even as you saw iron mixed with clay. ⁴²As the toes were partly iron and partly clay, so this kingdom will be partly strong and partly brittle. ⁴³And just as you saw the iron mixed with baked clay, so the people will be a mixture and will not remain united, any more than iron mixes with clay.

⁴⁴"In the time of those kings, the God of heaven will set up a kingdom that will never be destroyed, nor will it be left to another people. It will crush all those kingdoms and bring them to an end, but it will itself endure forever. ⁴⁵This is the meaning of the vision of the rock cut out of a mountain, but not by human hands—a rock that broke the iron, the bronze, the clay, the silver and the gold to pieces.

"The great God has shown the king what will take place in the future. The dream is true and its interpretation is trustworthy."

⁴⁶Then King Nebuchadnezzar fell prostrate before Daniel and paid him honor and ordered that an offering and incense be presented to him. ⁴⁷The king said to Daniel, "Surely your God is the God of gods and the Lord of kings and a revealer of mysteries, for you were able to reveal this mystery."

ROCK SOLID *promises*

"God is the God of gods and the Lord of kings and a revealer of mysteries." Daniel 2:47

Your Lord is smarter, stronger, and kinder than anyone else that tries to boss you around. He is the one real God.

⁴⁸Then the king placed Daniel in a high position and lavished many gifts on him. He made him ruler over the entire province of Babylon and placed him in charge of all its wise men. ⁴⁹Moreover, at Daniel's request the king appointed Shadrach, Meshach and Abednego administrators over the province of Babylon, while Daniel himself remained at the royal court.

The Image of Gold and the Blazing Furnace

3 King Nebuchadnezzar made an image of gold, sixty cubits high and six cubits wide,^a and set it up on the plain of Dura in the province of Babylon. ²He then summoned the satraps, prefects, governors, advisers, treasurers, judges, magistrates and all the other provincial officials to come to the dedication of the image he had set up. ³So the satraps, prefects, governors, advisers, treasurers, judges, magistrates and all the other provincial officials assembled for the dedication of the image that King Nebuchadnezzar had set up, and they stood before it.

⁴Then the herald loudly proclaimed, "Nations and peoples of every language, this is what you are commanded to do: ⁵As soon as you hear the sound of the horn, flute, zither, lyre, harp, pipe and all kinds of music, you must fall down and worship the image of gold that King Nebuchadnezzar has set up. ⁶Whoever does not fall down and worship will immediately be thrown into a blazing furnace."

⁷Therefore, as soon as they heard the sound of the horn, flute, zither, lyre, harp and all kinds of music, all the nations and peoples of every language fell down and worshiped the image of gold that King Nebuchadnezzar had set up.

⁸At this time some astrologers^b came forward and denounced the Jews. ⁹They said to King Nebuchadnezzar, "May the king live forever! ¹⁰Your Majesty has issued a decree that everyone who hears the sound of the horn, flute, zither, lyre, harp, pipe and all kinds of music must fall down and worship the image of gold, ¹¹and that whoever does not fall down and worship will be thrown into a blazing furnace. ¹²But there are some Jews whom you have set over the affairs of the province of Babylon—Shadrach, Meshach and Abednego—who pay no attention to you, Your Majesty. They neither serve your gods nor worship the image of gold you have set up."

¹³Furious with rage, Nebuchadnezzar summoned Shadrach, Meshach and Abednego. So these men were brought before the king, ¹⁴and Nebuchadnezzar said to them, "Is it true, Shadrach, Meshach and Abednego, that you do not serve my gods or worship the image of gold I have set up? ¹⁵Now when you hear the sound of the horn, flute, zither, lyre, harp, pipe and all kinds of music, if you are ready to fall down and worship the image I made, very good. But if you do not worship it, you will be thrown immediately into a blazing furnace. Then what god will be able to rescue you from my hand?"

¹⁶Shadrach, Meshach and Abednego replied to him, "King Nebuchadnezzar, we do not need to defend ourselves before you in this matter. ¹⁷If we are thrown into the blazing furnace, the God we serve is able to deliver us from it, and he will deliver us^c from Your Majesty's hand. ¹⁸But even if he does not, we want you to know, Your Majesty, that we will not serve your gods or worship the image of gold you have set up."

¹⁹Then Nebuchadnezzar was furious with Shadrach, Meshach and Abednego, and his attitude toward them changed. He ordered the furnace heated seven times hotter than usual ²⁰and commanded some of the strongest soldiers in his army to tie up Shadrach, Meshach and Abednego and throw them into the blazing furnace. ²¹So these men, wearing their robes, trousers, turbans and other clothes, were bound and thrown into the blazing furnace. ²²The king's command was so urgent and the furnace so hot that the flames of the fire killed the soldiers who took up Shadrach, Meshach and Abednego, ²³and these three men, firmly tied, fell into the blazing furnace.

²⁴Then King Nebuchadnezzar leaped to his feet in amazement and asked his advisers, "Weren't there three men that we tied up and threw into the fire?"

^a 1 That is, about 90 feet high and 9 feet wide or about 27 meters high and 2.7 meters wide ^b 8 Or *Chaldeans* ^c 17 Or *If the God we serve is able to deliver us, then he will deliver us from the blazing furnace and*

They replied, "Certainly, Your Majesty."
²⁵ He said, "Look! I see four men walking around in the fire, unbound and unharmed, and the fourth looks like a son of the gods."

²⁶ Nebuchadnezzar then approached the opening of the blazing furnace and shouted, "Shadrach, Meshach and Abednego, servants of the Most High God, come out! Come here!"

So Shadrach, Meshach and Abednego came out of the fire, ²⁷ and the satraps, prefects, governors and royal advisers crowded around them. They saw that the fire had not harmed their bodies, nor was a hair of their heads singed; their robes were not scorched, and there was no smell of fire on them.

²⁸ Then Nebuchadnezzar said, "Praise be to the God of Shadrach, Meshach and Abednego, who has sent his angel and rescued his servants! They trusted in him and defied the king's command and were willing to give up their lives rather than serve or worship any god except their own God. ²⁹ Therefore I decree that the people of any nation or language who say anything against the God of Shadrach, Meshach and Abednego be cut into pieces and their houses be turned into piles of rubble, for no other god can save in this way."

³⁰ Then the king promoted Shadrach, Meshach and Abednego in the province of Babylon.

Nebuchadnezzar's Dream of a Tree

4 ᵃ King Nebuchadnezzar,

To the nations and peoples of every language, who live in all the earth:

May you prosper greatly!

²It is my pleasure to tell you about the miraculous signs and wonders

ᵃ In Aramaic texts 4:1-3 is numbered 3:31-33, and 4:4-37 is numbered 4:1-34.

ROCK SOLID principles

Daniel 3:1–30

Stand for what's right no matter what.

"So Shelby—are you in?" Tyler asked. Every head in the room swung around to look at Shelby, who had just taken a bite of pizza. Caught off guard, she was glad to have a few seconds to chew before she was supposed to give an answer. Pretty much the whole band was mad at their director, and the trumpet section wanted to toss a homemade stink bomb on stage during the final concert of the year. "Uhhh, I can't do that," Shelby finally said. "I just can't pull that kind of prank on Mr. Dobbins. It's stupid and dangerous and will make him look like an idiot in front of everyone. It's not okay."

King Nebuchadnezzar of Babylon expected everyone in his kingdom to bow to a statue of himself. When three young followers of God stood up straight, he threatened to toss them in a blazing inferno. The guys didn't know if God would rescue them, but they decided it didn't matter. They vowed to keep doing right no matter what (see Daniel 3:16–18).

that the Most High God has performed for me.

³How great are his signs,
how mighty his wonders!
His kingdom is an eternal
kingdom;
his dominion endures from
generation to generation.

⁴I, Nebuchadnezzar, was at home in my palace, contented and prosperous. ⁵I had a dream that made me afraid. As I was lying in bed, the images and visions that passed through my mind terrified me. ⁶So I commanded that all the wise men of Babylon be brought before me to interpret the dream for me. ⁷When the magicians, enchanters, astrologers[a] and diviners came, I told them the dream, but they could not interpret it for me. ⁸Finally, Daniel came into my presence and I told him the dream. (He is called Belteshazzar, after the name of my god, and the spirit of the holy gods is in him.)

⁹I said, "Belteshazzar, chief of the magicians, I know that the spirit of the holy gods is in you, and no mystery is too difficult for you. Here is my dream; interpret it for me. ¹⁰These are the visions I saw while lying in bed: I looked, and there before me stood a tree in the middle of the land. Its height was enormous. ¹¹The tree grew large and strong and its top touched the sky; it was visible to the ends of the earth. ¹²Its leaves were beautiful, its fruit abundant, and on it was food for all. Under it the wild animals found shelter, and the birds lived in its branches; from it every creature was fed.

¹³"In the visions I saw while lying in bed, I looked, and there before me was a holy one, a messenger,[b] coming down from heaven. ¹⁴He called in a loud voice: 'Cut down the tree and trim off its branches; strip off its leaves and scatter its fruit. Let the animals flee from under it and the birds from its branches. ¹⁵But let the stump and its roots, bound with iron and bronze, remain in the ground, in the grass of the field.

"'Let him be drenched with the dew of heaven, and let him live with the animals among the plants of the earth. ¹⁶Let his mind be changed from that of a man and let him be given the mind of an animal, till seven times[c] pass by for him.

¹⁷"'The decision is announced by messengers, the holy ones declare the verdict, so that the living may know that the Most High is sovereign over all kingdoms on earth and gives them to anyone he wishes and sets over them the lowliest of people.'

¹⁸"This is the dream that I, King Nebuchadnezzar, had. Now, Belteshazzar, tell me what it means, for none of the wise men in my kingdom can interpret it for me. But you can, because the spirit of the holy gods is in you."

Daniel Interprets the Dream

¹⁹Then Daniel (also called Belteshazzar) was greatly perplexed for a time, and his thoughts terrified him. So the king said, "Belteshazzar, do not let the dream or its meaning alarm you."

Belteshazzar answered, "My lord, if only the dream applied to your enemies and its meaning to your adversaries! ²⁰The tree you saw, which grew large and strong, with its top touching the sky, visible to the whole earth, ²¹with beautiful leaves and abundant fruit, providing food for all, giving shelter to the wild animals, and having nesting places in its branches for the birds— ²²Your Majesty, you are that tree! You have become great and strong; your greatness has grown until it reaches the sky, and your dominion extends to distant parts of the earth.

---

^a 7 Or *Chaldeans*   ^b 13 Or *watchman*; also in verses 17 and 23   ^c 16 Or *years*; also in verses 23, 25 and 32

23 "Your Majesty saw a holy one, a messenger, coming down from heaven and saying, 'Cut down the tree and destroy it, but leave the stump, bound with iron and bronze, in the grass of the field, while its roots remain in the ground. Let him be drenched with the dew of heaven; let him live with the wild animals, until seven times pass by for him.'

24 "This is the interpretation, Your Majesty, and this is the decree the Most High has issued against my lord the king: 25 You will be driven away from people and will live with the wild animals; you will eat grass like the ox and be drenched with the dew of heaven. Seven times will pass by for you until you acknowledge that the Most High is sovereign over all kingdoms on earth and gives them to anyone he wishes. 26 The command to leave the stump of the tree with its roots means that your kingdom will be restored to you when you acknowledge that Heaven rules. 27 Therefore, Your Majesty, be pleased to accept my advice: Renounce your sins by doing what is right, and your wickedness by being kind to the oppressed. It may be that then your prosperity will continue."

The Dream Is Fulfilled

28 All this happened to King Nebuchadnezzar. 29 Twelve months later, as the king was walking on the roof of the royal palace of Babylon, 30 he said, "Is not this the great Babylon I have built as the royal residence, by my mighty power and for the glory of my majesty?"

31 Even as the words were on his lips, a voice came from heaven, "This is what is decreed for you, King Nebuchadnezzar: Your royal authority has been taken from you. 32 You will be driven away from people and will live with the wild animals; you will eat grass like the ox. Seven times will pass by for you until you acknowledge that the Most High is

sovereign over all kingdoms on earth and gives them to anyone he wishes."

33 Immediately what had been said about Nebuchadnezzar was fulfilled. He was driven away from people and ate grass like the ox. His body was drenched with the dew of heaven until his hair grew like the feathers of an eagle and his nails like the claws of a bird.

34 At the end of that time, I, Nebuchadnezzar, raised my eyes toward heaven, and my sanity was restored. Then I praised the Most High; I honored and glorified him who lives forever.

His dominion is an eternal dominion;
  his kingdom endures from
    generation to generation.
35 All the peoples of the earth
  are regarded as nothing.
He does as he pleases
  with the powers of heaven
  and the peoples of the earth.
No one can hold back his hand
  or say to him: "What have you
    done?"

36 At the same time that my sanity was restored, my honor and splendor were returned to me for the glory of my kingdom. My advisers and nobles sought me out, and I was restored to my throne and became even greater than before. 37 Now I, Nebuchadnezzar, praise and exalt and glorify the King of heaven, because everything he does is right and all his ways are just. And those who walk in pride he is able to humble.

The Writing on the Wall

5 King Belshazzar gave a great banquet for a thousand of his nobles and drank wine with them. 2 While Belshazzar was drinking his wine, he gave orders to bring in the gold and silver goblets that Nebuchadnezzar his father[a] had

---

[a] 2 Or *ancestor*; or *predecessor*; also in verses 11, 13 and 18

taken from the temple in Jerusalem, so that the king and his nobles, his wives and his concubines might drink from them. ³So they brought in the gold goblets that had been taken from the temple of God in Jerusalem, and the king and his nobles, his wives and his concubines drank from them. ⁴As they drank the wine, they praised the gods of gold and silver, of bronze, iron, wood and stone.

⁵Suddenly the fingers of a human hand appeared and wrote on the plaster of the wall, near the lampstand in the royal palace. The king watched the hand as it wrote. ⁶His face turned pale and he was so frightened that his legs became weak and his knees were knocking.

⁷The king summoned the enchanters, astrologers*a* and diviners. Then he said to these wise men of Babylon, "Whoever reads this writing and tells me what it means will be clothed in purple and have a gold chain placed around his neck, and he will be made the third highest ruler in the kingdom."

⁸Then all the king's wise men came in, but they could not read the writing or tell the king what it meant. ⁹So King Belshazzar became even more terrified and his face grew more pale. His nobles were baffled.

¹⁰The queen,*b* hearing the voices of the king and his nobles, came into the banquet hall. "May the king live forever!" she said. "Don't be alarmed! Don't look so pale! ¹¹There is a man in your kingdom who has the spirit of the holy gods in him. In the time of your father he was found to have insight and intelligence and wisdom like that of the gods. Your father, King Nebuchadnezzar, appointed him chief of the magicians, enchanters, astrologers and diviners. ¹²He did this because Daniel, whom the king called Belteshazzar, was found to have a keen mind and knowledge and understanding, and also the ability to interpret dreams, explain riddles and solve difficult problems. Call for Daniel, and he will tell you what the writing means."

¹³So Daniel was brought before the

king, and the king said to him, "Are you Daniel, one of the exiles my father the king brought from Judah? ¹⁴I have heard that the spirit of the gods is in you and that you have insight, intelligence and outstanding wisdom. ¹⁵The wise men and enchanters were brought before me to read this writing and tell me what it means, but they could not explain it. ¹⁶Now I have heard that you are able to give interpretations and to solve difficult problems. If you can read this writing and tell me what it means, you will be clothed in purple and have a gold chain placed around your neck, and you will be made the third highest ruler in the kingdom."

¹⁷Then Daniel answered the king, "You may keep your gifts for yourself and give your rewards to someone else. Nevertheless, I will read the writing for the king and tell him what it means.

¹⁸"Your Majesty, the Most High God gave your father Nebuchadnezzar sovereignty and greatness and glory and splendor. ¹⁹Because of the high position he gave him, all the nations and peoples of every language dreaded and feared him. Those the king wanted to put to death, he put to death; those he wanted to spare, he spared; those he wanted to promote, he promoted; and those he wanted to humble, he humbled. ²⁰But when his heart became arrogant and hardened with pride, he was deposed from his royal throne and stripped of his glory. ²¹He was driven away from people and given the mind of an animal; he lived with the wild donkeys and ate grass like the ox; and his body was drenched with the dew of heaven, until he acknowledged that the Most High God is sovereign over all kingdoms on earth and sets over them anyone he wishes.

²²"But you, Belshazzar, his son,*c* have not humbled yourself, though you knew all this. ²³Instead, you have set yourself up against the Lord of heaven. You had the goblets from his temple brought to you, and you and your nobles, your wives and your concubines drank wine from them.

---

a 7 Or *Chaldeans*; also in verse 11   *b* 10 Or *queen mother*   *c* 22 Or *descendant*; or *successor*

You praised the gods of silver and gold, of bronze, iron, wood and stone, which cannot see or hear or understand. But you did not honor the God who holds in his hand your life and all your ways. ²⁴Therefore he sent the hand that wrote the inscription.

²⁵"This is the inscription that was written:

MENE, MENE, TEKEL, PARSIN

²⁶"Here is what these words mean:

Mene^a: God has numbered the days of your reign and brought it to an end.
²⁷ Tekel^b: You have been weighed on the scales and found wanting.
²⁸ Peres^c: Your kingdom is divided and given to the Medes and Persians."

²⁹Then at Belshazzar's command, Daniel was clothed in purple, a gold chain was placed around his neck, and he was proclaimed the third highest ruler in the kingdom.

³⁰That very night Belshazzar, king of the Babylonians,^d was slain, ³¹and Darius the Mede took over the kingdom, at the age of sixty-two.^e

Daniel in the Den of Lions

6 ^f It pleased Darius to appoint 120 satraps to rule throughout the kingdom, ²with three administrators over them, one of whom was Daniel. The satraps were made accountable to them so that the king might not suffer loss. ³Now Daniel so distinguished himself among the administrators and the satraps by his exceptional qualities that the king planned to set him over the whole kingdom. ⁴At this, the administrators and the satraps tried to find grounds for charges against Daniel in his conduct of government affairs, but they were unable to do so. They could find no corruption in him, because he was trustworthy and neither corrupt nor negligent. ⁵Finally these men said, "We will never find any basis for charges against this man Daniel un-

less it has something to do with the law of his God."

⁶So these administrators and satraps went as a group to the king and said: "May King Darius live forever! ⁷The royal administrators, prefects, satraps, advisers and governors have all agreed that the king should issue an edict and enforce the decree that anyone who prays to any god or human being during the next thirty days, except to you, Your Majesty, shall be thrown into the lions' den. ⁸Now, Your Majesty, issue the decree and put it in writing so that it cannot be altered—in accordance with the law of the Medes and Persians, which cannot be repealed." ⁹So King Darius put the decree in writing.

¹⁰Now when Daniel learned that the decree had been published, he went home to his upstairs room where the windows opened toward Jerusalem. Three times a day he got down on his knees and prayed, giving thanks to his God, just as he had done before. ¹¹Then these men went as a group and found Daniel praying and asking God for help. ¹²So they went to the king and spoke to him about his royal decree: "Did you not publish a decree that during the next thirty days anyone who prays to any god or human being except to you, Your Majesty, would be thrown into the lions' den?"

The king answered, "The decree stands—in accordance with the law of the Medes and Persians, which cannot be repealed."

¹³Then they said to the king, "Daniel, who is one of the exiles from Judah, pays no attention to you, Your Majesty, or to the decree you put in writing. He still prays three times a day." ¹⁴When the king heard this, he was greatly distressed; he was determined to rescue Daniel and made every effort until sundown to save him.

^a 26 Mene can mean numbered or mina (a unit of money).   ^b 27 Tekel can mean weighed or shekel.   ^c 28 Peres (the singular of Parsin) can mean divided or Persia or a half mina or a half shekel.   ^d 30 Or Chaldeans   ^e 31 In Aramaic texts this verse (5:31) is numbered 6:1.   ^f In Aramaic texts 6:1-28 is numbered 6:2-29.

¹⁵Then the men went as a group to King Darius and said to him, "Remember, Your Majesty, that according to the law of the Medes and Persians no decree or edict that the king issues can be changed."

¹⁶So the king gave the order, and they brought Daniel and threw him into the lions' den. The king said to Daniel, "May your God, whom you serve continually, rescue you!"

¹⁷A stone was brought and placed over the mouth of the den, and the king sealed it with his own signet ring and with the rings of his nobles, so that Daniel's situation might not be changed. ¹⁸Then the king returned to his palace and spent the night without eating and without any entertainment being brought to him. And he could not sleep.

¹⁹At the first light of dawn, the king got up and hurried to the lions' den. ²⁰When he came near the den, he called to Daniel in an anguished voice, "Daniel, servant of the living God, has your God, whom you serve continually, been able to rescue you from the lions?"

²¹Daniel answered, "May the king live forever! ²²My God sent his angel, and he shut the mouths of the lions. They have not hurt me, because I was found innocent in his sight. Nor have I ever done any wrong before you, Your Majesty."

²³The king was overjoyed and gave orders to lift Daniel out of the den. And when Daniel was lifted from the den, no wound was found on him, because he had trusted in his God.

²⁴At the king's command, the men who had falsely accused Daniel were brought in and thrown into the lions' den, along with their wives and children. And before they reached the floor of the den, the lions overpowered them and crushed all their bones.

²⁵Then King Darius wrote to all the nations and peoples of every language in all the earth:

"May you prosper greatly!

²⁶"I issue a decree that in every part of my kingdom people must fear and reverence the God of Daniel.

"For he is the living God
   and he endures forever;
his kingdom will not be destroyed,
   his dominion will never end.

ROCK SOLID
promises

"He is the living God . . . his kingdom will not be destroyed."
Daniel 6:26

God is real. He existed before the world began. And he will never stop ruling the universe.

²⁷He rescues and he saves;
   he performs signs and wonders
      in the heavens and on the earth.
He has rescued Daniel
   from the power of the lions."

²⁸So Daniel prospered during the reign of Darius and the reign of Cyrus[a] the Persian.

Daniel's Dream of Four Beasts

7 In the first year of Belshazzar king of Babylon, Daniel had a dream, and visions passed through his mind as he was lying in bed. He wrote down the substance of his dream.

²Daniel said: "In my vision at night I looked, and there before me were the four winds of heaven churning up the great sea. ³Four great beasts, each different from the others, came up out of the sea.

⁴"The first was like a lion, and it had the wings of an eagle. I watched until its wings were torn off and it was lifted from the ground so that it stood on two feet like a human being, and the mind of a human was given to it.

⁵"And there before me was a second

_____
a 28 Or *Darius, that is, the reign of Cyrus*

beast, which looked like a bear. It was raised up on one of its sides, and it had three ribs in its mouth between its teeth. It was told, 'Get up and eat your fill of flesh!'

6 "After that, I looked, and there before me was another beast, one that looked like a leopard. And on its back it had four wings like those of a bird. This beast had four heads, and it was given authority to rule.

7 "After that, in my vision at night I looked, and there before me was a fourth beast—terrifying and frightening and very powerful. It had large iron teeth; it crushed and devoured its victims and trampled underfoot whatever was left. It was different from all the former beasts, and it had ten horns.

8 "While I was thinking about the horns, there before me was another horn, a little one, which came up among them; and three of the first horns were uprooted before it. This horn had eyes like the eyes of a human being and a mouth that spoke boastfully.

9 "As I looked,

"thrones were set in place,
    and the Ancient of Days took his
        seat.
His clothing was as white as snow;
    the hair of his head was white like
        wool.
His throne was flaming with fire,
    and its wheels were all ablaze.
10 A river of fire was flowing,
    coming out from before him.
Thousands upon thousands attended
        him;
    ten thousand times ten thousand
        stood before him.
The court was seated,
    and the books were opened.

11 "Then I continued to watch because of the boastful words the horn was speaking. I kept looking until the beast was slain and its body destroyed and thrown into the blazing fire. 12 (The other beasts had been stripped of their authority, but were allowed to live for a period of time.)

13 "In my vision at night I looked, and

there before me was one like a son of man,[a] coming with the clouds of heaven. He approached the Ancient of Days and was led into his presence. 14 He was given authority, glory and sovereign power; all nations and peoples of every language worshiped him. His dominion is an everlasting dominion that will not pass away, and his kingdom is one that will never be destroyed.

The Interpretation of the Dream

15 "I, Daniel, was troubled in spirit, and the visions that passed through my mind disturbed me. 16 I approached one of those standing there and asked him the meaning of all this.

"So he told me and gave me the interpretation of these things: 17 'The four great beasts are four kings that will rise from the earth. 18 But the holy people of the Most High will receive the kingdom and will possess it forever—yes, for ever and ever.'

19 "Then I wanted to know the meaning of the fourth beast, which was different from all the others and most terrifying, with its iron teeth and bronze claws—the beast that crushed and devoured its victims and trampled underfoot whatever was left. 20 I also wanted to know about the ten horns on its head and about the other horn that came up, before which three of them fell—the horn that looked more imposing than the others and that had eyes and a mouth that spoke boastfully. 21 As I watched, this horn was waging war against the holy people and defeating them, 22 until the Ancient of Days came and pronounced judgment in favor of the holy people of the Most High, and the time came when they possessed the kingdom.

23 "He gave me this explanation: 'The fourth beast is a fourth kingdom that will appear on earth. It will be different from

---

a 13 The Aramaic phrase *bar enash* means *human being*. The phrase *son of man* is retained here because of its use in the New Testament as a title of Jesus, probably based largely on this verse.

all the other kingdoms and will devour the whole earth, trampling it down and crushing it. ²⁴The ten horns are ten kings who will come from this kingdom. After them another king will arise, different from the earlier ones; he will subdue three kings. ²⁵He will speak against the Most High and oppress his holy people and try to change the set times and the laws. The holy people will be delivered into his hands for a time, times and half a time.ᵃ

²⁶" 'But the court will sit, and his power will be taken away and completely destroyed forever. ²⁷Then the sovereignty, power and greatness of all the kingdoms under heaven will be handed over to the holy people of the Most High. His kingdom will be an everlasting kingdom, and all rulers will worship and obey him.'

²⁸"This is the end of the matter. I, Daniel, was deeply troubled by my thoughts, and my face turned pale, but I kept the matter to myself."

Daniel's Vision of a Ram and a Goat

8 In the third year of King Belshazzar's reign, I, Daniel, had a vision, after the one that had already appeared to me. ²In my vision I saw myself in the citadel of Susa in the province of Elam; in the vision I was beside the Ulai Canal. ³I looked up, and there before me was a ram with two horns, standing beside the canal, and the horns were long. One of the horns was longer than the other but grew up later. ⁴I watched the ram as it charged toward the west and the north and the south. No animal could stand against it, and none could rescue from its power. It did as it pleased and became great.

⁵As I was thinking about this, suddenly a goat with a prominent horn between its eyes came from the west, crossing the whole earth without touching the ground. ⁶It came toward the two-horned ram I had seen standing beside the canal and charged at it in great rage. ⁷I saw it attack the ram furiously, striking the ram and shattering its two horns. The ram was powerless to stand against it; the goat

knocked it to the ground and trampled on it, and none could rescue the ram from its power. ⁸The goat became very great, but at the height of its power the large horn was broken off, and in its place four prominent horns grew up toward the four winds of heaven.

⁹Out of one of them came another horn, which started small but grew in power to the south and to the east and toward the Beautiful Land. ¹⁰It grew until it reached the host of the heavens, and it threw some of the starry host down to the earth and trampled on them. ¹¹It set itself up to be as great as the commander of the army of the Lord; it took away the daily sacrifice from the Lord, and his sanctuary was thrown down. ¹²Because of rebellion, the Lord's peopleᵇ and the daily sacrifice were given over to it. It prospered in everything it did, and truth was thrown to the ground.

¹³Then I heard a holy one speaking, and another holy one said to him, "How long will it take for the vision to be fulfilled— the vision concerning the daily sacrifice, the rebellion that causes desolation, the surrender of the sanctuary and the trampling underfoot of the Lord's people?"

¹⁴He said to me, "It will take 2,300 evenings and mornings; then the sanctuary will be reconsecrated."

The Interpretation of the Vision

¹⁵While I, Daniel, was watching the vision and trying to understand it, there before me stood one who looked like a man. ¹⁶And I heard a man's voice from the Ulai calling, "Gabriel, tell this man the meaning of the vision."

¹⁷As he came near the place where I was standing, I was terrified and fell prostrate. "Son of man,"ᶜ he said to me, "understand that the vision concerns the time of the end."

¹⁸While he was speaking to me, I was in a deep sleep, with my face to the

---

ᵃ 25 Or *for a year, two years and half a year*
ᵇ 12 Or *rebellion, the armies*   ᶜ 17 The Hebrew phrase *ben adam* means *human being*. The phrase *son of man* is retained as a form of address here because of its possible association with "Son of Man" in the New Testament.

ground. Then he touched me and raised me to my feet.

¹⁹He said: "I am going to tell you what will happen later in the time of wrath, because the vision concerns the appointed time of the end.ᵃ ²⁰The two-horned ram that you saw represents the kings of Media and Persia. ²¹The shaggy goat is the king of Greece, and the large horn between its eyes is the first king. ²²The four horns that replaced the one that was broken off represent four kingdoms that will emerge from his nation but will not have the same power.

²³"In the latter part of their reign, when rebels have become completely wicked, a fierce-looking king, a master of intrigue, will arise. ²⁴He will become very strong, but not by his own power. He will cause astounding devastation and will succeed in whatever he does. He will destroy those who are mighty, the holy people. ²⁵He will cause deceit to prosper, and he will consider himself superior. When they feel secure, he will destroy many and take his stand against the Prince of princes. Yet he will be destroyed, but not by human power.

²⁶"The vision of the evenings and mornings that has been given you is true, but seal up the vision, for it concerns the distant future."

²⁷I, Daniel, was worn out. I lay exhausted for several days. Then I got up and went about the king's business. I was appalled by the vision; it was beyond understanding.

Daniel's Prayer

9 In the first year of Darius son of Xerxesᵇ (a Mede by descent), who was made ruler over the Babylonianᶜ kingdom— ²in the first year of his reign, I, Daniel, understood from the Scriptures, according to the word of the LORD given to Jeremiah the prophet, that the desolation of Jerusalem would last seventy years. ³So I turned to the Lord God and pleaded with him in prayer and petition, in fasting, and in sackcloth and ashes.

⁴I prayed to the LORD my God and confessed:

"Lord, the great and awesome God, who keeps his covenant of love with those who love him and keep his commandments, ⁵we have sinned and done wrong. We have been wicked and have rebelled; we have turned away from your commands and laws. ⁶We have not listened to your servants the prophets, who spoke in your name to our kings, our princes and our ancestors, and to all the people of the land.

⁷"Lord, you are righteous, but this day we are covered with shame—the people of Judah and the inhabitants of Jerusalem and all Israel, both near and far, in all the countries where you have scattered us because of our unfaithfulness to you. ⁸We and our kings, our princes and our ancestors are covered with shame, LORD, because we have sinned against you. ⁹The Lord our God is merciful and forgiving, even though we have rebelled against him; ¹⁰we have not obeyed the LORD our God or kept the laws he gave us through his servants the prophets. ¹¹All Israel has transgressed your law and turned away, refusing to obey you.

"Therefore the curses and sworn judgments written in the Law of Moses, the servant of God, have been poured out on us, because we have sinned against you. ¹²You have fulfilled the words spoken against us and against our rulers by bringing on us great disaster. Under the whole heaven nothing has ever been done like what has been done to Jerusalem. ¹³Just as it is written in the Law of Moses, all this disaster has come on us, yet we have not sought the favor of the LORD our God by turning from our sins and giving attention to your truth. ¹⁴The LORD did not

---

ᵃ 19 Or *because the end will be at the appointed time*   ᵇ 1 Hebrew *Ahasuerus*
ᶜ 1 Or *Chaldean*

hesitate to bring the disaster on us, for the Lord our God is righteous in everything he does; yet we have not obeyed him.

[15] "Now, Lord our God, who brought your people out of Egypt with a mighty hand and who made for yourself a name that endures to this day, we have sinned, we have done wrong. [16] Lord, in keeping with all your righteous acts, turn away your anger and your wrath from Jerusalem, your city, your holy hill. Our sins and the iniquities of our ancestors have made Jerusalem and your people an object of scorn to all those around us.

[17] "Now, our God, hear the prayers and petitions of your servant. For your sake, Lord, look with favor on your desolate sanctuary. [18] Give ear, our God, and hear; open your eyes and see the desolation of the city that bears your Name. We do not make requests of you because we are righteous, but because of your great mercy. [19] Lord, listen! Lord, forgive! Lord, hear and act! For your sake, my God, do not delay, because your city and your people bear your Name."

The Seventy "Sevens"

[20] While I was speaking and praying, confessing my sin and the sin of my people Israel and making my request to the Lord my God for his holy hill— [21] while I was still in prayer, Gabriel, the man I had seen in the earlier vision, came to me in swift flight about the time of the evening sacrifice. [22] He instructed me and said to me, "Daniel, I have now come to give you insight and understanding. [23] As soon as you began to pray, a word went out, which I have come to tell you, for you are highly esteemed. Therefore, consider the word and understand the vision:

[24] "Seventy 'sevens'[a] are decreed for your people and your holy city to finish[b] transgression, to put an end to sin, to atone for wickedness, to bring in everlasting righteousness, to seal up vision and prophecy and to anoint the Most Holy Place.[c]

[25] "Know and understand this: From the time the word goes out to restore and rebuild Jerusalem until the Anointed One,[d] the ruler, comes, there will be seven 'sevens,' and sixty-two 'sevens.' It will be rebuilt with streets and a trench, but in times of trouble. [26] After the sixty-two 'sevens,' the Anointed One will be put to death and will have nothing.[e] The people of the ruler who will come will destroy the city and the sanctuary. The end will come like a flood: War will continue until the end, and desolations have been decreed. [27] He will confirm a covenant with many for one 'seven.'[f] In the middle of the 'seven'[f] he will put an end to sacrifice and offering. And at the temple[g] he will set up an abomination that causes desolation, until the end that is decreed is poured out on him.[b]"[i]

Daniel's Vision of a Man

10 In the third year of Cyrus king of Persia, a revelation was given to Daniel (who was called Belteshazzar). Its message was true and it concerned a great war.[j] The understanding of the message came to him in a vision.

[2] At that time I, Daniel, mourned for three weeks. [3] I ate no choice food; no meat or wine touched my lips; and I used no lotions at all until the three weeks were over.

[4] On the twenty-fourth day of the first month, as I was standing on the bank of the great river, the Tigris, [5] I looked up and there before me was a man dressed in linen, with a belt of fine gold from Uphaz around his waist. [6] His body was like topaz, his face like lightning, his eyes like flaming torches, his arms and legs like the

---

[a] 24 Or 'weeks'; also in verses 25 and 26
[b] 24 Or restrain   [c] 24 Or the most holy One
[d] 25 Or an anointed one; also in verse 26
[e] 26 Or death and will have no one; or death, but not for himself   [f] 27 Or 'week'
[g] 27 Septuagint and Theodotion; Hebrew wing   [h] 27 Or it   [i] 27 Or And one who causes desolation will come upon the wing of the abominable temple, until the end that is decreed is poured out on the desolated city   [j] 1 Or true and burdensome

gleam of burnished bronze, and his voice like the sound of a multitude.

⁷I, Daniel, was the only one who saw the vision; those who were with me did not see it, but such terror overwhelmed them that they fled and hid themselves. ⁸So I was left alone, gazing at this great vision; I had no strength left, my face turned deathly pale and I was helpless. ⁹Then I heard him speaking, and as I listened to him, I fell into a deep sleep, my face to the ground.

¹⁰A hand touched me and set me trembling on my hands and knees. ¹¹He said, "Daniel, you who are highly esteemed, consider carefully the words I am about to speak to you, and stand up, for I have now been sent to you." And when he said this to me, I stood up trembling.

¹²Then he continued, "Do not be afraid, Daniel. Since the first day that you set your mind to gain understanding and to humble yourself before your God, your words were heard, and I have come in response to them. ¹³But the prince of the Persian kingdom resisted me twenty-one days. Then Michael, one of the chief princes, came to help me, because I was detained there with the king of Persia. ¹⁴Now I have come to explain to you what will happen to your people in the future, for the vision concerns a time yet to come."

Daniel 9
Daniel kept himself pure.

You likely know Daniel as the guy tossed into a lion den for breaking the law by praying openly to the one true God (see Daniel 6:10–28). But there is much more to his story than that.

Daniel was forced from his home in Jerusalem when the Babylonians took a group of captives from the city in 605 BC. He was one of the "young men without any physical defect, handsome, showing aptitude for every kind of learning, well informed, quick to understand, and qualified to serve in the king's palace" (Daniel 1:4). In a faraway land he was taught the Babylonian language and fed food and wine from the king's table, all to prepare him for royal service.

Early on, however, Daniel had decided to fully keep God's law, even as he trained as a servant in a vast and bewildering foreign empire. He refused the king's food and requested a simple diet of vegetables and water that allowed him to keep pure according to God's dietary rules. Instead of fainting from hunger, Daniel outperformed all the other royal trainees. In every area of wisdom he and a few Jewish friends were "ten times better than all the magicians and enchanters in his whole kingdom" (Daniel 1:20).

Daniel's decision to obey God didn't happen at the instant he was about to be dropped into a lion cage. He committed every part of his life to God right from the start. He decided to live pure no matter what.

You can find Daniel in Ezekiel 14 and Matthew 24:15 as well as the book named after him.

UNSHAKEN people

¹⁵While he was saying this to me, I bowed with my face toward the ground and was speechless. ¹⁶Then one who looked like a man*ᵃ* touched my lips, and I opened my mouth and began to speak. I said to the one standing before me, "I am overcome with anguish because of the vision, my lord, and I feel very weak. ¹⁷How can I, your servant, talk with you, my lord? My strength is gone and I can hardly breathe."

¹⁸Again the one who looked like a man touched me and gave me strength. ¹⁹"Do not be afraid, you who are highly esteemed," he said. "Peace! Be strong now; be strong."

When he spoke to me, I was strengthened and said, "Speak, my lord, since you have given me strength."

²⁰So he said, "Do you know why I have come to you? Soon I will return to fight against the prince of Persia, and when I go, the prince of Greece will come; ²¹but first I will tell you what is written in the Book of Truth. (No one supports me against them except Michael, your prince.

11 ¹And in the first year of Darius the Mede, I took my stand to support and protect him.)

The Kings of the South and the North

²"Now then, I tell you the truth: Three more kings will arise in Persia, and then a fourth, who will be far richer than all the others. When he has gained power by his wealth, he will stir up everyone against the kingdom of Greece. ³Then a mighty king will arise, who will rule with great power and do as he pleases. ⁴After he has arisen, his empire will be broken up and parceled out toward the four winds of heaven. It will not go to his descendants, nor will it have the power he exercised, because his empire will be uprooted and given to others.

⁵"The king of the South will become strong, but one of his commanders will become even stronger than he and will rule his own kingdom with great power. ⁶After some years, they will become allies. The daughter of the king of the South will go to the king of the North to make an alliance, but she will not retain her power, and he and his power*ᵇ* will not last. In those days she will be betrayed, together with her royal escort and her father*ᶜ* and the one who supported her.

⁷"One from her family line will arise to take her place. He will attack the forces of the king of the North and enter his fortress; he will fight against them and be victorious. ⁸He will also seize their gods, their metal images and their valuable articles of silver and gold and carry them off to Egypt. For some years he will leave the king of the North alone. ⁹Then the king of the North will invade the realm of the king of the South but will retreat to his own country. ¹⁰His sons will prepare for war and assemble a great army, which will sweep on like an irresistible flood and carry the battle as far as his fortress.

¹¹"Then the king of the South will march out in a rage and fight against the king of the North, who will raise a large army, but it will be defeated. ¹²When the army is carried off, the king of the South will be filled with pride and will slaughter many thousands, yet he will not remain triumphant. ¹³For the king of the North will muster another army, larger than the first; and after several years, he will advance with a huge army fully equipped.

¹⁴"In those times many will rise against the king of the South. Those who are violent among your own people will rebel in fulfillment of the vision, but without success. ¹⁵Then the king of the North will come and build up siege ramps and will capture a fortified city. The forces of the South will be powerless to resist; even their best troops will not have the strength to stand. ¹⁶The invader will do as he pleases; no one will be able to stand against him. He will establish himself in the Beautiful Land and will have the power to destroy it. ¹⁷He will determine to come with the might of his entire king-

---

ᵃ 16 Most manuscripts of the Masoretic Text; one manuscript of the Masoretic Text, Dead Sea Scrolls and Septuagint *Then something that looked like a human hand*   *ᵇ 6* Or *offspring*   *ᶜ 6* Or *child* (see Vulgate and Syriac) dom and will make an alliance with the king of the South. And he will give him a daughter in marriage in order to overthrow the kingdom, but his plans*a* will not succeed or help him. ¹⁸Then he will turn his attention to the coastlands and will take many of them, but a commander will put an end to his insolence and will turn his insolence back on him. ¹⁹After this, he will turn back toward the fortresses of his own country but will stumble and fall, to be seen no more.

²⁰"His successor will send out a tax collector to maintain the royal splendor. In a few years, however, he will be destroyed, yet not in anger or in battle.

²¹"He will be succeeded by a contemptible person who has not been given the honor of royalty. He will invade the kingdom when its people feel secure, and he will seize it through intrigue. ²²Then an overwhelming army will be swept away before him; both it and a prince of the covenant will be destroyed. ²³After coming to an agreement with him, he will act deceitfully, and with only a few people he will rise to power. ²⁴When the richest provinces feel secure, he will invade them and will achieve what neither his fathers nor his forefathers did. He will distribute plunder, loot and wealth among his followers. He will plot the overthrow of fortresses—but only for a time.

²⁵"With a large army he will stir up his strength and courage against the king of the South. The king of the South will wage war with a large and very powerful army, but he will not be able to stand because of the plots devised against him. ²⁶Those who eat from the king's provisions will try to destroy him; his army will be swept away, and many will fall in battle. ²⁷The two kings, with their hearts bent on evil, will sit at the same table and lie to each other, but to no avail, because an end will still come at the appointed time. ²⁸The king of the North will return to his own country with great wealth, but his heart will be set against the holy covenant. He will take action against it and then return to his own country.

²⁹"At the appointed time he will invade the South again, but this time the outcome will be different from what it was before. ³⁰Ships of the western coastlands will oppose him, and he will lose heart. Then he will turn back and vent his fury against the holy covenant. He will return and show favor to those who forsake the holy covenant.

³¹"His armed forces will rise up to desecrate the temple fortress and will abolish the daily sacrifice. Then they will set up the abomination that causes desolation. ³²With flattery he will corrupt those who have violated the covenant, but the people who know their God will firmly resist him.

³³"Those who are wise will instruct many, though for a time they will fall by the sword or be burned or captured or plundered. ³⁴When they fall, they will receive a little help, and many who are not sincere will join them. ³⁵Some of the wise will stumble, so that they may be refined, purified and made spotless until the time of the end, for it will still come at the appointed time.

The King Who Exalts Himself

³⁶"The king will do as he pleases. He will exalt and magnify himself above every god and will say unheard-of things against the God of gods. He will be successful until the time of wrath is completed, for what has been determined must take place. ³⁷He will show no regard for the gods of his ancestors or for the one desired by women, nor will he regard any god, but will exalt himself above them all. ³⁸Instead of them, he will honor a god of fortresses; a god unknown to his ancestors he will honor with gold and silver, with precious stones and costly gifts. ³⁹He will attack the mightiest fortresses with the help of a foreign god and will greatly honor those who acknowledge him. He will make them rulers over many people and will distribute the land at a price.*b*

⁴⁰"At the time of the end the king of the South will engage him in battle, and the

a 17 Or *but she*   *b 39* Or *land for a reward*

king of the North will storm out against him with chariots and cavalry and a great fleet of ships. He will invade many countries and sweep through them like a flood. [41]He will also invade the Beautiful Land. Many countries will fall, but Edom, Moab and the leaders of Ammon will be delivered from his hand. [42]He will extend his power over many countries; Egypt will not escape. [43]He will gain control of the treasures of gold and silver and all the riches of Egypt, with the Libyans and Cushites[a] in submission. [44]But reports from the east and the north will alarm him, and he will set out in a great rage to destroy and annihilate many. [45]He will pitch his royal tents between the seas at[b] the beautiful holy mountain. Yet he will come to his end, and no one will help him.

The End Times

12 "At that time Michael, the great prince who protects your people, will arise. There will be a time of distress such as has not happened from the beginning of nations until then. But at that time your people—everyone whose name is found written in the book—will be delivered. [2]Multitudes who sleep in the dust of the earth will awake: some to everlasting life, others to shame and everlasting contempt. [3]Those who are wise[c] will shine like the brightness of the heavens, and those who lead many to righteousness, like the stars for ever and ever. [4]But you, Daniel, roll up and seal the words of the scroll until the time of the end. Many will go here and there to increase knowledge."

[5]Then I, Daniel, looked, and there before me stood two others, one on this bank of the river and one on the opposite bank. [6]One of them said to the man clothed in linen, who was above the waters of the river, "How long will it be before these astonishing things are fulfilled?"

[7]The man clothed in linen, who was above the waters of the river, lifted his right hand and his left hand toward heaven, and I heard him swear by him who

lives forever, saying, "It will be for a time, times and half a time.[d] When the power of the holy people has been finally broken, all these things will be completed."

[8]I heard, but I did not understand. So I asked, "My lord, what will the outcome of all this be?"

[9]He replied, "Go your way, Daniel, because the words are rolled up and sealed until the time of the end. [10]Many will be

[a] 43 That is, people from the upper Nile region
[b] 45 Or *the sea and*   [c] 3 Or *who impart wisdom*
[d] 7 Or *a year, two years and half a year*

Daniel 12:1–13

The Bible predicts the end of the world.

Daniel was puzzled when he thought about the visions God gave him of the future. He said, "I, Daniel, was troubled in spirit, and the visions that passed through my mind disturbed me" (Daniel 7:15). He had to confess, "I heard, but I did not understand" (Daniel 12:8). Daniel's four visions of the future in chapters 7—12 cover human history from his day until the end of time. Knowing that fact, however, doesn't make the revelations perfectly clear, although many Christians have tried to build timelines for the end of the world based on these chapters. You can be sure of one thing: God will make the meaning of a vision obvious at the right time, exactly when his followers need it. At the moment Daniel admitted he was confused, an angel promised him "those who are wise will understand" (Daniel 12:10).

Think: Why would God include these puzzling messages about the future in the Bible?

ROCK SOLID truths

purified, made spotless and refined, but the wicked will continue to be wicked. None of the wicked will understand, but those who are wise will understand.

¹¹"From the time that the daily sacrifice is abolished and the abomination that causes desolation is set up, there will be 1,290 days. ¹²Blessed is the one who waits for and reaches the end of the 1,335 days.

¹³"As for you, go your way till the end. You will rest, and then at the end of the days you will rise to receive your allotted inheritance."

BOOK OUTLINE

Hosea's experience in family life
(1:1 — 3:5)

Israel's sin
(4:1 — 6:3)

Punishment for Israel
(6:4 — 10:15)

God's judgment and mercy
(11:1 — 14:9)

The prophet Hosea was a citizen of the northern kingdom, Israel, which he commonly called Ephraim. He probably began his ministry before King Jeroboam II died in 753 BC and may have given his messages shortly before the fall of Samaria in 722 BC.

Chapters 1 – 3 tell about Hosea's love for his unfaithful wife, Gomer. Her unfaithfulness is a picture of Israel's unfaithfulness in her covenant relationship with God. Instead of responding in thankfulness and love to God for all their blessings, the Israelites used their crops as offerings to idols. The injustice and mistreatment of others reflected their lack of love for God as well as for their fellow citizens.

The word of the LORD that came to Hosea son of Beeri during the reigns of Uzziah, Jotham, Ahaz and Hezekiah, kings of Judah, and during the reign of Jeroboam son of Jehoash[a] king of Israel:

Hosea's Wife and Children

²When the LORD began to speak through Hosea, the LORD said to him, "Go, marry a promiscuous woman and have children with her, for like an adulterous wife this land is guilty of unfaithfulness to the LORD." ³So he married Gomer daughter of Diblaim, and she conceived and bore him a son.

⁴Then the LORD said to Hosea, "Call him Jezreel, because I will soon punish the house of Jehu for the massacre at Jezreel, and I will put an end to the kingdom of Israel. ⁵In that day I will break Israel's bow in the Valley of Jezreel."

⁶Gomer conceived again and gave birth to a daughter. Then the LORD said to Hosea, "Call her Lo-Ruhamah (which means "not loved"), for I will no longer show love to Israel, that I should at all forgive them. ⁷Yet I will show love to Judah; and I will save them—not by bow, sword or battle, or by horses and horsemen, but I, the LORD their God, will save them."

⁸After she had weaned Lo-Ruhamah, Gomer had another son. ⁹Then the LORD said, "Call him Lo-Ammi (which means "not my people"), for you are not my people, and I am not your God.[b]

¹⁰"Yet the Israelites will be like the sand on the seashore, which cannot be measured or counted. In the place where it was said to them, 'You are not my people,' they will be called 'children of the living God.' ¹¹The people of Judah and the people of Israel will come together; they will appoint one leader and will come up out of the land, for great will be the day of Jezreel.[c]

2 [d] "Say of your brothers, 'My people,' and of your sisters, 'My loved one.'

Israel Punished and Restored

²"Rebuke your mother, rebuke her,
   for she is not my wife,
   and I am not her husband.

Let her remove the adulterous look
   from her face
   and the unfaithfulness from
      between her breasts.
³Otherwise I will strip her naked
   and make her as bare as on the day
      she was born;
I will make her like a desert,
   turn her into a parched land,
   and slay her with thirst.
⁴I will not show my love to her
   children,
   because they are the children of
      adultery.
⁵Their mother has been unfaithful
   and has conceived them in disgrace.
She said, 'I will go after my lovers,
   who give me my food and my water,
   my wool and my linen, my olive oil
      and my drink.'
⁶Therefore I will block her path with
   thornbushes;
   I will wall her in so that she cannot
      find her way.
⁷She will chase after her lovers but not
   catch them;
   she will look for them but not find
      them.
Then she will say,
   'I will go back to my husband as at
      first,
   for then I was better off than now.'
⁸She has not acknowledged that I was
   the one
   who gave her the grain, the new
      wine and oil,
who lavished on her the silver and
   gold—
   which they used for Baal.

⁹"Therefore I will take away my grain
   when it ripens,
   and my new wine when it is ready.
I will take back my wool and my linen,
   intended to cover her naked body.
¹⁰So now I will expose her lewdness
   before the eyes of her lovers;
   no one will take her out of my hands.

---

[a] 1 Hebrew *Joash*, a variant of *Jehoash*
[b] 9 Or *your I AM*   [c] 11 In Hebrew texts 1:10,11 is numbered 2:1,2.   [d] In Hebrew texts 2:1-23 is numbered 2:3-25.

11 I will stop all her celebrations:
    her yearly festivals, her New Moons,
    her Sabbath days—all her
        appointed festivals.
12 I will ruin her vines and her fig trees,
    which she said were her pay from
        her lovers;
I will make them a thicket,
    and wild animals will devour them.
13 I will punish her for the days
    she burned incense to the Baals;
she decked herself with rings and
        jewelry,
    and went after her lovers,
but me she forgot,"
                declares the LORD.

14 "Therefore I am now going to allure
    her;
I will lead her into the wilderness
    and speak tenderly to her.
15 There I will give her back her vineyards,
    and will make the Valley of Achor*a*
        a door of hope.
There she will respond*b* as in the days
    of her youth,
    as in the day she came up out of
        Egypt.

16 "In that day," declares the LORD,
    "you will call me 'my husband';
you will no longer call me 'my
        master.'*c*
17 I will remove the names of the Baals
    from her lips;
    no longer will their names be
        invoked.
18 In that day I will make a covenant for
    them
    with the beasts of the field, the
        birds in the sky
    and the creatures that move along
        the ground.
Bow and sword and battle
    I will abolish from the land,
    so that all may lie down in safety.
19 I will betroth you to me forever;
    I will betroth you in*d* righteousness
        and justice,
    in*d* love and compassion.
20 I will betroth you in*d* faithfulness,
    and you will acknowledge the LORD.

ROCK SOLID truths

Hosea 2:14–20

God loves you deeply.

God had an odd plan for Hosea. The Lord told the prophet to go and marry "an adulterous wife," a prostitute who chased after other lovers (Hosea 1:2). That command makes no sense—until you hear what God planned to teach the nation through his prophet. God said his people were acting like an unfaithful wife hooking up with other men. That charge really hit home, especially because Israel followed false gods whose worship included sex with temple prostitutes to guarantee prosperity (see Hosea 4:11–14). When the Lord told Hosea to take Gomer as his wife, he painted a living picture of his own persistent love for Israel. The crazy drama taught everyone that God loved them no matter what. That's the same point the apostle Paul makes in the New Testament when he says God loves us even while we are sinners, long before we love him (Romans 5:8).

Think: Why does God love sinful people?

---

21 "In that day I will respond,"
    declares the LORD—
"I will respond to the skies,
    and they will respond to the earth;
22 and the earth will respond to the grain,
    the new wine and the olive oil,
    and they will respond to Jezreel.*e*
23 I will plant her for myself in the land;
    I will show my love to the one I
        called 'Not my loved one.'*f*

a 15 *Achor* means *trouble.*   *b* 15 Or *sing*
c 16 Hebrew *baal*   *d* 19,20 Or *with*
e 22 *Jezreel* means *God plants.*   *f* 23 Hebrew
Lo-Ruhamah (see 1:6)

I will say to those called 'Not my
people,'[a] 'You are my people';
and they will say, 'You are my God.'"

Hosea's Reconciliation With His Wife

3 The LORD said to me, "Go, show
your love to your wife again,
though she is loved by anoth-
er man and is an adulteress. Love her as
the LORD loves the Israelites, though they
turn to other gods and love the sacred raisin cakes."

[2] So I bought her for fifteen shekels[b] of
silver and about a homer and a lethek[c] of
barley. [3] Then I told her, "You are to live
with me many days; you must not be a prostitute or be intimate with any man, and I
will behave the same way toward you."

[4] For the Israelites will live many days
without king or prince, without sacrifice
or sacred stones, without ephod or household gods. [5] Afterward the Israelites will
return and seek the LORD their God and
David their king. They will come trembling to the LORD and to his blessings in
the last days.

The Charge Against Israel

4 Hear the word of the LORD, you
Israelites,
because the LORD has a charge
to bring
against you who live in the land:
"There is no faithfulness, no love,
no acknowledgment of God in the
land.
[2] There is only cursing,[d] lying and
murder,
stealing and adultery;
they break all bounds,
and bloodshed follows bloodshed.
[3] Because of this the land dries up,
and all who live in it waste away;
the beasts of the field, the birds in the
sky
and the fish in the sea are swept
away.

[4] "But let no one bring a charge,
let no one accuse another,
for your people are like those
who bring charges against a priest.

[5] You stumble day and night,
and the prophets stumble with you.
So I will destroy your mother—
[6] my people are destroyed from lack
of knowledge.

"Because you have rejected knowledge,
I also reject you as my priests;
because you have ignored the law of
your God,
I also will ignore your children.
[7] The more priests there were,
the more they sinned against me;
they exchanged their glorious God[e]
for something disgraceful.
[8] They feed on the sins of my people
and relish their wickedness.
[9] And it will be: Like people, like
priests.
I will punish both of them for their
ways
and repay them for their deeds.

[10] "They will eat but not have enough;
they will engage in prostitution but
not flourish,
because they have deserted the LORD
to give themselves [11] to prostitution;
old wine and new wine
take away their understanding.
[12] My people consult a wooden idol,
and a diviner's rod speaks to them.
A spirit of prostitution leads them
astray;
they are unfaithful to their God.
[13] They sacrifice on the mountaintops
and burn offerings on the hills,
under oak, poplar and terebinth,
where the shade is pleasant.
Therefore your daughters turn to
prostitution
and your daughters-in-law to
adultery.

[14] "I will not punish your daughters
when they turn to prostitution,

---

[a] 23 Hebrew *Lo-Ammi* (see 1:9)   [b] 2 That is,
about 6 ounces or about 170 grams   [c] 2 A
homer and a lethek possibly weighed about 430
pounds or about 195 kilograms.   [d] 2 That is,
to pronounce a curse on   [e] 7 Syriac (see also
an ancient Hebrew scribal tradition); Masoretic
Text *me; / I will exchange their glory*

nor your daughters-in-law
    when they commit adultery,
because the men themselves consort
        with harlots
    and sacrifice with shrine
            prostitutes—
    a people without understanding will
        come to ruin!

15 "Though you, Israel, commit adultery,
    do not let Judah become guilty.

"Do not go to Gilgal;
    do not go up to Beth Aven.*a*
    And do not swear, 'As surely as the
        LORD lives!'
16 The Israelites are stubborn,
    like a stubborn heifer.
How then can the LORD pasture them
    like lambs in a meadow?
17 Ephraim is joined to idols;
    leave him alone!
18 Even when their drinks are gone,
    they continue their prostitution;
    their rulers dearly love shameful
        ways.
19 A whirlwind will sweep them away,
    and their sacrifices will bring them
        shame.

Judgment Against Israel

5 "Hear this, you priests!
    Pay attention, you Israelites!
    Listen, royal house!
    This judgment is against you:
You have been a snare at Mizpah,
    a net spread out on Tabor.
2 The rebels are knee-deep in slaughter.
    I will discipline all of them.
3 I know all about Ephraim;
    Israel is not hidden from me.
Ephraim, you have now turned to
        prostitution;
    Israel is corrupt.

4 "Their deeds do not permit them
    to return to their God.
A spirit of prostitution is in their heart;
    they do not acknowledge the LORD.
5 Israel's arrogance testifies against them;
    the Israelites, even Ephraim,
        stumble in their sin;
    Judah also stumbles with them.

6 When they go with their flocks and
        herds
    to seek the LORD,
    they will not find him;
    he has withdrawn himself from
        them.
7 They are unfaithful to the LORD;
    they give birth to illegitimate
        children.
When they celebrate their New Moon
        feasts,
    he will devour*b* their fields.

8 "Sound the trumpet in Gibeah,
    the horn in Ramah.
Raise the battle cry in Beth Aven*a*;
    lead on, Benjamin.
9 Ephraim will be laid waste
    on the day of reckoning.
Among the tribes of Israel
    I proclaim what is certain.
10 Judah's leaders are like those
    who move boundary stones.
I will pour out my wrath on them
    like a flood of water.
11 Ephraim is oppressed,
    trampled in judgment,
    intent on pursuing idols.*c*
12 I am like a moth to Ephraim,
    like rot to the people of Judah.

13 "When Ephraim saw his sickness,
    and Judah his sores,
then Ephraim turned to Assyria,
    and sent to the great king for help.
But he is not able to cure you,
    not able to heal your sores.
14 For I will be like a lion to Ephraim,
    like a great lion to Judah.
I will tear them to pieces and go away;
    I will carry them off, with no one to
        rescue them.
15 Then I will return to my lair
    until they have borne their guilt
    and seek my face—
in their misery
    they will earnestly seek me."

*a 15,8 Beth Aven means house of wickedness (a
derogatory name for Bethel, which means house
of God).   b 7 Or Now their New Moon feasts /
will devour them and   c 11 The meaning of
the Hebrew for this word is uncertain.*

Israel Unrepentant

6 "Come, let us return to the Lord.
He has torn us to pieces
but he will heal us;
he has injured us
but he will bind up our wounds.
²After two days he will revive us;
on the third day he will restore us,
that we may live in his presence.
³Let us acknowledge the Lord;
let us press on to acknowledge him.
As surely as the sun rises,
he will appear;
he will come to us like the winter
rains,
like the spring rains that water the
earth."

⁴"What can I do with you, Ephraim?
What can I do with you, Judah?
Your love is like the morning mist,
like the early dew that disappears.
⁵Therefore I cut you in pieces with my
prophets,
I killed you with the words of my
mouth—
then my judgments go forth like the
sun.ᵃ
⁶For I desire mercy, not sacrifice,
and acknowledgment of God rather
than burnt offerings.
⁷As at Adam,ᵇ they have broken the
covenant;
they were unfaithful to me there.
⁸Gilead is a city of evildoers,
stained with footprints of blood.
⁹As marauders lie in ambush for a
victim,
so do bands of priests;
they murder on the road to Shechem,
carrying out their wicked schemes.
¹⁰I have seen a horrible thing in Israel:
There Ephraim is given to
prostitution,
Israel is defiled.

ᵃ 5 The meaning of the Hebrew for this line is
uncertain.   ᵇ 7 Or *Like Adam*; or *Like human
beings*

ROCK SOLID *principles*

Hosea 6:1–3

Come back to God.

Trevor couldn't remember the last time he read his Bible . . . or prayed . . . or even thought about God. A couple years ago he completely ditched church and his Christian friends for a different crowd. He tried to think back to the steps that put in him in such a bad spot, and none of it made sense. His new friends were always looking for a better high, and Trevor slid right into that groove. He discovered he got the biggest thrill from B & E, breaking and entering houses to steal whatever he could carry. As Trevor looked out a window in juvenile hall, he wondered if God would help him put his life back together.

Any kind of sin is like running far and fast from God. Before long, you create a huge gap between you and God—and you might wonder if God even wants you back. But he does. He wants to heal your hurts and breathe life back into your heart. When you wander from God, quit running. Turn around and "return to the Lord" (Hosea 6:1).

¹¹ "Also for you, Judah,
a harvest is appointed.

"Whenever I would restore the
fortunes of my people,

7 ¹whenever I would heal Israel,
the sins of Ephraim are exposed
and the crimes of Samaria
revealed.
They practice deceit,
thieves break into houses,
bandits rob in the streets;
² but they do not realize
that I remember all their evil deeds.
Their sins engulf them;
they are always before me.

³ "They delight the king with their
wickedness,
the princes with their lies.
⁴ They are all adulterers,
burning like an oven
whose fire the baker need not stir
from the kneading of the dough till
it rises.
⁵ On the day of the festival of our king
the princes become inflamed with
wine,
and he joins hands with the
mockers.
⁶ Their hearts are like an oven;
they approach him with intrigue.
Their passion smolders all night;
in the morning it blazes like a
flaming fire.
⁷ All of them are hot as an oven;
they devour their rulers.
All their kings fall,
and none of them calls on me.

⁸ "Ephraim mixes with the nations;
Ephraim is a flat loaf not turned
over.
⁹ Foreigners sap his strength,
but he does not realize it.
His hair is sprinkled with gray,
but he does not notice.
¹⁰ Israel's arrogance testifies against
him,
but despite all this
he does not return to the Lord his
God
or search for him.

¹¹ "Ephraim is like a dove,
easily deceived and senseless—
now calling to Egypt,
now turning to Assyria.
¹² When they go, I will throw my net
over them;
I will pull them down like the birds
in the sky.
When I hear them flocking together,
I will catch them.
¹³ Woe to them,
because they have strayed from me!
Destruction to them,
because they have rebelled against
me!
I long to redeem them
but they speak about me falsely.
¹⁴ They do not cry out to me from their
hearts
but wail on their beds.
They slash themselves,ᵃ appealing to
their gods
for grain and new wine,
but they turn away from me.
¹⁵ I trained them and strengthened their
arms,
but they plot evil against me.
¹⁶ They do not turn to the Most High;
they are like a faulty bow.
Their leaders will fall by the sword
because of their insolent words.
For this they will be ridiculed
in the land of Egypt.

Israel to Reap the Whirlwind

8 "Put the trumpet to your lips!
An eagle is over the house of the
Lord
because the people have broken my
covenant
and rebelled against my law.
² Israel cries out to me,
'Our God, we acknowledge you!'
³ But Israel has rejected what is good;
an enemy will pursue him.
⁴ They set up kings without my
consent;
they choose princes without my
approval.

ᵃ 14 Some Hebrew manuscripts and Septuagint;
most Hebrew manuscripts *They gather together*

With their silver and gold
they make idols for themselves
to their own destruction.
⁵ Samaria, throw out your calf-idol!
My anger burns against them.
How long will they be incapable of
purity?
⁶ They are from Israel!
This calf—a metalworker has made it;
it is not God.
It will be broken in pieces,
that calf of Samaria.

⁷ "They sow the wind
and reap the whirlwind.
The stalk has no head;
it will produce no flour.
Were it to yield grain,
foreigners would swallow it up.
⁸ Israel is swallowed up;
now she is among the nations
like something no one wants.
⁹ For they have gone up to Assyria
like a wild donkey wandering alone.
Ephraim has sold herself to lovers.
¹⁰ Although they have sold themselves
among the nations,
I will now gather them together.
They will begin to waste away
under the oppression of the mighty
king.

¹¹ "Though Ephraim built many altars
for sin offerings,
these have become altars for sinning.
¹² I wrote for them the many things of
my law,
but they regarded them as
something foreign.
¹³ Though they offer sacrifices as gifts
to me,
and though they eat the meat,
the Lᴏʀᴅ is not pleased with them.
Now he will remember their
wickedness
and punish their sins:
They will return to Egypt.
¹⁴ Israel has forgotten their Maker
and built palaces;
Judah has fortified many towns.
But I will send fire on their cities
that will consume their fortresses."

Punishment for Israel

9 Do not rejoice, Israel;
do not be jubilant like the other
nations.
For you have been unfaithful to your
God;
you love the wages of a prostitute
at every threshing floor.
² Threshing floors and winepresses will
not feed the people;
the new wine will fail them.
³ They will not remain in the Lᴏʀᴅ's
land;
Ephraim will return to Egypt
and eat unclean food in Assyria.
⁴ They will not pour out wine offerings
to the Lᴏʀᴅ,
nor will their sacrifices please him.
Such sacrifices will be to them like the
bread of mourners;
all who eat them will be unclean.
This food will be for themselves;
it will not come into the temple of
the Lᴏʀᴅ.

⁵ What will you do on the day of your
appointed festivals,
on the feast days of the Lᴏʀᴅ?
⁶ Even if they escape from destruction,
Egypt will gather them,
and Memphis will bury them.
Their treasures of silver will be taken
over by briers,
and thorns will overrun their tents.
⁷ The days of punishment are coming,
the days of reckoning are at hand.
Let Israel know this.
Because your sins are so many
and your hostility so great,
the prophet is considered a fool,
the inspired person a maniac.
⁸ The prophet, along with my God,
is the watchman over Ephraim,[a]
yet snares await him on all his paths,
and hostility in the house of his God.
⁹ They have sunk deep into corruption,
as in the days of Gibeah.
God will remember their wickedness
and punish them for their sins.

---

[a] 8 Or *The prophet is the watchman over Ephraim,
/ the people of my God*

¹⁰ "When I found Israel,
	it was like finding grapes in the
		desert;
	when I saw your ancestors,
		it was like seeing the early fruit on
			the fig tree.
	But when they came to Baal Peor,
		they consecrated themselves to that
			shameful idol
	and became as vile as the thing they
		loved.
¹¹ Ephraim's glory will fly away like a
		bird—
	no birth, no pregnancy, no
		conception.
¹² Even if they rear children,
	I will bereave them of every one.
	Woe to them
		when I turn away from them!
¹³ I have seen Ephraim, like Tyre,
	planted in a pleasant place.
	But Ephraim will bring out
		their children to the slayer."

¹⁴ Give them, LORD—
	what will you give them?
	Give them wombs that miscarry
	and breasts that are dry.

¹⁵ "Because of all their wickedness in
		Gilgal,
	I hated them there.
	Because of their sinful deeds,
		I will drive them out of my house.
	I will no longer love them;
		all their leaders are rebellious.
¹⁶ Ephraim is blighted,
	their root is withered,
		they yield no fruit.
	Even if they bear children,
		I will slay their cherished
			offspring."

¹⁷ My God will reject them
	because they have not obeyed him;
	they will be wanderers among the
		nations.

10

Israel was a spreading vine;
	he brought forth fruit for
		himself.
As his fruit increased,
	he built more altars;
as his land prospered,
	he adorned his sacred stones.
² Their heart is deceitful,
	and now they must bear their guilt.
The LORD will demolish their altars
	and destroy their sacred stones.

³ Then they will say, "We have no king
	because we did not revere the LORD.
But even if we had a king,
	what could he do for us?"
⁴ They make many promises,
	take false oaths
	and make agreements;
therefore lawsuits spring up
	like poisonous weeds in a plowed
		field.
⁵ The people who live in Samaria fear
	for the calf-idol of Beth Aven.ᵃ
Its people will mourn over it,
	and so will its idolatrous priests,
those who had rejoiced over its
		splendor,
	because it is taken from them into
		exile.
⁶ It will be carried to Assyria
	as tribute for the great king.
Ephraim will be disgraced;
	Israel will be ashamed of its foreign
		alliances.
⁷ Samaria's king will be destroyed,
	swept away like a twig on the
		surface of the waters.
⁸ The high places of wickednessᵇ will be
		destroyed—
	it is the sin of Israel.
Thorns and thistles will grow up
	and cover their altars.
Then they will say to the mountains,
	"Cover us!"
	and to the hills, "Fall on us!"

⁹ "Since the days of Gibeah, you have
		sinned, Israel,
	and there you have remained.ᶜ
Will not war again overtake
	the evildoers in Gibeah?

ᵃ 5 Beth Aven means house of wickedness (a
derogatory name for Bethel, which means house
of God).	ᵇ 8 Hebrew aven, a reference to
Beth Aven (a derogatory name for Bethel); see
verse 5.	ᶜ 9 Or there a stand was taken

¹⁰ When I please, I will punish them;
nations will be gathered against them
to put them in bonds for their
double sin.
¹¹ Ephraim is a trained heifer
that loves to thresh;
so I will put a yoke
on her fair neck.
I will drive Ephraim,
Judah must plow,
and Jacob must break up the ground.
¹² Sow righteousness for yourselves,
reap the fruit of unfailing love,
and break up your unplowed ground;
for it is time to seek the LORD,
until he comes
and showers his righteousness on you.

ROCK SOLID
promises

"It is time to seek the LORD."

Hosea 10:12

**Don't wait a moment longer to ditch sin
and chase God wholeheartedly. This is
the time.**

¹³ But you have planted wickedness,
you have reaped evil,
you have eaten the fruit of deception.
Because you have depended on your
own strength
and on your many warriors,
¹⁴ the roar of battle will rise against your
people,
so that all your fortresses will be
devastated—
as Shalman devastated Beth Arbel on
the day of battle,
when mothers were dashed to the
ground with their children.
¹⁵ So will it happen to you, Bethel,
because your wickedness is great.

When that day dawns,
the king of Israel will be completely
destroyed.

God's Love for Israel

11 "When Israel was a child, I
loved him,
and out of Egypt I called my son.
² But the more they were called,
the more they went away from me.*
They sacrificed to the Baals
and they burned incense to images.
³ It was I who taught Ephraim to walk,
taking them by the arms;
but they did not realize
it was I who healed them.
⁴ I led them with cords of human
kindness,
with ties of love.
To them I was like one who lifts
a little child to the cheek,
and I bent down to feed them.

⁵ "Will they not return to Egypt
and will not Assyria rule over them
because they refuse to repent?
⁶ A sword will flash in their cities;
it will devour their false prophets
and put an end to their plans.
⁷ My people are determined to turn
from me.
Even though they call me God
Most High,
I will by no means exalt them.

⁸ "How can I give you up, Ephraim?
How can I hand you over, Israel?
How can I treat you like Admah?
How can I make you like Zeboyim?
My heart is changed within me;
all my compassion is aroused.
⁹ I will not carry out my fierce anger,
nor will I devastate Ephraim again.
For I am God, and not a man—
the Holy One among you.
I will not come against their cities.
¹⁰ They will follow the LORD;
he will roar like a lion.
When he roars,
his children will come trembling
from the west.

ª 2 Septuagint; Hebrew them

UNSHAKEN God

God is persistent.

There are no pretty words to describe the sins exposed in the book of Hosea. By worshiping false gods—the Baals—Israel acted like a prostitute chasing down customers. Yet even as the nation ran from the Lord, he pursued them with reckless love. Israel was like a child God had raised ... taught to walk ... held ... led gently ... freed and fed. As Israel continued to run away, God still wanted Israel back. So how could the Lord continue to love a sinful people? Because he wanted his children to quit wrecking their lives and come home. God always chases down his own. It's his persistent love.

So ... How have you experienced God's persistence?

11 They will come from Egypt,
   trembling like sparrows,
   from Assyria, fluttering like doves.
I will settle them in their homes,"
   declares the Lord.

Israel's Sin

12 Ephraim has surrounded me with lies,
   Israel with deceit.
And Judah is unruly against God,
   even against the faithful Holy One.*

12

b 1 Ephraim feeds on the
   wind;
   he pursues the east wind
all day
and multiplies lies and violence.
He makes a treaty with Assyria
   and sends olive oil to Egypt.
2 The Lord has a charge to bring
   against Judah;
he will punish Jacob* according to
   his ways
and repay him according to his deeds.

3 In the womb he grasped his brother's
   heel;
   as a man he struggled with God.
4 He struggled with the angel and
   overcame him;
   he wept and begged for his favor.
He found him at Bethel
   and talked with him there—
5 the Lord God Almighty,
   the Lord is his name!
6 But you must return to your God;
   maintain love and justice,
   and wait for your God always.

7 The merchant uses dishonest scales
   and loves to defraud.
8 Ephraim boasts,
   "I am very rich; I have become
      wealthy.
With all my wealth they will not find
   in me
   any iniquity or sin."

9 "I have been the Lord your God
   ever since you came out of Egypt;
I will make you live in tents again,
   as in the days of your appointed
      festivals.
10 I spoke to the prophets,
   gave them many visions
   and told parables through them."

11 Is Gilead wicked?
   Its people are worthless!
Do they sacrifice bulls in Gilgal?
   Their altars will be like piles of
      stones
   on a plowed field.
12 Jacob fled to the country of Aram*d*;
   Israel served to get a wife,
   and to pay for her he tended
      sheep.
13 The Lord used a prophet to bring
   Israel up from Egypt,
   by a prophet he cared for him.
14 But Ephraim has aroused his bitter
      anger;

a 12 In Hebrew texts this verse (11:12) is numbered 12:1.   *b* In Hebrew texts 12:1-14 is numbered 12:2-15.   *c* 2 *Jacob* means *he grasps the heel*, a Hebrew idiom for *he takes advantage of* or *he deceives*.   *d* 12 That is, Northwest Mesopotamia

his Lord will leave on him the guilt
of his bloodshed
and will repay him for his contempt.

The Lord's Anger Against Israel

13 When Ephraim spoke, people
trembled;
he was exalted in Israel.
But he became guilty of Baal
worship and died.
² Now they sin more and more;
they make idols for themselves from
their silver,
cleverly fashioned images,
all of them the work of craftsmen.
It is said of these people,
"They offer human sacrifices!
They kiss*a* calf-idols!"
³ Therefore they will be like the
morning mist,
like the early dew that disappears,
like chaff swirling from a threshing
floor,
like smoke escaping through a
window.

⁴ "But I have been the Lord your God
ever since you came out of Egypt.
You shall acknowledge no God but me,
no Savior except me.
⁵ I cared for you in the wilderness,
in the land of burning heat.
⁶ When I fed them, they were satisfied;
when they were satisfied, they
became proud;
then they forgot me.
⁷ So I will be like a lion to them,
like a leopard I will lurk by the path.
⁸ Like a bear robbed of her cubs,
I will attack them and rip them
open;
like a lion I will devour them —
a wild animal will tear them apart.

⁹ "You are destroyed, Israel,
because you are against me, against
your helper.
¹⁰ Where is your king, that he may save
you?
Where are your rulers in all your
towns,
of whom you said,

'Give me a king and princes'?
¹¹ So in my anger I gave you a king,
and in my wrath I took him away.
¹² The guilt of Ephraim is stored up,
his sins are kept on record.
¹³ Pains as of a woman in childbirth
come to him,
but he is a child without wisdom;
when the time arrives,
he doesn't have the sense to come
out of the womb.

¹⁴ "I will deliver this people from the
power of the grave;
I will redeem them from death.
Where, O death, are your plagues?
Where, O grave, is your
destruction?

"I will have no compassion,
¹⁵ even though he thrives among his
brothers.
An east wind from the Lord will
come,
blowing in from the desert;
his spring will fail
and his well dry up.
His storehouse will be plundered
of all its treasures.
¹⁶ The people of Samaria must bear their
guilt,
because they have rebelled against
their God.
They will fall by the sword;
their little ones will be dashed to
the ground,
their pregnant women ripped
open."*b*

Repentance to Bring Blessing

14 *c* Return, Israel, to the Lord
your God.
Your sins have been your
downfall!
² Take words with you
and return to the Lord.
Say to him:
"Forgive all our sins

---

a 2 Or *"Men who sacrifice / kiss*   *b* 16 In
Hebrew texts this verse (13:16) is numbered
14:1.   *c* In Hebrew texts 14:1-9 is numbered
14:2-10.

and receive us graciously,
  that we may offer the fruit of our
    lips.[a]
[3] Assyria cannot save us;
  we will not mount warhorses.
We will never again say 'Our gods'
  to what our own hands have made,
    for in you the fatherless find
      compassion."

[4] "I will heal their waywardness
    and love them freely,
  for my anger has turned away from
    them.
[5] I will be like the dew to Israel;
  he will blossom like a lily.
Like a cedar of Lebanon
  he will send down his roots;
[6]   his young shoots will grow.
His splendor will be like an olive
    tree,
  his fragrance like a cedar of
    Lebanon.
[7] People will dwell again in his shade;
  they will flourish like the grain,
they will blossom like the vine—
  Israel's fame will be like the wine of
    Lebanon.
[8] Ephraim, what more have I[b] to do
    with idols?
  I will answer him and care for him.

ROCK SOLID *promises*

"I will heal their waywardness and love them freely." Hosea 14:4

Even when you walk away from God, he continues to love you. He works to change you. And he always welcomes you back.

I am like a flourishing juniper;
  your fruitfulness comes from me."
[9] Who is wise? Let them realize these
    things.
  Who is discerning? Let them
    understand.
The ways of the LORD are right;
  the righteous walk in them,
  but the rebellious stumble in them.

[a] 2 Or *offer our lips as sacrifices of bulls*
[b] 8 Or Hebrew; Septuagint *What more has Ephraim*

JOEL

Although the name Joel was common in the Old Testament, nothing is known about this prophet beyond what the book says—he was the son of Pethuel.

In this book Joel describes in detail a severe locust plague that ravaged Palestine. In this event he saw a sign for the final judgment and warned the people to turn to God in repentance. Joel announced that the "day of the LORD" was coming, a day that would bring even greater judgment.

The word of the LORD that came to Joel son of Pethuel.

An Invasion of Locusts

2 Hear this, you elders;
  listen, all who live in the land.
Has anything like this ever happened
    in your days
  or in the days of your ancestors?
3 Tell it to your children,
    and let your children tell it to their
      children,
    and their children to the next
      generation.
4 What the locust swarm has left
    the great locusts have eaten;
  what the great locusts have left
    the young locusts have eaten;
  what the young locusts have left
    other locusts*a* have eaten.

5 Wake up, you drunkards, and weep!
    Wail, all you drinkers of wine;
  wail because of the new wine,
    for it has been snatched from your
      lips.
6 A nation has invaded my land,
    a mighty army without number;
  it has the teeth of a lion,
    the fangs of a lioness.
7 It has laid waste my vines
    and ruined my fig trees.
  It has stripped off their bark
    and thrown it away,
    leaving their branches white.

8 Mourn like a virgin in sackcloth
    grieving for the betrothed of her
      youth.
9 Grain offerings and drink offerings
    are cut off from the house of the
      LORD.
  The priests are in mourning,
    those who minister before the
      LORD.
10 The fields are ruined,
    the ground is dried up;
  the grain is destroyed,
    the new wine is dried up,
    the olive oil fails.

11 Despair, you farmers,
    wail, you vine growers;

grieve for the wheat and the barley,
    because the harvest of the field is
      destroyed.
12 The vine is dried up
    and the fig tree is withered;
  the pomegranate, the palm and the
      apple*b* tree—
    all the trees of the field—are dried
      up.
  Surely the people's joy
    is withered away.

A Call to Lamentation

13 Put on sackcloth, you priests, and
      mourn;
  wail, you who minister before the
      altar.
  Come, spend the night in sackcloth,
    you who minister before my God;
  for the grain offerings and drink
      offerings
    are withheld from the house of your
      God.
14 Declare a holy fast;
    call a sacred assembly.
  Summon the elders
    and all who live in the land
  to the house of the LORD your God,
    and cry out to the LORD.

15 Alas for that day!
    For the day of the LORD is near;
  it will come like destruction from
      the Almighty.*c*

16 Has not the food been cut off
    before our very eyes—
  joy and gladness
    from the house of our God?
17 The seeds are shriveled
    beneath the clods.*d*
  The storehouses are in ruins,
    the granaries have been broken
      down,
    for the grain has dried up.
18 How the cattle moan!
    The herds mill about

---

a 4 The precise meaning of the four Hebrew words used here for locusts is uncertain.
b 12 Or possibly *apricot*   *c* 15 Hebrew *Shaddai*   *d* 17 The meaning of the Hebrew for this word is uncertain.

because they have no pasture;
  even the flocks of sheep are
    suffering.

¹⁹ To you, Lord, I call,
  for fire has devoured the pastures in
    the wilderness
  and flames have burned up all the
    trees of the field.
²⁰ Even the wild animals pant for you;
  the streams of water have dried up
  and fire has devoured the pastures
    in the wilderness.

An Army of Locusts

2 Blow the trumpet in Zion;
  sound the alarm on my holy hill.

Let all who live in the land tremble,
  for the day of the Lord is coming.
It is close at hand—
²   a day of darkness and gloom,
  a day of clouds and blackness.
Like dawn spreading across the
    mountains
  a large and mighty army comes,
such as never was in ancient times
  nor ever will be in ages to come.

³ Before them fire devours,
  behind them a flame blazes.
Before them the land is like the
    garden of Eden,
  behind them, a desert waste—
    nothing escapes them.
⁴ They have the appearance of horses;
  they gallop along like cavalry.
⁵ With a noise like that of chariots
  they leap over the mountaintops,
like a crackling fire consuming
    stubble,
  like a mighty army drawn up for
    battle.

⁶ At the sight of them, nations are in
    anguish;
  every face turns pale.
⁷ They charge like warriors;
  they scale walls like soldiers.
They all march in line,
  not swerving from their course.
⁸ They do not jostle each other;
  each marches straight ahead.

They plunge through defenses
  without breaking ranks.
⁹ They rush upon the city;
  they run along the wall.
They climb into the houses;
  like thieves they enter through the
    windows.

¹⁰ Before them the earth shakes,
  the heavens tremble,
the sun and moon are darkened,
  and the stars no longer shine.
¹¹ The Lord thunders
  at the head of his army;
his forces are beyond number,
  and mighty is the army that obeys
    his command.
The day of the Lord is great;
  it is dreadful.
  Who can endure it?

Rend Your Heart

¹² "Even now," declares the Lord,
  "return to me with all your
    heart,
  with fasting and weeping and
    mourning."

¹³ Rend your heart
  and not your garments.
Return to the Lord your God,
  for he is gracious and
    compassionate,
slow to anger and abounding in
    love,
  and he relents from sending
    calamity.
¹⁴ Who knows? He may turn and
    relent
  and leave behind a blessing—
grain offerings and drink offerings
  for the Lord your God.

¹⁵ Blow the trumpet in Zion,
  declare a holy fast,
  call a sacred assembly.
¹⁶ Gather the people,
  consecrate the assembly;
bring together the elders,
  gather the children,
  those nursing at the breast.
Let the bridegroom leave his room
  and the bride her chamber.

¹⁷ Let the priests, who minister before
the Lord,
weep between the portico and the
altar.
Let them say, "Spare your people,
Lord.
Do not make your inheritance an
object of scorn,
a byword among the nations.
Why should they say among the
peoples,
'Where is their God?'"

The Lord's Answer

¹⁸ Then the Lord was jealous for his
land
and took pity on his people.

¹⁹ The Lord replied*ᵃ* to them:

"I am sending you grain, new wine
and olive oil,
enough to satisfy you fully;
never again will I make you
an object of scorn to the nations.

²⁰ "I will drive the northern horde far
from you,
pushing it into a parched and barren
land;
its eastern ranks will drown in the
Dead Sea
and its western ranks in the
Mediterranean Sea.
And its stench will go up;
its smell will rise."

Surely he has done great things!
²¹ Do not be afraid, land of Judah;
be glad and rejoice.
Surely the Lord has done great
things!
²² Do not be afraid, you wild
animals,
for the pastures in the wilderness
are becoming green.
The trees are bearing their fruit;
the fig tree and the vine yield their
riches.
²³ Be glad, people of Zion,
rejoice in the Lord your God,
for he has given you the autumn rains
because he is faithful.

He sends you abundant showers,
both autumn and spring rains, as
before.
²⁴ The threshing floors will be filled
with grain;
the vats will overflow with new
wine and oil.

²⁵ "I will repay you for the years the
locusts have eaten—
the great locust and the young
locust,
the other locusts and the locust
swarm*ᵇ*—
my great army that I sent among you.
²⁶ You will have plenty to eat, until you
are full,
and you will praise the name of the
Lord your God,
who has worked wonders for you;
never again will my people be
shamed.
²⁷ Then you will know that I am in
Israel,
that I am the Lord your God,
and that there is no other;
never again will my people be shamed.

The Day of the Lord

²⁸ "And afterward,
I will pour out my Spirit on all
people.
Your sons and daughters will
prophesy,
your old men will dream dreams,
your young men will see visions.
²⁹ Even on my servants, both men and
women,
I will pour out my Spirit in those
days.
³⁰ I will show wonders in the heavens
and on the earth,
blood and fire and billows of
smoke.
³¹ The sun will be turned to darkness
and the moon to blood
before the coming of the great and
dreadful day of the Lord.

ᵃ 18,19 Or Lord will be jealous . . . / and take
pity . . . / *¹⁹ The Lord will reply*
ᵇ 25 The precise meaning of the four Hebrew
words used here for locusts is uncertain.

took my silver and my gold and carried off my finest treasures to your temples.[d] [6]You sold the people of Judah and Jerusalem to the Greeks, that you might send them far from their homeland.

[7]"See, I am going to rouse them out of the places to which you sold them, and I will return on your own heads what you have done. [8]I will sell your sons and daughters to the people of Judah, and they will sell them to the Sabeans, a nation far away." The LORD has spoken.

[9]Proclaim this among the nations:
    Prepare for war!
  Rouse the warriors!
    Let all the fighting men draw near
      and attack.
[10]Beat your plowshares into swords
    and your pruning hooks into
      spears.
  Let the weakling say,
    "I am strong!"
[11]Come quickly, all you nations from
      every side,
    and assemble there.

  Bring down your warriors, LORD!

[12]"Let the nations be roused;
    let them advance into the Valley
      of Jehoshaphat,
  for there I will sit
    to judge all the nations on every
      side.
[13]Swing the sickle,
    for the harvest is ripe.
  Come, trample the grapes,
    for the winepress is full
    and the vats overflow —
  so great is their wickedness!"

[14]Multitudes, multitudes
    in the valley of decision!
  For the day of the LORD is near
    in the valley of decision.
[15]The sun and moon will be
      darkened,
    and the stars no longer shine.

ROCK SOLID promises

"I will pour out my Spirit on all people."
Joel 2:28

The Holy Spirit isn't for someone else. It's for you. God will fill you with his Spirit to teach and empower you.

---

[32]And everyone who calls
    on the name of the LORD will be
      saved;
  for on Mount Zion and in
      Jerusalem
    there will be deliverance,
    as the LORD has said,
  even among the survivors
    whom the LORD calls.[a]

The Nations Judged

3[b] "In those days and at that time,
    when I restore the fortunes of
    Judah and Jerusalem,
[2]I will gather all nations
    and bring them down to the Valley
      of Jehoshaphat.[c]
  There I will put them on trial
    for what they did to my inheritance,
      my people Israel,
  because they scattered my people
      among the nations
    and divided up my land.
[3]They cast lots for my people
    and traded boys for prostitutes;
    they sold girls for wine to drink.

[4]"Now what have you against me, Tyre and Sidon and all you regions of Philistia? Are you repaying me for something I have done? If you are paying me back, I will swiftly and speedily return on your own heads what you have done. [5]For you

---

[a] 32 In Hebrew texts 2:28-32 is numbered 3:1-5.
[b] In Hebrew texts 3:1-21 is numbered 4:1-21.
[c] 2 Jehoshaphat means the LORD judges; also in verse 12.   [d] 5 Or palaces

Everyone answers to God.

The prophet Joel spoke a blistering warning from the Lord. First he described a recent attack of ravenous locusts, oversized grasshoppers that had devoured the nation's crops and left everyone hungry. Then Joel predicted a future event when God will judge evildoers. This terrifying "day of the LORD" will bring disaster like no one has ever seen, and as he envisions lush landscapes being scorched into wastelands, the prophet asks, "The day of the LORD is great; it is dreadful. Who can endure it?" (Joel 2:11). And in the final chapter of the book, Joel says exactly whom the Lord stands ready to judge—and it's everyone on earth! God says he will gather the world in "the Valley of Jehoshaphat," a name meaning "the Lord judges" (Joel 3:2). God will punish the world's great wickedness, and no one will escape answering to the Lord.

Think: Why can't God just overlook sin? Why does he hold people accountable?

ROCK SOLID truths

¹⁶The LORD will roar from Zion
    and thunder from Jerusalem;
    the earth and the heavens will
        tremble.
But the LORD will be a refuge for his
        people,
    a stronghold for the people of Israel.

Blessings for God's People

¹⁷"Then you will know that I, the LORD
        your God,
    dwell in Zion, my holy hill.
Jerusalem will be holy;
    never again will foreigners invade
        her.

¹⁸"In that day the mountains will drip
        new wine,
    and the hills will flow with milk;
    all the ravines of Judah will run
        with water.
A fountain will flow out of the LORD's
        house
    and will water the valley of acacias.ᵃ
¹⁹But Egypt will be desolate,
    Edom a desert waste,
because of violence done to the people
        of Judah,
    in whose land they shed innocent
        blood.
²⁰Judah will be inhabited forever
    and Jerusalem through all
        generations.
²¹Shall I leave their innocent blood
        unavenged?
    No, I will not."

    The LORD dwells in Zion!

ᵃ*18* Or *Valley of Shittim*

BOOK OUTLINE

The author's name, Amos, means "burden" or "burdenbearer." God called Amos, a shepherd, to be a prophet in the northern cities of Israel. During this time the people living in the northern kingdom were enjoying riches and wealth. Amos went to the people and announced God's judgment on them for turning away from God, for being cruel to the poor, and for living selfishly.

In a series of five visions, Amos saw the day of judgment coming soon. He warned the people to prepare themselves to meet God. For those who loved God, however, Amos had a word of hope. Some day the kingdom of David would be re-established and God's people would dwell in safety.

1 The words of Amos, one of the shepherds of Tekoa—the vision he saw concerning Israel two years before the earthquake, when Uzziah was king of Judah and Jeroboam son of Jehoash[a] was king of Israel.

² He said:

"The Lord roars from Zion
and thunders from Jerusalem;
the pastures of the shepherds dry up,
and the top of Carmel withers."

Judgment on Israel's Neighbors

³ This is what the Lord says:

"For three sins of Damascus,
even for four, I will not relent.
Because she threshed Gilead
with sledges having iron teeth,
⁴ I will send fire on the house of Hazael
that will consume the fortresses of
Ben-Hadad.
⁵ I will break down the gate of
Damascus;
I will destroy the king who is in[b]
the Valley of Aven[c]
and the one who holds the scepter in
Beth Eden.
The people of Aram will go into
exile to Kir,"
says the Lord.

⁶ This is what the Lord says:

"For three sins of Gaza,
even for four, I will not relent.
Because she took captive whole
communities
and sold them to Edom,
⁷ I will send fire on the walls of Gaza
that will consume her fortresses.
⁸ I will destroy the king[d] of Ashdod
and the one who holds the scepter
in Ashkelon.
I will turn my hand against Ekron,
till the last of the Philistines are
dead,"
says the Sovereign Lord.

⁹ This is what the Lord says:

"For three sins of Tyre,
even for four, I will not relent.

Because she sold whole communities
of captives to Edom,
disregarding a treaty of
brotherhood,
¹⁰ I will send fire on the walls of Tyre
that will consume her fortresses."

¹¹ This is what the Lord says:

"For three sins of Edom,
even for four, I will not relent.
Because he pursued his brother with a
sword
and slaughtered the women of the
land,
because his anger raged continually
and his fury flamed unchecked,
¹² I will send fire on Teman
that will consume the fortresses of
Bozrah."

¹³ This is what the Lord says:

"For three sins of Ammon,
even for four, I will not relent.
Because he ripped open the pregnant
women of Gilead
in order to extend his borders,
¹⁴ I will set fire to the walls of
Rabbah
that will consume her fortresses
amid war cries on the day of battle,
amid violent winds on a stormy
day.
¹⁵ Her king[e] will go into exile,
he and his officials together,"
says the Lord.

2 This is what the Lord says:

"For three sins of Moab,
even for four, I will not relent.
Because he burned to ashes
the bones of Edom's king,
² I will send fire on Moab
that will consume the fortresses
of Kerioth.[f]
Moab will go down in great tumult
amid war cries and the blast of the
trumpet.

---

[a] 1 Hebrew Joash, a variant of Jehoash
[b] 5 Or the inhabitants of   [c] 5 Aven means
wickedness.   [d] 8 Or inhabitants
[e] 15 Or / Molek   [f] 2 Or of her cities

3 I will destroy her ruler
   and kill all her officials with him,"
                        says the LORD.

4 This is what the LORD says:

"For three sins of Judah,
   even for four, I will not relent.
Because they have rejected the law of
   the LORD
   and have not kept his decrees,
because they have been led astray by
   false gods,*a*
   the gods*b* their ancestors followed,
5 I will send fire on Judah
   that will consume the fortresses of
   Jerusalem."

Judgment on Israel

6 This is what the LORD says:

"For three sins of Israel,
   even for four, I will not relent.
They sell the innocent for silver,
   and the needy for a pair of sandals.
7 They trample on the heads of the
   poor
   as on the dust of the ground
   and deny justice to the oppressed.
Father and son use the same girl
   and so profane my holy name.
8 They lie down beside every altar
   on garments taken in pledge.
In the house of their god
   they drink wine taken as fines.

9 "Yet I destroyed the Amorites before
   them,
   though they were tall as the cedars
   and strong as the oaks.
I destroyed their fruit above
   and their roots below.
10 I brought you up out of Egypt
   and led you forty years in the
   wilderness
   to give you the land of the
   Amorites.

11 "I also raised up prophets from among
   your children
   and Nazirites from among your
   youths.
Is this not true, people of Israel?"
                        declares the LORD.

12 "But you made the Nazirites drink
   wine
   and commanded the prophets not to
   prophesy.

13 "Now then, I will crush you
   as a cart crushes when loaded with
   grain.
14 The swift will not escape,
   the strong will not muster their
   strength,
   and the warrior will not save his
   life.
15 The archer will not stand his ground,
   the fleet-footed soldier will not get
   away,
   and the horseman will not save his
   life.
16 Even the bravest warriors
   will flee naked on that day,"
                        declares the LORD.

Witnesses Summoned Against Israel

3 Hear this word, people of Israel,
   the word the LORD has spoken
   against you—against the whole
family I brought up out of Egypt:

2 "You only have I chosen
   of all the families of the earth;
therefore I will punish you
   for all your sins."

3 Do two walk together
   unless they have agreed to do so?
4 Does a lion roar in the thicket
   when it has no prey?
Does it growl in its den
   when it has caught nothing?
5 Does a bird swoop down to a trap on
   the ground
   when no bait is there?
Does a trap spring up from the ground
   if it has not caught anything?
6 When a trumpet sounds in a city,
   do not the people tremble?
When disaster comes to a city,
   has not the LORD caused it?

7 Surely the Sovereign LORD does nothing
   without revealing his plan
   to his servants the prophets.

a 4 Or *by lies*   *b 4* Or *lies*

1067

⁸The lion has roared—
who will not fear?
The Sovereign LORD has spoken—
who can but prophesy?

⁹Proclaim to the fortresses of
Ashdod
and to the fortresses of Egypt:
"Assemble yourselves on the
mountains of Samaria;
see the great unrest within her
and the oppression among her
people."

¹⁰"They do not know how to do right,"
declares the LORD,
"who store up in their fortresses
what they have plundered and
looted."

¹¹Therefore this is what the Sovereign
LORD says:

"An enemy will overrun your land,
pull down your strongholds
and plunder your fortresses."

¹²This is what the LORD says:

"As a shepherd rescues from the lion's
mouth
only two leg bones or a piece of an
ear,
so will the Israelites living in Samaria
be rescued,
with only the head of a bed
and a piece of fabricᵃ from a
couch.ᵇ"

¹³"Hear this and testify against the descendants of Jacob," declares the Lord, the
LORD God Almighty.

¹⁴"On the day I punish Israel for her
sins,
I will destroy the altars of Bethel;
the horns of the altar will be cut off
and fall to the ground.
¹⁵I will tear down the winter house
along with the summer house;
the houses adorned with ivory will be
destroyed
and the mansions will be
demolished,"
declares the LORD.

Israel Has Not Returned to God

4 Hear this word, you cows of
Bashan on Mount Samaria,
you women who oppress the poor
and crush the needy
and say to your husbands, "Bring us
some drinks!"

²The Sovereign LORD has sworn by his
holiness:
"The time will surely come
when you will be taken away with
hooks,
the last of you with fishhooks.ᶜ

³You will each go straight out
through breaches in the wall,
and you will be cast out toward
Harmon,ᵈ"
declares the LORD.

⁴"Go to Bethel and sin;
go to Gilgal and sin yet more.
Bring your sacrifices every morning,
your tithes every three years.ᵉ
⁵Burn leavened bread as a thank
offering
and brag about your freewill
offerings—
boast about them, you Israelites,
for this is what you love to do,"
declares the Sovereign LORD.

⁶"I gave you empty stomachs in every
city
and lack of bread in every town,
yet you have not returned to me,"
declares the LORD.

⁷"I also withheld rain from you
when the harvest was still three
months away.
I sent rain on one town,
but withheld it from another.
One field had rain;
another had none and dried up.
⁸People staggered from town to town
for water

ᵃ 12 The meaning of the Hebrew for this phrase
is uncertain.   ᵇ 12 Or Israelites be rescued, /
those who sit in Samaria / on the edge of their beds /
and in Damascus on their couches.   ᶜ 2 Or away
in baskets, / the last of you in fish baskets
ᵈ 3 Masoretic Text; with a different word
division of the Hebrew (see Septuagint) out, you
mountain of oppression   ᵉ 4 Or days

but did not get enough to drink,
  yet you have not returned to me,"
    declares the LORD.

9 "Many times I struck your gardens
    and vineyards,
  destroying them with blight and
    mildew.
Locusts devoured your fig and olive
    trees,
  yet you have not returned to me,"
    declares the LORD.

10 "I sent plagues among you
    as I did to Egypt.
I killed your young men with the
    sword,
  along with your captured horses.
I filled your nostrils with the stench of
    your camps,
  yet you have not returned to me,"
    declares the LORD.

11 "I overthrew some of you
    as I overthrew Sodom and
    Gomorrah.
You were like a burning stick snatched
    from the fire,
  yet you have not returned to me,"
    declares the LORD.

12 "Therefore this is what I will do to
    you, Israel,
  and because I will do this to you,
    Israel,
  prepare to meet your God."

ROCK SOLID
promises

"Prepare to meet your God."

Amos 4:12

For a believer, meeting God isn't a threat: It's a loving promise.

---

13 He who forms the mountains,
  who creates the wind,
  and who reveals his thoughts to
    mankind,
who turns dawn to darkness,
  and treads on the heights of the
    earth—
  the LORD God Almighty is his
    name.

A Lament and Call to Repentance

5 Hear this word, Israel, this lament
  I take up concerning you:

2 "Fallen is Virgin Israel,
  never to rise again,
deserted in her own land,
  with no one to lift her up."

3 This is what the Sovereign LORD says
to Israel:

"Your city that marches out a
    thousand strong
  will have only a hundred left;
your town that marches out a hundred
    strong
  will have only ten left."

4 This is what the LORD says to Israel:

"Seek me and live;
5   do not seek Bethel,
do not go to Gilgal,
  do not journey to Beersheba.
For Gilgal will surely go into exile,
  and Bethel will be reduced to
    nothing.a"
6 Seek the LORD and live,
  or he will sweep through the tribes
    of Joseph like a fire;
it will devour them,
  and Bethel will have no one to
    quench it.

7 There are those who turn justice into
    bitterness
  and cast righteousness to the ground.

8 He who made the Pleiades and Orion,
  who turns midnight into dawn
  and darkens day into night,

a 5 Hebrew aven, a reference to Beth Aven (a
derogatory name for Bethel); see Hosea 4:15.

who calls for the waters of the sea
　　and pours them out over the face of
　　　the land—
　　the Lord is his name.
⁹ With a blinding flash he destroys the
　　stronghold
　　and brings the fortified city to ruin.

¹⁰ There are those who hate the one who
　　upholds justice in court
　　and detest the one who tells the
　　　truth.

¹¹ You levy a straw tax on the poor
　　and impose a tax on their grain.
Therefore, though you have built
　　stone mansions,
　　you will not live in them;
though you have planted lush
　　vineyards,
　　you will not drink their wine.
¹² For I know how many are your
　　offenses
　　and how great your sins.

There are those who oppress the
　　innocent and take bribes
　　and deprive the poor of justice in
　　　the courts.
¹³ Therefore the prudent keep quiet in
　　such times,
　　for the times are evil.

¹⁴ Seek good, not evil,
　　that you may live.
Then the Lord God Almighty will be
　　with you,
　　just as you say he is.
¹⁵ Hate evil, love good;
　　maintain justice in the courts.
Perhaps the Lord God Almighty will
　　have mercy
　　on the remnant of Joseph.

¹⁶ Therefore this is what the Lord, the
Lord God Almighty, says:

　"There will be wailing in all the
　　streets
　　and cries of anguish in every public
　　　square.
The farmers will be summoned to
　　weep
　　and the mourners to wail.

¹⁷ There will be wailing in all the
　　vineyards,
　　for I will pass through your midst,"
　　　　　　　says the Lord.

The Day of the Lord

¹⁸ Woe to you who long
　　for the day of the Lord!
Why do you long for the day of the
　　Lord?
　　That day will be darkness, not
　　　light.
¹⁹ It will be as though a man fled from a
　　lion
　　only to meet a bear,
as though he entered his house
　　and rested his hand on the wall
　　only to have a snake bite him.
²⁰ Will not the day of the Lord be
　　darkness, not light—
　　pitch-dark, without a ray of
　　　brightness?

²¹ "I hate, I despise your religious
　　festivals;
　　your assemblies are a stench to me.
²² Even though you bring me burnt
　　offerings and grain offerings,
　　I will not accept them.
Though you bring choice fellowship
　　offerings,
　　I will have no regard for them.
²³ Away with the noise of your songs!
　　I will not listen to the music of your
　　　harps.
²⁴ But let justice roll on like a river,
　　righteousness like a never-failing
　　　stream!

²⁵ "Did you bring me sacrifices and
　　offerings
　　forty years in the wilderness, people
　　　of Israel?
²⁶ You have lifted up the shrine of your
　　king,
　　the pedestal of your idols,
　　the star of your god*a*—
　　which you made for yourselves.

a 26 Or *lifted up Sakkuth your king / and Kaiwan
your idols, / your star-gods*; Septuagint *lifted up the
shrine of Molek / and the star of your god Rephan, /
their idols*

ROCK·SOLID
principles

Amos 5:21–24

Care for the poor.

"Really?" Paige was dumbstruck. "You all think we need another gaming system in the youth room? I mean—I'm into that as much as anyone—but can't we do something more significant with our money? Can't we give it somewhere or start something that helps someone besides us?" Paige's youth group was geared up to collect money for the youth program, with each grade preparing for its annual battle to see who could scavenge the most spare change. It didn't really matter who won, because everyone benefited from the fundraising—everyone in the group, that is. The money didn't do much good for anyone else.

God didn't think much of the religious habits of his people. They got together for large feasts. They burned up grain and sacrificial animals as payment for their sins. They sang loud enough for the noise to reach heaven. But the Lord couldn't stand any of it. He hates religious rituals if we don't deal justly with the poor or lead moral lives.

²⁷ Therefore I will send you into exile
    beyond Damascus,"
  says the Lord, whose name is God
    Almighty.

Woe to the Complacent

6 Woe to you who are complacent
    in Zion,
  and to you who feel secure on
    Mount Samaria,
you notable men of the foremost nation,
  to whom the people of Israel come!
² Go to Kalneh and look at it;
  go from there to great Hamath,
  and then go down to Gath in Philistia.
Are they better off than your two
    kingdoms?
  Is their land larger than yours?
³ You put off the day of disaster
  and bring near a reign of terror.
⁴ You lie on beds adorned with ivory
  and lounge on your couches.
You dine on choice lambs
  and fattened calves.

⁵ You strum away on your harps like
    David
  and improvise on musical
    instruments.
⁶ You drink wine by the bowlful
  and use the finest lotions,
  but you do not grieve over the ruin
    of Joseph.
⁷ Therefore you will be among the first
    to go into exile;
  your feasting and lounging will end.

The Lord Abhors the Pride of Israel

⁸ The Sovereign Lord has sworn by himself—the Lord God Almighty declares:

"I abhor the pride of Jacob
  and detest his fortresses;
I will deliver up the city
  and everything in it."

⁹ If ten people are left in one house, they too will die. ¹⁰ And if the relative who comes to carry the bodies out of the house

to burn them*a* asks anyone who might be hiding there, "Is anyone else with you?" and he says, "No," then he will go on to say, "Hush! We must not mention the name of the Lord."

11 For the Lord has given the command,
and he will smash the great house
into pieces
and the small house into bits.

12 Do horses run on the rocky crags?
Does one plow the sea*b* with oxen?
But you have turned justice into poison
and the fruit of righteousness into
bitterness—
13 you who rejoice in the conquest of Lo
Debar*c*
and say, "Did we not take Karnaim*d*
by our own strength?"

14 For the Lord God Almighty declares,
"I will stir up a nation against you,
Israel,
that will oppress you all the way
from Lebo Hamath to the valley of
the Arabah."

Locusts, Fire and a Plumb Line

7 This is what the Sovereign Lord showed me: He was preparing swarms of locusts after the king's share had been harvested and just as the late crops were coming up. 2 When they had stripped the land clean, I cried out, "Sovereign Lord, forgive! How can Jacob survive? He is so small!"

3 So the Lord relented.

"This will not happen," the Lord said.

4 This is what the Sovereign Lord showed me: The Sovereign Lord was calling for judgment by fire; it dried up the great deep and devoured the land. 5 Then I cried out, "Sovereign Lord, I beg you, stop! How can Jacob survive? He is so small!"

6 So the Lord relented.

"This will not happen either," the Sovereign Lord said.

7 This is what he showed me: The Lord was standing by a wall that had been built true to plumb,*e* with a plumb line*f* in his hand. 8 And the Lord asked me, "What do you see, Amos?"

"A plumb line," I replied.

Then the Lord said, "Look, I am setting a plumb line among my people Israel; I will spare them no longer.

9 "The high places of Isaac will be
destroyed
and the sanctuaries of Israel will be
ruined;
with my sword I will rise against
the house of Jeroboam."

Amos and Amaziah

10 Then Amaziah the priest of Bethel sent a message to Jeroboam king of Israel: "Amos is raising a conspiracy against you in the very heart of Israel. The land cannot bear all his words. 11 For this is what Amos is saying:

"'Jeroboam will die by the sword,
and Israel will surely go into exile,
away from their native land.'"

12 Then Amaziah said to Amos, "Get out, you seer! Go back to the land of Judah. Earn your bread there and do your prophesying there. 13 Don't prophesy anymore at Bethel, because this is the king's sanctuary and the temple of the kingdom."

14 Amos answered Amaziah, "I was neither a prophet nor the son of a prophet, but I was a shepherd, and I also took care of sycamore-fig trees. 15 But the Lord took me from tending the flock and said to me, 'Go, prophesy to my people Israel.' 16 Now then, hear the word of the Lord. You say,

"'Do not prophesy against Israel,
and stop preaching against the
descendants of Isaac.'

17 "Therefore this is what the Lord says:

"'Your wife will become a prostitute in
the city,

---

a 10 Or *to make a funeral fire in honor of the dead*
b 12 With a different word division of the Hebrew; Masoretic Text *plow there*   *c* 13 *Lo Debar* means *nothing*.   *d* 13 *Karnaim* means *horns; horn* here symbolizes strength.
e 7 The meaning of the Hebrew for this phrase is uncertain.   *f* 7 The meaning of the Hebrew for this phrase is uncertain; also in verse 8.

and your sons and daughters will
    fall by the sword.
Your land will be measured and
    divided up,
and you yourself will die in a pagan[a]
    country.
And Israel will surely go into exile,
    away from their native land.'"

A Basket of Ripe Fruit

8 This is what the Sovereign LORD showed me: a basket of ripe fruit. [2]"What do you see, Amos?" he asked.

"A basket of ripe fruit," I answered.

Then the LORD said to me, "The time is ripe for my people Israel; I will spare them no longer.

[3]"In that day," declares the Sovereign LORD, "the songs in the temple will turn to wailing.[b] Many, many bodies—flung everywhere! Silence!"

[4]Hear this, you who trample the needy
    and do away with the poor of the
      land,

[5]saying,

"When will the New Moon be over
    that we may sell grain,

---

[a] 17 Hebrew *an unclean*   [b] 3 Or "*the temple singers will wail*

Amos 7:10–17

Amos confronted injustice.

Life was good in Israel. Too good. The rich were getting richer by exploiting the poor. And during the reigns of Uzziah of Judah and Jeroboam of Israel, the prophet Amos roared out of nowhere to condemn this injustice.

Amos probably didn't dream of being a prophet. He came from Tekoa, a town near Bethlehem on the edge of the Judean wilderness. He called himself a shepherd and a tender of fig trees (see Amos 7:14) and probably knew poverty firsthand. But the Lord took him from tending the flock and said, "Go, prophesy to my people Israel" (Amos 7:15).

Maybe Amos considered preaching a message of encouragement to the masses struggling to survive. But we know he verbally attacked the highest levels of society. He told off the rich for doing nothing to help the poor. He blasted military leaders for trusting their weapons rather than God for protection. He preached to religious people and said the Lord hated their offerings and religious gatherings. And he thundered at everyone to work for justice: "Let justice roll on like a river, righteousness like a never-failing stream!" (Amos 5:24).

The people who heard Amos didn't like his words. The Bible doesn't say how long he preached, but his messages might have been over within a few days. The pagan priest Amaziah tossed him out of the temple and ordered him to go back home. Within two years King Jeroboam was dead, and less than thirty years later the Assyrians conquered Israel. But Amos did his best to right terrible wrongs.

You can find Amos in the book named for him.

UNSHAKEN*people*

and the Sabbath be ended
    that we may market wheat?"—
skimping on the measure,
    boosting the price
    and cheating with dishonest scales,
⁶buying the poor with silver
    and the needy for a pair of sandals,
    selling even the sweepings with the
        wheat.

⁷The Lord has sworn by himself, the
Pride of Jacob: "I will never forget anything they have done.

⁸"Will not the land tremble for this,
    and all who live in it mourn?
The whole land will rise like the Nile;
    it will be stirred up and then sink
    like the river of Egypt.

⁹"In that day," declares the Sovereign
Lord,

"I will make the sun go down at noon
    and darken the earth in broad
        daylight.
¹⁰I will turn your religious festivals into
        mourning
    and all your singing into weeping.
I will make all of you wear sackcloth
    and shave your heads.
I will make that time like mourning
    for an only son
    and the end of it like a bitter day.

¹¹"The days are coming," declares the
        Sovereign Lord,
    "when I will send a famine through
        the land—
not a famine of food or a thirst for
        water,
    but a famine of hearing the words of
        the Lord.
¹²People will stagger from sea to sea
    and wander from north to east,
searching for the word of the Lord,
    but they will not find it.

¹³"In that day

"the lovely young women and strong
        young men
    will faint because of thirst.
¹⁴Those who swear by the sin of
        Samaria—

who say, 'As surely as your god lives,
        Dan,'
or, 'As surely as the godᵃ of
        Beersheba lives'—
they will fall, never to rise again."

Israel to Be Destroyed

9 I saw the Lord standing by the altar, and he said:

"Strike the tops of the pillars
    so that the thresholds shake.
Bring them down on the heads of all
        the people;
    those who are left I will kill with
        the sword.
Not one will get away,
    none will escape.
²Though they dig down to the depths
        below,
    from there my hand will take them.
Though they climb up to the heavens
        above,
    from there I will bring them down.
³Though they hide themselves on the
        top of Carmel,
    there I will hunt them down and
        seize them.
Though they hide from my eyes at the
        bottom of the sea,
    there I will command the serpent to
        bite them.
⁴Though they are driven into exile by
        their enemies,
    there I will command the sword to
        slay them.

"I will keep my eye on them
    for harm and not for good."

⁵The Lord, the Lord Almighty—
he touches the earth and it melts,
    and all who live in it mourn;
the whole land rises like the Nile,
    then sinks like the river of Egypt;
⁶he builds his lofty palaceᵇ in the
        heavens
    and sets its foundationᶜ on the earth;

ᵃ 14 Hebrew *the way*   ᵇ 6 The meaning of
the Hebrew for this phrase is uncertain.
ᶜ 6 The meaning of the Hebrew for this word
is uncertain.

he calls for the waters of the sea
    and pours them out over the face of
      the land—
    the Lord is his name.

7 "Are not you Israelites
    the same to me as the Cushites*a*?"
                  declares the Lord.
"Did I not bring Israel up from Egypt,
    the Philistines from Caphtor*b*
    and the Arameans from Kir?

8 "Surely the eyes of the Sovereign
    Lord
    are on the sinful kingdom.
I will destroy it
    from the face of the earth.
Yet I will not totally destroy
    the descendants of Jacob,"
                  declares the Lord.
9 "For I will give the command,
    and I will shake the people of Israel
      among all the nations
as grain is shaken in a sieve,
    and not a pebble will reach the
      ground.
10 All the sinners among my people
    will die by the sword,
all those who say,
    'Disaster will not overtake or meet
      us.'

Israel's Restoration

11 "In that day

"I will restore David's fallen shelter—
    I will repair its broken walls

and restore its ruins—
    and will rebuild it as it used to be,
12 so that they may possess the remnant
    of Edom
    and all the nations that bear my
      name,*c*"
             declares the Lord,
          who will do these things.

13 "The days are coming," declares the
Lord,

"when the reaper will be overtaken by
    the plowman
    and the planter by the one treading
      grapes.
New wine will drip from the
    mountains
    and flow from all the hills,
14   and I will bring my people Israel
      back from exile.*d*

"They will rebuild the ruined cities
    and live in them.
They will plant vineyards and drink
    their wine;
they will make gardens and eat
    their fruit.
15 I will plant Israel in their own land,
    never again to be uprooted
    from the land I have given them,"
          says the Lord your God.

a 7 That is, people from the upper Nile region
b 7 That is, Crete   *c* 12 Hebrew; Septuagint
so that the remnant of people / and all the nations
that bear my name may seek me   *d* 14 Or *will*
restore the fortunes of my people Israel

OBADIAH

The name Obadiah means "servant of the Lord." Nothing more is known about this prophet than this short book containing his prophecy.

Obadiah is a book of prophecy against the nation of Edom. This country had invaded and plundered Jerusalem at least four times, so Obadiah announced God's judgment against them and prophesied that their kingdom would be destroyed.

The Edomites are never heard of again in history after the destruction of Jerusalem in AD 70.

Obadiah's Vision

¹The vision of Obadiah.

This is what the Sovereign LORD says about Edom—

We have heard a message from the
LORD:
  An envoy was sent to the nations to
  say,
"Rise, let us go against her for
  battle"—

²"See, I will make you small among the
  nations;
  you will be utterly despised.
³The pride of your heart has deceived
  you,
  you who live in the clefts of the
  rocks*
  and make your home on the
  heights,
you who say to yourself,
  'Who can bring me down to the
  ground?'
⁴Though you soar like the eagle
  and make your nest among the
  stars,
  from there I will bring you down,"
      declares the LORD.
⁵"If thieves came to you,
  if robbers in the night—
oh, what a disaster awaits you!—
  would they not steal only as much
  as they wanted?
If grape pickers came to you,
  would they not leave a few grapes?
⁶But how Esau will be ransacked,
  his hidden treasures pillaged!
⁷All your allies will force you to the
  border;
  your friends will deceive and
  overpower you;
those who eat your bread will set a
  trap for you,*
  but you will not detect it.

⁸"In that day," declares the LORD,
  "will I not destroy the wise men of
  Edom,
  those of understanding in the
  mountains of Esau?

⁹Your warriors, Teman, will be
  terrified,
  and everyone in Esau's mountains
  will be cut down in the slaughter.
¹⁰Because of the violence against your
  brother Jacob,
  you will be covered with shame;
  you will be destroyed forever.
¹¹On the day you stood aloof
  while strangers carried off his
  wealth
and foreigners entered his gates
  and cast lots for Jerusalem,
  you were like one of them.
¹²You should not gloat over your brother
  in the day of his misfortune,
nor rejoice over the people of Judah
  in the day of their destruction,
nor boast so much
  in the day of their trouble.
¹³You should not march through the
  gates of my people
  in the day of their disaster,
nor gloat over them in their calamity
  in the day of their disaster,
nor seize their wealth
  in the day of their disaster.
¹⁴You should not wait at the crossroads
  to cut down their fugitives,
nor hand over their survivors
  in the day of their trouble.

¹⁵"The day of the LORD is near
  for all nations.
As you have done, it will be done to
  you;
  your deeds will return upon your
  own head.
¹⁶Just as you drank on my holy hill,
  so all the nations will drink
  continually;
they will drink and drink
  and be as if they had never been.
¹⁷But on Mount Zion will be
  deliverance;
  it will be holy,
  and Jacob will possess his inheritance.
¹⁸Jacob will be a fire
  and Joseph a flame;

---

a 3 Or *of Sela*   *b 7* The meaning of the
Hebrew for this clause is uncertain.

Esau will be stubble,
    and they will set him on fire and
      destroy him.
There will be no survivors
    from Esau."
              The Lord has spoken.

¹⁹ People from the Negev will occupy
    the mountains of Esau,
and people from the foothills will
      possess
    the land of the Philistines.
They will occupy the fields of
      Ephraim and Samaria,
and Benjamin will possess Gilead.

²⁰ This company of Israelite exiles who
      are in Canaan
will possess the land as far as
      Zarephath;
the exiles from Jerusalem who are in
      Sepharad
will possess the towns of the
      Negev.
²¹ Deliverers will go up on[a] Mount
    Zion
to govern the mountains of Esau.
And the kingdom will be the
    Lord's.

[a] 21 Or *from*

JONAH

BOOK OUTLINE

God called Jonah to be a prophet during the reign of King Jeroboam II (793–753 BC). His job was to warn a foreign nation that God would destroy them if they didn't admit they were sinful and start obeying God. But Jonah didn't want that job. He didn't want to be nice to the people of the city of Nineveh in Assyria since they were the enemy.

So Jonah ran away, taking a ship to a far-away country. His trip ended in disaster. After his adventure, Jonah obeyed God, went to Nineveh to preach and warned the people about God's judgment. Jonah learned, to his dismay, that God would forgive even a heathen city if the people were sorry for their sins.

Jonah Flees From the LORD

1 The word of the LORD came to Jonah son of Amittai: ²"Go to the great city of Nineveh and preach against it, because its wickedness has come up before me."

³But Jonah ran away from the LORD and headed for Tarshish. He went down to Joppa, where he found a ship bound for that port. After paying the fare, he went aboard and sailed for Tarshish to flee from the LORD.

⁴Then the LORD sent a great wind on the sea, and such a violent storm arose that the ship threatened to break up. ⁵All the sailors were afraid and each cried out to his own god. And they threw the cargo into the sea to lighten the ship.

But Jonah had gone below deck, where he lay down and fell into a deep sleep. ⁶The captain went to him and said, "How can you sleep? Get up and call on your god! Maybe he will take notice of us so that we will not perish."

⁷Then the sailors said to each other, "Come, let us cast lots to find out who is responsible for this calamity." They cast lots and the lot fell on Jonah. ⁸So they asked him, "Tell us, who is responsible for making all this trouble for us? What kind of work do you do? Where do you come from? What is your country? From what people are you?"

⁹He answered, "I am a Hebrew and I worship the LORD, the God of heaven, who made the sea and the dry land."

¹⁰This terrified them and they asked, "What have you done?" (They knew he was running away from the LORD, because he had already told them so.)

¹¹The sea was getting rougher and rougher. So they asked him, "What should we do to you to make the sea calm down for us?"

¹²"Pick me up and throw me into the sea," he replied, "and it will become calm. I know that it is my fault that this great storm has come upon you."

¹³Instead, the men did their best to row back to land. But they could not, for the sea grew even wilder than before. ¹⁴Then they cried out to the LORD, "Please, LORD, do not let us die for taking this man's life. Do not hold us accountable for killing an innocent man, for you, LORD, have done as you pleased." ¹⁵Then they took Jonah and threw him overboard, and the raging sea grew calm. ¹⁶At this the men greatly feared the LORD, and they offered a sacrifice to the LORD and made vows to him.

Jonah 1:1–17

The Bible makes us think.

Some people see the book of Jonah as a giant fish story. God tells the prophet Jonah to go preach to the people of Nineveh, his most hated enemies. When the prophet takes off in the opposite direction, he ends up in the belly of a giant fish. Some readers call Jonah's story pure fiction. But Jesus clearly saw it as history, comparing the prophet's stay in the belly of the fish to his own death and resurrection (see Matthew 12:39–41). His point doesn't make sense unless Jonah was really inside the fish, and the people of Nineveh actually repented when they heard Jonah's message. Other readers object to God's plan to wipe out a sinful city. But in the book of Jonah we see "a gracious and compassionate God, slow to anger and abounding in love, a God who relents from sending calamity" (Jonah 4:2). Don't panic when the Bible pushes you to think. It's a nudge to figure out what it really says.

Think: What parts of the Bible puzzle you? How do you find answers for your questions?

ROCK SOLID *truths*

Jonah's Prayer

¹⁷Now the LORD provided a huge fish to swallow Jonah, and Jonah was in the belly of the fish three days and three nights.

2 *ᵃ* ¹From inside the fish Jonah prayed to the LORD his God. ²He said:

"In my distress I called to the LORD,
and he answered me.
From deep in the realm of the dead
I called for help,
and you listened to my cry.
³You hurled me into the depths,
into the very heart of the seas,
and the currents swirled about
me;
all your waves and breakers
swept over me.
⁴I said, 'I have been banished
from your sight;
yet I will look again
toward your holy temple.'

⁵The engulfing waters threatened me,ᵇ
the deep surrounded me;
seaweed was wrapped around my
head.
⁶To the roots of the mountains I sank
down;
the earth beneath barred me in
forever.
But you, LORD my God,
brought my life up from the pit.

⁷"When my life was ebbing away,
I remembered you, LORD,
and my prayer rose to you,
to your holy temple.

⁸"Those who cling to worthless idols
turn away from God's love for them.
⁹But I, with shouts of grateful praise,
will sacrifice to you.

ᵃ In Hebrew texts 2:1 is numbered 1:17, and 2:1-10 is numbered 2:2-11.   ᵇ 5 Or *waters were at my throat*

ROCK SOLID *principles*

Jonah 2:1 – 10

Reach out to your enemies.

Austin shook his head. No way was he going to help Jared. "But you can at least tutor him enough to get through math," Austin's mom pleaded. "Math is simple for you, but it baffles him." Not very long ago Austin and Jared had been best buddies of the neighborhood, but they were now sworn enemies. Austin couldn't remember ever doing anything bad to Jared, but Jared excelled at publicly humiliating Austin. So Austin didn't care if his ex-friend was about to flunk a grade, and it was no surprise that Jared's stupidity and laziness had finally caught up with him. "Don't ask again," Austin told his mom. "I'm not doing it."

God sent the prophet Jonah to the last place he wanted to go—to preach to his enemies in the totally wicked city of Nineveh. It took a wild ride in the belly of an enormous fish to convince Jonah to go. Loving your enemies might be the last thing you want to do, but it's one of the top things God requires (see Matthew 5:43–48).

What I have vowed I will make good.
I will say, 'Salvation comes from the
Lord.'"

¹⁰And the Lord commanded the fish,
and it vomited Jonah onto dry land.

Jonah Goes to Nineveh

3 Then the word of the Lord came
to Jonah a second time: ²"Go to
the great city of Nineveh and proclaim to it the message I give you."

³Jonah obeyed the word of the Lord
and went to Nineveh. Now Nineveh was
a very large city; it took three days to
go through it. ⁴Jonah began by going a
day's journey into the city, proclaiming,
"Forty more days and Nineveh will be
overthrown." ⁵The Ninevites believed
God. A fast was proclaimed, and all of
them, from the greatest to the least, put
on sackcloth.

⁶When Jonah's warning reached the
king of Nineveh, he rose from his throne,
took off his royal robes, covered himself
with sackcloth and sat down in the dust.
⁷This is the proclamation he issued in
Nineveh:

"By the decree of the king and his
nobles:

Do not let people or animals,
herds or flocks, taste anything; do
not let them eat or drink. ⁸But let
people and animals be covered with
sackcloth. Let everyone call urgently on God. Let them give up their
evil ways and their violence. ⁹Who
knows? God may yet relent and with
compassion turn from his fierce anger so that we will not perish."

¹⁰When God saw what they did and
how they turned from their evil ways, he
relented and did not bring on them the
destruction he had threatened.

Jonah's Anger at the Lord's Compassion

4 But to Jonah this seemed very
wrong, and he became angry. ²He
prayed to the Lord, "Isn't this
what I said, Lord, when I was still at
home? That is what I tried to forestall by
fleeing to Tarshish. I knew that you are a
gracious and compassionate God, slow to
anger and abounding in love, a God who
relents from sending calamity. ³Now,
Lord, take away my life, for it is better
for me to die than to live."

⁴But the Lord replied, "Is it right for
you to be angry?"

⁵Jonah had gone out and sat down at a
place east of the city. There he made himself a shelter, sat in its shade and waited
to see what would happen to the city.
⁶Then the Lord God provided a leafy
plant*ᵃ* and made it grow up over Jonah
to give shade for his head to ease his dis-
comfort, and Jonah was very happy about
the plant. ⁷But at dawn the next day God
provided a worm, which chewed the plant
so that it withered. ⁸When the sun rose,
God provided a scorching east wind, and
the sun blazed on Jonah's head so that he
grew faint. He wanted to die, and said, "It
would be better for me to die than to live."

⁹But God said to Jonah, "Is it right for
you to be angry about the plant?"

"It is," he said. "And I'm so angry I wish
I were dead."

¹⁰But the Lord said, "You have been
concerned about this plant, though you
did not tend it or make it grow. It sprang
up overnight and died overnight. ¹¹And
should I not have concern for the great
city of Nineveh, in which there are more
than a hundred and twenty thousand people who cannot tell their right hand from
their left—and also many animals?"

ᵃ 6 The precise identification of this plant is
uncertain; also in verses 7, 9 and 10.

MICAH

This book contains the writings of the prophet Micah who lived in the countryside of Judah during the reigns of Jotham, Ahaz and Hezekiah. Micah warned about God's judgment against the capital cities of both kingdoms, Jerusalem and Samaria, because of the sinfulness of their rulers, prophets and priests. The poor were oppressed and people's lives did not show that they belonged to a holy God.

But Micah promised the restoration of Zion and a kingdom of peace for those who trusted in God. He prophesied that a ruler born in Bethlehem would set up a kingdom that would last forever.

1 The word of the Lord that came to Micah of Moresheth during the reigns of Jotham, Ahaz and Hezekiah, kings of Judah—the vision he saw concerning Samaria and Jerusalem.

² Hear, you peoples, all of you,
	listen, earth and all who live in it,
that the Sovereign Lord may bear
	witness against you,
	the Lord from his holy temple.

Judgment Against Samaria and Jerusalem

³ Look! The Lord is coming from his
	dwelling place;
	he comes down and treads on the
	heights of the earth.
⁴ The mountains melt beneath him
	and the valleys split apart,
like wax before the fire,
	like water rushing down a slope.
⁵ All this is because of Jacob's
	transgression,
	because of the sins of the people of
	Israel.
What is Jacob's transgression?
	Is it not Samaria?
What is Judah's high place?
	Is it not Jerusalem?

⁶ "Therefore I will make Samaria a heap
	of rubble,
	a place for planting vineyards.
I will pour her stones into the valley
	and lay bare her foundations.
⁷ All her idols will be broken to pieces;
	all her temple gifts will be burned
	with fire;
	I will destroy all her images.
Since she gathered her gifts from the
	wages of prostitutes,
	as the wages of prostitutes they will
	again be used."

Weeping and Mourning

⁸ Because of this I will weep and wail;
	I will go about barefoot and naked.
I will howl like a jackal
	and moan like an owl.
⁹ For Samaria's plague is incurable;
	it has spread to Judah.

It has reached the very gate of my
	people,
	even to Jerusalem itself.
¹⁰ Tell it not in Gath[a];
	weep not at all.
In Beth Ophrah[b]
	roll in the dust.
¹¹ Pass by naked and in shame,
	you who live in Shaphir.[c]
Those who live in Zaanan[d]
	will not come out.
Beth Ezel is in mourning;
	it no longer protects you.
¹² Those who live in Maroth[e] writhe in
	pain,
	waiting for relief,
because disaster has come from the
	Lord,
	even to the gate of Jerusalem.
¹³ You who live in Lachish,
	harness fast horses to the chariot.
You are where the sin of Daughter
	Zion began,
	for the transgressions of Israel were
	found in you.
¹⁴ Therefore you will give parting gifts
	to Moresheth Gath.
The town of Akzib[f] will prove
	deceptive
	to the kings of Israel.
¹⁵ I will bring a conqueror against you
	who live in Mareshah.[g]
The nobles of Israel
	will flee to Adullam.
¹⁶ Shave your head in mourning
	for the children in whom you delight;
make yourself as bald as the vulture,
	for they will go from you into exile.

Human Plans and God's Plans

2 Woe to those who plan iniquity,
	to those who plot evil on their
	beds!
At morning's light they carry it out
	because it is in their power to do it.

---

[a] 10 *Gath* sounds like the Hebrew for *tell*.
[b] 10 *Beth Ophrah* means *house of dust*.
[c] 11 *Shaphir* means *pleasant*.   [d] 11 *Zaanan* sounds like the Hebrew for *come out*.
[e] 12 *Maroth* sounds like the Hebrew for *bitter*.
[f] 14 *Akzib* means *deception*.   [g] 15 *Mareshah* sounds like the Hebrew for *conqueror*.

²They covet fields and seize them,
and houses, and take them.
They defraud people of their homes,
they rob them of their inheritance.

³Therefore, the Lord says:

"I am planning disaster against this
people,
from which you cannot save
yourselves.
You will no longer walk proudly,
for it will be a time of calamity.
⁴In that day people will ridicule you;
they will taunt you with this
mournful song:
'We are utterly ruined;
my people's possession is divided
up.
He takes it from me!
He assigns our fields to traitors.'"

⁵Therefore you will have no one in the
assembly of the Lord
to divide the land by lot.

False Prophets

⁶"Do not prophesy," their prophets say.
"Do not prophesy about these
things;
disgrace will not overtake us."
⁷You descendants of Jacob, should it be
said,
"Does the Lord become[a]
impatient?
Does he do such things?"

"Do not my words do good
to the one whose ways are upright?
⁸Lately my people have risen up
like an enemy.
You strip off the rich robe
from those who pass by without a
care,
like men returning from battle.
⁹You drive the women of my people
from their pleasant homes.
You take away my blessing
from their children forever.
¹⁰Get up, go away!
For this is not your resting place,
because it is defiled,
it is ruined, beyond all remedy.

¹¹If a liar and deceiver comes and says,
'I will prophesy for you plenty of
wine and beer,'
that would be just the prophet for
this people!

Deliverance Promised

¹²"I will surely gather all of you,
Jacob;
I will surely bring together the
remnant of Israel.
I will bring them together like sheep
in a pen,
like a flock in its pasture;
the place will throng with people.
¹³The One who breaks open the way
will go up before them;
they will break through the gate
and go out.
Their King will pass through before
them,
the Lord at their head."

Leaders and Prophets Rebuked

3 Then I said,

"Listen, you leaders of Jacob,
you rulers of Israel.
Should you not embrace justice,
²   you who hate good and love evil;
who tear the skin from my people
and the flesh from their bones;
³who eat my people's flesh,
strip off their skin
and break their bones in pieces;
who chop them up like meat for the
pan,
like flesh for the pot?"

⁴Then they will cry out to the Lord,
but he will not answer them.
At that time he will hide his face from
them
because of the evil they have done.

⁵This is what the Lord says:

"As for the prophets
who lead my people astray,
they proclaim 'peace'
if they have something to eat,

---

[a] 7 Or *Is the Spirit of the* LORD

but prepare to wage war against anyone
who refuses to feed them.
⁶Therefore night will come over you,
without visions,
and darkness, without divination.
The sun will set for the prophets,
and the day will go dark for them.
⁷The seers will be ashamed
and the diviners disgraced.
They will all cover their faces
because there is no answer from
God."
⁸But as for me, I am filled with power,
with the Spirit of the LORD,
and with justice and might,
to declare to Jacob his transgression,
to Israel his sin.

⁹Hear this, you leaders of Jacob,
you rulers of Israel,
who despise justice
and distort all that is right;
¹⁰who build Zion with bloodshed,
and Jerusalem with wickedness.
¹¹Her leaders judge for a bribe,
her priests teach for a price,
and her prophets tell fortunes for
money.
Yet they look for the LORD's support
and say,
"Is not the LORD among us?
No disaster will come upon us."
¹²Therefore because of you,
Zion will be plowed like a field,
Jerusalem will become a heap of
rubble,
the temple hill a mound overgrown
with thickets.

The Mountain of the LORD

4 In the last days

the mountain of the LORD's
temple will be established
as the highest of the mountains;
it will be exalted above the hills,
and peoples will stream to it.

²Many nations will come and say,

"Come, let us go up to the mountain
of the LORD,
to the temple of the God of Jacob.

He will teach us his ways,
so that we may walk in his paths."
The law will go out from Zion,
the word of the LORD from
Jerusalem.
³He will judge between many
peoples
and will settle disputes for strong
nations far and wide.
They will beat their swords into
plowshares
and their spears into pruning
hooks.
Nation will not take up sword against
nation,
nor will they train for war
anymore.
⁴Everyone will sit under their own
vine
and under their own fig tree,
and no one will make them afraid,
for the LORD Almighty has spoken.
⁵All the nations may walk
in the name of their gods,
but we will walk in the name of the
LORD
our God for ever and ever.

The LORD's Plan

⁶"In that day," declares the LORD,

"I will gather the lame;
I will assemble the exiles
and those I have brought to grief.
⁷I will make the lame my remnant,
those driven away a strong nation.
The LORD will rule over them in
Mount Zion
from that day and forever.
⁸As for you, watchtower of the flock,
stronghold*a* of Daughter Zion,
the former dominion will be restored
to you;
kingship will come to Daughter
Jerusalem."

⁹Why do you now cry aloud—
have you no king*b*?
Has your ruler*c* perished,
that pain seizes you like that of a
woman in labor?

---

a 8 Or *hill*   *b 9* Or *King*   *c 9* Or *Ruler*

Micah 4:1–5

There is one true God.

Hundreds of years before Jesus told his disciples to "go and make disciples of all nations" (Matthew 28:19), the prophet Micah had a vision of the nations streaming to Jerusalem to worship. It's an outburst of spiritual passion that would astonish you if it happened in your hometown. People come to God so they can learn his ways and "walk in his paths" (Micah 4:2). When God settles disputes, the nations "beat their swords into plowshares" (Micah 4:3). Individuals enjoy peace and prosperity, "and no one will make them afraid" (Micah 4:4). And the scene wraps up with a pledge by true believers to live for the one true God. Like Micah says, "We will walk in the name of the LORD our God for ever and ever" (Micah 4:5). Micah's vision isn't yet a reality, and our world still struggles to figure out who Jesus is. So make sure you take a clear stand for the one true God.

Think: Why do you think there is one real God?

ROCK SOLID *truths*

They say, "Let her be defiled,
let our eyes gloat over Zion!"
¹² But they do not know
the thoughts of the LORD;
they do not understand his plan,
that he has gathered them like
sheaves to the threshing floor.
¹³ "Rise and thresh, Daughter Zion,
for I will give you horns of iron;
I will give you hooves of bronze,
and you will break to pieces many
nations."
You will devote their ill-gotten gains
to the LORD,
their wealth to the Lord of all the
earth.

A Promised Ruler From Bethlehem

5 *ᵃ* Marshal your troops now, city of
troops,
for a siege is laid against us.
They will strike Israel's ruler
on the cheek with a rod.

² "But you, Bethlehem Ephrathah,
though you are small among the
clans*ᵇ* of Judah,
out of you will come for me
one who will be ruler over Israel,
whose origins are from of old,
from ancient times."

³ Therefore Israel will be abandoned
until the time when she who is in
labor bears a son,
and the rest of his brothers return
to join the Israelites.

⁴ He will stand and shepherd his
flock
in the strength of the LORD,
in the majesty of the name of the
LORD his God.
And they will live securely, for then
his greatness
will reach to the ends of the earth.

⁵ And he will be our peace
when the Assyrians invade our
land
and march through our fortresses.

¹⁰ Writhe in agony, Daughter Zion,
like a woman in labor,
for now you must leave the city
to camp in the open field.
You will go to Babylon;
there you will be rescued.
There the LORD will redeem you
out of the hand of your enemies.

¹¹ But now many nations
are gathered against you.

ᵃ In Hebrew texts 5:1 is numbered 4:14, and 5:2-
15 is numbered 5:1-14.   *ᵇ 2* Or *rulers*

1087

We will raise against them seven
shepherds,
even eight commanders,
⁶who will rule*ᵃ* the land of Assyria
with the sword,
the land of Nimrod with drawn
sword.*ᵇ*
He will deliver us from the
Assyrians
when they invade our land
and march across our borders.

⁷The remnant of Jacob will be
in the midst of many peoples
like dew from the LORD,
like showers on the grass,
which do not wait for anyone
or depend on man.
⁸The remnant of Jacob will be among
the nations,
in the midst of many peoples,
like a lion among the beasts of the
forest,
like a young lion among flocks of
sheep,
which mauls and mangles as it goes,
and no one can rescue.
⁹Your hand will be lifted up in triumph
over your enemies,
and all your foes will be destroyed.

¹⁰"In that day," declares the LORD,

"I will destroy your horses from
among you
and demolish your chariots.
¹¹I will destroy the cities of your land
and tear down all your
strongholds.
¹²I will destroy your witchcraft
and you will no longer cast spells.
¹³I will destroy your idols
and your sacred stones from among
you;
you will no longer bow down
to the work of your hands.
¹⁴I will uproot from among you your
Asherah poles*ᶜ*
when I demolish your cities.
¹⁵I will take vengeance in anger and
wrath
on the nations that have not obeyed
me."

The LORD's Case Against Israel

6 Listen to what the LORD says:

"Stand up, plead my case before
the mountains;
let the hills hear what you have to say.

²"Hear, you mountains, the LORD's
accusation;
listen, you everlasting foundations
of the earth.
For the LORD has a case against his
people;
he is lodging a charge against Israel.

³"My people, what have I done to you?
How have I burdened you? Answer
me.
⁴I brought you up out of Egypt
and redeemed you from the land of
slavery.
I sent Moses to lead you,
also Aaron and Miriam.
⁵My people, remember
what Balak king of Moab plotted
and what Balaam son of Beor
answered.
Remember your journey from Shittim
to Gilgal,
that you may know the righteous
acts of the LORD."

⁶With what shall I come before the
LORD
and bow down before the exalted
God?
Shall I come before him with burnt
offerings,
with calves a year old?
⁷Will the LORD be pleased with
thousands of rams,
with ten thousand rivers of olive oil?
Shall I offer my firstborn for my
transgression,
the fruit of my body for the sin of
my soul?
⁸He has shown you, O mortal, what is
good.
And what does the LORD require of
you?

ᵃ 6 Or *crush*   *ᵇ 6* Or *Nimrod in its gates*
ᶜ 14 That is, wooden symbols of the goddess
Asherah

To act justly and to love mercy
   and to walk humbly[a] with your
      God.

Israel's Guilt and Punishment

⁹ Listen! The Lord is calling to the
   city—
   and to fear your name is wisdom—
   "Heed the rod and the One who
      appointed it.[b]
¹⁰ Am I still to forget your ill-gotten
      treasures, you wicked house,
   and the short ephah,[c] which is
      accursed?
¹¹ Shall I acquit someone with dishonest
      scales,
   with a bag of false weights?
¹² Your rich people are violent;
   your inhabitants are liars
   and their tongues speak deceitfully.
¹³ Therefore, I have begun to destroy
      you,
   to ruin[d] you because of your sins.

¹⁴ You will eat but not be satisfied;
   your stomach will still be empty.[e]
   You will store up but save nothing,
   because what you save[f] I will give
      to the sword.
¹⁵ You will plant but not harvest;
   you will press olives but not use the
      oil,
   you will crush grapes but not drink
      the wine.
¹⁶ You have observed the statutes of
      Omri
   and all the practices of Ahab's
      house;
   you have followed their traditions.

[a] 8 Or *prudently*   [b] 9 The meaning of the Hebrew for this line is uncertain.   [c] 10 An ephah was a dry measure.   [d] 13 Or *Therefore, I will make you ill and destroy you; / I will ruin*   [e] 14 The meaning of the Hebrew for this word is uncertain.   [f] 14 Or *You will press toward birth but not give birth, / and what you bring to birth*

ROCK SOLID *principles*

Micah 6:8

Keep it simple.

Madison felt crushed under all the expectations being heaped on her. A few months ago she signed up for an intense spiritual growth experience at church, but her youth pastor kept piling on requirements for the handful of hardcore students who signed up. Group members had to be in church each Sunday morning—no problem with that. But they were also required to attend a weekly Bible study and weekly leadership training meeting. Each had to start an evangelistic Bible study at school. And anyone who couldn't meet these obligations got the boot. Madison wondered how she would ever have time for family or friends or homework. And she felt like God had gotten misplaced in all the clutter.

The people of Israel had become experts in religion, but they lacked an authentic relationship with the Lord. They burned up endless offerings and bowed enough to create a breeze. But they missed the main point. The Lord wants us to keep faith real—to treat people fairly . . . to enjoy showing mercy . . . to happily obey our God.

Therefore I will give you over to ruin
and your people to derision;
you will bear the scorn of the
nations.*"*

Israel's Misery

7 What misery is mine!
I am like one who gathers
summer fruit
at the gleaning of the vineyard;
there is no cluster of grapes to eat,
none of the early figs that I crave.
² The faithful have been swept from the
land;
not one upright person remains.
Everyone lies in wait to shed blood;
they hunt each other with nets.
³ Both hands are skilled in doing evil;
the ruler demands gifts,
the judge accepts bribes,
the powerful dictate what they
desire —
they all conspire together.
⁴ The best of them is like a brier,
the most upright worse than a thorn
hedge.
The day God visits you has come,
the day your watchmen sound the
alarm.
Now is the time of your confusion.
⁵ Do not trust a neighbor;
put no confidence in a friend.
Even with the woman who lies in your
embrace
guard the words of your lips.
⁶ For a son dishonors his father,
a daughter rises up against her mother,
a daughter-in-law against her mother-
in-law —
a man's enemies are the members of
his own household.

⁷ But as for me, I watch in hope for the
LORD,
I wait for God my Savior;
my God will hear me.

Israel Will Rise

⁸ Do not gloat over me, my enemy!
Though I have fallen, I will rise.
Though I sit in darkness,
the LORD will be my light.

⁹ Because I have sinned against him,
I will bear the LORD's wrath,
until he pleads my case
and upholds my cause.
He will bring me out into the light;
I will see his righteousness.
¹⁰ Then my enemy will see it
and will be covered with shame,
she who said to me,
"Where is the LORD your God?"
My eyes will see her downfall;
even now she will be trampled
underfoot
like mire in the streets.

¹¹ The day for building your walls will
come,
the day for extending your
boundaries.
¹² In that day people will come to you
from Assyria and the cities of
Egypt,
even from Egypt to the Euphrates
and from sea to sea
and from mountain to mountain.
¹³ The earth will become desolate
because of its inhabitants,
as the result of their deeds.

Prayer and Praise

¹⁴ Shepherd your people with your staff,
the flock of your inheritance,
which lives by itself in a forest,
in fertile pasturelands.*b*
Let them feed in Bashan and Gilead
as in days long ago.

¹⁵ "As in the days when you came out of
Egypt,
I will show them my wonders."

¹⁶ Nations will see and be ashamed,
deprived of all their power.
They will put their hands over their
mouths
and their ears will become deaf.
¹⁷ They will lick dust like a snake,
like creatures that crawl on the
ground.
They will come trembling out of their
dens;

---

a 16 Septuagint; Hebrew *scorn due my people*
b 14 Or *in the middle of Carmel*

they will turn in fear to the L<small>ORD</small>
    our God
and will be afraid of you.
¹⁸ Who is a God like you,
    who pardons sin and forgives the
        transgression
    of the remnant of his inheritance?
You do not stay angry forever
    but delight to show mercy.
¹⁹ You will again have compassion on us;
    you will tread our sins underfoot
    and hurl all our iniquities into the
        depths of the sea.
²⁰ You will be faithful to Jacob,
    and show love to Abraham,
as you pledged on oath to our ancestors
    in days long ago.

ROCK SOLID *promises*

"You do not stay angry forever but delight to show mercy."

Micah 7:18

God hates evil, but your sins can't stop his love for you. He wants to show you mercy.

NAHUM

BOOK OUTLINE

Nahum was a prophet in the last half of the seventh century BC. He prophesied at the same time as Zephaniah, Jeremiah and Habakkuk.

Nahum is a book of prophecy against Nineveh, the capital of Assyria. The prophet describes the cruelty of the Assyrians as they conquered nation after nation. He predicts the siege and destruction of Nineveh and the end of the kingdom of Assyria.

Nahum's only advice to Judah was that they observe their religious festivals since the Assyrians would never again threaten Jerusalem.

1

A prophecy concerning Nineveh. The book of the vision of Nahum the Elkoshite.

The Lord's Anger Against Nineveh

²The Lord is a jealous and avenging God;
  the Lord takes vengeance and is filled with wrath.
The Lord takes vengeance on his foes
  and vents his wrath against his enemies.
³The Lord is slow to anger but great in power;
  the Lord will not leave the guilty unpunished.
His way is in the whirlwind and the storm,
  and clouds are the dust of his feet.
⁴He rebukes the sea and dries it up;
  he makes all the rivers run dry.
Bashan and Carmel wither
  and the blossoms of Lebanon fade.
⁵The mountains quake before him
  and the hills melt away.
The earth trembles at his presence,
  the world and all who live in it.
⁶Who can withstand his indignation?
  Who can endure his fierce anger?
His wrath is poured out like fire;
  the rocks are shattered before him.

⁷The Lord is good,
  a refuge in times of trouble.
He cares for those who trust in him,
⁸ but with an overwhelming flood
he will make an end of Nineveh;
  he will pursue his foes into the realm of darkness.

⁹Whatever they plot against the Lord
  he will bring*ᵃ* to an end;
  trouble will not come a second time.
¹⁰They will be entangled among thorns
  and drunk from their wine;
  they will be consumed like dry stubble.*ᵇ*
¹¹From you, Nineveh, has one come forth
  who plots evil against the Lord
  and devises wicked plans.

ROCK SOLID *promises*

"The Lord is good, a refuge in times of trouble. He cares for those who trust in him." Nahum 1:7

God gives you shelter even if no one else does. Before, during, and after trouble he cares for you.

¹²This is what the Lord says:

"Although they have allies and are numerous,
  they will be destroyed and pass away.
Although I have afflicted you, Judah,
  I will afflict you no more.
¹³Now I will break their yoke from your neck
  and tear your shackles away."

¹⁴The Lord has given a command concerning you, Nineveh:
  "You will have no descendants to bear your name.
I will destroy the images and idols
  that are in the temple of your gods.
I will prepare your grave,
  for you are vile."

¹⁵Look, there on the mountains,
  the feet of one who brings good news,
  who proclaims peace!
Celebrate your festivals, Judah,
  and fulfill your vows.
No more will the wicked invade you;
  they will be completely destroyed.*ᶜ*

ᵃ 9 Or *What do you foes plot against the Lord? / He will bring it   ᵇ 10* The meaning of the Hebrew for this verse is uncertain.   *ᶜ 15* In Hebrew texts this verse (1:15) is numbered 2:1.

Nineveh to Fall

2 [a] An attacker advances against
you, Nineveh.
Guard the fortress,
watch the road,
brace yourselves,
marshal all your strength!

2 The LORD will restore the splendor of
Jacob
like the splendor of Israel,
though destroyers have laid them
waste
and have ruined their vines.

3 The shields of the soldiers are red;
the warriors are clad in scarlet.
The metal on the chariots flashes
on the day they are made ready;
the spears of juniper are
brandished.[b]
4 The chariots storm through the streets,
rushing back and forth through the
squares.
They look like flaming torches;
they dart about like lightning.

5 Nineveh summons her picked troops,
yet they stumble on their way.
They dash to the city wall;
the protective shield is put in place.
6 The river gates are thrown open
and the palace collapses.
7 It is decreed[c] that Nineveh
be exiled and carried away.
Her female slaves moan like doves
and beat on their breasts.
8 Nineveh is like a pool
whose water is draining away.
"Stop! Stop!" they cry,
but no one turns back.
9 Plunder the silver!
Plunder the gold!
The supply is endless,
the wealth from all its treasures!
10 She is pillaged, plundered, stripped!
Hearts melt, knees give way,
bodies tremble, every face grows
pale.

11 Where now is the lions' den,
the place where they fed their
young,
where the lion and lioness went,
and the cubs, with nothing to fear?
12 The lion killed enough for his cubs
and strangled the prey for his mate,
filling his lairs with the kill
and his dens with the prey.

13 "I am against you,"
declares the LORD Almighty.
"I will burn up your chariots in
smoke,
and the sword will devour your
young lions.
I will leave you no prey on the
earth.
The voices of your messengers
will no longer be heard."

Woe to Nineveh

3 Woe to the city of blood,
full of lies,
full of plunder,
never without victims!
2 The crack of whips,
the clatter of wheels,
galloping horses
and jolting chariots!
3 Charging cavalry,
flashing swords
and glittering spears!
Many casualties,
piles of dead,
bodies without number,
people stumbling over the
corpses—
4 all because of the wanton lust of a
prostitute,
alluring, the mistress of sorceries,
who enslaved nations by her
prostitution
and peoples by her witchcraft.

5 "I am against you," declares the LORD
Almighty.
"I will lift your skirts over your
face.
I will show the nations your nakedness
and the kingdoms your shame.

---

[a] In Hebrew texts 2:1-13 is numbered 2:2-14.
[b] 3 Hebrew; Septuagint and Syriac *ready; / the
horsemen rush to and fro.*   [c] 7 The meaning of
the Hebrew for this word is uncertain.

⁶I will pelt you with filth,
   I will treat you with contempt
   and make you a spectacle.
⁷All who see you will flee from you and
      say,
   'Nineveh is in ruins—who will
      mourn for her?'
   Where can I find anyone to comfort
      you?"

⁸Are you better than Thebes,
   situated on the Nile,
   with water around her?
The river was her defense,
   the waters her wall.
⁹Cush*ᵃ* and Egypt were her boundless
      strength;
   Put and Libya were among her allies.
¹⁰Yet she was taken captive
   and went into exile.
Her infants were dashed to pieces
   at every street corner.
Lots were cast for her nobles,
   and all her great men were put in
      chains.
¹¹You too will become drunk;
   you will go into hiding
   and seek refuge from the enemy.

¹²All your fortresses are like fig trees
   with their first ripe fruit;
when they are shaken,
   the figs fall into the mouth of the
      eater.
¹³Look at your troops—
   they are all weaklings.
The gates of your land
   are wide open to your enemies;
   fire has consumed the bars of your
      gates.

¹⁴Draw water for the siege,
   strengthen your defenses!
Work the clay,
   tread the mortar,
   repair the brickwork!
¹⁵There the fire will consume you;
   the sword will cut you down—
   they will devour you like a swarm of
      locusts.
Multiply like grasshoppers,
   multiply like locusts!
¹⁶You have increased the number of
      your merchants
   till they are more numerous than
      the stars in the sky,
but like locusts they strip the land
   and then fly away.
¹⁷Your guards are like locusts,
   your officials like swarms of locusts
   that settle in the walls on a cold
      day—
but when the sun appears they fly
      away,
   and no one knows where.

¹⁸King of Assyria, your shepherds*ᵇ*
      slumber;
   your nobles lie down to rest.
Your people are scattered on the
      mountains
   with no one to gather them.
¹⁹Nothing can heal you;
   your wound is fatal.
All who hear the news about you
   clap their hands at your fall,
for who has not felt
   your endless cruelty?

ᵃ 9 That is, the upper Nile region   *ᵇ 18* That
is, rulers

HABAKKUK

BOOK OUTLINE

Habakkuk was written as a dialogue or conversation between God and the prophet. Habakkuk saw that the leaders in Judah were oppressing the poor, so he asked God the question: Why do you allow wicked people to prosper? When God told him that the Babylonians would come to punish Judah, Habakkuk became more concerned. He did not understand how God could use the Babylonians, who were actually more wicked than the wicked Israelites, to bring judgment on God's chosen people. God's answer was that the just would live by faith in God and that they had the assurance that God was doing what was right. God told Habakkuk that eventually he would judge the Babylonians too and he would bring justice to his chosen people. Habakkuk ends his book with a prayer of praise.

The prophecy that Habakkuk the prophet received.

Habakkuk's Complaint

²How long, Lord, must I call for help,
but you do not listen?
Or cry out to you, "Violence!"
but you do not save?
³Why do you make me look at injustice?
Why do you tolerate wrongdoing?
Destruction and violence are before me;
there is strife, and conflict abounds.
⁴Therefore the law is paralyzed,
and justice never prevails.
The wicked hem in the righteous,
so that justice is perverted.

The Lord's Answer

⁵"Look at the nations and watch—
and be utterly amazed.
For I am going to do something in your days
that you would not believe,
even if you were told.
⁶I am raising up the Babylonians,^a
that ruthless and impetuous people,
who sweep across the whole earth
to seize dwellings not their own.
⁷They are a feared and dreaded people;
they are a law to themselves
and promote their own honor.
⁸Their horses are swifter than leopards,
fiercer than wolves at dusk.
Their cavalry gallops headlong;
their horsemen come from afar.
They fly like an eagle swooping to devour;
⁹ they all come intent on violence.
Their hordes^b advance like a desert wind
and gather prisoners like sand.
¹⁰They mock kings
and scoff at rulers.

They laugh at all fortified cities;
by building earthen ramps they capture them.
¹¹Then they sweep past like the wind and go on—
guilty people, whose own strength is their god."

---

^a 6 Or *Chaldeans*   ^b 9 The meaning of the Hebrew for this word is uncertain.

Habakkuk 1:1–11

God loves honest questions.

Some people seem to think that believing in God and having faith means you can't ever question the Lord—who he is, how he acts, or what his promises truly mean. But God doesn't shy away from honest questions. Actually, he welcomes the chance to hear your thoughts, and he answers you through his Word and wise people. This entire book of Habakkuk is a back-and-forth conversation between God and his spokesperson. The prophet started with a major complaint, "How long, Lord, must I call for help, but you do not listen?" (Habakkuk 1:2). He challenged God with questions like "Why do you tolerate wrongdoing?" (Habakkuk 1:3). The Lord not only heard these questions but gave detailed answers. God knew Habakkuk wasn't just spouting off. The prophet wanted real answers to his deep questions, and he was willing to live by the truths the Lord told him.

Think: What hard questions do you have for God? Is he scared when you bring him your doubts? Why—or why not?

ROCK SOLID *truths*

Habakkuk's Second Complaint

¹² Lord, are you not from everlasting?
My God, my Holy One, you*ᵃ* will
never die.
You, Lord, have appointed them to
execute judgment;
you, my Rock, have ordained them
to punish.
¹³ Your eyes are too pure to look on evil;
you cannot tolerate wrongdoing.
Why then do you tolerate the
treacherous?
Why are you silent while the
wicked
swallow up those more righteous
than themselves?
¹⁴ You have made people like the fish in
the sea,
like the sea creatures that have no
ruler.
¹⁵ The wicked foe pulls all of them up
with hooks,
he catches them in his net,
he gathers them up in his dragnet;
and so he rejoices and is glad.
¹⁶ Therefore he sacrifices to his net
and burns incense to his dragnet,
for by his net he lives in luxury
and enjoys the choicest food.
¹⁷ Is he to keep on emptying his net,
destroying nations without mercy?

2 I will stand at my watch
and station myself on the
ramparts;
I will look to see what he will say to me,
and what answer I am to give to this
complaint.*ᵇ*

The Lord's Answer

² Then the Lord replied:

"Write down the revelation
and make it plain on tablets
so that a herald*ᶜ* may run with it.
³ For the revelation awaits an appointed
time;
it speaks of the end
and will not prove false.
Though it linger, wait for it;
it*ᵈ* will certainly come
and will not delay.

⁴ "See, the enemy is puffed up;
his desires are not upright—
but the righteous person will live
by his faithfulness*ᵉ*—
⁵ indeed, wine betrays him;
he is arrogant and never at rest.
Because he is as greedy as the grave
and like death is never satisfied,
he gathers to himself all the nations
and takes captive all the peoples.

⁶ "Will not all of them taunt him with
ridicule and scorn, saying,

"'Woe to him who piles up stolen
goods
and makes himself wealthy by
extortion!
How long must this go on?'
⁷ Will not your creditors suddenly
arise?
Will they not wake up and make
you tremble?
Then you will become their prey.
⁸ Because you have plundered many
nations,
the peoples who are left will
plunder you.
For you have shed human blood;
you have destroyed lands and cities
and everyone in them.

⁹ "Woe to him who builds his house by
unjust gain,
setting his nest on high
to escape the clutches of ruin!
¹⁰ You have plotted the ruin of many
peoples,
shaming your own house and
forfeiting your life.
¹¹ The stones of the wall will cry out,
and the beams of the woodwork
will echo it.

¹² "Woe to him who builds a city with
bloodshed
and establishes a town by
injustice!

ᵃ 12 An ancient Hebrew scribal tradition;
Masoretic Text *we*   *ᵇ 1* Or *and what to answer
when I am rebuked*   *ᶜ 2* Or *so that whoever
reads it*   *ᵈ 3* Or *Though he linger, wait for him;
/ he*   *ᵉ 4* Or *faith*

¹³ Has not the LORD Almighty determined
   that the people's labor is only fuel for the fire,
   that the nations exhaust themselves for nothing?
¹⁴ For the earth will be filled with the knowledge of the glory of the LORD
   as the waters cover the sea.

¹⁵ "Woe to him who gives drink to his neighbors,
   pouring it from the wineskin till they are drunk,
   so that he can gaze on their naked bodies!
¹⁶ You will be filled with shame instead of glory.
   Now it is your turn! Drink and let your nakedness be exposed[a]!
   The cup from the LORD's right hand is coming around to you,
   and disgrace will cover your glory.
¹⁷ The violence you have done to Lebanon will overwhelm you,
   and your destruction of animals will terrify you.
   For you have shed human blood;
   you have destroyed lands and cities and everyone in them.

¹⁸ "Of what value is an idol carved by a craftsman?
   Or an image that teaches lies?
   For the one who makes it trusts in his own creation;
   he makes idols that cannot speak.
¹⁹ Woe to him who says to wood, 'Come to life!'
   Or to lifeless stone, 'Wake up!'
   Can it give guidance?
   It is covered with gold and silver;
   there is no breath in it."

²⁰ The LORD is in his holy temple;
   let all the earth be silent before him.

Habakkuk's Prayer

3 A prayer of Habakkuk the prophet. On *shigionoth*.[b]

² LORD, I have heard of your fame;
   I stand in awe of your deeds, LORD.
   Repeat them in our day,
   in our time make them known;
   in wrath remember mercy.

³ God came from Teman,
   the Holy One from Mount Paran.[c]
His glory covered the heavens
   and his praise filled the earth.
⁴ His splendor was like the sunrise;
   rays flashed from his hand,
   where his power was hidden.
⁵ Plague went before him;
   pestilence followed his steps.
⁶ He stood, and shook the earth;
   he looked, and made the nations tremble.
The ancient mountains crumbled
   and the age-old hills collapsed—
   but he marches on forever.
⁷ I saw the tents of Cushan in distress,
   the dwellings of Midian in anguish.

⁸ Were you angry with the rivers, LORD?
   Was your wrath against the streams?
Did you rage against the sea
   when you rode your horses
   and your chariots to victory?
⁹ You uncovered your bow,
   you called for many arrows.
You split the earth with rivers;
¹⁰ the mountains saw you and writhed.
Torrents of water swept by;
   the deep roared
   and lifted its waves on high.

¹¹ Sun and moon stood still in the heavens
   at the glint of your flying arrows,
   at the lightning of your flashing spear.
¹² In wrath you strode through the earth
   and in anger you threshed the nations.
¹³ You came out to deliver your people,
   to save your anointed one.

---

[a] 16 Masoretic Text; Dead Sea Scrolls, Aquila, Vulgate and Syriac (see also Septuagint) *and stagger* [b] 1 Probably a literary or musical term [c] 3 The Hebrew has *Selah* (a word of uncertain meaning) here and at the middle of verse 9 and at the end of verse 13.

You crushed the leader of the land of
wickedness,
you stripped him from head to foot.
¹⁴With his own spear you pierced his
head
when his warriors stormed out to
scatter us,
gloating as though about to devour
the wretched who were in hiding.
¹⁵You trampled the sea with your horses,
churning the great waters.

¹⁶I heard and my heart pounded,
my lips quivered at the sound;
decay crept into my bones,
and my legs trembled.
Yet I will wait patiently for the day of
calamity
to come on the nation invading us.

¹⁷Though the fig tree does not bud
and there are no grapes on the
vines,
though the olive crop fails
and the fields produce no food,
though there are no sheep in the pen
and no cattle in the stalls,
¹⁸yet I will rejoice in the LORD,
I will be joyful in God my
Savior.

¹⁹The Sovereign LORD is my strength;
he makes my feet like the feet of a
deer,
he enables me to tread on the
heights.

For the director of music. On my
stringed instruments.

ROCK SOLID principles

Habakkuk 3:17–19

Be happy no matter what.

Sure, basketball is only a game. But William couldn't stop thinking about the moment an opposing player stuck an elbow in William's gut and broke from his coverage, spinning into a layup that scored the winning point and eliminated William's team from regional playoffs. William and his teammates battled all season to earn a spot in that game, and everything they worked for was cut short by a foul that never got called. That moment solidified what William had been thinking for so long. Why do cheaters win? Why doesn't anyone stop them? And why doesn't God rise up and demolish evildoers who always seem to get away with even bigger sins?

The prophet Habakkuk hammered God with hard questions like "Why don't you punish injustice?" (Habakkuk 1:2–4) and "Why do you tolerate sin?" (see Habakkuk 1:12–17). The prophet listened to God and decided to trust him — to be happy even if everything falls apart. Whether good or bad comes, God still controls your world.

ZEPHANIAH

ephaniah was a prophet during the reign of King Josiah
(640 – 609 BC). He warned that the day of the Lord would
bring judgment on Judah and Jerusalem and he called the
people to return to God.

Zephaniah also predicted that God would destroy Judah's
neighboring nations as well. With a note of hope, he promised that
God would bring his people home.

1 The word of the LORD that came to Zephaniah son of Cushi, the son of Gedaliah, the son of Amariah, the son of Hezekiah, during the reign of Josiah son of Amon king of Judah:

Judgment on the Whole Earth in the Day of the LORD

2 "I will sweep away everything
    from the face of the earth,"
            declares the LORD.
3 "I will sweep away both man and
        beast;
    I will sweep away the birds in the sky
        and the fish in the sea—
    and the idols that cause the wicked
        to stumble."[a]

    "When I destroy all mankind
        on the face of the earth,"
            declares the LORD,
4 "I will stretch out my hand against
        Judah
    and against all who live in
        Jerusalem.
    I will destroy every remnant of Baal
        worship in this place,
    the very names of the idolatrous
        priests—
5 those who bow down on the roofs
    to worship the starry host,
    those who bow down and swear by the
        LORD
    and who also swear by Molek,[b]
6 those who turn back from following
        the LORD
    and neither seek the LORD nor
        inquire of him."

7 Be silent before the Sovereign LORD,
    for the day of the LORD is near.
    The LORD has prepared a sacrifice;
    he has consecrated those he has
        invited.

8 "On the day of the LORD's sacrifice
    I will punish the officials
    and the king's sons
    and all those clad
        in foreign clothes.
9 On that day I will punish
    all who avoid stepping on the
        threshold,[c]

who fill the temple of their gods
    with violence and deceit.

10 "On that day,"
        declares the LORD,
    "a cry will go up from the Fish Gate,
    wailing from the New Quarter,
    and a loud crash from the hills.
11 Wail, you who live in the market
        district[d];
    all your merchants will be wiped
        out,
    all who trade with[e] silver will be
        destroyed.
12 At that time I will search Jerusalem
        with lamps
    and punish those who are
        complacent,
    who are like wine left on its dregs,
    who think, 'The LORD will do
        nothing,
    either good or bad.'
13 Their wealth will be plundered,
    their houses demolished.
    Though they build houses,
        they will not live in them;
    though they plant vineyards,
        they will not drink the wine."

14 The great day of the LORD is near—
    near and coming quickly.
    The cry on the day of the LORD is
        bitter;
    the Mighty Warrior shouts his
        battle cry.
15 That day will be a day of wrath—
    a day of distress and anguish,
    a day of trouble and ruin,
    a day of darkness and gloom,
    a day of clouds and blackness—
16   a day of trumpet and battle cry
    against the fortified cities
    and against the corner towers.

17 "I will bring such distress on all people
    that they will grope about like those
        who are blind,
    because they have sinned against
        the LORD.

---

a 3 The meaning of the Hebrew for this line is uncertain.   b 5 Hebrew *Malkam*
c 9 See 1 Samuel 5:5.   d 11 Or *the Mortar*
e 11 Or *in*

ROCK SOLID
promises

"The great day of the Lord is near — near and coming quickly."

Zephaniah 1:14

God rules and reigns right now. But one day the whole world will bow to him.

Their blood will be poured out like dust
    and their entrails like dung.
18 Neither their silver nor their gold
    will be able to save them
    on the day of the Lord's wrath."

In the fire of his jealousy
    the whole earth will be consumed,
for he will make a sudden end
    of all who live on the earth.

Judah and Jerusalem Judged Along With the Nations

Judah Summoned to Repent

2 Gather together, gather
    yourselves together,
    you shameful nation,
2 before the decree takes effect
    and that day passes like windblown
        chaff,
    before the Lord's fierce anger
        comes upon you,
    before the day of the Lord's wrath
        comes upon you.
3 Seek the Lord, all you humble of the
        land,
    you who do what he commands.
Seek righteousness, seek humility;
    perhaps you will be sheltered
    on the day of the Lord's anger.

Philistia

4 Gaza will be abandoned
    and Ashkelon left in ruins.

At midday Ashdod will be emptied
    and Ekron uprooted.
5 Woe to you who live by the sea,
    you Kerethite people;
the word of the Lord is against you,
    Canaan, land of the Philistines.
He says, "I will destroy you,
    and none will be left."
6 The land by the sea will become
        pastures
    having wells for shepherds
    and pens for flocks.
7 That land will belong
    to the remnant of the people of
        Judah;
    there they will find pasture.
In the evening they will lie down
    in the houses of Ashkelon.
The Lord their God will care for
        them;
    he will restore their fortunes.*

Moab and Ammon

8 "I have heard the insults of Moab
    and the taunts of the Ammonites,
who insulted my people
    and made threats against their land.
9 Therefore, as surely as I live,"
    declares the Lord Almighty,
    the God of Israel,
"surely Moab will become like
        Sodom,
    the Ammonites like Gomorrah —
a place of weeds and salt pits,
    a wasteland forever.
The remnant of my people will
        plunder them;
    the survivors of my nation will
        inherit their land."

10 This is what they will get in return for
        their pride,
    for insulting and mocking
    the people of the Lord Almighty.
11 The Lord will be awesome to them
    when he destroys all the gods of the
        earth.
Distant nations will bow down to
        him,
    all of them in their own lands.

a 7 Or *will bring back their captives*

Cush

12 "You Cushites,[a] too,
  will be slain by my sword."

Assyria

13 He will stretch out his hand against
      the north
  and destroy Assyria,
  leaving Nineveh utterly desolate
  and dry as the desert.
14 Flocks and herds will lie down there,
  creatures of every kind.
  The desert owl and the screech owl
  will roost on her columns.
  Their hooting will echo through the
      windows,
  rubble will fill the doorways,
  the beams of cedar will be exposed.
15 This is the city of revelry
  that lived in safety.
  She said to herself,
  "I am the one! And there is none
      besides me."
  What a ruin she has become,
  a lair for wild beasts!
  All who pass by her scoff
  and shake their fists.

Jerusalem

3 Woe to the city of oppressors,
  rebellious and defiled!
2 She obeys no one,
  she accepts no correction.
She does not trust in the LORD,
  she does not draw near to her God.
3 Her officials within her
  are roaring lions;
her rulers are evening wolves,
  who leave nothing for the
      morning.
4 Her prophets are unprincipled;
  they are treacherous people.
Her priests profane the sanctuary
  and do violence to the law.
5 The LORD within her is righteous;
  he does no wrong.
Morning by morning he dispenses his
      justice,
  and every new day he does not fail,
  yet the unrighteous know no
      shame.

Jerusalem Remains Unrepentant

6 "I have destroyed nations;
  their strongholds are demolished.
I have left their streets deserted,
  with no one passing through.
Their cities are laid waste;
  they are deserted and empty.
7 Of Jerusalem I thought,
  'Surely you will fear me
  and accept correction!'
Then her place of refuge[b] would not
      be destroyed,
  nor all my punishments come upon[c]
      her.
But they were still eager
  to act corruptly in all they did.
8 Therefore wait for me,"
  declares the LORD,
  "for the day I will stand up to
      testify.[d]
I have decided to assemble the nations,
  to gather the kingdoms
and to pour out my wrath on them—
  all my fierce anger.
The whole world will be consumed
  by the fire of my jealous anger.

Restoration of Israel's Remnant

9 "Then I will purify the lips of the
      peoples,
  that all of them may call on the
      name of the LORD
  and serve him shoulder to shoulder.
10 From beyond the rivers of Cush[e]
  my worshipers, my scattered people,
  will bring me offerings.
11 On that day you, Jerusalem, will not
      be put to shame
  for all the wrongs you have done
      to me,
because I will remove from you
  your arrogant boasters.
Never again will you be haughty
  on my holy hill.
12 But I will leave within you
  the meek and humble.

a 12 That is, people from the upper Nile region
b 7 Or her sanctuary   c 7 Or all those I
appointed over   d 8 Septuagint and Syriac;
Hebrew will rise up to plunder   e 10 That is,
the upper Nile region

The remnant of Israel
  will trust in the name of the Lord.
¹³They will do no wrong;
  they will tell no lies.
A deceitful tongue
  will not be found in their mouths.
They will eat and lie down
  and no one will make them afraid."

¹⁴Sing, Daughter Zion;
  shout aloud, Israel!
Be glad and rejoice with all your
    heart,
  Daughter Jerusalem!
¹⁵The Lord has taken away your
    punishment,
  he has turned back your enemy.
The Lord, the King of Israel, is with
    you;
  never again will you fear any harm.
¹⁶On that day
  they will say to Jerusalem,
"Do not fear, Zion;
  do not let your hands hang limp.
¹⁷The Lord your God is with you,
  the Mighty Warrior who saves.
He will take great delight in you;
  in his love he will no longer rebuke
    you,
  but will rejoice over you with
    singing."

¹⁸"I will remove from you
  all who mourn over the loss of your
    appointed festivals,
  which is a burden and reproach for
    you.
¹⁹At that time I will deal
  with all who oppressed you.
I will rescue the lame;
  I will gather the exiles.

UNSHAKEN God

Zephaniah 3:14–17

God is joyful.

The last time someone sang to you and you alone they were probably humming a lullaby. Or strumming a love song. But the picture here starts with God purifying the world of people who rebel against him. The Lord pours out his anger and punishes evildoers, then gathers his worshipers. The only people left in the city of Jerusalem are those who obey God gladly (see Zephaniah 3:1–13). And that's when the singing begins. God sings because he's crazy about his people. He calms them with his love. When he sees them he rejoices and bursts out in song. Got the picture? That's the joy God feels when he looks at you.

So … God sings to you. Is that awkward—or what?

I will give them praise and honor
  in every land where they have
    suffered shame.
²⁰At that time I will gather you;
  at that time I will bring you home.
I will give you honor and praise
  among all the peoples of the earth
when I restore your fortunesᵃ
  before your very eyes,"
            says the Lord.

ᵃ 20 Or I bring back your captives

HAGGAI

Eighteen years had passed since Cyrus's decree in 538 BC had allowed the Jews to return to Jerusalem from exile. Because they were busy building their own homes, the people still had not finished building God's temple.

Haggai's message was that the time had come to build the house of the Lord. Under the leadership of Zerubbabel and Joshua and with Haggai's prodding, the temple was rebuilt during the years 520 – 515 BC.

Haggai told the people that the glory of the temple they were building would be greater than that of the former temple, even though the building itself would be less to look at. This temple would be greater because God would fill this house with his glory.

A Call to Build the House of the LORD

In the second year of King Darius, on the first day of the sixth month, the word of the LORD came through the prophet Haggai to Zerubbabel son of Shealtiel, governor of Judah, and to Joshua son of Jozadak,*a* the high priest:

2 This is what the LORD Almighty says: "These people say, 'The time has not yet come to rebuild the LORD's house.'"

3 Then the word of the LORD came through the prophet Haggai: 4 "Is it a time for you yourselves to be living in your paneled houses, while this house remains a ruin?"

5 Now this is what the LORD Almighty says: "Give careful thought to your ways. 6 You have planted much, but harvested little. You eat, but never have enough. You drink, but never have your fill. You put on clothes, but are not warm. You earn wages, only to put them in a purse with holes in it."

7 This is what the LORD Almighty says: "Give careful thought to your ways. 8 Go up into the mountains and bring down timber and build my house, so that I may take pleasure in it and be honored," says the LORD. 9 "You expected much, but see, it turned out to be little. What you brought home, I blew away. Why?" declares the LORD Almighty. "Because of my house, which remains a ruin, while each of you is busy with your own house. 10 Therefore, because of you the heavens have withheld their dew and the earth its crops. 11 I called for a drought on the fields and the mountains, on the grain, the new wine, the olive oil and everything else the ground produces, on people and livestock, and on all the labor of your hands."

12 Then Zerubbabel son of Shealtiel, Joshua son of Jozadak, the high priest, and the whole remnant of the people obeyed the voice of the LORD their God and the message of the prophet Haggai, because

a 1 Hebrew *Jehozadak*, a variant of *Jozadak*; also in verses 12 and 14

ROCK SOLID *principles*

Haggai 1:1–11

Ditch the distractions.

Serena had big things she wanted to accomplish. If her days were like a big sheet of blank paper, she was smart enough to sketch in all the major features before she filled in the details. She had goals to do well at school, conquer flute, and win at a different sport each season. She sensed God was on board with all those activities. What was missing from her plan, however, were specific times she could focus on her relationship with God — some time each day, and a bigger chunk a couple times a week. And there was no place Serena was doing anything to serve others. Her schedule was packed with good goals. But it ended up looking like it was all about her.

The people of God had returned to Jerusalem after being held captive in Babylon. They had been home a long time — so long that they had planted large fields and built beautiful houses — but they had delayed building a house of worship. Until they paid attention to him, God said, their lives were doomed to be dry.

the Lord their God had sent him. And the people feared the Lord.

¹³Then Haggai, the Lord's messenger, gave this message of the Lord to the people: "I am with you," declares the Lord. ¹⁴So the Lord stirred up the spirit of Zerubbabel son of Shealtiel, governor of Judah, and the spirit of Joshua son of Jozadak, the high priest, and the spirit of the whole remnant of the people. They came and began to work on the house of the Lord Almighty, their God, ¹⁵on the twenty-fourth day of the sixth month.

The Promised Glory of the New House

2 In the second year of King Darius, ¹on the twenty-first day of the seventh month, the word of the Lord came through the prophet Haggai: ²"Speak to Zerubbabel son of Shealtiel, governor of Judah, to Joshua son of Jozadak,ᵃ the high priest, and to the remnant of the people. Ask them, ³'Who of you is left who saw this house in its former glory? How does it look to you now? Does it not seem to you like nothing? ⁴But now be strong, Zerubbabel,' declares the Lord. 'Be strong, Joshua son of Jozadak, the high priest. Be strong, all you people of the land,' declares the Lord, 'and work. For I am with you,' declares the Lord Almighty. ⁵'This is what I covenanted with you when you came out of Egypt. And my Spirit remains among you. Do not fear.'

⁶"This is what the Lord Almighty says: 'In a little while I will once more shake the heavens and the earth, the sea and the dry land. ⁷I will shake all nations, and what is desired by all nations will come, and I will fill this house with glory,' says the Lord Almighty. ⁸'The silver is mine and the gold is mine,' declares the Lord Almighty. ⁹'The glory of this present house will be greater than the glory of the former house,' says the Lord Almighty. 'And in this place I will grant peace,' declares the Lord Almighty."

Blessings for a Defiled People

¹⁰On the twenty-fourth day of the ninth month, in the second year of Darius, the word of the Lord came to the prophet Haggai: ¹¹"This is what the Lord Almighty says: 'Ask the priests what the law says: ¹²If

someone carries consecrated meat in the fold of their garment, and that fold touches some bread or stew, some wine, olive oil or other food, does it become consecrated?'"

The priests answered, "No."

¹³Then Haggai said, "If a person defiled by contact with a dead body touches one of these things, does it become defiled?"

"Yes," the priests replied, "it becomes defiled."

¹⁴Then Haggai said, "'So it is with this people and this nation in my sight,' declares the Lord. 'Whatever they do and whatever they offer there is defiled.

¹⁵"'Now give careful thought to this from this day onᵇ—consider how things were before one stone was laid on another in the Lord's temple. ¹⁶When anyone came to a heap of twenty measures, there were only ten. When anyone went to a wine vat to draw fifty measures, there were only twenty. ¹⁷I struck all the work of your hands with blight, mildew and hail, yet you did not return to me,' declares the Lord. ¹⁸'From this day on, from this twenty-fourth day of the ninth month, give careful thought to the day when the foundation of the Lord's temple was laid. Give careful thought: ¹⁹Is there yet any seed left in the barn? Until now, the vine and the fig tree, the pomegranate and the olive tree have not borne fruit.

"'From this day on I will bless you.'"

Zerubbabel the Lord's Signet Ring

²⁰The word of the Lord came to Haggai a second time on the twenty-fourth day of the month: ²¹"Tell Zerubbabel governor of Judah that I am going to shake the heavens and the earth. ²²I will overturn royal thrones and shatter the power of the foreign kingdoms. I will overthrow chariots and their drivers; horses and their riders will fall, each by the sword of his brother.

²³"'On that day,' declares the Lord Almighty, 'I will take you, my servant Zerubbabel son of Shealtiel,' declares the Lord, 'and I will make you like my signet ring, for I have chosen you,' declares the Lord Almighty."

ᵃ 2 Hebrew *Jehozadak*, a variant of *Jozadak*; also in verse 4   ᵇ 15 Or *to the days past*

ZECHARIAH

BOOK OUTLINE

Zechariah's prophecies began two months after Haggai's first message (520 BC). In his opening message Zechariah told the people who had just begun rebuilding the temple that they needed to listen to God's message through the prophets. They also needed to keep a close relationship with God so that there would be no further judgment.

This opening message is followed by visions that encouraged the builders when they were ready to give up. Zechariah comforted them by telling them God had a long-range plan for Israel.

In chapters 7 and 8 Zechariah called the people to obey God by acting fairly and mercifully to one another. God wanted obedience in his relationship with them.

Chapters 9 through 14 tell of the coming Messiah, the last judgment and the long-range growth of the final kingdom.

A Call to Return to the Lord

1 In the eighth month of the second year of Darius, the word of the Lord came to the prophet Zechariah son of Berekiah, the son of Iddo:

² "The Lord was very angry with your ancestors. ³ Therefore tell the people: This is what the Lord Almighty says: 'Return to me,' declares the Lord Almighty, 'and I will return to you,' says the Lord Almighty. ⁴ Do not be like your ancestors, to whom the earlier prophets proclaimed: This is what the Lord Almighty says: 'Turn from your evil ways and your evil practices.' But they would not listen or pay attention to me, declares the Lord. ⁵ Where are your ancestors now? And the prophets, do they live forever? ⁶ But did not my words and my decrees, which I commanded my servants the prophets, overtake your ancestors?

"Then they repented and said, 'The Lord Almighty has done to us what our ways and practices deserve, just as he determined to do.'"

The Man Among the Myrtle Trees

⁷ On the twenty-fourth day of the eleventh month, the month of Shebat, in the second year of Darius, the word of the Lord came to the prophet Zechariah son of Berekiah, the son of Iddo.

⁸ During the night I had a vision, and there before me was a man mounted on a red horse. He was standing among the myrtle trees in a ravine. Behind him were red, brown and white horses.

⁹ I asked, "What are these, my lord?"

The angel who was talking with me answered, "I will show you what they are."

¹⁰ Then the man standing among the myrtle trees explained, "They are the ones the Lord has sent to go throughout the earth."

¹¹ And they reported to the angel of the Lord who was standing among the myrtle trees, "We have gone throughout the earth and found the whole world at rest and in peace."

¹² Then the angel of the Lord said, "Lord Almighty, how long will you withhold mercy from Jerusalem and from the towns of Judah, which you have been angry with these seventy years?" ¹³ So the Lord spoke kind and comforting words to the angel who talked with me.

¹⁴ Then the angel who was speaking to me said, "Proclaim this word: This is what the Lord Almighty says: 'I am very jealous for Jerusalem and Zion, ¹⁵ and I am very angry with the nations that feel secure. I was only a little angry, but they went too far with the punishment.'

¹⁶ "Therefore this is what the Lord says: 'I will return to Jerusalem with mercy, and there my house will be rebuilt. And the measuring line will be stretched out over Jerusalem,' declares the Lord Almighty.

¹⁷ "Proclaim further: This is what the Lord Almighty says: 'My towns will again overflow with prosperity, and the Lord will again comfort Zion and choose Jerusalem.'"

Four Horns and Four Craftsmen

¹⁸ Then I looked up, and there before me were four horns. ¹⁹ I asked the angel who was speaking to me, "What are these?"

He answered me, "These are the horns that scattered Judah, Israel and Jerusalem."

²⁰ Then the Lord showed me four craftsmen. ²¹ I asked, "What are these coming to do?"

He answered, "These are the horns that scattered Judah so that no one could raise their head, but the craftsmen have come to terrify them and throw down these horns of the nations who lifted up their horns against the land of Judah to scatter its people."[a]

A Man With a Measuring Line

2[b] Then I looked up, and there before me was a man with a measuring line in his hand. ² I asked, "Where are you going?"

He answered me, "To measure Jerusalem, to find out how wide and how long it is."

³ While the angel who was speaking

---

[a] 21 In Hebrew texts 1:18-21 is numbered 2:1-4.
[b] In Hebrew texts 2:1-13 is numbered 2:5-17.

to me was leaving, another angel came to meet him ⁴and said to him: "Run, tell that young man, 'Jerusalem will be a city without walls because of the great number of people and animals in it. ⁵And I myself will be a wall of fire around it,' declares the LORD, 'and I will be its glory within.'

⁶"Come! Come! Flee from the land of the north," declares the LORD, "for I have scattered you to the four winds of heaven," declares the LORD.

⁷"Come, Zion! Escape, you who live in Daughter Babylon!" ⁸For this is what the LORD Almighty says: "After the Glorious One has sent me against the nations that have plundered you—for whoever touches you touches the apple of his eye— ⁹I will surely raise my hand against them so that their slaves will plunder them.ᵃ Then you will know that the LORD Almighty has sent me.

ROCK SOLID
promises

"Whoever touches you touches the apple of his eye." Zechariah 2:8

God protects you from harm, because you are as important to him as his own pupil.

---

¹⁰"Shout and be glad, Daughter Zion. For I am coming, and I will live among you," declares the LORD. ¹¹"Many nations will be joined with the LORD in that day and will become my people. I will live among you and you will know that the LORD Almighty has sent me to you. ¹²The LORD will inherit Judah as his portion in the holy land and will again choose Jerusalem. ¹³Be still before the LORD, all mankind, because he has roused himself from his holy dwelling."

Clean Garments for the High Priest

3 Then he showed me Joshua the high priest standing before the angel of the LORD, and Satanᵇ standing at his right side to accuse him. ²The LORD said to Satan, "The LORD rebuke you, Satan! The LORD, who has chosen Jerusalem, rebuke you! Is not this man a burning stick snatched from the fire?"

³Now Joshua was dressed in filthy clothes as he stood before the angel. ⁴The angel said to those who were standing before him, "Take off his filthy clothes."

Then he said to Joshua, "See, I have taken away your sin, and I will put fine garments on you."

⁵Then I said, "Put a clean turban on his head." So they put a clean turban on his head and clothed him, while the angel of the LORD stood by.

⁶The angel of the LORD gave this charge to Joshua: ⁷"This is what the LORD Almighty says: 'If you will walk in obedience to me and keep my requirements, then you will govern my house and have charge of my courts, and I will give you a place among these standing here.

⁸"'Listen, High Priest Joshua, you and your associates seated before you, who are men symbolic of things to come: I am going to bring my servant, the Branch. ⁹See, the stone I have set in front of Joshua! There are seven eyesᶜ on that one stone, and I will engrave an inscription on it,' says the LORD Almighty, 'and I will remove the sin of this land in a single day.

¹⁰"'In that day each of you will invite your neighbor to sit under your vine and fig tree,' declares the LORD Almighty."

The Gold Lampstand and the Two Olive Trees

4 Then the angel who talked with me returned and woke me up, like someone awakened from sleep. ²He asked me, "What do you see?"

I answered, "I see a solid gold lampstand with a bowl at the top and seven

---

ᵃ 8,9 Or *says after . . . eye:* ⁹*"I . . . plunder them."*
ᵇ 1 Hebrew *satan* means *adversary.*
ᶜ 9 Or *facets*

lamps on it, with seven channels to the lamps. ³Also there are two olive trees by it, one on the right of the bowl and the other on its left."

⁴I asked the angel who talked with me, "What are these, my lord?"

⁵He answered, "Do you not know what these are?"

"No, my lord," I replied.

⁶So he said to me, "This is the word of the LORD to Zerubbabel: 'Not by might nor by power, but by my Spirit,' says the LORD Almighty.

ROCK SOLID promises

" 'Not by might nor by power, but by my Spirit,' says the LORD Almighty."

Zechariah 4:6

God can do things bigger than your dreams. His Spirit infinitely overpowers every human strength or skill.

---

⁷"What are you, mighty mountain? Before Zerubbabel you will become level ground. Then he will bring out the capstone to shouts of 'God bless it! God bless it!' "

⁸Then the word of the LORD came to me: ⁹"The hands of Zerubbabel have laid the foundation of this temple; his hands will also complete it. Then you will know that the LORD Almighty has sent me to you.

¹⁰"Who dares despise the day of small things, since the seven eyes of the LORD that range throughout the earth will rejoice when they see the chosen capstone*a* in the hand of Zerubbabel?"

¹¹Then I asked the angel, "What are these two olive trees on the right and the left of the lampstand?"

¹²Again I asked him, "What are these two olive branches beside the two gold pipes that pour out golden oil?"

¹³He replied, "Do you not know what these are?"

"No, my lord," I said.

¹⁴So he said, "These are the two who are anointed to*b* serve the Lord of all the earth."

The Flying Scroll

5 I looked again, and there before me was a flying scroll.

²He asked me, "What do you see?"

I answered, "I see a flying scroll, twenty cubits long and ten cubits wide.*c*"

³And he said to me, "This is the curse that is going out over the whole land; for according to what it says on one side, every thief will be banished, and according to what it says on the other, everyone who swears falsely will be banished. ⁴The LORD Almighty declares, 'I will send it out, and it will enter the house of the thief and the house of anyone who swears falsely by my name. It will remain in that house and destroy it completely, both its timbers and its stones.' "

The Woman in a Basket

⁵Then the angel who was speaking to me came forward and said to me, "Look up and see what is appearing."

⁶I asked, "What is it?"

He replied, "It is a basket." And he added, "This is the iniquity*d* of the people throughout the land."

⁷Then the cover of lead was raised, and there in the basket sat a woman! ⁸He said, "This is wickedness," and he pushed her back into the basket and pushed its lead cover down on it.

⁹Then I looked up—and there before me were two women, with the wind in their wings! They had wings like those of a stork, and they lifted up the basket between heaven and earth.

¹⁰"Where are they taking the basket?" I asked the angel who was speaking to me.

a 10 Or *the plumb line*   *b 14* Or *two who bring oil and*   *c 2* That is, about 30 feet long and 15 feet wide or about 9 meters long and 4.5 meters wide   *d 6* Or *appearance*

[11] He replied, "To the country of Babylonia[a] to build a house for it. When the house is ready, the basket will be set there in its place."

Four Chariots

6 I looked up again, and there before me were four chariots coming out from between two mountains—mountains of bronze. [2] The first chariot had red horses, the second black, [3] the third white, and the fourth dappled—all of them powerful. [4] I asked the angel who was speaking to me, "What are these, my lord?"

[5] The angel answered me, "These are the four spirits[b] of heaven, going out from standing in the presence of the Lord of the whole world. [6] The one with the black horses is going toward the north country, the one with the white horses toward the west,[c] and the one with the dappled horses toward the south."

[7] When the powerful horses went out, they were straining to go throughout the earth. And he said, "Go throughout the earth!" So they went throughout the earth.

[8] Then he called to me, "Look, those going toward the north country have given my Spirit[d] rest in the land of the north."

A Crown for Joshua

[9] The word of the Lord came to me: [10] "Take silver and gold from the exiles Heldai, Tobijah and Jedaiah, who have arrived from Babylon. Go the same day to the house of Josiah son of Zephaniah. [11] Take the silver and gold and make a crown, and set it on the head of the high priest, Joshua son of Jozadak.[e] [12] Tell him this is what the Lord Almighty says: 'Here is the man whose name is the Branch, and he will branch out from his place and build the temple of the Lord. [13] It is he who will build the temple of the Lord, and he will be clothed with majesty and will sit and rule on his throne. And he[f] will be a priest on his throne. And there will be harmony between the two.' [14] The crown will be given to Heldai,[g] Tobijah, Jedaiah and Hen[h] son of Zephaniah as a memorial in the temple of the Lord. [15] Those who are far away will come and help to build the temple of the Lord, and you will know that the Lord Almighty has sent me to you. This will happen if you diligently obey the Lord your God."

Justice and Mercy, Not Fasting

7 In the fourth year of King Darius, the word of the Lord came to Zechariah on the fourth day of the ninth month, the month of Kislev. [2] The people of Bethel had sent Sharezer and Regem-Melek, together with their men, to entreat the Lord [3] by asking the priests of the house of the Lord Almighty and the prophets, "Should I mourn and fast in the fifth month, as I have done for so many years?"

[4] Then the word of the Lord Almighty came to me: [5] "Ask all the people of the land and the priests, 'When you fasted and mourned in the fifth and seventh months for the past seventy years, was it really for me that you fasted? [6] And when you were eating and drinking, were you not just feasting for yourselves? [7] Are these not the words the Lord proclaimed through the earlier prophets when Jerusalem and its surrounding towns were at rest and prosperous, and the Negev and the western foothills were settled?'"

[8] And the word of the Lord came again to Zechariah: [9] "This is what the Lord Almighty said: 'Administer true justice; show mercy and compassion to one another. [10] Do not oppress the widow or the fatherless, the foreigner or the poor. Do not plot evil against each other.'

[11] "But they refused to pay attention; stubbornly they turned their backs and covered their ears. [12] They made their hearts as hard as flint and would not listen to the law or to the words that the Lord Almighty had sent by his Spirit through the earlier prophets. So the Lord Almighty was very angry.

[13] "When I called, they did not listen; so when they called, I would not listen,'

---

[a] 11 Hebrew *Shinar*   [b] 5 Or *winds*
[c] 6 Or *horses after them*   [d] 8 Or *spirit*
[e] 11 Hebrew *Jehozadak*, a variant of *Jozadak*
[f] 13 Or *there*   [g] 14 Syriac; Hebrew *Helem*
[h] 14 Or *and the gracious one, the*

says the Lord Almighty. ¹⁴'I scattered them with a whirlwind among all the nations, where they were strangers. The land they left behind them was so desolate that no one traveled through it. This is how they made the pleasant land desolate.'"

The Lord Promises to Bless Jerusalem

8 The word of the Lord Almighty came to me. ²This is what the Lord Almighty says: "I am very jealous for Zion; I am burning with jealousy for her."

³This is what the Lord says: "I will return to Zion and dwell in Jerusalem. Then Jerusalem will be called the Faithful City, and the mountain of the Lord Almighty will be called the Holy Mountain."

⁴This is what the Lord Almighty says: "Once again men and women of ripe old age will sit in the streets of Jerusalem, each of them with cane in hand because of their age. ⁵The city streets will be filled with boys and girls playing there."

⁶This is what the Lord Almighty says: "It may seem marvelous to the remnant of this people at that time, but will it seem marvelous to me?" declares the Lord Almighty.

⁷This is what the Lord Almighty says: "I will save my people from the countries of the east and the west. ⁸I will bring them back to live in Jerusalem; they will be my people, and I will be faithful and righteous to them as their God."

⁹This is what the Lord Almighty says: "Now hear these words, 'Let your hands be strong so that the temple may be built.' This is also what the prophets said who were present when the foundation was laid for the house of the Lord Almighty. ¹⁰Before that time there were no wages for people or hire for animals. No one could go about their business safely because of their enemies, since I had turned everyone against their neighbor. ¹¹But now I will not deal with the remnant of this people as I did in the past," declares the Lord Almighty.

ROCK·SOLID *principles*

Zechariah 7:4–14

Treat everyone well.

No one could fault Reggie's choice of solid activities. His weeks were packed with spiritual commotion—youth group, a couple of small group Bible studies that met at friends' homes, doing drama for Sunday church services. Reggie had built a consistent habit of reading the Bible and praying each day. But his faith never got beyond church walls. He was fanatical about his own growth and helping other Christians get mature. But he was blind to the needs of his peers who weren't into God . . . to the kid next door with no dad . . . to the battered women looking for help at a shelter next to his school . . . to the hungry near and far. . .

God saw his people fasting and feasting. But whether they were going without food or throwing a holy party, the Lord knew their religious habits focused only on themselves. True devotion to God shows up in our care for widows and orphans, foreigners, and the needy (see Zechariah 7:10). If we really love God, we love like he does. We care especially for people that others overlook.

¹²"The seed will grow well, the vine will yield its fruit, the ground will produce its crops, and the heavens will drop their dew. I will give all these things as an inheritance to the remnant of this people. ¹³ Just as you, Judah and Israel, have been a curse*a* among the nations, so I will save you, and you will be a blessing.*b* Do not be afraid, but let your hands be strong."

¹⁴This is what the LORD Almighty says: "Just as I had determined to bring disaster on you and showed no pity when your ancestors angered me," says the LORD Almighty, ¹⁵"so now I have determined to do good again to Jerusalem and Judah. Do not be afraid. ¹⁶These are the things you are to do: Speak the truth to each other, and render true and sound judgment in your courts; ¹⁷do not plot evil against each other, and do not love to swear falsely. I hate all this," declares the LORD.

¹⁸The word of the LORD Almighty came to me.

¹⁹This is what the LORD Almighty says: "The fasts of the fourth, fifth, seventh and tenth months will become joyful and glad occasions and happy festivals for Judah. Therefore love truth and peace."

²⁰This is what the LORD Almighty says: "Many peoples and the inhabitants of many cities will yet come, ²¹and the inhabitants of one city will go to another and say, 'Let us go at once to entreat the LORD and seek the LORD Almighty. I myself am going.' ²²And many peoples and powerful nations will come to Jerusalem to seek the LORD Almighty and to entreat him."

²³This is what the LORD Almighty says: "In those days ten people from all languages and nations will take firm hold of one Jew by the hem of his robe and say, 'Let us go with you, because we have heard that God is with you.'"

Judgment on Israel's Enemies

9 A prophecy:

The word of the LORD is against
   the land of Hadrak
and will come to rest on
   Damascus—

for the eyes of all people and all the
   tribes of Israel
are on the LORD—*c*
² and on Hamath too, which borders
   on it,
and on Tyre and Sidon, though they
   are very skillful.
³ Tyre has built herself a stronghold;
   she has heaped up silver like dust,
   and gold like the dirt of the streets.
⁴ But the Lord will take away her
   possessions
   and destroy her power on the sea,
   and she will be consumed by fire.
⁵ Ashkelon will see it and fear;
   Gaza will writhe in agony,
   and Ekron too, for her hope will
     wither.
Gaza will lose her king
   and Ashkelon will be deserted.
⁶ A mongrel people will occupy Ashdod,
   and I will put an end to the pride of
     the Philistines.
⁷ I will take the blood from their
     mouths,
   the forbidden food from between
     their teeth.
Those who are left will belong to our
     God
   and become a clan in Judah,
   and Ekron will be like the Jebusites.
⁸ But I will encamp at my temple
   to guard it against marauding
     forces.
Never again will an oppressor overrun
     my people,
   for now I am keeping watch.

The Coming of Zion's King

⁹ Rejoice greatly, Daughter Zion!
   Shout, Daughter Jerusalem!
See, your king comes to you,
   righteous and victorious,
lowly and riding on a donkey,
   on a colt, the foal of a donkey.

---

a 13 That is, your name has been used in cursing (see Jer. 29:22); or, you have been regarded as under a curse.　　*b 13* Or *and your name will be used in blessings* (see Gen. 48:20); or *and you will be seen as blessed*　　*c 1* Or *Damascus. / For the eye of the LORD is on all people, / as well as on the tribes of Israel,*

¹⁰ I will take away the chariots from
  Ephraim
    and the warhorses from Jerusalem,
    and the battle bow will be broken.
  He will proclaim peace to the nations.
    His rule will extend from sea to sea
    and from the River^a to the ends of
      the earth.
¹¹ As for you, because of the blood of my
    covenant with you,
  I will free your prisoners from the
    waterless pit.

¹² Return to your fortress, you prisoners
    of hope;
  even now I announce that I will
    restore twice as much to you.
¹³ I will bend Judah as I bend my bow
    and fill it with Ephraim.
  I will rouse your sons, Zion,
    against your sons, Greece,
    and make you like a warrior's
      sword.

The Lord Will Appear

¹⁴ Then the Lord will appear over
    them;
  his arrow will flash like lightning.
  The Sovereign Lord will sound the
    trumpet;
  he will march in the storms of the
    south,
¹⁵ and the Lord Almighty will shield
    them.
  They will destroy
    and overcome with slingstones.
  They will drink and roar as with wine;
    they will be full like a bowl
  used for sprinkling^b the corners of
    the altar.
¹⁶ The Lord their God will save his
    people on that day
  as a shepherd saves his flock.
  They will sparkle in his land
    like jewels in a crown.
¹⁷ How attractive and beautiful they will
    be!
  Grain will make the young men
    thrive,
  and new wine the young women.

The Lord Will Care for Judah

10 Ask the Lord for rain in the
  springtime;
  it is the Lord who sends the
    thunderstorms.
  He gives showers of rain to all people,
    and plants of the field to everyone.
² The idols speak deceitfully,
    diviners see visions that lie;
  they tell dreams that are false,
    they give comfort in vain.

ROCK SOLID *truths*

Zechariah 9:9–10

The Bible tells the future.

You have to wonder what was running through the prophet Zechariah's head as he spoke these words about a future king. The Bible says the prophets "spoke from God as they were carried along by the Holy Spirit" (2 Peter 1:21), and through Zechariah the Holy Spirit was speaking a highly specific prediction about the coming king. He would enter Jerusalem "righteous and victorious, lowly and riding on a donkey, on a colt, the foal of a donkey" (Zechariah 9:9). Although Zechariah couldn't see it at the time, Jesus would fulfill that prophecy hundreds of years later by riding triumphantly into Jerusalem on the back of a young donkey, an event we call Palm Sunday (see Matthew 21:4–5). That's remarkable, but it's even more astounding that this is just one of several hundred places where the Bible reports specific facts about Jesus long before they happen.

Think: Why would God reveal specific future events like this?

---

^a 10 That is, the Euphrates   ^b 15 Or
bowl, / like

Therefore the people wander like
sheep
oppressed for lack of a shepherd.
³"My anger burns against the
shepherds,
and I will punish the leaders;
for the Lord Almighty will care
for his flock, the people of Judah,
and make them like a proud horse
in battle.
⁴From Judah will come the
cornerstone,
from him the tent peg,
from him the battle bow,
from him every ruler.
⁵Together they*ᵃ will be like warriors in
battle
trampling their enemy into the mud
of the streets.
They will fight because the Lord is
with them,
and they will put the enemy
horsemen to shame.

⁶"I will strengthen Judah
and save the tribes of Joseph.
I will restore them
because I have compassion on them.
They will be as though
I had not rejected them,
for I am the Lord their God
and I will answer them.
⁷The Ephraimites will become like
warriors,
and their hearts will be glad as with
wine.
Their children will see it and be
joyful;
their hearts will rejoice in the Lord.
⁸I will signal for them
and gather them in.
Surely I will redeem them;
they will be as numerous as before.
⁹Though I scatter them among the
peoples,
yet in distant lands they will
remember me.
They and their children will survive,
and they will return.
¹⁰I will bring them back from Egypt
and gather them from Assyria.

I will bring them to Gilead and
Lebanon,
and there will not be room enough
for them.
¹¹They will pass through the sea of
trouble;
the surging sea will be subdued
and all the depths of the Nile will
dry up.
Assyria's pride will be brought down
and Egypt's scepter will pass away.
¹²I will strengthen them in the Lord
and in his name they will live
securely,"
declares the Lord.

Open your doors, Lebanon,
so that fire may devour your
cedars!
²Wail, you juniper, for the cedar has
fallen;
the stately trees are ruined!
Wail, oaks of Bashan;
the dense forest has been cut
down!
³Listen to the wail of the shepherds;
their rich pastures are destroyed!
Listen to the roar of the lions;
the lush thicket of the Jordan is
ruined!

Two Shepherds

⁴This is what the Lord my God says: "Shepherd the flock marked for slaughter. ⁵Their buyers slaughter them and go unpunished. Those who sell them say, 'Praise the Lord, I am rich!' Their own shepherds do not spare them. ⁶For I will no longer have pity on the people of the land," declares the Lord. "I will give everyone into the hands of their neighbors and their king. They will devastate the land, and I will not rescue anyone from their hands."

⁷So I shepherded the flock marked for slaughter, particularly the oppressed of the flock. Then I took two staffs and called one Favor and the other Union, and I shepherded the flock. ⁸In one month I got rid of the three shepherds.

The flock detested me, and I grew weary

ᵃ 4,5 Or *ruler, all of them together.* / ⁵*They*

1117

of them ⁹and said, "I will not be your shepherd. Let the dying die, and the perishing perish. Let those who are left eat one another's flesh."

¹⁰Then I took my staff called Favor and broke it, revoking the covenant I had made with all the nations. ¹¹It was revoked on that day, and so the oppressed of the flock who were watching me knew it was the word of the LORD.

¹²I told them, "If you think it best, give me my pay; but if not, keep it." So they paid me thirty pieces of silver.

¹³And the LORD said to me, "Throw it to the potter"—the handsome price at which they valued me! So I took the thirty pieces of silver and threw them to the potter at the house of the LORD.

¹⁴Then I broke my second staff called Union, breaking the family bond between Judah and Israel.

¹⁵Then the LORD said to me, "Take again the equipment of a foolish shepherd. ¹⁶For I am going to raise up a shepherd over the land who will not care for the lost, or seek the young, or heal the injured, or feed the healthy, but will eat the meat of the choice sheep, tearing off their hooves.

¹⁷"Woe to the worthless shepherd,
    who deserts the flock!
May the sword strike his arm and his
    right eye!
May his arm be completely
    withered,
his right eye totally blinded!"

Jerusalem's Enemies to Be Destroyed

12 A prophecy: The word of the LORD concerning Israel.

The LORD, who stretches out the heavens, who lays the foundation of the earth, and who forms the human spirit within a person, declares: ²"I am going to make Jerusalem a cup that sends all the surrounding peoples reeling. Judah will be besieged as well as Jerusalem. ³On that day, when all the nations of the earth are gathered against her, I will make Jerusalem an immovable rock for all the nations. All who try to move it will injure themselves. ⁴On

that day I will strike every horse with panic and its rider with madness," declares the LORD. "I will keep a watchful eye over Judah, but I will blind all the horses of the nations. ⁵Then the clans of Judah will say in their hearts, 'The people of Jerusalem are strong, because the LORD Almighty is their God.'

⁶"On that day I will make the clans of Judah like a firepot in a woodpile, like a flaming torch among sheaves. They will consume all the surrounding peoples right and left, but Jerusalem will remain intact in her place.

⁷"The LORD will save the dwellings of Judah first, so that the honor of the house of David and of Jerusalem's inhabitants may not be greater than that of Judah. ⁸On that day the LORD will shield those who live in Jerusalem, so that the feeblest among them will be like David, and the house of David will be like God, like the angel of the LORD going before them. ⁹On that day I will set out to destroy all the nations that attack Jerusalem.

Mourning for the One They Pierced

¹⁰"And I will pour out on the house of David and the inhabitants of Jerusalem a spirit*ᵃ* of grace and supplication. They will look on*ᵇ* me, the one they have pierced, and they will mourn for him as one mourns for an only child, and grieve bitterly for him as one grieves for a firstborn son. ¹¹On that day the weeping in Jerusalem will be as great as the weeping of Hadad Rimmon in the plain of Megiddo. ¹²The land will mourn, each clan by itself, with their wives by themselves: the clan of the house of David and their wives, the clan of the house of Nathan and their wives, ¹³the clan of the house of Levi and their wives, the clan of Shimei and their wives, ¹⁴and all the rest of the clans and their wives.

Cleansing From Sin

13 "On that day a fountain will be opened to the house of David and the inhabitants of Jerusalem, to cleanse them from sin and impurity.

ᵃ 10 Or *the Spirit*   *ᵇ 10* Or *to*

2"On that day, I will banish the names of the idols from the land, and they will be remembered no more," declares the LORD Almighty. "I will remove both the prophets and the spirit of impurity from the land. 3And if anyone still prophesies, their father and mother, to whom they were born, will say to them, 'You must die, because you have told lies in the LORD's name.' Then their own parents will stab the one who prophesies.

4"On that day every prophet will be ashamed of their prophetic vision. They will not put on a prophet's garment of hair in order to deceive. 5Each will say, 'I am not a prophet. I am a farmer; the land has been my livelihood since my youth.'*a* 6If someone asks, 'What are these wounds on your body*b*?' they will answer, 'The wounds I was given at the house of my friends.'

The Shepherd Struck, the Sheep Scattered

7"Awake, sword, against my shepherd,
    against the man who is close to
        me!"
    declares the LORD Almighty.
"Strike the shepherd,
    and the sheep will be scattered,
    and I will turn my hand against the
        little ones.
8In the whole land," declares the LORD,
    "two-thirds will be struck down
        and perish;
    yet one-third will be left in it.
9This third I will put into the fire;
    I will refine them like silver
    and test them like gold.
They will call on my name
    and I will answer them;
I will say, 'They are my people,'
    and they will say, 'The LORD is our
        God.'"

The LORD Comes and Reigns

14 A day of the LORD is coming, Jerusalem, when your possessions will be plundered and divided up within your very walls.

2I will gather all the nations to Jeru-

---

salem to fight against it; the city will be captured, the houses ransacked, and the women raped. Half of the city will go into exile, but the rest of the people will not be taken from the city. 3Then the LORD will go out and fight against those nations, as he fights on a day of battle. 4On that day his feet will stand on the Mount of Olives, east of Jerusalem, and the Mount of Olives will be split in two from east to west, forming a great valley, with half of the mountain moving north and half moving south. 5You will flee by my mountain valley, for it will extend to Azel. You will flee as you fled from the earthquake*c* in the days of Uzziah king of Judah. Then the LORD my God will come, and all the holy ones with him.

6On that day there will be neither sunlight nor cold, frosty darkness. 7It will be a unique day—a day known only to the LORD—with no distinction between day and night. When evening comes, there will be light.

8On that day living water will flow out from Jerusalem, half of it east to the Dead Sea and half of it west to the Mediterranean Sea, in summer and in winter.

9The LORD will be king over the whole

---

a 5 Or *farmer; a man sold me in my youth*
b 6 Or *wounds between your hands*   *c* 5 Or *My mountain valley will be blocked and will extend to Azel. It will be blocked as it was blocked because of the earthquake*

earth. On that day there will be one LORD, and his name the only name.

¹⁰The whole land, from Geba to Rimmon, south of Jerusalem, will become like the Arabah. But Jerusalem will be raised up high from the Benjamin Gate to the site of the First Gate, to the Corner Gate, and from the Tower of Hananel to the royal winepresses, and will remain in its place. ¹¹It will be inhabited; never again will it be destroyed. Jerusalem will be secure.

¹²This is the plague with which the LORD will strike all the nations that fought against Jerusalem: Their flesh will rot while they are still standing on their feet, their eyes will rot in their sockets, and their tongues will rot in their mouths. ¹³On that day people will be stricken by the LORD with great panic. They will seize each other by the hand and attack one another. ¹⁴Judah too will fight at Jerusalem. The wealth of all the surrounding nations will be collected—great quantities of gold and silver and clothing. ¹⁵A similar plague will strike the horses and mules, the camels and donkeys, and all the animals in those camps.

¹⁶Then the survivors from all the nations that have attacked Jerusalem will go up year after year to worship the King, the LORD Almighty, and to celebrate the Festival of Tabernacles. ¹⁷If any of the peoples of the earth do not go up to Jerusalem to worship the King, the LORD Almighty, they will have no rain. ¹⁸If the Egyptian people do not go up and take part, they will have no rain. The LORDᵃ will bring on them the plague he inflicts on the nations that do not go up to celebrate the Festival of Tabernacles. ¹⁹This will be the punishment of Egypt and the punishment of all the nations that do not go up to celebrate the Festival of Tabernacles.

²⁰On that day HOLY TO THE LORD will be inscribed on the bells of the horses, and the cooking pots in the LORD's house will be like the sacred bowls in front of the altar. ²¹Every pot in Jerusalem and Judah will be holy to the LORD Almighty, and all who come to sacrifice will take some of the pots and cook in them. And on that day there will no longer be a Canaaniteᵇ in the house of the LORD Almighty.

ᵃ 18 Or part, then the LORD   ᵇ 21 Or merchant

MALACHI

This book records the messages of the prophet Malachi, who lived during the second half of the fifth century BC, after the temple had been rebuilt. The Jews had married foreign women, disobeyed God's rules for sacrifices, failed to give God what they should have, and forgotten God's covenant.

Malachi's chief concern was that the Israelites' relationship to God was not as it should be. They had forgotten God and treated him with dishonor. They failed to do what God required of them. Because of this, Malachi told the people God would judge them. But he also said that the God-fearing people did not need to worry because they would enjoy God's salvation forever.

1

A prophecy: The word of the LORD to Israel through Malachi.[a]

Israel Doubts God's Love

[2] "I have loved you," says the LORD.

"But you ask, 'How have you loved us?'

"Was not Esau Jacob's brother?" declares the LORD. "Yet I have loved Jacob, [3] but Esau I have hated, and I have turned his hill country into a wasteland and left his inheritance to the desert jackals."

[4] Edom may say, "Though we have been crushed, we will rebuild the ruins."

But this is what the LORD Almighty says: "They may build, but I will demolish. They will be called the Wicked Land, a people always under the wrath of the LORD. [5] You will see it with your own eyes and say, 'Great is the LORD—even beyond the borders of Israel!'

Breaking Covenant Through Blemished Sacrifices

[6] "A son honors his father, and a slave his master. If I am a father, where is the honor due me? If I am a master, where is the respect due me?" says the LORD Almighty.

"It is you priests who show contempt for my name.

"But you ask, 'How have we shown contempt for your name?'

[7] "By offering defiled food on my altar.

"But you ask, 'How have we defiled you?'

"By saying that the LORD's table is contemptible. [8] When you offer blind animals for sacrifice, is that not wrong? When you sacrifice lame or diseased animals, is that not wrong? Try offering them to your governor! Would he be pleased with you? Would he accept you?" says the LORD Almighty.

[9] "Now plead with God to be gracious to us. With such offerings from your hands, will he accept you?"—says the LORD Almighty.

[10] "Oh, that one of you would shut the temple doors, so that you would not light useless fires on my altar! I am not pleased with you," says the LORD Almighty, "and I will accept no offering from your hands.

[11] My name will be great among the nations, from where the sun rises to where it sets. In every place incense and pure offerings will be brought to me, because my name will be great among the nations," says the LORD Almighty.

[12] "But you profane it by saying, 'The Lord's table is defiled,' and, 'Its food is contemptible.' [13] And you say, 'What a burden!' and you sniff at it contemptuously," says the LORD Almighty.

"When you bring injured, lame or diseased animals and offer them as sacrifices, should I accept them from your hands?" says the LORD. [14] "Cursed is the cheat who has an acceptable male in his flock and vows to give it, but then sacrifices a blemished animal to the Lord. For I am a great king," says the LORD Almighty, "and my name is to be feared among the nations.

Additional Warning to the Priests

2

"And now, you priests, this warning is for you. [2] If you do not listen, and if you do not resolve to honor my name," says the LORD Almighty, "I will send a curse on you, and I will curse your blessings. Yes, I have already cursed them, because you have not resolved to honor me.

[3] "Because of you I will rebuke your descendants[b]; I will smear on your faces the dung from your festival sacrifices, and you will be carried off with it. [4] And you will know that I have sent you this warning so that my covenant with Levi may continue," says the LORD Almighty. [5] "My covenant was with him, a covenant of life and peace, and I gave them to him; this called for reverence and he revered me and stood in awe of my name. [6] True instruction was in his mouth and nothing false was found on his lips. He walked with me in peace and uprightness, and turned many from sin.

[7] "For the lips of a priest ought to preserve knowledge, because he is the messenger of the LORD Almighty and people seek instruction from his mouth. [8] But you have turned from the way and by your teaching have caused many to stumble;

---

[a] 1 Malachi means my messenger.   [b] 3 Or will blight your grain

you have violated the covenant with Levi," says the Lord Almighty. ⁹"So I have caused you to be despised and humiliated before all the people, because you have not followed my ways but have shown partiality in matters of the law."

Breaking Covenant Through Divorce

¹⁰Do we not all have one Father*ᵃ*? Did not one God create us? Why do we profane the covenant of our ancestors by being unfaithful to one another?

¹¹Judah has been unfaithful. A detestable thing has been committed in Israel and in Jerusalem: Judah has desecrated the sanctuary the Lord loves by marrying women who worship a foreign god. ¹²As for the man who does this, whoever he may be, may the Lord remove him from the tents of Jacob*ᵇ*—even though he brings an offering to the Lord Almighty.

¹³Another thing you do: You flood the Lord's altar with tears. You weep and wail because he no longer looks with favor on your offerings or accepts them with pleasure from your hands. ¹⁴You ask, "Why?" It is because the Lord is the witness between you and the wife of your youth. You have been unfaithful to her, though she is your partner, the wife of your marriage covenant.

¹⁵Has not the one God made you? You belong to him in body and spirit. And what does the one God seek? Godly offspring.*ᶜ* So be on your guard, and do not be unfaithful to the wife of your youth.

¹⁶"The man who hates and divorces his wife," says the Lord, the God of Israel, "does violence to the one he should protect,"*ᵈ* says the Lord Almighty.

ᵃ 10 Or *father   ᵇ 12* Or *¹²May the Lord remove from the tents of Jacob anyone who gives testimony in behalf of the man who does this   ᶜ 15* The meaning of the Hebrew for the first part of this verse is uncertain.   *ᵈ 16* Or *"I hate divorce," says the Lord, the God of Israel, "because the man who divorces his wife covers his garment with violence,"*

ROCK SOLID principles

Malachi 2:10–16

Stick to your spouse.

Karah thought her parents were madly in love. But she wasn't stupid. She saw how money stressed them out. So did her brother's struggles at school. And so did their problems getting along with her mom's family. But Karah always saw her mom and dad pull back together. What she couldn't see was her dad's secret affair with a woman from work. One evening he packed a suitcase like he was headed off on a business trip, then sat Karah and her brother down and announced he was moving out. Karah couldn't think of words. She started to cry. And over the next few months one main thought ran through her head: "It's not supposed to be this way."

God's people couldn't figure out why life wasn't going well. When they worshiped and prayed, it was as if the Lord wasn't paying attention. Then God explained his anger with their evil habits of marriage and divorce. God hates divorce (Malachi 2:16). Jesus echoed that thought when he answered a question about divorce in Matthew 19:3–9.

So be on your guard, and do not be unfaithful.

Breaking Covenant Through Injustice

¹⁷You have wearied the LORD with your words.

"How have we wearied him?" you ask.

By saying, "All who do evil are good in the eyes of the LORD, and he is pleased with them" or "Where is the God of justice?"

3 "I will send my messenger, who will prepare the way before me. Then suddenly the Lord you are seeking will come to his temple; the messenger of the covenant, whom you desire, will come," says the LORD Almighty.

²But who can endure the day of his coming? Who can stand when he appears? For he will be like a refiner's fire or a launderer's soap. ³He will sit as a refiner and purifier of silver; he will purify the Levites and refine them like gold and silver. Then the LORD will have men who will bring offerings in righteousness, ⁴and the offerings of Judah and Jerusalem will be acceptable to the LORD, as in days gone by, as in former years.

⁵"So I will come to put you on trial. I will be quick to testify against sorcerers, adulterers and perjurers, against those who defraud laborers of their wages, who oppress the widows and the fatherless, and deprive the foreigners among you of justice, but do not fear me," says the LORD Almighty.

Breaking Covenant by Withholding Tithes

⁶"I the LORD do not change. So you, the descendants of Jacob, are not destroyed. ⁷Ever since the time of your ancestors you have turned away from my decrees and have not kept them. Return to me, and I will return to you," says the LORD Almighty.

"But you ask, 'How are we to return?'

⁸"Will a mere mortal rob God? Yet you rob me.

"But you ask, 'How are we robbing you?'

"In tithes and offerings. ⁹You are under a curse—your whole nation—because you are robbing me. ¹⁰Bring the whole tithe into the storehouse, that there may be food in my house. Test me in this," says the LORD Almighty, "and see if I will not throw open the floodgates of heaven and pour out so much blessing that there will not be room enough to store it. ¹¹I will prevent pests from devouring your crops, and the vines in your fields will not drop their fruit before it is ripe," says the LORD Almighty. ¹²"Then all the nations will call you blessed, for yours will be a delightful land," says the LORD Almighty.

Israel Speaks Arrogantly Against God

¹³"You have spoken arrogantly against me," says the LORD.

"Yet you ask, 'What have we said against you?'

¹⁴"You have said, 'It is futile to serve God. What do we gain by carrying out his requirements and going about like mourners before the LORD Almighty? ¹⁵But now we call the arrogant blessed. Certainly evildoers prosper, and even when they put God to the test, they get away with it.'"

The Faithful Remnant

¹⁶Then those who feared the LORD talked with each other, and the LORD listened and heard. A scroll of remembrance was written in his presence concerning those who feared the LORD and honored his name.

¹⁷"On the day when I act," says the LORD Almighty, "they will be my treasured possession. I will spare them, just as a father has compassion and spares his son who serves him. ¹⁸And you will again see the distinction between the righteous and the wicked, between those who serve God and those who do not.

Judgment and Covenant Renewal

4 ᵃ "Surely the day is coming; it will burn like a furnace. All the arrogant and every evildoer will be stubble, and the day that is coming will set them on fire," says the LORD Almighty. "Not a root or a branch will be

---

ᵃ In Hebrew texts 4:1-6 is numbered 3:19-24.

left to them. ²But for you who revere my name, the sun of righteousness will rise with healing in its rays. And you will go out and frolic like well-fed calves. ³Then you will trample on the wicked; they will be ashes under the soles of your feet on the day when I act," says the LORD Almighty.

⁴"Remember the law of my servant Moses, the decrees and laws I gave him at Horeb for all Israel.

⁵"See, I will send the prophet Elijah to you before that great and dreadful day of the LORD comes. ⁶He will turn the hearts of the parents to their children, and the hearts of the children to their parents; or else I will come and strike the land with total destruction."

ROCK SOLID *promises*

"For you who revere my name, the sun of righteousness will rise with healing in its rays." Malachi 4:2

As you live in awe of God, he will comfort you like a bird gathers its chicks under its wings.

NEW TESTAMENT

MATTHEW

BOOK OUTLINE

Background and preparation
(1:1 — 4:25)

The Galilean ministry
(5:1 — 18:35)

The Sermon on the Mount
(5:1 — 7:29)

The ministry through miracles
(8:1 — 10:42)

Teaching through parables
(11:1 — 13:52)

Opposition and withdrawal
(13:53 — 16:12)

Jesus as the Son of God
(16:13 — 18:35)

The final period
(19:1 — 28:20)

Toward Jerusalem
(19:1 — 20:34)

The triumphal entry
(21:1 – 17)

Christ as teacher
(21:18 — 25:46)

Trial, death and burial
(26:1 — 27:66)

Resurrection and ascension
(28:1 – 20)

The book of Matthew tells of the good news that the long-awaited Messiah had come to save people — both Jews and Gentiles. Matthew, one of the twelve disciples, is believed to be the author of this book. It was probably written sometime before the Romans destroyed the temple in Jerusalem in AD 70.

Matthew uses much of the Gospel to show that Jesus is the promised Messiah of the Old Testament. Matthew frequently quotes the Old Testament and uses the phrase "kingdom of heaven." Because of this many people think he was writing his Gospel to Jewish people.

Matthew also presents Christ as the great teacher who helps us understand God's law and tells the people about the kingdom of God and what it is. Most of Christ's teachings are found in the following five places:

1. The Sermon on the Mount (5:1 — 7:27)
2. Instruction to the disciples (10:5 – 42)
3. Teaching through parables (13:3 – 52)
4. The meaning of discipleship (18:1 – 35)
5. Teachings about the end of time and the coming of the kingdom of heaven (24:4 — 25:46)

The Genealogy of Jesus the Messiah

This is the genealogy[a] of Jesus the Messiah[b] the son of David, the son of Abraham:

2 Abraham was the father of Isaac,
Isaac the father of Jacob,
Jacob the father of Judah and his brothers,
3 Judah the father of Perez and Zerah, whose mother was Tamar,
Perez the father of Hezron,
Hezron the father of Ram,
4 Ram the father of Amminadab,
Amminadab the father of Nahshon,
Nahshon the father of Salmon,
5 Salmon the father of Boaz, whose mother was Rahab,
Boaz the father of Obed, whose mother was Ruth,
Obed the father of Jesse,
6 and Jesse the father of King David.

David was the father of Solomon, whose mother had been Uriah's wife,
7 Solomon the father of Rehoboam,
Rehoboam the father of Abijah,
Abijah the father of Asa,
8 Asa the father of Jehoshaphat,
Jehoshaphat the father of Jehoram,
Jehoram the father of Uzziah,
9 Uzziah the father of Jotham,
Jotham the father of Ahaz,
Ahaz the father of Hezekiah,
10 Hezekiah the father of Manasseh,
Manasseh the father of Amon,
Amon the father of Josiah,
11 and Josiah the father of Jeconiah[c] and his brothers at the time of the exile to Babylon.

12 After the exile to Babylon:
Jeconiah was the father of Shealtiel,
Shealtiel the father of Zerubbabel,
13 Zerubbabel the father of Abihud,
Abihud the father of Eliakim,
Eliakim the father of Azor,
14 Azor the father of Zadok,
Zadok the father of Akim,
Akim the father of Elihud,
15 Elihud the father of Eleazar,
Eleazar the father of Matthan,
Matthan the father of Jacob,
16 and Jacob the father of Joseph, the husband of Mary, and Mary was the mother of Jesus who is called the Messiah.

17 Thus there were fourteen generations in all from Abraham to David, fourteen from David to the exile to Babylon, and fourteen from the exile to the Messiah.

Joseph Accepts Jesus as His Son

18 This is how the birth of Jesus the Messiah came about[d]: His mother Mary was pledged to be married to Joseph, but before they came together, she was found to be pregnant through the Holy Spirit. 19 Because Joseph her husband was faithful to the law, and yet[e] did not want to expose her to public disgrace, he had in mind to divorce her quietly.

20 But after he had considered this, an angel of the Lord appeared to him in a dream and said, "Joseph son of David, do not be afraid to take Mary home as your wife, because what is conceived in her is from the Holy Spirit. 21 She will give birth to a son, and you are to give him the name Jesus,[f] because he will save his people from their sins."

22 All this took place to fulfill what

---

[a] 1 Or is an account of the origin   [b] 1 Or Jesus Christ. Messiah (Hebrew) and Christ (Greek) both mean Anointed One; also in verse 18.   [c] 11 That is, Jehoiachin; also in verse 12   [d] 18 Or The origin of Jesus the Messiah was like this   [e] 19 Or was a righteous man and   [f] 21 Jesus is the Greek form of Joshua, which means the LORD saves.

ROCK SOLID promises

"You are to give him the name Jesus, because he will save his people from their sins."

Matthew 1:21

Jesus came not only to bring you forgiveness but also to rescue you from being stuck forever in sinful habits.

the Lord had said through the prophet: [23]"The virgin will conceive and give birth to a son, and they will call him Immanuel"[a] (which means "God with us").

[24]When Joseph woke up, he did what the angel of the Lord had commanded him and took Mary home as his wife. [25]But he did not consummate their marriage until she gave birth to a son. And he gave him the name Jesus.

The Magi Visit the Messiah

2 After Jesus was born in Bethlehem in Judea, during the time of King Herod, Magi[b] from the east came to Jerusalem [2]and asked, "Where is the one who has been born king of the Jews? We saw his star when it rose and have come to worship him."

[3]When King Herod heard this he was disturbed, and all Jerusalem with him. [4]When he had called together all the people's chief priests and teachers of the law, he asked them where the Messiah was to be born. [5]"In Bethlehem in Judea," they replied, "for this is what the prophet has written:

[6]"'But you, Bethlehem, in the land of Judah,
  are by no means least among the rulers of Judah;

[a] 23 Isaiah 7:14   [b] 1 Traditionally *wise men*

Matthew 1:18–25

Joseph trusted God.

The situation couldn't have been more traumatic for Joseph. The woman he loved and would soon marry was pregnant, and Joseph knew for certain the child wasn't his. Mary's apparent sexual sin could be punished by stoning, and Joseph determined to break their engagement, the ancient equivalent of divorce. Because Joseph was a good man, he planned to send Mary away without shaming her with a public scene (see Matthew 1:19).

Before Joseph could act on his decision, however, an angel appeared to him in a dream. The angel assured Joseph that Mary hadn't been with another man but was carrying a son conceived by the power of the Holy Spirit. The couple was to call the boy Jesus, meaning "the Lord saves," because "he will save his people from their sins" (Matthew 1:21).

Joseph was a carpenter or builder (see Matthew 13:55). He surely knew the Old Testament prophecy that God would send a Savior to be born to a virgin (see Isaiah 7:14). But he must have been shocked to have been swept up in God's miraculous plan. Joseph had to choose between rejecting the word of Mary and an angel or obeying God despite this astonishing news. Joseph chose to trust the Lord, raising God's Son as his own.

Jesus was almost a teenager the last time Joseph appears in the Bible (see Luke 2:41–49). You don't spot him in later accounts, even where Jesus' mother and siblings are mentioned (see Matthew 13:55–56). It's likely this good husband and father died before Jesus began his public preaching.

You can find Joseph in Matthew 1—2 and Luke 1—2.

UNSHAKEN *people*

for out of you will come a ruler
  who will shepherd my people
  Israel.'*"

⁷Then Herod called the Magi secretly and found out from them the exact time the star had appeared. ⁸He sent them to Bethlehem and said, "Go and search carefully for the child. As soon as you find him, report to me, so that I too may go and worship him."

⁹After they had heard the king, they went on their way, and the star they had seen when it rose went ahead of them until it stopped over the place where the child was. ¹⁰When they saw the star, they were overjoyed. ¹¹On coming to the house, they saw the child with his mother Mary, and they bowed down and worshiped him. Then they opened their treasures and presented him with gifts of gold, frankincense and myrrh. ¹²And having been warned in a dream not to go back to Herod, they returned to their country by another route.

The Escape to Egypt

¹³When they had gone, an angel of the Lord appeared to Joseph in a dream. "Get up," he said, "take the child and his mother and escape to Egypt. Stay there until I tell you, for Herod is going to search for the child to kill him."

¹⁴So he got up, took the child and his mother during the night and left for Egypt, ¹⁵where he stayed until the death of Herod. And so was fulfilled what the Lord had said through the prophet: "Out of Egypt I called my son."*

¹⁶When Herod realized that he had been outwitted by the Magi, he was furious, and he gave orders to kill all the boys in Bethlehem and its vicinity who were two years old and under, in accordance with the time he had learned from the Magi. ¹⁷Then what was said through the prophet Jeremiah was fulfilled:

¹⁸"A voice is heard in Ramah,
  weeping and great mourning,
Rachel weeping for her children
  and refusing to be comforted,
  because they are no more."*

The Return to Nazareth

¹⁹After Herod died, an angel of the Lord appeared in a dream to Joseph in Egypt ²⁰and said, "Get up, take the child and his mother and go to the land of Israel, for those who were trying to take the child's life are dead."

²¹So he got up, took the child and his mother and went to the land of Israel. ²²But when he heard that Archelaus was reigning in Judea in place of his father Herod, he was afraid to go there. Having been warned in a dream, he withdrew to the district of Galilee, ²³and he went and lived in a town called Nazareth. So was fulfilled what was said through the prophets, that he would be called a Nazarene.

John the Baptist Prepares the Way

3 In those days John the Baptist came, preaching in the wilderness of Judea ²and saying, "Repent, for the kingdom of heaven has come near." ³This is he who was spoken of through the prophet Isaiah:

"A voice of one calling in the
    wilderness,
'Prepare the way for the Lord,
  make straight paths for him.'"*

⁴John's clothes were made of camel's hair, and he had a leather belt around his waist. His food was locusts and wild honey. ⁵People went out to him from Jerusalem and all Judea and the whole region of the Jordan. ⁶Confessing their sins, they were baptized by him in the Jordan River.

⁷But when he saw many of the Pharisees and Sadducees coming to where he was baptizing, he said to them: "You brood of vipers! Who warned you to flee from the coming wrath? ⁸Produce fruit in keeping with repentance. ⁹And do not think you can say to yourselves, 'We have Abraham as our father.' I tell you that out of these stones God can raise up children for Abraham. ¹⁰The ax is already at the root of the trees, and every tree that does not produce good fruit will be cut down and thrown into the fire.

a 6 Micah 5:2,4   *b 15* Hosea 11:1
c 18 Jer. 31:15   *d 3* Isaiah 40:3

11 "I baptize you with[a] water for repentance. But after me comes one who is more powerful than I, whose sandals I am not worthy to carry. He will baptize you with[a] the Holy Spirit and fire. 12 His winnowing fork is in his hand, and he will clear his threshing floor, gathering his wheat into the barn and burning up the chaff with unquenchable fire."

The Baptism of Jesus

13 Then Jesus came from Galilee to the Jordan to be baptized by John. 14 But John tried to deter him, saying, "I need to be baptized by you, and do you come to me?"

15 Jesus replied, "Let it be so now; it is proper for us to do this to fulfill all righteousness." Then John consented.

16 As soon as Jesus was baptized, he went up out of the water. At that moment heaven was opened, and he saw the Spirit of God descending like a dove and alighting on him. 17 And a voice from heaven said, "This is my Son, whom I love; with him I am well pleased."

Jesus Is Tested in the Wilderness

4 Then Jesus was led by the Spirit into the wilderness to be tempted[b] by the devil. 2 After fasting forty days and forty nights, he was hungry. 3 The tempter came to him and said, "If you are the Son of God, tell these stones to become bread."

4 Jesus answered, "It is written: 'Man shall not live on bread alone, but on every word that comes from the mouth of God.'[c]"

5 Then the devil took him to the holy city and had him stand on the highest point of the temple. 6 "If you are the Son of God," he said, "throw yourself down. For it is written:

"'He will command his angels
concerning you,
and they will lift you up in their
hands,
so that you will not strike your foot
against a stone.'[d]"

7 Jesus answered him, "It is also written: 'Do not put the Lord your God to the test.'[e]"

ROCK SOLID promises

"Man shall not live on bread alone, but on every word that comes from the mouth of God." Matthew 4:4

Good things fill you up for a while, but you need to feast on God's Word.

8 Again, the devil took him to a very high mountain and showed him all the kingdoms of the world and their splendor. 9 "All this I will give you," he said, "if you will bow down and worship me."

10 Jesus said to him, "Away from me, Satan! For it is written: 'Worship the Lord your God, and serve him only.'[f]"

11 Then the devil left him, and angels came and attended him.

Jesus Begins to Preach

12 When Jesus heard that John had been put in prison, he withdrew to Galilee. 13 Leaving Nazareth, he went and lived in Capernaum, which was by the lake in the area of Zebulun and Naphtali— 14 to fulfill what was said through the prophet Isaiah:

15 "Land of Zebulun and land of
Naphtali,
the Way of the Sea, beyond the
Jordan,
Galilee of the Gentiles—
16 the people living in darkness
have seen a great light;
on those living in the land of the
shadow of death
a light has dawned."[g]

---

[a] 11 Or in   [b] 1 The Greek for tempted can also mean tested.   [c] 4 Deut. 8:3
[d] 6 Psalm 91:11,12   [e] 7 Deut. 6:16
[f] 10 Deut. 6:13   [g] 16 Isaiah 9:1,2

[17]From that time on Jesus began to preach, "Repent, for the kingdom of heaven has come near."

Jesus Calls His First Disciples

[18]As Jesus was walking beside the Sea of Galilee, he saw two brothers, Simon called Peter and his brother Andrew. They were casting a net into the lake, for they were fishermen. [19]"Come, follow me," Jesus said, "and I will send you out to fish for people." [20]At once they left their nets and followed him.

[21]Going on from there, he saw two other brothers, James son of Zebedee and his brother John. They were in a boat with their father Zebedee, preparing their nets. Jesus called them, [22]and immediately they left the boat and their father and followed him.

Jesus Heals the Sick

[23]Jesus went throughout Galilee, teaching in their synagogues, proclaiming the good news of the kingdom, and healing every disease and sickness among the people. [24]News about him spread all over Syria, and people brought to him all who were ill with various diseases, those suffering severe pain, the demon-possessed, those having seizures, and the paralyzed; and he healed them. [25]Large crowds from Galilee, the Decapolis,[a] Jerusalem, Judea and the region across the Jordan followed him.

Introduction to the Sermon on the Mount

5 Now when Jesus saw the crowds, he went up on a mountainside and sat down. His disciples came to him, [2]and he began to teach them.

The Beatitudes

He said:

[3]"Blessed are the poor in spirit,
  for theirs is the kingdom of heaven.
[4]Blessed are those who mourn,
  for they will be comforted.
[5]Blessed are the meek,
  for they will inherit the earth.

Matthew 4:23–25

Jesus did all kinds of miracles.

Suppose you knew nothing of Jesus. You pick up a Bible for the first time. You begin reading. You likely would be startled by accounts describing the miracles Jesus performed. The first four books of the New Testament relate many of Jesus' mind-boggling actions. He healed every kind of disease and sickness (see Matthew 4:23). He drove out evil spirits (see Mark 5:1–20). He multiplied five loaves of bread and two fish to feed a crowd of more than five thousand (see Luke 9:10–17). And he raised his good friend Lazarus from the dead (see John 11:1–44). Those examples and many more prove Jesus had power over every element of our world—the kind of wonder-working power only God possesses. While some people toss out all of the Bible's miracles as pure impossibilities, they still have to answer the evidence for the most well-documented miracle of all—the resurrection of Jesus from the dead.

Think: Do you believe that Jesus performed miracles? Why—or why not?

ROCK SOLID *truths*

---

[6]Blessed are those who hunger and
    thirst for righteousness,
  for they will be filled.
[7]Blessed are the merciful,
  for they will be shown mercy.
[8]Blessed are the pure in heart,
  for they will see God.

[a] 25 That is, the Ten Cities

9 Blessed are the peacemakers,
    for they will be called children of
    God.
10 Blessed are those who are
    persecuted because of
    righteousness,
    for theirs is the kingdom of
    heaven.

11 "Blessed are you when people insult you, persecute you and falsely say all kinds of evil against you because of me. 12 Rejoice and be glad, because great is your reward in heaven, for in the same way they persecuted the prophets who were before you.

Salt and Light

13 "You are the salt of the earth. But if the salt loses its saltiness, how can it be made salty again? It is no longer good for anything, except to be thrown out and trampled underfoot.

14 "You are the light of the world. A town built on a hill cannot be hidden. 15 Neither do people light a lamp and put it under a bowl. Instead they put it on its stand, and it gives light to everyone in the house. 16 In the same way, let your light shine before others, that they may see your good deeds and glorify your Father in heaven.

The Fulfillment of the Law

17 "Do not think that I have come to abolish the Law or the Prophets; I have not come to abolish them but to fulfill them. 18 For truly I tell you, until heaven and earth disappear, not the smallest letter, not the least stroke of a pen, will by any means disappear from the Law until everything is accomplished. 19 Therefore anyone who sets aside one of the least of these commands and teaches others accordingly will be called least in the kingdom of heaven, but whoever practices and teaches these commands will be called

ROCK SOLID principles

Matthew 5:1–16

Stand out.

Jesse came home from a month-long summer mission project radically altered by God, fully committed to obeying the Lord in every way he could. Back home he tried to explain to his long-time friends how the summer had impacted him—and how they too could meet Jesus. They gave him strange looks. They shut out his words. After months of awkward encounters and frustration, Jesse tried a new tactic with his friends. He was still ready to talk about Jesus, but it occurred to him that actions might be more persuasive than words. So instead of starting out by telling people about God, he looked for ways to first show them God's love. Instead of killing conversation, his kind actions got others asking questions.

When Jesus uttered the short statements called the "Beatitudes," he turned life upside-down, like putting poor people first and promising humble people the earth belongs to them. Jesus expects his followers to live according to those values. When they do, their actions season their world like salt. They shine in the darkness like bright city lights. They stand out.

great in the kingdom of heaven. ²⁰For I tell you that unless your righteousness surpasses that of the Pharisees and the teachers of the law, you will certainly not enter the kingdom of heaven.

Murder

²¹"You have heard that it was said to the people long ago, 'You shall not murder,ᵃ and anyone who murders will be subject to judgment.' ²²But I tell you that anyone who is angry with a brother or sisterᵇ,ᶜ will be subject to judgment. Again, anyone who says to a brother or sister, 'Raca,'ᵈ is answerable to the court. And anyone who says, 'You fool!' will be in danger of the fire of hell.

²³"Therefore, if you are offering your gift at the altar and there remember that your brother or sister has something against you, ²⁴leave your gift there in front of the altar. First go and be reconciled to them; then come and offer your gift.

²⁵"Settle matters quickly with your adversary who is taking you to court. Do it while you are still together on the way, or your adversary may hand you over to the judge, and the judge may hand you over to the officer, and you may be thrown into prison. ²⁶Truly I tell you, you will not get out until you have paid the last penny.

Adultery

²⁷"You have heard that it was said, 'You shall not commit adultery.'ᵉ ²⁸But I tell you that anyone who looks at a woman lustfully has already committed adultery with her in his heart. ²⁹If your right eye causes you to stumble, gouge it out and throw it away. It is better for you to lose one part of your body than for your whole body to be thrown into hell. ³⁰And if your right hand causes you to stumble, cut it off and throw it away. It is better for you to lose one part of your body than for your whole body to go into hell.

Divorce

³¹"It has been said, 'Anyone who divorces his wife must give her a certificate of divorce.'ᶠ ³²But I tell you that anyone who divorces his wife, except for sexual immorality, makes her the victim of adultery, and anyone who marries a divorced woman commits adultery.

Oaths

³³"Again, you have heard that it was said to the people long ago, 'Do not break your oath, but fulfill to the Lord the vows you have made.' ³⁴But I tell you, do not swear an oath at all: either by heaven, for it is God's throne; ³⁵or by the earth, for it is his footstool; or by Jerusalem, for it is the city of the Great King. ³⁶And do not swear by your head, for you cannot make even one hair white or black. ³⁷All you need to say is simply 'Yes' or 'No'; anything beyond this comes from the evil one.ᵍ

Eye for Eye

³⁸"You have heard that it was said, 'Eye for eye, and tooth for tooth.'ᵇ ³⁹But I tell you, do not resist an evil person. If anyone slaps you on the right cheek, turn to them the other cheek also. ⁴⁰And if anyone wants to sue you and take your shirt, hand over your coat as well. ⁴¹If anyone forces you to go one mile, go with them two miles. ⁴²Give to the one who asks you, and do not turn away from the one who wants to borrow from you.

Love for Enemies

⁴³"You have heard that it was said, 'Love your neighborⁱ and hate your enemy.' ⁴⁴But I tell you, love your enemies and pray for those who persecute you, ⁴⁵that you may be children of your Father in heaven. He causes his sun to rise on the evil and the good, and sends rain on the righteous and the unrighteous. ⁴⁶If you love those who love you, what reward will

ᵃ 21 Exodus 20:13   ᵇ 22 The Greek word for *brother or sister* (*adelphos*) refers here to a fellow disciple, whether man or woman; also in verse 23.   ᶜ 22 Some manuscripts *brother or sister without cause*   ᵈ 22 An Aramaic term of contempt   ᵉ 27 Exodus 20:14
ᶠ 31 Deut. 24:1   ᵍ 37 Or *from evil*
ᵇ 38 Exodus 21:24; Lev. 24:20; Deut. 19:21
ⁱ 43 Lev. 19:18

you get? Are not even the tax collectors doing that? ⁴⁷And if you greet only your own people, what are you doing more than others? Do not even pagans do that? ⁴⁸Be perfect, therefore, as your heavenly Father is perfect.

Giving to the Needy

6 "Be careful not to practice your righteousness in front of others to be seen by them. If you do, you will have no reward from your Father in heaven.

²"So when you give to the needy, do not announce it with trumpets, as the hypocrites do in the synagogues and on the streets, to be honored by others. Truly I tell you, they have received their reward in full. ³But when you give to the needy, do not let your left hand know what your right hand is doing, ⁴so that your giving may be in secret. Then your Father, who sees what is done in secret, will reward you.

Prayer

⁵"And when you pray, do not be like the hypocrites, for they love to pray standing in the synagogues and on the street corners to be seen by others. Truly I tell you, they have received their reward in full. ⁶But when you pray, go into your room, close the door and pray to your Father, who is unseen. Then your Father, who sees what is done in secret, will reward you. ⁷And when you pray, do not keep on babbling like pagans, for they think they will be heard because of their many words. ⁸Do not be like them, for your Father knows what you need before you ask him.

⁹"This, then, is how you should pray:

"'Our Father in heaven,
hallowed be your name,
¹⁰your kingdom come,
your will be done,
on earth as it is in heaven.
¹¹Give us today our daily bread.
¹²And forgive us our debts,
as we also have forgiven our debtors.
¹³And lead us not into temptation,ᵃ
but deliver us from the evil one.ᵇ'

¹⁴For if you forgive other people when they sin against you, your heavenly Father will also forgive you. ¹⁵But if you do not forgive others their sins, your Father will not forgive your sins.

Fasting

¹⁶"When you fast, do not look somber as the hypocrites do, for they disfigure their faces to show others they are fasting. Truly I tell you, they have received their reward in full. ¹⁷But when you fast, put oil on your head and wash your face, ¹⁸so that it will not be obvious to others that you are fasting, but only to your Father, who is unseen; and your Father, who sees what is done in secret, will reward you.

Treasures in Heaven

¹⁹"Do not store up for yourselves treasures on earth, where moths and vermin destroy, and where thieves break in and steal. ²⁰But store up for yourselves treasures in heaven, where moths and vermin

---

ᵃ *13* The Greek for *temptation* can also mean *testing.* ᵇ *13* Or *from evil*; some late manuscripts *one, / for yours is the kingdom and the power and the glory forever. Amen.*

ROCK SOLID *plans*

Matthew 6:19 – 34

Seek God first.

Maybe no one was surprised when Jesus said what amounted to "put God first." But then he added that when you "seek first his kingdom and his righteousness ... all these things will be given to you as well" (Matthew 6:33). In other words, when you make obeying God the most important thing in your life, everything else falls into the right place. God guarantees he will supply everything you truly need to live for him.

Your next step: Write down your biggest goals for life. Then figure out how to keep God at the top of your list.

do not destroy, and where thieves do not break in and steal. ²¹For where your treasure is, there your heart will be also.

²²"The eye is the lamp of the body. If your eyes are healthy,ᵃ your whole body will be full of light. ²³But if your eyes are unhealthy,ᵇ your whole body will be full of darkness. If then the light within you is darkness, how great is that darkness!

²⁴"No one can serve two masters. Either you will hate the one and love the other, or you will be devoted to the one and despise the other. You cannot serve both God and money.

Do Not Worry

²⁵"Therefore I tell you, do not worry about your life, what you will eat or drink; or about your body, what you will wear. Is not life more than food, and the body more than clothes? ²⁶Look at the birds of the air; they do not sow or reap or store away in barns, and yet your heavenly Father feeds them. Are you not much more valuable than they? ²⁷Can any one of you by worrying add a single hour to your lifeᶜ?

²⁸"And why do you worry about clothes? See how the flowers of the field grow. They do not labor or spin. ²⁹Yet I tell you that not even Solomon in all his splendor was dressed like one of these. ³⁰If that is how God clothes the grass of the field, which is here today and tomorrow is thrown into the fire, will he not much more clothe you—you of little faith? ³¹So do not worry, saying, 'What shall we eat?' or 'What shall we drink?' or 'What shall we wear?' ³²For the pagans run after all these things, and your heavenly Father knows that you need them. ³³But seek first his kingdom and his righteousness, and all these things will be given to you as well. ³⁴Therefore do not worry about tomorrow, for tomorrow will worry about itself. Each day has enough trouble of its own.

Judging Others

7 "Do not judge, or you too will be judged. ²For in the same way you judge others, you will be judged,

and with the measure you use, it will be measured to you.

³"Why do you look at the speck of sawdust in your brother's eye and pay no attention to the plank in your own eye? ⁴How

ᵃ 22 The Greek for *healthy* here implies *generous*. ᵇ 23 The Greek for *unhealthy* here implies *stingy*. ᶜ 27 Or *single cubit to your height*

Matthew 7:1–5

Judging isn't judgmental.

Everyone has heard the words "Do not judge, or you too will be judged" (Matthew 7:1). Almost everyone misuses those words, however, without bothering to understand what Jesus meant. Most assume he was saying, "Look the other way when someone does evil. Don't call anyone's actions sinful. Always be tolerant." But Jesus doesn't mean we should never point out evil or confront someone's sinful deeds. The Bible repeatedly trains us to know the difference between good and evil so we can escape sin and help others do the same. The apostle James wrote, "Whoever turns a sinner from the error of their way will save them from death" (James 5:20). Jesus wants us to actively discern right from wrong—but also to avoid the kind of judging that condemns others and constantly finds fault with them, an offense that's doubly bad if we pretend to be totally good and treat others like they are totally evil.

Think: When and how should you point out another person's sins?

ROCK SOLID truths

can you say to your brother, 'Let me take the speck out of your eye,' when all the time there is a plank in your own eye? [5] You hypocrite, first take the plank out of your own eye, and then you will see clearly to remove the speck from your brother's eye.

[6] "Do not give dogs what is sacred; do not throw your pearls to pigs. If you do, they may trample them under their feet, and turn and tear you to pieces.

Ask, Seek, Knock

[7] "Ask and it will be given to you; seek and you will find; knock and the door will be opened to you. [8] For everyone who asks receives; the one who seeks finds; and to the one who knocks, the door will be opened.

[9] "Which of you, if your son asks for bread, will give him a stone? [10] Or if he asks for a fish, will give him a snake? [11] If you, then, though you are evil, know how to give good gifts to your children, how much more will your Father in heaven give good gifts to those who ask him! [12] So in everything, do to others what you would have them do to you, for this sums up the Law and the Prophets.

The Narrow and Wide Gates

[13] "Enter through the narrow gate. For wide is the gate and broad is the road that leads to destruction, and many enter through it. [14] But small is the gate and narrow the road that leads to life, and only a few find it.

True and False Prophets

[15] "Watch out for false prophets. They come to you in sheep's clothing, but inwardly they are ferocious wolves. [16] By their fruit you will recognize them. Do people pick grapes from thornbushes, or figs from thistles? [17] Likewise, every good tree bears good fruit, but a bad tree bears bad fruit. [18] A good tree cannot bear bad fruit, and a bad tree cannot bear good fruit. [19] Every tree that does not bear good fruit is cut down and thrown into the fire. [20] Thus, by their fruit you will recognize them.

True and False Disciples

[21] "Not everyone who says to me, 'Lord, Lord,' will enter the kingdom of heaven, but only the one who does the will of my Father who is in heaven. [22] Many will say to me on that day, 'Lord, Lord, did we not prophesy in your name and in your name drive out demons and in your name perform many miracles?' [23] Then I will tell them plainly, 'I never knew you. Away from me, you evildoers!'

The Wise and Foolish Builders

[24] "Therefore everyone who hears these words of mine and puts them into practice is like a wise man who built his house on the rock. [25] The rain came down, the streams rose, and the winds blew and beat against that house; yet it did not fall, because it had its foundation on the rock.

ROCK SOLID promises

"Everyone who hears these words of mine and puts them into practice is like a wise man who built his house on the rock."
Matthew 7:24

Paying attention to God's words and putting them into action makes you unshakable.

[26] But everyone who hears these words of mine and does not put them into practice is like a foolish man who built his house on sand. [27] The rain came down, the streams rose, and the winds blew and beat against that house, and it fell with a great crash."

[28] When Jesus had finished saying these things, the crowds were amazed at his teaching, [29] because he taught as one who

had authority, and not as their teachers of the law.

Jesus Heals a Man With Leprosy

8 When Jesus came down from the mountainside, large crowds followed him. [2] A man with leprosy[a] came and knelt before him and said, "Lord, if you are willing, you can make me clean."

[3] Jesus reached out his hand and touched the man. "I am willing," he said. "Be clean!" Immediately he was cleansed of his leprosy. [4] Then Jesus said to him, "See that you don't tell anyone. But go, show yourself to the priest and offer the gift Moses commanded, as a testimony to them."

The Faith of the Centurion

[5] When Jesus had entered Capernaum, a centurion came to him, asking for help. [6] "Lord," he said, "my servant lies at home paralyzed, suffering terribly."

[7] Jesus said to him, "Shall I come and heal him?"

[8] The centurion replied, "Lord, I do not deserve to have you come under my roof. But just say the word, and my servant will be healed. [9] For I myself am a man under authority, with soldiers under me. I tell this one, 'Go,' and he goes; and that one, 'Come,' and he comes. I say to my servant, 'Do this,' and he does it."

[10] When Jesus heard this, he was amazed and said to those following him, "Truly I tell you, I have not found anyone in Israel with such great faith. [11] I say to you that many will come from the east and the west, and will take their places at the feast with Abraham, Isaac and Jacob in the kingdom of heaven. [12] But the subjects of the kingdom will be thrown outside, into the darkness, where there will be weeping and gnashing of teeth."

[13] Then Jesus said to the centurion, "Go! Let it be done just as you believed it would." And his servant was healed at that moment.

Jesus Heals Many

[14] When Jesus came into Peter's house, he saw Peter's mother-in-law lying in bed with a fever. [15] He touched her hand and the fever left her, and she got up and began to wait on him.

[16] When evening came, many who were demon-possessed were brought to him, and he drove out the spirits with a word and healed all the sick. [17] This was to fulfill what was spoken through the prophet Isaiah:

> "He took up our infirmities
>   and bore our diseases."[b]

The Cost of Following Jesus

[18] When Jesus saw the crowd around him, he gave orders to cross to the other side of the lake. [19] Then a teacher of the law came to him and said, "Teacher, I will follow you wherever you go."

[20] Jesus replied, "Foxes have dens and birds have nests, but the Son of Man has no place to lay his head."

[21] Another disciple said to him, "Lord, first let me go and bury my father."

[22] But Jesus told him, "Follow me, and let the dead bury their own dead."

Jesus Calms the Storm

[23] Then he got into the boat and his disciples followed him. [24] Suddenly a furious storm came up on the lake, so that the waves swept over the boat. But Jesus was sleeping. [25] The disciples went and woke him, saying, "Lord, save us! We're going to drown!"

[26] He replied, "You of little faith, why are you so afraid?" Then he got up and rebuked the winds and the waves, and it was completely calm.

[27] The men were amazed and asked, "What kind of man is this? Even the winds and the waves obey him!"

Jesus Restores Two Demon-Possessed Men

[28] When he arrived at the other side in the region of the Gadarenes,[c] two demon-

---

a 2 The Greek word traditionally translated *leprosy* was used for various diseases affecting the skin.   *b 17* Isaiah 53:4 (see Septuagint)
c 28 Some manuscripts *Gergesenes*; other manuscripts *Gerasenes*

ROCK SOLID
promises

"You of little faith, why are you so afraid?" Matthew 8:26

When you hold tight to Jesus, you don't have any reason to hang onto your fears.

___

possessed men coming from the tombs met him. They were so violent that no one could pass that way. ²⁹"What do you want with us, Son of God?" they shouted. "Have you come here to torture us before the appointed time?"

³⁰Some distance from them a large herd of pigs was feeding. ³¹The demons begged Jesus, "If you drive us out, send us into the herd of pigs."

³²He said to them, "Go!" So they came out and went into the pigs, and the whole herd rushed down the steep bank into the lake and died in the water. ³³Those tending the pigs ran off, went into the town and reported all this, including what had happened to the demon-possessed men. ³⁴Then the whole town went out to meet Jesus. And when they saw him, they pleaded with him to leave their region.

Jesus Forgives and Heals a Paralyzed Man

9 Jesus stepped into a boat, crossed over and came to his own town. ²Some men brought to him a paralyzed man, lying on a mat. When Jesus saw their faith, he said to the man, "Take heart, son; your sins are forgiven."

³At this, some of the teachers of the law said to themselves, "This fellow is blaspheming!"

⁴Knowing their thoughts, Jesus said, "Why do you entertain evil thoughts

in your hearts? ⁵Which is easier: to say, 'Your sins are forgiven,' or to say, 'Get up and walk'? ⁶But I want you to know that the Son of Man has authority on earth to forgive sins." So he said to the paralyzed man, "Get up, take your mat and go home." ⁷Then the man got up and went home. ⁸When the crowd saw this, they were filled with awe; and they praised God, who had given such authority to man.

The Calling of Matthew

⁹As Jesus went on from there, he saw a man named Matthew sitting at the tax collector's booth. "Follow me," he told him, and Matthew got up and followed him.

¹⁰While Jesus was having dinner at Matthew's house, many tax collectors and sinners came and ate with him and his disciples. ¹¹When the Pharisees saw this, they asked his disciples, "Why does your teacher eat with tax collectors and sinners?"

¹²On hearing this, Jesus said, "It is not the healthy who need a doctor, but the sick. ¹³But go and learn what this means: 'I desire mercy, not sacrifice.'ᵃ For I have not come to call the righteous, but sinners."

Jesus Questioned About Fasting

¹⁴Then John's disciples came and asked him, "How is it that we and the Pharisees fast often, but your disciples do not fast?"

¹⁵Jesus answered, "How can the guests of the bridegroom mourn while he is with them? The time will come when the bridegroom will be taken from them; then they will fast.

¹⁶"No one sews a patch of unshrunk cloth on an old garment, for the patch will pull away from the garment, making the tear worse. ¹⁷Neither do people pour new wine into old wineskins. If they do, the skins will burst; the wine will run out and the wineskins will be ruined. No, they pour new wine into new wineskins, and both are preserved."

ᵃ *13* Hosea 6:6

Matthew 9:9–13

Spend time with sinners.

Claire had watched Ariel take a long downhill slide from back in the day when they were best childhood friends. Ariel's story was a cliché. She hung with the wrong crowd ... tried alcohol and drugs ... got pregnant with a guy she barely knew. Claire's church friends told her to stay away from Ariel so she wouldn't get sucked into her unwise choices. But most days after school Claire stopped by for an hour to watch Ariel's baby. Claire wanted to give her old friend a break. Besides, Claire understood that people avoid big mistakes only because of God's help. If Claire hadn't discovered the Lord a few years back, she could easily have taken the same tough path as Ariel.

It's true you need to be on guard against getting dragged into doing wrong. But Jesus came to earth to love sinful people so much that they would want to be friends with God. He gave us the same job to do. You can't accomplish that task long-distance. You have to get close to people and love them no matter what. The test is whether you pull your friends closer to God—or they pull you into sin.

Jesus Raises a Dead Girl and Heals a Sick Woman

[18]While he was saying this, a synagogue leader came and knelt before him and said, "My daughter has just died. But come and put your hand on her, and she will live." [19]Jesus got up and went with him, and so did his disciples.

[20]Just then a woman who had been subject to bleeding for twelve years came up behind him and touched the edge of his cloak. [21]She said to herself, "If I only touch his cloak, I will be healed."

[22]Jesus turned and saw her. "Take heart, daughter," he said, "your faith has healed you." And the woman was healed at that moment.

[23]When Jesus entered the synagogue leader's house and saw the noisy crowd and people playing pipes, [24]he said, "Go away. The girl is not dead but asleep." But they laughed at him. [25]After the crowd had been put outside, he went in and took the girl by the hand, and she got up. [26]News of this spread through all that region.

Jesus Heals the Blind and the Mute

[27]As Jesus went on from there, two blind men followed him, calling out, "Have mercy on us, Son of David!"

[28]When he had gone indoors, the blind men came to him, and he asked them, "Do you believe that I am able to do this?"

"Yes, Lord," they replied.

[29]Then he touched their eyes and said, "According to your faith let it be done to you"; [30]and their sight was restored. Jesus warned them sternly, "See that no one knows about this." [31]But they went out and spread the news about him all over that region.

[32]While they were going out, a man who was demon-possessed and could not talk was brought to Jesus. [33]And when the demon was driven out, the man who had been mute spoke. The crowd was amazed

and said, "Nothing like this has ever been seen in Israel."

³⁴But the Pharisees said, "It is by the prince of demons that he drives out demons."

The Workers Are Few

³⁵Jesus went through all the towns and villages, teaching in their synagogues, proclaiming the good news of the kingdom and healing every disease and sickness. ³⁶When he saw the crowds, he had compassion on them, because they were harassed and helpless, like sheep without a shepherd. ³⁷Then he said to his disciples, "The harvest is plentiful but the workers are few. ³⁸Ask the Lord of the harvest, therefore, to send out workers into his harvest field."

Jesus Sends Out the Twelve

10 Jesus called his twelve disciples to him and gave them authority to drive out impure spirits and to heal every disease and sickness.

²These are the names of the twelve apostles: first, Simon (who is called Peter) and his brother Andrew; James son of Zebedee, and his brother John; ³Philip and Bartholomew; Thomas and Matthew the tax collector; James son of Alphaeus, and Thaddaeus; ⁴Simon the Zealot and Judas Iscariot, who betrayed him.

⁵These twelve Jesus sent out with the following instructions: "Do not go among the Gentiles or enter any town of the Samaritans. ⁶Go rather to the lost sheep of Israel. ⁷As you go, proclaim this message: 'The kingdom of heaven has come near.' ⁸Heal the sick, raise the dead, cleanse those who have leprosy,ᵃ drive out demons. Freely you have received; freely give.

⁹"Do not get any gold or silver or copper to take with you in your belts— ¹⁰no bag for the journey or extra shirt or sandals or a staff, for the worker is worth his keep. ¹¹Whatever town or village you enter, search there for some worthy person and stay at their house until you leave. ¹²As you enter the home, give it your greeting.

¹³If the home is deserving, let your peace rest on it; if it is not, let your peace return to you. ¹⁴If anyone will not welcome you or listen to your words, leave that home or town and shake the dust off your feet. ¹⁵Truly I tell you, it will be more bearable for Sodom and Gomorrah on the day of judgment than for that town.

¹⁶"I am sending you out like sheep among wolves. Therefore be as shrewd as snakes and as innocent as doves. ¹⁷Be on your guard; you will be handed over to the local councils and be flogged in the synagogues. ¹⁸On my account you will be brought before governors and kings as witnesses to them and to the Gentiles. ¹⁹But when they arrest you, do not worry about what to say or how to say it. At that time you will be given what to say, ²⁰for it will not be you speaking, but the Spirit of your Father speaking through you.

²¹"Brother will betray brother to death, and a father his child; children will rebel against their parents and have them put to death. ²²You will be hated by everyone because of me, but the one who stands firm to the end will be saved. ²³When you are persecuted in one place, flee to another. Truly I tell you, you will not finish going through the towns of Israel before the Son of Man comes.

²⁴"The student is not above the teacher, nor a servant above his master. ²⁵It is enough for students to be like their teachers, and servants like their masters. If the head of the house has been called Beelzebul, how much more the members of his household!

²⁶"So do not be afraid of them, for there is nothing concealed that will not be disclosed, or hidden that will not be made known. ²⁷What I tell you in the dark, speak in the daylight; what is whispered in your ear, proclaim from the roofs. ²⁸Do not be afraid of those who kill the body but cannot kill the soul. Rather, be afraid of the One who can destroy both soul and body in hell. ²⁹Are not two sparrows sold

---

ᵃ 8 The Greek word traditionally translated *leprosy* was used for various diseases affecting the skin.

for a penny? Yet not one of them will fall to the ground outside your Father's care.ᵃ ³⁰And even the very hairs of your head are all numbered. ³¹So don't be afraid; you are worth more than many sparrows.

³²"Whoever acknowledges me before others, I will also acknowledge before my Father in heaven. ³³But whoever disowns me before others, I will disown before my Father in heaven.

³⁴"Do not suppose that I have come to bring peace to the earth. I did not come to bring peace, but a sword. ³⁵For I have come to turn

"'a man against his father,
    a daughter against her mother,
a daughter-in-law against her mother-in-law—
³⁶   a man's enemies will be the members of his own household.'ᵇ

³⁷"Anyone who loves their father or mother more than me is not worthy of me; anyone who loves their son or daughter more than me is not worthy of me. ³⁸Whoever does not take up their cross and follow me is not worthy of me. ³⁹Whoever finds their life will lose it, and whoever loses their life for my sake will find it.

⁴⁰"Anyone who welcomes you welcomes me, and anyone who welcomes me welcomes the one who sent me. ⁴¹Whoever welcomes a prophet as a prophet will receive a prophet's reward, and whoever welcomes a righteous person as a righteous person will receive a righteous person's reward. ⁴²And if anyone gives even a cup of cold water to one of these little ones who is my disciple, truly I tell you, that person will certainly not lose their reward."

Jesus and John the Baptist

11 After Jesus had finished instructing his twelve disciples, he went on from there to teach and preach in the towns of Galilee.ᶜ

²When John, who was in prison, heard about the deeds of the Messiah, he sent his disciples ³to ask him, "Are you the one who is to come, or should we expect someone else?"

⁴Jesus replied, "Go back and report to John what you hear and see: ⁵The blind receive sight, the lame walk, those who have leprosyᵈ are cleansed, the deaf hear, the dead are raised, and the good news is proclaimed to the poor. ⁶Blessed is anyone who does not stumble on account of me."

⁷As John's disciples were leaving, Jesus began to speak to the crowd about John: "What did you go out into the wilderness to see? A reed swayed by the wind? ⁸If not, what did you go out to see? A man dressed in fine clothes? No, those who wear fine clothes are in kings' palaces. ⁹Then what did you go out to see? A prophet? Yes, I tell you, and more than a prophet. ¹⁰This is the one about whom it is written:

"'I will send my messenger ahead of you,
    who will prepare your way before you.'ᵉ

¹¹Truly I tell you, among those born of women there has not risen anyone greater than John the Baptist; yet whoever is least in the kingdom of heaven is greater than he. ¹²From the days of John the Baptist until now, the kingdom of heaven has been subjected to violence,ᶠ and violent people have been raiding it. ¹³For all the Prophets and the Law prophesied until John. ¹⁴And if you are willing to accept it, he is the Elijah who was to come. ¹⁵Whoever has ears, let them hear.

¹⁶"To what can I compare this generation? They are like children sitting in the marketplaces and calling out to others:

¹⁷"'We played the pipe for you,
    and you did not dance;
we sang a dirge,
    and you did not mourn.'

¹⁸For John came neither eating nor drinking, and they say, 'He has a demon.' ¹⁹The Son of Man came eating and drinking, and they say, 'Here is a glutton and a drunkard,

---

ᵃ 29 Or will; or knowledge   ᵇ 36 Micah 7:6
ᶜ 1 Greek in their towns   ᵈ 5 The Greek word traditionally translated leprosy was used for various diseases affecting the skin.
ᵉ 10 Mal. 3:1   ᶠ 12 Or been forcefully advancing

a friend of tax collectors and sinners.' But wisdom is proved right by her deeds."

Woe on Unrepentant Towns

²⁰Then Jesus began to denounce the towns in which most of his miracles had been performed, because they did not repent. ²¹"Woe to you, Chorazin! Woe to you, Bethsaida! For if the miracles that were performed in you had been performed in Tyre and Sidon, they would have repented long ago in sackcloth and ashes. ²²But I tell you, it will be more bearable for Tyre and Sidon on the day of judgment than for you. ²³And you, Capernaum, will you be lifted to the heavens? No, you will go down to Hades.ᵃ For if the miracles that were performed in you had been performed in Sodom, it would have remained to this day. ²⁴But I tell you that it will be more bearable for Sodom on the day of judgment than for you."

The Father Revealed in the Son

²⁵At that time Jesus said, "I praise you, Father, Lord of heaven and earth, because you have hidden these things from the wise and learned, and revealed them to little children. ²⁶Yes, Father, for this is what you were pleased to do.

²⁷"All things have been committed to me by my Father. No one knows the Son except the Father, and no one knows the Father except the Son and those to whom the Son chooses to reveal him.

²⁸"Come to me, all you who are weary and burdened, and I will give you rest. ²⁹Take my yoke upon you and learn from me, for I am gentle and humble in heart, and you will find rest for your souls. ³⁰For my yoke is easy and my burden is light."

Jesus Is Lord of the Sabbath

12 At that time Jesus went through the grainfields on the Sabbath. His disciples were hungry and began to pick some heads of grain and eat them. ²When the Pharisees saw this, they said to him, "Look! Your disciples are doing what is unlawful on the Sabbath."

ROCK SOLID *promises*

"Come to me, all you who are weary and burdened, and I will give you rest." Matthew 11:28

Jesus invites you to unload all your worries onto him. It's how you find real peace.

³He answered, "Haven't you read what David did when he and his companions were hungry? ⁴He entered the house of God, and he and his companions ate the consecrated bread—which was not lawful for them to do, but only for the priests. ⁵Or haven't you read in the Law that the priests on Sabbath duty in the temple desecrate the Sabbath and yet are innocent? ⁶I tell you that something greater than the temple is here. ⁷If you had known what these words mean, 'I desire mercy, not sacrifice,'ᵇ you would not have condemned the innocent. ⁸For the Son of Man is Lord of the Sabbath."

⁹Going on from that place, he went into their synagogue, ¹⁰and a man with a shriveled hand was there. Looking for a reason to bring charges against Jesus, they asked him, "Is it lawful to heal on the Sabbath?"

¹¹He said to them, "If any of you has a sheep and it falls into a pit on the Sabbath, will you not take hold of it and lift it out? ¹²How much more valuable is a person than a sheep! Therefore it is lawful to do good on the Sabbath."

¹³Then he said to the man, "Stretch out your hand." So he stretched it out and it was completely restored, just as sound as the other. ¹⁴But the Pharisees went out and plotted how they might kill Jesus.

ᵃ 23 That is, the realm of the dead
ᵇ 7 Hosea 6:6

God's Chosen Servant

[15] Aware of this, Jesus withdrew from that place. A large crowd followed him, and he healed all who were ill. [16] He warned them not to tell others about him. [17] This was to fulfill what was spoken through the prophet Isaiah:

[18] "Here is my servant whom I have chosen,
the one I love, in whom I delight;
I will put my Spirit on him,
and he will proclaim justice to the nations.
[19] He will not quarrel or cry out;
no one will hear his voice in the streets.
[20] A bruised reed he will not break,
and a smoldering wick he will not snuff out,
till he has brought justice through to victory.
[21] In his name the nations will put their hope."[a]

Jesus and Beelzebul

[22] Then they brought him a demon-possessed man who was blind and mute, and Jesus healed him, so that he could both talk and see. [23] All the people were astonished and said, "Could this be the Son of David?"

[24] But when the Pharisees heard this, they said, "It is only by Beelzebul, the prince of demons, that this fellow drives out demons."

[25] Jesus knew their thoughts and said to them, "Every kingdom divided against itself will be ruined, and every city or household divided against itself will not stand. [26] If Satan drives out Satan, he is divided against himself. How then can his kingdom stand? [27] And if I drive out demons by Beelzebul, by whom do your people drive them out? So then, they will be your judges. [28] But if it is by the Spirit of God that I drive out demons, then the kingdom of God has come upon you.

[29] "Or again, how can anyone enter a strong man's house and carry off his possessions unless he first ties up the strong man? Then he can plunder his house.

[30] "Whoever is not with me is against me, and whoever does not gather with me scatters. [31] And so I tell you, every kind of sin and slander can be forgiven, but blasphemy against the Spirit will not be forgiven. [32] Anyone who speaks a word against the Son of Man will be forgiven, but anyone who speaks against the Holy Spirit will not be forgiven, either in this age or in the age to come.

[a] 21 Isaiah 42:1-4

ROCK SOLID truths

Matthew 12:31–32

God can forgive every sin but one.

You sinned. Messed up badly. Disobeyed God on purpose, knowing deep down you were doing wrong. And now you worry if you crossed a holy line with God, sinning so terribly God will never forgive you. You might fret even more when you realize that Jesus said "Every kind of sin and slander can be forgiven, but blasphemy against the Spirit will not be forgiven" (Matthew 12:31). Jesus does say there is a sin that can't be forgiven, but it's no ordinary wrongdoing. It's speaking against the Holy Spirit. In this scene it's a sin committed by religious leaders so warped and beyond repentance that they said Jesus healed a demon-possessed man using Satan's power (see Matthew 12:22–24). God hates sin because of the pain it causes you, others, and him. But he's always ready to forgive. He wants you to admit your sin and get a fresh start (see 1 John 1:8–9).

Think: Why does God continue to forgive you when you do wrong?

[33] "Make a tree good and its fruit will be good, or make a tree bad and its fruit will be bad, for a tree is recognized by its fruit. [34] You brood of vipers, how can you who are evil say anything good? For the mouth speaks what the heart is full of. [35] A good man brings good things out of the good stored up in him, and an evil man brings evil things out of the evil stored up in him. [36] But I tell you that everyone will have to give account on the day of judgment for every empty word they have spoken. [37] For by your words you will be acquitted, and by your words you will be condemned."

The Sign of Jonah

[38] Then some of the Pharisees and teachers of the law said to him, "Teacher, we want to see a sign from you."

[39] He answered, "A wicked and adulterous generation asks for a sign! But none will be given it except the sign of the prophet Jonah. [40] For as Jonah was three days and three nights in the belly of a huge fish, so the Son of Man will be three days and three nights in the heart of the earth. [41] The men of Nineveh will stand up at the judgment with this generation and condemn it; for they repented at the preaching of Jonah, and now something greater than Jonah is here. [42] The Queen of the South will rise at the judgment with this generation and condemn it; for she came from the ends of the earth to listen to Solomon's wisdom, and now something greater than Solomon is here.

[43] "When an impure spirit comes out of a person, it goes through arid places seeking rest and does not find it. [44] Then it says, 'I will return to the house I left.' When it arrives, it finds the house unoccupied, swept clean and put in order. [45] Then it goes and takes with it seven other spirits more wicked than itself, and they go in and live there. And the final condition of that person is worse than the first. That is how it will be with this wicked generation."

Jesus' Mother and Brothers

[46] While Jesus was still talking to the crowd, his mother and brothers stood outside, wanting to speak to him. [47] Someone told him, "Your mother and brothers are standing outside, wanting to speak to you."

[48] He replied to him, "Who is my mother, and who are my brothers?" [49] Pointing to his disciples, he said, "Here are my mother and my brothers. [50] For whoever does the will of my Father in heaven is my brother and sister and mother."

The Parable of the Sower

13 That same day Jesus went out of the house and sat by the lake. [2] Such large crowds gathered around him that he got into a boat and sat in it, while all the people stood on the shore. [3] Then he told them many things in parables, saying: "A farmer went out to sow his seed. [4] As he was scattering the seed, some fell along the path, and the birds came and ate it up. [5] Some fell on rocky places, where it did not have much soil. It sprang up quickly, because the soil was shallow. [6] But when the sun came up, the plants were scorched, and they withered because they had no root. [7] Other seed fell among thorns, which grew up and choked the plants. [8] Still other seed fell on good soil, where it produced a crop—a hundred, sixty or thirty times what was sown. [9] Whoever has ears, let them hear."

[10] The disciples came to him and asked, "Why do you speak to the people in parables?"

[11] He replied, "Because the knowledge of the secrets of the kingdom of heaven has been given to you, but not to them. [12] Whoever has will be given more, and they will have an abundance. Whoever does not have, even what they have will be taken from them. [13] This is why I speak to them in parables:

"Though seeing, they do not see;
  though hearing, they do not hear or
    understand.

[14] In them is fulfilled the prophecy of Isaiah:

"'You will be ever hearing but never
    understanding;

you will be ever seeing but never
  perceiving.
¹⁵ For this people's heart has become
  calloused;
they hardly hear with their ears,
  and they have closed their eyes.
Otherwise they might see with their
  eyes,
  hear with their ears,
  understand with their hearts
and turn, and I would heal them.'ᵃ

¹⁶ But blessed are your eyes because they see, and your ears because they hear. ¹⁷ For truly I tell you, many prophets and righteous people longed to see what you see but did not see it, and to hear what you hear but did not hear it.

¹⁸ "Listen then to what the parable of the sower means: ¹⁹ When anyone hears the message about the kingdom and does not understand it, the evil one comes and snatches away what was sown in their heart. This is the seed sown along the path. ²⁰ The seed falling on rocky ground refers to someone who hears the word and at once receives it with joy. ²¹ But since they have no root, they last only a short time. When trouble or persecution comes because of the word, they quickly fall away. ²² The seed falling among the thorns refers to someone who hears the word, but the worries of this life and the deceitfulness of wealth choke the word, making it unfruitful. ²³ But the seed falling on good soil refers to someone who hears the word and understands it. This is the one who produces a crop, yielding a hundred, sixty or thirty times what was sown."

The Parable of the Weeds

²⁴ Jesus told them another parable: "The kingdom of heaven is like a man who sowed good seed in his field. ²⁵ But while everyone was sleeping, his enemy came and sowed weeds among the wheat, and went away. ²⁶ When the wheat sprouted and formed heads, then the weeds also appeared.

ᵃ 15 Isaiah 6:9,10 (see Septuagint)

ROCK SOLID principles

Matthew 13:1–23

Do the Word.

Jamal was his church's all-time winner of Bible quizzing, the kid who could quote more Bible verses from memory than most pastors. But there was a wild mismatch between what he knew and how he acted. It was like all the facts he memorized never sunk into his life, to that place deep inside where they would make a difference. Jamal got a shocking look at himself when some random guys at school joked about how stupid and boring church was. When Jamal mentioned that he happened to like his church, the guys were baffled. Watching the way he acted, they had no idea he even knew what church was.

Jesus told a simple story to make a big point. The things you learn in the Bible won't do you any good if you don't absorb them and act on them—not just the news of how Jesus makes you friends with God, but all his thoughts, plans, and commands for your life. Like the apostle James wrote, "Do not merely listen to the word, and so deceive yourselves. Do what it says." (James 1:22)

[27] "The owner's servants came to him and said, 'Sir, didn't you sow good seed in your field? Where then did the weeds come from?'

[28] " 'An enemy did this,' he replied.

"The servants asked him, 'Do you want us to go and pull them up?'

[29] " 'No,' he answered, 'because while you are pulling the weeds, you may uproot the wheat with them. [30] Let both grow together until the harvest. At that time I will tell the harvesters: First collect the weeds and tie them in bundles to be burned; then gather the wheat and bring it into my barn.' "

The Parables of the Mustard Seed and the Yeast

[31] He told them another parable: "The kingdom of heaven is like a mustard seed, which a man took and planted in his field. [32] Though it is the smallest of all seeds, yet when it grows, it is the largest of garden plants and becomes a tree, so that the birds come and perch in its branches."

[33] He told them still another parable: "The kingdom of heaven is like yeast that a woman took and mixed into about sixty pounds[a] of flour until it worked all through the dough."

[34] Jesus spoke all these things to the crowd in parables; he did not say anything to them without using a parable. [35] So was fulfilled what was spoken through the prophet:

"I will open my mouth in parables,
    I will utter things hidden since the
        creation of the world."[b]

The Parable of the Weeds Explained

[36] Then he left the crowd and went into the house. His disciples came to him and said, "Explain to us the parable of the weeds in the field."

[37] He answered, "The one who sowed the good seed is the Son of Man. [38] The field is the world, and the good seed stands for the people of the kingdom. The weeds are the people of the evil one, [39] and the enemy who sows them is the devil. The harvest is the end of the age, and the harvesters are angels.

[40] "As the weeds are pulled up and burned in the fire, so it will be at the end of the age. [41] The Son of Man will send out his angels, and they will weed out of his kingdom everything that causes sin and all who do evil. [42] They will throw them into the blazing furnace, where there will be weeping and gnashing of teeth. [43] Then the righteous will shine like the sun in the kingdom of their Father. Whoever has ears, let them hear.

The Parables of the Hidden Treasure and the Pearl

[44] "The kingdom of heaven is like treasure hidden in a field. When a man found it, he hid it again, and then in his joy went and sold all he had and bought that field.

[45] "Again, the kingdom of heaven is like a merchant looking for fine pearls. [46] When he found one of great value, he went away and sold everything he had and bought it.

The Parable of the Net

[47] "Once again, the kingdom of heaven is like a net that was let down into the lake and caught all kinds of fish. [48] When it was full, the fishermen pulled it up on the shore. Then they sat down and collected the good fish in baskets, but threw the bad away. [49] This is how it will be at the end of the age. The angels will come and separate the wicked from the righteous [50] and throw them into the blazing furnace, where there will be weeping and gnashing of teeth.

[51] "Have you understood all these things?" Jesus asked.

"Yes," they replied.

[52] He said to them, "Therefore every teacher of the law who has become a disciple in the kingdom of heaven is like the owner of a house who brings out of his storeroom new treasures as well as old."

A Prophet Without Honor

[53] When Jesus had finished these parables, he moved on from there. [54] Coming to his hometown, he began teaching the people in their synagogue, and they were

---

[a] 33 Or about 27 kilograms   [b] 35 Psalm 78:2

amazed. "Where did this man get this wisdom and these miraculous powers?" they asked. [55] "Isn't this the carpenter's son? Isn't his mother's name Mary, and aren't his brothers James, Joseph, Simon and Judas? [56] Aren't all his sisters with us? Where then did this man get all these things?" [57] And they took offense at him.

But Jesus said to them, "A prophet is not without honor except in his own town and in his own home."

[58] And he did not do many miracles there because of their lack of faith.

John the Baptist Beheaded

14 At that time Herod the tetrarch heard the reports about Jesus, [2] and he said to his attendants, "This is John the Baptist; he has risen from the dead! That is why miraculous powers are at work in him."

[3] Now Herod had arrested John and bound him and put him in prison because of Herodias, his brother Philip's wife, [4] for John had been saying to him: "It is not lawful for you to have her." [5] Herod wanted to kill John, but he was afraid of the people, because they considered John a prophet.

[6] On Herod's birthday the daughter of Herodias danced for the guests and pleased Herod so much [7] that he promised with an oath to give her whatever she asked. [8] Prompted by her mother, she said, "Give me here on a platter the head of John the Baptist." [9] The king was distressed, but because of his oaths and his dinner guests, he ordered that her request be granted [10] and had John beheaded in the prison. [11] His head was brought in on a platter and given to the girl, who carried it to her mother. [12] John's disciples came and took his body and buried it. Then they went and told Jesus.

Jesus Feeds the Five Thousand

[13] When Jesus heard what had happened, he withdrew by boat privately to a solitary place. Hearing of this, the crowds followed him on foot from the towns. [14] When Jesus landed and saw a large crowd, he had compassion on them and healed their sick.

[15] As evening approached, the disciples came to him and said, "This is a remote place, and it's already getting late. Send the crowds away, so they can go to the villages and buy themselves some food."

[16] Jesus replied, "They do not need to go away. You give them something to eat."

[17] "We have here only five loaves of bread and two fish," they answered.

[18] "Bring them here to me," he said. [19] And he directed the people to sit down on the grass. Taking the five loaves and the two fish and looking up to heaven, he gave thanks and broke the loaves. Then he gave them to the disciples, and the disciples gave them to the people. [20] They all ate and were satisfied, and the disciples picked up twelve basketfuls of broken pieces that were left over. [21] The number of those who ate was about five thousand men, besides women and children.

Jesus Walks on the Water

[22] Immediately Jesus made the disciples get into the boat and go on ahead of him to the other side, while he dismissed the crowd. [23] After he had dismissed them, he went up on a mountainside by himself to pray. Later that night, he was there alone, [24] and the boat was already a considerable distance from land, buffeted by the waves because the wind was against it.

[25] Shortly before dawn Jesus went out to them, walking on the lake. [26] When the disciples saw him walking on the lake, they were terrified. "It's a ghost," they said, and cried out in fear.

[27] But Jesus immediately said to them: "Take courage! It is I. Don't be afraid."

[28] "Lord, if it's you," Peter replied, "tell me to come to you on the water."

[29] "Come," he said.

Then Peter got down out of the boat, walked on the water and came toward Jesus. [30] But when he saw the wind, he was afraid and, beginning to sink, cried out, "Lord, save me!"

[31] Immediately Jesus reached out his hand and caught him. "You of little faith," he said, "why did you doubt?"

[32] And when they climbed into the boat,

ROCK SOLID *plans*

Matthew 14:22–36

Follow Jesus with faith.

The apostle Peter was a skilled fisherman who made his living on the Sea of Galilee. So he knew enough to feel terror when he saw someone stroll across the water in the dead of night. It turned out to be Jesus, who invited his close friend to do the impossible—to join him walking on the sea. Amazingly, Peter walked on the water too—at least until fear gripped him and took him down. Jesus told Peter that faith would have kept him from sinking.

Your next step: Ask a friend to pray with you for faith to try something hard—something you can't do without relying on God's power.

the wind died down. ³³Then those who were in the boat worshiped him, saying, "Truly you are the Son of God."

³⁴When they had crossed over, they landed at Gennesaret. ³⁵And when the men of that place recognized Jesus, they sent word to all the surrounding country. People brought all their sick to him ³⁶and begged him to let the sick just touch the edge of his cloak, and all who touched it were healed.

That Which Defiles

15 Then some Pharisees and teachers of the law came to Jesus from Jerusalem and asked, ²"Why do your disciples break the tradition of the elders? They don't wash their hands before they eat!"

³Jesus replied, "And why do you break the command of God for the sake of your tradition? ⁴For God said, 'Honor your father and mother'ᵃ and 'Anyone who curses their father or mother is to be put to death.'ᵇ ⁵But you say that if anyone declares that what might have been used to

help their father or mother is 'devoted to God,' ⁶they are not to 'honor their father or mother' with it. Thus you nullify the word of God for the sake of your tradition. ⁷You hypocrites! Isaiah was right when he prophesied about you:

⁸"'These people honor me with their
lips,
but their hearts are far from me.
⁹They worship me in vain;
their teachings are merely human
rules.'ᶜ"

¹⁰Jesus called the crowd to him and said, "Listen and understand. ¹¹What goes into someone's mouth does not defile them, but what comes out of their mouth, that is what defiles them."

¹²Then the disciples came to him and asked, "Do you know that the Pharisees were offended when they heard this?"

¹³He replied, "Every plant that my heavenly Father has not planted will be pulled up by the roots. ¹⁴Leave them; they are blind guides.ᵈ If the blind lead the blind, both will fall into a pit."

¹⁵Peter said, "Explain the parable to us."

¹⁶"Are you still so dull?" Jesus asked them. ¹⁷"Don't you see that whatever enters the mouth goes into the stomach and then out of the body? ¹⁸But the things that come out of a person's mouth come from the heart, and these defile them. ¹⁹For out of the heart come evil thoughts—murder, adultery, sexual immorality, theft, false testimony, slander. ²⁰These are what defile a person; but eating with unwashed hands does not defile them."

The Faith of a Canaanite Woman

²¹Leaving that place, Jesus withdrew to the region of Tyre and Sidon. ²²A Canaanite woman from that vicinity came to him, crying out, "Lord, Son of David, have mercy on me! My daughter is demon-possessed and suffering terribly."

²³Jesus did not answer a word. So his disciples came to him and urged him,

---

ᵃ 4 Exodus 20:12; Deut. 5:16 ᵇ 4 Exodus 21:17; Lev. 20:9 ᶜ 9 Isaiah 29:13 ᵈ 14 Some manuscripts *blind guides of the blind*

"Send her away, for she keeps crying out after us."

²⁴He answered, "I was sent only to the lost sheep of Israel."

²⁵The woman came and knelt before him. "Lord, help me!" she said.

²⁶He replied, "It is not right to take the children's bread and toss it to the dogs."

²⁷"Yes it is, Lord," she said. "Even the dogs eat the crumbs that fall from their master's table."

²⁸Then Jesus said to her, "Woman, you have great faith! Your request is granted." And her daughter was healed at that moment.

ROCK SOLID
promises

"Woman, you have great faith! Your request is granted."

Matthew 15:28

Jesus expects you to expect him to do amazing things in your life.

Jesus Feeds the Four Thousand

²⁹Jesus left there and went along the Sea of Galilee. Then he went up on a mountainside and sat down. ³⁰Great crowds came to him, bringing the lame, the blind, the crippled, the mute and many others, and laid them at his feet; and he healed them. ³¹The people were amazed when they saw the mute speaking, the crippled made well, the lame walking and the blind seeing. And they praised the God of Israel.

³²Jesus called his disciples to him and said, "I have compassion for these people; they have already been with me three days and have nothing to eat. I do not want to send them away hungry, or they may collapse on the way."

³³His disciples answered, "Where could we get enough bread in this remote place to feed such a crowd?"

³⁴"How many loaves do you have?" Jesus asked.

"Seven," they replied, "and a few small fish."

³⁵He told the crowd to sit down on the ground. ³⁶Then he took the seven loaves and the fish, and when he had given thanks, he broke them and gave them to the disciples, and they in turn to the people. ³⁷They all ate and were satisfied. Afterward the disciples picked up seven basketfuls of broken pieces that were left over. ³⁸The number of those who ate was four thousand men, besides women and children. ³⁹After Jesus had sent the crowd away, he got into the boat and went to the vicinity of Magadan.

The Demand for a Sign

16 The Pharisees and Sadducees came to Jesus and tested him by asking him to show them a sign from heaven.

²He replied, "When evening comes, you say, 'It will be fair weather, for the sky is red,' ³and in the morning, 'Today it will be stormy, for the sky is red and overcast.' You know how to interpret the appearance of the sky, but you cannot interpret the signs of the times.ᵃ ⁴A wicked and adulterous generation looks for a sign, but none will be given it except the sign of Jonah." Jesus then left them and went away.

The Yeast of the Pharisees and Sadducees

⁵When they went across the lake, the disciples forgot to take bread. ⁶"Be careful," Jesus said to them. "Be on your guard against the yeast of the Pharisees and Sadducees."

⁷They discussed this among themselves and said, "It is because we didn't bring any bread."

⁸Aware of their discussion, Jesus asked,

ᵃ *2,3* Some early manuscripts do not have *When evening comes . . . of the times.*

"You of little faith, why are you talking among yourselves about having no bread? ⁹Do you still not understand? Don't you remember the five loaves for the five thousand, and how many basketfuls you gathered? ¹⁰Or the seven loaves for the four thousand, and how many basketfuls you gathered? ¹¹How is it you don't understand that I was not talking to you about bread? But be on your guard against the yeast of the Pharisees and Sadducees." ¹²Then they understood that he was not telling them to guard against the yeast used in bread, but against the teaching of the Pharisees and Sadducees.

Peter Declares That Jesus Is the Messiah

¹³When Jesus came to the region of Caesarea Philippi, he asked his disciples, "Who do people say the Son of Man is?" ¹⁴They replied, "Some say John the Baptist; others say Elijah; and still others, Jeremiah or one of the prophets." ¹⁵"But what about you?" he asked. "Who do you say I am?" ¹⁶Simon Peter answered, "You are the Messiah, the Son of the living God." ¹⁷Jesus replied, "Blessed are you, Simon son of Jonah, for this was not revealed to you by flesh and blood, but by my Father in heaven. ¹⁸And I tell you that you are Peter,ᵃ and on this rock I will build my church, and the gates of Hadesᵇ will not overcome it. ¹⁹I will give you the keys of the kingdom of heaven; whatever you bind on earth will beᶜ bound in heaven, and whatever you loose on earth will beᶜ loosed in heaven." ²⁰Then he ordered his disciples not to tell anyone that he was the Messiah.

Jesus Predicts His Death

²¹From that time on Jesus began to explain to his disciples that he must go to Jerusalem and suffer many things at the hands of the elders, the chief priests and the teachers of the law, and that he must be killed and on the third day be raised to life. ²²Peter took him aside and began to re-

buke him. "Never, Lord!" he said. "This shall never happen to you!"

²³Jesus turned and said to Peter, "Get behind me, Satan! You are a stumbling block to me; you do not have in mind the concerns of God, but merely human concerns."

²⁴Then Jesus said to his disciples,

ᵃ 18 The Greek word for *Peter* means *rock*.
ᵇ 18 That is, the realm of the dead
ᶜ 19 Or *will have been*

Matthew 16:13–20
Jesus is the Messiah.

Jesus wanted to know what the crowds thought of him, but he wasn't trying to win a popularity contest. He asked his 12 closest followers, "Who do people say the Son of Man is?" (Matthew 16:13). They reported some people thought he was John the Baptist, come back from the dead (see Matthew 14:2; 16:14). Others thought Elijah or another Old Testament prophet had returned (see Malachi 4:5–6). Jesus kept poking, however, to learn what his own disciples thought. Peter finally answered, "You are the Messiah, the Son of the living God" (Matthew 16:16). As these guys heard Jesus preach and saw him in action, they concluded he was more than an ordinary man. He was "the Messiah," or "the Christ," the Savior sent from God. He was the "Son of the living God," someone with the same nature as God. Jesus didn't reject these immense insights. He congratulated Peter on figuring out the truth.

Think: How would you answer Jesus if he asked you, "Who do you say I am"?

ROCK SOLID truths

MATTHEW 16

"Whoever wants to be my disciple must deny themselves and take up their cross and follow me. ²⁵For whoever wants to save their life*a* will lose it, but whoever loses their life for me will find it. ²⁶What good will it be for someone to gain the whole world, yet forfeit their soul? Or what can anyone give in exchange for their soul? ²⁷For the Son of Man is going to come in his Father's glory with his angels, and then he will reward each person according to what they have done.

²⁸"Truly I tell you, some who are standing here will not taste death before they see the Son of Man coming in his kingdom."

The Transfiguration

17 After six days Jesus took with him Peter, James and John the brother of James, and led them up a high mountain by themselves. ²There he was transfigured before them. His face shone like the sun, and his clothes became as white as the light. ³Just then there appeared before them Moses and Elijah, talking with Jesus.

⁴Peter said to Jesus, "Lord, it is good for us to be here. If you wish, I will put up three shelters—one for you, one for Moses and one for Elijah."

⁵While he was still speaking, a bright cloud covered them, and a voice from the cloud said, "This is my Son, whom I love; with him I am well pleased. Listen to him!"

⁶When the disciples heard this, they fell facedown to the ground, terrified. ⁷But Jesus came and touched them. "Get up," he said. "Don't be afraid." ⁸When they looked up, they saw no one except Jesus.

⁹As they were coming down the mountain, Jesus instructed them, "Don't tell anyone what you have seen, until the Son of Man has been raised from the dead."

¹⁰The disciples asked him, "Why then do the teachers of the law say that Elijah must come first?"

¹¹Jesus replied, "To be sure, Elijah comes and will restore all things. ¹²But I tell you, Elijah has already come, and they did not recognize him, but have done to

him everything they wished. In the same way the Son of Man is going to suffer at their hands." ¹³Then the disciples understood that he was talking to them about John the Baptist.

Jesus Heals a Demon-Possessed Boy

¹⁴When they came to the crowd, a man approached Jesus and knelt before him. ¹⁵"Lord, have mercy on my son," he said. "He has seizures and is suffering greatly. He often falls into the fire or into the water. ¹⁶I brought him to your disciples, but they could not heal him."

¹⁷"You unbelieving and perverse generation," Jesus replied, "how long shall I stay with you? How long shall I put up with you? Bring the boy here to me." ¹⁸Jesus rebuked the demon, and it came out of the boy, and he was healed at that moment.

¹⁹Then the disciples came to Jesus in private and asked, "Why couldn't we drive it out?"

²⁰He replied, "Because you have so little faith. Truly I tell you, if you have faith as small as a mustard seed, you can say to this mountain, 'Move from here to there,' and it will move. Nothing will be impossible for you." [21]*b*

Jesus Predicts His Death a Second Time

²²When they came together in Galilee, he said to them, "The Son of Man is going to be delivered into the hands of men. ²³They will kill him, and on the third day he will be raised to life." And the disciples were filled with grief.

The Temple Tax

²⁴After Jesus and his disciples arrived in Capernaum, the collectors of the two-drachma temple tax came to Peter and asked, "Doesn't your teacher pay the temple tax?"

²⁵"Yes, he does," he replied.

When Peter came into the house, Jesus was the first to speak. "What do you think,

a 25 The Greek word means either *life* or *soul*; also in verse 26. *b 21* Some manuscripts include here words similar to Mark 9:29.

1154

Simon?" he asked. "From whom do the kings of the earth collect duty and taxes—from their own children or from others?"

²⁶"From others," Peter answered.

"Then the children are exempt," Jesus said to him. ²⁷"But so that we may not cause offense, go to the lake and throw out your line. Take the first fish you catch; open its mouth and you will find a four-drachma coin. Take it and give it to them for my tax and yours."

The Greatest in the Kingdom of Heaven

18 At that time the disciples came to Jesus and asked, "Who, then, is the greatest in the kingdom of heaven?"

²He called a little child to him, and placed the child among them. ³And he said: "Truly I tell you, unless you change and become like little children, you will never enter the kingdom of heaven. ⁴Therefore, whoever takes the lowly position of this child is the greatest in the kingdom of heaven. ⁵And whoever welcomes one such child in my name welcomes me.

Causing to Stumble

⁶"If anyone causes one of these little ones—those who believe in me—to stumble, it would be better for them to have a large millstone hung around their neck and to be drowned in the depths of the sea. ⁷Woe to the world because of the things that cause people to stumble! Such things must come, but woe to the person through whom they come! ⁸If your hand or your foot causes you to stumble, cut it off and throw it away. It is better for you to enter life maimed or crippled than to have two hands or two feet and be thrown into eternal fire. ⁹And if your eye causes you to stumble, gouge it out and throw it away. It is better for you to enter life with one eye than to have two eyes and be thrown into the fire of hell.

The Parable of the Wandering Sheep

¹⁰"See that you do not despise one of these little ones. For I tell you that their angels in heaven always see the face of my Father in heaven. [11]^a

¹²"What do you think? If a man owns a hundred sheep, and one of them wanders away, will he not leave the ninety-nine on the hills and go to look for the one that wandered off? ¹³And if he finds it, truly I tell you, he is happier about that one sheep than about the ninety-nine that did not wander off. ¹⁴In the same way your Father in heaven is not willing that any of these little ones should perish.

Dealing With Sin in the Church

¹⁵"If your brother or sister^b sins,^c go and point out their fault, just between the two of you. If they listen to you, you have won them over. ¹⁶But if they will not listen, take one or two others along, so that 'every matter may be established by the testimony of two or three witnesses.'^d ¹⁷If they still refuse to listen, tell it to the church; and if they refuse to listen even to the church, treat them as you would a pagan or a tax collector.

¹⁸"Truly I tell you, whatever you bind on earth will be^e bound in heaven, and whatever you loose on earth will be^e loosed in heaven.

¹⁹"Again, truly I tell you that if two of you on earth agree about anything they ask for, it will be done for them by my Father in heaven. ²⁰For where two or three gather in my name, there am I with them."

The Parable of the Unmerciful Servant

²¹Then Peter came to Jesus and asked, "Lord, how many times shall I forgive my brother or sister who sins against me? Up to seven times?"

²²Jesus answered, "I tell you, not seven times, but seventy-seven times.^f

²³"Therefore, the kingdom of heaven is like a king who wanted to settle accounts with his servants. ²⁴As he began the settlement, a man who owed him ten

---

^a 11 Some manuscripts include here the words of Luke 19:10.   ^b 15 The Greek word for *brother or sister* (*adelphos*) refers here to a fellow disciple, whether man or woman; also in verses 21 and 35.   ^c 15 Some manuscripts *sins against you*   ^d 16 Deut. 19:15   ^e 18 Or *will have been*   ^f 22 Or *seventy times seven*

Matthew 18:15–17

Work it out.

Playing attack on their school lacrosse team, Kate, Layla and Carly didn't have the option not to work together. If they didn't find a way to get along, their team could say goodbye to ever scoring another goal. After one especially intense spat, the three girls stopped talking — to each other, that is. Kate told the rest of the team about their disagreement and tried to enlist their support. Layla went straight to the coach with a long list of gripes. And Carly stormed away and walled herself off from everyone. None of the girls cared about anything except being right, and working things out was the last thing any of them wanted to do.

Jesus doesn't make you wonder about the best way to solve conflict. He says the first and most crucial step you can take is to talk directly to a person who offends you. If you need help after that, look for a mutual friend who can help you keep talking. If a conflict gets out of control, that's when you need input from a trusted authority — someone you respect at home, school, or church.

thousand bags of gold*a* was brought to him. ²⁵ Since he was not able to pay, the master ordered that he and his wife and his children and all that he had be sold to repay the debt.

²⁶ "At this the servant fell on his knees before him. 'Be patient with me,' he begged, 'and I will pay back everything.' ²⁷ The servant's master took pity on him, canceled the debt and let him go.

²⁸ "But when that servant went out, he found one of his fellow servants who owed him a hundred silver coins.*b* He grabbed him and began to choke him. 'Pay back what you owe me!' he demanded.

²⁹ "His fellow servant fell to his knees and begged him, 'Be patient with me, and I will pay it back.'

³⁰ "But he refused. Instead, he went off and had the man thrown into prison until he could pay the debt. ³¹ When the other servants saw what had happened, they were outraged and went and told their master everything that had happened.

³² "Then the master called the servant in. 'You wicked servant,' he said, 'I canceled all that debt of yours because you begged me to. ³³ Shouldn't you have had mercy on your fellow servant just as I had on you?' ³⁴ In anger his master handed him over to the jailers to be tortured, until he should pay back all he owed.

³⁵ "This is how my heavenly Father will treat each of you unless you forgive your brother or sister from your heart."

Divorce

19

When Jesus had finished saying these things, he left Galilee and went into the region of Judea to the other side of the Jordan. ² Large crowds followed him, and he healed them there.

³ Some Pharisees came to him to test

---

a 24 Greek *ten thousand talents*; a talent was worth about 20 years of a day laborer's wages.
b 28 Greek *a hundred denarii*; a denarius was the usual daily wage of a day laborer (see 20:2).

him. They asked, "Is it lawful for a man to divorce his wife for any and every reason?"

[4] "Haven't you read," he replied, "that at the beginning the Creator 'made them male and female,'[a] [5] and said, 'For this reason a man will leave his father and mother and be united to his wife, and the two will become one flesh'[b]? [6] So they are no longer two, but one flesh. Therefore what God has joined together, let no one separate."

ROCK SOLID *promises*

"What God has joined together, let no one separate." Matthew 19:6

No marriage is doomed to end in divorce because God is the one who glues a husband and wife together.

---

[7] "Why then," they asked, "did Moses command that a man give his wife a certificate of divorce and send her away?"

[8] Jesus replied, "Moses permitted you to divorce your wives because your hearts were hard. But it was not this way from the beginning. [9] I tell you that anyone who divorces his wife, except for sexual immorality, and marries another woman commits adultery."

[10] The disciples said to him, "If this is the situation between a husband and wife, it is better not to marry."

[11] Jesus replied, "Not everyone can accept this word, but only those to whom it has been given. [12] For there are eunuchs who were born that way, and there are eunuchs who have been made eunuchs by others—and there are those who choose to live like eunuchs for the sake of the kingdom of heaven. The one who can accept this should accept it."

The Little Children and Jesus

[13] Then people brought little children to Jesus for him to place his hands on them and pray for them. But the disciples rebuked them.

[14] Jesus said, "Let the little children come to me, and do not hinder them, for the kingdom of heaven belongs to such as these." [15] When he had placed his hands on them, he went on from there.

The Rich and the Kingdom of God

[16] Just then a man came up to Jesus and asked, "Teacher, what good thing must I do to get eternal life?"

[17] "Why do you ask me about what is good?" Jesus replied. "There is only One who is good. If you want to enter life, keep the commandments."

[18] "Which ones?" he inquired.

Jesus replied, "'You shall not murder, you shall not commit adultery, you shall not steal, you shall not give false testimony, [19] honor your father and mother,'[c] and 'love your neighbor as yourself.'[d]"

[20] "All these I have kept," the young man said. "What do I still lack?"

[21] Jesus answered, "If you want to be perfect, go, sell your possessions and give to the poor, and you will have treasure in heaven. Then come, follow me."

[22] When the young man heard this, he went away sad, because he had great wealth.

[23] Then Jesus said to his disciples, "Truly I tell you, it is hard for someone who is rich to enter the kingdom of heaven. [24] Again I tell you, it is easier for a camel to go through the eye of a needle than for someone who is rich to enter the kingdom of God."

[25] When the disciples heard this, they were greatly astonished and asked, "Who then can be saved?"

[26] Jesus looked at them and said, "With man this is impossible, but with God all things are possible."

[27] Peter answered him, "We have left

---

[a] 4 Gen. 1:27   [b] 5 Gen. 2:24
[c] 19 Exodus 20:12-16; Deut. 5:16-20
[d] 19 Lev. 19:18

everything to follow you! What then will there be for us?"

²⁸Jesus said to them, "Truly I tell you, at the renewal of all things, when the Son of Man sits on his glorious throne, you who have followed me will also sit on twelve thrones, judging the twelve tribes of Israel. ²⁹And everyone who has left houses or brothers or sisters or father or mother or wife*a* or children or fields for my sake will receive a hundred times as much and will inherit eternal life. ³⁰But many who are first will be last, and many who are last will be first.

The Parable of the Workers in the Vineyard

20 "For the kingdom of heaven is like a landowner who went out early in the morning to hire workers for his vineyard. ²He agreed to pay them a denarius*b* for the day and sent them into his vineyard.

³"About nine in the morning he went out and saw others standing in the marketplace doing nothing. ⁴He told them, 'You also go and work in my vineyard, and I will pay you whatever is right.' ⁵So they went.

"He went out again about noon and about three in the afternoon and did the same thing. ⁶About five in the afternoon he went out and found still others standing around. He asked them, 'Why have you been standing here all day long doing nothing?'

⁷"'Because no one has hired us,' they answered.

"He said to them, 'You also go and work in my vineyard.'

⁸"When evening came, the owner of the vineyard said to his foreman, 'Call the workers and pay them their wages, beginning with the last ones hired and going on to the first.'

⁹"The workers who were hired about five in the afternoon came and each received a denarius. ¹⁰So when those came who were hired first, they expected to receive more. But each one of them also received a denarius. ¹¹When they received it, they began to

grumble against the landowner. ¹²'These who were hired last worked only one hour,' they said, 'and you have made them equal to us who have borne the burden of the work and the heat of the day.'

¹³"But he answered one of them, 'I am not being unfair to you, friend. Didn't you agree to work for a denarius? ¹⁴Take your pay and go. I want to give the one who was hired last the same as I gave you. ¹⁵Don't I have the right to do what I want with my own money? Or are you envious because I am generous?'

¹⁶"So the last will be first, and the first will be last."

Jesus Predicts His Death a Third Time

¹⁷Now Jesus was going up to Jerusalem. On the way, he took the Twelve aside and said to them, ¹⁸"We are going up to Jerusalem, and the Son of Man will be delivered over to the chief priests and the teachers of the law. They will condemn him to death ¹⁹and will hand him over to the Gentiles to be mocked and flogged and crucified. On the third day he will be raised to life!"

A Mother's Request

²⁰Then the mother of Zebedee's sons came to Jesus with her sons and, kneeling down, asked a favor of him.

²¹"What is it you want?" he asked.

She said, "Grant that one of these two sons of mine may sit at your right and the other at your left in your kingdom."

²²"You don't know what you are asking," Jesus said to them. "Can you drink the cup I am going to drink?"

"We can," they answered.

²³Jesus said to them, "You will indeed drink from my cup, but to sit at my right or left is not for me to grant. These places belong to those for whom they have been prepared by my Father."

²⁴When the ten heard about this, they were indignant with the two brothers. ²⁵Jesus called them together and said,

---

a 29 Some manuscripts do not have *or wife*.
b 2 A denarius was the usual daily wage of a day laborer.

"You know that the rulers of the Gentiles lord it over them, and their high officials exercise authority over them. [26] Not so with you. Instead, whoever wants to become great among you must be your servant, [27] and whoever wants to be first must be your slave— [28] just as the Son of Man did not come to be served, but to serve, and to give his life as a ransom for many."

Two Blind Men Receive Sight

[29] As Jesus and his disciples were leaving Jericho, a large crowd followed him. [30] Two blind men were sitting by the roadside, and when they heard that Jesus was going by, they shouted, "Lord, Son of David, have mercy on us!"

[31] The crowd rebuked them and told them to be quiet, but they shouted all the louder, "Lord, Son of David, have mercy on us!"

[32] Jesus stopped and called them. "What do you want me to do for you?" he asked.

[33] "Lord," they answered, "we want our sight."

[34] Jesus had compassion on them and touched their eyes. Immediately they received their sight and followed him.

Jesus Comes to Jerusalem as King

21 As they approached Jerusalem and came to Bethphage on the Mount of Olives, Jesus sent two disciples, [2] saying to them, "Go to the village ahead of you, and at once you will find a donkey tied there, with her colt by her. Untie them and bring them to me. [3] If anyone says anything to you, say that the Lord needs them, and he will send them right away."

[4] This took place to fulfill what was spoken through the prophet:

[5] "Say to Daughter Zion,
'See, your king comes to you,
gentle and riding on a donkey,
and on a colt, the foal of a donkey.'"[a]

[6] The disciples went and did as Jesus had instructed them. [7] They brought the donkey and the colt and placed their cloaks on them for Jesus to sit on. [8] A very large crowd spread their cloaks on the road, while others cut branches from the trees and spread them on the road. [9] The crowds that went ahead of him and those that followed shouted,

"Hosanna[b] to the Son of David!"

"Blessed is he who comes in the name
of the Lord!"[c]

"Hosanna[b] in the highest heaven!"

[10] When Jesus entered Jerusalem, the whole city was stirred and asked, "Who is this?"

[11] The crowds answered, "This is Jesus, the prophet from Nazareth in Galilee."

Jesus at the Temple

[12] Jesus entered the temple courts and drove out all who were buying and selling there. He overturned the tables of the money changers and the benches of those selling doves. [13] "It is written," he said to them, "'My house will be called a house of prayer,'[d] but you are making it 'a den of robbers.'[e]"

[14] The blind and the lame came to him at the temple, and he healed them. [15] But when the chief priests and the teachers of the law saw the wonderful things he did and the children shouting in the temple courts, "Hosanna to the Son of David," they were indignant.

[16] "Do you hear what these children are saying?" they asked him.

"Yes," replied Jesus, "have you never read,

"'From the lips of children and infants
you, Lord, have called forth your
praise'[f]?"

[17] And he left them and went out of the city to Bethany, where he spent the night.

Jesus Curses a Fig Tree

[18] Early in the morning, as Jesus was on his way back to the city, he was hungry.

---

[a] 5 Zech. 9:9   [b] 9 A Hebrew expression meaning "Save!" which became an exclamation of praise; also in verse 15
[c] 9 Psalm 118:25,26   [d] 13 Isaiah 56:7
[e] 13 Jer. 7:11   [f] 16 Psalm 8:2 (see Septuagint)

¹⁹Seeing a fig tree by the road, he went up to it but found nothing on it except leaves. Then he said to it, "May you never bear fruit again!" Immediately the tree withered.

²⁰When the disciples saw this, they were amazed. "How did the fig tree wither so quickly?" they asked.

²¹Jesus replied, "Truly I tell you, if you have faith and do not doubt, not only can you do what was done to the fig tree, but also you can say to this mountain, 'Go, throw yourself into the sea,' and it will be done. ²²If you believe, you will receive whatever you ask for in prayer."

The Authority of Jesus Questioned

²³Jesus entered the temple courts, and, while he was teaching, the chief priests and the elders of the people came to him. "By what authority are you doing these things?" they asked. "And who gave you this authority?"

²⁴Jesus replied, "I will also ask you one question. If you answer me, I will tell you by what authority I am doing these things. ²⁵John's baptism—where did it come from? Was it from heaven, or of human origin?"

They discussed it among themselves and said, "If we say, 'From heaven,' he will ask, 'Then why didn't you believe him?' ²⁶But if we say, 'Of human origin'—we are afraid of the people, for they all hold that John was a prophet."

²⁷So they answered Jesus, "We don't know."

Then he said, "Neither will I tell you by what authority I am doing these things.

The Parable of the Two Sons

²⁸"What do you think? There was a man who had two sons. He went to the first and said, 'Son, go and work today in the vineyard.'

²⁹"'I will not,' he answered, but later he changed his mind and went.

³⁰"Then the father went to the other son and said the same thing. He answered, 'I will, sir,' but he did not go.

³¹"Which of the two did what his father wanted?"

"The first," they answered.

Jesus said to them, "Truly I tell you, the tax collectors and the prostitutes are entering the kingdom of God ahead of you. ³²For John came to you to show you the way of righteousness, and you did not believe him, but the tax collectors and the prostitutes did. And even after you saw this, you did not repent and believe him.

The Parable of the Tenants

³³"Listen to another parable: There was a landowner who planted a vineyard. He put a wall around it, dug a winepress in it and built a watchtower. Then he rented the vineyard to some farmers and moved to another place. ³⁴When the harvest time approached, he sent his servants to the tenants to collect his fruit.

³⁵"The tenants seized his servants; they beat one, killed another, and stoned a third. ³⁶Then he sent other servants to them, more than the first time, and the tenants treated them the same way. ³⁷Last of all, he sent his son to them. 'They will respect my son,' he said.

³⁸"But when the tenants saw the son, they said to each other, 'This is the heir. Come, let's kill him and take his inheritance.' ³⁹So they took him and threw him out of the vineyard and killed him.

⁴⁰"Therefore, when the owner of the vineyard comes, what will he do to those tenants?"

⁴¹"He will bring those wretches to a wretched end," they replied, "and he will rent the vineyard to other tenants, who will give him his share of the crop at harvest time."

⁴²Jesus said to them, "Have you never read in the Scriptures:

"'The stone the builders rejected
　has become the cornerstone;
the Lord has done this,
　and it is marvelous in our eyes'ᵃ?

⁴³"Therefore I tell you that the kingdom of God will be taken away from you and given to a people who will produce its fruit. ⁴⁴Anyone who falls on this stone

ᵃ 42 Psalm 118:22,23

will be broken to pieces; anyone on whom it falls will be crushed."[a]

⁴⁵When the chief priests and the Pharisees heard Jesus' parables, they knew he was talking about them. ⁴⁶They looked for a way to arrest him, but they were afraid of the crowd because the people held that he was a prophet.

The Parable of the Wedding Banquet

22 Jesus spoke to them again in parables, saying: ²"The kingdom of heaven is like a king who prepared a wedding banquet for his son. ³He sent his servants to those who had been invited to the banquet to tell them to come, but they refused to come.

⁴"Then he sent some more servants and said, 'Tell those who have been invited that I have prepared my dinner: My oxen and fattened cattle have been butchered, and everything is ready. Come to the wedding banquet.'

⁵"But they paid no attention and went off—one to his field, another to his business. ⁶The rest seized his servants, mistreated them and killed them. ⁷The king was enraged. He sent his army and destroyed those murderers and burned their city.

⁸"Then he said to his servants, 'The wedding banquet is ready, but those I invited did not deserve to come. ⁹So go to the street corners and invite to the banquet anyone you find.' ¹⁰So the servants went out into the streets and gathered all the people they could find, the bad as well as the good, and the wedding hall was filled with guests.

¹¹"But when the king came in to see the guests, he noticed a man there who was not wearing wedding clothes. ¹²He asked, 'How did you get in here without wedding clothes, friend?' The man was speechless.

¹³"Then the king told the attendants, 'Tie him hand and foot, and throw him outside, into the darkness, where there will be weeping and gnashing of teeth.'

¹⁴"For many are invited, but few are chosen."

Paying the Imperial Tax to Caesar

¹⁵Then the Pharisees went out and laid plans to trap him in his words. ¹⁶They sent their disciples to him along with the Herodians. "Teacher," they said, "we know that you are a man of integrity and that you teach the way of God in accordance with the truth. You aren't swayed by others, because you pay no attention to who they are. ¹⁷Tell us then, what is your opinion? Is it right to pay the imperial tax[b] to Caesar or not?"

¹⁸But Jesus, knowing their evil intent, said, "You hypocrites, why are you trying to trap me? ¹⁹Show me the coin used for paying the tax." They brought him a denarius, ²⁰and he asked them, "Whose image is this? And whose inscription?"

²¹"Caesar's," they replied.

Then he said to them, "So give back to Caesar what is Caesar's, and to God what is God's."

²²When they heard this, they were amazed. So they left him and went away.

Marriage at the Resurrection

²³That same day the Sadducees, who say there is no resurrection, came to him with a question. ²⁴"Teacher," they said, "Moses told us that if a man dies without having children, his brother must marry the widow and raise up offspring for him. ²⁵Now there were seven brothers among us. The first one married and died, and since he had no children, he left his wife to his brother. ²⁶The same thing happened to the second and third brother, right on down to the seventh. ²⁷Finally, the woman died. ²⁸Now then, at the resurrection, whose wife will she be of the seven, since all of them were married to her?"

²⁹Jesus replied, "You are in error because you do not know the Scriptures or the power of God. ³⁰At the resurrection people will neither marry nor be given in marriage; they will be like the angels in heaven. ³¹But about the resurrection of the dead—have you not read what God said to you, ³²'I am the God of Abraham, the God of Isaac, and the God of Jacob'[c]? He is not the God of the dead but of the living."

---

[a] 44 Some manuscripts do not have verse 44.
[b] 17 A special tax levied on subject peoples, not on Roman citizens   [c] 32 Exodus 3:6

33When the crowds heard this, they were astonished at his teaching.

The Greatest Commandment

34Hearing that Jesus had silenced the Sadducees, the Pharisees got together. 35One of them, an expert in the law, tested him with this question: 36"Teacher, which is the greatest commandment in the Law?"

37Jesus replied: "'Love the Lord your God with all your heart and with all your soul and with all your mind.'*a* 38This is the first and greatest commandment. 39And the second is like it: 'Love your neighbor as yourself.'*b* 40All the Law and the Prophets hang on these two commandments."

Whose Son Is the Messiah?

41While the Pharisees were gathered together, Jesus asked them, 42"What do you think about the Messiah? Whose son is he?"

"The son of David," they replied.

43He said to them, "How is it then that David, speaking by the Spirit, calls him 'Lord'? For he says,

44"'The Lord said to my Lord:
  "Sit at my right hand
  until I put your enemies
    under your feet."'*c*

45If then David calls him 'Lord,' how can he be his son?" 46No one could say a word in reply, and from that day on no one dared to ask him any more questions.

A Warning Against Hypocrisy

23 Then Jesus said to the crowds and to his disciples: 2"The teachers of the law and the Pharisees sit in Moses' seat. 3So you must be careful to do everything they tell you. But do not do what they do, for they do not practice what they preach. 4They tie up heavy, cumbersome loads and put them on other people's shoulders, but they themselves are not willing to lift a finger to move them.

5"Everything they do is done for people to see: They make their phylacteries*d* wide

and the tassels on their garments long; 6they love the place of honor at banquets and the most important seats in the synagogues; 7they love to be greeted with respect in the marketplaces and to be called 'Rabbi' by others.

8"But you are not to be called 'Rabbi,' for you have one Teacher, and you are all brothers. 9And do not call anyone on earth 'father,' for you have one Father, and he is in heaven. 10Nor are you to be called instructors, for you have one Instructor, the Messiah. 11The greatest among you will be your servant. 12For those who exalt themselves will be humbled, and those who humble themselves will be exalted.

Seven Woes on the Teachers of the Law and the Pharisees

13"Woe to you, teachers of the law and Pharisees, you hypocrites! You shut the door of the kingdom of heaven in people's faces. You yourselves do not enter, nor will you let those enter who are trying to. [14]*e*

15"Woe to you, teachers of the law and Pharisees, you hypocrites! You travel over land and sea to win a single convert, and when you have succeeded, you make them twice as much a child of hell as you are.

16"Woe to you, blind guides! You say, 'If anyone swears by the temple, it means nothing; but anyone who swears by the gold of the temple is bound by that oath.' 17You blind fools! Which is greater: the gold, or the temple that makes the gold sacred? 18You also say, 'If anyone swears by the altar, it means nothing; but anyone who swears by the gift on the altar is bound by that oath.' 19You blind men! Which is greater: the gift, or the altar that makes the gift sacred? 20Therefore, anyone who swears by the altar swears by it and by everything on it. 21And anyone who swears by the temple swears by it and by the one who dwells in it. 22And

a 37 Deut. 6:5   *b 39* Lev. 19:18
c 44 Psalm 110:1   *d 5* That is, boxes containing Scripture verses, worn on forehead and arm   *e 14* Some manuscripts include here words similar to Mark 12:40 and Luke 20:47.

anyone who swears by heaven swears by God's throne and by the one who sits on it.

²³"Woe to you, teachers of the law and Pharisees, you hypocrites! You give a tenth of your spices—mint, dill and cumin. But you have neglected the more important matters of the law—justice, mercy and faithfulness. You should have practiced the latter, without neglecting the former. ²⁴You blind guides! You strain out a gnat but swallow a camel.

²⁵"Woe to you, teachers of the law and Pharisees, you hypocrites! You clean the outside of the cup and dish, but inside they are full of greed and self-indulgence. ²⁶Blind Pharisee! First clean the inside of the cup and dish, and then the outside also will be clean.

²⁷"Woe to you, teachers of the law and Pharisees, you hypocrites! You are like whitewashed tombs, which look beautiful on the outside but on the inside are full of the bones of the dead and everything unclean. ²⁸In the same way, on the outside you appear to people as righteous but on the inside you are full of hypocrisy and wickedness.

²⁹"Woe to you, teachers of the law and Pharisees, you hypocrites! You build tombs for the prophets and decorate the graves of the righteous. ³⁰And you say, 'If we had lived in the days of our ancestors, we would not have taken part with them in shedding the blood of the prophets.' ³¹So you testify against yourselves that you are the descendants of those who murdered the prophets. ³²Go ahead, then, and complete what your ancestors started!

³³"You snakes! You brood of vipers! How will you escape being condemned to hell? ³⁴Therefore I am sending you prophets and sages and teachers. Some of them you will kill and crucify; others you will flog in your synagogues and pursue from town to town. ³⁵And so upon you will come all the righteous blood that has been shed on earth, from the blood of righteous Abel to the blood of Zechariah son of Berekiah, whom you murdered between the

Matthew 23:25–28

God hates hypocrisy.

Jesus blasted the Pharisees with the harshest words he could find. He labeled them "hypocrites," an ugly name that means "to play a part," or "to wear a mask" like an ancient actor. Jesus knew that these religious leaders weren't what they seemed. They sparkled like freshly washed cups and dishes on the outside, but they were full of filthy sins on the inside. They were like tombs that had been scrubbed clean but still reeked of death. Jesus said there was a fix for their hypocrisy. If they wanted to be truly spiritual, they should "First clean the inside of the cup and dish, and then the outside also will be clean" (Matthew 23:26). They needed to let God make their thoughts and attitudes clean, and then their actions would be truly pure as well. And if they didn't stop living as fakes, they could only expect "woe," calamity, and damnation sent by the Lord.

Think: Why does God get even angrier about hypocrisy than we do?

ROCK SOLID truths

temple and the altar. ³⁶Truly I tell you, all this will come on this generation.

³⁷"Jerusalem, Jerusalem, you who kill the prophets and stone those sent to you, how often I have longed to gather your children together, as a hen gathers her chicks under her wings, and you were not willing. ³⁸Look, your house is left to you desolate. ³⁹For I tell you, you will not see me again until you say, 'Blessed is he who comes in the name of the Lord.'ᵃ

ᵃ 39 Psalm 118:26

The Destruction of the Temple and Signs of the End Times

24 Jesus left the temple and was walking away when his disciples came up to him to call his attention to its buildings. [2] "Do you see all these things?" he asked. "Truly I tell you, not one stone here will be left on another; every one will be thrown down."

[3] As Jesus was sitting on the Mount of Olives, the disciples came to him privately. "Tell us," they said, "when will this happen, and what will be the sign of your coming and of the end of the age?"

[4] Jesus answered: "Watch out that no one deceives you. [5] For many will come in my name, claiming, 'I am the Messiah,' and will deceive many. [6] You will hear of wars and rumors of wars, but see to it that you are not alarmed. Such things must happen, but the end is still to come. [7] Nation will rise against nation, and kingdom against kingdom. There will be famines and earthquakes in various places. [8] All these are the beginning of birth pains.

[9] "Then you will be handed over to be persecuted and put to death, and you will be hated by all nations because of me. [10] At that time many will turn away from the faith and will betray and hate each other, [11] and many false prophets will appear and deceive many people. [12] Because of the increase of wickedness, the love of most will grow cold, [13] but the one who stands firm to the end will be saved. [14] And this gospel of the kingdom will be preached in the whole world as a testimony to all nations, and then the end will come.

[15] "So when you see standing in the holy place 'the abomination that causes desolation,'[a] spoken of through the prophet Daniel—let the reader understand— [16] then let those who are in Judea flee to the mountains. [17] Let no one on the housetop go down to take anything out of the house. [18] Let no one in the field go back to get their cloak. [19] How dreadful it will be in those days for pregnant women and nursing mothers! [20] Pray that your flight will not take place in winter or on the Sabbath. [21] For then there will be great distress, un-

equaled from the beginning of the world until now—and never to be equaled again.

[22] "If those days had not been cut short, no one would survive, but for the sake of the elect those days will be shortened. [23] At that time if anyone says to you, 'Look, here is the Messiah!' or, 'There he is!' do not believe it. [24] For false messiahs and false prophets will appear and perform great signs and wonders to deceive, if possible, even the elect. [25] See, I have told you ahead of time.

[26] "So if anyone tells you, 'There he is, out in the wilderness,' do not go out; or, 'Here he is, in the inner rooms,' do not believe it. [27] For as lightning that comes from the east is visible even in the west, so will be the coming of the Son of Man. [28] Wherever there is a carcass, there the vultures will gather.

[29] "Immediately after the distress of those days

> "'the sun will be darkened,
>   and the moon will not give its light;
> the stars will fall from the sky,
>   and the heavenly bodies will be
>   shaken.'[b]

[30] "Then will appear the sign of the Son of Man in heaven. And then all the peoples of the earth[c] will mourn when they see the Son of Man coming on the clouds of heaven, with power and great glory.[d] [31] And he will send his angels with a loud trumpet call, and they will gather his elect from the four winds, from one end of the heavens to the other.

[32] "Now learn this lesson from the fig tree: As soon as its twigs get tender and its leaves come out, you know that summer is near. [33] Even so, when you see all these things, you know that it[e] is near, right at the door. [34] Truly I tell you, this generation will certainly not pass away until all these things have happened. [35] Heaven and earth will pass away, but my words will never pass away.

---

[a] 15 Daniel 9:27; 11:31; 12:11
[b] 29 Isaiah 13:10; 34:4   [c] 30 Or the tribes of the land   [d] 30 See Daniel 7:13-14.
[e] 33 Or he

The Day and Hour Unknown

36 "But about that day or hour no one knows, not even the angels in heaven, nor the Son,[a] but only the Father. 37 As it was in the days of Noah, so it will be at the coming of the Son of Man. 38 For in the days before the flood, people were eating and drinking, marrying and giving in marriage, up to the day Noah entered the ark; 39 and they knew nothing about what would happen until the flood came and took them all away. That is how it will be at the coming of the Son of Man. 40 Two men will be in the field; one will be taken and the other left. 41 Two women will be grinding with a hand mill; one will be taken and the other left.

42 "Therefore keep watch, because you do not know on what day your Lord will come. 43 But understand this: If the owner of the house had known at what time of night the thief was coming, he would have kept watch and would not have let his house be broken into. 44 So you also must be ready, because the Son of Man will come at an hour when you do not expect him.

45 "Who then is the faithful and wise servant, whom the master has put in charge of the servants in his household to give them their food at the proper time? 46 It will be good for that servant whose master finds him doing so when he returns. 47 Truly I tell you, he will put him in charge of all his possessions. 48 But suppose that servant is wicked and says to himself, 'My master is staying away a long time,' 49 and he then begins to beat his fellow servants and to eat and drink with drunkards. 50 The master of that servant will come on a day when he does not expect him and at an hour he is not aware of. 51 He will cut him to pieces and assign him a place with the hypocrites, where there will be weeping and gnashing of teeth.

The Parable of the Ten Virgins

25 "At that time the kingdom of heaven will be like ten virgins who took their lamps and went out to meet the bridegroom.

2 Five of them were foolish and five were wise. 3 The foolish ones took their lamps but did not take any oil with them. 4 The wise ones, however, took oil in jars along with their lamps. 5 The bridegroom was a long time in coming, and they all became drowsy and fell asleep.

6 "At midnight the cry rang out: 'Here's the bridegroom! Come out to meet him!'

7 "Then all the virgins woke up and trimmed their lamps. 8 The foolish ones said to the wise, 'Give us some of your oil; our lamps are going out.'

9 " 'No,' they replied, 'there may not be enough for both us and you. Instead, go to those who sell oil and buy some for yourselves.'

10 "But while they were on their way to buy the oil, the bridegroom arrived. The virgins who were ready went in with him to the wedding banquet. And the door was shut.

11 "Later the others also came. 'Lord, Lord,' they said, 'open the door for us!'

12 "But he replied, 'Truly I tell you, I don't know you.'

13 "Therefore keep watch, because you do not know the day or the hour.

The Parable of the Bags of Gold

14 "Again, it will be like a man going on a journey, who called his servants and entrusted his wealth to them. 15 To one he gave five bags of gold, to another two bags, and to another one bag,[b] each according to his ability. Then he went on his journey. 16 The man who had received five bags of gold went at once and put his money to work and gained five bags more. 17 So also, the one with two bags of gold gained two more. 18 But the man who had received one bag went off, dug a hole in the ground and hid his master's money.

19 "After a long time the master of those servants returned and settled accounts with them. 20 The man who had received five bags of gold brought the other five.

---

[a] 36 Some manuscripts do not have *nor the Son.*
[b] 15 Greek *five talents . . . two talents . . . one talent*; also throughout this parable; a talent was worth about 20 years of a day laborer's wage.

'Master,' he said, 'you entrusted me with five bags of gold. See, I have gained five more.'

²¹"His master replied, 'Well done, good and faithful servant! You have been faithful with a few things; I will put you in charge of many things. Come and share your master's happiness!'

²²"The man with two bags of gold also came. 'Master,' he said, 'you entrusted me with two bags of gold; see, I have gained two more.'

²³"His master replied, 'Well done, good and faithful servant! You have been faithful with a few things; I will put you in charge of many things. Come and share your master's happiness!'

²⁴"Then the man who had received one bag of gold came. 'Master,' he said, 'I knew that you are a hard man, harvesting where you have not sown and gathering where you have not scattered seed. ²⁵So I was afraid and went out and hid your gold in the ground. See, here is what belongs to you.'

²⁶"His master replied, 'You wicked, lazy servant! So you knew that I harvest where I have not sown and gather where I have not scattered seed? ²⁷Well then, you should have put my money on deposit with the bankers, so that when I returned I would have received it back with interest.

²⁸"'So take the bag of gold from him and give it to the one who has ten bags. ²⁹For whoever has will be given more, and they will have an abundance. Whoever does not have, even what they have will be taken from them. ³⁰And throw that worthless servant outside, into the darkness, where there will be weeping and gnashing of teeth.'

The Sheep and the Goats

³¹"When the Son of Man comes in his glory, and all the angels with him, he will sit on his glorious throne. ³²All the nations will be gathered before him, and he will separate the people one from another as a shepherd separates the sheep from the goats. ³³He will put the sheep on his right and the goats on his left.

³⁴"Then the King will say to those on his right, 'Come, you who are blessed by my Father; take your inheritance, the kingdom prepared for you since the creation of the world. ³⁵For I was hungry and you gave me something to eat, I was thirsty and you gave me something to drink, I was a stranger and you invited me in, ³⁶I needed clothes and you clothed me, I was sick and you looked after me, I was in prison and you came to visit me.'

³⁷"Then the righteous will answer him, 'Lord, when did we see you hungry and feed you, or thirsty and give you something to drink? ³⁸When did we see you a stranger and invite you in, or needing clothes and clothe you? ³⁹When did we see you sick or in prison and go to visit you?'

⁴⁰"The King will reply, 'Truly I tell you, whatever you did for one of the least of these brothers and sisters of mine, you did for me.'

⁴¹"Then he will say to those on his left, 'Depart from me, you who are cursed, into the eternal fire prepared for the devil and his angels. ⁴²For I was hungry and you gave me nothing to eat, I was thirsty and you gave me nothing to drink, ⁴³I was a stranger and you did not invite me in, I needed clothes and you did not clothe me, I was sick and in prison and you did not look after me.'

⁴⁴"They also will answer, 'Lord, when did we see you hungry or thirsty or a stranger or needing clothes or sick or in prison, and did not help you?'

⁴⁵"He will reply, 'Truly I tell you, whatever you did not do for one of the least of these, you did not do for me.'

⁴⁶"Then they will go away to eternal punishment, but the righteous to eternal life."

The Plot Against Jesus

26 When Jesus had finished saying all these things, he said to his disciples, ²"As you know, the Passover is two days away—and the Son of Man will be handed over to be crucified."

³Then the chief priests and the elders

of the people assembled in the palace of the high priest, whose name was Caiaphas, ⁴and they schemed to arrest Jesus secretly and kill him. ⁵"But not during the festival," they said, "or there may be a riot among the people."

Jesus Anointed at Bethany

⁶While Jesus was in Bethany in the home of Simon the Leper, ⁷a woman came to him with an alabaster jar of very expensive perfume, which she poured on his head as he was reclining at the table.

⁸When the disciples saw this, they were indignant. "Why this waste?" they asked. ⁹"This perfume could have been sold at a high price and the money given to the poor."

¹⁰Aware of this, Jesus said to them, "Why are you bothering this woman? She has done a beautiful thing to me. ¹¹The poor you will always have with you,ᵃ but you will not always have me. ¹²When she poured this perfume on my body, she did it to prepare me for burial. ¹³Truly I tell you, wherever this gospel is preached throughout the world, what she has done will also be told, in memory of her."

Judas Agrees to Betray Jesus

¹⁴Then one of the Twelve—the one called Judas Iscariot—went to the chief priests ¹⁵and asked, "What are you willing to give me if I deliver him over to you?" So they counted out for him thirty pieces of silver. ¹⁶From then on Judas watched for an opportunity to hand him over.

The Last Supper

¹⁷On the first day of the Festival of Unleavened Bread, the disciples came to Jesus and asked, "Where do you want us to make preparations for you to eat the Passover?"

¹⁸He replied, "Go into the city to a certain man and tell him, 'The Teacher says: My appointed time is near. I am going to celebrate the Passover with my disciples at your house.'" ¹⁹So the disciples did as Jesus had directed them and prepared the Passover.

²⁰When evening came, Jesus was reclining at the table with the Twelve. ²¹And while they were eating, he said, "Truly I tell you, one of you will betray me."

²²They were very sad and began to say to him one after the other, "Surely you don't mean me, Lord?"

ᵃ *11* See Deut. 15:11.

Matthew 26:17–30

Communion remembers Jesus' death.

"Communion" is an act of worship where Christians consume bread and wine (or grape juice) to remember Jesus' death on the cross. Along with baptism (see Matthew 28:18–20), it's one of two "ordinances" or "sacraments" Jesus himself commanded us to practice until he comes back. The Lord gave instructions for communion the night before he died on the cross. He was sharing the Jewish Passover meal (see Exodus 12:1–14) with his closest followers, but he gave two elements of that meal a new meaning. He passed the bread and said, "Take and eat; this is my body" (Matthew 26:26). Then he handed around the cup and said, "This is my blood" (Matthew 26:28). The bread and wine were signs of a new "covenant" or "agreement" established by God. As payment for our sins, Jesus' body would be broken and his blood poured out. His death would make it possible for us to be forgiven and live forever with God.

Think: Why do we celebrate communion? What does it mean to you?

ROCK SOLID truths

²³Jesus replied, "The one who has dipped his hand into the bowl with me will betray me. ²⁴The Son of Man will go just as it is written about him. But woe to that man who betrays the Son of Man! It would be better for him if he had not been born."

²⁵Then Judas, the one who would betray him, said, "Surely you don't mean me, Rabbi?"

Jesus answered, "You have said so."

²⁶While they were eating, Jesus took bread, and when he had given thanks, he broke it and gave it to his disciples, saying, "Take and eat; this is my body."

²⁷Then he took a cup, and when he had given thanks, he gave it to them, saying, "Drink from it, all of you. ²⁸This is my blood of the*a* covenant, which is poured out for many for the forgiveness of sins. ²⁹I tell you, I will not drink from this fruit of the vine from now on until that day when I drink it new with you in my Father's kingdom."

³⁰When they had sung a hymn, they went out to the Mount of Olives.

Jesus Predicts Peter's Denial

³¹Then Jesus told them, "This very night you will all fall away on account of me, for it is written:

> "'I will strike the shepherd,
> and the sheep of the flock will be
> scattered.'*b*

³²But after I have risen, I will go ahead of you into Galilee."

³³Peter replied, "Even if all fall away on account of you, I never will."

³⁴"Truly I tell you," Jesus answered, "this very night, before the rooster crows, you will disown me three times."

³⁵But Peter declared, "Even if I have to die with you, I will never disown you." And all the other disciples said the same.

Gethsemane

³⁶Then Jesus went with his disciples to a place called Gethsemane, and he said to them, "Sit here while I go over there and pray." ³⁷He took Peter and the two sons of Zebedee along with him, and he began to be sorrowful and troubled. ³⁸Then he said to them, "My soul is overwhelmed with sorrow to the point of death. Stay here and keep watch with me."

³⁹Going a little farther, he fell with his face to the ground and prayed, "My Father, if it is possible, may this cup be taken from me. Yet not as I will, but as you will."

⁴⁰Then he returned to his disciples and found them sleeping. "Couldn't you men keep watch with me for one hour?" he asked Peter. ⁴¹"Watch and pray so that you will not fall into temptation. The spirit is willing, but the flesh is weak."

⁴²He went away a second time and prayed, "My Father, if it is not possible for this cup to be taken away unless I drink it, may your will be done."

⁴³When he came back, he again found them sleeping, because their eyes were heavy. ⁴⁴So he left them and went away once more and prayed the third time, saying the same thing.

⁴⁵Then he returned to the disciples and said to them, "Are you still sleeping and resting? Look, the hour has come, and the Son of Man is delivered into the hands of sinners. ⁴⁶Rise! Let us go! Here comes my betrayer!"

Jesus Arrested

⁴⁷While he was still speaking, Judas, one of the Twelve, arrived. With him was a large crowd armed with swords and clubs, sent from the chief priests and the elders of the people. ⁴⁸Now the betrayer had arranged a signal with them: "The one I kiss is the man; arrest him." ⁴⁹Going at once to Jesus, Judas said, "Greetings, Rabbi!" and kissed him.

⁵⁰Jesus replied, "Do what you came for, friend."*c*

Then the men stepped forward, seized Jesus and arrested him. ⁵¹With that, one of Jesus' companions reached for his sword, drew it out and struck the servant of the high priest, cutting off his ear.

⁵²"Put your sword back in its place,"

---

a 28 Some manuscripts *the new*   *b 31* Zech. 13:7
c 50 Or *"Why have you come, friend?"*

Jesus said to him, "for all who draw the sword will die by the sword. ⁵³Do you think I cannot call on my Father, and he will at once put at my disposal more than twelve legions of angels? ⁵⁴But how then would the Scriptures be fulfilled that say it must happen in this way?"

⁵⁵In that hour Jesus said to the crowd, "Am I leading a rebellion, that you have come out with swords and clubs to capture me? Every day I sat in the temple courts teaching, and you did not arrest me. ⁵⁶But this has all taken place that the writings of the prophets might be fulfilled." Then all the disciples deserted him and fled.

Jesus Before the Sanhedrin

⁵⁷Those who had arrested Jesus took him to Caiaphas the high priest, where the teachers of the law and the elders had assembled. ⁵⁸But Peter followed him at a distance, right up to the courtyard of the high priest. He entered and sat down with the guards to see the outcome.

⁵⁹The chief priests and the whole Sanhedrin were looking for false evidence against Jesus so that they could put him to death. ⁶⁰But they did not find any, though many false witnesses came forward.

Finally two came forward ⁶¹and declared, "This fellow said, 'I am able to destroy the temple of God and rebuild it in three days.'"

⁶²Then the high priest stood up and said to Jesus, "Are you not going to answer? What is this testimony that these men are bringing against you?" ⁶³But Jesus remained silent.

The high priest said to him, "I charge you under oath by the living God: Tell us if you are the Messiah, the Son of God."

⁶⁴"You have said so," Jesus replied. "But I say to all of you: From now on you will see the Son of Man sitting at the right hand of the Mighty One and coming on the clouds of heaven."[a]

⁶⁵Then the high priest tore his clothes and said, "He has spoken blasphemy! Why do we need any more witnesses? Look, now you have heard the blasphemy. ⁶⁶What do you think?"

"He is worthy of death," they answered.

⁶⁷Then they spit in his face and struck him with their fists. Others slapped him ⁶⁸and said, "Prophesy to us, Messiah. Who hit you?"

Peter Disowns Jesus

⁶⁹Now Peter was sitting out in the courtyard, and a servant girl came to him. "You also were with Jesus of Galilee," she said.

⁷⁰But he denied it before them all. "I don't know what you're talking about," he said.

⁷¹Then he went out to the gateway, where another servant girl saw him and said to the people there, "This fellow was with Jesus of Nazareth."

⁷²He denied it again, with an oath: "I don't know the man!"

⁷³After a little while, those standing there went up to Peter and said, "Surely you are one of them; your accent gives you away."

⁷⁴Then he began to call down curses, and he swore to them, "I don't know the man!"

Immediately a rooster crowed. ⁷⁵Then Peter remembered the word Jesus had spoken: "Before the rooster crows, you will disown me three times." And he went outside and wept bitterly.

Judas Hangs Himself

27 Early in the morning, all the chief priests and the elders of the people made their plans how to have Jesus executed. ²So they bound him, led him away and handed him over to Pilate the governor.

³When Judas, who had betrayed him, saw that Jesus was condemned, he was seized with remorse and returned the thirty pieces of silver to the chief priests and the elders. ⁴"I have sinned," he said, "for I have betrayed innocent blood."

"What is that to us?" they replied. "That's your responsibility."

⁵So Judas threw the money into the temple and left. Then he went away and hanged himself.

---

a 64 See Psalm 110:1; Daniel 7:13.

[6]The chief priests picked up the coins and said, "It is against the law to put this into the treasury, since it is blood money." [7]So they decided to use the money to buy the potter's field as a burial place for foreigners. [8]That is why it has been called the Field of Blood to this day. [9]Then what was spoken by Jeremiah the prophet was fulfilled: "They took the thirty pieces of silver, the price set on him by the people of Israel, [10]and they used them to buy the potter's field, as the Lord commanded me."[a]

Jesus Before Pilate

[11]Meanwhile Jesus stood before the governor, and the governor asked him, "Are you the king of the Jews?"

"You have said so," Jesus replied.

[12]When he was accused by the chief priests and the elders, he gave no answer. [13]Then Pilate asked him, "Don't you hear the testimony they are bringing against you?" [14]But Jesus made no reply, not even to a single charge—to the great amazement of the governor.

[15]Now it was the governor's custom at the festival to release a prisoner chosen by the crowd. [16]At that time they had a well-known prisoner whose name was Jesus[b] Barabbas. [17]So when the crowd had gathered, Pilate asked them, "Which one do you want me to release to you: Jesus Barabbas, or Jesus who is called the Messiah?" [18]For he knew it was out of self-interest that they had handed Jesus over to him.

[19]While Pilate was sitting on the judge's seat, his wife sent him this message: "Don't have anything to do with that innocent man, for I have suffered a great deal today in a dream because of him."

[20]But the chief priests and the elders persuaded the crowd to ask for Barabbas and to have Jesus executed.

[21]"Which of the two do you want me to release to you?" asked the governor.

"Barabbas," they answered.

[22]"What shall I do, then, with Jesus who is called the Messiah?" Pilate asked.

They all answered, "Crucify him!"

[23]"Why? What crime has he committed?" asked Pilate.

But they shouted all the louder, "Crucify him!"

[24]When Pilate saw that he was getting nowhere, but that instead an uproar was starting, he took water and washed his hands in front of the crowd. "I am innocent of this man's blood," he said. "It is your responsibility!"

[25]All the people answered, "His blood is on us and on our children!"

[26]Then he released Barabbas to them. But he had Jesus flogged, and handed him over to be crucified.

The Soldiers Mock Jesus

[27]Then the governor's soldiers took Jesus into the Praetorium and gathered the whole company of soldiers around him. [28]They stripped him and put a scarlet robe on him, [29]and then twisted together a crown of thorns and set it on his head. They put a staff in his right hand. Then they knelt in front of him and mocked him. "Hail, king of the Jews!" they said. [30]They spit on him, and took the staff and struck him on the head again and again. [31]After they had mocked him, they took off the robe and put his own clothes on him. Then they led him away to crucify him.

The Crucifixion of Jesus

[32]As they were going out, they met a man from Cyrene, named Simon, and they forced him to carry the cross. [33]They came to a place called Golgotha (which means "the place of the skull"). [34]There they offered Jesus wine to drink, mixed with gall; but after tasting it, he refused to drink it. [35]When they had crucified him, they divided up his clothes by casting lots. [36]And sitting down, they kept watch over him there. [37]Above his head they placed the written charge against him: THIS IS JESUS, THE KING OF THE JEWS.

[38]Two rebels were crucified with him, one on his right and one on his left. [39]Those who passed by hurled insults at him, shaking their heads [40]and saying,

[a] 10 See Zech. 11:12,13; Jer. 19:1-13; 32:6-9.
[b] 16 Many manuscripts do not have Jesus; also in verse 17.

"You who are going to destroy the temple and build it in three days, save yourself! Come down from the cross, if you are the Son of God!" [41] In the same way the chief priests, the teachers of the law and the elders mocked him. [42] "He saved others," they said, "but he can't save himself! He's the king of Israel! Let him come down now from the cross, and we will believe in him. [43] He trusts in God. Let God rescue him now if he wants him, for he said, 'I am the Son of God.'" [44] In the same way the rebels who were crucified with him also heaped insults on him.

The Death of Jesus

[45] From noon until three in the afternoon darkness came over all the land. [46] About three in the afternoon Jesus cried out in a loud voice, *"Eli, Eli,[a] lema sabachthani?"* (which means "My God, my God, why have you forsaken me?").[b] [47] When some of those standing there heard this, they said, "He's calling Elijah." [48] Immediately one of them ran and got a sponge. He filled it with wine vinegar, put it on a staff, and offered it to Jesus to drink. [49] The rest said, "Now leave him alone. Let's see if Elijah comes to save him." [50] And when Jesus had cried out again in a loud voice, he gave up his spirit.

[51] At that moment the curtain of the temple was torn in two from top to bottom. The earth shook, the rocks split [52] and the tombs broke open. The bodies of many holy people who had died were raised to life. [53] They came out of the tombs after Jesus' resurrection and[c] went into the holy city and appeared to many people.

[54] When the centurion and those with him who were guarding Jesus saw the earthquake and all that had happened, they were terrified, and exclaimed, "Surely he was the Son of God!"

[55] Many women were there, watching from a distance. They had followed Jesus from Galilee to care for his needs. [56] Among them were Mary Magdalene, Mary the mother of James and Joseph,[d] and the mother of Zebedee's sons.

ROCK SOLID *promises*

"Surely he was the Son of God!"

Matthew 27:54

People who watched Jesus die on the cross recognized him as the Son of God—one more solid reason you can be sure he's real.

The Burial of Jesus

[57] As evening approached, there came a rich man from Arimathea, named Joseph, who had himself become a disciple of Jesus. [58] Going to Pilate, he asked for Jesus' body, and Pilate ordered that it be given to him. [59] Joseph took the body, wrapped it in a clean linen cloth, [60] and placed it in his own new tomb that he had cut out of the rock. He rolled a big stone in front of the entrance to the tomb and went away. [61] Mary Magdalene and the other Mary were sitting there opposite the tomb.

The Guard at the Tomb

[62] The next day, the one after Preparation Day, the chief priests and the Pharisees went to Pilate. [63] "Sir," they said, "we remember that while he was still alive that deceiver said, 'After three days I will rise again.' [64] So give the order for the tomb to be made secure until the third day. Otherwise, his disciples may come and steal the body and tell the people that he has been raised from the dead. This last deception will be worse than the first."

[65] "Take a guard," Pilate answered. "Go, make the tomb as secure as you know how." [66] So they went and made the tomb

a 46 Some manuscripts *Eloi, Eloi*
b 46 Psalm 22:1   *c 53* Or *tombs, and after Jesus' resurrection they*   *d 56* Greek *Joses*, a variant of *Joseph*

secure by putting a seal on the stone and posting the guard.

Jesus Has Risen

28 After the Sabbath, at dawn on the first day of the week, Mary Magdalene and the other Mary went to look at the tomb.

[2] There was a violent earthquake, for an angel of the Lord came down from heaven and, going to the tomb, rolled back the stone and sat on it. [3] His appearance was like lightning, and his clothes were white as snow. [4] The guards were so afraid of him that they shook and became like dead men.

[5] The angel said to the women, "Do not be afraid, for I know that you are looking for Jesus, who was crucified. [6] He is not here; he has risen, just as he said. Come and see the place where he lay. [7] Then go quickly and tell his disciples: 'He has risen from the dead and is going ahead of you into Galilee. There you will see him.' Now I have told you."

[8] So the women hurried away from the tomb, afraid yet filled with joy, and ran to tell his disciples. [9] Suddenly Jesus met them. "Greetings," he said. They came to him, clasped his feet and worshiped him. [10] Then Jesus said to them, "Do not be afraid. Go and tell my brothers to go to Galilee; there they will see me."

The Guards' Report

[11] While the women were on their way, some of the guards went into the city and reported to the chief priests everything that had happened. [12] When the chief priests had met with the elders and devised a plan, they gave the soldiers a large sum of money, [13] telling them, "You are to say, 'His disciples came during the night and stole him away while we were asleep.' [14] If this report gets to the governor, we will satisfy him and keep you out of trouble." [15] So the soldiers took the money and did as they were instructed. And this story has been widely circulated among the Jews to this very day.

ROCK SOLID principles

Matthew 28:18–20

Go tell the news about Jesus.

Michael had heard plenty about sharing his faith. He knew he was supposed to tell everyone how they could be Christians, but he had a hard time seeing exactly why people needed God. Most looked happier than he was. Many had clearer plans. And not many seemed to be looking for friends. But one of the older guys at Michael's church had a different point of view. "Needing God isn't just about those things," Brandon explained. "It sounds like you haven't considered what God sees. He notices hurts and needs you can't see. He also knows your friends are separated from him because of sin. We all are. That's why we all need to know about Jesus, even if our lives look perfect from the outside."

In Matthew 28:18–20 Jesus spoke his "Great Commission" to all believers, commanding us to go throughout the world to tell others about him. That's not a job just for mature believers but for all of us. Check Acts 1:8 to see exactly where we get to go. You can be part of testifying about Jesus everywhere from your hometown to the far reaches of the planet.

The Great Commission

16Then the eleven disciples went to Galilee, to the mountain where Jesus had told them to go. 17When they saw him, they worshiped him; but some doubted. 18Then Jesus came to them and said, "All authority in heaven and on earth has been given to me. 19Therefore go and make disciples of all nations, baptizing them in the name of the Father and of the Son and of the Holy Spirit, 20and teaching them to obey everything I have commanded you. And surely I am with you always, to the very end of the age."

BOOK OUTLINE

Background and preparation
(1:1 – 13)

Ministry of healing and teaching
(1:14 — 8:26)

Jesus and his disciples
(8:27 — 10:45)

Jericho and Jerusalem
(10:46 — 13:37)

Passion and death of Christ
(14:1 — 15:47)

The resurrected Christ and his followers
(16:1 – 20)

MARK

Mark, the author of this Gospel, probably was the first to write down the events of Jesus' life. It is believed that he is the same person who worked for many years as a missionary with Paul and Barnabas.

The book of Mark, which stresses facts and actions rather than themes or topics, is the most exciting account of the life of Christ among the Gospels. Although it is the shortest of the four Gospels, it is often the most detailed. From the beginning Mark tells the stories of Christ's ministry, especially his miracles.

Mark shows Jesus as a man of action and authority. He spends one third of the book telling the events of Christ's last week on earth, ending with the Savior's death and resurrection.

John the Baptist Prepares the Way

1 The beginning of the good news about Jesus the Messiah,[a] the Son of God,[b] ²as it is written in Isaiah the prophet:

"I will send my messenger ahead
   of you,
who will prepare your
   way"[c]—
³"a voice of one calling in the
   wilderness,
'Prepare the way for the Lord,
   make straight paths for him.'"[d]

⁴And so John the Baptist appeared in the wilderness, preaching a baptism of repentance for the forgiveness of sins. ⁵The whole Judean countryside and all the people of Jerusalem went out to him. Confessing their sins, they were baptized by him in the Jordan River. ⁶John wore clothing made of camel's hair, with a leather belt around his waist, and he ate locusts and wild honey. ⁷And this was his message: "After me comes the one more powerful than I, the straps of whose sandals I am not worthy to stoop down and untie. ⁸I baptize you with[e] water, but he will baptize you with[e] the Holy Spirit."

The Baptism and Testing of Jesus

⁹At that time Jesus came from Nazareth in Galilee and was baptized by John in the Jordan. ¹⁰Just as Jesus was coming up out of the water, he saw heaven being torn open and the Spirit descending on him like a dove. ¹¹And a voice came from heaven: "You are my Son, whom I love; with you I am well pleased."

¹²At once the Spirit sent him out into the wilderness, ¹³and he was in the wilderness forty days, being tempted[f] by Satan. He was with the wild animals, and angels attended him.

Jesus Announces the Good News

¹⁴After John was put in prison, Jesus went into Galilee, proclaiming the good news of God. ¹⁵"The time has come," he said. "The kingdom of God has come near. Repent and believe the good news!"

UNSHAKEN God
MARK 1

Mark 1:9–11

God is complex.

You can get a good look at your complex God in this scene where Jesus was baptized. God the Son goes into the water. God the Holy Spirit descends in the form of a dove. And God the Father speaks from heaven. That's the consistent Bible picture of God as a "tri-unity" or "Trinity." While the word "Trinity" never appears in Scripture, it's how we make sense of the complex Biblical portrait of God as Father, Son, and Holy Spirit. They are the same yet separate, equal yet different, three persons yet so tightly united they are one being. The Trinity is simply who God is, and it proves that God is all about relationships at the very core of his being.

So … How would you explain to a non-Christian friend that God is "complex"? Why does it matter?

Jesus Calls His First Disciples

¹⁶As Jesus walked beside the Sea of Galilee, he saw Simon and his brother Andrew casting a net into the lake, for they were fishermen. ¹⁷"Come, follow me," Jesus said, "and I will send you out to fish for people." ¹⁸At once they left their nets and followed him.

¹⁹When he had gone a little farther, he saw James son of Zebedee and his brother John in a boat, preparing their nets. ²⁰Without delay he called them, and they left their father Zebedee in the boat with the hired men and followed him.

---

[a] 1 Or *Jesus Christ. Messiah* (Hebrew) and *Christ* (Greek) both mean *Anointed One.*   [b] 1 Some manuscripts do not have *the Son of God.*
[c] 2 Mal. 3:1   [d] 3 Isaiah 40:3   [e] 8 Or *in*
[f] 13 The Greek for *tempted* can also mean *tested.*

ROCK SOLID
promises

> " 'Come, follow me,' Jesus said, 'and I will send you out to fish for people.' "
>
> **Mark 1:17**

God not only wants you to follow him, but he wants you to invite others to chase after him too.

Jesus Drives Out an Impure Spirit

21 They went to Capernaum, and when the Sabbath came, Jesus went into the synagogue and began to teach. 22 The people were amazed at his teaching, because he taught them as one who had authority, not as the teachers of the law. 23 Just then a man in their synagogue who was possessed by an impure spirit cried out, 24 "What do you want with us, Jesus of Nazareth? Have you come to destroy us? I know who you are— the Holy One of God!"

25 "Be quiet!" said Jesus sternly. "Come out of him!" 26 The impure spirit shook the man violently and came out of him with a shriek.

27 The people were all so amazed that they asked each other, "What is this? A new teaching—and with authority! He even gives orders to impure spirits and they obey him." 28 News about him spread quickly over the whole region of Galilee.

Jesus Heals Many

29 As soon as they left the synagogue, they went with James and John to the home of Simon and Andrew. 30 Simon's mother-in-law was in bed with a fever, and they immediately told Jesus about her. 31 So he went to her, took her hand and helped her up. The fever left her and she began to wait on them.

32 That evening after sunset the people brought to Jesus all the sick and demon-possessed. 33 The whole town gathered at the door, 34 and Jesus healed many who had various diseases. He also drove out many demons, but he would not let the demons speak because they knew who he was.

Jesus Prays in a Solitary Place

35 Very early in the morning, while it was still dark, Jesus got up, left the house and went off to a solitary place, where he prayed. 36 Simon and his companions went to look for him, 37 and when they found him, they exclaimed: "Everyone is looking for you!"

38 Jesus replied, "Let us go somewhere else—to the nearby villages—so I can preach there also. That is why I have come." 39 So he traveled throughout Galilee, preaching in their synagogues and driving out demons.

Jesus Heals a Man With Leprosy

40 A man with leprosy[a] came to him and begged him on his knees, "If you are willing, you can make me clean."

41 Jesus was indignant.[b] He reached out his hand and touched the man. "I am willing," he said. "Be clean!" 42 Immediately the leprosy left him and he was cleansed.

43 Jesus sent him away at once with a strong warning: 44 "See that you don't tell this to anyone. But go, show yourself to the priest and offer the sacrifices that Moses commanded for your cleansing, as a testimony to them." 45 Instead he went out and began to talk freely, spreading the news. As a result, Jesus could no longer enter a town openly but stayed outside in lonely places. Yet the people still came to him from everywhere.

Jesus Forgives and Heals a Paralyzed Man

2 A few days later, when Jesus again entered Capernaum, the people heard that he had come home. 2 They gathered in such large numbers

---

[a] 40 The Greek word traditionally translated *leprosy* was used for various diseases affecting the skin. [b] 41 Many manuscripts *Jesus was filled with compassion*

that there was no room left, not even outside the door, and he preached the word to them. ³Some men came, bringing to him a paralyzed man, carried by four of them. ⁴Since they could not get him to Jesus because of the crowd, they made an opening in the roof above Jesus by digging through it and then lowered the mat the man was lying on. ⁵When Jesus saw their faith, he said to the paralyzed man, "Son, your sins are forgiven."

⁶Now some teachers of the law were sitting there, thinking to themselves, ⁷"Why does this fellow talk like that? He's blaspheming! Who can forgive sins but God alone?"

⁸Immediately Jesus knew in his spirit that this was what they were thinking in their hearts, and he said to them, "Why are you thinking these things? ⁹Which is easier: to say to this paralyzed man, 'Your sins are forgiven,' or to say, 'Get up, take your mat and walk'? ¹⁰But I want you to know that the Son of Man has authority on earth to forgive sins." So he said to the man, ¹¹"I tell you, get up, take your mat and go home." ¹²He got up, took his mat and walked out in full view of them all. This amazed everyone and they praised God, saying, "We have never seen anything like this!"

Jesus Calls Levi and Eats With Sinners

¹³Once again Jesus went out beside the lake. A large crowd came to him, and he began to teach them. ¹⁴As he walked along, he saw Levi son of Alphaeus sitting at the tax collector's booth. "Follow me," Jesus told him, and Levi got up and followed him.

¹⁵While Jesus was having dinner at Levi's house, many tax collectors and sinners were eating with him and his disciples, for there were many who followed him. ¹⁶When the teachers of the law who were Pharisees saw him eating with the sinners and tax collectors, they asked his disciples: "Why does he eat with tax collectors and sinners?"

¹⁷On hearing this, Jesus said to them, "It is not the healthy who need a doctor, but the sick. I have not come to call the righteous, but sinners."

Jesus Questioned About Fasting

¹⁸Now John's disciples and the Pharisees were fasting. Some people came and asked Jesus, "How is it that John's disciples and the disciples of the Pharisees are fasting, but yours are not?"

¹⁹Jesus answered, "How can the guests of the bridegroom fast while he is with them? They cannot, so long as they have him with them. ²⁰But the time will come when the bridegroom will be taken from them, and on that day they will fast.

²¹"No one sews a patch of unshrunk cloth on an old garment. Otherwise, the new piece will pull away from the old, making the tear worse. ²²And no one pours new wine into old wineskins. Otherwise, the wine will burst the skins, and both the wine and the wineskins will be ruined. No, they pour new wine into new wineskins."

Jesus Is Lord of the Sabbath

²³One Sabbath Jesus was going through the grainfields, and as his disciples walked along, they began to pick some heads of grain. ²⁴The Pharisees said to him, "Look, why are they doing what is unlawful on the Sabbath?"

²⁵He answered, "Have you never read what David did when he and his companions were hungry and in need? ²⁶In the days of Abiathar the high priest, he entered the house of God and ate the consecrated bread, which is lawful only for priests to eat. And he also gave some to his companions."

²⁷Then he said to them, "The Sabbath was made for man, not man for the Sabbath. ²⁸So the Son of Man is Lord even of the Sabbath."

Jesus Heals on the Sabbath

3 Another time Jesus went into the synagogue, and a man with a shriveled hand was there. ²Some of them were looking for a reason to accuse Jesus, so they watched him closely to see if he would heal him on the Sabbath. ³Jesus said to the man with the shriveled hand, "Stand up in front of everyone."

⁴Then Jesus asked them, "Which is

lawful on the Sabbath: to do good or to do evil, to save life or to kill?" But they remained silent.

⁵He looked around at them in anger and, deeply distressed at their stubborn hearts, said to the man, "Stretch out your hand." He stretched it out, and his hand was completely restored. ⁶Then the Pharisees went out and began to plot with the Herodians how they might kill Jesus.

Crowds Follow Jesus

⁷Jesus withdrew with his disciples to the lake, and a large crowd from Galilee followed. ⁸When they heard about all he was doing, many people came to him from Judea, Jerusalem, Idumea, and the regions across the Jordan and around Tyre and Sidon. ⁹Because of the crowd he told his disciples to have a small boat ready for him, to keep the people from crowding him. ¹⁰For he had healed many, so that those with diseases were pushing forward to touch him. ¹¹Whenever the impure spirits saw him, they fell down before him and cried out, "You are the Son of God." ¹²But he gave them strict orders not to tell others about him.

Jesus Appoints the Twelve

¹³Jesus went up on a mountainside and called to him those he wanted, and they came to him. ¹⁴He appointed twelve*a* that they might be with him and that he might send them out to preach ¹⁵and to have authority to drive out demons. ¹⁶These are the twelve he appointed: Simon (to whom he gave the name Peter), ¹⁷James son of Zebedee and his brother John (to them he gave the name Boanerges, which means "sons of thunder"), ¹⁸Andrew, Philip, Bartholomew, Matthew, Thomas, James son of Alphaeus, Thaddaeus, Simon the Zealot ¹⁹and Judas Iscariot, who betrayed him.

Jesus Accused by His Family and by Teachers of the Law

²⁰Then Jesus entered a house, and again a crowd gathered, so that he and his disciples were not even able to eat. ²¹When his family*b* heard about this, they went to take charge of him, for they said, "He is out of his mind."

²²And the teachers of the law who came down from Jerusalem said, "He is possessed by Beelzebul! By the prince of demons he is driving out demons."

²³So Jesus called them over to him and began to speak to them in parables: "How can Satan drive out Satan? ²⁴If a kingdom is divided against itself, that kingdom cannot stand. ²⁵If a house is divided against itself, that house cannot stand. ²⁶And if Satan opposes himself and is divided, he cannot stand; his end has come. ²⁷In fact, no one can enter a strong man's house without first tying him up. Then he can plunder the strong man's house. ²⁸Truly I tell you, people can be forgiven all their sins and every slander they utter, ²⁹but whoever blasphemes against the Holy Spirit will never be forgiven; they are guilty of an eternal sin."

³⁰He said this because they were saying, "He has an impure spirit."

³¹Then Jesus' mother and brothers arrived. Standing outside, they sent someone in to call him. ³²A crowd was sitting around him, and they told him, "Your mother and brothers are outside looking for you."

³³"Who are my mother and my brothers?" he asked.

³⁴Then he looked at those seated in a circle around him and said, "Here are my mother and my brothers! ³⁵Whoever does God's will is my brother and sister and mother."

The Parable of the Sower

4 Again Jesus began to teach by the lake. The crowd that gathered around him was so large that he got into a boat and sat in it out on the lake, while all the people were along the shore at the water's edge. ²He taught them many things by parables, and in his teaching said: ³"Listen! A farmer went out to sow his seed. ⁴As he was scattering the seed, some fell along the path, and the birds

a 14 Some manuscripts *twelve—designating them apostles—* *b 21* Or *his associates* plants were scorched, and they withered because they had no root. ⁷Other seed fell among thorns, which grew up and choked the plants, so that they did not bear grain. ⁸Still other seed fell on good soil. It came up, grew and produced a crop, some multiplying thirty, some sixty, some a hundred times."

⁹Then Jesus said, "Whoever has ears to hear, let them hear."

¹⁰When he was alone, the Twelve and the others around him asked him about the parables. ¹¹He told them, "The secret of the kingdom of God has been given to you. But to those on the outside everything is said in parables ¹²so that,

"'they may be ever seeing but never perceiving,
and ever hearing but never understanding;
otherwise they might turn and be forgiven!'^a"

¹³Then Jesus said to them, "Don't you understand this parable? How then will you understand any parable? ¹⁴The farmer sows the word. ¹⁵Some people are like seed along the path, where the word is sown. As soon as they hear it, Satan comes and takes away the word that was sown in them. ¹⁶Others, like seed sown on rocky places, hear the word and at once receive it with joy. ¹⁷But since they have no root, they last only a short time. When trouble or persecution comes because of the word, they quickly fall away. ¹⁸Still others, like seed sown among thorns, hear the word; ¹⁹but the worries of this life, the deceitfulness of wealth and the desires for other things come in and choke the word, making it unfruitful. ²⁰Others, like seed sown on good soil, hear the word, accept it, and produce a crop—some thirty, some sixty, some a hundred times what was sown."

A Lamp on a Stand

²¹He said to them, "Do you bring in a lamp to put it under a bowl or a bed? Instead, don't you put it on its stand? ²²For whatever is hidden is meant to be

^a 12 Isaiah 6:9,10

Mark 3:22–30
Demons are Satan's partners.

Demons are evil supernatural beings ruled by Satan. Throughout the Gospels and Acts you can see these unclean spirits inflicting people with terrible harm including deafness and muteness (see Mark 9:25), blindness (see Matthew 12:22), and physical deformities (see Luke 13:10–13). Demons caused uncontrollable behaviors (see Mark 1:23–24; Luke 9:37–39) and mental problems (see Matthew 8:28). While blaming demons for these afflictions might seem like nothing more than ancient ignorance, Jesus distinguished between affliction by demons and various sicknesses (see Matthew 4:24). Some Bible scholars today think demons are fallen angels (see 2 Peter 2:4), while others argue they are the offspring of angels and women before the flood of Noah (see Genesis 6:2). However demons originated, Jesus could free people from their power with a simple command (see Mark 1:25; 9:25), proving his dominance over Satan and all his evil forces. Jesus also gave his disciples authority to use his name to break demonic oppression (see Luke 10:17).

Think: Do you think demons just exist in horror movies— or are they real? How do you know this is true?

ROCK SOLID truths

came and ate it up. ⁵Some fell on rocky places, where it did not have much soil. It sprang up quickly, because the soil was shallow. ⁶But when the sun came up, the disclosed, and whatever is concealed is meant to be brought out into the open. ²³If anyone has ears to hear, let them hear."

²⁴"Consider carefully what you hear," he continued. "With the measure you use, it will be measured to you—and even more. ²⁵Whoever has will be given more; whoever does not have, even what they have will be taken from them."

The Parable of the Growing Seed

²⁶He also said, "This is what the kingdom of God is like. A man scatters seed on the ground. ²⁷Night and day, whether he sleeps or gets up, the seed sprouts and grows, though he does not know how. ²⁸All by itself the soil produces grain—first the stalk, then the head, then the full kernel in the head. ²⁹As soon as the grain is ripe, he puts the sickle to it, because the harvest has come."

The Parable of the Mustard Seed

³⁰Again he said, "What shall we say the kingdom of God is like, or what parable shall we use to describe it? ³¹It is like a mustard seed, which is the smallest of all seeds on earth. ³²Yet when planted, it grows and becomes the largest of all garden plants, with such big branches that the birds can perch in its shade."

³³With many similar parables Jesus spoke the word to them, as much as they could understand. ³⁴He did not say anything to them without using a parable. But when he was alone with his own disciples, he explained everything.

Jesus Calms the Storm

³⁵That day when evening came, he said to his disciples, "Let us go over to the other side." ³⁶Leaving the crowd behind, they took him along, just as he was, in the boat. There were also other boats with him. ³⁷A furious squall came up, and the waves broke over the boat, so that it was nearly swamped. ³⁸Jesus was in the stern, sleeping on a cushion. The disciples woke him and said to him, "Teacher, don't you care if we drown?"

³⁹He got up, rebuked the wind and said to the waves, "Quiet! Be still!" Then the wind died down and it was completely calm.

⁴⁰He said to his disciples, "Why are you so afraid? Do you still have no faith?"

⁴¹They were terrified and asked each other, "Who is this? Even the wind and the waves obey him!"

Jesus Restores a Demon-Possessed Man

5 They went across the lake to the region of the Gerasenes.ᵃ ²When Jesus got out of the boat, a man with an impure spirit came from the tombs to meet him. ³This man lived in the tombs, and no one could bind him anymore, not even with a chain. ⁴For he had often been chained hand and foot, but he tore the chains apart and broke the irons on his feet. No one was strong enough to subdue him. ⁵Night and day among the tombs and in the hills he would cry out and cut himself with stones.

⁶When he saw Jesus from a distance, he ran and fell on his knees in front of him. ⁷He shouted at the top of his voice, "What do you want with me, Jesus, Son of the Most High God? In God's name don't torture me!" ⁸For Jesus had said to him, "Come out of this man, you impure spirit!"

⁹Then Jesus asked him, "What is your name?"

"My name is Legion," he replied, "for we are many." ¹⁰And he begged Jesus again and again not to send them out of the area.

¹¹A large herd of pigs was feeding on the nearby hillside. ¹²The demons begged Jesus, "Send us among the pigs; allow us to go into them." ¹³He gave them permission, and the impure spirits came out and went into the pigs. The herd, about two thousand in number, rushed down the steep bank into the lake and were drowned.

¹⁴Those tending the pigs ran off and reported this in the town and countryside, and the people went out to see what had

---

ᵃ 1 Some manuscripts *Gadarenes*; other manuscripts *Gergesenes* happened. ¹⁵When they came to Jesus, they saw the man who had been possessed by the legion of demons, sitting there, dressed and in his right mind; and they were afraid. ¹⁶Those who had seen it told the people what had happened to the demon-possessed man—and told about the pigs as well. ¹⁷Then the people began to plead with Jesus to leave their region.

¹⁸As Jesus was getting into the boat, the man who had been demon-possessed begged to go with him. ¹⁹Jesus did not let him, but said, "Go home to your own people and tell them how much the Lord has done for you, and how he has had mercy on you." ²⁰So the man went away and began to tell in the Decapolis*a* how much Jesus had done for him. And all the people were amazed.

Jesus Raises a Dead Girl and Heals a Sick Woman

²¹When Jesus had again crossed over by boat to the other side of the lake, a large crowd gathered around him while he was by the lake. ²²Then one of the synagogue leaders, named Jairus, came, and when he saw Jesus, he fell at his feet. ²³He pleaded earnestly with him, "My little daughter is dying. Please come and put your hands on her so that she will be healed and live." ²⁴So Jesus went with him.

A large crowd followed and pressed around him. ²⁵And a woman was there who had been subject to bleeding for twelve years. ²⁶She had suffered a great deal under the care of many doctors and had spent all she had, yet instead of getting better she grew worse. ²⁷When she heard about Jesus, she came up behind him in the crowd and touched his cloak, ²⁸because she thought, "If I just touch his clothes, I will be healed." ²⁹Immediately her bleeding stopped and she felt in her body that she was freed from her suffering.

³⁰At once Jesus realized that power had gone out from him. He turned around in the crowd and asked, "Who touched my clothes?"

³¹"You see the people crowding against

you," his disciples answered, "and yet you can ask, 'Who touched me?'"

³²But Jesus kept looking around to see who had done it. ³³Then the woman, knowing what had happened to her, came and fell at his feet and, trembling with fear, told him the whole truth. ³⁴He said to her, "Daughter, your faith has healed you. Go in peace and be freed from your suffering."

³⁵While Jesus was still speaking, some people came from the house of Jairus, the synagogue leader. "Your daughter is dead," they said. "Why bother the teacher anymore?"

³⁶Overhearing*b* what they said, Jesus told him, "Don't be afraid; just believe."

³⁷He did not let anyone follow him except Peter, James and John the brother of James. ³⁸When they came to the home of the synagogue leader, Jesus saw a commotion, with people crying and wailing loudly. ³⁹He went in and said to them, "Why all this commotion and wailing? The child is not dead but asleep." ⁴⁰But they laughed at him.

After he put them all out, he took the child's father and mother and the disciples who were with him, and went in where the child was. ⁴¹He took her by the hand and said to her, "*Talitha koum!*" (which means "Little girl, I say to you, get up!"). ⁴²Immediately the girl stood up and began to walk around (she was twelve years old). At this they were completely astonished. ⁴³He gave strict orders not to let anyone know about this, and told them to give her something to eat.

A Prophet Without Honor

6 Jesus left there and went to his hometown, accompanied by his disciples. ²When the Sabbath came, he began to teach in the synagogue, and many who heard him were amazed.

"Where did this man get these things?" they asked. "What's this wisdom that has been given him? What are these remarkable miracles he is performing? ³Isn't this the carpenter? Isn't this Mary's son and

---

a 20 That is, the Ten Cities   *b 36* Or *Ignoring*

the brother of James, Joseph,^a Judas and Simon? Aren't his sisters here with us?" And they took offense at him.

⁴Jesus said to them, "A prophet is not without honor except in his own town, among his relatives and in his own home." ⁵He could not do any miracles there, except lay his hands on a few sick people and heal them. ⁶He was amazed at their lack of faith.

Jesus Sends Out the Twelve

Then Jesus went around teaching from village to village. ⁷Calling the Twelve to him, he began to send them out two by two and gave them authority over impure spirits.

⁸These were his instructions: "Take nothing for the journey except a staff— no bread, no bag, no money in your belts. ⁹Wear sandals but not an extra shirt. ¹⁰Whenever you enter a house, stay there until you leave that town. ¹¹And if any place will not welcome you or listen to you, leave that place and shake the dust off your feet as a testimony against them."

¹²They went out and preached that people should repent. ¹³They drove out many demons and anointed many sick people with oil and healed them.

John the Baptist Beheaded

¹⁴King Herod heard about this, for Jesus' name had become well known. Some were saying,^b "John the Baptist has been raised from the dead, and that is why miraculous powers are at work in him."

¹⁵Others said, "He is Elijah."

And still others claimed, "He is a prophet, like one of the prophets of long ago."

¹⁶But when Herod heard this, he said, "John, whom I beheaded, has been raised from the dead!"

¹⁷For Herod himself had given orders to have John arrested, and he had him bound and put in prison. He did this because of Herodias, his brother Philip's wife, whom he had married. ¹⁸For John had been saying to Herod, "It is not lawful for you to have your brother's wife." ¹⁹So Herodias nursed a grudge against John and wanted

to kill him. But she was not able to, ²⁰because Herod feared John and protected him, knowing him to be a righteous and holy man. When Herod heard John, he was greatly puzzled^c; yet he liked to listen to him.

²¹Finally the opportune time came. On his birthday Herod gave a banquet for his high officials and military commanders and the leading men of Galilee. ²²When the daughter of^d Herodias came in and danced, she pleased Herod and his dinner guests.

The king said to the girl, "Ask me for anything you want, and I'll give it to you." ²³And he promised her with an oath, "Whatever you ask I will give you, up to half my kingdom."

²⁴She went out and said to her mother, "What shall I ask for?"

"The head of John the Baptist," she answered.

²⁵At once the girl hurried in to the king with the request: "I want you to give me right now the head of John the Baptist on a platter."

²⁶The king was greatly distressed, but because of his oaths and his dinner guests, he did not want to refuse her. ²⁷So he immediately sent an executioner with orders to bring John's head. The man went, beheaded John in the prison, ²⁸and brought back his head on a platter. He presented it to the girl, and she gave it to her mother. ²⁹On hearing of this, John's disciples came and took his body and laid it in a tomb.

Jesus Feeds the Five Thousand

³⁰The apostles gathered around Jesus and reported to him all they had done and taught. ³¹Then, because so many people were coming and going that they did not even have a chance to eat, he said to them, "Come with me by yourselves to a quiet place and get some rest."

³²So they went away by themselves in a boat to a solitary place. ³³But many who

---

^a 3 Greek Joses, a variant of Joseph   ^b 14 Some early manuscripts He was saying   ^c 20 Some early manuscripts he did many things   ^d 22 Some early manuscripts When his daughter

saw them leaving recognized them and ran on foot from all the towns and got there ahead of them. ³⁴When Jesus landed and saw a large crowd, he had compassion on them, because they were like sheep without a shepherd. So he began teaching them many things.

³⁵By this time it was late in the day, so his disciples came to him. "This is a remote place," they said, "and it's already very late. ³⁶Send the people away so that they can go to the surrounding countryside and villages and buy themselves something to eat."

³⁷But he answered, "You give them something to eat."

They said to him, "That would take more than half a year's wages[a]! Are we to go and spend that much on bread and give it to them to eat?"

³⁸"How many loaves do you have?" he asked. "Go and see."

When they found out, they said, "Five—and two fish."

³⁹Then Jesus directed them to have all the people sit down in groups on the green grass. ⁴⁰So they sat down in groups of hundreds and fifties. ⁴¹Taking the five loaves and the two fish and looking up to heaven, he gave thanks and broke the

[a] 37 Greek *take two hundred denarii*

Mark 6:14–29

John the Baptist called the crowds to God.

The last words of the Old Testament promised God would send a prophet before the "great and dreadful day of the LORD" (Malachi 4:5). John the Baptist was that messenger of God, and he enters the scene even before Jesus appears at the first Christmas.

Note that John the Baptist isn't the same guy as John the close friend of Jesus, the author of the book of John. John the Baptist was born to Elizabeth, a close relative of Mary the mother of Jesus, making him a cousin of Jesus (see Luke 1:36). He grew up "strong in spirit," living in the desert (Luke 1:80). He wore clothes made of camel hair, surviving on jumbo grasshoppers and wild honey (see Matthew 3:4).

This man's most famous words were "Repent, for the kingdom of heaven has come near" (Matthew 3:2). He loudly warned everyone to leave their sins and to show their sorrow for sin by being baptized, getting dunked in the waters of the Jordan River (see Matthew 3:6). Some thought John was crazy—even demon possessed (see Matthew 11:17–18). But when John pointedly called people back to God, the crowds responded (see Matthew 3:5).

John spoke harsh words to religious leaders who came to him, exposing their hypocrisy and commanding them to truly repent (see Matthew 3:7–10). When he preached against the sins of the royal family, he was beheaded by King Herod, who gave his daughter John's head on a platter (see Mark 6:25–28).

You can also find John the Baptist in Matthew 3:1–17; Mathew 14:1–12; Luke 1:5–23; Luke 1:39–80; and Luke 3:1–20.

UNSHAKEN people

loaves. Then he gave them to his disciples to distribute to the people. He also divided the two fish among them all. ⁴²They all ate and were satisfied, ⁴³and the disciples picked up twelve basketfuls of broken pieces of bread and fish. ⁴⁴The number of the men who had eaten was five thousand.

Jesus Walks on the Water

⁴⁵Immediately Jesus made his disciples get into the boat and go on ahead of him to Bethsaida, while he dismissed the crowd. ⁴⁶After leaving them, he went up on a mountainside to pray.

⁴⁷Later that night, the boat was in the middle of the lake, and he was alone on land. ⁴⁸He saw the disciples straining at the oars, because the wind was against them. Shortly before dawn he went out to them, walking on the lake. He was about to pass by them, ⁴⁹but when they saw him walking on the lake, they thought he was a ghost. They cried out, ⁵⁰because they all saw him and were terrified.

Immediately he spoke to them and said, "Take courage! It is I. Don't be afraid." ⁵¹Then he climbed into the boat with them, and the wind died down. They were completely amazed, ⁵²for they had not understood about the loaves; their hearts were hardened.

⁵³When they had crossed over, they landed at Gennesaret and anchored there. ⁵⁴As soon as they got out of the boat, people recognized Jesus. ⁵⁵They ran throughout that whole region and carried the sick on mats to wherever they heard he was. ⁵⁶And wherever he went—into villages, towns or countryside—they placed the sick in the marketplaces. They begged him to let them touch even the edge of his cloak, and all who touched it were healed.

That Which Defiles

7 The Pharisees and some of the teachers of the law who had come from Jerusalem gathered around Jesus ²and saw some of his disciples eating food with hands that were defiled, that is, unwashed. ³(The Pharisees and all the Jews do not eat unless they give

their hands a ceremonial washing, holding to the tradition of the elders. ⁴When they come from the marketplace they do not eat unless they wash. And they observe many other traditions, such as the washing of cups, pitchers and kettles.ᵃ)

⁵So the Pharisees and teachers of the law asked Jesus, "Why don't your disciples live according to the tradition of the elders instead of eating their food with defiled hands?"

⁶He replied, "Isaiah was right when he prophesied about you hypocrites; as it is written:

> "'These people honor me with their lips,
> but their hearts are far from me.
> ⁷They worship me in vain;
> their teachings are merely human rules.'ᵇ

⁸You have let go of the commands of God and are holding on to human traditions."

⁹And he continued, "You have a fine way of setting aside the commands of God in order to observeᶜ your own traditions! ¹⁰For Moses said, 'Honor your father and mother,'ᵈ and, 'Anyone who curses their father or mother is to be put to death.'ᵉ ¹¹But you say that if anyone declares that what might have been used to help their father or mother is Corban (that is, devoted to God)— ¹²then you no longer let them do anything for their father or mother. ¹³Thus you nullify the word of God by your tradition that you have handed down. And you do many things like that."

¹⁴Again Jesus called the crowd to him and said, "Listen to me, everyone, and understand this. ¹⁵Nothing outside a person can defile them by going into them. Rather, it is what comes out of a person that defiles them." [16]ᶠ

¹⁷After he had left the crowd and entered the house, his disciples asked him

---

ᵃ 4 Some early manuscripts *pitchers, kettles and dining couches*   ᵇ 6,7 Isaiah 29:13   ᶜ 9 Some manuscripts *set up*   ᵈ 10 Exodus 20:12; Deut. 5:16   ᵉ 10 Exodus 21:17; Lev. 20:9
ᶠ 16 Some manuscripts include here the words of 4:23.

about this parable. [18]"Are you so dull?" he asked. "Don't you see that nothing that enters a person from the outside can defile them? [19]For it doesn't go into their heart but into their stomach, and then out of the body." (In saying this, Jesus declared all foods clean.)

[20]He went on: "What comes out of a person is what defiles them. [21]For it is from within, out of a person's heart, that evil thoughts come—sexual immorality, theft, murder, [22]adultery, greed, malice, deceit, lewdness, envy, slander, arrogance and folly. [23]All these evils come from inside and defile a person."

Jesus Honors a Syrophoenician Woman's Faith

[24]Jesus left that place and went to the vicinity of Tyre.[a] He entered a house and did not want anyone to know it; yet he could not keep his presence secret. [25]In fact, as soon as she heard about him, a woman whose little daughter was possessed by an impure spirit came and fell at his feet. [26]The woman was a Greek, born in Syrian Phoenicia. She begged Jesus to drive the demon out of her daughter.

[27]"First let the children eat all they want," he told her, "for it is not right to take the children's bread and toss it to the dogs."

[28]"Lord," she replied, "even the dogs under the table eat the children's crumbs."

[29]Then he told her, "For such a reply, you may go; the demon has left your daughter."

[30]She went home and found her child lying on the bed, and the demon gone.

Jesus Heals a Deaf and Mute Man

[31]Then Jesus left the vicinity of Tyre and went through Sidon, down to the Sea of Galilee and into the region of the Decapolis.[b] [32]There some people brought to him a man who was deaf and could hardly talk, and they begged Jesus to place his hand on him.

[33]After he took him aside, away from the crowd, Jesus put his fingers into the man's ears. Then he spit and touched the man's tongue. [34]He looked up to heaven and with a deep sigh said to him, "Ephphatha!" (which means "Be opened!"). [35]At this, the man's ears were opened, his tongue was loosened and he began to speak plainly.

[36]Jesus commanded them not to tell anyone. But the more he did so, the more they kept talking about it. [37]People were overwhelmed with amazement. "He has done everything well," they said. "He even makes the deaf hear and the mute speak."

Jesus Feeds the Four Thousand

8 During those days another large crowd gathered. Since they had nothing to eat, Jesus called his disciples to him and said, [2]"I have compassion for these people; they have already been with me three days and have nothing to eat. [3]If I send them home hungry, they will collapse on the way, because some of them have come a long distance."

[4]His disciples answered, "But where in this remote place can anyone get enough bread to feed them?"

[5]"How many loaves do you have?" Jesus asked.

"Seven," they replied.

[6]He told the crowd to sit down on the ground. When he had taken the seven loaves and given thanks, he broke them and gave them to his disciples to distribute to the people, and they did so. [7]They had a few small fish as well; he gave thanks for them also and told the disciples to distribute them. [8]The people ate and were satisfied. Afterward the disciples picked up seven basketfuls of broken pieces that were left over. [9]About four thousand were present. After he had sent them away, [10]he got into the boat with his disciples and went to the region of Dalmanutha.

[11]The Pharisees came and began to question Jesus. To test him, they asked him for a sign from heaven. [12]He sighed deeply and said, "Why does this generation ask for a sign? Truly I tell you, no sign will be given to it." [13]Then he left them,

[a] 24 Many early manuscripts *Tyre and Sidon*
[b] 31 That is, the Ten Cities

got back into the boat and crossed to the other side.

The Yeast of the Pharisees and Herod

¹⁴The disciples had forgotten to bring bread, except for one loaf they had with them in the boat. ¹⁵"Be careful," Jesus warned them. "Watch out for the yeast of the Pharisees and that of Herod."

¹⁶They discussed this with one another and said, "It is because we have no bread."

¹⁷Aware of their discussion, Jesus asked them: "Why are you talking about having no bread? Do you still not see or understand? Are your hearts hardened? ¹⁸Do you have eyes but fail to see, and ears but fail to hear? And don't you remember? ¹⁹When I broke the five loaves for the five thousand, how many basketfuls of pieces did you pick up?"

"Twelve," they replied.

²⁰"And when I broke the seven loaves for the four thousand, how many basketfuls of pieces did you pick up?"

They answered, "Seven."

²¹He said to them, "Do you still not understand?"

Jesus Heals a Blind Man at Bethsaida

²²They came to Bethsaida, and some people brought a blind man and begged Jesus to touch him. ²³He took the blind man by the hand and led him outside the village. When he had spit on the man's eyes and put his hands on him, Jesus asked, "Do you see anything?"

²⁴He looked up and said, "I see people; they look like trees walking around."

²⁵Once more Jesus put his hands on the man's eyes. Then his eyes were opened, his sight was restored, and he saw everything clearly. ²⁶Jesus sent him home, saying, "Don't even go into*a* the village."

Peter Declares That Jesus Is the Messiah

²⁷Jesus and his disciples went on to the villages around Caesarea Philippi. On the way he asked them, "Who do people say I am?"

²⁸They replied, "Some say John the Bap-

tist; others say Elijah; and still others, one of the prophets."

²⁹"But what about you?" he asked. "Who do you say I am?"

Peter answered, "You are the Messiah."

³⁰Jesus warned them not to tell anyone about him.

Jesus Predicts His Death

³¹He then began to teach them that the Son of Man must suffer many things and be rejected by the elders, the chief priests and the teachers of the law, and that he must be killed and after three days rise again. ³²He spoke plainly about this, and Peter took him aside and began to rebuke him.

³³But when Jesus turned and looked at his disciples, he rebuked Peter. "Get behind me, Satan!" he said. "You do not have in mind the concerns of God, but merely human concerns."

The Way of the Cross

³⁴Then he called the crowd to him along with his disciples and said: "Whoever wants to be my disciple must deny themselves and take up their cross and follow me. ³⁵For whoever wants to save their life*b* will lose it, but whoever loses their life for me and for the gospel will save it. ³⁶What good is it for someone to gain the whole world, yet forfeit their soul? ³⁷Or what can anyone give in exchange for their soul? ³⁸If anyone is ashamed of me and my words in this adulterous and sinful generation, the Son of Man will be ashamed of them when he comes in his Father's glory with the holy angels."

9 And he said to them, "Truly I tell you, some who are standing here will not taste death before they see that the kingdom of God has come with power."

The Transfiguration

²After six days Jesus took Peter, James and John with him and led them up a high mountain, where they were all alone.

---

a 26 Some manuscripts *go and tell anyone in*
b 35 The Greek word means either *life* or *soul*; also in verses 36 and 37.

ROCK SOLID *principles*

Mark 8:31–38

Grab your cross.

The band's lead singer spoke slowly, letting his words hang in the packed arena. "You can't live in a bubble," he said. "You can't go on an endless quest to make your life more and more comfortable. Following Jesus means going to unpleasant places and loving unlovable people. That's where Jesus spent all his time. That's where we need to be." Ashley felt the singer's words stab her. She liked her easy and predictable routine, but those words felt aimed right at her. She wasn't sure if God was trying to tell her something. If he was, she wanted to listen. No one had ever told Ashley that obeying Jesus could take her away from everything that made her life comfortable.

The Lord blasted his good friend Peter for trying to talk him out of dying on the cross. Then Jesus said that anyone who wants to follow him "must deny themselves and take up their cross and follow me" (Mark 8:34). Taking up your own cross means giving total control of your life to Jesus—going his way instead of your own. Even when it isn't comfortable.

There he was transfigured before them. [3]His clothes became dazzling white, whiter than anyone in the world could bleach them. [4]And there appeared before them Elijah and Moses, who were talking with Jesus.

[5]Peter said to Jesus, "Rabbi, it is good for us to be here. Let us put up three shelters—one for you, one for Moses and one for Elijah." [6](He did not know what to say, they were so frightened.)

[7]Then a cloud appeared and covered them, and a voice came from the cloud: "This is my Son, whom I love. Listen to him!"

[8]Suddenly, when they looked around, they no longer saw anyone with them except Jesus.

[9]As they were coming down the mountain, Jesus gave them orders not to tell anyone what they had seen until the Son of Man had risen from the dead. [10]They kept the matter to themselves, discussing what "rising from the dead" meant.

[11]And they asked him, "Why do the teachers of the law say that Elijah must come first?"

[12]Jesus replied, "To be sure, Elijah does come first, and restores all things. Why then is it written that the Son of Man must suffer much and be rejected? [13]But I tell you, Elijah has come, and they have done to him everything they wished, just as it is written about him."

Jesus Heals a Boy Possessed by an Impure Spirit

[14]When they came to the other disciples, they saw a large crowd around them and the teachers of the law arguing with them. [15]As soon as all the people saw Jesus, they were overwhelmed with wonder and ran to greet him.

[16]"What are you arguing with them about?" he asked.

[17]A man in the crowd answered, "Teacher, I brought you my son, who is possessed by a spirit that has robbed him

1187

of speech. [18]Whenever it seizes him, it throws him to the ground. He foams at the mouth, gnashes his teeth and becomes rigid. I asked your disciples to drive out the spirit, but they could not."

[19]"You unbelieving generation," Jesus replied, "how long shall I stay with you? How long shall I put up with you? Bring the boy to me."

[20]So they brought him. When the spirit saw Jesus, it immediately threw the boy into a convulsion. He fell to the ground and rolled around, foaming at the mouth.

[21]Jesus asked the boy's father, "How long has he been like this?"

"From childhood," he answered. [22]"It has often thrown him into fire or water to kill him. But if you can do anything, take pity on us and help us."

[23]"'If you can'?" said Jesus. "Everything is possible for one who believes."

[24]Immediately the boy's father exclaimed, "I do believe; help me overcome my unbelief!"

[25]When Jesus saw that a crowd was running to the scene, he rebuked the impure spirit. "You deaf and mute spirit," he said, "I command you, come out of him and never enter him again."

[26]The spirit shrieked, convulsed him violently and came out. The boy looked so much like a corpse that many said, "He's dead." [27]But Jesus took him by the hand and lifted him to his feet, and he stood up.

[28]After Jesus had gone indoors, his disciples asked him privately, "Why couldn't we drive it out?"

[29]He replied, "This kind can come out only by prayer.[a]"

Jesus Predicts His Death a Second Time

[30]They left that place and passed through Galilee. Jesus did not want anyone to know where they were, [31]because he was teaching his disciples. He said to them, "The Son of Man is going to be delivered into the hands of men. They will kill him, and after three days he will rise." [32]But they did not understand what he meant and were afraid to ask him about it.

[33]They came to Capernaum. When he was in the house, he asked them, "What were you arguing about on the road?" [34]But they kept quiet because on the way they had argued about who was the greatest.

[35]Sitting down, Jesus called the Twelve and said, "Anyone who wants to be first must be the very last, and the servant of all."

[36]He took a little child whom he placed among them. Taking the child in his arms, he said to them, [37]"Whoever welcomes one of these little children in my name welcomes me; and whoever welcomes me does not welcome me but the one who sent me."

Whoever Is Not Against Us Is for Us

[38]"Teacher," said John, "we saw someone driving out demons in your name and we told him to stop, because he was not one of us."

[39]"Do not stop him," Jesus said. "For no one who does a miracle in my name can in the next moment say anything bad about me, [40]for whoever is not against us is for us. [41]Truly I tell you, anyone who gives you a cup of water in my name because you belong to the Messiah will certainly not lose their reward.

Causing to Stumble

[42]"If anyone causes one of these little ones—those who believe in me—to stumble, it would be better for them if a large millstone were hung around their neck and they were thrown into the sea. [43]If your hand causes you to stumble, cut it off. It is better for you to enter life maimed than with two hands to go into hell, where the fire never goes out. [44][b] [45]And if your foot causes you to stumble, cut it off. It is better for you to enter life crippled than to have two feet and be thrown into hell. [46][b] [47]And if your eye causes you to stumble, pluck it out. It is better for you to enter the kingdom of God with one eye than

---

[a] 29 Some manuscripts *prayer and fasting*
[b] 44,46 Some manuscripts include here the words of verse 48.

to have two eyes and be thrown into hell, [48]where

> "'the worms that eat them do not die,
> and the fire is not quenched.'[a]

[49]Everyone will be salted with fire.

[50]"Salt is good, but if it loses its saltiness, how can you make it salty again? Have salt among yourselves, and be at peace with each other."

Divorce

10 Jesus then left that place and went into the region of Judea and across the Jordan. Again crowds of people came to him, and as was his custom, he taught them.

[2]Some Pharisees came and tested him by asking, "Is it lawful for a man to divorce his wife?"

[3]"What did Moses command you?" he replied.

[4]They said, "Moses permitted a man to write a certificate of divorce and send her away."

[5]"It was because your hearts were hard

that Moses wrote you this law," Jesus replied. [6]"But at the beginning of creation God 'made them male and female.'[b] [7]For this reason a man will leave his father and mother and be united to his wife,[c] [8]and the two will become one flesh.'[d] So they are no longer two, but one flesh. [9]Therefore what God has joined together, let no one separate."

[10]When they were in the house again, the disciples asked Jesus about this. [11]He answered, "Anyone who divorces his wife and marries another woman commits adultery against her. [12]And if she divorces her husband and marries another man, she commits adultery."

The Little Children and Jesus

[13]People were bringing little children to Jesus for him to place his hands on them, but the disciples rebuked them. [14]When Jesus saw this, he was indignant. He said to them, "Let the little children come to me, and do not hinder them, for the kingdom of God belongs to such as these. [15]Truly I tell you, anyone who will not receive the kingdom of God like a little child will never enter it." [16]And he took the children in his arms, placed his hands on them and blessed them.

The Rich and the Kingdom of God

[17]As Jesus started on his way, a man ran up to him and fell on his knees before him. "Good teacher," he asked, "what must I do to inherit eternal life?"

[18]"Why do you call me good?" Jesus answered. "No one is good—except God alone. [19]You know the commandments: 'You shall not murder, you shall not commit adultery, you shall not steal, you shall not give false testimony, you shall not defraud, honor your father and mother.'[e]"

[20]"Teacher," he declared, "all these I have kept since I was a boy."

[21]Jesus looked at him and loved him. "One thing you lack," he said. "Go, sell

ROCK SOLID *plans*

Mark 9:42–50

Untangle yourself.

Jesus sometimes uses oversized speech to make his point. Right here he says it's better to be lashed to a large grinding stone and tossed in the ocean than to make someone else sin. Or it's preferable to lose a body part than to let it drag you to hell. Jesus surely doesn't want you to do yourself harm. But you get the picture. He seriously expects you to get rid of anything in your life that pressures you to sin.

Your next step: Today when you feel tempted to do wrong, figure out what causes you to feel pressured—and take action to deal with it.

[a] 48 Isaiah 66:24   [b] 6 Gen. 1:27
[c] 7 Some early manuscripts do not have *and be united to his wife.*   [d] 8 Gen. 2:24
[e] 19 Exodus 20:12-16; Deut. 5:16-20

everything you have and give to the poor, and you will have treasure in heaven. Then come, follow me."

²²At this the man's face fell. He went away sad, because he had great wealth.

²³Jesus looked around and said to his disciples, "How hard it is for the rich to enter the kingdom of God!"

²⁴The disciples were amazed at his words. But Jesus said again, "Children, how hard it is*ᵃ* to enter the kingdom of God! ²⁵It is easier for a camel to go through the eye of a needle than for someone who is rich to enter the kingdom of God."

²⁶The disciples were even more amazed, and said to each other, "Who then can be saved?"

²⁷Jesus looked at them and said, "With man this is impossible, but not with God; all things are possible with God."

ROCK SOLID
promises

"All things are possible with God."
Mark 10:27

Jesus makes it possible for you to obey him no matter what seems to stand in your way.

²⁸Then Peter spoke up, "We have left everything to follow you!"

²⁹"Truly I tell you," Jesus replied, "no one who has left home or brothers or sisters or mother or father or children or fields for me and the gospel ³⁰will fail to receive a hundred times as much in this present age: homes, brothers, sisters, mothers, children and fields—along with persecutions—and in the age to come eternal life. ³¹But many who are first will be last, and the last first."

Jesus Predicts His Death a Third Time

³²They were on their way up to Jerusalem, with Jesus leading the way, and the disciples were astonished, while those who followed were afraid. Again he took the Twelve aside and told them what was going to happen to him. ³³"We are going up to Jerusalem," he said, "and the Son of Man will be delivered over to the chief priests and the teachers of the law. They will condemn him to death and will hand him over to the Gentiles, ³⁴who will mock him and spit on him, flog him and kill him. Three days later he will rise."

The Request of James and John

³⁵Then James and John, the sons of Zebedee, came to him. "Teacher," they said, "we want you to do for us whatever we ask."

³⁶"What do you want me to do for you?" he asked.

³⁷They replied, "Let one of us sit at your right and the other at your left in your glory."

³⁸"You don't know what you are asking," Jesus said. "Can you drink the cup I drink or be baptized with the baptism I am baptized with?"

³⁹"We can," they answered.

Jesus said to them, "You will drink the cup I drink and be baptized with the baptism I am baptized with, ⁴⁰but to sit at my right or left is not for me to grant. These places belong to those for whom they have been prepared."

⁴¹When the ten heard about this, they became indignant with James and John. ⁴²Jesus called them together and said, "You know that those who are regarded as rulers of the Gentiles lord it over them, and their high officials exercise authority over them. ⁴³Not so with you. Instead, whoever wants to become great among you must be your servant, ⁴⁴and whoever wants to be first must be slave of all. ⁴⁵For even the Son of Man did not come to be served, but to serve, and to give his life as a ransom for many."

ᵃ 24 Some manuscripts is for those who trust in riches

Blind Bartimaeus Receives His Sight

⁴⁶Then they came to Jericho. As Jesus and his disciples, together with a large crowd, were leaving the city, a blind man, Bartimaeus (which means "son of Timaeus"), was sitting by the roadside begging. ⁴⁷When he heard that it was Jesus of Nazareth, he began to shout, "Jesus, Son of David, have mercy on me!"

⁴⁸Many rebuked him and told him to be quiet, but he shouted all the more, "Son of David, have mercy on me!"

⁴⁹Jesus stopped and said, "Call him."

So they called to the blind man, "Cheer up! On your feet! He's calling you." ⁵⁰Throwing his cloak aside, he jumped to his feet and came to Jesus.

⁵¹"What do you want me to do for you?" Jesus asked him.

The blind man said, "Rabbi, I want to see."

⁵²"Go," said Jesus, "your faith has healed you." Immediately he received his sight and followed Jesus along the road.

Jesus Comes to Jerusalem as King

11 As they approached Jerusalem and came to Bethphage and Bethany at the Mount of Olives, Jesus sent two of his disciples, ²saying to them, "Go to the village ahead of you, and just as you enter it, you will find a colt tied there, which no one has ever ridden. Untie it and bring it here. ³If anyone asks you, 'Why are you doing this?' say, 'The Lord needs it and will send it back here shortly.'"

⁴They went and found a colt outside in the street, tied at a doorway. As they untied it, ⁵some people standing there asked, "What are you doing, untying that colt?" ⁶They answered as Jesus had told them to, and the people let them go. ⁷When they brought the colt to Jesus and threw their cloaks over it, he sat on it. ⁸Many people spread their cloaks on the road, while others spread branches they had cut in the fields. ⁹Those who went ahead and those who followed shouted,

"Hosanna!ᵃ"

"Blessed is he who comes in the name of the Lord!"ᵇ

¹⁰"Blessed is the coming kingdom of our father David!"

"Hosanna in the highest heaven!"

¹¹Jesus entered Jerusalem and went into the temple courts. He looked around at everything, but since it was already late, he went out to Bethany with the Twelve.

Jesus Curses a Fig Tree and Clears the Temple Courts

¹²The next day as they were leaving Bethany, Jesus was hungry. ¹³Seeing in the distance a fig tree in leaf, he went to find out if it had any fruit. When he reached it, he found nothing but leaves, because it was not the season for figs. ¹⁴Then he said to the tree, "May no one ever eat fruit from you again." And his disciples heard him say it.

¹⁵On reaching Jerusalem, Jesus entered the temple courts and began driving out those who were buying and selling there. He overturned the tables of the money changers and the benches of those selling doves, ¹⁶and would not allow anyone to carry merchandise through the temple courts. ¹⁷And as he taught them, he said, "Is it not written: 'My house will be called a house of prayer for all nations'ᶜ? But you have made it 'a den of robbers.'ᵈ"

¹⁸The chief priests and the teachers of the law heard this and began looking for a way to kill him, for they feared him, because the whole crowd was amazed at his teaching.

¹⁹When evening came, Jesus and his disciplesᵉ went out of the city.

²⁰In the morning, as they went along, they saw the fig tree withered from the roots. ²¹Peter remembered and said to Jesus, "Rabbi, look! The fig tree you cursed has withered!"

²²"Have faith in God," Jesus answered. ²³"Trulyᶠ I tell you, if anyone says to this

ᵃ 9 A Hebrew expression meaning "Save!" which became an exclamation of praise; also in verse 10   ᵇ 9 Psalm 118:25,26   ᶜ 17 Isaiah 56:7   ᵈ 17 Jer. 7:11   ᵉ 19 Some early manuscripts came, Jesus   ᶠ 22,23 Some early manuscripts "If you have faith in God," Jesus answered, ²³"truly

UNSHAKEN *God*

God is passionate.

People might picture Jesus as a guy who did nothing more than preach love (see Matthew 22:34–40) and bless babies (see Luke 18:15–17). That tender side of Jesus is real. But it's not the whole picture. Just as frequently Jesus takes a hard line on evil, and when Jesus flips tables in the temple you see a guy passionate about pure worship. He used the brute strength he built as a carpenter to take on people who had lined the temple with businesses swapping money and selling sacrificial animals. No one can ever accuse Jesus of not caring—from the welfare of little kids to the cause of right and wrong.

So ... Are you surprised by Jesus' actions in this temple scene? Why—or why not?

mountain, 'Go, throw yourself into the sea,' and does not doubt in their heart but believes that what they say will happen, it will be done for them. ²⁴Therefore I tell you, whatever you ask for in prayer, believe that you have received it, and it will be yours. ²⁵And when you stand praying, if you hold anything against anyone, forgive them, so that your Father in heaven may forgive you your sins." [26]*a*

The Authority of Jesus Questioned

²⁷They arrived again in Jerusalem, and while Jesus was walking in the temple courts, the chief priests, the teachers of the law and the elders came to him. ²⁸"By what authority are you doing these things?" they asked. "And who gave you authority to do this?"

²⁹Jesus replied, "I will ask you one question. Answer me, and I will tell you by what authority I am doing these things.

³⁰John's baptism—was it from heaven, or of human origin? Tell me!"

³¹They discussed it among themselves and said, "If we say, 'From heaven,' he will ask, 'Then why didn't you believe him?' ³²But if we say, 'Of human origin' . . ." (They feared the people, for everyone held that John really was a prophet.)

³³So they answered Jesus, "We don't know."

Jesus said, "Neither will I tell you by what authority I am doing these things."

The Parable of the Tenants

12 Jesus then began to speak to them in parables: "A man planted a vineyard. He put a wall around it, dug a pit for the winepress and built a watchtower. Then he rented the vineyard to some farmers and moved to another place. ²At harvest time he sent a servant to the tenants to collect from them some of the fruit of the vineyard. ³But they seized him, beat him and sent him away empty-handed. ⁴Then he sent another servant to them; they struck this man on the head and treated him shamefully. ⁵He sent still another, and that one they killed. He sent many others; some of them they beat, others they killed.

⁶"He had one left to send, a son, whom he loved. He sent him last of all, saying, 'They will respect my son.'

⁷"But the tenants said to one another, 'This is the heir. Come, let's kill him, and the inheritance will be ours.' ⁸So they took him and killed him, and threw him out of the vineyard.

⁹"What then will the owner of the vineyard do? He will come and kill those tenants and give the vineyard to others. ¹⁰Haven't you read this passage of Scripture:

"'The stone the builders rejected
    has become the cornerstone;
¹¹the Lord has done this,
    and it is marvelous in our eyes'*b*?"

¹²Then the chief priests, the teachers of the law and the elders looked for a way

a 26 Some manuscripts include here words similar to Matt. 6:15.   *b 11* Psalm 118:22,23 to arrest him because they knew he had spoken the parable against them. But they were afraid of the crowd; so they left him and went away.

Paying the Imperial Tax to Caesar

13 Later they sent some of the Pharisees and Herodians to Jesus to catch him in his words. 14 They came to him and said, "Teacher, we know that you are a man of integrity. You aren't swayed by others, because you pay no attention to who they are; but you teach the way of God in accordance with the truth. Is it right to pay the imperial tax[a] to Caesar or not? 15 Should we pay or shouldn't we?"

But Jesus knew their hypocrisy. "Why are you trying to trap me?" he asked. "Bring me a denarius and let me look at it." 16 They brought the coin, and he asked them, "Whose image is this? And whose inscription?"

"Caesar's," they replied.

17 Then Jesus said to them, "Give back to Caesar what is Caesar's and to God what is God's."

And they were amazed at him.

Marriage at the Resurrection

18 Then the Sadducees, who say there is no resurrection, came to him with a question. 19 "Teacher," they said, "Moses wrote for us that if a man's brother dies and leaves a wife but no children, the man must marry the widow and raise up offspring for his brother. 20 Now there were seven brothers. The first one married and died without leaving any children. 21 The second one married the widow, but he also died, leaving no child. It was the same with the third. 22 In fact, none of the seven left any children. Last of all, the woman died too. 23 At the resurrection[b] whose wife will she be, since the seven were married to her?"

24 Jesus replied, "Are you not in error because you do not know the Scriptures or the power of God? 25 When the dead rise, they will neither marry nor be given in marriage; they will be like the angels in heaven. 26 Now about the dead rising—

have you not read in the Book of Moses, in the account of the burning bush, how God said to him, 'I am the God of Abraham, the God of Isaac, and the God of Jacob'[c]? 27 He is not the God of the dead, but of the living. You are badly mistaken!"

The Greatest Commandment

28 One of the teachers of the law came and heard them debating. Noticing that Jesus had given them a good answer, he asked him, "Of all the commandments, which is the most important?"

29 "The most important one," answered Jesus, "is this: 'Hear, O Israel: The Lord our God, the Lord is one.[d] 30 Love the Lord your God with all your heart and with all your soul and with all your mind and with all your strength.'[e] 31 The second is this: 'Love your neighbor as yourself.'[f] There is no commandment greater than these."

32 "Well said, teacher," the man replied. "You are right in saying that God is one and there is no other but him. 33 To love him with all your heart, with all your understanding and with all your strength, and to love your neighbor as yourself is more important than all burnt offerings and sacrifices."

34 When Jesus saw that he had answered wisely, he said to him, "You are not far from the kingdom of God." And from then on no one dared ask him any more questions.

Whose Son Is the Messiah?

35 While Jesus was teaching in the temple courts, he asked, "Why do the teachers of the law say that the Messiah is the son of David? 36 David himself, speaking by the Holy Spirit, declared:

"'The Lord said to my Lord:
  "Sit at my right hand
until I put your enemies
    under your feet."'[g]

---

[a] 14 A special tax levied on subject peoples, not on Roman citizens   [b] 23 Some manuscripts *resurrection, when people rise from the dead,*
[c] 26 Exodus 3:6   [d] 29 Or *The Lord our God is one Lord*   [e] 30 Deut. 6:4,5   [f] 31 Lev. 19:18
[g] 36 Psalm 110:1

ROCK SOLID principles

Mark 12:28–31

Love God and people.

Daniel was into being a Christian in a big way. He sported Christian T-shirts, hung out at Christian events, read Christian books, and listened to Christian music. After a while it started to feel hollow, like he was pretending to be something he wasn't. One day a song he heard hit him like a slap in the face. He listened to it over and over until he caught the message. The biggest part of being a Christian, it said, is obeying the simple command to love God and love others. Daniel had missed the point of genuinely following Jesus. He had wrapped himself up in a Christian shell, but he needed to be a Christian from the inside out.

Jesus summed up all of the commands of the Bible when he said God's most important rule was to love him more than anything—and people almost as much. God wants you to love him "with all your heart and with all your soul and with all your mind and with all your strength." He wants you to love all people as much as you love yourself (Mark 12:30–31).

³⁷David himself calls him 'Lord.' How then can he be his son?"

The large crowd listened to him with delight.

Warning Against the Teachers of the Law

³⁸As he taught, Jesus said, "Watch out for the teachers of the law. They like to walk around in flowing robes and be greeted with respect in the marketplaces, ³⁹and have the most important seats in the synagogues and the places of honor at banquets. ⁴⁰They devour widows' houses and for a show make lengthy prayers. These men will be punished most severely."

The Widow's Offering

⁴¹Jesus sat down opposite the place where the offerings were put and watched the crowd putting their money into the temple treasury. Many rich people threw in large amounts. ⁴²But a poor widow came and put in two very small copper coins, worth only a few cents.

⁴³Calling his disciples to him, Jesus said, "Truly I tell you, this poor widow has put more into the treasury than all the others. ⁴⁴They all gave out of their wealth; but she, out of her poverty, put in everything—all she had to live on."

The Destruction of the Temple and Signs of the End Times

13 As Jesus was leaving the temple, one of his disciples said to him, "Look, Teacher! What massive stones! What magnificent buildings!"

²"Do you see all these great buildings?" replied Jesus. "Not one stone here will be left on another; every one will be thrown down."

³As Jesus was sitting on the Mount of Olives opposite the temple, Peter, James, John and Andrew asked him privately,

4 "Tell us, when will these things happen? And what will be the sign that they are all about to be fulfilled?"

5 Jesus said to them: "Watch out that no one deceives you. 6 Many will come in my name, claiming, 'I am he,' and will deceive many. 7 When you hear of wars and rumors of wars, do not be alarmed. Such things must happen, but the end is still to come. 8 Nation will rise against nation, and kingdom against kingdom. There will be earthquakes in various places, and famines. These are the beginning of birth pains.

9 "You must be on your guard. You will be handed over to the local councils and flogged in the synagogues. On account of me you will stand before governors and kings as witnesses to them. 10 And the gospel must first be preached to all nations. 11 Whenever you are arrested and brought to trial, do not worry beforehand about what to say. Just say whatever is given you at the time, for it is not you speaking, but the Holy Spirit.

12 "Brother will betray brother to death, and a father his child. Children will rebel against their parents and have them put to death. 13 Everyone will hate you because of me, but the one who stands firm to the end will be saved.

14 "When you see 'the abomination that causes desolation'[a] standing where it[b] does not belong—let the reader understand—then let those who are in Judea flee to the mountains. 15 Let no one on the housetop go down or enter the house to take anything out. 16 Let no one in the field go back to get their cloak. 17 How dreadful it will be in those days for pregnant women and nursing mothers! 18 Pray that this will not take place in winter, 19 because those will be days of distress unequaled from the beginning, when God created the world, until now—and never to be equaled again. 20 "If the Lord had not cut short those days, no one would survive. But for the sake of the elect, whom he has chosen, he has shortened them. 21 At that time if anyone says to you, 'Look, here is the Messi-

ah!' or, 'Look, there he is!' do not believe it. 22 For false messiahs and false prophets will appear and perform signs and wonders to deceive, if possible, even the elect. 23 So be on your guard; I have told you everything ahead of time.

24 "But in those days, following that distress,

"'the sun will be darkened,
and the moon will not give its light;
25 the stars will fall from the sky,
and the heavenly bodies will be
shaken.'[c]

26 "At that time people will see the Son of Man coming in clouds with great power and glory. 27 And he will send his angels and gather his elect from the four winds, from the ends of the earth to the ends of the heavens.

ROCK SOLID promises

"At that time people will see the Son of Man coming in clouds with great power and glory."

Mark 13:26

When Jesus shows up on earth a second time, no one will miss his arrival.

28 "Now learn this lesson from the fig tree: As soon as its twigs get tender and its leaves come out, you know that summer is near. 29 Even so, when you see these things happening, you know that it[b] is near, right at the door. 30 Truly I tell you, this generation will certainly not pass away until all these things have happened. 31 Heaven and earth will pass away, but my words will never pass away.

a 14 Daniel 9:27; 11:31; 12:11   b 14,29 Or he
c 25 Isaiah 13:10; 34:4

The Day and Hour Unknown

³²"But about that day or hour no one knows, not even the angels in heaven, nor the Son, but only the Father. ³³Be on guard! Be alert[a]! You do not know when that time will come. ³⁴It's like a man going away: He leaves his house and puts his servants in charge, each with their assigned task, and tells the one at the door to keep watch.

³⁵"Therefore keep watch because you do not know when the owner of the house will come back—whether in the evening, or at midnight, or when the rooster crows, or at dawn. ³⁶If he comes suddenly, do not let him find you sleeping. ³⁷What I say to you, I say to everyone: 'Watch!'"

Jesus Anointed at Bethany

14 Now the Passover and the Festival of Unleavened Bread were only two days away, and the chief priests and the teachers of the law were scheming to arrest Jesus secretly and kill him. ²"But not during the festival," they said, "or the people may riot."

³While he was in Bethany, reclining at the table in the home of Simon the Leper, a woman came with an alabaster jar of very expensive perfume, made of pure nard. She broke the jar and poured the perfume on his head.

⁴Some of those present were saying indignantly to one another, "Why this waste of perfume? ⁵It could have been sold for more than a year's wages[b] and the money given to the poor." And they rebuked her harshly.

⁶"Leave her alone," said Jesus. "Why are you bothering her? She has done a beautiful thing to me. ⁷The poor you will always have with you,[c] and you can help them any time you want. But you will not always have me. ⁸She did what she could. She poured perfume on my body beforehand to prepare for my burial. ⁹Truly I tell you, wherever the gospel is preached throughout the world, what she has done will also be told, in memory of her."

¹⁰Then Judas Iscariot, one of the Twelve, went to the chief priests to betray Jesus to them. ¹¹They were delighted to hear this and promised to give him money. So he watched for an opportunity to hand him over.

The Last Supper

¹²On the first day of the Festival of Unleavened Bread, when it was customary to sacrifice the Passover lamb, Jesus' disciples asked him, "Where do you want us to go and make preparations for you to eat the Passover?"

¹³So he sent two of his disciples, telling them, "Go into the city, and a man carrying a jar of water will meet you. Follow him. ¹⁴Say to the owner of the house he enters, 'The Teacher asks: Where is my guest room, where I may eat the Passover with my disciples?' ¹⁵He will show you a large room upstairs, furnished and ready. Make preparations for us there."

¹⁶The disciples left, went into the city and found things just as Jesus had told them. So they prepared the Passover.

¹⁷When evening came, Jesus arrived with the Twelve. ¹⁸While they were reclining at the table eating, he said, "Truly I tell you, one of you will betray me—one who is eating with me."

¹⁹They were saddened, and one by one they said to him, "Surely you don't mean me?"

²⁰"It is one of the Twelve," he replied, "one who dips bread into the bowl with me. ²¹The Son of Man will go just as it is written about him. But woe to that man who betrays the Son of Man! It would be better for him if he had not been born."

²²While they were eating, Jesus took bread, and when he had given thanks, he broke it and gave it to his disciples, saying, "Take it; this is my body."

²³Then he took a cup, and when he had given thanks, he gave it to them, and they all drank from it.

²⁴"This is my blood of the[d] covenant, which is poured out for many," he said to them. ²⁵"Truly I tell you, I will not drink

---

[a] 33 Some manuscripts *alert and pray*   [b] 5 Greek *than three hundred denarii*   [c] 7 See Deut. 15:11.   [d] 24 Some manuscripts *the new*

again from the fruit of the vine until that day when I drink it new in the kingdom of God."

²⁶When they had sung a hymn, they went out to the Mount of Olives.

Jesus Predicts Peter's Denial

²⁷"You will all fall away," Jesus told them, "for it is written:

> "'I will strike the shepherd,
>   and the sheep will be scattered.'ᵃ

²⁸But after I have risen, I will go ahead of you into Galilee."

²⁹Peter declared, "Even if all fall away, I will not."

³⁰"Truly I tell you," Jesus answered, "today—yes, tonight—before the rooster crows twiceᵇ you yourself will disown me three times."

³¹But Peter insisted emphatically, "Even if I have to die with you, I will never disown you." And all the others said the same.

Gethsemane

³²They went to a place called Gethsemane, and Jesus said to his disciples, "Sit here while I pray." ³³He took Peter, James and John along with him, and he began to be deeply distressed and troubled. ³⁴"My soul is overwhelmed with sorrow to the point of death," he said to them. "Stay here and keep watch."

³⁵Going a little farther, he fell to the ground and prayed that if possible the hour might pass from him. ³⁶"Abba,ᶜ Father," he said, "everything is possible for you. Take this cup from me. Yet not what I will, but what you will."

³⁷Then he returned to his disciples and found them sleeping. "Simon," he said to Peter, "are you asleep? Couldn't you keep watch for one hour? ³⁸Watch and pray so that you will not fall into temptation. The spirit is willing, but the flesh is weak."

³⁹Once more he went away and prayed the same thing. ⁴⁰When he came back, he again found them sleeping, because their eyes were heavy. They did not know what to say to him.

⁴¹Returning the third time, he said to them, "Are you still sleeping and resting?

Enough! The hour has come. Look, the Son of Man is delivered into the hands of sinners. ⁴²Rise! Let us go! Here comes my betrayer!"

Jesus Arrested

⁴³Just as he was speaking, Judas, one of the Twelve, appeared. With him was a crowd armed with swords and clubs, sent from the chief priests, the teachers of the law, and the elders.

⁴⁴Now the betrayer had arranged a signal with them: "The one I kiss is the man; arrest him and lead him away under guard." ⁴⁵Going at once to Jesus, Judas said, "Rabbi!" and kissed him. ⁴⁶The men seized Jesus and arrested him. ⁴⁷Then one of those standing near drew his sword and struck the servant of the high priest, cutting off his ear.

⁴⁸"Am I leading a rebellion," said Jesus, "that you have come out with swords and clubs to capture me? ⁴⁹Every day I was with you, teaching in the temple courts, and you did not arrest me. But the Scriptures must be fulfilled." ⁵⁰Then everyone deserted him and fled.

⁵¹A young man, wearing nothing but a linen garment, was following Jesus. When they seized him, ⁵²he fled naked, leaving his garment behind.

Jesus Before the Sanhedrin

⁵³They took Jesus to the high priest, and all the chief priests, the elders and the teachers of the law came together. ⁵⁴Peter followed him at a distance, right into the courtyard of the high priest. There he sat with the guards and warmed himself at the fire.

⁵⁵The chief priests and the whole Sanhedrin were looking for evidence against Jesus so that they could put him to death, but they did not find any. ⁵⁶Many testified falsely against him, but their statements did not agree.

⁵⁷Then some stood up and gave this false testimony against him: ⁵⁸"We heard him say, 'I will destroy this temple made with human hands and in three days will build

---

ᵃ 27 Zech. 13:7   ᵇ 30 Some early manuscripts do not have *twice*.   ᶜ 36 Aramaic for *father* another, not made with hands.'" ⁵⁹Yet even then their testimony did not agree.

⁶⁰Then the high priest stood up before them and asked Jesus, "Are you not going to answer? What is this testimony that these men are bringing against you?" ⁶¹But Jesus remained silent and gave no answer.

Again the high priest asked him, "Are you the Messiah, the Son of the Blessed One?"

⁶²"I am," said Jesus. "And you will see the Son of Man sitting at the right hand of the Mighty One and coming on the clouds of heaven."

⁶³The high priest tore his clothes. "Why do we need any more witnesses?" he asked. ⁶⁴"You have heard the blasphemy. What do you think?"

They all condemned him as worthy of death. ⁶⁵Then some began to spit at him; they blindfolded him, struck him with their fists, and said, "Prophesy!" And the guards took him and beat him.

Peter Disowns Jesus

⁶⁶While Peter was below in the courtyard, one of the servant girls of the high priest came by. ⁶⁷When she saw Peter warming himself, she looked closely at him.

"You also were with that Nazarene, Jesus," she said.

⁶⁸But he denied it. "I don't know or understand what you're talking about," he said, and went out into the entryway.ᵃ

⁶⁹When the servant girl saw him there, she said again to those standing around, "This fellow is one of them." ⁷⁰Again he denied it.

After a little while, those standing near said to Peter, "Surely you are one of them, for you are a Galilean."

⁷¹He began to call down curses, and he swore to them, "I don't know this man you're talking about."

⁷²Immediately the rooster crowed the second time.ᵇ Then Peter remembered the word Jesus had spoken to him: "Before the rooster crows twiceᶜ you will disown me three times." And he broke down and wept.

Jesus Before Pilate

15 Very early in the morning, the chief priests, with the elders, the teachers of the law and the whole Sanhedrin, made their plans. So they bound Jesus, led him away and handed him over to Pilate.

²"Are you the king of the Jews?" asked Pilate.

"You have said so," Jesus replied.

³The chief priests accused him of many things. ⁴So again Pilate asked him, "Aren't you going to answer? See how many things they are accusing you of."

⁵But Jesus still made no reply, and Pilate was amazed.

⁶Now it was the custom at the festival to release a prisoner whom the people requested. ⁷A man called Barabbas was in prison with the insurrectionists who had committed murder in the uprising. ⁸The crowd came up and asked Pilate to do for them what he usually did.

⁹"Do you want me to release to you the king of the Jews?" asked Pilate, ¹⁰knowing it was out of self-interest that the chief priests had handed Jesus over to him. ¹¹But the chief priests stirred up the crowd to have Pilate release Barabbas instead.

¹²"What shall I do, then, with the one you call the king of the Jews?" Pilate asked them.

¹³"Crucify him!" they shouted.

¹⁴"Why? What crime has he committed?" asked Pilate.

But they shouted all the louder, "Crucify him!"

¹⁵Wanting to satisfy the crowd, Pilate released Barabbas to them. He had Jesus flogged, and handed him over to be crucified.

The Soldiers Mock Jesus

¹⁶The soldiers led Jesus away into the palace (that is, the Praetorium) and called together the whole company of soldiers. ¹⁷They put a purple robe on him, then twisted together a crown of thorns and set

---

ᵃ 68 Some early manuscripts *entryway and the rooster crowed* ᵇ 72 Some early manuscripts do not have *the second time.* ᶜ 72 Some early manuscripts do not have *twice.*

it on him. ¹⁸ And they began to call out to him, "Hail, king of the Jews!" ¹⁹ Again and again they struck him on the head with a staff and spit on him. Falling on their knees, they paid homage to him. ²⁰ And when they had mocked him, they took off the purple robe and put his own clothes on him. Then they led him out to crucify him.

The Crucifixion of Jesus

²¹ A certain man from Cyrene, Simon, the father of Alexander and Rufus, was passing by on his way in from the country, and they forced him to carry the cross. ²² They brought Jesus to the place called Golgotha (which means "the place of the skull"). ²³ Then they offered him wine mixed with myrrh, but he did not take it. ²⁴ And they crucified him. Dividing up his clothes, they cast lots to see what each would get.

²⁵ It was nine in the morning when they crucified him. ²⁶ The written notice of the charge against him read: THE KING OF THE JEWS.

²⁷ They crucified two rebels with him, one on his right and one on his left. [28]ᵃ ²⁹ Those who passed by hurled insults at him, shaking their heads and saying, "So! You who are going to destroy the temple and build it in three days, ³⁰ come down from the cross and save yourself!" ³¹ In the same way the chief priests and the teachers of the law mocked him among themselves. "He saved others," they said, "but he can't save himself! ³² Let this Messiah, this king of Israel, come down now from the cross, that we may see and believe." Those crucified with him also heaped insults on him.

The Death of Jesus

³³ At noon, darkness came over the whole land until three in the afternoon. ³⁴ And at three in the afternoon Jesus cried out in a loud voice, *"Eloi, Eloi, lema sabachthani?"* (which means "My God, my God, why have you forsaken me?").ᵇ

³⁵ When some of those standing near heard this, they said, "Listen, he's calling Elijah."

³⁶ Someone ran, filled a sponge with wine vinegar, put it on a staff, and offered it to Jesus to drink. "Now leave him alone. Let's see if Elijah comes to take him down," he said.

³⁷ With a loud cry, Jesus breathed his last.

³⁸ The curtain of the temple was torn in two from top to bottom. ³⁹ And when the centurion, who stood there in front of Jesus, saw how he died,ᶜ he said, "Surely this man was the Son of God!"

⁴⁰ Some women were watching from a distance. Among them were Mary Magdalene, Mary the mother of James the younger and of Joseph,ᵈ and Salome. ⁴¹ In Galilee these women had followed him and cared for his needs. Many other women who had come up with him to Jerusalem were also there.

The Burial of Jesus

⁴² It was Preparation Day (that is, the day before the Sabbath). So as evening approached, ⁴³ Joseph of Arimathea, a prominent member of the Council, who was himself waiting for the kingdom of God, went boldly to Pilate and asked for Jesus' body. ⁴⁴ Pilate was surprised to hear that he was already dead. Summoning the centurion, he asked him if Jesus had already died. ⁴⁵ When he learned from the centurion that it was so, he gave the body to Joseph. ⁴⁶ So Joseph bought some linen cloth, took down the body, wrapped it in the linen, and placed it in a tomb cut out of rock. Then he rolled a stone against the entrance of the tomb. ⁴⁷ Mary Magdalene and Mary the mother of Joseph saw where he was laid.

Jesus Has Risen

16 When the Sabbath was over, Mary Magdalene, Mary the mother of James, and Salome bought spices so that they might go to anoint Jesus' body. ² Very early on the first day of the week, just after sunrise, they were on their way to the tomb ³ and they asked each other, "Who will roll the stone away from the entrance of the tomb?"

⁴ But when they looked up, they saw

ᵃ 28 Some manuscripts include here words similar to Luke 22:37.   ᵇ 34 Psalm 22:1
ᶜ 39 Some manuscripts *saw that he died with such a cry*   ᵈ 40 Greek *Joses,* a variant of *Joseph*; also in verse 47

that the stone, which was very large, had been rolled away. [5]As they entered the tomb, they saw a young man dressed in a white robe sitting on the right side, and they were alarmed.

[6]"Don't be alarmed," he said. "You are looking for Jesus the Nazarene, who was crucified. He has risen! He is not here. See the place where they laid him. [7]But go, tell his disciples and Peter, 'He is going ahead of you into Galilee. There you will see him, just as he told you.'"

[8]Trembling and bewildered, the women went out and fled from the tomb. They said nothing to anyone, because they were afraid.[a]

[The earliest manuscripts and some other ancient witnesses do not have verses 9–20.]

[9]When Jesus rose early on the first day of the week, he appeared first to Mary Magdalene, out of whom he had driven seven demons. [10]She went and told those who had been with him and who were mourning and weeping. [11]When they heard

[a] 8 Some manuscripts have the following ending between verses 8 and 9, and one manuscript has it after verse 8 (omitting verses 9-20): Then they quickly reported all these instructions to those around Peter. After this, Jesus himself also sent out through them from east to west the sacred and imperishable proclamation of eternal salvation. Amen.

Mark 15:33–41

Mary Magdalene broke loose from demons.

As Jesus hung dying on the cross, some women watched from a distance. They were women who had "followed him and cared for his needs" (Mark 15:42). Among these loyal friends was Mary Magdalene.

Mary's name "Magdalene" means she came from the town of Magdala on the Sea of Galilee. Some Bible readers assume Mary was the woman who washed Jesus' feet (see Luke 7:37–38) or the woman caught in adultery (see John 8:1–11), but the Bible doesn't identify her as the person in those scenes. What we know for sure is that Mary had been oppressed by seven demons, and she followed Jesus after he set her free (see Luke 8:2).

Mary watched as Jesus was put on trial, sentenced to die, cruelly beaten, and then executed on the cross. When Jesus rose from the dead, others saw the empty tomb before her. But Mary was the first person to meet the resurrected Jesus. As she wept at the tomb, she turned and saw a man she thought was a gardener. When she asked if he had moved the body of Jesus, he spoke just one word, "Mary!" Suddenly she recognized her risen friend and Lord. Mary wanted to hold on to Jesus, but he sent her to tell his other disciples he would soon ascend to heaven (see John 20:11–18). At first the guys who followed Jesus thought her words were "nonsense" (see Luke 24:10–11), but soon they too discovered Jesus had risen.

The fact that Jesus had a close female follower like Mary doesn't imply he was married to her, because the authors of the Bible would have no reason to hide that fact.

You can find Mary Magdalene in the gospels of Matthew, Luke and John. It's also likely she was present with the early disciples in Acts 1:14.

UNSHAKEN people

that Jesus was alive and that she had seen him, they did not believe it.

¹²Afterward Jesus appeared in a different form to two of them while they were walking in the country. ¹³These returned and reported it to the rest; but they did not believe them either.

¹⁴Later Jesus appeared to the Eleven as they were eating; he rebuked them for their lack of faith and their stubborn refusal to believe those who had seen him after he had risen.

¹⁵He said to them, "Go into all the world and preach the gospel to all creation. ¹⁶Whoever believes and is baptized will be saved, but whoever does not believe will be condemned. ¹⁷And these signs will accompany those who believe: In my name they will drive out demons; they will speak in new tongues; ¹⁸they will pick up snakes with their hands; and when they drink deadly poison, it will not hurt them at all; they will place their hands on sick people, and they will get well."

¹⁹After the Lord Jesus had spoken to them, he was taken up into heaven and he sat at the right hand of God. ²⁰Then the disciples went out and preached everywhere, and the Lord worked with them and confirmed his word by the signs that accompanied it.

BOOK OUTLINE

Luke, the longest of the Gospels, was written by the same author as the book of Acts. Luke's writing shows him to be a highly educated man, who wrote from a Greek background and viewpoint.

In this Gospel Luke shows that Jesus loved all kinds of people. He often wrote about and identified by name the women Christ met and spoke to. He also gave more attention to children than any other Gospel writer. In the parables especially, he wrote about the poor and oppressed. Jesus is portrayed as an actual person in history who "came to seek and to save the lost" (19:10).

The theme of joy is felt throughout this book—from the song of Mary and later the angels at Jesus' birth to the disciples who "returned to Jerusalem with great joy" after Christ's ascension. It is obvious that Luke wanted to tell others that Christ's coming brought joy as well as hope and salvation to a sinful world.

Introduction

Many have undertaken to draw up an account of the things that have been fulfilled*a* among us, ²just as they were handed down to us by those who from the first were eyewitnesses and servants of the word. ³With this in mind, since I myself have carefully investigated everything from the beginning, I too decided to write an orderly account for you, most excellent Theophilus, ⁴so that you may know the certainty of the things you have been taught.

The Birth of John the Baptist Foretold

⁵In the time of Herod king of Judea there was a priest named Zechariah, who belonged to the priestly division of Abijah; his wife Elizabeth was also a descendant of Aaron. ⁶Both of them were righteous in the sight of God, observing all the Lord's commands and decrees blamelessly. ⁷But they were childless because Elizabeth was not able to conceive, and they were both very old.

⁸Once when Zechariah's division was on duty and he was serving as priest before God, ⁹he was chosen by lot, according to the custom of the priesthood, to go into the temple of the Lord and burn incense. ¹⁰And when the time for the burning of incense came, all the assembled worshipers were praying outside.

¹¹Then an angel of the Lord appeared to him, standing at the right side of the altar of incense. ¹²When Zechariah saw him, he was startled and was gripped with fear. ¹³But the angel said to him: "Do not be afraid, Zechariah; your prayer has been heard. Your wife Elizabeth will bear you a son, and you are to call him John. ¹⁴He will be a joy and delight to you, and many will rejoice because of his birth, ¹⁵for he will be great in the sight of the Lord. He is never to take wine or other fermented drink, and he will be filled with the Holy Spirit even before he is born. ¹⁶He will bring back many of the people of Israel to the Lord their God. ¹⁷And he will go on before the Lord, in the spirit and power of Elijah, to turn the hearts of the parents to their children and the disobedient to the wisdom of the righteous—to make ready a people prepared for the Lord."

¹⁸Zechariah asked the angel, "How can I be sure of this? I am an old man and my wife is well along in years."

a 1 Or *been surely believed*

Luke 1:1–4

The Gospels are eyewitness accounts of Jesus.

You only have to read a few sentences into the book of Luke before you learn the author intends to give you an accurate report of the life of Jesus. Luke the doctor (see Colossians 4:14) was a traveling partner of the apostle Paul (see Acts 16:11). Luke says that many others have written about Jesus. But because he has carefully investigated the facts right from the start, he is uniquely qualified to give "an orderly account" (Luke 1:3). Significantly, this detail-minded doctor points out that he isn't collecting made-up stories but is getting reports from eyewitnesses, people who saw and heard Jesus firsthand. He presents these facts so his readers can know "the certainty of the things you have been taught" (Luke 1:4). That's amazing news. When you open the pages of Luke (and the other gospel books of Matthew, Mark, and John) you don't find fairy tales. You discover a reliable history of Jesus passed down from people who were there.

Think: Why does it matter that you learn about Jesus from eyewitnesses?

ROCK SOLID truths

1203

¹⁹The angel said to him, "I am Gabriel. I stand in the presence of God, and I have been sent to speak to you and to tell you this good news. ²⁰And now you will be silent and not able to speak until the day this happens, because you did not believe my words, which will come true at their appointed time."

²¹Meanwhile, the people were waiting for Zechariah and wondering why he stayed so long in the temple. ²²When he came out, he could not speak to them. They realized he had seen a vision in the temple, for he kept making signs to them but remained unable to speak.

²³When his time of service was completed, he returned home. ²⁴After this his wife Elizabeth became pregnant and for five months remained in seclusion. ²⁵"The Lord has done this for me," she said. "In these days he has shown his favor and taken away my disgrace among the people."

The Birth of Jesus Foretold

²⁶In the sixth month of Elizabeth's pregnancy, God sent the angel Gabriel to Nazareth, a town in Galilee, ²⁷to a virgin pledged to be married to a man named Joseph, a descendant of David. The virgin's name was Mary. ²⁸The angel went to her and said, "Greetings, you who are highly favored! The Lord is with you."

²⁹Mary was greatly troubled at his words and wondered what kind of greeting this might be. ³⁰But the angel said to her, "Do not be afraid, Mary; you have found favor with God. ³¹You will conceive and give birth to a son, and you are to call him Jesus. ³²He will be great and will be called the Son of the Most High. The Lord God will give him the throne of his father David, ³³and he will reign over Jacob's descendants forever; his kingdom will never end."

³⁴"How will this be," Mary asked the angel, "since I am a virgin?"

³⁵The angel answered, "The Holy Spirit will come on you, and the power of the Most High will overshadow you. So the holy one to be born will be called*a* the Son of God. ³⁶Even Elizabeth your relative is going to have a child in her old age, and she who was said to be unable to conceive is in her sixth month. ³⁷For no word from God will ever fail."

³⁸"I am the Lord's servant," Mary answered. "May your word to me be fulfilled." Then the angel left her.

Mary Visits Elizabeth

³⁹At that time Mary got ready and hurried to a town in the hill country of Judea, ⁴⁰where she entered Zechariah's home and greeted Elizabeth. ⁴¹When Elizabeth heard Mary's greeting, the baby leaped in her womb, and Elizabeth was filled with the Holy Spirit. ⁴²In a loud voice she exclaimed: "Blessed are you among women, and blessed is the child you will bear! ⁴³But why am I so favored, that the mother of my Lord should come to me? ⁴⁴As soon as the sound of your greeting reached my ears, the baby in my womb leaped for joy. ⁴⁵Blessed is she who has believed that the Lord would fulfill his promises to her!"

Mary's Song

⁴⁶And Mary said:

"My soul glorifies the Lord
⁴⁷   and my spirit rejoices in God my
        Savior,
⁴⁸for he has been mindful
        of the humble state of his servant.
    From now on all generations will call
        me blessed,
⁴⁹   for the Mighty One has done great
        things for me—
    holy is his name.
⁵⁰His mercy extends to those who fear
        him,
    from generation to generation.
⁵¹He has performed mighty deeds with
        his arm;
    he has scattered those who
        are proud in their inmost
        thoughts.
⁵²He has brought down rulers from
        their thrones
    but has lifted up the humble.

a 35 Or *So the child to be born will be called holy,*

⁵³He has filled the hungry with good
   things
   but has sent the rich away empty.
⁵⁴He has helped his servant Israel,
   remembering to be merciful
⁵⁵to Abraham and his descendants
   forever,
   just as he promised our ancestors."

⁵⁶Mary stayed with Elizabeth for about three months and then returned home.

ROCK SOLID promises

"He has filled the hungry with good things."
Luke 1:53

God remembers the poor. He promises to meet their needs. They are at the top of the list of people he loves.

The Birth of John the Baptist

⁵⁷When it was time for Elizabeth to have her baby, she gave birth to a son. ⁵⁸Her neighbors and relatives heard that the Lord had shown her great mercy, and they shared her joy.

⁵⁹On the eighth day they came to circumcise the child, and they were going to name him after his father Zechariah, ⁶⁰but his mother spoke up and said, "No! He is to be called John."

⁶¹They said to her, "There is no one among your relatives who has that name."

⁶²Then they made signs to his father, to find out what he would like to name the child. ⁶³He asked for a writing tablet, and to everyone's astonishment he wrote, "His name is John." ⁶⁴Immediately his mouth was opened and his tongue set free, and he began to speak, praising God. ⁶⁵All the neighbors were filled with awe, and throughout the hill country of Judea people were talking about all these things. ⁶⁶Everyone who heard this wondered about it, asking, "What then is this child going to be?" For the Lord's hand was with him.

Zechariah's Song

⁶⁷His father Zechariah was filled with the Holy Spirit and prophesied:

⁶⁸"Praise be to the Lord, the God of
   Israel,
   because he has come to his people
   and redeemed them.
⁶⁹He has raised up a horn[a] of salvation
   for us
   in the house of his servant David
⁷⁰(as he said through his holy prophets
   of long ago),
⁷¹salvation from our enemies
   and from the hand of all who hate
   us—
⁷²to show mercy to our ancestors
   and to remember his holy covenant,
⁷³   the oath he swore to our father
   Abraham:
⁷⁴to rescue us from the hand of our
   enemies,
   and to enable us to serve him
   without fear
⁷⁵   in holiness and righteousness before
   him all our days.

⁷⁶And you, my child, will be called a
   prophet of the Most High;
   for you will go on before the Lord
   to prepare the way for him,
⁷⁷to give his people the knowledge of
   salvation
   through the forgiveness of their sins,
⁷⁸because of the tender mercy of our God,
   by which the rising sun will come to
   us from heaven
⁷⁹to shine on those living in darkness
   and in the shadow of death,
   to guide our feet into the path of peace."

⁸⁰And the child grew and became strong in spirit[b]; and he lived in the wilderness until he appeared publicly to Israel.

ᵃ 69 Horn here symbolizes a strong king.
ᵇ 80 Or in the Spirit

The Birth of Jesus

In those days Caesar Augustus issued a decree that a census should be taken of the entire Roman world. ²(This was the first census that took place while*a* Quirinius was governor of Syria.) ³And everyone went to their own town to register.

⁴So Joseph also went up from the town of Nazareth in Galilee to Judea, to Bethlehem the town of David, because he belonged to the house and line of David. ⁵He went there to register with Mary, who was pledged to be married to him and was expecting a child. ⁶While they were there, the time came for the baby to be born, ⁷and she gave birth to her firstborn, a son. She wrapped him in cloths and placed him in a manger, because there was no guest room available for them.

⁸And there were shepherds living out in the fields nearby, keeping watch over their flocks at night. ⁹An angel of the Lord appeared to them, and the glory of the Lord shone around them, and they were terrified. ¹⁰But the angel said to them, "Do not be afraid. I bring you good news that will cause great joy for all the people. ¹¹Today in the town of David a Savior has been born to you; he is the Messiah, the Lord. ¹²This will be a sign to you: You will find a baby wrapped in cloths and lying in a manger."

¹³Suddenly a great company of the heavenly host appeared with the angel, praising God and saying,

¹⁴"Glory to God in the highest heaven,
and on earth peace to those on
whom his favor rests."

¹⁵When the angels had left them and gone into heaven, the shepherds said to one another, "Let's go to Bethlehem and see this thing that has happened, which the Lord has told us about."

¹⁶So they hurried off and found Mary and Joseph, and the baby, who was lying in the manger. ¹⁷When they had seen him, they spread the word concerning what had been told them about this child, ¹⁸and all who heard it were amazed at what the shepherds said to them. ¹⁹But Mary treasured up all these things and pondered them in her heart. ²⁰The shepherds returned, glorifying and praising God for all the things they had heard and seen, which were just as they had been told.

²¹On the eighth day, when it was time to circumcise the child, he was named Jesus, the name the angel had given him before he was conceived.

Jesus Presented in the Temple

²²When the time came for the purification rites required by the Law of Moses, Joseph and Mary took him to Jerusalem to present him to the Lord ²³(as it is written in the Law of the Lord, "Every firstborn male is to be consecrated to the Lord"*b*), ²⁴and to offer a sacrifice in keeping with what is said in the Law of the Lord: "a pair of doves or two young pigeons."*c*

²⁵Now there was a man in Jerusalem called Simeon, who was righteous and devout. He was waiting for the consolation of Israel, and the Holy Spirit was on him. ²⁶It had been revealed to him by the Holy Spirit that he would not die before he had seen the Lord's Messiah. ²⁷Moved by the Spirit, he went into the temple courts. When the parents brought in the child Jesus to do for him what the custom of the Law required, ²⁸Simeon took him in his arms and praised God, saying:

²⁹"Sovereign Lord, as you have
promised,
you may now dismiss*d* your servant
in peace.
³⁰For my eyes have seen your salvation,
³¹ which you have prepared in the
sight of all nations:
³²a light for revelation to the Gentiles,
and the glory of your people Israel."

³³The child's father and mother marveled at what was said about him. ³⁴Then Simeon blessed them and said to Mary, his mother: "This child is destined to cause the falling and rising of many in Is-

a 2 Or *This census took place before*
b 23 Exodus 13:2,12   *c 24* Lev. 12:8
d 29 Or *promised, / now dismiss*

rael, and to be a sign that will be spoken against, ³⁵so that the thoughts of many hearts will be revealed. And a sword will pierce your own soul too."

³⁶There was also a prophet, Anna, the daughter of Penuel, of the tribe of Asher. She was very old; she had lived with her husband seven years after her marriage, ³⁷and then was a widow until she was eighty-four.ᵃ She never left the temple but worshiped night and day, fasting and praying. ³⁸Coming up to them at that very moment, she gave thanks to God and spoke about the child to all who were looking forward to the redemption of Jerusalem.

³⁹When Joseph and Mary had done everything required by the Law of the Lord, they returned to Galilee to their own town of Nazareth. ⁴⁰And the child grew and became strong; he was filled with wisdom, and the grace of God was on him.

The Boy Jesus at the Temple

⁴¹Every year Jesus' parents went to Jerusalem for the Festival of the Passover. ⁴²When he was twelve years old, they went up to the festival, according to the custom. ⁴³After the festival was over,

ᵃ 37 Or *then had been a widow for eighty-four years.*

Luke 2:1–20

Mary the mother of Jesus was blessed.

Try to feel the confusion of Mary, the soon-to-be mother of Jesus. Just a poor girl from the town of Nazareth in the north of Israel, she was a virgin engaged to be married to a man named Joseph (see Luke 1:26–27). Without warning, an angel appeared to Mary and announced, "Greetings, you who are highly favored! The Lord is with you" (Luke 1:28).

Mary was startled, troubled by what the angel Gabriel might mean, but he told her to not be afraid. God was showing his goodness to her. Mary would soon become pregnant and give birth to a son. This child who would grow within her would be "the Son of the Most High" (Luke 1:32).

When Mary wondered out loud how a virgin could give birth to a child, the angel said that the child would be conceived by God's power, explaining that "no word from God will ever fail" (Luke 1:37). You know the rest of Mary's story, how Jesus was born on a trip to Bethlehem, several rough days of travel away from home. Baby Jesus entered the world in some sort of barn. Angels sang. Shepherds and magi worshiped him.

Mary's reaction to these unique and challenging events is astonishing. She calls herself blessed, because "the Mighty One has done great things for me" (Luke 1:49). Mary rejoiced that God had chosen her for a leading role in his world-changing plan—sending Jesus to be born, live, die, and rise to save humankind from sin.

You can find Mary in Matthew 1–2; Luke 1–2; Matthew 13:55–56; and John 19:25–27.

UNSHAKEN *people*

while his parents were returning home, the boy Jesus stayed behind in Jerusalem, but they were unaware of it. [44]Thinking he was in their company, they traveled on for a day. Then they began looking for him among their relatives and friends. [45]When they did not find him, they went back to Jerusalem to look for him. [46]After three days they found him in the temple courts, sitting among the teachers, listening to them and asking them questions. [47]Everyone who heard him was amazed at his understanding and his answers. [48]When his parents saw him, they were astonished. His mother said to him, "Son, why have you treated us like this? Your father and I have been anxiously searching for you."

[49]"Why were you searching for me?" he asked. "Didn't you know I had to be in my Father's house?"[a] [50]But they did not understand what he was saying to them.

[51]Then he went down to Nazareth with them and was obedient to them. But his mother treasured all these things in her heart. [52]And Jesus grew in wisdom and stature, and in favor with God and man.

John the Baptist Prepares the Way

3 In the fifteenth year of the reign of Tiberius Caesar—when Pontius Pilate was governor of Judea, Herod tetrarch of Galilee, his brother Philip tetrarch of Iturea and Traconitis, and Lysanias tetrarch of Abilene— [2]during the high-priesthood of Annas and Caiaphas, the word of God came to John son of Zechariah in the wilderness. [3]He went into all the country around the Jordan, preaching a baptism of repentance for the forgiveness of sins. [4]As it is written in the book of the words of Isaiah the prophet:

"A voice of one calling in the wilderness,
'Prepare the way for the Lord,
    make straight paths for him.
[5]Every valley shall be filled in,
    every mountain and hill made low.
The crooked roads shall become
        straight,
    the rough ways smooth.
[6]And all people will see God's
        salvation.'"[b]

Luke 2:52

Jesus was an actual human kid.

If Jesus grew up on your block, he would look like any other kid. Really. In fact, the Bible writers work hard to remind you he was a real human being. At his birth his mom and dad put him to bed in a food box used by animals (see Luke 2:6–7). Visiting shepherds and wise men meet a normal little guy (see Luke 2:16; Matthew 2:11). At times Jesus frustrated his parents (see Luke 2:41–51). And the Bible doesn't need many words to sum up the first dozen or so years of his life: "Jesus grew in wisdom and stature, and in favor with God and man" (Luke 2:52). As Jesus grew up he gained wisdom, the ability to navigate life. He grew in stature, not just physical height but also emotional maturity. Both God and people liked what they saw. It all proves that Jesus understands your life, because he's been there. He's one of us.

Think: How does the fact that Jesus was a real human being help you relate to him?

ROCK SOLID *truths*

---

[7]John said to the crowds coming out to be baptized by him, "You brood of vipers! Who warned you to flee from the coming wrath? [8]Produce fruit in keeping with repentance. And do not begin to say to yourselves, 'We have Abraham as our father.' For I tell you that out of these stones God can raise up children for Abraham. [9]The ax is already at the root of the trees, and every tree that does not produce good

---

[a] 49 Or *be about my Father's business*
[b] 6 Isaiah 40:3-5

fruit will be cut down and thrown into the fire."

¹⁰"What should we do then?" the crowd asked.

¹¹John answered, "Anyone who has two shirts should share with the one who has none, and anyone who has food should do the same."

¹²Even tax collectors came to be baptized. "Teacher," they asked, "what should we do?"

¹³"Don't collect any more than you are required to," he told them.

¹⁴Then some soldiers asked him, "And what should we do?"

He replied, "Don't extort money and don't accuse people falsely—be content with your pay."

¹⁵The people were waiting expectantly and were all wondering in their hearts if John might possibly be the Messiah. ¹⁶John answered them all, "I baptize you with*a* water. But one who is more powerful than I will come, the straps of whose sandals I am not worthy to untie. He will baptize you with*a* the Holy Spirit and fire. ¹⁷His winnowing fork is in his hand to clear his threshing floor and to gather the wheat into his barn, but he will burn up the chaff with unquenchable fire." ¹⁸And with many other words John exhorted the people and proclaimed the good news to them.

¹⁹But when John rebuked Herod the tetrarch because of his marriage to Herodias, his brother's wife, and all the other evil things he had done, ²⁰Herod added this to them all: He locked John up in prison.

The Baptism and Genealogy of Jesus

²¹When all the people were being baptized, Jesus was baptized too. And as he was praying, heaven was opened ²²and the Holy Spirit descended on him in bodily form like a dove. And a voice came from heaven: "You are my Son, whom I love; with you I am well pleased."

²³Now Jesus himself was about thirty years old when he began his ministry. He was the son, so it was thought, of Joseph,

the son of Heli, ²⁴the son of Matthat,
the son of Levi, the son of Melki,
the son of Jannai, the son of Joseph,
²⁵the son of Mattathias, the son of Amos,
the son of Nahum, the son of Esli,
the son of Naggai, ²⁶the son of Maath,
the son of Mattathias, the son of Semein,
the son of Josek, the son of Joda,
²⁷the son of Joanan, the son of Rhesa,
the son of Zerubbabel, the son of Shealtiel,
the son of Neri, ²⁸the son of Melki,
the son of Addi, the son of Cosam,
the son of Elmadam, the son of Er,
²⁹the son of Joshua, the son of Eliezer,
the son of Jorim, the son of Matthat,
the son of Levi, ³⁰the son of Simeon,
the son of Judah, the son of Joseph,
the son of Jonam, the son of Eliakim,
³¹the son of Melea, the son of Menna,
the son of Mattatha, the son of Nathan,
the son of David, ³²the son of Jesse,
the son of Obed, the son of Boaz,
the son of Salmon,*b* the son of Nahshon,
³³the son of Amminadab, the son of Ram,*c*
the son of Hezron, the son of Perez,
the son of Judah, ³⁴the son of Jacob,
the son of Isaac, the son of Abraham,
the son of Terah, the son of Nahor,
³⁵the son of Serug, the son of Reu,
the son of Peleg, the son of Eber,
the son of Shelah, ³⁶the son of Cainan,
the son of Arphaxad, the son of Shem,
the son of Noah, the son of Lamech,
³⁷the son of Methuselah, the son of Enoch,
the son of Jared, the son of Mahalalel,
the son of Kenan, ³⁸the son of Enosh,
the son of Seth, the son of Adam,
the son of God.

a 16 Or *in*   *b 32* Some early manuscripts *Sala*
c 33 Some manuscripts *Amminadab, the son of Admin, the son of Arni*; other manuscripts vary widely.

Jesus Is Tested in the Wilderness

4 Jesus, full of the Holy Spirit, left the Jordan and was led by the Spirit into the wilderness, ²where for forty days he was tempted[a] by the devil. He ate nothing during those days, and at the end of them he was hungry.

³The devil said to him, "If you are the Son of God, tell this stone to become bread."

⁴Jesus answered, "It is written: 'Man shall not live on bread alone.'[b]"

⁵The devil led him up to a high place and showed him in an instant all the kingdoms of the world. ⁶And he said to him, "I will give you all their authority and splendor; it has been given to me, and I can give it to anyone I want to. ⁷If you worship me, it will all be yours."

⁸Jesus answered, "It is written: 'Worship the Lord your God and serve him only.'[c]"

⁹The devil led him to Jerusalem and had him stand on the highest point of the temple. "If you are the Son of God," he said, "throw yourself down from here. ¹⁰For it is written:

"'He will command his angels
        concerning you
    to guard you carefully;
¹¹they will lift you up in their hands,
        so that you will not strike your foot
            against a stone.'[d]"

¹²Jesus answered, "It is said: 'Do not put the Lord your God to the test.'[e]"

¹³When the devil had finished all this tempting, he left him until an opportune time.

Jesus Rejected at Nazareth

¹⁴Jesus returned to Galilee in the power of the Spirit, and news about him spread through the whole countryside. ¹⁵He was teaching in their synagogues, and everyone praised him.

¹⁶He went to Nazareth, where he had been brought up, and on the Sabbath day he went into the synagogue, as was his custom. He stood up to read, ¹⁷and the scroll of the prophet Isaiah was handed to him. Unrolling it, he found the place where it is written:

¹⁸"The Spirit of the Lord is on me,
    because he has anointed me
        to proclaim good news to the
            poor.
He has sent me to proclaim freedom
        for the prisoners
    and recovery of sight for the blind,
to set the oppressed free,
¹⁹   to proclaim the year of the Lord's
            favor."[f]

²⁰Then he rolled up the scroll, gave it back to the attendant and sat down. The eyes of everyone in the synagogue were fastened on him. ²¹He began by saying to them, "Today this scripture is fulfilled in your hearing."

²²All spoke well of him and were amazed at the gracious words that came from his lips. "Isn't this Joseph's son?" they asked.

²³Jesus said to them, "Surely you will quote this proverb to me: 'Physician, heal yourself!' And you will tell me, 'Do here in your hometown what we have heard that you did in Capernaum.'"

²⁴"Truly I tell you," he continued, "no prophet is accepted in his hometown. ²⁵I assure you that there were many widows in Israel in Elijah's time, when the sky was shut for three and a half years and there was a severe famine throughout the land. ²⁶Yet Elijah was not sent to any of them, but to a widow in Zarephath in the region of Sidon. ²⁷And there were many in Israel with leprosy[g] in the time of Elisha the prophet, yet not one of them was cleansed—only Naaman the Syrian."

²⁸All the people in the synagogue were furious when they heard this. ²⁹They got up, drove him out of the town, and took him to the brow of the hill on which the town was built, in order to throw him off

---

[a] 2 The Greek for *tempted* can also mean *tested*.   [b] 4 Deut. 8:3   [c] 8 Deut. 6:13
[d] 11 Psalm 91:11,12   [e] 12 Deut. 6:16
[f] 19 Isaiah 61:1,2 (see Septuagint); Isaiah 58:6
[g] 27 The Greek word traditionally translated *leprosy* was used for various diseases affecting the skin.

the cliff. ³⁰But he walked right through the crowd and went on his way.

Jesus Drives Out an Impure Spirit

³¹Then he went down to Capernaum, a town in Galilee, and on the Sabbath he taught the people. ³²They were amazed at his teaching, because his words had authority.

³³In the synagogue there was a man possessed by a demon, an impure spirit. He cried out at the top of his voice, ³⁴"Go away! What do you want with us, Jesus of Nazareth? Have you come to destroy us? I know who you are—the Holy One of God!"

³⁵"Be quiet!" Jesus said sternly. "Come out of him!" Then the demon threw the man down before them all and came out without injuring him.

³⁶All the people were amazed and said to each other, "What words these are! With authority and power he gives orders to impure spirits and they come out!" ³⁷And the news about him spread throughout the surrounding area.

Jesus Heals Many

³⁸Jesus left the synagogue and went to the home of Simon. Now Simon's mother-in-law was suffering from a high fever, and they asked Jesus to help her. ³⁹So he bent over her and rebuked the fever, and

---

Luke 4

Luke gathered the facts about Jesus.

Although Luke wrote more than a quarter of the New Testament, he never mentioned his own name. But you first meet this man at the start of the book now known as the Gospel of Luke. He explains his goal of writing "an orderly account" of all the events surrounding Jesus (Luke 1:3). He didn't stop with facts about Jesus. He went on to tell the history of the early Christians, recording all the details in the second half of his story, the book of Acts.

That's Luke. He presents all the facts so his readers can be sure of what they believe.

Luke was a physician (see Colossians 4:14), who became friends with the apostle Paul and accompanied him on missionary trips across the Mediterranean. While the book of Luke and the first part of Acts were based on information he gathered from eyewitnesses (Luke 1:2), he likely was a participant in much of the action in Acts. Three times in the storyline he says "we," indicating he was present with Paul (see Acts 16:10–17; 20:5–21:18; 27:1—28:16). In the span before Paul died, the apostle said Luke was the only one with him (see 2 Timothy 4:11).

Because of Luke's mind for detail, people throughout history and across the world have been able to read highly accurate accounts of Jesus and the early church. And along the way you often see Luke reveal his doctor's heart for the needy, telling stories of the poor, sick, and outcast and how God met their needs.

You can find Luke in Luke 1:1–4 and in the background of Acts 16–28.

UNSHAKEN *people*

it left her. She got up at once and began to wait on them.

⁴⁰At sunset, the people brought to Jesus all who had various kinds of sickness, and laying his hands on each one, he healed them. ⁴¹Moreover, demons came out of many people, shouting, "You are the Son of God!" But he rebuked them and would not allow them to speak, because they knew he was the Messiah.

⁴²At daybreak, Jesus went out to a solitary place. The people were looking for him and when they came to where he was, they tried to keep him from leaving them. ⁴³But he said, "I must proclaim the good news of the kingdom of God to the other towns also, because that is why I was sent." ⁴⁴And he kept on preaching in the synagogues of Judea.

Jesus Calls His First Disciples

5 One day as Jesus was standing by the Lake of Gennesaret,ᵃ the people were crowding around him and listening to the word of God. ²He saw at the water's edge two boats, left there by the fishermen, who were washing their nets. ³He got into one of the boats, the one belonging to Simon, and asked him to put out a little from shore. Then he sat down and taught the people from the boat.

⁴When he had finished speaking, he said to Simon, "Put out into deep water, and let down the nets for a catch."

⁵Simon answered, "Master, we've worked hard all night and haven't caught anything. But because you say so, I will let down the nets."

⁶When they had done so, they caught such a large number of fish that their nets began to break. ⁷So they signaled their partners in the other boat to come and help them, and they came and filled both boats so full that they began to sink.

⁸When Simon Peter saw this, he fell at Jesus' knees and said, "Go away from me, Lord; I am a sinful man!" ⁹For he and all his companions were astonished at the catch of fish they had taken, ¹⁰and so were James and John, the sons of Zebedee, Simon's partners.

Then Jesus said to Simon, "Don't be afraid; from now on you will fish for people." ¹¹So they pulled their boats up on shore, left everything and followed him.

Jesus Heals a Man With Leprosy

¹²While Jesus was in one of the towns, a man came along who was covered with leprosy.ᵇ When he saw Jesus, he fell with his face to the ground and begged him, "Lord, if you are willing, you can make me clean."

¹³Jesus reached out his hand and touched the man. "I am willing," he said. "Be clean!" And immediately the leprosy left him.

¹⁴Then Jesus ordered him, "Don't tell anyone, but go, show yourself to the priest and offer the sacrifices that Moses commanded for your cleansing, as a testimony to them."

¹⁵Yet the news about him spread all the more, so that crowds of people came to hear him and to be healed of their sicknesses. ¹⁶But Jesus often withdrew to lonely places and prayed.

Jesus Forgives and Heals a Paralyzed Man

¹⁷One day Jesus was teaching, and Pharisees and teachers of the law were sitting there. They had come from every village of Galilee and from Judea and Jerusalem. And the power of the Lord was with Jesus to heal the sick. ¹⁸Some men came carrying a paralyzed man on a mat and tried to take him into the house to lay him before Jesus. ¹⁹When they could not find a way to do this because of the crowd, they went up on the roof and lowered him on his mat through the tiles into the middle of the crowd, right in front of Jesus.

²⁰When Jesus saw their faith, he said, "Friend, your sins are forgiven."

²¹The Pharisees and the teachers of the law began thinking to themselves, "Who is this fellow who speaks blasphemy? Who can forgive sins but God alone?"

²²Jesus knew what they were thinking

ᵃ 1 That is, the Sea of Galilee   ᵇ 12 The Greek word traditionally translated *leprosy* was used for various diseases affecting the skin.

and asked, "Why are you thinking these things in your hearts? ²³Which is easier: to say, 'Your sins are forgiven,' or to say, 'Get up and walk'? ²⁴But I want you to know that the Son of Man has authority on earth to forgive sins." So he said to the paralyzed man, "I tell you, get up, take your mat and go home." ²⁵Immediately he stood up in front of them, took what he had been lying on and went home praising God. ²⁶Everyone was amazed and gave praise to God. They were filled with awe and said, "We have seen remarkable things today."

Jesus Calls Levi and Eats With Sinners

²⁷After this, Jesus went out and saw a tax collector by the name of Levi sitting at his tax booth. "Follow me," Jesus said to him, ²⁸and Levi got up, left everything and followed him.

²⁹Then Levi held a great banquet for Jesus at his house, and a large crowd of tax collectors and others were eating with them. ³⁰But the Pharisees and the teachers of the law who belonged to their sect complained to his disciples, "Why do you eat and drink with tax collectors and sinners?"

³¹Jesus answered them, "It is not the healthy who need a doctor, but the sick. ³²I have not come to call the righteous, but sinners to repentance."

Jesus Questioned About Fasting

³³They said to him, "John's disciples often fast and pray, and so do the disciples of the Pharisees, but yours go on eating and drinking."

³⁴Jesus answered, "Can you make the friends of the bridegroom fast while he is with them? ³⁵But the time will come when the bridegroom will be taken from them; in those days they will fast."

³⁶He told them this parable: "No one tears a piece out of a new garment to patch an old one. Otherwise, they will have torn the new garment, and the patch from the new will not match the old. ³⁷And no one pours new wine into old wineskins. Otherwise, the new wine

Luke 5:27–32

God is loving to sinners.

The "Pharisees and the teachers of the law" were religious leaders with strict rules against associating with sinful people (Luke 5:30). So they were beyond shocked when Jesus hung out with people they deemed the worst of that society, people like tax collectors and prostitutes. Even more scandalous, Jesus ate with these sinners, an act of fellowship far deeper than merely sharing a meal in our culture. Jesus had frequent harsh words for the Pharisees, pointing out they were as guilty as everyone else (see Matthew 23:1–39). And Jesus gave a reason for seeking out sinful people. He was a spiritual doctor, and the Pharisees thought they were too healthy to need Jesus. But those so-called bad people were eager for his help.

So ... What would Jesus say to you—are you a good person or a bad person? Explain.

will burst the skins; the wine will run out and the wineskins will be ruined. ³⁸No, new wine must be poured into new wineskins. ³⁹And no one after drinking old wine wants the new, for they say, 'The old is better.'"

Jesus Is Lord of the Sabbath

6 One Sabbath Jesus was going through the grainfields, and his disciples began to pick some heads of grain, rub them in their hands and eat the kernels. ²Some of the Pharisees asked, "Why are you doing what is unlawful on the Sabbath?"

³Jesus answered them, "Have you never read what David did when he and his companions were hungry? ⁴He entered the house of God, and taking the consecrated bread, he ate what is lawful only

for priests to eat. And he also gave some to his companions." ⁵Then Jesus said to them, "The Son of Man is Lord of the Sabbath."

⁶On another Sabbath he went into the synagogue and was teaching, and a man was there whose right hand was shriveled. ⁷The Pharisees and the teachers of the law were looking for a reason to accuse Jesus, so they watched him closely to see if he would heal on the Sabbath. ⁸But Jesus knew what they were thinking and said to the man with the shriveled hand, "Get up and stand in front of everyone." So he got up and stood there.

⁹Then Jesus said to them, "I ask you, which is lawful on the Sabbath: to do good or to do evil, to save life or to destroy it?"

¹⁰He looked around at them all, and then said to the man, "Stretch out your hand." He did so, and his hand was completely restored. ¹¹But the Pharisees and the teachers of the law were furious and began to discuss with one another what they might do to Jesus.

The Twelve Apostles

¹²One of those days Jesus went out to a mountainside to pray, and spent the night praying to God. ¹³When morning came, he called his disciples to him and chose twelve of them, whom he also designated apostles: ¹⁴Simon (whom he named Peter), his brother Andrew, James, John, Philip, Bartholomew, ¹⁵Matthew, Thomas, James son of Alphaeus, Simon who was called the Zealot, ¹⁶Judas son of James, and Judas Iscariot, who became a traitor.

Blessings and Woes

¹⁷He went down with them and stood on a level place. A large crowd of his disciples was there and a great number of people from all over Judea, from Jerusalem, and from the coastal region around Tyre and Sidon, ¹⁸who had come to hear him and to be healed of their diseases. Those troubled by impure spirits were cured, ¹⁹and the people all tried to touch him, because power was coming from him and healing them all.

²⁰Looking at his disciples, he said:

"Blessed are you who are poor,
	for yours is the kingdom of God.
²¹Blessed are you who hunger now,
	for you will be satisfied.
Blessed are you who weep now,
	for you will laugh.

ROCK SOLID promises

"Blessed are you who weep now, for you will laugh." Luke 6:21

Sadness doesn't last forever. Jesus will lift your heart and make you laugh again.

²²Blessed are you when people hate you,
	when they exclude you and insult you
	and reject your name as evil,
		because of the Son of Man.

²³"Rejoice in that day and leap for joy, because great is your reward in heaven. For that is how their ancestors treated the prophets.

²⁴"But woe to you who are rich,
	for you have already received your
		comfort.
²⁵Woe to you who are well fed now,
	for you will go hungry.
Woe to you who laugh now,
	for you will mourn and weep.
²⁶Woe to you when everyone speaks
		well of you,
	for that is how their ancestors
		treated the false prophets.

Love for Enemies

²⁷"But to you who are listening I say: Love your enemies, do good to those who

hate you, ²⁸bless those who curse you, pray for those who mistreat you. ²⁹If someone slaps you on one cheek, turn to them the other also. If someone takes your coat, do not withhold your shirt from them. ³⁰Give to everyone who asks you, and if anyone takes what belongs to you, do not demand it back. ³¹Do to others as you would have them do to you.

³²"If you love those who love you, what credit is that to you? Even sinners love those who love them. ³³And if you do good to those who are good to you, what credit is that to you? Even sinners do that. ³⁴And if you lend to those from whom you expect repayment, what credit is that to you? Even sinners lend to sinners, expecting to be repaid in full. ³⁵But love your enemies, do good to them, and lend to them without expecting to get anything back. Then your reward will be great, and you will be children of the Most High, because he is kind to the ungrateful and wicked. ³⁶Be merciful, just as your Father is merciful.

Judging Others

³⁷"Do not judge, and you will not be judged. Do not condemn, and you will not be condemned. Forgive, and you will be forgiven. ³⁸Give, and it will be given to you. A good measure, pressed down, shaken together and running over, will be poured into your lap. For with the measure you use, it will be measured to you."

³⁹He also told them this parable: "Can the blind lead the blind? Will they not both fall into a pit? ⁴⁰The student is not above the teacher, but everyone who is fully trained will be like their teacher.

⁴¹"Why do you look at the speck of sawdust in your brother's eye and pay no attention to the plank in your own eye? ⁴²How can you say to your brother, 'Brother, let me take the speck out of your eye,' when you yourself fail to see the plank in your own eye? You hypocrite, first take the plank out of your eye, and then you will see clearly to remove the speck from your brother's eye.

A Tree and Its Fruit

⁴³"No good tree bears bad fruit, nor does a bad tree bear good fruit. ⁴⁴Each tree is recognized by its own fruit. People do not pick figs from thornbushes, or grapes from briers. ⁴⁵A good man brings good things out of the good stored up in his heart, and an evil man brings evil things out of the evil stored up in his heart. For the mouth speaks what the heart is full of.

The Wise and Foolish Builders

⁴⁶"Why do you call me, 'Lord, Lord,' and do not do what I say? ⁴⁷As for everyone who comes to me and hears my words and puts them into practice, I will show you what they are like. ⁴⁸They are like a man building a house, who dug down deep and laid the foundation on rock. When a flood came, the torrent struck that house but could not shake it, because it was well built. ⁴⁹But the one who hears my words and does not put them into practice is like a man who built a house on the ground without a foundation. The moment the torrent struck that house, it collapsed and its destruction was complete."

The Faith of the Centurion

7 When Jesus had finished saying all this to the people who were listening, he entered Capernaum. ²There a centurion's servant, whom his master valued highly, was sick and about to die. ³The centurion heard of Jesus and sent some elders of the Jews to him, asking him to come and heal his servant. ⁴When they came to Jesus, they pleaded earnestly with him, "This man deserves to have you do this, ⁵because he loves our nation and has built our synagogue." ⁶So Jesus went with them.

He was not far from the house when the centurion sent friends to say to him: "Lord, don't trouble yourself, for I do not deserve to have you come under my roof. ⁷That is why I did not even consider myself worthy to come to you. But say the word, and my servant will be healed. ⁸For I myself am a man under authority, with soldiers under me. I tell this one, 'Go,' and he goes; and that one, 'Come,' and he comes. I say to my servant, 'Do this,' and he does it."

⁹When Jesus heard this, he was amazed at him, and turning to the crowd following him, he said, "I tell you, I have not found such great faith even in Israel." ¹⁰Then the men who had been sent returned to the house and found the servant well.

Jesus Raises a Widow's Son

¹¹Soon afterward, Jesus went to a town called Nain, and his disciples and a large crowd went along with him. ¹²As he approached the town gate, a dead person was being carried out—the only son of his mother, and she was a widow. And a large crowd from the town was with her. ¹³When the Lord saw her, his heart went out to her and he said, "Don't cry."

¹⁴Then he went up and touched the bier they were carrying him on, and the bearers stood still. He said, "Young man, I say to you, get up!" ¹⁵The dead man sat up and began to talk, and Jesus gave him back to his mother.

¹⁶They were all filled with awe and praised God. "A great prophet has appeared among us," they said. "God has come to help his people." ¹⁷This news about Jesus spread throughout Judea and the surrounding country.

Jesus and John the Baptist

¹⁸John's disciples told him about all these things. Calling two of them, ¹⁹he sent them to the Lord to ask, "Are you the one who is to come, or should we expect someone else?"

²⁰When the men came to Jesus, they said, "John the Baptist sent us to you to ask, 'Are you the one who is to come, or should we expect someone else?'"

²¹At that very time Jesus cured many who had diseases, sicknesses and evil spirits, and gave sight to many who were blind. ²²So he replied to the messengers, "Go back and report to John what you have seen and heard: The blind receive sight, the lame walk, those who have leprosy*a* are cleansed, the deaf hear, the dead are raised, and the good news is proclaimed to the poor. ²³Blessed is anyone who does not stumble on account of me."

²⁴After John's messengers left, Jesus began to speak to the crowd about John: "What did you go out into the wilderness to see? A reed swayed by the wind? ²⁵If not, what did you go out to see? A man dressed in fine clothes? No, those who wear expensive clothes and indulge in luxury are in palaces. ²⁶But what did you go out to see? A prophet? Yes, I tell you, and more than a prophet. ²⁷This is the one about whom it is written:

"'I will send my messenger ahead of you,
who will prepare your way before
you.'*b*

²⁸I tell you, among those born of women there is no one greater than John; yet the one who is least in the kingdom of God is greater than he."

²⁹(All the people, even the tax collectors, when they heard Jesus' words, acknowledged that God's way was right, because they had been baptized by John. ³⁰But the Pharisees and the experts in the law rejected God's purpose for themselves, because they had not been baptized by John.)

³¹Jesus went on to say, "To what, then, can I compare the people of this generation? What are they like? ³²They are like children sitting in the marketplace and calling out to each other:

"'We played the pipe for you,
and you did not dance;
we sang a dirge,
and you did not cry.'

³³For John the Baptist came neither eating bread nor drinking wine, and you say, 'He has a demon.' ³⁴The Son of Man came eating and drinking, and you say, 'Here is a glutton and a drunkard, a friend of tax collectors and sinners.' ³⁵But wisdom is proved right by all her children."

Jesus Anointed by a Sinful Woman

³⁶When one of the Pharisees invited Jesus to have dinner with him, he went to the Pharisee's house and reclined at the

---

a 22 The Greek word traditionally translated *leprosy* was used for various diseases affecting the skin.　*b 27* Mal. 3:1

table. [37]A woman in that town who lived a sinful life learned that Jesus was eating at the Pharisee's house, so she came there with an alabaster jar of perfume. [38]As she stood behind him at his feet weeping, she began to wet his feet with her tears. Then she wiped them with her hair, kissed them and poured perfume on them.

[39]When the Pharisee who had invited him saw this, he said to himself, "If this man were a prophet, he would know who is touching him and what kind of woman she is—that she is a sinner."

[40]Jesus answered him, "Simon, I have something to tell you."

"Tell me, teacher," he said.

[41]"Two people owed money to a certain moneylender. One owed him five hundred denarii,[a] and the other fifty. [42]Neither of them had the money to pay him back, so he forgave the debts of both. Now which of them will love him more?"

[43]Simon replied, "I suppose the one who had the bigger debt forgiven."

"You have judged correctly," Jesus said.

[44]Then he turned toward the woman and said to Simon, "Do you see this woman? I came into your house. You did not give me any water for my feet, but she wet my feet with her tears and wiped them with her hair. [45]You did not give me a kiss, but this woman, from the time I entered, has not stopped kissing my feet. [46]You did not put oil on my head, but she has poured perfume on my feet. [47]Therefore, I tell you, her many sins have been forgiven—as her great love has shown. But whoever has been forgiven little loves little."

[48]Then Jesus said to her, "Your sins are forgiven."

[49]The other guests began to say among themselves, "Who is this who even forgives sins?"

[50]Jesus said to the woman, "Your faith has saved you; go in peace."

The Parable of the Sower

8 After this, Jesus traveled about from one town and village to another, proclaiming the good news of the kingdom of God. The Twelve were with him, [2]and also some women who had been cured of evil spirits and diseases: Mary (called Magdalene) from whom seven demons had come out; [3]Joanna the wife of Chuza, the manager of Herod's household; Susanna; and many others. These women were helping to support them out of their own means.

[4]While a large crowd was gathering and people were coming to Jesus from town after town, he told this parable: [5]"A farmer went out to sow his seed. As he was scattering the seed, some fell along the path; it was trampled on, and the birds ate it up. [6]Some fell on rocky ground, and when it came up, the plants withered because they had no moisture. [7]Other seed fell among thorns, which grew up with it and choked the plants. [8]Still other seed fell on good soil. It came up and yielded a crop, a hundred times more than was sown."

When he said this, he called out, "Whoever has ears to hear, let them hear."

[9]His disciples asked him what this parable meant. [10]He said, "The knowledge of the secrets of the kingdom of God has been given to you, but to others I speak in parables, so that,

"'though seeing, they may not see;
    though hearing, they may not
        understand.'[b]

ROCK SOLID
promises

"Your sins are forgiven."
Luke 7:48

Your sins might be monstrous and too many to count, but Jesus will forgive you if you ask.

---

[a] 41 A denarius was the usual daily wage of a day laborer (see Matt. 20:2).   [b] 10 Isaiah 6:9

¹¹"This is the meaning of the parable: The seed is the word of God. ¹²Those along the path are the ones who hear, and then the devil comes and takes away the word from their hearts, so that they may not believe and be saved. ¹³Those on the rocky ground are the ones who receive the word with joy when they hear it, but they have no root. They believe for a while, but in the time of testing they fall away. ¹⁴The seed that fell among thorns stands for those who hear, but as they go on their way they are choked by life's worries, riches and pleasures, and they do not mature. ¹⁵But the seed on good soil stands for those with a noble and good heart, who hear the word, retain it, and by persevering produce a crop.

A Lamp on a Stand

¹⁶"No one lights a lamp and hides it in a clay jar or puts it under a bed. Instead, they put it on a stand, so that those who come in can see the light. ¹⁷For there is nothing hidden that will not be disclosed, and nothing concealed that will not be known or brought out into the open. ¹⁸Therefore consider carefully how you listen. Whoever has will be given more; whoever does not have, even what they think they have will be taken from them."

Luke 8:1–3
Women disciples followed Jesus closely.

The tough male disciples known as "the Twelve" weren't the only followers of Jesus (see Matthew 10:2–4). The Bible also mentions Jesus sending out 72 to preach about the kingdom of God (see Luke 10:1). Sometimes there were crowds who chased after Jesus (see John 6:24). But don't miss the fact that Jesus' closest friends included "some women who had been cured of evil spirits and diseases" (Luke 8:2).

First in that list is Mary Magdalene, "from whom seven demons had come out" (Luke 8:3). Another, Joanna, was married to Chuza, who had the major responsibility of managing King Herod's household. No details are given about Susanna, who isn't mentioned elsewhere in the Bible. Along with these women, there were "many others" (Luke 8:3).

The female disciples of Jesus played significant roles in his life, providing financial support for him and his other followers out of their own pockets. Don't get the idea that these women trailed after Jesus and his men like rock band groupies. The fact that Jesus had close female followers doesn't imply Jesus acted sinfully. His enemies would have loudly condemned any sexual immorality.

The women disciples were loyal to Jesus to the end and beyond. They didn't follow for a time and then leave. While most of Jesus' other disciples fled, they watched Jesus suffer and die. One of them, Mary Magdalene, was the first person to encounter Jesus after the resurrection (see John 20:11–18).

You can find these women disciples in Mark 15:33–41 and Luke 8:1–3.

UNSHAKEN people

Jesus' Mother and Brothers

¹⁹ Now Jesus' mother and brothers came to see him, but they were not able to get near him because of the crowd. ²⁰ Someone told him, "Your mother and brothers are standing outside, wanting to see you."

²¹ He replied, "My mother and brothers are those who hear God's word and put it into practice."

Jesus Calms the Storm

²² One day Jesus said to his disciples, "Let us go over to the other side of the lake." So they got into a boat and set out. ²³ As they sailed, he fell asleep. A squall came down on the lake, so that the boat was being swamped, and they were in great danger.

²⁴ The disciples went and woke him, saying, "Master, Master, we're going to drown!"

He got up and rebuked the wind and the raging waters; the storm subsided, and all was calm. ²⁵ "Where is your faith?" he asked his disciples.

In fear and amazement they asked one another, "Who is this? He commands even the winds and the water, and they obey him."

Jesus Restores a Demon-Possessed Man

²⁶ They sailed to the region of the Gerasenes,ᵃ which is across the lake from Galilee. ²⁷ When Jesus stepped ashore, he was met by a demon-possessed man from the town. For a long time this man had not worn clothes or lived in a house, but had lived in the tombs. ²⁸ When he saw Jesus, he cried out and fell at his feet, shouting at the top of his voice, "What do you want with me, Jesus, Son of the Most High God? I beg you, don't torture me!" ²⁹ For Jesus had commanded the impure spirit to come out of the man. Many times it had seized him, and though he was chained hand and foot and kept under guard, he had broken his chains and had been driven by the demon into solitary places.

³⁰ Jesus asked him, "What is your name?"

"Legion," he replied, because many demons had gone into him. ³¹ And they begged Jesus repeatedly not to order them to go into the Abyss.

³² A large herd of pigs was feeding there on the hillside. The demons begged Jesus to let them go into the pigs, and he gave them permission. ³³ When the demons came out of the man, they went into the pigs, and the herd rushed down the steep bank into the lake and was drowned.

³⁴ When those tending the pigs saw what had happened, they ran off and reported this in the town and countryside, ³⁵ and the people went out to see what had happened. When they came to Jesus, they found the man from whom the demons had gone out, sitting at Jesus' feet, dressed and in his right mind; and they were afraid. ³⁶ Those who had seen it told the people how the demon-possessed man had been cured. ³⁷ Then all the people of the region of the Gerasenes asked Jesus to leave them, because they were overcome with fear. So he got into the boat and left.

³⁸ The man from whom the demons had gone out begged to go with him, but Jesus sent him away, saying, ³⁹ "Return home and tell how much God has done for you." So the man went away and told all over town how much Jesus had done for him.

Jesus Raises a Dead Girl and Heals a Sick Woman

⁴⁰ Now when Jesus returned, a crowd welcomed him, for they were all expecting him. ⁴¹ Then a man named Jairus, a synagogue leader, came and fell at Jesus' feet, pleading with him to come to his house ⁴² because his only daughter, a girl of about twelve, was dying.

As Jesus was on his way, the crowds almost crushed him. ⁴³ And a woman was there who had been subject to bleeding for twelve years,ᵇ but no one could heal her. ⁴⁴ She came up behind him and touched the edge of his cloak, and immediately her bleeding stopped.

ᵃ 26 Some manuscripts *Gadarenes*; other manuscripts *Gergesenes*; also in verse 37
ᵇ 43 Many manuscripts *years, and she had spent all she had on doctors*

⁴⁵"Who touched me?" Jesus asked.

When they all denied it, Peter said, "Master, the people are crowding and pressing against you."

⁴⁶But Jesus said, "Someone touched me; I know that power has gone out from me."

⁴⁷Then the woman, seeing that she could not go unnoticed, came trembling and fell at his feet. In the presence of all the people, she told why she had touched him and how she had been instantly healed. ⁴⁸Then he said to her, "Daughter, your faith has healed you. Go in peace."

⁴⁹While Jesus was still speaking, someone came from the house of Jairus, the synagogue leader. "Your daughter is dead," he said. "Don't bother the teacher anymore."

⁵⁰Hearing this, Jesus said to Jairus, "Don't be afraid; just believe, and she will be healed."

⁵¹When he arrived at the house of Jairus, he did not let anyone go in with him except Peter, John and James, and the child's father and mother. ⁵²Meanwhile, all the people were wailing and mourning for her. "Stop wailing," Jesus said. "She is not dead but asleep."

⁵³They laughed at him, knowing that she was dead. ⁵⁴But he took her by the hand and said, "My child, get up!" ⁵⁵Her spirit returned, and at once she stood up. Then Jesus told them to give her something to eat. ⁵⁶Her parents were astonished, but he ordered them not to tell anyone what had happened.

Jesus Sends Out the Twelve

9 When Jesus had called the Twelve together, he gave them power and authority to drive out all demons and to cure diseases, ²and he sent them out to proclaim the kingdom of God and to heal the sick. ³He told them: "Take nothing for the journey—no staff, no bag, no bread, no money, no extra shirt. ⁴Whatever house you enter, stay there until you leave that town. ⁵If people do not welcome you, leave their town and shake the dust off your feet as a testimony against them." ⁶So they set out and went from village to

village, proclaiming the good news and healing people everywhere.

⁷Now Herod the tetrarch heard about all that was going on. And he was perplexed because some were saying that John had been raised from the dead, ⁸others that Elijah had appeared, and still others that one of the prophets of long ago had come back to life. ⁹But Herod said, "I beheaded John. Who, then, is this I hear such things about?" And he tried to see him.

Jesus Feeds the Five Thousand

¹⁰When the apostles returned, they reported to Jesus what they had done. Then he took them with him and they withdrew by themselves to a town called Bethsaida, ¹¹but the crowds learned about it and followed him. He welcomed them and spoke to them about the kingdom of God, and healed those who needed healing.

¹²Late in the afternoon the Twelve came to him and said, "Send the crowd away so they can go to the surrounding villages and countryside and find food and lodging, because we are in a remote place here."

¹³He replied, "You give them something to eat."

They answered, "We have only five loaves of bread and two fish—unless we go and buy food for all this crowd." ¹⁴(About five thousand men were there.)

But he said to his disciples, "Have them sit down in groups of about fifty each." ¹⁵The disciples did so, and everyone sat down. ¹⁶Taking the five loaves and the two fish and looking up to heaven, he gave thanks and broke them. Then he gave them to the disciples to distribute to the people. ¹⁷They all ate and were satisfied, and the disciples picked up twelve basketfuls of broken pieces that were left over.

Peter Declares That Jesus Is the Messiah

¹⁸Once when Jesus was praying in private and his disciples were with him, he asked them, "Who do the crowds say I am?"

¹⁹They replied, "Some say John the Baptist; others say Elijah; and still oth-

ers, that one of the prophets of long ago has come back to life."

20 "But what about you?" he asked. "Who do you say I am?"

Peter answered, "God's Messiah."

Jesus Predicts His Death

21 Jesus strictly warned them not to tell this to anyone. 22 And he said, "The Son of Man must suffer many things and be rejected by the elders, the chief priests and the teachers of the law, and he must be killed and on the third day be raised to life."

23 Then he said to them all: "Whoever wants to be my disciple must deny themselves and take up their cross daily and follow me. 24 For whoever wants to save their life will lose it, but whoever loses their life for me will save it. 25 What good is it for someone to gain the whole world, and yet lose or forfeit their very self? 26 Whoever is ashamed of me and my words, the Son of Man will be ashamed of them when he comes in his glory and in the glory of the Father and of the holy angels.

27 "Truly I tell you, some who are standing here will not taste death before they see the kingdom of God."

The Transfiguration

28 About eight days after Jesus said this, he took Peter, John and James with him and went up onto a mountain to pray. 29 As he was praying, the appearance of his face

---

ROCK SOLID
promises

"Whoever wants to save their life will lose it, but whoever loses their life for me will save it." Luke 9:24

As soon as you choose to do life your own way, you have stopped following Jesus.

---

changed, and his clothes became as bright as a flash of lightning. 30 Two men, Moses and Elijah, appeared in glorious splendor, talking with Jesus. 31 They spoke about his departure,[a] which he was about to bring to fulfillment at Jerusalem. 32 Peter and his companions were very sleepy, but when they became fully awake, they saw his glory and the two men standing with him. 33 As the men were leaving Jesus, Peter said to him, "Master, it is good for us to be here. Let us put up three shelters—one for you, one for Moses and one for Elijah." (He did not know what he was saying.)

34 While he was speaking, a cloud appeared and covered them, and they were afraid as they entered the cloud. 35 A voice came from the cloud, saying, "This is my Son, whom I have chosen; listen to him." 36 When the voice had spoken, they found that Jesus was alone. The disciples kept this to themselves and did not tell anyone at that time what they had seen.

Jesus Heals a Demon-Possessed Boy

37 The next day, when they came down from the mountain, a large crowd met him. 38 A man in the crowd called out, "Teacher, I beg you to look at my son, for he is my only child. 39 A spirit seizes him and he suddenly screams; it throws him into convulsions so that he foams at the mouth. It scarcely ever leaves him and is destroying him. 40 I begged your disciples to drive it out, but they could not."

41 "You unbelieving and perverse generation," Jesus replied, "how long shall I stay with you and put up with you? Bring your son here."

42 Even while the boy was coming, the demon threw him to the ground in a convulsion. But Jesus rebuked the impure spirit, healed the boy and gave him back to his father. 43 And they were all amazed at the greatness of God.

Jesus Predicts His Death a Second Time

While everyone was marveling at all that Jesus did, he said to his disciples, 44 "Listen carefully to what I am about to

---

[a] 31 Greek exodos

tell you: The Son of Man is going to be delivered into the hands of men." ⁴⁵But they did not understand what this meant. It was hidden from them, so that they did not grasp it, and they were afraid to ask him about it.

⁴⁶An argument started among the disciples as to which of them would be the greatest. ⁴⁷Jesus, knowing their thoughts, took a little child and had him stand beside him. ⁴⁸Then he said to them, "Whoever welcomes this little child in my name welcomes me; and whoever welcomes me welcomes the one who sent me. For it is the one who is least among you all who is the greatest."

⁴⁹"Master," said John, "we saw someone driving out demons in your name and we tried to stop him, because he is not one of us."

⁵⁰"Do not stop him," Jesus said, "for whoever is not against you is for you."

Samaritan Opposition

⁵¹As the time approached for him to be taken up to heaven, Jesus resolutely set out for Jerusalem. ⁵²And he sent messengers on ahead, who went into a Samaritan village to get things ready for him; ⁵³but the people there did not welcome him, because he was heading for Jerusalem. ⁵⁴When the disciples James and John saw this, they asked, "Lord, do you want us to call fire down from heaven to destroy them*?" ⁵⁵But Jesus turned and rebuked them. ⁵⁶Then he and his disciples went to another village.

The Cost of Following Jesus

⁵⁷As they were walking along the road, a man said to him, "I will follow you wherever you go."

⁵⁸Jesus replied, "Foxes have dens and birds have nests, but the Son of Man has no place to lay his head."

⁵⁹He said to another man, "Follow me." But he replied, "Lord, first let me go and bury my father."

⁶⁰Jesus said to him, "Let the dead bury their own dead, but you go and proclaim the kingdom of God."

⁶¹Still another said, "I will follow you,

Lord; but first let me go back and say goodbye to my family."

⁶²Jesus replied, "No one who puts a hand to the plow and looks back is fit for service in the kingdom of God."

Jesus Sends Out the Seventy-Two

10 After this the Lord appointed seventy-two*ᵇ* others and sent them two by two ahead of him to every town and place where he was about to go. ²He told them, "The harvest is plentiful, but the workers are few. Ask the Lord of the harvest, therefore, to send out workers into his harvest field. ³Go! I am sending you out like lambs among wolves. ⁴Do not take a purse or bag or sandals; and do not greet anyone on the road.

⁵"When you enter a house, first say, 'Peace to this house.' ⁶If someone who promotes peace is there, your peace will rest on them; if not, it will return to you. ⁷Stay there, eating and drinking whatever they give you, for the worker deserves his wages. Do not move around from house to house.

⁸"When you enter a town and are welcomed, eat what is offered to you. ⁹Heal the sick who are there and tell them, 'The kingdom of God has come near to you.' ¹⁰But when you enter a town and are not welcomed, go into its streets and say, ¹¹'Even the dust of your town we wipe from our feet as a warning to you. Yet be sure of this: The kingdom of God has come near.' ¹²I tell you, it will be more bearable on that day for Sodom than for that town.

¹³"Woe to you, Chorazin! Woe to you, Bethsaida! For if the miracles that were performed in you had been performed in Tyre and Sidon, they would have repented long ago, sitting in sackcloth and ashes. ¹⁴But it will be more bearable for Tyre and Sidon at the judgment than for you. ¹⁵And you, Capernaum, will you be lifted to the heavens? No, you will go down to Hades.*ᶜ*

¹⁶"Whoever listens to you listens to me;

ᵃ 54 Some manuscripts *them, just as Elijah did*
ᵇ 1 Some manuscripts *seventy*; also in verse 17
ᶜ 15 That is, the realm of the dead

whoever rejects you rejects me; but whoever rejects me rejects him who sent me."

¹⁷The seventy-two returned with joy and said, "Lord, even the demons submit to us in your name."

¹⁸He replied, "I saw Satan fall like lightning from heaven. ¹⁹I have given you authority to trample on snakes and scorpions and to overcome all the power of the enemy; nothing will harm you. ²⁰However, do not rejoice that the spirits submit to you, but rejoice that your names are written in heaven."

²¹At that time Jesus, full of joy through the Holy Spirit, said, "I praise you, Father, Lord of heaven and earth, because you have hidden these things from the wise and learned, and revealed them to little children. Yes, Father, for this is what you were pleased to do.

²²"All things have been committed to me by my Father. No one knows who the Son is except the Father, and no one knows who the Father is except the Son and those to whom the Son chooses to reveal him."

²³Then he turned to his disciples and said privately, "Blessed are the eyes that see what you see. ²⁴For I tell you that many prophets and kings wanted to see what you see but did not see it, and to hear what you hear but did not hear it."

The Parable of the Good Samaritan

²⁵On one occasion an expert in the law stood up to test Jesus. "Teacher," he asked, "what must I do to inherit eternal life?"

²⁶"What is written in the Law?" he replied. "How do you read it?"

²⁷He answered, "'Love the Lord your God with all your heart and with all your soul and with all your strength and with all your mind'ᵃ; and, 'Love your neighbor as yourself.'ᵇ"

²⁸"You have answered correctly," Jesus replied. "Do this and you will live."

²⁹But he wanted to justify himself, so he asked Jesus, "And who is my neighbor?"

³⁰In reply Jesus said: "A man was going down from Jerusalem to Jericho, when he was attacked by robbers. They stripped him of his clothes, beat him and went away, leaving him half dead. ³¹A priest happened to be going down the same road, and when he saw the man, he passed by on the other side. ³²So too, a Levite, when he came to the place and saw him, passed by on the other side. ³³But a Samaritan, as he traveled, came where the man was; and when he saw him, he took pity on him. ³⁴He went to him and bandaged his wounds, pouring on oil and wine. Then he put the man on his own donkey, brought him to an inn and took care of him. ³⁵The next day he took out two denariiᶜ and gave them to the innkeeper. 'Look after him,' he said, 'and when I return, I will reimburse you for any extra expense you may have.'

³⁶"Which of these three do you think was a neighbor to the man who fell into the hands of robbers?"

³⁷The expert in the law replied, "The one who had mercy on him."

Jesus told him, "Go and do likewise."

At the Home of Martha and Mary

³⁸As Jesus and his disciples were on their way, he came to a village where a woman named Martha opened her home to him. ³⁹She had a sister called Mary, who sat at the Lord's feet listening to what he said. ⁴⁰But Martha was distracted by all the preparations that had to be made. She came to him and asked, "Lord, don't you care that my sister has left me to do the work by myself? Tell her to help me!"

⁴¹"Martha, Martha," the Lord answered, "you are worried and upset about many things, ⁴²but few things are needed—or indeed only one.ᵈ Mary has chosen what is better, and it will not be taken away from her."

Jesus' Teaching on Prayer

11 One day Jesus was praying in a certain place. When he finished, one of his disciples said to him, "Lord, teach us to pray, just as John taught his disciples."

ᵃ *27* Deut. 6:5   ᵇ *27* Lev. 19:18
ᶜ *35* A denarius was the usual daily wage of a day laborer (see Matt. 20:2).   ᵈ *42* Some manuscripts *but only one thing is needed*

²He said to them, "When you pray, say:

"'Father,ᵃ
hallowed be your name,
your kingdom come.ᵇ
³Give us each day our daily bread.
⁴Forgive us our sins,
    for we also forgive everyone who
        sins against us.ᶜ
And lead us not into temptation.ᵈ'"

⁵Then Jesus said to them, "Suppose you have a friend, and you go to him at midnight and say, 'Friend, lend me three loaves of bread; ⁶a friend of mine on a journey has come to me, and I have no food to offer him.' ⁷And suppose the one inside answers, 'Don't bother me. The door is already locked, and my children and I are in bed. I can't get up and give you anything.' ⁸I tell you, even though he will not get up and give you the bread because of friendship, yet because of your shameless audacityᵉ he will surely get up and give you as much as you need.

⁹"So I say to you: Ask and it will be given to you; seek and you will find; knock

ᵃ 2 Some manuscripts *Our Father in heaven*
ᵇ 2 Some manuscripts *come. May your will be done on earth as it is in heaven.*   ᶜ 4 Greek *everyone who is indebted to us*   ᵈ 4 Some manuscripts *temptation, but deliver us from the evil one*   ᵉ 8 Or *yet to preserve his good name*

Luke 10:38–42

Mary chose to spend time with Jesus.

Jesus' mother was named Mary. One of his closest followers—a formerly demon-possessed woman—was known as Mary Magdalene (see Mark 15:33–41). And yet another well-known Mary shows up in the Lord's life, Mary the sister of Martha and Lazarus.

Mary, Martha, and Lazarus were all good friends of Jesus. The book of John shows Jesus arriving at the siblings' home several days after Lazarus had died and been buried. Martha scolded Jesus for not coming in time to save her brother, but Jesus shared her grief. He wept for his friend, then raised Lazarus from the dead (see John 11:17–44).

Martha might look like an awful person when you see her in Luke 10, but don't forget that she is a woman with an unstoppable faith who trusted the Lord's power to heal and who openly worshiped him as God's Son (see John 11:27). Martha was serving as the host and doing what was culturally expected of her. But Martha was distracted by all the serving she had to do and was also irritated with her sister, Mary, for failing to pitch in.

Martha was too busy serving Jesus to take time to listen to his teaching. Mary instead chose to sit at his feet and soak up his every word. Jesus was so impressed with Mary that he told Martha her sister had made the very best choice. Martha wasn't doing anything evil. But by spending time with Jesus, Mary picked something way better.

You can find Mary in Luke 10:38–42; John 11:1–44; and John 12:1–3.

UNSHAKEN *people*

and the door will be opened to you. ¹⁰For everyone who asks receives; the one who seeks finds; and to the one who knocks, the door will be opened.

¹¹"Which of you fathers, if your son asks for*ᵃ* a fish, will give him a snake instead? ¹²Or if he asks for an egg, will give him a scorpion? ¹³If you then, though you are evil, know how to give good gifts to your children, how much more will your Father in heaven give the Holy Spirit to those who ask him!"

Jesus and Beelzebul

¹⁴Jesus was driving out a demon that was mute. When the demon left, the man who had been mute spoke, and the crowd was amazed. ¹⁵But some of them said, "By Beelzebul, the prince of demons, he is driving out demons." ¹⁶Others tested him by asking for a sign from heaven.

¹⁷Jesus knew their thoughts and said to them: "Any kingdom divided against itself will be ruined, and a house divided against itself will fall. ¹⁸If Satan is divided against himself, how can his kingdom stand? I say this because you claim that I drive out demons by Beelzebul. ¹⁹Now if I drive out demons by Beelzebul, by whom do your followers drive them out? So then, they will be your judges. ²⁰But if I drive out demons by the finger of God, then the kingdom of God has come upon you.

²¹"When a strong man, fully armed, guards his own house, his possessions are safe. ²²But when someone stronger attacks and overpowers him, he takes away the armor in which the man trusted and divides up his plunder.

²³"Whoever is not with me is against me, and whoever does not gather with me scatters.

²⁴"When an impure spirit comes out of a person, it goes through arid places seeking rest and does not find it. Then it says, 'I will return to the house I left.' ²⁵When it arrives, it finds the house swept clean and put in order. ²⁶Then it goes and takes seven other spirits more wicked than itself, and they go in and live there. And the final condition of that person is worse than the first."

Luke 11:1–13

God likes simple prayers.

The religious experts of Bible times excelled at long prayers (see Matthew 6:7; Luke 18:11–12). They had a habit of praying on street corners so everyone could see and applaud them (see Matthew 6:5). If everyone thought that was the best way to talk to God, people must have been astounded when Jesus taught his followers a very simple prayer. He starts by declaring that God is as close as a Father. He praises God's holiness. He invites the Father to rule his life. He asks God to supply his most basic needs. He admits the need for forgiveness for our own sins and for help forgiving the sins of others. Jesus finishes by asking for strength to avoid sin. Then he goes on to explain that God eagerly answers prayer, proving you don't need to beg God to hear you. You just need to talk to him.

Think: What do you pray for—or not—each day? How can you pray in a way that resembles Jesus' prayer?

ROCK SOLID truths

²⁷As Jesus was saying these things, a woman in the crowd called out, "Blessed is the mother who gave you birth and nursed you."

²⁸He replied, "Blessed rather are those who hear the word of God and obey it."

The Sign of Jonah

²⁹As the crowds increased, Jesus said, "This is a wicked generation. It asks for a

ᵃ 11 Some manuscripts *for bread, will give him a stone? Or if he asks for*

ROCK SOLID
promises

"Blessed rather are those who hear the word of God and obey it."

Luke 11:28

You don't experience God's blessings simply from reading the Bible. You need to live out his words.

sign, but none will be given it except the sign of Jonah. ³⁰For as Jonah was a sign to the Ninevites, so also will the Son of Man be to this generation. ³¹The Queen of the South will rise at the judgment with the people of this generation and condemn them, for she came from the ends of the earth to listen to Solomon's wisdom; and now something greater than Solomon is here. ³²The men of Nineveh will stand up at the judgment with this generation and condemn it, for they repented at the preaching of Jonah; and now something greater than Jonah is here.

The Lamp of the Body

³³"No one lights a lamp and puts it in a place where it will be hidden, or under a bowl. Instead they put it on its stand, so that those who come in may see the light. ³⁴Your eye is the lamp of your body. When your eyes are healthy,ᵃ your whole body also is full of light. But when they are unhealthy,ᵇ your body also is full of darkness. ³⁵See to it, then, that the light within you is not darkness. ³⁶Therefore, if your whole body is full of light, and no part of it dark, it will be just as full of light as when a lamp shines its light on you."

Woes on the Pharisees and the Experts in the Law

³⁷When Jesus had finished speaking, a Pharisee invited him to eat with him; so he went in and reclined at the table. ³⁸But the Pharisee was surprised when he noticed that Jesus did not first wash before the meal.

³⁹Then the Lord said to him, "Now then, you Pharisees clean the outside of the cup and dish, but inside you are full of greed and wickedness. ⁴⁰You foolish people! Did not the one who made the outside make the inside also? ⁴¹But now as for what is inside you—be generous to the poor, and everything will be clean for you.

⁴²"Woe to you Pharisees, because you give God a tenth of your mint, rue and all other kinds of garden herbs, but you neglect justice and the love of God. You should have practiced the latter without leaving the former undone.

⁴³"Woe to you Pharisees, because you love the most important seats in the synagogues and respectful greetings in the marketplaces.

⁴⁴"Woe to you, because you are like unmarked graves, which people walk over without knowing it."

⁴⁵One of the experts in the law answered him, "Teacher, when you say these things, you insult us also."

⁴⁶Jesus replied, "And you experts in the law, woe to you, because you load people down with burdens they can hardly carry, and you yourselves will not lift one finger to help them.

⁴⁷"Woe to you, because you build tombs for the prophets, and it was your ancestors who killed them. ⁴⁸So you testify that you approve of what your ancestors did; they killed the prophets, and you build their tombs. ⁴⁹Because of this, God in his wisdom said, 'I will send them prophets and apostles, some of whom they will kill and others they will persecute.' ⁵⁰Therefore this generation will be held responsible for the blood of all the prophets that has been shed since the beginning of the world, ⁵¹from the blood of Abel to the blood of Zechariah, who was killed between the altar and the sanctuary. Yes, I

ᵃ 34 The Greek for *healthy* here implies *generous*.
ᵇ 34 The Greek for *unhealthy* here implies *stingy*.

tell you, this generation will be held responsible for it all.

⁵²"Woe to you experts in the law, because you have taken away the key to knowledge. You yourselves have not entered, and you have hindered those who were entering."

⁵³When Jesus went outside, the Pharisees and the teachers of the law began to oppose him fiercely and to besiege him with questions, ⁵⁴waiting to catch him in something he might say.

Warnings and Encouragements

12 Meanwhile, when a crowd of many thousands had gathered, so that they were trampling on one another, Jesus began to speak first to his disciples, saying: "Be*a* on your guard against the yeast of the Pharisees, which is hypocrisy. ²There is nothing concealed that will not be disclosed, or hidden that will not be made known. ³What you have said in the dark will be heard in the daylight, and what you have whispered in the ear in the inner rooms will be proclaimed from the roofs.

⁴"I tell you, my friends, do not be afraid of those who kill the body and after that can do no more. ⁵But I will show you whom you should fear: Fear him who, after your body has been killed, has authority to throw you into hell. Yes, I tell you, fear him. ⁶Are not five sparrows sold for two pennies? Yet not one of them is forgotten by God. ⁷Indeed, the very hairs of your head are all numbered. Don't be afraid; you are worth more than many sparrows.

⁸"I tell you, whoever publicly acknowledges me before others, the Son of Man will also acknowledge before the angels of God. ⁹But whoever disowns me before others will be disowned before the angels of God. ¹⁰And everyone who speaks a word against the Son of Man will be forgiven, but anyone who blasphemes against the Holy Spirit will not be forgiven.

¹¹"When you are brought before synagogues, rulers and authorities, do not worry about how you will defend your-

selves or what you will say, ¹²for the Holy Spirit will teach you at that time what you should say."

The Parable of the Rich Fool

¹³Someone in the crowd said to him, "Teacher, tell my brother to divide the inheritance with me."

¹⁴Jesus replied, "Man, who appointed me a judge or an arbiter between you?" ¹⁵Then he said to them, "Watch out! Be on your guard against all kinds of greed; life does not consist in an abundance of possessions."

¹⁶And he told them this parable: "The ground of a certain rich man yielded an abundant harvest. ¹⁷He thought to himself, 'What shall I do? I have no place to store my crops.'

¹⁸"Then he said, 'This is what I'll do. I will tear down my barns and build bigger ones, and there I will store my surplus grain. ¹⁹And I'll say to myself, "You have plenty of grain laid up for many years. Take life easy; eat, drink and be merry."'

²⁰"But God said to him, 'You fool! This very night your life will be demanded from you. Then who will get what you have prepared for yourself?'

²¹"This is how it will be with whoever stores up things for themselves but is not rich toward God."

Do Not Worry

²²Then Jesus said to his disciples: "Therefore I tell you, do not worry about your life, what you will eat; or about your body, what you will wear. ²³For life is more than food, and the body more than clothes. ²⁴Consider the ravens: They do not sow or reap, they have no storeroom or barn; yet God feeds them. And how much more valuable you are than birds! ²⁵Who of you by worrying can add a single hour to your life*b*? ²⁶Since you cannot do this very little thing, why do you worry about the rest? ²⁷"Consider how the wild flowers grow. They do not labor or spin. Yet I tell you, not even Solomon in all his splendor was

a 1 Or *speak to his disciples, saying: "First of all, be*
b 25 Or *single cubit to your height*

dressed like one of these. ²⁸If that is how God clothes the grass of the field, which is here today, and tomorrow is thrown into the fire, how much more will he clothe you—you of little faith! ²⁹And do not set your heart on what you will eat or drink; do not worry about it. ³⁰For the pagan world runs after all such things, and your Father knows that you need them. ³¹But seek his kingdom, and these things will be given to you as well.

³²"Do not be afraid, little flock, for your Father has been pleased to give you the kingdom. ³³Sell your possessions and give to the poor. Provide purses for yourselves that will not wear out, a treasure in heaven that will never fail, where no thief comes near and no moth destroys. ³⁴For where your treasure is, there your heart will be also.

Watchfulness

³⁵"Be dressed ready for service and keep your lamps burning, ³⁶like servants waiting for their master to return from a wedding banquet, so that when he comes and knocks they can immediately open the door for him. ³⁷It will be good for those servants whose master finds them watching when he comes. Truly I tell you, he will dress himself to serve, will have them recline at the table and will come and wait on them. ³⁸It will be good for those servants whose master finds them ready, even if he comes in the middle of the night or toward daybreak. ³⁹But understand this: If the owner of the house had known at what hour the thief was coming, he would not have let his house be broken into. ⁴⁰You also must be ready, because the Son of Man will come at an hour when you do not expect him."

⁴¹Peter asked, "Lord, are you telling this parable to us, or to everyone?"

⁴²The Lord answered, "Who then is the faithful and wise manager, whom the master puts in charge of his servants to give them their food allowance at the

ROCK SOLID principles

Luke 12:22–34

Don't worry.

Abby flipped over in bed and stared at her alarm clock. She must have looked at it a hundred times during the night, and this time it said 3:47. Exhausted, she groaned and pounded her pillow. Abby was so tired of being tired. Part of her was growing more excited each day as she thought about her family's move to a new city. Her dad was getting a raise, she would get her own room, and the ocean was just a short drive away. But Abby's mind spun with questions. *Will anyone like me? Will school be too hard? What if we move and I figure out I would rather be back here?*

Worries might keep you awake at night. It can make you edgy during the day. Jesus says you can let go of your worries, trusting him to take care of burdens too big for you to lift. Like he said, "Who of you by worrying can add a single hour to your life?" (Luke 12:25). Tell God every one of your needs—big and small—and trust him to meet them at exactly the right time.

proper time? ⁴³It will be good for that servant whom the master finds doing so when he returns. ⁴⁴Truly I tell you, he will put him in charge of all his possessions. ⁴⁵But suppose the servant says to himself, 'My master is taking a long time in coming,' and he then begins to beat the other servants, both men and women, and to eat and drink and get drunk. ⁴⁶The master of that servant will come on a day when he does not expect him and at an hour he is not aware of. He will cut him to pieces and assign him a place with the unbelievers.

⁴⁷"The servant who knows the master's will and does not get ready or does not do what the master wants will be beaten with many blows. ⁴⁸But the one who does not know and does things deserving punishment will be beaten with few blows. From everyone who has been given much, much will be demanded; and from the one who has been entrusted with much, much more will be asked.

Not Peace but Division

⁴⁹"I have come to bring fire on the earth, and how I wish it were already kindled! ⁵⁰But I have a baptism to undergo, and what constraint I am under until it is completed! ⁵¹Do you think I came to bring peace on earth? No, I tell you, but division. ⁵²From now on there will be five in one family divided against each other, three against two and two against three. ⁵³They will be divided, father against son and son against father, mother against daughter and daughter against mother, mother-in-law against daughter-in-law and daughter-in-law against mother-in-law."

Interpreting the Times

⁵⁴He said to the crowd: "When you see a cloud rising in the west, immediately you say, 'It's going to rain,' and it does. ⁵⁵And when the south wind blows, you say, 'It's going to be hot,' and it is. ⁵⁶Hypocrites! You know how to interpret the appearance of the earth and the sky. How is it that you don't know how to interpret this present time?

⁵⁷"Why don't you judge for yourselves what is right? ⁵⁸As you are going with your adversary to the magistrate, try hard to be reconciled on the way, or your adversary may drag you off to the judge, and the judge turn you over to the officer, and the officer throw you into prison. ⁵⁹I tell you, you will not get out until you have paid the last penny."

Repent or Perish

13 Now there were some present at that time who told Jesus about the Galileans whose blood Pilate had mixed with their sacrifices. ²Jesus answered, "Do you think that these Galileans were worse sinners than all the other Galileans because they suffered this way? ³I tell you, no! But unless you repent, you too will all perish. ⁴Or those eighteen who died when the tower in Siloam fell on them—do you think they were more guilty than all the others living in Jerusalem? ⁵I tell you, no! But unless you repent, you too will all perish."

⁶Then he told this parable: "A man had a fig tree growing in his vineyard, and he went to look for fruit on it but did not find any. ⁷So he said to the man who took care of the vineyard, 'For three years now I've been coming to look for fruit on this fig tree and haven't found any. Cut it down! Why should it use up the soil?'

⁸"'Sir,' the man replied, 'leave it alone for one more year, and I'll dig around it and fertilize it. ⁹If it bears fruit next year, fine! If not, then cut it down.'"

Jesus Heals a Crippled Woman on the Sabbath

¹⁰On a Sabbath Jesus was teaching in one of the synagogues, ¹¹and a woman was there who had been crippled by a spirit for eighteen years. She was bent over and could not straighten up at all. ¹²When Jesus saw her, he called her forward and said to her, "Woman, you are set free from your infirmity." ¹³Then he put his hands on her, and immediately she straightened up and praised God.

¹⁴Indignant because Jesus had healed

on the Sabbath, the synagogue leader said to the people, "There are six days for work. So come and be healed on those days, not on the Sabbath."

[15] The Lord answered him, "You hypocrites! Doesn't each of you on the Sabbath untie your ox or donkey from the stall and lead it out to give it water? [16] Then should not this woman, a daughter of Abraham, whom Satan has kept bound for eighteen long years, be set free on the Sabbath day from what bound her?"

[17] When he said this, all his opponents were humiliated, but the people were delighted with all the wonderful things he was doing.

The Parables of the Mustard Seed and the Yeast

[18] Then Jesus asked, "What is the kingdom of God like? What shall I compare it to? [19] It is like a mustard seed, which a man took and planted in his garden. It grew and became a tree, and the birds perched in its branches."

[20] Again he asked, "What shall I compare the kingdom of God to? [21] It is like yeast that a woman took and mixed into about sixty pounds[a] of flour until it worked all through the dough."

The Narrow Door

[22] Then Jesus went through the towns and villages, teaching as he made his way to Jerusalem. [23] Someone asked him, "Lord, are only a few people going to be saved?"

He said to them, [24] "Make every effort to enter through the narrow door, because many, I tell you, will try to enter and will not be able to. [25] Once the owner of the house gets up and closes the door, you will stand outside knocking and pleading, 'Sir, open the door for us.'

"But he will answer, 'I don't know you or where you come from.'

[26] "Then you will say, 'We ate and drank with you, and you taught in our streets.'

[27] "But he will reply, 'I don't know you or where you come from. Away from me, all you evildoers!'

[28] "There will be weeping there, and gnashing of teeth, when you see Abraham, Isaac and Jacob and all the prophets in the kingdom of God, but you yourselves thrown out. [29] People will come from east and west and north and south, and will take their places at the feast in the kingdom of God. [30] Indeed there are those who are last who will be first, and first who will be last."

a 21 Or about 27 kilograms

Luke 13:22–30

Following Jesus isn't always popular.

The people who heard Jesus preach asked a significant question: "Lord, are only a few people going to be saved?" (Luke 13:23). Jesus gave an unpopular answer. Not everyone who tries to enter heaven will get in. A big crowd of people will be shut out, like people left standing outside a locked house. They claim to be friends with the homeowner, but he says he never met them. And that's the problem. Plenty of people claim to be Christians, but they never truly become his friend. They hang out in his presence—they might show up at church, for example—but they never begin a personal relationship with him on his terms. Jesus himself is "the narrow door" (Luke 13:24). He's the one way to heaven (see John 14:6). The gift of salvation is granted when you trust in Jesus and his death for your sins (see Ephesians 2:8–9). And many people ignore or reject that truth.

Think: Why is following Jesus not always a popular thing to do?

ROCK SOLID truths

Jesus' Sorrow for Jerusalem

³¹At that time some Pharisees came to Jesus and said to him, "Leave this place and go somewhere else. Herod wants to kill you."

³²He replied, "Go tell that fox, 'I will keep on driving out demons and healing people today and tomorrow, and on the third day I will reach my goal.' ³³In any case, I must press on today and tomorrow and the next day—for surely no prophet can die outside Jerusalem!

³⁴"Jerusalem, Jerusalem, you who kill the prophets and stone those sent to you, how often I have longed to gather your children together, as a hen gathers her chicks under her wings, and you were not willing. ³⁵Look, your house is left to you desolate. I tell you, you will not see me again until you say, 'Blessed is he who comes in the name of the Lord.'ᵃ"

Jesus at a Pharisee's House

14 One Sabbath, when Jesus went to eat in the house of a prominent Pharisee, he was being carefully watched. ²There in front of him was a man suffering from abnormal swelling of his body. ³Jesus asked the Pharisees and experts in the law, "Is it lawful to heal on the Sabbath or not?" ⁴But they remained silent. So taking hold of the man, he healed him and sent him on his way.

⁵Then he asked them, "If one of you has a childᵇ or an ox that falls into a well on the Sabbath day, will you not immediately pull it out?" ⁶And they had nothing to say.

⁷When he noticed how the guests picked the places of honor at the table, he told them this parable: ⁸"When someone invites you to a wedding feast, do not take the place of honor, for a person more distinguished than you may have been invited. ⁹If so, the host who invited both of you will come and say to you, 'Give this person your seat.' Then, humiliated, you will have to take the least important place. ¹⁰But when you are invited, take the lowest place, so that when your host comes, he will say to you, 'Friend, move up to a better place.' Then you will be honored in the presence of all the other guests. ¹¹For all those who exalt themselves will be humbled, and those who humble themselves will be exalted."

¹²Then Jesus said to his host, "When you give a luncheon or dinner, do not invite your friends, your brothers or sisters, your relatives, or your rich neighbors; if you do, they may invite you back and so you will be repaid. ¹³But when you give a banquet, invite the poor, the crippled, the lame, the blind, ¹⁴and you will be blessed. Although they cannot repay you, you will be repaid at the resurrection of the righteous."

The Parable of the Great Banquet

¹⁵When one of those at the table with him heard this, he said to Jesus, "Blessed is the one who will eat at the feast in the kingdom of God."

¹⁶Jesus replied: "A certain man was preparing a great banquet and invited many guests. ¹⁷At the time of the banquet he sent his servant to tell those who had been invited, 'Come, for everything is now ready.'

¹⁸"But they all alike began to make excuses. The first said, 'I have just bought a field, and I must go and see it. Please excuse me.'

¹⁹"Another said, 'I have just bought five yoke of oxen, and I'm on my way to try them out. Please excuse me.'

²⁰"Still another said, 'I just got married, so I can't come.'

²¹"The servant came back and reported this to his master. Then the owner of the house became angry and ordered his servant, 'Go out quickly into the streets and alleys of the town and bring in the poor, the crippled, the blind and the lame.'

²²"'Sir,' the servant said, 'what you ordered has been done, but there is still room.'

²³"Then the master told his servant, 'Go out to the roads and country lanes and compel them to come in, so that my house will be full. ²⁴I tell you, not one of

ᵃ 35 Psalm 118:26   ᵇ 5 Some manuscripts *donkey*

those who were invited will get a taste of my banquet.'"

The Cost of Being a Disciple

[25] Large crowds were traveling with Jesus, and turning to them he said: [26] "If anyone comes to me and does not hate father and mother, wife and children, brothers and sisters—yes, even their own life—such a person cannot be my disciple. [27] And whoever does not carry their cross and follow me cannot be my disciple.

[28] "Suppose one of you wants to build a tower. Won't you first sit down and estimate the cost to see if you have enough money to complete it? [29] For if you lay the foundation and are not able to finish it, everyone who sees it will ridicule you, [30] saying, 'This person began to build and wasn't able to finish.'

[31] "Or suppose a king is about to go to war against another king. Won't he first sit down and consider whether he is able with ten thousand men to oppose the one coming against him with twenty thousand? [32] If he is not able, he will send a delegation while the other is still a long way off and will ask for terms of peace. [33] In the same way, those of you who do not give up everything you have cannot be my disciples.

[34] "Salt is good, but if it loses its saltiness, how can it be made salty again? [35] It is fit neither for the soil nor for the manure pile; it is thrown out.

"Whoever has ears to hear, let them hear."

The Parable of the Lost Sheep

15 Now the tax collectors and sinners were all gathering around to hear Jesus. [2] But the Pharisees and the teachers of the law muttered, "This man welcomes sinners and eats with them."

[3] Then Jesus told them this parable: [4] "Suppose one of you has a hundred sheep and loses one of them. Doesn't he leave

ROCK SOLID *principles*

Luke 14:25–33

Count the cost of following.

Peter could hear the beer slosh in his backpack. A friend's older sister was glad to get him alcohol for a few bucks in profit, giving Peter and a couple friends the opportunity to throw a little party while his parents enjoyed a long evening out. Deep down Peter knew the beer was a bad idea. And illegal. And just plain wrong. Yet at the moment, all he could think about was getting buzzed and being a hero to his friends. Right now, that mattered more than obeying a bunch of Bible verses. Peter's biggest worry was whether the beer would fizz all over from getting shook so much.

Jesus said that being his disciple requires picking up your cross and following him. That means you give him complete control of your life and choose his way instead of your own, and that's no small decision. You calculate the cost of obeying Jesus, then decide you're willing to pay the price, no matter how high it gets. If you aren't willing to carry your cross, you can't be his disciple.

the ninety-nine in the open country and go after the lost sheep until he finds it? ⁵And when he finds it, he joyfully puts it on his shoulders ⁶and goes home. Then he calls his friends and neighbors together and says, 'Rejoice with me; I have found my lost sheep.' ⁷I tell you that in the same way there will be more rejoicing in heaven over one sinner who repents than over ninety-nine righteous persons who do not need to repent.

The Parable of the Lost Coin

⁸"Or suppose a woman has ten silver coins*a* and loses one. Doesn't she light a lamp, sweep the house and search carefully until she finds it? ⁹And when she finds it, she calls her friends and neighbors together and says, 'Rejoice with me; I have found my lost coin.' ¹⁰In the same way, I tell you, there is rejoicing in the presence of the angels of God over one sinner who repents."

ROCK SOLID
promises

"There is rejoicing in the presence of the angels of God over one sinner who repents." Luke 15:10

Heaven throws a party every time someone decides to ditch sin and starts to live for Jesus.

The Parable of the Lost Son

¹¹Jesus continued: "There was a man who had two sons. ¹²The younger one said to his father, 'Father, give me my share of the estate.' So he divided his property between them.

¹³"Not long after that, the younger son got together all he had, set off for a distant country and there squandered his wealth in wild living. ¹⁴After he had spent everything, there was a severe famine in that whole country, and he began to be in need. ¹⁵So he went and hired himself out to a citizen of that country, who sent him to his fields to feed pigs. ¹⁶He longed to fill his stomach with the pods that the pigs were eating, but no one gave him anything.

¹⁷"When he came to his senses, he said, 'How many of my father's hired servants have food to spare, and here I am starving to death! ¹⁸I will set out and go back to my father and say to him: Father, I have sinned against heaven and against you. ¹⁹I am no longer worthy to be called your son; make me like one of your hired servants.' ²⁰So he got up and went to his father.

"But while he was still a long way off, his father saw him and was filled with compassion for him; he ran to his son, threw his arms around him and kissed him.

²¹"The son said to him, 'Father, I have sinned against heaven and against you. I am no longer worthy to be called your son.'

²²"But the father said to his servants, 'Quick! Bring the best robe and put it on him. Put a ring on his finger and sandals on his feet. ²³Bring the fattened calf and kill it. Let's have a feast and celebrate. ²⁴For this son of mine was dead and is alive again; he was lost and is found.' So they began to celebrate.

²⁵"Meanwhile, the older son was in the field. When he came near the house, he heard music and dancing. ²⁶So he called one of the servants and asked him what was going on. ²⁷'Your brother has come,' he replied, 'and your father has killed the fattened calf because he has him back safe and sound.'

²⁸"The older brother became angry and refused to go in. So his father went out and pleaded with him. ²⁹But he answered his father, 'Look! All these years I've been slaving for you and never disobeyed your orders. Yet you never gave me even

a 8 Greek *ten drachmas*, each worth about a day's wages

a young goat so I could celebrate with my friends. ³⁰But when this son of yours who has squandered your property with prostitutes comes home, you kill the fattened calf for him!'

³¹"'My son,' the father said, 'you are always with me, and everything I have is yours. ³²But we had to celebrate and be glad, because this brother of yours was dead and is alive again; he was lost and is found.'"

The Parable of the Shrewd Manager

16 Jesus told his disciples: "There was a rich man whose manager was accused of wasting his possessions. ²So he called him in and asked him, 'What is this I hear about you? Give an account of your management, because you cannot be manager any longer.'

³"The manager said to himself, 'What shall I do now? My master is taking away my job. I'm not strong enough to dig, and I'm ashamed to beg— ⁴I know what I'll do so that, when I lose my job here, people will welcome me into their houses.'

⁵"So he called in each one of his master's debtors. He asked the first, 'How much do you owe my master?'

⁶"'Nine hundred gallons[a] of olive oil,' he replied.

"The manager told him, 'Take your bill, sit down quickly, and make it four hundred and fifty.'

⁷"Then he asked the second, 'And how much do you owe?'

"'A thousand bushels[b] of wheat,' he replied.

"He told him, 'Take your bill and make it eight hundred.'

⁸"The master commended the dishonest manager because he had acted shrewdly. For the people of this world are more shrewd in dealing with their own kind than are the people of the light. ⁹I tell you, use worldly wealth to gain friends for yourselves, so that when it is gone, you will be welcomed into eternal dwellings.

¹⁰"Whoever can be trusted with very little can also be trusted with much, and whoever is dishonest with very little will also be dishonest with much. ¹¹So if you have not been trustworthy in handling worldly wealth, who will trust you with true riches? ¹²And if you have not been trustworthy with someone else's property, who will give you property of your own?

¹³"No one can serve two masters. Either you will hate the one and love the other, or you will be devoted to the one and despise the other. You cannot serve both God and money."

¹⁴The Pharisees, who loved money, heard all this and were sneering at Jesus. ¹⁵He said to them, "You are the ones who justify yourselves in the eyes of others, but God knows your hearts. What people value highly is detestable in God's sight.

Additional Teachings

¹⁶"The Law and the Prophets were proclaimed until John. Since that time, the good news of the kingdom of God is being preached, and everyone is forcing their way into it. ¹⁷It is easier for heaven and earth to disappear than for the least stroke of a pen to drop out of the Law.

¹⁸"Anyone who divorces his wife and marries another woman commits adultery, and the man who marries a divorced woman commits adultery.

The Rich Man and Lazarus

¹⁹"There was a rich man who was dressed in purple and fine linen and lived in luxury every day. ²⁰At his gate was laid a beggar named Lazarus, covered with sores ²¹and longing to eat what fell from the rich man's table. Even the dogs came and licked his sores.

²²"The time came when the beggar died and the angels carried him to Abraham's side. The rich man also died and was buried. ²³In Hades, where he was in torment, he looked up and saw Abraham far away, with Lazarus by his side. ²⁴So he called to him, 'Father Abraham, have pity on me and send Lazarus to dip the tip of his finger in water and cool my tongue, because I am in agony in this fire.'

___
[a] 6 Or about 3,000 liters   [b] 7 Or about 30 tons

²⁵"But Abraham replied, 'Son, remember that in your lifetime you received your good things, while Lazarus received bad things, but now he is comforted here and you are in agony. ²⁶And besides all this, between us and you a great chasm has been set in place, so that those who want to go from here to you cannot, nor can anyone cross over from there to us.'

²⁷"He answered, 'Then I beg you, father, send Lazarus to my family, ²⁸for I have five brothers. Let him warn them, so that they will not also come to this place of torment.'

²⁹"Abraham replied, 'They have Moses and the Prophets; let them listen to them.'

³⁰"'No, father Abraham,' he said, 'but if someone from the dead goes to them, they will repent.'

³¹"He said to him, 'If they do not listen to Moses and the Prophets, they will not be convinced even if someone rises from the dead.'"

Sin, Faith, Duty

17 Jesus said to his disciples: "Things that cause people to stumble are bound to come, but woe to anyone through whom they come. ²It would be better for them to be thrown into the sea with a millstone tied around their neck than to cause one of these little ones to stumble. ³So watch yourselves.

"If your brother or sister*a* sins against you, rebuke them; and if they repent, forgive them. ⁴Even if they sin against you seven times in a day and seven times come back to you saying 'I repent,' you must forgive them."

⁵The apostles said to the Lord, "Increase our faith!"

⁶He replied, "If you have faith as small as a mustard seed, you can say to this mulberry tree, 'Be uprooted and planted in the sea,' and it will obey you.

⁷"Suppose one of you has a servant plowing or looking after the sheep. Will he say to the servant when he comes in from the field, 'Come along now and sit down to eat'? ⁸Won't he rather say, 'Pre-

pare my supper, get yourself ready and wait on me while I eat and drink; after that you may eat and drink'? ⁹Will he thank the servant because he did what he was told to do? ¹⁰So you also, when you have done everything you were told to do, should say, 'We are unworthy servants; we have only done our duty.'"

Jesus Heals Ten Men With Leprosy

¹¹Now on his way to Jerusalem, Jesus traveled along the border between Samaria and Galilee. ¹²As he was going into a village, ten men who had leprosy*b* met him. They stood at a distance ¹³and called out in a loud voice, "Jesus, Master, have pity on us!"

¹⁴When he saw them, he said, "Go, show yourselves to the priests." And as they went, they were cleansed.

¹⁵One of them, when he saw he was healed, came back, praising God in a loud voice. ¹⁶He threw himself at Jesus' feet and thanked him—and he was a Samaritan.

¹⁷Jesus asked, "Were not all ten cleansed? Where are the other nine? ¹⁸Has no one returned to give praise to God except this foreigner?" ¹⁹Then he said to him, "Rise and go; your faith has made you well."

The Coming of the Kingdom of God

²⁰Once, on being asked by the Pharisees when the kingdom of God would come, Jesus replied, "The coming of the kingdom of God is not something that can be observed, ²¹nor will people say, 'Here it is,' or 'There it is,' because the kingdom of God is in your midst."*c*

²²Then he said to his disciples, "The time is coming when you will long to see one of the days of the Son of Man, but you will not see it. ²³People will tell you, 'There he is!' or 'Here he is!' Do not go running off after them. ²⁴For the Son of

---

a 3 The Greek word for *brother or sister* (*adelphos*) refers here to a fellow disciple, whether man or woman.   *b 12* The Greek word traditionally translated *leprosy* was used for various diseases affecting the skin.   *c 21* Or *is within you*

Man in his day*a* will be like the lightning, which flashes and lights up the sky from one end to the other. ²⁵But first he must suffer many things and be rejected by this generation.

²⁶"Just as it was in the days of Noah, so also will it be in the days of the Son of Man. ²⁷People were eating, drinking, marrying and being given in marriage up to the day Noah entered the ark. Then the flood came and destroyed them all.

²⁸"It was the same in the days of Lot. People were eating and drinking, buying and selling, planting and building. ²⁹But the day Lot left Sodom, fire and sulfur rained down from heaven and destroyed them all.

³⁰"It will be just like this on the day the Son of Man is revealed. ³¹On that day no one who is on the housetop, with possessions inside, should go down to get them. Likewise, no one in the field should go back for anything. ³²Remember Lot's wife! ³³Whoever tries to keep their life will lose it, and whoever loses their life will preserve it. ³⁴I tell you, on that night two people will be in one bed; one will be taken and the other left. ³⁵Two women will be grinding grain together; one will be taken and the other left." [36]*b*

³⁷"Where, Lord?" they asked.

He replied, "Where there is a dead body, there the vultures will gather."

The Parable of the Persistent Widow

18 Then Jesus told his disciples a parable to show them that they should always pray and not give up. ²He said: "In a certain town there was a judge who neither feared God nor cared what people thought. ³And there was a widow in that town who kept

a 24 Some manuscripts do not have *in his day.*
b 36 Some manuscripts include here words similar to Matt. 24:40.

ROCK SOLID principles

Luke 17:11–19
Show gratitude.

Cassie had a seriously close call. After years of snowboarding she was maybe getting overconfident and even a bit careless, but as she lofted from a jump and flipped forward she rotated too far and slammed her body into ice-covered ground. A bruised lung and jolted kidney made her seep blood inside. The doctor said the same amount of blood on her brain could have been fatal—and said Cassie was lucky. But Cassie was convinced it wasn't merely luck that she would be able to get back to boarding in a couple weeks. God kept her from getting hurt worse, and she couldn't stop telling him thanks.

One day Jesus met ten men infected with a skin disease so serious they were kicked out of their homes and families. He sent them for an exam by the priests, who could confirm their cure. On the way, all ten men noticed a miraculous healing. All ten men knew who had made them well. Only one man did the right thing. He turned around, went back to Jesus, and said thanks.

coming to him with the plea, 'Grant me justice against my adversary.'

⁴"For some time he refused. But finally he said to himself, 'Even though I don't fear God or care what people think, ⁵yet because this widow keeps bothering me, I will see that she gets justice, so that she won't eventually come and attack me!'"

⁶And the Lord said, "Listen to what the unjust judge says. ⁷And will not God bring about justice for his chosen ones, who cry out to him day and night? Will he keep putting them off? ⁸I tell you, he will see that they get justice, and quickly. However, when the Son of Man comes, will he find faith on the earth?"

The Parable of the Pharisee and the Tax Collector

⁹To some who were confident of their own righteousness and looked down on everyone else, Jesus told this parable: ¹⁰"Two men went up to the temple to pray, one a Pharisee and the other a tax collector. ¹¹The Pharisee stood by himself and prayed: 'God, I thank you that I am not like other people—robbers, evildoers, adulterers—or even like this tax collector. ¹²I fast twice a week and give a tenth of all I get.'

¹³"But the tax collector stood at a distance. He would not even look up to heaven, but beat his breast and said, 'God, have mercy on me, a sinner.'

¹⁴"I tell you that this man, rather than the other, went home justified before God. For all those who exalt themselves will be humbled, and those who humble themselves will be exalted."

The Little Children and Jesus

¹⁵People were also bringing babies to Jesus for him to place his hands on them. When the disciples saw this, they rebuked them. ¹⁶But Jesus called the children to him and said, "Let the little children come to me, and do not hinder them, for the kingdom of God belongs to such as these. ¹⁷Truly I tell you, anyone who will not receive the kingdom of God like a little child will never enter it."

The Rich and the Kingdom of God

¹⁸A certain ruler asked him, "Good teacher, what must I do to inherit eternal life?"

¹⁹"Why do you call me good?" Jesus answered. "No one is good—except God alone. ²⁰You know the commandments: 'You shall not commit adultery, you shall not murder, you shall not steal, you shall not give false testimony, honor your father and mother.'[a]"

²¹"All these I have kept since I was a boy," he said.

²²When Jesus heard this, he said to him, "You still lack one thing. Sell everything you have and give to the poor, and you will have treasure in heaven. Then come, follow me."

²³When he heard this, he became very sad, because he was very wealthy. ²⁴Jesus looked at him and said, "How hard it is for the rich to enter the kingdom of God! ²⁵Indeed, it is easier for a camel to go through the eye of a needle than for someone who is rich to enter the kingdom of God."

²⁶Those who heard this asked, "Who then can be saved?"

²⁷Jesus replied, "What is impossible with man is possible with God."

²⁸Peter said to him, "We have left all we had to follow you!"

ᵃ 20 Exodus 20:12-16; Deut. 5:16-20

²⁹"Truly I tell you," Jesus said to them, "no one who has left home or wife or brothers or sisters or parents or children for the sake of the kingdom of God ³⁰will fail to receive many times as much in this age, and in the age to come eternal life."

Jesus Predicts His Death a Third Time

³¹Jesus took the Twelve aside and told them, "We are going up to Jerusalem, and everything that is written by the prophets about the Son of Man will be fulfilled. ³²He will be delivered over to the Gentiles. They will mock him, insult him and spit on him; ³³they will flog him and kill him. On the third day he will rise again."

³⁴The disciples did not understand any of this. Its meaning was hidden from them, and they did not know what he was talking about.

A Blind Beggar Receives His Sight

³⁵As Jesus approached Jericho, a blind man was sitting by the roadside begging. ³⁶When he heard the crowd going by, he asked what was happening. ³⁷They told him, "Jesus of Nazareth is passing by."

³⁸He called out, "Jesus, Son of David, have mercy on me!"

³⁹Those who led the way rebuked him and told him to be quiet, but he shouted all the more, "Son of David, have mercy on me!"

⁴⁰Jesus stopped and ordered the man to be brought to him. When he came near, Jesus asked him, ⁴¹"What do you want me to do for you?"

"Lord, I want to see," he replied.

⁴²Jesus said to him, "Receive your sight; your faith has healed you." ⁴³Immediately he received his sight and followed Jesus, praising God. When all the people saw it, they also praised God.

Zacchaeus the Tax Collector

19 Jesus entered Jericho and was passing through. ²A man was there by the name of Zacchaeus; he was a chief tax collector and was wealthy. ³He wanted to see who Jesus was, but because he was short he could not see over the crowd. ⁴So he ran ahead and climbed a sycamore-fig tree to see him, since Jesus was coming that way.

⁵When Jesus reached the spot, he looked up and said to him, "Zacchaeus, come down immediately. I must stay at your house today." ⁶So he came down at once and welcomed him gladly.

⁷All the people saw this and began to mutter, "He has gone to be the guest of a sinner."

⁸But Zacchaeus stood up and said to the Lord, "Look, Lord! Here and now I give half of my possessions to the poor, and if I have cheated anybody out of anything, I will pay back four times the amount."

⁹Jesus said to him, "Today salvation has come to this house, because this man, too, is a son of Abraham. ¹⁰For the Son of Man came to seek and to save the lost."

The Parable of the Ten Minas

¹¹While they were listening to this, he went on to tell them a parable, because he was near Jerusalem and the people thought that the kingdom of God was going to appear at once. ¹²He said: "A man of noble birth went to a distant country to have himself appointed king and then to return. ¹³So he called ten of his servants and gave them ten minas.[a] 'Put this money to work,' he said, 'until I come back.'

¹⁴"But his subjects hated him and sent a delegation after him to say, 'We don't want this man to be our king.'

¹⁵"He was made king, however, and returned home. Then he sent for the servants to whom he had given the money, in order to find out what they had gained with it.

¹⁶"The first one came and said, 'Sir, your mina has earned ten more.'

¹⁷"'Well done, my good servant!' his master replied. 'Because you have been trustworthy in a very small matter, take charge of ten cities.'

¹⁸"The second came and said, 'Sir, your mina has earned five more.'

¹⁹"His master answered, 'You take charge of five cities.'

²⁰"Then another servant came and said,

---

^a *13* A mina was about three months' wages.

'Sir, here is your mina; I have kept it laid away in a piece of cloth. [21] I was afraid of you, because you are a hard man. You take out what you did not put in and reap what you did not sow.'

[22] "His master replied, 'I will judge you by your own words, you wicked servant! You knew, did you, that I am a hard man, taking out what I did not put in, and reaping what I did not sow? [23] Why then didn't you put my money on deposit, so that when I came back, I could have collected it with interest?'

[24] "Then he said to those standing by, 'Take his mina away from him and give it to the one who has ten minas.'

[25] "'Sir,' they said, 'he already has ten!'

[26] "He replied, 'I tell you that to everyone who has, more will be given, but as for the one who has nothing, even what they have will be taken away. [27] But those enemies of mine who did not want me to be king over them—bring them here and kill them in front of me.'"

Jesus Comes to Jerusalem as King

[28] After Jesus had said this, he went on ahead, going up to Jerusalem. [29] As he approached Bethphage and Bethany at the hill called the Mount of Olives, he sent two of his disciples, saying to them, [30] "Go to the village ahead of you, and as you enter

---

Luke 19:1–10

Zacchaeus went looking for Jesus.

Jesus often ran into trouble with religious leaders for hanging out with "sinners," and his encounter with Zacchaeus shows Jesus at his best, making friends with a complete outcast.

Zacchaeus ranked among the lowest of the low in his society. It was bad enough that he was a tax collector—a guy who forced his fellow citizens to pay more than they owed and who worked as a traitor with the Romans controlling their country. But Zacchaeus was also a tax collector boss—a guy who grew wealthy from his own crimes and from the cut he took from other lowlifes who worked under him.

When the notorious Zacchaeus heard Jesus was passing through his city, he wanted to get a look. Too short to see over a crowd of shoulders and heads, he scaled a tree for a better view. When Jesus spotted him above all the other onlookers, he called Zacchaeus down by name and invited himself for dinner and lodging at the tax collector's home. Zacchaeus was so overwhelmed by Jesus that he instantly admitted his sin, promising to give away half of what he owned and pay back four times what he had stolen.

Zacchaeus went looking for Jesus, but Jesus also went looking for Zacchaeus. When people complained that Jesus had become friends with a sinner, Jesus replied that the whole reason he came to our world was to find and rescue all who need him—and that actually includes everybody.

You can find Zacchaeus only here in Luke 19:1–10, but you can find other tax collectors in Luke 5:27–29 and 18:9–14.

UNSHAKEN *people*

it, you will find a colt tied there, which no one has ever ridden. Untie it and bring it here. ³¹If anyone asks you, 'Why are you untying it?' say, 'The Lord needs it.'"

³²Those who were sent ahead went and found it just as he had told them. ³³As they were untying the colt, its owners asked them, "Why are you untying the colt?"

³⁴They replied, "The Lord needs it."

³⁵They brought it to Jesus, threw their cloaks on the colt and put Jesus on it. ³⁶As he went along, people spread their cloaks on the road.

³⁷When he came near the place where the road goes down the Mount of Olives, the whole crowd of disciples began joyfully to praise God in loud voices for all the miracles they had seen:

³⁸"Blessed is the king who comes in the name of the Lord!"ᵃ

"Peace in heaven and glory in the highest!"

³⁹Some of the Pharisees in the crowd said to Jesus, "Teacher, rebuke your disciples!"

⁴⁰"I tell you," he replied, "if they keep quiet, the stones will cry out."

⁴¹As he approached Jerusalem and saw the city, he wept over it ⁴²and said, "If you, even you, had only known on this day what would bring you peace—but now it is hidden from your eyes. ⁴³The days will come upon you when your enemies will build an embankment against you and encircle you and hem you in on every side. ⁴⁴They will dash you to the ground, you and the children within your walls. They will not leave one stone on another, because you did not recognize the time of God's coming to you."

Jesus at the Temple

⁴⁵When Jesus entered the temple courts, he began to drive out those who were selling. ⁴⁶"It is written," he said to them, "'My house will be a house of prayer'ᵇ; but you have made it 'a den of robbers.'ᶜ"

⁴⁷Every day he was teaching at the temple. But the chief priests, the teachers of the law and the leaders among the people were trying to kill him. ⁴⁸Yet they could not find any way to do it, because all the people hung on his words.

The Authority of Jesus Questioned

20 One day as Jesus was teaching the people in the temple courts and proclaiming the good news, the chief priests and the teachers of the law, together with the elders, came up to him. ²"Tell us by what authority you are doing these things," they said. "Who gave you this authority?"

³He replied, "I will also ask you a question. Tell me: ⁴John's baptism—was it from heaven, or of human origin?"

⁵They discussed it among themselves and said, "If we say, 'From heaven,' he will ask, 'Why didn't you believe him?' ⁶But if we say, 'Of human origin,' all the people will stone us, because they are persuaded that John was a prophet."

⁷So they answered, "We don't know where it was from."

⁸Jesus said, "Neither will I tell you by what authority I am doing these things."

The Parable of the Tenants

⁹He went on to tell the people this parable: "A man planted a vineyard, rented it to some farmers and went away for a long time. ¹⁰At harvest time he sent a servant to the tenants so they would give him some of the fruit of the vineyard. But the tenants beat him and sent him away empty-handed. ¹¹He sent another servant, but that one also they beat and treated shamefully and sent away empty-handed. ¹²He sent still a third, and they wounded him and threw him out.

¹³"Then the owner of the vineyard said, 'What shall I do? I will send my son, whom I love; perhaps they will respect him.'

¹⁴"But when the tenants saw him, they talked the matter over. 'This is the heir,' they said. 'Let's kill him, and the inheritance will be ours.' ¹⁵So they threw him out of the vineyard and killed him.

ᵃ 38 Psalm 118:26   ᵇ 46 Isaiah 56:7
ᶜ 46 Jer. 7:11

"What then will the owner of the vineyard do to them? [16] He will come and kill those tenants and give the vineyard to others."

When the people heard this, they said, "God forbid!"

[17] Jesus looked directly at them and asked, "Then what is the meaning of that which is written:

" 'The stone the builders rejected
has become the cornerstone'[a]?

[18] Everyone who falls on that stone will be broken to pieces; anyone on whom it falls will be crushed."

[19] The teachers of the law and the chief priests looked for a way to arrest him immediately, because they knew he had spoken this parable against them. But they were afraid of the people.

Paying Taxes to Caesar

[20] Keeping a close watch on him, they sent spies, who pretended to be sincere. They hoped to catch Jesus in something he said, so that they might hand him over to the power and authority of the governor. [21] So the spies questioned him: "Teacher, we know that you speak and teach what is right, and that you do not show partiality but teach the way of God in accordance with the truth. [22] Is it right for us to pay taxes to Caesar or not?"

[23] He saw through their duplicity and said to them, [24] "Show me a denarius. Whose image and inscription are on it?"

"Caesar's," they replied.

[25] He said to them, "Then give back to Caesar what is Caesar's, and to God what is God's."

[26] They were unable to trap him in what he had said there in public. And astonished by his answer, they became silent.

The Resurrection and Marriage

[27] Some of the Sadducees, who say there is no resurrection, came to Jesus with a question. [28] "Teacher," they said, "Moses wrote for us that if a man's brother dies and leaves a wife but no children, the man must marry the widow and raise up offspring for his brother. [29] Now there were

seven brothers. The first one married a woman and died childless. [30] The second [31] and then the third married her, and in the same way the seven died, leaving no children. [32] Finally, the woman died too. [33] Now then, at the resurrection whose wife will she be, since the seven were married to her?"

[34] Jesus replied, "The people of this age marry and are given in marriage. [35] But those who are considered worthy of taking part in the age to come and in the resurrection from the dead will neither marry nor be given in marriage, [36] and they can no longer die; for they are like the angels. They are God's children, since they are children of the resurrection. [37] But in the account of the burning bush, even Moses showed that the dead rise, for he calls the Lord 'the God of Abraham, and the God of Isaac, and the God of Jacob.'[b] [38] He is not the God of the dead, but of the living, for to him all are alive."

[a] 17 Psalm 118:22   [b] 37 Exodus 3:6

ROCK SOLID plans

Luke 20:20–26

Do your duty.

Jesus' enemies thought they had devised a perfect trap, forcing him to answer whether it was right to pay taxes to Caesar, emperor of Rome. If Jesus said yes, the crowds would turn on him for supporting the foreign power occupying their country. If he said no, the Lord would be charged with advocating political revolt. Jesus shrewdly used a Roman coin to prove that God deserves honor and that religious convictions don't exempt believers from the basic duties of citizenship.

Your next step: Brainstorm ways you can be a committed Christian and also contribute as a solid citizen to your community, country, and world.

[39] Some of the teachers of the law responded, "Well said, teacher!" [40] And no one dared to ask him any more questions.

Whose Son Is the Messiah?

[41] Then Jesus said to them, "Why is it said that the Messiah is the son of David? [42] David himself declares in the Book of Psalms:

"'The Lord said to my Lord:
"Sit at my right hand
[43] until I make your enemies
a footstool for your feet."' [a]

[44] David calls him 'Lord.' How then can he be his son?"

Warning Against the Teachers of the Law

[45] While all the people were listening, Jesus said to his disciples, [46] "Beware of the teachers of the law. They like to walk around in flowing robes and love to be greeted with respect in the marketplaces and have the most important seats in the synagogues and the places of honor at banquets. [47] They devour widows' houses and for a show make lengthy prayers. These men will be punished most severely."

The Widow's Offering

21 As Jesus looked up, he saw the rich putting their gifts into the temple treasury. [2] He also saw a poor widow put in two very small copper coins. [3] "Truly I tell you," he said, "this poor widow has put in more than all the others. [4] All these people gave their gifts out of their wealth; but she out of her poverty put in all she had to live on."

The Destruction of the Temple and Signs of the End Times

[5] Some of his disciples were remarking about how the temple was adorned with beautiful stones and with gifts dedicated to God. But Jesus said, [6] "As for what you see here, the time will come when not one stone will be left on another; every one of them will be thrown down."

[7] "Teacher," they asked, "when will these things happen? And what will be the sign that they are about to take place?"

[8] He replied: "Watch out that you are not deceived. For many will come in my name, claiming, 'I am he,' and, 'The time is near.' Do not follow them. [9] When you hear of wars and uprisings, do not be frightened. These things must happen first, but the end will not come right away."

[10] Then he said to them: "Nation will rise against nation, and kingdom against kingdom. [11] There will be great earthquakes, famines and pestilences in various places, and fearful events and great signs from heaven.

[12] "But before all this, they will seize you and persecute you. They will hand you over to synagogues and put you in prison, and you will be brought before kings and governors, and all on account of my name. [13] And so you will bear testimony to me. [14] But make up your mind not to worry beforehand how you will defend yourselves. [15] For I will give you words and wisdom that none of your adversaries will be able to resist or contradict. [16] You will be betrayed even by parents, brothers and sisters, relatives and friends, and they will put some of you to death. [17] Everyone will hate you because of me. [18] But not a hair of your head will perish. [19] Stand firm, and you will win life.

[a] 43 Psalm 110:1

ROCK SOLID promises

"I will give you words and wisdom that none of your adversaries will be able to resist or contradict."

Luke 21:15

People might baffle you with spiritual questions. Ask God to teach you how to answer.

20"When you see Jerusalem being surrounded by armies, you will know that its desolation is near. 21Then let those who are in Judea flee to the mountains, let those in the city get out, and let those in the country not enter the city. 22For this is the time of punishment in fulfillment of all that has been written. 23How dreadful it will be in those days for pregnant women and nursing mothers! There will be great distress in the land and wrath against this people. 24They will fall by the sword and will be taken as prisoners to all the nations. Jerusalem will be trampled on by the Gentiles until the times of the Gentiles are fulfilled.

25"There will be signs in the sun, moon and stars. On the earth, nations will be in anguish and perplexity at the roaring and tossing of the sea. 26People will faint from terror, apprehensive of what is coming on the world, for the heavenly bodies will be shaken. 27At that time they will see the Son of Man coming in a cloud with power and great glory. 28When these things begin to take place, stand up and lift up your heads, because your redemption is drawing near."

29He told them this parable: "Look at the fig tree and all the trees. 30When they sprout leaves, you can see for yourselves and know that summer is near. 31Even so, when you see these things happening, you know that the kingdom of God is near.

32"Truly I tell you, this generation will certainly not pass away until all these things have happened. 33Heaven and earth will pass away, but my words will never pass away.

34"Be careful, or your hearts will be weighed down with carousing, drunkenness and the anxieties of life, and that day will close on you suddenly like a trap. 35For it will come on all those who live on the face of the whole earth. 36Be always on the watch, and pray that you may be able to escape all that is about to happen, and that you may be able to stand before the Son of Man."

37Each day Jesus was teaching at the temple, and each evening he went out to spend the night on the hill called the Mount of Olives, 38and all the people came early in the morning to hear him at the temple.

Judas Agrees to Betray Jesus

22 Now the Festival of Unleavened Bread, called the Passover, was approaching, 2and the chief priests and the teachers of the law were looking for some way to get rid

Luke 21:25–33
Jesus is coming back to earth.

You know how Jesus got here—he was born to the Virgin Mary in some sort of animal shelter in the little town of Bethlehem (see Luke 2:4–7). You might not know what happened after he rose from the dead—he left earth and "ascended" to heaven as his disciples watched (see Acts 1:6–11). And there is a whole lot more to know about how he will come back—in a "second coming" no one will miss. At that time the sun will darken and stars will fall from the sky (see Matthew 24:29). Everyone will see Jesus "coming in a cloud with power and great glory" (Luke 21:27). His arrival will rescue believers from the ends of the earth (see Matthew 24:31). It will bring judgment for people who don't believe in him (see Matthew 25:31–46). No one can predict exactly when Jesus will come back (see Matthew 24:36), but our job is to live for him and be ready for his coming at any time (see Luke 21:34–36).

Think: Why look forward to Jesus' second coming?

ROCK SOLID truths

of Jesus, for they were afraid of the people. ³Then Satan entered Judas, called Iscariot, one of the Twelve. ⁴And Judas went to the chief priests and the officers of the temple guard and discussed with them how he might betray Jesus. ⁵They were delighted and agreed to give him money. ⁶He consented, and watched for an opportunity to hand Jesus over to them when no crowd was present.

The Last Supper

⁷Then came the day of Unleavened Bread on which the Passover lamb had to be sacrificed. ⁸Jesus sent Peter and John, saying, "Go and make preparations for us to eat the Passover."

⁹"Where do you want us to prepare for it?" they asked.

¹⁰He replied, "As you enter the city, a man carrying a jar of water will meet you. Follow him to the house that he enters, ¹¹and say to the owner of the house, 'The Teacher asks: Where is the guest room, where I may eat the Passover with my disciples?' ¹²He will show you a large room upstairs, all furnished. Make preparations there."

¹³They left and found things just as Jesus had told them. So they prepared the Passover.

¹⁴When the hour came, Jesus and his apostles reclined at the table. ¹⁵And he said to them, "I have eagerly desired to eat this Passover with you before I suffer. ¹⁶For I tell you, I will not eat it again until it finds fulfillment in the kingdom of God."

¹⁷After taking the cup, he gave thanks and said, "Take this and divide it among you. ¹⁸For I tell you I will not drink again from the fruit of the vine until the kingdom of God comes."

¹⁹And he took bread, gave thanks and broke it, and gave it to them, saying, "This is my body given for you; do this in remembrance of me."

²⁰In the same way, after the supper he took the cup, saying, "This cup is the new covenant in my blood, which is poured out for you.ᵃ ²¹But the hand of him who is going to betray me is with mine on the table. ²²The Son of Man will go as it has been decreed. But woe to that man who betrays him!" ²³They began to question among themselves which of them it might be who would do this.

²⁴A dispute also arose among them as to which of them was considered to be greatest. ²⁵Jesus said to them, "The kings of the Gentiles lord it over them; and those who exercise authority over them call themselves Benefactors. ²⁶But you are not to be like that. Instead, the greatest among you should be like the youngest, and the one who rules like the one who serves. ²⁷For who is greater, the one who is at the table or the one who serves? Is it not the one who is at the table? But I am among you as one who serves. ²⁸You are those who have stood by me in my trials. ²⁹And I confer on you a kingdom, just as my Father conferred one on me, ³⁰so that you may eat and drink at my table in my kingdom and sit on thrones, judging the twelve tribes of Israel.

³¹"Simon, Simon, Satan has asked to sift all of you as wheat. ³²But I have prayed for you, Simon, that your faith may not fail. And when you have turned back, strengthen your brothers."

³³But he replied, "Lord, I am ready to go with you to prison and to death."

³⁴Jesus answered, "I tell you, Peter, before the rooster crows today, you will deny three times that you know me."

³⁵Then Jesus asked them, "When I sent you without purse, bag or sandals, did you lack anything?"

"Nothing," they answered.

³⁶He said to them, "But now if you have a purse, take it, and also a bag; and if you don't have a sword, sell your cloak and buy one. ³⁷It is written: 'And he was numbered with the transgressors'ᵇ; and I tell you that this must be fulfilled in me. Yes, what is written about me is reaching its fulfillment."

³⁸The disciples said, "See, Lord, here are two swords."

"That's enough!" he replied.

ᵃ 19,20 Some manuscripts do not have given for you . . . poured out for you.   ᵇ 37 Isaiah 53:12

Jesus Prays on the Mount of Olives

³⁹Jesus went out as usual to the Mount of Olives, and his disciples followed him. ⁴⁰On reaching the place, he said to them, "Pray that you will not fall into temptation." ⁴¹He withdrew about a stone's throw beyond them, knelt down and prayed, ⁴²"Father, if you are willing, take this cup from me; yet not my will, but yours be done." ⁴³An angel from heaven appeared to him and strengthened him. ⁴⁴And being in anguish, he prayed more earnestly, and his sweat was like drops of blood falling to the ground.^a

⁴⁵When he rose from prayer and went back to the disciples, he found them asleep, exhausted from sorrow. ⁴⁶"Why are you sleeping?" he asked them. "Get up and pray so that you will not fall into temptation."

Jesus Arrested

⁴⁷While he was still speaking a crowd came up, and the man who was called Judas, one of the Twelve, was leading them. He approached Jesus to kiss him, ⁴⁸but Jesus asked him, "Judas, are you betraying the Son of Man with a kiss?"

⁴⁹When Jesus' followers saw what was going to happen, they said, "Lord, should we strike with our swords?" ⁵⁰And one of them struck the servant of the high priest, cutting off his right ear.

⁵¹But Jesus answered, "No more of this!" And he touched the man's ear and healed him.

⁵²Then Jesus said to the chief priests, the officers of the temple guard, and the elders, who had come for him, "Am I leading a rebellion, that you have come with swords and clubs? ⁵³Every day I was with you in the temple courts, and you did not lay a hand on me. But this is your hour— when darkness reigns."

Peter Disowns Jesus

⁵⁴Then seizing him, they led him away and took him into the house of the high priest. Peter followed at a distance. ⁵⁵And when some there had kindled a fire in the middle of the courtyard and had sat down together, Peter sat down with them. ⁵⁶A servant girl saw him seated there in the firelight. She looked closely at him and said, "This man was with him."

⁵⁷But he denied it. "Woman, I don't know him," he said.

⁵⁸A little later someone else saw him and said, "You also are one of them."

"Man, I am not!" Peter replied.

⁵⁹About an hour later another asserted, "Certainly this fellow was with him, for he is a Galilean."

⁶⁰Peter replied, "Man, I don't know what you're talking about!" Just as he was speaking, the rooster crowed. ⁶¹The Lord turned and looked straight at Peter. Then Peter remembered the word the Lord had spoken to him: "Before the rooster crows today, you will disown me three times." ⁶²And he went outside and wept bitterly.

The Guards Mock Jesus

⁶³The men who were guarding Jesus began mocking and beating him. ⁶⁴They blindfolded him and demanded, "Prophesy! Who hit you?" ⁶⁵And they said many other insulting things to him.

Jesus Before Pilate and Herod

⁶⁶At daybreak the council of the elders of the people, both the chief priests and the teachers of the law, met together, and Jesus was led before them. ⁶⁷"If you are the Messiah," they said, "tell us."

Jesus answered, "If I tell you, you will not believe me, ⁶⁸and if I asked you, you would not answer. ⁶⁹But from now on, the Son of Man will be seated at the right hand of the mighty God."

⁷⁰They all asked, "Are you then the Son of God?"

He replied, "You say that I am."

⁷¹Then they said, "Why do we need any more testimony? We have heard it from his own lips."

23 Then the whole assembly rose and led him off to Pilate. ²And they began to accuse him, saying, "We have found this man subverting our nation. He opposes

---

^a *43,44* Many early manuscripts do not have verses 43 and 44.

payment of taxes to Caesar and claims to be Messiah, a king."

³So Pilate asked Jesus, "Are you the king of the Jews?"

"You have said so," Jesus replied.

⁴Then Pilate announced to the chief priests and the crowd, "I find no basis for a charge against this man."

⁵But they insisted, "He stirs up the people all over Judea by his teaching. He started in Galilee and has come all the way here."

⁶On hearing this, Pilate asked if the man was a Galilean. ⁷When he learned that Jesus was under Herod's jurisdiction, he sent him to Herod, who was also in Jerusalem at that time.

⁸When Herod saw Jesus, he was greatly pleased, because for a long time he had been wanting to see him. From what he had heard about him, he hoped to see him perform a sign of some sort. ⁹He plied him with many questions, but Jesus gave him no answer. ¹⁰The chief priests and the teachers of the law were standing there, vehemently accusing him. ¹¹Then Herod and his soldiers ridiculed and mocked him. Dressing him in an elegant robe, they sent him back to Pilate. ¹²That day Herod and Pilate became friends—before this they had been enemies.

¹³Pilate called together the chief priests, the rulers and the people, ¹⁴and said to them, "You brought me this man as one who was inciting the people to rebellion. I have examined him in your presence and have found no basis for your charges against him. ¹⁵Neither has Herod, for he sent him back to us; as you can see, he has done nothing to deserve death. ¹⁶Therefore, I will punish him and then release him." [17]ᵃ

¹⁸But the whole crowd shouted, "Away with this man! Release Barabbas to us!" ¹⁹(Barabbas had been thrown into prison for an insurrection in the city, and for murder.)

²⁰Wanting to release Jesus, Pilate appealed to them again. ²¹But they kept shouting, "Crucify him! Crucify him!"

²²For the third time he spoke to them: "Why? What crime has this man committed? I have found in him no grounds for the death penalty. Therefore I will have him punished and then release him."

²³But with loud shouts they insistently demanded that he be crucified, and their shouts prevailed. ²⁴So Pilate decided to grant their demand. ²⁵He released the man who had been thrown into prison for insurrection and murder, the one they asked for, and surrendered Jesus to their will.

The Crucifixion of Jesus

²⁶As the soldiers led him away, they seized Simon from Cyrene, who was on his way in from the country, and put the cross on him and made him carry it behind Jesus. ²⁷A large number of people followed him, including women who mourned and wailed for him. ²⁸Jesus turned and said to them, "Daughters of Jerusalem, do not weep for me; weep for yourselves and for your children. ²⁹For the time will come when you will say, 'Blessed are the childless women, the wombs that never bore and the breasts that never nursed!' ³⁰Then

> "'they will say to the mountains, "Fall
> on us!"
> and to the hills, "Cover us!"'ᵇ

³¹For if people do these things when the tree is green, what will happen when it is dry?"

³²Two other men, both criminals, were also led out with him to be executed. ³³When they came to the place called the Skull, they crucified him there, along with the criminals—one on his right, the other on his left. ³⁴Jesus said, "Father, forgive them, for they do not know what they are doing."ᶜ And they divided up his clothes by casting lots.

³⁵The people stood watching, and the rulers even sneered at him. They said, "He saved others; let him save himself if he is God's Messiah, the Chosen One."

³⁶The soldiers also came up and mocked him. They offered him wine vinegar ³⁷and

ᵃ 17 Some manuscripts include here words similar to Matt. 27:15 and Mark 15:6. ᵇ 30 Hosea 10:8 ᶜ 34 Some early manuscripts do not have this sentence.

said, "If you are the king of the Jews, save yourself."

[38] There was a written notice above him, which read: THIS IS THE KING OF THE JEWS.

[39] One of the criminals who hung there hurled insults at him: "Aren't you the Messiah? Save yourself and us!"

[40] But the other criminal rebuked him. "Don't you fear God," he said, "since you are under the same sentence? [41] We are punished justly, for we are getting what our deeds deserve. But this man has done nothing wrong."

[42] Then he said, "Jesus, remember me when you come into your kingdom.[a]"

[43] Jesus answered him, "Truly I tell you, today you will be with me in paradise."

The Death of Jesus

[44] It was now about noon, and darkness came over the whole land until three in the afternoon, [45] for the sun stopped shining. And the curtain of the temple was torn in two. [46] Jesus called out with a loud voice, "Father, into your hands I commit my spirit."[b] When he had said this, he breathed his last.

[47] The centurion, seeing what had happened, praised God and said, "Surely this was a righteous man." [48] When all the people who had gathered to witness this sight saw what took place, they beat their breasts and went away. [49] But all those who knew him, including the women who had followed him from Galilee, stood at a distance, watching these things.

The Burial of Jesus

[50] Now there was a man named Joseph, a member of the Council, a good and upright man, [51] who had not consented to their decision and action. He came from the Judean town of Arimathea, and he himself was waiting for the kingdom of God. [52] Going to Pilate, he asked for Jesus' body. [53] Then he took it down, wrapped it in linen cloth and placed it in a tomb cut in the rock, one in which no one had yet been laid. [54] It was Preparation Day, and the Sabbath was about to begin.

[55] The women who had come with Jesus from Galilee followed Joseph and saw the tomb and how his body was laid in it. [56] Then they went home and prepared spices and perfumes. But they rested on the Sabbath in obedience to the commandment.

[a] 42 Some manuscripts *come with your kingly power*   [b] 46 Psalm 31:5

Luke 23:26–56

Jesus really died.

If you want to disprove the idea that Jesus rose from the dead, there is a potential shortcut. Just claim that he never died. Some critics of Christianity say that Jesus merely passed out or "swooned" on the cross, then regained consciousness in the cool air of the tomb where his body was placed. But you don't have to wonder if Jesus was really dead. Before Jesus went to the cross, he was beaten nearly to death with leather strips laced with bone and iron (see Matthew 27:26). He was stripped and nailed to the cross, a victim of the Roman Empire's most severe form of execution. He was able to breathe only when he pushed up against his nail-pierced feet. Executioners sometimes chose to break a victim's legs to speed death by suffocation, but within a few hours Jesus was dead (see John 19:31–33). A soldier pierced Jesus' side with his spear. His death is an indisputable fact, and it paid the penalty for our sins (see Isaiah 53:5).

Think: How would you answer someone who doubted that Jesus died on the cross?

ROCK SOLID *truths*

Jesus Has Risen

24

On the first day of the week, very early in the morning, the women took the spices they had prepared and went to the tomb. ²They found the stone rolled away from the tomb, ³but when they entered, they did not find the body of the Lord Jesus. ⁴While they were wondering about this, suddenly two men in clothes that gleamed like lightning stood beside them. ⁵In their fright the women bowed down with their faces to the ground, but the men said to them, "Why do you look for the living among the dead? ⁶He is not here; he has risen! Remember how he told you, while he was still with you in Galilee: ⁷'The Son of Man must be delivered over to the hands of sinners, be crucified and on the third day be raised again.'" ⁸Then they remembered his words.

ROCK SOLID
promises

"He is not here; he has risen!"

Luke 24:6

Jesus died on the cross and was buried. But he didn't stay in the grave. You serve a risen Lord!

---

⁹When they came back from the tomb, they told all these things to the Eleven and to all the others. ¹⁰It was Mary Magdalene, Joanna, Mary the mother of James, and the others with them who told this to the apostles. ¹¹But they did not believe the women, because their words seemed to them like nonsense. ¹²Peter, however, got up and ran to the tomb. Bending over, he saw the strips of linen lying by themselves, and he went away, wondering to himself what had happened.

On the Road to Emmaus

¹³Now that same day two of them were going to a village called Emmaus, about seven miles*ᵃ* from Jerusalem. ¹⁴They were talking with each other about everything that had happened. ¹⁵As they talked and discussed these things with each other, Jesus himself came up and walked along with them; ¹⁶but they were kept from recognizing him.

¹⁷He asked them, "What are you discussing together as you walk along?"

They stood still, their faces downcast. ¹⁸One of them, named Cleopas, asked him, "Are you the only one visiting Jerusalem who does not know the things that have happened there in these days?"

¹⁹"What things?" he asked.

"About Jesus of Nazareth," they replied. "He was a prophet, powerful in word and deed before God and all the people. ²⁰The chief priests and our rulers handed him over to be sentenced to death, and they crucified him; ²¹but we had hoped that he was the one who was going to redeem Israel. And what is more, it is the third day since all this took place. ²²In addition, some of our women amazed us. They went to the tomb early this morning ²³but didn't find his body. They came and told us that they had seen a vision of angels, who said he was alive. ²⁴Then some of our companions went to the tomb and found it just as the women had said, but they did not see Jesus."

²⁵He said to them, "How foolish you are, and how slow to believe all that the prophets have spoken! ²⁶Did not the Messiah have to suffer these things and then enter his glory?" ²⁷And beginning with Moses and all the Prophets, he explained to them what was said in all the Scriptures concerning himself.

²⁸As they approached the village to which they were going, Jesus continued on as if he were going farther. ²⁹But they urged him strongly, "Stay with us, for it is nearly evening; the day is almost over." So he went in to stay with them.

³⁰When he was at the table with them,

ᵃ 13 Or about 11 kilometers

he took bread, gave thanks, broke it and began to give it to them. ³¹Then their eyes were opened and they recognized him, and he disappeared from their sight. ³²They asked each other, "Were not our hearts burning within us while he talked with us on the road and opened the Scriptures to us?"

³³They got up and returned at once to Jerusalem. There they found the Eleven and those with them, assembled together ³⁴and saying, "It is true! The Lord has risen and has appeared to Simon." ³⁵Then the two told what had happened on the way, and how Jesus was recognized by them when he broke the bread.

Jesus Appears to the Disciples

³⁶While they were still talking about this, Jesus himself stood among them and said to them, "Peace be with you."

³⁷They were startled and frightened, thinking they saw a ghost. ³⁸He said to them, "Why are you troubled, and why do doubts rise in your minds? ³⁹Look at my hands and my feet. It is I myself! Touch me and see; a ghost does not have flesh and bones, as you see I have."

⁴⁰When he had said this, he showed them his hands and feet. ⁴¹And while they still did not believe it because of joy and amazement, he asked them, "Do you have anything here to eat?" ⁴²They gave him a piece of broiled fish, ⁴³and he took it and ate it in their presence.

⁴⁴He said to them, "This is what I told you while I was still with you: Everything must be fulfilled that is written about me in the Law of Moses, the Prophets and the Psalms."

⁴⁵Then he opened their minds so they could understand the Scriptures. ⁴⁶He told them, "This is what is written: The Messiah will suffer and rise from the dead on the third day, ⁴⁷and repentance for the forgiveness of sins will be preached in his name to all nations, beginning at Jerusalem. ⁴⁸You are witnesses of these things. ⁴⁹I am going to send you what my Father has promised; but stay in the city until you have been clothed with power from on high."

The Ascension of Jesus

⁵⁰When he had led them out to the vicinity of Bethany, he lifted up his hands and blessed them. ⁵¹While he was blessing them, he left them and was taken up into heaven. ⁵²Then they worshiped him and returned to Jerusalem with great joy. ⁵³And they stayed continually at the temple, praising God.

BOOK OUTLINE

JOHN

The fourth Gospel was written by John, one of Jesus' twelve disciples. He is referred to as "the disciple whom Jesus loved." John wrote this Gospel sometime between AD 90 and 100 so that "you may believe that Jesus is the Messiah, the Son of God, and that by believing you may have life in his name" (John 20:31).

Although the book of John gives a general outline of the life and work of Jesus Christ, it is very different from the other three Gospels. John reports five miracles that are not reported by the other authors. Only two miracles reported in the other Gospels are reported in John. This book contains no parables and stresses Jesus' relationships with individuals.

The purpose of this Gospel is to report the signs (called miracles in the other Gospels) that prove Christ is God and has supernatural powers. John focuses on proving that Jesus is the Son of God, but also shows that Jesus was human by including stories about Jesus being tired, sad, hungry and thirsty.

The Word Became Flesh

In the beginning was the Word, and the Word was with God, and the Word was God. [2] He was with God in the beginning. [3] Through him all things were made; without him nothing was made that has been made. [4] In him was life, and that life was the light of all mankind. [5] The light shines in the darkness, and the darkness has not overcome[a] it.

[6] There was a man sent from God whose name was John. [7] He came as a witness to testify concerning that light, so that through him all might believe. [8] He himself was not the light; he came only as a witness to the light.

[9] The true light that gives light to everyone was coming into the world. [10] He was in the world, and though the world was made through him, the world did not recognize him. [11] He came to that which was his own, but his own did not receive him. [12] Yet to all who did receive him, to those who believed in his name, he gave the right to become children of God— [13] children born not of natural descent, nor of human decision or a husband's will, but born of God.

[14] The Word became flesh and made his dwelling among us. We have seen his glory, the glory of the one and only Son, who came from the Father, full of grace and truth.

[15] (John testified concerning him. He cried out, saying, "This is the one I spoke about when I said, 'He who comes after me has surpassed me because he was before me.'") [16] Out of his fullness we have all received grace in place of grace already given. [17] For the law was given through Moses; grace and truth came through Jesus Christ. [18] No one has ever seen God, but the one and only Son, who is himself God and[b] is in closest relationship with the Father, has made him known.

John the Baptist Denies Being the Messiah

[19] Now this was John's testimony when the Jewish leaders[c] in Jerusalem sent priests and Levites to ask him who he was. [20] He did not fail to confess, but confessed freely, "I am not the Messiah."

[21] They asked him, "Then who are you? Are you Elijah?"

He said, "I am not."

"Are you the Prophet?"

He answered, "No."

[22] Finally they said, "Who are you? Give

John 1:1–3

Jesus is God.

The start of the Gospel of John doesn't use the name "Jesus," but within a few verses you discover exactly who the apostle John is writing about. John calls Jesus "the Word," a term both Jews and Greeks knew as the intelligence and force that created the universe. John reports several facts about the Word. The Word was around before the creation of the world, existing from all eternity. He was always with God, relating to him face-to-face, as an equal. And while the Word is distinct from God the Father, somehow he is also the same, possessing every trait and characteristic of God. This Word came to earth as a human being. John writes, "The Word became flesh and made his dwelling among us. We have seen his glory, the glory of the one and only Son" (John 1:14). Jesus isn't merely like God. He is God. But Jesus didn't stay in heaven. He came to earth to live—and to love you.

Think: How do you know that Jesus is God?

ROCK SOLID *truths*

---

a 5 Or *understood*   *b 18* Some manuscripts *but the only Son, who*   *c 19* The Greek term traditionally translated *the Jews* (*hoi Ioudaioi*) refers here and elsewhere in John's Gospel to those Jewish leaders who opposed Jesus; also in 5:10, 15, 16; 7:1, 11, 13; 9:22; 18:14, 28, 36; 19:7, 12, 31, 38; 20:19.

us an answer to take back to those who sent us. What do you say about yourself?"

²³John replied in the words of Isaiah the prophet, "I am the voice of one calling in the wilderness, 'Make straight the way for the Lord.'"ᵃ

²⁴Now the Pharisees who had been sent ²⁵questioned him, "Why then do you baptize if you are not the Messiah, nor Elijah, nor the Prophet?"

²⁶"I baptize withᵇ water," John replied, "but among you stands one you do not know. ²⁷He is the one who comes after me, the straps of whose sandals I am not worthy to untie."

²⁸This all happened at Bethany on the other side of the Jordan, where John was baptizing.

John Testifies About Jesus

²⁹The next day John saw Jesus coming toward him and said, "Look, the Lamb of God, who takes away the sin of the world! ³⁰This is the one I meant when I said, 'A man who comes after me has surpassed me because he was before me.' ³¹I myself did not know him, but the reason I came baptizing with water was that he might be revealed to Israel."

³²Then John gave this testimony: "I saw the Spirit come down from heaven as a dove and remain on him. ³³And I myself did not know him, but the one who sent me to baptize with water told me, 'The man on whom you see the Spirit come down and remain is the one who will baptize with the Holy Spirit.' ³⁴I have seen and I testify that this is God's Chosen One."ᶜ

John's Disciples Follow Jesus

³⁵The next day John was there again with two of his disciples. ³⁶When he saw Jesus passing by, he said, "Look, the Lamb of God!"

³⁷When the two disciples heard him say this, they followed Jesus. ³⁸Turning around, Jesus saw them following and asked, "What do you want?"

They said, "Rabbi" (which means "Teacher"), "where are you staying?"

³⁹"Come," he replied, "and you will see."

So they went and saw where he was staying, and they spent that day with him. It was about four in the afternoon.

⁴⁰Andrew, Simon Peter's brother, was one of the two who heard what John had said and who had followed Jesus. ⁴¹The first thing Andrew did was to find his brother Simon and tell him, "We have found the Messiah" (that is, the Christ). ⁴²And he brought him to Jesus.

Jesus looked at him and said, "You are Simon son of John. You will be called Cephas" (which, when translated, is Peterᵈ).

Jesus Calls Philip and Nathanael

⁴³The next day Jesus decided to leave for Galilee. Finding Philip, he said to him, "Follow me."

⁴⁴Philip, like Andrew and Peter, was from the town of Bethsaida. ⁴⁵Philip found Nathanael and told him, "We have found the one Moses wrote about in the Law, and about whom the prophets also wrote—Jesus of Nazareth, the son of Joseph."

⁴⁶"Nazareth! Can anything good come from there?" Nathanael asked.

"Come and see," said Philip.

⁴⁷When Jesus saw Nathanael approaching, he said of him, "Here truly is an Israelite in whom there is no deceit."

⁴⁸"How do you know me?" Nathanael asked.

Jesus answered, "I saw you while you were still under the fig tree before Philip called you."

⁴⁹Then Nathanael declared, "Rabbi, you are the Son of God; you are the king of Israel."

⁵⁰Jesus said, "You believeᵉ because I told you I saw you under the fig tree. You will see greater things than that." ⁵¹He then added, "Very truly I tell you,ᶠ youᶠ will see 'heaven open, and the angels of God ascending and descending on'ᵍ the Son of Man."

ᵃ 23 Isaiah 40:3   ᵇ 26 Or in; also in verses 31 and 33 (twice)   ᶜ 34 See Isaiah 42:1; many manuscripts is the Son of God.   ᵈ 42 Cephas (Aramaic) and Peter (Greek) both mean rock.   ᵉ 50 Or Do you believe . . . ?   ᶠ 51 The Greek is plural   ᵍ 51 Gen. 28:12

Jesus Changes Water Into Wine

2 On the third day a wedding took place at Cana in Galilee. Jesus' mother was there, ²and Jesus and his disciples had also been invited to the wedding. ³When the wine was gone, Jesus' mother said to him, "They have no more wine."

⁴"Woman,*ᵃ* why do you involve me?" Jesus replied. "My hour has not yet come."

⁵His mother said to the servants, "Do whatever he tells you."

⁶Nearby stood six stone water jars, the kind used by the Jews for ceremonial washing, each holding from twenty to thirty gallons.*ᵇ*

⁷Jesus said to the servants, "Fill the jars with water"; so they filled them to the brim.

⁸Then he told them, "Now draw some out and take it to the master of the banquet."

They did so, ⁹and the master of the banquet tasted the water that had been turned into wine. He did not realize where it had come from, though the servants who had drawn the water knew. Then he called the bridegroom aside ¹⁰and said, "Everyone brings out the choice wine first and then the cheaper wine after the guests have had

ᵃ 4 The Greek for *Woman* does not denote any disrespect.   *ᵇ 6* Or from about 75 to about 115 liters

---

John 1:35–42

Andrew introduced others to Jesus.

Andrew started out as a disciple of John the Baptist, the fiery messenger of God who prepared the way for Jesus by commanding people to turn from their sins (see John 1:19–34). One day as Jesus wandered by, John declared him to be "the Lamb of God," the sacrifice who would take the punishment for all human sin (John 1:36).

Andrew must have liked John's spiritual intensity, but as Andrew heard Jesus teach, he discovered something even better. He immediately left to hunt down his brother Simon Peter and tell him, "We have found the Messiah," the Savior sent from God (John 1:41). As soon as Andrew introduced him to Jesus, Peter joined in following Jesus.

That's the first instance in the New Testament of one person bringing another to Jesus, but it wasn't the last time Andrew helped someone meet the Savior. Some time later, a group of Greeks wanted to see Jesus. Long before Jesus commanded his disciples to go into the world to tell others about him (see Matthew 28:18–20), Andrew knew enough to connect them to the Savior (see John 12:20–22).

Christian tradition says Andrew continued to spread the news about Jesus for the rest of his life. Reports say he went to Scythia, an area now part of the country of Ukraine, and that he was killed for his faith, crucified on an X-shaped cross.

You can find Andrew in Matthew 10:2–4; Mark 1:16–18, 29; John 1:35–42; 6:5–9; 12:20–22; and Acts 1:13.

UNSHAKEN people

too much to drink; but you have saved the best till now."

[11] What Jesus did here in Cana of Galilee was the first of the signs through which he revealed his glory; and his disciples believed in him.

[12] After this he went down to Capernaum with his mother and brothers and his disciples. There they stayed for a few days.

Jesus Clears the Temple Courts

[13] When it was almost time for the Jewish Passover, Jesus went up to Jerusalem. [14] In the temple courts he found people selling cattle, sheep and doves, and others sitting at tables exchanging money. [15] So he made a whip out of cords, and drove all from the temple courts, both sheep and cattle; he scattered the coins of the money changers and overturned their tables. [16] To those who sold doves he said, "Get these out of here! Stop turning my Father's house into a market!" [17] His disciples remembered that it is written: "Zeal for your house will consume me."[a]

[18] The Jews then responded to him, "What sign can you show us to prove your authority to do all this?"

[19] Jesus answered them, "Destroy this temple, and I will raise it again in three days."

[20] They replied, "It has taken forty-six years to build this temple, and you are going to raise it in three days?" [21] But the temple he had spoken of was his body. [22] After he was raised from the dead, his disciples recalled what he had said. Then they believed the scripture and the words that Jesus had spoken.

[23] Now while he was in Jerusalem at the Passover Festival, many people saw the signs he was performing and believed in his name.[b] [24] But Jesus would not entrust himself to them, for he knew all people. [25] He did not need any testimony about mankind, for he knew what was in each person.

Jesus Teaches Nicodemus

3 Now there was a Pharisee, a man named Nicodemus who was a member of the Jewish ruling council. [2] He came to Jesus at night and said,

"Rabbi, we know that you are a teacher who has come from God. For no one could perform the signs you are doing if God were not with him."

[3] Jesus replied, "Very truly I tell you, no one can see the kingdom of God unless they are born again.[c]"

[4] "How can someone be born when they are old?" Nicodemus asked. "Surely they cannot enter a second time into their mother's womb to be born!"

[5] Jesus answered, "Very truly I tell you, no one can enter the kingdom of God unless they are born of water and the Spirit. [6] Flesh gives birth to flesh, but the Spirit[d] gives birth to spirit. [7] You should not be surprised at my saying, 'You[e] must be born again.' [8] The wind blows wherever it pleases. You hear its sound, but you cannot tell where it comes from or where it is going. So it is with everyone born of the Spirit."[f]

[9] "How can this be?" Nicodemus asked.

[10] "You are Israel's teacher," said Jesus, "and do you not understand these things? [11] Very truly I tell you, we speak of what we know, and we testify to what we have seen, but still you people do not accept our testimony. [12] I have spoken to you of earthly things and you do not believe; how then will you believe if I speak of heavenly things? [13] No one has ever gone into heaven except the one who came from heaven—the Son of Man.[g] [14] Just as Moses lifted up the snake in the wilderness, so the Son of Man must be lifted up,[b] [15] that everyone who believes may have eternal life in him."[i]

[16] For God so loved the world that he gave his one and only Son, that whoever believes in him shall not perish but have eternal life. [17] For God did not send his Son into the world to condemn the world, but to save the world through him. [18] Who-

---

[a] 17 Psalm 69:9   [b] 23 Or in him
[c] 3 The Greek for *again* also means *from above*; also in verse 7.   [d] 6 Or *but spirit*   [e] 7 The Greek is plural.   [f] 8 The Greek for *Spirit* is the same as that for *wind*.   [g] 13 Some manuscripts *Man, who is in heaven*   [b] 14 The Greek for *lifted up* also means *exalted*.
[i] 15 Some interpreters end the quotation with verse 21.

ROCK SOLID
promises

"For God so loved the world that he gave his one and only Son, that whoever believes in him shall not perish but have eternal life."

John 3:16

God loves you so much he sent Jesus to die and rise for you. Trust that fact and you will live forever.

ever believes in him is not condemned, but whoever does not believe stands condemned already because they have not believed in the name of God's one and only Son. ¹⁹This is the verdict: Light has come into the world, but people loved darkness instead of light because their deeds were evil. ²⁰Everyone who does evil hates the light, and will not come into the light for fear that their deeds will be exposed. ²¹But whoever lives by the truth comes into the light, so that it may be seen plainly that what they have done has been done in the sight of God.

John Testifies Again About Jesus

²²After this, Jesus and his disciples went out into the Judean countryside, where he spent some time with them, and baptized. ²³Now John also was baptizing at Aenon near Salim, because there was plenty of water, and people were coming and being baptized. ²⁴(This was before John was put in prison.) ²⁵An argument developed between some of John's disciples and a certain Jew over the matter of ceremonial washing. ²⁶They came to John and said to him, "Rabbi, that man who was with you on the other side of the Jordan—the one you testified about—look, he is baptizing, and everyone is going to him."

²⁷To this John replied, "A person can receive only what is given them from heav-en. ²⁸You yourselves can testify that I said, 'I am not the Messiah but am sent ahead of him.' ²⁹The bride belongs to the bridegroom. The friend who attends the bridegroom waits and listens for him, and is full of joy when he hears the bridegroom's voice. That joy is mine, and it is now complete. ³⁰He must become greater; I must become less."ᵃ

³¹The one who comes from above is above all; the one who is from the earth belongs to the earth, and speaks as one from the earth. The one who comes from heaven is above all. ³²He testifies to what he has seen and heard, but no one accepts his testimony. ³³Whoever has accepted it has certified that God is truthful. ³⁴For the one whom God has sent speaks the words of God, for Godᵇ gives the Spirit without limit. ³⁵The Father loves the Son and has placed everything in his hands. ³⁶Whoever believes in the Son has eternal life, but whoever rejects the Son will not see life, for God's wrath remains on them.

Jesus Talks With a Samaritan Woman

4 Now Jesus learned that the Pharisees had heard that he was gaining and baptizing more disciples than John— ²although in fact it was not Jesus who baptized, but his disciples. ³So he left Judea and went back once more to Galilee. ⁴Now he had to go through Samaria. ⁵So he came to a town in Samaria called Sychar, near the plot of ground Jacob had given to his son Joseph. ⁶Jacob's well was there, and Jesus, tired as he was from the journey, sat down by the well. It was about noon.

⁷When a Samaritan woman came to draw water, Jesus said to her, "Will you give me a drink?" ⁸(His disciples had gone into the town to buy food.)

⁹The Samaritan woman said to him, "You are a Jew and I am a Samaritan woman. How can you ask me for a drink?" (For Jews do not associate with Samaritans.ᶜ)

¹⁰Jesus answered her, "If you knew the gift of God and who it is that asks you for

---

ᵃ *30* Some interpreters end the quotation with verse 36.   ᵇ *34* Greek *he*   ᶜ *9* Or *do not use dishes Samaritans have used* a drink, you would have asked him and he would have given you living water."

¹¹ "Sir," the woman said, "you have nothing to draw with and the well is deep. Where can you get this living water? ¹² Are you greater than our father Jacob, who gave us the well and drank from it himself, as did also his sons and his livestock?"

¹³ Jesus answered, "Everyone who drinks this water will be thirsty again, ¹⁴ but whoever drinks the water I give them will never thirst. Indeed, the water I give them will become in them a spring of water welling up to eternal life."

¹⁵ The woman said to him, "Sir, give me this water so that I won't get thirsty and have to keep coming here to draw water."

¹⁶ He told her, "Go, call your husband and come back."

¹⁷ "I have no husband," she replied.

Jesus said to her, "You are right when you say you have no husband. ¹⁸ The fact is, you have had five husbands, and the man you now have is not your husband. What you have just said is quite true."

¹⁹ "Sir," the woman said, "I can see that you are a prophet. ²⁰ Our ancestors worshiped on this mountain, but you Jews claim that the place where we must worship is in Jerusalem."

²¹ "Woman," Jesus replied, "believe me, a time is coming when you will worship the Father neither on this mountain nor in Jerusalem. ²² You Samaritans worship what you do not know; we worship what we do know, for salvation is from the Jews. ²³ Yet a time is coming and has now come when the true worshipers will worship the Father in the Spirit and in truth, for they are the kind of worshipers the Father seeks. ²⁴ God is spirit, and his worshipers must worship in the Spirit and in truth."

²⁵ The woman said, "I know that Messiah" (called Christ) "is coming. When he comes, he will explain everything to us."

²⁶ Then Jesus declared, "I, the one speaking to you—I am he."

The Disciples Rejoin Jesus

²⁷ Just then his disciples returned and were surprised to find him talking with a

UNSHAKEN God

John 4:1–26

God is invisible.

Jesus caught the woman at the well off guard when he supernaturally perceived she had been married to five men and was now living with man number six (see John 4:16–18). She tried to pull Jesus into a religious debate, arguing that her ancestors served God on a certain mountain, Mount Gerizim, while the Jews honored him in Jerusalem. But Jesus had big news for her. He said that ultimately neither place mattered, because "God is spirit" (John 4:24). God isn't a physical being locked in to one location. Because God is spirit we can't see him, but it also means we can worship him anywhere.

So ... Would it be easier to believe in God if he were visible? What would be the downside of us being able to see him?

woman. But no one asked, "What do you want?" or "Why are you talking with her?"

²⁸ Then, leaving her water jar, the woman went back to the town and said to the people, ²⁹ "Come, see a man who told me everything I ever did. Could this be the Messiah?" ³⁰ They came out of the town and made their way toward him.

³¹ Meanwhile his disciples urged him, "Rabbi, eat something."

³² But he said to them, "I have food to eat that you know nothing about."

³³ Then his disciples said to each other, "Could someone have brought him food?"

³⁴ "My food," said Jesus, "is to do the will of him who sent me and to finish his work. ³⁵ Don't you have a saying, 'It's still four months until harvest'? I tell you, open your eyes and look at the fields! They are ripe for harvest. ³⁶ Even now the one who reaps draws a wage and harvests a crop for eternal life, so that the sower and the

reaper may be glad together. ³⁷Thus the saying 'One sows and another reaps' is true. ³⁸I sent you to reap what you have not worked for. Others have done the hard work, and you have reaped the benefits of their labor."

Many Samaritans Believe

³⁹Many of the Samaritans from that town believed in him because of the woman's testimony, "He told me everything I ever did." ⁴⁰So when the Samaritans came to him, they urged him to stay with them, and he stayed two days. ⁴¹And because of his words many more became believers.

⁴²They said to the woman, "We no longer believe just because of what you said; now we have heard for ourselves, and we know that this man really is the Savior of the world."

Jesus Heals an Official's Son

⁴³After the two days he left for Galilee. ⁴⁴(Now Jesus himself had pointed out that a prophet has no honor in his own country.) ⁴⁵When he arrived in Galilee, the Galileans welcomed him. They had seen all that he had done in Jerusalem at the Passover Festival, for they also had been there.

⁴⁶Once more he visited Cana in Galilee, where he had turned the water into wine. And there was a certain royal official whose son lay sick at Capernaum. ⁴⁷When this man heard that Jesus had arrived in Galilee from Judea, he went to him and begged him to come and heal his son, who was close to death.

⁴⁸"Unless you people see signs and wonders," Jesus told him, "you will never believe."

⁴⁹The royal official said, "Sir, come down before my child dies."

⁵⁰"Go," Jesus replied, "your son will live."

The man took Jesus at his word and departed. ⁵¹While he was still on the way, his servants met him with the news that his boy was living. ⁵²When he inquired as to the time when his son got better, they said to him, "Yesterday, at one in the afternoon, the fever left him."

⁵³Then the father realized that this was the exact time at which Jesus had said to him, "Your son will live." So he and his whole household believed.

⁵⁴This was the second sign Jesus performed after coming from Judea to Galilee.

The Healing at the Pool

5 Some time later, Jesus went up to Jerusalem for one of the Jewish festivals. ²Now there is in Jerusalem near the Sheep Gate a pool, which in Aramaic is called Bethesda^a and which is surrounded by five covered colonnades. ³Here a great number of disabled people used to lie—the blind, the lame, the paralyzed. [4]^b ⁵One who was there had been an invalid for thirty-eight years. ⁶When Jesus saw him lying there and learned that he had been in this condition for a long time, he asked him, "Do you want to get well?"

⁷"Sir," the invalid replied, "I have no one to help me into the pool when the water is stirred. While I am trying to get in, someone else goes down ahead of me."

⁸Then Jesus said to him, "Get up! Pick up your mat and walk." ⁹At once the man was cured; he picked up his mat and walked.

The day on which this took place was a Sabbath, ¹⁰and so the Jewish leaders said to the man who had been healed, "It is the Sabbath; the law forbids you to carry your mat."

¹¹But he replied, "The man who made me well said to me, 'Pick up your mat and walk.'"

¹²So they asked him, "Who is this fellow who told you to pick it up and walk?"

¹³The man who was healed had no idea who it was, for Jesus had slipped away into the crowd that was there.

^a 2 Some manuscripts *Bethzatha*; other manuscripts *Bethsaida*   ^b 3,4 Some manuscripts include here, wholly or in part, *paralyzed—and they waited for the moving of the waters. ⁴From time to time an angel of the Lord would come down and stir up the waters. The first one into the pool after each such disturbance would be cured of whatever disease they had.*

¹⁴Later Jesus found him at the temple and said to him, "See, you are well again. Stop sinning or something worse may happen to you." ¹⁵The man went away and told the Jewish leaders that it was Jesus who had made him well.

The Authority of the Son

¹⁶So, because Jesus was doing these things on the Sabbath, the Jewish leaders began to persecute him. ¹⁷In his defense Jesus said to them, "My Father is always at his work to this very day, and I too am working." ¹⁸For this reason they tried all the more to kill him; not only was he breaking the Sabbath, but he was even calling God his own Father, making himself equal with God.

¹⁹Jesus gave them this answer: "Very truly I tell you, the Son can do nothing by himself; he can do only what he sees his Father doing, because whatever the Father does the Son also does. ²⁰For the Father loves the Son and shows him all he does. Yes, and he will show him even greater works than these, so that you will be amazed. ²¹For just as the Father raises the dead and gives them life, even so the Son gives life to whom he is pleased to give it. ²²Moreover, the Father judges no one, but has entrusted all judgment to the Son, ²³that all may honor the Son just as they honor the Father. Whoever does not honor the Son does not honor the Father, who sent him.

²⁴"Very truly I tell you, whoever hears my word and believes him who sent me has eternal life and will not be judged but has crossed over from death to life. ²⁵Very truly I tell you, a time is coming and has now come when the dead will hear the voice of the Son of God and those who hear will live. ²⁶For as the Father has life in himself, so he has granted the Son also to have life in himself. ²⁷And he has given him authority to judge because he is the Son of Man.

²⁸"Do not be amazed at this, for a time is coming when all who are in their graves will hear his voice ²⁹and come out—those who have done what is good will rise to

live, and those who have done what is evil will rise to be condemned. ³⁰By myself I can do nothing; I judge only as I hear, and my judgment is just, for I seek not to please myself but him who sent me.

Testimonies About Jesus

³¹"If I testify about myself, my testimony is not true. ³²There is another who testifies in my favor, and I know that his testimony about me is true.

³³"You have sent to John and he has testified to the truth. ³⁴Not that I accept human testimony; but I mention it that you may be saved. ³⁵John was a lamp that burned and gave light, and you chose for a time to enjoy his light.

³⁶"I have testimony weightier than that of John. For the works that the Father has given me to finish—the very works that I am doing—testify that the Father has sent me. ³⁷And the Father who sent me has himself testified concerning me. You have never heard his voice nor seen his form, ³⁸nor does his word dwell in you, for you do not believe the one he sent. ³⁹You study*a* the Scriptures diligently because you think that in them you have eternal life. These are the very Scriptures that testify about me, ⁴⁰yet you refuse to come to me to have life.

⁴¹"I do not accept glory from human be-

a 39 Or *³⁹Study*

ROCK SOLID
promises

"Whoever hears my word and believes him who sent me has eternal life and will not be judged but has crossed over from death to life." John 5:24

Eternal life isn't a prize you get when you die. It starts now and lasts forever.

ings, [42]but I know you. I know that you do not have the love of God in your hearts. [43]I have come in my Father's name, and you do not accept me; but if someone else comes in his own name, you will accept him. [44]How can you believe since you accept glory from one another but do not seek the glory that comes from the only God[a]?

[45]"But do not think I will accuse you before the Father. Your accuser is Moses, on whom your hopes are set. [46]If you believed Moses, you would believe me, for he wrote about me. [47]But since you do not believe what he wrote, how are you going to believe what I say?"

Jesus Feeds the Five Thousand

6 Some time after this, Jesus crossed to the far shore of the Sea of Galilee (that is, the Sea of Tiberias), [2]and a great crowd of people followed him because they saw the signs he had performed by healing the sick. [3]Then Jesus went up on a mountainside and sat down with his disciples. [4]The Jewish Passover Festival was near.

[5]When Jesus looked up and saw a great crowd coming toward him, he said to Philip, "Where shall we buy bread for these people to eat?" [6]He asked this only to test him, for he already had in mind what he was going to do.

[7]Philip answered him, "It would take more than half a year's wages[b] to buy enough bread for each one to have a bite!"

[8]Another of his disciples, Andrew, Simon Peter's brother, spoke up, [9]"Here is a boy with five small barley loaves and two small fish, but how far will they go among so many?"

[10]Jesus said, "Have the people sit down." There was plenty of grass in that place, and they sat down (about five thousand men were there). [11]Jesus then took the loaves, gave thanks, and distributed to those who were seated as much as they wanted. He did the same with the fish.

[12]When they had all had enough to eat, he said to his disciples, "Gather the pieces that are left over. Let nothing be wasted."

[13]So they gathered them and filled twelve baskets with the pieces of the five barley loaves left over by those who had eaten.

[14]After the people saw the sign Jesus performed, they began to say, "Surely this is the Prophet who is to come into the world." [15]Jesus, knowing that they intended to come and make him king by force, withdrew again to a mountain by himself.

Jesus Walks on the Water

[16]When evening came, his disciples went down to the lake, [17]where they got into a boat and set off across the lake for Capernaum. By now it was dark, and Jesus had not yet joined them. [18]A strong wind was blowing and the waters grew rough. [19]When they had rowed about three or four miles,[c] they saw Jesus approaching the boat, walking on the water; and they were frightened. [20]But he said to them, "It is I; don't be afraid." [21]Then they were willing to take him into the boat, and immediately the boat reached the shore where they were heading.

[22]The next day the crowd that had stayed on the opposite shore of the lake realized that only one boat had been there, and that Jesus had not entered it with his disciples, but that they had gone away alone. [23]Then some boats from Tiberias landed near the place where the people had eaten the bread after the Lord had given thanks. [24]Once the crowd realized that neither Jesus nor his disciples were there, they got into the boats and went to Capernaum in search of Jesus.

Jesus the Bread of Life

[25]When they found him on the other side of the lake, they asked him, "Rabbi, when did you get here?"

[26]Jesus answered, "Very truly I tell you, you are looking for me, not because you saw the signs I performed but because you ate the loaves and had your fill. [27]Do not work for food that spoils, but for food that endures to eternal life, which the Son of

[a] 44 Some early manuscripts the Only One
[b] 7 Greek take two hundred denarii
[c] 19 Or about 5 or 6 kilometers

Man will give you. For on him God the Father has placed his seal of approval."

28 Then they asked him, "What must we do to do the works God requires?"

29 Jesus answered, "The work of God is this: to believe in the one he has sent."

30 So they asked him, "What sign then will you give that we may see it and believe you? What will you do? 31 Our ancestors ate the manna in the wilderness; as it is written: 'He gave them bread from heaven to eat.'ᵃ

32 Jesus said to them, "Very truly I tell you, it is not Moses who has given you the bread from heaven, but it is my Father who gives you the true bread from heaven. 33 For the bread of God is the bread that comes down from heaven and gives life to the world."

34 "Sir," they said, "always give us this bread."

35 Then Jesus declared, "I am the bread of life. Whoever comes to me will never go hungry, and whoever believes in me will never be thirsty. 36 But as I told you, you have seen me and still you do not believe. 37 All those the Father gives me will come to me, and whoever comes to me I will never drive away. 38 For I have come down from heaven not to do my will but to do the will of him who sent me. 39 And this is the will of him who sent me, that I shall lose none of all those he has given me, but raise them up at the last day. 40 For my Father's will is that everyone who looks to the Son and believes in him shall have eternal life, and I will raise them up at the last day."

41 At this the Jews there began to grumble about him because he said, "I am the bread that came down from heaven." 42 They said, "Is this not Jesus, the son of Joseph, whose father and mother we know? How can he now say, 'I came down from heaven'?"

43 "Stop grumbling among yourselves," Jesus answered. 44 "No one can come to me unless the Father who sent me draws them, and I will raise them up at the last day. 45 It is written in the Prophets: 'They will all be taught by God.'ᵇ Everyone who has heard the Father and learned from him comes to

me. 46 No one has seen the Father except the one who is from God; only he has seen the Father. 47 Very truly I tell you, the one who believes has eternal life. 48 I am the bread of life. 49 Your ancestors ate the manna in the wilderness, yet they died. 50 But here is the bread that comes down from heaven, which anyone may eat and not die. 51 I am the living bread that came down from heaven. Whoever eats this bread will live forever. This bread is my flesh, which I will give for the life of the world."

52 Then the Jews began to argue sharply among themselves, "How can this man give us his flesh to eat?"

53 Jesus said to them, "Very truly I tell you, unless you eat the flesh of the Son of Man and drink his blood, you have no life in you. 54 Whoever eats my flesh and drinks my blood has eternal life, and I will raise them up at the last day. 55 For my flesh is real food and my blood is real drink. 56 Whoever eats my flesh and drinks my blood remains in me, and I in them. 57 Just as the living Father sent me and I live because of the Father, so the one who feeds on me will live because of me. 58 This is the bread that came down from heaven. Your ancestors ate manna and died, but whoever feeds on this bread will live forever." 59 He said this while teaching in the synagogue in Capernaum.

Many Disciples Desert Jesus

60 On hearing it, many of his disciples said, "This is a hard teaching. Who can accept it?"

61 Aware that his disciples were grumbling about this, Jesus said to them, "Does this offend you? 62 Then what if you see the Son of Man ascend to where he was before! 63 The Spirit gives life; the flesh counts for nothing. The words I have spoken to you—they are full of the Spiritᶜ and life. 64 Yet there are some of you who do not believe." For Jesus had known from the beginning which of them did not believe and who would betray him. 65 He

ᵃ 31 Exodus 16:4; Neh. 9:15; Psalm 78:24,25
ᵇ 45 Isaiah 54:13   ᶜ 63 Or are Spirit; or are spirit

went on to say, "This is why I told you that no one can come to me unless the Father has enabled them."

⁶⁶From this time many of his disciples turned back and no longer followed him.

⁶⁷"You do not want to leave too, do you?" Jesus asked the Twelve.

⁶⁸Simon Peter answered him, "Lord, to whom shall we go? You have the words of eternal life. ⁶⁹We have come to believe and to know that you are the Holy One of God."

⁷⁰Then Jesus replied, "Have I not chosen you, the Twelve? Yet one of you is a devil!" ⁷¹(He meant Judas, the son of Simon Iscariot, who, though one of the Twelve, was later to betray him.)

Jesus Goes to the Festival of Tabernacles

7 After this, Jesus went around in Galilee. He did not want*a* to go about in Judea because the Jewish leaders there were looking for a way to kill him. ²But when the Jewish Festival of Tabernacles was near, ³Jesus' brothers said to him, "Leave Galilee and go to Judea, so that your disciples there may see the works you do. ⁴No one who wants to become a public figure acts in secret. Since you are doing these things, show yourself to the world." ⁵For even his own brothers did not believe in him.

⁶Therefore Jesus told them, "My time is not yet here; for you any time will do. ⁷The world cannot hate you, but it hates me because I testify that its works are evil. ⁸You go to the festival. I am not*b* going up to this festival, because my time has not yet fully come." ⁹After he had said this, he stayed in Galilee.

¹⁰However, after his brothers had left for the festival, he went also, not publicly, but in secret. ¹¹Now at the festival the Jewish leaders were watching for Jesus and asking, "Where is he?"

a 1 Some manuscripts *not have authority*
b 8 Some manuscripts *not yet*

ROCK SOLID *principles*

John 6:60–71

Don't stop following.

Chad felt like he had a thousand reasons to quit being a Christian. But the one that bugged him most was the idea that Jesus was the only way anyone could know God or get to heaven. No matter how much he thought about it, he couldn't figure out why his non-Christian friends should go to hell or why they needed the death of Jesus to make them friends with God. Some of Chad's best friends followed other faiths, and some weren't into religion at all. If they all could get along without Jesus, he reasoned, so could he.

The crowds happily patted their full stomachs when Jesus miraculously fed them (see John 6:1–15). They felt confusion when he declared himself "the bread of life" who would fill them up forever (John 6:35). And many walked away when he said they needed to eat his flesh (see John 6:53). They didn't understand he meant accepting his one-of-a-kind death on their behalf. Peter knew enough to stick with the Lord. He realized Jesus is the only source of eternal life.

¹²Among the crowds there was widespread whispering about him. Some said, "He is a good man."

Others replied, "No, he deceives the people." ¹³But no one would say anything publicly about him for fear of the leaders.

Jesus Teaches at the Festival

¹⁴Not until halfway through the festival did Jesus go up to the temple courts and begin to teach. ¹⁵The Jews there were amazed and asked, "How did this man get such learning without having been taught?"

¹⁶Jesus answered, "My teaching is not my own. It comes from the one who sent me. ¹⁷Anyone who chooses to do the will of God will find out whether my teaching comes from God or whether I speak on my own. ¹⁸Whoever speaks on their own does so to gain personal glory, but he who seeks the glory of the one who sent him is a man of truth; there is nothing false about him. ¹⁹Has not Moses given you the law? Yet not one of you keeps the law. Why are you trying to kill me?"

²⁰"You are demon-possessed," the crowd answered. "Who is trying to kill you?"

²¹Jesus said to them, "I did one miracle, and you are all amazed. ²²Yet, because Moses gave you circumcision (though actually it did not come from Moses, but from the patriarchs), you circumcise a boy on the Sabbath. ²³Now if a boy can be circumcised on the Sabbath so that the law of Moses may not be broken, why are you angry with me for healing a man's whole body on the Sabbath? ²⁴Stop judging by mere appearances, but instead judge correctly."

Division Over Who Jesus Is

²⁵At that point some of the people of Jerusalem began to ask, "Isn't this the man they are trying to kill? ²⁶Here he is, speaking publicly, and they are not saying a word to him. Have the authorities really concluded that he is the Messiah? ²⁷But we know where this man is from; when the Messiah comes, no one will know where he is from."

²⁸Then Jesus, still teaching in the temple courts, cried out, "Yes, you know me, and you know where I am from. I am not here on my own authority, but he who sent me is true. You do not know him, ²⁹but I know him because I am from him and he sent me."

³⁰At this they tried to seize him, but no one laid a hand on him, because his hour had not yet come. ³¹Still, many in the crowd believed in him. They said, "When the Messiah comes, will he perform more signs than this man?"

³²The Pharisees heard the crowd whispering such things about him. Then the chief priests and the Pharisees sent temple guards to arrest him.

³³Jesus said, "I am with you for only a short time, and then I am going to the one who sent me. ³⁴You will look for me, but you will not find me; and where I am, you cannot come."

³⁵The Jews said to one another, "Where does this man intend to go that we cannot find him? Will he go where our people live scattered among the Greeks, and teach the Greeks? ³⁶What did he mean when he said, 'You will look for me, but you will not find me,' and 'Where I am, you cannot come'?"

³⁷On the last and greatest day of the festival, Jesus stood and said in a loud voice, "Let anyone who is thirsty come to me and drink. ³⁸Whoever believes in me, as Scripture has said, rivers of living water will flow from within them."*a* ³⁹By this he meant the Spirit, whom those who believed in him were later to receive. Up to that time the Spirit had not been given, since Jesus had not yet been glorified.

⁴⁰On hearing his words, some of the people said, "Surely this man is the Prophet."

⁴¹Others said, "He is the Messiah."

Still others asked, "How can the Messiah come from Galilee? ⁴²Does not Scripture say that the Messiah will come from David's descendants and from Bethlehem, the town where David lived?" ⁴³Thus the people were divided because of Jesus. ⁴⁴Some wanted to seize him, but no one laid a hand on him.

a 37,38 Or me. And let anyone drink ³⁸who believes in me." As Scripture has said, "Out of him (or them) will flow rivers of living water."

ROCK SOLID
promises

"Whoever believes in me, as Scripture has said, rivers of living water will flow from within them."

John 7:38

When you commit yourself to Jesus, he quenches your thirst from the inside out.

Unbelief of the Jewish Leaders

⁴⁵ Finally the temple guards went back to the chief priests and the Pharisees, who asked them, "Why didn't you bring him in?"

⁴⁶ "No one ever spoke the way this man does," the guards replied.

⁴⁷ "You mean he has deceived you also?" the Pharisees retorted. ⁴⁸ "Have any of the rulers or of the Pharisees believed in him? ⁴⁹ No! But this mob that knows nothing of the law—there is a curse on them."

⁵⁰ Nicodemus, who had gone to Jesus earlier and who was one of their own number, asked, ⁵¹ "Does our law condemn a man without first hearing him to find out what he has been doing?"

⁵² They replied, "Are you from Galilee, too? Look into it, and you will find that a prophet does not come out of Galilee."

[The earliest manuscripts and many other ancient witnesses do not have John 7:53—8:11. A few manuscripts include these verses, wholly or in part, after John 7:36, John 21:25, Luke 21:38 or Luke 24:53.]

8 ⁵³ Then they all went home, ¹ but Jesus went to the Mount of Olives. ² At dawn he appeared again in the temple courts, where all the people gathered around him, and he sat down to teach them. ³ The teachers of the law and the Pharisees brought in a woman caught in adultery. They made her stand before the group ⁴ and said to Jesus, "Teacher, this woman was caught in the act of adultery. ⁵ In the Law Moses commanded us to stone such women. Now what do you say?" ⁶ They were using this question as a trap, in order to have a basis for accusing him.

But Jesus bent down and started to write on the ground with his finger. ⁷ When they kept on questioning him, he straightened up and said to them, "Let any one of you who is without sin be the first to throw a stone at her." ⁸ Again he stooped down and wrote on the ground.

⁹ At this, those who heard began to go away one at a time, the older ones first, until only Jesus was left, with the woman still standing there. ¹⁰ Jesus straightened up and asked her, "Woman, where are they? Has no one condemned you?"

¹¹ "No one, sir," she said.

"Then neither do I condemn you," Jesus declared. "Go now and leave your life of sin."

Dispute Over Jesus' Testimony

¹² When Jesus spoke again to the people, he said, "I am the light of the world. Whoever follows me will never walk in darkness, but will have the light of life."

¹³ The Pharisees challenged him, "Here you are, appearing as your own witness; your testimony is not valid."

¹⁴ Jesus answered, "Even if I testify on my own behalf, my testimony is valid, for I know where I came from and where I am going. But you have no idea where I come from or where I am going. ¹⁵ You judge by human standards; I pass judgment on no one. ¹⁶ But if I do judge, my decisions are true, because I am not alone. I stand with the Father, who sent me. ¹⁷ In your own Law it is written that the testimony of two witnesses is true. ¹⁸ I am one who testifies for myself; my other witness is the Father, who sent me."

¹⁹ Then they asked him, "Where is your father?"

"You do not know me or my Father," Jesus replied. "If you knew me, you would know my Father also." ²⁰ He spoke these words while teaching in the temple courts near the place where the offerings were put. Yet no one seized him, because his hour had not yet come.

Dispute Over Who Jesus Is

²¹Once more Jesus said to them, "I am going away, and you will look for me, and you will die in your sin. Where I go, you cannot come."

²²This made the Jews ask, "Will he kill himself? Is that why he says, 'Where I go, you cannot come'?"

²³But he continued, "You are from below; I am from above. You are of this world; I am not of this world. ²⁴I told you that you would die in your sins; if you do not believe that I am he, you will indeed die in your sins."

²⁵"Who are you?" they asked.

"Just what I have been telling you from the beginning," Jesus replied. ²⁶"I have much to say in judgment of you. But he who sent me is trustworthy, and what I have heard from him I tell the world."

²⁷They did not understand that he was telling them about his Father. ²⁸So Jesus said, "When you have lifted up[a] the Son of Man, then you will know that I am he and that I do nothing on my own but speak just what the Father has taught me. ²⁹The one who sent me is with me; he has not left me alone, for I always do what pleases him." ³⁰Even as he spoke, many believed in him.

Dispute Over Whose Children Jesus' Opponents Are

³¹To the Jews who had believed him, Jesus said, "If you hold to my teaching, you are really my disciples. ³²Then you will know the truth, and the truth will set you free."

³³They answered him, "We are Abraham's descendants and have never been slaves of anyone. How can you say that we shall be set free?"

³⁴Jesus replied, "Very truly I tell you, everyone who sins is a slave to sin. ³⁵Now a slave has no permanent place in the family, but a son belongs to it forever. ³⁶So if the Son sets you free, you will be free indeed. ³⁷I know that you are Abraham's descendants. Yet you are looking for a way to kill me, because you have no room for my word. ³⁸I am telling you what I have seen

in the Father's presence, and you are doing what you have heard from your father.[b]"

³⁹"Abraham is our father," they answered.

"If you were Abraham's children," said Jesus, "then you would[c] do what Abraham did. ⁴⁰As it is, you are looking for a way to kill me, a man who has told you the truth that I heard from God. Abraham did not do such things. ⁴¹You are doing the works of your own father."

"We are not illegitimate children," they protested. "The only Father we have is God himself."

⁴²Jesus said to them, "If God were your Father, you would love me, for I have come here from God. I have not come on my own; God sent me. ⁴³Why is my language not clear to you? Because you are unable to hear what I say. ⁴⁴You belong to your father, the devil, and you want to carry out your father's desires. He was a murderer from the beginning, not holding to the truth, for there is no truth in him. When he lies, he speaks his native language, for he is a liar and the father of lies. ⁴⁵Yet because I tell the truth, you do not believe me! ⁴⁶Can any of you prove me guilty of sin? If I am telling the truth, why don't you believe me? ⁴⁷Whoever belongs

---

[a] 28 The Greek for *lifted up* also means *exalted*.
[b] 38 Or *presence. Therefore do what you have heard from the Father.*   [c] 39 Some early manuscripts *"If you are Abraham's children," said Jesus, "then*

to God hears what God says. The reason you do not hear is that you do not belong to God."

Jesus' Claims About Himself

⁴⁸The Jews answered him, "Aren't we right in saying that you are a Samaritan and demon-possessed?"

⁴⁹"I am not possessed by a demon," said Jesus, "but I honor my Father and you dishonor me. ⁵⁰I am not seeking glory for myself; but there is one who seeks it, and he is the judge. ⁵¹Very truly I tell you, whoever obeys my word will never see death."

⁵²At this they exclaimed, "Now we know that you are demon-possessed! Abraham died and so did the prophets, yet you say that whoever obeys your word will never taste death. ⁵³Are you greater than our father Abraham? He died, and so did the prophets. Who do you think you are?"

⁵⁴Jesus replied, "If I glorify myself, my glory means nothing. My Father, whom you claim as your God, is the one who glorifies me. ⁵⁵Though you do not know him, I know him. If I said I did not, I would be a liar like you, but I do know him and obey his word. ⁵⁶Your father Abraham rejoiced at the thought of seeing my day; he saw it and was glad."

⁵⁷"You are not yet fifty years old," they said to him, "and you have seen Abraham!"

⁵⁸"Very truly I tell you," Jesus answered, "before Abraham was born, I am!" ⁵⁹At this, they picked up stones to stone him, but Jesus hid himself, slipping away from the temple grounds.

Jesus Heals a Man Born Blind

9 As he went along, he saw a man blind from birth. ²His disciples asked him, "Rabbi, who sinned, this man or his parents, that he was born blind?"

³"Neither this man nor his parents sinned," said Jesus, "but this happened so that the works of God might be displayed in him. ⁴As long as it is day, we must do the works of him who sent me. Night is coming, when no one can work. ⁵While I am in the world, I am the light of the world."

⁶After saying this, he spit on the ground, made some mud with the saliva, and put it on the man's eyes. ⁷"Go," he told him, "wash in the Pool of Siloam" (this word means "Sent"). So the man went and washed, and came home seeing.

⁸His neighbors and those who had formerly seen him begging asked, "Isn't

---

John 8:48–58

Jesus claimed to be God.

In the first lines of his book the apostle John declares that Jesus is God (see John 1:1–3). Near the end he says he wrote in order that "you may believe that Jesus is the Messiah, the Son of God" (John 20:31). John and every other New Testament author asserted or assumed that Jesus is God. But what did Jesus himself think? Some Bible critics argue he never directly said, "I am God." That argument forgets Jesus' unmistakable claim in John 8. When his opponents probed whether Jesus came from God or the devil, he said, "Before Abraham was born, I am" (John 8:58). Casual readers might miss his point, but Jesus claims to have existed before a key Old Testament hero. Even more importantly, he also applies to himself God's most holy name, "I am" (see Exodus 3:14). The people who heard Jesus instantly recognized he had declared himself to be God. They even picked up rocks to kill him for his claim.

Think: Why is it essential that Jesus himself claimed to be God?

ROCK SOLID *truths*

this the same man who used to sit and beg?" ⁹Some claimed that he was.

Others said, "No, he only looks like him."

But he himself insisted, "I am the man."

¹⁰"How then were your eyes opened?" they asked.

¹¹He replied, "The man they call Jesus made some mud and put it on my eyes. He told me to go to Siloam and wash. So I went and washed, and then I could see."

¹²"Where is this man?" they asked him. "I don't know," he said.

The Pharisees Investigate the Healing

¹³They brought to the Pharisees the man who had been blind. ¹⁴Now the day on which Jesus had made the mud and opened the man's eyes was a Sabbath. ¹⁵Therefore the Pharisees also asked him how he had received his sight. "He put mud on my eyes," the man replied, "and I washed, and now I see."

¹⁶Some of the Pharisees said, "This man is not from God, for he does not keep the Sabbath."

But others asked, "How can a sinner perform such signs?" So they were divided.

¹⁷Then they turned again to the blind man, "What have you to say about him? It was your eyes he opened."

The man replied, "He is a prophet."

¹⁸They still did not believe that he had been blind and had received his sight until they sent for the man's parents. ¹⁹"Is this your son?" they asked. "Is this the one you say was born blind? How is it that now he can see?"

²⁰"We know he is our son," the parents answered, "and we know he was born blind. ²¹But how he can see now, or who opened his eyes, we don't know. Ask him. He is of age; he will speak for himself." ²²His parents said this because they were afraid of the Jewish leaders, who already had decided that anyone who acknowledged that Jesus was the Messiah would be put out of the synagogue. ²³That was why his parents said, "He is of age; ask him."

²⁴A second time they summoned the man who had been blind. "Give glory to God by telling the truth," they said. "We know this man is a sinner."

²⁵He replied, "Whether he is a sinner or not, I don't know. One thing I do know. I was blind but now I see!"

²⁶Then they asked him, "What did he do to you? How did he open your eyes?"

²⁷He answered, "I have told you already and you did not listen. Why do you want to hear it again? Do you want to become his disciples too?"

²⁸Then they hurled insults at him and said, "You are this fellow's disciple! We are disciples of Moses! ²⁹We know that God spoke to Moses, but as for this fellow, we don't even know where he comes from."

³⁰The man answered, "Now that is remarkable! You don't know where he comes from, yet he opened my eyes. ³¹We know that God does not listen to sinners. He listens to the godly person who does his will. ³²Nobody has ever heard of opening the eyes of a man born blind. ³³If this man were not from God, he could do nothing."

³⁴To this they replied, "You were steeped in sin at birth; how dare you lecture us!" And they threw him out.

Spiritual Blindness

³⁵Jesus heard that they had thrown him out, and when he found him, he said, "Do you believe in the Son of Man?"

³⁶"Who is he, sir?" the man asked. "Tell me so that I may believe in him."

³⁷Jesus said, "You have now seen him; in fact, he is the one speaking with you."

³⁸Then the man said, "Lord, I believe," and he worshiped him.

³⁹Jesus said,ᵃ "For judgment I have come into this world, so that the blind will see and those who see will become blind."

⁴⁰Some Pharisees who were with him heard him say this and asked, "What? Are we blind too?"

⁴¹Jesus said, "If you were blind, you would not be guilty of sin; but now that you claim you can see, your guilt remains.

ᵃ 38,39 Some early manuscripts do not have *Then the man said . . .* ³⁹*Jesus said.*

The Good Shepherd and His Sheep

10 "Very truly I tell you Pharisees, anyone who does not enter the sheep pen by the gate, but climbs in by some other way, is a thief and a robber. [2]The one who enters by the gate is the shepherd of the sheep. [3]The gatekeeper opens the gate for him, and the sheep listen to his voice. He calls his own sheep by name and leads them out. [4]When he has brought out all his own, he goes on ahead of them, and his sheep follow him because they know his voice. [5]But they will never follow a stranger; in fact, they will run away from him because they do not recognize a stranger's voice." [6]Jesus used this figure of speech, but the Pharisees did not understand what he was telling them.

[7]Therefore Jesus said again, "Very truly I tell you, I am the gate for the sheep. [8]All who have come before me are thieves and robbers, but the sheep have not listened to them. [9]I am the gate; whoever enters through me will be saved.[a] They will come in and go out, and find pasture. [10]The thief comes only to steal and kill and destroy; I have come that they may have life, and have it to the full.

[11]"I am the good shepherd. The good shepherd lays down his life for the sheep. [12]The hired hand is not the shepherd and does not own the sheep. So when he sees the wolf coming, he abandons the sheep and runs away. Then the wolf attacks the flock and scatters it. [13]The man runs away because he is a hired hand and cares nothing for the sheep.

[14]"I am the good shepherd; I know my sheep and my sheep know me— [15]just as the Father knows me and I know the Father—and I lay down my life for the sheep. [16]I have other sheep that are not of this sheep pen. I must bring them also. They too will listen to my voice, and there shall be one flock and one shepherd. [17]The reason my Father loves me is that I lay down my life—only to take it up again. [18]No one takes it from me, but I lay it down of my own accord. I have authority to lay it down and authority to

take it up again. This command I received from my Father."

[19]The Jews who heard these words were again divided. [20]Many of them said, "He is demon-possessed and raving mad. Why listen to him?"

[21]But others said, "These are not the sayings of a man possessed by a demon. Can a demon open the eyes of the blind?"

Further Conflict Over Jesus' Claims

[22]Then came the Festival of Dedication[b] at Jerusalem. It was winter, [23]and Jesus was in the temple courts walking in Solomon's Colonnade. [24]The Jews who were there gathered around him, saying, "How long will you keep us in suspense? If you are the Messiah, tell us plainly."

[25]Jesus answered, "I did tell you, but you do not believe. The works I do in my

[a] 9 Or *kept safe*   [b] 22 That is, Hanukkah

UNSHAKEN *God*

John 10:1–13

God is life-giving.

Thumb through the book of John and you find multiple pictures of Jesus as a guy who gives life. He's the "bread of life" (John 6:35), "the way and the truth and the life" (John 14:6) and "the resurrection and the life" (John 11:25). In John 10 Jesus calls himself "the good shepherd" who "lays down his life for the sheep" (John 10:11). He declares, "I have come that they may have life, and have it to the full" (John 10:10). If you ever worry that God wants to spoil your life, count on all those words. The Lord doesn't promise you a perfect life. But he gives an abundant life filled with him—and a life that lasts forever.

So ... What kind of life does Jesus offer you? Do you want that life—or something else?

Father's name testify about me, ²⁶but you do not believe because you are not my sheep. ²⁷My sheep listen to my voice; I know them, and they follow me. ²⁸I give them eternal life, and they shall never perish; no one will snatch them out of my hand. ²⁹My Father, who has given them to me, is greater than all^a; no one can snatch them out of my Father's hand. ³⁰I and the Father are one."

³¹Again his Jewish opponents picked up stones to stone him, ³²but Jesus said to them, "I have shown you many good works from the Father. For which of these do you stone me?"

³³"We are not stoning you for any good work," they replied, "but for blasphemy, because you, a mere man, claim to be God."

³⁴Jesus answered them, "Is it not written in your Law, 'I have said you are "gods"'^b? ³⁵If he called them 'gods,' to whom the word of God came—and Scripture cannot be set aside— ³⁶what about the one whom the Father set apart as his very own and sent into the world? Why then do you accuse me of blasphemy because I said, 'I am God's Son'? ³⁷Do not believe me unless I do the works of my Father. ³⁸But if I do them, even though you do not believe me, believe the works, that you may know and understand that the Father is in me, and I in the Father." ³⁹Again they tried to seize him, but he escaped their grasp.

⁴⁰Then Jesus went back across the Jordan to the place where John had been baptizing in the early days. There he stayed, ⁴¹and many people came to him. They said, "Though John never performed a sign, all that John said about this man was true." ⁴²And in that place many believed in Jesus.

The Death of Lazarus

11 Now a man named Lazarus was sick. He was from Bethany, the village of Mary and her sister Martha. ²(This Mary, whose brother Lazarus now lay sick, was the same one who poured perfume on the Lord and wiped his feet with her hair.) ³So the sisters sent word to Jesus, "Lord, the one you love is sick."

⁴When he heard this, Jesus said, "This sickness will not end in death. No, it is for God's glory so that God's Son may be glorified through it." ⁵Now Jesus loved Martha and her sister and Lazarus. ⁶So when he heard that Lazarus was sick, he stayed where he was two more days, ⁷and then he said to his disciples, "Let us go back to Judea."

⁸"But Rabbi," they said, "a short while ago the Jews there tried to stone you, and yet you are going back?"

⁹Jesus answered, "Are there not twelve hours of daylight? Anyone who walks in the daytime will not stumble, for they see by this world's light. ¹⁰It is when a person walks at night that they stumble, for they have no light."

¹¹After he had said this, he went on to tell them, "Our friend Lazarus has fallen asleep; but I am going there to wake him up."

¹²His disciples replied, "Lord, if he sleeps, he will get better." ¹³Jesus had been speaking of his death, but his disciples thought he meant natural sleep.

¹⁴So then he told them plainly, "Lazarus is dead, ¹⁵and for your sake I am glad I was not there, so that you may believe. But let us go to him."

¹⁶Then Thomas (also known as Didymus^c) said to the rest of the disciples, "Let us also go, that we may die with him."

Jesus Comforts the Sisters of Lazarus

¹⁷On his arrival, Jesus found that Lazarus had already been in the tomb for four days. ¹⁸Now Bethany was less than two miles^d from Jerusalem, ¹⁹and many Jews had come to Martha and Mary to comfort them in the loss of their brother. ²⁰When Martha heard that Jesus was coming, she went out to meet him, but Mary stayed at home.

²¹"Lord," Martha said to Jesus, "if you had been here, my brother would not have died. ²²But I know that even now God will give you whatever you ask."

^a 29 Many early manuscripts *What my Father has given me is greater than all*   ^b 34 Psalm 82:6   ^c 16 *Thomas* (Aramaic) and *Didymus* (Greek) both mean *twin*.   ^d 18 Or about 3 kilometers

²³Jesus said to her, "Your brother will rise again."

²⁴Martha answered, "I know he will rise again in the resurrection at the last day."

²⁵Jesus said to her, "I am the resurrection and the life. The one who believes in me will live, even though they die; ²⁶and whoever lives by believing in me will never die. Do you believe this?"

ROCK SOLID
promises

"I am the resurrection and the life. The one who believes in me will live, even though they die."

John 11:25

If you believe in Jesus, death won't keep you down. You will rise again to live forever with him and all his friends.

---

²⁷"Yes, Lord," she replied, "I believe that you are the Messiah, the Son of God, who is to come into the world."

²⁸After she had said this, she went back and called her sister Mary aside. "The Teacher is here," she said, "and is asking for you." ²⁹When Mary heard this, she got up quickly and went to him. ³⁰Now Jesus had not yet entered the village, but was still at the place where Martha had met him. ³¹When the Jews who had been with Mary in the house, comforting her, noticed how quickly she got up and went out, they followed her, supposing she was going to the tomb to mourn there.

³²When Mary reached the place where Jesus was and saw him, she fell at his feet and said, "Lord, if you had been here, my brother would not have died."

³³When Jesus saw her weeping, and the Jews who had come along with her also weeping, he was deeply moved in spirit and troubled. ³⁴"Where have you laid him?" he asked.

"Come and see, Lord," they replied.

³⁵Jesus wept.

³⁶Then the Jews said, "See how he loved him!"

³⁷But some of them said, "Could not he who opened the eyes of the blind man have kept this man from dying?"

Jesus Raises Lazarus From the Dead

³⁸Jesus, once more deeply moved, came to the tomb. It was a cave with a stone laid across the entrance. ³⁹"Take away the stone," he said.

"But, Lord," said Martha, the sister of the dead man, "by this time there is a bad odor, for he has been there four days."

⁴⁰Then Jesus said, "Did I not tell you that if you believe, you will see the glory of God?"

⁴¹So they took away the stone. Then Jesus looked up and said, "Father, I thank you that you have heard me. ⁴²I knew that you always hear me, but I said this for the benefit of the people standing here, that they may believe that you sent me."

⁴³When he had said this, Jesus called in a loud voice, "Lazarus, come out!" ⁴⁴The dead man came out, his hands and feet wrapped with strips of linen, and a cloth around his face.

Jesus said to them, "Take off the grave clothes and let him go."

The Plot to Kill Jesus

⁴⁵Therefore many of the Jews who had come to visit Mary, and had seen what Jesus did, believed in him. ⁴⁶But some of them went to the Pharisees and told them what Jesus had done. ⁴⁷Then the chief priests and the Pharisees called a meeting of the Sanhedrin.

"What are we accomplishing?" they asked. "Here is this man performing many signs. ⁴⁸If we let him go on like this, everyone will believe in him, and then the Romans will come and take away both our temple and our nation."

⁴⁹Then one of them, named Caiaphas, who was high priest that year, spoke up, "You know nothing at all! ⁵⁰You do not realize that it is better for you that one

man die for the people than that the whole nation perish."

⁵¹He did not say this on his own, but as high priest that year he prophesied that Jesus would die for the Jewish nation, ⁵²and not only for that nation but also for the scattered children of God, to bring them together and make them one. ⁵³So from that day on they plotted to take his life.

⁵⁴Therefore Jesus no longer moved about publicly among the people of Judea. Instead he withdrew to a region near the wilderness, to a village called Ephraim, where he stayed with his disciples.

⁵⁵When it was almost time for the Jewish Passover, many went up from the country to Jerusalem for their ceremonial cleansing before the Passover. ⁵⁶They kept looking for Jesus, and as they stood in the temple courts they asked one another, "What do you think? Isn't he coming to the festival at all?" ⁵⁷But the chief priests and the Pharisees had given orders that anyone who found out where Jesus was should report it so that they might arrest him.

Jesus Anointed at Bethany

12 Six days before the Passover, Jesus came to Bethany, where Lazarus lived, whom Jesus had raised from the dead. ²Here a dinner was given in Jesus' honor. Martha served, while Lazarus was among those reclining at the table with him. ³Then Mary took about a pint[a] of pure nard, an expensive perfume; she poured it on Jesus' feet and wiped his feet with her hair. And the house was filled with the fragrance of the perfume.

⁴But one of his disciples, Judas Iscariot, who was later to betray him, objected, ⁵"Why wasn't this perfume sold and the money given to the poor? It was worth a year's wages.[b]" ⁶He did not say this because he cared about the poor but because he was a thief; as keeper of the money bag, he used to help himself to what was put into it.

⁷"Leave her alone," Jesus replied. "It was intended that she should save this perfume for the day of my burial. ⁸You will always have the poor among you,[c] but you will not always have me."

⁹Meanwhile a large crowd of Jews found out that Jesus was there and came, not only because of him but also to see Lazarus, whom he had raised from the dead. ¹⁰So the chief priests made plans to kill Lazarus as well, ¹¹for on account of him many of the Jews were going over to Jesus and believing in him.

Jesus Comes to Jerusalem as King

¹²The next day the great crowd that had come for the festival heard that Jesus was on his way to Jerusalem. ¹³They took palm branches and went out to meet him, shouting,

"Hosanna![d]"

"Blessed is he who comes in the name of the Lord!"[e]

"Blessed is the king of Israel!"

¹⁴Jesus found a young donkey and sat on it, as it is written:

¹⁵"Do not be afraid, Daughter Zion;
    see, your king is coming,
    seated on a donkey's colt."[f]

¹⁶At first his disciples did not understand all this. Only after Jesus was glorified did they realize that these things had been written about him and that these things had been done to him.

¹⁷Now the crowd that was with him when he called Lazarus from the tomb and raised him from the dead continued to spread the word. ¹⁸Many people, because they had heard that he had performed this sign, went out to meet him. ¹⁹So the Pharisees said to one another, "See, this is getting us nowhere. Look how the whole world has gone after him!"

Jesus Predicts His Death

²⁰Now there were some Greeks among those who went up to worship at the festival. ²¹They came to Philip, who was from

---

a 3 Or about 0.5 liter   *b 5* Greek *three hundred denarii*   *c 8* See Deut. 15:11.
d 13 A Hebrew expression meaning "Save!" which became an exclamation of praise
e 13 Psalm 118:25,26   *f 15* Zech. 9:9

Bethsaida in Galilee, with a request. "Sir," they said, "we would like to see Jesus." ²²Philip went to tell Andrew; Andrew and Philip in turn told Jesus.

²³Jesus replied, "The hour has come for the Son of Man to be glorified. ²⁴Very truly I tell you, unless a kernel of wheat falls to the ground and dies, it remains only a single seed. But if it dies, it produces many seeds. ²⁵Anyone who loves their life will lose it, while anyone who hates their life in this world will keep it for eternal life. ²⁶Whoever serves me must follow me; and where I am, my servant also will be. My Father will honor the one who serves me.

²⁷"Now my soul is troubled, and what shall I say? 'Father, save me from this hour'? No, it was for this very reason I came to this hour. ²⁸Father, glorify your name!"

Then a voice came from heaven, "I have glorified it, and will glorify it again." ²⁹The crowd that was there and heard it said it had thundered; others said an angel had spoken to him.

³⁰Jesus said, "This voice was for your benefit, not mine. ³¹Now is the time for judgment on this world; now the prince of this world will be driven out. ³²And I, when I am lifted up*^a from the earth, will draw all people to myself." ³³He said this to show the kind of death he was going to die.

³⁴The crowd spoke up, "We have heard from the Law that the Messiah will remain forever, so how can you say, 'The Son of Man must be lifted up'? Who is this 'Son of Man'?"

³⁵Then Jesus told them, "You are going to have the light just a little while longer. Walk while you have the light, before darkness overtakes you. Whoever walks in the dark does not know where they are going. ³⁶Believe in the light while you have the light, so that you may become children of light." When he had finished speaking, Jesus left and hid himself from them.

Belief and Unbelief Among the Jews

³⁷Even after Jesus had performed so many signs in their presence, they still would not believe in him. ³⁸This was to fulfill the word of Isaiah the prophet:

"Lord, who has believed our message
and to whom has the arm of the
Lord been revealed?"*^b

³⁹For this reason they could not believe, because, as Isaiah says elsewhere:

⁴⁰"He has blinded their eyes
and hardened their hearts,
so they can neither see with their eyes,
nor understand with their hearts,
nor turn—and I would heal them."*^c

⁴¹Isaiah said this because he saw Jesus' glory and spoke about him.

⁴²Yet at the same time many even among the leaders believed in him. But because of the Pharisees they would not openly acknowledge their faith for fear they would be put out of the synagogue; ⁴³for they loved human praise more than praise from God.

⁴⁴Then Jesus cried out, "Whoever believes in me does not believe in me only, but in the one who sent me. ⁴⁵The one who looks at me is seeing the one who sent me. ⁴⁶I have come into the world as a light, so that no one who believes in me should stay in darkness.

⁴⁷"If anyone hears my words but does not keep them, I do not judge that person. For I did not come to judge the world, but to save the world. ⁴⁸There is a judge for the one who rejects me and does not accept my words; the very words I have spoken will condemn them at the last day. ⁴⁹For I did not speak on my own, but the Father who sent me commanded me to say all that I have spoken. ⁵⁰I know that his command leads to eternal life. So whatever I say is just what the Father has told me to say."

Jesus Washes His Disciples' Feet

13 It was just before the Passover Festival. Jesus knew that the hour had come for him to leave this world and go to the Father. Having loved his own who were in the world, he loved them to the end.

---

^a 32 The Greek for *lifted up* also means *exalted.*
^b 38 Isaiah 53:1   *^c 40* Isaiah 6:10

²The evening meal was in progress, and the devil had already prompted Judas, the son of Simon Iscariot, to betray Jesus. ³Jesus knew that the Father had put all things under his power, and that he had come from God and was returning to God; ⁴so he got up from the meal, took off his outer clothing, and wrapped a towel around his waist. ⁵After that, he poured water into a basin and began to wash his disciples' feet, drying them with the towel that was wrapped around him.

⁶He came to Simon Peter, who said to him, "Lord, are you going to wash my feet?"

⁷Jesus replied, "You do not realize now what I am doing, but later you will understand."

⁸"No," said Peter, "you shall never wash my feet."

Jesus answered, "Unless I wash you, you have no part with me."

⁹"Then, Lord," Simon Peter replied, "not just my feet but my hands and my head as well!"

¹⁰Jesus answered, "Those who have had a bath need only to wash their feet; their whole body is clean. And you are clean, though not every one of you." ¹¹For he knew who was going to betray him, and that was why he said not every one was clean.

¹²When he had finished washing their feet, he put on his clothes and returned to his place. "Do you understand what I have done for you?" he asked them. ¹³"You call me 'Teacher' and 'Lord,' and rightly so, for that is what I am. ¹⁴Now that I, your Lord and Teacher, have washed your feet, you also should wash one another's feet. ¹⁵I have set you an example that you should do as I have done for you. ¹⁶Very truly I tell you, no servant is greater than his master, nor is a messenger greater than the one who sent him. ¹⁷Now that you know these things, you will be blessed if you do them.

Jesus Predicts His Betrayal

¹⁸"I am not referring to all of you; I know those I have chosen. But this is to

ROCK SOLID principles

John 13:1–17

Serve others like Jesus serves you.

As Tessa moved up a grade and into a new school, she wanted to leave a big part of her old self behind. Everyone knew her as a bratty, self-absorbed girl quick to slice her peers with razor-sharp words. Tessa knew she needed to take charge of her mouth, but she wasn't sure that was enough for anyone to believe she had changed. So she promised herself and God that she would change not just her words but her actions. She decided to start serving her classmates by looking for one way each day to be surprisingly kind. One act of service a day might not be much, but it was a start.

Washing feet was the job of the lowest household slave, a courtesy performed for guests. But in this scene it was Jesus the teacher and master who stripped off his outer clothes and wrapped himself in a towel, kneeling to clean the feet of 12 burly followers, guys who tramped along dirt roads wearing sandals. It's a shocking model of how we should serve each other.

fulfill this passage of Scripture: 'He who shared my bread has turned*a* against me.'*b*

¹⁹"I am telling you now before it happens, so that when it does happen you will believe that I am who I am. ²⁰Very truly I tell you, whoever accepts anyone I send accepts me; and whoever accepts me accepts the one who sent me."

²¹After he had said this, Jesus was troubled in spirit and testified, "Very truly I tell you, one of you is going to betray me."

²²His disciples stared at one another, at a loss to know which of them he meant. ²³One of them, the disciple whom Jesus loved, was reclining next to him. ²⁴Simon Peter motioned to this disciple and said, "Ask him which one he means."

²⁵Leaning back against Jesus, he asked him, "Lord, who is it?"

²⁶Jesus answered, "It is the one to whom I will give this piece of bread when I have dipped it in the dish." Then, dipping the piece of bread, he gave it to Judas, the son of Simon Iscariot. ²⁷As soon as Judas took the bread, Satan entered into him.

So Jesus told him, "What you are about to do, do quickly." ²⁸But no one at the meal understood why Jesus said this to him. ²⁹Since Judas had charge of the money, some thought Jesus was telling him to buy what was needed for the festival, or to give something to the poor. ³⁰As soon as Judas had taken the bread, he went out. And it was night.

Jesus Predicts Peter's Denial

³¹When he was gone, Jesus said, "Now the Son of Man is glorified and God is glorified in him. ³²If God is glorified in him,*c* God will glorify the Son in himself, and will glorify him at once.

³³"My children, I will be with you only a little longer. You will look for me, and just as I told the Jews, so I tell you now: Where I am going, you cannot come.

³⁴"A new command I give you: Love one another. As I have loved you, so you must love one another. ³⁵By this everyone will know that you are my disciples, if you love one another."

³⁶Simon Peter asked him, "Lord, where are you going?"

Jesus replied, "Where I am going, you cannot follow now, but you will follow later."

³⁷Peter asked, "Lord, why can't I follow you now? I will lay down my life for you."

³⁸Then Jesus answered, "Will you really lay down your life for me? Very truly I tell you, before the rooster crows, you will disown me three times!

Jesus Comforts His Disciples

14 "Do not let your hearts be troubled. You believe in God*d*; believe also in me. ²My Father's house has many rooms; if that were not so, would I have told you that I am going there to prepare a place for you? ³And if I go and prepare a place for you, I will come back and take you to be with me that you also may be where I am. ⁴You know the way to the place where I am going."

ROCK SOLID *promises*

"My Father's house has many rooms; if that were not so, would I have told you that I am going there to prepare a place for you?"

John 14:2

Jesus has a place reserved for you in heaven, and one day he will lead you home.

Jesus the Way to the Father

⁵Thomas said to him, "Lord, we don't know where you are going, so how can we know the way?"

⁶Jesus answered, "I am the way and the truth and the life. No one comes to the Father except through me. ⁷If you really

---

a 18 Greek *has lifted up his heel*
b 18 Psalm 41:9   *c 32* Many early manuscripts do not have *If God is glorified in him.*   *d 1* Or *Believe in God*

John 14:1–6

Jesus is the only way to heaven.

The disciples couldn't have been more baffled or sad when Jesus revealed he was leaving them. That tight-knit group thought they would be with their Lord forever, but now he was going away. Jesus explained, however, that the separation wouldn't last forever. He would go to his Father's house and prepare a home for them. But that left his disciples with a huge question. How would they get there? Jesus answered with some of his most famous words: "I am the way and the truth and the life. No one comes to the Father except through me" (John 14:6). Jesus didn't suggest he was one way among many to get to heaven. He declared himself the one and only path. He's the one person in the universe who died for human sins, made us friends with God, and opened the door to heaven (see Hebrews 10:19–22).

Think: Do you agree that Jesus is the only way to heaven? Why—or why not?

ROCK SOLID truths

the Father, living in me, who is doing his work. [11] Believe me when I say that I am in the Father and the Father is in me; or at least believe on the evidence of the works themselves. [12] Very truly I tell you, whoever believes in me will do the works I have been doing, and they will do even greater things than these, because I am going to the Father. [13] And I will do whatever you ask in my name, so that the Father may be glorified in the Son. [14] You may ask me for anything in my name, and I will do it.

Jesus Promises the Holy Spirit

[15] "If you love me, keep my commands. [16] And I will ask the Father, and he will give you another advocate to help you and be with you forever— [17] the Spirit of truth. The world cannot accept him, because it neither sees him nor knows him. But you know him, for he lives with you and will be[b] in you. [18] I will not leave you as orphans; I will come to you. [19] Before long, the world will not see me anymore, but you will see me. Because I live, you also will live. [20] On that day you will realize that I am in my Father, and you are in me, and I am in you. [21] Whoever has my commands and keeps them is the one who loves me. The one who loves me will be loved by my Father, and I too will love them and show myself to them."

[22] Then Judas (not Judas Iscariot) said, "But, Lord, why do you intend to show yourself to us and not to the world?"

[23] Jesus replied, "Anyone who loves me will obey my teaching. My Father will love them, and we will come to them and make our home with them. [24] Anyone who does not love me will not obey my teaching. These words you hear are not my own; they belong to the Father who sent me.

[25] "All this I have spoken while still with you. [26] But the Advocate, the Holy Spirit, whom the Father will send in my name, will teach you all things and will remind you of everything I have said to you. [27] Peace I leave with you; my peace I give you. I do not give to you as the world

know me, you will know[a] my Father as well. From now on, you do know him and have seen him."

[8] Philip said, "Lord, show us the Father and that will be enough for us."

[9] Jesus answered: "Don't you know me, Philip, even after I have been among you such a long time? Anyone who has seen me has seen the Father. How can you say, 'Show us the Father'? [10] Don't you believe that I am in the Father, and that the Father is in me? The words I say to you I do not speak on my own authority. Rather, it is

---

[a] 7 Some manuscripts *If you really knew me, you would know*   [b] 17 Some early manuscripts *and is*

gives. Do not let your hearts be troubled and do not be afraid.

28 "You heard me say, 'I am going away and I am coming back to you.' If you loved me, you would be glad that I am going to the Father, for the Father is greater than I. 29 I have told you now before it happens, so that when it does happen you will believe. 30 I will not say much more to you, for the prince of this world is coming. He has no hold over me, 31 but he comes so that the world may learn that I love the Father and do exactly what my Father has commanded me.

"Come now; let us leave."

The Vine and the Branches

15 "I am the true vine, and my Father is the gardener. 2 He cuts off every branch in me that bears no fruit, while every branch that does bear fruit he prunes*a* so that it will be even more fruitful. 3 You are already clean because of the word I have spoken to you. 4 Remain in me, as I also remain in you. No branch can bear fruit by itself; it must remain in the vine. Neither can you bear fruit unless you remain in me.

5 "I am the vine; you are the branches. If you remain in me and I in you, you will bear much fruit; apart from me you can do nothing. 6 If you do not remain in me, you are like a branch that is thrown away and withers; such branches are picked up,

ROCK SOLID *plans*

John 15:1 – 9

Get everything from Jesus.

Jesus knows you need even more than determination, a good education, and a few "lucky breaks" to thrive in life. He plans for you to stay connected to him for everything you need, commanding you to "remain" in him, a word that means to "stay" or "settle in" or "sink deeper." If you "remain" in Jesus, your life will be productive as surely as a branch naturally produces fruit when it stays connected to a vine. Without Jesus, "you can do nothing" (John 15:5).

Your next step: Ask God to show you areas where you're trying to do life without his help.

thrown into the fire and burned. 7 If you remain in me and my words remain in you, ask whatever you wish, and it will be done for you. 8 This is to my Father's glory, that you bear much fruit, showing yourselves to be my disciples.

9 "As the Father has loved me, so have I loved you. Now remain in my love. 10 If you keep my commands, you will remain in my love, just as I have kept my Father's commands and remain in his love. 11 I have told you this so that my joy may be in you and that your joy may be complete. 12 My command is this: Love each other as I have loved you. 13 Greater love has no one than this: to lay down one's life for one's friends. 14 You are my friends if you do what I command. 15 I no longer call you servants, because a servant does not know his master's business. Instead, I have called you friends, for everything that I learned from my Father I have made known to you. 16 You did not choose me, but I chose you and appointed you so that you might go and bear fruit — fruit that will last — and so that whatever you ask in

ROCK SOLID *promises*

"If you remain in me and I in you, you will bear much fruit; apart from me you can do nothing."

John 15:5

You won't accomplish the very best things without staying connected to Jesus.

a 2 The Greek for *he prunes* also means *he cleans.*

my name the Father will give you. [17]This is my command: Love each other.

The World Hates the Disciples

[18]"If the world hates you, keep in mind that it hated me first. [19]If you belonged to the world, it would love you as its own. As it is, you do not belong to the world, but I have chosen you out of the world. That is why the world hates you. [20]Remember what I told you: 'A servant is not greater than his master.'[a] If they persecuted me, they will persecute you also. If they obeyed my teaching, they will obey yours also. [21]They will treat you this way because of my name, for they do not know the one who sent me. [22]If I had not come and spoken to them, they would not be guilty of sin; but now they have no excuse for their sin. [23]Whoever hates me hates my Father as well. [24]If I had not done among them the works no one else did, they would not be guilty of sin. As it is, they have seen, and yet they have hated both me and my Father. [25]But this is to fulfill what is written in their Law: 'They hated me without reason.'[b]

The Work of the Holy Spirit

[26]"When the Advocate comes, whom I will send to you from the Father—the Spirit of truth who goes out from the Father—he will testify about me. [27]And you also must testify, for you have been with me from the beginning.

16 "All this I have told you so that you will not fall away. [2]They will put you out of the synagogue; in fact, the time is coming when anyone who kills you will think they are offering a service to God. [3]They will do such things because they have not known the Father or me. [4]I have told you this, so that when their time comes you will remember that I warned you about them.

I did not tell you this from the beginning because I was with you, [5]but now I am going to him who sent me. None of you asks me, 'Where are you going?' [6]Rather, you are filled with grief because I have said these things. [7]But very truly I tell you, it is for your good that I am going away. Unless I go away, the Advocate will not come to you; but if I go, I will send him to you. [8]When he comes, he will prove the world to be in the wrong about sin and righteousness and judgment: [9]about sin, because people do not believe in me; [10]about righteousness, because I am going to the Father, where you can see me no longer; [11]and about judgment, because the prince of this world now stands condemned.

[a] 20 John 13:16   [b] 25 Psalms 35:19; 69:4

John 16:7–13

God lives in you.

When Christians say Jesus lives "in their heart," little kids might picture a tiny Jesus hanging out inside them. Older people might think Jesus "living in them" is just a warm spiritual feeling. But God "indwelling" us is more than that. The Bible sometimes says the "Spirit of Christ" lives inside believers (Romans 8:9). More often it says the "Spirit of God" (Romans 8:9) or just the "Holy Spirit" is in us (1 Corinthians 6:19). Those phrases all mean the same thing: When we believe, God establishes a relationship with us that's so close that we become one with him. He's in us, and we're in him. God promised back in the Old Testament to send his Spirit to cause us to obey him (see Ezekiel 36:27), and Jesus said the Spirit will come to comfort and teach us. Whenever you change and become more like Jesus, that's a sign of the Spirit working in you (see Galatians 5:22–23).

Think: How do you know the Holy Spirit is in you? What does the Spirit do for you?

ROCK SOLID truths

12 "I have much more to say to you, more than you can now bear. 13 But when he, the Spirit of truth, comes, he will guide you into all the truth. He will not speak on his own; he will speak only what he hears, and he will tell you what is yet to come. 14 He will glorify me because it is from me that he will receive what he will make known to you. 15 All that belongs to the Father is mine. That is why I said the Spirit will receive from me what he will make known to you."

The Disciples' Grief Will Turn to Joy

16 Jesus went on to say, "In a little while you will see me no more, and then after a little while you will see me."

17 At this, some of his disciples said to one another, "What does he mean by saying, 'In a little while you will see me no more, and then after a little while you will see me,' and 'Because I am going to the Father'?" 18 They kept asking, "What does he mean by 'a little while'? We don't understand what he is saying."

19 Jesus saw that they wanted to ask him about this, so he said to them, "Are you asking one another what I meant when I said, 'In a little while you will see me no more, and then after a little while you will see me'? 20 Very truly I tell you, you will weep and mourn while the world rejoices. You will grieve, but your grief will turn to joy. 21 A woman giving birth to a child has pain because her time has come; but when her baby is born she forgets the anguish because of her joy that a child is born into the world. 22 So with you: Now is your time of grief, but I will see you again and you will rejoice, and no one will take away your joy. 23 In that day you will no longer ask me anything. Very truly I tell you, my Father will give you whatever you ask in my name. 24 Until now you have not asked for anything in my name. Ask and you will receive, and your joy will be complete.

25 "Though I have been speaking figuratively, a time is coming when I will no longer use this kind of language but will tell you plainly about my Father. 26 In that day you will ask in my name. I am not saying that I will ask the Father on your behalf. 27 No, the Father himself loves you because you have loved me and have believed that I came from God. 28 I came from the Father and entered the world; now I am leaving the world and going back to the Father."

29 Then Jesus' disciples said, "Now you are speaking clearly and without figures of speech. 30 Now we can see that you know all things and that you do not even need to have anyone ask you questions. This makes us believe that you came from God."

31 "Do you now believe?" Jesus replied. 32 "A time is coming and in fact has come when you will be scattered, each to your own home. You will leave me all alone. Yet I am not alone, for my Father is with me.

33 "I have told you these things, so that in me you may have peace. In this world you will have trouble. But take heart! I have overcome the world."

UNSHAKEN God

John 16:33

God is encouraging.

Jesus saw his own death looming and knew he would soon head back to heaven (see John 14:9,28–31). When he told his closest followers this news, they were crushed. So Jesus assured them he would lead them to heaven (see John 14:1–6). He explained the Holy Spirit would comfort them (see John 14:15–27). He said they could stay connected to him as they lived in a hostile world (see John 15:1–26). And then he explained his reason for sharing all these details, so that "in me you may have peace" (John 16:33). As followers of Jesus we won't escape troubles, but we can take heart. With Jesus we will overcome any problem.

So ... How can you best use the words of the Bible to get encouragement when you encounter trouble?

Jesus Prays to Be Glorified

17 After Jesus said this, he looked toward heaven and prayed:

"Father, the hour has come. Glorify your Son, that your Son may glorify you. ²For you granted him authority over all people that he might give eternal life to all those you have given him. ³Now this is eternal life: that they know you, the only true God, and Jesus Christ, whom you have sent. ⁴I have brought you glory on earth by finishing the work you gave me to do. ⁵And now, Father, glorify me in your presence with the glory I had with you before the world began.

Jesus Prays for His Disciples

⁶"I have revealed you[a] to those whom you gave me out of the world. They were yours; you gave them to me and they have obeyed your word. ⁷Now they know that everything you have given me comes from you. ⁸For I gave them the words you gave me and they accepted them. They knew with certainty that I came from you, and they believed that you sent me. ⁹I pray for them. I am not praying for the world, but for those you have given me, for they are yours. ¹⁰All I have is yours, and all you have is mine. And glory has come to me through them. ¹¹I will remain in the world no longer, but they are still in the world, and I am coming to you. Holy Father, protect them by the power of[b] your name, the name you gave me, so that they may be one as we are one. ¹²While I was with them, I protected them and kept them safe by[c] that name you gave me. None has been lost except the one doomed to destruction so that Scripture would be fulfilled.

¹³"I am coming to you now, but I say these things while I am still in the world, so that they may have the full measure of my joy within them. ¹⁴I have given them your word and the world has hated them, for they are not of the world any more than I am of the world. ¹⁵My prayer is not that you take them out of the world but that you protect them from the evil one. ¹⁶They are not of the world, even as I am not of it. ¹⁷Sanctify them by[d] the truth; your word is truth. ¹⁸As you sent me into the world, I have sent them into the world. ¹⁹For them I sanctify myself, that they too may be truly sanctified.

Jesus Prays for All Believers

²⁰"My prayer is not for them alone. I pray also for those who will believe in me through their message, ²¹that all of them may be one, Father, just as you are in me and I am in you. May they also be in us so that the world may believe that you have sent me. ²²I have given them the glory that you gave me, that they may be one as we are one— ²³I in them and you in me—so that they may be brought to complete unity. Then the world will know that you sent me and have loved them even as you have loved me.

²⁴"Father, I want those you have given me to be with me where I am, and to see my glory, the glory you have given me because you loved me before the creation of the world.

²⁵"Righteous Father, though the world does not know you, I know you, and they know that you have sent me. ²⁶I have made you[a] known to them, and will continue to make you known in order that the love you have for me may be in them and that I myself may be in them."

Jesus Arrested

18 When he had finished praying, Jesus left with his disciples and crossed the Kidron Valley. On the other side there was a garden, and he and his disciples went into it. ²Now Judas, who betrayed him, knew

---

a 6,26 Greek *your name*   *b 11* Or *Father, keep them faithful to*   *c 12* Or *kept them faithful to*   *d 17* Or *them to live in accordance with* the place, because Jesus had often met there with his disciples. ³So Judas came to the garden, guiding a detachment of soldiers and some officials from the chief priests and the Pharisees. They were carrying torches, lanterns and weapons.

⁴Jesus, knowing all that was going to happen to him, went out and asked them, "Who is it you want?"

⁵"Jesus of Nazareth," they replied.

"I am he," Jesus said. (And Judas the traitor was standing there with them.) ⁶When Jesus said, "I am he," they drew back and fell to the ground.

⁷Again he asked them, "Who is it you want?"

"Jesus of Nazareth," they said.

⁸Jesus answered, "I told you that I am he. If you are looking for me, then let these men go." ⁹This happened so that the words he had spoken would be fulfilled: "I have not lost one of those you gave me."ᵃ

¹⁰Then Simon Peter, who had a sword, drew it and struck the high priest's servant, cutting off his right ear. (The servant's name was Malchus.)

¹¹Jesus commanded Peter, "Put your sword away! Shall I not drink the cup the Father has given me?"

¹²Then the detachment of soldiers with its commander and the Jewish officials arrested Jesus. They bound him ¹³and brought him first to Annas, who was the father-in-law of Caiaphas, the high priest that year. ¹⁴Caiaphas was the one who had advised the Jewish leaders that it would be good if one man died for the people.

Peter's First Denial

¹⁵Simon Peter and another disciple were following Jesus. Because this disciple was known to the high priest, he went with Jesus into the high priest's courtyard, ¹⁶but Peter had to wait outside at the door. The other disciple, who was known to the high priest, came back, spoke to the servant girl on duty there and brought Peter in.

¹⁷"You aren't one of this man's disciples too, are you?" she asked Peter.

He replied, "I am not."

¹⁸It was cold, and the servants and officials stood around a fire they had made to

keep warm. Peter also was standing with them, warming himself.

The High Priest Questions Jesus

¹⁹Meanwhile, the high priest questioned Jesus about his disciples and his teaching.

²⁰"I have spoken openly to the world," Jesus replied. "I always taught in synagogues or at the temple, where all the Jews come together. I said nothing in secret. ²¹Why question me? Ask those who heard me. Surely they know what I said."

²²When Jesus said this, one of the officials nearby slapped him in the face. "Is this the way you answer the high priest?" he demanded.

²³"If I said something wrong," Jesus replied, "testify as to what is wrong. But if I spoke the truth, why did you strike me?" ²⁴Then Annas sent him bound to Caiaphas the high priest.

Peter's Second and Third Denials

²⁵Meanwhile, Simon Peter was still standing there warming himself. So they asked him, "You aren't one of his disciples too, are you?"

He denied it, saying, "I am not."

²⁶One of the high priest's servants, a relative of the man whose ear Peter had cut off, challenged him, "Didn't I see you with him in the garden?" ²⁷Again Peter denied it, and at that moment a rooster began to crow.

Jesus Before Pilate

²⁸Then the Jewish leaders took Jesus from Caiaphas to the palace of the Roman governor. By now it was early morning, and to avoid ceremonial uncleanness they did not enter the palace, because they wanted to be able to eat the Passover. ²⁹So Pilate came out to them and asked, "What charges are you bringing against this man?"

³⁰"If he were not a criminal," they replied, "we would not have handed him over to you."

³¹Pilate said, "Take him yourselves and judge him by your own law."

"But we have no right to execute

ᵃ 9 John 6:39

anyone," they objected. ³²This took place to fulfill what Jesus had said about the kind of death he was going to die.

³³Pilate then went back inside the palace, summoned Jesus and asked him, "Are you the king of the Jews?"

³⁴"Is that your own idea," Jesus asked, "or did others talk to you about me?"

³⁵"Am I a Jew?" Pilate replied. "Your own people and chief priests handed you over to me. What is it you have done?"

³⁶Jesus said, "My kingdom is not of this world. If it were, my servants would fight to prevent my arrest by the Jewish leaders. But now my kingdom is from another place."

³⁷"You are a king, then!" said Pilate.

Jesus answered, "You say that I am a king. In fact, the reason I was born and came into the world is to testify to the truth. Everyone on the side of truth listens to me."

³⁸"What is truth?" retorted Pilate. With this he went out again to the Jews gathered there and said, "I find no basis for a charge against him. ³⁹But it is your custom for me to release to you one prisoner at the time of the Passover. Do you want me to release 'the king of the Jews'?"

⁴⁰They shouted back, "No, not him! Give us Barabbas!" Now Barabbas had taken part in an uprising.

Jesus Sentenced to Be Crucified

19 Then Pilate took Jesus and had him flogged. ²The soldiers twisted together a crown of thorns and put it on his head. They clothed him in a purple robe ³and went up to him again and again, saying, "Hail, king of the Jews!" And they slapped him in the face.

⁴Once more Pilate came out and said to the Jews gathered there, "Look, I am bringing him out to you to let you know that I find no basis for a charge against him." ⁵When Jesus came out wearing the crown of thorns and the purple robe, Pilate said to them, "Here is the man!"

⁶As soon as the chief priests and their officials saw him, they shouted, "Crucify! Crucify!"

But Pilate answered, "You take him and crucify him. As for me, I find no basis for a charge against him."

⁷The Jewish leaders insisted, "We have a law, and according to that law he must die, because he claimed to be the Son of God."

⁸When Pilate heard this, he was even more afraid, ⁹and he went back inside the palace. "Where do you come from?" he asked Jesus, but Jesus gave him no answer. ¹⁰"Do you refuse to speak to me?" Pilate said. "Don't you realize I have power either to free you or to crucify you?"

¹¹Jesus answered, "You would have no power over me if it were not given to you from above. Therefore the one who handed me over to you is guilty of a greater sin."

¹²From then on, Pilate tried to set Jesus free, but the Jewish leaders kept shouting, "If you let this man go, you are no friend of Caesar. Anyone who claims to be a king opposes Caesar."

¹³When Pilate heard this, he brought Jesus out and sat down on the judge's seat at a place known as the Stone Pavement (which in Aramaic is Gabbatha). ¹⁴It was the day of Preparation of the Passover; it was about noon.

"Here is your king," Pilate said to the Jews.

¹⁵But they shouted, "Take him away! Take him away! Crucify him!"

"Shall I crucify your king?" Pilate asked.

"We have no king but Caesar," the chief priests answered.

¹⁶Finally Pilate handed him over to them to be crucified.

The Crucifixion of Jesus

So the soldiers took charge of Jesus. ¹⁷Carrying his own cross, he went out to the place of the Skull (which in Aramaic is called Golgotha). ¹⁸There they crucified him, and with him two others—one on each side and Jesus in the middle.

¹⁹Pilate had a notice prepared and fastened to the cross. It read: JESUS OF NAZARETH, THE KING OF THE JEWS. ²⁰Many of the Jews read this sign, for the place where Jesus was crucified was near the city, and the sign was written in Aramaic,

Latin and Greek. ²¹The chief priests of the Jews protested to Pilate, "Do not write 'The King of the Jews,' but that this man claimed to be king of the Jews."

²²Pilate answered, "What I have written, I have written."

²³When the soldiers crucified Jesus, they took his clothes, dividing them into four shares, one for each of them, with the undergarment remaining. This garment was seamless, woven in one piece from top to bottom.

²⁴"Let's not tear it," they said to one another. "Let's decide by lot who will get it."

This happened that the scripture might be fulfilled that said,

"They divided my clothes among them
and cast lots for my garment."[a]

So this is what the soldiers did.

²⁵Near the cross of Jesus stood his mother, his mother's sister, Mary the wife of Clopas, and Mary Magdalene. ²⁶When Jesus saw his mother there, and the disciple whom he loved standing nearby, he said to her, "Woman,[b] here is your son," ²⁷and to the disciple, "Here is your mother." From that time on, this disciple took her into his home.

[a] 24 Psalm 22:18   [b] 26 The Greek for *Woman* does not denote any disrespect.

John 19:25–27

John lived tight with Jesus.

While John never claimed he was Jesus' best friend, the New Testament book that bears his name repeatedly calls him "the disciple whom Jesus loved" (John 13:23; 19:26; 20:2; 21:7,20).

John followed Jesus right from the start, when the Lord called him away from his profession as a fisherman (see Mark 1:19–20). John witnessed the biggest events of Jesus' life, including the Transfiguration, where the Lord shone with heavenly splendor (see Matthew 17:1–8). The night before Jesus went to the cross, John leaned up against his friend as they and the other disciples shared a last supper together (see John 13:23). Along with Peter and James, John went with Jesus to the Garden of Gethsemane, where the Lord sweat drops of blood, agonizing in prayer (see Luke 22:44). As Jesus was dying on the cross, he trusted his good friend John with the job of caring for his mother, Mary (see John 19:25–27). And after Jesus rose from the dead, John ran along with Peter to see the empty tomb (see John 20:3–9).

Even after Jesus left earth and ascended to heaven, John continued as the Lord's loyal friend. John unashamedly defended his faith in Jesus to religious authorities (see Acts 3–4). He was eventually banished to the Island of Patmos, where he had a vision of Jesus and the end of the world and penned the book of Revelation (see Revelation 1:1).

You can find John in Matthew 20:20–24; Mark 1:19; Acts 8:14–25; and also in John 21:2, where he is called one of "the sons of Zebedee."

UNSHAKEN *people*

The Death of Jesus

²⁸Later, knowing that everything had now been finished, and so that Scripture would be fulfilled, Jesus said, "I am thirsty." ²⁹A jar of wine vinegar was there, so they soaked a sponge in it, put the sponge on a stalk of the hyssop plant, and lifted it to Jesus' lips. ³⁰When he had received the drink, Jesus said, "It is finished." With that, he bowed his head and gave up his spirit.

³¹Now it was the day of Preparation, and the next day was to be a special Sabbath. Because the Jewish leaders did not want the bodies left on the crosses during the Sabbath, they asked Pilate to have the legs broken and the bodies taken down. ³²The soldiers therefore came and broke the legs of the first man who had been crucified with Jesus, and then those of the other. ³³But when they came to Jesus and found that he was already dead, they did not break his legs. ³⁴Instead, one of the soldiers pierced Jesus' side with a spear, bringing a sudden flow of blood and water. ³⁵The man who saw it has given testimony, and his testimony is true. He knows that he tells the truth, and he testifies so that you also may believe. ³⁶These things happened so that the scripture would be fulfilled: "Not one of his bones will be broken,"ᵃ ³⁷and, as another scripture says, "They will look on the one they have pierced."ᵇ

The Burial of Jesus

³⁸Later, Joseph of Arimathea asked Pilate for the body of Jesus. Now Joseph was a disciple of Jesus, but secretly because he feared the Jewish leaders. With Pilate's permission, he came and took the body away. ³⁹He was accompanied by Nicodemus, the man who earlier had visited Jesus at night. Nicodemus brought a mixture of myrrh and aloes, about seventy-five pounds.ᶜ ⁴⁰Taking Jesus' body, the two of them wrapped it, with the spices, in strips of linen. This was in accordance with Jewish burial customs. ⁴¹At the place where Jesus was crucified, there was a garden, and in the garden a new tomb, in which no one had ever been laid. ⁴²Because it was the Jewish day of Preparation and since the tomb was nearby, they laid Jesus there.

The Empty Tomb

20 Early on the first day of the week, while it was still dark, Mary Magdalene went to the tomb and saw that the stone had been removed from the entrance. ²So she came running to Simon Peter and the other disciple, the one Jesus loved, and said, "They have taken the Lord out of the tomb, and we don't know where they have put him!"

³So Peter and the other disciple started for the tomb. ⁴Both were running, but the other disciple outran Peter and reached the tomb first. ⁵He bent over and looked in at the strips of linen lying there but did not go in. ⁶Then Simon Peter came along behind him and went straight into the tomb. He saw the strips of linen lying there, ⁷as well as the cloth that had been wrapped around Jesus' head. The cloth was still lying in its place, separate from the linen. ⁸Finally the other disciple, who had reached the tomb first, also went inside. He saw and believed. ⁹(They still did not understand from Scripture that Jesus had to rise from the dead.) ¹⁰Then the disciples went back to where they were staying.

Jesus Appears to Mary Magdalene

¹¹Now Mary stood outside the tomb crying. As she wept, she bent over to look into the tomb ¹²and saw two angels in white, seated where Jesus' body had been, one at the head and the other at the foot.

¹³They asked her, "Woman, why are you crying?"

"They have taken my Lord away," she said, "and I don't know where they have put him." ¹⁴At this, she turned around and saw Jesus standing there, but she did not realize that it was Jesus.

¹⁵He asked her, "Woman, why are you crying? Who is it you are looking for?"

ᵃ 36 Exodus 12:46; Num. 9:12; Psalm 34:20
ᵇ 37 Zech. 12:10   ᶜ 39 Or about 34 kilograms

Thinking he was the gardener, she said, "Sir, if you have carried him away, tell me where you have put him, and I will get him."

¹⁶Jesus said to her, "Mary."

She turned toward him and cried out in Aramaic, "Rabboni!" (which means "Teacher").

¹⁷Jesus said, "Do not hold on to me, for I have not yet ascended to the Father. Go instead to my brothers and tell them, 'I am ascending to my Father and your Father, to my God and your God.'"

¹⁸Mary Magdalene went to the disciples with the news: "I have seen the Lord!" And she told them that he had said these things to her.

Jesus Appears to His Disciples

¹⁹On the evening of that first day of the week, when the disciples were together, with the doors locked for fear of the Jewish leaders, Jesus came and stood among them and said, "Peace be with you!" ²⁰After he said this, he showed them his hands and side. The disciples were overjoyed when they saw the Lord.

²¹Again Jesus said, "Peace be with you! As the Father has sent me, I am sending you." ²²And with that he breathed on them and said, "Receive the Holy Spirit. ²³If you forgive anyone's sins, their sins are forgiven; if you do not forgive them, they are not forgiven."

Jesus Appears to Thomas

²⁴Now Thomas (also known as Didymus[a]), one of the Twelve, was not with the disciples when Jesus came. ²⁵So the other disciples told him, "We have seen the Lord!"

But he said to them, "Unless I see the nail marks in his hands and put my finger where the nails were, and put my hand into his side, I will not believe."

²⁶A week later his disciples were in the house again, and Thomas was with them. Though the doors were locked, Jesus came and stood among them and said, "Peace be with you!" ²⁷Then he said to Thomas, "Put your finger here; see my hands.

Reach out your hand and put it into my side. Stop doubting and believe."

²⁸Thomas said to him, "My Lord and my God!"

²⁹Then Jesus told him, "Because you have seen me, you have believed; blessed are those who have not seen and yet have believed."

a 24 Thomas (Aramaic) and *Didymus* (Greek) both mean *twin*.

John 20:1–31

Jesus rose from the dead.

Jesus didn't just die. He rose from the dead. He wasn't resurrected just as some sort of spirit, but as actual flesh and blood. And that fact is hugely important, a core truth about Jesus that believers have declared from the beginning. One of the most amazing sentences in the Bible is "He is not here; he has risen" (Matthew 28:6). Those words echo through all of the accounts of the risen Jesus. In John 20 you see Mary Magdalene, Simon Peter, and "the other disciple" (the John who wrote this book) all discover the empty tomb. Soon Jesus talks one-on-one to Mary. He then appears to his closest followers, and finally to Thomas, who genuinely doubted Jesus was alive. Because Jesus rose from the grave, he lives and rules as Lord. The resurrection proves Jesus is the Son of God (see Romans 1:4). And it shows that one day you too will rise and live forever (see John 11:25–26).

Think: How would your faith be different if Jesus was still in the grave?

ROCK SOLID truths

The Purpose of John's Gospel

[30]Jesus performed many other signs in the presence of his disciples, which are not recorded in this book. [31]But these are written that you may believe[a] that Jesus is the Messiah, the Son of God, and that by believing you may have life in his name.

Jesus and the Miraculous Catch of Fish

21 Afterward Jesus appeared again to his disciples, by the Sea of Galilee.[b] It happened this way: [2]Simon Peter, Thomas (also known as Didymus[c]), Nathanael from Cana in Galilee, the sons of Zebedee, and two other disciples were together. [3]"I'm going out to fish," Simon Peter told them, and they said, "We'll go with you." So they went out and got into the boat, but that night they caught nothing.

[4]Early in the morning, Jesus stood on the shore, but the disciples did not realize that it was Jesus.

[5]He called out to them, "Friends, haven't you any fish?"

"No," they answered.

[6]He said, "Throw your net on the right

a 31 Or *may continue to believe* *b 1* Greek *Tiberias* *c 2 Thomas* (Aramaic) and *Didymus* (Greek) both mean *twin.*

John 20:24–31

Thomas checked the facts about Jesus.

Thomas missed out the first time the disciples saw Jesus after he had risen from the dead. He was one of the Lord's twelve closest followers, but he wasn't with the other guys as they hid for fear of being killed. The doors of their hideaway were locked tight, but suddenly Jesus appeared among them. As he stood in their midst, they saw firsthand his resurrected body, complete with the wounds he suffered on the cross (see John 20:19–23).

Thomas refused to believe the other disciples had seen Jesus alive from the dead. He vowed he wouldn't accept their story as fact unless he touched the holes torn in Jesus' hands—the places where he was nailed to the cross. He wanted to put his hand in the Lord's side—a gaping hole where a Roman soldier's spear had pierced his dead body.

Not much later, Jesus again appeared in a locked room. But this time Thomas was present to meet the risen Jesus. The Lord dared him to touch his hands and side, but Thomas had seen enough. He exclaimed his belief in Jesus, declaring, "My Lord and my God!" (John 20:28). Thomas not only grasped that Jesus lives, but that he is God.

This tough-minded disciple often gets a bad reputation as "Doubting Thomas." But for everyone who wonders whether the Lord's disciples were gullible fools, Thomas offers evidence that Jesus really lives. He checked the facts about Jesus before he accepted them as truth.

You can find Thomas in Matthew 10:2–4; John 11:16; 14:1–7; 20:19–29; 21:2; and Acts 1:13.

UNSHAKEN people

side of the boat and you will find some." When they did, they were unable to haul the net in because of the large number of fish.

⁷Then the disciple whom Jesus loved said to Peter, "It is the Lord!" As soon as Simon Peter heard him say, "It is the Lord," he wrapped his outer garment around him (for he had taken it off) and jumped into the water. ⁸The other disciples followed in the boat, towing the net full of fish, for they were not far from shore, about a hundred yards.ᵃ ⁹When they landed, they saw a fire of burning coals there with fish on it, and some bread.

¹⁰Jesus said to them, "Bring some of the fish you have just caught." ¹¹So Simon Peter climbed back into the boat and dragged the net ashore. It was full of large fish, 153, but even with so many the net was not torn. ¹²Jesus said to them, "Come and have breakfast." None of the disciples dared ask him, "Who are you?" They knew it was the Lord. ¹³Jesus came, took the bread and gave it to them, and did the same with the fish. ¹⁴This was now the third time Jesus appeared to his disciples after he was raised from the dead.

Jesus Reinstates Peter

¹⁵When they had finished eating, Jesus said to Simon Peter, "Simon son of John, do you love me more than these?"

"Yes, Lord," he said, "you know that I love you."

Jesus said, "Feed my lambs."

¹⁶Again Jesus said, "Simon son of John, do you love me?"

He answered, "Yes, Lord, you know that I love you."

Jesus said, "Take care of my sheep."

¹⁷The third time he said to him, "Simon son of John, do you love me?"

Peter was hurt because Jesus asked him the third time, "Do you love me?" He said, "Lord, you know all things; you know that I love you."

Jesus said, "Feed my sheep. ¹⁸Very truly I tell you, when you were younger you dressed yourself and went where you wanted; but when you are old you will stretch out your hands, and someone else will dress you and lead you where you do not want to go." ¹⁹Jesus said this to indicate the kind of death by which Peter would glorify God. Then he said to him, "Follow me!"

²⁰Peter turned and saw that the disciple whom Jesus loved was following them. (This was the one who had leaned back against Jesus at the supper and had said, "Lord, who is going to betray you?") ²¹When Peter saw him, he asked, "Lord, what about him?"

²²Jesus answered, "If I want him to remain alive until I return, what is that to you? You must follow me." ²³Because of this, the rumor spread among the believers that this disciple would not die. But Jesus did not say that he would not die; he only said, "If I want him to remain alive until I return, what is that to you?"

²⁴This is the disciple who testifies to these things and who wrote them down. We know that his testimony is true.

²⁵Jesus did many other things as well. If every one of them were written down, I suppose that even the whole world would not have room for the books that would be written.

ᵃ 8 Or about 90 meters

BOOK OUTLINE

The book of Acts is a record of the acts of the apostles and is often called by that name. It can also be called "The Acts of the Holy Spirit" because it teaches about the coming and work of the Spirit in the early Christian church. Acts is the second part of Luke's history. It was written so we would have the true story of how the Christian church began and grew.

This book focuses on the work of two of the apostles—Peter and Paul. Peter is the central person involved in beginning the church in Jerusalem. Paul is the important missionary who traveled to nearby countries to tell others about Christ.

The book of Acts teaches three things about the early church: (1) what the message of the early church was; (2) how the Jews rejected this message and how God sent the apostles to the Gentiles, who accepted the gospel; and (3) how the early church was treated by the local and Roman governments.

Jesus Taken Up Into Heaven

1 In my former book, Theophilus, I wrote about all that Jesus began to do and to teach ²until the day he was taken up to heaven, after giving instructions through the Holy Spirit to the apostles he had chosen. ³After his suffering, he presented himself to them and gave many convincing proofs that he was alive. He appeared to them over a period of forty days and spoke about the kingdom of God. ⁴On one occasion, while he was eating with them, he gave them this command: "Do not leave Jerusalem, but wait for the gift my Father promised, which you have heard me speak about. ⁵For John baptized with*ᵃ* water, but in a few days you will be baptized with*ᵃ* the Holy Spirit."

⁶Then they gathered around him and asked him, "Lord, are you at this time going to restore the kingdom to Israel?"

⁷He said to them: "It is not for you to know the times or dates the Father has set by his own authority. ⁸But you will receive power when the Holy Spirit comes on you; and you will be my witnesses in Jerusalem, and in all Judea and Samaria, and to the ends of the earth."

⁹After he said this, he was taken up before their very eyes, and a cloud hid him from their sight.

¹⁰They were looking intently up into the sky as he was going, when suddenly two men dressed in white stood beside them. ¹¹"Men of Galilee," they said, "why do you stand here looking into the sky? This same Jesus, who has been taken from you into heaven, will come back in the same way you have seen him go into heaven."

Matthias Chosen to Replace Judas

¹²Then the apostles returned to Jerusalem from the hill called the Mount of Olives, a Sabbath day's walk*ᵇ* from the city. ¹³When they arrived, they went upstairs to the room where they were staying. Those present were Peter, John, James and Andrew; Philip and Thomas, Bartholomew and Matthew; James son of Alphaeus and Simon the Zealot, and Judas son of James. ¹⁴They all joined together constantly in prayer, along with the women and Mary the mother of Jesus, and with his brothers.

¹⁵In those days Peter stood up among the believers (a group numbering about a hundred and twenty) ¹⁶and said, "Brothers and sisters,*ᶜ* the Scripture had to be fulfilled in which the Holy Spirit spoke long ago through David concerning Judas, who served as guide for those who arrested Jesus. ¹⁷He was one of our number and shared in our ministry."

¹⁸(With the payment he received for his wickedness, Judas bought a field; there he fell headlong, his body burst open and all his intestines spilled out. ¹⁹Everyone in Jerusalem heard about this, so they called that field in their language Akeldama, that is, Field of Blood.)

²⁰"For," said Peter, "it is written in the Book of Psalms:

"'May his place be deserted; let there be no one to dwell in it,'*ᵈ*

ROCK SOLID
promises

"But you will receive power when the Holy Spirit comes on you; and you will be my witnesses in Jerusalem, and in all Judea and Samaria, and to the ends of the earth." Acts 1:8

God will give you everything you need to tell others about him, from your neighborhood to the other side of the world.

ᵃ 5 Or *in*   *ᵇ 12* That is, about 5/8 mile or about 1 kilometer   *ᶜ 16* The Greek word for *brothers and sisters (adelphoi)* refers here to believers, both men and women, as part of God's family; also in 6:3; 11:29; 12:17; 16:40; 18:18, 27; 21:7, 17; 28:14, 15.   *ᵈ 20* Psalm 69:25

Acts 1:1–11

Jesus returned to heaven.

The Bible doesn't leave any question where Jesus came from. Before he was born on earth as a human being, he existed in heaven, possessing all the majesty that belongs to him as God (see John 17:5). Then he "became flesh and made his dwelling among us" (John 1:14). Forty days after Jesus rose from the dead, he returned to heaven. As he was speaking with his disciples, "he was taken up before their very eyes, and a cloud hid him from their sight" (Acts 1:9). Luke explains, "While he was blessing them, he left them and was taken up into heaven" (Luke 24:51). Jesus will come again to earth, his "second coming." But for now he "has gone into heaven and is at God's right hand—with angels, authorities and powers in submission to him" (1 Peter 3:22). Being at "God's right hand" means he rules everything. That includes you.

Think: Is it good—or bad— that Jesus is in heaven right now? Why?

ROCK SOLID truths

and,

"'May another take his place of leadership.'*a*

21 Therefore it is necessary to choose one of the men who have been with us the whole time the Lord Jesus was living among us, 22 beginning from John's baptism to the time when Jesus was taken up from us. For one of these must become a witness with us of his resurrection." 23 So they nominated two men: Joseph

called Barsabbas (also known as Justus) and Matthias. 24 Then they prayed, "Lord, you know everyone's heart. Show us which of these two you have chosen 25 to take over this apostolic ministry, which Judas left to go where he belongs." 26 Then they cast lots, and the lot fell to Matthias; so he was added to the eleven apostles.

The Holy Spirit Comes at Pentecost

2 When the day of Pentecost came, they were all together in one place. 2 Suddenly a sound like the blowing of a violent wind came from heaven and filled the whole house where they were sitting. 3 They saw what seemed to be tongues of fire that separated and came to rest on each of them. 4 All of them were filled with the Holy Spirit and began to speak in other tongues*b* as the Spirit enabled them.

5 Now there were staying in Jerusalem God-fearing Jews from every nation under heaven. 6 When they heard this sound, a crowd came together in bewilderment, because each one heard their own language being spoken. 7 Utterly amazed, they asked: "Aren't all these who are speaking Galileans? 8 Then how is it that each of us hears them in our native language? 9 Parthians, Medes and Elamites; residents of Mesopotamia, Judea and Cappadocia, Pontus and Asia,*c* 10 Phrygia and Pamphylia, Egypt and the parts of Libya near Cyrene; visitors from Rome 11 (both Jews and converts to Judaism); Cretans and Arabs—we hear them declaring the wonders of God in our own tongues!" 12 Amazed and perplexed, they asked one another, "What does this mean?"

13 Some, however, made fun of them and said, "They have had too much wine."

Peter Addresses the Crowd

14 Then Peter stood up with the Eleven, raised his voice and addressed the crowd: "Fellow Jews and all of you who live in Jerusalem, let me explain this to you; listen carefully to what I say. 15 These people are not drunk, as you suppose. It's only nine in

a 20 Psalm 109:8   *b 4* Or *languages*; also in verse 11   *c 9* That is, the Roman province by that name the morning! ¹⁶No, this is what was spoken by the prophet Joel:

¹⁷"'In the last days, God says,
  I will pour out my Spirit on all
    people.
Your sons and daughters will prophesy,
  your young men will see visions,
  your old men will dream dreams.
¹⁸Even on my servants, both men and
    women,
  I will pour out my Spirit in those days,
    and they will prophesy.
¹⁹I will show wonders in the heavens
    above
  and signs on the earth below,
  blood and fire and billows of smoke.
²⁰The sun will be turned to darkness
    and the moon to blood
  before the coming of the great and
    glorious day of the Lord.
²¹And everyone who calls
  on the name of the Lord will be
    saved.'^a

²²"Fellow Israelites, listen to this: Jesus of Nazareth was a man accredited by God to you by miracles, wonders and signs, which God did among you through him, as you yourselves know. ²³This man was handed over to you by God's deliberate plan and foreknowledge; and you, with the help of wicked men,^b put him to death by nailing him to the cross. ²⁴But God raised him from the dead, freeing him from the agony of death, because it was impossible for death to keep its hold on him. ²⁵David said about him:

"'I saw the Lord always before me.
  Because he is at my right hand,
  I will not be shaken.
²⁶Therefore my heart is glad and my
    tongue rejoices;
  my body also will rest in hope,
²⁷because you will not abandon me to
    the realm of the dead,
  you will not let your holy one see
    decay.
²⁸You have made known to me the paths
    of life;
  you will fill me with joy in your
    presence.'^c

²⁹"Fellow Israelites, I can tell you confidently that the patriarch David died and was buried, and his tomb is here to this day. ³⁰But he was a prophet and knew that God had promised him on oath that he would place one of his descendants on his throne. ³¹Seeing what was to come, he spoke of the resurrection of the Messiah, that he was not abandoned to the realm of the dead, nor did his body see decay. ³²God has raised this Jesus to life, and we are all witnesses of it. ³³Exalted to the right hand of God, he has received from the Father the promised Holy Spirit and has poured out what you now see and hear. ³⁴For David did not ascend to heaven, and yet he said,

"'The Lord said to my Lord:
  "Sit at my right hand
³⁵until I make your enemies
  a footstool for your feet."'^d

³⁶"Therefore let all Israel be assured of this: God has made this Jesus, whom you crucified, both Lord and Messiah."

³⁷When the people heard this, they were cut to the heart and said to Peter and the other apostles, "Brothers, what shall we do?"

³⁸Peter replied, "Repent and be baptized, every one of you, in the name of Jesus Christ for the forgiveness of your sins. And you will receive the gift of the Holy Spirit. ³⁹The promise is for you and your children and for all who are far off—for all whom the Lord our God will call."

⁴⁰With many other words he warned them; and he pleaded with them, "Save yourselves from this corrupt generation." ⁴¹Those who accepted his message were baptized, and about three thousand were added to their number that day.

The Fellowship of the Believers

⁴²They devoted themselves to the apostles' teaching and to fellowship, to the breaking of bread and to prayer. ⁴³Everyone was filled with awe at the many wonders

---

^a 21 Joel 2:28-32   ^b 23 Or of those not having the law (that is, Gentiles)   ^c 28 Psalm 16:8-11 (see Septuagint)   ^d 35 Psalm 110:1

and signs performed by the apostles. ⁴⁴All the believers were together and had everything in common. ⁴⁵They sold property and possessions to give to anyone who had need. ⁴⁶Every day they continued to meet together in the temple courts. They broke bread in their homes and ate together with glad and sincere hearts, ⁴⁷praising God and enjoying the favor of all the people. And the Lord added to their number daily those who were being saved.

Peter Heals a Lame Beggar

3 One day Peter and John were going up to the temple at the time of prayer—at three in the afternoon. ²Now a man who was lame from birth was being carried to the temple gate called Beautiful, where he was put every day to beg from those going into the temple courts. ³When he saw Peter and John about to enter, he asked them for money. ⁴Peter looked straight at him, as did John. Then Peter said, "Look at us!" ⁵So

the man gave them his attention, expecting to get something from them.

⁶Then Peter said, "Silver or gold I do not have, but what I do have I give you. In the name of Jesus Christ of Nazareth, walk." ⁷Taking him by the right hand, he helped him up, and instantly the man's feet and ankles became strong. ⁸He jumped to his feet and began to walk. Then he went with them into the temple courts, walking and jumping, and praising God. ⁹When all the people saw him walking and praising God, ¹⁰they recognized him as the same man who used to sit begging at the temple gate called Beautiful, and they were filled with wonder and amazement at what had happened to him.

Peter Speaks to the Onlookers

¹¹While the man held on to Peter and John, all the people were astonished and came running to them in the place called Solomon's Colonnade. ¹²When Peter saw this, he said to them: "Fellow Isra-

ROCK SOLID principles

Acts 2:42–47

Get together with other Christians to grow.

No one in Jonah's youth group thought it would do much good to try to spread their faith to their friends. Even Jonah was skeptical. "No one wants to hear about Jesus," he said. "We're just going to turn our friends into enemies." One by one, however, new faces started showing up at the group's Bible study, each full of spiritual questions. Many met Jesus and stuck around. As the group started to ask, "What now?" Jonah's youth pastor pointed them to Acts 2. The group saw how early Christians talked about Jesus, added to their group, and got together to grow. The basics of growing together weren't hard to figure out.

These few short verses describe the amazing first days of the church. Three thousand people had just accepted the message of Jesus (see Acts 2:41). Now they devoted themselves to study ... doing life together ... eating together ... praying ... with the result that even more people met Jesus. If you want to get more of Jesus, first get together with other believers.

elites, why does this surprise you? Why do you stare at us as if by our own power or godliness we had made this man walk? [13] The God of Abraham, Isaac and Jacob, the God of our fathers, has glorified his servant Jesus. You handed him over to be killed, and you disowned him before Pilate, though he had decided to let him go. [14] You disowned the Holy and Righteous One and asked that a murderer be released to you. [15] You killed the author of life, but God raised him from the dead. We are witnesses of this. [16] By faith in the name of Jesus, this man whom you see and know was made strong. It is Jesus' name and the faith that comes through him that has completely healed him, as you can all see.

[17] "Now, fellow Israelites, I know that you acted in ignorance, as did your leaders. [18] But this is how God fulfilled what he had foretold through all the prophets, saying that his Messiah would suffer. [19] Repent, then, and turn to God, so that your sins may be wiped out, that times of refreshing may come from the Lord, [20] and that he may send the Messiah, who has been appointed for you — even Jesus. [21] Heaven must receive him until the time comes for God to restore everything, as he promised long ago through his holy prophets. [22] For Moses said, 'The Lord your God will raise up for you a prophet like me from among your own people; you must listen to everything he tells you. [23] Anyone who does not listen to him will be completely cut off from their people.'[a]

[24] "Indeed, beginning with Samuel, all the prophets who have spoken have foretold these days. [25] And you are heirs of the prophets and of the covenant God made with your fathers. He said to Abraham, 'Through your offspring all peoples on earth will be blessed.'[b] [26] When God raised up his servant, he sent him first to you to bless you by turning each of you from your wicked ways."

Peter and John Before the Sanhedrin

4 The priests and the captain of the temple guard and the Sadducees came up to Peter and John while they were speaking to the people. [2] They were greatly disturbed because the apostles were teaching the people, proclaiming in Jesus the resurrection of the dead. [3] They seized Peter and John and, because it was evening, they put them in jail until the next day. [4] But many who heard the message believed; so the number of men who believed grew to about five thousand.

[5] The next day the rulers, the elders and the teachers of the law met in Jerusalem. [6] Annas the high priest was there, and so were Caiaphas, John, Alexander and others of the high priest's family. [7] They had Peter and John brought before them and began to question them: "By what power or what name did you do this?"

[8] Then Peter, filled with the Holy Spirit, said to them: "Rulers and elders of the people! [9] If we are being called to account today for an act of kindness shown to a man who was lame and are being asked how he was healed, [10] then know this, you and all the people of Israel: It is by the name of Jesus Christ of Nazareth, whom you crucified but whom God raised from the dead, that this man stands before you healed. [11] Jesus is

" 'the stone you builders rejected,
    which has become the cornerstone.'[c]

[12] Salvation is found in no one else, for there is no other name under heaven given to mankind by which we must be saved."

[13] When they saw the courage of Peter and John and realized that they were unschooled, ordinary men, they were astonished and they took note that these men had been with Jesus. [14] But since they could see the man who had been healed standing there with them, there was nothing they could say. [15] So they ordered them to withdraw from the Sanhedrin and then conferred together. [16] "What are we going to do with these men?" they asked. "Everyone living in Jerusalem knows they have performed a notable sign, and we cannot deny it. [17] But to stop this thing from spreading any further among the people, we must warn them to speak no longer to anyone in this name."

[a] 23 Deut. 18:15,18,19   [b] 25 Gen. 22:18; 26:4   [c] 11 Psalm 118:22

[18] Then they called them in again and commanded them not to speak or teach at all in the name of Jesus. [19] But Peter and John replied, "Which is right in God's eyes: to listen to you, or to him? You be the judges! [20] As for us, we cannot help speaking about what we have seen and heard."

[21] After further threats they let them go. They could not decide how to punish them, because all the people were praising God for what had happened. [22] For the man who was miraculously healed was over forty years old.

Acts 4:1–22

Only Jesus saves.

Critics of Christianity fiercely deny that Christianity is the one true religion—and that Jesus is the one Savior for all people in all times and all places. While people might dislike these "exclusive" claims, they are an essential part of Bible teaching. Jesus himself said, "I am the way and the truth and the life. No one comes to the Father except through me" (John 14:6). When early Christians were persecuted by opposing religious leaders, Peter boldly declared that God raised Jesus from the dead and that "salvation is found in no one else, for there is no other name under heaven given to mankind by which we must be saved" (Acts 4:12). Jesus is the one way we get "salvation." He is the only way we can be forgiven, become friends with God, and begin to escape bad habits of sin.

Think: How would you convince a friend that faith in Jesus is the only way to be saved?

ROCK SOLID truths

The Believers Pray

[23] On their release, Peter and John went back to their own people and reported all that the chief priests and the elders had said to them. [24] When they heard this, they raised their voices together in prayer to God. "Sovereign Lord," they said, "you made the heavens and the earth and the sea, and everything in them. [25] You spoke by the Holy Spirit through the mouth of your servant, our father David:

"'Why do the nations rage
　and the peoples plot in vain?
[26] The kings of the earth rise up
　and the rulers band together
against the Lord
　and against his anointed one.'[a][b]

[27] Indeed Herod and Pontius Pilate met together with the Gentiles and the people of Israel in this city to conspire against your holy servant Jesus, whom you anointed. [28] They did what your power and will had decided beforehand should happen. [29] Now, Lord, consider their threats and enable your servants to speak your word with great boldness. [30] Stretch out your hand to heal and perform signs and wonders through the name of your holy servant Jesus."

[31] After they prayed, the place where they were meeting was shaken. And they were all filled with the Holy Spirit and spoke the word of God boldly.

The Believers Share Their Possessions

[32] All the believers were one in heart and mind. No one claimed that any of their possessions was their own, but they shared everything they had. [33] With great power the apostles continued to testify to the resurrection of the Lord Jesus. And God's grace was so powerfully at work in them all [34] that there were no needy persons among them. For from time to time those who owned land or houses sold them, brought the money from the sales [35] and put it at the apostles' feet, and it was distributed to anyone who had need.

[a] 26 That is, Messiah or Christ
[b] 26 Psalm 2:1,2

[36] Joseph, a Levite from Cyprus, whom the apostles called Barnabas (which means "son of encouragement"), [37] sold a field he owned and brought the money and put it at the apostles' feet.

Ananias and Sapphira

5 Now a man named Ananias, together with his wife Sapphira, also sold a piece of property. [2] With his wife's full knowledge he kept back part of the money for himself, but brought the rest and put it at the apostles' feet.

[3] Then Peter said, "Ananias, how is it that Satan has so filled your heart that you have lied to the Holy Spirit and have kept for yourself some of the money you received for the land? [4] Didn't it belong to you before it was sold? And after it was sold, wasn't the money at your disposal? What made you think of doing such a thing? You have not lied just to human beings but to God."

[5] When Ananias heard this, he fell down and died. And great fear seized all who heard what had happened. [6] Then some young men came forward, wrapped up his body, and carried him out and buried him.

[7] About three hours later his wife came in, not knowing what had happened. [8] Peter asked her, "Tell me, is this the price you and Ananias got for the land?"

"Yes," she said, "that is the price."

[9] Peter said to her, "How could you conspire to test the Spirit of the Lord? Listen! The feet of the men who buried your husband are at the door, and they will carry you out also."

[10] At that moment she fell down at his feet and died. Then the young men came in and, finding her dead, carried her out and buried her beside her husband. [11] Great fear seized the whole church and all who heard about these events.

The Apostles Heal Many

[12] The apostles performed many signs and wonders among the people. And all the believers used to meet together in Solomon's Colonnade. [13] No one else dared join them, even though they were highly regarded by the people. [14] Nevertheless, more and more men and women believed in the Lord and were added to their number. [15] As a result, people brought the sick into the streets and laid them on beds and mats so that at least Peter's shadow might fall on some of them as he passed by. [16] Crowds gathered also from the towns around Jerusalem, bringing their sick and those tormented by impure spirits, and all of them were healed.

The Apostles Persecuted

[17] Then the high priest and all his associates, who were members of the party of the Sadducees, were filled with jealousy. [18] They arrested the apostles and put them in the public jail. [19] But during the night an angel of the Lord opened the doors of the jail and brought them out. [20] "Go, stand in the temple courts," he said, "and tell the people all about this new life."

[21] At daybreak they entered the temple courts, as they had been told, and began to teach the people.

When the high priest and his associates arrived, they called together the Sanhedrin—the full assembly of the elders of Israel—and sent to the jail for the apostles. [22] But on arriving at the jail, the officers did not find them there. So they went back and reported, [23] "We found the jail securely locked, with the guards standing at the doors; but when we opened them, we found no one inside." [24] On hearing this report, the captain of the temple guard and the chief priests were at a loss, wondering what this might lead to.

[25] Then someone came and said, "Look! The men you put in jail are standing in the temple courts teaching the people." [26] At that, the captain went with his officers and brought the apostles. They did not use force, because they feared that the people would stone them.

[27] The apostles were brought in and made to appear before the Sanhedrin to be questioned by the high priest. [28] "We gave you strict orders not to teach in this name," he said. "Yet you have filled Jerusalem with your teaching and are determined to make us guilty of this man's blood."

²⁹Peter and the other apostles replied: "We must obey God rather than human beings! ³⁰The God of our ancestors raised Jesus from the dead—whom you killed by hanging him on a cross. ³¹God exalted him to his own right hand as Prince and Savior that he might bring Israel to repentance and forgive their sins. ³²We are witnesses of these things, and so is the Holy Spirit, whom God has given to those who obey him."

³³When they heard this, they were furious and wanted to put them to death. ³⁴But a Pharisee named Gamaliel, a teacher of the law, who was honored by all the people, stood up in the Sanhedrin and ordered that the men be put outside for a little while. ³⁵Then he addressed the Sanhedrin: "Men of Israel, consider carefully what you intend to do to these men. ³⁶Some time ago Theudas appeared, claiming to be somebody, and about four hundred men rallied to him. He was killed, all his followers were dispersed, and it all came to nothing. ³⁷After him, Judas the Galilean appeared in the days of the census and led a band of people in revolt. He too was killed, and all his followers were scattered. ³⁸Therefore, in the present case I advise you: Leave these men alone! Let them go! For if their purpose or activity is of human origin, it will fail.

Acts 5:17–42

Peter obeyed God rather than people.

The apostle Peter had been tossed in jail with his good friend John for preaching about Jesus—that is, until an angel sprung them free and told them to get back to spreading the news about Jesus. When the religious authorities again tried to halt their teaching, Peter refused, saying, "We must obey God rather than human beings!" (Acts 5:29).

That's Peter, a guy well known for his boldness. "Peter" means "rock," a name Jesus gave him to describe his confident character. Peter once jumped from a boat to walk across the Sea of Galilee with Jesus (Matthew 14:28). He was the first disciple to shout out that Jesus was "the Christ, the Son of the living God" (Matthew 16:16). And when soldiers approached to arrest Jesus prior to the cross, Peter cut off a servant's ear in an attempt to defend the Lord (Matthew 26:51).

When Jesus said Peter would deny being his friend not just once but three times, Peter swore he would never abandon Jesus (Matthew 26:30–35). Peter wept when the Lord's prediction came true (Matthew 26:69–75), and Jesus invited him to follow once again (John 21:15–23). After Jesus rose from the dead, Peter preached powerful messages about Jesus, even when it brought him opposition, beatings, and imprisonment.

Church history says Peter was killed on a cross in Rome in the 60s. He asked that he be hung upside-down because he felt unworthy to die as Jesus had.

You can find Peter in scenes from Matthew 4:16 to Acts 15:7 and in Galatians 1:18–2:14, and you can read his two letters, 1 Peter and 2 Peter.

UNSHAKEN people

³⁹But if it is from God, you will not be able to stop these men; you will only find yourselves fighting against God."

⁴⁰His speech persuaded them. They called the apostles in and had them flogged. Then they ordered them not to speak in the name of Jesus, and let them go.

⁴¹The apostles left the Sanhedrin, rejoicing because they had been counted worthy of suffering disgrace for the Name. ⁴²Day after day, in the temple courts and from house to house, they never stopped teaching and proclaiming the good news that Jesus is the Messiah.

The Choosing of the Seven

6 In those days when the number of disciples was increasing, the Hellenistic Jews*a* among them complained against the Hebraic Jews because their widows were being overlooked in the daily distribution of food. ²So the Twelve gathered all the disciples together and said, "It would not be right for us to neglect the ministry of the word of God in order to wait on tables. ³Brothers and sisters, choose seven men from among you who are known to be full of the Spirit and wisdom. We will turn this responsibility over to them ⁴and will give our attention to prayer and the ministry of the word."

⁵This proposal pleased the whole group. They chose Stephen, a man full of faith and of the Holy Spirit; also Philip, Procorus, Nicanor, Timon, Parmenas, and Nicolas from Antioch, a convert to Judaism. ⁶They presented these men to the apostles, who prayed and laid their hands on them.

⁷So the word of God spread. The number of disciples in Jerusalem increased rapidly, and a large number of priests became obedient to the faith.

Stephen Seized

⁸Now Stephen, a man full of God's grace and power, performed great wonders and signs among the people. ⁹Opposition arose, however, from members of the Synagogue of the Freedmen (as it

was called)—Jews of Cyrene and Alexandria as well as the provinces of Cilicia and Asia—who began to argue with Stephen. ¹⁰But they could not stand up against the wisdom the Spirit gave him as he spoke.

¹¹Then they secretly persuaded some men to say, "We have heard Stephen speak blasphemous words against Moses and against God."

¹²So they stirred up the people and the elders and the teachers of the law. They seized Stephen and brought him before the Sanhedrin. ¹³They produced false witnesses, who testified, "This fellow never stops speaking against this holy place and against the law. ¹⁴For we have heard him say that this Jesus of Nazareth will destroy this place and change the customs Moses handed down to us."

¹⁵All who were sitting in the Sanhedrin looked intently at Stephen, and they saw that his face was like the face of an angel.

Stephen's Speech to the Sanhedrin

7 Then the high priest asked Stephen, "Are these charges true?"

²To this he replied: "Brothers and fathers, listen to me! The God of glory appeared to our father Abraham while he was still in Mesopotamia, before he lived in Harran. ³'Leave your country and your people,' God said, 'and go to the land I will show you.'*b*

⁴"So he left the land of the Chaldeans and settled in Harran. After the death of his father, God sent him to this land where you are now living. ⁵He gave him no inheritance here, not even enough ground to set his foot on. But God promised him that he and his descendants after him would possess the land, even though at that time Abraham had no child. ⁶God spoke to him in this way: 'For four hundred years your descendants will be strangers in a country not their own, and they will be enslaved and mistreated. ⁷But I will punish the nation they serve as slaves,' God said, 'and afterward they will come out of that country and worship

me in this place.'[a] [8]Then he gave Abraham the covenant of circumcision. And Abraham became the father of Isaac and circumcised him eight days after his birth. Later Isaac became the father of Jacob, and Jacob became the father of the twelve patriarchs.

[9]"Because the patriarchs were jealous of Joseph, they sold him as a slave into Egypt. But God was with him [10]and rescued him from all his troubles. He gave Joseph wisdom and enabled him to gain the goodwill of Pharaoh king of Egypt. So Pharaoh made him ruler over Egypt and all his palace.

[11]"Then a famine struck all Egypt and Canaan, bringing great suffering, and our ancestors could not find food. [12]When Jacob heard that there was grain in Egypt, he sent our forefathers on their first visit. [13]On their second visit, Joseph told his brothers who he was, and Pharaoh learned about Joseph's family. [14]After this, Joseph sent for his father Jacob and his whole family, seventy-five in all. [15]Then Jacob went down to Egypt, where he and our ancestors died. [16]Their bodies were brought back to Shechem and placed in the tomb that Abraham had bought from the sons of Hamor at Shechem for a certain sum of money.

[17]"As the time drew near for God to fulfill his promise to Abraham, the number of our people in Egypt had greatly increased. [18]Then 'a new king, to whom Joseph meant nothing, came to power in Egypt.'[b] [19]He dealt treacherously with our people and oppressed our ancestors by forcing them to throw out their newborn babies so that they would die.

[20]"At that time Moses was born, and he was no ordinary child.[c] For three months he was cared for by his family. [21]When he was placed outside, Pharaoh's daughter took him and brought him up as her own son. [22]Moses was educated in all the wisdom of the Egyptians and was powerful in speech and action.

[23]"When Moses was forty years old, he decided to visit his own people, the Israelites. [24]He saw one of them being mistreated by an Egyptian, so he went to his defense and avenged him by killing the Egyptian. [25]Moses thought that his own people would realize that God was using him to rescue them, but they did not. [26]The next day Moses came upon two Israelites who were fighting. He tried to reconcile them by saying, 'Men, you are brothers; why do you want to hurt each other?'

[27]"But the man who was mistreating the other pushed Moses aside and said, 'Who made you ruler and judge over us? [28]Are you thinking of killing me as you killed the Egyptian yesterday?'[d] [29]When Moses heard this, he fled to Midian, where he settled as a foreigner and had two sons.

[30]"After forty years had passed, an angel appeared to Moses in the flames of a burning bush in the desert near Mount Sinai. [31]When he saw this, he was amazed at the sight. As he went over to get a closer look, he heard the Lord say: [32]'I am the God of your fathers, the God of Abraham, Isaac and Jacob.'[e] Moses trembled with fear and did not dare to look.

[33]"Then the Lord said to him, 'Take off your sandals, for the place where you are standing is holy ground. [34]I have indeed seen the oppression of my people in Egypt. I have heard their groaning and have come down to set them free. Now come, I will send you back to Egypt.'[f]

[35]"This is the same Moses they had rejected with the words, 'Who made you ruler and judge?' He was sent to be their ruler and deliverer by God himself, through the angel who appeared to him in the bush. [36]He led them out of Egypt and performed wonders and signs in Egypt, at the Red Sea and for forty years in the wilderness.

[37]"This is the Moses who told the Israelites, 'God will raise up for you a prophet like me from your own people.'[g] [38]He was in the assembly in the wilderness, with the angel who spoke to him on Mount Sinai,

---

[a] 7 Gen. 15:13,14   [b] 18 Exodus 1:8
[c] 20 Or was fair in the sight of God
[d] 28 Exodus 2:14   [e] 32 Exodus 3:6
[f] 34 Exodus 3:5,7,8,10   [g] 37 Deut. 18:15

and with our ancestors; and he received living words to pass on to us.

³⁹"But our ancestors refused to obey him. Instead, they rejected him and in their hearts turned back to Egypt. ⁴⁰They told Aaron, 'Make us gods who will go before us. As for this fellow Moses who led us out of Egypt—we don't know what has happened to him!'^a ⁴¹That was the time they made an idol in the form of a calf. They brought sacrifices to it and reveled in what their own hands had made. ⁴²But God turned away from them and gave them over to the worship of the sun, moon and stars. This agrees with what is written in the book of the prophets:

"'Did you bring me sacrifices and
        offerings
    forty years in the wilderness, people
        of Israel?
⁴³You have taken up the tabernacle of
        Molek
    and the star of your god Rephan,
        the idols you made to worship.
Therefore I will send you into exile'^b
        beyond Babylon.

⁴⁴"Our ancestors had the tabernacle of the covenant law with them in the wilderness. It had been made as God directed Moses, according to the pattern he had seen. ⁴⁵After receiving the tabernacle, our ancestors under Joshua brought it with them when they took the land from the nations God drove out before them. It remained in the land until the time of David, ⁴⁶who enjoyed God's favor and asked that he might provide a dwelling place for the God of Jacob.^c ⁴⁷But it was Solomon who built a house for him.

⁴⁸"However, the Most High does not live in houses made by human hands. As the prophet says:

⁴⁹"'Heaven is my throne,
    and the earth is my footstool.
What kind of house will you build for
        me?
                    says the Lord.
    Or where will my resting place be?
⁵⁰Has not my hand made all these
        things?'^d

⁵¹"You stiff-necked people! Your hearts and ears are still uncircumcised. You are just like your ancestors: You always resist the Holy Spirit! ⁵²Was there ever a prophet your ancestors did not persecute? They even killed those who predicted the coming of the Righteous One. And now you have betrayed and murdered him— ⁵³you who have received the law that was given through angels but have not obeyed it."

The Stoning of Stephen

⁵⁴When the members of the Sanhedrin heard this, they were furious and gnashed their teeth at him. ⁵⁵But Stephen, full of the Holy Spirit, looked up to heaven and saw the glory of God, and Jesus standing at the right hand of God. ⁵⁶"Look," he said, "I see heaven open and the Son of Man standing at the right hand of God."

⁵⁷At this they covered their ears and, yelling at the top of their voices, they all rushed at him, ⁵⁸dragged him out of the city and began to stone him. Meanwhile, the witnesses laid their coats at the feet of a young man named Saul.

⁵⁹While they were stoning him, Stephen prayed, "Lord Jesus, receive my spirit." ⁶⁰Then he fell on his knees and cried out, "Lord, do not hold this sin against them." When he had said this, he fell asleep.

8 And Saul approved of their killing him.

The Church Persecuted and Scattered

On that day a great persecution broke out against the church in Jerusalem, and all except the apostles were scattered throughout Judea and Samaria. ²Godly men buried Stephen and mourned deeply for him. ³But Saul began to destroy the church. Going from house to house, he dragged off both men and women and put them in prison.

Philip in Samaria

⁴Those who had been scattered preached the word wherever they went.

^a 40 Exodus 32:1   ^b 43 Amos 5:25-27 (see Septuagint)   ^c 46 Some early manuscripts *the house of Jacob*   ^d 50 Isaiah 66:1,2

⁵Philip went down to a city in Samaria and proclaimed the Messiah there. ⁶When the crowds heard Philip and saw the signs he performed, they all paid close attention to what he said. ⁷For with shrieks, impure spirits came out of many, and many who were paralyzed or lame were healed. ⁸So there was great joy in that city.

Simon the Sorcerer

⁹Now for some time a man named Simon had practiced sorcery in the city and amazed all the people of Samaria. He boasted that he was someone great, ¹⁰and all the people, both high and low, gave him their attention and exclaimed, "This man is rightly called the Great Power of God." ¹¹They followed him because he had amazed them for a long time with his sorcery. ¹²But when they believed Philip as he proclaimed the good news of the kingdom of God and the name of Jesus Christ, they were baptized, both men and women. ¹³Simon himself believed and was baptized. And he followed Philip everywhere, astonished by the great signs and miracles he saw.

¹⁴When the apostles in Jerusalem heard that Samaria had accepted the word of God, they sent Peter and John to Samaria. ¹⁵When they arrived, they prayed for the new believers there that they might receive

---

Acts 7:54–60

Stephen died for his faith.

When the first Christians got into a dispute over caring fairly for widows, they looked for respected people to administer daily supplies of food. Everyone was happy when early church leaders picked Stephen as one of the seven since he was a guy known for being "full of faith and of the Holy Spirit" (Acts 6:5).

Stephen wasn't just an organizer. He also did "great wonders and signs" that put God's power on display (Acts 6:8). He was so skilled at answering arguments against Christian beliefs that his opponents could do nothing to fight back but spread false rumors about him and hauled him in front of Jewish religious leaders (see Acts 6:9–15).

Others might have backed down and shut up, but Stephen fearlessly told the story of Jesus. He started at the beginning of the Old Testament story and continued through the crucifixion, slamming his accusers for their continual rebellion against God. When Stephen reported that he saw heaven splitting open and Jesus standing next to God, the rulers furiously gnashed their teeth, dragged Stephen away, and stoned him.

Stephen became the first martyr of the church, the first person killed for his belief in Jesus. His murder was the start of a period of persecution that forced believers out of Jerusalem. As they fled, they spread the news about Jesus to neighboring areas (see Acts 8:1–2). Because Stephen died for his faith, many others discovered eternal life.

You can find Stephen in Acts 6:1 — 7:60.

UNSHAKEN people

the Holy Spirit, ¹⁶because the Holy Spirit had not yet come on any of them; they had simply been baptized in the name of the Lord Jesus. ¹⁷Then Peter and John placed their hands on them, and they received the Holy Spirit.

¹⁸When Simon saw that the Spirit was given at the laying on of the apostles' hands, he offered them money ¹⁹and said, "Give me also this ability so that everyone on whom I lay my hands may receive the Holy Spirit."

²⁰Peter answered: "May your money perish with you, because you thought you could buy the gift of God with money! ²¹You have no part or share in this ministry, because your heart is not right before God. ²²Repent of this wickedness and pray to the Lord in the hope that he may forgive you for having such a thought in your heart. ²³For I see that you are full of bitterness and captive to sin."

²⁴Then Simon answered, "Pray to the Lord for me so that nothing you have said may happen to me."

²⁵After they had further proclaimed the word of the Lord and testified about Jesus, Peter and John returned to Jerusalem, preaching the gospel in many Samaritan villages.

Philip and the Ethiopian

²⁶Now an angel of the Lord said to Philip, "Go south to the road—the desert road—that goes down from Jerusalem to Gaza." ²⁷So he started out, and on his way he met an Ethiopian^a eunuch, an important official in charge of all the treasury of the Kandake (which means "queen of the Ethiopians"). This man had gone to Jerusalem to worship, ²⁸and on his way home was sitting in his chariot reading the Book of Isaiah the prophet. ²⁹The Spirit told Philip, "Go to that chariot and stay near it."

³⁰Then Philip ran up to the chariot and heard the man reading Isaiah the prophet. "Do you understand what you are reading?" Philip asked.

³¹"How can I," he said, "unless someone explains it to me?" So he invited Philip to come up and sit with him.

³²This is the passage of Scripture the eunuch was reading:

"He was led like a sheep to the slaughter,
and as a lamb before its shearer is silent,
so he did not open his mouth.

^a 27 That is, from the southern Nile region

ACTS 8

Acts 8:26–40
Baptism shows you believe in Jesus.

Philip was on a road outside Jerusalem when he met a man from Ethiopia. This non-Jewish man had already discovered the truth about the one true God. But he knew nothing of Jesus. Philip used the Old Testament to prove that Jesus was the Savior sent by God. As soon as the man believed, he had a question for Philip. "What can stand in the way of my being baptized?" (Acts 8:36). Baptism is the act of being dipped in water (or sprinkled with water) as a sign of belief in Jesus. Baptism symbolizes our death and resurrection with Jesus (see Romans 6:3–4). Along with communion (see Matthew 26:17–30), baptism is one of two "ordinances" or "sacraments" Jesus commanded us to practice until he comes back (see Matthew 28:18–20). While Christians disagree about how and when people should be baptized—and even on the details of exactly what baptism means—they agree Jesus made it an essential act for all believers.

Think: Why is baptism so important? What does your church teach about it?

ROCK SOLID truths

³³In his humiliation he was deprived of
justice.
Who can speak of his descendants?
For his life was taken from the
earth."ᵃ

³⁴The eunuch asked Philip, "Tell me,
please, who is the prophet talking about,
himself or someone else?" ³⁵Then Philip
began with that very passage of Scripture
and told him the good news about Jesus.

³⁶As they traveled along the road, they
came to some water and the eunuch said,
"Look, here is water. What can stand in
the way of my being baptized?" [37]ᵇ ³⁸And
he gave orders to stop the chariot. Then
both Philip and the eunuch went down
into the water and Philip baptized him.
³⁹When they came up out of the water, the Spirit of the Lord suddenly took
Philip away, and the eunuch did not see
him again, but went on his way rejoicing.
⁴⁰Philip, however, appeared at Azotus and
traveled about, preaching the gospel in all
the towns until he reached Caesarea.

Saul's Conversion

9 Meanwhile, Saul was still breathing out murderous threats against
the Lord's disciples. He went to
the high priest ²and asked him for letters
to the synagogues in Damascus, so that if
he found any there who belonged to the
Way, whether men or women, he might
take them as prisoners to Jerusalem. ³As
he neared Damascus on his journey, suddenly a light from heaven flashed around
him. ⁴He fell to the ground and heard a
voice say to him, "Saul, Saul, why do you
persecute me?"

⁵"Who are you, Lord?" Saul asked.

"I am Jesus, whom you are persecuting,"
he replied. ⁶"Now get up and go into the
city, and you will be told what you must do."

⁷The men traveling with Saul stood
there speechless; they heard the sound but
did not see anyone. ⁸Saul got up from the
ground, but when he opened his eyes he
could see nothing. So they led him by the
hand into Damascus. ⁹For three days he
was blind, and did not eat or drink anything.

¹⁰In Damascus there was a disciple
named Ananias. The Lord called to him
in a vision, "Ananias!"

"Yes, Lord," he answered.

¹¹The Lord told him, "Go to the house
of Judas on Straight Street and ask for a
man from Tarsus named Saul, for he is
praying. ¹²In a vision he has seen a man
named Ananias come and place his hands
on him to restore his sight."

¹³"Lord," Ananias answered, "I have
heard many reports about this man and all
the harm he has done to your holy people
in Jerusalem. ¹⁴And he has come here with
authority from the chief priests to arrest
all who call on your name."

¹⁵But the Lord said to Ananias, "Go!
This man is my chosen instrument to proclaim my name to the Gentiles and their
kings and to the people of Israel. ¹⁶I will
show him how much he must suffer for
my name."

¹⁷Then Ananias went to the house and
entered it. Placing his hands on Saul, he
said, "Brother Saul, the Lord—Jesus, who
appeared to you on the road as you were
coming here—has sent me so that you may
see again and be filled with the Holy Spirit." ¹⁸Immediately, something like scales
fell from Saul's eyes, and he could see again.
He got up and was baptized, ¹⁹and after
taking some food, he regained his strength.

Saul in Damascus and Jerusalem

Saul spent several days with the disciples in Damascus. ²⁰At once he began to
preach in the synagogues that Jesus is the
Son of God. ²¹All those who heard him
were astonished and asked, "Isn't he the
man who raised havoc in Jerusalem among
those who call on this name? And hasn't
he come here to take them as prisoners to
the chief priests?" ²²Yet Saul grew more
and more powerful and baffled the Jews
living in Damascus by proving that Jesus
is the Messiah.

ᵃ 33 Isaiah 53:7,8 (see Septuagint)
ᵇ 37 Some manuscripts include here *Philip said,
"If you believe with all your heart, you may." The
eunuch answered, "I believe that Jesus Christ is the
Son of God."*

²³After many days had gone by, there was a conspiracy among the Jews to kill him, ²⁴but Saul learned of their plan. Day and night they kept close watch on the city gates in order to kill him. ²⁵But his followers took him by night and lowered him in a basket through an opening in the wall.

²⁶When he came to Jerusalem, he tried to join the disciples, but they were all afraid of him, not believing that he really was a disciple. ²⁷But Barnabas took him and brought him to the apostles. He told them how Saul on his journey had seen the Lord and that the Lord had spoken to him, and how in Damascus he had preached fearlessly in the name of Jesus. ²⁸So Saul stayed with them and moved about freely in Jerusalem, speaking boldly in the name of the Lord. ²⁹He talked and debated with the Hellenistic Jews,ᵃ but they tried to kill him. ³⁰When the believers learned of this, they took him down to Caesarea and sent him off to Tarsus.

³¹Then the church throughout Judea, Galilee and Samaria enjoyed a time of peace and was strengthened. Living in the fear of the Lord and encouraged by the Holy Spirit, it increased in numbers.

ᵃ 29 That is, Jews who had adopted the Greek language and culture

Acts 9:1–31

Paul told the world about Jesus.

The first time you spot the apostle Paul in the New Testament, he is known by his Jewish name, Saul of Tarsus. He was still a young man when he held the coats of people hurling rocks at Stephen, the first Christian killed for his faith (see Acts 7:57).

Paul had been raised as "a Hebrew of Hebrews" (Philippians 3:5) and studied under Gamaliel, the best-known Jewish teacher of his day (see Acts 22:3). He became such a radical defender of his beliefs that religious leaders gave him orders to chase down Jews who had become believers in Jesus, handing Paul authority to imprison or kill any he found.

With Paul "breathing out murderous threats against the Lord's disciples" (Acts 9:1), he was knocked to the ground by a blinding light. Jesus himself spoke from heaven, asking, "Saul, Saul, why do you persecute me?" (Acts 9:4). The Lord gave Paul the assignment of taking the good news about Jesus to the Gentiles—non-Jewish peoples—everywhere (see Acts 9:15–16).

Paul traveled much of the Roman Empire spreading the word about Jesus. The book of Acts records four missionary trips that brought him difficulties ranging from shipwrecks and stonings to robbery and riots (see 2 Corinthians 11:24–29). Yet through Paul's preaching, countless people became believers, and his passionate letters to churches and individuals make up much of the New Testament. Tradition says Paul was killed for his faith under the emperor Nero between AD 64 and 67.

You can find Paul in Acts 7:57—28:31 and in his letters from Romans to Philemon. He tells his own story in Acts 26:1–23.

UNSHAKEN people

Aeneas and Dorcas

[32] As Peter traveled about the country, he went to visit the Lord's people who lived in Lydda. [33] There he found a man named Aeneas, who was paralyzed and had been bedridden for eight years. [34] "Aeneas," Peter said to him, "Jesus Christ heals you. Get up and roll up your mat." Immediately Aeneas got up. [35] All those who lived in Lydda and Sharon saw him and turned to the Lord.

[36] In Joppa there was a disciple named Tabitha (in Greek her name is Dorcas); she was always doing good and helping the poor. [37] About that time she became sick and died, and her body was washed and placed in an upstairs room. [38] Lydda was near Joppa; so when the disciples heard that Peter was in Lydda, they sent two men to him and urged him, "Please come at once!"

[39] Peter went with them, and when he arrived he was taken upstairs to the room. All the widows stood around him, crying and showing him the robes and other clothing that Dorcas had made while she was still with them.

[40] Peter sent them all out of the room; then he got down on his knees and prayed. Turning toward the dead woman, he said, "Tabitha, get up." She opened her eyes, and seeing Peter she sat up. [41] He took her by the hand and helped her to her feet. Then he called for the believers, especially the widows, and presented her to them alive. [42] This became known all over Joppa, and many people believed in the Lord. [43] Peter stayed in Joppa for some time with a tanner named Simon.

Cornelius Calls for Peter

10 At Caesarea there was a man named Cornelius, a centurion in what was known as the Italian Regiment. [2] He and all his family were devout and God-fearing; he gave generously to those in need and prayed to God regularly. [3] One day at about three in the afternoon he had a vision. He distinctly saw an angel of God, who came to him and said, "Cornelius!"

[4] Cornelius stared at him in fear. "What is it, Lord?" he asked.

The angel answered, "Your prayers and gifts to the poor have come up as a memorial offering before God. [5] Now send men to Joppa to bring back a man named Simon who is called Peter. [6] He is staying with Simon the tanner, whose house is by the sea."

[7] When the angel who spoke to him had gone, Cornelius called two of his servants and a devout soldier who was one of his attendants. [8] He told them everything that had happened and sent them to Joppa.

Peter's Vision

[9] About noon the following day as they were on their journey and approaching the city, Peter went up on the roof to pray. [10] He became hungry and wanted something to eat, and while the meal was being prepared, he fell into a trance. [11] He saw heaven opened and something like a large sheet being let down to earth by its four corners. [12] It contained all kinds of four-footed animals, as well as reptiles and birds. [13] Then a voice told him, "Get up, Peter. Kill and eat."

[14] "Surely not, Lord!" Peter replied. "I have never eaten anything impure or unclean."

[15] The voice spoke to him a second time, "Do not call anything impure that God has made clean."

[16] This happened three times, and immediately the sheet was taken back to heaven.

[17] While Peter was wondering about the meaning of the vision, the men sent by Cornelius found out where Simon's house was and stopped at the gate. [18] They called out, asking if Simon who was known as Peter was staying there.

[19] While Peter was still thinking about the vision, the Spirit said to him, "Simon, three[a] men are looking for you. [20] So get up and go downstairs. Do not hesitate to go with them, for I have sent them."

[21] Peter went down and said to the men,

---

[a] 19 One early manuscript two; other manuscripts do not have the number.

"I'm the one you're looking for. Why have you come?"

²²The men replied, "We have come from Cornelius the centurion. He is a righteous and God-fearing man, who is respected by all the Jewish people. A holy angel told him to ask you to come to his house so that he could hear what you have to say." ²³Then Peter invited the men into the house to be his guests.

Peter at Cornelius's House

The next day Peter started out with them, and some of the believers from Joppa went along. ²⁴The following day he arrived in Caesarea. Cornelius was expecting them and had called together his relatives and close friends. ²⁵As Peter entered the house, Cornelius met him and fell at his feet in reverence. ²⁶But Peter made him get up. "Stand up," he said, "I am only a man myself."

²⁷While talking with him, Peter went inside and found a large gathering of people. ²⁸He said to them: "You are well aware that it is against our law for a Jew

ROCK SOLID plans

Acts 10:9–23

Expect surprises.

The Old Testament is packed with lists of foods that believers were forbidden to eat, like the command against eating pork (see Leviticus 11:7–8). When Jesus came, he abolished these dietary laws, a point Peter learned in a vision where God told him to preach the gospel to non-Jews (see Acts 10:24–48). Peter was a long-time follower of Jesus, but he still had things to learn. No matter how long you follow Jesus, he will always surprise you. He wants to show you things you haven't even imagined.

Your next step: Whenever you open your Bible to read, ask God to teach you something fresh.

to associate with or visit a Gentile. But God has shown me that I should not call anyone impure or unclean. ²⁹So when I was sent for, I came without raising any objection. May I ask why you sent for me?"

³⁰Cornelius answered: "Three days ago I was in my house praying at this hour, at three in the afternoon. Suddenly a man in shining clothes stood before me ³¹and said, 'Cornelius, God has heard your prayer and remembered your gifts to the poor. ³²Send to Joppa for Simon who is called Peter. He is a guest in the home of Simon the tanner, who lives by the sea.' ³³So I sent for you immediately, and it was good of you to come. Now we are all here in the presence of God to listen to everything the Lord has commanded you to tell us."

³⁴Then Peter began to speak: "I now realize how true it is that God does not show favoritism ³⁵but accepts from every nation the one who fears him and does what is right. ³⁶You know the message God sent to the people of Israel, announcing the good news of peace through Jesus Christ, who is Lord of all. ³⁷You know what has happened throughout the province of Judea, beginning in Galilee after the baptism that John preached— ³⁸how God anointed Jesus of Nazareth with the Holy Spirit and power, and how he went around doing good and healing all who were under the power of the devil, because God was with him.

³⁹"We are witnesses of everything he did in the country of the Jews and in Jerusalem. They killed him by hanging him on a cross, ⁴⁰but God raised him from the dead on the third day and caused him to be seen. ⁴¹He was not seen by all the people, but by witnesses whom God had already chosen—by us who ate and drank with him after he rose from the dead. ⁴²He commanded us to preach to the people and to testify that he is the one whom God appointed as judge of the living and the dead. ⁴³All the prophets testify about him that everyone who believes in him receives forgiveness of sins through his name."

⁴⁴While Peter was still speaking these words, the Holy Spirit came on all who

heard the message. [45]The circumcised believers who had come with Peter were astonished that the gift of the Holy Spirit had been poured out even on Gentiles. [46]For they heard them speaking in tongues[a] and praising God.

Then Peter said, [47]"Surely no one can stand in the way of their being baptized with water. They have received the Holy Spirit just as we have." [48]So he ordered that they be baptized in the name of Jesus Christ. Then they asked Peter to stay with them for a few days.

Peter Explains His Actions

11 The apostles and the believers throughout Judea heard that the Gentiles also had received the word of God. [2]So when Peter went up to Jerusalem, the circumcised believers criticized him [3]and said, "You went into the house of uncircumcised men and ate with them."

[4]Starting from the beginning, Peter told them the whole story: [5]"I was in the city of Joppa praying, and in a trance I saw a vision. I saw something like a large sheet being let down from heaven by its four corners, and it came down to where I was. [6]I looked into it and saw four-footed animals of the earth, wild beasts, reptiles and birds. [7]Then I heard a voice telling me, 'Get up, Peter. Kill and eat.'

[8]"I replied, 'Surely not, Lord! Nothing impure or unclean has ever entered my mouth.'

[9]"The voice spoke from heaven a second time, 'Do not call anything impure that God has made clean.' [10]This happened three times, and then it was all pulled up to heaven again.

[11]"Right then three men who had been sent to me from Caesarea stopped at the house where I was staying. [12]The Spirit told me to have no hesitation about going with them. These six brothers also went with me, and we entered the man's house. [13]He told us how he had seen an angel appear in his house and say, 'Send to Joppa for Simon who is called Peter. [14]He will bring you a message through which you and all your household will be saved.'

[15]"As I began to speak, the Holy Spirit came on them as he had come on us at the beginning. [16]Then I remembered what the Lord had said: 'John baptized with[b] water, but you will be baptized with[b] the Holy Spirit.' [17]So if God gave them the same gift he gave us who believed in the Lord Jesus Christ, who was I to think that I could stand in God's way?"

[18]When they heard this, they had no further objections and praised God, saying, "So then, even to Gentiles God has granted repentance that leads to life."

The Church in Antioch

[19]Now those who had been scattered by the persecution that broke out when Stephen was killed traveled as far as Phoenicia, Cyprus and Antioch, spreading the word only among Jews. [20]Some of them, however, men from Cyprus and Cyrene, went to Antioch and began to speak to Greeks also, telling them the good news about the Lord Jesus. [21]The Lord's hand was with them, and a great number of people believed and turned to the Lord.

[22]News of this reached the church in Jerusalem, and they sent Barnabas to Antioch. [23]When he arrived and saw what the grace of God had done, he was glad and encouraged them all to remain true to the Lord with all their hearts. [24]He was a good man, full of the Holy Spirit and faith, and a great number of people were brought to the Lord.

[25]Then Barnabas went to Tarsus to look for Saul, [26]and when he found him, he brought him to Antioch. So for a whole year Barnabas and Saul met with the church and taught great numbers of people. The disciples were called Christians first at Antioch.

[27]During this time some prophets came down from Jerusalem to Antioch. [28]One of them, named Agabus, stood up and through the Spirit predicted that a severe famine would spread over the entire Roman world. (This happened during the reign of Claudius.) [29]The disciples, as each one was able, decided to provide help for

a 46 Or other languages   *b 16 Or in*

the brothers and sisters living in Judea. ³⁰This they did, sending their gift to the elders by Barnabas and Saul.

Peter's Miraculous Escape From Prison

12 It was about this time that King Herod arrested some who belonged to the church, intending to persecute them. ²He had James, the brother of John, put to death with the sword. ³When he saw that this met with approval among the Jews, he proceeded to seize Peter also. This happened during the Festival of Unleavened Bread. ⁴After arresting him, he put him in prison, handing him over to be guarded by four squads of four soldiers each. Herod intended to bring him out for public trial after the Passover.

⁵So Peter was kept in prison, but the church was earnestly praying to God for him.

⁶The night before Herod was to bring him to trial, Peter was sleeping between two soldiers, bound with two chains, and sentries stood guard at the entrance. ⁷Suddenly an angel of the Lord appeared and a light shone in the cell. He struck Peter on the side and woke him up. "Quick, get up!" he said, and the chains fell off Peter's wrists.

⁸Then the angel said to him, "Put on your clothes and sandals." And Peter did so. "Wrap your cloak around you and follow me," the angel told him. ⁹Peter followed him out of the prison, but he had no idea that what the angel was doing was really happening; he thought he was seeing a vision. ¹⁰They passed the first and second guards and came to the iron gate leading to the city. It opened for them by itself, and they went through it. When they had walked the length of one street, suddenly the angel left him.

¹¹Then Peter came to himself and said, "Now I know without a doubt that the Lord has sent his angel and rescued me from Herod's clutches and from everything the Jewish people were hoping would happen."

¹²When this had dawned on him, he went to the house of Mary the mother of John, also called Mark, where many people had gathered and were praying. ¹³Peter knocked at the outer entrance, and a servant named Rhoda came to answer the door. ¹⁴When she recognized Peter's voice, she was so overjoyed she ran back without opening it and exclaimed, "Peter is at the door!"

¹⁵"You're out of your mind," they told her. When she kept insisting that it was so, they said, "It must be his angel."

¹⁶But Peter kept on knocking, and

Acts 12:1–19

Following Jesus can bring persecution.

Jesus predicted his followers would suffer persecution—they would be mocked, insulted, hurt, imprisoned, killed, and more for being his friends. The Lord didn't sugarcoat anything when he said, "Everyone will hate you because of me" (Mark 13:13) and "Blessed are those who are persecuted because of righteousness" (Matthew 5:10). A man named Stephen was the first believer killed for his faith (see Acts 6:8—8:1), and before the apostle Paul became a believer, he led a movement to viciously hunt Christians to jail and kill them (see Acts 8:3; 9:1–6). Later in his life Paul became convinced that opposition is an inescapable part of following Jesus. He wrote, "For it has been granted to you on behalf of Christ not only to believe in him, but also to suffer for him" (Philippians 1:29). Persecution isn't a happy thought, but it continues to be a reality in many places around the world.

Think: When have you suffered because you believe in Jesus? How did you react?

ROCK SOLID truths

when they opened the door and saw him, they were astonished. [17]Peter motioned with his hand for them to be quiet and described how the Lord had brought him out of prison. "Tell James and the other brothers and sisters about this," he said, and then he left for another place.

[18]In the morning, there was no small commotion among the soldiers as to what had become of Peter. [19]After Herod had a thorough search made for him and did not find him, he cross-examined the guards and ordered that they be executed.

Herod's Death

Then Herod went from Judea to Caesarea and stayed there. [20]He had been quarreling with the people of Tyre and Sidon; they now joined together and sought an audience with him. After securing the support of Blastus, a trusted personal servant of the king, they asked for peace, because they depended on the king's country for their food supply.

[21]On the appointed day Herod, wearing his royal robes, sat on his throne and delivered a public address to the people. [22]They shouted, "This is the voice of a god, not of a man." [23]Immediately, because Herod did not give praise to God, an angel of the Lord struck him down, and he was eaten by worms and died.

[24]But the word of God continued to spread and flourish.

Barnabas and Saul Sent Off

[25]When Barnabas and Saul had finished their mission, they returned from[a] Jerusalem, taking with them John, also called Mark. [1]Now in the church at Antioch there were prophets and teachers: Barnabas, Simeon called Niger, Lucius of Cyrene, Manaen (who had been brought up with Herod the tetrarch) and Saul. [2]While they were worshiping the Lord and fasting, the Holy Spirit said, "Set apart for me Barnabas and Saul for the work to which I have called them." [3]So after they had fasted and prayed, they placed their hands on them and sent them off.

On Cyprus

[4]The two of them, sent on their way by the Holy Spirit, went down to Seleucia and sailed from there to Cyprus. [5]When they arrived at Salamis, they proclaimed the word of God in the Jewish synagogues. John was with them as their helper.

[6]They traveled through the whole island until they came to Paphos. There they met a Jewish sorcerer and false prophet named Bar-Jesus, [7]who was an attendant of the proconsul, Sergius Paulus. The proconsul, an intelligent man, sent for Barnabas and Saul because he wanted to hear the word of God. [8]But Elymas the sorcerer (for that is what his name means) opposed them and tried to turn the proconsul from the faith. [9]Then Saul, who was also called Paul, filled with the Holy Spirit, looked straight at Elymas and said, [10]"You are a child of the devil and an enemy of everything that is right! You are full of all kinds of deceit and trickery. Will you never stop perverting the right ways of the Lord? [11]Now the hand of the Lord is against you. You are going to be blind for a time, not even able to see the light of the sun."

Immediately mist and darkness came over him, and he groped about, seeking someone to lead him by the hand. [12]When the proconsul saw what had happened, he believed, for he was amazed at the teaching about the Lord.

In Pisidian Antioch

[13]From Paphos, Paul and his companions sailed to Perga in Pamphylia, where John left them to return to Jerusalem. [14]From Perga they went on to Pisidian Antioch. On the Sabbath they entered the synagogue and sat down. [15]After the reading from the Law and the Prophets, the leaders of the synagogue sent word to them, saying, "Brothers, if you have a word of exhortation for the people, please speak."

[16]Standing up, Paul motioned with his hand and said: "Fellow Israelites and you

[a] 25 Some manuscripts to

Gentiles who worship God, listen to me! ¹⁷The God of the people of Israel chose our ancestors; he made the people prosper during their stay in Egypt; with mighty power he led them out of that country; ¹⁸for about forty years he endured their conduct*a* in the wilderness; ¹⁹and he overthrew seven nations in Canaan, giving their land to his people as their inheritance. ²⁰All this took about 450 years.

"After this, God gave them judges until the time of Samuel the prophet. ²¹Then the people asked for a king, and he gave them Saul son of Kish, of the tribe of Benjamin, who ruled forty years. ²²After removing Saul, he made David their king. God testified concerning him: 'I have found David son of Jesse, a man after my own heart; he will do everything I want him to do.'

²³"From this man's descendants God has brought to Israel the Savior Jesus, as he promised. ²⁴Before the coming of Jesus, John preached repentance and baptism to all the people of Israel. ²⁵As John was completing his work, he said: 'Who do you suppose I am? I am not the one you are looking for. But there is one coming after me whose sandals I am not worthy to untie.'

²⁶"Fellow children of Abraham and you God-fearing Gentiles, it is to us that this message of salvation has been sent. ²⁷The people of Jerusalem and their rulers did not recognize Jesus, yet in condemning him they fulfilled the words of the prophets that are read every Sabbath. ²⁸Though they found no proper ground for a death sentence, they asked Pilate to have him executed. ²⁹When they had carried out all that was written about him, they took him down from the cross and laid him in a tomb. ³⁰But God raised him from the dead, ³¹and for many days he was seen by those who had traveled with him from Galilee to Jerusalem. They are now his witnesses to our people.

³²"We tell you the good news: What God promised our ancestors ³³he has fulfilled for us, their children, by raising up Jesus. As it is written in the second Psalm:

"'You are my son;
today I have become your father.'*b*

³⁴God raised him from the dead so that he will never be subject to decay. As God has said,

"'I will give you the holy and sure blessings promised to David.'*c*

³⁵So it is also stated elsewhere:

"'You will not let your holy one see decay.'*d*

³⁶"Now when David had served God's purpose in his own generation, he fell asleep; he was buried with his ancestors and his body decayed. ³⁷But the one whom God raised from the dead did not see decay.

³⁸"Therefore, my friends, I want you to know that through Jesus the forgiveness of sins is proclaimed to you. ³⁹Through

ROCK SOLID *promises*

"I want you to know that through Jesus the forgiveness of sins is proclaimed to you." Acts 13:38

God made a loud public vow to forgive your sins. He won't ever back out of his promise.

him everyone who believes is set free from every sin, a justification you were not able to obtain under the law of Moses. ⁴⁰Take care that what the prophets have said does not happen to you:

⁴¹"'Look, you scoffers,
wonder and perish,

a 18 Some manuscripts *he cared for them*
b 33 Psalm 2:7 *c 34* Isaiah 55:3
d 35 Psalm 16:10 (see Septuagint)

for I am going to do something in
your days
that you would never believe,
even if someone told you.'[a]"

[42] As Paul and Barnabas were leaving the synagogue, the people invited them to speak further about these things on the next Sabbath. [43] When the congregation was dismissed, many of the Jews and devout converts to Judaism followed Paul and Barnabas, who talked with them and urged them to continue in the grace of God.

[44] On the next Sabbath almost the whole city gathered to hear the word of the Lord. [45] When the Jews saw the crowds, they were filled with jealousy. They began to contradict what Paul was saying and heaped abuse on him.

[46] Then Paul and Barnabas answered them boldly: "We had to speak the word of God to you first. Since you reject it and do not consider yourselves worthy of eternal life, we now turn to the Gentiles. [47] For this is what the Lord has commanded us:

"'I have made you[b] a light for the
Gentiles,
that you[b] may bring salvation to the
ends of the earth.'[c]"

[48] When the Gentiles heard this, they were glad and honored the word of the Lord; and all who were appointed for eternal life believed.

[49] The word of the Lord spread through the whole region. [50] But the Jewish leaders incited the God-fearing women of high standing and the leading men of the city. They stirred up persecution against Paul and Barnabas, and expelled them from their region. [51] So they shook the dust off their feet as a warning to them and went to Iconium. [52] And the disciples were filled with joy and with the Holy Spirit.

In Iconium

14 At Iconium Paul and Barnabas went as usual into the Jewish synagogue. There they spoke so effectively that a great number of Jews and Greeks believed. [2] But the Jews who refused to believe stirred up the other Gentiles and poisoned their minds against the brothers. [3] So Paul and Barnabas spent considerable time there, speaking boldly for the Lord, who confirmed the message of his grace by enabling them to perform signs and wonders. [4] The people of the city were divided; some sided with the Jews, others with the apostles. [5] There was a plot afoot among both Gentiles and Jews, together with their leaders, to mistreat them and stone them. [6] But they found out about it and fled to the Lycaonian cities of Lystra and Derbe and to the surrounding country, [7] where they continued to preach the gospel.

In Lystra and Derbe

[8] In Lystra there sat a man who was lame. He had been that way from birth and had never walked. [9] He listened to Paul as he was speaking. Paul looked directly at him, saw that he had faith to be healed [10] and called out, "Stand up on your feet!" At that, the man jumped up and began to walk.

[11] When the crowd saw what Paul had done, they shouted in the Lycaonian language, "The gods have come down to us in human form!" [12] Barnabas they called Zeus, and Paul they called Hermes because he was the chief speaker. [13] The priest of Zeus, whose temple was just outside the city, brought bulls and wreaths to the city gates because he and the crowd wanted to offer sacrifices to them.

[14] But when the apostles Barnabas and Paul heard of this, they tore their clothes and rushed out into the crowd, shouting: [15] "Friends, why are you doing this? We too are only human, like you. We are bringing you good news, telling you to turn from these worthless things to the living God, who made the heavens and the earth and the sea and everything in them. [16] In the past, he let all nations go their own way. [17] Yet he has not left himself without testimony: He has shown kindness by giving you rain from heaven

[a] 41 Hab. 1:5   [b] 47 The Greek is singular.
[c] 47 Isaiah 49:6

and crops in their seasons; he provides you with plenty of food and fills your hearts with joy." [18] Even with these words, they had difficulty keeping the crowd from sacrificing to them.

ROCK SOLID promises

"He has shown kindness by giving you rain from heaven and crops in their seasons." Acts 14:17

God showers the whole world with gifts that prove his kindness to every person on earth.

[19] Then some Jews came from Antioch and Iconium and won the crowd over. They stoned Paul and dragged him outside the city, thinking he was dead. [20] But after the disciples had gathered around him, he got up and went back into the city. The next day he and Barnabas left for Derbe.

The Return to Antioch in Syria

[21] They preached the gospel in that city and won a large number of disciples. Then they returned to Lystra, Iconium and Antioch, [22] strengthening the disciples and encouraging them to remain true to the faith. "We must go through many hardships to enter the kingdom of God," they said. [23] Paul and Barnabas appointed elders[a] for them in each church and, with prayer and fasting, committed them to the Lord, in whom they had put their trust. [24] After going through Pisidia, they came into Pamphylia, [25] and when they had preached the word in Perga, they went down to Attalia.

[26] From Attalia they sailed back to Antioch, where they had been committed to the grace of God for the work they had now completed. [27] On arriving there, they gathered the church together and reported all that God had done through them and how he had opened a door of faith to the Gentiles. [28] And they stayed there a long time with the disciples.

The Council at Jerusalem

15 Certain people came down from Judea to Antioch and were teaching the believers: "Unless you are circumcised, according to the custom taught by Moses, you cannot be saved." [2] This brought Paul and Barnabas into sharp dispute and debate with them. So Paul and Barnabas were appointed, along with some other believers, to go up to Jerusalem to see the apostles and elders about this question. [3] The church sent them on their way, and as they traveled through Phoenicia and Samaria, they told how the Gentiles had been converted. This news made all the believers very glad. [4] When they came to Jerusalem, they were welcomed by the church and the apostles and elders, to whom they reported everything God had done through them.

[5] Then some of the believers who belonged to the party of the Pharisees stood up and said, "The Gentiles must be circumcised and required to keep the law of Moses."

[6] The apostles and elders met to consider this question. [7] After much discussion, Peter got up and addressed them: "Brothers, you know that some time ago God made a choice among you that the Gentiles might hear from my lips the message of the gospel and believe. [8] God, who knows the heart, showed that he accepted them by giving the Holy Spirit to them, just as he did to us. [9] He did not discriminate between us and them, for he purified their hearts by faith. [10] Now then, why do you try to test God by putting on the necks of Gentiles a yoke that neither we nor our ancestors have been able to bear? [11] No! We believe it is through the grace of our Lord Jesus that we are saved, just as they are."

a 23 Or Barnabas ordained elders; or Barnabas had elders elected

¹²The whole assembly became silent as they listened to Barnabas and Paul telling about the signs and wonders God had done among the Gentiles through them. ¹³When they finished, James spoke up. "Brothers," he said, "listen to me. ¹⁴Simon^a has described to us how God first intervened to choose a people for his name from the Gentiles. ¹⁵The words of the prophets are in agreement with this, as it is written:

¹⁶"'After this I will return
　and rebuild David's fallen tent.
Its ruins I will rebuild,
　and I will restore it,
¹⁷that the rest of mankind may seek the
　Lord,
　even all the Gentiles who bear my
　name,
says the Lord, who does these
　things'^b—
¹⁸　things known from long ago.^c

¹⁹"It is my judgment, therefore, that we should not make it difficult for the Gentiles who are turning to God. ²⁰Instead we should write to them, telling them to abstain from food polluted by idols, from sexual immorality, from the meat of strangled animals and from blood. ²¹For the law of Moses has been preached in every city from the earliest times and is read in the synagogues on every Sabbath."

The Council's Letter to Gentile Believers

²²Then the apostles and elders, with the whole church, decided to choose some of their own men and send them to Antioch with Paul and Barnabas. They chose Judas (called Barsabbas) and Silas, men who were leaders among the believers. ²³With them they sent the following letter:

The apostles and elders, your brothers,

To the Gentile believers in Antioch, Syria and Cilicia:

Greetings.

²⁴We have heard that some went out from us without our authorization and disturbed you, troubling your minds by what they said. ²⁵So we all agreed to choose some men and send them to you with our dear friends Barnabas and Paul— ²⁶men who have risked their lives for the name of our Lord Jesus Christ. ²⁷Therefore we are sending Judas and Silas to confirm by word of mouth what we are writing. ²⁸It seemed good to the Holy Spirit and to us not to burden you with anything beyond the following requirements: ²⁹You are to abstain from food sacrificed to idols, from blood, from the meat of strangled animals and from sexual immorality. You will do well to avoid these things.

Farewell.

³⁰So the men were sent off and went down to Antioch, where they gathered the church together and delivered the letter. ³¹The people read it and were glad for its encouraging message. ³²Judas and Silas, who themselves were prophets, said much to encourage and strengthen the believers. ³³After spending some time there, they were sent off by the believers with the blessing of peace to return to those who had sent them. [³⁴]^d ³⁵But Paul and Barnabas remained in Antioch, where they and many others taught and preached the word of the Lord.

Disagreement Between Paul and Barnabas

³⁶Some time later Paul said to Barnabas, "Let us go back and visit the believers in all the towns where we preached the word of the Lord and see how they are doing." ³⁷Barnabas wanted to take John, also called Mark, with them, ³⁸but Paul did not think it wise to take him, because he had deserted them in Pamphylia and had not continued with them in the work. ³⁹They had such a sharp disagreement

^a 14 Greek Simeon, a variant of Simon; that is, Peter　^b 17 Amos 9:11,12 (see Septuagint)　^c 17,18 Some manuscripts things'— /¹⁸the Lord's work is known to him from long ago　^d 34 Some manuscripts include here But Silas decided to remain there.

that they parted company. Barnabas took Mark and sailed for Cyprus, [40]but Paul chose Silas and left, commended by the believers to the grace of the Lord. [41]He went through Syria and Cilicia, strengthening the churches.

Timothy Joins Paul and Silas

16 Paul came to Derbe and then to Lystra, where a disciple named Timothy lived, whose mother was Jewish and a believer but whose father was a Greek. [2]The believers at Lystra and Iconium spoke well of him. [3]Paul wanted to take him along on the journey, so he circumcised him because of the Jews who lived in that area, for they all knew that his father was a Greek. [4]As they traveled from town to town, they delivered the decisions reached by the apostles and elders in Jerusalem for the people to obey. [5]So the churches were strengthened in the faith and grew daily in numbers.

Paul's Vision of the Man of Macedonia

[6]Paul and his companions traveled throughout the region of Phrygia and Galatia, having been kept by the Holy Spirit from preaching the word in the province of Asia. [7]When they came to the border of Mysia, they tried to enter Bithynia, but the Spirit of Jesus would not allow them to. [8]So they passed by Mysia and went down to Troas. [9]During the night Paul had a vision of a man of Macedonia standing and begging him, "Come over to Macedonia and help us." [10]After Paul had seen the vision, we got ready at once to leave for Macedonia, concluding that God had called us to preach the gospel to them.

Lydia's Conversion in Philippi

[11]From Troas we put out to sea and sailed straight for Samothrace, and the next day we went on to Neapolis. [12]From there we traveled to Philippi, a Roman colony and the leading city of that district[a] of Macedonia. And we stayed there several days.

[13]On the Sabbath we went outside the city gate to the river, where we expected to find a place of prayer. We sat down and began to speak to the women who had gathered there. [14]One of those listening was a woman from the city of Thyatira named Lydia, a dealer in purple cloth. She was a worshiper of God. The Lord opened her heart to respond to Paul's message. [15]When she and the members of her household were baptized, she invited us to her home. "If you consider me a believer in the Lord," she said, "come and stay at my house." And she persuaded us.

Paul and Silas in Prison

[16]Once when we were going to the place of prayer, we were met by a female slave who had a spirit by which she predicted the future. She earned a great deal of money for her owners by fortune-telling. [17]She followed Paul and the rest of us, shouting, "These men are servants of the Most High God, who are telling you the way to be saved." [18]She kept this up for many days. Finally Paul became so annoyed that he turned around and said to the spirit, "In the name of Jesus Christ I command you to come out of her!" At that moment the spirit left her.

[19]When her owners realized that their hope of making money was gone, they seized Paul and Silas and dragged them into the marketplace to face the authorities. [20]They brought them before the magistrates and said, "These men are Jews, and are throwing our city into an uproar [21]by advocating customs unlawful for us Romans to accept or practice."

[22]The crowd joined in the attack against Paul and Silas, and the magistrates ordered them to be stripped and beaten with rods. [23]After they had been severely flogged, they were thrown into prison, and the jailer was commanded to guard them carefully. [24]When he received these orders, he put them in the inner cell and fastened their feet in the stocks.

[25]About midnight Paul and Silas were praying and singing hymns to God, and the other prisoners were listening to them.

a 12 The text and meaning of the Greek for *the leading city of that district* are uncertain.

²⁶Suddenly there was such a violent earthquake that the foundations of the prison were shaken. At once all the prison doors flew open, and everyone's chains came loose. ²⁷The jailer woke up, and when he saw the prison doors open, he drew his sword and was about to kill himself because he thought the prisoners had escaped. ²⁸But Paul shouted, "Don't harm yourself! We are all here!"

²⁹The jailer called for lights, rushed in and fell trembling before Paul and Silas. ³⁰He then brought them out and asked, "Sirs, what must I do to be saved?"

³¹They replied, "Believe in the Lord Jesus, and you will be saved—you and your household." ³²Then they spoke the word of the Lord to him and to all the others in his house. ³³At that hour of the night the jailer took them and washed their wounds; then immediately he and all his household were baptized. ³⁴The jailer brought them into his house and set a meal before them; he was filled with joy because he had come to believe in God—he and his whole household.

³⁵When it was daylight, the magistrates sent their officers to the jailer with the order: "Release those men." ³⁶The jailer told Paul, "The magistrates have ordered that you and Silas be released. Now you can leave. Go in peace."

Acts 16:11–15

Lydia found the one true God.

Even before Jesus rose from the dead and Christians began to spread the good news about him around the world, there were non-Jewish people who had come to believe in the one true God. These converts were known as "God-fearers" because of their reverence for the God of Israel. They abandoned pagan gods and the sexual sin that was part of their worship, adopted Jewish beliefs, followed Old Testament commands, and gathered in synagogues, the local centers of worship.

Lydia was one of these people: "a worshiper of God" (Acts 16:14). The book of Acts pictures her as a wealthy businesswoman, a seller of beautifully dyed purple cloth from her hometown of Thyatira.

When Paul preached about Jesus, God made Lydia open to his message. She and her entire household believed and were baptized, becoming the first Christians in Philippi, a city in Greece, and therefore the first believers in all of Europe.

Lydia used her work to help God's kingdom grow. She invited Paul and his missionary partner, Silas, to stay at her house. They stayed with her again after their miraculous release from a Philippian jail.

You can find Lydia in Acts 16:11–15 and 16:40.

UNSHAKEN people

ROCK SOLID
promises

"Believe in the Lord Jesus, and you will be saved." Acts 16:31

To become friends with God, trust what Jesus did for you on the cross.

---

37 But Paul said to the officers: "They beat us publicly without a trial, even though we are Roman citizens, and threw us into prison. And now do they want to get rid of us quietly? No! Let them come themselves and escort us out."

38 The officers reported this to the magistrates, and when they heard that Paul and Silas were Roman citizens, they were alarmed. 39 They came to appease them and escorted them from the prison, requesting them to leave the city. 40 After Paul and Silas came out of the prison, they went to Lydia's house, where they met with the brothers and sisters and encouraged them. Then they left.

In Thessalonica

17 When Paul and his companions had passed through Amphipolis and Apollonia, they came to Thessalonica, where there was a Jewish synagogue. 2 As was his custom, Paul went into the synagogue, and on three Sabbath days he reasoned with them from the Scriptures, 3 explaining and proving that the Messiah had to suffer and rise from the dead. "This Jesus I am proclaiming to you is the Messiah," he said. 4 Some of the Jews were persuaded and joined Paul and Silas, as did a large number of God-fearing Greeks and quite a few prominent women.

5 But other Jews were jealous; so they rounded up some bad characters from the marketplace, formed a mob and started a riot in the city. They rushed to Jason's house in search of Paul and Silas in order to bring them out to the crowd.[a] 6 But when they did not find them, they dragged Jason and some other believers before the city officials, shouting: "These men who have caused trouble all over the world have now come here, 7 and Jason has welcomed them into his house. They are all defying Caesar's decrees, saying that there is another king, one called Jesus." 8 When they heard this, the crowd and the city officials were thrown into turmoil. 9 Then they made Jason and the others post bond and let them go.

In Berea

10 As soon as it was night, the believers sent Paul and Silas away to Berea. On arriving there, they went to the Jewish synagogue. 11 Now the Berean Jews were of more noble character than those in Thessalonica, for they received the message with great eagerness and examined the Scriptures every day to see if what Paul said was true. 12 As a result, many of them believed, as did also a number of prominent Greek women and many Greek men.

13 But when the Jews in Thessalonica learned that Paul was preaching the word of God at Berea, some of them went there too, agitating the crowds and stirring them up. 14 The believers immediately sent Paul to the coast, but Silas and Timothy stayed at Berea. 15 Those who escorted Paul brought him to Athens and then left with instructions for Silas and Timothy to join him as soon as possible.

In Athens

16 While Paul was waiting for them in Athens, he was greatly distressed to see that the city was full of idols. 17 So he reasoned in the synagogue with both Jews and God-fearing Greeks, as well as in the marketplace day by day with those who happened to be there. 18 A group of

a 5 Or the assembly of the people

Epicurean and Stoic philosophers began to debate with him. Some of them asked, "What is this babbler trying to say?" Others remarked, "He seems to be advocating foreign gods." They said this because Paul was preaching the good news about Jesus and the resurrection. [19] Then they took him and brought him to a meeting of the Areopagus, where they said to him, "May we know what this new teaching is that you are presenting? [20] You are bringing some strange ideas to our ears, and we would like to know what they mean." [21] (All the Athenians and the foreigners who lived there spent their time doing nothing but talking about and listening to the latest ideas.)

[22] Paul then stood up in the meeting of the Areopagus and said: "People of Athens! I see that in every way you are very religious. [23] For as I walked around and looked carefully at your objects of worship, I even found an altar with this inscription: TO AN UNKNOWN GOD. So you are ignorant of the very thing you worship—and this is what I am going to proclaim to you.

[24] "The God who made the world and everything in it is the Lord of heaven and earth and does not live in temples built by human hands. [25] And he is not served by human hands, as if he needed anything. Rather, he himself gives everyone life and breath and everything else. [26] From one man he made all the nations, that they should inhabit the whole earth; and he marked out their appointed times in history and the boundaries of their lands. [27] God did this so that they would seek him and perhaps reach out for him and find him, though he is not far from any one of us. [28] 'For in him we live and move and have our being.'[a] As some of your own poets have said, 'We are his offspring.'[b]

[29] "Therefore since we are God's offspring, we should not think that the di-

[a] 28 From the Cretan philosopher Epimenides
[b] 28 From the Cilician Stoic philosopher Aratus

ROCK SOLID *principles*

Acts 17:16–34

Take time to reason with people.

Amber looked down, not sure what to say next. Claire just wasn't getting it. Amber had told her own story of how she became a Christian. She covered the basics about Jesus' death and resurrection. She explained how putting trust in Jesus makes us friends with God and gives us a home forever in heaven. After all that, Claire seemed to be saying "that's nice ... for you." Amber decided she wouldn't stop talking about Jesus, but she would make an extra effort to figure out Claire, support her as the best friend ever, and answer every question she could. None of this felt easy, but Amber wasn't going to give up.

The apostle Paul preached Jesus even when he wasn't sure people would listen. He talked with pagan idol worshipers, brainy philosophers, and his own people, the Jews. He kept talking even when he didn't get quick results, like the scene where he "spoke boldly there for three months, arguing persuasively about the kingdom of God" (Acts 19:8). Paul gave people time to make up their minds about Jesus.

vine being is like gold or silver or stone—an image made by human design and skill. [30]In the past God overlooked such ignorance, but now he commands all people everywhere to repent. [31]For he has set a day when he will judge the world with justice by the man he has appointed. He has given proof of this to everyone by raising him from the dead."

[32]When they heard about the resurrection of the dead, some of them sneered, but others said, "We want to hear you again on this subject." [33]At that, Paul left the Council. [34]Some of the people became followers of Paul and believed. Among them was Dionysius, a member of the Areopagus, also a woman named Damaris, and a number of others.

In Corinth

18 After this, Paul left Athens and went to Corinth. [2]There he met a Jew named Aquila, a native of Pontus, who had recently come from Italy with his wife Priscilla, because Claudius had ordered all Jews to leave Rome. Paul went to see them, [3]and because he was a tentmaker as they were, he stayed and worked with them. [4]Every Sabbath he reasoned in the synagogue, trying to persuade Jews and Greeks.

[5]When Silas and Timothy came from Macedonia, Paul devoted himself exclusively to preaching, testifying to the Jews that Jesus was the Messiah. [6]But when they opposed Paul and became abusive, he shook out his clothes in protest and said to them, "Your blood be on your own heads! I am innocent of it. From now on I will go to the Gentiles."

[7]Then Paul left the synagogue and went next door to the house of Titius Justus, a worshiper of God. [8]Crispus, the synagogue leader, and his entire household believed in the Lord; and many of the Corinthians who heard Paul believed and were baptized.

[9]One night the Lord spoke to Paul in a vision: "Do not be afraid; keep on speaking, do not be silent. [10]For I am with you, and no one is going to attack and harm

ROCK SOLID *promises*

"Do not be afraid; keep on speaking, do not be silent. For I am with you." Acts 18:9–10

Don't fear tough opponents, because God will give you the right words to say.

you, because I have many people in this city." [11]So Paul stayed in Corinth for a year and a half, teaching them the word of God.

[12]While Gallio was proconsul of Achaia, the Jews of Corinth made a united attack on Paul and brought him to the place of judgment. [13]"This man," they charged, "is persuading the people to worship God in ways contrary to the law."

[14]Just as Paul was about to speak, Gallio said to them, "If you Jews were making a complaint about some misdemeanor or serious crime, it would be reasonable for me to listen to you. [15]But since it involves questions about words and names and your own law—settle the matter yourselves. I will not be a judge of such things." [16]So he drove them off. [17]Then the crowd there turned on Sosthenes the synagogue leader and beat him in front of the proconsul; and Gallio showed no concern whatever.

Priscilla, Aquila and Apollos

[18]Paul stayed on in Corinth for some time. Then he left the brothers and sisters and sailed for Syria, accompanied by Priscilla and Aquila. Before he sailed, he had his hair cut off at Cenchreae because of a vow he had taken. [19]They arrived at Ephesus, where Paul left Priscilla and Aquila. He himself went into the synagogue and reasoned with the Jews. [20]When they

asked him to spend more time with them, he declined. ²¹But as he left, he promised, "I will come back if it is God's will." Then he set sail from Ephesus. ²²When he landed at Caesarea, he went up to Jerusalem and greeted the church and then went down to Antioch.

²³After spending some time in Antioch, Paul set out from there and traveled from place to place throughout the region of Galatia and Phrygia, strengthening all the disciples.

²⁴Meanwhile a Jew named Apollos, a native of Alexandria, came to Ephesus. He was a learned man, with a thorough knowledge of the Scriptures. ²⁵He had been instructed in the way of the Lord, and he spoke with great fervor[a] and taught about Jesus accurately, though he knew only the baptism of John. ²⁶He began to speak boldly in the synagogue. When Priscilla and Aquila heard him, they invited him to their home and explained to him the way of God more adequately.

²⁷When Apollos wanted to go to Achaia, the brothers and sisters encouraged him and wrote to the disciples there to welcome him. When he arrived, he was a great help to those who by grace had believed. ²⁸For he vigorously refuted his Jewish opponents in public debate, prov-

[a] 25 Or *with fervor in the Spirit*

Acts 18:1–28

Aquila and Priscilla teamed up for God.

As the message about Jesus spread, people across the Roman Empire became believers, including Jews living in the capital of the empire, Rome. In AD 49, the emperor Claudius ordered all Jews to leave Rome, likely because of heated fights about Jesus between those who believed and those who didn't.

A husband and wife named Aquila and Priscilla left Rome and went to Corinth. Like the apostle Paul, they ran a business making tents (see Acts 18:3). While Paul stayed and worked with them, he also tried to persuade both Jews and Greeks to believe in Jesus. When the Jews opposed his message, Paul left Corinth to preach to Gentiles, or non-Jews. Aquila and Priscilla went with him.

The trio landed in Ephesus, where they met a man named Apollos. Even though Apollos was a gifted preacher, he apparently knew nothing about the death and resurrection of Jesus or the arrival of the Holy Spirit. Aquila and Priscilla "invited him to their home and explained to him the way of God more adequately" (Acts 18:26). Because of their help, he became an even better teacher, "proving from the Scriptures that Jesus was the Messiah" (Acts 18:28).

Aquila and Priscilla were able to return to Rome, probably after the death of Claudius in AD 54. Paul greeted them at the end of his letter to the Romans, thanking them for risking their lives for him (see Romans 16:3–4).

You can find Aquila and Priscilla in Acts 18:1–4 and 18–28 as well as Romans 16:3–4 and 2 Timothy 4:19.

UNSHAKEN people

ing from the Scriptures that Jesus was the Messiah.

Paul in Ephesus

19 While Apollos was at Corinth, Paul took the road through the interior and arrived at Ephesus. There he found some disciples ²and asked them, "Did you receive the Holy Spirit when*ᵃ* you believed?"

They answered, "No, we have not even heard that there is a Holy Spirit."

³So Paul asked, "Then what baptism did you receive?"

"John's baptism," they replied.

⁴Paul said, "John's baptism was a baptism of repentance. He told the people to believe in the one coming after him, that is, in Jesus." ⁵On hearing this, they were baptized in the name of the Lord Jesus. ⁶When Paul placed his hands on them, the Holy Spirit came on them, and they spoke in tongues*ᵇ* and prophesied. ⁷There were about twelve men in all.

⁸Paul entered the synagogue and spoke boldly there for three months, arguing persuasively about the kingdom of God. ⁹But some of them became obstinate; they refused to believe and publicly maligned the Way. So Paul left them. He took the disciples with him and had discussions daily in the lecture hall of Tyrannus. ¹⁰This went on for two years, so that all the Jews and Greeks who lived in the province of Asia heard the word of the Lord.

¹¹God did extraordinary miracles through Paul, ¹²so that even handkerchiefs and aprons that had touched him were taken to the sick, and their illnesses were cured and the evil spirits left them.

¹³Some Jews who went around driving out evil spirits tried to invoke the name of the Lord Jesus over those who were demon-possessed. They would say, "In the name of the Jesus whom Paul preaches, I command you to come out." ¹⁴Seven sons of Sceva, a Jewish chief priest, were doing this. ¹⁵One day the evil spirit answered them, "Jesus I know, and Paul I know about, but who are you?" ¹⁶Then the man who had the evil spirit jumped on

them and overpowered them all. He gave them such a beating that they ran out of the house naked and bleeding.

¹⁷When this became known to the Jews and Greeks living in Ephesus, they were all seized with fear, and the name of the Lord Jesus was held in high honor. ¹⁸Many of those who believed now came and openly confessed what they had done. ¹⁹A number who had practiced sorcery brought their scrolls together and burned them publicly. When they calculated the value of the scrolls, the total came to fifty thousand drachmas.*ᶜ* ²⁰In this way the word of the Lord spread widely and grew in power.

²¹After all this had happened, Paul decided*ᵈ* to go to Jerusalem, passing through Macedonia and Achaia. "After I have been there," he said, "I must visit Rome also." ²²He sent two of his helpers, Timothy and Erastus, to Macedonia, while he stayed in the province of Asia a little longer.

The Riot in Ephesus

²³About that time there arose a great disturbance about the Way. ²⁴A silversmith named Demetrius, who made silver shrines of Artemis, brought in a lot of business for the craftsmen there. ²⁵He called them together, along with the workers in related trades, and said: "You know, my friends, that we receive a good income from this business. ²⁶And you see and hear how this fellow Paul has convinced and led astray large numbers of people here in Ephesus and in practically the whole province of Asia. He says that gods made by human hands are no gods at all. ²⁷There is danger not only that our trade will lose its good name, but also that the temple of the great goddess Artemis will be discredited; and the goddess herself, who is worshiped throughout the province of Asia and the world, will be robbed of her divine majesty."

²⁸When they heard this, they were furious and began shouting: "Great is Artemis of the Ephesians!" ²⁹Soon the whole city

---

ᵃ 2 Or *after*   *ᵇ 6* Or *other languages*
ᶜ 19 A drachma was a silver coin worth about a day's wages.   *ᵈ 21* Or *decided in the Spirit*

was in an uproar. The people seized Gaius and Aristarchus, Paul's traveling companions from Macedonia, and all of them rushed into the theater together. [30]Paul wanted to appear before the crowd, but the disciples would not let him. [31]Even some of the officials of the province, friends of Paul, sent him a message begging him not to venture into the theater.

Acts 19:23–41

Man-made gods are no gods at all.

The business people in Ephesus were furious with the apostle Paul. When he arrived in the city and began preaching Jesus as the one-and-only Savior and Lord, residents and religious tourists stopped buying silver statues of the goddess Artemis and other spiritual trinkets. The craftsmen protested that their trade in hand-made idols was dying. They pointed out that the great Artemis was being insulted, and soon everyone would stop worshiping their beloved goddess. Their anger escalated into a riot that halted only when the city leader stepped in. He counseled calm and, if needed, legal action against Paul. That furor all started when Paul preached that "gods made by human hands are no gods at all" (Acts 19:26). People often bow to man-made objects, whether handcrafted idols, hot cars, pretty clothes, or anything else. But none of them compare to the one true God. He commands that we worship him alone (see Exodus 20:1–6).

Think: What have you made into a false god? How did/can you stop worshiping it?

ROCK SOLID truths

[32]The assembly was in confusion: Some were shouting one thing, some another. Most of the people did not even know why they were there. [33]The Jews in the crowd pushed Alexander to the front, and they shouted instructions to him. He motioned for silence in order to make a defense before the people. [34]But when they realized he was a Jew, they all shouted in unison for about two hours: "Great is Artemis of the Ephesians!"

[35]The city clerk quieted the crowd and said: "Fellow Ephesians, doesn't all the world know that the city of Ephesus is the guardian of the temple of the great Artemis and of her image, which fell from heaven? [36]Therefore, since these facts are undeniable, you ought to calm down and not do anything rash. [37]You have brought these men here, though they have neither robbed temples nor blasphemed our goddess. [38]If, then, Demetrius and his fellow craftsmen have a grievance against anybody, the courts are open and there are proconsuls. They can press charges. [39]If there is anything further you want to bring up, it must be settled in a legal assembly. [40]As it is, we are in danger of being charged with rioting because of what happened today. In that case we would not be able to account for this commotion, since there is no reason for it." [41]After he had said this, he dismissed the assembly.

Through Macedonia and Greece

20 When the uproar had ended, Paul sent for the disciples and, after encouraging them, said goodbye and set out for Macedonia. [2]He traveled through that area, speaking many words of encouragement to the people, and finally arrived in Greece, [3]where he stayed three months. Because some Jews had plotted against him just as he was about to sail for Syria, he decided to go back through Macedonia. [4]He was accompanied by Sopater son of Pyrrhus from Berea, Aristarchus and Secundus from Thessalonica, Gaius from Derbe, Timothy also, and Tychicus and Trophimus from the province of Asia. [5]These men went on ahead and waited for us at Troas. ⁶But we sailed from Philippi after the Festival of Unleavened Bread, and five days later joined the others at Troas, where we stayed seven days.

Eutychus Raised From the Dead at Troas

⁷On the first day of the week we came together to break bread. Paul spoke to the people and, because he intended to leave the next day, kept on talking until midnight. ⁸There were many lamps in the upstairs room where we were meeting. ⁹Seated in a window was a young man named Eutychus, who was sinking into a deep sleep as Paul talked on and on. When he was sound asleep, he fell to the ground from the third story and was picked up dead. ¹⁰Paul went down, threw himself on the young man and put his arms around him. "Don't be alarmed," he said. "He's alive!" ¹¹Then he went upstairs again and broke bread and ate. After talking until daylight, he left. ¹²The people took the young man home alive and were greatly comforted.

Paul's Farewell to the Ephesian Elders

¹³We went on ahead to the ship and sailed for Assos, where we were going to take Paul aboard. He had made this

Acts 20:7–12

Eutychus woke up.

Eutychus probably wasn't the first person to fall asleep during a sermon, and he certainly wasn't the last. But the Bible forever remembers him as the guy who dozed off during an especially long message from the apostle Paul.

"Eutychus" means "fortunate," and the name couldn't fit better. Eutychus and other believers had gathered in the city of Troas, a key city in what is now Turkey. They came together to share communion and listen to Paul preach one last time before he departed the next morning to sail toward Jerusalem.

Paul preached until midnight in a third-story room that must have been hot and stuffy from heat given off by "many lamps" (Acts 20:8). Young Eutychus sat in a window, likely looking for some fresh air. As Paul talked on and on, Eutychus sank into a deep sleep, then tumbled out of the window to the ground below and died. The apostle miraculously brought Eutychus back to life, then kept preaching until dawn.

The people who loved Eutychus were glad to get him back alive. And it's interesting the words of the Bible don't condemn this young guy for dozing off during a sermon. God not only made us but understands our weaknesses (see Hebrews 4:14–16).

You can find Eutychus only in this episode in Acts 20:7–12.

UNSHAKEN people

arrangement because he was going there on foot. [14]When he met us at Assos, we took him aboard and went on to Mitylene. [15]The next day we set sail from there and arrived off Chios. The day after that we crossed over to Samos, and on the following day arrived at Miletus. [16]Paul had decided to sail past Ephesus to avoid spending time in the province of Asia, for he was in a hurry to reach Jerusalem, if possible, by the day of Pentecost.

[17]From Miletus, Paul sent to Ephesus for the elders of the church. [18]When they arrived, he said to them: "You know how I lived the whole time I was with you, from the first day I came into the province of Asia. [19]I served the Lord with great humility and with tears and in the midst of severe testing by the plots of my Jewish opponents. [20]You know that I have not hesitated to preach anything that would be helpful to you but have taught you publicly and from house to house. [21]I have declared to both Jews and Greeks that they must turn to God in repentance and have faith in our Lord Jesus.

[22]"And now, compelled by the Spirit, I am going to Jerusalem, not knowing what will happen to me there. [23]I only know that in every city the Holy Spirit warns me that prison and hardships are facing me. [24]However, I consider my life worth nothing to me; my only aim is to finish the race and complete the task the Lord Jesus has given me—the task of testifying to the good news of God's grace.

[25]"Now I know that none of you among whom I have gone about preaching the kingdom will ever see me again. [26]Therefore, I declare to you today that I am innocent of the blood of any of you. [27]For I have not hesitated to proclaim to you the whole will of God. [28]Keep watch over yourselves and all the flock of which the Holy Spirit has made you overseers. Be shepherds of the church of God,[a] which he bought with his own blood.[b] [29]I know that after I leave, savage wolves will come in among you and will not spare the flock. [30]Even from your own number men will arise and distort the truth in order to draw away disciples after them. [31]So be on your guard! Remember that for three years I never stopped warning each of you night and day with tears.

[32]"Now I commit you to God and to the word of his grace, which can build you up and give you an inheritance among all those who are sanctified. [33]I have not coveted anyone's silver or gold or clothing. [34]You yourselves know that these hands of mine have supplied my own needs and the needs of my companions. [35]In everything I did, I showed you that by this kind of hard work we must help the weak, remembering the words the Lord Jesus himself said: 'It is more blessed to give than to receive.'"

[36]When Paul had finished speaking, he knelt down with all of them and prayed. [37]They all wept as they embraced him and kissed him. [38]What grieved them most was his statement that they would never see his face again. Then they accompanied him to the ship.

On to Jerusalem

21 After we had torn ourselves away from them, we put out to sea and sailed straight to Kos. The next day we went to Rhodes and from there to Patara. [2]We found a ship crossing over to Phoenicia, went on board and set sail. [3]After sighting Cyprus and passing to the south of it, we sailed on to Syria. We landed at Tyre, where our ship was to unload its cargo. [4]We sought out the disciples there and stayed with them seven days. Through the Spirit they urged Paul not to go on to Jerusalem. [5]When it was time to leave, we left and continued on our way. All of them, including wives and children, accompanied us out of the city, and there on the beach we knelt to pray. [6]After saying goodbye to each other, we went aboard the ship, and they returned home.

[7]We continued our voyage from Tyre and landed at Ptolemais, where we greeted the brothers and sisters and stayed with

---

[a] 28 Many manuscripts *of the Lord*
[b] 28 Or *with the blood of his own Son.*

them for a day. [8]Leaving the next day, we reached Caesarea and stayed at the house of Philip the evangelist, one of the Seven. [9]He had four unmarried daughters who prophesied.

[10]After we had been there a number of days, a prophet named Agabus came down from Judea. [11]Coming over to us, he took Paul's belt, tied his own hands and feet with it and said, "The Holy Spirit says, 'In this way the Jewish leaders in Jerusalem will bind the owner of this belt and will hand him over to the Gentiles.'"

[12]When we heard this, we and the people there pleaded with Paul not to go up to Jerusalem. [13]Then Paul answered, "Why are you weeping and breaking my heart? I am ready not only to be bound, but also to die in Jerusalem for the name of the Lord Jesus." [14]When he would not be dissuaded, we gave up and said, "The Lord's will be done."

[15]After this, we started on our way up to Jerusalem. [16]Some of the disciples from Caesarea accompanied us and brought us to the home of Mnason, where we were to stay. He was a man from Cyprus and one of the early disciples.

Paul's Arrival at Jerusalem

[17]When we arrived at Jerusalem, the brothers and sisters received us warmly. [18]The next day Paul and the rest of us went to see James, and all the elders were present. [19]Paul greeted them and reported in detail what God had done among the Gentiles through his ministry.

[20]When they heard this, they praised God. Then they said to Paul: "You see, brother, how many thousands of Jews have believed, and all of them are zealous for the law. [21]They have been informed that you teach all the Jews who live among the Gentiles to turn away from Moses, telling them not to circumcise their children or live according to our customs. [22]What shall we do? They will certainly hear that you have come, [23]so do what we tell you. There are four men with us who have made a vow. [24]Take these men, join in their purification rites and pay their expenses, so that they can have their heads shaved. Then everyone will know there is no truth in these reports about you, but that you yourself are living in obedience to the law. [25]As for the Gentile believers, we have written to them our decision that they should abstain from food sacrificed to idols, from blood, from the meat of strangled animals and from sexual immorality."

[26]The next day Paul took the men and purified himself along with them. Then he went to the temple to give notice of the date when the days of purification would end and the offering would be made for each of them.

Paul Arrested

[27]When the seven days were nearly over, some Jews from the province of Asia saw Paul at the temple. They stirred up the whole crowd and seized him, [28]shouting, "Fellow Israelites, help us! This is the man who teaches everyone everywhere against our people and our law and this place. And besides, he has brought Greeks into the temple and defiled this holy place." [29](They had previously seen Trophimus the Ephesian in the city with Paul and assumed that Paul had brought him into the temple.)

[30]The whole city was aroused, and the people came running from all directions. Seizing Paul, they dragged him from the temple, and immediately the gates were shut. [31]While they were trying to kill him, news reached the commander of the Roman troops that the whole city of Jerusalem was in an uproar. [32]He at once took some officers and soldiers and ran down to the crowd. When the rioters saw the commander and his soldiers, they stopped beating Paul.

[33]The commander came up and arrested him and ordered him to be bound with two chains. Then he asked who he was and what he had done. [34]Some in the crowd shouted one thing and some another, and since the commander could not get at the truth because of the uproar, he ordered that Paul be taken into

the barracks. [35] When Paul reached the steps, the violence of the mob was so great he had to be carried by the soldiers. [36] The crowd that followed kept shouting, "Get rid of him!"

Paul Speaks to the Crowd

[37] As the soldiers were about to take Paul into the barracks, he asked the commander, "May I say something to you?"

"Do you speak Greek?" he replied. [38] "Aren't you the Egyptian who started a revolt and led four thousand terrorists out into the wilderness some time ago?"

[39] Paul answered, "I am a Jew, from Tarsus in Cilicia, a citizen of no ordinary city. Please let me speak to the people."

[40] After receiving the commander's permission, Paul stood on the steps and motioned to the crowd. When they were all silent, he said to them in Arama-ic[a]: [1] "Brothers and fathers, listen now to my defense."

22

[2] When they heard him speak to them in Aramaic, they became very quiet.

Then Paul said: [3] "I am a Jew, born in Tarsus of Cilicia, but brought up in this city. I studied under Gamaliel and was thoroughly trained in the law of our ancestors. I was just as zealous for God as any of you are today. [4] I persecuted the followers of this Way to their death, arresting both men and women and throwing them into prison, [5] as the high priest and all the Council can themselves testify. I even obtained letters from them to their associates in Damascus, and went there to bring these people as prisoners to Jerusalem to be punished.

[6] "About noon as I came near Damascus, suddenly a bright light from heaven flashed around me. [7] I fell to the ground and heard a voice say to me, 'Saul! Saul! Why do you persecute me?'

[8] "'Who are you, Lord?' I asked.

"'I am Jesus of Nazareth, whom you are persecuting,' he replied. [9] My companions saw the light, but they did not understand the voice of him who was speaking to me.

[10] "'What shall I do, Lord?' I asked.

"'Get up,' the Lord said, 'and go into Damascus. There you will be told all that you have been assigned to do.' [11] My companions led me by the hand into Damascus, because the brilliance of the light had blinded me.

[12] "A man named Ananias came to see me. He was a devout observer of the law and highly respected by all the Jews living there. [13] He stood beside me and said, 'Brother Saul, receive your sight!' And at that very moment I was able to see him.

[14] "Then he said: 'The God of our ancestors has chosen you to know his will and to see the Righteous One and to hear words from his mouth. [15] You will be his witness to all people of what you have seen and heard. [16] And now what are you waiting for? Get up, be baptized and wash your sins away, calling on his name.'

[17] "When I returned to Jerusalem and was praying at the temple, I fell into a trance [18] and saw the Lord speaking to me. 'Quick!' he said. 'Leave Jerusalem immediately, because the people here will not accept your testimony about me.'

[19] "'Lord,' I replied, 'these people know that I went from one synagogue to another to imprison and beat those who believe in you. [20] And when the blood of your martyr[b] Stephen was shed, I stood there giving my approval and guarding the clothes of those who were killing him.'

[21] "Then the Lord said to me, 'Go; I will send you far away to the Gentiles.'"

Paul the Roman Citizen

[22] The crowd listened to Paul until he said this. Then they raised their voices and shouted, "Rid the earth of him! He's not fit to live!"

[23] As they were shouting and throwing off their cloaks and flinging dust into the air, [24] the commander ordered that Paul be taken into the barracks. He directed that he be flogged and interrogated in order to find out why the people were shouting at him like this. [25] As they stretched him out to flog him, Paul said to the centurion standing there, "Is it legal for you to

[a] 40 Or possibly *Hebrew*; also in 22:2
[b] 20 Or *witness*

flog a Roman citizen who hasn't even been found guilty?"

²⁶When the centurion heard this, he went to the commander and reported it. "What are you going to do?" he asked. "This man is a Roman citizen."

²⁷The commander went to Paul and asked, "Tell me, are you a Roman citizen?"

"Yes, I am," he answered.

²⁸Then the commander said, "I had to pay a lot of money for my citizenship."

"But I was born a citizen," Paul replied.

²⁹Those who were about to interrogate him withdrew immediately. The commander himself was alarmed when he realized that he had put Paul, a Roman citizen, in chains.

Paul Before the Sanhedrin

³⁰The commander wanted to find out exactly why Paul was being accused by the Jews. So the next day he released him and ordered the chief priests and all the members of the Sanhedrin to assemble. Then he brought Paul and had him stand before them.

23 Paul looked straight at the Sanhedrin and said, "My brothers, I have fulfilled my duty to God in all good conscience to this day." ²At this the high priest Ananias ordered those standing near Paul to strike him on the mouth. ³Then Paul said to him, "God will strike you, you whitewashed wall! You sit there to judge me according to the law, yet you yourself violate the law by commanding that I be struck!"

⁴Those who were standing near Paul said, "How dare you insult God's high priest!"

⁵Paul replied, "Brothers, I did not realize that he was the high priest; for it is written: 'Do not speak evil about the ruler of your people.'ᵃ"

⁶Then Paul, knowing that some of them were Sadducees and the others Pharisees, called out in the Sanhedrin, "My brothers, I am a Pharisee, descended from Pharisees. I stand on trial because of the hope of the resurrection of the dead." ⁷When he said this, a dispute broke out between the Pharisees and the Sadducees, and the assembly was divided. ⁸(The Sadducees say that there is no resurrection, and that there are neither angels nor spirits, but the Pharisees believe all these things.)

⁹There was a great uproar, and some of the teachers of the law who were Pharisees stood up and argued vigorously. "We find nothing wrong with this man," they said. "What if a spirit or an angel has spoken to him?" ¹⁰The dispute became so violent that the commander was afraid Paul would be torn to pieces by them. He ordered the troops to go down and take him away from them by force and bring him into the barracks.

¹¹The following night the Lord stood near Paul and said, "Take courage! As you have testified about me in Jerusalem, so you must also testify in Rome."

The Plot to Kill Paul

¹²The next morning some Jews formed a conspiracy and bound themselves with an oath not to eat or drink until they had killed Paul. ¹³More than forty men were involved in this plot. ¹⁴They went to the chief priests and the elders and said, "We have taken a solemn oath not to eat anything until we have killed Paul. ¹⁵Now then, you and the Sanhedrin petition the commander to bring him before you on the pretext of wanting more accurate information about his case. We are ready to kill him before he gets here."

¹⁶But when the son of Paul's sister heard of this plot, he went into the barracks and told Paul.

¹⁷Then Paul called one of the centurions and said, "Take this young man to the commander; he has something to tell him." ¹⁸So he took him to the commander.

The centurion said, "Paul, the prisoner, sent for me and asked me to bring this young man to you because he has something to tell you."

¹⁹The commander took the young man by the hand, drew him aside and asked, "What is it you want to tell me?"

²⁰He said: "Some Jews have agreed to

ᵃ 5 Exodus 22:28

ask you to bring Paul before the Sanhedrin tomorrow on the pretext of wanting more accurate information about him. ²¹Don't give in to them, because more than forty of them are waiting in ambush for him. They have taken an oath not to eat or drink until they have killed him. They are ready now, waiting for your consent to their request."

²²The commander dismissed the young man with this warning: "Don't tell anyone that you have reported this to me."

Paul Transferred to Caesarea

²³Then he called two of his centurions and ordered them, "Get ready a detachment of two hundred soldiers, seventy horsemen and two hundred spearmen*a* to go to Caesarea at nine tonight. ²⁴Provide horses for Paul so that he may be taken safely to Governor Felix."

²⁵He wrote a letter as follows:

²⁶Claudius Lysias,

To His Excellency, Governor Felix:

Greetings.

²⁷This man was seized by the Jews and they were about to kill him, but I came with my troops and rescued him, for I had learned that he is a Roman citizen. ²⁸I wanted to know why they were accusing him, so I brought him to their Sanhedrin. ²⁹I found that the accusation had to do with questions about their law, but there was no charge against him that deserved death or imprisonment. ³⁰When I was informed of a plot to be carried out against the man, I sent him to you at once. I also ordered his accusers to present to you their case against him.

³¹So the soldiers, carrying out their orders, took Paul with them during the night and brought him as far as Antipatris. ³²The next day they let the cavalry go on with him, while they returned to the barracks. ³³When the cavalry arrived in Caesarea, they delivered the letter to the governor and handed Paul over to him. ³⁴The governor read the letter and asked

what province he was from. Learning that he was from Cilicia, ³⁵he said, "I will hear your case when your accusers get here." Then he ordered that Paul be kept under guard in Herod's palace.

Paul's Trial Before Felix

24 Five days later the high priest Ananias went down to Caesarea with some of the elders and a lawyer named Tertullus, and they brought their charges against Paul before the governor. ²When Paul was called in, Tertullus presented his case before Felix: "We have enjoyed a long period of peace under you, and your foresight has brought about reforms in this nation. ³Everywhere and in every way, most excellent Felix, we acknowledge this with profound gratitude. ⁴But in order not to weary you further, I would request that you be kind enough to hear us briefly.

⁵"We have found this man to be a troublemaker, stirring up riots among the Jews all over the world. He is a ringleader of the Nazarene sect ⁶and even tried to desecrate the temple; so we seized him. [⁷]*b* ⁸By examining him yourself you will be able to learn the truth about all these charges we are bringing against him."

⁹The other Jews joined in the accusation, asserting that these things were true.

¹⁰When the governor motioned for him to speak, Paul replied: "I know that for a number of years you have been a judge over this nation; so I gladly make my defense. ¹¹You can easily verify that no more than twelve days ago I went up to Jerusalem to worship. ¹²My accusers did not find me arguing with anyone at the temple, or stirring up a crowd in the synagogues or anywhere else in the city. ¹³And they cannot prove to you the charges they are now making against me. ¹⁴However, I admit that I worship the God of our ancestors as a follower of the Way, which they call a sect. I believe

---

a 23 The meaning of the Greek for this word is uncertain.   *b 6-8* Some manuscripts include here *him, and we would have judged him in accordance with our law.* ⁷*But the commander Lysias came and took him from us with much violence,* ⁸*ordering his accusers to come before you.*

everything that is in accordance with the Law and that is written in the Prophets, [15] and I have the same hope in God as these men themselves have, that there will be a resurrection of both the righteous and the wicked. [16] So I strive always to keep my conscience clear before God and man.

[17] "After an absence of several years, I came to Jerusalem to bring my people gifts for the poor and to present offerings. [18] I was ceremonially clean when they found me in the temple courts doing this. There was no crowd with me, nor was I involved in any disturbance. [19] But there are some Jews from the province of Asia, who ought to be here before you and bring charges if they have anything against me. [20] Or these who are here should state what crime they found in me when I stood before the Sanhedrin— [21] unless it was this one thing I shouted as I stood in their presence: 'It is concerning the resurrection of the dead that I am on trial before you today.' "

[22] Then Felix, who was well acquainted with the Way, adjourned the proceedings. "When Lysias the commander comes," he said, "I will decide your case." [23] He ordered the centurion to keep Paul under guard but to give him some freedom and permit his friends to take care of his needs.

[24] Several days later Felix came with his wife Drusilla, who was Jewish. He sent for Paul and listened to him as he spoke about faith in Christ Jesus. [25] As Paul talked about righteousness, self-control and the judgment to come, Felix was afraid and said, "That's enough for now! You may leave. When I find it convenient, I will send for you." [26] At the same time he was hoping that Paul would offer him a bribe, so he sent for him frequently and talked with him.

[27] When two years had passed, Felix was succeeded by Porcius Festus, but because Felix wanted to grant a favor to the Jews, he left Paul in prison.

Paul's Trial Before Festus

25 Three days after arriving in the province, Festus went up from Caesarea to Jerusalem, [2] where the chief priests and the Jewish leaders appeared before him and presented the charges against Paul. [3] They requested Festus, as a favor to them, to have Paul transferred to Jerusalem, for they were preparing an ambush to kill him along the way. [4] Festus answered, "Paul is being held at Caesarea, and I myself am going there soon. [5] Let some of your leaders come with me, and if the man has done anything wrong, they can press charges against him there."

Acts 24:15

Death is not the end.

Death is certain—for everyone. Coming back to life is also certain—for everyone. The Bible teaches that all people will live again. As Paul says, "There will be a resurrection of both the righteous and the wicked" (Acts 24:15). After death, all people will face judgment (see Hebrews 9:27). Those who haven't trusted in Jesus will spend eternity separated from God in hell (see Matthew 25:41). But if you believe in Jesus, you can trust God's straightforward promise of heaven: "For God so loved the world that he gave his one and only Son, that whoever believes in him shall not perish but have eternal life" (John 3:16). The apostle Paul worried that Christians might face death with sadness and "grieve like the rest of mankind, who have no hope" (1 Thessalonians 4:13). But believers can see death in a radically better way. We can look forward to living with God and his people forever.

Think: Does the thought of heaven help you fear death any less? Why—or why not?

ROCK SOLID truths

⁶After spending eight or ten days with them, Festus went down to Caesarea. The next day he convened the court and ordered that Paul be brought before him. ⁷When Paul came in, the Jews who had come down from Jerusalem stood around him. They brought many serious charges against him, but they could not prove them.

⁸Then Paul made his defense: "I have done nothing wrong against the Jewish law or against the temple or against Caesar."

⁹Festus, wishing to do the Jews a favor, said to Paul, "Are you willing to go up to Jerusalem and stand trial before me there on these charges?"

¹⁰Paul answered: "I am now standing before Caesar's court, where I ought to be tried. I have not done any wrong to the Jews, as you yourself know very well. ¹¹If, however, I am guilty of doing anything deserving death, I do not refuse to die. But if the charges brought against me by these Jews are not true, no one has the right to hand me over to them. I appeal to Caesar!"

¹²After Festus had conferred with his council, he declared: "You have appealed to Caesar. To Caesar you will go!"

Festus Consults King Agrippa

¹³A few days later King Agrippa and Bernice arrived at Caesarea to pay their respects to Festus. ¹⁴Since they were spending many days there, Festus discussed Paul's case with the king. He said: "There is a man here whom Felix left as a prisoner. ¹⁵When I went to Jerusalem, the chief priests and the elders of the Jews brought charges against him and asked that he be condemned.

¹⁶"I told them that it is not the Roman custom to hand over anyone before they have faced their accusers and have had an opportunity to defend themselves against the charges. ¹⁷When they came here with me, I did not delay the case, but convened the court the next day and ordered the man to be brought in. ¹⁸When his accusers got up to speak, they did not charge him with any of the crimes I had expected. ¹⁹Instead, they had some points of dispute with him about their own religion and about a dead man named Jesus who Paul

claimed was alive. ²⁰I was at a loss how to investigate such matters; so I asked if he would be willing to go to Jerusalem and stand trial there on these charges. ²¹But when Paul made his appeal to be held over for the Emperor's decision, I ordered him held until I could send him to Caesar."

²²Then Agrippa said to Festus, "I would like to hear this man myself."

He replied, "Tomorrow you will hear him."

Paul Before Agrippa

²³The next day Agrippa and Bernice came with great pomp and entered the audience room with the high-ranking military officers and the prominent men of the city. At the command of Festus, Paul was brought in. ²⁴Festus said: "King Agrippa, and all who are present with us, you see this man! The whole Jewish community has petitioned me about him in Jerusalem and here in Caesarea, shouting that he ought not to live any longer. ²⁵I found he had done nothing deserving of death, but because he made his appeal to the Emperor I decided to send him to Rome. ²⁶But I have nothing definite to write to His Majesty about him. Therefore I have brought him before all of you, and especially before you, King Agrippa, so that as a result of this investigation I may have something to write. ²⁷For I think it is unreasonable to send a prisoner on to Rome without specifying the charges against him."

26 Then Agrippa said to Paul, "You have permission to speak for yourself."

So Paul motioned with his hand and began his defense: ²"King Agrippa, I consider myself fortunate to stand before you today as I make my defense against all the accusations of the Jews, ³and especially so because you are well acquainted with all the Jewish customs and controversies. Therefore, I beg you to listen to me patiently.

⁴"The Jewish people all know the way I have lived ever since I was a child, from the beginning of my life in my own country, and also in Jerusalem. ⁵They have known me for a long time and can testify, if they are willing, that I conformed to

the strictest sect of our religion, living as a Pharisee. ⁶And now it is because of my hope in what God has promised our ancestors that I am on trial today. ⁷This is the promise our twelve tribes are hoping to see fulfilled as they earnestly serve God day and night. King Agrippa, it is because of this hope that these Jews are accusing me. ⁸Why should any of you consider it incredible that God raises the dead?

⁹"I too was convinced that I ought to do all that was possible to oppose the name of Jesus of Nazareth. ¹⁰And that is just what I did in Jerusalem. On the authority of the chief priests I put many of the Lord's people in prison, and when they were put to death, I cast my vote against them. ¹¹Many a time I went from one synagogue to another to have them punished, and I tried to force them to blaspheme. I was so obsessed with persecuting them that I even hunted them down in foreign cities.

¹²"On one of these journeys I was going to Damascus with the authority and commission of the chief priests. ¹³About noon, King Agrippa, as I was on the road, I saw a light from heaven, brighter than the sun, blazing around me and my companions. ¹⁴We all fell to the ground, and I heard a voice saying to me in Aramaic,ᵃ 'Saul, Saul, why do you persecute me? It is hard for you to kick against the goads.'

¹⁵"Then I asked, 'Who are you, Lord?'

"'I am Jesus, whom you are persecuting,' the Lord replied. ¹⁶'Now get up and stand on your feet. I have appeared to you to appoint you as a servant and as a witness of what you have seen and will see of me. ¹⁷I will rescue you from your own people and from the Gentiles. I am sending you to them ¹⁸to open their eyes and turn them from darkness to light, and from the power of Satan to God, so that they may receive forgiveness of sins and a place among those who are sanctified by faith in me.'

¹⁹"So then, King Agrippa, I was not disobedient to the vision from heaven. ²⁰First to those in Damascus, then to those in Jerusalem and in all Judea, and then to the Gentiles, I preached that they should repent and turn to God and demonstrate their repentance by their deeds.

²¹That is why some Jews seized me in the temple courts and tried to kill me. ²²But God has helped me to this very day; so I

ᵃ *14* Or *Hebrew*

Acts 26:1–32

The New Testament records accurate history.

Scholars once argued that the New Testament was a completely unreliable source of history. They tried to discredit the Bible's historical statements in order to disprove its claims about Jesus. Modern scholars don't so easily dismiss Bible details. Luke—author of both Luke and Acts—is now widely recognized as an extremely accurate historian. Scholars once thought he was badly mistaken about details of Jesus' birth, for example, but later discoveries confirmed his statements about the use of ancient censuses and the identity of the governor Quirinius (see Luke 2:1–3). Throughout the book of Acts, Luke accurately uses titles and terms now confirmed by archaeologists. You can be sure your faith is grounded in reality, and Luke's accuracy shows your faith holds up to real-world scrutiny. Like the apostle Paul told Festus, "What I am saying is true and reasonable. The king is familiar with these things ... None of this has escaped his notice, because it was not done in a corner" (Acts 26:25–26).

Think: Who do you know who doubts the historical accuracy of the Bible? What can you tell them?

ROCK SOLID *truths*

stand here and testify to small and great alike. I am saying nothing beyond what the prophets and Moses said would happen— [23] that the Messiah would suffer and, as the first to rise from the dead, would bring the message of light to his own people and to the Gentiles."

[24] At this point Festus interrupted Paul's defense. "You are out of your mind, Paul!" he shouted. "Your great learning is driving you insane."

[25] "I am not insane, most excellent Festus," Paul replied. "What I am saying is true and reasonable. [26] The king is familiar with these things, and I can speak freely to him. I am convinced that none of this has escaped his notice, because it was not done in a corner. [27] King Agrippa, do you believe the prophets? I know you do."

[28] Then Agrippa said to Paul, "Do you think that in such a short time you can persuade me to be a Christian?"

[29] Paul replied, "Short time or long—I pray to God that not only you but all who are listening to me today may become what I am, except for these chains."

[30] The king rose, and with him the governor and Bernice and those sitting with them. [31] After they left the room, they began saying to one another, "This man is not doing anything that deserves death or imprisonment."

[32] Agrippa said to Festus, "This man could have been set free if he had not appealed to Caesar."

Paul Sails for Rome

27 When it was decided that we would sail for Italy, Paul and some other prisoners were handed over to a centurion named Julius, who belonged to the Imperial Regiment. [2] We boarded a ship from Adramyttium about to sail for ports along the coast of the province of Asia, and we put out to sea. Aristarchus, a Macedonian from Thessalonica, was with us.

[3] The next day we landed at Sidon; and Julius, in kindness to Paul, allowed him to go to his friends so they might provide for his needs. [4] From there we put out to sea

again and passed to the lee of Cyprus because the winds were against us. [5] When we had sailed across the open sea off the coast of Cilicia and Pamphylia, we landed at Myra in Lycia. [6] There the centurion found an Alexandrian ship sailing for Italy and put us on board. [7] We made slow headway for many days and had difficulty arriving off Cnidus. When the wind did not allow us to hold our course, we sailed to the lee of Crete, opposite Salmone. [8] We moved along the coast with difficulty and came to a place called Fair Havens, near the town of Lasea.

[9] Much time had been lost, and sailing had already become dangerous because by now it was after the Day of Atonement.[a] So Paul warned them, [10] "Men, I can see that our voyage is going to be disastrous and bring great loss to ship and cargo, and to our own lives also." [11] But the centurion, instead of listening to what Paul said, followed the advice of the pilot and of the owner of the ship. [12] Since the harbor was unsuitable to winter in, the majority decided that we should sail on, hoping to reach Phoenix and winter there. This was a harbor in Crete, facing both southwest and northwest.

The Storm

[13] When a gentle south wind began to blow, they saw their opportunity; so they weighed anchor and sailed along the shore of Crete. [14] Before very long, a wind of hurricane force, called the Northeaster, swept down from the island. [15] The ship was caught by the storm and could not head into the wind; so we gave way to it and were driven along. [16] As we passed to the lee of a small island called Cauda, we were hardly able to make the lifeboat secure, [17] so the men hoisted it aboard. Then they passed ropes under the ship itself to hold it together. Because they were afraid they would run aground on the sandbars of Syrtis, they lowered the sea anchor[b] and let the ship be driven along. [18] We took such a violent battering from the storm that the next day they began to throw the cargo overboard. [19] On the third day, they threw the ship's tackle overboard with their own hands.

---

[a] 9 That is, Yom Kippur   [b] 17 Or *the sails*

²⁰When neither sun nor stars appeared for many days and the storm continued raging, we finally gave up all hope of being saved.

²¹After they had gone a long time without food, Paul stood up before them and said: "Men, you should have taken my advice not to sail from Crete; then you would have spared yourselves this damage and loss. ²²But now I urge you to keep up your courage, because not one of you will be lost; only the ship will be destroyed. ²³Last night an angel of the God to whom I belong and whom I serve stood beside me ²⁴and said, 'Do not be afraid, Paul. You must stand trial before Caesar; and God has graciously given you the lives of all who sail with you.' ²⁵So keep up your courage, men, for I have faith in God that it will happen just as he told me. ²⁶Nevertheless, we must run aground on some island."

The Shipwreck

²⁷On the fourteenth night we were still being driven across the Adriatic*ᵃ* Sea, when about midnight the sailors sensed they were approaching land. ²⁸They took soundings and found that the water was a hundred and twenty feet*ᵇ* deep. A short time later they took soundings again and found it was ninety feet*ᶜ* deep. ²⁹Fearing that we would be dashed against the rocks, they dropped four anchors from the stern and prayed for daylight. ³⁰In an attempt to escape from the ship, the sailors let the lifeboat down into the sea, pretending they were going to lower some anchors from the bow. ³¹Then Paul said to the centurion and the soldiers, "Unless these men stay with the ship, you cannot be saved." ³²So the soldiers cut the ropes that held the lifeboat and let it drift away.

³³Just before dawn Paul urged them all to eat. "For the last fourteen days," he said, "you have been in constant suspense and have gone without food—you haven't eaten anything. ³⁴Now I urge you to take some food. You need it to survive. Not one of you will lose a single hair from his head." ³⁵After he said this, he took some bread and gave thanks to God in front of them all. Then he broke it and began to eat.

³⁶They were all encouraged and ate some food themselves. ³⁷Altogether there were 276 of us on board. ³⁸When they had eaten as much as they wanted, they lightened the ship by throwing the grain into the sea.

³⁹When daylight came, they did not recognize the land, but they saw a bay with a sandy beach, where they decided to run the ship aground if they could. ⁴⁰Cutting loose the anchors, they left them in the sea and at the same time untied the ropes that held the rudders. Then they hoisted the foresail to the wind and made for the beach. ⁴¹But the ship struck a sandbar and ran aground. The bow stuck fast and would not move, and the stern was broken to pieces by the pounding of the surf.

⁴²The soldiers planned to kill the prisoners to prevent any of them from swimming away and escaping. ⁴³But the centurion wanted to spare Paul's life and kept them from carrying out their plan. He ordered those who could swim to jump overboard first and get to land. ⁴⁴The rest were to get there on planks or on other pieces of the ship. In this way everyone reached land safely.

Paul Ashore on Malta

28 Once safely on shore, we found out that the island was called Malta. ²The islanders showed us unusual kindness. They built a fire and welcomed us all because it was raining and cold. ³Paul gathered a pile of brushwood and, as he put it on the fire, a viper, driven out by the heat, fastened itself on his hand. ⁴When the islanders saw the snake hanging from his hand, they said to each other, "This man must be a murderer; for though he escaped from the sea, the goddess Justice has not allowed him to live." ⁵But Paul shook the snake off into the fire and suffered no ill effects. ⁶The people expected him to swell up or suddenly fall dead; but after waiting a long time and seeing nothing unusual

ᵃ 27 In ancient times the name referred to an area extending well south of Italy.
ᵇ 28 Or about 37 meters   *ᶜ 28* Or about 27 meters

happen to him, they changed their minds and said he was a god.

[7] There was an estate nearby that belonged to Publius, the chief official of the island. He welcomed us to his home and showed us generous hospitality for three days. [8] His father was sick in bed, suffering from fever and dysentery. Paul went in to see him and, after prayer, placed his hands on him and healed him. [9] When this had happened, the rest of the sick on the island came and were cured. [10] They honored us in many ways; and when we were ready to sail, they furnished us with the supplies we needed.

Paul's Arrival at Rome

[11] After three months we put out to sea in a ship that had wintered in the island—it was an Alexandrian ship with the figurehead of the twin gods Castor and Pollux. [12] We put in at Syracuse and stayed there three days. [13] From there we set sail and arrived at Rhegium. The next day the south wind came up, and on the following day we reached Puteoli. [14] There we found some brothers and sisters who invited us to spend a week with them. And so we came to Rome. [15] The brothers and sisters there had heard that we were coming, and they traveled as far as the Forum of Appius and the Three Taverns to meet us. At the sight of these people Paul thanked God and was encouraged. [16] When we got to Rome, Paul was allowed to live by himself, with a soldier to guard him.

Paul Preaches at Rome Under Guard

[17] Three days later he called together the local Jewish leaders. When they had assembled, Paul said to them: "My brothers, although I have done nothing against our people or against the customs of our ancestors, I was arrested in Jerusalem and handed over to the Romans. [18] They examined me and wanted to release me, because I was not guilty of any crime deserving death. [19] The Jews objected, so I was compelled to make an appeal to Caesar. I certainly did not intend to bring any charge against my own people. [20] For this reason I have asked to see you and talk with you. It is because of the hope of Israel that I am bound with this chain."

[21] They replied, "We have not received any letters from Judea concerning you, and none of our people who have come from there has reported or said anything bad about you. [22] But we want to hear what your views are, for we know that people everywhere are talking against this sect."

[23] They arranged to meet Paul on a certain day, and came in even larger numbers to the place where he was staying. He witnessed to them from morning till evening, explaining about the kingdom of God, and from the Law of Moses and from the Prophets he tried to persuade them about Jesus. [24] Some were convinced by what he said, but others would not believe. [25] They disagreed among themselves and began to leave after Paul had made this final statement: "The Holy Spirit spoke the truth to your ancestors when he said through Isaiah the prophet:

[26] "'Go to this people and say,
"You will be ever hearing but never
    understanding;
  you will be ever seeing but never
    perceiving."
[27] For this people's heart has become
    calloused;
  they hardly hear with their ears,
  and they have closed their eyes.
Otherwise they might see with their
    eyes,
  hear with their ears,
  understand with their hearts
and turn, and I would heal them.'[a]

[28] "Therefore I want you to know that God's salvation has been sent to the Gentiles, and they will listen!" [29][b]

[30] For two whole years Paul stayed there in his own rented house and welcomed all who came to see him. [31] He proclaimed the kingdom of God and taught about the Lord Jesus Christ—with all boldness and without hindrance!

[a] 27 Isaiah 6:9,10 (see Septuagint)   [b] 29 Some manuscripts include here *After he said this, the Jews left, arguing vigorously among themselves.*

BOOK OUTLINE

ROMANS

This letter was written by Paul to the church in Rome in AD 56 or 57 as he was finishing his third missionary journey. Since Paul hoped to go to Jerusalem and then to Rome and Spain, he probably wrote this letter in preparation for his visit.

The theme of this letter is righteousness. Paul teaches in this letter that: (1) no human being is righteous; (2) Jesus Christ is perfectly righteous; (3) if we have faith in Jesus, we are freed from the power of sin, given a new life, and returned to a right relationship with God; (4) we should live Christian lives that are "holy and pleasing to God."

1 Paul, a servant of Christ Jesus, called to be an apostle and set apart for the gospel of God— [2]the gospel he promised beforehand through his prophets in the Holy Scriptures [3]regarding his Son, who as to his earthly life[a] was a descendant of David, [4]and who through the Spirit of holiness was appointed the Son of God in power[b] by his resurrection from the dead: Jesus Christ our Lord. [5]Through him we received grace and apostleship to call all the Gentiles to the obedience that comes from[c] faith for his name's sake. [6]And you also are among those Gentiles who are called to belong to Jesus Christ.

[7]To all in Rome who are loved by God and called to be his holy people:

Grace and peace to you from God our Father and from the Lord Jesus Christ.

Paul's Longing to Visit Rome

[8]First, I thank my God through Jesus Christ for all of you, because your faith is being reported all over the world. [9]God, whom I serve in my spirit in preaching the gospel of his Son, is my witness how constantly I remember you [10]in my prayers at all times; and I pray that now at last by God's will the way may be opened for me to come to you.

[11]I long to see you so that I may impart to you some spiritual gift to make you strong— [12]that is, that you and I may be mutually encouraged by each other's faith. [13]I do not want you to be unaware, brothers and sisters,[d] that I planned many times to come to you (but have been prevented from doing so until now) in order that I might have a harvest among you, just as I have had among the other Gentiles.

[14]I am obligated both to Greeks and non-Greeks, both to the wise and the foolish. [15]That is why I am so eager to preach the gospel also to you who are in Rome.

[16]For I am not ashamed of the gospel, because it is the power of God that brings salvation to everyone who believes: first to the Jew, then to the Gentile. [17]For in the gospel the righteousness of God is revealed—a righteousness that is by faith

ROCK SOLID promises

"I am not ashamed of the gospel, because it is the power of God that brings salvation to everyone who believes." Romans 1:16

Don't be embarrassed of Jesus and the cross. Faith in him is the only way God makes people right with himself.

from first to last,[e] just as it is written: "The righteous will live by faith."[f]

God's Wrath Against Sinful Humanity

[18]The wrath of God is being revealed from heaven against all the godlessness and wickedness of people, who suppress the truth by their wickedness, [19]since what may be known about God is plain to them, because God has made it plain to them. [20]For since the creation of the world God's invisible qualities—his eternal power and divine nature—have been clearly seen, being understood from what has been made, so that people are without excuse.

[21]For although they knew God, they neither glorified him as God nor gave thanks to him, but their thinking became futile and their foolish hearts were darkened. [22]Although they claimed to be wise, they became fools [23]and exchanged the glory of the immortal God for images made to look like a mortal human being and birds and animals and reptiles.

[24]Therefore God gave them over in the sinful desires of their hearts to sexual im-

[a] 3 Or *who according to the flesh*   [b] 4 Or *was declared with power to be the Son of God*
[c] 5 Or *that is*   [d] 13 The Greek word for *brothers and sisters* (*adelphoi*) refers here to believers, both men and women, as part of God's family; also in 7:1, 4; 8:12, 29; 10:1; 11:25; 12:1; 15:14, 30; 16:14, 17.   [e] 17 Or *is from faith to faith*   [f] 17 Hab. 2:4

purity for the degrading of their bodies with one another. [25]They exchanged the truth about God for a lie, and worshiped and served created things rather than the Creator—who is forever praised. Amen.

[26]Because of this, God gave them over to shameful lusts. Even their women exchanged natural sexual relations for unnatural ones. [27]In the same way the men also abandoned natural relations with women and were inflamed with lust for one another. Men committed shameful acts with other men, and received in themselves the due penalty for their error.

[28]Furthermore, just as they did not think it worthwhile to retain the knowledge of God, so God gave them over to a depraved mind, so that they do what ought not to be done. [29]They have become filled with every kind of wickedness, evil, greed and depravity. They are full of envy, murder, strife, deceit and malice. They are gossips, [30]slanderers, God-haters, insolent, arrogant and boastful; they invent ways of doing evil; they disobey their parents; [31]they have no understanding, no fidelity, no love, no mercy. [32]Although they know God's righteous decree that those who do such things deserve death, they not only continue to do these very things but also approve of those who practice them.

God's Righteous Judgment

2 You, therefore, have no excuse, you who pass judgment on someone else, for at whatever point you judge another, you are condemning yourself, because you who pass judgment do the same things. [2]Now we know that God's judgment against those who do such things is based on truth. [3]So when you, a mere human being, pass judgment on them and yet do the same things, do you think you will escape God's judgment? [4]Or do you show contempt for the riches of his kindness, forbearance and patience, not realizing that God's kindness is intended to lead you to repentance?

[5]But because of your stubbornness and your unrepentant heart, you are storing up wrath against yourself for the day of God's wrath, when his righteous judgment will be revealed. [6]God "will repay each person according to what they have done."[a] [7]To those who by persistence in doing good seek glory, honor and immortality, he will give eternal life. [8]But for those who are self-seeking and who reject the truth and follow evil, there will be wrath and anger. [9]There will be trouble and distress for every human being who does evil: first for

ROCK SOLID truths

Romans 1:18–32

People know right from wrong.

There is no nice way to say it. God is furious about the sins of humankind, "all the godlessness and wickedness of people" (Romans 1:18). We can fumble for excuses for our sinful thoughts, words, and actions, like claiming we don't know if we're doing wrong, but God puts the truth in plain sight. All we have to do is glance around at the world God created to witness his amazing power and character, but we "suppress the truth" (Romans 1:18). When we squash that inner voice nagging us with the real facts about God, our problem swells even bigger. Because we don't recognize God … or praise him … or thank him … all of our thinking gets messed up. We not only create fake gods, but our sins pile higher and higher as we "invent ways of doing evil" (Romans 1:30). Humankind deserves God's wrath, his judgment against evil. But God sent Jesus to save us.

Think: Why do people shut out their understanding of God—and of right and wrong?

[a] 6 Psalm 62:12; Prov. 24:12

the Jew, then for the Gentile; [10]but glory, honor and peace for everyone who does good: first for the Jew, then for the Gentile. [11]For God does not show favoritism.

[12]All who sin apart from the law will also perish apart from the law, and all who sin under the law will be judged by the law. [13]For it is not those who hear the law who are righteous in God's sight, but it is those who obey the law who will be declared righteous. [14](Indeed, when Gentiles, who do not have the law, do by nature things required by the law, they are a law for themselves, even though they do not have the law. [15]They show that the requirements of the law are written on their hearts, their consciences also bearing witness, and their thoughts sometimes accusing them and at other times even defending them.) [16]This will take place on the day when God judges people's secrets through Jesus Christ, as my gospel declares.

The Jews and the Law

[17]Now you, if you call yourself a Jew; if you rely on the law and boast in God; [18]if you know his will and approve of what is superior because you are instructed by the law; [19]if you are convinced that you are a guide for the blind, a light for those who are in the dark, [20]an instructor of the foolish, a teacher of little children, because you have in the law the embodiment of knowledge and truth— [21]you, then, who teach others, do you not teach yourself? You who preach against stealing, do you steal? [22]You who say that people should not commit adultery, do you commit adultery? You who abhor idols, do you rob temples? [23]You who boast in the law, do you dishonor God by breaking the law? [24]As it is written: "God's name is blasphemed among the Gentiles because of you."[a]

[25]Circumcision has value if you observe the law, but if you break the law, you have become as though you had not been circumcised. [26]So then, if those who are not circumcised keep the law's requirements, will they not be regarded as though they were circumcised? [27]The one who is not circumcised physically and yet obeys the law will condemn you who, even though you have the[b] written code and circumcision, are a lawbreaker.

[28]A person is not a Jew who is one only outwardly, nor is circumcision merely outward and physical. [29]No, a person is a Jew who is one inwardly; and circumcision is circumcision of the heart, by the Spirit, not by the written code. Such a person's praise is not from other people, but from God.

God's Faithfulness

3 What advantage, then, is there in being a Jew, or what value is there in circumcision? [2]Much in every way! First of all, the Jews have been entrusted with the very words of God.

[3]What if some were unfaithful? Will their unfaithfulness nullify God's faithfulness? [4]Not at all! Let God be true, and every human being a liar. As it is written:

"So that you may be proved right
　　when you speak
　and prevail when you judge."[c]

[5]But if our unrighteousness brings out God's righteousness more clearly, what shall we say? That God is unjust in bringing his wrath on us? (I am using a human argument.) [6]Certainly not! If that were so, how could God judge the world? [7]Someone might argue, "If my falsehood enhances God's truthfulness and so increases his glory, why am I still condemned as a sinner?" [8]Why not say—as some slanderously claim that we say—"Let us do evil that good may result"? Their condemnation is just!

No One Is Righteous

[9]What shall we conclude then? Do we have any advantage? Not at all! For we have already made the charge that Jews and Gentiles alike are all under the power of sin. [10]As it is written:

"There is no one righteous, not even
　　one;
[11]　there is no one who understands;
　　there is no one who seeks God.

---

[a] 24 Isaiah 52:5 (see Septuagint); Ezek. 36:20,22　[b] 27 Or who, by means of a　[c] 4 Psalm 51:4

¹²All have turned away,
  they have together become
    worthless;
there is no one who does good,
  not even one."ᵃ
¹³"Their throats are open graves;
  their tongues practice deceit."ᵇ
"The poison of vipers is on their
    lips."ᶜ
¹⁴ "Their mouths are full of cursing
    and bitterness."ᵈ
¹⁵"Their feet are swift to shed blood;
¹⁶ ruin and misery mark their ways,
¹⁷and the way of peace they do not
    know."ᵉ
¹⁸ "There is no fear of God before
    their eyes."ᶠ

¹⁹Now we know that whatever the law says, it says to those who are under the law, so that every mouth may be silenced and the whole world held accountable to God. ²⁰Therefore no one will be declared righteous in God's sight by the works of the law; rather, through the law we become conscious of our sin.

Righteousness Through Faith

²¹But now apart from the law the righteousness of God has been made known, to which the Law and the Prophets testify. ²²This righteousness is given through faith inᵍ Jesus Christ to all who believe. There is no difference between Jew and Gentile, ²³for all have sinned and fall short of the glory of God, ²⁴and all are justified freely by his grace through the redemption that came by Christ Jesus. ²⁵God presented Christ as a sacrifice of atonement,ᵇ through the shedding of his blood—to be received by faith. He did this to demonstrate his righteousness, because in his forbearance he had left the sins committed beforehand unpunished— ²⁶he did it to demonstrate his righteousness at the present time, so as to be just and the one who justifies those who have faith in Jesus.

²⁷Where, then, is boasting? It is excluded. Because of what law? The law that requires works? No, because of the law that requires faith. ²⁸For we maintain that a person is justified by faith apart from the works of the law. ²⁹Or is God the God of Jews only? Is he not the God of Gentiles too? Yes, of Gentiles too, ³⁰since there is only one God, who will justify the circumcised by faith and the uncircumcised

ᵃ 12 Psalms 14:1-3; 53:1-3; Eccles. 7:20
ᵇ 13 Psalm 5:9   ᶜ 13 Psalm 140:3
ᵈ 14 Psalm 10:7 (see Septuagint)
ᵉ 17 Isaiah 59:7,8   ᶠ 18 Psalm 36:1
ᵍ 22 Or through the faithfulness of   ᵇ 25 The Greek for sacrifice of atonement refers to the atonement cover on the ark of the covenant (see Lev. 16:15,16).

Romans 3:10–26

Being good won't get you into heaven.

Ask anyone around you why God should let them into heaven, and you're likely to hear "because I'm a good person." The Bible offers a couple comments on that thought. First, human goodness is overrated. God bluntly says, "There is no one righteous, not even one" (Romans 3:10). That doesn't mean people never make a positive impact in the world. But we consistently go our own way, and even the best people on the planet fall short of God's perfection (see Romans 3:23). Second, being good can't earn us friendship with God. No amount of good we do can make up for our sins. Our wrongdoing has earned the punishment of death (see Romans 6:23), so God sent Jesus as a sacrifice for our sins. The only way to get right with God is through faith in his blood (see Romans 3:25), trusting he died the death you deserve.

Think: Do you think people are really too sinful to get into heaven? Why—or why not?

ROCK SOLID truths

1335

through that same faith. ³¹Do we, then, nullify the law by this faith? Not at all! Rather, we uphold the law.

Abraham Justified by Faith

4 What then shall we say that Abraham, our forefather according to the flesh, discovered in this matter? ²If, in fact, Abraham was justified by works, he had something to boast about—but not before God. ³What does Scripture say? "Abraham believed God, and it was credited to him as righteousness."ᵃ

⁴Now to the one who works, wages are not credited as a gift but as an obligation. ⁵However, to the one who does not work but trusts God who justifies the ungodly, their faith is credited as righteousness. ⁶David says the same thing when he speaks of the blessedness of the one to whom God credits righteousness apart from works:

⁷"Blessed are those
    whose transgressions are forgiven,
    whose sins are covered.
⁸Blessed is the one
    whose sin the Lord will never count
        against them."ᵇ

⁹Is this blessedness only for the circumcised, or also for the uncircumcised? We have been saying that Abraham's faith was credited to him as righteousness. ¹⁰Under what circumstances was it credited? Was it after he was circumcised, or before? It was not after, but before! ¹¹And he received circumcision as a sign, a seal of the righteousness that he had by faith while he was still uncircumcised. So then, he is the father of all who believe but have not been circumcised, in order that righteousness might be credited to them. ¹²And he is then also the father of the circumcised who not only are circumcised but who also follow in the footsteps of the faith that our father Abraham had before he was circumcised.

¹³It was not through the law that Abraham and his offspring received the promise that he would be heir of the world, but through the righteousness that comes by faith. ¹⁴For if those who depend on the law are heirs, faith means nothing and the promise is worthless, ¹⁵because the law brings wrath. And where there is no law there is no transgression.

¹⁶Therefore, the promise comes by faith, so that it may be by grace and may be guaranteed to all Abraham's offspring—not only to those who are of the law but also to those who have the faith of Abraham. He is the father of us all. ¹⁷As it is written: "I have made you a father of many nations."ᶜ He is our father in the sight of God, in whom he believed—the God who gives life to the dead and calls into being things that were not.

¹⁸Against all hope, Abraham in hope believed and so became the father of many nations, just as it had been said to him, "So shall your offspring be."ᵈ ¹⁹Without weakening in his faith, he faced the fact that his body was as good as dead—since he was about a hundred years old—and that Sarah's womb was also dead. ²⁰Yet he did not waver through unbelief regarding the promise of God, but was strengthened in his faith and gave glory to God, ²¹being fully persuaded that God had power to do what he had promised. ²²This is why "it was credited to him as righteousness." ²³The words "it was credited to him" were written not for him alone, ²⁴but also for us, to whom God will credit righteousness—for us who believe in him who raised Jesus our Lord from the dead. ²⁵He was delivered over to death for our sins and was raised to life for our justification.

Peace and Hope

5 Therefore, since we have been justified through faith, weᵉ have peace with God through our Lord Jesus Christ, ²through whom we have gained access by faith into this grace in which we now stand. And weᶠ boast in the hope of the glory of God. ³Not only so, but weᶠ also glory in our sufferings, because we know that suffering produc-

ᵃ 3 Gen. 15:6; also in verse 22
ᵇ 8 Psalm 32:1,2   ᶜ 17 Gen. 17:5
ᵈ 18 Gen. 15:5   ᵉ 1 Many manuscripts
let us   ᶠ 2,3 Or let us

es perseverance; [4] perseverance, character; and character, hope. [5] And hope does not put us to shame, because God's love has been poured out into our hearts through the Holy Spirit, who has been given to us.

[6] You see, at just the right time, when we were still powerless, Christ died for the ungodly. [7] Very rarely will anyone die for a righteous person, though for a good person someone might possibly dare to die. [8] But God demonstrates his own love for us in this: While we were still sinners, Christ died for us.

ROCK SOLID
promises

"God demonstrates his own love for us in this: While we were still sinners, Christ died for us."
Romans 5:8

God loves us even before we come clean about our sin and begin to believe in him.

---

[9] Since we have now been justified by his blood, how much more shall we be saved from God's wrath through him! [10] For if, while we were God's enemies, we were reconciled to him through the death of his Son, how much more, having been reconciled, shall we be saved through his life! [11] Not only is this so, but we also boast in God through our Lord Jesus Christ, through whom we have now received reconciliation.

Death Through Adam, Life Through Christ

[12] Therefore, just as sin entered the world through one man, and death through sin, and in this way death came to all people, because all sinned—

[13] To be sure, sin was in the world before the law was given, but sin is not charged against anyone's account where there is no law. [14] Nevertheless, death reigned from the time of Adam to the time of Moses, even over those who did not sin by breaking a command, as did Adam, who is a pattern of the one to come.

[15] But the gift is not like the trespass. For if the many died by the trespass of the one man, how much more did God's grace and the gift that came by the grace of the one man, Jesus Christ, overflow to the many! [16] Nor can the gift of God be compared with the result of one man's sin: The judgment followed one sin and brought condemnation, but the gift followed many trespasses and brought justification. [17] For if, by the trespass of the one man, death reigned through that one man, how much more will those who receive God's abundant provision of grace and of the gift of righteousness reign in life through the one man, Jesus Christ!

[18] Consequently, just as one trespass resulted in condemnation for all people, so also one righteous act resulted in justification and life for all people. [19] For just as through the disobedience of the one man the many were made sinners, so also through the obedience of the one man the many will be made righteous.

[20] The law was brought in so that the trespass might increase. But where sin increased, grace increased all the more, [21] so that, just as sin reigned in death, so also grace might reign through righteousness to bring eternal life through Jesus Christ our Lord.

Dead to Sin, Alive in Christ

6 What shall we say, then? Shall we go on sinning so that grace may increase? [2] By no means! We are those who have died to sin; how can we live in it any longer? [3] Or don't you know that all of us who were baptized into Christ Jesus were baptized into his death? [4] We were therefore buried with him through baptism into death in order that, just as Christ was raised from the dead through the glory of the Father, we too may live a new life.

Romans 5:12–20

The existence of evil doesn't disprove God's existence.

God makes an easy target when people go looking for someone to blame for all the evil in the world. If God really rules the world, they reason, why doesn't he step in and fix all our problems? Some people struggle to answer that troubling question and get mad at God. Others conclude his lack of action proves he doesn't exist at all. The Bible offers a different explanation of evil. It isn't God's doing. It's a human choice that goes back to the beginning of time. The Bible names Adam as the first sinner. His choice to disobey God's command back in the Garden of Eden was the start of sin (see Genesis 3:1–24). We all joined in Adam's rebellion, and now we all suffer the same consequence, death. God isn't the cause of evil in the world. We are. And God acted to solve the problem of evil by sending Jesus, bringing forgiveness and a fresh start to anyone who wants it.

Think: Is God to blame for evil? Why—or why not?

ROCK SOLID *truths*

⁵For if we have been united with him in a death like his, we will certainly also be united with him in a resurrection like his. ⁶For we know that our old self was crucified with him so that the body ruled by sin might be done away with,ᵃ that we should no longer be slaves to sin— ⁷because anyone who has died has been set free from sin.

⁸Now if we died with Christ, we believe that we will also live with him. ⁹For we know that since Christ was raised from the dead, he cannot die again; death no longer has mastery over him. ¹⁰The death he died, he died to sin once for all; but the life he lives, he lives to God.

¹¹In the same way, count yourselves dead to sin but alive to God in Christ Jesus. ¹²Therefore do not let sin reign in your mortal body so that you obey its evil desires. ¹³Do not offer any part of yourself to sin as an instrument of wickedness, but rather offer yourselves to God as those who have been brought from death to life; and offer every part of yourself to him as an instrument of righteousness. ¹⁴For sin shall no longer be your master, because you are not under the law, but under grace.

Slaves to Righteousness

¹⁵What then? Shall we sin because we are not under the law but under grace? By no means! ¹⁶Don't you know that when you offer yourselves to someone as obedient slaves, you are slaves of the one you obey—whether you are slaves to sin, which leads to death, or to obedience, which leads to righteousness? ¹⁷But thanks be to God that, though you used to be slaves to sin, you have come to obey from your heart the pattern of teaching that has now claimed your allegiance. ¹⁸You have been set free from sin and have become slaves to righteousness.

¹⁹I am using an example from everyday life because of your human limitations. Just as you used to offer yourselves as slaves to impurity and to ever-increasing wickedness, so now offer yourselves as slaves to righteousness leading to holiness. ²⁰When you were slaves to sin, you were free from the control of righteousness. ²¹What benefit did you reap at that time from the things you are now ashamed of? Those things result in death! ²²But now that you have been set free from sin and have become slaves of God, the benefit you reap leads to holiness, and the result is eternal life. ²³For the wages of sin is death, but the gift of God is eternal life inᵇ Christ Jesus our Lord.

ᵃ 6 Or *be rendered powerless*   ᵇ 23 Or *through*

ROCK SOLID
promises

"For the wages of sin is death, but the gift of God is eternal life in Christ Jesus our Lord."

Romans 6:23

Sin has a punishment—death. Through Jesus you get a free gift—life forever.

Released From the Law, Bound to Christ

7 Do you not know, brothers and sisters—for I am speaking to those who know the law—that the law has authority over someone only as long as that person lives? ²For example, by law a married woman is bound to her husband as long as he is alive, but if her husband dies, she is released from the law that binds her to him. ³So then, if she has sexual relations with another man while her husband is still alive, she is called an adulteress. But if her husband dies, she is released from that law and is not an adulteress if she marries another man.

⁴So, my brothers and sisters, you also died to the law through the body of Christ, that you might belong to another, to him who was raised from the dead, in order that we might bear fruit for God. ⁵For when we were in the realm of the flesh,ᵃ the sinful passions aroused by the law were at work in us, so that we bore fruit for death. ⁶But now, by dying to what once bound us, we have been released from the law so that we serve in the new way of the Spirit, and not in the old way of the written code.

The Law and Sin

⁷What shall we say, then? Is the law sinful? Certainly not! Nevertheless, I would not have known what sin was had it not been for the law. For I would not have known what coveting really was if the law had not said, "You shall not covet."ᵇ ⁸But sin, seizing the opportunity afforded by the commandment, produced in me every kind of coveting. For apart from the law, sin was dead. ⁹Once I was alive apart from the law; but when the commandment came, sin sprang to life and I died. ¹⁰I found that the very commandment that was intended to bring life actually brought death. ¹¹For sin, seizing the opportunity afforded by the commandment, deceived me, and through the commandment put me to death. ¹²So then, the law is holy, and the commandment is holy, righteous and good.

¹³Did that which is good, then, become death to me? By no means! Nevertheless, in order that sin might be recognized as sin, it used what is good to bring about my death, so that through the commandment sin might become utterly sinful.

¹⁴We know that the law is spiritual; but I am unspiritual, sold as a slave to sin. ¹⁵I do not understand what I do. For what I want to do I do not do, but what I hate I do. ¹⁶And if I do what I do not want to do, I agree that the law is good. ¹⁷As it is, it is no longer I myself who do it, but it is sin living in me. ¹⁸For I know that good itself does not dwell in me, that is, in my sinful nature.ᶜ For I have the desire to do what is good, but I cannot carry it out. ¹⁹For I do not do the good I want to do, but the evil I do not want to do—this I keep on doing. ²⁰Now if I do what I do not want to do, it is no longer I who do it, but it is sin living in me that does it.

²¹So I find this law at work: Although I want to do good, evil is right there with me. ²²For in my inner being I delight in God's law; ²³but I see another law at work in me, waging war against the law of my mind and making me a prisoner of the law of sin at work within me. ²⁴What a

---

ᵃ 5 In contexts like this, the Greek word for *flesh* (*sarx*) refers to the sinful state of human beings, often presented as a power in opposition to the Spirit. ᵇ 7 Exodus 20:17; Deut. 5:21 ᶜ 18 Or *my flesh* wretched man I am! Who will rescue me from this body that is subject to death? [25]Thanks be to God, who delivers me through Jesus Christ our Lord!

So then, I myself in my mind am a slave to God's law, but in my sinful nature[a] a slave to the law of sin.

Life Through the Spirit

8 Therefore, there is now no condemnation for those who are in Christ Jesus, [2]because through Christ Jesus the law of the Spirit who gives life has set you[b] free from the law of sin and death. [3]For what the law was powerless to do because it was weakened by the flesh,[c] God did by sending his own Son in the likeness of sinful flesh to be a sin offering.[d] And so he condemned sin in the flesh, [4]in order that the righteous requirement of the law might be fully met in us, who do not live according to the flesh but according to the Spirit.

[5]Those who live according to the flesh have their minds set on what the flesh desires; but those who live in accordance with the Spirit have their minds set on what the Spirit desires. [6]The mind governed by the flesh is death, but the mind governed by the Spirit is life and peace. [7]The mind governed by the flesh is hostile to God; it does not submit to God's law, nor can it do so. [8]Those who are in the realm of the flesh cannot please God.

[9]You, however, are not in the realm of the flesh but are in the realm of the Spirit, if indeed the Spirit of God lives in you. And if anyone does not have the Spirit of Christ, they do not belong to Christ. [10]But if Christ is in you, then even though your body is subject to death because of sin, the Spirit gives life[e] because of righteousness. [11]And if the Spirit of him who raised Jesus from the dead is living in you, he who raised Christ from the dead will also give life to your mortal bodies because of[f] his Spirit who lives in you.

[12]Therefore, brothers and sisters, we have an obligation—but it is not to the flesh, to live according to it. [13]For if you live according to the flesh, you will die; but if by the Spirit you put to death the misdeeds of the body, you will live.

[14]For those who are led by the Spirit of God are the children of God. [15]The Spirit you received does not make you slaves, so that you live in fear again; rather, the Spirit you received brought about your adoption to sonship.[g] And by him we cry, "Abba,[h] Father." [16]The Spirit himself testifies with our spirit that we are God's children. [17]Now if we are children, then we are heirs—heirs of God and co-heirs with Christ, if indeed we share in his sufferings in order that we may also share in his glory.

Present Suffering and Future Glory

[18]I consider that our present sufferings are not worth comparing with the glory that will be revealed in us. [19]For the creation waits in eager expectation for the children of God to be revealed. [20]For the creation was subjected to frustration, not by its own choice, but by the will of the one who subjected it, in hope [21]that[i] the creation itself will be liberated from its bondage to decay and brought into the freedom and glory of the children of God.

[22]We know that the whole creation has been groaning as in the pains of childbirth right up to the present time. [23]Not only so, but we ourselves, who have the firstfruits of the Spirit, groan inwardly as we wait eagerly for our adoption to sonship, the redemption of our bodies. [24]For in this hope we were saved. But hope that is seen is no hope at all. Who hopes for what they already have? [25]But if we hope

---

[a] 25 Or in the flesh   [b] 2 The Greek is singular; some manuscripts me   [c] 3 In contexts like this, the Greek word for flesh (sarx) refers to the sinful state of human beings, often presented as a power in opposition to the Spirit; also in verses 4-13.   [d] 3 Or flesh, for sin   [e] 10 Or you, your body is dead because of sin, yet your spirit is alive   [f] 11 Some manuscripts bodies through   [g] 15 The Greek word for adoption to sonship is a term referring to the full legal standing of an adopted male heir in Roman culture; also in verse 23.   [h] 15 Aramaic for father   [i] 20,21 Or subjected it in hope. [21]For

for what we do not yet have, we wait for it patiently.

²⁶ In the same way, the Spirit helps us in our weakness. We do not know what we ought to pray for, but the Spirit himself intercedes for us through wordless groans. ²⁷ And he who searches our hearts knows the mind of the Spirit, because the Spirit intercedes for God's people in accordance with the will of God.

²⁸ And we know that in all things God works for the good of those who love him, who*a* have been called according to his purpose. ²⁹ For those God foreknew he also predestined to be conformed to the image of his Son, that he might be the firstborn among many brothers and sisters. ³⁰ And those he predestined, he also called; those he called, he also justified; those he justified, he also glorified.

More Than Conquerors

³¹ What, then, shall we say in response to these things? If God is for us, who can

---

ROCK SOLID
plans

Romans 8:28

Trust God to work for your good.

People like to quote Romans 8:28 as if it means God always makes everything okay. That's not what the Bible says. The message is that you won't escape tough times — like everyone else, you will endure "all things." No matter what you suffer, however, God always goes through it with you. He always works for your benefit. And he always keep you moving toward his ultimate goal of making you more like Jesus (see Romans 8:29 – 30).

Your next step: Think of a difficult situation you face right now and tell God you're counting on him to help you through it.

ROCK SOLID
promises

"We are more than conquerors through him who loved us."

Romans 8:37

God loves you, so nothing can overwhelm you. There is nothing in the world that can ever undo his love for you.

---

be against us? ³² He who did not spare his own Son, but gave him up for us all — how will he not also, along with him, graciously give us all things? ³³ Who will bring any charge against those whom God has chosen? It is God who justifies. ³⁴ Who then is the one who condemns? No one. Christ Jesus who died — more than that, who was raised to life — is at the right hand of God and is also interceding for us. ³⁵ Who shall separate us from the love of Christ? Shall trouble or hardship or persecution or famine or nakedness or danger or sword? ³⁶ As it is written:

> "For your sake we face death all day long;
> we are considered as sheep to be slaughtered."*b*

³⁷ No, in all these things we are more than conquerors through him who loved us. ³⁸ For I am convinced that neither death nor life, neither angels nor demons,*c* neither the present nor the future, nor any powers, ³⁹ neither height nor depth, nor anything else in all creation, will be able to separate us from the love of God that is in Christ Jesus our Lord.

a 28 Or *that all things work together for good to those who love God, who*; or *that in all things God works together with those who love him to bring about what is good — with those who*
b 36 Psalm 44:22   *c 38* Or *nor heavenly rulers*

Paul's Anguish Over Israel

9 I speak the truth in Christ—I am not lying, my conscience confirms it through the Holy Spirit— [2] I have great sorrow and unceasing anguish in my heart. [3] For I could wish that I myself were cursed and cut off from Christ for the sake of my people, those of my own race, [4] the people of Israel. Theirs is the adoption to sonship; theirs the divine glory, the covenants, the receiving of the law, the temple worship and the promises. [5] Theirs are the patriarchs, and from them is traced the human ancestry of the Messiah, who is God over all, forever praised![a] Amen.

God's Sovereign Choice

[6] It is not as though God's word had failed. For not all who are descended from Israel are Israel. [7] Nor because they are his descendants are they all Abraham's children. On the contrary, "It is through Isaac that your offspring will be reckoned."[b] [8] In other words, it is not the children by physical descent who are God's children, but it is the children of the promise who are regarded as Abraham's offspring. [9] For this was how the promise was stated: "At the appointed time I will return, and Sarah will have a son."[c]

[10] Not only that, but Rebekah's children were conceived at the same time by our father Isaac. [11] Yet, before the twins were born or had done anything good or bad—in order that God's purpose in election might stand: [12] not by works but by him who calls—she was told, "The older will serve the younger."[d] [13] Just as it is written: "Jacob I loved, but Esau I hated."[e]

[14] What then shall we say? Is God unjust? Not at all! [15] For he says to Moses,

"I will have mercy on whom I have
    mercy,
and I will have compassion on
    whom I have compassion."[f]

[16] It does not, therefore, depend on human desire or effort, but on God's mercy. [17] For Scripture says to Pharaoh: "I raised you up for this very purpose, that I might display my power in you and that my name might be proclaimed in all the earth."[g] [18] Therefore God has mercy on whom he wants to have mercy, and he hardens whom he wants to harden.

[19] One of you will say to me: "Then why does God still blame us? For who is able to resist his will?" [20] But who are you, a human being, to talk back to God? "Shall what is formed say to the one who formed it, 'Why did you make me like this?'"[b] [21] Does not the potter have the right to make out of the same lump of clay some pottery for special purposes and some for common use?

[22] What if God, although choosing to show his wrath and make his power known, bore with great patience the objects of his wrath—prepared for destruction? [23] What if he did this to make the riches of his glory known to the objects of his mercy, whom he prepared in advance for glory— [24] even us, whom he also called, not only from the Jews but also from the Gentiles? [25] As he says in Hosea:

"I will call them 'my people' who are
    not my people;
and I will call her 'my loved one'
    who is not my loved one,"[i]

[26] and,

"In the very place where it was said to
    them,
'You are not my people,'
there they will be called 'children of
    the living God.'"[j]

[27] Isaiah cries out concerning Israel:

"Though the number of the Israelites
    be like the sand by the sea,
only the remnant will be saved.
[28] For the Lord will carry out
    his sentence on earth with speed
    and finality."[k]

---

[a] 5 Or *Messiah, who is over all. God be forever praised!* Or *Messiah. God who is over all be forever praised!*   [b] 7 Gen. 21:12   [c] 9 Gen. 18:10,14   [d] 12 Gen. 25:23   [e] 13 Mal. 1:2,3   [f] 15 Exodus 33:19   [g] 17 Exodus 9:16   [b] 20 Isaiah 29:16; 45:9   [i] 25 Hosea 2:23   [j] 26 Hosea 1:10   [k] 28 Isaiah 10:22,23 (see Septuagint)

29 It is just as Isaiah said previously:

"Unless the Lord Almighty
    had left us descendants,
we would have become like Sodom,
    we would have been like Gomorrah."*a*

Israel's Unbelief

30 What then shall we say? That the Gentiles, who did not pursue righteousness, have obtained it, a righteousness that is by faith; 31 but the people of Israel, who pursued the law as the way of righteousness, have not attained their goal. 32 Why not? Because they pursued it not by faith but as if it were by works. They stumbled over the stumbling stone. 33 As it is written:

"See, I lay in Zion a stone that causes
    people to stumble
and a rock that makes them fall,
    and the one who believes in him
    will never be put to shame."*b*

10 Brothers and sisters, my heart's desire and prayer to God for the Israelites is that they may be saved. 2 For I can testify about them that they are zealous for God, but their zeal is not based on knowledge. 3 Since they did not know the righteousness of God and sought to establish their own, they did not submit to God's righteousness. 4 Christ is the culmination of the law so that there may be righteousness for everyone who believes.

5 Moses writes this about the righteousness that is by the law: "The person who does these things will live by them."*c* 6 But the righteousness that is by faith says: "Do not say in your heart, 'Who will ascend into heaven?'"*d* (that is, to bring Christ down) 7 "or 'Who will descend into the deep?'"*e* (that is, to bring Christ up from the dead). 8 But what does it say? "The word is near you; it is in your mouth and in your heart,"*f* that is, the message concerning faith that we proclaim: 9 If you declare with your mouth, "Jesus is Lord," and believe in your heart that God raised him from the dead, you will be saved. 10 For it is with your heart that you believe and are justified, and it is with your mouth that

you profess your faith and are saved. 11 As Scripture says, "Anyone who believes in him will never be put to shame."*g* 12 For there is no difference between Jew and Gentile—the same Lord is Lord of all and richly blesses all who call on him, 13 for, "Everyone who calls on the name of the Lord will be saved."*b*

a 29 Isaiah 1:9   *b 33* Isaiah 8:14; 28:16
c 5 Lev. 18:5   *d 6* Deut. 30:12   *e 7* Deut. 30:13
f 8 Deut. 30:14   *g 11* Isaiah 28:16 (see Septuagint)   *b 13* Joel 2:32

Romans 10:1–14

Salvation is simple.

The apostle Paul crisscrossed the Mediterranean world spreading the news about Jesus to people who had never heard of him. But he never lost his concern for his own people. The Jews tried to get right with God through "good works," attempting to perfectly follow Old Testament law. Paul preached that Jesus ended the system of trying to earn God's approval. Because no one can ever be good enough to earn salvation—a package that includes forgiveness, friendship with God, freedom from sin, and a home forever in heaven—we now get right with God by faith, not good deeds (see Ephesians 2:8–9). And faith isn't complicated. Paul explained, "If you declare with your mouth, 'Jesus is Lord,' and believe in your heart that God raised him from the dead, you will be saved" (Romans 10:9). Belief makes you right with God. Confessing your faith makes it real. It's simple.

Think: Is salvation through faith in Jesus too simple to work? Why—or why not?

ROCK SOLID truths

¹⁴How, then, can they call on the one they have not believed in? And how can they believe in the one of whom they have not heard? And how can they hear without someone preaching to them? ¹⁵And how can anyone preach unless they are sent? As it is written: "How beautiful are the feet of those who bring good news!"[a]

¹⁶But not all the Israelites accepted the good news. For Isaiah says, "Lord, who has believed our message?"[b] ¹⁷Consequently, faith comes from hearing the message, and the message is heard through the word about Christ. ¹⁸But I ask: Did they not hear? Of course they did:

"Their voice has gone out into all the earth,
their words to the ends of the world."[c]

ROCK SOLID
promises

"Faith comes from hearing the message, and the message is heard through the word about Christ." Romans 10:17

If you want to boost your faith in God, focus on the fact that Jesus lived, died, and rose for you.

---

¹⁹Again I ask: Did Israel not understand? First, Moses says,

"I will make you envious by those who are not a nation;
I will make you angry by a nation that has no understanding."[d]

²⁰And Isaiah boldly says,

"I was found by those who did not seek me;
I revealed myself to those who did not ask for me."[e]

²¹But concerning Israel he says,

"All day long I have held out my hands to a disobedient and obstinate people."[f]

The Remnant of Israel

11 I ask then: Did God reject his people? By no means! I am an Israelite myself, a descendant of Abraham, from the tribe of Benjamin. ²God did not reject his people, whom he foreknew. Don't you know what Scripture says in the passage about Elijah—how he appealed to God against Israel: ³"Lord, they have killed your prophets and torn down your altars; I am the only one left, and they are trying to kill me"[g]? ⁴And what was God's answer to him? "I have reserved for myself seven thousand who have not bowed the knee to Baal."[h] ⁵So too, at the present time there is a remnant chosen by grace. ⁶And if by grace, then it cannot be based on works; if it were, grace would no longer be grace.

⁷What then? What the people of Israel sought so earnestly they did not obtain. The elect among them did, but the others were hardened, ⁸as it is written:

"God gave them a spirit of stupor,
eyes that could not see
and ears that could not hear,
to this very day."[i]

⁹And David says:

"May their table become a snare and a trap,
a stumbling block and a retribution for them.
¹⁰May their eyes be darkened so they cannot see,
and their backs be bent forever."[j]

Ingrafted Branches

¹¹Again I ask: Did they stumble so as to fall beyond recovery? Not at all! Rath-

---

[a] *15* Isaiah 52:7   [b] *16* Isaiah 53:1
[c] *18* Psalm 19:4   [d] *19* Deut. 32:21
[e] *20* Isaiah 65:1   [f] *21* Isaiah 65:2
[g] *3* 1 Kings 19:10,14   [h] *4* 1 Kings 19:18
[i] *8* Deut. 29:4; Isaiah 29:10
[j] *10* Psalm 69:22,23

er, because of their transgression, salvation has come to the Gentiles to make Israel envious. [12]But if their transgression means riches for the world, and their loss means riches for the Gentiles, how much greater riches will their full inclusion bring!

[13]I am talking to you Gentiles. Inasmuch as I am the apostle to the Gentiles, I take pride in my ministry [14]in the hope that I may somehow arouse my own people to envy and save some of them. [15]For if their rejection brought reconciliation to the world, what will their acceptance be but life from the dead? [16]If the part of the dough offered as firstfruits is holy, then the whole batch is holy; if the root is holy, so are the branches.

[17]If some of the branches have been broken off, and you, though a wild olive shoot, have been grafted in among the others and now share in the nourishing sap from the olive root, [18]do not consider yourself to be superior to those other branches. If you do, consider this: You do not support the root, but the root supports you. [19]You will say then, "Branches were broken off so that I could be grafted in." [20]Granted. But they were broken off because of unbelief, and you stand by faith. Do not be arrogant, but tremble. [21]For if God did not spare the natural branches, he will not spare you either.

[22]Consider therefore the kindness and sternness of God: sternness to those who fell, but kindness to you, provided that you continue in his kindness. Otherwise, you also will be cut off. [23]And if they do not persist in unbelief, they will be grafted in, for God is able to graft them in again. [24]After all, if you were cut out of an olive tree that is wild by nature, and contrary to nature were grafted into a cultivated olive tree, how much more readily will these, the natural branches, be grafted into their own olive tree!

All Israel Will Be Saved

[25]I do not want you to be ignorant of this mystery, brothers and sisters, so that you may not be conceited: Israel has experienced a hardening in part until the full number of the Gentiles has come in, [26]and in this way[a] all Israel will be saved. As it is written:

> "The deliverer will come from Zion;
> he will turn godlessness away from Jacob.
> [27]And this is[b] my covenant with them when I take away their sins."[c]

[28]As far as the gospel is concerned, they are enemies for your sake; but as far as election is concerned, they are loved on account of the patriarchs, [29]for God's gifts and his call are irrevocable. [30]Just as you who were at one time disobedient to God have now received mercy as a result of their disobedience, [31]so they too have now become disobedient in order that they too may now[d] receive mercy as a result of God's mercy to you. [32]For God has bound everyone over to disobedience so that he may have mercy on them all.

Doxology

[33]Oh, the depth of the riches of the wisdom and[e] knowledge of God!
> How unsearchable his judgments, and his paths beyond tracing out!
> [34]"Who has known the mind of the Lord?
> Or who has been his counselor?"[f]
> [35]"Who has ever given to God, that God should repay them?"[g]
> [36]For from him and through him and for him are all things.
> To him be the glory forever! Amen.

A Living Sacrifice

12 Therefore, I urge you, brothers and sisters, in view of God's mercy, to offer your bodies as a living sacrifice, holy and pleasing

[a] 26 Or and so   [b] 27 Or will be
[c] 27 Isaiah 59:20,21; 27:9 (see Septuagint); Jer. 31:33,34   [d] 31 Some manuscripts do not have now.   [e] 33 Or riches and the wisdom and the   [f] 34 Isaiah 40:13   [g] 35 Job 41:11

to God—this is your true and proper worship. [2] Do not conform to the pattern of this world, but be transformed by the renewing of your mind. Then you will be able to test and approve what God's will is—his good, pleasing and perfect will.

Humble Service in the Body of Christ

[3] For by the grace given me I say to every one of you: Do not think of yourself more highly than you ought, but rather think of yourself with sober judgment, in accordance with the faith God has distributed to each of you. [4] For just as each of us has one body with many members, and these members do not all have the same function, [5] so in Christ we, though many, form one body, and each member belongs to all the others. [6] We have different gifts, according to the grace given to each of us. If your gift is prophesying, then prophesy in accordance with your[a] faith; [7] if it is serving, then serve; if it is teaching, then teach; [8] if it is to encourage, then give encouragement; if it is giving, then give generously; if it is to lead,[b] do it diligently; if it is to show mercy, do it cheerfully.

Love in Action

[9] Love must be sincere. Hate what is evil; cling to what is good. [10] Be devoted to one another in love. Honor one another above yourselves. [11] Never be lacking in zeal, but keep your spiritual fervor, serving the Lord. [12] Be joyful in hope, patient in affliction, faithful in prayer. [13] Share with the Lord's people who are in need. Practice hospitality.

[14] Bless those who persecute you; bless and do not curse. [15] Rejoice with those who rejoice; mourn with those who mourn. [16] Live in harmony with one another. Do not be proud, but be willing to associate with people of low position.[c] Do not be conceited.

[17] Do not repay anyone evil for evil. Be careful to do what is right in the eyes of everyone. [18] If it is possible, as far as it depends on you, live at peace with everyone. [19] Do not take revenge, my dear friends, but leave room for God's wrath, for it is written: "It is mine to avenge; I will repay,"[d] says the Lord. [20] On the contrary:

"If your enemy is hungry, feed him;
　　if he is thirsty, give him something
　　　　to drink.
In doing this, you will heap burning
　　　　coals on his head."[e]

[21] Do not be overcome by evil, but overcome evil with good.

Romans 12:1–2

God wants to give you a makeover.

You might figure you got enough of God when you put your trust in Jesus. But God hasn't gotten enough of you. He wants to transform you, making you over inside and out. It starts when you consider the Lord's phenomenal mercy, his grace and forgiveness. The appropriate response to his limitless love is to "offer your bodies as a living sacrifice, holy and pleasing to God—this is your true and proper worship" (Romans 12:1). Your job isn't merely to give God your body but every bit of yourself. God makes that possible by the "renewing of your mind" (Romans 12:2), so that you understand and want what God wants. As you let God teach you more and more about him, the more willing you are to obey. If you let God remake you, then you will worship him with your entire life.

Think: Are you ready for God to remake your life? What do you want to tell God about his plans?

ROCK SOLID truths

---

[a] 6 Or *the*　　[b] 8 Or *to provide for others*
[c] 16 Or *willing to do menial work*
[d] 19 Deut. 32:35　　[e] 20 Prov. 25:21,22

Submission to Governing Authorities

13 Let everyone be subject to the governing authorities, for there is no authority except that which God has established. The authorities that exist have been established by God. ²Consequently, whoever rebels against the authority is rebelling against what God has instituted, and those who do so will bring judgment on themselves. ³For rulers hold no terror for those who do right, but for those who do wrong. Do you want to be free from fear of the one in authority? Then do what is right and you will be commended. ⁴For the one in authority is God's servant for your good. But if you do wrong, be afraid, for rulers do not bear the sword for no reason. They are God's servants, agents of wrath to bring punishment on the wrongdoer. ⁵Therefore, it is necessary to submit to the authorities, not only because of possible punishment but also as a matter of conscience.

⁶This is also why you pay taxes, for the authorities are God's servants, who give their full time to governing. ⁷Give to everyone what you owe them: If you owe taxes, pay taxes; if revenue, then revenue; if respect, then respect; if honor, then honor.

Love Fulfills the Law

⁸Let no debt remain outstanding, except the continuing debt to love one another, for whoever loves others has fulfilled the law. ⁹The commandments, "You shall not commit adultery," "You shall not murder," "You shall not steal," "You shall not covet,"*ᵃ* and whatever other command there may be, are summed up in this one command: "Love your neighbor as yourself."*ᵇ* ¹⁰Love does no harm to a neighbor. Therefore love is the fulfillment of the law.

ᵃ 9 Exodus 20:13-15,17; Deut. 5:17-19,21
ᵇ 9 Lev. 19:18

ROCK SOLID *principles*

Romans 13:1–5

Show respect.

Garrett thought his safety-freak shop teacher was as dumb as a stump, like the blocks of wood he and his classmates were crafting into little foot stools. Garrett had spent endless hours with his dad sawing and hammering to renovate their old house, and he still had all his fingers. Even though Garrett hadn't used all the big machines in the school shop, he didn't feel any need to listen during his teacher's demonstrations. One day Garrett dropped a plank of wood on a table saw and shoved it toward the blade. An instant later the wood shot back like an overgrown spear, barely missing him before it cracked loudly into a wall.

You know it is right to submit to people in authority over you, from parents and police to teachers and bosses. That doesn't make obedience easy. So remember it was God who created the chain of command and put people over you. You can count on them to help you, even if they don't seem to deserve your respect. Every authority in your life "is God's servant for your good" (Romans 13:4).

The Day Is Near

[11] And do this, understanding the present time: The hour has already come for you to wake up from your slumber, because our salvation is nearer now than when we first believed. [12] The night is nearly over; the day is almost here. So let us put aside the deeds of darkness and put on the armor of light. [13] Let us behave decently, as in the daytime, not in carousing and drunkenness, not in sexual immorality and debauchery, not in dissension and jealousy. [14] Rather, clothe yourselves with the Lord Jesus Christ, and do not think about how to gratify the desires of the flesh.[a]

The Weak and the Strong

14 Accept the one whose faith is weak, without quarreling over disputable matters. [2] One person's faith allows them to eat anything, but another, whose faith is weak, eats only vegetables. [3] The one who eats everything must not treat with contempt the one who does not, and the one who does not eat everything must not judge the one who does, for God has accepted them. [4] Who are you to judge someone else's servant? To their own master, servants stand or fall. And they will stand, for the Lord is able to make them stand.

[5] One person considers one day more sacred than another; another considers every day alike. Each of them should be fully convinced in their own mind. [6] Whoever regards one day as special does so to the Lord. Whoever eats meat does so to the Lord, for they give thanks to God; and whoever abstains does so to the Lord and gives thanks to God. [7] For none of us lives for ourselves alone, and none of us dies for ourselves alone. [8] If we live, we live for the Lord; and if we die, we die for the Lord. So, whether we live or die, we belong to the Lord. [9] For this very reason, Christ died and returned to life so that he might be the Lord of both the dead and the living.

[10] You, then, why do you judge your brother or sister[b]? Or why do you treat them with contempt? For we will all stand before God's judgment seat. [11] It is written:

> " 'As surely as I live,' says the Lord,
> 'every knee will bow before me;
>   every tongue will acknowledge
>   God.' "[c]

[12] So then, each of us will give an account of ourselves to God.

[13] Therefore let us stop passing judgment on one another. Instead, make up your mind not to put any stumbling block or obstacle in the way of a brother or sister. [14] I am convinced, being fully persuaded in the Lord Jesus, that nothing is unclean in itself. But if anyone regards something as unclean, then for that person it is unclean. [15] If your brother or sister is distressed because of what you eat, you are no longer acting in love. Do not by your eating destroy someone for whom Christ died. [16] Therefore do not let what you know is good be spoken of as evil. [17] For the kingdom of God is not a matter of eating and drinking, but of righteousness, peace and joy in the Holy Spirit, [18] because anyone who serves Christ in this way is pleasing to God and receives human approval.

[19] Let us therefore make every effort to do what leads to peace and to mutual edification. [20] Do not destroy the work of God for the sake of food. All food is clean, but it is wrong for a person to eat anything that causes someone else to stumble. [21] It is better not to eat meat or drink wine or to do anything else that will cause your brother or sister to fall.

[22] So whatever you believe about these things keep between yourself and God. Blessed is the one who does not condemn himself by what he approves. [23] But whoever has doubts is condemned if they eat, because their eating is not from faith; and everything that does not come from faith is sin.[d]

---

[a] *14* In contexts like this, the Greek word for *flesh* (*sarx*) refers to the sinful state of human beings, often presented as a power in opposition to the Spirit.   [b] *10* The Greek word for *brother or sister* (*adelphos*) refers here to a believer, whether man or woman, as part of God's family; also in verses 13, 15 and 21.   [c] *11* Isaiah 45:23   [d] *23* Some manuscripts place 16:25-27 here; others after 15:33.

15 We who are strong ought to bear with the failings of the weak and not to please ourselves. ²Each of us should please our neighbors for their good, to build them up. ³For even Christ did not please himself but, as it is written: "The insults of those who insult you have fallen on me."ᵃ ⁴For everything that was written in the past was written to teach us, so that through the endurance taught in the Scriptures and the encouragement they provide we might have hope.

⁵May the God who gives endurance and encouragement give you the same attitude of mind toward each other that Christ Jesus had, ⁶so that with one mind and one voice you may glorify the God and Father of our Lord Jesus Christ.

⁷Accept one another, then, just as Christ accepted you, in order to bring praise to God. ⁸For I tell you that Christ has become a servant of the Jewsᵇ on behalf of God's truth, so that the promises made to the patriarchs might be confirmed ⁹and, moreover, that the Gentiles might glorify God for his mercy. As it is written:

"Therefore I will praise you among
    the Gentiles;
I will sing the praises of your
    name."ᶜ

¹⁰Again, it says,

"Rejoice, you Gentiles, with his
    people."ᵈ

¹¹And again,

"Praise the Lord, all you Gentiles;
    let all the peoples extol him."ᵉ

¹²And again, Isaiah says,

"The Root of Jesse will spring up,
    one who will arise to rule over the
        nations;
in him the Gentiles will hope."ᶠ

¹³May the God of hope fill you with all joy and peace as you trust in him, so that you may overflow with hope by the power of the Holy Spirit.

ROCK SOLID promises

"May the God of hope fill you with all joy and peace as you trust in him." Romans 15:13

Trusting God isn't just the right thing to do. It alters your mood in every good way.

Paul the Minister to the Gentiles

¹⁴I myself am convinced, my brothers and sisters, that you yourselves are full of goodness, filled with knowledge and competent to instruct one another. ¹⁵Yet I have written you quite boldly on some points to remind you of them again, because of the grace God gave me ¹⁶to be a minister of Christ Jesus to the Gentiles. He gave me the priestly duty of proclaiming the gospel of God, so that the Gentiles might become an offering acceptable to God, sanctified by the Holy Spirit.

¹⁷Therefore I glory in Christ Jesus in my service to God. ¹⁸I will not venture to speak of anything except what Christ has accomplished through me in leading the Gentiles to obey God by what I have said and done— ¹⁹by the power of signs and wonders, through the power of the Spirit of God. So from Jerusalem all the way around to Illyricum, I have fully proclaimed the gospel of Christ. ²⁰It has always been my ambition to preach the gospel where Christ was not known, so that I would not be building on someone else's foundation. ²¹Rather, as it is written:

ᵃ 3 Psalm 69:9   ᵇ 8 Greek circumcision
ᶜ 9 2 Samuel 22:50; Psalm 18:49
ᵈ 10 Deut. 32:43   ᵉ 11 Psalm 117:1
ᶠ 12 Isaiah 11:10 (see Septuagint)

"Those who were not told about him
will see,
and those who have not heard will
understand."[a]

²²This is why I have often been hindered
from coming to you.

Paul's Plan to Visit Rome

²³But now that there is no more place
for me to work in these regions, and since
I have been longing for many years to visit
you, ²⁴I plan to do so when I go to Spain.
I hope to see you while passing through
and to have you assist me on my journey
there, after I have enjoyed your company for a while. ²⁵Now, however, I am on
my way to Jerusalem in the service of the
Lord's people there. ²⁶For Macedonia and
Achaia were pleased to make a contribution for the poor among the Lord's people
in Jerusalem. ²⁷They were pleased to do it,
and indeed they owe it to them. For if the
Gentiles have shared in the Jews' spiritual
blessings, they owe it to the Jews to share
with them their material blessings. ²⁸So
after I have completed this task and have
made sure that they have received this
contribution, I will go to Spain and visit
you on the way. ²⁹I know that when I come
to you, I will come in the full measure of
the blessing of Christ.

³⁰I urge you, brothers and sisters, by
our Lord Jesus Christ and by the love
of the Spirit, to join me in my struggle
by praying to God for me. ³¹Pray that I
may be kept safe from the unbelievers in
Judea and that the contribution I take to
Jerusalem may be favorably received by
the Lord's people there, ³²so that I may
come to you with joy, by God's will, and
in your company be refreshed. ³³The God
of peace be with you all. Amen.

Personal Greetings

16 I commend to you our sister Phoebe, a deacon[b,c] of the
church in Cenchreae. ²I ask
you to receive her in the Lord in a way
worthy of his people and to give her any
help she may need from you, for she has

been the benefactor of many people, including me.

³Greet Priscilla[d] and Aquila, my co-
workers in Christ Jesus. ⁴They risked
their lives for me. Not only I but all
the churches of the Gentiles are
grateful to them.
⁵Greet also the church that meets at
their house.

Greet my dear friend Epenetus, who
was the first convert to Christ in the
province of Asia.
⁶Greet Mary, who worked very hard for
you.
⁷Greet Andronicus and Junia, my fellow
Jews who have been in prison with
me. They are outstanding among[e]
the apostles, and they were in Christ
before I was.
⁸Greet Ampliatus, my dear friend in the
Lord.
⁹Greet Urbanus, our co-worker in
Christ, and my dear friend Stachys.
¹⁰Greet Apelles, whose fidelity to Christ
has stood the test.

Greet those who belong to the household of Aristobulus.
¹¹Greet Herodion, my fellow Jew.

Greet those in the household of Narcis-
sus who are in the Lord.
¹²Greet Tryphena and Tryphosa, those
women who work hard in the Lord.

Greet my dear friend Persis, another
woman who has worked very hard in
the Lord.
¹³Greet Rufus, chosen in the Lord, and
his mother, who has been a mother
to me, too.
¹⁴Greet Asyncritus, Phlegon, Hermes,
Patrobas, Hermas and the other
brothers and sisters with them.
¹⁵Greet Philologus, Julia, Nereus and
his sister, and Olympas and all the
Lord's people who are with them.

---

[a] 21 Isaiah 52:15 (see Septuagint)
[b] 1 Or *servant*   [c] 1 The word *deacon* refers
here to a Christian designated to serve with the
overseers/elders of the church in a variety of
ways; similarly in Phil. 1:1 and 1 Tim. 3:8,12.
[d] 3 Greek *Prisca*, a variant of *Priscilla*
[e] 7 Or *are esteemed by*

¹⁶Greet one another with a holy kiss.

All the churches of Christ send greetings.

¹⁷I urge you, brothers and sisters, to watch out for those who cause divisions and put obstacles in your way that are contrary to the teaching you have learned. Keep away from them. ¹⁸For such people are not serving our Lord Christ, but their own appetites. By smooth talk and flattery they deceive the minds of naive people. ¹⁹Everyone has heard about your obedience, so I rejoice because of you; but I want you to be wise about what is good, and innocent about what is evil.

²⁰The God of peace will soon crush Satan under your feet.

The grace of our Lord Jesus be with you.

²¹Timothy, my co-worker, sends his greetings to you, as do Lucius, Jason and Sosipater, my fellow Jews.

²²I, Tertius, who wrote down this letter, greet you in the Lord.

²³Gaius, whose hospitality I and the whole church here enjoy, sends you his greetings.

Erastus, who is the city's director of public works, and our brother Quartus send you their greetings. [24]*a*

²⁵Now to him who is able to establish you in accordance with my gospel, the message I proclaim about Jesus Christ, in keeping with the revelation of the mystery hidden for long ages past, ²⁶but now revealed and made known through the prophetic writings by the command of the eternal God, so that all the Gentiles might come to the obedience that comes from^b faith— ²⁷to the only wise God be glory forever through Jesus Christ! Amen.

a 24 Some manuscripts include here *May the grace of our Lord Jesus Christ be with all of you. Amen.* *b 26* Or *that is*

Romans 16:25–27

God is wise.

In a world full of smart people, only God is wise. Even before the world began, the Lord had a mysterious plan to save humankind through Jesus Christ. He took hundreds of years to reveal his plot though his spokespeople, the prophets. When Jesus lived, died and rose, it proved the Lord's wisdom because he had opened a way "so that all the Gentiles might come to the obedience that comes from faith" (Romans 16:26). Not only is God the only one who can tell you how to be saved, but you can also expect him to know history before it happens (see Ezra 4:1–4) and to be aware of all the practical details of your life (see Psalm 127:1–2).

So … What difference will it make to you today that God is smarter than you—or anyone else in your world?

BOOK OUTLINE

This letter was written by Paul to the church in Corinth, probably in the winter of AD 55. While he was in Ephesus Paul sent this response to a letter he received from the Corinthian church.

The city of Corinth was a wealthy trading center located on the Mediterranean Sea. It was a city known throughout the Roman world for its wickedness. The new church in Corinth was having problems because the Christians struggled to act differently than the people around them.

The Christians in Corinth were not getting along with one another—they were taking sides. Some of them were living very sinful lives. Paul wrote this letter to scold them and teach them how Christians should act. He tried to teach the people practical lessons about the Christian life so they would know right from wrong.

Paul, called to be an apostle of Christ Jesus by the will of God, and our brother Sosthenes,

[2] To the church of God in Corinth, to those sanctified in Christ Jesus and called to be his holy people, together with all those everywhere who call on the name of our Lord Jesus Christ—their Lord and ours:

[3] Grace and peace to you from God our Father and the Lord Jesus Christ.

Thanksgiving

[4] I always thank my God for you because of his grace given you in Christ Jesus. [5] For in him you have been enriched in every way—with all kinds of speech and with all knowledge— [6] God thus confirming our testimony about Christ among you. [7] Therefore you do not lack any spiritual gift as you eagerly wait for our Lord Jesus Christ to be revealed. [8] He will also keep you firm to the end, so that you will be blameless on the day of our Lord Jesus Christ. [9] God is faithful, who has called you into fellowship with his Son, Jesus Christ our Lord.

A Church Divided Over Leaders

[10] I appeal to you, brothers and sisters,[a] in the name of our Lord Jesus Christ, that all of you agree with one another in what you say and that there be no divisions among you, but that you be perfectly united in mind and thought. [11] My brothers and sisters, some from Chloe's household have informed me that there are quarrels among you. [12] What I mean is this: One of you says, "I follow Paul"; another, "I follow Apollos"; another, "I follow Cephas[b]"; still another, "I follow Christ."

[13] Is Christ divided? Was Paul crucified for you? Were you baptized in the name of Paul? [14] I thank God that I did not baptize any of you except Crispus and Gaius, [15] so no one can say that you were baptized in my name. [16] (Yes, I also baptized the household of Stephanas; beyond that, I don't remember if I baptized anyone else.) [17] For Christ did not send me to baptize, but to preach the gospel—not with wisdom and eloquence, lest the cross of Christ be emptied of its power.

Christ Crucified Is God's Power and Wisdom

[18] For the message of the cross is foolishness to those who are perishing, but to us who are being saved it is the power of God. [19] For it is written:

"I will destroy the wisdom of the wise;
    the intelligence of the intelligent I
        will frustrate."[c]

[20] Where is the wise person? Where is the teacher of the law? Where is the philosopher of this age? Has not God made foolish the wisdom of the world? [21] For since in the wisdom of God the world through its wisdom did not know him, God was pleased through the foolishness of what was preached to save those who believe. [22] Jews demand signs and Greeks look for wisdom, [23] but we preach Christ crucified: a stumbling block to Jews and foolishness to Gentiles, [24] but to those whom God has called, both Jews and Greeks, Christ the power of God and the wisdom of God. [25] For the foolishness of God is wiser than human wisdom, and the weakness of God is stronger than human strength.

[26] Brothers and sisters, think of what you were when you were called. Not many of you were wise by human standards; not many were influential; not many were of noble birth. [27] But God chose the foolish things of the world to shame the wise; God chose the weak things of the world to shame the strong. [28] God chose the lowly things of this world and the despised things—and the things that are not—to nullify the things that are, [29] so that no one may boast before him. [30] It is because of him that you are in Christ Jesus, who

---

[a] 10 The Greek word for *brothers and sisters* (*adelphoi*) refers here to believers, both men and women, as part of God's family; also in verses 11 and 26; and in 2:1; 3:1; 4:6; 6:8; 7:24, 29; 10:1; 11:33; 12:1; 14:6, 20, 26, 39; 15:1, 6, 50, 58; 16:15, 20.   [b] 12 That is, Peter
[c] 19 Isaiah 29:14

1 Corinthians 1:18–25

The cross sounds crazy, but it means everything.

The fact that Jesus died on the cross for our sins is an indispensible part of Christian faith. But some people think the cross makes no sense. Some object that the vicious killing of one man can't make the rest of the human race right with God. Others see the cross as a sign of weakness, the last stop for a failed spiritual teacher. The apostle Paul had heard those objections. The Greeks of his day thought the cross wasn't very smart. They wanted a better plan. The Jews expected the Savior to establish an earthly kingdom. They expected miraculous signs proving Jesus was the Messiah sent by God. But Paul wouldn't stop preaching about the cross of Christ, because "to us who are being saved it is the power of God" (1 Corinthians 1:18). The cross only looks foolish to people who are perishing.

Think: Why does the cross not make sense to people you know? How can you explain it to them?

ROCK SOLID truths

Jesus Christ and him crucified. [3]I came to you in weakness with great fear and trembling. [4]My message and my preaching were not with wise and persuasive words, but with a demonstration of the Spirit's power, [5]so that your faith might not rest on human wisdom, but on God's power.

God's Wisdom Revealed by the Spirit

[6]We do, however, speak a message of wisdom among the mature, but not the wisdom of this age or of the rulers of this age, who are coming to nothing. [7]No, we declare God's wisdom, a mystery that has been hidden and that God destined for our glory before time began. [8]None of the rulers of this age understood it, for if they had, they would not have crucified the Lord of glory. [9]However, as it is written:

"What no eye has seen,
what no ear has heard,
and what no human mind has
conceived"[c]—
the things God has prepared for
those who love him—

[10]these are the things God has revealed to us by his Spirit.

The Spirit searches all things, even the deep things of God. [11]For who knows a person's thoughts except their own spirit within them? In the same way no one knows the thoughts of God except the Spirit of God. [12]What we have received is not the spirit of the world, but the Spirit who is from God, so that we may understand what God has freely given us. [13]This is what we speak, not in words taught us by human wisdom but in words taught by the Spirit, explaining spiritual realities with Spirit-taught words.[d] [14]The person without the Spirit does not accept the things that come from the Spirit of God but considers them foolishness, and cannot understand them because they are discerned only through the Spirit. [15]The person with the Spirit makes judgments

has become for us wisdom from God— that is, our righteousness, holiness and redemption. [31]Therefore, as it is written: "Let the one who boasts boast in the Lord."[a]

2 And so it was with me, brothers and sisters. When I came to you, I did not come with eloquence or human wisdom as I proclaimed to you the testimony about God.[b] [2]For I resolved to know nothing while I was with you except

[a] 31 Jer. 9:24   [b] 1 Some manuscripts proclaimed to you God's mystery   [c] 9 Isaiah 64:4   [d] 13 Or Spirit, interpreting spiritual truths to those who are spiritual

about all things, but such a person is not subject to merely human judgments, [16]for,

"Who has known the mind of the
  Lord
    so as to instruct him?"[a]

But we have the mind of Christ.

The Church and Its Leaders

3 Brothers and sisters, I could not address you as people who live by the Spirit but as people who are still worldly—mere infants in Christ. [2]I gave you milk, not solid food, for you were not yet ready for it. Indeed, you are still not ready. [3]You are still worldly. For since there is jealousy and quarreling among you, are you not worldly? Are you not acting like mere humans? [4]For when one says, "I follow Paul," and another, "I follow Apollos," are you not mere human beings?

[5]What, after all, is Apollos? And what is Paul? Only servants, through whom you came to believe—as the Lord has assigned to each his task. [6]I planted the seed, Apollos watered it, but God has been making it grow. [7]So neither the one who plants nor the one who waters is anything, but only God, who makes things grow. [8]The one who plants and the one who waters have one purpose, and they will each be rewarded according to their own labor. [9]For we are co-workers in God's service; you are God's field, God's building.

[10]By the grace God has given me, I laid a foundation as a wise builder, and someone else is building on it. But each one should build with care. [11]For no one can lay any foundation other than the one already laid, which is Jesus Christ. [12]If anyone builds on this foundation using gold, silver, costly stones, wood, hay or straw, [13]their work will be shown for what it is, because the Day will bring it to light. It will be revealed with fire, and the fire will test the quality of each person's work. [14]If what has been built survives, the builder will receive a reward. [15]If it is burned up, the builder will suffer loss but yet will be saved—even though only as one escaping through the flames.

[16]Don't you know that you yourselves are God's temple and that God's Spirit dwells in your midst? [17]If anyone destroys God's temple, God will destroy that person; for God's temple is sacred, and you together are that temple.

ROCK SOLID promises

"Don't you know that you yourselves are God's temple and that God's Spirit dwells in your midst?" 1 Corinthians 3:16

When you belong to God, the Holy Spirit moves into your life and makes you holy.

[18]Do not deceive yourselves. If any of you think you are wise by the standards of this age, you should become "fools" so that you may become wise. [19]For the wisdom of this world is foolishness in God's sight. As it is written: "He catches the wise in their craftiness"[b]; [20]and again, "The Lord knows that the thoughts of the wise are futile."[c] [21]So then, no more boasting about human leaders! All things are yours, [22]whether Paul or Apollos or Cephas[d] or the world or life or death or the present or the future—all are yours, [23]and you are of Christ, and Christ is of God.

The Nature of True Apostleship

4 This, then, is how you ought to regard us: as servants of Christ and as those entrusted with the mysteries God has revealed. [2]Now it is required that those who have been given a trust must prove faithful. [3]I care very little if I am judged by you or by any human court; indeed, I do not even judge myself. [4]My conscience is clear, but that

[a] 16 Isaiah 40:13   [b] 19 Job 5:13
[c] 20 Psalm 94:11   [d] 22 That is, Peter

does not make me innocent. It is the Lord who judges me. [5] Therefore judge nothing before the appointed time; wait until the Lord comes. He will bring to light what is hidden in darkness and will expose the motives of the heart. At that time each will receive their praise from God.

[6] Now, brothers and sisters, I have applied these things to myself and Apollos for your benefit, so that you may learn from us the meaning of the saying, "Do not go beyond what is written." Then you will not be puffed up in being a follower of one of us over against the other. [7] For who makes you different from anyone else? What do you have that you did not receive? And if you did receive it, why do you boast as though you did not?

[8] Already you have all you want! Already you have become rich! You have begun to reign—and that without us! How I wish that you really had begun to reign so that we also might reign with you! [9] For it seems to me that God has put us apostles on display at the end of the procession, like those condemned to die in the arena. We have been made a spectacle to the whole universe, to angels as well as to human beings. [10] We are fools for Christ, but you are so wise in Christ! We are weak, but you are strong! You are honored, we are dishonored! [11] To this very hour we go hungry and thirsty, we are in rags, we are brutally treated, we are homeless. [12] We work hard with our own hands. When we are cursed, we bless; when we are persecuted, we endure it; [13] when we are slandered, we answer kindly. We have become the scum of the earth, the garbage of the world—right up to this moment.

Paul's Appeal and Warning

[14] I am writing this not to shame you but to warn you as my dear children. [15] Even if you had ten thousand guardians in Christ, you do not have many fathers, for in Christ Jesus I became your father through the gospel. [16] Therefore I urge you to imitate me. [17] For this reason I have sent to you Timothy, my son whom I love, who is faithful in the Lord. He will remind you

of my way of life in Christ Jesus, which agrees with what I teach everywhere in every church.

[18] Some of you have become arrogant, as if I were not coming to you. [19] But I will come to you very soon, if the Lord is willing, and then I will find out not only how these arrogant people are talking, but what power they have. [20] For the kingdom of God is not a matter of talk but of power. [21] What do you prefer? Shall I come to you with a rod of discipline, or shall I come in love and with a gentle spirit?

Dealing With a Case of Incest

5 It is actually reported that there is sexual immorality among you, and of a kind that even pagans do not tolerate: A man is sleeping with his father's wife. [2] And you are proud! Shouldn't you rather have gone into mourning and have put out of your fellowship the man who has been doing this? [3] For my part, even though I am not physically present, I am with you in spirit. As one who is present with you in this way, I have already passed judgment in the name of our Lord Jesus on the one who has been doing this. [4] So when you are assembled and I am with you in spirit, and the power of our Lord Jesus is present, [5] hand this man over to Satan for the destruction of the flesh,[a,b] so that his spirit may be saved on the day of the Lord.

[6] Your boasting is not good. Don't you know that a little yeast leavens the whole batch of dough? [7] Get rid of the old yeast, so that you may be a new unleavened batch—as you really are. For Christ, our Passover lamb, has been sacrificed. [8] Therefore let us keep the Festival, not with the old bread leavened with malice and wickedness, but with the unleavened bread of sincerity and truth.

[9] I wrote to you in my letter not to associate with sexually immoral people— [10] not at all meaning the people of this world who are immoral, or the greedy

---

[a] 5 In contexts like this, the Greek word for *flesh* (*sarx*) refers to the sinful state of human beings, often presented as a power in opposition to the Spirit. [b] 5 Or *of his body*

and swindlers, or idolaters. In that case you would have to leave this world. ¹¹ But now I am writing to you that you must not associate with anyone who claims to be a brother or sister*a* but is sexually immoral or greedy, an idolater or slanderer, a drunkard or swindler. Do not even eat with such people.

¹²What business is it of mine to judge those outside the church? Are you not to judge those inside? ¹³ God will judge those outside. "Expel the wicked person from among you."*b*

Lawsuits Among Believers

6 If any of you has a dispute with another, do you dare to take it before the ungodly for judgment instead of before the Lord's people? ² Or do you not know that the Lord's people will judge the world? And if you are to judge the world, are you not competent to judge trivial cases? ³ Do you not know that we will judge angels? How much more the things of this life! ⁴ Therefore, if you have disputes about such matters, do you ask for a ruling from those whose way of life is scorned in the church? ⁵ I say this to shame you. Is it possible that there is nobody among you wise enough to judge a dispute between believers? ⁶ But instead, one brother takes another to court—and this in front of unbelievers!

⁷ The very fact that you have lawsuits among you means you have been completely defeated already. Why not rather be wronged? Why not rather be cheated? ⁸ Instead, you yourselves cheat and do wrong, and you do this to your brothers and sisters. ⁹ Or do you not know that wrongdoers will not inherit the kingdom of God? Do not be deceived: Neither the sexually immoral nor idolaters nor adulterers nor men who have sex with men*c* ¹⁰ nor thieves nor the greedy nor drunkards nor slanderers nor swindlers will inherit the kingdom of God. ¹¹ And that is what some of you were. But you were washed, you were sanctified, you were justified in the name of the Lord Jesus Christ and by the Spirit of our God.

Sexual Immorality

¹² "I have the right to do anything," you say—but not everything is beneficial. "I have the right to do anything"—but I will not be mastered by anything. ¹³ You say, "Food for the stomach and the stomach for food, and God will destroy them both." The body, however, is not meant for sexual immorality but for the Lord, and the Lord for the body. ¹⁴ By his power God raised the Lord from the dead, and he will raise us also. ¹⁵ Do you not know that your bodies are members of Christ himself? Shall I then take the members of Christ and unite them with a prostitute? Never! ¹⁶ Do you not know that he who unites himself with a prostitute is one with her in body? For it is said, "The two will become one flesh."*d* ¹⁷ But whoever is united with the Lord is one with him in spirit.*e*

¹⁸ Flee from sexual immorality. All other sins a person commits are outside

a 11 The Greek word for *brother or sister* (*adelphos*) refers here to a believer, whether man or woman, as part of God's family; also in 8:11, 13.   *b* 13 Deut. 13:5; 17:7; 19:19; 21:21; 22:21,24; 24:7   *c* 9 The words *men who have sex with men* translate two Greek words that refer to the passive and active participants in homosexual acts.   *d* 16 Gen. 2:24
e 17 Or *in the Spirit*

the body, but whoever sins sexually, sins against their own body. [19] Do you not know that your bodies are temples of the Holy Spirit, who is in you, whom you have received from God? You are not your own; [20] you were bought at a price. Therefore honor God with your bodies.

Concerning Married Life

7 Now for the matters you wrote about: "It is good for a man not to have sexual relations with a woman." [2] But since sexual immorality is occurring, each man should have sexual relations with his own wife, and each woman with her own husband. [3] The husband should fulfill his marital duty to his wife, and likewise the wife to her husband. [4] The wife does not have authority over her own body but yields it to her husband. In the same way, the husband does not have authority over his own body but yields it to his wife. [5] Do not deprive each other except perhaps by mutual consent and for a time, so that you may devote yourselves to prayer. Then come together again so that Satan will not tempt you because of your lack of self-control. [6] I say this as a concession, not as a command. [7] I wish that all of you were as I am. But each of you has your own gift from God; one has this gift, another has that.

[8] Now to the unmarried[a] and the widows I say: It is good for them to stay unmarried, as I do. [9] But if they cannot control themselves, they should marry, for it is better to marry than to burn with passion.

[10] To the married I give this command (not I, but the Lord): A wife must not separate from her husband. [11] But if she does, she must remain unmarried or else be reconciled to her husband. And a husband must not divorce his wife.

a 8 Or widowers

ROCK SOLID principles

1 Corinthians 6:12–20

Don't pollute your temple.

"I really don't see the problem with having some fun," Cameron always said. "Whatever I can get a girl to do, I will." But he couldn't ignore a painful outbreak of nasty blisters. A doctor confirmed he had herpes, a contagious sexually transmitted disease no drug could fix. Suddenly Cameron had a reason to get serious about God's commands about purity. And he realized a lifelong infection with no cure wasn't even the biggest of his problems. His real issue was the attitudes that got him into trouble — how he looked at girls, himself, and God. At least those were things he could still change.

The believers in Corinth lived among pagans who worshiped false gods through religious prostitution. They thought they could sin and then run to God for forgiveness. The apostle Paul said they were missing the point. God forbids sexual sin because it hurts everyone involved — even God, who lives in us through his Holy Spirit. When you sin with your body, you pollute your temple.

¹²To the rest I say this (I, not the Lord): If any brother has a wife who is not a believer and she is willing to live with him, he must not divorce her. ¹³And if a woman has a husband who is not a believer and he is willing to live with her, she must not divorce him. ¹⁴For the unbelieving husband has been sanctified through his wife, and the unbelieving wife has been sanctified through her believing husband. Otherwise your children would be unclean, but as it is, they are holy.

¹⁵But if the unbeliever leaves, let it be so. The brother or the sister is not bound in such circumstances; God has called us to live in peace. ¹⁶How do you know, wife, whether you will save your husband? Or, how do you know, husband, whether you will save your wife?

Concerning Change of Status

¹⁷Nevertheless, each person should live as a believer in whatever situation the Lord has assigned to them, just as God has called them. This is the rule I lay down in all the churches. ¹⁸Was a man already circumcised when he was called? He should not become uncircumcised. Was a man uncircumcised when he was called? He should not be circumcised. ¹⁹Circumcision is nothing and uncircumcision is nothing. Keeping God's commands is what counts. ²⁰Each person should remain in the situation they were in when God called them.

²¹Were you a slave when you were called? Don't let it trouble you—although if you can gain your freedom, do so. ²²For the one who was a slave when called to faith in the Lord is the Lord's freed person; similarly, the one who was free when called is Christ's slave. ²³You were bought at a price; do not become slaves of human beings. ²⁴Brothers and sisters, each person, as responsible to God, should remain in the situation they were in when God called them.

Concerning the Unmarried

²⁵Now about virgins: I have no command from the Lord, but I give a judg-ment as one who by the Lord's mercy is trustworthy. ²⁶Because of the present crisis, I think that it is good for a man to remain as he is. ²⁷Are you pledged to a woman? Do not seek to be released. Are you free from such a commitment? Do not look for a wife. ²⁸But if you do marry, you have not sinned; and if a virgin marries, she has not sinned. But those who marry will face many troubles in this life, and I want to spare you this.

²⁹What I mean, brothers and sisters, is that the time is short. From now on those who have wives should live as if they do not; ³⁰those who mourn, as if they did not; those who are happy, as if they were not; those who buy something, as if it were not theirs to keep; ³¹those who use the things of the world, as if not engrossed in them. For this world in its present form is passing away.

³²I would like you to be free from concern. An unmarried man is concerned about the Lord's affairs—how he can please the Lord. ³³But a married man is concerned about the affairs of this world—how he can please his wife— ³⁴and his interests are divided. An unmarried woman or virgin is concerned about the Lord's affairs: Her aim is to be devoted to the Lord in both body and spirit. But a married woman is concerned about the affairs of this world—how she can please her husband. ³⁵I am saying this for your own good, not to restrict you, but that you may live in a right way in undivided devotion to the Lord.

³⁶If anyone is worried that he might not be acting honorably toward the virgin he is engaged to, and if his passions are too strong[a] and he feels he ought to marry, he should do as he wants. He is not sinning. They should get married. ³⁷But the man who has settled the matter in his own mind, who is under no compulsion but has control over his own will, and who has made up his mind not to marry the virgin—this man also does the right thing. ³⁸So then, he who marries the virgin does

[a] 36 Or *if she is getting beyond the usual age for marriage*

right, but he who does not marry her does better.[a]

[39] A woman is bound to her husband as long as he lives. But if her husband dies, she is free to marry anyone she wishes, but he must belong to the Lord. [40] In my judgment, she is happier if she stays as she is — and I think that I too have the Spirit of God.

Concerning Food Sacrificed to Idols

8 Now about food sacrificed to idols: We know that "We all possess knowledge." But knowledge puffs up while love builds up. [2] Those who think they know something do not yet know as they ought to know. [3] But whoever loves God is known by God.[b]

[4] So then, about eating food sacrificed to idols: We know that "An idol is nothing at all in the world" and that "There is no God but one." [5] For even if there are so-called gods, whether in heaven or on earth (as indeed there are many "gods" and many "lords"), [6] yet for us there is but one God, the Father, from whom all things came and for whom we live; and there is but one Lord, Jesus Christ, through whom all things came and through whom we live.

[7] But not everyone possesses this knowledge. Some people are still so accustomed to idols that when they eat sacrificial food they think of it as having been sacrificed to a god, and since their conscience is weak, it is defiled. [8] But food does not bring us near to God; we are no worse if we do not eat, and no better if we do.

[9] Be careful, however, that the exercise of your rights does not become a stumbling block to the weak. [10] For if someone with a weak conscience sees you, with all your knowledge, eating in an idol's temple, won't that person be emboldened to eat what is sacrificed to idols? [11] So this weak brother or sister, for whom Christ died, is destroyed by your knowledge. [12] When you sin against them in this way and wound their weak conscience, you sin against Christ. [13] Therefore, if what I eat causes my brother or sister to fall into sin, I will never eat meat again, so that I will not cause them to fall.

Paul's Rights as an Apostle

9 Am I not free? Am I not an apostle? Have I not seen Jesus our Lord? Are you not the result of my work in the Lord? [2] Even though I may not be an apostle to others, surely I am to you! For you are the seal of my apostleship in the Lord.

[3] This is my defense to those who sit in judgment on me. [4] Don't we have the right to food and drink? [5] Don't we have the right to take a believing wife along with us, as do the other apostles and the Lord's brothers and Cephas[c]? [6] Or is it only I and Barnabas who lack the right to not work for a living?

[7] Who serves as a soldier at his own expense? Who plants a vineyard and does not eat its grapes? Who tends a flock and does not drink the milk? [8] Do I say this merely on human authority? Doesn't the Law say the same thing? [9] For it is written in the Law of Moses: "Do not muzzle an ox while it is treading out the grain."[d] Is it about oxen that God is concerned? [10] Surely he says this for us, doesn't he? Yes, this was written for us, because whoever plows and threshes should be able to do so in the hope of sharing in the harvest. [11] If we have sown spiritual seed among you, is it too much if we reap a material harvest from you? [12] If others have this right of support from you, shouldn't we have it all the more?

But we did not use this right. On the contrary, we put up with anything rather than hinder the gospel of Christ.

---

[a] 36-38 Or [36]*If anyone thinks he is not treating his daughter properly, and if she is getting along in years (or if her passions are too strong), and he feels she ought to marry, he should do as he wants. He is not sinning. He should let her get married.* [37]*But the man who has settled the matter in his own mind, who is under no compulsion but has control over his own will, and who has made up his mind to keep the virgin unmarried—this man also does the right thing.* [38]*So then, he who gives his virgin in marriage does right, but he who does not give her in marriage does better.*   [b] 2,3 An early manuscript and another ancient witness *think they have knowledge do not yet know as they ought to know.* [3]*But whoever loves truly knows.*   [c] 5 That is, Peter   [d] 9 Deut. 25:4

Life is sometimes gray, but truth is not.

A truth is "absolute" when it is true for all people in all times and all places. Most people agree that 2+2=4 is always true. But many would disagree with the claim that sex outside of marriage is wrong. They call that a "gray area," a matter of personal choice. Christians believe the Bible gives us God's absolute commands. They don't change. They aren't gray. But the Bible does recognize that gray areas exist. When early Christians couldn't agree whether it was okay to eat meat that had been sacrificed to idols, Paul left the choice up to their individual convictions. He told mature Christians not to do anything that would encourage less mature Christians to violate their consciences. When Christians today disagree — about things like media or dancing or alcohol — they owe it to each other to help each live fully for God, whatever choices they make.

Think: What choices in your life aren't gray? Which might be? Who helps you make those decisions?

ROCK SOLID truths

of this boast. ¹⁶For when I preach the gospel, I cannot boast, since I am compelled to preach. Woe to me if I do not preach the gospel! ¹⁷If I preach voluntarily, I have a reward; if not voluntarily, I am simply discharging the trust committed to me. ¹⁸What then is my reward? Just this: that in preaching the gospel I may offer it free of charge, and so not make full use of my rights as a preacher of the gospel.

Paul's Use of His Freedom

¹⁹Though I am free and belong to no one, I have made myself a slave to everyone, to win as many as possible. ²⁰To the Jews I became like a Jew, to win the Jews. To those under the law I became like one under the law (though I myself am not under the law), so as to win those under the law. ²¹To those not having the law I became like one not having the law (though I am not free from God's law but am under Christ's law), so as to win those not having the law. ²²To the weak I became weak, to win the weak. I have become all things to all people so that by all possible means I might save some. ²³I do all this for the sake of the gospel, that I may share in its blessings.

The Need for Self-Discipline

²⁴Do you not know that in a race all the runners run, but only one gets the prize? Run in such a way as to get the prize. ²⁵Everyone who competes in the games goes into strict training. They do it to get a crown that will not last, but we do it to get a crown that will last forever. ²⁶Therefore I do not run like someone running aimlessly; I do not fight like a boxer beating the air. ²⁷No, I strike a blow to my body and make it my slave so that after I have preached to others, I myself will not be disqualified for the prize.

Warnings From Israel's History

10 For I do not want you to be ignorant of the fact, brothers and sisters, that our ancestors were all under the cloud and that they all passed through the sea. ²They were all baptized

¹³Don't you know that those who serve in the temple get their food from the temple, and that those who serve at the altar share in what is offered on the altar? ¹⁴In the same way, the Lord has commanded that those who preach the gospel should receive their living from the gospel.

¹⁵But I have not used any of these rights. And I am not writing this in the hope that you will do such things for me, for I would rather die than allow anyone to deprive me

into Moses in the cloud and in the sea. ³They all ate the same spiritual food ⁴and drank the same spiritual drink; for they drank from the spiritual rock that accompanied them, and that rock was Christ. ⁵Nevertheless, God was not pleased with most of them; their bodies were scattered in the wilderness.

⁶Now these things occurred as examples to keep us from setting our hearts on evil things as they did. ⁷Do not be idolaters, as some of them were; as it is written: "The people sat down to eat and drink and got up to indulge in revelry."[a] ⁸We should not commit sexual immorality, as some of them did—and in one day twenty-three thousand of them died. ⁹We should not test Christ,[b] as some of them did—and were killed by snakes. ¹⁰And do not grumble, as some of them did—and were killed by the destroying angel.

¹¹These things happened to them as examples and were written down as warnings for us, on whom the culmination of the ages has come. ¹²So, if you think you are standing firm, be careful that you don't fall! ¹³No temptation[c] has overtaken you except what is common to mankind. And God is faithful; he will not let you be tempted[c] beyond what you can bear. But when you are tempted,[c] he will also provide a way out so that you can endure it.

ROCK SOLID
promises

"God is faithful; he will not let you be tempted beyond what you can bear. But when you are tempted, he will also provide a way out so that you can endure it."

1 Corinthians 10:13

No temptation ever looms so big that you can't say no. God always opens a way for you to escape the urge to sin.

Idol Feasts and the Lord's Supper

¹⁴Therefore, my dear friends, flee from idolatry. ¹⁵I speak to sensible people; judge for yourselves what I say. ¹⁶Is not the cup of thanksgiving for which we give thanks a participation in the blood of Christ? And is not the bread that we break a participation in the body of Christ? ¹⁷Because there is one loaf, we, who are many, are one body, for we all share the one loaf.

¹⁸Consider the people of Israel: Do not those who eat the sacrifices participate in the altar? ¹⁹Do I mean then that food sacrificed to an idol is anything, or that an idol is anything? ²⁰No, but the sacrifices of pagans are offered to demons, not to God, and I do not want you to be participants with demons. ²¹You cannot drink the cup of the Lord and the cup of demons too; you cannot have a part in both the Lord's table and the table of demons. ²²Are we trying to arouse the Lord's jealousy? Are we stronger than he?

The Believer's Freedom

²³"I have the right to do anything," you say—but not everything is beneficial. "I have the right to do anything"—but not everything is constructive. ²⁴No one should seek their own good, but the good of others.

²⁵Eat anything sold in the meat market without raising questions of conscience, ²⁶for, "The earth is the Lord's, and everything in it."[d]

²⁷If an unbeliever invites you to a meal and you want to go, eat whatever is put before you without raising questions of conscience. ²⁸But if someone says to you, "This has been offered in sacrifice," then do not eat it, both for the sake of the one who told you and for the sake of conscience. ²⁹I am referring to the other person's conscience, not yours. For why is my freedom being judged by another's conscience? ³⁰If I take part in the meal

---

[a] 7 Exodus 32:6   [b] 9 Some manuscripts test the Lord   [c] 13 The Greek for temptation and tempted can also mean testing and tested.   [d] 26 Psalm 24:1

with thankfulness, why am I denounced because of something I thank God for? [31] So whether you eat or drink or whatever you do, do it all for the glory of God. [32] Do not cause anyone to stumble, whether Jews, Greeks or the church of God— [33] even as I try to please everyone in every way. For I am not seeking my own good but the good of many, so that they may be saved. [1] Follow my example, as I follow the example of Christ.

On Covering the Head in Worship

[2] I praise you for remembering me in everything and for holding to the traditions just as I passed them on to you. [3] But I want you to realize that the head of every man is Christ, and the head of the woman is man,[a] and the head of Christ is God. [4] Every man who prays or prophesies with his head covered dishonors his head. [5] But every woman who prays or prophesies with her head uncovered dishonors her head—it is the same as having her head shaved. [6] For if a woman does not cover her head, she might as well have her hair cut off; but if it is a disgrace for a woman to have her hair cut off or her head shaved, then she should cover her head.

[7] A man ought not to cover his head,[b] since he is the image and glory of God; but woman is the glory of man. [8] For man did not come from woman, but woman from man; [9] neither was man created for woman, but woman for man. [10] It is for this reason that a woman ought to have authority over her own[c] head, because of the angels. [11] Nevertheless, in the Lord woman is not independent of man, nor is man independent of woman. [12] For as woman came from man, so also man is born of woman. But everything comes from God.

[13] Judge for yourselves: Is it proper for a woman to pray to God with her head uncovered? [14] Does not the very nature of things teach you that if a man has long hair, it is a disgrace to him, [15] but that if a woman has long hair, it is her glory? For long hair is given to her as a covering. [16] If anyone wants to be contentious about this, we have no other practice—nor do the churches of God.

Correcting an Abuse of the Lord's Supper

[17] In the following directives I have no praise for you, for your meetings do more harm than good. [18] In the first place, I hear that when you come together as a church, there are divisions among you, and to some extent I believe it. [19] No doubt there have to be differences among you to show which of you have God's approval. [20] So then, when you come together, it is not the Lord's Supper you eat, [21] for when you are eating, some of you go ahead with your own private suppers. As a result, one person remains hungry and another gets

ROCK SOLID *plans*

1 Corinthians 10:31

Glorify God.

The Bible has some major tests to make sure you're on track with the Lord. It says to love God "with all your heart and with all your soul and with all your strength" (Deuteronomy 6:5). It tells you to "Love your neighbor as yourself" (Matthew 22:39). And here's another significant one: Test your thoughts, words and actions—everything you do—to ensure you glorify God. You pass the test when you display his greatness, give him honor, and demonstrate that he deserves to rule all of you.

Your next step: Ask a mature Christian to help you spot areas of your life that don't glorify God.

---

a 3 Or of the wife is her husband
b 4-7 Or ⁴Every man who prays or prophesies with long hair dishonors his head. ⁵But every woman who prays or prophesies with no covering of hair dishonors her head—she is just like one of the "shorn women." ⁶If a woman has no covering, let her be for now with short hair; but since it is a disgrace for a woman to have her hair shorn or shaved, she should grow it again. ⁷A man ought not to have long hair
c 10 Or have a sign of authority on her

drunk. [22] Don't you have homes to eat and drink in? Or do you despise the church of God by humiliating those who have nothing? What shall I say to you? Shall I praise you? Certainly not in this matter!

[23] For I received from the Lord what I also passed on to you: The Lord Jesus, on the night he was betrayed, took bread, [24] and when he had given thanks, he broke it and said, "This is my body, which is for you; do this in remembrance of me." [25] In the same way, after supper he took the cup, saying, "This cup is the new covenant in my blood; do this, whenever you drink it, in remembrance of me." [26] For whenever you eat this bread and drink this cup, you proclaim the Lord's death until he comes.

[27] So then, whoever eats the bread or drinks the cup of the Lord in an unworthy manner will be guilty of sinning against the body and blood of the Lord. [28] Everyone ought to examine themselves before they eat of the bread and drink from the cup. [29] For those who eat and drink without discerning the body of Christ eat and drink judgment on themselves. [30] That is why many among you are weak and sick, and a number of you have fallen asleep. [31] But if we were more discerning with regard to ourselves, we would not come under such judgment. [32] Nevertheless, when we are judged in this way by the Lord, we are being disciplined so that we will not be finally condemned with the world.

[33] So then, my brothers and sisters, when you gather to eat, you should all eat together. [34] Anyone who is hungry should eat something at home, so that when you meet together it may not result in judgment.

And when I come I will give further directions.

Concerning Spiritual Gifts

12 Now about the gifts of the Spirit, brothers and sisters, I do not want you to be uninformed. [2] You know that when you were pagans, somehow or other you were influenced and led astray to mute idols. [3] Therefore I want you to know that no one who is speaking by the Spirit of God says, "Jesus be cursed," and no one can say, "Jesus is Lord," except by the Holy Spirit.

[4] There are different kinds of gifts, but the same Spirit distributes them. [5] There are different kinds of service, but the same Lord. [6] There are different kinds of working, but in all of them and in everyone it is the same God at work.

[7] Now to each one the manifestation of the Spirit is given for the common good.

ROCK SOLID
promises

"Now to each one the manifestation of the Spirit is given for the common good." 1 Corinthians 12:7

God gives you spiritual gifts so you can prove his love to people and help them get closer to him.

[8] To one there is given through the Spirit a message of wisdom, to another a message of knowledge by means of the same Spirit, [9] to another faith by the same Spirit, to another gifts of healing by that one Spirit, [10] to another miraculous powers, to another prophecy, to another distinguishing between spirits, to another speaking in different kinds of tongues,[a] and to still another the interpretation of tongues.[a] [11] All these are the work of one and the same Spirit, and he distributes them to each one, just as he determines.

Unity and Diversity in the Body

[12] Just as a body, though one, has many parts, but all its many parts form one body, so it is with Christ. [13] For we were all baptized by[b] one Spirit so as to form one body—whether Jews or Gentiles, slave or

[a] 10 Or languages; also in verse 28
[b] 13 Or with; or in

free—and we were all given the one Spirit to drink. ¹⁴Even so the body is not made up of one part but of many.

¹⁵Now if the foot should say, "Because I am not a hand, I do not belong to the body," it would not for that reason stop being part of the body. ¹⁶And if the ear should say, "Because I am not an eye, I do not belong to the body," it would not for that reason stop being part of the body. ¹⁷If the whole body were an eye, where would the sense of hearing be? If the whole body were an ear, where would the sense of smell be? ¹⁸But in fact God has placed the parts in the body, every one of them, just as he wanted them to be. ¹⁹If they were all one part, where would the body be? ²⁰As it is, there are many parts, but one body.

²¹The eye cannot say to the hand, "I don't need you!" And the head cannot say to the feet, "I don't need you!" ²²On the contrary, those parts of the body that seem to be weaker are indispensable, ²³and the parts that we think are less honorable we treat with special honor. And the parts that are unpresentable are treated with special modesty, ²⁴while our presentable parts need no special treatment. But God has put the body together, giving greater honor to the parts that lacked it, ²⁵so that there should be no division in the body, but that its parts should have equal concern for each other. ²⁶If one part suffers, every part suffers with it; if one part is honored, every part rejoices with it.

²⁷Now you are the body of Christ, and each one of you is a part of it. ²⁸And God has placed in the church first of all apostles, second prophets, third teachers, then miracles, then gifts of healing, of helping, of guidance, and of different kinds of tongues. ²⁹Are all apostles? Are all prophets? Are all teachers? Do all work miracles? ³⁰Do all have gifts of healing? Do all speak in tongues*ᵃ*? Do all interpret? ³¹Now eagerly desire the greater gifts.

Love Is Indispensable

And yet I will show you the most excellent way.

ROCK SOLID *plans*

1 Corinthians 12:12–31

Do your thing.

The first part of this famous Bible chapter informs you that God gave you a spiritual gift for the good of everyone around you (see 1 Corinthians 12:7). This second part illustrates how God's people fall apart when they don't use their gifts. If you fail to act on your unique gift—or neglect to get help from others and their variety of gifts—you're like a renegade body part trying to survive on its own. You won't make it. And everyone loses out when you don't do your thing.

Your next step: If you aren't sure about your spiritual gifts or how they can benefit others, check with your pastor for insights.

---

13 If I speak in the tongues*ᵇ* of men or of angels, but do not have love, I am only a resounding gong or a clanging cymbal. ²If I have the gift of prophecy and can fathom all mysteries and all knowledge, and if I have a faith that can move mountains, but do not have love, I am nothing. ³If I give all I possess to the poor and give over my body to hardship that I may boast,*ᶜ* but do not have love, I gain nothing.

⁴Love is patient, love is kind. It does not envy, it does not boast, it is not proud. ⁵It does not dishonor others, it is not self-seeking, it is not easily angered, it keeps no record of wrongs. ⁶Love does not delight in evil but rejoices with the truth. ⁷It always protects, always trusts, always hopes, always perseveres.

⁸Love never fails. But where there are prophecies, they will cease; where there are tongues, they will be stilled; where

ᵃ 30 Or *other languages*   *ᵇ 1* Or *languages*
ᶜ 3 Some manuscripts *body to the flames*

ROCK SOLID *promises*

"Love never fails."

1 Corinthians 13:8

True love never runs short of energy or determination. It does what it takes to get the job done.

there is knowledge, it will pass away. [9] For we know in part and we prophesy in part, [10] but when completeness comes, what is in part disappears. [11] When I was a child, I talked like a child, I thought like a child, I reasoned like a child. When I became a man, I put the ways of childhood behind me. [12] For now we see only a reflection as in a mirror; then we shall see face to face. Now I know in part; then I shall know fully, even as I am fully known.

[13] And now these three remain: faith, hope and love. But the greatest of these is love.

Intelligibility in Worship

14 Follow the way of love and eagerly desire gifts of the Spirit, especially prophecy. [2] For anyone who speaks in a tongue[a] does not speak to people but to God. Indeed, no one understands them; they utter mysteries by the Spirit. [3] But the one who prophesies speaks to people for their strengthening, encouraging and comfort. [4] Anyone who speaks in a tongue edifies themselves, but the one who prophesies edifies the church. [5] I would like every one of you to speak in tongues,[b] but I would rather have you prophesy. The one who prophesies is greater than the one who speaks in tongues,[b] unless someone interprets, so that the church may be edified.

[6] Now, brothers and sisters, if I come to you and speak in tongues, what good will I be to you, unless I bring you some revelation or knowledge or prophecy or word of instruction? [7] Even in the case of lifeless things that make sounds, such as the pipe or harp, how will anyone know what tune is being played unless there is a distinction in the notes? [8] Again, if the trumpet does not sound a clear call, who will get ready for battle? [9] So it is with you. Unless you speak intelligible words with your tongue, how will anyone know what you are saying? You will just be speaking into the air. [10] Undoubtedly there are all sorts of languages in the world, yet none of them is without meaning. [11] If then I do not grasp the meaning of what someone is saying, I am a foreigner to the speaker, and the speaker is a foreigner to me. [12] So it is with you. Since you are eager for gifts of the Spirit, try to excel in those that build up the church.

[13] For this reason the one who speaks in a tongue should pray that they may interpret what they say. [14] For if I pray in a tongue, my spirit prays, but my mind is unfruitful. [15] So what shall I do? I will pray with my spirit, but I will also pray with my understanding; I will sing with my spirit, but I will also sing with my understanding. [16] Otherwise when you are praising God in the Spirit, how can someone else, who is now put in the position of an inquirer,[c] say "Amen" to your thanksgiving, since they do not know what you are saying? [17] You are giving thanks well enough, but no one else is edified.

[18] I thank God that I speak in tongues more than all of you. [19] But in the church I would rather speak five intelligible words to instruct others than ten thousand words in a tongue.

[20] Brothers and sisters, stop thinking like children. In regard to evil be infants, but in your thinking be adults. [21] In the Law it is written:

a 2 Or *in another language*; also in verses 4, 13, 14, 19, 26 and 27   *b 5* Or *in other languages*; also in verses 6, 18, 22, 23 and 39
c 16 The Greek word for *inquirer* is a technical term for someone not fully initiated into a religion; also in verses 23 and 24.

"With other tongues
and through the lips of foreigners
I will speak to this people,
but even then they will not listen
to me,
says the Lord."[a]

[22]Tongues, then, are a sign, not for believers but for unbelievers; prophecy, however, is not for unbelievers but for believers. [23]So if the whole church comes together and everyone speaks in tongues, and inquirers or unbelievers come in, will they not say that you are out of your mind? [24]But if an unbeliever or an inquirer comes in while everyone is prophesying, they are convicted of sin and are brought under judgment by all, [25]as the secrets of their hearts are laid bare. So they will fall down and worship God, exclaiming, "God is really among you!"

Good Order in Worship

[26]What then shall we say, brothers and sisters? When you come together, each of you has a hymn, or a word of instruction, a revelation, a tongue or an interpretation. Everything must be done so that the church may be built up. [27]If anyone speaks in a tongue, two—or at the most three—should speak, one at a time, and someone must interpret. [28]If there is no interpreter, the speaker should keep quiet in the church and speak to himself and to God.

[29]Two or three prophets should speak, and the others should weigh carefully what is said. [30]And if a revelation comes to someone who is sitting down, the first speaker should stop. [31]For you can all prophesy in turn so that everyone may be instructed and encouraged. [32]The spirits of prophets are subject to the control of prophets. [33]For God is not a God of disorder but of peace—as in all the congregations of the Lord's people.

[34]Women[b] should remain silent in the churches. They are not allowed to speak, but must be in submission, as the law says. [35]If they want to inquire about something, they should ask their own husbands at home; for it is disgraceful for a woman to speak in the church.[c]

[36]Or did the word of God originate with you? Or are you the only people it has reached? [37]If anyone thinks they are a prophet or otherwise gifted by the Spirit, let them acknowledge that what I am writing to you is the Lord's command. [38]But if anyone ignores this, they will themselves be ignored.[d]

[39]Therefore, my brothers and sisters, be eager to prophesy, and do not forbid speaking in tongues. [40]But everything should be done in a fitting and orderly way.

The Resurrection of Christ

15 Now, brothers and sisters, I want to remind you of the gospel I preached to you, which you received and on which you have taken your stand. [2]By this gospel you are saved, if you hold firmly to the word I preached to you. Otherwise, you have believed in vain.

[3]For what I received I passed on to you as of first importance[e]: that Christ died for our sins according to the Scriptures, [4]that he was buried, that he was raised on the third day according to the Scriptures, [5]and that he appeared to Cephas,[f] and then to the Twelve. [6]After that, he appeared to more than five hundred of the brothers and sisters at the same time, most of whom are still living, though some have fallen asleep. [7]Then he appeared to James, then to all the apostles, [8]and last of all he appeared to me also, as to one abnormally born.

[9]For I am the least of the apostles and do not even deserve to be called an apostle, because I persecuted the church of God. [10]But by the grace of God I am what I am, and his grace to me was not without effect. No, I worked harder than all of them—yet not I, but the grace of God that was with me. [11]Whether, then, it is I or they, this is what we preach, and this is what you believed.

---

[a] 21 Isaiah 28:11,12   [b] 33,34 Or peace. As in all the congregations of the Lord's people, [34]women   [c] 34,35 In a few manuscripts these verses come after verse 40.   [d] 38 Some manuscripts But anyone who is ignorant of this will be ignored   [e] 3 Or you at the first   [f] 5 That is, Peter

1 Corinthians 15:1–8

Many people saw Jesus alive after his death.

Read this Bible passage word by word. Then memorize it. This handful of verses not only explains your core Christian beliefs but also gives you evidence to support them. The apostle Paul spells out the gospel that saves you: "Christ died for our sins according to the Scriptures … he was buried … he was raised on the third day according to the Scriptures" (1 Corinthians 15:3–4). That's the most important news you could ever know. And the news that Jesus rose from the dead comes backed up by more facts than most people know. Jesus appeared to his friend Peter, then the rest of his inner circle. He appeared to James and Paul. And he also appeared to more than five hundred believers at once, most whom were still living at the time Paul wrote this letter. If people doubted the reality of the resurrection, they could check the facts for themselves.

Think: What's significant about Jesus appearing to so many people after he rose from the dead?

ROCK SOLID *truths*

we have testified about God that he raised Christ from the dead. But he did not raise him if in fact the dead are not raised. ¹⁶For if the dead are not raised, then Christ has not been raised either. ¹⁷And if Christ has not been raised, your faith is futile; you are still in your sins. ¹⁸Then those also who have fallen asleep in Christ are lost. ¹⁹If only for this life we have hope in Christ, we are of all people most to be pitied.

²⁰But Christ has indeed been raised from the dead, the firstfruits of those who have fallen asleep. ²¹For since death came through a man, the resurrection of the dead comes also through a man. ²²For as in Adam all die, so in Christ all will be made alive. ²³But each in turn: Christ, the firstfruits; then, when he comes, those who belong to him. ²⁴Then the end will come, when he hands over the kingdom to God the Father after he has destroyed all dominion, authority and power. ²⁵For he must reign until he has put all his enemies under his feet. ²⁶The last enemy to be destroyed is death. ²⁷For he "has put everything under his feet."[a] Now when it says that "everything" has been put under him, it is clear that this does not include God himself, who put everything under Christ. ²⁸When he has done this, then the Son himself will be made subject to him who put everything under him, so that God may be all in all.

²⁹Now if there is no resurrection, what will those do who are baptized for the dead? If the dead are not raised at all, why are people baptized for them? ³⁰And as for us, why do we endanger ourselves every hour? ³¹I face death every day—yes, just as surely as I boast about you in Christ Jesus our Lord. ³²If I fought wild beasts in Ephesus with no more than human hopes, what have I gained? If the dead are not raised,

"Let us eat and drink,
    for tomorrow we die."[b]

³³Do not be misled: "Bad company corrupts good character."[c] ³⁴Come back to

The Resurrection of the Dead

¹²But if it is preached that Christ has been raised from the dead, how can some of you say that there is no resurrection of the dead? ¹³If there is no resurrection of the dead, then not even Christ has been raised. ¹⁴And if Christ has not been raised, our preaching is useless and so is your faith. ¹⁵More than that, we are then found to be false witnesses about God, for

[a] 27 Psalm 8:6   [b] 32 Isaiah 22:13
[c] 33 From the Greek poet Menander

your senses as you ought, and stop sinning; for there are some who are ignorant of God—I say this to your shame.

The Resurrection Body

35 But someone will ask, "How are the dead raised? With what kind of body will they come?" 36 How foolish! What you sow does not come to life unless it dies. 37 When you sow, you do not plant the body that will be, but just a seed, perhaps of wheat or of something else. 38 But God gives it a body as he has determined, and to each kind of seed he gives its own body. 39 Not all flesh is the same: People have one kind of flesh, animals have another, birds another and fish another. 40 There are also heavenly bodies and there are earthly bodies; but the splendor of the heavenly bodies is one kind, and the splendor of the earthly bodies is another. 41 The sun has one kind of splendor, the moon another and the stars another; and star differs from star in splendor.

42 So will it be with the resurrection of the dead. The body that is sown is perishable, it is raised imperishable; 43 it is sown in dishonor, it is raised in glory; it is sown in weakness, it is raised in power; 44 it is sown a natural body, it is raised a spiritual body.

If there is a natural body, there is also a spiritual body. 45 So it is written: "The first man Adam became a living being"[a]; the last Adam, a life-giving spirit. 46 The spiritual did not come first, but the natural, and after that the spiritual. 47 The first man was of the dust of the earth; the second man is of heaven. 48 As was the earthly man, so are those who are of the earth; and as is the heavenly man, so also are those who are of heaven. 49 And just as we have borne the image of the earthly man, so shall we[b] bear the image of the heavenly man.

50 I declare to you, brothers and sisters, that flesh and blood cannot inherit the kingdom of God, nor does the perishable inherit the imperishable. 51 Listen, I tell you a mystery: We will not all sleep, but we will all be changed— 52 in a flash, in the twinkling of an eye, at the last trumpet. For the trumpet will sound, the dead will be raised imperishable, and we will be changed. 53 For the perishable must clothe itself with the imperishable, and the mortal with immortality. 54 When the perishable has been clothed with the imperishable, and the mortal with immortality, then the saying that is written will come true: "Death has been swallowed up in victory."[c]

55 "Where, O death, is your victory?
Where, O death, is your sting?"[d]

56 The sting of death is sin, and the power of sin is the law. 57 But thanks be to God! He gives us the victory through our Lord Jesus Christ.

58 Therefore, my dear brothers and sisters, stand firm. Let nothing move you. Always give yourselves fully to the work of the Lord, because you know that your labor in the Lord is not in vain.

ROCK SOLID promises

"Always give yourselves fully to the work of the Lord, because you know that your labor in the Lord is not in vain." 1 Corinthians 15:58

You can be happy to serve God with every bit of yourself because he never wastes anything you do for him.

The Collection for the Lord's People

16 Now about the collection for the Lord's people: Do what I told the Galatian churches to do. 2 On the first day of every week, each one of you should set aside a sum of money in keeping with your income, saving it up,

a 45 Gen. 2:7   b 49 Some early manuscripts so let us   c 54 Isaiah 25:8   d 55 Hosea 13:14

so that when I come no collections will have to be made. ³Then, when I arrive, I will give letters of introduction to the men you approve and send them with your gift to Jerusalem. ⁴If it seems advisable for me to go also, they will accompany me.

Personal Requests

⁵After I go through Macedonia, I will come to you—for I will be going through Macedonia. ⁶Perhaps I will stay with you for a while, or even spend the winter, so that you can help me on my journey, wherever I go. ⁷For I do not want to see you now and make only a passing visit; I hope to spend some time with you, if the Lord permits. ⁸But I will stay on at Ephesus until Pentecost, ⁹because a great door for effective work has opened to me, and there are many who oppose me.

¹⁰When Timothy comes, see to it that he has nothing to fear while he is with you, for he is carrying on the work of the Lord, just as I am. ¹¹No one, then, should treat him with contempt. Send him on his way in peace so that he may return to me. I am expecting him along with the brothers.

¹²Now about our brother Apollos: I strongly urged him to go to you with the brothers. He was quite unwilling to go now, but he will go when he has the opportunity.

¹³Be on your guard; stand firm in the faith; be courageous; be strong. ¹⁴Do everything in love.

¹⁵You know that the household of Stephanas were the first converts in Achaia, and they have devoted themselves to the service of the Lord's people. I urge you, brothers and sisters, ¹⁶to submit to such people and to everyone who joins in the work and labors at it. ¹⁷I was glad when Stephanas, Fortunatus and Achaicus arrived, because they have supplied what was lacking from you. ¹⁸For they refreshed my spirit and yours also. Such men deserve recognition.

Final Greetings

¹⁹The churches in the province of Asia send you greetings. Aquila and Priscilla[a] greet you warmly in the Lord, and so does the church that meets at their house. ²⁰All the brothers and sisters here send you greetings. Greet one another with a holy kiss.

²¹I, Paul, write this greeting in my own hand.

²²If anyone does not love the Lord, let that person be cursed! Come, Lord[b]!

²³The grace of the Lord Jesus be with you.

²⁴My love to all of you in Christ Jesus. Amen.[c]

a 19 Greek *Prisca,* a variant of *Priscilla*
b 22 The Greek for *Come, Lord* reproduces an Aramaic expression (*Marana tha*) used by early Christians.   *c 24* Some manuscripts do not have *Amen.*

2 CORINTHIANS

Paul wrote this second letter to the Corinthians soon after the first letter. The divisions and problems he addressed in 1 Corinthians were still in the church at Corinth. Paul may have visited Corinth, but left quickly because some of the members in the church refused to believe that he was an apostle of God.

After returning to Macedonia, Paul was encouraged when Titus brought him the good news that the people in the Corinthian church had recognized their problems and sins and were willing to change. Paul then wrote his second letter to the Corinthians.

In the first part of his letter Paul tells the Corinthians how happy and thankful he was when he heard that they were sorry for the way they had acted and were now trying to live the way God wanted them to.

In the second part of his letter, Paul defends himself against the people who were angry with him and who were saying untrue things about him.

1 Paul, an apostle of Christ Jesus by the will of God, and Timothy our brother,

To the church of God in Corinth, together with all his holy people throughout Achaia:

[2] Grace and peace to you from God our Father and the Lord Jesus Christ.

Praise to the God of All Comfort

[3] Praise be to the God and Father of our Lord Jesus Christ, the Father of compassion and the God of all comfort, [4] who comforts us in all our troubles, so that we can comfort those in any trouble with the comfort we ourselves receive from God.

ROCK SOLID *promises*

"The God of all comfort ... comforts us in all our troubles, so that we can comfort those in any trouble with the comfort we ourselves receive from God."

2 Corinthians 1:3–4

God comforts you in your toughest experiences of life. And there is nothing better to do with that comfort than to pass it along.

[5] For just as we share abundantly in the sufferings of Christ, so also our comfort abounds through Christ. [6] If we are distressed, it is for your comfort and salvation; if we are comforted, it is for your comfort, which produces in you patient endurance of the same sufferings we suffer. [7] And our hope for you is firm, because we know that just as you share in our sufferings, so also you share in our comfort.

[8] We do not want you to be uninformed, brothers and sisters,[a] about the troubles we experienced in the province of Asia. We were under great pressure, far beyond our ability to endure, so that we despaired of life itself. [9] Indeed, we felt we had received the sentence of death. But this happened that we might not rely on ourselves but on God, who raises the dead. [10] He has delivered us from such a deadly peril, and he will deliver us again. On him we have set our hope that he will continue to deliver us, [11] as you help us by your prayers. Then many will give thanks on our behalf for the gracious favor granted us in answer to the prayers of many.

Paul's Change of Plans

[12] Now this is our boast: Our conscience testifies that we have conducted ourselves in the world, and especially in our relations with you, with integrity[b] and godly sincerity. We have done so, relying not on worldly wisdom but on God's grace. [13] For we do not write you anything you cannot read or understand. And I hope that, [14] as you have understood us in part, you will come to understand fully that you can boast of us just as we will boast of you in the day of the Lord Jesus.

[15] Because I was confident of this, I wanted to visit you first so that you might benefit twice. [16] I wanted to visit you on my way to Macedonia and to come back to you from Macedonia, and then to have you send me on my way to Judea. [17] Was I fickle when I intended to do this? Or do I make my plans in a worldly manner so that in the same breath I say both "Yes, yes" and "No, no"?

[18] But as surely as God is faithful, our message to you is not "Yes" and "No." [19] For the Son of God, Jesus Christ, who was preached among you by us—by me and Silas[c] and Timothy—was not "Yes" and "No," but in him it has always been "Yes." [20] For no matter how many promises God has made, they are "Yes" in Christ. And

a 8 The Greek word for *brothers and sisters* (*adelphoi*) refers here to believers, both men and women, as part of God's family; also in 8:1; 13:11. *b 12* Many manuscripts *holiness* *c 19* Greek *Silvanus*, a variant of *Silas* so through him the "Amen" is spoken by us to the glory of God. ²¹Now it is God who makes both us and you stand firm in Christ. He anointed us, ²²set his seal of ownership on us, and put his Spirit in our hearts as a deposit, guaranteeing what is to come.

²³I call God as my witness—and I stake my life on it—that it was in order to spare you that I did not return to Corinth. ²⁴Not that we lord it over your faith, but we work with you for your joy, because it is by faith you stand firm. ¹So I made up my mind that I would not make another painful visit to you. ²For if I grieve you, who is left to make me glad but you whom I have grieved? ³I wrote as I did, so that when I came I would not be distressed by those who should have made me rejoice. I had confidence in all of you, that you would all share my joy. ⁴For I wrote you out of great distress and anguish of heart and with many tears, not to grieve you but to let you know the depth of my love for you.

Forgiveness for the Offender

⁵If anyone has caused grief, he has not so much grieved me as he has grieved all of you to some extent—not to put it too severely. ⁶The punishment inflicted on him by the majority is sufficient. ⁷Now instead, you ought to forgive and comfort him, so that he will not be overwhelmed by excessive sorrow. ⁸I urge you, therefore, to reaffirm your love for him. ⁹Another reason I wrote you was to see if you would stand the test and be obedient in everything. ¹⁰Anyone you forgive, I also forgive. And what I have forgiven—if there was anything to forgive—I have forgiven in the sight of Christ for your sake, ¹¹in order that Satan might not outwit us. For we are not unaware of his schemes.

Ministers of the New Covenant

¹²Now when I went to Troas to preach the gospel of Christ and found that the Lord had opened a door for me, ¹³I still had no peace of mind, because I did not find my brother Titus there. So I said

ROCK SOLID *plans*

2 Corinthians 2:12–13

Watch for open doors.

The apostle Paul wanted to tell the citizens of Troas about Jesus, and when he reached that city, he found the circumstances were wide open for him to preach. He called it an "open door" from God. Sometimes the Lord springs open a door you're supposed to walk through. Other times he blocks your way. Don't jump to quick conclusions, however, about how God is using circumstances to lead you. Paul walked away from this open door, and sometimes it takes perseverance to push hard on doors that at first seem locked tight.

Your next step: Look for ways God wants to direct your life by opening and closing opportunities for you.

goodbye to them and went on to Macedonia.

¹⁴But thanks be to God, who always leads us as captives in Christ's triumphal procession and uses us to spread the aroma of the knowledge of him everywhere. ¹⁵For we are to God the pleasing aroma of Christ among those who are being saved and those who are perishing. ¹⁶To the one we are an aroma that brings death; to the other, an aroma that brings life. And who is equal to such a task? ¹⁷Unlike so many, we do not peddle the word of God for profit. On the contrary, in Christ we speak before God with sincerity, as those sent from God.

¹Are we beginning to commend ourselves again? Or do we need, like some people, letters of recommendation to you or from you? ²You yourselves are our letter, written on our hearts, known and read by everyone. ³You show that you are a letter from Christ, the result of our ministry, written not with ink but with the Spirit of the living God, not

on tablets of stone but on tablets of human hearts.

⁴Such confidence we have through Christ before God. ⁵Not that we are competent in ourselves to claim anything for ourselves, but our competence comes from God. ⁶He has made us competent as ministers of a new covenant—not of the letter but of the Spirit; for the letter kills, but the Spirit gives life.

The Greater Glory of the New Covenant

⁷Now if the ministry that brought death, which was engraved in letters on stone, came with glory, so that the Israelites could not look steadily at the face of Moses because of its glory, transitory though it was, ⁸will not the ministry of the Spirit be even more glorious? ⁹If the ministry that brought condemnation was glorious, how much more glorious is the ministry that brings righteousness! ¹⁰For what was glorious has no glory now in comparison with the surpassing glory. ¹¹And if what was transitory came with glory, how much greater is the glory of that which lasts!

¹²Therefore, since we have such a hope, we are very bold. ¹³We are not like Moses, who would put a veil over his face to prevent the Israelites from seeing the end of what was passing away. ¹⁴But their minds were made dull, for to this day the same veil remains when the old covenant is read. It has not been removed, because only in Christ is it taken away. ¹⁵Even to this day when Moses is read, a veil covers their hearts. ¹⁶But whenever anyone turns to the Lord, the veil is taken away. ¹⁷Now the Lord is the Spirit, and where the Spirit of the Lord is, there is freedom. ¹⁸And we all, who with unveiled faces contemplate*a* the Lord's glory, are being transformed into his image with ever-increasing glory, which comes from the Lord, who is the Spirit.

Present Weakness and Resurrection Life

4 Therefore, since through God's mercy we have this ministry, we do not lose heart. ²Rather, we have renounced secret and shameful ways; we

ROCK SOLID promises

"We ... are being transformed into his image with ever-increasing glory." **2 Corinthians 3:18**

God won't let you stay stuck in sin. Little by little he makes you look more and more like him.

do not use deception, nor do we distort the word of God. On the contrary, by setting forth the truth plainly we commend ourselves to everyone's conscience in the sight of God. ³And even if our gospel is veiled, it is veiled to those who are perishing. ⁴The god of this age has blinded the minds of unbelievers, so that they cannot see the light of the gospel that displays the glory of Christ, who is the image of God. ⁵For what we preach is not ourselves, but Jesus Christ as Lord, and ourselves as your servants for Jesus' sake. ⁶For God, who said, "Let light shine out of darkness,"*b* made his light shine in our hearts to give us the light of the knowledge of God's glory displayed in the face of Christ.

⁷But we have this treasure in jars of clay to show that this all-surpassing power is from God and not from us. ⁸We are hard pressed on every side, but not crushed; perplexed, but not in despair; ⁹persecuted, but not abandoned; struck down, but not destroyed. ¹⁰We always carry around in our body the death of Jesus, so that the life of Jesus may also be revealed in our body. ¹¹For we who are alive are always being given over to death for Jesus' sake, so that his life may also be revealed in our mortal body. ¹²So then, death is at work in us, but life is at work in you.

¹³It is written: "I believed; therefore I

a 18 Or *reflect*   *b 6* Gen. 1:3

1374

have spoken."[a] Since we have that same spirit of[b] faith, we also believe and therefore speak, [14]because we know that the one who raised the Lord Jesus from the dead will also raise us with Jesus and present us with you to himself. [15]All this is for your benefit, so that the grace that is reaching more and more people may cause thanksgiving to overflow to the glory of God.

[16]Therefore we do not lose heart. Though outwardly we are wasting away, yet inwardly we are being renewed day by day. [17]For our light and momentary troubles are achieving for us an eternal glory that far outweighs them all. [18]So we fix our eyes not on what is seen, but on what is unseen, since what is seen is temporary, but what is unseen is eternal.

Awaiting the New Body

5 For we know that if the earthly tent we live in is destroyed, we have a building from God, an eternal house in heaven, not built by human hands. [2]Meanwhile we groan, longing to be clothed instead with our heavenly dwelling, [3]because when we are clothed, we will not be found naked. [4]For while we are in this tent, we groan and are burdened, because we do not wish to be unclothed but to be clothed instead with our heavenly dwelling, so that what is mortal may be swallowed up by life. [5]Now the one who has fashioned us for this very purpose is God, who has given us the Spirit as a deposit, guaranteeing what is to come.

[6]Therefore we are always confident and know that as long as we are at home in the body we are away from the Lord. [7]For we live by faith, not by sight. [8]We are confident, I say, and would prefer to be away from the body and at home with the Lord. [9]So we make it our goal to please him, whether we are at home in the body or away from it. [10]For we must all appear before the judgment seat of Christ, so that each of us may receive what is due us for the things done while in the body, whether good or bad.

The Ministry of Reconciliation

[11]Since, then, we know what it is to fear the Lord, we try to persuade others. What

we are is plain to God, and I hope it is also plain to your conscience. [12]We are not trying to commend ourselves to you again, but are giving you an opportunity to take pride in us, so that you can answer those who take pride in what is seen rather than in what is in the heart. [13]If we are "out of our mind," as some say, it is for God; if we are in our right mind, it is for you. [14]For Christ's love compels us, because we are convinced that one died for all, and therefore all died. [15]And he died for all, that those who live should no longer live for themselves but for him who died for them and was raised again.

[16]So from now on we regard no one from a worldly point of view. Though we once regarded Christ in this way, we do so no longer. [17]Therefore, if anyone is in Christ, the new creation has come:[c] The old has gone, the new is here! [18]All this is

---

ROCK SOLID promises

"If anyone is in Christ, the new creation has come: The old has gone, the new is here!"

2 Corinthians 5:17

When you believe in Jesus, you become a new person from the inside out. You're forgiven and freed from sin.

---

from God, who reconciled us to himself through Christ and gave us the ministry of reconciliation: [19]that God was reconciling the world to himself in Christ, not counting people's sins against them. And he has committed to us the message of reconciliation. [20]We are therefore Christ's ambassadors, as though God were making his appeal through us. We implore you

---

[a] *13* Psalm 116:10 (see Septuagint)   [b] *13* Or *Spirit-given*   [c] *17* Or *Christ, that person is a new creation.*

on Christ's behalf: Be reconciled to God. [21] God made him who had no sin to be sin[a] for us, so that in him we might become the righteousness of God.

6 As God's co-workers we urge you not to receive God's grace in vain. [2] For he says,

"In the time of my favor I heard you,
and in the day of salvation I helped you."[b]

I tell you, now is the time of God's favor, now is the day of salvation.

Paul's Hardships

[3] We put no stumbling block in anyone's path, so that our ministry will not be discredited. [4] Rather, as servants of God we commend ourselves in every way: in great endurance; in troubles, hardships and distresses; [5] in beatings, imprisonments and riots; in hard work, sleepless nights and hunger; [6] in purity, understanding, patience and kindness; in the Holy Spirit and in sincere love; [7] in truthful speech and in the power of God; with weapons of righteousness in the right hand and in the left; [8] through glory and dishonor, bad report and good report; genuine, yet regarded as impostors; [9] known, yet regarded as unknown; dying, and yet we live on; beaten, and yet not killed; [10] sorrowful, yet always rejoicing; poor, yet making many rich; having nothing, and yet possessing everything.

[11] We have spoken freely to you, Corinthians, and opened wide our hearts to you. [12] We are not withholding our affection from you, but you are withholding yours from us. [13] As a fair exchange—I speak as to my children—open wide your hearts also.

Warning Against Idolatry

[14] Do not be yoked together with unbelievers. For what do righteousness and wickedness have in common? Or what fellowship can light have with darkness? [15] What harmony is there between Christ and Belial[c]? Or what does a believer have in common with an unbeliever? [16] What agreement is there between the temple of God and idols? For we are the temple of the living God. As God has said:

"I will live with them
and walk among them,
and I will be their God,
and they will be my people."[d]

ROCK SOLID truths

2 Corinthians 5:11–21

Jesus died for you so you would live for him.

Some thought the apostle Paul was crazy for traveling the known world to help people become friends with God. He couldn't stop sharing the amazing truth that God was "reconciling the world to himself in Christ, not counting people's sins against them" (2 Corinthians 5:19). It wasn't insanity, however, that drove Paul to give his whole life to God. Paul had a simple explanation. He said, "Christ's love compels us" (2 Corinthians 5:14). The love of Jesus propelled Paul into the world, and it should power how you do life. Jesus died not just for the big believers of the Bible, but for you. Paul says Jesus "died for all, that those who live should no longer live for themselves but for him who died for them and was raised again" (2 Corinthians 5:15). When you need a reminder of why you live for God, ponder the fact that Jesus died for you.

Think: How much does Jesus' death for you motivate you to live for him—or not?

---

[a] 21 Or *be a sin offering*   [b] 2 Isaiah 49:8
[c] 15 Greek *Beliar*, a variant of *Belial*
[d] 16 Lev. 26:12; Jer. 32:38; Ezek. 37:27

[17] Therefore,

"Come out from them
and be separate,
says the Lord.
Touch no unclean thing,
and I will receive you."[a]

[18] And,

"I will be a Father to you,
and you will be my sons and
daughters,
says the Lord Almighty."[b]

7 Therefore, since we have these promises, dear friends, let us purify ourselves from everything that contaminates body and spirit, perfecting holiness out of reverence for God.

Paul's Joy Over the Church's Repentance

[2] Make room for us in your hearts. We have wronged no one, we have corrupted no one, we have exploited no one. [3] I do not say this to condemn you; I have said before that you have such a place in our hearts that we would live or die with you. [4] I have spoken to you with great frankness; I take great pride in you. I am greatly encouraged; in all our troubles my joy knows no bounds.

[5] For when we came into Macedonia, we had no rest, but we were harassed at every turn—conflicts on the outside, fears within. [6] But God, who comforts the downcast, comforted us by the coming of Titus, [7] and not only by his coming but also by the comfort you had given him. He told us about your longing for me, your deep sorrow, your ardent concern for me, so that my joy was greater than ever.

[8] Even if I caused you sorrow by my letter, I do not regret it. Though I did regret it—I see that my letter hurt you,

[a] 17 Isaiah 52:11; Ezek. 20:34,41
[b] 18 2 Samuel 7:14; 7:8

ROCK SOLID *principles*

2 Corinthians 6:14–18

Don't glue yourself to unbelievers.

Alyssa couldn't stop sneaking glances at Evan, and she grabbed every chance she could to escape taking orders at the drive-through window to visit him back at the grill. She was obsessed. When Evan finally asked Alyssa out, she said yes. He was the greatest guy she had ever met, and she planned to get him interested in God. Alyssa passionately followed Jesus, but as months went by, it felt like she had less time and energy for God. Alyssa wasn't sure when her excitement about God started to fade, but the Lord didn't seem nearly as important as he once did.

Jesus made friends with everyone, even people regarded as the worst of his society, like tax collectors and prostitutes. Yet he never got lured away from God's purposes. The Lord wants you close to all kinds of people so you can help them meet God (see Matthew 9:9–13). But you can't glue yourself to someone who doesn't follow Jesus, as in dating or marrying a non-Christian (see Ezra 9:1–15) without being affected. Sooner or later you'll get pulled away from God.

but only for a little while— ⁹yet now I am happy, not because you were made sorry, but because your sorrow led you to repentance. For you became sorrowful as God intended and so were not harmed in any way by us. ¹⁰Godly sorrow brings repentance that leads to salvation and leaves no regret, but worldly sorrow brings death.

ROCK SOLID *promises*

"Godly sorrow brings repentance that leads to salvation and leaves no regret." 2 Corinthians 7:10

If you see and feel the true badness of doing wrong, you won't regret giving up sinful habits.

¹¹See what this godly sorrow has produced in you: what earnestness, what eagerness to clear yourselves, what indignation, what alarm, what longing, what concern, what readiness to see justice done. At every point you have proved yourselves to be innocent in this matter. ¹²So even though I wrote to you, it was neither on account of the one who did the wrong nor on account of the injured party, but rather that before God you could see for yourselves how devoted to us you are. ¹³By all this we are encouraged.

In addition to our own encouragement, we were especially delighted to see how happy Titus was, because his spirit has been refreshed by all of you. ¹⁴I had boasted to him about you, and you have not embarrassed me. But just as everything we said to you was true, so our boasting about you to Titus has proved to be true as well. ¹⁵And his affection for you is all the greater when he remembers that you were all obedient, receiving him with fear and trembling. ¹⁶I am glad I can have complete confidence in you.

The Collection for the Lord's People

8 And now, brothers and sisters, we want you to know about the grace that God has given the Macedonian churches. ²In the midst of a very severe trial, their overflowing joy and their extreme poverty welled up in rich generosity. ³For I testify that they gave as much as they were able, and even beyond their ability. Entirely on their own, ⁴they urgently pleaded with us for the privilege of sharing in this service to the Lord's people. ⁵And they exceeded our expectations: They gave themselves first of all to the Lord, and then by the will of God also to us. ⁶So we urged Titus, just as he had earlier made a beginning, to bring also to completion this act of grace on your part. ⁷But since you excel in everything—in faith, in speech, in knowledge, in complete earnestness and in the love we have kindled in youᵃ—see that you also excel in this grace of giving.

⁸I am not commanding you, but I want to test the sincerity of your love by comparing it with the earnestness of others. ⁹For you know the grace of our Lord Jesus Christ, that though he was rich, yet for your sake he became poor, so that you through his poverty might become rich.

¹⁰And here is my judgment about what is best for you in this matter. Last year you were the first not only to give but also to have the desire to do so. ¹¹Now finish the work, so that your eager willingness to do it may be matched by your completion of it, according to your means. ¹²For if the willingness is there, the gift is acceptable according to what one has, not according to what one does not have.

¹³Our desire is not that others might be relieved while you are hard pressed, but that there might be equality. ¹⁴At the present time your plenty will supply what they need, so that in turn their plenty will supply what you need. The goal is equality, ¹⁵as it is written: "The one who gathered much did not have too much, and the

ᵃ 7 Some manuscripts *and in your love for us*

one who gathered little did not have too little."[a]

Titus Sent to Receive the Collection

[16]Thanks be to God, who put into the heart of Titus the same concern I have for you. [17]For Titus not only welcomed our appeal, but he is coming to you with much enthusiasm and on his own initiative. [18]And we are sending along with him the brother who is praised by all the churches for his service to the gospel. [19]What is more, he was chosen by the churches to accompany us as we carry the offering, which we administer in order to honor the Lord himself and to show our eagerness to help. [20]We want to avoid any criticism of the way we administer this liberal gift. [21]For we are taking pains to do what is right, not only in the eyes of the Lord but also in the eyes of man.

[22]In addition, we are sending with them our brother who has often proved to us in many ways that he is zealous, and now even more so because of his great confidence in you. [23]As for Titus, he is my partner and co-worker among you; as for our brothers, they are representatives of the churches and an honor to Christ. [24]Therefore show these men the proof of your love and the reason for our pride in you, so that the churches can see it.

9 There is no need for me to write to you about this service to the Lord's people. [2]For I know your eagerness to help, and I have been boasting about it to the Macedonians, telling them that since last year you in Achaia were ready to give; and your enthusiasm has stirred most of them to action. [3]But I am sending the brothers in order that our boasting about you in this matter should not prove hollow, but that you may be ready, as I said you would be. [4]For if any Macedonians come with me and find you unprepared, we — not to say anything about you — would be ashamed of having been so confident. [5]So I thought it necessary to urge the brothers to visit you in advance and finish the arrangements for the generous gift you had promised. Then it will be

ready as a generous gift, not as one grudgingly given.

Generosity Encouraged

[6]Remember this: Whoever sows sparingly will also reap sparingly, and whoever sows generously will also reap generously. [7]Each of you should give what you have decided in your heart to give, not reluctantly or under compulsion, for God loves a cheerful giver. [8]And God is able to bless you abundantly, so that in all things at all times, having all that you need, you will abound in every good work. [9]As it is written:

> "They have freely scattered their gifts
>   to the poor;
>   their righteousness endures
>   forever."[b]

[10]Now he who supplies seed to the sower and bread for food will also supply and increase your store of seed and will enlarge

[a] 15 Exodus 16:18   [b] 9 Psalm 112:9

ROCK SOLID plans

2 Corinthians 9:1–15

Live generously.

The Christians at Corinth were eager givers, but the apostle Paul wanted them to follow through on their enthusiasm. He encouraged them to set aside money for suffering believers in Jerusalem, details you can find in 1 Corinthians 16:1–4 and 2 Corinthians 8:1–24. Paul describes giving as a must-do part of your faith, and he tells how to give God's way. True giving is generous ... sacrificial ... and cheerful. Like Jesus said, "It is more blessed to give than to receive" (Acts 20:35).

Your next step: Take your giving to the next level. Start giving ... or give more ... or build a more consistent habit of sharing what God gives you.

the harvest of your righteousness. [11]You will be enriched in every way so that you can be generous on every occasion, and through us your generosity will result in thanksgiving to God.

[12]This service that you perform is not only supplying the needs of the Lord's people but is also overflowing in many expressions of thanks to God. [13]Because of the service by which you have proved yourselves, others will praise God for the obedience that accompanies your confession of the gospel of Christ, and for your generosity in sharing with them and with everyone else. [14]And in their prayers for you their hearts will go out to you, because of the surpassing grace God has given you. [15]Thanks be to God for his indescribable gift!

Paul's Defense of His Ministry

10 By the humility and gentleness of Christ, I appeal to you—I, Paul, who am "timid" when face to face with you, but "bold" toward you when away! [2]I beg you that when I come I may not have to be as bold as I expect to be toward some people who think that we live by the standards of this world. [3]For though we live in the world, we do not wage war as the world does. [4]The weapons we fight with are not the weapons of the world. On the contrary, they have divine power to demolish strongholds. [5]We demolish arguments and every pretension that sets itself up against the knowledge of God, and we take captive every thought to make it obedient to Christ. [6]And we will be ready to punish every act of disobedience, once your obedience is complete.

[7]You are judging by appearances.[a] If anyone is confident that they belong to Christ, they should consider again that we belong to Christ just as much as they do. [8]So even if I boast somewhat freely about the authority the Lord gave us for building you up rather than tearing you down, I will not be ashamed of it. [9]I do not want to seem to be trying to frighten you with my letters. [10]For some say, "His letters are weighty and forceful, but in person he is unimpressive and his speaking amounts to nothing." [11]Such people should realize that what we are in our letters when we are absent, we will be in our actions when we are present.

[12]We do not dare to classify or compare ourselves with some who commend themselves. When they measure themselves by themselves and compare themselves with themselves, they are not wise. [13]We, how-

[a] 7 Or *Look at the obvious facts*

---

2 Corinthians 10:1–18

God's truth always wins.

Outside the city of Corinth was a hill nearly two thousand feet high, and perched on that hill was a military fort. That's the scene the apostle Paul had in mind when he told the Corinthians that spiritual weapons have "divine power to demolish strongholds" (2 Corinthians 10:4). Some of Paul's readers complained that Paul was timid, not to mention a bad speaker. Paul countered that he wasn't like other preachers who only cared about making themselves look good. The point to notice is that Paul refused to fight back with the brute force of ordinary worldly power. He counted instead on the strength of God's truth. That truth is able to defeat every lie that claims to be bigger or better than God. It corrects every thought that doesn't submit to Jesus. God's truth is strong enough to pull down even the most heavily guarded fortress.

Think: Why do Christians rely on truth to win fights—rather than fists or any other force?

ROCK SOLID *truths*

ever, will not boast beyond proper limits, but will confine our boasting to the sphere of service God himself has assigned to us, a sphere that also includes you. [14]We are not going too far in our boasting, as would be the case if we had not come to you, for we did get as far as you with the gospel of Christ. [15]Neither do we go beyond our limits by boasting of work done by others. Our hope is that, as your faith continues to grow, our sphere of activity among you will greatly expand, [16]so that we can preach the gospel in the regions beyond you. For we do not want to boast about work already done in someone else's territory. [17]But, "Let the one who boasts boast in the Lord."[a] [18]For it is not the one who commends himself who is approved, but the one whom the Lord commends.

Paul and the False Apostles

11 I hope you will put up with me in a little foolishness. Yes, please put up with me! [2]I am jealous for you with a godly jealousy. I promised you to one husband, to Christ, so that I might present you as a pure virgin to him. [3]But I am afraid that just as Eve was deceived by the serpent's cunning, your minds may somehow be led astray from your sincere and pure devotion to Christ. [4]For if someone comes to you and preaches a Jesus other than the Jesus we preached, or if you receive a different spirit from the Spirit you received, or a different gospel from the one you accepted, you put up with it easily enough.

[5]I do not think I am in the least inferior to those "super-apostles."[b] [6]I may indeed be untrained as a speaker, but I do have knowledge. We have made this perfectly clear to you in every way. [7]Was it a sin for me to lower myself in order to elevate you by preaching the gospel of God to you free of charge? [8]I robbed other churches by receiving support from them so as to serve you. [9]And when I was with you and needed something, I was not a burden to anyone, for the brothers who came from Macedonia supplied what

I needed. I have kept myself from being a burden to you in any way, and will continue to do so. [10]As surely as the truth of Christ is in me, nobody in the regions of Achaia will stop this boasting of mine. [11]Why? Because I do not love you? God knows I do!

[12]And I will keep on doing what I am doing in order to cut the ground from under those who want an opportunity to be considered equal with us in the things they boast about. [13]For such people are false apostles, deceitful workers, masquerading as apostles of Christ. [14]And no wonder, for Satan himself masquerades as an angel of light. [15]It is not surprising, then, if his servants also masquerade as servants of righteousness. Their end will be what their actions deserve.

Paul Boasts About His Sufferings

[16]I repeat: Let no one take me for a fool. But if you do, then tolerate me just as you would a fool, so that I may do a little boasting. [17]In this self-confident boasting I am not talking as the Lord would, but as a fool. [18]Since many are boasting in the way the world does, I too will boast. [19]You gladly put up with fools since you are so wise! [20]In fact, you even put up with anyone who enslaves you or exploits you or takes advantage of you or puts on airs or slaps you in the face. [21]To my shame I admit that we were too weak for that!

Whatever anyone else dares to boast about—I am speaking as a fool—I also dare to boast about. [22]Are they Hebrews? So am I. Are they Israelites? So am I. Are they Abraham's descendants? So am I. [23]Are they servants of Christ? (I am out of my mind to talk like this.) I am more. I have worked much harder, been in prison more frequently, been flogged more severely, and been exposed to death again and again. [24]Five times I received from the Jews the forty lashes minus one. [25]Three times I was beaten with rods, once I was pelted with stones, three times I was shipwrecked, I spent a night and a day in the

[a] 17 Jer. 9:24   [b] 5 Or *to the most eminent apostles*

open sea, ²⁶I have been constantly on the move. I have been in danger from rivers, in danger from bandits, in danger from my fellow Jews, in danger from Gentiles; in danger in the city, in danger in the country, in danger at sea; and in danger from false believers. ²⁷I have labored and toiled and have often gone without sleep; I have known hunger and thirst and have often gone without food; I have been cold and naked. ²⁸Besides everything else, I face daily the pressure of my concern for all the churches. ²⁹Who is weak, and I do not feel weak? Who is led into sin, and I do not inwardly burn?

³⁰If I must boast, I will boast of the things that show my weakness. ³¹The God and Father of the Lord Jesus, who is to be praised forever, knows that I am not lying. ³²In Damascus the governor under King Aretas had the city of the Damascenes guarded in order to arrest me. ³³But I was lowered in a basket from a window in the wall and slipped through his hands.

Paul's Vision and His Thorn

12 I must go on boasting. Although there is nothing to be gained, I will go on to visions and revelations from the Lord. ²I know a man in Christ who fourteen years ago was caught up to the third heaven. Whether it was in the body or out of the body I do not know—God knows. ³And I know that this man—whether in the body or apart from the body I do not know, but God knows— ⁴was caught up to paradise and heard inexpressible things, things that no one is permitted to tell. ⁵I will boast about a man like that, but I will not boast about myself, except about my weaknesses. ⁶Even if I should choose to boast, I would not be a fool, because I would be speaking the truth. But I refrain, so no one will think more of me than is warranted by what I do or say, ⁷or because of these surpassingly great revelations. Therefore, in order to keep me from becoming conceited, I was given a thorn in my flesh, a messenger of Satan, to torment me. ⁸Three times I pleaded with the Lord to take it away from me. ⁹But he said to me, "My grace is sufficient for you, for my power is made perfect in weakness." Therefore I will boast all the more gladly about my weaknesses, so that Christ's power may rest on me. ¹⁰That is why, for Christ's sake, I delight in weaknesses, in insults, in hardships, in persecutions, in difficulties. For when I am weak, then I am strong.

ROCK SOLID truths

2 Corinthians 11:23–29

Christianity isn't for sissies.

There is an idea floating around that Christianity is a religion of weaklings. That flawed belief ignores the determined grit of everyday Christians pressing on to obey Jesus. It also overlooks the enormous sufferings believers have endured for their faith. Need details? You can flip first to the great "hall of faith" in Hebrews 11, where you learn not only that Christians have triumphed but also that they have been tortured, chained and imprisoned, stoned, sawed in two, and killed by the sword. The apostle Paul offers his own list of pains he faced to take the good news about Jesus to the world. Five times he was lashed nearly to death. He was stoned, shipwrecked, and awash at sea. He went without sleep, food, or drink. Christians still suffer and die for their faith today, yet in the midst of terrible hardship God fills them with strength.

Think: Do you think it takes more guts to follow Jesus—or not follow him?

ROCK SOLID
promises

"My grace is sufficient for you, for my power is made perfect in weakness." 2 Corinthians 12:9

You don't have to pretend to be strong. When you admit you're weak, God carries you.

Paul's Concern for the Corinthians

[11] I have made a fool of myself, but you drove me to it. I ought to have been commended by you, for I am not in the least inferior to the "super-apostles,"[a] even though I am nothing. [12] I persevered in demonstrating among you the marks of a true apostle, including signs, wonders and miracles. [13] How were you inferior to the other churches, except that I was never a burden to you? Forgive me this wrong!

[14] Now I am ready to visit you for the third time, and I will not be a burden to you, because what I want is not your possessions but you. After all, children should not have to save up for their parents, but parents for their children. [15] So I will very gladly spend for you everything I have and expend myself as well. If I love you more, will you love me less? [16] Be that as it may, I have not been a burden to you. Yet, crafty fellow that I am, I caught you by trickery! [17] Did I exploit you through any of the men I sent to you? [18] I urged Titus to go to you and I sent our brother with him. Titus did not exploit you, did he? Did we not walk in the same footsteps by the same Spirit?

[19] Have you been thinking all along that we have been defending ourselves to you? We have been speaking in the sight of God as those in Christ; and everything we do, dear friends, is for your strengthening. [20] For I am afraid that when I come I may not find you as I want you to be, and you may not find me as you want me to be. I fear that there may be discord, jealousy, fits of rage, selfish ambition, slander, gossip, arrogance and disorder. [21] I am afraid that when I come again my God will humble me before you, and I will be grieved over many who have sinned earlier and have not repented of the impurity, sexual sin and debauchery in which they have indulged.

Final Warnings

13 This will be my third visit to you. "Every matter must be established by the testimony of two or three witnesses."[b] [2] I already gave you a warning when I was with you the second time. I now repeat it while absent: On my return I will not spare those who sinned earlier or any of the others, [3] since you are demanding proof that Christ is speaking through me. He is not weak in dealing with you, but is powerful among you. [4] For to be sure, he was crucified in weakness, yet he lives by God's power. Likewise, we are weak in him, yet by God's power we will live with him in our dealing with you.

[5] Examine yourselves to see whether you are in the faith; test yourselves. Do you not realize that Christ Jesus is in you— unless, of course, you fail the test? [6] And I trust that you will discover that we have not failed the test. [7] Now we pray to God that you will not do anything wrong—not so that people will see that we have stood the test but so that you will do what is right even though we may seem to have failed. [8] For we cannot do anything against the truth, but only for the truth. [9] We are glad whenever we are weak but you are strong; and our prayer is that you may be fully restored. [10] This is why I write these things when I am absent, that when I come I may not have to be harsh in my use of authority—the authority the Lord gave me for building you up, not for tearing you down.

[a] *11 Or the most eminent apostles*
[b] *1 Deut. 19:15*

Final Greetings

¹¹Finally, brothers and sisters, rejoice! Strive for full restoration, encourage one another, be of one mind, live in peace. And the God of love and peace will be with you.

¹²Greet one another with a holy kiss. ¹³All God's people here send their greetings.

¹⁴May the grace of the Lord Jesus Christ, and the love of God, and the fellowship of the Holy Spirit be with you all.

GALATIANS

BOOK OUTLINE

Introduction
(1:1–10)

Paul's authority from God
(1:11—2:21)

Legalism versus God's grace
(3:1—4:31)

The gospel in practice
(5:1—6:16)

Conclusion
(6:17,18)

Paul wrote this letter to the Christian churches in the Roman province of Galatia. False teachers called Judaizers were confusing the Galatians by teaching that Gentile Christians were not really saved unless they obeyed all the Jewish laws—such as being circumcised, eating special foods, and celebrating Jewish feast days. This group also said that Paul did not have God's authority and, therefore, was not to be listened to.

Paul begins the letter by telling the Galatians what gospel it is that he preaches and that his authority is from God. He continues by stating that we cannot be saved from our sins by obeying the law; we are saved only by believing in Jesus Christ. Christians are free to live by the law of love, not the Law of Moses. Faith, Paul says, must be shown in love and believers must live by the Spirit.

1

Paul, an apostle—sent not from men nor by a man, but by Jesus Christ and God the Father, who raised him from the dead— ²and all the brothers and sisters*a* with me,

To the churches in Galatia:

³Grace and peace to you from God our Father and the Lord Jesus Christ, ⁴who gave himself for our sins to rescue us from the present evil age, according to the will of our God and Father, ⁵to whom be glory for ever and ever. Amen.

No Other Gospel

⁶I am astonished that you are so quickly deserting the one who called you to live in the grace of Christ and are turning to a different gospel— ⁷which is really no gospel at all. Evidently some people are throwing you into confusion and are trying to pervert the gospel of Christ. ⁸But even if we or an angel from heaven should preach a gospel other than the one we preached to you, let them be under God's curse! ⁹As we have already said, so now I say again: If anybody is preaching to you a gospel other than what you accepted, let them be under God's curse!

¹⁰Am I now trying to win the approval of human beings, or of God? Or am I trying to please people? If I were still trying to please people, I would not be a servant of Christ.

Paul Called by God

¹¹I want you to know, brothers and sisters, that the gospel I preached is not of human origin. ¹²I did not receive it from any man, nor was I taught it; rather, I received it by revelation from Jesus Christ.

¹³For you have heard of my previous way of life in Judaism, how intensely I persecuted the church of God and tried to destroy it. ¹⁴I was advancing in Judaism beyond many of my own age among my people and was extremely zealous for the traditions of my fathers. ¹⁵But when God, who set me apart from my mother's womb and called me by his grace, was pleased ¹⁶to reveal his Son in me so that I might preach him among the Gentiles, my immediate re-

Galatians 1:1–10

There is only one gospel.

God gave the apostle Paul a job— preaching about "the Lord Jesus Christ, who gave himself for our sins to rescue us from the present evil age" (Galatians 1:3–4). But some of the people he had taught were getting mixed up. The Galatians had become Christians through the grace of God, receiving forgiveness as a gift they didn't deserve. Now they were giving up on grace and trying to keep Old Testament rules to earn God's approval and grow spiritually (see Galatians 3:1–5). That might sound like no big deal. But this wrongheaded belief couldn't save them and bring them home to heaven. So Paul reminded them of the real gospel. He even said that if ever he dared to teach anything other than the one true faith, he deserved to go to hell. Truth matters that much.

Think: Why is it so important we hang onto the true facts about Jesus and how to know God?

ROCK SOLID *truths*

sponse was not to consult any human being. ¹⁷I did not go up to Jerusalem to see those who were apostles before I was, but I went into Arabia. Later I returned to Damascus.

¹⁸Then after three years, I went up to Jerusalem to get acquainted with Cephas*b* and stayed with him fifteen days. ¹⁹I saw none of the other apostles—only James,

---

a 2 The Greek word for *brothers and sisters* (*adelphoi*) refers here to believers, both men and women, as part of God's family; also in verse 11; and in 3:15; 4:12, 28, 31; 5:11, 13; 6:1, 18.
b 18 That is, Peter

the Lord's brother. ²⁰I assure you before God that what I am writing you is no lie. ²¹Then I went to Syria and Cilicia. ²²I was personally unknown to the churches of Judea that are in Christ. ²³They only heard the report: "The man who formerly persecuted us is now preaching the faith he once tried to destroy." ²⁴And they praised God because of me.

Paul Accepted by the Apostles

2 Then after fourteen years, I went up again to Jerusalem, this time with Barnabas. I took Titus along also. ²I went in response to a revelation and, meeting privately with those esteemed as leaders, I presented to them the gospel that I preach among the Gentiles. I wanted to be sure I was not running and had not been running my race in vain. ³Yet not even Titus, who was with me, was compelled to be circumcised, even though he was a Greek. ⁴This matter arose because some false believers had infiltrated our ranks to spy on the freedom we have in Christ Jesus and to make us slaves. ⁵We did not give in to them for a moment, so that the truth of the gospel might be preserved for you.

⁶As for those who were held in high esteem—whatever they were makes no difference to me; God does not show favoritism—they added nothing to my message. ⁷On the contrary, they recognized that I had been entrusted with the task of preaching the gospel to the uncircumcised,ᵃ just as Peter had been to the circumcised.ᵇ ⁸For God, who was at work in Peter as an apostle to the circumcised, was also at work in me as an apostle to the Gentiles. ⁹James, Cephasᶜ and John, those esteemed as pillars, gave me and Barnabas the right hand of fellowship when they recognized the grace given to me. They agreed that we should go to the Gentiles, and they to the circumcised. ¹⁰All they asked was that we should continue to remember the poor, the very thing I had been eager to do all along.

Paul Opposes Cephas

¹¹When Cephas came to Antioch, I opposed him to his face, because he stood condemned. ¹²For before certain men came from James, he used to eat with the Gentiles. But when they arrived, he began to draw back and separate himself from the Gentiles because he was afraid of those who belonged to the circumcision group. ¹³The other Jews joined him in his hypocrisy, so that by their hypocrisy even Barnabas was led astray.

¹⁴When I saw that they were not acting in line with the truth of the gospel, I said to Cephas in front of them all, "You are a Jew, yet you live like a Gentile and not like a Jew. How is it, then, that you force Gentiles to follow Jewish customs?

¹⁵"We who are Jews by birth and not sinful Gentiles ¹⁶know that a person is not justified by the works of the law, but by faith in Jesus Christ. So we, too, have put our faith in Christ Jesus that we may be justified by faith inᵈ Christ and not by the works of the law, because by the works of the law no one will be justified.

¹⁷"But if, in seeking to be justified in Christ, we Jews find ourselves also among the sinners, doesn't that mean that Christ promotes sin? Absolutely not! ¹⁸If I rebuild what I destroyed, then I really would be a lawbreaker.

¹⁹"For through the law I died to the law so that I might live for God. ²⁰I have been crucified with Christ and I no longer live, but Christ lives in me. The life I now live in the body, I live by faith in the Son of God, who loved me and gave himself for me. ²¹I do not set aside the grace of God, for if righteousness could be gained through the law, Christ died for nothing!"ᵉ

Faith or Works of the Law

3 You foolish Galatians! Who has bewitched you? Before your very eyes Jesus Christ was clearly portrayed as crucified. ²I would like to learn just one thing from you: Did you receive the Spirit

ᵃ 7 That is, Gentiles   ᵇ 7 That is, Jews; also in verses 8 and 9   ᶜ 9 That is, Peter; also in verses 11 and 14   ᵈ 16 Or *but through the faithfulness of . . . justified on the basis of the faithfulness of*   ᵉ 21 Some interpreters end the quotation after verse 14.

ROCK SOLID
promises

"Christ lives in me. The life I now live in the body, I live by faith in the Son of God, who loved me and gave himself for me."

Galatians 2:20

Don't try to muscle your way through life. Count on Jesus to love you, live in you, and give you unstoppable power.

by the works of the law, or by believing what you heard? ³Are you so foolish? After beginning by means of the Spirit, are you now trying to finish by means of the flesh?ᵃ ⁴Have you experiencedᵇ so much in vain—if it really was in vain? ⁵So again I ask, does God give you his Spirit and work miracles among you by the works of the law, or by your believing what you heard? ⁶So also Abraham "believed God, and it was credited to him as righteousness."ᶜ

⁷Understand, then, that those who have faith are children of Abraham. ⁸Scripture foresaw that God would justify the Gentiles by faith, and announced the gospel in advance to Abraham: "All nations will be blessed through you."ᵈ ⁹So those who rely on faith are blessed along with Abraham, the man of faith.

¹⁰For all who rely on the works of the law are under a curse, as it is written: "Cursed is everyone who does not continue to do everything written in the Book of the Law."ᵉ ¹¹Clearly no one who relies on the law is justified before God, because "the righteous will live by faith."ᶠ ¹²The law is not based on faith; on the contrary, it says, "The person who does these things will live by them."ᵍ ¹³Christ redeemed us from the curse of the law by becoming a curse for us, for it is written: "Cursed is everyone who is hung on a pole."ʰ ¹⁴He redeemed us in order that the blessing given

to Abraham might come to the Gentiles through Christ Jesus, so that by faith we might receive the promise of the Spirit.

The Law and the Promise

¹⁵Brothers and sisters, let me take an example from everyday life. Just as no one can set aside or add to a human covenant that has been duly established, so it is in this case. ¹⁶The promises were spoken to Abraham and to his seed. Scripture does not say "and to seeds," meaning many people, but "and to your seed,"ⁱ meaning one person, who is Christ. ¹⁷What I mean is this: The law, introduced 430 years later, does not set aside the covenant previously established by God and thus do away with the promise. ¹⁸For if the inheritance depends on the law, then it no longer depends on the promise; but God in his grace gave it to Abraham through a promise.

¹⁹Why, then, was the law given at all? It was added because of transgressions until the Seed to whom the promise referred had come. The law was given through angels and entrusted to a mediator. ²⁰A mediator, however, implies more than one party; but God is one.

²¹Is the law, therefore, opposed to the promises of God? Absolutely not! For if a law had been given that could impart life, then righteousness would certainly have come by the law. ²²But Scripture has locked up everything under the control of sin, so that what was promised, being given through faith in Jesus Christ, might be given to those who believe.

Children of God

²³Before the coming of this faith,ʲ we were held in custody under the law, locked up until the faith that was to come would be revealed. ²⁴So the law was our guardian until Christ came that we might

---

ᵃ *3* In contexts like this, the Greek word for *flesh* (*sarx*) refers to the sinful state of human beings, often presented as a power in opposition to the Spirit.   ᵇ *4* Or *suffered*   ᶜ *6* Gen. 15:6   ᵈ *8* Gen. 12:3; 18:18; 22:18   ᵉ *10* Deut. 27:26   ᶠ *11* Hab. 2:4   ᵍ *12* Lev. 18:5   ʰ *13* Deut. 21:23   ⁱ *16* Gen. 12:7; 13:15; 24:7   ʲ *22,23* Or *through the faithfulness of Jesus . . . ²³Before faith came* be justified by faith. [25] Now that this faith has come, we are no longer under a guardian.

[26] So in Christ Jesus you are all children of God through faith, [27] for all of you who were baptized into Christ have clothed yourselves with Christ. [28] There is neither Jew nor Gentile, neither slave nor free, nor is there male and female, for you are all one in Christ Jesus. [29] If you belong to Christ, then you are Abraham's seed, and heirs according to the promise.

4 What I am saying is that as long as an heir is underage, he is no different from a slave, although he owns the whole estate. [2] The heir is subject to guardians and trustees until the time set by his father. [3] So also, when we were underage, we were in slavery under the elemental spiritual forces[a] of the world. [4] But when the set time had fully come, God sent his Son, born of a woman, born under the law, [5] to redeem those under the law, that we might receive adoption to sonship.[b] [6] Because you are his sons, God sent the Spirit of his Son into our hearts, the Spirit who calls out, "Abba,[c] Father." [7] So you are no longer a slave, but God's child; and since you are his child, God has made you also an heir.

Paul's Concern for the Galatians

[8] Formerly, when you did not know God, you were slaves to those who by nature are not gods. [9] But now that you know God—or rather are known by God—how is it that you are turning back to those weak and miserable forces[d]? Do you wish to be enslaved by them all over again? [10] You are observing special days and months and seasons and years! [11] I fear for you, that somehow I have wasted my efforts on you.

[12] I plead with you, brothers and sisters, become like me, for I became like you. You did me no wrong. [13] As you know, it was because of an illness that I first preached the gospel to you, [14] and even though my illness was a trial to you, you did not treat me with contempt or scorn. Instead, you welcomed me as if I were an angel of God, as if I were Christ Jesus himself. [15] Where, then, is your blessing of me now? I can testify that, if you could have done so, you would have torn out your eyes and given

---

[a] 3 Or *under the basic principles*   [b] 5 The Greek word for *adoption to sonship* is a legal term referring to the full legal standing of an adopted male heir in Roman culture.   [c] 6 Aramaic for *Father*   [d] 9 Or *principles*

ROCK SOLID truths

Galatians 3:26–28

Everyone is equal in Jesus.

Bible critics slam the apostle Paul for his stance on women within the church, pointing to passages he wrote about women teaching (see 1 Timothy 2:12) and covering their heads (see 1 Corinthians 11:5). Others take him to task for not attacking the practice of slavery (see Colossians 3:22). Many Christians read his comments on women as meant for a particular time and place, and they recognize that Paul alone couldn't dismantle slavery, a widespread form of indentured servitude involving a large number of people of the Roman Empire. The Bible also makes clear that all people are nothing less than equals. Paul himself wrote that "There is neither Jew nor Gentile, neither slave nor free, nor is there male and female, for you are all one in Christ Jesus" (Galatians 3:28). That was a radical stance in Paul's day, and nearly two thousand years later those words inspired American Christians to work to abolish the evil of slavery.

Think: Who do you see in your world who is treated as less than an equal? What can you do about that?

them to me. ¹⁶Have I now become your enemy by telling you the truth?

¹⁷Those people are zealous to win you over, but for no good. What they want is to alienate you from us, so that you may have zeal for them. ¹⁸It is fine to be zealous, provided the purpose is good, and to be so always, not just when I am with you. ¹⁹My dear children, for whom I am again in the pains of childbirth until Christ is formed in you, ²⁰how I wish I could be with you now and change my tone, because I am perplexed about you!

Hagar and Sarah

²¹Tell me, you who want to be under the law, are you not aware of what the law says? ²²For it is written that Abraham had two sons, one by the slave woman and the other by the free woman. ²³His son by the slave woman was born according to the flesh, but his son by the free woman was born as the result of a divine promise.

²⁴These things are being taken figuratively: The women represent two covenants. One covenant is from Mount Sinai and bears children who are to be slaves: This is Hagar. ²⁵Now Hagar stands for Mount Sinai in Arabia and corresponds to the present city of Jerusalem, because she is in slavery with her children. ²⁶But the Jerusalem that is above is free, and she is our mother. ²⁷For it is written:

"Be glad, barren woman,
    you who never bore a child;
shout for joy and cry aloud,
    you who were never in labor;
because more are the children of the
        desolate woman
    than of her who has a husband."ᵃ

²⁸Now you, brothers and sisters, like Isaac, are children of promise. ²⁹At that time the son born according to the flesh persecuted the son born by the power of the Spirit. It is the same now. ³⁰But what does Scripture say? "Get rid of the slave woman and her son, for the slave woman's son will never share in the inheritance with the free woman's son."ᵇ ³¹Therefore, brothers and sisters, we are not children of the slave woman, but of the free woman.

Freedom in Christ

5 It is for freedom that Christ has set us free. Stand firm, then, and do not let yourselves be burdened again by a yoke of slavery.

²Mark my words! I, Paul, tell you that if you let yourselves be circumcised, Christ will be of no value to you at all. ³Again I declare to every man who lets himself be circumcised that he is obligated to obey the whole law. ⁴You who are trying to be justified by the law have been alienated from Christ; you have fallen away from grace. ⁵For through the Spirit we eagerly await by faith the righteousness for which we hope. ⁶For in Christ Jesus neither circumcision nor uncircumcision has any value. The only thing that counts is faith expressing itself through love.

⁷You were running a good race. Who cut in on you to keep you from obeying the truth? ⁸That kind of persuasion does not come from the one who calls you. ⁹"A little yeast works through the whole batch of dough." ¹⁰I am confident in the Lord that you will take no other view. The one who is throwing you into confusion, whoever that may be, will have to pay the penalty. ¹¹Brothers and sisters, if I am still preaching circumcision, why am I still being persecuted? In that case the offense of the cross has been abolished. ¹²As for those agitators, I wish they would go the whole way and emasculate themselves!

Life by the Spirit

¹³You, my brothers and sisters, were called to be free. But do not use your freedom to indulge the fleshᶜ; rather, serve one another humbly in love. ¹⁴For the entire law is fulfilled in keeping this one command: "Love your neighbor as yourself."ᵈ ¹⁵If you bite and devour each other, watch out or you will be destroyed by each other.

ᵃ 27 Isaiah 54:1   ᵇ 30 Gen. 21:10   ᶜ 13 In contexts like this, the Greek word for *flesh* (*sarx*) refers to the sinful state of human beings, often presented as a power in opposition to the Spirit; also in verses 16, 17, 19 and 24; and in 6:8.
ᵈ 14 Lev. 19:18

¹⁶So I say, walk by the Spirit, and you will not gratify the desires of the flesh. ¹⁷For the flesh desires what is contrary to the Spirit, and the Spirit what is contrary to the flesh. They are in conflict with each other, so that you are not to do whatever[a] you want. ¹⁸But if you are led by the Spirit, you are not under the law.

ROCK SOLID *promises*

"Walk by the Spirit, and you will not gratify the desires of the flesh." Galatians 5:16

It's impossible to quit doing evil unless the Spirit works inside you. He makes you want to do good.

¹⁹The acts of the flesh are obvious: sexual immorality, impurity and debauchery; ²⁰idolatry and witchcraft; hatred, discord, jealousy, fits of rage, selfish ambition, dissensions, factions ²¹and envy; drunkenness, orgies, and the like. I warn you, as I did before, that those who live like this will not inherit the kingdom of God.

²²But the fruit of the Spirit is love, joy, peace, forbearance, kindness, goodness, faithfulness, ²³gentleness and self-control. Against such things there is no law. ²⁴Those who belong to Christ Jesus have crucified the flesh with its passions and desires. ²⁵Since we live by the Spirit, let us keep in step with the Spirit. ²⁶Let us not become conceited, provoking and envying each other.

Doing Good to All

6 Brothers and sisters, if someone is caught in a sin, you who live by the Spirit should restore that person gently. But watch yourselves, or you also may be tempted. ²Carry each other's bur-

---

Galatians 5:19–25

The Holy Spirit changes you.

The believers who received this letter from the apostle Paul were slipping into rule-following as a way to earn God's approval and grow spiritually. And Paul observed these folks had a lot of growing to do. He saw them biting and devouring each other (see Galatians 5:15) and listed all the ugly things that happened when they followed their sinful inclinations—from sexual immorality and drunkenness to idolatry, conflict, and selfish ambition. Paul told these feisty believers they would only break free from evil if they let the Holy Spirit lead them. The Holy Spirit changes us from the inside out, growing good qualities that make us more like Jesus. His work grows fruit like "love, joy, peace, forbearance, kindness, goodness, faithfulness, gentleness and self-control" (Galatians 5:22–23). Trying harder to follow rules won't change us. If we don't want to give in to sin, we need to get life from the Spirit.

Think: How do you rely on the Spirit to help you become more like Jesus?

ROCK SOLID truths

---

dens, and in this way you will fulfill the law of Christ. ³If anyone thinks they are something when they are not, they deceive themselves. ⁴Each one should test their own actions. Then they can take pride in themselves alone, without comparing themselves to someone else, ⁵for each one should carry their own load. ⁶Nevertheless, the one

---

[a] 17 Or *you do not do what*

Galatians 6:1–5

Pick up friends who stumble.

Seth saw instant changes in his good friend. Cody never wanted to talk about the day his dad died of a heart attack while coaching their soccer team. With Cody's dad gone, something snapped inside Cody. He dropped away from their crowd of guys and started hanging with a group famous for making trouble. When no one else wanted to try to help Cody, his old friend went to talk to him alone. Seth told Cody he couldn't even understand what Cody was going through ... the pain of losing his dad ... but it seemed like Cody was throwing away his own life and making his situation worse. Whatever it took, Seth was going to help.

We need each other to stay faithful in following Jesus. So when you see another Christian getting pulled into sin, your job is to pull that person free. There's only one exception. Watch out if you feel attracted to that same kind of sin, "or you also may be tempted" (Galatians 6:1). You have to be strong to pick up friends who stumble.

who receives instruction in the word should share all good things with their instructor.

[7] Do not be deceived: God cannot be mocked. A man reaps what he sows. [8] Whoever sows to please their flesh, from the flesh will reap destruction; whoever sows to please the Spirit, from the Spirit will reap eternal life. [9] Let us not become weary in doing good, for at the proper time we will reap a harvest if we do not give up. [10] Therefore, as we have opportunity, let us do good to all people, especially to those who belong to the family of believers.

Not Circumcision but the New Creation

[11] See what large letters I use as I write to you with my own hand!

[12] Those who want to impress people by means of the flesh are trying to compel you to be circumcised. The only reason they do this is to avoid being persecuted for the cross of Christ. [13] Not even those who are circumcised keep the law, yet they

want you to be circumcised that they may boast about your circumcision in the flesh. [14] May I never boast except in the cross of our Lord Jesus Christ, through which[a] the world has been crucified to me, and I

[a] 14 Or *whom*

"Let us not become weary in doing good, for at the proper time we will reap a harvest if we do not give up." Galatians 6:9

Keep doing right even when you would rather give up. God will make it worth the effort.

to the world. ¹⁵Neither circumcision nor uncircumcision means anything; what counts is the new creation. ¹⁶Peace and mercy to all who follow this rule—to*a* the Israel of God.

¹⁷From now on, let no one cause me trouble, for I bear on my body the marks of Jesus.

¹⁸The grace of our Lord Jesus Christ be with your spirit, brothers and sisters. Amen.

a 16 Or *rule and to*

EPHESIANS

BOOK OUTLINE

Ephesus was a large, important city that naturally became the center for the Christian churches in the area. Paul wrote this letter to the Ephesians during his two-year imprisonment in Rome (about AD 60). This letter was sent to all the Christian churches near Ephesus, not just to the church in the city.

One of Paul's themes in Ephesians is that of unity and God's purpose "to bring unity to all things in heaven and on earth under Christ." Because of this unity, Paul writes, all Christians are one family in Christ and should love each other. He gives believers instructions on how to live a life of love by addressing the husband-wife, parent-children, and slave-master relationships.

In this letter Paul also writes about the church—not a church building in a certain place but the church that is made up of all Christians who have ever lived—the universal church. He compares Christ's relationship with the church to the human body, a building and a wife.

Paul, an apostle of Christ Jesus by the will of God,

To God's holy people in Ephesus,*a* the faithful in Christ Jesus:

²Grace and peace to you from God our Father and the Lord Jesus Christ.

Praise for Spiritual Blessings in Christ

³Praise be to the God and Father of our Lord Jesus Christ, who has blessed us in the heavenly realms with every spiritual blessing in Christ. ⁴For he chose us in him before the creation of the world to be holy and blameless in his sight. In love

---

ROCK SOLID
promises

"He chose us in him before the creation of the world to be holy and blameless in his sight."

Ephesians 1:4

Even before the world began, God had a plan to make you his child, forgiven and totally devoted to him.

---

⁵he*b* predestined us for adoption to sonship*c* through Jesus Christ, in accordance with his pleasure and will— ⁶to the praise of his glorious grace, which he has freely given us in the One he loves. ⁷In him we have redemption through his blood, the forgiveness of sins, in accordance with the riches of God's grace ⁸that he lavished on us. With all wisdom and understanding, ⁹he*d* made known to us the mystery of his will according to his good pleasure, which he purposed in Christ, ¹⁰to be put into effect when the times reach their fulfillment—to bring unity to all things in heaven and on earth under Christ.

¹¹In him we were also chosen,*e* having been predestined according to the plan of him who works out everything in conformity with the purpose of his will, ¹²in order that we, who were the first to put our hope in Christ, might be for the praise of his glory. ¹³And you also were included in Christ when you heard the message of truth, the gospel of your salvation. When you believed, you were marked in him with a seal, the promised Holy Spirit, ¹⁴who is a deposit guaranteeing our inheritance until the redemption of those who are God's possession—to the praise of his glory.

Thanksgiving and Prayer

¹⁵For this reason, ever since I heard about your faith in the Lord Jesus and your love for all God's people, ¹⁶I have not stopped giving thanks for you, remembering you in my prayers. ¹⁷I keep asking that the God of our Lord Jesus Christ, the glorious Father, may give you the Spirit*f* of wisdom and revelation, so that you may know him better. ¹⁸I pray that the eyes of your heart may be enlightened in order that you may know the hope to which he has called you, the riches of his glorious inheritance in his holy people, ¹⁹and his incomparably great power for us who believe. That power is the same as the mighty strength ²⁰he exerted when he raised Christ from the dead and seated him at his right hand in the heavenly realms, ²¹far above all rule and authority, power and dominion, and every name that is invoked, not only in the present age but also in the one to come. ²²And God placed all things under his feet and appointed him to be head over everything for the church, ²³which is his body, the fullness of him who fills everything in every way.

---

a 1 Some early manuscripts do not have *in Ephesus.*   *b 4,5* Or *sight in love.* ⁵*He*
c 5 The Greek word for *adoption to sonship* is a legal term referring to the full legal standing of an adopted male heir in Roman culture.
d 8,9 Or *us with all wisdom and understanding.* ⁹*And he*   *e 11* Or *were made heirs*   *f 17* Or *a spirit*

Made Alive in Christ

2 As for you, you were dead in your transgressions and sins, ²in which you used to live when you followed the ways of this world and of the ruler of the kingdom of the air, the spirit who is now at work in those who are disobedient. ³All of us also lived among them at one time, gratifying the cravings of our flesh*a* and following its desires and thoughts. Like the rest, we were by nature deserving of wrath. ⁴But because of his great love for us, God, who is rich in mercy, ⁵made us alive with Christ even when we were dead in transgressions—it is by grace you have been saved. ⁶And God raised us up with Christ and seated us with him in the heavenly realms in Christ Jesus, ⁷in order that in the coming ages he might show the incomparable riches of his grace, expressed in his kindness to us in Christ Jesus. ⁸For it is by grace you have been saved, through faith—and this is not from yourselves, it is the gift of God— ⁹not by works, so that no one can boast. ¹⁰For we are God's handiwork, created in Christ Jesus to do good works, which God prepared in advance for us to do.

Jew and Gentile Reconciled Through Christ

¹¹Therefore, remember that formerly you who are Gentiles by birth and called "uncircumcised" by those who call themselves "the circumcision" (which is done in the body by human hands)— ¹²remember that at that time you were separate from Christ, excluded from citizenship in Israel and foreigners to the covenants of the promise, without hope and without God in the world. ¹³But now in Christ Jesus you who once were far away have been brought near by the blood of Christ.

¹⁴For he himself is our peace, who has made the two groups one and has destroyed the barrier, the dividing wall of hostility, ¹⁵by setting aside in his flesh the law with its commands and regulations. His purpose was to create in himself one new humanity out of the two, thus making peace, ¹⁶and in one body to reconcile both of them to God through the cross, by which he put to death their hostility. ¹⁷He came and preached peace to you who were far away and peace to those who were near. ¹⁸For through him we both have access to the Father by one Spirit.

¹⁹Consequently, you are no longer for-

---

a 3 In contexts like this, the Greek word for *flesh* (*sarx*) refers to the sinful state of human beings, often presented as a power in opposition to the Spirit.

Ephesians 2:1–10

You're saved by grace through faith.

If you ever wonder if you have what it takes to make yourself right with God and become all he wants you to be, think of a dead body. That's what we are before we meet Jesus. We are dead in our sins, our stubbornly disobedient ways. We follow Satan, we let sinful cravings control us, and we rightly deserve God's judgment. But then our loving and merciful God comes and makes us alive, making our dead bodies move. He gives us a seat of honor and showers riches on us. And we don't deserve any of this. God rescues us from death because of his grace—favor we don't deserve. He saves us through faith—because we understand and accept that Jesus paid for our sins on the cross. We can't save ourselves by doing good things. The only way we can be saved is "by grace" and "through faith" (Ephesians 2:8).

Think: What's the difference between trying to earn God's approval and being saved by grace through faith?

ROCK SOLID truths

ROCK SOLID *plans*

Ephesians 2:8–10

Be God's art.

God saves you "by grace," as a gift you don't deserve. He rescues you "through faith," when you trust that Jesus died on the cross for your sins. And he saves you "to do good works," impacting your world as a way of giving him thanks. Whenever you do good, you show off the fact that you're his "handiwork," a word that also means "masterpiece" or "work of art" (Ephesians 2:8,10). The Lord doesn't make you his friend so you can hang around and wait for heaven. Go do something. Be his art.

Your next step: Make a concrete plan to do good today.

eigners and strangers, but fellow citizens with God's people and also members of his household, ²⁰ built on the foundation of the apostles and prophets, with Christ Jesus himself as the chief cornerstone. ²¹ In him the whole building is joined together and rises to become a holy temple in the Lord. ²² And in him you too are being built together to become a dwelling in which God lives by his Spirit.

God's Marvelous Plan for the Gentiles

3 For this reason I, Paul, the prisoner of Christ Jesus for the sake of you Gentiles—

² Surely you have heard about the administration of God's grace that was given to me for you, ³ that is, the mystery made known to me by revelation, as I have already written briefly. ⁴ In reading this, then, you will be able to understand my insight into the mystery of Christ, ⁵ which was not made known to people in other generations as it has now been revealed by the Spirit to God's holy apostles and prophets. ⁶ This mystery is that through the gospel the Gentiles are heirs together with Israel, members together of one body, and sharers together in the promise in Christ Jesus.

⁷ I became a servant of this gospel by the gift of God's grace given me through the working of his power. ⁸ Although I am less than the least of all the Lord's people, this grace was given me: to preach to the Gentiles the boundless riches of Christ, ⁹ and to make plain to everyone the administration of this mystery, which for ages past was kept hidden in God, who created all things. ¹⁰ His intent was that now, through the church, the manifold wisdom of God should be made known to the rulers and authorities in the heavenly realms, ¹¹ according to his eternal purpose that he accomplished in Christ Jesus our Lord. ¹² In him and through faith in him we may approach God with freedom and confidence. ¹³ I ask you, therefore, not to be discouraged because of my sufferings for you, which are your glory.

A Prayer for the Ephesians

¹⁴ For this reason I kneel before the Father, ¹⁵ from whom every family*a* in heaven and on earth derives its name. ¹⁶ I pray that out of his glorious riches he may strengthen you with power through his Spirit in your inner being, ¹⁷ so that Christ may dwell in your hearts through faith. And I pray that you, being rooted and established in love, ¹⁸ may have power, together with all the Lord's holy people, to grasp how wide and long and high and deep is the love of Christ, ¹⁹ and to know this love that surpasses knowledge—that you may be filled to the measure of all the fullness of God.

²⁰ Now to him who is able to do immeasurably more than all we ask or imagine, according to his power that is at work within us, ²¹ to him be glory in the church and in Christ Jesus throughout all generations, for ever and ever! Amen.

a 15 The Greek for *family* (*patria*) is derived from the Greek for *father* (*pater*).

ROCK SOLID
promises

"Now to him who is able to do immeasurably more than all we ask or imagine, according to his power that is at work within us."

Ephesians 3:20

God answers your prayers in ways that are better than you can ever imagine, especially when your request is to know him more.

Unity and Maturity in the Body of Christ

4 As a prisoner for the Lord, then, I urge you to live a life worthy of the calling you have received. ²Be completely humble and gentle; be patient, bearing with one another in love. ³Make every effort to keep the unity of the Spirit through the bond of peace. ⁴There is one body and one Spirit, just as you were called to one hope when you were called; ⁵one Lord, one faith, one baptism; ⁶one God and Father of all, who is over all and through all and in all.

⁷But to each one of us grace has been given as Christ apportioned it. ⁸This is why it*ᵃ* says:

"When he ascended on high,
  he took many captives
  and gave gifts to his people."*ᵇ*

⁹(What does "he ascended" mean except that he also descended to the lower, earthly regions*ᶜ*? ¹⁰He who descended is the very one who ascended higher than all the heavens, in order to fill the whole universe.) ¹¹So Christ himself gave the apostles, the prophets, the evangelists, the pastors and teachers, ¹²to equip his people for works of service, so that the body of Christ may be built up ¹³until we all reach unity in the faith and in the knowledge of the Son of God and become mature, attaining to the whole measure of the fullness of Christ.

¹⁴Then we will no longer be infants, tossed back and forth by the waves, and blown here and there by every wind of teaching and by the cunning and craftiness of people in their deceitful scheming. ¹⁵Instead, speaking the truth in love, we will grow to become in every respect the mature body of him who is the head, that is, Christ. ¹⁶From him the whole body, joined and held together by every supporting ligament, grows and builds itself up in love, as each part does its work.

Instructions for Christian Living

¹⁷So I tell you this, and insist on it in the Lord, that you must no longer live as the Gentiles do, in the futility of their thinking. ¹⁸They are darkened in their understanding and separated from the life of God because of the ignorance that is in them due to the hardening of their hearts. ¹⁹Having lost all sensitivity, they have given themselves over to sensuality so as to indulge in every kind of impurity, and they are full of greed.

²⁰That, however, is not the way of life you learned ²¹when you heard about Christ and were taught in him in accordance with the truth that is in Jesus. ²²You were taught, with regard to your former way of life, to put off your old self, which is being corrupted by its deceitful desires; ²³to be made new in the attitude of your minds; ²⁴and to put on the new self, created to be like God in true righteousness and holiness.

²⁵Therefore each of you must put off falsehood and speak truthfully to your neighbor, for we are all members of one body. ²⁶"In your anger do not sin"*ᵈ*: Do not let the sun go down while you are still angry, ²⁷and do not give the devil a foothold. ²⁸Anyone who has been stealing must steal no longer, but must work, doing something useful with their own

ᵃ 8 Or *God*   *ᵇ 8* Psalm 68:18   *ᶜ 9* Or *the depths of the earth*   *ᵈ 26* Psalm 4:4 (see Septuagint) hands, that they may have something to share with those in need.

²⁹Do not let any unwholesome talk come out of your mouths, but only what is helpful for building others up according to their needs, that it may benefit those who listen. ³⁰And do not grieve the Holy Spirit of God, with whom you were sealed for the day of redemption. ³¹Get rid of all bitterness, rage and anger, brawling and slander, along with every form of malice. ³²Be kind and compassionate to one another, forgiving each other, just as in Christ God forgave you. ¹Follow God's example, therefore, as dearly loved children ²and walk in the way of love, just as Christ loved us and gave himself up for us as a fragrant offering and sacrifice to God.

³But among you there must not be even a hint of sexual immorality, or of any kind of impurity, or of greed, because these are improper for God's holy people. ⁴Nor should there be obscenity, foolish talk or coarse joking, which are out of place, but rather thanksgiving. ⁵For of this you can be sure: No immoral, impure or greedy person—such a person is an idolater—has any inheritance in the kingdom of Christ and of God.ᵃ ⁶Let no one deceive you with empty words, for because of such things God's wrath comes on those who are disobedient. ⁷Therefore do not be partners with them.

⁸For you were once darkness, but now you are light in the Lord. Live as children of light ⁹(for the fruit of the light consists in all goodness, righteousness and truth) ¹⁰and find out what pleases the Lord. ¹¹Have nothing to do with the fruitless deeds of darkness, but rather expose them. ¹²It is shameful even to mention what the disobedient do in secret. ¹³But everything exposed by the light becomes

ᵃ 5 Or *kingdom of the Messiah and God*

ROCK SOLID *principles*

Ephesians 4:29

Talk it up.

Danita was up for the challenge. She wanted to end the stream of ugly words she aimed at everyone around her. She made it a goal to put Ephesians 4:29 into action, only saying "what is helpful for building others up according to their needs, that it may benefit those who listen." So one day Danita recorded every putdown, complaint, and sarcastic remark she spoke to her family, friends, and everyone else. By the end of the day she had a list filling a notebook page and spilling onto the back. It took the rest of the week to work through her list and jot down what she could have said instead. Danita didn't like what she discovered, but she knew exactly what to work on.

Keep track of what you say and you might find yourself speaking a lot of words that tear down instead of build up. You can use Ephesians 4:29 as a filter for your mouth, making sure every word you speak passes its test. Check out Ephesians 5:3–5 too.

ROCK SOLID
promises

"You were once darkness, but now you are light in the Lord. Live as children of light ... and find out what pleases the Lord."

Ephesians 5:8 and 10

Sin darkened the deepest parts of your heart, but God lights up your whole life. Now live in his light.

---

visible—and everything that is illuminated becomes a light. [14]This is why it is said:

> "Wake up, sleeper,
>   rise from the dead,
>   and Christ will shine on you."

[15]Be very careful, then, how you live—not as unwise but as wise, [16]making the most of every opportunity, because the days are evil. [17]Therefore do not be foolish, but understand what the Lord's will is. [18]Do not get drunk on wine, which leads to debauchery. Instead, be filled with the Spirit, [19]speaking to one another with psalms, hymns, and songs from the Spirit. Sing and make music from your heart to the Lord, [20]always giving thanks to God the Father for everything, in the name of our Lord Jesus Christ.

Instructions for Christian Households

[21]Submit to one another out of reverence for Christ.

[22]Wives, submit yourselves to your own husbands as you do to the Lord. [23]For the husband is the head of the wife as Christ is the head of the church, his body, of which he is the Savior. [24]Now as the church submits to Christ, so also wives should submit to their husbands in everything.

[25]Husbands, love your wives, just as Christ loved the church and gave himself up for her [26]to make her holy, cleansing[a]

her by the washing with water through the word, [27]and to present her to himself as a radiant church, without stain or wrinkle or any other blemish, but holy and blameless. [28]In this same way, husbands ought to love their wives as their own bodies. He who loves his wife loves himself. [29]After all, no one ever hated their own body, but they feed and care for their body, just as Christ does the church— [30]for we are members of his body. [31]"For this reason a man will leave his father and mother and be united to his wife, and the two will become one flesh."[b] [32]This is a profound mystery—but I am talking about Christ and the church. [33]However, each one of you also must love his wife as he loves himself, and the wife must respect her husband.

6 Children, obey your parents in the Lord, for this is right. [2]"Honor your father and mother"—which is the first commandment with a promise— [3]"so that it may go well with you and that you may enjoy long life on the earth."[c]

[4]Fathers,[d] do not exasperate your children; instead, bring them up in the training and instruction of the Lord.

[5]Slaves, obey your earthly masters with respect and fear, and with sincerity of heart, just as you would obey Christ. [6]Obey them not only to win their favor when their eye is on you, but as slaves of Christ, doing the will of God from your heart. [7]Serve wholeheartedly, as if you were serving the Lord, not people, [8]because you know that the Lord will reward each one for whatever good they do, whether they are slave or free.

[9]And masters, treat your slaves in the same way. Do not threaten them, since you know that he who is both their Master and yours is in heaven, and there is no favoritism with him.

The Armor of God

[10]Finally, be strong in the Lord and in his mighty power. [11]Put on the full armor

---

[a] 26 Or *having cleansed*   [b] 31 Gen. 2:24
[c] 3 Deut. 5:16   [d] 4 Or *Parents*

of God, so that you can take your stand against the devil's schemes. ¹²For our struggle is not against flesh and blood, but against the rulers, against the authorities, against the powers of this dark world and against the spiritual forces of evil in the heavenly realms. ¹³Therefore put on the full armor of God, so that when the day of evil comes, you may be able to stand your ground, and after you have done everything, to stand. ¹⁴Stand firm then, with the belt of truth buckled around your waist, with the breastplate of righteousness in place, ¹⁵and with your feet fitted with the readiness that comes from the gospel of peace. ¹⁶In addition to all this, take up the shield of faith, with which you can extinguish all the flaming arrows of the evil one. ¹⁷Take the helmet of salvation and the sword of the Spirit, which is the word of God.

¹⁸And pray in the Spirit on all occasions with all kinds of prayers and requests. With this in mind, be alert and always keep on praying for all the Lord's people. ¹⁹Pray also for me, that whenever I speak, words may be given me so that I will fearlessly make known the mystery of the gospel, ²⁰for which I am an ambassador in chains. Pray that I may declare it fearlessly, as I should.

Final Greetings

²¹Tychicus, the dear brother and faithful servant in the Lord, will tell you everything, so that you also may know how I am and what I am doing. ²²I am sending him to you for this very purpose, that you may know how we are, and that he may encourage you.

²³Peace to the brothers and sisters,ᵃ and love with faith from God the Father and the Lord Jesus Christ. ²⁴Grace to all who love our Lord Jesus Christ with an undying love.ᵇ

ᵃ 23 The Greek word for *brothers and sisters* (*adelphoi*) refers here to believers, both men and women, as part of God's family.   ᵇ 24 Or *Grace and immortality to all who love our Lord Jesus Christ.*

ROCK SOLID truths

Ephesians 6:10–19

There's a spiritual world you can't see.

We think our problems have to do with tough circumstances and annoying people. But there is a bigger struggle going on. The Bible says there is an unseen world of "rulers" and "authorities" and "powers of this dark world" and "spiritual forces of evil in the heavenly realms" (Ephesians 6:12). These spiritual beings are more real than the characters in a role-playing game, but God doesn't tell us about them so they can steal all our attention. God wants us to be aware of the reality of Satan and his allies and to arm ourselves against them. We fight not with earthly weapons like guns and knives but with spiritual weapons like prayer, truth, righteousness, faith, and the power of God's Word and the Holy Spirit. We can't see the spiritual world. But we can battle evil and win.

Think: Do you believe that the spiritual world exists? How do you deal with it?

PHILIPPIANS

BOOK OUTLINE

The letter to the Philippians was written by Paul while he was in prison in Rome about AD 60. The church in Philippi had sent Epaphroditus to Paul with a gift. While Epaphroditus was in Rome, he became sick, and the Philippian Christians were worried about him. After he was better, Paul sent him back to Philippi with this letter.

Paul reveals his love for the Philippians throughout this letter, the most personal one of all his letters written to a church. Paul thanks the Philippians for their love and helpfulness.

Even though Paul was writing from prison, this letter is full of joy. The words "joy" or "rejoice" are used thirteen times. Paul gives his own testimony to the meaning of his present life when he writes "For to me, to live is Christ and to die is gain" (1:21).

As in his other letters, Paul encourages the people and instructs them to live in harmony with others and in obedience to God.

I Paul and Timothy, servants of Christ Jesus,

To all God's holy people in Christ Jesus at Philippi, together with the overseers and deacons[a]:

[2] Grace and peace to you from God our Father and the Lord Jesus Christ.

Thanksgiving and Prayer

[3] I thank my God every time I remember you. [4] In all my prayers for all of you, I always pray with joy [5] because of your partnership in the gospel from the first day until now, [6] being confident of this, that he who began a good work in you will carry it on to completion until the day of Christ Jesus.

ROCK SOLID *promises*

"He who began a good work in you will carry it on to completion until the day of Christ Jesus."

Philippians 1:6

God has an amazing spiritual growth plan for you, and he won't stop working until he's done.

[7] It is right for me to feel this way about all of you, since I have you in my heart and, whether I am in chains or defending and confirming the gospel, all of you share in God's grace with me. [8] God can testify how I long for all of you with the affection of Christ Jesus.

[9] And this is my prayer: that your love may abound more and more in knowledge and depth of insight, [10] so that you may be able to discern what is best and may be pure and blameless for the day of Christ, [11] filled with the fruit of righteousness that comes through Jesus Christ—to the glory and praise of God.

Paul's Chains Advance the Gospel

[12] Now I want you to know, brothers and sisters,[b] that what has happened to me has actually served to advance the gospel. [13] As a result, it has become clear throughout the whole palace guard[c] and to everyone else that I am in chains for Christ. [14] And because of my chains, most of the brothers and sisters have become confident in the Lord and dare all the more to proclaim the gospel without fear.

[15] It is true that some preach Christ out of envy and rivalry, but others out of goodwill. [16] The latter do so out of love, knowing that I am put here for the defense of the gospel. [17] The former preach Christ out of selfish ambition, not sincerely, supposing that they can stir up trouble for me while I am in chains. [18] But what does it matter? The important thing is that in every way, whether from false motives or true, Christ is preached. And because of this I rejoice.

Yes, and I will continue to rejoice, [19] for I know that through your prayers and God's provision of the Spirit of Jesus Christ what has happened to me will turn out for my deliverance.[d] [20] I eagerly expect and hope that I will in no way be ashamed, but will have sufficient courage so that now as always Christ will be exalted in my body, whether by life or by death. [21] For to me, to live is Christ and to die is gain. [22] If I am to go on living in the body, this will mean fruitful labor for me. Yet what shall I choose? I do not know! [23] I am torn between the two: I desire to depart and be with Christ, which is better by far; [24] but it is more necessary for you that I remain in the body. [25] Convinced of this, I know that I will remain, and I will continue with all of you for your progress and joy in the faith, [26] so that through my being with you again your boasting in Christ Jesus will abound on account of me.

[a] *1* The word *deacons* refers here to Christians designated to serve with the overseers/elders of the church in a variety of ways; similarly in Romans 16:1 and 1 Tim. 3:8,12.   [b] *12* The Greek word for *brothers and sisters* (*adelphoi*) refers here to believers, both men and women, as part of God's family; also in verse 14; and in 3:1, 13, 17; 4:1, 8, 21.   [c] *13* Or *whole palace*   [d] *19* Or *vindication*; or *salvation*

Life Worthy of the Gospel

[27]Whatever happens, conduct yourselves in a manner worthy of the gospel of Christ. Then, whether I come and see you or only hear about you in my absence, I will know that you stand firm in the one Spirit,[a] striving together as one for the faith of the gospel [28]without being frightened in any way by those who oppose you. This is a sign to them that they will be destroyed, but that you will be saved — and that by God. [29]For it has been granted to you on behalf of Christ not only to believe in him, but also to suffer for him, [30]since you are going through the same struggle you saw I had, and now hear that I still have.

Imitating Christ's Humility

2 Therefore if you have any encouragement from being united with Christ, if any comfort from his love, if any common sharing in the Spirit, if any tenderness and compassion, [2]then make my joy complete by being like-minded, having the same love, being one in spirit and of one mind. [3]Do nothing out of selfish ambition or vain conceit. Rather, in humility value others above yourselves, [4]not looking to your own interests but each of you to the interests of the others.

[5]In your relationships with one another, have the same mindset as Christ Jesus:

[6]Who, being in very nature[b] God,
did not consider equality with God
something to be used to his
own advantage;
[7]rather, he made himself nothing
by taking the very nature[c] of a servant,
being made in human likeness.
[8]And being found in appearance as a
man,
he humbled himself
by becoming obedient to death —
even death on a cross!

[a] 27 Or *in one spirit*   [b] 6 Or *in the form of*   [c] 7 Or *the form*

ROCK SOLID *principles*

Philippians 2:1 – 11

Think like Jesus.

Darnell floated through life with no worries. His mom cooked him breakfast, lunch, and dinner and kept his room tidy. His dad worked long hours to give the family almost everything they could wish for. An older sister even took charge of making sure Darnell did well at school. When Darnell's mom had to spend a couple years fighting cancer, the family scrambled, and clearly there were no more easy rides for the baby of the family. For the first time ever, Darnell had to think of the needs of his mom as well as the rest of his family. By the time his mom was feeling better, he had discovered there was a big world of needs he had never noticed.

Servanthood happens when you latch onto a new attitude. Start by reminding yourself exactly what Jesus has done for you — giving you comfort, friendship, compassion, and more. Then make a genuine choice to pass along those things to others — making their needs as important as your own. That's the attitude Jesus had.

⁹ Therefore God exalted him to the
highest place
and gave him the name that is
above every name,
¹⁰ that at the name of Jesus every knee
should bow,
in heaven and on earth and under
the earth,
¹¹ and every tongue acknowledge that
Jesus Christ is Lord,
to the glory of God the Father.

Do Everything Without Grumbling

¹² Therefore, my dear friends, as you
have always obeyed—not only in my
presence, but now much more in my absence—continue to work out your salva-
tion with fear and trembling, ¹³ for it is
God who works in you to will and to act
in order to fulfill his good purpose.

¹⁴ Do everything without grumbling or
arguing, ¹⁵ so that you may become blameless and pure, "children of God without
fault in a warped and crooked generation."^a
Then you will shine among them like stars
in the sky ¹⁶ as you hold firmly to the word
of life. And then I will be able to boast on
the day of Christ that I did not run or labor
in vain. ¹⁷ But even if I am being poured out
like a drink offering on the sacrifice and
service coming from your faith, I am glad
and rejoice with all of you. ¹⁸ So you too
should be glad and rejoice with me.

Timothy and Epaphroditus

¹⁹ I hope in the Lord Jesus to send
Timothy to you soon, that I also may be
cheered when I receive news about you. ²⁰ I
have no one else like him, who will show
genuine concern for your welfare. ²¹ For
everyone looks out for their own interests,
not those of Jesus Christ. ²² But you know
that Timothy has proved himself, because
as a son with his father he has served with
me in the work of the gospel. ²³ I hope,
therefore, to send him as soon as I see how
things go with me. ²⁴ And I am confident
in the Lord that I myself will come soon.

²⁵ But I think it is necessary to send
back to you Epaphroditus, my brother,
co-worker and fellow soldier, who is also

your messenger, whom you sent to take
care of my needs. ²⁶ For he longs for all of
you and is distressed because you heard
he was ill. ²⁷ Indeed he was ill, and almost
died. But God had mercy on him, and not
on him only but also on me, to spare me
sorrow upon sorrow. ²⁸ Therefore I am all
the more eager to send him, so that when
you see him again you may be glad and I
may have less anxiety. ²⁹ So then, welcome
him in the Lord with great joy, and honor
people like him, ³⁰ because he almost died
for the work of Christ. He risked his life to
make up for the help you yourselves could
not give me.

No Confidence in the Flesh

3 Further, my brothers and sisters,
rejoice in the Lord! It is no trouble
for me to write the same things to
you again, and it is a safeguard for you.
² Watch out for those dogs, those evildo-
ers, those mutilators of the flesh. ³ For it
is we who are the circumcision, we who
serve God by his Spirit, who boast in
Christ Jesus, and who put no confidence
in the flesh— ⁴ though I myself have reasons for such confidence.

If someone else thinks they have reasons to put confidence in the flesh, I
have more: ⁵ circumcised on the eighth
day, of the people of Israel, of the tribe of

^a 15 Deut. 32:5

ROCK SOLID promises

**"I consider everything a loss
because of the surpassing worth of
knowing Christ Jesus my Lord."**

Philippians 3:8

The world is full of amazing things—but
not one compares to knowing Jesus up
close.

Benjamin, a Hebrew of Hebrews; in regard to the law, a Pharisee; ⁶as for zeal, persecuting the church; as for righteousness based on the law, faultless.

⁷But whatever were gains to me I now consider loss for the sake of Christ. ⁸What is more, I consider everything a loss because of the surpassing worth of knowing Christ Jesus my Lord, for whose sake I have lost all things. I consider them garbage, that I may gain Christ ⁹and be found in him, not having a righteousness of my own that comes from the law, but that which is through faith in*a* Christ—the righteousness that comes from God on the basis of faith. ¹⁰I want to know Christ— yes, to know the power of his resurrection and participation in his sufferings, becoming like him in his death, ¹¹and so, somehow, attaining to the resurrection from the dead.

¹²Not that I have already obtained all this, or have already arrived at my goal, but I press on to take hold of that for which Christ Jesus took hold of me. ¹³Brothers and sisters, I do not consider myself yet to have taken hold of it. But one thing I do: Forgetting what is behind and straining toward what is ahead, ¹⁴I press on toward the goal to win the prize for which God has called me heavenward in Christ Jesus.

Following Paul's Example

¹⁵All of us, then, who are mature should take such a view of things. And if on some point you think differently, that too God will make clear to you. ¹⁶Only let us live up to what we have already attained.

¹⁷Join together in following my example, brothers and sisters, and just as you have us as a model, keep your eyes on those who live as we do. ¹⁸For, as I have often told you before and now tell you again even with tears, many live as enemies of the cross of Christ. ¹⁹Their destiny is destruction, their god is their stomach, and their glory is in their shame. Their mind is set on earthly things. ²⁰But our citizenship is in heaven. And we eagerly await a Savior from there, the Lord Jesus

Christ, ²¹who, by the power that enables him to bring everything under his control, will transform our lowly bodies so that they will be like his glorious body.

Closing Appeal for Steadfastness and Unity

4 Therefore, my brothers and sisters, you whom I love and long for, my joy and crown, stand firm in the Lord in this way, dear friends!

²I plead with Euodia and I plead with Syntyche to be of the same mind in the Lord. ³Yes, and I ask you, my true companion, help these women since they have contended at my side in the cause of the gospel, along with Clement and the rest of my co-workers, whose names are in the book of life.

Final Exhortations

⁴Rejoice in the Lord always. I will say it again: Rejoice! ⁵Let your gentleness be evident to all. The Lord is near. ⁶Do not

ROCK SOLID *plans*

Philippians 3:12–14

Get up and go on.

You might glance at the start of Philippians 3 and assume the apostle Paul has his spiritual life perfectly put together. He says, for example, that nothing on earth compares to "the surpassing worth of knowing Christ Jesus my Lord" (Philippians 3:8). But Paul admits he hasn't grabbed hold of every spiritual blessing God has for him (see Philippians 3:12–14). At times he stumbles like everyone else. Yet Paul knows exactly what to do when he falls short of God's plan. He gets up and goes on.

Your next step: Ask God for help letting go of your past failures, then give yourself a fresh start today.

a 9 Or through the faithfulness of

be anxious about anything, but in every situation, by prayer and petition, with thanksgiving, present your requests to God. ⁷And the peace of God, which transcends all understanding, will guard your hearts and your minds in Christ Jesus.

⁸Finally, brothers and sisters, whatever is true, whatever is noble, whatever is right, whatever is pure, whatever is lovely, whatever is admirable—if anything is excellent or praiseworthy—think about such things. ⁹Whatever you have learned or received or heard from me, or seen in me—put it into practice. And the God of peace will be with you.

Thanks for Their Gifts

¹⁰I rejoiced greatly in the Lord that at last you renewed your concern for me. Indeed, you were concerned, but you had no opportunity to show it. ¹¹I am not saying this because I am in need, for I have learned to be content whatever the circumstances. ¹²I know what it is to be in need, and I know what it is to have plenty. I have learned the secret of being content in any and every situation, whether well fed or hungry, whether living in plenty or in want. ¹³I can do all this through him who gives me strength.

ROCK SOLID *promises*

"I can do all this through him who gives me strength."

Philippians 4:13

You have God's colossal power inside you. So you can triumph in every good, bad, and boring circumstance you face.

ROCK SOLID *principles*

Philippians 4:6–9

Think right.

Kiara kept trying to stop thinking bad things about her boss, but she could easily dream up a dozen ways to make the store a better place to work, not to mention get customers to buy more clothes. It didn't help that the boss was her mom. There was no way Kiara could run away to a job somewhere else, and she was getting more miserable by the day. So she changed her tactics. She thanked God she had a job. She made a list of the good points of working in the family business. And she decided to keep sharing her ideas with her mom. But slowly. Like no more than one a week.

You can't make yourself quit thinking about bad things any more than you can force yourself not to picture a pink stuffed elephant. You instead need to push out the bad with better things. When your mind trips down evil paths, shift your focus to everything God likes—whatever is "true . . . noble . . . right . . . pure . . . lovely . . . admirable . . . excellent . . . praiseworthy" (Philippians 4:8).

¹⁴Yet it was good of you to share in my troubles. ¹⁵Moreover, as you Philippians know, in the early days of your acquaintance with the gospel, when I set out from Macedonia, not one church shared with me in the matter of giving and receiving, except you only; ¹⁶for even when I was in Thessalonica, you sent me aid more than once when I was in need. ¹⁷Not that I desire your gifts; what I desire is that more be credited to your account. ¹⁸I have received full payment and have more than enough. I am amply supplied, now that I have received from Epaphroditus the gifts you sent. They are a fragrant offering, an acceptable sacrifice, pleasing to God. ¹⁹And my God will meet all your needs according to the riches of his glory in Christ Jesus.

²⁰To our God and Father be glory for ever and ever. Amen.

Final Greetings

²¹Greet all God's people in Christ Jesus. The brothers and sisters who are with me send greetings. ²²All God's people here send you greetings, especially those who belong to Caesar's household.

²³The grace of the Lord Jesus Christ be with your spirit. Amen.*ª*

ª 23 Some manuscripts do not have *Amen.*

ROCK SOLID *promises*

"My God will meet all your needs according to the riches of his glory in Christ Jesus." Philippians 4:19

God will give you everything you really need, but not necessarily everything you want.

COLOSSIANS

BOOK OUTLINE

Greetings and appreciation
(1:1–8)

Christ and the believer
(1:9—2:5)

Dangerous rules
(2:6–23)

Rules for holy living
(3:1—4:6)

Greetings and conclusion
(4:7–18)

Colossians is the third letter Paul wrote from prison in Rome (about AD 60). Epaphras traveled from Colossae to Rome to tell Paul that false teachers were convincing the people that the Christian faith was incomplete. They were teaching the Colossians to worship angels and to follow special rules and ceremonies.

Paul wrote to the Colossians to oppose these false teachers. He reminded them that Jesus is supreme over everything, that Christ's death is all we need to be saved from our sins, and that through Christ we are free from man-made rules.

Paul, an apostle of Christ Jesus by the will of God, and Timothy our brother,

[2] To God's holy people in Colossae, the faithful brothers and sisters[a] in Christ:

Grace and peace to you from God our Father.[b]

Thanksgiving and Prayer

[3] We always thank God, the Father of our Lord Jesus Christ, when we pray for you, [4] because we have heard of your faith in Christ Jesus and of the love you have for all God's people— [5] the faith and love that spring from the hope stored up for you in heaven and about which you have already heard in the true message of the gospel [6] that has come to you. In the same way, the gospel is bearing fruit and growing throughout the whole world—just as it has been doing among you since the day you heard it and truly understood God's grace. [7] You learned it from Epaphras, our dear fellow servant,[c] who is a faithful minister of Christ on our[d] behalf, [8] and who also told us of your love in the Spirit.

[9] For this reason, since the day we heard about you, we have not stopped praying for you. We continually ask God to fill you with the knowledge of his will through all the wisdom and understanding that the Spirit gives,[e] [10] so that you may live a life worthy of the Lord and please him in every way: bearing fruit in every good work, growing in the knowledge of God, [11] being strengthened with all power according to his glorious might so that you may have great endurance and patience, [12] and giving joyful thanks to the Father, who has qualified you[f] to share in the inheritance of his holy people in the kingdom of light. [13] For he has rescued us from the dominion of darkness and brought us into the kingdom of the Son he loves, [14] in whom we have redemption, the forgiveness of sins.

The Supremacy of the Son of God

[15] The Son is the image of the invisible God, the firstborn over all creation. [16] For in him all things were created: things in heaven and on earth, visible and invisible, whether thrones or powers or rulers or authorities; all things have been created through him and for him. [17] He is before all things, and in him all things hold together. [18] And he is the head of the body, the church; he is the beginning and the firstborn from among the dead, so that in everything he might have the supremacy. [19] For God was pleased to have all his fullness dwell in him, [20] and through him to reconcile to himself all things, whether things on earth or things in heaven, by making peace through his blood, shed on the cross.

[21] Once you were alienated from God and were enemies in your minds because of[g] your evil behavior. [22] But now he has reconciled you by Christ's physical body through death to present you holy in his sight, without blemish and free from accusation— [23] if you continue in your faith, established and firm, and do not move from the hope held out in the gospel. This is the gospel that you heard and that has been proclaimed to every creature under heaven, and of which I, Paul, have become a servant.

Paul's Labor for the Church

[24] Now I rejoice in what I am suffering for you, and I fill up in my flesh what is still lacking in regard to Christ's afflictions, for the sake of his body, which is the church. [25] I have become its servant by the commission God gave me to present to you the word of God in its fullness— [26] the mystery that has been kept hidden for ages and generations, but is now disclosed to the Lord's people. [27] To them God has chosen to make known among the Gentiles the glorious riches of this

---

[a] 2 The Greek word for *brothers and sisters* (*adelphoi*) refers here to believers, both men and women, as part of God's family; also in 4:15.
[b] 2 Some manuscripts *Father and the Lord Jesus Christ*   [c] 7 Or *slave*   [d] 7 Some manuscripts *your*   [e] 9 Or *all spiritual wisdom and understanding*   [f] 12 Some manuscripts *us*
[g] 21 Or *minds, as shown by*

mystery, which is Christ in you, the hope of glory.

²⁸He is the one we proclaim, admonishing and teaching everyone with all wisdom, so that we may present everyone fully mature in Christ. ²⁹To this end I strenuously contend with all the energy Christ so powerfully works in me.

2 I want you to know how hard I am contending for you and for those at Laodicea, and for all who have not met me personally. ²My goal is that they may be encouraged in heart and united in love, so that they may have the full riches of complete understanding, in order that they may know the mystery of God, namely, Christ, ³in whom are hidden all the treasures of wisdom and knowledge. ⁴I tell you this so that no one may deceive you by fine-sounding arguments. ⁵For though I am absent from you in body, I am present with you in spirit and delight to see how disciplined you are and how firm your faith in Christ is.

Spiritual Fullness in Christ

⁶So then, just as you received Christ Jesus as Lord, continue to live your lives in him, ⁷rooted and built up in him, strengthened in the faith as you were taught, and overflowing with thankfulness.

⁸See to it that no one takes you captive through hollow and deceptive philosophy, which depends on human tradition and the elemental spiritual forces*a* of this world rather than on Christ.

⁹For in Christ all the fullness of the Deity lives in bodily form, ¹⁰and in Christ you have been brought to fullness. He is the head over every power and authority. ¹¹In him you were also circumcised with a circumcision not performed by human hands. Your whole self ruled by the flesh*b* was put off when you were circumcised by*c* Christ, ¹²having been buried with him in baptism, in which you were also raised with him through your faith in the working of God, who raised him from the dead.

¹³When you were dead in your sins and in the uncircumcision of your flesh, God made you*d* alive with Christ. He forgave us all our sins, ¹⁴having canceled the charge of our legal indebtedness, which stood against us and condemned us; he has taken it away, nailing it to the cross. ¹⁵And

---

a 8 Or *the basic principles*; also in verse 20
b 11 In contexts like this, the Greek word for *flesh* (*sarx*) refers to the sinful state of human beings, often presented as a power in opposition to the Spirit; also in verse 13. *c 11* Or *put off in the circumcision of* *d 13* Some manuscripts *us*

ROCK SOLID truths

Colossians 1:21–23

God shows us how to become his friend.

You might really want to tell your friends about Jesus, but you maybe aren't quite sure what to say beyond "Jesus died for your sins so you should believe in him." Try pointing them to this tight Bible passage. The apostle Paul was writing to the Colossians, helping them understand their own faith. Paul says we have a *problem*—sin. Doing wrong alienates us from God and makes us his enemies in what we think and do (see Colossians 1:21). But God has a *solution*—the death of Jesus on the cross. His death pays the penalty for our sins and reconciles us with God so we can stand before the Lord without guilt (see Colossians 1:22). And God requires a *response*—faith. He requires we trust that Jesus died for our sins. Sin breaks our relationship with God whether our wrongdoing seems big or small, whether everyone knows about our sins or no one does. But God provides a way out. Problem, solution, response—those are the facts your friends need to know.

Think: How would you explain to your friends how they can become a Christian?

having disarmed the powers and authorities, he made a public spectacle of them, triumphing over them by the cross.[a]

Freedom From Human Rules

¹⁶Therefore do not let anyone judge you by what you eat or drink, or with regard to a religious festival, a New Moon celebration or a Sabbath day. ¹⁷These are a shadow of the things that were to come; the reality, however, is found in Christ. ¹⁸Do not let anyone who delights in false humility and the worship of angels disqualify you. Such a person also goes into great detail about what they have seen; they are puffed up with idle notions by their unspiritual mind. ¹⁹They have lost connection with the head, from whom the whole body, supported and held together by its ligaments and sinews, grows as God causes it to grow.

²⁰Since you died with Christ to the elemental spiritual forces of this world, why, as though you still belonged to the world, do you submit to its rules: ²¹"Do not handle! Do not taste! Do not touch!"? ²²These rules, which have to do with things that are all destined to perish with use, are based on merely human commands and teachings. ²³Such regulations indeed have an appearance of wisdom, with their self-imposed worship, their false humility and their harsh treatment of the body, but they lack any value in restraining sensual indulgence.

Living as Those Made Alive in Christ

3 Since, then, you have been raised with Christ, set your hearts on things above, where Christ is, seated at the right hand of God. ²Set your minds on things above, not on earthly things. ³For you died, and your life is now hidden with Christ in God. ⁴When Christ, who is your[b] life, appears, then you also will appear with him in glory.

⁵Put to death, therefore, whatever belongs to your earthly nature: sexual im-

[a] 15 Or them in him   [b] 4 Some manuscripts our

ROCK SOLID principles

Colossians 3:12–14

Forgive.

When Josh heard that he should forgive others the way God had forgiven him, he thought he had that command down cold. He grew up in a Christian home and, in his own opinion, he had never done anything really awful. Since he never actually messed up, why should he let others off the hook for their bad behavior? When others wronged Josh, he was quick to call them on it. He made a point of explaining how they could do better next time. And only if they really groveled did he eventually mumble "I forgive you" and let it go.

God wants to change you so you show off amazing qualities like compassion, kindness, and forgiveness. He plans to teach you to put up with others and wrap everything in love. The secret to doing any of those things is getting them from God before you attempt to give them away. Only when you realize even your smallest sins truly offend God and need his forgiveness, for example, do you get power to forgive "as the Lord forgave you" (Colossians 3:13).

morality, impurity, lust, evil desires and greed, which is idolatry. ⁶Because of these, the wrath of God is coming.ᵃ ⁷You used to walk in these ways, in the life you once lived. ⁸But now you must also rid yourselves of all such things as these: anger, rage, malice, slander, and filthy language from your lips. ⁹Do not lie to each other, since you have taken off your old self with its practices ¹⁰and have put on the new self, which is being renewed in knowledge in the image of its Creator. ¹¹Here there is no Gentile or Jew, circumcised or uncircumcised, barbarian, Scythian, slave or free, but Christ is all, and is in all.

¹²Therefore, as God's chosen people, holy and dearly loved, clothe yourselves with compassion, kindness, humility, gentleness and patience. ¹³Bear with each other and forgive one another if any of you has a grievance against someone. Forgive as the Lord forgave you. ¹⁴And over all these virtues put on love, which binds them all together in perfect unity.

¹⁵Let the peace of Christ rule in your hearts, since as members of one body you were called to peace. And be thankful. ¹⁶Let the message of Christ dwell among you richly as you teach and admonish one another with all wisdom through psalms, hymns, and songs from the Spirit, singing to God with gratitude in your hearts. ¹⁷And whatever you do, whether in word or deed, do it all in the name of the Lord Jesus, giving thanks to God the Father through him.

Instructions for Christian Households

¹⁸Wives, submit yourselves to your husbands, as is fitting in the Lord.

¹⁹Husbands, love your wives and do not be harsh with them.

²⁰Children, obey your parents in everything, for this pleases the Lord.

²¹Fathers,ᵇ do not embitter your children, or they will become discouraged.

ᵃ 6 Some early manuscripts *coming on those who are disobedient*   ᵇ 21 Or *Parents*

ROCK SOLID *principles*

Colossians 3:20–21

Obey your parents.

Emily was barely 13 by the time both of her older sisters had left for college. She quickly concluded her parents had far too much time on their hands. As the only daughter left at home, she seemed to be getting extra scrutiny from her parents as they hovered over every detail of her life. At first Emily liked the extra attention, but after a while it seemed like her parents just wanted to catch her being bad. She started doing everything she could to evade their watchful eyes. And if she was going to get in trouble no matter what she did, she might as well go ahead and act out, she reasoned.

God tells you to obey your parents, then tells you why: "for this pleases the Lord" (Colossians 3:20). The Old Testament adds another motivation: "so that you may live long" (Exodus 20:12). Your job is to show your parents the honor they deserve, but God never says you can't respectfully dialogue. He also tells your parents not to "embitter" or discourage you (see Colossians 3:21).

[22] Slaves, obey your earthly masters in everything; and do it, not only when their eye is on you and to curry their favor, but with sincerity of heart and reverence for the Lord. [23] Whatever you do, work at it with all your heart, as working for the Lord, not for human masters, [24] since you know that you will receive an inheritance from the Lord as a reward. It is the Lord Christ you are serving. [25] Anyone who does wrong will be repaid for their wrongs, and there is no favoritism.

ROCK SOLID promises

"Whatever you do, work at it with all your heart, as working for the Lord, not for human masters ... It is the Lord Christ you are serving."

Colossians 3:23–24

No matter who you work for or what you do, God will always be your real boss.

---

4 Masters, provide your slaves with what is right and fair, because you know that you also have a Master in heaven.

Further Instructions

[2] Devote yourselves to prayer, being watchful and thankful. [3] And pray for us, too, that God may open a door for our message, so that we may proclaim the mystery of Christ, for which I am in chains. [4] Pray that I may proclaim it clearly, as I should. [5] Be wise in the way you act toward outsiders; make the most of every opportunity. [6] Let your conversation be always full of grace, seasoned with salt, so that you may know how to answer everyone.

Final Greetings

[7] Tychicus will tell you all the news about me. He is a dear brother, a faithful minister and fellow servant[a] in the Lord. [8] I am sending him to you for the express purpose that you may know about our[b] circumstances and that he may encourage your hearts. [9] He is coming with Onesimus, our faithful and dear brother, who is one of you. They will tell you everything that is happening here.

[10] My fellow prisoner Aristarchus sends you his greetings, as does Mark, the cousin of Barnabas. (You have received instructions about him; if he comes to you, welcome him.) [11] Jesus, who is called Justus, also sends greetings. These are the only Jews[c] among my co-workers for the kingdom of God, and they have proved a comfort to me. [12] Epaphras, who is one of you and a servant of Christ Jesus, sends greetings. He is always wrestling in prayer for you, that you may stand firm in all the will of God, mature and fully assured. [13] I vouch for him that he is working hard for you and for those at Laodicea and Hierapolis. [14] Our dear friend Luke, the doctor, and Demas send greetings. [15] Give my greetings to the brothers and sisters at Laodicea, and to Nympha and the church in her house.

[16] After this letter has been read to you, see that it is also read in the church of the Laodiceans and that you in turn read the letter from Laodicea.

[17] Tell Archippus: "See to it that you complete the ministry you have received in the Lord."

[18] I, Paul, write this greeting in my own hand. Remember my chains. Grace be with you.

---

[a] 7 Or *slave*; also in verse 12   [b] 8 Some manuscripts *that he may know about your*
[c] 11 Greek *only ones of the circumcision group*

1 THESSALONIANS

Paul started the church at Thessalonica on his second missionary journey. He taught there for about three weeks. Then the Jews opposed him so strongly he had to leave. On hearing from Timothy about the conditions in Thessalonica, Paul wrote this letter from Corinth to encourage the Thessalonians and to teach them more about Christianity (AD 51).

Paul praises the Thessalonians for being brave and not giving up their faith "in the midst of severe suffering" (1:6). He instructs them "how to live in order to please God" (4:1). And he teaches them about Jesus' second coming. He explains that the time of Jesus' coming is secret, so they should continue working until he comes.

1

Paul, Silas[a] and Timothy,

To the church of the Thessalonians in God the Father and the Lord Jesus Christ:

Grace and peace to you.

Thanksgiving for the Thessalonians' Faith

[2] We always thank God for all of you and continually mention you in our prayers. [3] We remember before our God and Father your work produced by faith, your labor prompted by love, and your endurance inspired by hope in our Lord Jesus Christ.

[4] For we know, brothers and sisters[b] loved by God, that he has chosen you, [5] because our gospel came to you not simply with words but also with power, with the Holy Spirit and deep conviction. You know how we lived among you for your sake. [6] You became imitators of us and of the Lord, for you welcomed the message in the midst of severe suffering with the joy given by the Holy Spirit. [7] And so you became a model to all the believers in Macedonia and Achaia. [8] The Lord's message rang out from you not only in Macedonia and Achaia—your faith in God has become known everywhere. Therefore we do not need to say anything about it, [9] for they themselves report what kind of reception you gave us. They tell how you turned to God from idols to serve the living and true God, [10] and to wait for his Son from heaven, whom he raised from the dead—Jesus, who rescues us from the coming wrath.

Paul's Ministry in Thessalonica

2

You know, brothers and sisters, that our visit to you was not without results. [2] We had previously suffered and been treated outrageously

[a] 1 Greek *Silvanus*, a variant of *Silas*   [b] 4 The Greek word for *brothers and sisters* (*adelphoi*) refers here to believers, both men and women, as part of God's family; also in 2:1, 9, 14, 17; 3:7; 4:1, 10, 13; 5:1, 4, 12, 14, 25, 27.

ROCK SOLID principles

1 Thessalonians 1:2–10

Be a role model.

Matt had gotten labeled "the guy who never did anything wrong." That wasn't meant as a compliment, and it wasn't true. Matt had become a Christian because he understood he needed God's forgiveness for things he had done—deeds more awful than anyone would imagine. He wasn't ready to tell everyone that part of his past, but he had decided to trust 2 Corinthians 5:17—that because of Jesus he was a new creation. God promised a fresh start. Matt took it. He hated the reputation of being "too good," but that just meant he needed to work hard to let others know not just his successes but his struggles. After all, a role model has to be real.

The new Thessalonian Christians hadn't merely heard the apostle Paul preach. When they saw God act, they dedicated themselves to God despite brutal persecution. News of their faith spread across their world, so that everyone heard how they turned from dead idols to serve the living God. Whatever your story of meeting God, you can be a role model who impacts others.

in Philippi, as you know, but with the help of our God we dared to tell you his gospel in the face of strong opposition. [3]For the appeal we make does not spring from error or impure motives, nor are we trying to trick you. [4]On the contrary, we speak as those approved by God to be entrusted with the gospel. We are not trying to please people but God, who tests our hearts. [5]You know we never used flattery, nor did we put on a mask to cover up greed—God is our witness. [6]We were not looking for praise from people, not from you or anyone else, even though as apostles of Christ we could have asserted our authority. [7]Instead, we were like young children[a] among you.

Just as a nursing mother cares for her children, [8]so we cared for you. Because we loved you so much, we were delighted to share with you not only the gospel of God but our lives as well. [9]Surely you remember, brothers and sisters, our toil and hardship; we worked night and day in order not to be a burden to anyone while we preached the gospel of God to you. [10]You are witnesses, and so is God, of how holy, righteous and blameless we were among you who believed. [11]For you know that we dealt with each of you as a father deals with his own children, [12]encouraging, comforting and urging you to live lives worthy of God, who calls you into his kingdom and glory.

[13]And we also thank God continually because, when you received the word of God, which you heard from us, you accepted it not as a human word, but as it actually is, the word of God, which is indeed at work in you who believe. [14]For you, brothers and sisters, became imitators of God's churches in Judea, which are in Christ Jesus: You suffered from your own people the same things those churches suffered from the Jews [15]who killed the Lord Jesus and the prophets and also drove us out. They displease God and are hostile to everyone [16]in their effort to keep us from speaking to the Gentiles so that they may be saved. In this way they always heap up their sins to the limit. The wrath of God has come upon them at last.[b]

Paul's Longing to See the Thessalonians

[17]But, brothers and sisters, when we were orphaned by being separated from you for a short time (in person, not in thought), out of our intense longing we made every effort to see you. [18]For we wanted to come to you—certainly I, Paul, did, again and again—but Satan blocked our way. [19]For what is our hope, our joy, or the crown in which we will glory in the presence of our Lord Jesus when he comes? Is it not you? [20]Indeed, you are our glory and joy.

3 So when we could stand it no longer, we thought it best to be left by ourselves in Athens. [2]We sent Timothy, who is our brother and co-worker in God's service in spreading the gospel of Christ, to strengthen and encourage you in your faith, [3]so that no one would be unsettled by these trials. For you know quite well that we are destined for them. [4]In fact, when we were with you, we kept telling you that we would be persecuted. And it turned out that way, as you well know. [5]For this reason, when I could stand it no longer, I sent to find out about your faith. I was afraid that in some way the tempter had tempted you and that our labors might have been in vain.

Timothy's Encouraging Report

[6]But Timothy has just now come to us from you and has brought good news about your faith and love. He has told us that you always have pleasant memories of us and that you long to see us, just as we also long to see you. [7]Therefore, brothers and sisters, in all our distress and persecution we were encouraged about you because of your faith. [8]For now we really live, since you are standing firm in the Lord. [9]How can we thank God enough for you in return for all the joy we have in the presence of our God because of you?

[a] 7 Some manuscripts were gentle
[b] 16 Or them fully

¹⁰Night and day we pray most earnestly that we may see you again and supply what is lacking in your faith.

¹¹Now may our God and Father himself and our Lord Jesus clear the way for us to come to you. ¹²May the Lord make your love increase and overflow for each other and for everyone else, just as ours does for you. ¹³May he strengthen your hearts so that you will be blameless and holy in the presence of our God and Father when our Lord Jesus comes with all his holy ones.

Living to Please God

4 As for other matters, brothers and sisters, we instructed you how to live in order to please God, as in fact you are living. Now we ask you and urge you in the Lord Jesus to do this more and more. ²For you know what instructions we gave you by the authority of the Lord Jesus.

³It is God's will that you should be sanctified: that you should avoid sexual immorality; ⁴that each of you should learn to control your own body*a* in a way that is holy and honorable, ⁵not in passionate lust like the pagans, who do not know God; ⁶and that in this matter no one should wrong or take advantage of a brother or sister.*b* The Lord will punish all those who commit such sins, as we told you and warned you before. ⁷For God did not call us to be impure, but to live a holy life. ⁸Therefore, anyone who rejects this instruction does not reject a human being but God, the very God who gives you his Holy Spirit.

⁹Now about your love for one another we do not need to write to you, for you yourselves have been taught by God to love each other. ¹⁰And in fact, you do love all of God's family throughout Macedonia. Yet we urge you, brothers and sisters, to do so more and more, ¹¹and to make it your ambition to lead a quiet life: You should mind your own business and work with your hands, just as we told you, ¹²so that your daily life may win the respect of outsiders and so that you will not be dependent on anybody.

Believers Who Have Died

¹³Brothers and sisters, we do not want you to be uninformed about those who sleep in death, so that you do not grieve like the rest of mankind, who have no hope. ¹⁴For we believe that Jesus died and rose again, and so we believe that God will bring with Jesus those who have fallen asleep in him. ¹⁵According to the Lord's word, we tell you that we who are still alive, who are left until the coming of the Lord, will certainly not precede those who have fallen asleep. ¹⁶For the Lord himself will come down from heaven, with a loud command, with the voice of the archangel and with the trumpet call of God, and the dead in Christ will rise first. ¹⁷After that, we who are still alive and are left will be caught up together with them in the clouds to meet the Lord in the air. And so we will be with the Lord forever. ¹⁸Therefore encourage one another with these words.

The Day of the Lord

5 Now, brothers and sisters, about times and dates we do not need to write to you, ²for you know very well that the day of the Lord will come like a thief in the night. ³While people are saying, "Peace and safety," destruction will come on them suddenly, as labor pains on a pregnant woman, and they will not escape.

⁴But you, brothers and sisters, are not in darkness so that this day should surprise you like a thief. ⁵You are all children of the light and children of the day. We do not belong to the night or to the darkness. ⁶So then, let us not be like others, who are asleep, but let us be awake and sober. ⁷For those who sleep, sleep at night, and those who get drunk, get drunk at night. ⁸But since we belong to the day, let us be sober, putting on faith and love as a breastplate, and the hope of salvation as a helmet. ⁹For God did not appoint us to suffer wrath but to receive salvation through our Lord Jesus

---

a 4 Or *learn to live with your own wife*; or *learn to acquire a wife*   *b* 6 The Greek word for *brother or sister* (*adelphos*) refers here to a believer, whether man or woman, as part of God's family.

ROCK SOLID *promises*

"God did not appoint us to suffer wrath but to receive salvation through our Lord Jesus Christ."

1 Thessalonians 5:9

God didn't create you to end up in hell. He wants you to trust Jesus and be saved.

Christ. [10]He died for us so that, whether we are awake or asleep, we may live together with him. [11]Therefore encourage one another and build each other up, just as in fact you are doing.

Final Instructions

[12]Now we ask you, brothers and sisters, to acknowledge those who work hard among you, who care for you in the Lord and who admonish you. [13]Hold them in the highest regard in love because of their work. Live in peace with each other. [14]And we urge you, brothers and sisters, warn those who are idle and disruptive, encourage the disheartened, help the weak, be patient with everyone. [15]Make sure that nobody pays back wrong for wrong, but always strive to do what is good for each other and for everyone else.

[16]Rejoice always, [17]pray continually, [18]give thanks in all circumstances; for this is God's will for you in Christ Jesus.

[19]Do not quench the Spirit. [20]Do not treat prophecies with contempt [21]but test them all; hold on to what is good, [22]reject every kind of evil.

ROCK SOLID *principles*

1 Thessalonians 5:16–18

Crowd out evil.

Isabella didn't have much time to get in trouble. She had plenty of school and sports and friends in her life, but for years she and her parents had been giving every spare moment to serving in a shelter for homeless families. Isabella had barely started school when her dad and mom began serving meals. It wasn't much later that Isabella was helping take care of children instead of needing to be babysat. Doing good had become such a major part of her life that diving into sin like many of her peers had no appeal. She couldn't understand why she needed do bad things when she could have so much fun doing good.

It's tough to commit evil when you're busy doing good. And in 1 Thessalonians 5:16–18, the apostle Paul passes along some commands that are all part of God's plan for you to do right. So "rejoice always," not faking cheeriness but being happy about God. You can "pray continually," both consistently and persistently. And God wants you to "give thanks in all circumstances," praising him in spite of bad times.

23 May God himself, the God of peace, sanctify you through and through. May your whole spirit, soul and body be kept blameless at the coming of our Lord Jesus Christ. 24 The one who calls you is faithful, and he will do it.

25 Brothers and sisters, pray for us. 26 Greet all God's people with a holy kiss. 27 I charge you before the Lord to have this letter read to all the brothers and sisters.

28 The grace of our Lord Jesus Christ be with you.

2 THESSALONIANS

BOOK OUTLINE

Paul's personal concern
(1:1–12)

Conditions for the Lord's coming
(2:1–17)

Strong advice and a blessing
(3:1–18)

Paul was in Corinth when he sent his second letter to the Thessalonians a few months after the first letter. Some people had misunderstood Paul's teaching on the second coming and were sure Jesus was coming very soon. In fact, they had stopped working and were just waiting for Jesus.

Paul writes the Thessalonians again and describes what Jesus' second coming will be like. He also reminds them to keep working hard until Jesus comes and to use their time wisely.

Paul, Silas[a] and Timothy,

To the church of the Thessalonians in God our Father and the Lord Jesus Christ:

[2] Grace and peace to you from God the Father and the Lord Jesus Christ.

Thanksgiving and Prayer

[3] We ought always to thank God for you, brothers and sisters,[b] and rightly so, because your faith is growing more and more, and the love all of you have for one another is increasing. [4] Therefore, among God's churches we boast about your perseverance and faith in all the persecutions and trials you are enduring.

[5] All this is evidence that God's judgment is right, and as a result you will be counted worthy of the kingdom of God, for which you are suffering. [6] God is just: He will pay back trouble to those who trouble you [7] and give relief to you who are troubled, and to us as well. This will happen when the Lord Jesus is revealed from heaven in blazing fire with his powerful angels. [8] He will punish those who do not know God and do not obey the gospel of our Lord Jesus. [9] They will be punished with everlasting destruction and shut out from the presence of the Lord and from the glory of his might [10] on the day he comes to be glorified in his holy people and to be marveled at among all those who have believed. This includes you, because you believed our testimony to you.

[11] With this in mind, we constantly pray for you, that our God may make you worthy of his calling, and that by his power he may bring to fruition your every desire for goodness and your every deed prompted by faith. [12] We pray this so that the name of our Lord Jesus may be glorified in you, and you in him, according to the grace of our God and the Lord Jesus Christ.[c]

The Man of Lawlessness

2 Concerning the coming of our Lord Jesus Christ and our being gathered to him, we ask you, brothers and sisters, [2] not to become easily unsettled or alarmed by the teaching allegedly from us—whether by a prophecy or by word of mouth or by letter—asserting that the day of the Lord has already come. [3] Don't let anyone deceive you in any way, for that day will not come until the

a 1 Greek *Silvanus*, a variant of *Silas*
b 3 The Greek word for *brothers and sisters* (*adelphoi*) refers here to believers, both men and women, as part of God's family; also in 2:1, 13, 15; 3:1, 6, 13.   *c* 12 Or *God and Lord, Jesus Christ*

2 Thessalonians 2:1–17

We must stand firm.

The book of Revelation talks about the "beast" whose number is 666 (Revelation 13:1–18). The apostle Paul mentions "the man of lawlessness" here (2 Thessalonians 2:3). John warns that the world is full of false teachers, antichrists that hint at the final antichrist (1 John 2:18). The antichrist will lead a worldwide rebellion by declaring himself to be God. With Satan's help he will perform counterfeit miracles and deceive the masses. People will die without God "because they refused to love the truth and so be saved" (2 Thessalonians 2:10). Paul told his readers that the "lawless one" hadn't yet come. They didn't have to live in fear, because one day Jesus would arrive and overthrow the antichrist. Until that time, they were to "stand firm and hold fast to the teachings" (2 Thessalonians 2:15). That's exactly what God wants you to do too.

Think: What does it mean to you to "stand firm" in your faith today?

ROCK SOLID truths

rebellion occurs and the man of lawlessness[a] is revealed, the man doomed to destruction. [4]He will oppose and will exalt himself over everything that is called God or is worshiped, so that he sets himself up in God's temple, proclaiming himself to be God.

[5]Don't you remember that when I was with you I used to tell you these things? [6]And now you know what is holding him back, so that he may be revealed at the proper time. [7]For the secret power of lawlessness is already at work; but the one who now holds it back will continue to do so till he is taken out of the way. [8]And then the lawless one will be revealed, whom the Lord Jesus will overthrow with the breath of his mouth and destroy by the splendor of his coming. [9]The coming of the lawless one will be in accordance with how Satan works. He will use all sorts of displays of power through signs and wonders that serve the lie, [10]and all the ways that wickedness deceives those who are perishing. They perish because they refused to love the truth and so be saved. [11]For this reason God sends them a powerful delusion so that they will believe the lie [12]and so that all will be condemned who have not believed the truth but have delighted in wickedness.

Stand Firm

[13]But we ought always to thank God for you, brothers and sisters loved by the Lord, because God chose you as firstfruits[b] to be saved through the sanctifying work of the Spirit and through belief in the truth. [14]He called you to this through our gospel, that you might share in the glory of our Lord Jesus Christ.

[15]So then, brothers and sisters, stand firm and hold fast to the teachings[c] we passed on to you, whether by word of mouth or by letter.

[16]May our Lord Jesus Christ himself and God our Father, who loved us and by his grace gave us eternal encouragement and good hope, [17]encourage your hearts and strengthen you in every good deed and word.

Request for Prayer

3 As for other matters, brothers and sisters, pray for us that the message of the Lord may spread rapidly and be honored, just as it was with you. [2]And pray that we may be delivered from wicked and evil people, for not everyone has faith. [3]But the Lord is faithful, and he will strengthen you and protect you from the evil one. [4]We have confidence in the Lord that you are doing and will continue to do the things we command. [5]May the Lord direct your hearts into God's love and Christ's perseverance.

ROCK SOLID promises

"The Lord is faithful, and he will strengthen and protect you from the evil one." 2 Thessalonians 3:3

God doesn't leave you unprotected, as easy prey for the devil. He makes you strong enough to beat every kind of evil.

Warning Against Idleness

[6]In the name of the Lord Jesus Christ, we command you, brothers and sisters, to keep away from every believer who is idle and disruptive and does not live according to the teaching[d] you received from us. [7]For you yourselves know how you ought to follow our example. We were not idle when we were with you, [8]nor did we eat anyone's food without paying for it. On the contrary, we worked night and day, laboring and toiling so that we would not be a burden to any of you. [9]We did this, not because we do not have the right to

---

[a] 3 Some manuscripts *sin*   [b] 13 Some manuscripts *because from the beginning God chose you*   [c] 15 Or *traditions*   [d] 6 Or *tradition*

such help, but in order to offer ourselves as a model for you to imitate. [10]For even when we were with you, we gave you this rule: "The one who is unwilling to work shall not eat."

[11]We hear that some among you are idle and disruptive. They are not busy; they are busybodies. [12]Such people we command and urge in the Lord Jesus Christ to settle down and earn the food they eat. [13]And as for you, brothers and sisters, never tire of doing what is good.

[14]Take special note of anyone who does not obey our instruction in this letter. Do not associate with them, in order that they may feel ashamed. [15]Yet do not regard them as an enemy, but warn them as you would a fellow believer.

Final Greetings

[16]Now may the Lord of peace himself give you peace at all times and in every way. The Lord be with all of you.

[17]I, Paul, write this greeting in my own hand, which is the distinguishing mark in all my letters. This is how I write.

[18]The grace of our Lord Jesus Christ be with you all.

ROCK SOLID principles

2 Thessalonians 3:6–15

Earn your keep.

Jacob knew the day was coming when his parents would stop handing him a weekly allowance, money he could spend mostly how he wanted. But it still shocked him when they sat him down and said they would give him a large bump in money each month—with a catch. With that cash Jacob had to take responsibility for most of his own expenses, everything from clothes and school supplies to entertainment and giving to good causes. It sounded like a lot of money, but Jacob found it wouldn't buy everything he wanted. Soon he started hunting for chores to make money and then for a part-time job. It was all part of his parents' plan.

Some of the Thessalonian believers were so convinced Jesus was coming back soon that they quit their jobs to hang out and wait for his return. It sounds deeply spiritual, but it was downright lazy. The apostle Paul wrote, "The one who is unwilling to work shall not eat" (2 Thessalonians 3:10). God designed work as a good part of life. We're to "never tire of doing what is good" (2 Thessalonians 3:13).

1 TIMOTHY

First and Second Timothy and Titus are commonly called the pastoral letters because they deal with the qualifications and duties of pastors. Paul wrote these letters to the young leaders in the Christian church.

Timothy was born at Lystra and had a Greek father and a Jewish mother (who taught him the Scriptures from childhood). He went with Paul on his second missionary journey and from then on helped Paul in his work. At the time Paul wrote this letter, Timothy was working as the teacher and leader of the church at Ephesus.

Timothy was quite young to have the important job of leading a church, so Paul wrote this very personal letter to him. In this letter Paul gives him help and advice for his work. He warns him of false teachers and their teachings that are opposite God's commands. Because of Paul's deep care for Timothy he offers him advice on how to be a man of God.

1 Paul, an apostle of Christ Jesus by the command of God our Savior and of Christ Jesus our hope,

[2] To Timothy my true son in the faith:

Grace, mercy and peace from God the Father and Christ Jesus our Lord.

Timothy Charged to Oppose False Teachers

[3] As I urged you when I went into Macedonia, stay there in Ephesus so that you may command certain people not to teach false doctrines any longer [4] or to devote themselves to myths and endless genealogies. Such things promote controversial speculations rather than advancing God's work—which is by faith. [5] The goal of this command is love, which comes from a pure heart and a good conscience and a sincere faith. [6] Some have departed from these and have turned to meaningless talk. [7] They want to be teachers of the law, but they do not know what they are talking about or what they so confidently affirm.

[8] We know that the law is good if one uses it properly. [9] We also know that the law is made not for the righteous but for lawbreakers and rebels, the ungodly and sinful, the unholy and irreligious, for those who kill their fathers or mothers, for murderers, [10] for the sexually immoral, for those practicing homosexuality, for slave traders and liars and perjurers—and for whatever else is contrary to the sound doctrine [11] that conforms to the gospel concerning the glory of the blessed God, which he entrusted to me.

The Lord's Grace to Paul

[12] I thank Christ Jesus our Lord, who has given me strength, that he considered me trustworthy, appointing me to his service. [13] Even though I was once a blasphemer and a persecutor and a violent man, I was shown mercy because I acted in ignorance and unbelief. [14] The grace of our Lord was poured out on me abundantly, along with the faith and love that are in Christ Jesus.

[15] Here is a trustworthy saying that deserves full acceptance: Christ Jesus came into the world to save sinners—of whom I am the worst. [16] But for that very reason I was shown mercy so that in me, the worst of sinners, Christ Jesus might display his immense patience as an example for those who would believe in him and receive eternal life. [17] Now to the King eternal, immortal, invisible, the only God, be honor and glory for ever and ever. Amen.

The Charge to Timothy Renewed

[18] Timothy, my son, I am giving you this command in keeping with the prophecies once made about you, so that by recalling them you may fight the battle well, [19] holding on to faith and a good conscience, which some have rejected and so have suffered shipwreck with regard to the faith. [20] Among them are Hymenaeus and Alexander, whom I have handed over to Satan to be taught not to blaspheme.

Instructions on Worship

2 I urge, then, first of all, that petitions, prayers, intercession and thanksgiving be made for all people— [2] for kings and all those in authority, that we may live peaceful and quiet lives in all godliness and holiness. [3] This is good, and pleases God our Savior, [4] who wants all people to be saved and to come to a knowledge of the truth. [5] For there is one God and one mediator between God and mankind, the man Christ Jesus, [6] who gave himself as a ransom for all people. This has now been witnessed to at the proper time. [7] And for this purpose I was appointed a herald and an apostle—I am telling the truth, I am not lying—and a true and faithful teacher of the Gentiles.

[8] Therefore I want the men everywhere to pray, lifting up holy hands without anger or disputing. [9] I also want the women to dress modestly, with decency and propriety, adorning themselves, not with elaborate hairstyles or gold or pearls or expensive clothes, [10] but with good deeds, appropriate for women who profess to worship God.

[11] A woman[a] should learn in quietness and full submission. [12] I do not permit a woman to teach or to assume authori-

---

[a] 11 Or *wife*; also in verse 12

1 Timothy 2:1–8

God wants all people to be saved.

God commands us to pray. He wants us to offer all kinds of prayers for all kinds of people, especially for kings and other government authorities, "that we may live peaceful and quiet lives in all godliness and holiness" (1 Timothy 2:2). Those words might sound like a shallow prayer asking God for a comfortable life of heading to church and singing hymns. Yet the peace, quiet, godliness, and holiness that please God have a vastly bigger purpose. The apostle Paul lays it out: The Lord wants all people to realize the truth and be saved. God sent Jesus to bridge the gap between himself and human beings, and he aches for all people to have a chance to respond to his love. Calm surroundings can help that happen. So pray hard for your world. Then don't waste the opportunity to tell others about Jesus.

Think: How can you help fulfill God's desire for all people to be saved?

ROCK SOLID truths

ty over a man;[a] she must be quiet. [13]For Adam was formed first, then Eve. [14]And Adam was not the one deceived; it was the woman who was deceived and became a sinner. [15]But women[b] will be saved through childbearing—if they continue in faith, love and holiness with propriety.

Qualifications for Overseers and Deacons

3 Here is a trustworthy saying: Whoever aspires to be an overseer desires a noble task. [2]Now the overseer is to be above reproach, faithful to his wife, temperate, self-controlled, respectable, hospitable, able to teach, [3]not given to drunkenness, not violent but gentle, not quarrelsome, not a lover of money. [4]He must manage his own family well and see that his children obey him, and he must do so in a manner worthy of full[c] respect. [5](If anyone does not know how to manage his own family, how can he take care of God's church?) [6]He must not be a recent convert, or he may become conceited and fall under the same judgment as the devil. [7]He must also have a good reputation with outsiders, so that he will not fall into disgrace and into the devil's trap.

[8]In the same way, deacons[d] are to be worthy of respect, sincere, not indulging in much wine, and not pursuing dishonest gain. [9]They must keep hold of the deep truths of the faith with a clear conscience. [10]They must first be tested; and then if there is nothing against them, let them serve as deacons.

[11]In the same way, the women[e] are to be worthy of respect, not malicious talkers but temperate and trustworthy in everything.

[12]A deacon must be faithful to his wife and must manage his children and his household well. [13]Those who have served well gain an excellent standing and great assurance in their faith in Christ Jesus.

Reasons for Paul's Instructions

[14]Although I hope to come to you soon, I am writing you these instructions so that, [15]if I am delayed, you will know how people ought to conduct themselves in God's household, which is the church of the living God, the pillar and foundation of the truth. [16]Beyond all question, the mystery from which true godliness springs is great:

[a] 12 Or over her husband   [b] 15 Greek she
[c] 4 Or him with proper   [d] 8 The word deacons refers here to Christians designated to serve with the overseers/elders of the church in a variety of ways; similarly in verse 12; and in Romans 16:1 and Phil. 1:1.   [e] 11 Possibly deacons' wives or women who are deacons

He appeared in the flesh,
    was vindicated by the Spirit,[a]
was seen by angels,
    was preached among the nations,
was believed on in the world,
    was taken up in glory.

4

The Spirit clearly says that in later times some will abandon the faith and follow deceiving spirits and things taught by demons. [2] Such teachings come through hypocritical liars, whose consciences have been seared as with a hot iron. [3] They forbid people to marry and order them to abstain from certain foods, which God created to be received with thanksgiving by those who believe and who know the truth. [4] For everything God created is good, and nothing is to be rejected if it is received with thanksgiving, [5] because it is consecrated by the word of God and prayer.

[6] If you point these things out to the brothers and sisters,[b] you will be a good

ROCK SOLID *plans*

1 Timothy 3:1–16

Prepare to lead.

The apostle Paul never feared telling people to follow his lead, like when he said, "Follow my example, as I follow the example of Christ" (1 Corinthians 11:1). He often described the gifts and character traits needed by Christian leaders. You might not consider yourself a leader, but people watch you no matter where you go or what you do or say. You have an influence on others, whether you realize it or not. God may want you to step up as a leader right now—and to get ready for him to use you as a full-grown leader.

Your next step: Study the list of leadership qualities in 1 Timothy 3 and make a plan to grow in one of those areas.

ROCK SOLID *promises*

"Physical training is of some value, but godliness has value for all things, holding promise for both the present life and the life to come." 1 Timothy 4:8

Physical workouts matter. Spiritual workouts matter even more. Their benefits start now and last forever.

minister of Christ Jesus, nourished on the truths of the faith and of the good teaching that you have followed. [7] Have nothing to do with godless myths and old wives' tales; rather, train yourself to be godly. [8] For physical training is of some value, but godliness has value for all things, holding promise for both the present life and the life to come. [9] This is a trustworthy saying that deserves full acceptance. [10] That is why we labor and strive, because we have put our hope in the living God, who is the Savior of all people, and especially of those who believe.

[11] Command and teach these things. [12] Don't let anyone look down on you because you are young, but set an example for the believers in speech, in conduct, in love, in faith and in purity. [13] Until I come, devote yourself to the public reading of Scripture, to preaching and to teaching. [14] Do not neglect your gift, which was given you through prophecy when the body of elders laid their hands on you.

[15] Be diligent in these matters; give yourself wholly to them, so that everyone may see your progress. [16] Watch your life and doctrine closely. Persevere in them,

[a] 16 Or *vindicated in spirit*   [b] 6 The Greek word for *brothers and sisters* (*adelphoi*) refers here to believers, both men and women, as part of God's family.

ROCK SOLID
principles

1 Timothy 4:12

Don't let anyone look down on you.

Hannah wanted to scream. She had gone to a meeting at church only to watch the adults argue for more than an hour about the best way to care for the church lawn. Hannah planned to talk to church leadership about their neighborhood, where countless young kids spent hours alone at home after school while their parents worked. Hannah wanted to start a free afterschool program offering both fun and tutoring, but she needed a few adults to be part of the program. When the adults sent her home without an answer, Hannah didn't know where to turn for help. She just knew she wasn't going to give up.

Paul knew people might not take his young friend Timothy seriously as he worked to lead the church. So Paul told Timothy to excel at the core areas of following Jesus, "in speech, in conduct, in love, in faith and in purity" (1 Timothy 4:12). If you want to be part of God's work in the world, that's the plan to follow.

because if you do, you will save both yourself and your hearers.

Widows, Elders and Slaves

5 Do not rebuke an older man harshly, but exhort him as if he were your father. Treat younger men as brothers, ²older women as mothers, and younger women as sisters, with absolute purity.

³Give proper recognition to those widows who are really in need. ⁴But if a widow has children or grandchildren, these should learn first of all to put their religion into practice by caring for their own family and so repaying their parents and grandparents, for this is pleasing to God. ⁵The widow who is really in need and left all alone puts her hope in God and continues night and day to pray and to ask God for help. ⁶But the widow who lives for pleasure is dead even while she lives. ⁷Give the people these instructions, so that no one may be open to blame. ⁸Any-

one who does not provide for their relatives, and especially for their own household, has denied the faith and is worse than an unbeliever.

⁹No widow may be put on the list of widows unless she is over sixty, has been faithful to her husband, ¹⁰and is well known for her good deeds, such as bringing up children, showing hospitality, washing the feet of the Lord's people, helping those in trouble and devoting herself to all kinds of good deeds.

¹¹As for younger widows, do not put them on such a list. For when their sensual desires overcome their dedication to Christ, they want to marry. ¹²Thus they bring judgment on themselves, because they have broken their first pledge. ¹³Besides, they get into the habit of being idle and going about from house to house. And not only do they become idlers, but also busybodies who talk nonsense, saying things they ought not to. ¹⁴So I counsel younger widows to marry, to have

children, to manage their homes and to give the enemy no opportunity for slander. ¹⁵Some have in fact already turned away to follow Satan.

¹⁶If any woman who is a believer has widows in her care, she should continue to help them and not let the church be burdened with them, so that the church can help those widows who are really in need.

¹⁷The elders who direct the affairs of the church well are worthy of double honor, especially those whose work is preaching and teaching. ¹⁸For Scripture says, "Do not muzzle an ox while it is treading out the grain,"ᵃ and "The worker deserves his wages."ᵇ ¹⁹Do not entertain an accusa-tion against an elder unless it is brought by two or three witnesses. ²⁰But those elders who are sinning you are to reprove before everyone, so that the others may take warning. ²¹I charge you, in the sight of God and Christ Jesus and the elect angels, to keep these instructions without partiality, and to do nothing out of favoritism.

²²Do not be hasty in the laying on of hands, and do not share in the sins of others. Keep yourself pure.

²³Stop drinking only water, and use a little wine because of your stomach and your frequent illnesses.

ᵃ *18* Deut. 25:4   ᵇ *18* Luke 10:7

---

1 Timothy 5

Timothy grew into leadership.

Most characters in the New Testament plotline pass in and out with little detail provided about their lives. But the Bible informs us that Timothy was born to a non-Jewish dad and a Jewish-Christian mom named Eunice, and he was the grandson of Lois. Both mother and grandmother fed his faith (see 2 Timothy 1:5), and the apostle Paul says Timothy knew the Scriptures "from infancy" (2 Timothy 3:15).

Paul calls Timothy "my true son in the faith" (1 Timothy 1:2), so it's likely that Timothy came to believe in Jesus because of the apostle's preaching. Timothy soon became Paul's close partner, going along on missionary trips (see Acts 16:3) but also staying in places like Thessalonica and Philippi to train Christians.

Timothy must not have been born a forceful guy. He might have been fearful in Corinth (see 1 Corinthians 16:10). Paul instructed Timothy not to let anyone look down on him because of his age (see 1 Timothy 4:12) and to flee youthful lusts (see 2 Timothy 2:22).

Across the years of life and work, God made Timothy strong. Like Paul told him, "The Spirit God gave us does not make us timid, but gives us power, love and self-discipline" (2 Timothy 1:7). Timothy must have taken that message to heart as he led the church in Ephesus and signed on to several of Paul's letters. He proves that a young person can be completely committed to God.

You can find Timothy in Acts 16–20; 1 Corinthians 4:17; Philippians 2:19–24; 1 Thessalonians 3:1–9; Hebrews 13:23 and throughout 1 and 2 Timothy.

UNSHAKEN people

[24]The sins of some are obvious, reaching the place of judgment ahead of them; the sins of others trail behind them. [25]In the same way, good deeds are obvious, and even those that are not obvious cannot remain hidden forever.

6 All who are under the yoke of slavery should consider their masters worthy of full respect, so that God's name and our teaching may not be slandered. [2]Those who have believing masters should not show them disrespect just because they are fellow believers. Instead, they should serve them even better because their masters are dear to them as fellow believers and are devoted to the welfare[a] of their slaves.

False Teachers and the Love of Money

These are the things you are to teach and insist on. [3]If anyone teaches otherwise and does not agree to the sound instruction of our Lord Jesus Christ and to godly teaching, [4]they are conceited and understand nothing. They have an unhealthy interest in controversies and quarrels about words that result in envy, strife, malicious talk, evil suspicions [5]and constant friction between people of corrupt mind, who have been robbed of the truth and who think that godliness is a means to financial gain.

[6]But godliness with contentment is great gain. [7]For we brought nothing into the world, and we can take nothing out of it. [8]But if we have food and clothing, we will be content with that. [9]Those who want to get rich fall into temptation and a trap and into many foolish and harmful desires that plunge people into ruin and destruction. [10]For the love of money is a root of all kinds of evil. Some people, eager for money, have wandered from the faith and pierced themselves with many griefs.

Final Charge to Timothy

[11]But you, man of God, flee from all this, and pursue righteousness, godliness, faith, love, endurance and gentleness. [12]Fight the good fight of the faith. Take hold of the eternal life to which you were called when you made your good confession in the presence of many witnesses. [13]In the sight of God, who gives life to everything, and of Christ Jesus, who while testifying before Pontius Pilate made the good confession, I charge you [14]to keep this command without spot or blame until the appearing of our Lord Jesus Christ, [15]which God will bring about in his own time—God, the blessed and only Ruler, the King of kings and Lord of lords, [16]who alone is immortal and who lives in unapproachable light, whom no one has seen or can see. To him be honor and might forever. Amen.

[17]Command those who are rich in this present world not to be arrogant nor to put their hope in wealth, which is so uncertain, but to put their hope in God, who richly provides us with everything for our enjoyment. [18]Command them to do good, to be rich in good deeds, and to be generous and willing to share. [19]In this way they will lay up treasure for themselves as a firm foundation for the coming age, so that they may take hold of the life that is truly life.

[20]Timothy, guard what has been entrusted to your care. Turn away from godless chatter and the opposing ideas of what is falsely called knowledge, [21]which some have professed and in so doing have departed from the faith.

Grace be with you all.

[a] 2 Or *and benefit from the service*

ROCK SOLID
promises

"Godliness with contentment is great gain." 1 Timothy 6:6

Chasing money gets you nowhere. Being happy with what you have beats being filthy rich.

2 TIMOTHY

BOOK OUTLINE

Paul probably was arrested sometime after writing 1 Timothy and Titus, so he wrote his second letter to Timothy from Rome where he was a prisoner.

In this letter Paul seems to know that he will never be released from prison and that he will soon die. This is why he writes to Timothy.

Paul expresses his desire to see Timothy again and encourages Timothy to continue the missionary work after his death. He gives Timothy more instructions on how to lead a church and warns him to stay away from false teachers. He urges Timothy to be faithful to true Christian teachings.

Paul, an apostle of Christ Jesus by the will of God, in keeping with the promise of life that is in Christ Jesus,

[2] To Timothy, my dear son:

Grace, mercy and peace from God the Father and Christ Jesus our Lord.

Thanksgiving

[3] I thank God, whom I serve, as my ancestors did, with a clear conscience, as night and day I constantly remember you in my prayers. [4] Recalling your tears, I long to see you, so that I may be filled with joy. [5] I am reminded of your sincere faith, which first lived in your grandmother Lois and in your mother Eunice and, I am persuaded, now lives in you also.

Appeal for Loyalty to Paul and the Gospel

[6] For this reason I remind you to fan into flame the gift of God, which is in you through the laying on of my hands. [7] For the Spirit God gave us does not make us timid, but gives us power, love and self-discipline. [8] So do not be ashamed of the testimony about our Lord or of me his prisoner. Rather, join with me in suffering for the gospel, by the power of God. [9] He has saved us and called us to a holy life — not because of anything we have done but because of his own purpose and grace. This grace was given us in Christ Jesus before the beginning of time, [10] but it has now been revealed through the appearing of our Savior, Christ Jesus, who has destroyed death and has brought life and immortality to light through the gospel. [11] And of this gospel I was appointed a herald and an apostle and a teacher. [12] That is why I am suffering as I am. Yet this is no cause for shame, because I know whom I have believed, and am convinced that he is able to guard what I have entrusted to him until that day.

[13] What you heard from me, keep as the pattern of sound teaching, with faith and love in Christ Jesus. [14] Guard the good deposit that was entrusted to you — guard it with the help of the Holy Spirit who lives in us.

Examples of Disloyalty and Loyalty

[15] You know that everyone in the province of Asia has deserted me, including Phygelus and Hermogenes.

[16] May the Lord show mercy to the household of Onesiphorus, because he often refreshed me and was not ashamed of my chains. [17] On the contrary, when he was in Rome, he searched hard for me until he found me. [18] May the Lord grant that he will find mercy from the Lord on that day! You know very well in how many ways he helped me in Ephesus.

The Appeal Renewed

You then, my son, be strong in the grace that is in Christ Jesus. [2] And the things you have heard me say in the presence of many witnesses entrust to reliable people who will also be qualified to teach others. [3] Join with me in suffering, like a good soldier of Christ Jesus. [4] No one serving as a soldier gets entangled in civilian affairs, but rather tries to please his commanding officer. [5] Similarly, anyone who competes as an athlete does not receive the victor's crown except by competing according to the rules. [6] The hardworking farmer should be the first to

ROCK SOLID promises

"For the Spirit God gave us does not make us timid, but gives us power, love and self-discipline."

2 Timothy 1:7

God doesn't want you to go through life afraid. Count on him to pump you full of boldness, love and determination.

receive a share of the crops. [7]Reflect on what I am saying, for the Lord will give you insight into all this.

[8]Remember Jesus Christ, raised from the dead, descended from David. This is my gospel, [9]for which I am suffering even to the point of being chained like a criminal. But God's word is not chained. [10]Therefore I endure everything for the sake of the elect, that they too may obtain the salvation that is in Christ Jesus, with eternal glory.

[11]Here is a trustworthy saying:

If we died with him,
  we will also live with him;
[12]if we endure,
  we will also reign with him.
If we disown him,
  he will also disown us;
[13]if we are faithless,
  he remains faithful,
  for he cannot disown himself.

Dealing With False Teachers

[14]Keep reminding God's people of these things. Warn them before God against quarreling about words; it is of no value, and only ruins those who listen. [15]Do your best to present yourself to God as one approved, a worker who does not need to be ashamed and who correctly handles the word of truth. [16]Avoid godless chatter, because those who indulge in it will become more and more ungodly. [17]Their teaching will spread like gangrene. Among them are Hymenaeus and Philetus, [18]who have departed from the truth. They say that the resurrection has already taken place, and they destroy the faith of some. [19]Nevertheless, God's solid foundation stands firm, sealed with this inscription: "The Lord knows those who are his," and, "Everyone who confesses the name of the Lord must turn away from wickedness."

[20]In a large house there are articles not only of gold and silver, but also of wood and clay; some are for special purposes and some for common use. [21]Those who cleanse themselves from the latter will be instruments for special purposes, made

1434

ROCK SOLID promises

"The Lord knows those who are his." 2 Timothy 2:19

Because God made you his child, he won't ever forget to care for you or keep you on the right path.

holy, useful to the Master and prepared to do any good work.

[22]Flee the evil desires of youth and pursue righteousness, faith, love and peace, along with those who call on the Lord out of a pure heart. [23]Don't have anything to do with foolish and stupid arguments, because you know they produce quarrels. [24]And the Lord's servant must not be quarrelsome but must be kind to everyone, able to teach, not resentful. [25]Opponents must be gently instructed, in the hope that God will grant them repentance leading them to a knowledge of the truth, [26]and that they will come to their senses and escape from the trap of the devil, who has taken them captive to do his will.

3 But mark this: There will be terrible times in the last days. [2]People will be lovers of themselves, lovers of money, boastful, proud, abusive, disobedient to their parents, ungrateful, unholy, [3]without love, unforgiving, slanderous, without self-control, brutal, not lovers of the good, [4]treacherous, rash, conceited, lovers of pleasure rather than lovers of God— [5]having a form of godliness but denying its power. Have nothing to do with such people.

[6]They are the kind who worm their way into homes and gain control over gullible women, who are loaded down with sins and are swayed by all kinds of evil desires,

ROCK·SOLID *principles*

2 Timothy 2:20–22

Hold tight to Christian friends.

David wouldn't think of taking the football field all by himself—one guy battling eleven opposing team members. As talented as David might be on his own, he would get smeared across the turf without his teammates. David hadn't figured out, however, that he couldn't survive as a follower of Christ on his own either. So his youth pastor put it in terms David could understand. He needed direction from a coach, equipment from a trainer, help from teammates, and encouragement from a cheering crowd. Without each of those things, David was doomed. He would get beat badly.

The apostle Paul wasn't down on being young. But he knew it isn't easy to fight against the flow to obey God and become useful to him. You need to flee evil ... plus choose to live right, believe big, show love and peace ... and you do all that best along with faith-filled friends (see 2 Timothy 2:22). Don't settle for apathetic Christians as your spiritual partners. Look for peers who truly rely on God for help.

---

[7] always learning but never able to come to a knowledge of the truth. [8] Just as Jannes and Jambres opposed Moses, so also these teachers oppose the truth. They are men of depraved minds, who, as far as the faith is concerned, are rejected. [9] But they will not get very far because, as in the case of those men, their folly will be clear to everyone.

A Final Charge to Timothy

[10] You, however, know all about my teaching, my way of life, my purpose, faith, patience, love, endurance, [11] persecutions, sufferings—what kinds of things happened to me in Antioch, Iconium and Lystra, the persecutions I endured. Yet the Lord rescued me from all of them. [12] In fact, everyone who wants to live a godly life in Christ Jesus will be persecuted, [13] while evildoers and impostors will go from bad to worse, deceiving and being deceived. [14] But as for you, continue in what you have learned and have become

convinced of, because you know those from whom you learned it, [15] and how from infancy you have known the Holy Scriptures, which are able to make you wise for salvation through faith in Christ Jesus. [16] All Scripture is God-breathed and is useful for teaching, rebuking, correcting and training in righteousness, [17] so that the servant of God[a] may be thoroughly equipped for every good work.

4 In the presence of God and of Christ Jesus, who will judge the living and the dead, and in view of his appearing and his kingdom, I give you this charge: [2] Preach the word; be prepared in season and out of season; correct, rebuke and encourage—with great patience and careful instruction. [3] For the time will come when people will not put up with sound doctrine. Instead, to suit their own desires, they will gather around them a great number of teachers to say what their

[a] 17 Or *that you, a man of God,*

2 Timothy 3:10–16

The Bible teaches you what you need to know.

Suppose you're stranded alone on a deserted tropical island. A crate drifts ashore and inside you discover one lone book. No one would blame you for hoping for a jungle survival guide. But God designed the Bible as an equally indispensable book. The apostle Paul reminded his young friend Timothy that Timothy has known the Scriptures from the days he was a baby. Paul encouraged Timothy to stick to the truth he has learned, pushing him to look to Scripture to discover life's most important facts. The Bible makes us "wise for salvation through faith in Christ Jesus" (2 Timothy 3:15), teaching us how to be friends with God. It offers help in "teaching, rebuking, correcting and training in righteousness" (2 Timothy 3:16), providing us with everything we need to obey God. And the Bible is "God-breathed" (2 Timothy 3:16), giving us information we can stake our lives on.

Think: How will the Bible be indispensable in your life today?

ROCK SOLID truths

fight, I have finished the race, I have kept the faith. ⁸Now there is in store for me the crown of righteousness, which the Lord, the righteous Judge, will award to me on that day—and not only to me, but also to all who have longed for his appearing.

Personal Remarks

⁹Do your best to come to me quickly, ¹⁰for Demas, because he loved this world, has deserted me and has gone to Thessalonica. Crescens has gone to Galatia, and Titus to Dalmatia. ¹¹Only Luke is with me. Get Mark and bring him with you, because he is helpful to me in my ministry. ¹²I sent Tychicus to Ephesus. ¹³When you come, bring the cloak that I left with Carpus at Troas, and my scrolls, especially the parchments.

¹⁴Alexander the metalworker did me a great deal of harm. The Lord will repay him for what he has done. ¹⁵You too should be on your guard against him, because he strongly opposed our message.

¹⁶At my first defense, no one came to my support, but everyone deserted me. May it not be held against them. ¹⁷But the Lord stood at my side and gave me strength, so that through me the message might be fully proclaimed and all the Gentiles might hear it. And I was delivered from the lion's mouth. ¹⁸The Lord will rescue me from every evil attack and

ROCK SOLID promises

"The Lord will rescue me from every evil attack and will bring me safely to his heavenly kingdom."

2 Timothy 4:18

You can't escape evil hassles, but God gets you through and leads you all the way to heaven.

itching ears want to hear. ⁴They will turn their ears away from the truth and turn aside to myths. ⁵But you, keep your head in all situations, endure hardship, do the work of an evangelist, discharge all the duties of your ministry.

⁶For I am already being poured out like a drink offering, and the time for my departure is near. ⁷I have fought the good

will bring me safely to his heavenly kingdom. To him be glory for ever and ever. Amen.

Final Greetings

[19] Greet Priscilla[a] and Aquila and the household of Onesiphorus. [20] Erastus stayed in Corinth, and I left Trophimus sick in Miletus. [21] Do your best to get here before winter. Eubulus greets you, and so do Pudens, Linus, Claudia and all the brothers and sisters.[b]

[22] The Lord be with your spirit. Grace be with you all.

[a] *19* Greek *Prisca*, a variant of *Priscilla*
[b] *21* The Greek word for *brothers and sisters* (*adelphoi*) refers here to believers, both men and women, as part of God's family.

BOOK OUTLINE

Introduction
(1:1–4)

Duties of elders and deacons
(1:5–16)

Duties of a pastor
(2:1 — 3:11)

Conclusion
(3:12–15)

Titus was another friend and helper of Paul's. He had traveled with Paul on several missionary journeys, and was working as the leader of the church on the island of Crete. This letter is similar to the two letters Paul wrote to Timothy.

The church in Crete was an unorganized church, made up of people who needed much instruction in being Christians. Paul tells Titus and the church how God's people should behave. He tells Titus to teach the people the truth of God and instructs him in how to be a good church leader.

Paul, a servant of God and an apostle of Jesus Christ to further the faith of God's elect and their knowledge of the truth that leads to godliness— [2] in the hope of eternal life, which God, who does not lie, promised before the beginning of time, [3] and which now at his appointed season he has brought to light through the preaching entrusted to me by the command of God our Savior,

[4] To Titus, my true son in our common faith:

Grace and peace from God the Father and Christ Jesus our Savior.

Appointing Elders Who Love What Is Good

[5] The reason I left you in Crete was that you might put in order what was left unfinished and appoint[a] elders in every town, as I directed you. [6] An elder must be blameless, faithful to his wife, a man whose children believe[b] and are not open to the charge of being wild and disobedient. [7] Since an overseer manages God's household, he must be blameless—not overbearing, not quick-tempered, not given to drunkenness, not violent, not pursuing dishonest gain. [8] Rather, he must be hospitable, one who loves what is good, who is self-controlled, upright, holy and disciplined. [9] He must hold firmly to the trustworthy message as it has been taught, so that he can encourage others by sound doctrine and refute those who oppose it.

Rebuking Those Who Fail to Do Good

[10] For there are many rebellious people, full of meaningless talk and deception, especially those of the circumcision group. [11] They must be silenced, because they are disrupting whole households by teaching things they ought not to teach—and that for the sake of dishonest gain. [12] One of Crete's own prophets has said it: "Cretans are always liars, evil brutes, lazy gluttons."[c] [13] This saying is true. Therefore rebuke them sharply, so that they will be sound in the faith [14] and will pay no attention to Jewish myths or to the merely human commands of those who reject the truth. [15] To the pure, all things are pure, but to those who are corrupted and do not believe, nothing is pure. In fact, both their minds and consciences are corrupted. [16] They claim to know God, but by their actions they deny him. They are detestable, disobedient and unfit for doing anything good.

Doing Good for the Sake of the Gospel

2 You, however, must teach what is appropriate to sound doctrine. [2] Teach the older men to be temperate, worthy of respect, self-controlled, and sound in faith, in love and in endurance.

[3] Likewise, teach the older women to be reverent in the way they live, not to be slanderers or addicted to much wine, but to teach what is good. [4] Then they can

---

UNSHAKEN God

Titus 1:1–3

God is truthful.

The apostle Paul wanted truth—and nothing but truth. If he didn't have the correct facts about everything Jesus accomplished by dying on the cross, then he couldn't pass along the "knowledge of the truth that leads to godliness" (Titus 1:1). His hearers would miss out on a faith and knowledge resting "in the hope of eternal life" (Titus 1:2). But Paul confidently preached about Jesus because he was convinced of one fact: God doesn't lie. The Lord entrusted Paul with the complete truth about Jesus and his intense care for the world, so everyone can count on the good news about Jesus—including you.

So … Why does it matter that God will never lie to you?

---

[a] 5 Or *ordain*   [b] 6 Or *children are trustworthy*
[c] 12 From the Cretan philosopher Epimenides

urge the younger women to love their husbands and children, [5]to be self-controlled and pure, to be busy at home, to be kind, and to be subject to their husbands, so that no one will malign the word of God.

[6]Similarly, encourage the young men to be self-controlled. [7]In everything set them an example by doing what is good. In your teaching show integrity, seriousness [8]and soundness of speech that cannot be condemned, so that those who oppose you may be ashamed because they have nothing bad to say about us.

[9]Teach slaves to be subject to their masters in everything, to try to please them, not to talk back to them, [10]and not to steal from them, but to show that they can be fully trusted, so that in every way they will make the teaching about God our Savior attractive.

[11]For the grace of God has appeared that offers salvation to all people. [12]It teaches us to say "No" to ungodliness and worldly passions, and to live self-controlled, upright and godly lives in this present age, [13]while we wait for the blessed hope—the appearing of the glory of our great God and Savior, Jesus Christ, [14]who gave himself for us to redeem us from all wickedness and to purify for himself a people that are his very own, eager to do what is good.

[15]These, then, are the things you should teach. Encourage and rebuke with all authority. Do not let anyone despise you.

Saved in Order to Do Good

3 Remind the people to be subject to rulers and authorities, to be obedient, to be ready to do whatever is good, [2]to slander no one, to be peaceable and considerate, and always to be gentle toward everyone.

[3]At one time we too were foolish, disobedient, deceived and enslaved by all kinds of passions and pleasures. We lived in malice and envy, being hated and hating one another. [4]But when the kindness and love of God our Savior appeared, [5]he

ROCK SOLID principles

Titus 2:11–15

Say no to sin.

Sarah pushed her boyfriend away. In fact, she pushed Chris right out of her life, breaking off their relationship when he kept pressuring her to get involved physically. Sarah knew it was hypocritical to sin on purpose and then go running to God for forgiveness. So she counted on God to give her strength to say no to sexual sin. She also looked to him for courage to say a permanent "No!" to Chris by refusing to go out with him anymore. It felt stupid to toy with temptation every time she saw Chris when she had the power to stop the temptation altogether.

You might think God's grace gives you an excuse to say yes to sin. It actually teaches you to say no to disobedience. God saves you not just so you can have a ticket to heaven after you die but so you can live for him right now. He "gave himself for us to redeem us from all wickedness and to purify for himself a people that are his very own, eager to do what is good" (Titus 2:14).

saved us, not because of righteous things we had done, but because of his mercy. He saved us through the washing of rebirth and renewal by the Holy Spirit, [6]whom he poured out on us generously through Jesus Christ our Savior, [7]so that, having been justified by his grace, we might become heirs having the hope of eternal life. [8]This is a trustworthy saying. And I want you to stress these things, so that those who have trusted in God may be careful to devote themselves to doing what is good. These things are excellent and profitable for everyone.

[9]But avoid foolish controversies and genealogies and arguments and quarrels about the law, because these are unprofitable and useless. [10]Warn a divisive person once, and then warn them a second time. After that, have nothing to do with them. [11]You may be sure that such people are warped and sinful; they are self-condemned.

ROCK SOLID
promises

"When the kindness and love of God our Savior appeared, he saved us, not because of righteous things we had done, but because of his mercy." Titus 3:4–5

God doesn't save you because you're a phenomenal person. His mercy powers his kind love for you.

Final Remarks

[12]As soon as I send Artemas or Tychicus to you, do your best to come to me at Nicopolis, because I have decided to winter there. [13]Do everything you can to help Zenas the lawyer and Apollos on their way and see that they have everything they need. [14]Our people must learn to devote themselves to doing what is good, in order to provide for urgent needs and not live unproductive lives.

[15]Everyone with me sends you greetings. Greet those who love us in the faith.

Grace be with you all.

PHILEMON

Philemon was a leader of the church at Colossae and a friend of Paul's. Philemon's slave, Onesimus, had stolen money from him and had run away to Rome. While he was there he met Paul and became a Christian.

Paul sends Onesimus back to Philemon with this letter. He begs Philemon to forgive Onesimus and to treat him as a brother in Christ instead of as a runaway slave.

This short letter, along with Ephesians, Colossians and Philippians are often called the prison letters because they were written while Paul was in prison in Rome (about AD 59–61).

¹Paul, a prisoner of Christ Jesus, and Timothy our brother,

To Philemon our dear friend and fellow worker— ²also to Apphia our sister and Archippus our fellow soldier—and to the church that meets in your home:

³Grace and peace to you* from God our Father and the Lord Jesus Christ.

Thanksgiving and Prayer

⁴I always thank my God as I remember you in my prayers, ⁵because I hear about your love for all his holy people and your faith in the Lord Jesus. ⁶I pray that your partnership with us in the faith may be effective in deepening your understanding of every good thing we share for the sake of Christ. ⁷Your love has given me great joy and encouragement, because you, brother, have refreshed the hearts of the Lord's people.

Paul's Plea for Onesimus

⁸Therefore, although in Christ I could be bold and order you to do what you ought to do, ⁹yet I prefer to appeal to you on the basis of love. It is as none other than Paul—an old man and now also a prisoner of Christ Jesus— ¹⁰that I appeal to you for my son Onesimus,ᵇ who became my son while I was in chains. ¹¹Formerly he was useless to you, but now he has become useful both to you and to me.

¹²I am sending him—who is my very heart—back to you. ¹³I would have liked to keep him with me so that he could take your place in helping me while I am in chains for the gospel. ¹⁴But I did not want to do anything without your consent, so that any favor you do would not seem forced but would be voluntary. ¹⁵Perhaps the reason he was separated from you for a little while was that you might have him back forever— ¹⁶no longer as a slave, but better than a slave, as a dear brother. He is very dear to me but even dearer to you, both as a fellow man and as a brother in the Lord.

¹⁷So if you consider me a partner, welcome him as you would welcome me. ¹⁸If he has done you any wrong or owes you anything, charge it to me. ¹⁹I, Paul, am writing this with my own hand. I will pay it back—not to mention that you owe me your very self. ²⁰I do wish, brother, that I may have some benefit from you in the Lord; refresh my heart in Christ. ²¹Confident of your obedience, I write to you, knowing that you will do even more than I ask.

²²And one thing more: Prepare a guest room for me, because I hope to be restored to you in answer to your prayers.

²³Epaphras, my fellow prisoner in Christ Jesus, sends you greetings. ²⁴And so do Mark, Aristarchus, Demas and Luke, my fellow workers.

²⁵The grace of the Lord Jesus Christ be with your spirit.

*3 The Greek is plural; also in verses 22 and 25; elsewhere in this letter "you" is singular.
ᵇ 10 Onesimus means useful.

HEBREWS

BOOK OUTLINE

Christ—God's complete revelation
(1:1–3)

Christ—superior to the angels
(1:4—2:18)

Christ—superior to Moses and Joshua
(3:1—4:13)

Christ—the superior intercessor or priest
(4:14—7:28)

Christ's superior covenant and sacrifice
(8:1—10:18)

The practical appeal
(10:19—12:29)

Concluding advice
(13:1–25)

Although the author of Hebrews is unknown, this book was probably written in the late AD 60s. During this time persecution was a real problem for the church in Rome. This letter was most likely written to the Jewish Christians in either Palestine or Rome who were ready to give up their faith and return to the Jewish beliefs because of persecution.

The book of Hebrews was written to teach Jewish Christians that Christ is from God and is better than angels, Moses, Joshua or any priest. He is the ultimate high priest "designated by God to be high priest in the order of Melchizedek" (5:10). The author states that after Christ's death, the Old Testament sacrifices were no longer needed because Christ made the final sacrifice for all sin by dying himself.

Chapter 11 is the famous chapter that summarizes the lives of men and women of faith in the Old Testament. These summaries reminded the people of their heritage and gave the persecuted Christians great hope. The author encourages his readers to "hold firmly to the faith we profess" (4:14) and to trust in God.

God's Final Word: His Son

In the past God spoke to our ancestors through the prophets at many times and in various ways, [2]but in these last days he has spoken to us by his Son, whom he appointed heir of all things, and through whom also he made the universe. [3]The Son is the radiance of God's glory and the exact representation of his being, sustaining all things by his powerful word. After he had provided purification for sins, he sat down at the right hand of the Majesty in heaven. [4]So he became as much superior to the angels as the name he has inherited is superior to theirs.

The Son Superior to Angels

[5]For to which of the angels did God ever say,

"You are my Son;
    today I have become your
        Father"[a]?

Or again,

"I will be his Father,
    and he will be my Son"[b]?

[6]And again, when God brings his firstborn into the world, he says,

"Let all God's angels worship him."[c]

[7]In speaking of the angels he says,

"He makes his angels spirits,
    and his servants flames of fire."[d]

[8]But about the Son he says,

"Your throne, O God, will last for
    ever and ever;
    a scepter of justice will be the
        scepter of your kingdom.
[9]You have loved righteousness and
    hated wickedness;
    therefore God, your God, has set
        you above your companions
    by anointing you with the oil of
        joy."[e]

[10]He also says,

"In the beginning, Lord, you laid the
    foundations of the earth,

and the heavens are the work of
    your hands.
[11]They will perish, but you remain;
    they will all wear out like a
        garment.
[12]You will roll them up like a robe;
    like a garment they will be
        changed.
But you remain the same,
    and your years will never end."[f]

[13]To which of the angels did God ever say,

"Sit at my right hand
    until I make your enemies
        a footstool for your feet"[g]?

[14]Are not all angels ministering spirits sent to serve those who will inherit salvation?

Warning to Pay Attention

We must pay the most careful attention, therefore, to what we have heard, so that we do not drift away. [2]For since the message spoken through angels was binding, and every violation and disobedience received its just punishment, [3]how shall we escape if we ignore so great a salvation? This salvation, which was first announced by the Lord, was confirmed to us by those who heard him. [4]God also testified to it by signs, wonders and various miracles, and by gifts of the Holy Spirit distributed according to his will.

Jesus Made Fully Human

[5]It is not to angels that he has subjected the world to come, about which we are speaking. [6]But there is a place where someone has testified:

"What is mankind that you are
    mindful of them,
    a son of man that you care for him?
[7]You made them a little[b] lower than
    the angels;

---

[a] 5 Psalm 2:7   [b] 5 2 Samuel 7:14;
1 Chron. 17:13   [c] 6 Deut. 32:43 (see Dead
Sea Scrolls and Septuagint)   [d] 7 Psalm 104:4
[e] 9 Psalm 45:6,7   [f] 12 Psalm 102:25-27
[g] 13 Psalm 110:1   [h] 7 Or them for a little while

you crowned them with glory and
honor
8   and put everything under their
feet."[a],[b]

In putting everything under them,[c] God
left nothing that is not subject to them.[c]
Yet at present we do not see everything
subject to them.[c] 9But we do see Jesus,
who was made lower than the angels for a
little while, now crowned with glory and
honor because he suffered death, so that
by the grace of God he might taste death
for everyone.

10In bringing many sons and daughters
to glory, it was fitting that God, for whom
and through whom everything exists,
should make the pioneer of their salvation
perfect through what he suffered. 11Both
the one who makes people holy and those
who are made holy are of the same family. So Jesus is not ashamed to call them
brothers and sisters.[d] 12He says,

"I will declare your name to my
brothers and sisters;
in the assembly I will sing your
praises."[e]

13And again,

"I will put my trust in him."[f]

And again he says,

"Here am I, and the children God has
given me."[g]

14Since the children have flesh and
blood, he too shared in their humanity so
that by his death he might break the power of him who holds the power of death—
that is, the devil— 15and free those who
all their lives were held in slavery by their
fear of death. 16For surely it is not angels
he helps, but Abraham's descendants.
17For this reason he had to be made like
them,[h] fully human in every way, in order that he might become a merciful and
faithful high priest in service to God, and
that he might make atonement for the sins
of the people. 18Because he himself suffered when he was tempted, he is able to
help those who are being tempted.

ROCK SOLID *promises*

"Because he himself suffered when he was tempted, he is able to help those who are being tempted."

Hebrews 2:18

Jesus hurts with you when you feel lured to do wrong, because he too was tempted. You can ask him for help.

Jesus Greater Than Moses

3 Therefore, holy brothers and sisters,
who share in the heavenly calling,
fix your thoughts on Jesus, whom
we acknowledge as our apostle and high
priest. 2He was faithful to the one who
appointed him, just as Moses was faithful
in all God's house. 3Jesus has been found
worthy of greater honor than Moses, just
as the builder of a house has greater honor
than the house itself. 4For every house is
built by someone, but God is the builder of
everything. 5"Moses was faithful as a servant in all God's house,"[i] bearing witness
to what would be spoken by God in the
future. 6But Christ is faithful as the Son
over God's house. And we are his house,
if indeed we hold firmly to our confidence
and the hope in which we glory.

Warning Against Unbelief

7So, as the Holy Spirit says:

"Today, if you hear his voice,
8   do not harden your hearts

a 6-8 Psalm 8:4-6   *b 7,8* Or *7You made him a
little lower than the angels;/ you crowned him with
glory and honor/ 8and put everything under his feet."*
c 8 Or *him*   *d 11* The Greek word for *brothers
and sisters (adelphoi)* refers here to believers, both
men and women, as part of God's family; also in
verse 12; and in 3:1, 12; 10:19; 13:22.
e 12 Psalm 22:22   *f 13* Isaiah 8:17
g 13 Isaiah 8:18   *h 17* Or *like his brothers*
i 5 Num. 12:7

as you did in the rebellion,
during the time of testing in the
wilderness,
[9] where your ancestors tested and tried
me,
though for forty years they saw
what I did.
[10] That is why I was angry with that
generation;
I said, 'Their hearts are always
going astray,
and they have not known my
ways.'
[11] So I declared on oath in my anger,
'They shall never enter my
rest.'"[a]

[12] See to it, brothers and sisters, that none of you has a sinful, unbelieving heart that turns away from the living God. [13] But encourage one another daily, as long as it is called "Today," so that none of you may be hardened by sin's deceitfulness. [14] We have come to share in Christ, if indeed we hold our original conviction firmly to the very end. [15] As has just been said:

"Today, if you hear his voice,
do not harden your hearts
as you did in the rebellion."[b]

[16] Who were they who heard and rebelled? Were they not all those Moses led out of Egypt? [17] And with whom was he angry for forty years? Was it not with those who sinned, whose bodies perished in the wilderness? [18] And to whom did God swear that they would never enter his rest if not to those who disobeyed? [19] So we see that they were not able to enter, because of their unbelief.

A Sabbath-Rest for the People of God

4 Therefore, since the promise of entering his rest still stands, let us be careful that none of you be found to have fallen short of it. [2] For we also have had the good news proclaimed to us, just as they did; but the message they heard was of no value to them, because they did not share the faith of those who obeyed.[c] [3] Now we who have believed enter that rest, just as God has said,

"So I declared on oath in my anger,
'They shall never enter my rest.'"[d]

And yet his works have been finished since the creation of the world. [4] For somewhere he has spoken about the seventh day in these words: "On the seventh day God rested from all his works."[e] [5] And again in the passage above he says, "They shall never enter my rest."

[6] Therefore since it still remains for some to enter that rest, and since those who formerly had the good news proclaimed to them did not go in because of their disobedience, [7] God again set a certain day, calling it "Today." This he did when a long time later he spoke through David, as in the passage already quoted:

"Today, if you hear his voice,
do not harden your hearts."[b]

[8] For if Joshua had given them rest, God would not have spoken later about another day. [9] There remains, then, a Sabbath-rest for the people of God; [10] for anyone who enters God's rest also rests from their works,[f] just as God did from his. [11] Let us, therefore, make every effort to enter that rest, so that no one will perish by following their example of disobedience.

[12] For the word of God is alive and active. Sharper than any double-edged sword, it penetrates even to dividing soul and spirit, joints and marrow; it judges the thoughts and attitudes of the heart. [13] Nothing in all creation is hidden from God's sight. Everything is uncovered and laid bare before the eyes of him to whom we must give account.

Jesus the Great High Priest

[14] Therefore, since we have a great high priest who has ascended into heaven,[g] Jesus the Son of God, let us hold firmly to the faith we profess. [15] For we do not have a high priest who is unable to empathize with our weaknesses, but we have

[a] 11 Psalm 95:7-11   [b] 15,7 Psalm 95:7,8
[c] 2 Some manuscripts *because those who heard did not combine it with faith*   [d] 3 Psalm 95:11; also in verse 5   [e] 4 Gen. 2:2   [f] 10 Or *labor*
[g] 14 Greek *has gone through the heavens*

Hebrews 4:12–13

The Bible reveals the real you.

Opening the Bible can often be like chatting with a friend to get encouragement. Or asking a teacher for instruction. Or seeking guidance from a parent. Yet reading Scripture can also feel like getting cut open by a surgeon. The Bible is no ordinary book. This "alive and active" book is powered by the Holy Spirit, making its message "sharper than any double-edged sword" (Hebrews 4:12). It slices open your innermost parts like a scalpel splitting your joints and bones, exposing not just your thoughts but your innermost feelings and intentions. You might wonder why you shouldn't skip over the parts of the Bible that pointedly tell you to quit sinning or challenge you to live more for God. Just remember that God never uses the Bible to cause pain for the sake of pain. Like a surgeon, he only hurts in order to heal.

Think: Do you avoid the challenging parts of the Bible? How can you make sure you don't skip those sections?

ROCK SOLID truths

astray, since he himself is subject to weakness. [3]This is why he has to offer sacrifices for his own sins, as well as for the sins of the people. [4]And no one takes this honor on himself, but he receives it when called by God, just as Aaron was.

[5]In the same way, Christ did not take on himself the glory of becoming a high priest. But God said to him,

"You are my Son;
today I have become your Father."[a]

[6]And he says in another place,

"You are a priest forever,
in the order of Melchizedek."[b]

[7]During the days of Jesus' life on earth, he offered up prayers and petitions with fervent cries and tears to the one who could save him from death, and he was heard because of his reverent submission. [8]Son though he was, he learned obedience from what he suffered [9]and, once made perfect, he became the source of eternal salvation for all who obey him [10]and was designated by God to be high priest in the order of Melchizedek.

Warning Against Falling Away

[11]We have much to say about this, but it is hard to make it clear to you because you no longer try to understand. [12]In fact, though by this time you ought to be teachers, you need someone to teach you the elementary truths of God's word all over again. You need milk, not solid food! [13]Anyone who lives on milk, being still an infant, is not acquainted with the teaching about righteousness. [14]But solid food is for the mature, who by constant use have trained themselves to distinguish good from evil.

6 Therefore let us move beyond the elementary teachings about Christ and be taken forward to maturity, not laying again the foundation of repentance from acts that lead to death,[c] and of faith in God, [2]instruction about cleansing rites,[d] the laying on of hands, the resur-

one who has been tempted in every way, just as we are—yet he did not sin. [16]Let us then approach God's throne of grace with confidence, so that we may receive mercy and find grace to help us in our time of need.

5 Every high priest is selected from among the people and is appointed to represent the people in matters related to God, to offer gifts and sacrifices for sins. [2]He is able to deal gently with those who are ignorant and are going

a 5 Psalm 2:7   *b 6* Psalm 110:4   *c 1* Or *from useless rituals*   *d 2* Or *about baptisms* rection of the dead, and eternal judgment. ³And God permitting, we will do so.

⁴It is impossible for those who have once been enlightened, who have tasted the heavenly gift, who have shared in the Holy Spirit, ⁵who have tasted the goodness of the word of God and the powers of the coming age ⁶and who have fallen[a] away, to be brought back to repentance. To their loss they are crucifying the Son of God all over again and subjecting him to public disgrace. ⁷Land that drinks in

---

ROCK SOLID promises

"God is not unjust; he will not forget your work and the love you have shown him as you have helped his people and continue to help them." **Hebrews 6:10**

God won't overlook how you pour your life into others—in the past, now, and in the future.

---

the rain often falling on it and that produces a crop useful to those for whom it is farmed receives the blessing of God. ⁸But land that produces thorns and thistles is worthless and is in danger of being cursed. In the end it will be burned.

⁹Even though we speak like this, dear friends, we are convinced of better things in your case—the things that have to do with salvation. ¹⁰God is not unjust; he will not forget your work and the love you have shown him as you have helped his people and continue to help them. ¹¹We want each of you to show this same diligence to the very end, so that what you hope for may be fully realized. ¹²We do not want you to become lazy, but to imitate those who through faith and patience inherit what has been promised.

The Certainty of God's Promise

¹³When God made his promise to Abraham, since there was no one greater for him to swear by, he swore by himself, ¹⁴saying, "I will surely bless you and give you many descendants."[b] ¹⁵And so after waiting patiently, Abraham received what was promised.

¹⁶People swear by someone greater than themselves, and the oath confirms what is said and puts an end to all argument.

Hebrews 4:15–16

You can count on help from Jesus.

God might be the last person you count on for help when you're in a tough spot. But he's actually the first one to run to. Better than anyone else on earth, Jesus knows exactly what you are going through. Surprisingly, he didn't get to take an easy path through life. The Bible says the fully-human Jesus was made "perfect" or "complete" through suffering (Hebrews 2:10). He isn't ashamed to be known as our "brother" (Hebrews 2:11). He shared our humanity, and he's like us "in every way" (Hebrews 2:14–17). He is our "great high priest," the one who stands watch in heaven reminding our enemies that our sins are forgiven (Hebrews 4:14). Because Jesus was tempted in every way like us—yet didn't give in to sin—we can go to him confidently. When we do, we always "receive mercy and find grace to help us in our time of need" (Hebrews 4:16).

Think: Why can you count on Jesus for help—no matter what you need?

ROCK SOLID truths

---

[a] 6 Or *age,* ⁶*if they fall*   [b] 14 Gen. 22:17

[17]Because God wanted to make the unchanging nature of his purpose very clear to the heirs of what was promised, he confirmed it with an oath. [18]God did this so that, by two unchangeable things in which it is impossible for God to lie, we who have fled to take hold of the hope set before us may be greatly encouraged. [19]We have this hope as an anchor for the soul, firm and secure. It enters the inner sanctuary behind the curtain, [20]where our forerunner, Jesus, has entered on our behalf. He has become a high priest forever, in the order of Melchizedek.

Melchizedek the Priest

7 This Melchizedek was king of Salem and priest of God Most High. He met Abraham returning from the defeat of the kings and blessed him, [2]and Abraham gave him a tenth of everything. First, the name Melchizedek means "king of righteousness"; then also, "king of Salem" means "king of peace." [3]Without father or mother, without genealogy, without beginning of days or end of life, resembling the Son of God, he remains a priest forever.

[4]Just think how great he was: Even the patriarch Abraham gave him a tenth of the plunder! [5]Now the law requires the descendants of Levi who become priests to collect a tenth from the people—that is, from their fellow Israelites—even though they also are descended from Abraham. [6]This man, however, did not trace his descent from Levi, yet he collected a tenth from Abraham and blessed him who had the promises. [7]And without doubt the lesser is blessed by the greater. [8]In the one case, the tenth is collected by people who die; but in the other case, by him who is declared to be living. [9]One might even say that Levi, who collects the tenth, paid the tenth through Abraham, [10]because when Melchizedek met Abraham, Levi was still in the body of his ancestor.

Jesus Like Melchizedek

[11]If perfection could have been attained through the Levitical priesthood—and indeed the law given to the people established that priesthood—why was there still need for another priest to come, one in the order of Melchizedek, not in the order of Aaron? [12]For when the priesthood is changed, the law must be changed also. [13]He of whom these things are said belonged to a different tribe, and no one from that tribe has ever served at the altar. [14]For it is clear that our Lord descended from Judah, and in regard to that tribe Moses said nothing about priests. [15]And what we have said is even more clear if another priest like Melchizedek appears, [16]one who has become a priest not on the basis of a regulation as to his ancestry but on the basis of the power of an indestructible life. [17]For it is declared:

> "You are a priest forever,
>   in the order of Melchizedek."[a]

[18]The former regulation is set aside because it was weak and useless [19](for the law made nothing perfect), and a better hope is introduced, by which we draw near to God.

[20]And it was not without an oath! Others became priests without any oath, [21]but he became a priest with an oath when God said to him:

> "The Lord has sworn
>   and will not change his mind:
>   'You are a priest forever.'"[a]

[22]Because of this oath, Jesus has become the guarantor of a better covenant.

[23]Now there have been many of those priests, since death prevented them from continuing in office; [24]but because Jesus lives forever, he has a permanent priesthood. [25]Therefore he is able to save completely[b] those who come to God through him, because he always lives to intercede for them.

[26]Such a high priest truly meets our need—one who is holy, blameless, pure, set apart from sinners, exalted above the heavens. [27]Unlike the other high priests, he does not need to offer sacrifices day after day, first for his own sins, and then

---

[a] 17,21 Psalm 110:4   [b] 25 Or forever

for the sins of the people. He sacrificed for their sins once for all when he offered himself. [28] For the law appoints as high priests men in all their weakness; but the oath, which came after the law, appointed the Son, who has been made perfect forever.

The High Priest of a New Covenant

8 Now the main point of what we are saying is this: We do have such a high priest, who sat down at the right hand of the throne of the Majesty in heaven, [2] and who serves in the sanctuary, the true tabernacle set up by the Lord, not by a mere human being.

[3] Every high priest is appointed to offer both gifts and sacrifices, and so it was necessary for this one also to have something to offer. [4] If he were on earth, he would not be a priest, for there are already priests who offer the gifts prescribed by the law. [5] They serve at a sanctuary that is a copy and shadow of what is in heaven. This is why Moses was warned when he was about to build the tabernacle: "See to it that you make everything according to the pattern shown you on the mountain."[a] [6] But in fact the ministry Jesus has received is as superior to theirs as the covenant of which he is mediator is superior to the old one, since the new covenant is established on better promises.

[7] For if there had been nothing wrong with that first covenant, no place would have been sought for another. [8] But God found fault with the people and said[b]:

"The days are coming, declares the Lord,
when I will make a new covenant
with the people of Israel
and with the people of Judah.
[9] It will not be like the covenant
I made with their ancestors
when I took them by the hand
to lead them out of Egypt,
because they did not remain faithful
to my covenant,
and I turned away from them,
declares the Lord.

[10] This is the covenant I will establish
with the people of Israel
after that time, declares the Lord.
I will put my laws in their minds
and write them on their hearts.
I will be their God,
and they will be my people.
[11] No longer will they teach their neighbor,
or say to one another, 'Know the Lord,'
because they will all know me,
from the least of them to the greatest.
[12] For I will forgive their wickedness
and will remember their sins no more."[c]

[13] By calling this covenant "new," he has made the first one obsolete; and what is obsolete and outdated will soon disappear.

Worship in the Earthly Tabernacle

9 Now the first covenant had regulations for worship and also an earthly sanctuary. [2] A tabernacle was set up. In its first room were the lampstand and the table with its consecrated bread; this was called the Holy Place. [3] Behind the second curtain was a room called the Most Holy Place, [4] which had the golden altar of incense and the gold-covered ark of the covenant. This ark contained the gold jar of manna, Aaron's staff that had budded, and the stone tablets of the covenant. [5] Above the ark were the cherubim of the Glory, overshadowing the atonement cover. But we cannot discuss these things in detail now.

[6] When everything had been arranged like this, the priests entered regularly into the outer room to carry on their ministry. [7] But only the high priest entered the inner room, and that only once a year, and never without blood, which he offered for himself and for the sins the people had committed in ignorance. [8] The Holy Spirit was showing by this that the way into the Most Holy Place had not yet been

---

[a] 5 Exodus 25:40   [b] 8 Some manuscripts may be translated *fault and said to the people.*
[c] 12 Jer. 31:31-34

disclosed as long as the first tabernacle was still functioning. [9]This is an illustration for the present time, indicating that the gifts and sacrifices being offered were not able to clear the conscience of the worshiper. [10]They are only a matter of food and drink and various ceremonial washings—external regulations applying until the time of the new order.

The Blood of Christ

[11]But when Christ came as high priest of the good things that are now already here,[a] he went through the greater and more perfect tabernacle that is not made with human hands, that is to say, is not a part of this creation. [12]He did not enter by means of the blood of goats and calves; but he entered the Most Holy Place once for all by his own blood, thus obtaining[b] eternal redemption. [13]The blood of goats and bulls and the ashes of a heifer sprinkled on those who are ceremonially unclean sanctify them so that they are outwardly clean. [14]How much more, then, will the blood of Christ, who through the eternal Spirit offered himself unblemished to God, cleanse our consciences from acts that lead to death,[c] so that we may serve the living God!

[15]For this reason Christ is the mediator of a new covenant, that those who are called may receive the promised eternal inheritance—now that he has died as a ransom to set them free from the sins committed under the first covenant.

[16]In the case of a will,[d] it is necessary to prove the death of the one who made it, [17]because a will is in force only when somebody has died; it never takes effect while the one who made it is living. [18]This is why even the first covenant was not put into effect without blood. [19]When Moses had proclaimed every command of the law to all the people, he took the blood of calves, together with water, scarlet wool and branches of hyssop, and sprinkled the scroll and all the people. [20]He said, "This is the blood of the covenant, which God has commanded you to keep."[e] [21]In the same way, he sprinkled with the blood

both the tabernacle and everything used in its ceremonies. [22]In fact, the law requires that nearly everything be cleansed with blood, and without the shedding of blood there is no forgiveness.

[23]It was necessary, then, for the copies of the heavenly things to be purified with these sacrifices, but the heavenly

[a] 11 Some early manuscripts *are to come*
[b] 12 Or *blood, having obtained*   [c] 14 Or *from useless rituals*   [d] 16 Same Greek word as *covenant*; also in verse 17   [e] 20 Exodus 24:8

Hebrews 9:11–28

Jesus died for your sin.

Old Testament law gave instructions for bulls and goats to be sacrificed once a year on the Day of Atonement to pay for people's sins (see Leviticus 16:1–34). For centuries the highest ranking priest offered these sacrifices as a bloody reminder of an enormous truth—that "without the shedding of blood there is no forgiveness" (Hebrews 9:22). These sacrifices, however, couldn't permanently fix the problem of sin. Like the New Testament says, "It is impossible for the blood of bulls and goats to take away sins" (Hebrews 10:4). So God gave humankind a better solution. He sent his Son, Jesus, to die on the cross. That death wasn't a random tragedy or the result of a sentence handed down by an ancient Roman government. Jesus died as part of God's plan. He "was sacrificed once to take away the sins of many" (Hebrews 9:28). His death was payment for your sins and the sins of every human being.

Think: Why did Jesus die?

ROCK SOLID truths

things themselves with better sacrifices than these. ²⁴For Christ did not enter a sanctuary made with human hands that was only a copy of the true one; he entered heaven itself, now to appear for us in God's presence. ²⁵Nor did he enter heaven to offer himself again and again, the way the high priest enters the Most Holy Place every year with blood that is not his own. ²⁶Otherwise Christ would have had to suffer many times since the creation of the world. But he has appeared once for all at the culmination of the ages to do away with sin by the sacrifice of himself. ²⁷Just as people are destined to die once, and after that to face judgment, ²⁸so Christ was sacrificed once to take away the sins of many; and he will appear a second time, not to bear sin, but to bring salvation to those who are waiting for him.

Christ's Sacrifice Once for All

10 The law is only a shadow of the good things that are coming— not the realities themselves. For this reason it can never, by the same sacrifices repeated endlessly year after year, make perfect those who draw near to worship. ²Otherwise, would they not have stopped being offered? For the worshipers would have been cleansed once for all, and would no longer have felt guilty for their sins. ³But those sacrifices are an annual reminder of sins. ⁴It is impossible for the blood of bulls and goats to take away sins.

⁵Therefore, when Christ came into the world, he said:

"Sacrifice and offering you did not desire,
    but a body you prepared for me;
⁶with burnt offerings and sin offerings
    you were not pleased.
⁷Then I said, 'Here I am—it is written
    about me in the scroll—
I have come to do your will, my
    God.'"ᵃ

⁸First he said, "Sacrifices and offerings, burnt offerings and sin offerings you did not desire, nor were you pleased with them"—though they were offered in ac-

cordance with the law. ⁹Then he said, "Here I am, I have come to do your will." He sets aside the first to establish the second. ¹⁰And by that will, we have been made holy through the sacrifice of the body of Jesus Christ once for all.

¹¹Day after day every priest stands and performs his religious duties; again and again he offers the same sacrifices, which can never take away sins. ¹²But when this priest had offered for all time one sacrifice for sins, he sat down at the right hand of God, ¹³and since that time he waits for his enemies to be made his footstool. ¹⁴For by one sacrifice he has made perfect forever those who are being made holy.

¹⁵The Holy Spirit also testifies to us about this. First he says:

¹⁶"This is the covenant I will make with
    them
    after that time, says the Lord.
I will put my laws in their hearts,
    and I will write them on their
      minds."ᵇ

¹⁷Then he adds:

"Their sins and lawless acts
    I will remember no more."ᶜ

¹⁸And where these have been forgiven, sacrifice for sin is no longer necessary.

A Call to Persevere in Faith

¹⁹Therefore, brothers and sisters, since we have confidence to enter the Most Holy Place by the blood of Jesus, ²⁰by a new and living way opened for us through the curtain, that is, his body, ²¹and since we have a great priest over the house of God, ²²let us draw near to God with a sincere heart and with the full assurance that faith brings, having our hearts sprinkled to cleanse us from a guilty conscience and having our bodies washed with pure water. ²³Let us hold unswervingly to the hope we profess, for he who promised is faithful. ²⁴And let us consider how we may spur one another on toward love and good deeds, ²⁵not giving up meeting together,

---

ᵃ 7 Psalm 40:6-8 (see Septuagint)
ᵇ 16 Jer. 31:33   ᶜ 17 Jer. 31:34

ROCK SOLID
promises

"Let us draw near to God with a sincere heart and with the full assurance that faith brings, having our hearts sprinkled to cleanse us from a guilty conscience."

Hebrews 10:22

Because of Jesus, you can get close to God without fear. Because you're forgiven, nothing stands between you and God.

as some are in the habit of doing, but encouraging one another—and all the more as you see the Day approaching.

²⁶If we deliberately keep on sinning after we have received the knowledge of the truth, no sacrifice for sins is left, ²⁷but only a fearful expectation of judgment and of raging fire that will consume the enemies of God. ²⁸Anyone who rejected the law of Moses died without mercy on the testimony of two or three witnesses. ²⁹How much more severely do you think someone deserves to be punished who has trampled the Son of God underfoot, who has treated as an unholy thing the blood of the covenant that sanctified them, and who has insulted the Spirit of grace? ³⁰For we know him who said, "It is mine to avenge; I will repay,"ᵃ and again, "The Lord will judge his people."ᵇ ³¹It is a dreadful thing to fall into the hands of the living God.

³²Remember those earlier days after you had received the light, when you endured in a great conflict full of suffering. ³³Sometimes you were publicly exposed to insult and persecution; at other times you stood side by side with those who were so treated. ³⁴You suffered along with those in prison and joyfully accepted the confiscation of your property, because you knew that you yourselves had better and lasting

possessions. ³⁵So do not throw away your confidence; it will be richly rewarded.

³⁶You need to persevere so that when you have done the will of God, you will receive what he has promised. ³⁷For,

"In just a little while,
    he who is coming will come
    and will not delay."ᶜ

³⁸And,

"But my righteousᵈ one will live by
    faith.
And I take no pleasure
    in the one who shrinks back."ᵉ

³⁹But we do not belong to those who shrink back and are destroyed, but to those who have faith and are saved.

Faith in Action

11 Now faith is confidence in what we hope for and assurance about what we do not see. ²This is what the ancients were commended for.

³By faith we understand that the universe was formed at God's command, so that what is seen was not made out of what was visible.

⁴By faith Abel brought God a better offering than Cain did. By faith he was commended as righteous, when God spoke well of his offerings. And by faith Abel still speaks, even though he is dead.

⁵By faith Enoch was taken from this life, so that he did not experience death: "He could not be found, because God had taken him away."ᶠ For before he was taken, he was commended as one who pleased God. ⁶And without faith it is impossible to please God, because anyone who comes to him must believe that he exists and that he rewards those who earnestly seek him.

⁷By faith Noah, when warned about things not yet seen, in holy fear built an ark to save his family. By his faith he condemned the world and became heir of the righteousness that is in keeping with faith.

ᵃ *30* Deut. 32:35   ᵇ *30* Deut. 32:36; Psalm 135:14   ᶜ *37* Isaiah 26:20; Hab. 2:3
ᵈ *38* Some early manuscripts *But the righteous*
ᵉ *38* Hab. 2:4 (see Septuagint)   ᶠ *5* Gen. 5:24

Hebrews 10:24–25

Share and care.

Shane hadn't cried in front of anyone since his dog had died years before. But as a group of guys and girls confronted his nonstop barrage of practical jokes and sarcastic words, he broke down. Sure, he felt ganged-up on. He wondered why it took a dozen people to point out his problem. Each person in the room explained how Shane had hurt them, then the group offered a couple suggestions of how he could act differently. Soon Shane felt the deep care of the whole group. They were all tired of his obnoxious behavior, but they also wanted to stop him from making himself an outcast.

It's impossible to "do" faith alone. You're like one part of a body that needs every part to function (see 1 Corinthians 12:1–31). You need partners to help you ditch evil and chase God (see 2 Timothy 2:22). God wants you to make getting together to grow with other Christians a habit you don't break. And when you're together, make it your priority to push one another to show love and do good.

[8] By faith Abraham, when called to go to a place he would later receive as his inheritance, obeyed and went, even though he did not know where he was going. [9] By faith he made his home in the promised land like a stranger in a foreign country; he lived in tents, as did Isaac and Jacob, who were heirs with him of the same promise. [10] For he was looking forward to the city with foundations, whose architect and builder is God. [11] And by faith even Sarah, who was past childbearing age, was enabled to bear children because she[a] considered him faithful who had made the promise. [12] And so from this one man, and he as good as dead, came descendants as numerous as the stars in the sky and as countless as the sand on the seashore.

[13] All these people were still living by faith when they died. They did not receive the things promised; they only saw them and welcomed them from a distance, admitting that they were foreigners and strangers on earth. [14] People who say such things show that they are looking for a country of their own. [15] If they had been thinking of the country they had left, they would have had opportunity to return. [16] Instead, they were longing for a better country—a heavenly one. Therefore God is not ashamed to be called their God, for he has prepared a city for them.

[17] By faith Abraham, when God tested him, offered Isaac as a sacrifice. He who had embraced the promises was about to sacrifice his one and only son, [18] even though God had said to him, "It is through Isaac that your offspring will be reckoned."[b] [19] Abraham reasoned that God could even raise the dead, and so in a manner of speaking he did receive Isaac back from death.

[20] By faith Isaac blessed Jacob and Esau in regard to their future.

[a] *11 Or By faith Abraham, even though he was too old to have children—and Sarah herself was not able to conceive—was enabled to become a father because he* [b] *18 Gen. 21:12*

²¹ By faith Jacob, when he was dying, blessed each of Joseph's sons, and worshiped as he leaned on the top of his staff.

²² By faith Joseph, when his end was near, spoke about the exodus of the Israelites from Egypt and gave instructions concerning the burial of his bones.

²³ By faith Moses' parents hid him for three months after he was born, because they saw he was no ordinary child, and they were not afraid of the king's edict.

²⁴ By faith Moses, when he had grown up, refused to be known as the son of Pharaoh's daughter. ²⁵ He chose to be mistreated along with the people of God rather than to enjoy the fleeting pleasures of sin. ²⁶ He regarded disgrace for the sake of Christ as of greater value than the treasures of Egypt, because he was looking ahead to his reward. ²⁷ By faith he left Egypt, not fearing the king's anger; he persevered because he saw him who is invisible. ²⁸ By faith he kept the Passover and the application of blood, so that the destroyer of the firstborn would not touch the firstborn of Israel.

²⁹ By faith the people passed through the Red Sea as on dry land; but when the Egyptians tried to do so, they were drowned.

³⁰ By faith the walls of Jericho fell, after the army had marched around them for seven days.

³¹ By faith the prostitute Rahab, because she welcomed the spies, was not killed with those who were disobedient.ᵃ

³² And what more shall I say? I do not have time to tell about Gideon, Barak, Samson and Jephthah, about David and Samuel and the prophets, ³³ who through faith conquered kingdoms, administered justice, and gained what was promised; who shut the mouths of lions, ³⁴ quenched the fury of the flames, and escaped the edge of the sword; whose weakness was turned to strength; and who became powerful in battle and routed foreign armies. ³⁵ Women received back their dead, raised to life again. There were others who were tortured, refusing to be released so that they might gain an even better resurrec-

tion. ³⁶ Some faced jeers and flogging, and even chains and imprisonment. ³⁷ They were put to death by stoning;ᵇ they were sawed in two; they were killed by the sword. They went about in sheepskins and goatskins, destitute, persecuted and mistreated— ³⁸ the world was not worthy of them. They wandered in deserts and mountains, living in caves and in holes in the ground.

³⁹ These were all commended for their faith, yet none of them received what had been promised, ⁴⁰ since God had planned something better for us so that only together with us would they be made perfect.

12 Therefore, since we are surrounded by such a great cloud of witnesses, let us throw off everything that hinders and the sin that so easily entangles. And let us run with perseverance the race marked out for us, ² fixing our eyes on Jesus, the pioneer and perfecter of faith. For the joy set before him he endured the cross, scorning its shame, and sat down at the right hand of the throne of God. ³ Consider him who endured such opposition from sinners, so that you will not grow weary and lose heart.

God Disciplines His Children

⁴ In your struggle against sin, you have not yet resisted to the point of shedding your blood. ⁵ And have you completely forgotten this word of encouragement that addresses you as a father addresses his son? It says,

"My son, do not make light of the
    Lord's discipline,
  and do not lose heart when he
    rebukes you,
⁶ because the Lord disciplines the one
    he loves,
  and he chastens everyone he accepts
    as his son."ᶜ

⁷ Endure hardship as discipline; God is treating you as his children. For what

---

ᵃ 31 Or *unbelieving*   ᵇ 37 Some early manuscripts *stoning; they were put to the test;*   ᶜ 5,6 Prov. 3:11,12 (see Septuagint)

ROCK SOLID *principles*

Hebrews 11:1—12:1

Keep the faith.

Belinda knew there had to be other genuine Christians at school, but she had no idea where they were. On some days school felt like a scene out of a science fiction movie, with everyone cloaked by invisibility shields. She knew plenty of classmates who went to church because they had to, but she hadn't found anyone who shared her deep passion for following Jesus. She kept sliding her faith into conversations to watch for a response, hoping to find a like-minded friend. In the meantime, she kept telling herself she wasn't alone. Millions of Christians had survived the loneliness she felt. They faced the same test—or worse—each day. And the Bible showed her countless real people who kept the faith no matter what.

You might feel like you're completely alone doing your faith, having to figure out how to follow Jesus all by yourself. But you can look for inspiration and tips from major believers of the past. Hebrews 11 is the Bible's "Hall of Faith," a collection displaying both the incredible achievements and heartbreaks of believers who have gone before you.

children are not disciplined by their father? ⁸If you are not disciplined—and everyone undergoes discipline—then you are not legitimate, not true sons and daughters at all. ⁹Moreover, we have all had human fathers who disciplined us and we respected them for it. How much more should we submit to the Father of spirits and live! ¹⁰They disciplined us for a little while as they thought best; but God disciplines us for our good, in order that we may share in his holiness. ¹¹No discipline seems pleasant at the time, but painful. Later on, however, it produces a harvest of righteousness and peace for those who have been trained by it.

¹²Therefore, strengthen your feeble arms and weak knees. ¹³"Make level paths for your feet,"[a] so that the lame may not be disabled, but rather healed.

Warning and Encouragement

¹⁴Make every effort to live in peace with everyone and to be holy; without holiness no one will see the Lord. ¹⁵See to it that no one falls short of the grace of God and that no bitter root grows up to cause trouble and defile many. ¹⁶See that no one is sexually immoral, or is godless like Esau, who for a single meal sold his inheritance rights as the oldest son. ¹⁷Afterward, as you know, when he wanted to inherit this blessing, he was rejected. Even though he sought the blessing with tears, he could not change what he had done.

The Mountain of Fear and the Mountain of Joy

¹⁸You have not come to a mountain that can be touched and that is burning with fire; to darkness, gloom and storm; ¹⁹to a trumpet blast or to such a voice speaking words that those who heard it begged that no further word be spoken to them, ²⁰because they could not bear what was commanded: "If even an animal touches the

[a] *13* Prov. 4:26

mountain, it must be stoned to death."[a] [21] The sight was so terrifying that Moses said, "I am trembling with fear."[b]

[22] But you have come to Mount Zion, to the city of the living God, the heavenly Jerusalem. You have come to thousands upon thousands of angels in joyful assembly, [23] to the church of the firstborn, whose names are written in heaven. You have come to God, the Judge of all, to the spirits of the righteous made perfect, [24] to Jesus the mediator of a new covenant, and to the sprinkled blood that speaks a better word than the blood of Abel.

[25] See to it that you do not refuse him who speaks. If they did not escape when they refused him who warned them on earth, how much less will we, if we turn away from him who warns us from heaven? [26] At that time his voice shook the earth, but now he has promised, "Once more I will shake not only the earth but also the heavens."[c] [27] The words "once more" indicate the removing of what can be shaken—that is, created things—so that what cannot be shaken may remain.

[28] Therefore, since we are receiving a kingdom that cannot be shaken, let us be thankful, and so worship God acceptably with reverence and awe, [29] for our "God is a consuming fire."[d]

Concluding Exhortations

13 Keep on loving one another as brothers and sisters. [2] Do not forget to show hospitality to strangers, for by so doing some people have shown hospitality to angels without knowing it. [3] Continue to remember those in prison as if you were together with them in prison, and those who are mistreated as if you yourselves were suffering.

[4] Marriage should be honored by all, and the marriage bed kept pure, for God will judge the adulterer and all the sexually immoral. [5] Keep your lives free from the love of money and be content with what you have, because God has said,

"Never will I leave you;
    never will I forsake you."[e]

ROCK SOLID promises

"Never will I leave you; never will I forsake you."   Hebrews 13:5

God won't ever leave you alone or lonely. You can't see him, but he's always with you.

[6] So we say with confidence,

"The Lord is my helper; I will not be afraid.
    What can mere mortals do to me?"[f]

[7] Remember your leaders, who spoke the word of God to you. Consider the outcome of their way of life and imitate their faith. [8] Jesus Christ is the same yesterday and today and forever.

[9] Do not be carried away by all kinds of strange teachings. It is good for our hearts to be strengthened by grace, not by eating ceremonial foods, which is of no benefit to those who do so. [10] We have an altar from which those who minister at the tabernacle have no right to eat.

[11] The high priest carries the blood of animals into the Most Holy Place as a sin offering, but the bodies are burned outside the camp. [12] And so Jesus also suffered outside the city gate to make the people holy through his own blood. [13] Let us, then, go to him outside the camp, bearing the disgrace he bore. [14] For here we do not have an enduring city, but we are looking for the city that is to come.

[15] Through Jesus, therefore, let us continually offer to God a sacrifice of praise—the fruit of lips that openly pro-

---

[a] 20 Exodus 19:12,13   [b] 21 See Deut. 9:19.
[c] 26 Haggai 2:6   [d] 29 Deut. 4:24
[e] 5 Deut. 31:6   [f] 6 Psalm 118:6,7

fess his name. [16]And do not forget to do good and to share with others, for with such sacrifices God is pleased.

[17]Have confidence in your leaders and submit to their authority, because they keep watch over you as those who must give an account. Do this so that their work will be a joy, not a burden, for that would be of no benefit to you.

[18]Pray for us. We are sure that we have a clear conscience and desire to live honorably in every way. [19]I particularly urge you to pray so that I may be restored to you soon.

Benediction and Final Greetings

[20]Now may the God of peace, who through the blood of the eternal covenant brought back from the dead our Lord Jesus, that great Shepherd of the sheep, [21]equip you with everything good for doing his will, and may he work in us what is pleasing to him, through Jesus Christ, to whom be glory for ever and ever. Amen.

[22]Brothers and sisters, I urge you to bear with my word of exhortation, for in fact I have written to you quite briefly.

[23]I want you to know that our brother Timothy has been released. If he arrives soon, I will come with him to see you.

[24]Greet all your leaders and all the Lord's people. Those from Italy send you their greetings.

[25]Grace be with you all.

BOOK OUTLINE

The heart of true religion
(1:1–27)

True faith in practice
(2:1 — 3:12)

True wisdom in practice
(3:13 — 5:12)

The prayer of faith
(5:13–20)

JAMES

The book of James may be the earliest of the New Testament letters, written about AD 48. This letter was written by James, the brother of Jesus, who was one of the leaders of the church in Jerusalem. The letter is addressed to Christians everywhere. Seven books of the New Testament, James through Jude, are called the general letters because they are addressed to Christians in general and not to a specific church.

James wrote this letter to teach Christians how to live Christ-like lives. He insists that if we have real faith, we will show it by acting like Christians. He gives practical advice on things like anger and quarreling, showing favoritism, controlling the tongue, boasting, patience and prayer.

James, a servant of God and of the Lord Jesus Christ,

To the twelve tribes scattered among the nations:

Greetings.

Trials and Temptations

²Consider it pure joy, my brothers and sisters,*a* whenever you face trials of many kinds, ³because you know that the testing of your faith produces perseverance. ⁴Let perseverance finish its work so that you may be mature and complete, not lacking anything. ⁵If any of you lacks wisdom, you should ask God, who gives generously to all without finding fault, and it will be given to you. ⁶But when you ask, you must believe and not doubt, because the one who doubts is like a wave of the sea, blown and tossed by the wind. ⁷That person should not expect to receive anything from the Lord. ⁸Such a person is double-minded and unstable in all they do.

ROCK SOLID
promises

"The testing of your faith produces perseverance." James 1:3

Every tough thing you face gives you an opportunity to prove you trust God.

⁹Believers in humble circumstances ought to take pride in their high position. ¹⁰But the rich should take pride in their humiliation—since they will pass away like a wild flower. ¹¹For the sun rises with scorching heat and withers the plant; its blossom falls and its beauty is destroyed. In the same way, the rich will fade away even while they go about their business.

¹²Blessed is the one who perseveres under trial because, having stood the test, that person will receive the crown of life that the Lord has promised to those who love him.

¹³When tempted, no one should say, "God is tempting me." For God cannot be tempted by evil, nor does he tempt anyone; ¹⁴but each person is tempted when they are dragged away by their own evil desire and enticed. ¹⁵Then, after desire has conceived, it gives birth to sin; and sin, when it is full-grown, gives birth to death.

¹⁶Don't be deceived, my dear brothers and sisters. ¹⁷Every good and perfect gift is from above, coming down from the Father of the heavenly lights, who does not change like shifting shadows. ¹⁸He chose to give us birth through the word of truth, that we might be a kind of firstfruits of all he created.

Listening and Doing

¹⁹My dear brothers and sisters, take note of this: Everyone should be quick to listen, slow to speak and slow to become angry, ²⁰because human anger does not produce the righteousness that God desires. ²¹Therefore, get rid of all moral filth and the evil that is so prevalent and humbly accept the word planted in you, which can save you.

²²Do not merely listen to the word, and so deceive yourselves. Do what it says. ²³Anyone who listens to the word but does not do what it says is like someone who looks at his face in a mirror ²⁴and, after looking at himself, goes away and immediately forgets what he looks like. ²⁵But whoever looks intently into the perfect law that gives freedom, and continues in it—not forgetting what they have heard, but doing it—they will be blessed in what they do.

a 2 The Greek word for *brothers and sisters* (*adelphoi*) refers here to believers, both men and women, as part of God's family; also in verses 16 and 19; and in 2:1, 5, 14; 3:10, 12; 4:11; 5:7, 9, 10, 12, 19.

ROCK SOLID *plans*

James 1:5–8

Ask God to guide you.

God might seem like the scariest of teachers—like you don't want to let him know you need help, much less stay after class to ask him a question. But when you lack wisdom, you can go right to the source of all insight because God's input comes with a nice surprise. The Lord never ever looks down on you for asking for help. Yet he does require one thing. He doesn't want you to be "double-minded" (James 1:8), wavering about whether you will obey what he tells you. So ask away. But be ready to follow his commands.

Your next step: Talk to God about a decision or a problem you have been afraid to bring up with him.

²⁶Those who consider themselves religious and yet do not keep a tight rein on their tongues deceive themselves, and their religion is worthless. ²⁷Religion that God our Father accepts as pure and faultless is this: to look after orphans and widows in their distress and to keep oneself from being polluted by the world.

Favoritism Forbidden

2 My brothers and sisters, believers in our glorious Lord Jesus Christ must not show favoritism. ²Suppose a man comes into your meeting wearing a gold ring and fine clothes, and a poor man in filthy old clothes also comes in. ³If you show special attention to the man wearing fine clothes and say, "Here's a good seat for you," but say to the poor man, "You stand there" or "Sit on the floor by my feet," ⁴have you not discriminated among yourselves and become judges with evil thoughts?

⁵Listen, my dear brothers and sisters:

Has not God chosen those who are poor in the eyes of the world to be rich in faith and to inherit the kingdom he promised those who love him? ⁶But you have dishonored the poor. Is it not the rich who are exploiting you? Are they not the ones who are dragging you into court? ⁷Are they not the ones who are blaspheming the noble name of him to whom you belong?

⁸If you really keep the royal law found in Scripture, "Love your neighbor as yourself,"ᵃ you are doing right. ⁹But if you show favoritism, you sin and are convicted by the law as lawbreakers. ¹⁰For whoever keeps the whole law and yet stumbles at just one point is guilty of breaking all of it. ¹¹For he who said, "You shall not commit adultery,"ᵇ also said, "You shall not murder."ᶜ If you do not commit adultery but do commit murder, you have become a lawbreaker.

¹²Speak and act as those who are going to be judged by the law that gives freedom, ¹³because judgment without mercy will be shown to anyone who has not been merciful. Mercy triumphs over judgment.

Faith and Deeds

¹⁴What good is it, my brothers and sisters, if someone claims to have faith but has no deeds? Can such faith save them? ¹⁵Suppose a brother or a sister is without clothes and daily food. ¹⁶If one of you says to them, "Go in peace; keep warm and well fed," but does nothing about their physical needs, what good is it? ¹⁷In the same way, faith by itself, if it is not accompanied by action, is dead.

¹⁸But someone will say, "You have faith; I have deeds."

Show me your faith without deeds, and I will show you my faith by my deeds. ¹⁹You believe that there is one God. Good! Even the demons believe that— and shudder.

²⁰You foolish person, do you want evidence that faith without deeds is uselessᵈ?

ᵃ 8 Lev. 19:18   ᵇ 11 Exodus 20:14; Deut. 5:18
ᶜ 11 Exodus 20:13; Deut. 5:17   ᵈ 20 Some early manuscripts *dead*

ROCK SOLID *principles*

James 2:1–7

Don't play favorites

Caleb cringed. The most awkward guy in his grade was headed his way, aiming right for the open spot at his lunch table. Sure enough, Ben sat down and spread out his lunch. For days Caleb had teased a girl he liked about meeting him for lunch, and he thought today was the day she would show up. Now that plan had clearly failed. Caleb turned away from Ben and acted intensely interested in the argument going on between his two guy friends at the table. For the next twenty minutes until the lunch period was over, Caleb did everything he could to ignore Ben and send him the message that he shouldn't sit with them ever again.

A well-dressed guy comes to church and gets the royal treatment. A shabby-looking guy walks in and gets ushered to the cheap seats. The Bible calls that "favoritism," judging and treating people according to their appearance, popularity, wealth, or anything else (see James 2:1). Whether it happens at church, school, or anywhere else, that's the exact opposite of welcoming people with God's love. Stop it!

²¹Was not our father Abraham considered righteous for what he did when he offered his son Isaac on the altar? ²²You see that his faith and his actions were working together, and his faith was made complete by what he did. ²³And the scripture was fulfilled that says, "Abraham believed God, and it was credited to him as righteousness,"[a] and he was called God's friend. ²⁴You see that a person is considered righteous by what they do and not by faith alone.

²⁵In the same way, was not even Rahab the prostitute considered righteous for what she did when she gave lodging to the spies and sent them off in a different direction? ²⁶As the body without the spirit is dead, so faith without deeds is dead.

Taming the Tongue

3 Not many of you should become teachers, my fellow believers, because you know that we who teach will be judged more strictly. ²We all stumble in many ways. Anyone who is never at fault in what they say is perfect, able to keep their whole body in check.

³When we put bits into the mouths of horses to make them obey us, we can turn the whole animal. ⁴Or take ships as an example. Although they are so large and are driven by strong winds, they are steered by a very small rudder wherever the pilot wants to go. ⁵Likewise, the tongue is a small part of the body, but it makes great boasts. Consider what a great forest is set on fire by a small spark. ⁶The tongue also is a fire, a world of evil among the parts of the body. It corrupts the whole body, sets the whole course of one's life on fire, and is itself set on fire by hell.

⁷All kinds of animals, birds, reptiles and sea creatures are being tamed and have been tamed by mankind, ⁸but no human being can tame the tongue. It is a restless evil, full of deadly poison.

[a] 23 Gen. 15:6

⁹With the tongue we praise our Lord and Father, and with it we curse human beings, who have been made in God's likeness. ¹⁰Out of the same mouth come praise and cursing. My brothers and sisters, this should not be. ¹¹Can both fresh water and salt water flow from the same spring? ¹²My brothers and sisters, can a fig tree bear olives, or a grapevine bear figs? Neither can a salt spring produce fresh water.

Two Kinds of Wisdom

¹³Who is wise and understanding among you? Let them show it by their good life, by deeds done in the humility that comes from wisdom. ¹⁴But if you harbor bitter envy and selfish ambition in your hearts, do not boast about it or deny the truth. ¹⁵Such "wisdom" does not come down from heaven but is earthly, unspiritual, demonic. ¹⁶For where you have envy and selfish ambition, there you find disorder and every evil practice.

¹⁷But the wisdom that comes from heaven is first of all pure; then peace-loving, considerate, submissive, full of mercy and good fruit, impartial and sincere. ¹⁸Peacemakers who sow in peace reap a harvest of righteousness.

Submit Yourselves to God

4 What causes fights and quarrels among you? Don't they come from your desires that battle within you? ²You desire but do not have, so you kill. You covet but you cannot get what you want, so you quarrel and fight. You do not have because you do not ask God. ³When you ask, you do not receive, because you ask with wrong motives, that you may spend what you get on your pleasures.

⁴You adulterous people,ᵃ don't you know that friendship with the world means enmity against God? Therefore, anyone who chooses to be a friend of the world becomes an enemy of God. ⁵Or do you think Scripture says without reason that he jealously longs for the spirit he has caused to dwell in us?ᵇ ⁶But he gives us more grace. That is why Scripture says:

"God opposes the proud
but shows favor to the humble."ᶜ

⁷Submit yourselves, then, to God. Resist the devil, and he will flee from you. ⁸Come near to God and he will come near to you. Wash your hands, you sinners, and purify your hearts, you double-minded. ⁹Grieve, mourn and wail. Change your laughter to mourning and your joy to gloom. ¹⁰Humble yourselves before the Lord, and he will lift you up.

ROCK SOLID promises

"Submit yourselves, then, to God. Resist the devil, and he will flee from you." James 4:7

Set your heart on obeying God, and the devil will get tired of trying to get you to sin. Sooner or later he will leave you alone.

¹¹Brothers and sisters, do not slander one another. Anyone who speaks against a brother or sisterᵈ or judges them speaks against the law and judges it. When you judge the law, you are not keeping it, but sitting in judgment on it. ¹²There is only one Lawgiver and Judge, the one who is able to save and destroy. But you—who are you to judge your neighbor?

Boasting About Tomorrow

¹³Now listen, you who say, "Today or tomorrow we will go to this or that city, spend a year there, carry on busi-

ᵃ 4 An allusion to covenant unfaithfulness; see Hosea 3:1. ᵇ 5 Or that the spirit he caused to dwell in us envies intensely; or that the Spirit he caused to dwell in us longs jealously ᶜ 6 Prov. 3:34 ᵈ 11 The Greek word for brother or sister (adelphos) refers here to a believer, whether man or woman, as part of God's family.

ROCK SOLID
plans

James 4:13–17

Include God.

You might be confident of all your abilities to win at life, like you can plan your work and work your plan. But watch out. Self-assurance easily turns into smugness, and the apostle James points out that God might have radically different plans for your future, even equating your life to a mist that could vanish by tomorrow. The Lord doesn't like being a tacked-on afterthought to your plans. He wants to help form your goals from the start, then stick with you until you succeed.

Your next step: Think of times you have left God out of your plans and decisions — and tell him you want to include him from now on.

ness and make money." ¹⁴Why, you do not even know what will happen tomorrow. What is your life? You are a mist that appears for a little while and then vanishes. ¹⁵Instead, you ought to say, "If it is the Lord's will, we will live and do this or that." ¹⁶As it is, you boast in your arrogant schemes. All such boasting is evil. ¹⁷If anyone, then, knows the good they ought to do and doesn't do it, it is sin for them.

Warning to Rich Oppressors

5 Now listen, you rich people, weep and wail because of the misery that is coming on you. ²Your wealth has rotted, and moths have eaten your clothes. ³Your gold and silver are corroded. Their corrosion will testify against you and eat your flesh like fire. You have hoarded wealth in the last days. ⁴Look! The wages you failed to pay the workers who mowed your fields are crying out against you. The cries of the harvesters have reached

the ears of the Lord Almighty. ⁵You have lived on earth in luxury and self-indulgence. You have fattened yourselves in the day of slaughter.ᵃ ⁶You have condemned and murdered the innocent one, who was not opposing you.

Patience in Suffering

⁷Be patient, then, brothers and sisters, until the Lord's coming. See how the farmer waits for the land to yield its valuable crop, patiently waiting for the autumn and spring rains. ⁸You too, be patient and stand firm, because the Lord's coming is near. ⁹Don't grumble against one another, brothers and sisters, or you will be judged. The Judge is standing at the door!

¹⁰Brothers and sisters, as an example of patience in the face of suffering, take the prophets who spoke in the name of the Lord. ¹¹As you know, we count as blessed those who have persevered. You have heard of Job's perseverance and have seen what the Lord finally brought about. The Lord is full of compassion and mercy.

¹²Above all, my brothers and sisters, do not swear — not by heaven or by earth or by anything else. All you need to say is a simple "Yes" or "No." Otherwise you will be condemned.

ᵃ 5 Or *yourselves as in a day of feasting*

ROCK SOLID
promises

"The prayer of a righteous person is powerful and effective."

James 5:16

Good people get results when they pray because they want what God wants.

The Prayer of Faith

¹³Is anyone among you in trouble? Let them pray. Is anyone happy? Let them sing songs of praise. ¹⁴Is anyone among you sick? Let them call the elders of the church to pray over them and anoint them with oil in the name of the Lord. ¹⁵And the prayer offered in faith will make the sick person well; the Lord will raise them up. If they have sinned, they will be forgiven. ¹⁶Therefore confess your sins to each other and pray for each other so that you may be healed. The prayer of a righteous person is powerful and effective.

¹⁷Elijah was a human being, even as we are. He prayed earnestly that it would not rain, and it did not rain on the land for three and a half years. ¹⁸Again he prayed, and the heavens gave rain, and the earth produced its crops.

¹⁹My brothers and sisters, if one of you should wander from the truth and someone should bring that person back, ²⁰remember this: Whoever turns a sinner from the error of their way will save them from death and cover over a multitude of sins.

BOOK OUTLINE

Greetings
(1:1,2)

Praise to God for salvation
(1:3–12)

Holy living
(1:13—2:12)

Conduct of the believer
(2:13—4:11)

Ministry through suffering
(4:12—5:11)

Conclusion
(5:12–14)

P eter, one of Jesus' twelve disciples, wrote this letter to the Christians who lived in the northern part of Asia Minor. These Christians were being persecuted for their faith, so Peter wrote to encourage them.

He urges them to remember how much Jesus suffered for them and to follow his example by trusting God to care for them. Because God chose them to be his people and his Son Jesus suffered and died for them, they should live holy lives. Peter also tells them how to handle suffering, live as Christians in this sinful world, and have hope for the future.

Peter, an apostle of Jesus Christ,

To God's elect, exiles scattered throughout the provinces of Pontus, Galatia, Cappadocia, Asia and Bithynia, ²who have been chosen according to the foreknowledge of God the Father, through the sanctifying work of the Spirit, to be obedient to Jesus Christ and sprinkled with his blood:

Grace and peace be yours in abundance.

Praise to God for a Living Hope

³Praise be to the God and Father of our Lord Jesus Christ! In his great mercy he has given us new birth into a living hope through the resurrection of Jesus Christ from the dead, ⁴and into an inheritance that can never perish, spoil or fade. This inheritance is kept in heaven for you, ⁵who through faith are shielded by God's power until the coming of the salvation that is ready to be revealed in the last time. ⁶In all this you greatly rejoice, though now for a little while you may have had to suffer grief in all kinds of trials. ⁷These have come so that the proven genuineness of your faith—of greater worth than gold, which perishes even though refined by fire—may result in praise, glory and honor when Jesus Christ is revealed. ⁸Though you have not seen him, you love him; and even though you do not see him now, you believe in him and are filled with an inexpressible and glorious joy, ⁹for you are receiving the end result of your faith, the salvation of your souls.

¹⁰Concerning this salvation, the prophets, who spoke of the grace that was to come to you, searched intently and with the greatest care, ¹¹trying to find out the time and circumstances to which the Spirit of Christ in them was pointing when he predicted the sufferings of the Messiah and the glories that would follow. ¹²It was

ROCK SOLID principles

1 Peter 1:3–9

Hang tough.

Emma tried to lift her arm and couldn't, not without screaming. She had lunged heroically for the volleyball, diving to bump the ball before it hit the floor. But as she landed on her shoulder, she heard a crack. She reached at the point of pain with her other hand, and one poke told her she had broken her collarbone. Emma started to cry, not because of the pain but because her volleyball season was finished. Emma's team was good—good enough to win the high school state championship. And her injury meant she would watch the season unfold from the sideline. Why did this have to happen?

God lavishes you with mercy. He saves you and remakes you. He has a home waiting for you in heaven. But for now "you may have had to suffer grief in all kinds of trials" (1 Peter 1:6). Those trials prove you possess authentic faith. Your triumphs give everyone reason to praise God. So trials can be a reason to grab God's joy. It sounds crazy. But it's true.

revealed to them that they were not serving themselves but you, when they spoke of the things that have now been told you by those who have preached the gospel to you by the Holy Spirit sent from heaven. Even angels long to look into these things.

Be Holy

¹³ Therefore, with minds that are alert and fully sober, set your hope on the grace to be brought to you when Jesus Christ is revealed at his coming. ¹⁴ As obedient children, do not conform to the evil desires you had when you lived in ignorance. ¹⁵ But just as he who called you is holy, so be holy in all you do; ¹⁶ for it is written: "Be holy, because I am holy."ᵃ

¹⁷ Since you call on a Father who judges each person's work impartially, live out your time as foreigners here in reverent fear. ¹⁸ For you know that it was not with perishable things such as silver or gold that you were redeemed from the empty way of life handed down to you from your ancestors, ¹⁹ but with the precious blood of Christ, a lamb without blemish or defect. ²⁰ He was chosen before the creation of the world, but was revealed in these last times for your sake. ²¹ Through him you believe in God, who raised him from the dead and glorified him, and so your faith and hope are in God.

²² Now that you have purified yourselves by obeying the truth so that you have sincere love for each other, love one another deeply, from the heart.ᵇ ²³ For you have been born again, not of perishable seed, but of imperishable, through the living and enduring word of God. ²⁴ For,

> "All people are like grass,
>   and all their glory is like the flowers of the field;
> the grass withers and the flowers fall,
> ²⁵   but the word of the Lord endures forever."ᶜ

And this is the word that was preached to you.

2 Therefore, rid yourselves of all malice and all deceit, hypocrisy, envy, and slander of every kind.

²Like newborn babies, crave pure spiritual milk, so that by it you may grow up in your salvation, ³ now that you have tasted that the Lord is good.

The Living Stone and a Chosen People

⁴ As you come to him, the living Stone—rejected by humans but chosen by God and precious to him— ⁵ you also, like living stones, are being built into a spiritual houseᵈ to be a holy priesthood, offering spiritual sacrifices acceptable to God through Jesus Christ. ⁶ For in Scripture it says:

> "See, I lay a stone in Zion,
>   a chosen and precious cornerstone,
> and the one who trusts in him
>   will never be put to shame."ᵉ

⁷ Now to you who believe, this stone is precious. But to those who do not believe,

> "The stone the builders rejected
>   has become the cornerstone,"ᶠ

⁸ and,

> "A stone that causes people to stumble
>   and a rock that makes them fall."ᵍ

They stumble because they disobey the message—which is also what they were destined for.

⁹ But you are a chosen people, a royal priesthood, a holy nation, God's special possession, that you may declare the praises of him who called you out of darkness into his wonderful light. ¹⁰ Once you were not a people, but now you are the people of God; once you had not received mercy, but now you have received mercy.

Living Godly Lives in a Pagan Society

¹¹ Dear friends, I urge you, as foreigners and exiles, to abstain from sinful desires, which wage war against your soul. ¹² Live such good lives among the pagans that, though they accuse you of doing wrong,

ᵃ *16* Lev. 11:44,45; 19:2   ᵇ *22* Some early manuscripts *from a pure heart*
ᶜ *25* Isaiah 40:6-8 (see Septuagint)   ᵈ *5* Or *into a temple of the Spirit*   ᵉ *6* Isaiah 28:16
ᶠ *7* Psalm 118:22   ᵍ *8* Isaiah 8:14

ROCK SOLID
promises

"You are a chosen people, a royal priesthood, a holy nation, God's special possession." 1 Peter 2:9

God chose you to be his child, and he connected you to a worldwide group of people who follow him.

they may see your good deeds and glorify God on the day he visits us.

[13] Submit yourselves for the Lord's sake to every human authority: whether to the emperor, as the supreme authority, [14] or to governors, who are sent by him to punish those who do wrong and to commend those who do right. [15] For it is God's will that by doing good you should silence the ignorant talk of foolish people. [16] Live as free people, but do not use your freedom as a cover-up for evil; live as God's slaves. [17] Show proper respect to everyone, love the family of believers, fear God, honor the emperor.

[18] Slaves, in reverent fear of God submit yourselves to your masters, not only to those who are good and considerate, but also to those who are harsh. [19] For it is commendable if someone bears up under the pain of unjust suffering because they are conscious of God. [20] But how is it to your credit if you receive a beating for doing wrong and endure it? But if you suffer for doing good and you endure it, this is commendable before God. [21] To this you were called, because Christ suffered for you, leaving you an example, that you should follow in his steps.

[22] "He committed no sin,
and no deceit was found in his
mouth."[a]

[23] When they hurled their insults at him, he did not retaliate; when he suffered, he made no threats. Instead, he entrusted himself to him who judges justly. [24] "He himself bore our sins" in his body on the cross, so that we might die to sins and live for righteousness; "by his wounds you have been healed." [25] For "you were like sheep going astray,"[b] but now you have returned to the Shepherd and Overseer of your souls.

3 Wives, in the same way submit yourselves to your own husbands so that, if any of them do not believe the word, they may be won over without words by the behavior of their wives, [2] when they see the purity and reverence of your lives. [3] Your beauty should not come from outward adornment, such as elaborate hairstyles and the wearing of gold jewelry or fine clothes. [4] Rather, it should be that of your inner self, the unfading beauty of a gentle and quiet spirit, which is of great worth in God's sight. [5] For this is the way the holy women of the past who put their hope in God used to adorn themselves. They submitted themselves to their own husbands, [6] like Sarah, who obeyed Abraham and called him her lord. You are her daughters if you do what is right and do not give way to fear.

[7] Husbands, in the same way be considerate as you live with your wives, and treat them with respect as the weaker partner and as heirs with you of the gracious gift of life, so that nothing will hinder your prayers.

Suffering for Doing Good

[8] Finally, all of you, be like-minded, be sympathetic, love one another, be compassionate and humble. [9] Do not repay evil with evil or insult with insult. On the contrary, repay evil with blessing, because to this you were called so that you may inherit a blessing. [10] For,

"Whoever would love life
and see good days

---

[a] *22* Isaiah 53:9   [b] *24,25* Isaiah 53:4,5,6 (see Septuagint)

must keep their tongue from evil
and their lips from deceitful speech.
¹¹They must turn from evil and do good;
they must seek peace and pursue it.
¹²For the eyes of the Lord are on the
righteous
and his ears are attentive to their
prayer,
but the face of the Lord is against
those who do evil."ᵃ

¹³Who is going to harm you if you are eager to do good? ¹⁴But even if you should suffer for what is right, you are blessed. "Do not fear their threats*ᵇ*; do not be frightened."*ᶜ* ¹⁵But in your hearts revere Christ as Lord. Always be prepared to give an answer to everyone who asks you to give the reason for the hope that you have. But do this with gentleness and respect, ¹⁶keeping a clear conscience, so that those who speak maliciously against your good behavior in Christ may be ashamed of their slander. ¹⁷For it is better, if it is God's will, to suffer for doing good than for doing evil. ¹⁸For Christ also suffered once for sins, the righteous for the unrighteous, to bring you to God. He was put to death in the body but made alive in the Spirit. ¹⁹After being made alive,*ᵈ* he went and made proclamation to the imprisoned spirits— ²⁰to those who were disobedient long ago when God waited patiently in the days of Noah while the ark was being built. In it only a few people, eight in all, were saved through water, ²¹and this water symbolizes baptism that now saves you also—not the removal of dirt from the body but the pledge of a clear conscience toward God.*ᵉ* It saves you by the resurrection of Jesus Christ, ²²who has gone into heaven and is at God's right hand—with angels, authorities and powers in submission to him.

Living for God

4 Therefore, since Christ suffered in his body, arm yourselves also with the same attitude, because whoever suffers in the body is done with sin. ²As a result, they do not live the rest of their earthly lives for evil human desires, but rather for the will of God. ³For

you have spent enough time in the past doing what pagans choose to do—living in debauchery, lust, drunkenness, orgies, carousing and detestable idolatry. ⁴They are surprised that you do not join them in their reckless, wild living, and they heap abuse on you. ⁵But they will have to give account to him who is ready to judge the living and the dead. ⁶For this is the reason the gospel was preached even to those who are now dead, so that they might be judged according to human standards in regard to the body, but live according to God in regard to the spirit.

⁷The end of all things is near. Therefore be alert and of sober mind so that you may pray. ⁸Above all, love each other deeply, because love covers over a multitude of sins. ⁹Offer hospitality to one another without grumbling. ¹⁰Each of you should use whatever gift you have received to serve others, as faithful stewards of God's grace in its various forms.

ᵃ 12 Psalm 34:12-16   ᵇ 14 Or *fear what they fear*   ᶜ 14 Isaiah 8:12   ᵈ 18,19 Or *but made alive in the spirit,* ¹⁹*in which also*   ᵉ 21 Or *but an appeal to God for a clear conscience*

ROCK SOLID *plans*

1 Peter 4:1–8

Live to do God's will.

Jesus was all about doing exactly what his Father wanted. He once said, "My food ... is to do the will of him who sent me and to finish his work" (John 4:34). Peter pointed out that Jesus lived "for the will of God" and that we're to have the same attitude (1 Peter 4:1–2). We all have spent enough time chasing sin (1 Peter 4:3), and it's time to live for God, starting now and never stopping.

Your next step: Talk to God and tell him your highest goal is do his will, obeying him as best you know how.

¹¹If anyone speaks, they should do so as one who speaks the very words of God. If anyone serves, they should do so with the strength God provides, so that in all things God may be praised through Jesus Christ. To him be the glory and the power for ever and ever. Amen.

Suffering for Being a Christian

¹²Dear friends, do not be surprised at the fiery ordeal that has come on you to test you, as though something strange were happening to you. ¹³But rejoice inasmuch as you participate in the sufferings of Christ, so that you may be overjoyed when his glory is revealed. ¹⁴If you are insulted because of the name of Christ, you are blessed, for the Spirit of glory and of God rests on you. ¹⁵If you suffer, it should

ROCK SOLID
promises

"If you are insulted because of the name of Christ, you are blessed, for the Spirit of glory and of God rests on you." 1 Peter 4:14

Don't get upset when you get trashed for following Jesus. Those unkind words mean you belong to God.

not be as a murderer or thief or any other kind of criminal, or even as a meddler. ¹⁶However, if you suffer as a Christian, do not be ashamed, but praise God that you bear that name. ¹⁷For it is time for judgment to begin with God's household; and if it begins with us, what will the outcome be for those who do not obey the gospel of God? ¹⁸And,

"If it is hard for the righteous to be saved,
what will become of the ungodly and the sinner?"ᵃ

¹⁹So then, those who suffer according to God's will should commit themselves to their faithful Creator and continue to do good.

To the Elders and the Flock

5 To the elders among you, I appeal as a fellow elder and a witness of Christ's sufferings who also will share in the glory to be revealed: ²Be shepherds of God's flock that is under your care, watching over them—not because you must, but because you are willing, as God wants you to be; not pursuing dishonest gain, but eager to serve; ³not lording it over those entrusted to you, but being examples to the flock. ⁴And when the Chief Shepherd appears, you will receive the crown of glory that will never fade away.

⁵In the same way, you who are younger, submit yourselves to your elders. All of you, clothe yourselves with humility toward one another, because,

"God opposes the proud
but shows favor to the humble."ᵇ

⁶Humble yourselves, therefore, under God's mighty hand, that he may lift you up in due time. ⁷Cast all your anxiety on him because he cares for you.

ᵃ *18* Prov. 11:31 (see Septuagint)
ᵇ *5* Prov. 3:34

ROCK SOLID
promises

"Cast all your anxiety on him because he cares for you." 1 Peter 5:7

You can't go wrong telling God about your worries. He cares about your every problem—big, small, or in-between.

[8] Be alert and of sober mind. Your enemy the devil prowls around like a roaring lion looking for someone to devour. [9] Resist him, standing firm in the faith, because you know that the family of believers throughout the world is undergoing the same kind of sufferings.

[10] And the God of all grace, who called you to his eternal glory in Christ, after you have suffered a little while, will himself restore you and make you strong, firm and steadfast. [11] To him be the power for ever and ever. Amen.

Final Greetings

[12] With the help of Silas,[a] whom I regard as a faithful brother, I have written to you briefly, encouraging you and testifying that this is the true grace of God. Stand fast in it.

[13] She who is in Babylon, chosen together with you, sends you her greetings, and so does my son Mark. [14] Greet one another with a kiss of love.

Peace to all of you who are in Christ.

[a] 12 Greek *Silvanus*, a variant of *Silas*

---

1 Peter 5:8-11

The devil wants to devour you.

Christians make two mistakes about the devil. They think about him too much, as if dealing with the master of evil should be the main focus of following Jesus. Or they think about him not at all, as if the devil has no part at all of our everyday lives. The apostle Peter offers a third option. He tells us to be "alert and of sober mind" (1 Peter 5:8). "Sober mind" means to be self-disciplined and to think straight. "Alert" is to watch out for anything that might make us stumble. Peter warns that the devil does prowl around like a lion looking for his next meal. He is both stealthy and vicious. But you choose to fight back by staying committed to God. The Lord will ultimately defeat the devil and make you strong. The devil is a real threat, but with God you have the power to chase him away (see 1 John 4:4).

Think: How do you see the devil trying to devour you? How do you fend him off?

ROCK SOLID *truths*

2 PETER

BOOK OUTLINE

Peter wrote this second letter about AD 66 to Christians he had written to earlier. They were living in the northern part of Asia Minor. These Christians were no longer being persecuted but were now in danger of being confused by false teachers.

Peter reminds the Christians that the best way to resist false teachers is to grow in the knowledge and practice of the Christian faith. He assures them that God will destroy the false teachers. Because Jesus will certainly keep his promise to come again, Peter reminds these Christians to live "holy and godly lives" (3:11).

Simon Peter, a servant and apostle of Jesus Christ,

To those who through the righteousness of our God and Savior Jesus Christ have received a faith as precious as ours:

²Grace and peace be yours in abundance through the knowledge of God and of Jesus our Lord.

Confirming One's Calling and Election

³His divine power has given us everything we need for a godly life through our knowledge of him who called us by his own glory and goodness. ⁴Through these he has given us his very great and precious promises, so that through them you may participate in the divine nature, having escaped the corruption in the world caused by evil desires.

⁵For this very reason, make every effort to add to your faith goodness; and to goodness, knowledge; ⁶and to knowledge, self-control; and to self-control, perseverance; and to perseverance, godliness; ⁷and to godliness, mutual affection; and to mutual affection, love. ⁸For if you possess these qualities in increasing measure, they will keep you from being ineffective and unproductive in your knowledge of our Lord Jesus Christ. ⁹But whoever does not have them is nearsighted and blind, forgetting that they have been cleansed from their past sins.

¹⁰Therefore, my brothers and sisters,*ᵃ* make every effort to confirm your calling and election. For if you do these things, you will never stumble, ¹¹and you will receive a rich welcome into the eternal kingdom of our Lord and Savior Jesus Christ.

Prophecy of Scripture

¹²So I will always remind you of these things, even though you know them and are firmly established in the truth you now have. ¹³I think it is right to refresh your memory as long as I live in the tent of this body, ¹⁴because I know that I will soon put it aside, as our Lord Jesus Christ has made clear to me. ¹⁵And I will make

every effort to see that after my departure you will always be able to remember these things.

¹⁶For we did not follow cleverly devised stories when we told you about the coming of our Lord Jesus Christ in power, but we were eyewitnesses of his majesty. ¹⁷He received honor and glory from God the Father when the voice came to him from the Majestic Glory, saying, "This is my

---

ᵃ 10 The Greek word for *brothers and sisters* (*adelphoi*) refers here to believers, both men and women, as part of God's family.

---

2 Peter 1:12–21

God wrote the Bible.

Knowing he wouldn't live much longer, the apostle Peter told his readers he was going to remind them once again of everything the Lord had taught him. He begins by stating he hadn't told made-up accounts of Jesus. He wrote, "We did not follow cleverly devised stories when we told you about the coming of our Lord Jesus Christ in power, but we were eyewitnesses of his majesty" (2 Peter 1:16). Peter accurately reported what he had seen. But there was more going on as Peter wrote this letter that would one day be included in the Bible. Peter was the human author, yet God was active in writing every word. Like Peter said, "For prophecy never had its origin in the human will, but prophets, though human, spoke from God as they were carried along by the Holy Spirit" (2 Peter 1:21). So Peter wrote this piece of the Bible. Even more importantly, so did God.

Think: How would you explain to a friend how the Bible was written?

ROCK SOLID truths

Son, whom I love; with him I am well pleased."*a* 18We ourselves heard this voice that came from heaven when we were with him on the sacred mountain.

19We also have the prophetic message as something completely reliable, and you will do well to pay attention to it, as to a light shining in a dark place, until the day dawns and the morning star rises in your hearts. 20Above all, you must understand that no prophecy of Scripture came about by the prophet's own interpretation of things. 21For prophecy never had its origin in the human will, but prophets, though human, spoke from God as they were carried along by the Holy Spirit.

False Teachers and Their Destruction

2 But there were also false prophets among the people, just as there will be false teachers among you. They will secretly introduce destructive heresies, even denying the sovereign Lord who bought them—bringing swift destruction on themselves. 2Many will follow their depraved conduct and will bring the way of truth into disrepute. 3In their greed these teachers will exploit you with fabricated stories. Their condemnation has long been hanging over them, and their destruction has not been sleeping.

4For if God did not spare angels when they sinned, but sent them to hell,*b* putting them in chains of darkness*c* to be held for judgment; 5if he did not spare the ancient world when he brought the flood on its ungodly people, but protected Noah, a preacher of righteousness, and seven others; 6if he condemned the cities of Sodom and Gomorrah by burning them to ashes, and made them an example of what is going to happen to the ungodly; 7and if he rescued Lot, a righteous man, who was distressed by the depraved conduct of the lawless 8(for that righteous man, living among them day after day, was tormented in his righteous soul by the lawless deeds he saw and heard)— 9if this is so, then the Lord knows how to rescue the godly from trials and to hold the unrighteous for punishment on the day of judgment.

10This is especially true of those who follow the corrupt desire of the flesh*d* and despise authority.

Bold and arrogant, they are not afraid to heap abuse on celestial beings; 11yet even angels, although they are stronger and more powerful, do not heap abuse on such beings when bringing judgment on them from*e* the Lord. 12But these people blaspheme in matters they do not understand. They are like unreasoning animals, creatures of instinct, born only to be caught and destroyed, and like animals they too will perish.

13They will be paid back with harm for the harm they have done. Their idea of pleasure is to carouse in broad daylight. They are blots and blemishes, reveling in their pleasures while they feast with you.*f* 14With eyes full of adultery, they never stop sinning; they seduce the unstable; they are experts in greed—an accursed brood! 15They have left the straight way and wandered off to follow the way of Balaam son of Bezer,*g* who loved the wages

---

a 17 Matt. 17:5; Mark 9:7; Luke 9:35
b 4 Greek *Tartarus*   *c* 4 Some manuscripts *in gloomy dungeons*   *d* 10 In contexts like this, the Greek word for *flesh* (*sarx*) refers to the sinful state of human beings, often presented as a power in opposition to the Spirit; also in verse 18.   *e* 11 Many manuscripts *beings in the presence of*   *f* 13 Some manuscripts *in their love feasts*   *g* 15 Greek *Bosor*

of wickedness. [16]But he was rebuked for his wrongdoing by a donkey—an animal without speech—who spoke with a human voice and restrained the prophet's madness.

[17]These people are springs without water and mists driven by a storm. Blackest darkness is reserved for them. [18]For they mouth empty, boastful words and, by appealing to the lustful desires of the flesh, they entice people who are just escaping from those who live in error. [19]They promise them freedom, while they themselves are slaves of depravity—for "people are slaves to whatever has mastered them." [20]If they have escaped the corruption of the world by knowing our Lord and Savior Jesus Christ and are again entangled in it and are overcome, they are worse off at the end than they were at the beginning. [21]It would have been better for them not to have known the way of righteousness, than to have known it and then to turn their backs on the sacred command that was passed on to them. [22]Of them the proverbs are true: "A dog returns to its vomit,"[a] and, "A sow that is washed returns to her wallowing in the mud."

The Day of the Lord

3 Dear friends, this is now my second letter to you. I have written both of them as reminders to stimulate you to wholesome thinking. [2]I want you to recall the words spoken in the past by the holy prophets and the command given by our Lord and Savior through your apostles.

[3]Above all, you must understand that in the last days scoffers will come, scoffing and following their own evil desires. [4]They will say, "Where is this 'coming' he promised? Ever since our ancestors died, everything goes on as it has since the beginning of creation." [5]But they deliberately forget that long ago by God's word the heavens came into being and the earth was formed out of water and by water. [6]By these waters also the world of that time was deluged and destroyed. [7]By the same word the present heavens

and earth are reserved for fire, being kept for the day of judgment and destruction of the ungodly.

[8]But do not forget this one thing, dear friends: With the Lord a day is like a thousand years, and a thousand years are like a day. [9]The Lord is not slow in keeping his promise, as some understand slowness. Instead he is patient with you, not wanting anyone to perish, but everyone to come to repentance.

[10]But the day of the Lord will come like a thief. The heavens will disappear with a roar; the elements will be destroyed by fire, and the earth and everything done in it will be laid bare.[b]

[11]Since everything will be destroyed in this way, what kind of people ought you to be? You ought to live holy and godly lives [12]as you look forward to the day of

[a] 22 Prov. 26:11   [b] 10 Some manuscripts *be burned up*

UNSHAKEN *God*

2 Peter 3:1–10

God is patient.

In the years toward the end of the apostle Peter's life, people had begun to scoff. They questioned why Jesus hadn't kept his promise to come back to earth (see Matthew 24:1–31; Acts 1:1–8). These doubters argued that everything in the world was going on just as it had since the dawn of time. But Peter argued that the Lord has a good reason for his delay. He hasn't yet returned because he is giving time for as many people as possible to believe in him, "not wanting anyone to perish, but everyone to come to repentance" (2 Peter 3:9). Because God loves us, he patiently waits for us.

So ... Does it bother you that Jesus seems to be taking a long time coming back? Why—or why not?

ROCK SOLID
promises

"The day of the Lord will come like a thief."　　2 Peter 3:10

People can try to predict when Jesus will return, but he will show up without warning and put an end to every kind of evil.

God and speed its coming.*a* That day will bring about the destruction of the heavens by fire, and the elements will melt in the heat. ¹³But in keeping with his promise we are looking forward to a new heaven and a new earth, where righteousness dwells.

¹⁴So then, dear friends, since you are looking forward to this, make every effort to be found spotless, blameless and at peace with him. ¹⁵Bear in mind that our Lord's patience means salvation, just as our dear brother Paul also wrote you with the wisdom that God gave him. ¹⁶He writes the same way in all his letters, speaking in them of these matters. His letters contain some things that are hard to understand, which ignorant and unstable people distort, as they do the other Scriptures, to their own destruction.

¹⁷Therefore, dear friends, since you have been forewarned, be on your guard so that you may not be carried away by the error of the lawless and fall from your secure position. ¹⁸But grow in the grace and knowledge of our Lord and Savior Jesus Christ. To him be glory both now and forever! Amen.

a 12 Or *as you wait eagerly for the day of God to come*

BOOK OUTLINE

1 JOHN

First, Second and Third John were written by John, Jesus' beloved disciple, who also wrote the fourth Gospel. All four books may have been written about the same time, probably about AD 90.

The first letter of John was written to warn Christians about dangerous false teachers who were trying to mislead them. These teachers were teaching that the man Jesus was not the Christ, the Son of God. They said that God did not become a man. John tells the Christians he is writing because it is very important for them to know and believe that Jesus Christ is both God and man.

John also encourages these Christians to keep their faith in Christ strong and to continue loving one another. He says Christians can know they are God's children if they love one another and if they obey God's commands.

The Incarnation of the Word of Life

That which was from the beginning, which we have heard, which we have seen with our eyes, which we have looked at and our hands have touched— this we proclaim concerning the Word of life. ²The life appeared; we have seen it and testify to it, and we proclaim to you the eternal life, which was with the Father and has appeared to us. ³We proclaim to you what we have seen and heard, so that you also may have fellowship with us. And our fellowship is with the Father and with his Son, Jesus Christ. ⁴We write this to make our*a* joy complete.

Light and Darkness, Sin and Forgiveness

⁵This is the message we have heard from him and declare to you: God is light; in him there is no darkness at all. ⁶If we claim to have fellowship with him and yet walk in the darkness, we lie and do not live out the truth. ⁷But if we walk in the light, as he is in the light, we have fellowship with one another, and the blood of Jesus, his Son, purifies us from all*b* sin.

⁸If we claim to be without sin, we deceive ourselves and the truth is not in us. ⁹If we confess our sins, he is faithful and just and will forgive us our sins and purify us from all unrighteousness. ¹⁰If we claim we have not sinned, we make him out to be a liar and his word is not in us.

My dear children, I write this to you so that you will not sin. But if anybody does sin, we have an advocate with the Father—Jesus Christ, the Righteous One. ²He is the atoning sacrifice for our sins, and not only for ours but also for the sins of the whole world.

Love and Hatred for Fellow Believers

³We know that we have come to know him if we keep his commands. ⁴Whoever says, "I know him," but does not do what

---

a 4 Some manuscripts *your*   *b* 7 Or *every*

ROCK SOLID *principles*

1 John 1:8–10

Get forgiveness.

Taylor might as well have her eyes shut tight and be wearing dark glasses covered by a blindfold. Not that she doesn't have other faults, but she is completely blind to her selfishness. Every sentence that spews from her mouth starts with "I." She streams her opinions to the whole planet, whether people ask for them or not. Taylor always has to go first, get the best, and take the most. She can't make it through a single day without creating a pile of hurt people, heaped up like garbage along her trail. Worst of all, everyone knows she claims to follow Jesus. People don't just dislike Taylor. Because of her, they don't think much of Jesus.

Anyone who claims to never sin is lying—or doesn't know what sin is. It's falling short of God's standards in what we think, say, or do—and it's a problem no matter how much we love Jesus. But God gives us a way to get clean every time we mess up: "If we confess our sins, he is faithful and just and will forgive us our sins and purify us from all unrighteousness" (1 John 1:9).

ROCK SOLID
promises

"He is the atoning sacrifice for our sins, and not only for ours but also for the sins of the whole world."

1 John 2:2

Jesus died on the cross to pay the penalty for your sins. He paid for the sins of every human who ever lived.

---

he commands is a liar, and the truth is not in that person. [5]But if anyone obeys his word, love for God[a] is truly made complete in them. This is how we know we are in him: [6]Whoever claims to live in him must live as Jesus did.

[7]Dear friends, I am not writing you a new command but an old one, which you have had since the beginning. This old command is the message you have heard. [8]Yet I am writing you a new command; its truth is seen in him and in you, because the darkness is passing and the true light is already shining.

[9]Anyone who claims to be in the light but hates a brother or sister[b] is still in the darkness. [10]Anyone who loves their brother and sister[c] lives in the light, and there is nothing in them to make them stumble. [11]But anyone who hates a brother or sister is in the darkness and walks around in the darkness. They do not know where they are going, because the darkness has blinded them.

Reasons for Writing

[12]I am writing to you, dear children,
  because your sins have been
    forgiven on account of his
      name.
[13]I am writing to you, fathers,
  because you know him who is from
    the beginning.

I am writing to you, young men,
  because you have overcome the evil
    one.
[14]I write to you, dear children,
  because you know the Father.
I write to you, fathers,
  because you know him who is from
    the beginning.
I write to you, young men,
  because you are strong,
  and the word of God lives in you,
  and you have overcome the evil
    one.

On Not Loving the World

[15]Do not love the world or anything in the world. If anyone loves the world, love for the Father[d] is not in them. [16]For everything in the world—the lust of the flesh, the lust of the eyes, and the pride of life—comes not from the Father but from the world. [17]The world and its desires pass away, but whoever does the will of God lives forever.

Warnings Against Denying the Son

[18]Dear children, this is the last hour; and as you have heard that the antichrist is coming, even now many antichrists have come. This is how we know it is the last hour. [19]They went out from us, but they did not really belong to us. For if they had belonged to us, they would have remained with us; but their going showed that none of them belonged to us.

[20]But you have an anointing from the Holy One, and all of you know the truth.[e] [21]I do not write to you because you do not know the truth, but because you do know it and because no lie comes from the truth. [22]Who is the liar? It is whoever denies that

---

[a] *5* Or *word, God's love*   [b] *9* The Greek word for *brother or sister* (*adelphos*) refers here to a believer, whether man or woman, as part of God's family; also in verse 11; and in 3:15, 17; 4:20; 5:16.   [c] *10* The Greek word for *brother and sister* (*adelphos*) refers here to a believer, whether man or woman, as part of God's family; also in 3:10; 4:20, 21.   [d] *15* Or *world, the Father's love*   [e] *20* Some manuscripts *and you know all things*

1 John 2:15

The world can lure you from God.

The apostle John understood love. He was "the disciple whom Jesus loved" (John 21:20). He wrote, "God is love" (1 John 4:8). He commanded, "Let us love one another" (1 John 4:7). And he was the guy who noticed that sometimes we fall in love with "the world" (1 John 2:15). John wasn't talking about caring too much for planet Earth or being affectionate toward people but rather being lured into an evil system opposed to God. Loving the world means getting caught up in "the lust of the flesh," wanting sinful pleasures. Or "the lust of the eyes," wanting what others have. Or "the pride of life," being proud of possessions or position (1 John 2:16). Love for the world is sinful because it gets in the way of doing God's will. Love for the world is foolish because none of those things will last.

Think: When are you most enticed by "the world"? What can you do to escape?

ROCK SOLID truths

Jesus is the Christ. Such a person is the antichrist—denying the Father and the Son. ²³No one who denies the Son has the Father; whoever acknowledges the Son has the Father also.

²⁴As for you, see that what you have heard from the beginning remains in you. If it does, you also will remain in the Son and in the Father. ²⁵And this is what he promised us—eternal life.

²⁶I am writing these things to you about those who are trying to lead you astray.

²⁷As for you, the anointing you received from him remains in you, and you do not need anyone to teach you. But as his anointing teaches you about all things and as that anointing is real, not counterfeit—just as it has taught you, remain in him.

God's Children and Sin

²⁸And now, dear children, continue in him, so that when he appears we may be confident and unashamed before him at his coming.

²⁹If you know that he is righteous, you know that everyone who does what is right has been born of him.

3 See what great love the Father has lavished on us, that we should be called children of God! And that is what we are! The reason the world does not know us is that it did not know him. ²Dear friends, now we are children of God, and what we will be has not yet been made known. But we know that when Christ appears,ᵃ we shall be like him, for we shall see him as he is. ³All who have this hope in him purify themselves, just as he is pure.

⁴Everyone who sins breaks the law; in fact, sin is lawlessness. ⁵But you know that he appeared so that he might take away our sins. And in him is no sin. ⁶No one who lives in him keeps on sinning. No one who continues to sin has either seen him or known him.

⁷Dear children, do not let anyone lead you astray. The one who does what is right is righteous, just as he is righteous. ⁸The one who does what is sinful is of the devil, because the devil has been sinning from the beginning. The reason the Son of God appeared was to destroy the devil's work. ⁹No one who is born of God will continue to sin, because God's seed remains in them; they cannot go on sinning, because they have been born of God. ¹⁰This is how we know who the children of God are and who the children of the devil are: Anyone who does not do what is right is not God's child, nor is anyone who does not love their brother and sister.

ᵃ 2 Or *when it is made known*

More on Love and Hatred

[11]For this is the message you heard from the beginning: We should love one another. [12]Do not be like Cain, who belonged to the evil one and murdered his brother. And why did he murder him? Because his own actions were evil and his brother's were righteous. [13]Do not be surprised, my brothers and sisters,[a] if the world hates you. [14]We know that we have passed from death to life, because we love each other. Anyone who does not love remains in death. [15]Anyone who hates a brother or sister is a murderer, and you know that no murderer has eternal life residing in him.

[16]This is how we know what love is: Jesus Christ laid down his life for us. And we ought to lay down our lives for our brothers and sisters. [17]If anyone has material possessions and sees a brother or sister in need but has no pity on them, how can the love of God be in that person? [18]Dear children, let us not love with words or speech but with actions and in truth.

[19]This is how we know that we belong to the truth and how we set our hearts at rest in his presence: [20]If our hearts condemn us, we know that God is greater than our hearts, and he knows everything. [21]Dear friends, if our hearts do not condemn us, we have confidence before God [22]and receive from him anything we ask, because we keep his commands and do what pleases him. [23]And this is his command: to believe in the name of his Son, Jesus Christ, and to love one another as he commanded us. [24]The one who keeps God's commands lives in him, and he in them. And this is how we know that he lives in us: We know it by the Spirit he gave us.

On Denying the Incarnation

4 Dear friends, do not believe every spirit, but test the spirits to see whether they are from God, because many false prophets have gone out into the world. [2]This is how you can recognize the Spirit of God: Every spirit that acknowledges that Jesus Christ has come in the flesh is from God, [3]but every spirit that does not acknowledge Jesus is not from God. This is the spirit of the antichrist, which you have heard is coming and even now is already in the world.

[4]You, dear children, are from God and have overcome them, because the one who is in you is greater than the one who is in the world. [5]They are from the world and

ROCK SOLID
promises

"The one who is in you is greater than the one who is in the world."

1 John 4:4

You might feel small and weak when the devil hassles you. But you have the infinitely powerful God living inside you.

therefore speak from the viewpoint of the world, and the world listens to them. [6]We are from God, and whoever knows God listens to us; but whoever is not from God does not listen to us. This is how we recognize the Spirit[b] of truth and the spirit of falsehood.

God's Love and Ours

[7]Dear friends, let us love one another, for love comes from God. Everyone who loves has been born of God and knows God. [8]Whoever does not love does not know God, because God is love. [9]This is how God showed his love among us: He sent his one and only Son into the world that we might live through him. [10]This is love: not that we loved God, but that he

[a] 13 The Greek word for *brothers and sisters* (*adelphoi*) refers here to believers, both men and women, as part of God's family; also in verse 16.
[b] 6 Or *spirit*

loved us and sent his Son as an atoning sacrifice for our sins. [11] Dear friends, since God so loved us, we also ought to love one another. [12] No one has ever seen God; but if we love one another, God lives in us and his love is made complete in us.

[13] This is how we know that we live in him and he in us: He has given us of his Spirit. [14] And we have seen and testify that the Father has sent his Son to be the Savior of the world. [15] If anyone acknowledges that Jesus is the Son of God, God lives in them and they in God. [16] And so we know and rely on the love God has for us.

God is love. Whoever lives in love lives in God, and God in them. [17] This is how love is made complete among us so that we will have confidence on the day of judgment: In this world we are like Jesus. [18] There is no fear in love. But perfect love drives out fear, because fear has to do with punishment. The one who fears is not made perfect in love.

[19] We love because he first loved us. [20] Whoever claims to love God yet hates a brother or sister is a liar. For whoever does not love their brother and sister, whom they have seen, cannot love God, whom they have not seen. [21] And he has given us this command: Anyone who loves God must also love their brother and sister.

Faith in the Incarnate Son of God

5 Everyone who believes that Jesus is the Christ is born of God, and everyone who loves the father loves his child as well. [2] This is how we know that we love the children of God: by loving God and carrying out his commands. [3] In fact, this is love for God: to keep his commands. And his commands are not burdensome, [4] for everyone born of God overcomes the world. This is the victory that has overcome the world, even our faith. [5] Who is it that overcomes the world? Only the one who believes that Jesus is the Son of God.

[6] This is the one who came by water and blood—Jesus Christ. He did not come by water only, but by water and blood. And it is the Spirit who testifies, because the Spirit is the truth. [7] For there are three that testify: [8] the[a] Spirit, the water and the blood; and the three are in agreement. [9] We accept human testimony, but God's testimony is greater because it is the testimony of God, which he has given about his Son. [10] Whoever believes in the Son of God accepts this testimony. Whoever does not believe God has made him out to be a liar, because they have not believed the testimony God has given about his Son. [11] And this is the testimony: God has given us eternal life, and this life is in his Son. [12] Whoever has the Son has life; whoever does not have the Son of God does not have life.

UNSHAKEN God

1 John 4:7–12

God is love.

Suppose you want to explain God to some friends and need to pick just a single word that best describes him. Of all the words you could choose to finish the sentence "God is ... ", one jumps to the top of the list. Love. It's the characteristic that sums up everything else you can ever say about the Lord. His love is more than a cold fact or theoretical idea. He invites you to experience his concern and care for you every second of every day, in every part of your life. And he sent Jesus "as an atoning sacrifice for our sins" (1 John 4:10) to prove his love for you, your friends, and every human being.

So ... Why is "love" the best word you can use to describe God—or not?

[a] 7,8 Late manuscripts of the Vulgate *testify in heaven: the Father, the Word and the Holy Spirit, and these three are one.* [8] *And there are three that testify on earth: the* (not found in any Greek manuscript before the fourteenth century)

Concluding Affirmations

¹³I write these things to you who believe in the name of the Son of God so that you may know that you have eternal life. ¹⁴This is the confidence we have in approaching God: that if we ask anything according to his will, he hears us. ¹⁵And if we know that he hears us—whatever we ask—we know that we have what we asked of him.

¹⁶If you see any brother or sister commit a sin that does not lead to death, you should pray and God will give them life. I refer to those whose sin does not lead to death. There is a sin that leads to death. I am not saying that you should pray about that. ¹⁷All wrongdoing is sin, and there is sin that does not lead to death.

¹⁸We know that anyone born of God does not continue to sin; the One who was born of God keeps them safe, and the evil one cannot harm them. ¹⁹We know that we are children of God, and that the whole world is under the control of the evil one. ²⁰We know also that the Son of God has come and has given us understanding, so that we may know him who is true. And we are in him who is true by being in his Son Jesus Christ. He is the true God and eternal life.

²¹Dear children, keep yourselves from idols.

ROCK SOLID
promises

"This is the confidence we have in approaching God: that if we ask anything according to his will, he hears us." 1 John 5:14

You can confidently expect God to give you what you ask—as long as you want what he wants.

2 JOHN

John wrote this letter "to the lady chosen by God and to her children." He might have meant either a Christian woman and her family or a church and its members.

In this letter John writes how important it is for Christians to love one another. He says that to love means to obey God's commandments, and God's commandments tell us to live lives of love.

John again emphasizes the importance of the doctrine that Jesus is God's Son and a human being. Christians should separate themselves from those who teach that Jesus is not God's Son.

¹The elder,

To the lady chosen by God and to her children, whom I love in the truth—and not I only, but also all who know the truth— ²because of the truth, which lives in us and will be with us forever:

³Grace, mercy and peace from God the Father and from Jesus Christ, the Father's Son, will be with us in truth and love.

⁴It has given me great joy to find some of your children walking in the truth, just as the Father commanded us. ⁵And now, dear lady, I am not writing you a new command but one we have had from the beginning. I ask that we love one another. ⁶And this is love: that we walk in obedience to his commands. As you have heard from the beginning, his command is that you walk in love.

⁷I say this because many deceivers, who do not acknowledge Jesus Christ as coming in the flesh, have gone out into the world. Any such person is the deceiver and the antichrist. ⁸Watch out that you do not lose what we*a* have worked for, but that you may be rewarded fully. ⁹Anyone who runs ahead and does not continue in the teaching of Christ does not have God; whoever continues in the teaching has both the Father and the Son. ¹⁰If anyone comes to you and does not bring this teaching, do not take them into your house or welcome them. ¹¹Anyone who welcomes them shares in their wicked work.

¹²I have much to write to you, but I do not want to use paper and ink. Instead, I hope to visit you and talk with you face to face, so that our joy may be complete.

¹³The children of your sister, who is chosen by God, send their greetings.

a 8 Some manuscripts *you*

3 JOHN

BOOK OUTLINE

Greeting
(1–4)

Encouragement for Gaius
(5–8)

A scolding for Diotrephes
(9,10)

Praise for Demetrius
(11,12)

Conclusion
(13–15)

John wrote this letter to his friend Gaius, a leader in the church. A man named Diotrephes in Gaius's church refused to welcome God's messengers. John writes this letter to praise and thank Gaius for his help and to scold Diotrephes for not cooperating. John promises to come to this church soon to deal with this matter himself.

¹The elder,

To my dear friend Gaius, whom I love in the truth.

²Dear friend, I pray that you may enjoy good health and that all may go well with you, even as your soul is getting along well. ³It gave me great joy when some believers came and testified about your faithfulness to the truth, telling how you continue to walk in it. ⁴I have no greater joy than to hear that my children are walking in the truth.

⁵Dear friend, you are faithful in what you are doing for the brothers and sisters,ᵃ even though they are strangers to you. ⁶They have told the church about your love. Please send them on their way in a manner that honors God. ⁷It was for the sake of the Name that they went out, receiving no help from the pagans. ⁸We ought therefore to show hospitality to such people so that we may work together for the truth.

⁹I wrote to the church, but Diotrephes, who loves to be first, will not welcome us. ¹⁰So when I come, I will call attention to what he is doing, spreading malicious nonsense about us. Not satisfied with that, he even refuses to welcome other believers. He also stops those who want to do so and puts them out of the church.

¹¹Dear friend, do not imitate what is evil but what is good. Anyone who does what is good is from God. Anyone who does what is evil has not seen God. ¹²Demetrius is well spoken of by everyone—and even by the truth itself. We also speak well of him, and you know that our testimony is true.

¹³I have much to write you, but I do not want to do so with pen and ink. ¹⁴I hope to see you soon, and we will talk face to face.

Peace to you. The friends here send their greetings. Greet the friends there by name.

ᵃ 5 The Greek word for *brothers and sisters* (*adelphoi*) refers here to believers, both men and women, as part of God's family.

BOOK OUTLINE

Introduction
(1,2)

Warnings against false teachers
(3–16)

Warning and conclusion
(17–25)

J ude, like James, was a brother of Jesus. He wrote to warn Christians about the same false teachers Peter wrote about in his second letter. These false teachers were not only teaching that Jesus was not the Son of God; they were also leading the people to live sinful lives. Jude warns that God will punish and destroy these false teachers just as he had punished sinners in the Old Testament.

¹Jude, a servant of Jesus Christ and a brother of James,

To those who have been called, who are loved in God the Father and kept for*a* Jesus Christ:

²Mercy, peace and love be yours in abundance.

The Sin and Doom of Ungodly People

³Dear friends, although I was very eager to write to you about the salvation we share, I felt compelled to write and urge you to contend for the faith that was once for all entrusted to God's holy people. ⁴For certain individuals whose condemnation was written about*b* long ago have secretly slipped in among you. They are ungodly people, who pervert the grace of our God into a license for immorality and deny Jesus Christ our only Sovereign and Lord.

⁵Though you already know all this, I want to remind you that the Lord*c* at one time delivered his people out of Egypt, but later destroyed those who did not believe. ⁶And the angels who did not keep their positions of authority but abandoned their proper dwelling—these he has kept in darkness, bound with everlasting chains for judgment on the great Day. ⁷In a similar way, Sodom and Gomorrah and the surrounding towns gave themselves up to sexual immorality and perversion. They serve as an example of those who suffer the punishment of eternal fire.

⁸In the very same way, on the strength of their dreams these ungodly people pollute their own bodies, reject authority and heap abuse on celestial beings. ⁹But even the archangel Michael, when he was disputing with the devil about the body of Moses, did not himself dare to condemn him for slander but said, "The Lord rebuke you!"*d* ¹⁰Yet these people slander whatever they do not understand, and the very things they do understand by instinct—as irrational animals do—will destroy them.

¹¹Woe to them! They have taken the way of Cain; they have rushed for profit into Balaam's error; they have been destroyed in Korah's rebellion.

¹²These people are blemishes at your love feasts, eating with you without the slightest qualm—shepherds who feed only themselves. They are clouds without rain, blown along by the wind; autumn trees, without fruit and uprooted—twice dead.

---

a 1 Or *by*; or *in*   *b* 4 Or *individuals who were marked out for condemnation*   *c* 5 Some early manuscripts *Jesus*   *d* 9 Jude is alluding to the Jewish *Testament of Moses* (approximately the first century A.D.).

Jude 1–25

The faith is worth fighting for.

Jude could no longer contain his worry. He intended to write a letter about "the salvation we share," covering details of what it means to know and follow Jesus (Jude 3). But instead he had to urge his readers to "contend for the faith that was once for all entrusted to God's holy people" (Jude 3). "Contend" is a word at the root of the English word "agonize." So Jude was telling everyone to snap awake and start passionately defending the true beliefs handed down from the apostles, Jesus' original disciples. Jude saw that false teachers had crept into the church, and they were using God's gracious forgiveness as an excuse to keep on sinning. You might be shy about arguing for the rightness of your beliefs, but there are all kinds of attractive teachings inside and outside the church that lead people to hell. So stick to your faith—and don't let others get duped by lies (Jude 22–23).

Think: When and how should you try to correct people's false beliefs?

ROCK SOLID truths

[13]They are wild waves of the sea, foaming up their shame; wandering stars, for whom blackest darkness has been reserved forever.

[14]Enoch, the seventh from Adam, prophesied about them: "See, the Lord is coming with thousands upon thousands of his holy ones [15]to judge everyone, and to convict all of them of all the ungodly acts they have committed in their ungodliness, and of all the defiant words ungodly sinners have spoken against him."[a] [16]These people are grumblers and faultfinders; they follow their own evil desires; they boast about themselves and flatter others for their own advantage.

A Call to Persevere

[17]But, dear friends, remember what the apostles of our Lord Jesus Christ foretold. [18]They said to you, "In the last times there will be scoffers who will follow their own ungodly desires." [19]These are the people who divide you, who follow mere natural instincts and do not have the Spirit.

[20]But you, dear friends, by building yourselves up in your most holy faith and praying in the Holy Spirit, [21]keep yourselves in God's love as you wait for the mercy of our Lord Jesus Christ to bring you to eternal life.

[22]Be merciful to those who doubt; [23]save others by snatching them from the fire; to others show mercy, mixed with fear—hating even the clothing stained by corrupted flesh.[b]

Doxology

[24]To him who is able to keep you from stumbling and to present you before his glorious presence without fault and with great joy— [25]to the only God our Savior be glory, majesty, power and authority, through Jesus Christ our Lord, before all ages, now and forevermore! Amen.

[a] 14,15 From the Jewish First Book of Enoch (approximately the first century B.C.)
[b] 22,23 The Greek manuscripts of these verses vary at several points.

REVELATION

BOOK OUTLINE

Christ reveals himself to John
(1:1–20)

Letters to the seven churches
(2:1—3:22)

The heavenly throne
(4:1—5:14)

The seven seals
(6:1—8:5)

The seven trumpets
(8:6—11:19)

Seven more signs
(12:1—14:20)

The bowls of wrath
(15:1—16:21)

Babylon judged
(17:1—19:10)

Beast and false prophet judged
(19:11–21)

Satan judged
(20:1–3)

Thousand-year reign
(20:4–6)

Rebellion and final judgment
(20:7–15)

New heaven, new earth, new Jerusalem
(21:1—22:5)

Conclusion
(22:6–21)

The apostle John wrote the book of Revelation during his exile on the island of Patmos. John's purpose in writing this book was to give hope and encouragement to the Christians who were suffering severe persecution for their faith in Jesus Christ. These Christians needed to know that God controls everything that happens here on earth.

Through imagery and symbols, John makes one thing very clear: Jesus Christ is the Lord and ruler over everyone and everything— even powerful human governments. Christ is clearly in control and will someday judge and punish what is evil, even Satan. He will also establish an everlasting kingdom with a new heaven and a new earth.

Prologue

The revelation from Jesus Christ, which God gave him to show his servants what must soon take place. He made it known by sending his angel to his servant John, ²who testifies to everything he saw—that is, the word of God and the testimony of Jesus Christ. ³Blessed is the one who reads aloud the words of this prophecy, and blessed are those who hear it and take to heart what is written in it, because the time is near.

Greetings and Doxology

⁴John,

To the seven churches in the province of Asia:

Grace and peace to you from him who is, and who was, and who is to come, and from the seven spirits*a* before his throne, ⁵and from Jesus Christ, who is the faithful witness, the firstborn from the dead, and the ruler of the kings of the earth.

To him who loves us and has freed us from our sins by his blood, ⁶and has made us to be a kingdom and priests to serve his God and Father—to him be glory and power for ever and ever! Amen.

⁷"Look, he is coming with the clouds,"*b*
    and "every eye will see him,
even those who pierced him";
    and all peoples on earth "will
        mourn because of him."*c*
            So shall it be! Amen.

⁸"I am the Alpha and the Omega," says the Lord God, "who is, and who was, and who is to come, the Almighty."

John's Vision of Christ

⁹I, John, your brother and companion in the suffering and kingdom and patient endurance that are ours in Jesus, was on the island of Patmos because of the word of God and the testimony of Jesus. ¹⁰On the Lord's Day I was in the Spirit, and I heard behind me a loud voice like a trumpet, ¹¹which said: "Write on a scroll what you see and send it to the seven churches: to Ephesus, Smyrna, Pergamum, Thyatira, Sardis, Philadelphia and Laodicea."

¹²I turned around to see the voice that was speaking to me. And when I turned I saw seven golden lampstands, ¹³and among the lampstands was someone like a son of man,*d* dressed in a robe reaching down to his feet and with a golden sash around his chest. ¹⁴The hair on his head was white like wool, as white as snow, and his eyes were like blazing fire. ¹⁵His feet were like bronze glowing in a furnace, and his voice was like the sound of rushing waters. ¹⁶In his right hand he held seven stars, and coming out of his mouth was a sharp, double-edged sword. His face was like the sun shining in all its brilliance.

¹⁷When I saw him, I fell at his feet as though dead. Then he placed his right hand on me and said: "Do not be afraid. I am the First and the Last. ¹⁸I am the Living One; I was dead, and now look, I am alive for ever and ever! And I hold the keys of death and Hades.

ROCK SOLID promises

"I am the Living One; I was dead, and now look, I am alive for ever and ever! And I hold the keys of death and Hades." Revelation 1:18

Jesus rose from the dead. He alone can let you into heaven or lock you in hell.

¹⁹"Write, therefore, what you have seen, what is now and what will take place later. ²⁰The mystery of the seven stars that you saw in my right hand and of the seven golden lampstands is this: The seven stars are the angels*e* of the seven churches,

---

a 4 That is, the sevenfold Spirit
b 7 Daniel 7:13   *c 7* Zech. 12:10
d 13 See Daniel 7:13.   *e 20* Or *messengers*

and the seven lampstands are the seven churches.

To the Church in Ephesus

 "To the angel[a] of the church in Ephesus write:

These are the words of him who holds the seven stars in his right hand and walks among the seven golden lampstands. [2]I know your deeds, your hard work and your perseverance. I know that you cannot tolerate wicked people, that you have tested those who claim to be apostles but are not, and have found them false. [3]You have persevered and have endured hardships for my name, and have not grown weary.

[4]Yet I hold this against you: You have forsaken the love you had at first. [5]Consider how far you have fallen! Repent and do the things you did at first. If you do not repent, I will come to you and remove your lampstand from its place. [6]But you have this in your favor: You hate the practices of the Nicolaitans, which I also hate.

[7]Whoever has ears, let them hear what the Spirit says to the churches. To the one who is victorious, I will give the right to eat from the tree of life, which is in the paradise of God.

To the Church in Smyrna

[8]"To the angel of the church in Smyrna write:

These are the words of him who is the First and the Last, who died and came to life again. [9]I know your afflictions and your poverty—yet you are rich! I know about the slander of those who say they are Jews and are not, but are a synagogue of Satan. [10]Do not be afraid of what you are about to suffer. I tell you, the devil will put some of you in prison to test you, and you will suffer persecution for ten days. Be faithful, even to the point of death, and I will give you life as your victor's crown.

ROCK SOLID *plans*

Revelation 2:1–7

Get back to basics.

Jesus himself speaks at the start of the book of Revelation, addressing the highs and lows of seven churches scattered across Asia Minor, now modern Turkey. He applauds the believers in Ephesus for their good deeds, rejection of evil and persistence in the face of hardship. But Jesus says they have forgotten the most important part of being a believer. They don't love him as much as they did when they first believed. He tells them to repent and get back to their first love.

Your next step: Ask a mature Christian how you can stay passionately dedicated to Jesus.

[11]Whoever has ears, let them hear what the Spirit says to the churches. The one who is victorious will not be hurt at all by the second death.

To the Church in Pergamum

[12]"To the angel of the church in Pergamum write:

These are the words of him who has the sharp, double-edged sword. [13]I know where you live—where Satan has his throne. Yet you remain true to my name. You did not renounce your faith in me, not even in the days of Antipas, my faithful witness, who was put to death in your city—where Satan lives.

[14]Nevertheless, I have a few things against you: There are some among you who hold to the teaching of Balaam, who taught Balak to entice the Israelites to sin so that they ate food sacrificed to idols and committed sexual immorality. [15]Likewise, you

[a] 1 Or *messenger*; also in verses 8, 12 and 18

also have those who hold to the teaching of the Nicolaitans. ¹⁶Repent therefore! Otherwise, I will soon come to you and will fight against them with the sword of my mouth.

¹⁷Whoever has ears, let them hear what the Spirit says to the churches. To the one who is victorious, I will give some of the hidden manna. I will also give that person a white stone with a new name written on it, known only to the one who receives it.

To the Church in Thyatira

¹⁸"To the angel of the church in Thyatira write:

These are the words of the Son of God, whose eyes are like blazing fire and whose feet are like burnished bronze. ¹⁹I know your deeds, your love and faith, your service and perseverance, and that you are now doing more than you did at first.

²⁰Nevertheless, I have this against you: You tolerate that woman Jezebel, who calls herself a prophet. By her teaching she misleads my servants into sexual immorality and the eating of food sacrificed to idols. ²¹I have given her time to repent of her immorality, but she is unwilling. ²²So I will cast her on a bed of suffering, and I will make those who commit adultery with her suffer intensely, unless they repent of her ways. ²³I will strike her children dead. Then all the churches will know that I am he who searches hearts and minds, and I will repay each of you according to your deeds.

²⁴Now I say to the rest of you in Thyatira, to you who do not hold to her teaching and have not learned Satan's so-called deep secrets, 'I will not impose any other burden on you, ²⁵except to hold on to what you have until I come.'

²⁶To the one who is victorious and does my will to the end, I will give authority over the nations— ²⁷that one 'will rule them with an iron scepter and will dash them to pieces like pottery'ᵃ—just as I have received authority from my Father. ²⁸I will also give that one the morning star. ²⁹Whoever has ears, let them hear what the Spirit says to the churches.

To the Church in Sardis

3 "To the angelᵇ of the church in Sardis write:

These are the words of him who holds the seven spiritsᶜ of God and the seven stars. I know your deeds; you have a reputation of being alive, but you are dead. ²Wake up! Strengthen what remains and is about to die, for I have found your deeds unfinished in the sight of my God. ³Remember, therefore, what you have received and heard; hold it fast, and repent. But if you do not wake up, I will come like a thief, and you will not know at what time I will come to you.

⁴Yet you have a few people in Sardis who have not soiled their clothes. They will walk with me, dressed in white, for they are worthy. ⁵The one who is victorious will, like them, be dressed in white. I will never blot out the name of that person from the book of life, but will acknowledge that name before my Father and his angels. ⁶Whoever has ears, let them hear what the Spirit says to the churches.

To the Church in Philadelphia

⁷"To the angel of the church in Philadelphia write:

These are the words of him who is holy and true, who holds the key of David. What he opens no one can shut, and what he shuts no one can open. ⁸I know your deeds. See, I have

---

ᵃ *27* Psalm 2:9   ᵇ *1* Or *messenger*; also in verses 7 and 14   ᶜ *1* That is, the sevenfold Spirit placed before you an open door that no one can shut. I know that you have little strength, yet you have kept my word and have not denied my name. ⁹I will make those who are of the synagogue of Satan, who claim to be Jews though they are not, but are liars—I will make them come and fall down at your feet and acknowledge that I have loved you. ¹⁰Since you have kept my command to endure patiently, I will also keep you from the hour of trial that is going to come on the whole world to test the inhabitants of the earth.

¹¹I am coming soon. Hold on to what you have, so that no one will take your crown. ¹²The one who is victorious I will make a pillar in the temple of my God. Never again will they leave it. I will write on them the name of my God and the name of the city of my God, the new Jerusalem, which is coming down out of heaven from my God; and I will also write on them my new name. ¹³Whoever has ears, let them hear what the Spirit says to the churches.

To the Church in Laodicea

¹⁴"To the angel of the church in Laodicea write:

These are the words of the Amen, the faithful and true witness, the ruler of God's creation. ¹⁵I know your deeds, that you are neither cold nor hot. I wish you were either one or the other! ¹⁶So, because you are lukewarm—neither hot nor cold—I am about to spit you out of my mouth. ¹⁷You say, 'I am rich; I have acquired wealth and do not need a thing.' But you do not realize that you are wretched, pitiful, poor, blind and naked. ¹⁸I counsel you to buy from me gold refined in the fire, so you can become rich; and white clothes to wear, so you can cover your shameful nakedness; and salve to put on your eyes, so you can see.

¹⁹Those whom I love I rebuke and discipline. So be earnest and repent. ²⁰Here I am! I stand at the door and knock. If anyone hears my voice and opens the door, I will come in and eat with that person, and they with me.

²¹To the one who is victorious, I will give the right to sit with me on my throne, just as I was victorious and sat down with my Father on his throne. ²²Whoever has ears, let them hear what the Spirit says to the churches."

The Throne in Heaven

4 After this I looked, and there before me was a door standing open in heaven. And the voice I had first heard speaking to me like a trumpet said, "Come up here, and I will show you what must take place after this." ²At once I was in the Spirit, and there before me was a throne in heaven with someone sitting on it. ³And the one who sat there had the appearance of jasper and ruby. A rainbow that shone like an emerald encircled the throne. ⁴Surrounding the throne were twenty-four other thrones, and seated on them were twenty-four elders. They were dressed in white and had crowns of gold on their heads. ⁵From the throne came flashes of lightning, rumblings and peals of thunder. In front of the throne, seven lamps were blazing. These are the seven spirits[a] of God. [6]Also in front of the throne there was what looked like a sea of glass, clear as crystal.

In the center, around the throne, were four living creatures, and they were covered with eyes, in front and in back. [7]The first living creature was like a lion, the second was like an ox, the third had a face like a man, the fourth was like a flying eagle. [8]Each of the four living creatures had six wings and was covered with eyes all around, even under its wings. Day and night they never stop saying:

> "'Holy, holy, holy
> is the Lord God Almighty,'[b]
> who was, and is, and is to come."

[9]Whenever the living creatures give glory, honor and thanks to him who sits on the throne and who lives for ever and ever, [10]the twenty-four elders fall down before him who sits on the throne and worship him who lives for ever and ever. They lay their crowns before the throne and say:

[11]"You are worthy, our Lord and God,
> to receive glory and honor and power,
> for you created all things,
> and by your will they were created
> and have their being."

The Scroll and the Lamb

5 Then I saw in the right hand of him who sat on the throne a scroll with writing on both sides and sealed with seven seals. [2]And I saw a mighty angel proclaiming in a loud voice, "Who is worthy to break the seals and open the scroll?" [3]But no one in heaven or on earth or under the earth could open the scroll or even look inside it. [4]I wept and wept because no one was found who was worthy to open the scroll or look inside. [5]Then one of the elders said to me, "Do not weep! See, the Lion of the tribe of Judah, the Root of David, has triumphed. He is able to open the scroll and its seven seals."

[6]Then I saw a Lamb, looking as if it had been slain, standing at the center of the

UNSHAKEN *God*

Revelation 4:1–11

God is worthy.

When the apostle John saw an open door into heaven, Jesus himself invited him to come close and see what would happen at the end of time (see Revelation 4:1). Suddenly John was swept into heaven, and he saw God sitting on his throne, surrounded with blazing brightness. The creatures around the Lord constantly worshiped him, and the end of this chapter tells why they never took a break. The Lord is "worthy," deserving "glory and honor and power" (Revelation 4:11). He created the world and keeps it running. So he deserves not only your praise-filled words but your obedience-filled life.

So ... Why does God deserve worship—and your life?

throne, encircled by the four living creatures and the elders. The Lamb had seven horns and seven eyes, which are the seven spirits[a] of God sent out into all the earth. [7]He went and took the scroll from the right hand of him who sat on the throne. [8]And when he had taken it, the four living creatures and the twenty-four elders fell down before the Lamb. Each one had a harp and they were holding golden bowls full of incense, which are the prayers of God's people. [9]And they sang a new song, saying:

> "You are worthy to take the scroll
> and to open its seals,
> because you were slain,
> and with your blood you purchased for God
> persons from every tribe and language and people and nation.

---

[a] 5,6 That is, the sevenfold Spirit
[b] 8 Isaiah 6:3

[10]You have made them to be a kingdom
and priests to serve our God,
and they will reign[a] on the earth."

[11]Then I looked and heard the voice of many angels, numbering thousands upon thousands, and ten thousand times ten thousand. They encircled the throne and the living creatures and the elders. [12]In a loud voice they were saying:

"Worthy is the Lamb, who was
slain,
to receive power and wealth and
wisdom and strength
and honor and glory and
praise!"

[13]Then I heard every creature in heaven and on earth and under the earth and on the sea, and all that is in them, saying:

"To him who sits on the throne and
to the Lamb
be praise and honor and glory and
power,
for ever and ever!"

[14]The four living creatures said, "Amen," and the elders fell down and worshiped.

The Seals

6 I watched as the Lamb opened the first of the seven seals. Then I heard one of the four living creatures say in a voice like thunder, "Come!" [2]I looked, and there before me was a white horse! Its rider held a bow, and he was given a crown, and he rode out as a conqueror bent on conquest.

[3]When the Lamb opened the second seal, I heard the second living creature say, "Come!" [4]Then another horse came out, a fiery red one. Its rider was given power to take peace from the earth and to make people kill each other. To him was given a large sword.

[5]When the Lamb opened the third seal, I heard the third living creature say, "Come!" I looked, and there before me was a black horse! Its rider was holding a pair of scales in his hand. [6]Then I heard what sounded like a voice among the four living creatures, saying, "Two pounds[b] of

wheat for a day's wages,[c] and six pounds[d] of barley for a day's wages,[c] and do not damage the oil and the wine!"

[7]When the Lamb opened the fourth seal, I heard the voice of the fourth living creature say, "Come!" [8]I looked, and there before me was a pale horse! Its rider was named Death, and Hades was following close behind him. They were given power over a fourth of the earth to kill by sword, famine and plague, and by the wild beasts of the earth.

[9]When he opened the fifth seal, I saw under the altar the souls of those who had been slain because of the word of God and the testimony they had maintained. [10]They called out in a loud voice, "How long, Sovereign Lord, holy and true, until you judge the inhabitants of the earth and avenge our blood?" [11]Then each of them was given a white robe, and they were told to wait a little longer, until the full number of their fellow servants, their brothers and sisters,[e] were killed just as they had been.

[12]I watched as he opened the sixth seal. There was a great earthquake. The sun turned black like sackcloth made of goat hair, the whole moon turned blood red, [13]and the stars in the sky fell to earth, as figs drop from a fig tree when shaken by a strong wind. [14]The heavens receded like a scroll being rolled up, and every mountain and island was removed from its place.

[15]Then the kings of the earth, the princes, the generals, the rich, the mighty, and everyone else, both slave and free, hid in caves and among the rocks of the mountains. [16]They called to the mountains and the rocks, "Fall on us and hide us[f] from the face of him who sits on the throne and from the wrath of the Lamb! [17]For the great day of their[g] wrath has come, and who can withstand it?"

---

[a] 10 Some manuscripts *they reign*
[b] 6 Or about 1 kilogram   [c] 6 Greek *a denarius*
[d] 6 Or about 3 kilograms   [e] 11 The Greek word for *brothers and sisters* (*adelphoi*) refers here to believers, both men and women, as part of God's family; also in 12:10; 19:10.   [f] 16 See Hosea 10:8.   [g] 17 Some manuscripts *his*

144,000 Sealed

7 After this I saw four angels standing at the four corners of the earth, holding back the four winds of the earth to prevent any wind from blowing on the land or on the sea or on any tree. ²Then I saw another angel coming up from the east, having the seal of the living God. He called out in a loud voice to the four angels who had been given power to harm the land and the sea: ³"Do not harm the land or the sea or the trees until we put a seal on the foreheads of the servants of our God." ⁴Then I heard the number of those who were sealed: 144,000 from all the tribes of Israel.

⁵From the tribe of Judah 12,000 were sealed,
from the tribe of Reuben 12,000,
from the tribe of Gad 12,000,
⁶from the tribe of Asher 12,000,
from the tribe of Naphtali 12,000,
from the tribe of Manasseh 12,000,
⁷from the tribe of Simeon 12,000,
from the tribe of Levi 12,000,
from the tribe of Issachar 12,000,
⁸from the tribe of Zebulun 12,000,
from the tribe of Joseph 12,000,
from the tribe of Benjamin 12,000.

The Great Multitude in White Robes

⁹After this I looked, and there before me was a great multitude that no one could count, from every nation, tribe, people and language, standing before the throne and before the Lamb. They were wearing white robes and were holding palm branches in their hands. ¹⁰And they cried out in a loud voice:

"Salvation belongs to our God,
who sits on the throne,
and to the Lamb."

¹¹All the angels were standing around the throne and around the elders and the four living creatures. They fell down on their faces before the throne and worshiped God, ¹²saying:

"Amen!
Praise and glory

ROCK SOLID promises

"Salvation belongs to our God, who sits on the throne, and to the Lamb." Revelation 7:10

No matter how chaotic your world feels, God rules from his heavenly throne. He's working to save the world.

and wisdom and thanks and honor
and power and strength
be to our God for ever and ever.
Amen!"

¹³Then one of the elders asked me, "These in white robes—who are they, and where did they come from?"

¹⁴I answered, "Sir, you know."

And he said, "These are they who have come out of the great tribulation; they have washed their robes and made them white in the blood of the Lamb. ¹⁵Therefore,

"they are before the throne of God
and serve him day and night in his
temple;
and he who sits on the throne
will shelter them with his
presence.
¹⁶'Never again will they hunger;
never again will they thirst.
The sun will not beat down on
them,'ᵃ
nor any scorching heat.
¹⁷For the Lamb at the center of the
throne
will be their shepherd;
'he will lead them to springs of living
water.'ᵃ
'And God will wipe away every tear
from their eyes.'ᵇ"

ᵃ *16,17* Isaiah 49:10   ᵇ *17* Isaiah 25:8

The Seventh Seal and the Golden Censer

8 When he opened the seventh seal, there was silence in heaven for about half an hour.

²And I saw the seven angels who stand before God, and seven trumpets were given to them.

³Another angel, who had a golden censer, came and stood at the altar. He was given much incense to offer, with the prayers of all God's people, on the golden altar in front of the throne. ⁴The smoke of the incense, together with the prayers of God's people, went up before God from the angel's hand. ⁵Then the angel took the censer, filled it with fire from the altar, and hurled it on the earth; and there came peals of thunder, rumblings, flashes of lightning and an earthquake.

The Trumpets

⁶Then the seven angels who had the seven trumpets prepared to sound them.

⁷The first angel sounded his trumpet, and there came hail and fire mixed with blood, and it was hurled down on the earth. A third of the earth was burned up, a third of the trees were burned up, and all the green grass was burned up.

⁸The second angel sounded his trumpet, and something like a huge mountain, all ablaze, was thrown into the sea. A third of the sea turned into blood, ⁹a third of the living creatures in the sea died, and a third of the ships were destroyed.

¹⁰The third angel sounded his trumpet, and a great star, blazing like a torch, fell from the sky on a third of the rivers and on the springs of water— ¹¹the name of the star is Wormwood.ᵃ A third of the waters turned bitter, and many people died from the waters that had become bitter.

¹²The fourth angel sounded his trumpet, and a third of the sun was struck, a third of the moon, and a third of the stars, so that a third of them turned dark. A third of the day was without light, and also a third of the night.

¹³As I watched, I heard an eagle that was flying in midair call out in a loud voice: "Woe! Woe! Woe to the inhabitants of the earth, because of the trumpet blasts about to be sounded by the other three angels!"

9 The fifth angel sounded his trumpet, and I saw a star that had fallen from the sky to the earth. The star was given the key to the shaft of the Abyss. ²When he opened the Abyss, smoke rose from it like the smoke from a gigantic furnace. The sun and sky were darkened by the smoke from the Abyss. ³And out of the smoke locusts came down on the earth and were given power like that of scorpions of the earth. ⁴They were told not to harm the grass of the earth or any plant or tree, but only those people who did not have the seal of God on their foreheads. ⁵They were not allowed to kill them but only to torture them for five months. And the agony they suffered was like that of the sting of a scorpion when it strikes. ⁶During those days people will seek death but will not find it; they will long to die, but death will elude them.

⁷The locusts looked like horses prepared for battle. On their heads they wore something like crowns of gold, and their faces resembled human faces. ⁸Their hair was like women's hair, and their teeth were like lions' teeth. ⁹They had breastplates like breastplates of iron, and the sound of their wings was like the thundering of many horses and chariots rushing into battle. ¹⁰They had tails with stingers, like scorpions, and in their tails they had power to torment people for five months. ¹¹They had as king over them the angel of the Abyss, whose name in Hebrew is Abaddon and in Greek is Apollyon (that is, Destroyer).

¹²The first woe is past; two other woes are yet to come.

¹³The sixth angel sounded his trumpet, and I heard a voice coming from the four horns of the golden altar that is before God. ¹⁴It said to the sixth angel who had the trumpet, "Release the four angels who are bound at the great river Euphrates." ¹⁵And the four angels who had been

---

ᵃ *11* Wormwood is a bitter substance.

kept ready for this very hour and day and month and year were released to kill a third of mankind. ¹⁶The number of the mounted troops was twice ten thousand times ten thousand. I heard their number.

¹⁷The horses and riders I saw in my vision looked like this: Their breastplates were fiery red, dark blue, and yellow as sulfur. The heads of the horses resembled the heads of lions, and out of their mouths came fire, smoke and sulfur. ¹⁸A third of mankind was killed by the three plagues of fire, smoke and sulfur that came out of their mouths. ¹⁹The power of the horses was in their mouths and in their tails; for their tails were like snakes, having heads with which they inflict injury.

²⁰The rest of mankind who were not killed by these plagues still did not repent of the work of their hands; they did not stop worshiping demons, and idols of gold, silver, bronze, stone and wood—idols that cannot see or hear or walk. ²¹Nor did they repent of their murders, their magic arts, their sexual immorality or their thefts.

Revelation 9

The end of time brings God's judgment.

People wonder if God will ever put an end to evil, and the Bible assures us he will. It starts with the fact that every human being has sinned and deserves God's punishment (see Romans 2:5–6), but faith in Jesus provides a way out of condemnation (see John 5:24). God delays his judgment to give more people time to reject sin and believe in Jesus (see 2 Peter 3:9), but the book of Revelation shows God judging the world at the end of time, detailing his outpouring of anger at sin and an end to his patience for people who won't repent. As you read a sample of these judgments in Revelation 9, don't miss the message at the end. It says that people who survived these terrible plagues "still did not repent" (Revelation 9:21) of worshiping false gods. Neither did they quit sins ranging from murder to magic to sexual immorality (Revelation 9:20). God has to stop evil because people won't.

Think: Why will God judge the world? Why does he wait to punish evil?

ROCK SOLID truths

The Angel and the Little Scroll

10 Then I saw another mighty angel coming down from heaven. He was robed in a cloud, with a rainbow above his head; his face was like the sun, and his legs were like fiery pillars. ²He was holding a little scroll, which lay open in his hand. He planted his right foot on the sea and his left foot on the land, ³and he gave a loud shout like the roar of a lion. When he shouted, the voices of the seven thunders spoke. ⁴And when the seven thunders spoke, I was about to write; but I heard a voice from heaven say, "Seal up what the seven thunders have said and do not write it down."

⁵Then the angel I had seen standing on the sea and on the land raised his right hand to heaven. ⁶And he swore by him who lives for ever and ever, who created the heavens and all that is in them, the earth and all that is in it, and the sea and all that is in it, and said, "There will be no more delay! ⁷But in the days when the seventh angel is about to sound his trumpet, the mystery of God will be accomplished, just as he announced to his servants the prophets."

⁸Then the voice that I had heard from heaven spoke to me once more: "Go, take the scroll that lies open in the hand of the angel who is standing on the sea and on the land."

⁹So I went to the angel and asked him to give me the little scroll. He said to me, "Take it and eat it. It will turn your stom-

ach sour, but 'in your mouth it will be as sweet as honey.'*[a]* [10] I took the little scroll from the angel's hand and ate it. It tasted as sweet as honey in my mouth, but when I had eaten it, my stomach turned sour. [11] Then I was told, "You must prophesy again about many peoples, nations, languages and kings."

The Two Witnesses

11 I was given a reed like a measuring rod and was told, "Go and measure the temple of God and the altar, with its worshipers. [2] But exclude the outer court; do not measure it, because it has been given to the Gentiles. They will trample on the holy city for 42 months. [3] And I will appoint my two witnesses, and they will prophesy for 1,260 days, clothed in sackcloth." [4] They are "the two olive trees" and the two lampstands, and "they stand before the Lord of the earth."*[b]* [5] If anyone tries to harm them, fire comes from their mouths and devours their enemies. This is how anyone who wants to harm them must die. [6] They have power to shut up the heavens so that it will not rain during the time they are prophesying; and they have power to turn the waters into blood and to strike the earth with every kind of plague as often as they want.

[7] Now when they have finished their testimony, the beast that comes up from the Abyss will attack them, and overpower and kill them. [8] Their bodies will lie in the public square of the great city — which is figuratively called Sodom and Egypt — where also their Lord was crucified. [9] For three and a half days some from every people, tribe, language and nation will gaze on their bodies and refuse them burial. [10] The inhabitants of the earth will gloat over them and will celebrate by sending each other gifts, because these two prophets had tormented those who live on the earth.

[11] But after the three and a half days the breath*[c]* of life from God entered them, and they stood on their feet, and terror struck those who saw them. [12] Then they heard a loud voice from heaven saying to them, "Come up here." And they went up to heaven in a cloud, while their enemies looked on.

[13] At that very hour there was a severe earthquake and a tenth of the city collapsed. Seven thousand people were killed in the earthquake, and the survivors were terrified and gave glory to the God of heaven.

[14] The second woe has passed; the third woe is coming soon.

The Seventh Trumpet

[15] The seventh angel sounded his trumpet, and there were loud voices in heaven, which said:

> "The kingdom of the world has become
>   the kingdom of our Lord and of his Messiah,
>   and he will reign for ever and ever."

[16] And the twenty-four elders, who were seated on their thrones before God, fell on their faces and worshiped God, [17] saying:

> "We give thanks to you, Lord God Almighty,
>   the One who is and who was,
> because you have taken your great power
>   and have begun to reign.
> [18] The nations were angry,
>   and your wrath has come.
> The time has come for judging the dead,
>   and for rewarding your servants the prophets
> and your people who revere your name,
>   both great and small —
> and for destroying those who destroy the earth."

[19] Then God's temple in heaven was opened, and within his temple was seen the ark of his covenant. And there came flashes of lightning, rumblings, peals of thunder, an earthquake and a severe hailstorm.

---

a 9 Ezek. 3:3   *b 4* See Zech. 4:3,11,14.
c 11 Or *Spirit* (see Ezek. 37:5,14)

The Woman and the Dragon

12 A great sign appeared in heaven: a woman clothed with the sun, with the moon under her feet and a crown of twelve stars on her head. ²She was pregnant and cried out in pain as she was about to give birth. ³Then another sign appeared in heaven: an enormous red dragon with seven heads and ten horns and seven crowns on its heads. ⁴Its tail swept a third of the stars out of the sky and flung them to the earth. The dragon stood in front of the woman who was about to give birth, so that it might devour her child the moment he was born. ⁵She gave birth to a son, a male child, who "will rule all the nations with an iron scepter."ᵃ And her child was snatched up to God and to his throne. ⁶The woman fled into the wilderness to a place prepared for her by God, where she might be taken care of for 1,260 days.

⁷Then war broke out in heaven. Michael and his angels fought against the dragon, and the dragon and his angels fought back. ⁸But he was not strong enough, and they lost their place in heaven. ⁹The great dragon was hurled down—that ancient serpent called the devil, or Satan, who leads the whole world astray. He was hurled to the earth, and his angels with him.

¹⁰Then I heard a loud voice in heaven say:

"Now have come the salvation and the
    power
and the kingdom of our God,
and the authority of his Messiah.
For the accuser of our brothers and
    sisters,
who accuses them before our God
    day and night,
has been hurled down.
¹¹They triumphed over him
    by the blood of the Lamb
    and by the word of their testimony;
they did not love their lives so much
    as to shrink from death.
¹²Therefore rejoice, you heavens
    and you who dwell in them!
But woe to the earth and the sea,
    because the devil has gone down to
        you!

He is filled with fury,
    because he knows that his time is
        short."

¹³When the dragon saw that he had been hurled to the earth, he pursued the woman who had given birth to the male child. ¹⁴The woman was given the two wings of a great eagle, so that she might fly to the place prepared for her in the wilderness, where she would be taken care of for a time, times and half a time, out of the serpent's reach. ¹⁵Then from his mouth the serpent spewed water like a river, to overtake the woman and sweep her away with the torrent. ¹⁶But the earth helped the woman by opening its mouth and swallowing the river that the dragon had spewed out of his mouth. ¹⁷Then the dragon was enraged at the woman and went off to wage war against the rest of her offspring—those who keep God's commands and hold fast their testimony about Jesus.

The Beast out of the Sea

13 The dragonᵇ stood on the shore of the sea. And I saw a beast coming out of the sea. It had ten horns and seven heads, with ten crowns on its horns, and on each head a blasphemous name. ²The beast I saw resembled a leopard, but had feet like those of a bear and a mouth like that of a lion. The dragon gave the beast his power and his throne and great authority. ³One of the heads of the beast seemed to have had a fatal wound, but the fatal wound had been healed. The whole world was filled with wonder and followed the beast. ⁴People worshiped the dragon because he had given authority to the beast, and they also worshiped the beast and asked, "Who is like the beast? Who can wage war against it?"

⁵The beast was given a mouth to utter proud words and blasphemies and to exercise its authority for forty-two months. ⁶It opened its mouth to blaspheme God, and to slander his name and his dwelling place and those who live in heaven. ⁷It was given power to wage war against God's

---

ᵃ *5* Psalm 2:9   ᵇ *1* Some manuscripts *And I*

holy people and to conquer them. And it was given authority over every tribe, people, language and nation. ⁸All inhabitants of the earth will worship the beast—all whose names have not been written in the Lamb's book of life, the Lamb who was slain from the creation of the world.ᵃ

⁹Whoever has ears, let them hear.

¹⁰"If anyone is to go into captivity,
     into captivity they will go.
If anyone is to be killedᵇ with the
     sword,
   with the sword they will be killed."ᶜ

This calls for patient endurance and faithfulness on the part of God's people.

The Beast out of the Earth

¹¹Then I saw a second beast, coming out of the earth. It had two horns like a lamb, but it spoke like a dragon. ¹²It exercised all the authority of the first beast on its behalf, and made the earth and its inhabitants worship the first beast, whose fatal wound had been healed. ¹³And it performed great signs, even causing fire to come down from heaven to the earth in full view of the people. ¹⁴Because of the signs it was given power to perform on behalf of the first beast, it deceived the inhabitants of the earth. It ordered them to set up an image in honor of the beast who was wounded by the sword and yet lived. ¹⁵The second beast was given power to give breath to the image of the first beast, so that the image could speak and cause all who refused to worship the image to be killed. ¹⁶It also forced all people, great and small, rich and poor, free and slave, to receive a mark on their right hands or on their foreheads, ¹⁷so that they could not buy or sell unless they had the mark, which is the name of the beast or the number of its name.

ᵃ 8 Or *written from the creation of the world in the book of life belonging to the Lamb who was slain*
ᵇ 10 Some manuscripts *anyone kills*
ᶜ 10 Jer. 15:2

ROCK SOLID *principles*

Revelation 13:1–10

Get your name in the book.

Thomas had been to the brink of a decision before. Unlike every other instance, however, this time he didn't feel forced to decide on the spot whether or not he believed in Jesus. Thomas had questions, but he had gotten them answered. He understood following Jesus could be costly, but he was willing to pay the price. So as a friend led him in a simple prayer, Thomas admitted to God that he was sinful. He prayed and said that Jesus had died for him on the cross and rose to prove he was really God. And Thomas promised he was ready to follow. A moment before, Thomas wasn't a Christian. Now he was.

The "book of life" is the heavenly list of people who have come to believe in Jesus as their Savior, trusting that he was (and is) all he claimed to be. Revelation 20:11–15 shows all people being judged at the end of time, where the Bible says, "Anyone whose name was not found written in the book of life was thrown into the lake of fire." If your name isn't in the book, now is the time to talk to God.

¹⁸This calls for wisdom. Let the person who has insight calculate the number of the beast, for it is the number of a man.^a That number is 666.

The Lamb and the 144,000

14 Then I looked, and there before me was the Lamb, standing on Mount Zion, and with him 144,000 who had his name and his Father's name written on their foreheads. ²And I heard a sound from heaven like the roar of rushing waters and like a loud peal of thunder. The sound I heard was like that of harpists playing their harps. ³And they sang a new song before the throne and before the four living creatures and the elders. No one could learn the song except the 144,000 who had been redeemed from the earth. ⁴These are those who did not defile themselves with women, for they remained virgins. They follow the Lamb wherever he goes. They were purchased from among mankind and offered as firstfruits to God and the Lamb. ⁵No lie was found in their mouths; they are blameless.

The Three Angels

⁶Then I saw another angel flying in midair, and he had the eternal gospel to proclaim to those who live on the earth—to every nation, tribe, language and people. ⁷He said in a loud voice, "Fear God and give him glory, because the hour of his judgment has come. Worship him who made the heavens, the earth, the sea and the springs of water."

⁸A second angel followed and said, "'Fallen! Fallen is Babylon the Great,'^b which made all the nations drink the maddening wine of her adulteries."

⁹A third angel followed them and said in a loud voice: "If anyone worships the beast and its image and receives its mark on their forehead or on their hand, ¹⁰they, too, will drink the wine of God's fury, which has been poured full strength into the cup of his wrath. They will be tormented with burning sulfur in the presence of the holy angels and of the Lamb. ¹¹And the smoke of their torment will rise for ever and ever.

There will be no rest day or night for those who worship the beast and its image, or for anyone who receives the mark of its name." ¹²This calls for patient endurance on the part of the people of God who keep his commands and remain faithful to Jesus.

¹³Then I heard a voice from heaven say, "Write this: Blessed are the dead who die in the Lord from now on."

"Yes," says the Spirit, "they will rest from their labor, for their deeds will follow them."

Harvesting the Earth and Trampling the Winepress

¹⁴I looked, and there before me was a white cloud, and seated on the cloud was one like a son of man^c with a crown of gold on his head and a sharp sickle in his hand. ¹⁵Then another angel came out of the temple and called in a loud voice to him who was sitting on the cloud, "Take your sickle and reap, because the time to reap has come, for the harvest of the earth is ripe." ¹⁶So he who was seated on the cloud swung his sickle over the earth, and the earth was harvested.

¹⁷Another angel came out of the temple in heaven, and he too had a sharp sickle. ¹⁸Still another angel, who had charge of the fire, came from the altar and called in a loud voice to him who had the sharp sickle, "Take your sharp sickle and gather the clusters of grapes from the earth's vine, because its grapes are ripe." ¹⁹The angel swung his sickle on the earth, gathered its grapes and threw them into the great winepress of God's wrath. ²⁰They were trampled in the winepress outside the city, and blood flowed out of the press, rising as high as the horses' bridles for a distance of 1,600 stadia.^d

Seven Angels With Seven Plagues

15 I saw in heaven another great and marvelous sign: seven angels with the seven last plagues—last, because with them God's

---

^a 18 Or *is humanity's number*   ^b 8 Isaiah 21:9
^c 14 See Daniel 7:13.   ^d 20 That is, about 180 miles or about 300 kilometers

wrath is completed. ²And I saw what looked like a sea of glass glowing with fire and, standing beside the sea, those who had been victorious over the beast and its image and over the number of its name. They held harps given them by God ³and sang the song of God's servant Moses and of the Lamb:

"Great and marvelous are your deeds,
    Lord God Almighty.
Just and true are your ways,
    King of the nations.ᵃ
⁴Who will not fear you, Lord,
    and bring glory to your name?
For you alone are holy.
All nations will come
    and worship before you,
for your righteous acts have been
    revealed."ᵇ

⁵After this I looked, and I saw in heaven the temple—that is, the tabernacle of the covenant law—and it was opened. ⁶Out of the temple came the seven angels with the seven plagues. They were dressed in clean, shining linen and wore golden sashes around their chests. ⁷Then one of the four living creatures gave to the seven angels seven golden bowls filled with the wrath of God, who lives for ever and ever. ⁸And the temple was filled with smoke from the glory of God and from his power, and no one could enter the temple until the seven plagues of the seven angels were completed.

The Seven Bowls of God's Wrath

16 Then I heard a loud voice from the temple saying to the seven angels, "Go, pour out the seven bowls of God's wrath on the earth."

²The first angel went and poured out his bowl on the land, and ugly, festering sores broke out on the people who had the mark of the beast and worshiped its image.

³The second angel poured out his bowl on the sea, and it turned into blood like that of a dead person, and every living thing in the sea died.

⁴The third angel poured out his bowl on the rivers and springs of water, and they became blood. ⁵Then I heard the angel in charge of the waters say:

"You are just in these judgments,
    O Holy One,
you who are and who were;
⁶for they have shed the blood of your
        holy people and your prophets,
    and you have given them blood to
        drink as they deserve."

⁷And I heard the altar respond:

"Yes, Lord God Almighty,
    true and just are your judgments."

⁸The fourth angel poured out his bowl on the sun, and the sun was allowed to scorch people with fire. ⁹They were seared by the intense heat and they cursed the name of God, who had control over these plagues, but they refused to repent and glorify him.

¹⁰The fifth angel poured out his bowl on the throne of the beast, and its kingdom was plunged into darkness. People gnawed their tongues in agony ¹¹and cursed the God of heaven because of their pains and their sores, but they refused to repent of what they had done.

¹²The sixth angel poured out his bowl on the great river Euphrates, and its water was dried up to prepare the way for the kings from the East. ¹³Then I saw three impure spirits that looked like frogs; they came out of the mouth of the dragon, out of the mouth of the beast and out of the mouth of the false prophet. ¹⁴They are demonic spirits that perform signs, and they go out to the kings of the whole world, to gather them for the battle on the great day of God Almighty.

¹⁵"Look, I come like a thief! Blessed is the one who stays awake and remains clothed, so as not to go naked and be shamefully exposed."

¹⁶Then they gathered the kings together to the place that in Hebrew is called Armageddon.

ᵃ 3 Some manuscripts *ages*   ᵇ 3,4 Phrases in this song are drawn from Psalm 111:2,3; Deut. 32:4; Jer. 10:7; Psalms 86:9; 98:2.

[17]The seventh angel poured out his bowl into the air, and out of the temple came a loud voice from the throne, saying, "It is done!" [18]Then there came flashes of lightning, rumblings, peals of thunder and a severe earthquake. No earthquake like it has ever occurred since mankind has been on earth, so tremendous was the quake. [19]The great city split into three parts, and the cities of the nations collapsed. God remembered Babylon the Great and gave her the cup filled with the wine of the fury of his wrath. [20]Every island fled away and the mountains could not be found. [21]From the sky huge hailstones, each weighing about a hundred pounds,[a] fell on people. And they cursed God on account of the plague of hail, because the plague was so terrible.

Babylon, the Prostitute on the Beast

17 One of the seven angels who had the seven bowls came and said to me, "Come, I will show you the punishment of the great prostitute, who sits by many waters. [2]With her the kings of the earth committed adultery, and the inhabitants of the earth were intoxicated with the wine of her adulteries."

[3]Then the angel carried me away in the Spirit into a wilderness. There I saw a woman sitting on a scarlet beast that was covered with blasphemous names and had seven heads and ten horns. [4]The woman was dressed in purple and scarlet, and was glittering with gold, precious stones and pearls. She held a golden cup in her hand, filled with abominable things and the filth of her adulteries. [5]The name written on her forehead was a mystery:

BABYLON THE GREAT
THE MOTHER OF PROSTITUTES
AND OF THE ABOMINATIONS OF THE
EARTH.

[6]I saw that the woman was drunk with the blood of God's holy people, the blood of those who bore testimony to Jesus.

When I saw her, I was greatly astonished. [7]Then the angel said to me: "Why are you astonished? I will explain to you the mystery of the woman and of the beast she rides, which has the seven heads and ten horns. [8]The beast, which you saw, once was, now is not, and yet will come up out of the Abyss and go to its destruction. The inhabitants of the earth whose names have not been written in the book of life from the creation of the world will

---

[a] 21 Or about 45 kilograms

Revelation 16

The Bible is complete.

The end of the book of Revelation warns against tampering with the words of the book by adding to them or taking away from them (see Revelation 22:18–19). It's a good caution for the rest of the Bible as well, because the collection or "canon" of Scripture is complete. The books of the Old Testament were composed over about a thousand years, ending around 400 BC, and the books of the New Testament were finished by about AD 95. Jewish believers recognized the 39 books that became our Old Testament, and early Christians reached unanimous agreement about the 27 New Testament books included in the Bible at a gathering of Christians in Carthage in AD 397. Note that books didn't become Scripture because believers said they were. Rather, books were recognized as Scripture because they displayed specific marks of inspiration by God. In other words, believers didn't invent the Bible. They recognized and included books God had clearly inspired.

Think: How is it helpful to know the contents of the Bible are complete?

ROCK SOLID truths

be astonished when they see the beast, because it once was, now is not, and yet will come.

⁹"This calls for a mind with wisdom. The seven heads are seven hills on which the woman sits. ¹⁰They are also seven kings. Five have fallen, one is, the other has not yet come; but when he does come, he must remain for only a little while. ¹¹The beast who once was, and now is not, is an eighth king. He belongs to the seven and is going to his destruction.

¹²"The ten horns you saw are ten kings who have not yet received a kingdom, but who for one hour will receive authority as kings along with the beast. ¹³They have one purpose and will give their power and authority to the beast. ¹⁴They will wage war against the Lamb, but the Lamb will triumph over them because he is Lord of lords and King of kings—and with him will be his called, chosen and faithful followers."

¹⁵Then the angel said to me, "The waters you saw, where the prostitute sits, are peoples, multitudes, nations and languages. ¹⁶The beast and the ten horns you saw will hate the prostitute. They will bring her to ruin and leave her naked; they will eat her flesh and burn her with fire. ¹⁷For God has put it into their hearts to accomplish his purpose by agreeing to hand over to the beast their royal authority, until God's words are fulfilled. ¹⁸The woman you saw is the great city that rules over the kings of the earth."

Lament Over Fallen Babylon

18 After this I saw another angel coming down from heaven. He had great authority, and the earth was illuminated by his splendor. ²With a mighty voice he shouted:

"'Fallen! Fallen is Babylon the
    Great!'ᵃ
She has become a dwelling for
    demons
and a haunt for every impure spirit,
    a haunt for every unclean bird,
    a haunt for every unclean and
        detestable animal.

³For all the nations have drunk
    the maddening wine of her
        adulteries.
The kings of the earth committed
    adultery with her,
    and the merchants of the earth
        grew rich from her excessive
            luxuries."

Warning to Escape Babylon's Judgment

⁴Then I heard another voice from heaven say:

"'Come out of her, my people,'ᵇ
    so that you will not share in her sins,
    so that you will not receive any of
        her plagues;
⁵for her sins are piled up to heaven,
    and God has remembered her
        crimes.
⁶Give back to her as she has given;
    pay her back double for what she
        has done.
    Pour her a double portion from her
        own cup.
⁷Give her as much torment and grief
    as the glory and luxury she gave
        herself.
In her heart she boasts,
    'I sit enthroned as queen.
I am not a widow;ᶜ
    I will never mourn.'
⁸Therefore in one day her plagues will
        overtake her:
    death, mourning and famine.
She will be consumed by fire,
    for mighty is the Lord God who
        judges her.

Threefold Woe Over Babylon's Fall

⁹"When the kings of the earth who committed adultery with her and shared her luxury see the smoke of her burning, they will weep and mourn over her. ¹⁰Terrified at her torment, they will stand far off and cry:

"'Woe! Woe to you, great city,
    you mighty city of Babylon!
In one hour your doom has come!'

ᵃ 2 Isaiah 21:9   ᵇ 4 Jer. 51:45   ᶜ 7 See
Isaiah 47:7,8.

¹¹"The merchants of the earth will weep and mourn over her because no one buys their cargoes anymore— ¹²cargoes of gold, silver, precious stones and pearls; fine linen, purple, silk and scarlet cloth; every sort of citron wood, and articles of every kind made of ivory, costly wood, bronze, iron and marble; ¹³cargoes of cinnamon and spice, of incense, myrrh and frankincense, of wine and olive oil, of fine flour and wheat; cattle and sheep; horses and carriages; and human beings sold as slaves.

¹⁴"They will say, 'The fruit you longed for is gone from you. All your luxury and splendor have vanished, never to be recovered.' ¹⁵The merchants who sold these things and gained their wealth from her will stand far off, terrified at her torment. They will weep and mourn ¹⁶and cry out:

"'Woe! Woe to you, great city,
     dressed in fine linen, purple and
          scarlet,
     and glittering with gold, precious
          stones and pearls!
¹⁷In one hour such great wealth has
     been brought to ruin!'

"Every sea captain, and all who travel by ship, the sailors, and all who earn their living from the sea, will stand far off. ¹⁸When they see the smoke of her burning, they will exclaim, 'Was there ever a city like this great city?' ¹⁹They will throw dust on their heads, and with weeping and mourning cry out:

"'Woe! Woe to you, great city,
     where all who had ships on the sea
          became rich through her wealth!
In one hour she has been brought to
          ruin!'

²⁰"Rejoice over her, you heavens!
     Rejoice, you people of God!
     Rejoice, apostles and prophets!
For God has judged her
     with the judgment she imposed on
          you."

The Finality of Babylon's Doom

²¹Then a mighty angel picked up a boulder the size of a large millstone and threw it into the sea, and said:

"With such violence
     the great city of Babylon will be
          thrown down,
     never to be found again.
²²The music of harpists and musicians,
     pipers and trumpeters,
     will never be heard in you again.
No worker of any trade
     will ever be found in you again.
The sound of a millstone
     will never be heard in you again.
²³The light of a lamp
     will never shine in you again.
The voice of bridegroom and bride
     will never be heard in you again.
Your merchants were the world's
     important people.
By your magic spell all the nations
     were led astray.
²⁴In her was found the blood of prophets
     and of God's holy people,
     of all who have been slaughtered on
          the earth."

Threefold Hallelujah Over Babylon's Fall

19 After this I heard what sounded like the roar of a great multitude in heaven shouting:

"Hallelujah!
Salvation and glory and power belong
     to our God,
²   for true and just are his judgments.
He has condemned the great
     prostitute
     who corrupted the earth by her
          adulteries.
He has avenged on her the blood of
     his servants."

³And again they shouted:

"Hallelujah!
The smoke from her goes up for ever
     and ever."

⁴The twenty-four elders and the four living creatures fell down and worshiped God, who was seated on the throne. And they cried:

"Amen, Hallelujah!"

⁵Then a voice came from the throne, saying:

"Praise our God,
    all you his servants,
you who fear him,
    both great and small!"

[6] Then I heard what sounded like a great multitude, like the roar of rushing waters and like loud peals of thunder, shouting:

"Hallelujah!
    For our Lord God Almighty reigns.
[7] Let us rejoice and be glad
    and give him glory!
For the wedding of the Lamb has come,
    and his bride has made herself ready.
[8] Fine linen, bright and clean,
    was given her to wear."

(Fine linen stands for the righteous acts of God's holy people.)

[9] Then the angel said to me, "Write this: Blessed are those who are invited to the wedding supper of the Lamb!" And he added, "These are the true words of God."

[10] At this I fell at his feet to worship him. But he said to me, "Don't do that! I am a fellow servant with you and with your brothers and sisters who hold to the testimony of Jesus. Worship God! For it is the Spirit of prophecy who bears testimony to Jesus."

The Heavenly Warrior Defeats the Beast

[11] I saw heaven standing open and there before me was a white horse, whose rider is called Faithful and True. With justice he judges and wages war. [12] His eyes are like blazing fire, and on his head are many crowns. He has a name written on him that no one knows but he himself. [13] He is dressed in a robe dipped in blood, and his name is the Word of God. [14] The armies of heaven were following him, riding on white horses and dressed in fine linen, white and clean. [15] Coming out of his mouth is a sharp sword with which to strike down the nations. "He will rule them with an iron scepter."[a] He treads the winepress of the fury of the wrath of God Almighty. [16] On his robe and on his thigh he has this name written:

KING OF KINGS AND LORD OF LORDS.

[17] And I saw an angel standing in the sun, who cried in a loud voice to all the birds flying in midair, "Come, gather together for the great supper of God, [18] so that you may eat the flesh of kings, generals, and the mighty, of horses and their riders, and the flesh of all people, free and slave, great and small."

[19] Then I saw the beast and the kings of the earth and their armies gathered together to wage war against the rider on the horse and his army. [20] But the beast was captured, and with it the false prophet who had performed the signs on its behalf. With these signs he had deluded those who had received the mark of the beast and worshiped its image. The two of them were thrown alive into the fiery lake of burning sulfur. [21] The rest were killed with the sword coming out of the mouth of the rider on the horse, and all the birds gorged themselves on their flesh.

The Thousand Years

20 And I saw an angel coming down out of heaven, having the key to the Abyss and holding in his hand a great chain. [2] He seized the dragon, that ancient serpent, who is the devil, or Satan, and bound him for a thousand years. [3] He threw him into the Abyss, and locked and sealed it over him, to keep him from deceiving the nations anymore until the thousand years were ended. After that, he must be set free for a short time.

[4] I saw thrones on which were seated those who had been given authority to judge. And I saw the souls of those who had been beheaded because of their testimony about Jesus and because of the word of God. They[b] had not worshiped the beast or its image and had not received its mark on their foreheads or their hands. They came to life and reigned with Christ a thousand years. [5] (The rest of the dead did not come to life until the thousand years were ended.) This is the first resurrection. [6] Blessed and holy are those who

[a] 15 Psalm 2:9   [b] 4 Or God; I also saw those who

share in the first resurrection. The second death has no power over them, but they will be priests of God and of Christ and will reign with him for a thousand years.

The Judgment of Satan

⁷When the thousand years are over, Satan will be released from his prison ⁸and will go out to deceive the nations in the four corners of the earth—Gog and Magog—and to gather them for bat-tle. In number they are like the sand on the seashore. ⁹They marched across the breadth of the earth and surrounded the camp of God's people, the city he loves. But fire came down from heaven and devoured them. ¹⁰And the devil, who deceived them, was thrown into the lake of burning sulfur, where the beast and the false prophet had been thrown. They will be tormented day and night for ever and ever.

The Judgment of the Dead

¹¹Then I saw a great white throne and him who was seated on it. The earth and the heavens fled from his presence, and there was no place for them. ¹²And I saw the dead, great and small, standing before the throne, and books were opened. Another book was opened, which is the book of life. The dead were judged according to what they had done as recorded in the books. ¹³The sea gave up the dead that were in it, and death and Hades gave up the dead that were in them, and each person was judged according to what they had done. ¹⁴Then death and Hades were thrown into the lake of fire. The lake of fire is the second death. ¹⁵Anyone whose name was not found written in the book of life was thrown into the lake of fire.

A New Heaven and a New Earth

21 Then I saw "a new heaven and a new earth,"ᵃ for the first heaven and the first earth had passed away, and there was no longer any sea. ²I saw the Holy City, the new Jerusalem, coming down out of heaven from God, prepared as a bride beautifully dressed for her husband. ³And I heard a loud voice from the throne saying, "Look! God's dwelling place is now among the people, and he will dwell with them. They will be his people, and God himself will be with them and be their God. ⁴'He will wipe every tear from their eyes. There will be no more death'ᵇ or mourning or crying or pain, for the old order of things has passed away."

ᵃ *1* Isaiah 65:17   ᵇ *4* Isaiah 25:8

ROCK SOLID truths

Revelation 20:7–15

Hell is real.

The Old Testament pictures a place called "Sheol" where people both good and evil go after death to receive either rewards or punishment (see Psalm 9:17). The New Testament fills out more facts when it describes a place called Gehenna as the location of punishment for evildoers. Gehenna was an actual valley outside Jerusalem used as a dump. Fire constantly smoldered there to consume all of the city's waste, including the bodies of dead criminals. Winds carried its terrible smell back to the city. And that's the Bible's picture of hell. It's a dump for anything unfit to enter heaven. Revelation pictures hell as "the fiery lake of burning sulfur" (Revelation 19:20), the final destination of Satan and people who don't know God. Hell brings permanent separation from God, his people, and anything good. Hell is real, but it's also a choice. Anyone can escape hell by believing in Jesus (see John 3:16–18).

Think: Do you think hell is a necessary way to deal with evil? Why—or why not?

⁵He who was seated on the throne said, "I am making everything new!" Then he said, "Write this down, for these words are trustworthy and true."

⁶He said to me: "It is done. I am the Alpha and the Omega, the Beginning and the End. To the thirsty I will give water without cost from the spring of the water of life. ⁷Those who are victorious will inherit all this, and I will be their God and they will be my children. ⁸But the cowardly, the unbelieving, the vile, the murderers, the sexually immoral, those who practice magic arts, the idolaters and all liars — they will be consigned to the fiery lake of burning sulfur. This is the second death."

The New Jerusalem, the Bride of the Lamb

⁹One of the seven angels who had the seven bowls full of the seven last plagues came and said to me, "Come, I will show you the bride, the wife of the Lamb." ¹⁰And he carried me away in the Spirit to a mountain great and high, and showed me the Holy City, Jerusalem, coming down out of heaven from God. ¹¹It shone with the glory of God, and its brilliance was like that of a very precious jewel, like a jasper, clear as crystal. ¹²It had a great, high wall with twelve gates, and with twelve angels at the gates. On the gates were written the names of the twelve tribes of Israel. ¹³There were three gates on the east, three on the north, three on the south and three on the west. ¹⁴The wall of the city had twelve foundations, and on them were the names of the twelve apostles of the Lamb.

¹⁵The angel who talked with me had a measuring rod of gold to measure the city, its gates and its walls. ¹⁶The city was laid out like a square, as long as it was wide. He measured the city with the rod and found it to be 12,000 stadia*a* in length, and as wide and high as it is long. ¹⁷The angel measured the wall using human measurement, and it was 144 cubits*b* thick.*c* ¹⁸The wall was made of jasper, and the city of pure gold, as pure as glass. ¹⁹The foundations

---

ROCK SOLID truths

Revelation 21:1–7

You can live with God and his people forever.

The apostle Paul said that if the best that Christians can hope for is life here on earth, "we are of all people most to be pitied" (1 Corinthians 15:19). That's not saying that following Jesus right now isn't good, but that being at home in heaven forever is so much better. The Bible pictures heaven as the future home of everyone who trusts in Jesus (see John 14:1–6). In heaven we will receive completely transformed bodies (see 2 Corinthians 5:1–5). And in heaven God's will is obeyed completely (see Matthew 6:10). If you trust in Jesus, you can look forward to an eternity filled with God and his people. Everything tough about this life will be gone, and "there will be no more death or mourning or crying or pain" (Revelation 21:4). God will be nearer to us than we can understand right now, and our eternity with him will be better than anything we can begin to imagine.

Think: What makes heaven so great?

---

of the city walls were decorated with every kind of precious stone. The first foundation was jasper, the second sapphire, the third agate, the fourth emerald, ²⁰the fifth onyx, the sixth ruby, the seventh chrysolite, the eighth beryl, the ninth topaz, the tenth turquoise, the eleventh jacinth, and

---

a 16 That is, about 1,400 miles or about 2,200 kilometers   *b 17* That is, about 200 feet or about 65 meters   *c 17* Or *high* the twelfth amethyst.*ᵃ ²¹The twelve gates were twelve pearls, each gate made of a single pearl. The great street of the city was of gold, as pure as transparent glass.

²²I did not see a temple in the city, because the Lord God Almighty and the Lamb are its temple. ²³The city does not need the sun or the moon to shine on it, for the glory of God gives it light, and the Lamb is its lamp. ²⁴The nations will walk by its light, and the kings of the earth will bring their splendor into it. ²⁵On no day will its gates ever be shut, for there will be no night there. ²⁶The glory and honor of the nations will be brought into it. ²⁷Nothing impure will ever enter it, nor will anyone who does what is shameful or deceitful, but only those whose names are written in the Lamb's book of life.

Eden Restored

22 Then the angel showed me the river of the water of life, as clear as crystal, flowing from the throne of God and of the Lamb ²down the middle of the great street of the city. On each side of the river stood the tree of life, bearing twelve crops of fruit, yielding its fruit every month. And the leaves of the tree are for the healing of the nations. ³No longer will there be any curse. The throne of God and of the Lamb will be in the city, and his servants will serve him. ⁴They will see his face, and his name will be on their foreheads. ⁵There will be no more night. They will not need the light of a lamp or the light of the sun, for the Lord God will give them light. And they will reign for ever and ever.

John and the Angel

⁶The angel said to me, "These words are trustworthy and true. The Lord, the God who inspires the prophets, sent his angel to show his servants the things that must soon take place."

⁷"Look, I am coming soon! Blessed is the one who keeps the words of the prophecy written in this scroll."

⁸I, John, am the one who heard and saw these things. And when I had heard and

ROCK SOLID promises

"Look, I am coming soon! Blessed is the one who keeps the words of the prophecy written in this scroll."

Revelation 22:7

Jesus awaits the right moment to come back to this world. In the meantime, he wants you to obey his commands.

seen them, I fell down to worship at the feet of the angel who had been showing them to me. ⁹But he said to me, "Don't do that! I am a fellow servant with you and with your fellow prophets and with all who keep the words of this scroll. Worship God!"

¹⁰Then he told me, "Do not seal up the words of the prophecy of this scroll, because the time is near. ¹¹Let the one who does wrong continue to do wrong; let the vile person continue to be vile; let the one who does right continue to do right; and let the holy person continue to be holy."

Epilogue: Invitation and Warning

¹²"Look, I am coming soon! My reward is with me, and I will give to each person according to what they have done. ¹³I am the Alpha and the Omega, the First and the Last, the Beginning and the End.

¹⁴"Blessed are those who wash their robes, that they may have the right to the tree of life and may go through the gates into the city. ¹⁵Outside are the dogs, those who practice magic arts, the sexually immoral, the murderers, the idolaters and everyone who loves and practices falsehood.

¹⁶"I, Jesus, have sent my angel to give youᵇ this testimony for the churches. I am

---

ᵃ 20 The precise identification of some of these precious stones is uncertain.   ᵇ 16 The Greek is plural.

the Root and the Offspring of David, and the bright Morning Star."

17 The Spirit and the bride say, "Come!" And let the one who hears say, "Come!" Let the one who is thirsty come; and let the one who wishes take the free gift of the water of life.

18 I warn everyone who hears the words of the prophecy of this scroll: If anyone adds anything to them, God will add to that person the plagues described in this scroll. 19 And if anyone takes words away from this scroll of prophecy, God will take away from that person any share in the tree of life and in the Holy City, which are described in this scroll.

20 He who testifies to these things says, "Yes, I am coming soon."

Amen. Come, Lord Jesus.

21 The grace of the Lord Jesus be with God's people. Amen.

STUDY HELPS

Table of
Weights and Measures

	BIBLICAL UNIT	APPROXIMATE AMERICAN EQUIVALENT	APPROXIMATE METRIC EQUIVALENT
WEIGHTS	talent (60 minas)	75 pounds	34 kilograms
	mina (50 shekels)	1 1/4 pounds	560 grams
	shekel (2 bekas)	2/5 ounce	11.5 grams
	pim (2/3 shekel)	1/4 ounce	7.8 grams
	beka (10 gerahs)	1/5 ounce	5.7 grams
	gerah	1/50 ounce	0.6 gram
	daric	1/3 ounce	8.4 grams
LENGTH	cubit	18 inches	45 centimeters
	span	9 inches	23 centimeters
	handbreadth	3 inches	7.5 centimeters
	stadion (pl. stadia)	600 feet	183 meters
CAPACITY			
Dry Measure	cor [homer] (10 ephahs)	6 bushels	220 liters
	lethek (5 ephahs)	3 bushels	110 liters
	ephah (10 omers)	3/5 bushel	22 liters
	seah (1/3 ephah)	7 quarts	7.5 liters
	omer (1/10 ephah)	2 quarts	2 liters
	cab (1/18 ephah)	1 quart	1 liter
Liquid Measure	bath (1 ephah)	6 gallons	22 liters
	hin (1/6 bath)	1 gallon	3.8 liters
	log (1/72 bath)	1/3 quart	0.3 liter

The figures of the table are calculated on the basis of a shekel equaling 11.5 grams, a cubit equaling 18 inches and an ephah equaling 22 liters. The quart referred to is either a dry quart (slightly larger than a liter) or a liquid quart (slightly smaller than a liter), whichever is applicable. The ton referred to in the footnotes is the American ton of 2,000 pounds. These weights are calculated relative to the particular commodity involved. Accordingly, the same measure of capacity in the text may be converted into different weights in the footnotes.

This table is based upon the best available information, but it is not intended to be mathematically precise; like the measurement equivalents in the footnotes, it merely gives approximate amounts and distances. Weights and measures differed somewhat at various times and places in the ancient world. There is uncertainty particularly about the ephah and the bath; further discoveries may shed more light on these units of capacity.

What Do I Read Today?

The Bible contains exciting action, characters with whom you can identify, and help for all the good and not-so-good situations in your life. All you have to do is read to find it all.

1. If you are reading the Bible for the first time:
   - Begin by reading the Gospel of Mark or the Gospel of John in the New Testament.
   - After reading one of these gospels, read the book of Acts or the book of Romans.
   - After reading Acts or Romans, pick an Old Testament book like Genesis or perhaps Psalms.
2. If you want to read through the entire Bible in one year:
   - Read three chapters each day, Monday through Saturday, and five chapters on Sunday.
3. If you want to read through the entire Bible in two years:
   - Read two chapters each day, Sunday through Saturday.

The following chart covers every book and chapter of the Bible. To keep track of what you have read, mark off each chapter as you complete it.

GENESIS ☐1 ☐2 ☐3 ☐4 ☐5 ☐6 ☐7 ☐8 ☐9 ☐10 ☐11 ☐12 ☐13 ☐14 ☐15 ☐16 ☐17 ☐18 ☐19 ☐20 ☐21 ☐22 ☐23 ☐24 ☐25 ☐26 ☐27 ☐28 ☐29 ☐30 ☐31 ☐32 ☐33 ☐34 ☐35 ☐36 ☐37 ☐38 ☐39 ☐40 ☐41 ☐42 ☐43 ☐44 ☐45 ☐46 ☐47 ☐48 ☐49 ☐50

EXODUS ☐1 ☐2 ☐3 ☐4 ☐5 ☐6 ☐7 ☐8 ☐9 ☐10 ☐11 ☐12 ☐13 ☐14 ☐15 ☐16 ☐17 ☐18 ☐19 ☐20 ☐21 ☐22 ☐23 ☐24 ☐25 ☐26 ☐27 ☐28 ☐29 ☐30 ☐31 ☐32 ☐33 ☐34 ☐35 ☐36 ☐37 ☐38 ☐39 ☐40

LEVITICUS ☐1 ☐2 ☐3 ☐4 ☐5 ☐6 ☐7 ☐8 ☐9 ☐10 ☐11 ☐12 ☐13 ☐14 ☐15 ☐16 ☐17 ☐18 ☐19 ☐20 ☐21 ☐22 ☐23 ☐24 ☐25 ☐26 ☐27

NUMBERS ☐1 ☐2 ☐3 ☐4 ☐5 ☐6 ☐7 ☐8 ☐9 ☐10 ☐11 ☐12 ☐13 ☐14 ☐15 ☐16 ☐17 ☐18 ☐19 ☐20 ☐21 ☐22 ☐23 ☐24 ☐25 ☐26 ☐27 ☐28 ☐29 ☐30 ☐31 ☐32 ☐33 ☐34 ☐35 ☐36

DEUTERONOMY ☐1 ☐2 ☐3 ☐4 ☐5 ☐6 ☐7 ☐8 ☐9 ☐10 ☐11 ☐12 ☐13 ☐14 ☐15 ☐16 ☐17 ☐18 ☐19 ☐20 ☐21 ☐22 ☐23 ☐24 ☐25 ☐26 ☐27 ☐28 ☐29 ☐30 ☐31 ☐32 ☐33 ☐34

JOSHUA ☐1 ☐2 ☐3 ☐4 ☐5 ☐6 ☐7 ☐8 ☐9 ☐10 ☐11 ☐12 ☐13 ☐14 ☐15 ☐16 ☐17 ☐18 ☐19 ☐20 ☐21 ☐22 ☐23 ☐24

JUDGES ☐1 ☐2 ☐3 ☐4 ☐5 ☐6 ☐7 ☐8 ☐9 ☐10 ☐11 ☐12 ☐13 ☐14 ☐15 ☐16 ☐17 ☐18 ☐19 ☐20 ☐21

RUTH ☐ 1 ☐ 2 ☐ 3 ☐ 4

1 SAMUEL ☐ 1 ☐ 2 ☐ 3 ☐ 4 ☐ 5 ☐ 6 ☐ 7 ☐ 8 ☐ 9 ☐ 10 ☐ 11 ☐ 12 ☐ 13 ☐ 14 ☐ 15 ☐ 16 ☐ 17 ☐ 18 ☐ 19 ☐ 20 ☐ 21 ☐ 22 ☐ 23 ☐ 24 ☐ 25 ☐ 26 ☐ 27 ☐ 28 ☐ 29 ☐ 30 ☐ 31

2 SAMUEL ☐ 1 ☐ 2 ☐ 3 ☐ 4 ☐ 5 ☐ 6 ☐ 7 ☐ 8 ☐ 9 ☐ 10 ☐ 11 ☐ 12 ☐ 13 ☐ 14 ☐ 15 ☐ 16 ☐ 17 ☐ 18 ☐ 19 ☐ 20 ☐ 21 ☐ 22 ☐ 23 ☐ 24

1 KINGS ☐ 1 ☐ 2 ☐ 3 ☐ 4 ☐ 5 ☐ 6 ☐ 7 ☐ 8 ☐ 9 ☐ 10 ☐ 11 ☐ 12 ☐ 13 ☐ 14 ☐ 15 ☐ 16 ☐ 17 ☐ 18 ☐ 19 ☐ 20 ☐ 21 ☐ 22

2 KINGS ☐ 1 ☐ 2 ☐ 3 ☐ 4 ☐ 5 ☐ 6 ☐ 7 ☐ 8 ☐ 9 ☐ 10 ☐ 11 ☐ 12 ☐ 13 ☐ 14 ☐ 15 ☐ 16 ☐ 17 ☐ 18 ☐ 19 ☐ 20 ☐ 21 ☐ 22 ☐ 23 ☐ 24 ☐ 251

1 CHRONICLES ☐ 1 ☐ 2 ☐ 3 ☐ 4 ☐ 5 ☐ 6 ☐ 7 ☐ 8 ☐ 9 ☐ 10 ☐ 11 ☐ 12 ☐ 13 ☐ 14 ☐ 15 ☐ 16 ☐ 17 ☐ 18 ☐ 19 ☐ 20 ☐ 21 ☐ 22 ☐ 23 ☐ 24 ☐ 25 ☐ 26 ☐ 27 ☐ 28 ☐ 29

2 CHRONICLES ☐ 1 ☐ 2 ☐ 3 ☐ 4 ☐ 5 ☐ 6 ☐ 7 ☐ 8 ☐ 9 ☐ 10 ☐ 11 ☐ 12 ☐ 13 ☐ 14 ☐ 15 ☐ 16 ☐ 17 ☐ 18 ☐ 19 ☐ 20 ☐ 21 ☐ 22 ☐ 23 ☐ 24 ☐ 25 ☐ 26 ☐ 27 ☐ 28 ☐ 29 ☐ 30 ☐ 31 ☐ 32 ☐ 33 ☐ 34 ☐ 35 ☐ 36

EZRA ☐ 1 ☐ 2 ☐ 3 ☐ 4 ☐ 5 ☐ 6 ☐ 7 ☐ 8 ☐ 9 ☐ 10

NEHEMIAH ☐ 1 ☐ 2 ☐ 3 ☐ 4 ☐ 5 ☐ 6 ☐ 7 ☐ 8 ☐ 9 ☐ 10 ☐ 11 ☐ 12 ☐ 13

ESTHER ☐ 1 ☐ 2 ☐ 3 ☐ 4 ☐ 5 ☐ 6 ☐ 7 ☐ 8 ☐ 9 ☐ 10

JOB ☐ 1 ☐ 2 ☐ 3 ☐ 4 ☐ 5 ☐ 6 ☐ 7 ☐ 8 ☐ 9 ☐ 10 ☐ 11 ☐ 12 ☐ 13 ☐ 14 ☐ 15 ☐ 16 ☐ 17 ☐ 18 ☐ 19 ☐ 20 ☐ 21 ☐ 22 ☐ 23 ☐ 24 ☐ 25 ☐ 26 ☐ 27 ☐ 28 ☐ 29 ☐ 30 ☐ 31 ☐ 32 ☐ 33 ☐ 34 ☐ 35 ☐ 36 ☐ 37 ☐ 38 ☐ 39 ☐ 40 ☐ 41 ☐ 42

PSALMS ☐ 1 ☐ 2 ☐ 3 ☐ 4 ☐ 5 ☐ 6 ☐ 7 ☐ 8 ☐ 9 ☐ 10 ☐ 11 ☐ 12 ☐ 13 ☐ 14 ☐ 15 ☐ 16 ☐ 17 ☐ 18 ☐ 19 ☐ 20 ☐ 21 ☐ 22 ☐ 23 ☐ 24 ☐ 25 ☐ 26 ☐ 27 ☐ 28 ☐ 29 ☐ 30 ☐ 31 ☐ 32 ☐ 33 ☐ 34 ☐ 35 ☐ 36 ☐ 37 ☐ 38 ☐ 39 ☐ 40 ☐ 41 ☐ 42 ☐ 43 ☐ 44 ☐ 45 ☐ 46 ☐ 47 ☐ 48 ☐ 49 ☐ 50 ☐ 51 ☐ 52 ☐ 53 ☐ 54 ☐ 55 ☐ 56 ☐ 57 ☐ 58 ☐ 59 ☐ 60 ☐ 61 ☐ 62 ☐ 63 ☐ 64 ☐ 65 ☐ 66 ☐ 67 ☐ 68 ☐ 69 ☐ 70 ☐ 71 ☐ 72 ☐ 73 ☐ 74 ☐ 75 ☐ 76 ☐ 77 ☐ 78 ☐ 79 ☐ 80 ☐ 81 ☐ 82 ☐ 83 ☐ 84 ☐ 85 ☐ 86 ☐ 87 ☐ 88 ☐ 89 ☐ 90 ☐ 91 ☐ 92 ☐ 93 ☐ 94 ☐ 95 ☐ 96 ☐ 97 ☐ 98 ☐ 99 ☐ 100 ☐ 101 ☐ 102 ☐ 103 ☐ 104 ☐ 105 ☐ 106 ☐ 107 ☐ 108 ☐ 109 ☐ 110 ☐ 111 ☐ 112 ☐ 113 ☐ 114 ☐ 115 ☐ 116 ☐ 117 ☐ 118 ☐ 119 ☐ 120 ☐ 121 ☐ 122 ☐ 123 ☐ 124 ☐ 125 ☐ 126 ☐ 127 ☐ 128 ☐ 129 ☐ 130 ☐ 131 ☐ 132 ☐ 133 ☐ 134 ☐ 135 ☐ 136 ☐ 137 ☐ 138 ☐ 139 ☐ 140 ☐ 141 ☐ 142 ☐ 143 ☐ 144 ☐ 145 ☐ 146 ☐ 147 ☐ 148 ☐ 149 ☐ 150

PROVERBS ☐ 1 ☐ 2 ☐ 3 ☐ 4 ☐ 5 ☐ 6 ☐ 7 ☐ 8 ☐ 9 ☐ 10 ☐ 11 ☐ 12 ☐ 13 ☐ 14 ☐ 15 ☐ 16 ☐ 17 ☐ 18 ☐ 19 ☐ 20 ☐ 21 ☐ 22 ☐ 23 ☐ 24 ☐ 25 ☐ 26 ☐ 27 ☐ 28 ☐ 29 ☐ 30 ☐ 31

ECCLESIASTES ☐ 1 ☐ 2 ☐ 3 ☐ 4 ☐ 5 ☐ 6 ☐ 7 ☐ 8 ☐ 9 ☐ 10 ☐ 11 ☐ 12

SONG OF SONGS ☐ 1 ☐ 2 ☐ 3 ☐ 4 ☐ 5 ☐ 6 ☐ 7 ☐ 8

ISAIAH ☐ 1 ☐ 2 ☐ 3 ☐ 4 ☐ 5 ☐ 6 ☐ 7 ☐ 8 ☐ 9 ☐ 10 ☐ 11 ☐ 12 ☐ 13 ☐ 14 ☐ 15 ☐ 16 ☐ 17 ☐ 18 ☐ 19 ☐ 20 ☐ 21 ☐ 22 ☐ 23 ☐ 24 ☐ 25 ☐ 26 ☐ 27 ☐ 28 ☐ 29 ☐ 30 ☐ 31 ☐ 32 ☐ 33 ☐ 34 ☐ 35 ☐ 36 ☐ 37 ☐ 38 ☐ 39 ☐ 40 ☐ 41 ☐ 42 ☐ 43 ☐ 44 ☐ 45 ☐ 46 ☐ 47 ☐ 48 ☐ 49 ☐ 50 ☐ 51 ☐ 52 ☐ 53 ☐ 54 ☐ 55 ☐ 56 ☐ 57 ☐ 58 ☐ 59 ☐ 60 ☐ 61 ☐ 62 ☐ 63 ☐ 64 ☐ 65 ☐ 66

JEREMIAH ☐ 1 ☐ 2 ☐ 3 ☐ 4 ☐ 5 ☐ 6 ☐ 7 ☐ 8 ☐ 9 ☐ 10 ☐ 11 ☐ 12 ☐ 13 ☐ 14 ☐ 15 ☐ 16 ☐ 17 ☐ 18 ☐ 19 ☐ 20 ☐ 21 ☐ 22 ☐ 23 ☐ 24 ☐ 25 ☐ 26 ☐ 27 ☐ 28 ☐ 29 ☐ 30 ☐ 31 ☐ 32 ☐ 33 ☐ 34 ☐ 35 ☐ 36 ☐ 37 ☐ 38 ☐ 39 ☐ 40 ☐ 41 ☐ 42 ☐ 43 ☐ 44 ☐ 45 ☐ 46 ☐ 47 ☐ 48 ☐ 49 ☐ 50 ☐ 51 ☐ 52

LAMENTATIONS ☐ 1 ☐ 2 ☐ 3 ☐ 4 ☐ 5

EZEKIEL ☐ 1 ☐ 2 ☐ 3 ☐ 4 ☐ 5 ☐ 6 ☐ 7 ☐ 8 ☐ 9 ☐ 10 ☐ 11 ☐ 12 ☐ 13 ☐ 14 ☐ 15 ☐ 16 ☐ 17 ☐ 18 ☐ 19 ☐ 20 ☐ 21 ☐ 22 ☐ 23 ☐ 24 ☐ 25 ☐ 26 ☐ 27 ☐ 28 ☐ 29 ☐ 30 ☐ 31 ☐ 32 ☐ 33 ☐ 34 ☐ 35 ☐ 36 ☐ 37 ☐ 38 ☐ 39 ☐ 40 ☐ 41 ☐ 42 ☐ 43 ☐ 44 ☐ 45 ☐ 46 ☐ 47 ☐ 48

DANIEL ☐ 1 ☐ 2 ☐ 3 ☐ 4 ☐ 5 ☐ 6 ☐ 7 ☐ 8 ☐ 9 ☐ 10 ☐ 11 ☐ 12

HOSEA ☐ 1 ☐ 2 ☐ 3 ☐ 4 ☐ 5 ☐ 6 ☐ 7 ☐ 8 ☐ 9 ☐ 10 ☐ 11 ☐ 12 ☐ 13 ☐ 14

JOEL ☐ 1 ☐ 2 ☐ 3

AMOS ☐ 1 ☐ 2 ☐ 3 ☐ 4 ☐ 5 ☐ 6 ☐ 7 ☐ 8 ☐ 9

OBADIAH ☐ Obadiah

JONAH ☐ 1 ☐ 2 ☐ 3 ☐ 4

MICAH ☐ 1 ☐ 2 ☐ 3 ☐ 4 ☐ 5 ☐ 6 ☐ 7

NAHUM ☐ 1 ☐ 2 ☐ 3

HABAKKUK ☐ 1 ☐ 2 ☐ 3

ZEPHANIAH ☐ 1 ☐ 2 ☐ 3

HAGGAI ☐ 1 ☐ 2

ZECHARIAH ☐ 1 ☐ 2 ☐ 3 ☐ 4 ☐ 5 ☐ 6 ☐ 7 ☐ 8 ☐ 9 ☐ 10 ☐ 11 ☐ 12 ☐ 13 ☐ 14

MALACHI ☐ 1 ☐ 2 ☐ 3 ☐ 4

MATTHEW ☐ 1 ☐ 2 ☐ 3 ☐ 4 ☐ 5 ☐ 6 ☐ 7 ☐ 8 ☐ 9 ☐ 10 ☐ 11 ☐ 12 ☐ 13 ☐ 14 ☐ 15 ☐ 16 ☐ 17 ☐ 18 ☐ 19 ☐ 20 ☐ 21 ☐ 22 ☐ 23 ☐ 24 ☐ 25 ☐ 26 ☐ 27 ☐ 28

MARK ☐ 1 ☐ 2 ☐ 3 ☐ 4 ☐ 5 ☐ 6 ☐ 7 ☐ 8 ☐ 9 ☐ 10 ☐ 11 ☐ 12 ☐ 13 ☐ 14 ☐ 15 ☐ 16

LUKE ☐ 1 ☐ 2 ☐ 3 ☐ 4 ☐ 5 ☐ 6 ☐ 7 ☐ 8 ☐ 9 ☐ 10 ☐ 11 ☐ 12 ☐ 13 ☐ 14 ☐ 15 ☐ 16 ☐ 17 ☐ 18 ☐ 19 ☐ 20 ☐ 21 ☐ 22 ☐ 23 ☐ 24

JOHN ☐ 1 ☐ 2 ☐ 3 ☐ 4 ☐ 5 ☐ 6 ☐ 7 ☐ 8 ☐ 9 ☐ 10 ☐ 11 ☐ 12 ☐ 13 ☐ 14 ☐ 15 ☐ 16 ☐ 17 ☐ 18 ☐ 19 ☐ 20 ☐ 21

ACTS ☐ 1 ☐ 2 ☐ 3 ☐ 4 ☐ 5 ☐ 6 ☐ 7 ☐ 8 ☐ 9 ☐ 10 ☐ 11 ☐ 12 ☐ 13 ☐ 14 ☐ 15 ☐ 16 ☐ 17 ☐ 18 ☐ 19 ☐ 20 ☐ 21 ☐ 22 ☐ 23 ☐ 24 ☐ 25 ☐ 26 ☐ 27 ☐ 28

ROMANS ☐ 1 ☐ 2 ☐ 3 ☐ 4 ☐ 5 ☐ 6 ☐ 7 ☐ 8 ☐ 9 ☐ 10 ☐ 11 ☐ 12 ☐ 13 ☐ 14 ☐ 15 ☐ 16

1 CORINTHIANS ☐ 1 ☐ 2 ☐ 3 ☐ 4 ☐ 5 ☐ 6 ☐ 7 ☐ 8 ☐ 9 ☐ 10 ☐ 11 ☐ 12 ☐ 13 ☐ 14 ☐ 15 ☐ 16

2 CORINTHIANS ☐ 1 ☐ 2 ☐ 3 ☐ 4 ☐ 5 ☐ 6 ☐ 7 ☐ 8 ☐ 9 ☐ 10 ☐ 11 ☐ 12 ☐ 13

GALATIANS ☐ 1 ☐ 2 ☐ 3 ☐ 4 ☐ 5 ☐ 6

EPHESIANS ☐ 1 ☐ 2 ☐ 3 ☐ 4 ☐ 5 ☐ 6

PHILIPPIANS ☐ 1 ☐ 2 ☐ 3 ☐ 4

COLOSSIANS ☐ 1 ☐ 2 ☐ 3 ☐ 4

1 THESSALONIANS ☐ 1 ☐ 2 ☐ 3 ☐ 4 ☐ 5

2 THESSALONIANS ☐ 1 ☐ 2 ☐ 3

1 TIMOTHY ☐ 1 ☐ 2 ☐ 3 ☐ 4 ☐ 5 ☐ 6

2 TIMOTHY ☐ 1 ☐ 2 ☐ 3 ☐ 4

TITUS ☐ 1 ☐ 2 ☐ 3

PHILEMON ☐ Philemon

HEBREWS ☐ 1 ☐ 2 ☐ 3 ☐ 4 ☐ 5 ☐ 6 ☐ 7 ☐ 8 ☐ 9 ☐ 10 ☐ 11 ☐ 12 ☐ 13

JAMES ☐ 1 ☐ 2 ☐ 3 ☐ 4 ☐ 5

Rock Solid TRUTHS
Index

ROCK SOLID TRUTHS INDEX

Rock Solid PROMISES
Index

Rock Solid PRINCIPLES Index

Rock Solid PLANS Index

Unshaken PEOPLE
Index

UNSHAKEN PEOPLE INDEX

Unshaken GOD
Index

God is...

Concordance

The NIV Concordance, created by John R. Kohlenberger III, has been developed specifically for use with the New International Version (NIV). Like all concordances, it is a special index that contains an alphabetical listing of words used in the Bible text.

This concordance contains 2,474 word entries, with more than 10,000 Scripture references. Each word entry is followed by significant Scripture references in which that particular word is found, as well as by a brief excerpt from the surrounding context. In the context, the entry word is abbreviated by its first letter in bold print. Other forms of the entry word and related words indexed in this concordance are in parentheses.

This concordance also contains 155 biographical entries for significant people in the Bible. The descriptive phrases replace the brief context surrounding each occurrence of the name. In those instances where more than one Bible character has the same name, that name is placed under one block entry, and each person is given a number (1), (2), etc.

Two entries are marked with an asterisk (*). LORD* and LORD'S* list occurrences of the proper name of God, *Yahweh,* spelled "Lᴏʀᴅ" and "Lᴏʀᴅ's" in the NIV. These entries are distinguished from LORD and LORD's, which list occurrences of the title "Lord" and "Lord's."

This concordance is a valuable tool for Bible study. While one of its key purposes is to help the reader find forgotten references to familiar verses, it can also be used to do word studies and to locate and trace biblical themes. Whenever you find a significant context, be sure to read at least the whole verse in the NIV to discover its fuller meaning in its larger context.

AARON
Priesthood of (Ex 28:1; Nu 17; Heb 5:1–4; 7), garments (Ex 28; 39), consecration (Ex 29), ordination (Lev 8).

Spokesman for Moses (Ex 4:14–16, 27–31; 7:1–2). Supported Moses' hands in battle (Ex 17:8–13). Built golden calf (Ex 32; Dt 9:20). Talked against Moses (Nu 12). Priesthood opposed (Nu 16); staff budded (Nu 17). Forbidden to enter land (Nu 20:1–12). Death (Nu 20:22–29; 33:38–39).

ABANDON
Dt	4: 31	he will not **a** or destroy you
1Ti	4: 1	in later times some will **a** the faith

ABBA
Ro	8: 15	And by him we cry, "**A**, Father."
Gal	4: 6	the Spirit who calls out, "**A**,

ABEL
Second son of Adam (Ge 4:2). Offered proper sacrifice (Ge 4:4; Heb 11:4). Murdered by Cain (Ge 4:8; Mt 23:35; Lk 11:51; 1Jn 3:12).

ABIGAIL
Wife of Nabal (1Sa 25:30); pled for his life with David (1Sa 25:14–35). Became David's wife (1Sa 25:36–42).

ABIJAH
Son of Rehoboam; king of Judah (1Ki 14:31—15:8; 2Ch 12:16—14:1).

ABILITY (ABLE)
Ezr	2: 69	According to their **a** they gave
2Co	1: 8	far beyond our **a** to endure,
	8: 3	were able, and even beyond their **a**.

ABIMELEK
1. King of Gerar who took Abraham's wife Sarah, believing her to be his sister (Ge 20). Later made a covenant with Abraham (Ge 21:22–33).

2. King of Gerar who took Isaac's wife Rebekah, believing her to be his sister (Ge 26:1–11). Later made a covenant with Isaac (Ge 26:12–31).

ABLE (ABILITY ENABLE ENABLED ENABLES)
Eze	7: 19	gold will not be **a** to deliver them
Da	3: 17	the God we serve is **a** to deliver us
Ro	8: 39	will be **a** to separate us
	14: 4	the Lord is **a** to make them stand.
	16: 25	to him who is **a** to establish you
2Co	9: 8	God is **a** to bless you abundantly,
Eph	3: 20	him who is **a** to do immeasurably
2Ti	1: 12	that he is **a** to guard what I have
	3: 15	which are **a** to make you wise
Heb	7: 25	he is **a** to save completely
Jude	: 24	To him who is **a** to keep you
Rev	5: 5	He is **a** to open the scroll and its

ABOLISH
Mt	5: 17	think that I have come to **a** the Law

ABOMINATION
Da	11: 31	set up the **a** that causes desolation.

1541

CONCORDANCE

ABOUND (ABOUNDING ABOUNDS)
2Co 9: 8 you will **a** in every good work.
Php 1: 9 your love may **a** more and more

ABOUNDING (ABOUND)
Ex 34: 6 to anger, **a** in love and faithfulness,
Ps 86: 5 **a** in love to all who call to you.

ABOUNDS (ABOUND)
2Co 1: 5 also our comfort **a** through Christ.

ABRAHAM
Covenant relation with the LORD (Ge 12:1–3; 13:14–17; 15; 17; 22:15–18; Ex 2:24; Ne 9:8; Ps 105; Mic 7:20; Lk 1:68–75; Ro 4; Heb 6:13–15).
Called from Ur, via Harran, to Canaan (Ge 12:1; Ac 7:2–4; Heb 11:8–10). Moved to Egypt, nearly lost Sarah to Pharoah (Ge 12:10–20). Divided the land with Lot (Ge 13). Saved Lot from four kings (Ge 14:1–16); blessed by Melchizedek (Ge 14:17–20; Heb 7:1–20). Declared righteous by faith (Ge 15:6; Ro 4:3; Gal 3:6–9). Fathered Ishmael by Hagar (Ge 16).
Name changed from Abram (Ge 17:5; Ne 9:7). Circumcised (Ge 17; Ro 4:9–12). Entertained three visitors (Ge 18); promised a son by Sarah (Ge 18:9–15; 17:16). Moved to Gerar; nearly lost Sarah to Abimelek (Ge 20). Fathered Isaac by Sarah (Ge 21:1–7; Ac 7:8; Heb 11:11–12); sent away Hagar and Ishmael (Ge 21:8–21; Gal 4:22–30). Tested by offering Isaac (Ge 22; Heb 11:17–19; Jas 2:21–24). Sarah died; bought field of Ephron for burial (Ge 23). Secured wife for Isaac (Ge 24). Death (Ge 25:7–11).

ABSALOM
Son of David by Maakah (2Sa 3:3; 1Ch 3:2). Killed Amnon for rape of his sister Tamar; banished by David (2Sa 13). Returned to Jerusalem; received by David (2Sa 14). Rebelled against David; seized kingdom (2Sa 15–17). Killed (2Sa 18).

ABSTAIN (ABSTAINS)
1Pe 2: 11 and exiles, to **a** from sinful desires,

ABSTAINS (ABSTAIN)
Ro 14: 6 and whoever **a** does so to the Lord

ABUNDANCE (ABUNDANT)
Lk 12: 15 not consist in an **a** of possessions."
Jude : 2 peace and love be yours in **a**.

ABUNDANT (ABUNDANCE)
Dt 28: 11 will grant you **a** prosperity—
Ps 145: 7 They celebrate your **a** goodness
Pr 28: 19 work their land will have **a** food,
Ro 5: 17 who receive God's **a** provision

ABUSE
2Pe 2: 11 do not heap **a** on such beings

ACCEPT (ACCEPTED ACCEPTS)
Ex 23: 8 "Do not **a** a bribe, for a bribe
Pr 10: 8 The wise in heart **a** commands,
19: 20 Listen to advice and **a** discipline,
Ro 15: 7 **A** one another, then, just as Christ
Jas 1: 21 humbly **a** the word planted in you,

ACCEPTED (ACCEPT)
Lk 4: 24 "no prophet is **a** in his hometown.

ACCEPTS (ACCEPT)
Ps 6: 9 the LORD **a** my prayer.
Jn 13: 20 whoever **a** anyone I send **a** me;

ACCOMPANY
Mk 16: 17 *these signs will **a** those who believe:*

ACCOMPLISH
Isa 55: 11 but will **a** what I desire and achieve

ACCORD
Nu 24: 13 not do anything of my own **a**,
Jn 10: 18 me, but I lay it down of my own **a**.

ACCOUNT (ACCOUNTABLE)
Mt 12: 36 will have to give **a** on the day
Ro 14: 12 of us will give an **a** of ourselves
Heb 4: 13 of him to whom we must give **a**.

ACCOUNTABLE (ACCOUNT)
Eze 33: 6 I will hold the watchman **a** for
Ro 3: 19 and the whole world held **a** to God.

ACCUSATION (ACCUSE)
1Ti 5: 19 not entertain an **a** against an elder

ACCUSE (ACCUSATION)
Pr 3: 30 Do not **a** anyone for no reason—
Lk 3: 14 money and don't **a** people falsely—

ACHAN
Sin at Jericho caused defeat at Ai; stoned (Jos 7; 22:20; 1Ch 2:7).

ACHE
Pr 14: 13 Even in laughter the heart may **a**,

ACKNOWLEDGE
Mt 10: 32 also **a** before my Father in heaven.
1Th 5: 12 **a** those who work hard among you,
Php 2: 11 every tongue **a** that Jesus Christ is
1Jn 4: 3 spirit that does not **a** Jesus is not

ACQUIT
Ex 23: 7 to death, for I will not **a** the guilty.

ACTION (ACTIONS ACTIVE ACTS)
Jas 2: 17 if it is not accompanied by **a**,

ACTIONS (ACTION)
Gal 6: 4 Each one should test their own **a**.
Titus 1: 16 God, but by their **a** they deny him.

ACTIVE (ACTION)
Heb 4: 12 For the word of God is alive and **a**.

ACTS (ACTION)
Ps 145: 12 people may know of your mighty **a**
150: 2 Praise him for his **a** of power;
Isa 64: 6 all our righteous **a** are like filthy

ADAM
First man (Ge 1:26—2:25; Ro 5:14; 1Ti 2:13). Sin of (Ge 3; Hos 6:7; Ro 5:12–21). Children of (Ge 4:1—5:5). Death of (Ge 5:5; Ro 5:12–21; 1Co 15:22).

ADD
Dt 12: 32 do not **a** to it or take away from it.
Pr 30: 6 Do not **a** to his words, or he will
Lk 12: 25 by worrying can **a** a single hour
Rev 22: 18 them, God will **a** to that person

ADMIRABLE
Php 4: 8 whatever is lovely, whatever is **a**—

ADMONISH
Col 3: 16 and **a** one another with all wisdom

ADOPTION
Ro 8: 23 wait eagerly for our **a** to sonship,
Eph 1: 5 he predestined us for **a** to sonship

ADORE
SS   1:   4   How right they are to **a** you!

ADORNMENT (ADORNS)
1Pe   3:   3   should not come from outward **a**,

ADORNS (ADORNMENT)
Ps   93:   5   holiness **a** your house for endless

ADULTERY
Ex   20: 14   "You shall not commit **a**.
Mt   5: 27   was said, 'You shall not commit **a**.'
      5: 28   lustfully has already committed **a**
      5: 32   a divorced woman commits **a**.
    15: 19   murder, **a**, sexual immorality, theft,

ADULTS
1Co   14: 20   but in your thinking be **a**.

ADVANCED
Job   32:   7   **a** years should teach wisdom.'

ADVANTAGE
Ex   22: 22   "Do not take **a** of the widow
Dt   24: 14   Do not take **a** of a hired worker
1Th   4:   6   should wrong or take **a** of a brother

ADVERSITY
Pr   17: 17   a brother is born for a time of **a**.

ADVICE
1Ki   12:   8   Rehoboam rejected the **a** the elders
    12: 14   he followed the **a** of the young men
Pr   12:   5   but the **a** of the wicked is deceitful.
    12: 15   to them, but the wise listen to **a**.
    19: 20   Listen to **a** and accept discipline,
    20: 18   Plans are established by seeking **a**;

ADVOCATE
Jn   14: 16   he will give you another **a** to help
    14: 26   But the **A**, the Holy Spirit,
1Jn   2:   1   sin, we have an **a** with the Father—

AFFECTION
2Pe   1:   7   and to godliness, mutual **a**; and to
             mutual **a**, love.

AFFLICTION
Ro   12: 12   patient in **a**, faithful in prayer.

AFRAID (FEAR)
Ge   26: 24   Do not be **a**, for I am with you;
Ex   3:   6   because he was **a** to look at God.
Ps   27:   1   of my life—of whom shall I be **a**?
    56:   3   When I am **a**, I put my trust in
Pr   3: 24   you lie down, you will not be **a**;
Jer   1:   8   Do not be **a** of them, for I am
Mt   8: 26   of little faith, why are you so **a**?"
    10: 28   Do not be **a** of those who kill
    10: 31   So don't be **a**; you are worth more
Mk   5: 36   said, Jesus told him, "Don't be **a**;
Jn   14: 27   hearts be troubled and do not be **a**.
Heb   13:   6   Lord is my helper; I will not be **a**.

AGED
Job   12: 12   Is not wisdom found among the **a**?
Pr   17:   6   children are a crown to the **a**,

AGREE
Mt   18: 19   earth **a** about anything they ask for,
Ro   7: 16   want to do, I **a** that the law is good.

AHAB
Son of Omri; king of Israel (1Ki 16:28—22:40), husband of Jezebel (1Ki 16:31). Promoted Baal worship

(1Ki 16:31–33); opposed by Elijah (1Ki 17:1; 18; 21), a prophet (1Ki 20:35–43), Micaiah (1Ki 22:1–28). Defeated Ben-Hadad (1Ki 20). Killed for failing to kill Ben-Hadad and for murder of Naboth (1Ki 20:35—21:40).

AHAZ
Son of Jotham; king of Judah, (2Ki 16; 2Ch 28; Isa 7).

AHAZIAH
1. Son of Ahab; king of Israel (1Ki 22:51–2Ki 1:18; 2Ch 20:35–37).
2. Son of Jehoram; king of Judah (2Ki 8:25–29; 9:14–29), also called Jehoahaz (2Ch 21:17—22:9; 25:23).

AIM
1Co   7: 34   Her **a** is to be devoted to the Lord

AIR
1Co   9: 26   not fight like a boxer beating the **a**.
Eph   2:   2   the ruler of the kingdom of the **a**,
1Th   4: 17   clouds to meet the Lord in the **a**.

ALABASTER
Mt   26:   7   him with an **a** jar of very expensive

ALERT
Jos   8:   4   far from it. All of you be on the **a**.
Mk   13: 33   Be **a**! You do not know
Eph   6: 18   be **a** and always keep on praying
1Pe   1: 13   with minds that are **a** and fully

ALIENATED
Gal   5:   4   the law have been **a** from Christ;

ALIVE (LIVE)
Ac   1:   3   convincing proofs that he was **a**.
Ro   6: 11   to sin but **a** to God in Christ Jesus.
1Co   15: 22   die, so in Christ all will be made **a**.
Heb   4: 12   the word of God is **a** and active.

ALMIGHTY (MIGHT)
Ge   17:   1   to him and said, "I am God **A**;
Job   11:   7   Can you probe the limits of the **A**?
    33:   4   the breath of the **A** gives me life.
Ps   91:   1   will rest in the shadow of the **A**.
Isa   6:   3   "Holy, holy, holy is the Lᴏʀᴅ **A**;

ALTAR
Ge   22:   9   Abraham built an **a** there
Ex   27:   1   "Build an **a** of acacia wood,
1Ki   18: 30   he repaired the **a** of the Lᴏʀᴅ,
2Ch   4:   1   a bronze **a** twenty cubits long,
     4: 19   the golden **a**; the tables

ALWAYS
Ps   16:   8   I keep my eyes **a** on the Lᴏʀᴅ.
    26:   3   for I have **a** been mindful of your
    51:   3   and my sin is **a** before me.
Mt   26: 11   The poor you will **a** have with you,
    28: 20   And surely I am with you **a**,
1Co   13:   7   It **a** protects, **a** trusts, **a** hopes,
Php   4:   4   Rejoice in the Lord **a**. I will say it
1Pe   3: 15   **A** be prepared to give an answer

AMAZIAH
Son of Joash; king of Judah (2Ki 14; 2Ch 25).

AMBASSADORS
2Co   5: 20   We are therefore Christ's **a**,

AMBITION
Ro   15: 20   It has always been my **a** to preach
1Th   4: 11   make it your **a** to lead a quiet life:

AMON
Son of Manasseh; king of Judah (2Ki 21:18–26; 1Ch 3:14; 2Ch 33:21–25).

ANANIAS
1. Husband of Sapphira; died for lying to God (Ac 5:1–11).
2. Disciple who baptized Saul (Ac 9:10–19).
3. High priest at Paul's arrest (Ac 22:30—24:1).

ANCESTORS
Heb 1: 1 spoke to our **a** through the prophets

ANCHOR
Heb 6: 19 We have this hope as an **a**

ANCIENT
Da 7: 9 and the **A** of Days took his seat.

ANDREW
Apostle; brother of Simon Peter (Mt 4:18; 10:2; Mk 1:16–18, 29; 3:18; 13:3; Lk 6:14; Jn 1:35–44; 6:8–9; 12:22; Ac 1:13).

ANGEL (ANGELS ARCHANGEL)
Ps 34: 7 The **a** of the LORD encamps
Ac 6: 15 his face was like the face of an **a**.
2Co 11: 14 Satan himself masquerades as an **a**
Gal 1: 8 or an **a** from heaven should preach

ANGELS (ANGEL)
Ps 8: 5 a little lower than the **a**
91: 11 command his **a** concerning you
Mt 18: 10 that their **a** in heaven always see
25: 41 fire prepared for the devil and his **a**.
Lk 20: 36 for they are like the **a**.
1Co 6: 3 you not know that we will judge **a**?
Heb 1: 4 the **a** as the name he has inherited
1: 14 Are not all **a** ministering spirits
2: 7 them a little lower than the **a**;
13: 2 hospitality to **a** without knowing it.
1Pe 1: 12 Even **a** long to look into these
2Pe 2: 4 if God did not spare **a** when they

ANGER (ANGERED ANGRY)
Ex 32: 10 that my **a** may burn against them
34: 6 slow to **a**, abounding in love
Dt 29: 28 In furious **a** and in great wrath
2Ki 22: 13 Great is the LORD's **a** that burns
Ps 30: 5 For his **a** lasts only a moment,
Pr 15: 1 wrath, but a harsh word stirs up **a**.

ANGERED (ANGER)
Pr 22: 24 do not associate with one easily **a**,
1Co 13: 5 it is not easily **a**, it keeps no record

ANGRY (ANGER)
Ps 2: 12 he will be **a** and your way will lead
Pr 29: 22 An **a** person stirs up conflict,
Jas 1: 19 to speak and slow to become **a**,

ANOINT
Ps 23: 5 You **a** my head with oil;
Jas 5: 14 **a** them with oil in the name

ANOTHER
1Pe 3: 8 love one **a**, be compassionate

ANT
Pr 6: 6 Go to the **a**, you sluggard;

ANTICHRIST
1Jn 2: 18 have heard that the **a** is coming,
2Jn : 7 person is the deceiver and the **a**.

ANTIOCH
Ac 11: 26 were called Christians first at **A**.

ANXIETY
Pr 12: 25 **A** weighs down the heart,
1Pe 5: 7 Cast all your **a** on him because he

ANXIOUS (ANXIETY)
Php 4: 6 Do not be **a** about anything,

APOLLOS
Christian from Alexandria, learned in the Scriptures; instructed by Aquila and Priscilla (Ac 18:24–28). Ministered at Corinth (Ac 19:1; 1Co 1:12; 3; Titus 3:13).

APOSTLES
See also Andrew, Bartholomew, James, John, Judas, Matthew, Nathanael, Paul, Peter, Philip, Simon, Thaddaeus, Thomas.
Ac 1: 26 so he was added to the eleven **a**.
2: 43 and signs performed by the **a**.
1Co 12: 28 placed in the church first of all **a**,
15: 9 For I am the least of the **a** and do
2Co 11: 13 For such people are false **a**,
Eph 2: 20 built on the foundation of the **a**

APPEAR (APPEARANCE APPEARING)
Mk 13: 22 false prophets will **a** and perform
2Co 5: 10 we must all **a** before the judgment
Col 3: 4 you also will **a** with him in glory.
Heb 9: 24 now to **a** for us in God's presence.
9: 28 and he will **a** a second time,

APPEARANCE (APPEAR)
1Sa 16: 7 People look at the outward **a**,

APPEARING (APPEAR)
2Ti 4: 8 to all who have longed for his **a**.
Titus 2: 13 the **a** of the glory of our great God

APPLY
Pr 22: 17 **a** your heart to what I teach,
23: 12 **A** your heart to instruction and

APPROACH
Eph 3: 12 we may **a** God with freedom
Heb 4: 16 then **a** God's throne of grace

APPROVED
2Ti 2: 15 to present yourself to God as one **a**,

AQUILA
Husband of Priscilla; co-worker with Paul, instructor of Apollos (Ac 18; Ro 16:3; 1Co 16:19; 2Ti 4:19).

ARARAT
Ge 8: 4 to rest on the mountains of **A**.

ARCHANGEL (ANGEL)
1Th 4: 16 with the voice of the **a**
Jude : 9 But even the **a** Michael, when he

ARCHITECT
Heb 11: 10 whose **a** and builder is God.

ARGUING
Php 2: 14 everything without grumbling or **a**,

ARK
Ge 6: 14 So make yourself an **a** of cypress
Dt 10: 5 put the tablets in the **a** I had made,
2Ch 35: 3 "Put the sacred **a** in the temple
Heb 9: 4 This **a** contained the gold jar

ARM (ARMY)
Nu 11: 23 "Is the Lord's **a** too short?
1Pe 4: 1 **a** yourselves also with the same

ARMAGEDDON
Rev 16: 16 place that in Hebrew is called **A**.

ARMOR (ARMY)
1Ki 20: 11 his **a** should not boast like one who
Eph 6: 11 Put on the full **a** of God, so that
6: 13 Therefore put on the full **a** of God,

ARMS (ARMY)
Dt 33: 27 underneath are the everlasting **a**.
Ps 18: 32 It is God who **a** me with strength
Pr 31: 20 She opens her **a** to the poor
Isa 40: 11 He gathers the lambs in his **a**
Mk 10: 16 And he took the children in his **a**,

ARMY (ARM ARMOR ARMS)
Ps 33: 16 king is saved by the size of his **a**;
Rev 19: 19 the rider on the horse and his **a**.

AROMA
2Co 2: 15 the pleasing **a** of Christ among
2: 16 one we are an **a** that brings death;
2: 16 to the other, an **a** that brings life.

ARRAYED
Ps 110: 3 **A** in holy splendor, your young
Isa 61: 10 **a** me in a robe of his righteousness,

ARROGANT
Ro 11: 20 Do not be **a**, but tremble.

ARROWS
Eph 6: 16 can extinguish all the flaming **a**

ASA
King of Judah (1Ki 15:8–24; 1Ch 3:10; 2Ch 14–16).

ASCENDED
Eph 4: 8 "When he **a** on high, he took many

ASCRIBE
1Ch 16: 28 **A** to the Lord, all you families
16: 28 **a** to the Lord glory and strength.
Job 36: 3 I will **a** justice to my Maker.
Ps 29: 2 **A** to the Lord the glory due his

ASHAMED (SHAME)
Lk 9: 26 Whoever is **a** of me and my words,
the Son of Man will be **a** of them
Ro 1: 16 For I am not **a** of the gospel,
2Ti 1: 8 So do not be **a** of the testimony
2: 15 worker who does not need to be **a**

ASSIGNED
Mk 13: 34 each with their **a** task, and tells
1Co 3: 5 as the Lord has **a** to each his task.
7: 17 whatever situation the Lord has **a**

ASSOCIATE
Pr 22: 24 do not **a** with one easily angered,
Ro 12: 16 be willing to **a** with people of low
1Co 5: 11 you must not **a** with anyone who
2Th 3: 14 Do not **a** with them, in order

ASSURANCE
Heb 10: 22 and with the full **a** that faith brings,

ASTRAY
Pr 10: 17 ignores correction leads others **a**.
Isa 53: 6 have gone **a**, each of us has turned
Jer 50: 6 their shepherds have led them **a**

ATHALIAH
Evil queen of Judah (2Ki 11; 2Ch 23).

ATHLETE
2Ti 2: 5 competes as an **a** does not receive

ATONEMENT
Ex 25: 17 "Make an **a** cover of pure gold—
30: 10 Once a year Aaron shall make **a**
Lev 17: 11 blood that makes **a** for one's life.
23: 27 this seventh month is the Day of **A**.
Nu 25: 13 God and made **a** for the Israelites."
Ro 3: 25 presented Christ as a sacrifice of **a**,
Heb 2: 17 that he might make **a** for the sins

ATTENTION
Pr 4: 1 pay **a** and gain understanding.
5: 1 My son, pay **a** to my wisdom,
22: 17 Pay **a** and turn your ear
Titus 1: 14 and will pay no **a** to Jewish myths

ATTITUDE (ATTITUDES)
Eph 4: 23 made new in the **a** of your minds;
1Pe 4: 1 yourselves also with the same **a**,

ATTITUDES (ATTITUDE)
Heb 4: 12 the thoughts and **a** of the heart.

ATTRACTIVE
Titus 2: 10 teaching about God our Savior **a**.

AUTHORITIES (AUTHORITY)
Ro 13: 5 it is necessary to submit to the **a**,
13: 6 for the **a** are God's servants,
Titus 3: 1 to be subject to rulers and **a**,
1Pe 3: 22 **a** and powers in submission to him.

AUTHORITY (AUTHORITIES)
Mt 7: 29 he taught as one who had **a**,
9: 6 the Son of Man has **a** on earth
28: 18 "All **a** in heaven and on earth has
Ro 13: 1 for there is no **a** except
13: 2 rebels against the **a** is rebelling
1Co 11: 10 ought to have **a** over her own head,
1Ti 2: 2 for kings and all those in **a**, that we
2: 12 to teach or to assume **a** over a man;
Heb 13: 17 your leaders and submit to their **a**,

AVENGE (VENGEANCE)
Dt 32: 35 It is mine to **a**; I will repay.

AVOID
Pr 20: 3 It is to one's honor to **a** strife,
20: 19 so **a** anyone who talks too much.
1Th 4: 3 you should **a** sexual immorality;
2Ti 2: 16 **A** godless chatter, because those
Titus 3: 9 But **a** foolish controversies

AWAKE
Ps 17: 15 when I **a**, I will be satisfied
1Th 5: 6 asleep, but let us be **a** and sober.

AWE (AWESOME)
Job 25: 2 "Dominion and **a** belong to God;
Ps 119:120 of you; I stand in **a** of your laws.
Isa 29: 23 will stand in **a** of the God of Israel.
Jer 33: 9 they will be in **a** and will tremble
Hab 3: 2 I stand in **a** of your deeds, Lord.
Mal 2: 5 me and stood in **a** of my name.
Mt 9: 8 saw this, they were filled with **a**;

1Pe 2: 25 For "you were like sheep going **a**,"
1Jn 3: 7 do not let anyone lead you **a**.

CONCORDANCE

Lk	7: 16	They were all filled with **a**
Ac	2: 43	Everyone was filled with **a**
Heb	12: 28	acceptably with reverence and **a**,

AWESOME (AWE)

Ge	28: 17	and said, "How **a** is this place!
Ex	15: 11	majestic in holiness, **a** in glory,
Dt	7: 21	is among you, is a great and **a** God.
	10: 17	God, mighty and **a**, who shows no
	28: 58	revere this glorious and **a** name—
Jdg	13: 6	looked like an angel of God, very **a**.
Ne	1: 5	the great and **a** God, who keeps his
	9: 32	God, mighty and **a**, who keeps his
Job	10: 16	again display your **a** power against
	37: 22	God comes in a majesty.
Ps	45: 4	your right hand achieve **a** deeds.
	47: 2	For the LORD Most High is **a**,
	66: 5	has done, his **a** deeds for mankind!
	68: 35	You, God, are **a** in your sanctuary;
	89: 7	he is more **a** than all who surround
	99: 3	praise your great and **a** name—
	111: 9	holy and **a** is his name.
	145: 6	tell of the power of your **a** works—
Da	9: 4	the great and **a** God, who keeps his

BAAL

1Ki	18: 25	Elijah said to the prophets of **B**,

BAASHA

King of Israel (1Ki 15:16—16:7; 2Ch 16:1–6).

BABIES (BABY)

Lk	18: 15	bringing **b** to Jesus for him to place
1Pe	2: 2	Like newborn **b**, crave pure

BABY (BABIES)

Isa	49: 15	"Can a mother forget the **b** at her
Lk	1: 44	the **b** in my womb leaped for joy.
	2: 12	You will find a **b** wrapped in cloths
Jn	16: 21	**b** is born she forgets the anguish

BABYLON

Ps	137: 1	By the rivers of **B** we sat and wept

BACKSLIDING

Jer	3: 22	I will cure you of **b**."
Eze	37: 23	save them from all their sinful **b**,

BAGS

Mt	25: 15	To one he gave five **b** of gold, to
		another two **b**, and to another one

BALAAM

Prophet who attempted to curse Israel (Nu 22–24; Dt 23:4–5; 2Pe 2:15; Jude 11). Killed (Nu 31:8; Jos 13:22).

BALM

Jer	8: 22	Is there no **b** in Gilead? Is there no

BANISH

Jer	25: 10	will **b** from them the sounds of joy

BANQUET

SS	2: 4	Let him lead me to the **b** hall,
Lk	14: 13	But when you give a **b**,

BAPTIZE (BAPTIZED)

Mt	3: 11	"I **b** you with water for repentance.
	3: 11	He will **b** you with the Holy Spirit
Mk	1: 8	I **b** you with water, but he will **b**
1Co	1: 17	For Christ did not send me to **b**,

BAPTIZED (BAPTIZE)

Mt	3: 6	they were **b** by him in the Jordan
Mk	1: 9	and was **b** by John in the Jordan.
	10: 38	be **b** with the baptism I am **b** with?"
	16: 16	*believes and is **b** will be saved,*
Jn	4: 2	in fact it was not Jesus who **b**,
Ac	1: 5	For John **b** with water, but in a few

BARABBAS

Mt	27: 17	release to you: Jesus **B**, or Jesus

BARBS

Nu	33: 55	remain will become **b** in your eyes

BARE

Heb	4: 13	and laid **b** before the eyes of him

BARNABAS

Disciple, originally Joseph (Ac 4:36), prophet (Ac 13:1), apostle (Ac 14:14). Brought Paul to apostles (Ac 9:27), Antioch (Ac 11:22–29; Gal 2:1–13), on the first missionary journey (Ac 13–14). Together at Jerusalem Council, they separated over John Mark (Ac 15). Later co-workers (1Co 9:6; Col 4:10).

BARTHOLOMEW

Apostle (Mt 10:3; Mk 3:18; Lk 6:14; Ac 1:13). Possibly also known as Nathanael (Jn 1:45–49; 21:2).

BATH

Jn	13: 10	who have had a **b** need only

BATHSHEBA

Wife of Uriah who committed adultery with and became wife of David (2Sa 11), mother of Solomon (2Sa 12:24; 1Ki 1–2; 1Ch 3:5).

BATTLE

2Ch	20: 15	For the **b** is not yours, but God's.
Ps	24: 8	mighty, the LORD mighty in **b**.
Ecc	9: 11	to the swift or the **b** to the strong,

BEAR (BEARING BIRTH BIRTHRIGHT BORE BORN FIRSTBORN NEWBORN)

Ge	4: 13	punishment is more than I can **b**.
Ps	38: 4	me like a burden too heavy to **b**.
Isa	53: 11	many, and he will **b** their iniquities.
Da	7: 5	beast, which looked like a **b**.
Mt	7: 18	A good tree cannot **b** bad fruit,
Jn	15: 2	branch that does **b** fruit he prunes
	15: 16	so that you might go and to **b** fruit—
Ro	15: 1	We who are strong ought to **b**
1Co	10: 13	tempted beyond what you can **b**.
Col	3: 13	**B** with each other and forgive one

BEARING (BEAR)

Eph	4: 2	patient, **b** with one another in love.
Col	1: 10	**b** fruit in every good work,

BEAST

Rev	13: 18	calculate the number of the **b**, for it

BEAT (BEATING)

Isa	2: 4	They will **b** their swords
Joel	3: 10	**B** your plowshares into swords

BEATING (BEAT)

1Co	9: 26	I do not fight like a boxer **b** the air.
1Pe	2: 20	if you receive a **b** for doing wrong

BEAUTIFUL (BEAUTY)

Ge	6: 2	the daughters of humans were **b**,
	12: 11	"I know what a **b** woman you are.
	12: 14	saw that Sarai was a very **b** woman.

Ge	24: 16	The woman was very **b**, a virgin;
	26: 7	of Rebekah, because she is **b**."
	29: 17	had a lovely figure and was **b**.
Pr	11: 22	snout is a **b** woman who shows no
Ecc	3: 11	He has made everything **b** in its
Isa	4: 2	the Branch of the Lord will be **b**
	52: 7	How **b** on the mountains are the
Eze	20: 6	and honey, the most **b** of all lands.
Zec	9: 17	How attractive and **b** they will be!
Mt	23: 27	which look **b** on the outside
	26: 10	She has done a **b** thing to me.
Ro	10: 15	"How **b** are the feet of those who

BEAUTY (BEAUTIFUL)

Ps	27: 4	to gaze on the **b** of the Lord
	45: 11	the king be enthralled by your **b**;
Pr	31: 30	is deceptive, and **b** is fleeting;
Isa	33: 17	Your eyes will see the king in his **b**
	53: 2	He had no **b** or majesty to attract
	61: 3	them a crown of **b** instead of ashes,
Eze	28: 12	full of wisdom and perfect in **b**.
1Pe	3: 4	unfading **b** of a gentle and quiet

BED

Heb	13: 4	and the marriage **b** kept pure,

BEELZEBUL

Lk	11: 15	said, "By **B**, the prince of demons,

BEER

Pr	20: 1	Wine is a mocker and **b** a brawler;

BEERSHEBA

Jdg	20: 1	all Israel from Dan to **B**

BEGINNING

Ge	1: 1	In the **b** God created the heavens
Ps	102: 25	In the **b** you laid the foundations
	111: 10	of the Lord is the **b** of wisdom;
Pr	1: 7	the Lord is the **b** of knowledge,
	4: 7	The **b** of wisdom is this:
Jn	1: 1	In the **b** was the Word,
1Jn	1: 1	That which was from the **b**,
Rev	21: 6	and the Omega, the **B** and the End.

BEHAVE (BEHAVIOR)

Ro	13: 13	us **b** decently, as in the daytime,

BEHAVIOR (BEHAVE)

Pr	1: 3	receiving instruction in prudent **b**,

BELIEVE (BELIEVED BELIEVER BELIEVERS BELIEVES BELIEVING)

Pr	14: 15	The simple **b** anything,
Mt	18: 6	those who **b** in me—
	21: 22	If you **b**, you will receive whatever
Mk	1: 15	Repent and **b** the good news!"
	9: 24	the boy's father exclaimed, "I do **b**;
	16: 17	*accompany those who b:*
Lk	8: 50	just **b**, and she will be healed."
	24: 25	how slow to **b** all that the prophets
Jn	1: 7	so that through him all might **b**.
	3: 18	does not **b** stands condemned
	6: 29	to **b** in the one he has sent."
	10: 38	even though you do not **b** me,
	11: 27	"I **b** that you are the Messiah,
	14: 1	You **b** in God; **b** also in me.
	14: 11	**B** me when I say that I am
	16: 30	This makes us **b** that you came
	16: 31	"Do you now **b**?" Jesus replied.
	17: 21	the world may **b** that you have sent
	20: 27	into my side. Stop doubting and **b**."

Jn	20: 31	may **b** that Jesus is the Messiah,
Ac	16: 31	They replied, "**B** in the Lord Jesus,
	24: 14	I **b** everything that is in accordance
Ro	3: 22	faith in Jesus Christ to all who **b**.
	4: 11	he is the father of all who **b**
	10: 9	**b** in your heart that God raised
	10: 14	how can they **b** in the one of whom
1Th	4: 14	For we **b** that Jesus died and rose
2Th	2: 11	delusion so that they will **b** the lie
1Ti	4: 10	and especially of those who **b**.
Titus	1: 6	a man whose children **b** and are
Heb	11: 6	comes to him must **b** that he exists
Jas	2: 19	You **b** that there is one God. Good!
		Even the demons **b** that—
1Jn	4: 1	Dear friends, do not **b** every spirit,

BELIEVED (BELIEVE)

Ge	15: 6	Abram **b** the Lord, and he
Jnh	3: 5	The Ninevites **b** God. A fast was
Jn	1: 12	to those who **b** in his name,
	2: 22	Then they **b** the scripture
	3: 18	already because they have not **b**
	20: 8	also went inside. He saw and **b**.
	20: 29	who have not seen and yet have **b**."
Ac	13: 48	were appointed for eternal life **b**.
Ro	4: 3	"Abraham **b** God, and it was
	10: 14	call on the one they have not **b** in?
1Co	15: 2	Otherwise, you have **b** in vain.
Gal	3: 6	So also Abraham "**b** God, and it
2Ti	1: 12	because I know whom I have **b**,
Jas	2: 23	that says, "Abraham **b** God, and it

BELIEVER (BELIEVE)

1Co	7: 12	brother has a wife who is not a **b**
2Co	6: 15	what does a **b** have in common

BELIEVERS (BELIEVE)

Ac	4: 32	All the **b** were one in heart
	5: 12	all the **b** used to meet together
1Co	6: 5	to judge a dispute between **b**?
1Ti	4: 12	set an example for the **b** in speech,
1Pe	2: 17	love the family of **b**, fear God,

BELIEVES (BELIEVE)

Mk	9: 23	is possible for one who **b**."
	11: 23	**b** that what they say will happen,
	16: 16	*Whoever b and is baptized*
Jn	3: 16	whoever **b** in him shall not perish
	3: 36	Whoever **b** in the Son has eternal
	5: 24	**b** him who sent me has eternal life
	6: 35	and whoever **b** in me will never be
	6: 40	and **b** in him shall have eternal life,
	6: 47	you, the one who **b** has eternal life.
	7: 38	Whoever **b** in me, as Scripture has
Ro	1: 16	salvation to everyone who **b**
	9: 33	the one who **b** in him will never be
	10: 4	righteousness for everyone who **b**.
1Jn	5: 1	Everyone who **b** that Jesus is
	5: 5	Only the one who **b** that Jesus is

BELIEVING (BELIEVE)

Jn	11: 26	whoever lives by **b** in me will never
	20: 31	by **b** you may have life in his name.

BELONG (BELONGS)

Dt	29: 29	The secret things **b** to the Lord
Job	25: 2	"Dominion and awe **b** to God;
Ps	47: 9	for the kings of the earth **b** to God;
	95: 4	and the mountain peaks **b** to him.
Jn	8: 44	You **b** to your father, the devil,

Jn 15: 19 As it is, you do not **b** to the world,
Ro 1: 6 those Gentiles who are called to **b**
7: 4 that you might **b** to another, to him
14: 8 we live or die, we **b** to the Lord.
Gal 5: 24 Those who **b** to Christ Jesus have
1Th 5: 8 But since we **b** to the day, let us be

BELONGS (BELONG)
Job 41: 11 Everything under heaven **b** to me.
Ps 111: 10 To him **b** eternal praise.
Eze 18: 4 For everyone **b** to me, the parent as
Jn 8: 47 Whoever **b** to God hears what God
Ro 12: 5 each member **b** to all the others.

BELOVED (LOVE)
Dt 33: 12 "Let the **b** of the Lord rest
SS 2: 16 My **b** is mine and I am his;
7: 10 I belong to my **b**, and his desire is

BELT
Isa 11: 5 Righteousness will be his **b**
Eph 6: 14 the **b** of truth buckled around your

BENEFICIAL (BENEFIT)
1Co 10: 23 but not everything is **b**.

BENEFIT (BENEFICIAL BENEFITS)
Ro 6: 22 the **b** you reap leads to holiness,
2Co 4: 15 All this is for your **b**,

BENEFITS (BENEFIT)
Ps 103: 2 my soul, and forget not all his **b**—
Jn 4: 38 and you have reaped the **b** of their

BENJAMIN
Twelfth son of Jacob by Rachel (Ge 35:16–24; 46:19–21; 1Ch 2:2). Jacob refused to send him to Egypt, but relented (Ge 42–45).

BEREAN
Ac 17: 11 the **B** Jews were of more noble

BESTOWS
Ps 84: 11 the Lord **b** favor and honor;

BETHLEHEM
Mt 2: 1 After Jesus was born in **B** in Judea,

BETRAY
Pr 25: 9 do not **b** another's confidence,

BIND (BINDS)
Dt 6: 8 and **b** them on your foreheads.
Pr 6: 21 **B** them always on your heart;
Isa 61: 1 He has sent me to **b**
Mt 16: 19 whatever you **b** on earth will be

BINDS (BIND)
Ps 147: 3 and **b** up their wounds.
Isa 30: 26 when the Lord **b** up the bruises

BIRDS
Mt 8: 20 "Foxes have dens and **b** have nests,

BIRTH (BEAR)
Ps 58: 3 Even from **b** the wicked go astray;
Mt 1: 18 This is how the **b** of Jesus
1Pe 1: 3 great mercy he has given us new **b**

BIRTHRIGHT (BEAR)
Ge 25: 34 up and left. So Esau despised his **b**.

BLAMELESS
Ge 17: 1 walk before me faithfully and be **b**.
Job 1: 1 This man was **b** and upright;

Ps 84: 11 from those whose walk is **b**.
119: 1 are those whose ways are **b**,
Pr 19: 1 poor whose walk is **b** than a fool
1Co 1: 8 so that you will be **b** on the day
Eph 5: 27 any other blemish, but holy and **b**.
Php 2: 15 that you may become **b** and pure,
1Th 3: 13 your hearts so that you will be **b**
5: 23 body be kept **b** at the coming of
Titus 1: 6 An elder must be **b**, faithful to his
Heb 7: 26 one who is holy, **b**, pure, set apart
2Pe 3: 14 spotless, **b** and at peace with him.

BLASPHEMES
Mk 3: 29 whoever **b** against the Holy Spirit

BLEMISH
1Pe 1: 19 Christ, a lamb without **b** or defect.

BLESS (BLESSED BLESSING BLESSINGS)
Ge 12: 3 I will **b** those who **b** you,
Ro 12: 14 **B** those who persecute you;

BLESSED (BLESS)
Ge 1: 22 God **b** them and said, "Be fruitful
2: 3 Then God **b** the seventh day
22: 18 all nations on earth will be **b**,
Ps 1: 1 **B** is the one who does not walk
2: 12 **B** are all who take refuge in him.
33: 12 **B** is the nation whose God is
41: 1 **B** are those who have regard
84: 5 **B** are those whose strength is
106: 3 **B** are those who act justly,
112: 1 **B** are those who fear the Lord,
118: 26 **B** is he who comes in the name
Pr 29: 18 **b** is the one who heeds wisdom's
31: 28 Her children arise and call her **b**;
Mt 5: 3 "**B** are the poor in spirit, for theirs
5: 4 **B** are those who mourn, for they
5: 5 **B** are the meek, for they will
5: 6 **B** are those who hunger and thirst
5: 7 **B** are the merciful, for they will
5: 8 **B** are the pure in heart, for they
5: 9 **B** are the peacemakers, for they
5: 10 **B** are those who are persecuted
5: 11 "**B** are you when people insult you,
Lk 1: 48 on all generations will call me **b**,
Jn 12: 13 "**B** is he who comes in the name
Ac 20: 35 'It is more **b** to give than
Titus 2: 13 while we wait for the **b** hope—
Jas 1: 12 **B** is the one who perseveres under
Rev 1: 3 **B** is the one who reads aloud
22: 14 "**B** are those who wash their robes,

BLESSING (BLESS)
Eze 34: 26 there will be showers of **b**.

BLESSINGS (BLESS)
Pr 10: 6 **B** crown the head of the righteous,

BLIND
Mt 15: 14 If the **b** lead the **b**, both will fall
23: 16 "Woe to you, **b** guides! You say,
Jn 9: 25 I do know. I was **b** but now I see!"

BLOOD
Ge 9: 6 "Whoever sheds human **b**, by humans
shall their **b** be shed;
Ex 12: 13 The **b** will be a sign for you
24: 8 "This is the **b** of the covenant
Lev 17: 11 For the life of a creature is in the **b**,

Lev	17: 11	it is the **b** that makes atonement
Ps	72: 14	for precious is their **b** in his sight.
Pr	6: 17	hands that shed innocent **b**,
Mt	26: 28	This is my **b** of the covenant,
Ro	3: 25	through the shedding of his **b**—
	5: 9	have now been justified by his **b**,
1Co	11: 25	cup is the new covenant in my **b**;
Eph	1: 7	we have redemption through his **b**,
	2: 13	brought near by the **b** of Christ.
Col	1: 20	by making peace through his **b**,
Heb	9: 12	once for all by his own **b**,
	9: 22	everything be cleansed with **b**,
1Pe	1: 19	but with the precious **b** of Christ,
1Jn	1: 7	and the **b** of Jesus, his Son,
Rev	1: 5	has freed us from our sins by his **b**,
	5: 9	with your **b** you purchased for God
	7: 14	them white in the **b** of the Lamb.
	12: 11	over him by the **b** of the Lamb

BLOT (BLOTS)
Ex	32: 32	**b** me out of the book you have
Ps	51: 1	to your great compassion **b** out my
Rev	3: 5	I will never **b** out the name

BLOTS (BLOT)
| Isa | 43: 25 | "I, even I, am he who **b** out your |

BLOWN
| Eph | 4: 14 | and **b** here and there by every wind |
| Jas | 1: 6 | the sea, **b** and tossed by the wind. |

BOAST
1Ki	20: 11	his armor should not **b** like one
Ps	44: 8	In God we make our **b** all day long,
Pr	27: 1	Do not **b** about tomorrow, for you
1Co	1: 31	"Let the one who boasts **b**
Gal	6: 14	May I never **b** except in the cross
Eph	2: 9	not by works, so that no one can **b**.

BOAZ
Wealthy Bethlehemite who showed favor to Ruth (Ru 2), married her (Ru 4). Ancestor of David (Ru 4:18–22; 1Ch 2:12–15), Jesus (Mt 1:5–16; Lk 3:23–32).

BODIES (BODY)
Ro	12: 1	to offer your **b** as a living sacrifice,
1Co	6: 15	not know that your **b** are members
	6: 19	not know that your **b** are temples
Eph	5: 28	to love their wives as their own **b**.

BODY (BODIES)
Zec	13: 6	are these wounds on your **b**?'
Mt	10: 28	can destroy both soul and **b** in hell.
	10: 28	be afraid of those who kill the **b**
	26: 26	"Take and eat; this is my **b**."
Jn	13: 10	their whole **b** is clean.
1Co	11: 24	"This is my **b**, which is for you;
	12: 12	Just as a **b**, though one, has many
Eph	5: 30	for we are members of his **b**.

BOLD (BOLDNESS)
| Pr | 21: 29 | The wicked put up a **b** front, |
| | 28: 1 | but the righteous are as **b** as a lion. |

BOLDNESS (BOLD)
| Ac | 4: 29 | to speak your word with great **b**. |

BONDAGE
| Ezr | 9: 9 | God has not forsaken us in our **b**. |

BOOK (BOOKS)
| Jos | 1: 8 | Keep this **B** of the Law always |

Ne	8: 8	They read from the **B** of the Law
Jn	20: 30	which are not recorded in this **b**.
Php	4: 3	whose names are in the **b** of life.
Rev	21: 27	are written in the Lamb's **b** of life.

BOOKS (BOOK)
| Ecc | 12: 12 | Of making many **b** there is no end, |

BORE (BEAR)
| Isa | 53: 4 | up our pain and **b** our suffering, |

BORN (BEAR)
Isa	9: 6	For to us a child is **b**, to us a son is
Jn	3: 7	my saying, 'You must be **b** again.'
1Pe	1: 23	For you have been **b** again,
1Jn	4: 7	Everyone who loves has been **b**
	5: 1	that Jesus is the Christ is **b** of God,

BORROWER
| Pr | 22: 7 | and the **b** is slave to the lender. |

BOUGHT
Ac	20: 28	which he **b** with his own blood.
1Co	6: 20	you were **b** at a price.
	7: 23	You were **b** at a price;
2Pe	2: 1	the sovereign Lord who **b** them—

BOUNDLESS
| Eph | 3: 8 | the Gentiles the **b** riches of Christ, |

BOW
Ps	95: 6	Come, let us **b** down in worship,
Isa	45: 23	Before me every knee will **b**;
Ro	14: 11	Lord, 'every knee will **b** before me;
Php	2: 10	name of Jesus every knee should **b**,

BRANCH (BRANCHES)
| Isa | 4: 2 | that day the **B** of the Lord will be |
| Jer | 33: 15 | I will make a righteous **B** sprout |

BRANCHES (BRANCH)
| Jn | 15: 5 | "I am the vine; you are the **b**. |

BRAVE
| 2Sa | 2: 7 | then, be strong and **b**, for Saul your |

BREAD
Dt	8: 3	that man does not live on **b** alone
Pr	30: 8	riches, but give me only my daily **b**.
Isa	55: 2	spend money on what is not **b**,
Mt	4: 4	'Man shall not live on **b** alone,
	6: 11	Give us today our daily **b**.
Jn	6: 35	Jesus declared, "I am the **b** of life.
	21: 13	took the **b** and gave it to them,
1Co	11: 23	the night he was betrayed, took **b**,

BREAK (BREAKING BROKEN)
Nu	30: 2	he must not **b** his word but must
Jdg	2: 1	'I will never **b** my covenant
Ps	2: 9	You will **b** them with a rod of iron;
Isa	42: 3	A bruised reed he will not **b**,
Mt	12: 20	A bruised reed he will not **b**,

BREAKING (BREAK)
| Jas | 2: 10 | just one point is guilty of **b** all of it. |

BREASTPIECE (BREASTPLATE)
| Ex | 28: 15 | "Fashion a **b** for making decisions |

BREASTPLATE (BREASTPIECE)
Isa	59: 17	He put on righteousness as his **b**,
Eph	6: 14	the **b** of righteousness in place,
1Th	5: 8	putting on faith and love as a **b**,

CONCORDANCE

BREATHED (GOD-BREATHED)
Ge 2: 7 **b** into his nostrils the breath of life,
Jn 20: 22 with that he **b** on them and said,

BRIBE
Ex 23: 8 "Do not accept a **b**, for a **b** blinds
Pr 6: 35 he will refuse a **b**, however great it

BRIDE
Rev 19: 7 and his **b** has made herself ready.

BRIGHTER (BRIGHTNESS)
Pr 4: 18 shining ever **b** till the full light

BRIGHTNESS (BRIGHTER)
2Sa 22: 13 Out of the **b** of his presence bolts
Da 12: 3 who are wise will shine like the **b**

BROAD
Mt 7: 13 gate and **b** is the road that leads

BROKEN (BREAK)
Ps 51: 17 My sacrifice, O God, is a **b** spirit;
Ecc 4: 12 of three strands is not quickly **b**.

BROKENHEARTED (HEART)
Ps 34: 18 The Lᴏʀᴅ is close to the **b**
109: 16 the poor and the needy and the **b**.
147: 3 He heals the **b** and binds up their
Isa 61: 1 He has sent me to bind up the **b**,

BROTHER (BROTHER'S BROTHERS)
Pr 17: 17 a **b** is born for a time of adversity.
18: 24 a friend who sticks closer than a **b**.
Mt 18: 15 "If your **b** or sister sins,
Mk 3: 35 Whoever does God's will is my **b**
Lk 17: 3 "If your **b** or sister sins against you,
1Co 8: 13 if what I eat causes my **b** or sister
1Jn 2: 10 who loves their **b** and sister

BROTHER'S (BROTHER)
Ge 4: 9 "Am I my **b** keeper?"

BROTHERS (BROTHER)
Mt 25: 40 did for one of the least of these **b**
Mk 10: 29 "no one who has left home or **b**
Heb 13: 1 Keep on loving one another as **b**

BUILD (BUILDING BUILDS BUILT)
Mt 16: 18 on this rock I will **b** my church,
Ac 20: 32 which can **b** you up and give you
1Co 3: 10 But each one should **b** with care.
14: 12 excel in those that **b** up the church.
1Th 5: 11 one another and **b** each other up,

BUILDING (BUILD)
1Co 3: 9 you are God's field, God's **b**.
2Co 10: 8 authority the Lord gave us for **b**
Eph 4: 29 only what is helpful for **b** others

BUILDS (BUILD)
Ps 127: 1 Unless the Lᴏʀᴅ **b** the house,
1Co 8: 1 puffs up while love **b** up.

BUILT (BUILD)
Mt 7: 24 is like a wise man who **b** his house
1Co 14: 26 so that the church may be **b** up.
Eph 2: 20 **b** on the foundation of the apostles
4: 12 that the body of Christ may be **b**

BURDEN (BURDENED BURDENS)
Ps 38: 4 overwhelmed me like a **b** too heavy
Mt 11: 30 my yoke is easy and my **b** is light."

BURDENED (BURDEN)
Gal 5: 1 do not let yourselves be **b** again

BURDENS (BURDEN)
Ps 68: 19 our Savior, who daily bears our **b**.
Gal 6: 2 Carry each other's **b**, and in this

BURIED
Ro 6: 4 We were therefore **b** with him
1Co 15: 4 that he was **b**, that he was raised

BURNING
Lev 6: 9 the fire must be kept **b** on the altar.
Ro 12: 20 you will heap **b** coals on his head."

BUSINESS
Da 8: 27 got up and went about the king's **b**.
1Th 4: 11 You should mind your own **b**

BUSY
1Ki 20: 40 While your servant was **b** here
2Th 3: 11 are not **b**; they are busybodies.
Titus 2: 5 pure, to be **b** at home, to be kind,

CAESAR
Mt 22: 21 give back to **C** what is Caesar's,

CAIN
Firstborn of Adam (Ge 4:1), murdered brother Abel
(Ge 4:1–16; 1Jn 3:12).

CALEB
Judahite who spied out Canaan (Nu 13:6); allowed
to enter land because of faith (Nu 13:30—14:38; Dt
1:36). Possessed Hebron (Jos 14:6—15:19).

CALF
Ex 32: 4 into an idol cast in the shape of a **c**,
Lk 15: 23 Bring the fattened **c** and kill it.

CALL (CALLED CALLING CALLS)
Ps 145: 18 Lᴏʀᴅ is near to all who **c** on him,
Pr 31: 28 children arise and **c** her blessed;
Isa 5: 20 Woe to those who **c** evil good
55: 6 **c** on him while he is near.
65: 24 Before they **c** I will answer;
Jer 33: 3 'C to me and I will answer you
Mt 9: 13 I have not come to **c** the righteous,
Ro 10: 12 richly blesses all who **c** on him,
11: 29 gifts and his **c** are irrevocable.
1Th 4: 7 For God did not **c** us to be impure,

CALLED (CALL)
1Sa 3: 5 and said, "Here I am; you **c** me."
2Ch 7: 14 my people, who are **c** by my name,
Ps 34: 6 This poor man **c**, and the Lᴏʀᴅ
Mt 21: 13 " 'My house will be a **c** a house
Ro 8: 30 And those he predestined, he also **c**;
those he **c**, he also justified;
1Co 7: 15 God has **c** us to live in peace.
Gal 5: 13 and sisters, were **c** to be free.
1Pe 2: 9 the praises of him who **c** you

CALLING (CALL)
Jn 1: 23 voice of one **c** in the wilderness,
Ac 22: 16 your sins away, **c** on his name.'
Eph 4: 1 worthy of the **c** you have received.
2Pe 1: 10 every effort to confirm your **c**

CALLS (CALL)
Joel 2: 32 everyone who **c** on the name
Jn 10: 3 He **c** his own sheep by name
Ro 10: 13 "Everyone who **c** on the name

CALM

Pr   29: 11   but the wise bring **c** in the end.

CAMEL

Mt   19: 24   easier for a **c** to go through the eye
        23: 24   strain out a gnat but swallow a **c**.

CANAAN

1Ch 16: 18   **C** as the portion you will inherit."

CANCELED

Col   2: 14   having **c** the charge of our legal

CAPITAL

Dt   21: 22   someone guilty of a **c** offense is put

CARE (CAREFUL CAREFULLY CARES CARING)

Ps   8:   4   human beings that you **c** for them?

Pr   29:   7   The righteous **c** about justice

Lk   10: 34   him to an inn and took **c** of him.

Jn   21: 16   Jesus said, "Take **c** of my sheep."

1Co   3: 10   But each one should build with **c**.

Eph   5: 29   but they feed and **c** for their body,

Heb   2:   6   a son of man that you **c** for him?

1Pe   5:   2   of God's flock that is under your **c**,

CAREFUL (CARE)

Ex   23: 13   "Be **c** to do everything I have said

Dt   6:   3   be **c** to obey so that it may go well

Jos   23:   6   be **c** to obey all that is written
        23: 11   So be very **c** to love the Lord

Pr   13: 24   one who loves their children is **c**

Mt   6:   1   "Be **c** not to practice your

Ro   12: 17   Be **c** to do what is right in the eyes

1Co   8:   9   Be **c**, however, that the exercise of

Eph   5: 15   Be very **c**, then, how you live—

CAREFULLY

Pr   12: 26   righteous choose their friends **c**,

CARES (CARE)

Ps   55: 22   Cast your **c** on the Lord and he

Na   1:   7   He **c** for those who trust in him,

1Th   2:   7   Just as a nursing mother **c** for her

1Pe   5:   7   on him because he **c** for you.

CARING (CARE)

1Ti   5:   4   practice by **c** for their own family

CARRIED (CARRY)

Ex   19:   4   and how I **c** you on eagles' wings

Heb 13:   9   Do not be **c** away by all kinds

2Pe   1: 21   God as they were **c** along

CARRIES (CARRY)

Dt   32: 11   to catch them and **c** them aloft.

Isa   40: 11   arms and **c** them close to his heart;

CARRY (CARRIED CARRIES)

Lk   14: 27   whoever does not **c** their cross

Gal   6:   2   **C** each other's burdens, and in this
         6:   5   each one should **c** their own load.

CAST

Ps   22: 18   them and **c** lots for my garment.
        55: 22   **C** your cares on the Lord and he

Jn   19: 24   them and **c** lots for my garment."

1Pe   5:   7   **C** all your anxiety on him because

CATTLE

Ps   50: 10   and the **c** on a thousand hills.

CAUGHT

1Th   4: 17   are left will be **c** up together

CAUSE (CAUSES)

Pr   24: 28   against your neighbor without **c**—

Ecc   8:   3   Do not stand up for a bad **c**, for he

Mt   18:   7   the things that **c** people to stumble!

Ro   14: 21   that will **c** your brother or sister

1Co 10: 32   Do not **c** anyone to stumble,

CAUSES (CAUSE)

Isa   8: 14   he will be a stone that **c** people

Mt   18:   6   "If anyone **c** one of these little

CEASE

Ps   46:   9   He makes wars **c** to the ends

CELEBRATE

Ps   2: 11   fear and **c** his rule with trembling.

CENSER

Lev 16: 12   is to take a **c** full of burning coals

CENTURION

Mt   8:   5   Capernaum, a **c** came to him,

CERTAINTY

Lk   1:   4   you may know the **c** of the things

Jn   17:   8   They knew with **c** that I came

CHAFF

Ps   1:   4   They are like **c** that the wind blows

CHAINED

2Ti   2:   9   But God's word is not **c**.

CHAMPION

Ps   19:   5   like a **c** rejoicing to run his course.

CHANGE (CHANGED)

1Sa 15: 29   does not lie or **c** his mind;

Ps 110:   4   has sworn and will not **c** his mind:

Jer   7:   5   If you really **c** your ways and your

Mal   3:   6   "I the Lord do not **c**. So you,

Mt   18:   3   unless you **c** and become like little

Heb   7: 21   has sworn and will not **c** his mind:

Jas   1: 17   lights, who does not **c** like shifting

CHANGED (CHANGE)

1Co 15: 51   not all sleep, but we will all be **c**—

CHARACTER

Ru   3: 11   that you are a woman of noble **c**.

Pr   31: 10   A wife of noble **c** who can find?

Ro   5:   4   perseverance, **c**; and **c**, hope.

1Co 15: 33   "Bad company corrupts good **c**."

CHARGE

Ro   8: 33   will bring any **c** against those

2Co   4:   7   the gospel of God to you free of **c**?

2Ti   4:   1   and his kingdom, I give you this **c**:

CHARIOTS

2Ki   6: 17   and **c** of fire all around Elisha.

Ps   20:   7   Some trust in **c** and some in horses

CHARM

Pr   31: 30   **C** is deceptive, and beauty is

CHASE

Pr   12: 11   who **c** fantasies have no sense.

CHATTER (CHATTERING)

1Ti   6: 20   Turn away from godless **c**

2Ti   2: 16   Avoid godless **c**, because those who

CHATTERING (CHATTER)

Pr   10:   8   but a **c** fool comes to ruin.
        10: 10   grief, and a **c** fool comes to ruin.

CONCORDANCE

CHEAT (CHEATED)
Mal 1: 14 "Cursed is the **c** who has
1Co 6: 8 you yourselves **c** and do wrong,

CHEATED (CHEAT)
Lk 19: 8 if I have **c** anybody out of anything,
1Co 6: 7 Why not rather be **c**?

CHEEK
Mt 5: 39 turn to them the other **c** also.

CHEERFUL (CHEERS)
Pr 15: 13 A happy heart makes the face **c**,
15: 15 the **c** heart has a continual feast.
17: 22 A **c** heart is good medicine,
2Co 9: 7 for God loves a **c** giver.

CHEERS (CHEERFUL)
Pr 12: 25 the heart, but a kind word **c** it up.

CHILD (CHILDHOOD CHILDLESS CHILDREN)
Pr 22: 15 Folly is bound up in the heart of a **c**,
23: 13 not withhold discipline from a **c**;
29: 15 but a **c** left undisciplined disgraces
Isa 9: 6 For to us a **c** is born, to us a son is
11: 6 and a little **c** will lead them.
66: 13 As a mother comforts her **c**, so will
Mt 18: 2 He called a little **c** to him,
Lk 1: 42 and blessed is the **c** you will bear!
1: 80 And the **c** grew and became strong
1Co 13: 11 When I was a **c**, I talked like a **c**,
1Jn 5: 1 loves the father loves his **c** as well.

CHILDHOOD (CHILD)
1Co 13: 11 I put the ways of **c** behind me.

CHILDLESS
Ps 113: 9 settles the **c** woman in her home

CHILDREN (CHILD)
Dt 4: 9 Teach them to your **c** and to their **c**
11: 19 Teach them to your **c**,
Ps 8: 2 Through the praise of **c** and infants
Pr 13: 24 spares the rod hates their **c**,
17: 6 parents are the pride of their **c**.
20: 11 Even small **c** are known by their
22: 6 Start **c** off on the way they should
29: 17 Discipline your **c**, and they will
31: 28 Her **c** arise and call her blessed;
Mt 7: 11 how to give good gifts to your **c**,
11: 25 and revealed them to little **c**.
18: 3 change and become like little **c**,
19: 14 said, "Let the little **c** come to me,
21: 16 " 'From the lips of **c** and infants
Mk 9: 37 these little **c** in my name welcomes
10: 14 them, "Let the little **c** come to me,
10: 16 And he took the **c** in his arms,
13: 12 **c** will rebel against their parents
Lk 10: 21 and revealed them to little **c**.
18: 16 said, "Let the little **c** come to me,
Jn 12: 36 so that you may become **c** of light."
Ro 8: 16 with our spirit that we are God's **c**.
2Co 12: 14 **c** should not have to save for
Eph 6: 1 **C**, obey your parents in the Lord,
6: 4 Fathers, do not exasperate your **c**;
Col 3: 20 **C**, obey your parents in everything,
3: 21 do not embitter your **c**, or they will
1Ti 3: 4 well and see that his **c** obey him,
3: 12 and must manage his **c** and his
5: 10 such as bringing up **c**,

Heb 12: 7 God is treating you as his **c**.
1Jn 3: 1 that we should be called **c** of God!

CHOOSE (CHOOSES CHOSE CHOSEN)
Dt 30: 19 Now **c** life, so that you and your
Jos 24: 15 **c** for yourselves this day whom you
Pr 8: 10 **C** my instruction instead of silver,
Jn 15: 16 You did not **c** me, but I chose you
Ac 15: 14 God first intervened to **c** a people

CHOOSES (CHOOSE)
Jn 7: 17 who **c** to do the will of God

CHOSE (CHOOSE)
Ge 13: 11 Lot **c** for himself the whole plain
Ps 33: 12 the people he **c** for his inheritance.
Jn 15: 16 but I **c** you and appointed you so
1Co 1: 27 But God **c** the foolish things
Eph 1: 4 For he **c** us in him before
2Th 2: 13 because God **c** you as firstfruits

CHOSEN (CHOOSE)
Isa 41: 8 whom I have **c**, you descendants
Mt 22: 14 many are invited, but few are **c**."
Lk 10: 42 Mary has **c** what is better, and it
23: 35 if he is God's Messiah, the **C** One."
Jn 15: 19 but I have **c** you out of the world.
1Pe 1: 20 He was **c** before the creation
2: 9 But you are a **c** people, a royal

CHRIST (CHRIST'S CHRISTIAN MESSIAH)
Jn 1: 41 found the Messiah" (that is, the **C**).
Ro 3: 22 faith in Jesus **C** to all who believe.
5: 6 powerless, **C** died for the ungodly.
5: 8 we were still sinners, **C** died for us.
5: 17 life through the one man, Jesus **C**!
6: 4 just as **C** was raised from the dead
8: 1 for those who are in **C** Jesus,
8: 9 does not have the Spirit of **C**, they do
not belong to **C**.
8: 35 separate us from the love of **C**?
10: 4 **C** is the culmination of the law so
14: 9 **C** died and returned to life so that
15: 3 even **C** did not please himself but,
1Co 1: 23 but we preach **C** crucified:
2: 2 while I was with you except Jesus **C**
3: 11 one already laid, which is Jesus **C**.
5: 7 For **C**, our Passover lamb, has been
8: 6 Jesus **C**, through whom all things
10: 4 them, and that rock was **C**.
10: 9 We should not test **C**, as some
11: 1 as I follow the example of **C**.
11: 3 that the head of every man is **C**,
11: 3 and the head of **C** is God.
12: 27 Now you are the body of **C**,
15: 3 that **C** died for our sins according
15: 14 And if **C** has not been raised,
15: 22 die, so in **C** all will be made alive.
15: 57 victory through our Lord Jesus **C**.
2Co 3: 3 show that you are a letter from **C**,
4: 5 but Jesus **C** as Lord, and ourselves
5: 10 before the judgment seat of **C**,
5: 17 if anyone is in **C**, the new creation
11: 2 to **C**, so that I might present you as
Gal 2: 20 I have been crucified with **C**
3: 13 **C** redeemed us from the curse
6: 14 in the cross of our Lord Jesus **C**,
Eph 1: 3 and Father of our Lord Jesus **C**,
3: 8 Gentiles the boundless riches of **C**,

Eph	4:	13	whole measure of the fullness of **C**.
	5:	2	just as **C** loved us and gave himself
	5:	23	head of the wife as **C** is the head
	5:	25	just as **C** loved the church and gave
	3:	15	Let the peace of **C** rule in your
Php	1:	21	to live is **C** and to die is gain.
	1:	27	manner worthy of the gospel of **C**.
	4:	19	to the riches of his glory in **C** Jesus.
Col	1:	27	which is **C** in you, the hope
	1:	28	present everyone fully mature in **C**.
	2:	6	as you received **C** Jesus as Lord,
	2:	17	the reality, however, is found in **C**.
	3:	15	Let the peace of **C** rule in your
2Th	2:	1	the coming of our Lord Jesus **C**
1Ti	1:	15	**C** Jesus came into the world to save
	2:	5	and mankind, the man **C** Jesus,
2Ti	2:	3	like a good soldier of **C** Jesus.
	3:	15	salvation through faith in **C** Jesus.
Titus	2:	13	our great God and Savior, Jesus **C**,
Heb	3:	14	We have come to share in **C**,
	9:	14	will the blood of **C**, who through
	9:	15	For this reason **C** is the mediator
	9:	28	so **C** was sacrificed once to take
	10:	10	of the body of Jesus **C** once for all.
	13:	8	Jesus **C** is the same yesterday
1Pe	1:	19	but with the precious blood of **C**,
	2:	21	called, because **C** suffered for you,
	3:	18	For **C** also suffered once for sins,
	4:	14	insulted because of the name of **C**,
1Jn	2:	22	whoever denies that Jesus is the **C**.
	3:	16	Jesus **C** laid down his life for us.
	5:	1	who believes that Jesus is the **C**
Rev	20:	4	reigned with **C** a thousand years.

CHRIST'S (CHRIST)

2Co	5:	14	For **C** love compels us, because we
	5:	20	We are therefore **C** ambassadors,
	12:	9	so that **C** power may rest on me.

CHRISTIAN (CHRIST)

1Pe	4:	16	if you suffer as a **C**, do not be

CHURCH

Mt	16:	18	and on this rock I will build my **c**,
	18:	17	if they refuse to listen even to the **c**,
Ac	20:	28	Be shepherds of the **c** of God,
1Co	5:	12	mine to judge those outside the **c**?
	14:	4	one who prophesies edifies the **c**.
	14:	12	excel in those that build up the **c**.
	14:	26	done so that the **c** may be built up.
Eph	5:	23	wife as Christ is the head of the **c**,
Col	1:	24	the sake of his body, which is the **c**.

CIRCUMCISED

Ge	17:	10	Every male among you shall be **c**.
Gal	2:	8	in Peter as an apostle to the **c**,

CIRCUMSTANCES

Php	4:	11	to be content whatever the **c**.
1Th	5:	18	give thanks in all **c**; for this is God's

CITIZENS (CITIZENSHIP)

Eph	2:	19	but fellow **c** with God's people

CITIZENSHIP (CITIZENS)

Php	3:	20	But our **c** is in heaven.

CITY

Heb	13:	14	here we do not have an enduring **c**,

CIVILIAN

2Ti	2:	4	a soldier gets entangled in **c** affairs,

CLAIM (CLAIMS)

Pr	25:	6	do not **c** a place among his great
1Jn	1:	6	If we **c** to have fellowship with him
	1:	8	If we **c** to be without sin,
	1:	10	If we **c** we have not sinned,

CLAIMS (CLAIM)

Jas	2:	14	if someone **c** to have faith but has
1Jn	2:	6	Whoever **c** to live in him must live
	2:	9	Anyone who **c** to be in the light

CLAP

Ps	47:	1	**C** your hands, all you nations;
Isa	55:	12	trees of the field will **c** their hands.

CLAY

Isa	45:	9	Does the **c** say to the potter,
	64:	8	We are the **c**, you are the potter;
Jer	18:	6	"Like **c** in the hand of the potter,
La	4:	2	are now considered as pots of **c**,
Da	2:	33	of iron and partly of baked **c**.
Ro	9:	21	the same lump of **c** some pottery
2Co	4:	7	this treasure in jars of **c** to show
2Ti	2:	20	and silver, but also of wood and **c**;

CLEAN

Lev	16:	30	you will be **c** from all your sins,
Ps	24:	4	one who has **c** hands and a pure
Mt	12:	44	swept **c** and put in order.
	23:	25	You **c** the outside of the cup
Mk	7:	19	this, Jesus declared all foods **c**.)
Jn	13:	10	you are **c**, though not every one
	15:	3	You are already **c** because
Ac	10:	15	impure that God has made **c**."
Ro	14:	20	All food is **c**, but it is wrong

CLING

Ps	63:	8	I **c** to you; your right hand upholds
Ro	12:	9	Hate what is evil; **c** to what is good.

CLOAK

2Ki	4:	29	"Tuck your **c** into your belt,

CLOSE (CLOSER)

Ps	34:	18	The LORD is **c**
Isa	40:	11	and carries them **c** to his heart;
Jer	30:	21	near and he will come **c** to me—

CLOSER (CLOSE)

Ex	3:	5	"Do not come any **c**," God said.
Pr	18:	24	friend who sticks **c** than a brother.

CLOTHE (CLOTHED CLOTHES CLOTHING)

Ps	45:	3	**c** yourself with splendor
Isa	52:	1	Zion, **c** yourself with strength!
Ro	13:	14	**c** yourselves with the Lord Jesus
Col	3:	12	**c** yourselves with compassion,
1Pe	5:	5	**c** yourselves with humility toward

CLOTHED (CLOTHE)

Ps	30:	11	my sackcloth and **c** me with joy,
Pr	31:	25	She is **c** with strength and dignity;
Lk	24:	49	the city until you have been **c**

CLOTHES (CLOTHE)

Mt	6:	25	food, and the body more than **c**?
	6:	28	"And why do you worry about **c**?
Jn	11:	44	"Take off the grave **c** and let him

CLOTHING (CLOTHE)

Dt	22:	5	nor a man wear women's **c**,
Mt	7:	15	They come to you in sheep's **c**,

CONCORDANCE

CLOUD (CLOUDS)
Ex   13: 21   them in a pillar of **c** to guide them
Isa 19: 1   the Lord rides on a swift **c** and is
Lk   21: 27   of Man coming in a **c** with power
Heb 12: 1   by such a great **c** of witnesses,

CLOUDS (CLOUD)
Ps   104: 3   He makes the **c** his chariot and
Da   7: 13   man, coming with the **c** of heaven.
Mk   13: 26   Man coming in **c** with great power
1Th   4: 17   them in the **c** to meet the Lord

CO-HEIRS (INHERIT)
Ro   8: 17   heirs of God and **c** with Christ,

COALS
Pr   25: 22   will heap burning **c** on his head,
Ro   12: 20   this, you will heap burning **c** on his

COAT
Lk   6: 29   If someone takes your **c**, do not

COLD
Pr   25: 25   Like **c** water to a weary soul is
Mt   10: 42   anyone gives even a cup of **c** water
     24: 12   the love of most will grow **c**,

COMFORT (COMFORTED COMFORTS)
Ps   23: 4   your rod and your staff, they **c** me.
     119: 52   ancient laws, and I find **c** in them.
     119: 76   May your unfailing love be my **c**,
Zec   1: 17   the Lord will again **c** Zion
1Co 14: 3   strengthening, encouraging and **c**.
2Co   1: 4   that we can **c** those in any trouble
      2: 7   you ought to forgive and **c** him,

COMFORTED (COMFORT)
Mt   5: 4   who mourn, for they will be **c**.

COMFORTS (COMFORT)
Job 29: 25   I was like one who **c** mourners.
Isa 49: 13   For the Lord **c** his people
     51: 12   "I, even I, am he who **c** you.
     66: 13   As a mother **c** her child, so will I
2Co   1: 4   who **c** us in all our troubles,
      7: 6   But God, who **c** the downcast,

COMMAND (COMMANDED COMMANDING
   COMMANDMENT COMMANDMENTS
   COMMANDS)
Ex   7: 2   You are to say everything I **c** you,
Nu   24: 13   to go beyond the **c** of the Lord—
Dt   4: 2   Do not add to what I **c** you and do
     30: 16   For I **c** you today to love
     32: 46   so that you may **c** your children
Ps   91: 11   he will **c** his angels concerning you
     148: 5   for at his **c** they were created,
Pr   6: 23   For this **c** is a lamp, this teaching is
     13: 13   whoever respects a **c** is rewarded.
Ecc   8: 2   Obey the king's **c**, I say,
Joel 2: 11   mighty is the army that obeys his **c**.
Jn   13: 34   "A new **c** I give you:
     15: 12   My **c** is this: Love each other as I
1Co 14: 37   I am writing to you is the Lord's **c**.
Gal   5: 14   is fulfilled in keeping this one **c**:
1Ti   1: 5   The goal of this **c** is love,
Heb 11: 3   the universe was formed at God's **c**,
1Jn   3: 23   And this is his **c**: to believe
2Jn   : 6   his **c** is that you walk in love.

COMMANDED (COMMAND)
Ps   33: 9   came to be; he **c**, and it stood firm.

COMMITTED

Mt   28: 20   to obey everything I have **c** you.
1Co   9: 14   way, the Lord has **c** that those who
1Jn   3: 23   and to love one another as he **c** us.

COMMANDING (COMMAND)
2Ti   2: 4   rather tries to please his **c** officer.

COMMANDMENT (COMMAND)
Jos 22: 5   be very careful to keep the **c**
Mt   22: 38   This is the first and greatest **c**.
Ro   7: 12   and the **c** is holy,
Eph   6: 2   is the first **c** with a promise—

COMMANDMENTS (COMMAND)
Ex   20: 6   those who love me and keep my **c**.
     34: 28   words of the covenant—the Ten **C**.
Dt   7: 9   those who love him and keep his **c**.
Ecc 12: 13   Fear God and keep his **c**, for this is
Da   9: 4   those who love him and keep his **c**,
Mt   22: 40   the Prophets hang on these two **c**."

COMMANDS (COMMAND)
Dt   11: 27   you obey the **c** of the Lord your
Ps   112: 1   who find great delight in his **c**.
     119: 47   in your **c** because I love them.
     119: 86   All your **c** are trustworthy;
     119: 98   Your **c** are always with me
     119:127   I love your **c** more than gold,
     119:143   me, but your **c** give me delight.
     119:172   word, for all your **c** are righteous.
Pr   3: 1   but keep my **c** in your heart,
     10: 8   The wise in heart accept **c**,
Mt   5: 19   teaches these **c** will be called great
Jn   14: 15   "If you love me, keep my **c**.
     14: 21   Whoever has my **c** and keeps them
Ac   17: 30   now he **c** all people everywhere
1Co   7: 19   Keeping God's **c** is what counts.
1Jn   5: 3   this is love for God: to keep his **c**. And
               his **c** are not burdensome.

COMMEND (COMMENDED COMMENDS)
Ecc   8: 15   So I **c** the enjoyment of life,
1Pe   2: 14   wrong and to **c** those who do right.

COMMENDED (COMMEND)
Ro   13: 3   do what is right and you will be **c**.
Heb 11: 39   These were all **c** for their faith,

COMMENDS (COMMEND)
2Co 10: 18   but the one whom the Lord **c**.

COMMIT (COMMITS COMMITTED)
Ex   20: 14   "You shall not **c** adultery.
Ps   37: 5   **C** your way to the Lord;
Mt   5: 27   was said, 'You shall not **c** adultery.'
Lk   23: 46   into your hands I **c** my spirit."
Ac   20: 32   "Now I **c** you to God
1Co 10: 8   We should not **c** sexual immorality,
1Pe   4: 19   to God's will should **c** themselves

COMMITS (COMMIT)
Pr   6: 32   a man who **c** adultery has no sense;
     29: 22   hot-tempered person **c** many sins.
Mt   19: 9   marries another woman **c** adultery."

COMMITTED (COMMIT)
Nu   5: 7   must confess the sin they have **c**.
1Ki   8: 61   may your hearts be fully **c**
2Ch 16: 9   those whose hearts are fully **c**
Mt   5: 28   lustfully has already **c** adultery
2Co   5: 19   And he has **c** to us the message
1Pe   2: 22   "He **c** no sin, and no deceit was

COMMON

Pr	22:	2	Rich and poor have this in **c**:
1Co	10:	13	has overtaken you except what is **c**
2Co	6:	14	and wickedness have in **c**?

COMPANION

Pr	13:	20	for a **c** of fools suffers harm.
	28:	7	a **c** of gluttons disgraces his father.
	29:	3	but a **c** of prostitutes squanders his

COMPANY

Pr	24:	1	the wicked, do not desire their **c**;
Jer	15:	17	I never sat in the **c** of revelers,
1Co	15:	33	"Bad **c** corrupts good character."

COMPARED (COMPARING)

Eze	31:	2	" 'Who can be **c** with you

COMPARING (COMPARED)

Ro	8:	18	present sufferings are not worth **c**
2Co	8:	8	of your love by **c** it
Gal	6:	4	without **c** themselves to someone

COMPASSION (COMPASSIONATE COMPASSIONS)

Ex	33:	19	I will have **c** on whom I will have **c**.
Ne	9:	19	your great **c** you did not abandon
	9:	28	in your **c** you delivered them time
Ps	51:	1	to your great **c** blot out my
	103:	4	pit and crowns you with love and **c**,
	103:	13	As a father has **c** on his children,
	145:	9	he has **c** on all he has made.
Isa	49:	13	will have **c** on his afflicted ones.
	49:	15	and have no **c** on the child she has
Hos	2:	19	and justice, in love and **c**.
	11:	8	all my **c** is aroused.
Jnh	3:	9	with **c** turn from his fierce anger so
Mt	9:	36	saw the crowds, he had **c** on them,
Mk	8:	2	"I have **c** for these people;
Ro	9:	15	I will have **c** on whom I have **c**."
Col	3:	12	clothe yourselves with **c**, kindness,
Jas	5:	11	The Lord is full of **c** and mercy.

COMPASSIONATE (COMPASSION)

Ne	9:	17	gracious and **c**, slow to anger
Ps	103:	8	The LORD is **c** and gracious,
	112:	4	for those who are gracious and **c**
Eph	4:	32	Be kind and **c** to one another,
1Pe	3:	8	love one another, be **c** and humble.

COMPASSIONS (COMPASSION)

La	3:	22	not consumed, for his **c** never fail.

COMPEL (COMPELLED COMPELS)

Lk	14:	23	lanes and **c** them to come in,

COMPELLED (COMPEL)

Ac	20:	22	"And now, **c** by the Spirit, I am
1Co	9:	16	boast, since I am **c** to preach.

COMPELS (COMPEL)

2Co	5:	14	For Christ's love **c** us, because we

COMPETENCE (COMPETENT)

2Co	3:	5	but our **c** comes from God.

COMPETENT (COMPETENCE)

Ro	15:	14	and **c** to instruct one another.
1Co	6:	2	are you not **c** to judge trivial cases?
2Co	3:	5	Not that we are **c** in ourselves
	3:	6	He has made us **c** as ministers

COMPETES

1Co	9:	25	Everyone who **c** in the games goes
2Ti	2:	5	anyone who **c** as an athlete does

COMPLACENT

Am	6:	1	Woe to you who are **c** in Zion,

COMPLETE

Jn	15:	11	in you and that your joy may be **c**.
	16:	24	will receive, and your joy will be **c**.
	17:	23	they may be brought to **c** unity.
Ac	20:	24	**c** the task the Lord Jesus has given
Php	2:	2	then make my joy **c** by being
Col	4:	17	it that you **c** the ministry you have
Jas	1:	4	so that you may be mature and **c**,
	2:	22	faith was made **c** by what he did.

CONCEAL (CONCEALED CONCEALS)

Ps	40:	10	I do not **c** your love and your
Pr	25:	2	It is the glory of God to **c** a matter;

CONCEALED (CONCEAL)

Jer	16:	17	me, nor is their sin **c** from my eyes.
Mt	10:	26	for there is nothing **c** that will not
Mk	4:	22	whatever is **c** is meant to be

CONCEALS (CONCEAL)

Pr	28:	13	Whoever **c** their sins does not

CONCEITED

Gal	5:	26	Let us not become **c**,
1Ti	6:	4	they are **c** and understand nothing.

CONCEIVE (CONCEIVED)

Isa	7:	14	The virgin will **c** and give birth
Mt	1:	23	"The virgin will **c** and give birth

CONCEIVED (CONCEIVE)

Mt	1:	20	because what is **c** in her is
1Co	2:	9	and what no human mind has **c**"—

CONCERN (CONCERNED)

Eze	36:	21	I had **c** for my holy name,
1Co	7:	32	I would like you to be free from **c**.
	12:	25	that its parts should have equal **c**
2Co	11:	28	of my **c** for all the churches.

CONCERNED (CONCERN)

Jnh	4:	10	"You have been **c** about this plant,
1Co	7:	32	An unmarried man is **c**

CONDEMN (CONDEMNATION CONDEMNED CONDEMNING CONDEMNS)

Job	40:	8	you **c** me to justify yourself?
Isa	50:	9	Who will **c** me? They will all wear
Lk	6:	37	Do not **c**, and you will not be
Jn	3:	17	Son into the world to **c** the world,
	12:	48	words I have spoken will **c** them
Ro	2:	27	yet obeys the law will **c** you who,
1Jn	3:	20	If our hearts **c** us, we know that

CONDEMNATION (CONDEMN)

Ro	5:	18	just as one trespass resulted in **c**
	8:	1	there is now no **c** for those who are
2Co	3:	9	that brought **c** was glorious,

CONDEMNED (CONDEMN)

Ps	34:	22	who takes refuge in him will be **c**.
Mt	12:	37	and by your words you will be **c**."
	23:	33	How will you escape being **c**
Jn	3:	18	Whoever believes in him is not **c**,
	16:	11	prince of this world now stands **c**.
Ro	14:	23	whoever has doubts is **c** if they eat,
1Co	11:	32	that we will not be finally **c**
Heb	11:	7	By his faith he **c** the world

CONCORDANCE

CONDEMNING (CONDEMN)
Pr   17: 15 the guilty and **c** the innocent—
Ro   2: 1 you are **c** yourself, because you

CONDEMNS (CONDEMN)
Pr   14: 34 exalts a nation, but sin **c** any people
Ro   8: 34 Who then is the one who **c**?

CONDUCT
Pr   20: 11 is their **c** really pure and upright?
       21: 8 but the **c** of the innocent is upright.
Ecc   6: 8 how to **c** themselves before others?
Jer   4: 18 "Your own **c** and actions have
       17: 10 each person according to their **c**,
Eze   7: 3 I will judge you according to your **c**
1Ti   3: 15 how people ought to **c** themselves

CONFESS (CONFESSION)
Lev 16: 21 and **c** over it all the wickedness
     26: 40 if they will **c** their sins and the sins
Nu   5: 7 **c** the sin they have committed.
Ps   38: 18 I **c** my iniquity; I am troubled by
Jas   5: 16 Therefore **c** your sins to each other
1Jn   1: 9 If we **c** our sins, he is faithful

CONFESSION (CONFESS)
2Co   9: 13 accompanies your **c** of the gospel

CONFIDENCE
Ps   71: 5 LORD, my **c** since my youth.
Pr   11: 13 A gossip betrays a **c**,
      25: 9 to court, do not betray another's **c**,
      31: 11 Her husband has full **c** in her
Isa   32: 17 will be quietness and **c** forever.
Jer   17: 7 in the LORD, whose **c** is in him.
Php   3: 3 and who put no **c** in the flesh—
Heb   4: 16 God's throne of grace with **c**,
     10: 19 since we have **c** to enter the Most
     10: 35 So do not throw away your **c**;
     11: 1 Now faith is **c** in what we hope
     13: 17 Have **c** in your leaders and submit
1Jn   5: 14 This is the **c** we have

CONFIRM
2Pe   1: 10 make every effort to **c** your calling

CONFLICT
Pr   6: 14 his heart—he always stirs up **c**.
      6: 19 a person who stirs up **c**
    10: 12 Hatred stirs up **c**, but love covers
    15: 18 A hot-tempered person stirs up **c**,
    16: 28 A perverse person stirs up **c**,
    28: 25 The greedy stir up **c**,
    29: 22 An angry person stirs up **c**,

CONFORM (CONFORMED)
Ro   12: 2 not **c** to the pattern of this world,
1Pe   1: 14 do not **c** to the evil desires you had

CONFORMED (CONFORM)
Ro   8: 29 predestined to be **c** to the image

CONQUERORS
Ro   8: 37 are more than **c** through him who

CONSCIENCE (CONSCIENCES)
Ro   13: 5 but also as a matter of **c**.
1Co   8: 7 a god, and since their **c** is weak,
      8: 12 this way and wound their weak **c**,
    10: 25 without raising questions of **c**,
    10: 29 being judged by another's **c**?
Heb 10: 22 to cleanse us from a guilty **c**
1Pe   3: 16 keeping a clear **c**, so that those who

CONSCIENCES (CONSCIENCE)
Ro   2: 15 hearts, their **c** also bearing witness,
1Ti   4: 2 whose **c** have been seared as
Titus 1: 15 their minds and **c** are corrupted.
Heb 9: 14 cleanse our **c** from acts that lead

CONSCIOUS
Ro   3: 20 through the law we become **c** of
1Pe   2: 19 unjust suffering because they are **c**

CONSECRATE (CONSECRATED)
Ex   13: 2 "**C** to me every firstborn male.
Lev 20: 7 "'**C** yourselves and be holy,

CONSECRATED (CONSECRATE)
Ex   29: 43 and the place will be **c** by my glory.
1Ti   4: 5 because it is **c** by the word of God

CONSIDER (CONSIDERATE CONSIDERED
   CONSIDERS)
1Sa 12: 24 **c** what great things he has done
Job 37: 14 stop and **c** God's wonders.
Ps   8: 3 When I **c** your heavens, the work
   143: 5 and **c** what your hands have done.
Lk   12: 24 **C** the ravens: They do not sow
     12: 27 "**C** how the wild flowers grow.
Php   3: 8 I **c** everything a loss because
Heb 10: 24 And let us **c** how we may spur one
Jas   1: 2 **C** it pure joy, my brothers
     1: 26 Those who **c** themselves religious

CONSIDERATE (CONSIDER)
Titus 3: 2 to be peaceable and **c**, and always
Jas   3: 17 then peace-loving, **c**, submissive,
1Pe   2: 18 only to those who are good and **c**,
      3: 7 the same way be **c** as you live

CONSIDERED (CONSIDER)
Job   1: 8 "Have you **c** my servant Job?
      2: 3 "Have you **c** my servant Job?
Ps   44: 22 we are **c** as sheep to be
          slaughtered.
Isa   53: 4 yet we **c** him punished by God,
Ro   8: 36 all day long; we are **c** as sheep to be

CONSIDERS (CONSIDER)
Pr   31: 16 She **c** a field and buys it; out of her
Ro   14: 5 One person **c** one day more sacred

CONSIST
Lk   12: 15 life does not **c** in an abundance

CONSOLATION
Ps   94: 19 within me, your **c** brought me joy.

CONSTRUCTIVE
1Co 10: 23 but not everything is **c**.

CONSUME (CONSUMING)
Jn   2: 17 "Zeal for your house will **c** me."

CONSUMING (CONSUME)
Dt   4: 24 For the LORD your God is a **c** fire,
Heb 12: 29 for our "God is a **c** fire."

CONTAIN
1Ki   8: 27 the highest heaven, cannot **c** you.
2Pe   3: 16 His letters **c** some things that are

CONTAMINATES
2Co   7: 1 from everything that **c** body

CONTEMPLATE
2Co   3: 18 unveiled faces **c** the Lord's glory,

CONTEMPT
Pr	14: 31	oppresses the poor shows **c** for
	17: 5	Whoever mocks the poor shows **c**
	18: 3	so does **c**, and with shame comes
Da	12: 2	others to shame and everlasting **c**.
Ro	2: 4	do you show **c** for the riches of his
Gal	4: 14	did not treat me with **c** or scorn.
1Th	5: 20	Do not treat prophecies with **c**

CONTEND
Jude : 3 urge you to **c** for the faith that was

CONTENT (CONTENTMENT)
Pr	13: 25	The righteous eat to their hearts' **c**,
Php	4: 11	to be **c** whatever the circumstances.
	4: 12	learned the secret of being **c** in any
1Ti	6: 8	clothing, we will be **c** with that.
Heb	13: 5	and be **c** with what you have,

CONTENTMENT (CONTENT)
1Ti 6: 6 But godliness with **c** is great gain.

CONTINUAL (CONTINUE)
Pr 15: 15 but the cheerful heart has a **c** feast.

CONTINUE (CONTINUAL)
Php	2: 12	**c** to work out your salvation
2Ti	3: 14	**c** in what you have learned and
1Jn	5: 18	born of God does not **c** to sin;
Rev	22: 11	let the one who does right **c** to do
	22: 11	let the holy person **c** to be holy."

CONTRITE
Ps	51: 17	a broken and **c** heart you, God,
Isa	57: 15	and to revive the heart of the **c**.
	66: 2	who are humble and **c** in spirit,

CONTROL (CONTROLLED SELF-CONTROL SELF-CONTROLLED)
1Co	7: 9	But if they cannot **c** themselves,
	7: 37	but has **c** over his own will,
1Th	4: 4	should learn to **c** your own body

CONTROLLED (CONTROL)
Ps 32: 9 understanding but must be **c** by bit

CONTROVERSIES
Titus 3: 9 But avoid foolish **c** and genealogies

CONVERSATION
Col 4: 6 Let your **c** be always full of grace,

CONVERT
1Ti 3: 6 He must not be a recent **c**, or he

CONVICTION
Heb 3: 14 we hold our original **c** firmly

CONVINCED (CONVINCING)
Ro	8: 38	I am **c** that neither death nor life,
2Ti	1: 12	am **c** that he is able to guard what I
	3: 14	have learned and have become **c** of,

CONVINCING (CONVINCED)
Ac 1: 3 and gave many **c** proofs that he was

CORNELIUS
Roman to whom Peter preached; first Gentile Christian (Ac 10).

CORNERSTONE (STONE)
Ps	118: 22	builders rejected has become the **c**;
Isa	28: 16	a precious **c** for a sure foundation;
Eph	2: 20	Christ Jesus himself as the chief **c**.
1Pe	2: 6	a chosen and precious **c**,
	2: 7	rejected has become the **c**,"

CORRECT (CORRECTING CORRECTION CORRECTS)
2Ti 4: 2 **c**, rebuke and encourage—

CORRECTING (CORRECT)
2Ti 3: 16 **c** and training in righteousness,

CORRECTION (CORRECT)
Pr	10: 17	but whoever ignores **c** leads others
	12: 1	but whoever hates **c** is stupid.
	15: 5	whoever heeds **c** shows prudence.
	15: 10	the one who hates **c** will die.

CORRECTS (CORRECT)
Job	5: 17	"Blessed is the one whom God **c**;
Pr	9: 7	Whoever **c** a mocker invites insults

CORRUPT (CORRUPTS)
Ge 6: 11 Now the earth was **c** in God's sight

CORRUPTS (CORRUPT)
Ecc	7: 7	into a fool, and a bribe **c** the heart.
1Co	15: 33	"Bad company **c** good character."
Jas	3: 6	It **c** the whole body, sets the whole

COST
Pr	4: 7	Though it **c** all you have,
Isa	55: 1	milk without money and without **c**.
Rev	21: 6	thirsty I will give water without **c**

COUNSEL (COUNSELOR)
1Ki	22: 5	"First seek the **c** of the LORD."
Pr	15: 22	Plans fail for lack of **c**,
Rev	3: 18	I **c** you to buy from me gold

COUNSELOR (COUNSEL)
Isa 9: 6 And he will be called Wonderful **C**,

COUNT (COUNTING COUNTS)
Ro	4: 8	Lord will never **c** against them."
	6: 11	**c** yourselves dead to sin but alive

COUNTING (COUNT)
2Co 5: 19 not **c** people's sins against them.

COUNTRY
Jn 4: 44 prophet has no honor in his own **c**.

COUNTS (COUNT)
Jn	6: 63	the flesh **c** for nothing.
1Co	7: 19	God's commands is what **c**.
Gal	5: 6	**c** is faith expressing itself through

COURAGE (COURAGEOUS)
Ac 23: 11 stood near Paul and said, "Take **c**!

COURAGEOUS (COURAGE)
Dt	31: 6	Be strong and **c**. Do not be afraid
Jos	1: 6	Be strong and **c**, because you will
1Co	16: 13	firm in the faith; be **c**; be strong.

COURSE
Ps	19: 5	a champion rejoicing to run his **c**.
Pr	15: 21	understanding keeps a straight **c**.

COURTS
Ps	84: 10	your **c** than a thousand elsewhere;
	100: 4	thanksgiving and his **c** with praise;

COVENANT (COVENANTS)
Ge	9: 9	"I now establish my **c** with you
Ex	19: 5	if you obey me fully and keep my **c**,
1Ch	16: 15	He remembers his **c** forever,
Job	31: 1	"I made a **c** with my eyes not
Jer	31: 31	I will make a new **c** with the people
1Co	11: 25	"This cup is the new **c** in my blood;

CONCORDANCE

Gal 4: 24 One **c** is from Mount Sinai
Heb 9: 15 Christ is the mediator of a new **c**,

COVENANTS (COVENANT)
Ro 9: 4 the **c**, the receiving of the law,
Gal 4: 24 The women represent two **c**.

COVER (COVER-UP COVERED COVERS)
Ps 91: 4 He will **c** you with his feathers,
Jas 5: 20 and **c** over a multitude of sins.

COVER-UP (COVER)
1Pe 2: 16 do not use your freedom as a **c**

COVERED (COVER)
Ps 32: 1 are forgiven, whose sins are **c**.
Isa 6: 2 With two wings they **c** their faces,
Ro 4: 7 are forgiven, whose sins are **c**.
1Co 11: 4 with his head **c** dishonors his head.

COVERS (COVER)
Pr 10: 12 conflict, but love **c** over all wrongs.
1Pe 4: 8 because love **c** over a multitude

COVET
Ex 20: 17 "You shall not **c** your neighbor's
Ro 13: 9 "You shall not **c**," and whatever

COWARDLY
Rev 21: 8 But the **c**, the unbelieving, the vile,

CRAFTINESS (CRAFTY)
1Co 3: 19 "He catches the wise in their **c**";

CRAFTY (CRAFTINESS)
Ge 3: 1 the serpent was more **c** than any
2Co 12: 16 Yet, **c** fellow that I am, I caught you

CRAVE
Pr 23: 3 Do not **c** his delicacies, for that
1Pe 2: 2 babies, **c** pure spiritual milk,

CREATE (CREATED CREATION CREATOR)
Ps 51: 10 **C** in me a pure heart, O God,
Isa 45: 18 he did not **c** it to be empty,

CREATED (CREATE)
Ge 1: 1 In the beginning God **c** the heavens
   1: 21 So God **c** the great creatures
   1: 27 So God **c** mankind in his own
   1: 27 male and female he **c** them.
Ps 148: 5 for at his command they were **c**,
Ro 1: 25 and served **c** things rather than
1Co 11: 9 neither was man **c** for woman,
Col 1: 16 For in him all things were **c**:
1Ti 4: 4 For everything God **c** is good,
Rev 10: 6 who **c** the heavens and all that is

CREATION (CREATE)
Mk 16: 15 *preach the gospel to all* **c**.
Jn 17: 24 because you loved me before the **c**
Ro 8: 19 For the **c** waits in eager expectation
   8: 39 nor anything else in all **c**, will be
2Co 5: 17 is in Christ, the new **c** has come:
Col 1: 15 God, the firstborn over all **c**.
1Pe 1: 20 He was chosen before the **c**
Rev 13: 8 was slain from the **c** of the world.

CREATOR (CREATE)
Ge 14: 22 Most High, **C** of heaven and earth,
Isa 42: 5 Lord says—the **C** of the heavens,
Ro 1: 25 created things rather than the **C**—

CREATURE (CREATURES)
Lev 17: 11 For the life of a **c** is in the blood,

CREATURES (CREATURE)
Ge 6: 19 into the ark two of all living **c**,
Ps 104: 24 the earth is full of your **c**.

CREDIT (CREDITED)
Ro 4: 24 whom God will **c** righteousness—
1Pe 2: 20 it to your **c** if you receive a beating

CREDITED (CREDIT)
Ge 15: 6 and he **c** it to him as righteousness.
Ro 4: 5 their faith is **c** as righteousness.
Gal 3: 6 it was **c** to him as righteousness."
Jas 2: 23 it was **c** to him as righteousness,"

CRIED (CRY)
Ps 18: 6 I **c** to my God for help.

CRIMSON
Isa 1: 18 though they are red as **c**, they shall

CRIPPLED
Mk 9: 45 to enter life **c** than to have two feet

CRITICISM
2Co 8: 20 want to avoid any **c** of the way we

CROOKED
Pr 10: 9 whoever takes **c** paths will be
Php 2: 15 fault in a warped and **c** generation."

CROSS
Mt 10: 38 Whoever does not take up their **c**
Lk 9: 23 take up their **c** daily and follow me.
Ac 2: 23 to death by nailing him to the **c**.
1Co 1: 17 lest the **c** of Christ be emptied of
Gal 6: 14 in the **c** of our Lord Jesus Christ,
Php 2: 8 even death on a **c**!
Col 1: 20 through his blood, shed on the **c**.
   2: 14 taken it away, nailing it to the **c**.
   2: 15 triumphing over them by the **c**.
Heb 12: 2 joy set before him he endured the **c**,

CROWD
Ex 23: 2 pervert justice by siding with the **c**,

CROWN (CROWNED CROWNS)
Pr 4: 9 and present you with a glorious **c**."
   10: 6 Blessings **c** the head
   12: 4 noble character is her husband's **c**,
   17: 6 Children's children are a **c**
Isa 61: 3 on them a **c** of beauty instead
Zec 9: 16 in his land like jewels in a **c**.
Mt 27: 29 then twisted together a **c** of thorns
1Co 9: 25 to get a **c** that will last forever.
2Ti 4: 8 store for me the **c** of righteousness,
Rev 2: 10 will give you life as your victor's **c**.

CROWNED (CROWN)
Ps 8: 5 the angels and **c** them with glory
Pr 14: 18 the prudent are **c** with knowledge.
Heb 2: 7 you **c** them with glory and honor

CROWNS (CROWN)
Rev 4: 10 They lay their **c** before the throne
   19: 12 fire, and on his head are many **c**.

CRUCIFIED (CRUCIFY)
Mt 20: 19 to be mocked and flogged and **c**.
   27: 38 Two rebels were **c** with him,
Lk 24: 7 be **c** and on the third day be raised
Jn 19: 18 they **c** him, and with him two
Ac 2: 36 Jesus, whom you **c**, both Lord
Ro 6: 6 that our old self was **c** with him so

1Co   1: 23   but we preach Christ **c**:
      2: 2   you except Jesus Christ and him **c**.
Gal   2: 20   I have been **c** with Christ and I no
      5: 24   Christ Jesus have **c** the flesh with

CRUCIFY (CRUCIFIED CRUCIFYING)
Mt   27: 22   They all answered, "**C** him!"
      27: 31   Then they led him away to **c** him.

CRUCIFYING (CRUCIFY)
Heb   6: 6   their loss they are **c** the Son of God

CRUSH (CRUSHED)
Ge   3: 15   he will **c** your head, and you will
Isa 53: 10   it was the Lord's will to **c** him
Ro 16: 20   peace will soon **c** Satan under your

CRUSHED (CRUSH)
Ps 34: 18   and saves those who are **c** in spirit.
Isa 53: 5   he was **c** for our iniquities;
2Co   4: 8   pressed on every side, but not **c**;

CRY (CRIED)
Ps 34: 15   and his ears are attentive to their **c**;
     40: 1   he turned to me and heard my **c**.
  130: 1   Out of the depths I **c** to you,

CULMINATION
Ro 10: 4   Christ is the **c** of the law so

CUP
Ps 23: 5   my head with oil; my **c** overflows.
Mt 10: 42   anyone gives even a **c** of cold water
    23: 25   You clean the outside of the **c**
    26: 39   may this **c** be taken from me.
1Co 11: 25   "This **c** is the new covenant in my

CURSE (CURSED)
Dt 11: 26   you today a blessing and a **c**—
    21: 23   is hung on a pole is under God's **c**.
Lk   6: 28   bless those who **c** you,
Gal   1: 8   to you, let them be under God's **c**!
     3: 13   redeemed us from the **c** of the law by
           becoming a **c** for us,
Rev 22: 3   No longer will there be any **c**.

CURSED (CURSE)
Ge   3: 17   "**C** is the ground because of you;
Dt 27: 15   "**C** is anyone who makes an idol—
    27: 16   "**C** is anyone who dishonors their
    27: 17   "**C** is anyone who moves their
    27: 18   "**C** is anyone who leads the blind
    27: 19   "**C** is anyone who withholds justice
    27: 20   "**C** is anyone who sleeps with his
    27: 21   "**C** is anyone who has sexual
    27: 22   "**C** is anyone who sleeps with his
    27: 23   "**C** is anyone who sleeps with his
    27: 24   "**C** is anyone who kills their
    27: 25   "**C** is anyone who accepts a bribe
    27: 26   "**C** is anyone who does not uphold
Ro   9: 3   I could wish that I myself were **c**
Gal   3: 10   "**C** is everyone who does not

CURTAIN
Ex 26: 33   Hang the **c** from the clasps
    26: 33   The **c** will separate the Holy Place
Lk 23: 45   the **c** of the temple was torn in two.
Heb 10: 20   way opened for us through the **c**,

CYMBAL
1Co 13: 1   a resounding gong or a clanging **c**.

DANCE (DANCING)
Ecc   3: 4   a time to mourn and a time to **d**,
Mt 11: 17   the pipe for you, and you did not **d**;

DANCING (DANCE)
Ps 30: 11   You turned my wailing into **d**;
  149: 3   Let them praise his name with **d**

DANGER
Pr 27: 12   The prudent see **d** and take refuge,
Ro   8: 35   or nakedness or **d** or sword?

DANIEL
    Hebrew exile to Babylon, name changed to Belteshazzar (Da 1:6–7). Refused to eat unclean food (Da 1:8–21). Interpreted Nebuchadnezzar's dreams (Da 2; 4), writing on the wall (Da 5). Thrown into lion's den (Da 6). Visions of (Da 7–12).

DARK (DARKEST DARKNESS)
Ro   2: 19   a light for those who are in the **d**,
2Pe   1: 19   it, as to a light shining in a **d** place,

DARKEST (DARK)
Ps 23: 4   though I walk through the **d** valley,

DARKNESS (DARK)
Ge   1: 4   he separated the light from the **d**.
2Sa 22: 29   the Lord turns my **d** into light.
Job 34: 22   utter **d**, where evildoers can hide.
Jn   3: 19   but people loved **d** instead of light
2Co   6: 14   fellowship can light have with **d**?
Eph   5: 8   For you were once **d**, but now you
1Pe   2: 9   out of **d** into his wonderful light.
1Jn   1: 5   in him there is no **d** at all.
     2: 9   a brother or sister is still in the **d**.

DAUGHTERS
Joel   2: 28   Your sons and **d** will prophesy,

DAVID
    Son of Jesse (Ru 4:17–22; 1Ch 2:13–15), ancestor of Jesus (Mt 1:1–17; Lk 3:31).
    Anointed king by Samuel (1Sa 16:1–13). Musician to Saul (1Sa 16:14–23; 18:10). Killed Goliath (1Sa 17). Relation with Jonathan (1Sa 18:1–4; 19–20; 23:16–18; 2Sa 1). Disfavor of Saul (1Sa 18:6—23:29). Spared Saul's life (1Sa 24; 26). Among Philistines (1Sa 21:10–14; 27–30). Lament for Saul and Jonathan (2Sa 1).
    Anointed king of Judah (2Sa 2:1–11); of Israel (2Sa 5:1–4; 1Ch 11:1–3). Promised eternal dynasty (2Sa 7; 1Ch 17; Ps 132). Adultery with Bathsheba (2Sa 11–12). Absalom's revolt (2Sa 14–18). Last words (2Sa 23:1–7). Death (1Ki 2:10–12; 1Ch 29:28).

DAWN
Ps 37: 6   righteous reward shine like the **d**,

DAY (DAYS)
Ge   1: 5   God called the light "**d**,"
Ex 20: 8   "Remember the Sabbath **d**
Lev 23: 28   because it is the **D** of Atonement,
Nu 14: 14   them in a pillar of cloud by **d**
Jos   1: 8   meditate on it **d** and night,
Ps 84: 10   Better is one **d** in your courts than
    96: 2   proclaim his salvation **d** after **d**.
  118: 24   The Lord has done it this very **d**;
Pr 27: 1   do not know what a **d** may bring.
Joel   2: 31   great and dreadful **d** of the Lord.
Ob   : 15   "The **d** of the Lord is near for all
Lk 11: 3   Give us each **d** our daily bread.

CONCORDANCE

Ac 17: 11 examined the Scriptures every **d**
2Co 4: 16 we are being renewed **d** by **d**.
1Th 5: 2 the **d** of the Lord will come like
2Pe 3: 8 With the Lord a **d** is like a thousand

DAYS (DAY)
Dt 17: 19 he is to read it all the **d** of his life so
Ps 23: 6 love will follow me all the **d** of my
90: 10 Our **d** may come to seventy years,
Ecc 12: 1 Creator in the **d** of your youth,
Joel 2: 29 I will pour out my Spirit in those **d**.
Mic 4: 1 In the last **d** the mountain
Heb 1: 2 in these last **d** he has spoken to us
2Pe 3: 3 that in the last **d** scoffers will come,

DEACONS
1Ti 3: 8 way, **d** are to be worthy of respect,

DEAD (DIE)
Dt 18: 11 or spiritist or who consults the **d**.
Mt 28: 7 'He has risen from the **d** and is
Ro 6: 11 count yourselves **d** to sin but alive
Eph 2: 1 you were **d** in your transgressions
1Th 4: 16 and the **d** in Christ will rise first.
Jas 2: 17 is not accompanied by action, is **d**.
2: 26 so faith without deeds is **d**.

DEATH (DIE)
Nu 35: 16 the murderer is to be put to **d**.
Ps 116: 15 of the Lord is the **d** of his faithful
Pr 8: 36 all who hate me love **d**."
14: 12 right, but in the end it leads to **d**.
Ecc 7: 2 for **d** is the destiny of everyone;
Isa 25: 8 he will swallow up **d** forever.
53: 12 he poured out his life unto **d**,
Jn 5: 24 but has crossed over from **d** to life.
Ro 5: 12 **d** through sin, and in this way **d**
6: 23 For the wages of sin is **d**,
8: 13 Spirit you put to **d** the misdeeds
1Co 15: 21 For since **d** came through a man,
15: 31 I face **d** every day—yes, just as
15: 55 "Where, O **d**, is your victory?
1Pe 3: 18 He was put to **d** in the body
Rev 1: 18 I hold the keys of **d** and Hades.
20: 6 The second **d** has no power over
20: 14 The lake of fire is the second **d**.
21: 4 There will be no more **d**'

DEBAUCHERY
Ro 13: 13 not in sexual immorality and **d**,
Eph 5: 18 drunk on wine, which leads to **d**.

DEBORAH
Prophetess who led Israel to victory over Canaanites (Jdg 4–5).

DEBT (DEBTORS DEBTS)
Ro 13: 8 except the continuing **d** to love

DEBTORS (DEBT)
Mt 6: 12 as we also have forgiven our **d**.

DEBTS (DEBT)
Dt 15: 1 seven years you must cancel **d**.
Mt 6: 12 And forgive us our **d**, as we

DECAY
Ps 16: 10 will you let your faithful one see **d**.
Ac 2: 27 will not let your holy one see **d**.

DECEIT (DECEIVE)
Mk 7: 22 greed, malice, **d**, lewdness, envy,

1Pe 2: 1 yourselves of all malice and all **d**,
2: 22 and no **d** was found in his mouth."

DECEITFUL (DECEIVE)
Jer 17: 9 The heart is **d** above all things
2Co 11: 13 are false apostles, **d** workers,

DECEITFULNESS (DECEIVE)
Mk 4: 19 the **d** of wealth and the desires
Heb 3: 13 of you may be hardened by sin's **d**.

DECEIVE (DECEIT DECEITFUL DECEITFULNESS
DECEIVED DECEIVES DECEPTIVE)
Lev 19: 11 " 'Do not **d** one another.
Pr 14: 5 An honest witness does not **d**,
Mt 24: 5 am the Messiah,' and will **d** many.
Ro 16: 18 flattery they **d** the minds of naive
1Co 3: 18 Do not **d** yourselves. If any of you
Gal 6: 3 they are not, they **d** themselves.
Eph 5: 6 no one **d** you with empty words,
Jas 1: 22 to the word, and so **d** yourselves.
Jas 1: 26 rein on their tongues **d** themselves,
1Jn 1: 8 we **d** ourselves and the truth is not

DECEIVED (DECEIVE)
Ge 3: 13 said, "The serpent **d** me, and I ate."
Gal 6: 7 Do not be **d**: God cannot be
1Ti 2: 14 And Adam was not the one **d**; it was
the woman who was **d**
2Ti 3: 13 to worse, deceiving and being **d**.
Jas 1: 16 Don't be **d**, my dear brothers

DECENCY
1Ti 2: 9 modestly, with **d** and propriety,

DECEPTIVE (DECEIVE)
Pr 31: 30 Charm is **d**, and beauty is fleeting;
Col 2: 8 through hollow and **d** philosophy,

DECLARE (DECLARED DECLARING)
1Ch 16: 24 **D** his glory among the nations,
Ps 19: 1 The heavens **d** the glory of God;
96: 3 **D** his glory among the nations,
Isa 42: 9 taken place, and new things I **d**;
Ro 10: 9 If you **d** with your mouth, "Jesus is

DECLARED (DECLARE)
Mk 7: 19 saying this, Jesus **d** all foods clean.)
Ro 2: 13 the law who will be **d** righteous.
3: 20 no one will be **d** righteous

DECLARING (DECLARE)
Ps 71: 8 **d** your splendor all day long.
Ac 2: 11 hear them **d** the wonders of God

DECREED (DECREES)
La 3: 37 it happen if the Lord has not **d** it?
Lk 22: 22 Son of Man will go as it has been **d**.

DECREES (DECREED)
Lev 10: 11 Israelites all the **d** the Lord has
Ps 119:112 on keeping your **d** to the very end.

DEDICATE (DEDICATION)
Pr 20: 25 It is a trap to **d** something rashly

DEDICATION (DEDICATE)
1Ti 5: 11 sensual desires overcome their **d**

DEED (DEEDS)
Col 3: 17 whether in word or **d**, do it all

DEEDS (DEED)
1Sa 2: 3 knows, and by him **d** are weighed.

Ps	65: 5	us with awesome and righteous **d**,
	66: 3	to God, "How awesome are your **d**!
	78: 4	next generation the praiseworthy **d**
	86: 10	you are great and do marvelous **d**;
	92: 4	For you make me glad by your **d**,
	111: 3	Glorious and majestic are his **d**,
Hab	3: 2	I stand in awe of your **d**, Lᴏʀᴅ.
Mt	5: 16	that they may see your good **d**
	11: 19	wisdom is proved right by her **d**."
Ac	26: 20	their repentance by their **d**.
Jas	2: 14	claims to have faith but has no **d**?
	2: 20	that faith without **d** is useless?
1Pe	2: 12	they may see your good **d**

DEEP (DEPTH)

1Co	2: 10	things, even the **d** things of God.
1Ti	3: 9	must keep hold of the **d** truths

DEER

Ps	42: 1	As the **d** pants for streams of water,

DEFEND (DEFENSE)

Ps	74: 22	Rise up, O God, and **d** your cause;
Pr	31: 9	**d** the rights of the poor and needy.
Jer	50: 34	He will vigorously **d** their cause so

DEFENSE (DEFEND)

Ps	35: 23	Awake, and rise to my **d**!
Php	1: 16	put here for the **d** of the gospel.

DEFERRED

Pr	13: 12	Hope **d** makes the heart sick,

DEFILE (DEFILED)

Da	1: 8	Daniel resolved not to **d** himself

DEFILED (DEFILE)

Isa	24: 5	The earth is **d** by its people;

DEFRAUD

Lev	19: 13	" 'Do not **d** or rob your neighbor.

DEITY

Col	2: 9	Christ all the fullness of the **D** lives

DELIGHT (DELIGHTS)

1Sa	15: 22	"Does the Lᴏʀᴅ **d** in burnt
Ps	1: 2	but whose **d** is in the law
	16: 3	noble ones in whom is all my **d**."
	35: 9	the Lᴏʀᴅ and **d** in his salvation.
	37: 4	Take **d** in the Lᴏʀᴅ, and he will
	43: 4	of God, to God, my joy and my **d**.
	51: 16	You do not **d** in sacrifice,
	119: 77	I may live, for your law is my **d**.
Isa	42: 1	my chosen one in whom I **d**;
	55: 2	you will **d** in the richest of fare.
	61: 10	I **d** greatly in the Lᴏʀᴅ;
Jer	9: 24	earth, for in these I **d**,"
	15: 16	they were my joy and my heart's **d**,
Mic	7: 18	angry forever but **d** to show mercy.
Zep	3: 17	He will take great **d** in you;
Mt	12: 18	the one I love, in whom I **d**;
1Co	13: 6	Love does not **d** in evil but rejoices
2Co	12: 10	for Christ's sake, I **d** in weaknesses,

DELIGHTS (DELIGHT)

Ps	22: 8	deliver him, since he **d** in him."
	35: 27	who **d** in the well-being of his
	36: 8	them drink from your river of **d**.
Pr	3: 12	he loves, as a father the son he **d** in.
	12: 22	**d** in people who are trustworthy.
	29: 17	will bring you the **d** you desire.

DELILAH

Woman who betrayed Samson (Jdg 16:4–22).

DELIVER (DELIVERANCE DELIVERED DELIVERER DELIVERS)

Ps	72: 12	he will **d** the needy who cry out,
	79: 9	**d** us and forgive our sins for your
Da	3: 17	the God we serve is able to **d** us
Mt	6: 13	but **d** us from the evil one.'
2Co	1: 10	that he will continue to **d** us,

DELIVERANCE (DELIVER)

Ps	3: 8	From the Lᴏʀᴅ comes **d**.
	32: 7	and surround me with songs of **d**.
	33: 17	A horse is a vain hope for **d**;

DELIVERED (DELIVER)

Ps	34: 4	he **d** me from all my fears.
Ro	4: 25	He was **d** over to death for our sins

DELIVERER (DELIVER)

Ps	18: 2	is my rock, my fortress and my **d**;
	40: 17	You are my help and my **d**;
	140: 7	my strong **d**, you shield my head
	144: 2	stronghold and my **d**, my shield,

DELIVERS (DELIVER)

Ps	34: 17	he **d** them from all their troubles.
	34: 19	the Lᴏʀᴅ **d** him from them all;
	37: 40	The Lᴏʀᴅ helps them and **d** them;

DEMANDED

Lk	12: 20	This very night your life will be **d**
	12: 48	been given much, much will be **d**;

DEMONS

Mt	12: 27	And if I drive out **d** by Beelzebul,
Mk	5: 15	been possessed by the legion of **d**,
Ro	8: 38	life, neither angels nor **d**,
Jas	2: 19	Good! Even the **d** believe that—

DEMONSTRATE (DEMONSTRATES)

Ac	26: 20	**d** their repentance by their deeds.
Ro	3: 26	he did it to **d** his righteousness

DEMONSTRATES (DEMONSTRATE)

Ro	5: 8	God **d** his own love for us in this:

DEN

Da	6: 16	and threw him into the lions' **d**.
Mt	21: 13	but you are making it 'a **d**

DENARIUS

Mk	12: 15	"Bring me a **d** and let me look

DENIED (DENY)

1Ti	5: 8	has **d** the faith and is worse than

DENIES (DENY)

1Jn	2: 23	No one who **d** the Son has

DENY (DENIED DENIES DENYING)

Ex	23: 6	"Do not **d** justice to your poor
Job	27: 5	till I die, I will not **d** my integrity;
La	3: 35	**d** people their rights before the
Lk	9: 23	be my disciple must **d** themselves
Titus	1: 16	but by their actions they **d** him.

DENYING (DENY)

Eze	22: 29	the foreigner, **d** them justice.
2Ti	3: 5	a form of godliness but **d** its power.
2Pe	2: 1	even **d** the sovereign Lord who

DEPART (DEPARTED)

Ge	49: 10	The scepter will not **d** from Judah,

CONCORDANCE

Job	1: 21	mother's womb, and naked I will **d**.
Mt	25: 41	to those on his left, '**D** from me,
Php	1: 23	I desire to **d** and be with Christ,

DEPARTED (DEPART)
1Sa	4: 21	"The Glory has **d** from Israel"—
Ps	119:102	I have not **d** from your laws,

DEPOSIT
2Co	1: 22	put his Spirit in our hearts as a **d**,
	5: 5	who has given us the Spirit as a **d**,
Eph	1: 14	who is a **d** guaranteeing our
2Ti	1: 14	Guard the good **d** that was entrusted

DEPRAVED (DEPRAVITY)
Ro	1: 28	God gave them over to a **d** mind,
2Pe	2: 7	was distressed by the **d** conduct

DEPRAVITY (DEPRAVED)
Ro	1: 29	of wickedness, evil, greed and **d**.

DEPRIVE
Dt	24: 17	Do not **d** the foreigner
Pr	18: 5	and so **d** the innocent of justice.
Isa	10: 2	to **d** the poor of their rights
	29: 21	with false testimony **d** the innocent
1Co	7: 5	Do not **d** each other except

DEPTH (DEEP)
Ro	8: 39	neither height nor **d**, nor anything
	11: 33	the **d** of the riches of the wisdom

DESERT See WILDERNESS

DESERTED (DESERTS)
Mt	26: 56	all the disciples **d** him and fled.
2Ti	1: 15	in the province of Asia has **d** me,

DESERTING (DESERTS)
Gal	1: 6	you are so quickly **d** the one who

DESERTS (DESERTED DESERTING)
Zec	11: 17	shepherd, who **d** the flock!

DESERVE (DESERVES)
Ps	103: 10	he does not treat us as our sins **d**
Jer	21: 14	I will punish you as your deeds **d**,
Mt	22: 8	those I invited did not **d** to come.
Ro	1: 32	those who do such things **d** death,

DESERVES (DESERVE)
Lk	10: 7	for the worker **d** his wages.
1Ti	5: 18	and "The worker **d** his wages."

DESIRABLE (DESIRE)
Pr	22: 1	name is more **d** than great riches;

DESIRE (DESIRABLE DESIRES)
Ge	3: 16	Your **d** will be for your husband,
Dt	5: 21	You shall not set your **d** on your
Ps	40: 6	and offering you did not **d**—
	40: 8	I **d** to do your will, my God;
	73: 25	earth has nothing I **d** besides you.
Pr	3: 15	nothing you **d** can compare
	10: 24	what the righteous **d** will be
	11: 23	The **d** of the righteous ends only
	19: 2	**D** without knowledge is not good
Isa	26: 8	and renown are the **d** of our hearts.
	53: 2	appearance that we should **d** him.
	55: 11	but will accomplish what I **d**
Hos	6: 6	For I **d** mercy, not sacrifice,
Mt	9: 13	'I **d** mercy, not sacrifice.'
Ro	7: 18	For I have the **d** to do what is good,
1Co	12: 31	Now eagerly **d** the greater gifts.

1Co	14: 1	and eagerly **d** gifts of the Spirit,
Php	1: 23	I **d** to depart and be with Christ,
Heb	13: 18	**d** to live honorably in every way.
Jas	1: 15	after **d** has conceived, it gives birth

DESIRES (DESIRE)
Ge	4: 7	it **d** to have you, but you must rule
1Ch	29: 18	keep these **d** and thoughts
Ps	34: 12	life and **d** to see many good days,
	37: 4	will give you the **d** of your heart.
	103: 5	who satisfies your **d** with good
	145: 19	He fulfills the **d** of those who fear
Pr	11: 6	the unfaithful are trapped by evil **d**.
	19: 22	What a person **d** is unfailing love;
Mk	4: 19	and the **d** for other things come
Ro	8: 5	minds set on what the Spirit **d**.
	13: 14	how to gratify the **d** of the flesh.
Gal	5: 16	and you will not gratify the **d**
	5: 17	For the flesh **d** what is contrary
1Ti	3: 1	to be an overseer **d** a noble task.
	6: 9	harmful **d** that plunge people
2Ti	2: 22	Flee the evil **d** of youth and pursue
Jas	1: 20	the righteousness that God **d**.
	4: 1	from your **d** that battle within you?
1Pe	2: 11	to abstain from sinful **d**,
1Jn	2: 17	The world and its **d** pass away,

DESOLATE
Isa	54: 1	the children of the **d** woman than

DESPAIR
Isa	61: 3	of praise instead of a spirit of **d**.
2Co	4: 8	perplexed, but not in **d**;

DESPISE (DESPISED DESPISES)
Job	42: 6	Therefore I **d** myself and repent
Pr	1: 7	fools **d** wisdom and instruction.
	3: 11	do not **d** the Lord's discipline,
	14: 21	It is a sin to **d** one's neighbor,
	15: 32	disregard discipline **d** themselves,
	23: 22	do not **d** your mother when she is
Zec	4: 10	"Who dares **d** the day of small
Lk	16: 13	devoted to the one and **d** the other.
Titus	2: 15	Do not let anyone **d** you.

DESPISED (DESPISE)
Ge	25: 34	and left. So Esau **d** his birthright.
Isa	53: 3	He was **d** and rejected by mankind,
1Co	1: 28	of this world and the **d** things—

DESPISES (DESPISE)
Pr	15: 20	but a foolish man **d** his mother.

DESTINED (DESTINY)
Lk	2: 34	"This child is **d** to cause the falling

DESTINY (DESTINED PREDESTINED)
Ps	73: 17	then I understood their final **d**.
Ecc	7: 2	for death is the **d** of everyone;

DESTITUTE
Pr	31: 8	for the rights of all who are **d**.
Heb	11: 37	in sheepskins and goatskins, **d**,

DESTROY (DESTROYED DESTROYS DESTRUCTION)
Pr	1: 32	complacency of fools will **d** them;
	11: 9	the godless **d** their neighbors,
Mt	10: 28	of the One who can **d** both soul

DESTROYED (DESTROY)
Job	19: 26	And after my skin has been **d**,
1Co	8: 11	is **d** by your knowledge.

1Co	15: 26	The last enemy to be **d** is death.
2Co	5: 1	if the earthly tent we live in is **d**,
Heb	10: 39	those who shrink back and are **d**,
2Pe	3: 10	the elements will be **d** by fire,

DESTROYS (DESTROY)

Pr	6: 32	whoever does so **d** himself.
	18: 9	his work is brother to one who **d**.
	28: 24	wrong," is partner to one who **d**.
Ecc	9: 18	but one sinner **d** much good.
1Co	3: 17	If anyone **d** God's temple, God will

DESTRUCTION (DESTROY)

Ps	1: 6	the way of the wicked leads to **d**.
Pr	16: 18	Pride goes before **d**, a haughty
Hos	13: 14	Where, O grave, is your **d**?
Mt	7: 13	broad is the road that leads to **d**,
Gal	6: 8	flesh, from the flesh will reap **d**;
2Th	1: 9	will be punished with everlasting **d**
1Ti	6: 9	that plunge people into ruin and **d**.
2Pe	2: 1	bringing swift **d** on themselves.
	3: 16	other Scriptures, to their own **d**.

DETERMINED (DETERMINES)

Job	14: 5	A person's days are **d**;
Isa	14: 26	This is the plan **d** for the whole
Da	11: 36	what has been **d** must take place.

DETERMINES (DETERMINED)

Ps	147: 4	He **d** the number of the stars
1Co	12: 11	them to each one, just as he **d**.

DETESTABLE (DETESTS)

Pr	21: 27	The sacrifice of the wicked is **d**—
	28: 9	even their prayers are **d**.
Isa	1: 13	Your incense is **d** to me.
Lk	16: 15	What people value highly is **d**
Titus	1: 16	They are **d**, disobedient and unfit

DETESTS (DETESTABLE)

Dt	22: 5	the LORD your God **d** anyone who
	23: 18	the LORD your God **d** them both.
	25: 16	the LORD your God **d** anyone who
Pr	11: 1	The LORD **d** dishonest scales,
	12: 22	The LORD **d** lying lips, but he
	15: 8	The LORD **d** the sacrifice
	15: 9	The LORD **d** the way
	15: 26	The LORD **d** the thoughts
	16: 5	The LORD **d** all the proud
	17: 15	The LORD **d** them both.
	20: 23	The LORD **d** differing weights,

DEVIL (DEVIL'S)

Mt	13: 39	the enemy who sows them is the **d**.
	25: 41	the eternal fire prepared for the **d**
Lk	4: 2	forty days he was tempted by the **d**.
	8: 12	then the **d** comes and takes away
Eph	4: 27	and do not give the **d** a foothold.
2Ti	2: 26	and escape from the trap of the **d**,
Jas	4: 7	Resist the **d**, and he will flee
1Pe	5: 8	Your enemy the **d** prowls around
1Jn	3: 8	who does what is sinful is of the **d**,
Rev	12: 9	that ancient serpent called the **d**,

DEVIL'S (DEVIL)

Eph	6: 11	your stand against the **d** schemes.
1Ti	3: 7	into disgrace and into the **d** trap.
1Jn	3: 8	was to destroy the **d** work.

DEVISED

2Pe	1: 16	we did not follow cleverly **d** stories

DEVOTE (DEVOTED DEVOTING DEVOTION DEVOUT)

Job	11: 13	"Yet if you **d** your heart to him
Jer	30: 21	who is he who will **d** himself to be
Col	4: 2	**D** yourselves to prayer,
1Ti	4: 13	**d** yourself to the public reading
Titus	3: 8	may be careful to **d** themselves

DEVOTED (DEVOTE)

Ezr	7: 10	For Ezra had **d** himself to the study
Ac	2: 42	They **d** themselves to the apostles'
Ro	12: 10	Be **d** to one another in love.
1Co	7: 34	Her aim is to be **d** to the Lord

DEVOTING (DEVOTE)

1Ti	5: 10	**d** herself to all kinds of good deeds.

DEVOTION (DEVOTE)

1Ch	28: 9	serve him with wholehearted **d**
1Co	7: 35	way in undivided **d** to the Lord.
2Co	11: 3	your sincere and pure **d** to Christ.

DEVOUR

2Sa	2: 26	to Joab, "Must the sword **d** forever?
Mk	12: 40	They **d** widows' houses
1Pe	5: 8	lion looking for someone to **d**.

DEVOUT (DEVOTE)

Lk	2: 25	Simeon, who was righteous and **d**.

DIE (DEAD DEATH DIED DIES)

Ge	2: 17	eat from it you will certainly **d**."
Ex	11: 5	Every firstborn son in Egypt will **d**,
Ru	1: 17	Where you **d** I will **d**, and there I
2Ki	14: 6	each will **d** for their own sin."
Pr	5: 23	For lack of discipline they will **d**,
	10: 21	many, but fools **d** for lack of sense.
	11: 7	placed in mortals **d** with them;
	15: 10	one who hates correction will **d**.
	23: 13	them with the rod, they will not **d**.
Ecc	3: 2	a time to be born and a time to **d**,
Isa	66: 24	the worms that eat them will not **d**,
Eze	3: 18	wicked person will **d** for their sin,
	18: 4	one who sins is the one who will **d**.
	33: 8	wicked person will **d** for their sin,
Mt	26: 52	all who draw the sword will **d**
Jn	11: 25	in me will live, even though they **d**;
	11: 26	by believing in me will never **d**.
Ro	5: 7	Very rarely will anyone **d**
	14: 8	and if we **d**, we **d** for the Lord.
1Co	15: 22	For as in Adam all **d**, so in Christ
Php	1: 21	to live is Christ and to **d** is gain.
Heb	9: 27	as people are destined to **d** once,
Rev	14: 13	Blessed are the dead who **d**

DIED (DIE)

Ro	5: 6	Christ **d** for the ungodly.
	6: 2	We are those who have **d** to sin;
	6: 8	Now if we **d** with Christ, we believe
	14: 15	someone for whom Christ **d**.
1Co	8: 11	for whom Christ **d**, is destroyed
	15: 3	that Christ **d** for our sins according
2Co	5: 14	one **d** for all, and therefore all **d**.
Col	3: 3	For you **d**, and your life is now
1Th	5: 10	He **d** for us so that, whether we are
2Ti	2: 11	If we **d** with him, we will also live
Heb	9: 15	that he has **d** as a ransom to set
Rev	2: 8	Last, who **d** and came to life again.

DIES (DIE)

Job	14: 14	If someone **d**, will they live again?
1Co	15: 36	does not come to life unless it **d**.

CONCORDANCE

DIFFERENCE (DIFFERENT)
Ro 10: 12 For there is no **d** between Jew

DIFFERENT (DIFFERENCE)
1Co 12: 4 There are **d** kinds of gifts,
2Co 11: 4 or a **d** gospel from the one you

DIGNITY
Pr 31: 25 She is clothed with strength and **d**;

DIGS
Pr 26: 27 Whoever **d** a pit will fall into it;

DILIGENCE (DILIGENT)
Heb 6: 11 show this same **d** to the very end,

DILIGENT (DILIGENCE)
Pr 21: 5 The plans of the **d** lead to profit as
1Ti 4: 15 Be **d** in these matters;

DIRECT (DIRECTS)
Ps 119: 35 **D** me in the path of your
   119:133 **D** my footsteps according to your
Jer 10: 23 it is not for them to **d** their steps.
2Th 3: 5 May the Lord **d** your hearts

DIRECTS (DIRECT)
Ps 42: 8 By day the Lord **d** his love,
Isa 48: 17 who **d** you in the way you should

DIRGE
Mt 11: 17 we sang a **d**, and you did not

DISAPPEAR
Mt 5: 18 until heaven and earth **d**,
Lk 16: 17 earth to **d** than for the least stroke

DISASTER
Ps 57: 1 your wings until the **d** has passed.
Pr 3: 25 Have no fear of sudden **d**
   17: 5 whoever gloats over **d** will not go
Isa 45: 7 I bring prosperity and create **d**;
Eze 7: 5 Unheard-of! See, it comes!

DISCERN (DISCERNING)
Ps 19: 12 But who can **d** their own errors?
   139: 3 You **d** my going out and my lying
Php 1: 10 you may be able to **d** what is best

DISCERNING (DISCERN)
Pr 14: 6 knowledge comes easily to the **d**.
   15: 14 The **d** heart seeks knowledge,
   17: 10 A rebuke impresses a **d** person
   17: 24 A **d** person keeps wisdom in view,
   17: 28 and **d** if they hold their tongues.
   19: 25 rebuke the **d**, and they will gain
   28: 11 and **d** sees how deluded they are.

DISCIPLE (DISCIPLES)
Mt 10: 42 of these little ones who is my **d**,
Lk 14: 27 and follow me cannot be my **d**.

DISCIPLES (DISCIPLE)
Mt 28: 19 go and make **d** of all nations,
Jn 8: 31 my teaching, you are really my **d**.
   13: 35 will know that you are my **d**, if you
Ac 11: 26 The **d** were called Christians first

DISCIPLINE (DISCIPLINED DISCIPLINES)
Ps 38: 1 your anger or **d** me in your wrath.
   39: 11 rebuke and **d** anyone for their sin,
   94: 12 Blessed is the one you **d**, Lord,
Pr 3: 11 do not despise the Lord's **d**
   5: 12 You will say, "How I hated **d**!
   5: 23 For lack of **d** they will die,

Pr 10: 17 Whoever heeds **d** shows the way
   12: 1 Whoever loves **d** loves knowledge,
   13: 18 Whoever disregards **d** comes
   13: 24 their children is careful to **d** them.
   15: 5 A fool spurns a parent's **d**,
   15: 32 disregard **d** despise themselves,
   19: 18 **D** your children, for in that there is
   19: 20 Listen to advice and accept **d**,
   22: 15 the rod of **d** will drive it far away.
   23: 13 Do not withhold **d** from a child;
   29: 17 **D** your children, and they will give
Heb 12: 5 do not make light of the Lord's **d**,
   12: 7 Endure hardship as **d**;
   12: 11 No **d** seems pleasant at the time,
Rev 3: 19 Those whom I love I rebuke and **d**.

DISCIPLINED (DISCIPLINE)
Jer 31: 18 'You **d** me like an unruly calf,
1Co 11: 32 we are being **d** so that we will not
Col 2: 5 delight to see how **d** you are
Titus 1: 8 upright, holy and **d**.
Heb 12: 7 For what children are not **d** by

DISCIPLINES (DISCIPLINE)
Dt 8: 5 so the Lord your God **d** you.
Pr 3: 12 because the Lord **d** those he
Heb 12: 6 the Lord **d** the one he loves,
   12: 10 but God **d** us for our good,

DISCLOSED
Lk 8: 17 nothing hidden that will not be **d**,

DISCOURAGED
Jos 1: 9 do not be **d**, for the Lord your
   10: 25 "Do not be afraid; do not be **d**.
1Ch 28: 20 Do not be afraid or **d**,
Isa 42: 4 or be **d** till he establishes justice
Col 3: 21 children, or they will become **d**.

DISCREDITED
2Co 6: 3 so that our ministry will not be **d**.

DISCRETION
1Ch 22: 12 May the Lord give you **d**
Pr 1: 4 knowledge and **d** to the young—
   2: 11 **D** will protect you,
   5: 2 that you may maintain **d** and your
   8: 12 I possess knowledge and **d**.
   11: 22 beautiful woman who shows no **d**.

DISCRIMINATED
Jas 2: 4 have you not **d** among yourselves

DISFIGURED
Isa 52: 14 his appearance was so **d** beyond

DISGRACE (DISGRACEFUL DISGRACES)
Pr 11: 2 then comes **d**, but with humility
   19: 26 is a child who brings shame and **d**.
Ac 5: 41 worthy of suffering **d** for the Name.
Heb 13: 13 the camp, bearing the **d** he bore.

DISGRACEFUL (DISGRACE)
Pr 10: 5 sleeps during harvest is a **d** son.
   17: 2 servant will rule over a **d** son

DISGRACES (DISGRACE)
Pr 28: 7 companion of gluttons **d** his father.
   29: 15 left undisciplined **d** its mother.

DISGUISE
Pr 26: 24 Enemies **d** themselves with their

DISHONEST
Pr	11: 1	The Lord detests **d** scales,
	29: 27	The righteous detest the **d**;
Lk	16: 10	whoever is **d** with very little will
1Ti	3: 8	wine, and not pursuing **d** gain.

DISHONOR (DISHONORS)
Lev	18: 7	" 'Do not **d** your father by having
Pr	30: 9	and so **d** the name of my God.
1Co	13: 5	It does not **d** others, it is not
	15: 43	it is sown in **d**, it is raised in glory;

DISHONORS (DISHONOR)
Dt	27: 16	is anyone who **d** their father

DISMAYED
Isa	41: 10	do not be **d**, for I am your God.

DISOBEDIENCE (DISOBEY)
Ro	5: 19	as through the **d** of the one man
	11: 32	has bound everyone over to **d** so
Heb	2: 2	and **d** received its just punishment,
	4: 6	did not go in because of their **d**,
	4: 11	by following their example of **d**.

DISOBEDIENT (DISOBEY)
2Ti	3: 2	proud, abusive, **d** to their parents,
Titus	1: 6	to the charge of being wild and **d**.
	1: 16	**d** and unfit for doing anything

DISOBEY (DISOBEDIENCE DISOBEDIENT)
Dt	11: 28	the curse if you **d** the commands
2Ch	24: 20	'Why do you **d** the Lord's
Ro	1: 30	of doing evil; they **d** their parents;

DISORDER
1Co	14: 33	For God is not a God of **d**
2Co	12: 20	slander, gossip, arrogance and **d**.
Jas	3: 16	there you find **d** and every evil

DISOWN
Pr	30: 9	I may have too much and **d** you
Mt	10: 33	will **d** before my Father in heaven.
	26: 35	to die with you, I will never **d** you."
2Ti	2: 12	If we **d** him, he will also **d** us;

DISPLAY (DISPLAYS)
Eze	39: 21	"I will **d** my glory among
1Ti	1: 16	Christ Jesus might **d** his immense

DISPLAYS (DISPLAY)
Isa	44: 23	Jacob, he **d** his glory in Israel.

DISPUTE (DISPUTES)
Pr	17: 14	the matter before a **d** breaks out.
1Co	6: 1	If any of you has a **d** with another,

DISPUTES (DISPUTE)
Pr	18: 18	Casting the lot settles **d** and keeps

DISQUALIFIED
1Co	9: 27	I myself will not be **d** for the prize.

DISREGARD
Pr	15: 32	Those who **d** discipline despise

DISREPUTE
2Pe	2: 2	will bring the way of truth into **d**.

DISSENSION
Ro	13: 13	debauchery, not in **d** and jealousy.

DISTINGUISH
1Ki	3: 9	and to **d** between right and wrong.
Heb	5: 14	have trained themselves to **d** good

DISTORT
2Co	4: 2	nor do we **d** the word of God.
2Pe	3: 16	ignorant and unstable people **d**,

DISTRESS (DISTRESSED)
Ps	18: 6	In my **d** I called to the Lord;
Jnh	2: 2	"In my **d** I called to the Lord,
Jas	1: 27	and widows in their **d** and to keep

DISTRESSED (DISTRESS)
Ro	14: 15	sister is **d** because of what you eat,

DIVIDED (DIVISION)
Mt	12: 25	"Every kingdom **d** against itself
Lk	23: 34	**d** up his clothes by casting lots.
1Co	1: 13	Is Christ **d**? Was Paul crucified

DIVINATION
Lev	19: 26	" 'Do not practice **d** or seek

DIVINE
Ro	1: 20	his eternal power and **d** nature—
2Co	10: 4	they have **d** power to demolish
2Pe	1: 4	may participate in the **d** nature,

DIVISION (DIVIDED DIVISIONS DIVISIVE)
Lk	12: 51	peace on earth? No, I tell you, but **d**.
1Co	12: 25	there should be no **d** in the body,

DIVISIONS (DIVISION)
Ro	16: 17	to watch out for those who cause **d**
1Co	1: 10	and that there be no **d** among you,
	11: 18	as a church, there are **d** among you,

DIVISIVE (DIVISION)
Titus	3: 10	Warn a **d** person once,

DIVORCE (DIVORCES)
Mt	19: 3	for a man to **d** his wife for any
1Co	7: 11	a husband must not **d** his wife.

DIVORCES (DIVORCE)
Mal	2: 16	man who hates and **d** his wife,"

DOCTOR
Mt	9: 12	"It is not the healthy who need a **d**,

DOCTRINE
1Ti	4: 16	Watch your life and **d** closely.
Titus	2: 1	what is appropriate to sound **d**.

DOMINION
Ps	22: 28	for **d** belongs to the Lord and he

DOOR
Ps	141: 3	keep watch over the **d** of my lips.
Mt	6: 6	close the **d** and pray to your Father,
	7: 7	and the **d** will be opened to you.
Rev	3: 20	I stand at the **d** and knock.

DOORKEEPER
Ps	84: 10	I would rather be a **d** in the house

DOUBLE-EDGED
Heb	4: 12	Sharper than any **d** sword,
Rev	1: 16	of his mouth was a sharp, **d** sword.
	2: 12	of him who has the sharp, **d** sword.

DOUBLE-MINDED (MIND)
Ps	119: 113	I hate **d** people, but I love your law.
Jas	1: 8	Such a person is **d** and unstable

DOUBT
Mt	14: 31	faith," he said, "why did you **d**?"
	21: 21	if you have faith and do not **d**,
Mk	11: 23	and does not **d** in their heart

CONCORDANCE

Jas 1: 6 you must believe and not **d**,
Jude : 22 Be merciful to those who **d**;

DOWNCAST
Ps 42: 5 Why, my soul, are you **d**?
2Co 7: 6 who comforts the **d**, comforted us

DRAW (DRAWING DRAWS)
Mt 26: 52 "for all who **d** the sword will die
Jn 12: 32 earth, will **d** all people to myself."
Heb 10: 22 let us **d** near to God with a sincere

DRAWING (DRAW)
Lk 21: 28 your redemption is **d** near."

DRAWS (DRAW)
Jn 6: 44 the Father who sent me **d** them,

DREADFUL
Heb 10: 31 It is a **d** thing to fall into the hands

DRESS
1Ti 2: 9 want the women to **d** modestly,

DRINK (DRUNK DRUNKARDS DRUNKENNESS)
Pr 5: 15 **D** water from your own cistern,
Lk 12: 19 eat, **d** and be merry." '
Jn 7: 37 who is thirsty come to me and **d**.
1Co 12: 13 were all given the one Spirit to **d**.

DRIVES
1Jn 4: 18 But perfect love **d** out fear,

DROP
Pr 17: 14 so **d** the matter before a dispute
Isa 40: 15 Surely the nations are like a **d**

DRUNK (DRINK)
Eph 5: 18 Do not get **d** on wine, which leads

DRUNKARDS (DRINK)
Pr 23: 21 for **d** and gluttons become poor,
1Co 6: 10 the greedy nor **d** nor slanderers

DRUNKENNESS (DRINK)
Lk 21: 34 **d** and the anxieties of life,
Ro 13: 13 not in carousing and **d**,
Gal 5: 21 and envy; **d**, orgies, and the like.
1Pe 4: 3 living in debauchery, lust, **d**, orgies,

DRY
Isa 53: 2 and like a root out of **d** ground.
Eze 37: 4 bones and say to them, '**D** bones,

DUST
Ge 2: 7 a man from the **d** of the ground
Ps 103: 14 he remembers that we are **d**.
Ecc 3: 20 come from **d**, and to **d** all return.

DUTY
Ecc 12: 13 for this is the **d** of all mankind.
Ac 23: 1 I have fulfilled my **d** to God in all
1Co 7: 3 husband should fulfill his marital **d**

DWELL (DWELLING DWELLS)
1Ki 8: 27 "But will God really **d** on earth?
Ps 23: 6 I will **d** in the house of the LORD
Isa 43: 18 do not **d** on the past.
Eph 3: 17 Christ may **d** in your hearts
Col 1: 19 to have all his fullness **d** in him,
 3: 16 of Christ **d** among you richly

DWELLING (DWELL)
Eph 2: 22 built together to become a **d**

DWELLS (DWELL)
1Co 3: 16 that God's Spirit **d** in your midst?

EAGER
Pr 31: 13 and flax and works with **e** hands.
1Pe 5: 2 dishonest gain, but **e** to serve;

EAGLE'S (EAGLES)
Ps 103: 5 your youth is renewed like the **e**.

EAGLES (EAGLE'S)
Isa 40: 31 They will soar on wings like **e**;

EAR (EARS)
1Co 2: 9 eye has seen, what no **e** has heard,
 12: 16 And if the **e** should say, "Because I

EARS (EAR)
Job 42: 5 My **e** had heard of you but now my
Ps 34: 15 and his **e** are attentive to their cry;
Pr 21: 13 Whoever shuts their **e** to the cry
2Ti 4: 3 to say what their itching **e** want

EARTH (EARTHLY)
Ge 1: 1 God created the heavens and the **e**.
Ps 24: 1 The **e** is the LORD's,
 108: 5 let your glory be over all the **e**.
Isa 6: 3 the whole **e** is full of his glory."
 51: 6 the **e** will wear out like a garment
 55: 9 the heavens are higher than the **e**,
 66: 1 throne, and the **e** is my footstool.
Jer 23: 24 "Do not I fill heaven and **e**?"
Hab 2: 20 let all the **e** be silent before him.
Mt 6: 10 will be done, on **e** as it is in heaven.
 16: 19 you bind on **e** will be bound
 24: 35 Heaven and **e** will pass away,
 28: 18 and on **e** has been given to me.
Lk 2: 14 on **e** peace to those on whom his
1Co 10: 26 for, "The **e** is the Lord's,
Php 2: 10 heaven and on **e** and under the **e**,
2Pe 3: 13 to a new heaven and a new **e**,

EARTHLY (EARTH)
Php 3: 19 Their mind is set on **e** things.
Col 3: 2 on things above, not on **e** things.

EAST
Ps 103: 12 as far as the **e** is from the west,

EASY
Mt 11: 30 For my yoke is **e** and my burden is

EAT (EATING)
Ge 2: 17 you must not **e** from the tree
Isa 55: 1 have no money, come, buy and **e**!
 65: 25 the lion will **e** straw like the ox,
Mt 26: 26 his disciples, saying, "Take and **e**;
Ro 14: 2 faith allows them to **e** anything,
1Co 8: 13 if what I **e** causes my brother
 10: 31 So whether you **e** or drink
2Th 3: 10 is unwilling to work shall not **e**."

EATING (EAT)
Ro 14: 17 kingdom of God is not a matter of **e**

EDICT
Heb 11: 23 they were not afraid of the king's **e**.

EDIFIES
1Co 14: 4 speaks in a tongue **e** themselves,

EFFECT
Isa 32: 17 its **e** will be quietness
Heb 9: 18 was not put into **e** without blood.

EFFORT
Lk 13: 24 "Make every **e** to enter through

Ro	9:	16	depend on human desire or **e**,
	14:	19	Let us therefore make every **e** to do
Eph	4:	3	Make every **e** to keep the unity
Heb	4:	11	make every **e** to enter that rest,
	12:	14	Make every **e** to live in peace
2Pe	1:	5	make every **e** to add to your faith
	3:	14	make every **e** to be found spotless,

ELAH
Son of Baasha; king of Israel (1Ki 16:6–14).

ELDERLY (ELDERS)
Lev 19: 32 show respect for the **e** and revere

ELDERS (ELDERLY)
1Ti 5: 17 The **e** who direct the affairs

ELECTION
Ro 9: 11 God's purpose in **e** might stand:
2Pe 1: 10 to confirm your calling and **e**.

ELI
High priest in youth of Samuel (1Sa 1–4). Blessed Hannah (1Sa 1:12–18); raised Samuel (1Sa 2:11–26).

ELIJAH
Prophet; predicted famine in Israel (1Ki 17:1; Jas 5:17). Fed by ravens (1Ki 17:2–6). Raised Sidonian widow's son (1Ki 17:7–24). Defeated prophets of Baal at Carmel (1Ki 18:16–46). Ran from Jezebel (1Ki 19:1–9). Prophesied death of Azariah (2Ki 1). Succeeded by Elisha (1Ki 19:19–21; 2Ki 2:1–18). Taken to heaven in whirlwind (2Ki 2:11–12).

Return prophesied (Mal 4:5–6); equated with John the Baptist (Mt 17:9–13; Mk 9:9–13; Lk 1:17). Appeared with Moses in transfiguration of Jesus (Mt 17:1–8; Mk 9:1–8).

ELISHA
Prophet; successor of Elijah (1Ki 19:16–21); inherited his cloak (2Ki 2:1–18). Miracles of (2Ki 2–6).

ELIZABETH
Mother of John the Baptist, relative of Mary (Lk 1:5–58).

EMBITTER
Col 3: 21 Fathers, do not **e** your children,

EMPEROR
1Pe 2: 17 of believers, fear God, honor the **e**.

EMPTY
Mt 12: 36 for every **e** word they have spoken.
Eph 5: 6 no one deceive you with **e** words,
1Pe 1: 18 you were redeemed from the **e** way

ENABLE (ABLE)
Lk 1: 74 to **e** us to serve him without fear
Ac 4: 29 **e** your servants to speak your word

ENABLED (ABLE)
Lev 26: 13 **e** you to walk with heads held high.
Jn 6: 65 me unless the Father has **e** them."

ENABLES (ABLE)
Php 3: 21 by the power that **e** him to bring

ENCAMPS
Ps 34: 7 the Lᴏʀᴅ **e** around those who fear

ENCOURAGE (ENCOURAGEMENT ENCOURAGING)
Ps 10: 17 you **e** them, and you listen to their
Ac 15: 32 said much to **e** and strengthen
Ro 12: 8 if it is to **e**, then give

1Th	4:	18	Therefore **e** one another with these
2Ti	4:	2	correct, rebuke and **e**—
Titus	2:	6	Similarly, **e** the young men to be
Heb	3:	13	But **e** one another daily, as long as

ENCOURAGEMENT (ENCOURAGE)
Ac 4: 36 (which means "son of **e**"),
Ro 15: 4 the **e** they provide we might have
15: 5 **e** give you the same attitude of
Heb 12: 5 completely forgotten this word of **e**

ENCOURAGING (ENCOURAGE)
1Co 14: 3 their strengthening, **e** and comfort.
Heb 10: 25 habit of doing, but **e** one another—

END
Ps 119: 33 that I may follow it to the **e**.
Pr 14: 12 right, but in the **e** it leads to death.
19: 20 the **e** you will be counted among
23: 32 In the **e** it bites like a snake
Ecc 12: 12 making many books there is no **e**,
Mt 10: 22 stands firm to the **e** will be saved.
Lk 21: 9 but the **e** will not come right away."
1Co 15: 24 Then the **e** will come, when he

ENDURANCE (ENDURE)
Ro 15: 4 so that through the **e** taught
15: 5 May the God who gives **e**
2Co 1: 6 you patient **e** of the same sufferings
Col 1: 11 might so that you may have great **e**
1Ti 6: 11 faith, love, **e** and gentleness.
Titus 2: 2 and sound in faith, in love and in **e**.

ENDURE (ENDURANCE ENDURES)
Ps 72: 17 May his name **e** forever;
Pr 12: 19 Truthful lips **e** forever, but a lying
27: 24 for riches do not **e** forever,
Ecc 3: 14 everything God does will **e** forever;
Mal 3: 2 who can **e** the day of his coming?
2Ti 2: 12 if we **e**, we will also reign with him.
Heb 12: 7 **E** hardship as discipline;
Rev 3: 10 kept my command to **e** patiently,

ENDURES (ENDURE)
Ps 112: 9 poor, their righteousness **e** forever;
136: 1 *His love* **e** *forever.*
Da 9: 15 yourself a name that **e** to this day,
1Pe 1: 25 but the word of the Lord **e** forever."

ENEMIES (ENEMY)
Ps 23: 5 before me in the presence of my **e**.
Mic 7: 6 a man's **e** are the members of his
Mt 5: 44 love your **e** and pray for those who
Lk 20: 43 until I make your **e** a footstool

ENEMY (ENEMIES ENMITY)
Pr 24: 17 Do not gloat when your **e** falls;
25: 21 If your **e** is hungry, give him food
27: 6 trusted, but an **e** multiplies kisses.
1Co 15: 26 The last **e** to be destroyed is death.
1Ti 5: 14 and to give the **e** no opportunity
Jas 4: 4 of the world becomes an **e** of God.

ENJOY (JOY)
Dt 6: 2 and so that you may **e** long life.
Eph 6: 3 and that you may **e** long life
Heb 11: 25 than to **e** the fleeting pleasures

ENJOYMENT (JOY)
Ecc 4: 8 why am I depriving myself of **e**?"
1Ti 6: 17 us with everything for our **e**.

CONCORDANCE

ENLIGHTENED (LIGHT)
Eph 1: 18 eyes of your heart may be **e** in
Heb 6: 4 for those who have once been **e**,

ENMITY (ENEMY)
Ge 3: 15 I will put **e** between you

ENOCH
Walked with God and taken by him (Ge 5:18–24; Heb 11:5). Prophet (Jude 14).

ENTANGLED (ENTANGLES)
2Ti 2: 4 soldier gets **e** in civilian affairs,
2Pe 2: 20 Jesus Christ and are again **e** in it

ENTANGLES (ENTANGLED)
Heb 12: 1 hinders and the sin that so easily **e**.

ENTER (ENTERED ENTERS ENTRANCE)
Ps 100: 4 **E** his gates with thanksgiving
Mt 5: 20 will certainly not **e** the kingdom
7: 13 "**E** through the narrow gate.
18: 8 It is better for you to **e** life maimed
Mk 10: 15 like a little child will never **e** it."
10: 23 the rich to **e** the kingdom of God!"

ENTERED (ENTER)
Ro 5: 12 just as sin **e** the world through one
Heb 9: 12 he **e** the Most Holy Place once

ENTERS (ENTER)
Mk 7: 18 that nothing that **e** a person
Jn 10: 2 The one who **e** by the gate is

ENTERTAIN
1Ti 5: 19 Do not **e** an accusation against

ENTHRALLED
Ps 45: 11 Let the king be **e** by your beauty;

ENTHRONED (THRONE)
1Sa 4: 4 who is **e** between the cherubim.
Ps 2: 4 The One **e** in heaven laughs;
102: 12 But you, LORD, sit **e** forever;
Isa 40: 22 He sits **e** above the circle

ENTICE
Pr 1: 10 if sinful men **e** you, do not give
2Pe 2: 18 they **e** people who are just escaping

ENTIRE
Gal 5: 14 For the **e** law is fulfilled in keeping

ENTRUSTED (TRUST)
1Ti 6: 20 guard what has been **e** to your care.
2Ti 1: 12 to guard what I have **e** to him until
1: 14 good deposit that was **e** to you—
Jude : 3 once for all **e** to God's holy people.

ENVY
Pr 3: 31 Do not **e** the violent or choose any
14: 30 to the body, but **e** rots the bones.
1Co 13: 4 It does not **e**, it does not boast,

EPHRAIM
1. Second son of Joseph (Ge 41:52; 46:20). Blessed as firstborn by Jacob (Ge 48).
2. Synonymous with Northern Kingdom (Isa 7:17; Hos 5).

EQUAL
Isa 40: 25 Or who is my **e**?" says the Holy
Jn 5: 18 Father, making himself **e** with God.
1Co 12: 25 its parts should have **e** concern

EQUIP (EQUIPPED)
Eph 4: 12 to **e** his people for works of service,
Heb 13: 21 **e** you with everything good

EQUIPPED (EQUIP)
2Ti 3: 17 God may be thoroughly **e** for every

ERROR
Jas 5: 20 the **e** of their way will save them

ESAU
Firstborn of Isaac, twin of Jacob (Ge 25:21–26). Also called Edom (Ge 25:30). Sold Jacob his birthright (Ge 25:29–34); lost blessing (Ge 27). Reconciled to Jacob (Gen 33).

ESCAPE (ESCAPING)
Ro 2: 3 think you will **e** God's judgment?
Heb 2: 3 how shall we **e** if we ignore so great

ESCAPING (ESCAPE)
1Co 3: 15 only as one **e** through the flames.

ESTABLISH (ESTABLISHED ESTABLISHES)
Ge 6: 18 But I will **e** my covenant with you,
1Ch 28: 7 I will **e** his kingdom forever if he is
Ro 10: 3 of God and sought to **e** their own,

ESTABLISHED (ESTABLISH)
Ps 8: 2 infants you have **e** a stronghold

ESTABLISHES (ESTABLISH)
Pr 16: 9 course, but the LORD **e** their steps.

ESTEEM (ESTEEMED)
Isa 53: 3 and we held him in low **e**.

ESTEEMED (ESTEEM)
Pr 22: 1 to be **e** is better than silver or gold.

ESTHER
Jewess who lived in Persia; cousin of Mordecai (Est 2:7). Chosen queen of Xerxes (Est 2:8–18). Foiled Haman's plan to exterminate the Jews (Est 3–4; 7–9).

ETERNAL (ETERNITY)
Ps 16: 11 with **e** pleasures at your right hand.
111: 10 To him belongs **e** praise.
119: 89 Your word, LORD, is **e**;
Isa 26: 4 the LORD himself, is the Rock **e**.
Mt 19: 16 good thing must I do to get **e** life?"
25: 41 the **e** fire prepared for the devil
25: 46 but the righteous to **e** life."
Jn 3: 15 who believes may have **e** life
3: 16 him shall not perish but have **e** life.
3: 36 believes in the Son has **e** life,
4: 14 of water welling up to **e** life."
5: 24 believes him who sent me has **e** life
6: 47 the one who believes has **e** life.
6: 68 You have the words of **e** life.
10: 28 I give them **e** life, and they shall
17: 3 Now this is **e** life: that they know
Ro 1: 20 his **e** power and divine nature—
6: 23 of God is **e** life in Christ Jesus our
2Co 4: 17 for us an **e** glory that far outweighs
4: 18 temporary, but what is unseen is **e**.
1Ti 1: 16 believe in him and receive **e** life.
1: 17 Now to the King **e**, immortal,
Heb 9: 12 thus obtaining **e** redemption.
1Jn 5: 11 God has given us **e** life, and this life
5: 13 you may know that you have **e** life.

ETERNITY (ETERNAL)
Ps	93: 2	you are from all **e**.
Ecc	3: 11	has also set **e** in the human heart;

ETHIOPIAN
Jer	13: 23	Can an **E** change his skin

EUNUCHS
Mt	19: 12	choose to live like **e** for the sake

EVANGELIST (EVANGELISTS)
2Ti	4: 5	do the work of an **e**, discharge all

EVANGELISTS (EVANGELIST)
Eph	4: 11	the **e**, the pastors and teachers,

EVE
2Co	11: 3	afraid that just as **E** was deceived
1Ti	2: 13	For Adam was formed first, then **E**.

EVEN-TEMPERED
Pr	17: 27	whoever has understanding is **e**.

EVER (EVERLASTING FOREVER)
Ex	15: 18	"The Lord reigns for **e** and **e**."
Dt	8: 19	you **e** forget the Lord your God
Ps	5: 11	you be glad; let them **e** sing for joy.
	10: 16	The Lord is King for **e** and **e**;
	25: 3	one who hopes in you will **e** be put
	45: 6	throne, O God, will last for **e** and **e**;
	52: 8	I trust in God's unfailing love for **e**
	89: 33	nor will I **e** betray my faithfulness.
	145: 1	I will praise your name for **e** and **e**.
Pr	4: 18	shining **e** brighter till the full light
	5: 19	may you **e** be intoxicated with her
Isa	66: 8	Who has **e** heard of such things?
Jer	31: 36	"will Israel **e** cease being a nation
Da	7: 18	possess it forever—yes, for **e** and **e**.'
	12: 3	like the stars for **e** and **e**.
Mk	4: 12	" 'they may be **e** seeing but never
Jn	1: 18	No one has **e** seen God, but
Rev	1: 18	now look, I am alive for **e** and **e**!
	22: 5	And they will reign for **e** and **e**.

EVER-INCREASING (INCREASE)
Ro	6: 19	to impurity and to **e** wickedness,
2Co	3: 18	into his image with **e** glory,

EVERLASTING (EVER)
Dt	33: 27	and underneath are the **e** arms.
Ne	9: 5	your God, who is from **e** to **e**."
Ps	90: 2	world, from **e** to **e** you are God.
	139: 24	in me, and lead me in the way **e**.
Isa	9: 6	Mighty God, **E** Father,
	33: 14	of us can dwell with **e** burning?"
	35: 10	**e** joy will crown their heads.
	45: 17	by the Lord with an **e** salvation;
	54: 8	**e** kindness I will have compassion
	55: 3	I will make an **e** covenant with you,
	63: 12	them, to gain for himself **e** renown,
Jer	31: 3	"I have loved you with an **e** love;
Da	9: 24	to bring in **e** righteousness, to seal
	12: 2	some to **e** life, others to shame and **e** contempt.
2Th	1: 9	will be punished with **e** destruction
Jude	: 6	bound with **e** chains for judgment

EVER-PRESENT
Ps	46: 1	and strength, an **e** help in trouble.

EVIDENCE (EVIDENT)
Jn	14: 11	on the **e** of the works themselves.

EVIDENT (EVIDENCE)
Php	4: 5	Let your gentleness be **e** to all.

EVIL (EVILDOER EVILDOERS)
Ge	2: 9	of the knowledge of good and **e**.
Job	1: 1	he feared God and shunned **e**.
	1: 8	a man who fears God and shuns **e**."
	34: 10	Far be it from God to do **e**,
Ps	23: 4	will fear no **e**, for you are with me;
	34: 14	Turn from **e** and do good;
	51: 4	and done what is **e** in your sight;
	97: 10	those who love the Lord hate **e**,
	101: 4	have nothing to do with what is **e**.
Pr	8: 13	To fear the Lord is to hate **e**;
	11: 27	**e** comes to one who searches for it.
Isa	5: 20	who call **e** good and good **e**,
	13: 11	I will punish the world for its **e**,
Hab	1: 13	Your eyes are too pure to look on **e**;
Mt	5: 45	He causes his sun to rise on the **e**
	6: 13	but deliver us from the **e** one.'
	7: 11	you are **e**, know how to give
	12: 35	an **e** man brings **e** things out of the **e**
Jn	17: 15	you protect them from the **e** one.
Ro	2: 9	for every human being who does **e**:
	12: 9	Hate what is **e**; cling to what is
	12: 17	Do not repay anyone **e** for **e**.
	16: 19	and innocent about what is **e**.
1Co	13: 6	Love does not delight in **e**
	14: 20	In regard to **e** be infants, but in
Eph	6: 16	all the flaming arrows of the **e** one.
1Th	5: 22	reject every kind of **e**.
1Ti	6: 10	of money is a root of all kinds of **e**.
2Ti	2: 22	Flee the **e** desires of youth
Jas	1: 13	For God cannot be tempted by **e**,
1Pe	2: 16	your freedom as a cover-up for **e**;
	3: 9	Do not repay **e** with **e** or insult
	3: 9	the contrary, repay **e** with blessing,

EVILDOER (EVIL)
Pr	24: 20	for the **e** has no future hope,

EVILDOERS (EVIL)
Pr	24: 19	Do not fret because of **e** or be

EXACT
Heb	1: 3	the **e** representation of his being,

EXALT (EXALTED EXALTS)
Ps	30: 1	I will **e** you, Lord, for you lifted
	34: 3	let us **e** his name together.
	118: 28	you are my God, and I will **e** you.
Isa	24: 15	**e** the name of the Lord, the God
Mt	23: 12	For those who **e** themselves will be

EXALTED (EXALT)
2Sa	22: 47	**E** be my God, the Rock, my Savior!
1Ch	29: 11	you are **e** as head over all.
Ne	9: 5	and may it be **e** above all blessing
Ps	21: 13	Be **e** in your strength, Lord;
	46: 10	I will be **e** among the nations,
	57: 5	Be **e**, O God, above the heavens;
	97: 9	you are **e** far above all gods.
	99: 2	he is **e** over all the nations.
	108: 5	Be **e**, O God, above the heavens;
	148: 13	the Lord, for his name alone is **e**;
Isa	6: 1	high and **e**, seated on a throne;
	12: 4	and proclaim that his name is **e**.
	33: 5	The Lord is **e**, for he dwells
Eze	21: 26	The lowly will be **e** and the **e** will

1569

CONCORDANCE

Mt	23:	12	who humble themselves will be **e**.
Php	1:	20	now as always Christ will be **e**
	2:	9	Therefore God **e** him to the highest

EXALTS (EXALT)

| Ps | 75: | 7 | He brings one down, he **e** another. |
| Pr | 14: | 34 | Righteousness **e** a nation, but sin |

EXAMINE (EXAMINED)

Ps	26:	2	try me, **e** my heart and my mind;
Jer	17:	10	search the heart and **e** the mind,
La	3:	40	Let us **e** our ways and test them,
1Co	11:	28	to **e** themselves before they eat
2Co	13:	5	**E** yourselves to see whether you

EXAMINED (EXAMINE)

| Ac | 17: | 11 | **e** the Scriptures every day to see |

EXAMPLE (EXAMPLES)

Jn	13:	15	I have set you an **e** that you should
1Co	11:	1	Follow my **e**, as I follow the **e**
1Ti	4:	12	set an **e** for the believers in speech,
Titus	2:	7	everything set them an **e** by doing
1Pe	2:	21	leaving you an **e**, that you should

EXAMPLES (EXAMPLE)

1Co	10:	6	Now these things occurred as **e**
	10:	11	things happened to them as **e**
1Pe	5:	3	to you, but being **e** to the flock.

EXASPERATE

| Eph | 6: | 4 | Fathers, do not **e** your children; |

EXCEL (EXCELLENT)

| 1Co | 14: | 12 | try to **e** in those that build |
| 2Co | 8: | 7 | you also **e** in this grace of giving. |

EXCELLENT (EXCEL)

1Co	12:	31	yet I will show you the most **e** way.
Php	4:	8	if anything is **e** or praiseworthy—
1Ti	3:	13	have served well gain an **e** standing
Titus	3:	8	These things are **e** and profitable

EXCHANGED

| Ro | 1: | 23 | **e** the glory of the immortal God |
| | 1: | 25 | **e** the truth about God for a lie, |

EXCUSE (EXCUSES)

| Jn | 15: | 22 | now they have no **e** for their sin. |
| Ro | 1: | 20 | made, so that people are without **e**. |

EXCUSES (EXCUSE)

| Lk | 14: | 18 | "But they all alike began to make **e**. |

EXISTS

| Heb | 2: | 10 | and through whom everything **e**, |
| | 11: | 6 | to him must believe that he **e** |

EXPECT (EXPECTATION)

| Mt | 24: | 44 | at an hour when you do not **e** him. |

EXPECTATION (EXPECT)

| Ro | 8: | 19 | waits in eager **e** for the children |
| Heb | 10: | 27 | but only a fearful **e** of judgment |

EXPEL

| 1Co | 5: | 13 | "**E** the wicked person from among |

EXPENSIVE

| 1Ti | 2: | 9 | or gold or pearls or **e** clothes, |

EXPLOIT

| Pr | 22: | 22 | Do not **e** the poor because they are |
| 2Co | 12: | 17 | I **e** you through any of the men |

1570

EXPOSE

| 1Co | 4: | 5 | and will **e** the motives of the heart. |
| Eph | 5: | 11 | of darkness, but rather **e** them. |

EXTENDS

| Pr | 31: | 20 | poor and **e** her hands to the needy. |
| Lk | 1: | 50 | His mercy **e** to those who fear him, |

EXTINGUISHED

| 2Sa | 21: | 17 | the lamp of Israel will not be **e**." |

EXTOL

Job	36:	24	Remember to **e** his work,
Ps	34:	1	I will **e** the LORD at all times;
	68:	4	**e** him who rides on the clouds;
	95:	2	thanksgiving and **e** him with music
	109:	30	mouth I will greatly **e** the LORD;
	111:	1	I will **e** the LORD with all my
	115:	18	it is we who **e** the LORD,
	117:	1	**e** him, all you peoples.
	145:	2	and **e** your name for ever
	145:	10	your faithful people **e** you.
	147:	12	**E** the LORD, Jerusalem;

EXTORT

| Lk | 3: | 14 | "Don't **e** money and don't accuse |

EYE (EYES)

Ex	21:	24	**e** for **e**, tooth for tooth,
Ps	94:	9	Does he who formed the **e** not see?
Mt	5:	29	If your right **e** causes you
	5:	38	have heard that it was said, '**E** for **e**,
	7:	3	speck of sawdust in your brother's **e**
1Co	2:	9	"What no **e** has seen, what no ear
Col	3:	22	not only when their **e** is on you
Rev	1:	7	and "every **e** will see him,

EYES (EYE)

Nu	33:	55	remain will become barbs in your **e**
Jos	23:	13	your backs and thorns in your **e**,
2Ch	16:	9	For the **e** of the LORD range
Job	31:	1	"I made a covenant with my **e** not
	36:	7	not take his **e** off the righteous;
Ps	119:	18	Open my **e** that I may see
	121:	1	I lift up my **e** to the mountains—
	141:	8	But my **e** are fixed on you,
Pr	3:	7	Do not be wise in your own **e**;
	4:	25	Let your **e** look straight ahead;
	15:	3	The **e** of the LORD are
Isa	6:	5	and my **e** have seen the King,
Hab	1:	13	Your **e** are too pure to look on evil;
Jn	4:	35	open your **e** and look at the fields;
2Co	4:	18	So we fix our **e** not on what is seen,
Heb	12:	2	fixing our **e** on Jesus, the pioneer
Jas	2:	5	who are poor in the **e** of the world
1Pe	3:	12	For the **e** of the Lord are
Rev	7:	17	away every tear from their **e**.' "
	21:	4	will wipe every tear from their **e**.

EZEKIEL

Priest called to be prophet to the exiles (Eze 1–3).

EZRA

Priest and teacher of the Law who led a return of exiles to Israel to reestablish temple and worship (Ezr 7–8). Corrected intermarriage of priests (Ezr 9–10). Read Law at celebration of Feast of Tabernacles (Neh 8).

FACE (FACES)

| Ge | 32: | 30 | "It is because I saw God **f** to **f**, |

Ex	34:	29	that his **f** was radiant because he
Nu	6:	25	the Lᴏʀᴅ make his **f** shine on you
1Ch	16:	11	and his strength; seek his **f** always.
2Ch	7:	14	and seek my **f** and turn from their
Ps	4:	6	Let the light of your **f** shine on us.
	27:	8	My heart says of you, "Seek his **f**!"
	31:	16	Let your **f** shine on your servant;
	105:	4	and his strength; seek his **f** always.
	119:135		Make your **f** shine on your servant
Isa	50:	7	Therefore have I set my **f** like flint,
Mt	17:	2	His **f** shone like the sun, and his
1Co	13:	12	in a mirror; then we shall see **f** to **f**.
2Co	4:	6	glory displayed in the **f** of Christ.
1Pe	3:	12	the **f** of the Lord is against those
Rev	1:	16	His **f** was like the sun shining in all

FACES (FACE)

2Co	3:	18	unveiled **f** contemplate the Lord's

FACTIONS

Gal	5:	20	rage, selfish ambition, dissensions,

FADE

1Pe	5:	4	of glory that will never **f** away.

FAIL (FAILING FAILINGS FAILS)

1Ch	28:	20	He will not **f** you or forsake you
2Ch	34:	33	they did not **f** to follow the Lᴏʀᴅ,
Ps	89:	28	my covenant with him will never **f**.
Pr	15:	22	Plans **f** for lack of counsel,
Isa	51:	6	my righteousness will never **f**.
La	3:	22	for his compassions never **f**.
2Co	13:	5	unless, of course, you **f** the test?

FAILING (FAIL)

1Sa	12:	23	I should sin against the Lᴏʀᴅ by **f**

FAILINGS (FAIL)

Ro	15:	1	to bear with the **f** of the weak

FAILS (FAIL)

1Co	13:	8	Love never **f**. But where there are

FAINT

Isa	40:	31	weary, they will walk and not be **f**.

FAIR

Pr	1:	3	doing what is right and just and **f**;
Col	4:	1	your slaves with what is right and **f**,

FAITH (FAITHFUL FAITHFULLY FAITHFULNESS FAITHLESS)

2Ch	20:	20	Have **f** in the Lᴏʀᴅ your God
	20:	20	have **f** in his prophets
Mt	9:	29	"According to your **f** let it be done
	17:	20	if you have **f** as small as a mustard
	24:	10	many will turn away from the **f**
Mk	11:	22	"Have **f** in God," Jesus answered.
Lk	7:	9	I have not found such great **f** even
	12:	28	will he clothe you—you of little **f**!
	17:	5	said to the Lord, "Increase our **f**!"
	18:	8	comes, will he find **f** on the earth?"
Ac	14:	9	him, saw that he had **f** to be healed
	14:	27	how he had opened a door of **f**
Ro	1:	12	encouraged by each other's **f**.
	1:	17	"The righteous will live by **f**."
	1:	17	righteousness that is by **f** from first
	3:	22	righteousness is given through **f**
	3:	25	of his blood—to be received by **f**.
	4:	5	their **f** is credited as righteousness.
	5:	1	we have been justified through **f**,

Ro	10:	17	**f** comes from hearing the message,
	14:	1	Accept the one whose **f** is weak,
	14:	23	that does not come from **f** is sin.
	16:	26	the obedience that comes from **f**—
1Co	13:	2	have a **f** that can move mountains,
	13:	13	three remain: **f**, hope and love.
	16:	13	stand firm in the **f**; be courageous;
2Co	5:	7	For we live by **f**, not by sight.
	13:	5	to see whether you are in the **f**;
Gal	2:	16	we may be justified by **f** in Christ
	2:	20	body, I live by **f** in the Son of God,
	3:	11	"the righteous will live by **f**."
	3:	24	that we might be justified by **f**.
Eph	2:	8	you have been saved, through **f**—
	4:	5	one Lord, one **f**, one baptism;
	6:	16	take up the shield of **f**,
Col	1:	23	if you continue in your **f**,
1Th	5:	8	be sober, putting on **f** and love as
1Ti	2:	15	if they continue in **f**,
	4:	1	later times some will abandon the **f**
	5:	8	has denied the **f** and is worse than
	6:	12	Fight the good fight of the **f**.
2Ti	3:	15	salvation through **f** in Christ Jesus.
	4:	7	finished the race, I have kept the **f**.
Phm	:	6	with us in the **f** may be effective
Heb	10:	38	my righteous one will live by **f**.
	11:	1	Now **f** is confidence in what we
	11:	3	By **f** we understand that the
	11:	5	By **f** Enoch was taken from this
	11:	6	without **f** it is impossible to please
	11:	7	By **f** Noah, when warned
	11:	7	By his **f** he condemned the world
	11:	8	By **f** Abraham, when called to go
	11:	17	By **f** Abraham, when God tested
	11:	20	By **f** Isaac blessed Jacob and Esau
	11:	21	By **f** Jacob, when he was dying,
	11:	22	By **f** Joseph, when his end was
	11:	24	By **f** Moses, when he had grown
	11:	31	By **f** the prostitute Rahab,
	12:	2	Jesus, the pioneer and perfecter of **f**.
Jas	2:	14	Can such **f** save them?
	2:	17	In the same way, **f** by itself, if it is
	2:	26	is dead, so **f** without deeds is dead.
2Pe	1:	5	effort to add to your **f** goodness;
1Jn	5:	4	overcome the world, even our **f**.
Jude	:	3	contend for the **f** that was once

FAITHFUL (FAITH)

Nu	12:	7	he is **f** in all my house.
Dt	7:	9	he is the **f** God, keeping his
	32:	4	A **f** God who does no wrong,
2Sa	22:	26	"To the **f** you show yourself **f**,
Ps	16:	10	will you let your **f** one see decay.
	25:	10	and **f** toward those who keep
	31:	23	Love the Lᴏʀᴅ, all his **f** people!
	33:	4	right and true; he is **f** in all he does.
	37:	28	just and will not forsake his **f** ones.
	97:	10	for he guards the lives of his **f** ones
	116:	15	is the death of his **f** servants.
	145:	13	all he promises and **f** in all he does.
	145:	17	in all his ways and **f** in all he does.
	146:	6	he remains **f** forever.
Pr	31:	26	and instruction is on her tongue.
Mt	25:	21	'Well done, good and **f** servant!
	25:	21	You have been **f** with a few things;
Ro	12:	12	patient in affliction, **f** in prayer.

CONCORDANCE

1Co	4: 2	been given a trust must prove **f**.
	10: 13	And God is **f**; he will not let you be
1Th	5: 24	The one who calls you is **f**, and he
1Ti	3: 2	to be above reproach, **f** to his wife,
2Ti	2: 13	he remains **f**, for he cannot disown
Heb	3: 6	Christ is **f** as the Son over God's
	10: 23	profess, for he who promised is **f**.
1Pe	4: 10	as **f** stewards of God's grace in its
	4: 19	themselves to their **f** Creator
1Jn	1: 9	he is **f** and just and will forgive us
Rev	1: 5	who is the **f** witness, the firstborn
	2: 10	Be **f**, even to the point of death,
	19: 11	whose rider is called **F** and True.

FAITHFULLY (FAITH)

Dt	11: 13	So if you **f** obey the commands
1Sa	12: 24	and serve him **f** with all your heart;
1Ki	2: 4	if they walk **f** before me with all

FAITHFULNESS (FAITH)

Ps	51: 6	you desired **f** even in the womb;
	57: 10	your **f** reaches to the skies.
	85: 10	Love and **f** meet together;
	86: 15	to anger, abounding in love and **f**.
	89: 1	make your **f** known through all
	89: 14	love and **f** go before you.
	91: 4	his **f** will be your shield
	117: 2	the **f** of the LORD endures forever.
	119: 75	and that in **f** you have afflicted me.
Pr	3: 3	Let love and **f** never leave you;
Isa	11: 5	and **f** the sash around his waist.
La	3: 23	new every morning; great is your **f**.
Hab	2: 4	righteous person will live by his **f**—
Ro	3: 3	their unfaithfulness nullify God's **f**?
Gal	5: 22	forbearance, kindness, goodness, **f**,

FAITHLESS (FAITH)

Ps	119:158	I look on the **f** with loathing,
Jer	3: 22	"Return, **f** people; I will cure you
2Ti	2: 13	if we are **f**, he remains faithful,

FALL (FALLEN FALLS)

Ps	37: 24	he will not **f**, for the LORD
	69: 9	of those who insult you **f** on me.
Pr	11: 28	who trust in their riches will **f**,
Lk	11: 17	a house divided against itself will **f**.
Jn	16: 1	you so that you will not **f** away.
Ro	3: 23	and **f** short of the glory of God,
	14: 4	own master, servants stand or **f**.

FALLEN (FALL)

2Sa	1: 19	How the mighty have **f**!
Isa	14: 12	How you have **f** from heaven,
1Co	15: 20	of those who have **f** asleep.
Gal	5: 4	you have **f** away from grace.
1Th	4: 15	precede those who have **f** asleep.
Heb	6: 6	and who have **f** away, to be brought

FALLS (FALL)

Pr	24: 17	Do not gloat when your enemy **f**;
Jn	12: 24	a kernel of wheat **f** to the ground

FALSE (FALSEHOOD FALSELY)

Ex	20: 16	shall not give **f** testimony against
	23: 1	"Do not spread **f** reports.
Pr	13: 5	The righteous hate what is **f**,
	19: 5	A **f** witness will not go unpunished,
Mt	7: 15	"Watch out for **f** prophets.
	19: 18	steal, you shall not give **f** testimony,
	24: 11	and many **f** prophets will appear

Php	1: 18	whether from **f** motives or true,
1Ti	1: 3	not to teach **f** doctrines any longer
2Pe	2: 1	there will be **f** teachers among you.

FALSEHOOD (FALSE)

Ps	119:163	and detest **f** but I love your law.
Pr	30: 8	Keep **f** and lies far from me;
Eph	4: 25	each of you must put off **f**

FALSELY (FALSE)

Lev	19: 12	"'Do not swear **f** by my name
Lk	3: 14	money and don't accuse people **f**—
1Ti	6: 20	ideas of what is **f** called knowledge,

FALTER

Pr	24: 10	If you **f** in a time of trouble,
Isa	42: 4	he will not **f** or be discouraged till

FAMILIES (FAMILY)

Ps	68: 6	God sets the lonely in **f**, he leads

FAMILY (FAMILIES)

Pr	31: 15	she provides food for her **f**
Lk	9: 61	go back and say goodbye to my **f**."
	12: 52	in one **f** divided against each other,
1Ti	3: 4	He must manage his own **f** well
	3: 5	know how to manage his own **f**,
	5: 4	practice by caring for their own **f**

FAMINE

Ge	41: 30	seven years of **f** will follow them.
Am	8: 11	I will send a **f** through the land—
Ro	8: 35	or persecution or **f** or nakedness

FAN

2Ti	1: 6	this reason I remind you to **f**

FAST

Dt	13: 4	serve him and hold **f** to him.
Jos	22: 5	to hold **f** to him and to serve him
	23: 8	to hold **f** to the LORD your God,
Ps	119: 31	I hold **f** to your statutes, LORD;
	139: 10	me, your right hand will hold me **f**.
Mt	6: 16	"When you **f**, do not look somber
1Pe	5: 12	the true grace of God. Stand **f** in it.

FATHER (FATHER'S FATHERLESS FATHERS)

Ge	2: 24	That is why a man leaves his **f**
	17: 4	You will be the **f** of many nations.
Ex	20: 12	"Honor your **f** and your mother,
	21: 15	"Anyone who attacks their **f**
	21: 17	"Anyone who curses their **f**
Lev	18: 7	"'Do not dishonor your **f**
	19: 3	must respect your mother and **f**,
Dt	5: 16	"Honor your **f** and your mother,
	21: 18	son who does not obey his **f**
Ps	27: 10	Though my **f** and mother forsake
	68: 5	A **f** to the fatherless, a defender
Pr	10: 1	A wise son brings joy to his **f**,
	23: 22	Listen to your **f**, who gave you life,
	23: 24	The **f** of a righteous child has great
	28: 7	of gluttons disgraces his **f**.
	29: 3	loves wisdom brings joy to his **f**,
Isa	9: 6	Everlasting **F**, Prince of Peace.
Mt	6: 9	"'Our **F** in heaven, hallowed be
	10: 37	"Anyone who loves their **f**
	15: 4	said, 'Honor your **f** and mother'
	19: 5	this reason a man will leave his **f**
Lk	12: 53	**f** against son and son against **f**,
	23: 34	Jesus said, "**F**, forgive them,
Jn	6: 44	unless the **F** who sent me draws

Jn	6: 46	from God; only he has seen the **F**.
	8: 44	You belong to your **f**, the devil,
	10: 30	I and the **F** are one."
	14: 6	comes to the **F** except through me.
	14: 9	who has seen me has seen the **F**.
Ro	4: 11	he is the **f** of all who believe
2Co	6: 18	And, "I will be a **F** to you, and you
Eph	6: 2	"Honor your **f** and mother"—
Heb	12: 7	are not disciplined by their **f**?

FATHER'S (FATHER)

Pr	13: 1	wise son heeds his **f** instruction,
	19: 13	A foolish child is a **f** ruin,
Lk	2: 49	know I had to be in my **F** house?"
Jn	2: 16	Stop turning my **F** house
	10: 29	can snatch them out of my **F** hand.
	14: 2	My **F** house has many rooms;

FATHERLESS (FATHER)

Dt	10: 18	He defends the cause of the **f**
	24: 17	the foreigner or the **f** of justice,
	24: 19	the foreigner, the **f** and the widow,
Ps	68: 5	A father to the **f**, a defender
Pr	23: 10	or encroach on the fields of the **f**,

FATHERS (FATHER)

Lk	11: 11	"Which of you **f**, if your son asks
Eph	6: 4	**F**, do not exasperate your children;
Col	3: 21	**F**, do not embitter your children,

FATHOM

Job	11: 7	"Can you **f** the mysteries of God?
Ps	145: 3	his greatness no one can **f**.
Ecc	3: 11	no one can **f** what God has done
Isa	40: 28	his understanding no one can **f**.
1Co	13: 2	of prophecy and can **f** all mysteries

FAULT (FAULTS)

Mt	18: 15	sins, go and point out their **f**,
Php	2: 15	of God without **f** in a warped
Jas	1: 5	generously to all without finding **f**,
Jude	: 24	his glorious presence without **f**

FAULTFINDERS

Jude	: 16	These people are grumblers and **f**;

FAULTS (FAULT)

Ps	19: 12	Forgive my hidden **f**.

FAVORITISM

Ex	23: 3	do not show **f** to a poor person
Lev	19: 15	to the poor or **f** to the great,
Ac	10: 34	true it is that God does not show **f**
Ro	2: 11	For God does not show **f**.
Gal	2: 6	God does not show **f**—
Eph	6: 9	heaven, and there is no **f** with him.
Col	3: 25	for their wrongs, and there is no **f**.
1Ti	5: 21	and to do nothing out of **f**.
Jas	2: 1	Lord Jesus Christ must not show **f**.
	2: 9	But if you show **f**, you sin and are

FEAR (AFRAID FEARS)

Dt	6: 13	**F** the Lord your God, serve him
	10: 12	you but to **f** the Lord your God,
	31: 12	learn to **f** the Lord your God
Ps	19: 9	The **f** of the Lord is pure,
	23: 4	the darkest valley, I will **f** no evil,
	27: 1	and my salvation—whom shall I **f**?
	91: 5	You will not **f** the terror of night,
	111: 10	The **f** of the Lord is
Pr	8: 13	To **f** the Lord is to hate evil;

Pr	9: 10	The **f** of the Lord is
	10: 27	The **f** of the Lord adds length
	14: 27	The **f** of the Lord is a fountain
	15: 33	instruction is to **f** the Lord,
	16: 6	through the **f** of the Lord evil is
	19: 23	The **f** of the Lord leads to life;
	29: 25	**F** of man will prove to be a snare,
Ecc	5: 7	Therefore **f** God.
Isa	11: 3	will delight in the **f** of the Lord.
	41: 10	So do not **f**, for I am with you;
Lk	12: 5	will show you whom you should **f**:
Php	2: 12	to work out your salvation with **f**
1Jn	4: 18	There is no **f** in love. But perfect love drives out **f**,

FEARS (FEAR)

Job	1: 8	a man who **f** God and shuns evil."
Ps	34: 4	he delivered me from all my **f**.
Pr	31: 30	a woman who **f** the Lord is to be
1Jn	4: 18	The one who **f** is not made perfect

FEED

Jn	21: 15	Jesus said, "**F** my lambs."
	21: 17	Jesus said, "**F** my sheep.
Ro	12: 20	"If your enemy is hungry, **f** him;
Jude	: 12	shepherds who **f** only themselves.

FEET (FOOT)

Ps	8: 6	you put everything under their **f**:
	22: 16	they pierce my hands and my **f**.
	40: 2	he set my **f** on a rock and gave me
	110: 1	enemies a footstool for your **f**."
	119:105	Your word is a lamp to my **f**
Ro	10: 15	"How beautiful are the **f** of those
1Co	12: 21	And the head cannot say to the **f**,
	15: 25	has put all his enemies under his **f**.
Heb	12: 13	"Make level paths for your **f**,"

FELLOWSHIP

2Co	6: 14	**f** can light have with darkness?
	13: 14	the **f** of the Holy Spirit be with you
1Jn	1: 6	If we claim to have **f** with him
	1: 7	light, we have **f** with one another,

FEMALE

Ge	1: 27	male and **f** he created them.
Gal	3: 28	nor is there male and **f**, for you are

FERVOR

Ro	12: 11	but keep your spiritual **f**,

FIDELITY

Ro	1: 31	no understanding, no **f**, no love,

FIELD (FIELDS)

Mt	6: 28	See how the flowers of the **f** grow.
	13: 38	The **f** is the world, and the good
1Co	3: 9	you are God's **f**, God's building.

FIELDS (FIELD)

Lk	2: 8	shepherds living out in the **f**
Jn	4: 35	open your eyes and look at the **f**!

FIERY (FIRE)

1Pe	4: 12	do not be surprised at the **f** ordeal

FIG (FIGS)

Ge	3: 7	so they sewed **f** leaves together

FIGHT (FOUGHT)

Ex	14: 14	The Lord will **f** for you;
Dt	1: 30	is going before you, will **f** for you,
	3: 22	the Lord your God himself will **f**

CONCORDANCE

Ne	4: 20	Our God will **f** for us!"
Ps	35: 1	**f** against those who **f** against me.
Jn	18: 36	my servants would **f** to prevent my
1Co	9: 26	I do not **f** like a boxer beating
2Co	10: 4	The weapons we **f** with are not
1Ti	1: 18	them you may **f** the battle well,
	6: 12	**F** the good **f** of the faith.
2Ti	4: 7	I have fought the good **f**, I have

FIGS (FIG)

Lk	6: 44	People do not pick **f**

FILL (FILLED FILLS FULL FULLNESS FULLY)

Ge	1: 28	**f** the earth and subdue it.
Ps	16: 11	you will **f** me with joy in your
	81: 10	wide your mouth and I will **f** it.
Pr	28: 19	chase fantasies will have their **f**
Hag	2: 7	and I will **f** this house with glory,'
Jn	6: 26	you ate the loaves and had your **f**.
Ac	2: 28	you will **f** me with joy in your
Ro	15: 13	May the God of hope **f** you with all

FILLED (FILL)

Ps	72: 19	may the whole earth be **f** with his
	119: 64	The earth is **f** with your love,
Isa	11: 9	for the earth will be **f**
Eze	43: 5	glory of the Lord **f** the temple.
Hab	2: 14	For the earth will be **f**
Lk	1: 15	he will be **f** with the Holy Spirit
	1: 41	Elizabeth was **f** with the Holy Spirit.
Jn	12: 3	the house was **f** with the fragrance
Ac	2: 4	of them were **f** with the Holy Spirit
	4: 8	Then Peter, **f** with the Holy Spirit,
	9: 17	and be **f** with the Holy Spirit."
	13: 9	called Paul, **f** with the Holy Spirit,
Eph	5: 18	Instead, be **f** with the Spirit,
Php	1: 11	**f** with the fruit of righteousness

FILLS (FILL)

Nu	14: 21	of the Lord **f** the whole earth,
Ps	107: 9	and **f** the hungry with good things.
Eph	1: 23	him who **f** everything in every way.

FILTHY

Isa	64: 6	all our righteous acts are like **f** rags;
Col	3: 8	and **f** language from your lips.

FIND (FINDS FOUND)

Nu	32: 23	be sure that your sin will **f** you out.
Dt	4: 29	you will **f** him if you seek him
1Sa	23: 16	and helped him **f** strength in God.
Ps	91: 4	under his wings you will **f** refuge;
	112: 1	Lord, who **f** great delight in his
Pr	14: 22	those who plan what is good **f** love
	31: 10	wife of noble character who can **f**?
Jer	6: 16	and you will **f** rest for your souls.
Mt	7: 7	seek and you will **f**;
	11: 29	and you will **f** rest for your souls.
	16: 25	loses their life for me will **f** it.
Lk	18: 8	will he **f** faith on the earth?"
Jn	10: 9	come in and go out, and **f** pasture.

FINDS (FIND)

Ps	62: 1	Truly my soul **f** rest in God;
	119:162	promise like one who **f** great spoil.
Pr	18: 22	He who **f** a wife **f** what is good
Mt	7: 8	the one who seeks **f**; and to the one
	10: 39	Whoever **f** their life will lose it,
Lk	12: 37	whose master **f** them watching
	15: 4	go after the lost sheep until he **f** it?

FINISH (FINISHED)

Jn	4: 34	him who sent me and to **f** his work.
	5: 36	that the Father has given me to **f**—
Ac	20: 24	my only aim is to **f** the race
2Co	8: 11	Now **f** the work, so that your eager
Gal	3: 3	are you now trying to **f** by means
Jas	1: 4	Let perseverance **f** its work so

FINISHED (FINISH)

Ge	2: 2	seventh day God had **f** the work he
Jn	19: 30	the drink, Jesus said, "It is **f**."
2Ti	4: 7	the good fight, I have **f** the race,

FIRE (FIERY)

Ex	13: 21	in a pillar of **f** to give them light,
Lev	6: 12	The **f** on the altar must be kept
Isa	30: 27	and his tongue is a consuming **f**.
Jer	23: 29	"Is not my word like **f**,"
Mt	3: 11	you with the Holy Spirit and **f**.
	5: 22	will be in danger of the **f** of hell.
	25: 41	the eternal **f** prepared for the devil
Mk	9: 43	hell, where the **f** never goes out.
Ac	2: 3	to be tongues of **f** that separated
1Co	3: 13	It will be revealed with **f**, and the **f**
Heb	12: 29	for our "God is a consuming **f**."
Jas	3: 5	what a great forest is set on **f**
2Pe	3: 10	the elements will be destroyed by **f**,
Jude	: 23	by snatching them from the **f**;
Rev	20: 14	**f**. The lake of **f** is the second death.

FIRM

Ex	14: 13	Stand **f** and you will see
2Ch	20: 17	stand **f** and see the deliverance
Ps	33: 11	plans of the Lord stand **f** forever,
	37: 23	The Lord makes **f** the steps
	40: 2	and gave me a **f** place to stand.
	89: 2	that your love stands **f** forever,
	119: 89	it stands **f** in the heavens.
Zec	8: 23	nations will take **f** hold of one Jew
Mk	13: 13	the one who stands **f** to the end
1Co	16: 13	on your guard; stand **f** in the faith;
2Co	1: 24	because it is by faith you stand **f**.
Eph	6: 14	Stand **f** then, with the belt of truth
Col	4: 12	that you may stand **f** in all the will
2Th	2: 15	stand **f** and hold fast to the teachings
2Ti	2: 19	God's solid foundation stands **f**,
Heb	6: 19	anchor for the soul, **f** and secure.
1Pe	5: 9	Resist him, standing **f** in the faith,

FIRST

Isa	44: 6	I am the **f** and I am the last;
	48: 12	I am the **f** and I am the last.
Mt	5: 24	**F** go and be reconciled to them;
	6: 33	But seek **f** his kingdom and his
	7: 5	**f** take the plank out of your own
	20: 27	wants to be **f** must be your slave—
	22: 38	This is the **f** and greatest
	23: 26	**F** clean the inside of the cup
Mk	13: 10	the gospel must **f** be preached to all
Ac	11: 26	disciples were called Christians **f**
Ro	1: 16	**f** to the Jew, then to the Gentile.
1Co	12: 28	in the church **f** of all apostles,
2Co	8: 5	They gave themselves **f** of all
1Ti	2: 13	For Adam was formed **f**, then Eve.
Jas	3: 17	comes from heaven is **f** of all pure;
1Jn	4: 19	We love because he **f** loved us.
3Jn	: 9	who loves to be **f**, will not welcome
Rev	1: 17	I am the **F** and the Last.
	2: 4	have forsaken the love you had at **f**.

FIRSTBORN (BEAR)
Ex | 11: | 5 | Every **f** son in Egypt will die,

FIRSTFRUITS
Ex | 23: | 19 | "Bring the best of the **f** of your soil

FISH
Mk | 1: | 17 | I will send you out to **f** for people."
Lk | 5: | 10 | from now on you will **f** for people."

FITTING
Ps | 33: | 1 | it is **f** for the upright to praise him.
  | 147: | 1 | how pleasant and **f** to praise him!
Pr | 19: | 10 | It is not **f** for a fool to live
  | 26: | 1 | in harvest, honor is not **f** for a fool.
1Co | 14: | 40 | everything should be done in a **f**
Col | 3: | 18 | your husbands, as is **f** in the Lord.
Heb | 2: | 10 | to glory, it was **f** that God,

FIX (FIXING)
Dt | 11: | 18 | **F** these words of mine in your
Pr | 4: | 25 | **f** your gaze directly before you.
2Co | 4: | 18 | So we **f** our eyes not on what is
Heb | 3: | 1 | calling, **f** your thoughts on Jesus,

FIXING (FIX)
Heb | 12: | 2 | **f** our eyes on Jesus, the pioneer

FLAME (FLAMES FLAMING)
2Ti | 1: | 6 | you to fan into **f** the gift of God,

FLAMES (FLAME)
1Co | 3: | 15 | only as one escaping through the **f**.

FLAMING (FLAME)
Eph | 6: | 16 | you can extinguish all the **f** arrows

FLASH
1Co | 15: | 52 | in a **f**, in the twinkling of an eye,

FLATTER (FLATTERING FLATTERY)
Ps | 12: | 2 | they **f** with their lips but harbor
Job | 32: | 21 | no partiality, nor will I **f** anyone;
Jude | : | 16 | **f** others for their own advantage.

FLATTERING (FLATTER)
Ps | 12: | 3 | May the Lord silence all **f** lips
Pr | 26: | 28 | it hurts, and a **f** mouth works ruin.

FLATTERY (FLATTER)
Ro | 16: | 18 | **f** they deceive the minds of naive
1Th | 2: | 5 | You know we never used **f**, nor did

FLAWLESS
2Sa | 22: | 31 | The Lord's word is **f**;
Job | 11: | 4 | 'My beliefs are **f** and I am pure
Ps | 12: | 6 | And the words of the Lord are **f**,
  | 18: | 30 | The Lord's word is **f**;
Pr | 30: | 5 | "Every word of God is **f**; he is
SS | 5: | 2 | my darling, my dove, my **f** one.

FLEE
Ps | 139: | 7 | Where can I **f** from your presence?
1Co | 6: | 18 | **F** from sexual immorality.
  | 10: | 14 | my dear friends, **f** from idolatry.
1Ti | 6: | 11 | man of God, **f** from all this,
2Ti | 2: | 22 | **F** the evil desires of youth
Jas | 4: | 7 | the devil, and he will **f** from you.

FLEETING
Ps | 89: | 47 | Remember how **f** is my life.
Pr | 31: | 30 | is deceptive, and beauty is **f**;

FLESH
Ge | 2: | 23 | bone of my bones and **f** of my **f**;
  | 2: | 24 | to his wife, and they become one **f**.

Job | 19: | 26 | yet in my **f** I will see God;
Eze | 11: | 19 | of stone and give them a heart of **f**.
  | 36: | 26 | of stone and give you a heart of **f**.
Mt | 26: | 41 | spirit is willing, but the **f** is weak."
Mk | 10: | 8 | and the two will become one **f**.'
Jn | 1: | 14 | The Word became **f** and made his
  | 6: | 51 | bread is my **f**, which I will give
Ro | 8: | 4 | do not live according to the **f** but
  | 8: | 8 | realm of the **f** cannot please God.
1Co | 6: | 16 | said, "The two will become one **f**."
Gal | 3: | 3 | trying to finish by means of the **f**?
  | 5: | 19 | The acts of the **f** are obvious:
  | 5: | 24 | crucified the **f** with its passions
Eph | 5: | 31 | and the two will become one **f**."
  | 6: | 12 | For our struggle is not against **f**

FLOCK (FLOCKS)
Isa | 40: | 11 | He tends his **f** like a shepherd:
Eze | 34: | 2 | not shepherds take care of the **f**?
Zec | 11: | 17 | shepherd, who deserts the **f**!
Mt | 26: | 31 | the sheep of the **f** will be scattered.'
Ac | 20: | 28 | all the **f** of which the Holy Spirit
1Pe | 5: | 2 | of God's **f** that is under your care,

FLOCKS (FLOCK)
Lk | 2: | 8 | keeping watch over their **f** at night.

FLOG
Ac | 22: | 25 | **f** a Roman citizen who hasn't even

FLOODGATES
Mal | 3: | 10 | will not throw open the **f** of heaven

FLOURISHING
Ps | 52: | 8 | am like an olive tree **f** in the house

FLOW (FLOWING)
Nu | 13: | 27 | and it does **f** with milk and honey!
Jn | 7: | 38 | of living water will **f** from within

FLOWERS
Isa | 40: | 7 | The grass withers and the **f** fall,
Lk | 12: | 27 | "Consider how the wild **f** grow.

FLOWING (FLOW)
Ex | 3: | 8 | a land **f** with milk and honey—

FOLDING
Pr | 6: | 10 | a little **f** of the hands to rest—

FOLLOW (FOLLOWS)
Ex | 23: | 2 | "Do not **f** the crowd in doing
Lev | 18: | 4 | laws and be careful to **f** my decrees.
Dt | 5: | 1 | Learn them and be sure to **f** them.
Ps | 23: | 6 | love will **f** me all the days of my
Mt | 16: | 24 | and take up their cross and **f** me.
Jn | 10: | 4 | his sheep **f** him because they know
1Co | 14: | 1 | **F** the way of love and eagerly desire
Eph | 5: | 1 | **F** God's example, therefore,
Rev | 14: | 4 | They **f** the Lamb wherever he goes.

FOLLOWS (FOLLOW)
Jn | 8: | 12 | Whoever **f** me will never walk

FOOD (FOODS)
Pr | 20: | 13 | awake and you will have **f** to spare.
  | 22: | 9 | for they share their **f** with the poor.
  | 25: | 21 | enemy is hungry, give him **f** to eat;
  | 31: | 15 | she provides **f** for her family
Da | 1: | 8 | to defile himself with the royal **f**
Jn | 6: | 27 | Do not work for **f** that spoils, but for **f** that endures to eternal life,

CONCORDANCE

1Co   8:   8   **f** does not bring us near to God;
1Ti   6:   8   But if we have **f** and clothing,
Jas   2: 15   sister is without clothes and daily **f.**

FOODS (FOOD)
Mk   7: 19   this, Jesus declared all **f** clean.)

FOOL (FOOLISH FOOLISHNESS FOOLS)
Ps   14:   1   The **f** says in his heart, "There
Pr   15:   5   A **f** spurns a parent's discipline,
      26:   5   Answer a **f** according to his folly,
Mt   5: 22   And anyone who says, 'You **f!**'

FOOLISH (FOOL)
Pr   10:   1   a **f** son brings grief to his mother.
      17: 25   A **f** son brings grief to his father
Mt   7: 26   practice is like a **f** man who built
      25:   2   Five of them were **f** and five were
1Co   1: 27   God chose the **f** things of the world

FOOLISHNESS (FOOL)
1Co   1: 18   of the cross is **f** to those who are
      1: 25   the **f** of God is wiser than human
      2: 14   Spirit of God but considers them **f,**
      3: 19   of this world is **f** in God's sight.

FOOLS (FOOL)
Pr   14:   9   **F** mock at making amends for sin,
      17: 28   Even **f** are thought wise if they
      18:   2   **F** find no pleasure in understanding
      28: 26   who trust in themselves are **f,**
1Co   4: 10   We are **f** for Christ, but you are so

FOOT (FEET FOOTHOLD)
Jos   1:   3   every place where you set your **f,**
Isa   1:   6   the sole of your **f** to the top of your
1Co 12: 15   Now if the **f** should say, "Because I

FOOTHOLD (FOOT)
Eph   4: 27   and do not give the devil a **f.**

FORBEARANCE
Ro   3: 25   his **f** he had left the sins committed
Gal   5: 22   love, joy, peace, **f,** kindness,

FORBID
1Co 14: 39   and do not **f** speaking in tongues.

FOREIGNER (FOREIGNERS)
Ex   22: 21   "Do not mistreat or oppress a **f,**

FOREIGNERS (FOREIGNER)
1Pe   2: 11   urge you, as **f** and exiles, to abstain

FOREKNEW (KNOW)
Ro   8: 29   those God **f** he also predestined
      11:   2   not reject his people, whom he **f.**

FOREVER (EVER)
1Ch 16: 15   He remembers his covenant **f,**
      16: 34   for he is good; his love endures **f.**
Ps   9:   7   The LORD reigns **f;**
      23:   6   dwell in the house of the LORD **f.**
      33: 11   plans of the LORD stand firm **f,**
      86: 12   I will glorify your name **f.**
      92:   8   But you, LORD, are **f** exalted.
     110:   4   "You are a priest **f,** in the order
     119:111   Your statutes are my heritage **f;**
Jn   6: 51   Whoever eats this bread will live **f.**
      14: 16   to help you and be with you **f**—
1Co   9: 25   do it to get a crown that will last **f.**
1Th   4: 17   And so we will be with the Lord **f.**
Heb 13:   8   the same yesterday and today and **f.**

1Pe   1: 25   the word of the Lord endures **f.**"
1Jn   2: 17   does the will of God lives **f.**

FORFEIT
Lk   9: 25   and yet lose or **f** their very self?

FORGAVE (FORGIVE)
Ps   32:   5   And you **f** the guilt of my sin.
Lk   7: 42   him back, so he **f** the debts of both.
Eph   4: 32   other, just as in Christ God **f** you.
Col   2: 13   He **f** us all our sins,
      3: 13   Forgive as the Lord **f** you.

FORGET (FORGETS FORGETTING)
Dt   6: 12   that you do not **f** the LORD,
Ps   103:   2   my soul, and **f** not all his benefits—
     137:   5   If I **f** you, Jerusalem, may my right
Isa 49: 15   Though she may **f,** I will not **f** you!
Heb   6: 10   will not **f** your work and the love

FORGETS (FORGET)
Jn   16: 21   is born she **f** the anguish because
Jas   1: 24   immediately **f** what he looks like.

FORGETTING (FORGET)
Php   3: 13   **F** what is behind and straining

FORGIVE (FORGAVE FORGIVENESS FORGIVING)
2Ch   7: 14   and I will **f** their sin and will heal
Ps   19: 12   **F** my hidden faults.
Mt   6: 12   And **f** us our debts, as we also have
      6: 14   if you **f** other people when they sin
      18: 21   many times shall I **f** my brother
Mk   11: 25   anything against anyone, **f** them,
Lk   11:   4   **F** us our sins, for we also **f** everyone
      23: 34   "Father, **f** them, for they do not
Col   3: 13   **F** as the Lord forgave you.
1Jn   1:   9   and will **f** us our sins and purify

FORGIVENESS (FORGIVE)
Ps   130:   4   But with you there is **f,** so that we
Ac   10: 43   in him receives **f** of sins through
Eph   1:   7   through his blood, the **f** of sins,
Col   1: 14   we have redemption, the **f** of sins,
Heb   9: 22   the shedding of blood there is no **f.**

FORGIVING (FORGIVE)
Ne   9: 17   But you are a **f** God,
Eph   4: 32   to one another, **f** each other, just as

FORMED
Ge   2:   7   the LORD God **f** a man
Ps   103: 14   for he knows how we are **f,**
Isa 45: 18   be empty, but **f** it to be inhabited—
Ro   9: 20   what is **f** say to the one who **f** it,
1Ti   2: 13   For Adam was **f** first, then Eve.
Heb 11:   3   that the universe was **f** at God's

FORSAKE (FORSAKEN)
Jos   1:   5   I will never leave you nor **f** you.
      24: 16   us to **f** the LORD to serve other
2Ch 15:   2   you, but if you **f** him, he will **f** you.
Ps   27: 10   Though my father and mother **f** me,
Isa 55:   7   Let the wicked **f** their ways
Heb 13:   5   will I leave you; never will I **f** you."

FORSAKEN (FORSAKE)
Ezr   9:   9   God has not **f** us in our bondage.
Ps   22:   1   God, my God, why have you **f** me?
      37: 25   I have never seen the righteous **f**
Mt   27: 46   my God, why have you **f** me?").
Rev   2:   4   You have **f** the love you had at first.

1576

FORTIFIED
Pr 18: 10 name of the Lord is a **f** tower;

FORTRESS
Ps 18: 2 is my rock, my **f** and my deliverer;
71: 3 me, for you are my rock and my **f**.

FOUGHT (FIGHT)
2Ti 4: 7 I have **f** the good fight, I have

FOUND (FIND)
1Ch 28: 9 If you seek him, he will be **f** by you;
Isa 55: 6 Seek the Lord while he may be **f**;
Da 5: 27 on the scales and **f** wanting.
Lk 15: 6 I have **f** my lost sheep.'
15: 9 I have **f** my lost coin.'
Ac 4: 12 Salvation is **f** in no one else,

FOUNDATION
Isa 28: 16 a precious cornerstone for a sure **f**;
1Co 3: 11 can lay any **f** other than the one
Eph 2: 20 built on the **f** of the apostles
2Ti 2: 19 God's solid **f** stands firm,

FOXES
Mt 8: 20 "**F** have dens and birds have nests,

FRANKINCENSE
Mt 2: 11 him with gifts of gold, **f** and myrrh.

FREE (FREED FREEDOM FREELY)
Ps 146: 7 The Lord sets prisoners **f**,
Jn 8: 32 truth, and the truth will set you **f**."
Ro 6: 18 You have been set **f** from sin
Gal 3: 28 neither slave nor **f**, nor is there
1Pe 2: 16 Live as **f** people, but do not use

FREED (FREE)
Rev 1: 5 has **f** us from our sins by his blood,

FREEDOM (FREE)
Ro 8: 21 brought into the **f** and glory
2Co 3: 17 the Spirit of the Lord is, there is **f**.
Gal 5: 13 But do not use your **f** to indulge
1Pe 2: 16 do not use your **f** as

FREELY (FREE)
Isa 55: 7 to our God, for he will **f** pardon.
Mt 10: 8 **F** you have received; **f** give.
Ro 3: 24 and all are justified **f** by his grace
Eph 1: 6 which he has **f** given us in the One

FRIEND (FRIENDS)
Ex 33: 11 face to face, as one speaks to a **f**.
Pr 17: 17 A **f** loves at all times, and a brother
18: 24 there is a **f** who sticks closer than
27: 6 Wounds from a **f** can be trusted,
27: 10 Do not forsake your **f** or a **f** of your
Jas 4: 4 to be a **f** of the world becomes

FRIENDS (FRIEND)
Pr 16: 28 and a gossip separates close **f**.
18: 24 who has unreliable **f** soon comes
Zec 13: 6 I was given at the house of my **f**.'
Jn 15: 13 to lay down one's life for one's **f**.

FRUIT (FRUITFUL)
Ps 1: 3 which yields its **f** in season
Pr 11: 30 The **f** of the righteous is a tree
Mt 7: 16 By their **f** you will recognize them.
Jn 15: 2 branch that does bear **f** he prunes
Gal 5: 22 But the **f** of the Spirit is love, joy,
Rev 22: 2 bearing twelve crops of **f**, yielding
its **f** every month.

FRUITFUL (FRUIT)
Ge 1: 22 "Be **f** and increase in number
Ps 128: 3 wife will be like a **f** vine within
Jn 15: 2 so that it will be even more **f**.

FULFILL (FULFILLED FULFILLMENT)
Ps 116: 14 I will **f** my vows to the Lord
Mt 5: 17 to abolish them but to **f** them.
1Co 7: 3 The husband should **f** his marital

FULFILLED (FULFILL)
Pr 13: 19 A longing **f** is sweet to the soul,
Mk 14: 49 But the Scriptures must be **f**."
Ro 13: 8 whoever loves others has **f** the law.

FULFILLMENT (FULFILL)
Ro 13: 10 Therefore love is the **f** of the law.

FULL (FILL)
Ps 127: 5 Blessed is the man whose quiver is **f**
Pr 31: 11 Her husband has **f** confidence in her
Isa 6: 3 the whole earth is **f** of his glory."
Lk 6: 45 speaks what the heart is **f** of.
Jn 10: 10 may have life, and have it to the **f**.
Ac 6: 3 who are known to be **f** of the Spirit

FULLNESS (FILL)
Col 1: 19 to have all his **f** dwell in him,
2: 9 in Christ all the **f** of the Deity lives

FULLY (FILL)
1Ki 8: 61 may your hearts be **f** committed
2Ch 16: 9 whose hearts are **f** committed
Ps 119: 4 precepts that are to be **f** obeyed.
119:138 righteous; they are **f** trustworthy.
1Co 15: 58 Always give yourselves **f**

FUTURE
Ps 37: 37 a **f** awaits those who seek peace.
Pr 23: 18 There is surely a **f** hope for you,
Ro 8: 38 neither the present nor the **f**,

GABRIEL
Angel who interpreted Daniel's visions (Da 8:16–26; 9:20–27); announced births of John (Lk 1:11–20), Jesus (Lk 1:26–38).

GAIN (GAINED)
Ps 60: 12 With God we will **g** the victory,
Mk 8: 36 for someone to **g** the whole world,
1Co 13: 3 but do not have love, I **g** nothing.
Php 1: 21 me, to live is Christ and to die is **g**.
3: 8 them garbage, that I may **g** Christ
1Ti 6: 6 with contentment is great **g**.
1Pe 5: 2 not pursuing dishonest **g**, but eager

GAINED (GAIN)
Ro 5: 2 through whom we have **g** access

GALILEE
Isa 9: 1 in the future he will honor **G**

GALL
Mt 27: 34 Jesus wine to drink, mixed with **g**;

GAP
Eze 22: 30 stand before me in the **g** on behalf

GARBAGE
Php 3: 8 I consider them **g**, that I may gain

GARDENER
Jn 15: 1 true vine, and my Father is the **g**.

CONCORDANCE

GARMENT (GARMENTS)
Ps	102: 26	they will all wear out like a **g**.
Mt	9: 16	the patch will pull away from the **g**,
Jn	19: 23	This **g** was seamless, woven in one
	19: 24	them and cast lots for my **g**."

GARMENTS (GARMENT)
Ge	3: 21	The LORD God made **g** of skin
Isa	61: 10	For he has clothed me with **g**
	63: 1	with his **g** stained crimson?

GATE (GATES)
Mt	7: 13	"Enter through the narrow **g**.
Jn	10: 9	I am the **g**; whoever enters through

GATES (GATE)
Ps	100: 4	Enter his **g** with thanksgiving
Mt	16: 18	the **g** of Hades will not overcome

GATHER (GATHERS)
Zec	14: 2	I will **g** all the nations to Jerusalem
Mt	12: 30	and whoever does not **g** with me
	23: 37	longed to **g** your children together,

GATHERS (GATHER)
Isa	40: 11	He **g** the lambs in his arms
Mt	23: 37	as a hen **g** her chicks under her

GAVE (GIVE)
Ezr	2: 69	their ability they **g** to the treasury
Job	1: 21	The LORD **g** and the LORD has
Jn	3: 16	so loved the world that he **g** his
2Co	8: 5	They **g** themselves first of all
Gal	2: 20	loved me and **g** himself for me.
1Ti	2: 6	who **g** himself as a ransom for all

GAZE
Ps	27: 4	to **g** on the beauty of the LORD
Pr	4: 25	fix your **g** directly before you.

GENEALOGIES
1Ti	1: 4	themselves to myths and endless **g**.

GENERATIONS
Ps	22: 30	**g** will be told about the Lord.
	102: 12	renown endures through all **g**.
	145: 13	dominion endures through all **g**.
Lk	1: 48	now on all **g** will call me blessed,
Eph	3: 5	other **g** as it has now been revealed

GENEROUS
Ps	112: 5	Good will come to those who are **g**
Pr	22: 9	The **g** will themselves be blessed,
2Co	9: 5	Then it will be ready as a **g** gift,
1Ti	6: 18	and to be **g** and willing to share.

GENTILE (GENTILES)
Ro	1: 16	first to the Jew, then to the **G**.
	10: 12	no difference between Jew and **G**—

GENTILES (GENTILE)
Isa	42: 6	for the people and a light for the **G**,
Ro	3: 9	**G** alike are all under the power
	11: 13	as I am the apostle to the **G**, I take
1Co	1: 23	block to Jews and foolishness to **G**,

GENTLE (GENTLENESS)
Pr	15: 1	A **g** answer turns away wrath,
Mt	11: 29	for I am **g** and humble in heart,
	21: 5	to you, **g** and riding on a donkey,
1Co	4: 21	I come in love and with a **g** spirit?
1Pe	3: 4	unfading beauty of a **g** and quiet

GENTLENESS (GENTLE)
2Co	10: 1	By the humility and **g** of Christ,
Gal	5: 23	**g** and self-control.
Php	4: 5	Let your **g** be evident to all.
Col	3: 12	kindness, humility, **g** and patience.
1Ti	6: 11	faith, love, endurance and **g**.
1Pe	3: 15	But do this with **g** and respect,

GETHSEMANE
Mt	26: 36	his disciples to a place called **G**,

GIDEON
Judge, also called Jerub-Baal; freed Israel from Midianites (Jdg 6–8; Heb 11:32). Given sign of fleece (Jdg 8:36–40).

GIFT (GIFTS)
Pr	21: 14	A **g** given in secret soothes anger,
Mt	5: 23	you are offering your **g** at the altar
Ac	2: 38	you will receive the **g** of the Holy
Ro	6: 23	the **g** of God is eternal life in Christ
1Co	7: 7	of you has your own **g** from God;
2Co	8: 12	the **g** is acceptable according
	9: 15	be to God for his indescribable **g**!
Eph	2: 8	yourselves, it is the **g** of God—
1Ti	4: 14	Do not neglect your **g**, which was
2Ti	1: 6	you to fan into flame the **g** of God,
Jas	1: 17	good and perfect **g** is from above,
1Pe	4: 10	should use whatever **g** you have

GIFTS (GIFT)
Ro	11: 29	for God's **g** and his call are
	12: 6	We have different **g**,
1Co	12: 4	There are different kinds of **g**,
	12: 31	Now eagerly desire the greater **g**.
	14: 1	and eagerly desire **g** of the Spirit,
	14: 12	Since you are eager for **g**

GILEAD
Jer	8: 22	Is there no balm in **G**? Is there no

GIVE (GAVE GIVEN GIVER GIVES GIVING)
Nu	6: 26	toward you and **g** you peace." '
1Sa	1: 11	forget your servant but **g** her a son,
	1: 11	I will **g** him to the LORD for all
2Ch	15: 7	be strong and do not **g** up, for your
Pr	21: 26	the righteous **g** without sparing.
	23: 26	**g** me your heart and let your eyes
	28: 27	Those who **g** to the poor will lack
	30: 8	but **g** me only my daily bread.
Eze	36: 26	I will **g** you a new heart and put
Mt	6: 11	**G** us today our daily bread.
	10: 8	Freely you have received; freely **g**.
	22: 21	them, "So **g** back to Caesar what is
Mk	8: 37	what can anyone **g** in exchange
Lk	6: 38	**G**, and it will be given to you.
	11: 13	Father in heaven **g** the Holy Spirit
Jn	10: 28	I **g** them eternal life, and they shall
	13: 34	"A new command I **g** you:
Ac	20: 35	'It is more blessed to **g** than
Ro	12: 8	encourage, then **g** encouragement;
	12: 8	if it is giving, then **g** generously;
	13: 7	**G** to everyone what you owe them:
	14: 12	then, each of us will **g** an account
2Co	9: 7	should **g** what you have decided
Rev	14: 7	voice, "Fear God and **g** him glory,

GIVEN (GIVE)
Nu	8: 16	Israelites who are to be **g** wholly
Ps	115: 16	but the earth he has **g** to mankind.

Isa	9:	6	a son is **g**, and the government
Mt	6:	33	all these things will be **g** to you as
	7:	7	"Ask and it will be **g** to you;
Lk	22:	19	saying, "This is my body **g** for you;
Jn	3:	27	can receive only what is **g** them
Ro	5:	5	Holy Spirit, who has been **g** to us.
1Co	4:	2	those who have been **g** a trust must
	12:	13	and we were all **g** the one Spirit
Eph	4:	7	of us grace has been **g** as Christ

GIVER (GIVE)

Pr	18:	16	ushers the **g** into the presence
2Co	9:	7	for God loves a cheerful **g**.

GIVES (GIVE)

Ps	119:130		unfolding of your words **g** light;
Pr	14:	30	A heart at peace **g** life to the body,
	15:	30	good news **g** health to the bones.
Isa	40:	29	He **g** strength to the weary
Mt	10:	42	anyone **g** even a cup of cold water
Jn	6:	63	The Spirit **g** life; the flesh counts
1Co	15:	57	He **g** us the victory through our
2Co	3:	6	the letter kills, but the Spirit **g** life.

GIVING (GIVE)

Ne	8:	8	**g** the meaning so that the people
Ps	19:	8	LORD are right, **g** joy to the heart.
Mt	6:	4	so that your **g** may be in secret.
2Co	8:	7	you also excel in this grace of **g**.

GLAD (GLADNESS)

Ps	31:	7	I will be **g** and rejoice in your love,
	46:	4	whose streams make **g** the city
	97:	1	LORD reigns, let the earth be **g**;
	118:	24	let us rejoice today and be **g**.
Zec	2:	10	"Shout and be **g**, Daughter Zion.
Mt	5:	12	Rejoice and be **g**, because great is

GLADNESS (GLAD)

Ps	45:	15	Led in with joy and **g**, they enter
	51:	8	Let me hear joy and **g**;
	100:	2	Worship the LORD with **g**;
Jer	31:	13	I will turn their mourning into **g**;

GLORIFIED (GLORY)

Jn	13:	31	"Now the Son of Man is **g** and God
			is **g** in him.
Ro	8:	30	those he justified, he also **g**.
2Th	1:	10	he comes to be **g** in his holy people

GLORIFY (GLORY)

Ps	34:	3	**G** the LORD with me; let us exalt
	86:	12	I will **g** your name forever.
Mt	5:	16	deeds and **g** your Father in heaven.
Jn	13:	32	God will **g** the Son in himself,
	17:	1	**G** your Son, that your Son may **g**

GLORIOUS (GLORY)

Ps	45:	13	All **g** is the princess within her
	111:	3	**G** and majestic are his deeds,
	145:	5	They speak of the **g** splendor
Isa	4:	2	the LORD will be beautiful and **g**,
	12:	5	LORD, for he has done **g** things;
	42:	21	to make his law great and **g**.
	63:	15	from your lofty throne, holy and **g**.
Mt	19:	28	Son of Man sits on his **g** throne,
Lk	9:	30	and Elijah, appeared in **g** splendor
Ac	2:	20	of the great and **g** day of the Lord.
2Co	3:	8	of the Spirit be even more **g**?
Php	3:	21	so that they will be like his **g** body.
Jude	:	24	you before his **g** presence without

GLORY (GLORIFIED GLORIFY GLORIOUS)

Ex	15:	11	awesome in **g**, working wonders?
	33:	18	said, "Now show me your **g**."
1Sa	4:	21	"The **G** has departed from Israel"
1Ch	16:	24	Declare his **g** among the nations,
	16:	28	ascribe to the LORD **g**
	29:	11	power and the **g** and the majesty
Ps	8:	5	crowned them with **g** and honor.
	19:	1	The heavens declare the **g** of God;
	24:	7	that the King of **g** may come in.
	29:	1	beings, ascribe to the LORD **g**
	34:	2	I will **g** in the LORD;
	72:	19	the whole earth be filled with his **g**.
	96:	3	Declare his **g** among the nations,
Pr	19:	11	is to one's **g** to overlook an offense.
	25:	2	It is the **g** of God to conceal
	25:	2	a matter is the **g** of kings.
Isa	6:	3	the whole earth is full of his **g**."
	42:	8	I will not yield my **g** to another
	48:	11	I will not yield my **g** to another.
Eze	43:	2	and I saw the **g** of the God of Israel
Mt	24:	30	of heaven, with power and great **g**.
	25:	31	the Son of Man comes in his **g**,
Mk	8:	38	in his Father's **g** with the holy
	13:	26	in clouds with great power and **g**.
Lk	2:	9	and the **g** of the Lord shone around
	2:	14	"**G** to God in the highest heaven,
Jn	1:	14	have seen his **g**, the **g** of the one
	17:	5	your presence with the **g** I had
	17:	24	and to see my **g**, the **g** you have
Ac	7:	2	God of **g** appeared to our father
Ro	1:	23	exchanged the **g** of the immortal
	3:	23	and fall short of the **g** of God,
	8:	18	with the **g** that will be revealed
	9:	4	theirs the divine **g**, the covenants,
1Co	10:	31	you do, do it all for the **g** of God.
	11:	7	since he is the image and **g** of God;
	11:	7	but woman is the **g** of man.
	15:	43	sown in dishonor, it is raised in **g**;
2Co	3:	10	what was glorious has no **g** now
	3:	18	faces contemplate the Lord's **g**,
	4:	17	us an eternal **g** that far outweighs
Php	4:	19	the riches of his **g** in Christ Jesus.
Col	1:	27	is Christ in you, the hope of **g**.
	3:	4	you also will appear with him in **g**.
1Ti	3:	16	on in the world, was taken up in **g**.
Titus	2:	13	appearing of the **g** of our great God
Heb	1:	3	The Son is the radiance of God's **g**
	2:	7	crowned them with **g** and honor
1Pe	1:	24	all their **g** is like the flowers
Rev	4:	11	to receive **g** and honor and power,
	21:	23	for the **g** of God gives it light,

GLUTTONS

Titus	1:	12	always liars, evil brutes, lazy **g**."

GNASHING

Mt	8:	12	will be weeping and **g** of teeth."

GNAT

Mt	23:	24	You strain out a **g** but swallow

GOAL

2Co	5:	9	So we make it our **g** to please him,
Php	3:	14	on toward the **g** to win the prize

GOAT (GOATS SCAPEGOAT)

Isa	11:	6	leopard will lie down with the **g**,

CONCORDANCE

GOATS (GOAT)
Nu 7: 17 five male **g** and five male lambs

GOD (GOD'S GODLINESS GODLY GODS)
Ge 1: 1 beginning **G** created the heavens
    1: 2 of **G** was hovering over the waters.
    1: 26 Then **G** said, "Let us make
    1: 27 So **G** created mankind in his own
    1: 31 **G** saw all that he had made, and it
    2: 3 Then **G** blessed the seventh day
    2: 22 the Lord **G** made a woman
    3: 21 The Lord **G** made garments
    3: 23 So the Lord **G** banished him
    5: 22 walked faithfully with **G** 300 years
    6: 2 sons of **G** saw that the daughters
    9: 16 everlasting covenant between **G**
   17: 1 to him and said, "I am **G** Almighty;
   21: 33 name of the Lord, the Eternal **G**.
   22: 8 "**G** himself will provide the lamb
   28: 12 the angels of **G** were ascending
   32: 28 because you have struggled with **G**
   32: 30 "It is because I saw **G** face to face,
   35: 10 **G** said to him, "Your name is
   41: 51 said, "It is because **G** has made me
   50: 20 me, but **G** intended it for good
Ex 2: 24 **G** heard their groaning and he
    3: 6 he said, "I am the **G** of your father,
    3: 6 because he was afraid to look at **G**.
    6: 7 know that I am the Lord your **G**,
    8: 10 is no one like the Lord our **G**.
   13: 18 So **G** led the people around
   15: 2 He is my **G**, and I will praise him,
   17: 9 with the staff of **G** in my hands."
   19: 3 Then Moses went up to **G**,
   20: 2 "I am the Lord your **G**,
   20: 5 the Lord your **G**, am a jealous **G**,
   20: 19 But do not have **G** speak to us
   22: 28 "Do not blaspheme **G** or curse
   31: 18 stone inscribed by the finger of **G**.
   34: 6 the compassionate and gracious **G**,
   34: 14 name is Jealous, is a jealous **G**.
Lev 18: 21 not profane the name of your **G**.
   19: 2 I, the Lord your **G**, am holy.
   26: 12 walk among you and be your **G**,
Nu 22: 38 I must speak only what **G** puts
   23: 19 **G** is not human, that he should lie,
Dt 1: 17 anyone, for judgment belongs to **G**.
    3: 22 the Lord your **G** himself will
    3: 24 For what **g** is there in heaven
    4: 24 **G** is a consuming fire, a jealous **G**.
    4: 31 the Lord your **G** is a merciful **G**;
    4: 39 day that the Lord is **G** in heaven
    5: 11 the name of the Lord your **G**,
    5: 14 is a sabbath to the Lord your **G**.
    5: 26 voice of the living **G** speaking
    6: 4 The Lord our **G**, the Lord is
    6: 5 Love the Lord your **G** with all
    6: 13 Fear the Lord your **G**, serve him
    6: 16 Do not put the Lord your **G**
    7: 9 is **G**; he is the faithful **G**,
    7: 12 the Lord your **G** will keep his
    7: 21 is a great and awesome **G**.
    8: 5 the Lord your **G** disciplines you.
   10: 12 what does the Lord your **G** ask you
          but to fear the Lord your **G**,
   10: 14 To the Lord your **G** belong

Dt 10: 17 For the Lord your **G** is **G** of gods
   11: 13 to love the Lord your **G**
   13: 3 The Lord your **G** is testing you
   13: 4 It is the Lord your **G** you must
   15: 6 the Lord your **G** will bless you
   19: 9 to love the Lord your **G**
   25: 16 the Lord your **G** detests anyone
   29: 29 things belong to the Lord our **G**,
   30: 2 return to the Lord your **G**
   30: 16 today to love the Lord your **G**,
   30: 20 you may love the Lord your **G**,
   31: 6 the Lord your **G** goes with you;
   32: 3 Oh, praise the greatness of our **G**!
   32: 4 A faithful **G** who does no wrong,
   33: 27 The eternal **G** is your refuge,
Jos 1: 9 the Lord your **G** will be with you
    14: 8 the Lord my **G** wholeheartedly.
    22: 5 to love the Lord your **G**, to walk
    22: 34 that the Lord is **G**.
    23: 11 careful to love the Lord your **G**.
    23: 14 the Lord your **G** gave you has
Jdg 16: 28 Please, **G**, strengthen me just once
Ru 1: 16 be my people and your **G** my **G**.
1Sa 2: 2 there is no Rock like our **G**.
    2: 3 for the Lord is a **G** who knows,
    2: 25 **G** may mediate for the offender;
   10: 26 men whose hearts **G** had touched.
   12: 12 the Lord your **G** was your king.
   17: 26 defy the armies of the living **G**?"
   17: 46 know that there is a **G** in Israel.
   30: 6 found strength in the Lord his **G**.
2Sa 14: 14 But that is not what **G** desires;
   22: 3 my **G** is my rock, in whom I take
   22: 31 "As for **G**, his way is perfect:
1Ki 4: 29 **G** gave Solomon wisdom and very
    8: 23 there is no **G** like you in heaven
    8: 27 "But will **G** really dwell on earth?
    8: 61 committed to the Lord our **G**,
   18: 21 If the Lord is **G**, follow him;
   18: 37 are **G**, and that you are turning
   20: 28 think the Lord is a **g** the hills
2Ki 19: 15 you alone are **G** over all
1Ch 16: 35 Cry out, "Save us, **G** our Savior;
   28: 2 for the footstool of our **G**, and I
   28: 9 acknowledge the **G** of your father,
   29: 10 Lord, the **G** of our father Israel,
   29: 17 my **G**, that you test the heart and
2Ch 2: 4 for the Name of the Lord my **G**
    5: 14 the Lord filled the temple of **G**.
    6: 18 will **G** really dwell on earth
   18: 13 can tell him only what my **G** says."
   20: 6 you not the **G** who is in heaven?
   25: 8 for **G** has the power to help
   30: 9 for the Lord your **G** is gracious
   33: 12 the favor of the Lord his **G**
Ezr 8: 22 "The gracious hand of our **G** is
    9: 6 my **G**, to lift up my face to you,
    9: 13 our **G**, you have punished us less
Ne 1: 5 the great and awesome **G**,
    8: 8 from the Book of the Law of **G**,
    9: 17 But you are a forgiving **G**,
    9: 32 "Now therefore, our **G**, the great **G**,
Job 1: 1 he feared **G** and shunned evil.
    2: 10 Shall we accept good from **G**,
    4: 17 mortal be more righteous than **G**?
    5: 17 is the one whom **G** corrects;

Job	11: 7	you fathom the mysteries of **G**?
	19: 26	yet in my flesh I will see **G**;
	22: 13	Yet you say, 'What does **G** know?
	25: 4	a mortal be righteous before **G**?
	33: 14	For **G** does speak—now one way,
	34: 12	unthinkable that **G** would do wrong,
	36: 26	How great is **G**—
	37: 22	**G** comes in awesome majesty.
Ps	18: 2	my **G** is my rock, in whom I take
	18: 28	my **G** turns my darkness into light.
	19: 1	The heavens declare the glory of **G**;
	22: 1	My **G**, my **G**, why have you
	29: 3	the **G** of glory thunders, the LORD
	31: 14	I say, "You are my **G**."
	40: 3	mouth, a hymn of praise to our **G**.
	40: 8	I desire to do your will, my **G**;
	42: 2	My soul thirsts for **G**, for the living
	42: 2	When can I go and meet with **G**?
	42: 11	Put your hope in **G**, for I will yet
	45: 6	O **G**, will last for ever and ever;
	46: 1	**G** is our refuge and strength,
	46: 10	"Be still, and know that I am **G**;
	47: 7	For **G** is the King of all the earth;
	50: 3	Our **G** comes and will not be silent
	51: 1	O **G**, according to your unfailing
	51: 10	O **G**, and renew a steadfast spirit
	51: 17	sacrifice, O **G**, is a broken spirit;
	62: 7	and my honor depend on **G**;
	65: 5	and righteous deeds, **G** our Savior,
	66: 1	Shout for joy to **G**, all the earth!
	66: 16	Come and hear, all you who fear **G**;
	68: 6	**G** sets the lonely in families,
	71: 17	my youth, **G**, you have taught
	71: 19	Who is like you, **G**?
	71: 22	harp for your faithfulness, my **G**;
	73: 26	but **G** is the strength of my heart
	77: 13	What **g** is as great as our **G**?
	78: 19	They spoke against **G**,
	81: 1	Sing for joy to **G** our strength;
	84: 2	my flesh cry out for the living **G**.
	84: 10	the house of my **G** than dwell
	86: 12	you, Lord my **G**, with all my heart;
	89: 7	of the holy ones is greatly feared;
	90: 2	to everlasting you are **G**.
	91: 2	fortress, my **G**, in whom I trust."
	95: 7	for he is our **G** and we are
	100: 3	Know that the LORD is **G**. It is he
	108: 1	My heart, O **G**, is steadfast;
	113: 5	Who is like the LORD our **G**,
	139: 23	Search me, **G**, and know my heart;
Pr	3: 4	a good name in the sight of **G**
	25: 2	It is the glory of **G** to conceal
	30: 5	"Every word of **G** is flawless;
Ecc	3: 11	can fathom what **G** has done
	11: 5	cannot understand the work of **G**,
	12: 13	of the matter: Fear **G** and keep his
Isa	9: 6	Mighty **G**, Everlasting Father,
	37: 16	you alone are **G** over all
	40: 3	in the desert a highway for our **G**.
	40: 8	the word of our **G** endures forever."
	40: 28	The LORD is the everlasting **G**,
	41: 10	not be dismayed, for I am your **G**.
	44: 6	apart from me there is no **G**.
	52: 7	who say to Zion, "Your **G** reigns!"
	55: 7	and to our **G**, for he will freely
	57: 21	says my **G**, "for the wicked."

Isa	59: 2	have separated you from your **G**;
	61: 10	my soul rejoices in my **G**.
	62: 5	so will your **G** rejoice over you.
Jer	23: 23	"Am I only a **G** nearby,"
	31: 33	I will be their **G**, and they will be
	32: 27	the LORD, the **G** of all mankind.
Eze	28: 13	You were in Eden, the garden of **G**;
Da	3: 17	the **G** we serve is able to deliver us
	9: 4	the great and awesome **G**,
Hos	12: 6	But you must return to your **G**;
Joel	2: 13	Return to the LORD your **G**, for he
Am	4: 12	Israel, prepare to meet your **G**."
Mic	6: 8	and to walk humbly with your **G**.
Na	1: 2	is a jealous and avenging **G**;
Zec	14: 5	Then the LORD my **G** will come,
Mal	3: 8	"Will a mere mortal rob **G**?
Mt	1: 23	(which means "**G** with us").
	5: 8	pure in heart, for they will see **G**.
	6: 24	You cannot serve both **G**
	19: 6	Therefore what **G** has joined
	19: 26	but with **G** all things are possible."
	22: 21	Caesar's, and to **G** what is God's."
	22: 37	" 'Love the Lord your **G** with all
	27: 46	(which means "My **G**, my **G**,
Mk	12: 29	The Lord our **G**, the Lord is one.
	16: 19	*at the right hand of* **G**.
Lk	1: 37	For no word from **G** will ever fail."
	1: 47	my spirit rejoices in **G** my Savior,
	10: 9	'The kingdom of **G** has come near
	10: 27	" 'Love the Lord your **G** with all
	18: 19	"No one is good—except **G** alone.
Jn	1: 1	and the Word was with **G**, and the
		Word was **G**.
	1: 18	No one has ever seen **G**, but
	1: 18	who is himself **G** and is in closest
	3: 16	For **G** so loved the world that he
	4: 24	**G** is spirit, and his worshipers must
	7: 17	to do the will of **G** will find
	14: 1	You believe in **G**;
	20: 28	said to him, "My Lord and my **G**!"
Ac	2: 24	But **G** raised him from the dead,
	5: 4	lied just to human beings but to **G**."
	5: 29	"We must obey **G** rather than
	7: 55	to heaven and saw the glory of **G**,
	17: 23	inscription: TO AN UNKNOWN **G**.
	20: 27	to you the whole will of **G**.
	20: 32	"Now I commit you to **G**
Ro	1: 17	righteousness of **G** is revealed—
	2: 11	For **G** does not show favoritism.
	3: 4	Let **G** be true, and every human
	3: 23	and fall short of the glory of **G**,
	4: 24	**G** will credit righteousness—
	5: 8	**G** demonstrates his own love for us
	6: 23	the gift of **G** is eternal life in Christ
	8: 28	in all things **G** works for the good
	11: 22	the kindness and sternness of **G**:
	14: 12	give an account of ourselves to **G**.
1Co	1: 20	not **G** made foolish the wisdom
	2: 9	the things **G** has prepared for those
	3: 6	it, but **G** has been making it grow.
	6: 20	Therefore honor **G** with your
	7: 24	they were in when **G** called them.
	8: 8	food does not bring us near to **G**;
	10: 13	**G** is faithful; he will not let you
	10: 31	you do, do it all for the glory of **G**.
	14: 33	For **G** is not a **G** of disorder

CONCORDANCE

1Co	15:	28	him, so that **G** may be all in all.
2Co	1:	9	not rely on ourselves but on **G**,
	2:	14	But thanks be to **G**, who always
	3:	5	our competence comes from **G**.
	4:	7	this all-surpassing power is from **G**
	5:	19	that **G** was reconciling the world
	5:	21	become the righteousness of **G**.
	6:	16	we are the temple of the living **G**.
	9:	7	for **G** loves a cheerful giver.
	9:	8	**G** is able to bless you abundantly,
Gal	2:	6	**G** does not show favoritism—
	6:	7	**G** cannot be mocked.
Eph	2:	10	**G** prepared in advance for us
	4:	6	one **G** and Father of all, who is
Php	2:	6	being in very nature **G**, did not
			consider equality with **G**
	4:	19	And my **G** will meet all your needs
1Th	2:	4	not trying to please people but **G**,
	4:	7	For **G** did not call us to be impure,
	4:	9	yourselves have been taught by **G**
	5:	9	For **G** did not appoint us to suffer
1Ti	2:	5	there is one **G** and one mediator
	4:	4	For everything **G** created is good,
	5:	4	for this is pleasing to **G**.
Titus	2:	13	of the glory of our great **G**
Heb	1:	1	the past **G** spoke to our ancestors
	4:	12	For the word of **G** is alive
	6:	10	**G** is not unjust; he will not forget
	10:	31	fall into the hands of the living **G**.
	11:	6	faith it is impossible to please **G**,
	12:	10	but **G** disciplines us for our good,
	12:	29	for our "**G** is a consuming fire."
	13:	15	us continually offer to **G** a sacrifice
Jas	1:	13	For **G** cannot be tempted by evil,
	2:	19	You believe that there is one **G**.
	2:	23	"Abraham believed **G**, and it was
	4:	4	the world becomes an enemy of **G**.
	4:	8	Come near to **G** and he will come
1Pe	4:	11	who speaks the very words of **G**.
2Pe	1:	21	from **G** as they were carried along
1Jn	1:	5	him and declare to you: **G** is light;
	2:	5	love for **G** is truly made complete
	3:	20	that **G** is greater than our hearts,
	4:	7	another, for love comes from **G**.
	4:	7	has been born of **G** and knows **G**.
	4:	9	This is how **G** showed his love
	4:	11	Dear friends, since **G** so loved us,
	4:	12	No one has ever seen **G**; but if we
	4:	16	Whoever lives in love lives in **G**,
Rev	4:	8	holy is the Lord **G** Almighty,'
	7:	17	**G** will wipe away every tear
	19:	6	For our Lord **G** Almighty reigns.

GOD-BREATHED (BREATHED)

2Ti	3:	16	All Scripture is **G** and is useful

GOD'S (GOD)

2Ch	20:	15	For the battle is not yours, but **G**.
Job	37:	14	stop and consider **G** wonders.
Ps	52:	8	I trust in **G** unfailing love for ever
	69:	30	I will praise **G** name in song
Mk	3:	35	Whoever does **G** will is my brother
Jn	10:	36	because I said, 'I am **G** Son'?
Ro	2:	3	think you will escape **G** judgment?
	2:	4	that **G** kindness is intended
	3:	3	nullify **G** faithfulness?
	7:	22	my inner being I delight in **G** law;

Ro	9:	16	desire or effort, but on **G** mercy.
	11:	29	for **G** gifts and his call are
	12:	2	test and approve what **G** will is—
	13:	6	for the authorities are **G** servants,
1Co	7:	19	Keeping **G** commands is what
2Co	6:	2	now is the time of **G** favor, now is
Eph	1:	7	with the riches of **G** grace
	5:	1	Follow **G** example, therefore,
1Th	4:	3	It is **G** will that you should be
	5:	18	for this is **G** will for you in Christ
1Ti	6:	1	so that **G** name and our teaching
2Ti	2:	19	**G** solid foundation stands firm,
Titus	1:	7	an overseer manages **G** household,
Heb	1:	3	The Son is the radiance of **G** glory
	9:	24	to appear for us in **G** presence.
	11:	3	was formed at **G** command,
1Pe	2:	15	For it is **G** will that by doing good
	3:	4	which is of great worth in **G** sight.

GODLINESS (GOD)

1Ti	2:	2	quiet lives in all **g** and holiness.
	4:	8	value, but **g** has value for all things,
	6:	6	**g** with contentment is great gain.
	6:	11	and pursue righteousness, **g**, faith,

GODLY (GOD)

2Co	7:	10	**G** sorrow brings repentance
	11:	2	jealous for you with a **g** jealousy.
2Ti	3:	12	live a **g** life in Christ Jesus will be
2Pe	3:	11	You ought to live holy and **g** lives

GODS (GOD)

Ex	20:	3	shall have no other **g** before me.
Ac	19:	26	by human hands are no **g** at all.

GOLD

Job	23:	10	tested me, I will come forth as **g**.
Ps	19:	10	precious than **g**, than much pure **g**;
	119:127		love your commands more than **g**,
Pr	22:	1	esteemed is better than silver or **g**.

GOLGOTHA

Jn	19:	17	(which in Aramaic is called **G**).

GOLIATH

Philistine giant killed by David (1Sa 17; 21:9).

GOOD

Ge	1:	4	God saw that the light was **g**,
	1:	31	he had made, and it was very **g**.
	2:	18	"It is not **g** for the man to be alone.
	50:	20	God intended it for **g**
Job	2:	10	Shall we accept **g** from God,
Ps	14:	1	there is no one who does **g**.
	34:	8	Taste and see that the Lᴏʀᴅ is **g**;
	37:	3	Trust in the Lᴏʀᴅ and do **g**;
	84:	11	no **g** thing does he withhold
	86:	5	are forgiving and **g**,
	103:	5	your desires with **g** things so
	119:	68	You are **g**, and what you do is **g**;
	133:	1	How **g** and pleasant it is
	147:	1	How **g** it is to sing praises to our
Pr	3:	4	and a **g** name in the sight of God
	11:	27	Whoever seeks **g** finds favor,
	13:	21	are rewarded with **g** things.
	17:	22	A cheerful heart is **g** medicine,
	18:	22	He who finds a wife finds what is **g**
	22:	1	A **g** name is more desirable than
	31:	12	She brings him **g**, not harm,
Isa	5:	20	Woe to those who call evil **g** and **g**

Isa	52:	7	the feet of those who bring **g** news,
Jer	6:	16	ask where the **g** way is, and walk
Mic	6:	8	shown you, O mortal, what is **g**.
Mt	5:	45	sun to rise on the evil and the **g**,
	7:	17	Likewise, every **g** tree bears **g** fruit,
	12:	35	A **g** man brings **g** things out of the **g**
	19:	17	"There is only One who is **g**.
	25:	21	'Well done, **g** and faithful servant!
Mk	3:	4	to do **g** or to do evil, to save life
	8:	36	What **g** is it for someone to gain
Lk	6:	27	do **g** to those who hate you,
Jn	10:	11	"I am the **g** shepherd.
Ro	8:	28	for the **g** of those who love him,
	10:	15	feet of those who bring **g** news!"
	12:	9	Hate what is evil; cling to what is **g**.
1Co	10:	24	their own **g**, but the **g** of others.
	15:	33	company corrupts **g** character."
2Co	9:	8	you will abound in every **g** work.
Gal	6:	9	us not become weary in doing **g**,
	6:	10	let us do **g** to all people,
Eph	2:	10	in Christ Jesus to do **g** works,
Php	1:	6	he who began a **g** work in you will
1Th	5:	21	test them all; hold on to what is **g**,
2Th	3:	13	never tire of doing what is **g**.
1Ti	3:	7	have a **g** reputation with outsiders,
	4:	4	For everything God created is **g**,
	6:	12	Fight the **g** fight of the faith.
	6:	18	do **g**, to be rich in **g** deeds,
2Ti	3:	17	equipped for every **g** work.
	4:	7	I have fought the **g** fight, I have
Heb	12:	10	but God disciplines us for our **g**,
1Pe	2:	3	you have tasted that the Lord is **g**.
	2:	12	Live such **g** lives among the pagans

GOSPEL

Ro	1:	16	For I am not ashamed of the **g**,
	15:	16	duty of proclaiming the **g** of God,
1Co	1:	17	to baptize, but to preach the **g**—
	9:	16	Woe to me if I do not preach the **g**!
	15:	1	to remind you of the **g** I preached
Gal	1:	7	trying to pervert the **g** of Christ.
Php	1:	27	a manner worthy of the **g** of Christ.
	1:	27	as one for the faith of the **g**

GOSSIP

Pr	11:	13	A **g** betrays a confidence,
	16:	28	and a **g** separates close friends.
	18:	8	of a **g** are like choice morsels;
	26:	20	without a **g** a quarrel dies down.
2Co	12:	20	slander, **g**, arrogance and disorder.

GOVERNED

Ro	8:	6	the mind **g** by the Spirit is life

GRACE (GRACIOUS)

Ps	45:	2	lips have been anointed with **g**,
Jn	1:	17	**g** and truth came through Jesus
Ac	20:	32	to God and to the word of his **g**,
Ro	3:	24	by his **g** through the redemption
	5:	15	that came by the **g** of the one man,
	5:	17	God's abundant provision of **g**
	5:	20	increased, **g** increased all the more,
	6:	14	are not under the law, but under **g**.
	11:	6	if it were, **g** would no longer be **g**.
2Co	6:	1	you not to receive God's **g** in vain.
	8:	9	you know the **g** of our Lord Jesus
	12:	9	to me, "My **g** is sufficient for you,
Gal	2:	21	I do not set aside the **g** of God,

Gal	5:	4	you have fallen away from **g**.
Eph	1:	7	with the riches of God's **g**
	2:	5	it is by **g** you have been saved.
	2:	7	the incomparable riches of his **g**,
	2:	8	For it is by **g** you have been saved,
Php	1:	7	all of you share in God's **g** with me.
Col	4:	6	conversation be always full of **g**,
2Th	2:	16	gave us eternal encouragement
2Ti	2:	1	be strong in the **g** that is in Christ
Titus	2:	11	For the **g** of God has appeared
	3:	7	having been justified by his **g**,
Heb	2:	9	the **g** of God he might taste death
	4:	16	approach God's throne of **g**
	4:	16	**g** to help us in our time of need.
Jas	4:	6	But he gives us more **g**. That is why
2Pe	3:	18	grow in the **g** and knowledge of

GRACIOUS (GRACE)

Nu	6:	25	face shine on you and be **g** to you;
Isa	30:	18	the Lord longs to be **g** to you;

GRAIN

Ecc	11:	1	Ship your **g** across the sea;
1Co	9:	9	an ox while it is treading out the **g**."

GRANTED

Php	1:	29	For it has been **g** to you on behalf

GRASS

Ps	103:	15	The life of mortals is like **g**,
1Pe	1:	24	the **g** withers and the flowers fall,

GRAVE (GRAVES)

Pr	7:	27	Her house is a highway to the **g**,
Hos	13:	14	Where, O **g**, is your destruction?

GRAVES (GRAVE)

Jn	5:	28	are in their **g** will hear his voice
Ro	3:	13	"Their throats are open **g**;

GREAT (GREATER GREATEST GREATNESS)

Ge	12:	2	"I will make you into a **g** nation,
Dt	10:	17	gods and Lord of lords, the **g** God,
2Sa	22:	36	your help has made me **g**.
Ps	19:	11	in keeping them there is **g** reward.
	89:	1	sing of the Lord's **g** love forever;
	103:	11	so **g** is his love for those who fear
	108:	4	For **g** is your love, higher than
	119:165		**G** peace have those who love your
	145:	3	**G** is the Lord and most worthy
Pr	23:	24	father of a righteous child has **g** joy
Isa	42:	21	his righteousness to make his law **g**
La	3:	23	**g** is your faithfulness.
Mk	10:	43	become **g** among you must be your
Lk	21:	27	in a cloud with power and **g** glory.
1Ti	6:	6	with contentment is **g** gain.
Titus	2:	13	appearing of the glory of our **g** God
Heb	2:	3	if we ignore so **g** a salvation?
1Jn	3:	1	See what **g** love the Father has

GREATER (GREAT)

Mk	12:	31	is no commandment **g** than these."
Jn	1:	50	You will see **g** things than that."
	15:	13	**G** love has no one than this:
1Co	12:	31	Now eagerly desire the **g** gifts.
Heb	11:	26	as of **g** value than the treasures
1Jn	3:	20	that God is **g** than our hearts,
	4:	4	is in you is **g** than the one who is

GREATEST (GREAT)

Mt	22:	38	is the first and **g** commandment.

CONCORDANCE

Lk	9: 48	least among you all who is the **g**."
1Co	13: 13	But the **g** of these is love.

GREATNESS (GREAT)

Ps	145: 3	his **g** no one can fathom.
	150: 2	praise him for his surpassing **g**.
Isa	9: 7	the **g** of his government and peace
	63: 1	forward in the **g** of his strength?

GREED (GREEDY)

Lk	12: 15	guard against all kinds of **g**;
Ro	1: 29	wickedness, evil, **g** and depravity.
Eph	5: 3	or of **g**, because these are improper
Col	3: 5	desires and **g**, which is idolatry.
2Pe	2: 14	they are experts in **g**—

GREEDY (GREED)

Pr	15: 27	The **g** bring ruin to their
1Co	6: 10	thieves nor the **g** nor drunkards
Eph	5: 5	No immoral, impure or **g** person—

GREEN

Ps	23: 2	makes me lie down in **g** pastures,

GREW (GROW)

Lk	2: 52	And Jesus **g** in wisdom and stature,
Ac	16: 5	in the faith and **g** daily in numbers.

GRIEF (GRIEVE)

Ps	10: 14	you consider their **g** and take it
Pr	14: 13	ache, and rejoicing may end in **g**.
La	3: 32	Though he brings **g**, he will show
Jn	16: 20	grieve, but your **g** will turn to joy.
1Pe	1: 6	have had to suffer **g** in all kinds

GRIEVE (GRIEF)

Eph	4: 30	do not **g** the Holy Spirit of God,
1Th	4: 13	so that you do not **g** like the rest

GROUND

Ge	3: 17	it,' "Cursed is the **g** because of you;
Ex	3: 5	where you are standing is holy **g**."
Eph	6: 13	you may be able to stand your **g**,

GROW (GREW)

Pr	13: 11	money little by little makes it **g**.
1Co	3: 6	it, but God has been making it **g**.
2Pe	3: 18	But **g** in the grace and knowledge

GRUMBLE (GRUMBLING)

1Co	10: 10	do not **g**, as some of them did—
Jas	5: 9	Don't **g** against one another,

GRUMBLING (GRUMBLE)

Jn	6: 43	"Stop **g** among yourselves,"
1Pe	4: 9	hospitality to one another without **g**.

GUARANTEEING (GUARANTOR)

2Co	1: 22	as a deposit, **g** what is to come.
Eph	1: 14	is a deposit **g** our inheritance until

GUARANTOR (GUARANTEEING)

Heb	7: 22	Jesus has become the **g** of a better

GUARD (GUARDIAN, GUARDIAN-REDEEMER)

Ps	141: 3	Set a **g** over my mouth, Lord;
Pr	4: 23	Above all else, **g** your heart,
	13: 3	Those who **g** their lips preserve
	21: 23	Those who **g** their mouths and
Isa	52: 12	God of Israel will be your rear **g**.
Mk	13: 33	Be on **g**! Be alert! You do not know
1Co	16: 13	Be on your **g**; stand firm
Php	4: 7	will **g** your hearts and your minds
1Ti	6: 20	**g** what has been entrusted to your

GUARDIAN (GUARD)

Gal	3: 25	come, we are no longer under a **g**.

GUARDIAN-REDEEMER (GUARD)

Ru	3: 9	since you are a **g** of our family."

GUIDE

Ex	13: 21	of cloud to **g** them on their way
	15: 13	In your strength you will **g** them
Ne	9: 19	cloud did not fail to **g** them on
Ps	25: 5	**G** me in your truth and teach me,
	48: 14	he will be our **g** even to the end.
	67: 4	and **g** the nations of the earth.
	73: 24	You **g** me with your counsel,
	139: 10	even there your hand will **g** me,
Pr	6: 22	When you walk, they will **g** you;
Isa	58: 11	The Lord will **g** you always;
Jn	16: 13	he will **g** you into all the truth.

GUILTY

Ex	34: 7	does not leave the **g** unpunished;
Jn	8: 46	Can any of you prove me **g** of sin?
Heb	10: 22	to cleanse us from a **g** conscience
Jas	2: 10	at just one point is **g** of breaking all

HADES

Mt	16: 18	the gates of **H** will not overcome it.
Lk	16: 23	In **H**, where he was in torment,

HAGAR

Servant of Sarah, wife of Abraham, mother of Ishmael (Ge 16:1–6; 25:12). Driven away by Sarah while pregnant (Ge 16:5–16); after birth of Isaac (Ge 21:9–21; Gal 4:21–31).

HAGGAI

Post-exilic prophet who encouraged rebuilding of the temple (Ezr 5:1; 6:14; Hag 1–2).

HAIR (HAIRS)

Lk	21: 18	not a **h** of your head will perish.
1Co	11: 6	for a woman to have her **h** cut off

HAIRS (HAIR)

Mt	10: 30	even the very **h** of your head are all

HALLELUJAH

Rev	19: 1,	multitude in heaven shouting: "**H**!

HALLOWED (HOLY)

Mt	6: 9	Father in heaven, **h** be your name,

HAND (HANDIWORK HANDS)

Ps	16: 8	With him at my right **h**, I will not
	37: 24	the Lord upholds him with his **h**.
	139: 10	even there your **h** will guide me,
Ecc	9: 10	Whatever your **h** finds to do, do it
Mt	6: 3	not let your left **h** know what your right **h** is doing,
Jn	10: 28	one will snatch them out of my **h**.
1Co	12: 15	say, "Because I am not a **h**, I do not

HANDIWORK (HAND)

Eph	2: 10	For we are God's **h**,

HANDS (HAND)

Ps	22: 16	they pierce my **h** and my feet.
	24: 4	one who has clean **h** and a pure
	31: 5	Into your **h** I commit my spirit;
	31: 15	My times are in your **h**;
Pr	10: 4	but diligent **h** bring wealth.
	31: 20	and extends her **h** to the needy.
Isa	55: 12	trees of the field will clap their **h**.

Isa 65: 2 out my **h** to an obstinate people,
Lk 23: 46 into your **h** I commit my spirit."
1Th 4: 11 business and work with your **h**,
1Ti 2: 8 lifting up holy **h** without anger
5: 22 not be hasty in the laying on of **h**,

HANNAH
Wife of Elkanah, mother of Samuel (1Sa 1). Prayer at dedication of Samuel (1Sa 2:1–10). Blessed (1Sa 2:18–21).

HAPPY
Ps 68: 3 may they be **h** and joyful.
Pr 15: 13 A **h** heart makes the face cheerful,
Ecc 3: 12 better for people than to be **h**
Jas 5: 13 Is anyone **h**? Let them sing songs

HARD (HARDEN HARDSHIP)
Ge 18: 14 Is anything too **h** for the Lord?
Ps 118: 5 When **h** pressed, I cried
Mt 19: 23 it is **h** for someone who is rich
1Co 4: 12 We work **h** with our own hands.
1Th 5: 12 those who work **h** among you,

HARDEN (HARD)
Ro 9: 18 he hardens whom he wants to **h**.
Heb 3: 8 do not **h** your hearts as you did

HARDHEARTED (HEART)
Dt 15: 7 do not be **h** or tightfisted toward

HARDSHIP (HARD)
Ro 8: 35 Shall trouble or **h** or persecution
2Ti 4: 5 endure **h**, do the work
Heb 12: 7 Endure **h** as discipline;

HARM
Ps 121: 6 the sun will not **h** you by day,
Pr 3: 29 not plot **h** against your neighbor,
31: 12 good, not **h**, all the days of her life.
Ro 13: 10 Love does no **h** to a neighbor.
1Jn 5: 18 and the evil one cannot **h** them.

HARMONY
Ro 12: 16 Live in **h** with one another.
2Co 6: 15 What **h** is there between Christ

HARVEST
Mt 9: 37 "The **h** is plentiful but the workers
Jn 4: 35 at the fields! They are ripe for **h**.
Gal 6: 9 at the proper time we will reap a **h**
Heb 12: 11 it produces a **h** of righteousness

HASTE (HASTY)
Pr 21: 5 lead to profit as surely as **h** leads
29: 20 you see someone who speaks in **h**?

HASTY (HASTE)
Pr 19: 2 how much more will **h** feet miss
Ecc 5: 2 do not be **h** in your heart to utter
1Ti 5: 22 Do not be **h** in the laying

HATE (HATED HATES HATRED)
Lev 19: 17 "'Do not **h** a fellow Israelite
Ps 5: 5 You **h** all who do wrong;
45: 7 righteousness and **h** wickedness;
97: 10 those who love the Lord **h** evil,
139: 21 Do I not **h** those who **h** you,
Pr 8: 13 To fear the Lord is to **h** evil; I **h**
Am 5: 15 **H** evil, love good;
Mt 5: 43 your neighbor and **h** your enemy.'
Lk 6: 27 do good to those who **h** you,
Ro 12: 9 **H** what is evil; cling to what is

HATED (HATE)
Mt 10: 22 be **h** by everyone because of me,
Ro 9: 13 "Jacob I loved, but Esau I **h**."
Eph 5: 29 all, no one ever **h** their own body,
Heb 1: 9 righteousness and **h** wickedness;

HATES (HATE)
Pr 6: 16 There are six things the Lord **h**,
13: 24 spares the rod **h** their children,
Mal 2: 16 "The man who **h** and divorces his
Jn 3: 20 Everyone who does evil **h** the light,
1Jn 2: 9 to be in the light but **h** a brother

HATRED (HATE)
Pr 10: 12 **H** stirs up conflict, but love covers

HAUGHTY
Pr 16: 18 destruction, a **h** spirit before a fall.

HAY
1Co 3: 12 costly stones, wood, **h** or straw,

HEAD (HEADS HOTHEADED)
Ge 3: 15 he will crush your **h**, and you will
Ps 23: 5 You anoint my **h** with oil;
Pr 25: 22 will heap burning coals on his **h**,
Isa 59: 17 the helmet of salvation on his **h**;
Mt 8: 20 of Man has no place to lay his **h**."
Ro 12: 20 will heap burning coals on his **h**."
1Co 11: 3 the **h** of every man is Christ, and the **h** of the woman is man, and the **h** of Christ is God.
12: 21 And the **h** cannot say to the feet,
Eph 5: 23 the husband is the **h** of the wife as Christ is the **h**
2Ti 4: 5 keep your **h** in all situations,
Rev 19: 12 fire, and on his **h** are many crowns.

HEADS (HEAD)
Lev 26: 13 you to walk with **h** held high.
Isa 35: 10 everlasting joy will crown their **h**.

HEAL (HEALED HEALING HEALS)
2Ch 7: 14 their sin and will **h** their land.
Ps 41: 4 **h** me, for I have sinned against
Mt 10: 8 **H** the sick, raise the dead,
Lk 4: 23 'Physician, **h** yourself!'
5: 17 Lord was with Jesus to **h** the sick.

HEALED (HEAL)
Isa 53: 5 him, and by his wounds we are **h**.
Mt 9: 22 he said, "your faith has **h** you."
14: 36 and all who touched it were **h**.
Ac 4: 10 that this man stands before you **h**.
14: 9 saw that he had faith to be **h**
Jas 5: 16 each other so that you may be **h**.
1Pe 2: 24 "by his wounds you have been **h**."

HEALING (HEAL)
Eze 47: 12 for food and their leaves for **h**."
Mal 4: 2 righteousness will rise with **h** in its
1Co 12: 9 to another gifts of **h** by that one
12: 30 Do all have gifts of **h**? Do all speak
Rev 22: 2 the tree are for the **h** of the nations.

HEALS (HEAL)
Ex 15: 26 for I am the Lord, who **h** you."
Ps 103: 3 your sins and **h** all your diseases,
147: 3 He **h** the brokenhearted and binds

HEALTH (HEALTHY)
Pr 3: 8 This will bring **h** to your body
15: 30 good news gives **h** to the bones.

HEALTHY (HEALTH)

| Mk | 2: | 17 | "It is not the **h** who need a doctor, |

HEAR (HEARD HEARING HEARS)

Dt	6:	4	**H**, O Israel: The LORD our God,
	31:	13	law, must **h** it and learn to fear
2Ch	7:	14	then I will **h** from heaven,
Ps	94:	9	he who fashioned the ear not **h**?
Isa	29:	18	day the deaf will **h** the words
	65:	24	they are still speaking I will **h**.
Mt	11:	15	Whoever has ears, let them **h**.
Jn	8:	47	The reason you do not **h** is that
2Ti	4:	3	what their itching ears want to **h**.

HEARD (HEAR)

Job	42:	5	My ears had **h** of you but now my
Isa	66:	8	Who has ever **h** of such things?
Mt	5:	21	"You have **h** that it was said
	5:	27	"You have **h** that it was said,
	5:	33	you have **h** that it was said
	5:	38	"You have **h** that it was said,
	5:	43	"You have **h** that it was said,
1Co	2:	9	what no ear has **h**, and what no
1Th	2:	13	which you **h** from us, you accepted
2Ti	1:	13	What you **h** from me, keep as
Jas	1:	25	not forgetting what they have **h**,

HEARING (HEAR)

| Ro | 10: | 17 | faith comes from **h** the message, |

HEARS (HEAR)

Jn	5:	24	whoever **h** my word and believes
1Jn	5:	14	according to his will, he **h** us.
Rev	3:	20	If anyone **h** my voice and opens

HEART (BROKENHEARTED HARDHEARTED HEARTS WHOLEHEARTEDLY)

Ex	25:	2	everyone whose **h** prompts them
Lev	19:	17	not hate a fellow Israelite in your **h**.
Dt	4:	29	him if you seek him with all your **h**
	6:	5	LORD your God with all your **h**
	10:	12	LORD your God with all your **h**
	15:	10	and do so without a grudging **h**;
	30:	6	you may love him with all your **h**
	30:	10	LORD your God with all your **h**
Jos	22:	5	and to serve him with all your **h**
1Sa	13:	14	sought out a man after his own **h**
	16:	7	but the LORD looks at the **h**."
2Ki	23:	3	and decrees with all his **h** and
1Ch	28:	9	for the LORD searches every **h**
2Ch	7:	16	eyes and my **h** will always be there.
Job	22:	22	and lay up his words in your **h**.
	37:	1	"At this my **h** pounds and leaps
Ps	14:	1	says in his **h**, "There is no God."
	19:	14	this meditation of my **h** be pleasing
	37:	4	will give you the desires of your **h**.
	45:	1	My **h** is stirred by a noble theme as
	51:	10	Create in me a pure **h**, O God,
	51:	17	a broken and contrite **h** you, God,
	66:	18	If I had cherished sin in my **h**,
	86:	11	give me an undivided **h**, that I may
	119:	11	in my **h** that I might not sin against
	139:	23	Search me, God, and know my **h**;
Pr	3:	5	Trust in the LORD with all your **h**
	4:	21	sight, keep them within your **h**;
	4:	23	guard your **h**, for everything you
	7:	3	write them on the tablet of your **h**.
	13:	12	Hope deferred makes the **h** sick,

Pr	14:	13	Even in laughter the **h** may ache,
	15:	30	eyes brings joy to the **h**, and good
	17:	22	A cheerful **h** is good medicine,
	24:	17	stumble, do not let your **h** rejoice,
	27:	19	the face, so one's life reflects the **h**.
Ecc	3:	11	also set eternity in the human **h**;
	8:	5	the wise **h** will know the proper
SS	4:	9	You have stolen my **h**, my sister,
Isa	40:	11	and carries them close to his **h**;
	57:	15	and to revive the **h** of the contrite.
Jer	17:	9	The **h** is deceitful above all things
	29:	13	when you seek me with all your **h**.
Eze	36:	26	I will give you a new **h** and put
Mt	5:	8	Blessed are the pure in **h**, for they
	6:	21	treasure is, there your **h** will be
	12:	34	mouth speaks what the **h** is full of.
	22:	37	the Lord your God with all your **h**
Lk	6:	45	mouth speaks what the **h** is full of.
Ro	2:	29	is circumcision of the **h**,
	10:	10	it is with your **h** that you believe
Eph	5:	19	music from your **h** to the Lord,
	6:	6	doing the will of God from your **h**.
Col	3:	23	you do, work at it with all your **h**,
1Pe	1:	22	one another deeply, from the **h**.

HEARTS (HEART)

Dt	11:	18	Fix these words of mine in your **h**
1Ki	8:	39	do, since you know their **h** (for you
	8:	61	may your **h** be fully committed
Ps	62:	8	pour out your **h** to him, for God is
Jer	31:	33	their minds and write it on their **h**.
Lk	16:	15	of others, but God knows your **h**.
	24:	32	"Were not our **h** burning within us
Jn	14:	1	"Do not let your **h** be troubled.
Ac	15:	9	for he purified their **h** by faith.
Ro	2:	15	of the law are written on their **h**,
1Co	14:	25	the secrets of their **h** are laid bare.
2Co	3:	2	written on our **h**, known and read
	3:	3	of stone but on tablets of human **h**.
	4:	6	shine in our **h** to give us the light
Eph	3:	17	may dwell in your **h** through faith.
Col	3:	1	Christ, set your **h** on things above,
Heb	3:	8	do not harden your **h** as you did
	10:	16	I will put my laws in their **h**, and I
1Jn	3:	20	that God is greater than our **h**,

HEAT

| 2Pe | 3: | 12 | and the elements will melt in the **h**. |

HEAVEN (HEAVENLY HEAVENS)

Ge	14:	19	Most High, Creator of **h** and earth.
1Ki	8:	27	even the highest **h**, cannot contain
2Ki	2:	1	take Elijah up to **h** in a whirlwind,
2Ch	7:	14	then I will hear from **h**, and I will
Isa	14:	12	How you have fallen from **h**,
	66:	1	"**H** is my throne, and the earth is
Da	7:	13	man, coming with the clouds of **h**.
Mt	6:	9	"'Our Father in **h**, hallowed be
	6:	20	up for yourselves treasures in **h**,
	16:	19	you the keys of the kingdom of **h**;
	16:	19	bind on earth will be bound in **h**,
	19:	23	is rich to enter the kingdom of **h**.
	24:	35	**H** and earth will pass away, but my
	26:	64	and coming on the clouds of **h**."
	28:	18	"All authority in **h** and on earth has
Mk	16:	19	*was taken up into* **h**
Lk	15:	7	**h** over one sinner who repents

Lk 18: 22 and you will have treasure in **h**.
Ro 10: 6 heart, 'Who will ascend into **h**?' "
2Co 5: 1 an eternal house in **h**, not built
12: 2 ago was caught up to the third **h**.
Php 2: 10 in **h** and on earth and under
3: 20 But our citizenship is in **h**.
1Th 1: 10 and to wait for his Son from **h**,
Heb 8: 5 a copy and shadow of what is in **h**.
9: 24 he entered **h** itself, now to appear
2Pe 3: 13 we are looking forward to a new **h**
Rev 21: 1 I saw "a new **h** and a new earth,"

HEAVENLY (HEAVEN)
2Co 5: 2 clothed instead with our **h** dwelling,
Eph 1: 3 who has blessed us in the **h** realms
1: 20 at his right hand in the **h** realms,
2Ti 4: 18 bring me safely to his **h** kingdom.
Heb 12: 22 of the living God, the **h** Jerusalem.

HEAVENS (HEAVEN)
Ge 1: 1 In the beginning God created the **h**
1Ki 8: 27 The **h**, even the highest heaven,
2Ch 2: 6 since the **h**, even the highest **h**,
Ps 8: 3 When I consider your **h**, the work
19: 1 The **h** declare the glory of God;
102: 25 the **h** are the work of your hands.
108: 4 is your love, higher than the **h**;
119: 89 it stands firm in the **h**.
139: 8 If I go up to the **h**, you are there;
Isa 51: 6 the **h** will vanish like smoke,
55: 9 "As the **h** are higher than the earth,
65: 17 will create new **h** and a new earth.
Joel 2: 30 I will show wonders in the **h**
Eph 4: 10 ascended higher than all the **h**,
2Pe 3: 10 The **h** will disappear with a roar;

HEBREW
Ge 14: 13 and reported this to Abram the **H**.

HEEDS
Pr 13: 1 A wise son **h** his father's
13: 18 whoever **h** correction is honored.
15: 5 but whoever **h** correction shows
15: 32 but the one who **h** correction gains

HEEL
Ge 3: 15 head, and you will strike his **h**."

HEIRS (INHERIT)
Ro 8: 17 **h** of God and co-heirs with Christ,
Gal 3: 29 and **h** according to the promise.
Eph 3: 6 gospel the Gentiles are **h** together
1Pe 3: 7 as **h** with you of the gracious gift

HELL
Mt 5: 22 will be in danger of the fire of **h**.
2Pe 2: 4 but sent them to **h**, putting them

HELMET
Isa 59: 17 and the **h** of salvation on his head;
Eph 6: 17 Take the **h** of salvation
1Th 5: 8 and the hope of salvation as a **h**.

HELP (HELPED HELPER HELPING HELPS)
2Sa 22: 36 You make your saving **h** my shield;
Ps 18: 6 I cried to my God for **h**.
30: 2 called to you for **h**, and you healed
46: 1 an ever-present **h** in trouble.
70: 4 long for your saving **h** always say,
79: 9 **H** us, God our Savior, for the glory
121: 1 where does my **h** come from?

Isa 41: 10 I will strengthen you and **h** you;
Jnh 2: 2 the realm of the dead I called for **h**,
Mk 9: 24 **h** me overcome my unbelief!"
Ac 16: 9 over to Macedonia and **h** us."

HELPED (HELP)
1Sa 7: 12 "Thus far the Lᴏʀᴅ has **h** us."

HELPER (HELP)
Ge 2: 18 I will make a **h** suitable for him."
Ps 10: 14 you are the **h** of the fatherless.
Heb 13: 6 confidence, "The Lord is my **h**;

HELPING (HELP)
Ac 9: 36 always doing good and **h** the poor.
1Co 12: 28 gifts of healing, of **h**, of guidance,
1Ti 5: 10 **h** those in trouble and devoting

HELPS (HELP)
Ro 8: 26 the Spirit **h** us in our weakness.

HEN
Mt 23: 37 as a **h** gathers her chicks under her

HERITAGE (INHERIT)
Ps 127: 3 Children are a **h** from the Lᴏʀᴅ,

HEROD
1. King of Judea who tried to kill Jesus (Mt 2; Lk 1:5).
2. Son of 1. Tetrarch of Galilee who arrested and beheaded John the Baptist (Mt 14:1–12; Mk 6:14–29; Lk 3:1, 19–20; 9:7–9); tried Jesus (Lk 23:6–15).
3. Grandson of 1. King of Judea who killed James (Ac 12:2); arrested Peter (Ac 12:3–19). Death (Ac 12:19–23).

HERODIAS
Wife of Herod the Tetrarch who persuaded her daughter to ask for John the Baptist's head (Mt 14:1–12; Mk 6:14–29).

HEZEKIAH
King of Judah. Restored the temple and worship (2Ch 29–31). Sought the Lᴏʀᴅ for help against Assyria (2Ki 18–19; 2Ch 32:1–23; Isa 36–37). Illness healed (2Ki 20:1–11; 2Ch 32:24–26; Isa 38). Judged for showing Babylonians his treasures (2Ki 20:12–21; 2Ch 32:31; Isa 39).

HID (HIDE)
Ge 3: 8 they **h** from the Lᴏʀᴅ God among
Ex 2: 2 child, she **h** him for three months.
Jos 6: 17 because she **h** the spies we sent.
Heb 11: 23 faith Moses' parents **h** him for

HIDDEN (HIDE)
Ps 19: 12 Forgive my **h** faults.
119: 11 I have **h** your word in my heart
Pr 2: 4 and search for it as for **h** treasure,
Isa 59: 2 your sins have **h** his face from you,
Mt 5: 14 A town built on a hill cannot be **h**.
13: 44 heaven is like treasure **h** in a field.
Col 1: 26 that has been kept **h** for ages
2: 3 in whom are **h** all the treasures
3: 3 and your life is now **h** with Christ

HIDE (HID HIDDEN)
Ps 17: 8 **h** me in the shadow of your wings
143: 9 Lᴏʀᴅ, for I **h** myself in you.

HIGH
Isa 57: 15 "I live in a **h** and holy place,

CONCORDANCE

HILL (HILLS)
Mt 5: 14 town built on a **h** cannot be hidden.

HILLS (HILL)
Ps 50: 10 and the cattle on a thousand **h**.

HINDER (HINDERS)
1Sa 14: 6 Nothing can **h** the LORD
Mt 19: 14 do not **h** them, for the kingdom
1Co 9: 12 anything rather than **h** the gospel
1Pe 3: 7 so that nothing will **h** your prayers.

HINDERS (HINDER)
Heb 12: 1 let us throw off everything that **h**

HINT
Eph 5: 3 you there must not be even a **h**

HOLD
Ex 20: 7 LORD will not **h** anyone guiltless
Lev 19: 13 "'Do not **h** back the wages
Jos 22: 5 to **h** fast to him and to serve him
Ps 73: 23 you **h** me by my right hand.
Pr 4: 4 "Take **h** of my words with all your
Isa 54: 2 tent curtains wide, do not **h** back;
Mk 11: 25 if you **h** anything against anyone,
Php 2: 16 as you **h** firmly to the word of life.
3: 12 which Christ Jesus took **h** of me.
Col 1: 17 and in him all things **h** together.
1Th 5: 21 test them all; **h** on to what is good,
1Ti 6: 12 Take **h** of the eternal life
Heb 10: 23 Let us **h** unswervingly to the hope

HOLINESS (HOLY)
Ex 15: 11 majestic in **h**, awesome in glory,
Ps 29: 2 the LORD in the splendor of his **h**.
96: 9 the LORD in the splendor of his **h**;
Ro 6: 19 to righteousness leading to **h**.
2Co 7: 1 perfecting **h** out of reverence
Eph 4: 24 God in true righteousness and **h**.
Heb 12: 10 in order that we may share in his **h**.
12: 14 without **h** no one will see the Lord.

HOLY (HALLOWED HOLINESS)
Ex 19: 6 kingdom of priests and a **h** nation.'
20: 8 the Sabbath day by keeping it **h**.
Lev 11: 44 and be **h**, because I am **h**.
20: 7 yourselves and be **h**, because I am
20: 26 You are to be **h** to me because I,
21: 8 LORD am **h**—I who make you **h**.
22: 32 Do not profane my **h** name,
Ps 24: 3 Who may stand in his **h** place?
77: 13 Your ways, God, are **h**. What god is
99: 3 great and awesome name—he is **h**.
99: 5 worship at his footstool; he is **h**.
99: 9 for the LORD our God is **h**.
111: 9 **h** and awesome is his name.
Isa 5: 16 the **h** God will be proved **h** by his
6: 3 "**H, h, h** is the LORD Almighty;
40: 25 who is my equal?" says the **H** One.
57: 15 who lives forever, whose name is **h**:
Eze 28: 25 I will be proved **h** through them
Da 9: 24 and to anoint the Most **H** Place.
Hab 2: 20 The LORD is in his **h** temple;
Ac 2: 27 will not let your **H** one see decay.
Ro 7: 12 the law is **h**, and the commandment is **h**,
12: 1 sacrifice, **h** and pleasing to God—
2Th 1: 10 to be glorified in his **h** people
2Ti 1: 9 saved us and called us to a **h** life—

2Ti 3: 15 you have known the **H** Scriptures,
Titus 1: 8 upright, **h** and disciplined.
1Pe 1: 15 is **h**, so be **h** in all you do;
1: 16 "Be **h**, because I am **h**."
2: 9 a royal priesthood, a **h** nation,
2Pe 3: 11 You ought to live **h** and godly lives
Rev 4: 8 "'**H, h, h** is the Lord God

HOME (HOMES)
Dt 6: 7 Talk about them when you sit at **h**
Ps 84: 3 Even the sparrow has found a **h**,
Pr 3: 33 he blesses the **h** of the righteous.
Mk 10: 29 "no one who has left **h** or brothers
Jn 14: 23 and make our **h** with them.
Titus 2: 5 pure, to be busy at **h**, to be kind,

HOMES (HOME)
Ne 4: 14 daughters, your wives and your **h**."
1Ti 5: 14 to manage their **h** and to give

HOMOSEXUALITY
1Ti 1: 10 for those practicing **h**, for slave

HONEST
Lev 19: 36 **h** weights, an **h** ephah and an **h** hin.
Dt 25: 15 must have accurate and **h** weights
Job 31: 6 let God weigh me in **h** scales and
Pr 12: 17 An **h** witness tells the truth,

HONEY
Ex 3: 8 a land flowing with milk and **h**—
Ps 19: 10 they are sweeter than **h**, than **h**
119:103 taste, sweeter than **h** to my mouth!

HONOR (HONORABLE HONORABLY HONORED HONORS)
Ex 20: 12 "**H** your father and your mother,
Nu 25: 13 he was zealous for the **h** of his God
Dt 5: 16 "**H** your father and your mother,
1Sa 2: 30 Those who **h** me I will **h**, but those
Ps 8: 5 crowned them with glory and **h**.
Pr 3: 9 **H** the LORD with your wealth,
11: 16 A kindhearted woman gains **h**,
15: 33 and humility comes before **h**.
20: 3 It is to one's **h** to avoid strife,
31: 31 **H** her for all that her hands have
Mt 15: 4 '**H** your father and mother'
Ro 12: 10 **H** one another above yourselves.
1Co 6: 20 Therefore **h** God with your bodies.
Eph 6: 2 "**H** your father and mother"—
1Ti 5: 17 church well are worthy of double **h**,
Heb 2: 7 crowned them with glory and **h**
Rev 4: 9 **h** and thanks to him who sits

HONORABLE (HONOR)
1Th 4: 4 body in a way that is holy and **h**,

HONORABLY (HONOR)
Heb 13: 18 and desire to live **h** in every way.

HONORED (HONOR)
Ps 12: 8 what is vile is **h** by the human race.
Pr 13: 18 but whoever heeds correction is **h**.
1Co 12: 26 if one part is **h**, every part rejoices
Heb 13: 4 Marriage should be **h** by all,

HONORS (HONOR)
Ps 15: 4 but **h** those who fear the LORD;
Pr 14: 31 is kind to the needy **h** God.
3Jn : 6 their way in a manner that **h** God.

HOOKS
| Isa | 2: | 4 | and their spears into pruning **h**. |
| Joel | 3: | 10 | and your pruning **h** into spears. |

HOPE (HOPES)
Job	13:	15	he slay me, yet will I **h** in him;
Ps	42:	5	Put your **h** in God, for I will yet
	62:	5	rest in God; my **h** comes from him.
	119:	74	for I have put my **h** in your word.
	130:	7	Israel, put your **h** in the LORD,
	147:	11	put their **h** in his unfailing love.
Pr	13:	12	**H** deferred makes the heart sick,
Isa	40:	31	but those who **h** in the LORD will
Ro	5:	4	and character, **h**.
	8:	24	But **h** that is seen is no **h** at all.
	12:	12	Be joyful in **h**, patient in affliction,
	15:	4	they provide we might have **h**.
1Co	13:	13	three remain: faith, **h** and love.
	15:	19	for this life we have **h** in Christ,
Col	1:	27	is Christ in you, the **h** of glory.
1Th	5:	8	and the **h** of salvation as a helmet.
1Ti	6:	17	to put their **h** in God, who richly
Titus	2:	13	while we wait for the blessed **h**—
Heb	6:	19	We have this **h** as an anchor
	11:	1	faith is confidence in what we **h**
1Jn	3:	3	All who have this **h** in him purify

HOPES (HOPE)
| 1Co | 13: | 7 | trusts, always **h**, always perseveres. |

HORSE
Ps	147:	10	is not in the strength of the **h**,
Pr	26:	3	A whip for the **h**, a bridle
Zec	1:	8	me was a man mounted on a red **h**.
Rev	6:	2	and there before me was a white **h**!
	6:	4	Then another **h** came out, a fiery
	6:	5	and there before me was a black **h**!
	6:	8	and there before me was a pale **h**!
	19:	11	and there before me was a white **h**,

HOSANNA
| Mt | 21: | 9 | shouted, "**H** to the Son of David!" |

HOSHEA
Last king of Israel (2Ki 15:30; 17:1–6).

HOSPITABLE (HOSPITALITY)
| 1Ti | 3: | 2 | respectable, **h**, able to teach, |
| Titus | 1: | 8 | he must be **h**, one who loves what |

HOSPITALITY (HOSPITABLE)
Ro	12:	13	people who are in need. Practice **h**.
1Ti	5:	10	showing **h**, washing the feet
Heb	13:	2	shown **h** to angels without knowing
1Pe	4:	9	Offer **h** to one another without

HOSTILE
| Ro | 8: | 7 | governed by the flesh is **h** to God; |

HOT
| 1Ti | 4: | 2 | have been seared as with a **h** iron. |
| Rev | 3: | 15 | that you are neither cold nor **h**. |

HOT-TEMPERED
Pr	15:	18	A **h** person stirs up conflict,
	19:	19	A **h** person must pay the penalty;
	22:	24	not make friends with a **h** person,
	29:	22	and a **h** person commits many sins.

HOTHEADED (HEAD)
| Pr | 14: | 16 | but a fool is **h** and yet feels secure. |

HOUR
Ecc	9:	12	one knows when their **h** will come:
Mt	6:	27	worrying add a single **h** to your life?
Lk	12:	40	an **h** when you do not expect him."
Jn	12:	23	"The **h** has come for the Son
	12:	27	this very reason I came to this **h**.

HOUSE (HOUSEHOLD HOUSEHOLDS STOREHOUSE)
Ex	20:	17	shall not covet your neighbor's **h**.
Ps	23:	6	in the **h** of the LORD forever.
	84:	10	in the **h** of my God than dwell
	122:	1	"Let us go to the **h** of the LORD."
	127:	1	Unless the LORD builds the **h**,
Pr	7:	27	Her **h** is a highway to the grave,
	21:	9	of the roof than share a **h**
Isa	56:	7	my **h** will be called a **h** of prayer
Zec	13:	6	I was given at the **h** of my friends.'
Mt	7:	24	is like a wise man who built his **h**
	12:	29	can anyone enter a strong man's **h**
	21:	13	" 'My **h** will be called a **h**
Mk	3:	25	If a **h** is divided against itself, that **h**
Lk	11:	17	a **h** divided against itself will fall.
Jn	2:	16	Stop turning my Father's **h**
	12:	3	the **h** was filled with the fragrance
	14:	2	My Father's **h** has many rooms;
Heb	3:	3	of a **h** has greater honor than the **h**

HOUSEHOLD (HOUSE)
Jos	24:	15	But as for me and my **h**, we will
Mic	7:	6	are the members of his own **h**.
Mt	10:	36	will be the members of his own **h**.'
	12:	25	or **h** divided against itself will not
1Ti	3:	12	manage his children and his **h** well.
	3:	15	to conduct themselves in God's **h**,

HOUSEHOLDS (HOUSE)
| Pr | 15: | 27 | The greedy bring ruin to their **h**, |

HUMAN (HUMANITY)
Ge	9:	6	"Whoever sheds **h** blood,
1Sa	15:	29	for he is not a **h** being, that he
Ac	5:	29	obey God rather than **h** beings!
2Pe	1:	21	never had its origin in the **h** will,

HUMANITY (HUMAN)
| Heb | 2: | 14 | he too shared in their **h** so |

HUMBLE (HUMBLED HUMILIATE HUMILIATING HUMILITY)
2Ch	7:	14	will **h** themselves and pray and
Ps	25:	9	He guides the **h** in what is right
Pr	3:	34	favor to the **h** and oppressed.
Isa	66:	2	those who are **h** and contrite
Mt	11:	29	for I am gentle and **h** in heart,
Eph	4:	2	Be completely **h** and gentle;
Jas	4:	10	**H** yourselves before the Lord,
1Pe	5:	6	**H** yourselves, therefore,

HUMBLED (HUMBLE)
| Mt | 23: | 12 | who exalt themselves will be **h**, |
| Php | 2: | 8 | he **h** himself by becoming obedient |

HUMILIATE (HUMBLE)
| Pr | 25: | 7 | for him to **h** you before his nobles. |

HUMILIATING (HUMBLE)
| 1Co | 11: | 22 | God by **h** those who have nothing? |

HUMILITY (HUMBLE)
| Pr | 11: | 2 | but with **h** comes wisdom. |
| | 15: | 33 | LORD, and **h** comes before honor. |

CONCORDANCE

2Co	10:	1	the **h** and gentleness of Christ,
Php	2:	3	in **h** value others above yourselves,
1Pe	5:	5	with **h** toward one another,

HUNGRY

Ps	107:	9	and fills the **h** with good things.
	146:	7	oppressed and gives food to the **h**.
Pr	25:	21	If your enemy is **h**, give him food
Eze	18:	7	his food to the **h** and provides
Mt	25:	35	For I was **h** and you gave me
Lk	1:	53	has filled the **h** with good things
Jn	6:	35	comes to me will never go **h**,
Ro	12:	20	"If your enemy is **h**, feed him;

HURT (HURTS)

Ecc	8:	9	lords it over others to his own **h**.
Mk	16:	18	*it will not **h** them*
Rev	2:	11	one who is victorious will not be **h**

HURTS (HURT)

| Ps | 15: | 4 | who keeps an oath even when it **h**, |
| Pr | 26: | 28 | A lying tongue hates those it **h**, |

HUSBAND (HUSBAND'S HUSBANDS)

1Co	7:	3	The **h** should fulfill his marital
	7:	3	and likewise the wife to her **h**.
	7:	4	her own body but yields it to her **h**.
	7:	4	the **h** does not have authority over
	7:	10	wife must not separate from her **h**.
	7:	11	And a **h** must not divorce his wife.
	7:	13	And if a woman has a **h** who is not
	7:	39	But if her **h** dies, she is free
2Co	11:	2	I promised you to one **h**, to Christ,
Eph	5:	23	For the **h** is the head of the wife as
	5:	33	and the wife must respect her **h**.

HUSBAND'S (HUSBAND)

| Pr | 12: | 4 | of noble character is her **h** crown, |

HUSBANDS (HUSBAND)

Eph	5:	22	yourselves to your own **h** as you do
	5:	25	**H**, love your wives, just as Christ
Titus	2:	4	the younger women to love their **h**
1Pe	3:	1	yourselves to your own **h** so that,
	3:	7	**H**, in the same way be considerate

HYMN

| 1Co | 14: | 26 | each of you has a **h**, or a word |

HYPOCRISY (HYPOCRITE HYPOCRITES)

| Mt | 23: | 28 | on the inside you are full of **h** |
| 1Pe | 2: | 1 | of all malice and all deceit, **h**, envy, |

HYPOCRITE (HYPOCRISY)

| Mt | 7: | 5 | You **h**, first take the plank |

HYPOCRITES (HYPOCRISY)

| Ps | 26: | 4 | deceitful, nor do I associate with **h**. |
| Mt | 6: | 5 | do not be like the **h**, for they love |

HYSSOP

| Ps | 51: | 7 | Cleanse me with **h**, and I will be |

IDLE (IDLENESS)

1Th	5:	14	those who are **i** and disruptive,
2Th	3:	6	away from every believer who is **i**
1Ti	5:	13	they get into the habit of being **i**

IDLENESS (IDLE)

| Pr | 31: | 27 | and does not eat the bread of **i**. |

IDOL (IDOLATRY IDOLS)

| Isa | 44: | 17 | From the rest he makes a god, his **i**; |
| 1Co | 8: | 4 | We know that "An **i** is nothing |

IDOLATRY (IDOL)

| Col | 3: | 5 | evil desires and greed, which is **i**. |

IDOLS (IDOL)

| 1Co | 8: | 1 | Now about food sacrificed to **i**: |

IGNORANT (IGNORE)

1Co	15:	34	there are some who are **i** of God—
Heb	5:	2	to deal gently with those who are **i**
1Pe	2:	15	good you should silence the **i** talk
2Pe	3:	16	**i** and unstable people distort,

IGNORE (IGNORANT IGNORES)

Dt	22:	1	not **i** it but be sure to take it back
Ps	9:	12	he does not **i** the cries
Heb	2:	3	escape if we **i** so great a salvation?

IGNORES (IGNORE)

| Pr | 10: | 17 | whoever **i** correction leads others |

ILLUMINATED

| Rev | 18: | 1 | and the earth was **i** by his splendor. |

IMAGE

Ge	1:	26	"Let us make mankind in our **i**,
	1:	27	God created mankind in his own **i**, in the **i** of God he created them;
Ro	8:	29	to be conformed to the **i** of his Son,
1Co	11:	7	since he is the **i** and glory of God;
2Co	3:	18	into his **i** with ever-increasing glory,
Col	1:	15	The Son is the **i** of the invisible
	3:	10	in knowledge in the **i** of its Creator.

IMAGINE

| Eph | 3: | 20 | more than all we ask or **i**, |

IMITATE (IMITATORS)

1Co	4:	16	Therefore I urge you to **i** me.
Heb	6:	12	but to **i** those who through faith
	13:	7	of their way of life and **i** their faith.
3Jn	:	11	do not **i** what is evil but what is

IMITATORS (IMITATE)

| 1Th | 1: | 6 | You became **i** of us and of the Lord, |
| | 2: | 14 | became **i** of God's churches |

IMMANUEL

| Isa | 7: | 14 | birth to a son, and will call him **I**. |
| Mt | 1: | 23 | they will call him **I**" (which means |

IMMORAL (IMMORALITY)

1Co	5:	9	to associate with sexually **i** people
	5:	10	the people of this world who are **i**,
	5:	11	or sister but is sexually **i** or greedy,
	6:	9	Neither the sexually **i** nor idolaters
Eph	5:	5	No **i**, impure or greedy person—
Heb	12:	16	See that no one is sexually **i**, or is
	13:	4	the adulterer and all the sexually **i**.
Rev	21:	8	the sexually **i**, those who practice
	22:	15	arts, the sexually **i**, the murderers,

IMMORALITY (IMMORAL)

Mt	5:	32	except for sexual **i**, makes her
	19:	9	except for sexual **i**, and marries
1Co	6:	13	is not meant for sexual **i**
	6:	18	Flee from sexual **i**. All other sins
	10:	8	We should not commit sexual **i**,
Gal	5:	19	sexual **i**, impurity and debauchery;
Eph	5:	3	must not be even a hint of sexual **i**,
1Th	4:	3	that you should avoid sexual **i**;
Jude	:	4	grace of our God into a license for **i**

IMMORTAL (IMMORTALITY)
Ro	1: 23	exchanged the glory of the **i** God
1Ti	1: 17	Now to the King eternal, **i**,
	6: 16	who alone is **i** and who lives

IMMORTALITY (IMMORTAL)
Ro	2: 7	and **i**, he will give eternal life.
1Co	15: 53	and the mortal with **i**.
2Ti	1: 10	and **i** to light through the gospel.

IMPERISHABLE
| 1Pe | 1: 23 | seed, but of **i**, through the living |

IMPORTANCE (IMPORTANT)
| 1Co | 15: 3 | I passed on to you as of first **i**: |

IMPORTANT (IMPORTANCE)
Mt	23: 23	have neglected the more **i** matters
Mk	12: 29	"The most **i** one," answered Jesus,
	12: 33	as yourself is more **i** than all burnt
Php	1: 18	The **i** thing is that in every way,

IMPOSSIBLE
Mt	17: 20	Nothing will be **i** for you."
Lk	18: 27	"What is **i** with man is possible
Heb	6: 18	in which it is **i** for God to lie,
	11: 6	without faith it is **i** to please God,

IMPROPER
| Eph | 5: 3 | because these are **i** for God's holy |

IMPURE (IMPURITY)
Ac	10: 15	"Do not call anything **i** that God
Eph	5: 5	No immoral, **i** or greedy person—
1Th	4: 7	For God did not call us to be **i**,
Rev	21: 27	Nothing **i** will ever enter it,

IMPURITY (IMPURE)
| Ro | 1: 24 | hearts to sexual **i** for the degrading |
| Eph | 5: 3 | or of any kind of **i**, or of greed, |

INCENSE
| Ex | 40: 5 | Place the gold altar of **i** in front |
| Ps | 141: 2 | my prayer be set before you like **i**; |

INCOME
| Ecc | 5: 10 | is never satisfied with their **i**. |
| 1Co | 16: 2 | of money in keeping with your **i**, |

INCOMPARABLE
| Eph | 2: 7 | ages he might show the **i** riches |

INCREASE (EVER-INCREASING INCREASED INCREASING)
Ge	1: 22	"Be fruitful and **i** in number and
Ps	62: 10	though your riches **i**, do not set
Lk	17: 5	said to the Lord, "**I** our faith!"
1Th	3: 12	May the Lord make your love **i**

INCREASED (INCREASE)
| Ac | 6: 7 | of disciples in Jerusalem **i** rapidly, |
| Ro | 5: 20 | where sin **i**, grace **i** all the more, |

INCREASING (INCREASE)
Ac	6: 1	the number of disciples was **i**,
2Th	1: 3	all of you have for one another is **i**.
2Pe	1: 8	these qualities in **i** measure,

INDEPENDENT
| 1Co | 11: 11 | in the Lord woman is not **i** of man, |
| | | nor is man **i** of woman. |

INDESCRIBABLE
| 2Co | 9: 15 | Thanks be to God for his **i** gift! |

INDISPENSABLE
| 1Co | 12: 22 | body that seem to be weaker are **i**, |

INEFFECTIVE
| 2Pe | 1: 8 | they will keep you from being **i** |

INEXPRESSIBLE
| 2Co | 12: 4 | up to paradise and heard **i** things, |
| 1Pe | 1: 8 | are filled with an **i** and glorious joy, |

INFANTS
| Mt | 21: 16 | the lips of children and **i** you, Lord, |
| 1Co | 14: 20 | In regard to evil be **i**, but in your |

INHERIT (CO-HEIRS HEIRS HERITAGE INHERITANCE)
Ps	37: 11	the meek will **i** the land and enjoy
	37: 29	The righteous will **i** the land
Mt	5: 5	the meek, for they will **i** the earth.
Mk	10: 17	"what must I do to **i** eternal life?"
1Co	15: 50	cannot **i** the kingdom of God,

INHERITANCE (INHERIT)
Dt	4: 20	to be the people of his **i**, as you
Pr	13: 22	A good person leaves an **i** for their
Eph	1: 14	deposit guaranteeing our **i** until
	5: 5	has any **i** in the kingdom of Christ
Heb	9: 15	receive the promised eternal **i**—
1Pe	1: 4	This **i** is kept in heaven for you,

INIQUITIES (INIQUITY)
Ps	78: 38	he forgave their **i** and did not
	103: 10	or repay us according to our **i**.
Isa	59: 2	your **i** have separated you from
Mic	7: 19	hurl all our **i** into the depths

INIQUITY (INIQUITIES)
| Ps | 51: 2 | Wash away all my **i** and cleanse me |
| Isa | 53: 6 | has laid on him the **i** of us all. |

INJUSTICE
| 2Ch | 19: 7 | the Lord our God there is no **i** |

INNOCENT
Pr	17: 26	a fine on the **i** is not good,
Mt	10: 16	shrewd as snakes and as **i** as doves.
	27: 4	said, "for I have betrayed **i** blood."
1Co	4: 4	clear, but that does not make me **i**.

INSCRIPTION
| Mt | 22: 20 | image is this? And whose **i**?" |

INSOLENT
| Ro | 1: 30 | **i**, arrogant and boastful; |

INSTITUTED
| Ro | 13: 2 | is rebelling against what God has **i**, |

INSTRUCT (INSTRUCTED INSTRUCTION)
Ps	32: 8	I will **i** you and teach you
Pr	9: 9	**I** the wise and they will be wiser
Ro	15: 14	and competent to **i** one another.

INSTRUCTED (INSTRUCT)
| 2Ti | 2: 25 | Opponents must be gently **i**, |

INSTRUCTION (INSTRUCT)
Pr	1: 3	for receiving **i** in prudent behavior,
	1: 7	but fools despise wisdom and **i**.
	1: 8	your father's **i** and do not forsake
	4: 1	Listen, my sons, to a father's **i**;
	4: 13	Hold on to **i**, do not let it go;
	6: 23	correction and **i** are the way to life,
	8: 10	Choose my **i** instead of silver,
	8: 33	Listen to my **i** and be wise;
	13: 1	A wise son heeds his father's **i**,

CONCORDANCE

Pr 13: 13 Whoever scorns **i** will pay for it,
16: 20 Whoever gives heed to **i** prospers,
16: 21 and gracious words promote **i**.
23: 12 Apply your heart to **i** and your ears
23: 23 wisdom, **i** and insight as well.
Isa 8: 20 Consult God's **i** and the testimony
1Co 14: 6 or prophecy or word of **i**?
14: 26 hymn, or a word of **i**, a revelation,
Eph 6: 4 in the training and **i** of the Lord.
1Th 4: 8 who rejects this **i** does not reject
2Th 3: 14 anyone who does not obey our **i**
1Ti 6: 3 sound **i** of our Lord Jesus Christ
2Ti 4: 2 with great patience and careful **i**.

INSULT (INSULTS)
Pr 12: 16 but the prudent overlook an **i**.
Mt 5: 11 are you when people **i** you,
Lk 6: 22 when they exclude you and **i** you
1Pe 3: 9 not repay evil with evil or **i** with **i**.

INSULTS (INSULT)
Pr 9: 7 corrects a mocker invites **i**;

INTEGRITY
1Ki 9: 4 walk before me faithfully with **i**
Job 2: 3 And he still maintains his **i**,
27: 5 till I die, I will not deny my **i**.
Pr 10: 9 Whoever walks in **i** walks securely,
11: 3 The **i** of the upright guides them,
29: 10 The bloodthirsty hate a person of **i**
Titus 2: 7 In your teaching show **i**,

INTELLIGENCE
Isa 29: 14 the **i** of the intelligent will vanish."
1Co 1: 19 the **i** of the intelligent I will

INTELLIGIBLE
1Co 14: 19 I would rather speak five **i** words

INTERCEDE (INTERCEDES INTERCESSION)
Heb 7: 25 him, because he always lives to **i**

INTERCEDES (INTERCEDE)
Ro 8: 26 the Spirit himself **i** for us through

INTERCESSION (INTERCEDE)
Isa 53: 12 and made **i** for the transgressors.
1Ti 2: 1 **i** and thanksgiving be made for all

INTEREST
Ne 5: 10 But let us stop charging **i**!

INTERESTS
1Co 7: 34 and his **i** are divided.
Php 2: 4 not looking to your own **i** but each of you to the **i** of the others.
2: 21 everyone looks out for their own **i**,

INTERMARRY (MARRY)
Dt 7: 3 Do not **i** with them. Do not give

INVESTIGATED
Lk 1: 3 I myself have carefully **i** everything

INVISIBLE
Ro 1: 20 of the world God's **i** qualities—
Col 1: 15 The Son is the image of the **i** God,
1Ti 1: 17 eternal, immortal, **i**, the only God,

INVITE (INVITED INVITES)
Lk 14: 13 you give a banquet, **i** the poor,

INVITED (INVITE)
Mt 22: 14 "For many are **i**, but few are
25: 35 I was a stranger and you **i** me in,

INVITES (INVITE)
1Co 10: 27 If an unbeliever **i** you to a meal

IRON
1Ti 4: 2 have been seared as with a hot **i**.
Rev 2: 27 'will rule them with an **i** scepter

IRREVOCABLE
Ro 11: 29 for God's gifts and his call are **i**.

ISAAC
Son of Abraham by Sarah (Ge 17:19; 21:1–7; 1Ch 1:28). Offered up by Abraham (Ge 22; Heb 11:17–19). Rebekah taken as wife (Ge 24). Fathered Esau and Jacob (Ge 25:19–26; 1Ch 1:34). Tricked into blessing Jacob (Ge 27). Father of Israel (Ex 3:6; Dt 29:13; Ro 9:10).

ISAIAH
Prophet to Judah (Isa 1:1). Called by the LORD (Isa 6).

ISHMAEL
Son of Abraham by Hagar (Ge 16; 1Ch 1:28). Blessed, but not son of covenant (Ge 17:18–21; Gal 4:21–31). Sent away by Sarah (Ge 21:8–21).

ISRAEL (ISRAELITES)
1. Name given to Jacob (see JACOB).
2. Corporate name of Jacob's descendants; often specifically Northern Kingdom.
Dt 6: 4 Hear, O **I**: The LORD our God,
1Sa 4: 21 "The Glory has departed from **I**"—
Isa 27: 6 **I** will bud and blossom and fill all
Jer 31: 10 'He who scattered **I** will gather
Eze 39: 23 that the people of **I** went into exile
Mk 12: 29 'Hear, O **I**: The Lord our God,
Lk 22: 30 judging the twelve tribes of **I**.
Ro 9: 6 all who are descended from **I** are **I**.
11: 26 and in this way all **I** will be saved.
Eph 3: 6 Gentiles are heirs together with **I**,

ISRAELITES (ISRAEL)
Ex 14: 22 the **I** went through the sea on dry
16: 35 The **I** ate manna forty years,
Hos 1: 10 "Yet the **I** will be like the sand
Ro 9: 27 number of the **I** be like the sand

ITCHING
2Ti 4: 3 say what their **i** ears want to hear.

JACOB
Second son of Isaac, twin of Esau (Ge 25:21–26; 1Ch 1:34). Bought Esau's birthright (Ge 25:29–34); tricked Isaac into blessing him (Ge 27:1–37). Abrahamic covenant perpetuated through (Ge 28:13–15; Mal 1:2). Vision at Bethel (Ge 28:10–22). Wives and children (Ge 29:1–30:24; 35:16–26; 1Ch 2–9). Wrestled with God; name changed to Israel (Ge 32:22–32). Sent sons to Egypt during famine (Ge 42–43). Settled in Egypt (Ge 46). Blessed Ephraim and Manasseh (Ge 48). Blessed sons (Ge 49:1–28; Heb 11:21). Death (Ge 49:29–33). Burial (Ge 50:1–14).

JAMES
1. Apostle; brother of John (Mt 4:21–22; 10:2; Mk 3:17; Lk 5:1–10). At transfiguration (Mt 17:1–13; Mk 9:1–13; Lk 9:28–36). Killed by Herod (Ac 12:2).
2. Apostle; son of Alphaeus (Mt 10:3; Mk 3:18; Lk 6:15).
3. Brother of Jesus (Mt 13:55; Mk 6:3; Lk 24:10;

Gal 1:19) and Judas (Jude 1). With believers before Pentecost (Ac 1:13). Leader of church at Jerusalem (Ac 12:17; 15; 21:18; Gal 2:9, 12). Author of epistle (Jas 1:1).

JAPHETH
Son of Noah (Ge 5:32; 1Ch 1:4–5). Blessed (Ge 9:18–28).

JARS
2Co   4:   7   we have this treasure in **j** of clay

JEALOUS (JEALOUSY)
Ex   20:   5   am a **j** God, punishing the children
      34: 14   whose name is **J**, is a **j** God.
Dt   4: 24   God is a consuming fire, a **j** God.
Joel   2: 18   Then the LORD was **j** for his land
Zec   1: 14   I am very **j** for Jerusalem and Zion,
2Co   11:   2   am **j** for you with a godly jealousy.

JEALOUSY (JEALOUS)
1Co   3:   3   For since there is **j** and quarreling
2Co   11:   2   I am jealous for you with a godly **j**.
Gal   5: 20   hatred, discord, **j**, fits of rage,

JEHOAHAZ
1. Son of Jehu; king of Israel (2Ki 13:1–9).
2. Son of Josiah; king of Judah (2Ki 23:31–34; 2Ch 36:1–4).

JEHOASH
Son of Jehoahaz; king of Israel (2Ki 13–14; 2Ch 25).

JEHOIACHIN
Son of Jehoiakim; king of Judah exiled by Nebuchadnezzar (2Ki 24:8–17; 2Ch 36:8–10; Jer 22:24–30; 24:1). Raised from prisoner status (2Ki 25:27–30; Jer 52:31–34).

JEHOIAKIM
Son of Josiah; king of Judah (2Ki 23:34—24:6; 2Ch 36:4–8; Jer 22:18–23; 36).

JEHORAM
Son of Jehoshaphat; king of Judah (2Ki 8:16–24).

JEHOSHAPHAT
Son of Asa; king of Judah (1Ki 22:41–50; 2Ki 3; 2Ch 17–20).

JEHU
King of Israel (1Ki 19:16–19; 2Ki 9–10).

JEPHTHAH
Judge from Gilead who delivered Israel from Ammon (Jdg 10:6—12:7). Made rash vow concerning his daughter (Jdg 11:30–40).

JEREMIAH
Prophet to Judah (Jer 1:1–3). Called by the LORD (Jer 1). Put in stocks (Jer 20:1–3). Threatened for prophesying (Jer 11:18–23; 26). Opposed by Hananiah (Jer 28). Scroll burned (Jer 36). Imprisoned (Jer 37). Thrown into cistern (Jer 38). Forced to Egypt with those fleeing Babylonians (Jer 43).

JEROBOAM
1. Official of Solomon; rebelled to become first king of Israel (1Ki 11:26–40; 12:1–20; 2Ch 10). Idolatry (1Ki 12:25–33); judgment for (1Ki 13–14; 2Ch 13).
2. Son of Jehoash; king of Israel (1Ki 14:23–29).

JERUSALEM
2Ki   23: 27   and I will reject **J**, the city I chose,

2Ch   6:   6   now I have chosen **J** for my Name
Ne   2: 17   let us rebuild the wall of **J**,
Ps   122:   6   Pray for the peace of **J**:
     125:   2   As the mountains surround **J**,
     137:   5   If I forget you, **J**, may my right
Isa   40:   9   You who bring good news to **J**,
      65: 18   for I will create **J** to be a delight
Joel   3: 17   **J** will be holy; never again will
Zep   3: 16   On that day they will say to **J**,
Zec   2:   4   man, '**J** will be a city without walls
       8:   8   I will bring them back to live in **J**;
      14:   8   living water will flow out from **J**,
Mt   23: 37   "**J**, **J**, you who kill the prophets
Lk   13: 34   "**J**, **J**, you who kill the prophets
      21: 24   **J** will be trampled
Jn   4: 20   where we must worship is in **J**."
Ac   1:   8   and you will be my witnesses in **J**,
Gal   4: 25   to the present city of **J**,
Rev   21:   2   the new **J**, coming down

JESUS
LIFE: Genealogy (Mt 1:1–17; Lk 3:21–37). Birth announced (Mt 1:18–25; Lk 1:26–45). Birth (Mt 2:1–12; Lk 2:1–40). Escape to Egypt (Mt 2:13–23). As a boy in the temple (Lk 2:41–52). Baptism (Mt 3:13–17; Mk 1:9–11; Lk 3:21–22; Jn 1:32–34). Temptation (Mt 4:1–11; Mk 1:12–13; Lk 4:1–13). Ministry in Galilee (Mt 4:12—18:35; Mk 1:14—9:50; Lk 4:14—13:9; Jn 1:35—2:11; 4; 6), Transfiguration (Mt 17:1–8; Mk 9:2–8; Lk 9:28–36), on the way to Jerusalem (Mt 19–20; Mk 10; Lk 13:10—19:27), in Jerusalem (Mt 21–25; Mk 11–13; Lk 19:28—21:38; Jn 2:12—3:36; 5; 7–12). Last supper (Mt 26:17–35; Mk 14:12–31; Lk 22:1–38; Jn 13–17). Arrest and trial (Mt 26:36—27:31; Mk 14:43—15:20; Lk 22:39—23:25; Jn 18:1—19:16). Crucifixion (Mt 27:32–66; Mk 15:21–47; Lk 23:26–55; Jn 19:28–42). Resurrection and appearances (Mt 28; Mk 16; Lk 24; Jn 20–21; Ac 1:1–11; 7:56; 9:3–6; 1Co 15:1–8; Rev 1:1–20).
MIRACLES. Healings: official's son (Jn 4:43–54), demoniac in Capernaum (Mk 1:23–26; Lk 4:33–35), Peter's mother-in-law (Mt 8:14–17; Mk 1:29–31; Lk 4:38–39), leper (Mt 8:2–4; Mk 1:40–45; Lk 5:12–16), paralytic (Mt 9:1–8; Mk 2:1–12; Lk 5:17–26), cripple (Jn 5:1–9), shriveled hand (Mt 12:10–13; Mk 3:1–5; Lk 6:6–11), centurion's servant (Mt 8:5–13; Lk 7:1–10), widow's son raised (Lk 7:11–17), demoniac (Mt 12:22–23; Lk 11:14), Gadarene demoniacs (Mt 8:28–34; Mk 5:1–20; Lk 8:26–39), woman's bleeding and Jairus' daughter (Mt 9:18–26; Mk 5:21–43; Lk 8:40–56), blind man (Mt 9:27–31), mute man (Mt 9:32–33), Canaanite woman's daughter (Mt 15:21–28; Mk 7:24–30), deaf man (Mk 7:31–37), blind man (Mk 8:22–26), demoniac boy (Mt 17:14–18; Mk 9:14–29; Lk 9:37–43), ten lepers (Lk 17:11–19), man born blind (Jn 9:1–7), Lazarus raised (Jn 11), crippled woman (Lk 13:11–17), man with dropsy (Lk 14:1–6), two blind men (Mt 20:29–34; Mk 10:46–52; Lk 18:35–43), Malchus' ear (Lk 22:50–51). Other Miracles: water to wine (Jn 2:1–11), catch of fish (Lk 5:1–11), storm stilled (Mt 8:23–27; Mk 4:37–41; Lk 8:22–25), 5,000 fed (Mt 14:15–21; Mk 6:35–44; Lk 9:10–17; Jn 6:1–14), walking on water (Mt 14:25–32; Mk 6:48–52; Jn 6:15–21), 4,000 fed (Mt 15:32–39; Mk 8:1–9), money from fish (Mt 17:24–27), fig tree cursed (Mt 21:18–22; Mk 11:12–14), catch of fish (Jn 21:1–14).

CONCORDANCE

MAJOR TEACHING: Sermon on the Mount (Mt 5–7; Lk 6:17–49), to Nicodemus (Jn 3), to Samaritan woman (Jn 4), Bread of Life (Jn 6:22–59), at Feast of Tabernacles (Jn 7–8), woes to Pharisees (Mt 23; Lk 11:37–54), Good Shepherd (Jn 10:1–18), Olivet Discourse (Mt 24–25; Mk 13; Lk 21:5–36), Upper Room Discourse (Jn 13–16).

PARABLES: Sower (Mt 13:3–23; Mk 4:3–25; Lk 8:5–18), seed's growth (Mk 4:26–29), wheat and weeds (Mt 13:24–30, 36–43), mustard seed (Mt 13:31–32; Mk 4:30–32), yeast (Mt 13:33; Lk 13:20–21), hidden treasure (Mt 13:44), valuable pearl (Mt 13:45–46), net (Mt 13:47–51), house owner (Mt 13:52), good Samaritan (Lk 10:25–37), unmerciful servant (Mt 18:15–35), lost sheep (Mt 18:10–14; Lk 15:4–7), lost coin (Lk 15:8–10), prodigal son (Lk 15:11–32), dishonest manager (Lk 16:1–13), rich man and Lazarus (Lk 16:19–31), persistent widow (Lk 18:1–8), Pharisee and tax collector (Lk 18:9–14), payment of workers (Mt 20:1–16), tenants and the vineyard (Mt 21:28–46; Mk 12:1–12; Lk 20:9–19), wedding banquet (Mt 22:1–14), faithful servant (Mt 24:45–51), ten virgins (Mt 25:1–13), talents (Mt 25:1–30; Lk 19:12–27).

DISCIPLES see APOSTLES. Call of (Jn 1:35–51; Mt 4:18–22; 9:9; Mk 1:16–20; 2:13–14; Lk 5:1–11, 27–28). Named Apostles (Mk 3:13–19; Lk 6:12–16). Twelve sent out (Mt 10; Mk 6:7–11; Lk 9:1–5). Seventy sent out (Lk 10:1–24). Defection of (Jn 6:60–71; Mt 26:56; Mk 14:50–52). Final commission (Mt 28:16–20; Jn 21:15–23; Ac 1:3–8).

Ac	2: 32	God has raised this **J** to life, and we
	9: 5	Saul asked. "I am **J**, whom you are
	15: 11	of our Lord **J** that we are saved,
	16: 31	"Believe in the Lord **J**, and you will
Ro	3: 24	redemption that came by Christ **J**.
	5: 17	life through the one man, **J** Christ!
	8: 1	for those who are in Christ **J**,
1Co	2: 2	I was with you except **J** Christ
	8: 6	and there is but one Lord, **J** Christ,
	12: 3	and no one can say, "**J** is Lord,"
2Co	4: 5	but **J** Christ as Lord, and ourselves
Gal	2: 16	of the law, but by faith in **J** Christ.
	3: 28	for you are all one in Christ **J**.
	5: 6	in Christ **J** neither circumcision
Eph	2: 10	in Christ **J** to do good works,
	2: 20	with Christ **J** himself as the chief
Php	1: 6	until the day of Christ **J**.
	2: 5	have the same mindset as Christ **J**:
	2: 10	name of **J** every knee should bow,
Col	3: 17	do it all in the name of the Lord **J**,
2Th	2: 1	the coming of our Lord **J** Christ
1Ti	1: 15	**J** came into the world to save
2Ti	3: 12	life in Christ **J** will be persecuted,
Titus	2: 13	our great God and Savior, **J** Christ,
Heb	2: 9	But we do see **J**, who was made
	3: 1	fix your thoughts on **J**, whom we
	4: 14	into heaven, **J** the Son of God,
	7: 22	**J** has become the guarantor
	7: 24	but because **J** lives forever, he has
	12: 2	fixing our eyes on **J**, the pioneer
2Pe	1: 16	of our Lord **J** Christ in power,
1Jn	1: 7	and the blood of **J**, his Son,
	2: 1	**J** Christ, the Righteous One.
	2: 6	to live in him must live as **J** did.
	4: 15	acknowledges that **J** is the Son
Rev	22: 20	Amen. Come, Lord **J**.

JEW (JEWS JUDAISM)

Zec	8: 23	take firm hold of one **J** by the hem
Ro	1: 16	first to the **J**, then to the Gentile.
	10: 12	there is no difference between **J**
1Co	9: 20	To the Jews I became like a **J**,
Gal	3: 28	There is neither **J** nor Gentile,

JEWELRY (JEWELS)

1Pe	3: 3	wearing of gold **j** or fine clothes.

JEWELS (JEWELRY)

Isa	61: 10	as a bride adorns herself with her **j**.
Zec	9: 16	in his land like **j** in a crown.

JEWS (JEW)

Mt	2: 2	who has been born king of the **J**?
	27: 11	him, "Are you the king of the **J**?"
Jn	4: 22	know, for salvation is from the **J**.
Ro	3: 29	Or is God the God of **J** only?
1Co	1: 22	**J** demand signs and Greeks look
	9: 20	To the **J** I became like a Jew, to win
	12: 13	whether **J** or Gentiles,
Rev	3: 9	claim to be **J** though they are not,

JEZEBEL

Sidonian wife of Ahab (1Ki 16:31). Promoted Baal worship (1Ki 16:32–33). Killed prophets of the LORD (1Ki 18:4, 13). Opposed Elijah (1Ki 19:1–2). Had Naboth killed (1Ki 21). Death prophesied (1Ki 21:17–24). Killed by Jehu (2Ki 9:30–37).

JOASH

Son of Ahaziah; king of Judah. Sheltered from Athaliah by Jehoiada (2Ki 11; 2Ch 22:10—23:21). Repaired temple (2Ki 12; 2Ch 24).

JOB

Wealthy man from Uz; feared God (Job 1:1–5). Righteousness tested by disaster (Job 1:6–22), personal affliction (Job 2). Maintained innocence in debate with three friends (Job 3–31), Elihu (Job 32–37). Rebuked by the LORD (Job 38–41). Vindicated and restored to greater stature by the LORD (Job 42). Example of righteousness (Eze 14:14, 20).

JOHN

1. Son of Zechariah and Elizabeth (Lk 1). Called the Baptist (Mt 3:1–12; Mk 1:2–8). Witness to Jesus (Mt 3:11–12; Mk 1:7–8; Lk 3:15–18; Jn 1:6–35; 3:27–30; 5:33–36). Doubts about Jesus (Mt 11:2–6; Lk 7:18–23). Arrest (Mt 4:12; Mk 1:14). Execution (Mt 14:1–12; Mk 6:14–29; Lk 9:7–9). Ministry compared to Elijah (Mt 11:7–19; Mk 9:11–13; Lk 7:24–35).

2. Apostle; brother of James (Mt 4:21–22; 10:2; Mk 3:17; Lk 5:1–10). At transfiguration (Mt 17:1–13; Mk 9:1–13; Lk 9:28–36). Desire to be greatest (Mk 10:35–45). Leader of church at Jerusalem (Ac 4:1–3; Gal 2:9). Elder who wrote epistles (2Jn 1; 3Jn 1). Prophet who wrote Revelation (Rev 1:1; 22:8).

3. Cousin of Barnabas, co-worker with Paul, (Ac 12:12—13:13; 15:37), see MARK.

JOIN (JOINED)

Pr	23: 20	not **j** those who drink too much
	24: 21	do not **j** with rebellious officials,
Ro	15: 30	to **j** me in my struggle by praying
2Ti	1: 8	**j** with me in suffering
2Ti	2: 3	**J** with me in suffering, like a good

JOINED (JOIN)

Mt	19: 6	Therefore what God has **j** together,
Mk	10: 9	Therefore what God has **j** together,

Eph 2: 21 the whole building is **j** together
4: 16 body, **j** and held together by every

JOINTS
Heb 4: 12 soul and spirit, **j** and marrow;

JOKING
Eph 5: 4 foolish talk or coarse **j**, which are

JONAH
Prophet in days of Jeroboam II (2Ki 14:25). Called to Nineveh; fled to Tarshish (Jnh 1:1–3). Cause of storm; thrown into sea (Jnh 1:4–16). Swallowed by fish (Jnh 1:17). Prayer (Jnh 2). Preached to Nineveh (Jnh 3). Attitude reproved by the Lord (Jnh 4). Sign of (Mt 12:39–41; Lk 11:29–32).

JONATHAN
Son of Saul (1Sa 13:16; 1Ch 8:33). Valiant warrior (1Sa 13–14). Relation to David (1Sa 18:1–4; 19–20; 23:16–18). Killed at Gilboa (1Sa 31). Mourned by David (2Sa 1).

JORAM
1. Son of Ahab; king of Israel (2Ki 3; 8–9; 2Ch 22).

JORDAN
Nu 34: 12 boundary will go down along the **J**
Jos 4: 22 'Israel crossed the **J** on dry ground.'
Mt 3: 6 baptized by him in the **J** River.

JOSEPH
1. Son of Jacob by Rachel (Ge 30:24; 1Ch 2:2). Favored by Jacob, hated by brothers (Ge 37:3–4). Dreams (Ge 37:5–11). Sold by brothers (Ge 37:12–36). Served Potiphar; imprisoned by false accusation (Ge 39). Interpreted dreams of Pharaoh's servants (Ge 40), of Pharaoh (Ge 41:4–40). Made greatest in Egypt (Ge 41:41–57). Sold grain to brothers (Ge 42–45). Brought Jacob and sons to Egypt (Ge 46–47). Sons Ephraim and Manasseh blessed (Ge 48). Blessed (Ge 49:22–26; Dt 33:13–17). Death (Ge 50:22–26; Ex 13:19; Heb 11:22). 12,000 from (Rev 7:8).
2. Husband of Mary, mother of Jesus (Mt 1:16–24; 2:13–19; Lk 1:27; 2; Jn 1:45).
3. Disciple from Arimathea, who gave his tomb for Jesus' burial (Mt 27:57–61; Mk 15:43–47; Lk 23:50–53).
4. Original name of Barnabas (Ac 4:36).

JOSHUA
1. Son of Nun; name changed from Hoshea (Nu 13:8, 16; 1Ch 7:27). Fought Amalekites under Moses (Ex 17:9–14). Servant of Moses on Sinai (Ex 24:13; 32:17). Spied Canaan (Nu 13). With Caleb, allowed to enter land (Nu 14:6, 30). Succeeded Moses (Dt 1:38; 31:1–8; 34:9).
Charged Israel to conquer Canaan (Jos 1). Crossed Jordan (Jos 3–4). Circumcised sons of wilderness wanderings (Jos 5). Conquered Jericho (Jos 6), Ai (Jos 7–8), five kings at Gibeon (Jos 10:1–28), southern Canaan (Jos 10:29–43), northern Canaan (Jos 11–12). Defeated at Ai (Jos 7). Deceived by Gibeonites (Jos 9). Renewed covenant (Jos 8:30–35; 24:1–27). Divided land among tribes (Jos 13–22). Last words (Jos 23). Death (Jos 24:28–31).
2. High priest during rebuilding of temple (Hag 1–2; Zec 3:1–9; 6:11).

JOSIAH
Son of Amon; king of Judah (2Ki 22–23; 2Ch 34–35).

JOTHAM
Son of Azariah (Uzziah); king of Judah (2Ki 15:32–38; 2Ch 26:21—27:9).

JOY (ENJOY ENJOYMENT JOYFUL OVERJOYED REJOICE REJOICES REJOICING)
Dt 16: 15 hands, and your **j** will be complete.
1Ch 16: 27 and **j** are in his dwelling place.
Ne 8: 10 for the **j** of the Lord is your
Est 9: 22 their sorrow was turned into **j**
Job 38: 7 and all the angels shouted for **j**?
Ps 4: 7 Fill my heart with **j** when their
21: 6 glad with the **j** of your presence.
30: 11 sackcloth and clothed me with **j**,
43: 4 God, to God, my **j** and my delight.
51: 12 to me the **j** of your salvation
66: 1 Shout for **j** to God, all the earth!
96: 12 all the trees of the forest sing for **j**.
107: 22 tell of his works with songs of **j**.
119:111 forever; they are the **j** of my heart.
Pr 10: 1 A wise son brings **j** to his father,
10: 28 The prospect of the righteous is **j**,
12: 20 those who promote peace have **j**.
15: 30 in a messenger's eyes brings **j**
Isa 35: 10 everlasting **j** will crown their heads
51: 11 Gladness and **j** will overtake them,
55: 12 You will go out in **j** and be led
Lk 1: 44 the baby in my womb leaped for **j**.
2: 10 will cause great **j** for all the people.
Jn 15: 11 and that your **j** may be complete.
16: 20 grieve, but your grief will turn to **j**.
2Co 8: 2 trial, their overflowing **j** and their
Php 2: 2 then make my **j** complete by being
4: 1 love and long for, my **j** and crown,
1Th 2: 19 our **j**, or the crown in which we
Phm : 7 Your love has given me great **j**
Heb 12: 2 the **j** set before him he endured
Jas 1: 2 Consider it pure **j**, my brothers
1Pe 1: 8 an inexpressible and glorious **j**,
2Jn : 4 It has given me great **j** to find some
3Jn : 4 I have no greater **j** than to hear

JOYFUL (JOY)
Ps 100: 2 come before him with **j** songs.
Pr 23: 25 may she who gave you birth be **j**!
Hab 3: 18 I will be **j** in God my Savior.

JUDAH
1. Son of Jacob by Leah (Ge 29:35; 35:23; 1Ch 2:1). Tribe of blessed as ruling tribe (Ge 49:8–12; Dt 33:7).
2. Name used for people and land of Southern Kingdom.

Jer 13: 19 All **J** will be carried into exile,
Zec 10: 4 From **J** will come the cornerstone,
Heb 7: 14 that our Lord descended from **J**,

JUDAISM (JEW)
Gal 1: 13 of my previous way of life in **J**,

JUDAS
1. Apostle (Lk 6:16; Jn 14:22; Ac 1:13). Probably also called Thaddaeus (Mt 10:3; Mk 3:18).
2. Brother of James and Jesus (Mt 13:55; Mk 6:3), also called Jude (Jude 1).
3. Apostle, also called Iscariot, who betrayed Jesus (Mt 10:4; 26:14–56; Mk 3:19; 14:10–50; Lk 6:16; 22:3–53; Jn 6:71; 12:4; 13:2–30; 18:2–11). Suicide of (Mt 27:3–5; Ac 1:16–25).

CONCORDANCE

JUDGE (JUDGED JUDGES JUDGING JUDGMENT)
Ge	18:	25	Will not the **J** of all the earth do
1Ch	16:	33	Lᴏʀᴅ, for he comes to **j** the earth.
Joel	3:	12	there I will sit to **j** all the nations
Mt	7:	1	"Do not **j**, or you too will be
Jn	7:	24	but instead **j** correctly."
	12:	47	For I did not come to **j** the world,
Ac	17:	31	set a day when he will **j** the world
1Co	4:	3	indeed, I do not even **j** myself.
	6:	2	the Lord's people will **j** the world?
2Ti	4:	1	who will **j** the living and the dead,
	4:	8	the righteous **J**, will award to me
Jas	4:	12	who are you to **j** your neighbor?
Rev	20:	4	who had been given authority to **j**.

JUDGED (JUDGE)
Mt	7:	1	"Do not judge, or you too will be **j**.
Jn	5:	24	will not be **j** but has crossed over
Jas	3:	1	who teach will be **j** more strictly.
Rev	20:	12	The dead were **j** according to what

JUDGES (JUDGE)
Jdg	2:	16	Then the Lᴏʀᴅ raised up **j**,
Ps	9:	8	and **j** the peoples with equity.
	58:	11	there is a God who **j** the earth."
Ro	2:	16	God **j** people's secrets through Jesus
Heb	4:	12	it **j** the thoughts and attitudes
Rev	19:	11	With justice he **j** and wages war.

JUDGING (JUDGE)
Mt	19:	28	**j** the twelve tribes of Israel.
Jn	7:	24	Stop **j** by mere appearances,
2Co	10:	7	You are **j** by appearances.

JUDGMENT (JUDGE)
Dt	1:	17	of anyone, for **j** belongs to God.
Ps	1:	5	the wicked will not stand in the **j**,
	119:	66	Teach me knowledge and good **j**,
Ecc	12:	14	God will bring every deed into **j**,
Isa	66:	16	his sword the Lᴏʀᴅ will execute **j**
Mt	5:	21	who murders will be subject to **j**.'
	10:	15	Gomorrah on the day of **j** than
	12:	36	the day of **j** for every empty word
Jn	5:	22	but has entrusted all **j** to the Son,
	16:	8	about sin and righteousness and **j**:
Ro	14:	10	will all stand before God's **j** seat.
	14:	13	Therefore let us stop passing **j**
1Co	11:	29	eat and drink **j** on themselves.
	11:	31	we would not come under such **j**.
2Co	5:	10	we must all appear before the **j** seat
Heb	9:	27	to die once, and after that to face **j**,
	10:	27	only a fearful expectation of **j**
1Pe	4:	17	For it is time for **j** to begin
Jude	:	6	everlasting chains for **j** on the great

JUST (JUSTICE JUSTIFICATION JUSTIFIED JUSTIFY JUSTLY)
Dt	32:	4	are perfect, and all his ways are **j**.
Ps	37:	28	For the Lᴏʀᴅ loves the **j** and will
	111:	7	of his hands are faithful and **j**;
Pr	1:	3	doing what is right and **j** and fair;
	2:	8	for he guards the course of the **j**
Da	4:	37	does is right and all his ways are **j**.
Ro	3:	26	time, so as to be **j** and the one who
Heb	2:	2	received its **j** punishment.
1Jn	1:	9	he is faithful and **j** and will forgive
Rev	16:	7	true and **j** are your judgments."

JUSTICE (JUST)
Ex	23:	2	do not pervert **j** by siding
Ex	23:	6	"Do not deny **j** to your poor people
Job	37:	23	in his **j** and great righteousness,
Ps	9:	16	Lᴏʀᴅ is known by his acts of **j**;
	11:	7	the Lᴏʀᴅ is righteous, he loves **j**;
	45:	6	a scepter of **j** will be the scepter
	101:	1	I will sing of your love and **j**;
Pr	21:	15	When **j** is done, it brings joy
	29:	4	By **j** a king gives a country stability,
	29:	26	is from the Lᴏʀᴅ that one gets **j**.
Isa	9:	7	and upholding it with **j**
	28:	17	I will make **j** the measuring line
	30:	18	For the Lᴏʀᴅ is a God of **j**.
	42:	1	and he will bring **j** to the nations.
	42:	4	be discouraged till he establishes **j**
	56:	1	"Maintain **j** and do what is right,
	61:	8	"For I, the Lᴏʀᴅ, love **j**;
Eze	34:	16	I will shepherd the flock with **j**.
Am	5:	15	maintain **j** in the courts.
	5:	24	But let **j** roll on like a river,
Zec	7:	9	'Administer true **j**; show mercy
Lk	11:	42	you neglect **j** and the love of God.

JUSTIFICATION (JUST)
Ac	13:	39	sin, a **j** you were not able to obtain
Ro	4:	25	sins and was raised to life for our **j**.
	5:	18	one righteous act resulted in **j**

JUSTIFIED (JUST)
Ro	3:	24	all are **j** freely by his grace through
	3:	28	that a person is **j** by faith apart
	5:	1	since we have been **j** through faith,
	5:	9	Since we have now been **j** by his
	8:	30	he called, he also **j**; those he **j**,
1Co	6:	11	you were **j** in the name of the Lord
Gal	2:	16	that a person is not **j** by the works
	3:	11	relies on the law is **j** before God,
	3:	24	came that we might be **j** by faith.

JUSTIFY (JUST)
Gal	3:	8	that God would **j** the Gentiles

JUSTLY (JUST)
Ps	106:	3	Blessed are those who act **j**,
Mic	6:	8	To act **j** and to love mercy

KEEP (KEEPER KEEPING KEEPS KEPT)
Ge	31:	49	"May the Lᴏʀᴅ **k** watch between
Ex	20:	6	love me and **k** my commandments.
Nu	6:	24	Lᴏʀᴅ bless you and **k** you;
Ps	18:	28	You, Lᴏʀᴅ, **k** my lamp burning;
	19:	13	**K** your servant also from willful
	121:	7	The Lᴏʀᴅ will **k** you from all
	141:	3	**k** watch over the door of my lips.
Pr	4:	24	**K** your mouth free of perversity;
	17:	28	are thought wise if they **k** silent,
Isa	26:	3	You will **k** in perfect peace those
Am	5:	13	Therefore the prudent **k** quiet
Mt	10:	10	staff, for the worker is worth his **k**.
Lk	12:	35	service and **k** your lamps burning,
Gal	5:	25	let us **k** in step with the Spirit.
Eph	4:	3	Make every effort to **k** the unity
1Ti	5:	22	the sins of others. **K** yourself pure.
2Ti	4:	5	you, **k** your head in all situations,
Heb	13:	5	**K** your lives free from the love
Jas	1:	26	and yet do not **k** a tight rein on
	2:	8	If you really **k** the royal law found
1Jn	5:	3	love for God: to **k** his commands.
Jude	:	24	To him who is able to **k** you

KEEPER (KEEP)
Ge   4: 9   "Am I my brother's **k**?"

KEEPING (KEEP)
Ex 20: 8   the Sabbath day by **k** it holy.
Ps 19: 11 in **k** them there is great reward.
Mt   3: 8   Produce fruit in **k** with repentance.
Lk   2: 8   **k** watch over their flocks at night.
1Co 7: 19 **K** God's commands is what counts.
2Pe 3: 9   Lord is not slow in **k** his promise,

KEEPS (KEEP)
1Co 13: 5   angered, it **k** no record of wrongs.
Jas   2: 10 For whoever **k** the whole law

KEPT (KEEP)
Ps 130: 3   Lord, **k** a record of sins, Lord,
2Ti   4: 7   finished the race, I have **k** the faith.
1Pe   1: 4   This inheritance is **k** in heaven

KEYS
Mt 16: 19 will give you the **k** of the kingdom

KILL (KILLS)
Mt 17: 23 will **k** him, and on the third day

KILLS (KILL)
Lev 24: 21 whoever **k** a human being is to be
2Co 3: 6   for the letter **k**, but the Spirit gives

KIND (KINDNESS KINDS)
Ge   1: 24 animals, each according to its **k**."
2Ch 10: 7   "If you will be **k** to these people
Pr 11: 17 Those who are **k** benefit themselves,
     12: 25 the heart, but a **k** word cheers it up.
     14: 21 blessed is the one who is **k**
     14: 31 whoever is **k** to the needy honors
     19: 17 Whoever is **k** to the poor lends
Da   4: 27 by being **k** to the oppressed.
Lk   6: 35 because he is **k** to the ungrateful
1Co 13: 4   Love is patient, love is **k**.
     15: 35 what **k** of body will they come?"
Eph 4: 32 Be **k** and compassionate to one
2Ti   2: 24 but must be **k** to everyone,
Titus 2: 5   to be **k**, and to be subject to their

KINDNESS (KIND)
Ac 14: 17 He has shown **k** by giving you rain
Ro 11: 22 but **k** to you, provided that you
            continue in his **k**.
Gal   5: 22 peace, forbearance, **k**, goodness,
Eph 2: 7   expressed in his **k** to us in Christ

KINDS (KIND)
1Co 12: 4   There are different **k** of gifts,
1Ti   6: 10 of money is a root of all **k** of evil.

KING (KINGDOM KINGS)
1. Kings of Judah and Israel: see Saul, David, Solomon.

2. Kings of Judah: see Rehoboam, Abijah, Asa, Jehoshaphat, Jehoram, Ahaziah, Athaliah (Queen), Joash, Amaziah, Uzziah, Jotham, Ahaz, Hezekiah, Manasseh, Amon, Josiah, Jehoahaz, Jehoiakim, Jehoiachin, Zedekiah.

3. Kings of Israel: see Jeroboam I, Nadab, Baasha, Elah, Zimri, Tibni, Omri, Ahab, Ahaziah, Joram, Jehu, Jehoahaz, Jehoash, Jeroboam II, Zechariah, Shallum, Menahem, Pekah, Pekahiah, Hoshea.

Jdg 17: 6   In those days Israel had no **k**;
1Sa 12: 12 'No, we want a **k** to rule over us'—

1Sa 12: 12 the Lord your God was your **k**.
Ps 24: 7   that the **K** of glory may come in.
Isa 32: 1   a **k** will reign in righteousness
Zec   9: 9   See, your **k** comes to you,
1Ti   6: 15 the **K** of kings and Lord of lords,
Rev 19: 16 thigh he has this name written: **k**

KINGDOM (KING)
Ex 19: 6   you will be for me a **k** of priests
1Ch 29: 11 Yours, Lord, is the **k**;
Ps 45: 6   justice will be the scepter of your **k**.
Da   4: 3   His **k** is an eternal **k**;
Mt   3: 2   for the **k** of heaven has come near."
      5: 3   spirit, for theirs is the **k** of heaven.
      6: 10 your **k** come, your will be done,
      6: 33 But seek first his **k** and his
      7: 21 Lord,' will enter the **k** of heaven,
     11: 11 the **k** of heaven is greater than he.
     13: 24 "The **k** of heaven is like a man who
     13: 31 "The **k** of heaven is like a mustard
     13: 33 "The **k** of heaven is like yeast
     13: 44 "The **k** of heaven is like treasure
     13: 45 the **k** of heaven is like a merchant
     13: 47 the **k** of heaven is like a net that
     16: 19 you the keys of the **k** of heaven;
     18: 23 the **k** of heaven is like a king who
     19: 24 who is rich to enter the **k** of God."
     24: 7   rise against nation, and **k** against **k**.
     24: 14 gospel of the **k** will be preached
     25: 34 the **k** prepared for you since
Mk   9: 47 you to enter the **k** of God with one
     10: 14 for the **k** of God belongs to such as
     10: 23 for the rich to enter the **k** of God!"
Lk 10: 9   'The **k** of God has come near
     12: 31 But seek his **k**, and these things
     17: 21 is,' because the **k** of God is in your
Jn   3: 5   one can enter the **k** of God unless
     18: 36 said, "My **k** is not of this world.
1Co 6: 9   wrongdoers will not inherit the **k**
     15: 24 when he hands over the **k** to God
Rev 1: 6   has made us to be a **k** and priests
     11: 15 "The **k** of the world has become

KINGS (KING)
Ps   2: 2   The **k** of the earth rise
   72: 11 May all **k** bow down to him and all
Da   7: 24 ten horns are ten **k** who will come
1Ti   2: 2   for **k** and all those in authority,
Rev 1: 5   and the ruler of the **k** of the earth.

KISS
Ps   2: 12 **K** his son, or he will be angry
Pr 24: 26 An honest answer is like a **k**
Lk 22: 48 the Son of Man with a **k**?"

KNEE (KNEES)
Isa 45: 23 Before me every **k** will bow;
Ro 14: 11 Lord, 'every **k** will bow before me;
Php   2: 10 name of Jesus every **k** should bow,

KNEES (KNEE)
Isa 35: 3   hands, steady the **k** that give way;
Heb 12: 12 your feeble arms and weak **k**.

KNEW (KNOW)
Job 23: 3   If only I **k** where to find him;
Jnh   4: 2   I **k** that you are a gracious
Mt   7: 23 tell them plainly, 'I never **k** you.

KNOCK

Mt	7:	7	**k** and the door will be opened
Rev	3:	20	I stand at the door and **k**.

KNOW (FOREKNEW KNEW KNOWING KNOWLEDGE KNOWN KNOWS)

Dt	18:	21	"How can we **k** when a message
Job	19:	25	I **k** that my redeemer lives,
	42:	3	things too wonderful for me to **k**.
Ps	46:	10	says, "Be still, and **k** that I am God;
	73:	11	Does the Most High **k** anything?"
	139:	1	LORD, and you **k** me.
	139:	23	Search me, God, and **k** my heart;
Pr	27:	1	you do not **k** what a day may bring.
Jer	24:	7	I will give them a heart to **k** me,
	31:	34	because they will all **k** me,
Mt	6:	3	let your left hand **k** what your right
	24:	42	because you do not **k** on what day
Lk	1:	4	so that you may **k** the certainty
Jn	3:	11	you, we speak of what we **k**, and we
	4:	22	worship what you do not **k**;
	9:	25	One thing I do **k**. I was blind
	10:	14	I **k** my sheep and my sheep **k** me—
	17:	3	that they **k** you, the only true God,
	21:	24	We **k** that his testimony is true.
Ac	1:	7	"It is not for you to **k** the times
Ro	6:	6	we **k** that our old self was crucified
	7:	18	I **k** that good itself does not dwell
	8:	28	we **k** that in all things God works
1Co	2:	2	I resolved to **k** nothing while I was
	6:	15	Do you not **k** that your bodies are
	6:	19	Do you not **k** that your bodies are
	8:	2	do not yet **k** as they ought to **k**.
	13:	12	Now I **k** in part; then I shall **k** fully,
	15:	58	because you **k** that your labor
Php	3:	10	I want to **k** Christ—yes, to **k**
2Ti	1:	12	because I **k** whom I have believed,
Jas	4:	14	do not even **k** what will happen
1Jn	2:	4	Whoever says, "I **k** him," but does
	3:	14	We **k** that we have passed
	3:	16	This is how we **k** what love is:
	5:	2	This is how we **k** that we love
	5:	13	may **k** that you have eternal life.

KNOWING (KNOW)

Ge	3:	5	will be like God, **k** good and evil."
Php	3:	8	worth of **k** Christ Jesus my Lord,

KNOWLEDGE (KNOW)

Ge	2:	9	the tree of the **k** of good and evil.
Job	42:	3	that obscures my plans without **k**?'
Ps	19:	2	night after night they reveal **k**.
	139:	6	Such **k** is too wonderful for me,
Pr	1:	7	of the LORD is the beginning of **k**,
	10:	14	The wise store up **k**, but the mouth
	12:	1	Whoever loves discipline loves **k**,
	13:	16	All who are prudent act with **k**,
	19:	2	Desire without **k** is not good—
Isa	11:	9	the **k** of the LORD as the waters
Hab	2:	14	will be filled with the **k** of the glory
Ro	11:	33	riches of the wisdom and **k** of God!
1Co	8:	1	But **k** puffs up while love builds up.
	8:	11	Christ died, is destroyed by your **k**.
	13:	2	can fathom all mysteries and all **k**,
2Co	2:	14	aroma of the **k** of him everywhere.
	4:	6	of the **k** of God's glory displayed
Eph	3:	19	know this love that surpasses **k**—

Col	2:	3	all the treasures of wisdom and **k**.
1Ti	6:	20	ideas of what is falsely called **k**,
2Pe	3:	18	grow in the grace and **k** of our Lord

KNOWN (KNOW)

Ps	16:	11	You make **k** to me the path of life;
	105:	1	make **k** among the nations what he
Isa	46:	10	I make **k** the end
Mt	10:	26	or hidden that will not be made **k**.
Ro	1:	19	since what may be **k** about God is
	11:	34	"Who has **k** the mind of the Lord?
	15:	20	the gospel where Christ was not **k**,
2Co	3:	2	our hearts, **k** and read by everyone.
2Pe	2:	21	than to have **k** it and then to turn

KNOWS (KNOW)

1Sa	2:	3	for the LORD is a God who **k**,
Job	23:	10	But he **k** the way that I take;
Ps	44:	21	since he **k** the secrets of the heart?
	94:	11	The LORD **k** all human plans; he **k**
Ecc	8:	7	Since no one **k** the future, who can
Mt	6:	8	your Father **k** what you need
	24:	36	about that day or hour no one **k**,
Ro	8:	27	searches our hearts **k** the mind
2Ti	2:	19	"The Lord **k** those who are his,"

LABAN

Brother of Rebekah (Ge 24:29–51), father of Rachel and Leah (Ge 29–31).

LABOR

Ex	20:	9	Six days you shall **l** and do all your
Isa	55:	2	your **l** on what does not satisfy?
Mt	6:	28	They do not **l** or spin.
1Co	3:	8	rewarded according to their own **l**.
	15:	58	know that your **l** in the Lord is not

LACK (LACKING LACKS)

Pr	15:	22	Plans fail for **l** of counsel,
Col	2:	23	but they **l** any value in restraining

LACKING (LACK)

Ro	12:	11	Never be **l** in zeal, but keep your
Jas	1:	4	and complete, not **l** anything.

LACKS (LACK)

Jas	1:	5	If any of you **l** wisdom, you should

LAID (LAY)

Isa	53:	6	and the LORD has **l** on him
1Co	3:	11	other than the one already **l**,
1Jn	3:	16	Jesus Christ **l** down his life for us.

LAKE

Rev	19:	20	into the fiery **l** of burning sulfur.
	20:	14	The **l** of fire is the second death.

LAMB (LAMB'S LAMBS)

Ge	22:	8	"God himself will provide the **l**
Ex	12:	21	and slaughter the Passover **l**.
Isa	11:	6	The wolf will live with the **l**,
	53:	7	he was led like a **l** to the slaughter,
Jn	1:	29	"Look, the **L** of God, who takes
1Co	5:	7	our Passover **l**, has been sacrificed.
1Pe	1:	19	a **l** without blemish or defect.
Rev	5:	6	Then I saw a **L**, looking as if it had
	5:	12	"Worthy is the **L**, who was slain,
	14:	4	as firstfruits to God and the **L**.

LAMB'S (LAMB)

Rev	21:	27	names are written in the **L** book

CONCORDANCE

LAMBS (LAMB)
Lk 10: 3 you out like **l** among wolves.
Jn 21: 15 Jesus said, "Feed my **l**."

LAMENT
2Sa 1: 17 took up this **l** concerning Saul

LAMP (LAMPS)
2Sa 22: 29 You, LORD, are my **l**;
Ps 18: 28 You, LORD, keep my **l** burning;
119:105 Your word is a **l** to my feet
Pr 31: 18 and her **l** does not go out at night.
Lk 8: 16 "No one lights a **l** and hides it
Rev 21: 23 gives it light, and the Lamb is its **l**.

LAMPS (LAMP)
Mt 25: 1 be like ten virgins who took their **l**
Lk 12: 35 service and keep your **l** burning,

LAND
Ge 1: 10 God called the dry ground "**l**,"
1: 11 said, "Let the **l** produce vegetation:
12: 7 your offspring I will give this **l**."
Ex 3: 8 a **l** flowing with milk and honey—
Nu 35: 33 Bloodshed pollutes the **l**,
Dt 34: 1 LORD showed him the whole **l**—
Jos 13: 2 "This is the **l** that remains:
14: 4 Levites received no share of the **l**
2Ch 7: 14 their sin and will heal their **l**.
7: 20 then I will uproot Israel from my **l**,
Eze 36: 24 bring you back into your own **l**.

LANGUAGE
Ge 11: 1 Now the whole world had one **l**
Jn 8: 44 speaks his native **l**, for he is
a liar
Ac 2: 6 heard their own **l** being spoken.
Col 3: 8 slander, and filthy **l** from your lips.
Rev 5: 9 God persons from every tribe and **l**

LAST (LASTING LASTS LATTER)
2Sa 23: 1 These are the **l** words of David:
Isa 44: 6 I am the first and I am the **l**;
Mt 19: 30 But many who are first will be **l**,
Mk 10: 31 will be **l**, and the **l** first."
Jn 15: 16 fruit that will **l**—and so
Ro 1: 17 that is by faith from first to **l**,
2Ti 3: 1 will be terrible times in the **l** days.
2Pe 3: 3 in the **l** days scoffers will come,
Rev 1: 17 I am the First and the **L**.
22: 13 the First and the **L**, the Beginning

LASTING (LAST)
Ex 12: 14 to the LORD—a **l** ordinance.
Lev 24: 8 of the Israelites, as a **l** covenant.
Nu 25: 13 have a covenant of a **l** priesthood,
Heb 10: 34 had better and **l** possessions.

LASTS (LAST)
Ps 30: 5 For his anger **l** only a moment,
2Co 3: 11 greater is the glory of that
which **l**!

LATTER (LAST)
Job 42: 12 The LORD blessed the **l** part

LAUGH (LAUGHS)
Ecc 3: 4 a time to weep and a time to **l**,

LAUGHS (LAUGH)
Ps 2: 4 The One enthroned in heaven **l**;
37: 13 but the Lord **l** at the wicked, for he

LAVISHED
Eph 1: 8 that he **l** on us. With all wisdom
1Jn 3: 1 See what great love the Father has **l**

LAW (LAWS)
Dt 31: 11 you shall read this **l** before them
31: 26 "Take this Book of the **L** and place
Jos 1: 8 Keep this Book of the **L** always
Ne 8: 8 from the Book of the **L** of God,
Ps 1: 2 delight is in the **l** of the LORD,
19: 7 The **l** of the LORD is perfect,
119: 18 may see wonderful things in your **l**.
119: 72 The **l** from your mouth is more
119: 97 Oh, how I love your **l**! I meditate
119:165 peace have those who love your **l**,
Jer 31: 33 "I will put my **l** in their minds
Mt 5: 17 that I have come to abolish the **L**
7: 12 you, for this sums up the **L**
22: 40 All the **L** and the Prophets hang
Lk 16: 17 stroke of a pen to drop out of the **L**.
Jn 1: 17 For the **l** was given through Moses;
Ro 2: 12 All who sin apart from the **l** will
2: 15 requirements of the **l** are written
5: 13 account where there is no **l**.
5: 20 The **l** was brought in so
6: 14 because you are not under the **l**,
7: 6 we have been released from the **l** so
7: 12 So then, the **l** is holy,
8: 3 For what the **l** was powerless to do
10: 4 Christ is the culmination of the **l**
13: 10 love is the fulfillment of the **l**.
Gal 3: 13 curse of the **l** by becoming a curse
3: 24 So the **l** was our guardian until
5: 3 he is obligated to obey the whole **l**.
5: 4 by the **l** have been alienated
5: 14 For the entire **l** is fulfilled
Heb 7: 19 (for the **l** made nothing perfect),
10: 1 The **l** is only a shadow of the good
Jas 1: 25 the perfect **l** that gives freedom,
2: 10 For whoever keeps the whole **l**

LAWLESSNESS
2Th 2: 3 occurs and the man of **l** is revealed,
2: 7 the secret power of **l** is already
1Jn 3: 4 sins breaks the law; in fact, sin is **l**.

LAWS (LAW)
Lev 25: 18 and be careful to obey my **l**,
Ps 119: 30 I have set my heart on your **l**.
119:120 fear of you; I stand in awe of your **l**.
Heb 8: 10 I will put my **l** in their minds
10: 16 I will put my **l** in their hearts, and I

LAY (LAID LAYING)
Job 22: 22 and **l** up his words in your heart.
Isa 28: 16 "See, I **l** a stone in Zion, a tested
Mt 8: 20 of Man has no place to **l** his head."
Jn 10: 15 and I **l** down my life for the sheep.
15: 13 to **l** down one's life for one's
1Co 3: 11 no one can **l** any foundation other
1Jn 3: 16 we ought to **l** down our lives for
Rev 4: 10 They **l** their crowns before

LAYING (LAY)
1Ti 5: 22 not be hasty in the **l** on of hands,
Heb 6: 1 not **l** again the foundation

LAZARUS
1. Poor man in Jesus' parable (Lk 16:19–31).

2. Brother of Mary and Martha whom Jesus raised from the dead (Jn 11:1—12:19).

LAZY
Pr	10: 4	**L** hands make for poverty,
Heb	6: 12	We do not want you to become **l**,

LEAD (LEADERS LEADS LED)
Ex	15: 13	love you will **l** the people you have
Ps	27: 11	**l** me in a straight path because
	61: 2	**l** me to the rock that is higher than I.
	139: 24	and **l** me in the way everlasting.
	143: 10	may your good Spirit **l** me on level
Ecc	5: 6	Do not let your mouth **l** you
Isa	11: 6	and a little child will **l** them.
Da	12: 3	those who **l** many to righteousness,
Mt	6: 13	And **l** us not into temptation,
1Jn	3: 7	do not let anyone **l** you astray.

LEADERS (LEAD)
Heb	13: 7	Remember your **l**, who spoke
	13: 17	Have confidence in your **l**

LEADS (LEAD)
Ps	23: 2	he **l** me beside quiet waters,
Pr	19: 23	The fear of the Lord **l** to life;
Isa	40: 11	he gently **l** those that have young.
Mt	7: 13	gate and broad is the road that **l**
Jn	10: 3	sheep by name and **l** them out.
Ro	14: 19	every effort to do what **l** to peace
2Co	2: 14	God, who always **l** us as captives

LEAH
Wife of Jacob (Ge 29:16–30); bore six sons and one daughter (Ge 29:31—30:21; 34:1; 35:23).

LEAN
Pr	3: 5	**l** not on your own understanding;

LEARN (LEARNED LEARNING)
Isa	1: 17	**L** to do right; seek justice.
Mt	11: 29	my yoke upon you and **l** from me,

LEARNED (LEARN)
Php	4: 11	I have **l** to be content whatever
2Ti	3: 14	know those from whom you **l** it,

LEARNING (LEARN)
Pr	1: 5	the wise listen and add to their **l**,
2Ti	3: 7	always **l** but never able to come

LED (LEAD)
Isa	53: 7	he was **l** like a lamb
Am	2: 10	I **l** you forty years in the wilderness
Ro	8: 14	For those who are **l** by the Spirit

LEFT
Jos	1: 7	turn from it to the right or to the **l**,
Pr	4: 27	Do not turn to the right or the **l**;
Mt	6: 3	do not let your **l** hand know what
	25: 33	on his right and the goats on his **l**.

LEGION
Mk	5: 9	"My name is **L**," he replied,

LEND (LENDS)
Dt	15: 8	freely **l** them whatever they need.
Ps	37: 26	are always generous and **l** freely;
Lk	6: 34	Even sinners **l** to sinners,

LENDS (LEND)
Pr	19: 17	kind to the poor **l** to the Lord,

LENGTH (LONG)
Pr	10: 27	fear of the Lord adds **l** to life,

LEPROSY
2Ki	7: 3	Now there were four men with **l**

LETTER (LETTERS)
Mt	5: 18	not the smallest **l**, not the least
2Co	3: 2	You yourselves are our **l**,
	3: 6	not of the **l** but of the Spirit; for the **l** kills,
2Th	3: 14	not obey our instruction in this **l**.

LETTERS (LETTER)
2Co	3: 7	which was engraved in **l** on stone,
	10: 10	"His **l** are weighty and forceful,
2Pe	3: 16	He writes the same way in all his **l**,

LEVEL
Ps	143: 10	good Spirit lead me on **l** ground.
Isa	26: 7	The path of the righteous is **l**;
Heb	12: 13	"Make **l** paths for your feet,"

LEVI (LEVITES)
1. Son of Jacob by Leah (Ge 29:34; 46:11; 1Ch 2:1). Tribe of blessed (Ge 49:5–7; Dt 33:8–11), chosen as priests (Nu 3–4), numbered (Nu 3:39; 26:62), allotted cities, but not land (Nu 18; 35; Dt 10:9; Jos 13:14; 21), land (Eze 48:8–22), 12,000 from (Rev 7:7).
2. See MATTHEW.

LEVITES (LEVI)
Nu	1: 53	The **L** are to be responsible
	8: 6	"Take the **L** from among all
	18: 21	"I give to the **L** all the tithes

LEWDNESS
Mk	7: 22	malice, deceit, **l**, envy, slander,

LIAR (LIE)
Pr	19: 22	better to be poor than a **l**.
Jn	8: 44	for he is a **l** and the father of lies.
Ro	3: 4	be true, and every human being a **l**.

LIBERATED
Ro	8: 21	the creation itself will be **l** from its

LIE (LIAR LIED LIES LYING)
Lev	19: 11	" 'Do not **l**. " 'Do not deceive
Nu	23: 19	that he should **l**, not a human
Dt	6: 7	when you **l** down and when you
Ps	23: 2	He makes me **l** down in green
Isa	11: 6	the leopard will **l** down
Eze	34: 14	There they will **l** down in good
Ro	1: 25	the truth about God for a **l**,
Col	3: 9	Do not **l** to each other, since you
Heb	6: 18	which it is impossible for God to **l**,

LIED (LIE)
Ac	5: 4	You have not **l** just to human

LIES (LIE)
Ps	34: 13	evil and your lips from telling **l**.
Jn	8: 44	for he is a liar and the father of **l**.

LIFE (LIVE)
Ge	2: 7	into his nostrils the breath of **l**,
	2: 9	of the garden were the tree of **l**
	9: 11	Never again will all **l** be destroyed
Ex	21: 23	injury, you are to take **l** for **l**,
Lev	17: 14	because the **l** of every creature is its
	24: 18	must make restitution—**l** for **l**.
Dt	30: 19	Now choose **l**, so that you and your

Ps	16: 11	make known to me the path of l;
	23: 6	will follow me all the days of my l,
	34: 12	Whoever of you loves l and desires
	39: 4	let me know how fleeting my l is.
	49: 7	one can redeem the l of another
	104: 33	I will sing to the Lord all my l;
Pr	6: 23	and instruction are the way to l,
	7: 23	little knowing it will cost him his l.
	8: 35	For those who find me find l
	11: 30	fruit of the righteous is a tree of l,
	21: 21	righteousness and love finds l,
Eze	37: 5	enter you, and you will come to l.
Da	12: 2	some to everlasting l,
Mt	6: 25	do not worry about your l,
	7: 14	and narrow the road that leads to l,
	10: 39	whoever loses their l for my sake
	16: 25	wants to save their l will lose it,
	20: 28	to give his l as a ransom for many."
Mk	10: 45	to give his l as a ransom for many."
Lk	12: 15	l does not consist in an abundance
	12: 22	do not worry about your l,
	14: 26	yes, even their own l—
Jn	1: 4	In him was l, and that l was the light
	3: 15	who believes may have eternal l
	3: 36	believes in the Son has eternal l,
	4: 14	of water welling up to eternal l."
	5: 24	has crossed over from death to l.
	6: 35	Jesus declared, "I am the bread of l.
	6: 47	the one who believes has eternal l.
	6: 68	You have the words of eternal l.
	10: 10	I have come that they may have l,
	10: 15	and I lay down my l for the sheep.
	10: 28	I give them eternal l, and they shall
	11: 25	"I am the resurrection and the l.
	14: 6	am the way and the truth and the l.
	15: 13	lay down one's l for one's friends.
	20: 31	by believing you may have l in his
Ac	13: 48	appointed for eternal l believed.
Ro	4: 25	was raised to l for our justification.
	6: 13	have been brought from death to l;
	6: 23	God is eternal l in Christ Jesus our
	8: 38	convinced that neither death nor l,
1Co	15: 19	If only for this l we have hope
2Co	3: 6	the letter kills, but the Spirit gives l.
Gal	2: 20	The l l now live in the body, l live
Eph	4: 1	to live a l worthy of the calling you
Php	2: 16	as you hold firmly to the word of l.
Col	1: 10	you may live a l worthy of the Lord
1Th	4: 12	your daily l may win the respect
1Ti	4: 8	the present l and the l to come.
	4: 16	Watch your l and doctrine closely.
	6: 19	take hold of the l that is truly l.
2Ti	3: 12	live a godly l in Christ Jesus will be
Jas	1: 12	person will receive the crown of l
	3: 13	Let them show it by their good l,
1Pe	3: 10	"Whoever would love l and see
2Pe	1: 3	a godly l through our knowledge
1Jn	3: 14	we have passed from death to l,
	5: 11	God has given us eternal l, and this l
Rev	13: 8	written in the Lamb's book of l,
	20: 12	was opened, which is the book of l.
	21: 27	are written in the Lamb's book of l.
	22: 2	side of the river stood the tree of l,

LIFT (LIFTED LIFTING)

Ps	121: 1	I l up my eyes to the mountains—
Ps	134: 2	L up your hands in the sanctuary
La	3: 41	Let us l up our hearts and our hands

LIFTED (LIFT)

Ps	40: 2	He l me out of the slimy pit,
Jn	3: 14	so the Son of Man must be l up,
	12: 32	I, when I am l up from the earth,

LIFTING (LIFT)

1Ti	2: 8	l up holy hands without anger

LIGHT (ENLIGHTENED)

Ge	1: 3	"Let there be l," and there was l.
2Sa	22: 29	Lord turns my darkness into l.
Job	38: 19	"What is the way to the abode of l?
Ps	4: 6	Let the l of your face shine on us.
	19: 8	are radiant, giving l to the eyes.
	27: 1	The Lord is my l and my
	56: 13	walk before God in the l of life.
	76: 4	You are radiant with l,
	104: 2	The Lord wraps himself in l as
	119:105	lamp to my feet and a l for my path.
	119:130	unfolding of your words gives l;
Isa	2: 5	let us walk in the l of the Lord.
	9: 2	in darkness have seen a great l;
	49: 6	also make you a l for the Gentiles,
Mt	4: 16	shadow of death a l has dawned."
	5: 16	way, let your l shine before others,
	11: 30	yoke is easy and my burden is l."
Jn	3: 19	L has come into the world,
	8: 12	he said, "I am the l of the world.
2Co	4: 6	made his l shine in our hearts
	6: 14	Or what fellowship can l have
	11: 14	masquerades as an angel of l.
1Ti	6: 16	and who lives in unapproachable l,
1Pe	2: 9	of darkness into his wonderful l.
1Jn	1: 5	God is l; in him there is no darkness
	1: 7	But if we walk in the l, as he is
Rev	21: 23	for the glory of God gives it l,

LIGHTNING

Da	10: 6	his face like l, his eyes like flaming
Mt	24: 27	For as l that comes from the east is
	28: 3	His appearance was like l, and his

LIKENESS

Ge	1: 26	in our l, so that they may rule over
Ps	17: 15	will be satisfied with seeing your l.
Isa	52: 14	his form marred beyond human l
Ro	8: 3	his own Son in the l of sinful flesh
Php	2: 7	a servant, being made in human l.
Jas	3: 9	who have been made in God's l.

LION

Isa	11: 7	and the l will eat straw like the ox.
1Pe	5: 8	around like a roaring l looking
Rev	5: 5	See, the L of the tribe of Judah,

LIPS

Ps	34: 1	his praise will always be on my l.
	119:171	May my l overflow with praise,
Pr	13: 3	who guard their l preserve their
	27: 2	an outsider, and not your own l.
Isa	6: 5	For I am a man of unclean l, and l
Mt	21: 16	read, " 'From the l of children
Col	3: 8	and filthy language from your l.

LISTEN (LISTENING)

Dt	30: 20	Lord your God, l to his voice,
Pr	1: 5	let the wise l and add to their
	12: 15	to them, but the wise l to advice.

CONCORDANCE

Jn 10: 27 My sheep I to my voice;
Jas 1: 19 Everyone should be quick to I,
1: 22 Do not merely I to the word,

LISTENING (LISTEN)
1Sa 3: 9 LORD, for your servant is I.'"
Pr 18: 13 To answer before I—that is folly

LIVE (ALIVE LIFE LIVES LIVING)
Ex 20: 12 that you may I long in the land
33: 20 face, for no one may see me and I."
Dt 8: 3 that man does not I on bread alone
Job 14: 14 If someone dies, will they I again?
Ps 119:175 Let me I that I may praise you,
Isa 55: 3 come to me; listen, that you may I.
Eze 37: 3 "Son of man, can these bones I?"
Hab 2: 4 the righteous person will I by his
Mt 4: 4 'Man shall not I on bread alone,
Ac 17: 24 not I in temples built by human
17: 28 'For in him we I and move and
Ro 1: 17 "The righteous will I by faith."
2Co 5: 7 For we I by faith, not by sight.
Gal 2: 20 The life I now I in the body,
5: 25 Since we I by the Spirit, let us keep
Php 1: 21 me, to I is Christ and to die is gain.
1Th 5: 13 L in peace with each other.
2Ti 3: 12 who wants to I a godly life
Heb 12: 14 Make every effort to I in peace
1Pe 1: 17 I out your time as foreigners here

LIVES (LIVE)
Job 19: 25 I know that my redeemer I,
Pr 11: 30 and the one who is wise saves I.
Isa 57: 15 he who I forever, whose name is
Da 3: 28 to give up their I rather than serve
Jn 14: 17 he I with you and will be in you.
Gal 2: 20 I no longer live, but Christ I in me.
Heb 13: 5 Keep your I free from the love
2Pe 3: 11 You ought to live holy and godly I
1Jn 3: 16 to lay down our I for our brothers
4: 16 Whoever I in love I in God,

LIVING (LIVE)
Ge 2: 7 life, and the man became a I being.
Jer 2: 13 the spring of I water, and have dug
Mt 22: 32 the God of the dead but of the I."
Jn 7: 38 said, rivers of I water will flow
Ro 12: 1 to offer your bodies as a I sacrifice,
Heb 10: 31 to fall into the hands of the I God.
Rev 1: 18 I am the L One; I was dead,

LOAD
Gal 6: 5 each one should carry their own I.

LOCUSTS
Mt 3: 4 His food was I and wild honey.

LOFTY
Ps 139: 6 for me, too I for me to attain.

LONELY
Ps 68: 6 God sets the I in families, he leads

LONG (LENGTH LONGED LONGING LONGS)
1Ki 18: 21 "How I will you waver between
Jn 9: 4 As I as it is day, we must do
Eph 3: 18 to grasp how wide and I and high
1Pe 1: 12 Even angels I to look into these

LONGED (LONG)
Mt 13: 17 righteous people I to see what you

Mt 23: 37 how often I have I to gather your
2Ti 4: 8 to all who have I for his appearing.

LONGING (LONG)
Pr 13: 19 A I fulfilled is sweet to the soul,
2Co 5: 2 I to be clothed instead with our

LONGS (LONG)
Isa 30: 18 Yet the LORD I to be gracious

LOOK (LOOKING LOOKS)
Job 31: 1 my eyes not to I lustfully at a young
Ps 34: 5 Those who I to him are radiant;
Pr 4: 25 Let your eyes I straight ahead;
Isa 60: 5 Then you will I and be radiant,
Hab 1: 13 Your eyes are too pure to I on evil;
Zec 12: 10 They will I on me, the one they
Mk 13: 21 is the Messiah!' or, 'L, there he is!'
Lk 24: 39 L at my hands and my feet. It is I
Jn 1: 36 by, he said, "L, the Lamb of God!"
4: 35 open your eyes and I at the fields!
19: 37 "They will I on the one they have
Jas 1: 27 to I after orphans and widows
1Pe 1: 12 Even angels long to I into these

LOOKING (LOOK)
Rev 5: 6 a Lamb, I as if it had been slain,

LOOKS (LOOK)
1Sa 16: 7 but the LORD I at the heart."
Lk 9: 62 puts a hand to the plow and I back
Php 2: 21 everyone I out for their own interests,

LORD (LORD'S LORDING)
Ne 4: 14 Remember the L, who is great
Job 28: 28 human race, "The fear of the L—
Ps 54: 4 the L is the one who sustains me.
62: 12 and with you, L, is unfailing love";
86: 5 You, L, are forgiving and good,
110: 1 The LORD says to my I:
147: 5 Great is our L and mighty in power
Isa 6: 1 died, I saw the L, high and exalted,
Da 9: 4 "L, the great and awesome God,
Mt 3: 3 'Prepare the way for the L,
4: 7 'Do not put the L your God
7: 21 "Not everyone who says to me, 'L,
22: 37 "'Love the L your God with all
22: 44 "'The L said to my L: "Sit at my
Mk 12: 11 the L has done this, and it is
12: 29 The L our God, the L is one.
Lk 2: 9 An angel of the L appeared to
6: 46 "Why do you call me, 'L, L,'
10: 27 "'Love the L your God with all
Ac 2: 21 on the name of the L will be saved.'
16: 31 "Believe in the L Jesus, and you
Ro 10: 9 "Jesus is L," and believe in your
10: 13 the name of the L will be saved."
12: 11 your spiritual fervor, serving the L.
14: 8 we live or die, we belong to the L.
1Co 1: 31 the one who boasts boast in the L."
3: 5 as the L has assigned to each his
7: 34 to be devoted to the L in both body
11: 23 The L Jesus, on the night he was
12: 3 "Jesus is L," except by the Holy
15: 57 victory through our L Jesus Christ.
16: 22 let that person be cursed! Come, L!
2Co 3: 17 Now the L is the Spirit, and where
8: 5 gave themselves first of all to the L,
10: 17 the one who boasts boast in the L."

Gal	6: 14	in the cross of our **L** Jesus Christ,
Eph	4: 5	one **L**, one faith, one baptism;
	5: 10	and find out what pleases the **L**.
	5: 19	music from your heart to the **L**,
Php	2: 11	acknowledge that Jesus Christ is **L**,
	3: 1	and sisters, rejoice in the **L**!
	4: 4	Rejoice in the **L** always. I will say it
Col	2: 6	as you received Christ Jesus as **L**,
	3: 17	do it all in the name of the **L** Jesus,
	3: 23	working for the **L**, not for human
	4: 17	you have received in the **L**."
1Th	3: 12	May the **L** make your love increase
	5: 2	day of the **L** will come like a thief
	5: 23	at the coming of our **L** Jesus Christ.
2Th	2: 1	the coming of our **L** Jesus Christ
2Ti	2: 19	"The **L** knows those who are his,"
Heb	12: 14	holiness no one will see the **L**.
	13: 6	confidence, "The **L** is my helper;
Jas	4: 10	Humble yourselves before the **L**,
1Pe	1: 25	the word of the **L** endures forever."
	2: 3	you have tasted that the **L** is good.
	3: 15	in your hearts revere Christ as **L**.
2Pe	1: 16	the coming of our **L** Jesus Christ
	2: 1	sovereign **L** who bought them—
	3: 9	The **L** is not slow in keeping his
Jude	: 14	the **L** is coming with thousands
Rev	4: 8	holy is the **L** God Almighty,'
	4: 11	"You are worthy, our **L** and God,
	17: 14	triumph over them because he is **L**
	22: 20	Amen. Come, **L** Jesus.

LORD'S (LORD)

Ac	21: 14	up and said, "The **L** will be done."
1Co	10: 26	"The earth is the **L**, and everything
	11: 26	you proclaim the **L** death until he
2Co	3: 18	faces contemplate the **L** glory,
2Ti	2: 24	And the **L** servant must not be
Jas	4: 15	"If it is the **L** will, we will live

LORDING (LORD)

1Pe	5: 3	not **I** it over those entrusted to you,

LORD* (LORD'S*; this is the proper name of God,
  Yahweh, spelled "LORD" in the NIV)

Ge	2: 4	when the **L** God made the earth
	2: 7	the **L** God formed a man
	3: 21	The **L** God made garments of skin
	7: 16	Then the **L** shut him in.
	15: 6	Abram believed the **L**, and he
	18: 14	Is anything too hard for the **L**?
	31: 49	"May the **L** keep watch between
Ex	3: 2	There the angel of the **L** appeared
	9: 12	But the **L** hardened Pharaoh's heart
	14: 30	That day the **L** saved Israel
	20: 2	"I am the **L** your God, who
	33: 11	The **L** would speak to Moses face
	40: 34	glory of the **L** filled the tabernacle.
Lev	19: 2	'Be holy because I, the **L** your God,
Nu	8: 5	The **L** said to Moses:
	14: 21	glory of the **L** fills the whole earth,
Dt	2: 7	The **L** your God has blessed you
	5: 9	for I, the **L** your God, am a jealous
	6: 4	The **L** our God, the **L** is one.
	6: 5	Love the **L** your God with all your
	6: 16	Do not put the **L** your God
	10: 14	**L** your God belong the heavens,
	10: 17	For the **L** your God is God of gods

Dt	11: 1	Love the **L** your God and keep his
	28: 1	If you fully obey the **L** your God
	30: 16	you today to love the **L** your God,
	30: 20	For the **L** is your life, and he will
	31: 6	for the **L** your God goes with you;
Jos	22: 5	to love the **L** your God, to walk
	24: 15	household, we will serve the **L**."
1Sa	1: 28	So now I give him to the **L**.
	2: 2	"There is no one holy like the **L**;
	7: 12	"Thus far the **L** has helped us."
	12: 22	his great name the **L** will not reject
	15: 22	as much as in obeying the **L**?
2Sa	22: 2	"The **L** is my rock, my fortress
1Ki	2: 3	and observe what the **L** your God
	8: 11	the glory of the **L** filled his temple.
	8: 61	fully committed to the **L** our God,
	18: 21	If the **L** is God, follow him;
2Ki	13: 23	But the **L** was gracious to them
1Ch	16: 8	Give praise to the **L**, proclaim his
	16: 23	Sing to the **L**, all the earth;
	28: 9	for the **L** searches every heart
	29: 11	Yours, **L**, is the kingdom;
2Ch	5: 14	the glory of the **L** filled the temple
	16: 9	the **L** range throughout the earth
	19: 6	for mere mortals but for the **L**,
	30: 9	for the **L** your God is gracious
Ne	1: 5	"**L**, the God of heaven, the great
Job	1: 21	The **L** gave and the **L** has taken
	38: 1	the **L** spoke to Job out of the storm.
	42: 9	did what the **L** told them;
Ps	1: 2	whose delight is in the law of the **L**,
	9: 9	The **L** is a refuge for the oppressed,
	12: 6	the words of the **L** are flawless.
	16: 8	I keep my eyes always on the **L**.
	19: 7	The law of the **L** is perfect,
	19: 14	heart be pleasing in your sight, **L**,
	23: 1	The **L** is my shepherd, I lack
	23: 6	dwell in the house of the **L** forever.
	27: 1	The **L** is the stronghold of my life
	27: 4	to gaze on the beauty of the **L**
	29: 1	ascribe to the **L** glory and strength.
	32: 2	one whose sin the **L** does not count
	33: 12	is the nation whose God is the **L**,
	33: 18	the eyes of the **L** are on those who
	34: 3	Glorify the **L** with me; let us exalt
	34: 7	of the **L** encamps around those
	34: 8	Taste and see that the **L** is good;
	34: 18	The **L** is close to the brokenhearted
	37: 4	Take delight in the **L**, and he will
	40: 1	I waited patiently for the **L**;
	47: 2	For the **L** Most High is awesome,
	48: 1	Great is the **L**, and most worthy
	55: 22	Cast your cares on the **L** and he
	75: 8	In the hand of the **L** is a cup full
	84: 11	For the **L** God is a sun and shield;
	86: 11	Teach me your way, **L**, that I may
	89: 5	heavens praise your wonders, **L**,
	95: 1	Come, let us sing for joy to the **L**;
	96: 1	Sing to the **L** a new song;
	98: 4	Shout for joy to the **L**, all the earth,
	100: 1	Shout for joy to the **L**, all the earth.
	103: 1	Praise the **L**, my soul; all my
	103: 8	The **L** is compassionate
	104: 1	Praise the **L**, my soul. **L** my God,
	107: 8	to the **L** for his unfailing love
	110: 1	The **L** says to my lord: "Sit at my

Ps	113:	4	The **L** is exalted over all the nations
	115:	1	Not to us, **L**, not to us but to your
	116:	15	the sight of the **L** is the death of his
	118:	1	Give thanks to the **L**, for he is good;
	118:	24	The **L** has done it this very day;
	121:	2	My help comes from the **L**,
	121:	5	The **L** watches over you—the **L** is
	125:	2	so the **L** surrounds his people both
	127:	1	Unless the **L** builds the house,
	127:	3	Children are a heritage from the **L**,
	130:	3	If you, **L**, kept a record of sins,
	135:	6	The **L** does whatever pleases him,
	136:	1	Give thanks to the **L**, for he is good.
	139:	1	You have searched me, **L**, and you
	144:	3	**L**, what are human beings that you
	145:	3	Great is the **L** and most worthy
	145:	18	The **L** is near to all who call on him,
Pr	1:	7	The fear of the **L** is the beginning
	3:	5	Trust in the **L** with all your heart
	3:	9	Honor the **L** with your wealth,
	3:	12	because the **L** disciplines those he
	3:	19	By wisdom the **L** laid the earth's
	5:	21	your ways are in full view of the **L**,
	6:	16	There are six things the **L** hates,
	10:	27	The fear of the **L** adds length to life,
	11:	1	The **L** detests dishonest scales,
	12:	22	The **L** detests lying lips, but he
	14:	26	Whoever fears the **L** has a secure
	15:	3	The eyes of the **L** are everywhere,
	16:	2	but motives are weighed by the **L**.
	16:	4	The **L** works out everything to its
	16:	9	but the **L** establishes their steps.
	16:	33	but its every decision is from the **L**.
	18:	10	name of the **L** is a fortified tower;
	18:	22	and receives favor from the **L**.
	19:	14	but a prudent wife is from the **L**.
	19:	17	is kind to the poor lends to the **L**,
	21:	3	acceptable to the **L** than sacrifice.
	21:	30	plan that can succeed against the **L**.
	21:	31	battle, but victory rests with the **L**.
	22:	2	The **L** is the Maker of them all.
	24:	18	or the **L** will see and disapprove
	31:	30	a woman who fears the **L** is to be
Isa	6:	3	holy, holy is the **L** Almighty;
	11:	2	The Spirit of the **L** will rest on him
	11:	9	of the **L** as the waters cover the sea.
	12:	2	The **L**, the **L** himself, is my strength
	24:	1	the **L** is going to lay waste the earth
	25:	8	The Sovereign **L** will wipe away
	29:	15	to hide their plans from the **L**,
	33:	6	the fear of the **L** is the key to this
	35:	10	those the **L** has rescued will return.
	40:	5	For the mouth of the **L** has spoken.
	40:	7	because the breath of the **L** blows
	40:	10	the Sovereign **L** comes with power,
	40:	28	The **L** is the everlasting God,
	40:	31	in the **L** will renew their strength.
	42:	8	"I am the **L**; that is my name!
	43:	11	I am the **L**, and apart from me
	44:	24	I am the **L**, the Maker of all things,
	45:	5	I am the **L**, and there is no other;
	45:	21	Was it not I, the **L**? And there is no
	51:	11	Those the **L** has rescued will return
	53:	6	the **L** has laid on him the iniquity
	53:	10	the will of the **L** will prosper in his
	55:	6	Seek the **L** while he may be found;

Isa	58:	8	of the **L** will be your rear guard.
	58:	11	The **L** will guide you always;
	59:	1	the arm of the **L** is not too short
	61:	3	a planting of the **L** for the display
	61:	10	I delight greatly in the **L**;
Jer	1:	9	Then the **L** reached out his hand
	9:	24	in these I delight," declares the **L**.
	16:	19	**L**, my strength and my fortress,
	17:	7	is the one who trusts in the **L**,
La	3:	40	and let us return to the **L**.
Eze	1:	28	of the likeness of the glory of the **L**.
Hos	1:	7	but I, the **L** their God, will save
	3:	5	return and seek the **L** their God
	6:	1	"Come, let us return to the **L**.
Joel	2:	1	for the day of the **L** is coming.
	2:	11	The day of the **L** is great;
	3:	14	day of the **L** is near in the valley
Am	5:	18	you who long for the day of the **L**!
Jnh	1:	3	But Jonah ran away from the **L**
Mic	4:	2	the word of the **L** from Jerusalem.
	6:	8	what does the **L** require of you?
Na	1:	2	The **L** is a jealous and avenging
	1:	3	The **L** is slow to anger but great
Hab	2:	14	of the **L** as the waters cover the sea.
	2:	20	The **L** is in his holy temple;
Zep	3:	17	The **L** your God is with you,
Zec	1:	17	and the **L** will again comfort Zion
	9:	16	The **L** their God will save his people
	14:	5	Then the **L** my God will come,
	14:	9	On that day there will be one **L**,
Mal	4:	5	and dreadful day of the **L** comes.

LORD'S* (LORD*; this is the proper name of God, Yahweh, spelled "LORD's" in the NIV)

Ex	34:	34	he entered the **L** presence to speak
Nu	14:	41	you disobeying the **L** command?
Dt	6:	18	is right and good in the **L** sight,
	32:	9	For the **L** portion is his people,
Jos	21:	45	all the **L** good promises to Israel
Ps	24:	1	The earth is the **L**,
	32:	10	the **L** unfailing love surrounds
	89:	1	I will sing of the **L** great love
	103:	17	the **L** love is with those who fear
Pr	3:	11	do not despise the **L** discipline,
Isa	24:	14	west they acclaim the **L** majesty.
	62:	3	a crown of splendor in the **L** hand,
Jer	48:	10	who is lax in doing the **L** work!
La	3:	22	Because of the **L** great love we are
Mic	4:	1	the mountain of the **L** temple will

LOSE (LOSES LOSS LOST)

1Sa	17:	32	"Let no one **I** heart on account
Mt	10:	39	Whoever finds their life will **I** it,
Lk	9:	25	and yet **I** or forfeit their very self?
Jn	6:	39	that I shall **I** none of all those
Heb	12:	3	will not grow weary and **I** heart.
	12:	5	not **I** heart when he rebukes you,

LOSES (LOSE)

Mt	5:	13	But if the salt **I** its saltiness,
Lk	15:	4	a hundred sheep and **I** one of them.
	15:	8	has ten silver coins and **I** one.

LOSS (LOSE)

Ro	11:	12	their **I** means riches for the Gentiles,
1Co	3:	15	the builder will suffer **I** but yet will
Php	3:	8	I consider everything a **I** because

LOST (LOSE)

Ps	73:	2	I had nearly I my foothold.
Jer	50:	6	"My people have been I sheep;
Eze	34:	4	the strays or searched for the I.
	34:	16	I will search for the I and bring
Lk	15:	4	go after the I sheep until he finds
	15:	6	I have found my I sheep.'
	15:	9	I have found my I coin.'
	15:	24	he was I and is found.'
	19:	10	came to seek and to save the I."
Php	3:	8	for whose sake I have I all things.

LOT (LOTS)

Nephew of Abraham (Ge 11:27; 12:5). Chose to live in Sodom (Ge 13). Rescued from four kings (Ge 14). Rescued from Sodom (Ge 19:1–29; 2Pe 2:7). Fathered Moab and Ammon by his daughters (Ge 19:30–38).

Est	3:	7	the I) was cast in the presence
	9:	24	the I) for their ruin and destruction.
Pr	16:	33	The I is cast into the lap, but its
	18:	18	Casting the I settles disputes
Ecc	3:	22	their work, because that is their I.
Ac	1:	26	cast lots, and the I fell to Matthias;

LOTS (LOT)

Ps	22:	18	them and cast I for my garment.
Mt	27:	35	divided up his clothes by casting I.

LOVE (BELOVED LOVED LOVELY LOVER LOVERS LOVES LOVING)

Ge	22:	2	son, your only son, whom you I—
Ex	15:	13	In your unfailing I you will lead
	20:	6	showing I to a thousand generations
	34:	6	abounding in I and faithfulness,
Lev	19:	18	but I your neighbor as yourself.
	19:	34	L them as yourself, for you were
Nu	14:	18	abounding in I and forgiving sin
Dt	5:	10	showing I to a thousand generations
	6:	5	L the LORD your God with all
	7:	13	He will I you and bless you
	10:	12	to I him, to serve the LORD your
	11:	13	to I the LORD your God
	13:	6	or the wife you I, or your closest
	30:	6	you may I him with all your heart
Jos	22:	5	to I the LORD your God, to walk
1Ki	3:	3	Solomon showed his I
	8:	23	you who keep your covenant of I
2Ch	5:	13	his I endures forever."
Ne	1:	5	covenant of I with those who I him
Ps	18:	1	I I you, LORD, my strength.
	23:	6	I will follow me all the days of my
	25:	6	your great mercy and I, for they are
	31:	16	save me in your unfailing I.
	32:	10	LORD's unfailing I surrounds
	33:	5	the earth is full of his unfailing I.
	33:	18	whose hope is in his unfailing I,
	36:	5	Your I, LORD,
	36:	7	How priceless is your unfailing I,
	45:	7	You I righteousness and hate
	51:	1	God, according to your unfailing I;
	57:	10	For great is your I,
	63:	3	Because your I is better than life,
	66:	20	prayer or withheld his I from me!
	77:	8	his unfailing I vanished forever?
	85:	7	Show us your unfailing I, LORD,
	85:	10	L and faithfulness meet together;
	86:	13	For great is your I toward me;

Ps	89:	1	sing of the LORD's great I forever;
	89:	33	but I will not take my I from him,
	92:	2	proclaiming your I in the morning
	94:	18	slipping," your unfailing I, LORD,
	100:	5	is good and his I endures forever;
	101:	1	I will sing of your I and justice;
	103:	4	crowns you with I and compassion,
	103:	8	slow to anger, abounding in I.
	103:	11	so great is his I for those who fear
	107:	8	to the LORD for his unfailing I
	108:	4	For great is your I, higher than
	116:	1	I I the LORD, for he heard my
	118:	1	he is good; his I endures forever.
	119:	47	your commands because I I them.
	119:	64	The earth is filled with your I,
	119:	76	May your unfailing I be my
	119:	97	Oh, how I I your law! I meditate
	119:	119	dross; therefore I I your statutes.
	119:	124	your servant according to your I
	119:	132	do to those who I your name.
	119:	159	See how I I your precepts;
	119:	163	detest falsehood but I I your law.
	119:	165	peace have those who I your law,
	122:	6	"May those who I you be secure.
	130:	7	for with the LORD is unfailing I
	136:	1	*His I endures forever.*
	143:	8	bring me word of your unfailing I,
	145:	8	slow to anger and rich in I.
	145:	20	LORD watches over all who I him,
	147:	11	put their hope in his unfailing I.
Pr	3:	3	Let I and faithfulness never leave
	4:	6	I her, and she will watch over you.
	5:	19	you ever be intoxicated with her I.
	8:	17	I I those who I me, and those who
	9:	8	rebuke the wise and they will I you.
	10:	12	but I covers over all wrongs.
	14:	22	those who plan what is good find I
	15:	17	with I than a fattened calf
	17:	9	Whoever would foster I covers
	19:	22	a person desires is unfailing I;
	20:	6	Many claim to have unfailing I,
	20:	13	Do not I sleep or you will grow
	20:	28	L and faithfulness keep a king safe;
	21:	21	righteousness and I finds life,
	27:	5	is open rebuke than hidden I.
Ecc	9:	6	Their I, their hate and their
	9:	9	whom you I, all the days of this
SS	2:	4	and let his banner over me be I.
	8:	6	for I is as strong as death,
	8:	7	Many waters cannot quench I;
Isa	5:	1	sing for the one I I a song about his
	16:	5	In I a throne will be established;
	38:	17	In your I you kept me from the pit
	54:	10	yet my unfailing I for you will not
	55:	3	my faithful I promised to David.
	61:	8	"For I, the LORD, I justice;
	63:	9	In his I and mercy he redeemed
Jer	5:	31	and my people I it this way.
	31:	3	loved you with an everlasting I;
	32:	18	You show I to thousands but bring
	33:	11	his I endures forever."
La	3:	22	of the LORD's great I we are not
	3:	32	so great is his unfailing I.
Eze	33:	32	more than one who sings I songs
Da	9:	4	covenant of I with those who I him
Hos	2:	19	and justice, in I and compassion.

CONCORDANCE

Hos	3: 1	**L** her as the Lord loves
	11: 4	of human kindness, with ties of **l**.
	12: 6	maintain **l** and justice, and wait
Joel	2: 13	slow to anger and abounding in **l**,
Am	5: 15	Hate evil, **l** good; maintain justice
Mic	3: 2	you who hate good and **l** evil;
	6: 8	to **l** mercy and to walk humbly
Zep	3: 17	his **l** he will no longer rebuke you,
Zec	8: 19	Therefore **l** truth and peace."
Mt	3: 17	said, "This is my Son, whom I **l**;
	5: 44	**l** your enemies and pray for those
	6: 24	will hate the one and **l** the other,
	17: 5	said, "This is my Son, whom I **l**;
	19: 19	'**l** your neighbor as yourself.' "
	22: 37	" '**L** the Lord your God with all
Lk	6: 32	"If you **l** those who **l** you,
	7: 42	which of them will **l** him more?"
	20: 13	I will send my son, whom I **l**;
Jn	13: 34	command I give you: **L** one another.
	13: 35	my disciples, if you **l** one another."
	14: 15	"If you **l** me, keep my commands.
	15: 13	Greater **l** has no one than this:
	15: 17	This is my command: **L** each other.
	21: 15	do you **l** me more than these?"
Ro	5: 5	because God's **l** has been poured
	5: 8	God demonstrates his own **l** for us
	8: 28	for the good of those who **l** him,
	8: 35	separate us from the **l** of Christ?
	8: 39	separate us from the **l** of God that
	12: 9	**L** must be sincere. Hate what is
	12: 10	Be devoted to one another in **l**.
	13: 8	continuing debt to **l** one another.
	13: 9	"**L** your neighbor as yourself."
	13: 10	Therefore **l** is the fulfillment
1Co	2: 9	prepared for those who **l** him—
	8: 1	puffs up while **l** builds up.
	13: 1	but do not have **l**, I am only
	13: 2	but do not have **l**, I am nothing.
	13: 3	but do not have **l**, I gain nothing.
	13: 4	**L** is patient, **l** is kind. It does not
	13: 6	**L** does not delight in evil
	13: 8	**L** never fails. But where there are
	13: 13	these three remain: faith, hope and **l**. But the greatest of these is **l**.
	14: 1	Follow the way of **l** and eagerly
	16: 14	Do everything in **l**.
2Co	5: 14	For Christ's **l** compels us,
	8: 8	sincerity of your **l** by comparing it
	8: 24	show these men the proof of your **l**
Gal	5: 6	is faith expressing itself through **l**.
	5: 13	serve one another humbly in **l**.
	5: 22	But the fruit of the Spirit is **l**, joy,
Eph	1: 4	holy and blameless in his sight. In **l**
	2: 4	But because of his great **l** for us,
	3: 17	being rooted and established in **l**,
	3: 18	high and deep is the **l** of Christ,
	3: 19	and to know this **l** that surpasses
	4: 2	bearing with one another in **l**.
	4: 15	speaking the truth in **l**, we will
	5: 2	and walk in the way of **l**, just as
	5: 25	Husbands, **l** your wives, just as
	5: 28	to **l** their wives as their own bodies.
	5: 33	must **l** his wife as he loves himself,
Php	1: 9	that your **l** may abound more
	2: 2	having the same **l**, being one
Col	1: 5	**l** that spring from the hope stored

Col	2: 2	in heart and united in **l**,
	3: 14	And over all these virtues put on **l**,
	3: 19	**l** your wives and do not be harsh
1Th	1: 3	your labor prompted by **l**, and your
	4: 9	been taught by God to **l** each other.
	5: 8	on faith and **l** as a breastplate,
2Th	3: 5	Lord direct your hearts into God's **l**
1Ti	1: 5	The goal of this command is **l**,
	2: 15	faith, **l** and holiness with propriety.
	4: 12	conduct, in **l**, in faith and in purity.
	6: 10	For the **l** of money is a root of all
	6: 11	faith, **l**, endurance and gentleness.
2Ti	1: 7	us power, **l** and self-discipline.
	2: 22	faith, **l** and peace, along with those
	3: 10	faith, patience, **l**, endurance,
Titus	2: 4	women to **l** their husbands
Phm	: 9	to appeal to you on the basis of **l**.
Heb	6: 10	the **l** you have shown him as you
	10: 24	may spur one another on toward **l**
	13: 5	your lives free from the **l** of money
Jas	1: 12	has promised to those who **l** him.
	2: 5	he promised those who **l** him?
	2: 8	"**L** your neighbor as yourself,"
1Pe	1: 22	you have sincere **l** for each other,
	2: 17	everyone, **l** the family of believers,
	3: 8	be sympathetic, **l** one another,
	3: 10	For, "Whoever would **l** life and see
	4: 8	Above all, **l** each other deeply,
	4: 8	because **l** covers over a multitude
	5: 14	Greet one another with a kiss of **l**.
2Pe	1: 7	and to mutual affection, **l**.
	1: 17	saying, "This is my Son, whom I **l**;
1Jn	2: 5	**l** for God is truly made complete
	2: 15	Do not **l** the world or anything
	3: 1	See what great **l** the Father has
	3: 10	who does not **l** their brother
	3: 11	We should **l** one another.
	3: 14	to life, because we **l** each other.
	3: 16	This is how we know what **l** is:
	3: 18	let us not **l** with words or speech
	3: 23	**l** one another as he commanded
	4: 7	one another, for **l** comes from God.
	4: 8	not know God, because God is **l**.
	4: 9	is how God showed his **l** among us:
	4: 10	This is **l**: not that we loved God,
	4: 11	us, we also ought to **l** one another.
	4: 12	but if we **l** one another, God lives
	4: 16	God is **l**. Whoever lives in **l** lives
	4: 17	This is how **l** is made complete
	4: 18	There is no fear in **l**. But perfect **l**
	4: 19	We **l** because he first loved us.
	4: 20	whoever does not **l** their brother
	4: 21	loves God must also **l** their brother
	5: 2	we know that we **l** the children
	5: 3	In fact, this is **l** for God: to keep his
2Jn	: 5	I ask that we **l** one another.
	: 6	his command is that you walk in **l**.
Jude	: 12	are blemishes at your **l** feasts,
	: 21	yourselves in God's **l** as you wait
Rev	2: 4	You have forsaken the **l** you had
	3: 19	Those whom I **l** I rebuke
	12: 11	they did not **l** their lives so much

LOVED (LOVE)

Ge	24: 67	she became his wife, and he **l** her;
	37: 3	Now Israel **l** Joseph more than any

Dt	7:	8	it was because the Lord I you
1Sa	1:	5	a double portion because he I her,
	20:	17	because he I him as he I himself.
Ps	44:	3	light of your face, for you I them.
Jer	2:	2	youth, how as a bride you I me
	31:	3	"I have I you with an everlasting
Hos	2:	23	to the one I called 'Not my I one.'
	3:	1	though she is I by another man
	9:	10	became as vile as the thing they I.
	11:	1	"When Israel was a child, I I him,
Mal	1:	2	"I have I you," says the Lord.
Mk	12:	6	one left to send, a son, whom he I.
Jn	3:	16	For God so I the world that he gave
	3:	19	people I darkness instead of light
	11:	5	Now Jesus I Martha and her sister
	12:	43	for they I human praise more than
	13:	1	in the world, he I them to the end.
	13:	23	the disciple whom Jesus I,
	13:	34	As I have I you, so you must love
	14:	21	The one who loves me will be I
	15:	9	"As the Father has I me, so have I I
	15:	12	Love each other as I have I you.
	19:	26	disciple whom he I standing
Ro	8:	37	conquerors through him who I us.
	9:	13	"Jacob I I, but Esau I hated."
	9:	25	'my I one' who is not my I one,"
	11:	28	they are I on account
Gal	2:	20	who I me and gave himself for me.
Eph	5:	2	just as Christ I us and gave himself
	5:	25	just as Christ I the church and gave
2Th	2:	16	who I us and by his grace gave us
2Ti	4:	10	for Demas, because he I this world,
Heb	1:	9	You have I righteousness and hated
1Jn	4:	10	not that we I God, but that he I us
	4:	11	since God so I us, we also ought
	4:	19	We love because he first I us.

LOVELY (LOVE)

Ps	84:	1	How I is your dwelling place,
SS	2:	14	voice is sweet, and your face is I.
	5:	16	sweetness itself; he is altogether I.
Php	4:	8	is pure, whatever is I, whatever is

LOVER (LOVE)

1Ti	3:	3	not quarrelsome, not a I of money.

LOVERS (LOVE)

2Ti	3:	2	People will be I of themselves,
	3:	3	brutal, not I of the good,
	3:	4	I of pleasure rather than I of God—

LOVES (LOVE)

Ps	11:	7	Lord is righteous, he I justice;
	33:	5	The Lord I righteousness
	34:	12	Whoever of you I life and desires
	127:	2	for he grants sleep to those he I.
Pr	3:	12	the Lord disciplines those he I,
	12:	1	Whoever I discipline I knowledge,
	17:	17	A friend I at all times, and
	17:	19	Whoever I a quarrel I sin;
	22:	11	One who I a pure heart and who
Mt	10:	37	"Anyone who I their father
Lk	7:	47	has been forgiven little I little."
Jn	3:	35	The Father I the Son and has
	10:	17	The reason my Father I me is that I
	14:	21	The one who I me will be loved
	14:	23	"Anyone who I me will obey my
Ro	13:	8	for whoever I others has fulfilled

2Co	9:	7	for God I a cheerful giver.
Eph	5:	28	He who I his wife I himself.
	5:	33	must love his wife as he I himself,
Heb	12:	6	the Lord disciplines the one he I,
1Jn	4:	7	Everyone who I has been born
	5:	1	who I the father I his child
3Jn	:	9	but Diotrephes, who I to be first,
Rev	1:	5	To him who I us and has freed us

LOVING (LOVE)

Ps	25:	10	All the ways of the Lord are I
Heb	13:	1	Keep on I one another as brothers
1Jn	5:	2	by I God and carrying out his

LOWLY

Job	5:	11	The I he sets on high, and those
Pr	29:	23	low, but the I in spirit gain honor.
Isa	57:	15	to revive the spirit of the I
Eze	21:	26	The I will be exalted and
Mt	18:	4	whoever takes the I position
1Co	1:	28	God chose the I things of this

LUKE

Co-worker with Paul (Col 4:14; 2Ti 4:11; Phm 24).

LUKEWARM

Rev	3:	16	So, because you are I—

LUST

Pr	6:	25	Do not I in your heart after her
Col	3:	5	impurity, I, evil desires and greed,
1Th	4:	5	not in passionate I like the pagans,
1Jn	2:	16	the I of the flesh, the I of the eyes,

LYING (LIE)

Pr	6:	17	haughty eyes, a I tongue,
	26:	28	A I tongue hates those it hurts,

MACEDONIA

Ac	16:	9	a vision of a man of M standing

MADE (MAKE)

Ge	1:	16	God m two great lights—
	1:	25	God m the wild animals according
	2:	22	the Lord God m a woman
2Ki	19:	15	You have m heaven and earth.
Ps	95:	5	for he m it, and his hands formed
	100:	3	It is he who m us, and we are his;
	139:	14	I am fearfully and wonderfully m;
Ecc	3:	11	He has m everything beautiful in
Mk	2:	27	"The Sabbath was m for man,
Jn	1:	3	Through him all things were m;
Ac	17:	24	"The God who m the world
Heb	1:	2	whom also he m the universe.
Rev	14:	7	Worship him who m the heavens,

MAGI

Mt	2:	1	M from the east came to Jerusalem

MAGOG

Eze	38:	2	of the land of M, the chief prince
	39:	6	I will send fire on M and on those
Rev	20:	8	Gog and M—and to gather them

MAIMED

Mt	18:	8	It is better for you to enter life m

MAJESTIC (MAJESTY)

Ex	15:	6	hand, Lord, was m in power.
	15:	11	m in holiness, awesome in glory,
Ps	8:	1	m is your name in all the earth!
	29:	4	the voice of the Lord is m.
	111:	3	Glorious and m are his deeds,

SS 6: 10 sun, **m** as the stars in procession?
2Pe 1: 17 came to him from the **M** Glory,

MAJESTY (MAJESTIC)
Ex 15: 7 your **m** you threw down those who
Dt 33: 26 and on the clouds in his **m**.
1Ch 16: 27 Splendor and **m** are before him;
Est 1: 4 the splendor and glory of his **m**.
Job 37: 22 God comes in awesome **m**.
40: 10 clothe yourself in honor and **m**.
Ps 45: 4 In your **m** ride forth victoriously
93: 1 Lord reigns, he is robed in **m**;
145: 5 the glorious splendor of your **m**—
Isa 53: 2 beauty or **m** to attract us to him,
Eze 31: 2 can be compared with you in **m**?
2Pe 1: 16 but we were eyewitnesses of his **m**.
Jude : 25 only God our Savior be glory, **m**,

MAKE (MADE MAKER MAKES MAKING)
Ge 1: 26 "Let us **m** mankind in our image,
2: 18 I will **m** a helper suitable for him."
12: 2 "I will **m** you into a great nation,
Ex 22: 3 steals must certainly **m** restitution,
Nu 6: 25 the Lord **m** his face shine on you
Ps 108: 1 sing and **m** music with all my soul.
Isa 14: 14 I will **m** myself like the Most
29: 16 formed it, "You did not **m** me"?
Jer 31: 31 "when I will **m** a new covenant
Mt 3: 3 Lord, **m** straight paths for him.' "
28: 19 go and **m** disciples of all nations,
Lk 13: 24 "**M** every effort to enter through
Ro 14: 19 Let us therefore **m** every effort to
2Co 5: 9 So we **m** it our goal to please him,
Eph 4: 3 **M** every effort to keep the unity
Col 4: 5 **m** the most of every opportunity.
1Th 4: 11 **m** it your ambition to lead a quiet
Heb 4: 11 **m** every effort to enter that rest,
12: 14 **M** every effort to live in peace
2Pe 1: 5 **m** every effort to add to your faith
3: 14 **m** every effort to be found spotless,

MAKER (MAKE)
Job 4: 17 man be more pure than his **M**?
36: 3 I will ascribe justice to my **M**.
Ps 95: 6 us kneel before the Lord our **M**;
Pr 22: 2 The Lord is the **M** of them all.
Isa 45: 9 to those who quarrel with their **M**,
54: 5 For your **M** is your husband—
Jer 10: 16 these, for he is the **M** of all things,

MAKES (MAKE)
1Co 3: 7 but only God, who **m** things grow.

MAKING (MAKE)
Ps 19: 7 are trustworthy, **m** wise the simple.
Ecc 12: 12 Of **m** many books there is no end,
Jn 5: 18 Father, **m** himself equal with God.
Eph 5: 16 **m** the most of every opportunity,

MALE
Ge 1: 27 **m** and female he created them.
Gal 3: 28 nor free, nor is there **m** and female,

MALICE (MALICIOUS)
Ro 1: 29 envy, murder, strife, deceit and **m**.
Col 3: 8 anger, rage, **m**, slander, and filthy
1Pe 2: 1 rid yourselves of all **m** and all

MALICIOUS (MALICE)
1Ti 3: 11 not **m** talkers but temperate
6: 4 envy, strife, **m** talk, evil suspicions

MAN (MANKIND MEN WOMAN WOMEN)
Ge 2: 7 the Lord God formed a **m**
2: 18 not good for the **m** to be alone.
2: 23 for she was taken out of **m**."
Dt 8: 3 **m** does not live on bread alone
1Sa 13: 14 sought out a **m** after his own heart
Ps 127: 5 Blessed is the **m** whose quiver is
Pr 30: 19 way of a **m** with a young woman.
Isa 53: 3 by mankind, a **m** of suffering,
Mt 19: 5 this reason a **m** will leave his father
Lk 4: 4 'M shall not live on bread alone.' "
Ro 5: 12 entered the world through one **m**,
1Co 7: 2 **m** should have sexual relations
11: 3 that the head of every **m** is Christ,
11: 3 and the head of the woman is **m**,
13: 11 When I became a **m**, I put the ways
Php 2: 8 being found in appearance as a **m**,
1Ti 2: 5 and mankind, the **m** Christ Jesus,
2: 12 or to assume authority over a **m**;

MANAGE
Jer 12: 5 how will you **m** in the thickets
1Ti 3: 4 He must **m** his own family well
3: 12 to his wife and must **m** his children
5: 14 to **m** their homes and to give

MANASSEH
1. Firstborn of Joseph (Ge 41:51; 46:20). Blessed (Ge 48).
2. Son of Hezekiah; king of Judah (2Ki 21:1–18; 2Ch 33:1–20).

MANGER
Lk 2: 12 in cloths and lying in a **m**."

MANKIND (MAN)
Ge 1: 26 "Let us make **m** in our image,

MANNA
Ex 16: 31 people of Israel called the bread **m**.
Dt 8: 16 He gave you **m** to eat
Jn 6: 49 Your ancestors ate the **m**
Rev 2: 17 I will give some of the hidden **m**.

MANNER
1Co 11: 27 in an unworthy **m** will be guilty
Php 1: 27 conduct yourselves in a **m** worthy

MARITAL (MARRY)
Ex 21: 10 of her food, clothing and **m** rights.
1Co 7: 3 husband should fulfill his **m** duty

MARK (MARKS)
Cousin of Barnabas (Col 4:10; 2Ti 4:11; Phm 24; 1Pe 5:13), see JOHN.

Ge 4: 15 the Lord put a **m** on Cain so
Rev 13: 16 to receive a **m** on their right hands

MARKS (MARK)
Jn 20: 25 "Unless I see the nail **m** in his
Gal 6: 17 I bear on my body the **m** of Jesus.

MARRED
Isa 52: 14 and his form **m** beyond human

MARRIAGE (MARRY)
Mt 22: 30 neither marry nor be given in **m**;
24: 38 marrying and giving in **m**,
Heb 13: 4 **M** should be honored by all,

MARRIED (MARRY)
Ro 7: 2 by law a **m** woman is bound to her

1Co 7: 33 But a **m** man is concerned
    7: 36 is not sinning. They should get **m**.

MARRIES (MARRY)
Mt 5: 32 anyone who **m** a divorced woman
   19: 9 and **m** another woman commits
Lk 16: 18 the man who **m** a divorced woman

MARRY (INTERMARRY MARITAL MARRIAGE
   MARRIED MARRIES)
Mt 22: 30 people will neither **m** nor be given
1Co 7: 9 they should **m**, for it is better to **m**
1Ti 5: 14 So I counsel younger widows to **m**,

MARTHA
   Sister of Mary and Lazarus (Lk 10:38–42; Jn 11; 12:2).

MARVELED
Lk 2: 33 mother **m** at what was said

MARY
   1. Mother of Jesus (Mt 1:16–25; Lk 1:27–56; 2:1–40). With Jesus at temple (Lk 2:41–52), at the wedding in Cana (Jn 2:1–5), questioning his sanity (Mk 3:21), at the cross (Jn 19:25–27). Among disciples after Ascension (Ac 1:14).
   2. Magdalene; former demoniac (Lk 8:2). Helped support Jesus' ministry (Lk 8:1–3). At the cross (Mt 27:56; Mk 15:40; Jn 19:25), burial (Mt 27:61; Mk 15:47). Saw angel after resurrection (Mt 28:1–10; Mk 16:1–9; Lk 24:1–12); also Jesus (Jn 20:1–18).
   3. Sister of Martha and Lazarus (Jn 11). Washed Jesus' feet (Jn 12:1–8).

MASQUERADES
2Co 11: 14 for Satan himself **m** as an angel

MASTER (MASTERED MASTERS)
Mt 10: 24 teacher, nor a servant above his **m**.
   24: 46 servant whose **m** finds him doing
   25: 21 "His **m** replied, 'Well done,
Ro 6: 14 For sin shall no longer be your **m**,
   14: 4 To their own **m**, servants stand
2Ti 2: 21 useful to the **M** and prepared to do

MASTERED (MASTER)
1Co 6: 12 but I will not be **m** by anything.
2Pe 2: 19 are slaves to whatever has **m** them."

MASTERS (MASTER)
Mt 6: 24 "No one can serve two **m**.
Eph 6: 5 obey your earthly **m** with respect
   6: 9 **m**, treat your slaves in the same
Titus 2: 9 be subject to their **m** in everything,

MATTHEW
   Apostle; former tax collector (Mt 9:9–13; 10:3; Mk 3:18; Lk 6:15; Ac 1:13). Also called Levi (Mk 2:14–17; Lk 5:27–32).

MATURE (MATURITY)
Eph 4: 13 of the Son of God and become **m**,
Php 3: 15 who are **m** should take such a view
Heb 5: 14 But solid food is for the **m**,
Jas 1: 4 its work so that you may be **m**

MATURITY (MATURE)
Heb 6: 1 Christ and be taken forward to **m**,

MEAL
1Co 10: 27 If an unbeliever invites you to a **m**
Heb 12: 16 single **m** sold his inheritance rights

MEANING
Ne 8: 8 and giving the **m** so that the people

MEANS
1Co 9: 22 by all possible **m** I might save some.

MEAT
Ro 14: 6 eats **m** does so to the Lord,
   14: 21 It is better not to eat **m** or drink

MEDIATOR
1Ti 2: 5 one God and one **m** between God
Heb 8: 6 which he is **m** is superior to the old
   9: 15 this reason Christ is the **m** of a new
   12: 24 to Jesus the **m** of a new covenant,

MEDICINE
Pr 17: 22 A cheerful heart is good **m**,

MEDITATE (MEDITATION)
Jos 1: 8 **m** on it day and night, so that you
Ps 119: 15 I **m** on your precepts and consider
   119: 78 but I will **m** on your precepts.
   119: 97 I **m** on it all day long.
   145: 5 I will **m** on your wonderful works.

MEDITATES (MEDITATE)
Ps 1: 2 who **m** on his law day and night.

MEDITATION (MEDITATE)
Ps 19: 14 this **m** of my heart be pleasing
   104: 34 May my **m** be pleasing to him, as I

MEDIUM
Lev 20: 27 or woman who is a **m** or spiritist

MEEK
Ps 37: 11 But the **m** will inherit the land
Mt 5: 5 Blessed are the **m**, for they will

MEET (MEETING)
Ps 85: 10 Love and faithfulness **m** together;
Am 4: 12 Israel, prepare to **m** your God."
1Th 4: 17 the clouds to **m** the Lord in the air.

MEETING (MEET)
Heb 10: 25 not giving up **m** together, as some

MELCHIZEDEK
Ge 14: 18 **M** king of Salem brought out bread
Ps 110: 4 a priest forever, in the order of **M**."
Heb 7: 11 one in the order of **M**,

MELT
2Pe 3: 12 the elements will **m** in the heat.

MEMBERS
Mic 7: 6 a man's enemies are the **m** of his
Ro 12: 4 of us has one body with many **m**,
1Co 6: 15 your bodies are **m** of Christ
Eph 4: 25 for we are all **m** of one body.
Col 3: 15 since as **m** of one body you were

MEN (MAN)
Ro 1: 27 **M** committed shameful acts with
      other **m**,
1Ti 2: 8 Therefore I want the **m** everywhere

MENAHEM
   King of Israel (2Ki 15:17–22).

MERCIFUL (MERCY)
Dt 4: 31 the Lᴏʀᴅ your God is a **m** God;
Ne 9: 31 for you are a gracious and **m** God.
Mt 5: 7 Blessed are the **m**, for they will be
Lk 6: 36 Be **m**, just as your Father is **m**.

Heb   2: 17   in order that he might become a **m**
Jude   : 22   Be **m** to those who doubt;

MERCY (MERCIFUL)
Ex   33: 19   have **m** on whom I will have **m**,
Ps   25: 6   LORD, your great **m** and love,
Isa   63: 9   his love and **m** he redeemed them;
Hos   6: 6   For I desire **m**, not sacrifice,
Mic   6: 8   to love **m** and to walk humbly
Hab   3: 2   in wrath remember **m**.
Mt   12: 7   mean, 'I desire **m**, not sacrifice,'
    23: 23   justice, **m** and faithfulness.
Ro   9: 15   "I will have **m** on whom I have **m**,
Eph   2: 4   love for us, God, who is rich in **m**,
Jas   2: 13   **M** triumphs over judgment.
1Pe   1: 3   In his great **m** he has given us new

MESSAGE
Isa   53: 1   Who has believed our **m**
Jn   12: 38   who has believed our **m**
Ro   10: 17   faith comes from hearing the **m**,
1Co   1: 18   the **m** of the cross is foolishness
2Co   5: 19   to us the **m** of reconciliation.

MESSIAH (MESSIAH)
Mt   1: 16   of Jesus who is called the **M**.
    16: 16   "You are the **M**, the Son
    22: 42   "What do you think about the **M**?
Jn   1: 41   "We have found the **M**" (that is,
    4: 25   that **M**" (called Christ) "is coming.
    20: 31   may believe that Jesus is the **M**,
Ac   2: 36   you crucified, both Lord and **M**."
    5: 42   the good news that Jesus is the **M**.
    9: 22   by proving that Jesus is the **M**.
    17: 3   proving that the **M** had to suffer
    18: 28   the Scriptures that Jesus was the **M**.
    26: 23   that the **M** would suffer and,

MESSIAHS (MESSIAH)
Mt   24: 24   For false **m** and false prophets will

METHUSELAH
Ge   5: 27   **M** lived a total of 969 years,

MICHAEL
    Archangel (Jude 9); warrior in angelic realm, protector of Israel (Da 10:13, 21; 12:1; Rev 12:7).

MIDWIVES
Ex   1: 17   The **m**, however, feared God

MIGHT (ALMIGHTY MIGHTY)
Jdg   16: 30   Then he pushed with all his **m**,
2Sa   6: 14   before the LORD with all his **m**,
Ps   21: 13   we will sing and praise your **m**.
Zec   4: 6   'Not by **m** nor by power, but by my
1Ti   6: 16   To him be honor and **m** forever.

MIGHTY (MIGHT)
Ex   6: 1   of my **m** hand he will let them go;
Dt   7: 8   he brought you out with a **m** hand
2Sa   1: 19   How the **m** have fallen!
    23: 8   the names of David's **m** warriors:
Ps   24: 8   and **m**, the LORD **m** in battle.
    50: 1   The **M** One, God, the LORD,
    89: 8   are **m**, and your faithfulness
    136: 12   a **m** hand and outstretched arm;
    147: 5   Great is our Lord and **m** in power;
Isa   9: 6   Wonderful Counselor, **M** God,
Zep   3: 17   you, the **M** Warrior who saves.
Eph   6: 10   in the Lord and in his **m** power.

MILE
Mt   5: 41   If anyone forces you to go one **m**,

MILK
Ex   3: 8   a land flowing with **m** and honey—
Isa   55: 1   buy wine and **m** without money
1Co   3: 2   I gave you **m**, not solid food,
Heb   5: 12   You need **m**, not solid food!
1Pe   2: 2   crave pure spiritual **m**, so that by it

MILLSTONE (STONE)
Lk   17: 2   with a **m** tied around their neck

MIND (DOUBLE-MINDED MINDFUL MINDS
    MINDSET)
1Sa   15: 29   does not lie or change his **m**;
1Ch   28: 9   devotion and with a willing **m**,
Ps   26: 2   me, examine my heart and my **m**;
Mt   22: 37   all your soul and with all your **m**.'
Ac   4: 32   believers were one in heart and **m**.
Ro   7: 25   then, I myself in my **m** am a slave
    8: 7   The **m** governed by the flesh is
    12: 2   by the renewing of your **m**.
1Co   2: 9   what no human **m** has conceived"
    14: 14   spirit prays, but my **m** is unfruitful.
2Co   13: 11   another, be of one **m**, live in peace.
Php   3: 19   Their **m** is set on earthly things.
1Th   4: 11   You should **m** your own business
Heb   7: 21   sworn and will not change his **m**:

MINDFUL (MIND)
Ps   8: 4   is mankind that you are **m** of them,
Lk   1: 48   he has been **m** of the humble state
Heb   2: 6   is mankind that you are **m** of them,

MINDS (MIND)
Ps   7: 9   the righteous God who probes **m**
Isa   26: 3   peace those whose **m** are steadfast,
Jer   31: 33   "I will put my law in their **m**
Eph   4: 23   new in the attitude of your **m**;
Col   3: 2   Set your **m** on things above,
Heb   8: 10   I will put my laws in their **m**
Rev   2: 23   he who searches hearts and **m**,

MINDSET (MIND)
Php   2: 5   have the same **m** as Christ Jesus:

MINISTERING (MINISTRY)
Heb   1: 14   Are not all angels **m** spirits sent

MINISTRY (MINISTERING)
Ac   6: 4   to prayer and the **m** of the word."
2Co   5: 18   gave us the **m** of reconciliation:
2Ti   4: 5   discharge all the duties of your **m**.

MIRACLES
1Ch   16: 12   done, his **m**, and the judgments he
Ps   77: 14   You are the God who performs **m**;
Mt   11: 20   most of his **m** had been performed,
    11: 21   the **m** that were performed in you
Mk   6: 2   What are these remarkable **m** he is
Ac   2: 22   accredited by God to you by **m**,
    19: 11   did extraordinary **m** through Paul,
1Co   12: 28   then **m**, then gifts of healing,
Heb   2: 4   wonders and various **m**, and by

MIRE
Ps   40: 2   slimy pit, out of the mud and **m**;
Isa   57: 20   whose waves cast up **m** and mud.

MIRIAM
    Sister of Moses and Aaron (Nu 26:59). Led dancing

at Red Sea (Ex 15:20–21). Struck with leprosy for criticizing Moses (Nu 12). Death (Nu 20:1).

MIRROR
Jas	1: 23	who looks at his face in a **m**

MISERY
Ex	3: 7	"I have indeed seen the **m** of my
Jdg	10: 16	he could bear Israel's **m** no longer.
Hos	5: 15	in their **m** they will earnestly seek
Ro	3: 16	ruin and **m** mark their ways,
Jas	5: 1	because of the **m** that is coming

MISLED
1Co	15: 33	Do not be **m**:

MISS
Pr	19: 2	more will hasty feet **m** the way!

MIST
Hos	6: 4	Your love is like the morning **m**,
Jas	4: 14	You are a **m** that appears for a little

MISUSE
Ex	20: 7	"You shall not **m** the name
Dt	5: 11	"You shall not **m** the name
Ps	139: 20	your adversaries **m** your name.

MOCK (MOCKED MOCKER MOCKERS MOCKING)
Ps	22: 7	All who see me **m** me;
Pr	14: 9	Fools **m** at making amends for sin,
Mk	10: 34	who will **m** him and spit on him,

MOCKED (MOCK)
Mt	27: 29	knelt in front of him and **m** him.
	27: 41	of the law and the elders **m** him.
Gal	6: 7	not be deceived: God cannot be **m**.

MOCKER (MOCK)
Pr	9: 7	corrects a **m** invites insults;
	9: 12	you are a **m**, you alone will suffer.
	20: 1	Wine is a **m** and beer a brawler;
	22: 10	Drive out the **m**, and out goes

MOCKERS (MOCK)
Ps	1: 1	take or sit in the company of **m**,

MOCKING (MOCK)
Isa	50: 6	I did not hide my face from **m**

MODEL
1Th	1: 7	And so you became a **m** to all
2Th	3: 9	to offer ourselves as a **m** for you

MOMENT
Job	20: 5	the joy of the godless lasts but a **m**.
Ps	30: 5	For his anger lasts only a **m**, but his
Isa	66: 8	a nation be brought forth in a **m**?
Gal	2: 5	We did not give in to them for a **m**,

MONEY
Ecc	5: 10	loves **m** never has enough;
Isa	55: 1	and you who have no **m**, come,
Mt	6: 24	You cannot serve both God and **m**.
Lk	9: 3	bag, no bread, no **m**, no extra shirt.
1Co	16: 2	you should set aside a sum of **m**
1Ti	3: 3	not quarrelsome, not a lover of **m**.
	6: 10	the love of **m** is a root of all kinds
2Ti	3: 2	themselves, lovers of **m**, boastful,
Heb	13: 5	your lives free from the love of **m**

MOON
Ps	121: 6	you by day, nor the **m** by night.
Joel	2: 31	the **m** to blood before the coming
1Co	15: 41	the **m** another and the stars

MORNING
Ge	1: 5	was evening, and there was **m**—
Dt	28: 67	In the **m** you will say, "If only it
Ps	5: 3	In the **m**, Lᴏʀᴅ, you hear my
2Pe	1: 19	and the **m** star rises in your hearts.
Rev	22: 16	of David, and the bright **M** Star."

MORTAL
1Co	15: 53	and the **m** with immortality.

MOSES
Levite; brother of Aaron (Ex 6:20; 1Ch 6:3). Put in basket into Nile; discovered and raised by Pharaoh's daughter (Ex 2:1–10). Fled to Midian after killing Egyptian (Ex 2:11–15). Married to Zipporah, fathered Gershom (Ex 2:16–22).

Called by the Lᴏʀᴅ to deliver Israel (Ex 3–4). Pharaoh's resistance (Ex 5). Ten plagues (Ex 7–11). Passover and Exodus (Ex 12–13). Led Israel through Red Sea (Ex 14). Song of deliverance (Ex 15:1–21). Brought water from rock (Ex 17:1–7). Raised hands to defeat Amalekites (Ex 17:8–16). Delegated judges (Ex 18; Dt 1:9–18).

Received Law at Sinai (Ex 19–23; 25–31; Jn 1:17). Announced Law to Israel (Ex 19:7–8; 24; 35). Broke tablets because of golden calf (Ex 32; Dt 9). Saw glory of the Lᴏʀᴅ (Ex 33–34). Supervised building of tabernacle (Ex 36–40). Set apart Aaron and priests (Lev 8–9). Numbered tribes (Nu 1–4; 26). Opposed by Aaron and Miriam (Nu 12). Sent spies into Canaan (Nu 13). Announced forty years of wandering for failure to enter land (Nu 14). Opposed by Korah (Nu 16). Forbidden to enter land for striking rock (Nu 20:1–13; Dt 1:37). Lifted bronze snake for healing (Nu 21:4–9; Jn 3:14). Final address to Israel (Dt 1–33). Succeeded by Joshua (Nu 27:12–23; Dt 34). Death (Dt 34:5–12).

"Law of Moses" (1Ki 2:3; Ezr 3:2; Mk 12:26; Lk 24:44). "Book of Moses" (2Ch 25:12; Ne 13:1). "Song of Moses" (Ex 15:1–21; Rev 15:3). "Prayer of Moses" (Ps 90).

MOTHS
Mt	6: 19	where **m** and vermin destroy,

MOTHER (MOTHER'S)
Ge	2: 24	why a man leaves his father and **m**
	3: 20	because she would become the **m**
Ex	20: 12	"Honor your father and your **m**,
Lev	20: 9	they have cursed their father or **m**,
Dt	5: 16	"Honor your father and your **m**,
	21: 18	does not obey his father and **m**
	27: 16	who dishonors their father or **m**."
1Sa	2: 19	Each year his **m** made him a little
Ps	113: 9	her home as a happy **m** of children.
Pr	23: 25	May your father and **m** rejoice;
	29: 15	left undisciplined disgraces its **m**.
	31: 1	utterance his **m** taught him.
Isa	49: 15	"Can a **m** forget the baby at her
	66: 13	As a **m** comforts her child, so will I
Mt	10: 37	or **m** more than me is not worthy
	15: 4	said, 'Honor your father and **m**'
	19: 5	a man will leave his father and **m**
Mk	7: 10	'Honor your father and **m**,' and,
	10: 19	honor your father and **m**.'"
Jn	19: 27	to the disciple, "Here is your **m**."

MOTHER'S (MOTHER)
Job	1: 21	"Naked I came from my **m** womb,
Pr	1: 8	do not forsake your **m** teaching.

CONCORDANCE

MOTIVES

Pr	16:	2	but **m** are weighed by the LORD.
1Co	4:	5	and will expose the **m** of the heart.
Php	1:	18	way, whether from false **m** or true,
1Th	2:	3	not spring from error or impure **m**,
Jas	4:	3	because you ask with wrong **m**,

MOUNTAIN (MOUNTAINS)

Mic	4:	2	let us go up to the **m** of the LORD,
Mt	17:	20	you can say to this **m**,

MOUNTAINS (MOUNTAIN)

Isa	52:	7	beautiful on the **m** are the feet
	55:	12	the **m** and hills will burst into song
1Co	13:	2	if I have a faith that can move **m**,

MOURN (MOURNING)

Ecc	3:	4	a time to **m** and a time to dance,
Isa	61:	2	of our God, to comfort all who **m**,
Mt	5:	4	Blessed are those who **m**, for they
Ro	12:	15	**m** with those who **m**.

MOURNING (MOURN)

Jer	31:	13	I will turn their **m** into gladness;
Rev	21:	4	There will be no more death' or **m**

MOUTH

Ps	19:	14	May these words of my **m** and this
	40:	3	He put a new song in my **m**,
	119:103		taste, sweeter than honey to my **m**!
Pr	27:	2	praise you, and not your own **m**;
Isa	51:	16	I have put my words in your **m**
Mt	12:	34	the **m** speaks what the heart is full
	15:	11	but what comes out of their **m**,
Ro	10:	9	If you declare with your **m**,

MUD

Ps	40:	2	slimy pit, out of the **m** and mire;
Isa	57:	20	whose waves cast up mire and **m**.
2Pe	2:	22	returns to her wallowing in the **m**."

MULTITUDE (MULTITUDES)

Isa	31:	1	who trust in the **m** of their chariots
1Pe	4:	8	because love covers over a **m**
Rev	7:	9	there before me was a great **m**

MULTITUDES (MULTITUDE)

Joel	3:	14	**M, m** in the valley of decision!

MURDER (MURDERER MURDERERS)

Ex	20:	13	"You shall not **m**.
Mt	15:	19	**m**, adultery, sexual immorality,
Ro	13:	9	"You shall not **m**," "You shall not
Jas	2:	11	commit adultery but do commit **m**,

MURDERER (MURDER)

Nu	35:	16	a **m**; the **m** is to be put to death.
Jn	8:	44	He was a **m** from the beginning,
1Jn	3:	15	hates a brother or sister is a **m**,

MURDERERS (MURDER)

1Ti	1:	9	kill their fathers or mothers, for **m**,
Rev	21:	8	vile, the **m**, the sexually immoral,

MUSIC

Ps	27:	6	sing and make **m** to the LORD.
	95:	2	and extol him with **m** and song.
	98:	4	burst into jubilant song with **m**,
	108:	1	sing and make **m** with all my soul.
Eph	5:	19	make **m** from your heart to the Lord,

MUSTARD

Mt	13:	31	kingdom of heaven is like a **m** seed,
	17:	20	you have faith as small as a **m** seed,

MUZZLE

Dt	25:	4	Do not **m** an ox while it is treading
Ps	39:	1	I will put a **m** on my mouth while
1Co	9:	9	Do not **m** an ox while it is treading

MYRRH

Mt	2:	11	gifts of gold, frankincense and **m**.
Mk	15:	23	offered him wine mixed with **m**,

MYSTERY

Ro	16:	25	the revelation of the **m** hidden
1Co	15:	51	Listen, I tell you a **m**: We will not
Eph	5:	32	This is a profound **m**—but I am
Col	1:	26	the **m** that has been kept hidden
1Ti	3:	16	the **m** from which true godliness

MYTHS

1Ti	4:	7	Have nothing to do with godless **m**

NADAB

Son of Jeroboam I; king of Israel (1Ki 15:25–32).

NAIL (NAILING)

Jn	20:	25	"Unless I see the **n** marks in his

NAILING (NAIL)

Ac	2:	23	him to death by **n** him to the cross.
Col	2:	14	has taken it away, **n** it to the cross.

NAKED

Ge	2:	25	Adam and his wife were both **n**,
Job	1:	21	womb, and **n** I will depart.
Isa	58:	7	you see the **n**, to clothe them,
2Co	5:	3	are clothed, we will not be found **n**.

NAME

Ex	3:	15	"This is my **n** forever, the **n** you
	20:	7	"You shall not misuse the **n**
Dt	5:	11	"You shall not misuse the **n**
	28:	58	this glorious and awesome **n**—
1Ki	5:	5	will build the temple for my **N**.'
2Ch	7:	14	people, who are called by my **n**,
Ps	34:	3	let us exalt his **n** together.
	103:	1	my inmost being, praise his holy **n**.
	147:	4	the stars and calls them each by **n**.
Pr	22:	1	A good **n** is more desirable than
	30:	4	What is his **n**, and what is the **n**
Isa	40:	26	and calls forth each of them by **n**.
	57:	15	who lives forever, whose **n** is holy:
Jer	14:	7	LORD, for the sake of your **n**.
Da	12:	1	everyone whose **n** is found written
Joel	2:	32	the **n** of the LORD will be saved;
Zec	14:	9	one LORD, and his **n** the only **n**.
Mt	1:	21	you are to give him the **n** Jesus,
	6:	9	in heaven, hallowed be your **n**,
	18:	20	where two or three gather in my **n**,
Jn	10:	3	He calls his own sheep by **n**
	16:	24	not asked for anything in my **n**.
Ac	4:	12	is no other **n** under heaven given
Ro	10:	13	on the **n** of the Lord will be saved."
Php	2:	9	the **n** that is above every **n**,
Col	3:	17	do it all in the **n** of the Lord Jesus,
Heb	1:	4	the angels as the **n** he has inherited
Rev	20:	15	whose **n** was not found written

NAOMI

Mother-in-law of Ruth (Ru 1). Advised Ruth to seek marriage with Boaz (Ru 2–4).

NARROW

Mt	7:	13	"Enter through the **n** gate.

NATHANAEL
Apostle (Jn 1:45–49; 21:2). Probably also called Bartholomew (Mt 10:3).

NATION (NATIONS)
Ge	12: 2	"I will make you into a great **n**,
Ps	33: 12	Blessed is the **n** whose God is
Pr	14: 34	Righteousness exalts a **n**, but sin
Isa	65: 1	a **n** that did not call on my name,
1Pe	2: 9	a holy **n**, God's special possession,
Rev	7: 9	could count, from every **n**, tribe,

NATIONS (NATION)
Ge	17: 4	You will be the father of many **n**.
	18: 18	and all **n** on earth will be blessed
Ex	19: 5	of all **n** you will be my treasured
Ne	1: 8	I will scatter you among the **n**,
Ps	96: 3	Declare his glory among the **n**,
Isa	40: 15	Surely the **n** are like a drop
Eze	36: 23	has been profaned among the **n**,
Hag	2: 7	what is desired by all **n** will come,
Zec	8: 23	**n** will take firm hold of one Jew
	14: 2	I will gather all the **n** to Jerusalem
Mt	28: 19	go and make disciples of all **n**,
Rev	21: 24	The **n** will walk by its light,

NATURAL (NATURE)
1Co	15: 44	it is sown a **n** body, it is raised

NATURE (NATURAL)
Php	2: 6	Who, being in very **n** God, did not

NAZARENE
Mt	2: 23	that he would be called a **N**.

NAZIRITE
Jdg	13: 7	because the boy will be a **N** of God

NECESSARY
Ro	13: 5	it is **n** to submit to the authorities,

NEED (NEEDS NEEDY)
Mt	6: 8	knows what you **n** before you ask
Ro	12: 13	the Lord's people who are in **n**.
1Co	12: 21	say to the hand, "I don't **n** you!"
1Jn	3: 17	sister in **n** but has no pity on them,

NEEDLE
Mt	19: 24	to go through the eye of a **n** than

NEEDS (NEED)
Isa	58: 11	he will satisfy your **n**
Php	4: 19	God will meet all your **n** according

NEEDY (NEED)
Pr	14: 21	is the one who is kind to the **n**.
	14: 31	is kind to the **n** honors God.
	31: 20	and extends her hands to the **n**.
Mt	6: 2	"So when you give to the **n**, do not

NEGLECT (NEGLECTED)
Ne	10: 39	"We will not **n** the house of our
Ps	119: 16	I will not **n** your word.
Ac	6: 2	for us to **n** the ministry of the word
1Ti	4: 14	not **n** your gift, which was given

NEGLECTED (NEGLECT)
Mt	23: 23	But you have **n** the more important

NEHEMIAH
Cupbearer of Artaxerxes (Ne 2:1); governor of Israel (Ne 8:9). Returned to Jerusalem to rebuild walls (Ne 2–6). With Ezra, reestablished worship (Ne 8). Prayer confessing nation's sin (Ne 9). Dedicated wall (Ne 12).

NEIGHBOR (NEIGHBOR'S)
Ex	20: 16	give false testimony against your **n**.
Lev	19: 18	people, but love your **n** as yourself.
Pr	27: 10	better a **n** nearby than a relative far
Mt	19: 19	and 'love your **n** as yourself.' "
Lk	10: 29	asked Jesus, "And who is my **n**?"
Ro	13: 10	Love does no harm to a **n**.

NEIGHBOR'S (NEIGHBOR)
Ex	20: 17	"You shall not covet your **n** house.
Dt	5: 21	"You shall not covet your **n** wife.
	19: 14	not move your **n** boundary stone
Pr	25: 17	Seldom set foot in your **n** house—

NEW
Ps	40: 3	He put a **n** song in my mouth,
Ecc	1: 9	there is nothing **n** under the sun.
Isa	65: 17	I will create **n** heavens and a **n**
Jer	31: 31	I will make a **n** covenant
Eze	36: 26	I will give you a **n** heart and put a **n** spirit in you;
Mt	9: 17	they pour **n** wine into **n** wineskins,
Lk	22: 20	"This cup is the **n** covenant in my
2Co	5: 17	in Christ, the **n** creation has come:
Eph	4: 24	and to put on the **n** self,
2Pe	3: 13	to a **n** heaven and a **n** earth,
1Jn	2: 8	Yet I am writing you a **n** command;

NEWBORN (BEAR)
1Pe	2: 2	Like **n** babies, crave pure spiritual

NEWS
Isa	52: 7	the feet of those who bring good **n**,
Mk	1: 15	Repent and believe the good **n**!"
Lk	2: 10	I bring you good **n** that will cause
Ac	5: 42	proclaiming the good **n** that Jesus
	17: 18	Paul was preaching the good **n**
Ro	10: 15	feet of those who bring good **n**!"

NICODEMUS
Pharisee who visited Jesus at night (Jn 3). Argued fair treatment of Jesus (Jn 7:50–52). With Joseph, prepared Jesus for burial (Jn 19:38–42).

NIGHT
Job	35: 10	Maker, who gives songs in the **n**,
Ps	1: 2	meditates on his law day and **n**.
	91: 5	You will not fear the terror of **n**,
Jn	3: 2	He came to Jesus at **n** and said,
1Th	5: 2	Lord will come like a thief in the **n**.
	5: 5	We do not belong to the **n**
Rev	21: 25	shut, for there will be no **n** there.

NOAH
Righteous man (Eze 14:14, 20) called to build ark (Ge 6–8; Heb 11:7; 1Pe 3:20; 2Pe 2:5). God's covenant with (Ge 9:1–17). Drunkenness of (Ge 9:18–23). Blessed sons, cursed Canaan (Ge 9:24–27).

NOBLE
Ru	3: 11	you are a woman of **n** character.
Ps	45: 1	by a **n** theme as I recite my verses
Pr	12: 4	**n** character is her husband's crown,
	31: 10	wife of **n** character who can find?
	31: 29	"Many women do **n** things, but
Isa	32: 8	But the **n** make **n** plans, and by **n**
Lk	8: 15	good soil stands for those with a **n**
Php	4: 8	whatever is **n**, whatever is right,

NOTHING
Ne	9: 21	they lacked **n**, their clothes did not

Jer 32: 17 **N** is too hard for you.
Jn 15: 5 apart from me you can do **n**.

NULLIFY
Ro 3: 31 we, then, **n** the law by this faith?

OATH
Dt 7: 8 and kept the **o** he swore to your

OBEDIENCE (OBEY)
2Ch 31: 21 of God's temple and in **o** to the law
Ro 1: 5 all the Gentiles to the **o** that comes
 6: 16 to death, or to **o**, which leads
2Jn : 6 that we walk in **o** to his commands.

OBEDIENT (OBEY)
Lk 2: 51 with them and was **o** to them.
Php 2: 8 himself by becoming **o** to death—
1Pe 1: 14 As **o** children, do not conform

OBEY (OBEDIENCE OBEDIENT OBEYED)
Ex 12: 24 "**O** these instructions as a lasting
Dt 6: 3 be careful to **o** so that it may go
 13: 4 Keep his commands and **o** him;
 21: 18 son who does not **o** his father
 30: 2 God and **o** him with all your heart
 32: 46 to **o** carefully all the words
1Sa 15: 22 To **o** is better than sacrifice,
Ps 119: 34 your law and **o** it with all my heart.
Mt 28: 20 to **o** everything I have commanded
Jn 14: 23 who loves me will **o** my teaching.
Ac 5: 29 must **o** God rather than human
Ro 6: 16 you are slaves of the one you **o**—
Gal 5: 3 he is obligated to **o** the whole law.
Eph 6: 1 **o** your parents in the Lord, for this
 6: 5 heart, just as you would **o** Christ.
Col 3: 20 **o** your parents in everything,
1Ti 3: 4 and see that his children **o** him,

OBEYED (OBEY)
Ps 119: 4 precepts that are to be fully **o**.
Jnh 3: 3 Jonah **o** the word of the LORD
Jn 17: 6 to me and they have **o** your word.
Heb 11: 8 as his inheritance, **o** and went,
1Pe 3: 6 who **o** Abraham and called him

OBLIGATED
Ro 1: 14 I am **o** both to Greeks
Gal 5: 3 that he is **o** to obey the whole law.

OBSCENITY
Eph 5: 4 Nor should there be **o**, foolish talk

OBSOLETE
Heb 8: 13 "new," he has made the first one **o**;

OBTAINED
Ro 9: 30 not pursue righteousness, have **o** it,
Php 3: 12 Not that I have already **o** all this,

OFFENSE (OFFENSIVE)
Pr 17: 9 would foster love covers over an **o**,
 19: 11 it is to one's glory to overlook an **o**.

OFFENSIVE (OFFENSE)
Ps 139: 24 See if there is any **o** way in me,

OFFER (OFFERED OFFERING OFFERINGS)
Ro 12: 1 **o** your bodies as a living sacrifice,
Heb 13: 15 let us continually **o** to God

OFFERED (OFFER)
Heb 7: 27 sins once for all when he **o** himself.

OFFERING (OFFER)
Ge 22: 8 provide the lamb for the burnt **o**,
Ps 40: 6 Sacrifice and **o** you did not desire
Isa 53: 10 the LORD makes his life an **o**
Mt 5: 23 if you are **o** your gift at the altar
Eph 5: 2 himself up for us as a fragrant **o**
Heb 10: 5 "Sacrifice and **o** you did not desire,

OFFERINGS (OFFER)
Mal 3: 8 we robbing you?' "In tithes and **o**.
Mk 12: 33 is more important than all burnt **o**

OFFICER
2Ti 2: 4 tries to please his commanding **o**.

OFFSPRING
Ge 3: 15 and between your **o** and hers;
 12: 7 "To your **o** I will give this land."

OIL
Ps 23: 5 You anoint my head with **o**;
Isa 61: 3 the **o** of joy instead of mourning,
Heb 1: 9 by anointing you with the **o** of joy."

OLIVE (OLIVES)
Zec 4: 3 Also there are two **o** trees by it,
Ro 11: 17 though a wild **o** shoot, have been
Rev 11: 4 They are "the two **o** trees"

OLIVES (OLIVE)
Jas 3: 12 can a fig tree bear **o**, or a grapevine

OMEGA
Rev 1: 8 "I am the Alpha and the **O**,"

OMRI
King of Israel (1Ki 16:21–26).

OPINIONS
1Ki 18: 21 will you waver between two **o**?
Pr 18: 2 but delight in airing their own **o**.

OPPORTUNITY
Ro 7: 11 sin, seizing the **o** afforded
Gal 6: 10 as we have **o**, let us do good to all
Eph 5: 16 making the most of every **o**,
Col 4: 5 make the most of every **o**.
1Ti 5: 14 to give the enemy no **o** for slander.

OPPOSES
Jas 4: 6 "God **o** the proud but shows favor
1Pe 5: 5 "God **o** the proud but shows favor

OPPRESS (OPPRESSED)
Ex 22: 21 "Do not mistreat or **o** a foreigner,
Zec 7: 10 Do not **o** the widow

OPPRESSED (OPPRESS)
Ps 9: 9 The LORD is a refuge for the **o**,
Isa 53: 7 He was **o** and afflicted, yet he did
Zec 10: 2 the people wander like sheep **o**

ORDERLY
1Co 14: 40 be done in a fitting and **o** way.

ORGIES
Gal 5: 21 drunkenness, **o**, and the like.
1Pe 4: 3 lust, drunkenness, **o**,

ORIGIN
2Pe 1: 21 For prophecy never had its **o**

ORPHANS
Jn 14: 18 I will not leave you as **o**;
Jas 1: 27 to look after **o** and widows in their

OUTCOME
Heb	13: 7	Consider the **o** of their way of life
1Pe	4: 17	what will the **o** be for those who do

OUTSIDERS
Col	4: 5	wise in the way you act toward **o**;
1Th	4: 12	daily life may win the respect of **o**
1Ti	3: 7	also have a good reputation with **o**,

OUTSTANDING
SS	5: 10	and ruddy, **o** among ten thousand.
Ro	13: 8	Let no debt remain **o**,

OUTSTRETCHED
Ex	6: 6	I will redeem you with an **o** arm
Jer	27: 5	power and **o** arm I made the earth
Eze	20: 33	with a mighty hand and an **o** arm

OUTWEIGHS
2Co	4: 17	an eternal glory that far **o** them all.

OVERCOME (OVERCOMES)
Mt	16: 18	and the gates of Hades will not **o** it.
Mk	9: 24	help me **o** my unbelief!"
Jn	16: 33	But take heart! I have **o** the world."
Ro	12: 21	Do not be **o** by evil, but **o** evil
1Jn	5: 4	is the victory that has **o** the world,

OVERCOMES (OVERCOME)
1Jn	5: 4	everyone born of God **o** the world.
	5: 5	Who is it that **o** the world?

OVERFLOW (OVERFLOWS)
Ps	119:171	May my lips **o** with praise, for you
Ro	15: 13	so that you may **o** with hope
2Co	4: 15	may cause thanksgiving to **o**
1Th	3: 12	love increase and **o** for each other

OVERFLOWS (OVERFLOW)
Ps	23: 5	anoint my head with oil; my cup **o**.

OVERJOYED (JOY)
Da	6: 23	The king was **o** and gave orders
Mt	2: 10	they saw the star, they were **o**.
Jn	20: 20	disciples were **o** when they saw
Ac	12: 14	she was so **o** she ran back without
1Pe	4: 13	that you may be **o** when his glory

OVERSEER (OVERSEERS)
1Ti	3: 1	to be an **o** desires a noble task.
	3: 2	Now the **o** is to be above reproach,
Titus	1: 7	Since an **o** manages God's

OVERSEERS (OVERSEER)
Ac	20: 28	the Holy Spirit has made you **o**.
Php	1: 1	together with the **o** and deacons:

OVERWHELMED
Ps	38: 4	My guilt has **o** me like a burden
	65: 3	When we were **o** by sins,
Mt	26: 38	"My soul is **o** with sorrow
Mk	7: 37	People were **o** with amazement.

OWE
Ro	13: 7	Give to everyone what you **o** them:
Phm	: 19	that you **o** me your very self.

OX
Dt	25: 4	Do not muzzle an **o** while it is
Isa	11: 7	the lion will eat straw like the **o**.
1Co	9: 9	"Do not muzzle an **o** while it is

PAGANS
Mt	5: 47	Do not even **p** do that?
1Pe	2: 12	such good lives among the **p** that,

PAIN (PAINFUL PAINS)
Job	33: 19	on a bed of **p** with constant distress
Jn	16: 21	to a child has **p** because her time

PAINFUL (PAIN)
Ge	3: 17	through **p** toil you will eat food
Heb	12: 11	seems pleasant at the time, but **p**.

PAINS (PAIN)
Ge	3: 16	"I will make your **p** in childbearing

PALMS
Isa	49: 16	engraved you on the **p** of my hands

PANTS
Ps	42: 1	As the deer **p** for streams of water, so my soul **p** for you,

PARADISE
Lk	23: 43	today you will be with me in **p**."
2Co	12: 4	was caught up to **p** and heard
Rev	2: 7	tree of life, which is in the **p** of God.

PARALYZED
Mk	2: 3	bringing to him a **p** man,

PARDON (PARDONS)
Isa	55: 7	and to our God, for he will freely **p**.

PARDONS (PARDON)
Mic	7: 18	like you, who **p** sin and forgives

PARENT (PARENT'S PARENTS)
Pr	17: 21	is no joy for the **p** of a godless fool.

PARENT'S (PARENT)
	15: 5	A fool spurns a **p** discipline,

PARENTS
Ex	20: 5	for the sin of the **p** to the third
Pr	17: 6	**p** are the pride of their children.
Lk	18: 29	sisters or **p** or children for the sake
	21: 16	You will be betrayed even by **p**,
Ro	1: 30	of doing evil; they disobey their **p**;
2Co	12: 14	not have to save up for their **p**,
Eph	6: 1	Children, obey your **p** in the Lord,
Col	3: 20	obey your **p** in everything,
2Ti	3: 2	disobedient to their **p**, ungrateful,

PARTIALITY
Dt	10: 17	who shows no **p** and accepts no
2Ch	19: 7	our God there is no injustice or **p**
Lk	20: 21	that you do not show **p** but teach

PARTICIPATION
1Co	10: 16	bread that we break a **p** in the body

PASS
Ex	12: 13	I see the blood, I will **p** over you.
La	1: 12	nothing to you, all you who **p** by?
Lk	21: 33	but my words will never **p** away.
1Co	13: 8	there is knowledge, it will **p** away.

PASSION (PASSIONS)
1Co	7: 9	to marry than to burn with **p**.

PASSIONS (PASSION)
Gal	5: 24	have crucified the flesh with its **p**
Titus	2: 12	to ungodliness and worldly **p**,

PASSOVER
Ex	12: 11	Eat it in haste; it is the Lord's **P**.
Dt	16: 1	celebrate the **P** of the Lord your
1Co	5: 7	For Christ, our **P** lamb, has been

CONCORDANCE

PAST
Isa 43: 18 do not dwell on the **p**.
Ro 15: 4 was written in the **p** was written
Heb 1: 1 the **p** God spoke to our ancestors

PASTORS
Eph 4: 11 the evangelists, the **p** and teachers,

PASTURE (PASTURES)
Ps 37: 3 dwell in the land and enjoy safe **p**.
100: 3 are his people, the sheep of his **p**.
Jer 50: 7 their verdant **p**, the LORD,
Eze 34: 13 I will **p** them on the mountains
Jn 10: 9 come in and go out, and find **p**.

PASTURES (PASTURE)
Ps 23: 2 He makes me lie down in green **p**,

PATCH
Mt 9: 16 No one sews a **p** of unshrunk cloth

PATH (PATHS)
Ps 27: 11 me in a straight **p** because of my
119: 9 person stay on the **p** of purity?
119:105 to my feet and a light for my **p**.
Pr 15: 19 the **p** of the upright is a highway.
15: 24 The **p** of life leads upward
Isa 26: 7 The **p** of the righteous is level;
Lk 1: 79 guide our feet into the **p** of peace."
2Co 6: 3 no stumbling block in anyone's **p**,

PATHS (PATH)
Ps 23: 3 He guides me along the right **p**
25: 4 ways, LORD, teach me your **p**.
Pr 3: 6 and he will make your **p** straight.
Ro 11: 33 and his **p** beyond tracing out!
Heb 12: 13 "Make level **p** for your feet,"

PATIENCE (PATIENT)
Pr 19: 11 A person's wisdom yields **p**; it is
2Co 6: 6 understanding, **p** and kindness;
Col 1: 11 may have great endurance and **p**,
3: 12 humility, gentleness and **p**.

PATIENT (PATIENCE PATIENTLY)
Pr 15: 18 the one who is **p** calms a quarrel.
Ro 12: 12 Be joyful in hope, **p** in affliction,
1Co 13: 4 Love is **p**, love is kind. It does not
Eph 4: 2 be **p**, bearing with one another
1Th 5: 14 help the weak, be **p** with everyone.

PATIENTLY (PATIENT)
Ps 40: 1 I waited **p** for the LORD;
Ro 8: 25 we do not yet have, we wait for it **p**.

PATTERN
Ro 5: 14 who is a **p** of the one to come.
12: 2 not conform to the **p** of this world,
2Ti 1: 13 keep as the **p** of sound teaching,

PAUL
Also called Saul (Ac 13:9). Pharisee from Tarsus (Ac 9:11; Php 3:5). Apostle (Gal 1). At stoning of Stephen (Ac 8:1). Persecuted Church (Ac 9:1–2; Gal 1:13). Vision of Jesus on road to Damascus (Ac 9:4–9; 26:12–18). In Arabia (Gal 1:17). Preached in Damascus; escaped death through the wall in a basket (Ac 9:19–25). In Jerusalem; sent back to Tarsus (Ac 9:26–30).
Brought to Antioch by Barnabas (Ac 11:22–26). First missionary journey to Cyprus and Galatia (Ac 13–14). Stoned at Lystra (Ac 14:19–20). At Jerusa-

lem council (Ac 15). Split with Barnabas over Mark (Ac 15:36–41).
Second missionary journey with Silas (Ac 16–20). Called to Macedonia (Ac 16:6–10). Freed from prison in Philippi (Ac 16:16–40). In Thessalonica (Ac 17:1–9). Speech in Athens (Ac 17:16–33). In Corinth (Ac 18). In Ephesus (Ac 19). Return to Jerusalem (Ac 20). Farewell to Ephesian elders (Ac 20:13–38). Arrival in Jerusalem (Ac 21:1–26). Arrested (Ac 21:27–36). Addressed crowds (Ac 22), Sanhedrin (Ac 23:1–11). Transferred to Caesarea (Ac 23:12–35). Trial before Felix (Ac 24), Festus (Ac 25:1–12). Before Agrippa (Ac 25:13—26:32). Voyage to Rome; shipwreck (Ac 27). Arrival in Rome (Ac 28).

PAY (REPAID REPAY)
Lev 26: 43 They will **p** for their sins because
Pr 22: 17 **P** attention and turn your ear
Mt 22: 17 Is it right to **p** the imperial tax
Ro 13: 6 This is also why you **p** taxes,
2Pe 1: 19 you will do well to **p** attention to it,

PEACE (PEACEMAKERS)
Nu 6: 26 toward you and give you **p**." '
Ps 34: 14 and do good; seek **p** and pursue it.
85: 10 righteousness and **p** kiss each
119:165 Great **p** have those who love your
122: 6 Pray for the **p** of Jerusalem:
Pr 14: 30 A heart at **p** gives life to the body,
17: 1 Better a dry crust with **p** and quiet
Isa 9: 6 Everlasting Father, Prince of **P**.
26: 3 in perfect **p** those whose minds are
48: 22 "There is no **p**," says the LORD,
Zec 9: 10 He will proclaim **p** to the nations.
Mt 10: 34 I did not come to bring **p**,
Lk 2: 14 and on earth **p** to those on whom
Jn 14: 27 **P** I leave with you; my **p** I give you.
16: 33 so that in me you may have **p**.
Ro 5: 1 we have **p** with God through our
1Co 7: 15 God has called us to live in **p**.
14: 33 is not a God of disorder but of **p**—
Gal 5: 22 Spirit is love, joy, **p**, forbearance,
Eph 2: 14 For he himself is our **p**, who has
Php 4: 7 the **p** of God, which transcends
Col 1: 20 by making **p** through his blood,
3: 15 Let the **p** of Christ rule in your
1Th 5: 3 people are saying, "**P** and safety,"
2Th 3: 16 the Lord of **p** himself give you **p**
2Ti 2: 22 love and **p**, along with those who
1Pe 3: 11 they must seek **p** and pursue it.
Rev 6: 4 power to take **p** from the earth

PEACEMAKERS (PEACE)
Mt 5: 9 Blessed are the **p**, for they will be
Jas 3: 18 **P** who sow in peace reap a harvest

PEARL (PEARLS)
Rev 21: 21 each gate made of a single **p**.

PEARLS (PEARL)
Mt 7: 6 do not throw your **p** to pigs.
13: 45 like a merchant looking for fine **p**.
1Ti 2: 9 or gold or **p** or expensive clothes,
Rev 21: 21 The twelve gates were twelve **p**,

PEKAH
King of Israel (2Ki 15:25–31; Isa 7:1).

PEKAHIAH
Son of Menahem; king of Israel (2Ki 15:22–26).

PEN
Mt 5: 18 not the least stroke of a **p**,

PENTECOST
Ac 2: 1 When the day of **P** came, they were

PEOPLE (PEOPLES)
Dt 32: 9 For the Lᴏʀᴅ's portion is his **p**,
Ru 1: 16 Your **p** will be my **p** and your God
2Ch 7: 14 if my **p**, who are called by my
Ps 133: 1 it is when God's **p** live together
Jer 24: 7 They will be my **p**, and I will be
Zec 2: 11 in that day and will become my **p**.
Mt 4: 19 I will send you out to fish for **p**."
Lk 2: 10 will cause great joy for all the **p**.
Jn 12: 32 earth, will draw all **p** to myself."
Ac 15: 14 to choose a **p** for his name
Ro 5: 12 and in this way death came to all **p**,
8: 27 for God's **p** in accordance
1Co 9: 22 I have become all things to all **p** so
2Co 6: 16 their God, and they will be my **p**."
Eph 1: 18 glorious inheritance in his holy **p**,
6: 18 keep on praying for all the Lord's **p**.
1Ti 2: 4 who wants all **p** to be saved
2Ti 2: 2 entrust to reliable **p** who will also
Titus 2: 14 himself a **p** that are his very own,
Heb 9: 27 Just as **p** are destined to die once,
1Pe 2: 9 But you are a chosen **p**, a royal
Rev 5: 8 which are the prayers of God's **p**.
19: 8 the righteous acts of God's holy **p**.)
21: 3 They will be his **p**, and God

PEOPLES (PEOPLE)
Da 7: 14 **p** of every language worshiped him
Mic 4: 1 the hills, and **p** will stream to it.

PERCEIVING
Isa 6: 9 be ever seeing, but never **p**.'

PERFECT (PERFECTER PERFECTION)
SS 6: 9 but my dove, my **p** one, is unique,
Isa 26: 3 in **p** peace those whose minds are
Mt 5: 48 Be **p**, therefore, as your heavenly
Father is **p**.
Ro 12: 2 his good, pleasing and **p** will.
2Co 12: 9 my power is made **p** in weakness."
Col 3: 14 binds them all together in **p** unity.
Heb 9: 11 more **p** tabernacle that is not made
10: 14 he has made **p** forever those who
Jas 1: 17 good and **p** gift is from above,
1: 25 looks intently into the **p** law
3: 2 never at fault in what they say is **p**,
1Jn 4: 18 But **p** love drives out fear,

PERFECTER (PERFECT)
Heb 12: 2 on Jesus, the pioneer and **p** of faith.

PERFECTION (PERFECT)
Ps 119: 96 To all **p** I see a limit, but your
Heb 7: 11 If **p** could have been attained

PERFORMS
Ps 77: 14 You are the God who **p** miracles;

PERISH (PERISHABLE)
Ps 102: 26 They will **p**, but you remain;
Lk 13: 3 you repent, you too will all **p**.
Jn 10: 28 eternal life, and they shall never **p**;
Col 2: 22 that are all destined to **p** with use,
Heb 1: 11 They will **p**, but you remain;
2Pe 3: 9 you, not wanting anyone to **p**,

PERISHABLE (PERISH)
1Co 15: 42 The body that is sown is **p**, it is

PERJURERS
1Ti 1: 10 for slave traders and liars and **p**—

PERMIT
1Ti 2: 12 I do not **p** a woman to teach

PERSECUTE (PERSECUTED PERSECUTION)
Mt 5: 11 **p** you and falsely say all kinds
Jn 15: 20 persecuted me, they will **p** you
Ac 9: 4 "Saul, Saul, why do you **p** me?"
Ro 12: 14 Bless those who **p** you; bless and

PERSECUTED (PERSECUTE)
1Co 4: 12 when we are **p**, we endure it;
2Ti 3: 12 godly life in Christ Jesus will be **p**,

PERSECUTION (PERSECUTE)
Ro 8: 35 trouble or hardship or **p** or famine

PERSEVERANCE (PERSEVERE)
Ro 5: 3 we know that suffering produces **p**;
5: 4 **p**, character; and character, hope.
Heb 12: 1 let us run with **p** the race marked
Jas 1: 3 testing of your faith produces **p**.
2Pe 1: 6 and to self-control, **p**; and to **p**,

PERSEVERE (PERSEVERANCE PERSEVERED PERSEVERES)
1Ti 4: 16 **P** in them, because if you do,
Heb 10: 36 You need to **p** so that when you

PERSEVERED (PERSEVERE)
Heb 11: 27 he **p** because he saw him who is
Jas 5: 11 count as blessed those who have **p**.
Rev 2: 3 You have **p** and have endured

PERSEVERES (PERSEVERE)
1Co 13: 7 trusts, always hopes, always **p**.
Jas 1: 12 one who **p** under trial because,

PERSUADE
2Co 5: 11 to fear the Lord, we try to **p** others.

PERVERSION (PERVERT)
Lev 18: 23 sexual relations with it; that is a **p**.
Jude : 7 up to sexual immorality and **p**.

PERVERT (PERVERSION)
Gal 1: 7 are trying to **p** the gospel of Christ.

PESTILENCE
Ps 91: 6 the **p** that stalks in the darkness,

PETER
Apostle, brother of Andrew, also called Simon (Mt 10:2; Mk 3:16; Lk 6:14; Ac 1:13), and Cephas (Jn 1:42). Confession of Christ (Mt 16:13–20; Mk 8:27–30; Lk 9:18–27). At transfiguration (Mt 17:1–8; Mk 9:2–8; Lk 9:28–36; 2Pe 1:16–18). Caught fish with coin (Mt 17:24–27). Denial of Jesus predicted (Mt 26:31–35; Mk 14:27–31; Lk 22:31–34; Jn 13:31–38). Denied Jesus (Mt 26:69–75; Mk 14:66–72; Lk 22:54–62; Jn 18:15–27). Commissioned by Jesus to shepherd his flock (Jn 21:15–23).

Speech at Pentecost (Ac 2). Healed beggar (Ac 3:1–10). Speech at temple (Ac 3:11–26), before Sanhedrin (Ac 4:1–22). In Samaria (Ac 8:14–25). Sent by vision to Cornelius (Ac 10). Announced salvation of Gentiles in Jerusalem (Ac 11; 15). Freed from prison (Ac 12). Inconsistency at Antioch (Gal 2:11–21). At Jerusalem Council (Ac 15).

PHARISEES
Mt　　5: 20　surpasses that of the **P**

PHILIP
　　1. Apostle (Mt 10:3; Mk 3:18; Lk 6:14; Jn 1:43–48; 14:8; Ac 1:13).
　　2. Deacon (Ac 6:1–7); evangelist in Samaria (Ac 8:4–25), to Ethiopian (Ac 8:26–40).

PHILOSOPHY
Col　　2: 8　through hollow and deceptive **p**,

PHYLACTERIES
Mt　　23: 5　They make their **p** wide

PHYSICAL
1Ti　　4: 8　For **p** training is of some value,
Jas　　2: 16　does nothing about their **p** needs,

PIECES
Ge　　15: 17　and passed between the **p**.
Jer　　34: 18　two and then walked between its **p**.

PIERCE (PIERCED)
Ps　　22: 16　they **p** my hands and my feet.

PIERCED (PIERCE)
Isa　　53: 5　he was **p** for our transgressions,
Zec　　12: 10　the one they have **p**, and they will
Jn　　19: 37　will look on the one they have **p**.”

PIGS
Mt　　7: 6　do not throw your pearls to **p**.

PILATE
　　Governor of Judea. Questioned Jesus (Mt 27:1–26; Mk 15:15; Lk 22:66—23:25; Jn 18:28—19:16); sent him to Herod (Lk 23:6–12); consented to his crucifixion when crowds chose Barabbas (Mt 27:15–26; Mk 15:6–15; Lk 23:13–25; Jn 19:1–10).

PILLAR
Ge　　19: 26　back, and she became a **p** of salt.
Ex　　13: 21　by night in a **p** of fire to give them
1Ti　　3: 15　the **p** and foundation of the truth.

PIT
Ps　　40: 2　He lifted me out of the slimy **p**,
　　103: 4　who redeems your life from the **p**
Mt　　15: 14　the blind, both will fall into a **p**.”

PITIED
1Co　　15: 19　we are of all people most to be **p**.

PLAGUE
2Ch　　6: 28　famine or **p** comes to the land,

PLAIN
Ro　　1: 19　God has made it **p** to them.

PLAN (PLANNED PLANS)
Pr　　14: 22　those who **p** what is good find love
Eph　　1: 11　to the **p** of him who works

PLANK
Mt　　7: 3　attention to the **p** in your own eye?
Lk　　6: 41　attention to the **p** in your own eye?

PLANNED (PLAN)
Ps　　40: 5　have done, the things you **p** for us.
Isa　　46: 11　what I have **p**, that I will do.
Heb　　11: 40　since God had **p** something better

PLANS (PLAN)
Ps　　20: 4　heart and make all your **p** succeed.
　　33: 11　But the **p** of the LORD stand firm

Pr　　20: 18　**P** are established by seeking advice;
Isa　　32: 8　But the noble make noble **p**,

PLANTED (PLANTS)
Ps　　1: 3　person is like a tree **p** by streams
Mt　　15: 13　Father has not **p** will be pulled
1Co　　3: 6　I **p** the seed, Apollos watered it,

PLANTS (PLANTED)
1Co　　3: 7　neither the one who **p** nor the one
　　9: 7　Who **p** a vineyard and does not eat

PLATTER
Mk　　6: 25　head of John the Baptist on a **p**.”

PLAYED
Lk　　7: 32　“ ‘We **p** the pipe for you, and you
1Co　　14: 7　what tune is being **p** unless there is

PLEADED
2Co　　12: 8　Three times I **p** with the Lord

PLEASANT (PLEASE)
Ps　　16: 6　lines have fallen for me in **p** places;
　　133: 1　and **p** it is when God’s people live
　　147: 1　how **p** and fitting to praise him!
Heb　　12: 11　No discipline seems **p** at the time,

PLEASE (PLEASANT PLEASED PLEASES PLEASING PLEASURE PLEASURES)
Pr　　20: 23　and dishonest scales do not **p** him.
Jer　　6: 20　your sacrifices do not **p** me.”
Jn　　5: 30　for I seek not to **p** myself but him
Ro　　8: 8　realm of the flesh cannot **p** God.
　　15: 2　Each of us should **p** our neighbors
1Co　　7: 32　how he can **p** the Lord.
　　10: 33　even as I try to **p** everyone in every
2Co　　5: 9　So we make it our goal to **p** him,
Gal　　1: 10　If I were still trying to **p** people,
1Th　　4: 1　you how to live in order to **p** God,
2Ti　　2: 4　tries to **p** his commanding officer.
Heb　　11: 6　faith it is impossible to **p** God,

PLEASED (PLEASE)
Mt　　3: 17　with him I am well **p**.”
1Co　　1: 21　God was **p** through the foolishness
Col　　1: 19　God was **p** to have all his fullness
Heb　　11: 5　commended as one who **p** God.
2Pe　　1: 17　with him I am well **p**.”

PLEASES (PLEASE)
Ps　　135: 6　The LORD does whatever **p** him,
Pr　　15: 8　the prayer of the upright **p** him.
Jn　　3: 8　The wind blows wherever it **p**.
　　8: 29　alone, for I always do what **p** him.”
Col　　3: 20　in everything, for this **p** the Lord.
1Ti　　2: 3　is good, and **p** God our Savior,
1Jn　　3: 22　his commands and do what **p** him.

PLEASING (PLEASE)
Ps　　104: 34　May my meditation be **p** to him,
Ro　　12: 1　living sacrifice, holy and **p** to God
Php　　4: 18　an acceptable sacrifice, **p** to God.
Heb　　13: 21　he work in us what is **p** to him,

PLEASURE (PLEASE)
Ps　　147: 10　His **p** is not in the strength
Pr　　21: 17　loves **p** will become poor;
Eze　　18: 32　For I take no **p** in the death
Eph　　1: 5　in accordance with his **p** and will—
　　1: 9　of his will according to his good **p**,
2Ti　　3: 4　lovers of **p** rather than lovers

PLEASURES (PLEASE)
Ps 16: 11 with eternal **p** at your right hand.
Heb 11: 25 than to enjoy the fleeting **p** of sin.
2Pe 2: 13 reveling in their **p** while they feast

PLENTIFUL
Mt 9: 37 "The harvest is **p** but the workers

PLOW (PLOWSHARES)
Lk 9: 62 "No one who puts a hand to the **p**

PLOWSHARES (PLOW)
Isa 2: 4 They will beat their swords into **p**
Joel 3: 10 Beat your **p** into swords and your

PLUNDER
Ex 3: 22 And so you will **p** the Egyptians."

POINT
Jas 2: 10 yet stumbles at just one **p** is guilty

POISON
Mk 16: 18 *and when they drink deadly p,*
Jas 3: 8 It is a restless evil, full of deadly **p.**

POLLUTE (POLLUTED)
Nu 35: 33 " 'Do not **p** the land where you
Jude : 8 these ungodly people **p** their own

POLLUTED (POLLUTE)
Ezr 9: 11 is a land **p** by the corruption
Pr 25: 26 a **p** well are the righteous who give
Ac 15: 20 to abstain from food **p** by idols,
Jas 1: 27 oneself from being **p** by the world.

PONDER
Ps 64: 9 of God and **p** what he has done.
   119: 95 me, but I will **p** your statutes.

POOR (POVERTY)
Dt 15: 4 need be no **p** people among you,
   15: 11 There will always be **p** people
Ps 34: 6 This **p** man called, and the LORD
   82: 3 uphold the cause of the **p**
   112: 9 freely scattered their gifts to the **p,**
Pr 13: 7 another pretends to be **p,** yet has
   14: 31 oppresses the **p** shows contempt
   19: 1 Better the **p** whose walk is
   19: 17 Whoever is kind to the **p** lends
   22: 2 Rich and **p** have this in common:
   22: 9 they share their food with the **p.**
   28: 6 Better the **p** whose walk is
   31: 20 She opens her arms to the **p**
Isa 61: 1 to proclaim good news to the **p.**
Mt 5: 3 "Blessed are the **p** in spirit,
   11: 5 good news is proclaimed to the **p.**
   19: 21 your possessions and give to the **p,**
   26: 11 The **p** you will always have
Mk 12: 42 a **p** widow came and put in two
Ac 10: 4 and gifts to the **p** have come up as
1Co 13: 3 If I give all I possess to the **p**
2Co 8: 9 yet for your sake he became **p,**
Jas 2: 2 and a **p** man in filthy old clothes

PORTION
Dt 32: 9 For the LORD's **p** is his people,
2Ki 2: 9 "Let me inherit a double **p** of your
La 3: 24 to myself, "The LORD is my **p;**

POSSESS (POSSESSING POSSESSION
  POSSESSIONS)
Nu 33: 53 for I have given you the land to **p.**

POSSESSING (POSSESS)
2Co 6: 10 nothing, and yet **p** everything.

POSSESSION (POSSESS)
Ge 15: 7 give you this land to take **p** of it."
Nu 13: 30 go up and take **p** of the land,
Eph 1: 14 of those who are God's **p**—

POSSESSIONS (POSSESS)
Lk 12: 15 not consist in an abundance of **p.**
2Co 12: 14 because what I want is not your **p**
1Jn 3: 17 If anyone has material **p** and sees

POSSIBLE
Mt 19: 26 but with God all things are **p.**"
Mk 9: 23 "Everything is **p** for one who
   10: 27 all things are **p** with God."
Ro 12: 18 If it is **p,** as far as it depends on you
1Co 9: 22 by all **p** means I might save some.

POT (POTSHERDS POTTER POTTERY)
2Ki 4: 40 of God, there is death in the **p!**"
Jer 18: 4 the potter formed it into another **p,**

POTSHERDS (POT)
Isa 45: 9 but **p** among the **p** on the ground.

POTTER (POT)
Isa 29: 16 Can the pot say to the **p,**
   45: 9 Does the clay say to the **p,**
   64: 8 We are the clay, you are the **p;**
Jer 18: 6 do with you, Israel, as this **p** does?"
Ro 9: 21 Does not the **p** have the right

POTTERY (POT)
Ro 9: 21 of clay some **p** for special purposes

POUR (POURED)
Ps 62: 8 **p** out your hearts to him, for God
Joel 2: 28 I will **p** out my Spirit on all people.
Mal 3: 10 **p** out so much blessing that there
Ac 2: 17 I will **p** out my Spirit on all people.

POURED (POUR)
Ac 10: 45 the Holy Spirit had been **p** out
Ro 5: 5 because God's love has been **p**

POVERTY (POOR)
Pr 14: 23 but mere talk leads only to **p.**
   21: 5 profit as surely as haste leads to **p.**
   30: 8 give me neither **p** nor riches,
Mk 12: 44 she, out of her **p,** put in everything
2Co 8: 2 their extreme **p** welled up in rich
   8: 9 you through his **p** might become

POWER (POWERFUL POWERS)
1Ch 29: 11 greatness and the **p** and the glory.
2Ch 32: 7 for there is a greater **p** with us than
Job 36: 22 "God is exalted in his **p.** Who is
Ps 63: 2 and beheld your **p** and your glory.
   68: 34 Proclaim the **p** of God,
   147: 5 Great is our Lord and mighty in **p;**
Pr 24: 5 The wise prevail through great **p,**
Isa 40: 10 Sovereign LORD comes with **p,**
Zec 4: 6 'Not by might nor by **p,** but by my
Mt 22: 29 the Scriptures or the **p** of God.
   24: 30 of heaven, with **p** and great glory.
Ac 1: 8 you will receive **p** when the Holy
   4: 33 With great **p** the apostles
   10: 38 with the Holy Spirit and **p,**
Ro 1: 16 because it is the **p** of God
1Co 1: 18 us who are being saved it is the **p**

1Co 15: 56 is sin, and the **p** of sin is the law.
2Co 12: 9 so that Christ's **p** may rest on me.
Eph 1: 19 his incomparably great **p** for us
Php 3: 10 to know the **p** of his resurrection
Col 1: 11 strengthened with all **p** according
2Ti 1: 7 us timid, but gives us **p,**
Heb 7: 16 of the **p** of an indestructible life.
Rev 4: 11 to receive glory and honor and **p,**
    19: 1 glory and **p** belong to our God,
    20: 6 second death has no **p** over them,

POWERFUL (POWER)
Ps 29: 4 The voice of the Lᴏʀᴅ is **p;**
Lk 24: 19 **p** in word and deed before God
2Th 1: 7 in blazing fire with his **p** angels.
Heb 1: 3 sustaining all things by his **p** word.
Jas 5: 16 prayer of a righteous person is **p**

POWERLESS
Ro 5: 6 when we were still **p,** Christ died
    8: 3 what the law was **p** to do because it

POWERS (POWER)
Ro 8: 38 present nor the future, nor any **p,**
1Co 12: 10 to another miraculous **p,**
Col 1: 16 whether thrones or **p** or rulers
    2: 15 And having disarmed the **p**

PRACTICE
Lev 19: 26 " 'Do not **p** divination or seek
Mt 23: 3 for they do not **p** what they preach.
Lk 8: 21 hear God's word and put it into **p.**"
Ro 12: 13 who are in need. **P** hospitality.
1Ti 5: 4 put their religion into **p** by caring

PRAISE (PRAISED PRAISES PRAISING)
Ex 15: 2 and I will **p** him, my father's God,
Dt 32: 3 Oh, **p** the greatness of our God!
Ru 4: 14 "**P** be to the Lᴏʀᴅ, who this day
2Sa 22: 47 **P** be to my Rock!
1Ch 16: 25 the Lᴏʀᴅ and most worthy of **p;**
2Ch 20: 21 to **p** him for the splendor of his
Ps 8: 2 Through the **p** of children
    33: 1 it is fitting for the upright to **p** him.
    34: 1 his **p** will always be on my lips.
    40: 3 mouth, a hymn of **p** to our God.
    48: 1 and most worthy of **p,** in the city
    68: 19 **P** be to the Lord, to God our Savior,
    89: 5 The heavens **p** your wonders,
    100: 4 give thanks to him and **p** his name.
    105: 2 Sing to him, sing **p** to him;
    106: 1 **P** the Lᴏʀᴅ. Give thanks
    119:175 Let me live that I may **p** you,
    139: 14 I **p** you because I am fearfully
    145: 21 Let every creature **p** his holy name
    146: 1 **P** the Lᴏʀᴅ. **P** the Lᴏʀᴅ, my soul.
    150: 2 **p** him for his surpassing greatness.
    150: 6 Let everything that has breath **p** the
        Lᴏʀᴅ. **P** the Lᴏʀᴅ.
Pr 27: 2 Let someone else **p** you, and not
    27: 21 but people are tested by their **p.**
    31: 31 let her works bring her **p** at the city
Mt 21: 16 Lord, have called forth your **p**'?"
Jn 12: 43 they loved human **p** more than **p** from
        God.
Eph 1: 6 to the **p** of his glorious grace,
    1: 12 might be for the **p** of his glory.
    1: 14 to the **p** of his glory.

Heb 13: 15 offer to God a sacrifice of **p**—
Jas 5: 13 Let them sing songs of **p.**

PRAISED (PRAISE)
1Ch 29: 10 David **p** the Lᴏʀᴅ in the presence
Ne 8: 6 Ezra **p** the Lᴏʀᴅ, the great God;
Da 2: 19 Then Daniel **p** the God of heaven
Ro 9: 5 who is God over all, forever **p!**
1Pe 4: 11 God may be **p** through Jesus Christ

PRAISES (PRAISE)
2Sa 22: 50 I will sing the **p** of your name.
Ps 47: 6 Sing **p** to God, sing **p;** sing **p**
    147: 1 good it is to sing **p** to our God,
Pr 31: 28 her husband also, and he **p** her:

PRAISING (PRAISE)
Ac 10: 46 speaking in tongues and **p** God.
1Co 14: 16 when you are **p** God in the Spirit,

PRAY (PRAYED PRAYER PRAYERS PRAYING)
Dt 4: 7 our God is near us whenever we **p**
1Sa 12: 23 the Lᴏʀᴅ by failing to **p** for you.
2Ch 7: 14 will humble themselves and **p**
Job 42: 8 My servant Job will **p** for you,
Ps 122: 6 **P** for the peace of Jerusalem:
Mt 5: 44 and **p** for those who persecute you,
    6: 5 for they love to **p** standing
    6: 9 "This, then, is how you should **p:**
    26: 36 here while I go over there and **p.**"
Lk 6: 28 you, **p** for those who mistreat you.
    18: 1 them that they should always **p**
    22: 40 them, "**P** that you will not fall
Ro 8: 26 not know what we ought to **p** for,
1Co 14: 13 in a tongue should **p** that they may
1Th 5: 17 **p** continually,
Jas 5: 13 Let them **p.** Is anyone happy?
    5: 16 **p** for each other so that you may be

PRAYED (PRAY)
1Sa 1: 27 I **p** for this child, and the Lᴏʀᴅ
Jnh 2: 1 From inside the fish Jonah **p**
Mk 14: 35 and **p** that if possible the hour

PRAYER (PRAY)
2Ch 30: 27 for their **p** reached heaven, his holy
Ezr 8: 23 about this, and he answered our **p.**
Ps 6: 9 the Lᴏʀᴅ accepts my **p.**
    86: 6 Hear my **p,** Lᴏʀᴅ; listen to my
Pr 15: 8 the **p** of the upright pleases him.
Isa 56: 7 house will be called a house of **p**
Mt 21: 13 house will be called a house of **p,**'
Mk 11: 24 whatever you ask for in **p,**
Jn 17: 15 My **p** is not that you take them
Ac 6: 4 will give our attention to **p**
Php 4: 6 every situation, by **p** and petition,
Jas 5: 15 the **p** offered in faith will make
1Pe 3: 12 and his ears are attentive to their **p,**

PRAYERS (PRAY)
1Ch 5: 20 He answered their **p,** because they
Mk 12: 40 and for a show make lengthy **p.**
1Pe 3: 7 so that nothing will hinder your **p.**
Rev 5: 8 which are the **p** of God's people.

PRAYING (PRAY)
Mk 11: 25 And when you stand **p,** if you hold
Jn 17: 9 I am not **p** for the world,
Ac 16: 25 Silas were **p** and singing hymns
Eph 6: 18 always keep on **p** for all the Lord's

1620

PREACH (PREACHED PREACHING)
Mt   23: 3   they do not practice what they **p**.
Mk   16: 15   *and **p** the gospel to all creation.*
Ac   9: 20   At once he began to **p**
Ro   10: 15   how can anyone **p** unless they are
      15: 20   to **p** the gospel where Christ was
1Co   1: 17   to baptize, but to **p** the gospel—
      1: 23   but we **p** Christ crucified:
      9: 14   that those who **p** the gospel should
      9: 16   Woe to me if I do not **p** the gospel!
2Co 10: 16   so that we can **p** the gospel
Gal   1: 8   heaven should **p** a gospel other
2Ti   4: 2   **P** the word; be prepared in season

PREACHED (PREACH)
Mk   13: 10   the gospel must first be **p** to all
Ac   8: 4   who had been scattered **p** the word
1Co   9: 27   so that after I have **p** to others,
      15: 1   remind you of the gospel I **p** to you
2Co 11: 4   a Jesus other than the Jesus we **p**,
Gal   1: 8   a gospel other than the one we **p**
Php   1: 18   false motives or true, Christ is **p**.
1Ti   3: 16   angels, was **p** among the nations,

PREACHING (PREACH)
Ro   10: 14   can they hear without someone **p**
1Co   9: 18   in **p** the gospel I may offer it free
1Ti   4: 13   of Scripture, to **p** and to teaching.
      5: 17   especially those whose work is **p**

PRECEPTS
Ps   19: 8   The **p** of the Lord are right,
     111: 7   all his **p** are trustworthy.
     111: 10   all who follow his **p** have good
     119: 40   How I long for your **p**!
     119: 69   I keep your **p** with all my heart.
     119:104   I gain understanding from your **p**;
     119:159   See how I love your **p**; preserve my

PRECIOUS
Ps   19: 10   They are more **p** than gold,
     116: 15   **P** in the sight of the Lord is
Pr   8: 11   for wisdom is more **p** than rubies,
Isa 28: 16   stone, a **p** cornerstone for a sure
1Pe   1: 19   but with the **p** blood of Christ,
      2: 6   a chosen and **p** cornerstone,
2Pe   1: 4   us his very great and **p** promises,

PREDESTINED (DESTINY)
Ro   8: 29   **p** to be conformed to the image
      8: 30   And those he **p**, he also called;
Eph   1: 5   he **p** us for adoption to sonship
      1: 11   been **p** according to the plan

PREDICTION
Jer 28: 9   Lord only if his **p** comes true."

PREPARE (PREPARED)
Ps   23: 5   You **p** a table before me
Am   4: 12   to you, Israel, **p** to meet your God."
Jn   14: 2   that I am going there to **p** a place

PREPARED (PREPARE)
Mt   25: 34   the kingdom **p** for you since
1Co   2: 9   the things God has **p** for those who
Eph   2: 10   which God **p** in advance for us
2Ti   4: 2   be **p** in season and out of season;
1Pe   3: 15   Always be **p** to give an answer

PRESENCE (PRESENT)
Ex   25: 30   Put the bread of the **P** on this table

Ezr   9: 15   not one of us can stand in your **p**."
Ps   31: 20   the shelter of your **p** you hide them
      89: 15   who walk in the light of your **p**,
      90: 8   secret sins in the light of your **p**.
     139: 7   Where can I flee from your **p**?
Jer   5: 22   "Should you not tremble in my **p**?
Heb   9: 24   now to appear for us in God's **p**.
Jude   : 24   before his glorious **p** without fault

PRESENT (PRESENCE)
2Co 11: 2   that I might **p** you as a pure virgin
Eph   5: 27   and to **p** her to himself as a radiant
2Ti   2: 15   Do your best to **p** yourself to God

PRESERVES
Ps   119: 50   Your promise **p** my life.

PRESS (PRESSED PRESSURE)
Php   3: 14   I **p** on toward the goal to win

PRESSED (PRESS)
Lk   6: 38   A good measure, **p** down,

PRESSURE (PRESS)
2Co   1: 8   We were under great **p**, far beyond
      11: 28   I face daily the **p** of my concern

PREVAILS
1Sa   2: 9   "It is not by strength that one **p**;

PRICE
Job 28: 18   the **p** of wisdom is beyond rubies.
1Co   6: 20   you were bought at a **p**.
      7: 23   You were bought at a **p**;

PRIDE (PROUD)
Pr   8: 13   I hate **p** and arrogance,
      16: 18   **P** goes before destruction,
Da   4: 37   those who walk in **p** he is able
Gal   6: 4   can take **p** in themselves alone,
Jas   1: 9   to take **p** in their high position.

PRIEST (PRIESTHOOD PRIESTS)
Heb   4: 14   a great high **p** who has ascended
      4: 15   do not have a high **p** who is unable
      7: 26   Such a high **p** truly meets our need
      8: 1   We do have such a high **p**, who sat

PRIESTHOOD (PRIEST)
Heb   7: 24   lives forever, he has a permanent **p**.
1Pe   2: 5   a spiritual house to be a holy **p**,
      2: 9   people, a royal **p**, a holy nation,

PRIESTS (PRIEST)
Ex   19: 6   you will be for me a kingdom of **p**
Rev   5: 10   a kingdom and **p** to serve our God,

PRINCE
Isa   9: 6   Everlasting Father, **P** of Peace.
Jn   12: 31   now the **p** of this world will be
Ac   5: 31   him to his own right hand as **P**

PRISON (PRISONER)
Isa 42: 7   blind, to free captives from **p**
Mt   25: 36   I was in **p** and you came to visit
Rev 20: 7   Satan will be released from his **p**

PRISONER (PRISON)
Ro   7: 23   making me a **p** of the law of sin
Eph   3: 1   the **p** of Christ Jesus for the sake

PRIVILEGE
2Co   8: 4   for the **p** of sharing in this service

CONCORDANCE

PRIZE
1Co 9: 24 Run in such a way as to get the **p**.
Php 3: 14 on toward the goal to win the **p**

PROCLAIM (PROCLAIMED)
1Ch 16: 23 **p** his salvation day after day.
Ps 19: 1 the skies **p** the work of his hands.
50: 6 the heavens **p** his righteousness,
68: 34 **P** the power of God, whose majesty
118: 17 will **p** what the LORD has done.
Zec 9: 10 He will **p** peace to the nations.
Ac 20: 27 I have not hesitated to **p** to you
Ro 10: 8 concerning faith that we **p**:
1Co 11: 26 cup, you **p** the Lord's death until

PROCLAIMED (PROCLAIM)
Ro 15: 19 I have fully **p** the gospel of Christ.
Col 1: 23 has been **p** to every creature under

PRODUCE (PRODUCES)
Mt 3: 8 **P** fruit in keeping with repentance.
3: 10 does not **p** good fruit will be cut

PRODUCES (PRODUCE)
Pr 30: 33 so stirring up anger **p** strife."
Ro 5: 3 that suffering **p** perseverance;
Heb 12: 11 it **p** a harvest of righteousness

PROFANE
Lev 22: 32 Do not **p** my holy name, for I must

PROFESS
1Ti 2: 10 for women who **p** to worship God.
Heb 4: 14 let us hold firmly to the faith we **p**.
10: 23 unswervingly to the hope we **p**,

PROMISE (PROMISED PROMISES)
1Ki 8: 20 LORD has kept the **p** he made:
Ac 2: 39 The **p** is for you and your children
Gal 3: 14 faith we might receive the **p**
1Ti 4: 8 holding **p** for both the present life
2Pe 3: 9 Lord is not slow in keeping his **p**,

PROMISED (PROMISE)
Ex 3: 17 I have **p** to bring you up out of
Dt 26: 18 his treasured possession as he **p**,
Ps 119: 57 I have **p** to obey your words.
Ro 4: 21 had power to do what he had **p**.
Heb 10: 23 we profess, for he who **p** is faithful.
2Pe 3: 4 say, "Where is this 'coming' he **p**?

PROMISES (PROMISE)
Jos 21: 45 of all the LORD's good **p** to Israel
Ro 9: 4 law, the temple worship and the **p**.
2Pe 1: 4 us his very great and precious **p**,

PROMPTED
1Th 1: 3 by faith, your labor **p** by love,
2Th 1: 11 and your every deed **p** by faith.

PROPHECIES (PROPHESY)
1Co 13: 8 But where there are **p**, they will
1Th 5: 20 Do not treat **p** with contempt

PROPHECY (PROPHESY)
1Co 14: 1 gifts of the Spirit, especially **p**.
2Pe 1: 20 that no **p** of Scripture came

PROPHESY (PROPHECIES PROPHECY PROPHESYING
PROPHET PROPHETS)
Joel 2: 28 Your sons and daughters will **p**,
Mt 7: 22 did we not **p** in your name
1Co 14: 39 be eager to **p**, and do not forbid

1622

PROPHESYING (PROPHESY)
Ro 12: 6 If your gift is **p**, then prophesy

PROPHET (PROPHESY)
Dt 18: 18 for them a **p** like you from among
Am 7: 14 neither a **p** nor the son of a **p**,
Mt 10: 41 Whoever welcomes a **p** as a **p** will
Lk 4: 24 "no **p** is accepted in his hometown.

PROPHETS (PROPHESY)
Ps 105: 15 do my **p** no harm."
Mt 5: 17 come to abolish the Law or the **P**;
7: 12 for this sums up the Law and the **P**.
24: 24 messiahs and false **p** will appear
Lk 24: 25 believe all that the **p** have spoken!
Ac 10: 43 All the **p** testify about him
1Co 12: 28 apostles, second **p**, third teachers,
14: 32 The spirits of **p** are subject
Eph 2: 20 foundation of the apostles and **p**,
Heb 1: 1 ancestors through the **p** at many
1Pe 1: 10 the **p**, who spoke of the grace

PROSPER (PROSPERITY PROSPERS)
Pr 28: 25 who trust in the LORD will **p**.

PROSPERITY (PROSPER)
Ps 73: 3 when I saw the **p** of the wicked.

PROSPERS (PROSPER)
Ps 1: 3 whatever they do **p**.

PROSTITUTE (PROSTITUTES)
1Co 6: 15 of Christ and unite them with a **p**?

PROSTITUTES (PROSTITUTE)
Mt 21: 31 **p** are entering the kingdom of God
Lk 15: 30 your property with **p** comes home,

PROSTRATE
Dt 9: 18 again I fell **p** before the LORD

PROTECT (PROTECTS)
Ps 32: 7 you will **p** me from trouble
Pr 2: 11 Discretion will **p** you,
Jn 17: 11 **p** them by the power of your name,

PROTECTS (PROTECT)
1Co 13: 7 It always **p**, always trusts,

PROUD (PRIDE)
Pr 16: 5 The LORD detests all the **p**
Ro 12: 16 Do not be **p**, but be willing
1Co 13: 4 envy, it does not boast, it is not **p**.

PROVE
1Co 4: 2 been given a trust must **p** faithful.

PROVIDE (PROVIDED PROVIDES)
Ge 22: 8 "God himself will **p** the lamb
Isa 43: 20 because I **p** water in the wilderness
1Ti 5: 8 Anyone who does not **p** for their

PROVIDED (PROVIDE)
Jnh 1: 17 Now the LORD **p** a huge fish
4: 6 the LORD God **p** a leafy plant
4: 7 dawn the next day God **p** a worm,
4: 8 rose, God **p** a scorching east wind,

PROVIDES (PROVIDE)
1Ti 6: 17 who richly **p** us with everything
1Pe 4: 11 do so with the strength God **p**,

PROVOKED
Ecc 7: 9 Do not be quickly **p** in your spirit,

PRUDENT
Pr	14: 15	the **p** give thought to their steps.
	19: 14	but a **p** wife is from the Lord.
Am	5: 13	Therefore the **p** keep quiet in such

PRUNING
Isa	2: 4	and their spears into **p** hooks.
Joel	3: 10	and your **p** hooks into spears.

PSALMS
Eph	5: 19	speaking to one another with **p**,
Col	3: 16	with all wisdom through **p**,

PUBLICLY
Ac	20: 20	have taught you **p** and from house

PUFFS
1Co	8: 1	knowledge **p** up while love builds

PUNISH (PUNISHED)
Ex	32: 34	to **p**, I will **p** them for their sin."
Pr	23: 13	if you **p** them with the rod,
Isa	13: 11	I will **p** the world for its evil,
1Pe	2: 14	by him to **p** those who do wrong

PUNISHED (PUNISH)
La	3: 39	should the living complain when **p**
2Th	1: 9	They will be **p** with everlasting
Heb	10: 29	to be **p** who has trampled the Son

PURE (PURIFIES PURIFY PURITY)
2Sa	22: 27	to the **p** you show yourself **p**,
Ps	24: 4	who has clean hands and a **p** heart,
	51: 10	Create in me a **p** heart, O God,
Pr	20: 9	can say, "I have kept my heart **p**;
Isa	52: 11	Come out from it and be **p**,
Hab	1: 13	Your eyes are too **p** to look on evil;
Mt	5: 8	Blessed are the **p** in heart, for they
2Co	11: 2	I might present you as a **p** virgin
Php	4: 8	whatever is **p**, whatever is lovely,
1Ti	5: 22	the sins of others. Keep yourself **p**.
Titus	1: 15	To the **p**, all things are **p**,
	2: 5	to be self-controlled and **p**, to be
Heb	13: 4	all, and the marriage bed kept **p**,
1Jn	3: 3	purify themselves, just as he is **p**.

PURGE
Pr	20: 30	and beatings **p** the inmost being.

PURIFIES (PURE)
1Jn	1: 7	of Jesus, his Son, **p** us from all sin.

PURIFY (PURE)
Titus	2: 14	to **p** for himself a people that are
1Jn	1: 9	and **p** us from all unrighteousness.
	3: 3	this hope in him **p** themselves,

PURITY (PURE)
Ps	119: 9	person stay on the path of **p**?
2Co	6: 6	in **p**, understanding,
1Ti	4: 12	conduct, in love, in faith and in **p**.

PURPOSE
Pr	19: 21	it is the Lord's **p** that prevails.
Isa	55: 11	achieve the **p** for which I sent it.
Ro	8: 28	been called according to his **p**.

PURSES
Lk	12: 33	Provide **p** for yourselves that will

PURSUE
Ps	34: 14	and do good; seek peace and **p** it.
2Ti	2: 22	of youth and **p** righteousness, faith,
1Pe	3: 11	they must seek peace and **p** it.

QUALITIES (QUALITY)
2Pe	1: 8	if you possess these **q** in increasing

QUALITY (QUALITIES)
1Co	3: 13	and the fire will test the **q** of each

QUARREL (QUARRELSOME)
Pr	15: 18	the one who is patient calms a **q**.
	17: 14	Starting a **q** is like breaching a dam
	17: 19	Whoever loves a **q** loves sin;

QUARRELSOME (QUARREL)
Pr	19: 13	**q** wife is like the constant dripping
1Ti	3: 3	gentle, not **q**, not a lover of money.
2Ti	2: 24	the Lord's servant must not be **q**

QUENCH
1Th	5: 19	Do not **q** the Spirit.

QUICK-TEMPERED
Titus	1: 7	not **q**, not given to drunkenness,

QUIET (QUIETNESS)
Ps	23: 2	he leads me beside **q** waters,
Lk	19: 40	"if they keep **q**, the stones will cry
1Ti	2: 2	peaceful and **q** lives in all godliness
1Pe	3: 4	beauty of a gentle and **q** spirit,

QUIETNESS (QUIET)
Isa	30: 15	in **q** and trust is your strength,
	32: 17	its effect will be **q** and confidence
1Ti	2: 11	woman should learn in **q** and full

QUIVER
Ps	127: 5	Blessed is the man whose **q** is full

RACE
Ecc	9: 11	The **r** is not to the swift or
1Co	9: 24	that in a **r** all the runners run,
2Ti	4: 7	I have finished the **r**, I have kept
Heb	12: 1	with perseverance the **r** marked

RACHEL
Daughter of Laban (Ge 29:16); wife of Jacob (Ge 29:28); bore two sons (Ge 30:22–24; 35:16–24; 46:19).

RADIANCE (RADIANT)
Heb	1: 3	The Son is the **r** of God's glory

RADIANT (RADIANCE)
Ex	34: 29	that his face was **r** because he had
Ps	34: 5	Those who look to him are **r**;
SS	5: 10	My beloved is **r** and ruddy,
Isa	60: 5	Then you will look and be **r**,
Eph	5: 27	her to himself as a **r** church,

RAIN (RAINBOW)
Mt	5: 45	and sends **r** on the righteous

RAINBOW (RAIN)
Ge	9: 13	I have set my **r** in the clouds, and it

RAISED (RISE)
Ro	4: 25	was **r** to life for our justification.
	10: 9	your heart that God **r** him
1Co	15: 4	he was **r** on the third day according

RAN (RUN)
Jnh	1: 3	But Jonah **r** away from the Lord

RANSOM
Mt	20: 28	to give his life as a **r** for many."
Heb	9: 15	he has died as a **r** to set them free

RAVENS
1Ki	17: 6	The **r** brought him bread and meat
Lk	12: 24	Consider the **r**: They do not sow

READ (READS)
Jos	8: 34	Joshua **r** all the words of the law—
Ne	8: 8	understood what was being **r**.
2Co	3: 2	hearts, known and **r** by everyone.

READS (READ)
Rev	1: 3	is the one who **r** aloud the words

REAL (REALITY)
Jn	6: 55	For my flesh is **r** food and my blood
		is **r** drink.

REALITY (REAL)
Col	2: 17	the **r**, however, is found in Christ.

REAP (REAPS)
Job	4: 8	evil and those who sow trouble **r** it.
2Co	9: 6	generously will also **r** generously.

REAPS (REAP)
Gal	6: 7	A man **r** what he sows.

REASON
1Pe	3: 15	asks you to give the **r** for the hope

REBEKAH
Sister of Laban, secured as bride for Isaac (Ge 24). Mother of Esau and Jacob (Ge 25:19–26). Taken by Abimelek as sister of Isaac; returned (Ge 26:1–11). Encouraged Jacob to trick Isaac out of blessing (Ge 27:1–17).

REBEL
Mt	10: 21	children will **r** against their parents

REBUKE (REBUKING)
Pr	9: 8	**r** the wise and they will love you.
	27: 5	Better is open **r** than hidden love.
Lk	17: 3	or sister sins against you, **r** them;
2Ti	4: 2	correct, **r** and encourage—
Rev	3: 19	Those whom I love I **r**

REBUKING (REBUKE)
2Ti	3: 16	and is useful for teaching, **r**,

RECEIVE (RECEIVED RECEIVES)
Ac	1: 8	you will **r** power when the Holy
	20: 35	more blessed to give than to **r**.' "
2Co	6: 17	no unclean thing, and I will **r** you."
Rev	4: 11	to **r** glory and honor and power,

RECEIVED (RECEIVE)
Mt	6: 2	they have **r** their reward in full.
	10: 8	Freely you have **r**; freely give.
1Co	11: 23	For I **r** from the Lord what I
Col	2: 6	just as you **r** Christ Jesus as Lord,
1Pe	4: 10	should use whatever gift you have **r**

RECEIVES (RECEIVE)
Mt	7: 8	For everyone who asks **r**;
Ac	10: 43	who believes in him **r** forgiveness

RECKONING
Isa	10: 3	What will you do on the day of **r**,

RECOGNIZE (RECOGNIZED)
Mt	7: 16	By their fruit you will **r** them.

RECOGNIZED (RECOGNIZE)
Mt	12: 33	be bad, for a tree is **r** by its fruit.
Ro	7: 13	in order that sin might be **r** as sin,

RECOMPENSE
Isa	40: 10	him, and his **r** accompanies him.

RECONCILE (RECONCILED RECONCILIATION)
Eph	2: 16	and in one body to **r** both of them

RECONCILED (RECONCILE)
Mt	5: 24	First go and be **r** to them;
Ro	5: 10	were **r** to him through the death
2Co	5: 18	who **r** us to himself through Christ

RECONCILIATION (RECONCILE)
Ro	5: 11	whom we have now received **r**.
	11: 15	For if their rejection brought **r**
2Co	5: 18	and gave us the ministry of **r**:
	5: 19	committed to us the message of **r**.

RECORD
Ps	130: 3	you, Lᴏʀᴅ, kept a **r** of sins, Lord,

RED
Isa	1: 18	though they are **r** as crimson,

REDEEM (REDEEMED REDEEMER REDEMPTION)
2Sa	7: 23	out to **r** as a people for himself,
Ps	49: 7	No one can **r** the life of another
Gal	4: 5	to **r** those under the law, that we

REDEEMED (REDEEM)
Gal	3: 13	Christ **r** us from the curse of the law
1Pe	1: 18	you were **r** from the empty way

REDEEMER (REDEEM)
Job	19: 25	I know that my **r** lives,

REDEMPTION (REDEEM)
Ps	130: 7	love and with him is full **r**.
Lk	21: 28	because your **r** is drawing near."
Ro	8: 23	to sonship, the **r** of our bodies.
Eph	1: 7	we have **r** through his blood,
Col	1: 14	in whom we have **r**, the forgiveness
Heb	9: 12	blood, thus obtaining eternal **r**.

REFUGE
Nu	35: 11	some towns to be your cities of **r**,
Dt	33: 27	The eternal God is your **r**,
Ru	2: 12	wings you have come to take **r**."
Ps	46: 1	God is our **r** and strength,
	91: 2	"He is my **r** and my fortress,

REHOBOAM
Son of Solomon (1Ki 11:43; 1Ch 3:10). Harsh treatment of subjects caused divided kingdom (1Ki 12:1–24; 14:21–31; 2Ch 10–12).

REIGN (REIGNS)
Ro	6: 12	not let sin **r** in your mortal body
1Co	15: 25	he must **r** until he has put all his
2Ti	2: 12	if we endure, we will also **r** with
Rev	20: 6	**r** with him for a thousand years.

REIGNS (REIGN)
Ex	15: 18	"The Lᴏʀᴅ **r** for ever and ever."

REJECTED (REJECTS)
Ps	118: 22	stone the builders **r** has become
Isa	53: 3	was despised and **r** by mankind,
1Ti	4: 4	nothing is to be **r** if it is received
1Pe	2: 4	**r** by humans but chosen by God
	2: 7	stone the builders **r** has become

REJECTS (REJECTED)
Lk	10: 16	whoever **r** me **r** him who sent me."
Jn	3: 36	whoever **r** the Son will not see life,

REJOICE (JOY)
Ps	66:	6	come, let us **r** in him.
	118:	24	let us **r** today and be glad.
Pr	5:	18	you **r** in the wife of your youth.
Lk	10:	20	but **r** that your names are written
	15:	6	together and says, '**R** with me;
Ro	12:	15	**R** with those who r;
Php	4:	4	**R** in the Lord always. I will say it again: **R**!

REJOICES (JOY)
Isa	61:	10	my soul **r** in my God.
Lk	1:	47	and my spirit **r** in God my Savior,
1Co	12:	26	is honored, every part **r** with it.
	13:	6	delight in evil but **r** with the truth.

REJOICING (JOY)
Ps	30:	5	night, but **r** comes in the morning.
Lk	15:	7	the same way there will be more **r**
Ac	5:	41	**r** because they had been counted

RELIABLE
2Ti	2:	2	entrust to **r** people who will also be

RELIGION
1Ti	5:	4	of all to put their **r** into practice
Jas	1:	27	**R** that God our Father accepts as

REMAIN (REMAINS)
Nu	33:	55	you allow to **r** will become barbs
Jn	15:	7	If you **r** in me and my words **r**
Ro	13:	8	Let no debt **r** outstanding,
1Co	13:	13	And now these three **r**:

REMAINS (REMAIN)
Ps	146:	6	he **r** faithful forever.
2Ti	2:	13	if we are faithless, he **r** faithful,
Heb	7:	3	Son of God, he **r** a priest forever.

REMEMBER (REMEMBERS REMEMBRANCE)
Ex	20:	8	"**R** the Sabbath day by keeping it
1Ch	16:	12	**R** the wonders he has done,
Ecc	12:	1	**R** your Creator in the days of your
Jer	31:	34	and will **r** their sins no more."
Gal	2:	10	we should continue to **r** the poor,
Php	1:	3	I thank my God every time I **r** you.
Heb	8:	12	and will **r** their sins no more."

REMEMBERS (REMEMBER)
Ps	103:	14	are formed, he **r** that we are dust.
	111:	5	he **r** his covenant forever.
Isa	43:	25	own sake, and **r** your sins no more.

REMEMBRANCE (REMEMBER)
1Co	11:	24	is for you; do this in **r** of me."

REMIND
Jn	14:	26	will **r** you of everything I have said

REMOVED
Ps	30:	11	you **r** my sackcloth and clothed me
	103:	12	so far has he **r** our transgressions
Jn	20:	1	that the stone had been **r**

RENEW (RENEWED RENEWING)
Ps	51:	10	and **r** a steadfast spirit within me.
Isa	40:	31	in the LORD will **r** their strength.

RENEWED (RENEW)
Ps	103:	5	that your youth is **r** like the eagle's.
2Co	4:	16	yet inwardly we are being **r** day

RENEWING (RENEW)
Ro	12:	2	transformed by the **r** of your mind.

RENOUNCE (RENOUNCES)
Da	4:	27	**R** your sins by doing what is right,

RENOUNCES (RENOUNCE)
Pr	28:	13	confesses and **r** them finds mercy.

RENOWN
Isa	63:	12	to gain for himself everlasting **r**,
Jer	32:	20	have gained the **r** that is still yours.

REPAID (PAY)
Lk	14:	14	you will be **r** at the resurrection
Col	3:	25	Anyone who does wrong will be **r**

REPAY (PAY)
Dt	32:	35	It is mine to avenge; I will **r**.
Ru	2:	12	May the LORD **r** you for what you
Ro	12:	19	I will **r**," says the Lord.
1Pe	3:	9	the contrary, **r** evil with blessing,

REPENT (REPENTANCE REPENTS)
Job	42:	6	I despise myself and **r** in dust
Jer	15:	19	"If you **r**, I will restore you that you
Mt	4:	17	time on Jesus began to preach, "**R**,
Lk	13:	3	But unless you **r**, you too will all
	17:	3	and if they **r**, forgive them.
Ac	2:	38	Peter replied, "**R** and be baptized,
	17:	30	all people everywhere to **r**.

REPENTANCE (REPENT)
Lk	3:	8	Produce fruit in keeping with **r**.
	5:	32	call the righteous, but sinners to **r**."
Ac	26:	20	demonstrate their **r** by their deeds.
2Co	7:	10	Godly sorrow brings **r** that leads

REPENTS (REPENT)
Lk	15:	10	of God over one sinner who **r**."

REPROACH
1Ti	3:	2	Now the overseer is to be above **r**,

REPUTATION
1Ti	3:	7	also have a good **r** with outsiders,

REQUESTS
Ps	20:	5	May the LORD grant all your **r**.
Php	4:	6	present your **r** to God.

REQUIRE
Mic	6:	8	what does the LORD **r** of you?

RESCUE (RESCUES)
Da	6:	20	been able to **r** you from the lions?"
2Pe	2:	9	the Lord knows how to **r** the godly

RESCUES (RESCUE)
1Th	1:	10	who **r** us from the coming wrath.

RESIST
Jas	4:	7	**R** the devil, and he will flee
1Pe	5:	9	**R** him, standing firm in the faith,

RESOLVED
Da	1:	8	Daniel **r** not to defile himself
1Co	2:	2	For I **r** to know nothing while I

RESPECT (RESPECTABLE)
Lev	19:	3	of you must **r** your mother
	19:	32	show **r** for the elderly and revere
Mal	1:	6	a master, where is the **r** due me?"
1Th	4:	12	that your daily life may win the **r**
1Ti	3:	4	do so in a manner worthy of full **r**.
1Pe	2:	17	Show proper **r** to everyone,
	3:	7	them with **r** as the weaker partner

RESPECTABLE (RESPECT)
| 1Ti | 3: 2 | self-controlled, **r**, hospitable, |

REST
Ex	31: 15	seventh day is a day of sabbath **r**,
Ps	91: 1	the Most High will **r** in the shadow
Jer	6: 16	and you will find **r** for your souls.
Mt	11: 28	burdened, and I will give you **r**.

RESTITUTION
| Ex | 22: 3 | who steals must certainly make **r**, |
| Lev | 6: 5 | must make **r** in full, add a fifth |

RESTORE
| Ps | 51: 12 | **R** to me the joy of your salvation |
| Gal | 6: 1 | by the Spirit should **r** that person |

RESURRECTION
Mt	22: 30	the **r** people will neither marry nor
Lk	14: 14	be repaid at the **r** of the righteous."
Jn	11: 25	said to her, "I am the **r** and the life.
Ro	1: 4	in power by his **r** from the dead:
1Co	15: 12	say that there is no **r** of the dead?
Php	3: 10	yes, to know the power of his **r**
Rev	20: 5	This is the first **r**.

RETRIBUTION
| Jer | 51: 56 | For the LORD is a God of **r**; |

RETURN
2Ch	30: 9	If you **r** to the LORD, then your
Ne	1: 9	but if you **r** to me and obey my
Isa	55: 11	It will not **r** to me empty, but will
Hos	6: 1	"Come, let us **r** to the LORD.
Joel	2: 12	"**r** to me with all your heart,

REVEALED (REVELATION)
Dt	29: 29	but the things **r** belong to us
Isa	40: 5	the glory of the LORD will be **r**,
Mt	11: 25	and **r** them to little children.
Ro	1: 17	the righteousness of God is **r**—
	8: 18	with the glory that will be **r** in us.

REVELATION (REVEALED)
| Gal | 1: 12 | I received it by **r** from Jesus Christ. |
| Rev | 1: 1 | The **r** from Jesus Christ, |

REVENGE (VENGEANCE)
| Lev | 19: 18 | " 'Do not seek **r** or bear a grudge |
| Ro | 12: 19 | Do not take **r**, my dear friends, |

REVERE (REVERENCE)
| Ps | 33: 8 | all the people of the world **r** him. |

REVERENCE (REVERE)
Lev	19: 30	and have **r** for my sanctuary.
Ps	5: 7	in **r** I bow down toward your holy
Col	3: 22	of heart and **r** for the Lord.
1Pe	3: 2	see the purity and **r** of your lives.

REVIVE
| Ps | 85: 6 | Will you not **r** us again, that your |
| Isa | 57: 15 | to **r** the spirit of the lowly and to **r** |

REWARD (REWARDED)
Ps	19: 11	in keeping them there is great **r**.
	127: 3	the LORD, offspring a **r** from him.
Pr	19: 17	he will **r** them for what they have
	25: 22	head, and the LORD will **r** you.
Jer	17: 10	to **r** each person according to their
Mt	5: 12	because great is your **r** in heaven,
	6: 5	they have received their **r** in full.
	16: 27	he will **r** each person according

| 1Co | 3: 14 | the builder will receive a **r**. |
| Rev | 22: 12 | My **r** is with me, and I will give |

REWARDED (REWARD)
Ru	2: 12	May you be richly **r** by the LORD,
Ps	18: 24	The LORD has **r** me according
Pr	14: 14	and the good **r** for theirs.
1Co	3: 8	and they will each be **r** according

RICH (RICHES)
Pr	23: 4	Do not wear yourself out to get **r**;
Jer	9: 23	or the **r** boast of their riches,
Mt	19: 23	for someone who is **r** to enter
2Co	6: 10	poor, yet making many **r**;
	8: 9	his poverty might become **r**.
1Ti	6: 17	Command those who are **r** in this

RICHES (RICH)
Ps	119: 14	statutes as one rejoices in great **r**.
Pr	30: 8	give me neither poverty nor **r**,
Isa	10: 3	Where will you leave your **r**?
Ro	9: 23	to make the **r** of his glory known
	11: 33	the depth of the **r** of the wisdom
Eph	2: 7	he might show the incomparable **r**
	3: 8	to the Gentiles the boundless **r**
Col	1: 27	among the Gentiles the glorious **r**

RID
Ge	21: 10	"Get **r** of that slave woman and her
1Co	5: 7	Get **r** of the old yeast, so that you
Gal	4: 30	"Get **r** of the slave woman and her

RIGHT (RIGHTS)
Ge	18: 25	not the Judge of all the earth do **r**?"
Ex	15: 26	God and do what is **r** in his eyes,
Dt	5: 32	do not turn aside to the **r**
Ps	16: 8	With him at my **r** hand, I will not
	19: 8	The precepts of the LORD are **r**,
	63: 8	your **r** hand upholds me.
	110: 1	"Sit at my **r** hand until I make your
Pr	4: 27	Do not turn to the **r** or the left;
	14: 12	There is a way that appears to be **r**,
Isa	1: 17	Learn to do **r**; seek justice.
Jer	23: 5	do what is just and **r** in the land.
Hos	14: 9	The ways of the LORD are **r**;
Mt	6: 3	know what your **r** hand is doing,
Jn	1: 12	he gave the **r** to become children
Ro	9: 21	Does not the potter have the **r**
	12: 17	careful to do what is **r** in the eyes
Eph	1: 20	and seated him at his **r** hand
Php	4: 8	whatever is **r**, whatever is pure,

RIGHTEOUS (RIGHTEOUSNESS)
Ps	34: 15	eyes of the LORD are on the **r**,
	37: 25	yet I have never seen the **r** forsaken
	119:137	You are **r**, LORD, and your laws
	143: 2	no one living is **r** before you.
Pr	3: 33	but he blesses the home of the **r**.
	11: 30	The fruit of the **r** is a tree of life,
	18: 10	the **r** run to it and are safe.
Isa	64: 6	all our **r** acts are like filthy rags;
Hab	2: 4	but the **r** person will live by his
Mt	5: 45	and sends rain on the **r**
	9: 13	For I have not come to call the **r**,
	13: 49	and separate the wicked from the **r**
	25: 46	but the **r** to eternal life."
Ro	1: 17	"The **r** will live by faith."
	3: 10	"There is no one **r**, not even one;
1Ti	1: 9	that the law is made not for the **r**

Jas 2: 24 is considered **r** by what they do
1Pe 3: 18 for sins, the **r** for the unrighteous,
1Jn 3: 7 is right is **r**, just as he is **r**.
Rev 19: 8 (Fine linen stands for the **r** acts

RIGHTEOUSNESS (RIGHTEOUS)
Ge 15: 6 and he credited it to him as **r**.
1Sa 26: 23 rewards everyone for their **r**
Ps   9: 8 He rules the world in **r** and judges
    45: 7 You love **r** and hate wickedness;
    85: 10 **r** and peace kiss each other.
    89: 14 **R** and justice are the foundation
   111: 3 deeds, and his **r** endures forever.
Pr 14: 34 **R** exalts a nation, but sin
    21: 21 Whoever pursues **r** and love finds
Isa 59: 17 He put on **r** as his breastplate,
Eze 18: 20 The **r** of the righteous will be
Da   9: 24 to bring in everlasting **r**, to seal
    12: 3 and those who lead many to **r**,
Mal 4: 2 the sun of **r** will rise with healing
Mt   5: 6 those who hunger and thirst for **r**,
     5: 20 you that unless your **r** surpasses
     6: 1 practice your **r** in front of others
     6: 33 seek first his kingdom and his **r**,
Ro   3: 25 He did this to demonstrate his **r**,
     4: 3 and it was credited to him as **r**."
     4: 9 faith was credited to him as **r**.
     6: 13 to him as an instrument of **r**.
2Co 5: 21 we might become the **r** of God.
Gal 2: 21 **r** could be gained through the law,
     3: 6 and it was credited to him as **r**."
Eph 6: 14 with the breastplate of **r** in place,
Php 3: 9 not having a **r** of my own
2Ti 3: 16 correcting and training in **r**,
     4: 8 is in store for me the crown of **r**,
Heb 11: 7 and became heir of the **r** that is
2Pe 2: 21 not to have known the way of **r**,

RIGHTS (RIGHT)
La   3: 35 deny people their **r** before the Most

RISE (RAISED)
Isa 26: 19 their bodies will **r**—let those who
Mt 27: 63 'After three days I will **r** again.'
Jn   5: 29 who have done what is good will **r**
1Th 4: 16 and the dead in Christ will **r** first.

ROAD
Mt   7: 13 gate and broad is the **r** that leads

ROBBERS
Jer 7: 11 Name, become a den of **r** to you?
Lk 19: 46 you have made it 'a den of **r**.' "
Jn 10: 8 come before me are thieves and **r**,

ROCK
Ps 18: 2 The LORD is my **r**, my fortress
    40: 2 he set my feet on a **r** and gave me
Mt   7: 24 man who built his house on the **r**.
    16: 18 on this **r** I will build my church,
Ro   9: 33 and a **r** that makes them fall,
1Co 10: 4 them, and that **r** was Christ.

ROD
Ps 23: 4 your **r** and your staff, they comfort
Pr 13: 24 Whoever spares the **r** hates their
    23: 13 if you punish them with the **r**,

ROOM (ROOMS)
Mt   6: 6 go into your **r**, close the door

Lk   2: 7 there was no guest **r** available
Jn 21: 25 the whole world would not have **r**

ROOMS (ROOM)
Jn 14: 2 My Father's house has many **r**;

ROOT
Isa 53: 2 and like a **r** out of dry ground.
1Ti 6: 10 the love of money is a **r** of all kinds

ROYAL
Jas 2: 8 If you really keep the **r** law found
1Pe 2: 9 are a chosen people, a **r** priesthood,

RUIN (RUINS)
Pr 18: 24 unreliable friends soon comes to **r**,
    19: 3 person's own folly leads to their **r**,
1Ti 6: 9 desires that plunge people into **r**

RUINS (RUIN)
2Ti 2: 14 value, and only **r** those who listen.

RULE (RULER RULERS RULES)
1Sa 12: 12 'No, we want a king to **r** over us'—
Ps 119:133 to your word; let no sin **r** over me.
Zec 9: 10 His **r** will extend from sea to sea
Col 3: 15 peace of Christ **r** in your hearts,
Rev 2: 27 that one 'will **r** them with an iron

RULER (RULE)
Eph 2: 2 of the **r** of the kingdom of the air,
1Ti 6: 15 the blessed and only **R**, the King

RULERS (RULE)
Ps   2: 2 and the **r** band together against
     8: 6 You made them **r** over the works
Col 1: 16 or powers or **r** or authorities;

RULES (RULE)
Ps 103: 19 heaven, and his kingdom **r** over all.
Lk 22: 26 and the one who **r** like the one who
2Ti 2: 5 by competing according to the **r**.

RUMORS
Mt 24: 6 You will hear of wars and **r** of wars,

RUN (RAN)
Isa 40: 31 they will **r** and not grow weary,
1Co 9: 24 **R** in such a way as to get the prize.
Heb 12: 1 let us **r** with perseverance the race

RUTH
        Moabitess; widow who went to Bethlehem with
mother-in-law Naomi (Ru 1). Gleaned in field of Boaz;
shown favor (Ru 2). Proposed marriage to Boaz (Ru 3).
Married (Ru 4:1–12); bore Obed, ancestor of David (Ru
4:13–22), Jesus (Mt 1:5).

SABBATH
Ex 20: 8 "Remember the **S** day by keeping it
Dt   5: 12 "Observe the **S** day by keeping it
Col 2: 16 New Moon celebration or a **S** day.

SACKCLOTH
Mt 11: 21 would have repented long ago in **s**

SACRED
Mt   7: 6 "Do not give dogs what is **s**;
1Co 3: 17 for God's temple is **s**, and you

SACRIFICE (SACRIFICED)
Ge 22: 2 **S** him there as a burnt offering
Ex 12: 27 'It is the Passover **s** to the LORD,
1Sa 15: 22 To obey is better than **s**,
Ps 51: 17 My **s**, O God, is a broken spirit;

CONCORDANCE

Hos	6: 6	not **s**, and acknowledgment of God
Mt	9: 13	'I desire mercy, not **s**.'
Ro	12: 1	to offer your bodies as a living **s**,
Heb	9: 26	away with sin by the **s** of himself.
	13: 15	offer to God a **s** of praise—
1Jn	2: 2	He is the atoning **s** for our sins,

SACRIFICED (SACRIFICE)

1Co	5: 7	our Passover lamb, has been **s**.
	8: 1	Now about food **s** to idols:
Heb	9: 28	so Christ was **s** once to take away

SADDUCEES

Mk	12: 18	Then the **S**, who say there is no

SAFE (SAVE)

Ps	37: 3	in the land and enjoy **s** pasture.
Pr	18: 10	the righteous run to it and are **s**.

SAFETY (SAVE)

Ps	4: 8	alone, LORD, make me dwell in **s**.
1Th	5: 3	"Peace and **s**," destruction will

SAINTS See FAITHFUL, [GOD'S, LORD'S] PEOPLE,

SAKE

Ps	44: 22	your **s** we face death all day long;
Php	3: 7	consider loss for the **s** of Christ.
Heb	11: 26	disgrace for the **s** of Christ as

SALT

Ge	19: 26	back, and she became a pillar of **s**.
Mt	5: 13	"You are the **s** of the earth.

SALVATION (SAVE)

Ex	15: 2	he has become my **s**.
1Ch	16: 23	proclaim his **s** day after day.
Ps	27: 1	The LORD is my light and my **s**—
	51: 12	Restore to me the joy of your **s**
	62: 2	Truly he is my rock and my **s**;
	85: 9	Surely his **s** is near those who fear
	96: 2	proclaim his **s** day after day.
Isa	25: 9	let us rejoice and be glad in his **s**."
	45: 17	the LORD with an everlasting **s**;
	51: 6	But my **s** will last forever,
	59: 17	and the helmet of **s** on his head;
	61: 10	has clothed me with garments of **s**
Jnh	2: 9	'**S** comes from the LORD.' "
Lk	2: 30	For my eyes have seen your **s**,
Jn	4: 22	we do know, for **s** is from the Jews.
Ac	4: 12	**S** is found in no one else, for there
	13: 47	that you may bring **s** to the ends
Ro	11: 11	**s** has come to the Gentiles to make
2Co	7: 10	brings repentance that leads to **s**
Eph	6: 17	Take the helmet of **s** and the sword
Php	2: 12	to work out your **s** with fear
1Th	5: 8	and the hope of **s** as a helmet.
2Ti	3: 15	make you wise for **s** through faith
Heb	2: 3	we escape if we ignore so great a **s**?
	6: 9	the things that have to do with **s**.
1Pe	1: 10	Concerning this **s**, the prophets,
	2: 2	by it you may grow up in your **s**,

SAMARITAN

Lk	10: 33	But a **S**, as he traveled, came where

SAMSON

Danite judge. Birth promised (Jdg 13). Married to Philistine (Jdg 14). Vengeance on Philistines (Jdg 15). Betrayed by Delilah (Jdg 16:1–22). Death (Jdg 16:23–31). Feats of strength: killed lion (Jdg 14:6), 30

Philistines (Jdg 14:19), 1,000 Philistines with jawbone (Jdg 15:13–17), carried off gates of Gaza (Jdg 16:3), pushed down temple of Dagon (Jdg 16:25–30).

SAMUEL

Ephraimite judge and prophet (Heb 11:32). Birth prayed for (1Sa 1:10–18). Dedicated to temple by Hannah (1Sa 1:21–28). Raised by Eli (1Sa 2:11, 18–26). Called as prophet (1Sa 3). Led Israel to victory over Philistines (1Sa 7). Asked by Israel for a king (1Sa 8). Anointed Saul as king (1Sa 9–10). Farewell speech (1Sa 12). Rebuked Saul for sacrifice (1Sa 13). Announced rejection of Saul (1Sa 15). Anointed David as king (1Sa 16). Protected David from Saul (1Sa 19:18–24). Death (1Sa 25:1). Returned from dead to condemn Saul (1Sa 28).

SANCTIFIED (SANCTIFY)

Ac	20: 32	among all those who are **s**.
Ro	15: 16	to God, **s** by the Holy Spirit.
1Co	6: 11	you were **s**, you were justified
	7: 14	husband has been **s** through his
Heb	10: 29	blood of the covenant that **s** them,

SANCTIFY (SANCTIFIED SANCTIFYING)

1Th	5: 23	peace, **s** you through and through.

SANCTIFYING (SANCTIFY)

2Th	2: 13	be saved through the **s** work

SANCTUARY

Ex	25: 8	"Then have them make a **s** for me,

SAND

Ge	22: 17	sky and as the **s** on the seashore.
Mt	7: 26	man who built his house on **s**.

SANDALS

Ex	3: 5	"Take off your **s**, for the place
Jos	5: 15	"Take off your **s**, for the place

SANG (SING)

Job	38: 7	while the morning stars **s** together
Rev	5: 9	And they **s** a new song, saying:

SARAH

Wife of Abraham, originally named Sarai; barren (Ge 11:29–31; 1Pe 3:6). Taken by Pharaoh as Abraham's sister; returned (Ge 12:10–20). Gave Hagar to Abraham; sent her away in pregnancy (Ge 16). Name changed; Isaac promised (Ge 17:15–21; 18:10–15; Heb 11:11). Taken by Abimelek as Abraham's sister; returned (Ge 20). Isaac born; Hagar and Ishmael sent away (Ge 21:1–21; Gal 4:21–31). Death (Ge 23).

SATAN

Job	1: 6	and **S** also came with them.
Zec	3: 2	to **S**, "The LORD rebuke you, **S**!
Mk	4: 15	**S** comes and takes away the word
2Co	11: 14	**S** himself masquerades as an angel
	12: 7	a messenger of **S**, to torment me.
Rev	12: 9	or **S**, who leads the whole world
	20: 2	**S**, and bound him for a thousand
	20: 7	**S** will be released from his prison

SATISFIED (SATISFY)

Isa	53: 11	he will see the light of life and be **s**;

SATISFIES (SATISFY)

Ps	103: 5	**s** your desires with good things

SATISFY (SATISFIED SATISFIES)

Isa	55: 2	and your labor on what does not **s**?

SAUL

1. Benjamite; anointed by Samuel as first king of Israel (1Sa 9–10). Defeated Ammonites (1Sa 11). Rebuked for offering sacrifice (1Sa 13:1–15). Defeated Philistines (1Sa 14). Rejected as king for failing to annihilate Amalekites (1Sa 15). Soothed from evil spirit by David (1Sa 16:14–23). Sent David against Goliath (1Sa 17). Jealousy and attempted murder of David (1Sa 18:1–11). Gave David Michal as wife (1Sa 18:12–30). Second attempt to kill David (1Sa 19). Anger at Jonathan (1Sa 20:26–34). Pursued David: killed priests at Nob (1Sa 22), went to Keilah and Ziph (1Sa 23), life spared by David at En Gedi (1Sa 24) and in his tent (1Sa 26). Rebuked by Samuel's spirit for consulting witch at Endor (1Sa 28). Wounded by Philistines; took his own life (1Sa 31; 1Ch 10).

2. See PAUL

SAVE (SAFE SAFETY SALVATION SAVED SAVIOR)

Isa	63: 1	proclaiming victory, mighty to **s**."
Mt	1: 21	because he will **s** his people
	16: 25	wants to **s** their life will lose it,
Lk	19: 10	came to seek and to **s** the lost."
Jn	3: 17	but to **s** the world through him.
1Ti	1: 15	came into the world to **s** sinners—
Jas	5: 20	of their way will **s** them from death

SAVED (SAVE)

Ps	34: 6	he **s** him out of all his troubles.
Isa	45: 22	"Turn to me and be **s**, all you ends
Joel	2: 32	the name of the LORD will be **s**;
Mk	13: 13	stands firm to the end will be **s**.
	16: 16	*believes and is baptized will be **s**,*
Jn	10: 9	enters through me will be **s**.
Ac	4: 12	mankind by which we must be **s**."
	16: 30	"Sirs, what must I do to be **s**?"
Ro	9: 27	the sea, only the remnant will be **s**.
	10: 9	him from the dead, you will be **s**.
1Co	3: 15	will suffer loss but yet will be **s**—
	15: 2	By this gospel you are **s**, if you hold
Eph	2: 5	it is by grace you have been **s**.
	2: 8	For it is by grace you have been **s**,
1Ti	2: 4	who wants all people to be **s**

SAVIOR (SAVE)

Ps	89: 26	Father, my God, the Rock my **S**.'
Isa	43: 11	and apart from me there is no **s**.
Hos	13: 4	no God but me, no **S** except me.
Lk	1: 47	and my spirit rejoices in God my **S**,
	2: 11	town of David a **S** has been born
Jn	4: 42	that this man really is the **S**.
Eph	5: 23	his body, of which he is the **S**.
1Ti	4: 10	God, who is the **S** of all people,
Titus	2: 10	about God our **S** attractive.
	2: 13	the glory of our great God and **S**,
	3: 4	and love of God our **S** appeared,
1Jn	4: 14	his Son to be the **S** of the world.
Jude	: 25	to the only God our **S** be glory,

SCALES

Lev	19: 36	Use honest **s** and honest weights,
Da	5: 27	You have been weighed on the **s**

SCAPEGOAT (GOAT)

Lev	16: 10	it into the wilderness as a **s**.

SCARLET

Isa	1: 18	"Though your sins are like **s**,

SCATTERED

Jer	31: 10	'He who **s** Israel will gather them
Ac	8: 4	who had been **s** preached the word

SCEPTER

Rev	19: 15	"He will rule them with an iron **s**."

SCHEMES

2Co	2: 11	For we are not unaware of his **s**.
Eph	6: 11	your stand against the devil's **s**.

SCOFFERS

2Pe	3: 3	that in the last days **s** will come,

SCORPION

Rev	9: 5	of the sting of a **s** when it strikes.

SCRIPTURE (SCRIPTURES)

Jn	10: 35	and **S** cannot be set aside—
1Ti	4: 13	yourself to the public reading of **S**,
2Ti	3: 16	All **S** is God-breathed and is useful
2Pe	1: 20	that no prophecy of **S** came

SCRIPTURES (SCRIPTURE)

Lk	24: 27	in all the **S** concerning himself.
Jn	5: 39	You study the **S** diligently because
Ac	17: 11	examined the **S** every day to see

SCROLL

Eze	3: 1	eat what is before you, eat this **s**;

SEA

Ex	14: 16	the Israelites can go through the **s**
Isa	57: 20	the wicked are like the tossing **s**,
Mic	7: 19	iniquities into the depths of the **s**.
Jas	1: 6	who doubts is like a wave of the **s**,
Rev	13: 1	I saw a beast coming out of the **s**.

SEAL (SEALS)

Jn	6: 27	God the Father has placed his **s**
2Co	1: 22	set his **s** of ownership on us,
Eph	1: 13	you were marked in him with a **s**,

SEALS (SEAL)

Rev	5: 2	"Who is worthy to break the **s**
	6: 1	opened the first of the seven **s**.

SEARCH (SEARCHED SEARCHES SEARCHING)

Ps	4: 4	beds, **s** your hearts and be silent.
	139: 23	**S** me, God, and know my heart;
Pr	2: 4	and **s** for it as for hidden treasure,
Jer	17: 10	"I the LORD **s** the heart
Eze	34: 16	I will **s** for the lost and bring back
Lk	15: 8	and **s** carefully until she finds it?

SEARCHED (SEARCH)

Ps	139: 1	You have **s** me, LORD, and you

SEARCHES (SEARCH)

Ro	8: 27	who **s** our hearts knows the mind
1Co	2: 10	The Spirit **s** all things, even the

SEARCHING (SEARCH)

Am	8: 12	east, **s** for the word of the LORD,

SEARED

1Ti	4: 2	whose consciences have been **s** as

SEASON

2Ti	4: 2	be prepared in **s** and out of **s**;

SEAT (SEATED SEATS)

Da	7: 9	and the Ancient of Days took his **s**.
2Co	5: 10	all appear before the judgment **s**

CONCORDANCE

SEATED (SEAT)
Ps   47: 8 God is **s** on his holy throne.
Isa   6: 1 high and exalted, **s** on a throne;
Col   3: 1 Christ is, **s** at the right hand of God.

SEATS (SEAT)
Lk   11: 43 you love the most important **s**

SECRET (SECRETS)
Dt   29: 29 The **s** things belong to the Lord
Jdg 16: 6 "Tell me the **s** of your great
Ps   90: 8 you, our **s** sins in the light of your
Pr   11: 13 but a trustworthy person keeps a **s**.
Mt   6: 4 so that your giving may be in **s**.
2Co   4: 2 we have renounced **s** and shameful
Php   4: 12 have learned the **s** of being content

SECRETS (SECRET)
Ps   44: 21 since he knows the **s** of the heart?
1Co 14: 25 as the **s** of their hearts are laid bare.

SECURE (SECURITY)
Ps 112: 8 Their hearts are **s**, they will have
Heb   6: 19 an anchor for the soul, firm and **s**.

SECURITY (SECURE)
Job 31: 24 or said to pure gold, 'You are my **s**,'

SEED (SEEDS)
Lk   8: 11 The **s** is the word of God.
1Co   3: 6 I planted the **s**, Apollos watered it,
2Co   9: 10 he who supplies **s** to the sower
Gal   3: 29 you are Abraham's **s**, and heirs
1Pe   1: 23 again, not of perishable **s**,

SEEDS (SEED)
Jn   12: 24 But if it dies, it produces many **s**.
Gal   3: 16 Scripture does not say "and to **s**,"

SEEK (SEEKS SELF-SEEKING)
Dt   4: 29 you will find him if you **s** him
1Ch 28: 9 If you **s** him, he will be found
2Ch   7: 14 pray and **s** my face and turn
Ps 119: 10 I **s** you with all my heart; do not let
Isa 55: 6 **S** the Lord while he may be
     65: 1 found by those who did not **s** me.
Mt   6: 33 But **s** first his kingdom and his
Lk   19: 10 For the Son of Man came to **s**
Ro   10: 20 found by those who did not **s** me;
1Co   7: 27 Do not **s** to be released.

SEEKS (SEEK)
Jn   4: 23 the kind of worshipers the Father **s**.

SEER
1Sa   9: 9 of today used to be called a **s**.)

SELF-CONTROL (CONTROL)
1Co   7: 5 tempt you because of your lack of **s**.
Gal   5: 23 gentleness and **s**.
2Pe   1: 6 and to knowledge, **s**; and to **s**,

SELF-CONTROLLED (CONTROL)
1Ti   3: 2 his wife, temperate, **s**, respectable,
Titus 1: 8 what is good, who is **s**, upright,
      2: 2 worthy of respect, **s**, and sound
      2: 5 to be **s** and pure, to be busy
      2: 6 encourage the young men to be **s**.
      2: 12 to live **s**, upright and godly lives

SELF-INDULGENCE
Mt   23: 25 inside they are full of greed and **s**.

SELF-SEEKING (SEEK)
1Co 13: 5 it is not **s**, it is not easily angered,

SELFISH
Ps 119: 36 statutes and not toward **s** gain.
Pr   18: 1 unfriendly person pursues **s** ends
Gal   5: 20 fits of rage, **s** ambition, dissensions,
Php   1: 17 preach Christ out of **s** ambition,
      2: 3 Do nothing out of **s** ambition
Jas   3: 14 envy and **s** ambition in your hearts,
      3: 16 you have envy and **s** ambition,

SEND (SENDING SENT)
Isa   6: 8 And I said, "Here am I. **S** me!"
Mt   9: 38 to **s** out workers into his harvest
Jn   16: 7 but if I go, I will **s** him to you.

SENDING (SEND)
Jn   20: 21 the Father has sent me, I am **s** you."

SENSES
Lk   15: 17 "When he came to his **s**, he said,
1Co 15: 34 Come back to your **s** as you ought,
2Ti   2: 26 that they will come to their **s**

SENSUAL
Col   2: 23 value in restraining **s** indulgence.

SENT (SEND)
Isa 55: 11 achieve the purpose for which I **s** it.
Mt   10: 40 me welcomes the one who **s** me.
Jn   4: 34 "is to do the will of him who **s** me
Ro   10: 15 anyone preach unless they are **s**?
1Jn   4: 10 **s** his Son as an atoning sacrifice

SEPARATE (SEPARATED SEPARATES)
Mt   19: 6 has joined together, let no one **s**."
Ro   8: 35 Who shall **s** us from the love
1Co   7: 10 A wife must not **s** from her
2Co   6: 17 "Come out from them and be **s**,

SEPARATED (SEPARATE)
Isa 59: 2 your iniquities have **s** you from

SEPARATES (SEPARATE)
Pr   16: 28 and a gossip **s** close friends.

SERPENT
Ge   3: 1 Now the **s** was more crafty than
Rev 12: 9 that ancient **s** called the devil,

SERVANT (SERVANTS)
1Sa   3: 10 "Speak, for your **s** is listening."
Mt   20: 26 great among you must be your **s**,
     25: 21 'Well done, good and faithful **s**!
Php   2: 7 by taking the very nature of a **s**,
2Ti   2: 24 And the Lord's **s** must not be

SERVANTS (SERVANT)
Lk   17: 10 do, should say, 'We are unworthy **s**;
Jn   15: 15 I no longer call you **s**,

SERVE (SERVICE SERVING)
Dt   10: 12 to **s** the Lord your God with all
Jos 22: 5 and to **s** him with all your heart
     24: 15 household, we will **s** the Lord."
Mt   4: 10 Lord your God, and **s** him only.'"
      6: 24 "No one can **s** two masters.
      6: 24 You cannot **s** both God and money.
     20: 28 but to **s**, and to give his life as
Eph   6: 7 **S** wholeheartedly, as if you were

SERVICE (SERVE)
1Co 12: 5 There are different kinds of **s**,
Eph   4: 12 to equip his people for works of **s**,

SERVING (SERVE)
Ro	12: 11	your spiritual fervor, **s** the Lord.
Eph	6: 7	as if you were **s** the Lord,
Col	3: 24	It is the Lord Christ you are **s**.
2Ti	2: 4	No one **s** as a soldier gets entangled

SEVEN (SEVENTH)
Ge	7: 2	Take with you **s** pairs of every kind
Jos	6: 4	march around the city **s** times,
1Ki	19: 18	Yet I reserve **s** thousand in Israel—
Pr	6: 16	hates, **s** that are detestable to him:
	24: 16	though the righteous fall **s** times,
Isa	4: 1	that day **s** women will take hold
Da	9: 25	comes, there will be **s** 'sevens,'
Mt	18: 21	sins against me? Up to **s** times?"
Lk	11: 26	takes **s** other spirits more wicked
Ro	11: 4	myself **s** thousand who have not
Rev	1: 4	To the **s** churches in the province
	1: 4	from the **s** spirits before his throne,
	6: 1	Lamb opened the first of the **s** seals.
	8: 2	I saw the **s** angels who stand before
	8: 2	and **s** trumpets were given to them.
	10: 4	And when the **s** thunders spoke,
	15: 7	to the **s** angels **s** golden bowls filled

SEVENTH (SEVEN)
| Ge | 2: 2 | so on the **s** day he rested from all |
| Ex | 23: 12 | but on the **s** day do not work, |

SEX (SEXUAL SEXUALLY)
| 1Co | 6: 9 | nor men who have **s** with men |

SEXUAL (SEX)
Mt	5: 32	except for **s** immorality, makes her
	19: 9	except for **s** immorality,
1Co	6: 13	is not meant for **s** immorality,
	6: 18	Flee from **s** immorality.
	7: 1	a man not to have **s** relations
	10: 8	should not commit **s** immorality,
Eph	5: 3	not be even a hint of **s** immorality,
1Th	4: 3	you should avoid **s** immorality;

SEXUALLY (SEX)
| 1Co | 5: 9 | associate with **s** immoral people— |
| | 6: 18 | but whoever sins **s**, sins against |

SHADOW
| Ps | 36: 7 | take refuge in the **s** of your wings. |
| Heb | 10: 1 | The law is only a **s** of the good |

SHALLUM
King of Israel (2Ki 15:10–16).

SHAME (ASHAMED)
Ps	22: 5	they trusted and were not put to **s**.
	34: 5	faces are never covered with **s**.
Pr	13: 18	discipline comes to poverty and **s**,
Heb	12: 2	scorning its **s**, and sat down

SHARE (SHARED)
Ge	21: 10	that woman's son will never **s**
Lk	3: 11	who has two shirts should **s**
Gal	4: 30	the slave woman's son will never **s**
	6: 6	the word should **s** all good things
Eph	4: 28	they may have something to **s**
1Ti	6: 18	to be generous and willing to **s**.
Heb	12: 10	order that we may **s** in his holiness.
	13: 16	to do good and to **s** with others,

SHARED (SHARE)
| Heb | 2: 14 | he too **s** in their humanity so |

SHARON
| SS | 2: 1 | I am a rose of **S**, a lily |

SHARPER
| Heb | 4: 12 | **S** than any double-edged sword, |

SHED (SHEDDING)
| Ge | 9: 6 | by humans shall their blood be **s**; |
| Col | 1: 20 | through his blood, **s** on the cross. |

SHEDDING (SHED)
| Heb | 9: 22 | without the **s** of blood there is no |

SHEEP
Ps	100: 3	are his people, the **s** of his pasture.
	119:176	I have strayed like a lost **s**.
Isa	53: 6	We all, like **s**, have gone astray,
Jer	50: 6	"My people have been lost **s**;
Eze	34: 11	I myself will search for my **s**
Mt	9: 36	helpless, like **s** without a shepherd.
Jn	10: 3	He calls his own **s** by name
	10: 15	and I lay down my life for the **s**.
	10: 27	My **s** listen to my voice;
	21: 17	Jesus said, "Feed my **s**.
1Pe	2: 25	For "you were like **s** going astray,"

SHELTER
| Ps | 61: 4 | take refuge in the **s** of your wings. |
| | 91: 1 | in the **s** of the Most High will rest |

SHEM
Son of Noah (Ge 5:32; 6:10). Blessed (Ge 9:26). Descendants (Ge 10:21–31; 11:10–32).

SHEPHERD (SHEPHERDS)
Ps	23: 1	The Lord is my **s**, I lack nothing.
Isa	40: 11	He tends his flock like a **s**:
Jer	31: 10	will watch over his flock like a **s**.'
Eze	34: 12	a **s** looks after his scattered flock
Zec	11: 17	"Woe to the worthless **s**,
Mt	9: 36	and helpless, like sheep without a **s**.
Jn	10: 11	"I am the good **s**. The good **s** lays
	10: 16	there shall be one flock and one **s**.
1Pe	5: 4	And when the Chief **S** appears,

SHEPHERDS (SHEPHERD)
Jer	23: 1	"Woe to the **s** who are destroying
Lk	2: 8	there were **s** living out in the fields
Ac	20: 28	Be **s** of the church of God,
1Pe	5: 2	Be **s** of God's flock that is under

SHIELD
| Ps | 28: 7 | Lord is my strength and my **s**; |
| Eph | 6: 16 | take up the **s** of faith, |

SHINE (SHONE)
Ps	4: 6	Let the light of your face **s** on us.
	80: 1	between the cherubim, **s** forth
Isa	60: 1	"Arise, **s**, for your light has come,
Da	12: 3	are wise will **s** like the brightness
Mt	5: 16	let your light **s** before others,
	13: 43	the righteous will **s** like the sun
2Co	4: 6	made his light **s** in our hearts
Eph	5: 14	the dead, and Christ will **s** on you."

SHIPWRECK (SHIPWRECKED)
| 1Ti | 1: 19 | so have suffered **s** with regard |

SHIPWRECKED (SHIPWRECK)
| 2Co | 11: 25 | three times I was **s**, I spent a night |

SHONE (SHINE)
| Mt | 17: 2 | His face **s** like the sun, and his |

Lk	2: 9	glory of the Lord **s** around them,
Rev	21: 11	It **s** with the glory of God, and its

SHORT

| Isa | 59: 1 | of the Lord is not too **s** to save, |
| Ro | 3: 23 | and fall **s** of the glory of God, |

SHOULDERS

| Isa | 9: 6 | the government will be on his **s**. |
| Lk | 15: 5 | finds it, he joyfully puts it on his **s** |

SHOWED

| 1Jn | 4: 9 | This is how God **s** his love among |

SHREWD

| Mt | 10: 16 | Therefore be as **s** as snakes and as |

SHUN

| Job | 28: 28 | and to **s** evil is understanding." |
| Pr | 3: 7 | fear the Lord and **s** evil. |

SICK

Pr	13: 12	Hope deferred makes the heart **s**,
Mt	9: 12	who need a doctor, but the **s**.
	25: 36	I was **s** and you looked after me,
Jas	5: 14	Is anyone among you **s**?

SICKLE

| Joel | 3: 13 | Swing the **s**, for the harvest is ripe. |

SIDE

Ps	91: 7	A thousand may fall at your **s**,
	124: 1	the Lord had not been on our **s**—
2Ti	4: 17	Lord stood at my **s** and gave me

SIGHT

Ps	90: 4	years in your **s** are like a day
	116: 15	in the **s** of the Lord is the death
2Co	5: 7	For we live by faith, not by **s**.
1Pe	3: 4	which is of great worth in God's **s**.

SIGN (SIGNS)

| Isa | 7: 14 | the Lord himself will give you a **s**: |

SIGNS (SIGN)

Mt	24: 24	and perform great **s** and wonders
Mk	16: 17	*these **s** will accompany those who*
Jn	3: 2	could perform the **s** you are doing
	9: 16	can a sinner perform such **s**?"
	20: 30	Jesus performed many other **s**
1Co	1: 22	Jews demand **s** and Greeks look

SILENT

Pr	17: 28	are thought wise if they keep **s**,
Isa	53: 7	as a sheep before its shearers is **s**,
Hab	2: 20	let all the earth be **s** before him.
1Co	14: 34	Women should remain **s**

SILVER

Pr	25: 11	of **s** is a ruling rightly given.
Hag	2: 8	'The **s** is mine and the gold is
1Co	3: 12	on this foundation using gold, **s**,

SIMON

1. See PETER.
2. Apostle, called the Zealot (Mt 10:4; Mk 3:18; Lk 6:15; Ac 1:13).
3. Samaritan sorcerer (Ac 8:9–24).

SIN (SINFUL SINNED SINNER SINNERS SINNING SINS)

Nu	5: 7	and must confess the **s** they have
	32: 23	sure that your **s** will find you out.
Dt	24: 16	each will die for their own **s**.

1Ki	8: 46	there is no one who does not **s**—
2Ch	7: 14	I will forgive their **s** and will heal
Ps	4: 4	Tremble and do not **s**; when you
	32: 2	is the one whose **s** the Lord does
	32: 5	And you forgave the guilt of my **s**.
	51: 2	iniquity and cleanse me from my **s**.
	66: 18	If I had cherished **s** in my heart,
	119: 11	that I might not **s** against you.
	119:133	to your word; let no **s** rule over me.
Isa	6: 7	taken away and your **s** atoned for."
Mic	7: 18	you, who pardons **s** and forgives
Jn	1: 29	who takes away the **s** of the world!
	8: 34	everyone who sins is a slave to **s**.
Ro	5: 12	just as **s** entered the world through
	5: 20	But where **s** increased,
	6: 11	count yourselves dead to **s** but alive
	6: 23	For the wages of **s** is death,
	14: 23	that does not come from faith is **s**.
2Co	5: 21	God made him who had no **s** to be **s**
Gal	6: 1	if someone is caught in a **s**,
Heb	9: 26	to do away with **s** by the sacrifice
	11: 25	to enjoy the fleeting pleasures of **s**.
	12: 1	and the **s** that so easily entangles.
1Pe	2: 22	"He committed no **s**, and no deceit
1Jn	1: 8	If we claim to be without **s**,
	3: 4	in fact, **s** is lawlessness.
	3: 5	away our sins. And in him is no **s**.
	3: 9	is born of God will continue to **s**,
	5: 18	born of God does not continue to **s**;

SINCERE

| Ro | 12: 9 | Love must be **s**. Hate what is evil; |
| Heb | 10: 22 | us draw near to God with a **s** heart |

SINFUL (SIN)

Ps	51: 5	Surely I was **s** at birth,
Ro	7: 5	the **s** passions aroused by the law
1Pe	2: 11	to abstain from **s** desires,

SINFUL NATURE see FLESH

SING (SANG SINGING SONG SONGS)

Ps	30: 4	**S** the praises of the Lord, you his
	47: 6	**S** praises to God, **s** praises; **s** praises
	59: 16	in the morning I will **s** of your love
	89: 1	I will **s** of the Lord's great love
	101: 1	I will **s** of your love and justice;
Eph	5: 19	**S** and make music from your heart

SINGING (SING)

| Ps | 63: 5 | **s** lips my mouth will praise you. |
| Ac | 16: 25 | were praying and **s** hymns to God, |

SINNED (SIN)

2Sa	12: 13	"I have **s** against the Lord."
Job	1: 5	"Perhaps my children have **s**
Ps	51: 4	have I **s** and done what is evil
Da	9: 5	we have **s** and done wrong.
Mic	7: 9	Because I have **s** against him, I will
Lk	15: 18	I have **s** against heaven and against
Ro	3: 23	for all have **s** and fall short
1Jn	1: 10	If we claim we have not **s**, we make

SINNER (SIN)

Ecc	9: 18	war, but one **s** destroys much good.
Lk	15: 7	heaven over one **s** who repents
	18: 13	said, 'God, have mercy on me, a **s**.'
Jas	5: 20	Whoever turns a **s** from the error
1Pe	4: 18	become of the ungodly and the **s**?"

SINNERS (SIN)
Ps	1: 1	stand in the way that **s** take or sit
Pr	23: 17	Do not let your heart envy **s**,
Mt	9: 13	come to call the righteous, but **s**."
Ro	5: 8	While we were still **s**, Christ died
1Ti	1: 15	came into the world to save **s**—

SINNING (SIN)
Ex	20: 20	be with you to keep you from **s**."
1Co	15: 34	senses as you ought, and stop **s**;
Heb	10: 26	If we deliberately keep on **s** after
1Jn	3: 6	one who lives in him keeps on **s**.
	3: 9	they cannot go on **s**, because they

SINS (SIN)
Ezr	9: 6	because our **s** are higher than our
Ps	19: 13	your servant also from willful **s**;
	32: 1	are forgiven, whose **s** are covered.
	103: 3	who forgives all your **s** and heals
	130: 3	LORD, kept a record of **s**, Lord,
Pr	28: 13	Whoever conceals their **s** does not
Isa	1: 18	"Though your **s** are like scarlet,
	43: 25	and remembers your **s** no more.
	59: 2	your **s** have hidden his face
Eze	18: 4	The one who **s** is the one who will
Mt	1: 21	will save his people from their **s**."
	18: 15	"If your brother or sister **s**,
Lk	11: 4	Forgive us our **s**, for we also forgive everyone who **s** against us.
	17: 3	your brother or sister **s** against you,
Ac	22: 16	be baptized and wash your **s** away,
1Co	15: 3	Christ died for our **s** according
Eph	2: 1	dead in your transgressions and **s**,
Col	2: 13	He forgave us all our **s**,
Heb	1: 3	he had provided purification for **s**,
	7: 27	He sacrificed for their **s** once for all
	8: 12	will remember their **s** no more."
	10: 12	for all time one sacrifice for **s**,
Jas	5: 16	Therefore confess your **s** to each
	5: 20	and cover over a multitude of **s**.
1Pe	2: 24	so that we might die to **s** and live
	3: 18	For Christ also suffered once for **s**,
1Jn	1: 9	If we confess our **s**, he is faithful
	1: 9	will forgive us our **s** and purify us
Rev	1: 5	freed us from our **s** by his blood,

SITS
Ps	99: 1	he **s** enthroned between
Isa	40: 22	He **s** enthroned above the circle
Mt	19: 28	Son of Man **s** on his glorious throne,
Rev	4: 9	thanks to him who **s** on the throne

SKIN
Job	19: 20	escaped only by the **s** of my teeth.
	19: 26	And after my **s** has been destroyed,
Jer	13: 23	Can an Ethiopian change his **s**

SLAIN (SLAY)
Rev	5: 12	who was **s**, to receive power

SLANDER (SLANDERED SLANDERERS)
Lev	19: 16	spreading **s** among your people.
1Ti	5: 14	the enemy no opportunity for **s**.
Titus	3: 2	to **s** no one, to be peaceable

SLANDERED (SLANDER)
1Co	4: 13	when we are **s**, we answer kindly.

SLANDERERS (SLANDER)
Ro	1: 30	**s**, God-haters, insolent,

1Co	6: 10	nor drunkards nor **s** nor swindlers
Titus	2: 3	not to be **s** or addicted to much

SLAUGHTER
Isa	53: 7	he was led like a lamb to the **s**,

SLAVE (SLAVERY SLAVES)
Ge	21: 10	"Get rid of that **s** woman and her
Mt	20: 27	wants to be first must be your **s**—
Jn	8: 34	everyone who sins is a **s** to sin.
1Co	12: 13	whether Jews or Gentiles, **s** or free
Gal	3: 28	Jew nor Gentile, neither **s** nor free,
	4: 30	the **s** woman's son will never share

SLAVERY (SLAVE)
Gal	4: 3	in **s** under the elemental spiritual

SLAVES (SLAVE)
Ro	6: 6	we should no longer be **s** to sin—
	6: 22	and have become **s** of God,
2Pe	2: 19	for "people are **s** to whatever has

SLAY (SLAIN)
Job	13: 15	Though he **s** me, yet will I hope

SLEEP (SLEEPING)
Ps	121: 4	Israel will neither slumber nor **s**.
1Co	15: 51	We will not all **s**, but we will all be

SLEEPING (SLEEP)
Mk	13: 36	do not let him find you **s**.

SLOW
Ex	34: 6	and gracious God, **s** to anger,
Jas	1: 19	**s** to speak and **s** to become angry,
2Pe	3: 9	The Lord is not **s** in keeping his

SLUGGARD (SLUGGARDS)
Pr	6: 6	Go to the ant, you **s**;

SLUGGARDS (SLUGGARD)
Pr	20: 4	**S** do not plow in season;

SLUMBER
Ps	121: 3	he who watches over you will not **s**;
Pr	6: 10	little **s**, a little folding of the hands
Ro	13: 11	for you to wake up from your **s**,

SNAKE (SNAKES)
Nu	21: 8	"Make a **s** and put it up on a pole;
Pr	23: 32	In the end it bites like a **s**
Jn	3: 14	lifted up the **s** in the wilderness,

SNAKES (SNAKE)
Mt	10: 16	Therefore be as shrewd as **s** and as
Mk	16: 18	*they will pick up* **s**

SNATCH (SNATCHING)
Jn	10: 28	no one will **s** them out of my hand.

SNATCHING (SNATCH)
Jude	: 23	save others by **s** them from the fire;

SNOW
Ps	51: 7	me, and I will be whiter than **s**.

SOAR
Isa	40: 31	They will **s** on wings like eagles;

SODOM
Ge	19: 24	rained down burning sulfur on **S**
Ro	9: 29	we would have become like **S**,

SOIL
Ge	4: 2	kept flocks, and Cain worked the **s**.
Mt	13: 23	the seed falling on good **s** refers

CONCORDANCE

SOLDIER — SPIN

SOLDIER
1Co 9: 7 Who serves as a **s** at his own
2Ti 2: 3 like a good **s** of Christ Jesus.

SOLE
Dt 28: 65 resting place for the **s** of your foot.
Isa 1: 6 From the **s** of your foot to the top

SOLID
2Ti 2: 19 God's **s** foundation stands firm,
Heb 5: 12 You need milk, not **s** food!

SOLOMON
Son of David by Bathsheba; king of Judah (2Sa 12:24; 1Ch 3:5, 10). Appointed king by David (1Ki 1); adversaries Adonijah, Joab, Shimei killed by Benaiah (1Ki 2). Asked for wisdom (1Ki 3; 2Ch 1). Judged between two prostitutes (1Ki 3:16–28). Built temple (1Ki 5–7; 2Ch 2–5); prayer of dedication (1Ki 8; 2Ch 6). Visited by Queen of Sheba (1Ki 10; 2Ch 9). Wives turned his heart from God (1Ki 11:1–13). Jeroboam rebelled against (1Ki 11:26–40). Death (1Ki 11:41–43; 2Ch 9:29–31).
Proverbs of (1Ki 4:32; Pr 1:1; 10:1; 25:1); psalms of (Ps 72; 127); song of (SS 1:1).

SON (SONS)
Ge 22: 2 said, "Take your **s**, your only **s**,
Ex 11: 5 Every firstborn **s** in Egypt will die,
Dt 21: 18 rebellious **s** who does not obey his
Ps 2: 7 He said to me, "You are my **s**;
    2: 12 Kiss his **s**, or he will be angry
Pr 10: 1 A wise **s** brings joy to his father,
Isa 7: 14 will conceive and give birth to a **s**,
Hos 11: 1 and out of Egypt I called my **s**.
Mt 2: 15 "Out of Egypt I called my **s**."
    3: 17 said, "This is my **S**, whom I love;
    11: 27 knows the **S** except the Father,
    11: 27 knows the Father except the **S**
    16: 16 Messiah, the **S** of the living God."
    17: 5 said, "This is my **S**, whom I love;
    20: 18 the **S** of Man will be delivered over
    24: 30 appear the sign of the **S** of Man
    24: 44 because the **S** of Man will come
    27: 54 "Surely he was the **S** of God!"
    28: 19 and of the **S** and of the Holy Spirit,
Mk 10: 45 even the **S** of Man did not come
    14: 62 you will see the **S** of Man sitting
Lk 9: 58 the **S** of Man has no place to lay his
    18: 8 when the **S** of Man comes, will he
    19: 10 For the **S** of Man came to seek
Jn 3: 14 so the **S** of Man must be lifted up,
    3: 16 that he gave his one and only **S**,
    17: 1 Glorify your **S**, that your **S** may
Ro 8: 29 conformed to the image of his **S**,
    8: 32 He who did not spare his own **S**,
1Co 15: 28 the **S** himself will be made subject
Gal 4: 30 for the slave woman's **s** will never
1Th 1: 10 and to wait for his **S** from heaven,
Heb 1: 2 days he has spoken to us by his **S**,
    10: 29 punished who has trampled the **S**
1Jn 1: 7 Jesus, his **S**, purifies us from all sin.
    4: 9 only **S** into the world that we might
    5: 5 believes that Jesus is the **S** of God.
    5: 11 eternal life, and this life is in his **S**.

SONG (SING)
Ps 40: 3 He put a new **s** in my mouth,

Ps 96: 1 Sing to the LORD a new **s**;
    149: 1 Sing to the LORD a new **s**,
Isa 49: 13 burst into **s**, you mountains!
    55: 12 hills will burst into **s** before you,
Rev 5: 9 And they sang a new **s**, saying:
    15: 3 sang the **s** of God's servant Moses

SONGS (SING)
Job 35: 10 Maker, who gives **s** in the night,
Ps 100: 2 come before him with joyful **s**.
Eph 5: 19 hymns, and **s** from the Spirit.
Jas 5: 13 Let them sing **s** of praise.

SONS (SON)
Joel 2: 28 **s** and daughters will prophesy,
2Co 6: 18 you will be my **s** and daughters,

SORROW
Jer 31: 12 garden, and they will **s** no more.
Ro 9: 2 I have great **s** and unceasing
2Co 7: 10 Godly **s** brings repentance that

SOUL (SOULS)
Dt 6: 5 and with all your **s** and with all
    10: 12 all your heart and with all your **s**,
Jos 22: 5 all your heart and with all your **s**."
Ps 23: 3 he refreshes my **s**. He guides me
    42: 1 of water, so my **s** pants for you,
    42: 11 Why, my **s**, are you downcast?
    103: 1 Praise the LORD, my **s**;
Pr 13: 19 A longing fulfilled is sweet to the **s**,
Mt 10: 28 of the One who can destroy both **s**
    16: 26 the whole world, yet forfeit their **s**?
    22: 37 with all your **s** and with all your
Heb 4: 12 it penetrates even to dividing **s**

SOULS (SOUL)
Jer 6: 16 and you will find rest for your **s**.
Mt 11: 29 and you will find rest for your **s**.

SOUND
1Co 14: 8 the trumpet does not **s** a clear call,
    15: 52 the trumpet will **s**, the dead will
2Ti 4: 3 will not put up with **s** doctrine.

SOVEREIGN
Da 4: 25 Most High is **s** over all kingdoms

SOW (SOWS)
Job 4: 8 and those who **s** trouble reap it.
Mt 6: 26 they do not **s** or reap or store away
2Pe 2: 22 "A **s** that is washed returns to her

SOWS (SOW)
2Co 9: 6 and whoever **s** generously will

SPARE (SPARES)
Ro 8: 32 He who did not **s** his own Son,
    11: 21 God did not **s** the natural branches,

SPARES (SPARE)
Pr 13: 24 Whoever **s** the rod hates their

SPEARS
Isa 2: 4 and their **s** into pruning hooks.
Joel 3: 10 and your pruning hooks into **s**.
Mic 4: 3 and their **s** into pruning hooks.

SPECTACLE
1Co 4: 9 have been made a **s** to the whole
Col 2: 15 he made a public **s** of them,

SPIN
Mt 6: 28 They do not labor or **s**.

1634

SPIRIT (SPIRITS SPIRITUAL)

Ge	1: 2	the **S** of God was hovering over
	6: 3	said, "My **S** will not contend
2Ki	2: 9	inherit a double portion of your **s**,"
Job	33: 4	The **S** of God has made me;
Ps	31: 5	Into your hands I commit my **s**;
	51: 10	and renew a steadfast **s** within me.
	51: 11	or take your Holy **S** from me.
	51: 17	My sacrifice, O God, is a broken **s**;
	139: 7	Where can I go from your **S**?
Isa	57: 15	to revive the **s** of the lowly
	63: 10	rebelled and grieved his Holy **S**.
Eze	11: 19	heart and put a new **s** in them;
	36: 26	a new heart and put a new **s** in you;
Joel	2: 28	I will pour out my **S** on all people.
Zec	4: 6	but by my **S**,' says the Lord
Mt	1: 18	to be pregnant through the Holy **S**.
	3: 11	He will baptize you with the Holy **S**
	3: 16	he saw the **S** of God descending
	4: 1	led by the **S** into the wilderness
	5: 3	"Blessed are the poor in **s**, for
	26: 41	The **s** is willing, but the flesh is
	28: 19	and of the Son and of the Holy **S**,
Lk	1: 80	child grew and became strong in **s**;
	11: 13	in heaven give the Holy **S** to those
Jn	4: 24	God is **s**, and his worshipers must worship in the **S**
	7: 39	that time the **S** had not been given,
	14: 26	the Holy **S**, whom the Father will
	16: 13	But when he, the **S** of truth, comes,
	20: 22	and said, "Receive the Holy **S**.
Ac	1: 5	will be baptized with the Holy **S**."
	2: 4	tongues as the **S** enabled them.
	2: 38	will receive the gift of the Holy **S**.
	6: 3	who are known to be full of the **S**
	19: 2	"Did you receive the Holy **S**
Ro	8: 9	if indeed the **S** of God lives in you.
	8: 26	the **S** helps us in our weakness.
1Co	2: 10	God has revealed to us by his **S**.
	2: 10	The **S** searches all things,
	2: 14	without the **S** does not accept
	3: 1	as people who live by the **S** but as
	6: 19	bodies are temples of the Holy **S**,
	12: 1	Now about the gifts of the **S**,
	12: 13	we were all baptized by one **S**
	12: 13	and we were all given the one **S**
	14: 1	and eagerly desire gifts of the **S**,
2Co	3: 6	the letter kills, but the **S** gives life.
	5: 5	who has given us the **S** as a deposit,
Gal	5: 16	say, walk by the **S**, and you will not
	5: 22	But the fruit of the **S** is love, joy,
	5: 25	Since we live by the **S**, let us keep
Gal	6: 1	who live by the **S** should restore
Eph	1: 13	with a seal, the promised Holy **S**,
	4: 30	do not grieve the Holy **S** of God,
	5: 18	Instead, be filled with the **S**,
	5: 19	hymns, and songs from the **S**.
	6: 17	of salvation and the sword of the **S**,
1Th	5: 19	Do not quench the **S**.
2Th	2: 13	the sanctifying work of the **S**
Heb	4: 12	even to dividing soul and **s**,
1Pe	3: 4	beauty of a gentle and quiet **s**,
2Pe	1: 21	were carried along by the Holy **S**.
1Jn	4: 1	do not believe every **s**, but test

SPIRITS (SPIRIT)

1Co	12: 10	another distinguishing between **s**,
1Co	14: 32	The **s** of prophets are subject
1Jn	4: 1	but test the **s** to see whether they

SPIRITUAL (SPIRIT)

Ro	12: 11	but keep your **s** fervor,
1Co	2: 13	the Spirit, explaining **s** realities
	15: 44	a natural body, it is raised a **s** body.
Eph	1: 3	realms with every **s** blessing
	6: 12	against the **s** forces of evil
1Pe	2: 2	crave pure **s** milk, so that by it you
	2: 5	offering **s** sacrifices acceptable

SPLENDOR

1Ch	16: 29	the Lord in the **s** of his holiness.
	29: 11	glory and the majesty and the **s**,
Job	37: 22	of the north he comes in golden **s**;
Ps	29: 2	the Lord in the **s** of his holiness.
	45: 3	clothe yourself with **s** and majesty.
	96: 6	**S** and majesty are before him;
	96: 9	the Lord in the **s** of his holiness;
	104: 1	you are clothed with **s** and majesty.
	145: 5	of the glorious **s** of your majesty—
Isa	61: 3	the Lord for the display of his **s**.
	63: 1	robed in **s**, striding forward
Lk	9: 30	Elijah, appeared in glorious **s**,
2Th	2: 8	and destroy by the **s** of his coming.

SPOIL

Ps	119:162	promise like one who finds great **s**.

SPOTLESS

2Pe	3: 14	make every effort to be found **s**,

SPREAD (SPREADING)

Ac	12: 24	the word of God continued to **s**
	19: 20	way the word of the Lord **s** widely

SPREADING (SPREAD)

1Th	3: 2	in God's service in **s** the gospel

SPRING

Jer	2: 13	forsaken me, the **s** of living water,
Jn	4: 14	in them a **s** of water welling
Jas	3: 12	can a salt **s** produce fresh water.

SPUR

Heb	10: 24	how we may **s** one another

SPURNS

Pr	15: 5	A fool **s** a parent's discipline,

STAFF

Ps	23: 4	your rod and your **s**, they comfort

STAKES

Isa	54: 2	your cords, strengthen your **s**.

STAND (STANDING STANDS)

Ex	14: 13	**S** firm and you will see
2Ch	20: 17	**s** firm and see the deliverance
Ps	1: 5	Therefore the wicked will not **s**
	40: 2	rock and gave me a firm place to **s**.
	119:120	fear of you; I **s** in awe of your laws.
Eze	22: 30	**s** before me in the gap on behalf
Zec	14: 4	day his feet will **s** on the Mount
Mt	12: 25	divided against itself will not **s**.
Ro	14: 10	we will all **s** before God's judgment
1Co	15: 58	dear brothers and sisters, **s** firm.
Eph	6: 14	**S** firm then, with the belt of truth
2Th	2: 15	firm and hold fast to the teachings
Jas	5: 8	be patient and **s** firm,
Rev	3: 20	I **s** at the door and knock.

CONCORDANCE

STANDING (STAND)
Ex	3: 5	where you are **s** is holy ground."
Jos	5: 15	the place where you are **s** is holy."
1Pe	5: 9	Resist him, **s** firm in the faith,

STANDS (STAND)
Ps	89: 2	that your love **s** firm forever,
	119: 89	it **s** firm in the heavens.
2Ti	2: 19	God's solid foundation **s** firm,

STAR (STARS)
| Nu | 24: 17 | A **s** will come out of Jacob; |
| Rev | 22: 16 | David, and the bright Morning **S**." |

STARS (STAR)
| Da | 12: 3 | like the **s** for ever and ever. |
| Php | 2: 15 | you will shine among them like **s** |

STEADFAST
Ps	51: 10	and renew a **s** spirit within me.
Isa	26: 3	peace those whose minds are **s**,
1Pe	5: 10	and make you strong, firm and **s**.

STEAL
Ex	20: 15	"You shall not **s**.
Mt	19: 18	you shall not **s**, you shall not give
Eph	4: 28	has been stealing must **s** no longer,

STEP (STEPS)
| Gal | 5: 25 | let us keep in **s** with the Spirit. |

STEPS (STEP)
Pr	16: 9	but the LORD establishes their **s**.
Jer	10: 23	it is not for them to direct their **s**.
1Pe	2: 21	that you should follow in his **s**.

STICKS
| Pr | 18: 24 | there is a friend who **s** closer than |

STIFF-NECKED
| Ex | 34: 9 | Although this is a **s** people, |

STILL
| Ps | 46: 10 | "Be **s**, and know that I am God; |
| Zec | 2: 13 | Be **s** before the LORD, |

STIRS
Pr	6: 19	a person who **s** up conflict
	10: 12	Hatred **s** up conflict, but love
	15: 1	wrath, but a harsh word **s** up anger.
	29: 22	An angry person **s** up conflict,

STONE (CAPSTONE CORNERSTONE MILLSTONE)
1Sa	17: 50	the Philistine with a sling and a **s**;
Isa	8: 14	and Judah he will be a **s** that causes
Eze	11: 19	remove from them their heart of **s**
Mk	16: 3	"Who will roll the **s** away
Lk	4: 3	God, tell this **s** to become bread."
Jn	8: 7	*the first to throw a **s** at her.*"
2Co	3: 3	not on tablets of **s** but on tablets

STORE
| Pr | 10: 14 | The wise **s** up knowledge, |
| Mt | 6: 19 | "Do not **s** up for yourselves |

STOREHOUSE (HOUSE)
| Mal | 3: 10 | Bring the whole tithe into the **s**, |

STRAIGHT
Pr	3: 6	and he will make your paths **s**.
	4: 25	Let your eyes look **s** ahead;
	15: 21	understanding keeps a **s** course.
Jn	1: 23	'Make **s** the way for the Lord.'"

STRAIN
| Mt | 23: 24 | You **s** out a gnat but swallow |

STRANGER
| Mt | 25: 35 | I was a **s** and you invited me in, |
| Jn | 10: 5 | But they will never follow a **s**; |

STRAPS
| Mk | 1: 7 | **s** of whose sandals I am not worthy |

STREAMS
Ps	1: 3	person is like a tree planted by **s**
	46: 4	a river whose **s** make glad the city
Ecc	1: 7	All **s** flow into the sea, yet the sea is

STRENGTH (STRONG)
Ex	15: 2	"The LORD is my **s** and my
Dt	6: 5	all your soul and with all your **s**.
2Sa	22: 33	It is God who arms me with **s**
Ne	8: 10	the joy of the LORD is your **s**."
Ps	28: 7	The LORD is my **s** and my shield;
	46: 1	God is our refuge and **s**,
	96: 7	ascribe to the LORD glory and **s**.
	118: 14	The LORD is my **s** and my
	147: 10	pleasure is not in the **s** of the horse,
Isa	40: 31	in the LORD will renew their **s**.
Mk	12: 30	all your mind and with all your **s**.'
1Co	1: 25	of God is stronger than human **s**.
Php	4: 13	this through him who gives me **s**.
1Pe	4: 11	do so with the **s** God provides,

STRENGTHEN (STRONG)
2Ch	16: 9	to **s** those whose hearts are fully
Ps	119: 28	**s** me according to your word.
Isa	35: 3	**S** the feeble hands, steady the
	41: 10	I will **s** you and help you;
Eph	3: 16	of his glorious riches he may **s** you
2Th	2: 17	and **s** you in every good deed
Heb	12: 12	**s** your feeble arms and weak knees.

STRIFE
| Pr | 20: 3 | It is to one's honor to avoid **s**, |
| | 22: 10 | out the mocker, and out goes **s**; |

STRIKE
Ge	3: 15	your head, and you will **s** his heel."
Zec	13: 7	"**S** the shepherd, and the sheep will
Mt	26: 31	"'I will **s** the shepherd,

STRONG (STRENGTH STRENGTHEN)
Dt	31: 6	Be **s** and courageous. Do not be
1Ki	2: 2	"So be **s**, act like a man,
Pr	31: 17	her arms are **s** for her tasks.
SS	8: 6	for love is as **s** as death, its jealousy
Lk	2: 40	And the child grew and became **s**;
Ro	15: 1	We who are **s** ought to bear the
1Co	1: 27	things of the world to shame the **s**.
	16: 13	in the faith; be courageous; be **s**.
2Co	12: 10	For when I am weak, then I am **s**.
Eph	6: 10	be **s** in the Lord and in his mighty

STRUGGLE
Ro	15: 30	join me in my **s** by praying to God
Eph	6: 12	For our **s** is not against flesh
Heb	12: 4	In your **s** against sin, you have not

STUDY
Ezr	7: 10	Ezra had devoted himself to the **s**
Ecc	12: 12	end, and much **s** wearies the body.
Jn	5: 39	You **s** the Scriptures diligently

STUMBLE (STUMBLING)
Ps	37: 24	though he may **s**, he will not fall,
	119:165	law, and nothing can make them **s**.
Isa	8: 14	be a stone that causes people to **s**
Jer	31: 9	a level path where they will not **s**,
Eze	7: 19	for it has caused them to **s** into sin.
1Co	10: 32	Do not cause anyone to **s**,
1Pe	2: 8	"A stone that causes people to **s**

STUMBLING (STUMBLE)
Ro	14: 13	your mind not to put any **s** block
1Co	8: 9	rights does not become a a **s** block
2Co	6: 3	We put no **s** block in anyone's path,

SUBDUE
| Ge | 1: 28 | fill the earth and **s** it. |

SUBJECT (SUBJECTED)
1Co	14: 32	of prophets are **s** to the control
	15: 28	the Son himself will be made **s**
Titus	2: 5	and to be **s** to their husbands,
	2: 9	slaves to be **s** to their masters
	3: 1	Remind the people to be **s** to rulers

SUBJECTED (SUBJECT)
| Ro | 8: 20 | the creation was **s** to frustration, |

SUBMISSION (SUBMIT)
| 1Co | 14: 34 | but must be in **s**, as the law says. |
| 1Ti | 2: 11 | learn in quietness and full **s**. |

SUBMISSIVE (SUBMIT)
| Jas | 3: 17 | considerate, **s**, full of mercy |

SUBMIT (SUBMISSION SUBMISSIVE SUBMITS)
Ro	13: 5	necessary to **s** to the authorities,
1Co	16: 16	to **s** to such people and to everyone
Eph	5: 21	**S** to one another out of reverence
Col	3: 18	**s** yourselves to your husbands, as is
Heb	12: 9	How much more should we **s**
	13: 17	leaders and **s** to their authority,
Jas	4: 7	**S** yourselves, then, to God.
1Pe	2: 18	reverent fear of God **s** yourselves

SUBMITS (SUBMIT)
| Eph | 5: 24 | Now as the church **s** to Christ, |

SUCCESSFUL
Jos	1: 7	that you may be **s** wherever you go.
2Ki	18: 7	he was **s** in whatever he undertook.
2Ch	20: 20	in his prophets and you will be **s**."

SUFFER (SUFFERED SUFFERING SUFFERINGS
  SUFFERS)
Isa	53: 10	to crush him and cause him to **s**,
Mk	8: 31	Son of Man must **s** many things
Lk	24: 26	the Messiah have to **s** these things
	24: 46	The Messiah will **s** and rise
Php	1: 29	believe in him, but also to **s** for him,
1Pe	4: 16	if you **s** as a Christian, do not be

SUFFERED (SUFFER)
Heb	2: 9	and honor because he **s** death,
	2: 18	Because he himself **s** when he was
1Pe	2: 21	called, because Christ **s** for you,

SUFFERING (SUFFER)
Isa	53: 3	a man of **s**, and familiar with pain.
Ac	5: 41	been counted worthy of **s** disgrace
2Ti	1: 8	join with me in **s** for the gospel,

SUFFERINGS (SUFFER)
| Ro | 8: 17 | if indeed we share in his **s** in order |

Ro	8: 18	that our present **s** are not worth
2Co	1: 5	share abundantly in the **s** of Christ,
Php	3: 10	and participation in his **s**,

SUFFERS (SUFFER)
| Pr | 13: 20 | for a companion of fools **s** harm. |
| 1Co | 12: 26 | If one part **s**, every part **s** with it; |

SUFFICIENT
| 2Co | 12: 9 | said to me, "My grace is **s** for you, |

SUITABLE
| Ge | 2: 18 | I will make a helper **s** for him." |

SUN
Ecc	1: 9	there is nothing new under the **s**.
Mal	4: 2	the **s** of righteousness will rise
Mt	5: 45	He causes his **s** to rise on the evil
	17: 2	His face shone like the **s**, and his
Rev	1: 16	His face was like the **s** shining in
	21: 23	The city does not need the **s**

SUPERIOR
| Heb | 1: 4 | as the name he has inherited is **s** |
| | 8: 6 | he is mediator is **s** to the old one, |

SUPREMACY
| Col | 1: 18 | in everything he might have the **s**. |

SURE
Nu	32: 23	you may be **s** that your sin will find
Dt	6: 17	Be **s** to keep the commands
	14: 22	Be **s** to set aside a tenth of all
Isa	28: 16	cornerstone for a **s** foundation;

SURPASS (SURPASSES SURPASSING)
| Pr | 31: 29 | noble things, but you **s** them all." |

SURPASSES (SURPASS)
| Mt | 5: 20 | that unless your righteousness **s** |
| Eph | 3: 19 | to know this love that **s** knowledge |

SURPASSING (SURPASS)
Ps	150: 2	praise him for his **s** greatness.
2Co	3: 10	in comparison with the **s** glory.
	9: 14	of the **s** grace God has given you.
Php	3: 8	a loss because of the **s** worth

SURROUNDED
| Heb | 12: 1 | since we are **s** by such a great cloud |

SUSPENDS
| Job | 26: 7 | he **s** the earth over nothing. |

SUSTAINING (SUSTAINS)
| Heb | 1: 3 | **s** all things by his powerful word. |

SUSTAINS (SUSTAINING)
Ps	18: 35	shield, and your right hand **s** me;
	146: 9	the foreigner and **s** the fatherless
	147: 6	The Lᴏʀᴅ **s** the humble but casts
Isa	50: 4	to know the word that **s** the weary.

SWALLOWED
| 1Co | 15: 54 | "Death has been **s** up in victory." |
| 2Co | 5: 4 | so that what is mortal may be **s** |

SWEAR
| Mt | 5: 34 | I tell you, do not **s** an oath at all: |

SWORD (SWORDS)
Ps	45: 3	Gird your **s** on your side,
Mt	10: 34	not come to bring peace, but a **s**.
	26: 52	all who draw the **s** will die by the **s**.
Lk	2: 35	a **s** will pierce your own soul too."

1637

Ro	13: 4	for rulers do not bear the **s** for no
Eph	6: 17	of salvation and the **s** of the Spirit,
Heb	4: 12	Sharper than any double-edged **s**,
Rev	1: 16	was a sharp, double-edged **s**.

SWORDS (SWORD)

Pr	12: 18	words of the reckless pierce like **s**,
Isa	2: 4	They will beat their **s**
Joel	3: 10	Beat your plowshares into **s**

SYMPATHETIC

1Pe	3: 8	be **s**, love one another,

SYNAGOGUE

Lk	4: 16	the Sabbath day he went into the **s**,
Ac	17: 2	Paul went into the **s**, and on three

TABERNACLE

Ex	40: 34	the glory of the Lᴏʀᴅ filled the **t**.

TABLE (TABLES)

Ps	23: 5	You prepare a **t** before me

TABLES (TABLE)

Ac	6: 2	word of God in order to wait on **t**.

TABLET (TABLETS)

Pr	3: 3	write them on the **t** of your heart.
	7: 3	write them on the **t** of your heart.

TABLETS (TABLET)

Ex	31: 18	Sinai, he gave him the two **t**
Dt	10: 5	put the **t** in the ark I had made,
2Co	3: 3	not on **t** of stone but on **t** of human

TAKE (TAKEN TAKES TAKING TOOK)

Dt	12: 32	do not add to it or **t** away from it.
	31: 26	"**T** this Book of the Law and place
Job	23: 10	But he knows the way that I **t**;
Ps	49: 17	for they will **t** nothing with them
	51: 11	or **t** your Holy Spirit from me.
Mt	10: 38	Whoever does not **t** up their cross
	11: 29	**T** my yoke upon you and learn
	16: 24	deny themselves and **t** up their cross

TAKEN (TAKE)

Lev	6: 4	they have stolen or **t** by extortion,
Isa	6: 7	your guilt is **t** away and your sin
Mt	24: 40	one will be **t** and the other left.
Mk	16: 19	*them, he was* **t** *up into heaven*
1Ti	3: 16	on in the world, was **t** up in glory.

TAKES (TAKE)

1Ki	20: 11	not boast like one who **t** it off.' "
Jn	1: 29	who **t** away the sin of the world!
Rev	22: 19	if anyone **t** words away from this

TAKING (TAKE)

Php	2: 7	nothing by **t** the very nature

TALENT See BAGS

TAME

Jas	3: 8	no human being can **t** the tongue.

TASK

Mk	13: 34	each with their assigned **t**, and tells
Ac	20: 24	complete the **t** the Lord Jesus has
1Co	3: 5	the Lord has assigned to each his **t**.
2Co	2: 16	And who is equal to such a **t**?

TASTE (TASTED)

Ps	34: 8	**T** and see that the Lᴏʀᴅ is good;
Col	2: 21	Do not **t**! Do not touch!"?
Heb	2: 9	God he might **t** death for everyone.

TASTED (TASTE)

1Pe	2: 3	you have **t** that the Lord is good.

TAUGHT (TEACH)

Mt	7: 29	because he **t** as one who had
1Co	2: 13	but in words **t** by the Spirit,
Gal	1: 12	it from any man, nor was I **t** it;

TAX (TAXES)

Mt	22: 17	to pay the imperial **t** to Caesar

TAXES (TAX)

Ro	13: 7	you owe them: If you owe **t**, pay **t**;

TEACH (TAUGHT TEACHER TEACHERS TEACHES TEACHING)

Ex	33: 13	**t** me your ways so I may know you
Dt	4: 9	**T** them to your children and to
	8: 3	to **t** you that man does not live
	11: 19	**T** them to your children,
1Sa	12: 23	I will **t** you the way that is good
Ps	32: 8	**t** you in the way you should go;
	51: 13	I will **t** transgressors your ways,
	90: 12	**T** us to number our days, that we
	143: 10	**T** me to do your will, for you are
Jer	31: 34	longer will they **t** their neighbor,
Lk	11: 1	"Lord, **t** us to pray, just as John
Jn	14: 26	will **t** you all things and will
1Ti	2: 12	I do not permit a woman to **t**
	3: 2	respectable, hospitable, able to **t**,
Titus	2: 1	**t** what is appropriate to sound
Heb	8: 11	longer will they **t** their neighbor,
Jas	3: 1	that we who **t** will be judged more
1Jn	2: 27	you do not need anyone to **t** you.

TEACHER (TEACH)

Mt	10: 24	"The student is not above the **t**,
	23: 8	for you have one **T**, and you are
Jn	13: 14	your Lord and **T**, have washed

TEACHERS (TEACH)

1Co	12: 28	prophets, third **t**, then miracles,
Eph	4: 11	the evangelists, the pastors and **t**,
Heb	5: 12	by this time you ought to be **t**,

TEACHES (TEACH)

1Ti	6: 3	If anyone **t** otherwise and does not

TEACHING (TEACH)

Pr	1: 8	and do not forsake your mother's **t**.
Mt	28: 20	**t** them to obey everything I have
Jn	7: 17	out whether my **t** comes from God
	14: 23	who loves me will obey my **t**.
1Ti	4: 13	of Scripture, to preaching and to **t**.
2Ti	3: 16	is God-breathed and is useful for **t**,
Titus	2: 7	In your **t** show integrity,

TEAR (TEARS)

Rev	7: 17	God will wipe away every **t**

TEARS (TEAR)

Ps	126: 5	Those who sow with **t** will reap
Php	3: 18	and now tell you again even with **t**,

TEETH (TOOTH)

Mt	8: 12	will be weeping and gnashing of **t**."

TEMPERATE

1Ti	3: 2	reproach, faithful to his wife, **t**,
	3: 11	not malicious talkers but **t**
Titus	2: 2	Teach the older men to be **t**,

TEMPEST

Ps	55: 8	shelter, far from the **t** and storm."

TEMPLE (TEMPLES)
1Ki	8:	27	How much less this **t** I have built!
Hab	2:	20	The Lᴏʀᴅ is in his holy **t**;
1Co	3:	16	that you yourselves are God's **t**
2Co	6:	16	For we are the **t** of the living God.

TEMPLES (TEMPLE)
| Ac | 17: | 24 | does not live in **t** built by human |
| 1Co | 6: | 19 | your bodies are **t** of the Holy Spirit, |

TEMPT (TEMPTATION TEMPTED)
| 1Co | 7: | 5 | Satan will not **t** you because of |

TEMPTATION (TEMPT)
Mt	6:	13	lead us not into **t**, but deliver us
	26:	41	pray so that you will not fall into **t**.
1Co	10:	13	No **t** has overtaken you except

TEMPTED (TEMPT)
Mt	4:	1	the wilderness to be **t** by the devil.
1Co	10:	13	not let you be **t** beyond what you
Heb	2:	18	he himself suffered when he was **t**,
	2:	18	able to help those who are being **t**.
	4:	15	but we have one who has been **t**
Jas	1:	13	For God cannot be **t** by evil,

TEN (TENTH TITHE TITHES)
Ex	34:	28	the **T** Commandments.
Ps	91:	7	side, **t** thousand at your right hand,
Mt	25:	28	give it to the one who has **t** bags.
Lk	15:	8	suppose a woman has **t** silver coins

TENTH (TEN)
| Dt | 14: | 22 | Be sure to set aside a **t** of all |

TERRIBLE (TERROR)
| 2Ti | 3: | 1 | There will be **t** times in the last |

TERROR (TERRIBLE)
Ps	91:	5	You will not fear the **t** of night,
Lk	21:	26	People will faint from **t**,
Ro	13:	3	rulers hold no **t** for those who do

TEST (TESTED TESTS)
Dt	6:	16	your God to the **t** as you did
Ps	139:	23	**t** me and know my anxious
Ro	12:	2	you will be able to **t** and approve
1Co	3:	13	the fire will **t** the quality of each
1Jn	4:	1	**t** the spirits to see whether they are

TESTED (TEST)
Ge	22:	1	Some time later God **t** Abraham.
Job	23:	10	when he has **t** me, I will come forth
Pr	27:	21	but people are **t** by their praise.
1Ti	3:	10	They must first be **t**;

TESTIFY (TESTIMONY)
| Jn | 5: | 39 | These are the very Scriptures that **t** |

TESTIMONY (TESTIFY)
Isa	8:	20	instruction and the **t** of warning.
Lk	18:	20	you shall not give false **t**,
2Ti	1:	8	be ashamed of the **t** about our Lord

TESTS (TEST)
| Pr | 17: | 3 | for gold, but the Lᴏʀᴅ **t** the heart. |
| 1Th | 2: | 4 | people but God, who **t** our hearts. |

THADDAEUS
Apostle (Mt 10:3; Mk 3:18); probably also known as Judas son of James (Lk 6:16; Ac 1:13).

THANKFUL (THANKS)
| Heb | 12: | 28 | let us be **t**, and so worship God |

THANKS (THANKFUL THANKSGIVING)
Ne	12:	31	assigned two large choirs to give **t**.
Ps	100:	4	give **t** to him and praise his name.
1Co	15:	57	But **t** be to God! He gives us
2Co	2:	14	But **t** be to God, who always leads
	9:	15	**T** be to God for his indescribable
1Th	5:	18	give **t** in all circumstances;

THANKSGIVING (THANKS)
Ps	95:	2	Let us come before him with **t**
	100:	4	Enter his gates with **t** and his
Php	4:	6	**t**, present your requests to God.
1Ti	4:	3	to be received with **t** by those who

THIEF (THIEVES)
| 1Th | 5: | 2 | of the Lord will come like a **t** |
| Rev | 16: | 15 | "Look, I come like a **t**! |

THIEVES (THIEF)
| 1Co | 6: | 10 | nor **t** nor the greedy nor drunkards |

THINK (THOUGHT THOUGHTS)
| Ro | 12: | 3 | Do not **t** of yourself more highly |
| Php | 4: | 8 | **t** about such things. |

THIRST (THIRSTY)
Ps	69:	21	food and gave me vinegar for my **t**.
Mt	5:	6	hunger and **t** for righteousness,
Jn	4:	14	the water I give them will never **t**.

THIRSTY (THIRST)
Isa	55:	1	all you who are **t**,
Jn	7:	37	"Let anyone who is **t** come to me
Rev	22:	17	Let the one who is **t** come;

THOMAS
Apostle (Mt 10:3; Mk 3:18; Lk 6:15; Jn 11:16; 14:5; 21:2; Ac 1:13). Doubted resurrection (Jn 20:24–28).

THORN (THORNS)
| 2Co | 12: | 7 | I was given a **t** in my flesh, |

THORNS (THORN)
Nu	33:	55	in your eyes and **t** in your sides.
Mt	27:	29	twisted together a crown of **t** and
Heb	6:	8	land that produces **t** and thistles is

THOUGHT (THINK)
| Pr | 14: | 15 | the prudent give **t** to their steps. |
| 1Co | 13: | 11 | I talked like a child, I **t** like a child, |

THOUGHTS (THINK)
Ps	139:	23	test me and know my anxious **t**.
Isa	55:	8	"For my **t** are not your **t**, neither
Heb	4:	12	it judges the **t** and attitudes

THREE
Ecc	4:	12	of **t** strands is not quickly broken.
Mt	12:	40	the Son of Man will be **t** days and **t** nights in the heart of the earth.
	18:	20	where two or **t** gather in my name,
	27:	63	said, 'After **t** days I will rise again.'
1Co	13:	13	And now these **t** remain:
	14:	27	or at the most **t**—should speak,
2Co	13:	1	testimony of two or **t** witnesses."

THRESHING
| 2Sa | 24: | 18 | altar to the Lᴏʀᴅ on the **t** floor |

THRONE (ENTHRONED)
2Sa	7:	16	your **t** will be established
Ps	45:	6	Your **t**, O God, will last for ever
	47:	8	God is seated on his holy **t**.
Isa	6:	1	high and exalted, seated on a **t**;

CONCORDANCE

Isa	66:	1	"Heaven is my **t**, and the earth is
Heb	4:	16	then approach God's **t** of grace
	12:	2	at the right hand of the **t** of God.
Rev	4:	10	They lay their crowns before the **t**
	20:	11	I saw a great white **t** and him who
	22:	3	The **t** of God and of the Lamb will

THROW

Jn	8:	7	*the first to **t** a stone at her."*
Heb	10:	35	So do not **t** away your confidence;
	12:	1	let us **t** off everything that hinders

THWART

Isa	14:	27	has purposed, and who can **t** him?

TIBNI

King of Israel (1Ki 16:21–22).

TIME (TIMES)

Est	4:	14	royal position for such a **t** as this?"
Da	7:	25	be delivered into his hands for a **t**,
			times and half a **t**.
Hos	10:	12	for it is **t** to seek the LORD,
Ro	9:	9	"At the appointed **t** I will return,
Heb	9:	28	and he will appear a second **t**,
	10:	12	had offered for all **t** one sacrifice
1Pe	4:	17	For it is **t** for judgment to begin

TIMES (TIME)

Ps	9:	9	a stronghold in **t** of trouble.
	31:	15	My **t** are in your hands;
	62:	8	Trust in him at all **t**, you people;
Pr	17:	17	A friend loves at all **t**,
Am	5:	13	in such **t**, for the **t** are evil.
Mt	18:	21	sins against me? Up to seven **t**?"
Ac	1:	7	"It is not for you to know the **t**
Rev	12:	14	care of for a time, **t** and half a time,

TIMID

2Ti	1:	7	God gave us does not make us **t**,

TIMOTHY

Believer from Lystra (Ac 16:1). Joined Paul on second missionary journey (Ac 16–20). Sent to settle problems at Corinth (1Co 4:17; 16:10). Led church at Ephesus (1Ti 1:3). Co-writer with Paul (1Th 1:1; 2Th 1:1; Phm 1).

TIRE (TIRED)

2Th	3:	13	never **t** of doing what is good.

TIRED (TIRE)

Ex	17:	12	When Moses' hands grew **t**,
Isa	40:	28	He will not grow **t** or weary,

TITHE (TEN)

Lev	27:	30	" 'A **t** of everything
Dt	12:	17	your own towns the **t** of your grain
Mal	3:	10	Bring the whole **t**

TITHES (TEN)

Mal	3:	8	"In **t** and offerings.

TITUS

Gentile co-worker of Paul (Gal 2:1–3; 2Ti 4:10); sent to Corinth (2Co 2:13; 7–8; 12:18), Crete (Titus 1:4–5).

TODAY

Mt	6:	11	Give us **t** our daily bread.
Lk	23:	43	**t** you will be with me in paradise."
Heb	3:	13	as long as it is called "**T**,"
	13:	8	Christ is the same yesterday and **t**

TOIL

Ge	3:	17	through painful **t** you will eat food

TOLERATE

Hab	1:	13	then do you **t** the treacherous?
Rev	2:	2	that you cannot **t** wicked people,

TOMB

Mt	27:	65	make the **t** as secure as you know
Lk	24:	2	the stone rolled away from the **t**,

TOMORROW

Pr	27:	1	not boast about **t**, for you do not
Isa	22:	13	drink," you say, "for **t** we die!"
Mt	6:	34	do not worry about **t**, for it
Jas	4:	13	"Today or **t** we will go to this

TONGUE (TONGUES)

Ps	39:	1	my ways and keep my **t** from sin;
Pr	12:	18	but the **t** of the wise brings healing.
1Co	14:	2	who speaks in a **t** does not speak
	14:	4	speaks in a **t** edifies themselves,
	14:	13	one who speaks in a **t** should pray
	14:	19	than ten thousand words in a **t**.
Php	2:	11	and every **t** acknowledge that Jesus
Jas	3:	8	no human being can tame the **t**.

TONGUES (TONGUE)

Isa	28:	11	strange **t** God will speak to this
Mk	16:	17	*they will speak in new **t**;*
Ac	2:	4	other **t** as the Spirit enabled them.
	10:	46	For they heard them speaking in **t**
	19:	6	they spoke in **t** and prophesied.
1Co	12:	30	Do all speak in **t**? Do all interpret?
	14:	18	I speak in **t** more than all of you.
	14:	39	and do not forbid speaking in **t**.
Jas	1:	26	rein on their **t** deceive themselves,

TOOK (TAKE)

1Co	11:	23	the night he was betrayed, **t** bread,
Php	3:	12	which Christ Jesus **t** hold of me.

TOOTH (TEETH)

Ex	21:	24	eye for eye, **t** for **t**, hand for hand,
Mt	5:	38	was said, 'Eye for eye, and **t** for **t**.'

TORMENTED

Rev	20:	10	They will be **t** day and night

TORN

Gal	4:	15	you would have **t** out your eyes
Php	1:	23	I am **t** between the two: I desire

TOUCH

Ps	105:	15	"Do not **t** my anointed ones;
Lk	24:	39	**T** me and see; a ghost does not
2Co	6:	17	**T** no unclean thing, and I will
Col	2:	21	Do not taste! Do not **t**!"?

TOUCHED (TOUCH)

1Sa	10:	26	men whose hearts God had **t**.
Mt	14:	36	cloak, and all who **t** it were healed.

TOWER

Ge	11:	4	a **t** that reaches to the heavens,
Pr	18:	10	name of the LORD is a fortified **t**;

TOWN (TOWNS)

Mt	5:	14	**t** built on a hill cannot be hidden.

TOWNS (TOWN)

Nu	35:	2	to give the Levites **t** to live
	35:	15	These six **t** will be a place of refuge

TRACING
Ro 11: 33 and his paths beyond **t** out!

TRADITION
Mt 15: 6 word of God for the sake of your **t**.
Col 2: 8 which depends on human **t**

TRAINING
1Co 9: 25 in the games goes into strict **t**.
2Ti 3: 16 correcting and **t** in righteousness,

TRAMPLED
Lk 21: 24 Jerusalem will be **t**
Heb 10: 29 to be punished who has **t** the Son

TRANCE
Ac 10: 10 was being prepared, he fell into a **t**.

TRANSCENDS
Php 4: 7 God, which **t** all understanding,

TRANSFIGURED
Mt 17: 2 There he was **t** before them.

TRANSFORM (TRANSFORMED)
Php 3: 21 will **t** our lowly bodies so that they

TRANSFORMED (TRANSFORM)
Ro 12: 2 be **t** by the renewing of your mind.
2Co 3: 18 are being **t** into his image

TRANSGRESSION (TRANSGRESSIONS
  TRANSGRESSORS)
Isa 53: 8 **t** of my people he was punished.
Ro 4: 15 where there is no law there is no **t**.

TRANSGRESSIONS (TRANSGRESSION)
Ps 32: 1 is the one whose **t** are forgiven,
 51: 1 great compassion blot out my **t**.
 103: 12 so far has he removed our **t** from
Isa 53: 5 But he was pierced for our **t**,
Eph 2: 1 you were dead in your **t** and sins,

TRANSGRESSORS (TRANSGRESSION)
Ps 51: 13 Then I will teach **t** your ways,
Isa 53: 12 and was numbered with the **t**.
 53: 12 and made intercession for the **t**.

TREADING
Dt 25: 4 Do not muzzle an ox while it is **t**
1Co 9: 9 "Do not muzzle an ox while it is **t**

TREASURE (TREASURED TREASURES)
Isa 33: 6 of the LORD is the key to this **t**.
Mt 6: 21 where your **t** is, there your heart
2Co 4: 7 But we have this **t** in jars of clay

TREASURED (TREASURE)
Dt 7: 6 to be his people, his **t** possession.
Lk 2: 19 But Mary **t** up all these things

TREASURES (TREASURE)
Mt 6: 19 store up for yourselves **t** on earth,
Col 2: 3 in whom are hidden all the **t**
Heb 11: 26 of greater value than the **t** of Egypt,

TREAT
Lev 22: 2 sons to **t** with respect the sacred
1Ti 5: 1 **T** younger men as brothers,
1Pe 3: 7 **t** them with respect as the weaker

TREATY
Dt 7: 2 Make no **t** with them, and show

TREE
Ge 2: 9 of the garden were the **t** of life

Ge 2: 9 and the **t** of the knowledge of good
Ps 1: 3 is like a **t** planted by streams
Mt 3: 10 every **t** that does not produce good
 12: 33 for a **t** is recognized by its fruit.
Rev 22: 14 may have the right to the **t** of life

TREMBLE (TREMBLING)
1Ch 16: 30 **T** before him, all the earth!
Ps 114: 7 **T**, earth, at the presence of the Lord,

TREMBLING (TREMBLE)
Ps 2: 11 fear and celebrate his rule with **t**.
Php 2: 12 out your salvation with fear and **t**,

TRESPASS
Ro 5: 17 if, by the **t** of the one man,

TRIALS
1Th 3: 3 one would be unsettled by these **t**.
Jas 1: 2 whenever you face **t** of many kinds,
2Pe 2: 9 how to rescue the godly from **t**

TRIBES
Ge 49: 28 All these are the twelve **t** of Israel,
Mt 19: 28 judging the twelve **t** of Israel.

TRIBULATION
Rev 7: 14 who have come out of the great **t**;

TRIUMPHAL (TRIUMPHING)
Isa 60: 11 their kings led in **t** procession.
2Co 2: 14 as captives in Christ's **t** procession

TRIUMPHING (TRIUMPHAL)
Col 2: 15 of them, **t** over them by the cross.

TROUBLE (TROUBLED TROUBLES)
Job 14: 1 are of few days and full of **t**.
Ps 46: 1 strength, an ever-present help in **t**.
 107: 13 they cried to the LORD in their **t**,
Pr 24: 10 If you falter in a time of **t**,
Mt 6: 34 Each day has enough **t** of its own.
Jn 16: 33 In this world you will have **t**.
Ro 8: 35 Shall **t** or hardship or persecution

TROUBLED (TROUBLE)
Jn 14: 1 "Do not let your hearts be **t**.
 14: 27 Do not let your hearts be **t** and do

TROUBLES (TROUBLE)
1Co 7: 28 those who marry will face many **t**
2Co 1: 4 who comforts us in all our **t**,
 4: 17 momentary **t** are achieving for us

TRUE (TRUTH)
Dt 18: 22 does not take place or come **t**,
1Sa 9: 6 and everything he says comes **t**.
Ps 119:160 All your words are **t**; all your
Jn 17: 3 the only **t** God, and Jesus Christ,
Ro 3: 4 Let God be **t**, and every human
Php 4: 8 whatever is **t**, whatever is noble,
Rev 22: 6 These words are trustworthy and **t**.

TRUMPET
1Co 14: 8 if the **t** does not sound a clear call,
 15: 52 twinkling of an eye, at the last **t**.

TRUST (ENTRUSTED TRUSTED TRUSTWORTHY)
Ps 20: 7 we **t** in the name of the LORD our
 37: 3 **T** in the LORD and do good;
 56: 4 in God I **t** and am not afraid.
 119: 42 taunts me, for I **t** in your word.
Pr 3: 5 **T** in the LORD with all your heart

CONCORDANCE

Isa 30: 15 in quietness and **t** is your strength,
1Co 4: 2 been given a **t** must prove faithful.

TRUSTED (TRUST)
Ps 26: 1 I have **t** in the LORD and have not
Isa 25: 9 we **t** in him, and he saved us.
Da 3: 28 They **t** in him and defied the king's
Lk 16: 10 "Whoever can be **t** with very little

TRUSTWORTHY (TRUST)
Ps 119:138 are righteous; they are fully **t**.
Pr 11: 13 but a **t** person keeps a secret.
Rev 22: 6 to me, "These words are **t** and true.

TRUTH (TRUE TRUTHFUL TRUTHS)
Isa 45: 19 I, the LORD, speak the **t**;
Zec 8: 16 Speak the **t** to each other,
Jn 4: 23 the Father in the Spirit and in **t**,
8: 32 Then you will know the **t**, and the **t**
14: 6 "I am the way and the **t** and the life.
16: 13 he will guide you into all the **t**.
18: 38 "What is **t**?" retorted Pilate.
Ro 1: 25 They exchanged the **t** about God
1Co 13: 6 in evil but rejoices with the **t**.
2Co 13: 8 against the **t**, but only for the **t**.
Eph 4: 15 Instead, speaking the **t** in love,
6: 14 belt of **t** buckled around your waist,
2Th 2: 10 because they refused to love the **t**
1Ti 2: 4 to come to a knowledge of the **t**.
3: 15 the pillar and foundation of the **t**.
2Ti 2: 15 correctly handles the word of **t**.
3: 7 to come to a knowledge of the **t**.
Heb 10: 26 received the knowledge of the **t**,
1Pe 1: 22 by obeying the **t** so that you have
2Pe 2: 2 and will bring the way of **t**
1Jn 1: 6 we lie and do not live out the **t**.
1: 8 ourselves and the **t** is not in us.

TRUTHFUL (TRUTH)
Jn 3: 33 it has certified that God is **t**.

TRUTHS (TRUTH)
1Ti 3: 9 keep hold of the deep **t** of the faith
Heb 5: 12 teach you the elementary **t** of God's

TRY (TRYING)
Ps 26: 2 and **t** me, examine my heart and
Isa 7: 13 Will you **t** the patience of my God
1Co 14: 12 **t** to excel in those that build
2Co 5: 11 the Lord, we **t** to persuade others.

TRYING (TRY)
2Co 5: 12 We are not **t** to commend ourselves
1Th 2: 4 We are not **t** to please people

TURN (TURNED TURNS)
Ex 32: 12 **T** from your fierce anger;
Dt 5: 32 do not **t** aside to the right
28: 14 Do not **t** aside from any
Jos 1: 7 do not **t** from it to the right
2Ch 7: 14 face and **t** from their wicked ways,
30: 9 He will not **t** his face from you
Ps 78: 6 they in **t** would tell their children.
Pr 22: 6 they are old they will not **t** from it.
Isa 29: 16 You **t** things upside down,
30: 21 Whether you **t** to the right
45: 22 "**T** to me and be saved, all you ends
55: 7 Let them **t** to the LORD, and he
Eze 33: 11 they **t** from their ways and live.
Mal 4: 6 He will **t** the hearts of the parents

Mt 5: 39 **t** to them the other cheek also.
10: 35 to **t** " 'a man against his father,
Jn 12: 40 understand with their hearts, nor **t**
Ac 3: 19 and **t** to God, so that your sins may
26: 18 and **t** them from darkness to light,
1Ti 6: 20 **T** away from godless chatter
1Pe 3: 11 must **t** from evil and do good;

TURNED (TURN)
Ps 30: 11 You **t** my wailing into dancing;
40: 1 he **t** to me and heard my cry.
Isa 53: 6 each of us has **t** to our own way;
Hos 7: 8 Ephraim is a flat loaf not **t** over.
Joel 2: 31 The sun will be **t** to darkness
Ro 3: 12 All have **t** away, they have together

TURNS (TURN)
2Sa 22: 29 the LORD **t** my darkness
Pr 15: 1 A gentle answer **t** away wrath,
Isa 44: 25 of the wise and **t** it into nonsense,
Jas 5: 20 Whoever **t** a sinner from the error

TWELVE
Ge 49: 28 All these are the **t** tribes of Israel,
Mt 10: 1 Jesus called his **t** disciples to him

TWINKLING
1Co 15: 52 a flash, in the **t** of an eye, at the last

UNAPPROACHABLE
1Ti 6: 16 immortal and who lives in **u** light,

UNBELIEF (UNBELIEVER UNBELIEVERS
UNBELIEVING)
Mk 9: 24 help me overcome my **u**!"
Ro 11: 20 they were broken off because of **u**,
Heb 3: 19 able to enter, because of their **u**.

UNBELIEVER (UNBELIEF)
1Co 7: 15 But if the **u** leaves, let it be so.
10: 27 If an **u** invites you to a meal
14: 24 if an **u** or an inquirer comes in
2Co 6: 15 have in common with an **u**?
1Ti 5: 8 the faith and is worse than an **u**.

UNBELIEVERS (UNBELIEF)
1Co 6: 6 and this in front of **u**!
2Co 6: 14 Do not be yoked together with **u**.

UNBELIEVING (UNBELIEF)
1Co 7: 14 the **u** husband has been sanctified
7: 14 and the **u** wife has been sanctified
Rev 21: 8 But the cowardly, the **u**, the vile,

UNCERTAIN
1Ti 6: 17 which is so **u**, but to put their hope

UNCHANGEABLE
Heb 6: 18 that, by two **u** things in which it is

UNCIRCUMCISED
1Sa 17: 26 Who is this **u** Philistine that he
Col 3: 11 or Jew, circumcised or **u**,

UNCIRCUMCISION
1Co 7: 19 is nothing and **u** is nothing.
Gal 6: 6 neither circumcision nor **u** has any

UNCLEAN
Isa 6: 5 For I am a man of **u** lips, and I live
Ro 14: 14 Jesus, that nothing is **u** in itself.
2Co 6: 17 Touch no **u** thing, and I will

UNCONCERNED
Eze 16: 49 were arrogant, overfed and **u**;

UNCOVERED
Heb 4: 13 Everything is **u** and laid bare

UNDERSTAND (UNDERSTANDING UNDERSTANDS)
Job 42: 3 Surely I spoke of things I did not **u**,
Ps 73: 16 When I tried to **u** all this,
  119:125 that I may **u** your statutes.
Lk 24: 45 so they could **u** the Scriptures.
Ac 8: 30 "Do you **u** what you are reading?"
Ro 7: 15 I do not **u** what I do. For what I
1Co 2: 14 and cannot **u** them because they
Eph 5: 17 but **u** what the Lord's will is.
2Pe 3: 16 some things that are hard to **u**,

UNDERSTANDING (UNDERSTAND)
Ps 119: 32 for you have broadened my **u**.
  119:104 I gain **u** from your precepts;
  147: 5 in power; his **u** has no limit.
Pr 3: 5 heart and lean not on your own **u**;
  4: 7 Though it cost all you have, get **u**.
  10: 23 a person of **u** delights in wisdom.
  11: 12 one who has **u** holds their tongue.
  15: 21 but whoever has **u** keeps a straight
  15: 32 one who heeds correction gains **u**.
Isa 40: 28 and his **u** no one can fathom.
Da 5: 12 a keen mind and knowledge and **u**,
Mk 4: 12 and ever hearing but never **u**;
  12: 33 with all your **u** and with all your
Php 4: 7 which transcends all **u**, will guard

UNDERSTANDS (UNDERSTAND)
1Ch 28: 9 every heart and **u** every desire

UNDIVIDED
1Ch 12: 33 to help David with **u** loyalty—
Ps 86: 11 give me an **u** heart, that I may fear
Eze 11: 19 I will give them an **u** heart and put
1Co 7: 35 in a right way in **u** devotion

UNDOING
Pr 18: 7 The mouths of fools are their **u**,

UNDYING
Eph 6: 24 Lord Jesus Christ with an **u** love.

UNFADING
1Pe 3: 4 the **u** beauty of a gentle and quiet

UNFAILING
Ps 33: 5 the earth is full of his **u** love.
  119: 76 May your **u** love be my comfort,
  143: 8 bring me word of your **u** love, for I
Pr 19: 22 What a person desires is **u** love;
La 3: 32 compassion, so great is his **u** love.

UNFAITHFUL
Lev 6: 2 is **u** to the Lord by deceiving
1Ch 10: 13 Saul died because he was **u**
Pr 13: 15 but the way of the **u** leads to their

UNFOLDING
Ps 119:130 The **u** of your words gives light;

UNGODLINESS
Titus 2: 12 It teaches us to say "No" to **u**

UNITED (UNITY)
Ro 6: 5 For if we have been **u** with him
Php 2: 1 from being **u** with Christ, if any
Col 2: 2 encouraged in heart and **u** in love,

UNITY (UNITED)
Ps 133: 1 God's people live together in **u**!
Eph 4: 3 keep the **u** of the Spirit through
  4: 13 until we all reach **u** in the faith
Col 3: 14 them all together in perfect **u**.

UNIVERSE
Heb 1: 2 through whom also he made the **u**.

UNKNOWN
Ac 17: 23 with this inscription: TO AN **u** GOD.

UNLEAVENED
Ex 12: 17 "Celebrate the Festival of **U** Bread,

UNPROFITABLE
Titus 3: 9 because these are **u** and useless.

UNPUNISHED
Ex 34: 7 Yet he does not leave the guilty **u**;
Pr 19: 5 A false witness will not go **u**,

UNREPENTANT
Ro 2: 5 stubbornness and your **u** heart,

UNRIGHTEOUS
Zep 3: 5 not fail, yet the **u** know no shame.
Mt 5: 45 rain on the righteous and the **u**.
1Pe 3: 18 the righteous for the **u**, to bring
2Pe 2: 9 to hold the **u** for punishment

UNSEARCHABLE
Ro 11: 33 How **u** his judgments, and his

UNSEEN
2Co 4: 18 temporary, but what is **u** is eternal.

UNSTABLE
Jas 1: 8 double-minded and **u** in all they
2Pe 2: 14 they seduce the **u**; they are experts
  3: 16 ignorant and **u** people distort,

UNTHINKABLE
Job 34: 12 It is **u** that God would do wrong,

UNVEILED
2Co 3: 18 with **u** faces contemplate the Lord's

UNWORTHY
Job 40: 4 "I am **u**—how can I reply to you?
Lk 17: 10 do, should say, 'We are **u** servants;

UPRIGHT
Job 1: 1 This man was blameless and **u**;
Pr 2: 7 He holds success in store for the **u**,
  15: 8 but the prayer of the **u** pleases him.
Titus 1: 8 who is self-controlled, **u**,
  2: 12 **u** and godly lives in this present

UPROOTED
Jude : 12 autumn trees, without fruit and **u**

USEFUL
2Ti 2: 21 **u** to the Master and prepared to do
  3: 16 God-breathed and is **u** for teaching

USELESS
1Co 15: 14 our preaching is **u** and so is your
Jas 2: 20 that faith without deeds is **u**?

UZZIAH
Son of Amaziah; king of Judah also known as Azariah (2Ki 15:1–7; 1Ch 6:24; 2Ch 26).

VAIN
Ps 33: 17 A horse is a **v** hope for deliverance;

1643

CONCORDANCE

Isa	65:	23	They will not labor in **v**, nor will
1Co	15:	2	Otherwise, you have believed in **v**.
	15:	58	your labor in the Lord is not in **v**.
2Co	6:	1	you not to receive God's grace in **v**.

VALLEY

Ps	23:	4	I walk through the darkest **v**,
Isa	40:	4	Every **v** shall be raised up,
Joel	3:	14	Lord is near in the **v** of decision.

VALUABLE (VALUE)

Lk	12:	24	how much more **v** you are than

VALUE (VALUABLE)

Mt	13:	46	When he found one of great **v**,
1Ti	4:	8	For physical training is of some **v**, but godliness has **v** for all things,
Heb	11:	26	as of greater **v** than the treasures

VEIL

Ex	34:	33	to them, he put a **v** over his face.
2Co	3:	14	to this day the same **v** remains

VENGEANCE (AVENGE REVENGE)

Isa	34:	8	For the Lord has a day of **v**,

VICTORIES (VICTORY)

Ps	18:	50	He gives his king great **v**;
	21:	1	great is his joy in the **v** you give!

VICTORIOUS (VICTORY)

Zec	9:	9	king comes to you, righteous and **v**,
Rev	2:	7	To the one who is **v**, I will give
	2:	11	The one who is **v** will not be hurt
	2:	17	To the one who is **v**, I will give
	2:	26	To the one who is **v** and does my
	3:	5	The one who is **v** will, like them,
	3:	12	The one who is **v** I will make
	3:	21	To the one who is **v**, I will give
	21:	7	Those who are **v** will inherit all

VICTORIOUSLY (VICTORY)

Ps	45:	4	In your majesty ride forth **v**

VICTORY (VICTORIES VICTORIOUS VICTORIOUSLY)

Ps	60:	12	With God we will gain the **v**,
1Co	15:	54	has been swallowed up in **v**."
	15:	57	He gives us the **v** through our Lord
1Jn	5:	4	This is the **v** that has overcome

VINDICATED

1Ti	3:	16	in the flesh, was **v** by the Spirit,

VINE

Jn	15:	1	"I am the true **v**, and my Father is

VINEGAR

Mk	15:	36	filled a sponge with wine **v**, put it

VIOLATION

Heb	2:	2	every **v** and disobedience received

VIOLENCE

Isa	60:	18	No longer will **v** be heard in your
Eze	45:	9	Give up your **v** and oppression

VIPERS

Ro	3:	13	"The poison of **v** is on their lips."

VIRGIN

Isa	7:	14	The **v** will conceive and give birth
Mt	1:	23	"The **v** will conceive and give birth
2Co	11:	2	I might present you as a pure **v**

VIRTUES

Col	3:	14	And over all these **v** put on love,

VISION

Ac	26:	19	disobedient to the **v** from heaven.

VOICE

Ps	95:	7	if only you would hear his **v**,
Isa	30:	21	your ears will hear a **v** behind you,
Jn	5:	28	are in their graves will hear his **v**
	10:	3	him, and the sheep listen to his **v**.
Heb	3:	7	"Today, if you hear his **v**,
Rev	3:	20	If anyone hears my **v** and opens

VOMIT

Pr	26:	11	As a dog returns to its **v**, so fools
2Pe	2:	22	"A dog returns to its **v**," and,

VOW

Nu	30:	2	a man makes a **v** to the Lord

WAGES

Lk	10:	7	you, for the worker deserves his **w**.
Ro	4:	4	**w** are not credited as a gift but as
	6:	23	the **w** of sin is death, but the gift

WAILING

Ps	30:	11	You turned my **w** into dancing;

WAIST

2Ki	1:	8	had a leather belt around his **w**."
Mt	3:	4	he had a leather belt around his **w**.

WAIT (WAITED WAITS)

Ps	27:	14	**W** for the Lord; be strong
	130:	5	I **w** for the Lord, my whole being
Isa	30:	18	Blessed are all who **w** for him!
Ac	1:	4	**w** for the gift my Father promised,
Ro	8:	23	groan inwardly as we **w** eagerly
1Th	1:	10	and to **w** for his Son from heaven,
Titus	2:	13	while we **w** for the blessed hope—

WAITED (WAIT)

Ps	40:	1	I **w** patiently for the Lord;

WAITS (WAIT)

Ro	8:	19	the creation **w** in eager expectation

WALK (WALKED)

Dt	11:	19	and when you **w** along the road,
Ps	1:	1	Blessed is the one who does not **w**
	23:	4	though I **w** through the darkest
	89:	15	**w** in the light of your presence,
Isa	2:	5	let us **w** in the light of the Lord.
	30:	21	saying, "This is the way; **w** in it."
	40:	31	weary, they will **w** and not be faint.
Jer	6:	16	and **w** in it, and you will find rest
Da	4:	37	those who **w** in pride he is able
Am	3:	3	Do two **w** together unless they
Mic	6:	8	and to **w** humbly with your God.
Mk	2:	9	say, 'Get up, take your mat and **w**'?
Jn	8:	12	Whoever follows me will never **w**
1Jn	1:	7	But if we **w** in the light, as he is
2Jn	:	6	his command is that you **w** in love.

WALKED (WALK)

Ge	5:	24	Enoch **w** faithfully with God;
Jos	14:	9	which your feet have **w** will be
Mt	14:	29	**w** on the water and came toward

WALL

Jos	6:	20	gave a loud shout, the **w** collapsed;
Ne	2:	17	let us rebuild the **w** of Jerusalem,
Rev	21:	12	a great, high **w** with twelve gates,

WALLOWING

2Pe	2:	22	returns to her **w** in the mud."

WANT (WANTED WANTING WANTS)
1Sa	8: 19	they said. "We **w** a king over us.
Lk	19: 14	say, 'We don't **w** this man to be our
Ro	7: 15	For what I **w** to do I do not do,
Php	3: 10	I **w** to know Christ—yes, to know

WANTED (WANT)
| 1Co | 12: 18 | of them, just as he **w** them to be. |

WANTING (WANT)
| Da | 5: 27 | weighed on the scales and found **w**. |
| 2Pe | 3: 9 | with you, not **w** anyone to perish, |

WANTS (WANT)
Mt	20: 26	whoever **w** to become great among
Mk	8: 35	For whoever **w** to save their life
Ro	9: 18	on whom he **w** to have mercy,
	9: 18	he hardens whom he **w** to harden.
1Ti	2: 4	who **w** all people to be saved

WAR (WARS)
Isa	2: 4	nor will they train for **w** anymore.
Da	9: 26	**W** will continue until the end,
2Co	10: 3	we do not wage **w** as the world
Rev	19: 11	justice he judges and wages **w**.

WARN (WARNED WARNINGS)
| Eze | 3: 19 | if you do **w** the wicked person |
| | 33: 9 | if you do **w** the wicked person |

WARNED (WARN)
| Ps | 19: 11 | By them your servant is **w**; |

WARNINGS (WARN)
| 1Co | 10: 11 | and were written down as **w** for us, |

WARS (WAR)
| Ps | 46: 9 | He makes **w** cease to the ends |
| Mt | 24: 6 | will hear of **w** and rumors of **w**, |

WASH (WASHED WASHING)
Ps	51: 7	**w** me, and I will be whiter than
Jn	13: 5	and began to **w** his disciples' feet,
Ac	22: 16	be baptized and **w** your sins away,
Rev	22: 14	are those who **w** their robes,

WASHED (WASH)
| 1Co | 6: 11 | But you were **w**, you were |
| Rev | 7: 14 | they have **w** their robes and made |

WASHING (WASH)
| Eph | 5: 26 | the **w** with water through the word, |
| Titus | 3: 5 | saved us through the **w** of rebirth |

WATCH (WATCHES WATCHING WATCHMAN)
Ge	31: 49	the Lord keep **w** between you
Jer	31: 10	them and will **w** over his flock like
Mt	24: 42	"Therefore keep **w**, because you do
	26: 41	"**W** and pray so that you will not
Lk	2: 8	keeping **w** over their flocks at night
1Ti	4: 16	**W** your life and doctrine closely.

WATCHES (WATCH)
| Ps | 1: 6 | For the Lord **w** over the way |
| | 121: 3 | he who **w** over you will not |

WATCHING (WATCH)
| Lk | 12: 37 | servants whose master finds them **w** |

WATCHMAN (WATCH)
| Eze | 3: 17 | I have made you a **w** for the people |

WATER (WATERED WATERS)
| Ps | 1: 3 | like a tree planted by streams of **w**, |
| | 22: 14 | I am poured out like **w**, and all my |

Pr	25: 21	if he is thirsty, give him **w** to drink.
Isa	49: 10	and lead them beside springs of **w**.
Jer	2: 13	broken cisterns that cannot hold **w**.
Zec	14: 8	On that day living **w** will flow
Mk	9: 41	anyone who gives you a cup of **w**
Jn	4: 10	he would have given you living **w**."
	7: 38	rivers of living **w** will flow
Eph	5: 26	washing with **w** through the word,
1Pe	3: 21	this **w** symbolizes baptism that
Rev	21: 6	thirsty I will give **w** without cost

WATERED (WATER)
| 1Co | 3: 6 | I planted the seed, Apollos **w** it, |

WATERS (WATER)
Ps	23: 2	he leads me beside quiet **w**,
Isa	58: 11	like a spring whose **w** never fail.
1Co	3: 7	nor the one who **w** is anything,

WAVE (WAVES)
| Jas | 1: 6 | the one who doubts is like a **w** |

WAVES (WAVE)
Isa	57: 20	whose **w** cast up mire and mud.
Mt	8: 27	the winds and the **w** obey him!"
Eph	4: 14	tossed back and forth by the **w**,

WAY (WAYS)
Dt	1: 33	to show you the **w** you should go.
2Sa	22: 31	"As for God, his **w** is perfect:
Job	23: 10	But he knows the **w** that I take;
Ps	1: 1	stand in the **w** that sinners take
	37: 5	Commit your **w** to the Lord;
	139: 24	and lead me in the **w** everlasting.
Pr	14: 12	is a **w** that appears to be right,
	22: 6	off on the **w** they should go,
Isa	30: 21	behind you, saying, "This is the **w**;
	53: 6	of us has turned to our own **w**;
Mt	3: 3	'Prepare the **w** for the Lord,
Jn	14: 6	"I am the **w** and the truth
1Co	10: 13	provide a **w** out so that you can
	12: 31	will show you the most excellent **w**.
Heb	4: 15	who has been tempted in every **w**,
	9: 8	the **w** into the Most Holy Place had
	10: 20	living **w** opened for us through

WAYS (WAY)
Ex	33: 13	teach me your **w** so I may know
Ps	25: 10	All the **w** of the Lord are loving
	51: 13	I will teach transgressors your **w**,
Pr	3: 6	in all your **w** submit to him, and he
	16: 17	who guard their **w** preserve their
Isa	55: 7	Let the wicked forsake their **w**
	55: 8	neither are your **w** my **w**,"
Jas	3: 2	We all stumble in many **w**.

WEAK (WEAKER WEAKNESS)
Mt	26: 41	spirit is willing, but the flesh is **w**."
Ro	14: 1	Accept the one whose faith is **w**,
1Co	1: 27	chose the **w** things of the world
	8: 9	a stumbling block to the **w**.
	9: 22	To the **w** I became **w**, to win the **w**.
2Co	12: 10	For when I am **w**, then I am strong.
Heb	12: 12	your feeble arms and **w** knees.

WEAKER (WEAK)
| 1Co | 12: 22 | seem to be **w** are indispensable, |
| 1Pe | 3: 7 | them with respect as the **w** partner |

WEAKNESS (WEAK)
| Ro | 8: 26 | way, the Spirit helps us in our **w**. |

CONCORDANCE

1Co	1:	25	**w** of God is stronger than human
2Co	12:	9	my power is made perfect in **w**."
Heb	5:	2	since he himself is subject to **w**.

WEALTH

Pr	3:	9	Honor the Lord with your **w**,
Mk	10:	22	away sad, because he had great **w**.
Lk	15:	13	and there squandered his **w** in wild

WEAPONS

2Co	10:	4	The **w** we fight with are not the **w**

WEARIES (WEARY)

Ecc	12:	12	and much study **w** the body.

WEARY (WEARIES)

Isa	40:	31	they will run and not grow **w**,
Mt	11:	28	all you who are **w** and burdened,
Gal	6:	9	not become **w** in doing good,

WEDDING

Mt	22:	11	who was not wearing **w** clothes.
Rev	19:	7	For the **w** of the Lamb has come,

WEEP (WEEPING WEPT)

Ecc	3:	4	a time to **w** and a time to laugh,
Lk	6:	21	Blessed are you who **w** now, for

WEEPING (WEEP)

Ps	30:	5	**w** may stay for the night,
	126:	6	Those who go out **w**, carrying seed
Mt	8:	12	where there will be **w** and gnashing

WELCOMES

Mt	18:	5	**w** one such child in my name **w** me.
2Jn	:	11	Anyone who **w** them shares in

WELL

Lk	17:	19	your faith has made you **w**."
Jas	5:	15	faith will make the sick person **w**;

WEPT (WEEP)

Ps	137:	1	and **w** when we remembered Zion.
Jn	11:	35	Jesus **w**.

WEST

Ps	103:	12	as far as the east is from the **w**,

WHIRLWIND (WIND)

2Ki	2:	1	to take Elijah up to heaven in a **w**,
Hos	8:	7	They sow the wind and reap the **w**.
Na	1:	3	His way is in the **w** and the storm,

WHITE (WHITER)

Isa	1:	18	scarlet, they shall be as **w** as snow;
Da	7:	9	His clothing was as **w** as snow;
Rev	1:	14	hair on his head was **w** like wool,
	3:	4	dressed in **w**, for they are worthy.
	20:	11	I saw a great **w** throne and him

WHITER (WHITE)

Ps	51:	7	wash me, and I will be **w** than snow.

WHOLE

Mt	16:	26	for someone to gain the **w** world,
	24:	14	in the **w** world as a testimony to all
Jn	13:	10	their **w** body is clean.
	21:	25	even the **w** world would not have
Ac	20:	27	proclaim to you the **w** will of God.
Ro	3:	19	and the **w** world held accountable
	8:	22	the **w** creation has been groaning
Gal	5:	3	he is obligated to obey the **w** law.
Eph	4:	13	attaining to the **w** measure
Jas	2:	10	For whoever keeps the **w** law
1Jn	2:	2	but also for the sins of the **w** world.

WHOLEHEARTEDLY (HEART)

Dt	1:	36	he followed the Lord **w**."
Eph	6:	7	Serve **w**, as if you were serving

WICKED (WICKEDNESS)

Ps	1:	1	does not walk in step with the **w**
	1:	5	Therefore the **w** will not stand
	73:	3	when I saw the prosperity of the **w**.
Pr	10:	20	the heart of the **w** is of little value.
	11:	21	The **w** will not go unpunished,
Isa	53:	9	was assigned a grave with the **w**,
	55:	7	Let the **w** forsake their ways
	57:	20	But the **w** are like the tossing sea,
Eze	3:	18	that **w** person will die for their sin,
	18:	23	any pleasure in the death of the **w**?
	33:	14	And if I say to a **w** person,

WICKEDNESS (WICKED)

Eze	28:	15	you were created till **w** was found

WIDE

Isa	54:	2	stretch your tent curtains **w**, do not
Mt	7:	13	For **w** is the gate and broad is
Eph	3:	18	to grasp how **w** and long and high

WIDOW (WIDOWS)

Dt	10:	18	cause of the fatherless and the **w**,
Lk	21:	2	saw a poor **w** put in two very small

WIDOWS (WIDOW)

Jas	1:	27	orphans and **w** in their distress

WIFE (WIVES)

Ge	2:	24	and mother and is united to his **w**,
	24:	67	So she became his **w**, and he loved
Ex	20:	17	shall not covet your neighbor's **w**,
Dt	5:	21	shall not covet your neighbor's **w**.
Pr	5:	18	you rejoice in the **w** of your youth.
	12:	4	A **w** of noble character is her
	18:	22	who finds a **w** finds what is good
	19:	13	quarrelsome **w** is like the constant
	31:	10	A **w** of noble character who can
Mt	19:	3	for a man to divorce his **w** for any
1Co	7:	2	sexual relations with his own **w**,
	7:	33	how he can please his **w**—
Eph	5:	23	head of the **w** as Christ is the head
	5:	33	must love his **w** as he loves himself,
	5:	33	the **w** must respect her husband.
1Ti	3:	2	faithful to his **w**, temperate,
Rev	21:	9	you the bride, the **w** of the Lamb."

WILD

Lk	15:	13	squandered his wealth in **w** living.
Ro	11:	17	and you, though a **w** olive shoot,

WILL (WILLING WILLINGNESS)

Ps	40:	8	I desire to do your **w**, my God;
	143:	10	Teach me to do your **w**, for you are
Isa	53:	10	Yet it was the Lord's **w** to crush
Mt	6:	10	kingdom come, your **w** be done,
	26:	39	Yet not as I **w**, but as you **w**."
Jn	7:	17	chooses to do the **w** of God **w** find
Ac	20:	27	to you the whole **w** of God.
Ro	12:	2	test and approve what God's **w** is—
1Co	7:	37	but has control over his own **w**,
Eph	5:	17	understand what the Lord's **w** is.
Php	2:	13	for it is God who works in you to **w**
1Th	4:	3	It is God's **w** that you should be
	5:	18	for this is God's **w** for you in Christ
Heb	9:	16	In the case of a **w**, it is necessary
	10:	7	I have come to do your **w**,

Jas 4: 15 "If it is the Lord's **w**, we **w** live
1Jn 5: 14 ask anything according to his **w**,
Rev 4: 11 by your **w** they were created

WILLING (WILL)
Ps 51: 12 salvation and grant me a **w** spirit,
Da 3: 28 were **w** to give up their lives rather
Mt 18: 14 Father in heaven is not **w** that any
23: 37 her wings, and you were not **w**.
26: 41 The spirit is **w**, but the flesh is

WILLINGNESS (WILL)
2Co 8: 12 For if the **w** is there, the gift is

WIN
Php 3: 14 on toward the goal to **w** the prize
1Th 4: 12 your daily life may **w** the respect

WIND (WHIRLWIND)
Jas 1: 6 the sea, blown and tossed by the **w**.

WINE
Pr 20: 1 **W** is a mocker and beer a brawler;
Isa 55: 1 buy **w** and milk without money
Mt 9: 17 Neither do people pour new **w**
Lk 23: 36 They offered him **w** vinegar
Ro 14: 21 drink **w** or to do anything else
Eph 5: 18 Do not get drunk on **w**, which

WINESKINS
Mt 9: 17 people pour new wine into old **w**.

WINGS
Ru 2: 12 under whose **w** you have come
Ps 17: 8 hide me in the shadow of your **w**
Isa 40: 31 They will soar on **w** like eagles;
Lk 13: 34 gathers her chicks under her **w**,

WIPE
Rev 7: 17 God will **w** away every tear

WISDOM (WISE)
1Ki 4: 29 God gave Solomon **w** and very
Ps 111: 10 the Lord is the beginning of **w**;
Pr 31: 26 She speaks with **w**, and faithful
Jer 10: 12 he founded the world by his **w**
Mt 11: 19 **w** is proved right by her deeds."
Lk 2: 52 And Jesus grew in **w** and stature,
Ro 11: 33 the depth of the riches of the **w**
Col 2: 3 are hidden all the treasures of **w**
Jas 1: 5 If any of you lacks **w**, you should

WISE (WISDOM WISER)
1Ki 3: 12 I will give you a **w** and discerning
Job 5: 13 He catches the **w** in their craftiness,
Ps 19: 7 trustworthy, making **w** the simple.
Pr 3: 7 Do not be **w** in your own eyes;
9: 8 rebuke the **w** and they will love
10: 1 A **w** son brings joy to his father,
11: 30 and the one who is **w** saves lives.
13: 20 Walk with the **w** and become **w**,
17: 28 Even fools are thought **w** if they
Da 12: 3 Those who are **w** will shine like
Mt 11: 25 hidden these things from the **w**
1Co 1: 27 things of the world to shame the **w**;
2Ti 3: 15 make you **w** for salvation through

WISER (WISE)
1Co 1: 25 of God is **w** than human wisdom,

WITHER (WITHERS)
Ps 1: 3 and whose leaf does not **w**—

WITHERS (WITHER)
Isa 40: 7 The grass **w** and the flowers fall,
1Pe 1: 24 the grass **w** and the flowers fall,

WITHHOLD
Ps 84: 11 no good thing does he **w** from
Pr 23: 13 Do not **w** discipline from a child;

WITNESS (WITNESSES)
Jn 1: 8 he came only as a **w** to the light.

WITNESSES (WITNESS)
Dt 19: 15 by the testimony of two or three **w**.
Ac 1: 8 and you will be my **w** in Jerusalem,

WIVES (WIFE)
Eph 5: 22 **W**, submit yourselves to your own
5: 25 love your **w**, just as Christ loved
1Pe 3: 1 **W**, in the same way submit

WOE
Isa 6: 5 "**W** to me!" I cried. "I am ruined!

WOLF
Isa 65: 25 The **w** and the lamb will feed

WOMAN (MAN)
Ge 2: 22 the Lord God made a **w**
3: 15 put enmity between you and the **w**,
Lev 20: 13 with a man as one does with a **w**,
Dt 22: 5 A **w** must not wear men's clothing,
Ru 3: 11 that you are a **w** of noble character.
Pr 31: 30 a **w** who fears the Lord is to be
Mt 5: 28 a **w** lustfully has already committed
Jn 8: 3 brought in a **w** caught
Ro 7: 2 by law a married **w** is bound to her
1Co 11: 3 and the head of the **w** is man,
11: 13 Is it proper for a **w** to pray to God
1Ti 2: 11 A **w** should learn in quietness

WOMEN (MAN)
Lk 1: 42 "Blessed are you among **w**,
1Co 14: 34 **W** should remain silent
1Ti 2: 9 I also want the **w** to dress modestly,
Titus 2: 3 teach the older **w** to be reverent
1Pe 3: 5 the way the holy **w** of the past

WOMB
Job 1: 21 I came from my mother's **w**,
Jer 1: 5 I formed you in the **w** I knew you,
Lk 1: 44 the baby in my **w** leaped for joy.

WONDERFUL (WONDERS)
Job 42: 3 things too **w** for me to know.
Ps 119: 18 that I may see **w** things in your law.
119: 27 I may meditate on your **w** deeds.
119:129 statutes are **w**; therefore I obey
139: 6 Such knowledge is too **w** for me,
Isa 9: 6 he will be called **W** Counselor,
1Pe 2: 9 out of darkness into his **w** light.

WONDERS (WONDERFUL)
Job 37: 14 stop and consider God's **w**.
Ps 17: 7 Show me the **w** of your great love,
31: 21 for he showed me the **w** of his love
Joel 2: 30 I will show **w** in the heavens
Ac 2: 19 I will show **w** in the heavens

WOOD
Isa 44: 19 Shall I bow down to a block of **w**?"
1Co 3: 12 costly stones, **w**, hay or straw,

WORD (WORDS)

Dt	8: 3	but on every **w** that comes
2Sa	22: 31	The Lord's **w** is flawless;
Ps	119: 9	By living according to your **w**.
	119: 11	I have hidden your **w** in my heart
	119:105	Your **w** is a lamp to my feet
Pr	12: 25	the heart, but a kind **w** cheers it up.
	30: 5	"Every **w** of God is flawless; he is
Isa	55: 11	so is my **w** that goes out from my
Jn	1: 1	In the beginning was the **W**, and the **W** was with God, and the **W** was God.
	1: 14	The **W** became flesh and made his
2Co	2: 17	we do not peddle the **w** of God
	4: 2	nor do we distort the **w** of God.
Eph	6: 17	of the Spirit, which is the **w** of God.
Php	2: 16	as you hold firmly to the **w** of life.
2Ti	2: 15	and who correctly handles the **w**
Heb	4: 12	the **w** of God is alive and active.
Jas	1: 22	Do not merely listen to the **w**,

WORDS (WORD)

Dt	11: 18	Fix these **w** of mine in your hearts
Ps	119:103	How sweet are your **w** to my taste,
	119:130	unfolding of your **w** gives light;
	119:160	All your **w** are true; all your
Pr	30: 6	Do not add to his **w**, or he will
Jer	15: 16	When your **w** came, I ate them;
Mt	24: 35	but my **w** will never pass away.
Jn	6: 68	You have the **w** of eternal life.
	15: 7	in me and my **w** remain in you,
1Co	14: 19	rather speak five intelligible **w**
Rev	22: 19	if anyone takes **w** away from this

WORK (HANDIWORK WORKER WORKERS WORKING WORKMAN)

Ex	23: 12	but on the seventh day do not **w**,
Nu	8: 11	be ready to do the **w** of the Lord.
Dt	5: 14	On it you shall not do any **w**,
Jer	48: 10	who is lax in doing the Lord's **w**!
Jn	6: 27	Do not **w** for food that spoils,
	9: 4	is coming, when no one can **w**.
1Co	3: 13	test the quality of each person's **w**.
Php	1: 6	he who began a good **w** in you will
	2: 12	continue to **w** out your salvation
Col	3: 23	you do, **w** at it with all your heart,
1Th	5: 12	those who **w** hard among you,
2Th	3: 10	is unwilling to **w** shall not eat."
2Ti	3: 17	equipped for every good **w**.
Heb	6: 10	he will not forget your **w**

WORKER (WORK)

Lk	10: 7	for the **w** deserves his wages.
1Ti	5: 18	and "The **w** deserves his wages."
2Ti	2: 15	a **w** who does not need to be

WORKERS (WORK)

Mt	9: 37	is plentiful but the **w** are few.
1Co	3: 9	For we are **c** in God's service;

WORKING (WORK)

Col	3: 23	all your heart, as **w** for the Lord,

WORKS (WORK)

Pr	31: 31	her **w** bring her praise at the city
Ro	8: 28	in all things God **w** for the good
Eph	2: 9	not by **w**, so that no one can boast.
	4: 12	to equip his people for **w** of service,

WORLD (WORLDLY)

Ps	50: 12	for the **w** is mine, and all that is
Isa	13: 11	I will punish the **w** for its evil,
Mt	5: 14	"You are the light of the **w**,
	16: 26	for someone to gain the whole **w**,
Mk	16: 15	*"Go into all the **w** and preach*
Jn	1: 29	who takes away the sin of the **w**!
	3: 16	God so loved the **w** that he gave his
	8: 12	he said, "I am the light of the **w**.
	15: 19	but I have chosen you out of the **w**. That is why the **w** hates you.
	16: 33	I have overcome the **w**."
	18: 36	said, "My kingdom is not of this **w**.
Ro	3: 19	and the whole **w** held accountable
1Co	3: 19	the wisdom of this **w** is foolishness
2Co	5: 19	that God was reconciling the **w**
	10: 3	For though we live in the **w**, we do
1Ti	6: 7	For we brought nothing into the **w**,
1Jn	2: 2	but also for the sins of the whole **w**.
	2: 15	not love the **w** or anything in the **w**.
Rev	13: 8	slain from the creation of the **w**.

WORLDLY (WORLD)

Titus	2: 12	to ungodliness and **w** passions,

WORMS

Mk	9: 48	where " 'the **w** that eat them do

WORRY (WORRYING)

Mt	6: 25	I tell you, do not **w** about your life,
	10: 19	do not **w** about what to say or how

WORRYING (WORRY)

Mt	6: 27	you by **w** add a single hour to your

WORSHIP

1Ch	16: 29	**W** the Lord in the splendor of his
Ps	95: 6	let us bow down in **w**, let us kneel
Mt	2: 2	it rose and have come to **w** him."
Jn	4: 24	his worshipers must **w** in the Spirit
Ro	12: 1	this is your true and proper **w**.

WORTH (WORTHY)

Job	28: 13	No mortal comprehends its **w**;
Pr	31: 10	She is **w** far more than rubies.
Mt	10: 31	you are **w** more than many
Ro	8: 18	sufferings are not **w** comparing
1Pe	1: 7	of greater **w** than gold,
	3: 4	which is of great **w** in God's sight.

WORTHLESS

Pr	11: 4	Wealth is **w** in the day of wrath,
Jas	1: 26	themselves, and their religion is **w**.

WORTHY (WORTH)

1Ch	16: 25	is the Lord and most **w** of praise;
Eph	4: 1	live a life **w** of the calling you have
Php	1: 27	in a manner **w** of the gospel
Rev	5: 2	"Who is **w** to break the seals

WOUNDS

Pr	27: 6	**W** from a friend can be trusted,
Isa	53: 5	and by his **w** we are healed.
Zec	13: 6	'What are these **w** on your body?'
1Pe	2: 24	"by his **w** you have been healed."

WRATH

2Ch	36: 16	at his prophets until the **w**
Ps	2: 5	anger and terrifies them in his **w**,
	76: 10	Surely your **w** against mankind
Pr	15: 1	A gentle answer turns away **w**,

CONCORDANCE

Jer	25: 15	cup filled with the wine of my **w**
Ro	1: 18	The **w** of God is being revealed
	5: 9	saved from God's **w** through him!
1Th	5: 9	God did not appoint us to suffer **w**
Rev	6: 16	and from the **w** of the Lamb!

WRESTLED

| Ge | 32: 24 | a man **w** with him till daybreak. |

WRITE (WRITING WRITTEN)

Dt	6: 9	**W** them on the doorframes of your
Pr	7: 3	**w** them on the tablet of your heart.
Heb	8: 10	minds and **w** them on their hearts.

WRITING (WRITE)

| 1Co | 14: 37 | what I am **w** to you is the Lord's |

WRITTEN (WRITE)

Jos	1: 8	be careful to do everything **w** in it.
Da	12: 1	everyone whose name is found **w**
Lk	10: 20	that your names are **w** in heaven."
Jn	20: 31	these are **w** that you may believe
1Co	4: 6	"Do not go beyond what is **w**."
2Co	3: 3	**w** not with ink but with the Spirit
Heb	12: 23	whose names are **w** in heaven.

WRONG (WRONGDOING WRONGED WRONGS)

Ex	23: 2	not follow the crowd in doing **w**.
Nu	5: 7	restitution for the **w** they have
Job	34: 12	unthinkable that God would do **w**,
1Th	5: 15	that nobody pays back **w** for **w**,

WRONGDOING (WRONG)

| Job | 1: 22 | not sin by charging God with **w**. |

WRONGED (WRONG)

| 1Co | 6: 7 | Why not rather be **w**? |

WRONGS (WRONG)

| Pr | 10: 12 | conflict, but love covers over all **w**. |
| 1Co | 13: 5 | angered, it keeps no record of **w**. |

YEARS

Ps	90: 4	A thousand **y** in your sight are like
	90: 10	Our days may come to seventy **y**,
2Pe	3: 8	the Lord a day is like a thousand **y**,
Rev	20: 2	and bound him for a thousand **y**.

YESTERDAY

| Heb | 13: 8 | Jesus Christ is the same **y** and today |

YOKE (YOKED)

| Mt | 11: 29 | Take my **y** upon you and learn |

YOKED (YOKE)

| 2Co | 6: 14 | Do not be **y** together |

YOUNG (YOUTH)

| Ps | 119: 9 | can a **y** person stay on the path |
| 1Ti | 4: 12 | down on you because you are **y**, |

YOUTH (YOUNG)

Ps	103: 5	your **y** is renewed like the eagle's.
Ecc	12: 1	your Creator in the days of your **y**,
2Ti	2: 22	Flee the evil desires of **y** and

ZEAL

| Jn | 2: 17 | **Z** for your house will consume me. |
| Ro | 12: 11 | Never be lacking in **z**, but keep |

ZECHARIAH

1. Son of Jeroboam II; king of Israel (2Ki 15:8–12).
2. Post-exilic prophet who encouraged rebuilding of temple (Ezr 5:1; 6:14; Zec 1:1).
3. Father of John the Baptist (Lk 1:13; 3:2).

ZEDEKIAH

Mattaniah, son of Josiah (1Ch 3:15), made king of Judah by Nebuchadnezzar (2Ki 24:17—25:7; 2Ch 36:10–14; Jer 37–39; 52:1–11).

ZERUBBABEL

Descendant of David (1Ch 3:19; Mt 1:3). Led return from exile (Ezr 2–3; Ne 7:7; Hag 1–2; Zec 4).

ZIMRI

King of Israel (1Ki 16:9–20).

ZION

Ps	137: 3	"Sing us one of the songs of **Z**!"
Jer	50: 5	They will ask the way to **Z** and
Ro	9: 33	I lay in **Z** a stone that causes people
	11: 26	"The deliverer will come from **Z**;

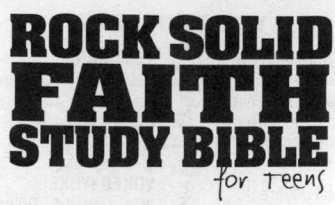

ROCK SOLID FAITH STUDY BIBLE
for teens

Project Management and Editorial:
Carol Postma

Proofreading:
Peachtree Editorial and Proofreading Service

Writer (work for hire):
Kevin Johnson

Cover Design:
Jody Langley

Interior Design:
Gayle Raymer

Typesetting Management:
Nancy Wilson

Typesetting:
Sherri Hoffman

Theological Review:
Terry Fisher, Master of Arts in Theology, Fuller Seminary

Production Management:
Phil Herich

GUARANTEE

WORLD OF THE PATRIARCHS

Possible location of Biblical "Ur of the Chaldeans," where Abraham's migration began.

Possible location of Sodom and Gomor'rah.

→ Abraham's Journey

EXODUS AND CONQUEST OF CANAAN

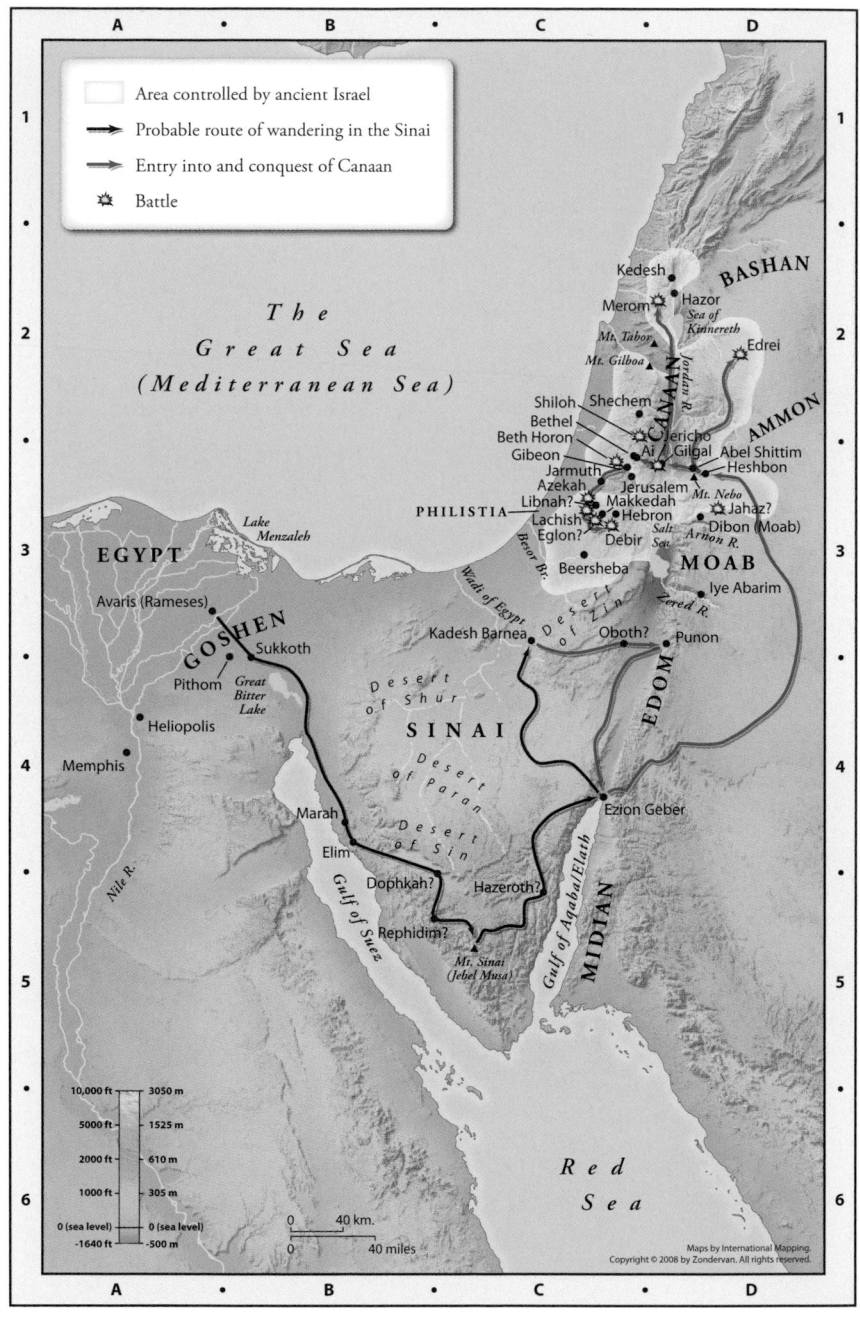

LAND OF THE TWELVE TRIBES

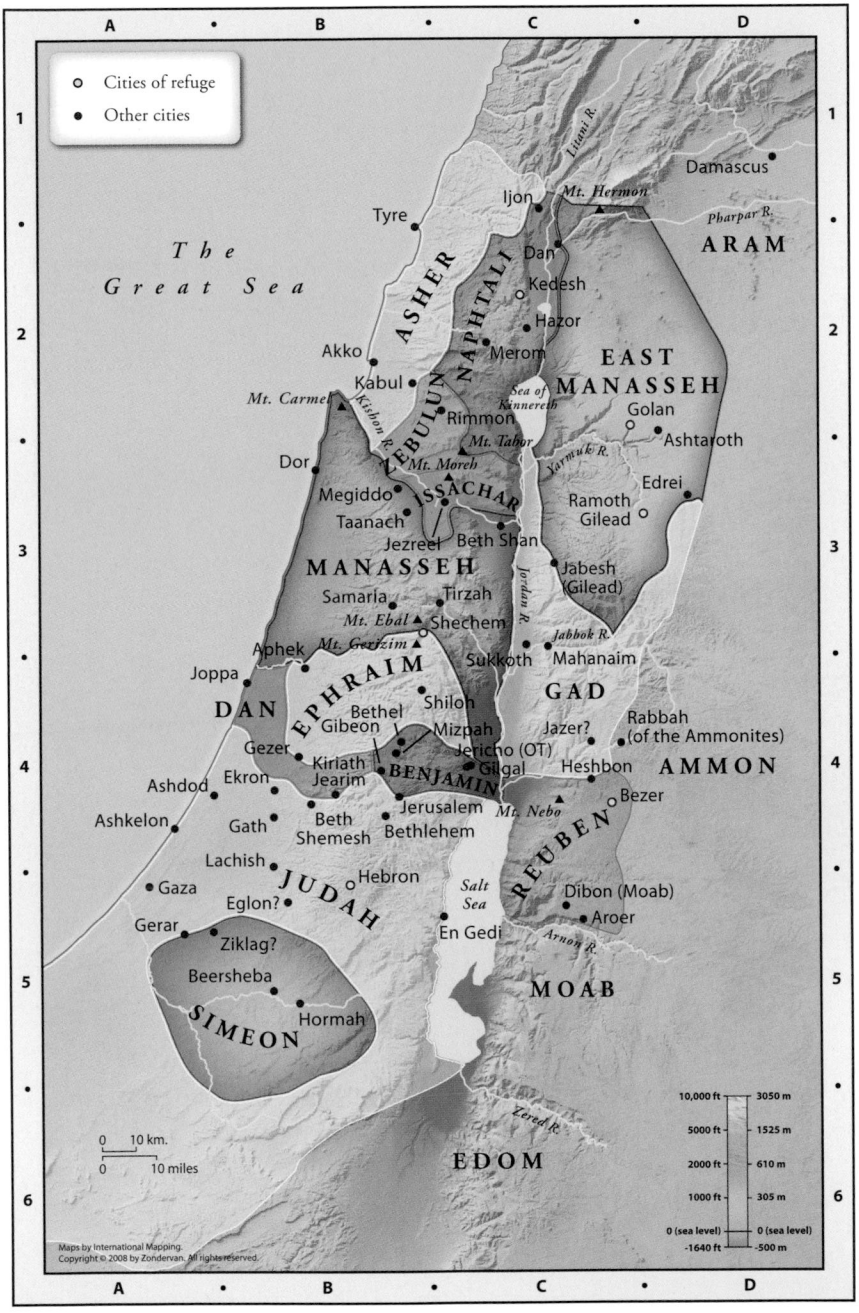

Cities of refuge

Other cities

Damascus

Tyre

Ijon   Mt. Hermon

Litani R.

Pharpar R.

ARAM

The Great Sea

ASHER   NAPHTALI   Dan

Kedesh

Hazor

Akko   Merom

EAST MANASSEH

Kabul

Mt. Carmel   ZEBULUN   *Kishon R.*   Rimmon   *Sea of Kinnereth*   Golan

Ashtaroth

Dor   *Mt. Tabor*

Mt. Moreh   ISSACHAR

Megiddo   *Mt. Ebal*   Edrei

Taanach   Ramoth Gilead

Jezreel   Beth Shan

MANASSEH   *Yarmuk R.*

Samaria   Tirzah   Jabesh (Gilead)

Mt. Ebal   Shechem

Aphek   *Mt. Gerizim*   *Jabbok R.*

Joppa   Sukkoth   Mahanaim

DAN   EPHRAIM   GAD

Shiloh   Rabbah (of the Ammonites)

Bethel   Mizpah   Jazer?

Gibeon   Jericho (OT)   Heshbon

Gezer   Kiriath Jearim   BENJAMIN   Gilgal   AMMON

Ashdod   Ekron   Bezer

Gath   Beth Shemesh   Jerusalem   *Mt. Nebo*

Ashkelon   Bethlehem   REUBEN

Lachish   *Salt Sea*   Dibon (Moab)

Gaza   Hebron   Aroer

Eglon?   JUDAH   En Gedi   *Arnon R.*

Gerar   Ziklag?

Beersheba   MOAB

SIMEON   Hormah

Zered R.

EDOM

0   10 km.

0   10 miles

10,000 ft	3050 m
5000 ft	1525 m
2000 ft	610 m
1000 ft	305 m
0 (sea level)	0 (sea level)
-1640 ft	-500 m

KINGDOM OF DAVID AND SOLOMON

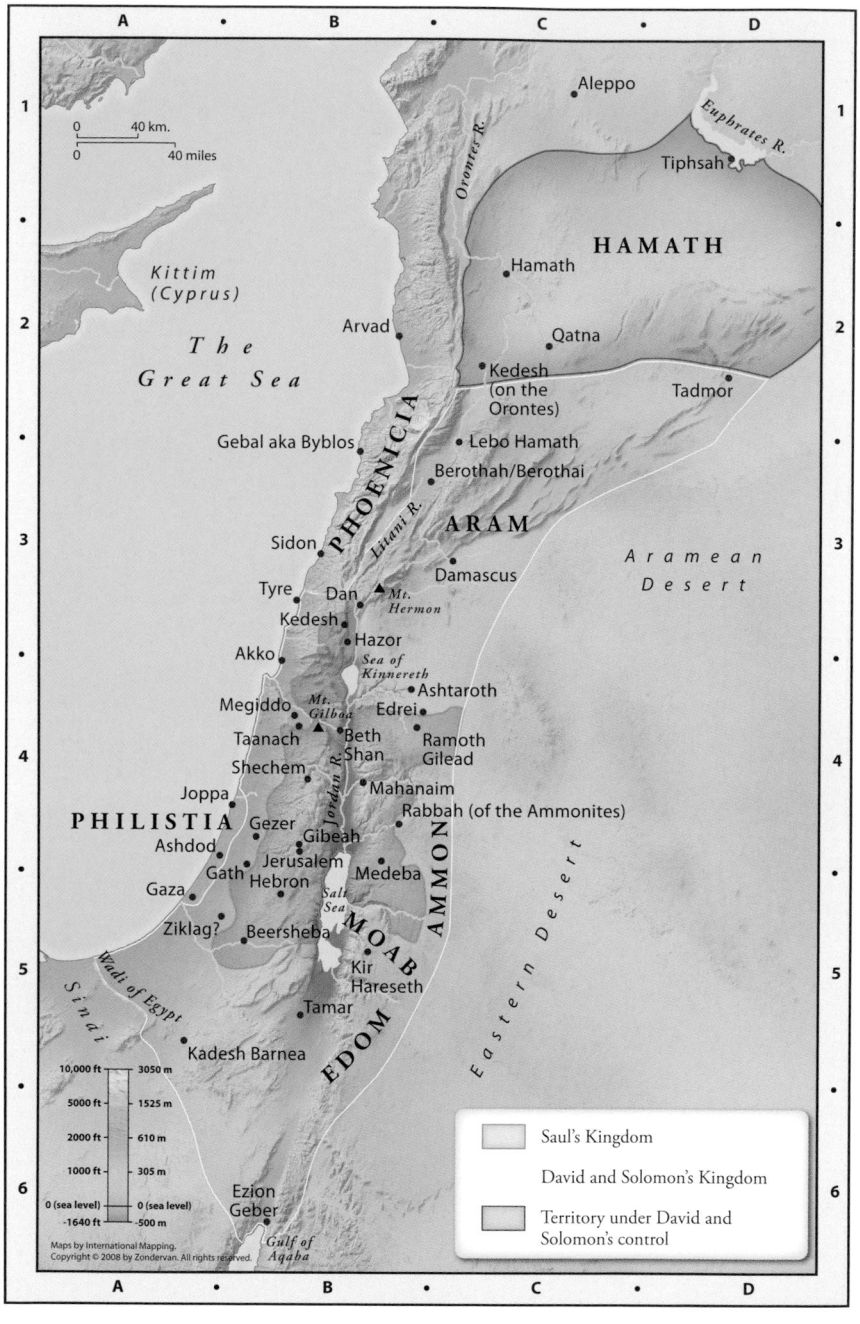

A · B · C · D

1

0   40 km.
0   40 miles

*Kittim
(Cyprus)*

*The
Great Sea*

HAMATH

Aleppo

Euphrates R.

Tiphsah

Hamath

Arvad

Qatna

Kedesh
(on the
Orontes)

Tadmor

Gebal aka Byblos

Lebo Hamath

Berothah/Berothai

PHOENICIA

Sidon

Litani R.

ARAM

*Aramean
Desert*

Tyre   Dan   ▲*Mt.
Hermon*

Damascus

Kedesh

Akko

Hazor

*Sea of
Kinnereth*

Megiddo   *Mt.
Gilboa*   Edrei

Ashtaroth

Taanach   Beth
Shan   Ramoth
Gilead

Shechem

Jordan R.

Joppa

PHILISTIA   Gezer

Mahanaim

Rabbah (of the Ammonites)

Ashdod

Gibeah

Gath   Jerusalem
Hebron

Medeba

Gaza

*Salt
Sea*

MOAB

AMMON

Eastern Desert

Ziklag?

Beersheba

Kir
Hareseth

Sinai

Wadi of Egypt

Tamar

EDOM

Kadesh Barnea

10,000 ft	3050 m
5000 ft	1525 m
2000 ft	610 m
1000 ft	305 m
0 (sea level)	0 (sea level)
-1640 ft	-500 m

Ezion
Geber

*Gulf of
Aqaba*

Maps by International Mapping.
Copyright © 2008 by Zondervan. All rights reserved.

Saul's Kingdom

David and Solomon's Kingdom

Territory under David and
Solomon's control

A · B · C · D

JESUS' MINISTRY

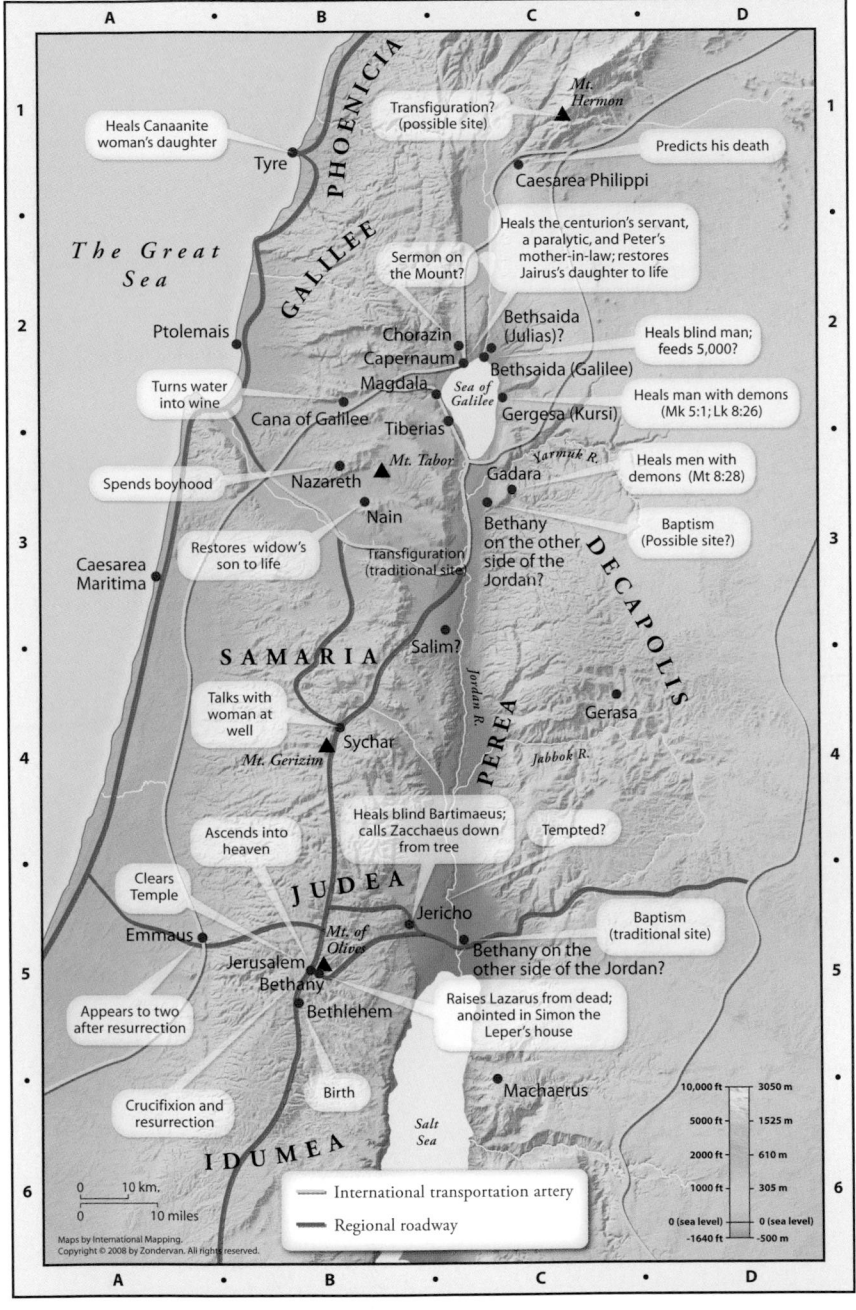

A • **B** • **C** • **D**

1

Heals Canaanite woman's daughter

Tyre

PHOENICIA

Transfiguration? (possible site)

Mt. *Hermon*

Predicts his death

Caesarea Philippi

The Great Sea

GALILEE

Sermon on the Mount?

Heals the centurion's servant, a paralytic, and Peter's mother-in-law; restores Jairus's daughter to life

2

Ptolemais

Chorazin

Capernaum

Magdala

Sea of Galilee

Cana of Galilee

Tiberias

Bethsaida (Julias)?

Bethsaida (Galilee)

Gergesa (Kursi)

Heals blind man; feeds 5,000?

Heals man with demons (Mk 5:1; Lk 8:26)

Turns water into wine

Mt. Tabor

Yarmuk R.

Gadara

Heals men with demons (Mt 8:28)

Spends boyhood

Nazareth

Nain

Bethany on the other side of the Jordan?

Baptism (Possible site?)

3

Caesarea Maritima

Restores widow's son to life

Transfiguration (traditional site)

DECAPOLIS

SAMARIA

Salim?

Talks with woman at well

Mt. Gerizim

Sychar

Jordan R.

PEREA

Gerasa

Jubbok R.

4

Ascends into heaven

Heals blind Bartimaeus; calls Zacchaeus down from tree

Tempted?

Clears Temple

JUDEA

Jericho

Baptism (traditional site)

Emmaus

Mt. of Olives

Bethany on the other side of the Jordan?

5

Jerusalem

Bethany

Bethlehem

Raises Lazarus from dead; anointed in Simon the Leper's house

Appears to two after resurrection

Crucifixion and resurrection

Birth

Salt Sea

Machaerus

IDUMEA

10,000 ft	3050 m
5000 ft	1525 m
2000 ft	610 m
1000 ft	305 m
0 (sea level)	0 (sea level)
-1640 ft	-500 m

6

0   10 km.

0   10 miles

Maps by International Mapping.
Copyright © 2008 by Zondervan. All rights reserved.

—— International transportation artery

—— Regional roadway

A • **B** • **C** • **D**

PAUL'S MISSIONARY JOURNEYS

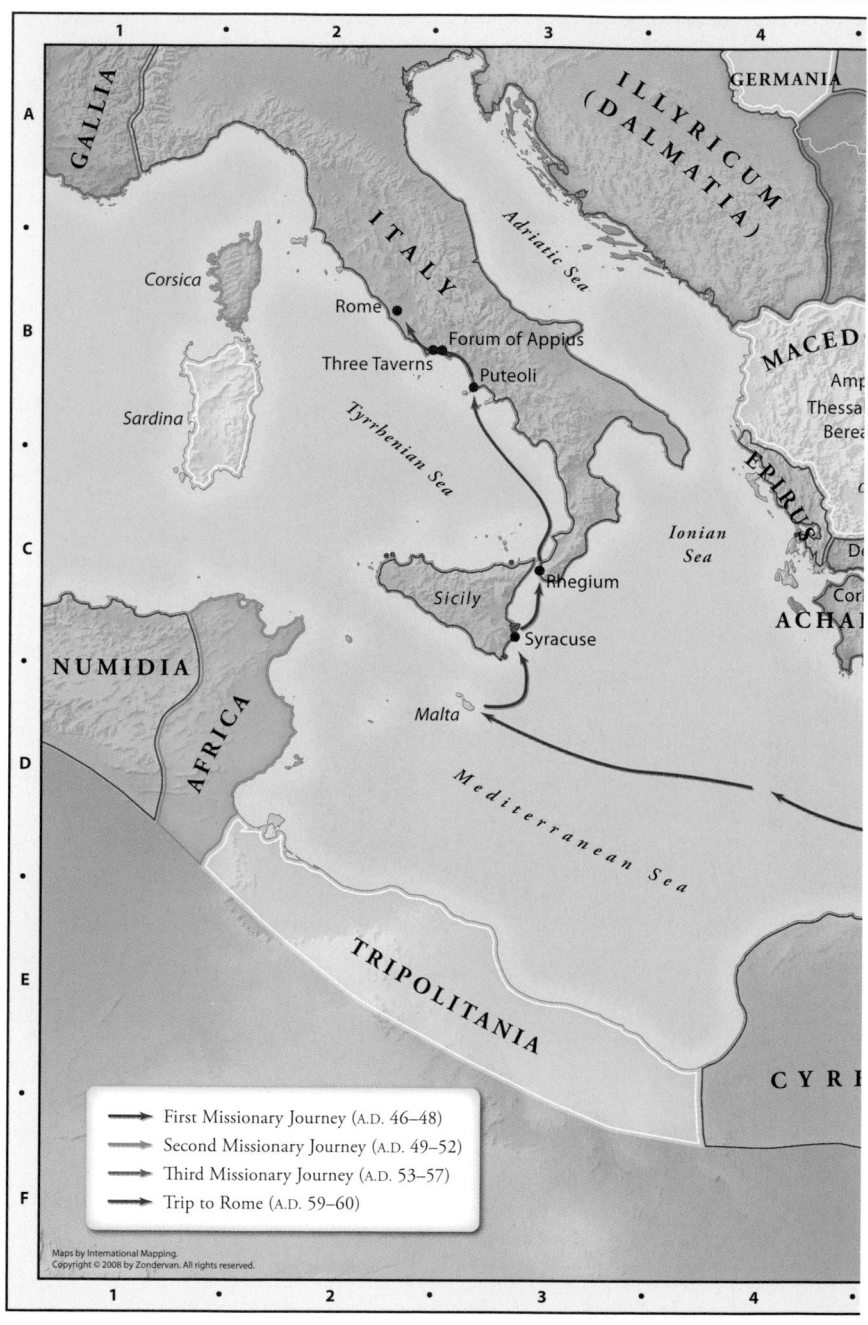

GALLIA

GERMANIA

ILLYRICUM
(DALMATIA)

ITALY

Adriatic Sea

Corsica

Rome

Forum of Appius

Three Taverns

Puteoli

MACED

Amp
Thessa
Berea

Sardina

Tyrrhenian Sea

EPIRUS

Ionian
Sea

Rhegium

Sicily

Cor

ACHA

NUMIDIA

AFRICA

Syracuse

Malta

Mediterranean Sea

TRIPOLITANIA

CYR

→ First Missionary Journey (A.D. 46–48)
→ Second Missionary Journey (A.D. 49–52)
→ Third Missionary Journey (A.D. 53–57)
→ Trip to Rome (A.D. 59–60)

JERUSALEM IN THE TIME OF JESUS

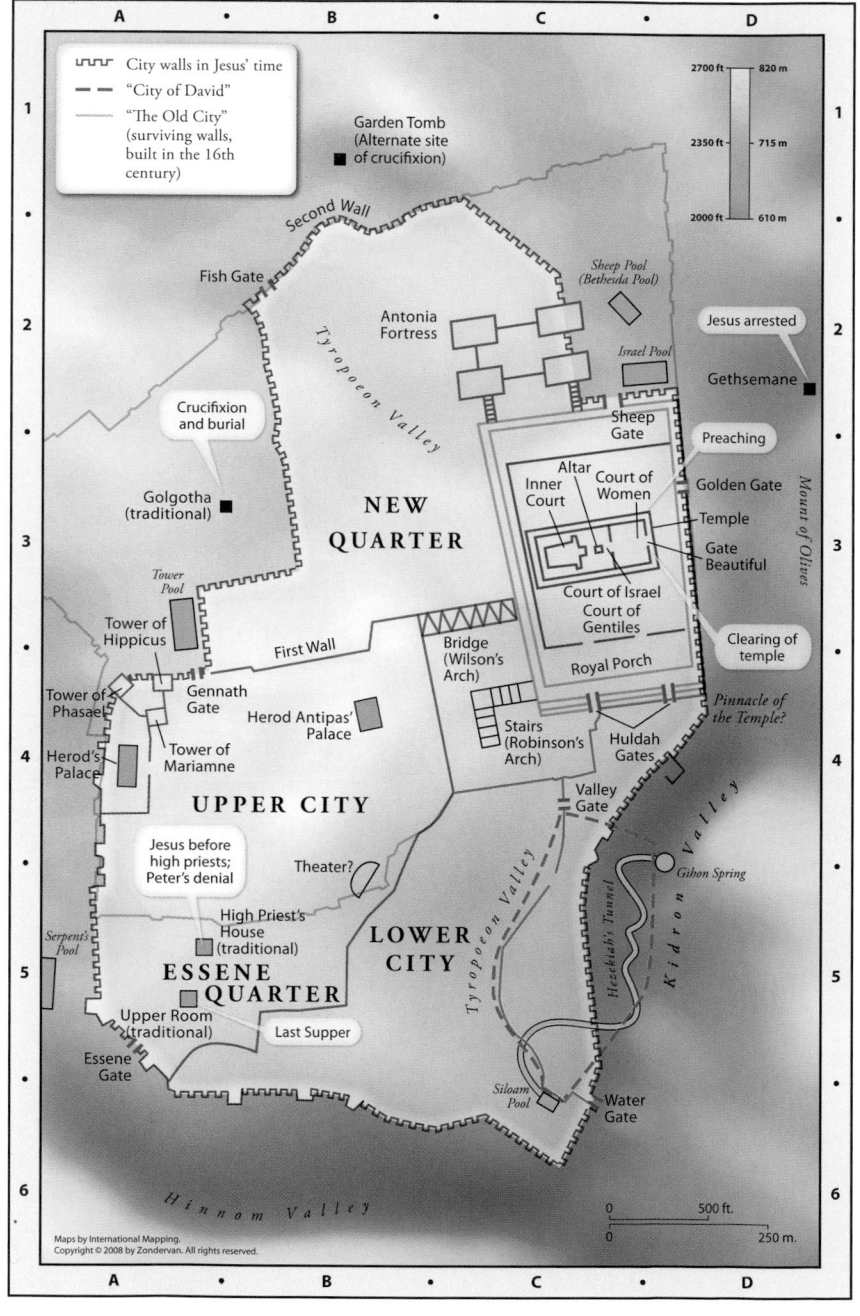

City walls in Jesus' time

"City of David"

"The Old City" (surviving walls, built in the 16th century)

Garden Tomb (Alternate site of crucifixion)

Second Wall

Fish Gate

Sheep Pool (Bethesda Pool)

Antonia Fortress

Israel Pool

Jesus arrested

Gethsemane

Tyropoeon Valley

Crucifixion and burial

Golgotha (traditional)

NEW QUARTER

Sheep Gate

Preaching

Altar

Inner Court

Court of Women

Golden Gate

Temple

Gate Beautiful

Court of Israel

Court of Gentiles

Mount of Olives

Tower Pool

Tower of Hippicus

First Wall

Bridge (Wilson's Arch)

Royal Porch

Clearing of temple

Pinnacle of the Temple?

Tower of Phasael

Gennath Gate

Herod Antipas' Palace

Stairs (Robinson's Arch)

Huldah Gates

Herod's Palace

Tower of Mariamne

UPPER CITY

Valley Gate

Jesus before high priests; Peter's denial

Theater?

LOWER CITY

Gihon Spring

High Priest's House (traditional)

Serpent's Pool

Hezekiah's Tunnel

Kidron Valley

ESSENE QUARTER

Tyropoeon Valley

Upper Room (traditional)

Last Supper

Essene Gate

Siloam Pool

Water Gate

Hinnom Valley

0   500 ft.

0   250 m.